arihant
SUCCESS AND NOTHING LESS
ARIHANT PRAKASHAN (SERIES), MEERUT

Skills in Mathematics

JEE Main & Advanced

Algebra

Dr. SK Goyal

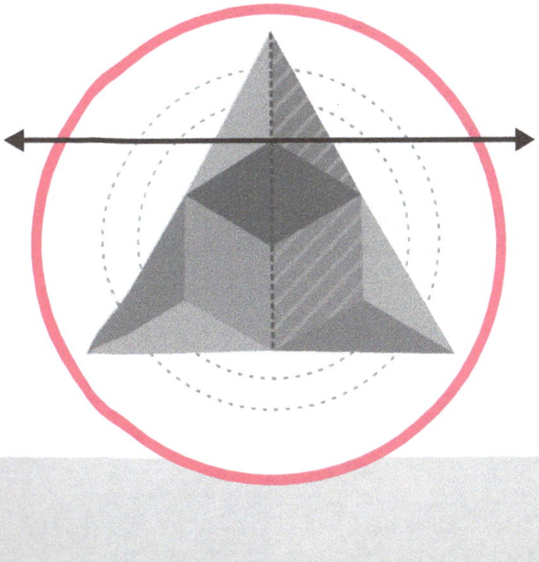

arihant
SUCCESS AND NOTHING LESS

Arihant Prakashan (Series), Meerut

Administrative & Production Offices

Regd. Office

'Ramchhaya' 4577/15, Agarwal Road, Darya Ganj, New Delhi -110002
Tele: 011- 47630600, 43518550

Head Office

Kalindi, TP Nagar, Meerut (UP) - 250002 Tel: 0121-7156203, 7156204

Sales & Support Offices

Agra, Ahmedabad, Bengaluru, Bareilly, Chennai, Delhi, Guwahati, Hyderabad, Jaipur, Jhansi, Kolkata, Lucknow, Nagpur & Pune.

PRICE: ₹ 795.00

PO No : TXT-XX-XXXXXXX-X-XX

Published by Arihant Publications (India) Ltd.

For further information about the books published by Arihant, log on to www.arihantbooks.com or e-mail at info@arihantbooks.com

Follow us on

Preface

It is a matter of great pride and honour for me to have received such an overwhelming response to the previous editions of this book from the readers. In a way, this has inspired me to revise this book thoroughly as per the changed pattern of JEE Main & Advanced. I have tried to make the contents more relevant as per the needs of students, many topics have been re-written, a lot of new problems of new types have been added. All possible efforts are made to remove all the printing errors that had crept in previous editions. The book is now in such a shape that the students would feel at ease while going through the problems, which will in turn clear their concepts too.

A Summary of changes that have been made in Revised & Enhanced Edition

- Theory has been completely updated so as to accommodate all the changes made in JEE Syllabus & Pattern in recent years.
- The most important point about this new edition is, now the whole text matter of each chapter has been divided into small milestones with practice exercise in each milestones. This will help reader in step by step learning
- Theory of each milestone is more precise with **JEE focus Points** and **JEE Spike**.
- **JEE Scanners** are incorporated in theory for more synced learning with JEE Main and Advanced PYQs.
- Just after completion of theory, Solved Examples of all JEE types have been given, providing the students a complete understanding of all the formats of JEE questions & the level of difficulty of questions generally asked in JEE.
- Along with exercises given with each Milestone, following three exercises have been given at the end of each chapter.
- Practice Milestone 1- JEE Main Pattern Exercises.
- Practice Milestone 2- JEE Advanced Pattern Exercises.
- Practice Milestone 3- Challenging Problems Exercises.
- Previous Years questions asked in JEE Main and Advanced have been incorporated in all the exercises.

However I have made the best efforts and put my all teaching experience in revising this book. Still I am looking forward to get the valuable suggestions and criticism from my own fraternity i.e. the fraternity of JEE teachers. I strongly believe that

"YOU CAN DO ANYTHING IF YOU SET YOUR MIND FOR IT. I ALWAYS BELIEVE THE MOST IMPORTANT FORMULA IS

COURAGE + DREAMS = SUCCESS"

I would also like to motivate the students to send their suggestions or the changes that they want to be incorporated in this book. All the suggestions given by you all will be kept in prime focus at the time of next revision of the book.

Dr SK Goyal

Enhanced Features

JEE Focus Points

- $e^{i\theta} + 1 = e^{i\theta/2} \cdot 2\cos\left(\frac{\theta}{2}\right)$ (Remember)
- $e^{i\theta} - 1 = e^{i\theta/2} \cdot 2i\sin\left(\frac{\theta}{2}\right)$ (Remember)
- $\frac{e^{i\theta} - 1}{e^{i\theta} + 1} = i\tan\left(\frac{\theta}{2}\right)$ (Remember)
- If $z = re^{i\theta}$; $|z| = r$, then $\arg(z) = \theta$, $\bar{z} = re^{-i\theta}$
- If $|z - z_0| = 1$, then $z - z_0 = e^{i\theta}$

Concept Inside Video

A collection of Key Points/Results prime from JEE Preparation point of View. These are further elaborated with support videos.

JEE SPIKE

Let $z = a + ib, a > 0, b > 0 = (a, b)$ (I quadrant)

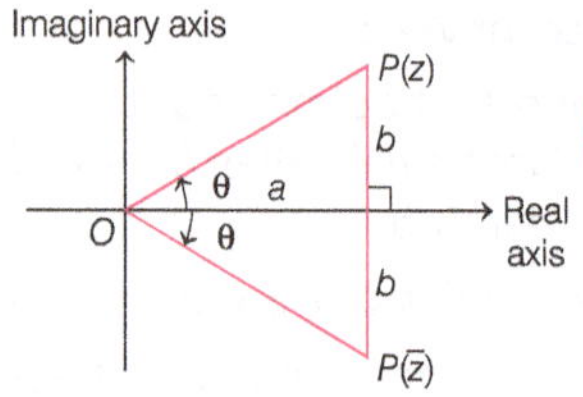

Concept Inside Video

Then, $\bar{z} = a - ib = (a, -b)$ (IV quadrant). Now,

(i) if z lies in I quadrant, then $\bar{z}$ lies in IV quadrant and *vice-versa*.

(ii) if z lies in II quadrant, then $\bar{z}$ lies in III quadrant and *vice-versa*.

Seggregated most valuable Pointers for JEE preparation

JEE SCANNER

Example Similar to PYQ Asked in JEE Main 2021

The least positive integer n such that $\frac{(1+i)^n}{(1-i)^{n-2}}$, $i = \sqrt{-1}$, *is a positive integer, is* ....

Sol. Given, $\frac{(1+i)^n}{(1-i)^{n-2}}$

For $n = 0$, $\frac{(1+i)^0}{(1-i)^{-2}} = (1-i)^2$

$= 1 - 1 - 2i = -2i$,

which is not a positive integer.

For $n = 1$, $\frac{(1+i)}{(1-i)^{-1}} = (1+i)(1-i)$

$= 1 - (-1) = 1 + 1 = 2$

Here, 2 is a positive integer.

$\therefore$ The least positive integer n is 1.

Skill Builder

The least positive integers n such that $\left(\frac{2i}{1+i}\right)^n$, $i = \sqrt{-1}$, is a positive integer, is ....

For Sol.

■ **For more practice** See Q.10 of Milestone Practice 1.1.

Unmatched Concept elevation tool helpful in syncing recent JEE Main & Advanced PYQs with theory and provide additional practice through Skill Builders.

Contents

1. COMPLEX NUMBER 1-108

Milestone 1 - IOTA, Definition of Complex Number, Algebra of Complex Number
- Integral Power of IOTA (*i*)
- Definition of Complex Number
- Algebraic Operations on Complex Numbers

Milestone 2 - Conjugate, Modulus and Argument of a Complex Number
- Conjugate of Complex Number
- Modulus of Complex Number
- Argument of Complex Number
- Trigonometric or Polar or Modulus Argument Form of Complex Number
- Euler's Form
- Logarithm of Complex Number

Milestone 3 - Square Root of Complex Number and De-Moivre's Theorem
- Square Root of Complex Number
- Solution of Complex Equation
- De-Moivre's Theorem
- Cube Root of Unity

Milestone 4 - Complex Number in Geometry
- Vector Representation of Complex Numbers
- Geometrical Representation of Algebraic Operation on Complex Numbers
- Rotation Theorem (Coni Method)
- Shifting the Origin in Case of Complex Numbers
- Inverse Points
- Use of Complex Numbers in Coordinate Geometry

Practice Milestones
- Practice Milestone 1 - JEE Main Pattern
- Practice Milestone 2 - JEE Advanced Pattern
- Practice Milestone 3 - Challenging Problems

2. THEORY OF EQUATION 109-206

Milestone 1 - Quadratic Equation
- Polynomial in One Variable
- Identity
- Quadratic Equation
- Nature of Roots
- Relation between Roots and Coefficients
- Transformation of Quadratic Equation
- Conditions for Common Roots
- Quadratic Expression
- Wavy Curve Method
- Condition for Resolution into Linear Factors
- Location of Roots

Milestone 2 - Theory of Equation
- Equation of Higher Degree
- Rational Algebraic Inequalities
- Irrational Equation
- Irrational Inequation
- Exponential Equations
- Exponential Inequations
- Logarithmic Equations
- Logarithmic Inequations

Practice Milestones
- Practice Milestone 1 - JEE Main Pattern
- Practice Milestone 2 - JEE Advanced Pattern
- Practice Milestone 3 - Challenging Problems

3. SEQUENCES AND SERIES 207-299

Milestone 1 - Arithmetic Progression
- Sequence
- Series
- Progression
- Arithmetic Progression

Milestone 2 - Geometric and Harmonic Progression
- Geometric Sequence or Geometric Progression (GP)
- Harmonic Sequence or Harmonic Progression (HP)

Milestone 3 - Mean
- Arithmetic Mean
- Geometric Mean
- Harmonic Mean
- Application to Problems of Maxima and Minima without Using Caculus

Milestone 4 - Some Special Series
- Arithmetico-Geometric Series (AGS)
- Sigma Notation
- Natural Numbers

Practice Milestones
- Practice Milestone 1 - JEE Main Pattern
- Practice Milestone 2 - JEE Advanced Pattern
- Practice Milestone 3 - Challenging Problems

4. LOGARITHMS 300-318

- Definition
- Properties of Logarithm
- Properties of Monotonocity of Logarithm
- Graphs of Logarithmic Functions
- Characteristic
- Mantissa

Practice Milestone
JEE Main Pattern

5. PERMUTATIONS AND COMBINATIONS 319-395

Milestone 1 - Fundamental Principle of Counting
- Fundamental Principle of Counting
- Factorial Notation
- Divisibility Test
- Principle of Inclusion and Exclusion

Milestone 2 - Permutation
- Permutation
- Number of Permutations Under Certain Conditions
- Circular Permutation
- Restricted Circular Permutations
- Rank in a Dictionary
- Gap Method

Milestone 3 - Combination
- Combination
- Restricted Combinations
- Combination from Identical Objects
- Arrangements in Groups
- Multinomial Theorem
- Geometrical Problem

Practice Milestones
- Practice Milestone 1 - JEE Main Pattern
- Practice Milestone 2 - JEE Advanced Pattern
- Practice Milestone 3 - Challenging Problems

6. BINOMIAL THEOREM 396-470

Milestone 1 - Types of Theorem
- Binomial Theorem For Positive Integral Index
- Middle Term
- Greatest Term
- Trinomial Expansion

Milestone 2 - Theory of Equation
- Two Important Theorems
- Divisibility Problems
- Use of Complex Numbers in Binomial Theorem
- Multinomial Theorem
- Use of Differentiation
- Use of Integration
- Binomial Inside Binomial
- Sum of the Series

Practice Milestones
- Practice Milestone 1 - JEE Main Pattern
- Practice Milestone 2 - JEE Advanced Pattern
- Practice Milestone 3 - Challenging Problems

7. MATRICES 471-554

Milestone 1 - Types and Algebra of Matrices
- Definition
- Types of Matrices
- Algebra of Matrices
- Product of Two Matrices
- Various Kind of Matrices

Milestone 2 - Transpose, Singular and Non-singular Matrices
- Transpose of a Matrix
- Expansion of Determinant
- Singular and Non-singular Matrices

Milestone 3 - Adjoint and Inverse of a Matrix
- Minors and Cofactors
- Adjoint of a Matrix
- Inverse of a Matrix (Reciprocal Matrix)
- Matrix Polynomial

Milestone 4 - Eigen Values and Cayley-Hamilton Theorem
- Solutions of Linear Simultaneous Equation Using Matrix Method
- Eigen Values or Characteristics Roots and Characteristics Vectors of a Square Matrix
- Cayley-Hamilton Theorem

Practice Milestones
- Practice Milestone 1 - JEE Main Pattern
- Practice Milestone 2 - JEE Advanced Pattern
- Practice Milestone 3 - Challenging Problems

8. DETERMINANTS 555-650

Milestone 1 - Determinant
- Definition of Determinant
- Expansion of Determinant
- Sarrus Rule for Expansion

Milestone 2 - Properties of Determinant
- Minors and Cofactors
- Use of Determinants in Coordinate Geometry
- Properties of Determinants

Milestone 3 - Solving a System of Linear Equations
- Examples on Largest Value of a Third Order Determinant
- Multiplication of Two Determinants of the Same Order
- System of Linear Equations
- Cramer's Rule
- Nature of Solutions of System of Linear Equations
- System of Homogeneous Linear Equations

Milestone 4 - Differentiation and Integration of Determinant
- Differentiation of Determinant
- Integration of Determinant
- Use of Σ in Determinant

Practice Milestones
- Practice Milestone 1 - JEE Main Pattern
- Practice Milestone 2 - JEE Advanced Pattern
- Practice Milestone 3 - Challenging Problems

9. PROBABILITY 651-717

Milestone 1 - Classical Probability
- Some Basic Definitions
- Mathematical or Priori
- Odds in Favour and Odds Against the Event

Milestone 2 - Conditional Probability
- Algebra of Probability
- Conditional Probability
- Independent Events

Milestone 3 - Important Theorems of Probability
- Total Probability Theorem
- Baye's Theorem or Inverse Probability
- Binomial Theorem on Probability
- Expectation
- Uncountable Uniform Spaces

Practice Milestones
- Practice Milestone 1 - JEE Main Pattern
- Practice Milestone 2 - JEE Advanced Pattern
- Practice Milestone 3 - Challenging Problems

10. STATISTICS 718-769

Milestone 1 - Measures of Central Tendecy
- Mean (Arithmetic Mean)
- Geometric Mean
- Harmonic Mean
- Median
- Mode
- Relation between Mean, Mode and Median

Milestone 2 - Measures of Dispersion
- Range
- Mean Deviation
- Standard Deviation
- Variance

Practice Milestones
- Practice Milestone 1 - JEE Main Pattern
- Practice Milestone 2 - JEE Advanced Pattern
- Practice Milestone 3 - Challenging Problems

11. SETS AND RELATIONS 770-824

Milestone 1 - Sets
- Definition of Set
- Representation of Set
- Different Types of Sets
- Laws of Algebra of Sets
- Venn Diagrams (Euler-Venn Diagrams)

Milestone 2 - Relations
- Ordered Pair
- Definition of Relation
- Ordered Relation
- Composition of Two Relations

Practice Milestones
- Practice Milestone 1 - JEE Main Pattern
- Practice Milestone 2 - JEE Advanced Pattern
- Practice Milestone 3 - Challenging Problems

Syllabus

JEE Main

Unit 1: Sets and Relations

Sets and their representation: Union, intersection and complement of sets and their algebraic properties; Power set; Relation, Type of relations, equivalence relations.

Unit 2: Complex Numbers and Quadratic Equations:

Complex numbers as ordered pairs of reals, Representation of complex numbers in the form $a + ib$ and their representation in a plane, Argand diagram, algebra of complex number, modulus, and argument (or amplitude) of a complex number.

Quadratic equations in real and complex number system and their solutions, Relations between roots and coefficient, nature of roots, the formation of quadratic equations with given roots.

Unit 3: Matrices and Determinants:

Matrices, algebra of matrices, type of matrices, determinants, and matrices of order two and three, evaluation of determinants, area of triangles using determinants, Adjoint and evaluation of inverse of a square matrix using determinants and test of consistency and solution of simultaneous linear equations in two or three variables using matrices.

Unit 4: Permutations and Combinations:

The fundamental principle of counting, permutation as an arrangement and combination as section, Meaning of $P(n,r)$ and $C(n,r)$, simple applications.

Unit 5: Binomial Theorem and its Simple Applications:

Binomial theorem for a positive integral index, general term, middle term and simple applications.

Unit 6: Sequence and Series:

Arithmetic and Geometric progressions, insertion of arithmetic, geometric means between two given numbers, Relation between AM and GM.

Unit 7: Statistics and Probability

Measures of discretion calculation of mean, median, mode of grouped and ungrouped data.
Calculation of standard deviation, variance and mean deviation for grouped and ungrouped data.

Probability Probability of an event, addition and multiplication theorems of probability, Baye's theorem, probability distribution of a random variate.

JEE Advanced

Sets and Relations

Sets and their representations, different kinds of sets (empty, finite and infinite), algebra of sets, intersection, complement, difference and symmetric difference of sets and their algebraic properties, De-Morgan's laws on union, intersection, difference (for finite number of sets) and practical problems based on them.

Cartesian product of finite sets, ordered pair, relations, domain and codomain of relations, equivalence relation.

Algebra

Algebra of complex numbers, addition, multiplication, conjugation, polar representation, properties of modulus and principal argument, triangle inequality, cube roots of unity, geometric interpretations.

Statement of fundamental theorem of algebra, Quadratic equations with real coefficients, relations between roots and coefficients, formation of quadratic equations with given roots, symmetric functions of roots.

Arithmetic and geometric progressions, arithmetic and geometric means, sums of finite arithmetic and geometric progressions, infinite geometric series, sum of the first n natural numbers, sums of squares and cubes of the first n natural numbers. Logarithms and their properties, permutations and combinations, binomial theorem for a positive integral index, properties of binomial coefficients.

Matrices

Matrices as a rectangular array of real numbers, equality of matrices, addition, multiplication by a scalar and product of matrices, transpose of a matrix, elementary row and column transformations, determinant of a square matrix of order up to three, adjoint of a matrix, inverse of a square matrix of order up to three, properties of these matrix operations, diagonal, symmetric and skew-symmetric matrices and their properties, solutions of simultaneous linear equations in two or three variables.

Probability and Statistics

Random experiment, sample space, different types of events (impossible, simple, compound), addition and multiplication rules of probability, conditional probability, independence of events, total probability, Bayes Theorem, computation of probability of events using permutations and combinations.

Measure of central tendency and dispersion, mean, median, mode, mean deviation, standard deviation and variance of grouped and ungrouped data, analysis of the frequency distribution with same mean but different variance, random variable, mean and variance of the random variable.

1

> As far as the laws of Mathematics refer to reality, they do not certain, and as far as they are certain, they do not refer to reality.
>
> **-Albert Einstein**

Complex Number

Learning Milestones

Milestone 1 Definition of Complex Number, Algebra of Complex Number

- Introduction
- Definition of Complex Number
- Algebraic Operations on Complex Numbers

Milestone 2 Conjugate, Modulus and Argument of a Complex Number

- Conjugate of Complex Number
- Modulus of Complex Number
- Argument of Complex Number
- Polar Form of Complex Number
- Euler's Form of Complex Number
- Logarithm of Complex Number

Milestone 3 Square Root of Complex Number and De-Moivre's Theorem

- Square Root of Complex Number
- Solution of Complex Equation
- De-Moivre's Theorem
- Cube Root of Unity

Milestone 4 Complex Number in Geometry

- Vector Representation of Complex Numbers
- Geometrical Representation of Algebraic Operation on Complex Numbers
- Rotation Theorem (Coni Method)
- Shifting the Origin in Case of Complex Numbers
- Inverse Points
- Use of Complex Numbers in Coordinate Geometry

Practice Milestones

Practice Milestone 1- JEE Main Pattern

Practice Milestone 2 - JEE Advanced Pattern

Practice Milestone 3 - Challenging Problems

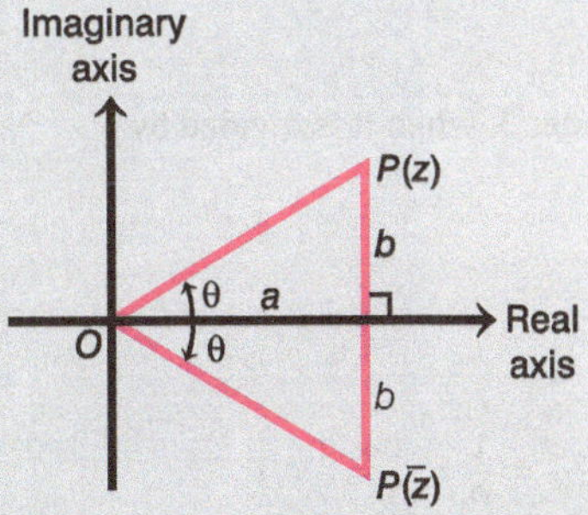

Milestone 1 Definition of Complex Number, Algebra of Complex Number

• Introduction • Definition of Complex Number • Algebraic Operations on Complex Numbers

1.1 Introduction

The square of any real number, whether positive, negative or zero, is always non-negative i.e. $x^2 \geq 0$ for all $x \in R$. Therefore, there will be no real value of x, which when squared, will give a negative number.

Thus, the equation $x^2+1=0$ is not satisfied for any real value of x. 'Euler' was the first Mathematician to introduce the symbol i (read 'Iota') for the square root of -1 with the property $i^2=-1$. The theory of complex number was later on developed by Gauss and Hamilton. According to Hamilton, 'Imaginary number is that number whose square is a negative number'. Hence, the equation $x^2+1=0$

$$\Rightarrow \qquad x^2=-1 \text{ or } x=\pm\sqrt{-1}$$

(in the sense of arithmetic, $\sqrt{-1}$ has no meaning)

Symbolically, $\sqrt{-1}$ is denoted by i (the first letter of the word 'Imaginary '.

$\therefore$ Solutions of $x^2+1=0$ are $x=\pm i$.

Also, i is the unit of complex number, since i is present in every complex number.

Generally, if a is positive quantity, then

$$\sqrt{-a}\times\sqrt{-a}=\sqrt{(-1)\times a}\times\sqrt{(-1)\times a}$$
$$=\sqrt{-1}\times\sqrt{a}\times\sqrt{-1}\times\sqrt{a}$$
$$=i\sqrt{a}\times i\sqrt{a}=i^2a=-a$$

JEE SPIKE

$\sqrt{-a}=i\sqrt{a}$, where a is positive quantity. Keeping this result in mind, the following computation is correct

$$\sqrt{-a}\sqrt{-b}=i\sqrt{a}\cdot i\sqrt{b}=i^2\sqrt{ab}=-\sqrt{ab}$$

where, a and b are positive real numbers.

But the computation, $\sqrt{-a}\sqrt{-b}=\sqrt{(-a)(-b)}=\sqrt{|a||b|}$ is wrong.

Because the property, $\sqrt{a}\sqrt{b}=\sqrt{ab}$ is valid only when atleast one of a and b is non-negative.

If a and b are both negative, then $\sqrt{a}\sqrt{b}=-\sqrt{|a||b|}$.

Example 1. Is the following computation correct? If not, give the correct computation.

$$\sqrt{-2}\sqrt{-3}=\sqrt{(-2)(-3)}=\sqrt{6}$$

Sol. No, if a and b are both negative real numbers, then

$\sqrt{a}\sqrt{b}=-\sqrt{|a||b|}$

Here, $a=-2$ and $b=-3$.

$$\therefore \qquad \sqrt{-2}\sqrt{-3}=-\sqrt{|(-2)||(-3)|}=-\sqrt{6}$$

Example 2. Explain the fallacy

$$-1=i\times i=\sqrt{-1}\times\sqrt{-1}=\sqrt{(-1)\times(-1)}=\sqrt{1}=1.$$

Sol. If a and b are both negative, then

$$\sqrt{a}\sqrt{b}=-\sqrt{|a||b|}$$
$$\therefore \qquad \sqrt{-1}\times\sqrt{-1}=-\sqrt{|-1||-1|}=-1$$

Integral Power of Iota (i)

If the power of iota is an integer, then

(i) $i^2=-1$ (ii) $i^3=-i$ (iii) $i^4=1$

(iv) $i^{4n+r}=i^r$, where $n\in N$ and $r=0, 1, 2, 3$

(v) $\frac{1}{i}=-i$

Example 3. Evaluate.

(i) i^{1998} (ii) i^{-9999} (iii) $(-\sqrt{-1})^{4n+3}, n\in N$

Sol. (i) 1998 leaves remainder 2, when it is divided by 4.
We can divide only last two digit to get remainder

i.e.
$$4\overline{)98}(24$$
$$\begin{array}{r} 8 \\ \hline 18 \\ 16 \\ \hline 2 \end{array}$$

$$\therefore \quad i^{1998}=i^2=-1$$

(ii) 9999 leaves remainder 3, when it is divided by 4

i.e.
$$4\overline{)99}(24$$
$$\begin{array}{r} 8 \\ \hline 19 \\ 16 \\ \hline 3 \end{array}$$

$$\therefore \qquad i^{-9999}=\frac{1}{i^{9999}}=\frac{1}{i^3}=\frac{i}{i^4}=\frac{i}{1}=i$$

(iii) $4n+3$ leaves remainder 3, when it is divided by 4

i.e. $4\overline{)4n+3}(n$
$\quad\underline{4n}$
$\quad\ 3$

$\therefore \quad i^{4n+3} = i^3 = -i$

Now, $(-\sqrt{-1})^{4n+3} = (-i)^{4n+3} = -(i)^{4n+3}$
$= -(-i)$
$= i$

JEE SPIKE

The Sum of Four Consecutive Powers of *i* (Iota) is Zero

If $n \in I$ and $i = \sqrt{-1}$, then

$$i^n + i^{n+1} + i^{n+2} + i^{n+3} = i^n(1 + i + i^2 + i^3)$$
$$= i^n(1 + i - 1 - i) = 0$$

Example 4. Find the value of $1 + i^2 + i^4 + i^6 + \ldots + i^{2n}$, where $i = \sqrt{-1}$ and $n \in N$.

Sol. $\because \quad 1 + i^2 + i^4 + i^6 + \ldots + i^{2n} = 1 - 1 + 1 - 1 + \ldots + (-1)^n$

***Case* I** If n is odd, then

$$1 + i^2 + i^4 + i^6 + \ldots + i^{2n} = 1 - 1 + 1 - 1 + \ldots + 1 - 1 = 0$$

***Case* II** If n is even, then

$$1 + i^2 + i^4 + i^6 + \ldots + i^{2n} = 1 - 1 + 1 - 1 + \ldots + 1 = 1$$

Example 5. If $a = \dfrac{1+i}{\sqrt{2}}$, where $i = \sqrt{-1}$, then find the value of a^{1929}.

Sol. $\because \quad a^2 = \left(\dfrac{1+i}{\sqrt{2}}\right)^2 = \left(\dfrac{1+i^2+2i}{2}\right)$

$$= \left(\frac{1-1+2i}{2}\right) = i$$

$\therefore \quad a^{1929} = a \cdot a^{1928} = a \cdot (a^2)^{964} = a\,(i)^{964}$

$$= a\,(i)^{4 \times 241}$$
$$= a \cdot (i^4)^{241} = a$$

Example 6. Find the value of

$$\frac{i^{492} + i^{490} + i^{488} + i^{486} + i^{484}}{i^{482} + i^{480} + i^{478} + i^{476} + i^{474}} - 2.$$

Sol. $\because \quad \dfrac{i^{492} + i^{490} + i^{488} + i^{486} + i^{484}}{i^{482} + i^{480} + i^{478} + i^{476} + i^{474}} - 2$

$$= \frac{i^{10}(i^{482} + i^{480} + i^{478} + i^{476} + i^{474})}{(i^{482} + i^{480} + i^{478} + i^{476} + i^{474})} - 2$$

$$= i^{10} - 2 = -1 - 2 = -3$$

JEE SCANNER

Example Similar to PYQ Asked in JEE Main 2021

The least positive integer n such that $\dfrac{(1+i)^n}{(1-i)^{n-2}}$, $i = \sqrt{-1}$, is a positive integer, is ....

Sol. Given, $\dfrac{(1+i)^n}{(1-i)^{n-2}}$

For $n = 0$, $\quad \dfrac{(1+i)^0}{(1-i)^{-2}} = (1-i)^2$

$$= 1 - 1 - 2i = -2i,$$

which is not a positive integer.

For $n = 1$, $\quad \dfrac{(1+i)}{(1-i)^{-1}} = (1+i)(1-i)$

$$= 1 - (-1) = 1 + 1 = 2$$

Here, 2 is a positive integer.

$\therefore$ The least positive integer n is 1.

Skill Builder

The least positive integers n such that $\left(\dfrac{2i}{1+i}\right)^n$, $i = \sqrt{-1}$, is a positive integer, is ....

For Sol.

■ **For more practice** See Q.10 of Milestone Practice 1.1.

Example 7. Dividing $f(z)$ by $z - i$, where $i = \sqrt{-1}$, we obtain the remainder i and dividing it by $z + i$, we get the remainder $1 + i$. Find the remainder upon the division of $f(z)$ by $z^2 + 1$.

Sol. $z - i = 0 \Rightarrow z = i$

Remainder, when $f(z)$ is divided by $(z - i) = i$

i.e. $\quad f(i) = i \quad \ldots$ (i)

and remainder, when $f(z)$ is divided by $(z + 1) = 1 + i$

i.e. $\quad f(-i) = 1 + i \quad [\because z + i = 0 \Rightarrow z = -i] \ldots$ (ii)

Since, $z^2 + 1$ is a quadratic expression, therefore remainder when $f(z)$ is divided by $z^2 + 1$, will be in general a linear expression.

Let $g(z)$ be the quotient and $az + b$ (where a and b are complex numbers) be the remainder, when $f(z)$ is divided by $z^2 + 1$.

Then, $\quad f(z) = (z^2 + 1)\,g(z) + az + b \quad \ldots$ (iii)

$\therefore \quad f(i) = (i^2 + 1)\,g(i) + ai + b = ai + b$

or $\quad ai + b = i \quad$ [from Eq. (i)] ... (iv)

and $\quad f(-i) = (i^2 + 1)\,g(-i) - ai + b = -ai + b$

or $\quad -ai + b = 1 + i \quad$ [from Eq. (ii)] ...(v)

From Eqs. (iv) and (v), we get

$$b = \frac{1}{2} + i \quad \text{and} \quad a = \frac{i}{2}$$

Hence, required remainder $= az + b$

$$= \frac{1}{2} iz + \frac{1}{2} + i$$

Example 8. Find the value of $\sum_{n=1}^{13} (i^n + i^{n+1})$ (where, $i = \sqrt{-1}$)

Sol. $\because \sum_{n=1}^{13} (i^n + i^{n+1}) = \sum_{n=1}^{13} i^n + \sum_{n=1}^{13} i^{n+1}$

$$= (i + 0) + (i^2 + 0)$$

$$= i - 1$$

$\left[\because \sum_{n=2}^{13} i^n = 0 \text{ and } \sum_{n=2}^{13} i^{n+1} = 0\right.$ (three sets of four consecutive powers of i)$\Big]$

Example 9. Find the value of $\sum_{n=0}^{100} i^{n!}$ (where, $i = \sqrt{-1}$).

Sol. $n!$ is divisible by 4, $\forall\, n \geq 4$.

$$\therefore \sum_{n=4}^{100} i^{n!} = \sum_{n=1}^{97} i^{(n+3)!}$$

$$= i^0 + i^0 + i^0 + \dots 97 \text{ times } = 97 \quad \text{...(i)}$$

$$\therefore \sum_{n=0}^{100} i^{n!} = \sum_{n=0}^{3} i^{n!} + \sum_{n=4}^{100} i^{n!}$$

$$= i^{0!} + i^{1!} + i^{2!} + i^{3!} + 97 \quad \text{[from Eq. (i)]}$$

$$= i^1 + i^1 + i^2 + i^6 + 97$$

$$= i + i - 1 - 1 + 97$$

$$= 95 + 2i$$

Example 10. Find the value of $\sum_{r=1}^{4n+7} i^r$ (where, $i = \sqrt{-1}$).

Sol. $\sum_{r=1}^{4n+7} i^r = i^1 + i^2 + i^3 + \sum_{r=4}^{4n+7} i^r = i - 1 - i + \sum_{r=1}^{4n+4} i^{r+3}$

$= -1 + 0$ [$(n+1)$ sets of four consecutive powers of i]

$= -1$

Example 11. Show that the polynomial $x^{4p} + x^{4q+1} + x^{4r+2} + x^{4s+3}$ is divisible by $x^3 + x^2 + x + 1$, where $p, q, r, s \in N$.

Sol. Let $f(x) = x^{4p} + x^{4q+1} + x^{4r+2} + x^{4s+3}$

and $x^3 + x^2 + x + 1 = (x^2 + 1)(x + 1)$

$$= (x + i)(x - i)(x + 1),$$

where $i = \sqrt{-1}$

Now, $f(i) = i^{4p} + i^{4q+1} + i^{4r+2} + i^{4s+3}$

$$= 1 + i + i^2 + i^3$$

$$= 0$$

[sum of four consecutive powers of i is zero]

$$f(-i) = (-i)^{4p} + (-i)^{4q+1} + (-i)^{4r+2} + (-i)^{4s+3}$$

$$= 1 + (-i)^1 + (-i)^2 + (-i)^3$$

$$= 1 - i - 1 + i$$

$$= 0$$

and $f(-1) = (-1)^{4p} + (-1)^{4q+1} + (-1)^{4r+2} + (-1)^{4s+3}$

$$= 1 - 1 + 1 - 1$$

$$= 0$$

Hence, by division theorem, $f(x)$ is divisible by $x^3 + x^2 + x + 1$.

1.2 Definition of Complex Number

A number of the form $a + ib$, where $a, b \in R$ and $i = \sqrt{-1}$, is called a **complex number.** It is denoted by z i.e. $z = a + ib$.

A complex number may also be defined as an ordered pair of real numbers; and may be denoted by the symbol (a, b). If we write $z = (a, b)$, then a is called the real part and b is the imaginary part of the complex number z and may be denoted by Re (z) and Im (z), respectively i.e., $a = \text{Re}(z)$ and $b = \text{Im}(z)$.

JEE Focus Points

- Every real number is a complex number.
- The set of real numbers (R) is a proper subset of the complex numbers (C) i.e. $R \subset C$. Hence, the complex number system is $N \subset W < I \subset Q < R \subset C$.
- Zero is both purely real and purely imaginary number.
- In case of purely imaginary number, real part must be zero and imaginary part may or may not be zero.
- Every real number is purely real and every purely real number is real but an imaginary number may not be purely imaginary, there is a purely imaginary number 0 which is not an imaginary number. An imaginary number is the form of $a + ib$, where b is a non-zero real number.

Representation of Complex Number on Argand Plane

A complex number $z = x + iy$ can be represented on Argand plane or Complex plane or Gaussian plane.

Let O be the origin and OX and OY be the X-axis and Y-axis, respectively. Corresponding to each complex number $x + iy$ there will be one and only one point $P(x, y)$ in the XY-plane.

Thus, each complex number $x+iy$ can be represented by a point $P(x,y)$ of the XY-plane and conversely corresponding to each point $P(x,y)$ of the XY-plane will be unique complex number $x+iy$. The XY-plane is called the argand plane or complex plane X-axis is called the real axis and Y-axis is imaginary axis.

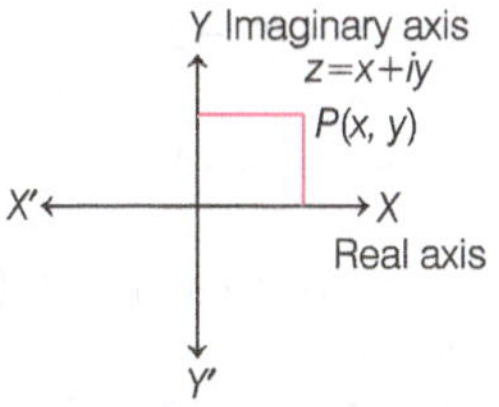

Equality of Complex Number

Two complex numbers are said to be equal, if and only if their real parts and imaginary parts are separately equal.

Thus, $a+ib=c+id$

$\Leftrightarrow \quad a=c$ and $b=d$

where, $a,b,c,d \in R$ and $i=\sqrt{-1}$.

i.e. $z_1 = z_2$

$\Leftrightarrow \quad \text{Re}(z_1)=\text{Re}(z_2)$ and $\text{Im}(z_1)=\text{Im}(z_2)$

JEE SPIKE

Inequality relation does not hold good in case of complex number having non-zero imaginary part.
i.e. $a+ib >$ or $< c+id$ is not define $b, d \neq 0$.
e.g. $9+6i > 3+2i$ makes no sense.

Example 12. Find the value of
(i) $(3y-2)+(5-4x)i=0$
(ii) $x+4yi=ix+y+3$

Sol. (i) Given, $(3y-2)+(5-4x)i=0$

$\Rightarrow \quad (3y-2)+(5-4x)i=0+0i$

Equating real and imaginary parts separately

$3y-2=0$ and $5-4x=0$

$\Rightarrow \quad y=\frac{2}{3}$ and $x=\frac{5}{4}$

(ii) Given, $x+4yi=ix+y+3$

$\Rightarrow \quad x+4yi=(y+3)+ix$

Equating real and imaginary part

$x=y+3$ and $4y=x$

$\Rightarrow \quad 4y=y+3$

$\Rightarrow \quad 3y=3, y=1$

and $\quad x=4y$

$\Rightarrow \quad x=4(1)=4$

$\therefore \quad x=4, y=1$

1.3 Algebraic Operations on Complex Numbers

Let two complex numbers be $z_1=a+ib$ and $z_2=c+id$, where $a,b,c,d \in R$ and $i=\sqrt{-1}$.

1. **Addition** $z_1+z_2=(a+ib)+(c+id)$
$= (a+c)+i(b+d)$
2. **Subtraction** $z_1-z_2=(a+ib)-(c+id)$
$=(a-c)+i(b-d)$
3. **Multiplication** $z_1\cdot z_2=(a+ib)\cdot(c+id)$
$=ac+iad+ibc+i^2bd$
$=ac+i(ad+bc)-bd$
$=(ac-bd)+i(ad+bc)$
4. **Division** $\frac{z_1}{z_2}=\frac{a+ib}{c+id}=\frac{(a+ib)}{(c+id)}\cdot\frac{(c-id)}{(c-id)}$

[multiplying numerator and denominator by $c-id$, where atleast one of c and d is non-zero]

$$=\frac{ac-iad+ibc-i^2bd}{(c)^2-(id)^2}=\frac{ac+i(bc-ad)+bd}{c^2-i^2d^2}$$

$$=\frac{(ac+bd)+i(bc-ad)}{c^2+d^2}$$

$$=\frac{(ac+bd)}{(c^2+d^2)}+i\frac{(bc-ad)}{(c^2+d^2)}$$

Properties of Algebraic Operations on Complex Numbers

Let z_1, z_2 and z_3 be any three complex numbers. Then, their algebraic operations satisfy the following properties :

Properties of Addition of Complex Numbers

(i) **Closure law** z_1+z_2 is a complex number.
(ii) **Commutative law** $z_1+z_2=z_2+z_1$
(iii) **Associative law** $(z_1+z_2)+z_3=z_1+(z_2+z_3)$
(iv) **Additive identity** $z+0=z=0+z$, then 0 is called the additive identity.
(v) **Additive inverse** $-z$ is called the additive inverse of z, i.e. $z+(-z)=0$.

Properties of Multiplication of Complex Numbers

(i) **Closure law** $z_1\cdot z_2$ is a complex number.
(ii) **Commutative law** $z_1\cdot z_2=z_2\cdot z_1$
(iii) **Associative law** $(z_1\cdot z_2)z_3=z_1(z_2\cdot z_3)$

(iv) **Multiplicative identity** $z \cdot 1 = z = 1 \cdot z$, then 1 is called the multiplicative identity.

(v) **Multiplicative inverse** If z is a non-zero complex number, then $\frac{1}{z}$ is called the multiplicative inverse of z i.e. $z.\ \frac{1}{z} = 1 = \frac{1}{z} \cdot z$

(vi) **Multiplication is distributive with respect to addition** $z_1(z_2 + z_3) = z_1 z_2 + z_1 z_3$

Example 13. If $z_1 = 2 + 3i$ and $z_2 = -1 + 2i$, then find

(i) $z_1 + z_2$ (ii) $z_1 - z_2$

(iii) $z_1 \cdot z_2$ (iv) $\frac{z_1}{z_2}$

Sol. We have, $z_1 = 2 + 3i$ and $z_2 = -1 + 2i$

(i) $z_1 + z_2 = (2 + 3i) + (-1 + 2i)$

$= (2 - 1) + (3 + 2)i = 1 + 5i$

(ii) $z_1 - z_2 = (2 + 3i) - (-1 + 2i)$

$= (2 - (-1)) + (3 - 2)i = 3 + i$

(iii) $z_1 \cdot z_2 = (2 + 3i)(-1 + 2i)$

$= -2 + 4i - 3i + 6i^2 = -2 + i - 6 = -8 + i$

(iv) $\frac{z_1}{z_2} = \frac{2 + 3i}{-1 + 2i}$

$= \frac{2 + 3i}{-1 + 2i} \times \frac{-1 - 2i}{-1 - 2i}$

$= \frac{-2 - 4i - 3i - 6i^2}{1 + 4} = \frac{4 - 7i}{5} = \frac{4}{5} - \frac{7}{5}i$

Example 14. $\frac{3 + 2i\sin\theta}{1 - 2i\sin\theta}$ will be purely imaginary, if $\theta =$

(a) $2n\pi \pm \frac{\pi}{3}, n \in I$ (b) $n\pi + \frac{\pi}{3}, n \in I$

(c) $n\pi \pm \frac{\pi}{3}, n \in I$ (d) None of these

Sol. (c) Let $z = \frac{3 + 2i\sin\theta}{1 - 2i\sin\theta} = \frac{3 + 2i\sin\theta}{1 - 2i\sin\theta} \times \frac{1 + 2i\sin\theta}{1 + 2i\sin\theta}$

$= \frac{3 + 6i\sin\theta + 2i\sin\theta - 4\sin^2\theta}{1 + 4\sin^2\theta}$

$= \frac{(3 - 4\sin^2\theta) + i(8\sin\theta)}{1 + 4\sin^2\theta}$

For z to be purely imaginary,

$\text{Re}(z) = 0 \Rightarrow 3 - 4\sin^2\theta = 0$

$\Rightarrow \sin^2\theta = \left(\frac{\sqrt{3}}{2}\right)^2 = \left(\sin\frac{\pi}{3}\right)^2$

$\Rightarrow \theta = n\pi \pm \frac{\pi}{3}, n \in I$

Example 15. Find the value of x and y if

$\frac{(1 + i)x - 2i}{3 + i} + \frac{(2 - 3i)y + i}{3 - i} = i.$

Sol. We have, $\frac{(1 + i)x - 2i}{3 + i} + \frac{(2 - 3i)y + i}{3 - i} = i$

$\Rightarrow [(1 + i)x - 2i](3 - i) + [(2 - 3i)y + i](3 + i) = (3 + i)(3 - i)i$

$\Rightarrow 3x + 3ix - 6i - ix + x - 2 + 6y - 9yi + 3i + 2iy + 3y - 1 = 10i$

$\Rightarrow (4x + 9y - 3) + i(2x - 7y - 3) = 10i$

On comparing, we get

$4x + 9y - 3 = 0$ and $2x - 7y - 3 = 10$

$\therefore x = 3, y = -1$

JEE SCANNER

Example Similar to PYQ Asked in JEE Main 2019

Let $\left(-3 - \frac{1}{4}i\right)^3 = \frac{x + iy}{64}$, where $i = \sqrt{-1}$ and x, y are real numbers, then $2y - x$ equal to

(a) -830 (b) 830 (c) 833 (d) -833

Sol. (b) Given, $\left(-3 - \frac{1}{4}i\right)^3 = (-3)^3 - \left(\frac{1}{4}i\right)^3 + \frac{9}{4}i\left(-3 - \frac{1}{4}i\right)$

$= -27 + \frac{1}{64}i - \frac{27}{4}i + \frac{9}{16}$

$= \frac{-423}{16} - \frac{431}{64}i$

$= \frac{-1692 - 431i}{64}$

$= \frac{-(1692 + 431i)}{64}$

$\therefore x = -1692$ and $y = -431$

$\Rightarrow 2y - x = 2(-431) + 1692$

$= -862 + 1692 = 830$

Skill Builder

For Sol.

Let $\left(\frac{1}{2} + 5i\right)^2 = \frac{x + iy}{4}$, where $i = \sqrt{-1}$ and x, y are real numbers, then $x + y$ equal to

(a) -79 (b) 79 (c) 110 (d) -110

■ **For more practice** See Q.11 of Milestone Practice 1.1.

Example 16. Find the value of $x^3 + 7x^2 - x + 16$, if $x = 1 + 2i$.

Sol. We have, $x = 1 + 2i \Rightarrow x - 1 = 2i$

$\Rightarrow (x - 1)^2 = -4 \Rightarrow x^2 - 2x + 5 = 0$

Now, $x^3 + 7x^2 - x + 16$

$$= x(x^2 - 2x + 5) + 9(x^2 - 2x + 5) + 12x - 29$$
$$= x(0) + 9(0) + 12x - 29$$
$$= 12x - 29 = 12(1 + 2i) - 29$$
$$= 12 + 24i - 29 = -17 + 24i$$

Example 17. Find the least positive integral value of n, for which $\left(\frac{1-i}{1+i}\right)^n$, where $i = \sqrt{-1}$, is purely imaginary with positive imaginary part.

Sol. $\left(\frac{1-i}{1+i}\right)^n = \left(\frac{1-i}{1+i} \times \frac{1-i}{1-i}\right)^n$

$$= \left(\frac{1 + i^2 - 2i}{2}\right)^n = \left(\frac{1 - 1 - 2i}{2}\right)^n$$

$$= (-i)^n = \text{Imaginary}$$

$\Rightarrow$ $n = 1, 3, 5, \ldots$ for positive imaginary part $n = 3$.

Example 18. Let z be a complex number satisfying the equation $z^2 - (3 + i)z + \lambda + 2i = 0$, where $\lambda \in R$ and $i = \sqrt{-1}$. Suppose the equation has a real root, find the non-real root.

Sol. Let α be the real root. Then,

$$\alpha^2 - (3 + i)\alpha + \lambda + 2i = 0$$

$\Rightarrow$ $(\alpha^2 - 3\alpha + \lambda) + i(2 - \alpha) = 0$

On comparing real and imaginary parts, we get

$$\alpha^2 - 3\alpha + \lambda = 0 \quad \text{...(i)}$$

$\Rightarrow$ $2 - \alpha = 0$ ...(ii)

From Eq. (ii), we get

$$\alpha = 2$$

Let other root be β.

Then, $\alpha + \beta = 3 + i$

$\Rightarrow$ $2 + \beta = 3 + i$

$\therefore$ $\beta = 1 + i$

Hence, the non-real root is $1 + i$.

Milestone Practice 1.1

1. Find the value of $(x - 1)^4$, if $x = 1 + i$.

2. $\sqrt{-9} \times \sqrt{\frac{-25}{9}}$ is equal to

   (a) 5 (b) -5 (c) $5i$ (d) $-5i$

3. If m, n, p and q are consecutive integers, then the value of $i^m + i^n + i^p + i^q$ is

   (a) 1 (b) 4
   (c) 0 (d) None of these

4. Which of the following is correct?

   (a) $1 + i > 2 - i$ (b) $2 + i > 1 + i$
   (c) $2 - i > 1 + i$ (d) None of these

5. Find the value of $i^{1+3+5+\ldots+(2n+1)}$, if

   (i) n is even (ii) n is odd

6. Evaluate $i + 2i^2 + 3i^3 + \ldots +$ upto 100 terms.

7. The value of $\sum_{n=0}^{50} i^{(2n+1)!}$ is

   (a) i (b) $47 - i$ (c) $48 + i$ (d) 1

8. If $z_1 = 3 - 2i$, $z_2 = 2 - i$, $z_3 = 2 + 5i$ and $z = z_1 + z_2 - 2z_3$, find Re(z) and Im(z).

9. If $x = -5 + 2\sqrt{-4}$, find the value of $x^4 + 9x^3 + 35x^2 - x + 4$.

10. Find the least positive integer n such that $\left(\frac{1-i}{1+i}\right)^{2n} = 1$.

11. If $\left(\frac{2}{3} + \frac{4}{5}i\right)^2 = \frac{a + bi}{225}$, where $i = \sqrt{-1}$ and a, b are real numbers, then find $\left(\frac{a+b}{2}\right)$.

12. If the roots of the equation $z^2 + (p + iq)x + r + is = 0$ are real where $p, q, r, s \in R$, then prove that $s^2 + q^2 r = pqs$.

13. If $S = \{i^n + i^{-n} : n \in Z\}$, then find S.

14. If $\sqrt{3} + i = (a + ib)(c + id)$, then $\tan^{-1}\frac{b}{a} + \tan^{-1}\frac{d}{c}$ is equal to

    (a) $\frac{\pi}{3} + 2n\pi, n \in Z$ (b) $n\pi + \frac{\pi}{6}, n \in Z$
    (c) $n\pi - \frac{\pi}{3}, n \in Z$ (d) $2n\pi - \frac{\pi}{3}, n \in Z$

Answer Key

1. (1)	2. (b)	3. (c)	4. (d)	5. (i) i (ii) 1	6. $50(1 - i)$	7. (c)
8. $(1, -13)$	9. -160	10. (2)	11. (98)	13. $\{-2, 0, 2\}$	14. (b)	

For Detailed Solution

Milestone 2 Conjugate, Modulus and Argument of a Complex Number

• Conjugate of Complex Number • Modulus of Complex Number • Argument of Complex Number
• Polar Form of Complex Number • Euler's Form of Complex Number • Logarithm of Complex Number

1.4 Conjugate of Complex Numbers

The complex numbers $z = (a, b) = a + ib$ and $\bar{z} = (a, -b) = a - ib$, where a and b are real numbers, $i = \sqrt{-1}$ and $b \neq 0$, are said to be complex conjugate of each other (here, the complex conjugate is obtained by just changing the sign of i).

Note that, sum $= (a + ib) + (a - ib) = 2a$, which is real.

And product $= (a + ib)(a - ib) = a^2 - (ib)^2$

$$= a^2 - i^2 b^2 = a^2 - (-1) b^2$$

$$= a^2 + b^2, \text{ which is real.}$$

Geometrically, $\bar{z}$ is the mirror image of z along real axis on argand plane.

JEE SPIKE

Let $z = a + ib, a > 0, b > 0 = (a, b)$ (I quadrant)

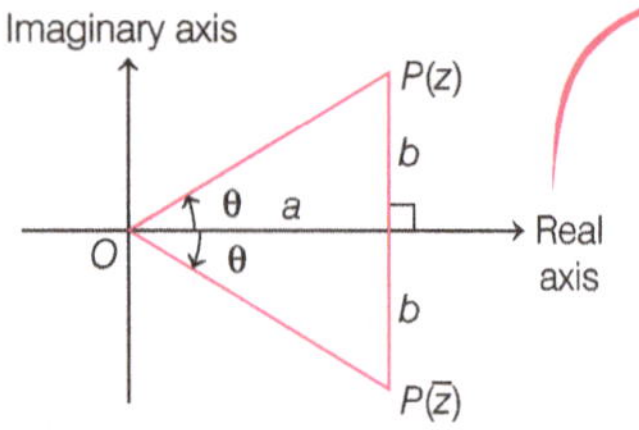

Concept Inside Video

Then, $\bar{z} = a - ib = (a, -b)$ (IV quadrant). Now,

(i) if z lies in I quadrant, then $\bar{z}$ lies in IV quadrant and *vice-versa*.

(ii) if z lies in II quadrant, then $\bar{z}$ lies in III quadrant and *vice-versa*.

Example 19. Find the conjugate of the complex number $z = \dfrac{1+3i}{1-2i}$.

Sol. We have, $z = \dfrac{1+3i}{1-2i} = \dfrac{1+3i}{1-2i} \times \dfrac{1+2i}{1+2i} = \dfrac{1+2i+3i-6}{1+4}$

$$= \frac{-5+5i}{5} = -1 + i$$

$\therefore \quad \bar{z} = -1 - i$

Properties of Conjugate Complex Numbers

Let z, z_1 and z_2 be complex numbers. Then,

(i) $\overline{(\bar{z})} = z$

(ii) $z + \bar{z} = 2\,\text{Re}\,(z)$

(iii) $z - \bar{z} = 2\,\text{Im}\,(z)$

(iv) $z + \bar{z} = 0 \Rightarrow z = -\bar{z}$
$\Rightarrow z$ is purely imaginary.

(v) $z - \bar{z} = 0 \Rightarrow z = \bar{z}$
$\Rightarrow z$ is purely real.

(vi) $\overline{z_1 \pm z_2} = \bar{z}_1 \pm \bar{z}_2$

In general,
$\overline{z_1 \pm z_2 \pm z_3 \pm \ldots \pm z_n} = \overline{z_1} \pm \overline{z_2} \pm \overline{z_3} \pm \ldots \pm \overline{z_n}$

(vii) $\overline{z_1 \cdot z_2} = \overline{z_1} \cdot \overline{z_2}$

In general, $\overline{z_1 \cdot z_2 \cdot z_3 \ldots z_n} = \overline{z_1} \cdot \overline{z_2} \cdot \overline{z_3} \ldots \overline{z_n}$

(viii) $\overline{\left(\dfrac{z_1}{z_2}\right)} = \dfrac{\bar{z}_1}{\bar{z}_2}, z_2 \neq 0$

(ix) $\overline{z^n} = (\bar{z})^n$

(x) $z_1 \overline{z_2} + \overline{z_1} z_2 = 2\,\text{Re}\,(z_1 \overline{z_2}) = 2\,\text{Re}\,(\overline{z_1} z_2)$

(xi) If $z = f(z_1, z_2)$, then $\bar{z} = f(\overline{z_1}, \overline{z_2})$

Example 20. If $(a + ib)^5 = p + iq$, where $i = \sqrt{-1}$, prove that $(b + ia)^5 = q + ip$.

Sol. $\because \quad (a + ib)^5 = p + iq$

$\therefore \quad \overline{(a + ib)^5} = \overline{p + iq}$

$\Rightarrow \quad (a - ib)^5 = (p - iq)$

$\Rightarrow \quad (-i^2 a - ib)^5 = (-i^2 p - iq) \qquad [\because i^2 = -1]$

$\Rightarrow \quad (-i)^5 (b + ia)^5 = (-i)(q + ip)$

$\Rightarrow \quad (-i)(b + ia)^5 = (-i)(q + ip)$

$\therefore \quad (b + ia)^5 = (q + ip)$

JEE SCANNER

Example Similar to PYQ Asked in JEE Main 2019

If $a > 0$ and $z = \dfrac{(1+i)^2}{a+i}$, has magnitude $\sqrt{\dfrac{2}{3}}$, then $\bar{z}$ is equal to

(a) $\dfrac{-1}{3} - \dfrac{\sqrt{5}}{3}i$ (b) $\dfrac{1}{3} - \dfrac{\sqrt{5}}{3}i$

(c) $\dfrac{1}{3} + \dfrac{\sqrt{5}}{3}i$ (d) $\dfrac{-1}{3} + \dfrac{\sqrt{5}}{3}i$

Sol. (b) Given, $z = \dfrac{(1+i)^2}{a+i} = \dfrac{2i}{a+i}$

$$= \frac{2i}{a+i} \times \frac{a-i}{a-i} = \frac{2ai+2}{a^2+1}$$

$$= \frac{2}{a^2+1} + \frac{2a}{a^2+1}i$$

$\because$ $|z| = \sqrt{\dfrac{2}{3}}$

$\Rightarrow$ $\sqrt{\dfrac{4}{(a^2+1)^2} + \dfrac{4a^2}{(a^2+1)^2}} = \sqrt{\dfrac{2}{3}}$

$\Rightarrow$ $\dfrac{4(a^2+1)}{(a^2+1)^2} = \dfrac{2}{3}$

$\Rightarrow$ $a^2 = 5$

$\therefore$ $z = \dfrac{2}{6} + \dfrac{2\sqrt{5}i}{6} = \dfrac{1}{3} + \dfrac{\sqrt{5}}{3}i \Rightarrow \bar{z} = \dfrac{1}{3} - \dfrac{\sqrt{5}}{3}i$

Skill Builder

If $a > 0$ and $z = \dfrac{(2+3i)^2}{a-i}$ has magnitude $\dfrac{1}{\sqrt{5}}$, then $\bar{z}$ is equal to

(a) $\dfrac{-52}{65} + \dfrac{91}{65}i$ (b) $\dfrac{52}{65} - \dfrac{91}{65}i$

(c) $\dfrac{-52}{65} - \dfrac{91}{65}i$ (d) $\dfrac{52}{65} + \dfrac{91}{65}i$

For Sol.

■ **For more practice** See Q.3 of Milestone Practice 1.2.

Example 21. Find real values of x and y for which the complex numbers $-3 + ix^2y$ and $x^2 + y + 4i$, where $i = \sqrt{-1}$, are conjugate to each other.

Sol. Given, $\overline{-3 + ix^2y} = x^2 + y + 4i$

$\Rightarrow$ $-3 - ix^2y = x^2 + y + 4i$

On comparing real and imaginary parts, we get

$$x^2 + y = -3 \quad \text{...(i)}$$

and $$-x^2y = 4 \quad \text{...(ii)}$$

From Eq. (ii), we get $x^2 = -\dfrac{4}{y}$

Then, $-\dfrac{4}{y} + y = -3$ $\left[\text{putting } x^2 = -\dfrac{4}{y} \text{ in Eq. (i)}\right]$

$y^2 + 3y - 4 = 0$

$\Rightarrow$ $(y+4)(y-1) = 0$

$\therefore$ $y = -4, 1$

For $y = -4$, $x^2 = 1$

$\Rightarrow$ $x = \pm 1$

For $y = 1$, $x^2 = -4$ [impossible]

$\therefore$ $x = \pm 1, y = -4$

Example 22. Find the condition on the complex constants α, β if $z^2 + \alpha z + \beta = 0$ has real roots.

Sol. We have, $z^2 + \alpha z + \beta = 0$ has real roots.

$\therefore$ $z = \bar{z}$

Now, $z^2 + \alpha z + \beta = 0$ ...(i)

$\therefore$ $\bar{z}^2 + \bar{\alpha}\,\bar{z} + \bar{\beta} = 0$

$\Rightarrow$ $z^2 + \bar{\alpha}\,z + \bar{\beta} = 0$ ...(ii)

On solving Eqs. (i) and (ii), we get

$$\frac{z^2}{\alpha\bar{\beta} - \bar{\alpha}\beta} = \frac{z}{\beta - \bar{\beta}} = \frac{1}{\bar{\alpha} - \alpha}$$

$\Rightarrow$ $z = \dfrac{\alpha\bar{\beta} - \bar{\alpha}\beta}{\beta - \bar{\beta}} = \dfrac{\beta - \bar{\beta}}{\bar{\alpha} - \alpha}$

$\Rightarrow$ $(\beta - \bar{\beta})^2 = (\bar{\alpha} - \alpha)(\alpha\bar{\beta} - \bar{\alpha}\beta)$

Example 23. If $(1+i)z = (1-i)\bar{z}$, then the value of $z + \bar{z}$ is

(a) $2t, \forall\, t \in R$

(b) $2it, \forall\, t \in R$

(c) $z - \bar{z}$

(d) None of the above

Sol. (a) We have, $(1+i)z = (1-i)\bar{z}$

$\Rightarrow$ $(1+i)z = \overline{(1+i)}\bar{z}$

$\Rightarrow$ $(1+i)z = \overline{(1+i)z}$

$\therefore$ $z(1+i)$ is purely real.

Now, $z(1+i) = \alpha, \alpha \in R$

$\Rightarrow$ $z = \dfrac{\alpha}{1+i}, \alpha \in R$

$\Rightarrow$ $z = \dfrac{\alpha(1-i)}{2}, \alpha \in R$

$\Rightarrow$ $z = t(1-i)$, where $t = \dfrac{\alpha}{2} \in R$

$\therefore$ $\bar{z} = t(1+i)$

Now, $z + \bar{z} = 2t, \forall\, t \in R$.

1.5 Modulus of a Complex Number

Let $z = x + iy$, then the length OP is called modulus of the complex number z denoted by $|z|$.

$$OP = r = |z| = \sqrt{x^2 + y^2}$$

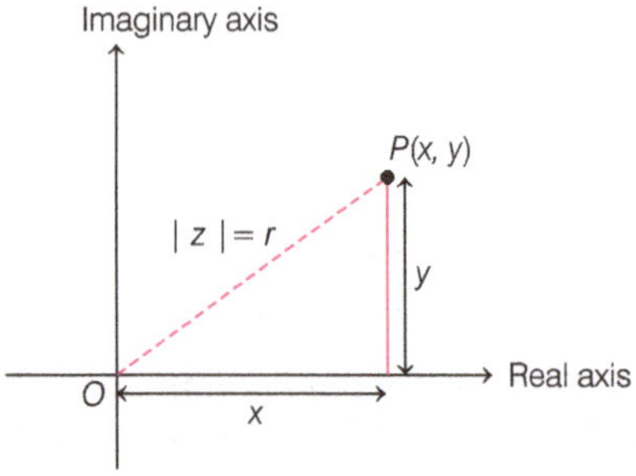

Example 24. Find the modulus of following complex numbers

(i) $3 + 4i$ (ii) $-4i$
(iii) 5 (iv) $8 - 6i$

Sol. (i) Let $z_1 = 3 + 4i$.

Then, $|z_1| = \sqrt{(3)^2 + (4)^2} = \sqrt{9 + 16} = 5$

(ii) Let $z_2 = -4i = 0 - 4i$.

Then, $|z_2| = \sqrt{(0)^2 + (-4)^2} = \sqrt{0 + 16} = 4$

(iii) Let $z_3 = 5 = 5 + 0i$.

Then, $|z_3| = \sqrt{(5)^2 + (0)^2} = \sqrt{25 + 0} = 5$

(iv) Let $z_4 = 8 - 6i$.

Then, $|z_4| = \sqrt{(8)^2 + (-6)^2} = \sqrt{64 + 36} = 10$

Properties of Modulus

(i) $|z| \geq 0 \Rightarrow |z| = 0$, iff $z = 0$ and $|z| > 0$, iff $z \neq 0$

(ii) $-|z| \leq \text{Re}(z) \leq |z|$ and $-|z| \leq \text{Im}(z) \leq |z|$

(iii) $|z| = |\bar{z}| = |-z| = |-\bar{z}|$

(iv) $z\bar{z} = |z|^2$

(v) $|z_1 z_2| = |z_1||z_2|$

In general, $|z_1 z_2 z_3 \ldots z_n| = |z_1||z_2||z_3| \ldots |z_n|$

(vi) $\left|\dfrac{z_1}{z_2}\right| = \dfrac{|z_1|}{|z_2|} \quad (z_2 \neq 0)$

(vii) $|z_1 \pm z_2| \leq |z_1| + |z_2|$

In general, $|z_1 \pm z_2 \pm z_3 \pm \ldots \pm z_n| \leq |z_1| + |z_2| + |z_3| + \ldots + |z_n|$

(viii) $|z_1 \pm z_2| \geq ||z_1| - |z_2||$

(ix) $|z^n| = |z|^n$

(x) $||z_1| - |z_2|| \leq |z_1 + z_2| \leq |z_1| + |z_2|$

Thus, $|z_1| + |z_2|$ is the greatest possible value of $|z_1 + z_2|$ and $||z_1| - |z_2||$ is the least possible value of $|z_1 + z_2|$.

(xi) $|z_1 \pm z_2|^2 = (z_1 \pm z_2)(\bar{z}_1 \pm \bar{z}_2)$

$= |z_1|^2 + |z_2|^2 \pm (z_1 \bar{z}_2 + \bar{z}_1 z_2)$

or $|z_1|^2 + |z_2|^2 \pm 2\,\text{Re}(z_1 \bar{z}_2)$

(xii) $z_1\bar{z}_2 + \bar{z}_1 z_2 = 2|z_1||z_2|\cos(\theta_1 - \theta_2)$, where $\theta_1 = \arg(z_1)$ and $\theta_2 = \arg(z_2)$

(xiii) $|z_1 + z_2|^2 = |z_1|^2 + |z_2|^2 \Leftrightarrow \dfrac{z_1}{z_2}$ is purely imaginary.

(xiv) $|z_1 + z_2|^2 + |z_1 - z_2|^2 = 2\{|z_1|^2 + |z_2|^2\}$

(xv) $|az_1 - bz_2|^2 + |bz_1 + az_2|^2 = (a^2 + b^2)(|z_1|^2 + |z_2|^2)$, where $a, b \in R$

(xvi) The multiplicative inverse of a non-zero complex number z is same as its reciprocal and is given by $\dfrac{1}{z} = \dfrac{\bar{z}}{z\bar{z}} = \dfrac{\bar{z}}{|z|^2}$.

(xvii) Unimodular i.e. unit modulus

If z is unimodular, then $|z| = 1$. In case of unimodular, let $z = \cos\theta + i\sin\theta, \theta \in R$ and $i = \sqrt{-1}$.

JEE Focus Points

- If $f(z)$ is unimodular, then $|f(z)| = 1$ and let $f(z) = \cos\theta + i\sin\theta, \theta \in R$ and $i = \sqrt{-1}$.
- $\dfrac{z}{|z|}$ is always a unimodular complex number, if $z \neq 0$.

Concept Inside Video

Example 25. If $z = \left[\dfrac{(3 + 4i)(1 + i)(1 + \sqrt{3}i)}{(1 - i)(4 - 3i)(2i)}\right]^2$, find $|z|$.

Sol. We have, $z = \left[\dfrac{(3 + 4i)(1 + i)(1 + \sqrt{3}i)}{(1 - i)(4 - 3i)(2i)}\right]^2$

$$\Rightarrow \quad |z| = \left[\left|\frac{(3 + 4i)(1 + i)(1 + \sqrt{3}i)}{(1 - i)(4 - 3i)(2i)}\right|\right]^2$$

$$= \left[\frac{|3 + 4i||1 + i||1 + \sqrt{3}i|}{|1 - i||4 - 3i||2i|}\right]^2 = \left[\frac{5 \times \sqrt{2} \times 2}{\sqrt{2} \times 5 \times 2}\right]^2 = 1$$

Example 26. If $z = x + iy$ such that $\text{Re}(z + 1) = |z - 1|$, then the value of $\dfrac{y^2}{x}$ is

(a) 1 (b) 2 (c) 3 (d) 4

Sol. (d) We have, $\text{Re}(z+1) = |z-1|$

$$\Rightarrow \quad \text{Re}(x+iy+1) = |x+iy-1|$$

$$\Rightarrow \quad x+1 = \sqrt{(x-1)^2+y^2}$$

$$\Rightarrow \quad (x+1)^2 = (x-1)^2 + y^2$$

$$\Rightarrow \quad x^2+2x+1 = x^2-2x+1+y^2$$

$$\Rightarrow \quad y^2 = 4x$$

$$\Rightarrow \quad \frac{y^2}{x} = 4$$

Example 27. If $|z_1| = 1, |z_2| = 2, |z_3| = 3$ and $|9z_1z_2 + 4z_3z_1 + z_2z_3| = 6$, find the value of $|z_1+z_2+z_3|$.

Sol. $\because \quad |z_1| = 1 \Rightarrow |z_1|^2 = 1$

$$\Rightarrow \quad z_1\bar{z}_1 = 1 \Rightarrow \frac{1}{z_1} = \bar{z}_1$$

$$|z_2| = 2 \Rightarrow |z_2|^2 = 4 \Rightarrow z_2\bar{z}_2 = 4 \Rightarrow \frac{4}{z_2} = \bar{z}_2$$

and $\quad |z_3| = 3 \Rightarrow |z_3|^2 = 9$

$$\Rightarrow \quad z_3\bar{z}_3 = 9 \Rightarrow \frac{9}{z_3} = \bar{z}_3$$

and given $|9z_1z_2 + 4z_3z_1 + z_2z_3| = 6$

$$\Rightarrow \quad |z_1z_2z_3|\left|\frac{9}{z_3} + \frac{4}{z_2} + \frac{1}{z_1}\right| = 6$$

$$\Rightarrow \quad |z_1||z_2||z_3||\bar{z}_3 + \bar{z}_2 + \bar{z}_1| = 6$$

$$\left[\because \frac{1}{z_1} = \bar{z}_1, \frac{4}{z_2} = \bar{z}_2 \text{ and } \frac{9}{z_3} = \bar{z}_3\right]$$

$$\Rightarrow \quad 1\cdot 2\cdot 3\,|\overline{z_1+z_2+z_3}| = 6$$

$$\therefore \quad |z_1+z_2+z_3| = 1 \qquad [\because |\bar{z}| = |z|]$$

Example 28. Prove that

$$|z_1| + |z_2| = \left|\frac{1}{2}(z_1+z_2) + \sqrt{z_1z_2}\right| + \left|\frac{1}{2}(z_1+z_2) - \sqrt{z_1z_2}\right|.$$

Sol. $\text{RHS} = \left|\frac{1}{2}(z_1+z_2) + \sqrt{z_1z_2}\right| + \left|\frac{1}{2}(z_1+z_2) - \sqrt{z_1z_2}\right|$

$$= \left|\frac{z_1+z_2+2\sqrt{z_1z_2}}{2}\right| + \left|\frac{z_1+z_2-2\sqrt{z_1z_2}}{2}\right|$$

$$= \frac{1}{2}\{|\sqrt{z_1}+\sqrt{z_2}|^2 + |\sqrt{z_1}-\sqrt{z_2}|^2\}$$

$$= \frac{1}{2}\cdot 2\{|\sqrt{z_1}|^2 + |\sqrt{z_2}|^2\} \qquad [\text{by property (xiv)}]$$

$$= |z_1| + |z_2| = \text{LHS}$$

JEE SCANNER

Example Similar to PYQ Asked in JEE Main 2019

If $z \neq 0$ be a complex number such that $|z| + z = 4 + 2i$ (where $i = \sqrt{-1}$). Then, $|z|$ is equal to

(a) $\frac{\sqrt{25}}{2}$ (b) $\frac{5}{2}$ (c) $\frac{\sqrt{21}}{4}$ (d) $\frac{5}{3}$

Sol. (b) Let $\quad z = x+iy$

$$\because \quad |z| + z = 4+2i$$

$$\sqrt{x^2+y^2} + x + iy = 4+2i$$

On comparing both sides, we get

$$\sqrt{x^2+y^2} + x = 4 \text{ and } y = 2$$

$$\Rightarrow \quad \sqrt{x^2+y^2} = 4-x$$

$$\Rightarrow \quad x^2+y^2 = (4-x)^2$$

$$\Rightarrow \quad x^2+y^2 = 16+x^2-8x$$

$$\Rightarrow \quad 4-16 = -8x$$

$$\Rightarrow \quad x = \frac{3}{2}$$

$$\Rightarrow \quad z = \frac{3}{2} + 2i$$

$$\therefore \quad |z| = \sqrt{\left(\frac{3}{2}\right)^2 + (2)^2} = \sqrt{\frac{9}{4}+4} = \sqrt{\frac{25}{4}} = \frac{5}{2}$$

Skill Builder

If $z \neq 0$ be a complex number such that $|z| - z = 3 - 7i$ (where $i = \sqrt{-1}$). Then, $|z|$ is

(a) $\frac{29}{3}$ (b) $\frac{\sqrt{29}}{3}$

(c) $\frac{-7}{3}$ (d) $\frac{29}{2}$

For Sol.

■ **For more practice** See Q.5 of Milestone Practice 1.2.

Example 29. z_1 and z_2 are two complex numbers, such that $\frac{z_1 - 2z_2}{2 - z_1\cdot\bar{z}_2}$ is unimodular, while z_2 is not unimodular. Find $|z_1|$.

Sol. Here, $\quad \left|\frac{z_1-2z_2}{2-z_1\bar{z}_2}\right| = 1 \qquad$ [by property (vi)]

$$\Rightarrow \quad \frac{|z_1-2z_2|}{|2-z_1\bar{z}_2|} = 1$$

$$\Rightarrow \quad |z_1-2z_2| = |2-z_1\bar{z}_2|$$

$$\Rightarrow \quad |z_1-2z_2|^2 = |2-z_1\bar{z}_2|^2$$

$$\Rightarrow (z_1 - 2z_2)\overline{(z_1 - 2z_2)} = (2 - z_1\bar{z}_2)\overline{(2 - z_1\bar{z}_2)}$$ [by property (iv)]

$$\Rightarrow (z_1 - 2z_2)(\bar{z}_1 - 2\bar{z}_2) = (2 - z_1\bar{z}_2)(2 - \bar{z}_1 z_2)$$

$$\Rightarrow z_1\bar{z}_1 - 2z_1\bar{z}_2 - 2z_2\bar{z}_1 + 4z_2\bar{z}_2 = 4 - 2\bar{z}_1 z_2 - 2z_1\bar{z}_2 + z_1\bar{z}_1 z_2\bar{z}_2$$

$$\Rightarrow |z_1|^2 + 4|z_2|^2 = 4 + |z_1|^2|z_2|^2$$

$$\Rightarrow |z_1|^2 - |z_1|^2 \cdot |z_2|^2 + 4|z_2|^2 - 4 = 0$$

$$\Rightarrow (|z_1|^2 - 4)(1 - |z_2|^2) = 0$$

But $|z_2| \neq 1$ [given]

$\therefore$ $|z_1|^2 = 4$

Hence, $|z_1| = 2$

Example 30. If $\theta_i \in [0, \pi/6]$, $i = 1, 2, 3, 4, 5$ and $\sin\theta_1 z^4 + \sin\theta_2 z^3 + \sin\theta_3 z^2 + \sin\theta_4 z + \sin\theta_5 = 2$, show that $\frac{3}{4} < |z| < 1$.

Sol. Given that

$$\sin\theta_1 z^4 + \sin\theta_2 z^3 + \sin\theta_3 z^2 + \sin\theta_4 z + \sin\theta_5 = 2$$

or $2 = |\sin\theta_1 z^4 + \sin\theta_2 z^3 + \sin\theta_3 z^2 + \sin\theta_4 z + \sin\theta_5|$

$$2 \le |\sin\theta_1 z^4| + |\sin\theta_2 z^3| + |\sin\theta_3 z^2| + |\sin\theta_4 z| + |\sin\theta_5|$$ [by property (vii)]

$$\Rightarrow 2 \le |\sin\theta_1||z^4| + |\sin\theta_2||z^3| + |\sin\theta_3||z^2| + |\sin\theta_4||z| + |\sin\theta_5|$$ [by property (v)]

$$\Rightarrow 2 \le |\sin\theta_1||z|^4 + |\sin\theta_2||z|^3 + |\sin\theta_3||z|^2 + |\sin\theta_4||z| + |\sin\theta_5|$$ [by property (ix)] ...(i)

But given, $\theta_i \in [0, \pi/6]$

$\therefore$ $\sin\theta_i \in \left[0, \frac{1}{2}\right]$ i.e. $0 \le \sin\theta_i \le \frac{1}{2}$

$\therefore$ Inequality Eq. (i) becomes,

$$2 \le \frac{1}{2}|z|^4 + \frac{1}{2}|z|^3 + \frac{1}{2}|z|^2 + \frac{1}{2}|z| + \frac{1}{2}$$

$$\Rightarrow 3 \le |z|^4 + |z|^3 + |z|^2 + |z|$$

$$\Rightarrow 3 \le |z| + |z|^2 + |z|^3 + |z|^4 < |z| + |z|^2 + |z|^3 + |z|^4 + \ldots + \infty$$

$$\Rightarrow 3 < |z| + |z|^2 + |z|^3 + |z|^4 + \ldots + \infty$$

$$\Rightarrow 3 < \frac{|z|}{1 - |z|}$$ [here, $|z| < 1$]

$$\Rightarrow 3 - 3|z| < |z| \Rightarrow 3 < 4|z|$$

$\therefore$ $|z| > \frac{3}{4}$

Hence, $\frac{3}{4} < |z| < 1$ [$\because |z| < 1$]

Example 31. If $|z - 2 + i| \le 2$, find the greatest and least values of $|z|$, where $i = \sqrt{-1}$.

Sol. Given that $|z - 2 + i| \le 2$ ...(i)

$\because$ $|z - 2 + i| \ge ||z| - |2 - i||$ [by property (x)]

$\therefore$ $|z - 2 + i| \ge ||z| - \sqrt{5}|$ ...(ii)

From Eqs. (i) and (ii), we get

$$||z| - \sqrt{5}| \le |z - 2 + i| \le 2$$

$\therefore$ $||z| - \sqrt{5}| \le 2$

$$\Rightarrow -2 \le |z| - \sqrt{5} \le 2$$

$$\Rightarrow \sqrt{5} - 2 \le |z| \le \sqrt{5} + 2$$

Hence, greatest value of $|z|$ is $\sqrt{5} + 2$ and least value of $|z|$ is $\sqrt{5} - 2$.

Example 32. If z is any complex number such that $|z + 4| \le 3$, find the greatest value of $|z + 1|$.

Sol. $\because |z + 1| = |(z + 4) - 3|$

$$= |(z + 4) + (-3)| \le |z + 4| + |-3|$$

$$= |z + 4| + 3$$

$$\le 3 + 3 = 6$$ [$\because |z + 4| \le 3$]

$\therefore$ $|z + 1| \le 6$

Hence, the greatest value of $|z + 1|$ is 6.

1.6 Argument of a Complex Number

Let $z = x + iy = (x, y)$ for all $x, y \in R$ and $i = \sqrt{-1}$.

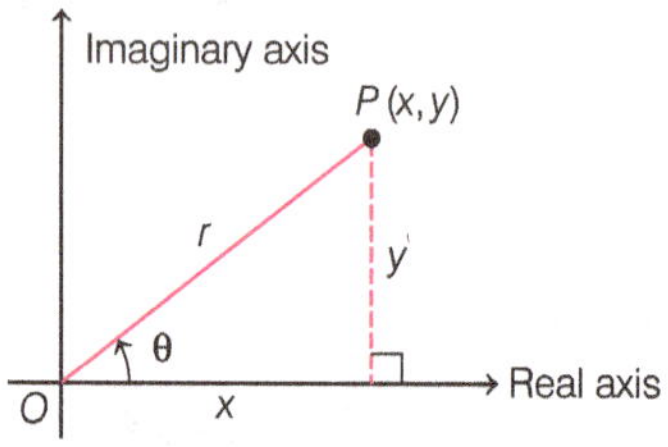

The length OP is called modulus of the complex number z denoted by $|z|$

i.e. $OP = r = |z| = \sqrt{(x^2 + y^2)}$

and if $(x, y) \neq (0, 0)$, then θ is called the argument or amplitude of z,

i.e. $\theta = \tan^{-1}\left(\frac{y}{x}\right)$ [angle made by OP with positive X-axis]

or $\arg(z) = \tan^{-1}(y/x)$

Also, argument of a complex number is not unique, since if θ is a value of the argument, so also is $2n\pi + \theta$, where $n \in I$.

But usually, we take only that value for which $0 \le \theta < 2\pi$. Any two arguments of a complex number differ by $2n\pi$.

Argument of z will be θ, $\pi - \theta$, $\pi + \theta$ and $2\pi - \theta$ according as the point z lies in I, II, III and IV quadrants respectively, where $\theta = \tan^{-1}\left|\frac{y}{x}\right|$.

Example 33. Find the arguments of $z_1 = 5 + 5i$, $z_2 = -4 + 4i$, $z_3 = -3 - 3i$ and $z_4 = 2 - 2i$, where $i = \sqrt{-1}$.

Sol. Since, z_1, z_2, z_3 and z_4 lies in I, II, III and IV quadrants respectively.

The arguments are given by

$$\arg(z_1) = \tan^{-1}\left|\frac{5}{5}\right| = \tan^{-1}1 = \pi/4$$

$$\arg(z_2) = \pi - \tan^{-1}\left|\frac{4}{-4}\right|$$

$$= \pi - \tan^{-1}1 = \pi - \frac{\pi}{4} = \frac{3\pi}{4}$$

$$\arg(z_3) = \pi + \tan^{-1}\left|\frac{-3}{-3}\right|$$

$$= \pi + \tan^{-1}1 = \pi + \frac{\pi}{4} = \frac{5\pi}{4}$$

and $\arg(z_4) = 2\pi - \tan^{-1}\left|\frac{-2}{2}\right|$

$$= 2\pi - \tan^{-1}1 = 2\pi - \frac{\pi}{4} = \frac{7\pi}{4}$$

Principal Value of the Argument

The value θ of the argument which satisfies the inequality $-\pi < \theta \le \pi$ is called the **principal value** of the argument.

If $z = x + iy = (x, y)$, $\forall\, x, y \in R$ and $i = \sqrt{-1}$, then $\arg(z) = \tan^{-1}\left(\frac{y}{x}\right)$ always gives the principal value. It depends on the quadrant in which the point (x, y) lies.

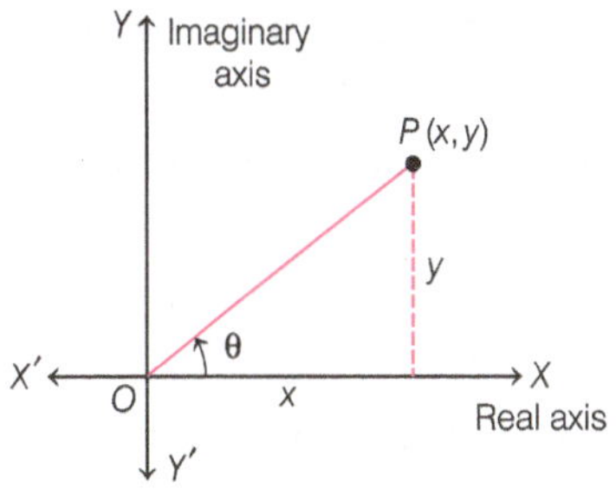

(i) $(x, y) \in$ first quadrant $x > 0, y > 0$.

The principal value of $\arg(z) = \theta = \tan^{-1}\left(\frac{y}{x}\right)$

It is an acute angle and positive.

(ii) $(x, y) \in$ second quadrant $x < 0, y > 0$.

The principal value of $\arg(z) = \theta = \pi - \tan^{-1}\left(\frac{y}{|x|}\right)$

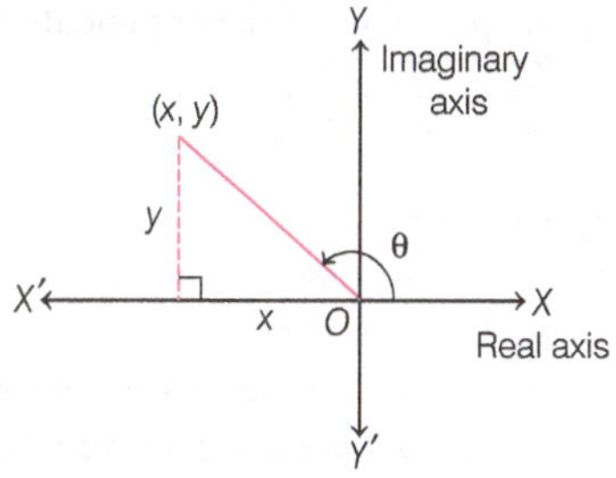

It is an obtuse angle and positive.

(iii) $(x, y) \in$ third quadrant $x < 0, y < 0$.

The principal value of $\arg(z) = \theta = -\pi + \tan^{-1}\left(\frac{y}{x}\right)$

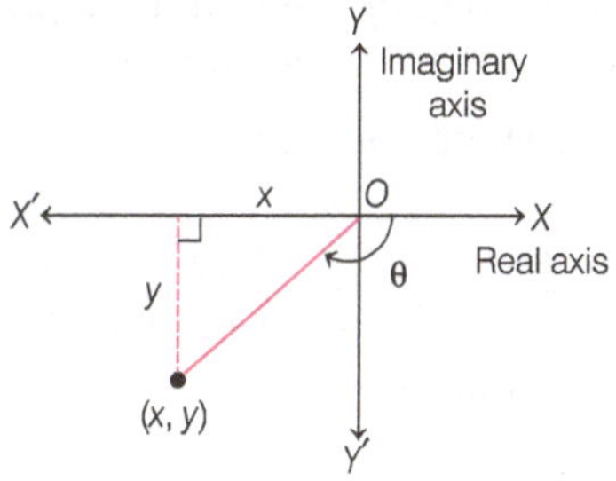

It is an obtuse angle and negative.

(iv) $(x, y) \in$ fourth quadrant $x > 0, y < 0$.

The principal value of $\arg(z) = \theta = -\tan^{-1}\left(\frac{|y|}{x}\right)$

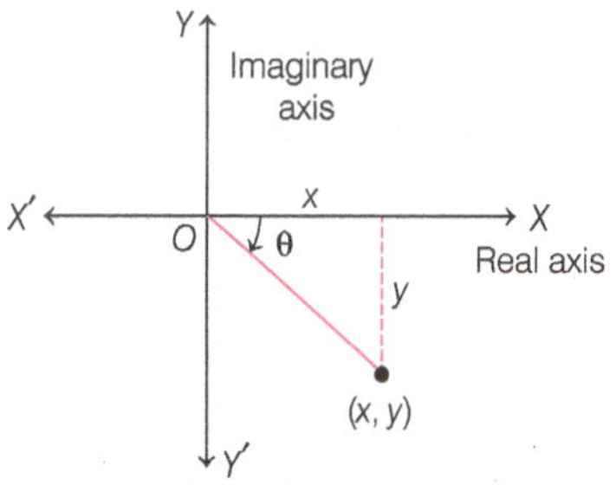

It is an acute angle and negative.

Example 34. Find the principal values of the arguments of $z_1 = 2 + 2i$, $z_2 = -3 + 3i$, $z_3 = -4 - 4i$ and $z_4 = 5 - 5i$, where $i = \sqrt{-1}$.

Sol. Since, z_1, z_2, z_3 and z_4 lies in I, II, III and IV quadrants respectively. The principal values of the arguments are given by

$$\tan^{-1}\left(\frac{2}{2}\right),\ \pi - \tan^{-1}\left(\frac{3}{|-3|}\right), -\pi + \tan^{-1}\left(\frac{-4}{-4}\right),$$

$$-\tan^{-1}\left(\frac{|-5|}{5}\right)$$

or $\tan^{-1} 1, \pi - \tan^{-1} 1, -\pi + \tan^{-1} 1, -\tan^{-1} 1$

or $\frac{\pi}{4}, \pi - \frac{\pi}{4}, -\pi + \frac{\pi}{4}, -\frac{\pi}{4}$ or $\frac{\pi}{4}, \frac{3\pi}{4}, -\frac{3\pi}{4}, -\frac{\pi}{4}$

Hence, the principal values of the arguments of z_1, z_2, z_3 and z_4 are $\frac{\pi}{4}, \frac{3\pi}{4}, -\frac{3\pi}{4}, -\frac{\pi}{4}$, respectively.

Concept Inside Video

JEE Focus Points

- Unless otherwise stated, amp (z) implies principal value of the argument.
- Argument of the complex number 0 is not defined.
- If $z_1 = z_2 \Leftrightarrow |z_1| = |z_2|$ and $\arg(z_1) = \arg(z_2)$.
- If $\arg(z) = \frac{\pi}{2}$ or $-\frac{\pi}{2}$, z is purely imaginary.
- If $\arg(z) = 0$ or π, z is purely real.

Example 35. Find the argument and the principal value of the argument of the complex number $z = \frac{2+i}{4i + (1+i)^2}$, where $i = \sqrt{-1}$.

Sol. Since, $z = \frac{2+i}{4i + (1+i)^2} = \frac{2+i}{4i + 1 + i^2 + 2i} = \frac{2+i}{6i} = \frac{1}{6} - \frac{1}{3}i$

$\therefore$ z lies in IV quadrant.

Here, $\theta = \tan^{-1} \left| \frac{-\frac{1}{3}}{\frac{1}{6}} \right| = \tan^{-1} 2$

$\therefore$ $\arg(z) = 2\pi - \theta = 2\pi - \tan^{-1} 2$

Hence, principal value of $\arg(z) = -\theta = -\tan^{-1} 2$.

Properties of Arguments

(i) $\arg(z_1 z_2) = \arg(z_1) + \arg(z_2) + 2k\pi, k \in I$

In general, $\arg(z_1 z_2 z_3 \ldots z_n)$
$= \arg(z_1) + \arg(z_2) + \arg(z_3) + \ldots + \arg(z_n) + 2k\pi$, $k \in I$.

(ii) $\arg\left(\frac{z_1}{z_2}\right) = \arg(z_1) - \arg(z_2) + 2k\pi, k \in I$

(iii) $\arg\left(\frac{z}{\bar{z}}\right) = 2\arg(z) + 2k\pi, k \in I$

(iv) $\arg(z^n) = n.\arg(z) + 2k\pi, k \in I$, where proper value of k must be chosen, so that RHS lies in $(-\pi, \pi]$.

(v) If $\arg\left(\frac{z_2}{z_1}\right) = \theta$, then $\arg\left(\frac{z_1}{z_2}\right) = 2n\pi - \theta$, where $n \in I$.

(vi) $\arg(\bar{z}) = -\arg(z)$

(vii) $\arg(z) - \arg(-z) = \pi, \arg(z) > 0$

(viii) $\arg(z) - \arg(-z) = -\pi, \arg(z) < 0$

Example 36. If $\arg(z_1) = \frac{17\pi}{18}$ and $\arg(z_2) = \frac{7\pi}{18}$, find the principal argument of $z_1 z_2$ and (z_1/z_2).

Sol. $\arg(z_1 z_2) = \arg(z_1) + \arg(z_2) + 2k\pi$

$$= \frac{17\pi}{18} + \frac{7\pi}{18} + 2k\pi$$

$$= \frac{4\pi}{3} + 2k\pi$$

$$= \frac{4\pi}{3} - 2\pi = -\frac{2\pi}{3} \quad \text{[for } k = -1]$$

and $\arg\left(\frac{z_1}{z_2}\right) = \arg(z_1) - \arg(z_2) + 2k\pi$

$$= \frac{17\pi}{18} - \frac{7\pi}{18} + 2k\pi$$

$$= \frac{10\pi}{18} + 2k\pi$$

$$= \frac{5\pi}{9} + 0 = \frac{5\pi}{9} \quad \text{[for } k = 0]$$

Example 37. If $z = \left[\frac{(3+4i)(1+i)(1+\sqrt{3}i)}{(1-i)(4-3i)(2i)}\right]^2$, then find amp$(z)$.

Sol. We have, $z = \left[\frac{(3+4i)(1+i)(1+\sqrt{3}i)}{(1-i)(4-3i)(2i)}\right]^2$

$\therefore$ amp$(z) = 2[$amp$(3+4i) + amp(1+i)$ + amp$(1+\sqrt{3}i)$ − amp$(1-i)$ − amp$(4-3i)$ − amp$(2i)] + 2k\pi, k \in Z$

$$= 2\left[\tan^{-1}\frac{4}{3} + \frac{\pi}{4} + \frac{\pi}{3} - \left(\frac{-\pi}{4}\right) - \tan^{-1}\left(\frac{-3}{4}\right) - \frac{\pi}{2}\right] + 2k\pi$$

$$= 2\left[\tan^{-1}\frac{4}{3} + \cot^{-1}\frac{4}{3} + \frac{\pi}{3}\right] + 2k\pi$$

$$= 2\left[\frac{\pi}{2} + \frac{\pi}{3}\right] + 2k\pi$$

$$= -\frac{\pi}{3} \quad [k = -1]$$

Example 38. If z_1 and z_2 are conjugate to each other, find the principal argument of $(-z_1 z_2)$.

Sol. $\because z_1$ and z_2 are conjugate to each other i.e., $z_2 = \bar{z}_1$, therefore, $z_1 z_2 = z_1 \bar{z}_1 = |z_1|^2$

$\therefore \arg(-z_1 z_2) = \arg(-|z_1|^2) = \arg$ [negative real number]
$= \pi$

Example 39. Let z be any non-zero complex number, then find the value of $\arg(z) + \arg(\bar{z})$.

Sol. $\arg(z) + \arg(\bar{z}) = \arg(z\bar{z})$
$= \arg(|z|^2) = \arg$ [positive real number]
$= 0$

Mixed Properties of Modulus and Arguments

(i) $|z_1+z_2|=|z_1|+|z_2| \Leftrightarrow \arg(z_1)=\arg(z_2)$

Proof

Let $\arg(z_1)=\theta$ and $\arg(z_2)=\phi$

$\therefore \quad |z_1+z_2|=|z_1|+|z_2|$

On squaring both sides, we get

$$|z_1+z_2|^2=|z_1|^2+|z_2|^2+2|z_1||z_2|$$

$$\Rightarrow |z_1|^2+|z_2|^2+2|z_1||z_2|\cos(\theta-\phi)=|z_1|^2+|z_2|^2+2|z_1||z_2|$$

$\Rightarrow \quad \cos(\theta-\phi)=1$

$\therefore \quad \theta-\phi=0$ or $\theta=\phi$

$\therefore \quad \arg(z_1)=\arg(z_2)$

(ii) $|z_1+z_2|=|z_1|-|z_2| \Leftrightarrow \arg(z_1)-\arg(z_2)=\pi$

Proof

$\because \quad |z_1+z_2|=|z_1|-|z_2|$

On squaring both sides, we get

$$|z_1+z_2|^2=|z_1|^2+|z_2|^2-2|z_1||z_2|$$

$$\Rightarrow |z_1|^2+|z_2|^2+2|z_1||z_2|\cos(\theta-\phi)=|z_1|^2+|z_2|^2-2|z_1||z_2|$$

$\Rightarrow \quad \cos(\theta-\phi)=-1$

$\therefore \quad \theta-\phi=\pi$

or $\arg(z_1)-\arg(z_2)=\pi$

(iii) $|z_1-z_2|=|z_1+z_2| \Leftrightarrow \arg(z_1)-\arg(z_2)=\pm\dfrac{\pi}{2}$, $\bar{z}_1 z_2$ and $\dfrac{z_1}{z_2}$ are purely imaginary.

Example 40. If $|z_1+z_2|^2=|z_1|^2+|z_2|^2$, then prove that $\dfrac{z_1}{z_2}$ is purely imaginary.

Sol. We have, $|z_1+z_2|^2=|z_1|^2+|z_2|^2$

$$\Rightarrow |z_1|^2+|z_2|^2+2|z_1||z_2|\cos(\arg(z_1)-\arg(z_2))=|z_1|^2+|z_2|^2$$

$\Rightarrow \quad \cos(\arg(z_1)-\arg(z_2))=0$

$\Rightarrow \quad \arg(z_1)-\arg(z_2)=\pm\dfrac{\pi}{2}$

$\Rightarrow \quad \arg\left(\dfrac{z_1}{z_2}\right)=\pm\dfrac{\pi}{2}$

$\therefore \dfrac{z_1}{z_2}$ is purely imaginary.

Example 41. If $|z_1|=|z_2|$ and $\arg(z_1/z_2)=\pi$, then find the value of z_1+z_2.

Sol. $\because \arg\left(\dfrac{z_1}{z_2}\right)=\pi$

$\Rightarrow \quad \arg(z_1)-\arg(z_2)=\pi \quad$ ...(i)

$\because \quad z_1=|z_1|(\cos(\arg z_1)+i\sin(\arg z_1)) \quad$ ...(ii)

and $\quad z_2=|z_2|(\cos(\arg z_2)+i\sin(\arg z_2)) \quad$ ...(iii)

From Eq. (ii), we get

$z_1=|z_2|(\cos(\pi+\arg(z_2))+i\sin(\pi+\arg(z_2)))$ [from Eq. (i) and $|z_1|=|z_2|$]

$=|z_2|(-\cos(\arg z_2)-i\sin(\arg z_2))=-z_2$ [from Eq. (iii)]

$\therefore z_1+z_2=0$

1.7 Polar Form of Complex Number

Let $z=x+iy$, where $x, y \in R$ and $i=\sqrt{-1}$, z is represented by $P(x, y)$ in the argand plane.

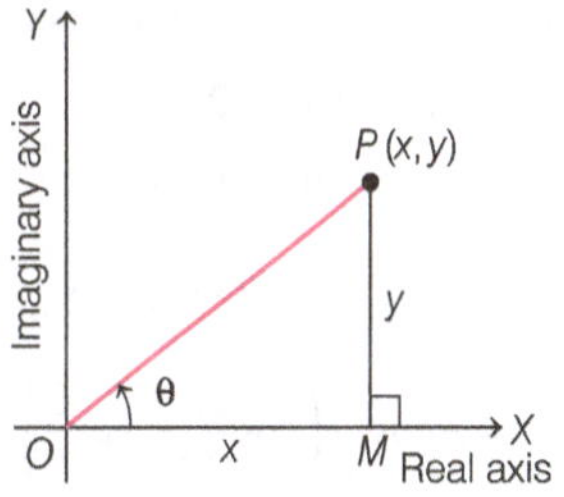

By geometrical representation,

$$OP=\sqrt{(x^2+y^2)}=|z|$$

$$\angle POM=\theta=\arg(z)$$

In ΔOPM, $\quad x=OP\cos(\angle POM)=|z|\cos(\arg z)$

and $\quad y=OP\sin(\angle POM)=|z|\sin(\arg z)$

$\because \quad z=x+iy$

$\therefore \quad z=|z|(\cos(\arg z)+i\sin(\arg z))$

or $\quad z=r(\cos\theta+i\sin\theta)$

$\quad \bar{z}=r(\cos\theta-i\sin\theta)$

where, $r=|z|$ and $\theta=$ principal value of $\arg(z)$.

JEE Focus Points

- $\cos\theta+i\sin\theta$ is also written as $CiS\,\theta$.
- Remember

$1=\cos 0+i\sin 0,\quad -1=\cos\pi+i\sin\pi$

$i=\cos\dfrac{\pi}{2}+i\sin\dfrac{\pi}{2},\quad -i=\cos\dfrac{\pi}{2}-i\sin\dfrac{\pi}{2}$

Example 42. Write the polar form of $-\frac{1}{2}-\frac{i\sqrt{3}}{2}$ (where, $i=\sqrt{-1}$).

Sol. Let $z=-\frac{1}{2}-\frac{i\sqrt{3}}{2}$. Since, $\left(-\frac{1}{2},-\frac{\sqrt{3}}{2}\right)$ lies in III quadrant.

$\therefore$ Principal value of $\arg(z)=-\pi+\tan^{-1}\left|\frac{-\sqrt{3}/2}{-1/2}\right|$

$$=-\pi+\tan^{-1}\sqrt{3}$$

$$=-\pi+\frac{\pi}{3}=-\frac{2\pi}{3}$$

and $|z|=\sqrt{\left(-\frac{1}{2}\right)^2+\left(-\frac{\sqrt{3}}{2}\right)^2}=\sqrt{\left(\frac{1}{4}+\frac{3}{4}\right)}=\sqrt{1}=1$

$\therefore$ Polar form of $z=|z|[\cos(\arg z)+i\sin(\arg z)]$

i.e. $-\frac{1}{2}-\frac{i\sqrt{3}}{2}=\left[\cos\left(-\frac{2\pi}{3}\right)+i\sin\left(-\frac{2\pi}{3}\right)\right]$

Example 43. If z is a point on the argand plane such that $|z-1|=1$, then prove that $\frac{z-2}{z}=i\tan(\arg z)$.

Sol. We have, $|z-1|=1$

Let $z-1=\cos\theta+i\sin\theta$

$\Rightarrow$ $z=1+\cos\theta+i\sin\theta$

$$=2\cos^2\frac{\theta}{2}+2i\sin\frac{\theta}{2}\cos\frac{\theta}{2}$$

$$=2\cos\frac{\theta}{2}\left(\cos\frac{\theta}{2}+i\sin\frac{\theta}{2}\right)$$

$\therefore$ $\arg(z)=\frac{\theta}{2}$

Again, $z-2=\cos\theta+i\sin\theta-1$

$$=-2\sin^2\frac{\theta}{2}+2i\sin\frac{\theta}{2}\cos\frac{\theta}{2}$$

$$=2i\sin\frac{\theta}{2}\left(\cos\frac{\theta}{2}+i\sin\frac{\theta}{2}\right)$$

$\therefore$ $$\frac{z-2}{z}=\frac{2i\sin\frac{\theta}{2}\left(\cos\frac{\theta}{2}+i\sin\frac{\theta}{2}\right)}{2\cos\frac{\theta}{2}\left(\cos\frac{\theta}{2}+i\sin\frac{\theta}{2}\right)}$$

$$=i\tan\frac{\theta}{2}$$

$$=i\tan(\arg(z))$$

1.8 Euler's Form of Complex Number

If $\theta\in R$ and $i=\sqrt{-1}$, then $e^{i\theta}=\cos\theta+i\sin\theta$ is known as Euler's identity.

Now, $e^{-i\theta}=\cos\theta-i\sin\theta$

Let $z=e^{i\theta}$

$\therefore$ $|z|=1$ and $\arg(z)=\theta$

Also, $e^{i\theta}+e^{-i\theta}=2\cos\theta$ and $e^{i\theta}-e^{-i\theta}=2i\sin\theta$

and if $\theta,\phi\in R$ and $i=\sqrt{-1}$, then

(i) $e^{i\theta}+e^{i\phi}=e^{i\left(\frac{\theta+\phi}{2}\right)}\cdot 2\cos\left(\frac{\theta-\phi}{2}\right)$

$\therefore$ $|e^{i\theta}+e^{i\phi}|=2\left|\cos\left(\frac{\theta-\phi}{2}\right)\right|$

and $\arg(e^{i\theta}+e^{i\phi})=\left(\frac{\theta+\phi}{2}\right)$

(ii) $e^{i\theta}-e^{i\phi}=e^{i\left(\frac{\theta+\phi}{2}\right)}\cdot 2i\sin\left(\frac{\theta-\phi}{2}\right)$

$\therefore$ $|e^{i\theta}-e^{i\phi}|=2\left|\sin\left(\frac{\theta-\phi}{2}\right)\right|$

and $\arg(e^{i\theta}-e^{i\phi})=\frac{\theta+\phi}{2}+\frac{\pi}{2}$ $\quad[\because i=e^{i\pi/2}]$

JEE Focus Points

- $e^{i\theta}+1=e^{i\theta/2}\cdot 2\cos\left(\frac{\theta}{2}\right)$ (Remember)
- $e^{i\theta}-1=e^{i\theta/2}\cdot 2i\sin\left(\frac{\theta}{2}\right)$ (Remember)
- $\frac{e^{i\theta}-1}{e^{i\theta}+1}=i\tan\left(\frac{\theta}{2}\right)$ (Remember)
- If $z=re^{i\theta}$; $|z|=r$, then $\arg(z)=\theta$, $\bar{z}=re^{-i\theta}$
- If $|z-z_0|=1$, then $z-z_0=e^{i\theta}$

Concept Inside Video

Example 44. Let z be a non-real complex number lying on $|z|=1$, prove that $z=\frac{1+i\tan\left(\frac{\arg(z)}{2}\right)}{1-i\tan\left(\frac{\arg(z)}{2}\right)}$.

(where, $i=\sqrt{-1}$).

Sol. Given, $|z|=1$

$\therefore$ $z=e^{i\theta}$ ...(i)

$\Rightarrow$ $\arg(z)=\theta$ ...(ii)

$$\text{RHS}=\frac{1+i\tan\left(\frac{\arg(z)}{2}\right)}{1-i\tan\left(\frac{\arg(z)}{2}\right)}=\frac{1+i\tan(\theta/2)}{1-i\tan(\theta/2)}\quad\text{[from Eq. (ii)]}$$

$$=\frac{\cos\theta/2+i\sin\theta/2}{\cos\theta/2-i\sin\theta/2}=\frac{e^{i\theta/2}}{e^{-i\theta/2}}$$

$$=e^{i\theta}=z=\text{LHS}\quad\text{[from Eq. (i)]}$$

JEE SCANNER

Example Similar to PYQ Asked in JEE Main 2023

The complex number $z = \dfrac{1+i}{\cos\dfrac{\pi}{3} + i\sin\dfrac{\pi}{3}}$ *is equal to*

(a) $\sqrt{2}\left(\cos\dfrac{\pi}{12} + i\sin\dfrac{\pi}{12}\right)$ (b) $\sqrt{2}\left(\cos\dfrac{\pi}{12} - i\sin\dfrac{\pi}{12}\right)$

(c) $\sqrt{2}\left(\cos\dfrac{\pi}{3} + i\sin\dfrac{\pi}{3}\right)$ (d) $\sqrt{2}\left(\cos\dfrac{\pi}{3} - i\sin\dfrac{\pi}{3}\right)$

Sol. (b) Given, $z = \dfrac{1+i}{\cos\dfrac{\pi}{3} + i\sin\dfrac{\pi}{3}}$

Let $z_1 = 1 + i \Rightarrow \arg(z_1) = \tan^{-1}\left|\dfrac{1}{1}\right|$

$\Rightarrow \quad \theta = \tan^{-1}(1) = \dfrac{\pi}{4}$

and $r = |z_1| = \sqrt{(1)^2 + (1)^2} = \sqrt{2}$

$\therefore \quad z_1 = |z_1|[\cos\theta + i\sin\theta] = \sqrt{2}\left[\cos\dfrac{\pi}{4} + i\sin\dfrac{\pi}{4}\right]$

$$\therefore \quad z = \frac{\sqrt{2}\left[\cos\dfrac{\pi}{4} + i\sin\dfrac{\pi}{4}\right]}{\cos\dfrac{\pi}{3} + i\sin\dfrac{\pi}{3}} = \frac{\sqrt{2}\,e^{i\frac{\pi}{4}}}{e^{i\frac{\pi}{3}}}$$

$$= \sqrt{2}e^{i\left(\frac{\pi}{4} - \frac{\pi}{3}\right)} = \sqrt{2}e^{-\frac{\pi}{12}i}$$

$$= \sqrt{2}\left[\cos\left(-\frac{\pi}{12}\right) + i\sin\left(\frac{-\pi}{12}\right)\right]$$

$$= \sqrt{2}\left[\cos\frac{\pi}{12} - i\sin\frac{\pi}{12}\right]$$

Skill Builder

The complex number $z = \dfrac{1-\sqrt{3}i}{\cos\dfrac{\pi}{6} + i\sin\dfrac{\pi}{6}}$ is equal to

(a) $2\cos\left(\dfrac{\pi}{2} - i\sin\dfrac{\pi}{2}\right)$ (b) $2\cos\left(\dfrac{\pi}{2} + i\sin\dfrac{\pi}{2}\right)$

(c) $2\cos\left(\dfrac{\pi}{3} - i\sin\dfrac{\pi}{3}\right)$ (d) $2\cos\left(\dfrac{\pi}{6} + i\sin\dfrac{\pi}{6}\right)$

For Sol.

■ **For more practice** See Q.14 of Milestone Practice 1.2.

Example 45. Prove that $\tan\left(i\ln\left(\dfrac{a-ib}{a+ib}\right)\right) = \dfrac{2ab}{a^2 - b^2}$ (where $a, b \in R^+$ and $i = \sqrt{-1}$).

Sol. $\because \quad \left|\dfrac{a-ib}{a+ib}\right| = \dfrac{|a-ib|}{|a+ib|} = 1 \qquad [\because |\bar{z}| = |z|]$

Let $\quad \dfrac{a-ib}{a+ib} = e^{i\theta} \qquad$ ...(i)

By componendo and dividendo, we get

$$\frac{(a-ib)-(a+ib)}{(a-ib)+(a+ib)} = \frac{e^{i\theta}-1}{e^{i\theta}+1} \Rightarrow \frac{-b}{a}i = i\tan(\theta/2)$$

or $\quad \tan\left(\dfrac{\theta}{2}\right) = -\dfrac{b}{a} \qquad$ ...(ii)

$$\therefore \quad \text{LHS} = \tan\left(i\ln\left(\frac{a-ib}{a+ib}\right)\right)$$

$= \tan(i\ln(e^{i\theta})) \qquad$ [from Eq. (i)]

$= \tan(i \cdot i\theta) = -\tan\theta$

$= -\dfrac{2\tan\theta/2}{1-\tan^2\theta/2} = -\dfrac{2(-b/a)}{1-(-b/a)^2} \qquad$ [from Eq. (ii)]

$= \dfrac{2ab}{a^2 - b^2} = \text{RHS}$

Applications of Euler's Form

If $x, y, \theta \in R$ and $i = \sqrt{-1}$, then

let $\quad z = x + iy \qquad$ [cartesian form]

$= |z|(\cos\theta + i\sin\theta) \qquad$ [polar form]

$= |z|e^{i\theta} \qquad$ [Euler's form]

(i) Product of Two Complex Numbers

Let two complex numbers be

$$z_1 = |z_1|e^{i\theta_1} \text{ and } z_2 = |z_2|e^{i\theta_2},$$

where $\theta_1, \theta_2 \in R$ and $i = \sqrt{-1}$

$$\therefore \quad z_1 \cdot z_2 = |z_1|e^{i\theta_1} \cdot |z_2|e^{i\theta_2} = |z_1||z_2|e^{i(\theta_1+\theta_2)}$$

$$= |z_1||z_2|(\cos(\theta_1+\theta_2) + i\sin(\theta_1+\theta_2))$$

Thus, $\quad |z_1 z_2| = |z_1||z_2|$

and $\quad \arg(z_1 z_2) = \theta_1 + \theta_2 = \arg(z_1) + \arg(z_2)$

(ii) Division of Two Complex Numbers

Let two complex numbers be

$$z_1 = |z_1|e^{i\theta_1} \text{ and } z_2 = |z_2|e^{i\theta_2},$$

where $\theta_1, \theta_2 \in R$ and $i = \sqrt{-1}$

$$\therefore \quad \frac{z_1}{z_2} = \frac{|z_1|e^{i\theta_1}}{|z_2|e^{i\theta_2}} = \frac{|z_1|}{|z_2|}e^{i(\theta_1-\theta_2)}$$

$$= \frac{|z_1|}{|z_2|}(\cos(\theta_1-\theta_2) + i\sin(\theta_1-\theta_2))$$

Thus, $\left|\dfrac{z_1}{z_2}\right| = \dfrac{|z_1|}{|z_2|}, (z_2 \neq 0)$

and $\arg\left(\dfrac{z_1}{z_2}\right) = \theta_1 - \theta_2 = \arg(z_1) - \arg(z_2)$

Example 46. If m and x are two real numbers and $i = \sqrt{-1}$, prove that $e^{2mi\cot^{-1}x}\left(\dfrac{xi+1}{xi-1}\right)^m = 1$.

Sol. Let $\cot^{-1} x = \theta$, then $\cot\theta = x$

$$\therefore \text{LHS} = e^{2mi\cot^{-1}x}\left(\frac{xi+1}{xi-1}\right)^m$$
$$= e^{2mi\theta}\left(\frac{i\cot\theta+1}{i\cot\theta-1}\right)^m$$
$$= e^{2mi\theta}\left(\frac{i(\cot\theta-i)}{i(\cot\theta+i)}\right)^m$$
$$= e^{2mi\theta}\left(\frac{\cos\theta - i\sin\theta}{\cos\theta+i\sin\theta}\right)^m$$
$$= e^{2mi\theta}\cdot\left(\frac{e^{-i\theta}}{e^{i\theta}}\right)^m$$
$$= e^{2mi\theta}\cdot(e^{-2i\theta})^m$$
$$= e^{2mi\theta}\cdot e^{-2mi\theta}$$
$$= e^0 = 1 = \text{RHS}$$

1.9 Logarithm of a Complex Number

$$\log_e(z) = \log_e(|z|e^{i\theta}) = \log_e|z| + \log_e(e^{i\theta})$$
$$= \log_e|z| + i\theta$$
$$= \log_e|z| + i\arg(z)$$

So, the general value of $\log_e(z)$

$$= \log_e(z) + 2n\pi i\,(-\pi < \arg z < \pi).$$

Example 47. Express $(1+i)^{-i}$, (where, $i = \sqrt{-1}$) in the form $A + iB$.

Sol. Let $A + iB = (1+i)^{-i}$

On taking logarithm both sides, we get

$$\log_e(A+iB) = -i\log_e(1+i)$$
$$= -i\log_e\left(\sqrt{2}\left(\frac{1}{\sqrt{2}} + \frac{i}{\sqrt{2}}\right)\right)$$
$$= -i\log_e\left(\sqrt{2}\left(\cos\frac{\pi}{4} + i\sin\frac{\pi}{4}\right)\right)$$
$$= -i\log_e(\sqrt{2}\,e^{i\pi/4})$$
$$= -i(\log_e\sqrt{2} + \log_e e^{i\pi/4})$$
$$= -i\left(\frac{1}{2}\log_e 2 + \frac{i\pi}{4}\right)$$
$$= -\frac{i}{2}\log_e 2 + \frac{\pi}{4}$$
$$\therefore A + iB = e^{-\frac{i}{2}\log_e 2 + \frac{\pi}{4}} = e^{\pi/4}\cdot e^{i\log_e 2^{-1/2}}$$
$$= e^{\pi/4}\cdot(\cos(\log_e 2^{-1/2}) + i\sin(\log_e 2^{-1/2}))$$
$$= e^{\pi/4}\cdot\cos\left(\log_e\left(\frac{1}{\sqrt{2}}\right)\right) + i\,e^{\pi/4}\sin\left(\log_e\left(\frac{1}{\sqrt{2}}\right)\right)$$

Example 48. If $\sin(\log_e i^i) = a + ib$, where $i = \sqrt{-1}$, hence find a and b, and $\cos(\log_e i^i)$.

Sol. $a + ib = \sin(\log_e i^i) = \sin(i\log_e i)$
$$= \sin(i(\log_e|i| + i\arg i))$$
$$= \sin(i(\log_e 1 + (i\pi/2)))$$
$$= \sin(i(0 + (i\pi/2)))$$
$$= \sin(-\pi/2) = -1$$

$\therefore$ $a = -1$ and $b = 0$

Now, $\cos(\log_e i^i) = \sqrt{1 - \sin^2(\log_e i^i)}$
$$= \sqrt{1-(-1)^2}$$
$$= \sqrt{(1-1)} = 0$$

Alternate Solution

$\because$ $i^i = (e^{i\pi/2})^i = e^{-\pi/2}$

$\therefore$ $\sin(\log_e i^i) = \sin(\log_e e^{-\pi/2}) = \sin\left(-\dfrac{\pi}{2}\log_e e\right)$

$= \sin(-\pi/2) = -1 = a + ib$ [given]

$\therefore$ $a = -1$ and $b = 0$

and $\cos(\log_e i^i) = \cos(\log_e e^{-\pi/2})$

$= \cos\left(-\dfrac{\pi}{2}\log_e e\right) = \cos\left(-\dfrac{\pi}{2}\right) = 0$

Example 49. Find the general value of $\log_2(5i)$, where $i = \sqrt{-1}$.

Sol. $\log_2 5i = \dfrac{\log_e 5i}{\log_e 2} = \dfrac{1}{\log_e 2}\{\log_e|5i| + i\arg(5i) + 2n\pi i\}$

$$= \frac{1}{\log_e 2}\left\{\log_e 5 + \frac{i\pi}{2} + 2n\pi i\right\}, n \in I$$

Milestone Practice 1.2

1. If $z_1 = 2-i$ and $z_2 = -2+i$, find

(i) $\text{Re}\left(\dfrac{z_1 z_2}{\bar{z}_1}\right)$ (ii) $\text{Im}\left(\dfrac{1}{z_1\bar{z}_1}\right)$

2. If $a+ib = \left(\dfrac{1-i}{1+i}\right)^{100}$, find a^2+b^2.

3. Find the conjugate of complex number z, if $z = \dfrac{(1-i)^2}{3a-i}$ and $|z| = \sqrt{\dfrac{2}{5}}$, where $a > 0$.

4. If z_1 and z_2 be complex numbers such that $z_1 \neq z_2$ and $|z_1| = |z_2|$. If z_1 has positive real part and z_2 has negative imaginary part, then $\dfrac{z_1+z_2}{z_1-z_2}$ may be

(a) purely imaginary
(b) real and positive
(c) real and negative
(d) None of the above

5. Find the modulus of z, if $|z| - z = 9 - 9i$, where $i = \sqrt{-1}$ and $z \neq 0$.

6. If $|z - i\text{Re}(z)| = |z - \text{Im}(z)|$, then prove that $(\text{Re}(z)) = \pm(\text{Im}(z))$.

7. If $z = x+iy$ and $w = \dfrac{1-iz}{z-i}$, then show that $|w| = 1$ $\Rightarrow z$ is purely real.

8. If $(\sqrt{8}+i)^{50} = 3^{49}(a+ib)$, find a^2+b^2.

9. Find the minimum value of $|z| + |z-2i|$.

10. Find the modulus and argument of complex number $\dfrac{1}{1+i}$.

11. Prove the following inequalities

(i) $\left|\dfrac{z}{|z|} - 1\right| \leq |\arg z|$

(ii) $|z-1| \leq |z||\arg z| + ||z|-1|$

12. Find the principal argument of the complex number $\sin\dfrac{6\pi}{5} + i\left(1+\cos\dfrac{6\pi}{5}\right)$.

13. If z_1 and z_2 both satisfy $z + \bar{z} = 2(z-1)$ and $\arg(z_1 - z_2) = \dfrac{\pi}{4}$, then find $\text{Im}(z_1+z_2)$.

14. The complex number $z = \dfrac{i-1}{\cos\dfrac{5\pi}{12} - i\sin\dfrac{5\pi}{12}}$ is

(a) $2\left(\cos\dfrac{\pi}{6} + i\sin\dfrac{\pi}{6}\right)$ (b) $\sqrt{2}\left(\cos\dfrac{\pi}{6} - i\sin\dfrac{\pi}{6}\right)$

(c) $\sqrt{2}\left(\cos\dfrac{\pi}{6} + i\sin\dfrac{\pi}{6}\right)$ (d) $2\left(\cos\dfrac{\pi}{6} - i\sin\dfrac{\pi}{6}\right)$

15. Find the polar form of the complex number $z = \dfrac{2+6\sqrt{3}i}{5+\sqrt{3}i}$.

16. If $z = i^{i^i}$, then find $|z|$.

17. If $z = re^{i\theta}$, prove that $|e^{iz}| = e^{-r\sin\theta}$

18. Find the real part of $(1-i)^{-i}$.

Answer Key

1. (i) $-\dfrac{2}{5}$ (ii) 0 **2.** 1 **3.** $\dfrac{1}{5} + \dfrac{3}{5}i$ **4.** (a) **5.** 9

8. 9 **9.** 2 **10.** $\dfrac{1}{\sqrt{2}}, -\dfrac{\pi}{4}$ **12.** $\arg(z) = \dfrac{9\pi}{10}$ **13.** 2

14. (c) **15.** $z = 2\left(\cos\dfrac{\pi}{3} + i\sin\dfrac{\pi}{3}\right)$ **16.** 1 **18.** $\text{Re}(z) = e^{-\frac{\pi}{4}}\cos\left(\dfrac{1}{2}\log 2\right)$

For Detailed Solution

Milestone 3 Square Root of Complex Number and De-Moivre's Theorem

- Square Root of Complex Number • Solution of Complex Equation • De-Moivre's Theorem
- Cube Root of Unity

1.10 Square Root of Complex Number

Let $z = x + iy$,

where $x, y \in R$ and $i = \sqrt{-1}$.

Suppose $\sqrt{(x+iy)} = a + ib$ ...(i)

On squaring both sides, we get

$$(x+iy) = (a^2 - b^2) + 2iab$$

On comparing the real and imaginary parts, we get

$$a^2 - b^2 = x \quad \text{...(ii)}$$

and $$2ab = y \quad \text{...(iii)}$$

$$\therefore \quad a^2 + b^2 = \sqrt{(a^2-b^2)^2 + 4a^2b^2} = \sqrt{(x^2+y^2)}$$

$$a^2 + b^2 = |z| \quad \text{...(iv)}$$

From Eqs. (ii) and (iv), we get

$$a = \pm\sqrt{\left(\frac{|z|+x}{2}\right)}, \; b = \pm\sqrt{\left(\frac{|z|-x}{2}\right)}$$

or $$a = \pm\sqrt{\left(\frac{|z|+\text{Re}(z)}{2}\right)}, \; b = \pm\sqrt{\left(\frac{|z|-\text{Re}(z)}{2}\right)}$$

Now, from Eq. (i), the required square roots,

$$\text{i.e. } \sqrt{z} = \begin{cases} \pm\left(\sqrt{\dfrac{|z|+\text{Re}(z)}{2}} + i\sqrt{\dfrac{|z|-\text{Re}(z)}{2}}\right), & \text{if Im}(z) > 0 \\ \pm\left(\sqrt{\dfrac{|z|+\text{Re}(z)}{2}} - i\sqrt{\dfrac{|z|-\text{Re}(z)}{2}}\right), & \text{if Im}(z) < 0 \end{cases}$$

JEE Focus Points

- $\sqrt{i} = \pm\left(\frac{1+i}{\sqrt{2}}\right)$
- $\sqrt{-i} = \pm\left(\frac{1-i}{\sqrt{2}}\right)$

Example 50. Find the square roots of the following

(i) $4 + 3i$

(ii) $-8 - 15i$

Sol. (i) Let $z = 4 + 3i$

$\therefore \quad |z| = 5, \text{Re}(z) = 4, \text{Im}(z) = 3 > 0$

$$\because \quad \sqrt{z} = \pm\left(\sqrt{\frac{|z|+\text{Re}(z)}{2}} + i\sqrt{\frac{|z|-\text{Re}(z)}{2}}\right)$$

$$\therefore \sqrt{(4+3i)} = \pm\left(\sqrt{\left(\frac{5+4}{2}\right)} + i\sqrt{\left(\frac{5-4}{2}\right)}\right) = \pm\left(\frac{3+i}{\sqrt{2}}\right)$$

(ii) Let $z = -8 - 15i$

$\therefore \quad |z| = 17, \text{Re}(z) = -8, \text{Im}(z) = -15 < 0$

$$\therefore \sqrt{(-8-15i)} = \pm\left(\sqrt{\left(\frac{17-8}{2}\right)} - i\sqrt{\left(\frac{17+8}{2}\right)}\right)$$

$$= \pm\left(\frac{3-5i}{\sqrt{2}}\right)$$

1.11 Solution of Complex Equations

Putting $z = x + iy$, where $x, y \in R$ and $i = \sqrt{-1}$ in the given equation and equating the real and imaginary parts, we get x and y, then required solution is $z = x + iy$.

Example 51. Solve the equation $z^2 + |z| = 0$.

Sol. Let $z = x + iy$, where $x, y \in R$ and $i = \sqrt{-1}$ ...(i)

$$\Rightarrow \quad z^2 = (x+iy)^2 = x^2 - y^2 + 2ixy$$

and $|z| = \sqrt{(x^2+y^2)}$

Then, given equation reduces to

$$x^2 - y^2 + 2ixy + \sqrt{(x^2+y^2)} = 0$$

On comparing the real and imaginary parts, we get

$$x^2 - y^2 + \sqrt{(x^2+y^2)} = 0 \quad \text{...(ii)}$$

and $$2xy = 0 \quad \text{...(iii)}$$

From Eq. (iii), let $x = 0$ and from Eq. (ii),

$$-y^2 + \sqrt{y^2} = 0$$

$$\Rightarrow \quad -|y|^2 + |y| = 0$$

$$\therefore \quad |y| = 0, 1$$

$$\Rightarrow \quad y = 0, \pm 1$$

From Eq. (iii), let $y = 0$ and from Eq. (ii),

$$x^2 + \sqrt{x^2} = 0$$

$$\Rightarrow \quad |x|^2 + |x| = 0$$

$$\Rightarrow \quad |x|^2 + |x| = 0$$

$$\Rightarrow \quad x = 0$$

$\therefore$ $x + iy$ are $0 + 0 \cdot i,\ 0 + i,\ 0 - i$

i.e. $z = 0, i, -i$ are the solutions of the given equation.

Example 52. Find the complex number z if $z\bar{z} = 2$ and $z + \bar{z} = 2$.

Sol. Let $z = x + iy$.

Then, $z\bar{z} = 2$

$$\Rightarrow \quad (x + iy)(x - iy) = 2$$

$$\Rightarrow \quad x^2 + y^2 = 2 \quad \text{...(i)}$$

Also, $z + \bar{z} = 2$

$$\Rightarrow (x + iy) + (x - iy) = 2$$

$$\Rightarrow \quad 2x = 2$$

$$\Rightarrow \quad x = 1 \quad \text{...(ii)}$$

From Eqs. (i) and (ii), we get

$$x = 1, y = \pm 1$$

$$\therefore \quad z = 1 + i \text{ or } 1 - i$$

Example 53. If $iz^3 + z^2 - z + i = 0$, then find $|z|$.

Sol. We have, $iz^3 + z^2 - z + i = 0$

$$\Rightarrow \quad iz(z^2 + i) + (z^2 + i) = 0$$

$$\Rightarrow \quad (z^2 + i)(iz + 1) = 0$$

$$\Rightarrow \quad z^2 + i = 0 \text{ or } iz + 1 = 0$$

Now, $z^2 + i = 0$

$$\Rightarrow \quad z^2 = -i$$

$$\Rightarrow \quad |z^2| = |-i|$$

$$\Rightarrow \quad |z|^2 = 1$$

$$\Rightarrow \quad |z| = 1$$

Again, $iz + 1 = 0$

$$\Rightarrow \quad z = -\frac{1}{i}$$

$$\Rightarrow \quad z = i$$

$$\Rightarrow \quad |z| = |i|$$

$$\Rightarrow \quad |z| = 1$$

So, $|z| = 1$

Example 54. If $|z + 1| = z + 2(1 + i)$, then

(a) $\text{Re}(z) = \frac{1}{2}, \text{Im}(z) = -2$ (b) $\text{Re}(z) = -\frac{1}{2}, \text{Im}(z) = 2$

(c) $\text{Re}(z) = 2, \text{Im}(z) = \frac{1}{2}$ (d) $\text{Re}(z) = -2, \text{Im}(z) = -\frac{1}{2}$

Sol. (a) Let $z = x + iy$.

Then, $|z + 1| = z + 2(1 + i)$

$$\Rightarrow \quad |(x + 1) + iy| = (x + 2) + (y + 2)i$$

$$\Rightarrow \quad \sqrt{(x + 1)^2 + y^2} = (x + 2) + (y + 2)i$$

$$\therefore \quad \sqrt{(x + 1)^2 + y^2} = x + 2 \text{ and } y + 2 = 0$$

$$\Rightarrow \quad (x + 1)^2 + y^2 = (x + 2)^2 \text{ and } y = -2$$

$$\Rightarrow \quad y^2 = 2x + 3 \text{ and } y = -2$$

$$\Rightarrow \quad 4 = 2x + 3 \text{ and } y = -2$$

$$\Rightarrow \quad x = \frac{1}{2} \text{ and } y = -2$$

$$\therefore \quad z = \frac{1}{2} - 2i$$

Example 55. Find the number of solutions of the equation $z^2 + |z|^2 = 0$.

Sol. $\because$ $z^2 + |z|^2 = 0$

or $z^2 + z\bar{z} = 0$

$$\Rightarrow \quad z(z + \bar{z}) = 0$$

$$\therefore \quad z = 0 \quad \text{...(i)}$$

and $z + \bar{z} = 0$

$$\Rightarrow \quad 2\text{Re}(z) = 0$$

$$\therefore \quad \text{Re}(z) = 0$$

If $z = x + iy$ $\quad [\because x = \text{Re}(z)]$

$$= 0 + iy, y \in R$$

and $i = \sqrt{-1}$ $\quad$ ...(ii)

On combining Eqs. (i) and (ii), then we can say that the given equation has infinite solutions.

Example 56. The number of complex numbers satisfying the equation $2|z|^2 + z^2 - 5 + i\sqrt{3} = 0$, where $i = \sqrt{-1}$, is

(a) 1 (b) 2

(c) 3 (d) 4

Sol. Let $z = x + iy$, where $x, y \in R$ and $i = \sqrt{-1}$

$$\Rightarrow \quad z^2 = (x + iy)^2 = x^2 - y^2 + 2ixy$$

and $|z| = \sqrt{(x^2 + y^2)}$

Then, given equation reduces to

$$2(x^2 + y^2) + x^2 - y^2 + 2ixy - 5 + i\sqrt{3} = 0$$

$$\Rightarrow \quad (3x^2 + y^2 - 5) + i(2xy + \sqrt{3}) = 0 = 0 + i \cdot 0$$

On comparing the real and imaginary parts, we get

$$3x^2 + y^2 - 5 = 0 \quad \text{...(i)}$$

and $2xy + \sqrt{3} = 0$ $\quad$ ...(ii)

On substituting the value of x from Eq. (ii) in Eq. (i), we get

$$3\left(-\frac{\sqrt{3}}{2y}\right)^2+y^2-5=0$$

$$\Rightarrow \quad \frac{9}{4y^2}+y^2=5$$

or $$4y^4-20y^2+9=0$$

$$\Rightarrow \quad (2y^2-9)(2y^2-1)=0$$

$$\therefore \quad y^2=\frac{9}{2}, y^2=\frac{1}{2} \text{ or } y=\pm\frac{3}{\sqrt{2}}, y=\pm\frac{1}{\sqrt{2}}$$

or $$y=-\frac{3}{\sqrt{2}}, \frac{3}{\sqrt{2}}, -\frac{1}{\sqrt{2}}, \frac{1}{\sqrt{2}}$$

From Eq. (ii), we get

$$x=\frac{1}{\sqrt{6}}, -\frac{1}{\sqrt{6}}, \sqrt{\frac{3}{2}}, -\sqrt{\frac{3}{2}}$$

$$\therefore \quad z=x+iy$$

$$=\frac{1}{\sqrt{6}}-\frac{3i}{\sqrt{2}}, -\frac{1}{\sqrt{6}}+\frac{3i}{\sqrt{2}}, \sqrt{\frac{3}{2}}-\frac{i}{\sqrt{2}}, -\sqrt{\frac{3}{2}}+\frac{i}{\sqrt{2}}$$

are the solutions of the given equation.

1.12 De-Moivre's Theorem

Statements

(i) If $\theta_1, \theta_2, \theta_3, \ldots, \theta_n \in R$ and $i=\sqrt{-1}$, then

$$(\cos\theta_1+i\sin\theta_1)(\cos\theta_2+i\sin\theta_2)(\cos\theta_3+i\sin\theta_3)\ldots(\cos\theta_n+i\sin\theta_n)$$
$$=\cos(\theta_1+\theta_2+\theta_3+\ldots+\theta_n)+i\sin(\theta_1+\theta_2+\theta_3+\ldots+\theta_n)$$

(ii) If $\theta \in R, n \in I$ (set of integers) and $i=\sqrt{-1}$, then

$$(\cos\theta+i\sin\theta)^n=\cos n\theta+i\sin n\theta$$

(iii) If $\theta \in R$, $n \in Q$ (set of rational numbers) and $i=\sqrt{-1}$, then $\cos n\theta+i\sin n\theta$ is one of the values of $(\cos\theta+i\sin\theta)^n$.

JEE Focus Points

- $(\cos\theta-i\sin\theta)^n=\cos n\theta-i\sin n\theta$
- $(\sin\theta+i\cos\theta)^n=i^n(\cos n\theta-i\sin n\theta)$
- $\dfrac{1}{\cos\theta+i\sin\theta}=(\cos\theta+i\sin\theta)^{-1}=\cos\theta-i\sin\theta$

Concept Inside Video

Example 57. If $z=\dfrac{\sqrt{3}}{2}-\dfrac{1}{2}i$, find z^6.

Sol. We have, $z=\dfrac{\sqrt{3}}{2}-\dfrac{1}{2}i=\cos\dfrac{\pi}{6}-i\sin\dfrac{\pi}{6}$

$$\therefore z^6=\left(\cos\frac{\pi}{6}-i\sin\frac{\pi}{6}\right)^6=\cos\left(6\times\frac{\pi}{6}\right)-i\sin\left(6\times\frac{\pi}{6}\right)$$
$$=\cos\pi-i\sin\pi=-1$$

Example 58. If $z_r=\cos\left(\dfrac{\pi}{3^r}\right)+i\sin\left(\dfrac{\pi}{3^r}\right)$, where $i=\sqrt{-1}$, prove that $z_1 z_2 z_3 \ldots$ upto infinity $=i$.

Sol. We have, $z_r=\cos\left(\dfrac{\pi}{3^r}\right)+i\sin\left(\dfrac{\pi}{3^r}\right)$

$$\therefore z_1 z_2 z_3 \ldots \infty=\cos\left(\frac{\pi}{3}+\frac{\pi}{3^2}+\frac{\pi}{3^3}+\ldots+\infty\right)+i\sin\left(\frac{\pi}{3}+\frac{\pi}{3^2}+\frac{\pi}{3^3}+\ldots+\infty\right)$$
$$=\cos\left(\frac{\frac{\pi}{3}}{1-\frac{1}{3}}\right)+i\sin\left(\frac{\frac{\pi}{3}}{1-\frac{1}{3}}\right)$$
$$=\cos\left(\frac{\pi}{2}\right)+i\sin\left(\frac{\pi}{2}\right)=0+i\cdot 1=i$$

Example 59. $\dfrac{(\cos\theta+i\sin\theta)^4}{(\sin\theta+i\cos\theta)^5}$ is equal to, where $i=\sqrt{-1}$, is

(a) $\cos 9\theta+i\sin 9\theta$ (b) $\cos 9\theta-i\sin 9\theta$
(c) $\sin 9\theta+i\cos 9\theta$ (d) $\sin 9\theta-i\cos 9\theta$

Sol. (d) $\because (\sin\theta+i\cos\theta)^5=(i)^5(\cos\theta-i\sin\theta)^5$
$$=i(\cos\theta+i\sin\theta)^{-5}$$
$$\therefore \frac{(\cos\theta+i\sin\theta)^4}{(\sin\theta+i\cos\theta)^5}=\frac{(\cos\theta+i\sin\theta)^4}{i(\cos\theta+i\sin\theta)^{-5}}$$
$$=\frac{(\cos\theta+i\sin\theta)^9}{i}=\frac{\cos 9\theta+i\sin 9\theta}{i}$$
$$=-i\cos 9\theta+\sin 9\theta=\sin 9\theta-i\cos 9\theta$$

Example 60. Solve the equation $z^{n-1}=\bar{z}$ $(n \in N)$.

Sol. Case I If $n=2$

$\therefore z^{2-1}=\bar{z} \Rightarrow z=\bar{z}$

$\therefore z$ is any real numbers

Case II If $n \neq 2$

$$\therefore \quad z^{n-1}=\bar{z} \Rightarrow |z^{n-1}|=|\bar{z}|$$
$$\Rightarrow |z|^{n-1}=|z| \Rightarrow |z|^{n-2}=1 \Rightarrow |z|=1$$

$\therefore z$ is unimodular complex number.

$\therefore z=\cos\theta+i\sin\theta$

Now, $z^{n-1}=\bar{z}$

$$\Rightarrow \quad (\cos\theta+i\sin\theta)^{n-1}=\cos\theta-i\sin\theta$$
$$\Rightarrow \quad (\cos\theta+i\sin\theta)^{n-1}=\frac{1}{\cos\theta+i\sin\theta}$$
$$\Rightarrow \quad (\cos\theta+i\sin\theta)^n=1$$
$$\Rightarrow \quad \cos n\theta+i\sin n\theta=1 \Rightarrow \cos n\theta=1 \text{ and } \sin n\theta=0$$
$$\Rightarrow \quad n\theta=2m\pi \Rightarrow \theta=\frac{2m\pi}{n}$$
$$\therefore z=\cos\left(\frac{2m\pi}{n}\right)+i\sin\left(\frac{2m\pi}{n}\right); m=0, 1, 2, \ldots, n-1$$

JEE SCANNER

Example Similar to PYQ Asked in JEE Main 2021

If $(1+\sqrt{3}i)^{100}=2^{99}(p+iq)$, then p and q are roots of the equation

(a) $x^2+(\sqrt{3}-1)x+\sqrt{3}=0$

(b) $x^2+(\sqrt{3}+1)x+\sqrt{3}=0$

(c) $x^2-(\sqrt{3}-1)x+\sqrt{3}=0$

(d) $x^2-(\sqrt{3}-1)x-\sqrt{3}=0$

Sol. (b) $\because \quad (1+\sqrt{3}i)^{100}=2^{99}(p+iq)$

$$\Rightarrow \left(2e^{i\frac{\pi}{3}}\right)^{100}=2^{99}(p+iq)$$

$$\Rightarrow 2^{100}\left(\cos\frac{100\pi}{3}+i\sin\frac{100\pi}{3}\right)=2^{99}(p+iq)$$

$$\Rightarrow 2\left(-\frac{1}{2}+i\left(\frac{-\sqrt{3}}{2}\right)\right)=p+iq$$

$$\Rightarrow p=-1 \text{ and } q=-\sqrt{3}$$

$\therefore\ p+q=-1-\sqrt{3}$ and $pq=\sqrt{3}$

Equation with roots -1 and $-\sqrt{3}$ is

$$x^2-(p+q)x+pq=x^2+(1+\sqrt{3})x+\sqrt{3}=0$$

Skill Builder

If $(1+i)^{50}=2^{48}(a+ib)$, then a and b are roots of the equation

(a) $2^{23}x^2-x=0$

(b) $2^{12}x^2-x=0$

(c) $2^{23}x^2+x=0$

(d) $2^{12}x^2+x=0$

For Sol.

■ **For more practice** See Q.4 of Milestone Practice 1.3.

1.13 Cube Root of Unity

Let $z=(1)^{1/3} \Rightarrow z^3=1 \Rightarrow z^3-1=0$

$\Rightarrow (z-1)(z^2+z+1)=0 \Rightarrow \quad z-1=0$ or $z^2+z+1=0$

$$\therefore \qquad z=1 \text{ or } z=\frac{-1\pm\sqrt{(1-4)}}{2}=\frac{-1\pm i\sqrt{3}}{2}$$

Therefore, $z=1, \dfrac{-1+i\sqrt{3}}{2}, \dfrac{-1-i\sqrt{3}}{2}$,

where $i=\sqrt{-1}$.

If second root is represented by ω (omega), third root will be ω^2.

$\therefore$ Cube roots of unity are $1, \omega, \omega^2$ and ω, ω^2 are called non-real complex cube roots of unity.

Properties of Cube Roots of Unity

(i) $1+\omega+\omega^2=0$ and $\omega^3=1$

(ii) **To find the value of $\omega^n\ (n>3)$.**

First divide n by 3. Let q be the quotient and r be the remainder.

$$\begin{array}{r} 3\,)\,n\,(q \\ -3q \\ \hline r \end{array}$$

i.e. $\qquad n=3q+r$, where $0\le r\le 2$

$$\therefore \qquad \omega^n=\omega^{3q+r}=(\omega^3)^q\cdot\omega^r=\omega^r$$

In general, $\boldsymbol{\omega^{3n}=1, \omega^{3n+1}=\omega, \omega^{3n+2}=\omega^2}$

(iii) $1+\omega^r+\omega^{2r}=\begin{cases}3, \text{ when } n \text{ is a multiple of } 3\\ 0, \text{ when } n \text{ is not a multiple of } 3\end{cases}$

(iv) Cube roots of -1 are $-1, -\omega$ and $-\omega^2$.

(v) $a+b\omega+c\omega^2=0 \Rightarrow \quad a=b=c$, if $a, b, c\in R$.

(vi) If a, b, c are non-zero numbers such that $a+b+c=0=a^2+b^2+c^2$, then $a:b:c=1:\omega:\omega^2$.

(vii) $\overline{\omega}=\omega^2, (\overline{\omega})^2=\omega$

(viii) $\sqrt{\omega}=\pm\omega^2, \sqrt{\omega^2}=\pm\omega$

(ix) $|\omega|=|\omega^2|=1$

(x) A complex number $a+ib$ (where $i=\sqrt{-1}$), for which $|a:b|=1:\sqrt{3}$ or $\sqrt{3}:1$ can always be expressed in terms of ω or ω^2.

e.g.

(a) $1+i\sqrt{3}=-(-1-i\sqrt{3}) \qquad [\because |1:\sqrt{3}|=1:\sqrt{3}]$

$$=-2\left(\frac{-1-i\sqrt{3}}{2}\right)$$

$$=-2\omega^2$$

(b) $\sqrt{3}+i=\dfrac{i(\sqrt{3}+i)}{i}$

$$=\frac{(-1+i\sqrt{3})}{i}$$

$$=\left(\frac{-1+i\sqrt{3}}{2}\right)\left(\frac{2}{i}\right) \qquad [\because |\sqrt{3}:1|=\sqrt{3}:1]$$

$$=\frac{2\omega}{i}=-2i\omega$$

(xi) The cube roots of unity when represented on complex plane lie on vertices of an equilateral triangle inscribed in a unit circle, having centre at origin. One vertex being on positive real axis.

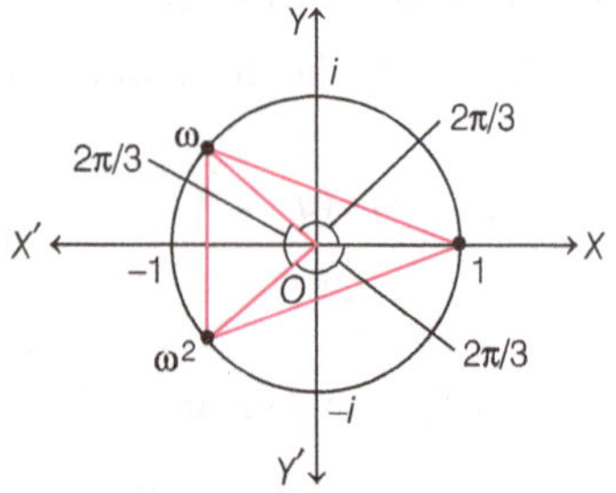

Example 61. If ω is an imaginary cube root of unity, then find

(i) $(1+\omega-\omega)^2$

(ii) $(1-\omega)(1-\omega^2)(1+\omega^4)(1+\omega^8)$

Sol. (i) $(1+\omega-\omega^2)^2=(-\omega^2-\omega^2)^2$

$$=(-2\omega^2)^2=4\omega^4=4\omega$$

(ii) $(1-\omega)(1-\omega^2)(1+\omega^4)(1+\omega^8)$

$$=(1-\omega)(1-\omega^2)(1+\omega)(1+\omega^2)$$
$$=(1-\omega^2)(1-\omega^4)$$
$$=(1-\omega^2)(1-\omega)$$
$$=1-\omega-\omega^2+\omega^3$$
$$=1-(\omega+\omega^2)+1$$
$$=1-(-1)+1=3$$

Example 62. Solve $(x-1)^3+27=0$.

Sol. We have, $(x-1)^3+27=0$

$$\Rightarrow \quad (x-1)^3=-27$$
$$\Rightarrow \quad (x-1)=(-27)^{\frac{1}{3}}$$
$$\Rightarrow \quad x-1=(-27)^{\frac{1}{3}}(1)^{\frac{1}{3}}$$
$$\Rightarrow \quad x-1=-3(1,\omega,\omega^2)$$
$$\Rightarrow \quad x-1=-3,-3\omega,-3\omega^2$$
$$\Rightarrow \quad x=-2,1-3\omega,1-3\omega^2$$

Important Relations in Terms of Cube Root of Unity

(i) $a^2+ab+b^2=(a-b\omega)(a-b\omega^2)$

(ii) $a^2-ab+b^2=(a+b\omega)(a+b\omega^2)$

(iii) $a^3+b^3=(a+b)(a+b\omega)(a+b\omega^2)$

(iv) $a^3-b^3=(a-b)(a-b\omega)(a-b\omega^2)$

(v) $a^2+b^2+c^2-ab-bc-ca$
$$=(a+b\omega+c\omega^2)(a+b\omega^2+c\omega)$$

(vi) $a^3+b^3+c^3-3abc$
$$=(a+b+c)(a+b\omega+c\omega^2)(a+b\omega^2+c\omega)$$

Example 63. If ω is a non-real complex cube root of unity, find the values of the following.

(i) ω^{1999}

(ii) ω^{-998}

(iii) $\left(\dfrac{-1+i\sqrt{3}}{2}\right)^{3n+2}$, $n\in N$ and $i=\sqrt{-1}$

(iv) $(1+\omega)(1+\omega^2)(1+\omega^4)(1+\omega^8)\ldots$ upto $2n$ factors

(v) $\left(\dfrac{\alpha+\beta\omega+\gamma\omega^2+\delta\omega^2}{\beta+\alpha\omega^2+\gamma\omega+\delta\omega}\right)$, where $\alpha,\beta,\gamma,\delta\in R$

(vi) $1\cdot(2-\omega)(2-\omega^2)+2\cdot(3-\omega)(3-\omega^2)$
$+3\cdot(4-\omega)(4-\omega^2)+\ldots+\ldots+(n-1)(n-\omega)(n-\omega^2)$

Sol. (i) $\omega^{1999}=\omega^{3\times 666+1}=\omega$

(ii) $\omega^{-998}=\dfrac{1}{\omega^{998}}=\dfrac{\omega}{\omega^{999}}=\omega$

(iii) $\left(\dfrac{-1+i\sqrt{3}}{2}\right)^{3n+2}=\omega^{3n+2}=\omega^{3n}\cdot\omega^2=(\omega^3)^n\cdot\omega^2$
$$=(1)^n\cdot\omega^2=\omega^2$$

(iv) $(1+\omega)(1+\omega^2)(1+\omega^4)(1+\omega^8)\ldots$ upto $2n$ factors
$=(1+\omega)(1+\omega^2)(1+\omega)(1+\omega^2)\ldots$ upto $2n$ factors
$=(-\omega^2)(-\omega)(-\omega^2)(-\omega)\ldots$ upto $2n$ factors
$=(\omega^3)(\omega^3)\ldots$ upto $2n$ factors $=1\cdot1\cdot1\cdot\ldots$upto $2n$ factors
$=(1)^{2n}=1$

(v) $\left(\dfrac{\alpha+\beta\omega+\gamma\omega^2+\delta\omega^2}{\beta+\alpha\omega^2+\gamma\omega+\delta\omega}\right)=\dfrac{\omega(\alpha+\beta\omega+\gamma\omega^2+\delta\omega^2)}{(\beta\omega+\alpha\omega^3+\gamma\omega^2+\delta\omega^2)}$
$$=\frac{\omega(\alpha+\beta\omega+\gamma\omega^2+\delta\omega^2)}{(\beta\omega+\alpha+\gamma\omega^2+\delta\omega^2)}=\omega$$

(vi) $\Sigma(n-1)(n-\omega)(n-\omega^2)=\Sigma(n^3-1)=\Sigma n^3-\Sigma 1$
$$=\left\{\frac{n(n+1)}{2}\right\}^2-n$$

Example 64. If α,β and γ are the roots of $x^3-3x^2+3x+7=0$, find the value of $\dfrac{\alpha-1}{\beta-1}+\dfrac{\beta-1}{\gamma-1}+\dfrac{\gamma-1}{\alpha-1}$.

Sol. We have, $\quad x^3-3x^2+3x+7=0$
$$\Rightarrow \quad (x-1)^3+8=0$$
$$\Rightarrow \quad (x-1)^3+2^3=0$$

$$\Rightarrow \quad (x-1+2)(x-1+2\omega)(x-1+2\omega^2)=0$$

$$\Rightarrow \quad (x+1)(x-1+2\omega)(x-1+2\omega^2)=0$$

$$\therefore \quad x=-1, 1-2\omega, 1-2\omega^2$$

$$\Rightarrow \quad \alpha=-1, \beta=1-2\omega, \gamma=1-2\omega^2$$

Then, $\dfrac{\alpha-1}{\beta-1}+\dfrac{\beta-1}{\gamma-1}+\dfrac{\gamma-1}{\alpha-1}=\dfrac{-2}{-2\omega}+\dfrac{-2\omega}{-2\omega^2}+\dfrac{-2\omega^2}{-2}$

$$=\frac{1}{\omega}+\frac{1}{\omega}+\omega^2$$

$$=\omega^2+\omega^2+\omega^2=3\omega^2$$

JEE SCANNER

Example Similar to PYQ Asked in JEE Main 2020

If a and b are real numbers such that $(3+\alpha)^3=a+b\alpha^2$, where $\alpha=\dfrac{-1+i\sqrt{3}}{2}$, then a − b is equal to ....

Sol. (19) Given, $\alpha=\dfrac{-1+i\sqrt{3}}{2}=\omega$

$$(3+\alpha)^3=a+b\alpha^2$$

$$\Rightarrow \quad (3+\omega)^3=a+b\omega^2$$

$$\Rightarrow \quad 27+\omega^3+27\omega+9\omega^2=a+b\omega^2$$

$$\Rightarrow \quad 27+1+27\omega+9\omega^2=a+b\omega^2 \qquad [\because \omega^3=1]$$

$$\Rightarrow \quad 1+27(1+\omega)+9\omega^2=a+b\omega^2$$

$$\Rightarrow \quad 1-27\omega^2+9\omega^2=a+b\omega^2 \qquad [\because 1+\omega+\omega^2=0]$$

$$\Rightarrow \quad 1-18\omega^2=a+b\omega^2$$

$$\Rightarrow \quad a=1 \text{ and } b=-18$$

$$\therefore \quad a-b=1-(-18)=19$$

Skill Builder

If *a* and *b* are real numbers such that $(3+\alpha)^4=a+b\omega$, where $\alpha=\dfrac{-1-i\sqrt{3}}{2}$, then $a-b$ is equal to ....

For Sol.

■ **For more practice** See Q.6 of Milestone Practice 1.3.

Example 65. If $z=\dfrac{\sqrt{3}+i}{2}$, where $i=\sqrt{-1}$, find the value of $(z^{101}+i^{103})^{105}$.

Sol. $\because \quad z=\dfrac{\sqrt{3}+i}{2}=\dfrac{1}{i}\left(\dfrac{i\sqrt{3}+i^2}{2}\right) \qquad [\because i^2=-1]$

$$=-i\left(\frac{-1+i\sqrt{3}}{2}\right)=-i\omega$$

$$\therefore \quad z^{101}=(-i\omega)^{101}=-i^{101}\cdot\omega^{101}=-i\omega^2$$

and $i^{103}=i^3=-i$

Then, $z^{101}+i^{103}=-i\omega^2-i=-i(\omega^2+1)$

$$=-i(-\omega)=i\omega$$

Hence, $(z^{101}+i^{103})^{105}=(i\omega)^{105}=i^{105}\cdot\omega^{105}=i\cdot 1=i$

Example 66. If $\left(\dfrac{3}{2}+\dfrac{i\sqrt{3}}{2}\right)^{50}=3^{25}(x-iy)$, where $x, y \in R$ and $i=\sqrt{-1}$, find the ordered pair of (x, y).

Sol. $\because \quad \dfrac{3}{2}+\dfrac{i\sqrt{3}}{2}=\sqrt{3}\left(\dfrac{\sqrt{3}+i}{2}\right)$

$$=\frac{\sqrt{3}}{i}\left(\frac{i\sqrt{3}+i^2}{2}\right)$$

$$=-i\sqrt{3}\left(\frac{-1+i\sqrt{3}}{2}\right)$$

$$=-i\sqrt{3}\,\omega$$

$$\therefore \left(\frac{3}{2}+\frac{i\sqrt{3}}{2}\right)^{50}=(-i\sqrt{3}\,\omega)^{50}=i^{50}\cdot 3^{25}\cdot\omega^{50}$$

$$=-1\cdot 3^{25}\cdot\omega^2=-3^{25}\cdot\left(\frac{-1-i\sqrt{3}}{2}\right)$$

$$=3^{25}\left(\frac{1}{2}+\frac{i\sqrt{3}}{2}\right)=3^{25}(x-iy) \qquad \text{[given]}$$

$$\therefore \quad x=\frac{1}{2}, y=-\frac{\sqrt{3}}{2}$$

$\Rightarrow$ Ordered pair is $\left(\dfrac{1}{2}, -\dfrac{\sqrt{3}}{2}\right)$.

*n*th Root of Unity

Let z be the nth root of unity, then

$$z=(1)^{1/n}=(\cos 0+i\sin 0)^{1/n}$$

$$=(\cos(2k\pi+0)+i\sin(2k\pi+0))^{1/n}$$

[where k is an integer]

$$=(\cos 2k\pi+i\sin 2k\pi)^{1/n}$$

$$\therefore \quad z=\cos\left(\frac{2k\pi}{n}\right)+i\sin\left(\frac{2k\pi}{n}\right)$$

where, $\quad k=0, 1, 2, 3, \ldots, (n-1)$

Let $\alpha=\cos\dfrac{2\pi}{n}+i\sin\dfrac{2\pi}{n}$, then, nth roots of unity are α^k $(k=0, 1, 2, 3, \ldots, n-1)$ i.e, then, nth roots of unity are $1, \alpha, \alpha^2, \alpha^3, \ldots, \alpha^{n-1}$ which are in GP with common ratio $=e^{2\pi i/n}$.

(a) **Sum of n, nth roots of unity**

$$1+\alpha+\alpha^2+\alpha^3+\ldots+\alpha^{n-1}=\frac{1\cdot(1-\alpha^n)}{(1-\alpha)}$$

$$=\frac{1-(\cos 2\pi+i\sin 2\pi)}{1-\alpha}$$

$$=\frac{1-(1+0)}{1-\alpha}=0$$

(b) **Product of n, nth roots of unity**

$$1\times\alpha\times\alpha^2\times\alpha^3\times\ldots\times\alpha^{n-1}=\alpha^{1+2+3+\ldots+(n-1)}$$

$$=\alpha^{\frac{(n-1)n}{2}}=\left(\cos\frac{2\pi}{n}+i\sin\frac{2\pi}{n}\right)^{\frac{(n-1)n}{2}}$$

$$=\cos(n-1)\pi+i\sin(n-1)\pi$$

$$=(\cos\pi+i\sin\pi)^{n-1}=(-1)^{n-1}\quad[\because n \text{ is even}]$$

Product $=1$ (n is odd)

(c) If α is an imaginary nth root of unity, then other roots are given by $\alpha^2, \alpha^3, \alpha^4, \ldots, \alpha^n$.

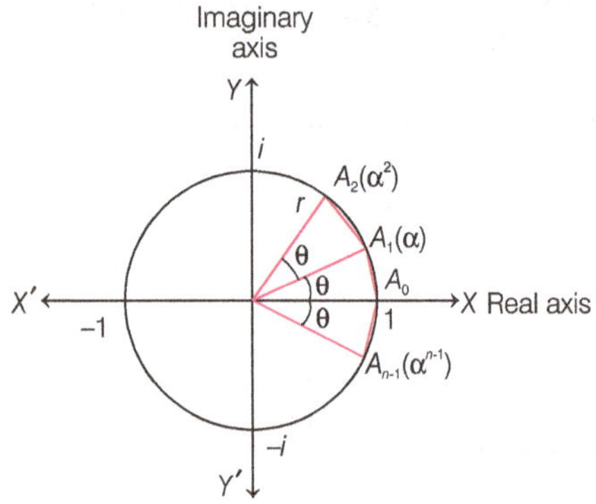

(d) $\because\ 1+\alpha+\alpha^2+\ldots+\alpha^{n-1}=0$

$$\Rightarrow \sum_{k=0}^{n-1}\alpha^k=0$$

or $$\sum_{k=0}^{n-1}\cos\left(\frac{2\pi k}{n}\right)+i\sum_{k=0}^{n-1}\sin\left(\frac{2\pi k}{n}\right)=0$$

$$\Rightarrow \sum_{k=0}^{n-1}\cos\left(\frac{2\pi k}{n}\right)=0$$

and $$\sum_{k=0}^{n-1}\sin\left(\frac{2\pi k}{n}\right)=0$$

These roots are located at the vertices of a regular plane polygon of n sides inscribed in a unit circle having centre at origin, one vertex being on positive real axis.

(e) $z^n-1=(z-1)(z-\alpha)(z-\alpha^2)\ldots(z-\alpha^{n-1})$.

JEE Focus Points

Concept Inside Video

- If $1, \alpha_1, \alpha_2, \alpha_3, \ldots, \alpha_{n-1}$ are the n, nth root of unity, then $(1)^p+(\alpha_1)^p+(\alpha_2)^p+\ldots+(\alpha_{n-1})^p$ $=\begin{cases}0, & \text{if } p \text{ is not an integral multiple of } n\\ n, & \text{if } p \text{ is an integral multiple of } n\end{cases}$
- $(1+\alpha_1)(1+\alpha_2)\ldots(1+\alpha_{n-1})=\begin{cases}0, & \text{if } n \text{ is even}\\ 1, & \text{if } n \text{ is odd}\end{cases}$
- $(1-\alpha_1)(1-\alpha_2)\ldots(1-\alpha_{n-1})=n$
- $z^n-1=(z-1)(z+1)\prod_{r=1}^{(n-2)/2}\left(z^2-2z\cos\frac{2r\pi}{n}+1\right)$, if '$n$' is even.
- $z^n+1=\prod_{r=0}^{(n-2)/2}\left(z^2-2z\cos\left(\frac{(2r+1)\pi}{n}\right)+1\right)$, if n is even.
- $z^n+1=(z+1)\prod_{r=0}^{(n-3)/2}\left(z^2-2z\cos\left(\frac{(2r+1)\pi}{n}\right)+1\right)$, if '$n$' is odd.

The Sum of the Following Series Should be Remembered

(i) $\cos\theta+\cos 2\theta+\cos 3\theta+\ldots+\cos n\theta$

$$=\frac{\sin\left(\frac{n\theta}{2}\right)}{\sin\left(\frac{\theta}{2}\right)}.\cos\left[\left(\frac{n+1}{2}\right)\theta\right]$$

(ii) $\sin\theta+\sin 2\theta+\sin 3\theta+\ldots+\sin n\theta$

$$=\frac{\sin\left(\frac{n\theta}{2}\right)}{\sin\left(\frac{\theta}{2}\right)}\cdot\sin\left[\left(\frac{n+1}{2}\right)\theta\right]$$

Example 67. Find all roots of the equation $x^6-x^5+x^4-x^3+x^2-x+1=0$.

Sol. $\because\ 1-x+x^2-x^3+x^4-x^5+x^6=0$

$$\Rightarrow 1\cdot\frac{[1-(-x)^7]}{1-(-x)}=0, 1+x\neq 0$$

or $1+x^7=0,\ x\neq -1$ or $x^7=-1$

$$\therefore x=(-1)^{1/7}=(\cos\pi+i\sin\pi)^{1/7}, i=\sqrt{-1}$$

$$=[\cos(2n+1)\pi+i\sin(2n+1)\pi]^{1/7}$$

$$=\cos\left(\frac{(2n+1)\pi}{7}\right)+i\sin\left(\frac{(2n+1)\pi}{7}\right)$$

for $n=0, 1, 2, 4, 5, 6$.

Example 68. If $1, \omega, \omega^2, \ldots, \omega^{n-1}$ are n, nth roots of unity, find the value of $(9-\omega)(9-\omega^2)\ldots(9-\omega^{n-1})$.

Sol. Let $x=(1)^{1/n} \Rightarrow x^n-1=0$

has n roots $1, \omega, \omega^2, \ldots, \omega^{n-1}$

$\therefore \quad x^n - 1 = (x-1)(x-\omega)(x-\omega^2)\ldots(x-\omega^{n-1})$

On putting $x = 9$ in both sides, we get

$$\frac{9^n - 1}{9-1} = (9-\omega)(9-\omega^2)(9-\omega^3)\ldots(9-\omega^{n-1})$$

or $\quad (9-\omega)(9-\omega^2)\ldots(9-\omega^{n-1}) = \dfrac{9^n-1}{8}$

Example 69. Find all roots of $x^5 - 1 = 0$.

Sol. $\because \quad x^5 - 1 = 0 \Rightarrow x^5 = 1$

$\therefore \quad x = (1)^{1/5} = (\cos 0 + i \sin 0)^{1/5}$, where $i = \sqrt{-1}$

$$= [\cos(2n\pi + 0) + i \sin(2n\pi + 0)]^{1/5}$$

$$= \cos\left(\frac{2n\pi}{5}\right) + i \sin\left(\frac{2n\pi}{5}\right), \text{ where } n = 0, 1, 2, 3, 4$$

$\therefore$ Roots are

$1, \cos\left(\frac{2\pi}{5}\right) + i \sin\left(\frac{2\pi}{5}\right), \cos\left(\frac{4\pi}{5}\right) + i \sin\left(\frac{4\pi}{5}\right),$

$\cos\left(\frac{6\pi}{5}\right) + i \sin\left(\frac{6\pi}{5}\right), \cos\left(\frac{8\pi}{5}\right) + i \sin\left(\frac{8\pi}{5}\right)$

Now, $\cos\left(\frac{6\pi}{5}\right) + i \sin\left(\frac{6\pi}{5}\right)$

$$= \cos\left(2\pi - \frac{4\pi}{5}\right) + i \sin\left(2\pi - \frac{4\pi}{5}\right)$$

$$= \cos\left(\frac{4\pi}{5}\right) - i \sin\left(\frac{4\pi}{5}\right)$$

and $\cos\left(\frac{8\pi}{5}\right) + i \sin\left(\frac{8\pi}{5}\right)$

$$= \cos\left(2\pi - \frac{2\pi}{5}\right) + i \sin\left(2\pi - \frac{2\pi}{5}\right)$$

$$= \cos\left(\frac{2\pi}{5}\right) - i \sin\left(\frac{2\pi}{5}\right)$$

Hence, roots are 1, $\cos\left(\frac{2\pi}{5}\right) \pm i \sin\left(\frac{2\pi}{5}\right)$

and $\cos\left(\frac{4\pi}{5}\right) \pm i \sin\left(\frac{4\pi}{5}\right)$.

JEE SPIKE

$$\frac{x^n - 1}{x - 1} = (x-\alpha)(x-\alpha^2)\ldots(x-\alpha^{n-1})$$

where $\alpha, \alpha^2, \ldots, \alpha^{n-1}$ are nth root of unity.

$$\therefore \lim_{x \to 1} \frac{x^n - 1}{x - 1} = \lim_{x \to 1} (x-\alpha)(x-\alpha^2)\ldots(x-\alpha^{n-1})$$

$$\Rightarrow \quad n = (1-\alpha)(1-\alpha^2)\ldots(1-\alpha^{n-1})$$

Concept Inside Video

Example 70. If $a = \cos\left(\frac{2\pi}{7}\right) + i \sin\left(\frac{2\pi}{7}\right)$, where $i = \sqrt{-1}$, find the quadratic equation whose roots are $\alpha = a + a^2 + a^4$ and $\beta = a^3 + a^5 + a^6$.

Sol. $\because \quad a = \cos\left(\frac{2\pi}{7}\right) + i \sin\left(\frac{2\pi}{7}\right)$

$\therefore \quad a^7 = \cos 2\pi + i \sin 2\pi = 1 + 0 = 1$ or $a = (1)^{1/7}$

$\therefore \quad 1, a, a^2, a^3, a^4, a^5, a^6$ are 7th roots of unity.

$\therefore \quad 1 + a + a^2 + a^3 + a^4 + a^5 + a^6 = 0 \qquad \ldots(i)$

$\Rightarrow \quad (a + a^2 + a^4) + (a^3 + a^5 + a^6) = -1$ or $\alpha + \beta = -1$

and $\alpha\beta = (a + a^2 + a^4)(a^3 + a^5 + a^6)$

$$= a^4 + a^6 + a^7 + a^5 + a^7 + a^8 + a^7 + a^9 + a^{10}$$

$$= a^4 + a^6 + 1 + a^5 + 1 + a + 1 + a^2 + a^3 \qquad [\because a^7 = 1]$$

$$= (1 + a + a^2 + a^3 + a^4 + a^5 + a^6) + 2$$

$$= 0 + 2 \qquad \text{[from Eq. (i)]}$$

$$= 2$$

Therefore, the required equation is

$$x^2 - (\alpha + \beta)x + \alpha\beta = 0 \text{ or } x^2 + x + 2 = 0$$

Example 71. The value of $\sum_{k=1}^{10}\left[\sin\left(\frac{2\pi k}{11}\right) - i \cos\left(\frac{2\pi k}{11}\right)\right]$, where $i = \sqrt{-1}$, is

(a) 1 (b) -1 (c) i (d) $-i$

Sol. $\sum_{k=1}^{10}\left[\sin\left(\frac{2\pi k}{11}\right) - i \cos\left(\frac{2\pi k}{11}\right)\right]$

$$= -i \sum_{k=1}^{10}\left[\cos\left(\frac{2\pi k}{11}\right) + i \sin\left(\frac{2\pi k}{11}\right)\right]$$

$$= -i\left\{\sum_{k=0}^{10}\left[\cos\left(\frac{2\pi k}{11}\right) + i \sin\left(\frac{2\pi k}{11}\right)\right] - 1\right\}$$

$$= -i(0 - 1) \qquad \text{[sum of 11, 11th roots of unity]}$$

$$= i$$

Example 72. If $n \geq 3$ and $1, \alpha_1, \alpha_2, \alpha_3, \ldots, \alpha_{n-1}$ are the n, nth roots of unity, then find the value of

$$\sum_{1 \le i < j \le n-1}\sum \alpha_i \alpha_j.$$

Sol. Let $\quad x = (1)^{1/n}$

$\therefore \quad x^n = 1$ or $x^n - 1 = 0$

$\therefore \quad 1 + \alpha_1 + \alpha_2 + \alpha_3 + \ldots + \alpha_{n-1} = 0$

or $\quad \alpha_1 + \alpha_2 + \alpha_3 + \ldots + \alpha_{n-1} = -1$

On squaring both sides, we get

$$\alpha_1^2 + \alpha_2^2 + \alpha_3^2 + \ldots + \alpha_{n-1}^2 + 2(\alpha_1\alpha_2 + \alpha_1\alpha_3 + \ldots + \alpha_1\alpha_{n-1} + \alpha_2\alpha_3 + \ldots + \alpha_2\alpha_{n-1} + \ldots + \alpha_{n-2}\alpha_{n-1}) = 1$$

or $1^2 + (\alpha_1)^2 + (\alpha_2)^2 + (\alpha_3)^2 + \ldots + (\alpha_{n-1})^2$

$$+ 2 \sum_{1 \le i < j \le n-1}\sum \alpha_i \alpha_j = 1 + 1^2$$

$$0 + 2 \sum_{1 \le i < j \le n-1}\sum \alpha_i \alpha_j = 2$$

[here, p is not a multiple of n]

$$\therefore \quad \sum_{1 \le i < j \le n-1}\sum \alpha_i \alpha_j = 1$$

JEE SCANNER

Example Similar to PYQ Asked in JEE Main 2022

If α, β, γ and δ are the roots of equation $x^4 + x^3 + x^2 + x + 1 = 0$, then $\alpha^{1991} + \beta^{1991} + \gamma^{1991} + \delta^{1991}$ is equal to

(a) 4

(b) 2

(c) -1

(d) 1

Sol. (c) Given, α, β, γ and δ are the roots of the equation

$$x^4 + x^3 + x^2 + x + 1 = 0$$

$\because \quad x^5 - 1 = (x - 1)(x^4 + x^3 + x^2 + x + 1)$

$\Rightarrow \quad x = 1 \text{ or } x^4 + x^3 + x^2 + x + 1 = 0$

$\Rightarrow \quad x^5 = 1$

$\because$ α, β, γ and δ are the 5th roots of unity.

$\Rightarrow \quad \alpha^5 = \beta^5 = \gamma^5 = \delta^5 = 1, \alpha + \beta + \gamma + \delta = 1$

$\therefore \alpha^{1991} + \beta^{1991} + \gamma^{1991} + \delta^{1991} = 1 \cdot \alpha + 1 \cdot \beta + 1 \cdot \gamma + \delta$

$= \alpha + \beta + \gamma + \delta$

$= -1$

Skill Builder

If z_1, z_2, z_3 and z_4 are fourth roots of unity, then $z_1^{12} + z_2^{13} + z_3^{14} + z_4^{15}$ is equal to

(a) 0 (b) $-1 + i$

(c) $-1 + 3i$ (d) $-1 - i$

For Sol.

■ **For more practice** See Q.11 of Milestone Practice 1.3.

Example 73. If $\alpha_0, \alpha_1, \alpha_2, \ldots, \alpha_{n-1}$ are the n, nth roots of the unity, then find the value of $\sum_{i=0}^{n-1} \frac{\alpha_i}{2 - \alpha_i}$.

Sol. Let $x = (1)^{1/n}$

$\Rightarrow x^n = 1$

$\therefore \quad x^n - 1 = 0$

or $\quad x^n - 1 = (x - \alpha_0)(x - \alpha_1)(x - \alpha_2) \ldots (x - \alpha_{n-1})$

$$= \prod_{i=0}^{n-1} (x - \alpha_i)$$

On taking logarithm both sides, we get

$$\log_e (x^n - 1) = \sum_{i=0}^{n-1} \log_e (x - \alpha_i)$$

On differentiating both sides w.r.t. x, we get

$$\frac{nx^{n-1}}{x^n - 1} = \sum_{i=0}^{n-1} \left(\frac{1}{x - \alpha_i} \right)$$

On putting $x = 2$, we get

$$\frac{n(2)^{n-1}}{2^n - 1} = \sum_{i=0}^{n-1} \frac{1}{(2 - \alpha_i)} \quad \ldots\text{(i)}$$

Now, $\sum_{i=0}^{n-1} \frac{\alpha_i}{(2 - \alpha_i)} = \sum_{i=0}^{n-1} \left(-1 + \frac{2}{2 - \alpha_i} \right)$

$= -\sum_{i=0}^{n-1} 1 + 2 \sum_{i=0}^{n-1} \frac{1}{(2 - \alpha_i)}$

$= -(n) + \frac{2 \cdot n \cdot 2^{n-1}}{2^n - 1}$ [from Eq. (i)]

$= -n + \frac{n \cdot 2^n}{2^n - 1} = \frac{n}{2^n - 1}$

Milestone Practice 1.3

1. Find the square root of $9 + 40i$.

2. Find the locus of z if $\text{Re}(z+1) = |z-1|$.

3. If $z = \left(\frac{\sqrt{3}}{2} + \frac{i}{2}\right)^5 + \left(\frac{\sqrt{3}}{2} - \frac{i}{2}\right)^5$, then prove that $\text{Im}(z) = 0$.

4. If $(\sqrt{3} + i)^{100} = 2^{98}(p + iq)$, then p and q are roots of the equation
   (a) $x^2 + (2 + 2\sqrt{3})x + 4\sqrt{3} = 0$
   (b) $x^2 - (-2 + 2\sqrt{3})x - 4\sqrt{3} = 0$
   (c) $x^2 + (2 - 2\sqrt{3})x + 4\sqrt{3} = 0$
   (d) $x^2 - (-2 - 2\sqrt{3})x + 4\sqrt{3} = 0$

5. Express $\left(-\frac{1}{2} + \frac{\sqrt{3}i}{2}\right)^{1000}$ in $a + ib$ form.

6. If m and n are real numbers such that $(2 + \alpha)^2 = m - n\alpha$, where $\alpha = \frac{-1 - i\sqrt{3}}{2}$, then find $\frac{m-n}{2}$.

7. Find the number of roots of the equation $z^{15} = 1$ satisfying $|\arg z| < \frac{\pi}{2}$.

8. Express $\frac{(\cos 2\theta - i\sin 2\theta)^4 (\cos 4\theta + i\sin 4\theta)^{-5}}{(\cos 3\theta + i\sin 3\theta)^{-2} (\cos 3\theta - i\sin 3\theta)^{-9}}$ in $a + ib$ form.

9. If $z = (a + ib)^5 + (b + ia)^5$, then prove that $\text{Re}(z) = \text{Im}(z)$ where $a, b \in R$.

10. When the polynomial $5x^3 + Mx + N$ is divided by $x^2 + x + 1$, then remainder is 0. Find M and N.

11. If the fourth roots of unity are z_1, z_2, z_3 and z_4, then $z_1^2 + z_2^2 + z_3^2 + z_4^2$ is equal to
    (a) 2
    (b) 0
    (c) 3
    (d) 4

12. If $1, z_1, z_2, z_3, \ldots, z_{n-1}$ are the nth roots of unity, then find $(1 - z_1)(1 - z_2)\ldots(1 - z_{n-1})$.

13. Express $\left(\frac{1 + \sin\alpha + i\cos\alpha}{1 + \sin\alpha - i\cos\alpha}\right)^n$ in standard form.

14. If α is one of the non-real imaginary seventh roots of unity, then form the quadratic equation whose roots are given by $\alpha + \alpha^2 + \alpha^4$ and $\alpha^3 + \alpha^5 + \alpha^6$.

Answer Key

1. $\pm(5 + 4i)$ 2. Parabola 4. (b) 5. $-\frac{1}{2} + \frac{\sqrt{3}}{2}i$ 6. (3) 7. 7
8. $\cos 49\theta - i\sin 49\theta$ 10. $M = 0, N = -5$ 11. (b) 12. n
13. $\sin n\alpha + i\cos n\alpha$ 14. $x^2 + x + 2 = 0$

For Detailed Solution

Milestone 4 Complex Number in Geometry

• Vector Representation of Complex Numbers • Geometrical Representation of Algebraic Operations on Complex Numbers • Rotation Theorem (Coni Method) • Shifting the Origin in Case of Complex Numbers • Inverse Points • Use of Complex Numbers in Coordinate Geometry

1.14 Vector Representation of Complex Numbers

If P is the point (x, y) on the argand plane corresponding to the complex number $z = x + iy$, where $x, y \in R$ and $i = \sqrt{-1}$.

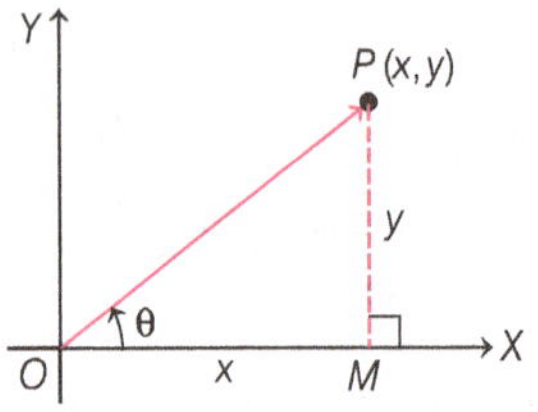

Then, $\mathbf{OP} = x\,\hat{\mathbf{i}} + y\,\hat{\mathbf{j}} \Rightarrow |\mathbf{OP}| = \sqrt{(x^2 + y^2)} = |z|$

and $\arg(z) =$ Direction of the vector $\mathbf{OP} = \tan^{-1}(y/x) = \theta$

Therefore, complex number z can also be represented by **OP**.

1.15 Geometrical Representation of Algebraic Operation on Complex Numbers

(a) Sum

Let the complex numbers $z_1 = x_1 + iy_1 = (x_1, y_1)$ and $z_2 = x_2 + iy_2 = (x_2, y_2)$ be represented by the points P and Q on the argand plane.

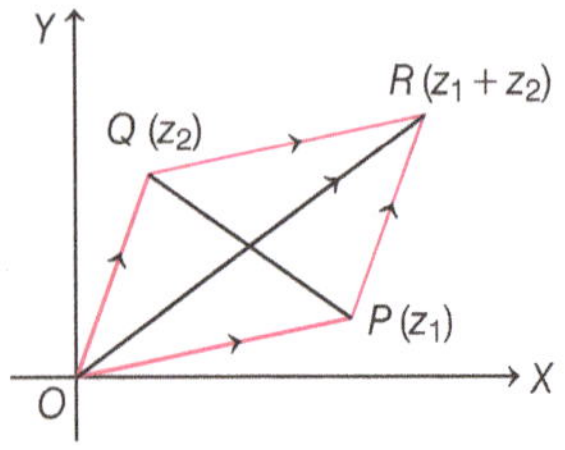

Complete the parallelogram $OPRQ$. Then, the mid-points of PQ and OR are the same.

The mid-point of $PQ = \left(\dfrac{x_1 + x_2}{2}, \dfrac{y_1 + y_2}{2}\right)$.

Hence, $R = (x_1 + x_2, y_1 + y_2)$

Therefore, complex number z can also be represented by

$$\mathbf{OR} = (x_1 + x_2) + i(y_1 + y_2) = (x_1 + iy_1) + (x_2 + iy_2)$$
$$= z_1 + z_2 = (x_1, y_1) + (x_2, y_2)$$

In vector notation, we have

$$z_1 + z_2 = \mathbf{OP} + \mathbf{OQ} = \mathbf{OP} + \mathbf{PR} = \mathbf{OR}$$

(b) Difference

We first represent $-z_2$ by Q', so that QQ' is bisected at O. Complete the parallelogram $OPRQ'$. Then, the point R represents the difference $z_1 - z_2$.

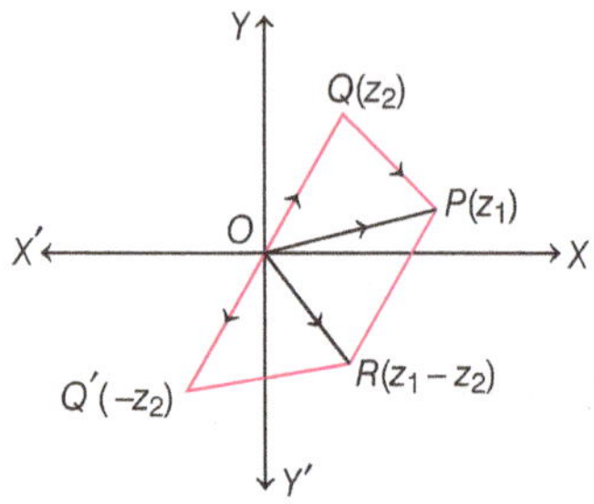

We see that $ORPQ$ is a parallelogram, so that

$$\mathbf{OR} = \mathbf{OP}$$

We have in vectorial notation,

$$z_1 - z_2 = \mathbf{OP} - \mathbf{OQ} = \mathbf{OP} + \mathbf{QO}$$
$$= \mathbf{OP} + \mathbf{PR} = \mathbf{OR} = \mathbf{QP}$$

(c) Product

Let $\quad z_1 = r_1(\cos\theta_1 + i\sin\theta_1) = r_1\, e^{i\theta_1}$

$\therefore \quad |z_1| = r_1$ and $\arg(z_1) = \theta_1$

and $\quad z_2 = r_2(\cos\theta_2 + i\sin\theta_2) = r_2\, e^{i\theta_2}$

$\therefore \quad |z_2| = r_2$ and $\arg(z_2) = \theta_2$

Then, $z_1 z_2 = r_1 r_2 (\cos\theta_1 + i\sin\theta_1)(\cos\theta_2 + i\sin\theta_2)$

$$= r_1 r_2 \{\cos(\theta_1 + \theta_2) + i\sin(\theta_1 + \theta_2)\}$$

$\therefore \quad |z_1 z_2| = r_1 r_2$ and $\arg(z_1 z_2) = \theta_1 + \theta_2$

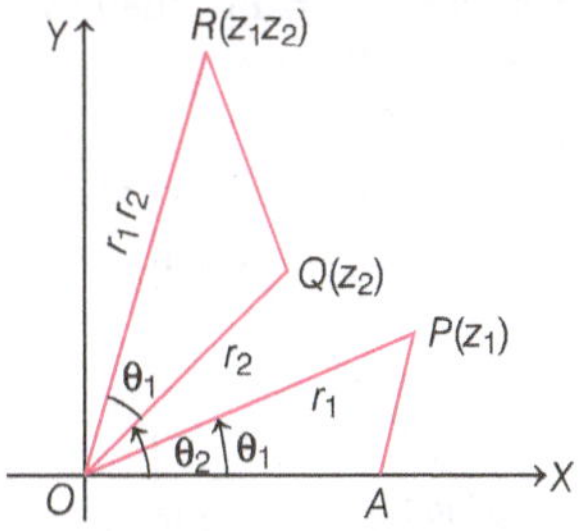

Let P and Q represent the complex numbers z_1 and z_2, respectively.

$$\therefore \quad OP = r_1, OQ = r_2$$

$$\angle POX = \theta_1 \quad \text{and} \quad \angle QOX = \theta_2$$

Take a point A on the real axis OX, such that $OA = 1$ unit. Complete the $\angle OPA$

Now, taking OQ as the base, construct a ΔOQR similar to ΔOPA, so that $\dfrac{OR}{OQ} = \dfrac{OP}{OA}$

i.e. $\quad OR = OP \cdot OQ = r_1 r_2 \quad$ [since, $OA = 1$ unit]

and $\quad \angle ROX = \angle ROQ + \angle QOX = \theta_1 + \theta_2$

Hence, R is the point representing product of complex numbers z_1 and z_2.

(d) Division

Let $\quad z_1 = r_1 (\cos\theta_1 + i\sin\theta_1) = r_1 e^{i\theta_1}$

$\therefore \quad |z_1| = r_1$ and $\arg(z_1) = \theta_1$

and $\quad z_2 = r_2 (\cos\theta_2 + i\sin\theta_2) = r_2 e^{i\theta_2}$

$\therefore \quad |z_2| = r_2$ and $\arg(z_2) = \theta_2$

Then, $\dfrac{z_1}{z_2} = \dfrac{r_1}{r_2} \cdot \dfrac{(\cos\theta_1 + i\sin\theta_1)}{(\cos\theta_2 + i\sin\theta_2)} \quad [z_2 \neq 0, r_2 \neq 0]$

$$\frac{z_1}{z_2} = \frac{r_1}{r_2}[\cos(\theta_1 - \theta_2) + i\sin(\theta_1 - \theta_2)]$$

$$\therefore \quad \left|\frac{z_1}{z_2}\right| = \frac{r_1}{r_2}, \arg\left(\frac{z_1}{z_2}\right) = \theta_1 - \theta_2$$

Let P and Q represent the complex numbers z_1 and z_2, respectively.

$\therefore \; OP = r_1, OQ = r_2, \; \angle POX = \theta_1$ and $\angle QOX = \theta_2$

Let OS be new position of OP, take a point A on the real axis OX, such that $OA = 1$ unit and through A draw a line making with OA an angle equal to the $\angle OQP$ and meeting OS in R.

Then, R represented by (z_1 / z_2).

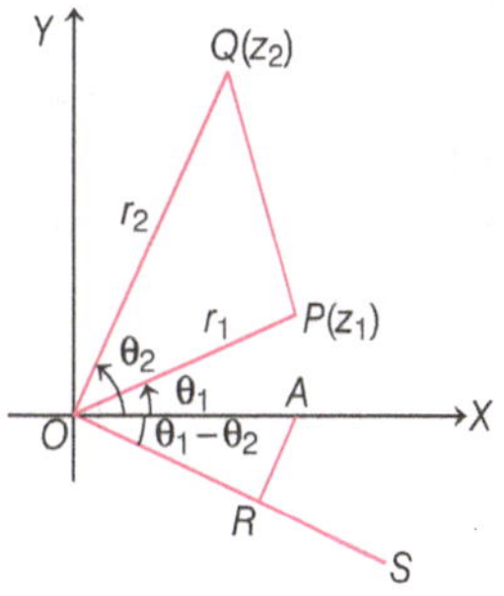

Now, in similar ΔOPQ and ΔOAR,

$$\frac{OR}{OA} = \frac{OP}{OQ}$$

$$\Rightarrow \quad OR = \frac{r_1}{r_2}$$

Since, $OA = 1$ and $\angle AOR = \angle POR - \angle POX = \theta_2 - \theta_1$

Hence, the vectorial angle of R is $-(\theta_2 - \theta_1)$ i.e. $\theta_1 - \theta_2$.

JEE Focus Points

Concept Inside Video

- Multiplication by i

  Since, $z = r(\cos\theta + i\sin\theta)$

  and $i = \left(\cos\dfrac{\pi}{2} + i\sin\dfrac{\pi}{2}\right)$

  $\therefore \quad iz = r\left[\cos\left(\dfrac{\pi}{2} + \theta\right) + i\sin\left(\dfrac{\pi}{2} + \theta\right)\right]$

  Hence, multiplication of z with i, then vector for z rotates a right angle in the positive sense.
- Thus, to multiply a vector by (-1) is to turn it through two right angles.
- Thus, to multiply a vector by $(\cos\theta + i\sin\theta)$ is to turn it through the angle θ in the positive sense.
- If θ_1 and θ_2 are the principal values of z_1 and z_2, then $\theta_1 + \theta_2$ and $\theta_1 - \theta_2$ are not necessarily the principal value of $\arg(z_1 z_2)$ and $\arg(z_1 / z_2)$.

1.16 Rotation Theorem (Coni Method)

Let z_1, z_2 and z_3 be the affixes of three points A, B and C respectively taken on argand plane.

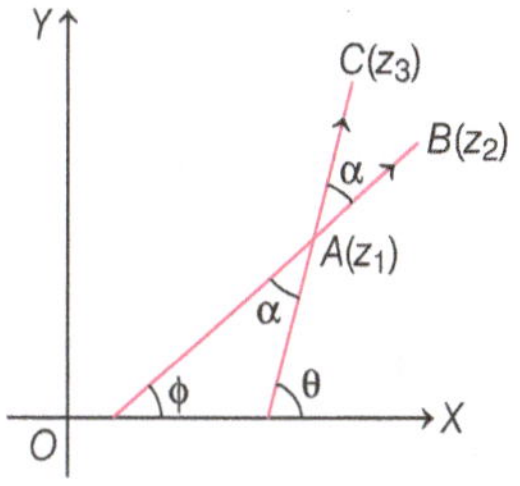

Then, we have $\mathbf{AC} = z_3 - z_1$ and $\mathbf{AB} = z_2 - z_1$

and let $\arg \mathbf{AC} = \arg (z_3 - z_1) = \theta$

and $\arg \mathbf{AB} = \arg (z_2 - z_1) = \phi$

Let $\angle CAB = \alpha$

$$\angle CAB = \alpha = \theta - \phi = \arg \mathbf{AC} - \arg \mathbf{AB}$$
$$= \arg (z_3 - z_1) - \arg (z_2 - z_1)$$
$$= \arg \left(\frac{z_3 - z_1}{z_2 - z_1} \right)$$

or angle between AC and AB

$$= \arg \left(\frac{\text{affix of } C - \text{affix of } A}{\text{affix of } B - \text{affix of } A} \right)$$

For any complex number z, we have

$$z = |z| e^{i(\arg z)}$$

Similarly, $$\left(\frac{z_3 - z_1}{z_2 - z_1} \right) = \left| \frac{z_3 - z_1}{z_2 - z_1} \right| e^{i\left[\arg \left(\frac{z_3 - z_1}{z_2 - z_1} \right)\right]}$$

or $$\frac{z_3 - z_1}{z_2 - z_1} = \frac{|z_3 - z_1|}{|z_2 - z_1|} e^{i(\angle CAB)} = \frac{AC}{AB} e^{i\alpha}$$

JEE Focus Points

- Here, only principal values of the arguments are considered.
- $\arg \left(\frac{z_1 - z_2}{z_3 - z_4} \right) = \theta$, if AB coincides with CD, then

  $\arg \left(\frac{z_1 - z_2}{z_3 - z_4} \right) = 0$ or π, so that $\frac{z_1 - z_2}{z_3 - z_4}$ is real. It follows that if $\frac{z_1 - z_2}{z_3 - z_4}$ is real, then the points A, B, C and D are collinear.

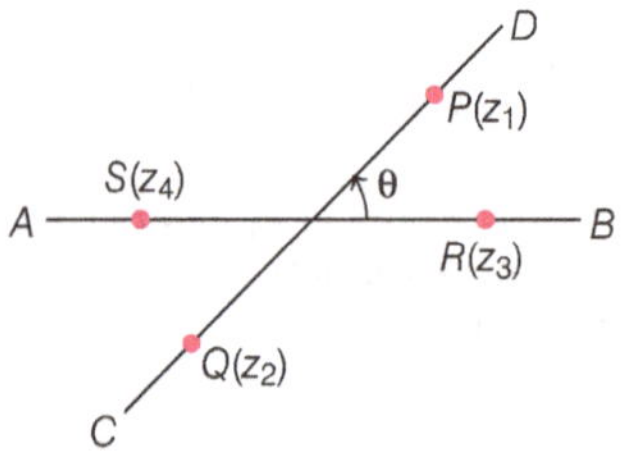

Concept Inside Video

- If AB is perpendicular to CD, then

  $\arg \left(\frac{z_1 - z_2}{z_3 - z_4} \right) = \pm \frac{\pi}{2}$, so $\frac{z_1 - z_2}{z_3 - z_4}$ is purely imaginary.
- It follows that, if $z_1 - z_2 = \pm k (z_3 - z_4)$, where k is purely imaginary number, then AB and CD are perpendicular to each other.

Triangle with vertices z_1, z_2, z_3, then

- $(z_1 - z_2)^2 + (z_2 - z_3)^2 + (z_3 - z_1)^2 = 0$
- $(z_1 - z_2)^2 = (z_2 - z_3)(z_3 - z_1)$
- $\sum (z_1 - z_2)(z_2 - z_3) = 0$
- $\sum \frac{1}{(z_1 - z_2)} = 0$

Example 74. Complex numbers z_1, z_2 and z_3 are the vertices A, B, C respectively of an isosceles right angled triangle with right angle at C. Show that $(z_1 - z_2)^2 = 2(z_1 - z_3)(z_3 - z_2)$.

Sol. Since, $\angle ACB = 90°$ and $AC = BC$, then by Coni method

$$\frac{z_1 - z_3}{z_2 - z_3} = \frac{AC}{BC} e^{i\pi/2} = i$$

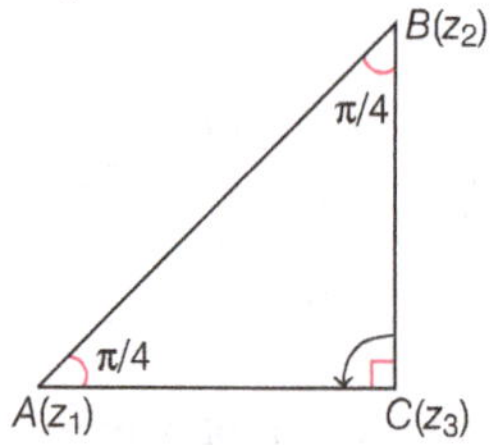

$$\Rightarrow \quad z_1 - z_3 = i(z_2 - z_3)$$

On squaring both sides, we get

$$(z_1 - z_3)^2 = -(z_2 - z_3)^2$$
$$\Rightarrow \quad z_1^2 + z_3^2 - 2z_1z_3 = -(z_2^2 + z_3^2 - 2z_2z_3)$$
$$\Rightarrow \quad z_1^2 + z_2^2 - 2z_1z_2 = 2(z_1z_3 - z_1z_2 - z_3^2 + z_2z_3)$$

Therefore, $(z_1 - z_2)^2 = 2(z_1 - z_3)(z_3 - z_2)$

Example 75. Complex numbers z_1, z_2, z_3 are the vertices of A, B, C respectively of an equilateral triangle. Show that

$$z_1^2 + z_2^2 + z_3^2 = z_1z_2 + z_2z_3 + z_3z_1.$$

Sol. Let $AB = BC = CA = a$

$\because \quad \angle ABC = \frac{\pi}{3}$

From Coni method, $\frac{z_1 - z_2}{z_3 - z_2} = \frac{a}{a} e^{i\pi/3}$ ...(i)

and $\angle BAC = \frac{\pi}{3}$

From Coni method, $\frac{z_3 - z_1}{z_2 - z_1} = \frac{a}{a} e^{i\pi/3}$ ...(ii)

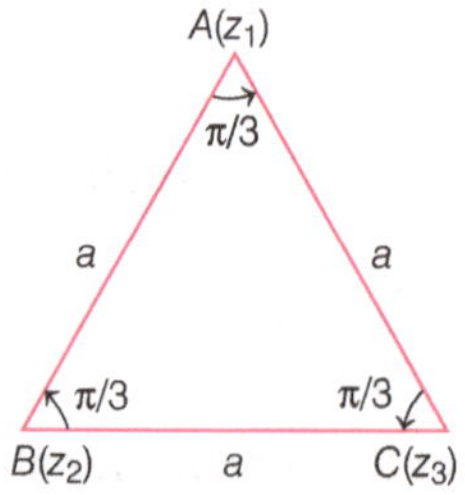

From Eqs. (i) and (ii), we get

$$\frac{z_1 - z_2}{z_3 - z_2} = \frac{z_3 - z_1}{z_2 - z_1}$$
$$\Rightarrow \quad (z_1 - z_2)(z_2 - z_1) = (z_3 - z_1)(z_3 - z_2)$$
$$\Rightarrow \quad z_1^2 + z_2^2 + z_3^2 = z_1z_2 + z_2z_3 + z_3z_1$$

Complex Number as a Rotating Arrow in the Argand Plane

Let $z = r(\cos\theta + i\sin\theta) = re^{i\theta}$ ...(i)

be a complex number representing a point P in the argand plane.

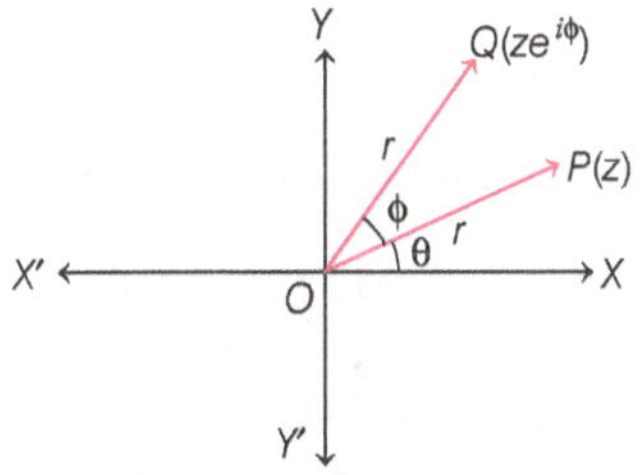

Then, $OP = |z| = r$ and $\angle POX = \theta$

Now, consider complex number $z_1 = ze^{i\phi}$

or $\quad z_1 = re^{i\theta} \cdot e^{i\phi} = re^{i(\theta+\phi)}$ [from Eq. (i)]

Clearly, the complex number z_1 represents a point Q in the argand plane, when $OQ = r$ and $\angle QOX = \theta + \phi$

Clearly, multiplication of z with $e^{i\phi}$ rotates the vector **OP** through angle ϕ in anti-clockwise sense. Similarly, multiplication of z with $e^{-i\phi}$ will rotate the vector **OP** in clockwise sense.

JEE Focus Points

Concept Inside Video

- If z_1, z_2 and z_3 are the affixes of the three points A, B and C, such that
$$AC = AB \text{ and } \angle CAB = \theta.$$
Therefore, **AB** $= z_2 - z_1$, **AC** $= z_3 - z_1$.
Then, **AC** will be obtained by rotating **AB** through an angle θ in anti- clockwise sense and therefore,
$$\mathbf{AC} = \mathbf{AB}\, e^{i\theta}$$
or $\quad (z_3 - z_1) = (z_2 - z_1)\, e^{i\theta}$
or $\quad \dfrac{z_3 - z_1}{z_2 - z_1} = e^{i\theta}$

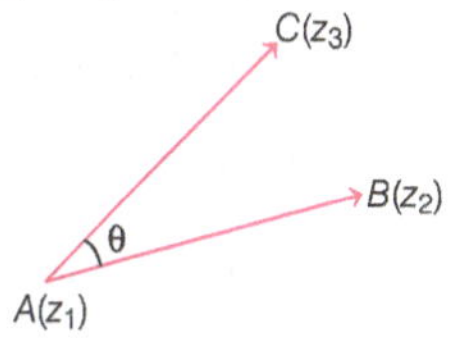

- If A, B and C are three points in argand plane, such that $AC = AB$ and $\angle CAB = \theta$, then use the rotation about A to find $e^{i\theta}$, but if $AC \neq AB$, then use Coni method.

Example 76. Let z_1 and z_2 be roots of the equation $z^2 + pz + q = 0$, where the coefficients p and q may be complex numbers. Let A and B represent z_1 and z_2 in the complex plane. If $\angle AOB = \alpha \neq 0$ and $OA = OB$, where O is the origin, prove that $p^2 = 4q\cos^2(\alpha/2)$.

Sol. Clearly, **OB** is obtained by rotating **OA** through angle α.

$\therefore \quad \mathbf{OB} = \mathbf{OA}\, e^{i\alpha}$

$\Rightarrow \quad z_2 = z_1 e^{i\alpha}$

$\Rightarrow \quad \dfrac{z_2}{z_1} = e^{i\alpha}$ ...(i)

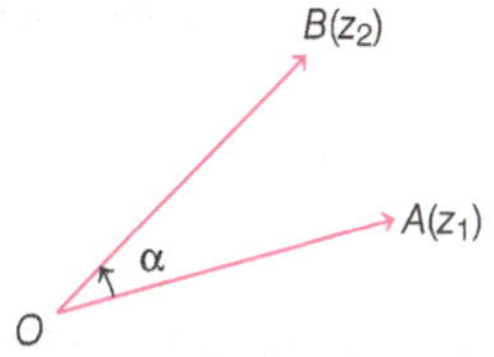

or $\quad \dfrac{z_2}{z_1} + 1 = (e^{i\alpha} + 1)$

$\Rightarrow \quad \dfrac{(z_1 + z_2)}{z_1} = e^{i\alpha/2} \cdot 2\cos(\alpha/2)$

On squaring both sides, we get

$$\frac{(z_1+z_2)^2}{z_1^2} = e^{i\alpha} \cdot (4\cos^2\alpha/2)$$

$\Rightarrow \quad \dfrac{(z_1+z_2)^2}{z_1^2} = \dfrac{z_2}{z_1} \cdot (4\cos^2\alpha/2)$ [from Eq. (i)]

$$(z_1 + z_2)^2 = 4z_1z_2\cos^2(\alpha/2)$$

$$(-p)^2 = 4q\cos^2(\alpha/2)$$

$\left[\begin{array}{l} \because z_1 \text{ and } z_2 \text{ are the roots of } z^2 + pz + q = 0 \\ \therefore z_1 + z_2 = -p \text{ and } z_1 z_2 = q \end{array}\right]$

or $\quad p^2 = 4q\cos^2(\alpha/2)$

1.17 Shifting the Origin in Case of Complex Numbers

Let O be the origin and P be a point with affix z_0.

Let a point Q has affix z with respect to the coordinate system passing through O.

When origin is shifted to the point $P(z_0)$, then the new affix Z of the point Q with respect to new origin P is given by $Z = z - z_0$.

i.e. to shift the origin at z_0, we should replace z by $Z + z_0$.

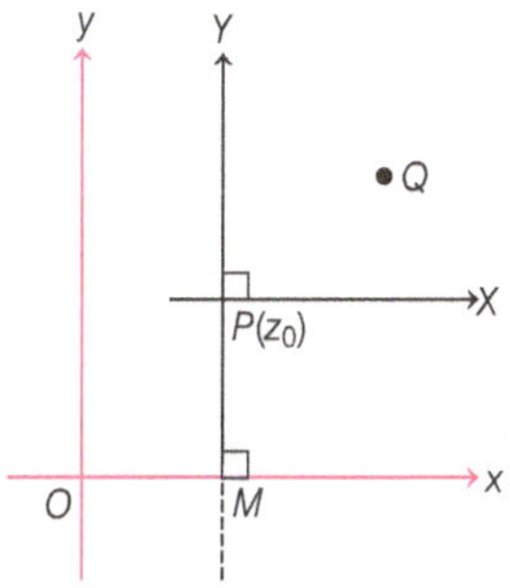

Example 77. If z_1, z_2 and z_3 are the vertices of an equilateral triangle with z_0 as its circumcentre, then changing origin to z_0, show that $Z_1^2+Z_2^2+Z_3^2=0$, where Z_1, Z_2, Z_3 are new complex numbers of the vertices.

Sol. In an equilateral triangle, the circumcentre and the centroid are the same point.

So, $$z_0 = \frac{z_1+z_2+z_3}{3}$$

$\therefore \quad z_1+z_2+z_3 = 3z_0$ ...(i)

To shift the origin at z_0, we have to replace z_1, z_2, z_3 and z_0 by $Z_1+z_0, Z_2+z_0, Z_3+z_0$ and $0+z_0$.

Then, Eq. (i) becomes

$$(Z_1+z_0)+(Z_2+z_0)+(Z_3+z_0)=3(0+z_0)$$

$\Rightarrow \quad Z_1+Z_2+Z_3=0$

On squaring, we get

$$Z_1^2+Z_2^2+Z_3^2+2(Z_1Z_2+Z_2Z_3+Z_3Z_1)=0 \quad \text{...(ii)}$$

But triangle with vertices Z_1, Z_2 and Z_3 is equilateral, then

$$Z_1^2+Z_2^2+Z_3^2=Z_1Z_2+Z_2Z_3+Z_3Z_1 \quad \text{...(iii)}$$

From Eqs. (ii) and (iii), we get

$$3(Z_1^2+Z_2^2+Z_3^2)=0$$

Therefore, $\quad Z_1^2+Z_2^2+Z_3^2=0$

1.18 Inverse Points

(a) Inverse Points with respect to a Line

Two points P and Q are said to be the inverse points with respect to the line RS. If Q is the image of P in RS, i.e. if the line RS is the right bisector of PQ.

Example 78. Show that z_1, z_2 are the inverse points with respect to the line $z\bar{a}+a\bar{z}=b$, if $z_1\bar{a}+a\bar{z}_2=b$.

Sol. Let RS be the line represented by the equation,

$$z\bar{a}+a\bar{z}=b \quad \text{...(i)}$$

Let P and Q are the inverse points with respect to the line RS. The point Q is the reflection (inverse) of the point P in the line RS, if the line RS is the right bisector of PQ. Take any point z in the line RS, then lines joining z to P and z to Q are equal.

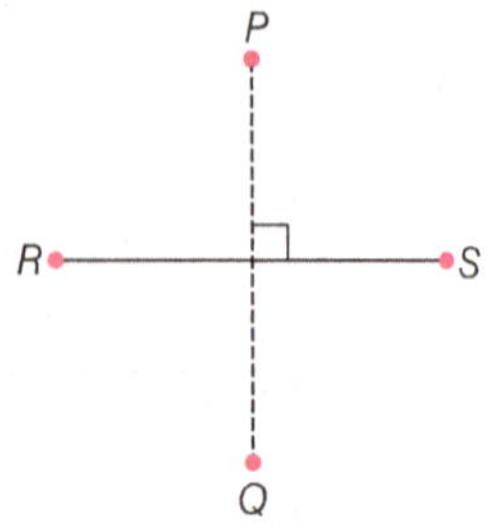

i.e. $\quad |z-z_1|=|z-z_2|$ or $|z-z_1|^2=|z-z_2|^2$

i.e. $\quad (z-z_1)(\bar{z}-\bar{z}_1)=(z-z_2)(\bar{z}-\bar{z}_2)$

$\Rightarrow \quad z(\bar{z}_2-\bar{z}_1)+\bar{z}(z_2-z_1)+(z_1\bar{z}_1-z_2\bar{z}_2)=0$ ...(ii)

Hence, Eqs. (i) and (ii) are identical, therefore, comparing coefficients, we get

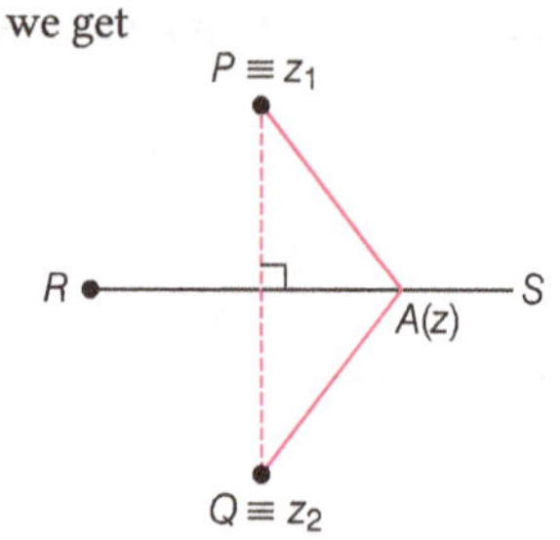

$$\frac{\bar{a}}{\bar{z}_2-\bar{z}_1}=\frac{a}{z_2-z_1}=\frac{-b}{z_1\bar{z}_1-z_2\bar{z}_2}$$

So that $$\frac{z_1\bar{a}}{z_1(\bar{z}_2-\bar{z}_1)}=\frac{a\bar{z}_2}{\bar{z}_2(z_2-z_1)}=\frac{-b}{z_1\bar{z}_1-z_2\bar{z}_2}=\frac{z_1\bar{a}+a\bar{z}_2-b}{0}$$

[by ratio and proportion rule]

$$z_1\bar{a}+a\bar{z}_2-b=0 \quad \text{or} \quad z_1\bar{a}+a\bar{z}_2=b$$

(b) Inverse Points with respect to a Circle

If C is the centre of the circle and P, Q are the inverse points with respect to the circle, then three points C, P, Q are collinear and also $CP \cdot CQ = r^2$, where r is the radius of the circle.

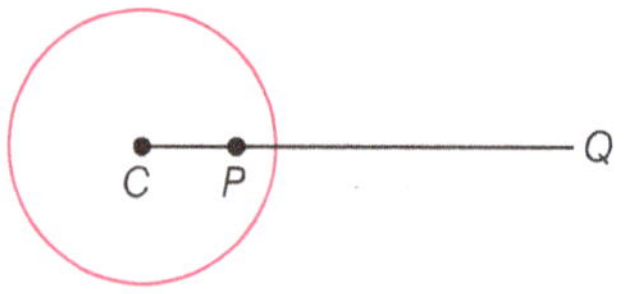

Example 79. Show that inverse of a point a with respect to the circle $|z-c|=R$ (a and c are complex numbers, centre c and radius R) is the point $c+\dfrac{R^2}{\bar{a}-\bar{c}}$.

Sol. Let a' be the inverse point of a with respect to the circle $|z-c|=R$, then by definition,

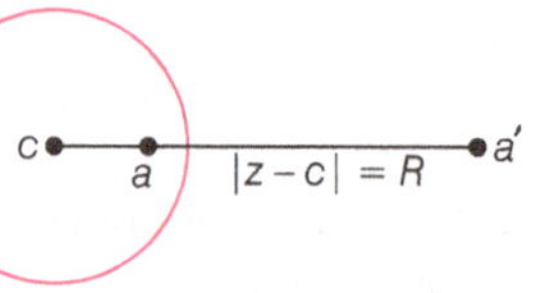

The points c, a, a' are collinear.

We have, $\arg(a' - c) = \arg(a - c)$

$$= -\arg(\bar{a} - \bar{c}) \qquad [\because \arg \bar{z} = -\arg z]$$

$$\Rightarrow \arg(a' - c) + \arg(\bar{a} - \bar{c}) = 0$$

$$\Rightarrow \arg\{(a' - c)(\bar{a} - \bar{c})\} = 0$$

$\therefore$ $(a' - c)(\bar{a} - \bar{c})$ is purely real and positive.

By definition, $|a' - c||a - c| = R^2 \qquad [\because CP \cdot CQ = r^2]$

$$\Rightarrow |a' - c||\bar{a} - \bar{c}| = R^2 \qquad [\because |z| = |\bar{z}|]$$

$$\Rightarrow |(a' - c)(\bar{a} - \bar{c})| = R^2$$

$$\Rightarrow (a' - c)(\bar{a} - \bar{c}) = R^2$$

$[\because (a' - c)(\bar{a} - \bar{c})$ is purely real and positive$]$

$$\Rightarrow a' - c = \frac{R^2}{\bar{a} - \bar{c}}$$

$$\Rightarrow a' = c + \frac{R^2}{\bar{a} - \bar{c}}$$

1.19 Use of Complex Numbers in Coordinate Geometry

(a) Distance Formula

The distance between two points $P(z_1)$ and $Q(z_2)$ is given by

$$PQ = |z_2 - z_1| = |\text{affix of } Q - \text{affix of } P|$$

JEE Focus Points

- The distance of a point z from origin, $|z - 0| = |z|$
- Three points $A(z_1)$, $B(z_2)$ and $C(z_3)$ are collinear, then $AB + BC = AC$
  i.e. $|z_1 - z_2| + |z_2 - z_3| = |z_1 - z_3|$.

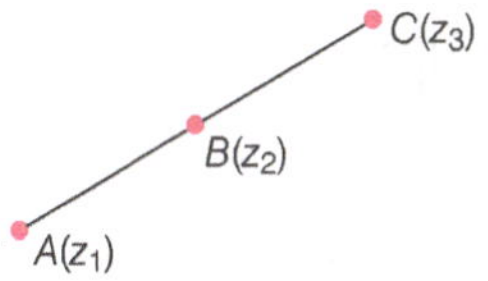

Example 80. Show that the points representing the complex numbers $(3 + 2i)$, $(2 - i)$ and $-7i$, where $i = \sqrt{-1}$, are collinear.

Sol. Let $z_1 = 3 + 2i$, $z_2 = 2 - i$ and $z_3 = -7i$.

Then, $|z_1 - z_2| = |1 + 3i| = \sqrt{10}$,

$$|z_2 - z_3| = |2 + 6i| = \sqrt{40} = 2\sqrt{10}$$

and $|z_1 - z_3| = |3 + 9i| = \sqrt{90} = 3\sqrt{10}$

$$\therefore \quad |z_1 - z_2| + |z_2 - z_3| = |z_1 - z_3|$$

Hence, the points $(3 + 2i)$, $(2 - i)$ and $-7i$ are collinear.

(b) Equation of the Perpendicular Bisector

If $P(z_1)$ and $Q(z_2)$ are two fixed points and $R(z)$ is moving point, such that it is always at equal distance from $P(z_1)$ and $Q(z_2)$.

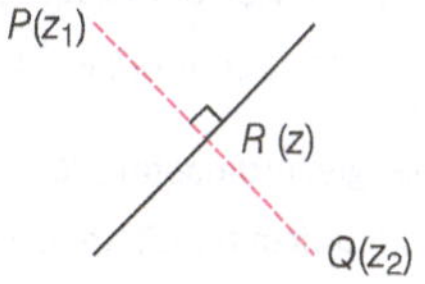

i.e. $\qquad PR = QR$

or $\qquad |z - z_1| = |z - z_2|$

or $\qquad z(\bar{z}_1 - \bar{z}_2) + \bar{z}(z_1 - z_2) = z_1\bar{z}_1 - z_2\bar{z}_2$

or $\qquad z(\bar{z}_1 - \bar{z}_2) + \bar{z}(z_1 - z_2) = |z_1|^2 - |z_2|^2$

Hence, z lies on the perpendicular bisectors of z_1 and z_2.

Example 81. Find the perpendicular bisector of $3 + 4i$ and $-5 + 6i$, where $i = \sqrt{-1}$.

Sol. Let $z_1 = 3 + 4i$ and $z_2 = -5 + 6i$

If z is moving point, such that it is always equal distance from z_1 and z_2.

i.e. $\qquad |z - z_1| = |z - z_2|$

or $\qquad z(\bar{z}_1 - \bar{z}_2) + \bar{z}(z_1 - z_2) = |z_1|^2 - |z_2|^2$

$$\Rightarrow z((3 - 4i) - (-5 - 6i)) + \bar{z}((3 + 4i) - (-5 + 6i)) = 25 - 61$$

Hence, $(8 + 2i)z + (8 - 2i)\bar{z} + 36 = 0$

which is required perpendicular bisector.

(c) Section Formula

If $R(z)$ divides the joining of $P(z_1)$ and $Q(z_2)$ in the ratio $m_1 : m_2$ $(m_1, m_2 > 0)$.

(i) If $R(z)$ divides the segment PQ internally in the ratio of $m_1 : m_2$, then

$$z = \frac{m_1 z_2 + m_2 z_1}{m_1 + m_2}$$

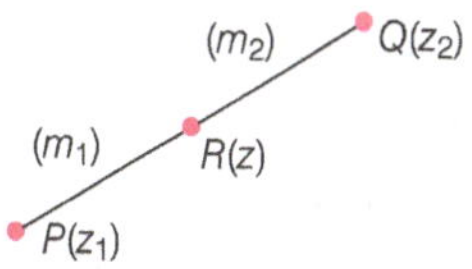

(ii) If $R(z)$ divides the segment PQ externally in the ratio of $m_1 : m_2$, then

$$z = \frac{m_1 z_2 - m_2 z_1}{m_1 - m_2}$$

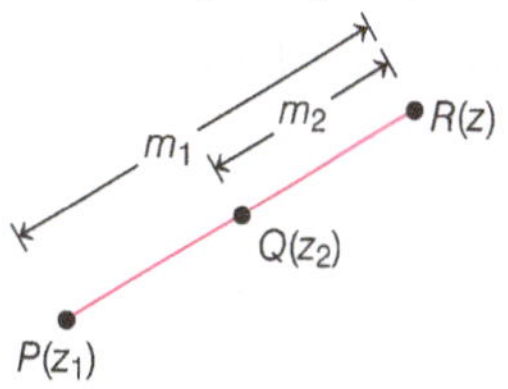

JEE Focus Points

- If $R(z)$ is the mid-point of PQ, then affix of R is $\frac{z_1 + z_2}{2}$.
- If z_1, z_2 and z_3 are affixes of the vertices of a triangle, then affix of its centroid is $\frac{z_1 + z_2 + z_3}{3}$.
- In acute angle triangle, orthocentre (O), nine point centre (N), centroid (G) and circumcentre (C) are collinear and $\frac{OG}{GC} = \frac{2}{1}$, $\frac{ON}{NG} = \frac{1}{1}$.
- If z_1, z_2, z_3 and z_4 are the affixes of the vertices of a parallelogram taken in order, then $z_1 + z_3 = z_2 + z_4$.

Concept Inside Video

Example 82. If z_1, z_2 and z_3 are the affixes of the vertices of a triangle having its circumcentre at the origin. If z is the affix of its orthocentre, prove that $z_1 + z_2 + z_3 - z = 0$.

Sol. We know that orthocentre O, centroid G and circumcentre C of a triangle are collinear, such that G divides OC in the ratio 2 : 1. Since, affix of G is $\frac{z_1 + z_2 + z_3}{3}$ and C is the origin.

Therefore, by section formula, we get

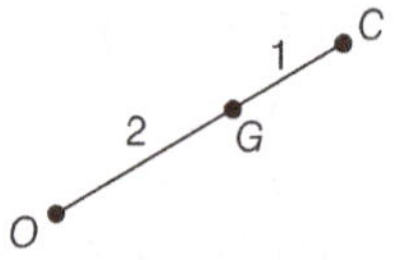

$$\Rightarrow \quad \frac{z_1 + z_2 + z_3}{3} = \frac{2 \cdot 0 + 1 \cdot z}{2 + 1}$$

$$\Rightarrow \quad z_1 + z_2 + z_3 = z$$

Therefore, $z_1 + z_2 + z_3 - z = 0$

Example 83. Let z_1, z_2 and z_3 be three complex numbers and $a, b, c \in R$, such that $a + b + c = 0$ and $az_1 + bz_2 + cz_3 = 0$, then show that z_1, z_2 and z_3 are collinear.

Sol. Given, $\quad a + b + c = 0 \quad$ ...(i)

and $\quad az_1 + bz_2 + cz_3 = 0 \quad$ ...(ii)

$\Rightarrow \quad az_1 + bz_2 - (a + b) z_3 = 0 \quad$ [from Eq. (i)]

or $\quad z_3 = \frac{az_1 + bz_2}{a + b}$

It follows that z_3 divides the line segment joining z_1 and z_2 internally in the ratio $b : a$. (If a, b are of same sign and opposite sign, then externally.)

Hence, z_1, z_2 and z_3 are collinear.

(d) Area of Triangle

(i) If z_1, z_2 and z_3 are the affixes of the vertices of a triangle, then its area $= \frac{1}{4} \left| \begin{vmatrix} z_1 & \bar{z}_1 & 1 \\ z_2 & \bar{z}_2 & 1 \\ z_3 & \bar{z}_3 & 1 \end{vmatrix} \right|$

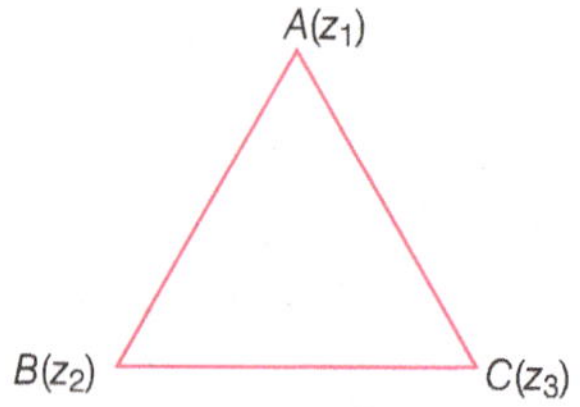

(ii) The area of the triangle with vertices $z, \omega z$ and $z + \omega z$ is $\frac{\sqrt{3}}{4} |z|^2$, where ω is the cube root of unity.

Example 84. Show that the area of the triangle on the argand plane formed by the complex numbers z, iz and $z + iz$ is $\frac{1}{2}|z|^2$, where $i = \sqrt{-1}$.

Sol. Required area $= \frac{1}{4} \left| \begin{vmatrix} z & \bar{z} & 1 \\ iz & \overline{iz} & 1 \\ z + iz & \overline{z + iz} & 1 \end{vmatrix} \right|$

$$= \frac{1}{4} \left| \begin{vmatrix} z & \bar{z} & 1 \\ iz & \overline{iz} & 1 \\ z + iz & \bar{z} + \overline{iz} & 1 \end{vmatrix} \right|$$

$$= \frac{1}{4} \left| \begin{vmatrix} z & \bar{z} & 1 \\ iz & -i\bar{z} & 1 \\ z + iz & \bar{z} - i\bar{z} & 1 \end{vmatrix} \right|$$

On applying $R_3 \to R_3 - (R_1 + R_2)$, we get

$$\text{Area} = \frac{1}{4} \left| \begin{vmatrix} z & \bar{z} & 1 \\ iz & -i\bar{z} & 1 \\ 0 & 0 & -1 \end{vmatrix} \right|$$

$$= \frac{1}{4} |(-1)(-iz\bar{z} - iz\bar{z})|$$

$$= \frac{1}{4} |2iz\bar{z}|$$

$$= \frac{1}{2} |i| |z\bar{z}|$$

$$= \frac{1}{2} |z|^2$$

(e) Equation of a Straight Line

(i) Parametric form

Equation of the straight line joining the points having affixes z_1 and z_2 is $z = tz_1 + (1-t)z_2$, where $t \in R \sim \{0\}$.

Proof $\because\ z = tz_1 + (1-t)z_2 = \dfrac{tz_1 + (1-t)z_2}{t + (1-t)}$

Hence, z divides the line joining z_1 and z_2 in the ratio $1-t : t$. Thus, the points z_1, z_2, z are collinear.

(ii) Non-parametric form

Equation of the straight line joining the points having affixes z_1 and z_2 is

$$\begin{vmatrix} z & \bar{z} & 1 \\ z_1 & \bar{z}_1 & 1 \\ z_2 & \bar{z}_2 & 1 \end{vmatrix} = 0$$

or $z(\bar{z}_1 - \bar{z}_2) - \bar{z}(z_1 - z_2) + z_1\bar{z}_2 - \bar{z}_1 z_2 = 0$

Proof Equation of the straight line joining points having affixes z_1 and z_2 is

$$z = tz_1 + (1-t)z_2, \text{ where } t \in R \sim \{0\}$$

$\Rightarrow \quad z - z_2 = t(z_1 - z_2)$ ...(i)

and $\quad \overline{z - z_2} = t(\overline{z_1 - z_2})$

or $\quad \bar{z} - \bar{z}_2 = t(\bar{z}_1 - \bar{z}_2)$ ...(ii)

From Eqs. (i) and (ii), we get

$$\frac{z - z_2}{\bar{z} - \bar{z}_2} = \frac{z_1 - z_2}{\bar{z}_1 - \bar{z}_2} \Rightarrow \frac{z - z_2}{z_1 - z_2} = \frac{\bar{z} - \bar{z}_2}{\bar{z}_1 - \bar{z}_2}$$

$$\Rightarrow \begin{vmatrix} z - z_2 & \bar{z} - \bar{z}_2 & 0 \\ z_1 - z_2 & \bar{z}_1 - \bar{z}_2 & 0 \\ z_2 & \bar{z}_2 & 1 \end{vmatrix} = 0$$

Now, applying $R_1 \to R_1 + R_3$ and $R_2 \to R_2 + R_3$, we get

$$\begin{vmatrix} z & \bar{z} & 1 \\ z_1 & \bar{z}_1 & 1 \\ z_2 & \bar{z}_2 & 1 \end{vmatrix} = 0$$

or $z(\bar{z}_1 - \bar{z}_2) - \bar{z}(z_1 - z_2) + z_1\bar{z}_2 - \bar{z}_1 z_2 = 0$

Alternate proof

Let $P(z)$ be an arbitrary point on the line, which pass through $A(z_1)$ and $B(z_2)$.

$\therefore \quad \angle BAP = 0$ or π

$\therefore \quad \arg\left(\dfrac{z - z_1}{z_2 - z_1}\right) = 0$ or π [by rotation theorem]

$\Rightarrow \dfrac{z - z_1}{z_2 - z_1}$ is purely real.

$$\therefore \quad \left(\frac{z - z_1}{z_2 - z_1}\right) = \left(\overline{\frac{z - z_1}{z_2 - z_1}}\right) \Rightarrow \frac{z - z_1}{z_2 - z_1} = \frac{\bar{z} - \bar{z}_1}{\bar{z}_2 - \bar{z}_1}$$

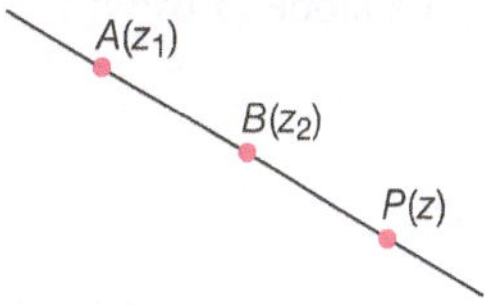

$$z(\bar{z}_1 - \bar{z}_2) - \bar{z}(z_1 - z_2) + z_1\bar{z}_2 - \bar{z}_1 z_2 = 0$$

or

$$\begin{vmatrix} z & \bar{z} & 1 \\ z_1 & \bar{z}_1 & 1 \\ z_2 & \bar{z}_2 & 1 \end{vmatrix} = 0$$

JEE SPIKE

If z_1, z_2 and z_3 are collinear, $\begin{vmatrix} z_1 & \bar{z}_1 & 1 \\ z_2 & \bar{z}_2 & 1 \\ z_3 & \bar{z}_3 & 1 \end{vmatrix} = 0$

or $\quad \sum \bar{z}_1(z_2 - z_3) = 0$

(iii) General form

The general equation of a straight line is of the form $\bar{a}z + a\bar{z} + b = 0$, where a is a complex number and b is a real number.

Proof The equation of a straight line passing through points having affixes z_1 and z_2 is given by

$$z(\bar{z}_1 - \bar{z}_2) - \bar{z}(z_1 - z_2) + z_1\bar{z}_2 - \bar{z}_1 z_2 = 0 \quad \text{...(i)}$$

On multiplying Eq. (i) by i (where, $i = \sqrt{-1}$), we get

$$zi(\bar{z}_1 - \bar{z}_2) - \bar{z}\,i(z_1 - z_2) + i(z_1\bar{z}_2 - \bar{z}_1 z_2) = 0$$

$$\Rightarrow \bar{z}\{-i(z_1 - z_2)\} + z\{i(\bar{z}_1 - \bar{z}_2)\} + i(z_1\bar{z}_2 - \bar{z}_1 z_2) = 0$$

$$\Rightarrow \bar{z}\{-i(z_1 - z_2)\} + z\{\overline{-i(z_1 - z_2)}\} + \{i(2i\,\text{Im}(z_1\bar{z}_2))\} = 0$$

$$\Rightarrow \bar{z}\{-i(z_1 - z_2)\} + z\{\overline{-i(z_1 - z_2)}\} + \{(-2\,\text{Im}(z_1\bar{z}_2)\} = 0$$

$$\Rightarrow \quad \bar{z}a + z\bar{a} + b = 0,$$

where, $a = -i(z_1 - z_2), b = -2\,\text{Im}(z_1\bar{z}_2)$

Hence, the general equation of a straight line is of the form $\bar{a}z + a\bar{z} + b = 0$,

where a is complex number and b is a real number.

(iv) Slope of the line $\bar{a}z + a\bar{z} + b = 0$

Let $A(z_1)$ and $B(z_2)$ be two points on the line $\bar{a}z + a\bar{z} + b = 0$, then

$$\bar{a}z_1 + a\bar{z}_1 + b = 0$$

and $\quad \bar{a}z_2 + a\bar{z}_2 + b = 0$

$\therefore \quad \bar{a}(z_1 - z_2) + a(\bar{z}_1 - \bar{z}_2) = 0$

$\Rightarrow \quad \dfrac{z_1 - z_2}{\bar{z}_1 - \bar{z}_2} = -\dfrac{a}{\bar{a}}$ [remember]

Complex slope of $AB = -\dfrac{a}{\bar{a}} = -\dfrac{\text{Coefficient of } \bar{z}}{\text{Coefficient of } z}$

Thus, the complex slope of the line $\bar{a}\,z + a\,\bar{z} + b = 0$ is $-\dfrac{a}{\bar{a}}$.

Important Theorem

If α_1 and α_2 are the complex slopes of two lines on the argand plane, then prove that the lines are

(i) perpendicular, if $\alpha_1 + \alpha_2 = 0$.

(ii) parallel, if $\alpha_1 = \alpha_2$.

Proof Let z_1 and z_2 be the affixes of two points on one line with complex slope α_1 and z_3 and z_4 be the affixes of two points another line with complex slope α_2. Then,

$$\alpha_1 = \frac{z_1 - z_2}{\bar{z}_1 - \bar{z}_2} \text{ and } \alpha_2 = \frac{z_3 - z_4}{\bar{z}_3 - \bar{z}_4} \quad \text{...(i)}$$

(i) If the lines are perpendicular, then

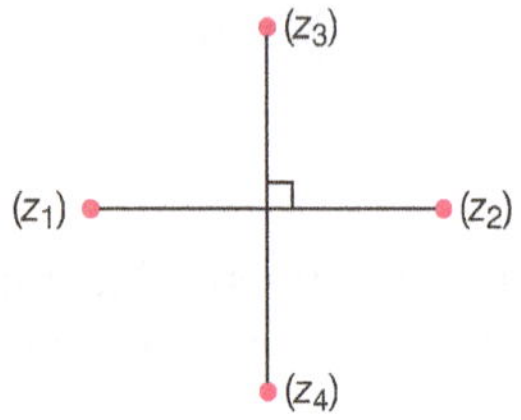

$$\frac{(z_1 - z_2)}{|z_1 - z_2|} = \frac{(z_3 - z_4)}{|z_3 - z_4|} e^{i\pi/2}$$

$$\Rightarrow \quad \frac{(z_1 - z_2)^2}{|z_1 - z_2|^2} = \frac{(z_3 - z_4)^2}{|z_3 - z_4|^2} e^{i\pi}$$

$$\Rightarrow \quad \frac{(z_1 - z_2)^2}{(z_1 - z_2)(\bar{z}_1 - \bar{z}_2)} = \frac{(z_3 - z_4)^2}{(z_3 - z_4)(\bar{z}_3 - \bar{z}_4)} e^{i\pi}$$

$$\Rightarrow \quad \frac{(z_1 - z_2)}{(\bar{z}_1 - \bar{z}_2)} = \frac{(z_3 - z_4)}{(\bar{z}_3 - \bar{z}_4)}(-1)$$

$$\Rightarrow \quad \alpha_1 = -\alpha_2 \quad \text{[from Eq. (i)]}$$

$$\therefore \quad \alpha_1 + \alpha_2 = 0$$

(ii) If the lines are parallel, then

$$\frac{z_1 - z_2}{|z_1 - z_2|} = \frac{z_3 - z_4}{|z_3 - z_4|} e^0$$

$$\Rightarrow \quad \frac{(z_1 - z_2)^2}{|z_1 - z_2|^2} = \frac{(z_3 - z_4)^2}{|z_3 - z_4|^2}$$

$$\Rightarrow \quad \frac{(z_1 - z_2)^2}{(z_1 - z_2)(\bar{z}_1 - \bar{z}_2)} = \frac{(z_3 - z_4)^2}{(z_3 - z_4)(\bar{z}_3 - \bar{z}_4)}$$

$$\Rightarrow \quad \frac{(z_1 - z_2)}{(\bar{z}_1 - \bar{z}_2)} = \frac{(z_3 - z_4)}{(\bar{z}_3 - \bar{z}_4)}$$

$$\Rightarrow \quad \alpha_1 = \alpha_2$$

JEE Focus Points

- The real slope of the line $\bar{a}\,z + a\bar{z} + b = 0$ is $-\dfrac{\text{Re }(a)}{\text{Im }(a)}$, i.e. $-\dfrac{\text{Re (coefficient of } \bar{z})}{\text{Im (coefficient of } \bar{z})}$.
- The equation of a line parallel to the line $\bar{a}\,z + a\bar{z} + b = 0$ is $\bar{a}\,z + a\bar{z} + \lambda = 0$, where $\lambda \in R$.
- The equation of a line perpendicular to the line $\bar{a}\,z + a\,\bar{z} + b = 0$ is $\bar{a}\,z - a\,\bar{z} + i\lambda = 0$ where, $\lambda \in R$ and $i = \sqrt{-1}$

Concept Inside Video

(v) Length of perpendicular from a given point on a given line

The length of perpendicular from a point $P(z_1)$ to the line $\bar{a}\,z + a\,\bar{z} + b = 0$ is given by $\dfrac{|\bar{a}z_1 + a\bar{z}_1 + b|}{2|a|}$.

Proof Let PM be perpendicular from P on the line $\bar{a}\,z + a\,\bar{z} + b = 0$ and let the affix of M be z_2, then

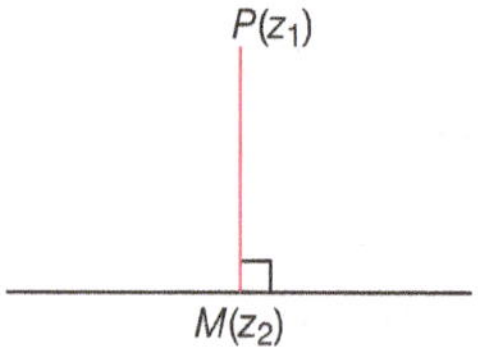

$$PM = |z_1 - z_2|$$

$$\bar{a}\,z + a\,\bar{z} + b = 0$$

and $M(z_2)$ lies on $\bar{a}\,z + a\,\bar{z} + b = 0$, then

$$\bar{a}\,z_2 + a\,\bar{z}_2 + b = 0 \quad \text{...(i)}$$

Since, PM perpendicular to the line $(\bar{a}\,z + a\,\bar{z} + b = 0)$.

Therefore, $\dfrac{z_1 - z_2}{\bar{z}_1 - \bar{z}_2} + \left(-\dfrac{a}{\bar{a}}\right) = 0$

$\Rightarrow \quad \bar{a}\,z_1 - \bar{a}\,z_2 - a\,\bar{z}_1 + a\,\bar{z}_2 = 0$

$\Rightarrow \quad \bar{a}\,z_1 + a\,\bar{z}_1 + b = 2\,a\,\bar{z}_1 + \bar{a}\,z_2 - a\,\bar{z}_2 + b$

$= 2\,a\,\bar{z}_1 - a\bar{z}_2 + (\bar{a}z_2 + b)$

$= 2\,a\,\bar{z}_1 - a\,\bar{z}_2 - a\,\bar{z}_2 \quad [\because \bar{a}\,z_2 + b = -a\,\bar{z}_2]$

$= 2\,a\,(\bar{z}_1 - \bar{z}_2)$

or $\quad |\bar{a}\,z_1 + a\,\bar{z}_1 + b| = 2|a||\bar{z}_1 - \bar{z}_2|$

$= 2|a||z_1 - z_2| \quad [\because |\bar{z}| = |z|]$

$= 2|a|PM$

$$\therefore \quad PM = \frac{|\bar{a}\,z_1 + a\,\bar{z}_1 + b|}{2|a|}$$

Example 85. Show that the point a' is the reflection of the point a in the line $z\bar{b}+\bar{z}b+c=0$, if $a'\bar{b}+\bar{a}b+c=0$.

Sol. Since, a' is the reflection of point a through the line.

So, the mid-point of PQ

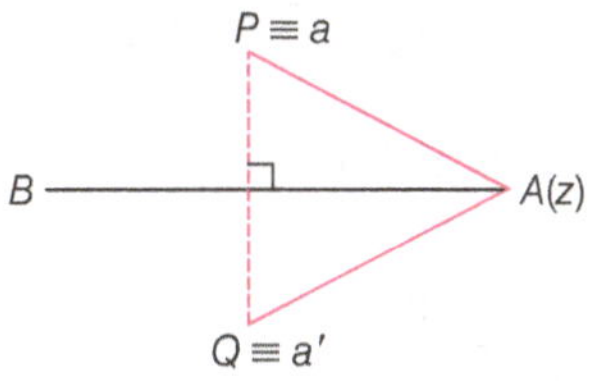

i.e., $\dfrac{a+a'}{2}$ lies on $z\bar{b}+\bar{z}b+c=0$

or $\bar{b}\left(\dfrac{a+a'}{2}\right)+b\left(\dfrac{\bar{a}+\bar{a}'}{2}\right)+c=0$

$$\Rightarrow \quad \bar{b}(a+a')+b(\bar{a}+\bar{a}')+2c=0 \qquad \text{...(i)}$$

Since, $PQ \perp AB$. Therefore,

Complex slope of PQ + Complex slope of $AB = 0$

$$\Rightarrow \quad \frac{a-a'}{\bar{a}-\bar{a}'}+\left(-\frac{b}{\bar{b}}\right)=0$$

$$\Rightarrow \quad \bar{b}(a-a')-b(\bar{a}-\bar{a}')=0 \qquad \text{...(ii)}$$

On subtracting Eq. (ii) from Eq. (i), we get

$$a'\bar{b}+\bar{a}b+c=0$$

Alternate Solution

Equation of perpendicular bisector of PQ is

$$z(\bar{a}'-\bar{a})+\bar{z}(a'-a)-a'\bar{a}'+a\bar{a}=0 \qquad \text{...(i)}$$

and given line $\quad z\bar{b}+\bar{z}b+c=0 \qquad \text{...(ii)}$

Since, Eqs. (i) and (ii) are identical, we have

$$\frac{\bar{a}'-\bar{a}}{\bar{b}}=\frac{a'-a}{b}=\frac{a\bar{a}-a'\bar{a}'}{c}=k \qquad \text{[say]}$$

$\because \quad \bar{a}'-\bar{a}=\bar{b}k,\ a'-a=bk$

and $\quad a\bar{a}-a'\bar{a}'=ck$

Now, $\quad a'\bar{b}+\bar{a}b=\left\{a'\left(\dfrac{\bar{a}'-\bar{a}}{k}\right)+\bar{a}\left(\dfrac{a'-a}{k}\right)\right\}$

$$=\frac{1}{k}\{a'\bar{a}'-a\bar{a}\}=\frac{1}{k}(-ck)=-c$$

Hence, $\quad a'\bar{b}+\bar{a}b+c=0$

(f) Circle

The equation of a circle whose centre is at point affix z_0 and radius r, is $|z-z_0|=r$.

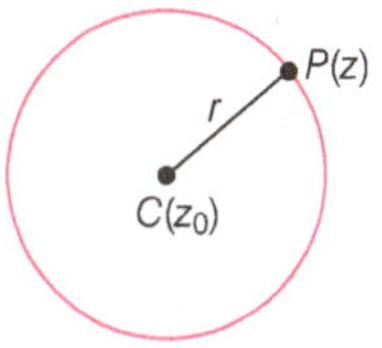

JEE Focus Points

- If the centre of the circle is at origin and radius r, then its equation is $|z|=r$.
- $|z-z_0|<r$ represents interior of a circle $|z-z_0|>r$ represent exterior of the circle $|z-z_0|=r$.
- $r<|z-z_0|<R$, this region is known as annulus.

Concept Inside Video

(i) General Equation of a Circle

The general equation of the circle is $z\bar{z}+\bar{a}z+a\bar{z}+b=0$, where a is a complex number and $b\in R$, having centre at $(-a)$ and radius $=\sqrt{|a|^2-b}$.

Proof The equation of circle having centre at z_0 and radius r is

$$|z-z_0|=r$$

$$\Rightarrow \quad |z-z_0|^2=r^2$$

$$\Rightarrow \quad (z-z_0)(\bar{z}-\bar{z}_0)=r^2$$

$$\Rightarrow \quad z\bar{z}-z\bar{z}_0-z_0\bar{z}+z_0\bar{z}_0=r^2$$

$$\Rightarrow \quad z\bar{z}+(-\bar{z}_0)z+(-z_0)\bar{z}+|z_0|^2-r^2=0$$

$$\Rightarrow \quad z\bar{z}+\bar{a}z+a\bar{z}+b=0$$

where, $\quad a=-z_0$ and $b=|z_0|^2-r^2$

$$\Rightarrow \quad z\bar{z}+\bar{a}z+a\bar{z}+b=0$$

where, $b\in R$ represents a circle having centre at $(-a)$ and radius $=\sqrt{|z_0|^2-b}=\sqrt{|a|^2-b}$.

Rule to Find the Centre and Radius of a Circle

Rules to find the centre and radius whose equation is given

(i) Make the coefficient of $z\bar{z}$ equal to 1 and right hand side equal to zero.

(ii) The centre of circle will be $=(-a)$
$=(-$ Coefficient of $\bar{z})$.

(iii) Radius $=\sqrt{(|a|^2-\text{constant term})}$

Example 86. Find the centre and radius of the circle $2z\bar{z}+(3-i)z+(3+i)\bar{z}-7=0$, where $i=\sqrt{-1}$.

Sol. The given equation can be written as

$$z\bar{z}+\left(\frac{3-i}{2}\right)z+\left(\frac{3+i}{2}\right)\bar{z}-\frac{7}{2}=0$$

So, it represent a circle with centre at $-\left(\dfrac{3+i}{2}\right)$ and radius

$$=\sqrt{\left(\left|-\left(\frac{3+i}{2}\right)\right|^2+\frac{7}{2}\right)}=\sqrt{\left(\frac{9}{4}+\frac{1}{4}+\frac{7}{2}\right)}=\sqrt{6}$$

JEE SCANNER

Example Similar to PYQ Asked in JEE Main 2023

If the centre and radius of circle $\left|\dfrac{z-3}{z-4}\right|=3$ *are respectively* (α, β) *and* γ, *then* $8(\alpha+\beta+\gamma)$ *is equal to*

(a) 36 (b) 33 (c) 99 (d) 37

Sol. (a) $\because \left|\dfrac{z-3}{z-4}\right|=3$

$$\Rightarrow |z-3|=3|z-4|$$
$$\Rightarrow |x+iy-3|=3|x+iy-4|$$
$$\Rightarrow \sqrt{(x-3)^2+y^2}=3\sqrt{(x-4)^2+y^2}$$
$$\Rightarrow (x-3)^2+y^2=9[(x-4)^2+y^2]$$
$$\Rightarrow x^2-6x+9+y^2=9(x^2-8x+16+y^2)$$
$$\Rightarrow x^2-6x+9+y^2=9x^2-72x+144+9y^2$$
$$\Rightarrow 8x^2+8y^2-66x+135=0$$
$$\Rightarrow x^2+y^2-\frac{66}{8}x+\frac{135}{8}=0$$
$$\Rightarrow x^2-\frac{66}{8}x+y^2+\frac{135}{8}=0$$
$$\Rightarrow x^2-2\cdot x\cdot\frac{33}{8}+\frac{1089}{64}+y^2+\frac{135}{8}-\frac{1089}{64}=0$$
$$\Rightarrow \left(x-\frac{33}{8}\right)^2+y^2-\frac{9}{64}=0$$
$$\Rightarrow \left(x-\frac{33}{8}\right)^2+y^2=\frac{9}{64}=\left(\frac{3}{8}\right)^2$$

$\therefore$ Center $(\alpha,\beta)=\left(\dfrac{33}{8},0\right)$ and radius $(\gamma)=\dfrac{3}{8}$

$$\therefore \quad 8(\alpha+\beta+\gamma)=8\left(\frac{33}{8}+0+\frac{3}{8}\right)=36$$

Skill Builder

If the centre and radius of circle $\left|\dfrac{z-5}{z-2}\right|=2$ are respectively (m,n) and r, then $m+n-r$ is

(a) 1 (b) -1

(c) 0 (d) 2

For Sol.

■ **For more practice** See Q.6 of Milestone Practice 1.1.

(ii) Equation of Circle Through Three Non-Collinear Points

Let $A(z_1), B(z_2), C(z_3)$ be three points on the circle and $P(z)$ be any point on the circle, then

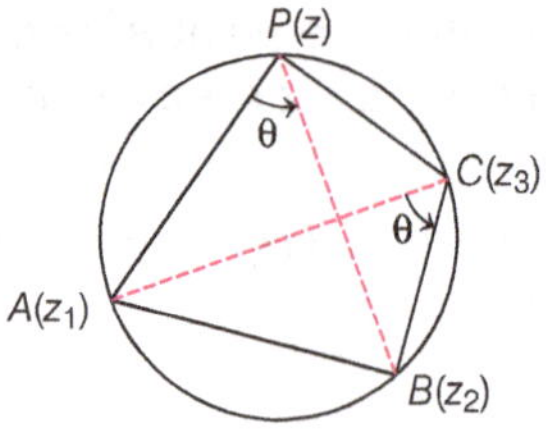

$$\angle ACB=\angle APB$$

Using Coni method,

in ΔACB, $\dfrac{z_2-z_3}{z_1-z_3}=\dfrac{BC}{CA}e^{i\theta}$ ...(i)

in ΔAPB, $\dfrac{z_2-z}{z_1-z}=\dfrac{BP}{AP}e^{i\theta}$ ...(ii)

From Eqs. (i) and (ii), we get

$$\frac{(z-z_1)(z_2-z_3)}{(z-z_2)(z_1-z_3)}=\text{Real} \quad ...(iii)$$

JEE SPIKE

If four points z_1, z_2, z_3, z_4 are concyclic, then

$\dfrac{(z_4-z_1)(z_2-z_3)}{(z_4-z_2)(z_1-z_3)}=$ real [replacing z by z_4 in Eq. (iii)]

or $\arg\left[\dfrac{(z_2-z_3)(z_4-z_1)}{(z_1-z_3)(z_4-z_2)}\right]=\pi, 0.$

(iii) Equation of Circle in Diametric Form

If end points of diameter represented by $A(z_1)$ and $B(z_2)$ and $P(z)$ is any point on circle.

$\therefore \quad \angle APB=90^\circ$

$\therefore$ Complex slope of PA + Complex slope of $PB=0$

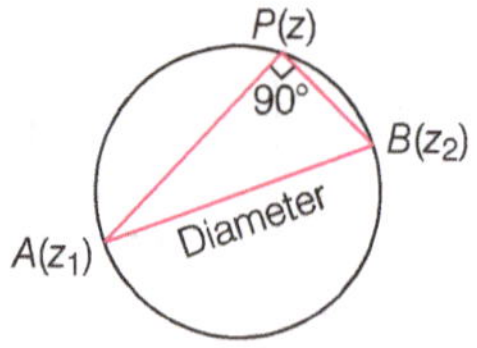

$$\Rightarrow \left(\frac{z-z_1}{\bar{z}-\bar{z}_1}\right)+\left(\frac{z-z_2}{\bar{z}-\bar{z}_2}\right)=0$$

Hence, $(z-z_1)(\bar{z}-\bar{z}_2)+(z-z_2)(\bar{z}-\bar{z}_1)=0$

which is required equation of circle in diametric form.

(iv) Other Forms of Circle

(a) Equation of all circles which are orthogonal to $|z-z_1|=r_1$ and $|z-z_2|=r_2$.

Let the circle be $|z-\alpha|=r$ cut given circles orthogonally.

$\therefore \quad r^2+r_1^2=|\alpha-z_1|^2 \quad$ ...(i)

and $\quad r^2+r_2^2=|\alpha-z_2|^2 \quad$ ...(ii)

On solving,

$r_2^2-r_1^2=\alpha(\bar{z}_1-\bar{z}_2)+\bar{\alpha}(z_1-z_2)+|z_2|^2-|z_1|^2$

and let $\alpha=a+ib$, $i=\sqrt{-1}$, $a, b\in R$

(b) **Apollonius circle** $\left|\dfrac{z-z_1}{z-z_2}\right|=k\neq 1$

It is the circle with join of z_3 and z_4 as a diameter, where $z_3=\dfrac{z_1+kz_2}{1+k}$, $z_4=\dfrac{z_1-kz_2}{1-k}$ for $k=1$, the circle reduces to the straight line which is perpendicular bisector of the line segment from z_1 to z_2.

(c) **Circular arc** $\arg\left(\dfrac{z-z_1}{z-z_2}\right)=\alpha$

This is an arc of a circle in which the chord joining z_1 and z_2 subtends angle α at any point on the arc.

If $\alpha=\pm\dfrac{\pi}{2}$, then locus of z is a circle with the join of z_1 and z_2 as diameter. If $\alpha=0$ or π, then locus is a straight line through the points z_1 and z_2.

(d) The equation $|z-z_1|^2+|z-z_2|^2=k$, will represent a circle, if $k\geq\dfrac{1}{2}|z_1-z_2|^2$.

Example 87. Find all circles which are orthogonal to $|z|=1$ and $|z-1|=4$.

Sol. Let $\quad |z-\alpha|=k \quad$ ...(i)

(where, $\alpha=a+ib$ and $a, b, k\in R$ and $i=\sqrt{-1}$) be a circle which cuts the circles

$|z|=1 \quad$ ...(ii)

and $\quad |z-1|=4 \quad$ ...(iii)

Orthogonally, then using the property that the sum of squares of their radii is equal to square of distance between centres. Thus, the circle (i) will cut the circles (ii) and (iii) orthogonally, if

$$k^2+1=|\alpha-0|^2=\alpha\bar{\alpha}$$

and
$$k^2+16=|\alpha-1|^2=(\alpha-1)(\bar{\alpha}-1)$$
$$=\alpha\bar{\alpha}-(\alpha+\bar{\alpha})+1$$

$\therefore \quad 1-(\alpha+\bar{\alpha})-15=0$

$\Rightarrow \quad \alpha+\bar{\alpha}=-14$

$\therefore \quad 2a=-14$

$\Rightarrow \quad a=-7$

$\Rightarrow \quad \alpha=a+ib=-7+ib$

Also, $\quad k^2=|\alpha|^2-1$

$\quad =(-7)^2+b^2-1=b^2+48$

$\Rightarrow \quad k=\sqrt{(b^2+48)}$

Therefore, required family of circles is given by

$$|z+7-ib|=\sqrt{(48+b^2)}.$$

(g) Equation of Parabola

Now, for parabola

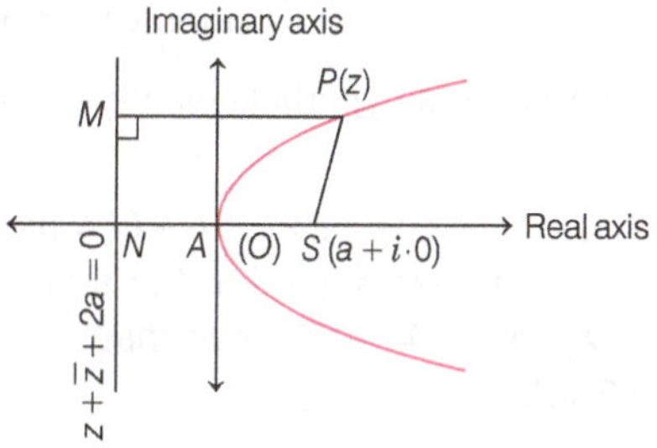

$$SP=PM$$

$$|z-a|=\frac{|z+\bar{z}+2a|}{2}$$

or $\quad z\bar{z}-4a(z+\bar{z})=\dfrac{1}{2}\{z^2+(\bar{z})^2\}$

where, $a\in R$ (focus), directrix is $z+\bar{z}+2a=0$.

(h) Equation of Ellipse

For ellipse

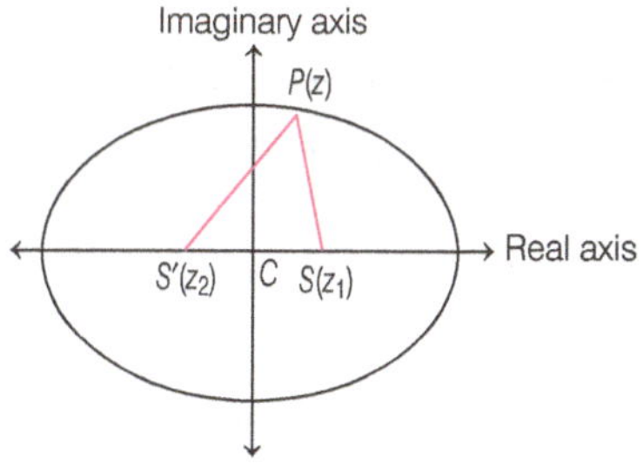

$$SP+S'P=2a$$

$\Rightarrow \quad |z-z_1|+|z-z_2|=2a$

where, $2a>|z_1-z_2|$ [since, eccentricity < 1]

Then, point z describes an ellipse having foci at z_1 and z_2 and $a\in R^+$.

(i) Equation of Hyperbola

For hyperbola

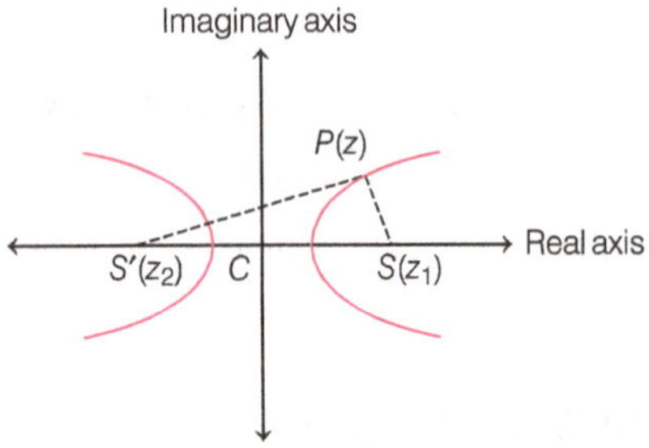

$$SP - S'P = 2a \Rightarrow |z - z_1| - |z - z_2| = 2a$$

where, $2a < |z_1 - z_2|$ [since, eccentricity > 1]

Then, point z describes a hyperbola having foci at z_1 and z_2 and $a \in R^+$.

Example 88. Let $z_1 = 10 + 6i$, $z_2 = 4 + 6i$, where $i = \sqrt{-1}$. If z is a complex number, such that the argument of $(z - z_1)/(z - z_2)$ is $\pi/4$, then prove that $|z - 7 - 9i| = 3\sqrt{2}$.

Sol. $\because$ $\arg\left(\dfrac{z - z_1}{z - z_2}\right) = \dfrac{\pi}{4}$

It is clear that z, z_1, z_2 are non-collinear points. Always a circle passes through z, z_1 and z_2. Let z_0 be the centre of the circle.

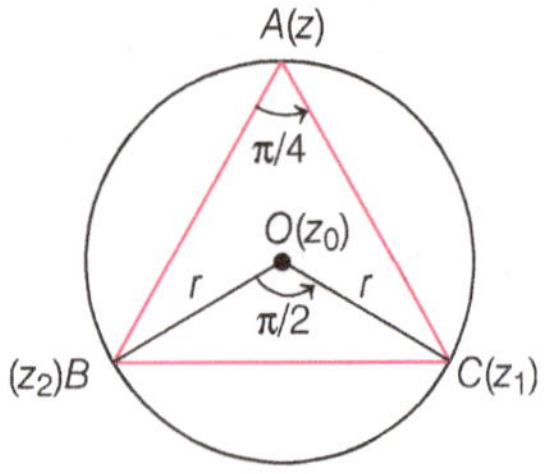

On applying rotation theorem in ΔBOC,

$$\frac{z_1 - z_0}{z_2 - z_0} = \frac{OC}{OB} e^{(i\pi/2)} = i \quad [\because OC = OB]$$

$\Rightarrow$ $(z_1 - z_0) = i(z_2 - z_0)$

$\Rightarrow$ $10 + 6i - z_0 = i(4 + 6i - z_0)$

$\Rightarrow$ $16 + 2i = (1 - i) z_0$

or $z_0 = \dfrac{(16 + 2i)}{(1 - i)} \cdot \dfrac{(1 + i)}{(1 + i)} = \dfrac{16 + 16i + 2i + 2i^2}{2}$

$= \dfrac{14 + 18i}{2} = 7 + 9i$

and radius, $r = OC = |z_0 - z_1| = |7 + 9i - 10 - 6i|$

$= |-3 + 3i|$

$= \sqrt{(9 + 9)} = 3\sqrt{2}$

Hence, required equation is

$$|z - z_0| = r \Rightarrow |z - 7 - 9i| = 3\sqrt{2}$$

Example 89. If $|z - 2 + i| \le 2$, where $i = \sqrt{-1}$, then find the greatest and least value of $|z|$.

Sol. $\because$ Radius = 2 units

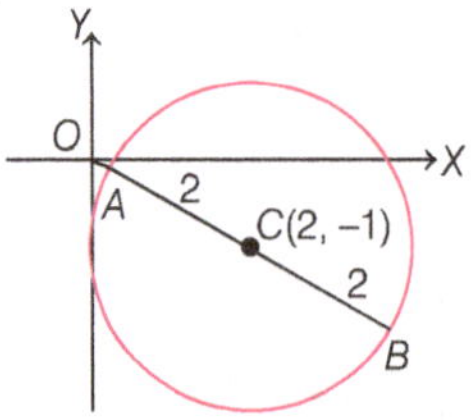

i.e. $AC = CB = 2$ units

$\therefore$ Least value of $|z| = OA = OC - AC = \sqrt{5} - 2$

and greatest value of $|z| = OB = OC + CB = \sqrt{5} + 2$

Hence, greatest value of $|z|$ is $\sqrt{5} + 2$ and least value of $|z|$ is $\sqrt{5} - 2$.

Example 90. In the argand plane, the vector $z = 4 - 3i$, where $i = \sqrt{-1}$, is turned in the clockwise sense through 180° and stretched three times. Then, find the complex number represented by the new vector.

Sol. $\because$ $z = 4 - 3i \Rightarrow |z| = \sqrt{(4)^2 + (-3)^2} = 5$

Let z_1 be the new vector obtained by rotating z in the clockwise sense through 180°, therefore

$$z_1 = z\, e^{-i\pi} = -z = -(4 - 3i) = -4 + 3i.$$

The unit vector in the direction of z_1 is $-\dfrac{4}{5} + \dfrac{3}{5}i$.

Therefore, required vector $= 3|z|\left(-\dfrac{4}{5} + \dfrac{3}{5}i\right)$

$= 15\left(-\dfrac{4}{5} + \dfrac{3}{5}i\right)$

$= -12 + 9i$

Alternate Solution

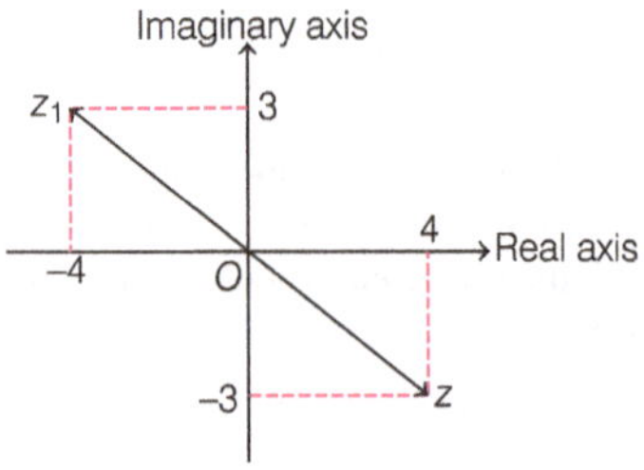

Here, $z_1 = -4 + 3i$

Hence, $3z_1 = -12 + 9i$

Example 91. $ABCD$ is a rhombus. Its diagonals AC and BD intersect at the point M and satisfy $BD = 2AC$. If the points D and M represents the complex numbers $1 + i$ and $2 - i$, where $i = \sqrt{-1}$, respectively, find A.

Sol. Let $A \equiv z$

$\because$ $BD = 2AC$ or $DM = 2\,AM$

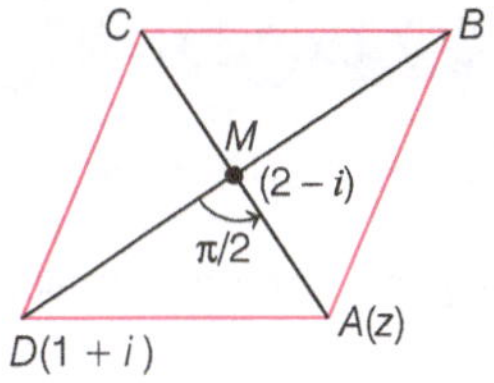

Now, in ΔDMA,

Applying Coni method, we have

$$\frac{z-(2-i)}{(1+i)-(2-i)} = \frac{AM}{DM} e^{i\pi/2} = \frac{1}{2} i$$

$$\Rightarrow \quad z - 2 + i = \frac{i}{2}(-1+2i) = -\frac{i}{2} - 1 \text{ or } z = 1 - \frac{3}{2} i$$

$$\therefore \quad A \equiv 1 - \frac{3}{2} i \text{ or } 3 - \frac{i}{2}$$

[if positions of A and C interchange]

If $\left| z \pm \frac{b}{z} \right| = a$, then the greatest and least values of $|z|$ are $\frac{a+\sqrt{(a^2+4|b|)}}{2}$ and $\frac{-a+\sqrt{(a^2+4|b|)}}{2}$, respectively.

Proof $$\left| z \pm \frac{b}{z} \right| \ge \left| |z| - \left| \frac{b}{z} \right| \right|$$

$$\Rightarrow \quad a \ge \left| |z| - \frac{|b|}{|z|} \right| \text{ or } -a \le |z| - \frac{|b|}{|z|} \le a$$

Now, $$|z| - \frac{|b|}{|z|} \le a \Rightarrow |z|^2 - a|z| - |b| \le 0$$

$$\therefore \quad \frac{a-\sqrt{(a^2+4|b|)}}{2} \le |z| \le \frac{a+\sqrt{(a^2+4|b|)}}{2}$$

or $$0 \le |z| \le \frac{a+\sqrt{(a^2+4|b|)}}{2} \quad \text{...(i)}$$

and $$|z| - \frac{|b|}{|z|} \ge -a \Rightarrow |z|^2 + a|z| - |b| \ge 0$$

$$\therefore \quad |z| \ge \frac{-a+\sqrt{(a^2+4|b|)}}{2} \quad \text{...(ii)}$$

From Eqs. (i) and (ii), we get

$$\frac{-a+\sqrt{(a^2+4|b|)}}{2} \le |z| \le \frac{a+\sqrt{(a^2+4|b|)}}{2}$$

Hence, the greatest value of $|z|$ is $\frac{a+\sqrt{(a^2+4|b|)}}{2}$

and the least value of $|z|$ is $\frac{-a+\sqrt{(a^2+4|b|)}}{2}$.

Corollary For $b = 1$, $\left| z \pm \frac{1}{z} \right| = a$

Then, $$\frac{-a+\sqrt{(a^2+4)}}{2} \le |z| \le \frac{a+\sqrt{(a^2+4)}}{2}$$

Example 92. Find the maximum and minimum values of $|z|$ satisfying $\left| z + \frac{1}{z} \right| = 2$.

Sol. Here, $b = 1$ and $a = 2$

$\therefore$ Maximum and minimum values of $|z|$ are $\frac{2+\sqrt{(4+4)}}{2}$ and $\frac{-2+\sqrt{(4+4)}}{2}$ i.e. $1+\sqrt{2}$ and $-1+\sqrt{2}$, respectively.

Example 93. If $\left| z + \frac{4}{z} \right| = 2$, find the maximum and minimum values of $|z|$.

Sol. Here, $b = 4$ and $a = 2$.

$\therefore$ Maximum and minimum values of $|z|$ are

$$\frac{2+\sqrt{(4+16)}}{2} \text{ and } \frac{-2+\sqrt{(4+16)}}{2}$$

i.e. $1+\sqrt{5}$ and $-1+\sqrt{5}$, respectively.

Example 94. If $|z| \ge 3$, then determine the least value of $\left| z + \frac{1}{z} \right|$.

Sol. $\because$ $$\left| z + \frac{1}{z} \right| \ge \left| |z| - \left| \frac{1}{z} \right| \right| = \left| |z| - \frac{1}{|z|} \right| \quad \text{...(i)}$$

$\because$ $$|z| \ge 3 \Rightarrow \frac{1}{|z|} \le \frac{1}{3}$$

or $$-\frac{1}{|z|} \ge -\frac{1}{3}$$

$\therefore$ $$|z| - \frac{1}{|z|} \ge 3 - \frac{1}{3} = \frac{8}{3}$$

$\Rightarrow$ $$|z| - \frac{1}{|z|} \ge \frac{8}{3}$$

or $$\left| |z| - \frac{1}{|z|} \right| \ge \frac{8}{3} \quad \text{...(ii)}$$

From Eqs. (i) and (ii), we get

$$\left| z + \frac{1}{z} \right| \ge \frac{8}{3}$$

$\therefore$ Least value of $\left| z + \frac{1}{z} \right|$ is $\frac{8}{3}$.

Milestone Practice 1.4

1. Find the locus of the points representing the complex number z for which $|z+5|^2 - |z-5|^2 = 10$.

2. Prove that the triangle formed by the points 1, $\frac{1+i}{\sqrt{2}}$ and i as vertices in the Argand diagram is isosceles.

3. If $|z| = 2$ and $\frac{z_1 - z_3}{z_2 - z_3} = \frac{z-2}{z+2}$, then prove that z_1, z_2, z_3 are vertices of right-angled triangle.

4. What is locus of w if $w = \frac{3}{z}$ and $|z-1| = 1$?

5. Find centre and radius of circle having equation $z\bar{z} + (1-i)z + (1+i)\bar{z} - 1 = 0$.

6. Find the centre and radius of circle, if $\left|\frac{z-7}{z-3}\right| = 4$.

7. If the equation $|z-a| + |z-b| = 3$ represents an ellipse and $a, b \in C$, where a is fixed, then find the locus of b.

8. If $|z-3i| + |z-4| = k$ represents ellipse, find the range of k.

Answer Key

1. Straight line
4. Perpendicular bisector
5. Centre $= (1+i)$, radius $= \sqrt{3}$
6. $\left(\frac{41}{15}, 0\right), \frac{16}{15}$
7. b lies inside the circle
8. $k \in (5, \infty)$

For Detailed Solution

JEE Pattern EXAMPLES

Single Option Correct Type Questions

Example 1 *If a, b, c, a_1, b_1 and c_1 are non-zero complex numbers satisfying $\frac{a}{a_1}+\frac{b}{b_1}+\frac{c}{c_1}=1+\ i$ and $\frac{a_1}{a}+\frac{b_1}{b}+\frac{c_1}{c}=0$, where $i=\sqrt{-1}$, the value of $\frac{a^2}{a_1^2}+\frac{b^2}{b_1^2}+\frac{c^2}{c_1^2}$ is*

(a) $2i$ (b) $2+2i$
(c) 2 (d) None of these

Sol. (a) We have, $\frac{a}{a_1}+\frac{b}{b_1}+\frac{c}{c_1}=1+i$

On squaring both sides, we get

$$\frac{a^2}{a_1^2}+\frac{b^2}{b_1^2}+\frac{c^2}{c_1^2}+2\left(\frac{ab}{a_1b_1}+\frac{bc}{b_1c_1}+\frac{ca}{c_1a_1}\right)=1+i^2+2i$$

$$\Rightarrow \frac{a^2}{a_1^2}+\frac{b^2}{b_1^2}+\frac{c^2}{c_1^2}+2\frac{abc}{a_1b_1c_1}\left(\frac{c_1}{c}+\frac{a_1}{a}+\frac{b_1}{b}\right)=1-1+2i$$

$$\Rightarrow \frac{a^2}{a_1^2}+\frac{b^2}{b_1^2}+\frac{c^2}{c_1^2}+0=2i$$

$$\therefore \frac{a^2}{a_1^2}+\frac{b^2}{b_1^2}+\frac{c^2}{c_1^2}=2i$$

Example 2 *If $|z|=1$ and $\omega=\frac{z-1}{z+1}$ (where $z\neq-1$), then $\text{Re}(\omega)$ is*

(a) 0 (b) $-\frac{1}{|z+1|^2}$

(c) $\left|\frac{z}{z+1}\right|\cdot\frac{1}{|z+1|^2}$ (d) $\frac{\sqrt{2}}{|z+1|^2}$

Sol. (a) We have, $|z|=1$.

Let $z=e^{i\theta}$,

where $\theta\in R$ and $i=\sqrt{-1}$.

Then, $\omega=\frac{z-1}{z+1}=\frac{e^{i\theta}-1}{e^{i\theta}+1}=i\tan\left(\frac{\theta}{2}\right)$

$\therefore$ $\text{Re}(\omega)=0$

JEE SCANNER

Example 3 Similar to PYQ Asked in JEE Main 2024

If z is a complex number such that $|z|\geq 3$, then the minimum value of $\left|z+\frac{(6+8i)}{2z}\right|$ is

(a) 2 (b) $\frac{4}{3}$ (c) $\frac{5}{3}$ (d) 10

Sol. (b) Given that $|z|\geq 3$

Now, $\left|z+\frac{(6+8i)}{2z}\right|\geq\left||z|-\frac{|(6+8i)|}{|2z|}\right|$

The least value occurs when $|z|=3$

$$\therefore \left|z+\frac{(6+8i)}{2z}\right|\geq\left||z|-\frac{|6+8i|}{2|z|}\right|$$

$$=\left|3-\frac{\sqrt{36+64}}{2\times 3}\right|$$

$$=\left|3-\frac{10}{6}\right|=\left|3-\frac{5}{3}\right|$$

$$=\left|\frac{4}{3}\right|=\left|\frac{4}{3}+0i\right|=\sqrt{\left(\frac{4}{3}\right)^2}=\frac{4}{3}$$

Skill Builder

If z is a complex number such that $|z|\geq 2$, then the minimum value of $\left|z+\frac{1}{2}\right|$ is

(a) $\frac{4}{3}$ (b) $\frac{3}{2}$
(c) $\frac{5}{3}$ (d) $\frac{5}{2}$

For Sol.

Example 4 *Let z and ω be complex numbers. If $\text{Re}(z)=|z-2|$, $\text{Re}(\omega)=|\omega-2|$ and $\arg(z-\omega)=\frac{\pi}{3}$, the value of $\text{Im}(z+\omega)$ is*

(a) $\frac{1}{\sqrt{3}}$ (b) $\frac{2}{\sqrt{3}}$ (c) $\sqrt{3}$ (d) $\frac{4}{\sqrt{3}}$

Sol. (d) Let $z = x + iy,\ x, y \in R$ and $i = \sqrt{-1}$

$\because \quad \text{Re}(z) = |z - 2|$

$\Rightarrow \quad x = \sqrt{(x-2)^2 + y^2} \Rightarrow y^2 = 4(x-1)$

$\therefore z = 1 + t^2 + 2ti$, parametric form and let $\omega = p + iq$

Similarly, $\quad \omega = 1 + s^2 + 2si$

$\therefore \quad z - \omega = (t^2 - s^2) + 2i(t - s)$

$\Rightarrow \quad \arg(z - \omega) = \dfrac{\pi}{3}$ [given]

$\therefore \quad \tan^{-1}\left(\dfrac{2}{t+s}\right) = \dfrac{\pi}{3} \Rightarrow \dfrac{2}{t+s} = \sqrt{3} \Rightarrow (t+s) = \dfrac{2}{\sqrt{3}}$

Now, $\quad z + \omega = 2 + t^2 + s^2 + 2i(t+s)$

$\therefore \quad \text{Im}(z + \omega) = 2(t+s) = \dfrac{4}{\sqrt{3}}$

Example 5 *If $8iz^3 + 12z^2 - 18z + 27i = 0$, then $|z|$ is equal to*

(a) $\dfrac{3}{2}$ (b) $\dfrac{2}{3}$ (c) 1 (d) $\dfrac{3}{4}$

Sol. (a) We have, $8iz^3 + 12z^2 - 18z + 27i = 0$

$\Rightarrow \quad 4iz^2(2z - 3i) - 9(2z - 3i) = 0$

$\Rightarrow \quad (2z - 3i)(4iz^2 - 9) = 0$

$\Rightarrow \quad z = \dfrac{3i}{2}$ and $z^2 = \dfrac{9}{4i}$

$\Rightarrow \quad |z| = \dfrac{3}{2}$ and $|z^2| = \dfrac{9}{4} \Rightarrow |z| = \dfrac{3}{2}$

Example 6 *Let z, ω be complex numbers such that $\bar{z} + i\bar{\omega} = 0$ and $\arg(z\omega) = \pi$. Then, $\arg(z)$ is equal to*

(a) $\dfrac{\pi}{4}$ (b) $\dfrac{\pi}{2}$ (c) $\dfrac{3\pi}{4}$ (d) $\dfrac{5\pi}{4}$

Sol. (c) We have, $\quad \bar{z} + i\bar{\omega} = 0$

$\Rightarrow \quad z - i\omega = 0$

$\Rightarrow \quad z = i\omega$

Now, $\quad \arg(z\omega) = \pi$

$\Rightarrow \quad \arg(z) + \arg(\omega) = \pi$

$\Rightarrow \quad \arg(z) + \arg\left(\dfrac{z}{i}\right) = \pi$

$\Rightarrow \quad \arg(z) + \arg(z) - \arg(i) = \pi \Rightarrow 2\arg(z) - \dfrac{\pi}{2} = \pi$

$\Rightarrow \quad 2\arg(z) = \dfrac{3\pi}{2} \Rightarrow \arg(z) = \dfrac{3\pi}{4}$

Example 7 *If z_1, z_2, z_3 are the vertices of an equilateral ΔABC such that $|z_1 - i| = |z_2 - i| = |z_3 - i|$, then $|z_1 + z_2 + z_3|$ is equal to*

(a) $3\sqrt{3}$ (b) $\sqrt{3}$ (c) 3 (d) $\dfrac{1}{3\sqrt{3}}$

Decoding the Question

We know that for an equilateral triangle, its circumcentre and centroid coincides.

Sol. (c) We have, $|z_1 - i| = |z_2 - i| = |z_3 - i|$

$\therefore$ z_1, z_2, z_3 lie on the circle whose centre is i.

Also, given that the triangle is equilateral.

$\therefore \quad \dfrac{z_1 + z_2 + z_3}{3} = i$

$\Rightarrow \quad z_1 + z_2 + z_3 = 3i \Rightarrow |z_1 + z_2 + z_3| = 3$

Example 8 *The locus of z which satisfies the inequality $\log_{0.3}|z - 1| > \log_{0.3}|z - i|$ is given by*

(a) $x + y < 0$ (b) $x + y > 0$

(c) $x - y > 0$ (d) $x - y < 0$

Sol. (c) We have, $\log_{0.3}|z - 1| > \log_{0.3}|z - i|$

$\Rightarrow \quad |z - 1| < |z - i| \Rightarrow |z - 1|^2 < |z - i|^2$

$\Rightarrow \quad (z - 1)(\bar{z} - 1) < (z - i)(\bar{z} + i)$

$\Rightarrow \quad z\bar{z} - z - \bar{z} + 1 < z\bar{z} + iz - i\bar{z} + 1$

$\Rightarrow \quad (1 + i)z + (1 - i)\bar{z} > 0 \Rightarrow (z + \bar{z}) + i(z - \bar{z}) > 0$

$\Rightarrow \quad 2x + 2i^2 y > 0$ $[z = x + iy]$

$\Rightarrow \quad x - y > 0$

Example 9 *The common roots of $x^{12} - 1 = 0$ and $x^4 + x^2 + 1 = 0$ are*

(a) ω, ω^2 (b) $-\omega, -\omega^2$

(c) $\pm\omega, \pm\omega^2$ (d) $\omega, -\omega^2$

Sol. (c) We have, $x^{12} - 1 = (x^6 + 1)(x^6 - 1)$

$= (x^6 + 1)(x^2 - 1)(x^4 + x^2 + 1)$

$\therefore$ Common roots are given by

$x^4 + x^2 + 1 = 0$

$\Rightarrow \quad x^2 = \dfrac{-1 \pm \sqrt{1 - 4}}{2} \Rightarrow x^2 = \dfrac{-1 \pm \sqrt{3}i}{2}$

$\Rightarrow \quad x^2 = \omega, \omega^2$

$\Rightarrow \quad x^2 = \omega^4, \omega^2$ $[\because \omega = \omega^4]$

$\Rightarrow \quad x = \pm\omega^2, \pm\omega$

Example 10 *The mirror image of the curve $\arg\left(\dfrac{z - 3}{z - i}\right) = \dfrac{\pi}{6}, i = \sqrt{-1}$ in the real axis, is*

(a) $\arg\left(\dfrac{z + 3}{z + i}\right) = \dfrac{\pi}{6}$ (b) $\arg\left(\dfrac{z - 3}{z + i}\right) = \dfrac{\pi}{6}$

(c) $\arg\left(\dfrac{z + i}{z + 3}\right) = \dfrac{\pi}{6}$ (d) $\arg\left(\dfrac{z + i}{z - 3}\right) = \dfrac{\pi}{6}$

Sol. (d) $\because$ The image of z in the real axis is $\bar{z}$.

The image is given by

$$\arg\left(\frac{\bar{z}-3}{\bar{z}-i}\right)=\frac{\pi}{6}$$

$$\Rightarrow \quad -\arg\left(\frac{z-3}{z+i}\right)=\frac{\pi}{6} \qquad [\because \arg(\bar{z})=-\arg(z)]$$

$$\Rightarrow \quad \arg\left(\frac{z+i}{z-3}\right)=\frac{\pi}{6} \qquad \left[\because \arg\left(\frac{z_1}{z_2}\right)=-\arg\left(\frac{z_2}{z_1}\right)\right]$$

JEE SCANNER

Example 11 Similar to PYQ Asked in JEE Main 2024

If $S=\{z\in C: |z-3|=|z+3|=|z+3i|=|z-3i|\}$, then $n(S)$ is

(a) 0 (b) 1 (c) 2 (d) 3

Sol. (b) Given that $|z-3|=|z+3|=|z+3i|=|z-3i|$

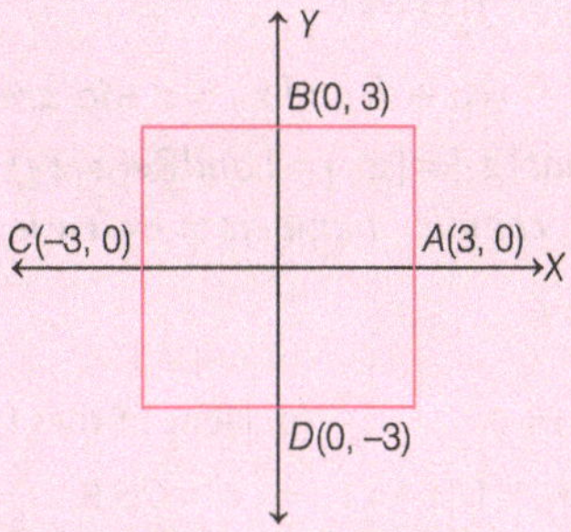

Since, $ABCD$ is a square.

Hence, the intersection of its diagonal is the only point whose distance from A, B, C and D will be same.

So, $n(S)=1$

Skill Builder

If $P=\{z\in C: |z-2i|=|z+3i|=|z-4|\}$, then $n(S)$ is

(a) 1 (b) 2

(c) 3 (d) 4

For Sol.

Example 12 *The mirror image of the curve $\arg\left(\frac{z+i}{z-1}\right)=\frac{\pi}{4}$, $i=\sqrt{-1}$ in the line $x-y=0$, is*

(a) $\arg\left(\frac{z+i}{z+1}\right)=\frac{\pi}{4}$ (b) $\arg\left(\frac{z+1}{z-i}\right)=\frac{\pi}{4}$

(c) $\arg\left(\frac{z-i}{z+1}\right)=\frac{\pi}{4}$ (d) $\arg\left(\frac{z+i}{z-1}\right)=\frac{\pi}{4}$

Sol. (c) $\because$ The image of z in the line $y=x$ is $i\bar{z}$.

$\therefore$ The image of the given curve is

$$\arg\left(\frac{i\bar{z}+i}{i\bar{z}-1}\right)=\frac{\pi}{4} \Rightarrow \arg\left(\frac{\bar{z}+1}{\bar{z}+i}\right)=\frac{\pi}{4}$$

$$\Rightarrow \quad -\arg\left(\frac{z+1}{z-i}\right)=\frac{\pi}{4} \qquad [\because \arg(\bar{z})=-\arg(z)]$$

$$\Rightarrow \quad \arg\left(\frac{z-i}{z+1}\right)=\frac{\pi}{4} \qquad \left[\because \arg\left(\frac{z_1}{z_2}\right)=-\arg\left(\frac{z_2}{z_1}\right)\right]$$

Example 13 *If $z+\frac{1}{z}=1$ and $a=z^{2017}+\frac{1}{z^{2017}}$ and b is the last digit of the number $2^{2^n}-1$, when the integer $n>1$, the value of a^2+b^2 is*

(a) 23 (b) 24 (c) 26 (d) 27

Sol. (c) $\because z+\frac{1}{z}=1 \Rightarrow z^2-z+1=0$

$$\therefore \quad z=\frac{-(-1)\pm\sqrt{(1-4)}}{2}=-\omega,-\omega^2$$

[ω is cube root of unity]

and $z^{2017}=(-\omega)^{2017}=-\omega$,

$z^{2017}=(-\omega^2)^{2017}=-\omega^2$

$$\therefore \quad a=z^{2017}+\frac{1}{z^{2017}}=-\left(\omega+\frac{1}{\omega}\right)=-\left(\frac{\omega^2+1}{\omega}\right)=1$$

and $2^{2^n}=2^{4\cdot 2^{n-2}}=16^{2^{n-2}}$ has last digit 6.

$\therefore \quad b=6-1=5$

Hence, $a^2+b^2=1^2+5^2=26$

Example 14 *If ω is complex cube root of unity and a, b, c are such that $\frac{1}{a+\omega}+\frac{1}{b+\omega}+\frac{1}{c+\omega}=2\omega^2$ and $\frac{1}{a+\omega^2}+\frac{1}{b+\omega^2}+\frac{1}{c+\omega^2}=2\omega$, then the value of $\frac{1}{a+1}+\frac{1}{b+1}+\frac{1}{c+1}$ is equal to*

(a) -2 (b) -1 (c) 1 (d) 2

Sol. (d) $\because \frac{1}{a+\omega}+\frac{1}{b+\omega}+\frac{1}{c+\omega}=2\omega^2=\frac{2}{\omega}$

and $\frac{1}{a+\omega^2}+\frac{1}{b+\omega^2}+\frac{1}{c+\omega^2}=2\omega=\frac{2}{\omega^2}$

It is clear that, ω and ω^2 are the roots of the equation

$$\frac{1}{a+x}+\frac{1}{b+x}+\frac{1}{c+x}=\frac{2}{x} \qquad \text{...(i)}$$

$\Rightarrow \quad x\sum(b+x)(c+x)=2(a+x)(b+x)(c+x)$

$\Rightarrow \quad x^3-(ab+bc+ca)x-2abc=0$

$\because$ Coefficient of $x^2=0$ and the sum of roots $=0$

$\Rightarrow \quad \alpha+\omega+\omega^2=0 \Rightarrow \alpha-1=0$

$\therefore \quad \alpha=1$

$\therefore$ Third root is 1.

From Eq. (i), we get

$$\frac{1}{a+1}+\frac{1}{b+1}+\frac{1}{c+1}=2$$

JEE SCANNER

Example 15 Similar to PYQ Asked in JEE Main 2024

If $z = x + iy$, $xy \neq 0$, satisfies the equation $z^2 + 4i\bar{z} = 0$, then $|z^2|$ is equal to

(a) 9 (b) 16 (c) 25 (d) 4

Sol. (b) Let $z = x + iy$

Now, $z^2 = -4i\bar{z} \Rightarrow |z^2| = |-4i\bar{z}|$

$\Rightarrow |z^2| = |-4i| \cdot |\bar{z}| \Rightarrow |z|^2 = 4|z|$

$\Rightarrow |z|^2 - 4|z| = 0 \Rightarrow |z|(|z| - 4) = 0$

$\Rightarrow |z| = 0$ or $|z| - 4 = 0$

$\therefore |z| = 4$ [$\because |z| = 0$ is not possible]

Thus, $|z|^2 = 4^2 = 16$

Skill Builder

If $z = x + iy$, $xy \neq 0$, satisfies the equation $4z + 2\bar{z} = 12$, then $|z|^3$ is equal to

(a) 8 (b) 27

(c) 64 (d) 125

For Sol.

Example 16 *If a, b and c are distinct integers and $\omega(\neq 1)$ is a cube root of unity, then the minimum value of $|a + b\omega + c\omega^2| + |a + b\omega^2 + c\omega|$, is*

(a) $2\sqrt{3}$ (b) 3 (c) $4\sqrt{2}$ (d) 2

Sol. (a) Let $z = a + b\omega + c\omega^2$.

Then, $|z|^2 = z\bar{z} = (a + b\omega + c\omega^2)(a + b\bar{\omega} + \overline{c\omega^2})$

$= (a + b\omega + c\omega^2)(a + b\omega^2 + c\omega)$

$= a^2 + b^2 + c^2 - ab - bc - ca$

$= \frac{1}{2}[(a-b)^2 + (b-c)^2 + (c-a)^2]$

$\Rightarrow |z|^2 \geq \frac{1}{2} \times 6 = 3$ $\left[\begin{array}{l}\because a \neq b \neq c \\ \therefore |a-b| \geq 1, |b-c| \geq 1 \\ \text{and } |a-c| \geq 2\end{array}\right]$

$\therefore |z| \geq \sqrt{3}$

$\therefore |a + b\omega + c\omega^2| + |a + b\omega^2 + c\omega|$

$= |a + b\omega + c\omega^2| + |a + b\omega^2 + \overline{c\omega}|$

$= |a + b\omega + c\omega^2| + |a + b\omega + c\omega^2|$

$= 2|a + b\omega + c\omega^2| = 2|z| \geq 2\sqrt{3}$

Hence, the minimum value of $|a + b\omega + c\omega^2| + |a + b\omega^2 + c\omega|$ is $2\sqrt{3}$.

More than One Correct Option Type Questions

Example 17 *If $x = 2 + 5i$ and $2\left(\frac{1}{1!9!} + \frac{1}{3!7!}\right) + \frac{1}{5!5!} = \frac{2^a}{b!}$ and $f(x) = x^3 - 5x^2 + 33x - 19$, then*

(a) $a = 10, b = 9$ (b) $a = 9, b = 10$

(c) $f(x) = a$ (d) $f(x) = b$

Sol. (b, d) We have, $2\left(\frac{1}{1!9!} + \frac{1}{3!7!}\right) + \frac{1}{5!5!} = \frac{2^a}{b!}$

$\Rightarrow \frac{2}{1!9!} + \frac{2}{3!7!} + \frac{1}{5!5!} = \frac{2^a}{b!}$

$\Rightarrow \frac{1}{10!}\left(\frac{2!10!}{1!9!} + \frac{2!10!}{3!7!} + \frac{10!}{5!5!}\right) = \frac{2^a}{b!}$

$\Rightarrow \frac{1}{10!}(2 \times {}^{10}C_1 + 2 \times {}^{10}C_3 + {}^{10}C_5) = \frac{2^a}{b!}$

$\Rightarrow \frac{1}{10!}({}^{10}C_1 + {}^{10}C_1 + {}^{10}C_3 + {}^{10}C_3 + {}^{10}C_5) = \frac{2^a}{b!}$

$\Rightarrow \frac{1}{10!}({}^{10}C_1 + {}^{10}C_9 + {}^{10}C_3 + {}^{10}C_7 + {}^{10}C_5) = \frac{2^a}{b!} \Rightarrow \frac{2^{10-1}}{10!} = \frac{2^a}{b!}$

$\therefore a = 9, b = 10$

Again, $x = 2 + 5i$

$\Rightarrow (x-2)^2 = -25 \Rightarrow x^2 - 4x + 29 = 0$

$\therefore x^3 - 5x^2 + 33x - 19 = (x-1)(x^2 - 4x + 29) + 10$

$= 0 + 10 = 10 = b$

$\therefore f(x) = b$

Example 18 *If $z_1 = a + ib$ and $z_2 = c + id$ are complex numbers such that $|z_1| = |z_2| = 1$ and $\text{Re}(z_1\bar{z}_2) = 0$, where $i = \sqrt{-1}$, then the complex numbers $\omega_1 = a + ic$ and $\omega_2 = b + id$ satisfy*

(a) $|\omega_1| = 1$ (b) $|\omega_2| = 1$

(c) $\text{Re}(\omega_1\bar{\omega}_2) = 0$ (d) None of these

Sol. (a, b, c) $\because |z_1| = 1, |z_2| = 1 \Rightarrow z_1 = CiS\,\theta, z_2 = CiS\,\phi$

$\text{Re}(z_1\bar{z}_2) = \text{Re}(CiS(\theta - \phi)) = 0$ [given]

$\Rightarrow \cos(\theta - \phi) = 0 \Rightarrow \theta - \phi = \frac{\pi}{2} \Rightarrow \phi = \theta - \frac{\pi}{2}$

and $a = \cos\theta, b = \sin\theta, c = \cos\phi, d = \sin\phi$

$\therefore \omega_1 = a + ic = \cos\theta + i\cos\phi = \cos\theta + i\sin\theta$ $\left[\because \phi = \theta - \frac{\pi}{2}\right]$

and $\omega_2 = b + id = \sin\theta + i\sin\phi = \sin\theta - i\cos\theta$ $\left[\because \phi = \theta - \frac{\pi}{2}\right]$

$\therefore |\omega_1| = 1, |\omega_2| = 1$

and $\text{Re}(\omega_1\bar{\omega}_2) = \text{Re}(\cos\theta + i\sin\theta)(\sin\theta + i\cos\theta) = 0$

Example 19 *The complex numbers z_1, z_2, z_3 satisfying $(z_2 - z_3) = (1+i)(z_1 - z_3)$, where $i = \sqrt{-1}$, are vertices of a triangle which is*

(a) equilateral (b) isosceles

(c) right angled (d) scalene

Sol. (b, c) $\because (z_2 - z_3) = (1+i)(z_1 - z_3)$

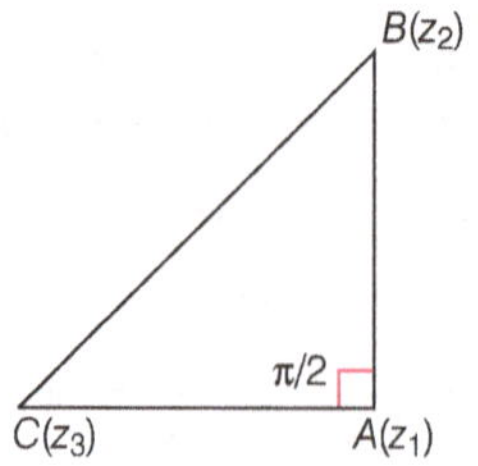

$\Rightarrow \quad (z_2 - z_1) = i(z_1 - z_3)$

$\Rightarrow \quad (z_2 - z_1) = -i(z_3 - z_1)$

or $\quad (z_3 - z_1) = i(z_2 - z_1) \Rightarrow \dfrac{z_3 - z_1}{z_2 - z_1} = e^{i\pi/2}$

AC is obtained by rotating AB about A through $\dfrac{\pi}{2}$ anti-clockwise.

$\therefore \quad AB = AC, \angle CAB = \dfrac{\pi}{2}$

Hence, z_1, z_2, z_3 form isosceles right angled triangle.

Example 20 *If z satisfies the inequality $|z-1| < |z+1|$, then one has*

(a) $|z - 2 - i| < |z + 2 - i|, i = \sqrt{-1}$

(b) $|\arg(z + i)| < \dfrac{\pi}{2}, i = \sqrt{-1}$

(c) $\text{Re}(z) < 0$

(d) $\text{Im}(i\bar{z}) > 0, i = \sqrt{-1}$

Sol. (a, b, d) On putting $z = x + iy$ in the given relation, we have

$$(x-1)^2 + y^2 < (x+1)^2 + y^2$$

$\Rightarrow \quad x > 0$

i.e. $\quad \text{Re}(z) > 0 \quad$ ...(i)

and on putting $z = x + iy$ in alternate (a), then

$$(x-2)^2 + (y-1)^2 < (x+2)^2 + (y-1)^2$$

$\Rightarrow \quad x > 0 \quad$ [from Eq. (i)]

which is true.

$\therefore$ Real part of $(z + i) = x > 0$,

then $\arg(z + i)$ lies between $-\dfrac{\pi}{2}$ and $\dfrac{\pi}{2}$

and hence $|\arg(z+i)| < \dfrac{\pi}{2}$

and $\quad \text{Im}(i\bar{z}) = \text{Im}(i(x - iy)) = \text{Im}(y + ix)$

$\quad = x > 0 \quad$ [from Eq. (i)]

which is true.

Example 21 *The equation $z^2 - i|z-1|^2 = 0$, where $i = \sqrt{-1}$, has*

(a) no real root
(b) no purely imaginary root
(c) all roots inside $|z| = 1$
(d) atleast two roots

Sol. (a, b, c) On putting $z = x + iy$, we have

$$(x+iy)^2 - i|x + iy - 1|^2 = 0$$

$\Rightarrow \quad x^2 - y^2 + 2ixy - i((x-1)^2 + y^2) = 0$

On comparing real and imaginary parts, we get

$$x^2 - y^2 = 0 \text{ and } 2xy = (x-1)^2 + y^2$$

***Case* I** When $y = x$, then $2xy = (x-1)^2 + y^2$ reduces to

$$2x^2 = (x-1)^2 + x^2$$

$\Rightarrow \quad 0 = -2x + 1$

$\therefore \quad x = \dfrac{1}{2} = y$

$\Rightarrow \quad z = x + iy = \dfrac{1+i}{2} \quad$ ...(i)

***Case* II** When $y = -x$, then $2xy = (x-1)^2 + y^2$ reduces to $-2x^2 = (x-1)^2 + x^2$

$\Rightarrow (x-1)^2 + 3x^2 = 0$ which is not possible. ...(ii)

From Eqs. (i) and (ii), we get $z = \dfrac{1+i}{2}$

i.e. no real and no purely imaginary roots

and $\quad |z| = \dfrac{1}{\sqrt{2}} < 1$

Example 22 *Let z_1 and z_2 be two complex numbers represented by points on circles $|z_1| = 1$ and $|z_2| = 2$ respectively, then*

(a) $\max.|2z_1 + z_2| = 4$
(b) $\min.|z_1 - z_2| = 1$
(c) $\left|z_2 + \dfrac{1}{z_1}\right| \le 3$
(d) $\left|z_1 + \dfrac{2}{z_2}\right| \le 2$

Decoding the Question

For two complex numbers z_1 and z_2,

$$||z_1| - |z_2|| \le |z_1 + z_2| \le |z_1| + |z_2|$$

Sol. (a, b, c, d) $\because \quad |z_1| = 1$ and $|z_2| = 2$

$\therefore \quad |2z_1 + z_2| \le |2z_1| + |z_2| = 2|z_1| + |z_2|$

$\Rightarrow \quad |2z_1 + z_2| \le 2|z_1| + |z_2| = 2 + 2 = 4$

$\therefore \quad |2z_1 + z_2| \le 4$

$\Rightarrow \quad \max.|2z_1 + z_2| = 4 \quad$ [alternate (a)]

and $\quad |z_1 - z_2| \ge ||z_1| - |z_2|| = |1 - 2| = 1$

$\Rightarrow \quad |z_1 - z_2| \ge 1$

$\therefore \quad \min.|z_1 - z_2| = 1 \quad$ [alternate (b)]

$$\left|z_2 + \frac{1}{z_1}\right| \le |z_2| + \left|\frac{1}{z_1}\right| = |z_2| + \frac{1}{|z_1|} = 2 + \frac{1}{1} = 3$$

$\therefore \quad \left|z_2 + \dfrac{1}{z_1}\right| \le 3 \quad$ [alternate (c)]

and $\quad \left|z_1 + \dfrac{2}{z_2}\right| \le |z_1| + \left|\dfrac{2}{z_2}\right| = |z_1| + \dfrac{2}{|z_2|} = 1 + \dfrac{2}{2} = 2$

$\therefore \quad \left|z_1 + \dfrac{2}{z_2}\right| \le 2 \quad$ [alternate (d)]

Example 23 *If $|z-1| + |z+1| = 4$, then*

(a) locus of z is ellipse and $e = \dfrac{1}{2}$

(b) area bounded by figure is $2\pi\sqrt{3}$

(c) locus of z is a circle

(d) None of the above

Sol. (a, b) We have, $|z - \bar{z}_1| + |z - \bar{z}_2| = k$ represent ellipse such that $|\bar{z}_1 - \bar{z}_2| < k$ and $e = \dfrac{|z_1 - z_2|}{k}$.

So, z has locus of ellipse.

Now, on comparing

$$z_1 = 1, z_2 = -1 \text{ and } k = 4$$

$\therefore \quad e = \dfrac{|z_1 - z_2|}{k} = \dfrac{2}{4} = \dfrac{1}{2}$

Also, $\quad \text{area} = \pi ab$

$(\text{Area})^2 = \pi^2 a^2 b^2 = \pi^2 a^2 (1 - e^2) a^2 = \pi^2 a^4 (1 - e^2)$

$= \pi^2 (2)^4 \left(1 - \dfrac{1}{4}\right) \quad \left[\because a = \dfrac{k}{2}\right]$

$= \pi^2 \times 16 \times \dfrac{3}{4} = 12\pi^2$

$\therefore \quad \text{Area} = 2\sqrt{3}\pi$

Example 24 *If α is a complex number such that $\alpha z^2 + z + \overline{\alpha} = 0$ has a real root, then*

(a) $\alpha + \overline{\alpha} = 1$
(b) $\alpha + \overline{\alpha} = 0$
(c) $\alpha + \overline{\alpha} = -1$
(d) the absolute value of real root is 1

Sol. (a, c, d) We have, $\alpha z^2 + z + \overline{\alpha} = 0$

Let $\alpha = p + iq$

$\therefore \quad (p + iq) z^2 + z + p - iq = 0$

$\Rightarrow \quad p \cdot z^2 + z + p = 0$ and $z^2 q - q = 0 \quad$ [z is real]

$\therefore \quad z = \pm 1$

$\therefore \quad \alpha \pm 1 + \overline{\alpha} = 0 \Rightarrow \alpha + \overline{\alpha} = \pm 1$ and $|z| = 1$

Passage Based Questions

Passage I

(Ex. Nos. 25 to 26)

Let P be a point denoting a complex number z on the complex plane.

i.e. $\quad z = \text{Re}(z) + i\,\text{Im}(z)$, where $i = \sqrt{-1}$

If $\quad \text{Re}(z) = x$ and $\text{Im}(z) = y$, then $z = x + iy$

Example 25 *If P moves such that*

$$|\text{Re}(z)| + |\text{Im}(z)| = a \ (a \in R^+)$$

The locus of P is

(a) a parallelogram which is not a rhombus
(b) a rhombus which is not a square
(c) a rectangle which is not a square
(d) a square

Sol. (d) $\because \quad |\text{Re}(z)| + |\text{Im}(z)| = a \Rightarrow |x| + |y| = a$

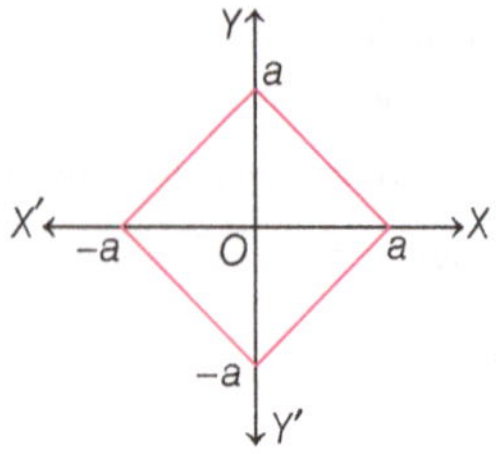

$\therefore$ Locus of P is a square.

Example 26 *The area of the circle inscribed in the region denoted by $|\text{Re}(z)| + |\text{Im}(z)| = 10$ equals to*

(a) 50π sq units
(b) 100π sq units
(c) 55 sq units
(d) 110 sq units

Sol. (a) From above, $a = 10$

Diameter of circle = Distance between sides of square

= Length of side of square $= a\sqrt{2} = 10\sqrt{2}$

or $\quad 2r = 10\sqrt{2} \Rightarrow r = 5\sqrt{2}$

$\therefore$ Area of a circle $= \pi r^2 = 50\pi$ sq units

Passage II

(Ex. Nos. 27 to 28)

If a, b, c are distinct non-zero complex numbers such that $|a| = |b| = |c|$.

Example 27 *If z_1 and z_2 are the roots of $az^2 + bz + c = 0$ such that $|z_1| = 2$, then the value of $(16z_2 + z_1)$ is equal to*

(a) $\dfrac{c}{b}$ (b) $\dfrac{-4c}{b}$ (c) $\dfrac{4c}{b}$ (d) $\dfrac{-c}{b}$

Sol. (b) Let z_1 and z_2 be the roots of the given equation.

$\therefore z_1 + z_2 = \dfrac{-b}{a}$ and $z_1 z_2 = \dfrac{c}{a}$

Now, $|z_1| = 2$

$|z_1 z_2| = \left|\dfrac{c}{a}\right| = 1 \Rightarrow |z_2| = \dfrac{1}{2}$

$\Rightarrow \quad |z_1 + z_2| = \left|\dfrac{-b}{a}\right| = 1 \Rightarrow (z_1 + z_2)(\overline{z}_1 + \overline{z}_2) = 1$

$\Rightarrow (z_1 + z_2)\left(\dfrac{4}{z_1} + \dfrac{1}{4z_2}\right) = 1 \Rightarrow (z_1 + z_2)\left(\dfrac{16z_2 + z_1}{4z_1 z_2}\right) = 1$

$\Rightarrow \quad 16z_2 + z_1 = \dfrac{\dfrac{4c}{a}}{\dfrac{-b}{a}} = \dfrac{-4c}{b}$

Example 28 *If $az^2 + bz + c = 0$ and $bz^2 + cz + a = 0$ have a root of modulus 1, then the equation $az^2 + bz + c = 0$ and $bz^2 + cz + a = 0$*

(a) have both roots common
(b) have exactly one root common
(c) can not have common root
(d) cannot be determined

Sol. (a) $az^2 + bz + c = 0$ and $bz^2 + cz + a = 0$ have a root of modulus 1.

$z_1 + z_2 = \dfrac{-b}{a}; z_1 z_2 = \dfrac{c}{a}$

$\Rightarrow \quad |z_1||z_2| = 1 \Rightarrow |z_2| = |z_1| = 1 \Rightarrow |z_1 + z_2| = 1$

$\Rightarrow \quad (z_1 + z_2)\left(\dfrac{1}{z_1} + \dfrac{1}{z_2}\right) = 1 \Rightarrow (z_1 + z_2)^2 = z_1 z_2$

$$\Rightarrow \qquad b^2 = ac \qquad \ldots\text{(i)}$$

Similarly, for second equation, we get

$$c^2 = ab \qquad \ldots\text{(ii)}$$

From Eqs. (i) and (ii), we get

$$a^3 = b^3 = c^3$$

$\Rightarrow a, b, c$ are $z_0, z_0\omega, z_0\omega^2$.

$\Rightarrow$ Ratio of coefficients of two equations are same.

$\Rightarrow$ Both roots are same.

Stem Based Questions

Stem I

(Ex. Nos. 29 to 30)

Let A, B, C be three sets of complex number as defined below.

$$A = \{z : \text{Im}(z) \geq 1\},\ B = \{z : |z - 2 - i| = 3\}$$

and $\quad C = \{z : \text{Re}((1 - i)\,z) = \sqrt{2}\}$.

Example 29 ■ *The number of elements in the set $A \cap B \cap C$ is ....*

Sol. (1) Let $z = x + iy$

Set A corresponds to the region, $y \geq 1$ ...(i)

Set B consists of points lying on the circle, centre at (2, 1) and radius 3

i.e. $\qquad x^2 + y^2 - 4x - 2y = 4$ ...(ii)

Set C consists of points lying on $x + y = \sqrt{2}$ ...(iii)

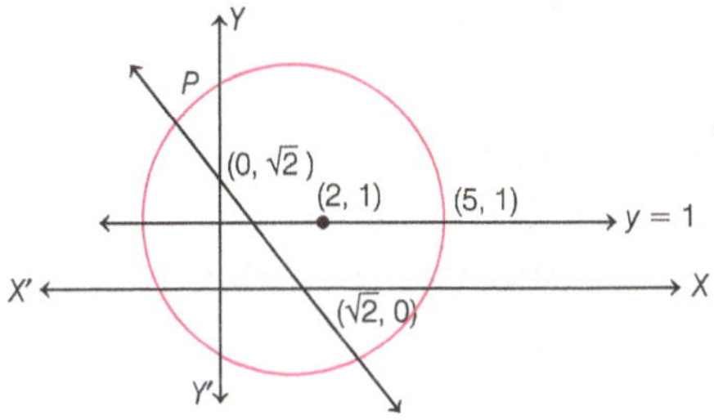

Clearly, there is only one point of intersection of the line $x + y = \sqrt{2}$ and circle $x^2 + y^2 - 4x - 2y = 4$.

Example 30 ■ *Let z be any point in $A \cap B \cap C$, then the value of $|z + 1 - i|^2 + |z - 5 - i|^2$ is ....*

Sol. (36) $|z + 1 - i|^2 + |z - 5 - i|^2$

$$= (x + 1)^2 + (y - 1)^2 + (x - 5)^2 + (y - 1)^2$$

$$= 2(x^2 + y^2 - 4x - 2y) + 28$$

$$= 2(4) + 28 = 36 \qquad [\because x^2 + y^2 - 4x - 2y = 4]$$

Stem II

(Ex. Nos. 31 to 32)

Let ω be the complex number representing the point $M\left(\dfrac{-1}{2}, \dfrac{\sqrt{3}}{2}\right)$ and $a, b, c, \alpha, \beta, \gamma$ be non-zero complex numbers such that

$$a + b + c = \alpha,\ a + b\omega + c\omega^2 = \beta,\ a + b\omega^2 + c\omega = \gamma$$

Example 31 ■ *If $|\alpha|^2 + |\beta|^2 + |\gamma|^2 = \lambda(|a|^2 + |b|^2 + |c|^2)$, then λ is equal to ....*

Sol. (3) Given, $a + b + c = \alpha$, $a + b\omega + c\omega^2 = \beta$, $a + b\omega^2 + c\omega = \gamma$

$$|\alpha|^2 + |\beta|^2 + |\gamma|^2 = \alpha\bar{\alpha} + \beta\bar{\beta} + \gamma\bar{\gamma} \qquad [\because \bar{\omega} = \omega^2]$$

Now, $\alpha\bar{\alpha} = (a + b + c)(\bar{a} + \bar{b} + \bar{c}) \qquad [\bar{\omega}^2 = \omega]$

$$= |a|^2 + |b|^2 + |c|^2 + a\bar{b} + a\bar{c} + b\bar{a} + b\bar{c} + c\bar{a} + c\bar{b}$$

$\beta\bar{\beta} = (a + b\omega + c\omega^2)(\bar{a} + \bar{b}\omega^2 + \bar{c}\omega)$

$$= |a|^2 + |b|^2 + |c|^2 + a\bar{b}\omega^2 + a\bar{c}\omega + b\bar{a}\omega + b\bar{c}\omega^2 + c\bar{a}\omega^2 + c\bar{b}\omega$$

$\gamma\bar{\gamma} = (a + b\omega^2 + c\omega)(\bar{a} + \bar{b}\omega + \bar{c}\omega^2)$

$$= |a|^2 + |b|^2 + |c|^2 + a\bar{b}\omega + a\bar{c}\omega^2 + b\bar{a}\omega^2 + b\bar{c}\omega + c\bar{b}\omega^2$$

So, $\alpha\bar{\alpha} + \beta\bar{\beta} + \gamma\bar{\gamma} = 3(|a|^2 + |b|^2 + |c|^2)$

$$+ (a\bar{b} + a\bar{c} + b\bar{a} + b\bar{c} + c\bar{a} + c\bar{b})(1 + \omega + \omega^2)$$

$$= 3(|a|^2 + |b|^2 + |c|^2) \qquad [\because 1 + \omega + \omega^2 = 0]$$

So, $\lambda = 3$

Example 32 ■ *Number of distinct complex numbers z satisfying the equation*

$$(z + 1)\begin{vmatrix} z + \omega^2 & 1 \\ 1 & z + \omega \end{vmatrix} + \omega\begin{vmatrix} 1 & \omega \\ z + \omega & \omega^2 \end{vmatrix} + \omega^2\begin{vmatrix} \omega & z + \omega^2 \\ \omega^2 & 1 \end{vmatrix} = 0 \text{ is equal to ....}$$

Sol. (1) $(z + 1)\begin{vmatrix} z + \omega^2 & 1 \\ 1 & z + \omega \end{vmatrix} + \omega\begin{vmatrix} 1 & \omega \\ z + \omega & \omega^2 \end{vmatrix} + \omega^2\begin{vmatrix} \omega^2 & z + \omega^2 \\ \omega^2 & 1 \end{vmatrix} = 0$

As, $1 + \omega + \omega^2 = 0$, $\omega^4 = \omega$

$$\Rightarrow (z + 1)(z^2 + z(\omega + \omega^2) + \omega^3 - 1) + \omega(\omega^2 - z\omega - \omega^2) + \omega^2(\omega - z\omega^2 - \omega^4) = 0$$

$$\Rightarrow \qquad (z + 1)(z^2 - z) + z(-\omega^2 - \omega) = 0$$

$$\Rightarrow \qquad z^3 - z^2 + z^2 - z + z = 0$$

$$\Rightarrow \qquad z^3 = 0$$

$\Rightarrow z = 0$ only 1 complex number.

Single Integer Answer Type Questions

Example 33 ■ *If M and m are the greatest value and least value of $|z_1 + z_2|$, if $z_1 = 24 + 7i$ and $|z_2| = 6$, then $\dfrac{M - m}{2}$ is equal to ....*

Sol. (6) We have, $z_1 = 24 + 7i$

$$\therefore |z_1| = \sqrt{(24)^2 + (7)^2} = 25$$

Now, $\qquad ||z_1| - |z_2|| \leq |z_1 + z_2| \leq |z_1| + |z_2|$

$$\Rightarrow \qquad |25 - 6| \leq |z_1 + z_2| \leq 25 + 6$$

$$\Rightarrow \quad 19 \le |z_1 + z_2| \le 31$$

$$\therefore \quad M = 31, m = 19$$

$$\therefore \quad \frac{M - m}{2} = \frac{31 - 19}{2} = 6$$

Example 34 *If ω is the imaginary cube root of unity, then the number of pairs of integers (a, b) such that $|a\omega + b| = 1$ is ....*

Sol. (6) We have, $|a\omega + b| = 1$

$$\Rightarrow \quad |a\omega + b|^2 = 1 \Rightarrow (a\omega + b)(a\bar{\omega} + b) = 1$$

$$\Rightarrow a^2 + ab(\omega + \bar{\omega}) + b^2 = 1$$

$$\Rightarrow \quad a^2 - ab + b^2 = 1$$

$$\Rightarrow \quad (a - b)^2 + ab = 1$$

Now, if $(a - b)^2 = 0$ and $ab = 1$, then (a, b): $(1, 1)$ and $(-1, -1)$

If $(a - b)^2 = 1$ and $ab = 0$, then

$$(a, b) : (0, 1), (1, 0), (0, -1), (-1, 0)$$

Hence, there are 6 ordered pairs.

Example 35 *If $z_1, z_2 \in C$, $z_1^2 + z_2^2 \in R$, $z_1(z_1^2 - 3z_2^2) = 2$ and $z_2(3z_1^2 - z_2^2) = 11$, the value of $z_1^2 + z_2^2$ is*

Sol. (5) We have, $\quad z_1(z_1^2 - 3z_2^2) = 2 \quad$ ...(i)

and $\quad z_2(3z_1^2 - z_2^2) = 11 \quad$ ...(ii)

multiplying Eq. (ii) by i $(\sqrt{-1})$ and then adding in Eq. (i), we get

$$z_1^3 - 3z_1 z_2^2 + i(3z_1^2 z_2 - z_2^3) = 2 + 11i$$

$$\Rightarrow \quad (z_1 + iz_2)^3 = 2 + 11i \quad \text{...(iii)}$$

Again, multiplying Eq. (ii) by $(-i)$ and then adding in Eq. (i), we get

$$z_1^3 - 3z_1 z_2^2 - i(3z_1^2 z_2 - z_2^3) = 2 - 11i$$

$$\Rightarrow \quad (z_1 - iz_2)^3 = 2 - 11i \quad \text{...(iv)}$$

Now, on multiplying Eqs. (iii) and (iv), we get

$$(z_1^2 + z_2^2)^3 = 4 + 121 = 125 = 5^3$$

$$\therefore \quad z_1^2 + z_2^2 = 5$$

Example 36 *The number of solutions of the equations $|z - (4 + 8i)| = \sqrt{10}$ and $|z - (3 + 5i)| + |z - (5 + 11i)| = 4\sqrt{5}$, where $i = \sqrt{-1}$.*

Sol. (2) Here, $|z - (4 + 8i)| = \sqrt{10}$

represents a circle with centre (4, 8) and radius $\sqrt{10}$.

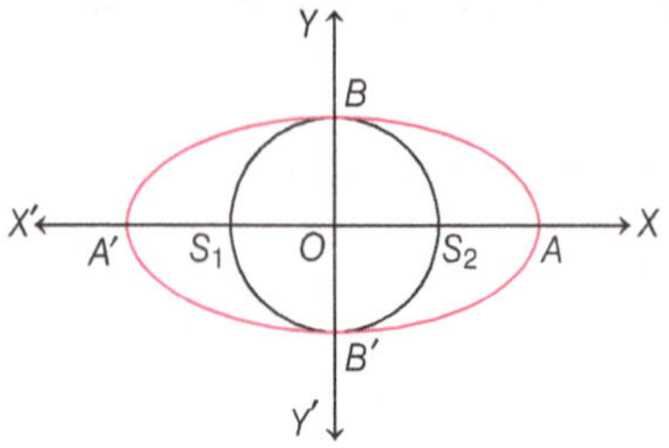

Also, $\quad |z - (3 + 5i)| + |z - (5 + 11i)| = 4\sqrt{5}$

represents an ellipse.

$$\therefore \quad |(3 + 5i) - (5 + 11i)| = \sqrt{4 + 36} = \sqrt{40} < 4\sqrt{5}$$

with foci $S_1(3, 5)$ and S_2 (5, 11).

Distance between foci $= S_1S_2 = \sqrt{40} = 2\sqrt{10}$

$= $ Diameter of circle

i.e. $\quad 2ae = 2\sqrt{10}$

$$\Rightarrow \quad ae = \sqrt{10} \text{ and } 2a = 4\sqrt{5} \Rightarrow a = 2\sqrt{5}$$

$$\therefore \quad e = \frac{ae}{a} = \frac{1}{\sqrt{2}}$$

Now, $\quad b = a\sqrt{(1 - e^2)} = 2\sqrt{5}\sqrt{\left(1 - \frac{1}{2}\right)} = \sqrt{10} =$ Radius of circle

$\therefore$ Centre of the ellipse = Mid-point of S_1 and S_2

$$= \frac{3 + 5i + 5 + 11i}{2} = 4 + 8i \text{ i.e. } (4, 8)$$

which coincides with the centre of the circle and length of minor-axis is equal to the radius of the circle. Hence, there are only (2) two solutions of the given equations.

Numerical Value Type Questions

Example 37 *Let z be a non-real complex number which satisfies the equation $z^{23} = 1$. Then, the value of $\sum_{k=1}^{22} \frac{1}{1 + z^{8k} + z^{16k}}$ is ....*

Sol. (15) $\sum_{k=1}^{22} \frac{1}{1 + z^{8k} + z^{16k}}$

$$= \sum_{k=1}^{22} \frac{z^{8k} - 1}{(z^{8k} - 1)(z^{16k} + z^{8k} + 1)}$$

$$= \sum_{k=1}^{22} \frac{z^{8k} - 1}{z^{24k} - 1}$$

$$= \sum_{k=1}^{22} \frac{z^{8k} - 1}{z^k - 1} \quad [\because z^{24k} = z^{23k} \cdot z^k = 1 \cdot z^k = z^k]$$

$$= \sum_{k=1}^{22} (1 + z^k + z^{2k} + \ldots + z^{7k})$$

$$= 22 + (0 - 1) \times 7 = 22 - 7 = 15$$

Example 38 *If ω is a complex cube root of unity and $a + b = 21$, $a^3 + b^3 = 8001$, then the value of $(a\omega^2 + b\omega)(a\omega + b\omega^2)$ is equal to ....*

Sol. (381) We have, $(a\omega^2 + b\omega)(a\omega + b\omega^2) = a^2 - ab + b^2$

$$= \frac{(a + b)(a^2 - ab + b^2)}{(a + b)}$$

$$= \frac{a^3 + b^3}{a + b}$$

$$= \frac{8001}{21} = 381$$

Example 39 *If the area of the triangle on the complex plane formed by the points z, $z+iz$ and iz is 200, then the value of $|3z|$ is equal to ....*

Sol. (60) Let $z = x + iy$

$\therefore \; z + iz = (x+iy) + i(x+iy) = (x-y) + i(x+y)$

and $\quad iz = i(x+iy) = -y + ix$

Now, area of triangle $=200$

$$\therefore \quad \frac{1}{2}\begin{vmatrix} x & y & 1 \\ x-y & x+y & 1 \\ -y & x & 1 \end{vmatrix} = 200$$

$$\Rightarrow \quad \begin{vmatrix} x-y & x+y & 2 \\ x-y & x+y & 1 \\ -y & x & 1 \end{vmatrix} = 400$$

$$\Rightarrow \quad \begin{vmatrix} 0 & 0 & 1 \\ x-y & x+y & 1 \\ -y & x & 1 \end{vmatrix} = 400$$

$\Rightarrow \quad x(x-y) + y(x+y) = 400$

$\Rightarrow \quad x^2 + y^2 = 400$

$\Rightarrow \quad |z|^2 = 400$

$\Rightarrow \quad |z| = 20$

$\therefore \quad |3z| = 3|z| = 3 \times 20 = 60$

Example 40 *If α, β are the roots of $x^2 - 2x + 4 = 0$, then the value of $\alpha^6 + \beta^6$ is ......*

Sol. (128) We have, $x^2 - 2x + 4 = 0$

$$\Rightarrow \quad x = \frac{2 \pm \sqrt{4-16}}{2} = \frac{2 \pm 2\sqrt{3}i}{2} = 1 \pm \sqrt{3}i = 2\left(\frac{1}{2} \pm \frac{\sqrt{3}}{2}i\right) = 2\left(\cos\frac{\pi}{3} \pm i\sin\frac{\pi}{3}\right)$$

$$\therefore \quad \alpha = 2\left(\cos\frac{\pi}{3} + i\sin\frac{\pi}{3}\right)$$

and $\quad \beta = 2\left(\cos\frac{\pi}{3} - i\sin\frac{\pi}{3}\right)$

Now, $\alpha^6 + \beta^6 = 2^6[\cos 2\pi + i\sin 2\pi + \cos 2\pi - i\sin 2\pi]$

$= 2^6 \times 2\cos 2\pi$

$= 2^7$

$= 128$

Matching Type Questions

Example 41 *Match the Column I with Column II.*

	Column I		Column II
A.	If $|z-i| < 1$, then the value of $|z + 12 - 6i|$ is less than	(p)	0
B.	If $\omega \neq 1$ is a cube root of unity, then the value of $4 + 5\omega^{2002} + 3\omega^{2009}$ is	(q)	14
C.	$\omega^{2n} + \omega^n + 1$ (n is a positive integer and not a multiple of 3)	(r)	1
D.	If $|z| \le 1, |\omega| \le 1$ and $|z + i\omega| = |z - i\overline{\omega}| = 2$, then $\text{Im}(z) + 1$ equals to	(s)	$\sqrt{3}i$

Sol. (A) $\to$ (q), (B) $\to$ (s), (C) $\to$ (p), (D) $\to$ (r)

(A) $|z - 12 - 6i| = |(z-i) + (12-5i)|$

$\le |z-i| + |12-5i|$

$< 1 + \sqrt{144+25}$

$= 1 + 13 = 14$

$\therefore |z - 12 - 6i| < 14$

(B) $4 + 5\omega^{2002} + 3\omega^{2009} = 4 + 5\omega + 3\omega^2 \quad [\because \omega^3 = 1]$

$= 1 + 2\omega + 3(1 + \omega + \omega^2) = 1 + 2\omega$

$= 1 + 2\left(\frac{-1+\sqrt{3}i}{2}\right) \quad \left[\because \omega = \frac{-1+i\sqrt{3}}{2}\right]$

$= 1 - 1 + \sqrt{3}i = \sqrt{3}i$

(C) Let $n > 0$ and $n \neq 3m$ for all integers m.

Then, $n = 3m+1$ or $3m+2$

If $n = 3m+1 \Rightarrow \omega^{2n} + \omega^n + 1 = \omega^{6m+2} + \omega^{3m+1} + 1$

$= \omega^2 + \omega + 1 = 0$

If $n = 3m+2 \Rightarrow \omega^{2n} + \omega^n + 1 = \omega^{6m+4} + \omega^{3m+2} + 1$

$= \omega + \omega^2 + 1 = 0$

(D) Given, $\quad 2 = |z + i\omega| \le |z| + |\omega|$

$\Rightarrow \quad |z| + |\omega| \ge 2 \quad$ ...(i)

Also, $\quad |z| \le 1, |\omega| \le 1$

$\Rightarrow \quad |z| + |\omega| \le 2 \quad$ ...(ii)

From Eqs. (i) and (ii), we get

$|z| = |\omega| = 1$

Now, $\quad |z + i\omega|^2 = |z - i\overline{\omega}|^2$

$\Rightarrow \quad (z + i\omega)(\overline{z} - i\overline{\omega}) = (z - i\overline{\omega})(\overline{z} + i\omega)$

$\Rightarrow \quad \overline{z}\omega - z\overline{\omega} + \overline{z}\,\overline{\omega} - \omega z = 0$

$\Rightarrow \quad (\overline{z} - z)(\omega + \overline{\omega}) = 0$

$\Rightarrow \quad \overline{z} = z, \; \omega + \overline{\omega} = 0$

$\Rightarrow \text{Im}(z) = 0, \text{Re}(\omega) = 0$

Thus, $\text{Im}\, z + 1 = 0 + 1 = 1$

Example 42 *Match the Column I with Column II.*

	Column I		Column II
A.	If $\omega \neq 1$ is a cube roots of unity, then the value of $\frac{1}{3}(1-\omega)(1-\omega^2)(1-\omega^4)(1-\omega^8)$ is	(p)	12
B.	If $z^2 + z + 1 = 0$, then the value of $\left(z+\frac{1}{z}\right)^2 + \left(z^2+\frac{1}{z^2}\right)^2 + \ldots + \left(z^6+\frac{1}{z^6}\right)^2$	(q)	9
C.	The square of least positive integer n such that $(1+\omega^2)^n = (1+\omega^4)^n$ is	(r)	0
D.	If $\omega \neq 1$ is a cube roots of unity, $\frac{1}{5+4\omega} + \frac{1}{3+\omega} - \frac{1}{2+\omega}$ is equal to	(s)	3

Sol. (A) → (s), (B) → (p), (C) → (q), (D) → (r)

(A) We have, $\omega^3 = 1, 1 + \omega + \omega^2 = 0$

Now, $\frac{1}{3}(1-\omega)(1-\omega^2)(1-\omega^4)(1-\omega^8)$

$$= \frac{1}{3}(1-\omega)^2(1-\omega^2)^2 = \frac{1}{3}[(1-\omega)(1-\omega^2)]^2$$

$$= \frac{1}{3}[1-\omega-\omega^2+\omega^3]^2 = \frac{1}{3}(1+1+1)^2 = 3$$

(B) Since, $z^2 + z + 1 = 0 \Rightarrow z = \omega, \omega^2$

$$\therefore \left(z+\frac{1}{z}\right)^2 + \left(z^2+\frac{1}{z^2}\right)^2 + \ldots + \left(z^6+\frac{1}{z^6}\right)^2$$

$$= (\omega+\omega^2)^2 + (\omega+\omega^2)^2 + \left(\omega^3+\frac{1}{\omega^3}\right)^2 + (\omega+\omega^2)^2 + (\omega+\omega^2)^2 + \left(\omega^6+\frac{1}{\omega^6}\right)^2$$

$$= 4(\omega+\omega^2)^2 + 2\left(\omega^3+\frac{1}{\omega^3}\right)^2 = 4(1) + 2(2^2) = 12$$

(C) We have, $(1+\omega^2)^n = (1+\omega^4)^n$

$\Rightarrow \quad (1+\omega^2)^n = (1+\omega)^n \quad [\because \omega^3 = 1]$

$\Rightarrow \quad (-\omega)^n = (-\omega^2)^n \quad [\because 1+\omega+\omega^2 = 0]$

$\Rightarrow \quad \omega^n = \omega^{2n}$

The least such positive n is 3.

$\therefore$ The square of least such positive n is 9.

(D) We have,

$$\frac{1}{5+4\omega} + \frac{1}{3+\omega} - \frac{1}{2+\omega} = \frac{1}{5+4\omega} + \frac{2+\omega-3-\omega}{(3+\omega)(2+\omega)}$$

$$= \frac{1}{5+4\omega} + \frac{(-1)}{6+5\omega+\omega^2}$$

$$= \frac{1}{5+4\omega} - \frac{1}{5+4\omega}$$

$$= 0$$

EXERCISE 1

JEE Main Pattern

Single Option Correct Type Questions

1. If n is an odd integer, then $(1+i)^{6n}+(1-i)^{6n}$ is equal to
(a) 0 (b) 2
(c) -2 (d) None of these

2. If $\text{Im}\left(\frac{2z+1}{iz+1}\right)=-2$, then the locus of z is
(a) parabola (b) line
(c) circle (d) None of these

3. The least positive integer n such that $\left(\frac{2i}{1+i}\right)^n$ is a positive integer, is
(a) 2 (b) 4 (c) 6 (d) 8

4. For positive integers n_1 and n_2, the value of $(1+i)^{n_1}+(1+i^3)^{n_1}+(1+i^5)^{n_2}+(1+i^7)^{n_2}$ is
(a) purely real (b) purely imaginary
(c) zero (d) None of these

5. For any complex number z, the minimum value of $\frac{\text{Im}(z^5)}{(\text{Im}\,z)^5}$ is
(a) 4 (b) -4 (c) 2 (d) -2

6. If $z=\frac{1+i}{\sqrt{2}}$, then the value of z^{1929} is
(a) $1+i$ (b) -1 (c) $\frac{1+i}{2}$ (d) $\frac{1+i}{\sqrt{2}}$

7. If α, β, γ are three distinct non-zero complex numbers such that $|\beta|=\frac{1}{|\gamma|}$, then the value of $\left|\frac{\beta\gamma-\alpha}{1-\bar{\alpha}\beta\gamma}\right|$ is equal to
(a) $\frac{3}{2}$ (b) $\frac{1}{2}$ (c) 1 (d) 2

8. If $\omega=\alpha+i\beta, \beta\neq 0, z\neq 1$ and $\left(\frac{\omega-\bar{\omega}z}{1-z}\right)$ is purely real, then $|z|$ is equal to
(a) 1 (b) 2 (c) 4 (d) 8

9. Let z be a complex number such that $z^2-(3+i)z+m+2i=0$, $m\in R$. If equation has a real root, then value of m is
(a) 0 (b) 1 (c) 2 (d) 3

10. If $z=\frac{(\sqrt{3}+i)^{17}}{(1-i)^{50}}$, then Re($z$) is equal to
(a) 2^9 (b) 2^{-9} (c) -2^9 (d) -2^{-9}

11. The area of the region bounded by $|\arg z|\leq\frac{\pi}{4}$ and $|z-1|<|z-3|$ is (in sq unit)
(a) 2 (b) 4 (c) 6 (d) 8

12. Value of $e^{2mi\theta}\left(\frac{i\cot\theta+1}{i\cot\theta-1}\right)^m$ is equal to
(a) 0 (b) 1
(c) -1 (d) None to these

13. The sum of squares of all roots of the equation $x^8-x^7+x^6-x^5+x^4-x^3+x^2-x+1=0$ is
(a) 0 (b) 1 (c) -1 (d) -8

14. The points A, B and C represent the complex numbers $z_1, z_2, (1-i)z_1+iz_2$ respectively, on the complex plane (where, $i=\sqrt{-1}$). The ΔABC is
(a) isosceles but not right angled
(b) right angled but not isosceles
(c) isosceles and right angled
(d) None of the above

15. The system of equations $|z+1-i|=\sqrt{2}$ and $|z|=3$ has (where, $i=\sqrt{-1}$)
(a) no solution (b) one solution
(c) two solutions (d) None of these

16. The centre of the circle represented by $|z+1|=2|z-1|$ on the complex plane, is
(a) 0 (b) $\frac{5}{3}$
(c) $\frac{1}{3}$ (d) None of these

17. If $x=9^{1/3}\cdot 9^{1/9}\cdot 9^{1/27}\ldots\infty$, $y=4^{1/3}\cdot 4^{-1/9}\cdot 4^{1/27}\ldots\infty$ and $z=\sum_{r=1}^{\infty}(1+i)^{-r}$, where $i=\sqrt{-1}$, then $\arg(x+yz)$ is equal to
(a) 0 (b) $-\tan^{-1}\left(\frac{\sqrt{2}}{3}\right)$
(c) $-\tan^{-1}\left(\frac{2}{\sqrt{3}}\right)$ (d) $\pi-\tan^{-1}\left(\frac{\sqrt{2}}{3}\right)$

18. If centre of a regular hexagon is at origin and one of the vertices on Argand diagram is $1+2i$, where $i=\sqrt{-1}$, then its perimeter is

(a) $2\sqrt{5}$ (b) $4\sqrt{5}$ (c) $6\sqrt{5}$ (d) $8\sqrt{5}$

19. Let $|z_r - r| \le r, \forall\ r = 1, 2, 3, \ldots, n$, then $\left|\sum_{r=1}^{n} z_r\right|$ is less than

(a) n (b) $2n$

(c) $n(n+1)$ (d) $\dfrac{n(n+1)}{2}$

20. If $\arg\left(\dfrac{z_1 - \dfrac{z}{|z|}}{\dfrac{z}{|z|}}\right) = \dfrac{\pi}{2}$ and $\left|\dfrac{z}{|z|} - z_1\right| = 3$, then $|z_1|$ equals to

(a) $\sqrt{3}$ (b) $2\sqrt{2}$ (c) $\sqrt{10}$ (d) $\sqrt{26}$

21. If $1, z_1, z_2, z_3, \ldots, z_{n-1}$ are the n, nth roots of unity, then the value of $\sum_{r=1}^{n-1} \dfrac{1}{(3-z_r)}$, is

(a) $\dfrac{n \cdot 3^{n-1}}{3^n - 1} - \dfrac{1}{2}$ (b) $\dfrac{n \cdot 3^{n-1}}{3^n - 1} - 1$

(c) $\dfrac{n \cdot 3^{n-1}}{3^n - 1} + 1$ (d) None of these

22. If $z = (3+7i)(\lambda + i\mu)$, when $\lambda, \mu \in I - \{0\}$ and $i = \sqrt{-1}$, is purely imaginary, then minimum value of $|z|^2$ is

(a) 0 (b) 58 (c) $\dfrac{3364}{3}$ (d) 3364

23. If $z^3 + (3+2i)z + (-1+ia) = 0$, where $i=\sqrt{-1}$, has one real root, the value of a lies in the interval $a \in R$

(a) $(-2, -1)$ (b) $(-1, 0)$

(c) $(0, 1)$ (d) $(1, 2)$

24. If m and n are the smallest positive integers satisfying the relation $\left(2\, CiS\, \dfrac{\pi}{6}\right)^m = \left(4\, CiS\, \dfrac{\pi}{4}\right)^n$, where $i=\sqrt{-1}$, $(m+n)$ equals to

(a) 60 (b) 72 (c) 96 (d) 120

25. Number of imaginary complex numbers satisfying the equation, $z^2 = \bar{z} \cdot 2^{1-|z|}$ is

(a) 0 (b) 1

(c) 2 (d) 3

Numerical Value Type Questions

26. If the complex numbers x and y satisfy $x^3 - y^3 = 98i$, $x - y = 7i$ and $xy = a + ib$, $a, b \in R$, then $(a+b)$ is equal to ……… .

27. Let $z = 9 + ib$, $b \in R - \{0\}$. If $\text{Im}(z^2) = \text{Im}(z^3)$, then $\dfrac{b}{3}$ is equal to ………

28. If $z + \sqrt{2}\,|z+1| + i = 0$, then $|z|^2$ is equal to ………

29. The number of solutions of the equation $z^2 + 8\bar{z} = 0$ is ……… .

30. If $x = \omega - \omega^2 - 2$, then the value of $x^4 + 3x^3 + 2x^2 - 11x - 6$ is ……… .

31. If z_1, z_2 and z_3 are three points lying on the circle $|z| = 2$, then minimum value of $|z_1 + z_2|^2 + |z_2 + z_3|^2 + |z_3 + z_1|^2$ is ……….

32. If $\left(\cos\dfrac{\pi}{2} + i\sin\dfrac{\pi}{2}\right)\left(\cos\dfrac{\pi}{2^2} + i\sin\dfrac{\pi}{2^2}\right)\ldots$ to $\infty = \lambda$, then $|100\lambda - 1|$ is equal to ……… .

33. The number of values of z (real or complex) simultaneously satisfying the system of equations

$$1 + z + z^2 + z^3 + \ldots + z^{17} = 0$$

and $$1 + z + z^2 + z^3 + \ldots + z^{13} = 0 \text{ is}$$

34. Number of complex numbers z satisfying $z^3 = \bar{z}$ is ………

35. Number of complex numbers z, such that $|z| = 1$ and $\left|\dfrac{z}{\bar{z}} + \dfrac{\bar{z}}{z}\right| = 1$ is ………

36. If $z = \dfrac{\pi}{4}(1+i)^4\left(\dfrac{1-\sqrt{\pi}\,i}{\sqrt{\pi}+i} + \dfrac{\sqrt{\pi}-i}{1+\sqrt{\pi}\,i}\right)$, where $i=\sqrt{-1}$, then $\left(\dfrac{|z|}{\text{amp}\,(z)}\right)$ equals to ………

37. Suppose A is a complex number and $n \in N$, such that $A^n = (A+1)^n = 1$, then the least value of n is ………

38. Let $z_r; r = 1, 2, 3, \ldots, 50$ be the roots of the equation $\sum_{r=0}^{50} (z)^r = 0$. If $\sum_{r=1}^{50} \dfrac{1}{(z_r - 1)} = -5\lambda$, then λ equals to ………

39. If $P = \sum_{p=1}^{32} (3p+2)\left(\sum_{q=1}^{10}\left(\sin\dfrac{2q\pi}{11} - i\cos\dfrac{2q\pi}{11}\right)\right)^p$, where $i=\sqrt{-1}$ and if $(1+i)P = n(n!)$, $n \in N$, then the value of n is ……… .

40. The least positive integer n for which $\left(\dfrac{1+i}{1-i}\right)^n = \dfrac{2}{\pi}\sin^{-1}\left(\dfrac{1+x^2}{2x}\right)$, where $x > 0$ and $i = \sqrt{-1}$ is ……… .

Previous Year Questions

41. Let z be a complex number such that the real part of $\frac{z-2i}{z+2i}$ is zero. Then, the maximum value of $|z-(6+8i)|$ is equal to **[Single Correct Type, 2024 Main]**

(a) 10 (b) 8 (c) 12 (d) ∞

42. The sum of all possible value of $\theta \in [-\pi, 2\pi]$, for which $\frac{1+i\cos\theta}{1-2i\cos\theta}$ is purely imaginary, is equal to **[Single Correct Type, 2024 Main]**

(a) 4π (b) 5π (c) 3π (d) 2π

43. Let z be a complex number such that $|z+2|=1$ and $\operatorname{Im}\left(\frac{z+1}{z+2}\right)=\frac{1}{5}$. Then, the value of $|\operatorname{Re}(\overline{z+2})|$ is **[Single Correct Type, 2024 Main]**

(a) $\frac{24}{5}$ (b) $\frac{2\sqrt{6}}{5}$ (c) $\frac{1+\sqrt{6}}{5}$ (d) $\frac{\sqrt{6}}{5}$

44. If $z=x+iy$, $xy \neq 0$, satisfies the equation $z^2+i\bar{z}=0$, then $|z^2|$ is equal to **[Single Correct Type, 2024 Main]**

(a) 4 (b) $\frac{1}{4}$ (c) 9 (d) 1

45. If $z=\frac{1}{2}-2i$ is such that $|z+1|=\alpha z+\beta(1+i)$, $i=\sqrt{-1}$ and $\alpha, \beta \in R$, then $\alpha+\beta$ is equal to **[Single Correct Type, 2024 Main]**

(a) -4 (b) -1 (c) 2 (d) 3

46. If the set $R=\{(a,b): a+5b=42,\ a, b \in N\}$ has m elements and $\sum_{n=1}^{m}(1-i^{n!})=x+iy$, where $i=\sqrt{-1}$, then the value of $m+x+y$ is **[Single Correct Type, 2024 Main]**

(a) 12 (b) 5 (c) 4 (d) 8

47. Let α and β be the sum and the product of all the non-zero solutions of the equation $(\bar{z})^2+|z|=0$, $z \in C$. Then, $4(\alpha^2+\beta^2)$ is equal to **[Single Correct Type, 2024 Main]**

(a) 6 (b) 2 (c) 4 (d) 8

48. Let $S=\{z \in C: |z-1|=1 \text{ and } (\sqrt{2}-1)(z+\bar{z})-i(z-\bar{z})=2\sqrt{2}\}$. Let $z_1, z_2 \in S$ be such that $|z_1|=\max_{z\in S}|z|$ and $|z_2|=\min_{z\in S}|z|$. Then, $|\sqrt{2}z_1-z_2|^2$ equals **[Single Correct Type, 2024 Main]**

(a) 4 (b) 3
(c) 2 (d) 1

49. Let z_1 and z_2 be two complex numbers such that $z_1+z_2=5$ and $z_1^3+z_2^3=20+15i$. Then, $|z_1^4+z_2^4|$ equals **[Single Correct Type, 2024 Main]**

(a) 75 (b) $25\sqrt{3}$
(c) $30\sqrt{3}$ (d) $15\sqrt{15}$

50. Consider the following two statements :

Statement I For any two non-zero complex numbers z_1, z_2 $(|z_1|+|z_2|)\left|\frac{z_1}{|z_1|}+\frac{z_2}{|z_2|}\right| \leq 2(|z_1|+|z_2|)$ and

Statement II If x, y, z are three distinct complex numbers and a, b, c are three positive real numbers such that $\frac{a}{|y-z|}=\frac{b}{|z-x|}=\frac{c}{|x-y|}$, then $\frac{a^2}{y-z}+\frac{b^2}{z-x}+\frac{c^2}{x-y}=1$. **[Single Correct Type, 2024 Main]**

Between the above two statements.

(a) Both Statement I and Statement II are incorrect.
(b) Statement I is incorrect but Statement II is correct.
(c) Both Statement I and Statement II are correct.
(d) Statement I is correct but Statement II is incorrect.

51. If z is a complex number, then the number of common roots of the equations $z^{1985}+z^{100}+1=0$ and $z^3+2z^2+2z+1=0$ is equal to **[Single Correct Type, 2024 Main]**

(a) 2 (b) 1
(c) 3 (d) 0

52. If z_1 and z_2 are two distinct complex number such that $\left|\frac{z_1-2z_2}{\frac{1}{2}-z_1\bar{z}_2}\right|=2$, then **[Single Correct Type, 2024 Main]**

(a) both z_1 and z_2 lie on the same circle
(b) z_1 lies on a circle of radius $\frac{1}{2}$ and z_2 lies on a circle of radius 1.
(c) either z_1 lies on a circle of radius $\frac{1}{2}$ or z_2 lies on a circle of radius 1.
(d) either z_1 lies on a circle of radius 1 or z_2 lies on a circle of radius $\frac{1}{2}$

53. If z is a complex number such that $|z| \geq 1$, then the minimum value of $\left|z+\frac{1}{2}(3+4i)\right|$ is **[Single Correct Type, 2024 Main]**

(a) $\frac{5}{2}$ (b) 3
(c) 2 (d) $\frac{3}{2}$

54. If $S=\{z \in C: |z-i|=|z+i|=|z-1|\}$, then $n(S)$ is **[Single Correct Type, 2024 Main]**

(a) 0 (b) 2
(c) 1 (d) 3

55. Let $S_1 = \{z \in C : |z| \le 5\}$,
$S_2 = \left\{z \in C : \text{Im}\left(\frac{z+1-\sqrt{3}i}{1-\sqrt{3}i}\right) \ge 0\right\}$ and $S_3 = \{z \in C :$ $\text{Re}(z) \ge 0\}$. Then, the area of the region $S_1 \cap S_2 \cap S_3$ is
[Single Correct Type, 2024 Main]
(a) $\frac{125\pi}{24}$ (b) $\frac{125\pi}{12}$
(c) $\frac{125\pi}{4}$ (d) $\frac{125\pi}{6}$

56. The area (in sq units) of the region
$S = \{z \in C: |z-1| \le 2; (z+\bar{z}) + i(z-\bar{z}) \le 2,$ $\text{Im}(z) \ge 0\}$ is **[Single Correct Type, 2024 Main]**
(a) $\frac{7\pi}{4}$ (b) $\frac{3\pi}{2}$ (c) $\frac{17\pi}{8}$ (d) $\frac{7\pi}{3}$

57. If 2 and 6 are the roots of the equation $ax^2 + bx + 1 = 0$, then the quadratic equation whose roots are $\frac{1}{2a+b}$ and $\frac{1}{6a+b}$, is **[Single Correct Type, 2024 Main]**
(a) $x^2 + 8x + 12 = 0$ (b) $2x^2 + 11x + 12 = 0$
(c) $x^2 + 10x + 16 = 0$ (d) $4x^2 + 14x + 12 = 0$

58. Let $S = \{x \in R : (\sqrt{3} + \sqrt{2})^x + (\sqrt{3} - \sqrt{2})^x = 10\}$. Then, the number of elements in S, is
[Single Correct Type, 2024 Main]
(a) 0 (b) 1 (c) 4 (d) 2

59. Let S be the set of positive integral values of a for which $\frac{ax^2 + 2(a+1)x + 9a + 4}{x^2 - 8x + 32} < 0, \forall x \in R$. Then, the number of elements in S is **[Single Correct Type, 2024 Main]**
(a) 1 (b) 3 (c) ∞ (d) 0

60. If α denotes the number of solutions of $|1-i|^x = 2^x$ and $\beta = \left(\frac{|z|}{\arg(z)}\right)$, where $z = \frac{\pi}{4}(1+i)^4 \left[\frac{1-\sqrt{\pi}i}{\sqrt{\pi}+i} + \frac{\sqrt{\pi}-i}{1+\sqrt{\pi}i}\right]$, $i = \sqrt{-1}$, then the distance of the point (α, β) from the line $4x - 3y = 7$ is ....
[Numerical Value Type, 2024 Main]

61. Let α, β be the roots of the equation $x^2 - \sqrt{6}x + 3 = 0$ such that $\text{Im}(\alpha) > \text{Im}(\beta)$. Let a, b be integers not divisible by 3 and n be a natural number such that $\frac{\alpha^{99}}{\beta} + \alpha^{98} = 3^n(a+ib)$, $i = \sqrt{-1}$. Then, $n + a + b$ is equal to .... **[Numerical Value Type, 2024 Main]**

62. The sum of the square of the modulus of the elements in the set $\{z = a + ib : a, b \in z, z \in C, |z-1| \le 1,$ $|z-5| \le |z-5i|\}$ is ....
[Numerical Value Type, 2024 Main]

63. Let $P = \{z \in C : |z+2-3i| \le 1\}$ and $Q = \{z \in C : z(1+i) + \bar{z}(1-i) \le -8\}$. Let in $P \cap Q$, $|z-3+2i|$ be maximum and minimum at z_1 and z_2, respectively. If $|z_1|^2 + 2|z_2|^2 = \alpha + \beta\sqrt{2}$, where α, β are integers, then $\alpha + \beta$ equals .... **[Numerical Value Type, 2024 Main]**

64. Let the complex numbers α and $1/\bar{\alpha}$ lie on the circles $|z - z_0|^2 = 4$ and $|z - z_0|^2 = 16$ respectively, where $z_0 = 1 + i$. Then, the value of $100|\alpha|^2$ is ....
[Numerical Value Type, 2024 Main]

65. Let $A = \left\{\theta \in (0, 2\pi) : \frac{1+2i\sin\theta}{1-i\sin\theta} \text{ is purely imaginary}\right\}$. Then the sum of the elements in A is
[Single Correct Type, 2023 Main]
(a) 2π (b) π
(b) 3π (d) 4π

66. Let w_1 be the point obtained by the rotation of $z_1 = 5 + 4i$ about the origin through a right angle in the anti-clockwise direction, and w_2 be the point obtained by the rotation of $z_2 = 3 + 5i$ about the origin through a right angle in the clockwise direction. Then, the principal argument of $w_1 - w_2$ is equal to
[Single Correct Type, 2023 Main]
(a) $\pi + \tan^{-1}\frac{8}{9}$ (b) $\pi - \tan^{-1}\frac{8}{9}$
(c) $\pi - \tan^{-1}\frac{33}{5}$ (d) $-\pi + \tan^{-1}\frac{33}{5}$

67. If the set $\left\{\text{Re}\left(\frac{z - \bar{z} + z\bar{z}}{2 - 3z + 5\bar{z}}\right) : z \in C, \text{Re}(z) = 3\right\}$ is equal to the interval $(\alpha, \beta]$, then $24(\beta - \alpha)$ is equal to
[Single Correct Type, 2023 Main]
(a) 36 (b) 30
(c) 27 (d) 42

68. Let $S = \{z \in C : \bar{z} = i(z^2 + \text{Re}(\bar{z}))\}$. Then, $\sum_{z \in S} |z|^2$ is equal to **[Single Correct Type, 2023 Main]**
(a) 3 (b) $\frac{7}{2}$ (c) $\frac{5}{2}$ (d) 4

69. For $a \in C$, let $A = \{z \in C : \text{Re}(a + \bar{z}) > \text{Im}(\bar{a} + z)\}$ and $B = \{z \in C : \text{Re}(a + \bar{z}) < \text{Im}(\bar{a} + z)\}$. Then, among the two statements :
(S1) If $\text{Re}(a), \text{Im}(a) > 0$, then the set A contains all the real numbers.
(S2) If $\text{Re}(a), \text{Im}(a) < 0$, then the set B contains all the real numbers. **[Single Correct Type, 2023 Main]**
(a) both are true (b) both are false
(c) only (S2) is true (d) only (S1) is true

70. Let $S = \left\{ z = x + iy : \dfrac{2z - 3i}{4z + 2i} \text{ is a real number} \right\}$.

Then, which of the following is not correct?

[Single Correct Type, 2023 Main]

(a) $(x, y) = \left(0, -\dfrac{1}{2}\right)$ (b) $y + x^2 + y^2 \neq -\dfrac{1}{4}$

(c) $x = 0$ (d) $y \in \left(-\infty, -\dfrac{1}{2}\right) \cup \left(-\dfrac{1}{2}, \infty\right)$

71. Let the complex number $z = x + iy$ be such that $\dfrac{2z - 3i}{2z + i}$ is purely imaginary. If $x + y^2 = 0$, then $y^4 + y^2 - y$ is equal to **[Single Correct Type, 2023 Main]**

(a) $\dfrac{2}{3}$ (b) $\dfrac{3}{2}$ (c) $\dfrac{3}{4}$ (d) $\dfrac{4}{5}$

72. Let $a \neq b$ two non-zero real numbers. Then the number of elements in the set $X = \{z \in C : \text{Re}(az^2 + bz) = a$ and $\text{Re}(bz^2 + az) = b\}$ is equal to

[Single Correct Type, 2023 Main]

(a) 2 (b) 1 (c) 3 (d) 0

73. Let a, b be two real numbers such that $ab < 0$. If the complex number $\dfrac{1 + ai}{b + i}$ is of unit modulus and $a + ib$ lies on the circle $|z - 1| = |2z|$, then a possible value of $\dfrac{1 + [a]}{4b}$, where $[t]$ is greatest integer function is

[Single Correct Type, 2023 Main]

(a) $-\dfrac{1}{2}$ (b) $\dfrac{1}{2}$ (c) -1 (d) 1

74. If the centre and radius of the circle $\left|\dfrac{z - 2}{z - 3}\right| = 2$ are respectively, (α, β) and γ, then $3(\alpha + \beta + \gamma)$ is equal to

[Single Correct Type, 2023 Main]

(a) 9 (b) 10 (c) 11 (d) 12

75. For two non-zero complex numbers z_1 and z_2, if $\text{Re}(z_1 z_2) = 0$ and $\text{Re}(z_1 + z_2) = 0$, then which of the following are possible? **[Single Correct Type, 2023 Main]**

A. $\text{Im}(z_1) > 0$ and $\text{Im}(z_2) > 0$

B. $\text{Im}(z_1) < 0$ and $\text{Im}(z_2) > 0$

C. $\text{Im}(z_1) > 0$ and $\text{Im}(z_2) < 0$

D. $\text{Im}(z_1) < 0$ and $\text{Im}(z_2) < 0$

Choose the correct answer from the options given below.

(a) B and D (b) A and B

(c) A and C (d) B and C

76. The complex number $z = \dfrac{i - 1}{\cos \dfrac{\pi}{3} + i \sin \dfrac{\pi}{3}}$ is equal to

[Single Correct Type, 2023 Main]

(a) $\sqrt{2}\left(\cos \dfrac{5\pi}{12} + i \sin \dfrac{5\pi}{12}\right)$ (b) $\cos \dfrac{\pi}{12} - i \sin \dfrac{\pi}{12}$

(c) $\sqrt{2}\left(\cos \dfrac{\pi}{12} + i \sin \dfrac{\pi}{12}\right)$ (d) $\sqrt{2}i\left(\cos \dfrac{5\pi}{12} - i \sin \dfrac{5\pi}{12}\right)$

77. Let $p, q \in R$ and $(1 - \sqrt{3}i)^{200} = 2^{199}(p + iq)$, $i = \sqrt{-1}$. Then, $p + q + q^2$ and $p - q + q^2$ are roots of the equation

[Single Correct Type, 2023 Main]

(a) $x^2 - 4x + 1 = 0$ (b) $x^2 - 4x - 1 = 0$

(c) $x^2 + 4x - 1 = 0$ (d) $x^2 + 4x + 1 = 0$

78. For all $z \in C$ on the curve $C_1 : |z| = 4$, let the locus of the point $z + \dfrac{1}{z}$ be the curve C_2. Then,

[Single Correct Type, 2023 Main]

(a) the curves C_1 and C_2 intersect at 4 points

(b) the curves C_1 and C_2 intersect at 2 points

(c) the curve C_2 lies inside C_1

(d) the curve C_1 lies inside C_2

79. Let z be a complex number such that $\left|\dfrac{z - 2i}{z + i}\right| = 2, z \neq -i$.

Then, z lies on the circle of radius 2 and centre

[Single Correct Type, 2023 Main]

(a) (2, 0) (b) (0, 0)

(c) (0, – 2) (d) (0, 2)

80. Let C be the circle in the complex plane with centre $z_0 = \dfrac{1}{2}(1 + 3i)$ and radius $r = 1$. Let $z_1 = 1 + i$ and the complex number z_2 be outside the circle C such that $|z_1 - z_0||z_2 - z_0| = 1$. If z_0, z_1 and z_2 are collinear, then the smaller value of $|z_2|^2$ is equal to

[Single Correct Type, 2023 Main]

(a) $\dfrac{13}{2}$ (b) $\dfrac{7}{2}$ (c) $\dfrac{5}{2}$ (d) $\dfrac{3}{2}$

81. Let $z_1 = 2 + 3i$ and $z_2 = 3 + 4i$. The set $S = \{z \in C : |z - z_1|^2 - |z - z_2|^2 = |z_1 - z_2|^2\}$ represents a **[Single Correct Type, 2023 Main]**

(a) hyperbola with the length of the transverse axis 7

(b) straight line with the sum of its intercepts on the co-ordinate axes equals 18

(c) straight line with the sum of its intercepts on the co-ordinate axes equals 14

(d) hyperbola with eccentricity 2

82. The set of all $a \in R$ for which the equation $x|x-1|+|x+2|+a=0$ has exactly one real root, is
[Single Correct Type, 2023 Main]

(a) $(-\infty, \infty)$ (b) $(-6, -3)$
(c) $(-6, \infty)$ (d) $(-\infty, -3)$

83. The number of integral values of k, for which one root of the equation $2x^2 - 8x + k = 0$ lies in the interval (1, 2) and its other root lies in the interval (2, 3), is
[Single Correct Type, 2023 Main]

(a) 3 (b) 2
(c) 0 (d) 1

84. The equation $x^2 - 4x + [x] + 3 = x[x]$, where $[x]$ denotes the greatest integer function, has
[Single Correct Type, 2023 Main]

(a) a unique solution in $(-\infty, \infty)$
(b) no solution
(c) a unique solution in $(-\infty, 1)$
(d) exactly two solutions in $(-\infty, \infty)$

85. Let $S = \left\{z \in C - \{i, 2i\} : \frac{z^2 + 8iz - 15}{z^2 - 3iz - 2} \in R\right\}$. If $\alpha - \frac{13}{11} i \in S$, $\alpha \in R - \{0\}$, then $242\alpha^2$ is equal to ....
[Numerical Value Type, 2023 Main]

86. Let $z = 1 + i$ and $z_1 = \frac{1 + i\bar{z}}{\bar{z}(1-z) + \frac{1}{z}}$. Then, $\frac{12}{\pi} \arg(z_1)$ is equal to ....
[Numerical Value Type, 2023 Main]

87. Let $\alpha = 8 - 14i$, $A = \left\{z \in c : \frac{\alpha z - \bar{\alpha}\bar{z}}{z^2 - (\bar{z})^2 - 112i} = 1\right\}$ and $B = \{z \in c : |z + 3i| = 4\}$. Then, $\sum_{z \in A \cap B} (\text{Re } z - \text{Im } z)$ is equal to ....
[Numerical Value Type, 2023 Main]

88. For $\alpha, \beta, z \in C$ and $\lambda > 1$, if $\sqrt{\lambda - 1}$ is the radius of the circle $|z - \alpha|^2 + |z - \beta|^2 = 2\lambda$, then $|\alpha - \beta|$ is equal to ....
[Numerical Value Type, 2023 Main]

89. If $z = 2 + 3i$, then $z^5 + (\bar{z})^5$ is equal to
[Single Correct Type, 2022 Main]

(a) 244 (b) 224 (c) 245 (d) 265

90. Let z_1 and z_2 be two complex numbers such that $\overline{z_1} = i\,\overline{z_2}$ and $\arg\left(\frac{z_1}{\overline{z_2}}\right) = \pi$. Then,
[Single Correct Type, 2022 Main]

(a) $\arg z_2 = \frac{\pi}{4}$ (b) $\arg z_2 = -\frac{3\pi}{4}$
(c) $\arg z_1 = \frac{\pi}{4}$ (d) $\arg z_1 = -\frac{3\pi}{4}$

91. Let $A = \{z \in C : 1 \le |z - (1+i)| \le 2\}$ and $B = \{z \in A : |z - (1-i)| = 1\}$. Then, B
[Single Correct Type, 2022 Main]

(a) is an empty set
(b) contains exactly two elements
(c) contains exactly three elements
(d) is an infinite set

92. Let S be the set of all (α, β), $\pi < \alpha, \beta < 2\pi$, for which the complex number $\frac{1 - i\sin\alpha}{1 + 2i\sin\alpha}$ is purely imaginary and $\frac{1 + i\cos\beta}{1 - 2i\cos\beta}$ is purely real. Let $Z_{\alpha\beta} = \sin 2\alpha + i \cos 2\beta$, $(\alpha, \beta) \in S$. Then, $\sum_{(\alpha, \beta) \in S} \left(iz_{\alpha\beta} + \frac{1}{i\bar{z}_{\alpha\beta}}\right)$ is equal to
[Single Correct Type, 2022 Main]

(a) 3 (b) $3i$ (c) 1 (d) $2 - i$

93. For $n \in N$, let $S_n = \left\{z \in C : |z - 3 + 2i| = \frac{n}{4}\right\}$ and $T_n = \left\{z \in C : |z - 2 + 3i| = \frac{1}{n}\right\}$. Then, the number of elements in the set $\{n \in N : S_n \cap T_n = \phi\}$ is
[Single Correct Type, 2022 Main]

(a) 0 (b) 2 (c) 3 (d) 4

94. Let α be a root of the equation $1 + x^2 + x^4 = 0$. Then, the value of $\alpha^{1011} + \alpha^{2022} - \alpha^{3033}$ is equal to
[Single Correct Type, 2022 Main]

(a) 1 (b) α (c) $1 + \alpha$ (d) $1 + 2\alpha$

95. Let the minimum value v_0 of $v = |z|^2 + |z - 3|^2 + |z - 6i|^2$, $z \in C$ is attained at $z = z_0$. Then, $|2z_0^2 - \bar{z}_0^3 + 3|^2 + v_0^2$ is equal to
[Single Correct Type, 2022 Main]

(a) 1000 (b) 1024 (c) 1105 (d) 1196

96. For $z \in C$ if the minimum value of $(|z - 3\sqrt{2}| + |z - p\sqrt{2}i|)$ is $5\sqrt{2}$, then a value of p is
[Single Correct Type, 2022 Main]

(a) 3 (b) $\frac{7}{2}$ (c) 4 (d) $\frac{9}{2}$

97. The number of points of intersection of $|z - (4 + 3i)| = 2$ and $|z| + |z - 4| = 6$, $z \in C$ is
[Single Correct Type, 2022 Main]

(a) 0 (b) 1 (c) 2 (d) 3

98. Let a circle C in complex plane pass through the points $z_1 = 3 + 4i$, $z_2 = 4 + 3i$ and $z_3 = 5i$. If $z\,(\ne z_1)$ is a point on C such that the line through z and z_1 is perpendicular to the line through z_2 and z_3, then $\arg(z)$ is equal to
[Single Correct Type, 2022 Main]

(a) $\tan^{-1}\left(\frac{2}{\sqrt{5}}\right) - \pi$ (b) $\tan^{-1}\left(\frac{24}{7}\right) - \pi$
(c) $\tan^{-1}(3) - \pi$ (d) $\tan^{-1}\left(\frac{3}{4}\right) - \pi$

99. Let $S = \{z = x + iy : |z - 1 + i| \geq |z|, |z| < 2, |z + i| = |z - 1|\}$. Then, the set of all values of x, for which $w = 2x + iy \in S$ for some $y \in R$, is **[Single Correct Type, 2022 Main]**

(a) $\left(-\sqrt{2}, \frac{1}{2\sqrt{2}}\right]$ (b) $\left(-\frac{1}{\sqrt{2}}, \frac{1}{4}\right]$

(c) $\left(-\sqrt{2}, \frac{1}{2}\right]$ (d) $\left(-\frac{1}{\sqrt{2}}, \frac{1}{2\sqrt{2}}\right]$

100. Let arg (z) represent the principal argument of the complex number z. Then, $|z| = 3$ and $\arg(z - 1) - \arg(z + 1) = \pi / 4$ intersect **[Single Correct Type, 2022 Main]**

(a) exactly at one point (b) exactly at two points

(c) nowhere (d) at infinitely many points

101. The area of the polygon, whose vertices are the non-real roots of the equation $\bar{z} = iz^2$ is **[Single Correct Type, 2022 Main]**

(a) $\frac{3\sqrt{3}}{4}$ (b) $\frac{3\sqrt{3}}{2}$ (c) $\frac{3}{2}$ (d) $\frac{3}{4}$

102. Let $A = \left\{z \in C : \left|\frac{z+1}{z-1}\right| < 1\right\}$ and $B = \left\{z \in C : \arg\left(\frac{z-1}{z+1}\right) = \frac{2\pi}{3}\right\}$. Then, $A \cap B$ is **[Single Correct Type, 2022 Main]**

(a) a portion of a circle centred at $\left(0, -\frac{1}{\sqrt{3}}\right)$ that lies in the second and third quadrants only

(b) a portion of a circle centred at $\left(0, -\frac{1}{\sqrt{3}}\right)$ that lies in the second quadrant only

(c) an empty set

(d) a portion of a circle of radius $\frac{2}{\sqrt{3}}$ that lies in the third quadrant only

103. Let $f(x) = ax^2 + bx + c$ be such that $f(1) = 3$, $f(-2) = \lambda$ and $f(3) = 4$. If $f(0) + f(1) + f(-2) + f(3) = 14$, then λ is equal to **[Single Correct Type, 2022 Main]**

(a) -4 (b) $\frac{13}{2}$

(c) $\frac{23}{2}$ (d) 4

104. Let $a, b \in R$ be such that the equation $ax^2 - 2bx + 15 = 0$ has a repeated root α. If α and β are the roots of the equation $x^2 - 2bx + 21 = 0$, then $\alpha^2 + \beta^2$ is equal to **[Single Correct Type, 2022 Main]**

(a) 37 (b) 58

(c) 68 (d) 92

105. The number of elements in the set $\{z = a + ib \in C : a, b \in z$ and $1 < |z - 3 + 2i| < 4\}$ is .... **[Numerical Value Type, 2022 Main]**

106. Let $z = a + ib, b \neq 0$ be complex numbers satisfying $z^2 = \bar{z} \cdot 2^{1-|Z|}$. Then, the least value of $n \in N$, such that $z^n = (z+1)^n$, is equal to .... **[Numerical Value Type, 2022 Main]**

107. Let $S = \{z \in C : |z - 2| \leq 1, z(1 + i) + \bar{z}(1 - i) \leq 2\}$. Let $|z - 4i|$ attains minimum and maximum values, respectively, at $z_1 \in S$ and $z_2 \in S$. If $5(|z_1|^2 + |z_2|^2) = \alpha + \beta\sqrt{5}$, where α and β are integers, then the value of $\alpha + \beta$ is equal to ...... **[Numerical Value Type, 2022 Main]**

108. If z and w are two complex numbers such that $|zw| = 1$ and $\arg(z) - \arg(w) = 3\pi/2$, then $\arg\left(\frac{1 - 2\bar{z}w}{1 + 3\bar{z}w}\right)$ is

(Here, arg (z) denotes the principal argument of complex number z) **[Single Correct Type, 2021 Main]**

(a) $\frac{\pi}{4}$ (b) $-\frac{3\pi}{4}$ (c) $-\frac{\pi}{4}$ (d) $\frac{3\pi}{4}$

109. Let n denote the number of solutions of the equation $z^2 + 3\bar{z} = 0$, where z is a complex number. Then, the value of $\sum_{k=0}^{\infty} \frac{1}{n^k}$ is equal to **[Single Correct Type, 2021 Main]**

(a) 1 (b) $\frac{4}{3}$ (c) $\frac{3}{2}$ (d) 2

110. If the real part of the complex number $(1 - \cos\theta + 2i\sin\theta)^{-1}$ is 1/5 for $\theta \in (0, \pi)$, then the value of the integral $\int_0^\theta \sin x \, dx$ is equal to **[Single Correct Type, 2021 Main]**

(a) 1 (b) 2 (c) -1 (d) 0

111. Let $z = \frac{1 - i\sqrt{3}}{2}$, $i = \sqrt{-1}$. Then the value of

$$21 + \left(z + \frac{1}{z}\right)^3 + \left(z^2 + \frac{1}{z^2}\right)^3 + \left(z^3 + \frac{1}{z^3}\right)^3 + \ldots + \left(z^{21} + \frac{1}{z^{21}}\right)^3$$

[Single Correct Type, 2021 Main]

(a) 12 (b) 13 (c) 18 (d) 20

112. Let a complex number be $w = 1 - \sqrt{3}i$. Let another complex number z be such that $|zw| = 1$ and $\arg(z) - \arg(w) = \pi/2$. Then the area of the triangle with vertices origin, z and w, is equal to **[Single Correct Type, 2021 Main]**

(a) 4 (b) $\frac{1}{2}$ (c) $\frac{1}{4}$ (d) 2

113. If z is a complex number such that $\frac{z - i}{z - 1}$ is purely imaginary, then the minimum value of $|z - (3 + 3i)|$ is **[Single Correct Type, 2021 Main]**

(a) $2\sqrt{2} - 1$ (b) $3\sqrt{2}$ (c) $6\sqrt{2}$ (d) $2\sqrt{2}$

114. The point $P(a, b)$ undergoes the following three transformations successively

(A) Reflection about the line $y = x$.

(B) Translation through 2 units along the positive direction of X-axis.

(C) Rotation through angle $\pi/4$ about the origin in the anti-clockwise direction.

If the coordinates of the final position of the point P are $\left(-\frac{1}{\sqrt{2}}, \frac{7}{\sqrt{2}}\right)$, then the value of $2a + b$ is equal to **[Single Correct Type, 2021 Main]**

(a) 13 (b) 9 (c) 5 (d) 7

115. Let C be the set of all complex numbers. Let $S_1 = \{z \in C : |z - 2| \le 1\}$ and $S_2 = \{z \in C : z(1 + i) + \bar{z}(1 - i) \ge 4\}$.

Then, the maximum value of $\left|z - \frac{5}{2}\right|^2$ for $z \in S_1 \cap S_2$ is equal to **[Single Correct Type, 2021 Main]**

(a) $\frac{3 + 2\sqrt{2}}{4}$ (b) $\frac{5 - 2\sqrt{2}}{2}$

(c) $\frac{3 + 2\sqrt{2}}{2}$ (d) $\frac{5 + 2\sqrt{2}}{4}$

116. Let the lines $(2 - i)z = (2 + i)\bar{z}$ and $(2 + i)z + (i - 2)\bar{z} - 4i = 0$, (here $i^2 = -1$) be normal to a circle C. If the line $iz + \bar{z} + 1 + i = 0$ is tangent to this circle C, then its radius is **[Single Correct Type, 2021 Main]**

(a) $\frac{3}{\sqrt{2}}$ (b) $\frac{1}{2\sqrt{2}}$ (c) $3\sqrt{2}$ (d) $\frac{3}{2\sqrt{2}}$

117. Let $[x]$ denote the greatest integer less than or equal to x. Then, the values of $x \in R$ satisfying the equation $[e^x]^2 + [e^x + 1] - 3 = 0$ lie in the interval **[Single Correct Type, 2021 Main]**

(a) $\left[0, \frac{1}{e}\right)$ (b) $[\log_e 2, \log_e 3)$

(c) $[1, e)$ (d) $[0, \log_e 2)$

118. If for the complex numbers z satisfying $|z - 2 - 2i| \le 1$ the maximum value of $|3iz + 6|$ is attained at $a + ib$, then $a + b$ is equal to .... **[Numerical Value Type, 2021 Main]**

119. The least positive integer n such that $\frac{(2i)^n}{(1 - i)^{n-2}}$, $i = \sqrt{-1}$, is a positive integer, is .... **[Numerical Value Type, 2021 Main]**

120. Let z_1, z_2 be the roots of the equation $z^2 + az + 12 = 0$ and z_1, z_2 form an equilateral triangle with origin. Then, the value of $|a|$ is .... **[Numerical Value Type, 2021 Main]**

121. The value of $\left(\frac{1 + \sin\frac{2\pi}{9} + i\cos\frac{2\pi}{9}}{1 + \sin\frac{2\pi}{9} - i\cos\frac{2\pi}{9}}\right)^3$ is **[Single Correct Type, 2020 Main]**

(a) $-\frac{1}{2}(\sqrt{3} - i)$ (b) $-\frac{1}{2}(1 - i\sqrt{3})$

(c) $\frac{1}{2}(\sqrt{3} - i)$ (d) $\frac{1}{2}(1 - i\sqrt{3})$

EXERCISE 2 — JEE Advanced Pattern

Single Option Correct Type Questions

1. If one root of equation $z^2 - az + a - 1 = 0$ is $(1 + i)$, where $a \in C$, then the other root is

(a) purely real (b) purely imaginary

(c) complex (d) None of these

2. Let $z = \frac{\cos\theta + i\sin\theta}{\cos\theta - i\sin\theta}$, $\frac{\pi}{4} < \theta < \frac{\pi}{2}$. Then, $\arg(z)$ is equal to

(a) 2θ (b) $2\theta - \pi$

(c) $\pi + 2\theta$ (d) None of these

3. The value of $\{\sin(\log i^i)\}^3 + \{\cos(\log i^i)\}^3$ is

(a) 1 (b) -1 (c) 2 (d) $2i$

4. If $z = a + ib$ such that $\arg(z - 1) = \arg(z + 3i)$, then the value of $(a - 1) : b$ is

(a) $1 : 2$ (b) $2 : 1$

(c) $1 : 3$ (d) $3 : 1$

5. The locus of point z satisfying $\text{Re}\left(\frac{1}{z}\right) = k$, $k \in R - \{0\}$, is

(a) straight line (b) circle

(c) ellipse (d) hyperbola

6. If $|z| = 4$ and $\omega = \frac{z - 4}{z + 4}$, then $\text{Re}(\omega)$ is equal to

(a) 0 (b) 4 (c) $\frac{1}{4}$ (d) $-\frac{1}{4}$

7. If $\arg(z^{1/3}) = \frac{1}{2}\arg(z^2 + \bar{z}z^{1/3})$, then $|z|$ is equal to
(a) 1 (b) 2 (c) 3 (d) 4

8. If $z + \frac{1}{z} = 2(\cos\theta + i\sin\theta)$, then $|z - i|$ is equal to
(a) 1 (b) $\sqrt{2}$ (c) $\frac{1}{\sqrt{2}}$ (d) 2

9. If z is a complex number satisfying $|z|^2 - |z| - 2 < 0$, then the value of $|z^2 + z\sin\theta|$, $\forall$ values of θ, is
(a) > 4 (b) < 4 (c) > 6 (d) < 6

10. If $\cos(1 - i) = a + ib$, where $a, b \in R$ and $i = \sqrt{-1}$, then
(a) $a = \frac{1}{2}\left(e - \frac{1}{e}\right)\cos 1,\ b = \frac{1}{2}\left(e + \frac{1}{e}\right)\sin 1$
(b) $a = \frac{1}{2}\left(e + \frac{1}{e}\right)\cos 1,\ b = \frac{1}{2}\left(e - \frac{1}{e}\right)\sin 1$
(c) $a = \frac{1}{2}\left(e + \frac{1}{e}\right)\cos 1,\ b = \frac{1}{2}\left(e + \frac{1}{e}\right)\sin 1$
(d) $a = \frac{1}{2}\left(e - \frac{1}{e}\right)\cos 1,\ b = \frac{1}{2}\left(e - \frac{1}{e}\right)\sin 1$

11. Number of roots of the equation $z^{10} - z^5 - 992 = 0$, where real parts are negative, is
(a) 3 (b) 4 (c) 5 (d) 6

12. If z and $\bar{z}$ represent adjacent vertices of a regular polygon of n sides with centre at origin and if $\frac{\text{Im}(z)}{\text{Re}(z)} = \sqrt{2} - 1$, the value of n is equal to
(a) 2 (b) 4 (c) 6 (d) 8

13. If $\prod_{p=1}^{r} e^{ip\theta} = 1$, where $\prod$ denotes the continued product and $i = \sqrt{-1}$, the most general value of θ is
(a) $\frac{2n\pi}{r(r-1)}, n \in I$ (b) $\frac{2n\pi}{r(r+1)}, n \in I$
(c) $\frac{4n\pi}{r(r-1)}, n \in I$ (d) $\frac{4n\pi}{r(r+1)}, n \in I$
(where, n is an integer)

14. The centre of a square $ABCD$ is at $z = 0$, A is z_1. Then, the centroid of ΔABC is
(a) $z_1(\cos\pi \pm i\sin\pi)$ (b) $\frac{z_1}{3}(\cos\pi \pm i\sin\pi)$
(c) $z_1\left(\cos\frac{\pi}{2} \pm i\sin\frac{\pi}{2}\right)$ (d) $\frac{z_1}{3}\left(\cos\frac{\pi}{2} \pm i\sin\frac{\pi}{2}\right)$
(where, $i = \sqrt{-1}$)

15. Let a and b be two fixed non-zero complex numbers and z is a variable complex number. If the lines $a\bar{z} + \bar{a}z + 1 = 0$ and $b\bar{z} + \bar{b}z - 1 = 0$ are mutually perpendicular, then
(a) $ab + \bar{a}\bar{b} = 0$ (b) $ab - \bar{a}\bar{b} = 0$
(c) $\bar{a}b - a\bar{b} = 0$ (d) $a\bar{b} + \bar{a}b = 0$

16. If $\alpha = \cos\left(\frac{8\pi}{11}\right) + i\sin\left(\frac{8\pi}{11}\right)$, where $i = \sqrt{-1}$, then $\text{Re}(\alpha + \alpha^2 + \alpha^3 + \alpha^4 + \alpha^5)$ is
(a) $\frac{1}{2}$ (b) $-\frac{1}{2}$
(c) 0 (d) None of these

17. The set of points in an Argand diagram which satisfy both $|z| \le 4$ and $0 \le \arg(z) \le \frac{\pi}{3}$, is
(a) a circle and a line (b) a radius of a circle
(c) a sector of a circle (d) an infinite part line

18. Let α and β be two distinct complex numbers, such that $|\alpha| = |\beta|$. If real part of α is positive and imaginary part of β is negative, then the complex number $(\alpha + \beta)/(\alpha - \beta)$ may be
(a) zero (b) real and negative
(c) real and positive (d) purely imaginary

19. The complex number z, satisfies the condition $\left|z - \frac{25}{z}\right| = 24$. The maximum distance from the origin of coordinates to the point z, is
(a) 25 (b) 30
(c) 32 (d) None of these

More than One Correct Option Type Questions

20. If $z_0 = \frac{1+i}{2}$, then the value of $(1 + z_0)(1 + z_0^2)\ldots(1 + z_0^{2n})$ must be
(a) $2^{2^{n+1}}$ (b) $(1 + i)\left(1 - \frac{1}{2^{2^n}}\right)$, if $n > 1$
(c) $\frac{5}{4}(1 + i)$, if $n = 1$ (d) 0

21. If z is complex number lying in the first quadrant such that $\text{Re}(z) + \text{Im}(z) = 3$, then for maximum value of $(\text{Re}(z))^2\ \text{Im}(z)$,
(a) $\text{Re}(z) = 2, \text{Im}(z) = 1$ (b) $\text{Re}(z) = 1, \text{Im}(z) = 2$
(c) maximum value $= 4$ (d) maximum value $= 2$

22. If z is a complex number such that $|z|^2 + 2(z + \bar{z}) + 3i(z - \bar{z}) + 4 = 0$, then complex number $z + 3 + 2i$ lies on a circle with
(a) centre $(1 + 5i)$ (b) centre $(1 - 5i)$
(c) radius 2 (d) radius 4

23. If $\left|z - \frac{4}{z}\right| = 2$, then
(a) $|z|_{\max} = 4 - \sqrt{5}$ (b) $|z|_{\min} = 1 - \sqrt{5}$
(c) $|z|_{\max} = 1 + \sqrt{5}$ (d) $|z|_{\min} = 0$

24. If $(\sqrt{3} - i)^n = 2^n$, $n \in Z$, then value of n can be
(a) 4 (b) 12
(c) 24 (d) 36

25. Let $z = i^i$. Then,

(a) $\text{Re}(z) = -\frac{\pi}{2}$ (b) $\text{Re}(z) = e^{-\frac{\pi}{2}}$

(c) $\text{Im}(z) = -\frac{\pi}{2}$ (d) $\text{Im}(z) = 0$

26. If $\frac{z+1}{z+i}$ is a purely imaginary number (where $i = \sqrt{-1}$), then z lies on a

(a) straight line

(b) circle

(c) circle with radius $= \frac{1}{\sqrt{2}}$

(d) circle passing through the origin

27. If z satisfies $|z-1| < |z+3|$, then $\omega = 2z + 3 - i$ (where, $i = \sqrt{-1}$) satisfies

(a) $|\omega - 5 - i| < |\omega + 3 + i|$

(b) $|\omega - 5| < |\omega + 3|$

(c) $\text{Im}(i\omega) > 1$

(d) $|\arg(\omega - 1)| < \frac{\pi}{2}$

28. If the complex number is $(1 + ri)^3 = \lambda(1 + i)$, when $i = \sqrt{-1}$, for some real λ, the value of r can be

(a) $\cos\frac{\pi}{5}$ (b) $\text{cosec}\frac{3\pi}{2}$

(c) $\cot\frac{\pi}{12}$ (d) $\tan\frac{\pi}{12}$

29. If $z \in C$, which of the following relation(s) represents a circle on an Argand diagram?

(a) $|z-1| + |z+1| = 3$ (b) $|z-3| = 2$

(c) $|z-2+i| = \frac{7}{3}$ (d) $(z-3+i)(\bar{z}-3-i) = 5$

(where, $i = \sqrt{-1}$)

30. If $1, z_1, z_2, z_3, \ldots, z_{n-1}$ be the n, nth roots of unity and ω be a non-real complex cube root of unity, then $\prod_{r=1}^{n-1} (\omega - z_r)$ can be equal to

(a) $1 + \omega$ (b) -1 (c) 0 (d) 1

31. If z is a complex number which simultaneously satisfies the equations $3|z-12| = 5|z-8i|$ and $|z-4| = |z-8|$, where $i = \sqrt{-1}$, then $\text{Im}(z)$ can be

(a) 8 (b) 17 (c) 7 (d) 15

32. If $|z-3| = \min\{|z-1|, |z-5|\}$, then $\text{Re}(z)$ is equal to

(a) 2 (b) 2.5 (c) 3.5 (d) 4

33. If $\arg(z+a) = \frac{\pi}{6}$ and $\arg(z-a) = \frac{2\pi}{3}$ $(a \in R^+)$, then

(a) $|z| = a$ (b) $|z| = 2a$

(c) $\arg(z) = \frac{\pi}{3}$ (d) $\arg(z) = \frac{\pi}{2}$

34. z_1 and z_2 are the roots of the equation $z^2 - az + b = 0$, where $|z_1| = |z_2| = 1$ and a, b are non-zero complex numbers, then

(a) $|a| \le 1$ (b) $|a| \le 2$

(c) $\arg(a) = \arg(b^2)$ (d) $\arg(a^2) = \arg(b)$

35. If the equation $z^3 + (3+i)z^2 - 3z - (m+i) = 0$, where $i = \sqrt{-1}$ and $m \in R$, has atleast one real root, value of m is

(a) 1 (b) 2 (c) 3 (d) 5

36. If $z^3 + (3+2i)z + (-1+ia) = 0$, where $i = \sqrt{-1}$, has one real root, the value of a lies in the interval $(a \in R)$

(a) $(-2, 1)$ (b) $(-1, 0)$

(c) $(0, 1)$ (d) $(-2, 3)$

Passage Based Questions

Passage I

(Q. Nos. 37 to 38)

- Consider the equation of line $L: (2-i)z + (2+i)\bar{z} + 3 = 0$

Lines L_1 and L_2 passes through the point $(-1, 4)$ and makes an angle of 45° with L.

37. Equation of line L_1 is

(a) $(1+3i)z + (1-i)\bar{z} - 22 = 0$

(b) $(1-3i)z + (1+3i)\bar{z} - 22 = 0$

(c) $(1+3i)z + (1-i)\bar{z} + 22 = 0$

(d) $(1-3i)z + (1+3i)\bar{z} + 22 = 0$

38. Equation of line L_2 is

(a) $(3+i)z + (3-i)\bar{z} + 14 = 0$

(b) $(1+3i)z + (1-3i)\bar{z} + 14 = 0$

(c) $(3+i)z + (3-i)\bar{z} - 14 = 0$

(d) $(1+3i)z + (1-3i)\bar{z} - 14 = 0$

Passage II

(Q. Nos. 39 to 40)

- The roots of the equation $x^3 + 3ax^2 + 3bx + c = 0$ are z_1, z_2, z_3 which corresponds to the points A, B, C on the Gaussion plane.

39. Centroid of the ΔABC is

(a) a (b) b (c) $-a$ (d) $-b$

40. If ΔABC is equilateral, then

(a) $a^2 = b$ (b) $a = b^2$

(c) $a^2 = c$ (d) $b^2 = c$

Passage III

(Q. Nos. 41 to 42)

- $\arg(\bar{z}) + \arg(-z) = \begin{cases} \pi, & \text{if } \arg(z) < 0 \\ -\pi, & \text{if } \arg(z) > 0 \end{cases}$, where $-\pi < \arg(z) \le \pi$.

41. Let z_1 and z_2 be two non-zero complex numbers, such that $|z_1| = |z_2|$ and $\arg(z_1 z_2) = \pi$, then z_1 is equal to

(a) z_2 (b) $\bar{z}_2$ (c) $-z_2$ (d) $-\bar{z}_2$

42. If $\arg(4z_1) - \arg(5z_2) = \pi$, then $\left|\frac{z_1}{z_2}\right|$ is equal to

(a) $\frac{2}{5}$ (b) $\frac{5}{4}$ (c) $\frac{1}{5}$ (d) $\frac{3}{4}$

Stem Based Questions

Stem I

(Q. Nos. 43 to 44)

- Sum of four consecutive powers of i (iota) is zero. i.e. $i^n + i^{n+1} + i^{n+2} + i^{n+3} = 0, \forall n \in I$.

43. If $\sum_{r=-2}^{95} i^r + \sum_{r=0}^{50} i^{r!} = a + ib$, where $i = \sqrt{-1}$, the unit place digit of $a^{2011} + b^{2012}$, is equal to ....

44. If $\sum_{r=4}^{100} i^{r!} + \prod_{r=1}^{101} i^r = a + ib$, where $i = \sqrt{-1}$, then $a + 75b$, is equal to ....

Stem II

(Q. Nos. 45 to 46)

- For any two complex numbers z_1 and z_2,

$$|z_1 - z_2| \ge \begin{cases} |z_1| - |z_2| \\ |z_2| - |z_1| \end{cases}$$

and equality holds iff origin z_1 and z_2 are collinear and z_1, z_2 lie on the same side of the origin.

45. If $\left|z + \frac{2}{z}\right| = 4$ and sum of greatest and least values of $|z|$ is λ, then λ^2 is equal to ....

46. If $\left|z - \frac{3}{z}\right| = 6$ and sum of greatest and least values of $|z|$ is 2λ, then λ^2 is equal to ....

Single Integer Type Questions

47. If complex number $z (z \ne 2)$ satisfies the equation $z^2 = 4z + |z|^2 + \frac{16}{|z|^3}$, then the value of $|z|^4$ is ......

48. Let $|z| = 2$ and $\omega = \frac{z+1}{z-1}$, $z, \omega \in C$. Then, product of least and greatest value of modulus of ω is ......

49. Suppose that z is a complex number that satisfies $|z - 2 - 2i| \le 1$. The maximum value of $|2iz + 4|$ is equal to ....

50. If z satisfies the condition $\arg(z + i) = \frac{\pi}{4}$. Then, the minimum value of $|z + 1 - i| + |z - 2 + 3i|$ is ....

51. Given that $1 + 2|z|^2 = |z^2 + 1|^2 + 2|z + 1|^2$, then the value of $|z(z + 1)|$ is ....

Numerical Value Type Questions

52. Let $z_1 = (8 + i)\sin\theta + (7 + 4i)\cos\theta$ and $z_2 = (1 + 8i)\sin\theta + (4 + 7i)\cos\theta$. If $z_1 z_2 = a + ib$ and M is the greatest value of $(a + b)$, then value of M is ......

53. Let $A = \{a \in R :$ equation $(1 + 2i)x^3 - 2(3 + i)x^2 + (5 - 4i)x + 2a^2 = 0$ has atleast one root$\}$. Then, $\Sigma a^2 =$ ....

54. If m is the minimum value of $|z|^2 + |z - 3|^2 + |z - 6i|^2$, then value of m is ....

55. If ω is complex cube root of unity and $(4 + 5\omega + 6\omega^2)^{n^2+2} + (6 + 5\omega^2 + 4\omega)^{n^2+2} + (5 + 6\omega + 4\omega^2)^{n^2+2} = 0$ and $n \in [1, 100]$, then number of values of n is ....

56. If z, z_1 and z_2 are complex numbers such that $z = z_1 z_2$ and $|\bar{z}_2 - z_1| \le 1$, then maximum value of $|z| - \text{Re}(z)$ is ....

Matching Type Questions

57. Match the Column I with Column II.

	Column I		Column II
A.	If $\left|z - \frac{1}{z}\right| = 2$ and if greatest and least values of $|z|$ are G and L respectively, then $G^2 + L^2$, is	(p)	5
B.	If $\left|z + \frac{2}{z}\right| = 4$ and if greatest and least values of $|z|$ are G and L respectively, then $G - L$, is	(q)	3
C.	If $\left|z - \frac{3}{z}\right| = 6$ and if greatest and least values of $|z|$ are G and L respectively, then GL is	(r)	6
D.	If $\left|z + \frac{4}{z}\right| = 3$ and if greatest and least values of $|z|$ are G and L respectively, then $G + L$ is	(s)	4

58. Match the Column I with Column II.

	Column I		Column II
A.	If $z = 1 + i$, then $5(z^4 - 4z^3 + 7z^2 - 6z + 3)$ is equal to	(p)	7
B.	If $\omega \neq 1$ is a cube root of unity and $(1 + \omega)^7 = A + B\omega$, then A and B are	(q)	5
C.	If $\lvert z - i \rvert \leq 2$ and $z_1 = 5 + 3i$, then maximum value of $\lvert iz + z_1 \rvert$ is	(r)	10
D.	If $\lvert z_1 \rvert = 1$ and $\lvert z_2 \rvert = 2$, then $\lvert z_1 + z_2 \rvert^2 + \lvert z_1 - z_2 \rvert^2$ is equal to	(s)	1, 1

59. Match the Column I with Column II.

	Column I		Column II
A.	The set of points z satisfying $\lvert z - i\lvert z \rvert \rvert = \lvert z + i\lvert z \rvert \rvert$, where $i = \sqrt{-1}$, is contained in or equal to	(p)	an ellipse with eccentricity 4/5
B.	The set of points z satisfying $\lvert z + 4 \rvert + \lvert z - 4 \rvert = 10$ is contained in or equal to	(q)	the set of points z = satisfying $\text{Im}(z) = 0$
C.	If $\lvert w \rvert = 2$, the set of points $z = w - \frac{1}{w}$ is contained in or equal to	(r)	the set of points z satisfying $\lvert \text{Im}(z) \rvert \leq 1$
D.	If $\lvert w \rvert = 1$, the set of points $z = w + \frac{1}{w}$ is contained in or equal to	(s)	the set of points of satisfying $\lvert \text{Re}(z) \rvert \leq 2$
		(t)	the set of points z satisfying $\lvert z \rvert \leq 3$

Previous Year Questions

60. Let $A = \left\{ \frac{1967 + 1686i \sin \theta}{7 - 3i \cos \theta} : \theta \in R \right\}$. If A contains exactly one positive integer n, then find the value of n.

[Numerical Value Type, 2023 Adv.]

61. Let z be a complex number satisfying $|z|^3 + 2z^2 + 4\bar{z} - 8 = 0$, where $\bar{z}$ denotes the complex conjugate of z. Let the imaginary part of z be non-zero. Match each entry in **List-I** to the correct entries in **List-II.** **[Matching Type, 2023 Adv.]**

	List-I		List-II
A.	$|z|^2$ is equal to	(p)	12
B.	$|z - \bar{z}|^2$ is equal to	(q)	4
C.	$|z|^2 + |z + \bar{z}|^2$ is equal to	(r)	8
D.	$|z + 1|^2$ is equal to	(s)	10
		(t)	7

The correct option is

	A	B	C	D		A	B	C	D
(a)	p	r	t	s	(b)	q	p	r	t
(c)	q	s	t	p	(d)	q	r	t	s

62. Let $\bar{z}$ denote the complex conjugate of a complex number z. If z is a non-zero complex number for which both real and imaginary parts of $(\bar{z})^2 + \frac{1}{z^2}$ are integers, then which of the following is/are possible value(s) of $|z|$? **[More than One Option Correct, 2022 Adv.]**

(a) $\left(\frac{43 + 3\sqrt{205}}{2}\right)^{1/4}$ (b) $\left(\frac{7 + \sqrt{33}}{4}\right)^{1/4}$

(c) $\left(\frac{9 + \sqrt{65}}{4}\right)^{1/4}$ (d) $\left(\frac{7 + \sqrt{13}}{6}\right)^{1/4}$

63. Let z be a complex number with non-zero imaginary part. If $\frac{2 + 3z + 4z^2}{2 - 3z + 4z^2}$ is a real number, then find the value of $|z|^2$. **[Numerical Value Type, 2022 Adv.]**

64. Let $\bar{z}$ denote the complex conjugate of a complex number then find z and let $i = \sqrt{-1}$. In the set of complex numbers, then find the number of distinct roots of the equation $\bar{z} - z^2 = i(\bar{z} + z^2)$.

[Numerical Value Type, 2022 Adv.]

65. Let $\theta_1, \theta_2, \ldots, \theta_{10}$ be positive valued angles (in radian) such that $\theta_1 + \theta_2 + \ldots + \theta_{10} = 2\pi$. Define the complex numbers $z_1 = e^{i\theta_1}$, $z_k = z_{k-1}e^{i\theta_k}$ for $k = 2, 3, \ldots, 10$, where $i = \sqrt{-1}$. Consider the Statements P and Q given below :

$P : |z_2 - z_1| + |z_3 - z_2| + \ldots + |z_{10} - z_9| + |z_1 - z_{10}| \leq 2\pi$

$Q : |z_2^2 - z_1^2| + |z_3^2 - z_2^2| + \ldots + |z_{10}^2 - z_9^2| + |z_1^2 - z_{10}^2| \leq 4\pi$

Then, **[Single Correct Type, 2021 Adv.]**

(a) P is true and Q is false (b) Q is true and P is false

(c) Both P and Q are true (d) Both P and Q are false

66. For any complex number $w = c + id$, let $\arg(w) \in (-\pi, \pi]$, where $i = \sqrt{-1}$. Let α and β be real numbers such that for all complex numbers $z = x + iy$ satisfying $\arg\left(\frac{z + \alpha}{z + \beta}\right) = \frac{\pi}{4}$, the ordered pair (x, y) lies on the circle $x^2 + y^2 + 5x - 3y + 4 = 0$ Then, which of the following statements is (are) true?

[More than One Option Correct, 2021 Adv.]

(a) $\alpha = -1$

(b) $\alpha\beta = 4$

(c) $\alpha\beta = -4$

(d) $\beta = 4$

67. Let S be the set of all complex numbers z satisfying $|z^2 + z + 1| = 1$. Then, which of the following statements is/are true? **[More than One Option Correct, 2020 Adv.]**

(a) $|z + 1/2| \le 1/2, \forall z \in S$
(b) $|z| \le 2, \forall z \in S$
(c) $|z + 1/2| \ge 1/2, \forall z \in S$
(d) The set S has exactly four elements

68. For a complex number z, let $\text{Re}(z)$ denote the real part of z. Let S be the set of all complex numbers z satisfying $z^4 - |z|^4 = 4iz^2$, where $i = \sqrt{-1}$. Then, the minimum possible value of $|z_1 - z_2|^2$, where $z_1, z_2 \in S$ with $\text{Re}(z_1) > 0$ and $\text{Re}(z_2) < 0$ is

[Numerical Value Type, 2020 Adv.]

EXERCISE 3

Challenging Problems

1. Let S denotes the real part of the complex number $z = \dfrac{5+2i}{2-5i} + \dfrac{20+5i}{7+6i} + 3i$, where $i = \sqrt{-1}$, K denotes the sum of the imaginary parts of the roots of the equation $z^2 - 8(1-i)z + 63 - 16i = 0$ and G denotes the value of $\sum_{r=4}^{2012} i^r$, where $i = \sqrt{-1}$, find the value of $S - K + G$.

2. If $|z - 1| = 1$, where z is a point on the argand plane, show that $\dfrac{z-2}{z} = i\tan(\arg z)$, where $i = \sqrt{-1}$.

3. If $\arg(z^{1/3}) = \dfrac{1}{2}\arg(z^2 + \bar{z}z^{1/3})$, find the value of $|z|$.

4. C is the complex numbers $f: C \to R$ is defined by $f(z) = |z^3 - z + 2|$. Find the maximum value of $f(z)$, if $|z| = 1$.

5. If $\alpha = e^{2\pi i/7}$, where $i = \sqrt{-1}$ and $f(x) = A_0 + \sum_{k=1}^{20} A_k x^k$, then find the value of $f(x) + f(\alpha x) + f(\alpha^2 x) + \ldots + f(\alpha^6 x)$ independent of α.

6. Show that all the roots of the equation $a_1 z^3 + a_2 z^2 + a_3 z + a_4 = 3$, (where $|a_i| \le 1, i = 1, 2, 3, 4$) lie outside the circle with centre at origin and radius $\dfrac{2}{3}$.

7. If A, B and C represent the complex numbers z_1, z_2 and z_3 respectively on the complex plane and the angles at B and C are each equal to $\dfrac{1}{2}(\pi - \alpha)$, then prove that $(z_2 - z_3)^2 = 4(z_3 - z_1)(z_1 - z_2)\sin^2\left(\dfrac{\alpha}{2}\right)$.

8. If z_1 and z_2 are two complex numbers such that $\left|\dfrac{z_1 - z_2}{z_1 + z_2}\right| = 1$, then prove that $\dfrac{iz_1}{z_2} = k$, where k is a real number. Find the angle between the lines from the origin to the points $z_1 + z_2$ and $z_1 - z_2$ in terms of k.

9. If $z = x + iy$ is a complex number with rationals x and y and $|z| = 1$, then show that $|z^{2n} - 1|$ is a rational number for every $n \in N$.

10. If a is a complex number such that $|a| = 1$, then find the value of a, so that equation $az^2 + z + 1 = 0$ has one purely imaginary root.

11. If $n \in N > 1$, find the sum of real parts of the roots of the equation $z^n = (z+1)^n$.

12. Among the complex numbers z which satisfies $|z - 25i| \le 15$, find the complex numbers z having

(i) least positive argument.
(ii) maximum positive argument.
(iii) least modulus.
(iv) maximum modulus.

13. Interpret the following equations geometrically on the Argand plane.

(i) $|z - 1| + |z + 1| = 4$ (ii) $\arg(z + i) - \arg(z - i) = \dfrac{\pi}{2}$

(iii) $1 < |z - 2 - 3i| < 4$ (iv) $\dfrac{\pi}{4} < \arg(z) < \dfrac{\pi}{3}$

(v) $\log_{\cos \pi/3}\left\{\dfrac{|z-1|+4}{3|z-1|-2}\right\} > 1$

14. If α and β are the roots of $z + \dfrac{1}{z} = 2(\cos\theta + i\sin\theta)$, where $0 < \theta < \pi$ and $i = \sqrt{-1}$, show that $|\alpha - i| = |\beta - i|$.

Answer Key

Exercise 1

1. (a)	2. (b)	3. (d)	4. (a)	5. (b)	6. (d)	7. (c)	8. (a)	9. (c)	10. (d)
11. (b)	12. (b)	13. (c)	14. (c)	15. (a)	16. (b)	17. (b)	18. (c)	19. (c)	20. (c)
21. (a)	22. (d)	23. (b)	24. (b)	25. (c)	26. (21)	27. (5)	28. (5)	29. (3)	30. (1)
31. (12)	32. (101)	33. (1)	34. (5)	35. (8)	36. (4)	37. (6)	38. (5)	39. (4)	40. (4)
41. (c)	42. (c)	43. (b)	44. (d)	45. (d)	46. (a)	47. (c)	48. (c)	49. (a)	50. (d)
51. (a)	52. (d)	53. (d)	54. (c)	55. (b)	56. (b)	57. (a)	58. (d)	59. (d)	60. (3)
61. (49)	62. (9)	63. (36)	64. (20)	65. (d)	66. (b)	67. (b)	68. (d)	69. (b)	70. (a)
71. (c)	72. (d)	73. (*)	74. (d)	75. (d)	76. (a)	77. (a)	78. (a)	79. (c)	80. (c)
81. (c)	82. (a)	83. (d)	84. (a)	85. (1680)	86. (9)	87. (14)	88. (2)	89. (a)	90. (c)
91. (d)	92. (c)	93. (d)	94. (a)	95. (a)	96. (c)	97. (c)	98. (b)	99. (b)	100. (c)
101. (a)	102. (b)	103. (d)	104. (b)	105. (40)	106. (6)	107. (26)	108. (b)	109. (b)	110. (a)
111. (b)	112. (b)	113. (d)	114. (b)	115. (d)	116. (d)	117. (d)	118. (5)	119. (6)	120. (6)
121. (a)									

Exercise 2

1. (a)	2. (a)	3. (b)	4. (c)	5. (b)	6. (a)	7. (a)	8. (b)	9. (d)	10. (b)
11. (c)	12. (d)	13. (d)	14. (d)	15. (d)	16. (b)	17. (c)	18. (d)	19. (a)	20. (b,c)
21. (a,c)	22. (a,d)	23. (c,d)	24. (b,c,d)	25. (b,d)	26. (b,c,d)	27. (b,c,d)	28. (b,c,d)	29. (b,c,d)	30. (a,c,d)
31. (a,b)	32. (a,d)	33. (a,c)	34. (b,d)	35. (a,d)	36. (a,b,d)	37. (b)	38. (a)	39. (c)	40. (a)
41. (d)	42. (b)	43. (5)	44. (22)	45. (24)	46. (12)	47. (4)	48. (1)	49. (3)	50. (5)
51. (1)	52. (125)	53. (18)	54. (30)	55. (33)	56. (0.5)	57. (A) → (r), (B) → (s), (C) → (q), (D) → (p)			
58. (A) → (q), (B) → (s), (C) → (p), (D) → (r)				59. (A) → (q), (B) → (p), (C) → (p), (D) → (q,s)					
60. (281)	61. (b)	62. (a)	63. (0.5)	64. (4)	65. (c)	66. (b,d)	67. (b,c)	68. (8)	

Solutions

Exercise 1 - JEE Main Pattern

1. We have, $(1+i)^{6n}+(1-i)^{6n}=[(1+i)^2]^{3n}+[(1-i)^2]^{3n}$

$$=(2i)^{3n}+(-2i)^{3n}$$
$$=2^{3n}[i^{3n}+(-i)^{3n}]$$
$$=2^{3n}[i^{3n}-i^{3n}] \qquad [\because n\in \text{odd}]$$
$$=0$$

2. Let $z=x+iy$, then

$$\frac{2z+1}{iz+1}=\frac{2(x+iy)+1}{i(x+iy)+1}$$
$$=\frac{(2x+1)+i2y}{(1-y)+ix}$$
$$=\frac{(2x+1)+i2y}{(1-y)+ix}\times\frac{(1-y)-ix}{(1-y)-ix}$$
$$=\frac{[(2x+1)(1-y)+2xy]+i[2y(1-y)-x(2x+1)]}{(1-y)^2+x^2}$$

Now, $\text{Im}\left(\frac{2z+1}{iz+1}\right)=-2$

$\therefore$ $\frac{2y(1-y)-x(2x+1)}{(1-y)^2+x^2}=-2$

$\Rightarrow$ $2y-2y^2-2x^2-x=-2-2y^2+4y-2x^2$

$\Rightarrow$ $x-2y-2=0$

which is a straight line.

3. We have, $\left(\frac{2i}{1+i}\right)^n=\left(\frac{2i(1-i)}{(1+i)(1-i)}\right)^n$

$$=\left(\frac{2i-2i^2}{1+1}\right)^n$$
$$=\left(\frac{2(i-i^2)}{2}\right)^n$$
$$=(1+i)^n$$
$$=[(1+i)^2]^{\frac{n}{2}}=(2i)^{\frac{n}{2}}$$

$\therefore$ $n=8$

4. We have, $(1+i)^{n_1}+(1+i^3)^{n_1}+(1+i^5)^{n_2}+(1+i^7)^{n_2}$

$$=(1+i)^{n_1}+(1-i)^{n_1}+(1+i)^{n_2}+(1-i)^{n_2}$$
$$=[(1+i)^{n_1}+\overline{(1+i)^{n_1}}]+[(1+i)^{n_2}+\overline{(1+i)^{n_2}}]$$
$$=\text{Purely real} \qquad [\because z+\bar{z}=\text{Purely real}]$$

5. Let $z=a+ib$

$\therefore$ $z^5=(a+ib)^5$

$$=a^5+5a^4ib+10a^3i^2b^2+10a^2i^3b^3+5ai^4b^4+i^5b^5$$

$\therefore$ $\text{Im}(z^5)=5a^4b-10a^2b^3+b^5$

Now, let $y=\frac{\text{Im}(z^5)}{(\text{Im } z)^5}$

$$=\frac{5a^4b-10a^2b^3+b^5}{b^5}$$
$$=5\left[\left(\frac{a}{b}\right)^4-2\left(\frac{a}{b}\right)^2+\frac{1}{5}\right]$$
$$=5\left[\left(\left(\frac{a}{b}\right)^2-1\right)^2+\frac{1}{5}-1\right]$$
$$=5\left[\left(\left(\frac{a}{b}\right)^2-1\right)^2\right]-4$$

$\therefore$ $y_{\min}=-4$

6. We have, $z=\frac{1+i}{\sqrt{2}}$

$\therefore$ $z^2=\frac{(1+i)^2}{2}=\frac{2i}{2}=i$

$\therefore$ $z^{1929}=z^{1928}\cdot z$

$$=(z^2)^{964}\cdot z$$
$$=(i)^{964}\cdot z$$
$$=(i^4)^{241}\cdot z$$
$$=z$$
$$=\frac{1+i}{\sqrt{2}}$$

7. We have, $|\beta|=\frac{1}{|\gamma|}\Rightarrow|\beta\gamma|=1$

Now, $\left|\frac{\beta\gamma-\alpha}{1-\bar{\alpha}\beta\gamma}\right|=\left|\frac{\beta\gamma-\alpha}{|\beta\gamma|^2-\bar{\alpha}\beta\gamma}\right|$

$$=\left|\frac{\beta\gamma-\alpha}{(\beta\gamma)(\overline{\beta\gamma})-\bar{\alpha}\beta\gamma}\right|$$
$$=\left|\frac{\beta\gamma-\alpha}{\beta\gamma(\overline{\beta\gamma}-\bar{\alpha})}\right|$$
$$=\left|\frac{\beta\gamma-\alpha}{\beta\gamma(\overline{\beta\gamma-\alpha})}\right|$$
$$=\frac{|\beta\gamma-\alpha|}{|\beta\gamma||(\overline{\beta\gamma-\alpha})|}$$
$$=1$$

8. Let $z_1=\frac{\omega-\bar{\omega}z}{1-z}$

Since, z_1 is purely real.

$\therefore \quad z_1 = \bar{z}_1$

$\Rightarrow \quad \dfrac{\omega - \bar{\omega}z}{1-z} = \dfrac{\bar{\omega} - \omega\bar{z}}{1-\bar{z}}$

$\Rightarrow \quad \omega - \omega\bar{z} - \bar{\omega}z + \bar{\omega}z\bar{z} = \bar{\omega} - \omega\bar{z} - \bar{\omega}z + \omega z\bar{z}$

$\Rightarrow (\omega - \bar{\omega}) + (\bar{\omega} - \omega)|z|^2 = 0$

$\Rightarrow \quad (\omega - \bar{\omega})(1 - |z|^2) = 0$

$\Rightarrow \quad 1 - |z|^2 = 0 \qquad [\omega - \bar{\omega} \neq 0, \beta \neq 0]$

$\Rightarrow \quad |z| = 1$

9. Let α be the real root.

Then, $\quad \alpha^2 - (3+i)\alpha + m + 2i = 0$

$\Rightarrow \quad (\alpha^2 - 3\alpha + m) + i(2-\alpha) = 0$

$\Rightarrow \quad \alpha^2 - 3\alpha + m = 0$ and $2 - \alpha = 0$

$\Rightarrow \quad \alpha^2 - 3\alpha + m = 0$ and $\alpha = 2$

$\therefore \quad 4 - 6 + m = 0$

$\Rightarrow \quad m = 2$

10. We have, $\quad z = \dfrac{(\sqrt{3}+i)^{17}}{(1-i)^{50}}$

$= \dfrac{i^{17}(1-\sqrt{3}i)^{17}}{((1-i)^2)^{25}}$

$= \dfrac{-i^{17}(-1+\sqrt{3}i)^{17}}{(-2i)^{25}}$

$= \dfrac{-i \times 2^{17}\left(\dfrac{-1+\sqrt{3}i}{2}\right)^{17}}{-(2)^{25} i^{25}}$

$= \dfrac{1}{2^8 i^{24}}\omega^{17} = \dfrac{1}{2^8}\omega^{17} = \dfrac{1}{2^8}\omega^2$

$= \dfrac{1}{2^8}\left(\dfrac{-1-\sqrt{3}i}{2}\right)$

$= \dfrac{1}{2^9}(-1-\sqrt{3}i)$

$\therefore \quad \text{Re}(z) = -2^{-9}$

11. We have, $|\arg z| \leq \dfrac{\pi}{4} \Rightarrow -\dfrac{\pi}{4} \leq \arg(z) \leq \dfrac{\pi}{4}$

Again, $\quad |z-1| < |z-3|$

$\Rightarrow |(x-1)+iy| < |(x-3)+iy| \qquad$ [let $z = x + iy$]

$\Rightarrow (x-1)^2 + y^2 < (x-3)^2 + y^2 \Rightarrow x < 2$

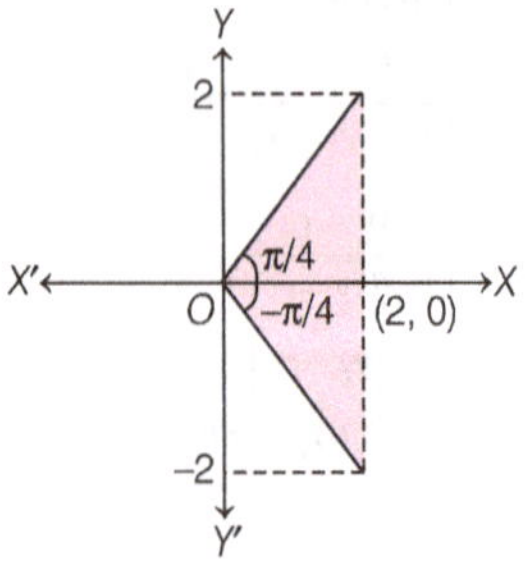

$\therefore$ Required area $= \dfrac{1}{2} \times (4)(2) = 4$ sq units

12. We have, $e^{2mi\theta}\left(\dfrac{i\cot\theta + 1}{i\cot\theta - 1}\right)^m = e^{2mi\theta}\left[\dfrac{i(\cot\theta - i)}{i(\cot\theta + i)}\right]^m$

$= e^{2mi\theta}\left(\dfrac{\cos\theta - i\sin\theta}{\cos\theta + i\sin\theta}\right)^m$

$= e^{2mi\theta}\left(\dfrac{e^{-i\theta}}{e^{i\theta}}\right)^m$

$= e^{2mi\theta} \cdot e^{-2mi\theta}$

$= 1$

13. We have, $x^8 - x^7 + x^6 - x^5 + x^4 - x^3 + x^2 - x + 1 = 0$

$\Rightarrow (x+1)(x^8 - x^7 + x^6 - x^5 + x^4 - x^3 + x^2 - x + 1) = 0$

$\Rightarrow \quad x^9 + 1 = 0$

$\Rightarrow \quad x = (-1)^{\frac{1}{9}}$

$\therefore$ The roots are 9th roots of -1, $x \neq -1$.

Let $\alpha_1, \alpha_2, \ldots, \alpha_8$ be the complex roots, then

$(-1)^2 + \alpha_1^2 + \alpha_2^2 + \ldots + \alpha_8^2 = 0$

$\Rightarrow \quad \alpha_1^2 + \alpha_2^2 + \ldots + \alpha_8^2 = -1$

14. $\because \quad A \equiv z_1, B \equiv z_2, C \equiv (1-i)z_1 + iz_2$

$\therefore \quad AB = |z_1 - z_2|$

$BC = |z_2 - (1-i)z_1 - iz_2| = |(1-i)(z_2 - z_1)|$

$= \sqrt{2}\,|z_1 - z_2|$

and $\quad CA = |(1-i)z_1 + iz_2 - z_1| = |-i(z_1 - z_2)|$

$= |-i||z_1 - z_2|$

$= |z_1 - z_2|$

It is clear that, $AB = CA$ and $(AB)^2 + (CA)^2 = (BC)^2$

$\therefore \quad \Delta ABC$ is isosceles and right angled.

15. Centre and radius of circle $|z| = 3 \qquad$ ...(i)

are $C_1 \equiv 0$, $r_1 = 3$

and centre and radius of circle

$|z + 1 - i| = \sqrt{2} \qquad$ ...(ii)

and $\quad C_2 = -1 + i, r_2 = \sqrt{2}$

$\because \quad |C_1C_2| = |-1+i| = \sqrt{2}$

and $\quad |C_1C_2| < r_1 - r_2$

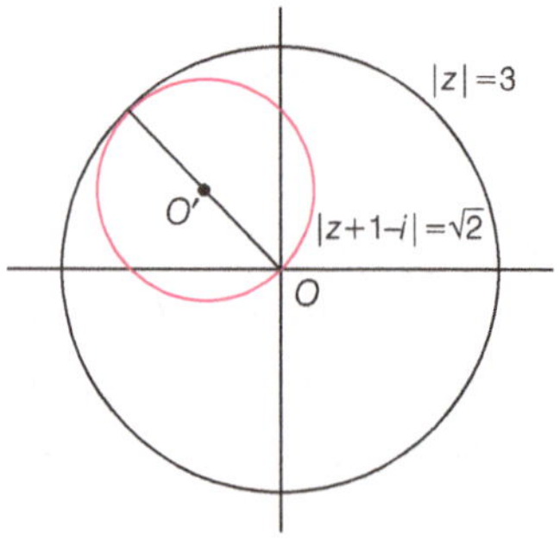

Hence, circle (ii) completely inside circle (i)

$\therefore$ Number of solutions = 0

16. We have, $|z+1| = 2|z-1|$

Put $\quad z = x + iy$, we get

$$(x+1)^2 + y^2 = 4[(x-1)^2 + y^2]$$

$$\Rightarrow \quad 3x^2 + 3y^2 - 10x + 3 = 0$$

$$\Rightarrow \quad x^2 + y^2 - \frac{10}{3}x + 1 = 0 \quad \text{...(i)}$$

On comparing Eq. (i) with the standard equation

$$x^2 + y^2 + 2gx + 2fy + c = 0$$

$$\Rightarrow \quad g = -\frac{10}{6} = -\frac{5}{3} \text{ and } f = 0$$

$\therefore$ Required centre of circle $\equiv (-g, -f) \equiv \left(\frac{5}{3}, 0\right)$

i.e. $\quad \frac{5}{3} + 0 \cdot i = \frac{5}{3}$

17. $\because \quad x = 9^{1/3} \cdot 9^{1/9} \cdot 9^{1/27} \dots \infty$

$$= 9^{1/3 + 1/9 + 1/27 + \dots \infty} = 9^{\frac{1/3}{1-1/3}} = 9^{1/2} = 3$$

$$y = 4^{1/3} \cdot 4^{-1/9} \cdot 4^{1/27} \dots \infty = 4^{1/3 - 1/9 + 1/27 \dots \infty}$$

$$= 4^{\frac{1/3}{1+1/3}} = 4^{1/4} = \sqrt{2}$$

and $z = \sum_{r=1}^{\infty} (1+i)^{-r} = \frac{1}{(1+i)} + \frac{1}{(1+i)^2} + \frac{1}{(1+i)^3} + \dots \infty$

$$= \frac{\frac{1}{(1+i)}}{1 - \frac{1}{(1+i)}} = \frac{1}{i} = -i$$

Now, $x + yz = 3 - i\sqrt{2}$

$\therefore \arg(x + yz) = \arg(3 - i\sqrt{2}) = -\tan^{-1}\left(\frac{\sqrt{2}}{3}\right)$

18. $\because \quad A_1 \equiv 1 + 2i$

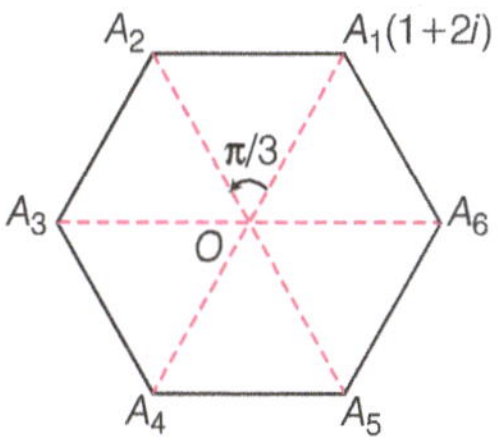

$\therefore \quad A_2 = (1+2i)\, e^{i\pi/3}$

$$= (1+2i)\left(\frac{1}{2} + \frac{i\sqrt{3}}{2}\right) = \frac{1}{2} + \frac{i\sqrt{3}}{2} + i - \sqrt{3}$$

$$= \left(\frac{1}{2} - \sqrt{3}\right) + i\left(\frac{\sqrt{3}}{2} + 1\right)$$

$$\therefore |A_1A_2| = \left|1 + 2i - \left(\frac{1}{2} - \sqrt{3}\right) - i\left(\frac{\sqrt{3}}{2} + 1\right)\right|$$

$$= \left|\frac{1}{2} + \sqrt{3} + i\left(1 - \frac{\sqrt{3}}{2}\right)\right|$$

$$= \sqrt{\left(\frac{1}{2} + \sqrt{3}\right)^2 + \left(1 - \frac{\sqrt{3}}{2}\right)^2} = \sqrt{5}$$

$\therefore \quad$ Perimeter $= 6\,|A_1A_2| = 6\sqrt{5}$

19. We have, $\left|\sum_{r=1}^{n} z_r\right| = \left|\sum_{r=1}^{n} ((z_r - r) + r)\right| \le \sum_{r=1}^{n} (|z_r - r| + |r|)$

$$= \sum_{r=1}^{n} |z_r - r| + \sum_{r=1}^{n} |r| \le \sum_{r=1}^{n} r + \sum_{r=1}^{n} |r| \quad \text{[given]}$$

$$= \frac{n(n+1)}{2} + \frac{n(n+1)}{2} = n(n+1)$$

$$\therefore \quad \left|\sum_{r=1}^{n} z_r\right| \le n(n+1)$$

20. We have, $\arg\left(\frac{z_1 - \frac{z}{|z|}}{\frac{z}{|z|}}\right) = \frac{\pi}{2}$ and $\left|\frac{z}{|z|} - z_1\right| = 3$

which implies the following diagram

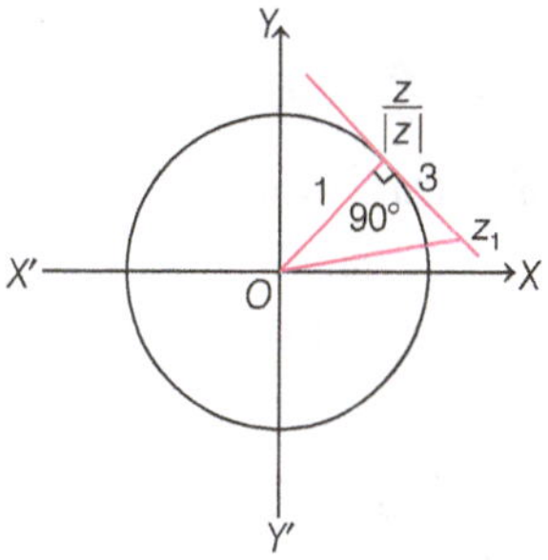

$$\Rightarrow \quad \left|\frac{z}{|z|} - z_1\right| = 3 \Rightarrow |z_1| = \sqrt{9+1} = \sqrt{10}$$

21. Since, $1, z_1, z_2, z_3, \dots, z_{n-1}$ are the n, nth roots of unity.

$$\therefore \quad (z^n - 1) = (z-1)(z-z_1)(z-z_2)(z-z_3)\dots(z-z_{n-1})$$

$$= (z-1)\prod_{r=1}^{n-1}(z - z_r)$$

Taking log on both sides, we get

$$\log_e(z^n - 1) = \log_e(z-1) + \sum_{r=1}^{n-1} \log_e(z - z_r)$$

On differentiating both sides w.r.t.z, we get

$$\frac{nz^{n-1}}{(z^n - 1)} - \frac{1}{(z-1)} = \sum_{r=1}^{n-1} \frac{1}{(z - z_r)}$$

Putting $z = 3$, we get

$$\sum_{r=1}^{n-1} \frac{1}{(3 - z_r)} = \frac{n \cdot 3^{n-1}}{(3^n - 1)} - \frac{1}{2}$$

22. We have, $\quad z = (3 + 7i)(\lambda + i\mu)$

$$= (3\lambda - 7\mu) + i(7\lambda + 3\mu)$$

Since, z is purely imaginary.

$\therefore \quad 3\lambda - 7\mu = 0$

$\Rightarrow \quad \dfrac{\lambda}{\mu} = \dfrac{7}{3}$

$\because \quad \lambda, \mu \in I - \{0\}$

For minimum value $\lambda = 7, \mu = 3$

$\therefore \quad |z|^2 = |(3+7i)(\lambda + i\mu)|^2$

$= |3+7i|^2 |\lambda + i\mu|^2 = 58(\lambda^2 + \mu^2)$

$= 58(7^2 + 3^2)$

$= (58)^2 = 3364$

23. Let $z = \alpha$ be a real roots of equation.

$$z^3 + (3+2i)z + (-1+ia) = 0$$

$\Rightarrow \quad \alpha^3 + (3+2i)\alpha + (-1+ia) = 0$

$\Rightarrow \quad (\alpha^3 + 3\alpha - 1) + i(a + 2\alpha) = 0$

On comparing the real and imaginary parts, we get

$$\alpha^3 + 3\alpha - 1 = 0 \text{ and } a + 2\alpha = 0$$

$\Rightarrow \quad \alpha = -\dfrac{a}{2}$

$\Rightarrow \quad -\dfrac{a^3}{8} - \dfrac{3a}{2} - 1 = 0$

$\Rightarrow \quad a^3 + 12a + 8 = 0$

Let $\quad f(a) = a^3 + 12a + 8$

$\Rightarrow \quad f(-1) < 0$ and $f(0) > 0$

$\therefore \quad a \in (-1, 0)$

24. $CiS\dfrac{\pi}{6} = \cos\dfrac{\pi}{6} + i\sin\dfrac{\pi}{6}$

$= \left(\dfrac{\sqrt{3}+i}{2}\right) = \dfrac{1}{i}\left(\dfrac{-1+i\sqrt{3}}{2}\right) = \dfrac{\omega}{i} = -i\omega$

$\therefore \quad \left(2\,CiS\dfrac{\pi}{6}\right)^m = (-2i\omega)^m = ((-2i\omega)^3)^{m/3} = (8i)^{m/3}$

and $\left(4\,CiS\dfrac{\pi}{4}\right)^n = \left(4\left(\cos\dfrac{\pi}{4} + i\sin\dfrac{\pi}{4}\right)\right)^n = (2\sqrt{2}(1+i))^n$

$= (8(1+i)^2)^{n/2} = (16i)^{n/2}$

Thus, $\quad (8i)^{m/3} = (16i)^{n/2}$

which is satisfy only when $m = 48$ and $n = 24$

$\therefore \quad m + n = 72$

25. We have, $\quad z^2 = \bar{z} \cdot 2^{1-|z|}$

$\Rightarrow \quad z^3 = z \cdot \bar{z} \cdot 2^{1-|z|} = |z|^2 \cdot 2^{1-|z|}$

Taking modulus on both sides, we get

$$|z|^3 = |z|^2 \cdot 2^{1-|z|}$$

$\Rightarrow \quad |z| = 2^{1-|z|}$

$\Rightarrow \quad |z| = 1$

$\Rightarrow \quad z^3 = 1$

$\Rightarrow \quad z = 1, \omega, \omega^2$

But 1 is not imaginary.

Hence, $z = \omega$ or ω^2

Hence, total number of solutions = 2

26. We have, $\quad x^3 - y^3 = 98i$

$\Rightarrow \quad (x-y)^3 + 3xy(x-y) = 98i$

$\Rightarrow \quad (7i)^3 + 3xy(7i) = 98i$

$\Rightarrow \quad -343i + 21xyi = 98i$

$\Rightarrow \quad 21xyi = 441i$

$\Rightarrow \quad xy = 21$

$\Rightarrow \quad a + ib = 21$

$\Rightarrow \quad a = 21, \; b = 0$

$\therefore \quad a + b = 21$

27. We have, $z = 9 + ib$

$\Rightarrow \quad z^2 = 81 - b^2 + 18ib$

and $\quad z^3 = 729 + 243bi - 27b^2 - b^3 i$

Now, $\quad \text{Im}(z^2) = \text{Im}(z^3)$

$\Rightarrow \quad 18b = 243b - b^3$

$\Rightarrow \quad b^3 + 18b - 243b = 0 \Rightarrow b = 15$

$\therefore \quad \dfrac{b}{3} = 5$

28. Let $z = x + iy$,

Then, $\quad z + \sqrt{2}\,|z+1| + i = 0$

$\Rightarrow \quad x + iy + \sqrt{2}\,|x + iy + 1| + i = 0$

$\Rightarrow \quad x + \sqrt{2(x+1)^2 + 2y^2} + (y+1)i = 0$

$\therefore \quad x + \sqrt{2(x+1)^2 + 2y^2} = 0$ and $y + 1 = 0$

$\Rightarrow x + \sqrt{2(x+1)^2 + 2y^2} = 0$ and $y = -1$

$\Rightarrow \quad x + \sqrt{2(x+1)^2 + 2} = 0$

$\Rightarrow \quad 2(x+1)^2 + 2 = x^2$

$\Rightarrow \quad x^2 + 4x + 4 = 0$

$\Rightarrow \quad x = -2$

$\therefore \quad z = -2 - i$

$\therefore \quad |z| = \sqrt{4+1} = \sqrt{5}$

$\Rightarrow \quad |z|^2 = 5$

29. We have, $\quad z^2 + 8\bar{z} = 0$

$\Rightarrow \quad z^2 = -8\bar{z}$

$\Rightarrow \quad |z^2| = |-8\bar{z}|$

$\Rightarrow \quad |z|^2 = 8|\bar{z}| \Rightarrow |z|^2 = 8|z|$

$\Rightarrow \quad |z| = 8 \Rightarrow |z|^2 = 64$

$\Rightarrow \quad z\bar{z} = 64 \Rightarrow \bar{z} = \dfrac{64}{z}$

$\therefore \quad z^2 + 8 \times \dfrac{64}{z} = 0 \Rightarrow z^3 + 512 = 0$

$\Rightarrow \quad z^3 = -512 \Rightarrow z = (-512)^{\frac{1}{3}}$

$\Rightarrow \quad z = -8(1, \omega, \omega^2)$

$\Rightarrow \quad z = -8, -8\omega, -8\omega^2$

Thus, there are 3 solutions.

30. We have, $x = \omega - \omega^2 - 2$

$\Rightarrow \quad x + 2 = \omega - \omega^2$

On squaring both sides, we get

$$(x+2)^2 = (\omega - \omega^2)^2$$

$$\Rightarrow \quad x^2 + 4x + 4 = \omega^2 - 2\omega^3 + \omega^4$$

$$\Rightarrow \quad x^2 + 4x + 4 = (\omega + \omega^2) - 2$$

$$\Rightarrow \quad x^2 + 4x + 4 = -1 - 2$$

$$\Rightarrow \quad x^2 + 4x + 7 = 0$$

Now, $x^4 + 3x^3 + 2x^2 - 11x - 6 = (x^2 + 4x + 7)(x^2 - x - 1) + 1$

$= 1$

31. We have, $|z_1| = |z_2| = |z_3| = 2$

Now, $\quad |z_1 + z_2 + z_3|^2 \geq 0$

$$\Rightarrow \quad (z_1 + z_2 + z_3)(\bar{z}_1 + \bar{z}_2 + \bar{z}_3) \geq 0$$

$$\Rightarrow \quad \Sigma |z_1|^2 + \Sigma(z_1\bar{z}_2 + \bar{z}_1 z_2) \geq 0$$

$$\Rightarrow \quad 2\Sigma |z_1|^2 + \Sigma(z_1\bar{z}_2 + \bar{z}_1 z_2) \geq \Sigma |z_1|^2$$

$$\Rightarrow \quad \Sigma |z_1 + z_2|^2 \geq 3 \times (2)^2$$

$$\Rightarrow |z_1 + z_2|^2 + |z_2 + z_3|^2 + |z_3 + z_1|^2 \geq 12$$

32. We have, $\lambda = \left(\cos\frac{\pi}{2} + i\sin\frac{\pi}{2}\right)\left(\cos\frac{\pi}{2^2} + i\sin\frac{\pi}{2^2}\right)\ldots\infty$

$$= \cos\left(\frac{\pi}{2} + \frac{\pi}{2^2} + \ldots\infty\right) + i\sin\left(\frac{\pi}{2} + \frac{\pi}{2^2} + \ldots\infty\right)$$

$$= \cos\left(\frac{\frac{\pi}{2}}{1 - \frac{1}{2}}\right) + i\sin\left(\frac{\frac{\pi}{2}}{1 - \frac{1}{2}}\right)$$

$$= \cos\pi + i\sin\pi = -1$$

$\therefore \ |100\lambda - 1| = |-100 - 1| = 101$

33. $\because \quad 1 + z + z^2 + z^3 + \ldots + z^{17} = 0$

$$\therefore \quad \frac{1 \cdot (1 - z^{18})}{(1 - z)} = 0$$

$$\Rightarrow \quad 1 - z^{18} = 0, 1 - z \neq 0$$

$$\therefore \quad z^{18} = 1, z \neq 1 \quad \ldots(\text{i})$$

and $\quad 1 + z + z^2 + z^3 + \ldots + z^{13} = 0$

$$\therefore \quad \frac{1 \cdot (1 - z^{14})}{(1 - z)} = 0$$

$$\Rightarrow \quad 1 - z^{14} = 0, 1 - z \neq 0$$

$$\therefore \quad z^{14} = 1, z \neq 1 \quad \ldots(\text{ii})$$

From Eqs. (i) and (ii), we get

$$z^{14} \cdot z^4 = 1 \Rightarrow 1 \cdot z^4 = 1$$

$$\therefore \quad z^4 = 1$$

Then, $\quad z = 1, -1, i, -i$

$\because \quad z \neq 1$

$\therefore \quad z = -1, i, -i$

Hence, only $z = -1$ satisfy both Eqs. (i) and (ii).

$\therefore$ Number of values of z is 1.

34. We have, $\quad z^3 = \bar{z} \quad \ldots(\text{i})$

$$\Rightarrow \quad |z|^3 = |\bar{z}| = |z|$$

$$\Rightarrow \quad |z|(|z|^2 - 1) = 0$$

$$\Rightarrow \quad |z| = 0 \text{ and } |z|^2 = 1$$

Now, $|z|^2 = 1$

$$\Rightarrow \quad z\bar{z} = 1 \Rightarrow \bar{z} = \frac{1}{z}$$

On putting this value in Eq. (i), we get

$$z^3 = \frac{1}{z}$$

$$\Rightarrow \quad z^4 = 1 \quad \ldots(\text{ii})$$

Clearly, Eq. (ii) has 4 solutions.

Therefore, the required number of solutions is 5.

35. Let $\quad z = x + iy$

$$\because \quad |z| = 1 \quad \ldots(\text{i})$$

$$\therefore \quad x^2 + y^2 = 1$$

and $\quad \left|\frac{z}{\bar{z}} + \frac{\bar{z}}{z}\right| = 1$

$$\Rightarrow \quad \left|\frac{x+iy}{x-iy} + \frac{x-iy}{x+iy}\right| = 1$$

$$\Rightarrow \quad \left|\frac{(x+iy)^2 + (x-iy)^2}{x^2 + y^2}\right| = 1$$

$$\Rightarrow \quad \left|\frac{2(x^2 - y^2)}{1}\right| = 1 \quad [\text{from Eq. (i)}]$$

$$\Rightarrow \quad x^2 - y^2 = \pm\frac{1}{2} \quad \ldots(\text{ii})$$

From Eqs. (i) and (ii), we get

$$2x^2 = 1 \pm \frac{1}{2} = \frac{1}{2}, \frac{3}{2}$$

$$\Rightarrow \quad x^2 = \frac{1}{4}, \frac{3}{4}$$

$$\Rightarrow \quad x = \pm\frac{1}{2}, \pm\frac{\sqrt{3}}{2}$$

For $x = \frac{1}{2}, y = \pm\frac{\sqrt{3}}{2}$ $\quad$ [from Eq. (i)]

For $x = -\frac{1}{2}, y = \pm\frac{\sqrt{3}}{2}$ $\quad$ [from Eq. (i)]

For $x = \frac{\sqrt{3}}{2}, y = \pm\frac{1}{2}$ $\quad$ [from Eq. (i)]

For $x = -\frac{\sqrt{3}}{2}, y = \pm\frac{1}{2}$ $\quad$ [from Eq. (i)]

$\therefore$ Solutions are $\frac{1}{2} \pm \frac{i\sqrt{3}}{2}, -\frac{1}{2} \pm \frac{i\sqrt{3}}{2}, \frac{\sqrt{3}}{2} \pm \frac{i}{2}, -\frac{\sqrt{3}}{2} \pm \frac{i}{2}$

Hence, number of solutions is 8.

36. $\because \quad (1+i)^4 = [(1+i)^2]^2$

$$= (1 + i^2 + 2i)^2 = (1 - 1 + 2i)^2$$

$$= 4i^2 = -4 \quad \ldots(\text{i})$$

and $\frac{1-\sqrt{\pi}\,i}{\sqrt{\pi}+i}+\frac{\sqrt{\pi}-i}{1+\sqrt{\pi}\,i}$

$$=\frac{(1-\sqrt{\pi}\,i)(\sqrt{\pi}-i)}{\pi+1}+\frac{(\sqrt{\pi}-i)(1-\sqrt{\pi}\,i)}{1+\pi}$$

$$=\frac{\sqrt{\pi}-i-\pi i-\sqrt{\pi}+\sqrt{\pi}-\pi i-i-\sqrt{\pi}}{\pi+1}$$

$$=\frac{-2\pi i-2i}{\pi+1}=-2i \quad \text{...(ii)}$$

Given, $z=\frac{\pi}{4}(1+i)^4\left(\frac{1-\sqrt{\pi}\,i}{\sqrt{\pi}+i}+\frac{\sqrt{\pi}-i}{1+\sqrt{\pi}\,i}\right)$

$$=\frac{\pi}{4}(-4)(-2i)=2\pi i \quad \text{[from Eqs. (i) and (ii)]}$$

Now, $\left(\frac{|z|}{\text{amp}(z)}\right)=\frac{2\pi}{\pi/2}=4$

37. $\because$ $A^n=1$

$\Rightarrow$ $A=(1)^{1/n}=e^{2\pi r i/n}, r=0,1,2,\ldots,n-1$

$\therefore$ $A=1, e^{2\pi i/n}, e^{4\pi i/n}, e^{6\pi i/n},\ldots, e^{2\pi(n-1)i/n}$

and $(A+1)^n=1 \Rightarrow A+1=(1)^{1/n}=e^{2\pi pi/n}$

$\Rightarrow$ $A=e^{2\pi pi/n}-1=e^{p\pi i/n}\cdot 2i\sin\left(\frac{\pi p}{n}\right)$,

$p=0,1,2,\ldots,n-1$

$\therefore$ $A=0, e^{\pi i/n}\cdot 2i\sin\left(\frac{\pi}{n}\right), e^{2\pi i/n}\,2i\sin\left(\frac{2\pi}{n}\right),\ldots,$

$e^{\pi i(n-1)/n}\cdot 2i\sin\left(\frac{\pi(n-1)}{n}\right)$

For $n=6$,

$e^{4\pi i/n}=e^{4\pi i/6}=e^{2\pi i/3}$

$$=\cos\frac{2\pi}{3}+i\sin\frac{2\pi}{3}=-\frac{1}{2}+\frac{i\sqrt{3}}{2}$$

and $e^{\pi i/n}\cdot 2i\sin\left(\frac{\pi}{n}\right)=e^{\pi i/6}\cdot 2i\sin\left(\frac{\pi}{6}\right)$

$$=\left(\cos\frac{\pi}{6}+i\sin\frac{\pi}{6}\right)\cdot i$$

$$=\left(\frac{\sqrt{3}}{2}+\frac{i}{2}\right)i$$

$$=-\frac{1}{2}+\frac{i\sqrt{3}}{2}$$

Hence, the least value of n is 6.

38. Given, $z_1, z_2, z_3, \ldots, z_{50}$ are the roots of the equation

$\sum_{r=0}^{50}(z)^r=0$, then

$$\sum_{r=0}^{50}(z)^r=(z-z_1)(z-z_2)(z-z_3)\ldots(z-z_{50})$$

$$=\prod_{r=1}^{50}(z-z_r)$$

Taking log on both sides on base e, we get

$$\log_e\left(\sum_{r=0}^{50}(z)^r\right)=\sum_{r=1}^{50}\log_e(z-z_r)$$

On differentiating both sides w.r.t. z, we get

$$\frac{\sum_{r=0}^{50}r(z)^{r-1}}{\sum_{r=0}^{50}(z)^r}=\sum_{r=1}^{50}\frac{1}{(z-z_r)}$$

On putting $z=1$ in both sides, we get

$$\frac{\sum_{r=0}^{50}r}{\sum_{r=0}^{50}1}=\sum_{r=1}^{50}\frac{1}{(1-z_r)}$$

$\Rightarrow$ $\frac{(1+2+3+\ldots+50)}{51}=-\sum_{r=1}^{50}\frac{1}{(z_r-1)}=-(-5\lambda)$ [given]

$\Rightarrow$ $\frac{\frac{50}{2}\times 51}{51}=5\lambda$

$\Rightarrow$ $\lambda=5$

39. $\because$ $\sum_{q=1}^{10}\left(\sin\frac{2q\pi}{11}-i\cos\frac{2q\pi}{11}\right)$

$$=-i\sum_{q=1}^{10}\left(\cos\frac{2q\pi}{11}+i\sin\frac{2q\pi}{11}\right)$$

$$=-i\left\{\sum_{q=0}^{10}\left(\cos\frac{2q\pi}{11}+i\sin\frac{2q\pi}{11}\right)-1\right\}$$

$=-i$ {(sum of 11, 11th roots of unity) -1}

$=-i(0-1)=i$

$\because$ $P=\sum_{p=1}^{32}(3p+2)\left(\sum_{q=1}^{10}\left(\sin\frac{2q\pi}{11}-i\cos\frac{2q\pi}{11}\right)\right)^p$

$$=\sum_{p=1}^{32}(3p+2)(i)^p=3\sum_{p=1}^{32}p(i)^p+2\sum_{p=1}^{32}(i)^p$$

$$=3\sum_{p=1}^{32}p(i)^p+0=3S \text{ (say)}$$

where, $S=\sum_{p=1}^{32}p(i)^p$

$$S=1\cdot i+2\cdot i^2+3\cdot i^3+\ldots+31\cdot i^{31}+32\cdot i^{32}$$

$$iS=1\cdot i^2+2\cdot i^3+\ldots+31\cdot i^{32}+32i^{33}$$

$$(1-i)S=(i+i^2+i^3+\ldots+i^{32})-32i^{33}$$

$$=(0)-32i$$

$\therefore$ $S=-\frac{32i\cdot(1+i)}{(1-i)\cdot(1+i)}$

$$=-16(i-1)=16(1-i)$$

$\therefore$ $P=3S=48(1-i)$

Given, $(1+i)P=n(n!)$

$\Rightarrow$ $(1+i)\cdot 48(1-i)=n(n!)$

$\Rightarrow$ $96=n(n!)$

$\Rightarrow$ $4(4!)=n(n!)$

$\therefore$ $n=4$

40. $\because \quad \frac{1+i}{1-i} = \frac{(1+i)^2}{(1-i)(1+i)} = \frac{1+i^2+2i}{2} = i$

Given, $\left(\frac{1+i}{1-i}\right)^n = \frac{2}{\pi}\sin^{-1}\left(\frac{1+x^2}{2x}\right)$

$\Rightarrow \quad i^n = \frac{2}{\pi}\sin^{-1}\left(\frac{1+x^2}{2x}\right)$

$\Rightarrow \quad \sin^{-1}\left(\frac{1+x^2}{2x}\right) = \frac{\pi}{2}(i)^n$

$\Rightarrow \quad \frac{1+x^2}{2x} = \sin\left(\frac{\pi}{2}(i)^n\right)$ ...(i)

Now, AM $\ge$ GM

$\frac{x+\frac{1}{x}}{2} \ge 1 \Rightarrow \frac{x^2+1}{2x} \ge 1$

$\Rightarrow \quad \sin\left(\frac{\pi}{2}(i)^n\right) \ge 1$

Since, $-1 \le \sin\theta \le 1$

$\therefore \quad \sin\left(\frac{\pi}{2}(i)^n\right) = 1 \Rightarrow n = 4, 8, 12, 16, \ldots$

$\therefore$ Least positive integer, $n = 4$

41. $\text{Re}\left(\frac{z-2i}{z+2i}\right) = 0$

$\Rightarrow \quad \frac{z-2i}{z+2i} + \overline{\left(\frac{z-2i}{z+2i}\right)} = 0$

$\Rightarrow \quad \frac{(z-2i)(\bar{z}-2i)+(z+2i)(\bar{z}+2i)}{(z+2i)(\bar{z}-2i)} = 0$

$\Rightarrow z\bar{z} - 2i\bar{z} - 2iz - 4 + z\bar{z} + 2iz + 2\bar{z}i - 4 = 0$

$\Rightarrow \quad 2|z|^2 = 8$

$\Rightarrow \quad |z|^2 = 4 \Rightarrow |z| = 2$

$\therefore |z-(6+8i)|_{\min} = 10 + 2 = 12$

42. $z = \frac{1+i\cos\theta}{1-2i\cos\theta}$

$= \frac{1+i\cos\theta}{1-2i\cos\theta} \times \frac{1+2i\cos\theta}{1+2i\cos\theta}$

$= \frac{1+2i\cos\theta + i\cos\theta - 2\cos^2\theta}{1+4\cos^2\theta}$

$= \frac{1-2\cos^2\theta}{1+4\cos^2\theta} + i\,\frac{3\cos\theta}{1+4\cos^2\theta}$

$\because z$ is purely imaginary

So, $\frac{1-2\cos^2\theta}{1+4\cos^2\theta} = 0$

$\Rightarrow \quad 1 - 2\cos^2\theta = 0 \quad [\because 1 + 4\cos^2\theta \ne 0]$

$\Rightarrow \quad \cos\theta = \pm\frac{1}{\sqrt{2}}$

So, $\theta = -\frac{3\pi}{4}, -\frac{\pi}{4}, \frac{\pi}{4}, \frac{3\pi}{4}, \frac{5\pi}{4}, \frac{7\pi}{4}$

Sum of all values $= \frac{12\pi}{4} = 3\pi$

43. Let $z = x + iy$

Given, $I_m\left(\frac{z+1}{z+2}\right) = \frac{1}{5}$

$\Rightarrow \quad \text{Im}\left(\frac{(x+1)+iy}{(x+2)+iy}\right) = \frac{1}{5}$

$\Rightarrow \text{Im}\left(\frac{((x+1)+iy)\times((x+2)-iy)}{((x+2)+iy)((x+2)-iy)}\right) = \frac{1}{5}$

$\Rightarrow \quad \frac{y(x+2)-y(x+1)}{(x+2)^2+y^2} = \frac{1}{5}$

and $|z+2| = 1$

$\Rightarrow \quad (x+2)^2 + y^2 = 1$

So, $y(x+2) - y(x+1) = \frac{1}{5} \Rightarrow y = \frac{1}{5}$

$\because \quad (x+2)^2 + y^2 = 1$

$\Rightarrow \quad (x+2)^2 = 1 - \frac{1}{25} = \frac{24}{25}$

$\Rightarrow \quad x + 2 = \frac{2\sqrt{6}}{5}$ ...(i)

$\Rightarrow \quad |\text{Re}\overline{(z+2)}| = |\text{Re}(\bar{z}+2)| = (x+2)$

By using Eq. (i),

$|\text{Re}\overline{(z+2)}| = \frac{2\sqrt{6}}{5}$

44. We have, $z^2 + i\bar{z} = 0$

$\Rightarrow \quad z^2 = -i\bar{z} \Rightarrow |z^2| = |-iz|$

$\Rightarrow \quad |z^2| = |z|$

$\therefore \quad |z|^2 - |z| = 0$

$\Rightarrow \quad |z|(|z|-1) = 0$

$|z| = 0$ [not comparable]

$\therefore \quad |z| = 1$

So, $|z^2| = 1$

45. We have, $z = \frac{1}{2} - 2i$

and $|z+1| = \alpha z + \beta(1+i)$

$\Rightarrow \left|\frac{1}{2} - 2i + 1\right| = \alpha\left(\frac{1}{2} - 2i\right) + \beta(1+i)$

$\Rightarrow \quad \left|\frac{3}{2} - 2i\right| = \frac{\alpha}{2} - 2\alpha i + \beta + \beta i$

$\Rightarrow \quad \left|\frac{3}{2} - 2i\right| = \left(\frac{\alpha}{2} + \beta\right) + (\beta - 2\alpha)i$

$\Rightarrow \quad \sqrt{\frac{9}{4} + 4} = \left(\frac{\alpha}{2} + \beta\right) + (\beta - 2\alpha)i$

$\Rightarrow \quad \beta - 2\alpha = 0$ and $\frac{\alpha}{2} + \beta = \frac{5}{2}$

$\Rightarrow \quad \beta = 2\alpha$ and $\frac{\alpha}{2} + 2\alpha = \frac{5}{2} \Rightarrow \alpha = 1$

Also, $\beta = 2$

$\therefore \quad \alpha + \beta = 1 + 2 = 3$

46. $a + 5b = 42 \Rightarrow b = \dfrac{42 - a}{5}$

So, $(a, b) = \{(2, 8), (7, 7), (12, 6), (17, 5), (22, 4), (27, 3), (32, 2), (37, 1)\}$

$\Rightarrow$ 8 pairs

So, $m = 8$

So, $\sum_{n=1}^{8}(1 - i^{n!}) = \sum_{n=1}^{8} 1 - \sum_{n=1}^{8} i^{n!}$

$= 8 - (i + (-1) + (-1) + 1 + 1 + 1 + 1 + 1)$
$= 8 - (i + 3) = 5 - i = x + iy$

So, $x = 5, y = -1$

Therefore, $x + y + m = 5 - 1 + 8 = 12$

47. Given, $(\bar{z})^2 + |z| = 0$ ... (i)

Let $z = x + iy$

So, $\bar{z} = x - iy$

From Eq. (i), $(x - iy)^2 + |x + iy| = 0$

$\Rightarrow (x^2 - y^2) + \sqrt{x^2 + y^2} - 2xyi = 0$

On equating real and imaginary part from both sides, we get

$2xy = 0$ ...(ii)

and $x^2 - y^2 + \sqrt{x^2 + y^2} = 0$ ...(iii)

From Eq. (i), there are two cases arises.

Case I When $x = 0$ and $y \neq 0$

From Eq. (iii),

$-y^2 + |y| = 0 \Rightarrow |y| = y^2 = |y|^2$

$\Rightarrow$ $y = 0, \pm 1$ but $y \neq 0$

So, $y = \pm 1$

$\therefore$ $z = 0 + i$ or $z = 0 - i$ i.e. $z = i$ or $z = -i$

Case II When $x \neq 0$ and $y = 0$

From Eq. (iii),

$x^2 + |x| = 0$

$\Rightarrow$ $x = 0$ only which is not possible because $x \neq 0$.

Hence, $z = \pm i$ (finally)

Now, $\alpha = i - i = 0$

and $\beta = (i)(-i) = -i^2 = -(-1) = 1$

Therefore, $4(\alpha^2 + \beta^2) = 4(0 + 1) = 4$

48. Given, $|z - 1| = 1$

$(x - 1)^2 + y^2 = 1$ ...(i)

and $(\sqrt{2} - 1)(z + \bar{z}) - i(z - \bar{z}) = 2\sqrt{2}$

$(\sqrt{2} - 1)(2x) - i(2iy) = 2\sqrt{2}$

$[\because z + \bar{z} = 2x, z - \bar{z} = 2yi]$

$2(\sqrt{2} - 1)x + 2y = 2\sqrt{2}$

$(\sqrt{2} - 1)x + y = \sqrt{2}$ ...(ii)

On solving Eqs. (i) and (ii), we get

$x = 1, \dfrac{1}{2 - \sqrt{2}}$

When $x = 1$, then $y = 1$

$\therefore$ $z_2 = 1 + i$

and when $x = \dfrac{1}{2 - \sqrt{2}}$, then $y = \sqrt{2} - \dfrac{1}{\sqrt{2}}$

$\therefore$ $z_1 = 1 + \dfrac{1}{\sqrt{2}} + \dfrac{i}{\sqrt{2}}$

$\therefore$ $|\sqrt{2}z_1 - z_2|^2 = z\left|\sqrt{2}\left(1 + \dfrac{1}{\sqrt{2}}\right) + i - 1 - i\right|^2 = (\sqrt{2})^2 = 2$

49. Given, $z_1 + z_2 = 5$

$\Rightarrow$ $z_1^3 + z_2^3 = 20 + 15i$

$\Rightarrow$ $z_1^3 + z_2^3 = (z_1 + z_2)((z_1 + z_2)^2 - 3z_1z_2)$

$\Rightarrow$ $20 + 15i = 5(5^2 - 3z_1z_2)$

$\Rightarrow$ $4 + 3i = 25 - 3z_1z_2$

$\Rightarrow$ $z_1z_2 = 7 - i$

$\Rightarrow$ $z_1 + z_2 = 5$

$\Rightarrow$ $(z_1 + z_2)^2 = 5^2 \Rightarrow z_1^2 + z_2^2 + 2z_1z_2 = 25$

$\Rightarrow z_1^2 + z_2^2 + 14 - 2i = 25 \Rightarrow z_1^2 + z_2^2 = 11 + 2i$

Squaring both sides,

$(z_1^2 + z_2^2)^2 = (11 + 2i)^2$

$\Rightarrow$ $z_1^4 + z_2^4 + 2(z_1z_2)^2 = 121 - 4 + 44i$

$\Rightarrow$ $z_1^4 + z_2^4 + 2(7 - i)^2 = 117 + 44i$

$\Rightarrow$ $z_1^4 + z_2^4 + 2(49 - 1 - 14i) = 117 + 44i$

$\Rightarrow$ $z_1^4 + z_2^4 = 21 + 72i$

$\therefore$ $|z_1^4 + z_2^4| = \sqrt{21^2 + 72^2} = 75$

50. **Statement I**

We know that

$$\left|\frac{z_1}{|z_1|} + \frac{z_2}{|z_2|}\right| \leq \left|\frac{z_1}{|z_1|}\right| + \left|\frac{z_2}{|z_2|}\right|$$

$$\Rightarrow \left|\frac{z_1}{|z_1|} + \frac{z_2}{|z_2|}\right| \leq \frac{|z_1|}{|z_1|} + \frac{|z_2|}{|z_2|}$$

$$\Rightarrow \left|\frac{z_1}{|z_1|} + \frac{z_2}{|z_2|}\right| \leq 2$$

$$\Rightarrow (|z_1| + |z_2|)\left|\frac{z_1}{|z_1|} + \frac{z_2}{|z_2|}\right| \leq 2(|z_1| + |z_2|)$$

$\therefore$ Statement I is correct.

Statement II

We have, $\dfrac{a}{|y - z|} = \dfrac{b}{|z - x|} = \dfrac{c}{|x - y|}$

$\Rightarrow$ $\dfrac{a^2}{|y - z|^2} = \dfrac{b^2}{|z - x|^2} = \dfrac{c^2}{|x - y|^2} = k$

$\Rightarrow$ $a^2 = k(|y - z|^2) = k(y - z)(\overline{y - z})$

$= k(y - z)(\bar{y} - \bar{z})$

$b^2 = k(|z - x|^2) = k(z - x)(\bar{z} - \bar{x})$

and $c^2 = k(|x - y|^2) = k(x - y)(\bar{x} - \bar{y})$

$\therefore \dfrac{a^2}{y - z} + \dfrac{b^2}{z - x} + \dfrac{c^2}{x - y} = k(\bar{y} - \bar{z}) + k(\bar{z} - \bar{x}) + k(\bar{x} - \bar{y})$

$= k(\bar{y} - \bar{z} + \bar{z} - \bar{x} + \bar{x} - \bar{y})$

$= k(0) = 0$

$\therefore$ Statement II is incorrect.

51. Given, $z^3 + 2z^2 + 2z + 1 = 0$ ...(i)

$$(z + 1)(z^2 + z + 1) = 0$$

$$\Rightarrow \quad z = -1, z^2 + z + 1 = 0$$

$$z = \omega, \omega^2$$

$\because$ Eq. (i) have common roots with

$$z^{1985} + z^{100} + 1 = 0$$

Put $z = -1 \Rightarrow -1 + 1 + 1 = 0 \Rightarrow 1 = 0$ [false]

$\therefore$ -1 is not common root.

Put $z = \omega$

$$\Rightarrow \quad \omega^{1985} + \omega^{100} + 1 = 0$$

$$\Rightarrow \quad \omega^2 + \omega + 1 = 0 \quad \text{[true]}$$

$\therefore$ ω is common root.

Put $z = \omega^2$

$$\Rightarrow \quad \omega^{3970} + \omega^{200} + 1 = 0$$

$$\Rightarrow \quad \omega + \omega^2 + 1 = 0 \quad \text{[true]}$$

$\therefore$ ω^2 is also common root.

Now, number of common roots = 2

52. According to the question,

$$\left|\frac{z_1 - 2z_2}{\frac{1}{2} - z_1\bar{z}_2}\right| = 2 \Rightarrow \frac{|z_1 - 2z_2|}{\left|\frac{1}{2} - z_1\bar{z}_2\right|} = 2$$

[$\because$ modulus is distributive]

$$\Rightarrow \quad |z_1 - 2z_2| = 2\left|\frac{1}{2} - z_1\bar{z}_2\right|$$

Squaring both sides,

$$|z_1 - 2z_2|^2 = |1 - 2z_1\bar{z}_2|^2$$

$$\Rightarrow (z_1 - 2z_2)(\bar{z}_1 - 2\bar{z}_2) = (1 - 2z_1\bar{z}_2)(1 - 2\bar{z}_1 z_2) \quad [\because |z|^2 = z\bar{z}]$$

$$\Rightarrow |z_1|^2 + 4|z_2|^2 - 2\bar{z}_1 z_2 - 2z_1\bar{z}_2$$

$$= 1 - 2\bar{z}_1 z_2 - 2z_1\bar{z}_2 + 4|z_1|^2|z_2|^2$$

$$\Rightarrow |z_1|^2 + 4|z_2|^2 - 4|z_1|^2|z_2|^2 - 1 = 0$$

$$\Rightarrow \quad (|z_1|^2 - 1)(1 - 4|z_2|^2) = 0$$

$$\Rightarrow \quad |z_1| = 1 \text{ and } |z_2| = \frac{1}{2}$$

53. If $|z| \geq 1 \Rightarrow z$ lie out side or on circle $|z| = 1$

$\left|z + \frac{3}{2} + 2i\right| \Rightarrow$ distance of z from $\left(-\frac{3}{2}, -2\right)$

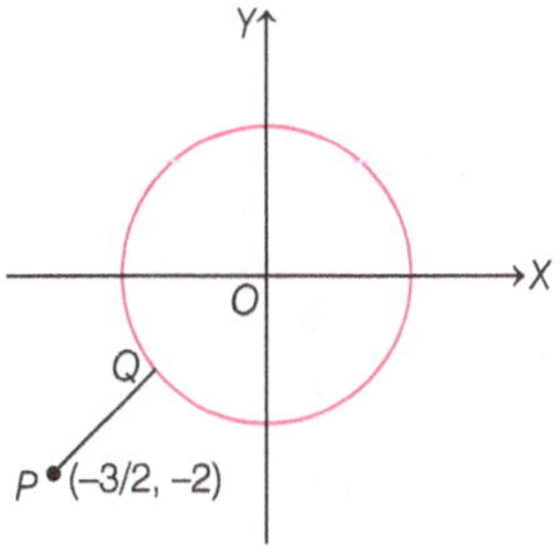

So, minimum value of PQ

$$= PO - QO$$

$$= \sqrt{\left(\frac{-3}{2} - 0\right)^2 + (-2 - 0)^2} - 1$$

$$= \sqrt{\frac{9}{4} + 4} - 1 \quad [\because \cos\theta = 1]$$

$$= \sqrt{\frac{25}{4}} - 1 = \frac{5}{2} - 1 = \frac{3}{2}$$

So, minimum value of $\left|z + \frac{1}{2}(3 + 4i)\right|$ is $\frac{3}{2}$.

54. Given, $|z - i| = |z + i| = |z - 1|$ ...(i)

From Eq. (i), we observe that, geometrically, z will be circumcentre of triangle with vertices $A(1)$, $B(i)$, $C(-i)$ as shown in figure below

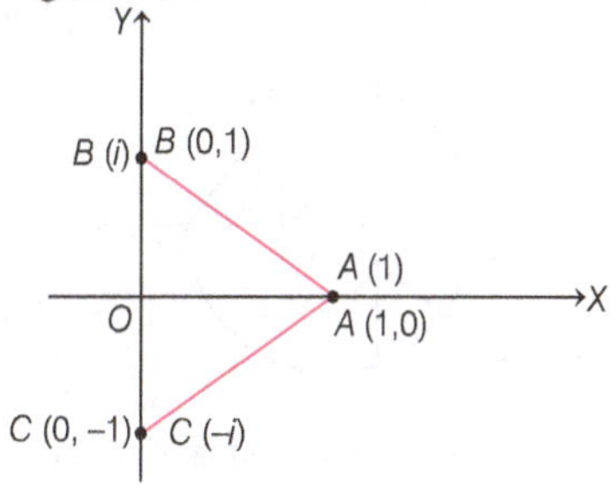

So, only one element exists in the set S.

Hence, $n(S) = 1$

55. $S_1 : \{z \in C : |z| \leq 5\}$

$$\Rightarrow \quad x^2 + y^2 \leq 25$$

$$S_2 = \left\{z \in C : \operatorname{Im}\frac{(z + 1 - \sqrt{3}i)}{1 - \sqrt{3}i} \geq 0\right\}$$

$$\operatorname{Im}\left(\frac{z}{1 - \sqrt{3}i} + \frac{(1 - \sqrt{3}i)}{1 - \sqrt{3}i}\right) \geq 0$$

$$\operatorname{Im}\left(\frac{z}{1 - \sqrt{3}i} + 1\right) \geq 0$$

$$\operatorname{Im}\left(\frac{z}{1 - \sqrt{3}i} \times \frac{1 + \sqrt{3}i}{1 + \sqrt{3}i}\right) \geq 0$$

$$\operatorname{Im}(x + iy)(1 + \sqrt{3}i) \geq 0$$

$$\Rightarrow \quad \sqrt{3}x + y \geq 0, \theta \Rightarrow 120°$$

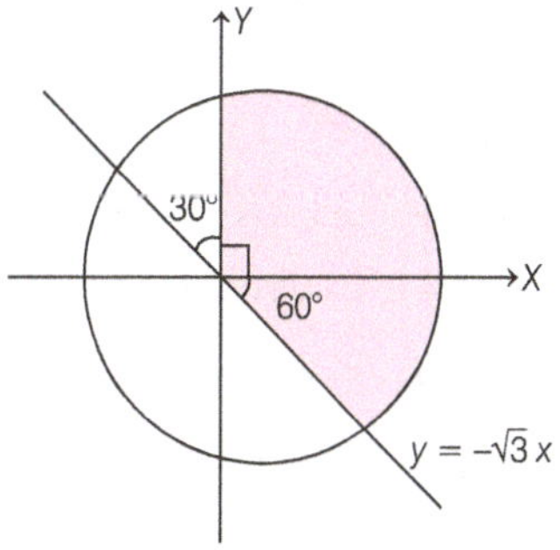

$S_3 : z \in C : \text{Re}(z) \geq 0\} \Rightarrow x \geq 0$

$\therefore \text{Area} = \dfrac{\pi r^2 (150°)}{360} = \pi \times \dfrac{5 \times 5 \times 150}{360}$

$= \pi \dfrac{5 \times 5 \times 5}{12} = \dfrac{125\pi}{12}$

56. $|z - 1| \leq 2,$

$z + \bar{z} + i(z - \bar{z}) \leq 2, \text{Im}(z) \geq 0$

Let $z = x + iy$ and $\bar{z} = x - iy$

$|(x - 1) + iy| \leq 2$

$(x - 1)^2 + y^2 = 4$

Centre of circle (1, 0)

Radius = 2;

$\text{Im}\, z + \bar{z} + i(z - \bar{z}) \leq 2$

$\Rightarrow \quad 2x + i(2iy) \leq 2 \Rightarrow 2x - 2y \leq 2$

$\Rightarrow x - y \leq 1$ and $\text{Im}(z) \geq 0, y \geq 0$

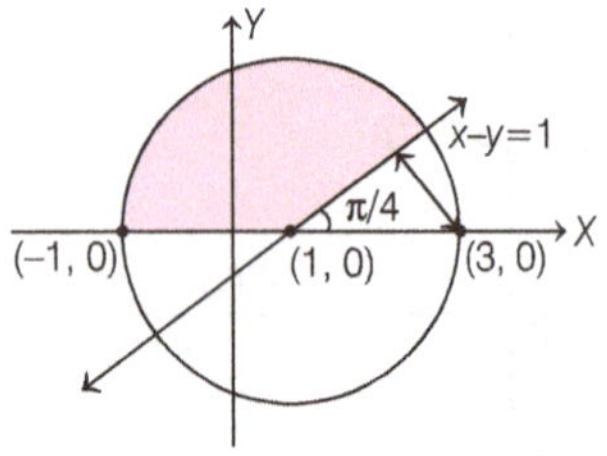

Required = Area of semicircle − Area of sector

$= \dfrac{\pi (r^2)}{2} - \dfrac{\pi r^2 \theta}{360}$

$= \dfrac{\pi (2)^2}{2} - \dfrac{\pi (2)^2 \times 45°}{360°}$

$= 2\pi - \dfrac{\pi}{2} = \dfrac{3\pi}{2}$

57. Given 2 and 6 are the roots of the equation $ax^2 + bx + 1 = 0$

$\therefore \text{Sum of roots} = -\dfrac{b}{a} = 8$

$\text{Product of roots} = \dfrac{1}{a} = 12$

$\Rightarrow \quad a = \dfrac{1}{12}$ so, $b = -\dfrac{2}{3}$

Now, $2a + b = \dfrac{2}{12} - \dfrac{2}{3} = -\dfrac{1}{2}$

and $6a + b = \dfrac{6}{12} - \dfrac{2}{3} = -\dfrac{1}{6}$

Now, $\dfrac{1}{2a + b} + \dfrac{1}{6a + b} = -2 - 6 = -8$

and $\left(\dfrac{1}{2a + b}\right)\left(\dfrac{1}{6a + b}\right) = 12$

$\therefore$ Required quadratic equation is $x^2 + 8x + 12 = 0.$

58. Given, $(\sqrt{3} + \sqrt{2})^x + (\sqrt{3} - \sqrt{2})^x = 10$

Let $(\sqrt{3} + \sqrt{2})^x = t \Rightarrow (\sqrt{3} - \sqrt{2})^x = \dfrac{1}{t}$

$t + \dfrac{1}{t} = 10$

$t^2 - 10t + 1 = 0$

$t = \dfrac{10 \pm \sqrt{96}}{2} = 5 \pm 2\sqrt{6}$

$(\sqrt{3} + \sqrt{2})^x = (\sqrt{3} \pm \sqrt{2})^2$

$x = \pm 2$

$\therefore$ Number of solution = 2

59. $\dfrac{ax^2 + 2(a + 1)x + 9a + 4}{x^2 - 8x + 32} < 0, \forall x \in R$

$\Rightarrow \dfrac{ax^2 + 2(a + 1)x + 9a + 4}{(x - 4)^2 + 16} < 0, \forall\, x \in R$

$\Rightarrow ax^2 + 2(a + 1)x + 9a + 4 < 0, \forall\, x \in R$

coefficient of $x^2 < 0$ and $D < 0$

$a < 0$ and $D < 0$

$\therefore$ No positive integral values of a

Hence, $\quad |S| = 0$

60. $|1 - i|^x = 2^x$

$(\sqrt{2})^x = 2^x$

$2^{\frac{x}{2}} = 2^x \Rightarrow x = 0$

Number of solution $(\alpha) = 1.$

Now, $z = \dfrac{\pi}{4}(1 + i)^4 \left(\dfrac{1 - \sqrt{\pi} i}{\sqrt{\pi} + i} + \dfrac{\sqrt{\pi} - i}{1 + \sqrt{\pi} i}\right)$

$= \dfrac{\pi}{4}(1 + i)^4 \left(\dfrac{1 + \pi + \pi + 1}{(\sqrt{\pi} + i)(1 + \sqrt{\pi} i)}\right)$

$= \dfrac{\pi}{4}(1 + 4i + 6i^2 + 4i^3 + 1)\left(\dfrac{2 + 2\pi}{(\pi + 1)}\right)$

$= \dfrac{\pi}{2} \dfrac{(1 + 4i - 6 - 4i + 1)}{i}$

$= \dfrac{\pi}{2} \dfrac{(-4)}{i} = \dfrac{\pi}{2}\left(\dfrac{4i^2}{i}\right) = 2\pi i \qquad [\because i^2 = -1]$

$z = 2\pi i$

$\beta = \dfrac{|z|}{\arg(z)} = \dfrac{2\pi}{\frac{\pi}{2}} = 4$

Point $(\alpha, \beta) = (1, 4)$

Distance between (α, β) and $4x - 3y - 7 = 0$

$D = \left|\dfrac{4 - 12 - 7}{5}\right| = 3$

61. α and β are roots of equation

$x^2 - \sqrt{6}x + 3 = 0$

$x = \dfrac{\sqrt{6} \pm \sqrt{6 - 12}}{2} = \dfrac{\sqrt{6} \pm \sqrt{6} i}{2} = \dfrac{\sqrt{6}}{2}(1 \pm i)$

$\text{Im}(\alpha) > \text{Im}(\beta)$

$\alpha = \dfrac{\sqrt{6}}{2}(1 + i), \beta = \dfrac{\sqrt{6}}{2}(1 - i)$

$\alpha = \dfrac{\sqrt{6}}{2} \sqrt{2} \cdot e^{i\frac{\pi}{4}} = \sqrt{3}\, e^{i\frac{\pi}{4}}$

$$\alpha^{98} = (\sqrt{3})^{98} (e^{i\,98 \times \frac{\pi}{4}})$$

$$= 3^{49} [e^{i\left(49\frac{\pi}{2}\right)}]$$

$$= 3^{49} \left(0 + i \sin 49 \frac{\pi}{2}\right)$$

$$= i\,(3^{49})$$

$$\therefore \quad \frac{\alpha^{99}}{\beta} + \alpha^{98} = \alpha^{98}\left(\frac{\alpha}{\beta} + 1\right)$$

$$\Rightarrow i\left[3^{49}\left(\frac{1+i}{1-i} + 1\right)\right] = i\,(3)^{49}\left(\frac{1+i+1-i}{1-i}\right)$$

$$= \frac{i}{1-i}(3)^{49}(2)$$

$$= \frac{i}{1-i} \times \left(\frac{1+i}{1+i}\right)(3)^{49}\,(2)$$

$$= \frac{i-1}{1+1} \cdot (3^{49}) \cdot 2$$

$$= 3^{49}(-1+i)$$

$\therefore \quad a = -1, b = 1, n = 49$

$n + a + b = 49$

62. Given, $|z - 1| \le 1$

Let $z = x + iy$

So, $\quad |(x-1) + iy| \le 1$

$\Rightarrow \quad \sqrt{(x-1)^2 + y^2} \le 1$

$\Rightarrow \quad (x-1)^2 + y^2 \le 1 \quad$ ...(i)

Also, $\quad |z - 5| \le |z - 5i|$

$\Rightarrow \quad (x-5)^2 + (y)^2 \le x^2 + (y-5)^2$

$\Rightarrow \quad -10x \le -10y \Rightarrow x \ge y \quad$ ...(ii)

On solving Eqs. (i) and (ii), we get

$(x-1)^2 + x^2 = 1$

$\Rightarrow \quad 2x^2 - 2x = 0$

$\Rightarrow \quad x(x-1) = 0$

$\Rightarrow \quad x = 0$ or 1

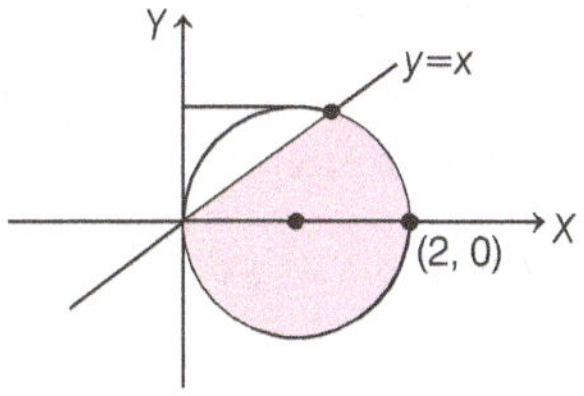

$\therefore \quad y = 0$ or 1

Points (0, 0), (1, 0), (2, 0), (1, 1), (1, – 1)

So, $0 + 1 + 4 + 1 + 1 + 1 + 1 = 9$

[as, $z_1 = 0 + 0i, z_2 = 1 + 0i, z_3 = 2 + 0i, z_4 = 1 + i, z_5 = 1 - i$]

63. $(x+2)^2 + (y-3)^2 = 1$

$L_1 : x + y - 1 = 0$

$L_2 : x - y + 4 = 0$

On solving circle and L_1, we get

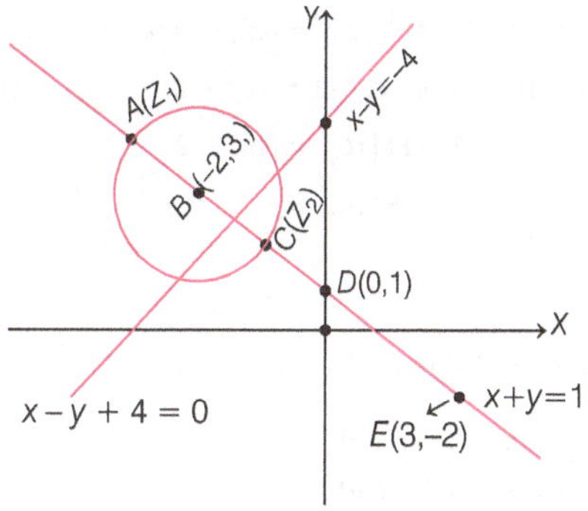

$$A\left(0 + (2\sqrt{2}+1)\left(\frac{-1}{\sqrt{2}}\right), 1 + (2\sqrt{2}+1)\frac{1}{\sqrt{2}}\right)$$

$$A\left(\frac{-(2\sqrt{2}+1)}{\sqrt{2}}, \frac{3\sqrt{2}+1}{\sqrt{2}}\right)$$

On solving circle and C_2, we get $C\left(\frac{-3}{2}, \frac{5}{2}\right)$

$$|z_1|^2 + 2|z_2|^2 = \frac{(2\sqrt{2}+1)^2}{2} + \frac{(3\sqrt{2}+1)^2}{2} + 2\left(\frac{9}{4} + \frac{25}{4}\right)$$

$$= \frac{28 + 10\sqrt{2} + 34}{2} = 31 + 5\sqrt{2}$$

$\alpha = 31, \beta = 5$

Hence, $\alpha + \beta = 36$

64. Given, α and $\frac{1}{\alpha}$ are two complex numbers.

Also, α lie on $|z - z_0|^2 = 4$

and $\quad \frac{1}{\alpha}$ lie on $|z - z_0|^2 = 16$

Now, α satisfies $\quad |z - z_0|^2 = 4$

$\Rightarrow \quad |\alpha - z_0|^2 = 4$

$\Rightarrow \quad (\alpha - z_0)\,\overline{(\alpha - z_0)} = 4 \quad [\because z\bar{z} = |z|^2]$

$\Rightarrow \quad (\alpha - z_0)(\bar{\alpha} - \bar{z}_0) = 4 \quad [\because \overline{z_1 \pm z_2} = \bar{z}_1 \pm \bar{z}_2]$

$\Rightarrow \quad \alpha\bar{\alpha} - \alpha\bar{z}_0 - \bar{\alpha}z_0 - z_0\bar{z}_0 = 4$

$\Rightarrow |\alpha|^2 - \alpha\bar{z}_0 - \bar{\alpha}z_0 + |\bar{z}_0|^2 = 4$

$\Rightarrow \quad |\alpha|^2 - \alpha\bar{z}_0 - \bar{\alpha}z_0 + 2 = 4$

[Given, $z_0 = 1 + i \therefore |z_0|^2 = 1^2 + 1^2 = 2$]

$\Rightarrow \quad \alpha\bar{z}_0 + \alpha z_0 = |\alpha|^2 - 2 \quad$ ...(i)

Also, $\frac{1}{\alpha}$ satisfies $\quad |z - z_0|^2 = 16$

$$\Rightarrow \quad \left|\frac{1}{\alpha} - z_0\right|^2 = 16$$

$$\Rightarrow \quad \left|\frac{1 - \alpha z_0}{\alpha}\right|^2 = 16$$

$\Rightarrow \quad (1 - \alpha z_0)\,\overline{(1 - \alpha z_0)} = 16\,|\bar{\alpha}|^2$

$\Rightarrow \quad (1 - \alpha z_0)(1 - \bar{\bar{\alpha}}\,\bar{z}_0) = 16\,|\alpha|^2 \quad [\because |z|^2 = |\bar{z}|^2]$

$\Rightarrow \quad (1 - \bar{\alpha}z_0)(1 - \alpha\bar{z}_0) = 16\,|\alpha|^2 \quad [\because \bar{\bar{z}} = z]$

$\Rightarrow (1 - \alpha\bar{z}_0 - \bar{\alpha}z_0 + \alpha\bar{\alpha}\, z_0\bar{z}) = 16|\alpha|^2$

$\Rightarrow \quad 1 - 16|\alpha|^2 + |\alpha|^2 \cdot |z_0|^2 = \alpha\bar{z}_0 + \bar{\alpha}z_0$

$\Rightarrow \quad 1 - 16|\alpha|^2 + |\alpha|^2 \cdot 2 = |\alpha|^2 - 2$ [from Eq. (i)]

$\Rightarrow \quad 1 - 14|\alpha|^2 = |\alpha|^2 - 2$

$\Rightarrow \quad 15|\alpha|^2 = 3$

$\Rightarrow \quad |\alpha|^2 = \frac{1}{5}$

Hence, $100|\alpha|^2 = 100 \times \frac{1}{5} = 20$

65. $z = \frac{1 + 2i\sin\theta}{1 - i\sin\theta} \times \frac{1 + i\sin\theta}{1 + i\sin\theta}$

$= \frac{(1 - 2\sin^2\theta) + i(3\sin\theta)}{1 + \sin^2\theta}$

According to the question,

$\text{Re}(z) = 0$

$\Rightarrow \quad 1 - 2\sin^2\theta = 0$

$\Rightarrow \quad \sin\theta = \pm\frac{1}{\sqrt{2}}$

$\because \quad \theta \in (0, 2\pi)$

$\therefore \quad \theta = \frac{\pi}{4}, \frac{3\pi}{4}, \frac{5\pi}{4}, \frac{7\pi}{4}$

$\Rightarrow \quad A = \left\{\frac{\pi}{4}, \frac{3\pi}{4}, \frac{5\pi}{4}, \frac{7\pi}{4}\right\}$

$\therefore \quad \text{Sum} = 4\pi$

66. We have, point w_1 obtained by rotation of z_1 about origin through 90° in anti-clockwise direction and point w_2 obtained by rotation of z_2 about origin through 90° in clockwise direction.

$\Rightarrow \quad w_1 = z_1 i$

and $\quad w_2 = z_2(-i)$

$w_1 = (5 + 4i)i$

and $\quad w_2 = (3 + 5i)(-i)$

$\Rightarrow \quad w_1 = -4 + 5i$ and $w_2 = 5 - 3i$

$w_1 - w_2 = -4 + 5i - 5 + 3i = -9 + 8i$

$\therefore$ Principal argument $= \pi - \tan^{-1}(8/9)$.

67. Let $w = \left(\frac{z - \bar{z} + z\bar{z}}{2 - 3z + 5\bar{z}}\right), z \in C,$

where $z = x + iy$

Since, $\text{Re}(z) = 3$

$\Rightarrow \quad z = 3 + iy \Rightarrow \bar{z} = 3 - iy$

$w = \left(\frac{z - \bar{z} + z\bar{z}}{2 - 3z + 5\bar{z}}\right)$

$= \left(\frac{(3 + iy) - (3 - iy) + (3 + iy)(3 - iy)}{2 - 3(3 + iy) + 5(3 - iy)}\right)$

$= \left(\frac{2iy + 9 + y^2}{2 - 9 - 3iy + 15 - 5iy}\right)$

$= \left(\frac{(9 + y^2) + i(2y)}{8 - 8iy}\right)$

$= \frac{[(9 + y^2) + i(2y)](1 + iy)}{8(1 - iy)(1 + iy)}$

$= \frac{(9 + y^2) + i(2y) + iy(9 + y^2) - 2y^2}{8(1 + y^2)}$

$\therefore \quad w = \frac{(9 + y^2 - 2y^2) + i\{2y + 9y + y^3\}}{8(1 + y^2)}$

$\text{Re}(w) = \frac{9 - y^2}{8(1 + y^2)}$

$= \frac{1}{8}\left[\frac{10 - (1 + y^2)}{1 + y^2}\right] = \frac{1}{8}\left[\frac{10}{1 + y^2} - 1\right]$

Since, $\quad 1 + y^2 \in [1, \infty)$

$\Rightarrow \quad \frac{1}{1 + y^2} \in (0, 1] \Rightarrow \frac{10}{1 + y^2} \in (0, 10]$

$\Rightarrow \quad \frac{10}{1 + y^2} - 1 \in (-1, 9]$

$\Rightarrow \quad \frac{1}{8}\left(\frac{10}{1 + y^2} - 1\right) \in \left(-\frac{1}{8}, \frac{9}{8}\right]$

$\because \quad \frac{1}{8}\left(\frac{10}{1 - y^2} - 1\right) \in (\alpha, \beta]$ [Given]

$\therefore \quad \alpha = -\frac{1}{8}, \beta = \frac{9}{8}$

Now, $\quad 24(\beta - \alpha) = 24\left(\frac{9}{8} + \frac{1}{8}\right) = 24\left(\frac{10}{8}\right)$

$= 30$

68. Given that

$S = \{z \in C : \bar{z} = i(z^2 + Re(\bar{z}))\}$

Let $z = x + iy, x \in R, y \in R$

So, $\bar{z} = x - iy$

Now, $\quad \bar{z} = i(z^2 + Re(\bar{z}))$

$\Rightarrow \quad x - iy = i(x^2 - y^2 + 2ixy + Re(x - iy))$

$\Rightarrow \quad x - iy = i(x^2 - y^2 + x + i(2xy))$

Now, comparing both sides, we get

$x = -2xy$ ...(i)

and $\quad -y = x^2 - y^2 + x$ ...(ii)

From Eq. (i),

$x(1 + 2y) = 0 \Rightarrow x = 0,\ y = -\frac{1}{2}$

On putting $x = 0$ in Eq. (ii), we get

$y^2 = y \Rightarrow y = 0, 1$

If $y = -\frac{1}{2} \Rightarrow -\left(-\frac{1}{2}\right) = x^2 - \frac{1}{4} + x$

$\Rightarrow \quad \frac{1}{4} + \frac{1}{2} = x^2 + x \Rightarrow \frac{3}{4} = x^2 + x$

$\Rightarrow \quad 4x^2 + 4x - 3 = 0$

$\Rightarrow \quad (2x + 3)(2x - 1) = 0$

$\Rightarrow \quad x = -\frac{3}{2}$ and $x = \frac{1}{2}$

Thus, (0, 0), (0, 1), $\left(-\frac{3}{2}, -\frac{1}{2}\right), \left(\frac{1}{2}, -\frac{1}{2}\right)$.

All the points belongs to S.

So, $\sum_{z \in S} |z|^2 = 0 + 1 + \left(\frac{9}{4} + \frac{1}{4}\right) + \left(\frac{1}{4} + \frac{1}{4}\right) = 1 + \frac{5}{2} + \frac{1}{2} = \frac{8}{2} = 4$

$\therefore \sum_{z \in S} |z|^2 = 4$

69. We have, $A = \{z \in C : \text{Re}(a + \bar{z}) > \text{Im}(\bar{a} + z)\}, a \in C$

and $B = \{z \in C : \text{Re}(a + \bar{z}) < \text{Im}(\bar{a} + z)\}$

Let $a = x_1 + iy_1$ and $z = x + iy$

For set A, $\text{Re}(a + \bar{z}) > \text{Im}(\bar{a} + z)$

$\Rightarrow \text{Re}(x_1 + iy_1 + x - iy) > \text{Im}(x_1 - iy_1 + x + iy)$

$\Rightarrow \text{Re}((x_1 + x) + i(y_1 - y)) > \text{Im}((x_1 + x) + i(y - y_1))$

$\Rightarrow (x_1 + x) > (y - y_1)$

Take, $x_1 = 2, y_1 = 10, x = -12, y = 0$, for these values given inequality is not valid.

So, $S1$ is false.

Again for set B,

$\text{Re}(a + \bar{z}) < \text{Im}(\bar{a} + z)$

$\Rightarrow \text{Re}(x_1 + iy_1 + x - iy) < \text{Im}(x_1 - iy_1 + x + iy)$

$\Rightarrow \text{Re}((x_1 + x) + i(y_1 - y)) < \text{Im}((x_1 + x) + (y - y_1))$

$\Rightarrow x_1 + x < y - y_1$

For $x_1 = -2, y_1 = -10, x = 12, y = 0$, the given inequality is not valid.

So, $S2$ is also false.

Thus, $S1$ and $S2$ both false.

70. We have, $S = \left\{z = x + iy : \frac{2z - 3i}{4z + 2i} \text{ is a real number}\right\}$

$$\frac{2z - 3i}{4z + 2i} \in R$$

$$\Rightarrow \frac{2(x + iy) - 3i}{4(x + iy) + 2i} \in R$$

$$\Rightarrow \frac{2x + i(2y - 3)}{4x + i(4y + 2)} \in R$$

$$\Rightarrow \frac{2x + i(2y - 3)}{4x + i(4y + 2)} \times \frac{4x - i(4y + 2)}{4x - i(4y + 2)} \in R$$

$$\Rightarrow \frac{8x^2 + 8y^2 - 8y - 6 + i[-2x(4y + 2) + 4x(2y - 3)]}{(4x)^2 + (4y + 2)^2} \in R$$

The expression will be real if imaginary part is 0.

$$-2x(4y + 2) + 4x(2y - 3) = 0$$

$$\Rightarrow x = 0$$

Also, $(4x)^2 + (4y + 2)^2 \neq 0$

$$\Rightarrow y + x^2 + y^2 \neq \frac{-1}{4}$$

If $x = 0$, then $y \neq -\frac{1}{2}$

$$y \in \left(-\infty, -\frac{1}{2}\right) \cup \left(-\frac{1}{2}, \infty\right)$$

71. We have, $z = x + iy$ such that $\frac{2z - 3i}{2z + i}$ is purely imaginary.

Now, $\left(\frac{2z - 3i}{2z + i}\right) + \left(\overline{\frac{2z - 3i}{2z + i}}\right) = 0$

$$\Rightarrow \frac{2z - 3i}{2z + i} + \frac{2\bar{z} + 3i}{2\bar{z} - i} = 0$$

$$\Rightarrow (2z - 3i)(2\bar{z} - i) + (2\bar{z} + 3i)(2z + i) = 0$$

$$\Rightarrow \{4|z|^2 - 6i\bar{z} - 2iz - 3\} + \{4|z|^2 + 6iz + 2i\bar{z} - 3\} = 0$$

$$\Rightarrow 8|z|^2 - 4i\bar{z} + 4iz - 6 = 0$$

$$\Rightarrow 8(x^2 + y^2) - 4i(x - iy) + 4i(x + iy) - 6 = 0$$

$$\Rightarrow 8(x^2 + y^2) - 4ix - 4y + 4ix - 4y - 6 = 0$$

$$\Rightarrow 8(x^2 + y^2) - 8y - 6 = 0$$

$$\Rightarrow 4(x^2 + y^2) - 4y - 3 = 0$$

[Given that $x + y^2 = 0 \Rightarrow x = -y^2$]

$$\Rightarrow 4(y^4 + y^2) - 4y = 3$$

$$\Rightarrow y^4 + y^2 - y = \frac{3}{4}$$

Hence, required answer is $\frac{3}{4}$.

72. Let $z = x + iy$

$\Rightarrow z^2 = x^2 - y^2 + 2ixy$

$\therefore az^2 + bz = a(x^2 - y^2 + 2ixy) + b(x + iy)$

$= a(x^2 - y^2) + bx + 2aixy + biy$

$\because \text{Re}(az^2 + bz) = a$

$\Rightarrow a(x^2 - y^2) + bx = a$

$\Rightarrow x^2 - y^2 + \frac{b}{a}x = 1$ ...(i)

and $bz^2 + az = b(x^2 - y^2 + 2ixy) + a(x + iy)$

$= b(x^2 - y^2) + ax + 2bixy + aiy$

$\because \text{Re}(bz^2 + az) = b$

$\Rightarrow b(x^2 - y^2) + ax = b$

$\Rightarrow x^2 - y^2 + \frac{a}{b}x = 1$ ...(ii)

On subtracting Eq. (ii) from Eq. (i), we get

$$\frac{b}{a}x - \frac{a}{b}x = 0 \Rightarrow \left(\frac{b}{a} - \frac{a}{b}\right)x = 0$$

$$\Rightarrow x = 0 \text{ or } \frac{b}{a} - \frac{a}{b} = 0$$

$$\Rightarrow b^2 - a^2 = 0 \Rightarrow a = \pm b$$

$$\Rightarrow a = -b \text{ (since } a \neq b)$$

From Eq. (i), when $x = 0$, then

$$0 - y^2 = 1 \Rightarrow y^2 = -1$$

$$\Rightarrow y \in \phi \Rightarrow z \in \phi$$

has no solution.

when, $a = -b$, then $x^2 - y^2 - x = 1$

has infinite many solutions.

73. We have, $\left|\dfrac{1+ai}{b+i}\right| = 1$

$\Rightarrow \quad |1+ai| = |b+i|$

$\Rightarrow \quad \sqrt{1+a^2} = \sqrt{b^2+1}$

$\Rightarrow \quad 1+a^2 = b^2+1$

$\Rightarrow \quad a^2 = b^2$

$\Rightarrow \quad a = \pm b$

$\Rightarrow \quad a = -b \qquad [\because ab < 0] \ldots\text{(i)}$

Again, $a+ib$ lies on $|z-1| = |2z|$

$\therefore \quad |a+ib-1| = |2(a+ib)|$

$\Rightarrow \quad |a-ia-1| = |2(a-ia)|$

$\Rightarrow \quad |(a-1)-ia| = 2|a-ia|$

$\Rightarrow \quad \sqrt{(a-1)^2+(-a)^2} = 2\sqrt{(a)^2+(-a)^2}$

$\Rightarrow \quad a^2-2a+1+a^2 = 8a^2$

$\Rightarrow \quad 6a^2+2a-1 = 0$

$\Rightarrow \quad a = \dfrac{-2\pm\sqrt{4+24}}{12}$

$= \dfrac{-2\pm 2\sqrt{7}}{12} = \dfrac{-1\pm\sqrt{7}}{6}$

Now, when $a = \dfrac{-1+\sqrt{7}}{6}$, then $[a] = 0$ and when $a = \dfrac{-1-\sqrt{7}}{6}$, then $[a] = -1$.

$\therefore \quad \dfrac{1+[a]}{4b} = \dfrac{1+0}{4b}$ or $\dfrac{1-1}{4b} = \dfrac{1}{4b}$ or 0

74. Let $z = x+iy$

We have, $\left|\dfrac{z-2}{z-3}\right| = 2 \Rightarrow \left|\dfrac{x+iy-2}{x+iy-3}\right| = 2$

$\Rightarrow \quad \dfrac{\sqrt{(x-2)^2+y^2}}{\sqrt{(x-3)^2+y^2}} = 2$

$\Rightarrow \quad (x-2)^2+y^2 = 4[(x-3)^2+y^2]$

$\Rightarrow \quad x^2-4x+4+y^2 = 4[x^2-6x+9+y^2]$

$\Rightarrow \quad x^2+y^2-\dfrac{20}{3}x+\dfrac{32}{3} = 0$

$\therefore$ Centre of circle is $\left(-\dfrac{1}{2}\times\left(\dfrac{-20}{3}\right), -\dfrac{1}{2}\times(0)\right)$ i.e. $\left(\dfrac{10}{3}, 0\right)$

And radius of circle $= \sqrt{\left(\dfrac{10}{3}\right)^2+(0)^2-\dfrac{32}{3}}$

$= \sqrt{\dfrac{100}{9}-\dfrac{32}{3}}$

$= \sqrt{\dfrac{100-96}{9}} = \dfrac{2}{3}$

$\therefore \quad \alpha = \dfrac{10}{3}, \beta = 0, \gamma = \dfrac{2}{3}$

So, $3(\alpha+\beta+\gamma) = 3\left(\dfrac{10}{3}+0+\dfrac{2}{3}\right) = 10+2 = 12$

75. We have non-zero complex numbers z_1 and z_2.

Let $z_1 = x_1+iy_1; z_2 = x_2+iy_2, x_1, x_2, y_1, y_2 \in R$

$\therefore z_1 z_2 = (x_1+iy_1)(x_2+iy_2)$

$= x_1x_2+ix_1y_2+iy_1x_2+i^2y_1y_2$

$= (x_1x_2-y_1y_2)+i(x_1y_2+y_1x_2) \qquad [\because i^2 = -1]$

Now, $\operatorname{Re}(z_1\cdot z_2) = 0$

$\Rightarrow \quad x_1x_2-y_1y_2 = 0$

$\Rightarrow \quad x_1x_2 = y_1y_2 \qquad \ldots\text{(i)}$

And $\quad z_1+z_2 = (x_1+iy_1)+(x_2+iy_2)$

$= (x_1+x_2)+i(y_1+y_2)$

Now, $\operatorname{Re}(z_1+z_2) = 0$

$\Rightarrow \quad x_1+x_2 = 0$

$\Rightarrow \quad x_1 = -x_2 \qquad \ldots\text{(ii)}$

From Eqs. (i) and (ii), we get

$y_1y_2 = -x_2^2$

$\because \quad x_2 \in R$

$\therefore \quad -x_2^2 < 0 \Rightarrow y_1, y_2 < 0$

i.e. $y_1 > 0$ and $y_2 < 0$ or $y_1 < 0$ and $y_2 > 0$

$\Rightarrow \operatorname{Im}(z_1) > 0$ and $\operatorname{Im}(z_2) < 0$

or $\operatorname{Im}(z_1) < 0$ and $\operatorname{Im}(z_2) > 0$

76. We have, $z = \dfrac{i-1}{\cos\dfrac{\pi}{3}+i\sin\dfrac{\pi}{3}} = \dfrac{-1+i}{\cos\dfrac{\pi}{3}+i\sin\dfrac{\pi}{3}}$

$= \dfrac{\sqrt{2}\left(-\dfrac{1}{\sqrt{2}}+\dfrac{1}{\sqrt{2}}i\right)}{\cos\dfrac{\pi}{3}+i\sin\dfrac{\pi}{3}} = \dfrac{\sqrt{2}\left(\cos\dfrac{3\pi}{4}+i\sin\dfrac{3\pi}{4}\right)}{\cos\dfrac{\pi}{3}+i\sin\dfrac{\pi}{3}}$

$= \dfrac{\sqrt{2}\,e^{i3\pi/4}}{e^{i\pi/3}} = \sqrt{2}\,e^{i\left(\frac{3\pi}{4}-\frac{\pi}{3}\right)} = \sqrt{2}\,e^{i\frac{5\pi}{12}}$

$= \sqrt{2}\left(\cos\dfrac{5\pi}{12}+i\sin\dfrac{5\pi}{12}\right)$

Alternate Solution

$$z = \frac{i-1}{\cos\frac{\pi}{3}+i\sin\frac{\pi}{3}} = \frac{i-1}{\frac{1}{2}+\frac{\sqrt{3}}{2}i}\times\frac{\frac{1}{2}-\frac{\sqrt{3}}{2}i}{\frac{1}{2}-\frac{\sqrt{3}}{2}i}$$

$$= \frac{\frac{\sqrt{3}-1}{2}+\frac{\sqrt{3}+1}{2}i}{\left(\frac{1}{2}\right)^2-\left(\frac{\sqrt{3}}{2}i\right)^2} = \frac{\sqrt{3}-1}{2}+\frac{\sqrt{3}+1}{2}i$$

Here, $r\cos\theta = \dfrac{\sqrt{3}-1}{2}$, $r\sin\theta = \dfrac{\sqrt{3}+1}{2}$

$\therefore \quad \tan\theta = \dfrac{\sqrt{3}+1}{\sqrt{3}-1} \Rightarrow \theta = \dfrac{5\pi}{12}$

and $\quad r^2 = 2 \Rightarrow r = \sqrt{2}$

$\therefore \quad z = \sqrt{2}\left(\cos\dfrac{5\pi}{12}+i\sin\dfrac{5\pi}{12}\right)$

77. **Decoding the Question**

By De-moivre's formula, mathematical statement for any real number x, we have

$$(\cos x + \sin x)^n = \cos(nx) + i\sin(nx)$$

Given, $(1-\sqrt{3}i)^{200} = 2^{199}(p+iq)$

$\Rightarrow \left[2\left(\frac{1}{2}-\frac{\sqrt{3}}{2}\right)i\right]^{200} = 2^{199}(p+iq)$

$\Rightarrow \frac{2^{200}}{2^{199}}\left[\cos\frac{\pi}{3} - i\sin\frac{\pi}{3}\right]^{200} = p+iq$

$\Rightarrow 2\left[\cos\frac{200\pi}{3} + i\sin\left(-\frac{200\pi}{3}\right)\right] = p+iq$

(using De-moivre's theorem) [$\because \sin(-\theta) = -\sin\theta$]

$\Rightarrow 2\left[-\frac{1}{2} - i\frac{\sqrt{3}}{2}\right] = p+iq$

$\Rightarrow -1-\sqrt{3}i = p+iq$

So, $p=-1, q=-\sqrt{3}$

Let $x_1 = p+q+q^2 = (-1)+(-\sqrt{3})+(-\sqrt{3})^2 = 2-\sqrt{3}$

and $x_2 = p-q+q^2 = (-1)-(-\sqrt{3})+(-\sqrt{3})^2 = 2+\sqrt{3}$

Now, sum of roots $= x_1+x_2 = 4$

and product of roots $= x_1x_2 = 1$

Hence, the required equation whose roots are x_1 and x_2 is given by

$$x^2-(x_1+x_2)x+x_1x_2 = 0$$

$\Rightarrow x^2-4x+1=0$

78. Let $w = z+\frac{1}{z} = 4e^{i\theta}+\frac{1}{4}e^{-i\theta}$

$\Rightarrow w = \frac{17}{4}\cos\theta + i\frac{15}{4}\sin\theta$

So, locus of w is ellipse

$$\frac{x^2}{\left(\frac{17}{4}\right)^2}+\frac{y^2}{\left(\frac{15}{4}\right)^2}=1$$

Locus of z is circle $x^2+y^2=16$

So, intersect at 4 points.

79. Given, $\left|\frac{z-2i}{z+i}\right| = 2, z \neq -i$

Let's suppose $z = x+iy$

So, $\left|\frac{x+iy-2i}{x+iy+i}\right| = 2$

$\Rightarrow \left|\frac{x+i(y-2)}{x+i(y+1)}\right| = 2$

$\Rightarrow |x+i(y-2)| = 2|x+i(y+1)|$

So, $\sqrt{x^2+(y-2)^2} = 2\sqrt{x^2+(y+1)^2}$

Now, squaring both the sides, we get

$$x^2+y^2-4y+4 = 4(x^2+y^2+2y+1)$$

$\Rightarrow 3x^2+3y^2+12y=0$

or $x^2+y^2+4y=0$

$\Rightarrow x^2+y^2+4y+4=4$

$\Rightarrow x^2+(y+2)^2=4$

$\therefore$ Centre $=(0,-2)$

80. In cartesian plane, circle has centre $A\left(\frac{1}{2},\frac{3}{2}\right)$ and radius 1 units and $P(z_1) = (1,1)$

Let $Q(z_2) = (h,k)$

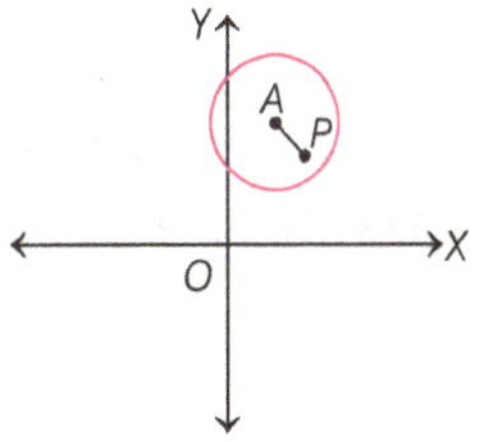

Now, $|z_1-z_0| = AP = \sqrt{\left(1-\frac{1}{2}\right)^2+\left(1-\frac{3}{2}\right)^2} = \frac{1}{\sqrt{2}}$

$\therefore |z_2-z_0| = \frac{1}{|z_1-z_0|} = \sqrt{2}$

Now, slope of AP, $\tan\theta = \frac{\frac{3}{2}-1}{\frac{1}{2}-1} = -1$

$\therefore \sin\theta = \frac{1}{\sqrt{2}}, \cos\theta = \frac{-1}{\sqrt{2}}$

Since b, z_0, z_1, z_2 are collinear.

$\therefore A, P, Q$ are collinear.

Using parametric form of line for Q,

$$\frac{h-\frac{1}{2}}{\cos\theta} = \pm\sqrt{2}, \frac{k-\frac{3}{2}}{\sin\theta} = \pm\sqrt{2}$$

$\Rightarrow \frac{h-\frac{1}{2}}{\left(-\frac{1}{\sqrt{2}}\right)} = \pm\sqrt{2}, \frac{k-\frac{3}{2}}{\left(\frac{1}{\sqrt{2}}\right)} = \pm\sqrt{2}$

$\Rightarrow h = -\frac{1}{2}$ or $\frac{3}{2}$ and $k = \frac{5}{2}$ or $\frac{1}{2}$

$\therefore Q = \left(-\frac{1}{2},\frac{5}{2}\right)$ or $\left(\frac{3}{2},\frac{1}{2}\right)$

Now, $(OQ)^2 = \left(\frac{-1}{2}\right)^2+\left(\frac{5}{2}\right)^2$ or $\left(\frac{3}{2}\right)^2+\left(\frac{1}{2}\right)^2$

i.e. $(OQ)^2 = \frac{13}{2}$ or $\frac{5}{2}$

$\Rightarrow |z_2|^2 = \frac{13}{2}$ or $\frac{5}{2}$

$\therefore$ Similar value of $|z_2|^2 = \frac{5}{2}$

81. Given, $z_1 = 2 + 3i, z_2 = 3 + 4i$

$$S = \{z \in C : |z - z_1|^2 - |z - z_2|^2 = |z_1 - z_2|^2\}$$

Let $z = x + iy$

$\therefore \quad |z - z_1| = |(x + iy) - (2 + 3i)|$

$= \sqrt{(x-2)^2 + (y-3)^2}$

$\therefore \quad |z - z_2| = |(x + iy) - (3 + 4i)|$

$= \sqrt{(x-3)^2 + (y-4)^2}$

and $|z_1 - z_2| = |(2 + 3i) - (3 + 4i)|$

$= |-1 - i| = \sqrt{1+1} = \sqrt{2}$

$\therefore \ |z - z_1|^2 - |z - z_2|^2 = |z_1 - z_2|^2$

$\Rightarrow \quad [(x-2)^2 + (y-3)^2] - [(x-3)^2 + (y-4)^2] = 2$

$\Rightarrow (x^2 + y^2 - 4x - 6y + 13) - (x^2 + y^2 - 6x - 8y + 25) = 2$

$\Rightarrow \quad 2x + 2y = 14$

$\Rightarrow \quad x + y = 7$

$\Rightarrow \quad \dfrac{x}{7} + \dfrac{y}{7} = 1$

x-intercept = y-intercept = 7

Sum of intercept on axes = 14

82. Let $f(x) = x|x-1| + |x+2| + \alpha$

$\therefore \ f(x) = 0$

$\Rightarrow \ x|x-1| + |x+2| + \alpha = 0$

$\Rightarrow \quad x|x-1| + |x+2| = -\alpha$

Now, $x|x-1| + |x+2|$

$$= \begin{cases} x^2 + 2 & x \ge 1 \\ -x^2 + 2x + 2 & -2 \le x < 1 \\ -x^2 - 2 & x < -2 \end{cases}$$

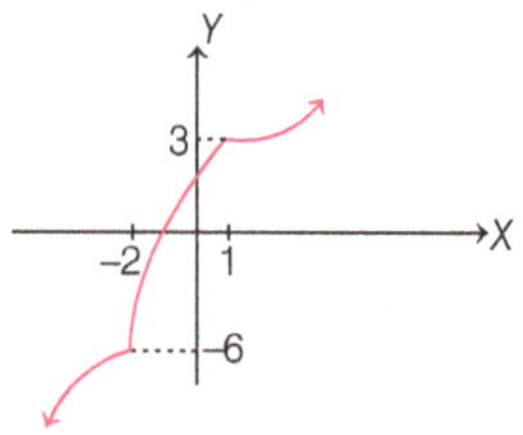

Thus, $-\alpha \in R$

Hence, the set of all $\alpha \in R$ for which the eqution $x|x-1| + |x+2| + a = 0$ has exactly one real root is $(-\infty, \infty)$.

83. Let $f(x) = 2x^2 - 8x + k$.

Since, one root lies in the interval (1, 2) and other in (2, 3), then

$$f(1) > 0, f(2) < 0, f(3) > 0$$

Now, $\quad f(1) > 0$

$\Rightarrow \quad k > 6, \ f(2) < 0$

$\Rightarrow \quad k < 8$ and $f(3) > 0$

$\Rightarrow \quad k > 6$

$\therefore \quad k \in (6, 8)$

So, integral value of $k = 7$.

Hence, there is only one integral value of k.

84. Given equation involving GIF is

$$x^2 - 4x + [x] + 3 = x[x]$$

$\Rightarrow \quad x^2 - 4x + 3 = x[x] - [x]$

$\Rightarrow \quad (x-1)(x-3) = [x](x-1)$

$\Rightarrow \quad (x-1)\{(x-3) - [x]\} = 0$

$\Rightarrow \quad (x-1) = 0$ or $(x-3) = [x]$

$\Rightarrow \quad x = 1$ or $x - 3 = [x] \Rightarrow x - [x] = 3$

$\Rightarrow \quad \{x\} = 3,$

where $\{\cdot\}$ represents fractional part function.

As we know that $0 \le \{x\} < 1$

So, $\{x\} = 3$ is not possible.

So, only one solution $x = 1$ in $(-\infty, \infty)$.

85. Given that $S = \left\{z \in C - \{i, 2i\} : \dfrac{z^2 + 8iz - 15}{z^2 - 3iz - 2} \in R\right\}$

Now, $\quad \dfrac{z^2 + 8iz - 15}{z^2 - 3iz - 2} \in R$

$\Rightarrow \quad 1 + \dfrac{11iz - 13}{z^2 - 3iz - 2} \in R$

Let $\quad z = \alpha - \dfrac{13}{11} i \in S$ [given]

So, this implies, $(z^2 - 3iz - 2)$ is imaginary.

Now, put, $z = x + iy \Rightarrow \{x^2 - y^2 + 3y - 2 + (2xy - 3x)i\} = 0$

[if z is imaginary $\Rightarrow$ Re $z = 0$]

$\therefore \quad x^2 - y^2 + 3y - 2 = 0$

$\Rightarrow \quad x^2 = y^2 - 3y + 2 = (y-2)(y-1)$

Since, $z = \alpha - \dfrac{13}{11} i$

So, $\quad x = \alpha, y = -\dfrac{13}{11}$

$\therefore \quad \alpha^2 = \left(-\dfrac{13}{11} - 2\right)\left(\dfrac{-13}{11} - 1\right)$

$= \left(\dfrac{-35}{11}\right) \times \left(\dfrac{-24}{11}\right)$

$\alpha^2 = \dfrac{24 \times 35}{121}$

$242\alpha^2 = 242 \times \dfrac{24 \times 35}{121} = 48 \times 35 = 1680$

86. Given, $\quad z = 1 + i \Rightarrow \bar{z} = 1 - i$

and $\quad z_1 = \dfrac{1 + i\bar{z}}{\bar{z}(1 - z) + \dfrac{1}{z}}$

$= \dfrac{1 + i(1 - i)}{(1 - i)(1 - 1 - i) + \dfrac{1}{1 + i}}$

$= \dfrac{2 + i}{\dfrac{-3i - 1}{2}} = \dfrac{4 + 2i}{-3i - 1}$

$z_1 = \dfrac{-(4 + 2i)(3i - 1)}{(3i)^2 - (1)^2}$

$\Rightarrow \quad z_1 = \dfrac{-12i + 4 - 6i^2 + 2i}{-9-1} = \dfrac{-10i + 10}{-10} = \dfrac{-10(i-1)}{-10}$

$\Rightarrow \quad z_1 = i - 1 = -1 + i$

$\therefore \quad \arg(z_1) = \dfrac{3\pi}{4} \qquad \left[\because \arg(z_1) = \tan^{-1}\left(\dfrac{b}{a}\right)\right]$

Hence, $\dfrac{12}{\pi}\arg(z_1) = \dfrac{12}{\pi} \times \dfrac{3\pi}{4} = 9$

87. Let $\alpha = 8 - 14i$, $A = \left\{z \in c : \dfrac{\alpha z - \bar{\alpha}\bar{z}}{z^2 - (\bar{z})^2 - 112i} = 1\right\}$

and $B = \{z \in c : |z + 3i| = 4\}$

Let $z = a + ib$

Now, on putting $z = a + ib$ and $8 - 14i = \alpha$ in A, we get

$(8-14i)(a+ib) - (8+14i)(a-ib) = (a+ib)^2 - (a-ib)^2 - 112i$

$\Rightarrow \quad i4(4b - 7a) = i(4ab - 112)$

$\Rightarrow \quad 4b - 7a = ab - 28 \qquad \text{...(i)}$

Rewriting Eq. (i) as,

$4b - ab = 7a - 28 \Rightarrow b = -7$

Again, if we rewrite Eq. (i) as,

$4b - ab = 7a - 28$

$\Rightarrow \quad 4b + 28 = 7a + ab \Rightarrow a = 4$

So, elements of A can be seen as $4 + ib$ and $a - 7i$ types.

Elements of $B = \{z \in c : |z + 3i| = 4\}$

So, elements from the set $A \cap B$ can be seen as, $4 - 3i$ and $-7i$

Because, $\quad B = \{z \notin c : |z + 3i| = 4\}$

$\Rightarrow |a + ib + 3i| = 4 \Rightarrow a^2 + (b+3)^2 = 16$

For, $a = 4, b = -3 \quad b = -7, a = 0$

So, $\sum_{z \in A \cap B} (\text{Re}\, z - \text{Im}\, z) = [4 - (-3)] + [0 - (-7)] = 7 + 7 = 14$

88. Given, equation of circle is

$|z - \alpha|^2 + |z - \beta|^2 = 2\lambda$

$\therefore \quad 2\lambda = |\alpha - \beta|^2 \qquad \text{...(i)}$

For circle, $|z - z_1|^2 + |z - z_2|^2 = |z_1 - z_2|^2$

$\therefore$ Radius, $\quad r = \dfrac{|z_1 - z_2|}{2} = \dfrac{|\alpha - \beta|}{2} = \sqrt{\lambda - 1}$

$\Rightarrow \quad |\alpha - \beta| = 2\sqrt{\lambda - 1}$

$\Rightarrow \quad |\alpha - \beta|^2 = 4(\lambda - 1)$

$\Rightarrow \quad 2\lambda = 4(\lambda - 1) \qquad$ [using Eq. (i)]

$\Rightarrow \quad 2\lambda = 4 \Rightarrow \lambda = 2$

$\Rightarrow \quad |\alpha - \beta|^2 = 4 \Rightarrow |\alpha - \beta| = 2$

89. $z = 2 + 3i$

$z^5 + (\bar{z})^5 = (2+3i)^5 + (2-3i)^5$

$= (T_1 + T_2 + T_3 + T_4 + T_5 + T_6)$
$\quad + (T_1 - T_2 + T_3 - T_4 + T_5 - T_6)$

$= 2(T_1 + T_3 + T_5)$

$= 2({}^5C_0 2^5 (3i)^0 + {}^5C_2 2^3 (3i)^2 + {}^5C_4 2 (3i)^4)$

$= 2(32 - 10 \times 8 \times 9 + 5 \times 2 \times 81)$

$= 2(842 - 720) = 2 \times 122 = 244$

90. Given, $\quad \bar{z}_1 = i\bar{z}_2$

$\Rightarrow \quad \bar{z}_1 / \bar{z}_2 = i$

$\Rightarrow \quad z_1 / z_2 = -i$

$\Rightarrow \quad z_1 = -iz_2$

$\Rightarrow \quad \arg(z_1) = -\dfrac{\pi}{2} + \arg(z_2) \qquad \text{... (i)}$

Also, $\quad \arg\left(\dfrac{z_1}{\bar{z}_2}\right) = \pi$

$\arg(z_1) - \arg(\bar{z}_2) = \pi$

$\arg(z_1) + \arg(z_2) = \pi \qquad \text{... (ii)}$

On substituting value of $\arg(z_1)$ in Eq. (ii), we get

$-\dfrac{\pi}{2} + \arg(z_2) + \arg(z_2) = \pi$

$\Rightarrow \quad \arg(z_2) = \dfrac{3\pi}{4}; \arg(z_1) = -\dfrac{\pi}{2} + \dfrac{3\pi}{4} = \dfrac{\pi}{4}$

91. Given that

$A = \{z \in C : 1 \le |z - (1+i)| \le 2\}$

and $\quad B = \{z \in A : |z - (1-i)| = 1\}$.

Here, A represents all those points lying inside the region of circle having radius greater than or equal to 1 or less than or equal to 2 and B represents all these points lying inside the circle having radius 1.

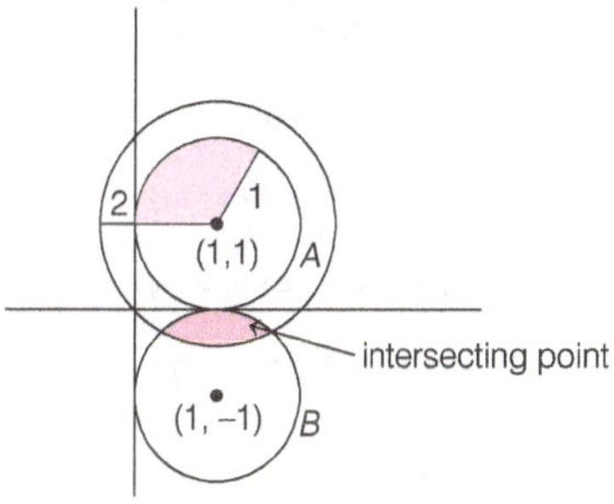

Clearly, from the above diagram, the set B has infinite point in it.

So, B is an infinite set.

92. $\alpha \in (\pi, 2\pi)$ and $\beta \in (\pi, 2\pi)$

$\dfrac{1 - i\sin\alpha}{1 + 2i\sin\alpha} + \dfrac{1 + i\sin\alpha}{1 - 2i\sin\alpha} = 0$

$\left[\because \dfrac{1 - i\sin\alpha}{1 + 2i\sin\alpha} \text{ is purely imaginary}\right]$

$\Rightarrow \quad 1 - 2\sin^2\alpha = 0$

$\Rightarrow \quad \alpha = \dfrac{5\pi}{4} \text{ or } \dfrac{7\pi}{4}$

$\therefore \quad \dfrac{1 + i\cos\beta}{1 - 2i\cos\beta} - \dfrac{1 - i\cos\beta}{1 + 2i\cos\beta} = 0 \left[\because \dfrac{1 + i\cos\beta}{1 - 2i\cos\beta} \text{ is purely real}\right]$

$\Rightarrow \quad 2\cos\beta + \cos\beta = 0$

$\therefore \quad \beta = \dfrac{3\pi}{2}$

$\therefore \quad (\alpha, \beta) = \left(\dfrac{5\pi}{4}, \dfrac{3\pi}{2}\right) \text{ or } \left(\dfrac{7\pi}{4}, \dfrac{3\pi}{2}\right)$

$\therefore \quad z_{\alpha\beta} = (1 - i) \text{ or } (-1 - i)$

$\therefore \sum_{(\alpha,\beta)\in S} \left(iz_{\alpha\beta} + \frac{1}{i\bar{z}_{\alpha\beta}} \right) = i + 1 + \frac{1}{i-1} + 1 - i - \frac{1}{i+1}$

$= 2 + \frac{-i+1+1+i}{-2} = 1$

93. **Decoding the Question**

The equation of circle whose centre is (x_0, y_0) i.e., z_0 and radius r is $(x - x_0)^2 + (y - y_0)^2 = r^2$ or $|z - z_0| = r$

$\therefore$ If $z = a + ib$, then $\arg z = \theta = \tan^{-1}\left(\frac{b}{a}\right)$

Given, $S_n = \left\{ z \in C : |z - 3 + 2i| = \frac{n}{4} \right\}$ represents a circle with centre $C_1(3, -2)$ and radius $r_1 = n/4$.

Also, $T_n = \left\{ z \in C : |z - 2 + 3i| = \frac{1}{n} \right\}$ also represent a circle with centre $C_2(2, -3)$ and radius $r_2 = 1/n$

Case I Since, $S_n \cap T_n = \phi$ [given]

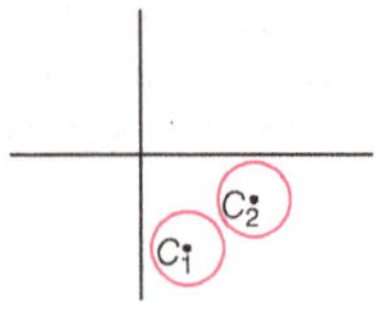

Thus, $C_1C_2 > r_1 + r_2$

$\Rightarrow \sqrt{(3-2)^2 + (-2+3)^2} > \frac{n}{4} + \frac{1}{n} \Rightarrow \sqrt{2} > \frac{n^2 + 4}{4n}$

$\Rightarrow \quad n^2 - 4\sqrt{2}n + 4 < 0 \Rightarrow n = 2\sqrt{2} \pm 2$

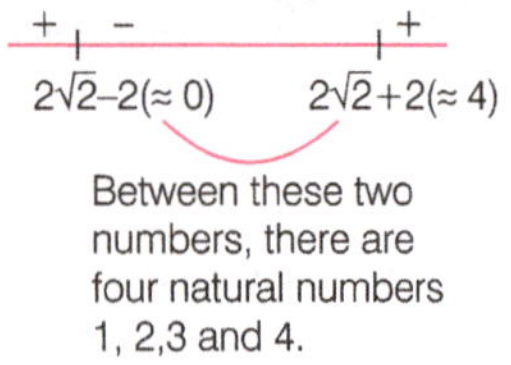

Thus, we get 4 values of n.

Case II

Since, $S_n \cap T_n = \phi$

$\Rightarrow \quad C_1C_2 < |r_1 - r_2| \Rightarrow \sqrt{2} < \left| \frac{n}{4} - \frac{1}{n} \right|$

$\Rightarrow \quad 4\sqrt{2} < \frac{|n^2 - 4|}{n}$ $[\because 4\sqrt{2} \approx 5.6]$

Clearly, the above relation hold for $n \geq N$.

Thus, here n may take infinite values $\geq N$.

94. **Decoding the Question**

For cube roots of unity

$\because x^3 = 1 \Rightarrow x^3 - 1 = 0$

$(x - 1)(x^2 + x - 1) = 0 \Rightarrow x = 1 \text{ or } x^2 + x - 1 = 0$

$x = \frac{-1 \pm \sqrt{1-4}}{2}; \ x = \frac{-1 + i\sqrt{3}}{2}, \frac{-1 - i\sqrt{3}}{2}$ and 1

$\omega = \frac{-1 + i\sqrt{3}}{2}, \omega^2 = \frac{-1 - i\sqrt{3}}{2}$ and $\omega^2 + \omega = -1$

Given, $x^4 + x^2 + 1 = 0$

$\Rightarrow \quad (x^2 + x + 1)(x^2 - x + 1) = 0$

$\Rightarrow \quad x^2 + x + 1 = 0 \text{ or } x^2 - x + 1 = 0$

$\Rightarrow \quad x = \frac{-1 \pm i\sqrt{3}}{2}$

or $\quad x = \frac{1 \pm i\sqrt{3}}{2}$

$\Rightarrow \quad x = \omega, \omega^2$

or $\quad x = -\omega, -\omega^2$

$\therefore \quad x = \pm\omega, \pm\omega^2$

Therefore, $\alpha^{1011} + \alpha^{2022} - \alpha^{3033} = 1 + 1 - 1 = 1$

[when $x = \alpha = \omega$ or ω^2, $\because \omega^3 = 1$]

$\alpha^{1011} + \alpha^{2022} - \alpha^{3033} = -1 + 1 - (-1)$

[when $x = \alpha = -\omega$ or $-\omega^2$]

$= 1$

95. $v = |z|^2 + |z - 3|^2 + |z - 6i|^2$

Let $z = x + iy$

$v = x^2 + y^2 + (x-3)^2 + y^2 + x^2 + (y-6)^2$

$= 3x^2 + 3y^2 - 6x - 12y + 45$

$= 3[(x-1)^2 + (y-2)^2 + 10]$

$\therefore \quad v_0 = 3 \times 10 = 30$ at $x = 1, y = 2$

$\therefore \quad z_0 = 1 + 2i$

$\therefore \quad |2z_0^2 - \bar{z}_0^3 + 3|^2 + v_0^2$

$= |2(1 + 4i - 4) - (1 - 6i - 12 + 8i) + 3|^2 + 900$

$= |8 + 6i|^2 + 900$

$= 100 + 900 = 1000$

96. We know that, $|z - z_1| + |z - z_2| \geq |z_1 - z_2|$

where $z_1 = (3\sqrt{2}, 0)$ and $z_2 = (0, p\sqrt{2})$

Now, distance between two points z_1 and z_2, which is minimising and distance given by $5\sqrt{2}$.

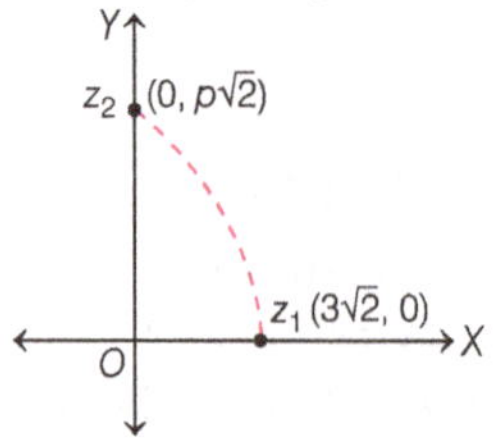

According to question,

$|z_1 - z_2| = 5\sqrt{2}$

$\Rightarrow \quad \sqrt{(3\sqrt{2})^2 + (p\sqrt{2})^2} = 5\sqrt{2}$

$\Rightarrow \quad \sqrt{18 + 2p^2} = 5\sqrt{2}$

$\Rightarrow \quad 18 + 2p^2 = 50$ [on squaring both sides]

$\Rightarrow \quad p^2 = 16$

$\Rightarrow \quad p = \pm 4$

Thus, the value of p is 4.

97. $|z-(4+3i)|=2$ respresents a circle with centre (4, 3) and radius 2 units.

$|z-(0+i0)|+|z-(4+i0)|=6$ represents an ellipse with foci (0, 0) and (4, 0) and the length of major axis equals 6 and length of semi-major axis $2\sqrt{5}$ and (4, 2) lies inside the both curve.

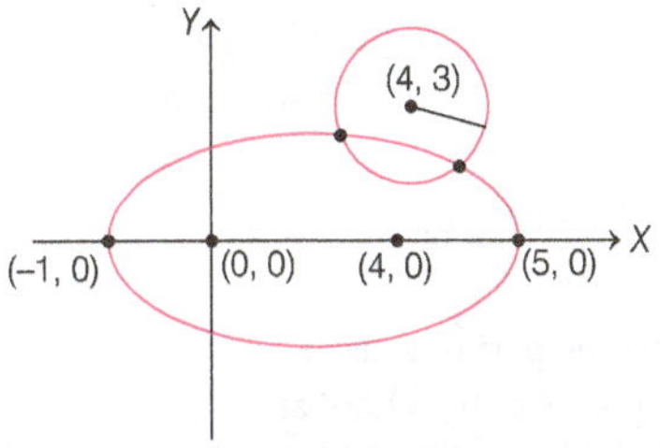

$\therefore$ Number of point of intersection = 2

98. The equation of circle that passes through the points z_1, z_2 and z_3 is $x^2+y^2=25$

Coordinates of z_1, z_2 and z_3 are (3, 4), (4, 3) and (0, 5) respectively.

Slope of $z_2\,z_3=\dfrac{5-3}{0-4}=-\dfrac{1}{2}$

Slope of $z\,z_1\times$ slope of $z_2\,z_3=-1$

[$\because zz_1$ is perpendicular to $z_2\,z_3$]

$\therefore$ Slope of $zz_1=2$

Equation of line $zz_1: y-4=2(x-3) \Rightarrow y=2x-2$

Substitute the value of y in equation of circle

$$x^2+(2x-2)^2=25$$

$$\Rightarrow \quad x^2+4x^2+4-8x=25$$

$$\Rightarrow \quad (x-3)(5x+7)=0 \Rightarrow x=3 \text{ or } -\frac{7}{5}$$

If $x=3$, then $y=4$ [not possible as $z\neq z_1$]

If $x=-\dfrac{7}{5}$, then $y=-\dfrac{14}{5}-2\Rightarrow\dfrac{-24}{5}$

Coordinate of z is $\left(-\dfrac{7}{5},-\dfrac{24}{5}\right)$.

$$\text{Argument}=-\left[\pi-\tan^{-1}\left|\frac{y}{x}\right|\right]=-\pi+\tan^{-1}\left|\frac{24}{7}\right|$$

99. $S=\{z=x+iy:|z-1+i|\geq|z|, |z|<2, |z+i|=|z-1|\}$

Case I $\quad |z-1+i|\geq|z|$

$$\Rightarrow \quad |x+iy-1+i|\geq|x+iy|$$

$$\Rightarrow \quad |x-1+i(y+1)|\geq|x+iy|$$

$$\Rightarrow \quad \sqrt{(x-1)^2+(y+1)^2}\geq\sqrt{x^2+y^2}$$

$$\Rightarrow \quad -2x+2y+2\geq 0 \Rightarrow -x+y+1\geq 0$$

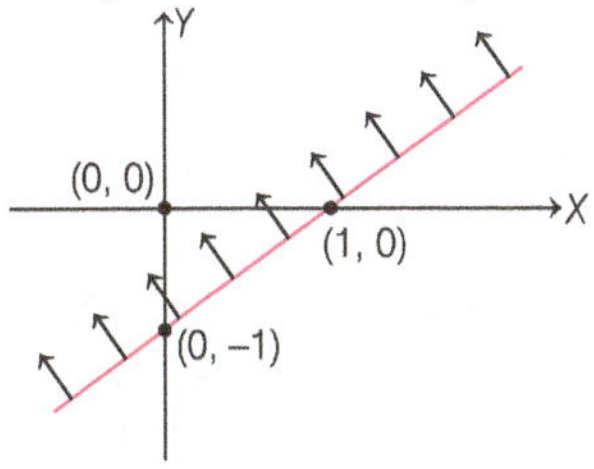

Case II $\quad |z|<2 \Rightarrow |x+iy|<2$

$$\Rightarrow \sqrt{x^2+y^2}<2 \Rightarrow x^2+y^2<4$$

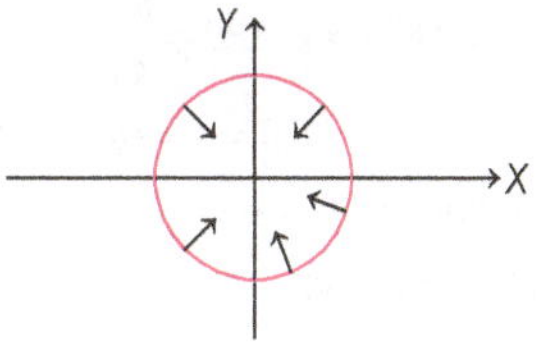

Case III $\quad |z+i|=|z-1|$

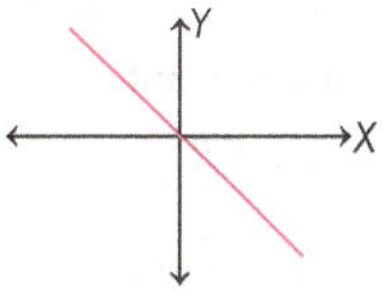

$$\Rightarrow \quad |x+iy+i|=|x+iy-1|$$

$$\Rightarrow \quad \sqrt{x^2+(y+1)^2}=\sqrt{(x-1)^2+y^2}$$

$$\Rightarrow \quad 2y=-2x \Rightarrow x+y=0$$

From Cases I, II and III,

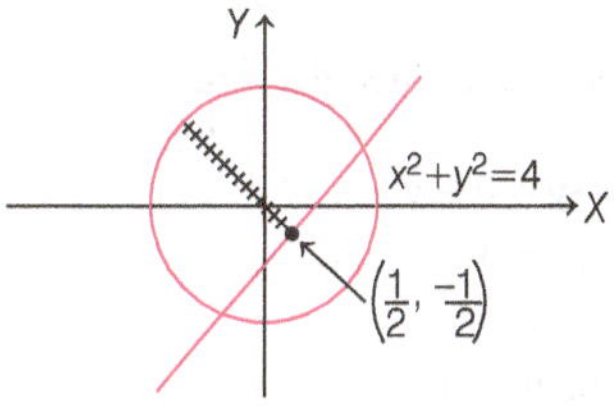

So, $\quad w=2x+iy\in S$

$\therefore \quad 2x\leq\dfrac{1}{2}\Rightarrow x\leq\dfrac{1}{4}$ ...(i)

Now, $\quad (2x)^2+(2x)^2<4$

$$x^2<\frac{1}{2}\Rightarrow x^2-\left(\frac{1}{\sqrt{2}}\right)^2<0$$

$\Rightarrow \quad x\in\left(\dfrac{-1}{\sqrt{2}},\dfrac{1}{\sqrt{2}}\right)$ ... (ii)

From Eqs. (i) and (ii),

$$x\in\left(-\frac{1}{\sqrt{2}},\frac{1}{4}\right]$$

100. Let $\arg(z-1)-\arg(z+1)=\dfrac{\pi}{4}$

$\therefore |z|=3$ represents a circle having radius 3 and centre at $z=0$, i.e. at (0, 0).

Now, $\arg(z-1)-\arg(z+1)=\dfrac{\pi}{4}$

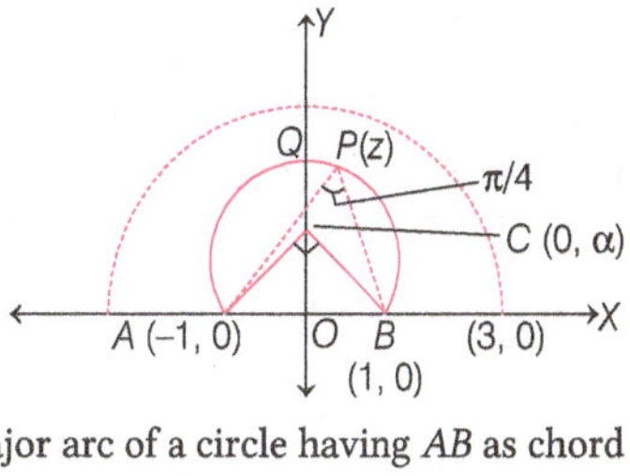

z is on major arc of a circle having AB as chord as shown in above figure.

$$\angle ACB = 2\angle APB$$

and $\angle ACO = \angle OCB$

$\therefore$ $\angle OCB = \angle APB = \dfrac{\pi}{4}$

$\Rightarrow$ $OC = OB = 1 = \alpha$

In right ΔOCB, radius $= BC = \sqrt{2}$

$\therefore$ $OQ = \alpha + \text{radius} = 1 + \sqrt{2}$

Another circle of radius 3 and centre (0, 0) does not intersect the circle of radius $\sqrt{2}$ and centre $(0, \sqrt{2})$.

Hence, there is no common point.

101. Let $z = x + iy, x, y \in R$

Given, $\bar{z} = iz^2$

$\Rightarrow$ $x - iy = i(x + iy)^2$

$\Rightarrow$ $x - iy = i(x^2 - y^2 + 2ixy)$

$\Rightarrow$ $x - iy = -2xy + i(x^2 - y^2)$

On equating real and imaginary parts from both sides, we get

$$x = -2xy, \ -y = x^2 - y^2$$

$\Rightarrow x(1 + 2y) = 0 \Rightarrow x = 0$ or $y = -\dfrac{1}{2}$

At $x = 0$, $-y = 0 - y^2$

$\Rightarrow$ $y - y^2 = 0$

$\Rightarrow$ $y = 0, 1$

Coordinates (0, 0) (0, 1).

At $y = \dfrac{-1}{2}$, $\dfrac{1}{2} = x^2 - \dfrac{1}{4}$

$\Rightarrow$ $x^2 = \dfrac{3}{4}$

$\Rightarrow$ $x = \pm\dfrac{\sqrt{3}}{2}$

Coordinates $\left(\dfrac{\sqrt{3}}{2}, \dfrac{-1}{2}\right)\left(\dfrac{-\sqrt{3}}{2}, \dfrac{-1}{2}\right)$

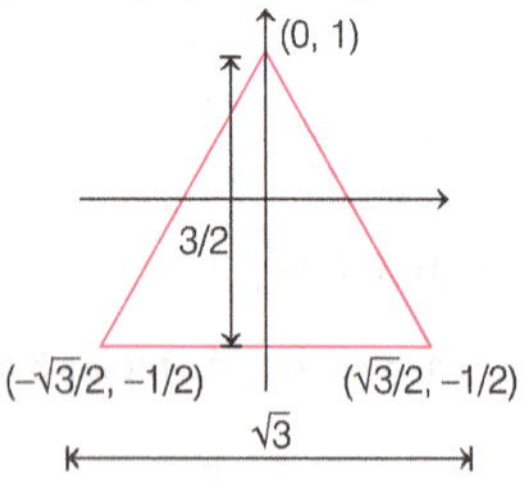

$\therefore$ Area $= \dfrac{1}{2} \times b \times h = \dfrac{1}{2} \times \sqrt{3} \times \dfrac{3}{2} = \dfrac{3\sqrt{3}}{4}$ sq. units

102. **Decoding the Question**

If $z = x + iy$, then $|z|^2 = x^2 + y^2$

Given, $A = \left\{z \in C : \left|\dfrac{z+1}{z-1}\right| < 1\right\}$

and $B = \left\{z \in C : \arg\left(\dfrac{z-1}{z+1}\right) = \dfrac{2\pi}{3}\right\}$

Then, $\left|\dfrac{z+1}{z-1}\right| < 1$

$\Rightarrow$ $|z + 1| < |z - 1|$

$\Rightarrow$ $(x + 1)^2 + y^2 < (x - 1)^2 + y^2$ $[\because z = x + iy]$

$\Rightarrow$ $(x + 1)^2 - (x - 1)^2 < 0$

$\Rightarrow$ $(x + 1 + x - 1)(x + 1 - x + 1) < 0$

$\Rightarrow$ $(2x)(2) < 0$

$\Rightarrow$ $x < 0$ ...(i)

Now, $\arg\left(\dfrac{z-1}{z+1}\right) = \dfrac{2\pi}{3}$

It represents the part of a circle, where end points of the chord are (1, 0) and (−1, 0) i.e., lying on the X-axis.

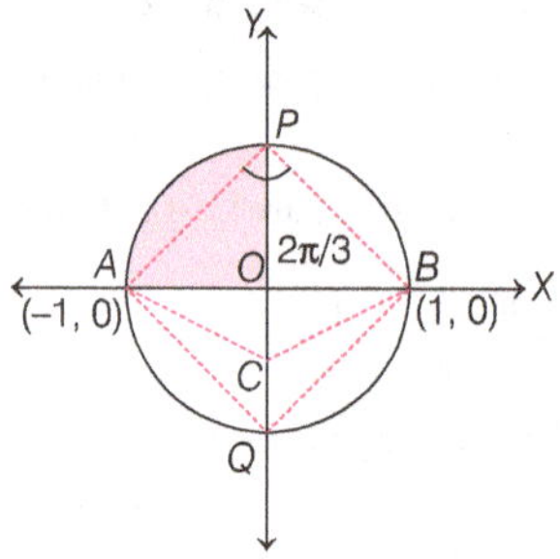

$\angle APB = \dfrac{2\pi}{3}$ because in this case the obtuse angle lies in the minor segment of the circle.

O is the mid-point of AB.

$\angle AQB = \pi - \dfrac{2\pi}{3} = \dfrac{\pi}{3}$ $[\because \angle APB + \angle AQB = \pi]$

$\angle ACB = \dfrac{2\pi}{3}$ $[\because \angle ACB = 2\angle AQB]$

$\therefore$ $\angle OCB = \dfrac{1}{2}\angle ACB = \dfrac{\pi}{3}$

In ΔOCB, $OB = 1$, $\angle OCB = \dfrac{\pi}{3}$

$$\tan\frac{\pi}{3} = \frac{OB}{OC} \Rightarrow OC = \frac{1}{\sqrt{3}}$$

$\therefore$ $C \equiv \left(0, -\dfrac{1}{\sqrt{3}}\right)$

Thus, from Eq. (i), we can say that $A \cap B$ is a portion of a circle centred at $\left(0, -\dfrac{1}{\sqrt{3}}\right)$ that lies in second quadrant only.

103. $f(x) = ax^2 + bx + c$

$f(1) = a + b + c = 3$ ...(i)

$f(3) = 9a + 3b + c = 4$ ...(ii)

$f(0) + f(1) + f(-2) + f(3) = 14$

$\Rightarrow$ $c + 3 + \lambda + 4 = 14$

$\Rightarrow$ $c + \lambda = 7$ ...(iii)

Also, $c + a + b + c + 4a - 2b + c + 9a + 3b + c = 14$

$\Rightarrow$ $14a + 2b + 4c = 14$

$\Rightarrow$ $7a + b + 2c = 7$ ...(iv)

From Eqs. (i) and (iv),

$$6a + c = 4 \quad \text{...(v)}$$

From Eqs. (i) and (ii),

$$6a - 2c = -5 \text{...(vi)}$$

From Eqs. (v) and (vi),

$$3c = 9 \Rightarrow c = 3$$

From Eq. (iii),

$$3 + \lambda = 7 \Rightarrow \lambda = 4$$

104. $ax^2 - 2bx + 15 = 0$ has repeated roots α.

So, $2\alpha = \frac{2b}{a}, \alpha^2 = \frac{15}{a} \Rightarrow \alpha = \frac{15}{b}$

As α and β are the roots of equation $x^2 - 2bx + 21 = 0$

$$\alpha + \beta = 2b \Rightarrow \frac{15}{b} + \beta = 2b$$

$$\Rightarrow \quad \beta = 2b - \frac{15}{b} = \frac{2b^2 - 15}{b}$$

Also, $\alpha\beta = 21 \Rightarrow \frac{15}{b} \times \frac{(2b^2 - 15)}{b} = 21$

$$\Rightarrow \quad 10b^2 - 75 = 7b^2 \Rightarrow b = \pm 5$$

$$\Rightarrow \quad \alpha = \pm 3 \text{ and } \beta = \frac{2 \times 25 - 15}{\pm 5} = \pm 7$$

$$\therefore \quad \alpha^2 + \beta^2 = 9 + 49 = 58$$

105. Given a relation

$$1 < |z - 3 + 2i| < 4$$

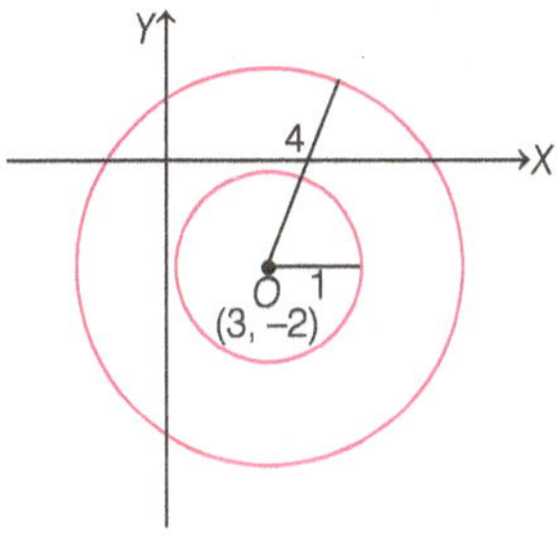

Let $z = a + ib$

$$1 < (a - 3)^2 + (b + 2)^2 < 16$$

$(0, \pm 2), (\pm 2, 0), (\pm 1, \pm 2), (\pm 2, \pm 1)$

$(\pm 2, \pm 3), (\pm 3, \pm 2), (\pm 1, \pm 1), (\pm 2, \pm 2)$

$(\pm 3, 0), (0, \pm 3), (\pm 3, \pm 1), (\pm 1, \pm 3)$

Total number of points $= 2 \times 4 + 4 \times 8 = 40$

106. Given, $z^2 = \bar{z} \cdot 2^{1 - |z|}$

$$|z^2| = |\bar{z}| \cdot 2^{1 - |z|}$$

$$|z|^2 = |\bar{z}| \times 2^{1 - |z|}$$

$$|z| = 2^{1 - |z|}$$

This is possible, when $|z| = 1$, as $|z| \neq 0$

$$\sqrt{a^2 + b^2} = 1 \Rightarrow a^2 + b^2 = 1$$

Again, $z^2 = \bar{z} \cdot 2^{1 - |z|}$

$$(a + ib)^2 = (a - ib) \times 2^{1-1} \quad [\because |z| = 1]$$

$$\Rightarrow a^2 + i^2b^2 + 2abi = a - ib$$

$$\Rightarrow \quad a^2 - b^2 + 2abi = a - ib$$

Comparing the real parts and imaginary part, we get

$$a^2 - b^2 = a \text{ and } 2ab = -b$$

$$\Rightarrow \quad 2a = -1 \text{ or } a = -\frac{1}{2} \quad [\because b \neq 0]$$

Now, $\frac{1}{4} - b^2 = -\frac{1}{2}$

$$\Rightarrow \quad b^2 = \frac{3}{4} \text{ or } b = \pm \frac{\sqrt{3}}{2}$$

$$\therefore \quad z = -\frac{1}{2} \pm \frac{\sqrt{3}}{2} i, \text{ i.e. } z = \omega \text{ and } \omega^2$$

$$z^n = (z + 1)^n \Rightarrow \left(\frac{z + 1}{z}\right)^n = 1$$

$$\Rightarrow \quad \left(1 + \frac{1}{z}\right)^n = 1 \Rightarrow \left(1 + \frac{1}{\omega}\right)^n = 1$$

$$\Rightarrow \quad (1 + \omega^2)^n = 1 \Rightarrow (-\omega)^n = 1 \quad [\because 1 + \omega + \omega^2 = 0]$$

$\therefore$ The minimum value of n is 6.

107. $S = \{z \in C : |z - 2| \leq 1, z(1 + i) + \bar{z}(1 - i) \leq 2\}$

and $5(|z_1|^2 + |z_2|^2) = \alpha + \beta\sqrt{5}$

Converting to cartesian form

$$|z - 2| \leq 1 \equiv (x - 2)^2 + (y - 0)^2 \leq 1$$

$\Rightarrow$ Circle centred at (2, 0) and radius = 1

$$z(1 + i) + \bar{z}(1 - i) \leq 2$$

$$\Rightarrow \quad (x + iy)(1 + i) + (x - iy)(1 - i) \leq 2$$

$$\Rightarrow \quad x + ix + iy - y + x - ix - iy - y \leq 2$$

$$\Rightarrow \quad 2x - 2y \leq 2$$

$$\Rightarrow \quad x - y \leq 1 \Rightarrow y \geq x - 1$$

Region above line $y = x - 1$.

The required common region.

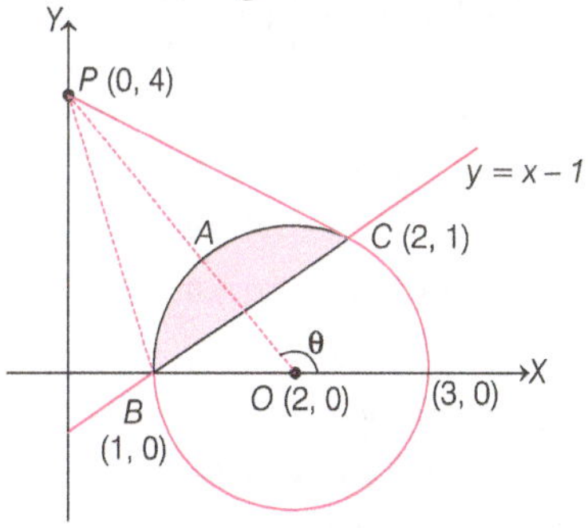

$4i \equiv (0, 4)$, $B \equiv (1, 0)$ and $C \equiv (2, 1)$

$PB = \sqrt{17}$, $PC = \sqrt{13}$

$\therefore$ Maximum is PB and minimum is PA.

Line $PA : y - 0 = \frac{0 - 4}{2 - 0}(x - 2) \Rightarrow y = -2(x - 2)$

On solving $y = -2(x - 2)$ and $(x - 2)^2 + y^2 = 1$, we get

$$(x - 2)^2 + 4(x - 2)^2 = 1$$

$$\Rightarrow \quad (x - 2)^2 = \frac{1}{5} \Rightarrow x = 2 \pm \frac{1}{\sqrt{5}}$$

$$\therefore \quad A \equiv \left(2 - \frac{1}{\sqrt{5}}, \frac{2}{\sqrt{5}}\right)$$

Minimum: $z_1 = \left(2 - \frac{1}{\sqrt{5}}\right) + \frac{2i}{\sqrt{5}}$

Maximum : $z_2 = 1 + 0i$

$$|z_1|^2 = \frac{25 - 4\sqrt{5}}{5} = 5 - \frac{4}{\sqrt{5}}$$

and $\quad |z_2|^2 = 1$

$$\therefore \quad 5(|z_1|^2 + |z_2|^2) = 5\left[5 - \frac{4}{\sqrt{5}} + 1\right]$$

$$= 30 - 4\sqrt{5} = \alpha + \beta\sqrt{5}$$

$$\therefore \quad \alpha + \beta = 30 - 4 = 26$$

108. $|zw| = 1, \arg(z) - \arg(w) = \frac{3\pi}{2}$

Let $\quad z = re^{i\theta} \Rightarrow \bar{z} = re^{-i\theta}$

$$w = \frac{1}{r}e^{i\left(\theta - \frac{3\pi}{2}\right)}$$

$$\Rightarrow \quad w\bar{z} = \frac{1}{r}e^{i\left(\theta - \frac{3\pi}{2}\right)} \cdot re^{-i\theta}$$

$$\Rightarrow \quad w\bar{z} = e^{i\left(\theta - \frac{3\pi}{2} - \theta\right)} = e^{-i\frac{3\pi}{2}}$$

$$\Rightarrow \quad w\bar{z} = \cos\left(\frac{-3\pi}{2}\right) + i\sin\left(\frac{-3\pi}{2}\right)$$

$$\Rightarrow \quad w\bar{z} = 0 + i \Rightarrow w\bar{z} = i$$

$$\Rightarrow \quad \left(\frac{1 - 2w\bar{z}}{1 + 3w\bar{z}}\right) = \left(\frac{1 - 2i}{1 + 3i} \times \frac{1 - 3i}{1 - 3i}\right)$$

$$= \frac{1 - 2i - 3i + 6i^2}{10} = \frac{-5 - 5i}{10}$$

$$\therefore \quad \arg\left(\frac{1 - 2w\bar{z}}{1 - 3w\bar{z}}\right) = -\left(\pi - \frac{\pi}{4}\right) = -\frac{3\pi}{4}$$

109. Given, $z^2 + 3\bar{z} = 0$

On putting $z = x + iy$, we get

$$(x^2 - y^2) + i(2xy) + 3(x - iy) = 0$$

$$\Rightarrow \quad (x^2 - y^2 + 3x) + i(2xy - 3y) = 0$$

$$\begin{cases} x^2 - y^2 + 3x = 0 \\ y(2x - 3) = 0 \end{cases}$$

$$y = 0 \text{ or } x = 3/2$$

If $y = 0$, then $x^2 + 3x = 0 \Rightarrow x = 0, -3$

So, (0, 0) and (−3, 0) are solutions, when $y = 0$.

If $x = 3/2$, then

$$\frac{9}{4} - y^2 + \frac{9}{2} = 0 \Rightarrow y = \pm\frac{3\sqrt{3}}{2}$$

$$\therefore \quad (x, y) = \left(\frac{3}{2}, \frac{3\sqrt{3}}{2}\right) \text{ and } \left(\frac{3}{2}, -\frac{3\sqrt{3}}{2}\right)$$

There are 4 solutions.

$$\sum_{k=0}^{\infty}\left(\frac{1}{n^k}\right) = 1 + \frac{1}{4} + \frac{1}{4^2} + \dots\infty$$

$$= \frac{1}{1 - 1/4} = \frac{4}{3}$$

110. Let $z = (1 - \cos\theta + 2i\sin\theta)^{-1}$

$$\Rightarrow \quad z = \frac{1}{1 - \cos\theta + 2i\sin\theta}$$

$$= \frac{1}{1 - \cos\theta + 2i\sin\theta} \times \frac{1 - \cos\theta - 2i\sin\theta}{1 - \cos\theta - 2i\sin\theta}$$

$$= \frac{(1 - \cos\theta) - 2i\sin\theta}{(1 - \cos\theta)^2 - (2i\sin\theta)^2}$$

$$= \frac{2\sin^2\frac{\theta}{2} - 4i\sin\frac{\theta}{2}\cos\frac{\theta}{2}}{4\sin^4\frac{\theta}{2} + 16\sin^2\frac{\theta}{2}\cos^2\frac{\theta}{2}}$$

$$= \frac{\sin\frac{\theta}{2} - 2i\cos\frac{\theta}{2}}{2\sin\frac{\theta}{2}\left(\sin^2\frac{\theta}{2} + 4\cos^2\frac{\theta}{2}\right)}$$

$$\text{Now, } \operatorname{Re}(z) = \frac{\sin\frac{\theta}{2}}{2\sin\frac{\theta}{2}\left(\sin^2\frac{\theta}{2} + 4\cos^2\frac{\theta}{2}\right)}$$

$$= \frac{1}{2\left(1 + 3\cos^2\frac{\theta}{2}\right)}$$

Given, $\quad \operatorname{Re}(z) = \frac{1}{5}$

$$\Rightarrow \quad \frac{1}{2\left(1 + 3\cos^2\frac{\theta}{2}\right)} = \frac{1}{5}$$

$$\Rightarrow \quad \cos\frac{\theta}{2} = \pm\frac{1}{\sqrt{2}}$$

$$\therefore \quad \frac{\theta}{2} = n\pi \pm \frac{\pi}{4}$$

$$\therefore \quad \theta = 2n\pi \pm \frac{\pi}{2}$$

Given, range is $\theta \in (0, \pi)$.

$$\therefore \quad \theta = \frac{\pi}{2}$$

$$\text{Now, } \int_0^{\theta}\sin x\,dx = \int_0^{\frac{\pi}{2}}\sin x\,dx$$

$$\int_0^{\frac{\pi}{2}}\sin x\,dx = [-\cos x]_0^{\pi/2} = -(0 - 1) = 1$$

111. $21 + \left(z + \frac{1}{z}\right)^3 + \left(z^2 + \frac{1}{z^2}\right)^3 + \dots + \left(z^{21} + \frac{1}{z^{21}}\right)^3$

Let $z = -\omega = \frac{1 - i\sqrt{3}}{2}$

$$= 21 + \left(-\omega - \frac{1}{\omega}\right)^3 + \left(\omega^2 + \frac{1}{\omega^2}\right)^3 + \dots + \left(-\omega^{21} - \frac{1}{\omega^{21}}\right)^3$$

$$= 21 - 8 = 13 \qquad [\because \omega^2 + \omega + 1 = 0 \text{ and } \omega^3 = 1]$$

112. Given, $\quad w = 1 - \sqrt{3}i$

$$\Rightarrow \quad |w| = \sqrt{(1)^2 + (-\sqrt{3})^2} = \sqrt{1 + 3} = 2$$

and $|zw| = 1 \Rightarrow |z||w| = 1$

$\Rightarrow \quad |z| = \dfrac{1}{|w|} = \dfrac{1}{2}$

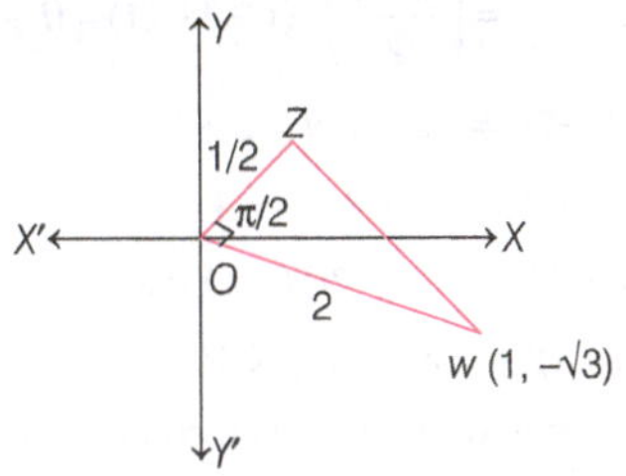

$\therefore$ Area of triangle $= \dfrac{1}{2} \times \dfrac{1}{2} \times 2 = \dfrac{1}{2}$

113. Let $z = x + iy$

$$\frac{z-i}{z-1} = \frac{x+i(y-1)}{(x-1)+iy} \times \frac{(x-1)-iy}{(x-1)-iy}$$

$$= \frac{x(x-1)+y(y-1)}{(x-1)^2+y^2} + i\left[\frac{(x-1)(y-1)-xy}{(x-1)^2+y^2}\right]$$

As $\dfrac{z-i}{z-1}$ is purely imaginary,

$$x^2 + y^2 - x - y = 0$$

$$\Rightarrow \quad \left(x - \frac{1}{2}\right)^2 + \left(y - \frac{1}{2}\right)^2 = \frac{1}{4}$$

This is a circle with centre (1/2, 1/2), radius $= 1/2$ which passes through origin as shown in the figure.

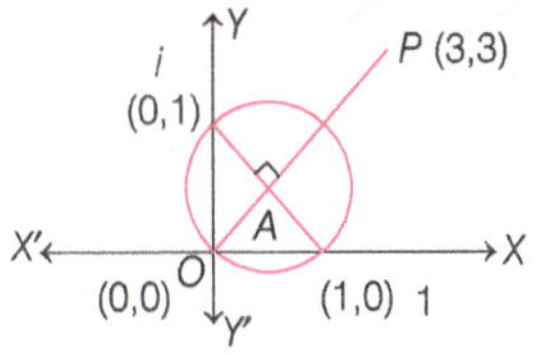

Minimum $|z - (3+3i)| = OP - OA$

$$= \sqrt{(3-0)^2 + (3-0)^2} - \sqrt{\left(\frac{1}{2} - 0\right)^2 + \left(\frac{1}{2} - 0\right)^2}$$

$$= 3\sqrt{2} - \sqrt{2}$$

$$= 2\sqrt{2}$$

114.

> **Decoding the Question**
>
> A complex rotation can be denoted as $|z|e^{i\theta}$ where θ is a real number in radius. θ denotes the rotation of the complex number in an anti-clockwise or counter clockwise direction and $-\theta$ for the clockwise direction.

The image of $P(a, b)$ along $y = x$ is $Q(b, a)$.

Translating it 2 units along the positive direction of X-axis, it becomes $R(b+2, a)$.

Then, rotation through $\dfrac{\pi}{4}$ about the origin in the anticlockwise direction, the final position of the point P is $\left(-\dfrac{1}{\sqrt{2}}, \dfrac{7}{\sqrt{2}}\right)$.

Now, applying rotational theorem,

$$-\frac{1}{\sqrt{2}} + \frac{7}{\sqrt{2}}i = [(b+2) + ai] \cdot \left(\cos\frac{\pi}{4} + i\sin\frac{\pi}{4}\right)$$

$$\Rightarrow \quad -\frac{1}{\sqrt{2}} + \frac{7}{\sqrt{2}}i = \left(\frac{b+2}{\sqrt{2}} - \frac{a}{\sqrt{2}}\right) + i\left(\frac{b+2}{\sqrt{2}} + \frac{a}{\sqrt{2}}\right)$$

$$\Rightarrow \quad -\frac{1}{\sqrt{2}} + \frac{7}{\sqrt{2}}i = \left(\frac{b-a+2}{\sqrt{2}}\right) + i\left(\frac{a+b+2}{\sqrt{2}}\right)$$

So, $\quad \dfrac{b-a+2}{\sqrt{2}} = -\dfrac{1}{\sqrt{2}}$

$\Rightarrow \quad b - a = -3 \quad$ ...(i)

and $\quad \dfrac{a+b+2}{\sqrt{2}} = \dfrac{7}{\sqrt{2}} \Rightarrow a + b = 5 \quad$ ...(ii)

Adding Eqs. (i) and (ii),

$$2b = 2 \Rightarrow b = 1$$

Substitute the value of b in Eq. (ii),

$$a = 4$$

Now, $2a + b = 2 \times 4 + 1 = 9$

115. Let $S_1 = \{z \in C : |z - 2| \le 1\}$

and $S_2 = \{z \in C : z(1+i) + \bar{z}(1-i) \ge 4\}$

Now, $|z - 2| \le 1$

Let $\quad z = x + iy$

$\Rightarrow |x + iy - 2| \le 1 \Rightarrow (x-2)^2 + y^2 \le 1$

Also, $\quad z(1+i) + \bar{z}(1-i) \ge 4$

$\Rightarrow (x+iy)(1+i) + (x-iy)(1-i) \ge 4$

$\Rightarrow \quad 2x - 2y \ge 4 \Rightarrow x - y \ge 2$

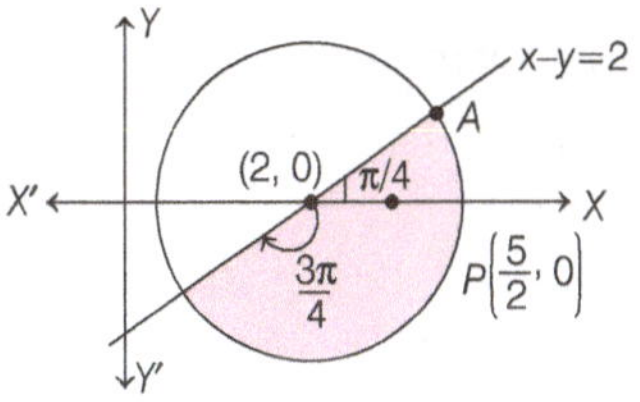

Let point on circle be $A(2 + \cos\theta, \sin\theta)$,

$$\theta \in \left[-\frac{3\pi}{4}, \frac{\pi}{4}\right]$$

$$(AP)^2 = \left(2 + \cos\theta - \frac{5}{2}\right)^2 + \sin^2\theta$$

$$\Rightarrow (AP)^2 = \cos^2\theta + \frac{1}{4} - \cos\theta + \sin^2\theta$$

$$\Rightarrow (AP)^2 = \frac{5}{4} - \cos\theta$$

For $(AP)^2$ to be maximum, $\theta = -\dfrac{3\pi}{4}$

$$(AP)^2 = \frac{5}{4} + \frac{1}{\sqrt{2}} = \frac{5 + 2\sqrt{2}}{4}$$

116. Given, $(2-i)z = (2+i)\bar{z}$

Let $z = x + iy$, then $\bar{z} = x - iy$

$\Rightarrow \quad (2-i)(x+iy) = (2+i)(x-iy)$

$\Rightarrow \quad 2x - ix + 2iy + y = 2x + ix - 2iy + y$

$\Rightarrow \quad 2ix - 4iy = 0$

$\therefore$ Equation of line

$$L_1 \Rightarrow x - 2y = 0 \quad \text{... (i)}$$

Also, $(2+i)z + (i-2)\bar{z} - 4i = 0$

$\Rightarrow (2+i)(x+iy) + (i-2)(x-iy) - 4i = 0$

$\Rightarrow 2x + ix + 2iy - y + ix - 2x + y + 2iy - 4i = 0$

$\Rightarrow 2ix + 4iy - 4i = 0$

$\therefore$ Equation of line

$$L_2 \Rightarrow x + 2y - 2 = 0 \quad \text{... (ii)}$$

From Eqs. (i) and (ii),

$$4y = 2 \text{ or } y = \frac{1}{2} \text{ and } x = 1$$

Hence, centre $= (1, 1/2)$

Equation of third line

$$L_3 \Rightarrow iz + \bar{z} + 1 + i = 0$$

$\Rightarrow i(x+iy) + (x-iy) + 1 + i = 0$

$\Rightarrow ix - y + x - iy + 1 + i = 0$

$\Rightarrow (x - y + 1) + i(x - y + 1) = 0$

$\therefore$ Radius = Distance of point (1, 1/2) to the line

$$x - y + 1 = 0$$

$$\therefore \quad r = \frac{\left|1 - \frac{1}{2} + 1\right|}{\sqrt{1^2 + 1^2}} = \frac{3}{2\sqrt{2}}$$

117. $[e^x]^2 + [e^x + 1] - 3 = 0$

$\Rightarrow [e^x]^2 + [e^x] + 1 - 3 = 0$

$\Rightarrow [e^x]^2 + [e^x] - 2 = 0$

$\Rightarrow ([e^x] - 1)([e^x] + 2) = 0$

$[e^x] = 1 \text{ or } [e^x] = -2$

$[e^x] = -2$ is not possible as $e^x > 0$.

$\Rightarrow [e^x] = 1$

$\Rightarrow 1 \le e^x < 2$

$\Rightarrow 0 \le x < \log_e 2$

118. $|z - 2 - 2i| \le 1$

$\Rightarrow z$ lies inside the circle with centre at $2 + 2i$ and radius = 1, as shown in figure.

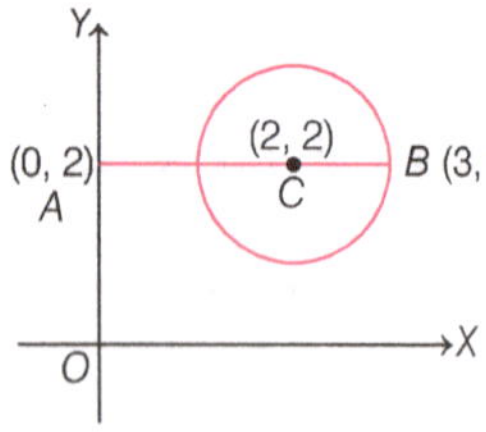

$$|3iz + 6| = |3i|\left|z + \frac{6}{3i}\right| = 3|z - 2i|$$

This is distance of z from $2i$.

$\therefore z = 3 + 2i = a + ib \Rightarrow a + b = 5$

119. We have, $\dfrac{(2i)^n}{(1-i)^{n-2}} = \dfrac{(2i)^n}{(1-i)^n(1-i)^{-2}}$

$$= \left(\frac{2i}{1-i}\right)^n (1-i)^2$$

$$= \left[\frac{2i(1+i)}{(1-i)(1+i)}\right]^n (1 + i^2 - 2i)$$

$$= \left(\frac{2i-2}{2}\right)^n (1 - 1 - 2i) = (i-1)^n(-2i)$$

If $n = 1, (i-1)(-2i) = -2i^2 + 2i = 2 + 2i$

If $n = 2, -2i(i-1)^2 = -2i(-2i) = -4$

If $n = 4, -2i(i-1)^4 = -2i(-2i)(-2i) = 8i$

If $n = 6, -2i(i-1)^6 = -2i(-2i)(-2i)(-2i) = 16$

So, least value of n for which given complex is positive is 6.

120. Given, z_1, z_2 are the roots of

$$z^2 + az + 12 = 0$$

$$\therefore \quad z_1 + z_2 = \frac{-a}{1} = -a$$

and $\quad z_1 z_2 = \dfrac{12}{1} = 12$

Now, z_1, z_2 and origin forms an equilateral triangle.

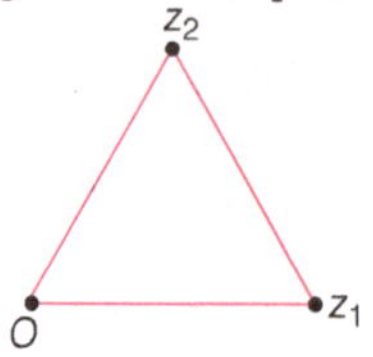

$\therefore \quad z_1^2 + z_2^2 + 0^2 = z_1z_2 + 0 + 0$

$\Rightarrow z_1^2 + z_2^2 = z_1z_2$

$\Rightarrow z_1^2 + z_2^2 + 2z_1z_2 = z_1z_2 + 2z_1z_2$

$\Rightarrow (z_1 + z_2)^2 = 3z_1z_2$

$\Rightarrow (-a)^2 = 3 \times (12)$

$\Rightarrow a^2 = 36$

$\Rightarrow |a|^2 = 36$

$\Rightarrow |a| = \pm 6$

But $|a| \ge 0$

$\therefore \quad |a| = 6$

121. **Decoding the Question**

De Moivre's theorem : It states that for any integer n, $(\cos\theta + i\sin\theta)^n = \cos(n\theta) + i\sin(n\theta)$ where n is positive integer and 'i' is the imaginary unit and n is a rational number.

Given expression, $\left(\dfrac{1 + \sin\frac{2\pi}{9} + i\cos\frac{2\pi}{9}}{1 + \sin\frac{2\pi}{9} - i\cos\frac{2\pi}{9}}\right)^3$

$$= \left[\frac{\left(\sin^2\frac{2\pi}{9} - i^2\cos^2\frac{2\pi}{9}\right) + \left(\sin\frac{2\pi}{9} + i\cos\frac{2\pi}{9}\right)}{1 + \sin\frac{2\pi}{9} - i\cos\frac{2\pi}{9}}\right]^3$$

$$= \left[\frac{\left(\sin\frac{2\pi}{9} + i\cos\frac{2\pi}{9}\right)\cdot\left\{\sin\frac{2\pi}{9} - i\cos\frac{2\pi}{9} + 1\right\}}{1 + \sin\frac{2\pi}{9} - i\cos\frac{2\pi}{9}}\right]^3$$

$$= \left(\sin\frac{2\pi}{9} + i\cos\frac{2\pi}{9}\right)^3 = \left(-i^2\sin\frac{2\pi}{9} + i\cos\frac{2\pi}{9}\right)^3$$

$$= i^3\left[\cos\frac{2\pi}{9} - i\sin\frac{2\pi}{9}\right]^3 = -i\left[\cos\left(-\frac{2\pi}{9}\right) + i\sin\left(-\frac{2\pi}{9}\right)\right]^3$$

$$= -i\left[\cos\frac{2\pi}{3} - i\sin\frac{2\pi}{3}\right]$$

[according the De-Moivre's theorem]

$$= -i\left[\left(-\frac{1}{2}\right) - i\frac{\sqrt{3}}{2}\right] = -\frac{\sqrt{3}}{2} + \frac{i}{2}$$

$$= -\frac{1}{2}(\sqrt{3} - i)$$

Exercise 2 - JEE Advanced Pattern

1. We have, $z^2 - az + a - 1 = 0$

Since, $z = 1 + i$ is root.

$\therefore \quad (1 + i)^2 - a(1 + i) + a - 1 = 0$

$\Rightarrow \quad 2i - a - ai + a - 1 = 0$

$\Rightarrow \quad -ai = 1 - 2i$

$\Rightarrow \quad a = 2 + i$

$\therefore \quad z^2 - (2 + i)z + 2 + i - 1 = 0$

$\Rightarrow \quad z^2 - (2 + i)z + (1 + i) = 0$

Let other root be α, then

$$(1 + i)\alpha = \frac{1 + i}{1}$$

$\Rightarrow \quad \alpha = 1$

2. We have, $z = \dfrac{\cos\theta + i\sin\theta}{\cos\theta - i\sin\theta}$

$= (\cos\theta + i\sin\theta)^2$

$= \cos 2\theta + i\sin 2\theta$

Now, $\dfrac{\pi}{4} < \theta < \dfrac{\pi}{2}$

$\Rightarrow \quad \dfrac{\pi}{2} < 2\theta < \pi$

$\Rightarrow \quad \cos 2\theta < 0$ and $\sin 2\theta > 0$

Let $\tan\alpha = \left|\dfrac{\text{Im}(z)}{\text{Re}(z)}\right|$.

Then, $\tan\alpha = |\tan 2\theta| = -\tan 2\theta$ $\quad [\because \tan 2\theta < 0]$

$\Rightarrow \quad \tan\alpha = \tan(\pi - 2\theta)$

$\Rightarrow \quad \alpha = \pi - 2\theta$

Since, $z \in$ II quadrant

$\therefore \arg(z) = \pi - \alpha = \pi - (\pi - 2\theta) = 2\theta$

3. We have, $\log z = \log|z| + i\arg(z)$

$$\therefore \quad \log i^i = i\log i = i\left[\log 1 + i\frac{\pi}{2}\right] = -\frac{\pi}{2}$$

Now, $\{\sin(\log i^i)\}^3 + \{\cos(\log i^i)\}^3$

$$= \left(\sin\left(-\frac{\pi}{2}\right)\right)^3 + \left(\cos\left(-\frac{\pi}{2}\right)\right)^3 = -1$$

4. We have, $\arg(z - 1) = \arg(z + 3i)$

$\Rightarrow \quad \arg((a - 1) + ib) = \arg(a + (b + 3)i)$

$\Rightarrow \quad \tan^{-1}\dfrac{b}{a - 1} = \tan^{-1}\dfrac{b + 3}{a}$

$\Rightarrow \quad \dfrac{b}{a - 1} = \dfrac{b + 3}{a}$

$\Rightarrow \quad ab = ab + 3a - b - 3$

$\Rightarrow \quad 3a - 3 = b$

$\Rightarrow \quad \dfrac{a - 1}{b} = \dfrac{1}{3}$

$\therefore \quad (a - 1) : b = 1 : 3$

5. Let $z = x + iy$

$$\therefore \quad \frac{1}{z} = \frac{1}{x + iy} = \frac{x - iy}{x^2 + y^2} = \frac{x}{x^2 + y^2} - \frac{y}{x^2 + y^2}i$$

Now, $\text{Re}\left(\dfrac{1}{z}\right) = k$

$\Rightarrow \quad \dfrac{x}{x^2 + y^2} = k$

$\Rightarrow \quad x^2 + y^2 - \dfrac{1}{k}x = 0,$

which is a circle.

6. We have, $|z| = 4$

$\Rightarrow \quad |z|^2 = 16$

$\Rightarrow \quad z \cdot \bar{z} = 16$

$\Rightarrow \quad \bar{z} = \dfrac{16}{z}$

Now, $2\text{Re}(\omega) = \omega + \bar{\omega}$

$$= \frac{z - 4}{z + 4} + \frac{\bar{z} - 4}{\bar{z} + 4}$$

$$= \frac{z - 4}{z + 4} + \frac{\frac{16}{z} - 4}{\frac{16}{z} + 4}$$

$$= \frac{z - 4}{z + 4} + \frac{4 - z}{4 + z}$$

$$= \frac{z - 4}{z + 4} - \frac{z - 4}{z + 4} = 0$$

$\therefore \text{Re}(\omega) = 0$

7. We have, $\arg(z^{1/3}) = \dfrac{1}{2}\arg(z^2 + \bar{z}z^{1/3})$

$\Rightarrow \quad 2\arg(z^{1/3}) = \arg(z^2 + \bar{z}z^{1/3})$

$\Rightarrow \quad \arg(z^{2/3}) = \arg(z^2 + \bar{z}z^{1/3})$ $\quad$ [by property]

$\Rightarrow \quad \arg(z^2 + \bar{z}z^{1/3}) - \arg(z^{2/3}) = 0$

$\Rightarrow \quad \arg\left(\dfrac{z^2 + \bar{z}z^{1/3}}{z^{2/3}}\right) = 0$ $\quad$ [by property]

$$\Rightarrow \quad \arg\left(z^{4/3} + \frac{\bar{z}}{z^{1/3}}\right) = 0$$

$\Rightarrow z^{4/3} + \dfrac{\bar{z}}{z^{1/3}}$ is purely real.

$$\Rightarrow \quad \text{Im}\left(z^{4/3} + \frac{\bar{z}}{z^{1/3}}\right) = 0$$

$$\Rightarrow \quad \frac{\left(z^{4/3} + \frac{\bar{z}}{z^{1/3}}\right) - \overline{\left(z^{4/3} + \frac{\bar{z}}{z^{1/3}}\right)}}{2i} = 0$$

$$\Rightarrow \quad z^{4/3} + \frac{\bar{z}}{z^{1/3}} = (\bar{z})^{4/3} + \frac{(\bar{\bar{z}})}{(\bar{z})^{1/3}}$$

$$\Rightarrow \quad z^{4/3} + \frac{(\bar{z})(\bar{z})^{1/3}}{|z|^{2/3}} = (\bar{z})^{4/3} + \frac{z(z)^{1/3}}{|z|^{2/3}}$$

$$[\because z^{1/3}(\bar{z})^{1/3} = (z\bar{z})^{1/3} = |z|^{2/3}]$$

$$\Rightarrow z^{4/3} - (\bar{z})^{4/3} - \frac{1}{|z|^{2/3}}((z)^{4/3} - (\bar{z})^{4/3}) = 0$$

$$\Rightarrow \quad \{z^{4/3} - (\bar{z})^{4/3}\}\left[1 - \frac{1}{|z|^{2/3}}\right] = 0$$

$$\therefore \quad |z|^{2/3} = 1 \qquad [\because z \neq \bar{z}]$$

Therefore, $\quad |z| = 1$

8. We have, $z + \dfrac{1}{z} = 2(\cos\theta + i\sin\theta)$

$$\Rightarrow \quad z + \frac{1}{z} = 2e^{i\theta}$$

$$\Rightarrow z^2 - 2e^{i\theta}z + 1 = 0$$

$$\therefore \quad z = \frac{2e^{i\theta} \pm \sqrt{4e^{2i\theta} - 4}}{2} = e^{i\theta} \pm \sqrt{e^{2i\theta} - 1} = e^{i\theta} \pm \sqrt{e^{i\theta} \cdot 2i\sin\theta}$$

Now, $z - i = e^{i\theta} - i \pm \sqrt{e^{i\theta} \cdot 2i\sin\theta}$

$$= (e^{i\theta} - e^{i\pi/2}) \pm \sqrt{e^{i\left(\theta + \frac{\pi}{2}\right)}} \cdot 2\sin\theta$$

$$= e^{i\left(\frac{\theta}{2} + \frac{\pi}{4}\right)} \cdot 2i\sin\left(\frac{\theta}{2} - \frac{\pi}{4}\right) \pm e^{i\left(\frac{\theta}{2} + \frac{\pi}{4}\right)}\sqrt{2\sin\theta}$$

$$= e^{i\left(\frac{\theta}{2} + \frac{\pi}{4}\right)}\left\{2i\sin\left(\frac{\theta}{2} - \frac{\pi}{4}\right) \pm \sqrt{2\sin\theta}\right\}$$

$$\therefore \quad |z - i| = 1 \cdot \sqrt{4\sin^2\left(\frac{\theta}{2} - \frac{\pi}{4}\right) + 2\sin\theta}$$

$$= \sqrt{2\left(1 - \cos\left(\theta - \frac{\pi}{2}\right)\right) + 2\sin\theta}$$

$$= \sqrt{2 - 2\sin\theta + 2\sin\theta}$$

$$= \sqrt{2}$$

9. We have, $|z|^2 - |z| - 2 < 0$

$$\Rightarrow \quad (|z| - 2)(|z| + 1) < 0$$

$$\Rightarrow \quad |z| - 2 < 0$$

$$\Rightarrow \quad |z| < 2$$

Now, $\quad |z^2 + z\sin\theta| \le |z|^2 + |z||\sin\theta|$

$$< |z|^2 + |z|$$

$$< 4 + 2$$

$$< 6$$

10. We have,

$$a + ib = \cos(1 - i)$$

$$= \cos 1 \cos i + \sin 1 \sin i$$

$$= \cos 1 \cosh 1 + \sin 1\, i\sinh 1$$

$$[\because \cos i = \cosh 1, \sin i \cdot 1 = i\sinh 1]$$

$$= \cos 1\left(\frac{e + e^{-1}}{2}\right) + i\sin 1\left(\frac{e - e^{-1}}{2}\right)$$

$$= \frac{1}{2}\left(e + \frac{1}{e}\right)\cos 1 + i \cdot \frac{1}{2}\left(e - \frac{1}{e}\right)\sin 1$$

$$\therefore \quad a = \frac{1}{2}\left(e + \frac{1}{e}\right)\cos 1$$

and $\quad b = \dfrac{1}{2}\left(e - \dfrac{1}{e}\right)\sin 1$

11. Given that, $z^{10} - z^5 - 992 = 0$

Let $\quad t = z^5$

$$\Rightarrow \quad t^2 - t - 992 = 0$$

$$\Rightarrow \quad t = \frac{1 \pm \sqrt{1 + 3968}}{2} = \frac{1 \pm 63}{2} = 32, -31$$

$$\therefore \quad z^5 = 32$$

and $\quad z^5 = -31$

But the real part is negative.

Therefore $z^5 = 32$ does not hold.

$\therefore$ Number of solutions is 5.

12. From Coni method,

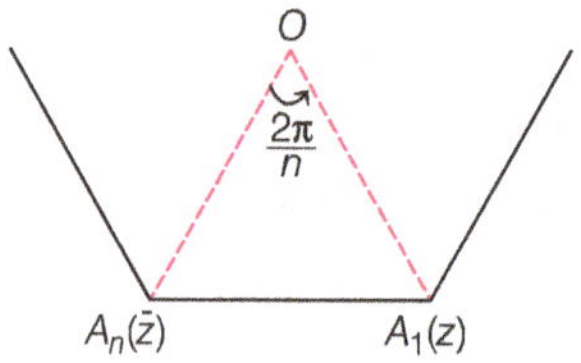

$$\frac{z - 0}{\bar{z} - 0} = e^{2\pi i/n} \text{ or } \frac{z}{\bar{z}} = e^{2\pi i/n} \qquad \ldots \text{(i)}$$

But given $\quad \dfrac{\text{Im}(z)}{\text{Re}(z)} = \sqrt{2} - 1$

$$\Rightarrow \quad \frac{\frac{z - \bar{z}}{2i}}{\frac{z + \bar{z}}{2}} = \sqrt{2} - 1 \Rightarrow \frac{1}{i}\left(\frac{\frac{z}{\bar{z}} - 1}{\frac{z}{\bar{z}} + 1}\right) = \sqrt{2} - 1$$

$$\Rightarrow \quad \left(\frac{e^{2\pi i/n} - 1}{e^{2\pi i/n} + 1}\right) = i(\sqrt{2} - 1) \qquad \text{[from Eq. (i)]}$$

$$\Rightarrow \quad i\tan\left(\frac{\pi}{n}\right) = i(\sqrt{2} - 1) \Rightarrow \tan\left(\frac{\pi}{n}\right) = \tan\left(\frac{\pi}{8}\right)$$

$$\therefore \quad n = 8$$

13. We have, $\prod_{p=1}^{r} e^{ip\theta} = 1$

$$\Rightarrow \quad e^{i\theta} \cdot e^{2i\theta} \cdot e^{3i\theta} \ldots e^{ri\theta} = 1$$

$$\Rightarrow \quad e^{i\theta(1+2+3+\ldots+r)} = 1$$

$$\Rightarrow \quad e^{i\theta\left(\frac{r(r+1)}{2}\right)} = 1$$

or $\cos\left\{\frac{r(r+1)}{2}\theta\right\} + i\sin\left\{\frac{r(r+1)}{2}\theta\right\} = 1 + i \cdot 0$

On comparing, we get

$$\cos\left\{\frac{r(r+1)}{2}\theta\right\} = 1 \text{ and } \sin\left\{\frac{r(r+1)}{2}\theta\right\} = 0$$

$$\Rightarrow \quad \frac{r(r+1)}{2}\theta = 2m\pi \text{ and } \frac{r(r+1)}{2}\theta = m_1\pi$$

$$\Rightarrow \quad \theta = \frac{4m\pi}{r(r+1)} \text{ and } \theta = \frac{2m_1\pi}{r(r+1)}$$

where, $m, m_1 \in I$

Hence, $\theta = \frac{4n\pi}{r(r+1)}, n \in I$.

14. Since, affix of A is z_1.

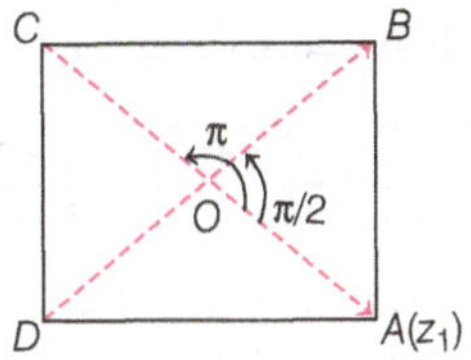

$\therefore \overrightarrow{OA} = z_1$ and $\overrightarrow{OB}$ and $\overrightarrow{OC}$ are obtained by rotating $\overrightarrow{OA}$ through $\frac{\pi}{2}$ and π.

Therefore, $\overrightarrow{OB} = iz_1$ and $\overrightarrow{OC} = -z_1$.

Hence, centroid of $\Delta ABC = \frac{z_1 + iz_1 + (-z_1)}{3}$

$$= \frac{i}{3}z_1$$

$$= \frac{z_1}{3}\left(\cos\frac{\pi}{2} + i\sin\frac{\pi}{2}\right)$$

If A, B and C are taken in clockwise, then centroid of ΔABC

$$= \frac{1}{3}z_1\left(\cos\frac{\pi}{2} - i\sin\frac{\pi}{2}\right)$$

$$\therefore \quad \text{Centroid of } \Delta ABC = \frac{z_1}{3}\left(\cos\frac{\pi}{2} \pm i\sin\frac{\pi}{2}\right)$$

15. The complex slope of the line $a\bar{z} + \bar{a}z + 1 = 0$ is $\alpha = -\frac{a}{\bar{a}}$ and the complex slope of the line $b\bar{z} + \bar{b}z - 1 = 0$ is $\beta = -\frac{b}{\bar{b}}$

Since, both lines are mutually perpendicular, then

$$\therefore \quad \alpha + \beta = 0$$

$$\Rightarrow \quad -\frac{a}{\bar{a}} - \frac{b}{\bar{b}} = 0$$

$$\Rightarrow \quad a\bar{b} + \bar{a}b = 0$$

16. We have, $\alpha = \cos\left(\frac{8\pi}{11}\right) + i\sin\left(\frac{8\pi}{11}\right)$

Now, $\text{Re}(\alpha + \alpha^2 + \alpha^3 + \alpha^4 + \alpha^5)$

$$= \frac{\alpha + \alpha^2 + \alpha^3 + \alpha^4 + \alpha^5 + \bar{\alpha} + \bar{\alpha}^2 + \bar{\alpha}^3 + \bar{\alpha}^4 + \bar{\alpha}^5}{2}$$

$$= \frac{-1 + (1 + \alpha + \alpha^2 + \alpha^3 + \alpha^4 + \alpha^5 + \bar{\alpha} + \bar{\alpha}^2 + \bar{\alpha}^3 + \bar{\alpha}^4 + \bar{\alpha}^5}{2}$$

$$= \frac{-1+0}{2} \quad \text{[sum of 11 roots of unity]}$$

$$= -\frac{1}{2}$$

17. $$|z| \le 4 \quad \ldots(\text{i})$$

and $$0 \le \arg(z) \le \frac{\pi}{3} \quad \ldots(\text{ii})$$

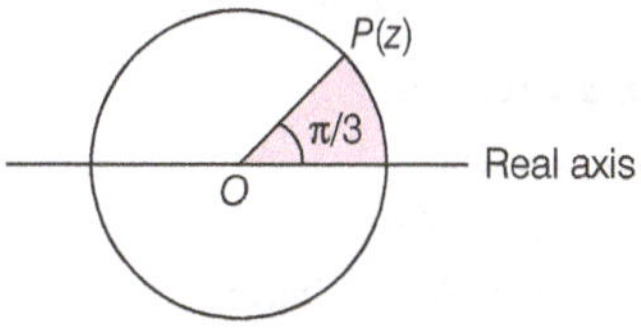

which implies the set of points in an argand plane, is a sector of a circle.

18. Let $\alpha = re^{i\theta}, \beta = re^{i\phi}$ $\quad [\because |\alpha| = |\beta|, \text{given}]$

where, $\theta \in \left(-\frac{\pi}{2}, \frac{\pi}{2}\right)$ and $\phi \in (-\pi, 0)$

$$\therefore \quad \frac{\alpha+\beta}{\alpha-\beta} = \frac{re^{i\theta} + re^{i\phi}}{re^{i\theta} - re^{i\phi}} = \frac{e^{i\left(\frac{\theta+\phi}{2}\right)} \cdot 2\cos\left(\frac{\theta-\phi}{2}\right)}{e^{i\left(\frac{\theta+\phi}{2}\right)} \cdot 2i\sin\left(\frac{\theta-\phi}{2}\right)}$$

$$= -i\cot\left(\frac{\theta-\phi}{2}\right)$$

= Purely imaginary

19. We have, $|z| = \left|z + \frac{25}{z} - \frac{25}{z}\right| \le \left|z + \frac{25}{z}\right| + \left|\frac{25}{-z}\right|$

$$\Rightarrow \quad |z| \le 24 + \frac{25}{|z|}$$

$$\Rightarrow \quad |z|^2 - 24|z| - 25 \le 0 \Rightarrow (|z| - 25)(|z| + 1) \le 0$$

$$\therefore \quad |z| - 25 \le 0 \quad [\because |z| + 1 > 0]$$

$$\Rightarrow \quad |z| \le 25 \text{ or } |z - 0| \le 25$$

Hence, the maximum distance from the origin of coordinates to the point z is 25.

20. Let $S = (1 + z_0)(1 + z_0^2)(1 + z_0^{2^2}) \ldots (1 + z_0^{2^n})$

If $n = 1$, then

$$S = (1 + z_0)(1 + z_0^2)$$

$$= \left(1 + \frac{1+i}{2}\right)\left(1 + \frac{i}{2}\right)$$

$$= \left(\frac{3+i}{2}\right)\left(\frac{2+i}{2}\right)$$

$$= \frac{5+5i}{4} = \frac{5}{4}(1+i)$$

If $n > 1$, then

$$(1 - z_0)S = (1 - z_0^2)(1 + z_0^2)(1 + z_0^{2^2}) \ldots (1 + z_0^{2^n})$$
$$= (1 - z_0^{2^2})(1 + z_0^{2^2}) \ldots (1 + z_0^{2^n})$$
$$= 1 - z_0^{2^{n+1}}$$

Now, $z_0^2 = \dfrac{i}{2}$

$\therefore$ $$z_0^{2^{n+1}} = (z_0^2)^{2^n} = \left(\frac{i}{2}\right)^{2^n}$$
$$= \frac{1}{2^{2^n}} \quad [\because 2^n \text{ is divisible by } 4]$$

$\therefore$ $$(1 - z_0)S = \frac{1}{2^{2^n}}$$

$\Rightarrow$ $$S = \left(1 - \frac{1}{2^{2^n}}\right) \times \frac{1}{1 - z_0} = (1 + i)\left(1 - \frac{1}{2^{2^n}}\right)$$

21. Let $z = a + ib, a > 0, b > 0$.

Then, $a + b = 3$

$\Rightarrow$ $b = 3 - a$

Let $P = (\text{Re}(z))^2 \text{ Im}(z)$

$$= a^2 b$$
$$= a^2(3 - a) = 3a^2 - a^3$$

$\therefore \dfrac{dP}{da} = 6a - 3a^2$ and $\dfrac{d^2p}{da^2} = 6 - 6a$

For maximum or minimum value of P,

$$\frac{dP}{da} = 0 \Rightarrow 6a - 3a^2 = 0 \Rightarrow a = 0, 2$$

Now, $\left.\dfrac{d^2P}{da^2}\right|_{a=0} = 6$ and $\left.\dfrac{d^2P}{da^2}\right|_{a=2} = -6$

$\therefore$ At $a = 2, b = 1$, P is maximum and $P_{\max} = 4$.

22. We have, $|z|^2 + 2(z + \bar{z}) + 3i(z - \bar{z}) + 4 = 0$

$\Rightarrow$ $$z\bar{z} + (2 + 3i)z + (2 - 3i)\bar{z} + 4 = 0$$

It represents a circle with centre $(-2, 3)$ and radius $= \sqrt{4 + 9 - 4} = 3$

$\therefore$ $|z - (-2 + 3i)| = 4$

$\Rightarrow$ $|z + 2 - 3i| = 4$

$\Rightarrow$ $|z + 3 + 2i - 1 - 5i| = 4$

$\therefore (z + 3 + 2i)$ lies on a circle with centre $(1 + 5i)$ and radius 4.

23. We have, $$|z| = \left|z - \frac{4}{z} + \frac{4}{z}\right|$$

$\Rightarrow$ $$|z| \le \left|z - \frac{4}{z}\right| + \left|\frac{4}{z}\right|$$

$\Rightarrow$ $$|z| \le 2 + \frac{4}{|z|}$$

$\Rightarrow$ $$|z|^2 \le 2|z| + 4$$

$\Rightarrow$ $|z|^2 - 2|z| - 4 \le 0 \Rightarrow (|z| - 1 + \sqrt{5})(|z| - 1 - \sqrt{5}) \le 0$

$\Rightarrow$ $$1 - \sqrt{5} \le |z| \le 1 + \sqrt{5}$$

$\Rightarrow$ $$0 \le |z| \le 1 + \sqrt{5} \quad [\because |z| \ge 0]$$

24. We have, $(\sqrt{3} - i)^n = 2^n$

$\Rightarrow$ $$\left(\frac{\sqrt{3} - i}{2}\right)^n = 1$$

$\Rightarrow$ $$i^n\left(-\frac{1}{2} - \frac{\sqrt{3}}{2}i\right)^n = 1$$

$\Rightarrow$ $$i^n \omega^{2n} = 1$$

$\Rightarrow i^n = 1$ and $\omega^{2n} = 1$

$\because$ n is a multiple of 4 and 3 both.

$\therefore$ n is a multiple of 12.

25. We have, $z = i^i \Rightarrow \log z = i \log i = i \log(0 + i)$

$$= i\left[\log 1 + i\frac{\pi}{2}\right] \quad \left[\because |i| = 1, \arg(i) = \frac{\pi}{2}\right]$$
$$= -\frac{\pi}{2}$$

$\therefore$ $$z = e^{-\frac{\pi}{2}}$$

So, $\text{Re}(z) = e^{-\frac{\pi}{2}}, \text{Im}(z) = 0$

26. $\because \dfrac{z + 1}{z + i}$ is a purely imaginary number.

$\therefore$ $$\left(\overline{\frac{z + 1}{z + i}}\right) = -\left(\frac{z + 1}{z + i}\right) \Rightarrow \frac{\bar{z} + 1}{\bar{z} - i} = -\left(\frac{z + 1}{z + i}\right)$$

$\Rightarrow$ $$(\bar{z} + 1)(z + i) + (\bar{z} - i)(z + 1) = 0$$

$\Rightarrow$ $$2z\bar{z} + \bar{z}(1 + i) + z(1 - i) = 0$$

$\Rightarrow$ $$z\bar{z} + \left(\frac{1 + i}{2}\right)\bar{z} + \left(\frac{1 - i}{2}\right)z = 0$$

which is a circle and passing through the origin

and radius $= \sqrt{\left|\dfrac{1 + i}{2}\right|^2 - 0} = \left|\dfrac{1 + i}{2}\right| = \dfrac{1}{\sqrt{2}}$

27. Given, $|z - 1| < |z + 3|$

$\Rightarrow$ $|z - 1|^2 < |z + 3|^2$

$\Rightarrow$ $|z|^2 + 1 - 2\text{ Re}(z) < |z|^2 + 9 + 2\text{ Re}(3z)$

$\Rightarrow$ $2\text{ Re}(4z) > -8$

$\Rightarrow$ $\text{Re}(4z) > -4$

$\Rightarrow$ $$\frac{4z + 4\bar{z}}{2} > -4$$

$\therefore$ $z + \bar{z} > -2$

and $\omega = 2z + 3 - i$

$\therefore$ $$\omega + \bar{\omega} = 2z + 3 - i + 2\bar{z} + 3 + i$$
$$= 2(z + \bar{z}) + 6 > -4 + 6$$

$\Rightarrow$ $\omega + \bar{\omega} > 2$

Option (a) $|\omega - 5 - i| < |\omega + 3 + i|$

$\Rightarrow |2z + 3 - i - 5 - i| < |2z + 3 - i + 3 + i|$

$\Rightarrow$ $|2z - 2 - 2i| < |2z + 6|$

$\Rightarrow$ $|z - 1 - i| < |z + 3|$

which is false.

Option (b) $|\omega - 5| < |\omega + 3|$

$\Rightarrow$ $|2z + 3 - i - 5| < |2z + 3 - i + 3|$

$\Rightarrow \quad |2z-2-i|<|2z+6-i|$

$\Rightarrow \quad \left|z-1-\frac{i}{2}\right|<\left|z+3-\frac{i}{2}\right|$

$\Rightarrow \quad |z-1|<|z+3|$

which is true.

Option (c) $\quad \text{Im}(i\omega)>1$

$\Rightarrow \quad \frac{i\omega-\overline{i\omega}}{2i}>1$

$\Rightarrow \quad \frac{i\omega+i\overline{\omega}}{2i}>1$

$\Rightarrow \quad \omega+\overline{\omega}>2$

which is true.

Option (d) $\quad |\arg(\omega-1)|<\frac{\pi}{2}$

$\Rightarrow \quad |\arg(2z+3-i-1)|<\frac{\pi}{2}$

$\Rightarrow \quad |\arg(2z+2-i)|<\frac{\pi}{2}$

$\Rightarrow \quad \left|\tan^{-1}\left(\frac{\text{Im}(2z+2-i)}{\text{Re}(2z+2-i)}\right)\right|<\frac{\pi}{2}$

$\therefore \quad \text{Re}(2z+2-i)>0$

$\Rightarrow \quad \frac{(2z+2-i)+(2\overline{z}+2+i)}{2}>0$

$\Rightarrow \quad z+\overline{z}+2>0$

$\Rightarrow \quad z+\overline{z}>-2$

which is true.

28. $\therefore (1+ri)^3=\lambda(1+i)$

$\Rightarrow \quad 1+(ri)^3+3(1)^2ri+3(1)(ri)^2=\lambda(1+i)$

$\Rightarrow \quad 1-r^3i+3ri-3r^2=\lambda+i\lambda$

On comparing real and imaginary parts, we get

$$1-3r^2=\lambda$$

and $\quad -r^3+3r=\lambda$

Then, $\quad -r^3+3r=1-3r^2$

$\Rightarrow \quad r^3-3r^2-3r+1=0$

$\Rightarrow \quad (r^3+1)-3r(r+1)=0$

$\Rightarrow \quad (r+1)(r^2-r+1-3r)=0$

$\Rightarrow \quad (r+1)(r^2-4r+1)=0$

$\therefore \quad r=-1, 2\pm\sqrt{3}$

$\Rightarrow \quad r=\text{cosec}\frac{3\pi}{2}, \tan\frac{\pi}{12}, \cot\frac{\pi}{12}$

29. Option (a) $|z-1|+|z+1|=3$

Here, $|1-(-1)|<3$

i.e. $2<3$, which is an ellipse.

Option (b) $|z-3|=2$

It is a circle with centre 3 and radius 2.

Option (c) $|z-2+i|=\frac{7}{3}$

It is a circle with centre $(2-i)$ and radius $\frac{7}{3}$.

Option (d) $\quad (z-3+i)(\overline{z}-3-i)=5$

$\Rightarrow \quad (z-3+i)\overline{(z-3+i)}=5$

$\Rightarrow \quad |z-3+i|^2=5 \Rightarrow |z-3+i|=\sqrt{5}$

It is a circle with centre at $(3-i)$ and radius $\sqrt{5}$.

30. Since, $1, z_1, z_2, z_3, \ldots, z_{n-1}$ are the n, nth roots of unity.

Therefore,

$$z^n-1=(z-1)(z-z_1)(z-z_2)\ldots(z-z_{n-1})$$

$\Rightarrow \quad \frac{z^n-1}{z-1}=(z-z_1)(z-z_2)\ldots(z-z_{n-1})$

$$=\prod_{r=1}^{n-1}(z-z_r)$$

Now, putting $z=\omega$, we get

$$\prod_{r=1}^{n-1}(\omega-z_r)=\frac{\omega^n-1}{\omega-1}$$

$$=\begin{cases}0, & \text{if } n=3r, r\in Z\\ 1, & \text{if } n=3r+1, r\in Z\\ 1+\omega, & \text{if } n=3r+2, r\in Z\end{cases}$$

31. $\because \quad 3|z-12|=5|z-8i|$

$\therefore 9|z-12|^2=25|z-8i|^2$

$\Rightarrow \quad 9(z-12)(\overline{z}-12)=25(z-8i)(\overline{z}+8i)$

$\Rightarrow \quad 9(z\overline{z}-12(z+\overline{z})+144)=25(z\overline{z}+8i(z-\overline{z})+64)$

$\Rightarrow \quad 16z\overline{z}+108(z+\overline{z})+200(z-\overline{z})i+304=0$

$\Rightarrow \quad 16(x^2+y^2)+216x-400y+304=0$

$\Rightarrow \quad 2(x^2+y^2)+27x-50y+38=0 \quad$ ...(i)

and $\quad |z-4|=|z-8| \Rightarrow |z-4|^2=|z-8|^2$

$\Rightarrow \quad |z|^2+16-2\,\text{Re}(4z)=|z|^2+64-2\,\text{Re}(8z)$

$\Rightarrow \quad 8\,\text{Re}(z)=48$

$\therefore \quad \text{Re}(z)=6 \Rightarrow x=6 \quad$ ...(ii)

From Eqs. (i) and (ii), we get

$$2(36+y^2)+162-50y+38=0$$

$\Rightarrow \quad y^2-25y+136=0$

$\Rightarrow \quad (y-17)(y-8)=0$

$\Rightarrow \quad y=17, 8$

$\therefore \quad \text{Im}(z)=17, 8$

32. $\because |z-3|=\min\{|z-1|, |z-5|\}$

***Case* I** If $|z-3|=|z-1|$

On squaring both sides, we get

$$|z-3|^2=|z-1|^2$$

$\Rightarrow \quad |z|^2+9-2\,\text{Re}(3z)=|z|^2+1-2\,\text{Re}(z)$

$\Rightarrow \quad 4\,\text{Re}(z)=8$

$\Rightarrow \quad \text{Re}(z)=2$

***Case* II** If $|z-3|=|z-5|$

On squaring both sides, we get

$$|z-3|^2=|z-5|^2$$

$\Rightarrow \quad |z|^2+9-2\,\text{Re}(3z)=|z|^2+25-2\,\text{Re}(5z)$

$\Rightarrow \quad 4\,\text{Re}(z)=16 \Rightarrow \text{Re}(z)=4$

33.

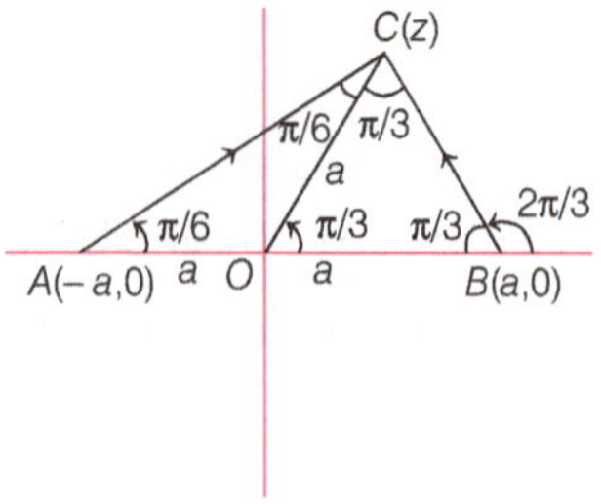

From figure, it is clear that z lies on the point of intersection of the rays from A and B.

$\because \angle ACB = 90°$ and OBC is an equilateral triangle.

Hence, $OC = a$

$\Rightarrow |z - 0| = a$ or $|z| = a$

and $\arg(z) = \arg(z - 0) = \dfrac{\pi}{3}$

34. $\because z_1 + z_2 = a, z_1z_2 = b$

and given $|z_1| = |z_2| = 1$

Let $z_1 = e^{i\theta}$ and $z_2 = e^{i\phi}$

$\because |a| = |z_1 + z_2| \le |z_1| + |z_2| = 1 + 1 = 2$

$\therefore |a| \le 2$

Also, $\arg(a) = \arg(z_1 + z_2) = \arg(e^{i\theta} + e^{i\phi}) = \dfrac{\theta + \phi}{2}$

and $\arg(b) = \arg(z_1z_2) = \arg(e^{i\theta + \phi)}) = \theta + \phi$

$\therefore 2\arg(a) = \arg(b) \Rightarrow \arg(a^2) = \arg(b)$

35. Let $z = \alpha$ be a real root of equation

$$z^3 + (3 + i)z^2 - 3z - (m + i) = 0$$

$\Rightarrow \alpha^3 + (3 + i)\alpha^2 - 3\alpha - (m + i) = 0$

$\Rightarrow (\alpha^3 + 3\alpha^2 - 3\alpha - m) + i(\alpha^2 - 1) = 0$

On comparing real and imaginary parts, we get

$$\alpha^3 + 3\alpha^2 - 3\alpha - m = 0$$

and $\alpha^2 - 1 = 0 \Rightarrow \alpha = \pm 1$

For $\alpha = 1$, we get

$$1 + 3 - 3 - m = 0 \Rightarrow m = 1$$

For $\alpha = -1$, we get

$$-1 + 3 + 3 - m = 0 \Rightarrow m = 5$$

36. Let $z = \alpha$ be a real root of equation

$$z^3 + (3 + 2i)z + (-1 + ia) = 0$$

$\Rightarrow \alpha^3 + (3 + 2i)\alpha + (-1 + ia) = 0$

$\Rightarrow (\alpha^3 + 3\alpha - 1) + i(a + 2\alpha) = 0$

On comparing real and imaginary parts, we get

$$\alpha^3 + 3\alpha - 1 = 0$$

and $a + 2\alpha = 0 \Rightarrow \alpha = -\dfrac{a}{2}$

$\Rightarrow -\dfrac{a^3}{8} - \dfrac{3a}{2} - 1 = 0 \Rightarrow a^3 + 12a + 8 = 0$

Let $f(a) = a^3 + 12a + 8$

$\therefore f(-1) < 0, f(0) > 0, f(-2) < 0$

$f(1) > 0$ and $f(3) > 0$

$\Rightarrow a \in (-2,1)$ or $a \in (-1,0)$ or $a \in (-2,3)$

Solutions (Q.Nos. 37-38)

Let $z = x + iy$

$\therefore \text{Re}(z) = x = \dfrac{z + \bar{z}}{2}$ ...(i)

and $\text{Im}(z) = y = \dfrac{z - \bar{z}}{2i}$ ...(ii)

The equation $(2 - i)z + (2 + i)\bar{z} + 3 = 0$ can be written as

$$2(z + \bar{z}) - i(z - \bar{z}) + 3 = 0$$

or $4x + 2y + 3 = 0$

$\therefore$ Slope of the given line, $m = -2$

Let slope of the required line be m_1, then

$\tan 45° = \left|\dfrac{m_1 - m}{1 + m_1m}\right| \Rightarrow 1 = \left|\dfrac{m_1 + 2}{1 - 2m_1}\right| \Rightarrow \pm 1 = \dfrac{m_1 + 2}{1 - 2m_1}$

$\therefore m_1 = -\dfrac{1}{3}, 3$

$\therefore$ Equation of straight lines through $(-1, 4)$ and having slopes $-\dfrac{1}{3}$ and 3 are $y - 4 = -\dfrac{1}{3}(x + 1)$ and $y - 4 = 3(x + 1)$

$\Rightarrow x + 3y - 11 = 0$ and $3x - y + 7 = 0$

Using Eqs. (i) and (ii), then equations of lines are

$$\frac{z + \bar{z}}{2} + \frac{3(z - \bar{z})}{2i} - 11 = 0$$

and $\dfrac{3(z + \bar{z})}{2} - \dfrac{(z - \bar{z})}{2i} + 7 = 0$

i.e., $(1 - 3i)z + (1 + 3i)\bar{z} - 22 = 0$

and $(3 + i)z + (3 - i)\bar{z} + 14 = 0$

37. (b) **38.** (a)

Solutions (Q.Nos. 39-40)

Since, z_1, z_2 and z_3 are the roots of

$$x^3 + 3ax^2 + 3bx + c = 0,$$

we get $z_1 + z_2 + z_3 = -3a$

$\Rightarrow \dfrac{z_1 + z_2 + z_3}{3} = -a$

and $z_1z_2 + z_2z_3 + z_3z_1 = 3b$

Hence, the centroid of the ΔABC is the point of affix $(-a)$.

Now, the triangle will be equilateral, if

$$z_1^2 + z_2^2 + z_3^2 = z_1z_2 + z_2z_3 + z_3z_1$$

$\Rightarrow (z_1 + z_2 + z_3)^2 = 3(z_1z_2 + z_2z_3 + z_3z_1)$

$\Rightarrow (-3a)^2 = 3(3b)$

Therefore, the condition is $a^2 = b$.

39. (c) **40.** (a)

Solutions (Q.Nos. 41-42)

41. $\because \arg(z_1z_2) = \pi$

$\Rightarrow \arg(z_1) + \arg(z_2) = \pi$

$\Rightarrow \arg(z_1) - \arg(\bar{z}_2) = \pi$

Given, $|z_1| = |z_2|$

$\therefore |z_1| = |\bar{z}_2| = |z_2|$

Then, $z_1 + \bar{z}_2 = 0$

$\Rightarrow z_1 = -\bar{z}_2$

42. $\arg(4z_1) - \arg(5z_2) = \pi$

is possible only when $|4z_1| = |5z_2|$

$$\Rightarrow \quad \left|\frac{z_1}{z_2}\right| = \frac{5}{4} = 1.25$$

and also $\quad 4z_1 + 5z_2 = 0 \Rightarrow \frac{z_1}{z_2} = -\frac{5}{4}$

$$\therefore \quad \left|\frac{z_1}{z_2}\right| = \frac{5}{4}$$

41. (d) **42.** (b)

Solutions (Q.Nos. 43-44)

43. $\therefore \sum_{r=-2}^{95} i^r + \sum_{r=0}^{50} i^{r!}$

$$= \sum_{r=1}^{98} i^{r-3} + \left(i^{0!} + i^{1!} + i^{2!} + i^{3!} + \sum_{r=4}^{50} i^{r!}\right)$$

$$= (i^{-2} + i^{-1} + 0) + \left(i^1 + i^1 + i^2 + i^6 + \sum_{r=1}^{47} i^{(r+3)!}\right)$$

$$= (-1 - i) + (i + i - 1 - 1 + (i^0 + i^0 + i^0 + \ldots 47 \text{ times}))$$

$$= (-1 - i) + (2i - 2 + 47)$$

$$= 44 + i = a + ib \quad \text{[given]}$$

$\therefore \quad a = 44, b = 1$

Unit place digit of $a^{2011} = (44)^{2011}$

$$= (44)((44)^2)^{1005} = (44)(1936)^{1005}$$

$$= (\text{Unit place of } 44) \times (\text{Unit place digit of } (1936)^{1005})$$

$$= \text{Unit place of } (4 \times 6) = 4$$

and unit place digit of $b^{2012} = (1)^{2012} = 1$

Hence, the unit place digit of $a^{2011} + b^{2012} = 4 + 1 = 5$.

44. $\because \sum_{r=4}^{100} i^{r!} + \prod_{r=1}^{101} i^r$

$$= \sum_{r=1}^{97} i^{(r+3)!} + i^1 \cdot i^2 \cdot i^3 \ldots i^{101}$$

$$= (i^0 + i^0 + i^0 + \ldots 97 \text{ times}) + i^{1+2+3+\ldots+101}$$

$$= 97 + i^{5151} = 97 + i^3 = 97 - i$$

$\therefore \quad a = 97$ and $b = -1$

Hence, $a + 75b = 97 - 75 = 22$

Solutions (Q.Nos. 45-46)

If $\left|z \pm \frac{a}{z}\right| = b$, where $a, b > 0$

$$\therefore \quad \left|z \pm \frac{a}{z}\right| \le |z| + \frac{a}{|z|}$$

$$\Rightarrow \quad b \le |z| + \frac{a}{|z|}$$

$$\Rightarrow \quad |z|^2 - b|z| + a \ge 0$$

$$\therefore \quad |z| \le \frac{b - \sqrt{b^2 - 4a}}{2}$$

and $\quad |z| \ge \dfrac{b + \sqrt{b^2 - 4a}}{2}$ ...(i)

Also, $\quad \left|z \pm \frac{a}{z}\right| \ge \left||z| - \frac{a}{|z|}\right|$

$$\Rightarrow \quad b \ge \left||z| - \frac{a}{|z|}\right|$$

$$\Rightarrow \quad -b \le |z| - \frac{a}{|z|} \le b$$

$$\Rightarrow \quad -b|z| \le |z|^2 - a \le b|z|$$

***Case* I** $-b|z| \le |z|^2 - a$

$\Rightarrow |z|^2 + b|z| - a \ge 0$

$$\therefore \quad |z| \le \frac{-b - \sqrt{b^2 + 4a}}{2}$$

and $\quad |z| \ge \dfrac{-b + \sqrt{b^2 - 4a}}{2}$

***Case* II** $|z|^2 - a \le b|z|$

$\Rightarrow |z|^2 - b|z| - a \le 0$

$$\therefore \quad \frac{b - \sqrt{b^2 + 4a}}{2} \le |z| \le \frac{b + \sqrt{b^2 + 4a}}{2}$$

From Case I and Case II, we get

$$\frac{-b + \sqrt{b^2 + 4a}}{2} \le |z| \le \frac{b + \sqrt{b^2 + 4a}}{2} \quad \text{...(ii)}$$

From Eqs. (i) and (ii), we get

$$\frac{-b + \sqrt{b^2 + 4a}}{2} \le |z| \le \frac{b + \sqrt{(b^2 + 4a)}}{2}$$

$\therefore$ The greatest value of $|z|$ is $\dfrac{b + \sqrt{b^2 + 4a}}{2}$

and the least value of $|z|$ is $\dfrac{-b + \sqrt{b^2 + 4a}}{2}$.

45. Here, $a = 2$ and $b = 4$

$\lambda =$ Sum of the greatest and least value of $|z|$.

$$= \sqrt{b^2 + 4a} = \sqrt{16 + 8} = \sqrt{24}$$

$$\therefore \quad \lambda^2 = 24$$

46. Here, $a = 3$ and $b = 6$

$\lambda =$ Sum of the greatest and least value of $|z|$

$$= \sqrt{b^2 + 4a} = \sqrt{36 + 12} = \sqrt{48} = 4\sqrt{3}$$

$$\Rightarrow \quad \lambda = 2\sqrt{3}$$

$$\therefore \quad \lambda^2 = 12$$

47. We have, $|z|^2 + \dfrac{16}{|z|^3} = z^2 - 4z = \bar{z}^2 - 4\bar{z}$

$\Rightarrow (z - \bar{z})(z + \bar{z} - 4) = 0$

$$\Rightarrow \quad z = \bar{z} = x (x \ne 2)$$

So, $x^2 = 4x + x^2 + \dfrac{16}{|x|^3}$

$\Rightarrow \quad x = \dfrac{-4}{|x|^3} \Rightarrow x = -\sqrt{2}$

$\therefore \quad z = -\sqrt{2}$

$\therefore \quad |z|^4 = 4$

48. Let $z = a + ib$

Given, $|z| = 2 \Rightarrow a^2 + b^2 = 4 \Rightarrow a, b \in [-2, 2]$

Now, $\omega = \dfrac{(a+1) + ib}{(a-1) + ib}$

$\Rightarrow |\omega| = \sqrt{\dfrac{(a+1)^2 + b^2}{(a-1)^2 + b^2}} = \sqrt{\dfrac{a^2 + b^2 + 2a + 1}{a^2 + b^2 - 2a + 1}} = \sqrt{\dfrac{5 + 2a}{5 - 2a}}$

$\therefore \quad |\omega|_{max} = \sqrt{\dfrac{5+4}{1}} = 3$ (when $a = 2$)

and $|\omega|_{min} = \sqrt{\dfrac{5-4}{9}} = \dfrac{1}{3}$ (when $a = -2$)

$\therefore$ Required product = 1

49. We have, $|z - 2 - 2i| \le 1$

which denotes the region inside a circle with centre (2, 2) and radius 1.

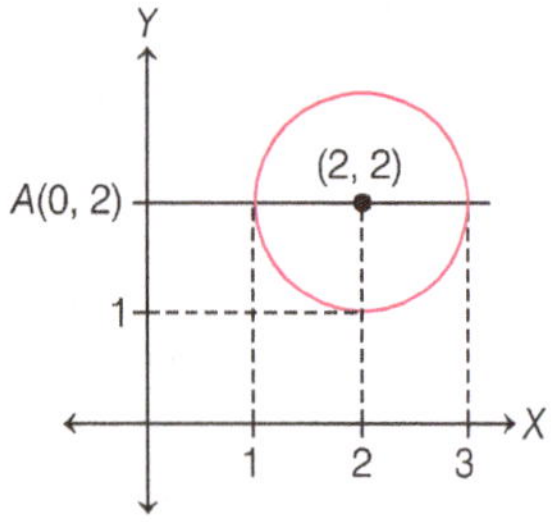

Now, $|2iz + 4| = |2i(z - 2i)|$

$= |2i||z - 2i|$

$= 2|z - 2i|$

$|z - 2i|$ = Distance of z from $A(0,2)$

$\therefore$ Maximum value is 3.

50. Locus given by equation $\arg(z + i) = \dfrac{\pi}{4}$ is a ray CD as shown in given figure.

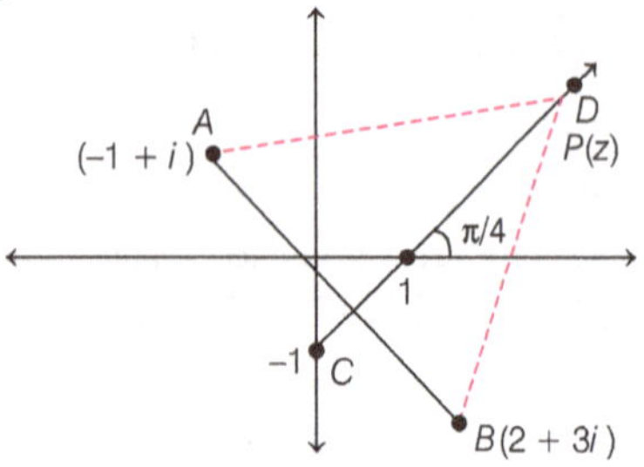

Complex number z moves on ray CD.

Now, $|z - (-1 + i)| + |z - (2 - 3i)| = PA + PB$

Clearly, $PA + PB$ is minimum when P is at C.

So, $(PA + PB)_{min} = AB = 5$

51. We have, $1 + 2|z|^2 = |z^2 + 1|^2 + 2|z + 1|^2$

$\Rightarrow \quad 1 + 2z\bar{z} = (z^2 + 1)(\bar{z}^2 + 1) + 2(z + 1)(\bar{z} + 1)$

$\Rightarrow \quad (z\bar{z})^2 + 2(z + \bar{z}) + z^2 + \bar{z}^2 + 2 = 0$

$\Rightarrow \quad (z\bar{z} - 1)^2 + (z + \bar{z} + 1)^2 = 0$

$\Rightarrow \quad z\bar{z} = 1 \Rightarrow \bar{z} = \dfrac{1}{z}$

and $\quad z + \bar{z} + 1 = 0 \Rightarrow z + \dfrac{1}{z} + 1 = 0$

$\Rightarrow \quad z^2 + z = -1 \Rightarrow |z^2 + z| = 1$

52. We have, $z_1 = (8\sin\theta + 7\cos\theta) + i(\sin\theta + 4\cos\theta)$

$z_2 = (\sin\theta + 4\cos\theta) + i(8\sin\theta + 4\cos\theta)$

$\therefore \quad z_1 = x + iy$ and $z_2 = y + ix$,

where $x = 8\sin\theta + 7\cos\theta$ and $y = \sin\theta + 4\cos\theta$

Now, $\quad z_1 z_2 = (xy - xy) + i(x^2 + y^2) = i(x^2 + y^2)$

$\Rightarrow \quad a + ib = i(x^2 + y^2)$

$\Rightarrow \quad a = 0, b = x^2 + y^2$

Now, $x^2 + y^2 = (8\sin\theta + 7\cos\theta)^2 + (\sin\theta + 4\cos\theta)^2$

$= 65 + 60\sin 2\theta$

$\therefore \quad z_1 z_2|_{max} = 125$

53. $A \equiv (1 + 2i)x^3 - 2(3 + i)x^2 + (5 - 4i)x + 2a^2 = 0$

Let α be the real root.

Then, $(1 + 2i)\alpha^3 - 2(3 + i)\alpha^2 + (5 - 4i)\alpha + 2a^2 = 0$

Equating imaginary part, we get

$2\alpha^3 - 2\alpha^2 - 4\alpha = 0$

$\Rightarrow \quad 2\alpha(\alpha^2 - \alpha - 2) = 0$

$\Rightarrow \quad \alpha = 0, -1, 2$

Now, equating real part, we get

$\alpha^3 - 6\alpha^2 + 5\alpha + 2a^2 = 0$

When $\alpha = 0 \Rightarrow a = 0$

$\alpha = -1 \Rightarrow a = \pm\sqrt{6}$

$\alpha = 2 \Rightarrow a = \pm\sqrt{3}$

$\therefore \Sigma a^2 = (0)^2 + (\sqrt{6})^2 + (-\sqrt{6})^2 + (\sqrt{3})^2 + (-\sqrt{3})^2 = 18$

54. Let $z = x + iy$

Now, let $E = z\bar{z} + (z - 3)(\bar{z} - 3) + (z - 6i)(\bar{z} + 6i)$

$= 3z\bar{z} - 3(z + \bar{z}) + 9 + 6(z - \bar{z})i + 36$

$= 3(x^2 + y^2) - 6x - 12y + 45$

$= 3[x^2 + y^2 - 2x - 4y + 15]$

$= 3[(x - 1)^2 + (y - 2)^2 + 10]$

$\therefore \quad E_{min} = 30$

55. $(4 + 5\omega + 6\omega^2)^{n^2 + 2} + (6 + 5\omega^2 + 4\omega)^{n^2 + 2} + (5 + 6\omega + 4\omega)^{n^2 + 2} = 0$

$\Rightarrow \quad (4 + 5\omega + 6\omega^2)^{n^2 + 2}[1 + \omega^{n^2 + 2} + \omega^{2n^2 + 4}] = 0$

$\Rightarrow \quad n = 3\lambda, n \ne 3\lambda + 1, 3\lambda + 2$

$\therefore \quad n = 3, 6, 9, 12, \ldots, 99$

So, number of values of n is 33.

56. We know that $|\bar{z}_2 - \bar{z}_1|^2 = |z_2|^2 + |z_1|^2 - 2\,\text{Re}(z_1 z_2)$

$$= (|z_2| - |z_1|)^2 + 2(|z| - \text{Re}(z))$$

$$\therefore \quad |z| - \text{Re}(z) = \frac{|\bar{z}_2 - z_1|^2}{2} - \frac{(|z_2| - |z_1|^2)}{2}$$

$$\le \frac{1}{2} - \frac{(|z_2| - |z_1|)^2}{2} \le \frac{1}{2}$$

$$\therefore \quad (|z| - \text{Re}(z))_{\max} = 0.5$$

57. If $\left|z \pm \frac{a}{z}\right| = b$, where $a > 0$ and $b > 0$, then

$$\frac{-b + \sqrt{b^2 + 4a}}{2} \le |z| \le \frac{b + \sqrt{b^2 + 4a}}{2}$$

(A) Here, $a = 1$ and $b = 2$

Then, $-1 + \sqrt{2} \le |z| \le 1 + \sqrt{2}$

$\therefore \quad G = 1 + \sqrt{2}$ and $L = -1 + \sqrt{2}$

$\Rightarrow \quad G^2 + L^2 = (\sqrt{2} + 1)^2 + (\sqrt{2} - 1)^2 = 2(2 + 1) = 6$

(B) Here, $a = 2$ and $b = 4$

Then, $-2 + \sqrt{6} \le |z| \le 2 + \sqrt{6}$

$\therefore \quad G = 2 + \sqrt{6}$

and $\quad L = -2 + \sqrt{6} \Rightarrow G - L = 4$

(C) Here, $a = 3$ and $b = 6$

Then, $-3 + 2\sqrt{3} \le |z| \le 3 + 2\sqrt{3}$

$\therefore \quad G = 3 + 2\sqrt{3}$ and $L = -3 + 2\sqrt{3}$

$\Rightarrow \quad G \times L = (2\sqrt{3} + 3)(2\sqrt{3} - 3) = 12 - 9 = 3$

(D) Here, $a = 4$, $b = 3$

Then, $\dfrac{-3 + \sqrt{9 + 16}}{2} \le |z| \le \dfrac{3 + \sqrt{9 + 16}}{2} \Rightarrow 1 \le |z| \le 4$

Here, $G = 4$, $L = 1$

$\therefore G + L = 4 + 1 = 5$

58. (A) If $z = 1 + i$, then

$$(z - 1)^4 = i^4$$

$$\Rightarrow \quad z^4 - 4z^3 + 6z^2 - 4z + 1 = 1$$

$$\Rightarrow (z^4 - 4z^3 + 7z^2 - 6z + 3) - z^2 + 2z - 2 = 1$$

$$\Rightarrow \quad z^4 - 4z^3 + 7z^2 - 6z + 3 = z^2 - 2z + 3$$

$$= (z - 1)^2 + 2$$

$$= i^2 + 2 = 1$$

$$\therefore 5(z^4 - 4z^3 + 7z^2 - 6z + 3) = 5$$

(B) Given that $(1 + \omega)^7 = A + B\omega$

$$\Rightarrow \quad A + B\omega = (1 + \omega)(1 + \omega)^6$$

$$= (1 + \omega)(-\omega^2)^6 \quad [\because 1 + \omega = -\omega^2]$$

$$= (1 + \omega)(\omega^{12}) = (1 + \omega)(\omega^3)^4$$

$$= (1 + \omega) \quad [\because \omega^3 = 1]$$

$$\therefore \quad A + B\omega = 1 + \omega$$

Thus, $A = 1$, $B = 1$

(C) Given, $|z - i| \le 2$ and $z_1 = 5 + 3i$

$$|iz + z_1| = |iz - i^2 + i^2 + z_1|$$

$$= |i(z - i) + 5 + 3i - 1|$$

$$= |i(z - i) + 4 + 3i|$$

$$\le |i(z - i)| + |4 + 3i|$$

$$\le |i||z - i| + \sqrt{16 + 9} \le 2 + 5$$

$$= 7$$

$\therefore$ The maximum value of $|zi + z_1|$ is 7.

(D) $|z_1 + z_2|^2 + |z_1 - z_2|^2 = 2(|z_1|^2 + |z_2|^2)$

$$= 2(1 + 4) = 10$$

59. $|z - i|z|| = |z + i|z||$

(A) Putting $z = x + iy$, we get $y\sqrt{x^2 + y^2} = 0$

i.e. $\text{Im}(z) = 0$

(B) $2ae = 8, 2a = 10 \Rightarrow 10e = 8 \Rightarrow e = \frac{4}{5}$

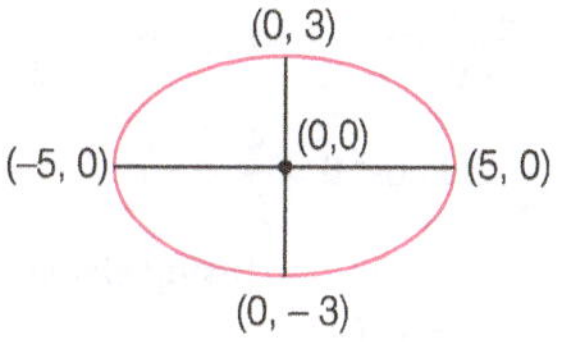

$$\therefore \quad b^2 = 25\left(1 - \frac{16}{25}\right) = 9 \Rightarrow \frac{x^2}{25} + \frac{y^2}{9} = 1$$

(C) $z = 2(\cos\theta + i\sin\theta) - \dfrac{1}{2(\cos\theta + i\sin\theta)}$

$$= 2(\cos\theta + i\sin\theta) - \frac{1}{2}(\cos\theta - i\sin\theta)$$

$$z = \frac{3}{2}\cos\theta + \frac{5}{2}i\sin\theta$$

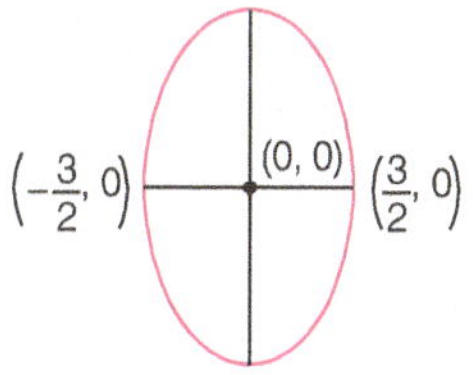

Let $z = x + iy$, then

$$x = \frac{3}{2}\cos\theta \text{ and } y = \frac{5}{2}\sin\theta$$

$$\Rightarrow \quad \left(\frac{2x}{3}\right)^2 + \left(\frac{2y}{5}\right)^2 = 1$$

$$\Rightarrow \quad \frac{4x^2}{9} + \frac{4y^2}{25} = 1$$

$$\Rightarrow \quad \frac{x^2}{9/4} + \frac{y^2}{25/4} = 1 \Rightarrow \frac{9}{4} = \frac{25}{4}(1 - e^2)$$

$$\therefore \quad e^2 = 1 - \frac{9}{25} = \frac{16}{25} \Rightarrow e = \frac{4}{5}$$

(D) Let $w = \cos\theta + i\sin\theta$, then

$$z = x + iy = w + \frac{1}{w}$$

$$\Rightarrow \quad x + iy = 2\cos\theta$$

$$\therefore \quad x = 2\cos\theta \text{ and } y = 0$$

60. **Method I**

Given, $$A = \frac{1967 + 1686\, i\sin\theta}{7 - 3i\cos\theta}$$

$$= \frac{281\,(7 + 6i\sin\theta)}{7 - 3i\cos\theta} \times \frac{7 + 3i\cos\theta}{7 + 3i\cos\theta}$$

$$= \frac{281(49 - 18\sin\theta\cdot\cos\theta + i(21\cos\theta + 42\sin\theta))}{49 + 9\cos^2\theta}$$

$$\Rightarrow \quad A = \frac{281(49 - 9\sin 2\theta)}{49 + 9\cos^2\theta} + i\left(\frac{281(21\cos\theta + 42\sin\theta)}{49 + 9\cos^2\theta}\right)$$

For A contains exactly one positive integer, A must be purely real, i.e. imaginary part of A must be equal to zero and this occurred when $21\cos\theta + 42\sin\theta = 0$

$$\Rightarrow \quad 21\cos\theta = -42\sin\theta$$

$$\Rightarrow \quad \frac{\sin\theta}{\cos\theta} = \frac{21}{-42} \Rightarrow \tan\theta = -\frac{1}{2}$$

So, $\sin 2\theta = -\frac{4}{5}$ and $\cos^2\theta = \frac{4}{5}$

[using elementary trigonometry]

Now, real part of $A = \text{Re}(A)$

$$= \frac{281(49 - 9\sin 2\theta)}{49 + 9\cos^2\theta}$$

$$= \frac{281\left(49 - 9\times\left(-\frac{4}{5}\right)\right)}{49 + 9\times\frac{4}{5}}$$

$$= 281 \times \left(\frac{49 + \frac{36}{5}}{49 + \frac{36}{5}}\right) = 281$$

$= a$, positive integer.

Method II

$$A = \frac{1967 + 1686\, i\sin\theta}{7 - 3i\cos\theta}$$

$$= \frac{(281\times 7) + (281\times 6)\, i\sin\theta}{7 - 3i\cos\theta} = 281\left(\frac{7 + 6i\sin\theta}{7 - 3i\cos\theta}\right)$$

$$= 281\left(\frac{7 - 3i\cos\theta + 3i\cos\theta + 6i\sin\theta}{7 - 3i\cos\theta}\right)$$

$$A = 281\left(\frac{7 - 3i\cos\theta}{7 - 3i\cos\theta} + \frac{3i\cos\theta + 6i\sin\theta}{7 - 3i\cos\theta}\right)$$

$$\Rightarrow A = 281\left(1 + \frac{3i(\cos\theta + 2\sin\theta)}{7 - 3i\cos\theta}\right)$$

For A to be purely real, we must have $\cos\theta + 2\sin\theta = 0$ so that $\frac{3i(\cos\theta + 2\sin\theta)}{7 - 3i\cos\theta}$ becomes zero.

$\Rightarrow \tan\theta = -\frac{1}{2}$ which is possible because $\theta \in R$.

So, exactly one + ve integer $= 281 \times 1 = 281$

61. Let $z = x + iy$, then $\bar{z} = x - iy$

and $|z| = \sqrt{x^2 + y^2} = (x^2 + y^2)^{\frac{1}{2}}$, where $y \neq 0$

Given, $$|z|^3 + 2z^2 + 4\bar{z} - 8 = 0 \quad \text{...(i)}$$

On taking conjugate both sides, we get

$$|z|^3 + 2\bar{z}^2 + 4z - 8 = 0 \quad \text{... (ii)}$$

$[\because |z| = |\bar{z}| \text{ and } \bar{\bar{z}} = z]$

On subtracting Eq. (ii) from Eq. (i), we get

$$2(z^2 - \bar{z}^2) + 4(\bar{z} - z) = 0$$

$$\Rightarrow \quad 2(z^2 - \bar{z}^2) - 4(\bar{z} - z) = 0$$

$$\Rightarrow \quad (z - \bar{z})\,[2(z + \bar{z}) - 4] = 0$$

Since, imaginary part of $z = y \neq 0$

$\therefore z = \bar{z}$ (Not possible) i.e. $z - \bar{z} = 0$ is not possible.

So, $$2(z + \bar{z}) - 4 = 0$$

$$\Rightarrow \quad 2(x + iy + x - iy) - 4 = 0$$

$$\Rightarrow \quad 4x - 4 = 0 \Rightarrow x = 1$$

$$\therefore \quad z = 1 + iy, \text{ then } \bar{z} = 1 - iy$$

and $|z| = \sqrt{1 + y^2}$

Putting above values in Eq. (i), we get

$$(1 + y^2)^{\frac{3}{2}} + 2(1 - y^2 + 2\,iy) + 4(1 - iy) - 8 = 0$$

$$\Rightarrow \quad (1 + y^2)^{\frac{3}{2}} + 2(1 - y^2) = 4$$

$$\Rightarrow \quad (1 + y^2)^{\frac{3}{2}} = 2(1 + y^2)$$

$$\Rightarrow \quad (1 + y^2)(\sqrt{1 + y^2} - 2) = 0$$

$\because y^2 + 1$ never be equal to zero.

$$\therefore \quad \sqrt{1 + y^2} = 2 \Rightarrow 1 + y^2 = 4 \Rightarrow y \pm \sqrt{3}$$

Hence, $z = 1 \pm \sqrt{3}i$

(A) $|z|^2 = 1 + y^2 = 1 + (\pm\sqrt{3})^2 = 1 + 3 = 4$

(B) $|z - \bar{z}|^2 = |1 + iy - (1 - iy)|^2 = |2iy|^2 = 4y^2 = 4\times 3 = 12$

(C) $|z|^2 + |z + \bar{z}|^2 = 4 + |(1 + iy) + (1 - iy)|^2$

$$= 4 + |2|^2 = 4 + 4 = 8$$

(D) $|z + 1|^2 = |1 + iy + 1|^2 = 4 + y^2 = 4 + 3 = 7$

62. Let $z = x + iy$

$$(\bar{z})^2 + 1/z^2 = a + ib, a, b \in I$$

$$\Rightarrow \quad (\bar{z})^2 + \frac{(\bar{z})^2}{z^2\,\bar{z}^2} = a + ib, a, b \in I$$

$$\Rightarrow \quad \bar{z}^2\left(1 + \frac{1}{|z|^4}\right) = a + ib \qquad [|z|^4 \to \text{ real number}]$$

$$\Rightarrow \quad \{x^2 - y^2 - i(2xy)\}\left(1 + \frac{1}{|z|^4}\right) = a + ib$$

On comparing,

$$(x^2 - y^2)\left(1 + \frac{1}{|z|^4}\right) = a \quad \text{...(i)}$$

and $$-2xy\left(1 + \frac{1}{|z|^4}\right) = b \quad \text{...(ii)}$$

On squaring and adding Eqs. (i) and (ii), we get

$$(x^4 + y^4 - 2x^2y^2 + 4x^2y^2)\left(1 + \frac{1}{|z|^4}\right)^2 = a^2 + b^2$$

$$\Rightarrow \quad (x^2 + y^2)^2\left(1 + \frac{1}{|z|^4}\right)^2 = a^2 + b^2$$

$$\Rightarrow \quad |z|^4\left(1 + \frac{1}{|z|^4}\right)^2 = a^2 + b^2$$

$$\Rightarrow \quad \left(|z|^2 + \frac{1}{|z|^2}\right)^2 = a^2 + b^2$$

$$\Rightarrow \quad |z|^4 + \frac{1}{|z|^4} + 2 = a^2 + b^2$$

For option (a), $|z| = \left(\frac{43 + 3\sqrt{205}}{2}\right)^{1/4}$

$$\Rightarrow \quad |z|^4 = \left(\frac{43 + 3\sqrt{205}}{2}\right)$$

$$\Rightarrow \quad \frac{1}{|z|^4} = \frac{2}{43 + 3\sqrt{205}} = \frac{(43 - 3\sqrt{205})}{2}$$

$$|z|^4 + \frac{1}{|z|^4} + 2 = 45 \Rightarrow a^2 + b^2 = 45$$

Only possible, if $a = \pm 3, b = \pm 6$ or $a = \pm 6, b = \pm 3$

Option (a) is correct.

For option (b),

$$|z|^4 = \frac{7 + \sqrt{33}}{4}, \frac{1}{|z|^4} = \frac{4}{7 + \sqrt{33}}$$

$$= \frac{7 - \sqrt{33}}{4} |z|^4 + \frac{1}{|z|^4} + 2$$

$$= \frac{7}{2} + 2 = \frac{11}{2}$$

$$\Rightarrow \quad a^2 + b^2 = \frac{11}{2}$$

Sum of two integers cannot be $\frac{11}{2}$, so wrong option.

For option (c),

$$|z|^4 = \frac{9 + \sqrt{65}}{4}, \frac{1}{|z|^4} = \frac{9 - \sqrt{65}}{4}$$

$$|z|^4 + \frac{1}{|z|^4} + 2 = \frac{9}{2} + 2 = \frac{13}{2}$$

$$a^2 + b^2 = \frac{13}{2}$$

Sum of two integers cannot be $\frac{13}{2}$, so wrong option.

For option (d),

$$|z|^4 = \frac{7 + \sqrt{13}}{6}, \frac{1}{|z|^4} = \frac{7 - \sqrt{13}}{6}$$

$$|z|^4 + \frac{1}{|z|^4} + 2 = \frac{7}{3} + 2 = \frac{13}{3} = a^2 + b^2$$

Sum of two integers cannot be $\frac{13}{2}$, so wrong option.

63. Given, z is a complex number with non-zero imaginary part.

Let $$\omega = \frac{4z^2 + 3z + 2}{4z^2 - 3z + 2}$$

$$= 1 + \frac{6z}{4z^2 - 3z + 2} = 1 + \frac{6}{4z - 3 + \frac{2}{z}}$$

$$= 1 + \frac{6}{2\left(2z + \frac{1}{z}\right) - 3}$$

Since, $\omega = \frac{4z^2 + 3z + 2}{4z^2 - 3z + 2}$ is a real number.

$\therefore 2z + \frac{1}{z}$ is a real number.

$$\Rightarrow \quad 2z + \frac{1}{\bar{z}} = 2\bar{z} + \frac{1}{\bar{z}} \quad [\because \text{If } \alpha \text{ is real, then } \bar{z} = \alpha]$$

$$\Rightarrow \quad 2(z - \bar{z}) + \frac{1}{z} - \frac{1}{\bar{z}} = 0$$

$$\Rightarrow \quad 2(z - \bar{z}) + \frac{\bar{z} - z}{z\bar{z}} = 0$$

$$\Rightarrow \quad 2(z - \bar{z}) + \frac{\bar{z} - z}{|z|^2} = 0 \quad [\because |z|^2 = z\bar{z}]$$

$$\Rightarrow (z - \bar{z})\left(2 - \frac{1}{|z|^2}\right) = 0$$

Since, $z \neq \bar{z}$ [Given]

So, $|z|^2 = \frac{1}{2} \Rightarrow |z|^2 = 0.50$

64. Given, $\bar{z} - z^2 = i(\bar{z} + z^2)$

$$\Rightarrow \quad \bar{z}(1 - i) = z^2(1 + i)$$

$$\Rightarrow \quad |\bar{z}||1 - i| = |z|^2|1 + i| \quad \text{[taking modulus on both sides]}$$

$$\Rightarrow \quad |\bar{z}|\sqrt{2} = |z|^2\sqrt{2}$$

$$\Rightarrow \quad |z| = |z|^2 \quad [\because |z| = |\bar{z}|]$$

$$\Rightarrow \quad |z|(|z| - 1) = 0 \Rightarrow |z| = 0 \text{ or } |z| = 1$$

Since, $|z| = 0 \Rightarrow z = 0$, which satisfied the given equation.

Again $|z| = 1$, then from given equation,

$$\bar{z} - z^2 = i(\bar{z} + z^2)$$

$$\Rightarrow \quad |z|^2\left(\frac{1 - i}{1 + i}\right) = z^3 \Rightarrow \frac{(1 - i)(1 - i)}{2} = z^3 \quad [\because |z| = 1]$$

$$\Rightarrow \quad z^3 = -i, \text{ since this is cubic equation.}$$

So, it has three distinct roots.

So, total number of the distinct roots of given equation is $(1 + 3) = 4$

65. $\because$ Length of direct distance $\le$ length of arc

i.e. $|z_2 - z_1|$ = length of line $AB \le$ length of arc AB.

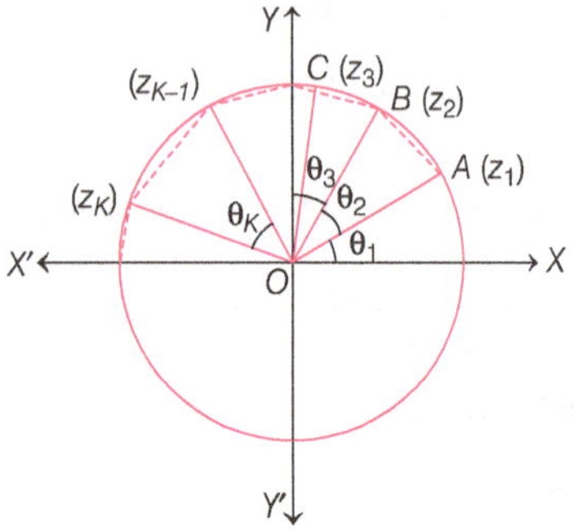

$|z_3 - z_2|$ = length of line $BC \le$ length of arc BC.

$\therefore$ Sum of length of these 10 lines $\le$ sum of length of arcs (i.e. 2π)

[because $\theta_1 + \theta_2 + \theta_3 + \ldots + \theta_{10} = 2\pi$, given]

$\therefore |z_2 - z_1| + |z_3 - z_2| + \ldots + |z_1 - z_{10}| \le 2\pi \to P$ is true.

And $|z_k^2 - z_{k-1}^2| = |z_k - z_{k-1}||z_k + z_{k-1}|$

As we know that

$|z_k + z_{k-1}| \le |z_k| + |z_{k-1}| \le 2$

$\therefore |z_2^2 - z_1^2| + |z_3^2 - z_2^2| + \ldots + |z_1^2 - z_{10}^2| \le 2$

$(|z_2 - z_1| + |z_3 - z_2| + \ldots + |z_1 - z_{10}|)$

$\le 2(2\pi) \le 4\pi \to Q$ is true.

66. Circle $x^2 + y^2 + 5x - 3y + 4 = 0$ cuts the real axis (X-axis) at $(-4, 0), (-1, 0)$.

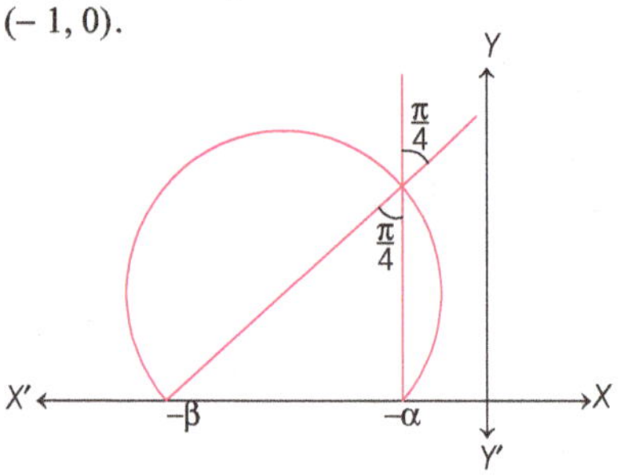

$\arg\left(\frac{z+\alpha}{z+\beta}\right) = \frac{\pi}{4}$ implies z is on arc and $(-\alpha, 0)$ and $(-\beta, 0)$ subtend $\frac{\pi}{4}$ on z.

So, $\alpha = 1$ and $\beta = 4$

Hence, $\alpha\beta = 1 \times 4 = 4$ and $\beta = 4$

67. It is given that the complex number z, satisfying

$$|z^2 + z + 1| = 1$$

$$\Rightarrow \quad ||z^2 + z| - 1| \le |(z^2 + z) + 1| \quad [\because ||z_1| - |z_2|| \le |z_1 - z_2|]$$

$$\Rightarrow \quad |z^2 + z| - 1 \le 1$$

$$\Rightarrow \quad |z^2 + z| \le 2$$

$$\because \quad ||z^2| - |z|| \le |z^2 + z|$$

$$\Rightarrow \quad ||z^2| - |z|| \le |z^2 + z| \le 2$$

which is only possible.

When $|z| \le 2$.

$$\because \quad \left|\left(z + \frac{1}{2}\right)^2 + \frac{3}{4}\right| \le \left|\left|z + \frac{1}{2}\right|^2 + \frac{3}{4}\right|$$

$$\Rightarrow \quad 1 \le \left|\left|z + \frac{1}{2}\right|^2 + \frac{3}{4}\right|$$

$$\Rightarrow \quad \left|z + \frac{1}{2}\right|^2 + \frac{3}{4} \ge 1$$

$$\Rightarrow \quad \left|z + \frac{1}{2}\right|^2 \ge \frac{1}{4}$$

$$\Rightarrow \quad \left|z + \frac{1}{2}\right| \ge \frac{1}{2} \quad \ldots \text{(ii)}$$

From Eqs. (i) and (ii), we get

$$\frac{1}{2} \le \left|z + \frac{1}{2}\right| \le 2, \forall z \in S$$

68. For a complex number z, it is given that

$$z^4 - |z|^4 = 4iz^2$$

$$\Rightarrow \quad z^4 - z^2\bar{z}^2 = 4iz^2$$

$$\Rightarrow \quad z^2(z - \bar{z})(z + \bar{z}) = 4iz^2$$

So, either $z^2 = 0$ or $(z - \bar{z})(z + \bar{z}) = 4i$

Now, **Case I** If $z^2 = 0$ and $z = x + iy$

So, $\quad x^2 - y^2 + 2ixy = 0$

$\Rightarrow \quad x^2 - y^2 = 0$

and $\quad xy = 0$

$\Rightarrow \quad x = y = 0$

$\Rightarrow \quad z = 0,$

which is not possible according to given conditions.

Case II If $(z - \bar{z})(z + \bar{z}) = 4i$

and $\quad z = x + iy$

So, $(2iy)(2x) = 4i$

$\Rightarrow xy = 1$ is an equation of rectangular hyperbola and for minimum value of $|\bar{z}_1 - \bar{z}_2|^2$, the z_1 and z_2 must be vertices of the rectangular hyperbola.

Therefore, $z_1 = 1 + i$ and $z_2 = -1 - i$

$\therefore$ Minimum value of $|z_1 - z_2|^2 = (1+1)^2 + (1+1)^2$

$4 + 4 = 8$

Exercise 3 - Challenging Problems

1. For S, $\quad z = \frac{(5+2i)}{(2-5i)} + \frac{(20+5i)}{(7+6i)} + 3i$

$$= \frac{(5+2i)(2+5i)}{29} + \frac{(20+5i)(7-6i)}{85} + 3i$$

$$= \frac{0+29i}{29} + \frac{170-85i}{85} + 3i$$

$$= i + 2 - i + 3i$$

$$= 2 + 3i$$

$\therefore$ Re$(z) = 2$

$\therefore \quad S = 2$

For K,

Put $z = x + iy$ in the given equation, then

$$(x+iy)^2 - 8(1-i)(x+iy) + 63 - 16i = 0$$

On comparing the real and imaginary parts, we get

$$x^2 - y^2 - 8(x+y) + 63 = 0 \quad \text{...(i)}$$

and $$xy + 4(x-y) = 8 \quad \text{...(ii)}$$

On substituting the value of x from Eq. (ii) in Eq. (i), we get

$$y^4 + 16y^3 + \ldots = 0$$

$\therefore$ $$K = -16$$

For G, $G = \sum_{r=4}^{2012} i^r = \sum_{r=1}^{2009} i^{r+3} = i^{1+3} + 0 = 1$

$\therefore$ $S - K + G = 2 - (-16) + 1 = 19$

2. Given, $|z-1| = 1 \Rightarrow |z-1|^2 = 1$

$\Rightarrow$ $(z-1)(\bar{z}-1) = 1 \Rightarrow z\bar{z} - z - \bar{z} = 0$

$\Rightarrow$ $(z + \bar{z}) = z\bar{z}$

$\Rightarrow$ $\dfrac{z}{\bar{z}} + 1 = z$

$\Rightarrow$ $\dfrac{z}{\bar{z}} = z - 1$ ...(i)

Now, RHS $= i\tan(\arg z) = i\left(\dfrac{\text{Im}(z)}{\text{Re}(z)}\right)$

$$= i\left\{\frac{\frac{z-\bar{z}}{2i}}{\frac{z+\bar{z}}{2}}\right\} = i\left(\frac{z-\bar{z}}{i(z+\bar{z})}\right)$$

$$= \frac{z-\bar{z}}{z+\bar{z}} = \frac{\frac{z}{\bar{z}} - 1}{\frac{z}{\bar{z}} + 1} = \frac{(z-1)-1}{(z-1)+1} = \frac{z-2}{z} \quad \text{[from Eq. (i)]}$$

$= \text{LHS}$

Alternate Solution

We have, $|z-1| = 1$ i.e. $(z-1)$ is unimodular, so we can take

$$z - 1 = \cos\theta + i\sin\theta$$

$\therefore$ $$z - 2 = -1 + \cos\theta + i\sin\theta$$

$$= -2\sin^2\frac{\theta}{2} + 2i\sin\frac{\theta}{2}\cos\frac{\theta}{2}$$

$$= 2i^2\sin^2\frac{\theta}{2} + 2i\sin\frac{\theta}{2}\cos\frac{\theta}{2}$$

or $$z - 2 = 2i\sin\frac{\theta}{2}\left(\cos\frac{\theta}{2} + i\sin\frac{\theta}{2}\right) \quad \text{...(i)}$$

and $$z = 1 + \cos\theta + i\sin\theta$$

$$= 2\cos^2\frac{\theta}{2} + 2i\sin\frac{\theta}{2}\cos\frac{\theta}{2}$$

$$z = 2\cos\frac{\theta}{2}\left(\cos\frac{\theta}{2} + i\sin\frac{\theta}{2}\right) \quad \text{...(ii)}$$

From Eqs. (i) and (ii), we get

$$\frac{z-2}{z} = i\tan\frac{\theta}{2}$$

Therefore, $\dfrac{z-2}{z} = i\tan(\arg z)$ [$\because \arg(z) = \theta/2$ from Eq. (ii)]

3. We have, $\arg(z^{1/3}) = \dfrac{1}{2}\arg(z^2 + \bar{z}z^{1/3})$

$\Rightarrow$ $2\arg(z^{1/3}) = \arg(z^2 + \bar{z}z^{1/3})$

$\Rightarrow$ $\arg(z^{2/3}) = \arg(z^2 + \bar{z}z^{1/3})$ [by property]

$\Rightarrow$ $\arg(z^2 + \bar{z}z^{1/3}) - \arg(z^{2/3}) = 0$

$\Rightarrow$ $\arg\left(\dfrac{z^2 + \bar{z}z^{1/3}}{z^{2/3}}\right) = 0$ [by property]

$\Rightarrow$ $\arg\left(z^{4/3} + \dfrac{\bar{z}}{z^{1/3}}\right) = 0$

$\Rightarrow$ $z^{4/3} + \dfrac{\bar{z}}{z^{1/3}}$ is purely real.

$\Rightarrow$ $\text{Im}\left(z^{4/3} + \dfrac{\bar{z}}{z^{1/3}}\right) = 0$

$\Rightarrow$ $\dfrac{\left(z^{4/3} + \dfrac{\bar{z}}{z^{1/3}}\right) - \overline{\left(z^{4/3} + \dfrac{\bar{z}}{z^{1/3}}\right)}}{2i} = 0$

$\Rightarrow$ $z^{4/3} + \dfrac{\bar{z}}{z^{1/3}} = (\bar{z})^{4/3} + \dfrac{(\bar{\bar{z}})}{(\bar{z})^{1/3}}$

$\Rightarrow$ $z^{4/3} + \dfrac{(\bar{z})(\bar{z})^{1/3}}{|z|^{2/3}} = (\bar{z})^{4/3} + \dfrac{z(z)^{1/3}}{|z|^{2/3}}$

[$\because z^{1/3}(\bar{z})^{1/3} = (z\bar{z})^{1/3} = |z|^{2/3}$]

$\Rightarrow$ $z^{4/3} - (\bar{z})^{4/3} - \dfrac{1}{|z|^{2/3}}((z)^{4/3} - (\bar{z})^{4/3}) = 0$

$\Rightarrow$ $\{z^{4/3} - (\bar{z})^{4/3}\}\left[1 - \dfrac{1}{|z|^{2/3}}\right] = 0$

$\therefore$ $|z|^{2/3} = 1$ [$\because z \neq \bar{z}$]

Therefore, $|z| = 1$

4. $\because$ $|z| = 1$

$\therefore$ $z = e^{i\theta}$

$\therefore$ $f(e^{i\theta}) = |e^{3i\theta} - e^{i\theta} + 2| = |e^{2i\theta}(e^{i\theta} - e^{-i\theta}) + 2|$

$= |e^{2i\theta} \cdot 2i\sin\theta + 2|$

$= |(\cos 2\theta + i\sin 2\theta) \cdot 2i\sin\theta + 2|$

$= |(2 - 2\sin 2\theta\sin\theta) + 2i\sin\theta\cos 2\theta|$

$= 2|(1 - \sin 2\theta\sin\theta) + i\sin\theta\cos 2\theta|$

$= 2\sqrt{(1 - \sin 2\theta\sin\theta)^2 + (\sin\theta\cos 2\theta)^2}$

$= 2\sqrt{(1 + \sin^2\theta - 2\sin\theta\sin 2\theta)}$

$= 2\sqrt{1 + \sin^2\theta(1 - 4\cos\theta)}$

$= 2\sqrt{1 + (1-\cos\theta)(1+\cos\theta)(1 - 4\cos\theta)}$

For maximum value, $\cos\theta = -\dfrac{1}{2}$ $\left[\because \cos\theta \neq -1, 1, \dfrac{1}{4}\right]$

$\therefore$ Maximum value of $f(z) = 2 \cdot \sqrt{1 + \left(\dfrac{3}{2}\right)\left(\dfrac{1}{2}\right)(3)} = \sqrt{13}$

5. $\because \quad \alpha = e^{2\pi i/7}$

$\therefore \quad \alpha^7 = e^{2\pi i} = \cos 2\pi + i\sin 2\pi = 1 + 0 = 1$ or $\alpha = (1)^{1/7}$

$\therefore$ $1, \alpha, \alpha^2, \alpha^3, \alpha^4, \alpha^5, \alpha^6$ are the seven, 7th roots of unity.

$$\because \quad f(x) = A_0 + \sum_{k=1}^{20} A_k x^k = \sum_{k=0}^{20} A_k x^k$$

Now, $f(x) + f(\alpha x) + f(\alpha^2 x) + \ldots + f(\alpha^6 x)$

$$= \sum_{k=0}^{20} A_k x^k [((1)^k + (\alpha)^k + (\alpha^2)^k + \ldots + (\alpha^6)^k]$$

$$= A_0 x^0 (7) + A_7 x^7 (7) + A_{14} x^{14} (7)$$

$$= 7(A_0 + A_7 x^7 + A_{14} x^{14})$$

$$\left[\because (1)^k + (\alpha)^k + (\alpha^2)^k + \ldots + (\alpha^6)^k = \begin{cases} 7, k \text{ is multiple of } 7 \\ 0, k \text{ is not multiple of } 7 \end{cases}\right]$$

6. Given that, $a_1 z^3 + a_2 z^2 + a_3 z + a_4 = 3$

We have, $|3| = |a_1 z^3 + a_2 z^2 + a_3 z + a_4|$

$$3 \le |a_1 z^3| + |a_2 z^2| + |a_3 z| + |a_4|$$

$$\Rightarrow 3 \le |a_1||z^3| + |a_2||z^2| + |a_3||z| + |a_4|$$

$$\Rightarrow 3 \le |a_1||z|^3 + |a_2||z|^2 + |a_3||z| + |a_4|$$

$$\Rightarrow 3 \le |z|^3 + |z|^2 + |z| + 1 \qquad [\because |a_i| \le 1]$$

$$\Rightarrow 3 \le 1 + |z| + |z|^2 + |z|^3 < 1 + |z| + |z|^2 + |z|^3 + \ldots$$

$$\Rightarrow 3 < 1 + |z| + |z|^2 + |z|^3 + \ldots$$

$$= \frac{1}{1 - |z|}$$

$$\Rightarrow \quad 3 < \frac{1}{1 - |z|}$$

$$\Rightarrow \quad 1 - |z| < \frac{1}{3}$$

$$\Rightarrow \quad \frac{2}{3} - |z| < 0$$

$$\Rightarrow \quad |z| > 2/3 \text{ or } |z - 0| > 2/3$$

Hence, all the roots lie in the exterior of circle, $|z - 0| = 2/3$.

7. It is given that,

$$\angle ABC = \angle ACB = \frac{\pi}{2} - \frac{\alpha}{2}$$

$$\Rightarrow \quad \angle A = \alpha$$

$$\therefore \quad AC = AB \qquad \ldots(\text{i})$$

So, ΔABC is an isosceles triangle.

Considering rotation of AB about A through angle α, we get

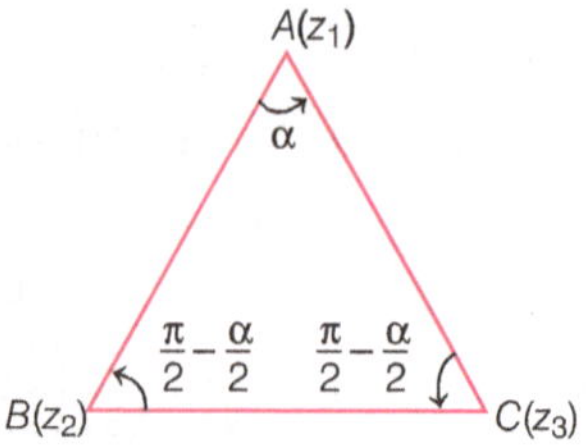

$$\Rightarrow \quad \frac{z_3 - z_1}{z_2 - z_1} = e^{i\alpha}$$

$$\Rightarrow \quad \frac{z_3 - z_1}{z_2 - z_1} = \cos\alpha + i\sin\alpha \qquad \ldots(\text{ii})$$

$$\Rightarrow \quad \frac{z_3 - z_1}{z_2 - z_1} - 1 = \cos\alpha - 1 + i\sin\alpha$$

$$\Rightarrow \quad \frac{z_3 - z_2}{z_2 - z_1} = -2\sin^2\frac{\alpha}{2} + 2i\sin\frac{\alpha}{2}\cos\frac{\alpha}{2}$$

$$\text{or} \quad \frac{z_3 - z_2}{z_2 - z_1} = 2i\sin\frac{\alpha}{2}\left(\cos\frac{\alpha}{2} + i\sin\frac{\alpha}{2}\right) \qquad \ldots(\text{iii})$$

On squaring both sides, we get

$$\frac{(z_3 - z_2)^2}{(z_2 - z_1)^2} = -4\sin^2\frac{\alpha}{2}\left(\cos\frac{\alpha}{2} + i\sin\frac{\alpha}{2}\right)^2$$

$$= -4\sin^2\frac{\alpha}{2}(\cos\alpha + i\sin\alpha)$$

[from De-Moivre's theorem]

$$\frac{(z_3 - z_2)^2}{(z_2 - z_1)^2} = -4\sin^2\frac{\alpha}{2}\left(\frac{z_3 - z_1}{z_2 - z_1}\right) \qquad [\text{from Eq. (ii)}]$$

Therefore, $(z_2 - z_3)^2 = 4\sin^2(\alpha/2)(z_3 - z_1)(z_1 - z_2)$

8. (i) Given, $\left|\dfrac{z_1 - z_2}{z_1 + z_2}\right| = 1$

$$\Rightarrow \quad \left|\frac{\frac{z_1}{z_2} - 1}{\frac{z_1}{z_2} + 1}\right| = 1$$

$$\Rightarrow \quad \left|\frac{z_1}{z_2} - 1\right| = \left|\frac{z_1}{z_2} + 1\right| \qquad \ldots(\text{i})$$

On squaring Eq. (i) both sides, we have

$$\left|\frac{z_1}{z_2}\right|^2 + 1 - 2\,\text{Re}\left(\frac{z_1}{z_2}\right) = \left|\frac{z_1}{z_2}\right|^2 + 1 + 2\,\text{Re}\left(\frac{z_1}{z_2}\right)$$

$$\Rightarrow \quad 4\,\text{Re}\left(\frac{z_1}{z_2}\right) = 0$$

$\Rightarrow \dfrac{z_1}{z_2}$ is purely imaginary number

$\Rightarrow \dfrac{z_1}{z_2}$ can be written as $i\dfrac{z_1}{z_2} = k$, where k is a real number.

(ii) Let θ be the angle between $z_1 - z_2$ and $z_1 + z_2$, then

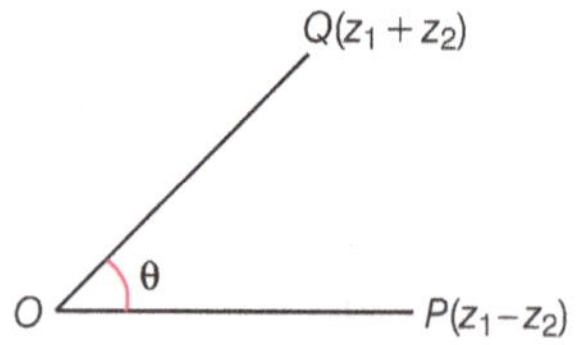

$$\theta = \arg\left(\frac{z_1 + z_2}{z_1 - z_2}\right) = \arg\left(\frac{\frac{z_1}{z_2} + 1}{\frac{z_1}{z_2} - 1}\right) = \arg\left(\frac{-ik + 1}{-ik - 1}\right)$$

$$= \arg\left(\frac{-1 + ik}{1 + ik}\right) = \arg\left(\frac{k^2 - 1 + 2ik}{k^2 + 1}\right)$$

Therefore, $\theta = \tan^{-1}\left(\dfrac{2k}{k^2 - 1}\right)$

9. Since, $|z| = 1$, where z is unimodular

$\therefore \quad z = \cos\theta + i\sin\theta$

As x and y are rational, $\cos\theta, \sin\theta$ are rationals

$$\therefore \quad \left| z^{2n} - 1 \right| = \left| z^n \left(z^n - \frac{1}{z^n} \right) \right| = |z|^n \left| z^n - z^{-n} \right|$$

$$= 1\,|2i\sin n\theta| = 2\,|\sin n\theta|$$

Since, $\sin n\theta$ is rational, therefore $\left| z^{2n} - 1 \right|$ is a rational number.

10. We have, $az^2 + z + 1 = 0$ ...(i)

On taking conjugate both sides, we get

$$\overline{az^2 + z + 1} = \overline{0}$$

$\Rightarrow \quad \bar{a}(\bar{z})^2 + \bar{z} + 1 = 0 \Rightarrow \bar{a}\,(-z)^2 + (-z) + 1 = 0$

[since, z is purely imaginary, $\bar{z} = -z$]

or $\quad \bar{a}\,z^2 - z + 1 = 0$ ...(ii)

Eliminating z from Eqs. (i) and (ii) by cross-multiplication rule, we get

$$(\bar{a} - a)^2 + 2\,(a + \bar{a}) = 0$$

On dividing each by 4, we get

$$\left(\frac{\bar{a} - a}{2} \right)^2 + \left(\frac{a + \bar{a}}{2} \right) = 0 \Rightarrow -\left(\frac{a - \bar{a}}{2i} \right)^2 + \left(\frac{a + \bar{a}}{2} \right) = 0$$

or $\quad -(\text{Im}\,(a))^2 + \text{Re}\,(a) = 0$ ...(iii)

Given, $\quad |a| = 1$

Let $\quad a = \cos\alpha + i\sin\alpha$

$\therefore \quad \text{Re}\,(a) = \cos\alpha, \text{Im}\,(a) = \sin\alpha$

Then, from Eq. (iii), we get

$$-\sin^2\alpha + \cos\alpha = 0 \quad \text{or} \quad \cos^2\alpha + \cos\alpha - 1 = 0$$

$$\therefore \quad \cos\alpha = \frac{-1 \pm \sqrt{1 + 4}}{2}$$

Only feasible value of $\cos\alpha = \dfrac{\sqrt{5} - 1}{2}$

Hence, $a = \cos\alpha + i\sin\alpha$, where $\alpha = \cos^{-1}\left(\dfrac{\sqrt{5} - 1}{2} \right)$

11. The equation $z^n = (z + 1)^n$ will have exactly $n - 1$ roots.

We have, $\left(\dfrac{z + 1}{z} \right)^n = 1 \Rightarrow \left| \left(\dfrac{z + 1}{z} \right)^n \right| = |1|$

$\Rightarrow \quad \dfrac{|z + 1|}{|z|} = 1 \Rightarrow |z + 1| = |z|$

$\Rightarrow \quad |z - (-1)| = |z - 0|$

Therefore, z lies on the right bisector of the segment connecting the points $0 + i \cdot 0$ and $-1 + 0 \cdot i$.

Thus, $\text{Re}\,(z) = -\dfrac{1}{2}$.

Hence, roots are collinear and will have their real parts equal to $-\dfrac{1}{2}$

Hence, sum of the real parts of roots is $\left(-\dfrac{1}{2}(n - 1) \right)$.

12. The complex numbers z satisfying the condition

$$|z - 25i| \le 15 \quad \text{...(i)}$$

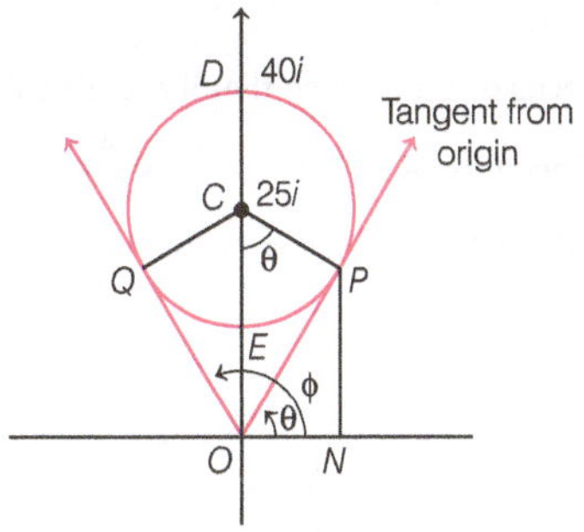

are represented by the points inside and on the circle of radius 15 and centre at the point $C\,(0, 25)$.

The complex numbers having least positive argument and maximum positive arguments in this region are the points of contact of tangents drawn from origin to the circle.

Here, θ = Least positive argument

and $\quad \phi$ = Maximum positive argument

$\therefore$ In $\quad \Delta OCP, OP = \sqrt{(OC)^2 - (CP)^2} = \sqrt{(25)^2 - (15)^2} = 20$

and $\quad \sin\theta = \dfrac{OP}{OC} = \dfrac{20}{25} = \dfrac{4}{5}$

$\therefore \quad \tan\theta = \dfrac{4}{3} \Rightarrow \theta = \tan^{-1}\left(\dfrac{4}{3} \right)$

Thus, complex number at P has modulus 20 and argument $\theta = \tan^{-1}\left(\dfrac{4}{3} \right)$

$\therefore \quad z_P = 20\,(\cos\theta + i\sin\theta) = 20\left(\dfrac{3}{5} + i\,\dfrac{4}{5} \right)$

$\therefore \quad z_P = 12 + 16i$

Similarly, $\quad z_Q = -12 + 16i$

From the figure, E is the point with least modulus and D is the point with maximum modulus.

Hence, $\quad z_E = \overrightarrow{\mathbf{OE}} = \overrightarrow{\mathbf{OC}} - \overrightarrow{\mathbf{EC}} = 25i - 15i = 10i$

and $\quad z_D = \overrightarrow{\mathbf{OD}} = \overrightarrow{\mathbf{OC}} + \overrightarrow{\mathbf{CD}} = 25i + 15i = 40i$

13. (i) Since, $|z - 1| + |z + 1| = 4$

i.e. (distance of z from the point $1 + 0 \cdot i$) + (distance of z from the point $-1 + 0 \cdot i$) = 4 (constant)

i.e. The sum of the distances of z from two fixed points $1 + 0 \cdot i$ and $-1 + 0 \cdot i$ is constant, which is the definition of an ellipse.

Therefore, locus of z satisfying the given condition will be an ellipse with foci at $1 + 0 \cdot i$ and $-1 + 0 \cdot i$ and centre at origin.

(ii) Given that, $\arg(z + i) - \arg(z - i) = \dfrac{\pi}{2}$

or $\quad \arg\left(\dfrac{z + i}{z - i} \right) = \dfrac{\pi}{2}$ ...(i)

Let the points A and B have affixes i and $-i$ and the point P has affix z.

Then, Eq. (i) can be written as

$$\angle BPA = \frac{\pi}{2} \qquad \left[\because \angle BPA = \arg\left(\frac{z+i}{z-i}\right)\right]$$

Thus, locus of $P(z)$ is such that the angle subtended at P by the line joining points A and B is $\frac{\pi}{2}$.

This is the definition of a circle with diameter AB.

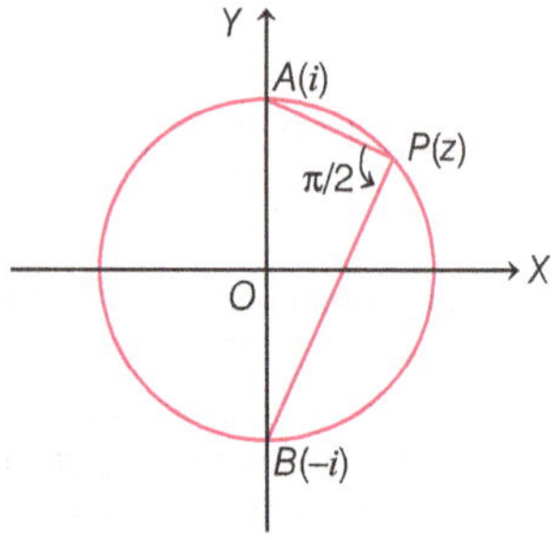

Therefore, locus of point z is a circle with diameter AB and centre at origin with radius 1.

(iii) We have, $1 < |z - 2 - 3i| < 4$ represents a circle with centre at $(2, 3)$ and radius $r \in (1, 4)$.

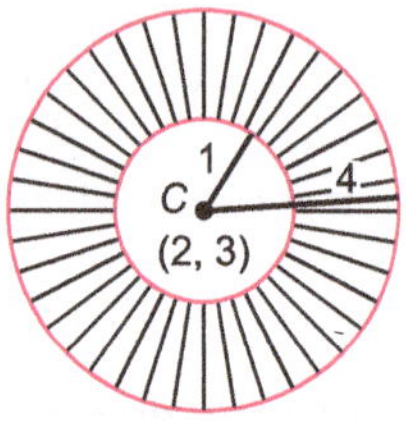

Since, $|z - 2 - 3i| > 1$ represents the region in the plane outside the circle.

$\therefore \qquad |z - 2 - 3i| = 1 \qquad$ ...(i)

and $|z - 2 - 3i| < 4$ represents the region inside circle.

$\therefore \qquad |z - 2 - 3i| = 4 \qquad$ ...(ii)

Hence, $1 < |z - 2 - 3i| < 4$ represent the angular space between the two circles (i) and (ii).

(iv) We have, $\frac{\pi}{4} < \arg(z) < \frac{\pi}{3}$

Let $z = x + iy \Rightarrow \arg(z) = \tan^{-1}\left(\frac{y}{x}\right)$

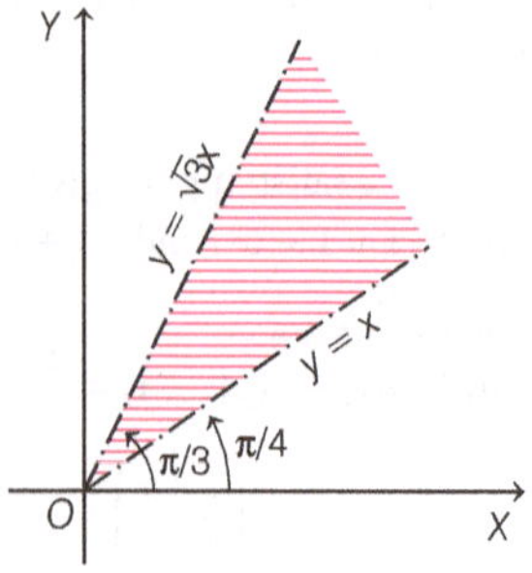

The given inequality can be written as

$$\frac{\pi}{4} < \tan^{-1}\left(\frac{y}{x}\right) < \frac{\pi}{3}$$

$$\Rightarrow \quad \tan\frac{\pi}{4} < \frac{y}{x} < \tan\frac{\pi}{3}$$

$$\Rightarrow \quad 1 < \frac{y}{x} < \sqrt{3}$$

$$\Rightarrow \quad x < y < \sqrt{3}\,x$$

This inequality represents the region between the lines $y = x$ and $y = \sqrt{3}x$

(v) We have, $\log_{\cos \pi/3}\left\{\frac{|z-1|+4}{3|z-1|-2}\right\} > 1$

or $\quad \log_{1/2}\left\{\frac{|z-1|+4}{3|z-1|-2}\right\} > 1$

$$\Rightarrow \quad \frac{|z-1|+4}{3|z-1|-2} < \frac{1}{2}$$

or $\quad 2|z-1| + 8 < 3|z-1| - 2$

$$\Rightarrow \quad |z-1| > 10$$

Hence, the inequality represents exterior of a circle of radius 10 with centre at $(1, 0)$.

14. Since, $z + \frac{1}{z} = 2(\cos\theta + i\sin\theta)$

$$\therefore \quad z + \frac{1}{z} = 2e^{i\theta}$$

$$\Rightarrow \quad z^2 - 2e^{i\theta}z + 1 = 0$$

$$\Rightarrow \quad z = \frac{2e^{i\theta} \pm \sqrt{(4e^{2i\theta} - 4)}}{2}$$

$$\Rightarrow \quad z = e^{i\theta} \pm \sqrt{(e^{2i\theta} - 1)}$$

$$\Rightarrow \quad z = e^{i\theta} \pm \sqrt{e^{i\theta} \cdot 2i\sin\theta}$$

$$\Rightarrow \quad z - i = e^{i\theta} - i \pm \sqrt{e^{i\theta} \cdot 2i\sin\theta}$$

$$= (e^{i\theta} - e^{i\pi/2}) \pm \sqrt{e^{i(\theta+\pi/2)} \cdot 2\sin\theta}$$

$$= e^{i\left(\frac{\theta}{2}+\frac{\pi}{4}\right)} \cdot 2i\sin\left(\frac{\theta}{2}-\frac{\pi}{4}\right) \pm e^{i(\theta/2+\pi/4)} \cdot \sqrt{2\sin\theta}$$

$$= e^{i(\theta/2+\pi/4)}\left\{2i\sin\left(\frac{\theta}{2}-\frac{\pi}{4}\right) \pm \sqrt{2\sin\theta}\right\}$$

$$\therefore \quad |z - i| = 1 \cdot \sqrt{4\sin^2\left(\frac{\theta}{2}-\frac{\pi}{4}\right) + 2\sin\theta}$$

$$= \sqrt{2\left(1 - \cos\left(\theta - \frac{\pi}{2}\right)\right) + 2\sin\theta}$$

$$= \sqrt{2 - 2\sin\theta + 2\sin\theta}$$

$$= \sqrt{2}$$

$$\Rightarrow \quad |\alpha - i| = |\beta - i| = \sqrt{2}$$

[here, α, β are two values of $z - i$]

2

> *Mathematics is not about numbers, equations, computations or algorithms. It is about understanding.*
>
> **–William Paul Thurston**

Theory of Equation

Learning Milestones

Milestone 1 Quadratic Equation

- Polynomial in One Variable
- Identity
- Quadratic Equation
- Nature of Roots
- Relation between Roots and Coefficients
- Transformation of Quadratic Equation
- Conditions for Common Roots
- Quadratic Expression
- Wavy Curve Method
- Condition for Resolution into Linear Factors
- Location of Roots

Milestone 2 Theory of Equation

- Equation of Higher Degree
- Rational Algebraic Inequalities
- Irrational Equation
- Irrational Inequation
- Exponential Equations
- Exponential Inequations
- Logarithmic Equations
- Logarithmic Inequations

Practice Milestones

Practice Milestone 1- JEE Main Pattern

Practice Milestone 2 - JEE Advanced Pattern

Practice Milestone 3 - Challenging Problems

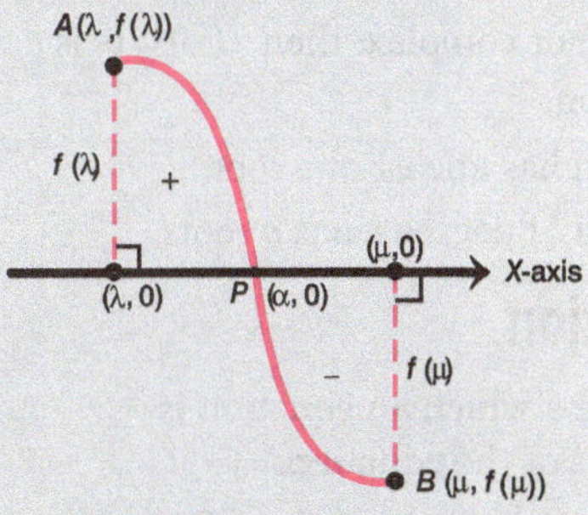

Milestone 1 Quadratic Equation

• Polynomial in One Variable • Identity • Quadratic Equation • Nature of Roots • Relation between Roots and Coefficients • Transformation of Quadratic Equation • Conditions of Common Roots • Quadratic Expression • Wavy Curve Method • Condition for Resolution into Linear Factors • Location of Roots

2.1 Polynomial in One Variable

An algebraic expression containing many terms of the form cx^n, n being a non-negative integer is called a polynomial,

i.e. $f(x) = a_0 \cdot x^n + a_1 \cdot x^{n-1} + a_2 \cdot x^{n-2} + \dots + a_{n-1} \cdot x + a_n,$

where x is a variable, $a_0, a_1, a_2, \dots, a_n$ are constants and $a_0 \neq 0$.

1. Real Polynomial

Let $a_0, a_1, a_2, \dots, a_n$ be real numbers and x is a real variable.

Then, $f(x) = a_0 \cdot x^n + a_1 \cdot x^{n-1} + a_2 \cdot x^{n-2} + \dots + a_{n-1} \cdot x + a_n$

is called a real polynomial of real variable (x) with real coefficients.

e.g. $5x^3 - 3x^2 + 7x - 4$, $x^2 - 3x + 1$, etc., are real polynomials.

2. Complex Polynomial

Let $a_0, a_1, a_2, \dots, a_n$ are complex numbers and x is a varying complex number.

Then, $f(x) = a_0 \cdot x^n + a_1 \cdot x^{n-1} + a_2 \cdot x^{n-2} + \dots + a_{n-1} \cdot x + a_n$

is called a complex polynomial or a polynomial of complex variable with complex coefficients.

e.g. $x^3 - 7ix^2 + (3-2i)x + 13$, $3x^2 - (2+3i)x + 5i$, etc. (where $i = \sqrt{-1}$) are complex polynomials.

3. Rational Expression or Rational Function

An expression of the form $\dfrac{P(x)}{Q(x)}$, where $P(x)$ and $Q(x)$ are polynomials in x, is called a rational expression.

As a particular case when $Q(x)$ is a non-zero constant, $\dfrac{P(x)}{Q(x)}$ reduces to a polynomial.

Thus, every polynomial is a rational expression but a rational expression may or may not be a polynomial.

e.g.

(i) $x^2 - 7x + 8$ (ii) $\dfrac{2}{x-3}$

(iii) $\dfrac{x^3 - 6x^2 + 11x - 6}{(x-4)}$ (iv) $x + \dfrac{3}{x}$ or $\dfrac{x^2+3}{x}$

4. Degree of Polynomial

The highest power of variable (x) present in the polynomial is called the degree of the polynomial.

e.g.

$f(x) = a_0 \cdot x^n + a_1 \cdot x^{n-1} + a_2 \cdot x^{n-2} + \dots + a_{n-1} \cdot x + a_n$

is a polynomial in x of degree n.

JEE SPIKE

A polynomial of degree one is generally called a linear polynomial. Polynomials of degree 2, 3, 4 and 5 are known as quadratic, cubic, biquadratic and pentic polynomials, respectively.

5. Polynomial Equation

If $f(x)$ is a polynomial, real or complex, then $f(x) = 0$ is called a polynomial equation.

(i) A polynomial equation has atleast one root.

(ii) A polynomial equation of degree n has n roots.

6. Roots of an Equation

The values of the variable for which an equation is satisfied are called the roots of the equation.

If $x = \alpha$ is a root of the equation $f(x) = 0$, then $f(\alpha) = 0$.

7. Solution Set

The set of all roots of an equation in a given domain is called the solution set of the equation.

e.g. The roots of the equation

$x^3 - 2x^2 - 5x + 6 = 0$ are $1, -2, 3$, the solution set is $\{1, -2, 3\}$.

JEE Focus Points

- A polynomial equation of degree one is called a **linear equation** i.e. $ax + b = 0$, where $a, b \in C$, set of all complex numbers and $a \neq 0$.
- A polynomial equation of degree two is called a **quadratic equation** i.e. $ax^2 + bx + c$, where $a, b, c \in C$ and $a \neq 0$.
- A polynomial equation of degree three is called a **cubic equation** i.e. $ax^3 + bx^2 + cx + d = 0$, where $a, b, c, d \in C$ and $a \neq 0$.
- A polynomial equation of degree four is called a **biquadratic equation** i.e. $ax^4 + bx^3 + cx^2 + dx + e = 0$, where $a, b, c, d, e \in C$ and $a \neq 0$.
- A polynomial equation of degree five is called a **pentic equation** i.e. $ax^5 + bx^4 + cx^3 + dx^2 + ex + f = 0$, where $a, b, c, d, e, f \in C$ and $a \neq 0$.
- The real roots of an equation $F(x) = 0$ are the values of x, where the curve $y = F(x)$ crosses X-axis.
- Solve or solving an equation means finding its solution set or obtaining all its roots.

Example 1. A polynomial in x of degree 3 vanishes when $x = 1$ and $x = -2$ and has the values 4 and 28 when $x = -1$ and $x = 2$, respectively. Find the value of polynomial when $x = 3$.

Sol. We have,

$$f(x) = (x-1)(x+2)(ax+b)$$

Now, $f(-1) = 4$ and $f(2) = 28$

$\therefore (-1-1)(-1+2)(-a+b) = 4$

$\Rightarrow \quad a - b = 2$

and $(2-1)(2+2)(2a+b) = 28$

$\Rightarrow \quad 2a + b = 7$

$\therefore \quad a = 3, b = 1$

Thus, $f(x) = (x-1)(x+2)(3x+1)$

$\therefore \quad f(3) = (3-1)(3+2)(9+1)$

$= 100$

Remainder Theorem

The remainder theorem states that if a polynomial $P(x)$ is divided by a linear polynomial $(x - a)$, then the remainder is equal to $P(a)$.

Example 2. Let $a \neq 0$ and $P(x)$ be a polynomial of degree greater than 2. If $P(x)$ leaves remainder a and $-a$ when divided, respectively, by $x + a$ and $x - a$, then find the remainder when $P(x)$ is divided by $x^2 - a^2$.

Sol. We have, $P(a) = -a$ and $P(-a) = a$

Let the remainder, when $P(x)$ is divided by $x^2 - a^2$ be $Ax + B$.

$\therefore P(x) = Q(x)(x^2 - a^2) + Ax + B$, where $Q(x)$ is quotient.

Now, $\quad P(a) = Aa + B$

$\Rightarrow \quad Aa + B = -a$

and $\quad P(-a) = -Aa + B \Rightarrow -Aa + B = a$

$\therefore \quad B = 0, A = -1$

So, required remainder $= -x$

Factor Theorem

Factor theorem states that for any polynomial $P(x)$, if $P(a) = 0$, then $P(x)$ is divisible by $x - a$.

Example 3. If $x^2 + x - 6$ is a factor of

$$2x^4 + x^3 - ax^2 + bx + a + b - 1,$$

then find the values of a and b.

Sol. We have, $x^2 + x - 6 = (x+3)(x-2)$

Let $P(x) = 2x^4 + x^3 - ax^2 + bx + a + b - 1$

Since, $x^2 + x - 6$ is a factor of $P(x)$

$\therefore \quad P(-3) = 0$

$\Rightarrow \quad 134 - 8a - 2b = 0$

$\Rightarrow \quad 4a + b = 67 \quad$ ...(i)

and $\quad P(2) = 0$

$\Rightarrow \quad 39 - 3a + 3b = 0$

$\Rightarrow \quad a - b = 13 \quad$ ...(ii)

On solving Eqs. (i) and (ii), we get

$$a = 16, b = 3$$

2.2 Identity

If two expressions are equal for all values of x, then the statement of equality between the two expressions is called an identity.

e.g. $(x+1)^2 = x^2 + 2x + 1$ is an identity in x.

or

If $f(x) = 0$ is satisfied by every value of x in the domain of $f(x)$, then it is called an identity.

e.g. $f(x) = (x+1)^2 - (x^2 + 2x + 1) = 0$ is an identity in the domain C, as it is satisfied by every complex number.

or

If $f(x) = a_0 \cdot x^n + a_1 \cdot x^{n-1} + a_2 \cdot x^{n-2} + \ldots + a_{n-1} \cdot x + a_n = 0$

have more than n distinct roots, it is an identity, then

$$a_0 = a_1 = a_2 = \ldots = a_{n-1} = a_n = 0$$

e.g. If $ax^2 + bx + c = 0$ is satisfied by more than two values of x, then $a = b = c = 0$.

or

In an identity in x coefficients of similar powers of x on the two sides are equal.

e.g. If $ax^4 + bx^3 + cx^2 + dx + e = 5x^4 - 3x^3 + 4x^2 - 7x - 9$ be an identity in x, then $a = 5, b = -3, c = 4, d = -7, e = -9$.

Thus, an identity in x satisfied by all values of x, where as an equation in x is satisfied by some particular values of x.

Example 4. If equation

$$(\lambda^2 - 5\lambda + 6)x^2 + (\lambda^2 - 3\lambda + 2)x + (\lambda^2 - 4) = 0$$

is satisfied by more than two values of x, then find the parameter λ.

Sol. If an equation of degree two is satisfied by more than two values of unknown, then it must be an identity. Then, we must have

$$\lambda^2 - 5\lambda + 6 = 0, \lambda^2 - 3\lambda + 2 = 0, \lambda^2 - 4 = 0$$

$$\Rightarrow \quad \lambda = 2, 3 \text{ and } \lambda = 2, 1 \text{ and } \lambda = 2, -2$$

Common value of λ which satisfies each condition is $\lambda = 2$.

Example 5. Show that

$$\frac{(x+b)(x+c)}{(b-a)(c-a)} + \frac{(x+c)(x+a)}{(c-b)(a-b)} + \frac{(x+a)(x+b)}{(a-c)(b-c)} = 1$$

is an identity.

Sol. Given relation is

$$\frac{(x+b)(x+c)}{(b-a)(c-a)} + \frac{(x+c)(x+a)}{(c-b)(a-b)} + \frac{(x+a)(x+b)}{(a-c)(b-c)} = 1 \quad \text{...(i)}$$

When $x = -a$, then

$$\text{LHS of Eq. (i)} = \frac{(b-a)(c-a)}{(b-a)(c-a)} = 1 = \text{RHS of Eq. (i)}$$

When $x = -b$, then

$$\text{LHS of Eq. (i)} = \frac{(c-b)(a-b)}{(c-b)(a-b)} = 1 = \text{RHS of Eq. (i)}$$

and when $x = -c$, then

$$\text{LHS of Eq. (i)} = \frac{(a-c)(b-c)}{(a-c)(b-c)} = 1 = \text{RHS of Eq. (i)}.$$

Thus, highest power of x occurring in relation of Eq. (i) is 2 and this relation is satisfied by three distinct values of $x (= -a, -b, -c)$.

Therefore, it cannot be an equation and hence it is an identity.

Graphical Interpretation of Zero of an Expression and Roots of an Equation

The zeroes of an expression are the x-coordinates of the points where the graph of expression intersects the X-axis.

e.g. Let graph of a polynomial $P(x)$ is given as

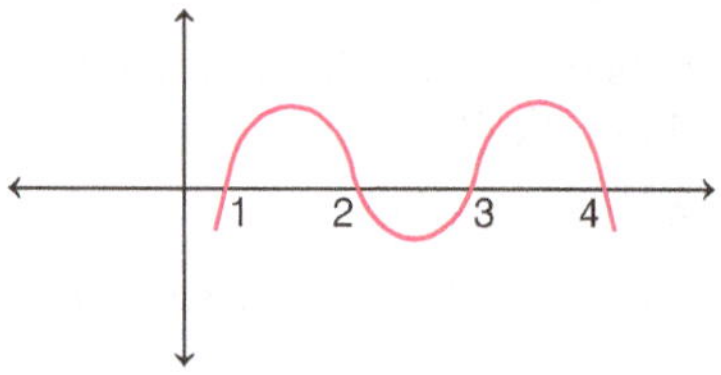

Since, graph intersects X-axis at $x = 1, 2, 3, 4$ which are zeroes of $P(x)$ or roots of the equation $P(x) = 0$.

Solving an Equation

While solving an equation $P(x) = 0$, always we take those values of variable which lies within the domain of equation.

Example 6. Solve

(i) $\dfrac{x^2 - 2x - 3}{x + 1} = 0$ (ii) $(x^3 - 4x)\sqrt{x^2 - 1} = 0$

Sol. (i) We have, $\dfrac{x^2 - 2x - 3}{x + 1} = 0$

$$\Rightarrow \quad x^2 - 2x - 3 = 0, x \neq -1$$

$$\Rightarrow (x-3)(x+1) = 0, x \neq -1$$

$$\Rightarrow \quad x = 3, -1, x \neq -1$$

So, $x = 3$

(ii) We have, $(x^3 - 4x)\sqrt{x^2 - 1} = 0$

It is solvable for $x^2 - 1 \geq 0$

$$\Rightarrow \quad x \in (-\infty, -1] \cup [1, \infty)$$

Now, $(x^3 - 4x)\sqrt{x^2 - 1} = 0$

$$\Rightarrow x(x-2)(x+2)\sqrt{x^2 - 1} = 0$$

$$\Rightarrow \quad x = 0, 2, -2, -1, 1$$

But $x \in (-\infty, -1] \cup [1, \infty)$

$$\therefore \quad x = -1, -2, 1, 2$$

Linear Equation

An equation of the form

$$ax + b = 0 \quad \text{...(i)}$$

where $a, b \in R$ and $a \neq 0$, is a linear equation.

Eq. (i) has an unique root equal to $-\dfrac{b}{a}$.

Example 7. Solve the equation $\dfrac{x}{2} + \dfrac{(3x-1)}{6} = 1 - \dfrac{x}{2}$

Sol. We have, $\dfrac{x}{2} + \dfrac{(3x-1)}{6} = 1 - \dfrac{x}{2}$

$$\Rightarrow \quad \frac{x}{2} + \frac{x}{2} + \frac{x}{2} = 1 + \frac{1}{6} \Rightarrow \frac{3x}{2} = \frac{7}{6} \Rightarrow x = \frac{7}{9}$$

Example 8. Solve the equation $(a-3)x+5=a+2$.

Sol. *Case I* For $a \neq 3$, this equation is linear, then

$(a-3)\,x=(a-3)$.

$$\therefore \qquad x=\frac{(a-3)}{(a-3)}=1$$

Case II For $a=3$,

$$0\cdot x+5=3+2$$

$$\Rightarrow \qquad 5=5$$

Therefore, any real number is its solution.

2.3 Quadratic Equations

An equation in which the highest power of the unknown quantity is 2, is called a quadratic equation.

Quadratic equations are of two types :

1. Purely Quadratic Equation

A quadratic equation in which the term containing the first degree of the unknown quantity is absent, is called a purely quadratic equation.

i.e. $\qquad ax^2+c=0,$

where $a, c \in C$ and $a \neq 0$.

2. Adfected Quadratic Equation

A quadratic equation in which it contains the terms of first as well as second degrees of the unknown quantity, is called an adfected (or complete) quadratic equation.

i.e. $\qquad ax^2+bx+c=0,$

where $a, b, c \in C$ and $a \neq 0, b \neq 0$.

Standard Quadratic Equation

An equation of the form

$$ax^2+bx+c=0 \qquad \text{...(i)}$$

where $a, b, c \in C$ and $a \neq 0$, is called a standard quadratic equation.

The numbers a, b, c are called the coefficients of this equation.

A root of the quadratic Eq. (i) is a complex number α, such that $a\alpha^2+b\alpha+c=0$.

Recall that $D=b^2-4ac$ is the discriminant of the Eq. (i) and its roots are given by the following formula.

$$x=\frac{-b\pm\sqrt{D}}{2a} \qquad \text{[Shridharacharya method]}$$

2.4 Nature of Roots

1. If $a, b, c \in R$ and $a \neq 0$, then
   (i) If $D<0$, then Eq. (i) has non-real complex roots.
   (ii) If $D>0$, then Eq. (i) has real and distinct roots, namely
   $$x_1=\frac{-b+\sqrt{D}}{2a},\ x_2=\frac{-b-\sqrt{D}}{2a} \text{ and then}$$
   $$ax^2+bx+c=a(x-x_1)(x-x_2). \qquad \text{...(ii)}$$
   (iii) If $D=0$, then Eq. (i) has real and equal roots, then
   $x_1=x_2=-\dfrac{b}{2a}$ and then
   $$ax^2+bx+c=a(x-x_1)^2. \qquad \text{...(iii)}$$
   To represent the quadratic ax^2+bx+c in form Eqs. (ii) or (iii), is to expand it into linear factors.
   (iv) If $D \geq 0$, then Eq. (i) has real roots.
   (v) If D_1 and D_2 be the discriminants of two quadratic equations, then
   (a) If $D_1+D_2 \geq 0$, then
   - atleast one of D_1 and $D_2 \geq 0$.
   - if $D_1<0$, then $D_2>0$ and if $D_1>0$, then $D_2<0$.

   (b) If $D_1+D_2<0$, then
   - atleast one of D_1 and $D_2<0$.
   - if $D_1<0$, then $D_2>0$ and if $D_1>0$, then $D_2<0$.
2. If $a, b, c \in Q$ and D is a perfect square of a rational number, the roots are rational and in case it is not a perfect square, the roots are irrational.
3. If $a, b, c \in R$ and $p+iq$ is one root of Eq. (i) $(q \neq 0)$, then the other must be the conjugate $(p-iq)$ and *vice-versa* (where, $p, q \in R$ and $i=\sqrt{-1}$).
4. If $a, b, c \in Q$ and $p+\sqrt{q}$ is one root of Eq. (i), then the other must be the conjugate $p-\sqrt{q}$ and *vice-versa* (where, p is a rational and $\sqrt{q}$ is a surd).
5. If $a=1$ and $b, c \in I$ and the roots of Eq. (i) are rational numbers, these roots must be integers.
6. If $a+b+c=0$ and a, b, c are rational, 1 is a root of the Eq. (i) and roots of the Eq. (i) are rational.
7. $a^2+b^2+c^2-ab-bc-ca=\dfrac{1}{2}$
   $\{(a-b)^2+(b-c)^2+(c-a)^2\}$
   $$=-\{(a-b)(b-c)+(b-c)(c-a)+(c-a)(a-b)\}$$

Example 9. Find all values of the parameter a for which the quadratic equation

$$(a+1)x^2+2(a+1)x+a-2=0$$

(i) has two distinct roots.
(ii) has no roots.
(iii) has two equal roots.

Sol. By the hypothesis, this equation is quadratic and therefore $a \neq -1$ and the discriminant of this equation,

$$D = 4(a+1)^2 - 4(a+1)(a-2)$$
$$= 4(a+1)(a+1-a+2)$$
$$= 12(a+1)$$

(i) For $a > (-1)$, then $D > 0$, this equation has two distinct roots.
(ii) For $a < (-1)$, then $D < 0$, this equation has no roots.
(iii) This equation cannot have two equal roots. Since, $D = 0$ only for $a = -1$ and this contradicts the hypothesis.

Example 10. Solve for x,

$$(5+2\sqrt{6})^{x^2-3}+(5-2\sqrt{6})^{x^2-3}=10.$$

Sol. $\because$ $(5+2\sqrt{6})(5-2\sqrt{6})=1$

$\therefore$ $(5-2\sqrt{6}) = \dfrac{1}{(5+2\sqrt{6})}$

$\therefore$ $(5+2\sqrt{6})^{x^2-3}+(5-2\sqrt{6})^{x^2-3}=10$

reduces to $(5+2\sqrt{6})^{x^2-3}+\left(\dfrac{1}{5+2\sqrt{6}}\right)^{x^2-3}=10$

Put $(5+2\sqrt{6})^{x^2-3}=t$, then $t+\dfrac{1}{t}=10$

$\Rightarrow$ $t^2-10t+1=0$

or $t = \dfrac{10 \pm \sqrt{(100-4)}}{2} = (5 \pm 2\sqrt{6})$

$\Rightarrow$ $(5+2\sqrt{6})^{x^2-3} = (5\pm 2\sqrt{6}) = (5+2\sqrt{6})^{\pm 1}$

$\therefore$ $x^2-3=\pm 1$

$\Rightarrow$ $x^2-3=1$ or $x^2-3=-1$

$\Rightarrow$ $x^2=4$ or $x^2=2$

Hence, $x=\pm 2, \pm\sqrt{2}$

Example 11. Find all roots of the equation $x^4+2x^3-16x^2-22x+7=0$, if one root is $2+\sqrt{3}$.

Sol. All coefficients are real, irrational roots will occur in conjugate pairs.

Hence, another root is $2-\sqrt{3}$.

$\therefore$ Product of these roots $=(x-2-\sqrt{3})(x-2+\sqrt{3})$
$=(x-2)^2-3=x^2-4x+1$

On dividing $x^4+2x^3-16x^2-22x+7$ by x^2-4x+1, then the other quadratic factor is x^2+6x+7.

Then, the given equation reduce in the form

$$(x^2-4x+1)(x^2+6x+7)=0$$

$\therefore$ $x^2+6x+7=0$

Then, $x = \dfrac{-6\pm\sqrt{36-28}}{2} = -3\pm\sqrt{2}$

Hence, the other roots are $2-\sqrt{3}, -3\pm\sqrt{2}$.

2.5 Relation between Roots and Coefficients

1. **Relation between roots and coefficients of quadratic equation** If roots of the equation $ax^2+bx+c=0\ (a\neq 0)$ be real and distinct and $\alpha<\beta$, then $\alpha = \dfrac{-b+\sqrt{D}}{2a}, \beta = \dfrac{-b-\sqrt{D}}{2a}$.

   (i) Sum of roots

   $$= S = \alpha+\beta = -\frac{b}{a} = -\frac{\text{Coefficient of } x}{\text{Coefficient of } x^2}$$

   (ii) Product of roots

   $$= P = \alpha\beta = \frac{c}{a} = \frac{\text{Constant term}}{\text{Coefficient of } x^2}$$

   (iii) Difference of roots

   $$= D' = \alpha-\beta = \frac{\sqrt{D}}{a} = \frac{\sqrt{\text{Discriminant}}}{\text{Coefficient of } x^2}$$

2. **Formation of an equation with given roots** A quadratic equation whose roots are α and β, is given by $(x-\alpha)(x-\beta)=0$ or $x^2-(\alpha+\beta)x+\alpha\beta=0$

   i.e. x^2-(Sum of roots) $x+$Product of roots $=0$

   $\therefore$ $x^2-Sx+P=0.$

3. **Symmetric function of roots** A function of α and β is said to be symmetric function, if it remains unchanged, when α and β are interchanged.

   e.g. $\alpha^3+3\alpha^2\beta+3\alpha\beta^2+\beta^3$ is a symmetric function of α and β, whereas $\alpha^3-\beta^3+5\alpha\beta$ is not a symmetric function of α and β. In order to find the value of a symmetric function in terms of $\alpha+\beta, \alpha\beta$ and $\alpha-\beta$ and also in terms of a, b and c.

   (i) $\alpha^2+\beta^2=(\alpha+\beta)^2-2\alpha\beta$

   $$=\left(-\frac{b}{a}\right)^2-2\left(\frac{c}{a}\right)=\frac{b^2-2ac}{a^2}$$

(ii) $\alpha^2 - \beta^2 = (\alpha+\beta)(\alpha-\beta)$

$$= \left(-\frac{b}{a}\right)\left(\frac{\sqrt{D}}{a}\right) = -\frac{b\sqrt{D}}{a^2}$$

(iii) $\alpha^3 + \beta^3 = (\alpha+\beta)^3 - 3\alpha\beta(\alpha+\beta)$

$$= \left(-\frac{b}{a}\right)^3 - 3\left(\frac{c}{a}\right)\left(-\frac{b}{a}\right) = -\left(\frac{b^3 - 3abc}{a^3}\right)$$

(iv) $\alpha^3 - \beta^3 = (\alpha-\beta)^3 + 3\alpha\beta(\alpha-\beta)$

$$= \left(\frac{\sqrt{D}}{a}\right)^3 + 3\left(\frac{c}{a}\right)\left(\frac{\sqrt{D}}{a}\right) = \frac{\sqrt{D}(D+3ac)}{a^3}$$

(v) $\alpha^4 + \beta^4 = (\alpha^2+\beta^2)^2 - 2\alpha^2\beta^2$

$$= \left(\frac{b^2 - 2ac}{a^2}\right)^2 - 2\left(\frac{c}{a}\right)^2$$

$$= \frac{b^4 + 2a^2c^2 - 4acb^2}{a^4}$$

(vi) $\alpha^4 - \beta^4 = (\alpha^2+\beta^2)(\alpha^2-\beta^2) = -\dfrac{b\sqrt{D}(b^2-2ac)}{a^4}$

(vii) $\alpha^5 + \beta^5 = (\alpha^2+\beta^2)(\alpha^3+\beta^3) - \alpha^2\beta^2(\alpha+\beta)$

$$= \left(\frac{b^2-2ac}{a^2}\right)\left(-\frac{(b^3-3abc)}{a^3}\right) - \frac{c^2}{a^2}\left(-\frac{b}{a}\right)$$

$$= \frac{-(b^5 - 5ab^3c + 5a^2bc^2)}{a^5}$$

(viii) $\alpha^5 - \beta^5 = (\alpha^2+\beta^2)(\alpha^3-\beta^3) + \alpha^2\beta^2(\alpha-\beta)$

$$= \left(\frac{b^2-2ac}{a^2}\right)\left(\frac{\sqrt{D}(D+3ac)}{a^3}\right) + \left(\frac{c}{a}\right)^2\left(\frac{\sqrt{D}}{a}\right)$$

$$= \frac{\sqrt{D}(b^4 - 3acb^2 + 3a^2c^2)}{a^5}$$

Example 12. If one root of the equation $x^2 - \sqrt{5}x - 19 = 0$ is $\dfrac{9+\sqrt{5}}{2}$, then find the other root.

Sol. All coefficients of the given equation are not rational, then

other root $\neq \dfrac{9-\sqrt{5}}{2}$.

Let other root be α, sum of roots $= \sqrt{5}$

$$\Rightarrow \quad \frac{9+\sqrt{5}}{2} + \alpha = \sqrt{5}$$

$$\Rightarrow \quad \alpha = \frac{-9+\sqrt{5}}{2}$$

Hence, other root is $\dfrac{-9+\sqrt{5}}{2}$.

Example 13. If the difference between the corresponding roots of the equations $x^2 + ax + b = 0$ and $x^2 + bx + a = 0$ $(a \neq b)$ is the same, find the value of $a + b$.

Sol. Let α, β be the roots of $x^2 + ax + b = 0$ and γ, δ be the roots of $x^2 + bx + a = 0$, then given

$$\alpha - \beta = \gamma - \delta$$

$$\Rightarrow \quad \frac{\sqrt{a^2-4b}}{1} = \frac{\sqrt{b^2-4a}}{1} \qquad \left[\because \alpha - \beta = \frac{\sqrt{D}}{a}\right]$$

$$\Rightarrow \quad a^2 - 4b = b^2 - 4a$$

$$\Rightarrow \quad (a^2 - b^2) + 4(a - b) = 0$$

$$\Rightarrow \quad (a-b)(a+b+4) = 0$$

$$\because \quad a - b \neq 0$$

$$\therefore \quad a + b + 4 = 0 \text{ or } a + b = -4.$$

Example 14. If $a + b + c = 0$ and a, b, c are rational. Prove that the roots of the equation $(b+c-a)x^2 + (c+a-b)x + (a+b-c) = 0$ are rational.

Sol. Given equation is

$$(b+c-a)x^2 + (c+a-b)x + (a+b-c) = 0 \quad \text{...(i)}$$

$\because (b+c-a) + (c+a-b) + (a+b-c) = a+b+c = 0$

$\therefore$ $x = 1$ is a root of Eq. (i), let other root of Eq. (i) is α, then

$$\text{Product of roots} = \frac{a+b-c}{b+c-a}$$

$$\Rightarrow \quad 1 \times \alpha = \frac{-c-c}{-a-a} \qquad [\because a+b+c=0]$$

$$\therefore \quad \alpha = \frac{c}{a} \qquad \text{[rational]}$$

Hence, both roots of Eq. (i) are rational.

Alternate Solution

Let $b + c - a = A, c + a - b = B, a + b - c = C$

Then, $A + B + C = 0$ $\quad [\because a + b + c = 0]$ ...(ii)

Now, Eq. (i) becomes

$$Ax^2 + Bx + C = 0 \quad \text{...(iii)}$$

Discriminant of Eq. (iii),

$$D = B^2 - 4AC$$

$$= (-C - A)^2 - 4AC \qquad [\because A + B + C = 0]$$

$$= (C + A)^2 - 4AC$$

$$= (C - A)^2 = (2a - 2c)^2$$

$$= 4(a - c)^2 = \text{A perfect square}$$

Hence, roots of Eq. (i) are rational.

Example 15. If the roots of equation

$$a(b-c)x^2 + b(c-a)x + c(a-b) = 0$$

be equal, prove that a, b, c are in HP.

Sol. Given equation is

$$a(b-c)x^2 + b(c-a)x + c(a-b) = 0 \quad \text{...(i)}$$

Here, coefficient of x^2 + coefficient of x + constant term = 0

i.e. $a(b-c)+b(c-a)+c(a-b)=0$

Then, 1 is a root of Eq. (i). Since, its roots are equal. Therefore, its other root will be also equal to 1.

Then, product of roots $= 1\times 1 = \dfrac{c(a-b)}{a(b-c)} \Rightarrow ab-ac = ca-bc$

$\therefore \quad b = \dfrac{2ac}{a+c}$

Hence, a, b and c are in HP.

Example 16. If α,β are the roots of the equation $\lambda(x^2-x)+x+5=0$. If λ_1 and λ_2 are two values of λ for which the roots α,β are related by $\dfrac{\alpha}{\beta}+\dfrac{\beta}{\alpha}=\dfrac{4}{5}$, find the value of $\dfrac{\lambda_1}{\lambda_2}+\dfrac{\lambda_2}{\lambda_1}$.

Sol. The given equation can be written as

$$\lambda x^2-(\lambda-1)x+5=0$$

$\because$ α,β are the roots of this equation.

$$\therefore \quad \alpha+\beta=\frac{\lambda-1}{\lambda} \text{ and } \alpha\beta=\frac{5}{\lambda}$$

But given $\dfrac{\alpha}{\beta}+\dfrac{\beta}{\alpha}=\dfrac{4}{5}$

$$\Rightarrow \quad \frac{\alpha^2+\beta^2}{\alpha\beta}=\frac{4}{5}$$

$$\Rightarrow \quad \frac{(\alpha+\beta)^2-2\alpha\beta}{\alpha\beta}=\frac{4}{5}$$

$$\Rightarrow \quad \frac{\dfrac{(\lambda-1)^2}{\lambda^2}-\dfrac{10}{\lambda}}{\dfrac{5}{\lambda}}=\frac{4}{5}$$

$$\Rightarrow \quad \frac{(\lambda-1)^2-10\lambda}{5\lambda}=\frac{4}{5}$$

$$\Rightarrow \quad \lambda^2-12\lambda+1=4\lambda$$

$$\Rightarrow \quad \lambda^2-16\lambda+1=0$$

It is a quadratic equation in λ, let roots be λ_1 and λ_2, then

$$\lambda_1+\lambda_2=16 \text{ and } \lambda_1\lambda_2=1$$

$$\therefore \quad \frac{\lambda_1}{\lambda_2}+\frac{\lambda_2}{\lambda_1}=\frac{\lambda_1^2+\lambda_2^2}{\lambda_1\lambda_2}=\frac{(\lambda_1+\lambda_2)^2-2\lambda_1\lambda_2}{\lambda_1\lambda_2}$$

$$=\frac{(16)^2-2(1)}{1}=254$$

Example 17. If α,β are the roots of the equation $x^2-px+q=0$, find the quadratic equation the roots of which are $(\alpha^2-\beta^2)(\alpha^3-\beta^3)$ and $\alpha^3\beta^2+\alpha^2\beta^3$.

Sol. Since, α,β are the roots of $x^2-px+q=0$.

$$\therefore \quad \alpha+\beta=p, \alpha\beta=q \Rightarrow \alpha-\beta=\sqrt{(p^2-4q)}$$

Now, $(\alpha^2-\beta^2)(\alpha^3-\beta^3)$

$$=(\alpha+\beta)(\alpha-\beta)(\alpha-\beta)(\alpha^2+\alpha\beta+\beta^2)$$

$$=(\alpha+\beta)(\alpha-\beta)^2\{(\alpha+\beta)^2-\alpha\beta\}$$

$$=p(p^2-4q)(p^2-q)$$

and $\alpha^3\beta^2+\alpha^2\beta^3=\alpha^2\beta^2(\alpha+\beta)=pq^2$

$$S = \text{Sum of roots} = p(p^2-4q)(p^2-q)+pq^2$$

$$=p(p^4-5p^2q+5q^2)$$

$$P = \text{Product of roots} = p^2q^2(p^2-4q)(p^2-q)$$

$\therefore$ Required equation is $x^2-Sx+P=0$

i.e. $x^2-p(p^4-5p^2q+5q^2)x+p^2q^2(p^2-4q)(p^2-q)=0$

JEE SCANNER

Example Similar to PYQ Asked in JEE Main 2022

Let α and β be the roots of the equation $x^2-5x-1=0$, then the value of $\dfrac{\alpha^{15}+\alpha^{11}+\beta^{15}+\beta^{11}}{\alpha^{13}+\beta^{13}}$ is ....

Sol. (27) We have, α and β are roots of the equation $x^2-5x-1=0$.

$$\therefore \quad \alpha+\beta=5, \alpha\beta=-1$$

Now, $\dfrac{\alpha^{15}+\beta^{15}+\alpha^{11}+\beta^{11}}{\alpha^{13}+\beta^{13}}=\dfrac{\alpha^{15}+\beta^{15}+\alpha^2\beta^2(\alpha^{11}+\beta^{11})}{\alpha^{13}+\beta^{13}}$

$[\because \alpha\beta=-1 \Rightarrow \alpha^2\beta^2=1]$

$$=\frac{\alpha^{15}+\alpha^{13}\beta^2+\beta^{15}+\alpha^2\beta^{13}}{\alpha^{13}+\beta^{13}}$$

$$=\frac{\alpha^{13}[\alpha^2+\beta^2]+\beta^{13}[\alpha^2+\beta^2]}{\alpha^{13}+\beta^{13}}$$

$$=\frac{(\alpha^2+\beta^2)(\alpha^{13}+\beta^{13})}{\alpha^{13}+\beta^{13}}=\alpha^2+\beta^2$$

$$=(\alpha+\beta)^2-2\alpha\beta=25+2=27$$

Skill Builder

For Sol.

If α,β are the roots of the equation $2x^2-5x+2=0$ and the value of $\dfrac{\alpha^3}{\beta}+\dfrac{\beta^3}{\alpha}-2\alpha\beta=\dfrac{m}{n}$, then $m-n$ is equal to ....

■ **For more practice** See Q.5 of Milestone Practice 2.1.

2.6 Transformation of Quadratic Equations

Let α, β be the roots of the equation $ax^2 + bx + c = 0$, then the equation

(i) whose roots are $\alpha + k, \beta + k$, is

$a(x-k)^2 + b(x-k) + c = 0$ [replace x by $(x-k)$]

(ii) whose roots are $\alpha - k, \beta - k$, is

$a(x+k)^2 + b(x+k) + c = 0$ [replace x by $(x+k)$]

(iii) whose roots are $\alpha k, \beta k$, is

$ax^2 + kbx + k^2c = 0$ $\left[\text{replace } x \text{ by} \left(\frac{x}{k}\right)\right]$

(iv) whose roots are $\frac{\alpha}{k}, \frac{\beta}{k}$, is

$ak^2x^2 + bkx + c = 0$ [replace x by xk]

(v) whose roots are $-\alpha, -\beta$, is

$ax^2 - bx + c = 0$ [replace x by $(-x)$]

(vi) whose roots are $\frac{1}{\alpha}, \frac{1}{\beta}$, is

$cx^2 + bx + a = 0$ $\left[\text{replace } x \text{ by} \left(\frac{1}{x}\right)\right]$

(vii) whose roots are $-\frac{1}{\alpha}, -\frac{1}{\beta}$, is

$cx^2 - bx + a = 0$ $\left[\text{replace } x \text{ by} \left(-\frac{1}{x}\right)\right]$

(viii) whose roots are $\frac{k}{\alpha}, \frac{k}{\beta}$, is

$cx^2 + kbx + k^2a = 0$ $\left[\text{replace } x \text{ by} \left(\frac{k}{x}\right)\right]$

(ix) whose roots are $p\alpha + q, p\beta + q$, is

$a\left(\frac{x-q}{p}\right)^2 + b\left(\frac{x-q}{p}\right) + c = 0$ $\left[\text{replace } x \text{ by} \left(\frac{x-q}{p}\right)\right]$

(x) whose roots are $\alpha^n, \beta^n, n \in N$, is

$a(x^{1/n})^2 + b(x^{1/n}) + c = 0$ [replace x by $(x^{1/n})$]

(xi) whose roots are $\alpha^{1/n}, \beta^{1/n}, n \in N$ is

$a(x^n)^2 + b(x^n) + c = 0$ [replace x by (x^n)]

Example 18. If α, β be the roots of the equation $x^2 - px + q = 0$, then find the equation whose roots are $\frac{q}{p-\alpha}$ and $\frac{q}{p-\beta}$.

Sol. Let $\frac{q}{p-\alpha} = x \Rightarrow \alpha = p - \frac{q}{x}$

So, we replacing x by $p - \frac{q}{x}$ in the given equation, we get

$$\left(p - \frac{q}{x}\right)^2 - p\left(p - \frac{q}{x}\right) + q = 0$$

$$\Rightarrow \quad p^2 + \frac{q^2}{x^2} - \frac{2pq}{x} - p^2 + \frac{pq}{x} + q = 0$$

$$\Rightarrow \quad q - \frac{pq}{x} + \frac{q^2}{x^2} = 0$$

or $qx^2 - pqx + q^2 = 0$ or $x^2 - px + q = 0$

is the required equation whose roots are $\frac{q}{p-\alpha}$ and $\frac{q}{p-\beta}$.

Example 19. If α and β are the roots of $ax^2 + bx + c = 0$, then find the roots of the equation $ax^2 - bx(x-1) + c(x-1)^2 = 0$.

Sol. $\because \quad ax^2 - bx(x-1) + c(x-1)^2 = 0$ ...(i)

$$\Rightarrow \quad a\left(\frac{x}{x-1}\right)^2 - b\left(\frac{x}{x-1}\right) + c = 0$$

$$\text{or} \quad a\left(\frac{x}{1-x}\right)^2 + b\left(\frac{x}{1-x}\right) + c = 0$$

Now, α, β are the roots of $ax^2 + bx + c = 0$.

Then, $\alpha = \frac{x}{1-x}$ and $\beta = \frac{x}{1-x}$

$$\Rightarrow \quad x = \frac{\alpha}{\alpha+1} \text{ and } x = \frac{\beta}{\beta+1}$$

Hence, $\frac{\alpha}{\alpha+1}, \frac{\beta}{\beta+1}$ are the roots of the Eq. (i).

Example 20. If α, β be the roots of the equation $3x^2 + 2x + 1 = 0$, then find value of $\left(\frac{1-\alpha}{1+\alpha}\right)^3 + \left(\frac{1-\beta}{1+\beta}\right)^3$.

Sol. Let $\frac{1-\alpha}{1+\alpha} = x \Rightarrow \alpha = \frac{1-x}{1+x}$

So, replacing x by $\frac{1-x}{1+x}$ in the given equation, we get

$$3\left(\frac{1-x}{1+x}\right)^2 + 2\left(\frac{1-x}{1+x}\right) + 1 = 0 \Rightarrow x^2 - 2x + 3 = 0 \quad \text{...(i)}$$

It is clear that $\frac{1-\alpha}{1+\alpha}$ and $\frac{1-\beta}{1+\beta}$ are the roots of Eq. (i).

$$\therefore \quad \left(\frac{1-\alpha}{1+\alpha}\right) + \left(\frac{1-\beta}{1+\beta}\right) = 2 \quad \text{...(ii)}$$

$$\text{and} \quad \left(\frac{1-\alpha}{1+\alpha}\right)\left(\frac{1-\beta}{1+\beta}\right) = 3 \quad \text{...(iii)}$$

$$\therefore \quad \left(\frac{1-\alpha}{1+\alpha}\right)^3 + \left(\frac{1-\beta}{1+\beta}\right)^3 = \left(\frac{1-\alpha}{1+\alpha} + \frac{1-\beta}{1+\beta}\right)^3 - 3\left(\frac{1-\alpha}{1+\alpha}\right)\left(\frac{1-\beta}{1+\beta}\right)\left(\frac{1-\alpha}{1+\alpha} + \frac{1-\beta}{1+\beta}\right) = 2^3 - 3 \cdot 3 \cdot 2$$

$$= 8 - 18 = -10$$

Roots Under Special Cases

Consider the quadratic equation $ax^2 + bx + c = 0$ ...(i)

where $a, b, c \in R$ and $a \neq 0$. Then, the following hold good :

(i) If roots of Eq. (i) are equal in magnitude but opposite in sign, then sum of roots is zero as well as $D > 0$, i.e. $b = 0$ and $D > 0$.

(ii) If roots of Eq. (i) are reciprocal to each other, then product of roots is 1 as well as $D \geq 0$ i.e. $a = c$ and $D \geq 0$.

(iii) If roots of Eq. (i) are of opposite signs, then product of roots < 0 as well as $D > 0$ i.e. $a > 0, c < 0$ and $D > 0$ or $a < 0, c > 0$ and $D > 0$.

(iv) If both roots of Eq. (i) are positive, then sum and product of roots > 0 as well as $D \geq 0$ i.e. $a > 0, b < 0, c > 0$ and $D \geq 0$ or $a < 0, b > 0, c < 0$ and $D \geq 0$.

(v) If both roots of Eq. (i) are negative, then sum of roots < 0, product of roots > 0 as well as $D \geq 0$ i.e. $a > 0, b > 0, c > 0$ and $D \geq 0$ or $a < 0, b < 0, c < 0$ and $D \geq 0$.

(vi) If atleast one root of Eq. (i) is positive, then either one root is positive or both roots are positive i.e. point (iii) $\cup$ (iv).

(vii) If atleast one root of Eq. (i) is negative, then either one root is negative or both roots are negative i.e. point (iii) $\cup$ (v).

(viii) If greater root in magnitude of Eq. (i) is positive, then sign of b = sign of $c \neq$ sign of a.

(ix) If greater root in magnitude of Eq. (i) is negative, then sign of a = sign of $b \neq$ sign of c.

(x) If both roots of Eq. (i) are zero, then $b = c = 0$.

(xi) If roots of Eq. (i) are 0 and $\left(-\frac{b}{a}\right)$, then $c = 0$.

(xii) If roots of Eq. (i) are 1 and $\frac{c}{a}$, then $a + b + c = 0$.

Example 21. For what values of m, the equation $x^2 + 2(m-1)x + m + 5 = 0$ has $(m \in R)$

(i) roots are equal in magnitude but opposite in sign?
(ii) roots are reciprocals to each other?
(iii) roots are opposite in sign?
(iv) both roots are positive?
(v) both roots are negative?
(vi) atleast one root is positive?
(vii) atleast one root is negative?

Sol. Here, $a = 1, b = 2(m-1)$ and $c = m + 5$

$\therefore \quad D = b^2 - 4ac = 4(m-1)^2 - 4(m+5) = 4(m^2 - 3m - 4)$

$\therefore \quad D = 4(m-4)(m+1)$ and here $a = 1 > 0$

(i) $b = 0$ and $D > 0$

$\Rightarrow 2(m-1) = 0$ and $4(m-4)(m+1) > 0$

$\Rightarrow m = 1$ and $m \in (-\infty, -1) \cup (4, \infty)$

$\therefore \quad m \in \phi$ [null set]

(ii) $a = c$ and $D \geq 0$

$\Rightarrow 1 = m + 5$ and $4(m-4)(m+1) \geq 0$

$\Rightarrow m = -4$ and $m \in (-\infty, -1] \cup [4, \infty)$

$\therefore \quad m = -4$

(iii) $a > 0, c < 0$ and $D > 0$

$\Rightarrow 1 > 0, m + 5 < 0$ and $4(m-4)(m+1) > 0$

$\Rightarrow m < -5$ and $m \in (-\infty, -1) \cup (4, \infty)$

$\therefore \quad m \in (-\infty, -5)$

(iv) $a > 0, b < 0, c > 0$ and $D \geq 0$

$\Rightarrow 1 > 0, 2(m-1) < 0, m + 5 > 0$

and $4(m-4)(m+1) \geq 0$

$\Rightarrow m < 1, m > -5$ and $m \in (-\infty, -1] \cup [4, \infty)$

$\Rightarrow m \in (-5, -1]$

(v) $a > 0, b > 0, c > 0$ and $D \geq 0$

$\Rightarrow 1 > 0, 2(m-1) > 0, m + 5 > 0$

and $4(m-4)(m+1) \geq 0$

$\Rightarrow m > 1, m > -5$ and $m \in (-\infty, -1] \cup [4, \infty)$

$\therefore \quad m \in [4, \infty)$

(vi) Either one root is positive or both roots are positive i.e. part (iii) $\cup$ (iv)

$\Rightarrow m \in (-\infty, -5) \cup (-5, -1]$

(vii) Either one root is negative or both roots are negative i.e. part (iii) $\cup$ (v)

$\Rightarrow m \in (-\infty, -5) \cup [4, \infty)$

2.7 Conditions for Common Roots

1. Only One Root is Common

Consider two quadratic equations

$$ax^2 + bx + c = 0 \text{ and } a'x^2 + b'x + c' = 0$$

[where $a, a' \neq 0$ and $ab' - a'b \neq 0$]

Let α be a common root, then

$$a\alpha^2 + b\alpha + c = 0 \text{ and } a'\alpha^2 + b'\alpha + c' = 0.$$

On solving these two equations by cross-multiplication, we have

$$\frac{\alpha^2}{bc' - b'c} = \frac{\alpha}{ca' - c'a} = \frac{1}{ab' - a'b}$$

From first two relations, we get

$$\alpha = \frac{bc' - b'c}{ca' - c'a} \quad \text{...(i)}$$

and from last two relations, we get

$$\alpha = \frac{ca' - c'a}{ab' - a'b} \quad \text{...(ii)}$$

From Eqs. (i) and (ii), we get

$$\frac{bc' - b'c}{ca' - c'a} = \frac{ca' - c'a}{ab' - a'b}$$

$$\Rightarrow \quad (ab' - a'b)(bc' - b'c) = (ca' - c'a)^2$$

$$\text{or} \quad \begin{vmatrix} a & b \\ a' & b' \end{vmatrix} \times \begin{vmatrix} b & c \\ b' & c' \end{vmatrix} = \begin{vmatrix} c & a \\ c' & a' \end{vmatrix}^2 \quad \text{[remember]}$$

This is the required condition for one root of two quadratic equations to be common.

2. Both Roots are Common

Let α, β be the common roots of the equations $ax^2 + bx + c = 0$ and $a'x^2 + b'x + c' = 0$, then

$$\alpha + \beta = -\frac{b}{a} = -\frac{b'}{a'} \Rightarrow \frac{a}{a'} = \frac{b}{b'} \quad \text{...(iii)}$$

$$\text{and} \quad \alpha\beta = \frac{c}{a} = \frac{c'}{a'} \Rightarrow \frac{a}{a'} = \frac{c}{c'} \quad \text{...(iv)}$$

From Eqs. (iii) and (iv), we get $\frac{a}{a'} = \frac{b}{b'} = \frac{c}{c'}$

This is the required condition for both roots of two quadratic equations to be identical.

JEE SPIKE

To find the common root between the two equations, make the same coefficient of x^2 in both equations and then subtract of the two equations.

Concept Inside Video

Example 22. Find the value of λ, so that the equations $x^2 - x - 12 = 0$ and $\lambda x^2 + 10x + 3 = 0$ may have one root in common. Also, find the common root.

Sol. $\because \quad x^2 - x - 12 = 0 \Rightarrow (x - 4)(x + 3) = 0$

$\therefore \quad x = 4, -3$

If $x = 4$ is a common root, then

$$\lambda(4)^2 + 10(4) + 3 = 0$$

$$\therefore \quad \lambda = -\frac{43}{16}$$

and if $x = -3$ is a common root, then

$$\lambda(-3)^2 + 10(-3) + 3 = 0$$

$$\therefore \quad \lambda = 3$$

Hence, for $\lambda = -\frac{43}{16}$, common root is $x = 4$

and for $\lambda = 3$, common root is $x = -3$.

Example 23. If a, b, c are in GP, show that the equations $ax^2 + 2bx + c = 0$ and $dx^2 + 2ex + f = 0$ have a common root, if $\frac{a}{d}, \frac{b}{e}, \frac{c}{f}$ are in HP.

Sol. Given equations are

$$ax^2 + 2bx + c = 0 \quad \text{...(i)}$$

$$\text{and} \quad dx^2 + 2ex + f = 0 \quad \text{...(ii)}$$

Since, a, b, c are in GP.

$$\therefore \quad b^2 = ac \text{ or } b = \sqrt{ac}$$

From Eq. (i), $ax^2 + 2\sqrt{ac}\,x + c = 0$

$$\text{or} \quad (\sqrt{a}\,x + \sqrt{c})^2 = 0 \quad \text{or} \quad x = -\frac{\sqrt{c}}{\sqrt{a}}$$

$\because$ Given Eqs. (i) and (ii) have a common root.

Hence, $x = -\frac{\sqrt{c}}{\sqrt{a}}$ also satisfied Eq. (ii), then

$$d\left(\frac{c}{a}\right) - 2e\frac{\sqrt{c}}{\sqrt{a}} + f = 0$$

$$\Rightarrow \quad \frac{d}{a} - \frac{2e}{\sqrt{ac}} + \frac{f}{c} = 0$$

$$\text{or} \quad \frac{d}{a} - \frac{2e}{b} + \frac{f}{c} = 0 \quad [\because b = \sqrt{ac}]$$

$$\text{or} \quad \frac{d}{a} + \frac{f}{c} = \frac{2e}{b}$$

$\therefore \quad \frac{d}{a}, \frac{e}{b}, \frac{f}{c}$ are in AP.

Hence, $\frac{a}{d}, \frac{b}{e}, \frac{c}{f}$ are in HP.

2.8 Quadratic Expression

An expression of the form $ax^2 + bx + c$, where $a, b, c \in R$ and $a \neq 0$ is called a quadratic expression in x. So, in general quadratic expression is represented by

$$f(x) = ax^2 + bx + c \quad \text{or} \quad y = ax^2 + bx + c.$$

Graph of a Quadratic Expression

We have, $\quad y = ax^2 + bx + c = f(x), \quad [a \neq 0]$

$$\Rightarrow \quad y = a\left[\left(x + \frac{b}{2a}\right)^2 - \frac{D}{4a^2}\right]$$

$$\text{or} \quad \left(y + \frac{D}{4a}\right) = a\left(x + \frac{b}{2a}\right)^2$$

Now, let $y + \frac{D}{4a} = Y$ and $x + \frac{b}{2a} = X$

$$\therefore \quad Y = aX^2 \Rightarrow X^2 = \frac{Y}{a}$$

1. The shape of the curve $y = f(x)$ is parabolic.
2. The axis of parabola is $X = 0$ or $x + \frac{b}{2a} = 0$

   or $x = -\frac{b}{2a}$ i.e. parallel to Y-axis.
3. (i) If $\frac{1}{a} > 0 \Rightarrow a > 0$, the parabola open upwards.

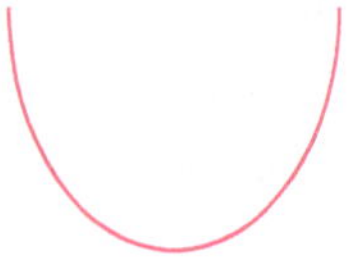

   (ii) If $\frac{1}{a} < 0 \Rightarrow a < 0$, the parabola open downwards.

4. **Intersection with axes**

   (i) Intersection with X-axis

   For X-axis, $y = 0$.

   $\therefore \quad ax^2 + bx + c = 0 \Rightarrow x = \frac{-b \pm \sqrt{D}}{2a}$

   For $D > 0$, parabola cuts X-axis in two real and distinct points

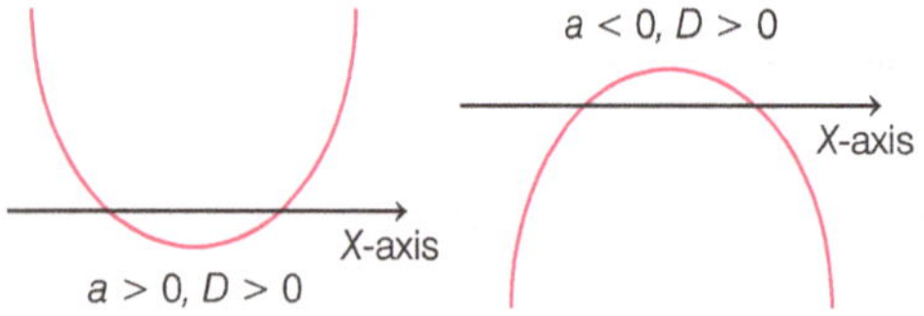

   For $D = 0$, parabola touches X-axis in one point i.e. $x = -\frac{b}{2a}$.

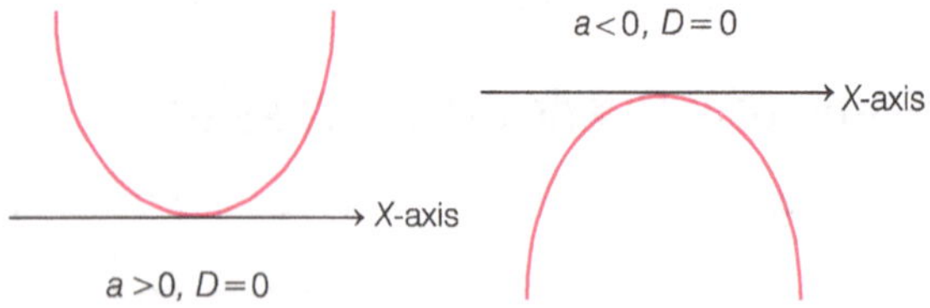

   For $D < 0$, parabola does not cut X-axis i.e. imaginary values of x.

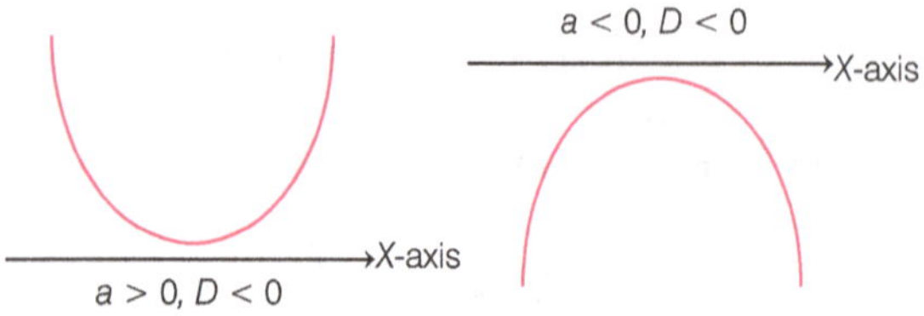

   (ii) **Intersection with Y-axis**

   For Y-axis, $x = 0$.

   $\therefore \quad y = c$

5. **Greatest and least values of $f(x)$**

   Vertex of the parabola $X^2 = \frac{1}{a}Y$ is

   $X = 0, Y = 0$

   $\Rightarrow \quad x + \frac{b}{2a} = 0, y + \frac{D}{4a} = 0$ or $x = -\frac{b}{2a}, y = -\frac{D}{4a}$

   Hence, vertex of $y = ax^2 + bx + c$ is $\left(-\frac{b}{2a}, -\frac{D}{4a}\right)$.

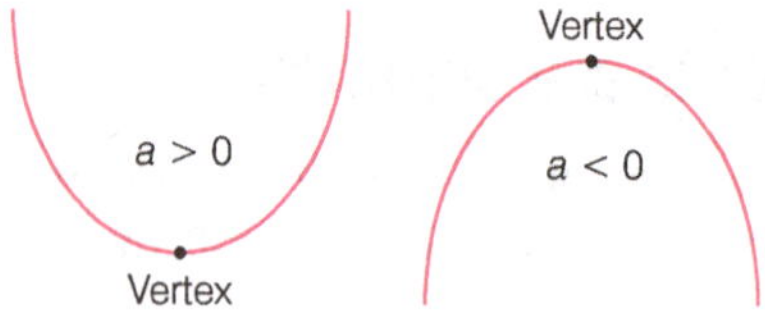

   For $a > 0$, $f(x)$ has least value at $x = -\frac{b}{2a}$.

   This least value is given by $f\left(-\frac{b}{2a}\right) = -\frac{D}{4a}$

   or $\quad y_{\text{least}} = -\frac{D}{4a}$.

   $\therefore$ Range of $y = ax^2 + bx + c$ is $\left[-\frac{D}{4a}, \infty\right)$.

   For $a < 0$, $f(x)$ has greatest value at $x = -\frac{b}{2a}$.

   This greatest value is given by $f\left(-\frac{b}{2a}\right) = -\frac{D}{4a}$

   or $\quad y_{\text{greatest}} = -\frac{D}{4a}$

   $\therefore$ Range of $y = ax^2 + bx + c$ is $\left(-\infty, -\frac{D}{4a}\right]$

Sign of Quadratic Expression

Let $f(x) = ax^2 + bx + c$ or $y = ax^2 + bx + c$,

where $a, b, c \in R$ and $a \neq 0$, for some values of x, $f(x)$ may be positive, negative or zero. This gives the following cases :

1. **$a > 0$ and $D < 0$.**

   So, $f(x) > 0$ for all $x \in R$,

   i.e. $f(x)$ is positive for all real values of x.

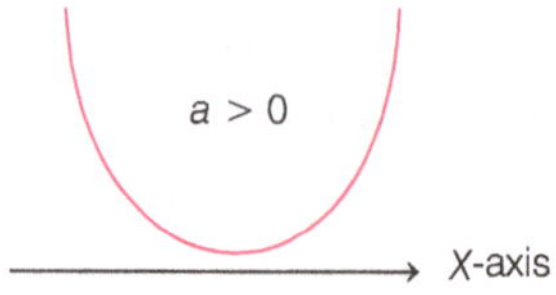

2. **$a<0$ and $D<0$**. So, $f(x)<0$ for all $x \in R$,

   i.e. $f(x)$ is negative for all real values of x.

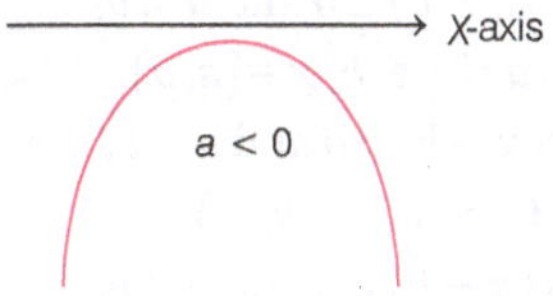

3. **$a>0$ and $D=0$**. So, $f(x) \geq 0$ for all $x \in R$,

   i.e. $f(x)$ is positive for all real values of x except at vertex, where $f(x)=0$.

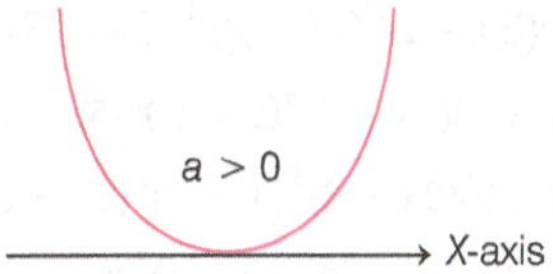

4. **$a<0$ and $D=0$**. So, $f(x) \leq 0$ for all $x \in R$,

   i.e. $f(x)$ is negative for all real values of x except at vertex, where $f(x)=0$.

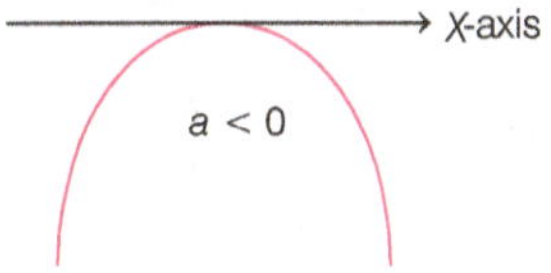

5. **$a>0$ and $D>0$**.

   Let $f(x)=0$ have two real roots α and β $(\alpha<\beta)$, then $f(x)>0$ for all $x \in(-\infty, \alpha) \cup(\beta, \infty)$ and $f(x)<0$ for all $x \in(\alpha, \beta)$.

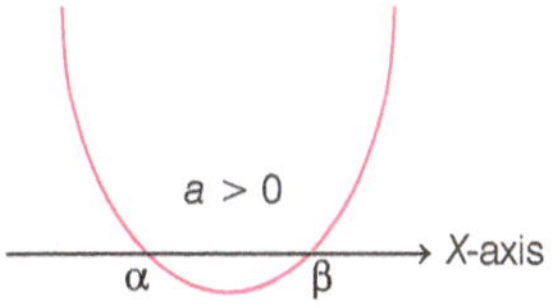

6. **$a<0$ and $D>0$**

   Let $f(x)=0$ have two real roots α and β $(\alpha<\beta)$, then $f(x)<0$ for all $x \in(-\infty, \alpha) \cup(\beta, \infty)$ and $f(x)>0$ for all $x \in(\alpha, \beta)$.

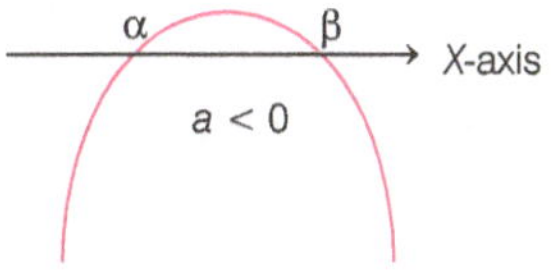

Example 24. Find the least value of n such that

$$(n-2)x^2+8x+n+4>0, \forall\, x \in R, n \in N.$$

Sol. $(n-2)x^2+8x+n+4>0, \forall\, x \in R$

$\Rightarrow D=64-4(n-2)(n+4)<0, n-2>0$

$\Rightarrow \quad 16-(n^2+2n-8)<0, n>2$

$\Rightarrow \quad n^2+2n-24>0, n>2$

$\Rightarrow \quad (n+6)(n-4)>0, n>2$

$\Rightarrow \quad n>4, n>2$

$\therefore \quad n \geq 5$.

So, least value of n is 5.

2.9 Wavy Curve Method (Generalised Method of Intervals)

Wave Curve Method is used for solving inequalities of the form

$$f(x)=\frac{(x-a_1)^{k_1}(x-a_2)^{k_2}\ldots(x-a_m)^{k_m}}{(x-b_1)^{p_1}(x-b_2)^{p_2}\ldots(x-b_n)^{p_n}}>0$$

$(<0, \geq 0 \text{ or } \leq 0)$,

where, $k_1, k_2, \ldots, k_m, p_1, p_2, \ldots, p_n$ are natural numbers and such that $a_i \neq b_j$, where $i=1,2, \ldots, m$ and $j=1,2, \ldots, n$.

We use the following methods:

1. Solve $(x-a_1)^{k_1}(x-a_2)^{k_2} \ldots(x-a_m)^{k_m}=0$ and

   $(x-b_1)^{p_1}(x-a_2)^{p_2} \ldots(x-b_n)^{p_n}=0$, then we get

   $x=a_1, a_2, \ldots, a_m, b_1, b_2, \ldots, b_n$ [critical points]

2. Assume $a_1<a_2<\ldots<a_m<b_1<b_2<\ldots<b_n$

   Plot them on the real line. Arrange inked (black) circles (●) and un-inked (white) circles (○), such that

	$a_1\ a_2 \ldots a_m$	$b_1\ b_2 \ldots b_n$
If $f(x)>0$	○ ○ ... ○	○ ○ ... ○
$f(x)<0$	○ ○ ... ○	○ ○ ... ○
$f(x) \geq 0$	● ● ... ●	○ ○ ... ○
$f(x) \leq 0$	● ● ... ●	○ ○ ... ○

3. Obviously, b_n is the greatest root. If in all brackets before x positive sign and expression has also positive sign, then wave start from right to left, beginning above the number line, i.e.

   $$+\frac{(x-a_1)^{k_1}(x-a_2)^{k_2}\ldots(x-a_m)^{k_m}}{(x-b_1)^{p_1}(x-b_2)^{p_2}\ldots(x-b_n)^{p_n}}, \text{ then}$$

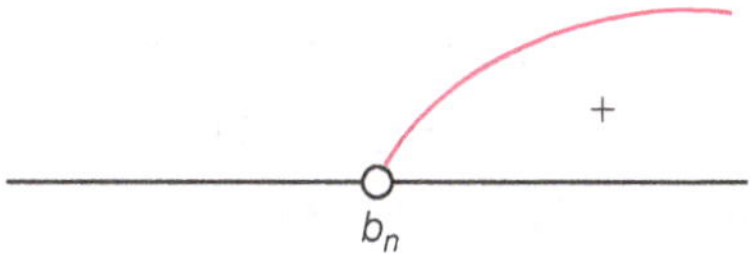

and if in all brackets before x positive sign and expression has negative sign, then wave start from right to left, beginning below the number line, i.e.

$$-\frac{(x-a_1)^{k_1}(x-a_2)^{k_2}\dots(x-a_m)^{k_m}}{(x-b_1)^{p_1}(x-b_2)^{p_2}\dots(x-b_n)^{p_n}}, \text{ then}$$

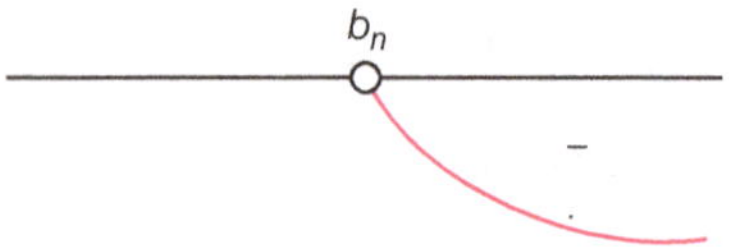

4. If roots occur even times, then sign remain same from right to left side of the roots and if roots occur odd times, then sign will change from right to left through the roots of

$$x = a_1, a_2, \dots, a_m, b_1, b_2, \dots, b_n.$$

5. The solution of $f(x) > 0$ or $f(x) \geq 0$ is the union of all intervals in which we have put the plus sign and the solution of $f(x) < 0$ or $f(x) \leq 0$ is the union of all intervals in which we have put the minus sign.

Important Results

1. The point where denominator is zero or function approaches infinity, will never be included in the answer.
2. For $x^2 < a^2$ or $|x| < a \Leftrightarrow -a < x < a$
   i.e. $x \in (-a, a)$
3. For $0 < x^2 < a^2$ or $0 < |x| < a$
   $\Leftrightarrow \quad -a < x < a \sim \{0\}$
   i.e. $x \in (-a, a) \sim \{0\}$
4. For $x^2 \geq a^2$ or $|x| \geq a \Leftrightarrow x \leq -a$ or $x \geq a$
   i.e. $x \in (-\infty, -a] \cup [a, \infty)$
5. For $x^2 > a^2$ or $|x| > a \Leftrightarrow x < -a$ or $x > a$
   i.e. $x \in (-\infty, -a) \cup (a, \infty)$
6. For $a^2 \leq x^2 \leq b^2$ or $a \leq |x| \leq b$
   $\Leftrightarrow \quad a \leq x \leq b$ or $-b \leq x \leq -a$
   i.e. $x \in [-b, -a] \cup [a, b]$
7. For $a^2 < x^2 \leq b^2$ or $a < |x| \leq b$
   $\Leftrightarrow \quad a < x \leq b$ or $-b \leq x < -a$
   i.e. $x \in [-b, -a) \cup (a, b]$
8. For $a^2 \leq x^2 < b^2$ or $a \leq |x| < b$
   $\Leftrightarrow \quad a \leq x < b$ or $-b < x \leq -a$
   i.e. $x \in (-b, -a] \cup [a, b)$
9. For $a^2 < x^2 < b^2$ or $a < |x| < b$
   $\Leftrightarrow \quad a < x < b$ or $-b < x < -a$
   i.e. $x \in (-b, -a) \cup (a, b)$
10. For $(x-a)(x-b) < 0$ and $a < b$, then $a < x < b$
    i.e. $x \in (a, b)$
11. If $(x-a)(x-b) \leq 0$ and $a < b$,
    then $a \leq x \leq b$, $x \in [a, b]$
12. If $(x-a)(x-b) > 0$ and $a < b$, then $x < a$ or $x > b$
    i.e. $x \in (-\infty, a) \cup (b, \infty)$
13. If $(x-a)(x-b) \geq 0$ and $a < b$,
    then $x \leq a$ or $x \geq b$
    i.e. $x \in (-\infty, a] \cup [b, \infty)$

Example 25. Solve the inequality

$$(x+3)(3x-2)^5(7-x)^3(5x+8)^2 \geq 0.$$

Sol. We have, $(x+3)(3x-2)^5(7-x)^3(5x+8)^2 \geq 0$

$\Rightarrow \quad -(x+3)(3x-2)^5(x-7)^3(5x+8)^2 \geq 0$

$\Rightarrow \quad (x+3)(3x-2)^5(x-7)^3(5x+8)^2 \leq 0$

[take before x, + ve sign in all brackets]

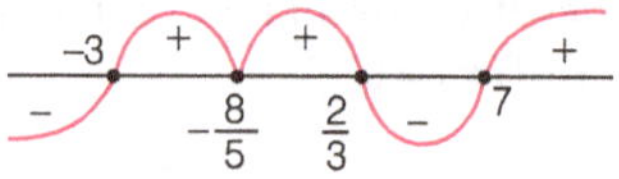

The critical points are $(-3), \left(-\frac{8}{5}\right), \frac{2}{3}, 7.$

Hence, $x \in (-\infty, -3] \cup \left[\frac{2}{3}, 7\right] \cup \left\{-\frac{8}{5}\right\}.$

Example 26. Solve the inequality

$$\frac{(x-2)^{10000}(x+1)^{253}\left(x-\frac{1}{2}\right)^{971}(x+8)^4}{x^{500}(x-3)^{75}(x+2)^{93}} \geq 0$$

Sol. We have, $\dfrac{(x-2)^{10000}(x+1)^{253}\left(x-\frac{1}{2}\right)^{971}(x+8)^4}{x^{500}(x-3)^{75}(x+2)^{93}} \geq 0$

The critical points are $(-8), (-2), (-1), 0, \frac{1}{2}, 2, 3.$

$[\because x \neq -2, 0, 3]$

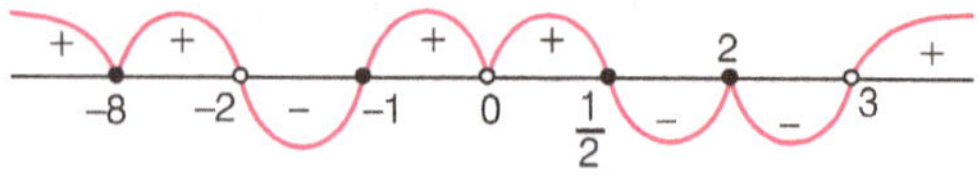

Hence, $x \in (-\infty, -8] \cup [-8, -2) \cup [-1, 0) \cup \left(0, \frac{1}{2}\right] \cup (3, \infty)$

or $\quad x \in (-\infty, -2) \cup [-1, 0) \cup \left(0, \frac{1}{2}\right] \cup (3, \infty)$

Example 27. Let $f(x) = \dfrac{(x-3)(x+2)(x+6)}{(x+1)(x-5)}$.

Find intervals, where $f(x)$ is positive or negative.

Sol. We have, $f(x) = \dfrac{(x-3)(x+2)(x+6)}{(x+1)(x-5)}$

The critical points are $(-6), (-2), (-1), 3, 5$

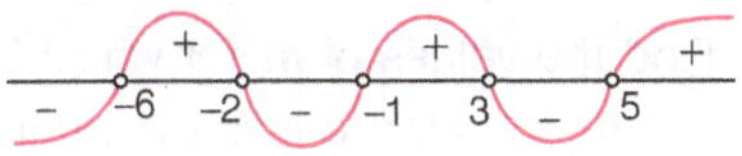

For $f(x) > 0,\ x \in (-6, -2) \cup (-1, 3) \cup (5, \infty)$

For $f(x) < 0,\ x \in (-\infty, -6) \cup (-2, -1) \cup (3, 5)$

Example 28. Find the set of all x for which

$$\frac{2x}{(2x^2+5x+2)} > \frac{1}{(x+1)}.$$

Sol. We have, $\dfrac{2x}{(2x^2+5x+2)} > \dfrac{1}{(x+1)}$

$$\Rightarrow \quad \frac{2x}{(x+2)(2x+1)} - \frac{1}{(x+1)} > 0$$

$$\Rightarrow \quad \frac{(2x^2+2x)-(2x^2+5x+2)}{(x+2)(x+1)(2x+1)} > 0$$

$$\Rightarrow \quad -\frac{(3x+2)}{(x+2)(x+1)(2x+1)} > 0$$

$$\text{or} \quad \frac{(3x+2)}{(x+2)(x+1)(2x+1)} < 0$$

The critical points are $(-2), (-1), \left(-\dfrac{2}{3}\right), \left(-\dfrac{1}{2}\right)$.

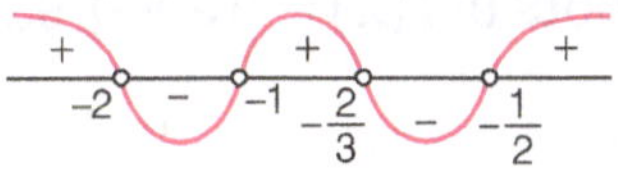

Hence, $x \in (-2, -1) \cup \left(-\dfrac{2}{3}, -\dfrac{1}{2}\right)$

Example 29. For what values of the parameter k in the inequality $\left|\dfrac{x^2+kx+1}{x^2+x+1}\right| < 3$, satisfied for all real values of x?

Sol. We have, $\left|\dfrac{x^2+kx+1}{x^2+x+1}\right| < 3$

$$\Rightarrow \quad -3 < \frac{x^2+kx+1}{x^2+x+1} < 3$$

Since, $x^2+x+1 = \left(x+\dfrac{1}{2}\right)^2 + \dfrac{3}{4} > 0$

$$\therefore \quad -3(x^2+x+1) < x^2+kx+1 < 3(x^2+x+1)$$

$$\therefore \quad 4x^2+(k+3)x+4 > 0 \quad \text{...(i)}$$

$$\text{and} \quad 2x^2-(k-3)x+2 > 0 \quad \text{...(ii)}$$

$$\because \quad 4 > 0 \text{ and } 2 > 0$$

The inequality (i) will be valid, if

$$(k+3)^2 - 4\cdot 4\cdot 4 < 0$$

$$\Rightarrow \quad (k+3)^2 < 64$$

$$\text{or} \quad -8 < k+3 < 8$$

$$\text{or} \quad -11 < k < 5 \quad \text{...(iii)}$$

and the inequality (ii) will be valid, if

$$(k-3)^2 - 4\cdot 2\cdot 2 < 0$$

$$\text{or} \quad (k-3)^2 < 16$$

$$\text{or} \quad -4 < k-3 < 4$$

$$\text{or} \quad -1 < k < 7 \quad \text{...(iv)}$$

The conditions (iii) and (iv) will hold simultaneously, if

$$-1 < k < 5$$

2.10 Condition for Resolution into Linear Factors

The quadratic function

$$f(x, y) = ax^2 + 2hxy + by^2 + 2gx + 2fy + c$$

may be resolved into two linear factors, iff

$$\Delta = abc + 2fgh - af^2 - bg^2 - ch^2 = 0$$

i.e. $\begin{vmatrix} a & h & g \\ h & b & f \\ g & f & c \end{vmatrix} = 0$

Example 30. Find the value of m for which the expression $12x^2 - 10xy + 2y^2 + 11x - 5y + m$ can be resolved into two rational linear factors.

Sol. Comparing the given expression with $ax^2 + 2hxy + by^2 + 2gx + 2fy + c$, we have

$$a = 12, h = -5, b = 2, g = \frac{11}{2}, f = \left(-\frac{5}{2}\right), c = m$$

The given expression will have two linear factors, if and only if

$$abc + 2fgh - af^2 - bg^2 - ch^2 = 0$$

$$\text{or } (12)(2)(m) + 2\left(-\frac{5}{2}\right)\left(\frac{11}{2}\right)(-5) - (12)\left(-\frac{5}{2}\right)^2 - (2)\left(\frac{11}{2}\right)^2 - (m)(-5)^2 = 0$$

$$\Rightarrow \quad 24m + \frac{275}{2} - 75 - \frac{121}{2} - 25m = 0 \text{ or } m = 2$$

Example 31. If the expression $ax^2 + by^2 + cz^2 + 2ayz + 2bzx + 2cxy$ can be resolved into two rational factors, prove that

$$a^3 + b^3 + c^3 = 3abc.$$

Sol. Given expression is

$$ax^2 + by^2 + cz^2 + 2ayz + 2bzx + 2cxy \quad \text{...(i)}$$

$$= z^2\left[a\left(\frac{x}{z}\right)^2 + b\left(\frac{y}{z}\right)^2 + c + 2a\left(\frac{y}{z}\right) + 2b\left(\frac{x}{z}\right) + 2c\left(\frac{x}{z}\right)\left(\frac{y}{z}\right)\right]$$

$$= z^2\,[aX^2 + bY^2 + c + 2aY + 2bX + 2cXY]$$

where, $\frac{x}{z} = X$ and $\frac{y}{z} = Y$

Expression (i) will have two rational linear factors in x, y and z, if expression

$aX^2 + bY^2 + 2cXY + 2bX + 2aY + c$ will have two linear factors, if

$$abc + 2abc - aa^2 - bb^2 - cc^2 = 0$$

or $$a^3 + b^3 + c^3 = 3abc$$

Example 32. Find the linear factors of

$$x^2 - 5xy + 4y^2 + x + 2y - 2.$$

Sol. Given expression is $x^2 - 5xy + 4y^2 + x + 2y - 2$ ...(i)

Its corresponding equation is

$$x^2 - 5xy + 4y^2 + x + 2y - 2 = 0$$

or $$x^2 - x(5y - 1) + 4y^2 + 2y - 2 = 0$$

$$\therefore \quad x = \frac{(5y-1) \pm \sqrt{(5y-1)^2 - 4\cdot 1\cdot(4y^2 + 2y - 2)}}{2}$$

$$= \frac{(5y-1) \pm \sqrt{(9y^2 - 18y + 9)}}{2} = \frac{(5y-1) \pm \sqrt{(3y-3)^2}}{2}$$

$$= \frac{(5y-1) \pm (3y-3)}{2} = 4y - 2, y + 1$$

$\therefore$ The required linear factors are $(x - 4y + 2)$ and $(x - y - 1)$.

2.11 Location of Roots (Interval in which Roots Lie)

Let $f(x) = ax^2 + bx + c$, $a, b, c \in R$, $a \neq 0$ and α, β be the roots of $f(x) = 0$. Suppose $k, k_1, k_2 \in R$ and $k_1 < k_2$. Then, the following hold good :

1. Conditions for Number k (If both the roots of $f(x) = 0$ are less than k)

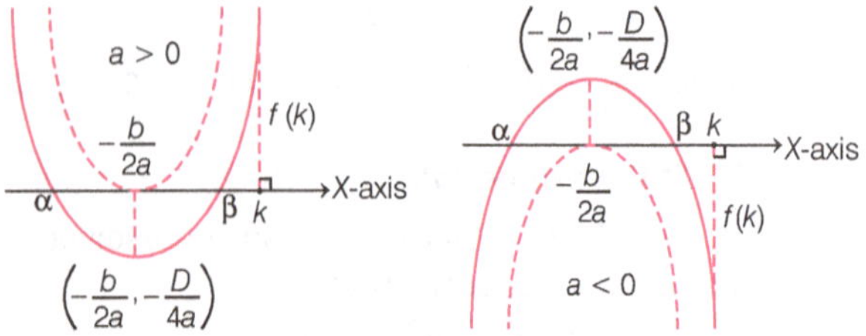

(i) $D \geq 0$ (roots may be equal)

(ii) $af(k) > 0$

(iii) $k > -\frac{b}{2a}$, where $\alpha \leq \beta$.

Example 33. Find the values of m, for which both roots of equation $x^2 - mx + 1 = 0$ are less than unity.

Sol. Let $f(x) = x^2 - mx + 1$, as both roots of $f(x) = 0$ are less than 1, we can take $D \geq 0$, $af(1) > 0$ and $-\frac{b}{2a} < 1$.

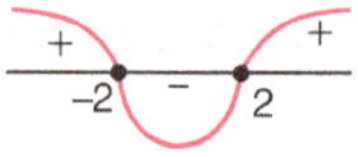

(i) **Consider $D \geq 0$** $(-m)^2 - 4\cdot 1\cdot 1 \geq 0$

$\Rightarrow \quad (m + 2)(m - 2) \geq 0$

$\Rightarrow \quad m \in (-\infty, -2] \cup [2, \infty)$ ...(i)

(ii) **Consider $af(1) > 0$** $1(1 - m + 1) > 0$

$\Rightarrow \quad m - 2 < 0 \Rightarrow m < 2 \Rightarrow m \in (-\infty, 2)$ ...(ii)

(iii) **Consider $\left(-\frac{b}{2a} < 1\right)$**

$\frac{m}{2} < 1 \Rightarrow m < 2 \Rightarrow m \in (-\infty, 2)$ ...(iii)

Hence, the values of m satisfying Eqs. (i), (ii) and (iii) at the same time are $m \in (-\infty, -2]$.

2. Conditions for a Number k (If both the roots of $f(x) = 0$ are greater than k)

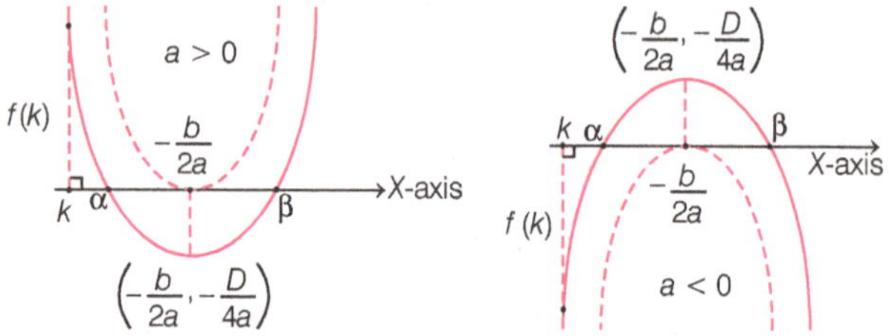

(i) $D \geq 0$ (roots may be equal)

(ii) $af(k) > 0$

(iii) $k < -\frac{b}{2a}$, where $\alpha \leq \beta$.

Example 34. For what values of $m \in R$, both roots of the equation $x^2 - 6mx + 9m^2 - 2m + 2 = 0$ exceed 3?

Sol. Let $f(x) = x^2 - 6mx + 9m^2 - 2m + 2$

As both roots of $f(x) = 0$ are greater than 3, we can take $D \geq 0$, $af(3) > 0$ and $-\frac{b}{2a} > 3$.

(i) **Consider $D \geq 0$**

$(-6m)^2 - 4\cdot 1(9m^2 - 2m + 2) \geq 0 \Rightarrow 8m - 8 \geq 0$

$\therefore \quad m \geq 1$ or $m \in [1, \infty)$ ...(i)

(ii) **Consider $af(3) > 0$**

$$1 \cdot (9 - 18m + 9m^2 - 2m + 2) > 0$$

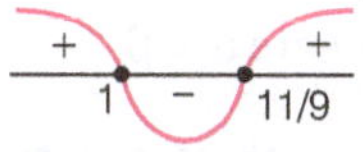

$\Rightarrow \quad 9m^2 - 20m + 11 > 0 \Rightarrow (9m - 11)(m - 1) > 0$

$\Rightarrow \quad \left(m - \frac{11}{9}\right)(m - 1) > 0$

$\Rightarrow \quad m \in (-\infty, 1) \cup \left(\frac{11}{9}, \infty\right)$ ...(ii)

(iii) **Consider $\left(-\frac{b}{2a} > 3\right)$**

$\frac{6m}{2} > 3 \Rightarrow m > 1 \Rightarrow m \in (1, \infty)$ ...(iii)

Hence, the values of m satisfying Eqs. (i), (ii) and (iii) at the same time are $m \in \left(\frac{11}{9}, \infty\right)$.

3. Conditions for a Number k (If k lies between the roots of $f(x) = 0$)

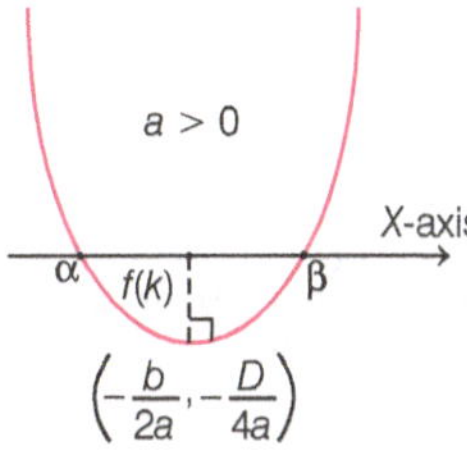

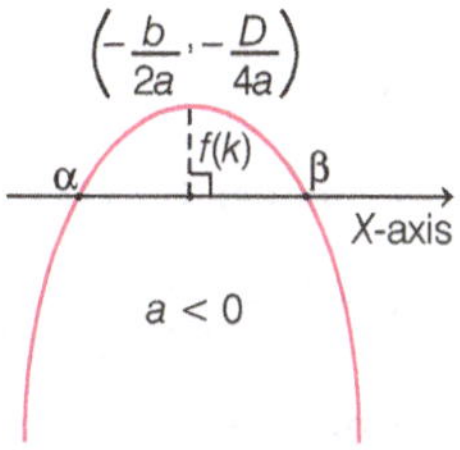

(i) $D > 0$ (ii) $af(k) < 0$, where $\alpha < \beta$

Example 35. Find all values of p, so that 6 lies between roots of the equation $x^2 + 2(p - 3)x + 9 = 0$.

Sol. Let $f(x) = x^2 + 2(p - 3)x + 9$, as 6 lies between the roots of $f(x) = 0$, we can take $D > 0$ and $af(6) < 0$

(i) **Consider $D > 0$**

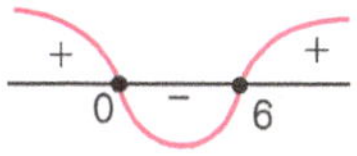

$\{2(p - 3)\}^2 - 4 \cdot 1 \cdot 9 > 0 \Rightarrow (p - 3)^2 - 9 > 0$

$\Rightarrow \quad p(p - 6) > 0$

$\Rightarrow \quad p \in (-\infty, 0) \cup (6, \infty)$ ...(i)

(ii) **Consider $af(6) < 0$**

$1 \cdot \{36 + 12(p - 3) + 9\} < 0 \Rightarrow 12p + 9 < 0$

$\Rightarrow \quad p + \frac{3}{4} < 0 \Rightarrow p \in \left(-\infty, -\frac{3}{4}\right)$ ...(ii)

Hence, the values of p satisfying Eqs. (i) and (ii) at the same time are $p \in \left(-\infty, -\frac{3}{4}\right)$.

4. Conditions for Numbers k_1 and k_2 (If exactly one root of $f(x) = 0$ lies in the interval (k_1, k_2))

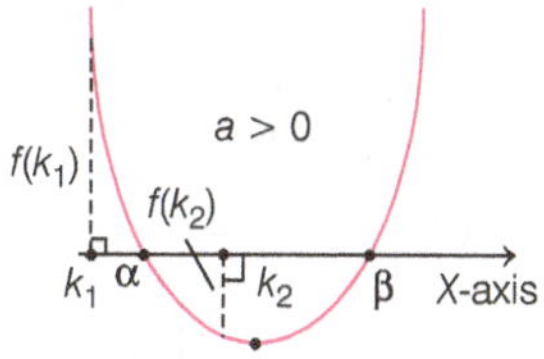

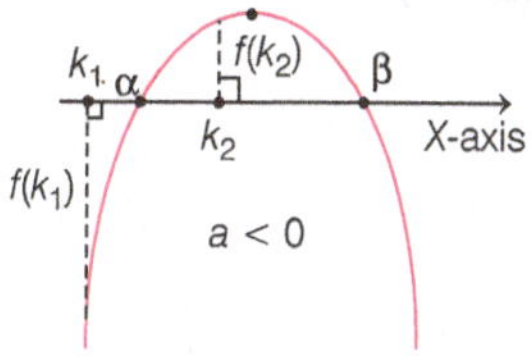

(i) $D > 0$

(ii) $f(k_1)f(k_2) < 0$, where $\alpha < \beta$.

JEE SCANNER

Example Similar to PYQ Asked in JEE Main 2022

The values of m, for which exactly one root of the equation $x^2 - 2mx + m^2 - 1 = 0$ lies in the interval $(-2, 4)$ is ....

(a) (4, 5) (b) (–3, –1)

(c) (–3, –1) ∪ (3, 5) (d) (–2, 3)

Sol. (c) Let $f(x) = x^2 - 2mx + m^2 - 1$, as exactly one root of $f(x) = 0$ lies in the interval $(-2, 4)$, we can take $D > 0$ and $f(-2)f(4) < 0$.

(i) **Consider $D > 0$**

$(-2m)^2 - 4 \cdot 1(m^2 - 1) > 0$

$\Rightarrow \quad 4 > 0$

$\therefore \quad m \in R$ ...(i)

(ii) **Consider $f(-2)f(4) < 0$**

$(4 + 4m + m^2 - 1)(16 - 8m + m^2 - 1) < 0$

$\Rightarrow \quad (m^2 + 4m + 3)(m^2 - 8m + 15) < 0$

$\Rightarrow \quad (m + 1)(m + 3)(m - 3)(m - 5) < 0$

$\Rightarrow \quad (m + 3)(m + 1)(m - 3)(m - 5) < 0$

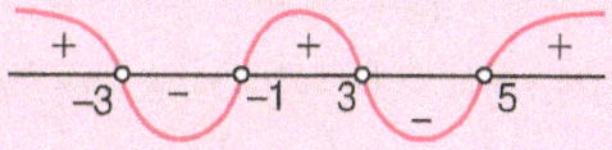

$\therefore \quad m \in (-3, -1) \cup (3, 5)$ ...(ii)

Hence, the values of m satisfying Eqs. (i) and (ii) at the same time are $m \in (-3, -1) \cup (3, 5)$.

Skill Builder

The values of a, for which exactly one root of the equation $x^2 - (a + 1)x + 2a = 0$ lies in the interval (0, 3) is ....

(a) (–∞, 0) ∪ (6, ∞)

(b) (–∞, 0)

(c) (6, ∞)

(d) (–∞, 0] ∪ [6, ∞)

For Sol.

■ **For more practice** See Q.9 of Milestone Practice 2.1.

5. Conditions for Numbers k_1 and k_2 (If both roots $f(x)=0$ are confined between k_1 and k_2)

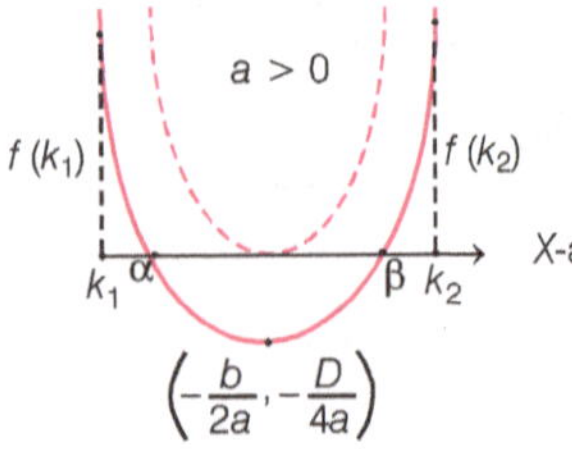

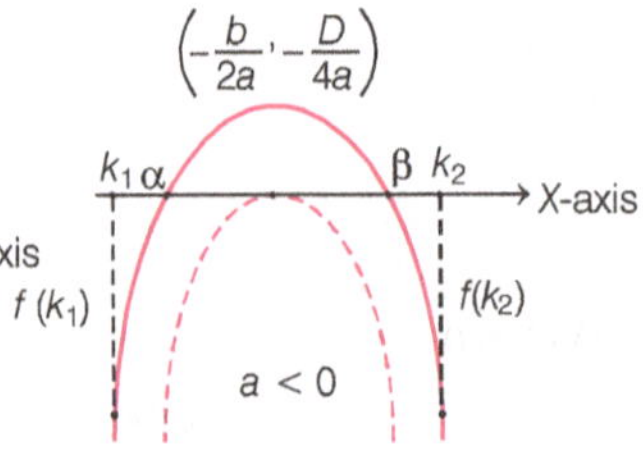

(i) $D \geq 0$ (roots may be equal)

(ii) $af(k_1) > 0$

(iii) $af(k_2) > 0$

(iv) $k_1 < -\dfrac{b}{2a} < k_2$, where $\alpha \leq \beta$ and $k_1 < k_2$.

Example 36. Find all values of a for which the equation $4x^2 - 2x + a = 0$ has two roots lie in the interval $(-1, 1)$.

Sol. Let $f(x) = 4x^2 - 2x + a$ as both roots of the equation, $f(x) = 0$ are lie between $(-1, 1)$, we can take $D \geq 0$, $af(-1) > 0$, $af(1) > 0$ and $-1 < \dfrac{1}{4} < 1$.

(i) **Consider $D \geq 0$**

$$(-2)^2 - 4 \cdot 4 \cdot a \geq 0 \Rightarrow a \leq \frac{1}{4} \quad \text{...(i)}$$

(ii) **Consider $af(-1) > 0$**

$$4(4 + 2 + a) > 0$$

$$\Rightarrow \quad a > -6$$

$$\Rightarrow \quad a \in (-6, \infty) \quad \text{...(ii)}$$

(iii) **Consider $af(1) > 0$**

$$4(4 - 2 + a) > 0 \Rightarrow a > -2$$

$$\Rightarrow \quad a \in (-2, \infty) \quad \text{...(iii)}$$

Hence, the values of a satisfying Eqs. (i), (ii) and (iii) at the same time are $a \in \left(-2, \dfrac{1}{4}\right]$.

6. Conditions for Numbers k_1 and k_2 (If k_1 and k_2 lie between the roots of $f(x)=0$)

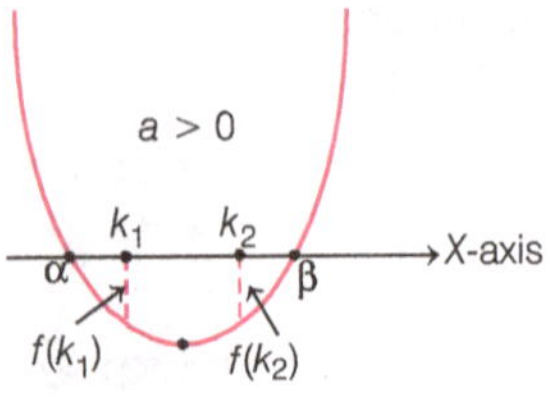

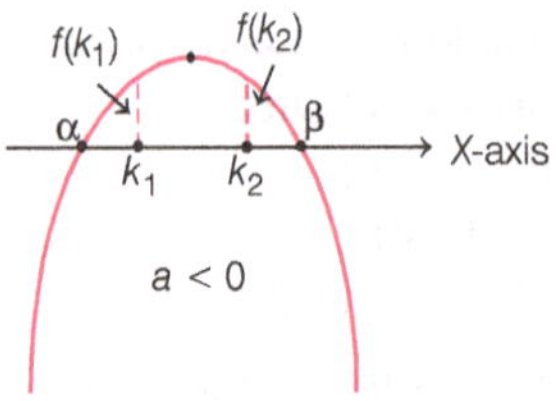

(i) $D > 0$

(ii) $af(k_1) < 0$

(iii) $af(k_2) < 0$, where $\alpha < \beta$.

Example 37. Find the values of a for which one root of equation $(a-5)x^2 - 2ax + a - 4 = 0$ is smaller than 1 and the other greater than 2.

Sol. The given equation can be written as

$$x^2 - \left(\frac{2a}{a-5}\right)x + \left(\frac{a-4}{a-5}\right) = 0, \ a \neq 5.$$

Now, let $f(x) = x^2 - \left(\dfrac{2a}{a-5}\right)x + \left(\dfrac{a-4}{a-5}\right)$

As 1 and 2 lie between the roots of $f(x) = 0$, we can take $D > 0$, $1 \cdot f(1) < 0$ and $1 \cdot f(2) < 0$.

(i) **Consider $D > 0$**

$$\left(-\left(\frac{2a}{a-5}\right)\right)^2 - 4 \cdot 1 \cdot \left(\frac{a-4}{a-5}\right) > 0$$

$$\Rightarrow \quad \frac{36\left(a - \dfrac{20}{9}\right)}{(a-5)^2} > 0 \quad [\because a \neq 5]$$

$$\text{or} \quad a > \frac{20}{9} \quad \text{...(i)}$$

(ii) **Consider $1 \cdot f(1) < 0$**

$$1^2 - \left(\frac{2a}{a-5}\right) + \left(\frac{a-4}{a-5}\right) < 0 \Rightarrow \frac{9}{(a-5)} > 0 \text{ or } a > 5 \quad \text{...(ii)}$$

(iii) **Consider $1 \cdot f(2) < 0$**

$$4 - \frac{4a}{(a-5)} + \left(\frac{a-4}{a-5}\right) < 0$$

$$\Rightarrow \quad \frac{(4a - 20 - 4a + a - 4)}{(a-5)} < 0 \Rightarrow \frac{(a-24)}{(a-5)} < 0$$

$$\text{or} \quad 5 < a < 24 \quad \text{...(iii)}$$

Hence, the values of a satisfying Eqs. (i), (ii) and (iii) at the same time are $a \in (5, 24)$.

Example 38. Let $x^2 - (m-3)x + m = 0$ $(m \in R)$ be a quadratic equation. Find the value of m for which

(i) both the roots are smaller than 2.

(ii) both the roots are greater than 2.

(iii) one root is smaller than 2 and the other root is greater than 2.

(iv) exactly one root lies in the interval (1, 2).

(v) both the roots lie in the interval (1, 2).

(vi) one root is greater than 2 and the other root is smaller than 1.

(vii) atleast one root lie in the interval (1, 2).

(viii) atleast one root is greater than 2.

Sol. Let $f(x) = x^2 - (m-3)x + m$

Here, $a = 1, b = -(m-3), c = m$

and $D = b^2 - 4ac = (m-3)^2 - 4m$

$= m^2 - 10m + 9 = (m-1)(m-9)$

and x-coordinate of vertex $= -\dfrac{b}{2a} = \dfrac{(m-3)}{2}$

(i) **Both the roots are smaller than 2**

$D \geq 0$

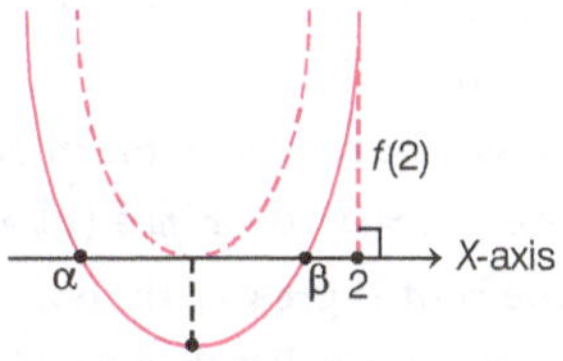

i.e. $(m-1)(m-9) \geq 0$

$\therefore \quad m \in (-\infty, 1] \cup [9, \infty)$ ...(i)

$f(2) > 0$

i.e. $4 - 2(m-3) + m > 0$

$\Rightarrow \quad m < 10$

$\therefore \quad m \in (-\infty, 10)$ ...(ii)

and x-coordinate of vertex < 2

i.e. $\dfrac{(m-3)}{2} < 2 \Rightarrow m < 7$

$\therefore \quad m \in (-\infty, 7)$ ...(iii)

On combining Eqs. (i), (ii) and (iii), we get

$m \in (-\infty, 1]$

(ii) **Both the roots are greater than 2**

$D \geq 0$

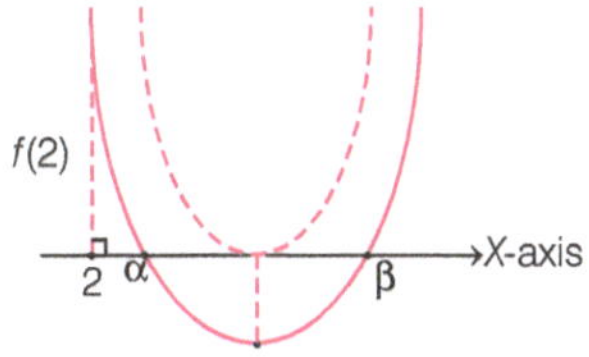

i.e. $(m-1)(m-9) \geq 0$

$\therefore \quad m \in (-\infty, 1] \in [9, \infty)$ ...(i)

$f(2) > 0$

i.e. $4 - 2(m-3) + m > 0$

$\Rightarrow \quad m < 10$

$\therefore \quad m \in (-\infty, 10)$ ...(ii)

and x-coordinate of vertex > 2

i.e. $\dfrac{(m-3)}{2} > 2 \Rightarrow m > 7$

$\therefore \quad m \in (7, \infty)$ ...(iii)

On combining Eqs. (i), (ii) and (iii), we get

$m \in [9, 10)$

(iii) **One root is smaller than 2 and the other root is greater than 2**

$D > 0$

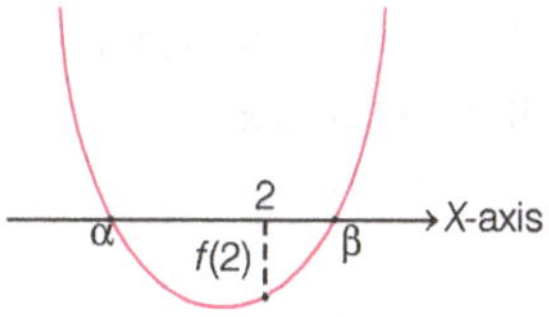

i.e., $(m-1)(m-9) > 0$

$\therefore \quad m \in (-\infty, 1) \cup (9, \infty)$ ...(i)

$f(2) < 0$

i.e. $4 - 2(m-3) + m < 0$

$\therefore \quad m > 10$

$\therefore \quad m \in (10, \infty)$ ...(ii)

On combining Eqs. (i) and (ii), we get

$m \in (10, \infty)$.

(iv) **Exactly one root lies in the interval (1, 2)**

$D > 0$

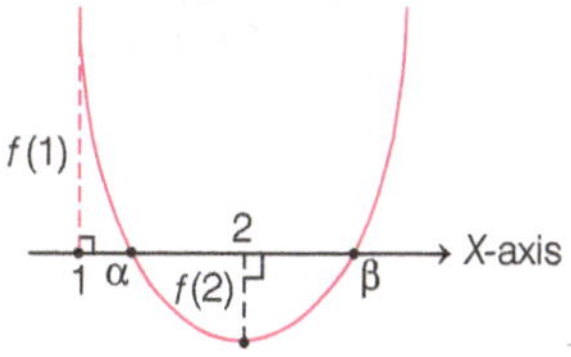

i.e. $(m-1)(m-9) > 0$

$\therefore \quad m \in (-\infty, 1) \cup (9, \infty)$ ...(i)

$f(1) f(2) < 0$

$(1 - (m-3) + m)(4 - 2(m-3) + m) < 0$

$\Rightarrow \quad 4(-m + 10) < 0$

$\Rightarrow \quad m - 10 > 0 \Rightarrow m > 10$

$\therefore \quad m \in (10, \infty)$ ...(ii)

On combining Eqs. (i) and (ii), we get

$m \in (10, \infty)$

(v) **Both the roots lie in the interval (1, 2)**

$D \geq 0$

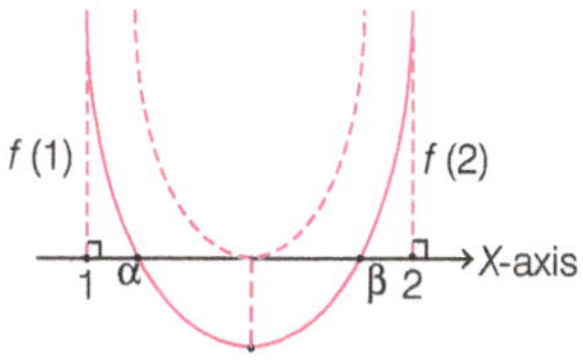

i.e. $(m-1)(m-9) \geq 0$

$\therefore \quad m \in (-\infty, 1] \cup [9, \infty)$ ...(i)

$f(1) > 0$

i.e. $(1 - (m-3) + m) > 0 \Rightarrow 4 > 0$

$\therefore \quad m \in R$ ...(ii)

$f(2) > 0$

i.e. $4 - 2(m-3) + m > 0$

$\Rightarrow \quad m < 10$

$\therefore \quad m \in (-\infty, 10)$ ...(iii)

$1 < x$-coordinate of vertex < 2

i.e. $1 < \dfrac{(m-3)}{2} < 2$

$\Rightarrow \quad 2 < m - 3 < 4$

or $\quad 5 < m < 7$

$\therefore \quad m \in (5, 7)$ ...(iv)

On combining Eqs. (i), (ii), (iii) and (iv), we get

$m \in \phi$

(vi) **One root is greater than 2 and the other root is smaller than 1**

$D > 0$

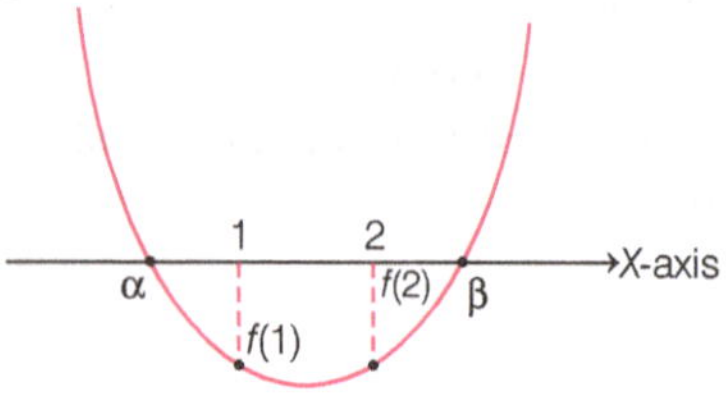

i.e. $(m-1)(m-9) > 0$

$\therefore \quad m \in (-\infty, 1) \cup (9, \infty)$ ...(i)

$f(1) < 0$

i.e. $4 < 0$, which is not possible.

Thus, no such 'm' exists.

(vii) **At least one root lie in the interval (1, 2)**

Case I Exactly one root lies in (1, 2)

$m \in (10, \infty)$ [from (iv) part]

Case II Both roots lie in the interval (1, 2).

$m \in \phi$ [from (v) part]

Hence, at least one root lie in the interval (1, 2)

$m \in (10, \infty) \cup \phi$ or $m \in (10, \infty)$

(viii) **Atleast one root is greater than 2**

Case I One root is smaller than 2 and the other root is greater than 2.

Then, $m \in (10, \infty)$ [from (iii) part]

Case II Both the roots are greater than 2, then $m \in [9, 10)$. [from (ii) part]

Hence, atleast one root is greater than 2.

$\therefore \quad m \in (10, \infty) \cup [9, 10)$ or $m \in [9, 10) \cup (10, \infty)$

Milestone Practice 2.1

1. Let $f(x)$ be a quadratic polynomial satisfying $f(2)+f(4)=0$. If unity is one root of $f(x)=0$, then find the other root.

2. If $(a^2-1)\,x^2+(a-1)\,x+(a^2-4a+3)=0$ is an identity in x, then find the value of a.

3. Solve $x=\sqrt{6+\sqrt{6+\sqrt{6+\ldots\infty}}}$

4. If the roots of the equation $x^2-8x+a^2-6a=0$ are real distinct, then find all possible values of a.

5. If α and β are the roots of the equation $4x^2+2x-1=0$, find the value of $\dfrac{\alpha^2+\beta^2-\alpha\beta}{(\alpha^3+\beta^3)}$.

6. If α,β are the roots of the equation $2x^2-3x-6=0$, find equation whose roots are α^2+2 and β^2+2.

7. If $x^2+px+q=0$ and $x^2+qx+p=0$, $(p\neq q)$ have a common root, show that $1+p+q=0$. Also, show that their other roots are the roots of the equation $x^2+x+pq=0$.

8. Find the range of $\dfrac{6x^2-22x+21}{5x^2-18x+17}$ for real x.

9. Find the values of a, for which exactly one root of the equation $x^2-ax+(a-1)=0$ lies in the interval $(-1,3)$.

10. If $x^2+px+q=0$ is the quadratic equation, whose roots are $a-2$ and $b-2$, where a and b are the roots of $x^2-3x+1=0$, then
    (a) $p=1, q=-5$ (b) $p=1, q=1$
    (c) $p=1, q=-1$ (d) None of these

11. For what positive values of m, the equation $(1+m)x^2-2(1+3m)x+(1+8m)=0$ has equal roots.

12. If the roots of the equation $x^2-2ax+a^2+a-3=0$ are real and less than 3, then
    (a) $a<2$ (b) $a>4$ (c) $3<a\leq 4$ (d) $2\leq a<3$

13. If the equations $k(6x^2+3)+rx+2x^2-1=0$ and $6k(2x^2+1)+px+4x^2-2=0$ have both the roots are common, then the value of $r+p$ is ....

14. Find the number of integral values of 'a' for which the expression $\dfrac{x^2-ax+11}{x^2-5x+4}$ can assume all real values.

15. If x is real, the expression $\dfrac{x+2}{2x^2+3x+6}$ takes all value in the interval
    (a) $\left(\dfrac{1}{13},\dfrac{1}{3}\right)$ (b) $\left[\dfrac{-1}{13},\dfrac{1}{3}\right]$
    (c) $\left(\dfrac{-1}{3},\dfrac{1}{13}\right)$ (d) None of these

Answer Key

1. $\dfrac{7}{2}$	2. 1	3. 3	4. $(-2, 8)$	5. (-2)
6. $4x^2-49x+118=0$	8. $\left[1,\dfrac{5}{4}\right]$	9. $(-\infty,0)\cup(4,\infty)$	10. (c)	11. 0, 3
12. (a)	13. $\dfrac{3p}{2}$	14. 6	15. (b)	

For Detailed Solution

Milestone 2 Theory of Equation

• Equation of Higher Degree • Rational Algebraic Inequalities • Irrational Equation • Irrational Inequation • Exponential Equations • Exponential Inequations • Logarithmic Equations • Logarithmic Inequations

2.12 Equations of Higher Degree

The equation $a_0 x^n + a_1 x^{n-1} + a_2 x^{n-2} + \ldots + a_{n-1} x + a_n = 0$,

where $a_0, a_1, a_2, \ldots, a_{n-1}, a_n$ are constants but $a_0 \neq 0$, is a polynomial equation of degree n. It has n and only n roots. Let $\alpha_1, \alpha_2, \alpha_3, \ldots, \alpha_{n-1}, \alpha_n$ be n roots, then

- $\Sigma\alpha_1 = \alpha_1 + \alpha_2 + \alpha_3 + \ldots + \alpha_{n-1} + \alpha_n = (-1)^1 \dfrac{a_1}{a_0}$ [sum of all roots]
- $\Sigma\alpha_1\alpha_2 = \alpha_1\alpha_2 + \alpha_1\alpha_3 + \ldots + \alpha_1\alpha_n + \alpha_2\alpha_3 + \ldots + \alpha_2\alpha_n + \ldots + \alpha_{n-1}\alpha_n$
  $= (-1)^2 \dfrac{a_2}{a_0}$ [sum of products taken two at a time]
- $\Sigma\alpha_1\alpha_2\alpha_3 = (-1)^3 \dfrac{a_3}{a_0}$ [sum of products taken three at a time]
- $\alpha_1\alpha_2\alpha_3 \ldots \alpha_n = (-1)^n \dfrac{a_n}{a_0}$ [product of all roots]

In general, $\Sigma\alpha_1\alpha_2\alpha_3 \ldots \alpha_p = (-1)^p \dfrac{a_p}{a_0}$

Concept Inside Video

JEE Focus Points

- A polynomial equation of degree n has n roots (real or imaginary).
- If all the coefficients, i.e. $a_0, a_1, a_2, \ldots, a_n$ are real, then the imaginary roots occur in pairs, i.e. number of imaginary roots is always even.
- If the degree of a polynomial equation is odd, then atleast one of the roots will be real.
- $(x-\alpha_1)(x-\alpha_2)(x-\alpha_3) \ldots (x-\alpha_n)$
  $= x^n + (-1)^1 \Sigma\alpha_1 \cdot x^{n-1} + (-1)^2 \Sigma\alpha_1\alpha_2 \cdot x^{n-2} + \ldots + (-1)^n \alpha_1\alpha_2\alpha_3 \ldots \alpha_n$

In Particular

(i) For $n=3$, if α, β, γ are the roots of the equation $ax^3 + bx^2 + cx + d = 0$, where a, b, c, d are constants and $a \neq 0$, then $\Sigma\alpha = \alpha + \beta + \gamma = (-1)^1 \dfrac{b}{a} = -\dfrac{b}{a}$,

$$\Sigma\alpha\beta = \alpha\beta + \beta\gamma + \gamma\alpha = (-1)^2 \frac{c}{a} = \frac{c}{a}$$

and $$\alpha\beta\gamma = (-1)^3 \frac{d}{a} = -\frac{d}{a}$$

or $ax^3 + bx^2 + cx + d = a(x-\alpha)(x-\beta)(x-\gamma)$
$= a(x^3 - \Sigma\alpha \cdot x^2 + \Sigma\alpha\beta \cdot x - \alpha\beta\gamma)]$

(ii) For $n = 4$, if $\alpha, \beta, \gamma, \delta$ are the roots of the equation $ax^4 + bx^3 + cx^2 + dx + e = 0$, where a, b, c, d, e are constants and $a \neq 0$, then

$$\Sigma\alpha = \alpha + \beta + \gamma + \delta = (-1)^1 \frac{b}{a} = -\frac{b}{a},$$

$$\Sigma\alpha\beta = (\alpha+\beta)(\gamma+\delta) + \alpha\beta + \gamma\delta = (-1)^2 \frac{c}{a} = \frac{c}{a},$$

$$\Sigma\alpha\beta\gamma = \alpha\beta(\gamma+\delta) + \gamma\delta(\alpha+\beta) = (-1)^3 \frac{d}{a} = -\frac{d}{a}$$

and $\alpha\beta\gamma\delta = (-1)^4 \dfrac{e}{a} = \dfrac{e}{a}$

or $ax^4 + bx^3 + cx^2 + dx + e$
$= a(x-\alpha)(x-\beta)(x-\gamma)(x-\delta)$
$= a(x^4 - \Sigma\alpha \cdot x^3 + \Sigma\alpha\beta \cdot x^2 - \Sigma\alpha\beta\gamma \cdot x + \alpha\beta\gamma\delta)$

Example 39. Find the conditions, if roots of the equation $x^3 - px^2 + qx - r = 0$ are in

(i) AP (ii) GP (iii) HP

Sol. (i) Let roots of the given equation are $A - D, A, A + D$, then

$$A - D + A + A + D = p \Rightarrow A = \frac{p}{3}$$

Now, A is the roots of the given equation, then it must be satisfy

$$A^3 - pA^2 + qA - r = 0$$

$$\Rightarrow \quad \left(\frac{p}{3}\right)^3 - p\left(\frac{p}{3}\right)^2 + q\left(\frac{p}{3}\right) - r = 0$$

$$\Rightarrow \quad p^3 - 3p^3 + 9qp - 27r = 0$$

or $\quad 2p^3 - 9pq + 27r = 0,$

which is the required condition.

(ii) Let roots of the given equation are $\frac{A}{R}$, A, AR, then

$$\frac{A}{R}\cdot A \cdot AR = (-1)^3 \cdot \left(-\frac{r}{1}\right) = r$$

$$\Rightarrow \quad A^3 = r$$

$$\Rightarrow \quad A = r^{\frac{1}{3}}$$

Now, A is the root of the given equation, then

$$A^3 - pA^2 + qA - r = 0$$

$$\Rightarrow \quad r - p(r)^{2/3} + q(r)^{1/3} - r = 0$$

or $\quad p(r)^{2/3} = q(r)^{1/3}$

or $\quad p^3r^2 = q^3r$

or $\quad p^3r = q^3$

which is the required condition.

(iii) Given equation is

$$x^3 - px^2 + qx - r = 0 \quad \text{...(i)}$$

On replacing x by $\frac{1}{x}$ in Eq. (i), then

$$\left(\frac{1}{x}\right)^3 - p\left(\frac{1}{x}\right)^2 + q\left(\frac{1}{x}\right) - r = 0$$

$$\Rightarrow \quad rx^3 - qx^2 + px - 1 = 0 \quad \text{...(ii)}$$

Now, roots of Eq. (ii) are in AP.

Let roots of Eq. (ii) are $A - P$, A, $A + P$, then

$$A - P + A + A + P = \frac{q}{r}$$

or $\quad A = \frac{q}{3r}$

$\because A$ is a root of Eq. (ii), then

$$rA^3 - qA^2 + pA - 1 = 0$$

$$\Rightarrow \quad r\left(\frac{q}{3r}\right)^3 - q\left(\frac{q}{3r}\right)^2 + p\left(\frac{q}{3r}\right) - 1 = 0$$

$$\Rightarrow \quad q^3 - 3q^3 + 9pqr - 27r^2 = 0$$

$$\Rightarrow \quad 2q^3 - 9pqr + 27r^2 = 0,$$

which is the required condition.

Example 40. Solve $6x^3 - 11x^2 + 6x - 1 = 0$, if roots of the equation are in HP.

Sol. Put $x = \frac{1}{y}$ in the given equation, then

$$\frac{6}{y^3} - \frac{11}{y^2} + \frac{6}{y} - 1 = 0$$

$$\Rightarrow \quad y^3 - 6y^2 + 11y - 6 = 0 \quad \text{...(i)}$$

Now, roots of Eq. (i) are in AP.

Let the roots be $\alpha - \beta, \alpha, \alpha + \beta$.

Then, sum of roots $= \alpha - \beta + \alpha + \alpha + \beta = 6$

$$\Rightarrow \quad 3\alpha = 6$$

$$\therefore \quad \alpha = 2$$

Product of roots $= (\alpha - \beta)\cdot\alpha\cdot(\alpha + \beta) = 6$

$\Rightarrow \quad (2 - \beta)2(2 + \beta) = 6 \ \Rightarrow \ 4 - \beta^2 = 3$

$$\therefore \quad \beta = \pm 1$$

$\therefore$ Roots of Eqs. (i) are 1, 2, 3 or 3, 2, 1.

Hence, roots of the given equation are $1, \frac{1}{2}, \frac{1}{3}$ or $\frac{1}{3}, \frac{1}{2}, 1$.

Example 41. If α, β, γ are the roots of the equation $x^3 - px^2 + qx - r = 0$, find

(i) $\Sigma\alpha^2$. (ii) $\Sigma\alpha^2\beta$. (iii) $\Sigma\alpha^3$.

Sol. Since, α, β, γ are the roots of $x^3 - px^2 + qx - r = 0$.

$$\therefore \quad \Sigma\alpha = p, \Sigma\alpha\beta = q \text{ and } \alpha\beta\gamma = r$$

(i) $\because \ \Sigma\alpha \cdot \Sigma\alpha = p \cdot p$

$$\Rightarrow \quad (\alpha + \beta + \gamma)(\alpha + \beta + \gamma) = p^2$$

$$\Rightarrow \quad \alpha^2 + \beta^2 + \gamma^2 + 2(\alpha\beta + \beta\gamma + \gamma\alpha) = p^2$$

or $\quad \Sigma\alpha^2 + 2\Sigma\alpha\beta = p^2$

or $\quad \Sigma\alpha^2 = p^2 - 2q$

(ii) $\because \ \Sigma\alpha \cdot \Sigma\alpha\beta = p \cdot q$

$$\Rightarrow (\alpha + \beta + \gamma)\cdot(\alpha\beta + \beta\gamma + \gamma\alpha) = pq$$

$$\Rightarrow \alpha^2\beta + \alpha\beta\gamma + \alpha^2\gamma + \beta^2\alpha + \beta^2\gamma + \alpha\beta\gamma + \alpha\beta\gamma + \gamma^2\beta + \gamma^2\alpha = pq$$

$$\Rightarrow \quad (\alpha^2\beta + \alpha^2\gamma + \beta^2\alpha + \beta^2\gamma + \gamma^2\alpha + \gamma^2\beta) + 3\alpha\beta\gamma = pq$$

or $\quad \Sigma\alpha^2\beta + 3r = pq$

or $\quad \Sigma\alpha^2\beta = pq - 3r$

(iii) $\because \ \Sigma\alpha^2 \cdot \Sigma\alpha = (p^2 - 2q)\cdot p$ [from result (i)]

$$\Rightarrow \quad (\alpha^2 + \beta^2 + \gamma^2)(\alpha + \beta + \gamma) = p^3 - 2pq$$

$$\Rightarrow \quad \alpha^3 + \beta^3 + \gamma^3 + (\alpha^2\beta + \alpha^2\gamma + \beta^2\alpha + \beta^2\gamma + \gamma^2\alpha + \gamma^2\beta) = p^3 - 2pq$$

$$\Rightarrow \quad \Sigma\alpha^3 + \Sigma\alpha^2\beta = p^3 - 2pq$$

$\Rightarrow \quad \Sigma\alpha^3 + pq - 3r = p^3 - 2pq$ [from result (ii)]

or $\quad \Sigma\alpha^3 = p^3 - 3pq + 3r$

Example 42. If α, β, γ are the roots of the cubic equation $x^3 + qx + r = 0$, then find the equation whose roots are $(\alpha - \beta)^2, (\beta - \gamma)^2, (\gamma - \alpha)^2$.

Sol. $\because \alpha, \beta, \gamma$ are the roots of the cubic equation

$$x^3 + qx + r = 0 \quad \text{...(i)}$$

Then, $\Sigma\alpha = 0, \Sigma\alpha\beta = q, \alpha\beta\gamma = -r$ ...(ii)

If y is a root of the required equation, then

$$y = (\alpha - \beta)^2 = (\alpha + \beta)^2 - 4\alpha\beta$$

$$= (\alpha + \beta + \gamma - \gamma)^2 - \frac{4\alpha\beta\gamma}{\gamma}$$

$$= (0 - \gamma)^2 + \frac{4r}{\gamma} \quad \text{[from Eq. (ii)]}$$

$$\Rightarrow \quad y = \gamma^2 + \frac{4r}{\gamma}$$

[replacing γ by x which is a root of Eq. (i)]

$$\therefore \quad y = x^2 + \frac{4r}{x} \text{ or } x^3 - yx + 4r = 0 \quad \text{...(iii)}$$

The required equation is obtained by eliminating x between Eqs. (i) and (iii).

Now, subtracting Eq. (iii) from Eq. (i), we get

$$(q + y)x - 3r = 0 \text{ or } x = \frac{3r}{q + y}$$

On substituting the value of x in Eq. (i), we get

$$\left(\frac{3r}{q + y}\right)^3 + q\left(\frac{3r}{q + y}\right) + r = 0$$

Thus, $y^3 + 6qy^2 + 9q^2y + (4q^3 + 27r^2) = 0$

which is the required equation.

Some Results on Roots of a Polynomial Equation

1. Every equation of an odd degree has atleast one real root, whose sign is opposite to that of its last term, provided that the coefficient of the first term is positive.
2. Every equation of an even degree has atleast two real roots, one positive and one negative, whose last term is negative, provided that the coefficient of the first term is positive.
3. If an equation has no odd powers of x, then all roots of the equation are complex provided all the coefficients of the equation have positive sign.
4. If $x = \alpha$ is root repeated m times in $f(x) = 0$ ($f(x) = 0$ is an nth degree equation in x), then $f(x) = (x - \alpha)^m g(x)$ where, $g(x)$ is a polynomial of degree $(n - m)$ and the root $x = \alpha$ is repeated $(m - 1)$ time in $f'(x) = 0$, $(m - 2)$ times in $f''(x) = 0, \ldots, (m - (m - 1))$ times in $f^{m-1}(x) = 0$.
5. Let $f(x) = 0$ be a polynomial equation and λ, μ are two real numbers. Then, $f(x) = 0$ will have atleast one real root or an odd number of roots between λ and μ, if $f(\lambda)$ and $f(\mu)$ are of opposite signs.

   But if $f(\lambda)$ and $f(\mu)$ are of same signs, then either $f(x) = 0$ has no real roots or an even number of roots between λ and μ.

JEE SCANNER

Example Similar to PYQ Asked in JEE Main 2024

If α and β are the roots of the equation $x^2 - x + 2 = 0$ and $S_n = 2024\alpha^n + 2025\beta^n$, then

(a) $S_{10} = 2S_9 - S_8$
(b) $S_{10} = S_9 - 2S_8$
(c) $2S_{10} = S_9 - S_8$
(d) $S_{10} = S_9 + 2S_8$

Sol. (b) Given quadratic equation is

$$x^2 - x + 2 = 0 \quad \text{...(i)}$$

Also, given α and β are roots of Eq. (i)

and $S_n = 2024\alpha^n + 2025\beta^n$

Since, α and β are roots of Eq. (i)

So, $\alpha^2 - \alpha + 2 = 0$ and $\beta^2 - \beta + 2 = 0$

$$\Rightarrow \quad \alpha^2 = \alpha - 2 \text{ and } \beta^2 = \beta - 2$$

$$\Rightarrow \quad \alpha^{n-2}\alpha^2 = \alpha^{n-2}(\alpha - 2)$$

$$\text{and} \quad \beta^{n-2}\beta^2 = \beta^{n-2}(\beta - 2)$$

$$\Rightarrow \quad \alpha^n = \alpha^{n-1} - 2\alpha^{n-2} \quad \text{...(ii)}$$

$$\text{and} \quad \beta^n = \beta^{n-1} - 2\beta^{n-2} \quad \text{...(iii)}$$

Given, $S_n = 2024\alpha^n + 2025\beta^n$

$$= 2024(\alpha^{n-1} - 2\alpha^{n-2}) + 2025(\beta^{n-1} - 2\beta^{n-2})$$

[From Eqs. (ii) and (iii)]

$$S_n = 2024\alpha^{n-1} + 2025\beta^{n-1} - 2(2024\alpha^{n-2} + 2025\beta^{n-2})$$

$$S_n = S_{n-1} - 2S_{n-2} \quad \text{...(iv)}$$

On putting $n = 10$ in Eq. (iv), we have

$$S_{10} = S_9 - 2S_8$$

Skill Builder

If α and β are the roots of the equation $x^2 - x - 3 = 0$ and $S_n = 2025\alpha^n + 2026\beta^n$, then

(a) $S_6 = S_5 + S_4$
(b) $S_6 = S_5 + 3S_4$
(c) $3S_6 = S_5 + S_4$
(d) $S_6 = S_5 - 3S_4$

For Sol.

- **For more practice** See Q.4 of Milestone Practice 2.2.

Illustration by Graphs

Since, $f(x)$ be a polynomial in x, then graph of $y = f(x)$ will be continuous in every interval.

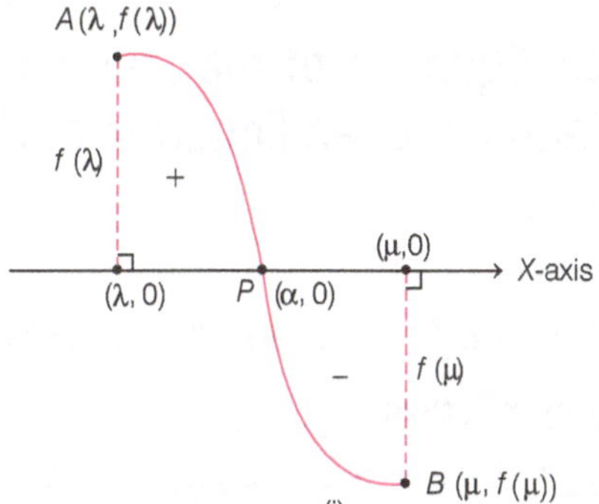

(i)

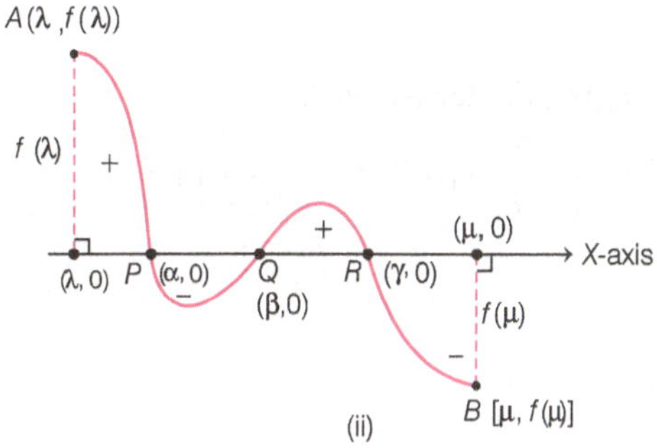

(ii)

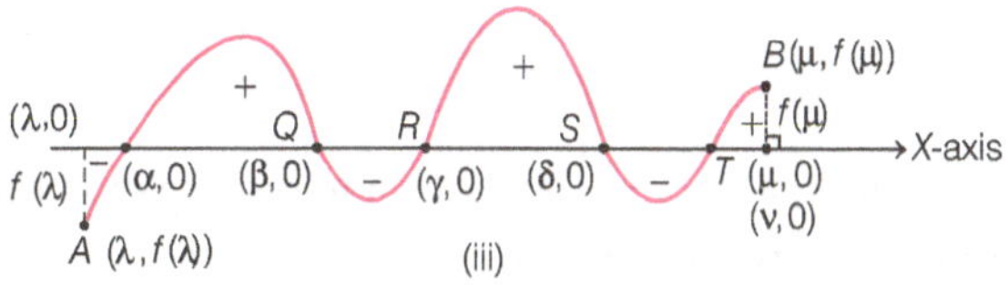

(iii)

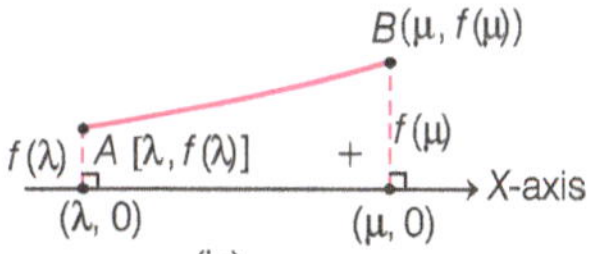

(iv)

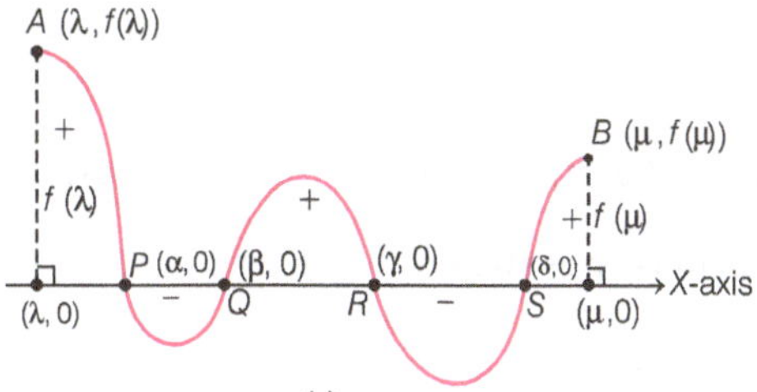

(v)

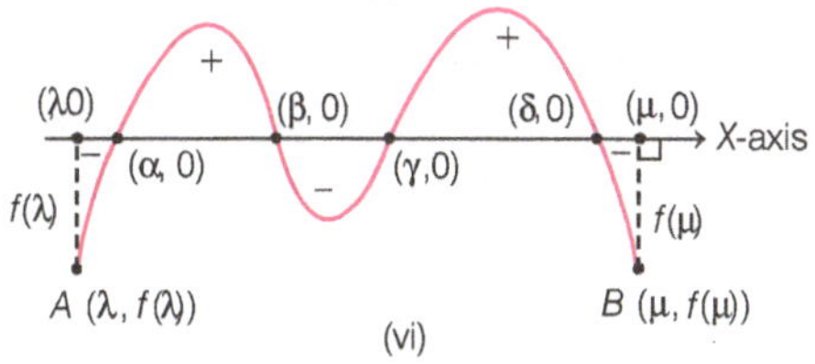

(vi)

(a) In figure (i), (ii) and (iii), $f(\lambda)$ and $f(\mu)$ have opposite signs and equation $f(x) = 0$, has one, three, five roots between λ and μ, respectively.

(b) In figure (iv), (v) and (vi), $f(\lambda)$ and $f(\mu)$ have same signs and equation $f(x) = 0$, has no, four and four roots between λ and μ, respectively.

Example 43. If a, b, c are real numbers, $a \neq 0$. If α is root of $a^2x^2 + bx + c = 0$, β is a root of $a^2x^2 - bx - c = 0$ and $0 < \alpha < \beta$, show that the equation $a^2x^2 + 2bx + 2c = 0$ has a root γ that always satisfies $\alpha < \gamma < \beta$.

Sol. Since, α is a root of $a^2x^2 + bx + c = 0$.

Then, $\quad a^2\alpha^2 + b\alpha + c = 0 \quad$ ...(i)

and β is a root of $\quad a^2x^2 - bx - c = 0$,

then $\quad a^2\beta^2 - b\beta - c = 0 \quad$ ...(ii)

Let $\quad f(x) = a^2x^2 + 2bx + 2c$

$\therefore \quad f(\alpha) = a^2\alpha^2 + 2b\alpha + 2c$

$= a^2\alpha^2 - 2a^2\alpha^2 \quad$ [from Eq. (i)]

$= -a^2\alpha^2$

$\Rightarrow \quad f(\alpha) < 0$

and $\quad f(\beta) = a^2\beta^2 + 2b\beta + 2c$

$= a^2\beta^2 + 2a^2\beta^2 \quad$ [from Eq. (ii)]

$= 3a^2\beta^2$

$\Rightarrow \quad f(\beta) > 0$

Since, $f(\alpha)$ and $f(\beta)$ are of opposite signs, then it is clear that a root γ of the equation $f(x) = 0$ lies between α and β.

Hence, $\quad \alpha < \gamma < \beta \quad [\because \alpha < \beta]$

Example 44. If $a < b < c < d$, then show that $(x - a)(x - c) + 3(x - b)(x - d) = 0$ has real and distinct roots.

Sol. Let $\quad f(x) = (x - a)(x - c) + 3(x - b)(x - d)$

Then, $f(a) = 0 + 3(a - b)(a - d) > 0 \quad [\because a - b < 0, a - d < 0]$

and $\quad f(b) = (b - a)(b - c) + 0 < 0 \quad [\because b - a > 0, b - c < 0]$

Thus, one root will lie between a and b.

and $\quad f(c) = 0 + 3(c - b)(c - d) < 0 \quad [\because c - b > 0, c - d < 0]$

and $\quad f(d) = (d - a)(d - c) + 0 > 0 \quad [\because d - a > 0, d - c > 0]$

Thus, one root will lie between c and d. Hence, roots of equation are real and distinct.

6. Let $f(x) = 0$ be a polynomial equation, then

(a) the number of positive roots of a polynomial equation $f(x) = 0$ (arranged in decreasing order of the degree) cannot exceed the number of changes of signs in $f(x) = 0$ as we move from left to right.

e.g. Consider the equation

$$2x^3 - x^2 - x + 1 = 0.$$

The number of changes of signs from left to right is 2 (+ to –, then – to +). Then, number of positive roots cannot exceed 2.

(b) The number of negative roots of a polynomial equation $f(x)=0$ cannot exceed the number of changes of signs in $f(-x)$.
e.g. Consider the equation

$$5x^4+3x^3-2x^2+5x-8=0$$

Let $f(x)=5x^4+3x^3-2x^2+5x-8$

$\therefore\ f(-x)=5x^4-3x^3-2x^2-5x-8$

The number of changes of signs from left to right is (+ to –). Then number of negative roots cannot exceed 1.

(c) If equation $f(x)=0$ have atmost r positive roots and atmost t negative roots, then equation $f(x)=0$ will have atmost $(r+t)$ real roots, i.e. it will have atleast $n-(r+t)$ imaginary roots, where n is the degree of polynomial.
e.g. Consider the equation

$$5x^6-8x^3+3x^5+5x^2+8=0$$

The given equation can be written as

$$5x^6+3x^5-8x^3+5x^2+8=0$$

Let $f(x)=5x^6+3x^5-8x^3+5x^2+8$

Here, $f(x)$ has two changes in signs.
So, $f(x)$ has atmost two positive real roots
and $f(-x)=5x^6-3x^5+8x^3+5x^2+8$
Here, $f(-x)$ has two changes in signs.
So, $f(x)$ has atmost two negative real roots.
and $x=0$ cannot be root of $f(x)=0$.

Hence, $f(x)=0$ has atmost four real roots, therefore atleast two imaginary roots.

7. **Rolle's Theorem** If $f(x)$ is continuous function in the interval $[a, b]$ and differentiable in interval (a, b) and $f(a)=f(b)$, then equation $f'(x)=0$ will have atleast one root between a and b. Since, every polynomial $f(x)$ is always continuous and differentiable in every interval. Therefore, Rolle's theorem is always applicable to polynomial function in every interval $[a, b]$ if $f(a)=f(b)$.

Example 45. If $2a+3b+6c=0$; $a, b, c\in R$, then show that the equation $ax^2+bx+c=0$ has atleast one root between 0 and 1.

Sol. Given, $2a+3b+6c=0 \Rightarrow \frac{a}{3}+\frac{b}{2}+c=0$ ...(i)

Let $f'(x)=ax^2+bx+c$,

Then, $f(x)=\frac{ax^3}{3}+\frac{bx^2}{2}+cx+d$

Now, $f(0)=d$ and $f(1)=\frac{a}{3}+\frac{b}{2}+c+d$

$=0+d$ [from Eq. (i)]

Since, $f(x)$ is a polynomial of three degree, then $f(x)$ is continuous and differentiable everywhere and $f(0)=f(1)$, then by Rolle's theorem $f'(x)=0$ i.e. $ax^2+bx+c=0$ has atleast one real root between 0 and 1.

Reciprocal Equation of the Standard Form can be Reduced to an Equation of Half Its Dimensions

Let the equation be

$$ax^{2m}+bx^{2m-1}+cx^{2m-2}+\ldots+kx^m+\ldots+cx^2+bx+a=0$$

On dividing by x^m, then

$$ax^m+bx^{m-1}+cx^{m-2}+\ldots+k+\ldots+\frac{c}{x^{m-2}}+\frac{b}{x^{m-1}}+\frac{a}{x^m}=0$$

On rearranging the terms, we have

$$a\left(x^m+\frac{1}{x^m}\right)+b\left(x^{m-1}+\frac{1}{x^{m-1}}\right)+c\left(x^{m-2}+\frac{1}{x^{m-2}}\right)+\ldots+k=0$$

Now, $x^{p+1}+\frac{1}{x^{p+1}}=\left(x^p+\frac{1}{x^p}\right)\left(x+\frac{1}{x}\right)-\left(x^{p-1}+\frac{1}{x^{p-1}}\right)$

Hence, writing z for $x+\frac{1}{x}$ and given to p succession the values 1, 2, 3, .., we obtain

$$x^2+\frac{1}{x^2}=z^2-2$$

$$x^3+\frac{1}{x^3}=z(z^2-2)-z=z^3-3z$$

$$x^4+\frac{1}{x^4}=z(z^3-3z)-(z^2-2)=z^4-4z^2+2$$

and so on and **generally $x^m+\frac{1}{x^m}$ is of m dimensions in z and therefore the equation in z is of m dimensions.**

Example 46. Solve the equation

$$2x^4+x^3-11x^2+x+2=0.$$

Sol. Since, $x=0$ is not a solution of the given equation.
On dividing by x^2 in both sides of the given equation, we get

$$2\left(x^2+\frac{1}{x^2}\right)+\left(x+\frac{1}{x}\right)-11=0 \quad \text{...(i)}$$

Put $x + \frac{1}{x} = y$ in Eq. (i), then Eq. (i) reduce in the form

$$2(y^2 - 2) + y - 11 = 0$$

$$\Rightarrow \quad 2y^2 + y - 15 = 0$$

$$\therefore \quad y_1 = -3 \text{ and } y_2 = \frac{5}{2}$$

Consequently, the original equation is equivalent to the collection of equations

$$\left[\begin{array}{l} x + \frac{1}{x} = -3 \\ x + \frac{1}{x} = \frac{5}{2} \end{array}\right.,$$

we find that, $x_1 = \frac{-3 - \sqrt{5}}{2}$, $x_2 = \frac{-3 + \sqrt{5}}{2}$, $x_3 = \frac{1}{2}$, $x_4 = 2$

Equations which can be Reduced to Linear, Quadratic and Biquadratic Equations

TYPE I

An equation of the form

$$(x - a)(x - b)(x - c)(x - d) = A$$

where, $a < b < c < d$, $b - a = d - c$, can be solved by a change of variable.

i.e. $y = \frac{(x-a) + (x-b) + (x-c) + (x-d)}{4}$

$$y = x - \frac{(a + b + c + d)}{4}$$

Example 47. Solve the equation

$$(12x - 1)(6x - 1)(4x - 1)(3x - 1) = 5.$$

Sol. The given equation can be written as

$$\left(x - \frac{1}{12}\right)\left(x - \frac{1}{6}\right)\left(x - \frac{1}{4}\right)\left(x - \frac{1}{3}\right) = \frac{5}{12 \cdot 6 \cdot 4 \cdot 3} \quad \text{...(i)}$$

Since, $\frac{1}{12} < \frac{1}{6} < \frac{1}{4} < \frac{1}{3}$ and $\frac{1}{6} - \frac{1}{12} = \frac{1}{3} - \frac{1}{4}$

We can introduced a new variable,

$$y = \frac{1}{4}\left[\left(x - \frac{1}{12}\right) + \left(x - \frac{1}{6}\right) + \left(x - \frac{1}{4}\right) + \left(x - \frac{1}{3}\right)\right]$$

$$y = x - \frac{5}{24}$$

On substituting $x = y + \frac{5}{24}$ in Eq. (i), we get

$$\left(y + \frac{3}{24}\right)\left(y + \frac{1}{24}\right)\left(y - \frac{1}{24}\right)\left(y - \frac{3}{24}\right) = \frac{5}{12 \cdot 6 \cdot 4 \cdot 3}$$

$$\Rightarrow \quad \left[y^2 - \left(\frac{1}{24}\right)^2\right]\left[y^2 - \left(\frac{3}{24}\right)^2\right] = \frac{5}{12 \cdot 6 \cdot 4 \cdot 3}$$

Hence, we find that

$$y^2 = \frac{49}{24^2}$$

i.e. $y_1 = \frac{7}{24}$ and $y_2 = -\frac{7}{24}$

Hence, the corresponding roots of the original equation are $-\frac{1}{12}$ and $\frac{1}{2}$.

TYPE II

An equation of the form

$$(x - a)(x - b)(x - c)(x - d) = Ax^2$$

where, $ab = cd$ can be reduced to a collection of two quadratic equations by a change of variable $y = x + \frac{ab}{x}$.

Example 48. Solve the equation

$$(x + 2)(x + 3)(x + 8)(x + 12) = 4x^2.$$

Sol. Since, $(-2)(-12) = (-3)(-8)$, so we can write given equation as

$$(x + 2)(x + 12)(x + 3)(x + 8) = 4x^2$$

$$\Rightarrow \quad (x^2 + 14x + 24)(x^2 + 11x + 24) = 4x^2 \quad \text{...(i)}$$

Now, $x = 0$ is not a root of given equation.

On dividing by x^2 in both sides of Eq. (i), we get

$$\left(x + \frac{24}{x} + 14\right)\left(x + \frac{24}{x} + 11\right) = 4 \quad \text{...(ii)}$$

Put $x + \frac{24}{x} = y$, then Eq. (ii) can be reduced in the form

$(y + 14)(y + 11) = 4$ or $y^2 + 25y + 150 = 0$

$$\therefore \quad y_1 = -15 \text{ and } y_2 = -10$$

Thus, the original equation is equivalent to the collection of equations

$$\left[\begin{array}{l} x + \frac{24}{x} = -15, \\ x + \frac{24}{x} = -10, \end{array}\right.$$

i.e. $\left[\begin{array}{l} x^2 + 15x + 24 = 0 \\ x^2 + 10x + 24 = 0 \end{array}\right.$

On solving these collection, we get

$$x_1 = \frac{-15 - \sqrt{129}}{2}, \; x_2 = \frac{-15 + \sqrt{129}}{2},$$

$$x_3 = -6, \; x_4 = -4$$

TYPE III

An equation of the form

$$(x - a)^4 + (x - b)^4 = A$$

can also be solved by a change of variable, i.e. making a substitution $y = \frac{(x - a) + (x - b)}{2}$.

Example 49. Solve the equation

$$(6-x)^4+(8-x)^4=16.$$

Sol. After a change of variable,

$$y=\frac{(6-x)+(8-x)}{2}$$

$$\therefore \quad y=7-x \quad \text{or} \quad x=7-y$$

Now, put $x=7-y$ in given equation, we get

$$(y-1)^4+(y+1)^4=16$$

$$\Rightarrow \quad y^4+6y^2-7=0$$

$$\Rightarrow \quad (y^2+7)(y^2-1)=0 \Rightarrow y^2+7\neq 0$$

[$\because$ y gives imaginary values]

$$\therefore \quad y^2-1=0$$

Then, $y_1=-1$ and $y_2=1$

Thus, $x_1=8$ and $x_2=6$ are the roots of the given equation.

2.13 Rational Algebraic Inequalities

Consider the following types of rational algebraic inequalities

$$\frac{P(x)}{Q(x)}>0,\ \frac{P(x)}{Q(x)}<0,\ \frac{P(x)}{Q(x)}\geq 0,\ \frac{P(x)}{Q(x)}\leq 0$$

If $P(x)$ and $Q(x)$ can be resolved in linear factors, then use *Wavy curve method*, otherwise we use the following statements for solving inequalities of this kind.

(1) $$\frac{P(x)}{Q(x)}>0 \Rightarrow \{P(x)\,Q(x)>0 \Rightarrow \begin{cases} P(x)>0, Q(x)>0 \\ \text{or} \\ P(x)<0, Q(x)<0 \end{cases}$$

(2) $$\frac{P(x)}{Q(x)}<0 \Rightarrow \{P(x)\,Q(x)<0 \Rightarrow \begin{cases} P(x)>0, Q(x)<0 \\ \text{or} \\ P(x)<0, Q(x)>0 \end{cases}$$

(3) $$\frac{P(x)}{Q(x)}\geq 0 \Rightarrow \begin{cases} P(x)\,Q(x)\geq 0 \\ Q(x)\neq 0 \end{cases} \Rightarrow \begin{cases} P(x)\geq 0, Q(x)>0 \\ \text{or} \\ P(x)\leq 0, Q(x)<0 \end{cases}$$

(4) $$\frac{P(x)}{Q(x)}\leq 0 \Rightarrow \begin{cases} P(x)\,Q(x)\leq 0 \\ Q(x)\neq 0 \end{cases} \Rightarrow \begin{cases} P(x)\geq 0, Q(x)<0 \\ \text{or} \\ P(x)\leq 0, Q(x)>0 \end{cases}$$

Example 50. Find all values of a for which the set of all solutions of the system $\begin{cases} \dfrac{x^2+ax-2}{x^2-x+1}<2 \\ \dfrac{x^2+ax-2}{x^2-x+1}>-3 \end{cases}$ is the entire number line.

Sol. The system is equivalent to

$$\begin{cases} \dfrac{x^2-(a+2)x+4}{x^2-x+1}>0 \\ \dfrac{4x^2+(a-3)x+1}{x^2-x+1}>0 \end{cases}$$

Since, $x^2-x+1=\left(x-\frac{1}{2}\right)^2+\frac{3}{4}>0$, this system is equivalent to $\begin{cases} x^2-(a+2)x+4>0 \\ 4x^2+(a-3)x+1>0 \end{cases}$

Hence, the discriminants of the both equations of this system are negative.

i.e. $$\begin{cases} (a+2)^2-16<0 \\ (a-3)^2-16<0 \end{cases} \Rightarrow (a+6)(a-2)<0$$

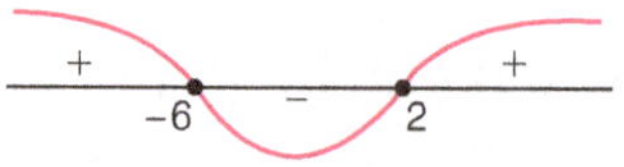

i.e. $$x\in(-6,2) \qquad \text{...(i)}$$

$$\Rightarrow \quad (a+1)(a-7)<0$$

i.e. $$x\in(-1,7) \qquad \text{...(ii)}$$

Hence, from Eqs. (i) and (ii), we get

$$x\in(-1,2)$$

Equations Containing Absolute Values

By definition, $|x|=x$, if $x\geq 0\,|x|=-x$, if $x<0$

Example 51. Solve the equation

$$\left|\frac{x^2-8x+12}{x^2-10x+21}\right|=-\frac{x^2-8x+12}{x^2-10x+21}.$$

Sol. This equation has the form $|f(x)|=-f(x)$

when, $f(x)=\dfrac{x^2-8x+12}{x^2-10x+21}$

such an equation is equivalent to the collection of systems

$$\begin{cases} f(x)=-f(x), \text{ if } f(x)\geq 0 \\ f(x)=f(x), \text{ if } f(x)<0 \end{cases}$$

The first system is equivalent to $f(x)=0$ and the second system is equivalent to $f(x)<0$ the combining both systems, we get

$$f(x)\leq 0$$

$$\therefore \quad \frac{x^2-8x+12}{x^2-10x+21}\leq 0 \Rightarrow \frac{(x-2)(x-6)}{(x-3)(x-7)}\leq 0$$

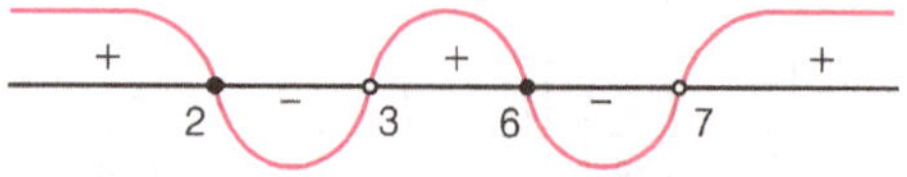

Hence, by *Wavy curve method*, $x\in[2,3)\cup[6,7)$

Example 52. Solve the equation $|x-|4-x||-2x=4$.

Sol. This equation is equivalent to the collection of systems

$$\left[\begin{array}{l}|x-(4-x)|-2x=4, \text{ if } 4-x\geq 0\\ |x+(4-x)|-2x=4, \text{ if } 4-x<0\end{array}\right.$$

$$\Rightarrow \left[\begin{array}{ll}|2x-4|-2x=4, & \text{if } x\leq 4\\ 4-2x=4, & \text{if } x>4\end{array}\right. \quad ...(i)$$

The second system of this collection gives

$$x=0 \text{ but } x>4$$

Hence, second system has no solution.

The first system of collection Eq. (i) is equivalent to the system of collection

$$\left[\begin{array}{l}2x-4-2x=4, \text{ if } 2x\geq 4\\ -2x+4-2x=4, \text{ if } 2x<4\end{array}\right.$$

$$\Rightarrow \left[\begin{array}{l}-4=4, \text{ if } x\geq 2\\ -4x=0, \text{ if } x<2\end{array}\right.$$

The first system is failed and second system gives $x=0$.

Hence, $x=0$ is unique solution of the given equation.

Important Forms Containing Absolute Values

Form 1 **The equation of the form**

$$|f(x)+g(x)|=|f(x)|+|g(x)|$$

is equivalent of the system $f(x)\,g(x)\geq 0$.

Example 53. Solve the equation

$$\left|\frac{x}{x-1}\right|+|x|=\frac{x^2}{|x-1|}.$$

Sol. Let $f(x)=\dfrac{x}{x-1}$ and $g(x)=x$,

Then, $f(x)+g(x)=\dfrac{x}{x-1}+x=\dfrac{x^2}{x-1}$

$\therefore$ The given equation can be reduced in the form

$$|f(x)|+|g(x)|=|f(x)+g(x)|$$

Hence, $f(x)\cdot g(x)\geq 0$

$$\Rightarrow \frac{x^2}{x-1}\geq 0$$

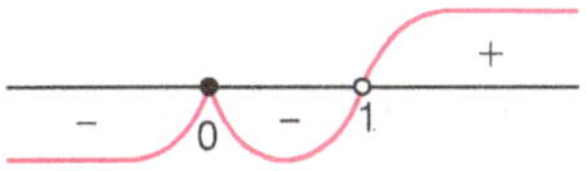

From *Wavy curve method*, $x\in(1,\infty)\cup\{0\}$.

Form 2 **The equation of the form**

$$|f_1(x)|+|f_2(x)|+\ldots+|f_n(x)|=g(x) \quad ...(i)$$

where, $f_1(x), f_2(x),\ldots, f_n(x), g(x)$ are functions of x and $g(x)$ may be constant.

Equations of this form solved by the **method of intervals**. We first find all critical points of $f_1(x), f_2(x),\ldots, f_n(x)$, if coefficient of x is positive, then graph start with positive sign (+) and if coefficient of x is negative, then graph start with negative sign (–). Then, using the definition of the absolute value, we pass from Eq. (i) to a collection of systems which do not contain the absolute value symbols.

Example 54. Solve the equation

$$|x-1|+|7-x|+2|x-2|=4.$$

Sol. Here, critical points are 1, 2, 7 using the method of intervals, we find intervals when the expressions $x-1, 7-x$ and $x-2$ are of constant signs.

i.e. $x<1, 1<x<2, 2<x<7, x>7$

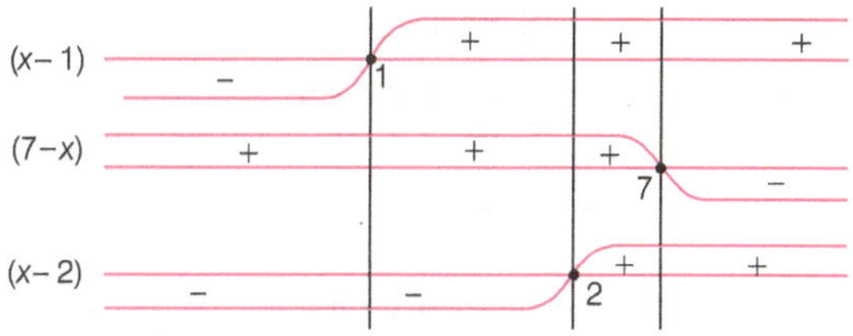

Thus, the given equation is equivalent to the collection of four systems,

$$\left[\begin{array}{l}\begin{cases}x<1\\ -(x-1)+(7-x)-2(x-2)=4\end{cases}\\ \begin{cases}1\leq x<2\\ (x-1)+(7-x)-2(x-2)=4\end{cases}\\ \begin{cases}2\leq x<7\\ (x-1)+(7-x)+2(x-2)=4\end{cases}\\ \begin{cases}x\geq 7\\ (x-1)-(7-x)+2(x-2)=4\end{cases}\end{array}\right. \Rightarrow \left[\begin{array}{l}\begin{cases}x<1\\ x=2\end{cases}\\ \begin{cases}1\leq x<2\\ x=3\end{cases}\\ \begin{cases}2\leq x<7\\ x=1\end{cases}\\ \begin{cases}x\geq 7\\ x=4\end{cases}\end{array}\right.$$

From the collection of four systems, the given equation has no solution.

Inequations Containing Absolute Values

By definition, $|x|<a\Rightarrow -a<x<a\,(a>0)$

$|x|\leq a\Rightarrow -a\leq x\leq a$

$|x|>a\Rightarrow x<-a$ and $x>a$

and $|x|\geq a\Rightarrow x\leq -a$ and $x\geq a$.

Example 55. Solve the inequation $\left|1-\dfrac{|x|}{1+|x|}\right|\geq\dfrac{1}{2}.$

Sol. The given inequation is equivalent to the collection of systems

$$\left[\begin{array}{l}\left|1-\dfrac{x}{1+x}\right|\geq\dfrac{1}{2}, \text{ if } x\geq 0\\ \left|1+\dfrac{x}{1-x}\right|\geq\dfrac{1}{2}, \text{ if } x<0\end{array}\right. \Rightarrow \left[\begin{array}{l}\dfrac{1}{|1+x|}\geq\dfrac{1}{2}, \text{ if } x\geq 0\\ \dfrac{1}{|1-x|}\geq\dfrac{1}{2}, \text{ if } x<0\end{array}\right.$$

$$\Rightarrow \begin{cases} \dfrac{1}{1+x} \ge \dfrac{1}{2}, \text{ if } x \ge 0 \\ \dfrac{1}{1-x} \ge \dfrac{1}{2}, \text{ if } x < 0 \end{cases} \Rightarrow \begin{cases} \dfrac{1-x}{1+x} \ge 0, \text{ if } x \ge 0 \\ \dfrac{1+x}{1-x} \ge 0, \text{ if } x < 0 \end{cases}$$

$$\Rightarrow \begin{cases} \dfrac{x-1}{x+1} \le 0, \text{ if } x \ge 0 \\ \dfrac{x+1}{x-1} \le 0, \text{ if } x < 0 \end{cases}$$

For $\dfrac{x-1}{x+1} \le 0$, if $x \ge 0$

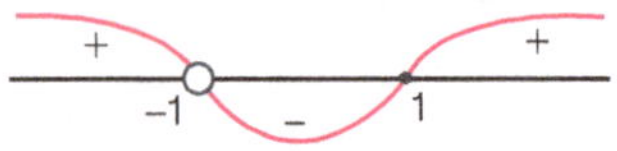

$\therefore \quad 0 \le x \le 1 \quad$ ...(i)

For $\dfrac{x+1}{x-1} \le 0$, if $x < 0$

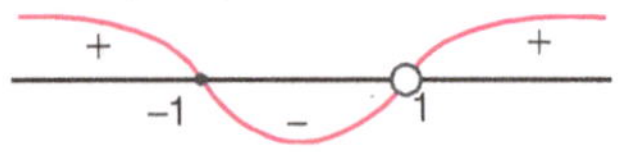

$\therefore \quad -1 \le x < 0 \quad$ ...(ii)

Hence, from Eqs. (i) and (ii), the solution of the given equation is $x \in [-1, 1]$.

Alternate Solution

$$\left|1 - \frac{|x|}{1+|x|}\right| \ge \frac{1}{2} \Rightarrow \left|\frac{1}{1+|x|}\right| \ge \frac{1}{2}$$

$$\Rightarrow \frac{1}{1+|x|} \ge \frac{1}{2} \Rightarrow 1 + |x| \le 2 \text{ or } |x| \le 1$$

$$\therefore \quad -1 \le x \le 1 \text{ or } x \Rightarrow [-1, 1]$$

Equations Involving Greatest Integer, Least Integer and Fractional Part

1. Greatest Integer

$[x]$ denotes the greatest integer less than or equal to x i.e. $[x] \le x$. It is also known as **floor** of x.

Thus, $[3.5779] = 3, [0.89] = 0, [3] = 3$

$[-8.7285] = -9$

$[-0.6] = -1$

$[-7] = -7$

In general, if n is an integer and x is any real number between n and $n+1$.

i.e. $n \le x < n+1$, then $[x] = n$

Properties of Greatest Integer

(i) $[x \pm n] = [x] \pm n, n \in I$

(ii) $[-x] = -[x], x \in I$

(iii) $[-x] = -1 - [x], x \notin I$

(iv) $[x] - [-x] = 2n$, if $x = n, n \in I$

(v) $[x] - [-x] = 2n + 1$, if $x = n + \{x\}, n \in I$ and $0 < \{x\} < 1$

(vi) $[x] \ge n \Rightarrow x \ge n, n \in I$

(vii) $[x] > n \Rightarrow x \ge n + 1, n \in I$

(viii) $[x] \le n \Rightarrow x < n + 1, n \in I$

(ix) $[x] < n \Rightarrow x < n, n \in I$

(x) $n_2 \le [x] \le n_1 \Rightarrow n_2 \le x < n_1 + 1, n_1, n_2 \in I$

(xi) $[x + y] \ge [x] + [y]$

(xii) $\left[\dfrac{[x]}{n}\right] = \left[\dfrac{x}{n}\right], n \in N$

(xiii) $\left[\dfrac{n+1}{2}\right] + \left[\dfrac{n+2}{4}\right] + \left[\dfrac{n+4}{8}\right] + \left[\dfrac{n+8}{16}\right] + \ldots = n, n \in N$

(xiv) $[x] + \left[x + \dfrac{1}{n}\right] + \left[x + \dfrac{2}{n}\right] + \ldots + \left[x + \dfrac{n-1}{n}\right] = [nx]$, $n \in N$

Graph of $y = [x]$

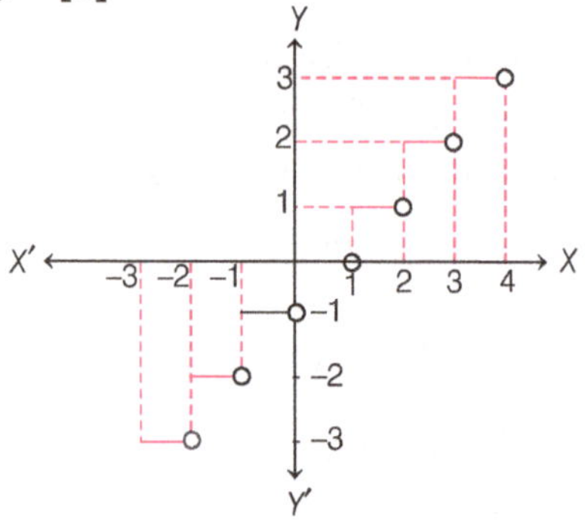

JEE SPIKE

Domain and Range of $[x]$ are R and I, respectively.

Example 56. If $[x]$ denotes the integral part of x for real x, then find the value of

$$\left[\frac{1}{4}\right] + \left[\frac{1}{4} + \frac{1}{200}\right] + \left[\frac{1}{4} + \frac{1}{100}\right] + \left[\frac{1}{4} + \frac{3}{200}\right] + \ldots + \left[\frac{1}{4} + \frac{199}{200}\right].$$

Sol. The given expression can be written as

$$\left[\frac{1}{4}\right] + \left[\frac{1}{4} + \frac{1}{200}\right] + \left[\frac{1}{4} + \frac{2}{200}\right] + \left[\frac{1}{4} + \frac{3}{200}\right] + \ldots + \left[\frac{1}{4} + \frac{199}{200}\right]$$

$$= \left[200 \cdot \frac{1}{4}\right] \quad \text{[from property (xiv)]}$$

$$= [50] = 50$$

Example 57. Let $[a]$ denotes the larger integer not exceeding the real number a. If x and y satisfy the equations $y = 2[x] + 3$ and $y = 3[x - 2]$ simulaneously, determine $[x + y]$.

Sol. We have, $y = 2[x] + 3 = 3[x - 2]$ ...(i)

$\Rightarrow \quad 2[x] + 3 = 3([x] - 2)$ [from property (i)]

$\Rightarrow \quad 2[x] + 3 = 3[x] - 6$

$\Rightarrow \quad [x] = 9$

From Eq. (i),

$$y = 2 \times 9 + 3 = 21$$

$\therefore \quad [x + y] = [x + 21]$

$$= [x] + 21 = 9 + 21 = 30$$

Hence, the value of $[x + y]$ is 30.

2. Least Integer

(x) or $\lceil x \rceil$ denotes the least integer greater than or equal to x i.e. $(x) \geq x$ or $\lceil x \rceil \geq x$. It is also known as **ceilling** of x.

Thus, $(3.578) = 4$, $(0.87) = 1$, $(4) = 4$

$\lceil -8.239 \rceil = -8$, $\lceil -0.7 \rceil = 0$

In general, if n is an integer and x is any real number between n and $n + 1$

i.e. $n < x \leq n + 1$, then $(x) = n + 1$

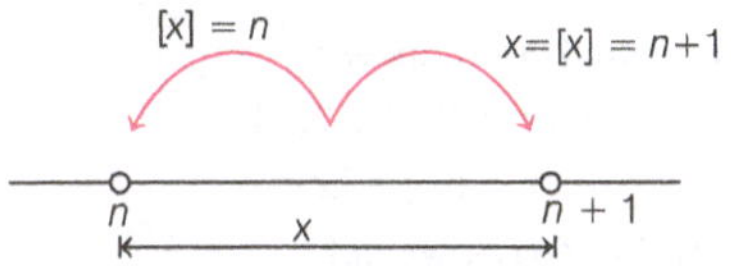

Relation between Greatest Integer and Least Integer

$$(x) = \begin{cases} [x], & x \in I \\ [x] + 1, & x \notin I \end{cases}$$

i.e. If $x \in I$, then $x = [x] = (x)$. [remember]

Graph of $y = (x) = \lceil x \rceil$

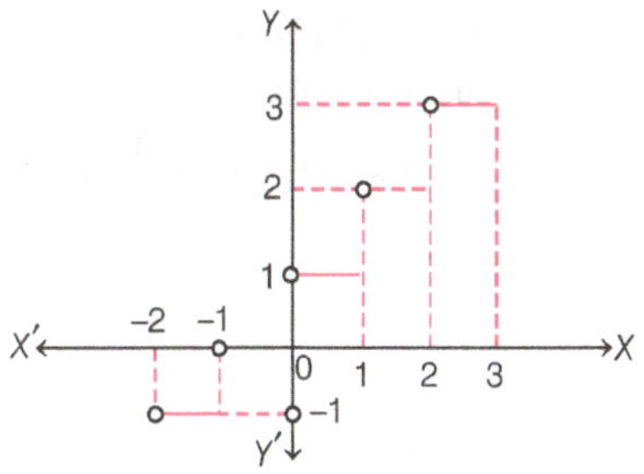

JEE Focus Points

- If $(x) = n$, then $(n - 1) < x \leq n$
- Domain and Range of (x) are R and I, respectively.

Example 58. If $[x]$ and (x) are the integral part of x and nearest integer to x, then solve $(x)[x] = 1$.

Sol. ***Case* I** If $x \in I$, then $x = [x] = (x)$

$\therefore$ Given equation convert in $x^2 = 1$.

$\therefore \quad x = (\pm 1)$

***Case* II** If $x \notin I$, then $(x) = [x] + 1$

$\therefore$ Given equation convert in

$$([x] + 1)[x] = 1$$

$\Rightarrow \quad [x]^2 + [x] - 1 = 0$

or $\quad [x] = \dfrac{-1 \pm \sqrt{5}}{2}$ [impossible]

$\therefore \quad x = \pm 1$

Example 59. Find the solution set of $(x)^2 + (x + 1)^2 = 25$, where (x) is the least integer greater than or equal to x.

Sol. ***Case* I** If $x \in I$, then $x = (x) = [x]$

Then, $(x)^2 + (x + 1)^2 = 25$ reduces to

$\Rightarrow \quad x^2 + (x + 1)^2 = 25$

$\Rightarrow \quad 2x^2 + 2x - 24 = 0$

$\Rightarrow \quad x^2 + x - 12 = 0$

$\Rightarrow \quad (x + 4)(x - 3) = 0$

$\therefore \quad x = -4, 3$ ...(i)

***Case* II** If $x \notin I$, then $(x) = [x] + 1$

Then, $(x)^2 + (x + 1)^2 = 25$ reduces to

$$\{[x] + 1\}^2 + \{[x + 1] + 1\}^2 = 25$$

$\Rightarrow \quad \{[x] + 1\}^2 + \{[x] + 2\}^2 = 25$

$\Rightarrow \quad 2[x]^2 + 6[x] - 20 = 0$

$\Rightarrow \quad [x]^2 + 3[x] - 10 = 0$

$\Rightarrow \quad \{[x] + 5\}\{[x] - 2\} = 0$

$\therefore \quad [x] = -5$ and $[x] = 2$

$\Rightarrow \quad x \in [-5, -4) \cup [2, 3)$

$\because \quad x \notin I$,

$\therefore \quad x \in (-5, -4) \cup (2, 3)$ ...(ii)

On combining Eqs. (i) and (ii), we get

$$x \in (-5, -4] \cup (2, 3]$$

3. Fractional Part

$\{x\}$ denotes the fractional part of x, i.e. $0 \leq \{x\} < 1$.

Thus, $\{2 \cdot 7\} = 0.7$, $\{5\} = 0$, $\{-3.72\} = 0.28$

If x is a real number, then $x = [x] + \{x\}$

i.e. $x = n + f$, where $n \in I$ and $0 \leq f < 1$

Properties of Fractional Part of x

(i) $\{x \pm n\} = \{x\}, n \in I$

(ii) If $0 \leq x < 1$, then $\{x\} = x$

Graph of $y = \{x\}$

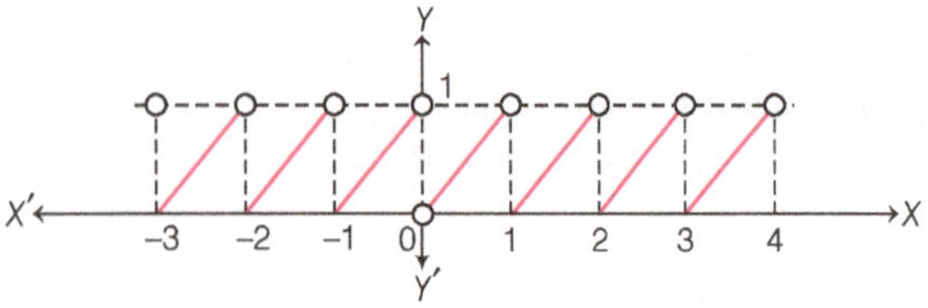

JEE Focus Points

- For proper fraction $0 < \{x\} < 1$.
- Domain and range of $\{x\}$ are R and $[0, 1)$, respectively.
- $\{-5.238\} = \{-5-0.238\} = \{-5-1+1-0.238\}$
  $= \{-6+0.762\} = \{\bar{6}.762\} = 0.762$

Example 60. If $\{x\}$ and $[x]$ represent fractional and integral part of x respectively, find the value of

$$[x] + \sum_{r=1}^{2000} \frac{\{x+r\}}{2000}.$$

Sol. $[x] + \sum_{r=1}^{2000} \frac{\{x+r\}}{2000} = [x] + \sum_{r=1}^{2000} \frac{\{x\}}{2000}$ [from property (i)]

$$= [x] + \frac{\{x\}}{2000} \sum_{r=1}^{2000} 1 = [x] + \frac{\{x\}}{2000} \times 2000$$

$$= [x] + \{x\} = x$$

Example 61. If $\{x\}$ and $[x]$ represent fractional and integral part of x respectively, then solve the equation $x - 1 = (x - [x])(x - \{x\})$.

Sol. $\because \quad x = [x] + \{x\}, 0 \le \{x\} < 1$

Thus, given equation reduces to

$$[x] + \{x\} - 1 = \{x\}[x]$$

$\Rightarrow \quad \{x\}[x] - [x] - \{x\} + 1 = 0$

$\Rightarrow \quad ([x] - 1)(\{x\} - 1) = 0$

Now, $\quad \{x\} - 1 \ne 0 \quad [\because 0 \le \{x\} < 1]$

$\therefore \quad [x] - 1 = 0 \Rightarrow [x] = 1$

$\therefore \quad x \in [1, 2)$

Problem Solving Cycle

If a problem has $x, |x|, [x], (x), \{x\}$, then first solve $|x|$, then problem convert in $x, [x], (x), \{x\}$.

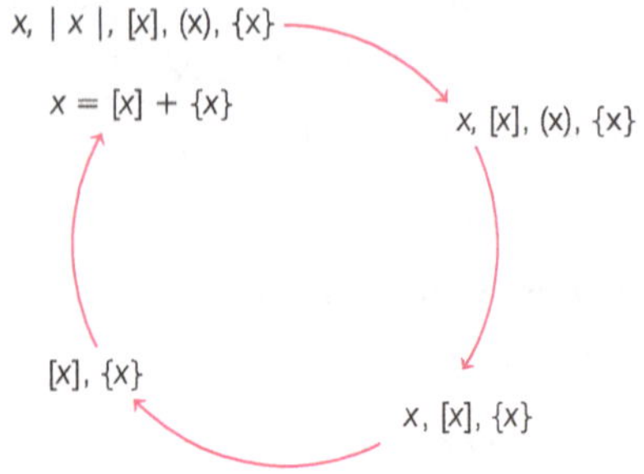

Secondly, solve $(x) = \begin{cases} [x], & x \in I \\ [x]+1, & x \notin I \end{cases}$

Then, problem convert in $x, [x], \{x\}$.

Now, put $\quad x = [x] + \{x\}$

Then, problem convert in $[x]$ and $\{x\}$. ...(i)

Since, $0 \le \{x\} < 1$, then we get $[x]$

From Eq. (i), we get $\{x\}$

Hence, final solution is $x = [x] + \{x\}$.

Example 62. Let $\{x\}$ and $[x]$ denotes the fractional and integral part of a real number (x), respectively. Solve $|2x-1| = 3[x] + 2\{x\}$.

Sol. ***Case* I** $2x - 1 \ge 0$ or $x \ge \frac{1}{2}$

Then, given equation convert to

$$2x - 1 = 3[x] + 2\{x\} \quad \text{...(i)}$$

$\because \quad x = [x] + \{x\}$ ...(ii)

From Eqs. (i) and (ii), we get

$$2([x] + \{x\}) - 1 = 3[x] + 2\{x\}$$

$\therefore \quad [x] = -1$

$\therefore \quad -1 \le x < 0$

No solution $\quad \left[\because x \ge \frac{1}{2}\right]$

***Case* II** $2x - 1 < 0$ or $x < \frac{1}{2}$

Then, given equation reduces to

$$1 - 2x = 3[x] + 2\{x\} \quad \text{...(iii)}$$

$\because \quad x = [x] + \{x\}$ ...(iv)

From Eqs. (iii) and (iv), we get

$$1 - 2([x] + \{x\}) = 3[x] + 2\{x\} \Rightarrow 1 - 5[x] = 4\{x\}$$

$\therefore \quad \{x\} = \frac{1 - 5[x]}{4}$ ...(v)

Now, $\quad 0 \le \{x\} < 1$

$\Rightarrow \quad 0 \le \frac{1 - 5[x]}{4} < 1$

$\Rightarrow \quad 0 \le 1 - 5[x] < 4$

$\Rightarrow \quad 0 \ge -1 + 5[x] > -4$

$\Rightarrow \quad 1 \ge 5[x] > -3$ or $-\frac{3}{5} < [x] \le \frac{1}{5}$

$\therefore \quad [x] = 0$

From Eq. (v), $\quad \{x\} = \frac{1}{4}$

$\therefore \quad x = 0 + \frac{1}{4} = \frac{1}{4}$

Example 63. Solve the equation $(x)^2 = [x]^2 + 2x$, where $[x]$ and (x) are integers just less than or equal to x and just greater than or equal to x, respectively.

Sol. ***Case* I** If $x \in I$, then

$$x = [x] = (x)$$

The given equation reduces to

$$x^2 = x^2 + 2x$$

$\Rightarrow$ $\quad 2x = 0$ or $x = 0$ ...(i)

***Case* II** If $x \notin I$, then $(x) = [x] + 1$

The given equation reduces to

$$([x] + 1)^2 = [x]^2 + 2x$$

$\Rightarrow$ $\quad 1 = 2(x - [x])$ or $\{x\} = \frac{1}{2}$

$\therefore$ $\quad x = [x] + \frac{1}{2} = n + \frac{1}{2}, n \in I$ ...(ii)

Hence, the solution of the original equation is $x = 0, n + \frac{1}{2}$, $n \in I$.

Example 64. Solve the system of equations in x, y and z satisfying the following equations:

$$x + [y] + \{z\} = 3 \cdot 1$$
$$\{x\} + y + [z] = 4 \cdot 3$$
$$[x] + \{y\} + z = 5 \cdot 4$$

where, $[\cdot]$ and $\{\cdot\}$ denotes the greatest integer and fractional parts, respectively.

Sol. $\because [x] + \{x\} = x$, $[y] + \{y\} = y$ and $[z] + \{z\} = z$,

On adding all the three given equations, we get

$$2(x + y + z) = 12.8$$

$\Rightarrow$ $\quad x + y + z = 6.4$ ...(i)

Now, adding first two equations, we get

$$x + y + z + [y] + \{x\} = 7.4$$

$\Rightarrow$ $\quad 6.4 + [y] + \{x\} = 7.4$ [from Eq. (i)]

$\Rightarrow$ $\quad [y] + \{x\} = 1$

$\therefore$ $\quad [y] = 1$ and $\{x\} = 0$ ...(ii)

On adding last two equations, we get

$$x + y + z + \{y\} + [z] = 9.7$$

$\quad \{y\} + [z] = 3.3$ [from Eq. (i)]

$\therefore$ $\quad [z] = 3$ and $\{y\} = 0.3$ ...(iii)

On adding first and last equations, we get

$$x + y + z + [x] + \{z\} = 8.5$$

$\Rightarrow$ $\quad [x] + \{z\} = 2.1$ [from Eq. (i)]

$\therefore$ $\quad [x] = 2, \{z\} = 0.1$ ...(iv)

From Eqs. (ii), (iii) and (iv), we get

$$x = [x] + \{x\} = 2 + 0 = 2$$

$$y = [y] + \{y\} = 1 + 0.3 = 1.3$$

and $\quad z = [z] + \{z\} = 3 + 0.1 = 3.1$

Roots of Equation with the Help of Graphs

Here, we will discuss some examples to find the roots of equations with the help of graphs.

Important Graphs

1. $y = ax^3 + bx^2 + cx + d$

$a > 0$ $\qquad a < 0$

2. $x = ay^3 + by^2 + cy + d$

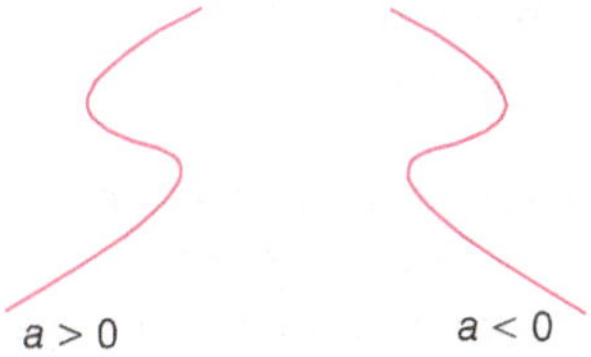

$a > 0$ $\qquad a < 0$

3. $y = ax^4 + bx^3 + cx^2 + dx + e$

$a > 0$ $\qquad a < 0$

Example 65. Solve the equation $x^3 - [x] = 3$, where $[x]$ denotes the greatest integer less than or equal to x.

Sol. We have, $x^3 - [x] = 3 \Rightarrow x^3 - 3 = [x]$

Let $f(x) = x^3 - 3$ and $g(x) = [x]$.

It is clear from the graphs, the point of intersection of two curves $y = f(x)$ and $y = g(x)$ lies between (1, 0) and (2, 0).

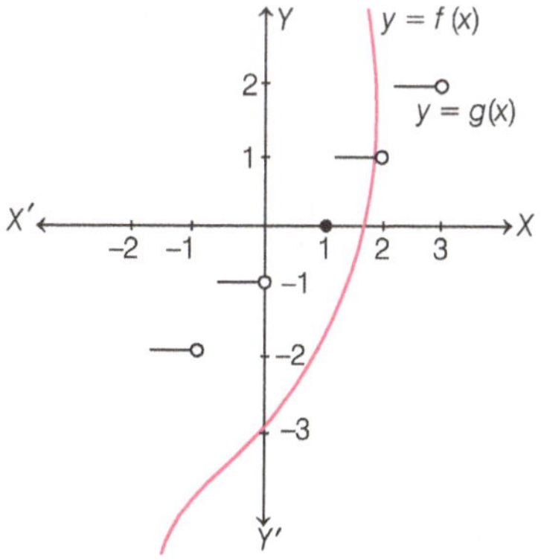

$\therefore$ $\quad 1 < x < 2$

We have, $f(x) = x^3 - 3$ and $g(x) = 1$

or $\quad x^3 - 3 = 1 \Rightarrow x^3 = 4$

$\therefore$ $\quad x = (4)^{1/3}$

Hence, $x = 4^{1/3}$ is the solution of the equation $x^3 - [x] = 3$.

Alternate Solution

$\because \quad x = [x] + f, 0 \le f < 1,$

Then, given equation reduces to

$$x^3 - (x - f) = 3 \Rightarrow x^3 - x = 3 - f$$

Hence, it follows that

$$2 < x^3 - x \le 3$$

$$\Rightarrow \quad 2 < x(x+1)(x-1) \le 3$$

Further for $x \ge 2$, we have $x(x+1)(x-1) \ge 6 > 3$

For $x < -1$, we have $x(x+1)(x-1) < 0 < 2$

For $x = -1$, we have $x(x+1)(x-1) = 0 < 2$

For $-1 < x \le 0$, we have $x(x+1)(x-1) \le -x < 1$

and for $0 < x \le 1$, we have $x(x+1)(x-1) < x < x^3 \le 1$

Therefore, x must be $1 < x < 2$

$\therefore \quad [x] = 1$

Now, the original equation can be written as

$$x^3 - 1 = 3 \Rightarrow x^3 = 4$$

Hence, $x = 4^{1/3}$ is the solution of the given equation.

Example 66. Solve the equation $x^3 - 3x - a = 0$ for different values of a.

Sol. We have, $x^3 - 3x - a = 0 \Rightarrow x^3 - 3x = a$

Let $f(x) = x^3 - 3x$ and $g(x) = a$

$\because \quad f'(x) = 0$

$\Rightarrow \quad 3x^2 - 3 = 0$

$\Rightarrow \quad x = -1, 1$

$f''(x) = 6x$

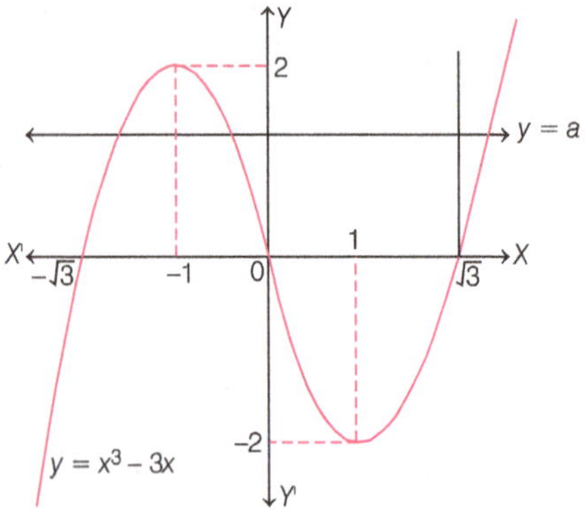

$\therefore \quad f''(-1) = -6 < 0$ and $f''(1) = 6 > 0$

$\therefore$ $f(x)$ local maximum at $x = (-1)$ and local minimum at $x = 1$ and $f(-1) = 2$ and $f(1) = -2$ and $y = g(x) = a$ is a straight line parallel to X-axis.

Following cases arise

Case I When $a > 2$,

In this case $y = f(x)$ and $y = g(x)$ intersects at only one point, so $x^3 - 3x - a = 0$ has only one real root.

Case II When $a = 2$,

In this case $y = f(x)$ and $y = g(x)$ intersects at two points, so $x^3 - 3x - a = 0$ has three real roots, two are equal and one different.

Case III When $-2 < a < 2$,

In this case $y = f(x)$ and $y = g(x)$ intersects at three points, so $x^3 - 3x - a = 0$ has three distinct real roots.

Case IV When $a = -2$,

In this case $y = f(x)$ and $y = g(x)$ touch at one point and intersect at other point, so $x^3 - 3x - a = 0$ has three real roots, two are equal and one different.

Case V When $a < -2$,

In this case $y = f(x)$ and $y = g(x)$ intersects at only one point, so $x^3 - 3x - a = 0$ has only one real root.

Example 67. Show that the equation $x^3 + 2x^2 + x + 5 = 0$ has only one real root, such that $[\alpha] = -3$, where $[x]$ denotes the integral part of x.

Sol. We have, $x^3 + 2x^2 + x + 5 = 0$

$\Rightarrow \quad x^3 + 2x^2 + x = -5$

Let $\quad f(x) = x^3 + 2x^2 + x$ and $g(x) = -5$

$\because \quad f'(x) = 0 \Rightarrow 3x^2 + 4x + 1 = 0$

$\Rightarrow \quad x = -1, -\frac{1}{3}$ and $f''(x) = 6x + 4$

$\therefore \quad f''(-1) = -2 < 0$ and $f''\left(-\frac{1}{3}\right) = -2 + 4 = 2 > 0$

$\therefore$ $f(x)$ local maximum at $x = -1$ and local minimum at $x = -\frac{1}{3}$

and $\quad f(-1) = 0, f\left(-\frac{1}{3}\right) = -\frac{4}{27}$

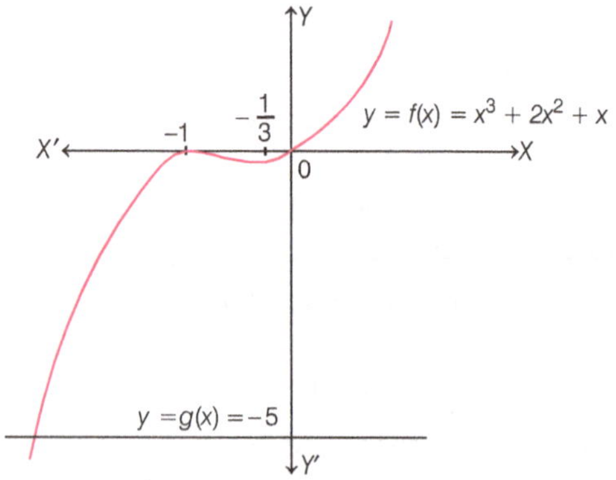

and $\quad f(-2) = -2$ and $f(-3) = -12$

Therefore, x must lie between (-3) and (-2).

i.e. $\quad -3 < \alpha < -2 \Rightarrow [\alpha] = -3$

Example 68. Find all values of the parameter k for which all the roots of the equation $x^4+4x^3-8x^2+k=0$ are real.

Sol. We have, $x^4+4x^3-8x^2+k=0$

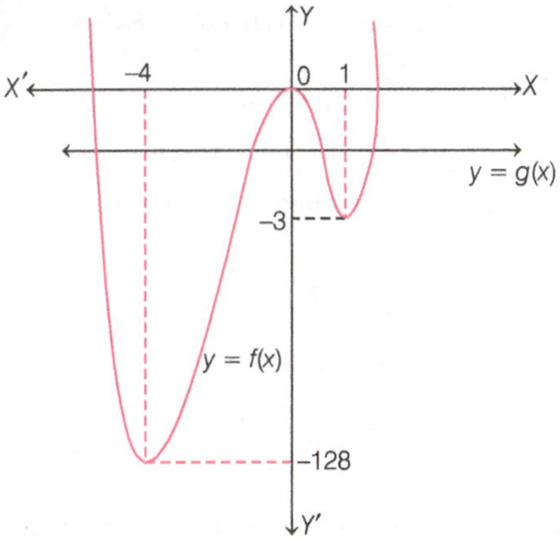

$\Rightarrow \quad x^4+4x^3-8x^2=-k$

Let $\quad f(x)=x^4+4x^3-8x^2$ and $g(x)=-k$

$\because \quad f'(x)=0$

$\Rightarrow \quad 4x^3+12x^2-16x=0$

$\Rightarrow \quad x=-4,0,1$

and $\quad f''(x)=12x^2+24x-16$

$\therefore \; f''(-4)=80,\; f''(0)=-16,\; f''(1)=20$

$\therefore f(x)$ has local minimum at $x=-4$ and $x=1$ and local maximum at $x=0$

and $\quad f(-4)=-128,\, f(0)=0,\, f(1)=-3.$

Following cases arise

Case I When $-k>0$ i.e. $k<0$

In this case $y=x^4+4x^3-8x^2$ and $y=(-k)$ intersect at two points, so $x^4+4x^3-8x^2+k=0$ has two real roots.

Case II When $-k=0$ and $-k=-3$, i.e. $k=0,3$

In this case $y=x^4+4x^3-8x^2$ and $y=-k$ intersect at four points, so $x^4+4x^3-8x^2+k=0$ has two distinct real roots and two equal roots.

Case III When $-3<-k<0$, i.e. $0<k<3$

In this case $y=x^4+4x^3-8x^2$ and $y=-k$ intersect at four distinct points, so $x^4+4x^3-8x^2+k=0$ has four distinct real roots.

Case IV When $-128<-k<-3$, i.e. $3<k<128$

In this case $y=x^4+4x^3-8x^2$ and $y=-k$ intersect at two distinct points, so $x^4+4x^3-8x^2+k=0$ has two distinct real roots.

Case V When $-k=-128$ i.e. $k=128$

In this case $y=x^4+4x^3-8x^2$ and $y=-k$ touch at one point, so $x^4+4x^3-8x^2+k=0$ has two real and equal roots.

Case VI When $-k<-128$, i.e. $k>128$

In this case $y=x^4+4x^3-8x^2$ and $y=-k$ do not intersect, so there is no real root.

Example 69. Let $-1\le p\le 1$, show that the equation $4x^3-3x-p=0$ has a unique root in the interval $\left[\frac{1}{2},1\right]$ and identify it.

Sol. We have, $4x^3-3x-p=0$

$\Rightarrow \quad 4x^3-3x=p$

Let $\quad f(x)=4x^3-3x$ and $g(x)=p$

$\therefore \quad f'(x)=0$

$\Rightarrow \quad 12x^2-3=0$

$\Rightarrow \quad x=\frac{1}{2},-\frac{1}{2}$ and $f''(x)=24x$

$\therefore \quad f''\left(-\frac{1}{2}\right)=-12<0$

and $\quad f''\left(\frac{1}{2}\right)=12>0$

$\therefore\; f(x)$ has local maximum at $\left(x=-\frac{1}{2}\right)$

and local minimum at $\left(x=\frac{1}{2}\right)$.

Also, $f\left(-\frac{1}{2}\right)=-\frac{4}{8}+\frac{3}{2}=1$

and $\quad f\left(\frac{1}{2}\right)=\frac{4}{8}-\frac{3}{2}=-1$

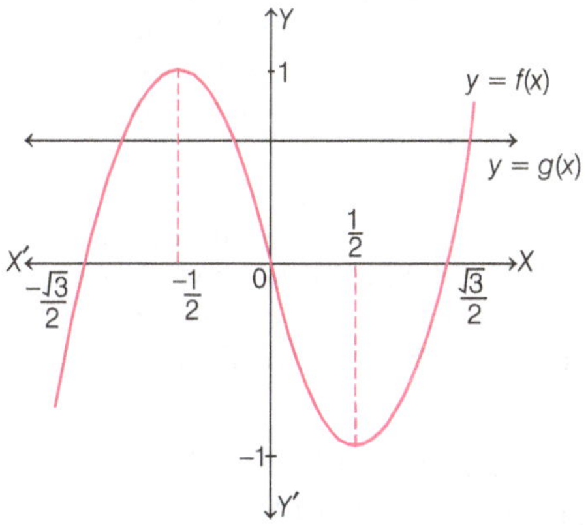

We observe that the line $y=g(x)=p$, where $-1\le p\le 1$ intersect the curve $y=f(x)$ exactly at point $\alpha\in\left[\frac{1}{2},1\right]$.

Hence, $4x^3-3x-p=0$ has exactly one root in the interval $\left[\frac{1}{2},1\right]$.

Alternate Solution

Let $\phi(x) = 4x^3 - 3x - p$

$\therefore$ $\phi'(x) = 12x^2 - 3 = 12\left(x + \frac{1}{2}\right)\left(x - \frac{1}{2}\right)$

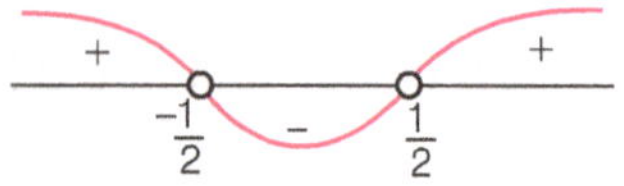

Clearly, $\phi'(x) > 0$ for $x \in \left[\frac{1}{2}, 1\right]$.

Hence, $\phi(x)$ can have atmost one root in $\left[\frac{1}{2}, 1\right]$.

Also, $\phi\left(\frac{1}{2}\right) = -1 - p$ and $\phi(1) = 1 - p$

$\therefore$ $\phi\left(\frac{1}{2}\right)\phi(1) = -(1 - p^2) = (p^2 - 1) \le 0$ $\quad [\because -1 \le p \le 1]$

Since, $\phi(x)$ being a polynomial, continuous on $\left[\frac{1}{2}, 1\right]$ and $\phi\left(\frac{1}{2}\right)\phi(1) \le 0$. Therefore, by intermediate value theorem $\phi(x)$ has atleast one root in $\left[\frac{1}{2}, 1\right]$.

Hence, $\phi(x)$ has exactly one root in $\left[\frac{1}{2}, 1\right]$.

2.14 Irrational Equations

Here, we consider equations of the type which contain the unknown under the radical sign and the value under the radical sign is known as radicand.

- If roots are all even (i.e. $\sqrt{x}, \sqrt[4]{x}, \sqrt[6]{x}, \ldots$, etc) of an equation are arithmetic. In other words, if the radicand is negative (i.e. $x < 0$), then the root is imaginary, if the radicand is zero, then the root is also zero and if the radicand is positive, then the value of the root is also positive.
- If roots are all odd (i.e. $\sqrt[3]{x}, \sqrt[5]{x}, \sqrt[7]{x}, \ldots$ etc) of an equation, then it is defined for all real values of the radicand. If the radicand is negative, then the root is negative, if the radicand is zero, then the root is zero and if the radicand is positive, then the root is positive.

Some Standard Formulae to Solve Irrational Equations

If f and g be functions of $x, k \in N$. Then,

1. $\sqrt[2k]{f}\,\sqrt[2k]{g} = \sqrt[2k]{fg}, f \ge 0, g \ge 0$
2. $\sqrt[2k]{f} / \sqrt[2k]{g} = \sqrt[2k]{(f/g)}, f \ge 0, g > 0$
3. $|f|\sqrt[2k]{g} = \sqrt[2k]{(f^{2k} g)}, g \ge 0$
4. $\sqrt[2k]{(f/g)} = \sqrt[2k]{|f|} / \sqrt[2k]{|g|}, fg \ge 0, g \ne 0$
5. $\sqrt[2k]{fg} = \sqrt[2k]{|f|}\,\sqrt[2k]{g}, fg \ge 0$

Example 70. Prove that the following equations has no solutions.

(i) $\sqrt{(2x+7)} + \sqrt{(x+4)} = 0$ (ii) $\sqrt{(x-4)} = -5$

(iii) $\sqrt{(6-x)} - \sqrt{(x-8)} = 2$ (iv) $\sqrt{-2-x} = \sqrt[5]{(x-7)}$

(v) $\sqrt{x} + \sqrt{(x+16)} = 3$ (vi) $7\sqrt{x} + 8\sqrt{-x} + \frac{15}{x^3} = 98$

(vii) $\sqrt{(x-3)} - \sqrt{x+9} = \sqrt{(x-1)}$

Sol. (i) We have, $\sqrt{(2x+7)} + \sqrt{(x+4)} = 0$

This equation is defined for $2x + 7 \ge 0$

and $x + 4 \ge 0$

$\Rightarrow \begin{cases} x \ge -\frac{7}{2} \\ x \ge -4 \end{cases}$

$\therefore$ $x \ge -\frac{7}{2}$

For $x \ge -\frac{7}{2}$, the left hand side of the original equation is positive, but right hand side is zero. Therefore, the equation has no roots.

(ii) We have, $\sqrt{(x-4)} = -5$

The equation is defined for $x - 4 \ge 0$

$\therefore$ $x \ge 4$

For $x \ge 4$, the left hand side of the original equation is positive, but right hand side is negative.

Therefore, the equation has no roots.

(iii) We have, $\sqrt{(6-x)} - \sqrt{x-8} = 2$

The equation is defined for

$6 - x \ge 0$ and $x - 8 \ge 0$

$\therefore \begin{cases} x \le 6 \\ x \ge 8 \end{cases}$

Consequently, there is no x for which both expressions would have sense. Therefore, the equation has no roots.

(iv) We have, $\sqrt{(-2-x)} = \sqrt[5]{(x-7)}$

This equation is defined for

$-2 - x \ge 0 \Rightarrow x \le -2$

For $x \le -2$ the left hand side is positive, but right hand side is negative.

Therefore, the equation has no roots.

(v) We have, $\sqrt{x} + \sqrt{(x+16)} = 3$

The equation is defined for

$x \ge 0$ and $x + 16 \ge 0$

$\Rightarrow \begin{cases} x \ge 0 \\ x \ge -16 \end{cases}$

Hence, $x \ge 0$

For $x \ge 0$ the left hand side ≥ 4, but right hand side is 3. Therefore, the equation has no roots.

(vi) We have, $7\sqrt{x} + 8\sqrt{-x} + \frac{15}{x^3} = 98$

For $x < 0$, the expression $7\sqrt{x}$ is meaningless,

For $x > 0$, the expression $8\sqrt{-x}$ is meaningless

and for $x = 0$, the expression $\frac{15}{x^3}$ is meaningless.

Consequently, the left hand side of the original equation is meaningless for any $x \in R$. Therefore, the equation has no roots.

(vii) We have, $\sqrt{(x-3)} - \sqrt{(x+9)} = \sqrt{x-1}$

This equation is defined for

$$\begin{cases} x - 3 \geq 0 \\ x + 9 \geq 0 \\ x - 1 \geq 0 \end{cases} \Rightarrow \begin{cases} x \geq 3 \\ x \geq -9 \\ x \geq 1 \end{cases}$$

Hence, $x \geq 3$

For $x \geq 3$, $\sqrt{x-3} < \sqrt{x+9}$ i.e. $\sqrt{(x-3)} - \sqrt{(x+9)} < 0$

Hence, for $x \geq 3$, the left hand side of the original equation is negative and right hand side is positive. Therefore, the equation has no roots.

Some Standard Forms to Solve Irrational Equations

Form 1 **An equation of the form**

$f^{2n}(x) = g^{2n}(x), n \in N$ is equivalent to $f(x) = g(x)$.

Then, find the roots of this equation. If root of this equation satisfies the original equation, then its root of the original equation, otherwise, we say that this root is its **extraneous root**.

JEE SPIKE

Squaring an Equation May Give Extraneous Roots

Squaring should be avoided as for as possible. If squaring is necessary, then the roots found after squaring must be checked whether they satisfy the original equation or not. If some values of x which do not satisfy the original equation. These values of x are called extraneous roots and are rejected.

Concept Inside Video

Example 71. Solve the equation $3\sqrt{(x+3)} - \sqrt{(x-2)} = 7$.

Sol. We have, $3\sqrt{(x+3)} - \sqrt{x-2} = 7$

$$\Rightarrow \quad 3\sqrt{(x+3)} = 7 + \sqrt{(x-2)}$$

On squaring both sides of the equation, we obtain

$$9x + 27 = 49 + x - 2 + 14\sqrt{x-2}$$

$$\Rightarrow \quad 8x - 20 = 14\sqrt{(x-2)}$$

$$(4x - 10) = 7\sqrt{x-2}$$

Again, squaring both sides, we obtain

$$16x^2 + 100 - 80x = 49x - 98$$

$$\Rightarrow \quad 16x^2 - 129x + 198 = 0$$

$$\Rightarrow \quad (x-6)\left(x - \frac{33}{16}\right) = 0$$

$$x_1 = 6 \text{ and } x_2 = \frac{33}{16}$$

Hence, $x_1 = 6$ satisfies the original equation, but $x_2 = \frac{33}{16}$ does not satisfy the original equation.

$\therefore$ $x_2 = \frac{33}{16}$ is the extraneous root.

Form 2 **An equation in the form $\sqrt[2n]{f(x)} = g(x), n \in N$ is equivalent to the system $\begin{cases} g(x) \geq 0 \\ f(x) = g^{2n}(x) \end{cases}$**

Example 72. Solve the equation $\sqrt{(6 - 4x - x^2)} = x + 4$.

Sol. We have, $\sqrt{(6 - 4x - x^2)} = x + 4$

This equation is equivalent to the system

$$\begin{cases} x + 4 \geq 0 \\ 6 - 4x - x^2 = (x+4)^2 \end{cases}$$

$$\Rightarrow \quad \begin{cases} x \geq -4 \\ x^2 + 6x + 5 = 0 \end{cases}$$

On solving the equation $x^2 + 6x + 5 = 0$

We find that, $x_1 = (-1)$ and $x_2 = (-5)$ only $x_1 = (-1)$ satisfies the condition $x \geq -4$.

Consequently, the number -1 is the only solution of the given equation.

Form 3 **An equation in the form**

$$\sqrt[3]{f(x)} + \sqrt[3]{g(x)} = h(x) \quad \text{...(i)}$$

where $f(x)$, $g(x)$ are the functions of x, but $h(x)$ is a function of x or constant, can be solved as follows cubing both sides of the equation, we obtain

$$f(x) + g(x) + 3\sqrt[3]{f(x)\,g(x)}\,(\sqrt[3]{f(x)} + \sqrt[3]{g(x)}) = h^3(x)$$

$$\Rightarrow \quad f(x) + g(x) + 3\sqrt[3]{f(x)\,g(x)}\,(h(x)) = h^3(x)$$

[from Eq. (i)]

We find its roots and then substituting, then into the original equation, we choose those which are the roots of the original equation.

Example 73. Solve the equation $\sqrt[3]{(2x-1)} + \sqrt[3]{(x-1)} = 1$.

Sol. We have, $\sqrt[3]{(2x-1)} + \sqrt[3]{(x-1)} = 1$ ...(i)

Cubing both sides of Eq. (i), we obtain

$$2x - 1 + x - 1 + 3 \cdot \sqrt[3]{(2x-1)(x-1)}$$
$$(\sqrt[3]{(2x-1)} + \sqrt[3]{(x-1)}) = 1$$

$$\Rightarrow \quad 3x - 2 + 3 \cdot \sqrt[3]{(2x^2 - 3x + 1)}\,(1) = 1 \quad \text{[from Eq. (i)]}$$

$$\Rightarrow \qquad 3\cdot\sqrt[3]{(2x^2-3x+1)} = 3-3x$$

$$\Rightarrow \qquad \sqrt[3]{(2x^2-3x+1)} = (1-x)$$

Again, cubing both sides, we obtain

$$2x^2-3x+1=(1-x)^3$$

$$\Rightarrow \qquad (2x-1)(x-1)=(1-x)^3$$

$$\Rightarrow \qquad (2x-1)(x-1)=-(x-1)^3$$

$$\Rightarrow \qquad (x-1)\{2x-1+(x-1)^2\}=0 \Rightarrow (x-1)(x^2)=0$$

$$\therefore \qquad x_1=0 \text{ and } x_2=1$$

$\because x_1=0$ is not satisfies the Eq. (i), then $x_1=0$ is an extraneous root of the Eq. (i), thus $x_2=1$ is the only root of the original equation.

Form 4 **An equation of the form**

$$\sqrt[n]{a-f(x)}+\sqrt[n]{b+f(x)}=g(x).$$

Let $\qquad u=\sqrt[n]{a-f(x)}, v=\sqrt[n]{b+f(x)}$

Then, the given equation reduces to the solution of the system of algebraic equations.

$$\begin{cases} u+v=g(x) \\ u^n+v^n=a+b \end{cases}$$

Example 74. Solve the equation

$$\sqrt{(2x^2+5x-2)}-\sqrt{2x^2+5x-9}=1.$$

Sol. Let $\quad u=\sqrt{(2x^2+5x-2)}$ and $v=\sqrt{(2x^2+5x-9)}$

$\therefore \quad u^2=2x^2+5x-2$ and $v^2=2x^2+5x-9$

Then, the given equation reduces to the solution of the system of algebraic equations.

$$u-v=1$$

$$u^2-v^2=7 \Rightarrow (u+v)(u-v)=7$$

$$\Rightarrow \qquad u+v=7 \qquad [\because u-v=1]$$

We get, $\qquad u=4, v=3$

$$\therefore \qquad \sqrt{2x^2+5x-2}=4$$

$$\therefore \qquad 2x^2+5x-18=0$$

$$\therefore \qquad x_1=2 \text{ and } x_2=-9/2$$

Both roots satisfies the original equation.

Hence, $x_1=2$ and $x_2=-9/2$ are the roots of the original equation.

2.15 Irrational Inequations

We consider, here inequations which contain the unknown under the radical sign.

Some Standard Forms to Solve Irrational Inequations

Form 1 An inequation of the form

$$\sqrt[2n]{f(x)}<\sqrt[2n]{g(x)}, n\in N$$

is equivalent to the system $\begin{cases} f(x)\ge 0 \\ g(x)>f(x) \end{cases}$

and inequation of the form $\sqrt[2n+1]{f(x)}<\sqrt[2n+1]{g(x)}, n\in N$

is equivalent to the inequation $f(x)<g(x)$.

Example 75. Solve the inequation

$$\sqrt[5]{\left[\frac{3}{x+1}+\frac{7}{x+2}\right]}<\sqrt[5]{\frac{6}{x-1}}.$$

Sol. The given inequation is equivalent to

$$\frac{3}{x+1}+\frac{7}{x+2}<\frac{6}{x-1}$$

$$\Rightarrow \qquad \frac{4x^2-15x-25}{(x+1)(x+2)(x-1)}<0$$

$$\Rightarrow \qquad \frac{(x+5/4)(x-5)}{(x+1)(x+2)(x-1)}<0$$

From Wavy Curve Method :

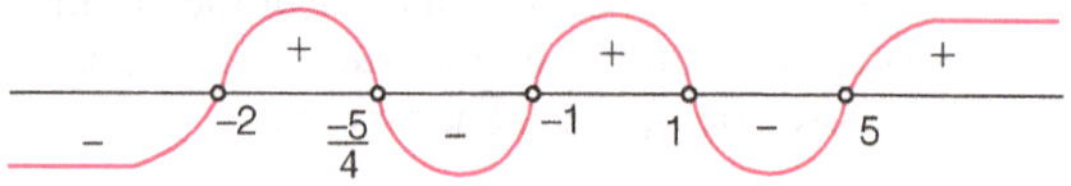

$$x\in(-\infty,-2)\cup\left(-\frac{5}{4},-1\right)\cup(1,5)$$

Form 2 **An inequation of the form**

$$\sqrt[2n]{f(x)}<g(x), n\in N.$$

is equivalent to the system $\begin{cases} f(x)\ge 0 \\ g(x)>0 \\ f(x)<g^{2n}(x), \end{cases}$

and inequation of the form

$$\sqrt[2n+1]{f(x)}<g(x), n\in N$$

is equivalent to the inequation $f(x)<g^{2n+1}(x)$.

Example 76. Solve the inequation $\sqrt{(x+14)}<(x+2)$.

Sol. We have, $\sqrt{(x+14)}<(x+2)$

This inequation is equivalent to the system

$$\begin{cases} x+14\ge 0 \\ x+2>0 \\ x+14<(x+2)^2 \end{cases} \Rightarrow \begin{cases} x\ge -14 \\ x>-2 \\ x^2+3x-10>0 \end{cases}$$

$$\Rightarrow \begin{cases} x\ge -14 \\ x>-2 \\ (x+5)(x-2)>0 \end{cases} \Rightarrow \begin{cases} x\ge -14 \\ x>-2 \\ x<-5 \text{ and } x>2 \end{cases}$$

On combining all three inequation of the system, we get

$$x>2, \text{ i.e. } x\in(2,\infty)$$

Form 3 **An inequation of the form**

$$\sqrt[2n]{f(x)} > g(x), n \in N$$

is equivalent to the collection of two systems of inequations

i.e. $\begin{cases} g(x) \geq 0 \\ f(x) > g^{2n}(x) \end{cases}$ and $\begin{cases} g(x) < 0 \\ f(x) \geq 0 \end{cases}$

and inequation of the form $\sqrt[2n+1]{f(x)} > g(x), n \in N$

is equivalent to the inequation $f(x) > g^{2n+1}(x)$.

Example 77. Solve the inequation

$$\sqrt{(-x^2 + 4x - 3)} > 6 - 2x.$$

Sol. We have, $\sqrt{(-x^2 + 4x - 3)} > 6 - 2x$

This inequation is equivalent to the collection of two systems, of inequations

i.e. $\begin{cases} 6 - 2x \geq 0 \\ -x^2 + 4x - 3 > (6 - 2x)^2 \end{cases}$ and $\begin{cases} 6 - 2x < 0 \\ -x^2 + 4x - 3 \geq 0 \end{cases}$

$\Rightarrow \begin{cases} x \leq 3 \\ (x - 3)(5x - 13) < 0 \end{cases}$ and $\begin{cases} x > 3 \\ (x - 1)(x - 3) \leq 0 \end{cases}$

$\Rightarrow \begin{cases} x \leq 3 \\ \frac{13}{5} < x < 3 \end{cases}$ and $\begin{cases} x > 3 \\ 1 \leq x < 3 \end{cases}$

The second system has no solution and the first system has solution in the interval $\left(\frac{13}{5} < x < 3\right)$.

Hence, $x \in \left(\frac{13}{5}, 3\right)$ is the set of solution of the original inequation.

2.16 Exponential Equations

If we have an equation of the form $a^x = b \, (a > 0)$, then

(i) $x \in \phi$, if $b \leq 0$

(ii) $x = \log_a b$, if $b > 0, a \neq 1$

(iii) $x \in \phi$, if $a = 1, b \neq 1$

(iv) $x \in R$, if $a = 1, b = 1$ (since, $1^x = 1 \Rightarrow 1 = 1, x \in R$)

Example 78. Solve the equation

$$\sqrt{(6 - x)} \, (3^{x^2 - 7.2x + 3.9} - 9\sqrt{3}) = 0.$$

Sol. We have, $\sqrt{(6 - x)} \, (3^{x^2 - 7.2x + 3.9} - 9\sqrt{3}) = 0$

This equation is defined for

$6 - x \geq 0$ i.e. $x \leq 6$ ...(i)

This equation is equivalent to the collection of equations

$\sqrt{6 - x} = 0$ and $3^{x^2 - 7.2x + 3.9} - 9\sqrt{3} = 0$

$\therefore \quad x_1 = 6$ and $3^{x^2 - 7.2x + 3.9} = 3^{2.5}$

Then, $x^2 - 7.2x + 3.9 = 2.5$

$x^2 - 7.2x + 1.4 = 0$

We find that $x_2 = \frac{1}{5}$ and $x_3 = 7$

Hence, solution of the original equation are [which satisfies Eq. (i)]

$$x_1 = 6, x_2 = \frac{1}{5}.$$

Some Standard Forms to Solve Exponential Equations

Form 1 **An equation in the form $a^{f(x)} = 1, a > 0, a \neq 1$**

is equivalent to the equation $f(x) = 0$

Example 79. Solve the equation $5^{x^2 + 3x + 2} = 1$.

Sol. This equation is equivalent to

$x^2 + 3x + 2 = 0 \Rightarrow (x + 1)(x + 2) = 0$

$\therefore \quad x_1 = -1, x_2 = -2$

consequently, this equation has two roots $x_1 = -1$ and $x_2 = -2$.

Form 2 **An equation in the form $f(a^x) = 0$**

is equivalent to the equation $f(t) = 0$, where $t = a^x$.

If $t_1, t_2, t_3, \ldots, t_k$ are the roots of $f(t) = 0$, then

$$a^x = t_1, a^x = t_2, a^x = t_3, \ldots, a^x = t_k$$

Example 80. Solve the equation $5^{2x} - 24 \cdot 5^x - 25 = 0$.

Sol. Let $5^x = t$, then the given equation can reduce in the form

$t^2 - 24t - 25 = 0$

$\Rightarrow \quad (t - 25)(t + 1) = 0$

$\Rightarrow \quad t \neq -1,$

$\therefore \quad t = 25,$

then $\quad 5^x = 25 = 5^2,$

then $\quad x = 2$

Hence, $x_1 = 2$ is only one root of the original equation.

Form 3 **An equation of the form**

$$\alpha a^{f(x)} + \beta b^{f(x)} + \gamma c^{f(x)} = 0,$$

where $\alpha, \beta, \gamma \in R$ and $\alpha, \beta, \gamma \neq 0$ and the bases satisfy the condition $b^2 = ac$ is equivalent to the equation

$$\alpha t^2 + \beta t + \gamma = 0,$$

where $t = (a / b)^{f(x)}$

If roots of this equation are t_1 and t_2, then

$$(a / b)^{f(x)} = t_1 \text{ and } (a / b)^{f(x)} = t_2$$

Example 81. Solve the equation

$$64 \cdot 9^x - 84 \cdot 12^x + 27 \cdot 16^x = 0.$$

Sol. Here, $9 \times 16 = (12)^2$.

Then, we divide its both sides by 12^x and obtain

$\Rightarrow \quad 64 \cdot \left(\frac{3}{4}\right)^x - 84 + 27 \cdot \left(\frac{4}{3}\right)^x = 0$ ...(i)

Let $\left(\frac{3}{4}\right)^x = t$, then Eq. (i) reduce in the form

$$64t^2 - 84t + 27 = 0$$

$$\therefore \quad t_1 = \frac{3}{4} \text{ and } t_2 = \frac{9}{16}$$

Then, $\left(\frac{3}{4}\right)^x = \left(\frac{3}{4}\right)^1$ and $\left(\frac{3}{4}\right)^x = \left(\frac{3}{4}\right)^2$

$\therefore \quad x_1 = 1$ and $x_2 = 2$

Hence, roots of the original equation are $x_1 = 1$ and $x_2 = 2$.

Form 4 **An equation in the form**

$$\alpha \cdot a^{f(x)} + \beta \cdot b^{f(x)} + c = 0,$$

where $\alpha, \beta, c \in R$ and $\alpha, \beta, c \neq 0$ and $ab = 1$ (a and b are inverse positive numbers) is equivalent to the equation

$$\alpha t^2 + ct + \beta = 0, \text{ where } t = a^{f(x)}.$$

If roots of this equation are t_1 and t_2, then $a^{f(x)} = t_1$ and $a^{f(x)} = t_2$.

Example 82. Solve the equation $15 \cdot 2^{x+1} + 15 \cdot 2^{2-x} = 135$.

Sol. This equation rewrite in the form

$$30.2^x + \frac{60}{2^x} = 135$$

Let $\quad t = 2^x$,

Then, $\quad 30t^2 - 135t + 60 = 0$

$\Rightarrow \quad 6t^2 - 27t + 12 = 0$

$\Rightarrow \quad 6t^2 - 24t - 3t + 12 = 0$

$\Rightarrow \quad (t-4)(6t-3) = 0$

Then, $\quad t_1 = 4$ and $t_2 = \frac{1}{2}$

Thus, given equation is equivalent to

$$2^x = 4 \text{ and } 2^x = \frac{1}{2}$$

Then, $\quad x_1 = 2$ and $x_2 = -1$

Hence, roots of the original equation are $x_1 = 2$ and $x_2 = -1$.

Form 5 **An equation of the form $a^{f(x)} + b^{f(x)} = c$,**

where $a, b, c \in R$ and a, b, c satisfies the condition $a^2 + b^2 = c$, then solution of this equation is $f(x) = 2$ and no other solution of this equation.

Example 83. Solve the equation

$$3^{x-4} + 5^{x-4} = 34.$$

Sol. Here, $3^2 + 5^2 = 34$, then given equation has a solution $x - 4 = 2$.

$\therefore \; x_1 = 6$ is a root of the original equation.

Form 6 **An equation of the form $\{f(x)\}^{g(x)}$ is equivalent to the equation**

$$\{f(x)\}^{g(x)} = 10^{g(x) \log f(x)},$$

where $f(x) > 0$.

Example 84. Solve the equation $5^x \sqrt[x]{8^{x-1}} = 500$.

Sol. We have, $\quad 5^x \sqrt[x]{8^{x-1}} = 5^3 \cdot 2^2$

$\Rightarrow \quad 5^x \cdot 8^{\left(\frac{x-1}{x}\right)} = 5^3 \cdot 2^2 \Rightarrow 5^x \cdot 2^{\frac{3x-3}{x}} = 5^3 \cdot 2^2$

$\Rightarrow \quad 5^{x-3} \cdot 2^{\left(\frac{x-3}{x}\right)} = 1 \Rightarrow (5.2^{1/x})^{(x-3)} = 1$

is equivalent to the equation

$$10^{(x-3)\log(5 \cdot 2^{1/x})} = 1$$

$\Rightarrow (x-3)\log(5 \cdot 2^{1/x}) = 0$

Thus, original equation is equivalent to the collection of equations

$$x - 3 = 0, \; \log(5 \cdot 2^{1/x}) = 0$$

$\therefore \quad x_1 = 3, 5 \cdot 2^{1/x} = 1$

$\Rightarrow \quad 2^{1/x} = \left(\frac{1}{5}\right)$

$\therefore \quad x_2 = -\log_5 2$

Hence, roots of the original equation are $x_1 = 3$ and $x_2 = -\log_5 2$.

2.17 Exponential Inequations

When we solve exponential inequation $a^{f(x)} > b \; (a > 0)$, we have

(i) $x \in D_f$, if $b \leq 0$

(ii) If $b > 0$, then we have $f(x) > \log_a b$, if $a > 1$ and $f(x) < \log_a b$, if $0 < a < 1$ for $a = 1$, then $b < 1$.

JEE SPIKE

The inequation $a^{f(x)} \leq b$ has no solution for $b \leq 0$, $a > 0$, $a \neq 1$.

Example 85. Solve the inequation $3^{x+2} > \left(\frac{1}{9}\right)^{1/x}$.

Sol. We have,

$$3^{x+2} > (3^{-2})^{1/x}$$

$\Rightarrow \quad 3^{x+2} > 3^{-2/x}$

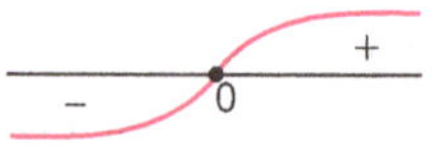

Here, base $3>1$

$$\Rightarrow \quad x+2>-\frac{2}{x}$$

$$\Rightarrow \quad \frac{x^2+2x+2}{x}>0$$

$$\Rightarrow \quad \frac{(x+1)^2+1}{x}>0$$

$$\Rightarrow \quad x>0$$

$$\therefore \quad x\in(0,\infty)$$

Some Standard Forms to Solve Exponential Inequations

Form 1 **An inequation of the form**

$$f(a^x)\geq 0 \quad \text{or } f(a^x)\leq 0$$

is equivalent to the system of collection

$$\begin{cases} t>0, & \text{where } t=a^x \\ f(t)\geq 0 \text{ or } & f(t)\leq 0 \end{cases}$$

Example 86. Solve the inequation $4^{x+1}-16^x<2\log_4 8$.

Sol. Let $4^x=t$, then given inequation reduce in the form

$$4t-t^2>2\cdot\frac{3}{2}$$

$$\Rightarrow \quad t^2-4t+3<0$$

$$\Rightarrow \quad (t-1)(t-3)<0$$

$$\Rightarrow \quad 1<t<3 \qquad [\because t>0]$$

$$\Rightarrow \quad 1<4^x<3$$

$$\Rightarrow \quad 0<x<\log_4 3$$

$$\therefore \quad x\in(0,\log_4 3)$$

Form 2 **An inequation of the form**

$$\alpha a^{f(x)}+\beta b^{f(x)}+\gamma c^{f(x)}\geq 0$$

or

$$\alpha a^{f(x)}+\beta b^{f(x)}+\gamma c^{f(x)}\leq 0$$

where $\alpha,\beta,\gamma\in R$ and $\alpha,\beta,\gamma\neq 0$ and the bases satisfy the condition $b^2=ac$ is equivalent to the inequation

$$\alpha t^2+\beta t+\gamma\geq 0 \quad \text{or} \quad \alpha t^2+\beta t+\gamma\leq 0,$$

where $t=(a/b)^{f(x)}$.

Form 3 **An inequation of the form**

$$\alpha a^{f(x)}+\beta b^{f(x)}+\gamma\geq 0$$

or

$$\alpha a^{f(x)}+\beta b^{f(x)}+\gamma\leq 0$$

where $\alpha,\beta,\gamma\in R$ and $\alpha,\beta,\gamma\neq 0$ and $ab=1$(a and b are inverse (+ve) numbers) is equivalent to the inequation

$$\alpha t^2+\beta t+\gamma\geq 0 \quad \text{or} \quad \alpha t^2+\beta t+\gamma\leq 0$$

where $\quad t=a^{f(x)}$

Form 4 **If an inequation of the exponential form reduces to the solution of homogeneous algebraic inequation, i.e.**

$$a_0 f^n(x)+a_1 f^{n-1}(x)\,g(x)+a_2 f^{n-2}(x)g^2(x)+\ldots$$
$$+a_{n-1}f(x)\,g^{n-1}(x)+a_n\,g^n(x)\geq 0,$$

where $a_0,a_1,a_2,\ldots,a_n$ are constants ($a_0\neq 0$) and $f(x)$ and $g(x)$ are functions of x.

Example 87. Solve the inequation

$$2^{2x^2-10x+3}+6^{x^2-5x+1}\geq 3^{2x^2-10x+3}.$$

Sol. The given inequation is equivalent to

$$8\cdot 2^{2(x^2-5x)}+6\cdot 2^{x^2-5x}\cdot 3^{x^2-5x}-27\cdot 3^{2(x^2-5x)}\geq 0$$

Let $\quad 2^{x^2-5x}=f(x)$ and $3^{x^2-5x}=g(x)$,

then $\quad 8\cdot f^2(x)+6f(x)\cdot g(x)-27g^2(x)\geq 0$

On dividing in each by $g^2(x)$. $\qquad [\because g(x)>0]$

Then, $8\left(\frac{f(x)}{g(x)}\right)^2+6\left(\frac{f(x)}{g(x)}\right)-27\geq 0$

and let $\quad \frac{f(x)}{g(x)}=t \qquad [\because t>0]$

Then, $\quad 8t^2+6t-27\geq 0\Rightarrow\left(t-\frac{3}{2}\right)\left(t+\frac{9}{4}\right)\geq 0$

$$\Rightarrow \quad t\geq\frac{3}{2} \text{ and } t\leq-\frac{9}{4}$$

The second inequation has no root. $\qquad [\because t>0]$

From the first inequation, $t>3/2$

$$\left(\frac{2}{3}\right)^{x^2-5x}\geq\left(\frac{2}{3}\right)^{-1} \qquad \left[\because \frac{2}{3}<1\right]$$

$$\Rightarrow \quad x^2-5x\leq -1 \Rightarrow x^2-5x+1\leq 0$$

$$\therefore \quad \frac{5-\sqrt{21}}{2}\leq x\leq\frac{5+\sqrt{21}}{2}$$

Hence, $x\in\left[\frac{5-\sqrt{21}}{2},\frac{5+\sqrt{21}}{2}\right]$.

2.18 Logarithmic Equations

If we have an equation of the form

$$\log_a f(x)=b,\ (a>0),\ a\neq 1$$

is equivalent to the equation

$$f(x)=a^b \quad (f(x)>0).$$

Example 88. Solve the equation $\log_3(5+4\log_3(x-1))=2$.

Sol. We have, $\log_3(5+4\log_3(x-1))=2$

is equivalent to the equation (here, base $\neq 1,>0$).

$\therefore \quad 5 + 4\log_3(x-1) = 3^2$

$\Rightarrow \quad \log_3(x-1) = 1 \Rightarrow x - 1 = 3^1$

$\therefore \quad x = 4$

Hence, $x_1 = 4$ is the solution of the original equation.

Some Standard Formulae to Solve Logarithmic Equations

f and g are some functions and $a > 0, a \neq 1$, then if $f > 0, g > 0$, we have

(i) $\log_a(fg) = \log_a f + \log_a g$

(ii) $\log_a(f/g) = \log_a f - \log_a g$

(iii) $\log_a f^{2\alpha} = 2\alpha \log_a |f|$

(iv) $\log_{a^\beta} f^\alpha = \dfrac{\alpha}{\beta}\log_a f$

(v) $f^{\log_a g} = g^{\log_a f}$

(vi) $a^{\log_a f} = f$

Example 89. Solve the equation $2x^{\log_4 3} + 3^{\log_4 x} = 27$.

Sol. The domain of the admissible values of the equation is $x > 0$.

The given equation is equivalent to

$2.3^{\log_4 x} + 3^{\log_4 x} = 27$ [from above result (v)]

$\Rightarrow \quad 3.3^{\log_4 x} = 27$

$\Rightarrow \quad 3^{\log_4 x} = 9$

$\Rightarrow \quad 3^{\log_4 x} = 3^2 \Rightarrow \log_4 x = 2$

$\Rightarrow \quad x_1 = 4^2 = 16$ is its only root.

Some Standard Forms to Solve Logarithmic Equations

Form 1 An equation of the form $\log_x a = b, a > 0$ has

(i) Only root $x = a^{1/b}$, if $a \neq 1$ and $b \neq 0$.

(ii) Any positive root different from unity, if $a = 1$ and $b = 0$.

(iii) No roots, if $a = 1, b \neq 0$.

(iv) No roots, if $a \neq 1, b = 0$.

Example 90. Solve the equation $\log_{(\log_5 x)} 5 = 2$.

Sol. We have, $\log_{(\log_5 x)} 5 = 2$

Base of logarithm > 0 and $\neq 1$.

$\therefore \quad \log_5 x > 0$ and $\log_5 x \neq 1$

$\Rightarrow \quad x > 1$ and $x \neq 5$

$\therefore$ The original equation is equivalent to

$\log_5 x = 5^{1/2} = \sqrt{5}$

$\therefore \quad x_1 = 5^{\sqrt{5}}$

Hence, $5^{\sqrt{5}}$ is the only root of the original equation.

Form 2 Equations of the form

(i) $f(\log_a x) = 0, a > 0, a \neq 1$ and

(ii) $g(\log_x A) = 0, A > 0$

Then, Eq. (i) is equivalent to

$f(t) = 0$, where $t = \log_a x$

If $t_1, t_2, t_3, \ldots, t_k$ are the roots of $f(t) = 0$, then

$\log_a x = t_1, \log_a x = t_2, \ldots, \log_a x = t_k$

and Eq. (ii) is equivalent to $f(y) = 0$, where $y = \log_x A$.

If $y_1, y_2, y_3, \ldots, y_k$ are the roots of $f(y) = 0$, then

$\log_x A = y_1, \log_x A = y_2, \ldots, \log_x A = y_k$

Example 91. Solve the equation $\dfrac{1 - 2(\log x^2)^2}{\log x - 2(\log x)^2} = 1$.

Sol. The given equation can rewrite in the form

$$\frac{1 - 2(2\log x)^2}{\log x - 2(\log x)^2} = 1$$

$$\Rightarrow \quad \frac{1 - 8(\log x)^2}{\log x - 2(\log x)^2} - 1 = 0$$

Let $\quad \log x = t$,

then $\dfrac{1 - 8t^2}{t - 2t^2} - 1 = 0 \Rightarrow \dfrac{1 - 8t^2 - t + 2t^2}{t - 2t^2} = 0$

$$\Rightarrow \quad \frac{1 - t - 6t^2}{(t - 2t^2)} = 0 \Rightarrow \frac{(1 + 2t)(1 - 3t)}{t(1 - 2t)} = 0$$

$$\Rightarrow \quad \begin{cases} t = -\frac{1}{2} \\ t = \frac{1}{3} \end{cases} \Rightarrow \begin{cases} \log x = -\frac{1}{2} \\ \log x = \frac{1}{3} \end{cases} \Rightarrow \begin{cases} x_1 = 10^{-1/2} \\ x_2 = 10^{1/3} \end{cases}$$

Hence, $x_1 = \dfrac{1}{\sqrt{10}}$ and $x_2 = \sqrt[3]{10}$ are the roots of the original equation.

Example 92. Solve the equation $\log_x^3 10 - 6\log_x^2 10 + 11\log_x 10 - 6 = 0$.

Sol. Put $\log_x 10 = t$ in the given equation, we get

$t^3 - 6t^2 + 11t - 6 = 0 \Rightarrow (t-1)(t-2)(t-3) = 0$,

then $\begin{cases} t = 1 \\ t = 2 \\ t = 3 \end{cases}$

It follows that

$$\begin{cases} \log_x 10 = 1 \\ \log_x 10 = 2 \\ \log_x 10 = 3 \end{cases} \Rightarrow \begin{cases} x = 10 \\ x^2 = 10 \\ x^3 = 10 \end{cases} \Rightarrow \begin{cases} x = 10 \\ x = \sqrt{10} \\ x = \sqrt[3]{10} \end{cases} \quad [\because x > 0 \text{ and } \neq 1]$$

$\therefore x_1 = 10, x_2 = \sqrt{10}$ and $x_3 = \sqrt[3]{10}$ are the roots of the original equation.

Form 3 Equations of the form

(i) $\log_a f(x) = \log_a g(x), a > 0, a \neq 1$ is equivalent to two ways.

Method I $\begin{cases} g(x) > 0 \\ f(x) = g(x) \end{cases}$, Method II $\begin{cases} f(x) > 0 \\ f(x) = g(x) \end{cases}$

(ii) $\log_{f(x)} A = \log_{g(x)} A, A > 0$ is equivalent to two ways.

Method I $\begin{cases} g(x) > 0 \\ g(x) \neq 1 \\ f(x) = g(x) \end{cases}$, Method II $\begin{cases} f(x) > 0 \\ f(x) \neq 1 \\ f(x) = g(x) \end{cases}$

Example 93. Solve the equation

$$\log_{1/3}\left[2\left(\frac{1}{2}\right)^x - 1\right] = \log_{1/3}\left[\left(\frac{1}{4}\right)^x - 4\right].$$

Sol. The given equation is equivalent to

$$\begin{cases} 2\left(\frac{1}{2}\right)^x - 1 > 0 \\ 2\left(\frac{1}{2}\right)^x - 1 = \left(\frac{1}{4}\right)^x - 4 \end{cases}$$

$$\Rightarrow \begin{cases} \left(\frac{1}{2}\right)^x > \frac{1}{2} \\ \left(\frac{1}{2}\right)^{2x} - 2\left(\frac{1}{2}\right)^x - 3 = 0 \end{cases}$$

$$\Rightarrow \begin{cases} x < 1 \\ \left[\left(\frac{1}{2}\right)^x - 3\right]\left[\left(\frac{1}{2}\right)^x + 1\right] = 0 \end{cases}$$

$$\Rightarrow \begin{cases} x < 1 \\ \left(\frac{1}{2}\right)^x = 3, \left(\frac{1}{2}\right)^x + 1 \neq 0 \end{cases} \Rightarrow \begin{cases} x < 1 \\ x = (-\log_2 3) \end{cases}$$

Hence, $x_1 = -\log_2 3$ is the root of the original equation.

Example 94. Solve the equation $\log_{\left(\frac{2+x}{10}\right)} 7 = \log_{\left(\frac{2}{x+1}\right)} 7.$

Sol. The given equation is equivalent to

$$\begin{cases} \frac{2}{x+1} > 0 \\ \frac{2}{x+1} \neq 1 \\ \frac{2+x}{10} = \frac{2}{x+1} \end{cases} \Rightarrow \begin{cases} x + 1 > 0 \\ x \neq 1 \\ x = -6, 3 \end{cases}$$

$\therefore$ $x_1 = 3$ is root of the original equation.

Form 4 Equations of the form

(i) $\log_{f(x)} g(x) = \log_{f(x)} h(x)$ is equivalent to two ways.

Method I $\begin{cases} g(x) > 0 \\ f(x) > 0 \\ f(x) \neq 1 \\ g(x) = h(x) \end{cases}$, Method II $\begin{cases} h(x) > 0 \\ f(x) > 0 \\ f(x) \neq 1 \\ g(x) = h(x) \end{cases}$

(ii) $\log_{g(x)} f(x) = \log_{h(x)} f(x)$ is equivalent to two ways.

Method I $\begin{cases} f(x) > 0 \\ g(x) > 0 \\ g(x) \neq 1 \\ g(x) = h(x) \end{cases}$, Method II $\begin{cases} f(x) > 0 \\ h(x) > 0 \\ h(x) \neq 1 \\ g(x) = h(x) \end{cases}$

Example 95. Solve the equation

$\log_{(x^2-1)}(x^3 + 6) = \log_{(x^2-1)}(2x^2 + 5x).$

Sol. This equation is equivalent to the system

$$\begin{cases} 2x^2 + 5x > 0 \\ x^2 - 1 > 0 \\ x^2 - 1 \neq 1 \\ x^3 + 6 = 2x^2 + 5x \end{cases} \Rightarrow \begin{cases} x < -\frac{5}{2} \text{ and } x > 0 \\ x < -1 \text{ and } x > 1 \\ x \neq \pm\sqrt{2} \\ x = -2, 1, 3 \end{cases}$$

Hence, $x_1 = 3$ is only root of the original equation.

Example 96. Solve the equation

$\log_{(x^3+6)}(x^2 - 1) = \log_{(2x^2+5x)}(x^2 - 1).$

Sol. This equation is equivalent to

$$\begin{cases} x^2 - 1 > 0 \\ 2x^2 + 5x > 0 \\ 2x^2 + 5x \neq 1 \\ x^3 + 6 = 2x^2 + 5x \end{cases} \Rightarrow \begin{cases} x < -1 \text{ and } x > 1 \\ x < -\frac{5}{2} \text{ and } x > 0 \\ x \neq \frac{-5 \pm \sqrt{33}}{4} \\ x = -2, 1, 3 \end{cases}$$

Hence, $x_1 = 3$ is only root of the original equation.

Form 5 **An equation of the form**

$\log_{h(x)}(\log_{g(x)} f(x)) = 0$ is equivalent to the system

$$\begin{cases} h(x) > 0 \\ h(x) \neq 1 \\ g(x) > 0 \\ g(x) \neq 1 \\ f(x) = g(x) \end{cases}$$

Example 97. Solve the equation

$\log_{x^2-6x+8}[\log_{2x^2-2x+8}(x^2 + 5x)] = 0.$

Sol. This equation is equivalent to the system

$$\begin{cases} x^2 - 6x + 8 > 0 \\ x^2 - 6x + 8 \neq 1 \\ 2x^2 - 2x - 8 > 0 \\ 2x^2 - 2x - 8 \neq 1 \\ x^2 + 5x = 2x^2 - 2x - 8 \end{cases}$$

Solve the equations of this system

$$\Rightarrow \begin{cases} x < 2 \text{ and } x > 4 \\ x \neq 3 \pm \sqrt{2} \\ x < \dfrac{1-\sqrt{17}}{2} \text{ and } x > \dfrac{1+\sqrt{17}}{2} \\ x \neq \dfrac{1 \pm \sqrt{19}}{2} \\ x = -1, 8 \end{cases}$$

$x = -1$, does not satisfy the third relation of this system. Hence, $x_1 = 8$ is only root of the original equation.

Form 6 **An equation of the form**

$2m \log_a f(x) = \log_a g(x), a > 0, a \neq 1, m \in N$ **is** equivalent to the system

$$\begin{cases} f(x) > 0 \\ f^{2m}(x) = g(x) \end{cases}$$

Example 98. Solve the equation

$$2\log 2x = \log (7x - 2 - 2x^2).$$

Sol. This equation is equivalent to the system

$$\begin{cases} 2x > 0 \\ (2x)^2 = 7x - 2 - 2x^2 \end{cases}$$

$$\Rightarrow \begin{cases} x > 0 \\ 6x^2 - 7x + 2 = 0 \end{cases}$$

$$\Rightarrow \begin{cases} x > 0 \\ (x - 1/2)(x - 2/3) = 0 \end{cases} \Rightarrow \begin{cases} x = 1/2 \\ x = 2/3 \end{cases}$$

Hence, $x_1 = 1/2$ and $x_2 = 2/3$ are the roots of the original equation.

Form 7 **An equation of the form**

$$(2m+1)\log_a f(x) = \log_a g(x), a > 0, a \neq 1, m \in N$$

is equivalent to the system $\begin{cases} g(x) > 0 \\ f^{2m+1}(x) = g(x) \end{cases}$.

Example 99. Solve the equation
$\log (3x^2 + x - 2) = 3\log (3x - 2)$.

Sol. This equation is equivalent to the system

$$\begin{cases} 3x^2 + x - 2 > 0 \\ 3x^2 + x - 2 = (3x - 2)^3 \end{cases}$$

$$\Rightarrow \begin{cases} (x - 2/3)(x + 1) > 0 \\ (x - 2/3)(9x^2 - 13x + 3) = 0 \end{cases}$$

$$\Rightarrow \begin{cases} x < 2/3 \text{ and } x > -1 \\ x = \dfrac{2}{3}, x = \dfrac{13 \pm \sqrt{61}}{18} \end{cases}$$

Original equation has the only root $x_1 = \dfrac{13 - \sqrt{61}}{18}$.

Form 8 **An equation of the form**

$$\log_a f(x) + \log_a g(x) = \log_a m(x), a > 0, a \neq 1$$

is equivalent to the system

$$\begin{cases} f(x) > 0 \\ g(x) > 0 \\ f(x)\, g(x) = m(x) \end{cases}$$

Example 100. Solve the equation
$2\log_3 x + \log_3 (x^2 - 3) = \log_3 0.5 + 5^{\log_5 (\log_3 8)}$

Sol. This equation can be written as

$$\log_3 x^2 + \log_3(x^2 - 3) = \log_3 0.5 + \log_3 8$$

$$\log_3 x^2 + \log_3(x^2 - 3) = \log_3(4)$$

This is equivalent to the system

$$\begin{cases} x^2 > 0 \\ x^2 - 3 > 0 \\ x^2(x^2 - 3) = 4 \end{cases} \Rightarrow \begin{cases} x < 0 \text{ and } x > 0 \\ x < -\sqrt{3} \text{ and } x > \sqrt{3} \\ (x^2 - 4)(x^2 + 1) = 0 \end{cases}$$

$$\Rightarrow \qquad x^2 - 4 = 0 \qquad [\because x^2 + 1 \neq 0]$$

$$\therefore \qquad x = \pm 2, \text{ but } x > 0$$

Consequently, $x_1 = 2$ is only root of the original equation.

Form 9 **An equation of the form**

$\log_a f(x) - \log_a g(x) = \log_a h(x) - \log_a t(x), a > 0, a \neq 1$

is equivalent to the equation

$\log_a f(x) + \log_a t(x) = \log_a g(x) + \log_a h(x)$,

which is equivalent to the system

$$\begin{cases} f(x) > 0 \\ t(x) > 0 \\ g(x) > 0 \\ h(x) > 0 \\ f(x) \cdot t(x) = g(x) \cdot h(x) \end{cases}$$

Example 101. Solve the equation

$$\log_2 (3 - x) - \log_2 \left(\frac{\sin \frac{3\pi}{4}}{5 - x} \right) = \frac{1}{2} + \log_2 (x + 7).$$

Sol. This equation is equivalent to

$$\log_2(3 - x) = \log_2 \left(\frac{\sin \frac{3\pi}{4}}{5 - x} \right) + \frac{1}{2}\log_2 2 + \log_2(x + 7)$$

$$\Rightarrow \log_2(3 - x) = \log_2 \left(\frac{1}{\sqrt{2}(5 - x)} \right) + \log_2 \sqrt{2} + \log_2(x + 7)$$

which is equivalent to the system

$$\begin{cases} 3-x>0 \\ \dfrac{1}{\sqrt{2}(5-x)}>0 \\ x+7>0 \\ (3-x)=\dfrac{\sqrt{2}(x+7)}{\sqrt{2}\,(5-x)} \end{cases}$$

$$\Rightarrow \begin{cases} x<3 \\ x<5 \\ x>-7 \\ (x-1)(x-8)=0 \end{cases}$$

Hence, $x_1 = 1$ is only root of the original equation.

2.19 Logarithmic Inequations

When we solve logarithmic inequations

(i) $\begin{cases} \log_a f(x) > \log_a g(x) \\ a>1 \end{cases} \Rightarrow \begin{cases} g(x)>0 \\ a>1 \\ f(x)>g(x) \end{cases}$

(ii) $\begin{cases} \log_a f(x) > \log_a g(x) \\ 0<a<1 \end{cases} \Rightarrow \begin{cases} f(x)>0 \\ 0<a<1 \\ f(x)<g(x) \end{cases}$

Example 102. Solve the inequation

$$\log_{2x+3} x^2 < \log_{2x+3}(2x+3).$$

Sol. This inequation is equivalent to the collection of the systems

$$\left[\begin{array}{l} \begin{cases} 2x+3>1 \\ x^2<2x+3 \end{cases} \\ \begin{cases} 0<2x+3<1 \\ x^2>2x+3 \end{cases} \end{array}\right. \Rightarrow \left[\begin{array}{l} \begin{cases} x>-1 \\ (x-3)(x+1)<0 \end{cases} \\ \begin{cases} -\dfrac{3}{2}<x<-1 \\ (x-3)(x+1)>0 \end{cases} \end{array}\right.$$

$$\Rightarrow \left[\begin{array}{l} \begin{cases} x>-1 \\ -1<x<3 \end{cases} \Rightarrow -1<x<3 \\ \begin{cases} -\dfrac{3}{2}<x<-1 \\ x<-1 \text{ and } x>3 \end{cases} \Rightarrow -\dfrac{3}{2}<x<-1 \end{array}\right.$$

Hence, the solution of the original inequation is

$$x \in \left(-\frac{3}{2}, -1\right) \cup (-1, 3).$$

Canonical Logarithmic Inequalities

1. $\begin{cases} \log_a x>0 \\ a>1 \end{cases} \Rightarrow \begin{cases} x>1 \\ a>1 \end{cases}$

2. $\begin{cases} \log_a x>0 \\ 0<a<1 \end{cases} \Rightarrow \begin{cases} 0<x<1 \\ 0<a<1 \end{cases}$

3. $\begin{cases} \log_a x<0 \\ a>1 \end{cases} \Rightarrow \begin{cases} 0<x<1 \\ a>1 \end{cases}$

4. $\begin{cases} \log_a x<0 \\ 0<a<1 \end{cases} \Rightarrow \begin{cases} x>1 \\ 0<a<1 \end{cases}$

Some Standard Forms to Solve Logarithmic Inequations

Form 1 **Inequations of the form**

Forms	Collection of systems
(a) $\log_{g(x)} f(x)>0 \Leftrightarrow$	$\begin{cases} f(x)>1, \\ g(x)>1, \end{cases} \begin{cases} 0<f(x)<1 \\ 0<g(x)<1 \end{cases}$
(b) $\log_{g(x)} f(x)\ge 0 \Leftrightarrow$	$\begin{cases} f(x)\ge 1, \\ g(x)>1, \end{cases} \begin{cases} 0<f(x)\le 1 \\ 0<g(x)<1 \end{cases}$
(c) $\log_{g(x)} f(x)<0 \Leftrightarrow$	$\begin{cases} f(x)>1, \\ 0<g(x)<1, \end{cases} \begin{cases} 0<f(x)<1 \\ g(x)>1 \end{cases}$
(d) $\log_{g(x)} f(x)\le 0 \Leftrightarrow$	$\begin{cases} f(x)\ge 1, \\ 0<g(x)<1, \end{cases} \begin{cases} 0<f(x)\le 1 \\ g(x)>1 \end{cases}$

Example 103. Solve the inequation

$$\log_{\left(\frac{x^2-12x+30}{10}\right)}\left(\log_2 \frac{2x}{5}\right)>0.$$

Sol. This inequation is equivalent to the collection of two systems

$$\begin{cases} \dfrac{x^2-12x+30}{10}>1, \\ \log_2\left(\dfrac{2x}{5}\right)>1, \end{cases}$$

$$\begin{cases} 0<\dfrac{x^2-12x+30}{10}<1 \\ 0<\log_2\left(\dfrac{2x}{5}\right)<1 \end{cases}$$

On solving the first system, we have

$$\Rightarrow \begin{cases} x^2-12x+20>0 \\ \dfrac{2x}{5}>2 \end{cases}$$

$$\Leftrightarrow \begin{cases} (x-10)(x-2)>0 \\ x>5 \end{cases}$$

$$\Leftrightarrow \begin{cases} x<2 \text{ and } x>10 \\ x>5 \end{cases}$$

Therefore, the system has solution $x>10$.

On solving the second system, we have

$$\Rightarrow \begin{cases} 0 < x^2 - 12x + 30 < 10 \\ 1 < \dfrac{2x}{5} < 2 \end{cases}$$

$$\Leftrightarrow \begin{cases} x^2 - 12x + 30 > 0 \text{ and } x^2 - 12x + 20 < 0 \\ 5/2 < x < 5 \end{cases}$$

$$\Leftrightarrow \begin{cases} x < 6 - \sqrt{6} \text{ and } x > 6 + \sqrt{6} \text{ and } 2 < x < 10 \\ 0 < x < 5 \end{cases}$$

Therefore, the system has solution $2 < x < 6 - \sqrt{6}$ combining both systems, then solution of the original inequations is

$x \in (2, 6 - \sqrt{6}) \cup (10, \infty)$.

Form 2 Inequations of the form

Forms		Collection of systems
(a) $\log_{\phi(x)} f(x) > \log_{\phi(x)} g(x)$	$\Leftrightarrow$	$\begin{cases} f(x) > g(x), \\ g(x) > 0, \\ \phi(x) > 1, \end{cases}$ $\begin{cases} f(x) < g(x) \\ f(x) > 0 \\ 0 < \phi(x) < 1 \end{cases}$
(b) $\log_{\phi(x)} f(x) \ge \log_{\phi(x)} g(x)$	$\Leftrightarrow$	$\begin{cases} f(x) \ge g(x), \\ g(x) > 0, \\ \phi(x) > 1, \end{cases}$ $\begin{cases} f(x) \le g(x) \\ f(x) > 0 \\ 0 < \phi(x) < 1 \end{cases}$
(c) $\log_{\phi(x)} f(x) < \log_{\phi(x)} g(x)$	$\Leftrightarrow$	$\begin{cases} f(x) < g(x), \\ f(x) > 0, \\ \phi(x) > 1, \end{cases}$ $\begin{cases} f(x) > g(x) \\ g(x) > 0 \\ 0 < \phi(x) < 1 \end{cases}$
(d) $\log_{\phi(x)} f(x) \le \log_{\phi(x)} g(x)$	$\Leftrightarrow$	$\begin{cases} f(x) \le g(x), \\ f(x) > 0, \\ \phi(x) > 1, \end{cases}$ $\begin{cases} f(x) \ge g(x) \\ g(x) > 0 \\ 0 < \phi(x) < 1 \end{cases}$

Example 104. Solve the inequation $\log_{(x-3)}(2(x^2 - 10x + 24)) \ge \log_{(x-3)}(x^2 - 9)$.

Sol. This inequation is equivalent to the collection of systems

$$\begin{cases} 2(x^2 - 10x + 24) \ge x^2 - 9, \\ x^2 - 9 > 0, \\ x - 3 > 1, \end{cases}$$

$$\begin{cases} 2(x^2 - 10x + 24) \le x^2 - 9 \\ 2(x^2 - 10x + 24) > 0 \\ 0 < x - 3 < 1 \end{cases}$$

On solving the first system, we have

$$\begin{cases} x^2 - 20x + 57 \ge 0, \\ (x + 3)(x - 3) > 0, \\ x > 4, \end{cases}$$

$$\Leftrightarrow \begin{cases} x \in (-\infty, 10 - \sqrt{43}] \cup [10 + \sqrt{43}, \infty) \\ x \in (-\infty, -3) \cup (3, \infty) \\ x \in (4, \infty) \end{cases}$$

Therefore, the system has solution

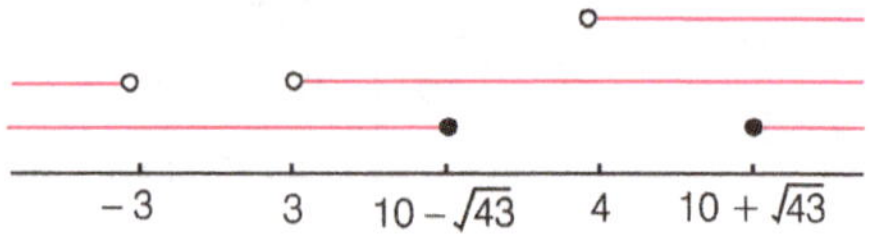

$$x \ge 10 + \sqrt{43}$$

i.e. $\quad x \in [10 + \sqrt{43}, \infty)$

On solving the second system, we have

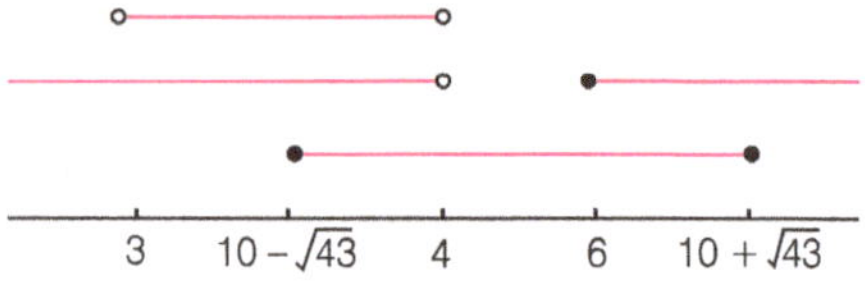

$$\begin{cases} x^2 - 20x + 57 \le 0, \\ (x - 6)(x - 4) > 0, \\ 3 < x < 4, \end{cases}$$

$$\Leftrightarrow \begin{cases} x \in [10 - \sqrt{43}, 10 + \sqrt{43}] \\ x \in (-\infty, 4) \cup (6, \infty) \\ x \in (3, 4) \end{cases}$$

Therefore, the system has solution

$$10 - \sqrt{43} \le x < 4,$$

i.e., $\quad x \in [10 - \sqrt{43}, 4)$

On combining the both systems, the solution of the original inequation is

$$x \in [10 - \sqrt{43}, 4) \cup [10 + \sqrt{43}, \infty).$$

Milestone Practice 2.2

1. Solve the equation $x^3 - 13x^2 + 15x + 189 = 0$, if one root exceeds the other by 2.

2. Solve $x^2 - 3|x| + 2 = 0$.

3. Find the value of k for which $\dfrac{kx^2 + 3x + 4}{x^2 + 2x + 2} < 5$.

4. If α and β are the roots of the equation $x^2 - x - 5 = 0$ and $S_n = 2029\alpha^n + 2026\beta^n$, then
   (a) $S_{13} = S_{12} + S_{11}$
   (b) $S_{13} = S_{12} - 5S_{11}$
   (c) $S_{13} = 5S_{12} + S_{11}$
   (d) $S_{13} = S_{12} + 5S_{11}$

5. Solve $3^{x^2 - x} + 4^{x^2 - x} = 25$.

6. Find the set of all values of x satisfying $3^{2x} - 3^x - 6 > 0$.

7. Find the number of real solutions of the equation $\sqrt{3x^2 - 7x - 30} - \sqrt{2x^2 - 7x - 5} = x + 5$

8. Solve $12x^4 - 56x^3 + 89x^2 - 56x + 12 = 0$

9. Find the value of x, if $[x]^2 = [x + 2]$.

10. Find the solution set of the inequation $5^x + (2\sqrt{3})^{2x} \geq 13^x$.

11. If α, β and γ are the roots of $x^3 - x^2 - 1 = 0$, then the value of $\sum\left(\dfrac{1+\alpha}{1-\alpha}\right) + \Pi\left(\dfrac{\alpha+1}{1-\alpha}\right)$ is equal to ......

12. If $x^2 + px + 1$ is a factor of the expression $ax^3 + bx + c$, then $a^2 - c^2$ is equal to ....

13. The product of all the solutions of the equation $(x + 2)^2 - |x + 2| = 0$ is ....

14. The set of all x satisfying $\left(\dfrac{1}{2}\right)^{x^2 - 2x} < \dfrac{1}{8}$ is given by
   (a) $0 < x < 1$
   (b) $x < 3$
   (c) $1 < x < 2$
   (d) $-1 < x < 3$

15. The number of real solutions of $\sqrt{x^2 - 4x + 3} + \sqrt{x^2 - 9} = \sqrt{4x^2 - 14x + 6}$ is ......

16. For $a > 0$, solve the equation $2\log_x a + \log_{ax} a + 3\log_{a^2x} a = 0$.

17. Find all value of the parameter 'a' for which the inequality $1 + \log_5(x^2 + 1) \geq \log_5(ax^2 + 4x + a)$ is valid for all real x.

Answer Key

1. 7, 9, -3
2. $\pm 1, \pm 2$
3. $k < \dfrac{71}{24}$
4. (d)
5. $-1, 2$
6. $(1, \infty)$
7. 0
8. $\dfrac{13}{6}, \dfrac{5}{2}, 2, \dfrac{1}{2}$
9. $[-1, 0) \cup [2, 3)$
10. $(-\infty, 2]$
11. 15
12. ab
13. (-6)
14. (d)
15. (1)
16. $a^{-4/3}, a^{-1/2}$
17. $(2, 3]$

For Detailed Solution

JEE Pattern EXAMPLES

Single Option Correct Type Questions

Example 1 *The harmonic mean of the roots of the equation* $(5+\sqrt{2})\,x^2-(4+\sqrt{5})\,x+(8+2\sqrt{5})=0$, *is*

(a) 2 (b) 4 (c) 6 (d) 8

Decoding the Question

For two numbers a and b,

Harmonic mean of a and $b = \dfrac{2ab}{a+b}$

Sol. (b) Let α, β are roots of given equation.

$$\alpha+\beta=\frac{4+\sqrt{5}}{5+\sqrt{2}} \text{ and } \alpha\beta=\frac{8+2\sqrt{5}}{5+\sqrt{2}}$$

$$\therefore \text{ HM of } \alpha,\beta=\frac{2\alpha\beta}{\alpha+\beta}=\frac{2\left(\dfrac{8+2\sqrt{5}}{5+\sqrt{2}}\right)}{\left(\dfrac{4+\sqrt{5}}{5+\sqrt{2}}\right)}=\frac{2\times 2(4+\sqrt{5})}{4+\sqrt{5}}=4$$

Example 2 *If the roots of the equation* $x^3-px^2+qx-r=0$ *are in AP, then*

(a) $2p^3=9pq-27r$ (b) $2q^3=9pq-27r$

(c) $p^3=9pq-27r$ (d) $2p^3=9pq+27r$

Sol. (a) Let the roots of the given equation be $a-d, a, a+d$.

Then, $a-d+a+a+d=p \Rightarrow a=\dfrac{p}{3}$

Since, a is root of the equation.

$$\therefore \quad a^3-pa^2+qa-r=0$$

$$\Rightarrow \quad \frac{p^3}{27}-\frac{p^3}{9}+\frac{pq}{3}-r=0 \qquad \left[\because a=\frac{p}{3}\right]$$

$$\Rightarrow p^3-3p^3+9pq-27r=0$$

$$\Rightarrow \quad 2p^3-9pq+27r=0$$

$$\Rightarrow \quad 2p^3=9pq-27r$$

Example 3 *If the roots of the quadratic equation* $x^2-4x-\log_3 a=0$ *are real, then the least value of a is*

(a) 81 (b) $\dfrac{1}{81}$ (c) $\dfrac{1}{64}$ (d) 64

Sol. (b) It is given,

Roots are real.

$$\therefore \quad D \ge 0$$

$$\Rightarrow 16+4\log_3 a \ge 0$$

$$\Rightarrow \quad \log_3 a \ge -4$$

$$\Rightarrow \quad a \ge 3^{-4} \Rightarrow a \ge \frac{1}{81}$$

So, least value of a is $\dfrac{1}{81}$.

Example 4 *The ratio of the roots of the equation* $ax^2+bx+c=0$ *is same as the ratio of the roots of the equation* $px^2+qx+r=0$. *If* D_1 and D_2 *are the discriminant of* $ax^2+bx+c=0$ *and* $px^2+qx+r=0$, *then* $D_1:D_2=$

(a) $\dfrac{a^2}{p^2}$ (b) $\dfrac{b^2}{q^2}$

(c) $\dfrac{c^2}{r^2}$ (d) None of these

Sol. (b) Let α_1, β_1 be the roots of $ax^2+bx+c=0$ and α_2, β_2 be the roots of $px^2+qx+r=0$

$$\text{Then,} \quad \frac{\alpha_1}{\beta_1}=\frac{\alpha_2}{\beta_2}$$

$$\Rightarrow \quad \frac{\alpha_1+\beta_1}{\alpha_1-\beta_1}=\frac{\alpha_2+\beta_2}{\alpha_2-\beta_2}$$

[by componendo and dividendo rule]

$$\Rightarrow \quad \frac{(\alpha_1+\beta_1)^2}{(\alpha_1-\beta_1)^2}=\frac{(\alpha_2+\beta_2)^2}{(\alpha_2-\beta_2)^2}$$

$$\Rightarrow \quad \frac{(\alpha_1+\beta_1)^2}{(\alpha_1+\beta_1)^2-4\alpha_1\beta_1}=\frac{(\alpha_2+\beta_2)^2}{(\alpha_2+\beta_2)^2-4\alpha_2\beta_2}$$

$$\Rightarrow \quad \frac{b^2/a^2}{\dfrac{b^2-4ac}{a^2}}=\frac{q^2/p^2}{\dfrac{q^2-4pr}{p^2}}$$

$$\Rightarrow \quad \frac{b^2}{D_1}=\frac{q^2}{D_2}$$

$$\Rightarrow \quad \frac{D_1}{D_2}=\frac{b^2}{q^2}$$

Example 5 *The equation* $\left|\frac{x}{x-1}\right| + |x| = \frac{x^2}{|x-1|}$ *has*

(a) exactly one solution
(b) exactly two solutions
(c) at most two solutions
(d) infinite number of solutions

Decoding the Question

For $a, b \in R$, $|a+b| = |a| + |b| \Leftrightarrow ab \ge 0$

Sol. (d) We have,

$$\left|\frac{x}{x-1}\right| + |x| = \frac{x^2}{|x-1|}$$

$$\Rightarrow \quad \left|\frac{x}{x-1}\right| + |x| = \left|\frac{x^2}{x-1}\right|$$

$$\Rightarrow \quad \left|\frac{x}{x-1}\right| + |x| = \left|\frac{x^2 - x + x}{x-1}\right|$$

$$\Rightarrow \quad \left|\frac{x}{x-1}\right| + |x| = \left|\frac{x(x-1) + x}{x-1}\right|$$

$$\Rightarrow \quad \left|\frac{x}{x-1}\right| + |x| = \left|\frac{x}{x-1} + x\right|$$

$$\Rightarrow \quad \frac{x}{x-1} \times x \ge 0 \Rightarrow \frac{x^2}{x-1} \ge 0$$

$$\Rightarrow \quad x - 1 \ge 0 \Rightarrow x \ge 1$$

$\therefore \; x \in [1, \infty)$

So, equation has infinite solutions.

Example 6 *If* α *and* $\beta (\alpha < \beta)$, *are the roots of the equation* $x^2 + bx + c = 0$, *where* $c < 0 < b$, *then*

(a) $0 < \alpha < \beta$
(b) $\alpha < 0 < \beta < |\alpha|$
(c) $\alpha < \beta < 0$
(d) $\alpha < 0 < |\alpha| < \beta$

Sol. (b) $\because \quad \alpha + \beta = -b, \; \alpha\beta = c \quad$ ...(i)

$\because \quad c < 0 \Rightarrow \alpha\beta < 0$

Let $\quad \alpha < 0, \beta > 0$

$\therefore \quad |\alpha| = -\alpha$ and $\alpha < 0 < \beta \quad [\because \alpha < \beta]$ ...(ii)

From Eq. (i), we get

$$-|\alpha| + \beta < 0$$

$\Rightarrow \quad \beta < |\alpha| \quad$ ...(iii)

From Eqs. (ii) and (iii), we get

$$\alpha < 0 < \beta < |\alpha|$$

Example 7 *Let* α, β *be the roots of the equation* $x^2 - x + p = 0$ *and* γ, δ *be the roots of the equation* $x^2 - 4x + q = 0$. *If* α, β, γ and δ *are in GP, the integral values of p and q respectively, are*

(a) $-2, -32$ (b) $-2, 3$ (c) $-6, 3$ (d) $-6, -32$

Sol. (a) Let r be the common ratio of the GP, then

$$\beta = \alpha r, \gamma = \alpha r^2 \text{ and } \delta = \alpha r^3$$

$\therefore \quad \alpha + \beta = 1 \Rightarrow \alpha + \alpha r = 1$

or $\quad \alpha(1 + r) = 1 \quad$ ...(i)

and $\quad \alpha\beta = p \Rightarrow \alpha(\alpha r) = p$

or $\quad \alpha^2 r = p \quad$ ...(ii)

and $\quad \gamma + \delta = 4 \Rightarrow \alpha r^2 + \alpha r^3 = 4$

or $\quad \alpha r^2(1 + r) = 4 \quad$ ...(iii)

and $\quad \gamma\delta = q$

$\Rightarrow \quad (\alpha r^2)(\alpha r^3) = q$

or $\quad \alpha^2 r^5 = q \quad$ ...(iv)

On dividing Eq. (iii) by Eq. (i), we get

$$r^2 = 4$$

$\Rightarrow \quad r = -2, 2$

If we take $r = 2$, then α is not integer, so we take $r = -2$.

On substituting $r = -2$ in Eq. (i), we get $\alpha = -1$

Now, from Eqs. (ii) and (iv), we get

$$p = \alpha^2 r = (-1)^2(-2) = -2$$

and $\quad q = \alpha^2 r^5 = (-1)^2(-2)^5 = -32$

Hence, $\quad (p, q) = (-2, -32)$

Example 8 *Let* $f(x) = \int_1^x \sqrt{(2 - t^2)}\, dt$, *the real roots of the equation* $x^2 - f'(x) = 0$ *are*

(a) ± 1 (b) $\pm \frac{1}{\sqrt{2}}$ (c) $\pm \frac{1}{2}$ (d) 0 and 1

Sol. (a) We have,

$$f(x) = \int_1^x \sqrt{(2 - t^2)}\, dt$$

$\Rightarrow \quad f'(x) = \sqrt{(2 - x^2)}$

$\therefore \quad x^2 - f'(x) = 0$

$\Rightarrow \quad x^2 - \sqrt{(2 - x^2)} = 0$

$\Rightarrow \quad x^4 + x^2 - 2 = 0$

$\Rightarrow \quad x^2 = 1, -2$

$\Rightarrow \quad x = \pm 1 \quad$ [only for real value of x]

Example 9 *If* $x^2 + 3x + 5 = 0$ *and* $ax^2 + bx + c = 0$ *have a common root and* $a, b, c \in N$, *the minimum value of* $a + b + c$ *is*

(a) 3 (b) 9 (c) 6 (d) 12

Sol. (b) $\because$ Roots of the equation $x^2 + 3x + 5 = 0$ are non-real. Thus, given equations will have two common roots.

$\Rightarrow \quad \frac{a}{1} = \frac{b}{3} = \frac{c}{5} = \lambda \quad$ [say]

$\therefore \quad a + b + c = 9\lambda$

Thus, minimum value of $a + b + c = 9 \quad [\because a, b, c \in N]$

Example 10 *If $x_1, x_2, x_3, \ldots, x_n$ are the roots of the equation $x^n + ax + b = 0$, the value of $(x_1 - x_2)(x_1 - x_3)(x_1 - x_4)\ldots(x_1 - x_n)$ is*

(a) $nx_1 + b$ (b) $n(x_1)^{n-1}$

(c) $n(x_1)^{n-1} + a$ (d) $n(x_1)^{n-1} + b$

Sol. (c) $\because x^n + ax + b = (x - x_1)(x - x_2)(x - x_3)\ldots(x - x_n)$

$$\Rightarrow (x - x_2)(x - x_3)\ldots(x - x_n) = \frac{x^n + ax + b}{x - x_1}$$

On taking $\lim\limits_{x \to x_1}$ both sides, we get

$$(x_1 - x_2)(x_1 - x_3)\ldots(x_1 - x_n) = \lim_{x \to x_1} \frac{x^n + ax + b}{x - x_1} \quad \left[\frac{0}{0}\text{form}\right]$$

$$= \lim_{x \to x_1} \frac{nx^{n-1} + a}{1}$$

$$= n(x_1)^{n-1} + a$$

Example 11 *If α, β are the roots of the equation $ax^2 + bx + c = 0$ and $A_n = \alpha^n + \beta^n$, then $a A_{n+2} + bA_{n+1} + cA_n$ is equal to*

(a) 0 (b) 1

(c) $a + b + c$ (d) abc

Sol. (a) $\because \alpha + \beta = -\frac{b}{a}$ and $\alpha\beta = \frac{c}{a}$

$$\therefore \quad A_{n+2} = \alpha^{n+2} + \beta^{n+2}$$

$$= (\alpha + \beta)(\alpha^{n+1} + \beta^{n+1}) - \alpha\beta^{n+1} - \beta\alpha^{n+1}$$

$$= (\alpha + \beta)(\alpha^{n+1} + \beta^{n+1}) - \alpha\beta(\alpha^n + \beta^n)$$

$$= -\frac{b}{a} A_{n+1} - \frac{c}{a} A_n$$

$$\Rightarrow a A_{n+2} + b A_{n+1} + c A_n = 0$$

Example 12 *If x and y are positive integers such that $xy + x + y = 71$, $x^2y + xy^2 = 880$, then $x^2 + y^2$ is equal to*

(a) 125 (b) 137 (c) 146 (d) 152

Sol. (c) $\because \; xy + x + y = 71$

$\Rightarrow xy + (x + y) = 71$

and $\quad x^2y + xy^2 = 880$

$\Rightarrow \quad xy\,(x + y) = 880$

$\Rightarrow xy$ and $(x + y)$ are the roots of the quadratic equation.

$$t^2 - 71t + 880 = 0$$

$$\Rightarrow \quad (t - 55)(t - 16) = 0$$

$$\Rightarrow \quad t = 55, 16$$

$$\therefore \quad x + y = 16$$

and $\quad xy = 55$

So, $x^2 + y^2 = (x + y)^2 - 2xy = (16)^2 - 110 = 146$

JEE SCANNER

Example 13 Similar to PYQ Asked in JEE Main 2024

If $2 + \sqrt{3}$ is a root of quadratic equation $x^2 + ax + b = 0$, then quadratic equation whose roots are $\frac{1}{a+b}$ and $\frac{2}{ab}$ is

(a) $x^2 - 4x + 1 = 0$

(b) $6x^2 + 5x + 1 = 0$

(c) $2x^2 - 5x + 4 = 0$

(d) None of the above

Sol. (b) $x^2 + ax + b = 0$, is a quadratic equation whose one root is $2 + \sqrt{3}$, so another root will be $2 - \sqrt{3}$.

$\because$ Conjugate roots occur in pair.

For $x^2 + ax + b = 0$

Sum of roots $= -a$

$$\Rightarrow \quad 2 + \sqrt{3} + 2 - \sqrt{3} = -a$$

$$\Rightarrow \quad 4 = -a$$

$$\Rightarrow \quad a = -4$$

Product of roots $= b$

$$\Rightarrow \quad (2 + \sqrt{3})(2 - \sqrt{3}) = b$$

$$\Rightarrow \quad 4 - 3 = b$$

$$\Rightarrow \quad b = 1$$

Now, $\quad \frac{1}{a+b} = \frac{1}{-3}, \frac{2}{ab} = \frac{2}{-4} = -\frac{1}{2}$

Sum of roots $= \frac{-1}{3} - \frac{1}{2} = \frac{-5}{6}$

Product of roots $= \frac{-1}{2} \times \frac{-1}{3} = \frac{1}{6}$

Quadratic equation whose roots are $\frac{1}{a+b}$ and $\frac{2}{ab}$ is

$x^2 -$ (sum of roots) $x +$ product of roots $= 0$

$$\Rightarrow \quad x^2 - \left(\frac{-5}{6}\right)x + \frac{1}{6} = 0$$

$$\Rightarrow \quad 6x^2 + 5x + 1 = 0$$

Skill Builder

If α, β are roots of $x^2 - 7x + b = 0$ and they are real and differ by one, then a quadratic equation whose roots are $\alpha^2 + \beta^2$ and $\alpha\beta$ is ......

(a) $x^2 - 37x + 300 = 0$

(b) $x^2 - 7x + 12 = 0$

(c) $x^2 - 25x + 12 = 0$

(d) None of the above

For Sol.

Example 14 *If α, β are the roots of the equation $x^2 - 3x + 5 = 0$ and γ, δ are the roots of the equation $x^2 + 5x - 3 = 0$, then the equation whose roots are $\alpha\gamma + \beta\delta$ and $\alpha\delta + \beta\gamma$, is*

(a) $x^2 - 15x - 158 = 0$ (b) $x^2 + 15x - 158 = 0$

(c) $x^2 - 15x + 158 = 0$ (d) $x^2 + 15x + 158 = 0$

Sol. (d) $\because \quad \alpha + \beta = 3, \alpha\beta = 5, \gamma + \delta = (-5), \gamma\delta = (-3)$

Sum of roots $= (\alpha\gamma + \beta\delta) + (\alpha\delta + \beta\gamma)$

$= (\alpha + \beta)(\gamma + \delta) = 3 \times (-5) = (-15)$

Product of roots $= (\alpha\gamma + \beta\delta)(\alpha\delta + \beta\gamma)$

$= \alpha^2\gamma\delta + \alpha\beta\gamma^2 + \beta\alpha\delta^2 + \beta^2\gamma\delta$

$= \gamma\delta(\alpha^2 + \beta^2) + \alpha\beta(\gamma^2 + \delta^2)$

$= -3(\alpha^2 + \beta^2) + 5(\gamma^2 + \delta^2)$

$= -3[(\alpha + \beta)^2 - 2\alpha\beta] + 5[(\gamma + \delta)^2 - 2\gamma\delta]$

$= -3[9 - 10] + 5[25 + 6] = 158$

$\therefore$ Required equation is $x^2 + 15x + 158 = 0$.

Example 15 *The number of roots of the equation*

$$\frac{1}{x} + \frac{1}{\sqrt{(1 - x^2)}} = \frac{35}{12} \text{ is}$$

(a) 0 (b) 1 (c) 2 (d) 3

Sol. (d) Let $\frac{1}{x} = u$ and $\frac{1}{\sqrt{(1 - x^2)}} = v$, then

$$u + v = \frac{35}{12} \text{ and } u^2 + v^2 = u^2v^2$$

$$\Rightarrow \quad (u + v)^2 = \left(\frac{35}{12}\right)^2$$

$$\Rightarrow \quad u^2 + v^2 + 2uv = \left(\frac{35}{12}\right)^2$$

$$\Rightarrow \quad u^2v^2 + 2uv = \left(\frac{35}{12}\right)^2 \quad [\because u^2 + v^2 = u^2v^2]$$

$$\Rightarrow \quad u^2v^2 + 2uv - \left(\frac{35}{12}\right)^2 = 0$$

$$\Rightarrow \quad \left(uv + \frac{49}{12}\right)\left(uv - \frac{25}{12}\right) = 0$$

$$\Rightarrow \quad uv = -\frac{49}{12}, uv = \frac{25}{12}$$

***Case* I** If $uv = -\frac{49}{12}$, then

$$\frac{1}{x} \cdot \frac{1}{\sqrt{(1 - x^2)}} = -\frac{49}{12} \quad [\text{here } x < 0]$$

$$\Rightarrow \quad x^4 - x^2 + \frac{(12)^2}{(49)^2} = 0 \Rightarrow x = -\frac{(5 + \sqrt{73})}{14}, \frac{-5 + \sqrt{73}}{14}$$

But for $x < 0, y > 0$, $x = \frac{-(5 + \sqrt{73})}{14}$

***Case* II** If $uv = \frac{25}{12}$, then

$$\frac{1}{x} \cdot \frac{1}{\sqrt{(1 - x^2)}} = \frac{25}{12} \quad [\text{here } x > 0]$$

$$\Rightarrow \quad x^4 - x^2 + \frac{(12)^2}{(25)^2} = 0$$

$$\Rightarrow \quad \left(x^2 - \frac{9}{25}\right)\left(x^2 - \frac{16}{25}\right) = 0 \Rightarrow x = \frac{3}{5}, \frac{4}{5}$$

On combining both cases,

$$x = -\frac{(5 + \sqrt{73})}{14}, \frac{3}{5}, \frac{4}{5}$$

Hence, number of roots = 3

Example 16 *The sum of the roots of the equation $2^{33x - 2} + 2^{11x + 2} = 2^{22x + 1} + 1$ is*

(a) $\frac{1}{11}$ (b) $\frac{2}{11}$ (c) $\frac{3}{11}$ (d) $\frac{4}{11}$

Decoding the Question

For a cubic polynomial $ax^3 + bx^2 + cx + d = 0$, if α, β and γ are the roots of the equation, then

$$\alpha + \beta + \gamma = -\frac{b}{a}, \alpha\beta + \beta\gamma + \gamma\alpha = \frac{c}{a}, \alpha\beta\gamma = \frac{-d}{a}$$

Sol. (b) Let $2^{11x} = t$, given equation reduces to

$$\frac{t^3}{4} + 4t = 2t^2 + 1$$

$$\Rightarrow \quad t^3 - 8t^2 + 16t - 4 = 0 \Rightarrow t_1 \cdot t_2 \cdot t_3 = 4$$

$$\Rightarrow \quad 2^{11x_1} \cdot 2^{11x_2} \cdot 2^{11x_3} = 4 \Rightarrow 2^{11(x_1 + x_2 + x_3)} = 2^2$$

$$\Rightarrow \quad 11(x_1 + x_2 + x_3) = 2$$

$$\therefore \quad x_1 + x_2 + x_3 = \frac{2}{11}$$

More than One Correct Option Type Questions

Example 17 *For the equation $2x^2 - 6\sqrt{2}x - 1 = 0$*

(a) roots are rational

(b) roots are irrational

(c) if one root is $(p + \sqrt{q})$, the other is $(-p + \sqrt{q})$

(d) if one root is $(p + \sqrt{q})$, the other is $(p - \sqrt{q})$

Sol. (b, c) As the coefficients are not rational, irrational roots need not appear in conjugate pair.

Here, $\alpha + \beta = 3\sqrt{2}$ and $\alpha\beta = -\frac{1}{2}$

Let $\alpha = p + \sqrt{q}$, then other root $\beta = -p + \sqrt{q}$.

Example 18 *Given that α, γ are roots of the equation $Ax^2 - 4x + 1 = 0$ and β, δ the roots of the equation $Bx^2 - 6x + 1 = 0$, such that α, β, γ and δ are in HP, then*

(a) $A = 3$ (b) $A = 4$ (c) $B = 2$ (d) $B = 8$

Sol. (a,d) Since, α, β, γ and δ are in HP, hence $\frac{1}{\alpha}, \frac{1}{\beta}, \frac{1}{\gamma}$ and $\frac{1}{\delta}$ are in AP and they may be taken as $a-3d$, $a-d$, $a+d$ and $a+3d$. Replacing x by $\frac{1}{x}$, we get the equation whose roots are $a-3d$, $a+d$ is $x^2-4x+A=0$ and equation whose roots are $a-d$, $a+3d$ is $x^2-6x+B=0$, then

$$(a-3d)+(a+d)=4 \Rightarrow 2(a-d)=4$$

and $$(a-d)+(a+3d)=6 \Rightarrow 2(a+d)=6$$

∴ $$a=\frac{5}{2} \text{ and } d=\frac{1}{2}$$

Now, $$A=(a-3d)(a+d)=\left(\frac{5}{2}-\frac{3}{2}\right)\left(\frac{5}{2}+\frac{1}{2}\right)=3$$

and $$B=(a-d)(a+3d)=\left(\frac{5}{2}-\frac{1}{2}\right)\left(\frac{5}{2}+\frac{3}{2}\right)=8$$

Example 19 *If $|ax^2+bx+c|\le 1$ for all x in [0, 1], then*

(a) $|a|\le 8$ (b) $|b|>8$

(c) $|c|\le 1$ (d) $|a|+|b|+|c|\le 17$

Sol. (a,c,d) On putting $x=0, 1$ and $\frac{1}{2}$, we get

$$|c|\le 1 \quad \text{...(i)}$$

$$|a+b+c|\le 1 \quad \text{...(ii)}$$

and $$|a+2b+4c|\le 4 \quad \text{...(iii)}$$

From Eqs. (i), (ii) and (iii), we get

$$|b|\le 8 \text{ and } |a|\le 8$$

$$\Rightarrow \quad |a|+|b|+|c|\le 17$$

Example 20 *If $\cos^4\theta+p, \sin^4\theta+p$ are the roots of the equation $x^2+a(2x+1)=0$ and $\cos^2\theta+q, \sin^2\theta+q$ are the roots of the equation $x^2+4x+2=0$ then a is equal to*

(a) -2 (b) -1 (c) 1 (d) 2

Sol. (b,d) ∵ $$\cos^4\theta-\sin^4\theta=\cos 2\theta$$

$$\Rightarrow \quad \cos^4\theta-\sin^4\theta=\cos^2\theta-\sin^2\theta$$

$$\Rightarrow (\cos^4\theta+p)-(\sin^4\theta+p)=(\cos^2\theta+q)-(\sin^2\theta+q)$$

$$\Rightarrow \quad \frac{\sqrt{4a^2-4a}}{1}=\frac{\sqrt{16-8}}{1} \quad \left[\because \alpha-\beta=\frac{\sqrt{D}}{a}\right]$$

$$\Rightarrow \quad 4a^2-4a=8 \text{ or } a^2-a-2=0$$

or $$(a-2)(a+1)=0 \text{ or } a=2,-1$$

Example 21 *If α, β, γ are the roots of $x^3-x^2+ax+b=0$ and β, γ, δ are the roots of $x^3-4x^2+mx+n=0$. If α, β, γ and δ are in AP with common difference d then*

(a) $a=m$ (b) $a=m-5$ (c) $n=b-a-2$ (d) $b=m+n-3$

Sol. (b,c,d) ∵ α,β,γ,δ are in AP with common difference d, then

$$\beta=\alpha+d, \gamma=\alpha+2d \text{ and } \delta=\alpha+3d \quad \text{...(i)}$$

Given, α,β,γ are the roots of $x^3-x^2+ax+b=0$, then

$$\alpha+\beta+\gamma=1 \quad \text{...(ii)}$$

$$\alpha\beta+\beta\gamma+\gamma\alpha=a \quad \text{...(iii)}$$

$$\alpha\beta\gamma=-b \quad \text{...(iv)}$$

Also, β,γ,δ are the roots of $x^3-4x^2+mx+n=0$, then

$$\beta+\gamma+\delta=4 \quad \text{...(v)}$$

$$\beta\gamma+\gamma\delta+\delta\beta=m \quad \text{...(vi)}$$

$$\beta\gamma\delta=-n \quad \text{...(vii)}$$

From Eqs. (i) and (ii), we get

$$3\alpha+3d=1 \quad \text{...(viii)}$$

and from Eqs. (i) and (v), we get

$$3\alpha+6d=4 \quad \text{...(ix)}$$

From Eqs. (viii) and (ix), we get

$$d=1, \alpha=-\frac{2}{3}$$

Now, from Eq. (i), we get

$$\beta=\frac{1}{3}, \gamma=\frac{4}{3} \text{ and } \delta=\frac{7}{3}$$

From Eqs. (iii), (iv), (vi) and (vii), we get

$$a=-\frac{2}{3}, b=\frac{8}{27}, m=\frac{13}{3}, n=-\frac{28}{27}$$

∴ $a=m-5, n=b-a-2$ and $b=m+n-3$

JEE SCANNER

Example 22 Similar to PYQ Asked in JEE Main 2024

The number of positive integral values of k which are less than 7, for which $\frac{kx^2+(2k+1)x+k}{-x^2+4x-7}<0, \forall x \in R$ is

(a) 4 (b) 6 (c) 7 (d) 2

Sol. (b) $-x^2+4x-7$ have leading coefficient negative and $D=4^2-4(-1)(-7)=-12$ also negative.

So, value of $-x^2+4x-7$ is always negative for $x \in R$.

Now, solve $$\frac{kx^2+(2k+1)x+k}{-x^2+4x-7}<0, \forall x \in R$$

$$\Rightarrow \quad kx^2+(2k+1)x+k>0$$

If $k>0$ and $D<0$

$$(2k+1)^2-4(k)(k)>0 \Rightarrow 4k^2+1+4k-4k^2>0$$

$$\Rightarrow \quad 1+4k>0 \Rightarrow k>-\frac{1}{4}$$

Value of $k=\{1, 2, 3, 4, 5, 6\}$

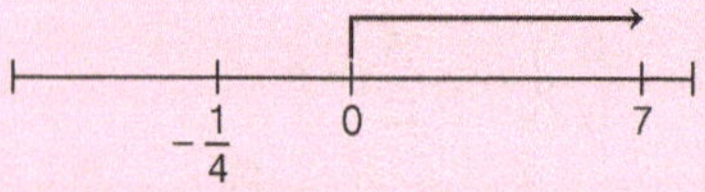

Number of positive values of k is 6.

Skill Builder

Let $\frac{kx^2+(4k+1)x+4k}{x^2+x+1}<0$, for all real values of x, then the number of integral value of k less then 10 is

(a) Infinite (b) 8

(c) 10 (d) None of these

For Sol.

Example 23 *Let S be the set of all non-zero real numbers α such that the quadratic equation $\alpha x^2 - x + \alpha = 0$ has two distinct real roots x_1 and x_2 satisfying the inequality $|x_1 - x_2| < 1$. Which of the following interval(s) is/are a subset of S?*

(a) $\left(-\frac{1}{2}, -\frac{1}{\sqrt{5}}\right)$ (b) $\left(-\frac{1}{\sqrt{5}}, 0\right)$

(c) $\left(0, \frac{1}{\sqrt{5}}\right)$ (d) $\left(\frac{1}{\sqrt{5}}, \frac{1}{2}\right)$

Sol. (a,d) Given, x_1 and x_2 are roots of $\alpha x^2 - x + \alpha = 0$.

$\therefore \quad x_1 + x_2 = \frac{1}{\alpha}$ and $x_1 x_2 = 1$

Also, $\quad |x_1 - x_2| < 1$

$\Rightarrow \quad |x_1 - x_2|^2 < 1 \Rightarrow (x_1 - x_2)^2 < 1$

or $\quad (x_1 + x_2)^2 - 4x_1x_2 < 1$

$\Rightarrow \quad \frac{1}{\alpha^2} - 4 < 1$ or $\frac{1}{\alpha^2} < 5$

$\Rightarrow \quad 5\alpha^2 - 1 > 0$

or $(\sqrt{5}\alpha - 1)(\sqrt{5}\alpha + 1) > 0$

$\therefore \quad \alpha \in \left(-\infty, -\frac{1}{\sqrt{5}}\right) \cup \left(\frac{1}{\sqrt{5}}, \infty\right)$ ...(i)

Also, $\quad D > 0$

$\Rightarrow \quad 1 - 4\alpha^2 > 0$ or $\alpha \in \left(-\frac{1}{2}, \frac{1}{2}\right)$ ...(ii)

From Eqs. (i) and (ii), we get

$$\alpha \in \left(-\frac{1}{2}, \frac{-1}{\sqrt{5}}\right) \cup \left(\frac{1}{\sqrt{5}}, \frac{1}{2}\right)$$

Example 24 *Let $a \in R$ and $f : R \to R$ be given by $f(x) = x^5 - 5x + a$. Then,*

(a) $f(x)$ has three real roots, if $a > 4$
(b) $f(x)$ has only one real root, if $a > 4$
(c) $f(x)$ has three real roots, if $a < -4$
(d) $f(x)$ has three real roots, if $-4 < a < 4$

Sol. (b,d) Let $y = x^5 - 5x$

(i) As $x \to \infty, y \to \infty$ and as $x \to -\infty, y \to -\infty$

(ii) Also, at $x = 0$, $y = 0$, thus the curve passes through the origin.

(iii) $\frac{dy}{dx} = 5x^4 - 5 = 5(x^4 - 1)$

$= 5(x^2 - 1)(x^2 + 1)$

$= 5(x - 1)(x + 1)(x^2 + 1)$

Now, $\frac{dy}{dx} > 0$ in $(-\infty, -1) \cup (1, \infty)$, thus $f(x)$ is increasing in these intervals.

Also, $\frac{dy}{dx} < 0$ in $(-1, 1)$, thus decreasing in $(-1, 1)$.

(iv) Also, at $x = -1$, dy/dx changes its sign from + ve to –ve.

$\therefore x = -1$ is point of local maxima.

Similarly, $x = 1$ is point of local minima.

Local maximum value, $y = (-1)^5 - 5(-1) = 4$

Local minimum value, $y = (1)^5 - 5(1) = -4$

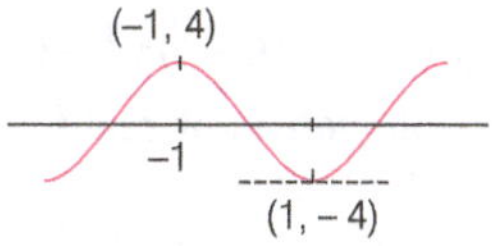

Now, let $y = -a$

As evident from the graph, if $a \in (-4, 4)$

Then, $f(x)$ has three real roots and if $-a > 4$ or $-a < -4$, then $f(x)$ has one real root.

i.e. for $a < -4$ or $a > 4$, $f(x)$ has one real root.

Passage Based Questions

Passage I

(Ex. Nos. 25 and 26)

If G and L are the greatest and least values of the expression $\frac{x^2 - x + 1}{x^2 + x + 1}$, $x \in R$ respectively, then

Example 25 *The least value of $G^5 + L^5$ is*

(a) 0 (b) 2 (c) 16 (d) 32

Sol. (b) Let $\quad y = \frac{x^2 - x + 1}{x^2 + x + 1}$

$\Rightarrow \quad x^2 y + xy + y = x^2 - x + 1$

$\Rightarrow \quad (y - 1)x^2 + (y + 1)x + y - 1 = 0 \quad [\because x \in R]$

$\therefore \quad (y + 1)^2 - 4 \cdot (y - 1)(y - 1) \geq 0 \quad [\because b^2 - 4ac \geq 0]$

$\Rightarrow \quad (y + 1)^2 - (2y - 2)^2 \geq 0$

$\Rightarrow \quad (3y - 1)(y - 3) \leq 0$

$\therefore \quad \frac{1}{3} \leq y \leq 3$

$\Rightarrow \quad G = 3$ and $L = \frac{1}{3}$

$\therefore \quad GL = 1$

Now, $\quad AM \geq GM$

$\frac{G^5 + L^5}{2} \geq (GL)^{1/5} = (1)^{1/5} = 1$

$\Rightarrow \quad \frac{G^5 + L^5}{2} \geq 1$ or $G^5 + L^5 \geq 2$

$\therefore$ Minimum value of $G^5 + L^5$ is 2.

Example 26 *G and L are the roots of the equation*

(a) $3x^2 - 10x + 3 = 0$ (b) $4x^2 - 17x + 4 = 0$

(c) $x^2 - 7x + 10 = 0$ (d) $x^2 - 5x + 6 = 0$

Sol. (a) Equation whose roots are G and L, is

$$x^2 - (G + L)x + GL = 0$$

$$\Rightarrow \quad x^2 - \frac{10}{3}x + 1 = 0 \text{ or } 3x^2 - 10x + 3 = 0$$

Passage II

(Ex. Nos. 27 and 28)

Consider the equation $x^4 - (k-1)x^2 + (2-k) = 0$. The complete set of possible values of real k for which the equation has

Example 27 *Four distinct real roots is*

(a) $(-\infty, 2)$ (b) $(2\sqrt{2} - 1, 2)$

(c) $(\sqrt{2} - 1, \sqrt{2} + 1)$ (d) $(1, \infty)$

Sol. (b) Given, $x^4 - (k-1)x^2 + (2-k) = 0$

Let $x^2 = t$

Then, $t^2 - (k-1)t + (2-k) = 0$

For distinct real root $D > 0$,

$$\therefore \quad (k-1)^2 - 4(2-k) > 0$$

$$\Rightarrow \quad k^2 + 1 - 2k - 8 + 4k > 0$$

$$\Rightarrow \quad k^2 + 2k - 7 > 0$$

$$\Rightarrow \quad k < -1 - 2\sqrt{2}, k > -1 + 2\sqrt{2}$$

Thus, $k \in (-\infty, -1 - 2\sqrt{2}) \cup (2\sqrt{2} - 1, \infty)$ ...(i)

Also, sum of roots > 0

$$k - 1 > 0$$

$$\Rightarrow \quad k > 1$$

$$\Rightarrow \quad k \in (1, \infty) \quad \text{...(ii)}$$

and product of roots > 0

$$\Rightarrow \quad (2 - k) > 0$$

$$\Rightarrow \quad k < 2$$

$$\Rightarrow \quad k \in (-\infty, 2) \quad \text{...(iii)}$$

From Eqs. (i), (ii) and (iii), we get

$$(2\sqrt{2} - 1, 2)$$

Example 28 *Three distinct real root is*

(a) $\{2\}$ (b) $\{2\sqrt{2} - 1\}$

(c) $\{2\sqrt{2}\}$ (d) $\{\sqrt{5} - 1\}$

Sol. (a) For equation $x^4 - (k-1)x^2 + (2-k) = 0$ will have three distinct real roots iff

$$t_1 = 0, t_2 > 0 \quad [\because \text{ where } t_1 \text{ and } t_2 \text{ are the root}]$$

Now, $f(0) = 0^4 - (k-1) \cdot 0 + (2-k) = 0$

$$\Rightarrow \quad 2 - k = 0$$

$$\Rightarrow \quad k = 2 \quad \text{...(i)}$$

and $\quad \frac{-b}{2a} > 0 \Rightarrow \frac{k-1}{2} > 0 \Rightarrow k > 1$ ...(ii)

From Eqs. (i) and (ii), we get

$$k = 2$$

Stem Based Questions

Stem I

(Ex. Nos. 29 to 30)

Let a, b, c and d are real numbers in GP. Suppose u, v, w satisfy the system of equations $u + 2v + 3w = 6$, $4u + 5v + 6w = 12$ and $6u + 9v = 4$. Further, consider the expressions

$$f(x) = \left(\frac{1}{u} + \frac{1}{v} + \frac{1}{w}\right)x^2 + [(b-c)^2 + (c-a)^2 + (d-b)^2]$$

$x + u + v + w = 0$ and $g(x) = 20x^2 + 10(a-d)^2 x - 9 = 0$.

Example 29 *$(u + v + w)$ is equal to ....*

Sol. (2) Now, $u + 2v + 3w = 6$ ...(i)

$$4u + 5v + 6w = 12 \quad \text{...(ii)}$$

and $\quad 6u + 9v = 4$ ...(iii)

From Eqs. (i) and (ii), we get

$$2u + v = 0 \quad \text{...(iv)}$$

On solving Eqs. (iii) and (iv), we get

$$u = -\frac{1}{3}, v = \frac{2}{3}$$

Now, from Eq. (i), we get $w = \frac{5}{3}$

$$\therefore \quad v + u + w = -\frac{1}{3} + \frac{2}{3} + \frac{5}{3} = 2$$

Example 30 *If roots of $f(x) = 0$ be $\alpha (= 2), \beta (= 4)$, the 8 (sum of roots of $g(x) = 0$) will be ....*

Sol. (6) Now, $f(x) = \left(\frac{1}{u} + \frac{1}{v} + \frac{1}{w}\right)x^2 + [(b-c)^2 + (c-a)^2 + (d-b)^2]x + u + v + w = 0$

$$\Rightarrow \quad f(x) = -\frac{9}{10}x^2 + (a-d)^2 x + 2 = 0$$

[$\because$ a, b, c, d are in GP]

$$\Rightarrow \quad f(x) = -9x^2 + 10(a-d)^2 x + 20 = 0 \quad \text{...(v)}$$

Given, roots of $f(x) = 0$ are α and β.

Now, replace x by $\frac{1}{x}$ in Eq. (v), then

$$\frac{-9}{x^2} + \frac{10(a-d)^2}{x} + 20 = 0$$

$$\Rightarrow \quad 20x^2 + 10(a-d)^2 x - 9 = 0 \Rightarrow g(x) = 0$$

$\therefore$ Roots of $g(x) = 0$ are $\frac{1}{\alpha}, \frac{1}{\beta}$.

$$\text{Required result} = 8\left(\frac{1}{2} + \frac{1}{4}\right) = 8 \times \frac{4+2}{8} = 6$$

Stem II

(Ex. Nos. 31 to 32)

Let $f:[-1,1]\rightarrow R$ be defined as $f(x)=ax^2+bx+c$ for all $x\in[-1,1]$, where $a, b, c\in R$ such that $f(-1)=2$, $f'(-1)=1$ and for $x\in[-1,1]$, the maximum value of $f''(x)$ is $\frac{1}{2}$. If $f(x)\le\alpha$, then

Example 31 *The sum of maximum and minimum value of $f(x)$ is ....*

Sol. (7) Given, $f:[-1,1]\rightarrow R$ defined by $f(x)=ax^2+bx+c$

Also, $f(-1)=2$, $f'(-1)=1$, $f''(x)=\frac{1}{2}$

$$\because \quad f(x)=ax^2+bx+c$$

$$\Rightarrow \quad f'(x)=2ax+b$$

$$\text{and} \quad f''(x)=2a$$

But $f''(x)=\frac{1}{2} \Rightarrow 2a=\frac{1}{2}\Rightarrow a=\frac{1}{4}$

Now, $f'(-1)=2a(-1)+b=1$

$$-2a+b=1$$

$$b=1+2\left(\frac{1}{4}\right)=\frac{3}{2}$$

And $f(-1)=a-b+c=2$

$$\frac{1}{4}-\frac{3}{2}+c=2$$

$$c=\frac{13}{4}$$

Thus, $f(x)=\frac{1}{4}x^2+\frac{3}{2}x+\frac{13}{4}=\frac{1}{4}[(x+3)^2+4]$

For $x\in[-1,1]$

$$f(x)_{\min}=\frac{1}{4}[(-1+3)^2+4]=2$$

$$f(x)_{\max}=\frac{1}{4}[(1+3)^2+4]=5$$

Now, $f(x)_{\min}+f(x)_{\max}=2+5=7$

Example 32 *The least value of α is equal to ....*

Sol. (5) Since, $f(x)_{\min}=2$

and $f(x)_{\max}=5$

$$\therefore \quad 2\le f(x)\le 5$$

Also, $f(x)\le\alpha \Rightarrow \alpha=5$

Thus, the least value of α is equal to 5.

Single Integer Answer Type Questions

Example 33 *If equations $x^3+5x^2+px+q=0$ and $x^3+7x^2+px+r=0$ have two roots in common and third roots of equations are x_1 and x_2, then the value of $\frac{x_1x_2}{7}$ is ...*

Sol. (5) Let roots of $x^3+5x^2+px+q=0$ be α, β, x_1

$$\therefore \quad \alpha+\beta+x_1=-5 \quad \text{...(i)}$$

$$\alpha\beta+\beta x_1+\alpha x_1=p \quad \text{...(ii)}$$

Roots of $x^3+7x^2+px+r=0$ be α, β, x_2.

$$\therefore \quad \alpha+\beta+x_2=-7 \quad \text{...(iii)}$$

$$\alpha\beta+\beta x_2+\alpha x_2=p \quad \text{...(iv)}$$

From Eqs. (ii) and (iv), we have

$$(x_1-x_2)(\alpha+\beta)=0$$

$$\therefore \quad \alpha+\beta=0 \quad [x_1\ne x_2]$$

$$\therefore \quad x_1=-5 \text{ and } x_2=-7$$

So, $\frac{x_1x_2}{7}=\frac{35}{7}=5$

Example 34 *The sum of all possible values of x for which $f(x)=x^3-8x^2+20x-13$ is a prime number, is*

Sol. (9) We have, $f(x)=x^3-8x^2+20x-13$

$$\therefore \quad f(1)=1-8+20-13=0$$

So, $f(x)=(x-1)(x^2-7x+13)$

For $f(x)$ to be prime atleast one of the factors must be prime.

$$\therefore \quad x-1=1 \text{ or } x^2-7x+13=1$$

$$\Rightarrow \quad x=2 \text{ or } x-7x+12=0$$

$$\Rightarrow \quad x=2 \text{ or } x=3, 4$$

$$\therefore \quad x=2, 3, 4$$

So, required sum = 9

Example 35 *If the roots of the equation $10x^3-cx^2-54x-27=0$ are in harmonic progression, then the value of c is ....*

Sol. (9) Given, roots of the equation

$$10x^3-cx^2-54x-27=0 \text{ are in HP.} \quad \text{...(i)}$$

Now, replacing x by $\frac{1}{x}$ in Eq. (i), we get

$$27x^3+54x^2+cx-10=0 \quad \text{...(ii)}$$

Hence, the roots of Eq. (ii) are in AP.

Let $a-d$, a and $a+d$ are the roots of Eq. (ii).

Then, $a-d+a+a+d=-\frac{54}{27}$

$$\Rightarrow \quad a=-\frac{2}{3} \quad \text{...(iii)}$$

Since, a is a root of Eq. (ii), then

$$27a^3+54a^2+ca-10=0$$

$$\Rightarrow \quad 27\left(-\frac{8}{27}\right)+54\left(\frac{4}{9}\right)+c\left(-\frac{2}{3}\right)-10=0 \quad \text{[from Eq. (iii)]}$$

$$\Rightarrow \quad 6-\frac{2c}{3}=0 \text{ or } c=9$$

Example 36 *If a root of the equation $n^2\sin^2 x-2\sin x-(2n+1)=0$ lies in $[0, \pi/2]$, the minimum positive integer value of n is ....*

Sol. (3) $\because \; n^2\sin^2 x - 2\sin x - (2n+1) = 0$

$$\Rightarrow \quad \sin x = \frac{2 \pm \sqrt{4 + 4n^2(2n+1)}}{2n^2}$$

[by Shridharacharya method]

$$= \frac{1 \pm \sqrt{(2n^3 + n^2 + 1)}}{n^2}$$

$$\because \quad 0 \le \sin x \le 1 \quad [\because x \in [0, \pi/2]]$$

$$\Rightarrow \quad 0 \le \frac{1 + \sqrt{(2n^3 + n^2 + 1)}}{n^2} \le 1$$

$$\Rightarrow \quad 0 \le 1 + \sqrt{(2n^3 + n^2 + 1)} \le n^2$$

$$\Rightarrow \quad \sqrt{(2n^3 + n^2 + 1)} \le (n^2 - 1) \quad [\because n > 1]$$

On squaring both sides, we get

$$2n^3 + n^2 + 1 \le n^4 - 2n^2 + 1$$

$$\Rightarrow \quad n^4 - 2n^3 - 3n^2 \ge 0 \Rightarrow n^2 - 2n - 3 \ge 0$$

$$\Rightarrow \quad (n-3)(n+1) \ge 0 \Rightarrow n \ge 3$$

$$\therefore \quad n = 3, 4, 5, \ldots$$

Hence, the minimum positive integer value of n is 3.

Numerical Value Type Questions

Example 37 *If α, β are the roots of $x^2 + x + 2 = 0$ and γ, δ are the roots of $x^2 + 3x + 4 = 0$, then $(\alpha+\gamma)(\alpha+\delta)(\beta+\gamma)(\beta+\delta)$ is equal to ....*

Sol. (44) Since, $\alpha + \beta = -1, \alpha\beta = 2, \gamma + \delta = -3, \gamma\delta = 4$

$$\therefore \; (\alpha+\gamma)(\alpha+\delta)(\beta+\gamma)(\beta+\delta) = (\alpha^2 - 3\alpha + 4)(\beta^2 - 3\beta + 4)$$

$$= 4 - 3\alpha\beta^2 + 4\beta^2 - 3\alpha^2\beta + 9\alpha\beta - 12\beta + 4\alpha^2 - 12\alpha + 16$$

$$= 4 - 3(2)\beta + 4\beta^2 + 4\alpha^2 - 3(2)\alpha + 9(2) - 12(\beta + \alpha) + 16$$

$$= 4 - 6\beta + 4(\alpha^2 + \beta^2) - 6\alpha + 18 + 12 + 16$$

$$= 50 + 6 + 4[(\alpha+\beta)^2 - 2\alpha\beta]$$

$$= 56 - 12 = 44$$

Example 38 *If $x^2 - 5x + 1 = 0$, then $x^5 + \dfrac{1}{x^5}$ is equal to ......*

Sol. (2525) $x + \dfrac{1}{x} = 5 \Rightarrow x^2 + \dfrac{1}{x^2} = 5^2 - 2 = 23$

and $\quad x^3 + \dfrac{1}{x^3} = 5^3 - 3 \times 5 = 110$

Now, $\left(x^2 + \dfrac{1}{x^2}\right)\left(x^3 + \dfrac{1}{x^3}\right) = 23 \times 110 = 2530$

$$\therefore \quad x^5 + \frac{1}{x^5} = 2530 - \left(x + \frac{1}{x}\right) = 2525$$

Example 39 *If one root of the equation $x^2 - \lambda x + 12 = 0$ is even prime while $x^2 + \lambda x + \mu = 0$ has equal roots, then μ is equal to ....*

Sol. (16) We know that only even prime is 2, then

$$(2)^2 - \lambda(2) + 12 = 0$$

$$\Rightarrow \quad \lambda = 8 \quad \ldots(\text{i})$$

and $x^2 + \lambda x + \mu = 0$ has equal roots.

$$\therefore \quad \lambda^2 - 4\mu = 0 \quad [\because D = 0]$$

$$\Rightarrow \quad (8)^2 - 4\mu = 0 \quad [\text{from Eq. (i)}]$$

$$\Rightarrow \quad \mu = 16$$

Example 40 *The possible positive values of $b, b \in R$ for which the equations $2017x^2 + bx + 7102 = 0$ and $7102x^2 + bx + 2017 = 0$ have a common root is ....*

Sol. (9119) Let the common root be a.

$$\therefore \quad 2017a^2 + ba + 7102 = 0 \quad \ldots(\text{i})$$

$$\text{and} \quad 7102a^2 + ba + 2017 = 0 \quad \ldots(\text{ii})$$

On subtracting Eq. (ii) from Eq. (i), we get

$$-5085a^2 + 5085 = 0$$

$$\Rightarrow \quad a^2 = 1$$

$$\Rightarrow \quad a = \pm 1$$

If $a = 1$, $\quad 2017 + b + 7102 = 0 \quad$ [from Eq. (i)]

$$\Rightarrow \quad b = -9119$$

and if $a = -1$, $\quad 2017 - b + 7102 = 0 \quad$ [from Eq. (ii)]

$$\Rightarrow \quad b = 9119$$

$$\therefore \quad b = 9119$$

Example 41 *If α and β are the roots of the equation $x^2 - p(x+1) - c = 0$, then the value of $\dfrac{\alpha^2 + 2\alpha + 1}{\alpha^2 + 2\alpha + c} + \dfrac{\beta^2 + 2\beta + 1}{\beta^2 + 2\beta + c}$ is ....*

Sol. (1) Given that $f(x) = x^2 - p(x+1) - c = 0 = x^2 - px - p - c$

(α and β are the roots of the equation)

$$\therefore \quad \alpha + \beta = -(-p) = p \quad \ldots(\text{i})$$

$$\alpha\beta = -p - c \quad \ldots(\text{ii})$$

$$\frac{\alpha^2 + 2\alpha + 1}{\alpha^2 + 2\alpha + c} + \frac{\beta^2 + 2\beta + 1}{\beta^2 + 2\beta + c}$$

$$= \frac{(\alpha+1)^2}{\alpha^2 + 2\alpha - p - \alpha\beta} + \frac{(\beta+1)^2}{\beta^2 + 2\beta - p - \alpha\beta} \quad [\text{from Eq. (ii)}]$$

$$= \frac{(\alpha+1)^2}{\alpha^2 + 2\alpha - \alpha - \beta - \alpha\beta} + \frac{(\beta+1)^2}{\beta^2 + 2\beta - \alpha - \beta - \alpha\beta} \quad [\text{from Eq. (i)}]$$

$$= \frac{(\alpha+1)^2}{(\alpha-\beta)(\alpha+1)} + \frac{(\beta+1)^2}{(\beta-\alpha)(\beta+1)}$$

$$= \frac{(\alpha+1)}{(\alpha-\beta)} - \frac{(\beta+1)}{(\alpha-\beta)}$$

$$= \frac{\alpha + 1 - \beta - 1}{(\alpha-\beta)} = \frac{\alpha-\beta}{\alpha-\beta} = 1$$

Matching Type Questions

Example 42 *Column I contains rational algebraic expressions and Column II contains possible integers which lie in their range. Match the entries of Column I with one or more entries of the elements of Column II.*

Column I		Column II
(A) $y = \dfrac{x^2 - 2x + 9}{x^2 + 2x + 9}, x \in R$	(p)	1
(B) $y = \dfrac{x^2 - 3x + 3}{2x - 3}, x \in R$	(q)	3
(C) $y = \dfrac{2x^2 - 2x + 4}{x^2 - 4x + 3}, x \in R$	(r)	− 4
(D) The number of real solutions of the equation $x^2 - 3\|x\| + 2 = 0$ is	(s)	− 9

Sol. (A) → (p); (B) → (p, q, r, s); (C) → (p, q, s); (D) → (p)

(A) $y = \dfrac{x^2 - 2x + 9}{x^2 + 2x + 9} \Rightarrow x^2y + 2xy + 9y = x^2 - 2x + 9$

$\Rightarrow \quad (y - 1)x^2 + 2x(y + 1) + 9(y - 1) = 0$

$\because \quad x \in R$

$\therefore \quad 4(y + 1)^2 - 4 \cdot 9 \cdot (y - 1)^2 \geq 0$

$\Rightarrow \quad (y + 1)^2 - (3y - 3)^2 \geq 0$

$\Rightarrow \quad (4y - 2)(-2y + 4) \geq 0$

$\Rightarrow \quad (2y - 1)(y - 2) \leq 0$

$\therefore \quad \dfrac{1}{2} \leq y \leq 2 \Rightarrow y = 1, 2$

(B) $\because \quad y = \dfrac{x^2 - 3x + 3}{2x - 3} \Rightarrow 2xy - 3y = x^2 - 3x + 3$

$\Rightarrow \quad x^2 - x(3 + 2y) + 3y + 3 = 0$

$\because \quad x \in R$

$\therefore \quad (3 + 2y)^2 - 4 \cdot 1 \cdot (3y + 3) \geq 0 \Rightarrow 4y^2 - 3 \geq 0$

$\therefore \quad y = 1, 2, \ldots$ and $y = -1, -2, \ldots$

(C) $\because \quad y = \dfrac{2x^2 - 2x + 4}{x^2 - 4x + 3}$

$\Rightarrow \quad x^2y - 4xy + 3y = 2x^2 - 2x + 4$

$\Rightarrow \quad x^2(y - 2) + 2x(1 - 2y) + 3y - 4 = 0$

$\because \quad x \in R$

$\therefore \quad 4(1 - 2y)^2 - 4(y - 2)(3y - 4) \geq 0$

$\Rightarrow \quad (4y^2 - 4y + 1) - (3y^2 - 10y + 8) \geq 0$

$\Rightarrow \quad y^2 + 6y - 7 \geq 0$

$\Rightarrow \quad (y + 7)(y - 1) \geq 0$

$\therefore \quad y \leq -7$ or $y \geq 1$

(D) Given, $x^2 - 3|x| + 2 = 0$

$\Rightarrow \quad |x|^2 - 3|x| + 2 = 0 \Rightarrow (|x| - 2)(|x| - 1) = 0$

$\Rightarrow \quad |x| = 1, 2$ or $x = \pm 1, \pm 2$

Example 43 *Entries of Column I are to be matched with one or more entries of Column II.*

	Column I		Column II
(A)	If $a + b + 2c = 0$ but $c \neq 0$, then $ax^2 + bx + c = 0$ has	(p)	atleast one root in $(-2, 0)$
(B)	If $a, b, c \in R$ such that $2a - 3b + 6c = 0$, then equation has	(q)	atleast one root in $(-1, 0)$
(C)	Let a, b, c be non-zero real numbers such that $\int_0^1 (1 + \cos^8 x)(ax^2 + bx + c)dx = \int_0^2 (1 + \cos^8 x)(ax^2 + bx + c)dx$, the equation $ax^2 + bx + c = 0$ has	(r)	atleast one root in $(-1, 1)$
(D)	If $4a + 2b + c = 0$, then equation $3ax^2 + 2bx + c = 0$ has	(s)	atleast one root in $(0, 1)$
		(t)	atleast one root in $(0, 2)$

Sol. (A) → (s); (B) → (q); (C) → (t); (D) → (t)

(A) Let $\quad f(x) = ax^2 + bx + c$

Then, $\quad f(1) = a + b + c = -c \quad [\because a + b + 2c = 0]$

and $\quad f(0) = c$

$\therefore \quad f(0)f(1) = -c^2 < 0 \quad [\because c \neq 0]$

$\therefore$ Equation $f(x) = 0$ has a root in $(0, 1)$.

(B) Let $\quad f'(x) = ax^2 + bx + c$

$\therefore \quad f(x) = \dfrac{ax^3}{3} + \dfrac{bx^2}{2} + cx + d$

$\therefore \quad f(0) = d$

and $\quad f(-1) = -\dfrac{a}{3} + \dfrac{b}{2} - c + d = -\left(\dfrac{2a - 3b + 6c}{6}\right) + d$

$= 0 + d = d \quad [\because 2a - 3b + 6c = 0]$

Hence, $\quad f(0) = f(-1)$

Hence, $\quad f'(x) = 0$ has atleast one root in $(-1, 0)$.

(C) Let $\quad f(x) = \int (1 + \cos^8 x)(ax^2 + bx + c)dx$

Given, $f(1) - f(0) = f(2) - f(0)$

$\Rightarrow \quad f(1) = f(2)$

$\Rightarrow \quad f'(x) = 0$ has atleast one root in $(0,2)$.

$\Rightarrow (1 + \cos^8 x)(ax^2 + bx + c) = 0$ has atleast one root in $(0,2)$.

$\Rightarrow \quad ax^2 + bx + c = 0$ has atleast one root in $(0, 2)$

(D) Let $f(x) = ax^3 + bx^2 + cx + d$

$f(0) = d, \; f(2) = 2(4a + 2b + c) + d = d$

$\because f(0) = f(2)$

$\Rightarrow f'(x) = 0$ has atleast one root in $(0, 2)$.

EXERCISE 1
JEE Main Pattern

Single Option Correct Type Questions

1. The sum of the non-real roots of the equation $(x^2 + x - 2)(x^2 + x - 3) = 12$ is
(a) -1 (b) 1 (c) -6 (d) 6

2. The curve $y = (\lambda + 1)x^2 + 2$ intersects the curve $y = \lambda x + 3$ in exactly one point, if λ equals to
(a) $-2, 2$ (b) 1 (c) -2 (d) 2

3. If the roots of the equation $x^2 + 2ax + b = 0$ are real and distinct and they differ by at most $2m$, then $b \in$
(a) $(a^2, a^2 + m^2)$ (b) $(a^2 - m^2, a^2)$
(c) $[a^2 - m^2, a^2)$ (d) None of these

4. If α, β are the roots of the equation $ax^2 + bx + c = 0$, then the value of $\frac{(a\alpha^2 + c)}{a\alpha + b} + \frac{a\beta^2 + c}{a\beta + b}$ is
(a) $\frac{b(b^2 - 2ac)}{4a}$ (b) $\frac{b^2 - 4ac}{2a}$
(c) $\frac{b(b^2 - 2ac)}{a^2c}$ (d) None of these

5. If the roots of the equation $ax^2 - bx + c = 0$ are α, β, then the roots of the equation $b^2cx^2 - ab^2x + a^3 = 0$ are
(a) $\frac{1}{\alpha^3 + \alpha\beta}, \frac{1}{\beta^3 + \alpha\beta}$ (b) $\frac{1}{\alpha^2 + \alpha\beta}, \frac{1}{\beta^2 + \alpha\beta}$
(c) $\frac{1}{\alpha^4 + \alpha\beta}, \frac{1}{\beta^4 + \alpha\beta}$ (d) None of these

6. If the equation $x^2 - 3px + 2q = 0$ and $x^2 - 3ax + 2b = 0$ have a common roots and the other roots of the second equation is the reciprocal of the other roots of the first, then $(2q - 2b)^2 =$
(a) $36pa(q - b)^2$ (b) $18pa(q - b)^2$
(c) $36bq(p - a)^2$ (d) $18pq(p - a)$

7. If both the roots of the equation $x^2 - 6ax + 2 - 2a + 9a^2 = 0$ exceeds 3, then
(a) $a > \frac{9}{11}$ (b) $a \geq \frac{11}{9}$
(c) $a > \frac{11}{9}$ (d) $a < \frac{11}{9}$

8. The number of real solutions of the equation $\frac{x^2}{1 - |x - 5|} = 1$, is
(a) 4 (b) 2
(c) 1 (d) None of these

9. The equation $||x - 1| + a| = 4$ can have real solutions for x if a belongs to
(a) $(-\infty, 4]$ (b) $(-\infty, -4]$ (c) $(4, \infty)$ (d) $[-4, 4]$

10. The solution set of the inequation $4^{-x + 0.5} - 7(2^{-x}) - 4 < 0$ is
(a) R (b) $(-2, \infty)$ (c) $(2, \infty)$ (d) $\left(2, \frac{7}{2}\right)$

11. If a, b, c are real and $a \neq b$, the roots of the equation $2(a - b)x^2 - 11(a + b + c)x - 3(a - b) = 0$ are
(a) real and equal (b) real and unequal
(c) purely imaginary (d) None of these

12. The graph of a quadratic polynomial $y = ax^2 + bx + c$; $a, b, c \in R$ is as shown.

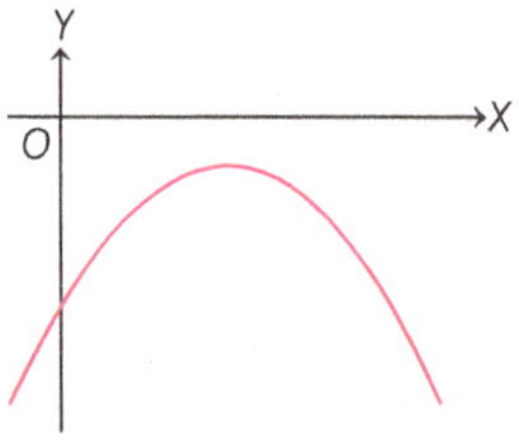

Which one of the following is not correct?
(a) $b^2 - 4ac < 0$
(b) $\frac{c}{a} < 0$
(c) c is negative
(d) Abscissa corresponding to the vertex is $\left(-\frac{b}{2a}\right)$

13. There is only one real value of 'a' for which the quadratic equation $ax^2 + (a + 3)x + a - 3 = 0$ has two positive integral solutions. The product of these two solutions is
(a) 9 (b) 8 (c) 6 (d) 12

14. If for all real values of a one root of the equation $x^2 - 3ax + f(a) = 0$ is double of the other, $f(x)$ is equal to

(a) $2x$ (b) x^2 (c) $2x^2$ (d) $2\sqrt{x}$

15. A quadratic equation the product of whose roots x_1 and x_2 is equal to 4 and satisfying the relation $\frac{x_1}{x_1 - 1} + \frac{x_2}{x_2 - 1} = 2$, is

(a) $x^2 - 2x + 4 = 0$ (b) $x^2 - 4x + 4 = 0$
(c) $x^2 + 2x + 4 = 0$ (d) $x^2 + 4x + 4 = 0$

16. If both roots of the quadratic equation $x^2 - 2ax + a^2 - 1 = 0$ lie in $(-2, 2)$, which one of the following can be $[a]$? (where $[\cdot]$ denotes the greatest integer function)

(a) -1 (b) 1 (c) 2 (d) 3

17. If $(-2, 7)$ is the highest point on the graph of $y = -2x^2 - 4ax + \lambda$, then λ equals

(a) 31 (b) 11 (c) -1 (d) $-\frac{1}{3}$

18. If the roots of the quadratic equation $(4p - p^2 - 5)x^2 - (2p - 1)x + 3p = 0$ lie on either side of unity, the number of integral values of p is

(a) 1 (b) 2 (c) 3 (d) 4

19. Solution set of the equation $3^{2x^2} - 2 \cdot 3^{x^2 + x + 6} + 3^{2(x+6)} = 0$ is

(a) $\{-3, 2\}$ (b) $\{6, -1\}$ (c) $\{-2, 3\}$ (d) $\{1, -6\}$

20. Consider two quadratic expressions $f(x) = ax^2 + bx + c$ and $g(x) = ax^2 + px + q$ $(a, b, c, p, q \in R, b \neq p)$ such that their discriminants are equal. If $f(x) = g(x)$ has a root $x = \alpha$, then

(a) α will be AM of the roots of $f(x) = 0$ and $g(x) = 0$
(b) α will be AM of the roots of $f(x) = 0$
(c) α will be AM of the roots of $f(x) = 0$ or $g(x) = 0$
(d) α will be AM of the roots of $g(x) = 0$

21. If x_1 and x_2 are the arithmetic and harmonic means of the roots of the equation $ax^2 + bx + c = 0$, the quadratic equation whose roots are x_1 and x_2, is

(a) $abx^2 + (b^2 + ac)x + bc = 0$
(b) $2abx^2 + (b^2 + 4ac)x + 2bc = 0$
(c) $2abx^2 + (b^2 + ac)x + bc = 0$
(d) None of the above

22. $f(x)$ is a cubic polynomial $x^3 + ax^2 + bx + c$ such that $f(x) = 0$ has three distinct integral roots and $f(g(x)) = 0$ does not have real roots, where $g(x) = x^2 + 2x - 5$, the minimum value of $a + b + c$ is

(a) 504 (b) 532 (c) 719 (d) 764

23. The value of the positive integer n for which the quadratic equation $\sum_{k=1}^{n} (x + k - 1)(x + k) = 10n$ has solutions α and $\alpha + 1$ for some α, is

(a) 7 (b) 11 (c) 17 (d) 25

24. If one root of the equation $x^2 - \lambda x + 12 = 0$ is even prime, while $x^2 + \lambda x + \mu = 0$ has equal roots, then μ is

(a) 8 (b) 16 (c) 24 (d) 32

25. Number of real roots of the equation $\sqrt{x} + \sqrt{x - \sqrt{(1 - x)}} = 1$ is

(a) 0 (b) 1 (c) 2 (d) 3

26. The value of $\sqrt{7 + \sqrt{7 - \sqrt{7 + \sqrt{7 - \dots}}}}$ upto ∞ is

(a) 5 (b) 4 (c) 3 (d) 2

27. For any real x, the expression $2(k - x)[x + \sqrt{x^2 + k^2}]$ cannot exceed

(a) k^2 (b) $2k^2$
(c) $3k^2$ (d) None of these

28. Given that, for all $x \in R$, the expression $\frac{x^2 - 2x + 4}{x^2 + 2x + 4}$ lies between $\frac{1}{3}$ and 3, the values between which the expression $\frac{9 \cdot 3^{2x} + 6 \cdot 3^x + 4}{9 \cdot 3^{2x} - 6 \cdot 3^x + 4}$ lies, are

(a) 3 and 1 (b) $\frac{3}{2}$ and 2
(c) -1 and 1 (d) 0 and 2

29. Let α, β, γ be the roots of the equation $(x - a)(x - b)(x - c) = d$, $d \neq 0$, the roots of the equation $(x - \alpha)(x - \beta)(x - \gamma) + d = 0$ are

(a) a, b, d (b) b, c, d
(c) a, b, c (d) $a + d, b + d, c + d$

30. If one root of the equation $ix^2 - 2(1 + i)x + 2 - i = 0$ is $(3 - i)$, where $i = \sqrt{-1}$, the other root is

(a) $3 + i$ (b) $3 + \sqrt{-1}$
(c) $-1 + i$ (d) $-1 - i$

Numerical Value Type Questions

31. Sum of the values of x satisfying the equation $\sqrt{2x + \sqrt{2x + 4}} = 4$ is ....

32. The quadratic equation $x^2 + mx + n = 0$ has roots which are twice those of $x^2 + px + m = 0$ and m, n and $p \neq 0$. Then, the value of $\frac{n}{p}$ is ....

33. All the values of k for which the quadratic polynomial $f(x) = -2x^2 + kx + k^2 + 5$ has two distinct zeroes and only one of them satisfying $0 < x < 2$, lie in the interval (a, b). Then, the value of $a + 10b$ is

34. a, b, c are all different and non-zero real numbers in AP. If the roots of quadratic equation $ax^2 + bx + c = 0$ are α and β such that $\frac{1}{\alpha} + \frac{1}{\beta}, \alpha + \beta$ and $\alpha^2 + \beta^2$ are in GP, then the value of $\frac{a}{c}$ is

35. If the equations $x^2 + ax + 12 = 0$, $x^2 + bx + 15 = 0$ and $x^2 + (a + b)x + 36 = 0$ have a common positive root, then the value of $|b - a|$ is

36. The least positive value of $\frac{x^2 + 2x + 4}{x + 2}$, is

37. If α, β, γ are the roots of the equation $x^3 + 4x + 1 = 0$, then the value of $\Sigma (\alpha + \beta)^{-1}$ is

38. The value of 'a' for which the equation $4 \operatorname{cosec}^2 \pi (a + x) + a^2 - 4a = 0$ has a real solution, is

39. The number of solutions of $|[x] - 2x| = 4$, is

40. If $\sqrt{x + 5} + \sqrt{x + 21} = \sqrt{6x + 40}$, then the sum of all values of x is

41. The sum of all the real roots of the equation $|x - 2|^2 + |x - 2| - 2 = 0$ is

42. The harmonic mean of the roots of the equation $(5 + \sqrt{2})x^2 - (4 + \sqrt{5})x + 8 + 2\sqrt{5} = 0$ is

43. If product of the real roots of the equation,

$$x^2 - ax + 30 = 2\sqrt{(x^2 - ax + 45)}, a > 0,$$

is λ and minimum value of sum of roots of the equation is μ. The value of (μ) (where $(\cdot)$ denotes the least integer function) is

44. The minimum value of $\dfrac{\left(x + \frac{1}{x}\right)^6 - \left(x^6 + \frac{1}{x^6}\right) - 2}{\left(x + \frac{1}{x}\right)^3 + x^3 + \frac{1}{x^3}}$ is (for $x > 0$)

45. Let a, b, c, d are distinct real numbers and a, b are the roots of the quadratic equation $x^2 - 2cx - 5d = 0$. If c and d are the roots of the quadratic equation $x^2 - 2ax - 5b = 0$, the sum of the digits of numerical values of $a + b + c + d$ is

Previous Year Questions

46. If 2 and 6 are the roots of the equation $ax^2 + bx + 1 = 0$, then the quadratic equation whose roots are $\frac{1}{2a + b}$ and $\frac{1}{6a + b}$, is **[Single Correct Type, 2024 Main]**
(a) $x^2 + 8x + 12 = 0$ (b) $2x^2 + 11x + 12 = 0$
(c) $x^2 + 10x + 16 = 0$ (d) $4x^2 + 14x + 12 = 0$

47. Let $S = \{x \in R : (\sqrt{3} + \sqrt{2})^x + (\sqrt{3} - \sqrt{2})^x = 10\}$. Then, the number of elements in S, is **[Single Correct Type, 2024 Main]**
(a) 0 (b) 1 (c) 4 (d) 2

48. Let S be the set of positive integral values of a for which $\frac{ax^2 + 2(a + 1)x + 9a + 4}{x^2 - 8x + 32} < 0, \forall x \in R$. Then, the number of elements in S is **[Single Correct Type, 2024 Main]**
(a) 1 (b) 3 (c) ∞ (d) 0

49. Let α, β be the roots of the equation $x^2 + 2\sqrt{2}x - 1 = 0$. The quadratic equation, whose roots are $\alpha^4 + \beta^4$ and $\frac{1}{10}(\alpha^6 + \beta^6)$, is **[Single Correct Type, 2024 Main]**
(a) $x^2 - 195x + 9506 = 0$ (b) $x^2 - 190x + 9466 = 0$
(c) $x^2 - 180x + 9506 = 0$ (d) $x^2 - 195x + 9466 = 0$

50. Let α, β be the distinct roots of the equation $x^2 - (t^2 - 5t + 6)x + 1 = 0, t \in R$ and $a_n = \alpha^n + \beta^n$.
Then, the minimum value of $\frac{a_{2023} + a_{2025}}{a_{2024}}$ is **[Single Correct Type, 2024 Main]**
(a) $\frac{-1}{4}$ (b) $\frac{1}{2}$ (c) $\frac{-1}{2}$ (d) $\frac{1}{4}$

51. Let α and β be the roots of the equation $px^2 + qx - r = 0$, where $p \neq 0$. If p, q and r are the consecutive terms of a non-constant GP and $\frac{1}{\alpha} + \frac{1}{\beta} = \frac{3}{4}$, then the value of $(\alpha - \beta)^2$ is **[Single Correct Type, 2024 Main]**
(a) 9 (b) $\frac{20}{3}$ (c) 8 (d) $\frac{80}{9}$

52. The number of distinct real roots of the equation $|x + 1||x + 3| - 4|x + 2| + 5 = 0$, is .... **[Numerical Value Type, 2024 Main]**

53. Let x_1, x_2, x_3, x_4 be the solution of the equation $4x^4 + 8x^3 - 17x^2 - 12x + 9 = 0$ and $(4 + x_1^2)(4 + x_2^2)(4 + x_3^2)(4 + x_4^2) = \frac{125}{16}m$. Then, the value of m is .... **[Numerical Value Type, 2024 Main]**

54. The number of real solutions of the equation $x|x+5|+2|x+7|-2=0$ is ......
[Numerical Value Type, 2024 Main]

55. If α satisfies the equation $x^2+x+1=0$ and $(1+\alpha)^7=A+B\alpha+C\alpha^2$, $A, B, C \ge 0$, then $5(3A-2B-C)$ is equal to .... **[Numerical Value Type, 2024 Main]**

56. The set of all $a \in R$ for which the equation $x|x-1|+|x+2|+a=0$ has exactly one real root, is
[Single Correct Type, 2023 Main]
(a) $(-\infty, \infty)$ (b) $(-6, -3)$
(c) $(-6, \infty)$ (d) $(-\infty, -3)$

57. The equation $x^2-4x+[x]+3=x[x]$, where $[x]$ denotes the greatest integer function, has
[Single Correct Type, 2023 Main]
(a) a unique solution in $(-\infty, \infty)$
(b) no solution
(c) a unique solution in $(-\infty, 1)$
(d) exactly two solutions in $(-\infty, \infty)$

58. The number of real solutions of the equation
$3\left(x^2+\frac{1}{x^2}\right)-2\left(x+\frac{1}{x}\right)+5=0$, is
[Single Correct Type, 2023 Main]
(a) 2 (b) 0 (c) 4 (d) 3

59. Let α, β be the roots of the equation $x^2-\sqrt{2}x+2=0$. Then, $\alpha^{14}+\beta^{14}$ is equal to
[Single Correct Type, 2023 Main]
(a) -128 (b) $-128\sqrt{2}$
(c) $-64\sqrt{2}$ (d) -64

60. Let α, β be the roots of the quadratic equation $x^2+\sqrt{6}x+3=0$. Then, $\frac{\alpha^{23}+\beta^{23}+\alpha^{14}+\beta^{14}}{\alpha^{15}+\beta^{15}+\alpha^{10}+\beta^{10}}$ is equal to **[Single Correct Type, 2023 Main]**
(a) 81 (b) 72 (c) 9 (d) 729

61. Let $S=\{x : x \in R$ and
$$(\sqrt{3}+\sqrt{2})^{x^2-4}+(\sqrt{3}-\sqrt{2})^{x^2-4}=10\}.$$
Then, $n(S)$ is equal to **[Single Correct Type, 2023 Main]**
(a) 4 (b) 2 (c) 0 (d) 6

62. If a and b are the roots of the equation $x^2-7x-1=0$, then the value of $\frac{a^{21}+b^{21}+a^{17}+b^{17}}{a^{19}+b^{19}}$ is equal to ....
[Numerical Value Type, 2023 Main]

63. Let $a \in R$ and let α, β be the roots of the equation $x^2+60^{\frac{1}{4}}x+a=0$. If $\alpha^4+\beta^4=-30$, then the product of all possible values of a is............ .
[Numerical Value Type, 2023 Main]

64. The number of distinct real roots of the equation $x^7-7x-2=0$ is **[Single Correct Type, 2022 Main]**
(a) 5 (b) 7 (c) 1 (d) 3

65. The sum of all the real roots of the equation $(e^{2x}-4)(6e^{2x}-5e^x+1)=0$ is
[Single Correct Type, 2022 Main]
(a) $\log_e 3$ (b) $-\log_e 3$
(c) $\log_e 6$ (d) $-\log_e 6$

66. Let α and β be the roots of the equation $x^2-\sqrt{2}x+\sqrt{6}=0$ and $\frac{1}{\alpha^2}+1, \frac{1}{\beta^2}+1$ be the roots of the equation $x^2+ax+b=0$. Then, the roots of the equation $x^2-(a+b-2)x+(a+b+2)=0$ are
[Single Correct Type, 2022 Main]
(a) non-real complex number
(b) real and both negative
(c) real and both positive
(d) real and exactly one of them is positive

67. Let α and β $(\alpha>\beta)$ be the roots of the quadratic equation $x^2-x-4=0$.
If $P_n=\alpha^n-\beta^n$, $n \in N$, then
$\frac{P_{15}P_{16}-P_{14}P_{16}-P_{15}^2+P_{14}P_{15}}{P_{13}P_{14}}$ is equal to ....
[Numerical Value Type, 2022 Main]

68. If for some $p, q, r \in R$, not all have same sign, one of the roots of the equation $(p^2+q^2)x^2-2q(p+r)x+q^2+r^2=0$ is also a root of the equation $x^2+2x-8=0$, then $\frac{q^2+r^2}{p^2}$ is equal to .... **[Numerical Value Type, 2022 Main]**

69. Let $[x]$ denote the greatest integer less than or equal to x. Then, the values of $x \in R$ satisfying the equation $[e^x]^2+[e^x+1]-3=0$ lie in the interval
[Single Correct Type, 2021 Main]
(a) $\left[0, \frac{1}{e}\right)$ (b) $[\log_e 2, \log_e 3)$
(c) $[1, e)$ (d) $[0, \log_e 2)$

70. The value of $3+\cfrac{1}{4+\cfrac{1}{3+\cfrac{1}{4+\cfrac{1}{3+\ldots\infty}}}}$ is equal to
[Single Correct Type, 2021 Main]
(a) $1.5+\sqrt{3}$ (b) $2+\sqrt{3}$
(c) $3+2\sqrt{3}$ (d) $4+\sqrt{3}$

71. Let p and q be two positive numbers, such that $p+q=2$ and $p^4+q^4=272$. Then, p and q are roots of the equation

[Single Correct Type, 2021 Main]

(a) $x^2-2x+136=0$ (b) $x^2-2x+16=0$
(c) $x^2-2x+8=0$ (d) $x^2-2x+2=0$

72. The sum of the roots of the equation $x+1-2\log_2(3+2^x)+2\log_4(10-2^{-x})=0$ is

[Single Correct Type, 2021 Main]

(a) $\log_2 14$ (b) $\log_2 11$ (c) $\log_2 12$ (d) $\log_2 13$

73. The sum of all integral values of $k\,(k\neq 0)$ for which the equation $\frac{2}{x-1}-\frac{1}{x-2}=\frac{2}{k}$ in x has no real roots, is ....

[Numerical Value Type, 2021 Main]

74. If α and β are the roots of the equation, $7x^2-3x-2=0$, then the value of $\frac{\alpha}{1-\alpha^2}+\frac{\beta}{1-\beta^2}$ is equal to

[Single Correct Type, 2020 Main]

(a) $\frac{27}{32}$ (b) $\frac{1}{24}$ (c) $\frac{3}{8}$ (d) $\frac{27}{16}$

75. If the equation $x^2+bx+45=0$ $(b\in R)$ has conjugate complex roots and they satisfy $|z+1|=2\sqrt{10}$, then

[Single Correct Type, 2020 Main]

(a) $b^2+b=72$ (b) $b^2+b=12$
(c) $b^2-b=30$ (d) $b^2-b=42$

76. The set of all real values of λ for which the quadratic equations, $(\lambda^2+1)x^2-4\lambda x+2=0$ always have exactly one root in the interval (0, 1) is

[Single Correct Type, 2020 Main]

(a) (0, 2) (b) (−3, −1)
(c) (2, 4] (d) (1, 3]

77. If α and β are the roots of the equation $x^2+px+2=0$ and $\frac{1}{\alpha}$ and $\frac{1}{\beta}$ are the roots of the equation $2x^2+2qx+1=0$, then $\left(\alpha-\frac{1}{\alpha}\right)\left(\beta-\frac{1}{\beta}\right)\left(\alpha+\frac{1}{\beta}\right)\left(\beta+\frac{1}{\alpha}\right)$ is equal to

[Single Correct Type, 2020 Main]

(a) $\frac{9}{4}(9+q^2)$ (b) $\frac{9}{4}(9-q^2)$
(c) $\frac{9}{4}(9+p^2)$ (d) $\frac{9}{4}(9-p^2)$

78. The number of real roots of the equation, $e^{4x}+e^{3x}-4e^{2x}+e^x+1=0$ is

[Single Correct Type, 2020 Main]

(a) 3 (b) 4
(c) 1 (d) 2

79. The least positive value of a for which the equation, $2x^2+(a-10)x+33/2=2a$ has real roots is ....

[Numerical Value Type, 2020 Main]

EXERCISE 2

JEE Advanced Pattern

Single Option Correct Type Questions

1. The number of solutions of $|[x]-2x|=4$, where $[x]$ denotes the greatest integer $\leq x$ is
(a) infinite (b) 4 (c) 3 (d) 2

2. If x^2+x+1 is a factor of ax^3+bx^2+cx+d, the real root of $ax^3+bx^2+cx+d=0$ is
(a) $-\frac{d}{a}$ (b) $\frac{d}{a}$
(c) $\frac{a}{d}$ (d) None of these

3. The value of x which satisfy the equation $\sqrt{(5x^2-8x+3)}-\sqrt{(5x^2-9x+4)}=\sqrt{(2x^2-2x)}-\sqrt{(2x^2-3x+1)}$, is
(a) 3 (b) 2 (c) 1 (d) 0

4. The roots of the equation
$$(a+\sqrt{b})^{x^2-15}+(a-\sqrt{b})^{x^2-15}=2a,$$
where $a^2-b=1$, are
(a) $\pm 2, \pm\sqrt{3}$ (b) $\pm 4, \pm\sqrt{14}$
(c) $\pm 3, \pm\sqrt{5}$ (d) $\pm 6, \pm\sqrt{20}$

5. The number of pairs (x, y) which will satisfy the equation $x^2-xy+y^2=4(x+y-4)$, is
(a) 1 (b) 2
(c) 4 (d) None of these

6. The number of positive integral solutions of $x^4-y^4=3789108$ is
(a) 0 (b) 1
(c) 2 (d) 4

7. The value of 'a' for which the equation $x^3+ax+1=0$ and $x^4+ax^2+1=0$, have a common root, is
(a) $a=2$ (b) $a=-2$
(c) $a=0$ (d) None of these

8. The necessary and sufficient condition for the equation $(1-a^2)x^2+2ax-1=0$ to have roots lying in the interval $(0, 1)$, is
(a) $a>0$ (b) $a<0$
(c) $a>2$ (d) None of these

9. Solution set of $x-\sqrt{1-|x|}<0$, is
(a) $\left[-1, \frac{-1+\sqrt{5}}{2}\right)$ (b) $[-1, 1]$
(c) $\left[-1, \frac{-1+\sqrt{5}}{2}\right]$ (d) $\left(-1, \frac{-1+\sqrt{5}}{2}\right)$

10. If the quadratic equations $ax^2+2cx+b=0$ and $ax^2+2bx+c=0 (b\neq c)$ have a common root, $a+4b+4c$, is equal to
(a) -2 (b) -1
(c) 0 (d) 1

11. If $a, b, c\in I$ and $ax^2+bx+c=0$ has irrational root and $\lambda\in Q=\frac{p}{q}$, where $f(x)=ax^2+bx+c$, then $|f(\lambda)|$
(a) $\geq\frac{1}{q^2}$ (b) $<\frac{1}{q^2}$
(c) Cannot be discussed (d) None of these

12. If $(ax^2+c)y+(a'x^2+c')=0$ and x is a rational function of y and ac is negative, then
(a) $ac'+a'c=0$ (b) $\frac{a}{a'}=\frac{c}{c'}$
(c) $a^2+c^2=a'^2+c'^2$ (d) $aa'+cc'=1$

13. If α and β are the roots of $ax^2+c=bx$, then the equation $(a+cy)^2=b^2y$ in y has the roots
(a) $\alpha\beta^{-1}$ and $\alpha^{-1}\beta$ (b) α^{-2} and β^{-2}
(c) α^{-1} and β^{-1} (d) α^2 and β^2

14. If α and β are the roots of $x^2+px+q=0$ and γ, δ are the roots of $x^2+px+r=0$, then $\frac{(\alpha-\gamma)(\alpha-\delta)}{(\beta-\gamma)(\beta-\delta)}$ is equal to
(a) 1 (b) q
(c) r (d) $q+r$

15. The equation $x^2\cdot 2^{|x-3|+4}+2^{x-1}=x^2\cdot 2^{x+1}+2^{|x-3|+2}$ has
(a) no solution
(b) two solutions
(c) $x=\pm\frac{1}{2}$ and $x\geq 3$
(d) $x\geq 3$

More than One Correct Option Type Questions

16. If $0 < a < b < c$ and the roots α, β of the equation $ax^2 + bx + c = 0$ are non-real complex numbers, then

(a) $|\alpha| = |\beta|$ (b) $|\alpha| > 1$
(c) $|\beta| < 1$ (d) None of these

17. If A, G and H are the arithmetic mean, geometric mean and harmonic mean between unequal positive integers. Then, the equation $Ax^2 - |G|x - H = 0$ has

(a) both roots are fractions
(b) atleast one root which is negative fraction
(c) exactly one positive root
(d) atleast one root which is an integer

18. The given graph of $y = ax^2 + bx + c$ shows that

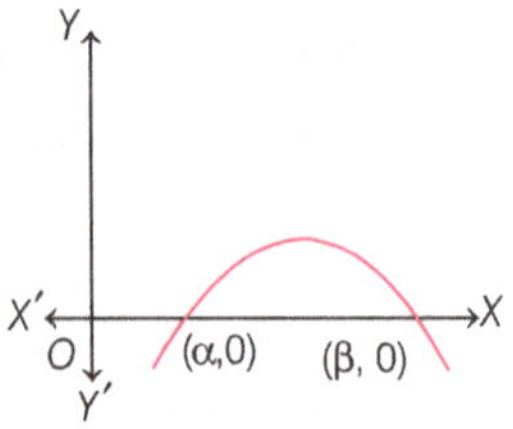

(a) $a < 0$
(b) $b^2 < 4ac$
(c) $c > 0$
(d) a and b are of opposite signs

19. If the equation $ax^2 + bx + c = 0\ (a > 0)$ has two roots α and β such that $\alpha < -2$ and $\beta > 2$, then

(a) $b^2 - 4ac > 0$ (b) $c < 0$
(c) $a + |b| + c < 0$ (d) $4a + 2|b| + c < 0$

20. If roots of the equation $x^3 + bx^2 + cx - 1 = 0$ from an increasing GP, then

(a) $b + c = 0$
(b) $b \in (-\infty, -3)$
(c) one of the roots is 1
(d) one root is smaller than one and one root is more than one

21. Let $f(x) = ax^2 + bx + c$, where $a, b, c \in R$, $a \neq 0$. Suppose $|f(x)| \leq 1, \forall\ x \in [0, 1]$, then

(a) $|a| \leq 8$ (b) $|b| \leq 8$
(c) $|c| \leq 1$ (d) $|a| + |b| + |c| \leq 17$

22. $\cos\alpha$ is a root of the equation $25x^2 + 5x - 12 = 0$, $-1 < x < 0$, the value of $\sin 2\alpha$ is

(a) $\frac{24}{25}$ (b) $-\frac{12}{25}$ (c) $-\frac{24}{25}$ (d) $\frac{20}{25}$

23. If $a, b, c \in R\ (a \neq 0)$ and $a + 2b + 4c = 0$, then equation $ax^2 + bx + c = 0$ has

(a) atleast one positive root
(b) atleast one non-integral root
(c) both integral roots
(d) no irrational root

24. If $x^3 + 3x^2 - 9x + \lambda$ is of the form $(x - \alpha)^2 (x - \beta)$, then λ is equal to

(a) 27 (b) -27
(c) 5 (d) -5

25. If the equation whose roots are the squares of the roots of the cubic $x^3 - ax^2 + bx - 1 = 0$ is identical with the given cubic equation, then

(a) $a = b = 0$
(b) $a = 0, b = 3$
(c) $a = b = 3$
(d) a, b are roots of $x^2 + x + 2 = 0$

Passage Based Questions

Passage I

(Q. Nos. 26 and 27)

- If G and L are the greatest and least values of the expression $\frac{2x^2 - 3x + 2}{2x^2 + 3x + 2}$, $x \in R$ respectively.

26. G and L are the roots of the equation

(a) $5x^2 - 26x + 5 = 0$ (b) $7x^2 - 50x + 7 = 0$
(c) $9x^2 - 82x + 9 = 0$ (d) $11x^2 - 122x + 11 = 0$

27. If $L^2 < \lambda < G^2, \lambda \in N$, the sum of all values of λ is

(a) 1035 (b) 1081 (c) 1225 (d) 1176

Passage II

(Q. Nos. 28 and 29)

- If roots of the equation $x^4 - 12x^3 + cx^2 + dx + 81 = 0$ are positive.

28. The value of c is

(a) -27 (b) 27 (c) -54 (d) 54

29. The value of d is

(a) -27 (b) -54 (c) -81 (d) -108

Passage III

(Q. Nos. 30 and 31)

- In the given figure, vertices of ΔABC lie on $y = f(x) = ax^2 + bx + c$. The ΔABC is right angled isosceles triangle whose hypotenuse $AC = 4\sqrt{2}$ units.

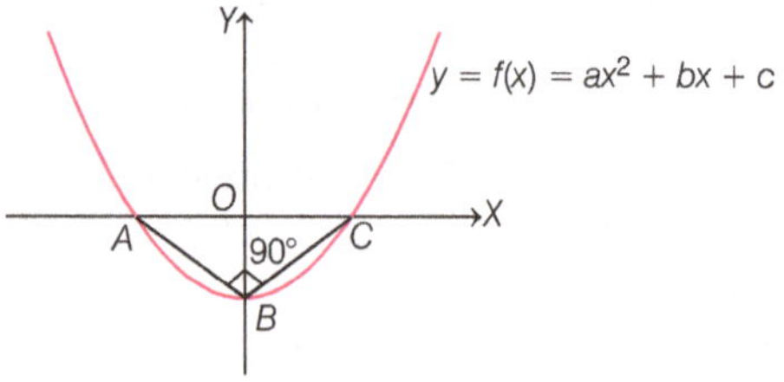

30. Minimum value of $y = f(x)$ is

(a) $-4\sqrt{2}$ (b) $-2\sqrt{2}$ (c) 0 (d) $2\sqrt{2}$

31. Number of integral value of λ for which $\frac{\lambda}{2}$ lies between the roots of $f(x) = 0$, is

(a) 9 (b) 10 (c) 11 (d) 12

Passage IV
(Q. Nos. 32 and 33)

- Let $f(x) = x^2 + bx + c$ and $g(x) = x^2 + b_1x + c_1$. Let the real roots of $f(x) = 0$ be α, β and real roots of $g(x) = 0$ be $\alpha + k, \beta + k$ for same constant k. The least value of $f(x)$ is $-\frac{1}{4}$ and least value of $g(x)$ occurs at $x = \frac{7}{2}$.

32. The least value of $g(x)$ is

(a) -1 (b) $-\frac{1}{2}$ (c) $-\frac{1}{3}$ (d) $-\frac{1}{4}$

33. The roots of $g(x) = 0$ are

(a) 3, 4 (b) -3, 4 (c) $-3, -4$ (d) $3, -4$

Passage V
(Q. Nos. 34 and 35)

- If $\alpha, \beta, \gamma, \delta$ are the roots of the equation $x^4 + Ax^3 + Bx^2 + Cx + D = 0$ such that $\alpha\beta = \gamma\delta = k$ and A, B, C, D are the roots of $x^4 - 2x^3 + 4x^2 + 6x - 21 = 0$ such that $A + B = 0$.

34. The value of $\frac{C}{A}$ is

(a) $-\frac{k}{2}$ (b) $-k$ (c) $\frac{k}{2}$ (d) k

35. The value of $(\alpha + \beta)(\gamma + \delta)$ in terms of B and k is

(a) $B - 2k$ (b) $B - k$ (c) $B + k$ (d) $B + 2k$

Stem Based Questions

Stem I
(Q. Nos. 36 and 37)

- If $ax^2 - bx + c = 0$ have two distinct roots lying in the interval $(0, 1)$; $a, b, c \in N$.

36. The least value of a is ....

37. The least value of b is ....

Stem II
(Q. Nos. 38 and 39)

- If $2x^3 + ax^2 + bx + 4 = 0$ (a and b are positive real numbers) has three real roots.

38. The minimum value of a^3 is ....

39. The minimum value of b^3 is ....

Single Integer Type Questions

40. If the maximum and minimum values of $y = \frac{x^2 - 3x + c}{x^2 + 3x + c}$ are 7 and $\frac{1}{7}$ respectively, the value of c is

41. Number of solutions of the equation $\sqrt{x^2} - \sqrt{(x-1)^2} + \sqrt{(x-2)^2} = \sqrt{5}$ is

42. If α and β are the complex roots of the equation $(1 + i)x^2 + (1 - i)x - 2i = 0$, where $i = \sqrt{-1}$, the value of $|\alpha - \beta|^2$ is

43. If α, β be the roots of the equation $4x^2 - 16x + c = 0, c \in R$ such that $1 < \alpha < 2$ and $2 < \beta < 3$, then the number of integral values of c, are

44. Let r, s and t be the roots of the equation $8x^3 + 1001x + 2008 = 0$ and if $99\lambda = (r + s)^3 + (s + t)^3 + (t + r)^3$, the value of $[\lambda]$ is (where $[\cdot]$ denotes the greatest integer function)

Numerical Value Type Questions

45. For the equation $3x^2 + px + 3 = 0, p > 0$, if one of the root is square of the other, then $154\,p$ is equal to ....

46. Let α and β be the roots of equation $x^2 - 6x - 2 = 0$. If $a_n = \alpha^n - \beta^n$, for $n \ge 1$, then the value of $7052 \left(\frac{a_{10} - 2a_8}{2a_9}\right)$ is ....

47. Let $a, b \in R$ and $ab \ne 1$. If $6a^2 + 20a + 15 = 0$ and $15b^2 + 20b + 6 = 0$, then the value of $\frac{4030b^3}{ab^2 - 9(ab+1)^3}$ is ....

48. If α and β are the roots of the equation $x^2 - 6x + 12 = 0$ and the value of $(\alpha - 2)^{24} - \frac{(\beta - 6)^8}{\alpha^8} + 1$ is 4^a, then the value of a is ....

49. The sum of the roots of the equation $2^{x+2} \cdot 27^{\frac{x}{x-1}} = 9$ are given by $-a - \log_b c$. Then, the value of $\frac{ac}{b}$ is ....

Matching Type Questions

50. Column I contains rational algebraic expressions and Column II contains possible integers which lie in their range. Match the entries of Column I with one or more entries of the elements of Column II.

Column I		Column II	
(A)	$y = \dfrac{x^2 - 2x + 4}{x^2 + 2x + 4}, x \in R$	(p)	1
(B)	$y = \dfrac{2x^2 + 4x + 1}{x^2 + 4x + 2}, x \in R$	(q)	−1
(C)	$y = \dfrac{x^2 - 3x + 4}{x - 3}, x \in R$	(r)	2
(D)	$y = \dfrac{x^2 + x + 1}{x^2 + 4x + 3}, x \in R$	(s)	3
		(t)	8

51. Match the following coumns.

Column I	Column II
(A) If a, b, c, d are four non-zero real numbers such that $(d + a - b)^2 + (d + b - c)^2 = 0$ and the roots of the equation $a(b - c)x^2 + b(c - a)x + c(a - b) = 0$ are real and equal, then	(p) $a + b + c = 0$
(B) If the equation $ax^2 + bx + c = 0$ and $x^3 - 3x^2 + 3x - 1 = 0$ have a common real root, then	(q) a, b, c are in AP
(C) Let a, b, c be positive real numbers such that the expression $bx^2 + (\sqrt{(a + c)^2 + 4b^2})x + (a + c)$ is non-negative, $\forall x \in R$, then	(r) a, b, c are in GP
(D) Let $a, b, c \in R$ be such that $b^2 - ac \ge 0$, then the equation $ax^2 + 2bx + c = 0$ has equal roots, then	(s) a, b, c are in HP

52. Match the following coumns.

Column I		Column II	
(A)	The equation $x^3 - 6x^2 + 9x + \lambda = 0$ have exactly one root is $(1, 3)$, then $\|[\lambda + 1]\|$ is (where $[\cdot]$ denotes the greatest integer function)	(p)	0
(B)	If $-3 < \dfrac{x^2 - \lambda x - 2}{x^2 + x + 1} < 2, \forall x \in R$, then $\|[\lambda]\|$ is (where $[\cdot]$ denotes the greatest integer function)	(q)	1
(C)	If $x^2 + \lambda x + 1 = 0$ and $(b - c)x^2 + (c - a)x + (a - b) = 0$ have both the roots common, then $\|[\lambda - 1]\|$, (where $[\cdot]$ denotes the greatest integer function)	(r)	2
(D)	The sum of values of x satisfying the equation $(31 + 8\sqrt{15})^{x^2-3} + 1 = (32 + 8\sqrt{15})^{x^2-3}$ is	(s)	3

Previous Year Questions

53. The product of all positive real values of x satisfying the equation $x^{(16(\log_5 x)^3 - 68 \log_5 x)} = 5^{-16}$ is ....

[Numerical Value Type, 2022 Adv.]

54. For $x \in R$, the number of real roots of the equation $3x^2 - 4|x^2 - 1| + x - 1 = 0$ is ....

[Numerical Value Type, 2022 Adv.]

55. Suppose a, b denote the distinct real roots of the quadratic polynomial $x^2 + 20x - 2020$ and suppose c, d denote the distinct complex roots of the quadratic polynomial $x^2 - 20x + 2020$. Then the value of $ac(a - c) + ad(a - d) + bc(b - c) + bd(b - d)$ is

[Single Correct Type, 2020 Adv.]

(a) 0
(b) 8000
(c) 8080
(d) 16000

EXERCISE 3

Challenging Problems

Subjective Type Questions

1. For what values of m, the equation $(1+m)x^2-2(1+3m)x+(1+8m)=0$ has $(m \in R)$
   (i) both roots are imaginary?
   (ii) both roots are equal?
   (iii) both roots are real and distinct?
   (iv) both roots are positive?
   (v) both roots are negative?
   (vi) roots are opposite in sign?
   (vii) roots are equal in magnitude but opposite in sign?
   (viii) atleast one root is positive?
   (ix) atleast one root is negative?
   (x) roots are in the ratio $2:3$?

2. For what values of m, then equation $2x^2-2(2m+1)x+m(m+1)=0$ has $(m \in R)$
   (i) both roots are smaller than 2?
   (ii) both roots are greater than 2?
   (iii) both roots lie in the interval $(2, 3)$?
   (iv) exactly one root lie in the interval $(2, 3)$?
   (v) one root is smaller than 1 and the other root is greater than 1?
   (vi) one root is greater than 3 and the other root is smaller than 2?
   (vii) atleast one root lies in the interval $(2, 3)$?
   (viii) atleast one root is greater than 2?
   (ix) atleast one root is smaller than 2?
   (x) roots α and β, such that both 2 and 3 lie between α and β?

3. If r is the ratio of the roots of the equation $ax^2+bx+c=0$, show that $\frac{(r+1)^2}{r}=\frac{b^2}{ac}$.

4. If the roots of the equation $\frac{1}{x+p}+\frac{1}{x+q}=\frac{1}{r}$ are equal in magnitude but opposite in sign, show that $p+q=2r$ and that the product of the roots is equal to $\left(-\frac{p^2+q^2}{2}\right)$.

5. If one root of the quadratic equation $ax^2+bx+c=0$ is equal to the nth power of the other, then show that $(ac^n)^{\frac{1}{n+1}}+(a^nc)^{\frac{1}{n+1}}+b=0$.

6. If α, β are the roots of the equation $ax^2+bx+c=0$ and γ, δ those of equation $lx^2+mx+n=0$, then find the equation whose roots are $\alpha\gamma+\beta\delta$ and $\alpha\delta+\beta\gamma$.

7. If the equation $x^2-2px+q=0$ has two equal roots, then the equation $(1+y)x^2-2(p+y)x+(q+y)=0$ will have its roots real and distinct only, when y is negative and p is not unity.

8. Solve the equation
$$(2+\sqrt{3})^{x^2-2x+1}+(2-\sqrt{3})^{x^2-2x-1}=\frac{101}{10(2-\sqrt{3})}.$$

9. Solve the equation $x^2+\left(\frac{x}{x-1}\right)^2=8$.

10. Solve the equation
$$\sqrt{(x+8)+2\sqrt{(x+7)}}+\sqrt{(x+1)-\sqrt{(x+7)}}=4.$$

11. Find all values of a for which the inequation $4^{x^2}+2(2a+1)2^{x^2}+4a^2-3>0$ is satisfied for any x.

12. Solve the inequation
$$\log_{x^2+2x-3}\left(\frac{|x+4|-|x|}{x-1}\right)>0.$$

13. Solve the system $|x^2-2x|+y=1, x^2+|y|=1$.

14. If α, β, γ are the roots of the cubic $x^3-px^2+qx-r=0$. Find the equations whose roots are
   (i) $\beta\gamma+\frac{1}{\alpha}, \gamma\alpha+\frac{1}{\beta}, \alpha\beta+\frac{1}{\gamma}$
   (ii) $(\beta+\gamma-\alpha), (\gamma+\alpha-\beta), (\alpha+\beta-\gamma)$
   Also, find the value of $(\beta+\gamma-\alpha)(\gamma+\alpha-\beta)(\alpha+\beta-\gamma)$.

15. If $A_1, A_2, A_3, \ldots, A_n, a_1, a_2, a_3, \ldots, a_n, a, b, c \in R$, show that the roots of the equation

$$\frac{A_1^2}{x-a_1}+\frac{A_2^2}{x-a_2}+\frac{A_3^2}{x-a_3}+\ldots+\frac{A_n^2}{x-a_n} = ab^2+c^2x+ac$$ are real.

16. For what values of the parameter a the equation $x^4+2ax^3+x^2+2ax+1=0$ has atleast two distinct negative roots?

17. How many real solutions of the equation $6x^2-77[x]+147=0$, where $[x]$ is the integral part of x?

18. If α, β are the roots of the equation $x^2-2x-a^2+1=0$ and γ, δ are the roots of the equation $x^2-2(a+1)x+a(a-1)=0$, such that $\alpha, \beta \in (\gamma, \delta)$, find the value of '$a$'.

19. If the equation $x^4+px^3+qx^2+rx+5=0$ has four positive real roots, find the minimum value of pr.

Answer Key

Exercise 1

1. (a)	2. (c)	3. (c)	4. (c)	5. (b)	6. (c)	7. (c)	8. (d)	9. (b)	10. (b)
11. (b)	12. (b)	13. (b)	14. (c)	15. (a)	16. (a)	17. (c)	18. (b)	19. (c)	20. (a)
21. (b)	22. (c)	23. (b)	24. (b)	25. (b)	26. (c)	27. (b)	28. (b)	29. (c)	30. (d)
31. (6)	32. (8)	33. (7)	34. (3)	35. (1)	36. (2)	37. (4)	38. (2)	39. (4)	40. (4)
41. (4)	42. (4)	43. (9)	44. (6)	45. (3)	46. (a)	47. (d)	48. (d)	49. (a)	50. (a)
51. (d)	52. (2)	53. (221)	54. (3)	55. (5)	56. (a)	57. (a)	58. (b)	59. (a)	60. (a)
61. (a)	62. (51)	63. (45)	64. (d)	65. (b)	66. (b)	67. (16)	68. (272)	69. (d)	70. (a)
71. (b)	72. (b)	73. (66)	74. (d)	75. (c)	76. (d)	77. (d)	78. (c)	79. (8)	

Exercise 2

1. (b)	2. (a)	3. (c)	4. (b)	5. (a)	6. (a)	7. (b)	8. (c)	9. (a)	10. (c)
11. (a)	12. (b)	13. (b)	14. (a)	15. (c)	16. (a,b)	17. (b,c)	18. (a,d)	19. (a,b,c,d)	20. (a,b,c,d)
21. (a,b,c,d)	22. (a,c)	23. (a,b)	24. (b,c)	25. (a,c,d)	26. (b)	27. (d)	28. (d)	29. (d)	30. (b)
31. (c)	32. (d)	33. (a)	34. (d)	35. (a)	36. (5)	37. (5)	38. (432)	39. (864)	40. (4)
41. (2)	42. (5)	43. (3)	44. (7)	45. (462)	46. (21156)	47. (12)	48. (12)	49. (1.5)	

50. A → (p, r, s); B → (p, q, r, s, t); C → (q, t); D → (p, q, r, s, t)

51. A → (q, r, s); B → (p); C → (q); D → (r)

52. A → (p, q, r, s); B → (p, q); C → (s); D → (p)

53. 1 54. (4) 55. (d)

Solutions

Exercise 1 - JEE Main Pattern

1. Put $x^2 + x = y$.

Then, $(y-2)(y-3) = 12$

$\Rightarrow \quad y^2 - 5y + 6 = 12$

$\Rightarrow \quad y^2 - 5y - 6 = 0$

$\Rightarrow \quad (y-6)(y+1) = 0$

$\Rightarrow \quad y = 6, -1$

$\Rightarrow \quad x^2 + x = 6$ or $x^2 + x = -1$

$\Rightarrow \quad x^2 + x - 6 = 0$ or $x^2 + x + 1 = 0$

$\Rightarrow \quad x = -3, 2 \quad$ [roots of $x^2 + x + 1$ are non-real]

So, required sum $= -1$

2. We have, $\quad (\lambda + 1)x^2 + 2 = \lambda x + 3$

$\Rightarrow \quad (\lambda + 1)x^2 - \lambda x - 1 = 0$

Since, both curves intersect at one point

$\therefore \quad D = 0$

$\Rightarrow \lambda^2 + 4(\lambda + 1) = 0$

$\Rightarrow \quad (\lambda + 2)^2 = 0$

$\Rightarrow \quad \lambda = -2$

3. Let the roots be α and β.

$\therefore \alpha + \beta = -2a$ and $\alpha\beta = b$

Now, we have

$|\alpha - \beta| \le 2m$

$\Rightarrow \quad |\alpha - \beta|^2 \le 4m^2$

$\Rightarrow \quad (\alpha + \beta)^2 - 4\alpha\beta \le 4m^2$

$\Rightarrow \quad 4a^2 - 4b \le 4m^2$

$\Rightarrow \quad b \ge a^2 - m^2$

Also, $\quad D > 0$

$\Rightarrow \quad 4a^2 - 4b > 0$

$\Rightarrow \quad b < a^2$

$\therefore \quad b \in [a^2 - m^2, a^2)$

4. We have, $\quad a\alpha^2 + b\alpha + c = 0$

and $\quad a\beta^2 + b\beta + c = 0$

$\Rightarrow a\alpha^2 + c = -b\alpha$ and $a\beta^2 + c = -b\beta$

$\Rightarrow a\alpha + b = -\dfrac{c}{\alpha}$ and $a\beta + b = -\dfrac{c}{\beta}$

Now, $\dfrac{a\alpha^2 + c}{a\alpha + b} + \dfrac{a\beta^2 + c}{a\beta + c} = \dfrac{-b\alpha}{-\dfrac{c}{\alpha}} + \dfrac{-b\beta}{-\dfrac{c}{\beta}}$

$= \dfrac{b}{c}(\alpha^2 + \beta^2)$

$= \dfrac{b}{c}((\alpha + \beta)^2 - 2\alpha\beta)$

$= \dfrac{b}{c}\left(\dfrac{b^2}{a^2} - \dfrac{2c}{a}\right)$

$= \dfrac{b}{ca^2}(b^2 - 2ac)$

5. We have, $\quad b^2cx^2 - ab^2x + a^3 = 0$

$\Rightarrow \quad \dfrac{c}{a^3}(b^2cx^2 - ab^2x + a^3) = 0$

$\Rightarrow \quad \dfrac{b^2c^2}{a^3}x^2 - \dfrac{b^2c}{a^2}x + c = 0$

$\Rightarrow \quad a\left(\dfrac{bc}{a^2}x\right)^2 - b\left(\dfrac{bc}{a^2}x\right) + c = 0$

$\Rightarrow \quad \dfrac{bc}{a^2}x = \alpha, \beta$

$\Rightarrow \quad (\alpha + \beta)\alpha\beta x = \alpha, \beta$

$\Rightarrow \quad x = \dfrac{1}{(\alpha + \beta)\alpha}, \dfrac{1}{(\alpha + \beta)\beta}$

6. Let α and β be roots of equation $x^2 - 3px + 2q = 0$

and $\alpha, \dfrac{1}{\beta}$ are roots of equation $x^2 - 3ax + 2b = 0$

$\therefore \quad \alpha + \beta = 3p, \alpha\beta = 2q$

and $\quad \alpha + \dfrac{1}{\beta} = 3a, \dfrac{\alpha}{\beta} = 2b$

$\therefore \quad (2q - 2b)^2 = \left(\alpha\beta - \dfrac{\alpha}{\beta}\right)^2$

$= \alpha^2\left(\beta - \dfrac{1}{\beta}\right)^2$

$= \dfrac{\alpha}{\beta}\cdot\beta\alpha\left[(\alpha + \beta) - \left(\alpha + \dfrac{1}{\beta}\right)\right]^2$

$= (2b)(2q)[3p - 3a]^2$

$= 36bq(p - a)^2$

7. Let $f(x) = x^2 - 6ax + 2 - 2a + 9a^2$

Since, both roots greater than 3, then $D \ge 0$, x-coordinate of vertex > 3, $f(3) > 0$

$\Rightarrow \quad 36a^2 - 8 + 8a - 36a^2 \ge 0, 3a > 3, 9a^2 - 20a + 11 = 0$

$\Rightarrow a \ge 1, a > 1, (9a - 11)(a - 1) > 0$

$\Rightarrow a \ge 1, a > 1, a \in (-\infty, 1) \cup \left(\dfrac{11}{9}, \infty\right)$

$\therefore \ a > \dfrac{11}{9}$

8. We have, $\dfrac{x^2}{1-|x-5|}=1$

$\Rightarrow \quad x^2 = 1 - |x-5|$

$\Rightarrow \quad x^2 - 1 = -|x-5|$

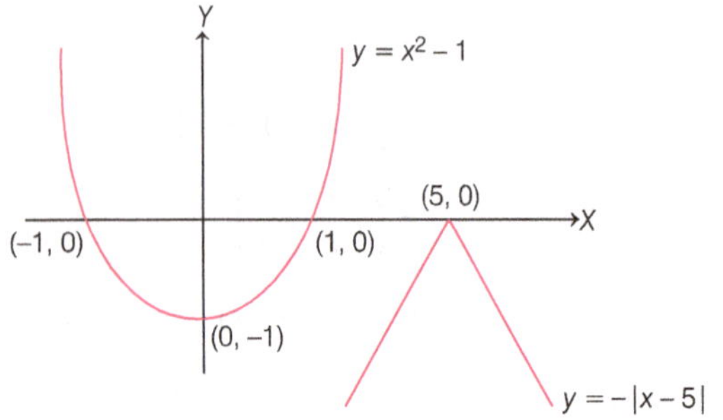

Since, both curves do not intersect each other, so given equation has no solution.

9. We have, $||x-1|+a|=4$

$\Rightarrow \quad |x-1|+a=\pm 4$

$\Rightarrow \quad |x-1| = \pm 4 - a$

For real solutions, $\pm 4 - a \ge 0$

$\Rightarrow \quad 4-a \ge 0$ and $-4-a \ge 0$

$\Rightarrow \quad a \le 4$ and $a \le -4$

$\Rightarrow \quad a \le -4$

$\Rightarrow \quad a \in (-\infty, -4]$

10. We have, $4^{-x+0.5} - 7(2^{-x}) - 4 < 0$

$\Rightarrow \quad 4^{-x} \times 2 - 7 \times 2^{-x} - 4 < 0$

$\Rightarrow \quad 2(2^{-x})^2 - 7(2^{-x}) - 4 < 0$

$\Rightarrow \quad 2y^2 - 7y - 4 < 0$, where $y = 2^{-x}$

$\Rightarrow \quad (2y+1)(y-4) < 0$

$\Rightarrow \quad y - 4 < 0 \qquad [2y+1 = 2\cdot 2^{-x} + 1 > 0]$

$\Rightarrow \quad y < 4$

$\Rightarrow \quad 2^{-x} < 4$

$\Rightarrow \quad 2^{-x} < 2^2$

$\Rightarrow \quad -x < 2$

$\Rightarrow \quad x > -2$

$\therefore \quad x \in (-2, \infty)$

11. We have, $2(a-b)x^2 - 11(a+b+c)x - 3(a-b) = 0$

$\therefore \quad D = \{-11(a+b+c)\}^2 - 4\cdot 2(a-b)\cdot(-3)(a-b)$

$= 121(a+b+c)^2 + 24(a-b)^2 > 0$

Therefore, the roots are real and unequal.

12. Here, $a < 0$

Cut-off Y-axis, $x = 0$

$\Rightarrow \quad y = c < 0 \qquad$ [from graph]

$\therefore \quad c < 0$

x-coordinate of vertex > 0

$\Rightarrow \quad -\dfrac{b}{2a} > 0$

$\Rightarrow \quad \dfrac{b}{a} < 0$

But $\quad a < 0$

$\therefore \quad b > 0$

and y-coordinate of vertex < 0

$\Rightarrow \quad -\dfrac{D}{4a} < 0 \Rightarrow \dfrac{D}{4a} > 0$

$\therefore \quad D < 0 \qquad [\because a < 0]$

i.e. $\quad b^2 - 4ac < 0$

$\therefore \quad \dfrac{c}{a} > 0 \qquad [\because c < 0, a < 0]$

13. Sum of the roots $= -\dfrac{(a+3)}{a} = I^+ \qquad$ [let]

$\therefore \quad a = \left(-\dfrac{3}{I^+ + 1}\right) \qquad$ ...(i)

Product of the roots $= \alpha\beta = \dfrac{a-3}{a} = I^+ + 2 \qquad$ ...(ii)

and $\quad D = (a+3)^2 - 4a(a-3)$

$= \dfrac{9}{(I^+ + 1)^2}\{(I^+ - 2)^2 - 12\} \qquad$ [from Eq. (i)]

D must be perfect square, then $I^+ = 6$

From Eq. (ii),

Product of the roots $= I^+ + 2 = 6 + 2 = 8$

14. Let α be one root of

$x^2 - 3ax + f(a) = 0$

$\Rightarrow \quad \alpha + 2\alpha = 3a \Rightarrow 3\alpha = 3a$

$\Rightarrow \quad \alpha = a \qquad$ ...(i)

and $\quad \alpha \cdot 2\alpha = f(a)$

$\Rightarrow \quad f(a) = 2\alpha^2 = 2a^2 \qquad$ [using Eq. (i)]

$\Rightarrow \quad f(x) = 2x^2$

15. $\because \quad x_1 x_2 = 4 \qquad$ ...(i)

and $\quad \dfrac{x_1}{x_1 - 1} + \dfrac{x_2}{x_2 - 1} = 2$

$\Rightarrow \quad 2x_1x_2 - x_1 - x_2 = 2(x_1x_2 - x_1 - x_2 + 1)$

$\Rightarrow \quad 8 - x_1 - x_2 = 2(4 - x_1 - x_2 + 1) \qquad$ [from Eq. (i)]

or $\quad x_1 + x_2 = 2 \qquad$ ...(ii)

From Eqs. (i) and (ii), required equation is

$x^2 - (x_1 + x_2)x + x_1x_2 = 0$

or $\quad x^2 - 2x + 4 = 0$

16. Let $f(x) = x^2 - 2ax + a^2 - 1$

Now, four cases arise:

Case I $D \ge 0$

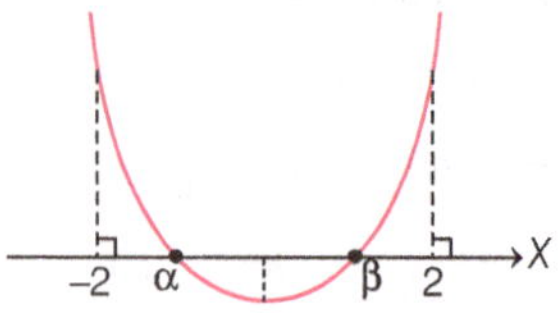

$\Rightarrow \quad (-2a)^2 - 4\cdot 1(a^2 - 1) \ge 0$

$\Rightarrow \quad 4 \ge 0$

$\therefore \quad a \in R$

Case II $f(-2) > 0$

$$\Rightarrow \quad 4 + 4a + a^2 - 1 > 0$$
$$\Rightarrow \quad a^2 + 4a + 3 > 0$$
$$\Rightarrow \quad (a+1)(a+3) > 0$$
$$\therefore \quad a \in (-\infty, -3) \cup (-1, \infty)$$

Case III $f(2) > 0$

$$\Rightarrow \quad 4 - 4a + a^2 - 1 > 0 \Rightarrow a^2 - 4a + 3 > 0$$
$$\Rightarrow \quad (a-1)(a-3) > 0$$
$$\therefore \quad a \in (-\infty, 1) \cup (3, \infty)$$

Case IV $-2 <$ x-coordinate of vertex < 2

$$\Rightarrow \quad -2 < a < 2$$
$$\therefore \quad a \in (-2, 2)$$

Combining all cases, we get $a \in (-1, 1)$

Hence, $[a] = -1, 0$

17. We have, $-\left(\dfrac{-4a}{2(-2)}\right) = -2$

$$\Rightarrow \quad a = 2$$
$$\therefore \quad y = -2x^2 - 8x + \lambda \qquad \text{...(i)}$$

Since, Eq. (i) passes through points $(-2, 7)$

$$\therefore \quad 7 = -2(-2)^2 - 8(-2) + \lambda$$
$$\Rightarrow \quad 7 = -8 + 16 + \lambda$$
$$\therefore \quad \lambda = -1$$

18. Since, the coefficient of $x^2 = (4p - p^2 - 5) < 0$

Therefore, the graph is open downward.

According to the question, 1 must lie between the roots.

Hence, $f(1) > 0$

$$\Rightarrow \quad 4p - p^2 - 5 - 2p + 1 + 3p > 0$$
$$\Rightarrow \quad -p^2 + 5p - 4 > 0$$
$$\Rightarrow \quad p^2 - 5p + 4 < 0$$
$$\Rightarrow \quad (p-4)(p-1) < 0$$
$$\Rightarrow \quad 1 < p < 4$$
$$\therefore \quad p = 2, 3$$

Hence, number of integral values of p is 2.

19. We have, $3^{2x^2} - 2 \cdot 3^{x^2 + x + 6} + 3^{2(x+6)} = 0$

$$\Rightarrow \quad (3^{x^2} - 3^{x+6})^2 = 0$$
$$\Rightarrow \quad 3^{x^2} - 3^{x+6} = 0$$
$$\Rightarrow \quad 3^{x^2} = 3^{x+6}$$
$$\Rightarrow \quad x^2 = x + 6$$
$$\Rightarrow \quad x^2 - x - 6 = 0$$
$$\Rightarrow \quad (x-3)(x+2) = 0$$
$$\therefore \quad x = \{-2, 3\}$$

20. Given, $b^2 - 4ac = p^2 - 4aq$ ...(i)

and $f(x) = g(x)$

$$\Rightarrow \quad ax^2 + bx + c = ax^2 + px + q$$
$$\Rightarrow \quad (b-p)x = q - c$$
$$\therefore \quad x = \frac{q-c}{b-p} = \alpha \qquad \text{[given] ...(ii)}$$

From Eq. (i), we get

$$(b+p)(b-p) + 4a(q-c) = 0$$
$$\Rightarrow \quad (b+p)(b-p) + 4a\alpha(b-p) = 0 \qquad \text{[from Eq. (ii)]}$$
$$\text{or} \quad \alpha = -\frac{(b+p)}{4a} \qquad [\because b \neq p]$$
$$= \frac{\left(-\dfrac{b}{a}\right) + \left(-\dfrac{p}{a}\right)}{4}$$
$$= \frac{\begin{bmatrix}\text{Sum of the roots of } (f(x) = 0) \\ + \text{ Sum of the roots of } (g(x) = 0)\end{bmatrix}}{4}$$
$$= \text{AM of the roots of } f(x) = 0$$
$$\text{and} \quad g(x) = 0$$

21. Let α and β be the roots of $ax^2 + bx + c = 0$.

$$\therefore \quad x_1 = \frac{\alpha + \beta}{2} = -\frac{b}{2a}$$
$$\text{and} \quad x_2 = \frac{2\alpha\beta}{\alpha + \beta} = \frac{2 \cdot \dfrac{c}{a}}{-\dfrac{b}{a}} = -\frac{2c}{b}$$

$\therefore$ The required equation is

$$x^2 - \left[\left(-\frac{b}{2a}\right) + \left(-\frac{2c}{b}\right)\right]x + \frac{2bc}{2ab} = 0$$

i.e. $$2abx^2 + (b^2 + 4ac)x + 2bc = 0$$

22. Let α_1, α_2 and α_3 be the roots of $f(x) = 0$, such that

$$\alpha_1 < \alpha_2 < \alpha_3$$

and $g(x)$ can take all values from $[-6, \infty)$.

$$\because \quad g(x) = (x+1)^2 - 6 \geq -6$$
$$\therefore \quad \alpha_3 \leq -7, \alpha_2 \leq -8, \alpha_1 \leq -9$$
$$\because \quad \alpha_1 + \alpha_2 + \alpha_3 = -a$$
$$\Rightarrow \quad -a \leq -24$$
$$\Rightarrow \quad a \geq 24$$
$$\alpha_1\alpha_2 + \alpha_2\alpha_3 + \alpha_3\alpha_1 = b$$
$$\Rightarrow \quad b \geq 191$$
$$\text{and} \quad \alpha_1\alpha_2\alpha_3 = -c$$
$$\Rightarrow \quad -c \leq -504$$
$$\Rightarrow \quad c \geq 504$$
$$\therefore \quad a + b + c \geq 719$$

Hence, minimum value of $a + b + c$ is 719.

23. $\because \displaystyle\sum_{k=1}^{n} (x + k - 1)(x + k) = 10n$

$$\Rightarrow \quad \sum_{k=1}^{n} x^2 + x(2k-1) + (k-1)k = 10n$$
$$\Rightarrow \quad nx^2 + x(1 + 3 + 5 + \ldots + (2n-1)) + (0 + 1 \cdot 2 + 2 \cdot 3 + 3 \cdot 4 + \ldots + (n-1)n) = 10n$$
$$\Rightarrow nx^2 + x \cdot \frac{n}{2}(1 + 2n - 1) + \left(\frac{n(n+1)(2n+1)}{6} - \frac{n(n+1)}{2}\right) = 10n$$
$$\Rightarrow \quad nx^2 + n^2x + \frac{n(n^2-1)}{3} = 10n$$

$\Rightarrow \quad x^2 + nx + \frac{(n^2-31)}{3} = 0$ [dividing by n]

$\because \quad (\alpha+1) - \alpha = \frac{\sqrt{D}}{1}$

$1 = \sqrt{D}$

$\Rightarrow \quad D = 1$

$\Rightarrow \quad n^2 - 4\cdot 1\cdot \frac{(n^2-31)}{3} = 1$

$\Rightarrow \quad 3n^2 - 4n^2 + 124 = 3$

$\Rightarrow \quad n^2 = 121$

$\therefore \quad n = 11$

24. Since, 2 is only even prime.

Therefore, we have

$2^2 - \lambda\cdot 2 + 12 = 0$

$\Rightarrow \quad \lambda = 8$

$\therefore \quad x^2 + \lambda x + \mu = 0$

$\Rightarrow \quad x^2 + 8x + \mu = 0$ ...(i)

But Eq. (i) has equal roots.

$\therefore \quad D = 0$

$\Rightarrow \quad 8^2 - 4\cdot 1\cdot \mu = 0$

$\Rightarrow \quad \mu = 16$

25. We have, $\sqrt{x} + \sqrt{x - \sqrt{(1-x)}} = 1$

$\Rightarrow \quad \sqrt{x - \sqrt{1-x}} = 1 - \sqrt{x}$

On squaring both sides, we get

$x - \sqrt{1-x} = 1 + x - 2\sqrt{x}$

$\Rightarrow \quad -\sqrt{1-x} = 1 - 2\sqrt{x}$

Again, squaring on both sides, we get

$1 - x = 1 + 4x - 4\sqrt{x}$

$4\sqrt{x} = 5x$

$\Rightarrow \quad \sqrt{x} = \frac{4}{5}$

$\Rightarrow \quad x = \frac{16}{25}$ [on squaring both sides]

Hence, the number of real solutions is 1.

26. Let $x = \sqrt{7 + \sqrt{7 - \sqrt{7 + \sqrt{7 - \ldots\infty}}}}$

$\Rightarrow \quad x = \sqrt{7 + \sqrt{7 - x}}$ [on squaring both sides]

$\Rightarrow \quad x^2 - 7 = \sqrt{7 - x}$

$\Rightarrow \quad (x^2-7)^2 = 7 - x$ [again, squaring on both sides]

$\Rightarrow \quad x^4 - 14x^2 + x + 42 = 0$

$\Rightarrow \quad (x-3)(x^3 + 3x^2 - 5x - 14) = 0$

$\Rightarrow \quad (x-3)(x+2)(x^2 + x - 7) = 0$

$\Rightarrow \quad x = 3, -2, \frac{-1 \pm \sqrt{29}}{2}$

$\therefore \quad x = 3$ $[\because x > \sqrt{7}]$

27. Let $y = 2(k-x)(x + \sqrt{(x^2+k^2)})$

$\Rightarrow \quad y - 2(k-x)x = 2(k-x)\sqrt{(x^2+k^2)}$

On squaring both sides, we get

$\Rightarrow \quad y^2 + 4(k-x)^2x^2 - 4xy(k-x) = 4(k-x)^2(x^2+k^2)$

$\Rightarrow \quad y^2 - 4xy(k-x) = 4(k-x)^2k^2$

$\Rightarrow \quad 4(k^2 - y)x^2 - 4(2k^3 - ky)x - y^2 + 4k^4 = 0$

Since, x is real.

$\therefore \quad D \ge 0$

$\Rightarrow \quad 16(2k^3 - ky)^2 - 4\cdot 4(k^2-y)(4k^4 - y^2) \ge 0$

[using, $b^2 - 4ac \ge 0$]

$\Rightarrow \quad 4k^6 + k^2y^2 - 4k^4y - (-k^2y^2 + 4k^6 + y^3 - 4yk^4) \ge 0$

$\Rightarrow \quad 2k^2y^2 - y^3 \ge 0$

$\Rightarrow \quad y^2(y - 2k^2) \le 0$

$\therefore \quad y \le 2k^2$

28. We have, $\frac{1}{3} < \frac{x^2 - 2x + 4}{x^2 + 2x + 4} < 3, \forall\, x \in R$

$\frac{1}{3} < \frac{x^2 + 2x + 4}{x^2 - 2x + 4} < 3, \forall\, x \in R$

Let $y = \frac{9\cdot 3^{2x} + 6\cdot 3^x + 4}{9\cdot 3^{2x} - 6\cdot 3^x + 4} = \frac{(3^{x+1})^2 + 2\cdot 3^{x+1} + 4}{(3^{x+1})^2 - 2\cdot 3^{x+1} + 4}$

$= \frac{t^2 + 2t + 4}{t^2 - 2t + 4}$, where $t = 3^{x+1}$

$\Rightarrow \quad (y-1)t^2 - 2(y+1)t + 4(y-1) = 0$

By the given condition, for every $t \in R$,

$\frac{1}{3} < y < 3$ ...(i)

But $\quad t = 3^{x+1} > 0$

We have, product of the roots $= 4 > 0$, which is true.

And sum of the roots $= \frac{2(y+1)}{(y-1)} > 0 \Rightarrow \frac{y+1}{y-1} > 0$

$\therefore \quad y \in (-\infty, -1) \cup (1, \infty)$ ...(ii)

From Eqs. (i) and (ii), we get

$1 < y < 3$

29. Since α, β and γ are the roots of

$(x-a)(x-b)(x-c) = d$

$\Rightarrow \quad (x-a)(x-b)(x-c) - d = (x-\alpha)(x-\beta)(x-\gamma)$

$\Rightarrow \quad (x-\alpha)(x-\beta)(x-\gamma) + d = (x-a)(x-b)(x-c)$

$\Rightarrow$ a, b and c are the roots of

$(x-\alpha)(x-\beta)(x-\gamma) + d = 0$

30. Since, all the coefficients of given equation are not real.

Therefore, other root $\ne 3 + i$.

Let other root be α.

Then, sum of the roots $= \frac{2(1+i)}{i} \Rightarrow \alpha + 3 - i = \frac{2(1+i)}{i}$

$\Rightarrow \quad \alpha + 3 - i = 2 - 2i$

$\therefore \quad \alpha = -1 - i$

31. We have,

$$\sqrt{2x+\sqrt{2x+4}}=4$$

$\Rightarrow \quad \sqrt{2x+4}=16-2x$

$\Rightarrow \quad 2x+4=4(8-x)^2$

$\Rightarrow \quad 2x^2-33x+126=0$

$\Rightarrow \quad (2x-21)(x-6)=0 \Rightarrow x=6, \frac{21}{2}$

But $x=\frac{21}{2}$ does not satisfy the given equation.

So, $x=6$, hence sum $=6$

32. α, β are roots of equation $x^2+px+m=0$

Then, $2\alpha, 2\beta$ are roots of equation $x^2+mx+n=0$

$\therefore \quad 2(\alpha+\beta)=-m, 4\alpha\beta=n$

and $\quad \alpha+\beta=-p, \alpha\beta=m$

$\therefore \quad 4m=n$ and $2p=m$

So, $\frac{n}{p}=\frac{4m}{(m/2)}=8$

33. For distinct real roots,

$$D>0$$

$\Rightarrow \quad k^2+8(k^2+5)>0$

$\Rightarrow \quad k\in R$

But $\quad f(0)>0$, so $f(2)<0$

$\Rightarrow \quad -8+2k+k^2+5<0$

$\Rightarrow \quad k^2+2k-3<0$

$\Rightarrow \quad (k+3)(k-1)<0$

$\Rightarrow \quad k\in(-3,1)$

$\therefore \quad a=-3, b=1$

So, $a+10b=-3+10=7$

34. We have,

$$(\alpha+\beta)^2=\left(\frac{1}{\alpha}+\frac{1}{\beta}\right)(\alpha^2+\beta^2)$$

$\Rightarrow \quad (\alpha+\beta)^2=\frac{(\alpha+\beta)(\alpha^2+\beta^2)}{\alpha\beta}$

$\Rightarrow \quad (\alpha+\beta)\alpha\beta=(\alpha+\beta)^2-2\alpha\beta$

$\Rightarrow \quad -\frac{b}{a}\times\frac{c}{a}=\frac{b^2}{a^2}-\frac{2c}{a}$

$\Rightarrow \quad -bc=b^2-2ac \Rightarrow b^2+bc-2ac=0$

$\Rightarrow \left(\frac{a+c}{2}\right)^2+\left(\frac{a+c}{2}\right)c-2ac=0$

$\left[a, b, c \text{ are in AP} \Rightarrow b=\frac{a+c}{2}\right]$

$\Rightarrow \quad a^2-4ac+3c^2=0$

$\Rightarrow \quad (a-c)(a-3c)=0$

$\Rightarrow \quad a=c, 3c$

$\Rightarrow \quad a=3c \quad [a\neq c]$

$\Rightarrow \quad \frac{a}{c}=3$

35. We have,

$x^2+ax+12=0 \quad$ ...(i)

$x^2+bx+15=0 \quad$ ...(ii)

$x^2+(a+b)x+36=0 \quad$ ...(iii)

On adding Eqs. (i) and (ii), we get

$2x^2+(a+b)x+27=0 \quad$ ...(iv)

On subtracting Eq. (iii) from Eq. (iv), we get

$$x^2-9=0$$

$\Rightarrow \quad x=\pm 3$

Thus, the common positive root is 3.

$\therefore \quad 9+12+3a=0$ and $9+3b+15=0$

$\Rightarrow \quad a=-7$ and $b=-8$

$\therefore \quad |b-a|=|-8+7|=1$

36. Let $y=\frac{x^2+2x+4}{x+2}$

$\Rightarrow x^2+(2-y)x+2(2-y)=0$

Since, x is real.

$\therefore \quad D\geq 0$

$\Rightarrow \quad (2-y)^2-8(2-y)\geq 0$

$\Rightarrow \quad (2-y)(2-y-8)\geq 0$

$\Rightarrow \quad (2-y)(6+y)\leq 0$

$\Rightarrow \quad (y-2)(y+6)\geq 0$

$\Rightarrow \quad y\leq -6, y\geq 2$

So, least positive value of y is 2.

37. We have,

$\alpha+\beta+\gamma=0, \alpha\beta+\beta\gamma+\gamma\alpha=4, \alpha\beta\gamma=-1$

$\therefore \quad \Sigma(\alpha+\beta)^{-1}=\frac{1}{\alpha+\beta}+\frac{1}{\beta+\gamma}+\frac{1}{\gamma+\alpha}$

$=\frac{1}{-\gamma}+\frac{1}{-\alpha}+\frac{1}{-\beta}$

$=-\left(\frac{\alpha\beta+\beta\gamma+\gamma\alpha}{\alpha\beta\gamma}\right)$

$=-\left(\frac{4}{-1}\right)$

$=4$

38. We have, $4\operatorname{cosec}^2\pi(a+x)+a^2-4a=0$

$\Rightarrow \quad 4a-a^2=4\operatorname{cosec}^2\pi(a+x)$

$\Rightarrow \quad 4a-a^2\geq 4 \quad [\because 4\operatorname{cosec}^2\pi(a+x)\geq 4]$

$\Rightarrow \quad a^2-4a+4\leq 0$

$\Rightarrow \quad (a-2)^2\leq 0 \Rightarrow a=2$

39. We have,

$$|[x]-2x|=4$$

If $x\in Z$, then $|x-2x|=4$

$\Rightarrow \quad |x|=4$

$\Rightarrow \quad x=\pm 4$

If $x \notin Z$, then $x = n + \lambda$, $n \in Z$ and $0 < \lambda < 1$

$\therefore \quad |[x] - 2x| = 4$

$\Rightarrow \quad |n - 2(n + \lambda)| = 4$

$\Rightarrow \quad n + 2\lambda = \pm 4$

$\Rightarrow \quad n = \pm 4 - 2\lambda$

This is only possible, when $\lambda = \frac{1}{2}$

$\therefore \quad n = \pm 4 - 1$

$\Rightarrow \quad n = 3, -5$

$\Rightarrow \quad x = 3 + \frac{1}{2}, -5 + \frac{1}{2}$

$\Rightarrow \quad x = \frac{7}{2}, -\frac{9}{2}$

40. We have, $\sqrt{x+5} + \sqrt{x+21} = \sqrt{6x+40}$

$\Rightarrow x + 5 + x + 21 + 2\sqrt{(x+5)(x+21)} = 6x + 40$

$\Rightarrow \quad \sqrt{(x+5)(x+21)} = 2x + 7$

$\Rightarrow \quad (x+5)(x+21) = (2x+7)^2$

$\Rightarrow \quad 3x^2 + 2x - 56 = 0$

$\Rightarrow \quad (3x + 14)(x - 4) = 0$

$\Rightarrow \quad x = \frac{-14}{3}, 4$

But $x = \frac{-14}{3}$ does not satisfy the original equation.

$\therefore \quad x = 4$

So, required sum is 4.

41. The given equation is $|x-2|^2 + |x-2| - 2 = 0$.

There are two cases:

***Case* I** If $x \geq 2$, then $(x-2)^2 + x - 2 - 2 = 0$

$\Rightarrow \quad x^2 - 3x = 0$

$\Rightarrow \quad x(x-3) = 0 \Rightarrow x = 0, 3$

Here, 0 is not possible.

$\therefore \quad x = 3$

***Case* II** If $x < 2$, then

$(x-2)^2 - x + 2 - 2 = 0$

$\Rightarrow \quad x^2 - 5x + 4 = 0$

$\Rightarrow \quad (x-1)(x-4) = 0$

$\Rightarrow \quad x = 1, 4$

Here, 4 is not possible.

$\therefore \quad x = 1$

$\therefore$ The sum of roots $= 1 + 3 = 4$

Alternate Solution

Let $|x - 2| = y$.

Then, we get $\quad y^2 + y - 2 = 0$

$\Rightarrow \quad (y-1)(y+2) = 0$

$\Rightarrow \quad y = 1, -2$

But -2 is not possible.

Hence, $\quad |x - 2| = 1$

$\Rightarrow \quad x = 1, 3$

$\therefore$ Sum of the roots $= 1 + 3 = 4$

42. We have, $(5 + \sqrt{2})x^2 - (4 + \sqrt{5})x + 8 + 2\sqrt{5} = 0$

$\therefore$ Sum of the roots $= \frac{4 + \sqrt{5}}{5 + \sqrt{2}}$

and product of the roots $= \frac{8 + 2\sqrt{5}}{5 + \sqrt{2}}$

$\therefore$ The harmonic mean of the roots

$$= \frac{2 \times \text{Product of the roots}}{\text{Sum of the roots}} = \frac{2 \times (8 + 2\sqrt{5})}{(4 + \sqrt{5})} = 4$$

43. Let $x^2 - ax + 30 = y$

$\therefore \quad y = 2\sqrt{y + 15} \quad$ ...(i)

$\Rightarrow \quad y^2 - 4y - 60 = 0 \Rightarrow (y - 10)(y + 6) = 0$

$\therefore \quad y = 10, -6$

$\Rightarrow \quad y = 10, y \neq -6 \quad [\because y > 0]$

Now, $\quad x^2 - ax + 30 = 10$

$\Rightarrow \quad x^2 - ax + 20 = 0$

Given, $\quad \alpha\beta = \lambda = 20$

$\therefore \quad \frac{\alpha + \beta}{2} \geq \sqrt{\alpha\beta} = \sqrt{20}$

$\Rightarrow \quad \alpha + \beta \geq 2\sqrt{20}$ or $\mu = 4\sqrt{5}$

$\therefore$ Minimum value of μ is $4\sqrt{5}$.

i.e. $\quad \mu = 4\sqrt{5} = 8.9 \Rightarrow (\mu) = 9$

44. $\because N^r = \left(x + \frac{1}{x}\right)^6 - \left(x^6 + \frac{1}{x^6}\right) - 2$

$$= \left(x + \frac{1}{x}\right)^6 - \left(x^3 + \frac{1}{x^3}\right)^2 = \left(\left(x + \frac{1}{x}\right)^3 + \left(x^3 + \frac{1}{x^3}\right)\right)$$
$$\left(\left(x + \frac{1}{x}\right)^3 - \left(x^3 + \frac{1}{x^3}\right)\right)$$

$$= D^r \cdot \left(3\left(x + \frac{1}{x}\right)\right)$$

$\therefore \quad \frac{N^r}{D^r} = 3\left(x + \frac{1}{x}\right) \geq 6$

Hence, minimum value of $\frac{N^r}{D^r}$ is 6.

45. $\quad a + b = 2c \quad$ ...(i)

$ab = -5d \quad$ ...(ii)

$c + d = 2a \quad$ ...(iii)

$cd = -5b \quad$ ...(iv)

From Eqs. (i) and (iii), we get

$a + b + c + d = 2(a + c)$

$\therefore \quad a + c = b + d \quad$ ...(v)

From Eqs. (i) and (iii), we get

$b - d = 3(c - a) \quad$ ...(vi)

Also, a is a root of $\quad x^2 - 2cx - 5d = 0$

$\therefore \quad a^2 - 2ac - 5d = 0 \quad$ ...(vii)

And c is a root of $\quad c^2 - 2ac - 5b = 0 \quad$ ...(viii)

From Eqs. (vii) and (viii), we get

$$a^2 - c^2 - 5(d-b) = 0$$

$\Rightarrow \quad (a+c)(a-c) + 5(b-d) = 0$

$\Rightarrow \quad (a+c)(a-c) + 15(c-a) = 0 \quad$ [from Eq. (vi)]

$\Rightarrow \quad (a-c)(a+c-15) = 0$

$\therefore \quad a + c = 15, a - c \neq 0$

From Eq. (v), we get $b + d = 15$

$\therefore \quad a+b+c+d = a+c+b+d = 15+15 = 30$

$\Rightarrow$ Sum of digits of $a+b+c+d = 3+0 = 3$

46. Given 2 and 6 are the roots of the equation $ax^2 + bx + 1 = 0$

$\therefore$ Sum of roots $= -\dfrac{b}{a} = 8$

Product of roots $= \dfrac{1}{a} = 12$

$\Rightarrow \quad a = \dfrac{1}{12}$ so, $b = -\dfrac{2}{3}$

Now, $2a + b = \dfrac{2}{12} - \dfrac{2}{3} = -\dfrac{1}{2}$ and $6a + b = \dfrac{6}{12} - \dfrac{2}{3} = -\dfrac{1}{6}$

Now, $\dfrac{1}{2a+b} + \dfrac{1}{6a+b} = -2-6 = -8$ and $\left(\dfrac{1}{2a+b}\right)\left(\dfrac{1}{6a+b}\right) = 12$

$\therefore$ Required quadratic equation is

$$x^2 + 8x + 12 = 0$$

47. Given, $(\sqrt{3}+\sqrt{2})^x + (\sqrt{3}-\sqrt{2})^x = 10$

Let $(\sqrt{3}+\sqrt{2})^x = t \Rightarrow (\sqrt{3}-\sqrt{2})^x = \dfrac{1}{t}$

$$t + \frac{1}{t} = 10$$

$$t^2 - 10t + 1 = 0$$

$$t = \frac{10 \pm \sqrt{96}}{2} = 5 \pm 2\sqrt{6}$$

$$(\sqrt{3}+\sqrt{2})^x = (\sqrt{3} \pm \sqrt{2})^2$$

$$x = \pm 2$$

$\therefore$ Number of solution $= 2$

48. $\dfrac{ax^2 + 2(a+1)x + 9a + 4}{x^2 - 8x + 32} < 0, \forall x \in R$

$\Rightarrow \quad \dfrac{ax^2 + 2(a+1)x + 9a + 4}{(x-4)^2 + 16} < 0, \forall x \in R$

$\Rightarrow \quad ax^2 + 2(a+1)x + 9a + 4 < 0, \forall x \in R$

coefficient of $x^2 < 0$ and $D < 0$

$$a < 0 \text{ and } D < 0$$

$\therefore$ No positive integral values of a.

Hence, $|S| = 0$

49. **Decoding the Question**

First use $\alpha^4 + \beta^4 = (\alpha^2 + \beta^2)^2 - 2\alpha^2\beta^2$
$= ((\alpha+\beta)^2 - 2\alpha\beta)^2 - 2\alpha^2\beta^2$

and then $\alpha^6 + \beta^6 = (\alpha^3 + \beta^3)^2 - 2\alpha^3\beta^3$
$= (\alpha+\beta)[(\alpha+\beta)^2 - 3\alpha\beta]^2 - 2(\alpha\beta)^3$

Given α and β are the roots of the given quadratic equation.

$$x^2 + 2\sqrt{2}x - 1 = 0$$

$$\alpha + \beta = -2\sqrt{2}, \alpha\beta = -1$$

Now, $\alpha^4 + \beta^4 = (\alpha^2 + \beta^2)^2 - 2\alpha^2\beta^2$

$= \{(\alpha+\beta)^2 - 2\alpha\beta\}^2 - 2(\alpha\beta)^2$

$= (8+2)^2 - 2(-1)^2 = 100 - 2 = 98$

and $\alpha^6 + \beta^6 = (\alpha^3 + \beta^3)^2 - 2\alpha^3\beta^3$

$= [(\alpha+\beta)\{(\alpha+\beta)^2 - 3\alpha\beta\}^2] - 2(\alpha\beta)^3$

$= [(-2\sqrt{2})(8+3)]^2 - 2(-1)^3 = (8)(121) + 2 = 970$

$\therefore \quad \dfrac{\alpha^6 + \beta^6}{10} = 97$

Hence, required quadratic equation is

$$x^2 - (98+97)x + (98)(97) = 0$$

$\Rightarrow \quad x^2 - 195x + 9506 = 0$

50. **Decoding the Question**

Here, we use Newton's formula i.e. if $ax^2 + bx + c = 0$ be any quadratic eqation and α, β be its roots, then

$\therefore \quad aS_n + bS_{n-1} + cS_{n-2} = 0$

where $\quad S_n = \alpha^n \pm \beta^n; n \in N$

By using Newton's formula in given quadratic equation

$\Rightarrow x^2 - (t^2 - 5t + 6)x + 1 = 0$ can be expressed as

$\Rightarrow \quad a_{2025} - (t^2 - 5t + 6)a_{2024} + a_{2023} = 0$

On rearranging

$\Rightarrow \quad \dfrac{a_{2025} + a_{2023}}{a_{2024}} = t^2 - 5t + 6$

$\Rightarrow \quad \dfrac{a_{2025} + a_{2023}}{a_{2024}} = t^2 - 5t + \dfrac{25}{4} - \dfrac{25}{4} + 6$

$\Rightarrow \quad \dfrac{a_{2025} + a_{2023}}{a_{2024}} = \left(t - \dfrac{5}{2}\right)^2 - \dfrac{1}{4}$

Minimum value of any square is 0

$\therefore$ Minimum value of $\dfrac{a_{2025} + a_{2023}}{a_{2024}} = 0 - \dfrac{1}{4} = -\dfrac{1}{4}$

51. We have, $px^2 + qx - r = 0$

Given that, p, q and r be the consecutive terms of a non-constant GP, then let

$$p = \frac{a}{r_1}, q = a, r = ar_1$$

and given, $\dfrac{1}{\alpha} + \dfrac{1}{\beta} = \dfrac{3}{4}$

$\Rightarrow \quad \dfrac{\alpha+\beta}{\alpha\beta} = \dfrac{3}{4} \Rightarrow \dfrac{-\dfrac{q}{p}}{-\dfrac{r}{p}} = \dfrac{3}{4}$

$\Rightarrow \quad \dfrac{q}{r} = \dfrac{3}{4} \Rightarrow \dfrac{1}{r_1} = \dfrac{3}{4} \Rightarrow r_1 = \dfrac{4}{3} \quad$ ...(i)

Now, $(\alpha-\beta)^2=(\alpha+\beta)^2-4\alpha\beta$

$$=\left(\frac{-q}{p}\right)^2-4\left(\frac{-r}{p}\right)=(r_1)^2+4(r_1^2)=5r_1^2$$

$$=5\left(\frac{4}{3}\right)^2 \quad \text{[from Eq. (i)]}$$

$$=\frac{80}{9}$$

Alternate Solution

$\because$ p, q, r in GP.

$\therefore$ $q^2=pr$

$\because$ $\frac{1}{\alpha}+\frac{1}{\beta}=\frac{3}{4}$

$\Rightarrow$ $\frac{\alpha+\beta}{\alpha\beta}=\frac{3}{4}$

$\therefore$ $\frac{q}{r}=\frac{3}{4}$

Now, $|\alpha-\beta|=\frac{\sqrt{q^2+4pr}}{|p|}$

$$(\alpha-\beta)^2=\frac{q^2+4pr}{p^2}$$

$$=\frac{5q^2}{p^2}=\frac{5q^2r^2}{q^4}=\frac{5r^2}{q^2}=5\times\frac{16}{9}=\frac{80}{9}$$

52. $|x+1||x+3|-4|x+2|+5=0$

Case I $x\le -3$

$(x+1)(x+3)+4(x+2)+5=0$

$\Rightarrow$ $x^2+4x+3+4x+13=0$

$\Rightarrow$ $x^2+8x+16=0$

$\Rightarrow$ $(x+4)^2=0 \Rightarrow x=-4$

Case II $-3\le x\le -2$

$-x^2-4x-3+4x+8+5=0$

$\Rightarrow$ $-x^2+10=0 \Rightarrow x=\pm\sqrt{10}$

Case III $-2\le x\le -1$

$-x^2-4x-3-4x-8+5=0$

$\Rightarrow$ $-x^2-8x-6=0$

$\Rightarrow$ $x=-4\pm\sqrt{10}$

Case IV $x\ge -1$

$x^2+4x+3-4x-8+5=0$

$\Rightarrow$ $x^2=0\Rightarrow x=0$

Hence, number of solutions $=2$

53. $4x^4+8x^3-17x^2-12x+9$

$$=4(x-x_1)(x-x_2)(x-x_3)(x-x_4)$$

Now, lets substitute $x=2i$ in above equation

$\Rightarrow 64-64i+68-24i+9=4(2i-x_1)(2i-x_2)(2i-x_3)(2i-x_4)$

$\Rightarrow$ $141-88i=4(2i-x_1)(2i-x_2)(2i-x_3)(2i-x_4)$ ...(i)

On putting $x=-2i$, we get

$141+88i=4(-2i-x_1)(-2i-x_2)(-2i-x_3)(-2i-x_4)$ ...(ii)

On multiple Eq. (i) by Eq. (ii), we get

$(141)^2+(88)^2=16(4+x_1^2)(4+x_2^2)(4+x_3^2)(4+x_4^2)$

$\Rightarrow (4+x_1^2)(4+x_2^2)(4+x_3^2)(4+x_4^2)=\frac{27625}{16}$

According to the question,

$$\frac{27625}{16}=\frac{125}{16}m \Rightarrow m=221$$

54. $x|x+5|+2|x+7|-2=0$

Case I $x\le -7$

We get $-x^2-5x-2x-14-2=0 \Rightarrow x^2+7x+16=0$

$D=49-64<0$

No real roots

Case II $-7<x<-5$

$-x^2-5x+2x+14-2=0$

$-x^2-3x+12=0$

$$x=\frac{-3\pm\sqrt{57}}{2}$$

$+$: $\frac{-3+\sqrt{57}}{2}$ $\qquad$ $-$: $\frac{-3-\sqrt{57}}{2}$

Rejected

Case III $x\ge -5$

$x^2+7x+12=0$

$x=-3,-4$

Number of real solution $=3$

55. Since, α satisfies the equation $x^2+x+1=0$.

So, $\alpha=\omega,\omega^2$ [which are roots of $x^2+x+1=0$]

Let $\alpha=\omega$.

Then, $(1+\alpha)^7=-\omega^{14}=-\omega^2=1+\omega$

$=A+B\alpha+C\alpha^2=A+B\omega+C\omega^2$

So, $A=1, B=1$ and $C=0$

$\therefore$ $5(3A-2B-C)=5(3-2-0)=5$

56. Let $f(x)=x|x-1|+|x+2|+\alpha$

$\therefore$ $f(x)=0$

$\Rightarrow$ $x|x-1|+|x+2|+\alpha=0$

$\Rightarrow$ $x|x-1|+|x+2|=-\alpha$

Now, $x|x-1|+|x+2|=\begin{cases}x^2+2 & x\ge 1\\ -x^2+2x+2 & -2\le x<1\\ -x^2-2 & x<-2\end{cases}$

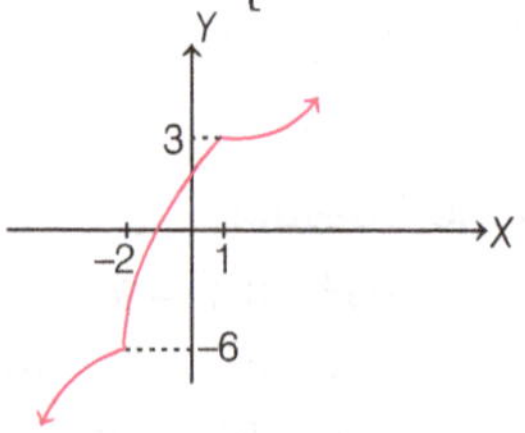

Thus, $-\alpha\in IR$

Hence, the set of all $\alpha\in R$ for which the eqution $x|x-1|+|x+2|+a=0$ has exactly one real root is $(-\infty,\infty)$.

57. Given equation involving GIF is

$$x^2 - 4x + [x] + 3 = x[x]$$

$$\Rightarrow \quad x^2 - 4x + 3 = x[x] - [x]$$

$$\Rightarrow \quad (x-1)(x-3) = [x](x-1)$$

$$\Rightarrow \quad (x-1)\{(x-3) - [x]\} = 0$$

$$\Rightarrow \quad (x-1) = 0 \text{ or } (x-3) = [x]$$

$$\Rightarrow \quad x = 1 \text{ or } x - 3 = [x] \Rightarrow x - [x] = 3$$

$\Rightarrow \{x\} = 3$, where $\{\cdot\}$ represents fractional part function.

As we know that $0 \le \{x\} < 1$

So, $\{x\} = 3$ is not possible.

So, only one solution $x = 1$ in $(-\infty, \infty)$.

58. Given equation is

$$3\left(x^2 + \frac{1}{x^2}\right) - 2\left(x + \frac{1}{x}\right) + 5 = 0$$

$$3\left\{\left(x + \frac{1}{x}\right)^2 - 2\right\} - 2\left(x + \frac{1}{x}\right) + 5 = 0$$

Let $x + \frac{1}{x} = t$;

$\therefore 3(t^2 - 2) - 2t + 5 = 0 \Rightarrow 3t^2 - 6 - 2t + 5 = 0$

$$\Rightarrow \quad 3t^2 - 2t - 1 = 0 \Rightarrow (3t+1)(t-1) = 0$$

$$\therefore \quad t = 1, -\frac{1}{3}$$

$$\therefore \quad x + \frac{1}{x} = 1, \; x + \frac{1}{x} = \frac{-1}{3}$$

$$x^2 - x + 1 = 0; \; x^2 + 1 = -\frac{x}{3} \Rightarrow 3x^2 + 3 + x = 0$$

$\because \quad D = b^2 - 4ac$

$\therefore D_1 = (-1)^2 - 4 \times 1 \times 1, = 1 - 4 = -3 < 0$

and $D_2 = 1^2 - 4 \times 3 \times 3 = 1 - 36 = -35 < 0$

No real solution.

Hence, there will not be any real solution.

59. Given equation is

$$x^2 - \sqrt{2}x + 2 = 0 \qquad \text{...(i)}$$

Apply the quadratic formula,

$$x = \frac{\sqrt{2} \pm \sqrt{2-8}}{2} = \frac{\sqrt{2} \pm \sqrt{6}i}{2}$$

Since, α, β are roots of Eq. (i), we get

$$\alpha = \frac{\sqrt{2} + \sqrt{6}i}{2}, \beta = \frac{\sqrt{2} - \sqrt{6}i}{2}$$

$$\Rightarrow \quad \alpha = \sqrt{2}\, e^{i\pi/3} \Rightarrow \beta = \sqrt{2}e^{-i\frac{\pi}{3}}$$

$$[\because e^{i\theta} = \cos\theta + i\sin\theta]$$

Now, $\alpha^{14} = (\sqrt{2})^{14}\, e^{\frac{14\pi}{3}i} = 2^7 \cdot e^{\frac{2\pi i}{3}} = 128\left\{\cos\frac{2\pi}{3} + i\sin\frac{2\pi}{3}\right\}$

Similarly, $\beta^{14} = 128\left\{\cos\frac{2\pi}{3} - i\sin\frac{2\pi}{3}\right\}$

$$\therefore \quad \alpha^{14} + \beta^{14} = 2 \times 128 \times \cos\frac{2\pi}{3} = 2 \times 128 \times \left(-\frac{1}{2}\right) = -128$$

60. $x^2 + \sqrt{6}x + 3 = 0$

$$\Rightarrow \quad x = \frac{-\sqrt{6} \pm \sqrt{6 - 4\cdot 3}}{2} = \frac{-\sqrt{6} \pm \sqrt{-6}}{2} = \frac{-\sqrt{6} \pm \sqrt{6}i}{2}$$

$$= \frac{\sqrt{6}}{2}(-1 \pm i) = \sqrt{3}\left(\frac{-1}{\sqrt{2}} \pm \frac{i}{\sqrt{2}}\right)$$

Let $\alpha = \sqrt{3}\left(-\frac{1}{\sqrt{2}} + \frac{i}{\sqrt{2}}\right), \beta = \sqrt{3}\left(-\frac{1}{\sqrt{2}} - \frac{i}{\sqrt{2}}\right)$

$$\Rightarrow \quad \alpha = \sqrt{3}\left(\cos\left(\frac{3\pi}{4}\right) + i\sin\left(\frac{3\pi}{4}\right)\right),$$

$$\beta = \sqrt{3}\left(\cos\left(\frac{5\pi}{4}\right) + i\sin\left(\frac{5\pi}{4}\right)\right)$$

$$\Rightarrow \quad \alpha = \sqrt{3}\, e^{i\left(\frac{3\pi}{4}\right)}, \beta = \sqrt{3}e^{i\left(\frac{5\pi}{4}\right)}$$

$$\Rightarrow \quad \alpha^4 = (\sqrt{3})^4\, e^{i(3\pi)} = 9(\cos(3\pi) + i\sin(3\pi)) = -9$$

and $\beta^4 = (\sqrt{3})^4\, e^{i(5\pi)} = 9(\cos(5\pi) + i\sin(5\pi)) = -9$

$$\therefore \frac{\alpha^{23} + \beta^{23} + \alpha^{14} + \beta^{14}}{\alpha^{15} + \beta^{15} + \alpha^{10} + \beta^{10}} = \frac{(\alpha^4)^5 \cdot \alpha^3 + (\beta^4)^5 \cdot \beta^3 + (\alpha^4)^3 \cdot \alpha^2 + (\beta^4)^3 \cdot \beta^2}{(\alpha^4)^3 \cdot \alpha^3 + (\beta^4)^3 \cdot \beta^3 + (\alpha^4)^2 \cdot \alpha^2 + (\beta^4)^2 \cdot \beta^2}$$

$$= \frac{(-9)^5(\alpha^3 + \beta^3) + (-9)^3(\alpha^2 + \beta^2)}{(-9)^3(\alpha^3 + \beta^3) + (-9)^2(\alpha^2 + \beta^2)} \qquad \text{...(i)}$$

Now, $\alpha + \beta = -\sqrt{6}, \alpha\beta = 3$

$$\Rightarrow \quad \alpha^2 + \beta^2 = (\alpha + \beta)^2 - 2\alpha\beta$$

$$= (-\sqrt{6})^2 - 2 \cdot 3 = 0$$

$\therefore$ Eq. (i) becomes $= \dfrac{(-9)^5(\alpha^3 + \beta^3)}{(-9)^3(\alpha^3 + \beta^3)} = (-9)^2 = 81$

61. We have, $(\sqrt{3} + \sqrt{2})^{x^2 - 4} + (\sqrt{3} - \sqrt{2})^{x^2 - 4} = 10$

Let $(\sqrt{3} + \sqrt{2})^{x^2 - 4} = y$, then $(\sqrt{3} - \sqrt{2})^{x^2 - 4}$

$$= \left[\frac{(\sqrt{3} - \sqrt{2})(\sqrt{3} + \sqrt{2})}{(\sqrt{3} + \sqrt{2})}\right]^{x^2 - 4}$$

$$= \left[\frac{3 - 2}{\sqrt{3} + \sqrt{2}}\right]^{x^2 - 4} = \frac{1}{(\sqrt{3} + \sqrt{2})^{x^2 - 4}} = \frac{1}{y}$$

$$\therefore \quad y + \frac{1}{y} = 10 \Rightarrow y^2 - 10y + 1 = 0$$

$$\Rightarrow \quad y = \frac{10 \pm \sqrt{100 - 4}}{2}$$

$$= \frac{10 \pm 4\sqrt{6}}{2} = 5 \pm 2\sqrt{6}$$

Now, $y = 5 + 2\sqrt{6}$

$$\Rightarrow (\sqrt{3} + \sqrt{2})^{x^2 - 4} = 5 + 2\sqrt{6}$$

$$\Rightarrow (\sqrt{3} + \sqrt{2})^{x^2 - 4} = (\sqrt{3} + \sqrt{2})^2$$

$$\Rightarrow \quad x^2 - 4 = 2$$

$$\Rightarrow \quad x = \pm\sqrt{6}$$

Again, $y = 5 - 2\sqrt{6}$

$\Rightarrow (\sqrt{3} + \sqrt{2})^{x^2 - 4} = 5 - 2\sqrt{6}$

$\Rightarrow (\sqrt{3} + \sqrt{2})^{x^2 - 4} = (\sqrt{3} - \sqrt{2})^2$

$\Rightarrow (\sqrt{3} + \sqrt{2})^{x^2 - 4} = (\sqrt{3} + \sqrt{2})^{-2}$

$\Rightarrow \quad x^2 - 4 = -2 \Rightarrow x = \pm\sqrt{2}$

$\therefore S = \{-\sqrt{6}, -\sqrt{2}, \sqrt{2}, \sqrt{6}\}$

So, $n(S) = 4$

62. We have, a and b are the roots of the equation

$$x^2 - 7x - 1 = 0$$

$$\Rightarrow \quad a^2 - 7a - 1 = 0$$

$$\Rightarrow \quad a^2 - 1 = 7a \quad \text{...(i)}$$

On squaring both sides, we get

$$a^4 + 1 = 51a^2$$

Similarly, $b^4 + 1 = 51b^2$ ...(ii)

Now, $\dfrac{a^{21} + b^{21} + a^{17} + b^{17}}{a^{19} + b^{19}}$

$$= \frac{a^{17}(a^4 + 1) + b^{17}(b^4 + 1)}{a^{19} + b^{19}}$$

$$= \frac{a^{17}(51a^2) + b^{17}(51b^2)}{a^{19} + b^{19}} \quad [\because \text{from Eqs. (i) and (ii)}]$$

$$= \frac{51[a^{19} + b^{19}]}{a^{19} + b^{19}} = 51$$

63. Given, $a \in R$, and α, β are root's of $x^2 + 60^{1/4}x + a = 0$

Sum of roots $= \alpha + \beta = -(60)^{1/4}$

Product of root's $= \alpha\beta = a$

And $\quad \alpha^4 + \beta^4 = -30$

So, $(\alpha^2 + \beta^2)^2 - 2\alpha^2\beta^2 = -30$

Now, $[(\alpha + \beta)^2 - 2\alpha\beta]^2 - 2(\alpha\beta)^2 = -30$

$\Rightarrow \quad [\{-(60)^{1/4}\}^2 - 2(a)]^2 - 2(a)^2 = -30$

$\Rightarrow \quad [\sqrt{60} - 2a]^2 - 2a^2 = -30$

$\Rightarrow \quad 60 + 4a^2 - 4a\sqrt{60} - 2a^2 = -30$

$\Rightarrow \quad 2a^2 - 4a\sqrt{60} + 90 = 0$

Or $\quad a^2 - 2a\sqrt{60} + 45 = 0$

It's a quadratic equation, so we will get 2 values of a or 2 roots of the equation.

So, product of root's $= \dfrac{45}{1} = 45$

64. Given that $x^7 - 7x - 2 = 0$

Let $f(x) = x^7 - 7x - 2$

On differentiating w.r.t. x, we get

$$f'(x) = 7x^6 - 7 = 7(x^6 - 1)$$

Now, $f'(x) = 0$

$\Rightarrow 7(x^6 - 1) = 0$

$\Rightarrow \quad x = \pm 1$

Now, $f(-1) = -1 + 7 - 2 = 4 > 0$ and $f(1) = 1 - 7 - 2 = -8 < 0$

So, roughly sketch of $f(x)$ will be

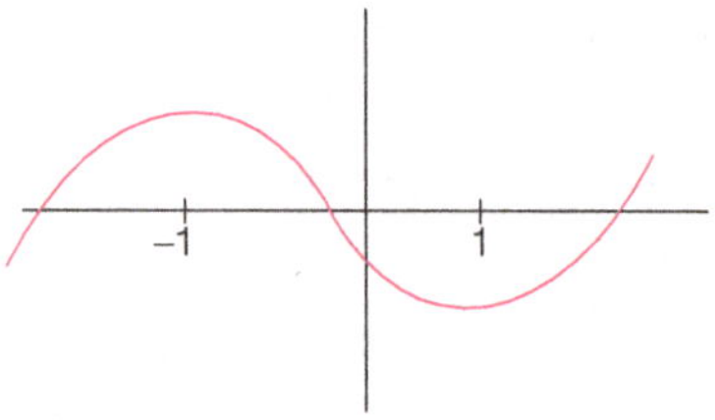

So, the number of real roots of $f(x) = 0$ is 3.

65. Given that $(e^{2x} - 4)(6e^{2x} - 5e^x + 1) = 0$

Let $e^x = p$

Thus, $\quad (p^2 - 4)(6p^2 - 5p + 1) = 0$

$\Rightarrow (p + 2)(p - 2)(2p - 1)(3p - 1) = 0 \Rightarrow p = -2, 2, 1/2, 1/3$

$\therefore \quad e^x = -2$	$e^x = 2$	$e^x = \dfrac{1}{2}$	$e^x = \dfrac{1}{3}$
This is not possible to take.	$\Rightarrow x = \log_e 2$	$\Rightarrow x = -\log_e 2$	$\Rightarrow x = -\log_e 3$

Thus, all the real roots of the above equation are

$$\log_e 2, -\log_e 2, -\log_e 3$$

Sum of these real roots $= \log_e 2 - \log_e 2 - \log_e 3 = -\log_e 3$

66. Given, α and β are the roots of the equation

$$x^2 - \sqrt{2}x + \sqrt{6} = 0$$

$$\alpha + \beta = \sqrt{2} \text{ and } \alpha\beta = \sqrt{6}$$

Now, $\dfrac{1}{\alpha^2} + 1 + \dfrac{1}{\beta^2} + 1 = \dfrac{\alpha^2 + \beta^2}{(\alpha\beta)^2} + 2$

$$= \frac{(\alpha + \beta)^2 - 2\alpha\beta}{(\alpha\beta)^2} + 2$$

$$= \frac{2 - 2\sqrt{6}}{6} + 2 = \frac{14 - 2\sqrt{6}}{6}$$

$\therefore \left(\dfrac{1}{\alpha^2} + 1\right)\left(\dfrac{1}{\beta^2} + 1\right) = \dfrac{1}{(\alpha\beta)^2} + \dfrac{\alpha^2 + \beta^2}{(\alpha\beta)^2} + 1$

$$= \frac{1}{6} + \frac{2 - 2\sqrt{6}}{6} + 1 = \frac{9 - 2\sqrt{6}}{6}$$

The equation whose roots are $\left(\dfrac{1}{\alpha^2} + 1, \dfrac{1}{\beta^2} + 1\right)$ is

$$x^2 - \left(\frac{14 - 2\sqrt{6}}{6}\right)x + \frac{9 - 2\sqrt{6}}{6} = 0$$

Here, $a = \dfrac{2\sqrt{6} - 14}{6}, b = \dfrac{9 - 2\sqrt{6}}{6}$

$$a + b = \frac{2\sqrt{6} - 14 + 9 - 2\sqrt{6}}{6} = -\frac{5}{6}$$

$\therefore x^2 - (a + b - 2)x + (a + b + 2) = 0$

$\Rightarrow x^2 - \left(-\dfrac{5}{6} - 2\right)x + \left(-\dfrac{5}{6} + 2\right) = 0 \Rightarrow x^2 + \dfrac{17}{6}x + \dfrac{7}{6} = 0$

$\Rightarrow \quad 6x^2 + 17x + 7 = 0 \Rightarrow x = -\dfrac{1}{2}, -\dfrac{7}{3}$

$\therefore$ Both roots are real and negative.

67. Given, α and β are roots of the equation $x^2 - x - 4 = 0$ and $\alpha > \beta$.

$$\alpha^2 - \alpha = 4 \text{ and } \beta^2 - \beta = 4$$

$$P_n = \alpha^n - \beta^n, n \in N$$

Then, $\dfrac{P_{15}P_{16} - P_{14}P_{16} - P_{15}^2 + P_{14}P_{15}}{P_{13}P_{14}}$

$$= \frac{P_{15}P_{16} - P_{15}^2 - P_{14}P_{16} + P_{14}P_{15}}{P_{13}P_{14}}$$

$$= \frac{P_{15}(P_{16} - P_{15}) - P_{14}(P_{16} - P_{15})}{P_{13}P_{14}}$$

$$= \frac{(P_{16} - P_{15})(P_{15} - P_{14})}{P_{13}P_{14}}$$

$$= \frac{[(\alpha^{16} - \beta^{16}) - (\alpha^{15} - \beta^{15})][(\alpha^{15} - \beta^{15}) - (\alpha^{14} - \beta^{14})]}{(\alpha^{13} - \beta^{13})(\alpha^{14} - \beta^{14})}$$

$$= \frac{[\alpha^{14}(\alpha^2 - \alpha) - \beta^{14}(\beta^2 - \beta)][\alpha^{13}(\alpha^2 - \alpha) - \beta^{13}(\beta^2 - \beta)]}{(\alpha^{13} - \beta^{13})(\alpha^{14} - \beta^{14})}$$

$$= \frac{4(\alpha^{14} - \beta^{14}) \cdot 4(\alpha^{13} - \beta^{13})}{(\alpha^{13} - \beta^{13})(\alpha^{14} - \beta^{14})} = 16$$

68.

> **Decoding the Question**
>
> Let $ax^2 + bx + c = 0$ and $dx^2 + ex + f = 0$ have a common roots α (say). Then, $a\alpha^2 + b\alpha + c = 0$ and $d\alpha^2 + e\alpha + f = 0$

Given, the equations $(p^2 + q^2)x^2 - 2q(p + r)x + q^2 + r^2 = 0$ and $x^2 + 2x - 8 = 0$ has a common root.

$$x^2 + 2x - 8 = 0$$

$\Rightarrow$ $x^2 + 4x - 2x - 8 = 0 \Rightarrow x = -4, 2$

Now, $(p^2 + q^2)x^2 - 2pqx - 2qrx + q^2 + r^2 = 0$

$\Rightarrow (p^2x^2 - 2pqx + q^2) + (q^2x^2 - 2qrx + r^2) = 0$

$\Rightarrow$ $(px - q)^2 + (qx - r)^2 = 0$

$\Rightarrow$ $px - q = 0$ and $qx - r = 0$

$\Rightarrow$ $x = \dfrac{q}{p}$ and $x = \dfrac{r}{q}$

As p, q and r are not all having same sign,

$$x \neq 2, x = \frac{q}{p} = \frac{r}{q} = -4,$$

$$q = -4p \text{ and } r = -4q$$

Also, $r = -4(-4p) = 16p$

Now, $\dfrac{q^2 + r^2}{p^2} = \dfrac{16p^2 + 256p^2}{p^2} = \dfrac{272p^2}{p^2} = 272$

69. $[e^x]^2 + [e^x + 1] - 3 = 0 \Rightarrow [e^x]^2 + [e^x] + 1 - 3 = 0$

$\Rightarrow$ $[e^x]^2 + [e^x] - 2 = 0 \Rightarrow ([e^x] - 1)([e^x] + 2) = 0$

$$[e^x] = 1 \text{ or } [e^x] = -2$$

$[e^x] = -2$ is not possible as $e^x > 0$.

$\Rightarrow$ $[e^x] = 1$

$\Rightarrow$ $1 \le e^x < 2$

$\Rightarrow$ $0 \le x < \log_e 2$

70. Let $x = 3 + \cfrac{1}{4 + \cfrac{1}{3 + \cfrac{1}{4 + \cfrac{1}{3 + \dots \infty}}}}$

So, $x = 3 + \cfrac{1}{4 + \cfrac{1}{x}} = 3 + \cfrac{1}{\cfrac{4x + 1}{x}} = 3 + \dfrac{x}{4x + 1}$

$\Rightarrow$ $(x - 3) = \dfrac{x}{4x + 1}$

$\Rightarrow$ $4x^2 - 12x - 3 = 0 \Rightarrow x = \dfrac{3 \pm 2\sqrt{3}}{2}$

$\Rightarrow$ $x = \dfrac{3}{2} \pm \sqrt{3} = 1.5 \pm \sqrt{3}$

But from above, $x > 0$.

$\therefore$ Only positive value of x is accepted.

$\therefore$ $x = 1.5 + \sqrt{3}$

71. Given, p, q are positive numbers.

$$p + q = 2 \quad \text{...(i)}$$

$$p^4 + q^4 = 272$$

$\Rightarrow$ $(p^2 + q^2)^2 - 2p^2q^2 = 272$

$\Rightarrow$ $[(p + q)^2 - 2pq]^2 - 2p^2q^2 = 272$

$\Rightarrow$ $[(2)^2 - 2pq]^2 - 2p^2q^2 = 272$ [from Eq. (i)]

$\Rightarrow$ $(4 - 2pq)^2 - 2p^2q^2 = 272$

$\Rightarrow$ $16 + 4p^2q^2 - 16pq - 2p^2q^2 = 272$

$\Rightarrow$ $2p^2q^2 - 16pq - 256 = 0$

$\Rightarrow$ $p^2q^2 - 8pq - 128 = 0$

$\therefore$ $pq = \dfrac{8 \pm \sqrt{64 + 4 \times 128}}{2 \times 1} = \dfrac{8 \pm \sqrt{576}}{2} = \dfrac{8 \pm 24}{2}$

$\therefore$ $pq = 16, -8$

Here, $pq = -8$ is not possible as p and q are positive.

$\therefore$ $pq = 16$

Now, the equation whose roots are p and q is

$$x^2 - (p + q)x + pq = 0 \Rightarrow x^2 - 2x + 16 = 0$$

72. $x + 1 - 2\log_2(3 + 2^x) + 2\log_4(10 - 2^{-x}) = 0$

$\Rightarrow$ $x + 1 - 2\log_2(3 + 2^x) + \log_2\left(\dfrac{10 \cdot 2^x - 1}{2^x}\right) = 0$

$\Rightarrow x + 1 - 2\log_2(3 + 2^x) + \log_2(10 \cdot 2^x - 1) - x = 0$

$\Rightarrow$ $1 + \log_2\left(\dfrac{10 \cdot 2^x - 1}{(3 + 2^x)^2}\right) = 0$

$\Rightarrow$ $\dfrac{10 \cdot 2^x - 1}{9 + (2^x)^2 + 6 \cdot 2^x} = \dfrac{1}{2}$

$\Rightarrow$ $(2^x)^2 - 14 \cdot 2^x + 11 = 0$

Let $2^x = y \Rightarrow y^2 - 14y + 11 = 0$

$$y = \frac{14 \pm \sqrt{152}}{2} = 7 \pm \frac{\sqrt{152}}{2}$$

$$y_1 = 7 + \frac{\sqrt{152}}{2},\ y_2 = 7 - \frac{\sqrt{152}}{2}$$

$$\Rightarrow \quad 2^{x_1} = 7 + \frac{\sqrt{152}}{2},\ 2^{x_2} = 7 - \frac{\sqrt{152}}{2}$$

$$\Rightarrow \quad x_1 = \log_2\left(7 + \frac{\sqrt{152}}{2}\right),\ x_2 = \log_2\left(7 - \frac{\sqrt{152}}{2}\right)$$

$\therefore$ Sum of roots $= x_1 + x_2$

$$= \log_2\left(49 - \frac{152}{4}\right) = \log_2 11$$

73. $$\frac{2}{x-1} - \frac{1}{x-2} = \frac{2}{k}$$

$$\Rightarrow \quad x \in R - \{1, 2\}$$

$$k(2x - 4 - x + 1) = 2(x^2 - 3x + 2)$$

$$k(x-3) = 2(x^2 - 3x + 2)$$

$$2x^2 - (6+k)x + 3k + 4 = 0$$

For no real roots $b^2 - 4ac < 0$

$$\therefore \quad (k+6)^2 - 8\cdot(3k+4) < 0$$

$$\Rightarrow \quad k^2 - 12k + 4 < 0 \Rightarrow (k-6)^2 - 32 < 0$$

$$\Rightarrow \quad (k-6)^2 < 32 \Rightarrow -4\sqrt{2} < k - 6 < 4\sqrt{2}$$

$$\Rightarrow \quad 6 - 4\sqrt{2} < k < 6 + 4\sqrt{2}$$

Integral $k \in \{1, 2, 3, 4, \ldots, 11\}$

Sum $= 66$

74. Given quadratic equation $7x^2 - 3x - 2 = 0$ has roots α and β.

So, $\alpha + \beta = \frac{3}{7}$ and $\alpha\beta = -\frac{2}{7}$.

Now, $$\frac{\alpha}{1-\alpha^2} + \frac{\beta}{1-\beta^2}$$

$$= \frac{\alpha - \alpha\beta^2 + \beta - \beta\alpha^2}{1 - (\alpha^2 + \beta^2) + \alpha^2\beta^2}$$

$$= \frac{(\alpha+\beta) - \alpha\beta(\alpha+\beta)}{1 - [(\alpha+\beta)^2 - 2\alpha\beta] + (\alpha\beta)^2}$$

$$= \frac{\frac{3}{7} + \frac{2}{7}\left(\frac{3}{7}\right)}{1 - \left[\left(\frac{3}{7}\right)^2 + \frac{4}{7}\right] + \frac{4}{49}}$$

$$= \frac{21+6}{49-37+4} = \frac{27}{16}$$

75. It is given that roots of quadratic equation $x^2 + bx + 45 = 0, b \in R$ has conjugate complex roots, now let roots are $\alpha + i\beta$ and $\alpha - i\beta$.

$\therefore$ Sum of roots $= 2\alpha = -b$ ...(i)

and product of roots $= \alpha^2 + \beta^2 = 45$ ...(ii)

$\because$ Roots $\alpha \pm i\beta$ satisfy $|z + 1| = 2\sqrt{10}$,

So $\quad (\alpha + 1)^2 + \beta^2 = 40$

$\Rightarrow \alpha^2 + 2\alpha + 1 + \beta^2 = 40$

From Eq. (ii), on putting the value of $\alpha^2 + \beta^2$, we get

$$45 + 2\alpha + 1 = 40$$

$$\Rightarrow \quad 2\alpha = -6 \Rightarrow \alpha = -3$$

From Eq. (i), we get

$$-b = 2(-3) \quad [\because \alpha = -3]$$

$$\Rightarrow \quad b = 6$$

$$\therefore \quad b^2 + b = 36 + 6 = 42 \text{ and } b^2 - b = 36 - 6 = 30$$

76. Given quadratic equations $f(x) = (\lambda^2 + 1)x^2 - 4\lambda x + 2 = 0$ have exactly one root in the interval (0, 1).

So, $D > 0 \Rightarrow 16\lambda^2 - 4(\lambda^2 + 1)2 > 0$

$$\Rightarrow \quad 8\lambda^2 - 8 > 0$$

$$\Rightarrow \quad \lambda^2 > 1$$

$$\Rightarrow \quad \lambda \in (-\infty, -1) \cup (1, \infty) \quad \text{...(i)}$$

and $$f(0)f(1) < 0$$

$$\Rightarrow \quad 2(\lambda^2 + 1 - 4\lambda + 2) < 0$$

$$\Rightarrow \quad \lambda^2 - 4\lambda + 3 < 0$$

$$\Rightarrow \quad (\lambda - 3)(\lambda - 1) < 0$$

$$\Rightarrow \quad \lambda \in (1, 3) \quad \text{...(ii)}$$

From Eqs. (i) and (ii), we get

$$\lambda \in (1, 3)$$

And if $\lambda = 3$, then the quadratic equation is

$$10x^2 - 12x + 2 = 0$$

$$\Rightarrow \quad 5x^2 - 6x + 1 = 0 \Rightarrow x = 1, 1/5$$

$\because$ The root $x = 1/5 \in (0, 1)$ for $\lambda = 3$

$\therefore \lambda \in (1, 3]$.

77. Given quadratic equations having roots α and β is

$x^2 + px + 2 = 0$, so $\alpha + \beta = -p$ and $\alpha\beta = 2$

and $\frac{1}{\alpha}$ and $\frac{1}{\beta}$ are the roots of the equation.

$$2x^2 + 2qx + 1 = 0, \text{ so } \frac{1}{\alpha} + \frac{1}{\beta} = -q$$

So, $$\left(\alpha - \frac{1}{\alpha}\right)\left(\beta - \frac{1}{\beta}\right)\left(\alpha + \frac{1}{\beta}\right)\left(\beta + \frac{1}{\alpha}\right)$$

$$= \left(\alpha\beta - \frac{\alpha}{\beta} - \frac{\beta}{\alpha} + \frac{1}{\alpha\beta}\right)\left(\alpha\beta + 1 + 1 + \frac{1}{\alpha\beta}\right)$$

$$= \left(2 - \frac{\alpha^2 + \beta^2}{\alpha\beta} + \frac{1}{2}\right)\left(2 + 1 + 1 + \frac{1}{2}\right)$$

$$= \left[\frac{5}{2} - \frac{(\alpha+\beta)^2 - 2\alpha\beta}{2}\right]\left[\frac{9}{2}\right]$$

$$= \frac{9}{4}(5 - (-p)^2 + 4) = \frac{9}{4}(9 - p^2)$$

78. Given equation is $e^{4x} + e^{3x} - 4e^{2x} + e^x + 1 = 0$

Let $e^x = y > 0$, so $y^4 + y^3 - 4y^2 + y + 1 = 0$

$$\Rightarrow \quad \left(y^2 + \frac{1}{y^2}\right) + \left(y + \frac{1}{y}\right) - 4 = 0 \text{ [on dividing by } y^2]$$

$$\Rightarrow \quad \left(y + \frac{1}{y}\right)^2 + \left(y + \frac{1}{y}\right) - 6 = 0$$

Again, let $y + \frac{1}{y} = t$, then $t^2 + t - 6 = 0$

$\Rightarrow \quad (t-2)(t+3) = 0$

$\Rightarrow \quad t = -3, 2$

$\therefore \quad y + \frac{1}{y} = -3 \text{ or } 2$

$\Rightarrow e^x + \frac{1}{e^x} = -3 \text{ or } 2 \Rightarrow e^x + \frac{1}{e^x} = 2$

$\left[\because e^x > 0 \Rightarrow e^x + \frac{1}{e^x} \neq -3 \, \forall x \in R\right]$

$\Rightarrow (e^x - 1)^2 = 0 \Rightarrow e^x = 1 \Rightarrow x = 0$

$\therefore$ Number of real roots of given equation is 1.

79. Since, the quadratic equation $2x^2 + (a-10)x + \frac{33}{2} = 2a$ has real roots.

So, $D \geq 0$

$\Rightarrow \quad (a-10)^2 - 4(2)\left(\frac{33}{2} - 2a\right) \geq 0$

$\Rightarrow \quad a^2 - 20a + 100 - 4(33 - 4a) \geq 0$

$\Rightarrow \quad a^2 - 4a - 32 \geq 0$

$\Rightarrow \quad (a+4)(a-8) \geq 0$

$\Rightarrow \quad a \in (-\infty, -4] \cup [8, \infty)$

$\therefore$ The least positive value of a for which the given quadratic equation has real roots is 8.

Exercise 2 - JEE Advanced Pattern

1. We have, $\quad |[x] - 2x| = 4$

$\Rightarrow \quad |[x] - 2([x] + \{x\})| = 4$

$\Rightarrow \quad |-[x] + 2\{x\}| = 4$

which is possible only when

$2\{x\} = 0, 1$

If $\{x\} = 0$, then $[x] = \pm 4$ and then $x = -4, 4$ and if $\{x\} = \frac{1}{2}$, then

$[x] + 1 = \pm 4$

$\Rightarrow \quad [x] = 3, -5$

$\therefore \quad x = 3 + \frac{1}{2} \text{ and } -5 + \frac{1}{2}$

$\Rightarrow \quad x = \frac{7}{2}, -\frac{9}{2} \Rightarrow x = -4, -\frac{9}{2}, \frac{7}{2}, 4$

2. We know that $x^2 + x + 1$ is a factor of $ax^3 + bx^2 + cx + d$.

Hence, roots of $x^2 + x + 1 = 0$ are also roots of $ax^3 + bx^2 + cx + d = 0$.

Since, ω and ω^2 $\left(\text{where, } \omega = -\frac{1}{2} + \frac{\sqrt{3}i}{2} \text{ and } \omega^2 = -\frac{1}{2} - \frac{\sqrt{3}}{2}i\right)$

are two complex roots of $x^2 + x + 1 = 0$. Therefore, ω and ω^2 are two complex roots of $ax^3 + bx^2 + cx + d = 0$.

We know that, a cubic equation has atleast one real root. Let real root be α.

Then, $\alpha \cdot \omega \cdot \omega^2 = -\frac{d}{a} \Rightarrow \alpha = -\frac{d}{a}$

3. We have, $\sqrt{(5x^2 - 8x + 3)} - \sqrt{(5x^2 - 9x + 4)}$

$= \sqrt{(2x^2 - 2x)} - \sqrt{(2x^2 - 3x + 1)}$

$\Rightarrow \sqrt{(5x-3)(x-1)} - \sqrt{(5x-4)(x-1)}$

$= \sqrt{2x(x-1)} - \sqrt{(2x-1)(x-1)}$

$\Rightarrow \sqrt{x-1}\,(\sqrt{5x-3} - \sqrt{5x-4}) = \sqrt{x-1}\,(\sqrt{2x} - \sqrt{2x-1})$

$\Rightarrow \quad \sqrt{x-1} = 0 \Rightarrow x = 1$

4. We have, $\quad (a + \sqrt{b})(a - \sqrt{b}) = a^2 - b = 1 \quad$ [given]

$\therefore \quad (a + \sqrt{b})^{x^2 - 15} + (a - \sqrt{b})^{x^2 - 15} = 2a$

$\Rightarrow \quad (a + \sqrt{b})^{x^2 - 15} + \frac{1}{(a + \sqrt{b})^{x^2 - 15}} = 2a$

Let $\quad y = (a + \sqrt{b})^{x^2 - 15}$

$\Rightarrow \quad y + \frac{1}{y} = 2a \Rightarrow y^2 - 2ay + 1 = 0$

$\Rightarrow \quad y = \frac{2a \pm \sqrt{4a^2 - 4}}{2} = a \pm \sqrt{a^2 - 1}$

$\therefore \quad y = a \pm \sqrt{b} = (a + \sqrt{b})^{\pm 1} \quad [\because a^2 - b = 1]$

$\Rightarrow (a + \sqrt{b})^{x^2 - 15} = (a + \sqrt{b})^{\pm 1}$

$\therefore \quad x^2 - 15 = \pm 1$

$\Rightarrow \quad x^2 = 15 \pm 1 \Rightarrow x^2 = 16, 14$

$\Rightarrow \quad x = \pm 4, \pm \sqrt{14}$

5. We have,

$x^2 - xy + y^2 = 4(x + y - 4)$

$\Rightarrow \quad x^2 - x(y + 4) + y^2 - 4y + 16 = 0$

$\because \quad x \in R$

$\therefore \quad (-(y+4))^2 - 4 \cdot 1 \cdot (y^2 - 4y + 16) \geq 0 \quad [\text{using, } b^2 - 4ac \geq 0]$

$\Rightarrow \quad y^2 + 8y + 16 - 4y^2 + 16y - 64 \geq 0$

$\Rightarrow \quad 3y^2 - 24y + 48 \leq 0$

$\Rightarrow \quad y^2 - 8y + 16 \leq 0$

$\Rightarrow \quad (y-4)^2 \leq 0$

$\therefore \quad (y-4)^2 = 0$

$\therefore \quad y = 4$

Then, $\quad x^2 - 4x + 16 = 4(x + 4 - 4)$

$\Rightarrow \quad x^2 - 8x + 16 = 0 \Rightarrow (x-4)^2 = 0 \Rightarrow x = 4$

Number of pairs is 1 i.e. (4, 4).

6. Since, 3789108 is an even integer. Therefore, $x^4 - y^4$ is also an even integer.

So, either both x and y are even integers or both of them are odd integers.

Now, $\quad x^4 - y^4 = (x - y)(x + y)(x^2 + y^2)$

$\Rightarrow x - y, x + y, x^2 + y^2$ must be even integers.

Therefore, $(x - y)(x + y)(x^2 + y^2)$ must be divisible by 8. But 3789108 is not divisible by 8.

Hence, the given equation has no solution.

$\therefore$ Number of solutions = 0

7. We have,

$$x^3 + ax + 1 = 0$$

or $$x^4 + ax^2 + x = 0 \quad \text{...(i)}$$

and $$x^4 + ax^2 + 1 = 0 \quad \text{...(ii)}$$

From Eqs. (i) and (ii), we get

$$x - 1 = 0$$

$$\Rightarrow \quad x = 1$$

which is a common root.

$$\therefore \quad 1 + a + 1 = 0$$

$$\Rightarrow \quad a = -2$$

8. $\because (1 - a^2)\, x^2 + 2ax - 1 = 0$

$$1 - a^2 \neq 0$$

$$x^2 + \left(\frac{2a}{1 - a^2}\right)x - \left(\frac{1}{1 - a^2}\right) = 0$$

Let $f(x) = x^2 + \left(\frac{2a}{1 - a^2}\right)x - \left(\frac{1}{(1 - a^2)}\right)$

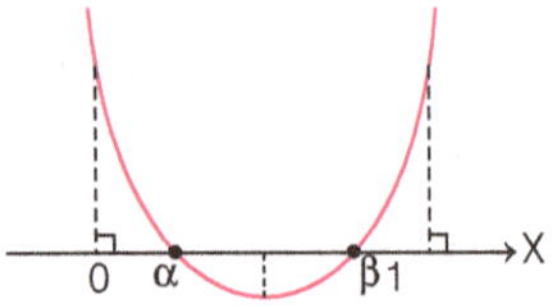

The following cases arise:

***Case* I** $D \geq 0$

$$\left(\frac{2a}{1 - a^2}\right)^2 - 4 \cdot 1 \cdot \left(\frac{-1}{1 - a^2}\right) \geq 0$$

$$\Rightarrow \quad \frac{4a^2}{(1 - a^2)^2} + \frac{4}{(1 - a^2)} \geq 0$$

$$\Rightarrow \quad \frac{4a^2 + 4 - 4a^2}{(1 - a^2)^2} \geq 0$$

$$\Rightarrow \quad \frac{4}{(1 - a^2)^2} \geq 0 \quad \text{[always true]}$$

***Case* II** $f(0) > 0$

$$\Rightarrow \quad \frac{-1}{(1 - a^2)} > 0 \Rightarrow \frac{1}{1 - a^2} < 0$$

$$\Rightarrow \quad 1 - a^2 < 0$$

$$\therefore \quad a \in (-\infty, -1) \cup (1, \infty)$$

***Case* III** $f(1) > 0$

$$\Rightarrow \quad 1 + \frac{2a}{(1 - a^2)} - \frac{1}{(1 - a^2)} > 0$$

$$\Rightarrow \quad \frac{1 - a^2 + 2a - 1}{(1 - a^2)} > 0 \Rightarrow \frac{a^2 - 2a}{1 - a^2} < 0$$

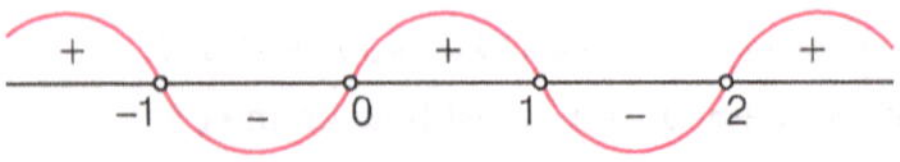

$$\Rightarrow \quad \frac{a(a - 2)}{(a + 1)(a - 1)} > 0$$

$$\therefore \quad a \in (-\infty, -1) \cup (0, 1) \cup (2, \infty)$$

***Case* IV** $0 <$ x-coordinate of vertex < 1

$$\Rightarrow \quad 0 < -\frac{2a}{2(1 - a^2)} < 1 \Rightarrow 0 < \frac{a}{a^2 - 1} < 1$$

$$\Rightarrow \quad 0 < \frac{a}{(a + 1)(a - 1)} \text{ and } 1 - \frac{a}{a^2 - 1} > 0$$

$$\Rightarrow \quad \frac{a}{(a + 1)(a - 1)} > 0$$

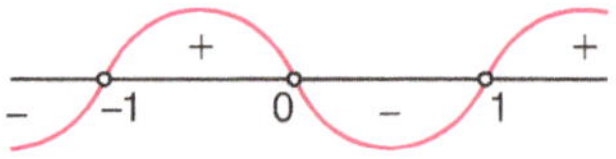

$$\Rightarrow \quad a \in (-1, 0) \cup (1, \infty)$$

and $$\frac{\left(a - \frac{1 + \sqrt{5}}{2}\right)\left(a - \frac{1 - \sqrt{5}}{2}\right)}{(a + 1)(a - 1)} > 0$$

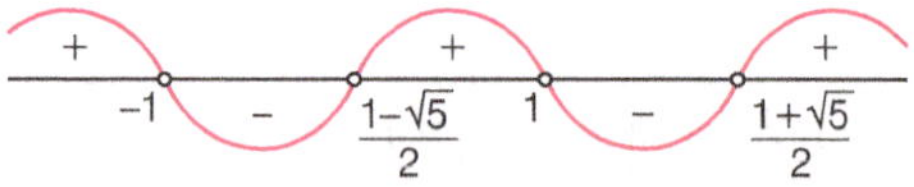

and $a \in (-\infty, -1) \cup \left(\frac{1 - \sqrt{5}}{2}, 1\right) \cup \left(\frac{1 + \sqrt{5}}{2}, \infty\right)$

$$\therefore \quad a \in \left(\frac{1 - \sqrt{5}}{2}, 0\right) \cup \left(\frac{1 + \sqrt{5}}{2}, \infty\right)$$

Combining all cases, we get

$$a > 2$$

9. We have, $\quad x - \sqrt{1 - |x|} < 0 \quad \text{...(i)}$

which is defined only when

$$1 - |x| \geq 0$$

$$\Rightarrow \quad |x| \leq 1$$

$$\Rightarrow \quad x \in [-1, 1]$$

Now, from Eq. (i), we get

$$x < \sqrt{1 - |x|}$$

***Case* I** If $x \geq 0$, i.e. $0 \leq x \leq 1$

$$x - \sqrt{(1 - |x|)} < 0$$

$$\Rightarrow \quad x < \sqrt{(1 - x)}$$

On squaring both sides, we get

$$x^2 + x - 1 < 0$$

$$\Rightarrow \quad \frac{-1 - \sqrt{5}}{2} < x < \frac{-1 + \sqrt{5}}{2}$$

But $\quad x \geq 0$

$$\therefore \quad x \in \left[0, \frac{-1 + \sqrt{5}}{2}\right)$$

***Case* II** If $x < 0$, i.e. $-1 \leq x < 0$

$$x - \sqrt{(1 + x)} < 0$$

$$\Rightarrow \quad x < \sqrt{1 + x} \quad \text{[always true]}$$

$$x \in [-1, 0)$$

Combining both cases, we get

$$x \in \left[-1, \frac{-1 + \sqrt{5}}{2}\right)$$

10. We have, $(a\cdot 2b - 2c\cdot a)(2c\cdot c - b\cdot 2b) = (ba - ca)^2$

$$\Rightarrow \quad 2a(b-c)\cdot 2(c^2-b^2) = a^2(b-c)^2$$

$$\Rightarrow \quad 4a(c-b)(c+b) = a^2(b-c) \quad [\because b \neq c]$$

$$\Rightarrow \quad 4a(c+b) = -a^2$$

$$\Rightarrow \quad a + 4b + 4c = 0$$

11. Let $f(x) = ax^2 + bx + c$

Since, coefficients are integers and one root is irrational, then both the roots are irrational.

$\therefore$ For any $\lambda \in Q$, $f(\lambda) \neq 0$

$\Rightarrow f(\lambda) > 0$ or $f(\lambda) < 0$, but $f(\lambda) \neq 0$

$$\therefore \quad |f(\lambda)| > 0$$

or $$\left| a\frac{p^2}{q^2} + b\frac{p}{q} + c \right| > 0$$

or $$\frac{1}{q^2}|ap^2 + bpq + cq^2| > 0 \quad \text{...(i)}$$

As $a, b, c, p, q \in$ integers

$$\therefore \quad |ap^2 + bpq + cq^2| \geq 1 \quad \text{...(ii)}$$

$$\Rightarrow \quad |f(\lambda)| = \frac{1}{q^2}|ap^2 + bpq + cq^2| \geq \frac{1}{q^2} \quad \text{[from Eqs. (i) and (ii)]}$$

12. Given, $(ax^2 + c)y + (a'x^2 + c') = 0$

or $\quad x^2(ay + a') + (cy + c') = 0$

If x is rational, then the discriminant of the above equation must be perfect square.

Hence, $0 - 4(ay + a')(cy + c')$ must be a perfect square.

$\Rightarrow -acy^2 - (ac' + a'c)y - a'c'$ must be a perfect square.

$$\Rightarrow \quad (ac' + a'c)^2 - 4aca'c' = 0 \quad [\because D = 0]$$

$$\Rightarrow \quad (ac' - a'c)^2 = 0 \Rightarrow ac' = a'c$$

$$\Rightarrow \quad \frac{a}{a'} = \frac{c}{c'}$$

13. We have, $ax^2 - bx + c = 0$

$$\alpha + \beta = \frac{b}{a} \text{ and } \alpha\beta = \frac{c}{a}$$

Also, $(a + cy)^2 = b^2y$

$$\Rightarrow \quad c^2y^2 - (b^2 - 2ac)y + a^2 = 0$$

$$\Rightarrow \quad \left(\frac{c}{a}\right)^2 y^2 - \left\{\left(\frac{b}{a}\right)^2 - 2\left(\frac{c}{a}\right)\right\}y + 1 = 0$$

$$\Rightarrow \quad (\alpha\beta)^2y^2 - (\alpha^2 + \beta^2)y + 1 = 0$$

$$\Rightarrow \quad y^2 - (\alpha^{-2} + \beta^{-2})y + \alpha^{-2}\beta^{-2} = 0$$

$$\Rightarrow \quad (y - \alpha^{-2})(y - \beta^{-2}) = 0$$

Hence, the roots are α^{-2} and β^{-2}.

14. α and β be the roots of $x^2 + px + q = 0$

γ and δ be the roots of $x^2 + px + r = 0$

$$\Rightarrow \quad \alpha + \beta = -p$$

and $$\alpha\beta = q$$

$$\Rightarrow \quad \gamma + \delta = -p$$

$$\gamma\delta = r$$

Now, $(\alpha - \gamma)(\alpha - \delta) = \alpha^2 - \alpha(\gamma + \delta) + \gamma\delta$

$$= \alpha^2 - \alpha(\alpha + \beta) + r = -\alpha\beta + r = -q + r$$

By symmetry, $(\beta - \gamma)(\beta - \delta) = -q + r$

Hence, $\dfrac{(\alpha - \gamma)(\alpha - \delta)}{(\beta - \gamma)(\beta - \delta)} = 1$

15. Here, $x^2 \cdot 2^{|x-3|+4} + 2^{x-1} = x^2 \cdot 2^{x+1} + 2^{|x-3|+2}$

If $\quad x - 3 \geq 0$

$$\Rightarrow \quad x^2 \cdot 2^{x-3+4} + 2^{x-1} = x^2 \cdot 2^{x+1} + 2^{x-3+2}$$

$$\Rightarrow \quad x^2 \cdot 2^{x+1} + 2^{x-1} = x^2 \cdot 2^{x+1} + 2^{x-1}$$

which is always true for $x \geq 3$.

Again, if $x - 3 < 0$

$$x^2 \cdot 2^{-(x-3)+4} + 2^{x-1} = x^2 \cdot 2^{x+1} + 2^{-(x-3)+2}$$

$$\Rightarrow \quad x^2 \cdot 2^{7-x} + 2^{x-1} = x^2 \cdot 2^{x+1} + 2^{5-x}$$

$$\Rightarrow \quad x^2 \cdot 2^{7-x} - 2^{5-x} = x^2 \cdot 2^{x+1} - 2^{x-1}$$

$$\Rightarrow \quad 2^{5-x}(x^2 \cdot 2^2 - 1) = 2^{x-1}(x^2 \cdot 2^2 - 1)$$

$$\Rightarrow (2^{5-x} - 2^{x-1})(4x^2 - 1) = 0$$

$$\Rightarrow \quad x^2 = \frac{1}{4} \text{ and } 5 - x = x - 1$$

$$\Rightarrow \quad x = \pm\frac{1}{2} \text{ and } x = 3$$

$\therefore$ Solution set is $x = \pm\frac{1}{2}$ and $x \geq 3$

16. $0 < a < b < c, \alpha + \beta = \left(-\dfrac{b}{a}\right)$ and $\alpha\beta = \dfrac{c}{a}$

For non-real complex roots,

$$b^2 - 4ac < 0$$

$$\Rightarrow \quad \frac{b^2}{a^2} - \frac{4c}{a} < 0$$

$$\Rightarrow \quad (\alpha + \beta)^2 - 4\alpha\beta < 0 \Rightarrow (\alpha - \beta)^2 < 0$$

$$\because \quad 0 < a < b < c$$

$\therefore$ Roots are conjugate, then $|\alpha| = |\beta|$

But $\quad \alpha\beta = \dfrac{c}{a}$

$$|\alpha\beta| = \left|\frac{c}{a}\right| > 1 \quad \left[\because a < c, \therefore \frac{c}{a} > 1\right]$$

$$\Rightarrow \quad |\alpha||\beta| > 1$$

$$\Rightarrow \quad |\alpha|^2 > 1 \text{ or } |\alpha| > 1$$

17. Given equation is

$$Ax^2 - |G|x - H = 0 \quad \text{...(i)}$$

$\therefore \quad$ Discriminant $= (-|G|)^2 - 4A(-H)$

$$= G^2 + 4AH = G^2 + 4G^2 \quad [\because G^2 = AH]$$

$$= 5G^2 > 0$$

$\therefore$ Roots of Eq. (i) are real and distinct.

$\because \quad A = \dfrac{a+b}{2} > 0, G = \sqrt{ab} > 0, H = \dfrac{2ab}{a+b} > 0$

[$\because$ a and b are two unequal positive integers]

Let α and β be the roots of Eq. (i).

Then, $\alpha + \beta = \frac{|G|}{A} > 0$

and $\alpha\beta = -\frac{H}{A} < 0$

and $\alpha - \beta = \frac{\sqrt{D}}{A} = \frac{G\sqrt{5}}{A} > 0$

$\therefore$ $\alpha = \frac{|G| + G\sqrt{5}}{2A} > 0$

and $\beta = \frac{|G| - G\sqrt{5}}{2A} < 0$

Exactly one positive root and atleast one root which is negative fraction.

18. It is clear from graph that the equation $y = ax^2 + bx + c = 0$ has two real and distinct roots. Therefore,

$$b^2 - 4ac > 0 \quad \text{...(i)}$$

$\because$ Parabola open downwards.

$\therefore$ $a < 0$

and $y = ax^2 + bx + c$ cuts-off Y-axis at, $x = 0$.

$\therefore$ $y = c < 0$

$\Rightarrow$ $c < 0$

and x-coordinate of vertex > 0

$\Rightarrow$ $-\frac{b}{2a} > 0 \Rightarrow \frac{b}{a} < 0$

$\Rightarrow$ $b > 0$ $\quad [\because a < 0]$

It is clear that a and b are of opposite signs.

19. Let $y = ax^2 + bx + c$

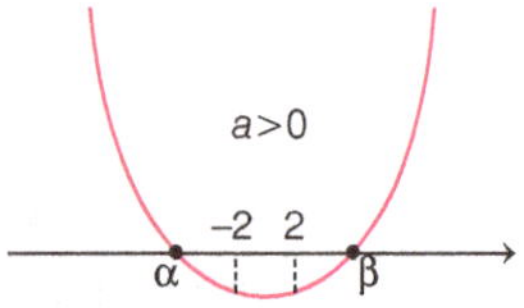

Consider the following cases:

***Case* I** $D > 0$

$\Rightarrow$ $b^2 - 4ac > 0$

***Case* II** $af(-2) < 0$

$\Rightarrow$ $a(4a - 2b + c) < 0$

$\Rightarrow$ $4a - 2b + c < 0$

***Case* III** $af(2) > 0$

$\Rightarrow$ $a(4a + 2b + c) > 0$

$\Rightarrow$ $4a + 2b + c > 0$

Combining *Case* II and *Case* III, we get

$$4a + 2|b| + c < 0$$

Also, at $x = 0$, $y < 0 \Rightarrow c < 0$

Also, since for $-2 < x < 2$,

$$y < 0$$

$\Rightarrow$ $ax^2 + bx + c < 0$

For $x = 1$, $a + b + c < 0$ ...(i)

and for $x = -1$, $a - b + c < 0$ ...(ii)

Combining Eqs. (i) and (ii), we get

$$a + |b| + c < 0$$

20. Let the roots be $\frac{a}{r}$, a and ar, where $a > 0, r > 1$

$\therefore$ Product of the roots $= 1$

$\Rightarrow$ $\frac{a}{r} \cdot a \cdot ar = 1$

$\Rightarrow$ $a^3 = 1$

$\therefore$ $a = 1$ $\quad$ [one root is 1]

Now, roots are $\frac{1}{r}$, 1 and r.

Then, $\frac{1}{r} + 1 + r = -b$

$\Rightarrow$ $\frac{1}{r} + r = -b - 1$ ...(i)

$\because$ $r + \frac{1}{r} > 2$

$\Rightarrow$ $-b - 1 > 2$

$\Rightarrow$ $b < -3$ $\quad$ [from Eq. (i)]

or $b \in (-\infty, -3)$

Also, $\frac{1}{r} \cdot 1 + 1 \cdot r + r \cdot \frac{1}{r} = c$

$\Rightarrow$ $\frac{1}{r} + r + 1 = c = -b$ $\quad$ [from Eq. (i)]

$\therefore$ $b + c = 0$

Now, first root $= \frac{1}{r} < 1$ $\quad$ [$\because$ one root is smaller than one]

Second root $= 1$

Third root $= r > 1$ $\quad$ [$\because$ one root is greater than one]

21. We have, $f(x) = ax^2 + bx + c$

$a, b, c \in R$ $\quad [\because a \neq 0]$

On putting $x = 0, 1, \frac{1}{2}$, we get

$$|c| \le 1$$

$$|a + b + c| \le 1$$

and $\left|\frac{1}{4}a + \frac{1}{2}b + c\right| \le 1$

$\Rightarrow$ $-1 \le c \le 1$,

$$-1 \le a + b + c \le 1$$

and $-4 \le a + 2b + 4c \le 4$

$\Rightarrow$ $-4 \le 4a + 4b + 4c \le 4$

and $-4 \le -a - 2b - 4c \le 4$

On adding, we get

$$-8 \le 3a + 2b \le 8$$

Also, $-8 \le a + 2b \le 8$

$\therefore$ $-16 \le 2a \le 16$

$\Rightarrow$ $|a| \le 8$

$\because$ $-1 \le -c \le 1, -8 \le -a \le 8$

We get, $-16 \le 2b \le 16$

$\Rightarrow$ $|b| \le 8$

$\therefore$ $|a| + |b| + |c| \le 17$

22. $\because \quad x = \dfrac{-5 \pm \sqrt{25 + 1200}}{50} = \dfrac{-5 \pm 35}{50} = \dfrac{30}{50}, \dfrac{-40}{50}$

or $\quad \cos \alpha = \dfrac{3}{5}, \dfrac{-4}{5}$

But $\quad -1 < x < 0$

$\therefore \quad \cos \alpha = -\dfrac{4}{5}$ [lies in II and III quadrants]

$\therefore \quad \sin \alpha = \dfrac{3}{5}$ [lies in II quadrant]

$\therefore \quad \sin \alpha = -\dfrac{3}{5}$ [lies in III quadrant]

$\therefore \quad \sin 2\alpha = 2 \cdot \sin\alpha \cdot \cos \alpha = -\dfrac{24}{25}$ [lies in II quadrant]

$\therefore \quad \sin 2\alpha = 2 \cdot \sin\alpha \cdot \cos\alpha = \dfrac{24}{25}$ [lies in III quadrant]

23. $\because a + 2b + 4c = 0$

$\therefore \quad a\left(\dfrac{1}{2}\right)^2 + b\left(\dfrac{1}{2}\right) + c = 0$

It is clear that one root is $\dfrac{1}{2}$.

Let other root be α.

Then, $\quad \alpha + \dfrac{1}{2} = -\dfrac{b}{a} \Rightarrow \alpha = -\dfrac{1}{2} - \dfrac{b}{a}$

which depends upon a and b.

24. Since, $f(x) = x^3 + 3x^2 - 9x + \lambda = (x - \alpha)^2(x - \beta)$

$\therefore \alpha$ is a double root.

$\therefore f'(x) = 0$ has also one root α.

i.e. $3x^2 + 6x - 9 = 0$ has one root α.

$\therefore \quad x^2 + 2x - 3 = 0$ or $(x + 3)(x - 1) = 0$

has the root α which can either -3 or 1.

If $\alpha = 1$, then $f(1) = 0$ gives $\lambda - 5 = 0 \Rightarrow \lambda = 5$.

If $\alpha = -3$, then $f(-3) = 0$ gives

$-27 + 27 + 27 + \lambda = 0 \Rightarrow \lambda = -27$

25. We have, $\quad x^3 - ax^2 + bx - 1 = 0 \quad$ ...(i)

Then, $\quad \alpha^2 + \beta^2 + \gamma^2 = (\alpha + \beta + \gamma)^2 - 2(\alpha\beta + \beta\gamma + \gamma\alpha)$

$= a^2 - 2b$

$\alpha^2\beta^2 + \beta^2\gamma^2 + \gamma^2\alpha^2 = (\alpha\beta + \beta\gamma + \gamma\alpha)^2$

$- 2\alpha\beta\gamma(\alpha + \beta + \gamma) = b^2 - 2a$

and $\quad \alpha^2\beta^2\gamma^2 = 1$

Therefore, the equation whose roots are α^2, β^2 and γ^2, is

$x^3 - (a^2 - 2b)x^2 + (b^2 - 2a)x - 1 = 0 \quad$ ...(ii)

Since, Eqs. (i) and (ii) are indentical, therefore

$a^2 - 2b = a$ and $b^2 - 2a = b$

Eliminating b, we have

$\dfrac{(a^2 - a)^2}{4} - 2a = \dfrac{a^2 - a}{2}$

$\Rightarrow \quad a\{a(a - 1)^2 - 8 - 2(a - 1)\} = 0$

$\Rightarrow \quad a(a^3 - 2a^2 - a - 6) = 0$

$\Rightarrow \quad a(a - 3)(a^2 + a + 2) = 0$

$\Rightarrow \quad a = 0$ or $a = 3$ or $a^2 + a + 2 = 0$

$\Rightarrow \quad b = 0$ or $b = 3$

or $\quad b^2 + b + 2 = 0$

$\therefore \quad a = b = 0$

or $\quad a = b = 3$

or a and b are roots of $x^2 + x + 2 = 0$.

Sol. (26 to 27)

Let $\quad y = \dfrac{2x^2 - 3x + 2}{2x^2 + 3x + 2}$

$\Rightarrow \quad 2x^2y + 3xy + 2y = 2x^2 - 3x + 2$

$\Rightarrow 2(y - 1)x^2 + 3(y + 1)x + 2(y - 1) = 0$

As $x \in R$

$\therefore \quad D \geq 0$

$\Rightarrow \quad 9(y + 1)^2 - 4 \cdot 2(y - 1) \cdot 2(y - 1) \geq 0$

$\Rightarrow \quad 9(y + 1)^2 - 16(y - 1)^2 \geq 0$

$\Rightarrow \quad (3y + 3)^2 - (4y - 4)^2 \geq 0$

$\Rightarrow \quad (7y - 1)(7 - y) \geq 0$

$\Rightarrow \quad (7y - 1)(y - 7) \leq 0$

$\therefore \quad \dfrac{1}{7} \leq y \leq 7$

$\therefore \quad G = 7$ and $L = \dfrac{1}{7}$

$\therefore \quad GL = 1$

Now, $\quad \dfrac{G^{100} + L^{100}}{2} \geq (GL)^{100} \Rightarrow \dfrac{G^{100} + L^{100}}{2} \geq 1$

$\Rightarrow \quad G^{100} + L^{100} \geq 2$

26. The quadratic equation having roots G and L, is

$x^2 - (G + L)x + GL = 0$

$\Rightarrow \quad x^2 - \dfrac{50}{7}x + 1 = 0$

$\Rightarrow \quad 7x^2 - 50x + 7 = 0$

27. We have, $\quad L^2 < \lambda < G^2$

$\Rightarrow \quad \left(\dfrac{1}{7}\right)^2 < \lambda < 7^2$

$\Rightarrow \quad \dfrac{1}{49} < \lambda < 49$

$\Rightarrow \quad \lambda = 1, 2, 3, \ldots, 48$ as $\lambda \in N$

$\therefore$ Sum of all values of $\lambda = 1 + 2 + 3 + \ldots + 48 = \dfrac{48 \times 49}{2} = 1176$

Sol. (28 to 29)

Let roots be $\alpha, \beta, \gamma, \delta > 0$.

$\therefore \quad \alpha + \beta + \gamma + \delta = 12$

$(\alpha + \beta)(\gamma + \delta) + \alpha\beta + \gamma\delta = c$

$\alpha\beta(\gamma + \delta) + \gamma\delta(\alpha + \beta) = -d$

$\alpha\beta\gamma\delta = 81$

$\because \quad AM = \frac{\alpha + \beta + \gamma + \delta}{4} = 3$

and $\quad GM = (\alpha\beta\gamma\delta)^{1/4} = (81)^{1/4} = 3$

$\therefore \quad AM = GM$

$\Rightarrow \quad \alpha = \beta = \gamma = \delta = 3$

28. $c = (\alpha + \beta)(\gamma + \delta) + \alpha\beta + \gamma\delta$

$= (3 + 3)(3 + 3) + 3 \cdot 3 + 3 \cdot 3$

$= 36 + 18 = 54$

29. $\because \alpha\beta(\gamma + \delta) + \gamma\delta(\alpha + \beta) = -d$

$\therefore \quad d = -\{3 \cdot 3 \cdot (3 + 3) + 3 \cdot 3 \cdot (3 + 3)\} = -108$

Sol. (30 to 31)

Given that, $AC = 4\sqrt{2}$ units

$\therefore \quad AB = BC = \frac{AC}{\sqrt{2}} = 4$ units

and $\quad OB = \sqrt{(BC)^2 - (OC)^2}$

$= \sqrt{(4)^2 - (2\sqrt{2})^2} \quad \left[\because OC = \frac{AC}{2}\right]$

$= 2\sqrt{2}$ units

$\therefore$ Vertices are $A \equiv (-2\sqrt{2}, 0)$,

$B \equiv (0, -2\sqrt{2})$

and $\quad C \equiv (2\sqrt{2}, 0)$

30. Minimum value of $y = \frac{x^2}{2\sqrt{2}} - 2\sqrt{2}$ is at $x = 0$.

$\therefore \quad (y)_{\min} = -2\sqrt{2}$

31. $f(x) = 0$

$\Rightarrow \quad \frac{x^2}{2\sqrt{2}} - 2\sqrt{2} = 0 \Rightarrow x = \pm 2\sqrt{2}$

Given, $\quad -2\sqrt{2} < \frac{\lambda}{2} < 2\sqrt{2}$

or $\quad -4\sqrt{2} < \lambda < 4\sqrt{2}$

$\therefore$ Initial values of λ are $-5, -4, -3, -2, -1, 0, 1, 2, 3, 4, 5$.

$\therefore$ Number of integral values is 11.

Sol. (32 to 33)

We have, $\quad (\alpha - \beta) = (\alpha + k) - (\beta + k)$

$\Rightarrow \quad \frac{\sqrt{b^2 - 4c}}{1} = \frac{\sqrt{b_1^2 - 4c_1}}{1}$

$\Rightarrow \quad b^2 - 4c = b_1^2 - 4c_1 \quad$ ...(i)

Given, least value of $f(x) = -\frac{1}{4} - \frac{(b^2 - 4c)}{4 \times 1} = -\frac{1}{4}$

$\Rightarrow \quad b^2 - 4c = 1$

$\therefore \quad b^2 - 4c = 1 = b_1^2 - 4c_1 \quad$ [from Eq. (i)] ...(ii)

Also, given least value of $g(x)$ occurs at $x = \frac{7}{2}$.

$\therefore \quad -\frac{b_1}{2 \times 1} = \frac{7}{2}$

$\therefore \quad b_1 = -7$

32. Least value of $g(x) = -\frac{b_1^2 - 4c_1}{4 \times 1} = -\frac{1}{4}$ [from Eq. (ii)]

33. $\because g(x) = 0$

$\therefore \quad x^2 + b_1 x + c_1 = 0$

$\Rightarrow \quad x = \frac{-b_1 \pm \sqrt{b_1^2 - 4c_1}}{2} = \frac{7 \pm 1}{2} = 3, 4$

$\therefore$ Roots of $g(x) = 0$ are 3, 4.

Sol. (34 to 35)

$\therefore \quad \alpha + \beta + \gamma + \delta = -A \quad$ ...(i)

$(\alpha + \beta)(\gamma + \delta) + \alpha\beta + \gamma\delta = B \quad$ ...(ii)

$\alpha\beta(\gamma + \delta) + \gamma\delta(\alpha + \beta) = -C \quad$ ...(iii)

and $\quad \alpha\beta\gamma\delta = D \quad$ ...(iv)

34. $\because \quad \frac{C}{A} = \frac{\alpha\beta(\gamma + \delta) + \gamma\delta(\alpha + \beta)}{\alpha + \beta + \gamma + \delta}$

$= \frac{k(\gamma + \delta) + k(\alpha + \beta)}{\alpha + \beta + \gamma + \delta} \quad [\because \alpha\beta = \gamma\delta = k]$

$= k \quad$ ...(v)

35. From Eq. (ii), we get

$(\alpha + \beta)(\gamma + \delta) = B - (\alpha\beta + \gamma\delta) = B - 2k \quad [\because \alpha\beta = \gamma\delta = k]$

Sol. (36 to 37)

Let $f(x) = ax^2 - bx + c$ has two distinct roots α and β.

Then, $f(x) = a(x - \alpha)(x - \beta)$.

Since, $f(0)$ and $f(1)$ are of same sign.

Therefore, $\quad c(a - b + c) > 0$

$\Rightarrow \quad c(a - b + c) \geq 1$

$\therefore \quad a^2\alpha\beta(1 - \alpha)(1 - \beta) \geq 1$

But $\quad \alpha(1 - \alpha) = \frac{1}{4} - \left(\frac{1}{2} - \alpha\right)^2 \leq \frac{1}{4}$

$\therefore \quad a^2\alpha\beta(1 - \alpha)(1 - \beta) < \frac{a^2}{16}$

$\Rightarrow \quad \frac{a^2}{16} > 1$

$\Rightarrow \quad a > 4 \quad [\because \alpha \neq \beta]$

$\Rightarrow \quad a \geq 5$ as $a \in I$

Also, $\quad b^2 - 4ac \geq 0$

$\Rightarrow \quad b^2 \geq 4ac \geq 20$

$\Rightarrow \quad b \geq 5$

Next, $a \geq 5$, $b \geq 5$, we get

$c \geq 1$

$\therefore \quad abc \geq 25$

$\therefore \quad \log_5 abc \geq \log_5 25 = 2$

36. Least value of a is 5.

37. Least value of b is 5.

Sol. (38 to 39)

Let α, β and γ be the roots of $2x^3 + ax^2 + bx + 4 = 0$.

$\therefore \quad \alpha + \beta + \gamma = -\frac{a}{2}$

$\alpha\beta + \beta\gamma + \gamma\alpha = \frac{b}{2}$ and $\alpha\beta\gamma = -2$

38. $\because$ AM $\geq$ GM

$$\therefore \quad \frac{(-\alpha)+(-\beta)+(-\gamma)}{3} \geq \{(-\alpha)(-\beta)(-\gamma)\}^{1/3}$$

$$\Rightarrow \quad \frac{\frac{a}{2}}{3} \geq (2)^{1/3}$$

$$\therefore \quad a \geq 6\,(2)^{1/3} \quad \text{...(i)}$$

$$\text{or} \quad a^3 \geq 432$$

Hence, minimum value of a^3 is 432.

39. $\because$ AM $\geq$ GM

$$\therefore \quad \frac{(-\alpha)(-\beta)+(-\beta)(-\gamma)+(-\gamma)(-\alpha)}{3}$$

$$\geq \{(-\alpha)(-\beta)(-\beta)(-\gamma)(-\gamma)(-\alpha)\}^{1/3}$$

$$\Rightarrow \quad \frac{b/2}{3} \geq (4)^{1/3}$$

$$\Rightarrow \quad b \geq 6\,(4)^{1/3} \quad \text{...(ii)}$$

$$\text{or} \quad b^3 \geq 864$$

Hence, minimum value of b^3 is 864.

40. $\because \quad y = \dfrac{x^2-3x+c}{x^2+3x+c}$

$$\Rightarrow \quad x^2(y-1)+3x(y+1)+c(y-1)=0$$

$$\because \quad x \in R$$

$$\therefore \quad 9(y+1)^2 - 4c(y-1)^2 \geq 0$$

$$(2\sqrt{c}y - 2\sqrt{c})^2 - (3y+3)^2 \leq 0$$

$$\Rightarrow \{(2\sqrt{c}+3)y - (2\sqrt{c}-3)\}\{(2\sqrt{c}-3)y - (2\sqrt{c}+3)\} \leq 0$$

$$\text{or} \quad \frac{2\sqrt{c}-3}{2\sqrt{c}+3} \leq y \leq \frac{2\sqrt{c}+3}{2\sqrt{c}-3}$$

$$\text{But given,} \quad \frac{2\sqrt{c}+3}{2\sqrt{c}-3} = 7$$

$$\Rightarrow \quad 2\sqrt{c}+3 = 14\sqrt{c}-21$$

$$\text{or} \quad 12\sqrt{c} = 24$$

$$\text{or} \quad \sqrt{c} = 2$$

$$\therefore \quad c = 4$$

41. We have, $\sqrt{x^2} - \sqrt{(x-1)^2} + \sqrt{(x-2)^2} = \sqrt{5}$

$$\Rightarrow \quad |x| - |x-1| + |x-2| = \sqrt{5}$$

***Case* I** If $x < 0$, then

$$-x + (x-1) - (x-2) = \sqrt{5}$$

$$x = 1 - \sqrt{5}$$

***Case* II** If $0 \leq x < 1$, then

$$x + (x-1) - (x-2) = \sqrt{5}$$

$\Rightarrow \quad x = \sqrt{5} - 1$, which is not possible.

***Case* III** If $1 \leq x < 2$, then

$$x - (x-1) - (x-2) = \sqrt{5}$$

$\Rightarrow \quad x = 3 - \sqrt{5}$, which is not possible.

***Case* IV** If $x > 2$, then

$$x - (x-1) + (x-2) = \sqrt{5}$$

$$\Rightarrow \quad x = 1 + \sqrt{5}$$

Hence, number of solutions is 2.

42. $\because \quad (1+i)x^2 + (1-i)x - 2i = 0$

$$\Rightarrow \quad x^2 + \frac{(1-i)}{(1+i)}x - \frac{2i}{(1+i)} = 0$$

$$\Rightarrow \quad x^2 - ix - (1+i) = 0$$

$$\therefore \quad \alpha+\beta = i, \text{ and } \alpha\beta = -(1+i)$$

$$\therefore \quad \alpha - \beta = \sqrt{(\alpha+\beta)^2 - 4\alpha\beta}$$

$$= \sqrt{i^2 + 4(1+i)} = \sqrt{(3+4i)}$$

$$|\alpha-\beta| = \sqrt{\sqrt{9+16}} = \sqrt{5}$$

$$\therefore \quad |\alpha-\beta|^2 = 5$$

43. $\because \quad 4x^2 - 16x + c = 0$

$$\Rightarrow \quad x^2 - 4x + \frac{c}{4} = 0$$

$$\text{Let} \quad f(x) = x^2 - 4x + \frac{c}{4}$$

Then, the following cases arises :

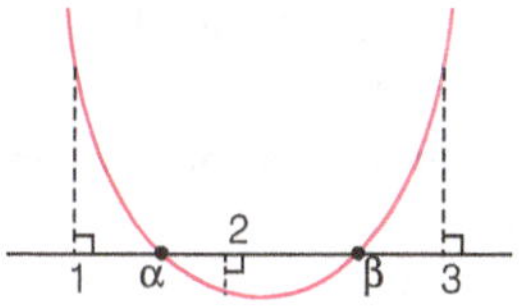

***Case* I** $\quad D > 0$

$$\Rightarrow \quad 16 - c > 0$$

$$\therefore \quad c < 16$$

***Case* II** $\quad f(1) > 0$

$$\Rightarrow \quad 1 - 4 + \frac{c}{4} > 0$$

$$\Rightarrow \quad \frac{c}{4} > 3$$

$$\therefore \quad c > 12$$

***Case* III** $\quad f(2) < 0$

$$\Rightarrow \quad 4 - 8 + \frac{c}{4} < 0$$

$$\Rightarrow \quad \frac{c}{4} < 4$$

$$\therefore \quad c < 16$$

***Case* IV** $\quad f(3) > 0$

$$\Rightarrow \quad 9 - 12 + \frac{c}{4} > 0$$

$$\Rightarrow \quad \frac{c}{4} > 3 \Rightarrow c > 12$$

Combining all cases, we get

$$12 < c < 16$$

Thus, integral values of c are 13, 14 and 15.

Hence, number of integral values of c is 3.

44. We have, $r + s + t = 0$ ...(i)

$$rs + st + tr = \frac{1001}{8} \quad \text{...(ii)}$$

and $$rst = -\frac{2008}{8} = -251 \quad \text{...(iii)}$$

Now, $(r+s)^3 + (s+t)^3 + (t+r)^3 = (-t)^3 + (-r)^3 + (-s)^3$ $[\because r + s + t = 0]$

$$= -(t^3 + r^3 + s^3) = -3\,rst \quad [\because r + s + t = 0]$$

$$= -3(-251) = 753$$

Now, $99\,\lambda = (r+s)^3 + (s+t)^3 + (t+r)^3 = 753$

$\therefore$ $$\lambda = \frac{753}{99} = 7.6$$

$\therefore$ $[\lambda] = 7$

45. Let α, α^2 be the roots of $3x^2 + px + 3 = 0$

Now, sum of roots $S = \alpha + \alpha^2 = -p/3$,

Product of roots $P = \alpha^3 = 1$

$\Rightarrow$ $\alpha = 1, \omega, \omega^2$

Now, $\alpha + \alpha^2 = -p/3$

$\Rightarrow$ $\omega + \omega^2 = -p/3$

$\Rightarrow$ $-1 = -p/3 \Rightarrow p = 3$

$\therefore$ $154p = 154 \times 3 = 462$

46. Given, α and β are the roots of the equation $x^2 - 6x - 2 = 0$.

$\therefore$ $a_n = \alpha^n - \beta^n$ for $n \ge 1$

$a_{10} = \alpha^{10} - \beta^{10}$

$a_8 = \alpha^8 - \beta^8$

$a_9 = \alpha^9 - \beta^9$

Now, consider

$$\frac{a_{10} - 2a_8}{2a_9} = \frac{\alpha^{10} - \beta^{10} - 2(\alpha^8 - \beta^8)}{2(\alpha^9 - \alpha^9)} = \frac{\alpha^8(\alpha^2 - 2) - \beta^8(\beta^2 - 2)}{2(\alpha^9 - \beta^9)}$$

$$= \frac{\alpha^8 \cdot 6\alpha - \beta^8 6\beta}{2(\alpha^9 - \beta^9)} = \frac{6\alpha^9 - 6\beta^9}{2(\alpha^9 - \beta^9)} = \frac{6}{2} = 3$$

$\left[\begin{array}{l} \because \alpha \text{ and } \beta \text{ are the roots of} \\ \quad x^2 - 6x - 2 = 0 \text{ or } x^2 = 6x + 2 \\ \Rightarrow \quad \alpha^2 = 6\alpha + 2 \Rightarrow \alpha^2 - 2 = 6\alpha \\ \text{and} \quad \beta^2 = 6\beta + 2 \Rightarrow \beta^2 - 2 = 6\beta \end{array}\right]$

Now, $7052\left(\dfrac{a_{10} - 2a_8}{2a_9}\right) = 3 \times 7052 = 21156$

Alternate Solution

Since, α and β are the roots of the equation

$x^2 - 6x - 2 = 0$ or $x^2 = 6x + 2$

$\therefore$ $\alpha^2 = 6\alpha + 2 \Rightarrow \alpha^{10} = 6\alpha^9 + 2\alpha^8$ ...(i)

Similarly, $\beta^{10} = 6\beta^9 + 2\beta^8$ ...(ii)

On subtracting Eq. (ii) from Eq. (i), we get

$$\alpha^{10} - \beta^{10} = 6(\alpha^9 - \beta^9) + 2(\alpha^8 - \beta^8) \quad [\because a_n = \alpha^n - \beta^n]$$

$\Rightarrow$ $a_{10} = 6a_9 + 2a_8 \Rightarrow a_{10} - 2a_8 = 6a_9$

47. From the given relations, we can say that a and $\frac{1}{b}$ are the roots of the equation $6x^2 + 20x + 15 = 0$

$\therefore$ $$a + \frac{1}{b} = -\frac{10}{3} \text{ and } \frac{a}{b} = \frac{5}{2}$$

$$\frac{b^3}{ab^2 - 9(ab+1)^3} = \frac{1}{a \cdot \frac{1}{b} - 9\left(a + \frac{1}{b}\right)^3} = \frac{1}{\frac{5}{2} + 9 \cdot \frac{1000}{27}} = \frac{6}{2015}$$

$\therefore$ $$\frac{4030b^3}{ab^2 - 9(ab+1)^3} = \frac{4030 \times 6}{2015} = 12$$

48. We have, $\alpha^2 - 6\alpha + 12 = 0$

$\therefore$ $6(\alpha - 2) = \alpha^2$

and $\beta^2 - 6\beta + 12 = 0$

$\therefore$ $\beta(\beta - 6) + 12 = 0$

So, $$(\alpha - 2)^{24} - \frac{(\beta - 6)^8}{\alpha^8} + 1 = (\alpha - 2)^{24} - \frac{12^8}{\alpha^8\beta^8} + 1$$

$$= (\alpha - 2)^{24} - \frac{12^8}{12^8} + 1$$

$$= (\alpha - 2)^{24}$$

$$= (3 \pm \sqrt{3}i - 2)^{24} \quad [\because \alpha = 3 \pm \sqrt{3}i]$$

$$= (1 \pm \sqrt{3}i)^{24}$$

$$= \left\{2\left(\cos\frac{\pi}{3} \pm i\sin\frac{\pi}{3}\right)\right\}^{24}$$

$$= 2^{24}(\cos\pi + i\,\sin 8\pi) = 4^{12}$$

$\therefore$ $a = 12$

49. $\because 2^{x+2} \cdot 27^{\frac{x}{x-1}} = 9 \Rightarrow 2^{x+2} \cdot 3^{\frac{3x}{x-1}} = 9$

Taking log both sides, we get

$$(x+2)\log 2 + \frac{3x}{x-1}\log 3 = \log 9$$

$\Rightarrow$ $$(x+2)\log 2 + \frac{3x}{x-1}\log 3 = 2\log 3$$

$\Rightarrow$ $$(x+2)\log 2 + \left(\frac{3x}{x-1} - 2\right)\log 3 = 0$$

$\Rightarrow$ $$(x+2)\log 2 + \left(\frac{x+2}{x-1}\right)\log 3 = 0$$

$\Rightarrow$ $$(x+2)\left[\log 2 + \frac{1}{x-1}\log 3\right] = 0$$

$\Rightarrow$ $$x = -2 \text{ or } \frac{1}{x-1}\log 3 + \log 2 = 0$$

$\Rightarrow$ $$x = -2 \text{ or } \frac{1}{x-1} = -\frac{\log 2}{\log 3} \Rightarrow x = -2 \text{ or } 1 - x = \frac{\log 3}{\log 2}$$

$\Rightarrow$ $x = -2$ or $x = +1 - \log_2 3$

$\therefore$ The sum of roots $= -2 + 1 - \log_2 3 = -1 - \log_2 3$

On comparing, we get

$a = 1, b = 2$ and $c = 3$

Thus, $$\frac{ac}{b} = \frac{1 \cdot 3}{2} = \frac{3}{2} = 1.5$$

50. **(A)** We have, $y = \dfrac{x^2 - 2x + 4}{x^2 + 2x + 4}$

$\Rightarrow x^2(y-1) + 2(y+1)x + 4(y-1) = 0$

As $x \in R$, we get

$$D \geq 0$$

$$\Rightarrow \quad 4(y+1)^2 - 16(y-1)^2 \geq 0$$

$$\Rightarrow \quad 3y^2 - 10y + 3 \leq 0$$

$$\Rightarrow \quad (y-3)(3y-1) \leq 0$$

$$\Rightarrow \quad \frac{1}{3} \leq y \leq 3$$

(B) We have, $y = \dfrac{2x^2 + 4x + 1}{x^2 + 4x + 2}$

$\Rightarrow x^2(y-2) + 4(y-1)x + 2y - 1 = 0$

As $x \in R$, we get

$$D \geq 0$$

$$\Rightarrow \quad 16(y-1)^2 - 4(y-2)(2y-1) \geq 0$$

$$\Rightarrow \quad 4(y-1)^2 - (y-2)(2y-1) \geq 0$$

$$\Rightarrow \quad 2y^2 - 3y + 2 \geq 0$$

$$\Rightarrow \quad y^2 - \frac{3}{2}y + 1 \geq 0$$

$$\Rightarrow \quad \left(y - \frac{3}{4}\right)^2 + \frac{7}{16} \geq 0$$

$$\therefore \quad y \in R$$

(C) We have, $y = \dfrac{x^2 - 3x + 4}{x - 3}$

$$\Rightarrow \quad x^2 - (3+y)x + 3y + 4 = 0$$

As $x \in R$, we get

$$D \geq 0$$

$$\Rightarrow \quad (3+y)^2 - 4(3y+4) \geq 0$$

$$\Rightarrow \quad y^2 - 6y - 7 \geq 0$$

$$\Rightarrow \quad (y+1)(y-7) \geq 0$$

$$\Rightarrow \quad y \in (-\infty, -1] \cup [7, \infty)$$

(D) We have, $y = \dfrac{x^2 + x + 1}{x^2 + 4x + 3}$

$\Rightarrow x^2(y-1) + (4y-1)x + (3y-1) = 0$

As $x \in R$, we get

$$(-(4y-1))^2 - 4(y-1)(3y-1) \geq 0$$

$$\Rightarrow \quad 16y^2 - 8y + 1 - 12y^2 + 16y - 4 \geq 0$$

$$\Rightarrow \quad 4y^2 + 8y - 3 \geq 0$$

$$\Rightarrow \quad y^2 + 2y - \frac{3}{4} \geq 0$$

So, $y \in \left(-\infty, -1 - \dfrac{\sqrt{7}}{2}\right] \cup \left[-1 + \dfrac{\sqrt{7}}{2}, \infty\right)$

51. **(A)** $\because (d + a - b)^2 + (d + b - c)^2 = 0$

which is possible only when

$$d + a - b = 0, d + b - c = 0$$

$$\Rightarrow \quad b - a = c - b$$

$$\Rightarrow \quad 2b = a + c$$

$\therefore$ a, b and c are in AP. ...(i)

$\because \quad a(b-c) + b(c-a) + c(a-b) = 0$

$\therefore$ $x = 1$ is a root of

$a(b-c)x^2 + b(c-a)x + c(a-b) = 0$ ...(ii)

Given, roots [Eq. (ii)] are equal.

$$\therefore \quad 1 \times 1 = \frac{c(a-b)}{a(b-c)}$$

$$\Rightarrow \quad a(b-c) = c(a-b) \text{ or } b = \frac{2ac}{a+c}$$

$\therefore$ a, b and c are in HP. ...(iii)

From Eqs. (i) and (ii), we get

$$a = b = c$$

$\therefore$ a, b and c are in AP, GP and HP.

(B) $\because \quad x^3 - 3x^2 + 3x - 1 = 0 \Rightarrow (x-1)^3 = 0$

$$\therefore \quad x = 1, 1, 1$$

$\Rightarrow$ Common root, $x = 1$

$$\therefore \quad a(1)^2 + b(1) + c = 0$$

$$\Rightarrow \quad a + b + c = 0$$

(C) Given, $bx^2 + (\sqrt{(a+c)^2 + 4b^2})\,x + (a+c) \geq 0$

$$\therefore \quad D \leq 0$$

$$\Rightarrow \quad (a+c)^2 + 4b^2 - 4b(a+c) \leq 0$$

$$\Rightarrow \quad (a+c-2b)^2 \leq 0$$

$$\text{or} \quad (a+c-2b)^2 = 0$$

$$\therefore \quad a + c = 2b$$

Hence a, b and c are in AP.

(D) $\because$ $ax^2 + 2bx + c = 0$

$\therefore D = 4(b^2 - ac) \geq 0$

Now, roots are equal,

$$\therefore \quad D = 0$$

$$\Rightarrow \quad 4(b^2 - ac) = 0 \Rightarrow b^2 = ac$$

$\Rightarrow$ a, b, c are in GP.

52. **(A)** Let $y = f(x) = x^3 - 6x^2 + 9x + \lambda$

$f'(x) = 3x^2 - 12x + 9 = 0$

$\therefore \quad x = 1, 3$

$f''(x) = 6x - 12$

$f''(1) < 0$ and $f''(3) > 0$

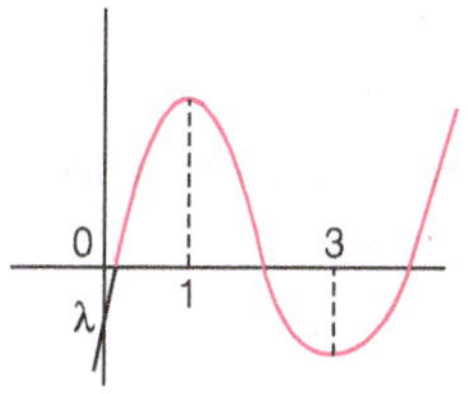

Also, $f(0) < 0 \Rightarrow \lambda < 0$ ...(i)

$f(1) > 0$

$\Rightarrow 1 - 6 + 9 + \lambda > 0$

$\Rightarrow \lambda > -4$ ...(ii)

and $f(3) < 0$

$\Rightarrow 27 - 54 + 27 + \lambda < 0$

$\Rightarrow \lambda < 0$ ...(iii)

From Eqs. (i), (ii) and (iii), we get

$-4 < \lambda < 0$

$\Rightarrow -3 < \lambda + 1 < 1$

$\therefore [\lambda + 1] = -3, -2, -1, 0$

$\therefore |[\lambda + 1]| = 3, 2, 1, 0$

(B) $\because x^2 + x + 1 > 0, \forall x \in R$

Given, $-3 < \dfrac{x^2 - \lambda x - 2}{x^2 + x + 1} < 2$

$\Rightarrow -3x^2 - 3x - 3 < x^2 - \lambda x - 2 < 2x^2 + 2x + 2$

$\Rightarrow 4x^2 - (\lambda - 3)x + 1 > 0$

and $x^2 + (\lambda + 2)x + 4 > 0$

$\therefore (\lambda - 3)^2 - 4 \cdot 4 \cdot 1 < 0$

and $(\lambda + 2)^2 - 4 \cdot 1 \cdot 4 < 0$

$\Rightarrow (\lambda - 3)^2 - 4^2 < 0$

and $(\lambda + 2)^2 - 4^2 < 0$

$\Rightarrow -4 < \lambda - 3 < 4$

and $-4 < \lambda + 2 < 4$

or $-1 < \lambda < 7$

and $-6 < \lambda < 2$

We get, $-1 < \lambda < 2$

$\therefore [\lambda] = -1, 0, 1$

$\Rightarrow |[\lambda]| = 0, 1$

(C) $\because (b - c) + (c - a) + (a - b) = 0$

$\therefore x = 1$ is a root of

$(b - c)x^2 + (c - a)x + (a - b) = 0$

Also, $x = 1$ satisfies

$x^2 + \lambda x + 1 = 0$

$\Rightarrow 1 + \lambda + 1 = 0$

$\therefore \lambda = -2$

Now, $\lambda - 1 = -3$

$[\lambda - 1] = -3$

$\Rightarrow |[\lambda - 1]| = 3$

(D) Given, $(31 + 8\sqrt{15})^{x^2-3} + 1 = (32 + 8\sqrt{15})^{x^2-3}$

$\Rightarrow (31 + 8\sqrt{15})^{x^2-3} + 1^{x^2-3} = (32 + 8\sqrt{15})^{x^2-3}$

$\Rightarrow x^2 - 3 = 1$ or $x = \pm 2$

$\therefore$ Sum of values of $x = +2 - 2 = 0$

53. Taking log with base 5 on the both sides,

$(16(\log_5 x)^3 - 68(\log_5 x))$

$(\log_5 x) = -16$

Let $(\log_5 x) = y$

$16y^4 - 68y^2 + 16 = 0$

$\Rightarrow 4y^4 - 16y^2 - y^2 + 4 = 0$

$\Rightarrow (4y^2 - 1)(y^2 - 4) = 0$

$\Rightarrow y = \pm \dfrac{1}{2}, \pm 2$

So, $\log_5 x = \pm \dfrac{1}{2}$ or ± 2

$\Rightarrow x = 5^{\frac{1}{2}}, 5^{\frac{-1}{2}}, 5^2, 5^{-2}$

$\therefore$ Product $= 5^{\frac{1}{2}} \cdot 5^{\frac{-1}{2}} \cdot 5^2 \cdot 5^{-2} = 1$

54. Given, $3x^2 - 4|x^2 - 1| + x - 1 = 0$ ...(i)

For $-1 \le x \le 1$ i.e. $x \in [-1, 1]$

From Eq. (i) , we get

$3x^2 - 4(-x^2 + 1) + x - 1 = 0$

$\Rightarrow 3x^2 + 4x^2 - 4 + x - 1 = 0$

$\Rightarrow 7x^2 + x - 5 = 0$

$\Rightarrow x = \dfrac{-1 \pm \sqrt{1 + 140}}{(2 \times 7)}$

Here, both values of x are acceptable.

For $|x| > |$ i.e. $x \in (-\infty, -1) \cup (1, \infty)$

From Eq. (i), we get

$3x^2 - 4(x^2 - 1) + x - 1 = 0 \Rightarrow x^2 - x - 3 = 0$

$\Rightarrow x = \dfrac{1 \pm \sqrt{1 + 12}}{2}$

Again here, both values of x are acceptable.

Hence, total number of solutions is 4.

55. Given quadratic polynomials, $x^2 + 20x - 2020$ and $x^2 - 20x + 2020$ having a, b distinct real and c, d distinct complex roots respectively.

So, $a + b = -20, ab = -2020$

and $c + d = 20, cd = 2020$

Now, $ac(a - c) + ad(a - d) + bc(b - c) + bd(b - d)$

$= a^2(c + d) - a(c^2 + d^2) + b^2(c + d) - b(c^2 + d^2)$

$= (c + d)(a^2 + b^2) - (c^2 + d^2)(a + b)$

$= (c + d)[(a + b)^2 - 2ab] - (a + b)\ [(c + d)^2 - 2cd]$

$= 20\ [(20)^2 + 4040] + 20\ [(20)^2 - 4040]$

$= 2 \times 20 \times (20)^2 = 40 \times 400 = 16000$

Exercise 3 - Challenging Problems

1. $\because (1 + m)x^2 - 2(1 + 3m)x + (1 + 8m) = 0$

$\therefore D = 4(1 + 3m)^2 - 4(1 + m)(1 + 8m) = 4m(m - 3)$

(i) Both roots are imaginary.

$\therefore D < 0$

$\Rightarrow 4m(m - 3) < 0$

$\Rightarrow 0 < m < 3$ or $m \in (0, 3)$

(ii) Both roots are equal.

$\therefore \quad D = 0$

$\Rightarrow \quad 4m(m-3) = 0 \Rightarrow m = 0, 3$

(iii) Both roots are real and distinct.

$\therefore \quad D > 0$

$\Rightarrow \quad 4m(m-3) > 0$

$\Rightarrow \quad m < 0$ or $m > 3$

$\therefore \quad m \in (-\infty, 0) \cup (3, \infty)$

(iv) Both roots are positive.

***Case* I** Sum of the roots > 0

$$\Rightarrow \quad \frac{2(1+3m)}{(1+m)} > 0$$

$$\Rightarrow \quad m \in (-\infty, -1) \cup \left(-\frac{1}{3}, \infty\right)$$

***Case* II** Product of the roots > 0

$$\Rightarrow \quad \frac{(1+8m)}{(1+m)} > 0$$

$$m \in (-\infty, -1) \cup \left(-\frac{1}{8}, \infty\right)$$

***Case* III** $\quad D \geq 0$

$\Rightarrow \quad 4m(m-3) \geq 0$

$$m \in (-\infty, 0] \cup [3, \infty)$$

Combining all Cases, we get

$$m \in (-\infty, -1) \cup [3, \infty)$$

(v) Both roots are negative.

Consider the following cases:

***Case* I** Sum of the roots $< 0 \Rightarrow \dfrac{2(1+3m)}{(1+m)} < 0$

$$\Rightarrow \quad m \in \left(-1, -\frac{1}{3}\right)$$

***Case* II** Product of the roots $> 0 \quad \Rightarrow \quad \dfrac{(1+8m)}{(1+m)} > 0$

$$\Rightarrow \quad m \in (-\infty, 1) \cup \left(-\frac{1}{8}, \infty\right)$$

***Case* III** $D \geq 0$

$4m(m-3) \geq 0 \quad \Rightarrow m \in (-\infty, 0] \cup [3, \infty)$

Combining all cases, we get

$m \in \phi$

(vi) Roots are opposite in sign, then

***Case* I** Consider the following cases:

Product of the roots < 0

$$\Rightarrow \quad \frac{(1+8m)}{(1+m)} < 0$$

$$m \in \left(-1, -\frac{1}{8}\right)$$

***Case* II** $\quad D > 0 \Rightarrow 4m(m-3) > 0$

$\Rightarrow \quad m \in (-\infty, 0) \cup (3, \infty)$

Combining all cases, we get

$$m \in \left(-1, -\frac{1}{8}\right)$$

(vii) Roots are equal in magnitude but opposite in sign, then Consider the following cases:

***Case* I** Sum of the roots = 0

$$\Rightarrow \quad \frac{2(1+3m)}{(1+m)} = 0 \Rightarrow m = -\frac{1}{3}, m \neq 1$$

***Case* II** $\quad D > 0$

$\Rightarrow \quad 4m(m-3) > 0$

$\Rightarrow \quad m \in (-\infty, 0) \cup (3, \infty)$

Combining all cases, we get

$$m = -\frac{1}{3}$$

(viii) Atleast one root is positive, then either one root is positive or both roots are positive. i.e. part (iv) $\cup$ (vi)

or $\quad m \in (-\infty, -1) \cup \left(-1, -\dfrac{1}{8}\right) \cup [3, \infty)$

(ix) Atleast one root is negative, then either one root is negative or both roots are negative.

i.e. part (v) $\cup$ (vi) $\quad$ or $\quad m \in \left(-1, -\dfrac{1}{8}\right)$

(x) Let roots be 2α and 3α. Then,

Consider the following cases:

***Case* I** Sum of the roots $= 2\alpha + 3\alpha = \dfrac{2(1+3m)}{(1+m)}$

$$\Rightarrow \quad \alpha = \frac{2(1+3m)}{5(1+m)} \quad \text{...(i)}$$

***Case* II** Product of the roots $= 2\alpha \cdot 3\alpha = \dfrac{(1+8m)}{(1+m)}$

$$\Rightarrow \quad 6\alpha^2 = \frac{(1+8m)}{(1+m)} \quad \text{...(ii)}$$

From Eqs. (i) and (ii), we get

$$6\left\{\frac{2(1+3m)}{5(1+m)}\right\}^2 = \frac{(1+8m)}{(1+m)}$$

$$\Rightarrow \quad 24(1+3m)^2 = 25(1+8m)(1+m)$$

$$\Rightarrow \quad 24(9m^2+6m+1) = 25(8m^2+9m+1)$$

$$16m^2 - 81m - 1 = 0$$

or $$m = \frac{81 \pm \sqrt{(-81)^2 + 64}}{32}$$

$$\Rightarrow \quad m = \frac{81 \pm \sqrt{6625}}{32}$$

2. $\because \quad 2x^2 - 2(2m+1)x + m(m+1) = 0 \quad [\because m \in R]$

$$\therefore \quad D = [-2(2m+1)]^2 - 8m(m+1) \quad [D = b^2 - 4ac]$$

$$= 4\{(2m+1)^2 - 2m(m+1)\}$$

$$= 4(2m^2 + 2m + 1)$$

$$= 8\left(m^2 + m + \frac{1}{2}\right) = 8\left\{\left(m + \frac{1}{2}\right)^2 + \frac{1}{4}\right\} > 0$$

or $\quad D > 0, \forall m \in R \quad$ ...(i)

$$x\text{-coordinate of vertex} = -\frac{b}{2a} = \frac{2(2m+1)}{4}$$

$$= \left(m + \frac{1}{2}\right) \quad \text{...(ii)}$$

and let

$$f(x) = x^2 - (2m+1)x + \frac{1}{2}m(m+1) \quad \text{...(iii)}$$

(i) Both roots are smaller than 2.

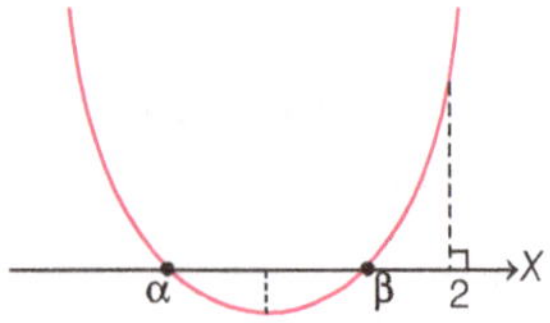

Consider the following cases:

***Case* I** $D \geq 0$

$\therefore \quad m \in R$ [from Eq. (i)]

***Case* II** x-coordinate of vertex < 2.

$\Rightarrow \quad m + \frac{1}{2} < 2$ [from Eq. (ii)]

or $\quad m < \frac{3}{2}$

***Case* III** $f(2) > 0$

$\Rightarrow \quad 4 - (2m + 1) 2 + \frac{1}{2} m (m + 1) > 0$

$\Rightarrow \quad m^2 - 7m + 4 > 0$

$\therefore \quad m \in \left(-\infty, \frac{7 - \sqrt{33}}{2} \right) \cup \left(\frac{7 + \sqrt{33}}{2}, \infty \right)$

Combining all cases, we get

$$m \in \left(-\infty, \frac{7 - \sqrt{33}}{2} \right)$$

(ii) Both roots are greater than 2.

Consider the following cases:

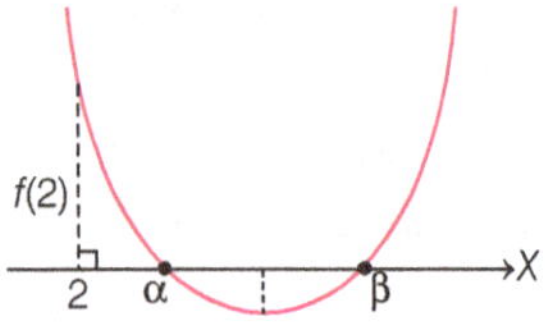

***Case* I** $D \geq 0$

$\therefore \quad m \in R$ [from Eq. (i)]

***Case* II** x-coordinate of vertex > 2

$\Rightarrow \quad m + \frac{1}{2} > 2$ [from Eq. (ii)]

$\therefore \quad m > \frac{3}{2}$

***Case* III** $f(2) > 0$

$m \in \left(-\infty, \frac{7 - \sqrt{33}}{2} \right) \cup \left(7 + \frac{\sqrt{33}}{2}, \infty \right)$ [from part (i)]

Combining all cases, we get

$$m \in \left(\frac{7 + \sqrt{33}}{2}, \infty \right)$$

(iii) Both roots lie in the interval (2, 3).

Consider the following cases:

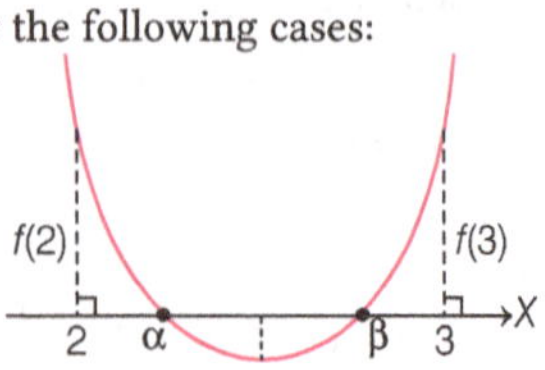

***Case* I** $D \geq 0$

$\therefore \quad m \in R$ [from Eq. (i)]

***Case* II** $f(2) > 0$

$\therefore \quad m \in \left(-\infty, \frac{7 - \sqrt{33}}{2} \right) \cup \left(\frac{7 + \sqrt{33}}{2}, \infty \right)$ [from part (i)]

***Case* III** $f(3) > 0$

$\Rightarrow \quad 9 - 3(2m + 1) + \frac{1}{2} m (m + 1) > 0$

or $\quad m^2 - 11m + 12 > 0$

$\therefore \quad m \in \left(-\infty, \frac{11 - \sqrt{73}}{2} \right) \cup \left(\frac{11 + \sqrt{73}}{2}, \infty \right)$

***Case* IV** $2 <$ x-coordinate of vertex < 3

$\Rightarrow \quad 2 < m + \frac{1}{2} < 3$

or $\quad \frac{3}{2} < m < \frac{5}{2}$ or $m \in \left(\frac{3}{2}, \frac{5}{2} \right)$

Combining all cases, we get

$$m \in \phi$$

(iv) Exactly one root lie in the interval (2,3) .

Consider the following cases:

***Case* I** $D > 0$

$\therefore \quad m \in R$ [from Eq. (i)]

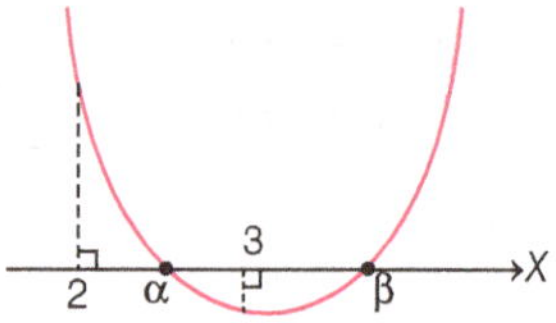

***Case* II** $f(2)\, f(3) < 0$

$$\left(4 - 2(2m + 1) + \frac{1}{2} m (m + 1) \right) \left(9 - 3(2m + 1) + \frac{1}{2} m (m + 1) \right) < 0$$

$\Rightarrow \quad (m^2 - 7m + 4)(m^2 - 11m + 12) < 0$

$\Rightarrow \quad \left(m - \frac{7 - \sqrt{33}}{2} \right) \left(m - \frac{7 + \sqrt{33}}{2} \right) \left(m - \frac{11 - \sqrt{73}}{2} \right) \left(m - \frac{11 + \sqrt{73}}{2} \right) < 0$

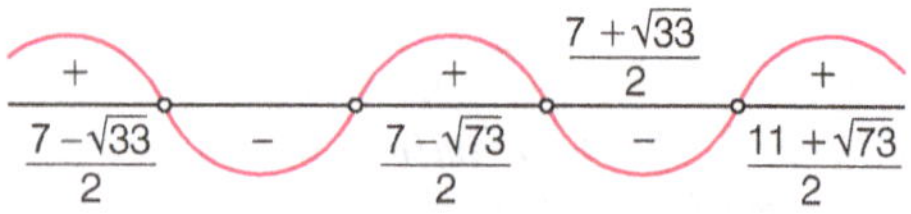

$\therefore \quad m \in \left(\frac{7 - \sqrt{33}}{2}, \frac{11 - \sqrt{73}}{2} \right) \cup \left(\frac{7 + \sqrt{33}}{2}, \frac{11 + \sqrt{73}}{2} \right)$

Combining all cases, we get

$$m \in \left(\frac{7 - \sqrt{33}}{2}, \frac{11 - \sqrt{73}}{2} \right) \cup \left(\frac{7 + \sqrt{33}}{2}, \frac{11 + \sqrt{73}}{2} \right)$$

(v) One root is smaller than 1 and the other root is greater than 1.

Consider the following cases:

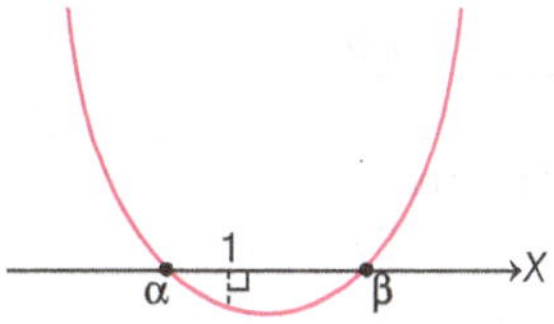

***Case* I** $D > 0$

$\therefore \quad m \in R$ [from Eq. (i)]

***Case* II** $f(1) < 0$

$\Rightarrow \quad 1 - (2m + 1) + \frac{1}{2} m (m + 1) < 0$ [from Eq. (iii)]

$\Rightarrow \quad m^2 - 3m < 0 \Rightarrow m(m - 3) < 0$

$\therefore \quad m \in (0, 3)$

Combining both cases, we get

$$m \in (0, 3)$$

(vi) One root is greater than 3 and the other root is smaller than 2.

Consider the following cases:

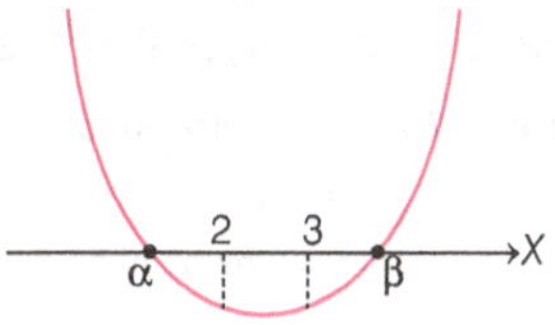

***Case* I** $D > 0$

$\therefore \quad m \in R$ [from Eq. (i)]

***Case* II** $f(2) < 0$

$\Rightarrow \quad m^2 - 7m + 4 < 0$

$\therefore \quad \frac{7 - \sqrt{33}}{2} < m < \frac{7 + \sqrt{33}}{2}$

$\therefore \quad m \in \left(\frac{7 - \sqrt{33}}{2}, \frac{7 + \sqrt{33}}{2} \right)$

***Case* III** $f(3) < 0$

$\Rightarrow \quad m^2 - 11m + 12 < 0$

$\therefore \quad \frac{11 - \sqrt{73}}{2} < m < \frac{11 + \sqrt{73}}{2}$

$\therefore \quad m \in \left(\frac{11 - \sqrt{73}}{2}, \frac{11 + \sqrt{73}}{2} \right)$

Combining all cases, we get

$$m \in \left(\frac{7 - \sqrt{33}}{2}, \frac{7 + \sqrt{33}}{2} \right)$$

(vii) Atleast one root lies in the interval (2, 3).

i.e. part (iv) $\cup$ (iii)

$\therefore \quad m \in \left(\frac{7 - \sqrt{33}}{2}, \frac{11 - \sqrt{73}}{2} \right) \cup \left(\frac{7 + \sqrt{33}}{2}, \frac{11 + \sqrt{73}}{2} \right)$

(viii) Atleast one root is greater than 2.

i.e. (Exactly one root is greater than 2) $\cup$ (Both roots are greater than 2)

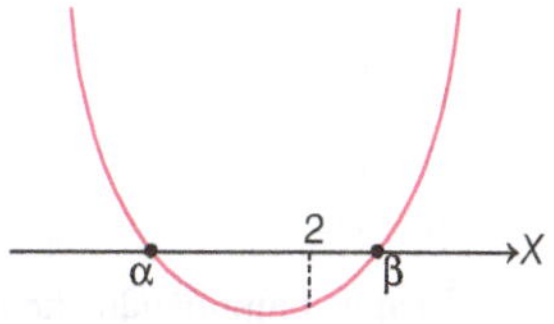

or(Exactly one root is greater than 2) $\cup (b)$ ...(i)

Consider the following cases:

***Case* I** $D > 0$

$\therefore \quad m \in R$ [from Eq. (i)]

***Case* II** $f(2) < 0$

$\Rightarrow \quad m^2 - 7m + 4 < 0$

$\therefore \quad m \in \left(\frac{7 - \sqrt{33}}{2}, \frac{7 + \sqrt{33}}{2} \right)$

Combining both cases, we get

$$m \in \left(\frac{7 - \sqrt{33}}{2}, \frac{7 + \sqrt{33}}{2} \right) \quad \text{...(ii)}$$

Finally from Eqs. (I) and (II), we get

$$m \in \left(\frac{7 - \sqrt{33}}{2}, \frac{7 + \sqrt{33}}{2} \right) \cup \left(\frac{7 + \sqrt{33}}{2}, \infty \right)$$

(ix) Atleast one root is smaller than 2.

i.e. (Exactly one root is smaller than 2) $\cup$(Both roots are smaller than 2) or part (viii) (II) $\cup$ (i)

We get, $m \in \left(-\infty, \frac{7 - \sqrt{33}}{2} \right) \cup \left(\frac{7 - \sqrt{33}}{2}, \frac{7 + \sqrt{33}}{2} \right)$

(x) Both 2 and 3 lie between α and β.

Consider the following cases:

***Case* I** $D > 0$

$\therefore \quad m \in R$ [from Eq. (i)]

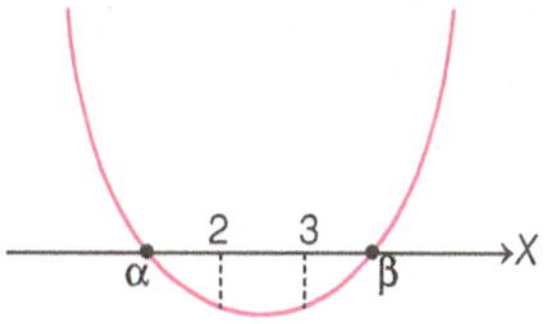

***Case* II** $f(2) < 0$

$\Rightarrow \quad m^2 - 7m + 4 < 0$

$\therefore \quad m \in \left(\frac{7 - \sqrt{33}}{2}, \frac{7 + \sqrt{33}}{2} \right)$

***Case* III** $f(3) < 0$

$\Rightarrow \quad m^2 - 11m + 12 < 0$

$\therefore \quad m \in \left(\frac{11 - \sqrt{73}}{2}, \frac{11 + \sqrt{73}}{2} \right)$

Combining all cases, we get

$$m \in \left(\frac{11 - \sqrt{73}}{2}, \frac{7 + \sqrt{33}}{2} \right)$$

3. $\because \quad \dfrac{\alpha}{\beta} = r$

$\Rightarrow \quad \dfrac{\alpha + \beta}{\alpha - \beta} = \dfrac{r+1}{r-1}$

[using componendo and dividendo method]

$\Rightarrow \quad \dfrac{-b/a}{\dfrac{\sqrt{D}}{a}} = \dfrac{r+1}{r-1}$

$\Rightarrow \quad b(1-r) = (1+r)\sqrt{D}$

On squaring both sides, we get

$\Rightarrow \quad b^2(1-r)^2 = (1+r)^2(b^2 - 4ac)$

or $\quad (1+r)^2 \cdot 4ac = b^2(4r)$

or $\quad \dfrac{(1+r)^2}{r} = \dfrac{b^2}{ac}$

4. We have, $\quad \dfrac{1}{x+p} + \dfrac{1}{x+q} = \dfrac{1}{r}$

$\Rightarrow \quad \dfrac{(x+q)+(x+p)}{x^2+(p+q)x+pq} = \dfrac{1}{r}$

$\Rightarrow \quad x^2 + (p+q-2r)x + pq - (p+q)r = 0$

Now, since the roots are equal in magnitudes, but opposite in sign. Therefore,

Sum of the roots = 0

$\Rightarrow \quad p + q - 2r = 0$

$\Rightarrow \quad p + q = 2r \qquad$ ...(i)

and product of the roots $= pq - (p+q)r$

$= pq - (p+q)\left(\dfrac{p+q}{2}\right) \qquad$ [from Eq. (i)]

$= \dfrac{2pq - p^2 - q^2 - 2pq}{2} = -\dfrac{p^2+q^2}{2}$

5. Let α be one root of the equation $ax^2 + bx + c = 0$.

Then, other root be α^n.

$\therefore \quad \alpha + \alpha^n = -\dfrac{b}{a} \qquad$ ...(i)

and $\quad \alpha \cdot \alpha^n = \dfrac{c}{a}$

$\Rightarrow \quad \alpha^{n+1} = \dfrac{c}{a} \Rightarrow \alpha = \left(\dfrac{c}{a}\right)^{\frac{1}{n+1}}$

$\therefore$ From Eq. (i), we get

$$\left(\frac{c}{a}\right)^{\frac{1}{n+1}} + \left(\frac{c}{a}\right)^{\frac{n}{n+1}} = -\frac{b}{a}$$

$\Rightarrow \quad (c)^{\frac{1}{n+1}} \cdot a^{-\frac{1}{n+1}+1} + (c^n)^{\frac{1}{n+1}} \cdot a^{-\frac{n}{n+1}+1} + b = 0$

$\Rightarrow \quad c^{\frac{1}{n+1}} \cdot a^{\frac{n}{n+1}} + (c^n)^{\frac{1}{n+1}} \cdot a^{\frac{1}{n+1}} + b = 0$

$\Rightarrow \quad (a^n c)^{\frac{1}{n+1}} + (c^n a)^{\frac{1}{n+1}} + b = 0$

6. We have, $\quad \alpha + \beta = -\dfrac{b}{a}$

$\alpha\beta = \dfrac{c}{a} \quad \Rightarrow \gamma + \delta = -\dfrac{m}{l}$ and $\gamma\delta = \dfrac{n}{l}$

Now, sum of the roots

$= (\alpha\gamma + \beta\delta) + (\alpha\delta + \beta\gamma) = (\alpha + \beta)\gamma + (\alpha + \beta)\delta$

$= (\alpha + \beta)(\gamma + \delta)$

$= \left(-\dfrac{b}{a}\right)\left(-\dfrac{m}{l}\right) = \dfrac{mb}{al}$

and product of the roots

$= (\alpha\gamma + \beta\delta)(\alpha\delta + \beta\gamma)$

$= (\alpha^2 + \beta^2)\gamma\delta + \alpha\beta(\gamma^2 + \delta^2)$

$= \{(\alpha+\beta)^2 - 2\alpha\beta\}\gamma\delta + \alpha\beta\{(\gamma+\delta)^2 - 2\gamma\delta\}$

$= \left\{\left(-\dfrac{b}{a}\right)^2 - \dfrac{2c}{a}\right\}\dfrac{n}{l} + \dfrac{c}{a}\left\{\left(-\dfrac{m}{l}\right)^2 - \dfrac{2n}{l}\right\}$

$= \left\{\dfrac{b^2 - 2ac}{a^2}\right\}\dfrac{n}{l} + \dfrac{c}{a}\left\{\dfrac{m^2 - 2nl}{l^2}\right\}$

$= \dfrac{(b^2 - 2ac)\,ln + (m^2 - 2nl)\,ac}{a^2l^2}$

$\therefore$ Required equation is

$$x^2 - \left(\frac{mb}{al}\right)x + \frac{(b^2 - 2ac)\,ln + (m^2 - 2nl)\,ac}{a^2l^2} = 0$$

$\Rightarrow \quad a^2l^2x^2 - mbalx + (b^2 - 2ac)\,ln + (m^2 - 2nl)\,ac = 0$

7. Since, roots of $x^2 - 2px + q = 0$ are equal.

$\therefore \quad D = 0$

i.e. $\quad (-2p)^2 - 4q = 0$ or $p^2 = q \qquad$ ...(i)

Now, $(1+y)x^2 - 2(p+y)x + (q+y) = 0$

$\therefore$ Discriminant $= 4(p+y)^2 - 4(1+y)(q+y)$

$= 4(p^2 + 2py + y^2 - q - y - qy - y^2)$

$= 4[(2p - q - 1)y + p^2 - q]$

$= 4[(2p - p^2 - 1)y + 0] \qquad$ [from Eq. (i)]

$= -4(p-1)^2y$

$> 0 \qquad [\because y < 0$ and $p \neq 1]$

Hence, roots of $(1+y)x^2 - 2(p+y)x + (q+y) = 0$ are real and distinct.

8. $\because \quad (2+\sqrt{3})^{x^2-2x+1} + (2-\sqrt{3})^{x^2-2x-1} = \dfrac{101}{10(2-\sqrt{3})}$

$\Rightarrow \quad (2+\sqrt{3})^{x^2-2x} \cdot (2+\sqrt{3})(2-\sqrt{3})$

$+ (2-\sqrt{3})^{x^2-2x-1} \cdot (2-\sqrt{3}) = \dfrac{101}{10}$

$\Rightarrow \quad (2+\sqrt{3})^{x^2-2x} + (2-\sqrt{3})^{x^2-2x} = \dfrac{101}{10}$

or $\quad (2+\sqrt{3})^{x^2-2x} + \dfrac{1}{(2+\sqrt{3})^{x^2-2x}} = \dfrac{101}{10} \qquad$ ...(i)

$\left[\because 2 - \sqrt{3} = \dfrac{1}{2+\sqrt{3}}\right]$

Let $(2+\sqrt{3})^{x^2-2x} = \lambda$, then Eq. (i) reduces to

$$\lambda + \frac{1}{\lambda} = \frac{101}{10}$$

$\Rightarrow \quad 10\lambda^2 - 101\lambda + 10 = 0$ or $(\lambda - 10)(10\lambda - 1) = 0$

$\therefore \quad \lambda = 10, \frac{1}{10}$

$\Rightarrow \quad (2+\sqrt{3})^{x^2-2x} = 10, 10^{-1}$

$\Rightarrow \quad x^2 - 2x = \log_{2+\sqrt{3}} 10, -\log_{2+\sqrt{3}} 10$

$\Rightarrow \quad (x-1)^2 = 1 + \log_{2+\sqrt{3}} 10, 1 - \log_{2+\sqrt{3}} 10$

$\therefore \quad (x-1)^2 = 1 + \log_{2+\sqrt{3}} 10$

$[\because (x-1)^2 \neq 1 - \log_{2+\sqrt{3}} 10]$

$\Rightarrow \quad x = 1 \pm \sqrt{(1 + \log_{2+\sqrt{3}} 10)}$

$\Rightarrow \quad x_1 = 1 + \sqrt{(1 + \log_{2+\sqrt{3}} 10)}$

$x_2 = 1 - \sqrt{(1 + \log_{2+\sqrt{3}} 10)}$

9. We have, $\quad x^2 + \left(\frac{x}{x-1}\right)^2 = 8$

$\Rightarrow \quad \left(x + \frac{x}{x-1}\right)^2 - 2 \cdot x \cdot \frac{x}{(x-1)} = 8$

$\Rightarrow \quad \left(\frac{x^2}{x-1}\right)^2 - 2\left(\frac{x^2}{x-1}\right) - 8 = 0 \quad \text{...(i)}$

Let $y = \frac{x^2}{x-1}$. Then, Eq. (i) reduces to

$y^2 - 2y - 8 = 0$

$\Rightarrow \quad (y-4)(y+2) = 0$

$\therefore \quad y = 4, -2$

If $y = 4$, then $\quad 4 = \frac{x^2}{x-1}$

or $\quad x^2 - 4x + 4 = 0$

or $\quad (x-2)^2 = 0$

or $\quad x = 2$

$\therefore \quad x_1 = 2$

and if $y = -2$, then $\quad -2 = \frac{x^2}{x-1}$

or $\quad x^2 + 2x - 2 = 0$

$\therefore \quad x = \frac{-2 \pm \sqrt{(4+8)}}{2}$

$\Rightarrow \quad x = -1 \pm \sqrt{3}$

$\therefore \quad x_2 = -1 + \sqrt{3}, x_3 = -1 - \sqrt{3}$

10. We have, $\sqrt{x + 8 + 2\sqrt{(x+7)}} + \sqrt{(x+1) - \sqrt{(x+7)}} = 4 \quad \text{...(i)}$

Let $\quad \sqrt{(x+7)} = \lambda \quad \text{...(ii)}$

or $\quad x = \lambda^2 - 7$

Then, Eq. (i) reduces to

$\sqrt{(\lambda^2 - 7 + 8 + 2\lambda)} + \sqrt{(\lambda^2 - 7 + 1 - \lambda)} = 4$

$\Rightarrow \quad (\lambda + 1) + \sqrt{(\lambda^2 - \lambda - 6)} = 4$

or $\quad \sqrt{(\lambda^2 - \lambda - 6)} = 3 - \lambda$

On squaring both sides, we get

$\lambda^2 - \lambda - 6 = 9 + \lambda^2 - 6\lambda$

$\Rightarrow \quad 5\lambda = 15$

$\therefore \quad \lambda = 3$

$\Rightarrow \quad \sqrt{(x+7)} = 3 \quad$ [from Eq. (ii)]

or $\quad x + 7 = 9$

$\therefore \quad x = 2$

and $x = 2$ satisfies Eq. (i).

Hence, $x_1 = 2$

11. We have, $\quad 4^{x^2} + 2(2a+1) 2^{x^2} + 4a^2 - 3 > 0 \quad \text{...(i)}$

On putting $t = 2^{x^2}$ in the Eq. (i), we get

$t^2 + 2(2a+1)t + 4a^2 - 3 > 0$

Let $\quad f(t) = t^2 + 2(2a+1)t + 4a^2 - 3 \quad [\because t > 0, \therefore 2^{x^2} > 0]$

$\because \quad f(t) > 0$

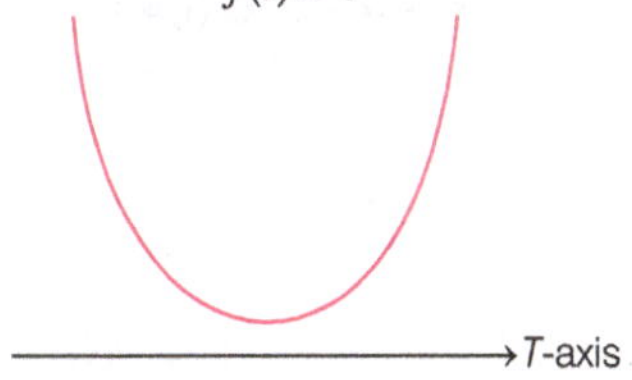

Consider the following cases:

***Case* I** Sum of the roots > 0

$-2\frac{(2a+1)}{1} > 0$

$\therefore \quad a \in \left(-\infty, -\frac{1}{2}\right)$

***Case* II** Product of the roots > 0

$\Rightarrow \quad \frac{4a^2 - 3}{1} > 0$

or $\quad a^2 > \frac{3}{4}$

or $\quad a \in \left(-\infty, -\frac{\sqrt{3}}{2}\right) \cup \left(\frac{\sqrt{3}}{2}, \infty\right)$

***Case* III** $\quad D < 0$

$\Rightarrow \quad 4(2a+1)^2 - 4 \cdot 1 \cdot (4a^2 - 3) < 0$

$\Rightarrow \quad 4a + 4 < 0$

$\therefore \quad a < -1$

or $\quad a \in (-\infty, -1)$

Combining all cases, we get

$a \in (-\infty, -1) \cup \left(\frac{\sqrt{3}}{2}, \infty\right)$

12. We have, $\quad \log_{x^2+2x-3}\left(\frac{|x+4| - |x|}{x-1}\right) > 0$

The given inequation is valid for

$\frac{|x+4| - |x|}{(x-1)} > 0$

and $\quad x^2 + 2x - 3 > 0, \neq 1 \quad \text{...(i)}$

Now, consider the following cases:

***Case* I** If $0 < x^2 + 2x - 3 < 1$

$\Rightarrow \quad 4 < x^2 + 2x + 1 < 5$

$\Rightarrow \quad 4 < (x+1)^2 < 5$

$\Rightarrow \quad -\sqrt{5} < (x+1) < -2 \text{ or } 2 < x+1 < \sqrt{5}$

$\Rightarrow \quad -\sqrt{5} - 1 < x < -3 \text{ or } 1 < x < \sqrt{5} - 1$

$\therefore \quad x \in (-\sqrt{5} - 1, -3) \cup (1, \sqrt{5} - 1)$ ...(ii)

Then, $\dfrac{|x+4| - |x|}{(x-1)} < 1$

Now, $x < -4$, then $\dfrac{-(x+4) + x}{(x-1)} < 1$

$\Rightarrow \quad 1 + \dfrac{4}{x-1} > 0 \Rightarrow \dfrac{(x+3)}{(x-1)} > 0$

$\therefore \quad x \in (-\infty, -3) \cup (1, \infty)$

$\Rightarrow \quad x \in (-\infty, -4)$ $[\because x < -4]$ ...(iii)

$-4 \le x < 0$, then $\dfrac{x+4+x}{(x-1)} - 1 < 0$

$\Rightarrow \quad \dfrac{(x+5)}{(x-1)} < 0$

$\therefore \quad x \in (-5, 1)$

$\Rightarrow \quad x \in [-4, 0)$ $[\because -4 \le x < 0]$ ...(iv)

and $\quad x \ge 0$, then $\dfrac{(x+4) - x}{(x-1)} < 1$

$\Rightarrow \quad 1 - \dfrac{4}{x-1} > 0$

$\Rightarrow \quad \dfrac{(x-5)}{(x-1)} > 0$

$\therefore \quad x \in (-\infty, 1) \cup (5, \infty)$

$\Rightarrow \quad x \in [0, 1) \cup (5, \infty)$ $[\because x \ge 0]$ ...(v)

From Eqs. (iii), (iv) and (v), we get

$x \in (-\infty, 1) \cup (5, \infty)$ ...(vi)

Now, common values in Eqs. (ii) and (iv) is

$x \in (-\sqrt{5} - 1, -3)$ ...(vii)

***Case* II** If $x^2 + 2x - 3 > 1$

$\Rightarrow \quad x^2 + 2x + 1 > 5 \Rightarrow (x+1)^2 > 5$

$\Rightarrow \quad x + 1 < -\sqrt{5}$

or $\quad x + 1 > \sqrt{5}$

$\therefore \quad x \in (-\infty, -1 - \sqrt{5}) \cup (\sqrt{5} - 1, \infty)$ ...(viii)

Then, $\dfrac{|x+4| - |x|}{(x-1)} > 1$

Now, $\quad x < -4$, then $\dfrac{-4}{x-1} > 1$

$\Rightarrow \quad 1 + \dfrac{4}{x-1} < 0$

$\Rightarrow \quad \dfrac{x+3}{x-1} < 0$

$\therefore \quad x \in (-3, 1)$

which is false. $[\because x < -4]$

$-4 \le x < 0$, then $\dfrac{2x+4}{(x-1)} - 1 > 0$

$\Rightarrow \quad \dfrac{(x+5)}{(x-1)} > 0$

$\therefore \quad x \in (-\infty, -5) \cup (1, \infty)$

which is false. $[\because -4 \le x < 0]$

and $\quad x \ge 0$, then $\dfrac{4}{x-1} > 1$

$\Rightarrow \quad 1 - \dfrac{4}{x-1} < 0$

$\Rightarrow \quad \dfrac{x-5}{x-1} < 0$

$\therefore \quad x \in (1, 5)$ ...(ix)

which is false. $[\because x \ge 0]$

Now, common values in Eq. (viii) and (ix) is

$\therefore \quad x \in (\sqrt{5} - 1, 5)$ ...(x)

Combining Eqs. (viii) and (x), we get

$x \in (-\sqrt{5} - 1, -3) \cup (\sqrt{5} - 1, 5)$

13. Let $y \ge 0$, then $|y| = y$

and then given system reduces to

$|x^2 - 2x| + y = 1$ ...(i)

and $\quad x^2 + y = 1$ ...(ii)

From Eqs. (i) and (ii), we get

$x^2 = |x^2 - 2x|$

$\Rightarrow \quad x^2 = |x||x-2|$

Now, $\quad x < 0, \quad 0 \le x < 2, \quad x \ge 2$

$x^2 = x(x-2), \quad x^2 = -x(x-2)$

$x^2 = x(x-2)$

$\therefore \quad x = 0$

$\Rightarrow \quad x(x + x - 2) = 0$

$\therefore \quad x = 0$

fail $\therefore x = 0, 1$ fail

$\Rightarrow \quad x = 0, 1$, then $y = 1, 0$

$\therefore$ Solutions are (0, 1) and (1, 0).

If $y < 0$ then $|y| = -y$ and then given system reduces to

$|x^2 - 2x| + y = 1$ ...(iii)

and $\quad x^2 - y = 1$ ...(iv)

From Eqs. (iii) and (iv), we get

$|x^2 - 2x| + x^2 = 2$

$\Rightarrow \quad |x||x-2| + x^2 = 2$

Now, $\quad x < 0, \quad 0 \le x < 2, \quad x \ge 2$

$x(x-2) + x^2 = 2$

$-x(x-2) + x^2 = 2$

$x(x-2) + x^2 = 2$

$\Rightarrow \quad 2x^2 - 2x - 2 = 0 \Rightarrow 2x = 2$

$\Rightarrow \quad x^2 - x - 1 = 0$

$\Rightarrow \quad x^2 - x - 1 = 0$

$\therefore \quad x = 1$

$\therefore \quad x = \dfrac{1 \pm \sqrt{5}}{2}$

$\therefore \quad x = \dfrac{1+\sqrt{5}}{2}$ fail $\Rightarrow x = \dfrac{1-\sqrt{5}}{2} \quad [\because x < 0]$

$\Rightarrow \quad x = \dfrac{1-\sqrt{5}}{2}, 1$, then $y = \dfrac{1-\sqrt{5}}{2}, 0$

$\therefore$ Solutions are $\left(\dfrac{1-\sqrt{5}}{2}, \dfrac{1-\sqrt{5}}{2}\right)$ and $(1, 0)$.

Hence, all pairs $(0, 1), (1, 0)$ and $\left(\dfrac{1-\sqrt{5}}{2}, \dfrac{1-\sqrt{5}}{2}\right)$ are solutions of the original system of equations.

14. Given, α, β and γ are the roots of the cubic equation

$$x^3 - px^2 + qx - r = 0 \quad \text{...(i)}$$

$\therefore \quad \alpha + \beta + \gamma = p, \ \alpha\beta + \beta\gamma + \gamma\alpha = q, \ \alpha\beta\gamma = r$

(i) Let $\quad y = \beta\gamma + \dfrac{1}{\alpha} \Rightarrow y = \dfrac{\alpha\beta\gamma + 1}{\alpha} = \dfrac{r+1}{\alpha}$

$\therefore \quad \alpha = \dfrac{r+1}{y}$

From Eq. (i), we get

$$\alpha^3 - p\alpha^2 + q\alpha - r = 0$$

$$\Rightarrow \quad \frac{(r+1)^3}{y^3} - \frac{p(r+1)^2}{y^2} + \frac{q(r+1)}{y} - r = 0$$

or $\quad ry^3 - q(r+1)y^2 + p(r+1)^2 y - (r+1)^3 = 0$

(ii) Let $y = \beta + \gamma - \alpha = (\alpha + \beta + \gamma) - 2\alpha = p - 2\alpha$

$\therefore \quad \alpha = \dfrac{p-y}{2}$

From Eq. (i), we get

$$\alpha^3 - p\alpha^2 + q\alpha - r = 0$$

$$\Rightarrow \quad \frac{(p-y)^3}{8} - \frac{p(p-y)^2}{4} + \frac{q(p-y)}{2} - r = 0$$

or $\quad y^3 - py^2 + (4q - p^2)y + (8r - 4pq + p^3) = 0$

Also, product of roots $= -(8r - 4pq + p^3)$

15. Assume $\alpha + i\beta$ is a complex root of the given equation, then conjugate of this root, i.e. $\alpha - i\beta$ is also root of this equation. On putting $x = \alpha + i\beta$ and $x = \alpha - i\beta$ in the given equation, we get

$$\frac{A_1^2}{\alpha + i\beta - a_1} + \frac{A_2^2}{\alpha + i\beta - a_2} + \frac{A_3^2}{\alpha + i\beta - a_3} + \ldots + \frac{A_n^2}{\alpha + i\beta - a_n} = ab^2 + c^2(\alpha + i\beta) + ac \quad \text{...(i)}$$

and $$\frac{A_1^2}{\alpha - i\beta - a_1} + \frac{A_2^2}{\alpha - i\beta - a_2} + \frac{A_3^2}{\alpha - i\beta - a_3} + \ldots + \frac{A_n^2}{\alpha - i\beta - a_n} = ab^2 + c^2(\alpha - i\beta) + ac \quad \text{...(ii)}$$

On subtracting Eq. (i) from Eq. (ii), we get

$$2i\beta \left[\frac{A_1^2}{(\alpha - a_1)^2 + \beta^2} + \frac{A_2^2}{(\alpha - a_2)^2 + \beta^2} + \frac{A_3^2}{(\alpha - a_3)^2 + \beta^2} + \ldots + \frac{A_n^2}{(\alpha - a_n)^2 + \beta^2} + c^2\right] = 0$$

The expression in bracket $\neq 0$

$\therefore \quad 2i\beta = 0 \Rightarrow \beta = 0$

Hence, all roots of the given equation are real.

16. Given equation is

$$x^4 + 2ax^3 + x^2 + 2ax + 1 = 0 \quad \text{...(i)}$$

On dividing by x^2, we get

$$x^2 + 2ax + 1 + \frac{2a}{x} + \frac{1}{x^2} = 0$$

$$\Rightarrow \quad \left(x^2 + \frac{1}{x^2}\right) + 2a\left(x + \frac{1}{x}\right) + 1 = 0$$

$$\Rightarrow \quad \left(x + \frac{1}{x}\right)^2 - 2 + 2a\left(x + \frac{1}{x}\right) + 1 = 0$$

or $$\left(x + \frac{1}{x}\right)^2 + 2a\left(x + \frac{1}{x}\right) - 1 = 0$$

or $\quad y^2 + 2ay - 1 = 0$, where $y = x + \dfrac{1}{x}$

$$\therefore \quad y = \frac{-2a \pm \sqrt{(4a^2 + 4)}}{2} = -a \pm \sqrt{(a^2 + 1)}$$

Taking '+' sign, we get

$$y = -a + \sqrt{(a^2 + 1)}$$

$$\Rightarrow \quad x + \frac{1}{x} = -a + \sqrt{(a^2 + 1)}$$

or $$x^2 + (a - \sqrt{(a^2 + 1)})\,x + 1 = 0 \quad \text{...(ii)}$$

Taking '–' sign, we get $\quad y = -a - \sqrt{(a^2 + 1)}$

$$\Rightarrow \quad x + \frac{1}{x} = -a - \sqrt{(a^2 + 1)}$$

or $$x^2 + (a + \sqrt{(a^2 + 1)})\,x + 1 = 0 \quad \text{...(iii)}$$

Let α, β be the roots of Eq. (ii) and γ, δ be the roots of Eq. (iii).

Then, $\quad \alpha + \beta = \sqrt{(a^2 + 1)} - a$

and $\quad \alpha\beta = 1$

and $\quad \gamma + \delta = -\sqrt{(a^2 + 1)} - a$

and $\quad \gamma\delta = 1$

Clearly, $\alpha + \beta > 0$ and $\alpha\beta > 0$

$\therefore$ Either α, β will be imaginary or both real and positive according to the Eq. (i) has atleast two distinct negative roots. Therefore, both γ and δ must be negative.

Therefore,

(i) $\gamma\delta > 0$, which is true as $\gamma\delta = 1$.

(ii) $\quad \gamma + \delta < 0$

$\Rightarrow \quad -(a + \sqrt{(a^2 + 1)}) < 0$

$\Rightarrow \quad a + \sqrt{(a^2 + 1)} > 0$, which is true for all a.

$\therefore \quad a \in R$

(iii) $\quad D > 0$

$\therefore \quad (a + \sqrt{(a^2 + 1)})^2 - 4 > 0$

$\Rightarrow \quad (a + \sqrt{(a^2 + 1)} + 2)(a + \sqrt{(a^2 + 1)} - 2) > 0$

$\because \quad a + \sqrt{(a^2 + 1)} + 2 > 0$

$\therefore \quad a + \sqrt{(a^2 + 1)} - 2 > 0$

$\Rightarrow \quad \sqrt{(a^2 + 1)} > 2 - a$

$$\Rightarrow \quad \begin{cases} a \ge 2 \\ \text{or } a^2 + 1 > (2-a)^2, \text{ if } a < 2 \end{cases}$$

$$\Rightarrow \quad \begin{cases} a \ge 2 \\ \text{or } a > \frac{3}{4}, \text{ if } a < 2 \end{cases} \Rightarrow \begin{cases} a \ge 2 \\ \text{or } \frac{3}{4} < a < 2 \end{cases}$$

Hence, $\frac{3}{4} < a < \infty$ or $a \in \left(\frac{3}{4}, \infty\right)$

17. We have, $6x^2 - 77[x] + 147 = 0$

$\Rightarrow \quad \dfrac{6x^2 + 147}{77} = [x]$

$\Rightarrow \quad (0.078)\,x^2 = [x] - 1.9$

$\because \quad (0.078)\,x^2 > 0 \Rightarrow x^2 > 0$

$\therefore \quad [x] - 1.9 > 0$ or $[x] > 1.9$

$\therefore \quad [x] = 2, 3, 4, 5, \ldots$

If $[x] = 2$, i.e. $2 \le x < 3$

Then, $x^2 = \dfrac{2 - 1.9}{0.078} = 1.28$

$\therefore \quad x = 1.13$ [fail]

If $[x] = 3$, i.e. $3 \le x < 4$

Then, $x^2 = \dfrac{3 - 1.9}{0.078} = 14.1$

$\therefore \quad x = 3.75$ [true]

If $[x] = 4$, i.e. $4 \le x < 5$

Then, $x^2 = \dfrac{4 - 1.9}{0.078} = 26.9$

$\therefore \quad x = 5.18$ [fail]

If $[x] = 5$, i.e. $5 \le x < 6$

Then, $x^2 = \dfrac{5 - 1.9}{0.078} = 39.7$

$\therefore \quad x = 6.3$ [fail]

If $[x] = 6$, i.e. $6 \le x < 7$

Then, $x^2 = \dfrac{6 - 1.9}{0.078} = \dfrac{4.1}{0.078} = 52.56$

$\therefore \quad x = 7.25$ [fail]

If $[x] = 7$, i.e. $7 \le x < 8$

Then, $x^2 = \dfrac{7 - 1.9}{0.078} = \dfrac{5.1}{0.078} = 65.38$

$\therefore \quad x = 8.08$ [fail]

If $[x] = 8$, i.e. $8 \le x < 9$

Then, $x^2 = \dfrac{8 - 1.9}{0.078} = \dfrac{6.1}{0.078} = 78.2$

$\therefore \quad x = 8.8$ [true]

If $[x] = 9$, i.e. $9 \le x < 10$

Then, $x^2 = \dfrac{9 - 1.9}{0.078} = \dfrac{7.1}{0.078} = 91.03$

$\therefore \quad x = 9.5$ [true]

If $[x] = 10$, i.e. $10 \le x < 11$

Then, $x^2 = \dfrac{10 - 1.9}{0.078} = \dfrac{8.1}{0.078} = 103.8$

$\therefore \quad x = 10.2$ [true]

If $[x] = 11$, i.e. $11 \le x < 12$

Then, $x^2 = \dfrac{11 - 1.9}{0.078} = \dfrac{9.1}{0.078} = 116.7$

$\therefore \quad x = 10.8$ [fail]

Other values are fail.

Hence, number of solutions is four.

18. Since, the given equation is

$$x^2 - 2x - a^2 + 1 = 0 \Rightarrow (x-1)^2 = a^2$$

$\therefore \quad x - 1 \ne a$ or $x = 1 \pm a$

$\Rightarrow \quad \alpha = 1 + a$ and $\beta = 1 - a$

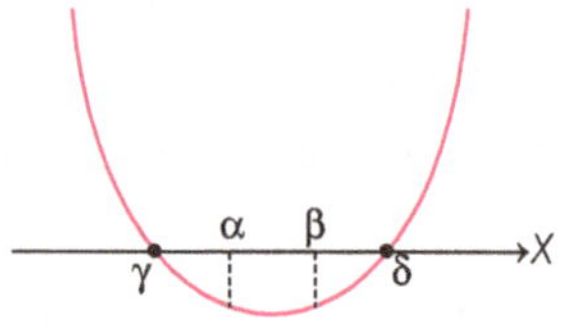

Let $f(x) = x^2 - 2(a+1)\,x + a\,(a-1)$, thus the following conditions hold good:

Consider the following cases:

Case I $\quad D > 0$

$\Rightarrow \quad 4\,(a+1)^2 - 4a\,(a-1) > 0$

$\Rightarrow \quad 3a + 1 > 0$

$\therefore \quad a > -\dfrac{1}{3}$

Case II $\quad f(\alpha) < 0 \Rightarrow f(1+a) < 0$

$\Rightarrow (1+a)^2 - 2\,(1+a)\,(1+a) + a\,(a-1) < 0$

$\Rightarrow \quad -(1+a)^2 + a\,(a-1) < 0$

$\Rightarrow \quad -3a - 1 < 0 \Rightarrow a > -\dfrac{1}{3}$

Case III $\quad f(s) = 0 \Rightarrow f(1-a) < 0$

$\Rightarrow (1-a)^2 - 2\,(a+1)\,(1-a) + a\,(a-1) < 0$

$\Rightarrow \quad (4a+1)\,(a-1) < 0$

$\therefore \quad -\dfrac{1}{4} < a < 1$

Combining all cases we get

$$a \in \left(-\frac{1}{4}, 1\right)$$

19. $pr = (-p)\,(-r)$

$= (\alpha + \beta + \gamma + \delta)(\alpha\beta\gamma + \alpha\beta\delta + \gamma\delta\alpha + \gamma\delta\beta)$

$= \alpha^2\beta\gamma + \alpha^2\beta\delta + \alpha^2\gamma\delta + \alpha\beta\gamma\delta + \beta^2\gamma\alpha$

$+ \beta^2\alpha\delta + \alpha\beta\gamma\delta + \beta^2\gamma\delta + \gamma^2\alpha\beta + \alpha\beta\gamma\delta$

$+ \gamma^2\delta\alpha + \gamma^2\delta\beta + \alpha\beta\gamma\delta + \alpha\beta\delta^2 + \gamma\alpha\delta^2 + \gamma\beta\delta^2$

$\because \quad \text{AM} \ge \text{GM}$

$\Rightarrow \quad \dfrac{pr}{16} \ge (\alpha^{16}\beta^{16}\gamma^{16}\delta^{16})^{1/16} = \alpha\beta\gamma\delta = 5$

$\Rightarrow \quad \dfrac{pr}{16} \ge 5$ or $pr \ge 80$

$\therefore$ Minimum value of pr is 80.

> *If people do not believe that mathematics is simple, it is only because they do not realize how complicated life is.*
>
> **–John Von Neumann**

3 Sequences and Series

Learning Milestones

Milestone 1 Arithmetic Progression
- Sequence
- Series
- Progression
- Arithmetic Progression

Milestone 2 Geometric and Harmonic Progression
- Geometric Sequence or Geometric Progression (GP)
- Harmonic Sequence or Harmonic Progression (HP)

Milestone 3 Arithmetic Mean, Geometric Mean and Harmonic Mean
- Arithmetic Mean
- Geometric Mean
- Harmonic Mean
- Application to Solve Problems of Maxima and Minima without Using Caculus

Milestone 4 Some Special Series
- Arithmetico-Geometric Series (AGS)
- Sigma Notation
- Natural Numbers

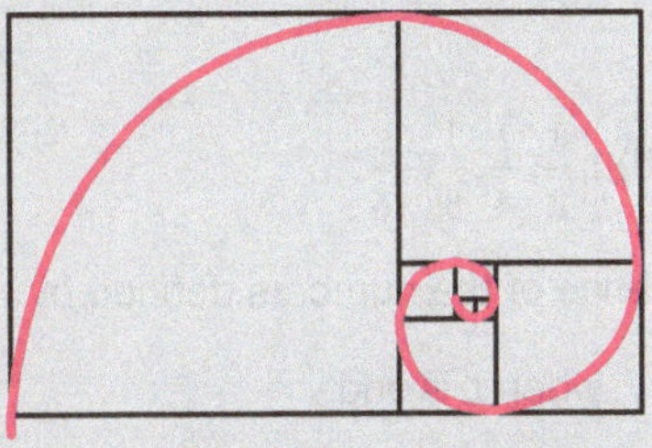

Practice Milestones

Practice Milestone 1- JEE Main Pattern

Practice Milestone 2 - JEE Advanced Pattern

Practice Milestone 3 - Challenging Problems

Milestone 1 Arithmetic Progression

• Sequence • Series • Progression • Arithmetic Progression

3.1 Sequence

A succession of numbers arranged in a definite order or arrangement according to some well-defined law is called a sequence.

Or

A sequence is a function of natural numbers (N) with codomain is the set of real numbers (R) [complex numbers (C)]. If range is subset of real numbers (complex numbers), it is called a real sequence (complex sequence).

Or

A mapping $f: N \to C$, then $f(n) = t_n, n \in N$ is called a sequence to be denoted it by

$$\{f(1), f(2), f(3), \ldots\} = \{t_1, t_2, t_3, \ldots\} = \{t_n\}.$$

The nth term of a sequence is denoted by $T_n, t_n, a_n, a(n), u_n$, etc.

JEE SPIKE

The term of sequence $a_1, a_2, a_3, \ldots$ is generally written as $\{a_n\}$.

e.g.

(i) 1, 3, 5, 7, ... is a sequence, because each term (except first) is obtained by adding 2 to the previous term or $T_n = 2n - 1, n \in N$.

(ii) 1, 2, 3, 5, 8, 13, ... is a sequence, because each term (except first two) is obtained by taking the sum of preceding two terms.

Or

If $T_1 = 1, T_2 = 2, T_{n+2} = T_n + T_{n+1}, n \geq 1$

(iii) 2, 3, 5, 7, 11, 13, 17, 19, ... is a sequence.

Here, we cannot express $T_n, n \in N$ by an algebraic formula.

Recursive Formula

A formula to determine the other terms of the sequence in terms of its preceding terms is known as recursive formula.

e.g. If $T_1 = 1$ and $T_{n+1} = 6T_n, n \in N$.

Then, $T_2 = 6T_1 = 6 \cdot 1 = 6$

$T_3 = 6T_2 = 6 \cdot 6 = 36$

$T_4 = 6T_3 = 6 \cdot 36 = 216 \ldots$

Then, sequence is 1, 6, 36, 216,...

Example 1. Write the first three terms of the sequence defined by $a_n = n(n+4)$.

Sol. We have,

$$a_n = n(n+4)$$

$\therefore$ $a_1 = 1(1+4) = 5$

$a_2 = 2(2+4) = 12$

$a_3 = 3(3+4) = 21$

So, first three terms are 5, 12, 21.

Types of Sequences

There are two types of sequences

1. Finite Sequence

A sequence is said to be finite sequence, if it has finite number of terms. A finite sequence is described by $a_1, a_2, a_3, \ldots, a_n$ or $T_1, T_2, T_3, \ldots, T_n$, where $n \in N$.

e.g.

(i) 3, 5, 7, 9, ..., 37

(ii) 2, 6, 18, 54, ..., 4374

2. Infinite Sequence

A sequence is said to be an infinite sequence, if it has infinite number of terms. An infinite sequence is described by $a_1, a_2, a_3, \ldots$ or $T_1, T_2, T_3, \ldots$

e.g.

(i) $1, \frac{1}{3}, \frac{1}{9}, \frac{1}{27}, \ldots$ (ii) $1, \frac{1}{2}, \frac{1}{4}, \frac{1}{8}, \frac{1}{16}, \ldots$

Example 2. Find the sequence of the numbers defined by

$$a_n = \begin{cases} \frac{1}{n}, & \text{when } n \text{ is odd} \\ -\frac{1}{n}, & \text{when } n \text{ is even} \end{cases}$$

Sol. When n is odd, $a_n = \frac{1}{n}$

$\therefore \quad a_1 = 1, a_3 = \frac{1}{3}, a_5 = \frac{1}{5}, \ldots$

When n is even, $a_n = -\frac{1}{n}$

$\therefore \quad a_2 = -\frac{1}{2}, a_4 = -\frac{1}{4}, a_6 = -\frac{1}{6}, \ldots$

So, sequence is

$$1, -\frac{1}{2}, \frac{1}{3}, -\frac{1}{4}, \frac{1}{5}, -\frac{1}{6}, \ldots$$

Example 3. If $f: N \to R$, where $f(n) = a_n = \frac{n}{(2n+1)^2}$, write the sequence in ordered pair form.

Sol. Here, $a_n = \frac{n}{(2n+1)^2}$

On putting $n = 1, 2, 3, 4, \ldots$ successively, we get

$$a_1 = \frac{1}{(2\cdot 1+1)^2} = \frac{1}{9}, \quad a_2 = \frac{2}{(2\cdot 2+1)^2} = \frac{2}{25}$$

$$a_3 = \frac{3}{(2\cdot 3+1)^2} = \frac{3}{49}, \quad a_4 = \frac{4}{(2\cdot 4+1)^2} = \frac{4}{81}$$

$$\vdots \qquad \vdots \qquad \vdots$$

Hence, we obtain the sequence $\frac{1}{9}, \frac{2}{25}, \frac{3}{49}, \frac{4}{81}, \ldots$

Now, the sequence in ordered pair form is

$$\left\{\left(1, \frac{1}{9}\right), \left(2, \frac{2}{25}\right), \left(3, \frac{3}{49}\right), \left(4, \frac{4}{81}\right), \ldots\right\}$$

Example 4. The Fibonacci sequence is defined by $a_1 = 1 = a_2, a_n = a_{n-1} + a_{n-2}, n > 2$. Find $\frac{a_{n+1}}{a_n}$ for $n = 1, 2, 3, 4, 5$.

Sol. $\because \quad a_1 = 1 = a_2$

$\therefore \quad a_3 = a_2 + a_1 = 1 + 1 = 2,$

$a_4 = a_3 + a_2 = 2 + 1 = 3$

$a_5 = a_4 + a_3 = 3 + 2 = 5$

and $\quad a_6 = a_5 + a_4 = 5 + 3 = 8$

$\therefore \quad \frac{a_2}{a_1} = 1, \frac{a_3}{a_2} = \frac{2}{1} = 2$

$\frac{a_4}{a_3} = \frac{3}{2}, \frac{a_5}{a_4} = \frac{5}{3}$ and $\frac{a_6}{a_5} = \frac{8}{5}$

3.2 Series

In a sequence, the sum of the directed terms is called a series.

e.g. If 1, 4, 7, 10, 13, 16,... is a sequence, then its sum i.e. $1 + 4 + 7 + 10 + 13 + 16 + \ldots$ is a series.

In general, if $T_1, T_2, T_3, \ldots, T_n, \ldots$ denote a sequence, then the symbolic expression $T_1 + T_2 + T_3 + \ldots + T_n + \ldots$ is called a series associated with the given sequence.

Each member of the series is called its term.

In a series, $T_1 + T_2 + T_3 + \ldots + T_r + \ldots$, the sum of first n terms is denoted by S_n. Thus,

$$S_n = T_1 + T_2 + T_3 + \ldots + T_n$$
$$= \sum_{r=1}^{n} T_r = \sum T_n$$

If S_n denotes the sum of n terms of a sequence.

Then, $\quad S_n - S_{n-1} = (T_1 + T_2 + T_3 + \ldots + T_n) - (T_1 + T_2 + \ldots + T_{n-1}) = T_n$

Thus, $\quad T_n = S_n - S_{n-1}$

Types of Series

There are two types of series

1. Finite Series

A series having finite number of terms is called a finite series.

e.g.

(i) $3 + 5 + 7 + 9 + \ldots + 21$

(ii) $2 + 6 + 18 + 54 + \ldots + 4374$

2. Infinite Series

A series having an infinite number of terms is called an infinite series.

e.g.

(i) $1 + \frac{1}{3} + \frac{1}{9} + \frac{1}{27} + \ldots$

(ii) $1 + \frac{1}{2} + \frac{1}{4} + \frac{1}{8} + \ldots$

Example 5. Find the first four terms of the sequence, $a_n = 5n - 1$ and write down the corresponding series.

Sol. We have, $a_n = 5n - 1$

$\therefore \quad a_1 = 5 \times 1 - 1 = 4, a_2 = 5 \times 2 - 1 = 9$

$a_3 = 5 \times 3 - 1 = 14, a_4 = 5 \times 4 - 1 = 19$

Hence, first four terms are 4, 9, 14, 19.

The corresponding series is $4 + 9 + 14 + 19 + \ldots$

Example 6. If the sum of n terms of a series is $2n^2 + 5n$ for all values of n, find its 7th term.

Sol. Given, $S_n = 2n^2 + 5n$

$\Rightarrow \quad S_{n-1} = 2(n-1)^2 + 5(n-1) = 2n^2 + n - 3$

$\therefore \quad T_n = S_n - S_{n-1} = (2n^2 + 5n) - (2n^2 + n - 3) = 4n + 3$

Hence, $T_7 = 4 \times 7 + 3 = 31$

Example 7.

(i) Write $\sum_{r=1}^{n}(r^2+2)$ in expanded form.

(ii) Write the series $\frac{1}{3}+\frac{2}{4}+\frac{3}{5}+\frac{4}{6}+\ldots+\frac{n}{n+2}$ in sigma form.

Sol. (i) On putting $r = 1, 2, 3, 4, \ldots, n$ in (r^2+2), we get

$$3, 6, 11, 18, \ldots, (n^2+2)$$

Hence, $\sum_{r=1}^{n}(r^2+2) = 3+6+11+18+\ldots+(n^2+2)$

(ii) The rth term of series $= \frac{r}{r+2}$.

Hence, the given series can be written as

$$\frac{1}{3}+\frac{2}{4}+\frac{3}{5}+\frac{4}{6}+\ldots+\frac{n}{n+2} = \sum_{r=1}^{n}\left(\frac{r}{r+2}\right)$$

3.3. Progression

If the terms of a sequence can be described by an explicit formula, then the sequence is called a progression.

Or

A sequence is said to be progression, if its terms increases or decreases, respectively numerically.

e.g. The following sequences are progression

(i) $1, 3, 5, 7, \ldots$ (ii) $\frac{1}{2}, \frac{1}{6}, \frac{1}{18}, \frac{1}{54}, \ldots$

(iii) $1, -\frac{1}{3}, \frac{1}{9}, -\frac{1}{27}, \ldots$ (iv) $1, 8, 27, 256, \ldots$

(v) $8, -4, 2, -1, \frac{1}{2}, \ldots$

The sequences (iii) and (v) are progressions, because

$$|1| > \left|-\frac{1}{3}\right| > \left|\frac{1}{9}\right| > \left|-\frac{1}{27}\right| > \ldots \text{ i.e. } 1 > \frac{1}{3} > \frac{1}{9} > \frac{1}{27} > \ldots$$

and $|8| > |-4| > |2| > |-1| > \left|\frac{1}{2}\right| > \ldots$ i.e. $8 > 4 > 2 > 1 > \frac{1}{2} > \ldots$

3.4 Arithmetic Progression (AP)

An arithmetic progression is a sequence in which the difference between any term and its just preceding term (i.e. term before it) is constant throughout. This constant is called the common difference (abbreviated as CD) and is generally denoted by 'd'.

Or

An arithmetic progression is a sequence whose terms increase or decrease by a fixed number. This fixed number is called the common difference of the AP.

A finite or infinite sequence $\{t_1, t_2, t_3, \ldots, t_n\}$ or $\{t_1, t_2, t_3, \ldots\}$ is said to be an arithmetic progression (AP), if $t_k - t_{k-1} = d$, a constant independent of k, for $k \geq 2$.

The constant d is called the common difference of the AP.

i.e. $d = t_2 - t_1 = t_3 - t_2 = \ldots = t_n - t_{n-1}$

JEE Focus Points

- If a be the first term and d be the common difference, then AP can be written as
  $a, a+d, a+2d, \ldots, a+(n-1)d, \ldots, \forall n \in N$.
- If we add the common difference to any term of AP, we get the next following term and if we subtract it from any term, we get the preceding term.
- The common difference of an AP may be **positive, zero, negative or imaginary.**
- **Constant AP** common difference of an AP is equal to zero.
- **Increasing AP** common difference of an AP is greater than zero.
- **Decreasing AP** common difference of an AP is less than zero.
- **Imaginary AP** common difference of an AP is imaginary.
- If the nth term of a sequence is an expression of first degree in n. e.g. $t_n = An + B$, where A, B are constants, then that sequence will be in AP for $t_n - t_{n-1} = (An+B) - [A(n-1)+B] = A[n-(n-1)] = A =$ constant $=$ Common difference or coefficient of n in t_n. Students are advised to consider the above point as a behaviour of standard result.

Algorithm to determine whether a sequence is an AP or not

***Step* I** Obtain t_n (the nth term of the sequence).

***Step* II** Replace n by $n-1$ in t_n to get t_{n-1}.

***Step* III** Calculate $t_n - t_{n-1}$.

If $t_n - t_{n-1}$ is independent of n, the given sequence is an AP otherwise it is not an AP.

Example 8. Show that the sequence $<t_n>$ defined by $t_n = 5n+4$ is an AP, also find its common difference.

Sol. We have, $t_n = 5n+4$

On replacing n by $(n-1)$, we get

$$t_{n-1} = 5(n-1)+4 \Rightarrow t_{n-1} = 5n-1$$

$$\therefore \quad t_n - t_{n-1} = (5n+4)-(5n-1) = 5$$

Clearly, $t_n - t_{n-1}$ is independent of n and is equal to 5.

So, the given sequence is an AP with common difference 5.

Example 9. Show that the sequence $<t_n>$ defined by $t_n = 3n^2+2$ is not an AP.

Sol. We have, $t_n = 3n^2+2$

On replacing n by $(n-1)$, we get

$$t_{n-1} = 3(n-1)^2+2$$

$$\Rightarrow \quad t_{n-1} = 3n^2 - 6n + 5$$

$$\therefore \quad t_n - t_{n-1} = (3n^2 + 2) - (3n^2 - 6n + 5)$$

$$= 6n - 3$$

Clearly, $t_n - t_{n-1}$ is not independent of n and therefore it is not constant. So, the given sequence is not an AP.

General Term of an AP

Let a be the first term, d be the common difference and l be the last term of an AP having n terms, where $n \in N$.

Then, AP can be written as $a, a+d, a+2d, \ldots, l-2d, l-d, l$

(i) *n*th Term of an AP from Beginning

1st term from beginning $= t_1 = a = a + (1-1)\,d$

2nd term from beginning $= t_2 = a + d = a + (2-1)\,d$

3rd term from beginning $= t_3 = a + 2d = a + (3-1)\,d$

$\vdots \quad \vdots \quad \vdots \quad \vdots$

n th term from beginning $= t_n = a + (n-1)\,d, \forall\, n \in N$

Hence, nth term of an AP from beginning

$= t_n = a + (n-1)\,d = l$ [last term]

(ii) *n*th Term of an AP from End

1st term from end $= t'_1 = l = l - (1-1)\,d$

2nd term from end $= t'_2 = l - d = l - (2-1)\,d$

3rd term from end $= t'_3 = l - 2d = l - (3-1)\,d$

$\vdots \quad \vdots \quad \vdots \quad \vdots$

nth term from end $= t'_n = l - (n-1)\,d, \forall\, n \in N$

Hence, nth term of an AP from end $t'_n = l - (n-1)\,d = a$

[first term]

Now, it is clear that

$t_n + t'_n = a + (n-1)\,d + l - (n-1)\,d = a + l$

or $\quad t_n + t'_n = a + l$

i.e. In a finite AP, the sum of the terms equidistant from the beginning and end is always same and is equal to the sum of first and last term.

JEE Focus Points

- nth term is also called the **general term**.
- If last term of AP is t_n and **common difference** be d, then terms of AP from end are $t_n, t_n - d, t_n - 2d, \ldots$
- If in a sequence, the terms are alternatively positive and negative, then it cannot be an AP.
- Common difference of AP $= \dfrac{l-a}{n-1}$, where, a = first term of AP, l = last term of AP and n = number of terms of AP.
- If t_n, t_{n+1}, t_{n+2} are three consecutive terms of an AP, then $2t_{n+1} = t_n + t_{n+2}$.
- In particular, if a, b and c are in AP, then $2b = a + c$.

Example 10. If $(x+1), 3x$ and $(4x+2)$ are first three terms of an AP, then its 5th term is

(a) 14 (b) 19

(c) 24 (d) 28

Sol. (c) We have, $(x+1), 3x, (4x+2)$ are in AP.

$$\Rightarrow \quad 3x - (x+1) = (4x+2) - 3x$$

$$\Rightarrow \quad 2x - 1 = x + 2 \Rightarrow x = 3$$

$$\therefore \quad a = x + 1 = 4$$

$$\text{and} \quad d = 3x - (x+1) = 9 - 4 = 5$$

$$\text{So,} \quad a_5 = a + 4d = 4 + 4 \times 5 = 24$$

JEE SCANNER

Example Similar to PYQ Asked in JEE Main 2024

For $x \ge 0$, the least value of k, for which $6^{1+x} + 6^{2+x}$, $\frac{k}{3}$, $36^x + 36^{-x}$ are three consecutive terms of an AP, is equal to

(a) 22 (b) 33 (c) 44 (d) 66

Sol. (d) Since $6^{1+x} + 6^{2+x}, \frac{k}{3}, 36^x + 36^{-x}$ are in AP.

$$\therefore \quad 2 \times \frac{k}{3} = (6^{1+x} + 6^{2+x}) + (36^x + 36^{-x})$$

$$= 6 \cdot 6^x + 6^2 \cdot 6^x + 36^x + 36^{-x}$$

$$= 6^x \cdot 6(1+6) + 6^{2x} + 6^{-2x}$$

$$= \underbrace{6^x \cdot 6 \cdot 7}_{\ge 42} + \underbrace{6^{2x} + 6^{-2x}}_{\ge 2}$$

$$\therefore \quad \frac{2k}{3} \ge 42 + 2$$

$$\Rightarrow \quad \frac{2k}{3} \ge 44 \Rightarrow k \ge 66 \Rightarrow k = 66$$

Skill Builder

For $x \ge 0$, the least value of k, for which $4^x + 4^{-x}$, $\frac{k}{4}$, $6^x + 6^{-x}$ are three consecutive terms of an AP, is equal to

(a) 2 (b) 6

(c) 8 (d) 7

For Sol.

■ **For more practice** See Q.13 of Milestone Practice 3.1.

Example 11. Find the term of the series $20, 19\frac{1}{4}, 18\frac{1}{2}, 17\frac{3}{4}, \ldots$ which is numerically the smallest.

Sol. The given sequence is an AP in which first term, $a = 20$ and common difference, $d = -\frac{3}{4}$. Let the nth term of the given AP be the first negative term.

Then, $t_n < 0 \Rightarrow a + (n-1)d < 0$

$$\Rightarrow \quad 20 + (n-1)\left(-\frac{3}{4}\right) < 0$$

$$\Rightarrow \quad 80 - 3n + 3 < 0$$

$$\Rightarrow \quad n > \frac{83}{3} \text{ or } n > 27\frac{2}{3}$$

$$\Rightarrow \quad n = 28$$

Thus, 28th term of the given sequence is the first negative term and 27th is smallest positive term.

Now, $a_{27} = a + 26d = 20 + 26 \times \left(-\frac{3}{4}\right) = \frac{1}{2}$

and $a_{28} = a + 27d = 20 + 27 \times \left(-\frac{3}{4}\right) = -\frac{1}{4}$

So, $\frac{1}{2}$ is numerically smallest.

Example 12. If the mth term of an AP is $\frac{1}{n}$ and the nth term is $\frac{1}{m}$, then find mnth term of an AP.

Sol. If A and B are constants, then rth term of AP is

$$t_r = Ar + B$$

Given, $t_m = \frac{1}{n}$

$$\Rightarrow \quad Am + B = \frac{1}{n} \quad \text{...(i)}$$

and $t_n = \frac{1}{m} \Rightarrow An + B = \frac{1}{m}$ ...(ii)

From Eqs. (i) and (ii), we get

$$A = \frac{1}{mn} \text{ and } B = 0$$

mnth term $= t_{mn} = Amn + B = \frac{1}{mn} \cdot mn + 0 = 1$

Hence, mnth term of the given AP is 1.

Example 13. If $|x-1|$, 3 and $|x-3|$ are first three terms of an increasing AP, then find the 6th term of an AP.

Sol. ***Case* I** For $x < 1$,

$$|x-1| = -(x-1)$$

and $|x-3| = -(x-3)$

$\therefore 1 - x, 3$ and $3 - x$ are in AP.

$$\Rightarrow \quad 6 = 1 - x + 3 - x$$

$$\Rightarrow \quad x = -1$$

Then, first three terms are 2, 3, 4, which is an increasing AP.

$\therefore$ 6th term is 7. $[\because d = 1]$

***Case* II** For $1 < x < 3$,

$$|x-1| = x - 1$$

and $|x-3| = -(x-3) = 3 - x$

$\therefore x - 1, 3$ and $3 - x$ are in AP.

$$\Rightarrow \quad 6 = x - 1 + 3 - x$$

$$\Rightarrow \quad 6 = 2 \quad \text{[impossible]}$$

***Case* III** For $x > 3$, $|x-1| = x-1$ and $|x-3| = x-3$

$\therefore x - 1, 3$ and $x - 3$ are in AP.

$$\Rightarrow \quad 6 = x - 1 + x - 3 \Rightarrow x = 5$$

Then, first three terms are 4, 3, 2, which is a decreasing AP.

Example 14. In the sequence 1, 2, 2, 3, 3, 3, 4, 4, 4, ..., where n consecutive terms have the value n, find the 150th term of the sequence.

Sol. Let the 150th term $= n$.

Then, $1 + 2 + 3 + \ldots + (n-1) < 150 < 1 + 2 + 3 + \ldots + n$

$$\Rightarrow \quad \frac{(n-1)n}{2} < 150 < \frac{n(n+1)}{2}$$

$$\Rightarrow \quad n(n-1) < 300 < n(n+1)$$

Taking first two members

$$n(n-1) < 300$$

$$\Rightarrow \quad n^2 - n - 300 < 0$$

$$\Rightarrow \quad \left(n - \frac{1}{2}\right)^2 < 300 + \frac{1}{4}$$

$$\Rightarrow \quad 0 < n < \frac{1}{2} + \frac{\sqrt{1201}}{2}$$

$$\Rightarrow \quad 0 < n < 17.8 \quad \text{...(i)}$$

and taking last two members,

$$n(n+1) > 300$$

$$\Rightarrow \quad \left(n + \frac{1}{2}\right)^2 > 300 + \frac{1}{4}$$

$$\therefore \quad n > -\frac{1}{2} + \frac{\sqrt{1201}}{2} \Rightarrow n > 16.8 \quad \text{...(ii)}$$

From Eqs. (i) and (ii), we get

$$16.8 < n < 17.8 \Rightarrow n = 17$$

Example 15. If a_1, a_2, a_3, a_4 and a_5 are in AP with common difference $\neq 0$, find the value of $\sum_{i=1}^{5} a_i$ when $a_3 = 2$.

Sol. $\because a_1, a_2, a_3, a_4$ and a_5 are in AP, we have

$$a_1 + a_5 = a_2 + a_4 = a_3 + a_3 \quad [\because t_n + t'_n = a + l]$$

$$a_1 + a_5 = a_2 + a_4 = 4 \quad [\because a_3 = 2]$$

$$a_1 + a_2 + a_3 + a_4 + a_5 = 4 + 2 + 4 = 10$$

$$\Rightarrow \quad \sum_{i=1}^{5} a_i = 10$$

Example 16. If $a_1, a_2, \ldots, a_n$ are in AP, where $a_i > 0$ for all i, then show that

$$\frac{1}{\sqrt{a_1} + \sqrt{a_2}} + \frac{1}{\sqrt{a_2} + \sqrt{a_3}} + \ldots + \frac{1}{\sqrt{a_{n-1}} + \sqrt{a_n}} = \frac{n-1}{\sqrt{a_1} + \sqrt{a_n}}.$$

Sol. Let $a_1, a_2, a_3, \ldots, a_n$ be in AP with common difference d.

$\therefore a_2 - a_1 = a_3 - a_2 = \ldots = a_n - a_{n-1} = d$

Now, $\frac{1}{\sqrt{a_1}+\sqrt{a_2}} + \frac{1}{\sqrt{a_2}+\sqrt{a_3}} + \ldots + \frac{1}{\sqrt{a_{n-1}}+\sqrt{a_n}}$

$$= \frac{\sqrt{a_2}-\sqrt{a_1}}{a_2-a_1} + \frac{\sqrt{a_3}-\sqrt{a_2}}{a_3-a_2} + \ldots + \frac{\sqrt{a_n}-\sqrt{a_{n-1}}}{a_n-a_{n-1}}$$

$$= \frac{\sqrt{a_2}-\sqrt{a_1}}{d} + \frac{\sqrt{a_3}-\sqrt{a_2}}{d} + \ldots + \frac{\sqrt{a_n}-\sqrt{a_{n-1}}}{d}$$

$$= \frac{\sqrt{a_n}-\sqrt{a_1}}{d} = \frac{a_n - a_1}{d[\sqrt{a_n}+\sqrt{a_1}]}$$

$$= \frac{(n-1)d}{d[\sqrt{a_n}+\sqrt{a_1}]} = \frac{n-1}{\sqrt{a_n}+\sqrt{a_1}}$$

Sum of *n* Terms of an AP

Let a be the first term, d be the common difference, l be the last term of an AP having n terms and S_n be the sum of n terms, then

$$S_n = a + (a+d) + (a+2d) + \ldots + (l-2d) + (l-d) + l \quad \ldots\text{(i)}$$

Reversing the right hand terms

$$S_n = l + (l-d) + (l-2d) + \ldots + (a+2d) + (a+d) + a \quad \ldots\text{(ii)}$$

On adding Eqs. (i) and (ii), we get

$$2S_n = (a+l) + (a+l) + (a+l) + \ldots + (a+l) + (a+l) + (a+l)$$

$$= (a+l) + (a+l) + \ldots \text{ upto } n \text{ terms} = n(a+l)$$

$$\therefore \quad \boldsymbol{S_n = \frac{n}{2}(a+l)} \quad \ldots\text{(iii)}$$

Now, if we substitute the value of l *viz.*, $l = a + (n-1)d$, in this formula, we get

$$S_n = \frac{n}{2}[a + a + (n-1)d] = \frac{n}{2}[2a + (n-1)d]$$

$$\therefore \quad S_n = \frac{n}{2}[2a + (n-1)d]$$

If we substitute the value of a *viz.*,

$$l = a + (n-1)d$$

or $\quad a = l - (n-1)d$ in Eq. (iii)

Then, $\quad S_n = \frac{n}{2}[2l - (n-1)d]$

If we substitute the value of $a + l$ *viz.*,

$t_n + t'_n = a + l$ in Eq. (iii)

Then, $\quad \boldsymbol{S_n = \frac{n}{2}(t_n + t'_n)}$

***Corollary* I** Sum of first n natural numbers

i.e. $1 + 2 + 3 + 4 + \ldots + n$

Here, $\quad a = 1$ and $d = 1$

$$\therefore \quad S = \frac{n}{2}[2 \cdot 1 + (n-1) \cdot 1] = \frac{n(n+1)}{2}$$

***Corollary* II** Sum of first n odd natural numbers

i.e. $1 + 3 + 5 + \ldots$

Here, $a = 1$ and $d = 2$

$$\therefore \quad S = \frac{n}{2}[2 \times 1 + (n-1) \times 2] = n^2$$

***Corollary* III** Sum of first n even natural numbers

i.e. $2 + 4 + 6 + \ldots$

Here, $a = 2$ and $d = 2$

$$\therefore \quad S = \frac{n}{2}[2 \times 2 + (n-1) \times 2] = n(n+1)$$

***Corollary* IV** If sum of first n terms is S_n, then sum of next m terms is $S_{m+n} - S_n$.

Example 17. The sum of all three digit natural numbers, which are divisible by 7 is

(a) 80336 (b) 70336

(c) 60336 (d) 50336

Sol. (b) The three digit numbers which are divisible by 7 are 105, 112, 119, ..., 994.

Clearly, it is an AP with $a = 105$, $d = 7$, $a_n = 994$.

Now, $\quad a_n = 994$

$\Rightarrow \quad a + (n-1)d = 994$

$\Rightarrow \quad 105 + (n-1) \times 7 = 994$

$\Rightarrow \quad n = 128$

$\therefore$ Required sum $= \frac{n}{2}[2a + (n-1)d]$

$$= \frac{128}{2}[2 \times 105 + (128-1) \times 7] = 70336$$

Example 18. The degree of the expansion $(1+x)(1+x^6)(1+x^{11})\ldots(1+x^{101})$ is

(a) 1007 (b) 1070

(c) 1071 (d) 1017

Sol. (c) We have, $(1+x)(1+x^6)(1+x^{11})\ldots(1+x^{101})$

$$= (1 + x + x^6 + x^{1+6})(1+x^{11})\ldots(1+x^{101})$$

$$= (1 + x + x^6 + x^7 + x^{11} + x^{12} + x^{17} + x^{1+6+11}) \ldots (1+x^{101})$$

$$= (1 + x + \ldots + x^{1+6+11+\ldots+101})$$

So, degree $= 1 + 6 + 11 + \ldots + 101$, which is an AP with $a = 1$, $d = 5$, $a_n = 101$.

Now, $a_n = 101$

$\Rightarrow \quad a + (n-1)d = 101$

$\Rightarrow \quad 1 + (n-1) \times 5 = 101 \Rightarrow n = 21$

$\therefore$ Degree $= \frac{21}{2}[1 + 101] = 21 \times 51 = 1071$

Example 19. How many terms of the series $20 + 19\frac{1}{3} + 18\frac{2}{3} + \ldots$ must be taken to make 300?

Sol. Here, given series is an AP with first term $a = 20$ and the common difference, $d = -\frac{2}{3}$.

Let the sum of n terms of the series be 300.

Then, $$S_n = \frac{n}{2}\{2a + (n-1)d\}$$

$$\Rightarrow \quad 300 = \frac{n}{2}\left\{2 \times 20 + (n-1)\left(-\frac{2}{3}\right)\right\}$$

$$\Rightarrow \quad 300 = \frac{n}{3}\{60 - n + 1\}$$

$$\Rightarrow \quad n^2 - 61n + 900 = 0 \Rightarrow (n-25)(n-36) = 0$$

$$\Rightarrow \quad n = 25 \text{ or } n = 36$$

$\therefore$ Sum of 25 terms = Sum of 36 terms = 300

Example 20. Find the arithmetic progression consisting of 10 terms, if the sum of the terms occupying the even places is equal to 15 and the sum of those occupying the odd places is equal to $12\frac{1}{2}$.

Sol. Let the successive terms of an AP be $t_1, t_2, t_3, \ldots, t_9, t_{10}$.

By hypothesis,

$$t_2 + t_4 + t_6 + t_8 + t_{10} = 15$$

$$\Rightarrow \quad \frac{5}{2}(t_2 + t_{10}) = 15$$

$$\Rightarrow \quad t_2 + t_{10} = 6$$

$$\Rightarrow \quad (a+d) + (a+9d) = 6 \Rightarrow 2a + 10d = 6 \quad \ldots\text{(i)}$$

and $$t_1 + t_3 + t_5 + t_7 + t_9 = 12\frac{1}{2} \Rightarrow \frac{5}{2}(t_1 + t_9) = \frac{25}{2}$$

$$\Rightarrow \quad t_1 + t_9 = 5 \Rightarrow a + a + 8d = 5$$

$$\Rightarrow \quad 2a + 8d = 5 \quad \ldots\text{(ii)}$$

From Eqs. (i) and (ii), we get $d = \frac{1}{2}$ and $a = \frac{1}{2}$

Hence, the AP is $\frac{1}{2}, 1, 1\frac{1}{2}, 2, 2\frac{1}{2}, \ldots$

Example 21. Find the sum of first 24 terms of an AP $t_1, t_2, t_3, \ldots$, if it is known that $t_1 + t_5 + t_{10} + t_{15} + t_{20} + t_{24} = 225$.

Sol. We know that in an AP the sums of the terms equidistant from the beginning and end is always same and is equal to the sum of first and last term.

Then, $t_1 + t_{24} = t_5 + t_{20} = t_{10} + t_{15}$

but given $$t_1 + t_5 + t_{10} + t_{15} + t_{20} + t_{24} = 225$$

$$\Rightarrow \quad (t_1 + t_{24}) + (t_5 + t_{20}) + (t_{10} + t_{15}) = 225$$

$$\Rightarrow \quad 3(t_1 + t_{24}) = 225$$

$$\Rightarrow \quad t_1 + t_{24} = 75$$

$$\therefore \quad S_{24} = \frac{24}{2}(t_1 + t_{24}) = 12 \times 75 = 900$$

Example 22. If $(1 + 3 + 5 + \ldots + p) + (1 + 3 + 5 + \ldots + q) = (1 + 3 + 5 + \ldots + r)$, where each set of parentheses contains the sum of consecutive odd integers as shown, then find the smallest possible value of $p + q + r$ (where, $p > 6$).

Sol. We know that $1 + 3 + 5 + \ldots + (2n-1) = n^2$

Thus, the given equation can be written as

$$\left(\frac{p+1}{2}\right)^2 + \left(\frac{q+1}{2}\right)^2 = \left(\frac{r+1}{2}\right)^2$$

$$\Rightarrow \quad (p+1)^2 + (q+1)^2 = (r+1)^2$$

Therefore, $(p+1, q+1, r+1)$ form a Pythagorean triplet as $p > 6 \Rightarrow p + 1 > 7$

The first Pythagorean triplet containing a number > 7 is (6, 8, 10).

$$\Rightarrow \quad p + 1 = 8, q + 1 = 6, r + 1 = 10$$

$$\Rightarrow \quad p + q + r = 21$$

JEE SCANNER

Example Similar to PYQ Asked in JEE Main 2024

The sum of the series $1 + \frac{1}{1+2} + \frac{1}{1+2+3} + \ldots$ *upto 10 terms, is*

(a) $\frac{11}{10}$ (b) $\frac{20}{11}$ (c) $\frac{40}{13}$ (d) $\frac{15}{8}$

Sol. (b) Let $S = 1 + \frac{1}{1+2} + \frac{1}{1+2+3} + \ldots$ upto 10 terms

So, $n = 10$

General term $$T_n = \frac{1}{\frac{n(n+1)}{2}} = \frac{2}{n(n+1)} = 2\left[\frac{1}{n} - \frac{1}{n+1}\right]$$

So, $S = T_1 + T_2 + T_3 + \ldots + T_{10}$

$$= 2\left[1 - \frac{1}{2}\right] + 2\left[\frac{1}{2} - \frac{1}{3}\right] + 2\left[\frac{1}{3} - \frac{1}{4}\right] + \ldots + 2\left[\frac{1}{10} - \frac{1}{11}\right]$$

$$= 2\left[1 - \frac{1}{2} + \frac{1}{2} - \frac{1}{3} + \frac{1}{3} - \frac{1}{4} + \frac{1}{4} - \frac{1}{5} + \ldots + \frac{1}{10} - \frac{1}{11}\right]$$

$$= 2\left[1 - \frac{1}{11}\right] = 2 \times \frac{10}{11} = \frac{20}{11}$$

$$\therefore \quad S = \frac{20}{11}$$

Skill Builder

For Sol.

The sum of series S upto 20 terms is $S = 1 + \frac{1}{2}(1+2) + \frac{1}{3}(1+2+3) + \ldots$

(a) 110 (b) 111 (c) 115 (d) 120

■ **For more practice** See Q.14 of Milestone Practice 3.1.

Important Results with Proof

1. If S_n, t_n and d are sum of n terms, nth term and common difference of an AP respectively, then

$$d = t_n - t_{n-1} \quad [n \geq 2]$$
$$t_n = S_n - S_{n-1} \quad [n \geq 2]$$
$$d = S_n - 2S_{n-1} + S_{n-2} \quad [n \geq 3]$$

Proof

$\because \quad S_n = t_1 + t_2 + t_3 + \ldots + t_{n-1} + t_n$

$\Rightarrow \quad S_n = S_{n-1} + t_n$

$\therefore \quad t_n = S_n - S_{n-1}$

but $\quad d = t_n - t_{n-1}$

$\quad = (S_n - S_{n-1}) - (S_{n-1} - S_{n-2})$

$\therefore \quad d = S_n - 2S_{n-1} + S_{n-2}$

2. A sequence is an AP if and only if the sum of its n terms is of the form $An^2 + Bn$, where A and B are constants independent of n.

In this case, the nth term and common difference of the AP are $A(2n-1)+B$ and $2A$, respectively.

Proof As $S_n = An^2 + Bn$

$\therefore \quad S_{n-1} = A(n-1)^2 + B(n-1)$

$\therefore \quad t_n = S_n - S_{n-1}$

$\quad = (An^2 + Bn) - [A(n-1)^2 + B(n-1)]$

$\quad = A[n^2 - (n-1)^2] + B$

$\quad t_n = A(2n-1) + B$

$\Rightarrow \quad t_{n-1} = A[2(n-1)-1] + B$

$\quad = A(2n-3) + B$

Now, $t_n - t_{n-1} = [A(2n-1)+B] - [A(2n-3)+B]$

$\quad = 2A \quad$ [a constant]

Hence, the sequence is an AP.

Conversely, consider an AP with first term a and common difference d.

Sum of first n terms $= \dfrac{n}{2}[2a + (n-1)d]$

$$= \frac{dn^2}{2} + \left(a - \frac{d}{2}\right)n = An^2 + Bn,$$

where, $A = \dfrac{d}{2}, B = a - \dfrac{d}{2}$

Hence, $S_n = An^2 + Bn$, where A and B are constants independent of n.

Hence, the converse is true.

Corollary $\because \quad S_n = An^2 + Bn$

$\therefore \quad t_n = A(2n-1) + B$

$t_n = A$ (replacing n^2 by $2n-1$) + Coefficient of n

and $\quad d = 2A$

i.e. $\quad d = 2 \quad$ [coefficient of n^2]

	S_n	t_n	d
1.	$5n^2 + 3n$	$5(2n-1) + 3 = 10n - 2$	10
2.	$-7n^2 + 2n$	$-7(2n-1) + 2 = -14n + 9$	-14
3.	$-9n^2 - 4n$	$-9(2n-1) - 4 = -18n + 5$	-18
4.	$4n^2 - n$	$4(2n-1) - 1 = 8n - 5$	8

3. If $S_n = an^2 + bn + c$, where S_n denotes the sum of n terms of a series, then whole series is not an AP. It is AP from the second term onwards.

Proof As $\quad S_n = an^2 + bn + c$ for $n \geq 1$, we get

$$S_{n-1} = a(n-1)^2 + b(n-1) + c \text{ for } n \geq 2$$

Now, $\quad t_n = S_n - S_{n-1}$

$\Rightarrow \quad t_n = a(2n-1) + b, n \geq 2$

$\therefore \quad t_{n-1} = a[2(n-1)-1] + b, n \geq 3$

$\Rightarrow \quad t_{n-1} = a(2n-3) + b, n \geq 3$

$\therefore \quad t_n - t_{n-1} = 2a = \text{constant}, n \geq 3$

$\therefore \quad t_3 - t_2 = t_4 - t_3 = t_5 - t_4 = \ldots$

But $\quad t_2 - t_1 = (S_2 - S_1) - S_1 = S_2 - 2S_1$

$\quad = (4a + 2b + c) - 2(a + b + c)$

$\quad = (2a - c) \quad [\because S_1 = t_1]$

$\therefore \quad t_2 - t_1 \neq t_3 - t_2$

Hence, the whole series is not an AP. It is AP from the second term onwards.

Ratio of Sums is Given

1. If ratio of the sums of m and n terms of an AP is given by $\dfrac{S_m}{S_n} = \dfrac{Am^2 + Bm}{An^2 + Bn}$

where A, B are constants and $A \neq 0$.

$\therefore \quad S_m = (Am^2 + Bm)k,$

$\quad S_n = (An^2 + Bn)k$

$\Rightarrow \quad t_m = S_m - S_{m-1} = [A(2m-1) + B]k$

$\quad t_n = S_n - S_{n-1} = [A(2n-1) + B]k$

$$\therefore \quad \frac{t_m}{t_n} = \frac{A(2m-1) + B}{A(2n-1) + B}$$

Example 23. The ratio of sums of m and n terms of an AP is $m^2 : n^2$. The ratio of the mth and nth terms is

(a) $(2m+1):(2n-1)$ (b) $m:n$

(c) $(2m-1):(2n-1)$ (d) None of these

Sol. (c) Here, $\frac{S_m}{S_n} = \frac{m^2}{n^2}$ $[\because A = 1, B = 0]$

$\therefore \frac{t_m}{t_n} = \frac{(2m-1)}{(2n-1)}$

$\Rightarrow t_m : t_n = (2m-1):(2n-1)$

2. If ratio of the sums of n terms of two AP's is given by

$$\frac{S_n}{S'_n} = \frac{An+B}{Cn+D}$$

where, A, B, C, D are constants and $A, C \neq 0$

$\therefore \quad S_n = n(An+B)k, \; S'_n = n(Cn+D)k$

$\Rightarrow \quad t_n = [A(2n-1)+B]k, \; t'_n = [C(2n-1)+D]k$

$\Rightarrow \quad d = t_n - t_{n-1} = 2A, \; d' = t'_n - t'_{n-1} = 2C$

$\therefore \quad \frac{t_n}{t'_n} = \frac{A(2n-1)+B}{C(2n-1)+D}$ and $\frac{d}{d'} = \frac{A}{C}$

Note If $A = 0, C = 0$

Then, $\frac{S_n}{S'_n} = \frac{B}{D} \Rightarrow \frac{t_n}{t'_n} = \frac{B}{D}$ and $\frac{d}{d'} = \frac{0}{0}$ = not defined

JEE SPIKE

If $\frac{t_n}{t'_n} = \frac{an+b}{cn+d}$

where, a, b, c, d are constants and $a, c \neq 0$,

then $\frac{S_n}{S'_n} = \frac{a\left(\frac{n+1}{2}\right)+b}{c\left(\frac{n+1}{2}\right)+d}$

Example 24. The sums of n terms of two arithmetic progressions are in the ratio $(7n+1):(4n+17)$. Find the ratio of their nth terms and also common differences.

Sol. Given, $S_n : S'_n = (7n+1):(4n+17)$

Here, $A = 7, B = 1, C = 4$ and $D = 17$

$\therefore \frac{t_n}{t'_n} = \frac{7(2n-1)+1}{4(2n-1)+17} = \frac{14n-6}{8n+13}$

and $\frac{d}{d'} = \frac{A}{C} = \frac{7}{4}$

Hence, $t_n : t'_n = (14n-6):(8n+13)$ and $d : d' = 7:4$

Example 25. The sums of n terms of two AP's are in the ratio $(3n-13):(5n+21)$. Find the ratio of their 24th terms.

Sol. Given, $S_n : S'_n = (3n-13):(5n+21)$

Here, $A = 3, B = -13, C = 5$ and $D = 21$

$\therefore \frac{t_{24}}{t'_{24}} = \frac{3(2\times 24-1)-13}{5(2\times 24-1)+21} = \frac{128}{256} = \frac{1}{2}$

$\therefore t_{24} : t'_{24} = 1:2$

Properties of Arithmetic Progression

1. If $a_1, a_2, a_3, \ldots$ are in AP with common difference d, then $a_1 \pm k, a_2 \pm k, a_3 \pm k, \ldots$ are also in AP with common difference d.

2. If $a_1, a_2, a_3, \ldots$ are in AP with common difference d, then $a_1k, a_2k, a_3k, \ldots$ and $\frac{a_1}{k}, \frac{a_2}{k}, \frac{a_3}{k}, \ldots$ are also in AP $(k \neq 0)$ with common differences kd and $\frac{d}{k}$, respectively.

3. If $a_1, a_2, a_3, \ldots$ and $b_1, b_2, b_3, \ldots$ are two AP's with common differences d_1 and d_2, respectively. Then, $a_1 \pm b_1, a_2 \pm b_2, a_3 \pm b_3, \ldots$ are also in AP with common difference $(d_1 \pm d_2)$.

4. If $a_1, a_2, a_3, \ldots$ and $b_1, b_2, b_3, \ldots$ are two AP's with common differences d_1 and d_2 respectively, then $a_1b_1, a_2b_2, a_3b_3, \ldots$ and $\frac{a_1}{b_1}, \frac{a_2}{b_2}, \frac{a_3}{b_3}, \ldots$ are not in AP.

5. If $a_1, a_2, a_3, \ldots, a_n$ are in AP, then
$$a_r = \frac{a_{r-k} + a_{r+k}}{2}, \forall\, k, 0 \leq k \leq n-r$$

6. If three numbers in AP whose sum is given are to be taken as $\alpha-\beta, \alpha, \alpha+\beta$ and if five numbers in AP whose sum is given, are to be taken as $\alpha-2\beta, \alpha-\beta, \alpha, \alpha+\beta, \alpha+2\beta$, etc.

   In general If $(2r+1)$ numbers in AP whose sum is given, are to be taken as $(r \in N)$.

   $\alpha - r\beta, \alpha-(r-1)\beta, \ldots, \alpha-\beta, \alpha, \alpha+\beta, \ldots, \alpha+(r-1)\beta, \alpha+r\beta$

7. If four numbers in AP whose sum is given, are to be taken as $\alpha-3\beta, \alpha-\beta, \alpha+\beta, \alpha+3\beta$ and if six numbers in AP, whose sum is given are to be taken as $\alpha-5\beta, \alpha-3\beta, \alpha-\beta, \alpha+\beta, \alpha+3\beta, \alpha+5\beta$, etc.

   In general If $2r$ numbers in AP whose sum is given, are to be taken as $(r \in N)$.

   $\alpha-(2r-1)\beta, \alpha-(2r-3)\beta, \ldots, \alpha-3\beta, \alpha-\beta, \alpha+\beta, \alpha+3\beta, \ldots, \alpha+(2r-3)\beta, \alpha+(2r-1)\beta$

Example 26. If $S_1, S_2, S_3, \ldots, S_p$ are the sums of n terms of p AP's whose first terms are $1, 2, 3, \ldots, p$ and common differences are $1, 2, 3, \ldots, (2p-1)$ respectively, show that $S_1 + S_2 + S_3 + \ldots + S_p = \frac{1}{2} np(np+1)$.

Sol. $\because 1, 2, 3, \ldots, p$ are in AP.

Then, $2 \cdot 1, 2 \cdot 2, 2 \cdot 3, \ldots, 2p$ are also in AP ...(i)

[multiplying 2 to each term]

and $1, 3, 5, \ldots, (2p-1)$ are in AP.

Then, $(n-1)\cdot 1, (n-1)\cdot 3, (n-1)\cdot 5, \ldots, (n-1)(2p-1)$ are also in AP. ...(ii)

[multiplying $(n-1)$ to each term]

From Eqs. (i) and (ii), we get

$2\cdot 1 + (n-1)\cdot 1, 2\cdot 2 + (n-1)\cdot 3, 2\cdot 3 + (n-1)\cdot 5, \ldots,$

$2p + (n-1)(2p-1)$ are also in AP. ...(iii)

[adding corresponding terms of Eqs. (i) and (ii)]

From Eq. (iii),

$$\frac{n}{2}\{2\cdot 1 + (n-1)\cdot 1\}, \frac{n}{2}\{2\cdot 2 + (n-1)\cdot 3\}, \frac{n}{2}\{2\cdot 3 + (n-1)\cdot 5\}, \ldots,$$

$\frac{n}{2}\{2p + (n-1)(2p-1)\}$ are also in AP

[multiplying $\frac{n}{2}$ to each term]

i.e. $S_1, S_2, S_3, \ldots, S_p$ are in AP.

$$\therefore \; S_1 + S_2 + S_3 + \ldots + S_p = \frac{p}{2}\{S_1 + S_p\}$$

$$= \frac{p}{2}\left\{\frac{n}{2}[2\cdot 1 + (n-1)\cdot 1] + \frac{n}{2}[2\cdot p + (n-1)(2p-1)]\right\}$$

$$= \frac{np}{4}\{2 + (n-1) + 2p + (n-1)(2p-1)\}$$

$$= \frac{np}{4}(2np+2) = \frac{1}{2}np(np+1)$$

Alternate Solution

Here, $S_1 = 1 + 2 + 3 + \ldots$ upto n terms $= \frac{n(n+1)}{2}$

$S_2 = 2 + 5 + 8 + \ldots$ upto n terms $= \frac{n}{2}[2\cdot 2 + (n-1)3]$

$= \frac{n(3n+1)}{2}$

Similarly, $S_3 = 3 + 8 + 13 + \ldots$ upto n terms $= \frac{n(5n+1)}{2}$, etc.

Now, $S_1 + S_2 + S_3 + \ldots + S_p$

$= \frac{n(n+1)}{2} + \frac{n(3n+1)}{2} + \frac{n(5n+1)}{2} + \ldots$ upto p terms

$= \frac{n}{2}[(n + 3n + 5n + \ldots \text{upto } p \text{ terms}) + (1 + 1 + 1 + \ldots \text{upto } p \text{ terms})]$

$= \frac{n}{2}\left[\frac{p}{2}(2n + (p-1)2n) + p\right]$

$= \frac{np}{2}[n + n(p-1) + 1] = \frac{1}{2}np(np+1)$

Example 27. Let α and β be roots of the equation $x^2 - 2x + A = 0$ and let γ and δ be the roots of the equation $x^2 - 18x + B = 0$. If $\alpha < \beta < \gamma < \delta$ are in arithmetic progression, then find the values of A and B.

Sol. $\because \alpha, \beta, \gamma, \delta$ are in AP.

Let $\beta = \alpha + d, \gamma = \alpha + 2d, \delta = \alpha + 3d, d > 0$

[here, sum of $\alpha, \beta, \gamma, \delta$ is not given]

Given, $\alpha + \beta = 2, \alpha\beta = A$

$\Rightarrow \quad 2\alpha + d = 2, \alpha\beta = A$ ...(i)

and $\gamma + \delta = 18, \gamma\delta = B$

$\Rightarrow \quad 2\alpha + 5d = 18, \gamma\delta = B$ ...(ii)

From Eqs. (i) and (ii), we get

$d = 4, \alpha = -1$

$\therefore \quad \beta = 3, \gamma = 7, \delta = 11$

$\Rightarrow \quad A = \alpha\beta = (-1)(3) = -3$

and $B = \gamma\delta = (7)(11) = 77$

Example 28. The digits of a positive integer having three digits are in AP and their sum is 15. The number obtained by reversing the digits is 594 less than the original number. Find the number.

Sol. Let the digit in the unit's place be $a - d$, digit in the ten's place be a and the digit in the hundred's place be $a + d$.

Sum of digits $= a - d + a + a + d = 15$ [given]

$\Rightarrow \quad 3a = 15$

$\therefore \quad a = 5$ ...(i)

$\therefore$ Original number $= (a-d) + 10a + 100(a+d)$

$= 111a + 99d = 555 + 99d$

and number formed by reversing the digits

$= (a+d) + 10a + 100(a-d)$

$= 111a - 99d = 555 - 99d$

Given, $(555 + 99d) - (555 - 99d) = 594$

$\Rightarrow \quad 198d = 594$

$\therefore \quad d = 3$

Hence, original number $= 555 + 99 \times 3 = 852$

Example 29. If three positive real numbers are in AP such that $abc = 4$, then find the minimum value of b.

Sol. $\because a, b, c$ are in AP.

Let $a = A - D, b = A, c = A + D$

Then, $a = b - D, c = b + D$

Now, $abc = 4$

$(b - D)b(b + D) = 4$

$\Rightarrow \quad b(b^2 - D^2) = 4$

$\Rightarrow \quad b^2 - D^2 < b^2$

$\Rightarrow \quad b(b^2 - D^2) < b^3 \Rightarrow 4 < b^3$

$\therefore \quad b > (4)^{1/3}$ or $b > (2)^{2/3}$

Hence, the minimum value of b is $(2)^{2/3}$.

JEE SCANNER

Example Similar to PYQ Asked in JEE Main 2024

The number of terms common to the two AP's 3, 7, 11, ..., 407 and 2, 9, 16, ..., 709 is ....

Sol. Given, AP are 3, 7, 11, ..., 407 and 2, 9, 16, ..., 709

Let $S_1 = 3, 7, 11, \ldots, 407$

Here, $a = 3$ and $d = 4$ and let $S_2 = 2, 9, 16, \ldots, 709$

Here, $a = 2$ and $d = 7$

Here, we observe that first common term is 23.

Let the number of common terms be n.

They will be in AP with common difference = 28 (i.e. LCM (4, 7))

Now, the last term cannot be greater than 407

$\therefore \quad a_n \le 407$

$\Rightarrow \quad a + (n-1)d \le 407$

$\Rightarrow \quad 23 + (n-1)28 \le 407$

$\Rightarrow \quad (n-1)28 \le 384$

$\Rightarrow \quad (n-1) \le \dfrac{384}{28}$

$\Rightarrow \quad n \le 14.7$

$\therefore \quad n = 14$

Skill Builder

The number of terms common to the two AP's 3, 7, 11, ..., 404 and 4, 7, 10, ..., 403 is ....

For Sol.

■ **For more practice** See Q.9 of Milestone Practice 3.1.

Example 30. If a, b, c, d are distinct integers form an increasing AP such that $d = a^2 + b^2 + c^2$, then find the value of $a + b + c + d$.

Sol. Here, sum of numbers i.e. $a + b + c + d$ is not given.

Let $\quad b = a + D, c = a + 2D, d = a + 3D, \forall\ D \in N$

According to hypothesis,

$$a + 3D = a^2 + (a + D)^2 + (a + 2D)^2$$

$$\Rightarrow \quad 5D^2 + 3(2a - 1)D + 3a^2 - a = 0 \qquad \text{...(i)}$$

$$\therefore \quad D = \frac{-3(2a-1) \pm \sqrt{9(2a-1)^2 - 20(3a^2 - a)}}{10}$$

$$= \frac{-3(2a-1) \pm \sqrt{(-24a^2 - 16a + 9)}}{10}$$

Now, $\quad -24a^2 - 16a + 9 \ge 0$

$\Rightarrow \quad 24a^2 + 16a - 9 \le 0$

$\Rightarrow \quad -\dfrac{1}{3} - \dfrac{\sqrt{70}}{12} \le a \le -\dfrac{1}{3} + \dfrac{\sqrt{70}}{12}$

$\Rightarrow \quad a = -1, 0 \qquad [\because a \in I]$

When $a = 0$ from Eq. (i), $D = 0, \dfrac{3}{5}$ (not possible $\because D \in N$) and for $a = -1$

From Eq. (i), $\quad D = 1, \dfrac{4}{5}$

$\therefore \quad D = 1 \qquad [\because D \in N]$

$\therefore \quad a = -1, b = 0, c = 1, d = 2$

Then, $\quad a + b + c + d = -1 + 0 + 1 + 2 = 2$

Example 31. If $\sec(\alpha - 2\beta)$, $\sec\alpha$ and $\sec(\alpha + 2\beta)$ are distinct terms in arithmetic progression, then find the value of $\dfrac{\cos^2\alpha}{\cos^2\beta}$ is

(a) 1 (b) 2 (c) 3 (d) $\dfrac{1}{2}$

Sol. (b) $2\sec\alpha = \sec(\alpha - 2\beta) + \sec(\alpha + 2\beta)$

$$\Rightarrow \quad \frac{2}{\cos\alpha} = \frac{1}{\cos(\alpha - 2\beta)} + \frac{1}{\cos(\alpha + 2\beta)}$$

$$\Rightarrow \quad \frac{2}{\cos\alpha} = \frac{2\cos\alpha \cdot \cos 2\beta}{\cos(\alpha - 2\beta)\cos(\alpha + 2\beta)}$$

$$\Rightarrow \quad \cos 2\alpha + \cos 4\beta = 2\cos^2\alpha \cos 2\beta$$

$$\Rightarrow \quad (2\cos^2\alpha - 1) + (2\cos^2 2\beta - 1) = 2\cos^2\alpha \cos 2\beta$$

$$\Rightarrow \quad \cos^2\alpha + \cos^2 2\beta - 1 = \cos^2\alpha \cos 2\beta$$

$$\Rightarrow \quad \cos^2\alpha(1 - \cos 2\beta) = (1 - \cos 2\beta)(1 + \cos 2\beta) = 2\cos^2\beta$$

$$\Rightarrow \quad \frac{\cos^2\alpha}{\cos^2\beta} = 2$$

Example 32. Let $s_1, s_2, s_3 \ldots$ and $t_1, t_2, t_3 \ldots$ are two arithmetic sequences, such that $s_1 = t_1 \ne 0$; $s_2 = 2t_2$ and $\sum_{i=1}^{10} s_i = \sum_{i=1}^{15} t_i$. Then, the value of $\dfrac{s_2 - s_1}{t_2 - t_1}$ is

(a) $\dfrac{8}{3}$ (b) $\dfrac{3}{2}$ (c) $\dfrac{19}{8}$ (d) 2

Sol. (c) Given, $s_1 + s_2 + s_3 + \ldots + s_{10} = t_1 + t_2 + t_3 + \ldots + t_{15}$

Let Ist sequence is

$$a_1, a_1 + d_1, a_1 + 2d_1, \ldots$$

and IInd is $a_1, a_1 + d_2, a_1 + 2d_2, \ldots \qquad$ (since $s_1 = t_1$)

Given, $s_2 = 2t_2$

$\therefore \quad a_1 + d_1 = 2(a_1 + d_2)$

$\therefore \quad a_1 = d_1 - 2d_2 \qquad \text{...(i)}$

We have to find $\dfrac{s_2 - s_1}{t_2 - t_1} = \dfrac{d_1}{d_2} = ?$

Now, $\dfrac{10}{2}[2a_1 + 9d_1] = \dfrac{15}{2}[2a_1 + 14d_2]$

This gives, $a_1 = 9d_1 - 21d_2 \qquad \text{...(ii)}$

From Eqs. (i) and (ii), we get

$$\frac{d_1}{d_2} = \frac{19}{8}$$

Example 33. The sequence $\{a_n\}$ is defined by formula $a_{n+1} = a_n^2 - 2a_n + 2$ for $n > 0$ and $a_0 = 4$, then value of a_{10} is equal to

(a) $1 + 2^{1024}$ (b) 4^{1024}
(c) $1 + 3^{1024}$ (d) 6^{1024}

Sol. (c)

$$a_{n+1} - 1 = (a_n - 1)^2$$
$$a_n - 1 = (a_{n-1} - 1)^2$$
$$a_2 - 1 = (a_1 - 1)^2$$
$$a_1 - 1 = (a_0 - 1)^2$$
$$\Rightarrow (a_n - 1)(a_{n-1} - 1)^2 (a_{n-2} - 1)^{2^2} \ldots (a_1 - 1)^{2^{n-1}}$$
$$= (a_{n-1} - 1)^2 (a_{n-2} - 1)^{2^2} \ldots (a_0 - 1)^{2^n}$$
$$\Rightarrow \quad (a_n - 1) = 3^{2^n} \Rightarrow a_{10} - 1 = 3^{1024} \Rightarrow (a_n - 1) = (a_0 - 1)^{2^n}$$
$$\therefore \quad a_{10} = 1 + 3^{1024}$$

Milestone Practice 3.1

1. Let $\{a_n\}$, $n \geq 1$ be a sequence, such that $a_1 = 1$ and $3a_{n+1} - 3a_n = 1$ for all $n \geq 1$. Then, find the value of a_{2002}.

2. If $\log 2, \log (2^n - 1), \log (2^n + 3)$ are in AP, then the value of n is equal to

(a) $\frac{5}{2}$ (b) $\log_2 5$ (c) $\log_3 5$ (d) $\frac{3}{2}$

3. If 5 times 5th term of an AP is equal to 8 times the 8th term, then 13th term is equal to

(a) -1 (b) 0 (c) 13 (d) 40

4. If the 9th terms of an AP is zero, the ratio of its 29th and 19th term is

(a) $1:2$ (b) $2:1$ (c) $1:3$ (d) $3:1$

5. For an AP $a_1, a_2, a_3, \ldots$, if $a_3 + a_5 + a_8 = 11$ and $a_4 + a_2 = -2$, then the value of $a_1 + a_6 + a_7$ is

(a) -8 (b) 5 (c) 7 (d) 9

6. If the sum of n terms of an AP is $2n^2 + 5n$, then find its 12th term.

7. If S_n denotes the sum of n terms of AP, then $S_{n+3} - 3S_{n+2} + 3S_{n+1} - S_n$ is equal to

(a) $2S_n$ (b) S_{n+1}
(c) $3S_n$ (d) 0

8. If a_n be the nth term of an AP and if $a_7 = 15$, then the value of the common difference that would make $a_2 a_7 a_{12}$ greater is

(a) 9 (b) $\frac{9}{4}$
(c) 0 (d) 18

9. For the two AP's $S_1: 2, 7, 12, 17, \ldots$, 500 terms and $S_2: 1, 8, 15, 22, \ldots$, 300 terms, the last common term is

(a) 2087 (b) 2094
(c) 2497 (d) None of these

10. If the AP whose common difference is non-zero, the sum of first $3n$ terms is equal to the sum of next n terms. Then, the ratio of the sum of the first $2n$ terms to the sum of next $2n$ terms is

(a) $\frac{1}{2}$ (b) $\frac{1}{3}$ (c) $\frac{1}{4}$ (d) $\frac{1}{5}$

11. If n is even, then $1^2 - 2^2 + 3^2 - 4^2 + \ldots$ upto n terms is equal to

(a) $\frac{n(n+1)}{2}$ (b) $\frac{n(n-1)}{2}$
(c) $\frac{-n(n+1)}{2}$ (d) $\frac{-n(n-1)}{2}$

12. If a, b, c, d are distinct integers in an AP, such that $d = a^2 + b^2 + c^2$, then the value of $a + b + c + d$ is equal to

(a) 0 (b) 1 (c) 2 (d) 3

13. For $x \geq 0$, the least value of K, for which $4^{1+x} + 4^{2+x}, \frac{K}{2}, 14^x + 14^{-x}$ are three consecutive terms of an AP, is equal to

(a) 11 (b) 22 (c) 20 (d) 10

14. Find the sum of the series $1 + 5 + 12 + 22 + 35 + \ldots$ upto 40 terms is

(a) 64000 (b) 60000
(c) 32800 (d) 40800

Answer Key

1. (668)	2. (b)	3. (b)	4. (b)	5. (c)
6. (51)	7. (d)	8. (c)	9. (a)	10. (d)
11. (c)	12. (c)	13. (b)	14. (c)	

For Detailed Solution

Milestone 2 Geometric and Harmonic Progression

• Geometric Sequence or Geometric Progression (GP) • Harmonic Sequence or Harmonic Progression (HP)

3.5 Geometric Sequence or Geometric Progression (GP)

A geometric progression is a sequence, if the ratio of any term and its just preceding term is constant throughout. This constant quantity is called the common ratio and is generally denoted by 'r'.

Or

A geometric progression (GP) is a sequence of numbers, whose first term is non-zero and each of the term is obtained by multiplying its just preceding term by a constant quantity. This constant quantity is called common ratio of the GP.

Let $t_1, t_2, t_3, \ldots, t_n; t_1, t_2, t_3, \ldots$ be respectively a finite or an infinite sequence. Assume that none of t_n''s is 0 and that $\frac{t_k}{t_{k-1}} = r$, a constant (i.e. independent of k).

For $k = 2, 3, 4, \ldots, n$ or $k = 2, 3, 4, \ldots$ as the case may be. We then call $\{t_k\}_{k=1}^{n}$ or $\{t_k\}_{k=1}^{\infty}$ as the case may be a geometric progression (GP). The constant ratio r is called the common ratio (CR) of the GP.

i.e. $r = \frac{t_2}{t_1} = \frac{t_3}{t_2} = \ldots = \frac{t_n}{t_{n-1}}$

If $t_1 = a$ is the first term of a GP, then

$t_2 = ar,\ t_3 = t_2 r = ar^2,\ t_4 = t_3 r = ar^3, \ldots,$

$t_n = t_{n-1} r = ar^{n-1}$

It follows that, given that first term a and the common ratio r, the GP can be rewritten as $a, ar, ar^2, \ldots, ar^{n-1}$ (standard GP) or $a, ar, ar^2, \ldots, ar^{n-1}, \ldots$ (standard GP) according as it is finite or infinite.

Important Results

1. In a GP, neither $a = 0$ nor $r = 0$.
2. In a GP, no term can be equal to '0'.
3. If in a GP, the terms are alternatively positive and negative, then its common ratio is always negative.
4. If we multiply the common ratio with any term of GP, we get the next following term and if we divide any term by the common ratio, we get the preceding term.
5. The common ratio of GP may be positive, negative or imaginary.
6. If common ratio of GP is equal to unity, then GP is known as constant GP.
7. If common ratio of GP is imaginary or real, then GP is known as imaginary GP.
8. **Increasing and Decreasing GP**
   For a GP to be increasing or decreasing $r > 0$. If $r < 0$, terms of GP are alternatively positive and negative and so neither increasing nor decreasing.

a	$a > 0$	$a > 0$	$a < 0$	$a < 0$
r	$0 < r < 1$	$r > 1$	$r > 1$	$0 < r < 1$
Result	Decreasing	Increasing	Decreasing	Increasing

Example 34. Check whether the given GP is increasing or decreasing.

(i) 1, 2, 4, 8, 16, ... (ii) 9, 3, 1, $\frac{1}{3}, \frac{1}{9}, \ldots$

(iii) $-2, -6, -18, \ldots$ (iv) $-8, -4, -2, -1, -\frac{1}{2}, \ldots$

(v) $5, -10, 20, \ldots$ (vi) 5, 5, 5, 5,...

(vii) $1, 1+i, 2i, -2+2i, \ldots; i = \sqrt{-1}$

Sol. (i) Here, $a = 1$

and $r = \frac{2}{1} = \frac{4}{2} = \frac{8}{4} = \frac{16}{8} = \ldots = 2$ i.e. $a = 1$ and $r = 2$

Increasing GP $(a > 0, r > 1)$

(ii) Here, $a = 9$

and $r = \frac{3}{9} = \frac{1}{3} = \frac{\frac{1}{3}}{1} = \frac{\frac{1}{9}}{\frac{1}{3}} = \ldots = \frac{1}{3}$ i.e. $a = 9, r = \frac{1}{3}$

Decreasing GP $(a > 0, 0 < r < 1)$

(iii) Here, $a = -2$

and $r = \frac{-6}{-2} = \frac{-18}{-6} = \ldots = 3$

i.e. $a = -2, r = 3$

Decreasing GP $(a < 0, r > 1)$

(iv) Here, $a = -8$

and $r = \frac{-4}{-8} = \frac{-2}{-4} = \frac{-1}{-2} = \frac{-\frac{1}{2}}{-1} = ... = \frac{1}{2}$

i.e. $a = -8, r = \frac{1}{2}$

Increasing GP $(a < 0, 0 < r < 1)$

(v) Here, $a = 5$

and $r = \frac{-10}{5} = \frac{20}{-10} = ... = -2$ i.e. $a = 5, r = -2$

Neither increasing nor decreasing $(r < 0)$

(vi) Here, $a = 5$

and $r = \frac{5}{5} = \frac{5}{5} = \frac{5}{5} = ... = 1$ i.e. $a = 5, r = 1$

Constant GP $(r = 1)$

(vii) Here, $a = 1$

and $r = \frac{1+i}{1} = \frac{2i}{1+i} = \frac{-2+2i}{2i} = ...$

$$= (1+i) = \frac{2i(1-i)}{(1+i)(1-i)} = \frac{(-1+i)i}{i^2} = ...$$

$$= (1+i) = (i+1) = (1+i) = ...$$

i.e. $a = 1, r = 1 + i$

Imaginary GP $(r = \text{imaginary})$

Example 35. Show that the sequence $< t_n >$ defined by $t_n = \frac{2^{2n-1}}{3}$ for all values of $n \in N$ is a GP. Also, find its common ratio.

Sol. We have, $t_n = \frac{2^{2n-1}}{3}$

On replacing n by $n - 1$, we get

$$t_{n-1} = \frac{2^{2n-3}}{3} \Rightarrow \frac{t_n}{t_{n-1}} = \frac{\frac{2^{2n-1}}{3}}{\frac{2^{2n-3}}{3}} = 2^2 = 4$$

Clearly, $\frac{t_n}{t_{n-1}}$ is independent of n and is equal to 4. So, the given sequence is a GP with common ratio 4.

Example 36. Show that the sequence $< t_n >$ defined by $t_n = 2 \cdot 3^n + 1$ is not a GP.

Sol. We have, $t_n = 2 \cdot 3^n + 1$

On replacing n by $(n-1)$ in t_n, we get

$$t_{n-1} = 2 \cdot 3^{n-1} + 1$$

$$\Rightarrow \quad t_{n-1} = \frac{(2 \cdot 3^n + 3)}{3}$$

$$\therefore \quad \frac{t_n}{t_{n-1}} = \frac{(2 \cdot 3^n + 1)}{\frac{(2 \cdot 3^n + 3)}{3}} = \frac{3(2 \cdot 3^n + 1)}{(2 \cdot 3^n + 3)}$$

Clearly, $\frac{t_n}{t_{n-1}}$ is not independent of n and is therefore not constant. So, the given sequence is not a GP.

General Term of a GP

Let a be the first term, r be the common ratio and l be the last term of a GP having n terms. Then, GP can be written as $a, ar, ar^2, ..., \frac{l}{r^2}, \frac{l}{r}, l$

(i) *n*th Term of a GP from Beginning

1st term from beginning $= t_1 = a = ar^{1-1}$

2nd term from beginning $= t_2 = ar = ar^{2-1}$

3rd term from beginning $= t_3 = ar^2 = ar^{3-1}$

$\vdots \quad \vdots \quad \vdots \quad \vdots \quad \vdots$

nth term from beginning $= t_n = ar^{n-1}, \forall n \in N$

Hence, n th term of a GP from beginning

$$t_n = ar^{n-1} = l \quad \text{[last term]}$$

(ii) *n*th Term of a GP from End

1st term from end $= t'_1 = l = \frac{l}{r^{1-1}}$

2nd term from end $= t'_2 = \frac{l}{r} = \frac{l}{r^{2-1}}$

3rd term from end $= t'_3 = \frac{l}{r^2} = \frac{l}{r^{3-1}}$

$\vdots \quad \vdots \quad \vdots \quad \vdots$

nth term from end $= t'_n = \frac{l}{r^{n-1}}, \forall n \in N$

Hence, nth term of a GP from end

$$= t'_n = \frac{l}{r^{n-1}} = a \quad \text{[first term]}$$

Now, it is clear that $t_k \times t'_k = ar^{k-1} \times \frac{l}{r^{k-1}} = a \times l$

or $\quad t_k \times t'_k = a \times l, \forall 1 \le k \le n$

i.e. in a finite GP of n terms, the product of the k th term from the beginning and the k th term form the end is independent of k and equals the product of the first and last terms.

JEE Focus Points

- nth term is also called the general term.
- If last term of GP be t_n and CR is r, then terms of GP from end are $t_n, \frac{t_n}{r}, \frac{t_n}{r^2}, \ldots$
- If in a GP, the terms are alternatively positive and negative, then its common ratio is always negative.
- If a and l represent first and last term of a GP respectively, then common ratio of GP $= r = \left(\frac{l}{a}\right)^{\frac{1}{n-1}}$
- If t_n, t_{n+1}, t_{n+2} are three consecutive terms of a GP, then
$$\frac{t_{n+1}}{t_n} = \frac{t_{n+2}}{t_{n+1}} \Rightarrow t_{n+1}^2 = t_n\, t_{n+2}$$
In particular, if a, b, c are in GP, then $\frac{b}{a} = \frac{c}{b} \Rightarrow b^2 = ac$
On squaring, $\frac{b^2}{a^2} = \frac{c^2}{b^2}$
Hence, a^2, b^2, c^2 are also in GP.

Concept Inside Video

Example 37. If first term of a GP is a, third term is b and $(n+1)$th term is c. The $(2n+1)$th term of a GP is

(a) $c\sqrt{\frac{b}{a}}$ (b) $\frac{bc}{a}$ (c) abc (d) $\frac{c^2}{a}$

Sol. (d) Let common ratio $= r$

$$\therefore \quad b = ar^2 \Rightarrow r = \sqrt{\frac{b}{a}}$$

Also, $$c = ar^n \Rightarrow r^n = \frac{c}{a}$$

$$\therefore \quad t_{2n+1} = ar^{2n} = a(r^n)^2 = a\left(\frac{c}{a}\right)^2 = \frac{c^2}{a}.$$

Example 38. The $(m+n)$th and $(m-n)$th terms of a GP are p and q, respectively. Then, the mth term of the GP is

(a) $p\left(\frac{q}{p}\right)^{\frac{m}{2n}}$ (b) $\sqrt{pq}$

(c) $\sqrt{\frac{p}{q}}$ (d) None of these

Sol. (b) Let a be the first term and r be the common ratio, then

$$t_{m+n} = p \Rightarrow ar^{m+n-1} = p \quad \ldots(i)$$
$$t_{m-n} = q \Rightarrow ar^{m-n-1} = q \quad \ldots(ii)$$

From Eqs. (i) and (ii), we get

$$ar^{m+n-1} \times ar^{m-n-1} = p \times q$$
$$\Rightarrow \quad a^2 r^{2m-2} = pq \Rightarrow ar^{m-1} = \sqrt{pq}$$
$$\Rightarrow \quad t_m = \sqrt{pq}$$

JEE SCANNER

Example Similar to PYQ Asked in JEE Main 2024

Let 4th, 10th and 18th term of a non-constant AP be respectively the 1st, 2nd and 3rd terms of a GP. If the first term is 2, then the sum of its first 10 terms is equal to

(a) 20 (b) 26 (c) 30 (d) 35

Sol. (b) Since, 4th, 10th and 18th terms of a non-constant AP are in GP.

$\therefore (2+3d), (2+9d)$ and $(2+17d)$ are in GP $\quad [\because a = 2]$

$$\therefore \quad (2+9d)^2 = (2+3d)(2+17d)$$
$$\Rightarrow \quad 4 + 81d^2 + 36d = 4 + 34d + 6d + 51d^2$$
$$\Rightarrow \quad 30d^2 = 40d - 36d$$
$$\Rightarrow \quad 30d = 4$$
$$\Rightarrow \quad d = \frac{4}{30} = \frac{2}{15}$$
$$\therefore \quad a = 2 \text{ and } d = \frac{2}{15}$$

Thus, $S_{10} = \frac{10}{2}\left[2 \times 2 + (10-1) \times \frac{2}{15}\right] = 5\left[4 + 9 \times \frac{2}{15}\right] = 26$

$$\therefore \quad S_{10} = 26$$

Skill Builder

Let 2nd, 8th and 30th term of a non-constant AP be, respectively the 1st, 2nd and 3rd terms of a GP. If the first term of the AP is 5, then the sum of its first 30 term is equal to

(a) 1690 (b) 1790
(c) 1890 (d) 1990

For Sol.

■ **For more practice** See Q.13 of Milestone Practice 3.2.

Example 39. If $\sin\theta, \sqrt{2}(\sin\theta + 1), 6\sin\theta + 6$ are in GP, then the fifth term is

(a) 81
(b) $81\sqrt{2}$
(c) 162
(d) $162\sqrt{2}$

Sol. (c) $[\sqrt{2}(\sin\theta + 1)]^2 = \sin\theta(6\sin\theta + 6)$

$$\Rightarrow (\sin\theta + 1)[2(\sin\theta + 1) - 6\sin\theta] = 0$$

We get, $\sin\theta = -1, \frac{1}{2}$

$$\therefore \quad \sin\theta = \frac{1}{2} \quad [\sin\theta = -1 \text{ is not possible}]$$

Then, first term $= a = \sin\theta = \frac{1}{2}$

and common ratio $= r = \dfrac{\sqrt{2}\left(\frac{1}{2}+1\right)}{\left(\frac{1}{2}\right)} = 3\sqrt{2}$

$\therefore \quad t_5 = ar^4 = \frac{1}{2}(3\sqrt{2})^4 = 162$

Example 40. If a, b, c are real numbers such that $3(a^2+b^2+c^2+1) = 2(a+b+c+ab+bc+ca)$, then a, b, c are in

(a) AP only (b) GP only

(c) GP and AP (d) None of these

Sol. (c) Given, $3(a^2+b^2+c^2+1) = 2(a+b+c+ab+bc+ca)$

$\Rightarrow \quad 2(a^2+b^2+c^2-ab-bc-ca) + (a^2+b^2+c^2-2a-2b-2c+3) = 0$

$\Rightarrow \quad \{(a-b)^2+(b-c)^2+(c-a)^2\} + \{(a-1)^2+(b-1)^2+(c-1)^2\} = 0$

$\Rightarrow a-b = b-c = c-a = 0$ and $a-1 = b-1 = c-1 = 0$

$\Rightarrow \quad a = b = c = 1$

$\Rightarrow$ a, b, c are in GP and AP.

Sum of n Terms of a GP

Let a be the first term, r be the common ratio, l be the last term of a GP having n terms and S_n the sum of n terms, then

$$S_n = a + ar + ar^2 + \ldots + \frac{l}{r^2} + \frac{l}{r} + l \qquad \ldots(\text{i})$$

On multiplying both sides by r (the common ratio)

$$rS_n = ar + ar^2 + ar^3 + \ldots + \frac{l}{r} + l + lr \qquad \ldots(\text{ii})$$

On subtracting Eq. (ii) from Eq. (i), we have

$$S_n - rS_n = a - lr \text{ or } S_n(1-r) = a - lr$$

$$\therefore \quad S_n = \frac{a-lr}{1-r}, \text{ when } r<1$$

$$S_n = \frac{lr-a}{r-1}, \text{ when } r>1$$

Now, $\quad l = t_n = ar^{n-1}$

Then, above formula can be written as

$$S_n = \frac{a(1-r^n)}{(1-r)} \text{ when } r<1, S_n = \frac{a(r^n-1)}{(r-1)},$$

when $r > 1$

If $r = 1$, the above formulae cannot be used. But, then the GP reduces to $a, a, a, \ldots$

$\therefore \quad S_n = a + a + a + \ldots n$ times $= na$

Sum of Infinite Number of Terms of a GP, when the Numerical Value of the Common Ratio is Less than Unity, i.e. It is a Proper Fraction.

If a be the first term, r be the common ratio of a GP, then

$$S_n = \frac{a(1-r^n)}{(1-r)} = \frac{a}{(1-r)} - \frac{ar^n}{(1-r)}$$

Let $-1 < r < 1$ i.e. $|r| < 1$, then $\lim_{n\to\infty} r^n \to 0$

Let S_∞ denote the sum of infinite number of terms of the GP, then

$$S_\infty = \frac{a}{(1-r)}, \text{ where } -1<r<1$$

Recurring Decimal

Recurring decimal is a very good example of an infinite geometric series and its value can be obtained by means of infinite geometric series as follows

$0.3\overline{27} = 0.327272727\ldots$ to infinity

$= 0.3 + 0.027 + 0.00027 + 0.0000027 + \ldots$ upto infinity

$= \frac{3}{10} + \frac{27}{10^3} + \frac{27}{10^5} + \frac{27}{10^7} + \ldots$ upto infinity

$= \frac{3}{10} + \frac{27}{10^3}\left(1 + \frac{1}{10^2} + \frac{1}{10^4} + \ldots \text{ upto infinity}\right)$

$= \frac{3}{10} + \frac{27}{10^3}\left(\dfrac{1}{1-\frac{1}{10^2}}\right)$

$= \frac{3}{10} + \frac{27}{990} = \frac{297+27}{990} = \frac{324}{990}$ [rational number]

Aliter (Best method)

Let P denotes the figure which do not recur and suppose these are p in number, Q denotes the recurring period consisting of q figures. Let R denotes the value of the recurring decimal.

Then, $\quad R = 0 \cdot PQQQ\ldots$

$\therefore \quad 10^p \times R = P \cdot QQQ\ldots$

and $\quad 10^{p+q} \times R = PQ \cdot QQQ\ldots$

$\therefore$ Therefore, by subtraction $R = \dfrac{PQ-P}{(10^{p+q}-10^p)}$.

***Corollary* I** If $R = 0 \cdot QQQ\ldots$

Then, $R = \dfrac{Q}{10^q - 1}$ (when Q denote the recurring period consisting of q figures)

e.g. If $R = 0.\bar{3}$, then $R = \dfrac{3}{10^1-1} = \dfrac{1}{3}$

***Corollary* II** The value of recurring decimal is always rational number.

Example 41. Find the value of $0.32\overline{58}$.

Sol. Let $R = 0.32\overline{58}$

$\Rightarrow \quad R = 0.3258585858\ldots \quad \ldots(\text{i})$

Here, number of figures which are not recurring is 2 and number of figures which are recurring is also 2.

Then, $100R = 32.58585858\ldots \quad \ldots(\text{ii})$

and $10000R = 3258.58585858\ldots \quad \ldots(\text{iii})$

On subtracting Eq. (ii) from Eq. (iii), we get

$$9900R = 3226$$

$$\therefore \quad R = \frac{3226}{9900}$$

Hence, $R = \frac{1613}{4950}$

Shortcut Methods for Recurring Decimals

1. The numerator of the vulgar fraction is obtained by subtracting the non-recurring figure from the given figure.
2. The denominator consists of as many 9's as there are recurring figure and as many zero as there are non-recurring figure.

e.g.

(i) $0.36\overline{54} = \frac{3654 - 36}{9900} = \frac{3618}{9900}$

(ii) $1.3\overline{27} = 1 + 0.3\overline{27} = 1 + \frac{327 - 3}{990} = \frac{1314}{990}$

(iii) $0.\bar{3} = \frac{3 - 0}{9} = \frac{1}{3}$

Example 42. Find the sum upto n terms of the series $a + aa + aaa + aaaa + \ldots, \ \forall a \in N$ and $1 \le a \le 9$.

Sol. Let $S = a + aa + aaa + aaaa + \ldots$ upto n terms

$= a(1 + 11 + 111 + 1111 + \ldots \text{ upto } n \text{ terms})$

$= \frac{a}{9}(9 + 99 + 999 + 9999 + \ldots \text{ upto } n \text{ terms})$

$= \frac{a}{9}\{(10^1 - 1) + (10^2 - 1) + (10^3 - 1) + (10^4 - 1) + \ldots \text{ upto } n \text{ terms}\}$

$= \frac{a}{9}\{(10 + 10^2 + 10^3 + \ldots \text{ upto } n \text{ terms}) - (1 + 1 + 1 + \ldots n \text{ times})\}$

$= \frac{a}{9}\left\{\frac{10(10^n - 1)}{10 - 1} - n\right\}$

$= \frac{a}{9}\left\{\frac{10}{9}(10^n - 1) - n\right\}$ [Remember]

Concept Inside Video

JEE Focus Points

- For $a = 1$, $1 + 11 + 111 + \ldots = \frac{1}{9}\left\{\frac{10}{9}(10^n - 1) - n\right\}$
- For $a = 2$, $2 + 22 + 222 + \ldots = \frac{2}{9}\left\{\frac{10}{9}(10^n - 1) - n\right\}$
- For $a = 3$, $3 + 33 + 333 + \ldots = \frac{3}{9}\left\{\frac{10}{9}(10^n - 1) - n\right\}$
- For $a = 4$, $4 + 44 + 444 + \ldots = \frac{4}{9}\left\{\frac{10}{9}(10^n - 1) - n\right\}$
- For $a = 5$, $5 + 55 + 555 + \ldots = \frac{5}{9}\left\{\frac{10}{9}(10^n - 1) - n\right\}$
- For $a = 6$, $6 + 66 + 666 + \ldots = \frac{6}{9}\left\{\frac{10}{9}(10^n - 1) - n\right\}$
- For $a = 7$, $7 + 77 + 777 + \ldots = \frac{7}{9}\left\{\frac{10}{9}(10^n - 1) - n\right\}$
- For $a = 8$, $8 + 88 + 888 + \ldots = \frac{8}{9}\left\{\frac{10}{9}(10^n - 1) - n\right\}$
- For $a = 9$, $9 + 99 + 999 + \ldots = \frac{9}{9}\left\{\frac{10}{9}(10^n - 1) - n\right\}$

Example 43. Find the sum upto n terms of the series $0.b + 0.bb + 0.bbb + 0.bbbb + \ldots, \forall b \in N$ and $1 \le b \le 9$.

Sol. Let $S = 0.b + 0.bb + 0.bbb + 0.bbbb + \ldots$ upto n terms

$= b(0.1 + 0.11 + 0.111 + 0.1111 + \ldots \text{ upto } n \text{ terms})$

$= \frac{b}{9}(0.9 + 0.99 + 0.999 + 0.9999 + \ldots \text{ upto } n \text{ terms})$

$= \frac{b}{9}\{(1 - 0.1) + (1 - 0.01) + (1 - 0.001) + (1 - 0.0001) + \ldots \text{ upto } n \text{ terms}\}$

$= \frac{b}{9}\{(1 + 1 + 1 + 1 + \ldots \text{ upto } n \text{ times}) - (0.1 + 0.01 + 0.001 + 0.0001 + \ldots \text{ upto } n \text{ terms})\}$

$= \frac{b}{9}\left\{n - \left(\frac{1}{10} + \frac{1}{10^2} + \frac{1}{10^3} + \frac{1}{10^4} + \ldots \text{ upto } n \text{ terms}\right)\right\}$

$= \frac{b}{9}\left\{n - \frac{\frac{1}{10}\left(1 - \left(\frac{1}{10}\right)^n\right)}{1 - \frac{1}{10}}\right\}$

$= \frac{b}{9}\left\{n - \frac{1}{9}\left[1 - \left(\frac{1}{10}\right)^n\right]\right\}$ [Remember]

JEE Focus Points

- For $b=1$,

$$0.1+0.11+0.111+\ldots=\frac{1}{9}\left\{n-\frac{1}{9}\left[1-\left(\frac{1}{10}\right)^n\right]\right\}$$

Concept Inside Video

- For $b=2, 0.2+0.22+0.222+\ldots=\frac{2}{9}\left\{n-\frac{1}{9}\left[1-\left(\frac{1}{10}\right)^n\right]\right\}$
- For $b=3, 0.3+0.33+0.333+\ldots=\frac{3}{9}\left\{n-\frac{1}{9}\left[1-\left(\frac{1}{10}\right)^n\right]\right\}$
- For $b=4, 0.4+0.44+0.444+\ldots=\frac{4}{9}\left\{n-\frac{1}{9}\left[1-\left(\frac{1}{10}\right)^n\right]\right\}$
- For $b=5, 0.5+0.55+0.555+\ldots=\frac{5}{9}\left\{n-\frac{1}{9}\left[1-\left(\frac{1}{10}\right)^n\right]\right\}$
- For $b=6, 0.6+0.66+0.666+\ldots=\frac{6}{9}\left\{n-\frac{1}{9}\left[1-\left(\frac{1}{10}\right)^n\right]\right\}$
- For $b=7, 0.7+0.77+0.777+\ldots=\frac{7}{9}\left\{n-\frac{1}{9}\left[1-\left(\frac{1}{10}\right)^n\right]\right\}$
- For $b=8, 0.8+0.88+0.888+\ldots=\frac{8}{9}\left\{n-\frac{1}{9}\left[1-\left(\frac{1}{10}\right)^n\right]\right\}$
- For $b=9, 0.9+0.99+0.999+\ldots=\frac{9}{9}\left\{n-\frac{1}{9}\left[1-\left(\frac{1}{10}\right)^n\right]\right\}$

Example 44. If N, the set of natural numbers is partitioned into groups $S_1=\{1\}, S_2=\{2,3\}$, $S_3=\{4,5,6,7\}, S_4=\{8,9,10,11,12,13,14,15\},\ldots$, then find the sum of the numbers in S_{50}.

Sol. The number of terms in the groups are $1, 2, 2^2, 2^3, \ldots$

$\therefore$ The number of terms in the 50th group $=2^{50-1}=2^{49}$

$\because$ The first term of 1st group $=1=2^0=2^{1-1}$

The first term of 2nd group $=2=2^1=2^{2-1}$

The first term of 3rd group $=4=2^2=2^{3-1}$

$\vdots \quad \vdots \quad \vdots \quad \vdots \quad \vdots$

The first term of 50th group $=2^{50-1}=2^{49}$

$$\therefore \quad S_{50}=\frac{2^{49}}{2}\{2\times 2^{49}+(2^{49}-1)\times 1\}=2^{48}(2^{50}+2^{49}-1)$$

$$=2^{48}[2^{49}(2+1)-1]=2^{48}(3\cdot 2^{49}-1)$$

Example 45. If $S_n=1+\frac{1}{2}+\frac{1}{2^2}+\ldots+\frac{1}{2^{n-1}}$, then calculate the least value of n such that $2-S_n<\frac{1}{100}$.

Sol. Given, $S_n=1+\frac{1}{2}+\frac{1}{2^2}+\ldots+\frac{1}{2^{n-1}}=\dfrac{1\cdot\left[1-\left(\frac{1}{2}\right)^n\right]}{\left(1-\frac{1}{2}\right)}$

$$\Rightarrow \quad S_n=2-\frac{1}{2^{n-1}}$$

$$\Rightarrow \quad 2-S_n=\frac{1}{2^{n-1}}<\frac{1}{100} \quad \left[\because 2-S_n<\frac{1}{100}\right]$$

$$\Rightarrow \quad 2^{n-1}>100>2^6 \Rightarrow 2^{n-1}>2^6$$

$$\therefore \quad n-1>6 \Rightarrow n>7$$

Hence, the least value of n is 8.

Example 46. If $x=1+a+a^2+a^3+\ldots+\infty$ and $y=1+b+b^2+b^3+\ldots+\infty$ show that $1+ab+a^2b^2+a^3b^3+\ldots+\infty=\frac{xy}{x+y-1}$, where $0<a<1$ and $0<b<1$.

Sol. Given, $x=1+a+a^2+a^3+\ldots+\infty=\frac{1}{1-a}$

$$\Rightarrow \quad x-ax=1$$

$$\therefore \quad a=\left(\frac{x-1}{x}\right) \quad \ldots(i)$$

and $\quad y=1+b+b^2+b^3+\ldots+\infty$

Similarly, $\quad b=\left(\frac{y-1}{y}\right) \quad \ldots(ii)$

Since, $\quad 0<a<1, 0<b<1$

$\therefore \quad 0<ab<1$

Now, $1+ab+a^2b^2+a^3b^3+\ldots+\infty=\frac{1}{1-ab}$

$$=\frac{1}{1-\left(\frac{x-1}{x}\right)\left(\frac{y-1}{y}\right)} \quad \text{[from Eqs. (i) and (ii)]}$$

$$=\frac{xy}{xy-xy+x+y-1}$$

Hence, $1+ab+a^2b^2+a^3b^3+\ldots+\infty=\frac{xy}{x+y-1}$

Properties of Geometric Progression

1. If $a_1, a_2, a_3, \ldots$ are in GP with common ratio r, then $a_1k, a_2k, a_3k, \ldots$ and $\frac{a_1}{k}, \frac{a_2}{k}, \frac{a_3}{k}, \ldots$ are also in GP $(k\neq 0)$ with common ratio r.
2. If $a_1, a_2, a_3, \ldots$ are in GP with common ratio r, then $a_1\pm k, a_2\pm k, a_3\pm k, \ldots$ are not in GP $(k\neq 0)$.
3. If $a_1, a_2, a_3, \ldots$ are in GP with common ratio r, then
   (i) $\frac{1}{a_1}, \frac{1}{a_2}, \frac{1}{a_3}, \ldots$ are also in GP with common ratio $\frac{1}{r}$.
   (ii) $a_1^n, a_2^n, a_3^n, \ldots$ are also in GP with common ratio r^n and $n\in Q$.

(iii) $\log a_1, \log a_2, \log a_3, \dots$ are in AP $(a_i > 0, \forall\, i)$
In this case, the converse also holds good.

4. If $a_1, a_2, a_3, \dots$ and $b_1, b_2, b_3, \dots$ are two GP's with common ratios r_1 and r_2, respectively. Then,

(i) $a_1b_1, a_2b_2, a_3b_3, \dots$ and $\frac{a_1}{b_1}, \frac{a_2}{b_2}, \frac{a_3}{b_3}, \dots$ are also in GP with common ratios r_1r_2 and $\frac{r_1}{r_2}$, respectively.

(ii) $a_1 \pm b_1, a_2 \pm b_2, a_3 \pm b_3, \dots$ are not in GP.

5. If $a_1, a_2, a_3, \dots, a_{n-2}, a_{n-1}, a_n$ are in GP. Then,

(i) $a_1a_n = a_2a_{n-1} = a_3a_{n-2} = \dots$

(ii) $a_r = \sqrt{a_{r-k}\, a_{r+k}}, \forall\, k, 0 \le k \le n-r$

(iii) $\frac{a_2}{a_1} = \frac{a_3}{a_2} = \frac{a_4}{a_3} = \dots = \frac{a_n}{a_{n-1}}$

$\Rightarrow \quad a_2^2 = a_3a_1, a_3^2 = a_2a_4, \dots$

Also, $a_2 = a_1r, a_3 = a_1r^2,$

$a_4 = a_1r^3, \dots, a_n = a_1r^{n-1}$

where, r is the common ratio of GP.

6. If three numbers in GP whose product is given are to be taken as $\frac{a}{r}, a, ar$ and if five numbers in GP whose product is given are to be taken as $\frac{a}{r^2}, \frac{a}{r}, a, ar, ar^2$, etc.

In general If $(2m+1)$ numbers in GP whose product is given are to be taken as $(m \in N)$

$$\frac{a}{r^m}, \frac{a}{r^{m-1}}, \dots, \frac{a}{r}, a, ar, \dots, ar^{m-1}, ar^m$$

7. If four numbers in GP whose product is given are to be taken as $\frac{a}{r^3}, \frac{a}{r}, ar, ar^3$ and if six numbers in GP whose product is given are to be taken as $\frac{a}{r^5}, \frac{a}{r^3}, \frac{a}{r}, ar, ar^3, ar^5$, etc.

In general If $(2m)$ numbers in GP whose product is given are to be taken as $(m \in N)$

$$\frac{a}{r^{2m-1}}, \frac{a}{r^{2m-3}}, \dots, \frac{a}{r^3}, \frac{a}{r}, ar, ar^3, \dots, ar^{2m-3}, ar^{2m-1}$$

Example 47. If $S_1, S_2, S_3, \dots, S_p$ are the sum of infinite geometric series whose first terms are 1, 2, 3, ..., p and whose common ratios are $\frac{1}{2}, \frac{1}{3}, \frac{1}{4}, \dots, \frac{1}{p+1}$ respectively, prove that $S_1 + S_2 + S_3 + \dots + S_p = \frac{p(p+3)}{2}$.

Sol. $\because \quad S_p = \frac{p}{1 - \frac{1}{p+1}} = (p+1)$

$\therefore \quad S_1 = 2, S_2 = 3, S_3 = 4, \dots$

$\therefore \quad \text{LHS} = S_1 + S_2 + S_3 + \dots + S_p$

$= 2 + 3 + 4 + \dots + (p+1) = \frac{p}{2}(4 + p - 1)$

$= \frac{p(p+3)}{2} = \text{RHS}$

Example 48. Let x_1 and x_2 be the roots of the equation $x^2 - 3x + A = 0$ and let x_3 and x_4 be the roots of the equation $x^2 - 12x + B = 0$. It is known that the numbers x_1, x_2, x_3, x_4 (in that order) form an increasing GP. Find A and B.

Sol. $\because x_1, x_2, x_3, x_4$ are in GP.

Let $x_2 = x_1r, x_3 = x_1r^2, x_4 = x_1r^3$

[here, product of x_1, x_2, x_3, x_4 are not given]

Given, $x_1 + x_2 = 3, x_1x_2 = A$

$\Rightarrow \quad x_1(1+r) = 3, x_1^2 r = A$ ...(i)

and $x_3 + x_4 = 12, x_3x_4 = B$

$\Rightarrow x_1r^2(1+r) = 12, x_1^2 r^5 = B$ ...(ii)

From Eqs. (i) and (ii), we get

$r^2 = 4 \Rightarrow r = 2$ [for increasing GP]

From Eq. (i), $x_1 = 1$

Now, $A = x_1^2 r = 1^2 \cdot 2 = 2$ [from Eq. (i)]

and $B = x_1^2 r^5 = 1^2 \cdot 2^5 = 32$ [from Eq. (ii)]

Example 49. Suppose a, b, c are in AP and a^2, b^2, c^2 are in GP, if $a > b > c$ and $a + b + c = \frac{3}{2}$, then find the values of a and c.

Sol. Since, a, b, c are in AP and sum of a, b, c is given.

Let $a = b - D, c = b + D$ $[D < 0][\because a > b > c]$

and given $a + b + c = \frac{3}{2} \Rightarrow b - D + b + b + D = \frac{3}{2}$

$\therefore \quad b = \frac{1}{2}$

Then, $a = \frac{1}{2} - D$ and $c = \frac{1}{2} + D$

Also, given a^2, b^2, c^2 are in GP, then $(b^2)^2 = a^2c^2$

$\Rightarrow \quad \pm b^2 = ac \Rightarrow \pm\frac{1}{4} = \frac{1}{4} - D^2$

$\Rightarrow \quad D^2 = \frac{1}{4} \pm \frac{1}{4} = \frac{1}{2}$ $[\because D \ne 0]$

$\therefore \quad D = \pm\frac{1}{\sqrt{2}} \Rightarrow D = -\frac{1}{\sqrt{2}}$ $[\because D < 0]$

Hence, $a = \frac{1}{2} + \frac{1}{\sqrt{2}}$ and $c = \frac{1}{2} - \frac{1}{\sqrt{2}}$

Example 50. If the continued product of three numbers in GP is 216 and the sum of their products in pairs is 156, then find the sum of three numbers.

Sol. Here, product of three numbers in GP is given.

$\therefore$ Let the three numbers be $\frac{a}{r}, a, ar$.

Then, $\frac{a}{r}\cdot a\cdot ar = 216 \Rightarrow a^3 = 216$

$\therefore \quad a = 6$

Sum of the products in pairs = 156

$$\Rightarrow \frac{a}{r}\cdot a + a\cdot ar + ar\cdot\frac{a}{r} = 156$$

$$\Rightarrow a^2\left(\frac{1}{r} + r + 1\right) = 156 \Rightarrow 36\left(\frac{1+r^2+r}{r}\right) = 156$$

$$\Rightarrow 3\left(\frac{1+r+r^2}{r}\right) = 13 \Rightarrow 3r^2 - 10r + 3 = 0$$

$$\Rightarrow (3r-1)(r-3) = 0 \Rightarrow r = \frac{1}{3} \text{ or } r = 3$$

On putting the values of a and r, the required numbers are 18, 6, 2 or 2, 6, 18. Hence, the sum of numbers is 26.

Example 51. Find a three-digit number whose consecutive digits form a GP. If we subtract 792 from this number, we get a number consisting of the same digits written in the reverse order. Now, if we increase the second digit of the required number by 2, then the resulting digits will form an AP.

Sol. Let the three digits be a, ar, ar^2, then according to hypothesis

$$100a + 10ar + ar^2 - 792 = 100ar^2 + 10ar + a$$

$$\Rightarrow 99a(1-r^2) = 792$$

$$\Rightarrow a(1+r)(1-r) = 8 \quad \text{...(i)}$$

and $a, ar+2, ar^2$ are in AP.

Then, $2(ar+2) = a + ar^2$

$$\Rightarrow a(r^2 - 2r + 1) = 4 \Rightarrow a(r-1)^2 = 4 \quad \text{...(ii)}$$

On dividing Eq. (i) by Eq. (ii), we get

$$\frac{r+1}{r-1} = -2 \Rightarrow r = \frac{1}{3}$$

From Eq. (ii), $a = 9$

Thus, digits are 9, 3, 1 and so the required number is 931.

Examples on Application of Progression in Geometrical Figures

Example 52. A square is drawn by joining the mid-points of the sides of a given square. A third square is drawn inside the second square in the same way and this process continues indefinitely. If a side of the first square is 16 cm, then determine the sum of the areas of all the squares.

Sol. Let a be the side length of square, then

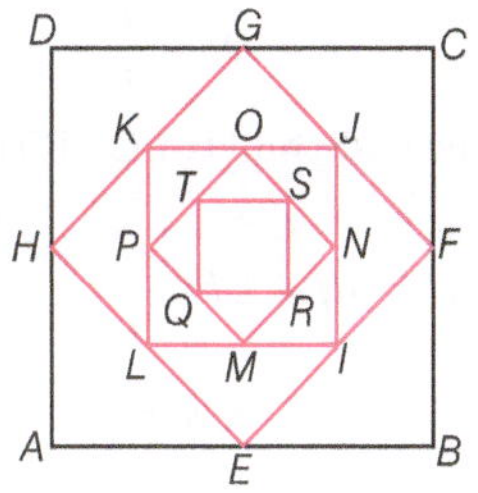

$$AB = BC = CD = DA = a$$

$\because E, F, G, H$ are the mid-points of AB, BC, CD and DA, respectively.

$$\therefore \quad EF = FG = GH = HE = \frac{a}{\sqrt{2}}$$

and I, J, K, L are the mid-points of EF, FG, GH and HE, respectively.

$$\therefore \quad IJ = JK = KL = LI = \frac{a}{2}$$

Similarly, $MN = NO = OP = PM = \frac{a}{2\sqrt{2}}$ and

$$QR = RS = ST = TQ = \frac{a}{4}, \dots$$

S = Sum of areas

$= ABCD + EFGH + IJKL + MNOP + QRST + \dots$

$$= a^2 + \left(\frac{a}{\sqrt{2}}\right)^2 + \left(\frac{a}{2}\right)^2 + \left(\frac{a}{2\sqrt{2}}\right)^2 + \dots$$

$$= a^2\left(1 + \frac{1}{2} + \frac{1}{4} + \frac{1}{8} + \dots\right)$$

$$= a^2\left(\frac{1}{1-\frac{1}{2}}\right) = 2a^2 = 2(16)^2 \quad [\because a = 16 \text{ cm}]$$

$= 512$ sq cm

Example 53. One side of an equilateral triangle is 24 cm. The mid-points of its sides are joined to form another triangle whose mid-points, in turn, are joined to form still another triangle. This process continues, indefinitely. Find the sum of the perimeters of all the triangles.

Sol. Let a be the side length of equilateral triangle, then $AB = BC = CA = a$

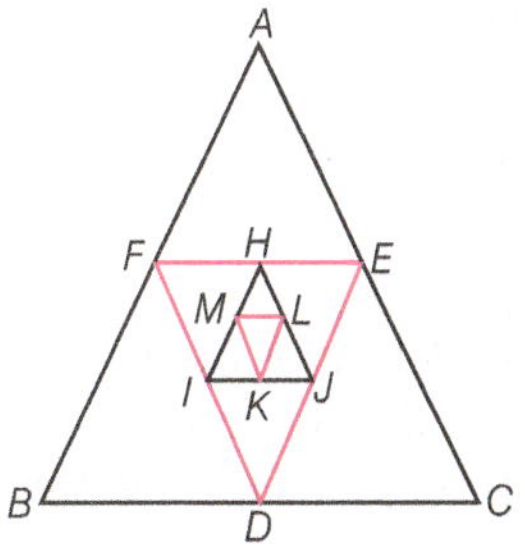

$\because D, E, F$ are the mid-points of BC, CA and AB, respectively.

$\therefore \quad EF = FD = DE = \dfrac{a}{2}$

and H, I, J are the mid-points of EF, FD and DE, respectively.

$\therefore \quad IJ = JH = HI = \dfrac{a}{4}$

Similarly, $\quad KL = ML = KM = \dfrac{a}{8}, \ldots$

$P = \text{Sum of perimeters} = 3\left(a + \dfrac{a}{2} + \dfrac{a}{4} + \dfrac{a}{8} + \ldots\right)$

$= 3\left(\dfrac{a}{1 - \dfrac{1}{2}}\right) = 6a = 6 \times 24 = 144 \text{ cm} \quad [\because a = 24 \text{ cm}]$

Example 54. Let $S_1, S_2, \ldots$ be squares such that for each $n \geq 1$, the length of a side of S_n equals the length of a diagonal of S_{n+1}. If the length of a side of S_1 is 10 cm and the area of S_n less than 1 sq cm. Then, find the value of n.

Sol. We have, length of a side of

S_n = length of diagonal of S_{n+1}

$\Rightarrow$ Length of a side of $S_n = \sqrt{2}$ (length of a side of S_{n+1})

$\Rightarrow \dfrac{\text{Length of a side of } S_{n+1}}{\text{Length of a side of } S_n} = \dfrac{1}{\sqrt{2}}$, for all $n \geq 1$

$\Rightarrow$ Sides of $S_1, S_2, S_3, \ldots$ form a GP with common ratio $\dfrac{1}{\sqrt{2}}$ and first term 10.

$\therefore \quad \text{Side of } S_n = 10\left(\dfrac{1}{\sqrt{2}}\right)^{n-1} = \dfrac{10}{2^{\frac{(n-1)}{2}}}$

$\Rightarrow$ Area of $S_n = (\text{Side})^2 = \dfrac{100}{2^{n-1}}$

Now, given area of $S_n < 1$

$\Rightarrow \quad \dfrac{100}{2^{n-1}} < 1 \Rightarrow 2^{n-1} > 100 > 2^6$

$\Rightarrow \quad 2^{n-1} > 2^6$

$\Rightarrow \quad n - 1 > 6$

$\therefore \quad n > 7$ or $n \geq 8$

Example 55. The line $x + y = 1$ meets X-axis at A and Y-axis at B, P is the mid-point of AB, P_1 is the foot of perpendicular from P to OA, M_1 is that from P_1 to OP; P_2 is that from M_1 to OA, M_2 is that from P_2 to OP; P_3 is that from M_2 to OA and so on. If P_n denotes the nth foot of the perpendicular on OA, then find OP_n.

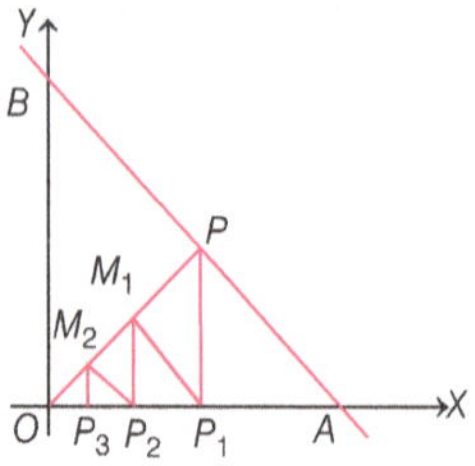

Sol. We have,

$(OM_{n-1})^2 = (OP_n)^2 + (P_n M_{n-1})^2$

$= (OP_n)^2 + (OP_n)^2 = 2(OP_n)^2 = 2\alpha_n^2$ [say]

Also, $(OP_{n-1})^2 = (OM_{n-1})^2 + (P_{n-1}M_{n-1})^2$

$\Rightarrow \quad \alpha_{n-1}^2 = 2\alpha_n^2 + \dfrac{1}{2}\alpha_{n-1}^2$

$\Rightarrow \quad \alpha_n^2 = \dfrac{1}{4}\alpha_{n-1}^2$

$\Rightarrow \quad \alpha_n = \dfrac{1}{2}\alpha_{n-1}$

$\Rightarrow \quad OP_n = \alpha_n = \dfrac{1}{2}\alpha_{n-1} = \dfrac{1}{2^2}\alpha_{n-2} = \ldots = \dfrac{1}{2^n}$

$\therefore \quad OP_n = \left(\dfrac{1}{2}\right)^n$

Use of GP in Solving Practical Problems

In this part, we will see how the formulae relating to GP can be made use in solving practical problems.

Example 56. Dipesh writes letters to four of his friends. He asks each of them to copy the letter and mail to four different persons with the request that they continue the chain similarly. Assuming that the chain is not broken and that it costs 25 paise to mail one letter, find the total money spent on postage till the 8th set of letters is mailed.

Sol. Number of letters in the 1st set = 4
(These are letters sent by Dipesh)

Number of letters in the 2nd set = 4 + 4 + 4 + 4 = 16

Number of letters in the 3rd set

= 4 + 4 + 4 + ... + 16 terms = 64

⋮ ⋮ ⋮ ⋮

The number of letters sent in the 1st set, 2nd set, 3rd set, ... are respectively 4, 16, 64, ... which is a GP with $a = 4$,

$r = \dfrac{16}{4} = \dfrac{64}{16} = 4$

$\therefore$ Total number of letters in all the first 8 sets

$= \dfrac{4(4^8 - 1)}{4 - 1} = 87380$

$\therefore$ Total money spent on letters $= 87380 \times \dfrac{25}{100} = ₹21845$

Example 57. An insect starts from a point and travels in a straight path 1 mm in the first second and half of the distance covered in the previous second in the succeeding second. In how much time would it reach a point 3 mm away from its starting point.

Sol. Distance covered by the insect in the 1st second = 1 mm

Distance covered by it in the 2nd second $= 1 \times \dfrac{1}{2} = \dfrac{1}{2}$ mm

Distance covered by it in the 3rd second $= \frac{1}{2} \times \frac{1}{2} = \frac{1}{4}$ mm

$\vdots \quad \vdots \quad \vdots \quad \vdots$

The distance covered by the insect in 1st second, 2nd second, 3rd second, ... are respectively $1, \frac{1}{2}, \frac{1}{4}, \ldots$, which are in GP with $a = 1, r = \frac{1}{2}$. Let time taken by the insect in covering 3 mm be n seconds.

$\therefore 1 + \frac{1}{2} + \frac{1}{4} + \ldots + n$ terms $= 3$

$$\Rightarrow \quad \frac{1 \cdot \left[1 - \left(\frac{1}{2}\right)^n\right]}{1 - \frac{1}{2}} = 3$$

$$\Rightarrow \quad 1 - \left(\frac{1}{2}\right)^n = \frac{3}{2}$$

$$\Rightarrow \quad \left(\frac{1}{2}\right)^n = -\frac{1}{2}$$

$$\Rightarrow \quad 2^n = -2$$

which is impossible because $2^n > 0$

$\therefore$ Our supposition is wrong.

$\therefore$ There is no $n \in N$, for which the insect could never travels 3 mm in n seconds.

Hence, it will never possible to cover 3 mm.

Example 58. The pollution in a normal atmosphere is less than 0.01%. Due to leakage of a gas from a factory, the pollution is increased to 20%. If every day 80% of the pollution is neutralised, in how many days the atmosphere will be normal?

Sol. Let the pollution on 1st day is increased by 20%.

The pollution on 2nd day $= 20 \times 20\% = 20\,(0.20)$

The pollution on 3rd day $= 20\,(0.20)^2$

$\vdots \quad \vdots \quad \vdots \quad \vdots$

Let in n days the atmosphere will be normal

$$\therefore \quad 20\,(0.20)^{n-1} < 0.01$$

$$\Rightarrow \quad \left(\frac{2}{10}\right)^{n-1} < \frac{1}{2000}$$

Taking logarithm with base 10 both sides, we get

$$(n-1)(\log 2 - \log 10) < \log 1 - \log 2000$$

$$\Rightarrow \quad (n-1)(0.3010 - 1) < 0 - (0.3010 + 3)$$

$$\Rightarrow \quad n - 1 > \frac{3.3010}{0.6990}$$

$$\Rightarrow \quad n > 5.722$$

Hence, the atmosphere will be normal in 6 days.

3.6 Harmonic Sequence or Harmonic Progression (HP)

A Harmonic Progression (HP) is a sequence, if the reciprocals of its terms are in Arithmetic Progression (AP)

i.e. $t_1, t_2, t_3, \ldots$ is HP if and only if $\frac{1}{t_1}, \frac{1}{t_2}, \frac{1}{t_3}, \ldots$ is an AP.

e.g. The sequence

(i) $\frac{1}{2}, \frac{1}{5}, \frac{1}{8}, \ldots$ (ii) $2, \frac{5}{2}, \frac{10}{3}, \ldots$

(iii) $\frac{1}{a}, \frac{1}{a+d}, \frac{1}{a+2d}, \ldots$ are HP's.

JEE Focus Points

Concept Inside Video

- No term of HP can be zero.
- The most general or standard HP is
  $$\frac{1}{a}, \frac{1}{a+d}, \frac{1}{a+2d}, \frac{1}{a+3d}, \ldots$$
- A HP may also be defined as a series in which every three consecutive terms (say I, II, III) satisfy this relation $\frac{\text{I} - \text{II}}{\text{II} - \text{III}} = \frac{\text{I}}{\text{III}}$.
- $$\frac{1}{n\text{th term of HP from beginning}} + \frac{1}{n\text{th term of HP from end}}$$
  $$= a + l = \frac{1}{\text{first term of HP}} + \frac{1}{\text{last term of HP}}$$
- There is no general formula for the sum of any number of quantities in HP and are generally solved by inverting the terms and making use of the corresponding AP.

Example 59. If a, b, c are in HP, then show that $\frac{a-b}{b-c} = \frac{a}{c}$.

Sol. Since, a, b, c are in HP, therefore

$\frac{1}{a}, \frac{1}{b}, \frac{1}{c}$ are in AP

i.e. $\frac{1}{b} - \frac{1}{a} = \frac{1}{c} - \frac{1}{b}$ or $\frac{a-b}{ab} = \frac{b-c}{bc}$ or $\frac{a-b}{b-c} = \frac{a}{c}$

Example 60. Find the first term of a HP whose second term is $\frac{5}{4}$ and the third term is $\frac{1}{2}$.

Sol. Let a be the first term. Then, $a, \frac{5}{4}, \frac{1}{2}$ are in HP.

Then, $$\frac{a - \frac{5}{4}}{\frac{5}{4} - \frac{1}{2}} = \frac{a}{\frac{1}{2}} \quad \text{[from above note]}$$

$$\Rightarrow \quad \frac{4a - 5}{5 - 2} = 2a \Rightarrow 4a - 5 = 6a \text{ or } 2a = -5$$

$$\therefore \quad a = -\frac{5}{2}$$

(i) nth Term of HP from Beginning

Let a be the first term, d be the common difference of an AP. Then, nth term of an AP from beginning $= a + (n-1)\,d$

Hence, the nth term of HP from beginning

$$= \frac{1}{a + (n-1)\,d}, \forall\, n \in N$$

(ii) nth Term of HP from End

Let l be the last term, d be the common difference of an AP. Then, nth term of an AP from end $= l - (n-1)\,d$

Hence, the nth term of HP from end $= \dfrac{1}{l - (n-1)\,d}, \forall\, n \in N$

Example 61. If $\dfrac{1}{a} + \dfrac{1}{c} + \dfrac{1}{a-b} + \dfrac{1}{c-b} = 0$, then prove that a, b, c are in HP, unless $b \neq a + c$.

Sol. We have, $\dfrac{1}{a} + \dfrac{1}{c} + \dfrac{1}{a-b} + \dfrac{1}{c-b} = 0$

$$\Rightarrow \left(\frac{1}{a} + \frac{1}{c-b}\right) + \left(\frac{1}{c} + \frac{1}{a-b}\right) = 0$$

$$\Rightarrow \frac{(c-b+a)}{a\,(c-b)} + \frac{(a-b+c)}{c\,(a-b)} = 0$$

$$\Rightarrow (a+c-b)\left[\frac{1}{a(c-b)} + \frac{1}{c(a-b)}\right] = 0$$

$$\Rightarrow (a+c-b)\,[2ac - b\,(a+c)] = 0$$

If $a + c - b \neq 0$, then

$$2ac - b\,(a+c) = 0$$

or $$b = \frac{2ac}{a+c}$$

Therefore, a, b, c are in HP and if $2ac - b\,(a+c) \neq 0$, then $a + c - b = 0$ i.e. $b = a + c$.

Example 62. If $a_1, a_2, a_3, \ldots, a_n$ are in HP, then prove that $a_1 a_2 + a_2 a_3 + a_3 a_4 + \ldots + a_{n-1} a_n = (n-1)\, a_1 a_n$

Sol. Given, $a_1, a_2, a_3, \ldots, a_n$ are in HP.

$$\therefore \quad \frac{1}{a_1}, \frac{1}{a_2}, \frac{1}{a_3}, \ldots, \frac{1}{a_n} \text{ are in AP.}$$

Let D be the common difference of the AP, then

$$\frac{1}{a_2} - \frac{1}{a_1} = \frac{1}{a_3} - \frac{1}{a_2} = \frac{1}{a_4} - \frac{1}{a_3} = \ldots = \frac{1}{a_n} - \frac{1}{a_{n-1}} = D$$

$$\Rightarrow \frac{a_1 - a_2}{a_1 a_2} = \frac{a_2 - a_3}{a_2 a_3} = \frac{a_3 - a_4}{a_3 a_4} = \ldots = \frac{a_{n-1} - a_n}{a_{n-1} a_n} = D$$

$$\Rightarrow a_1 a_2 = \frac{a_1 - a_2}{D}, a_2 a_3 = \frac{a_2 - a_3}{D}, a_3 a_4 = \frac{a_3 - a_4}{D},$$

$$\ldots, a_{n-1} a_n = \frac{a_{n-1} - a_n}{D}$$

On adding all such expressions, we get

$$a_1 a_2 + a_2 a_3 + a_3 a_4 + \ldots + a_{n-1} a_n = \frac{a_1 - a_n}{D} = \frac{a_1 a_n}{D}\left(\frac{1}{a_n} - \frac{1}{a_1}\right)$$

$$= \frac{a_1 a_n}{D}\left[\frac{1}{a_1} + (n-1)\,D - \frac{1}{a_1}\right] = (n-1)\, a_1 a_n$$

Hence, $a_1 a_2 + a_2 a_3 + a_3 a_4 + \ldots + a_{n-1} a_n = (n-1)\, a_1 a_n$

JEE Focus Points

In particular case,

- when $n = 4$, then $a_1 a_2 + a_2 a_3 + a_3 a_4 = 3 a_1 a_4$
- when $n = 6$, then $a_1 a_2 + a_2 a_3 + a_3 a_4 + a_4 a_5 + a_5 a_6 = 5\, a_1 a_6$

Example 63. The sum of three numbers in HP is 37 and the sum of their reciprocals is $\dfrac{1}{4}$. Find the numbers.

Sol. Three numbers in HP can be taken as $\dfrac{1}{a-d}, \dfrac{1}{a}, \dfrac{1}{a+d}$.

Then, $$\frac{1}{a-d} + \frac{1}{a} + \frac{1}{a+d} = 37 \quad \ldots\text{(i)}$$

and $$a - d + a + a + d = \frac{1}{4}$$

$$\therefore \quad a = \frac{1}{12}$$

From Eq. (i), $$\frac{12}{1-12d} + 12 + \frac{12}{1+12d} = 37$$

$$\Rightarrow \frac{12}{1-12d} + \frac{12}{1+12d} = 25 \Rightarrow \frac{24}{1-144d^2} = 25$$

$$\Rightarrow 1 - 144d^2 = \frac{24}{25} \text{ or } d^2 = \frac{1}{25 \times 144}$$

$$\therefore \quad d = \pm\frac{1}{60}$$

$\therefore\ a - d, a, a + d$ are $\dfrac{1}{15}, \dfrac{1}{12}, \dfrac{1}{10}$ or $\dfrac{1}{10}, \dfrac{1}{12}, \dfrac{1}{15}$.

Hence, three numbers in HP are 15, 12, 10 or 10, 12, 15.

Example 64. If pth, qth and rth terms of a HP be respectively a, b and c, then prove that $(q-r)\,bc + (r-p)\,ca + (p-q)\,ab = 0$.

Sol. Let A and D be the first term and common difference of the corresponding AP. Now, a, b, c are respectively the pth, qth and rth terms of HP.

$\therefore \dfrac{1}{a}, \dfrac{1}{b}, \dfrac{1}{c}$ will be respectively the p th, q th and r th terms of the corresponding AP.

$$\Rightarrow \frac{1}{a} = A + (p-1)\,D \quad \ldots\text{(i)}$$

$$\frac{1}{b} = A + (q-1)\,D \quad \ldots\text{(ii)}$$

$$\frac{1}{c} = A + (r-1)\,D \quad \ldots\text{(iii)}$$

On subtracting Eq. (iii) from Eq. (ii), we get

$$\frac{1}{b}-\frac{1}{c}=(q-r)D \Rightarrow bc(q-r)=\frac{(c-b)}{D}=-\frac{(b-c)}{D}$$

Similarly,

$$(r-p)ca=-\frac{(c-a)}{D} \text{ and } (p-q)ab=-\frac{(a-b)}{D}$$

So, LHS $=(q-r)bc+(r-p)ca+(p-q)ab$

$$=-\frac{1}{D}\{b-c+c-a+a-b\}=0=\text{RHS}$$

Theorem Relating to the Three Series

If a, b, c are three consecutive terms of a series, then

if $\frac{a-b}{b-c}=\frac{a}{a}$, then a, b, c are in AP.

if $\frac{a-b}{b-c}=\frac{a}{b}$, then a, b, c are in GP and if $\frac{a-b}{b-c}=\frac{a}{c}$, then a, b, c are in HP.

Mixed Examples on AP, GP and HP

Example 65. If a, b, c are in AP and a^2, b^2, c^2 be in HP. Then, prove that $-\frac{a}{2}, b, c$ are in GP or else $a=b=c$.

Sol. Given, a, b, c are in AP.

$$\therefore \quad b=\frac{a+c}{2} \quad \text{...(i)}$$

and a^2, b^2, c^2 are in HP.

$$\therefore \quad b^2=\frac{2a^2c^2}{a^2+c^2} \quad \text{...(ii)}$$

From Eq. (ii),

$$b^2\{(a+c)^2-2ac\}=2a^2c^2$$

$$\Rightarrow \quad b^2\{(2b)^2-2ac\}=2a^2c^2 \quad \text{[from Eq. (i)]}$$

$$\Rightarrow \quad 2b^4-acb^2-a^2c^2=0$$

$$\Rightarrow \quad (2b^2+ac)(b^2-ac)=0$$

$$\Rightarrow \quad 2b^2+ac=0 \text{ or } b^2-ac=0$$

If $2b^2+ac=0$, then $b^2=-\frac{1}{2}ac$ or $-\frac{a}{2}, b, c$ are in GP

and if $b^2-ac=0 \Rightarrow a, b, c$ are in GP.

But given, a, b, c are in AP.

which is possible only when $a=b=c$

Example 66. If a, b, c are in HP, b, c, d are in GP and c, d, e are in AP, then show that $e=\frac{ab^2}{(2a-b)^2}$.

Sol. Given, a, b, c are in HP.

$$\therefore \quad b=\frac{2ac}{a+c} \text{ or } c=\frac{ab}{2a-b} \quad \text{...(i)}$$

Given, b, c, d are in GP.

$$\therefore \quad c^2=bd \quad \text{...(ii)}$$

and given, c, d, e are in AP.

$$\therefore \quad d=\frac{c+e}{2} \Rightarrow e=2d-c$$

$$e=\left(\frac{2c^2}{b}-c\right) \quad \text{[from Eq. (ii)] ...(iii)}$$

From Eqs. (i) and (iii),

$$e=\frac{2}{b}\left(\frac{ab}{2a-b}\right)^2-\left(\frac{ab}{2a-b}\right)$$

$$=\frac{ab}{(2a-b)^2}\{2a-(2a-b)\}=\frac{ab^2}{(2a-b)^2}$$

Example 67. If a, b, c, d and e be five real numbers such that a, b, c are in AP; b, c, d are in GP; c, d, e are in HP. If $a=2$ and $e=18$, then find all possible values of b, c and d.

Sol. Given, a, b, c are in AP,

$$\therefore \quad b=\frac{a+c}{2} \quad \text{...(i)}$$

b, c, d are in GP,

$$\therefore \quad c^2=bd \quad \text{...(ii)}$$

and c, d, e are in HP.

$$\therefore \quad d=\frac{2ce}{c+e} \quad \text{...(iii)}$$

Now, substituting the values of b and d in Eq. (ii), then

$$c^2=\left(\frac{a+c}{2}\right)\left(\frac{2ce}{c+e}\right)$$

$$\Rightarrow \quad c(c+e)=e(a+c) \Rightarrow c^2=ae \quad \text{...(iv)}$$

Given, $a=2, e=18$

From Eq. (iv), $c^2=(2)(18)=36$

$\therefore \quad c=\pm 6$

From Eq. (i), $b=\frac{2\pm 6}{2}=4$ or -2

and from Eq. (ii), $d=\frac{c^2}{b}=\frac{36}{b}=\frac{36}{4}$ or $\frac{36}{-2}$

$\therefore \quad d=9$ or -18

Hence, $c=6, b=4, d=9$ or $c=-6, b=-2, d=-18$

Example 68. If three positive numbers a, b and c are in AP, GP and HP as well, then find their values.

Sol. Since, a, b, c are in AP, GP and HP as well

$$\therefore \quad b=\frac{a+c}{2} \quad \text{...(i)}$$

$$b^2=ac \quad \text{...(ii)}$$

$$\text{and} \quad b=\frac{2ac}{a+c} \quad \text{...(iii)}$$

From Eqs. (i) and (ii), we have

$$\left(\frac{a+c}{2}\right)^2=ac \Rightarrow (a+c)^2=4ac$$

$$\Rightarrow \quad (a+c)^2-4ac=0 \Rightarrow (a-c)^2=0$$

$$\therefore \quad a=c \quad \text{...(iv)}$$

On putting $c=a$ in Eq. (i), we get

$$b=\frac{a+a}{2}=a \quad \text{...(v)}$$

From Eqs. (iv) and (v), $a=b=c$, thus the three numbers will be equal.

Milestone Practice 3.2

1. If $x, 2x+2, 3x+3$ are in GP, the fourth term is
(a) 27 (b) −27 (c) 13.5 (d) −13.5

2. The third term of a GP is 4. Then the product of the first five terms is
(a) 64 (b) 128 (c) 512 (d) 1024

3. If $(m+n)$th term of a GP is a and its $(m-n)$th term is b, $a>0$, $b>0$, then m th term is equal to
(a) ab (b) $\sqrt{ab}$ (c) $\frac{1}{ab}$ (d) $\frac{1}{\sqrt{ab}}$

4. If a, G, b are in GP, then the value of $\frac{1}{G^2-a^2}+\frac{1}{G^2-b^2}$ is equal to
(a) G (b) $\frac{1}{G}$ (c) G^2 (d) $\frac{1}{G^2}$

5. $\frac{1}{2}+\frac{1}{3^2}+\frac{1}{2^3}+\frac{1}{3^4}+\frac{1}{2^5}+\frac{1}{3^6}+\dots\infty=$
(a) $\frac{11}{18}$ (b) $\frac{19}{24}$ (c) $\frac{5}{12}$ (d) $\frac{1}{6}$

6. The number of GP containing 27, 8, 12 as three of its term is
(a) 1 (b) 2
(c) infinite (d) can't be possible.

7. If a is the AM of b and c and the possible two GM are G_1 and G_2, then $G_1^3+G_2^3$ is equal to
(a) abc (b) $2abc$ (c) $3abc$ (d) $4abc$

8. If an infinite GP has second term x and its sum is 4, then $x \in$
(a) $(-8, 1)-\{0\}$ (b) $[-8, 1)-\{0\}$
(c) $(-8, 1]-\{0\}$ (d) None of these

9. If $\frac{a-x}{px}=\frac{a-y}{qy}=\frac{a-z}{rz}$ and p, q, r are in AP, then x, y, z are in
(a) AP (b) GP
(c) HP (d) None of these

10. Let $a_1, a_2, a_3, \dots$ and $b_1, b_2, b_3, \dots$ be two GP with $a_1=2\sqrt{3}$ and $b_1=\frac{52}{9}\sqrt{3}$. If $3a_{99}b_{99}=104$, then the value of $a_1b_1+a_2b_2+\dots+a_nb_n$ is, when $n=102$
(a) 3536 (b) 5336 (c) 3563 (d) 5363

11. If the 20th term of a HP is 1 and the 30th term is $-\frac{1}{17}$, then its largest term is
(a) 18th (b) 19th (c) 20th (d) 21th

12. If $\sum_{r=1}^{20} r^3=a$, $\sum_{r=1}^{20} r^2=b$, then sum of product 1, 2, ..., 20 taking two at a time is
(a) $\frac{a-b}{2}$ (b) $\frac{a^2-b^2}{2}$ (c) $a-b$ (d) a^2-b^2

13. Let 2nd, 5th and 9th term of a non-constant AP be respectively the 1st, 2nd and 3rd terms of a GP. If the first term is 3, then the sum of its first 20 terms is equal to
(a) $\frac{525}{4}$ (b) 600 (c) $\frac{730}{7}$ (d) $\frac{300}{7}$

14. Let a, b, c, d, e are non-zero and distinct positive real numbers. If a, b, c are in AP, b, c, d are in GP and c, d, e are in HP, then a, c, e are in
(a) AP (b) GP
(c) HP (d) Nothing can be said

15. If $(1.5)^{30}=k$, then the value of $\sum_{n=2}^{29}(1.5)^n$ is equal to
(a) $2k-3$ (b) $k+1$ (c) $2k+7$ (d) $2k-\frac{9}{2}$

16. If $\log_2 4$, $\log_{\sqrt{2}} 8$ and $\log_3 9^{k-1}$ are consecutive terms of a geometric sequence, then the number of integers that satisfy the system of inequalities $x^2-x>6$ and $|x|<k^2$ is
(a) 193 (b) 194 (c) 195 (d) 196

17. If T_k denotes the kth term of HP from beginning and $\frac{T_2}{T_6}=9$, then $\frac{T_{10}}{T_4}$ equals
(a) $\frac{17}{5}$ (b) $\frac{5}{17}$ (c) $\frac{7}{19}$ (d) $\frac{19}{7}$

18. $x_1, x_2, \dots, x_{2n}$ are in AP, then $\sum_{r=1}^{2n}(-1)^{r+1}x_r^2$ is equal to
(a) $\frac{n}{2n-1}(x_1^2-x_{2n}^2)$ (b) $\frac{2n}{2n-1}(x_1^2-x_{2n}^2)$
(c) $\frac{n}{n-1}(x_1^2-x_{2n}^2)$ (d) $\frac{n}{2n+1}(x_1^2-x_{2n}^2)$

Answer Key

1. (d)	2. (d)	3. (b)	4. (d)	5. (b)	6. (c)
7. (b)	8. (c)	9. (c)	10. (a)	11. (c)	12. (a)
13. (a)	14. (b)	15. (d)	16. (a)	17. (b)	18. (a)

For Detailed Solution

Milestone 3 Arithmetic Mean, Geometric Mean and Harmonic Mean

- Arithmetic Mean
- Geometric Mean
- Harmonic Mean
- Application to Solve Problems of Maxima and Minima without using Calculus

3.7 Arithmetic Mean

If three terms are in AP, then the middle term is called the **Arithmetic Mean** (or shortly written as AM) between the other two, so if a, b, c are in AP, then b is the AM of a and c.

(i) Single AM of n Positive Numbers

Let n positive numbers be $a_1, a_2, a_3, \ldots, a_n$ and A be the AM of these numbers, then

$$A = \frac{a_1 + a_2 + a_3 + \ldots + a_n}{n}$$

In particular Let a and b be two given numbers and A be the AM between them, then a, A, b are in AP.

$$\therefore \qquad A = \frac{a+b}{2}$$

JEE Focus Points

- AM of $2a, 3b, 5c$ is $\frac{2a+3b+5c}{3}$.
- AM of $a_1, a_2, a_3, \ldots, a_{n-1}, a_n$ is $\frac{a_1 + a_2 + a_3 + \ldots + a_{n-1} + a_n}{n}$.

(ii) Insert n-Arithmetic Mean Between Two Numbers

Let a and b be two given numbers and $A_1, A_2, A_3, \ldots, A_n$ are AM's between them.

Then, $a, A_1, A_2, A_3, \ldots, A_n, b$ will be in AP.

Now, $\quad b = (n+2)$ th term $= a + (n+2-1)\,d$

$$\therefore \qquad d = \left(\frac{b-a}{n+1}\right)$$

[Remember] [where, d = common difference] ...(i)

$$\therefore \quad A_1 = a + d,\ A_2 = a + 2d,\ \ldots,\ A_n = a + nd$$

$$\Rightarrow \quad A_1 = a + \left(\frac{b-a}{n+1}\right),\ A_2 = a + 2\left(\frac{b-a}{n+1}\right), \ldots,$$

$$\Rightarrow \quad A_n = a + n\left(\frac{b-a}{n+1}\right)$$

***Corollary* I The sum of n AM's between two given quantities is equal to n times the AM between them.**

Let two numbers be a and b and $A_1, A_2, A_3, \ldots, A_n$ are n AM's between them.

Then, $a, A_1, A_2, A_3, \ldots, A_n, b$ will be in AP.

$\therefore$ Sum of n AM's between a and b

$$= A_1 + A_2 + A_3 + \ldots + A_n$$

$$= \frac{n}{2}(A_1 + A_n) \qquad [\because A_1, A_2, A_3, \ldots, A_n \text{ are in AP}]$$

$$= \frac{n}{2}(a + d + a + nd)$$

$$= \frac{n}{2}[2a + (n+1)\,d]$$

$$= \frac{n}{2}(2a + b - a) \qquad [\text{from Eq. (i)}]$$

$$= n\left(\frac{a+b}{2}\right) = n \cdot (\text{AM between } a \text{ and } b)$$

[Remember]

Aliter I $A_1 + A_2 + A_3 + \ldots + A_n$

$$= (a + A_1 + A_2 + A_3 + \ldots + A_n + b) - (a+b)$$

$$= \frac{(n+2)}{2}(a+b) - (a+b) = n\left(\frac{a+b}{2}\right)$$

$$= n \cdot (\text{AM between } a \text{ and } b)$$

Aliter II

[This method is applicable only when n is even]

$$A_1 + A_2 + A_3 + \ldots + A_{n-2} + A_{n-1} + A_n$$

$$= (A_1 + A_n) + (A_2 + A_{n-1}) + (A_3 + A_{n-2}) + \ldots \text{ upto } \frac{n}{2} \text{ terms}$$

$$= (a+b) + (a+b) + (a+b) + \ldots \text{ upto } \frac{n}{2} \text{ times}$$

$$[\because T_n + T'_n = a + l]$$

$$= \frac{n}{2}(a+b) = n\left(\frac{a+b}{2}\right) = n \cdot (\text{AM between } a \text{ and } b)$$

Corollary II The sum of m AM's between any two numbers is to the sum of n AM's between them as $m : n$.

Let two numbers be a and b.

$\therefore$ Sum of m AM's between a and $b = m$ (AM of a and b) ...(i)

Similarly, sum of n AM's between a and $b = n$ (AM of a and b) ...(ii)

$$\therefore \quad \frac{\text{Sum of } m \text{ AM's}}{\text{Sum of } n \text{ AM's}} = \frac{m(\text{AM of } a \text{ and } b)}{n(\text{AM of } a \text{ and } b)} = \frac{m}{n}$$

Example 69. If a, b, c are in AP and p is the AM between a and b and q is the AM between b and c, then show that b is the AM between p and q.

Sol. $\because$ a, b, c are in AP.

$$\therefore \quad 2b = a + c \quad \text{...(i)}$$

$\because$ p is the AM between a and b.

$$\therefore \quad p = \frac{a+b}{2} \quad \text{...(ii)}$$

$\because$ q is the AM between b and c.

$$\therefore \quad q = \frac{b+c}{2} \quad \text{...(iii)}$$

On adding Eqs. (ii) and (iii), then

$$p + q = \frac{a+b}{2} + \frac{b+c}{2} = \frac{a+c+2b}{2} = \frac{2b+2b}{2} \quad \text{[using Eq. (i)]}$$

$$\therefore \quad p + q = 2b \text{ or } b = \frac{p+q}{2}$$

Hence, b is the AM between p and q.

Example 70. Find n, so that $\dfrac{a^{n+1} + b^{n+1}}{a^n + b^n}$ $(a \neq b)$ be the AM between a and b.

Sol. $\because$
$$\frac{a^{n+1} + b^{n+1}}{a^n + b^n} = \frac{a+b}{2}$$

$$\Rightarrow \quad \frac{b^{n+1}\left[\left(\frac{a}{b}\right)^{n+1} + 1\right]}{b^n\left[\left(\frac{a}{b}\right)^n + 1\right]} = \frac{b}{2}\left[\left(\frac{a}{b}\right) + 1\right]$$

$$\Rightarrow \quad 2\left[\left(\frac{a}{b}\right)^{n+1} + 1\right] = \left[\left(\frac{a}{b}\right)^n + 1\right]\left(\frac{a}{b} + 1\right)$$

Let $\quad \dfrac{a}{b} = \lambda$

$$\therefore \quad 2\lambda^{n+1} + 2 = (\lambda^n + 1)(\lambda + 1)$$

$$\Rightarrow \quad 2\lambda^{n+1} + 2 = \lambda^{n+1} + \lambda^n + \lambda + 1$$

$$\Rightarrow \quad \lambda^{n+1} - \lambda^n - \lambda + 1 = 0 \Rightarrow (\lambda^n - 1)(\lambda - 1) = 0$$

$$\lambda - 1 \neq 0 \quad [\because a \neq b]$$

$$\therefore \quad \lambda^n - 1 = 0 \Rightarrow \lambda^n = 1 = \lambda^0$$

$$\Rightarrow \quad n = 0$$

Example 71. There are n AM's between 3 and 54 such that 8th mean is to $(n-2)$th mean equal to 3 : 5. Find n.

Sol. Let $A_1, A_2, A_3, \ldots, A_n$ be n AM's between 3 and 54.

If d be the common difference, then

$$d = \frac{54-3}{n+1} = \frac{51}{n+1} \quad \text{...(i)}$$

According to the example,

$$\frac{A_8}{A_{n-2}} = \frac{3}{5}$$

$$\Rightarrow \quad 5(3 + 8d) = 3[3 + (n-2)d]$$

$$\Rightarrow \quad 6 = d(3n - 46)$$

$$\Rightarrow \quad 6 = (3n - 46)\frac{51}{(n+1)} \quad \text{[from Eq. (i)]}$$

$$\Rightarrow \quad 6n + 6 = 153n - 2346$$

$$\Rightarrow \quad 147n = 2352$$

$$\therefore \quad n = 16$$

Example 72. If 11 AM's are inserted between 28 and 10, then find the three middle terms in the series.

Sol. Let $A_1, A_2, A_3, \ldots, A_{11}$ be 11 AM's between 28 and 10.

If d be the common difference, then

$$d = \frac{10-28}{12} = -\frac{3}{2}$$

Total means = 11 (odd)

$$\therefore \quad \text{Middle mean} = \left(\frac{11+1}{2}\right)\text{th} = 6\text{th} = A_6$$

Then, three middle terms are A_5, A_6 and A_7.

$$\therefore \quad A_5 = 28 + 5d = 28 - \frac{15}{2} = \frac{41}{2}$$

$$A_6 = 28 + 6d = 28 - 9 = 19$$

and
$$A_7 = 28 + 7d = 28 - \frac{21}{2} = \frac{35}{2}$$

Example 73. If a, b, c are in AP, then show that $a^2(b+c) + b^2(c+a) + c^2(a+b) = \dfrac{2}{9}(a+b+c)^3$.

Sol. $\because$ a, b, c are in AP.

$$\therefore \quad b = \frac{a+c}{2} \text{ i.e. } 2b = a + c \quad \text{...(i)}$$

$$\begin{aligned}
\text{LHS} &= a^2(b+c) + b^2(c+a) + c^2(a+b) \\
&= (a^2b + a^2c) + b^2(2b) + (c^2a + c^2b) \\
&= b(a^2 + c^2) + ac(a+c) + 2b^3 \\
&= b[(a+c)^2 - 2ac] + ac(2b) + 2b^3 \\
&= b(a+c)^2 + 2b^3 = b(2b)^2 + 2b^3 = 6b^3
\end{aligned}$$

$$\text{RHS} = \frac{2}{9}(a+b+c)^3 = \frac{2}{9}(2b+b)^3 = \frac{2}{9} \times 27b^3 = 6b^3$$

Hence, LHS = RHS

3.8 Geometric Mean

If three terms are in GP, then the middle term is called the **Geometric Mean** (or shortly written as GM) between the other two, so if a, b, c are in GP, then b is the GM of a and c.

(i) Single GM of n Positive Numbers

Let n positive numbers be $a_1, a_2, a_3, \ldots, a_n$ and G be the GM of these numbers, then $G = (a_1 a_2 a_3 \ldots a_n)^{1/n}$

In particular Let a and b be two numbers and G be the GM between them, then a, G, b are in GP.

Hence, $G = \sqrt{ab}$; $a > 0, b > 0$

JEE Focus Points

- If $a < 0$, $b < 0$, then $G = -\sqrt{ab}$
- If $a < 0$, $b > 0$ or $a > 0$, $b < 0$, then GM between a and b does not exist.

Concept Inside Video

e.g.

(i) The GM between 4 and 9 is given by

$$G = \sqrt{4 \times 9} = 6$$

(ii) The GM between -4 and -9 is given by

$$G = \sqrt{-4 \times -9} = -6$$

(iii) The GM between -4 and 9 or 4 and -9 does not exist.

i.e. $\sqrt{(-4) \times 9} = \sqrt{-1}\sqrt{36} = 6i$

and $\sqrt{4 \times (-9)} = \sqrt{-1}\sqrt{36} = 6i$

(ii) Insert n-Geometric Mean Between Two Numbers

Let a and b be two given numbers and $G_1, G_2, G_3, \ldots, G_n$ are n GM's between them.

Then, $a, G_1, G_2, G_3, \ldots, G_n, b$ will be in GP.

Now, $b = (n+2)$ th term $= ar^{n+2-1}$

$$\therefore \quad r = \left(\frac{b}{a}\right)^{\frac{1}{n+1}} \quad \text{[where } r = \text{common ratio] [Remember]} \quad \ldots\text{(i)}$$

$$\therefore \quad G_1 = ar, G_2 = ar^2, \ldots, G_n = ar^n$$

$$\Rightarrow \quad G_1 = a\left(\frac{b}{a}\right)^{\frac{1}{n+1}}, G_2 = a\left(\frac{b}{a}\right)^{\frac{2}{n+1}}, \ldots, G_n = a\left(\frac{b}{a}\right)^{\frac{n}{n+1}}$$

Corollary **The product of n geometric means between a and b is equal to the nth power of the geometric mean between a and b.**

Let two numbers be a and b and $G_1, G_2, G_3, \ldots, G_n$ are n GM's between them.

Then, $a, G_1, G_2, G_3, \ldots, G_n, b$ will be in GP.

$\therefore$ Product of n GM's between a and b

$$= G_1 G_2 G_3 \ldots G_n = (ar)(ar^2)(ar^3)\ldots(ar^n)$$

$$= a^{1+1+1+\ldots+1} \cdot r^{1+2+3+\ldots+n}$$

$$= a^n \cdot r^{\frac{n(n+1)}{2}} = a^n \cdot \left[\left(\frac{b}{a}\right)^{\frac{1}{n+1}}\right]^{\frac{n(n+1)}{2}} \quad \text{[from Eq. (i)]}$$

$$= a^n \left(\frac{b}{a}\right)^{\frac{n}{2}} = a^{n/2} b^{n/2} = (\sqrt{ab})^n$$

$$= (\text{GM of } a \text{ and } b)^n \quad \text{[Remember]}$$

Aliter [This method is applicable only when n is even]

$$G_1 G_2 G_3 \ldots G_{n-2}\, G_{n-1}\, G_n = (G_1\, G_n)(G_2 G_{n-1})(G_3 G_{n-2}) \ldots \frac{n}{2} \text{ factors}$$

$$= (ab)(ab)(ab)\ldots\frac{n}{2} \text{ factors} \quad [\because T_n \times T_n' = a \times l]$$

$$= (ab)^{n/2} = (\sqrt{ab})^n = (\text{GM of } a \text{ and } b)^n$$

Example 74. Insert five geometric means between $\frac{1}{3}$ and 9 and verify that their product is the fifth power of the geometric mean between $\frac{1}{3}$ and 9.

Sol. Let G_1, G_2, G_3, G_4, G_5 be 5 GM's between $\frac{1}{3}$ and 9.

Then, $\frac{1}{3}, G_1, G_2, G_3, G_4, G_5, 9$ are in GP.

Here, $r = \text{common ratio} = \left(\dfrac{9}{\frac{1}{3}}\right)^{1/6} = 3^{\frac{1}{2}} = \sqrt{3}$

$$\therefore \quad G_1 = ar = \frac{1}{3}\cdot\sqrt{3} = \frac{1}{\sqrt{3}}$$

$$G_2 = ar^2 = \frac{1}{3}\cdot 3 = 1$$

$$G_3 = ar^3 = \frac{1}{3}\cdot 3\sqrt{3} = \sqrt{3}$$

$$G_4 = ar^4 = \frac{1}{3}\cdot 9 = 3$$

$$G_5 = ar^5 = \frac{1}{3}\cdot 9\sqrt{3} = 3\sqrt{3}$$

Now, product $= G_1 \times G_2 \times G_3 \times G_4 \times G_5$

$$= \frac{1}{\sqrt{3}} \times 1 \times \sqrt{3} \times 3 \times 3\sqrt{3} = 9\sqrt{3} = (3)^{\frac{5}{2}} = \left(\sqrt{\frac{1}{3} \times 9}\right)^5$$

$$= \left(\text{GM of } \frac{1}{3} \text{ and } 9\right)^5$$

Example 75. If a be one AM and G_1 and G_2 be two geometric means between b and c, then prove that $G_1^3 + G_2^3 = 2abc$.

Sol. Given, $a =$ AM between b and c

$$\Rightarrow \quad a = \frac{b+c}{2} \Rightarrow 2a = b + c \quad \text{...(i)}$$

Again, b, G_1, G_2, c are in GP.

$$\therefore \quad \frac{G_1}{b} = \frac{G_2}{G_1} = \frac{c}{G_2} \Rightarrow b = \frac{G_1^2}{G_2}, c = \frac{G_2^2}{G_1}$$

$$\text{and} \quad G_1 G_2 = bc \quad \text{...(ii)}$$

From Eqs. (i) and (ii),

$$2a = \frac{G_1^2}{G_2} + \frac{G_2^2}{G_1} = \frac{G_1^3 + G_2^3}{G_1 G_2} = \frac{G_1^3 + G_2^3}{bc} \quad [\because G_1G_2 = bc]$$

$$\Rightarrow \quad G_1^3 + G_2^3 = 2abc$$

Example 76. Find n, so that $\dfrac{a^{n+1} + b^{n+1}}{a^n + b^n}$ $(a \neq b)$ be the GM between a and b.

Sol. $\because \quad \dfrac{a^{n+1} + b^{n+1}}{a^n + b^n} = \sqrt{ab}$

$$\Rightarrow \quad \frac{b^{n+1}\left[\left(\frac{a}{b}\right)^{n+1} + 1\right]}{b^n\left[\left(\frac{a}{b}\right)^n + 1\right]} = b\sqrt{\frac{a}{b}} \Rightarrow \frac{\left(\frac{a}{b}\right)^{n+1} + 1}{\left(\frac{a}{b}\right)^n + 1} = \left(\frac{a}{b}\right)^{\frac{1}{2}}$$

$$\text{Let} \quad \frac{a}{b} = \lambda$$

$$\Rightarrow \quad \frac{\lambda^{n+1} + 1}{\lambda^n + 1} = \lambda^{\frac{1}{2}} \Rightarrow \lambda^{n+1} + 1 = \lambda^{n+\frac{1}{2}} + \lambda^{\frac{1}{2}}$$

$$\Rightarrow \quad \lambda^{n+\frac{1}{2}}(\lambda^{\frac{1}{2}} - 1) - (\lambda^{\frac{1}{2}} - 1) = 0$$

$$\Rightarrow \quad (\lambda^{\frac{1}{2}} - 1)(\lambda^{n+\frac{1}{2}} - 1) = 0$$

$$\Rightarrow \quad \lambda^{\frac{1}{2}} - 1 \neq 0 \quad [\because a \neq b]$$

$$\therefore \quad \lambda^{n+\frac{1}{2}} - 1 = 0$$

$$\Rightarrow \quad \lambda^{n+\frac{1}{2}} = 1 = \lambda^0$$

$$\Rightarrow \quad n + \frac{1}{2} = 0 \text{ or } n = -\frac{1}{2}$$

An Important Theorem

Let a and b be two real, positive and unequal numbers and A, G are arithmetic and geometric means between them, then

(i) a and b are the roots of the equation

$$x^2 - 2Ax + G^2 = 0 \quad \text{[Remember]}$$

(ii) a and b are given by $A \pm \sqrt{(A+G)(A-G)}$ [Remember]

(iii) $A > G$ [Remember]

Proof $\because$ A is the AM between a and b, then

$$A = \frac{a+b}{2} \Rightarrow a + b = 2A \quad \text{...(i)}$$

and G is the GM between a and b, then

$$G = \sqrt{ab} \Rightarrow ab = G^2 \quad \text{...(ii)}$$

$\therefore$ a and b are the roots of the equation, then

$x^2 -$ (sum of roots) $x +$ product of roots $= 0$

$$\Rightarrow \quad x^2 - (a+b)x + ab = 0$$

i.e. $x^2 - 2Ax + G^2 = 0$ is the required equation.

$$\Rightarrow \quad x = \frac{2A \pm \sqrt{(-2A)^2 - 4 \cdot 1 \cdot G^2}}{2 \cdot 1} = A \pm \sqrt{(A^2 - G^2)}$$

$$\therefore \quad x = A \pm \sqrt{(A+G)(A-G)}$$

Now, for a and b to be real, positive and unequal numbers

$$(A+G)(A-G) > 0 \Rightarrow (A - G) > 0$$

$$\therefore \quad A > G$$

Concept Inside Video

JEE Focus Points

- If a and b are real and positive numbers, then $A \geq G$
- If $a_1, a_2, a_3, \ldots, a_n$ are n positive numbers, then AM $\geq$ GM

  i.e. $\dfrac{a_1 + a_2 + a_3 + \ldots + a_n}{n} \geq (a_1 a_2 a_3 \ldots a_n)^{1/n}$
- (i) If $a > 0, b > 0$ or $a < 0, b < 0$ and $\lambda_1 > 0, \lambda_2 > 0$, then

  $$\lambda_1 \frac{a}{b} + \lambda_2 \frac{b}{a} \geq 2\sqrt{\lambda_1 \lambda_2}$$

  if $\dfrac{a}{b} = x > 0$ and $\lambda_1 = \lambda_2 = 1$, then $x + \dfrac{1}{x} \geq 2$

  (ii) If $a > 0, b < 0$ or $a < 0, b > 0$ and $\lambda_1 > 0, \lambda_2 > 0$, then

  $$\lambda_1 \frac{a}{b} + \lambda_2 \frac{b}{a} \leq -2\sqrt{\lambda_1 \lambda_2}$$

  if $\dfrac{a}{b} = x < 0$ and $\lambda_1 > 0, \lambda_2 > 0$, then, $x + \dfrac{1}{x} \leq -2$.

JEE SCANNER

Example Similar to PYQ Asked in JEE Main 2024

If x, y and z be in arithmetic progression and $x-3, y, z+4$ are in geometric progression, with two arithmetic mean of x, y and z is 12 and $x<17$, then the cube of the geometric mean of a, b and c is

(a) 1331 (b) 1728 (c) 1440 (d) 3126

Sol. (b) Since, x, y and z are in AP

and $x-3, y, z+4$ are in GP

and $\frac{x+y+z}{3}=12$

$\therefore \quad 2y = x+z$ ...(i)

and $y^2=(x-3)(z+4)$ ...(ii)

and $x+y+z=36$

$\Rightarrow \quad 3y=36$ [from Eq. (i)]

$\Rightarrow \quad y=12$ ...(iv)

$\Rightarrow \quad x+z=24$ ...(v)

From Eq. (ii), we have

$$144=(x-3)(24-x+4)=(x-3)(28-x)$$
$$=28x-x^2-84+3x=-x^2+31x-84$$

$\Rightarrow \quad x^2-31x+228=0$

$\Rightarrow \quad (x-19)(x-12)=0 \Rightarrow x=12$ or $x=19$

$\therefore \quad x=12$ $[\because x<17]$

and $z=24-12=12$

$\therefore \quad x=12, y=12, z=12$

Now, $[(abc)^{1/3}]^3=[(12\times12\times12)^{1/3}]^3=[(12^3)^{1/3}]^3=1728$

Skill Builder

Let three real numbers a, b, c be in arithmetic progression and $a+z$, b and $c+2$ in geometric progression. If $a>10$ and the arithmetic mean of a, b and c is 8, then the cube of the geometric mean of a, b and c is

For Sol.

(a) 200 (b) 224

(c) 320 (d) 480

■ **For more practice** See Q.19 of Milestone Practice 3.3.

3.9 Harmonic Mean

If three terms are in HP, then the middle term is called the **Harmonic Mean** (or shortly written as HM) between the other two, so if a, b, c are in HP, then b is the HM of a and c.

(i) Single HM of n Positive Numbers

Let n positive numbers be $a_1, a_2, a_3, \ldots, a_n$ and H be the HM of these numbers, then

$$H=\frac{n}{\left(\frac{1}{a_1}+\frac{1}{a_2}+\frac{1}{a_3}+\ldots+\frac{1}{a_n}\right)}$$

In particular Let a and b be two given numbers and H be the HM between them a, H, b are in HP.

Hence, $H=\frac{2}{\frac{1}{a}+\frac{1}{b}}$ i.e. $H=\frac{2ab}{(a+b)}$

JEE SPIKE

HM of a, b, c is $\frac{3}{\frac{1}{a}+\frac{1}{b}+\frac{1}{c}}$ or $\frac{3abc}{ab+bc+ca}$.

Caution The AM between two numbers a and b is $\frac{a+b}{2}$.

It does not follow that HM between the same numbers is $\frac{2}{a+b}$. The HM is the reciprocals of $\frac{\frac{1}{a}+\frac{1}{b}}{2}$ i.e. $\frac{2ab}{(a+b)}$.

(ii) Insert n-Harmonic Mean Between Two Numbers

Let a and b be two given numbers and $H_1, H_2, H_3, \ldots, H_n$ are n HM's between them.

Then, $a, H_1, H_2, H_3, \ldots, H_n, b$ will be in HP, if D be the common difference of the corresponding AP.

$\therefore b=(n+2)$ th term of HP.

$$=\frac{1}{(n+2)\text{th term of corresponding AP}}=\frac{1}{\frac{1}{a}+(n+2-1)D}$$

$$\Rightarrow \quad D=\frac{\frac{1}{b}-\frac{1}{a}}{(n+1)} \quad \text{[Remember]}$$

$$\therefore \quad \frac{1}{H_1}=\frac{1}{a}+D, \frac{1}{H_2}=\frac{1}{a}+2D, \ldots, \frac{1}{H_n}=\frac{1}{a}+nD$$

$$\Rightarrow \quad \frac{1}{H_1}=\frac{1}{a}+\frac{(a-b)}{ab(n+1)}, \frac{1}{H_2}=\frac{1}{a}+\frac{2(a-b)}{ab(n+1)}, \ldots, \frac{1}{H_n}=\frac{1}{a}+\frac{n(a-b)}{ab(n+1)}$$

Corollary **The sum of reciprocals of n harmonic means between two given numbers is n times the reciprocal of single HM between them.**

Let two numbers be a and b and $H_1, H_2, H_3, \ldots, H_n$ are n HM's between them. Then, $a, H_1, H_2, H_3, \ldots, H_n, b$ will be in HP.

$$\therefore \quad \frac{1}{H_1}+\frac{1}{H_2}+\frac{1}{H_3}+\ldots+\frac{1}{H_n}=\frac{n}{2}\left(\frac{1}{H_1}+\frac{1}{H_n}\right)$$

$$\left[\because S_n=\frac{n}{2}(a+l)\right]$$

$$= \frac{n}{2}\left(\frac{1}{a} + D + \frac{1}{b} - D\right) = \frac{n}{2}\left(\frac{1}{a} + \frac{1}{b}\right)$$

$$= \frac{n}{\left(\dfrac{2}{\frac{1}{a} + \frac{1}{b}}\right)} = \frac{n}{(\text{HM of } a \text{ and } b)}$$

Aliter [This method is applicable only when n is even]

$$\frac{1}{H_1} + \frac{1}{H_2} + \frac{1}{H_3} + \ldots + \frac{1}{H_{n-2}} + \frac{1}{H_{n-1}} + \frac{1}{H_n}$$

$$= \left(\frac{1}{H_1} + \frac{1}{H_n}\right) + \left(\frac{1}{H_2} + \frac{1}{H_{n-1}}\right) + \left(\frac{1}{H_3} + \frac{1}{H_{n-2}}\right) + \ldots \text{ upto } \frac{n}{2} \text{ terms}$$

$$= \left(\frac{1}{a} + D + \frac{1}{b} - D\right) + \left(\frac{1}{a} + 2D + \frac{1}{b} - 2D\right) + \left(\frac{1}{a} + 3D + \frac{1}{b} - 3D\right) + \ldots \text{upto } \frac{n}{2} \text{ terms}$$

$$= \left(\frac{1}{a} + \frac{1}{b}\right) + \left(\frac{1}{a} + \frac{1}{b}\right) + \left(\frac{1}{a} + \frac{1}{b}\right) + \ldots \text{ upto } \frac{n}{2} \text{ terms}$$

$$= \frac{n}{2}\left(\frac{1}{a} + \frac{1}{b}\right) = \frac{n}{\left(\dfrac{2}{\frac{1}{a} + \frac{1}{b}}\right)} = \frac{n}{(\text{HM of } a \text{ and } b)}$$

Example 77. If $a_1, a_2, a_3, \ldots, a_{10}$ be in AP and $h_1, h_2, h_3, \ldots, h_{10}$ be in HP. If $a_1 = h_1 = 2$ and $a_{10} = h_{10} = 3$, then find the value of $a_4 h_7$.

Sol. $\because$ $a_1, a_2, a_3, \ldots, a_{10}$ are in AP.

If d be the common difference, then

$$d = \frac{a_{10} - a_1}{9} = \frac{3 - 2}{9} = \frac{1}{9}$$

$$\therefore \quad a_4 = a_1 + 3d = 2 + \frac{3}{9} = 2 + \frac{1}{3} = \frac{7}{3} \quad \ldots\text{(i)}$$

and given $h_1, h_2, h_3, \ldots, h_{10}$ are in HP.

If D be common difference of corresponding AP.

Then, $$D = \frac{\frac{1}{h_{10}} - \frac{1}{h_1}}{9} = \frac{\frac{1}{3} - \frac{1}{2}}{9} = -\frac{1}{54}$$

$$\therefore \quad \frac{1}{h_7} = \frac{1}{h_1} + 6D = \frac{1}{2} - \frac{6}{54} = \frac{1}{2} - \frac{1}{9} = \frac{7}{18}$$

$$\Rightarrow \quad h_7 = \frac{18}{7}$$

Hence, $a_4 \cdot h_7 = \frac{7}{3} \times \frac{18}{7} = 6$

Example 78. Insert 6 harmonic means between 3 and $\frac{6}{23}$.

Sol. Let $H_1, H_2, H_3, H_4, H_5, H_6$ be 6 HM's between 3 and $\frac{6}{23}$.

Then, $3, H_1, H_2, H_3, H_4, H_5, H_6, \frac{6}{23}$ are in HP.

$\Rightarrow$ $\frac{1}{3}, \frac{1}{H_1}, \frac{1}{H_2}, \frac{1}{H_3}, \frac{1}{H_4}, \frac{1}{H_5}, \frac{1}{H_6}, \frac{23}{6}$ are in AP.

Let common difference of this AP be D.

$$\therefore \quad D = \frac{\frac{23}{6} - \frac{1}{3}}{7} = \frac{(23 - 2)}{7 \times 6} = \frac{21}{7 \times 6} = \frac{1}{2}$$

$$\therefore \quad \frac{1}{H_1} = \frac{1}{3} + D = \frac{1}{3} + \frac{1}{2} = \frac{5}{6}$$

$$\Rightarrow \quad H_1 = \frac{6}{5}$$

$$\frac{1}{H_2} = \frac{1}{3} + 2D = \frac{1}{3} + 1 = \frac{4}{3} \Rightarrow H_2 = \frac{3}{4}$$

$$\frac{1}{H_3} = \frac{1}{3} + 3D = \frac{1}{3} + \frac{3}{2} = \frac{11}{6} \Rightarrow H_3 = \frac{6}{11}$$

$$\frac{1}{H_4} = \frac{1}{3} + 4D = \frac{1}{3} + 2 = \frac{7}{3} \Rightarrow H_4 = \frac{3}{7}$$

$$\frac{1}{H_5} = \frac{1}{3} + 5D = \frac{1}{3} + \frac{5}{2} = \frac{17}{6} \Rightarrow H_5 = \frac{6}{17}$$

and $$\frac{1}{H_6} = \frac{1}{3} + 6D = \frac{1}{3} + 3 = \frac{10}{3} \Rightarrow H_6 = \frac{3}{10}$$

$\therefore$ HM's are $\frac{6}{5}, \frac{3}{4}, \frac{6}{11}, \frac{3}{7}, \frac{6}{17}, \frac{3}{10}$.

Important Theorem 1

Let a and b be two real, positive and unequal numbers and A, G and H are arithmetic, geometric and harmonic means respectively between them, then

(i) A, G, H form a GP i.e. $G^2 = AH$ [Remember]

(ii) $A > G > H$ [Remember]

Proof

(i) $\because$ $$A = \frac{a + b}{2}, G = \sqrt{ab} \text{ and } H = \frac{2ab}{a + b}$$

Now, $$AH = \left(\frac{a + b}{2}\right)\left(\frac{2ab}{a + b}\right) = ab = G^2$$

Therefore, $G^2 = AH$ i.e. A, G, H are in GP.

(ii) $\because$ $A > G$ [from important theorem of GM] ...(i)

or $\frac{A}{G} > 1 \Rightarrow \frac{G}{H} > 1$ $\left[\because \frac{A}{G} = \frac{G}{H} \Rightarrow G^2 = AH\right]$

$\Rightarrow$ $G > H$ ...(ii)

From Eqs. (i) and (ii), we get

$$A > G > H$$

JEE Focus Points

- The result $AH = G^2$ will be true for n numbers, if they are in GP.
- If $a_1, a_2, a_3, \ldots, a_n$ are n positive numbers, then AM ≥ GM ≥ HM i.e.

$$\frac{a_1 + a_2 + \ldots + a_n}{n} \geq (a_1 a_2 \ldots a_n)^{1/n} \geq \frac{n}{\left(\frac{1}{a_1} + \frac{1}{a_2} + \ldots + \frac{1}{a_n}\right)}$$

Concept Inside Video

Sign of equality (AH = GM = HM) holds when numbers are equal i.e. $a_1 = a_2 = \ldots = a_n$.

Important Theorem 2

If A, G, H are arithmetic, geometric and harmonic means of three given numbers a, b and c, then the equation having a, b, c as its roots is

$$\boldsymbol{x^3 - 3Ax^2 + \frac{3G^3}{H}x - G^3 = 0} \quad \text{[remember]}$$

Proof ∵ $A = \text{AM of } a, b, c = \dfrac{a+b+c}{3}$

i.e., $a + b + c = 3A$ ...(i)

$G = \text{GM of } a, b, c = (abc)^{1/3}$

i.e. $abc = G^3$ ...(ii)

and $H = \text{HM of } a, b, c$

$$= \frac{3}{\frac{1}{a} + \frac{1}{b} + \frac{1}{c}}$$

$$= \frac{3abc}{ab + bc + ca} = \frac{3G^3}{ab + bc + ca} \quad \text{[from Eq. (ii)]}$$

i.e. $ab + bc + ca = \dfrac{3G^3}{H}$ ...(iii)

∴ a, b, c are the roots of the equation

$$x^3 - (a + b + c)\,x^2 + (ab + bc + ca)\,x - abc = 0$$

i.e. $$x^3 - 3Ax^2 + \frac{3G^3}{H}x - G^3 = 0$$

[from Eqs. (i), (ii) and (iii)]

Geometrical Proof of $A > G > H$

Let $OA = a$ unit and $OB = b$ unit and AB be a diameter of semi-circle. Draw tangent OT to the circle and TM perpendicular to AB.

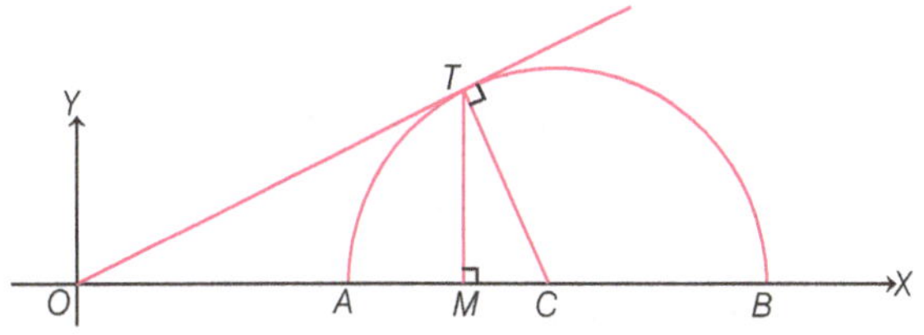

Let C be the centre of the semi-circle.

$$\because \frac{OA + OB}{2} = \frac{(OC - AC) + (OC + CB)}{2}$$

$$= \frac{2\,OC}{2} = OC \quad [\because AC = CB = \text{radius of circle}]$$

∴ $OC = \dfrac{a+b}{2}$ [i.e. OC = arithmetic mean]

⇒ $A = \dfrac{a+b}{2}$

Now, from geometry

$$(OT)^2 = OA \times OB = ab = G^2$$

∴ $OT = G$, the geometric mean

Now, from similar ΔOMT and ΔOTC, we have

$$\frac{OM}{OT} = \frac{OT}{OC} \text{ or } OM = \frac{(OT)^2}{OC} = \frac{ab}{\frac{a+b}{2}} = \frac{2ab}{a+b}$$

∴ $OM = H$, the harmonic mean

Also, it is clear from the figure, that

$$OC > OT > OM \text{ i.e. } A > G > H$$

Example 79. If $A^x = G^y = H^z$, where A, G, H are AM, GM and HM between two given quantities, then prove that x, y, z are in HP.

Sol. Let $A^x = G^y = H^z = k$

Then, $A = k^{1/x}, G = k^{1/y}, H = k^{1/z}$

∵ $G^2 = AH \Rightarrow (k^{1/y})^2 = k^{1/x} \cdot k^{1/z}$

⇒ $k^{2/y} = k^{1/x + 1/z} \Rightarrow \dfrac{2}{y} = \dfrac{1}{x} + \dfrac{1}{z} \Rightarrow \dfrac{1}{x}, \dfrac{1}{y}, \dfrac{1}{z}$ are in AP.

Hence, x, y, z are in HP.

Example 80. The harmonic mean of two numbers is 4, their arithmetic mean A and geometric mean G satisfy the relation $2A + G^2 = 27$. Find the numbers.

Sol. Let the numbers be a and b.

Given, $H = 4$

∵ $G^2 = AH = 4A$ ...(i)

and given $2A + G^2 = 27$

⇒ $2A + 4A = 27$ [from Eq. (i)]

∴ $A = \dfrac{9}{2}$

From Eq. (i), $G^2 = 4 \times \dfrac{9}{2} = 18$

Now, from important theorem of GM

$$a, b = A \pm \sqrt{(A^2 - G^2)}$$

$$= \frac{9}{2} \pm \sqrt{\left(\frac{81}{4} - 18\right)} = \frac{9}{2} \pm \frac{3}{2} = 6, 3 \text{ or } 3, 6$$

Example 81. If the geometric mean is $\frac{1}{n}$ times the harmonic mean between two numbers, then show that the ratio of the two numbers is

$$1+\sqrt{(1-n^2)}:1-\sqrt{(1-n^2)}.$$

Sol. Let the two numbers be a and b.

Given, $G=\frac{1}{n}H$ ...(i)

Now, $G^2 = AH$

$\Rightarrow \frac{H^2}{n^2} = AH$ [from Eq. (i)]

$\therefore A = \frac{H}{n^2}$ ...(ii)

Now, from important theorem of GM

$$a, b = A \pm \sqrt{(A^2 - G^2)}$$

$$= \frac{H}{n^2} \pm \sqrt{\left(\frac{H^2}{n^4} - \frac{H^2}{n^2}\right)}$$

$$= \frac{H}{n^2}[1 \pm \sqrt{(1-n^2)}]$$

$$\therefore \frac{a}{b} = \frac{\frac{H}{n^2}[1+\sqrt{(1-n^2)}]}{\frac{H}{n^2}[1-\sqrt{(1-n^2)}]}$$

$$\therefore a:b = 1+\sqrt{(1-n^2)}:1-\sqrt{(1-n^2)}$$

Example 82. If three positive unequal quantities a, b, c be in HP, then prove that $a^n + c^n > 2b^n, n \in N$.

Sol. $\because G > H$

$\therefore \sqrt{ac} > b$

$\Rightarrow (ac)^{\frac{n}{2}} > b^n$ or $a^{\frac{n}{2}} c^{\frac{n}{2}} > b^n$ ...(i)

Also, $(a^{\frac{n}{2}} - c^{\frac{n}{2}})^2 > 0 \Rightarrow a^n + c^n - 2a^{\frac{n}{2}} c^{\frac{n}{2}} > 0$

$\Rightarrow a^n + c^n > 2a^{\frac{n}{2}} c^{\frac{n}{2}} > 2b^n$ [from Eq. (i)]

$\therefore a^n + c^n > 2b^n$

3.10 Application to Solve Problems of Maxima and Minima without Using Calculus

Suppose that $a_1, a_2, a_3, \ldots, a_n$ are n positive variables and k is constant, then

(i) If $a_1 + a_2 + a_3 + \ldots + a_n = k$ (constant), the value of $a_1 a_2 a_3 \ldots a_n$ is greatest when $a_1 = a_2 = a_3 = \ldots = a_n$, so that the greatest value of $a_1 a_2 a_3 \ldots a_n$ is $\left(\frac{k}{n}\right)^n$.

Proof $\because$ AM $\geq$ GM

$$\therefore \frac{a_1 + a_2 + a_3 + \ldots + a_n}{n} \geq (a_1 a_2 a_3 \ldots a_n)^{1/n}$$

$$\Rightarrow \frac{k}{n} \geq (a_1 a_2 a_3 \ldots a_n)^{1/n} \text{ or } (a_1 a_2 a_3 \ldots a_n) \leq \left(\frac{k}{n}\right)^n$$

Here, $a_1 = a_2 = a_3 = \ldots = a_n$

$\therefore$ Greatest value of $a_1 a_2 a_3 \ldots a_n$ is $\left(\frac{k}{n}\right)^n$.

Example 83. Find the greatest value of xyz for positive values of x, y, z subject to the condition $yz + zx + xy = 12$.

Sol. Given, $yz + zx + xy = 12$ (constant), the value of $(yz)(zx)(xy)$ is greatest when $yz = zx = xy$

Here, $n = 3$ and $k = 12$

Hence, greatest value of $(yz)(zx)(xy)$ is $\left(\frac{12}{3}\right)^3$ i.e. 64.

$\therefore$ Greatest value of $x^2y^2z^2$ is 64.

Thus, greatest value of xyz is 8.

> **Alternate Solution**
>
> Given, $yz + zx + xy = 12$, the value of $(yz)(zx)(xy)$ is greatest, when
>
> $yz = zx = xy = c$ [say]
>
> Since, $yz + zx + xy = 12$
>
> $\therefore c + c + c = 12 \Rightarrow 3c = 12$ or $c = 4$
>
> $\therefore yz = zx = xy = 4$
>
> Hence, greatest value of $(yz)(zx)(xy)$ is $4 \cdot 4 \cdot 4$
>
> i.e. greatest value of $x^2y^2z^2$ is 64.
>
> Hence, greatest value of xyz is 8.

Example 84. Find the greatest value of x^3y^4, if $2x + 3y = 7$ and $x \geq 0, y \geq 0$.

Sol. To find the greatest value of x^3y^4 or $(x)(x)(x)(y)(y)(y)(y)$

Here, x repeats 3 times and y repeats 4 times.

Given, $2x + 3y = 7$, then multiplying and dividing coefficients of x and y by 3 and 4, respectively.

Rewrite $3\left(\frac{2x}{3}\right) + 4\left(\frac{3y}{4}\right) = 7$

or $\underset{1}{\left(\frac{2x}{3}\right)} + \underset{2}{\left(\frac{2x}{3}\right)} + \underset{3}{\left(\frac{2x}{3}\right)} + \underset{4}{\left(\frac{3y}{4}\right)} + \underset{5}{\left(\frac{3y}{4}\right)} + \underset{6}{\left(\frac{3y}{4}\right)} + \underset{7}{\left(\frac{3y}{4}\right)} = 7$

Here, $k = 7$ and $n = 7$

Hence, greatest value of

$$\left(\frac{2x}{3}\right)\left(\frac{2x}{3}\right)\left(\frac{2x}{3}\right)\left(\frac{3y}{4}\right)\left(\frac{3y}{4}\right)\left(\frac{3y}{4}\right)\left(\frac{3y}{4}\right) \text{ is } \left(\frac{7}{7}\right)^7.$$

or greatest value of $\frac{2^3 \cdot 3^4}{3^3 \cdot 4^4} x^3y^4$ is 1.

Thus, greatest value of x^3y^4 is $\frac{32}{3}$.

(ii) If $a_1a_2a_3 \dots a_n = k$ (constant), the value of $a_1 + a_2 + a_3 + \dots + a_n$ is least when $a_1 = a_2 = a_3 = \dots = a_n$, so that the least of $a_1 + a_2 + a_3 + \dots + a_n$ is $n(k)^{1/n}$.

Proof $\because$ AM $\geq$ GM

$$\therefore \quad \frac{a_1 + a_2 + a_3 + \dots + a_n}{n} \geq (a_1a_2a_3 \dots a_n)^{1/n} = (k)^{1/n}$$

$$\Rightarrow \quad \frac{a_1 + a_2 + a_3 + \dots + a_n}{n} \geq (k)^{1/n}$$

or $\quad a_1 + a_2 + a_3 + \dots + a_n \geq n(k)^{1/n}$

Here, $a_1 = a_2 = a_3 = \dots = a_n$

$\therefore$ Least value of $a_1 + a_2 + a_3 + \dots + a_n$ is $n(k)^{1/n}$

Example 85. Find the least value of $3x + 4y$ for positive values of x and y, subject to the condition $x^2y^3 = 6$.

Sol. Given, $x^2y^3 = 6$ or $(x)(x)(y)(y)(y) = 6$

Here, x repeats 2 times and y repeats 3 times

$$\therefore \quad 3x + 4y = 2\left(\frac{3x}{2}\right) + 3\left(\frac{4y}{3}\right)$$

$$= \left(\frac{3x}{2}\right) + \left(\frac{3x}{2}\right) + \left(\frac{4y}{3}\right) + \left(\frac{4y}{3}\right) + \left(\frac{4y}{3}\right)$$

1 2 3 4 5

[$\because$ multiply and divide coefficient of x and y by 2 and 3 respectively and write $x^2y^3 = 6$]

$$\Rightarrow \left(\frac{3x}{2}\right)\left(\frac{3x}{2}\right)\left(\frac{4y}{3}\right)\left(\frac{4y}{3}\right)\left(\frac{4y}{3}\right) = \frac{3^2}{2^2} \times \frac{4^3}{3^3} \times 6 = 32$$

Here, $n = 5$ and $k = 32$

Hence, least value of $\frac{3x}{2} + \frac{3x}{2} + \frac{4y}{3} + \frac{4y}{3} + \frac{4y}{3}$

$$= 5(32)^{1/5} = 10$$

i.e. least value of $3x + 4y = 10$

Example 86. Find the minimum value of $bcx + cay + abz$, when $xyz = abc$.

Sol. To find the minimum value of $bcx + cay + abz$,

write, $\quad xyz = abc \quad$ [given]

or $\quad (bcx)(cay)(abz) = a^3b^3c^3 = k \quad$ [constant]

Here, $\quad n = 3$

Hence, minimum value of $bcx + cay + abz = n(k)^{1/n}$

$$= 3(a^3b^3c^3)^{1/3} = 3abc$$

An Important Result

If $a_i > 0, i = 1, 2, 3, \dots, n$ which are not identical, then

(i) $\dfrac{a_1^m + a_2^m + \dots + a_n^m}{n} > \left(\dfrac{a_1 + a_2 + \dots + a_n}{n}\right)^m$; If $m < 0$

or $m > 1$

(ii) $\dfrac{a_1^m + a_2^m + \dots + a_n^m}{n} < \left(\dfrac{a_1 + a_2 + \dots + a_n}{n}\right)^m$;

If $0 < m < 1$

Example 87. If a, b, c be positive real numbers, prove that $\frac{a}{b+c} + \frac{b}{c+a} + \frac{c}{a+b} \geq \frac{3}{2}$.

Sol. Arithmetic mean of (-1) th powers $\geq (-1)$ th power of arithmetic mean

$$\frac{\left(\frac{b+c}{a+b+c}\right)^{-1} + \left(\frac{c+a}{a+b+c}\right)^{-1} + \left(\frac{a+b}{a+b+c}\right)^{-1}}{3} \geq \left(\frac{\frac{b+c}{a+b+c} + \frac{c+a}{a+b+c} + \frac{a+b}{a+b+c}}{3}\right)^{-1}$$

$$\Rightarrow \quad \frac{\frac{a+b+c}{b+c} + \frac{a+b+c}{c+a} + \frac{a+b+c}{a+b}}{3} \geq \left(\frac{2}{3}\right)^{-1}$$

$$\Rightarrow \quad \frac{a}{b+c} + 1 + \frac{b}{c+a} + 1 + \frac{c}{a+b} + 1 \geq \frac{9}{2}$$

$$\Rightarrow \quad \frac{a}{b+c} + \frac{b}{c+a} + \frac{c}{a+b} \geq \frac{9}{2} - 3$$

or $$\frac{a}{b+c} + \frac{b}{c+a} + \frac{c}{a+b} \geq \frac{3}{2}$$

Example 88. If a and b are positive and $a + b = 1$, show that $\left(a + \frac{1}{a}\right)^2 + \left(b + \frac{1}{b}\right)^2 > \frac{25}{2}$.

Sol. Since, AM of 2nd powers > 2nd power of AM

$$\therefore \quad \frac{\left(a + \frac{1}{a}\right)^2 + \left(b + \frac{1}{b}\right)^2}{2} > \left(\frac{a + \frac{1}{a} + b + \frac{1}{b}}{2}\right)^2$$

$$= \frac{1}{4}(a + b + a^{-1} + b^{-1})^2 = \frac{1}{4}(1 + a^{-1} + b^{-1})^2 \quad [\because a + b = 1]$$

$$\therefore \quad \left(a + \frac{1}{a}\right)^2 + \left(b + \frac{1}{b}\right)^2 > \frac{1}{2}(1 + a^{-1} + b^{-1})^2 \quad \dots(i)$$

Again, $$\frac{a^{-1} + b^{-1}}{2} > \left(\frac{a+b}{2}\right)^{-1} = \left(\frac{1}{2}\right)^{-1} = 2$$

or $$\frac{a^{-1} + b^{-1}}{2} > 2$$

$$\Rightarrow \quad a^{-1} + b^{-1} > 4$$

$$\therefore \quad (1 + a^{-1} + b^{-1}) > 5 \text{ or } (1 + a^{-1} + b^{-1})^2 > 25$$

$$\Rightarrow \quad \frac{1}{2}(1 + a^{-1} + b^{-1})^2 > \frac{25}{2} \quad \dots(ii)$$

From Eqs. (i) and (ii), we get

$$\left(a + \frac{1}{a}\right)^2 + \left(b + \frac{1}{b}\right)^2 > \frac{25}{2}$$

Milestone Practice 3.3

1. The product of 3 GM between 4 and $\frac{1}{4}$ is
(a) 1 (b) −1 (c) 2 (d) −2

2. The AM and HM between two numbers are 27 and 12, then their GM is
(a) 3 (b) 6 (c) 9 (d) 18

3. Let $A_1, A_2, A_3, \ldots, A_{10}$ are 10 AM between 1 and 10, then $\sum_{i=1}^{10} A_i$ is equal to
(a) 50 (b) 55 (c) 60 (d) 65

4. HM of the roots of the equation $x^2 - 10x + 11 = 0$ is
(a) $\frac{1}{5}$ (b) $\frac{5}{21}$ (c) $\frac{21}{20}$ (d) $\frac{11}{5}$

5. The minimum value of $4^x + 4^{2-x}$, $x \in R$ is
(a) 0 (b) 2 (c) 4 (d) 8

6. If $0 < \theta < \pi$, then the minimum value of $3\sin\theta + \operatorname{cosec}^3\theta$, is
(a) 0 (b) 2 (c) 4 (d) 8

7. The minimum value of $(a + b + c)\left(\frac{1}{a} + \frac{1}{b} + \frac{1}{c}\right)$ is
(a) 3 (b) 6 (c) 9 (d) 12

8. If $a + b + c = 5, (a, b, c > 0)$ and greatest value of $a^3b^2c^4$ is $2^{k_1} \cdot 3^{k_2} \cdot 5^{k_3}$, then $k_1 + k_2 + k_3$ is equal to
(a) 1 (b) 2 (c) 3 (d) 4

9. If x, y, z are positive reals satisfying $xyz = 32$, then the minimum value of $x^2 + 4xy + 4y^2 + 2z^2$ is
(a) 92 (b) 96 (c) 48 (d) 44

10. If α, β and γ are the negative roots of the equation $27x^3 + 216x^2 + 36px + 32p = 0$, $p \in R - \{0\}$, then $\left|\frac{p}{\gamma}\right|$ equals
(a) 2 (b) 6 (c) 8 (d) 64

11. For $a, b > 0$, let g_1, g_2, g_3 and g_4 be geometric means between a and b, then the roots of the equation $(g_2 g_3)x^2 - \left(\frac{g_2}{g_1 + g_3}\right)x - g_1 g_4 = 0$ are
(a) both negative (b) both positive
(c) one negative and one positive (d) imaginary

12. If a, b, c, d are positive real numbers, such that $a + b + c + d = 2$, then $M = (a + b)(c + d)$ satisfies the relation
(a) $0 < M \leq 1$ (b) $1 \leq M \leq 2$
(c) $2 \leq M \leq 3$ (d) $3 \leq M \leq 4$

13. If there positive real numbers a, b, c in AP, such that $abc = 4$, then minimum value of b is
(a) $2^{1/3}$ (b) $2^{2/3}$ (c) $2^{1/2}$ (d) $2^{3/2}$

14. The value of xyz is $\frac{15}{2}$ or $\frac{18}{5}$ according as the series a, x, y, z, b is arithmetic or harmonic, then ab is equal to
(a) 1 (b) 2 (c) 3 (d) 4

15. If the AM of two numbers a and b, $a > b > 0$ is twice their GM, then $\frac{a}{b}$ is equal to
(a) $2+\sqrt{3}$ (b) $7+2\sqrt{3}$ (c) $4+2\sqrt{3}$ (d) $7+4\sqrt{3}$

16. If p and q are positive real number such that $p^2 + q^2 = 1$, then the maximum value of $(p + q)$ is
(a) $\frac{1}{2}$ (b) $\frac{1}{\sqrt{2}}$ (c) $\sqrt{2}$ (d) 2

17. For ΔABC, if $81 + 144a^4 + 16b^4 + 9c^4 = 144abc$ (where notations have their usual meaning), then which is incorrect?
(a) $a > b > c$ (b) $a < b < c$
(c) Area of $\Delta ABC = \frac{4}{9}$ (d) ΔABC is right angle

18. The least value of $\alpha \in R$ for which $4\alpha x^2 + \frac{1}{x} \geq 1$ for all $x > 0$ is
(a) $\frac{1}{64}$ (b) $\frac{1}{32}$ (c) $\frac{1}{27}$ (d) $\frac{1}{25}$

19. Let three real numbers a, b, c be in arithmetic progression and $a - 2, b, c + 2$ be in geometric progression. If $a > 0$ and the arithmetic mean of a, b and c is 9, then cube of the geometric mean of a, b and c is
(a) 583 (b) 549 (c) 512 (d) 693

Answer Key

1. (a)	2. (d)	3. (b)	4. (d)	5. (d)	6. (c)
7. (c)	8. (d)	9. (b)	10. (b)	11. (c)	12. (a)
13. (c)	14. (c)	15. (d)	16. (c)	17. (b)	18. (c)
19. (d)					

For Detailed Solution

Milestone 4 Some Special Series

• Arithmetico-Geometric Series (AGS) • Sigma Notation • Natural Numbers

3.11 Arithmetico-Geometric Series (AGS)

A series formed by multiplying the corresponding terms of an AP and a GP is called **Arithmetico - Geometric Series** (or shortly written as AGS)

e.g. $1+4+7+10+\ldots$ is an AP and $1+x+x^2+x^3+\ldots$ is a GP.

Multiplying together the corresponding terms of these series, we get

$$1+4x+7x^2+10x^3+\ldots$$

which is an Arithmetico-Geometric Series.

Again, $a+(a+d)+(a+2d)+\ldots+[a+(n-1)d]$ is a typical AP and $1+r+r^2+\ldots+r^{n-1}$ is a typical GP.

Multiplying together the corresponding terms of these series, we get

$$a+(a+d)r+(a+2d)r^2+\ldots+[a+(n-1)d]r^{n-1}$$

which is called a standard Arithmetico-Geometric series.

Sum of *n* Terms of an Arithmetico-Geometric Series

Let the series be

$a+(a+d)r+(a+2d)r^2+\ldots+[a+(n-1)d]r^{n-1}$

Let S_n denotes the sum to n terms, then

$$S_n=a+(a+d)r+(a+2d)r^2+\ldots+[a+(n-2)d]r^{n-2}+[a+(n-1)d]r^{n-1} \quad \ldots(i)$$

Multiplying both sides of Eq. (i) by r, we get

$$rS_n=ar+(a+d)r^2+(a+2d)r^3+\ldots+[a+(n-2)d]r^{n-1}+[a+(n-1)d]r^n \quad \ldots(ii)$$

Subtracting Eq. (ii) from Eq. (i), we get

$$(1-r)S_n=a+(dr+dr^2+\ldots+dr^{n-1})-[a+(n-1)d]r^n$$

$$=a+\frac{dr(1-r^{n-1})}{(1-r)}-[a+(n-1)d]r^n$$

$$\therefore\ S_n=\frac{a}{(1-r)}+\frac{dr(1-r^{n-1})}{(1-r)^2}-\frac{[a+(n-1)d]r^n}{(1-r)} \quad \ldots(iii)$$

Note The above result (iii) is not used as standard formula in any examination. You should follow all steps as shown above.

To Deduce the Sum upto Infinity from the Sum upto *n* Terms of an Arithmetico - Geometric Series, when $|r|<1$

From Eq. (iii), we have

$$S_n=\frac{a}{1-r}+\frac{dr}{(1-r)^2}-\frac{dr^n}{(1-r)^2}-\frac{[a+(n-1)d]r^n}{(1-r)}$$

If $|r|<1$, when $n\to\infty$, $r^n\to 0$

and $\frac{dr^n}{(1-r)^2}$ and $\frac{[a+(n-1)d]r^n}{(1-r)}$ both $\to 0$

$$\therefore\ S_\infty=\frac{a}{(1-r)}+\frac{dr}{(1-r)^2}$$

Independent method Let S_∞ denotes the sum to infinity, then

$$S_\infty=a+(a+d)r+(a+2d)r^2+(a+3d)r^3+\ldots \text{ upto } \infty \quad \ldots(iv)$$

Multiplying both sides of Eq. (iv) by r, we get

$$rS_\infty=ar+(a+d)r^2+(a+2d)r^3+\ldots\text{upto } \infty \quad \ldots(v)$$

Subtracting Eq. (v) from Eq. (iv), we get

$$(1-r)S_\infty=a+(dr+dr^2+dr^3+\ldots\text{ upto } \infty)$$

$$=a+\frac{dr}{(1-r)}$$

$$\therefore\ S_\infty=\frac{a}{(1-r)}+\frac{dr}{(1-r)^2}$$

Example 89. Find the sum of the series

$1+\frac{4}{5}+\frac{7}{5^2}+\frac{10}{5^3}+\ldots$

(i) to n terms. (ii) to infinity.

Sol. The given series can be written as

$$1+4\left(\frac{1}{5}\right)+7\left(\frac{1}{5}\right)^2+10\left(\frac{1}{5}\right)^3+\ldots$$

The series is an Arithmetico-Geometric series, since each term is formed by multiplying corresponding terms of the series 1, 4, 7, ... which are in AP and $1, \frac{1}{5}, \frac{1}{5^2}, \ldots$ which are in GP.

$$\therefore \quad T_n = [n\text{ th term of } 1, 4, 7, \ldots]\left[n\text{th term of } 1, \frac{1}{5}, \left(\frac{1}{5}\right)^2, \ldots\right]$$

$$= [1+(n-1)3]\times 1\cdot\left(\frac{1}{5}\right)^{n-1} = (3n-2)\left(\frac{1}{5}\right)^{n-1}$$

$$\therefore T_{n-1} = (3n-5)\left(\frac{1}{5}\right)^{n-2}$$

(i) Let sum of n terms of the series is denoted by S_n.

Then, $S_n = 1+4\left(\frac{1}{5}\right)+7\left(\frac{1}{5}\right)^2+\ldots$

$$+(3n-5)\left(\frac{1}{5}\right)^{n-2}+(3n-2)\left(\frac{1}{5}\right)^{n-1} \quad \ldots\text{(i)}$$

On multiplying both the sides of Eq. (i) by $\frac{1}{5}$, we get

$$\therefore \quad \frac{1}{5}S_n = \frac{1}{5}+4\left(\frac{1}{5}\right)^2+7\left(\frac{1}{5}\right)^3+\ldots+(3n-5)\left(\frac{1}{5}\right)^{n-1}$$

$$+(3n-2)\left(\frac{1}{5}\right)^n \quad \ldots\text{(ii)}$$

On subtracting Eq. (ii) from Eq. (i), we get

$$\left(1-\frac{1}{5}\right)S_n = 1+3\left[\frac{1}{5}+\left(\frac{1}{5}\right)^2+\left(\frac{1}{5}\right)^3+\ldots+\left(\frac{1}{5}\right)^{n-1}\right]$$

$$-(3n-2)\left(\frac{1}{5}\right)^n$$

or $$\frac{4}{5}S_n = 1+3\left[\left(\frac{1}{5}\right)+\left(\frac{1}{5}\right)^2+\left(\frac{1}{5}\right)^3+\ldots+(n-1)\text{ terms}\right]$$

$$-(3n-2)\left(\frac{1}{5}\right)^n$$

$$= 1+3\left\{\frac{\frac{1}{5}\left[1-\left(\frac{1}{5}\right)^{n-1}\right]}{1-\frac{1}{5}}\right\}-(3n-2)\left(\frac{1}{5}\right)^n$$

$$= 1+\frac{3}{4}\left\{1-\left(\frac{1}{5}\right)^{n-1}\right\}-(3n-2)\left(\frac{1}{5}\right)^n$$

$$\therefore \quad S_n = \frac{5}{4}+\frac{15}{16}\left[1-\left(\frac{1}{5}\right)^{n-1}\right]-\frac{(3n-2)}{4}\left(\frac{1}{5}\right)^{n-1}$$

$$= \frac{35}{16}-\frac{(12n+7)}{16}\left(\frac{1}{5}\right)^{n-1}$$

(ii) $$S_\infty = 1+4\left(\frac{1}{5}\right)+7\left(\frac{1}{5}\right)^2+10\left(\frac{1}{5}\right)^3+\ldots\text{ upto }\infty \quad \ldots\text{(iii)}$$

On multiplying both sides of Eq. (i) by $\frac{1}{5}$, we get

$$\frac{1}{5}S_\infty = \left(\frac{1}{5}\right)+4\left(\frac{1}{5}\right)^2+7\left(\frac{1}{5}\right)^3+\ldots\text{ upto }\infty \quad \ldots\text{(iv)}$$

On subtracting Eq. (iv) from Eq. (iii), we get

$$\left(1-\frac{1}{5}\right)S_\infty = 1+3\left[\left(\frac{1}{5}\right)+\left(\frac{1}{5}\right)^2+\left(\frac{1}{5}\right)^3+\ldots\text{upto }\infty\right]$$

$$= 1+3\left(\frac{\frac{1}{5}}{1-\frac{1}{5}}\right) = 1+\frac{3}{4}$$

$$\Rightarrow \quad \frac{4}{5}S_\infty = \frac{7}{4}$$

$$\therefore \quad S_\infty = \frac{35}{16}$$

Example 90. If the sum to infinity of the series $1+4x+7x^2+10x^3+\ldots$ is $\frac{35}{16}$, find x.

Sol. Let $S_\infty = 1+4x+7x^2+10x^3+\ldots$ upto ∞ ...(i)

On multiplying both sides of Eq. (i) by x we get

$$x\,S_\infty = x+4x^2+7x^3+10x^4+\ldots\text{ upto }\infty \quad \ldots\text{(ii)}$$

On subtracting Eq. (ii) from Eq. (i), we get

$$(1-x)\,S_\infty = 1+3x+3x^2+3x^3+\ldots\text{ upto }\infty$$

$$= 1+3(x+x^2+x^3+\ldots\text{upto }\infty) = 1+3\left(\frac{x}{1-x}\right) = \frac{(1+2x)}{(1-x)}$$

$$\therefore \quad S_\infty = \frac{(1+2x)}{(1-x)^2} = \frac{35}{16} \quad \left[\because S_\infty = \frac{35}{16}\right]$$

$$\Rightarrow \quad 16+32x = 35-70x+35x^2$$

$$\Rightarrow \quad 35x^2-102x+19 = 0$$

$$\Rightarrow \quad (7x-19)(5x-1) = 0$$

$$x \neq \frac{19}{7}$$

[$\because$ for infinity series common ratio $-1 < x < 1$]

Hence, $x = \frac{1}{5}$

Example 91. Find the sum of the series $1+2^2x+3^2x^2+4^2x^3+\ldots$ up to ∞, $|x|<1$.

Sol. Here, the numbers $1^2, 2^2, 3^2, 4^2, \ldots$ i.e. 1, 4, 9, 16, … are not in AP but $1, 4-1=3, 9-4=5, 16-9=7, \ldots$ are in AP.

Let $S_\infty = 1+2^2x+3^2x^2+4^2x^3+\ldots$ upto ∞

$$=1+4x+9x^2+16x^3+\ldots \text{ upto } \infty \quad \ldots\text{(i)}$$

On multiplying both sides of Eq. (i) by x, we get

$$xS_\infty = x+4x^2+9x^3+16x^4+\ldots \text{ upto } \infty \quad \ldots\text{(ii)}$$

On subtracting Eq. (ii) from Eq. (i), we get

$$(1-x)S_\infty = 1+3x+5x^2+7x^3+\ldots \text{ upto } \infty \quad \ldots\text{(iii)}$$

Again, multiplying both sides of Eq. (iii) by x, we get

$$x(1-x)S_\infty = x+3x^2+5x^3+7x^4+\ldots \text{ upto } \infty \quad \ldots\text{(iv)}$$

On subtracting Eq. (iv) from Eq. (iii), we get

$$(1-x)(1-x)S_\infty = 1+2x+2x^2+2x^3+\ldots \text{ upto } \infty$$

$$=1+2(x+x^2+x^3+\ldots \text{ upto } \infty)$$

$$=1+2\left(\frac{x}{1-x}\right)=\frac{(1+x)}{(1-x)}$$

$$\therefore \quad S_\infty = \frac{(1+x)}{(1-x)^3}$$

3.12 Sigma (Σ) Notation

Σ is a letter of greek alphabets and it is called 'sigma'. The symbol sigma (Σ) represents the sum of similar terms. Usually sum of n terms of any series is represented by placing Σ the nth term of the series. But if we have to find the sum of k terms of a series whose nth term is u_n, this will be represented by $\sum_{n=1}^{k} u_n$.

e.g. $\sum_{n=1}^{n=9} n$, i.e. $\sum_{1}^{9} n$ only means the sum of n similar terms when n varies from 1 to 9.

Thus, $\sum_{1}^{9} n = 1+2+3+4+5+6+7+8+9$

JEE SPIKE

Shortly Σ is written in place of $\sum_{1}^{n}$.

Properties of Sigma Notation

1. $\sum_{r=1}^{n} T_r = T_1+T_2+T_3+\ldots+T_n$, when T_n is the general term of the series.

2. $\sum_{r=1}^{n}(T_r \pm T_r') = \sum_{r=1}^{n} T_r \pm \sum_{r=1}^{n} T_r'$

[sigma operator is distributive over addition and subtraction]

3. $\sum_{r=1}^{n} T_r T_r' \neq \left(\sum_{r=1}^{n} T_r\right)\left(\sum_{r=1}^{n} T_r'\right)$

[sigma operator is not distributive over multiplication]

4. $\sum_{r=1}^{n}\left(\frac{T_r}{T_r'}\right) \neq \frac{\left(\sum_{r=1}^{n} T_r\right)}{\left(\sum_{r=1}^{n} T_r'\right)}$

[sigma operator is not distributive over division]

5. $\sum_{r=1}^{n} aT_r = a\sum_{r=1}^{n} T_r$ [where a is constant]

6. $\sum_{j=1}^{n}\sum_{i=1}^{n} T_i T_j = \left(\sum_{i=1}^{n} T_i\right)\left(\sum_{j=1}^{n} T_j\right)$

[where i and j are independent]

Examples on Sigma Notation

(i) $\sum_{i=1}^{m} a = a+a+a+\ldots$ upto m times $= am$

(ii) $\sum a = a+a+a+\ldots$ upto n times $= an$

i.e. $\sum 5 = 5n$, $\sum 3 = 3n$

(iii) $\sum_{i=1}^{5}(i^2-3i) = \sum_{i=1}^{5} i^2 - 3\sum_{i=1}^{5} i$

$$=(1^2+2^2+3^2+4^2+5^2)-3(1+2+3+4+5)$$

$$=55-45=10$$

(iv) $\sum_{r=1}^{3}\left(\frac{r+1}{2r+4}\right) = \left(\frac{1+1}{2\cdot1+4}\right)+\left(\frac{2+1}{2\cdot2+4}\right)+\left(\frac{3+1}{2\cdot3+4}\right)$

$$=\frac{2}{6}+\frac{3}{8}+\frac{4}{10}=\frac{40+45+48}{120}=\frac{133}{120}=1\frac{13}{120}$$

Important Theorems on Σ (Sigma) Operator

Theorem 1 $\sum_{r=1}^{n} f(r+1)-f(r) = f(n+1)-f(1)$

Theorem 2

$$\sum_{r=1}^{n} f(r+2)-f(r) = f(n+2)+f(n+1)-f(2)-f(1)$$

Proof (Theorem 1) $\sum_{r=1}^{n} f(r+1)-f(r)$

$$=[f(2)-f(1)]+[f(3)-f(2)]+[f(4)-f(3)]+\ldots+[f(n+1)-f(n)]$$

$$=f(n+1)-f(1)$$

Proof (Theorem 2)

$$\sum_{r=1}^{n} f(r+2)-f(r)=\sum_{r=1}^{n}[f(r+2)-f(r+1)]+[f(r+1)-f(r)]$$

$$=\sum_{r=1}^{n} f(r+2)-f(r+1)+\sum_{r=1}^{n} f(r+1)-f(r)$$

$$=[f(n+2)-f(2)]+[f(n+1)-f(1)] \quad \text{[from Theorem 1]}$$

$$=f(n+2)+f(n+1)-f(2)-f(1)$$

JEE Focus Points

- $\sum_{r=1}^{n} f(r+k)-f(r)=\sum_{m=1}^{k} f(n+m)-\sum_{m=1}^{k} f(m), \forall\ k \in N$
- $\sum_{r=1}^{n} f(2r+1)-f(2r-1)=f(2n+1)-f(1)$
- $\sum_{r=1}^{n} f(2r)-f(2r-2)=f(2n)-f(0)$

Concept Inside Video

3.13 Natural Numbers

The positive integers 1, 2, 3, ... are called natural numbers. These form an AP with first term and common difference, each equal to unity.

(i) Sum of the First *n* Natural Numbers

$$1+2+3+\ldots+n=\frac{n(n+1)}{2}=\Sigma n$$

$$\Rightarrow \quad \Sigma n=\frac{n(n+1)}{2} \quad \text{[remember]}$$

(ii) Sum of the First *n* Odd Natural Numbers

$$1+3+5+\ldots \text{ upto } n \text{ terms}=\frac{n}{2}[2\cdot 1+(n-1)\cdot 2]=n^2$$

$$\Rightarrow \quad \sum(2n-1)=n^2 \quad \text{[remember]}$$

(iii) Sum of the Squares of the First *n* Natural Numbers

$$1^2+2^2+3^2+\ldots+n^2=\sum n^2=\frac{n(n+1)(2n+1)}{6}$$

Proof We know that $r^3-(r-1)^3=3r^2-3r+1$

Taking $\sum_{r=1}^{n}$ on both sides, we get

$$\sum_{r=1}^{n} r^3-(r-1)^3=3\sum_{r=1}^{n} r^2-3\sum_{r=1}^{n} r+\sum_{r=1}^{n} 1$$

$$\Rightarrow \quad n^3-0^3=3\sum n^2-3\sum n+n \quad \ldots\text{(i)}$$

[from important Theorem 1]

Substituting the value of $\sum n$ in Eq. (i), we get

$$\Rightarrow \quad n^3=3\sum n^2-\frac{3\cdot n(n+1)}{2}+n$$

$$\Rightarrow \quad 3\sum n^2=n^3+\frac{3n(n+1)}{2}-n=\frac{n}{2}(2n^2+3n+1)$$

$$=\frac{n(n+1)(2n+1)}{2}$$

$$\Rightarrow \quad \sum n^2=\frac{n(n+1)(2n+1)}{6} \quad \text{[remember]}$$

Independent Proof We know that

$$(2r+1)^3-(2r-1)^3=24r^2+2$$

Taking $\sum_{r=1}^{n}$ on both sides, we get

$$\sum_{r=1}^{n}(2r+1)^3-(2r-1)^3=\sum_{r=1}^{n}(24r^2+2)$$

$$\Rightarrow \quad (2n+1)^3-1^3=24\sum_{r=1}^{n} r^2+2\sum_{r=1}^{n} 1$$

$$\Rightarrow \quad (2n+1)^3-1=24\sum n^2+2n$$

$$\Rightarrow \quad (2n+1)^3-(2n+1)=24\sum n^2$$

$$\Rightarrow \quad (2n+1)[(2n+1)^2-1]=24\sum n^2$$

$$\Rightarrow \quad (2n+1)(2n+1+1)(2n+1-1)=24\sum n^2$$

$$\Rightarrow \quad \sum n^2=\frac{n(n+1)(2n+1)}{6} \quad \text{[remember]}$$

(iv) Sum of the Cubes of the First n Natural Numbers

$$1^3+2^3+3^3+\ldots+n^3=\Sigma n^3=(\Sigma n)^2=\left\{\frac{n(n+1)}{2}\right\}^2$$

Proof We know that

$$r^4-(r-1)^4=4r^3-6r^2+4r-1$$

Taking $\sum_{r=1}^{n}$ on both sides, we get

$$\sum_{r=1}^{n} r^4-(r-1)^4=4\sum_{r=1}^{n} r^3-6\sum_{r=1}^{n} r^2+4\sum_{r=1}^{n} r-\sum_{r=1}^{n} 1$$

$$\Rightarrow \quad n^4 - 0^4 = 4\sum n^3 - 6\sum n^2 + 4\sum n - n \quad ...(i)$$

[from important theorem 1]

Substituting the values of $\sum n^2$ and $\sum n$ in Eq. (i), we get

$$\Rightarrow \quad n^4 = 4\sum n^3 - \frac{6\,n(n+1)(2n+1)}{6} + \frac{4n(n+1)}{2} - n$$

$$\Rightarrow 4\sum n^3 = n^4 + n(n+1)(2n+1) - 2n(n+1) + n$$

$$= n[n^3 + (n+1)(2n+1) - 2(n+1) + 1]$$

$$= n(n^3 + 2n^2 + n)$$

$$= n^2(n+1)^2$$

$$\therefore \quad \sum n^3 = \left\{\frac{n(n+1)}{2}\right\}^2 = (\sum n)^2 \quad \text{[Remember]}$$

Independent Proof We know that

$$r^2(r+1)^2 - r^2(r-1)^2 = 4r^3$$

Taking $\sum_{r=1}^{n}$ on both sides, we get

$$\sum_{r=1}^{n} r^2(r+1)^2 - r^2(r-1)^2 = 4\sum_{r=1}^{n} r^3$$

$$\Rightarrow \quad n^2(n+1)^2 - 1^2 \cdot 0^2 = 4\sum n^3$$

[from important Theorem 1]

$$\Rightarrow \quad \sum n^3 = \left\{\frac{n(n+1)}{2}\right\}^2 = (\sum n)^2 \quad \text{[Remember]}$$

Corollary $1^3 + 2^3 + 3^3 + \ldots + n^3 = (1 + 2 + 3 + \ldots + n)^2$

(v) Sum of the Powers Four of the First *n* Natural Numbers

$$1^4 + 2^4 + 3^4 + \ldots + n^4 = \sum n^4$$

$$= \frac{n(n+1)(2n+1)(3n^2+3n-1)}{30}$$

Proof We know that

$$r^5 - (r-1)^5 = 5r^4 - 10r^3 + 10r^2 - 5r + 1$$

Taking $\sum_{r=1}^{n}$ on both sides, we get

$$\sum_{r=1}^{n} r^5 - (r-1)^5 = 5\sum_{r=1}^{n} r^4 - 10\sum_{r=1}^{n} r^3 + 10\sum_{r=1}^{n} r^2 - 5\sum_{r=1}^{n} r + \sum_{r=1}^{n} 1$$

$$\Rightarrow \quad n^5 - 0^5 = 5\sum n^4 - 10\sum n^3 + 10\sum n^2 - 5\sum n + n \quad ...(i)$$

[from important Theorem 1]

Substituting the values of $\sum n, \sum n^2, \sum n^3$ in Eq. (i), we get

$$\Rightarrow \quad n^5 = 5\sum n^4 - \frac{10\,n^2(n+1)^2}{4} + \frac{10\,n(n+1)(2n+1)}{6} - \frac{5n(n+1)}{2} + n$$

$$\therefore \quad 5\sum n^4 = n\left\{n^4 + \frac{5n(n+1)^2}{2} - \frac{5(n+1)(2n+1)}{3} + \frac{5(n+1)}{2} - 1\right\}$$

$$= \frac{n}{6}\{6n^4 + 15n(n^2+2n+1) - 10(2n^2+3n+1) + 15n + 15 - 6\}$$

$$\Rightarrow \quad \sum n^4 = \frac{n}{30}(6n^4 + 15n^3 + 10n^2 - 1)$$

$$= \frac{n(n+1)(2n+1)(3n^2+3n-1)}{30}$$

JEE SPIKE

If nth term of a sequence is given by $T_n = an^3 + bn^2 + cn + d$, where a, b, c, d are constants.
Then, sum of n terms, $S_n = \Sigma T_n = a\Sigma n^3 + b\,\Sigma n^2 + c\,\Sigma n + d\,\Sigma 1$
This can be evaluated using the above results.

Example 92. Find the sum to n terms of the series $1^2 + 3^2 + 5^2 + \ldots$ upto n terms.

Sol. Let T_n be the nth term of this series, then

$$T_n = [1 + (n-1)2]^2 = (2n-1)^2 = 4n^2 - 4n + 1$$

$\therefore$ Sum of n terms, $S_n = \Sigma T_n = 4\Sigma n^2 - 4\Sigma n + \Sigma 1$

$$= \frac{4n(n+1)(2n+1)}{6} - \frac{4n(n+1)}{2} + n$$

$$= \frac{n}{3}(4n^2 + 6n + 2 - 6n - 6 + 3)$$

$$= \frac{n(4n^2-1)}{3}$$

Example 93. Find the sum to n terms of the series $1\cdot 2^2 + 2\cdot 3^2 + 3\cdot 4^2 + \ldots$.

Sol. Let T_n be the nth term of this series, then

T_n = (nth term of 1, 2, 3, ...) (nth term of $2^2, 3^2, 4^2, \ldots$)

$$= n(n+1)^2 = n^3 + 2n^2 + n$$

$\therefore$ Sum of n terms $S_n = \Sigma T_n$

$$= \Sigma n^3 + 2\Sigma n^2 + \Sigma n$$

$$= \left\{\frac{n(n+1)}{2}\right\}^2 + 2\left\{\frac{n(n+1)(2n+1)}{6}\right\} + \frac{n(n+1)}{2}$$

$$= \frac{n(n+1)}{2}\left\{\frac{n(n+1)}{2} + \frac{2(2n+1)}{3} + 1\right\}$$

$$= \frac{n(n+1)}{12}(3n^2 + 3n + 8n + 4 + 6)$$

$$= \frac{n(n+1)(3n^2 + 11n + 10)}{12} = \frac{n(n+1)(n+2)(3n+5)}{12}$$

Example 94. Find the sum of n terms of the series whose nth terms is (i) $n(n-1)(n+1)$ (ii) $n^2 + 3^n$.

Sol. (i) We have, $T_n = n(n-1)(n+1) = n^3 - n$

$\therefore$ Sum of n terms $S_n = \Sigma T_n = \Sigma n^3 - \Sigma n$

$$= \left\{\frac{n(n+1)}{2}\right\}^2 - \left\{\frac{n(n+1)}{2}\right\}$$

$$= \frac{n(n+1)}{2}\left\{\frac{n(n+1)}{2} - 1\right\}$$

$$= \frac{n(n+1)(n-1)(n+2)}{4}$$

(ii) We have, $T_n = n^2 + 3^n$

$\therefore$ Sum of n terms $S_n = \Sigma T_n = \Sigma n^2 + \Sigma 3^n$

$$= \Sigma n^2 + (3^1 + 3^2 + 3^3 + \dots + 3^n)$$

$$= \frac{n(n+1)(2n+1)}{6} + \frac{3(3^n - 1)}{(3-1)}$$

$$= \frac{n(n+1)(2n+1)}{6} + \frac{3}{2}(3^n - 1)$$

Example 95. Find the sum of the series $\frac{1^3}{1} + \frac{1^3 + 2^3}{1+3} + \frac{1^3 + 2^3 + 3^3}{1+3+5} + \dots$ upto n terms.

Sol. Let T_n be the nth term of the given series. Then,

$$T_n = \frac{(1^3 + 2^3 + 3^3 + \dots + n^3)}{(1 + 3 + 5 + \dots + (2n-1))} = \frac{\left\{\frac{n(n+1)}{2}\right\}^2}{\frac{n}{2}(1 + 2n - 1)}$$

$$= \frac{(n+1)^2}{4} = \frac{1}{4}(n^2 + 2n + 1)$$

Let S_n denotes the sum of n terms of the given series. Then,

$$S_n = \Sigma T_n = \frac{1}{4}\Sigma(n^2 + 2n + 1)$$

$$= \frac{1}{4}(\Sigma n^2 + 2\Sigma n + \Sigma 1)$$

$$= \frac{1}{4}\left\{\frac{n(n+1)(2n+1)}{6} + \frac{2n(n+1)}{2} + n\right\}$$

$$= \frac{n}{24}\{2n^2 + 3n + 1 + 6n + 6 + 6\}$$

Hence, $S_n = \dfrac{n(2n^2 + 9n + 13)}{24}$

Example 96. Show that

$$\frac{1 \cdot 2^2 + 2 \cdot 3^2 + \dots + n \cdot (n+1)^2}{1^2 \cdot 2 + 2^2 \cdot 3 + \dots + n^2 \cdot (n+1)} = \frac{3n+5}{3n+1}.$$

Sol. Let T_n and T_n' be the nth terms of the series in numerator and denominator of LHS. Then,

$\therefore \quad T_n = n(n+1)^2$ and $T_n' = n^2(n+1)$

$$\therefore \text{LHS} = \frac{\Sigma T_n}{\Sigma T_n'} = \frac{\Sigma n(n+1)^2}{\Sigma n^2(n+1)} = \frac{\Sigma(n^3 + 2n^2 + n)}{\Sigma(n^3 + n^2)}$$

$$= \frac{\Sigma n^3 + 2\Sigma n^2 + \Sigma n}{\Sigma n^3 + \Sigma n^2}$$

$$= \frac{\left\{\frac{n(n+1)}{2}\right\}^2 + 2\left\{\frac{n(n+1)(2n+1)}{6}\right\} + \left\{\frac{n(n+1)}{2}\right\}}{\left\{\frac{n(n+1)}{2}\right\}^2 + \left\{\frac{n(n+1)(2n+1)}{6}\right\}}$$

$$= \frac{\frac{n(n+1)}{2}\left\{\frac{n(n+1)}{2} + \frac{2(2n+1)}{3} + 1\right\}}{\frac{n(n+1)}{2}\left\{\frac{n(n+1)}{2} + \frac{(2n+1)}{3}\right\}}$$

$$= \frac{\frac{1}{6}(3n^2 + 3n + 8n + 4 + 6)}{\frac{1}{6}(3n^2 + 3n + 4n + 2)}$$

$$= \frac{(3n^2 + 11n + 10)}{(3n^2 + 7n + 2)} = \frac{(3n+5)(n+2)}{(3n+1)(n+2)} = \frac{(3n+5)}{(3n+1)} = \text{RHS}$$

Example 97. Find the sum of the series $1 \cdot 2 \cdot 3 + 2 \cdot 3 \cdot 4 + 3 \cdot 4 \cdot 5 + \dots$ upto n terms.

Sol. Here, T_n = {nth term of 1, 2, 3, ...} × {nth term of 2, 3, 4, ...} × {nth term of 3, 4, 5, ...}

$\therefore \quad T_n = n(n+1)(n+2) = n^3 + 3n^2 + 2n$

$\therefore \quad S_n$ = Sum of n terms of the series

$$= \Sigma T_n = \Sigma n^3 + 3\Sigma n^2 + 2\Sigma n$$

$$= \left\{\frac{n(n+1)}{2}\right\}^2 + 3\left\{\frac{n(n+1)(2n+1)}{6}\right\} + 2\left\{\frac{n(n+1)}{2}\right\}$$

$$= \frac{n(n+1)}{2}\left\{\frac{n(n+1)}{2} + (2n+1) + 2\right\}$$

$$= \frac{n(n+1)}{4}(n^2 + n + 4n + 2 + 4)$$

$$= \frac{n(n+1)(n+2)(n+3)}{4}$$

Example 98. Find sum to n terms of the series

$$1 + (2+3) + (4+5+6) + \dots.$$

Sol. Now, number of terms in first bracket is 1, in the second bracket is 2, in the third bracket is 3, etc. Therefore, the number of terms in the nth bracket will be n.

Let the sum of the given series of n terms = S

$\therefore$ Number of terms in $S = 1+2+3+\ldots+n = \dfrac{n(n+1)}{2}$

Also, the first term of S is 1 and common difference is also 1.

$$\therefore \quad S = \frac{\left\{\frac{n(n+1)}{2}\right\}}{2}\left[2\cdot 1+\left(\frac{n(n+1)}{2}-1\right)\cdot 1\right]$$

$$= \frac{n(n+1)}{8}(4+n^2+n-2) = \frac{n(n+1)(n^2+n+2)}{8}$$

Method of Differences

If the differences of the successive terms of a series are in AP or GP, we can find the nth term of the series by the following steps.

***Step* I** Denote the nth term and the sum of the series upto n terms of the series by T_n and S_n, respectively.

***Step* II** Rewrite the given series with each term shifted by one place to the right.

***Step* III** Then, subtract the second expression of S_n from the first expression to obtain T_n.

Example 99. Find the nth term and sum of n terms of the series, $1+5+12+22+35+\ldots$.

Sol. The sequence of differences between successive terms is 4, 7, 10, 13,... . Clearly, it is an AP with common difference 3. So, let the nth term of the given series be T_n and sum of n terms be S_n.

Then, $S_n = 1+5+12+22+35+\ldots+T_{n-1}+T_n$ ...(i)

$S_n = 1+5+12+22+\ldots+T_{n-1}+T_n$ ...(ii)

Subtracting Eq. (ii) from Eq. (i), we get

$$0 = 1+4+7+10+13+\ldots+(T_n-T_{n-1})-T_n$$

$$\Rightarrow \quad T_n = 1+4+7+10+13+\ldots n \text{ terms}$$

$$= \frac{n}{2}\{2\cdot 1+(n-1)3\} = \frac{1}{2}(3n^2-n)$$

Hence, $T_n = \dfrac{3}{2}n^2 - \dfrac{1}{2}n$

$$\therefore \text{ Sum of } n \text{ terms } S_n = \Sigma T_n = \frac{3}{2}\Sigma n^2 - \frac{1}{2}\Sigma n$$

$$= \frac{3}{2}\left(\frac{n(n+1)(2n+1)}{6}\right) - \frac{1}{2}\left(\frac{n(n+1)}{2}\right)$$

$$= \frac{n(n+1)}{4}(2n+1-1)$$

$$= \frac{1}{2}n^2(n+1) = \frac{1}{2}(n^3+n^2)$$

Example 100. Find the nth term and sum of n terms of the series, $1+3+7+15+31+\ldots$.

Sol. The sequence of differences between successive terms is 2, 4, 8, 16, ... Clearly, it is a GP with common ratio 2. So, let the nth term and sum of the series upto n terms of the series be T_n and S_n, respectively.

Then, $S_n = 1+3+7+15+31+\ldots+T_{n-1}+T_n$ ...(i)

$S_n = 1+3+7+15+\ldots+T_{n-1}+T_n$ ...(ii)

Subtracting Eq. (ii) from Eq. (i), we get

$$0 = 1+2+4+8+16+\ldots+(T_n-T_{n-1})-T_n$$

$$\Rightarrow \quad T_n = 1+2+4+8+16+\ldots \text{ upto } n \text{ terms}$$

$$= \frac{1\cdot(2^n-1)}{2-1}$$

Hence, $T_n = (2^n - 1)$

$$\therefore \text{ Sum of } n \text{ terms, } S_n = \Sigma T_n = \Sigma(2^n-1) = \Sigma 2^n - \Sigma 1$$

$$= (2+2^2+2^3+\ldots+2^n) - n$$

$$= \frac{2\cdot(2^n-1)}{(2-1)} - n = 2^{n+1}-2-n$$

Example 101. Find the nth term of the series $1+4+10+20+35+\ldots$

Sol. The sequence of first consecutive differences is 3, 6, 10, 15, ... and second consecutive differences is 3, 4, 5, ... Clearly, it is an AP with common difference 1. So, let the nth term and sum of the series upto n terms of the series be T_n and S_n, respectively.

Then,

$S_n = 1+4+10+20+35+\ldots+T_{n-1}+T_n$ ...(i)

$S_n = 1+4+10+20+\ldots+T_{n-1}+T_n$ ...(ii)

Subtracting Eq. (ii) from Eq. (i), we get

$$0 = 1+3+6+10+15+\ldots+(T_n-T_{n-1})-T_n$$

$$\Rightarrow \quad T_n = 1+3+6+10+15+\ldots \text{ upto } n \text{ terms}$$

or $T_n = 1+3+6+10+15+\ldots+t_{n-1}+t_n$ ...(iii)

$T_n = 1+3+6+10+\ldots+t_{n-1}+t_n$ ...(iv)

Now, subtracting Eq. (iv) from Eq. (iii), we get

$$0 = 1+2+3+4+5+\ldots+(t_n-t_{n-1})-t_n$$

or $t_n = 1+2+3+4+5+\ldots$ upto n terms

$$= \Sigma n = \frac{n(n+1)}{2}$$

$$\therefore \quad T_n = \Sigma t_n = \frac{1}{2}(\Sigma n^2 + \Sigma n)$$

$$= \frac{1}{2}\left(\frac{n(n+1)(2n+1)}{6} + \frac{n(n+1)}{2}\right)$$

$$= \frac{1}{2}\cdot\frac{n(n+1)}{6}(2n+1+3) = \frac{1}{6}n(n+1)(n+2)$$

Example 102. Find the nth term of the series $1+5+18+58+179+\ldots$

Sol. The sequence of first consecutive differences is 4, 13, 40, 121, ... and second consecutive differences is 9, 27, 81, ... Clearly, it is a GP with common ratio 3. So, let the nth term and sum of the series upto n terms of the series be T_n and S_n, respectively.

Then, $S_n = 1+5+18+58+179+\ldots+T_{n-1}+T_n$ ...(i)

$S_n = 1+5+18+58+\ldots+T_{n-1}+T_n$ ...(ii)

Subtracting Eq. (ii) from Eq. (i), we get

$$0 = 1 + 4 + 13 + 40 + 121 + \dots + (T_n - T_{n-1}) - T_n$$

$\Rightarrow \quad T_n = 1 + 4 + 13 + 40 + 121 + \dots$ upto n terms

or $\quad T_n = 1 + 4 + 13 + 40 + 121 + \dots + t_{n-1} + t_n \quad \dots\text{(iii)}$

$\quad T_n = \quad 1 + 4 + 13 + 40 + \dots + t_{n-1} + t_n \quad \dots\text{(iv)}$

Now, subtracting Eq. (iv) from Eq. (iii), we get

$$0 = 1 + 3 + 9 + 27 + 81 + \dots + (t_n - t_{n-1}) - t_n$$

or $\quad t_n = 1 + 3 + 9 + 27 + 81 + \dots$ upto n terms

$$= \frac{1\cdot(3^n - 1)}{(3-1)} = \frac{1}{2}(3^n - 1)$$

$$\therefore \quad T_n = \Sigma t_n = \frac{1}{2}(\Sigma 3^n - \Sigma 1)$$

$$= \frac{1}{2}\{(3 + 3^2 + 3^3 + \dots + 3^n) - n\}$$

$$= \frac{1}{2}\left\{\frac{3(3^n - 1)}{(3-1)} - n\right\} = \frac{3}{4}(3^n - 1) - \frac{1}{2}n$$

Method of Differences (Shortcut) to find nth term of a Series

The nth term of the series can be written directly on the basis of successively differences, we use the following steps to find the nth term or T_n of the given sequence.

***Step* I** If the first consecutive differences of the given sequence are in AP, then take

$T_n = a(n-1)(n-2) + b(n-1) + c$, where a, b, c are constants. Determine a, b, c by putting $n = 1, 2, 3$ and putting the values of T_1, T_2, T_3.

***Step* II** If the first consecutive differences of the given sequence are in GP, then take

$T_n = ar^{n-1} + bn + c$, where a, b, c are constants and r is the common ratio of GP. Determine a, b, c by putting $n = 1, 2, 3$ and putting the values of T_1, T_2, T_3.

***Step* III** If the differences of the differences computed in Step I are in AP, then take

$T_n = a(n-1)(n-2)(n-3) + b(n-1)(n-2) + c(n-1) + d$, where a, b, c, d are constants.Determine by putting $n = 1, 2, 3, 4$ and putting the values of T_1, T_2, T_3, T_4.

***Step* IV** If the differences of the differences computed in Step I are in GP with common ratio r, then take

$T_n = ar^{n-1} + bn^2 + cn + d$, where a, b, c, d are constants. Determine by putting $n = 1, 2, 3, 4$ and putting the values of T_1, T_2, T_3, T_4.

Example 103. Find the nth term and sum of n terms of the series $2 + 4 + 7 + 11 + 16 + \dots$.

Sol. The sequence of first consecutive differences is 2, 3, 4, 5, ... Clearly, it is an AP.

Then, nth term of the given series be

$$T_n = a(n-1)(n-2) + b(n-1) + c \quad \dots\text{(i)}$$

On putting $n = 1, 2, 3$, we get

$$2 = c, \; 4 = b + c, 7 = 2a + 2b + c$$

After solving, we get $a = \frac{1}{2}, b = 2, c = 2$

On putting the values of a, b, c in Eq. (i), we get

$$T_n = \frac{1}{2}(n-1)(n-2) + 2(n-1) + 2 = \frac{1}{2}(n^2 + n + 2)$$

Hence, sum of series $S_n = \Sigma T_n = \frac{1}{2}(\Sigma n^2 + \Sigma n + 2\Sigma 1)$

$$= \frac{1}{2}\left(\frac{n(n+1)(2n+1)}{6} + \frac{n(n+1)}{2} + 2n\right)$$

$$= \frac{1}{6}n(n^2 + 3n + 8)$$

Example 104. Find the nth term and sum of n terms of the series $5 + 7 + 13 + 31 + 85 + \dots$.

Sol. The sequence of first consecutive differences is 2, 6, 18, 54, ... Clearly, it is a GP with common ratio 3. Then, nth term of the given series be

$$T_n = a(3)^{n-1} + bn + c \quad \dots\text{(i)}$$

On putting $n = 1, 2, 3$, we get

$$5 = a + b + c \quad \dots\text{(ii)}$$

$$7 = 3a + 2b + c \quad \dots\text{(iii)}$$

$$13 = 9a + 3b + c \quad \dots\text{(iv)}$$

On solving these equations, we get

$$a = 1, b = 0, c = 4$$

On putting the values of a, b, c in Eq. (i), we get

$$T_n = 3^{n-1} + 4$$

Hence, sum of the series

$$S_n = \Sigma T_n = \Sigma(3^{n-1} + 4) = \Sigma(3^{n-1}) + 4\Sigma 1$$

$$= (1 + 3 + 3^2 + \dots + 3^{n-1}) + 4n$$

$$= 1\cdot\frac{(3^n - 1)}{(3-1)} + 4n = \frac{1}{2}(3^n + 8n - 1)$$

Example 105. Find the nth term of the series $1 + 2 + 5 + 12 + 25 + 46 + \dots$.

Sol. The sequence of first consecutive differences is 1, 3, 7, 13, 21, ... The sequence of the second consecutive differences is 2, 4, 6, 8, ... Clearly, it is an AP. Then, nth term of the given series be

$$T_n = a(n-1)(n-2)(n-3) + b(n-1)(n-2) + c(n-1) + d \quad \dots\text{(i)}$$

On putting $n = 1, 2, 3, 4$, we get

$$1 = d \quad \dots\text{(ii)}$$

$$2 = c + d \quad \dots\text{(iii)}$$

$$5 = 2b + 2c + d \quad \dots\text{(iv)}$$

$$12 = 6a + 6b + 3c + d \quad \dots\text{(v)}$$

After, solving these equations, we get

$$a = \frac{1}{3}, b = 1, c = 1, d = 1$$

On putting the values of a, b, c, d in Eq. (i), we get

$$T_n = \frac{1}{3}(n^3 - 6n^2 + 11n - 6) + (n^2 - 3n + 2) + (n - 1) + 1$$

$$= \frac{1}{3}(n^3 - 3n^2 + 5n) = \frac{n}{3}(n^2 - 3n + 5)$$

Example 106. Find the nth term of the series $2 + 5 + 12 + 31 + 86 + \dots$.

Sol. The sequence of first consecutive differences is 3, 7, 19, 55, ... The sequence of the second consecutive differences is 4, 12, 36, ... Clearly, it is a GP with common ratio 3. Then, nth term of the given series be

$$T_n = a(3)^{n-1} + bn^2 + cn + d \qquad \dots\text{(i)}$$

On putting $n = 1, 2, 3, 4$, we get

$$2 = a + b + c + d \qquad \dots\text{(ii)}$$

$$5 = 3a + 4b + 2c + d \qquad \dots\text{(iii)}$$

$$12 = 9a + 9b + 3c + d \qquad \dots\text{(iv)}$$

$$31 = 27a + 16b + 4c + d \qquad \dots\text{(v)}$$

After, solving these equations, we get

$$a = 1, b = 0, c = 1, d = 0$$

On putting the values of a, b, c, d in Eq. (i), we get

$$T_n = 3^{n-1} + n$$

Method of Differences (Maha Shortcut)

To find $t_1 + t_2 + t_3 + \dots + t_{n-1} + t_n$

Let $S_n = t_1 + t_2 + t_3 + \dots + t_{n-1} + t_n$

Then, $\Delta t_1, \Delta t_2, \Delta t_3, \dots, \Delta t_{n-1}$ [1st order differences]

$\Delta^2 t_1, \Delta^2 t_2, \Delta^2 t_3, \dots, \Delta^2 t_{n-1}$ [2nd order differences]

$\vdots \quad \vdots \quad \vdots$

$$\therefore\ t_n = {}^{n-1}C_0\, t_1 + {}^{n-1}C_1\, \Delta t_1 + {}^{n-1}C_2\, \Delta^2 t_1 + \dots + {}^{n-1}C_{r-1}\, \Delta^{r-1} t_1$$

and $S_n = {}^nC_1\, t_1 + {}^nC_2\, \Delta t_1 + {}^nC_3\, \Delta^2 t_1 + \dots + {}^nC_r\, \Delta^r t_1$

where, $\Delta t_1 = t_2 - t_1, \Delta t_2 = t_3 - t_2$, etc.

$\Delta^2 t_1 = \Delta t_2 - \Delta t_1, \Delta^3 t_1 = \Delta^2 t_2 - \Delta^2 t_1$, etc.

Example 107. Find the nth term and sum to n terms of the series $12 + 40 + 90 + 168 + 280 + 432 + \dots$.

Sol. Let $S_n = 12 + 40 + 90 + 168 + 280 + 432 + \dots$, then

1st order differences are 28, 50, 78, 112, 152, ...
(i.e. $\Delta t_1, \Delta t_2, \Delta t_3, \dots$)

and 2nd order differences are
22, 28, 34, 40, ... (i.e. $\Delta^2 t_1, \Delta^2 t_2, \Delta^2 t_3, \dots$)

and 3rd order differences are
6, 6, 6, 6,... (i.e. $\Delta^3 t_1, \Delta^3 t_2, \Delta^3 t_3, \dots$)

and 4th order differences are
0, 0, 0, 0, ... (i.e. $\Delta^4 t_1, \Delta^4 t_2, \Delta^4 t_3, \dots$)

$$\therefore\ t_n = 12 \cdot {}^{n-1}C_0 + 28 \cdot {}^{n-1}C_1 + 22 \cdot {}^{n-1}C_2 + 6 \cdot {}^{n-1}C_3$$

$$= 12 + 28(n-1) + \frac{22(n-1)(n-2)}{2} + \frac{6(n-1)(n-2)(n-3)}{1 \cdot 2 \cdot 3}$$

$$= n^3 + 5n^2 + 6n$$

and $S_n = 12 \cdot {}^nC_1 + 28 \cdot {}^nC_2 + 22 \cdot {}^nC_3 + 6 \cdot {}^nC_4$

$$= 12n + \frac{28n(n-1)}{2} + \frac{22n(n-1)(n-2)}{1 \cdot 2 \cdot 3} + \frac{6 \cdot n(n-1)(n-2)(n-3)}{1 \cdot 2 \cdot 3 \cdot 4}$$

$$= \frac{n}{12}(n+1)(3n^2 + 23n + 46)$$

V_n Method

To find the sum of the series of the forms

I. $a_1 a_2 \dots a_r + a_2 a_3 \dots a_{r+1} + \dots + a_n a_{n+1} \dots a_{n+r-1}$

II. $\dfrac{1}{a_1 a_2 \dots a_r} + \dfrac{1}{a_2 a_3 \dots a_{r+1}} + \dots + \dfrac{1}{a_n a_{n+1} \dots a_{n+r-1}}$

where, $a_1, a_2, a_3, \dots, a_n, \dots$ are in AP.

***Solution of form* I** Let S_n be the sum and T_n be the nth term of the series, then

$$S_n = a_1 a_2 \dots a_r + a_2 a_3 \dots a_{r+1} + \dots + a_n a_{n+1} + \dots + a_{n+r-1}$$

$$\therefore\ T_n = a_n a_{n+1} a_{n+2} \dots a_{n+r-2}\, a_{n+r-1} \qquad \dots\text{(i)}$$

Let $V_n = a_n a_{n+1} a_{n+2} \dots a_{n+r-2}\, a_{n+r-1}\, a_{n+r}$

[taking one extra factor in T_n for V_n]

$$\therefore\ V_{n-1} = a_{n-1} a_n\, a_{n+1} \dots a_{n+r-3}\, a_{n+r-2}\, a_{n+r-1}$$

$$\Rightarrow\ V_n - V_{n-1} = a_n a_{n+1} a_{n+2} \dots a_{n+r-1}(a_{n+r} - a_{n-1})$$

$$= T_n(a_{n+r} - a_{n-1}) \qquad \text{[from Eq. (i)]} \dots\text{(ii)}$$

Let d be the common difference of AP, then

$$a_n = a_1 + (n-1)d$$

Then, from Eq. (ii)

$$V_n - V_{n-1} = T_n[\{a_1 + (n+r-1)d\} - \{a_1 + (n-2)d\}] = (r+1)\,d\,T_n$$

$$\Rightarrow\ T_n = \frac{1}{(r+1)d}(V_n - V_{n-1})$$

$$\therefore\ S_n = \Sigma T_n = \sum_{n=1}^{n} T_n = \frac{1}{(r+1)d}\sum_{n=1}^{n}(V_n - V_{n-1})$$

$$= \frac{1}{(r+1)d}(V_n - V_0)$$

[from important Theorem 1 of Σ]

$$= \frac{1}{(r+1)(a_2 - a_1)}(a_n a_{n+1} \dots a_{n+r} - a_0 a_1 \dots a_r)$$

***Corollary* I** If $a_1, a_2, a_3, \ldots, a_n, \ldots$ are in AP, then

(i) For $r=2$, $a_1a_2 + a_2a_3 + \ldots + a_na_{n+1} = \dfrac{1}{3(a_2-a_1)}(a_na_{n+1}a_{n+2} - a_0a_1a_2)$

(ii) For $r=3$,

$$a_1a_2a_3 + a_2a_3a_4 + \ldots + a_na_{n+1}a_{n+2} = \frac{1}{4(a_2-a_1)}(a_na_{n+1}a_{n+2}a_{n+3} - a_0a_1a_2a_3)$$

***Corollary* II**

(i) $1\cdot 2 + 2\cdot 3 + \ldots + n(n+1) = \dfrac{1}{3}\{n(n+1)(n+2) - 0\cdot 1\cdot 2\} = \dfrac{n(n+1)(n+2)}{3}$

(ii) $1\cdot 3\cdot 5\cdot 7 + 3\cdot 5\cdot 7\cdot 9 + \ldots + (2n-1)\cdot(2n+1)(2n+3)\cdot(2n+5)$

$$= \frac{1}{11}\{(2n-1)(2n+1)(2n+3)(2n+5)(2n+7) - (-1)\cdot 1\cdot 3\cdot 5\cdot 7\}$$

$$= \frac{1}{11}\{(2n-1)(2n+1)(2n+3)(2n+5)(2n+7) + 105\}$$

***Solution of form* II** Let d be the common difference of AP, then $a_n = a_1 + (n-1)d$

Let sum of the series and nth term are denoted by S_n and T_n, respectively. Then,

$$S_n = \frac{1}{a_1a_2\ldots a_r} + \frac{1}{a_2a_3\ldots a_{r+1}} + \ldots + \frac{1}{a_na_{n+1}\ldots a_{n+r-1}}$$

$$\therefore \quad T_n = \frac{1}{a_na_{n+1}a_{n+2}\ldots a_{n+r-2}\,a_{n+r-1}} \quad \ldots\text{(i)}$$

$$\text{Let} \quad V_n = \frac{1}{a_{n+1}\,a_{n+2}\ldots a_{n+r-2}\,a_{n+r-1}} \quad \ldots\text{(ii)}$$

[leaving first factor from denominator of T_n]

$$\text{So,} \quad V_{n-1} = \frac{1}{a_na_{n+1}\ldots a_{n+r-3}\,a_{n+r-2}}$$

$$\Rightarrow V_n - V_{n-1} = \frac{1}{a_{n+1}\,a_{n+2}\ldots a_{n+r-2}\,a_{n+r-1}} - \frac{1}{a_na_{n+1}\ldots a_{n+r-3}\,a_{n+r-2}}$$

$$= \frac{a_n - a_{n+r-1}}{a_na_{n+1}\,a_{n+2} - a_{n+r-2}\,a_{n+r-1}}$$

$= T_n\,(a_n - a_{n+r-1})$ [from Eq. (i)]

$= T_n\,[\{a_1 + (n-1)d\} - \{a_1 + (n+r-2)d\}]$

$= d(1-r)T_n$

$$\therefore \quad T_n = \frac{(V_n - V_{n-1})}{d(1-r)}$$

$$\therefore \quad S_n = \Sigma T_n = \sum_{n=1}^{n}\frac{(V_n - V_{n-1})}{d(1-r)} = \frac{1}{d(1-r)}(V_n - V_0)$$

[from important Theorem 1 of Σ]

$$= \frac{1}{(a_2-a_1)(1-r)}\left\{\frac{1}{a_{n+1}\,a_{n+2}\ldots a_{n+r-2}\,a_{n+r-1}} - \frac{1}{a_1\,a_2\ldots a_{r-2}\,a_{r-1}}\right\}$$

Hence, the sum of n terms is $S_n = \dfrac{1}{(r-1)(a_2-a_1)}\left\{\dfrac{1}{a_1a_2\ldots a_{r-1}} - \dfrac{1}{a_{n+1}\,a_{n+2}\ldots a_{n+r-1}}\right\}$

***Corollary* I** If $a_1, a_2, a_3, \ldots, a_n, \ldots$ are in AP, then

(i) For $r=2$,

$$\frac{1}{a_1a_2} + \frac{1}{a_2a_3} + \ldots + \frac{1}{a_na_{n+1}} = \frac{1}{(a_2-a_1)}\left\{\frac{1}{a_1} - \frac{1}{a_{n+1}}\right\} = \frac{1}{d}\left(\frac{a_{n+1}-a_1}{a_1\,a_{n+1}}\right)$$

$$= \frac{1}{d}\left(\frac{a_1 + nd - a_1}{a_1a_{n+1}}\right) = \frac{n}{a_1\,a_{n+1}}$$

(ii) For $r=3$, $\dfrac{1}{a_1a_2a_3} + \dfrac{1}{a_2a_3a_4} + \ldots + \dfrac{1}{a_n\,a_{n+1}\,a_{n+2}}$

$$= \frac{1}{2(a_2-a_1)}\left\{\frac{1}{a_1a_2} - \frac{1}{a_{n+1}\,a_{n+2}}\right\}$$

(iii) For $r=4$,

$$\frac{1}{a_1a_2a_3a_4} + \frac{1}{a_2a_3a_4a_5} + \ldots + \frac{1}{a_na_{n+1}a_{n+2}a_{n+3}} = \frac{1}{3(a_2-a_1)}\left\{\frac{1}{a_1a_2a_3} - \frac{1}{a_{n+1}\,a_{n+2}\,a_{n+3}}\right\}$$

***Corollary* II**

(i) $\dfrac{1}{1\cdot 2} + \dfrac{1}{2\cdot 3} + \dfrac{1}{3\cdot 4} + \ldots + \dfrac{1}{n(n+1)} = \dfrac{n}{n+1}$

(ii) $\dfrac{1}{1\cdot 2\cdot 3} + \dfrac{1}{2\cdot 3\cdot 4} + \dfrac{1}{3\cdot 4\cdot 5} + \ldots + \dfrac{1}{n(n+1)(n+2)}$

$$= \frac{1}{2}\left\{\frac{1}{1\cdot 2} - \frac{1}{(n+1)(n+2)}\right\} = \frac{1}{4} - \frac{1}{2(n+1)(n+2)}$$

(iii) $\dfrac{1}{1\cdot 3\cdot 5\cdot 7} + \dfrac{1}{3\cdot 5\cdot 7\cdot 9} + \ldots + \dfrac{1}{(2n-1)(2n+1)(2n+3)(2n+5)}$

$$= \frac{1}{6}\left\{\frac{1}{1\cdot 3\cdot 5} - \frac{1}{(2n+1)(2n+3)(2n+5)}\right\}$$

$$= \frac{1}{90} - \frac{1}{6(2n+1)(2n+3)(2n+5)}$$

Example 108. Find the sum upto n terms of the series $1\cdot4\cdot7\cdot10+4\cdot7\cdot10\cdot13+7\cdot10\cdot13\cdot16+\dots$

Sol. Let T_n be the nth term of the given series.

$\therefore T_n =$ (nth term of 1, 4, 7, ...) (nth term of 4, 7, 10, ...) (nth term of 7, 10, 13, ...) (nth term of 10, 13, 16, ...)

$$T_n = (3n-2)(3n+1)(3n+4)(3n+7) \quad \text{...(i)}$$

$$\therefore V_n = (3n-2)(3n+1)(3n+4)(3n+7)(3n+10)$$

$$V_{n-1} = (3n-5)(3n-2)(3n+1)(3n+4)(3n+7)$$

$$\Rightarrow \quad V_n = (3n+10)\,T_n \quad \text{[from Eq. (i)]}$$

and $\quad V_{n-1} = (3n-5)\,T_n$

$$\therefore \quad V_n - V_{n-1} = 15\,T_n$$

$$\therefore \quad T_n = \frac{1}{15}(V_n - V_{n-1})$$

$$\therefore \quad S_n = \Sigma T_n = \sum_{n=1}^{n}\frac{1}{15}(V_n - V_{n-1}) = \frac{1}{15}(V_n - V_0)$$

[from important Theorem 1 of Σ]

$$= \frac{1}{15}\{(3n-2)(3n+1)(3n+4)(3n+7)(3n+10) - (-2)(1)(4)(7)(10)\}$$

$$= \frac{1}{15}\{(3n-2)(3n+1)(3n+4)(3n+7)(3n+10)+560\}$$

Time Saving Technique

$$S_n = \frac{1}{(\text{last factor of III term} - \text{first factor of I term})}$$

[taking one extra factor in T_n in last – Taking one extra factor in I term in start]

$$= \frac{1}{(16-1)}\{(3n-2)(3n+1)(3n+4)(3n+7)(3n+10) - (-2)\cdot1\cdot4\cdot7\cdot10\}$$

$$= \frac{1}{15}\{(3n-2)(3n+1)(3n+4)(3n+7)(3n+10)+560\}$$

Example 109. Find the sum to n terms of the series $\frac{1}{1\cdot3\cdot5\cdot7\cdot9}+\frac{1}{3\cdot5\cdot7\cdot9\cdot11}+\frac{1}{5\cdot7\cdot9\cdot11\cdot13}+\dots$. Also, find the sum to infinity terms.

Sol. Let T_n be the nth term of the given series.

Then, $\quad T_n = \dfrac{1}{(2n-1)(2n+1)(2n+3)(2n+5)(2n+7)} \quad$ ...(i)

$$\therefore \quad V_n = \frac{1}{(2n+1)(2n+3)(2n+5)(2n+7)}$$

[leaving first factor from denominator of T_n]

$$V_{n-1} = \frac{1}{(2n-1)(2n+1)(2n+3)(2n+5)}$$

$$\Rightarrow \quad V_n - V_{n-1} = \frac{1}{(2n+1)(2n+3)(2n+5)(2n+7)} - \frac{1}{(2n-1)(2n+1)(2n+3)(2n+5)}$$

$$= \frac{(2n-1)-(2n+7)}{(2n-1)(2n+1)(2n+3)(2n+5)(2n+7)}$$

$$= -8\,T_n \quad \text{[from Eq. (i)]}$$

$$\therefore \quad T_n = -\frac{1}{8}(V_n - V_{n-1})$$

$$\therefore \quad S_n = \Sigma T_n = \sum_{n=1}^{n} T_n = -\frac{1}{8}\sum_{n=1}^{n}(V_n - V_{n-1}) = -\frac{1}{8}(V_n - V_0)$$

[from important Theorem 1 of Σ]

$$= \frac{1}{8}(V_0 - V_n)$$

$$= \frac{1}{8}\left\{\frac{1}{1\cdot3\cdot5\cdot7} - \frac{1}{(2n+1)(2n+3)(2n+5)(2n+7)}\right\}$$

$$= \frac{1}{840} - \frac{1}{8(2n+1)(2n+3)(2n+5)(2n+7)}$$

and $\quad S_\infty = \dfrac{1}{840} - \dfrac{1}{\infty} = \dfrac{1}{840} - 0 = \dfrac{1}{840}$

Example 110. If $\sum_{r=1}^{n} T_r = \dfrac{n(n+1)(n+2)(n+3)}{12}$, where T_r denotes the rth term of the series. Find $\lim_{n\to\infty}\sum_{r=1}^{n}\dfrac{1}{T_r}$.

Sol. We have, $T_n = \sum_{r=1}^{n} T_r - \sum_{r=1}^{n-1} T_r$

$$= \frac{n(n+1)(n+2)(n+3)}{12} - \frac{(n-1)n(n+1)(n+2)}{12}$$

$$= \frac{n(n+1)(n+2)}{12}[(n+3)-(n-1)] = \frac{n(n+1)(n+2)}{3}$$

$$\frac{1}{T_n} = \frac{3}{n(n+1)(n+2)}$$

$$\therefore \quad \lim_{n\to\infty}\sum_{r=1}^{n}\frac{1}{T_r} = \lim_{n\to\infty}\sum_{r=1}^{n}\frac{3}{r(r+1)(r+2)}$$

$$= 3\lim_{n\to\infty}\sum_{r=1}^{n}\frac{1}{r(r+1)(r+2)}$$

$$= 3\lim_{n\to\infty}\left(\frac{1}{1\cdot2\cdot3}+\frac{1}{2\cdot3\cdot4}+\frac{1}{3\cdot4\cdot5}+\dots+\frac{1}{n(n+1)(n+2)}\right)$$

Maha Shortcut Method

$$= 3\lim_{n\to\infty}\frac{1}{2}\left(\frac{1}{1\cdot2} - \frac{1}{(n+1)(n+2)}\right) = \frac{3}{2}\left(\frac{1}{2}-0\right) = \frac{3}{4}$$

Milestone Practice 3.4

1. The sum of the first n terms of the series $\frac{1}{2}+\frac{3}{4}+\frac{7}{8}+\frac{15}{16}+\dots$ is

(a) $2^n - n - 1$ (b) $1-2^{-n}$
(c) $n+2^{-n}-1$ (d) $2^n - 1$

2. $2^{1/4}.4^{1/8}.8^{1/16}.16^{1/32}\dots$ is equal to

(a) 1 (b) $\frac{3}{2}$
(c) 2 (d) $\frac{5}{2}$

3. The limiting sum of infinite series $\frac{1}{10}+\frac{2}{10^2}+\frac{3}{10^3}+\dots$ whose nth terms is $\frac{n}{10^n}$ is equal to

(a) $\frac{1}{9}$ (b) $\frac{10}{81}$
(c) $\frac{1}{8}$ (d) $\frac{17}{72}$

4. 99th term of the series $2+7+14+23+34+\dots$ is

(a) 9998 (b) 9999
(c) 10000 (d) 100000

5. The sum of the series $\frac{1}{1\cdot2}-\frac{1}{2\cdot3}+\frac{1}{3\cdot4}\dots$ upto ∞ is equal to

(a) $\log_e\left(\frac{4}{e}\right)$ (b) $2\log_e 2$
(c) $\log_e 2-1$ (d) $\log_e 2$

6. $\frac{1}{1\cdot2}+\frac{1}{2\cdot3}+\frac{1}{3\cdot4}+\dots+\frac{1}{n(n+1)}$ equals

(a) $\frac{1}{n(n+1)}$ (b) $\frac{n}{n+1}$
(c) $\frac{2n}{n+1}$ (d) $\frac{2}{n(n+1)}$

7. Sum of the n terms of the series $\frac{3}{1^2}+\frac{5}{1^2+2^2}+\frac{7}{1^2+2^2+3^2}+\dots$ is

(a) $\frac{2n}{n+1}$ (b) $\frac{4n}{n+1}$ (c) $\frac{6n}{n+1}$ (d) $\frac{9n}{n+1}$

8. If $t_n=\frac{1}{4}(n+2)(n+3)$ for $n=1,2,3,\dots$, then $\frac{1}{t_1}+\frac{1}{t_2}+\frac{1}{t_3}+\dots+\frac{1}{t_{2003}}$ equals

(a) $\frac{4006}{3006}$ (b) $\frac{4003}{3007}$
(c) $\frac{4006}{3008}$ (d) $\frac{4006}{3009}$

9. The value of $\frac{1}{(1+a)(2+a)}+\frac{1}{(2+a)(3+a)}+\frac{1}{(3+a)(4+a)}+\dots$ upto ∞ is (where, a is constant)

(a) $\frac{1}{1+a}$ (b) $\frac{2}{1+a}$
(c) ∞ (d) None of these

10. If $f(x)$ is a function satisfying $f(x+y)=f(x)f(y)$ for all $x, y \in N$ such that $f(1)=3$ and $\sum_{x=1}^{n} f(x)=120$. Then, the value of n is

(a) 4 (b) 5
(c) 6 (d) None of these

11. If the sum of the first n terms of an AP is cn^2, then the sum of squares of these n terms is

(a) $\frac{n(4n^2-1)c^2}{6}$ (b) $\frac{n(4n^2+1)c^2}{3}$
(c) $\frac{n(4n^2-1)c^2}{3}$ (d) $\frac{n(4n^2+1)c^2}{6}$

Answer Key

1. (c)	2. (c)	3. (b)	4. (a)	5. (a)	6. (b)
7. (c)	8. (d)	9. (a)	10. (a)	11. (c)	

For Detailed Solution

JEE Pattern
EXAMPLES

Single Option Correct Type Questions

Example 1 *If the sides of a right-angled triangle are in AP, then the sines of the acute angles are*

(a) $\frac{3}{5}, \frac{4}{5}$ (b) $\frac{1}{\sqrt{3}}, \sqrt{\frac{2}{3}}$

(c) $\frac{1}{2}, \frac{\sqrt{3}}{2}$ (d) None of these

Sol. (a) Let $\angle C = 90°$ and $\angle B = 90° - \angle A$

The sides are $a - d$, a and $a + d$

Now, $(a + d)^2 = a^2 + (a - d)^2$

$\Rightarrow$ $4ad - a^2 = 0 \Rightarrow a = 4d$

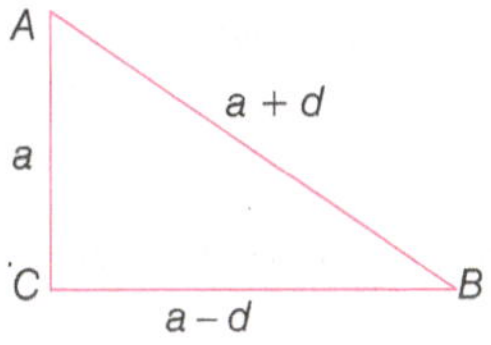

$\therefore$ The sides are $3d$, $4d$, $5d$.

Clearly, $\sin A = \frac{BC}{AB} = \frac{a - d}{a + d} = \frac{3d}{5d} = \frac{3}{5}$

and $\sin B = \frac{AC}{AB} = \frac{a}{a + d} = \frac{4d}{5d} = \frac{4}{5}$

Example 2 *Let* $F(n + 1) = \frac{2F(n) + 1}{2}$, *for* $n = 1, 2, 3, \dots$ *and* $F(1) = 2$. *Then,* $F(101)$ *is equal to*

(a) 50 (b) 52

(c) 54 (d) None of these

Sol. (b) Given, $F(n + 1) = \frac{2F(n) + 1}{2}$

$\Rightarrow$ $F(n + 1) - F(n) = \frac{1}{2}$

Hence, the given series in an AP with $a = 2, d = \frac{1}{2}$

$\therefore$ $F(101) = a_{101} = a + 100d$

$= 2 + 100 \times \frac{1}{2}$

$= 52$

JEE SCANNER

Example 3 Similar to PYQ Asked in JEE Main 2024

The 8th term from the end of the progression $\sqrt{2}, \sqrt{18}, \sqrt{50}, \sqrt{98}, \dots, \sqrt{1682}$ is

(a) $\sqrt{400}$ (b) $\sqrt{450}$ (c) $\sqrt{242}$ (d) $\sqrt{392}$

Sol. (b) Given, progression is

$\sqrt{2}, \sqrt{18}, \sqrt{50}, \sqrt{98}, \dots, \sqrt{1682}$

i.e. $\sqrt{2}, 3\sqrt{2}, 5\sqrt{2}, 7\sqrt{2}, \dots, 29\sqrt{2}$

So, here $a_1 = \sqrt{2}, d = 3\sqrt{2} - \sqrt{2} = 2\sqrt{2}$

and last term (t_n) or $l = 29\sqrt{2}$

As, we know that,

$t_n = a + (n - 1)\, d$

$\Rightarrow$ $29\sqrt{2} = \sqrt{2} + (n - 1)\, 2\sqrt{2}$

$\Rightarrow$ $(n - 1)\, 2\sqrt{2} = 28\sqrt{2}$

$\Rightarrow$ $n - 1 = 14$

$\Rightarrow$ $n = 15$

Since, rth term from end $= (n - r + 1)$th term from the beginning

$\Rightarrow$ 8th term from the end $= (15 - 8 + 1)$th term from the beginning $=$ 8th term from the beginning.

Hence, $t_8 = a_1 + (8 - 1)\, d$

$= \sqrt{2} + 7 \times 2\sqrt{2}$

$= \sqrt{2} + 14\sqrt{2}$

$= 15\sqrt{2}$

$= \sqrt{450}$

Skill Builder

The 35th term from the end of the progression 20, 17, 14, 11, ..., −127 is

(a) −20 (b) −25

(c) −30 (d) −35

For Sol.

Example 4 *The positive integer n for which* $2 \times 2^2 + 3 \times 2^3 + 4 \times 2^4 + \dots + n \times 2^n = 2^{n + 10}$ *is*

(a) 510 (b) 511

(c) 512 (d) 513

Sol. (d) We have, $2^{n+10} = 2\times2^2 + 3\times2^3 + 4\times2^4 + \ldots + n\times2^n$ ...(i)

$\Rightarrow 2(2^{n+10}) = 2\times2^3 + 3\times2^4 + \ldots + (n-1)\,2^n + n\times2^{n+1}$ ...(ii)

On subtracting Eq. (ii) from Eq. (i), we get

$$\therefore \quad -2^{n+10} = 2\times2^2 + 2^3 + 2^4 + \ldots + 2^n - n\times2^{n+1}$$

$$= 8 + \frac{8(2^{n-2}-1)}{2-1} - n\times2^{n+1}$$

$$= 8 + 2^{n+1} - 8 - n\times2^{n+1}$$

$$= 2^{n+1} - n\times2^{n+1}$$

$$\therefore \quad 2^{10} = 2n - 2$$

$$\Rightarrow \quad n = 513$$

JEE SCANNER

Example 5 Similar to PYQ Asked in JEE Main 2024

Let S_n denote the sum of first n terms of an arithmetic progression. If $S_{15} = 1350$ and $S_{10} = 1000$, then $S_9 - S_5$ is

(a) 208 (b) 368

(c) 460 (d) 944

Sol. (b) $S_{15} = 1350$ and $S_{10} = 1000$

$$S_{15} = \frac{15}{2}[2a + 14d] = 1350$$

$\Rightarrow \quad a + 7d = 90$ ...(i)

and $\quad S_{10} = \frac{10}{2}[2a + 9d] = 1000$

$\Rightarrow \quad 2a + 9d = 200$ ...(ii)

On solving Eqs. (i) and (ii), we get

$$a = 118,\ d = -4$$

Now $\quad S_9 - S_5 = \frac{9}{2}[2a + 8d] - \frac{5}{2}[2a + 4d]$

$$= \frac{1}{2}[18a + 72d - 10a - 20d]$$

$$= \frac{1}{2}[8a + 52d]$$

$$= \frac{1}{2}[8\times118 + 52\times-4]$$

$$= \frac{1}{2}[944 - 208]$$

$$= 368$$

Skill Builder

Let S_n denote the sum of first n terms of an arithmetic progression. If $S_{20} = 320$ and $S_5 = 50$. Then, $\frac{S_{12}}{S_8}$ is

(a) $\frac{5}{4}$ (b) $\frac{12}{5}$

(c) $\frac{12}{7}$ (d) $\frac{8}{7}$

For Sol.

Example 6 *If $x = 1 - x + x^2 - x^3 + x^4 - x^5 + \ldots\infty$, then $x =$*

(a) $2\cos 36^\circ$ (b) $2\cos 144^\circ$

(c) $2\sin 18^\circ$ (d) $2\cos 18^\circ$

Sol. (c) We have, $x = 1 - x + x^2 - x^3 + x^4 - x^5 + \ldots\infty$

$$\therefore \quad x = \frac{1}{1-(-x)} \Rightarrow x = \frac{1}{1+x}$$

$$\Rightarrow \quad x^2 + x - 1 = 0 \Rightarrow x = \frac{-1\pm\sqrt{5}}{2}$$

$$\Rightarrow \quad x = \frac{-1+\sqrt{5}}{2} \quad [\text{for infinite GP, } |r| < 1]$$

$$\therefore \quad x = 2\sin 18^\circ$$

Example 7 *In a GP the first, third and fifth terms may be considered as the first, fourth and sixteenth terms of an AP. Then the fourth term of the AP, knowing that its first term is 5, is*

(a) 10 (b) 12 (c) 16 (d) 20

Sol. (d) We have, $a = 5,\ ar^2 = a + 3d,\ ar^4 = a + 15d$

$$\therefore \quad 5r^2 = 5 + 3d,\ 5r^4 = 5 + 15d$$

$$\Rightarrow \quad r^4 = 1 + 3d$$

$$\Rightarrow \quad 25r^4 = 25 + 75d$$

$$\Rightarrow \quad (5 + 3d)^2 = 25 + 75d$$

$$\Rightarrow \quad 25 + 30d + 9d^2 = 25 + 75d$$

$$\Rightarrow \quad 9d^2 - 45d = 0 \Rightarrow d = 5, 0 \quad [d = 0 \text{ is not possible}]$$

$$\therefore \quad d = 5$$

$$\therefore \quad T_4 = a + 3d = 5 + 15 = 20$$

Example 8 *If $b - c,\ 2b - \lambda,\ b - a$ are in HP, then $a - \frac{\lambda}{2}$, $b - \frac{\lambda}{2}$, $c - \frac{\lambda}{2}$ are is*

(a) AP (b) GP

(c) HP (d) None of these

Sol. (b) $(2b - \lambda) = \frac{2(b-c)(b-a)}{(b-c)+(b-a)}$

$$\Rightarrow \quad (2b-\lambda)[(2b-(a+c)] = 2[b^2 - (a+c)b + ac]$$

$$\Rightarrow \quad 2b^2 - 2b\lambda + \lambda(a+c) - 2ac = 0$$

$$\Rightarrow \quad b^2 - b\lambda + \frac{\lambda}{2}(a+c) - ac = 0$$

$$\Rightarrow \left(b - \frac{\lambda}{2}\right)^2 - \frac{\lambda^2}{4} + \frac{\lambda}{2}(a+c) - ac = 0$$

$$\Rightarrow \quad \left(b - \frac{\lambda}{2}\right)^2 = \frac{\lambda^2}{4} - \frac{\lambda}{2}(a+c) + ac$$

$$\Rightarrow \quad \left(b - \frac{\lambda}{2}\right)^2 = \left(a - \frac{\lambda}{2}\right)\left(c - \frac{\lambda}{2}\right)$$

Hence, $a - \frac{\lambda}{2},\ b - \frac{\lambda}{2},\ c - \frac{\lambda}{2}$ are in GP.

JEE SCANNER

Example 9 Similar to PYQ Asked in JEE Main 2024

If the sum of the series $1-(1+d)\times\frac{1}{3}+(1+2d)\times\frac{1}{9}-(1+3d)\times\frac{1}{27}+\ldots$ *is equal to* $\frac{9}{16}$*. Then, 2d is equal to*

(a) $\frac{1}{2}$ (b) 1 (c) 2 (d) 4

Sol. (c) Given, $1-(1+d)\frac{1}{3}+(1+2d)\frac{1}{9}-(1+3d)\frac{1}{27}+\ldots=\frac{9}{16}$

$$\Rightarrow \underbrace{\left(1-\frac{1}{3}+\frac{1}{9}-\frac{1}{27}+\ldots\right)}_{S_1}-d\underbrace{\left(\frac{1}{3}-\frac{2}{9}+\frac{3}{27}-\ldots\right)}_{S_2}=\frac{9}{16} \quad \ldots\text{(i)}$$

Now, $S_1=1-\frac{1}{3}+\frac{1}{9}-\frac{1}{27}+\ldots$

$$=\left(\frac{-1}{3}\right)^0+\left(\frac{-1}{3}\right)^1+\left(\frac{-1}{3}\right)^2+\left(\frac{-1}{3}\right)^3+\ldots$$

$a=1$ and $r=\frac{-1}{3}$

$\therefore$ Sum, $S_1=\frac{1}{1-\left(\frac{-1}{3}\right)}=\frac{1}{1+\frac{1}{3}}=\frac{3}{4}$

and $S_2=\frac{1}{3}-\frac{2}{9}+\frac{3}{27}-\ldots=\frac{1}{3}-\frac{2}{3^2}+\frac{3}{3^3}-\ldots$

$\Rightarrow \frac{S_2}{3}=\frac{1}{3^2}-\frac{2}{3^3}+\frac{3}{3^4}-\ldots$

Now, $S_2+\frac{S_2}{3}=\frac{1}{3}-\frac{1}{3^2}+\frac{1}{3^3}-\ldots$

$\Rightarrow \frac{4S_2}{3}=\frac{1}{3}\left(1-\frac{1}{3}+\frac{1}{3^2}-\ldots\right)$

$\Rightarrow \frac{4S_2}{3}=\frac{1}{3}\cdot\left(\frac{3}{4}\right)=\frac{1}{4}$

$\Rightarrow S_2=\frac{3}{16}$

Now, $S_1-dS_2=\frac{9}{16}\Rightarrow\frac{3}{4}-d\frac{3}{16}=\frac{9}{16}$

$\Rightarrow \frac{3d}{16}=\frac{3}{4}-\frac{9}{16}=\frac{12-9}{16}=\frac{3}{16}$

$\Rightarrow \frac{3d}{16}=\frac{3}{16}\Rightarrow d=1$

$\therefore d=1$

Thus, $2d=2\times1=2$

Skill Builder

If the sum of the series $3+(3+d)\frac{1}{4}+(3+2d)\frac{1}{4^2}+\ldots$ is $4\frac{8}{9}$. Then, the value of d is

(a) 2 (b) 3
(c) 4 (d) 5

For Sol.

Example 10 *Let* $a_1, a_2, a_3, \ldots, a_{10}$ *are in GP with* $a_{51}=25$ *and* $\sum_{i=1}^{101}a_i=125$*, then the value of* $\sum_{i=1}^{101}\left(\frac{1}{a_i}\right)$ *equals*

(a) 5 (b) $\frac{1}{5}$ (c) $\frac{1}{25}$ (d) $\frac{1}{125}$

Sol. (b) Let 1st term be a_1 and common ratio be r, then

$$\sum_{i=1}^{101}\frac{1}{a_i}=125$$

$\Rightarrow (a_1+a_1r+a_1r^2+\ldots+a_1r^{100})=125$

$\Rightarrow \frac{a_1(1-r^{101})}{(1-r)}=125$ [let $0<r<1$] ...(i)

$$\therefore \sum_{i=1}^{101}\frac{1}{a_i}=\frac{1}{a_i}+\frac{1}{a_ir}+\frac{1}{a_ir^2}+\ldots+\frac{1}{a_ir^{100}}=\frac{\frac{1}{a_i}\left[\left(\frac{1}{r}\right)^{101}-1\right]}{\left(\frac{1}{r}-1\right)}$$

$\left[\text{here } \frac{1}{r}>1\right]$

$$=\frac{(1-r^{101})}{a_1r^{100}(1-r)}=\frac{1}{a_1r^{100}}\times\frac{125}{a_1} \quad \text{[from Eq. (i)]}$$

$$=\frac{125}{(a_1r^{50})^2}=\frac{125}{(a_{51})^2}=\frac{125}{(25)^2}=\frac{1}{5}$$

Example 11 *If* $x=111\ldots1$ *(20 digits),* $y=333\ldots3$ *(10 digits) and* $z=222\ldots2$ *(10 digits), then* $\frac{x-y^2}{z}$ *equals*

(a) $\frac{1}{2}$ (b) 1 (c) 2 (d) 4

Sol. (b) $\because x=\frac{1}{9}(999\ldots9)=\frac{1}{9}(10^{20}-1)$,

$y=\frac{1}{3}(999\ldots9)=\frac{1}{3}(10^{10}-1)$

and $z=\frac{2}{9}(999\ldots9)=\frac{2}{9}(10^{10}-1)$]

$$\therefore \frac{x-y^2}{z}=\frac{\frac{1}{9}(10^{20}-1)-\frac{1}{9}(10^{10}-1)^2}{\frac{2}{9}(10^{10}-1)}$$

$$=\frac{10^{10}+1-(10^{10}-1)}{2}=1$$

Example 12 *Consider the sequence* 1, 2, 2, 3, 3, 3, ..., *where n occurs n times. The number that occurs as* 2011th *terms is*

(a) 61 (b) 62 (c) 63 (d) 64

Sol. (c) Here, sequence is of the form 1, 2, 2, 3, 3, 3, 3, ... $\underbrace{n\ldots n}_{n \text{ times}}$

Thus, the series becomes $1+2+3+\ldots+n$

Now, $1+2+3+\ldots+n=2011$

$\Rightarrow \quad \frac{n}{2}[2\times 1+(n-1)d]=2011$

$\Rightarrow \quad \frac{n(n+1)}{2}=2011$

$\Rightarrow \quad n(n+1)=4022$

Thus, for $n(n+1)\ge 4022$

We have, $n=63$ (least value)

$\therefore \quad n=63$

Example 13 *Let* $S=\sum_{r=1}^{117}\frac{1}{2[\sqrt{r}]+1}$, *where* $[\cdot]$ *denotes the greatest integer function and if* $S=\frac{p}{q}$, *when p and q are coprimes, the value of* $p+q$ *is*

(a) 20 (b) 76 (c) 19 (d) 69

Sol. (b) $\because \quad S=\sum_{r=1}^{117}\frac{1}{2[\sqrt{r}]+1}$

$$=\frac{3}{2\cdot1+1}+\frac{5}{2\cdot2+1}+\frac{7}{2\cdot3+1}+\ldots+\frac{19}{2\cdot9+1}+\frac{18}{2\cdot10+1}$$

$$=9+\frac{18}{21}=9+\frac{6}{7}=\frac{69}{7}$$

$\therefore \quad p=69$ and $q=7 \Rightarrow p+q=69+7=76$

Example 14 *If a, b, c are non-zero real numbers, then the minimum value of the expression*

$$\frac{(a^8+4a^4+1)(b^4+3b^2+1)(c^2+2c+2)}{a^4b^2} \text{ equals}$$

(a) 12 (b) 24 (c) 30 (d) 60

Sol. (c) Let $P=\frac{(a^8+4a^4+1)(b^4+3b^2+1)(c^2+2c+2)}{a^4b^2}$

$$=\left(a^4+4+\frac{1}{a^4}\right)\left(b^2+3+\frac{1}{b^2}\right)\{(c+1)^2+1\}$$

$\because \quad a^4+4+\frac{1}{a^4}\ge 6,\ b^2+3+\frac{1}{b^2}\ge 5$ and $(c+1)^2+1\ge 1$

$$\left[\because x+\frac{1}{x}\ge 2 \text{ for } x>0\right]$$

$\therefore \quad P\ge 6\cdot5\cdot1=30 \Rightarrow P\ge 30$

Hence, the required minimum value is 30.

Example 15 *If the sum of m consecutive odd integers is* m^4, *then the first integer is*

(a) m^3+m+1 (b) m^3+m-1
(c) m^3-m-1 (d) m^3-m+1

Sol. (d) Let $2a+1, 2a+3, 2a+5, \ldots$ be the AP, then

$$m^4=(2a+1)+(2a+3)+(2a+5)+\ldots \text{ upto } m \text{ terms}$$

$$=\frac{m}{2}\{2(2a+1)+(m-1)\cdot2\}=m(2a+1+m-1)$$

$\Rightarrow \quad m^3=(2a+1)+m-1$

$\therefore \quad 2a+1=m^3-m+1$

Example 16 *The value of* $\sum_{r=1}^{\infty}\frac{(4r+5)5^{-r}}{r(5r+5)}$ *is*

(a) $\frac{1}{5}$ (b) $\frac{2}{5}$ (c) $\frac{1}{25}$ (d) $\frac{2}{125}$

Sol. (a) $\sum_{r=1}^{\infty}\frac{(4r+5)5^{-r}}{r(5r+5)}=\lim_{n\to\infty}\sum_{r=1}^{n}\left(\frac{(5r+5)-r}{r(5r+5)}\right)\cdot\frac{1}{5^r}$

$$=\lim_{n\to\infty}\sum_{r=1}^{n}\left(\frac{1}{r}-\frac{1}{5r+5}\right)\frac{1}{5^r}$$

$$=\lim_{n\to\infty}\sum_{r=1}^{n}\left(\frac{1}{r\cdot5^r}-\frac{1}{(r+1)5^{r+1}}\right)$$

$$=\lim_{n\to\infty}\left(\frac{1}{5}-\frac{1}{(n+1)5^{n+1}}\right)=\frac{1}{5}-0=\frac{1}{5}$$

Example 17 *Let* λ *be the greatest integer for which* $5p^2-16, 2p\lambda, \lambda^2$ *are distinct consecutive terms of an AP, where* $p\in R$. *If the common difference of the AP is* $\left(\frac{m}{n}\right)$, $m, n\in N$ *and m, n are relative prime, the value of* $m+n$ *is*

(a) 133 (b) 138 (c) 143 (d) 148

Sol. (a) $\because 5p^2-16, 2p\lambda, \lambda^2$ are in AP, then

$$4p\lambda=5p^2-16+\lambda^2$$

$\Rightarrow \quad 5p^2-4p\lambda+\lambda^2-16=0 \quad \ldots(i)$

$\therefore \quad B^2-4AC\ge 0 \quad [\because p\in R]$

$\Rightarrow \quad 16\lambda^2-4\cdot5\cdot(\lambda^2-16)\ge 0$

$\Rightarrow \quad -\lambda^2+80\ge 0$ or $\lambda^2\le 80$

$\Rightarrow \quad -\sqrt{80}\le\lambda\le\sqrt{80}$

$\therefore \quad \lambda=8 \quad$ [greatest integer]

From Eq. (i), $\quad 5p^2-32p+48=0$

$\Rightarrow \quad (p-4)(5p-12)=0$

$\therefore \quad p=4, p=\frac{12}{5}$

$\Rightarrow \quad p=\frac{12}{5}, p\ne 4$

[for $p=4$ all terms are equal]

Now, common difference $=\lambda^2-2p\lambda$

$$=64-16\times\frac{12}{5}=64\left(1-\frac{3}{5}\right)=\frac{128}{5}=\frac{m}{n}$$

[given]

$\therefore \quad m=128$ and $n=5$

Hence, $m+n=133$

Example 18 *If* 2λ, λ *and* $[\lambda^2-14]$, $\lambda\in R-\{0\}$ *and [.] denotes the greatest integer function are the first three terms of a GP in order, then the 51th term of the sequence,* $1, 3\lambda, 6\lambda, 10\lambda, \ldots$ *is*

(a) 5104 (b) 5304
(c) 5504 (d) 5704

Sol. (b) $\because 2\lambda, \lambda, [\lambda^2 - 14]$ are in GP, then

$$\lambda^2 = 2\lambda[\lambda^2 - 14] \Rightarrow \frac{\lambda}{2} = [\lambda^2 - 14]$$

$\therefore$ λ must be an even integer.

Hence, $\lambda = 4$

Now, required sequence 1,12, 24, 40, ...

or 1, $4(1+2)$, $4(1+2+3)$, $4(1+2+3+4)$, ...

$\therefore$ 51th term $= 4(1+2+3+...+51)$

$$= 4 \cdot \frac{51}{2}(1+51) = 4 \cdot 51 \cdot 26 = 5304$$

JEE SCANNER

Example 19 Similar to PYQ Asked in JEE Main 2024

Let the range of the function $f(x) = \frac{1}{\sin(x) + \cos(x) - 2}$, $x \in R$ be $[a, b]$. If α and β are respectively the AM and GM of a and b, then $\alpha^2 - \beta^2$ is equal to

(a) $\frac{1}{\sqrt{2}}$ (b) 1 (c) $\frac{1}{2}$ (d) -2

Sol. (c) Given, $f(x) = \frac{1}{\sin x + \cos x - 2}$

Since, $\sin x + \cos x \in [-\sqrt{2}, \sqrt{2}]$

$\therefore$ $\sin x + \cos x - 2 \in [-\sqrt{2} - 2, \sqrt{2} - 2]$

$$\Rightarrow \frac{1}{\sin x + \cos x - 2} \in \left[\frac{1}{\sqrt{2}-2}, \frac{1}{-\sqrt{2}-2}\right]$$

$$\therefore \quad a = \frac{1}{\sqrt{2}-2} = \frac{\sqrt{2}+2}{-2} \text{ and } b = \frac{1}{-\sqrt{2}-2} = \frac{\sqrt{2}-2}{2}$$

$$\text{Thus, } \alpha = \frac{a+b}{2} = \frac{1}{2}\left[\frac{\sqrt{2}+2}{-2} + \frac{\sqrt{2}-2}{2}\right]$$

$$= \frac{1}{2}\left[-\frac{\sqrt{2}}{2} - 1 + \frac{\sqrt{2}}{2} - 1\right] = -1$$

$$\text{and } \quad \beta = \sqrt{ab} = \sqrt{\frac{(\sqrt{2}+2)}{-2} \times \frac{\sqrt{2}-2}{2}} = \sqrt{\frac{2-4}{-4}} = \sqrt{\frac{-2}{-4}} = \frac{1}{\sqrt{2}}$$

$$\text{Therefore, } \alpha^2 - \beta^2 = (-1)^2 - \left(\frac{1}{\sqrt{2}}\right)^2 = 1 - \frac{1}{2} = \frac{1}{2}$$

Skill Builder

Let the range of the function $f(x) = \frac{1}{2\sin x + 2\cos x + 2}$, $x \in R$ be $[a, b]$. If α and β are respectively the AM and GM of a and b, then $\frac{\alpha^2}{\beta^2}$ is equal to

(a) i (b) π

(c) -1 (d) $\frac{1}{2}$

For Sol.

More than One Correct Option Type Questions

Example 20 *For an increasing AP $a_1, a_2, \ldots, a_n$, if $a_1 + a_3 + a_5 = -12$ and $a_1 a_3 a_5 = 80$, then which of the following is/are true?*

(a) $a_1 = -10$ (b) $a_2 = -1$

(c) $a_3 = -4$ (d) $a_5 = 2$

Sol. (a, c, d) We have, $a_1 + a_3 + a_5 = -12$

$\Rightarrow$ $a + a + 2d + a + 4d = -12$ $[d > 0]$

$\Rightarrow$ $a + 2d = -4$

Also, $a_1 a_3 a_5 = 80$

$\Rightarrow$ $a(a + 2d)(a + 4d) = 80$

$\Rightarrow$ $(-4 - 2d)(-4)(-4 + 2d) = 80$

$\Rightarrow$ $(4 + 2d)(4 - 2d) = -20 \Rightarrow 16 - 4d^2 = -20$

$\Rightarrow$ $4d^2 = 36 \Rightarrow d = \pm 3$

$\therefore$ $d = 3$ $[d > 0]$

$a = -4 - 2d = -4 - 6 = -10$

$\therefore$ $a_1 = -10$

$a_2 = -7$

$a_3 = -4$

$a_5 = 2$

Example 21 *If the sum of an infinite GP : $p, 1, \frac{1}{p}, \frac{1}{p^2} \ldots$ is $\frac{9}{2}$, then the value of p is*

(a) 2 (b) $\frac{3}{2}$ (c) 3 (d) $\frac{9}{2}$

Sol. (b, c) We have, $S_\infty = \frac{9}{2}, a = p, r = \frac{1}{p}$

$$\therefore \quad S_\infty = \frac{9}{2} \Rightarrow \frac{p}{1 - \frac{1}{p}} = \frac{9}{2}$$

$$\Rightarrow \quad 2p^2 - 9p + 9 = 0 \Rightarrow p = \frac{3}{2}, 3$$

Example 22 *If a, b and c are in GP and x, y are respectively the AM between a, b and b, c, then*

(a) $\frac{a}{x} + \frac{c}{y} = 2$ (b) $\frac{a}{x} + \frac{c}{y} = \frac{c}{a}$

(c) $\frac{1}{x} + \frac{1}{y} = \frac{2}{b}$ (d) $\frac{1}{x} + \frac{1}{y} = \frac{2}{ac}$

Sol. (a, c) a, b, c are in GP.

$\therefore$ $b^2 = ac$

x is AM of a and b.

Hence, $2x = a + b$

y is AM of b and c.

Hence, $2y = b + c$

$$\therefore \frac{a}{x} + \frac{c}{y} = a \times \frac{2}{a+b} + c \times \frac{2}{b+c} = 2\left[\frac{ab + ac + ac + bc}{ab + ac + b^2 + bc}\right] = 2$$

$[\because b^2 = ac]$

Again, $\frac{1}{x}+\frac{1}{y}=\frac{2}{a+b}+\frac{2}{b+c}$

$$=\frac{2(a+c+2b)}{ab+ac+b^2+bc}$$

$$=\frac{2(a+c+2b)}{ab+2b^2+bc}=\frac{2(a+c+2b)}{b(a+2b+c)}=\frac{2}{b}$$

Example 23 *The first three terms of a sequence are 3, −1, −1. The next terms are*

(a) 2 (b) 3 (c) $-\frac{5}{27}$ (d) $-\frac{5}{9}$

Sol. (b, d) The given sequence is not an AP or GP or HP. It is an AGP, $3, (3+d)r, (3+2d)r^2, \ldots$

$\Rightarrow \quad (3+d)r=-1, (3+2d)r^2=-1$

Eliminating r, we get $\quad (3+d)^2=-(3+2d)$

$\Rightarrow \quad d^2+8d+12=0 \Rightarrow d=-2,-6,$

Then, $\quad r=-1, \frac{1}{3}$

$\therefore$ Next term is $(3+3d)r^3=3, -\frac{5}{9}$

Example 24 *There are two numbers a and b whose product is 192 and the quotient of AM by HM of their greatest common divisor and least common multiple is $\frac{169}{48}$. The smaller of a and b is*

(a) 2 (b) 4 (c) 6 (d) 12

Sol. (b, d) If $G=$ GCD of a and b, $L=$ LCM of a and b, we have

$GL=ab=192 \quad \ldots$(i)

$\frac{\text{AM}}{\text{HM}}$ of G and L is $\left(\frac{G+L}{2}\right)\left(\frac{G+L}{2GL}\right)=\frac{169}{48}$

$\Rightarrow \quad (G+L)^2=\frac{169}{12}GL=\frac{169}{12}\times 192=13^2\cdot 4^2$

$\Rightarrow \quad G+L=52$ but $GL=192$

$\Rightarrow \quad G=4, L=48$

$\Rightarrow \quad a=4, b=48$

or $\quad a=12, b=16$

Example 25 *Consider a series*

$$\frac{1}{2}+\frac{1}{2^2}+\frac{2}{2^3}+\frac{3}{2^4}+\frac{5}{2^5}+\ldots+\frac{\lambda n}{2^n}.$$

If S_n denotes its sum to n terms, then S_n cannot be

(a) 2 (b) 3 (c) 4 (d) 5

Decoding the Question

For a arithmetic-geometric series,

$S_n=a+(a+d)r+(a+2d)r^2+\ldots+(a+(n-1)d)r^{n-1}$,

the sum of n terms is

$$S_n=\frac{a}{1-r}+d\left[\frac{r(1-r^{n-1})}{1-r}\right]-\frac{a+(n-1)d}{r^n}$$

Sol. (a, b, c, d)

$\because \quad S_n=\frac{1}{2}+\frac{1}{2^2}+\frac{2}{2^3}+\frac{3}{2^4}+\frac{5}{2^5}+\ldots+\frac{\lambda_n}{2^n}$

$$=\frac{3}{4}+\frac{1}{4}\left(\frac{1}{2}+\frac{1}{2^2}+\frac{2}{2^3}+\frac{3}{2^4}+\frac{5}{2^5}+\ldots+\frac{\lambda_n}{2^n}\right)$$

$$+\frac{1}{2}\left(\frac{1}{2}+\frac{1}{2^2}+\frac{2}{2^3}+\ldots+\frac{\lambda_n}{2^n}\right)-\frac{1}{4}-\frac{\lambda_n}{2^{n+2}}-\frac{\lambda_n}{2^{n+1}}$$

$\Rightarrow \quad S_n=\frac{3}{4}+\frac{1}{4}S_n+\frac{1}{2}S_n-\frac{1}{4}-\frac{\lambda_n}{2^{n+2}}-\frac{\lambda_n}{2^{n+1}}$

$\Rightarrow \frac{1}{4}S_n=\frac{1}{2}-\frac{\lambda_n}{2^{n+2}}-\frac{\lambda_n}{2^{n+1}} \Rightarrow S_n=2-\frac{\lambda_n}{2^n}-\frac{\lambda_n}{2^{n-1}}<2$

Example 26 *If $S_r=\sqrt{r+\sqrt{r+\sqrt{r+\sqrt{\ldots\infty}}}}$, $r>0$, then which the following is/are correct.*

(a) S_2, S_6, S_{12}, S_{20} are in AP

(b) S_4, S_9, S_{16} are irrational

(c) $(2S_4-1)^2, (2S_5-1)^2\ (2S_6-1)^2$ are in AP

(d) S_2, S_{12}, S_{56} are in GP

Sol. (a, b, c, d)

$\because S_r=\sqrt{r+\sqrt{r+\sqrt{+\sqrt{\ldots\infty}}}}=\sqrt{r+S_r}$

$\Rightarrow \quad S_r^2-S_r-r=0$

$\therefore \quad S_r=\frac{1+\sqrt{(1+4r)}}{2} \quad [\because r>0]$

Alternate (a) S_2, S_6, S_{12}, S_{20} i.e. 2, 3, 4, 5 are in AP.

Alternate (b) S_4, S_9, S_{16} i.e. $\frac{1+\sqrt{17}}{2}, \frac{1+\sqrt{37}}{2}, \frac{1+\sqrt{65}}{2}$ are irrationals.

Alternate (c) $(2S_4-1)^2, (2S_5-1)^2 (2S_6-1)^2$ i.e. 17, 21, 25 are in AP.

Alternate (d) S_2, S_{12}, S_{56} i.e. 2, 4, 8 are in GP.

Example 27 *If $\frac{1}{a}, \frac{1}{b}, \frac{1}{c}$ are in AP and a, b, −2c are in GP, where a, b, c are non-zero, then*

(a) $a^3+b^3+c^3=3abc$ (b) $-2a, b, -2c$ are in AP

(c) $-2a, b, -2c$ are in GP (d) $a^2, b^2, 4c^2$ are in GP

Sol. (a, b, d)

$\because \quad \frac{1}{a}, \frac{1}{b}, \frac{1}{c}$ are in AP $\Rightarrow a, b, c$ are in HP

$\therefore \quad b=\frac{2ac}{a+c} \quad \ldots$(i)

and $a, b, -2c$ are in GP, then $b^2=-2ac$ ...(ii)

From Eqs. (i) and (ii), we get

$$b=\frac{-b^2}{a+c} \Rightarrow a+b+c=0 \quad [\because b\neq 0]$$

$\therefore \quad a^3+b^3+c^3=3abc$ and $a, b, -2c$ are in GP

$\Rightarrow \quad a^2, b^2, 4c^2$ are also in GP and $a+b+c=0$

$\Rightarrow \quad 2b=-2a-2c$

$\therefore \quad -2a, b, -2c$ are in AP.

Passage Based Questions

Passage I

(Ex. Nos. 28 to 29)

Consider a sequence whose sum to n terms is given by the quadratic function $S_n = 3n^2 + 5n$.

Example 28 *The nature of the given series is*

(a) AP (b) GP (c) HP (d) AGP

Sol. (a) $\because$ $S_n = 3n^2 + 5n$

$\therefore$ $T_n = S_n - S_{n-1} = (3n^2 + 5n) - [3(n-1)^2 + 5(n-1)]$

$= 3(2n - 1) + 5 = 6n + 2$

The nth term is a linear function in n. Hence, sequence must be an AP.

Example 29 *For the given sequence, the number 5456 is the*

(a) 153 th term (b) 932 th term

(c) 707 th term (d) 909 th term

Sol. (d) Given, $T_n = 5456 \Rightarrow 6n + 2 = 5456 \Rightarrow 6n = 5454$

$\therefore$ $n = 909$

$\therefore$ The number 5456 is the 909th term.

Passage II

(Ex. Nos. 30 to 31)

Let r be the number of identical terms in the two AP's. Form the sequence of identical terms, it will be an AP, then the rth term of this AP make $t_r \le$ the smaller of the last term of the two AP's.

Example 30 *The number of terms common to two AP's 3, 7, 11, ..., 407 and 2, 9, 16, ..., 709 is*

(a) 14 (b) 21 (c) 28 (d) 35

Decoding the Question

For two different AP's with common difference d_1 and d_2, the sequence with common terms of both AP's has common difference is LCM of d_1 and d_2.

Sol. (a) Sequence 3, 7, 11, ... , 407 has common difference = 4 and sequence 2, 9, 16, ... , 709 has common difference = 7.

Hence, the sequence with common terms has common difference is LCM of 4 and 7 which is 28.

The first common term is 23.

Hence, the sequence is 23, 51, 79, ... , 387 which has 14 terms.

Example 31 *The 10th common term between the series $3 + 7 + 11 + \dots$ and $1 + 6 + 11 + \dots$ is*

(a) 189 (b) 191 (c) 211 (d) 213

Sol. (b) Series 3 + 7 + 11 + ... has common difference = 4 and series 1 + 6 + 11 + ... has common difference = 5.

Hence, the series with common terms has common difference is LCM of 4 and 5 which is 20.

The first common terms is 11.

Hence, the series is 11 + 31 + 51 + 71 + ...

$\therefore$ $t_{10} = 11 + (10 - 1)(20) = 191$

Alternate Solution

t_n for $3 + 7 + 11 + \dots = 3 + (n-1)(4) = 4n - 1$

and t_m for $1 + 6 + 11 + \dots = 1 + (m-1)(5) = 5m - 4$

For a common term, $4n - 1 = 5m - 4$ i.e. $4n = 5m - 3$

For $m = 3$, $n = 3$ gives the first common term i.e., 11.

For $m = 7$, $n = 8$ gives the second common term i.e. 31.

For $m = 11$, $n = 13$ gives the third common term i.e. 51.

Hence, the common term series is 11 + 31 + 51 + ...

$\therefore$ $t_{10} = 11 + (10 - 1)20 = 191$

Passage III

(Ex. Nos. 32 to 33)

We are giving the concept of arithmetic mean of mth power. Let $a_1, a_2, a_3, \dots, a_n$ be n positive real numbers (not all equal) and m be a real number. Then,

$$\frac{a_1^m + a_2^m + a_3^m + \dots + a_n^m}{n} > \left(\frac{a_1 + a_2 + a_3 + \dots + a_n}{n}\right)^m,$$

if $m \in R \sim [0, 1]$

However, if $m \in (0, 1)$, then

$$\frac{a_1^m + a_2^m + a_3^m + \dots + a_n^m}{n} < \left(\frac{a_1 + a_2 + a_3 + \dots + a_n}{n}\right)^m$$

Obviously, if $m = \{0, 1\}$, then

$$\frac{a_1^m + a_2^m + a_3^m + \dots + a_n^m}{n} = \left(\frac{a_1 + a_2 + a_3 + \dots + a_n}{n}\right)^m.$$

Example 32 *If $x > 0, y > 0, z > 0$ and $x + y + z = 1$, the minimum value of $\frac{x}{2-x} + \frac{y}{2-y} + \frac{z}{2-z}$, is*

(a) 0.2 (b) 0.4 (c) 0.6 (d) 0.8

Sol. (c) Since, AM of (-1)th powers $\ge (-1)$th powers of AM

$$\therefore \frac{(2-x)^{-1} + (2-y)^{-1} + (2-z)^{-1}}{3} \ge \left(\frac{2 - x + 2 - y + 2 - z}{3}\right)^{-1}$$

$$= \left[\frac{6 - (x + y + z)}{3}\right]^{-1} = \left(\frac{6-1}{3}\right)^{-1} = \frac{3}{5} \quad [\because x + y + z = 1]$$

$$\Rightarrow \frac{(2-x)^{-1} + (2-y)^{-1} + (2-z)^{-1}}{3} \ge \frac{3}{5}$$

$$\text{or} \quad \frac{1}{3}\left[\frac{1}{2-x} + \frac{1}{2-y} + \frac{1}{2-z}\right] \ge \frac{3}{5}$$

$$\Rightarrow \frac{1}{2-x} + \frac{1}{2-y} + \frac{1}{2-z} \ge \frac{9}{5}$$

$$\text{or} \quad \frac{2}{2-x} + \frac{2}{2-y} + \frac{2}{2-z} \ge \frac{18}{5}$$

$$\text{or} \quad 1 + \frac{x}{2-x} + 1 + \frac{y}{2-y} + 1 + \frac{z}{2-z} \ge \frac{18}{5}$$

$$\text{or} \quad \frac{x}{2-x} + \frac{y}{2-y} + \frac{z}{2-z} \ge \frac{18}{5} - 3$$

Hence, $\frac{x}{2-x}+\frac{y}{2-y}+\frac{z}{2-z} \geq \frac{3}{5}=0.6$

$\Rightarrow \quad \frac{x}{2-x}+\frac{y}{2-y}+\frac{z}{2-z} \geq 0.6$

Thus, minimum value of $\frac{x}{2-x}+\frac{y}{2-y}+\frac{z}{2-z}$ is 0.6.

Example 33 *If $\sum_{i=1}^{n} a_i^2=\lambda$, $\forall\, a_i \geq 0$ and if greatest and least values of $\left(\sum_{i=1}^{n} a_i\right)^2$ are λ_1 and λ_2 respectively, then $(\lambda_1-\lambda_2)$ is*

(a) $n\lambda$ (b) $(n-1)\lambda$
(c) $(n+2)\lambda$ (d) $(n+1)\lambda$

Sol. (b) $\because$ AM of 2nd powers $\geq$ 2nd power of AM

$\therefore \quad \frac{a_1^2+a_2^2+a_3^2+\ldots+a_n^2}{n} \geq \left(\frac{a_1+a_2+a_3+\ldots+a_n}{n}\right)^2$

$\Rightarrow \quad \frac{\lambda}{n} \geq \left(\frac{\sum_{i=1}^{n} a_i}{n}\right)^2$

$\therefore \quad \left(\sum_{i=1}^{n} a_i\right)^2 \leq n\lambda \quad \ldots(i)$

Also, $(a_1+a_2+a_3+\ldots+a_n)^2=a_1^2+a_2^2+a_3^2+\ldots+a_n^2+2\sum a_1 a_2$

$=\lambda+2\sum a_1 a_2 \geq \lambda$

$\therefore \quad \left(\sum_{i=1}^{n} a_i\right)^2 \geq \lambda \quad \ldots(ii)$

From Eqs. (i) and (ii), we get

$\lambda \leq \left(\sum_{i=1}^{n} a_i\right)^2 \leq n\lambda$

$\therefore \quad \lambda_1=n\lambda$ and $\lambda_2=\lambda$

Then, $\lambda_1-\lambda_2=(n-1)\lambda$

Stem Based Questions

Stem I

(Ex. Nos. 34 to 35)

There are two sets A and B each of which consists of three numbers in AP whose sum is 15 and where D and d are the common differences such that $D=1+d, d>0$. If $p=7(q-p)$, where p and q are the product of the numbers respectively in the two series.

Example 34 *The value of p is ....*

Example 35 *The value of q is ....*

Sol. (Q. Nos. 34 to 35)

Let $A=\{A-D, A, A+D\}$,
$B=\{a-d, a, a+d\}$

According to the question,

$A-D+A+A+D=15$

$\Rightarrow \quad 3A=15$

$\Rightarrow \quad A=5 \quad \ldots(i)$

and $a-d+a+a+d=15$

$\Rightarrow \quad a=5 \quad \ldots(ii)$

and $D=1+d \quad \ldots(iii)$

$p=(A-D)A(A+D)$

$p=A(A^2-D^2)$

$p=5(25-D^2) \quad \ldots(iv)$

Similarly, $q=5(25-d^2) \quad \ldots(v)$

Given that $p=7(q-p)$

$8p=7q$

From Eqs. (iv) and (v), we get

$8\times5(25-D^2)=7\times5(25-d^2)$

$200-8D^2=175-7d^2$

$25=8D^2-7d^2$

$25=8(1+d)^2-7d^2 \quad$ [from Eq. (iii)]

$25=8+8d^2+16d-7d^2$

$17-d^2-16d=0$

$d^2+16d-17=0$

$(d+17)(d-1)=0$

$d=-17$ or $d=1$

$\Rightarrow \quad d=1 \quad [\because d>0]$

$\Rightarrow \quad D=2$

34. $p=5(25-D^2)=5(25-4)=5(21)=105$

35. $q=5(25-d^2)=5(25-1)=120$

Stem II

(Ex. Nos. 36 to 37)

There are two sets A and B each of which consists of three numbers in GP whose product is 64 and R and r are the common ratios such that $R=r+2$. If $\frac{p}{q}=\frac{3}{2}$, where p and q are sum of numbers taken two at a time respectively in the two sets.

Example 36 *The value of q is*

Example 37 *The value of r^R+R^r is*

Sol. (Q. Nos. 36 to 37)

Let $A=\left\{\frac{A}{R}, A, AR\right\}; \quad B=\left\{\frac{a}{r}, a, ar\right\}$

According to the question, $\frac{A}{R} \cdot A \cdot AR = 64$

$$\Rightarrow \quad A^3 = 64 \Rightarrow A = 4 \quad \text{...(i)}$$

$$\frac{a}{r} \cdot a \cdot ar = 64 \Rightarrow a^3 = 64 \Rightarrow a = 4 \quad \text{...(ii)}$$

and $\quad R = r + 2 \quad$ ...(iii)

$$p = \frac{A}{R} \cdot A + A \cdot AR + AR \cdot \frac{A}{R}$$

$$= \frac{A^2}{R} + A^2R + A^2 = \frac{16}{R} + 16R + 16$$

$$q = \frac{a}{r} \cdot a + a \cdot ar + ar \cdot \frac{a}{r}$$

$$= \frac{a^2}{r} + a^2r + a^2 = \frac{16}{r} + 16r + 16$$

Given that $\quad \frac{p}{q} = \frac{3}{2}$

So, $$\frac{(16 + 16R^2 + 16R)\, r}{(16 + 16r^2 + 16r)\, R} = \frac{3}{2}$$

$$\frac{(1 + R^2 + R)\, r}{(1 + r^2 + r)\, R} = \frac{3}{2}$$

From Eq. (iii), $\quad R = r + 2$

$$\Rightarrow \quad \frac{(1 + r^2 + 4 + 4r + r + 2)\, r}{(1 + r + r^2)(r + 2)} = \frac{3}{2}$$

$$\Rightarrow \quad \frac{r^3 + 5r^2 + 7r}{r^3 + 3r^2 + 3r + 2} = \frac{3}{2}$$

$$\Rightarrow \quad r^3 - r^2 - 5r + 6 = 0$$

$$\Rightarrow \quad (r - 2)(r^2 + r - 3) = 0$$

$$\Rightarrow \quad r = 2 \text{ or } r = \frac{-1 \pm \sqrt{13}}{2}$$

So, $\quad R = 4$

36. $q = 16\left(\frac{1}{r} + r + 1\right) = 16\left(\frac{1}{2} + 2 + 1\right) = \frac{16}{2} \times 7 = 8 \times 7 = 56$

37. $r^R + R^r = (4)^2 + (2)^4 = 16 + 16 = 32$

Single Integer Answer Type Questions

Example 38 *A sequence of positive terms $A_1, A_2, A_3, \ldots, A_n$ satisfies the relation $A_{n+1} = \frac{3(1 + A_n)}{(3 + A_n)}$. Least integral value of A_1 for which the sequence is decreasing can be ....*

Sol. (2) $\because \quad A_{n+1} = \frac{3(1 + A_n)}{(3 + A_n)}$.

For $n = 1$, $A_2 = \frac{3(1 + A_1)}{(3 + A_1)}$, for $n = 2$, $A_3 = \frac{3(1 + A_2)}{(3 + A_2)}$

$$= \frac{3\left(1 + \frac{3(1 + A_1)}{(3 + A_1)}\right)}{3 + \frac{3(1 + A_1)}{(3 + A_1)}} = \frac{6 + 4A_1}{4 + 2A_1} = \frac{3 + 2A_1}{2 + A_1}$$

$\because$ Given, sequence can be written as

$$A_1, \frac{3(1 + A_1)}{(3 + A_1)}, \frac{(3 + 2A_1)}{(2 + A_1)}, \ldots$$

Given, $A_1 > 0$ and sequence is decreasing, then

$$A_1 > \frac{3(1 + A_1)}{(3 + A_1)}, \frac{3(1 + A_1)}{(3 + A_1)} > \frac{(3 + 2A_1)}{(2 + A_1)}$$

$$\Rightarrow \quad A_1^2 > 3 \text{ or } A_1 > \sqrt{3}$$

$\therefore \quad A_1 = 2 \quad$ [least integral value of A_1]

Example 39 *When the ninth term of an AP is divided by its second term we get 5 as the quotient, when the thirteenth term is divided by sixth term the quotient is 2 and the remainder is 5, then the second term is ....*

Sol. (7) Let a be the first term and d be the common difference, then $T_9 = 5\, T_2$

$$\Rightarrow \quad (a + 8d) = 5(a + d)$$

$\therefore \quad 4a = 3d \quad$ ...(i)

and $\quad T_{13} = T_6 \times 2 + 5$

$$\Rightarrow \quad a + 12d = 2(a + 5d) + 5$$

$\Rightarrow \quad 2d = a + 5 \quad$ ...(ii)

From Eqs. (i) and (ii), we get

$$a = 3$$

and $\quad d = 4$

$\therefore \quad T_2 = a + d = 7$

Example 40 *Let fourth term of an AP be 6 and mth term be 18. If AP has integral terms only, then the numbers of such AP is ......*

Sol. (9) We have, $\quad a_4 = a + 3d = 6 \quad$ ...(i)

and $\quad a_m = a + (m - 1)\, d = 18$

$\Rightarrow \quad (m - 4)\, d = 12 \quad$ [from Eq. (i)]

Since, terms are integers, we have

$$m - 4 = \pm 1, \pm 2, \pm 3, \pm 4, \pm 6, \pm 12$$

But $m > 0$

$\therefore \quad m - 4 = \pm 1, \pm 2, \pm 3, 4, 6, 12$

So, there are 9 possible values of m.

Example 41 *The difference between the sum of the first k terms of the series $1^3 + 2^3 + 3^3 + \ldots + n^3$ and the sum of the first k terms of the series $1 + 2 + 3 + \ldots + n$ is 1980. The value of k is ......*

Sol. (9) We have,

$$\left(\frac{k(k + 1)}{2}\right)^2 - \frac{k(k + 1)}{2} = 1980$$

$$\Rightarrow \quad \frac{k(k + 1)}{2}\left[\frac{k(k + 1)}{2} - 1\right] = 1980$$

$$\Rightarrow \quad k(k + 1)(k^2 + k - 2) = 1980 \times 4$$

$$\Rightarrow \quad (k - 1)\, k(k + 1)(k + 2) = 11 \times 10 \times 9 \times 8$$

$\therefore \quad k = 9$

Numerical Value Type Questions

Example 42 *The value of the sum*

$$\sum_{i=1}^{20} i\left(\frac{1}{i}+\frac{1}{i+1}+\frac{1}{i+2}+\ldots+\frac{1}{20}\right) \text{ is ......}$$

Sol. (115) Given sum is

$$1\left(\frac{1}{1}+\frac{1}{2}+\frac{1}{3}+\ldots+\frac{1}{20}\right)+2\left(\frac{1}{2}+\frac{1}{3}+\ldots+\frac{1}{20}\right)$$

$$+3\left(\frac{1}{3}+\ldots+\frac{1}{20}\right)+20\left(\frac{1}{20}\right)$$

$$=\frac{1}{1}(1)+\frac{1}{2}(1+2)+\frac{1}{3}(1+2+3)+\ldots$$

$$+\frac{1}{20}(1+2+3+\ldots+20)$$

$$=\sum_{r=1}^{20}\frac{1}{r}\cdot\frac{r(r+1)}{2}=\frac{1+1}{2}+\frac{2+1}{2}+\frac{3+1}{2}+\ldots+\frac{20+1}{2}$$

$$=\frac{1}{2}\left[\frac{20}{2}(4+19)\right]=115$$

Example 43 *Let $a_n = 16, 4, 1, \ldots$ be a GP. Define P_n as the product of the first n terms. The value of $\sum_{n=1}^{\infty}\sqrt[n]{P_n}$ is ......*

Sol. (32) For the GP $a, ar, ar^2, \ldots$

$$P_n=(a)(ar)(ar^2)\ldots(ar^{n-1})=a^n r^{n(n-1)/2}$$

$$\therefore \quad S=\sum_{n=1}^{\infty}\sqrt[n]{P_n}=\sum_{n=1}^{\infty}ar^{(n-1)/2}$$

Now, $\sum_{n=1}^{\infty}ar^{(n-1)/2}=a[1+\sqrt{r}+r+r\sqrt{r}+\ldots\infty]=\dfrac{a}{1-\sqrt{r}}$

Now, $\quad a=16, r=\dfrac{1}{4}$

$$\therefore \quad S=\frac{16}{1-\frac{1}{2}}=32$$

Example 44 *The sides of a right angled triangle are in arithmetic progression. If the triangle has area 24, then what is the length of its smallest side?*

Sol. (6) Let the sides are $a-d$, a and $a+d$. Then, $a(a-d)=48$

and $a^2-2ad+d^2+a^2=a^2+2ad+d^2$ [by Pythagoras theorem]

$\Rightarrow \quad a^2=4ad \Rightarrow a=4d$

Thus, $\quad a=8, d=2$

Hence, $\quad a-d=6$

Example 45 *The sum of 20 terms of the series $1\cdot3^2+2\cdot5^2+3\cdot7^2+\ldots$ is ....*

Sol. (188090) We have,

$$T_n=[n\text{th term of } 1, 2, 3, \ldots]\times[n\text{th terms of } 3, 5, 7, \ldots]^2$$

$$=n(2n+1)^2=n(4n^2+1+4n)=4n^3+4n^2+n$$

$$\therefore \quad S_n=\Sigma T_n=4\,\Sigma n^3+4\Sigma n^2+\Sigma n$$

$$=4\left(\frac{n(n+1)}{2}\right)^2+4\cdot\frac{n(n+1)(2n+1)}{6}+\frac{n(n+1)}{2}$$

$$=n^2(n+1)^2+\frac{2}{3}n(n+1)(2n+1)+\frac{n(n+1)}{2}$$

Thus, $S_{20}=20^2\times21^2+\dfrac{2}{3}\times20\times21\times41+\dfrac{1}{2}\times20\times21$

$$=188090$$

Example 46 *Let a, b, c be positive integer such that $\frac{b}{a}$ is an integer. If a, b, c are in geometric progression and the arithmetic mean of a, b, c is b + 2, then the value of $\dfrac{2(a^2+a-14)}{a+1}$ is ....*

Sol. (8) Since, $\quad \dfrac{a+b+c}{3}=b+2$

$$\Rightarrow \quad a+c=3(b+2)-b$$

$$=2(b+3)$$

Also, a, b, c are in GP.

Let the common ratio be r.

$$\Rightarrow \quad a+ar^2=2(ar+3)$$

$$\Rightarrow \quad a=\frac{6}{1+r^2-2r}$$

$$\Rightarrow \quad a=\frac{6}{(r-1)^2}$$

Since, both a and r will be an integer, so only possible solution is

$$r=2 \text{ and } a=6$$

Now, $\dfrac{2(a^2+a-14)}{a+1}=\dfrac{2(36+6-14)}{7}=2\times4=8$

Matching Type Questions

Example 47 *Match the following columns.*

	Column I		Column II
(A)	If $a_1, a_2, a_3, \ldots$ are in AP and $a_1+a_6+a_{10}+a_{21}+a_{25}+a_{30}=120$, then $\sum_{i=1}^{30}a_i$ is	(p)	400
(B)	If $a_1, a_2, a_3, \ldots$ are in AP and $a_1+a_5+a_9+a_{13}+a_{17}+a_{21}+a_{25}=112$, then $\sum_{i=1}^{25}a_i$ is	(q)	600
(C)	If $a_1, a_2, a_3, \ldots$ are in AP and $a_1+a_4+a_7+a_{10}+a_{13}+a_{16}=375$, then $\sum_{i=1}^{16}a_i$ is	(r)	1260
(D)	If $a_1, a_2, a_3, \ldots$ are in AP and $a_1+a_{10}+a_{15}+a_{16}+a_{21}+a_{30}=252$, then $\sum_{i=1}^{30}a_i$ is	(s)	1000

Sol. (A) → (q); (B) → (p); (C) → (s); (D) → (r)

(A) ∵ $a_1, a_2, a_3, \ldots$ are in AP.

∴ $a_1 + a_{30} = a_6 + a_{25} = a_{10} + a_{21} = \lambda$ [say]

∵ $a_1 + a_6 + a_{10} + a_{21} + a_{25} + a_{30} = 120$

∴ $3\lambda = 120 \Rightarrow \lambda = 40$

Then, $\sum_{i=1}^{30} a_i = \frac{30}{2}(a_1 + a_{30}) = 15 \times \lambda = 15 \times 40 = 600$

(B) ∵ $a_1, a_2, a_3, \ldots$ are in AP.

∴ $a_1 + a_{25} = a_5 + a_{21} = a_9 + a_{17} = a_{13} + a_{13} = \lambda$ [say]

∵ $a_1 + a_5 + a_9 + a_{13} + a_{17} + a_{21} + a_{25} = 112$

∴ $3\lambda + \frac{\lambda}{2} = 112$

⇒ $\frac{7\lambda}{2} = 112 \Rightarrow \lambda = 32$

Then, $\sum_{i=1}^{25} a_i = \frac{25}{2}(a_1 + a_{25}) = \frac{25}{2} \times 32 = 400$

(C) ∵ $a_1, a_2, a_3, \ldots$ are in AP.

∴ $a_1 + a_{16} = a_4 + a_{13} = a_7 + a_{10} = \lambda$ [say]

∵ $a_1 + a_4 + a_7 + a_{10} + a_{13} + a_{16} = 375$

∴ $3\lambda = 375 \Rightarrow \lambda = 125$

Then, $\sum_{i=1}^{16} a_i = \frac{16}{2}(a_1 + a_{16}) = 8 \times \lambda = 8 \times 125 = 1000$

(D) ∵ $a_1, a_2, \ldots$ are in AP.

∴ $a_1 + a_{30} = a_{10} + a_{21} = a_{15} + a_{16} = \lambda$

∵ $a_1 + a_{10} + a_{15} + a_{16} + a_{21} + a_{30} = 252$

⇒ $3\lambda = 252$

⇒ $\lambda = 84$

Then, $\sum_{i=1}^{30} a_i = \frac{30}{2}[a_1 + a_{30}] = 15 \times \lambda$

$= 15 \times 84$

$= 1260$

Example 48 *Match the following columns.*

	Column I		Column II
(A)	If $a > 0, b > 0, c > 0$ and the minimum value of $a(b^2 + c^2) + b(c^2 + a^2) + c(a^2 + b^2)$ is λabc, then λ is	(p)	3
(B)	If a, b, c are positive, $a + b + c = 1$ and the minimum value of $\left(\frac{1}{a} - 1\right)\left(\frac{1}{b} - 1\right)\left(\frac{1}{c} - 1\right)$ is λ, then λ is	(q)	4
(C)	If $a > 0, b > 0, c > 0, s = a + b + c$ and the minimum value of $\frac{2s}{s-a} + \frac{2s}{s-b} + \frac{2s}{s-c}$ is $(\lambda - 1)$, then λ is	(r)	6
(D)	If $a > 0, b > 0, c > 0, a, b, c$ are in GP and the minimum value of $a^3 + b^3 + c^3$ is λabc, then λ is	(s)	8
		(t)	10

Sol. (A) → (r); (B) → (s); (C) → (t); (D) → (p)

(A) ∵ AM ≥ GM

∴ $\frac{ab^2 + ac^2 + bc^2 + ba^2 + ca^2 + cb^2}{6} \geq (ab^2 \cdot ac^2 \cdot bc^2 \cdot ba^2 \cdot ca^2 \cdot cb^2)^{1/6} = abc$

∴ $a(b^2 + c^2) + b(c^2 + a^2) + c(a^2 + b^2) \geq 6\,abc$

⇒ $\lambda = 6$

(B) ∵ AM ≥ GM

For b, c, we get $\frac{(b+c)}{2} \geq \sqrt{bc} \Rightarrow (b+c) \geq 2\sqrt{bc}$ ...(i)

For c, a, we get

$\frac{(c+a)}{2} \geq \sqrt{ca} \Rightarrow (c+a) \geq 2\sqrt{ca}$ ...(ii)

and for a, b, we get

$\frac{(a+b)}{2} \geq \sqrt{ab} \Rightarrow (a+b) \geq 2\sqrt{ab}$ ...(iii)

On multiplying Eqs. (i), (ii) and (iii), we get

$(b+c)(c+a)(a+b) \geq 8abc$

⇒ $(1-a)(1-b)(1-c) \geq 8abc$ [∵ $a + b + c = 1$]

⇒ $\left(\frac{1}{a} - 1\right)\left(\frac{1}{b} - 1\right)\left(\frac{1}{c} - 1\right) \geq 8$

∴ $\lambda = 8$

(C) ∵ AM ≥ HM

$$\frac{(s-a) + (s-b) + (s-c)}{3} \geq \frac{3}{\frac{1}{s-a} + \frac{1}{s-b} + \frac{1}{s-c}}$$

$$\Rightarrow \frac{3s - (a+b+c)}{3} \geq \frac{3}{\frac{1}{s-a} + \frac{1}{s-b} + \frac{1}{s-c}}$$

$$\Rightarrow \frac{3s - s}{3} \geq \frac{3}{\left(\frac{1}{s-a} + \frac{1}{s-b} + \frac{1}{s-c}\right)}$$

$$\Rightarrow \frac{2s}{s-a} + \frac{2s}{s-b} + \frac{2s}{s-c} \geq 9$$

Here, $\lambda - 1 = 9$

∴ $\lambda = 10$

(D) Since, AM ≥ GM

∴ $\frac{a^3 + b^3 + c^3}{3} \geq (a^3 b^3 c^3)^{\frac{1}{3}}$

$\Rightarrow a^3 + b^3 + c^3 \geq 3abc$

⇒ $\lambda = 3$

EXERCISE 1

JEE Main Pattern

Single Option Correct Type Questions

1. If the terms $\sqrt{a-x}, \sqrt{x}, \sqrt{a+x}$ are in AP, all are integrals, where $a, x > 0$, then the least composite value of a is

(a) 19 (b) 20 (c) 21 (d) 22

2. The value of $0.2^{\log_{\sqrt{5}}\left(\frac{1}{4}+\frac{1}{8}+\frac{1}{16}+\dots\right)}$ is

(a) 4 (b) log 4
(c) log 2 (d) None of these

3. If $x, 2y, 3z$ are in AP, where the distinct numbers x, y, z are in GP, then the common ratio of the GP is

(a) 3 (b) $\frac{1}{3}$ (c) 2 (d) $\frac{1}{4}$

4. The sum of an infinite GP is 57 and the sum of their cubes is 9747, then the common ratio of the GP is

(a) $\frac{1}{3}$ (b) $\frac{2}{3}$
(c) $\frac{1}{6}$ (d) None of these

5. The 15th term of the series $2\frac{1}{2}+1\frac{7}{13}+1\frac{1}{9}+\frac{20}{23}+\dots$ is

(a) $\frac{10}{39}$ (b) $\frac{10}{21}$
(c) $\frac{10}{23}$ (d) None of these

6. If $a^2+b^2, ab+bc$ and b^2+c^2 are in GP, then a, b, c are in

(a) AP (b) GP
(c) HP (d) None of these

7. If $1-\frac{1}{3}+\frac{1}{5}-\frac{1}{7}+\frac{1}{9}-\frac{1}{11}+\dots=\frac{\pi}{4}$, then the value of $\frac{1}{1\times 3}+\frac{1}{5\times 7}+\frac{1}{9\times 11}+\dots$ is

(a) $\frac{\pi}{8}$ (b) $\frac{\pi}{6}$ (c) $\frac{\pi}{4}$ (d) $\frac{\pi}{36}$

8. If S_n denotes the sum of first n terms of an AP and $\frac{S_{3n}-S_{n-1}}{S_{2n}-S_{2n-1}}=31$, then the value of n is

(a) 21 (b) 15
(c) 16 (d) 19

9. Consider the ten numbers $ar, ar^2, ar^3, \dots, ar^{10}$. If their sum is 18 and the sum of their reciprocal is 6, then the product of these ten numbers is

(a) 81 (b) 243 (c) 343 (d) 324

10. The minimum value of $\frac{x^4+y^4+z^2}{xyz}$ for positive real numbers x, y, z is

(a) $\sqrt{2}$ (b) $2\sqrt{2}$ (c) $4\sqrt{2}$ (d) $8\sqrt{2}$

11. $\frac{1\times 2}{3!}+\frac{2\times 2^2}{4!}+\frac{3\times 2^3}{5!}+\dots+\frac{20\times 2^{20}}{22!}=$

(a) $\frac{2^{21}}{22!}$ (b) $1-\frac{2^{21}}{22!}$ (c) $\frac{2^{22}}{22!}$ (d) $1-\frac{2^{22}}{22!}$

12. If the numbers x, y, z are in HP, then $\frac{\sqrt{yz}}{\sqrt{y}+\sqrt{z}}, \frac{\sqrt{xz}}{\sqrt{x}+\sqrt{z}}, \frac{\sqrt{xy}}{\sqrt{x}+\sqrt{y}}$ are in

(a) AP (b) GP
(c) HP (d) None of these

13. If $a_1, a_2, \dots$ are in HP and $f_k=\sum_{r=1}^{n} a_r - a_k$, then $2^{\alpha_1}, 2^{\alpha_2}, 2^{\alpha_3}, 2^{\alpha_4}, \dots$ are in $\left\{\text{where } \alpha_1=\frac{a_1}{f_1}, \alpha_2=\frac{a_2}{f_2}, \alpha_3=\frac{a_3}{f_3}, \dots\right\}$

(a) AP (b) GP
(c) HP (d) None of these

14. Let S_n $(1\le n\le 9)$ denotes the sum of n terms of the series $1+22+333+\dots+\underbrace{999\dots9}_{9\text{ times}}$, then for $2\le n\le 9$

(a) $S_n-S_{n-1}=\frac{1}{9}(10^n-n^2+n)$ (b) $S_n=\frac{1}{9}(10^n-n^2+2n-2)$
(c) $9(S_n-S_{n-1})=n(10^n-1)$ (d) None of these

15. If a, b, c are in GP, then the equations

$$ax^2+2bx+c=0 \text{ and } dx^2+2ex+f=0$$

have a common root, if $\frac{d}{a}, \frac{e}{b}, \frac{f}{c}$ are in

(a) AP (b) GP
(c) HP (d) None of these

16. Sum of the first n terms of the series

$\frac{1}{2}+\frac{3}{4}+\frac{7}{8}+\frac{15}{16}+\ldots$ is equal to

(a) 2^n-n-1 (b) $1-2^{-n}$ (c) $n+2^{-n}-1$ (d) 2^n-1

17. If in a ΔPQR, $\sin P, \sin Q, \sin R$ are in AP, then

(a) the altitudes are in AP (b) the altitudes are in HP
(c) the medians are in GP (d) the medians are in AP

18. Let $a_1, a_2, \ldots, a_{10}$ be in AP and $h_1, h_2, \ldots, h_{10}$ be in HP. If $a_1=h_1=2$ and $a_{10}=h_{10}=3$, then a_4h_7 is

(a) 2 (b) 3 (c) 5 (d) 6

19. If $I_n=\int_0^\pi \frac{1-\sin 2nx}{1-\cos 2x}dx$, then $I_1, I_2, I_3, \ldots$ are in

(a) AP (b) GP
(c) HP (d) None of these

20. If $a(b-c)x^2+b(c-a)xy+c(a-b)y^2$ is a perfect square, the quantities a, b, c are in

(a) AP (b) GP
(c) HP (d) None of these

21. The sum to infinity of the series,

$1+2\left(1-\frac{1}{n}\right)+3\left(1-\frac{1}{n}\right)^2+\ldots$ is

(a) n^2 (b) $n(n+1)$
(c) $n\left(1+\frac{1}{n}\right)^2$ (d) None of these

22. If $\log_3 2, \log_3(2^x-5)$ and $\log_3\left(2^x-\frac{7}{2}\right)$ are in AP, x is equal to

(a) 2 (b) 3 (c) 4 (d) 2, 3

23. Let a, b, c be three positive prime numbers. The progression in which $\sqrt{a}, \sqrt{b}, \sqrt{c}$ can be three terms (not necessarily consecutive), is

(a) AP (b) GP
(c) HP (d) None of these

24. If n is an odd integer greater than or equal to 1, the value of $n^3-(n-1)^3+(n-2)^3-\ldots+(-1)^{n-1}1^3$ is

(a) $\frac{(n+1)^2(2n-1)}{4}$ (b) $\frac{(n-1)^2(2n-1)}{4}$
(c) $\frac{(n+1)^2(2n+1)}{4}$ (d) None of these

Numerical Value Type Questions

25. The 5th and 8th terms of a GP of real numbers are 7! and 8! respectively. If the sum of first n terms of the GP is 2205, then the value of n is ......

26. If $a^{2008}-2a+1=0$ and $S=1+a+a^2+\ldots+a^{2007}$, then the value of S is ......

27. If $a, b>0$ such that $a^3+b^3=2$, then minimum value of $a+b$ is ......

28. Let a, b, c be positive integers such that $\frac{b}{a}$ is an integer. If a, b, c are in GP and AM of a, b, c is $b+2$, then the value of $\frac{a^2+a-14}{a+1}$ is ......

29. The sides of a right angled triangle are in AP. If the area of triangle is 24, then the length of its smallest side is ......

30. if $a, b, c, d \in R^+-\{1\}$, then the minimum value of $\log_d a+\log_b d+\log_a c+\log_c b$ is ......

31. If AM between two positive numbers exceeds their GM by 2 and the GM exceeds their HM by $\frac{8}{5}$, then the HCF of the numbers is ......

32. The value of $9^{\frac{1}{3}+\frac{1}{9}+\frac{1}{27}+\ldots\infty}$ is ......

33. If $1+\frac{4}{7}+\frac{9}{49}+\frac{16}{343}+\ldots\infty$ is equal to $\frac{7^\alpha}{3^\beta}$, then $\alpha+\beta$ is equal to ......

34. Let $a+ar_1+ar_1^2+\ldots\infty$ and $a+ar_2+ar_2^2+\ldots\infty$ be two infinite series of positive numbers with the same first term. The sum of the first series is r_1 and the sum of the second series is r_2. Then the value of (r_1+r_2) is ......

35. For $a, b>0$, let $5a-b, 2a+b, a+2b$ be in AP and $(b+1)^2, ab+1, (a-1)^2$ are in GP, then the value of $(a^{-1}+b^{-1})$ is ......

36. The least value of $\frac{4x^2+8x+13}{6(1+x)}$, $x\geq 0$, is ......

37. If $S=1+\left(1+\frac{1}{5}\right)\left(\frac{1}{2}\right)+\left(1+\frac{1}{5}+\frac{1}{5^2}\right)\left(\frac{1}{2^2}\right)+\ldots\infty$, then the value of $\frac{20}{S}$ is equal to ......

38. The harmonic mean H between two numbers a and b is $\frac{21}{5}$, their AM 'A' and GM 'G' satisfy the relation $3A+G^2=36$. Then the value of (a^2+b^2-51) is ......

39. The first and second terms of a GP are x^{-4} and x^n respectively. If x^{52} is the 8th term, then the value of n is ......

Previous Year Questions

40. A software company sets up m number of computer systems to finish an assignment in 17 days. If 4 computer systems crashed on the start of the second day, 4 more computer systems crashed on the start of the third day and so on, then it took 8 more days to finish the assignment. The value of m is equal to **[Single Correct Type, 2024 Main]**

(a) 125 (b) 180 (c) 160 (d) 150

41. For $x \geq 0$, the least value of K, for which $4^{1+x} + 4^{1-x}$, $\frac{K}{2}$, $16^x + 16^{-x}$ are three consecutive terms of an AP, is equal to **[Single Correct Type, 2024 Main]**

(a) 10 (b) 16 (c) 4 (d) 8

42. Let S_n denote the sum of the first n terms of an arithmetic progression. If $S_{10} = 390$ and the ratio of the tenth and the fifth terms is 15 : 7, then $S_{15} - S_5$ is equal to **[Single Correct Type, 2024 Main]**

(a) 690 (b) 790 (c) 890 (d) 800

43. The number of common terms in the progressions 4, 9, 14, 19, ..., up to 25th term and 3, 6, 9, 12, ..., up to 37th term is **[Single Correct Type, 2024 Main]**

(a) 5 (b) 8 (c) 9 (d) 7

44. If in a GP of 64 terms, the sum of all the terms is 7times the sum of the odd terms of the GP, then the common ratio of the GP is equal to **[Single Correct Type, 2024 Main]**

(a) 7 (b) 6 (c) 5 (d) 4

45. If a function f satisfies $f(m+n) = f(m) + f(n)$ for all m, $n \in N$ and $f(1) = 1$, then the largest natural number λ such that $\sum_{k=1}^{2022} f(\lambda + k) \leq (2022)^2$ is equal to .... **[Numerical Value Type, 2024 Main]**

46. Let $a_1, a_2, a_3, \ldots$ be a GP of increasing positive numbers. Let the sum of its 6th and 8th terms be 2 and the product of its 3rd and 5th terms be $\frac{1}{9}$. Then, $6(a_2 + a_4)(a_4 + a_6)$ is equal to **[Single Correct Type, 2023 Main]**

(a) $2\sqrt{2}$ (b) 3 (c) $3\sqrt{3}$ (d) 2

47. Let the first term a and the common ratio r of a geometric progression be positive integers. If the sum of squares of its first three terms is 33033, then the sum of these three terms is equal to **[Single Correct Type, 2023 Main]**

(a) 210 (b) 220
(c) 231 (d) 241

48. Let A_1 and A_2 be two arithmetic means and G_1, G_2, G_3 be three geometric means of two distinct positive numbers. Then, $G_1^4 + G_2^4 + G_3^4 + G_1^2 G_3^2$ is equal to **[Single Correct Type, 2023 Main]**

(a) $(A_1 + A_2)^2 G_1 G_3$ (b) $2(A_1 + A_2) G_1^2 G_3^2$
(c) $(A_1 + A_2) G_1^2 G_3^2$ (d) $2(A_1 + A_2) G_1 G_3$

49. Let $0 < z < y < x$ be three real numbers such that $\frac{1}{x}, \frac{1}{y}, \frac{1}{z}$ are in an arithmetic progression and $x, \sqrt{2y}, z$ are in a geometric progression. If $xy + yz + zx = \frac{3}{\sqrt{2}} xyz$, then $3(x+y+z)^2$ is equal to .... **[Numerical Value Type, 2023 Main]**

50. Let α, β and γ be three positive real numbers. Let $f(x) = \alpha x^5 + \beta x^3 + \gamma x$, $x \in R$ and $g : R \to R$ be such that $g(f(x)) = x$ for all $x \in R$. If $a_1, a_2, a_3, \ldots\ldots a_n$ be in arithmetic progression with mean zero, then the value of $f\left(g\left(\frac{1}{n}\sum_{i=1}^{n} f(a_i)\right)\right)$ is equal to **[Single Correct Type, 2022 Main]**

(a) 0 (b) 3 (c) 9 (d) 27

51. For p and $q \in R$, consider the real valued function $f(x) = (x-p)^2 - q$, $x \in R$ and $q > 0$, let a_1, a_2, a_3 and a_4 be in an arithmetic progression with mean p and positive common difference. If $|f(a_i)| = 500$ for all $i = 1, 2, 3$ and 4, then the absolute difference between the roots of $f(x) = 0$ is .... **[Numerical Value Type, 2022 Main]**

52. If $x, y \in R$, $x > 0$, $y = \log_{10} x + \log_{10} x^{1/3} + \log_{10} x^{1/9} + \ldots$ upto ∞ terms and $\frac{2+4+6+\ldots+2y}{3+6+9+\ldots+3y} = \frac{4}{\log_{10} x}$, then the ordered pair (x, y) is equal to **[Single Correct Type, 2021 Main]**

(a) $(10^6, 6)$ (b) $(10^6, 9)$ (c) $(10^2, 3)$ (d) $(10^4, 6)$

53. In an increasing geometric series, the sum of the second and the sixth term is 25 / 2 and the product of the third and fifth term is 25. Then, the sum of 4th, 6th and 8th terms is equal to **[Single Correct Type, 2021 Main]**

(a) 30 (b) 26 (c) 35 (d) 32

54. If $|x| < 1, |y| < 1$ and $x \neq y$, then the sum to infinity of the following series $(x+y) + (x^2 + xy + y^2) + (x^3 + x^2 y + xy^2 + y^3) + \ldots$ is **[Single Correct Type, 2020 Main]**

(a) $\frac{x+y+xy}{(1+x)(1+y)}$ (b) $\frac{x+y-xy}{(1-x)(1-y)}$
(c) $\frac{x+y+xy}{(1-x)(1-y)}$ (d) $\frac{x+y-xy}{(1+x)(1+y)}$

55. If m arithmetic means (AM's) and three geometric means (GMs) are inserted between 3 and 243 such that 4th AM is equal to 2nd GM, then m is equal to .... **[Numerical Value Type, 2024 Main]**

EXERCISE 2
JEE Advanced Pattern

Single Option Correct Type Questions

1. The number of terms of an AP is even; the sum of the odd terms is 24, and of the even terms is 30, and the last term exceeds the first by $\frac{21}{2}$, then the number of terms in the series is
(a) 8 (b) 4
(c) 6 (d) 10

2. If a, b and c are in AP and $b-a$, $c-b$ and a are in GP, then $a:b:c$ is
(a) $1:2:3$ (b) $1:3:5$
(c) $2:3:4$ (d) $1:2:4$

3. ABC is a right-angled triangle in which $\angle B = 90°$ and $BC = a$. In n points $L_1, L_2, \dots, L_n$ on AB is divided in $(n+1)$ equal parts and $L_1M_1, L_2M_2, \dots, L_nM_n$ are line segments parallel to BC and $M_1, M_2, \dots, M_n$ are on AC, then the sum of the lengths of $L_1M_1, L_2M_2, \dots, L_nM_n$ is
(a) $\frac{a(n+1)}{2}$ (b) $\frac{a(n-1)}{2}$
(c) $\frac{an}{2}$ (d) None of these

4. The sum of 20 terms of a series of which every even term is 2 times the term before it and every odd term is 3 times the term before it, the first term being unity is
(a) $\left(\frac{2}{7}\right)(6^{10}-1)$ (b) $\frac{3}{7}(6^{10}-1)$
(c) $\frac{3}{5}(6^{10}-1)$ (d) None of these

5. If the sides of a right angled triangle form an AP, the sines of the acute angles are
(a) $\frac{3}{5}, \frac{4}{5}$ (b) $\sqrt{3}, \frac{1}{3}$
(c) $\sqrt{\frac{\sqrt{5}-1}{2}}, \sqrt{\frac{\sqrt{5}+1}{2}}$ (d) $\frac{\sqrt{3}}{2}, \frac{1}{2}$

6. The sixth term of an AP is equal to 2. The value of the common difference of the AP which makes the product $a_1 a_4 a_5$ least, is given by
(a) $\frac{8}{5}$ (b) $\frac{5}{4}$
(c) $\frac{2}{3}$ (d) None of these

7. If the arithmetic progression whose common difference is non-zero, the sum of first $3n$ terms is equal to the sum of the next n terms. The ratio of the sum of the first $2n$ terms to the next $2n$ terms is
(a) $\frac{1}{5}$ (b) $\frac{2}{3}$
(c) $\frac{3}{4}$ (d) None of these

8. The coefficient of x^{n-2} in the polynomial $(x-1)(x-2)(x-3)\dots(x-n)$, is
(a) $\frac{n(n^2+2)(3n+1)}{24}$ (b) $\frac{n(n^2-1)(3n+2)}{24}$
(c) $\frac{n(n^2+1)(3n+4)}{24}$ (d) None of these

9. Consider the pattern shown below
Row 1 1
Row 2 3 5
Row 3 7 9 11
Row 4 13 15 17, 19, etc.
The number at the end of row 60 is
(a) 3659 (b) 3519
(c) 3681 (d) 3731

10. Let a_n be the nth term of an AP. If $\sum_{r=1}^{100} a_{2r} = \alpha$ and $\sum_{r=1}^{100} a_{2r-1} = \beta$, the common difference of the AP is
(a) $\alpha - \beta$ (b) $\beta - \alpha$
(c) $\frac{\alpha - \beta}{2}$ (d) None of these

11. If a_1, a_2, a_3, a_4, a_5 are in HP, then $a_1a_2 + a_2a_3 + a_3a_4 + a_4a_5$ is equal to
(a) $2a_1a_5$ (b) $3a_1a_5$ (c) $4a_1a_5$ (d) $6a_1a_5$

12. If a, b, c and d are four positive real numbers such that $abcd = 1$, the minimum value of $(1+a)(1+b)(1+c)(1+d)$ is
(a) 1 (b) 4 (c) 16 (d) 64

13. If a, b, c are in AP and $(a+2b-c)(2b+c-a)(c+a-b) = \lambda abc$, then λ is
(a) 1 (b) 2
(c) 4 (d) None of these

14. If $a_1, a_2, a_3, \dots$ are in GP with first term a and common ratio r, then

$\frac{a_1 a_2}{a_1^2 - a_2^2} + \frac{a_2 a_3}{a_2^2 - a_3^2} + \frac{a_3 a_4}{a_3^2 - a_4^2} + \dots + \frac{a_{n-1} a_n}{a_{n-1}^2 - a_n^2}$ is equal to

(a) $\frac{nr}{1 - r^2}$ (b) $\frac{(n-1) r}{1 - r^2}$ (c) $\frac{nr}{1 - r}$ (d) $\frac{(n-1) r}{1 - r}$

15. The sum of the first ten terms of an AP is four times the sum of the first five terms, the ratio of the first term to the common difference is

(a) $\frac{1}{2}$ (b) 2 (c) $\frac{1}{4}$ (d) 4

16. If $\cos (x - y)$, $\cos x$ and $\cos (x + y)$ are in HP, the $\cos x \sec \left(\frac{y}{2}\right)$ is equal to

(a) $\pm \sqrt{2}$ (b) $\frac{1}{\sqrt{2}}$

(c) $-\frac{1}{\sqrt{2}}$ (d) None of these

17. If 11 AM's are inserted between 28 and 10, the number of integral AM's is

(a) 5 (b) 6 (c) 7 (d) 8

18. If x, y, z are in GP $(x, y, z > 1)$, then $\frac{1}{2x + \ln x}, \frac{1}{4x + \ln y}, \frac{1}{6x + \ln z}$ are in

(a) AP (b) GP

(c) HP (d) None of these

19. The minimum value of the quantity $\frac{(a^2 + 3a + 1)(b^2 + 3b + 1)(c^2 + 3c + 1)}{abc}$, where $a, b, c \in R^+$, is

(a) $\frac{11^3}{2^3}$ (b) 125 (c) 25 (d) 27

20. Let $a_1, a_2, \dots$ be in AP and $q_1, q_2, \dots$ be in GP. If $a_1 = q_1 = 2$ and $a_{10} = q_{10} = 3$, then

(a) $a_7 q_{19}$ is not an integer (b) $a_{19} q_7$ is an integer

(c) $a_7 q_{19} = a_{19} q_{10}$ (d) None of these

More than One Correct Option Type Questions

21. In an AP whose first term is α and common difference is β; $\alpha, \beta \neq 0$, the ratio r of the sum of the first n terms to the sum of n terms succeeding them, does not depend on n. Then, which of the following is/are correct?

(a) $\alpha : \beta = 2 : 1$.

(b) If α and β are roots of the equation $ax^2 + bx + c = 0$, then $2b^2 = 9ac$.

(c) The sum of infinite GP, $1 + r + r^2 + \dots$ is $\frac{3}{2}$.

(d) If $\alpha = 1$, then sum of 10 terms of AP is 100.

22. For the series, $S = 1 + \frac{1}{1+3}(1+2)^2 + \frac{1}{1+3+5}(1+2+3)^2 + \frac{1}{1+3+5+7}(1+2+3+4)^2 + \dots$

(a) $a_7 = 16$ (b) $a_7 = 18$

(c) $S_{10} = \frac{505}{4}$ (d) $S_{10} = \frac{405}{4}$

23. If $\frac{1}{a}, \frac{1}{b}, \frac{1}{c}$ are in AP and $a, b, -2c$ are in GP, where a, b, c are non-zero, then

(a) $a^3 + b^3 + c^3 = 3abc$

(b) $-2a, b, -2c$ are in AP

(c) $a^2, b^2, 4c^2$ are in GP

(d) Roots of equation $ax^2 + bx + c$ are real

24. If $\frac{1}{b-a} + \frac{1}{b-c} = \frac{1}{a} + \frac{1}{c}$, then

(a) a, b, c are in HP (b) a, b, c are in AP

(c) $b = a + c$ (d) $3a = b + c$

25. If $a(n) = 1 + \frac{1}{2} + \frac{1}{3} + \frac{1}{4} + \dots + \frac{1}{2^n - 1}$, then

(a) $a(100) < 100$ (b) $a(100) > 100$

(c) $a(200) > 100$ (d) $a(200) < 100$

26. If the first and $(2n - 1)$ th term of an AP, GP and HP are equal and their nth terms are a, b and c respectively, then

(a) $a = b = c$ (b) $a \geq b \geq c$

(c) $a + c = b$ (d) $ac - b^2 = 0$

27. For $0 < \phi < \frac{\pi}{2}$, if $x = \sum_{n=0}^{\infty} \cos^{2n} \phi$, $y = \sum_{n=0}^{\infty} \sin^{2n} \phi$ and $z = \sum_{n=0}^{\infty} \cos^{2n} \phi \sin^{2n} \phi$, then

(a) $xyz = xz + y$ (b) $xyz = xy + z$

(c) $xyz = x + y + z$ (d) $xyz = yz + x$

28. If a, b, c are in AP and a^2, b^2, c^2 are in HP, then which of the following could hold true?

(a) $-\frac{a}{2}, b, c$ are in GP (b) $a = b = c$

(c) a^3, b^3, c^3 are in GP (d) None of these

29. If the sum of n consecutive odd numbers is $25^2 - 11^2$, then

(a) $n = 14$ (b) $n = 16$

(c) first odd number is 23 (d) last odd number is 49

30. The GM of two positive numbers is 6. Their AM is A and HM is H satisfy the equation $90A + 5H = 918$, then A may be equal to

(a) $\frac{1}{5}$ (b) 5 (c) $\frac{5}{2}$ (d) 10

31. If the sum to n terms of the series

$$\frac{1}{1\cdot3\cdot5\cdot7}+\frac{1}{3\cdot5\cdot7\cdot9}+\frac{1}{5\cdot7\cdot9\cdot11}+\ldots \text{ is } \frac{1}{90}-\frac{\lambda}{f(n)}, \text{ then}$$

(a) $f(0)=15$ (b) $f(1)=105$

(c) $f(\lambda)=\frac{640}{27}$ (d) $\lambda=\frac{1}{3}$

32. Let $E=\frac{1}{1^2}+\frac{1}{2^2}+\frac{1}{3^2}+\ldots$, then

(a) $E<\frac{3}{2}$ (b) $E>\frac{3}{2}$

(c) $E<2$ (d) $E>2$

33. Let S_n $(n\geq 1)$ be a sequence of sets defined by

$$S_1=\{0\}, S_2=\left\{\frac{3}{2},\frac{5}{2}\right\}, S_3=\left\{\frac{8}{3},\frac{11}{3},\frac{14}{3}\right\},$$

$$S_4=\left\{\frac{15}{4},\frac{19}{4},\frac{23}{4},\frac{27}{4}\right\}, \ldots, \text{ then}$$

(a) third element in S_{20} is $\frac{439}{20}$

(b) third element in S_{20} is $\frac{431}{20}$

(c) sum of the elements in S_{20} is 589

(d) sum of the elements in S_{20} is 609

34. Let a sequence $\{a_n\}$ be defined by

$$a_n=\frac{1}{n+1}+\frac{1}{n+2}+\frac{1}{n+3}+\ldots+\frac{1}{3n}, \text{ then}$$

(a) $a_2=\frac{11}{12}$

(b) $a_2=\frac{19}{20}$

(c) $a_{n+1}-a_n=\frac{(9n+5)}{(3n+1)(3n+2)(3n+3)}$

(d) $a_{n+1}-a_n=\frac{-2}{3(n+1)}$

35. Let $S_n(x)=\left(x^{n-1}+\frac{1}{x^{n-1}}\right)+2\left(x^{n-2}+\frac{1}{x^{n-2}}\right)+\ldots$

$+(n-1)\left(x+\frac{1}{x}\right)+n$, then

(a) $S_1(x)=1$ (b) $S_1(x)=x+\frac{1}{x}$

(c) $S_{100}(x)=\frac{1}{x^{99}}\left(\frac{x^{100}-1}{x-1}\right)^2$ (d) $S_{100}(x)=\frac{1}{x^{100}}\left(\frac{x^{100}-1}{x-1}\right)^2$

36. All the terms of an AP are natural numbers and the sum of the first 20 terms is greater than 1072 and less than 1162. If the sixth term is 32, then

(a) first term is 7

(b) first term is 12

(c) common difference is 4

(d) common difference is 5

Passage Based Questions

Passage I

(Q. Nos. 37 to 38)

- S_n be the sum of n terms of the series $\frac{8}{5}+\frac{16}{65}+\frac{24}{325}+\ldots$

37. The value of $\lim_{n\to\infty} S_n$ is

(a) 0 (b) $\frac{1}{2}$ (c) 2 (d) 4

38. The value of S_8, is

(a) $\frac{288}{145}$ (b) $\frac{1088}{545}$ (c) $\frac{81}{41}$ (d) $\frac{107}{245}$

Passage II

(Q. Nos. 39 to 40)

- Two consecutive numbers from 1, 2, 3, ..., n are removed. The arithmetic mean of the remaining numbers is $\frac{105}{4}$.

39. The value of n lies in

(a) (41, 51) (b) (52, 62) (c) (63, 73) (d) (74, 84)

40. The removed numbers

(a) are less than 10 (b) lies between 10 to 30

(c) lies between 30 to 70 (d) greater than 70

Passage III

(Q. Nos. 41 to 42)

Suppose α, β *are roots of* $ax^2+bx+c=0$ *and* γ, δ *are roots of* $Ax^2+Bx+C=0$.

41. If $\alpha, \beta, \gamma, \delta$ are in AP, then common difference of AP is

(a) $\frac{1}{4}\left(\frac{b}{a}-\frac{B}{A}\right)$ (b) $\frac{1}{3}\left(\frac{b}{a}-\frac{B}{A}\right)$

(c) $\frac{1}{2}\left(\frac{c}{a}-\frac{B}{A}\right)$ (d) $\frac{1}{3}\left(\frac{c}{a}-\frac{C}{A}\right)$

42. If a, b, c are in GP as well as $\alpha, \beta, \gamma, \delta$ are in GP, then A, B, C are in

(a) AP only (b) GP only

(c) AP and GP (d) None of these

Passage IV

(Q. Nos. 43 to 44)

- Suppose p is the first of $n (n>1)$ arithmetic means between two positive numbers a and b and q the first of n harmonic means between the same two numbers.

43. The value of p is

(a) $\frac{na+b}{n+1}$ (b) $\frac{nb+a}{n+1}$ (c) $\frac{na-b}{n+1}$ (d) $\frac{nb-a}{n+1}$

44. The value of q is

(a) $\frac{(n-1)ab}{nb+a}$

(b) $\frac{(n+1)ab}{nb+a}$

(c) $\frac{(n+1)ab}{na+b}$

(d) $\frac{(n-1)ab}{na+b}$

Stem Based Questions

Stem I

(Q. Nos. 45 to 46)

- The numbers 1, 3, 6, 10, 15, 21, 28, ... are called triangular numbers. Let t_n denotes the nth triangular number such that $t_n = t_{n-1} + n, \forall n \ge 2$.

45. The value of t_{50} is ....

46. The number of positive integers lying between t_{100} and t_{101} are ....

Stem II

(Q. Nos. 47 to 48)

- Let $A_1, A_2, A_3, \ldots, A_m$ be arithmetic means between -3 and 828 and $G_1, G_2, G_3, \ldots, G_n$ be geometric means between 1 and 2187. Product of geometric means is 3^{35} and sum of arithmetic means is 14025.

47. The value of n is ....

48. The value of m is ....

Single Integer Type Questions

49. Let a, b, c, d be positive real numbers with $a < b < c < d$. Given that a, b, c, d are the first four terms of an AP and a, b, d are in GP. The value of $\frac{ad}{bc}$ is $\frac{p}{q}$, where p and q are prime numbers, then the value of q is ......

50. If the coefficient of x in the expansion of $\prod_{r=1}^{110}(1+rx)$ is $\lambda(1+10)(1+10+10^2)$, then the value of λ is ......

51. A 3-digit palindrome is a 3-digit number (not starting with zero) which reads the same backwards as forwards *For example*, 242. The sum of all even 3-digit palindromes is $2^{n_1} \cdot 3^{n_2} \cdot 5^{n_3} \cdot 7^{n_4} \cdot 11^{n_5}$, value of $n_1 + n_2 + n_3 + n_4 + n_5$ is ......

52. If n is a positive integer satisfying the equation $2 + (6 \cdot 2^2 - 4 \cdot 2) + (6 \cdot 3^2 - 4 \cdot 3) + \ldots + (6 \cdot n^2 - 4 \cdot n) = 140$, then the value of n is ......

53. Let $S(x) = 1 + x - x^2 - x^3 + x^4 + x^5 - x^6 - x^7 + \ldots + \infty$, where $0 < x < 1$. If $S(x) = \frac{\sqrt{2}+1}{2}$, then the value of $(x+1)^2$ is ......

Numerical Value Type Questions

54. The sequence $a_1, a_2, a_3, \ldots$ is a geometric sequence with common ratio r. The sequence $b_1, b_2, b_3, \ldots$ is also a geometric sequence. If $b_1 = 1, b_2 = \sqrt[4]{7} - \sqrt[4]{28} + 1, a_1 = \sqrt[4]{28}$ and $\sum_{n=1}^{\infty} \frac{1}{a_n} = \sum_{n=1}^{\infty} b_n$, then the value of $(1 + r^2 + r^4)^2$ is ....

55. Let (a_1, b_1) and (a_2, b_2) are the pair of real numbers such that 10, a, b, ab constitute an arithmetic progression. Then, the value of $\left(\frac{2a_1a_2 + b_1b_2}{100}\right)$ is ......

56. If one root of $Ax^3 + Bx^2 + Cx + D = 0$, $A \ne 0$, is the arithmetic mean of the other two roots, then the relation $2B^3 + \lambda ABC + \mu A^2 D = 0$ holds good. Then, the value of $2\lambda + \mu^2$ is ......

57. If $|x| > 1$, then sum of the series $\frac{1}{1+x} + \frac{2}{1+x^2} + \frac{2^2}{1+x^4} + \frac{2^3}{1+x^8} + \ldots$ upto ∞ is $\frac{1}{x-\lambda}$, then the value of 10λ is ....

58. Three non-zero real numbers form an AP and the squares of these numbers taken in same order form a GP. If the possible common ratios are $(3 \pm \sqrt{k})$, where $k \in N$, then the value of $\left[\frac{k^2}{3}\right]$ is ......

(where [ ] denotes the greatest integer function).

59. Let a, b, c, d be four distinct real numbers in AP. Then, the smallest positive value of k satisfying

$2(a-b) + k(b-c)^2 + (c-a)^3$
$= 2(a-d) + (b-d)^2 + (c-d)^3$ is ......

60. A person drops a ball from an 80 m tall building and each time the ball bounces, it rebounds to $x\%$ of its previous height. If the ball travels a total distance of 320 m, then the value of x is ......

61. Let S_k be sum of an infinite GP whose first term is k and common ratio is $\frac{1}{k+1}$. Then $\sum_{k=1}^{10} S_k$ is equal to ......

Matching Type Questions

62. Match the following columns.

Column I		Column II	
(A)	a, b, c, d are in AP, then	(p)	$a+d>b+c$
(B)	a, b, c, d are in GP, then	(q)	$ad>bc$
(C)	a, b, c, d are in HP, then	(r)	$\frac{1}{a}+\frac{1}{d}>\frac{1}{b}+\frac{1}{c}$
(D)	$\frac{1}{a}, \frac{1}{b}, \frac{1}{c}, \frac{1}{d}$ are in GP, then	(s)	$ad=bc$

63. Match the following columns.

Column I		Column II	
(A)	For an AP $a_1, a_2, a_3, \ldots, a_n, \ldots$; $a_1=\frac{5}{2}$; $a_{10}=16$. If $a_1+a_2+\ldots+a_n=110$, then 'n' equals	(p)	9
(B)	The interior angles of a convex non-equiangular polygon of 9 sides are in AP. The least positive integer that limits the upper value of the common difference between the measures of the angles in degrees is	(q)	10
(C)	For an increasing GP, $a_1, a_2, a_3, \ldots, a_n, \ldots$; $a_6=4a_4$; $a_9-a_7=192$, if $a_4+a_5+a_6+\ldots+a_n=1016$, then n equals	(r)	11
(D)	If α and β are roots of the equation $x^2-8x+4=0$ and $\alpha, a_1, a_2, \ldots, a_5, \beta$ in GP, then $\sum_{i=1}^{5}\log_2 a_i$ equal to	(s)	5

64. Match the following columns.

Column I		Column II	
(A)	The sequence $a, b, 10, c, d$ is an arithmetic progression, then the value of $a+b+c+d$ is	(p)	10
(B)	The sides of right triangle form a three term geometric sequence. The shortest side has length 2. The length of the hypotenuse is of the form $a+\sqrt{b}$, where $a\in N$ and $\sqrt{b}$ is surd, then a^2+b^2 equals	(q)	20
(C)	The sum of first three consecutive numbers of an infinite GP is 70. If the two extremes be multiplied each by 4 and the mean by 5. The products are in AP. The second term of the GP is	(r)	26
(D)	The diagonals of a parallelogram have a measure of 4 m and 6 m. They cut off forming an angle of 60°. If the perimeter of the parallelogram is $2(\sqrt{a}+\sqrt{b})$ where $a, b\in N$, then the arithmetic mean of a, b and 4 is	(s)	40

65. Match the following columns.

Column I		Column II	
(A)	If $4a^2+9b^2+16c^2=2(3ab+6bc+4ca)$, where a, b, c are non-zero numbers, then a, b, c are in	(p)	AP
(B)	If $17a^2+13b^2+5c^2=(3ab+15bc+5ca)$, where a, b, c are non-zero numbers, then a, b, c are in	(q)	GP
(C)	If $a^2+9b^2+25c^2=abc\left(\frac{15}{a}+\frac{5}{b}+\frac{3}{c}\right)$, where a, b, c are non-zero numbers, then a, b, c are in	(r)	HP
(D)	If $(a^2+b^2+c^2)p^2-2p(ab+bc+ca)+(a^2+b^2+c^2)\le 0$, where a, b, c, p are non-zero numbers, then a, b, c are in		

Previous Year Questions

66. Let $7\overbrace{5\ldots5}^{r}7$ denote the $(r+2$ digit number where the first and the last digits are 7 and the remaining r digits are 5. Consider the sum $S=77+757+7557+\ldots+7\overbrace{5\ldots5}^{98}7$. If $S=\frac{7\overbrace{5\ldots5}^{99}7+m}{n}$, where m and n are natural numbers less than 3000, then the value of $m+n$ is ....

[Numerical Value Type, 2023 Adv.]

67. Let $a_1, a_2, a_3, \ldots$ be an arithmetic progression with $a_1=7$ and common difference 8. Let $T_1, T_2, T_3, \ldots$ be such that $T_1=3$ and $T_{n+1}-T_n=a_n$ for $n\ge 1$. Then, which of the following is/are TRUE ?

[More than One Option Correct, 2022 Adv.]

(a) $T_{20}=1604$

(b) $\sum_{k=1}^{20} T_k=10510$

(c) $T_{30}=3454$

(d) $\sum_{k=1}^{30} T_k=35610$

68. Let $l_1, l_2, \ldots, l_{100}$ be consecutive terms of an arithmetic progression with common difference d_1, and let $w_1, w_2, \ldots, w_{100}$ be consecutive terms of another arithmetic progression with common difference d_2, where $d_1 d_2 = 10$. For each $i = 1, 2, \ldots, 100$, let R_i be a rectangle with length l_i, width w_i and area A_i. If $A_{51} - A_{50} = 1000$, then the value of $A_{100} - A_{90}$ is .... **[Numerical Value Type, 2022 Adv.]**

69. Let m be the minimum possible value of $\log_3(3^{y_1} + 3^{y_2} + 3^{y_3})$, where y_1, y_2, y_3 are real numbers for which $y_1 + y_2 + y_3 = 9$. Let M be the maximum possible value of $(\log_3 x_1 + \log_3 x_2 + \log_3 x_3)$, where x_1, x_2, x_3 are positive real numbers for which $x_1 + x_2 + x_3 = 9$. Then, the value of $\log_2(m^3) + \log_3(M^2)$ is .... **[Numerical Value Type, 2020 Adv.]**

70. Let $a_1, a_2, a_3, \ldots$ be a sequence of positive integers in arithmetic progression with common difference 2. Also, let $b_1, b_2, b_3, \ldots$ be a sequence of positive integers in geometric progression with common ratio 2. If $a_1 = b_1 = c$, then the number of all possible values of c, for which the equality
$$2(a_1 + a_2 + \ldots + a_n) = b_1 + b_2 + \ldots + b_n$$
holds for some positive integer n, is ...... **[Numerical Value Type, 2020 Adv.]**

EXERCISE 3
Challenging Problems

1. Find the sum of n terms of the series $(a+b) + (a^2 + ab + b^2) + (a^3 + a^2b + ab^2 + b^3) + \ldots$, where $a \neq 1, b \neq 1$ and $a \neq b$.

2. Let a, b, c are respectively the sums of the first n terms, the next n terms and the next n terms of a GP. Show that a, b, c are in GP.

3. If $\frac{1}{1^2} + \frac{1}{2^2} + \frac{1}{3^2} + \ldots$ upto $\infty = \frac{\pi^2}{6}$, find

(i) $\frac{1}{1^2} + \frac{1}{3^2} + \frac{1}{5^2} + \ldots$ upto ∞

(ii) $1 - \frac{1}{2^2} + \frac{1}{3^2} - \frac{1}{4^2} + \ldots$ upto ∞

4. If $t_1 = 1, t_r - t_{r-1} = 2^{r-1}, r \geq 2$, find $\sum_{r=1}^{n} t_r$.

5. Prove that $I_1, I_2, I_3, \ldots$ form an AP, if

(i) $I_n = \int_0^{\pi} \frac{\sin 2nx}{\sin x}\, dx$ (ii) $I_n = \int_0^{\pi} \left(\frac{\sin nx}{\sin x}\right)^2 dx$

6. If three unequal numbers are in HP and their squares are in AP, show that they are in the ratio
$$1 + \sqrt{3} : -2 : 1 - \sqrt{3}$$
or
$$1 - \sqrt{3} : -2 : 1 + \sqrt{3}.$$

7. If $a_1, a_2, a_3, \ldots, a_n$ are in AP with $a_1 = 0$, prove that
$$\frac{a_3}{a_2} + \frac{a_4}{a_3} + \ldots + \frac{a_n}{a_{n-1}} - a_2\left(\frac{1}{a_2} + \frac{1}{a_3} + \ldots + \frac{1}{a_{n-2}}\right) = \frac{a_{n-1}}{a_2} + \frac{a_2}{a_{n-1}}$$

8. If $\theta_1, \theta_2, \theta_3, \ldots, \theta_n$ are in AP whose common difference is d, then show that
$$\sin d \,\{\sec \theta_1 \sec \theta_2 + \sec \theta_2 \sec \theta_3 + \ldots + \sec \theta_{n-1} \sec \theta_n\} = \tan \theta_n - \tan \theta_1$$

9. Evaluate $S = \sum_{n=0}^{n} \frac{2^n}{(a^{2^n} + 1)}$ (where $a > 1$).

10. Find the sum to infinite terms of the series $\tan^{-1}\left(\frac{1}{3}\right)+\tan^{-1}\left(\frac{2}{9}\right)+\ldots+\tan^{-1}\left(\frac{2^{n-1}}{1+2^{2n-1}}\right)+\ldots$

11. If S_1, S_2, S_3 denote the sum of n terms of 3 arithmetic series whose first terms are unity and their common difference are in HP, prove that $n=\frac{2S_3S_1-S_1S_2-S_2S_3}{S_1-2S_2+S_3}$.

12. Three friends whose ages form a GP divide a certain sum of money in proportion to their ages. If they do that three years later, when the youngest is half the age of the oldest, then he will receive ₹ 105 more than he gets now and the middle friend will get ₹ 15 more than he gets now. Find the ages of the friends.

Answer Key

Exercise 1

1. (b)	2. (a)	3. (b)	4. (b)	5. (a)	6. (b)	7. (a)	8. (b)	9. (b)	10. (b)
11. (b)	12. (a)	13. (d)	14. (c)	15. (a)	16. (c)	17. (b)	18. (d)	19. (a)	20. (c)
21. (a)	22. (b)	23. (d)	24. (a)	25. (3)	26. (2)	27. (2)	28. (4)	29. (6)	30. (4)
31. (4)	32. (3)	33. (5)	34. (1)	35. (6)	36. (2)	37. (9)	38. (7)	39. (4)	40. (d)
41. (a)	42. (b)	43. (d)	44. (b)	45. (1010)	46. (b)	47. (c)	48. (a)	49. (150)	50. (a)
51. (50)	52. (b)	53. (c)	54. (b)	55. (39)					

Exercise 2

1. (b)	2. (a)	3. (c)	4. (c)	5. (a)	6. (c)	7. (a)	8. (b)	9. (a)	10. (d)
11. (c)	12. (c)	13. (c)	14. (b)	15. (a)	16. (a)	17. (a)	18. (c)	19. (b)	20. (c)
21. (b,c,d)	22. (a,c)	23. (a,b,c,d)	24. (a,c)	25. (a,c)	26. (b,d)	27. (b,c)	28. (a,b)	29. (a,c,d)	30. (a,d)
31. (a,b,c)	32. (b,c)	33. (a,c)	34. (b,c)	35. (a,c)	36. (a,d)	37. (c)	38. (a)	39. (a)	40. (a)
41. (a)	42. (b)	43. (a)	44. (b)	45. (1275)	46. (100)	47. (10)	48. (34)	49. (3)	50. (5)
51. (8)	52. (4)	53. (2)	54. (49)	55. (0.3)	56. (711)	57. (10)	58. (21)	59. (16)	60. (60)

61. (65) 62. (A) → (r); (B) → (p, r); (C) → (p,q); (D) → (s) 63. (A) → (r); (B) → (p); (C) → (q); (D) → (s)

64. (A) → (s); (B) → (r); (C) → (q); (D) → (p) 65. (A) → (r); (B) → (p); (C) → (r); (D) → (q)

66. (1219) 67. (b,c) 68. (18900) 69. (8) 70. (1)

Solutions

Exercise 1 - JEE Main Pattern

1. We have, $\sqrt{a-x}, \sqrt{x}, \sqrt{a+x}$ are in AP

$$\Rightarrow \quad 2\sqrt{x} = \sqrt{a-x} + \sqrt{a+x}$$
$$\Rightarrow \quad 4x = a - x + a + x + 2\sqrt{a^2 - x^2}$$
$$\Rightarrow \quad 2x - a = \sqrt{a^2 - x^2}$$
$$\Rightarrow \quad 4x^2 - 4ax + a^2 = a^2 - x^2$$
$$\Rightarrow \quad 5x^2 = 4ax \Rightarrow a = \frac{5x}{4}$$

Now, x must be perfect square as $\sqrt{x}$ is an integer.

$\therefore \quad x = 1, 4, 9, 16, \ldots$

For $x = 1, a = \frac{5}{4}$

$x = 4, a = 5$

$x = 9, a = \frac{45}{4}$

$x = 16, a = 20$

and so on.

$\therefore$ Least composite value of a is 20.

2.

> **Decoding the Question**
> Use sum of infinite terms of GP
> i.e. $a + ar + ar^2 = \frac{a}{1-r}, |r| < 1$

We have, $\frac{1}{4} + \frac{1}{8} + \frac{1}{16} + \ldots = \frac{\frac{1}{4}}{1 - \frac{1}{2}} = \frac{1}{2}$

$$\therefore 0.2^{\log_{\sqrt{5}}\left(\frac{1}{4}+\frac{1}{8}+\frac{1}{16}+\ldots\right)} = 0.2^{\log_{\sqrt{5}}\frac{1}{2}} = \left(\frac{1}{5}\right)^{\log_{\sqrt{5}}\frac{1}{2}}$$
$$= (5^{-1})^{2\log_5\frac{1}{2}} = 5^{-2\log_5\frac{1}{2}} = 5^{\log_5 4} = 4$$

3. x, y, z are in GP. Let r be the common ratio. Then,

$y = xr, z = xr^2$

Now, $x, 2y, 3z$ are in AP

$$\therefore \quad 4y = x + 3z$$
$$\Rightarrow \quad 4xr = x + 3xr^2$$
$$\Rightarrow \quad 3r^2 - 4r + 1 = 0 \Rightarrow (3r-1)(r-1) = 0$$
$$\Rightarrow \quad r = \frac{1}{3} \quad [x, y, z \text{ are distinct so } r \neq 1]$$

4. Let a be the first term and r be the common ratio. Then,

$$\frac{a}{1-r} = 57 \text{ and } \frac{a^3}{1-r^3} = 9747$$

$$\therefore \quad \frac{a^3}{(1-r)^3} \times \frac{1-r^3}{a^3} = \frac{(57)^3}{9747}$$
$$\Rightarrow \quad \frac{1-r^3}{(1-r)^3} = 19$$
$$\Rightarrow \quad \frac{1+r+r^2}{(1-r)^2} = 19$$
$$\Rightarrow \quad 18r^2 - 39r + 18 = 0$$
$$\Rightarrow \quad (3r-2)(2r-3) = 0$$
$$\Rightarrow \quad r = \frac{2}{3} \quad [\because r \neq 3/2 \text{ as } |r| < 1]$$

5. Reciprocals of the terms of the series are

$$\frac{2}{5}, \frac{13}{20}, \frac{9}{10}, \frac{23}{20}, \ldots \text{ or } \frac{8}{20}, \frac{13}{20}, \frac{18}{20}, \frac{23}{20}, \ldots$$

$$\therefore n\text{th term of reciprocal series} = \frac{8 + (n-1)5}{20} = \frac{5n+3}{20}$$

$$\therefore 15\text{th term of given series} = \frac{20}{5 \times 15 + 3} = \frac{20}{78} = \frac{10}{39}$$

6. We have, $a^2 + b^2, ab + bc, b^2 + c^2$ are in GP

$$(ab + bc)^2 = (a^2 + b^2)(b^2 + c^2)$$
$$\Rightarrow \quad a^2b^2 + b^2c^2 + 2ab^2c = a^2b^2 + a^2c^2 + b^4 + b^2c^2$$
$$\Rightarrow \quad b^4 - 2ab^2c + a^2c^2 = 0$$
$$\Rightarrow \quad (b^2 - ac)^2 = 0 \Rightarrow b^2 = ac$$

$\therefore$ a, b, c are in GP.

7. We have, $1 - \frac{1}{3} + \frac{1}{5} - \frac{1}{7} + \frac{1}{9} - \frac{1}{11} + \ldots = \frac{\pi}{4}$

$$\Rightarrow \quad \frac{3-1}{1 \times 3} + \frac{7-5}{5 \times 7} + \frac{11-9}{9 \times 11} + \ldots = \frac{\pi}{4}$$
$$\Rightarrow \quad 2\left(\frac{1}{1 \times 3} + \frac{1}{5 \times 7} + \frac{1}{9 \times 11} + \ldots\right) = \frac{\pi}{4}$$
$$\Rightarrow \quad \frac{1}{1 \times 3} + \frac{1}{5 \times 7} + \frac{1}{9 \times 11} + \ldots = \frac{\pi}{8}$$

8. We know that

$$S_{3n} - S_{n-1} = \frac{3n}{2}[2a + (3n-1)d] - \frac{n-1}{2}[2a + (n-2)d]$$
$$= a[3n - n + 1] + \frac{d}{2}[3n(3n-1) - (n-1)(n-2)]$$
$$= (2n+1)a + \frac{d}{2}[9n^2 - 3n - n^2 + 3n - 2]$$
$$= (2n+1)a + d(4n^2 - 1)$$
$$= (2n+1)[a + (2n-1)d] = (2n+1)a_{2n}$$

Also, $S_{2n} - S_{2n-1} = a_{2n}$

$\therefore \quad \dfrac{S_{3n} - S_{n-1}}{S_{2n} - S_{2n-1}} = \dfrac{(2n+1)\,a_{2n}}{a_{2n}} = 2n+1$

$\therefore \quad 2n + 1 = 31 \Rightarrow n = 15$

9. We have, $\dfrac{ar(r^{10}-1)}{r-1} = 18$ and $\dfrac{\frac{1}{ar}\left(1-\frac{1}{r^{10}}\right)}{1-\frac{1}{r}} = 6$

Now, $\dfrac{\frac{1}{ar}\left(1-\frac{1}{r^{10}}\right)}{1-\frac{1}{r}} = 6 \Rightarrow \dfrac{r^{10}-1}{ar^{10}(r-1)} = 6$

$\Rightarrow \quad \dfrac{ar(r^{10}-1)}{a^2r^{11}(r-1)} = 6 \Rightarrow \dfrac{18}{a^2r^{11}} = 6$

$\Rightarrow \quad a^2r^{11} = 3$

Now, required product $= (ar)(ar^2)\dots(ar^{10})$

$= a^{10}r^{1+2+3+\dots+10}$

$= a^{10}r^{55} = (a^2r^{11})^5 = 3^5$

$= 243$

10. Using AM ≥ GM, we have

$$\frac{x^4+y^4}{2} \ge \sqrt{x^4y^4} \Rightarrow x^4 + y^4 \ge 2x^2y^2$$

and $\quad \dfrac{2x^2y^2+z^2}{2} \ge \sqrt{2x^2y^2z^2}$

$\Rightarrow \quad 2x^2y^2 + z^2 \ge 2\sqrt{2}\,xyz$

$\therefore \quad \dfrac{2x^2y^2+z^2}{xyz} \ge 2\sqrt{2} \Rightarrow \dfrac{x^4+y^4+z^2}{xyz} \ge 2\sqrt{2}$

11. We have, $T_r = \dfrac{r \times 2^r}{(r+2)!} = \dfrac{(r+2-2)\times 2^r}{(r+2)!} = \dfrac{2^r}{(r+1)!} - \dfrac{2^{r+1}}{(r+2)!}$

$\therefore$ Required sum $= \displaystyle\sum_{r=1}^{20}\left[\frac{2^r}{(r+1)!} - \frac{2^{r+1}}{(r+2)!}\right]$

$= \dfrac{2}{2!} - \dfrac{2^{21}}{22!} = 1 - \dfrac{2^{21}}{22!}$

12. $\because$ x, y, z are in HP.

$\therefore \quad \dfrac{1}{x}, \dfrac{1}{y}, \dfrac{1}{z}$ are in AP.

$\therefore \quad \dfrac{1}{x} - \dfrac{1}{y} = \dfrac{1}{y} - \dfrac{1}{z}$ ...(i)

$\dfrac{\sqrt{yz}}{\sqrt{y}+\sqrt{z}} = \dfrac{1}{\frac{1}{\sqrt{y}} + \frac{1}{\sqrt{z}}} = a$ [say]

$\dfrac{\sqrt{zx}}{\sqrt{x}+\sqrt{z}} = \dfrac{1}{\frac{1}{\sqrt{z}} + \frac{1}{\sqrt{x}}} = b$ [say]

and $\quad \dfrac{\sqrt{xy}}{\sqrt{x}+\sqrt{y}} = \dfrac{1}{\frac{1}{\sqrt{x}} + \frac{1}{\sqrt{y}}} = c$ [say]

$$\because \frac{a-b}{b-c} = \frac{\dfrac{1}{\frac{1}{\sqrt{y}}+\frac{1}{\sqrt{z}}} - \dfrac{1}{\frac{1}{\sqrt{z}}+\frac{1}{\sqrt{x}}}}{\dfrac{1}{\frac{1}{\sqrt{z}}+\frac{1}{\sqrt{x}}} - \dfrac{1}{\frac{1}{\sqrt{x}}+\frac{1}{\sqrt{y}}}} = \frac{\frac{1}{x}-\frac{1}{y}}{\frac{1}{y}-\frac{1}{z}} = 1 \quad \text{[from Eq. (i)]}$$

Hence, $\dfrac{\sqrt{yz}}{\sqrt{y}+\sqrt{z}}, \dfrac{\sqrt{zx}}{\sqrt{z}+\sqrt{x}}, \dfrac{\sqrt{xy}}{\sqrt{x}+\sqrt{y}}$ are in AP.

13. $\because$ $a_1, a_2, a_3, \dots$ are in HP.

$\Rightarrow \quad \dfrac{1}{a_1}, \dfrac{1}{a_2}, \dfrac{1}{a_3}, \dots$ are in AP. ...(i)

$\because \quad f_k = \displaystyle\sum_{r=1}^{n} a_r - a_k$

$\Rightarrow \quad a_k + f_k = \displaystyle\sum_{r=1}^{n} a_r = \lambda$ [say]

$\Rightarrow \quad a_1 + f_1 = a_2 + f_2 = a_3 + f_3 = \dots = \lambda$

From Eq. (i), $\dfrac{\lambda}{a_1}, \dfrac{\lambda}{a_2}, \dfrac{\lambda}{a_3}, \dots$ are also in AP.

$\Rightarrow \quad \dfrac{a_1+f_1}{a_1}, \dfrac{a_2+f_2}{a_2}, \dfrac{a_3+f_3}{a_3}, \dots$ are also in AP.

Subtracting 1 from each term, we get

$\dfrac{f_1}{a_1}, \dfrac{f_2}{a_2}, \dfrac{f_3}{a_3}, \dots$ are also in AP.

$\Rightarrow \quad \dfrac{1}{\alpha_1}, \dfrac{1}{\alpha_2}, \dfrac{1}{\alpha_3}, \dots$ are in AP.

$\therefore \quad \alpha_1, \alpha_2, \alpha_3, \dots$ are in HP.

$\therefore \quad 2^{\alpha_1}, 2^{\alpha_2}, 2^{\alpha_3}, \dots$ are not in AP/GP/HP.

14. $\because \quad S_n = 1 + 22 + 333 + \dots + \underbrace{nnnn\dots n}_{n \text{ terms}}$

$\therefore \quad S_n - S_{n-1} = \underbrace{nnnn\dots n}_{n \text{ times}} = n\,\underbrace{(111\dots 1)}_{n \text{ times}}$

$= n(10^{n-1} + 10^{n-2} + \dots + 10 + 1) = \dfrac{n(10^n - 1)}{10 - 1}$

$\therefore \quad 9(S_n - S_{n-1}) = n(10^n - 1)$

15. Given that a, b, c are in GP.

Then, $\quad b^2 = ac$ ...(i)

and equations $ax^2 + 2bx + c = 0$

and $dx^2 + 2ex + f = 0$ have a common root. ...(A)

Now, $\quad ax^2 + 2bx + c = 0$

$\Rightarrow \quad ax^2 + 2\sqrt{ac}\,x + c = 0$ [by Eq. (i)]

$\Rightarrow \quad (\sqrt{a}x + \sqrt{c})^2 = 0$

$\Rightarrow \quad \sqrt{a}x + \sqrt{c} = 0$

$\Rightarrow \quad x = -\dfrac{\sqrt{c}}{\sqrt{a}}$ [repeated]

By the condition (A), $\left(-\dfrac{\sqrt{c}}{\sqrt{a}}\right)$ be the root of $dx^2 - 2ex + f = 0$

So, it satisfy the equation

$$d\left(-\sqrt{\frac{c}{a}}\right)^2 + 2e\left(-\sqrt{\frac{c}{a}}\right) + f = 0$$

$$\Rightarrow \quad \frac{dc}{a} - 2e\frac{\sqrt{c}}{\sqrt{a}} + f = 0 \Rightarrow \frac{d}{a} - \frac{2e}{\sqrt{ac}} + \frac{f}{c} = 0$$

$$\Rightarrow \quad \frac{d}{a} - \frac{2e}{b} + \frac{f}{c} = 0 \Rightarrow \frac{d}{a} + \frac{f}{c} = 2\left(\frac{e}{b}\right)$$

So, $\frac{d}{a}, \frac{e}{b}, \frac{f}{c}$ are in AP.

16. $\because \quad S_n = \frac{1}{2} + \frac{3}{4} + \frac{7}{8} + \frac{15}{16} + \dots n$ up to terms

$$= \left(1 - \frac{1}{2}\right) + \left(1 - \frac{1}{4}\right) + \left(1 - \frac{1}{8}\right) + \dots n \text{ up to terms}$$

$$= \left(1 - \frac{1}{2}\right) + \left(1 - \frac{1}{2^2}\right) + \left(1 - \frac{1}{2^3}\right) + \dots + \left(1 - \frac{1}{2^n}\right)$$

$$= n - \frac{1}{2}\left(1 + \frac{1}{2} + \frac{1}{2^2} + \dots + \frac{1}{2^{n-1}}\right)$$

$$= n - \frac{1}{2} \times \frac{1\left[1 - \left(\frac{1}{2}\right)^n\right]}{\left(1 - \frac{1}{2}\right)}$$

$\left[\text{by sum GP, } S_n = \frac{a(1 - r^n)}{1 - r}, \text{if } 0 < r < 1\right]$

$$= n - 1 + \frac{1}{2^n} = n - 1 + 2^{-n}$$

17. Let the triangle be ΔPQR.

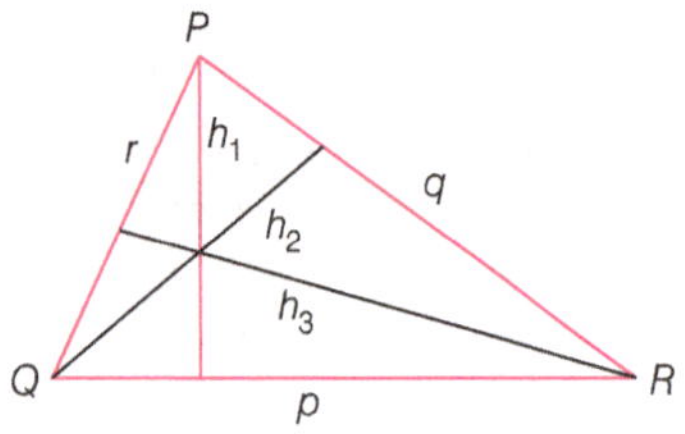

$\therefore \quad \Delta = \frac{1}{2} \times p \times h_1$ $\quad [h_1, h_2, h_3$ are altitudes$]$

$\Rightarrow \quad h_1 = \frac{2\Delta}{p}$ ...(i)

Similarly, $\quad h_2 = \frac{2\Delta}{q}$ ...(ii)

and $\quad h_3 = \frac{2\Delta}{r}$ ...(iii)

According to the question, $\sin P, \sin Q, \sin R$ are in AP.

Then, kp, kq, kr are in AP [by sine rule]

$\Rightarrow p, q, r$ are in AP.

$\Rightarrow \quad \frac{2\Delta}{h_1}, \frac{2\Delta}{h_2}, \frac{2\Delta}{h_3}$ are in AP. [by Eqs. (i), (ii) and (iii)]

$\Rightarrow \frac{1}{h_1}, \frac{1}{h_2}, \frac{1}{h_3}$ are in AP.

$\Rightarrow h_1, h_2, h_3$ are in HP.

$\Rightarrow$ Altitudes are in HP.

18. Given that, $a_1, a_2, \dots, a_{10}$ be in AP.

Let d be the common difference of AP.

$$\therefore \quad d = \frac{a_{10} - a_1}{10 - 1}$$

$$d = \frac{3 - 2}{9} \quad [\text{given that, } a_1 = h_1 = 2 \text{ and } a_{10} = h_{10} = 3]$$

$$d = \frac{1}{9}$$

$$\therefore \quad a_4 = a_1 + 3d = 2 + \frac{3}{9} = 2 + \frac{1}{3} = \frac{7}{3}$$

Now, $h_1, h_2, \dots, h_{10}$ be in HP.

So, common difference of respective AP.

$$D = \frac{\frac{1}{h_{10}} - \frac{1}{h_1}}{10 - 1} = \frac{\frac{1}{3} - \frac{1}{2}}{9} = \frac{-1}{9 \times 6} = \frac{-1}{54}$$

So, $\quad \frac{1}{h_7} = \frac{1}{h_1} + 6D \Rightarrow \frac{1}{h_7} = \frac{1}{2} + 6\left(\frac{-1}{54}\right) = \frac{1}{2} - \frac{1}{9}$

$$\frac{1}{h_7} = \frac{7}{18} \Rightarrow h_7 = \frac{18}{7}$$

So, $\quad a_4 h_7 = \frac{7}{3} \times \frac{18}{7} = 6$

19. $\because I_n = \int_0^\pi \frac{1 - \sin 2nx}{1 - \cos 2x} dx \Rightarrow I_n = \int_0^\pi \frac{1 - \sin 2nx}{2\sin^2 x} dx$

$\Rightarrow I_{n+1} + I_{n-1} - 2I_n$

$$= \frac{1}{2}\int_0^\pi \frac{[1 - \sin 2(n+1)x + 1 - \sin 2(n-1)x - 2 + 2\sin 2nx]}{\sin^2 x} dx$$

$$= \frac{1}{2}\int_0^\pi \frac{[\sin 2nx - \sin 2(n+1)x] + [\sin 2nx - \sin 2(n-1)x]}{\sin^2 x} dx$$

$$= \frac{1}{2}\int_0^\pi \frac{-2\cos(2n+1)x \sin(x) + 2\cos(2n-1)x \sin x}{\sin^2 x} dx$$

$$= \int_0^\pi \frac{\sin x[\cos(2n-1)x - \cos(2n+1)x]}{\sin^2 x} dx$$

$$= \int_0^\pi \frac{2\sin 2nx \sin x}{\sin x} dx = 2\int_0^\pi \sin 2nx\, dx = \frac{2}{2n}[-\cos 2nx]_0^\pi$$

$$= -\frac{1}{n}(1 - 1) = 0$$

$\therefore \quad I_{n+1} + I_{n-1} = 2I_n$

$\Rightarrow \quad I_{n-1}, I_n, I_{n+1}$ are in AP.

$\therefore \quad I_1, I_2, I_3, \dots$ are in AP.

20. Given that

$a(b - c)x^2 + b(c - a)xy + c(a - b)y^2$ is perfect square.

$$\therefore \quad b^2(c - a)^2 = 4a(b - c) \cdot c(a - b)$$

$$\Rightarrow \quad b^2(c - a)^2 = 4ac(a - b)(b - c)$$

$$\Rightarrow \quad [a(b - c) + c(a - b)]^2 = 4ac(a - b)(b - c)$$

$[\because a(b - c) + b(c - a) + c(a - b) = 0]$

$$\Rightarrow \quad [a(b - c) - c(a - b)]^2 = 0$$

$$\Rightarrow \quad a(b - c) - c(a - b) = 0$$

$$\Rightarrow \quad ab - ac - ca + bc = 0 \Rightarrow b(a + c) = 2ac$$

$$\Rightarrow \quad b = \frac{2ac}{a + b}$$

$\Rightarrow a, b, c$ are in HP.

21. Let $S = 1 + 2\left(1 - \frac{1}{n}\right) + 3\left(1 - \frac{1}{n}\right)^2 + \ldots + \infty$

$$\left(1 - \frac{1}{n}\right)S = \left(1 - \frac{1}{n}\right) + 2\left(1 - \frac{1}{n}\right)^2 + \ldots + \infty$$

$$S\left(1 - 1 + \frac{1}{n}\right) = 1 + \left(1 - \frac{1}{n}\right) + \left(1 - \frac{1}{n}\right)^2 + \ldots + \infty$$

$\Rightarrow \quad \frac{S}{n} = \frac{1}{1 - \left(1 - \frac{1}{n}\right)}$ $\quad \left[\text{for GP, } S_\infty = \frac{a}{1-r}\right]$

$\Rightarrow \quad S = \frac{n}{\frac{1}{n}}$

$\Rightarrow \quad S = n^2$

22. $\because \log_3 2, \log_3 (2^x - 5)$ and $\log_3\left(2^x - \frac{7}{2}\right)$ are in AP. ...(i)

For defined, $2^x - 5 > 0$ and $2^x - \frac{7}{2} > 0$

$\therefore \quad 2^x > 5$ ...(ii)

From Eq. (i), 2, $2^x - 5$, $2^x - \frac{7}{2}$ are in GP.

$\therefore \quad (2^x - 5)^2 = 2 \cdot \left(2^x - \frac{7}{2}\right)$

$\Rightarrow \quad 2^{2x} - 12 \cdot 2^x + 32 = 0$

$\Rightarrow \quad (2^x - 8)(2^x - 4) = 0$

$\therefore \quad 2^x = 8, 4$

$\Rightarrow \quad 2^x = 8 = 2^3, 2^x \neq 4$ [from Eq. (ii)]

$\therefore \quad x = 3$

23. $\because a, b, c$ are positive prime numbers.

Let $\sqrt{a}, \sqrt{b}, \sqrt{c}$ are 3 terms of AP. [not necessarily consecutive]

Then, $\sqrt{a} = A + (p-1)D$ ...(i)

$\sqrt{b} = A + (q-1)D$ ...(ii)

$\sqrt{c} = A + (r-1)D$ ...(iii)

[A and D be the first term and common difference of AP]

$\sqrt{a} - \sqrt{b} = (p-q)D$ ...(iv)

$\sqrt{b} - \sqrt{c} = (q-r)D$ ...(v)

$\sqrt{c} - \sqrt{a} = (r-p)D$ ...(vi)

On dividing Eq. (iv) by Eq. (v), we get

$$\frac{\sqrt{a} - \sqrt{b}}{\sqrt{b} - \sqrt{c}} = \frac{p-q}{q-r} \quad \text{...(vii)}$$

Since, p, q, r are natural numbers and a, b, c are positive prime numbers, so Eq. (vii) does not hold.

So, $\sqrt{a}, \sqrt{b}$ and $\sqrt{c}$ cannot be the 3 terms of AP.

[not necessarily consecutive]

Similarly, we can show that $\sqrt{a}, \sqrt{b}, \sqrt{c}$ cannot be any 3 terms of GP and HP. [not necessarily, consecutive]

24.

Decoding the Question

Use formula, $1 + 2 + 3 + 4 + \ldots + n = \frac{n(n+1)}{2}$

and $1^3 + 2^3 + 3^3 + \ldots + n^3 = \left[\frac{n(n+1)}{2}\right]^2$

Given that n is an odd integer greater than or equal to 1.

$$S_n = n^3 - (n-1)^3 + (n-2)^3 - \ldots + (-1)^{n-1}1^3$$

$$= 1^3 - 2^3 + \ldots + (n-2)^3 - (n-1)^3 + n^3$$

[$\because n$ is odd integer, so $(n-1)$ is even integer]

$$= (1^3 + 2^3 + \ldots + n^3) - 2 \cdot 2^3\left(1^3 + 2^3 + \ldots + \frac{n-1}{2}\text{ terms}\right)$$

$$= \left[\frac{n(n+1)}{2}\right]^2 - 16 \cdot \left[\frac{\frac{n-1}{2}\left(\frac{n-1}{2} + 1\right)}{2}\right]^2$$

$$= \frac{n^2(n+1)^2}{4} - \frac{4(n-1)^2(n+1)^2}{16}$$

$$= \frac{(n+1)^2}{4}[n^2 - (n-1)^2]$$

$$= \frac{(n+1)^2}{4} \cdot (2n-1)(1) = \frac{(2n-1)(n+1)^2}{4}$$

25. Let first term and common ratio of GP are a and r respectively.

Then $ar^4 = 7!$ and $ar^7 = 8!$

$\therefore \quad r^3 = 8 \Rightarrow r = 2$

$\therefore \quad a \times 2^4 = 7! \Rightarrow a = \frac{5040}{16} = 315$

Now, $S_n = 2205$

$\Rightarrow \quad \frac{315(2^n - 1)}{2 - 1} = 2205 \Rightarrow 2^n - 1 = 7 \Rightarrow n = 3$

26. We have, $S = 1 + a + a^2 + \ldots + a^{2007}$

$$= \frac{1 \cdot (a^{2008} - 1)}{a - 1} = \frac{2a - 1 - 1}{a - 1} \quad [\because a^{2008} - 2a + 1 = 0]$$

$$= \frac{2(a-1)}{(a-1)} = 2$$

27. We know that $\frac{a^m + b^m}{2} \geq \left(\frac{a+b}{2}\right)^m$

$\therefore \quad \frac{(a^3)^{1/3} + (b^3)^{1/3}}{2} \geq \left(\frac{a^3 + b^3}{2}\right)^{1/3}$

$\Rightarrow \quad \frac{a+b}{2} \geq \left(\frac{2}{2}\right)^{1/3}$

$\Rightarrow \quad a + b \geq 2$

28. We have, $b^2 = ac \Rightarrow c = \frac{b^2}{a}$

Also, $\frac{a+b+c}{3} = b + 2 \Rightarrow a - 2b + c = 6$

$\Rightarrow \quad a - 2b + \frac{b^2}{a} = 6$

$$\Rightarrow \quad 1 - 2\frac{b}{a} + \left(\frac{b}{a}\right)^2 = \frac{6}{a}$$

$$\Rightarrow \quad \left(1 - \frac{b}{a}\right)^2 = \frac{6}{a}$$

Since, $\frac{b}{a}$ is an integer.

$\therefore \left(1 - \frac{b}{a}\right)^2$ is also an integer.

So, $\frac{6}{a}$ is also on integer.

$$\therefore \quad a = 6$$

Now, $\frac{a^2 + a - 14}{a + 1} = \frac{36 + 6 - 14}{6 + 1} = 4$

29. Let the sides be $a - d, a, a + d, d > 0$

Now, $a^2 + (a - d)^2 = (a + d)^2 \Rightarrow a = 4d$

$\therefore$ Sides are $3d$, $4d$, $5d$.

Now, area of triangle = 24

$$\Rightarrow \quad \frac{1}{2} \times 3d \times 4d = 24 \Rightarrow d^2 = 4 \Rightarrow d = 2$$

$\therefore$ Sides are 6, 8, 10.

Thus, the smallest side length is 6.

30. We know that AM $\geq$ GM

$$\Rightarrow \quad \frac{\log_d a + \log_c b + \log_a c + \log_b d}{4} \geq (\log_d a \times \log_c b \times \log_a c \times \log_b d)^{1/4}$$

$$\Rightarrow \quad \log_d a + \log_c b + \log_a c + \log_b d \geq 4$$

$\therefore$ The minimum value is 4.

31. We have, $A - G = 2, G - H = \frac{8}{5}$

Now, $G^2 = AH = (G + 2)\left(G - \frac{8}{5}\right)$

$$\Rightarrow \quad G^2 = G^2 - \frac{8}{5}G + 2G - \frac{16}{5}$$

$$\Rightarrow \quad \frac{16}{5} = \frac{2}{5}G$$

$$\Rightarrow \quad G = 8$$

$$\therefore \quad A = 10, H = \frac{32}{5}$$

Now, $G = 8 \Rightarrow ab = 64$ and $A = 10$

$$\Rightarrow \quad a + b = 20$$

$$\therefore \quad a = 16, b = 4$$

So, HCF $(a, b) = 4$

32. Let $S = \frac{1}{3} + \frac{1}{9} + \frac{1}{27} + \ldots \infty$

$$= \frac{\frac{1}{3}}{1 - \frac{1}{3}} = \frac{1}{2}$$

$$\therefore \quad 9^{\frac{1}{3} + \frac{1}{9} + \frac{1}{27} + \ldots \infty} = 9^S = 9^{1/2} = 3$$

33. **Decoding the Question**

Use the concept of arithmetic geometric infinite series.

Let $S = 1 + 4\lambda + 9\lambda^2 + 16\lambda^3 + \ldots \infty$, where $\lambda = \frac{1}{7}$ ...(i)

$\Rightarrow \lambda S = \lambda + 4\lambda^2 + 9\lambda^3 + \ldots \infty$ ...(ii)

Subtracting Eq. (ii) from Eq. (i), we get

$$(1 - \lambda) S = 1 + 3\lambda + 5\lambda^2 + 7\lambda^3 + \ldots \infty \quad \text{...(iii)}$$

$$\Rightarrow \quad \lambda(1 - \lambda) S = \lambda + 3\lambda^2 + 5\lambda^3 + \ldots \infty \quad \text{...(iv)}$$

Subtracting Eq. (iv) from Eq. (iii), we get

$$(1 - \lambda)^2 S = 1 + 2\lambda + 2\lambda^2 + 2\lambda^3 + \ldots \infty$$

$$\Rightarrow \quad (1 - \lambda)^2 S = 1 + \frac{2\lambda}{1 - \lambda} \Rightarrow (1 - \lambda)^2 S = \frac{1 + \lambda}{1 - \lambda}$$

$$\Rightarrow \quad S = \frac{1 + \lambda}{(1 - \lambda)^3} = \frac{1 + \frac{1}{7}}{\left(1 - \frac{1}{7}\right)^3} = \frac{49}{27} = \frac{7^2}{3^3}$$

$\therefore \quad \alpha = 2, \beta = 3$

So, $\alpha + \beta = 5$

34. We have, $a + ar_1 + ar_1^2 + \ldots \infty = r_1$

and $a + ar_2 + ar_2^2 + \ldots \infty = r_2$

$$\Rightarrow \quad \frac{a}{1 - r_1} = r_1 \text{ and } \frac{a}{1 - r_2} = r_2$$

$\Rightarrow r_1^2 - r_1 + a = 0$ and $r_2^2 - r_2 + a = 0$

so, r_1 and r_2 are the roots of the equation

$$x^2 - x + a = 0$$

$$\therefore \quad r_1 + r_2 = \frac{-(-1)}{1} = 1$$

35. $5a - b, 2a + b, a + 2b$ are in AP

$$\therefore \quad 2(2a + b) = 5a - b + a + 2b \Rightarrow b = 2a$$

Again, $(b + 1)^2, ab + 1, (a - 1)^2$ are in GP

$$\therefore \quad (ab + 1)^2 = (b + 1)^2 (a - 1)^2$$

On putting $b = 2a$, we get

$$(2a^2 + 1)^2 = (2a + 1)^2 (a - 1)^2$$

$$\Rightarrow \quad a = 0, -2, \frac{1}{4} \Rightarrow a = \frac{1}{4} \qquad [\because a, b > 0]$$

$$\therefore \quad b = \frac{1}{2}$$

So, $a^{-1} + b^{-1} = 4 + 2 = 6$

36. Let $f(x) = \frac{4x^2 + 8x + 13}{6(1 + x)} = \frac{4(x + 1)^2 + 9}{6(1 + x)}$

$$= \frac{2(x + 1)}{3} + \frac{3}{2(1 + x)}$$

Now, we know that

AM $\geq$ GM

$$\Rightarrow \quad \frac{\frac{2(x + 1)}{3} + \frac{3}{2(1 + x)}}{2} \geq \sqrt{\frac{2(x + 1)}{3} \times \frac{3}{2(1 + x)}}$$

$$\Rightarrow \quad \frac{2(x + 1)}{3} + \frac{3}{2(1 + x)} \geq 2 \Rightarrow f(x) \geq 2$$

Thus, the least value is 2.

37. We have, $S = 1 + \left(1+\frac{1}{5}\right)\left(\frac{1}{2}\right) + \left(1+\frac{1}{5}+\frac{1}{5^2}\right)\left(\frac{1}{2^2}\right) + \dots \infty$ ...(i)

$\Rightarrow \quad \frac{S}{2} = \frac{1}{2} + \left(1+\frac{1}{5}\right)\left(\frac{1}{2^2}\right) + \dots \infty$ ...(ii)

Subtracting Eq. (ii) from Eq. (i), we get

$\frac{1}{2}S = 1 + \frac{1}{5}\times\frac{1}{2} + \frac{1}{5^2}\times\frac{1}{2^2} + \dots \infty$

$\Rightarrow \quad \frac{1}{2}S = \frac{1}{1-\frac{1}{10}} \Rightarrow \frac{1}{2}S = \frac{10}{9}$

$\Rightarrow \quad \frac{20}{S} = 9$

38. We have, $\quad H = \frac{21}{5}, 3A + G^2 = 36$

$\Rightarrow \quad 3A + AH = 36 \Rightarrow 3A + \frac{21}{5}A = 36$

$\Rightarrow \quad A = 5$

$\therefore \quad a + b = 10$

Again, $H = \frac{21}{5}$

$\Rightarrow \quad \frac{2ab}{a+b} = \frac{21}{5} \Rightarrow 2ab = \frac{21}{5}\times 10 = 42$

Now, $\quad a^2 + b^2 = (a+b)^2 - 2ab$

$= 100 - 42$

$= 58$

$\therefore \quad a^2 + b^2 - 51 = 7$

39. We have, $\quad r = \frac{a_2}{a_1} = \frac{x^n}{x^{-4}} = x^{n+4}$

Also, $\quad a_8 = x^{52}$

$\Rightarrow \quad ar^7 = x^{52}$

$\Rightarrow \quad x^{-4}\times(x^{n+4})^7 = x^{52}$

$\Rightarrow \quad x^{7n+24} = x^{52}$

$\Rightarrow \quad 7n + 24 = 52 \Rightarrow n = 4$

40. $17m = m + (m-4) + (m - 4\times 2) + \dots + (m - 4\times 24)$

$\Rightarrow \quad 17m = 25m - 4(1 + 2 + \dots + 24)$

$\Rightarrow \quad 8m = \frac{4\cdot 24\cdot 25}{2} \Rightarrow m = 150$

41. $4^{1+x} + 4^{1-x}, \frac{K}{2}, 16^x + 16^{-x} \to$ AP

$K = 4^{1+x} + 4^{1-x} + 16^x + 16^{-x}$

$= 4\left(4^x + \frac{1}{4^x}\right) + \left(4^{2x} + \frac{1}{4^{2x}}\right)$

$\because \quad P + \frac{1}{P} \geq 2$ for all $P > 0$

$\therefore \quad K_{\min} = 4\times 2 + 2 = 10$

42. Given that $\quad S_{10} = 390$ and $\frac{a_{10}}{a_5} = \frac{15}{7}$

$S_{10} = \frac{10}{2}[2a + 9d] = 390$

$\Rightarrow \quad 2a + 9d = 78$ ...(i)

$\frac{a_{10}}{a_5} = \frac{a+9d}{a+4d} = \frac{15}{7}$

$\Rightarrow \quad 7a + 63d = 15a + 60d$

$\Rightarrow \quad 8a = 3d$ ...(ii)

On solving Eqs. (i) and (ii), we get

$a = 3, d = 8$

Now, $\quad S_{15} - S_5 = \frac{15}{2}[2a + 14d] - \frac{5}{2}[2a + 4d]$

$= \frac{5}{2}[6a + 42d - 2a - 4d]$

$= \frac{5}{2}[4a + 38d] = 5(2a + 19d)$

$= 5(6 + 19\times 8) = 790$

43. First progression is 4, 9, 14, 19, ... upto 25th term.

Second progression is 3, 6, 9, 12, ... upto 37th term.

Now, T_{25} (for first) $= 4 + (25-1)\times 5 = 4 + 120 = 124$

and T_{37} (for second) $= 3 + (37-1)\times 3 = 3 + 108 = 111$

Let d_1 = common difference of 1st sequence = 5

d_2 = common difference of 2nd sequence = 3

So, first common term = 9

and common difference of common series = 15

(which is LCM of d_1 and d_2)

Hence, common terms are 9, 24, 39, 54, 69, 84, 99.

Thus, total number of common terms = 7

44. Let a be the first term and r be the common ratio of the GP

$\therefore (a + ar + ar^2 + \dots + ar^{63}) = 7(a + ar^2 + \dots + ar^{62})$

$\Rightarrow \quad \frac{a(1-r^{64})}{1-r} = \frac{7a(1-r^{64})}{1-r^2}$

$\Rightarrow \quad 1 = \frac{7}{1+r} \Rightarrow 1 + r = 7 \Rightarrow r = 6$

45. Given, $\quad f(m+n) = f(m) + f(n)$

So, $\quad f(x) = mx$

$\because \quad f(1) = 1 \Rightarrow 1 = m\times 1 \Rightarrow m = 1$

$\therefore \quad f(x) = x$

Now, $\sum_{k=1}^{2022} f(\lambda + k) \leq (2022)^2 \Rightarrow \sum_{k=1}^{2022}(\lambda + k) \leq (2022)^2$

$\Rightarrow (\lambda + \lambda + \lambda + \dots + \lambda) + (1 + 2 + 3 + \dots + 2022) \leq (2022)^2$

(2022 terms)

$\Rightarrow \quad 2022\lambda + \frac{2022\times 2023}{2} \leq (2022)^2$

$\Rightarrow \quad \lambda \leq 2022 - \frac{2023}{2}$

$\Rightarrow \quad \lambda \leq \frac{2021}{2} = 1010.5$

Thus, the largest natural number λ is 1010.

46. Let $a_1, a_2, a_3, \dots$ be a GP of increasing positive numbers and given that sum of its 6th and 8th terms be 2.

So, $\quad ar^5 + ar^7 = 2$ ...(i)

and also given that, product of its 3rd and 5th terms be $\frac{1}{9}$.

So, $(ar^2)(ar^4) = \frac{1}{9} \Rightarrow a^2r^6 = \frac{1}{9}$ ...(ii)

Since, $r > 0$

So, from Eq. (i), we get $ar^5(1 + r^2) = 2$ ...(iii)

and from Eq. (ii), we get $(ar^3)^2 = \frac{1}{9}$

$\Rightarrow \quad ar^3 = \pm \frac{1}{3}$

Since, $r > 0$ and $a > 0 \Rightarrow ar > 0$, so $ar^3 = \frac{1}{3}$

From Eq. (iii), we get $ar^3 \cdot r^2 (1 + r^2) = 2$

$\Rightarrow \quad \frac{1}{3}(r^2 + r^4) = 2$

$\Rightarrow \quad r^4 + r^2 - 6 = 0$

$\Rightarrow \quad r^2 = 2, \ r^2 = -3$ (not possible)

$\Rightarrow \quad r = \sqrt{2} \Rightarrow a = \frac{1}{6\sqrt{2}}$

Now, $6(a_2 + a_4)(a_4 + a_6) = 6(ar + ar^3)(ar^3 + ar^5)$

$= 6a^2r^4(1 + r^2)^2$

$= 6 \times \frac{1}{36 \times 2} \times 4 \times (1 + 2)^2$

$= \frac{1}{12} \times 4 \times 9 = 3$

47. Given that the first term a and common ratio r of a geometric progression be positive integer. So their first three terms are a, ar, ar^2

$a^2 + a^2r^2 + a^2r^4 = 33033$

$\Rightarrow \quad a^2(1 + r^2 + r^4) = 3 \times 7 \times 11 \times 11 \times 13$

$= 3 \times 7 \times 13 \times 11^2$

$\therefore \quad a^2 = 11^2$

$\Rightarrow \quad a = 11$ and $1 + r^2 + r^4 = 273$

$\Rightarrow \quad r^2 + r^4 = 272$

$\Rightarrow \quad r^4 + r^2 - 272 = 0$

$\Rightarrow \quad (r^2 + 17)(r^2 - 16) = 0$

$\Rightarrow \quad r^2 = -17$ and $r^2 - 16 = 0$ [$\because r^2 = -17$ not possible]

$\Rightarrow \quad r = \pm 4 \Rightarrow r = 4 \ (r > 0)$

So, sum of these first three terms are $a + ar + ar^2$

$\Rightarrow \quad 11 + 44 + 176 = 231$

48. a, A_1, A_2, b in AP

$\frac{a+b}{2} = \frac{A_1 + A_2}{2}$

$\Rightarrow \quad a + b = A_1 + A_2$ ...(i)

a, G_1, G_2, G_3, b in GP

$ab = a(ar^4) = (ar)(ar^3) = G_1G_3$ ...(ii)

$b = ar^4 \Rightarrow \sqrt[4]{\frac{b}{a}} = r$

$G_1 = ar = a\sqrt[4]{\frac{b}{a}},$

$G_2 = ar^2 = a \cdot \left(\sqrt[4]{\frac{b}{a}}\right)^2 = a\sqrt{\frac{b}{a}}$

$G_3 = ar^3 = a\left(\sqrt[4]{\frac{b}{a}}\right)^3 = a\left(\frac{b}{a}\right)^{3/4}$

$G_1^4 + G_2^4 + G_3^4 + G_1^2G_3^2$

$= \left(a\left(\frac{b}{a}\right)^{1/4}\right)^4 + \left(a\left(\frac{b}{a}\right)^{1/2}\right)^4 + \left[a\left(\frac{b}{a}\right)^{3/4}\right]^4$

$+ \left[a\left(\frac{b}{a}\right)^{1/4}\right]^2\left[a\left(\frac{b}{a}\right)^{3/4}\right]^2$

$= a^4 \times \frac{b}{a} + a^4 \times \frac{b^2}{a^2} + a^4 \times \frac{b^3}{a^3}$

$+ a^2\frac{b^{1/2}}{a^{1/2}} \times \frac{a^2 \times b \times b^{1/2}}{a \times a^{1/2}}$

$= a^3b + a^2b^2 + ab^3 + a^2b^2$

$= a^2b(a + b) + ab^2(a + b)$

$= (a + b)(a^2b + ab^2)$

$= (a + b)[ab(a + b)]$

$= (A_1 + A_2)(A_1 + A_2)ab$ [from Eqs. (i) and (ii)]

$= (A_1 + A_2)^2G_1G_3$

49. $\frac{1}{x}, \frac{1}{y}, \frac{1}{z}$ are in AP.

$\Rightarrow \quad \frac{2}{y} = \frac{1}{x} + \frac{1}{z}$ ...(i)

$x, \sqrt{2}y, z$ are in GP $\Rightarrow (\sqrt{2}y)^2 = xz$

$\Rightarrow \quad 2y^2 = xz$ ...(ii)

$xy + yz + zx = \frac{3}{\sqrt{2}}xyz$

$\Rightarrow \quad \frac{1}{z} + \frac{1}{x} + \frac{1}{y} = \frac{3}{\sqrt{2}}$ ...(iii)

From Eqs. (i) and (iii), $\frac{2}{y} + \frac{1}{y} = \frac{3}{\sqrt{2}} \Rightarrow y = \sqrt{2}$

From Eq. (ii), $2(\sqrt{2})^2 = xz \Rightarrow xz = 4$ ...(iv)

From Eq. (iii), $\frac{1}{z} + \frac{1}{x} + \frac{1}{\sqrt{2}} = \frac{3}{\sqrt{2}} \Rightarrow \frac{x+z}{xz} = \sqrt{2}$

$\Rightarrow \quad x + z = 4\sqrt{2}$ [$\because xz = 4$]

$\therefore \quad 3(x + y + z)^2 = 3(4\sqrt{2} + \sqrt{2})^2 = 3 \times 50 = 150$

50. It is given that

$\frac{a_1 + a_2 + \dots + a_n}{n} = 0$ i.e. $\frac{1}{n}\sum_{i=1}^{n} a_i = 0$

Now, $\sum_{i=1}^{n} f(a_i) = \alpha(a_1^5 + a_2^5 + \dots a_n^5) + \beta(a_1^3 + a_2^3 + \dots + a_n^3) + \gamma(a_1 + a_2 + \dots a_n)$

$= 0\alpha + 0\beta + 0\gamma = 0$

[as first and last, second and second last and so on are equal in magnitude and opposite in sign]

According to the question, $g(f(x)) = x$

$\Rightarrow g$ is inverse of f and f is inverse of g.

$$\therefore \quad f\left(g\left(\frac{1}{n}\sum_{i=1}^{n} f(a_i)\right)\right) = \frac{1}{n}\sum_{i=1}^{n} f(a_i) = 0$$

51. $\because a_1, a_2, a_3$ and a_4 are in AP and its mean is p.

$\therefore \quad a_1 = p - 3d, a_2 = p - d, a_3 = p + d, a_4 = p + 3d$ where, $d > 0$

$\because \quad |f(a_i)| = 500$ [given]

$|9d^2 - q| = 500$ and $|d^2 - q| = 500$ ... (i)

Either $9d^2 - q = d^2 - q$ or $9d^2 - q = q - d^2$

$\Rightarrow d = 0$ not acceptable because $d > 0$

$\therefore \quad 9d^2 - q = q - d^2$

$\Rightarrow \quad 10d^2 = 2q \Rightarrow 5d^2 - q = 0$

$\Rightarrow \quad d^2 = \frac{q}{5}$

From Eq. (i),

$$\left|9 \cdot \frac{q}{5} - q\right| = 500 \Rightarrow 4q = 2500 \Rightarrow q = 625$$

Roots of $f(x) = 0$ are $p + \sqrt{q}$ and $p - \sqrt{q}$.

$\therefore$ Absolute difference between roots $= |2\sqrt{q}| = 50$

52. Given, $\dfrac{2 + 4 + 6 + \ldots + 2y}{3 + 6 + 9 + \ldots + 3y} = \dfrac{4}{\log_{10} x}$

$\Rightarrow \quad \dfrac{2(1 + 2 + 3 + \ldots + y)}{3(1 + 2 + 3 + \ldots + y)} = \dfrac{4}{\log_{10} x}$

$\Rightarrow \quad \dfrac{2}{3} = \dfrac{4}{\log_{10} x}$

$\Rightarrow \quad \log_{10} x = 6 \Rightarrow \quad x = 10^6$

Now, $y = \log_{10} x + \log_{10} x^{\frac{1}{3}} + \log_{10} x^{\frac{1}{9}} + \ldots$ upto ∞ terms.

$= \log_{10}\left(x \cdot x^{\frac{1}{3}} \cdot x^{\frac{1}{9}} \ldots \infty \text{ terms}\right)$

$= \log_{10} x^{1 + \frac{1}{3} + \frac{1}{9} + \ldots \infty \text{ terms}} = \log_{10} x^{\frac{1}{1 - \frac{1}{3}}} = \log_{10} x^{3/2}$

$= \log_{10}(10^6)^{\frac{3}{2}}$ $[\because x = 10^6]$

$\Rightarrow \quad y = 6 \times \frac{3}{2} = 9$

$\therefore \quad x = 10^6, y = 9, (x, y) = (10^6, 9)$

53. Let the first term of geometric series be a and common ratio be r.

Given that $T_2 + T_6 = 25/2$

$\Rightarrow \quad ar(1 + r^4) = 25/2$ ... (i)

Also, $(T_3)(T_5) = 25$

$\Rightarrow \quad a^2r^6 = 25$ ...(ii)

On squaring Eq. (i), we get

$$a^2r^2(1 + r^4)^2 = \left(\frac{25}{2}\right)^2 \quad \text{...(iii)}$$

On dividing Eq. (iii) by Eq. (ii), we get

$$\frac{a^2r^2(1 + r^4)^2}{a^2r^6} = \frac{(25)^2}{4(25)}$$

$\Rightarrow \quad \dfrac{(1 + r^4)^2}{r^4} = \dfrac{25}{4}$

$\Rightarrow \quad 4(1 + r^4)^2 = 25r^4$

$\Rightarrow \quad 4(1 + r^8 + 2r^4) = 25r^4$

$\Rightarrow \quad 4r^8 - 17r^4 + 4 = 0$

$\Rightarrow \quad (r^4 - 4)(4r^4 - 1) = 0$

Gives, $\quad r^4 = 4$ or $r^4 = 1/4$

We have to find sum of 4th, 6th and 8th term, i.e.

$T_4 + T_6 + T_8 = ar^3 + ar^5 + ar^7$

$= ar^3(1 + r^2 + r^4)$ ...(iv)

Using Eq. (ii), $ar^3 = 5$

Also, we take $r^4 = 4$ because given series is increasing and $r^2 = 2$.

$\therefore \quad T_4 + T_6 + T_8 = 5(1 + 2 + 4)$

$= 5(7)$

$= 35$

54. Given series of infinite terms, if $|x| < 1, |y| < 1$ and $x \neq y$ is

$$S = (x + y) + (x^2 + xy + y^2) + (x^3 + x^2y + xy^2 + y^3) + \ldots$$

On multiplying $(x - y)$ both sides, we get

$(x - y)S = (x^2 - y^2) + (x^3 - y^3) + (x^4 - y^4) + \ldots$

$= [x^2 + x^3 + x^4 + \ldots] - [y^2 + y^3 + y^4 + \ldots]$

$= \dfrac{x^2}{1 - x} - \dfrac{y^2}{1 - y}$ as $|x| < 1$ and $|y| < 1$

$= \dfrac{(x^2 - y^2) - (x^2y - y^2x)}{(1 - x)(1 - y)}$

$\Rightarrow \quad (x - y)S = \dfrac{(x - y)[(x + y) - xy]}{(1 - x)(1 - y)}$

$\Rightarrow \quad S = \dfrac{x + y - xy}{(1 - x)(1 - y)}$

55. The 4th AM out of m AMs inserted between 3 and 243 is

$$A_4 = 3 + 4\frac{243 - 3}{m + 1} \quad \text{...(i)}$$

and the 2nd GM out of three GMs inserted between 3 and 243 is

$$G_2 = 3\left(\left(\frac{243}{3}\right)^{\frac{1}{3+1}}\right)^2 = 3(81)^{1/2} = 27$$

$\because \quad A_4 = G_2$

$\Rightarrow \quad 3 + 4\left(\dfrac{240}{m + 1}\right) = 27$

$\Rightarrow \quad m + 1 = 40$

$\Rightarrow \quad m = 39$

Exercise 2 - JEE Advanced Pattern

1. Let the series have $2n$ terms and the series is

$$a, a + d, a + 2d, \ldots, a + (2n-1)d$$

Now, we have

$$a_1 + a_3 + a_5 + \ldots + a_{2n-1} = 24$$

$$\Rightarrow \quad \frac{n}{2}[2a + (n-1)2d] = 24$$

$$\Rightarrow \quad n[a + (n-1)d] = 24 \quad \ldots\text{(i)}$$

Also, $\quad a_2 + a_4 + a_6 + \ldots + a_{2n} = 30$

$$\Rightarrow \quad \frac{n}{2}[2(a+d) + (n-1)2d] = 30$$

$$\Rightarrow \quad n[a + d + (n-1)d] = 30 \quad \ldots\text{(ii)}$$

Again, $a_{2n} - a = \frac{21}{2}$

$$\Rightarrow \quad a + (2n-1)d - a = \frac{21}{2}$$

$$\Rightarrow \quad (2n-1)d = \frac{21}{2} \quad \ldots\text{(iii)}$$

From Eqs. (i) and (ii), we get

$$nd = 6 \quad \ldots\text{(iv)}$$

From Eqs. (iii) and (iv), we get

$$\frac{2n-1}{n} = \frac{21}{12} \Rightarrow n = 4$$

2. We have, $2b = a + c$

and $\quad (c-b)^2 = (b-a)a$

$$\Rightarrow \quad (b-a)^2 = (b-a)a$$

$$\Rightarrow \quad b = 2a \Rightarrow c = 3a$$

$$\therefore \quad a : b : c = 1 : 2 : 3$$

3.

Decoding the Question

Apply if ΔABC and ΔPQR are similar, then

$$\frac{AB}{PQ} = \frac{AC}{PR} = \frac{BC}{QR}$$

$$\frac{AL_1}{AB} = \frac{L_1M_1}{BC} \Rightarrow \frac{1}{n+1} = \frac{L_1M_1}{a} \Rightarrow L_1M_1 = \frac{a}{n+1}$$

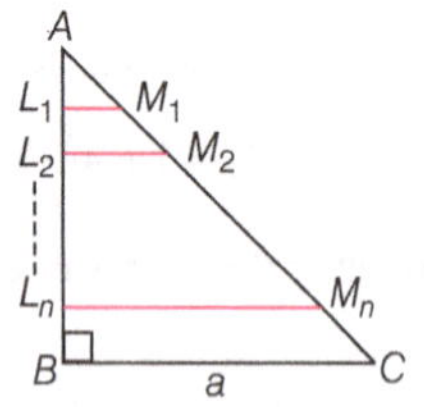

Again, $\quad \frac{AL_2}{AB} = \frac{L_2M_2}{BC} \Rightarrow \frac{2}{n+1} = \frac{L_2M_2}{a}$

$$\Rightarrow \quad L_2M_2 = \frac{2a}{n+1}$$

and so on.

$$\therefore \quad \text{Required sum} = \frac{a}{n+1} + \frac{2a}{n+1} + \frac{3a}{n+1} + \ldots + \frac{na}{n+1}$$

$$= \frac{a}{n+1} \times \frac{n(n+1)}{2} = \frac{an}{2}$$

4. The series is

$$1 + 2 + 2\times 3 + 2^2 \times 3 + 2^2 \times 3^2 + 2^3 \times 3^2 + \ldots \text{ upto 20 terms}$$

$$= (1 + 2\times 3 + 2^2 \times 3^2 + \ldots \text{ upto 10 terms})$$

$$+ (2 + 2^2 \times 3 + 2^3 \times 3^2 + \ldots \text{ to 10 terms})$$

$$= \frac{1(2^{10}3^{10} - 1)}{6-1} + \frac{2(2^{10}3^{10}-1)}{6-1} = \frac{3}{5}(6^{10} - 1)$$

5. Let the sides of right angled triangle be $(a-d), a, (a+d)\ (a > d)$.

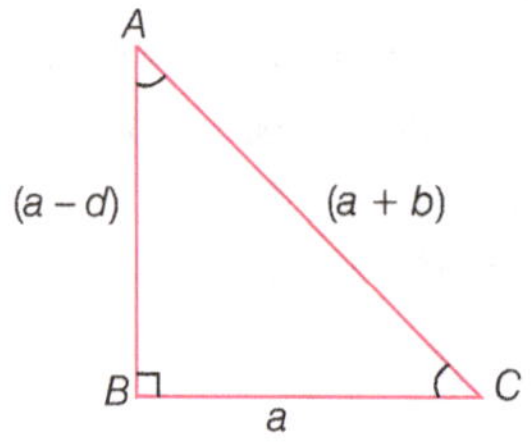

By Pythagoras theorem,

$$(a+d)^2 = a^2 + (a-d)^2$$

$$a^2 + d^2 + 2ad = a^2 + a^2 + d^2 - 2ad$$

$$a^2 = 4ad$$

$$a = 4d \quad [\text{since } a \neq 0] \ \ldots\text{(i)}$$

According to the question,

$$\sin A = \frac{a}{a+d} = \frac{4d}{5d} = \frac{4}{5}$$

$$\sin C = \frac{a-d}{a+d} = \frac{3d}{5d} = \frac{3}{5}$$

6. $T_6 = 2$

Let d be common difference of AP and a be the first term of AP.

$$T_6 = 2$$

$$\Rightarrow \quad a + 5d = 2 \quad \ldots\text{(i)}$$

Let $\quad A = a_1 a_4 a_5$

$$A = a(a+3d)(a+4d)$$

[using $T_n = a + (n-1)d$ and from Eq. (i) $a = 2 - 5d$]

$$A = (2-5d)(2-2d)(2-d)$$

$$A = 8 - 32d + 34d^2 - 10d^3$$

For max and min values of A, $\frac{dA}{dd} = 0$

$$-30d^2 + 68d - 32 = 0 \Rightarrow 15d^2 - 34d + 16 = 0$$

$$15d^2 - (24d + 10d) + 16 = 0$$

$$15d^2 - 24d - 10d + 16 = 0$$

$$3d(5d-8) - 2(5d-8) = 0$$

$$(5d-8)(3d-2) = 0$$

$$d = \frac{8}{5} \text{ or } d = \frac{2}{3}$$

For $\quad d = \frac{2}{3}, \ \frac{d^2A}{dd^2} > 0$

So, $\quad A$ is least for $d = \frac{2}{3}$.

7. Given, common difference $\neq 0$

$$S_{3n} = S_{4n} - S_{3n}$$

$$\Rightarrow \quad 2 \cdot S_{3n} = S_{4n} \qquad [\text{ let } S_n = Pn^2 + Qn]$$

$$\Rightarrow 2 \cdot [P(3n)^2 + Q(3n)] = P(4n)^2 + Q(4n)$$

$$\Rightarrow \quad 2Pn^2 + 2Qn = 0$$

$$\text{or} \quad Q = -nP \qquad \text{...(i)}$$

$$\therefore \frac{S_{2n}}{S_{4n} - S_{2n}} = \frac{P(2n)^2 + Q(2n)}{[P(4n)^2 + Q(4n)] - [P(2n)^2 + Q(2n)]}$$

$$= \frac{2n(2nP + Q)}{12Pn^2 + 2nQ} = \frac{2nP + Q}{6nP + Q}$$

$$= \frac{2nP - nP}{6nP - nP} = \frac{1}{5} \qquad [\text{from Eq. (i)}]$$

8. Let $f(x) = (x-1)(x-2)(x-3)\ldots(x-n)$

$$= x^n - S_1 x^{n-1} + S_2 x^{n-2} - \ldots + (-1)^n (1 \cdot 2 \cdot 3 \ldots n)$$

So, coefficient of x^{n-2} in $f(x) = S_2 = (1 \cdot 2 + 1 \cdot 3 + \ldots)$

= Sum of product of first n natural number taken 2 at time

$$= \frac{1}{2}[(1 + 2 + \ldots + n)^2 - (1^2 + 2^2 + \ldots + n^2)]$$

$$= \frac{1}{2}\left[\left\{\frac{n(n+1)}{2}\right\}^2 - \frac{n(n+1)(2n+1)}{6}\right]$$

$$= \frac{1}{2} \cdot \frac{n(n+1)}{2}\left[\frac{n(n+1)}{2} - \frac{2n+1}{3}\right]$$

$$= \frac{1}{2} \cdot \frac{n(n+1)}{2}\left[\frac{3n^2 + 3n - 4n - 2}{6}\right]$$

$$= \frac{n(n+1)(3n^2 - n - 2)}{24} = \frac{n(n+1)(3n+2)(n-1)}{24}$$

$$= \frac{n(n^2-1)(3n+2)}{24}$$

9. If last term of nth row is T_n, then

Let $S = 1 + 5 + 11 + 19 + \ldots + T_n$

$$S = \quad 1 + 5 + 11 + \ldots + T_{n-1} + T_n$$

$$0 = 1 + 4 + 6 + 8 + \ldots + n \text{ terms} - T_n$$

$$T_n = 1 + 2(2 + 3 + 4 + \ldots + (n-1) \text{ terms})$$

$$= 1 + 2\frac{(n-1)}{2}[2 \cdot 2 + (n-2) \cdot 1]$$

$$= 1 + (n-1)(n+2) = 1 + n^2 + n - 2$$

$$\Rightarrow T_n = n^2 + n - 1$$

$$\therefore T_{60} = (60)^2 + 60 - 1 = 3600 + 59 = 3659$$

10. Given that $\sum_{r=1}^{100} a_{2r} = \alpha \Rightarrow a_2 + a_4 + \ldots + a_{200} = \alpha$ ...(i)

and $\sum_{r=1}^{100} a_{2r-1} = \beta \Rightarrow a_1 + a_3 + \ldots + a_{199} = \beta$

On subtracting Eq. (ii) from Eq. (i), we get

$$(a_2 - a_1) + (a_4 - a_3) + \ldots + (a_{200} - a_{199}) = \alpha - \beta$$

$$d + d + \ldots \text{ up to 100 terms} = \alpha - \beta$$

[beacause a_n be the nth term of AP with common difference d]

$$100\, d = \alpha - \beta \Rightarrow d = \frac{\alpha - \beta}{100}$$

11. Given that, a_1, a_2, a_3, a_4, a_5 are in HP.

$\therefore \frac{1}{a_1}, \frac{1}{a_2}, \frac{1}{a_3}, \frac{1}{a_4}, \frac{1}{a_5}$ are in AP.

$$\Rightarrow \frac{1}{a_2} - \frac{1}{a_1} = \frac{1}{a_3} - \frac{1}{a_2} = \frac{1}{a_4} - \frac{1}{a_3} = \frac{1}{a_5} - \frac{1}{a_4} = d \qquad [\text{say}]$$

$$\therefore \quad a_1 - a_2 = a_1 a_2 d \Rightarrow a_2 - a_3 = a_2 a_3 d$$

$$a_3 - a_4 = a_3 a_4 d \Rightarrow a_4 - a_5 = a_4 a_5 d$$

On adding all, we get

$$a_1 a_2 + a_2 a_3 + a_3 a_4 + a_4 a_5 = \frac{a_1 - a_5}{d} = a_1 a_5 \left(\frac{\frac{1}{a_5} - \frac{1}{a_1}}{d}\right) = 4\, a_1 a_5$$

12.

> **Decoding the Question**
>
> Apply AM $\geq$ GM
>
> i.e. $\left(\frac{x_1 + x_2 + x_3 + \ldots + x_n}{n}\right) \geq (x_1 x_2 x_3 \ldots x_n)^{1/n}$

$$\because (1+a)(1+b)(1+c)(1+d)$$

$$= 1 + a + b + c + d + ab + ac + ad + bc + bd + cd$$

$$+ abc + abd + cda + cdb + abcd \qquad [16 \text{ terms}]$$

$\therefore$ AM $\geq$ GM

$$\frac{(1+a)(1+b)(1+c)(1+d)}{16} \geq (a^8 b^8 c^8 d^8)^{1/16}$$

$$= (abcd)^{1/2} = (1)^{1/2} = 1 \qquad [\because abcd = 1]$$

$$\Rightarrow \frac{(1+a)(1+b)(1+c)(1+d)}{16} \geq 1$$

$$\Rightarrow (1+a)(1+b)(1+c)(1+d) \geq 16$$

$\therefore$ Minimum value of $(1+a)(1+b)(1+c)(1+d)$ is 16.

13. $\because a, b, c$ are in AP.

$$\therefore \quad 2b = a + c \qquad \text{...(i)}$$

Now, $(a + 2b - c)(2b + c - a)(c + a - b)$

$$= (a + a + c - c)(a + c + c - a)(2b - b) \qquad [\text{from Eq. (i)}]$$

$$= (2a)(2c)(b) = 4abc$$

$$\therefore \quad \lambda = 4$$

14. $a_1, a_2, \ldots, a_n$ are in GP with first term a and common ratio r.

$$S_n = \underbrace{\frac{a_1 a_2}{a_1^2 - a_2^2} + \frac{a_2 a_3}{a_2^2 - a_3^2} + \ldots + \frac{a_{n-1} a_n}{a_{n-1}^2 - a_n^2}}_{(n-1) \text{ times}} \qquad \text{...(i)}$$

$$T_n = \frac{a_{n-1} a_n}{a_{n-1}^2 - a_n^2} = \frac{a_{n-1} a_n}{(a_{n-1} - a_n)(a_{n-1} + a_n)}$$

$$= \frac{1}{\left(1 - \frac{a_n}{a_{n-1}}\right)\left(1 + \frac{a_{n-1}}{a_n}\right)}$$

$$= \frac{1}{(1-r)\left(1 + \frac{1}{r}\right)} = \frac{r}{(r+1)(1-r)} \qquad [\text{ by GP}]$$

$$\therefore S_n = \sum_{n=2}^{n} T_n = \sum_{n=2}^{n} \frac{r}{(1-r^2)} = \frac{(n-1)r}{(1-r^2)}$$

15. According to the question, for AP

$$S_{10} = 4\,S_5$$

$$\frac{10}{2}(2a + 9d) = 4\cdot\frac{5}{2}(2a + 4d) \qquad \left[\text{by } S_n = \frac{n}{2}[2a + (n-1)\,d]\right]$$

$$10a + 45d = 20a + 40d$$

$$\Rightarrow \quad 10a = 5d \Rightarrow \frac{a}{d} = \frac{1}{2}$$

16. $\because \cos(x-y), \cos x, \cos(x+y)$ are in HP.

$$\therefore \quad \cos x = \frac{2\cos(x-y)\cos(x+y)}{\cos(x-y) + \cos(x+y)}$$

$$\Rightarrow \quad \cos x = \frac{2(\cos^2 x - \sin^2 y)}{2\cos x \cos y}$$

$$\Rightarrow \quad \cos^2 x \cos y = \cos^2 x - \sin^2 y$$

$$\Rightarrow \quad \cos^2 x(1 - \cos y) = \sin^2 y = (1 + \cos y)(1 - \cos y)$$

$$\Rightarrow \quad \cos^2 x = (1 + \cos y) \qquad [\because 1 - \cos y \neq 0]$$

$$\Rightarrow \quad \cos^2 x = 2\cos^2 \frac{y}{2} \Rightarrow \cos^2 x \sec^2\left(\frac{y}{2}\right) = 2$$

$$\therefore \quad \cos x \sec\left(\frac{y}{2}\right) = \pm\sqrt{2}$$

17. Let 11 AM's are $A_1, A_2, A_3, \ldots, A_{11}$.

Given, $28, A_1, A_2, A_3, \ldots, A_{11}, 10$ are in AP.

$$\therefore \quad d = \frac{10 - 28}{12} = -\frac{3}{2}$$

$$\therefore \quad A_i = 28 + id = 28 - \frac{3}{2}i$$

It is clear that $A_2, A_4, A_6, A_8, A_{10}$ are integral AM's.

Hence, number of integral AM's are 5.

18. $\because x, y, z$ are in GP. $\qquad [x, y, z > 1]$

$\therefore$ $\ln x, \ln y, \ln z$ are in AP.

and $2x, 4x, 6x$ are also in AP. $\qquad [x > 1]$

By property, $2x + \ln x, 4x + \ln y, 6x + \ln z$ are also in AP.

$$\therefore \quad \frac{1}{2x + \ln x}, \frac{1}{4x + \ln y}, \frac{1}{6x + \ln z} \text{ are in HP.}$$

19. Let $\quad A = \dfrac{(a^2 + 3a + 1)(b^2 + 3b + 1)(c^2 + 3c + 1)}{abc}$

$$= \left(\frac{a^2 + 3a + 1}{a}\right)\left(\frac{b^2 + 3b + 1}{b}\right)\left(\frac{c^2 + 3c + 1}{c}\right)$$

$$= \left(a + 3 + \frac{1}{a}\right)\left(b + 3 + \frac{1}{b}\right)\left(c + 3 + \frac{1}{c}\right),$$

where $a, b, c \in R^+$.

Applying AM $\geq$ GM on a and $\frac{1}{a}$,

$$a + \frac{1}{a} \geq 2 \Rightarrow a + \frac{1}{b} + 3 \geq 5$$

Similarly, $b + \frac{1}{b} \geq 2 \Rightarrow b + \frac{1}{b} + 3 \geq 5$

and $\quad c + \frac{1}{c} \geq 2 \Rightarrow c + \frac{1}{c} + 3 \geq 5$

$$\therefore \quad \left(a + \frac{1}{a} + 3\right)\left(b + \frac{1}{b} + 3\right)\left(c + \frac{1}{c} + 3\right) \geq 125$$

So, $\quad A \geq 5\cdot5\cdot5 \Rightarrow A \geq 125$

Minimum value of A is 125.

20. $a_1, a_2, \ldots,$ are in AP and $q_1, q_2, \ldots$ are in GP.

$$a_1 = q_1 = 2 \text{ and } a_{10} = q_{10} = 3$$

Let d be the common diference of AP

i.e. $\quad d = \dfrac{3-2}{9} = \dfrac{1}{9}$

Then, $\quad a_7 = a_1 + 6d = 2 + 6d = 2 + 6 \times \frac{1}{9} = \frac{8}{3}$

$$a_{19} = a_1 + 18d = 2 + 18d$$

$$= 2 + 18 \times \frac{1}{9} = \frac{36}{9} = 4$$

Let r be the common ratio of GP i.e. $r = \left(\frac{3}{2}\right)^{1/9}$

Then, $\quad q_7 = q_1 r^6 = 2r^6 = 2\cdot\left(\frac{3}{2}\right)^{6\times\frac{1}{9}} = 2\left(\frac{3}{2}\right)^{2/3}$

$$q_{10} = q_1 r^9 = 2r^9 = 2\cdot\left(\frac{3}{2}\right)^{9\times\frac{1}{9}} = 3$$

$$q_{19} = q_1 \cdot r^{18} = 2\cdot r^{18} = 2\cdot\left(\frac{3}{2}\right)^{18\times\frac{1}{9}} = 2\left(\frac{3}{2}\right)^{18/9} = \frac{9}{2}$$

(a) $a_7 q_{19} = \frac{8}{3} \times \frac{9}{2} = 12$, which is an integer.

(b) $a_{19} q_7 = 4 \times 2 \times \left(\frac{3}{2}\right)^{2/3} = 8\left(\frac{3}{2}\right)^{2/3}$, which is not an integer.

(c) $a_7 q_{19} = \frac{8}{3} \times \frac{9}{2} = 12$; $a_{19} q_{10} = 4 \times 3 = 12$

21. Let S_n denote the sum of first n terms of AP. So,

$$r = \frac{S_n}{S_{2n} - S_n} = \frac{1}{\frac{S_{2n}}{S_n} - 1} \text{ is independent of } n.$$

Therefore, $\frac{S_{2n}}{S_n}$ is independent of n.

$$\text{Now, } \frac{S_{2n}}{S_n} = \frac{\frac{2n}{2}(2\alpha + (2n-1)\beta)}{\frac{n}{2}(2\alpha + (n-1)\beta)} = \frac{2(2\alpha - \beta + 2n\beta)}{(2\alpha - \beta + n\beta)}$$

This ratio is independent of n if $2\alpha - \beta$

$$\therefore \quad \alpha : \beta = 1 : 2$$

$$\therefore \quad r = \frac{1}{4-1} = \frac{1}{3}$$

α and β are roots of the equation

$$ax^2 + bx + c = 0$$

$$\therefore \quad 2\alpha + \alpha = -\frac{b}{a} \text{ and } 2\alpha\cdot\alpha = \frac{c}{a}$$

$$\therefore \quad 2\left(-\frac{b}{3a}\right)^2 = \frac{c}{a} \Rightarrow 2b^2 = 9ac$$

Now, $1 + r + r^2 + \ldots = \dfrac{1}{1-\alpha} = \dfrac{1}{1-\dfrac{1}{3}} = \dfrac{3}{2}$

Again, $\alpha = 1, \beta = 2$

$\therefore$ Sum of 10 terms of AP $= \dfrac{10}{2}(2 \times 1 + (10-1) \times 2) = 100$

22. (a, c) $S = 1 + \dfrac{1}{1+3}(1+2)^2 + \dfrac{1}{1+3+5}(1+2+3)^2$

$$+ \frac{1}{1+3+5+7}(1+2+3+4)^2 + \ldots$$

$$\therefore \quad a_r = \frac{1}{r^2}(1+2+3+\ldots+r)^2$$

$$= \frac{1}{r^2}\left(\frac{r(r+1)}{2}\right)^2 = \left(\frac{r+1}{2}\right)^2 = \frac{r^2+2r+1}{4}$$

$$\therefore \quad a_7 = \frac{7^2 + 2 \times 7 + 1}{4} = 16$$

and $\quad S_{10} = \sum_{r=1}^{10} a_r$

$$= \frac{1}{4}\left\{\frac{10(10+1)(20+1)}{6} + 10(10+1) + 10\right\} = \frac{505}{4}$$

23. We have, $\quad b = \dfrac{2ac}{a+c}$ and $b^2 = -2ac$

$$\therefore \quad b = \frac{-b^2}{a+c} \Rightarrow a + b + c$$

$$\Rightarrow \quad 2b = -2a - 2c$$

$\therefore -2a, b, -2c$ are in AP.

Also, $a^3 + b^3 + c^3 = 3abc$

Again, $b^2 = -2ac \Rightarrow b^4 = 4a^2c^2$

$\therefore a^2, b^2, 4c^2$ are in GP.

Since, $a + b + c = 0$, equation $ax^2 + bx + c = 0$ has one root $x = 1$.

So, equation has real roots.

24. We have,

$$\frac{1}{b-a} + \frac{1}{b-c} = \frac{1}{a} + \frac{1}{c}$$

$$\Rightarrow \quad \frac{1}{b-a} - \frac{1}{c} = \frac{1}{a} - \frac{1}{b-c} \Rightarrow \frac{c-b+a}{c(b-a)} = \frac{b-c-a}{a(b-c)}$$

$$\Rightarrow \quad c - b + a = 0 \text{ or } \frac{1}{c(b-a)} = \frac{1}{a(c-b)}$$

$$\Rightarrow \quad b = a + c \text{ or } bc - ac = ac - ab$$

$$\Rightarrow \quad b = a + c \text{ or } b = \frac{2ac}{a+c}$$

25. $\because \quad a(n) = 1 + \dfrac{1}{2} + \dfrac{1}{3} + \ldots + \dfrac{1}{2^n - 1}$

$$= 1 + \left(\frac{1}{2} + \frac{1}{3}\right) + \left(\frac{1}{4} + \frac{1}{5} + \frac{1}{6} + \frac{1}{7}\right)$$

$$+ \left(\frac{1}{8} + \ldots + \frac{1}{15}\right) + \ldots + \frac{1}{2^n - 1}$$

$$= 1 + \left(\frac{1}{2} + \frac{1}{2^2 - 1}\right) + \left(\frac{1}{2^2} + \frac{1}{5} + \frac{1}{6} + \frac{1}{2^3 - 1}\right) + \ldots + \frac{1}{2^n - 1}$$

$\therefore \quad a(n) < 1 + 1 + \ldots +$ n terms

$\Rightarrow \quad a(n) < n$

$\Rightarrow \quad a(100) < 100$

Also, $a(n) = 1 + \dfrac{1}{2} + \left(\dfrac{1}{3} + \dfrac{1}{4}\right) + \left(\dfrac{1}{5} + \dfrac{1}{6} + \dfrac{1}{7} + \dfrac{1}{8}\right) + \ldots + \dfrac{1}{2^n - 1}$

$$= 1 + \frac{1}{2} + \left(\frac{1}{2^1 + 1} + \frac{1}{2^2}\right) + \left(\frac{1}{2^2 + 1} + \frac{1}{6} + \frac{1}{7} + \frac{1}{2^3}\right)$$

$$+ \ldots + \left(\frac{1}{2^{n-1} + 1} + \ldots + \frac{1}{2^n}\right) - \frac{1}{2^n}$$

$$a(n) > 1 + \frac{1}{2} + \frac{2}{4} + \frac{4}{8} + \ldots + \frac{2^{n-1}}{2^n} - \frac{1}{2^n}$$

$$a(n) > \left(1 - \frac{1}{2^n}\right) + \frac{n}{2} \Rightarrow a(n) > \frac{n}{2}$$

$\therefore \ a(200) > 100$

26.

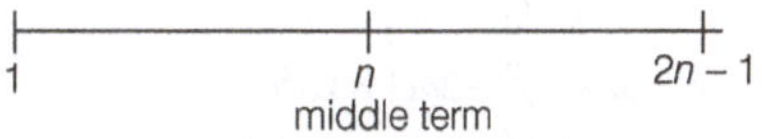

In a AP of $(2n - 1)$ terms, nth term $= a$

In a GP of $(2n - 1)$ terms, nth term $= b$

In a HP of $(2n - 1)$ terms, nth term $= c$

a, b, c will be arithmetic mean, geometric mean, harmonic mean, respectively.

So, $a \geq b \geq c$ and $b^2 = ac$

27.

> **Decoding the Question**
>
> Apply sum of infinite terms of GP
>
> i.e. $\quad a + ar + ar^2 + \ldots + \infty = \dfrac{a}{1-r}$

$$\because \quad 0 < \phi < \frac{\pi}{2}$$

$$\therefore \quad 0 < \sin\phi < 1 \text{ and } 0 < \cos\phi < 1$$

$$\therefore \quad x = \sum_{n=0}^{\infty} \cos^{2n}\phi = 1 + \cos^2\phi + \cos^4\phi + \ldots + \infty$$

$$= \frac{1}{1 - \cos^2\phi} = \frac{1}{\sin^2\phi}$$

or $\quad \sin^2\phi = \dfrac{1}{x} \qquad \ldots$(i)

and $\quad y = \sum_{n=0}^{\infty} \sin^{2n}\phi = 1 + \sin^2\phi + \sin^4\phi + \ldots + \infty$

$$= \frac{1}{1 - \sin^2\phi}$$

$$= \frac{1}{\cos^2\phi}$$

or $\quad \cos^2\phi = \dfrac{1}{y} \qquad \ldots$(ii)

From Eqs. (i) and (ii), we get

$$\sin^2\phi + \cos^2\phi = \frac{1}{x} + \frac{1}{y} \Rightarrow 1 = \frac{1}{x} + \frac{1}{y}$$

$\therefore \quad xy = x + y \quad$ ...(iii)

and $\quad z = \sum_{n=0}^{\infty} \cos^{2n}\phi \sin^{2n}\phi$

$$= 1 + \cos^2\phi \sin^2\phi + \cos^4\phi \sin^4\phi + \dots$$

$$= \frac{1}{1 - \sin^2\phi \cos^2\phi} = \frac{1}{1 - \frac{1}{xy}}$$

[from Eqs. (i) and (ii)]

$\Rightarrow \quad z = \frac{xy}{xy - 1} \Rightarrow xyz = z + xy$

and $\quad xyz = z + x + y \quad$ [from Eq. (iii)]

28. $\because$ a, b, c are in AP $\Rightarrow b = \frac{a + c}{2}$ ...(i)

and a^2, b^2, c^2 are in HP.

$\Rightarrow \quad b^2 = \frac{2a^2c^2}{a^2 + c^2}$ ...(ii)

$\Rightarrow \quad b^2 \{a^2 + c^2\} = 2a^2c^2$

$\Rightarrow \quad b^2 \{(a + c)^2 - 2ac\} = 2a^2c^2$ [from Eq. (i)]

$\Rightarrow \quad b^2 (4b^2 - 2ac) = 2a^2c^2$

$\Rightarrow \quad 2b^4 - ac(b^2) - a^2c^2 = 0$

$\Rightarrow \quad (b^2 - ac)(2b^2 + ac) = 0$

If $\quad b^2 - ac = 0$

a, b, c are in GP.

But given a, b, c are in AP.

$\therefore \quad a = b = c$

and if $\quad 2b^2 + ac = 0$

Then, $\frac{-a}{2}, b, c$ are in GP.

29. Let n consecutive odd numbers be

$$2k + 1, 2k + 3, 2k + 5, \dots, 2k + 2n - 1$$

According to question, sum of these n numbers

$$= \frac{n}{2}[2k + 1 + 2k + 2n - 1] = n(2k + n)$$

$$= n^2 + 2kn = (n + k)^2 - k^2$$

Given that $(n + k)^2 - k^2 = 25^2 - 11^2$

$\Rightarrow \quad n + k = 25$ and $k = 11 \quad \Rightarrow \quad n = 14$ and $k = 11$

So, first term $= 2k + 1 = 23$

Last term $= 2k + 2n - 1 = 22 + 28 - 1 = 22 + 27 = 49$

30. $\because \quad G = 6$ and $G^2 = AH$

$\Rightarrow \quad H = \frac{36}{A}$

Given, $\quad 90A + 5H = 918$

$\Rightarrow \quad 90A + 5 \times \frac{36}{A} = 918 \Rightarrow 5A + \frac{10}{A} = 51$

$\Rightarrow \quad 5A^2 - 51A + 10 = 0 \Rightarrow (A - 10)(5A - 1) = 0$

$\therefore \quad A = 10, \frac{1}{5}$

31. $\because \quad T_n = \frac{1}{(2n - 1)(2n + 1)(2n + 3)(2n + 5)}$

$\therefore \quad S_n = \sum_{n=1}^{n} T_n a$

$$S_n = \frac{1}{6}\sum_{n=1}^{n} \frac{(2n + 5) - (2n - 1)}{(2n - 1)(2n + 1)(2n + 3)(2n + 5)}$$

$$= \frac{1}{6}\sum_{n=1}^{n}\left(\frac{1}{(2n - 1)(2n + 1)(2n + 3)} - \frac{1}{(2n + 1)(2n + 3)(2n + 5)}\right)$$

$$= \frac{1}{6}\left(\frac{1}{1\cdot3\cdot5} - \frac{1}{(2n + 1)(2n + 3)(2n + 5)}\right)$$

$$= \frac{1}{90} - \frac{\frac{1}{6}}{(2n + 1)(2n + 3)(2n + 5)}$$

$\therefore \quad \lambda = \frac{1}{6}$

and $\quad f(n) = (2n + 1)(2n + 3)(2n + 5)$

$\therefore \quad f(0) = 15 \Rightarrow f(1) = 105$

and $\quad f(\lambda) = f\left(\frac{1}{6}\right) = \left(\frac{1}{3} + 1\right)\left(\frac{1}{3} + 3\right)\left(\frac{1}{3} + 5\right) = \frac{640}{27}$

32. $\quad E = \frac{1}{1^2} + \frac{1}{2^2} + \frac{1}{3^2} + \dots$

$$E < 1 + \frac{1}{(1)(2)} + \frac{1}{(2)(3)} + \dots$$

$$E < 1 + \left(1 - \frac{1}{2}\right) + \left(\frac{1}{2} - \frac{1}{3}\right) + \dots$$

$E < 2 \quad$ ...(i)

$$E > 1 + \frac{1}{(2)(3)} + \frac{1}{(3)(4)} + \dots$$

$$E > 1 + \left(\frac{1}{2} - \frac{1}{3}\right) + \left(\frac{1}{3} - \frac{1}{4}\right) + \dots$$

$$E > 1 + \frac{1}{2}; \quad E > \frac{3}{2}$$

33. $\because \quad S_1 = \{0\}$

$$S_2 = \left\{\frac{3}{2}, \frac{5}{2}\right\}$$

$$S_3 = \left\{\frac{8}{3}, \frac{11}{3}, \frac{14}{3}\right\}$$

$$S_4 = \left\{\frac{15}{4}, \frac{19}{4}, \frac{23}{4}, \frac{27}{4}\right\}$$

$\vdots \quad \vdots \quad \vdots$

Let $\quad S = 3 + 8 + 15 + \dots + T_{19}$

$\quad\;\; S = \quad 3 + 8 + \dots + T_{18} + T_{19}$

$0 = 3 + 5 + 7 + \dots + 19$ terms $- T_{19}$

$T_{19} = 3 + 5 + 7 + \dots + 19$ terms

$\therefore \quad T_{19} = \frac{19}{2}(6 + 18 \times 2) = \frac{19}{2} \times 42 = 399$

$$S_{20} = \left\{\frac{399}{20}, \frac{419}{20}, \frac{439}{20}, \dots\right\}$$

$\therefore$ Third element of $S_{20} = \dfrac{439}{20}$

Sum of elements of $S_{20} = \dfrac{20}{2} \times \dfrac{1}{2}[2 \times 399 + 19 \times 20]$

$= 399 + 190 = 589$

34. $\because$ $a_n = \dfrac{1}{n+1} + \dfrac{1}{n+2} + \dfrac{1}{n+3} + \dots + \dfrac{1}{3n}$

$$a_n = \frac{1}{n+1} + \frac{1}{n+2} + \frac{1}{n+3} + \dots + \frac{1}{n+2n}$$

$$a_n = \sum_{\alpha=1}^{2n} \frac{1}{n+\alpha}$$

$$a_2 = \sum_{\alpha=1}^{4} \frac{1}{2+\alpha} = \frac{1}{3} + \frac{1}{4} + \frac{1}{5} + \frac{1}{6}$$

$$= \frac{20+15+12+10}{60}$$

$$= \frac{57}{60} = \frac{19}{20}$$

Now, $a_{n+1} - a_n = \left(\dfrac{1}{n+2} + \dfrac{1}{n+3} + \dots + \dfrac{1}{3n+3}\right)$

$$- \left(\frac{1}{n+1} + \frac{1}{n+2} + \dots + \frac{1}{3n}\right)$$

$$= \frac{1}{3n+1} + \frac{1}{3n+2} + \frac{1}{3n+3} - \frac{1}{n+1}$$

$$= \frac{1}{3n+1} + \frac{1}{3n+2} - \frac{2}{3(n+1)}$$

$$= \frac{9n^2 + 15n + 6 + 9n^2 + 12n + 3 - 18n^2 - 18n - 4}{(3n+1)(3n+2)(3n+3)}$$

$$= \frac{9n+5}{(3n+1)(3n+2)(3n+3)}$$

35. $S_n(x) = \left(x^{n-1} + \dfrac{1}{x^{n-1}}\right) + 2\left(x^{n-2} + \dfrac{1}{x^{n-2}}\right)$

$$+ \dots + (n-1)\left(x + \frac{1}{x}\right) + n$$

Let $S' = x^{n-1} + 2x^{n-2} + 3x^{n-3} + \dots + (n-1)x$

$$\frac{S'}{x} = \quad x^{n-2} + 2x^{n-3} + \dots + (n-2)x + (n-1)$$

$\quad - \quad - \quad - \quad - \quad - \quad -$

$$S'\left(1 - \frac{1}{x}\right) = x^{n-1} + x^{n-2} + x^{n-3} + \dots + x - (n-1)$$

$$S' \frac{(x-1)}{x} = \frac{x \cdot (x^{n-1} - 1)}{(x-1)} - (n-1)$$

$\Rightarrow$ $$S' = \frac{x^2}{(x-1)^2}(x^{n-1} - 1) - \frac{(n-1)x}{(x-1)}$$

$$S'' = \frac{1}{x^{n-1}} + \frac{2}{x^{n-2}} + \dots + \frac{(n-1)}{x}$$

$\Rightarrow$ $$S'' = \frac{1}{x^n}[x + 2x^2 + \dots + (n-1)x^{n-1}]$$

$$= \frac{1}{x^n} \frac{[(n-1)x^n - nx^{n-1} + 1]}{(x-1)^2} \quad \text{[similarly as above]}$$

$\therefore$ $S_n(x) = S' + S'' + n$

$\Rightarrow$ $S_n(x) = \dfrac{1}{x^{(n-1)}}\left(\dfrac{x^n - 1}{x - 1}\right)^2$ ...(i)

For $n = 1, S_1(x) = 1$

$$S_{100}(x) = \frac{1}{x^{99}}\left(\frac{x^{100} - 1}{x - 1}\right)^2$$

36. Let the AP start with n and common difference d, then according to question,

$n + 5d = 32 \Rightarrow n = 32 - 5d$ ...(i)

and $1072 < n + (n+d) + \dots + (n+19d) < 1162$

$$1072 < 20n + \frac{19 \times 20}{2}d < 1162$$

$$1072 < 640 - 100d + 190d < 1162$$

$$432 < 90d < 522$$

$$4.8 < d < 5.8$$

Let d is natural number, so $d = 5$

$\therefore$ $n = 32 - 5 \times 5 = 7$

First term is 7 and common difference is 5.

Sol. (Q. Nos. 37 to 38)

Let $S_n = \dfrac{8}{5} + \dfrac{16}{65} + \dfrac{24}{325} + \dots$

$$T_r = \frac{8r}{4r^4 + 1} = \frac{8r}{(2r^2 + 2r + 1)(2r^2 - 2r + 1)}$$

$$= 2\left[\frac{(2r^2 + 2r + 1) - (2r^2 - 2r + 1)}{(2r^2 + 2r + 1)(2r^2 - 2r + 1)}\right]$$

$$= 2\left[\frac{1}{2r^2 - 2r + 1} - \frac{1}{2r^2 + 2r + 1}\right]$$

37. $\lim\limits_{n \to \infty} S_n = \lim\limits_{n \to \infty} \sum\limits_{r=1}^{n} T_r$

$$= \lim_{n \to \infty} \sum_{r=1}^{n} 2\left(\frac{1}{2r^2 - 2r + 1} - \frac{1}{2r^2 + 2r + 1}\right)$$

$$= 2 \lim_{n \to \infty}\left(1 - \frac{1}{2n^2 + 2n + 1}\right) = 2(1 - 0) = 2$$

38. $S_8 = \sum\limits_{r=1}^{8} T_r = 2\sum\limits_{r=1}^{8}\left(\dfrac{1}{2r^2 - 2r + 1} - \dfrac{1}{2r^2 + 2r + 1}\right)$

$$= 2\left(1 - \frac{1}{2(8)^2 + 2(8) + 1}\right) = 2\left(1 - \frac{1}{145}\right) = \frac{288}{145}$$

Sol. (Q. Nos. 39-40)

Let p and $(p+1)$ be removed numbers from 1, 2, 3, ... n, then Sum of the remaining numbers

$$= \frac{n(n+1)}{2} - (2p+1)$$

From given condition,

$$\frac{105}{4} = \frac{\dfrac{n(n+1)}{2} - (2p+1)}{(n-2)}$$

$\Rightarrow$ $$2n^2 - 103n - 8p + 206 = 0$$

Since, n and p are integers, so n must be even.

Let $n = 2r$, we get

$$p = \frac{4r^2 + 103(1-r)}{4}$$

Since, p is an integer, then $(1-r)$ must be divisible by 4.

Let $r = 1 + 4t$, we get

$$n = 2 + 8t \text{ and } p = 16t^2 - 95t + 1$$

Now, $1 \le p < n$

$\Rightarrow$ $1 \le 16t^2 - 95t + 1 < 8t + 2$

$\Rightarrow$ $t = 6 \Rightarrow n = 50$ and $p = 7$

39. Hence, the value of n lies in $(41, 51)$.

40. Hence, removed numbers are 7 and 8.

Sol. (Q. Nos. 41 to 42)

$\because$ $$\alpha + \beta = -\frac{b}{a}, \alpha\beta = \frac{c}{a}, \alpha - \beta = \frac{\sqrt{b^2 - 4ac}}{a}$$

and $$\gamma + \delta = -\frac{B}{A}, \gamma\delta = \frac{C}{A}, \gamma - \delta = \frac{\sqrt{B^2 - 4AC}}{A}$$

41. Since, α, β, γ are in AP.

Let $\beta = \alpha + D, \gamma = \alpha + 2D$ and $\delta = \alpha + 3D$

$\because$ $$\alpha + \beta = \frac{-b}{a} \Rightarrow \alpha + \alpha + D = -\frac{b}{a}$$

or $$2\alpha + D = -\frac{b}{a} \quad \text{...(i)}$$

and $$\gamma + \delta = -\frac{B}{A} \Rightarrow 2\alpha + 5D = -\frac{B}{A} \quad \text{...(ii)}$$

From Eqs. (i) and (ii), we get

$$4D = \left(-\frac{B}{A} + \frac{b}{a}\right) \text{ or } D = \frac{1}{4}\left(\frac{b}{a} - \frac{B}{A}\right)$$

42. Since, $\alpha, \beta, \gamma, \delta, \ldots$ are in GP.

$\therefore$ $$\frac{\beta}{\alpha} = \frac{\gamma}{\beta} = \frac{\delta}{\gamma} \Rightarrow \frac{\beta}{\alpha} = \frac{\delta}{\gamma} \Rightarrow \frac{\alpha}{\gamma} = \frac{\beta}{\delta}$$

$\Rightarrow$ $$\frac{\alpha + \beta}{\gamma + \delta} = \sqrt{\frac{\alpha\beta}{\gamma\delta}}$$

$\Rightarrow$ $$\frac{-\frac{b}{a}}{-\frac{B}{A}} = \sqrt{\frac{\frac{c}{a}}{\frac{C}{A}}} \Rightarrow \frac{b^2A^2}{a^2B^2} = \frac{cA}{aC}$$

$\Rightarrow$ $$\frac{ac\,A^2}{aB^2} = \frac{cA}{C} \Rightarrow B^2 = AC$$

Hence, A, B, C are in GP.

Sol. (Q. Nos. 43 to 44)

For $n > 1$, we have $n + 1 > n - 1$

$\Rightarrow$ $$\frac{n+1}{n-1} > 1 \Rightarrow p\left(\frac{n+1}{n-1}\right)^2 > p \quad [\because p > 0] \text{ ...(i)}$$

Now, $p = a + d$

Since, a, p, b, are in AP.

And $$d = \frac{b-a}{n+1}$$

43. $$p = a + \frac{(b-a)}{n+1} = \frac{na + b}{n+1}$$

44. $$\frac{1}{q} = \frac{1}{a} + D = \frac{1}{a} + \frac{\frac{1}{b} - \frac{1}{a}}{n+1}$$

$\Rightarrow$ $$q = \frac{ab\,(n+1)}{a + bn}$$

Sol. (Q. Nos. 45 to 46)

Given sequence, 1, 3, 6, 10, 15, 21, 28, ...

where $t_n = t_{n-1} + n, \forall\, n \ge 2$

So, $$t_n = [t_{n-2} + (n-1)] + n$$
$$= t_{n-3} + (n-2) + (n-1) + n$$
$$\vdots \qquad \vdots \qquad \vdots$$
$$t_n = t_1 + 2 + 3 + \ldots + (n-1) + n$$
$$t_n = 1 + 2 + 3 + \ldots + n$$
$$t_n = \frac{n\,(n+1)}{2} \quad \text{...(i)}$$

45. $$t_{50} = \frac{50 \times 51}{2} = 25 \times 51 = 1275$$

46. $$t_{100} = \frac{100 \times 101}{2} = 5050$$

$$t_{101} = \frac{101 \times 102}{2} = 101 \times 51 = 5151$$

Number of positive integers lying between t_{100} and t_{101}

$$= 5151 - 5050 - 1$$
$$= 101 - 1 = 100$$

Sol. (Q. Nos. 47 to 48)

$A_1, A_2, A_3, \ldots, A_m$ are arithmetic means between -3 and 828.

So, $$A_1 + A_2 + \ldots + A_m = m\frac{(a+b)}{2}$$

$\Rightarrow$ $$A_1 + A_2 + \ldots + A_m = m\left(\frac{-3 + 288}{2}\right)$$

$\Rightarrow$ $$14025 = m\left(\frac{825}{2}\right)$$

[given that sum of AM's = 14025]

$\Rightarrow$ $m = 17 \times 2$

$\therefore$ $m = 34$ ...(i)

Now, $G_1, G_2, \ldots, G_n$ be the GM's between 1 and 2187.

$\therefore$ $$G_1G_2G_3 \ldots G_n = (ab)^{n/2}$$

$\Rightarrow$ $$3^{35} = (1 \times 2187)^{n/2} \Rightarrow 3^{35} = 3^{7n/2}$$

So, $$35 = \frac{7n}{2}$$

$\Rightarrow$ $n = 10$ ...(ii)

47. $n = 10$ [by Eq. (ii)]

48. $m = 34$ [by Eq. (i)]

49. a, b, c, d are positive real numbers with

$$a < b < c < d \quad \text{...(A)}$$

According to the question, a, b, c, d are in AP.

$\Rightarrow$ $b = a + \alpha, c = a + 2\alpha$ and $d = a + 3\alpha$ ...(i)

α be the common difference

and a, b, d are in GP.

$$\Rightarrow \quad b^2 = ad \quad \quad ...(ii)$$

From Eqs. (i) and (ii), we get

$$(a+\alpha)^2 = a(a+3\alpha)$$

$$\Rightarrow \quad a^2 + \alpha^2 + 2a\alpha = a^2 + 3a\alpha$$

$$\Rightarrow \quad \alpha^2 = a\alpha$$

$$\Rightarrow \quad a(\alpha - a) = 0$$

$$\Rightarrow \quad \alpha = 0 \text{ or } \alpha = a$$

$a \neq 0$ by (A), so $\alpha = a$

From Eq. (i), $b = 2a$, $c = 3a$ and $d = 4a$

$$\frac{ad}{bc} = \frac{a \cdot 4a}{2a \cdot 3a} = \frac{2}{3} = \left(\frac{p}{q}\right)$$

where, p and q are prime numbers.

So, $\quad q = 3$

50. $\because \sum_{r=1}^{110} (1+rx) = (1+x)(1+2x)(1+3x)...(1+110x)$

$$= 1^{110} + (x + 2x + 3x + ... + 110x)\, 1^{109} + ...$$

So, coefficient of x in

$$\sum_{r=1}^{110} (1+rx) = (1+2+3+...+110) = \frac{110 \times 111}{2} = 55 \times 111$$

$$= 6105$$

Now, $\lambda(1+10)(1+10+10^2) = \lambda(11)(111)$

$$\Rightarrow \quad \lambda(111)(11) = 6105 \Rightarrow \lambda = 5$$

51. Let number of the form palindrome be $\alpha\beta\alpha$.

Now, If $\alpha\beta\alpha$ is even, then α may be 2, 4, 6, 8 and β take values 0, 1, 2, ..., 9.

So, total number of palindrome (even) $= 10 \times 4 = 40$

To find the sum of all even 3 digit plaindrome

So, sum of number start with 2

$$= (200+2) \times 10 + (0+1+2+3+...+9) \times 10$$

$$= 2020 + 450 = 2470$$

Sum of number start with 4 $= (404) \times 10 + 450$

Similarly, sum of number start with 6 $= (606) \times 10 + 450$

Similarly, sum of number start with 8 $= (808) \times 10 + 450$

$\therefore$ Total sum $= (202 + 404 + 606 + 808) \times 10 + 450 \times 4$

$$= 20200 + 1800 = 22000 = 2^4 \times 5^3 \times 11$$

On comparing $2^4 \times 5^3 \times 11^1$ with

$$2^{n_1} \times 3^{n_2} \times 5^{n_3} \times 7^{n_4} \times 11^{n_5},$$

$$n_1 = 4,\ n_2 = 3,\ n_3 = 0,\ n_4 = 0,\ n_5 = 1$$

Now, $\quad n_1 + n_2 + n_3 + n_4 + n_5 = 8$

52. $\because 2 + (6 \cdot 2^2 - 4 \cdot 2) + (6 \cdot 3^2 - 4 \cdot 3) + ... + (6 \cdot n^2 - 4 \cdot n) = 140$

$$\Rightarrow \quad 2 + 6(2^2 + 3^2 + ... + n^2) - 4 \cdot (2 + 3 + ... + n) = 140$$

$$\Rightarrow \quad 2 + 6\left(\frac{n(n+1)(2n-1)}{6} - 1\right) - 4\left(\frac{n(n+1)}{2} - 1\right) = 140$$

$$\Rightarrow \quad 2 + n(n+1)(2n+1) - 6 - 2n(n+1) + 4 = 140$$

$$\Rightarrow \quad n(n+1)(2n+1) - 2n(n+1) - 140 = 0$$

$$\Rightarrow \quad 2n^3 + 3n^2 + n - 2n^2 - 2n - 140 = 0$$

$$\Rightarrow \quad 2n^3 + n^2 - n - 140 = 0$$

$$\Rightarrow \quad (n-4)(2n^2 + 9n + 35) = 0$$

$$\Rightarrow \quad n = 4 \text{ or } 2n^2 + 9n + 35 = 0$$

$$\Rightarrow \quad 2n^2 + 9n + 35 = 0$$

$$\Rightarrow \quad n = \frac{-9 \pm \sqrt{81 - 280}}{4}$$

$$\therefore \quad n = \frac{9 \pm \sqrt{-199}}{4} \quad \text{[complex values]}$$

Only positive integer value of n is 4.

53. $S(x) = 1 + x - x^2 - x^3 + x^4 + x^5 - x^6 - x^7 + ... + \infty$

where $x \in (0, 1)$

$$S(x) = (1+x) - x^2(1+x) + x^4(1+x) - x^6(1+x) + ... + \infty$$

$$\Rightarrow S(x) = (1+x)[1 - x^2 + x^4 - x^6 + ... + \infty]$$

$$\Rightarrow S(x) = (1+x)\left(\frac{1}{1+x^2}\right) \quad \left[\because S_\infty = \frac{a}{1-r} \text{ for GP}\right]$$

According to the question,

$$S(x) = \frac{\sqrt{2}+1}{2}$$

So, $$\frac{1+x}{1+x^2} = \frac{\sqrt{2}+1}{2}$$

$$\Rightarrow \quad 2 + 2x = (\sqrt{2}+1)x^2 + \sqrt{2} + 1$$

$$\Rightarrow \quad (\sqrt{2}+1)x^2 - 2x - 2 + \sqrt{2} + 1 = 0$$

$$\Rightarrow \quad (\sqrt{2}+1)x^2 - 2x + \sqrt{2} - 1 = 0$$

$$\Rightarrow \quad (\sqrt{2}+1)x^2 - 2x + \frac{1}{\sqrt{2}+1} = 0$$

$$\Rightarrow \quad [(\sqrt{2}+1)x]^2 - 2(\sqrt{2}+1)x + 1 = 0$$

$$\Rightarrow \quad [(\sqrt{2}+1)x - 1]^2 = 0$$

$$\Rightarrow \quad x = \frac{1}{\sqrt{2}+1} \quad \text{[repeated]}$$

So, $$x = \sqrt{2} - 1$$

$$\therefore \quad (x+1)^2 = 2$$

54. $a_1, a_2, a_3, ...$ are in GP with common ratio r

and $b_1, b_2, b_3, ...$ is also a GP i.e. $b_1 = 1$

$$b_2 = \sqrt[4]{7} - \sqrt[4]{28} + 1,\ a_1 = \sqrt[4]{28}$$

and $$\sum_{n=1}^{\infty} \frac{1}{a_n} = \sum_{n=1}^{\infty} b_n$$

$$\frac{1}{a_1} + \frac{1}{a_2} + \frac{1}{a_3} + ... + \infty = b_1 + b_2 + b_3 + ... + \infty$$

$$\Rightarrow \frac{1}{\sqrt[4]{28}} + \frac{1}{\sqrt[4]{28}\, r} + \frac{1}{\sqrt[4]{28}\, r^2} + ... + \infty$$

$$= 1 + (\sqrt[4]{7} - \sqrt[4]{28} + 1) + (\sqrt[4]{7} - \sqrt[4]{28} + 1)^2 + ... + \infty$$

$$\Rightarrow \quad \frac{\frac{1}{\sqrt[4]{28}}}{1 - \frac{1}{r}} = \frac{1}{1 - \sqrt[4]{7} + \sqrt[4]{28} - 1}$$

$$\Rightarrow \quad \frac{r}{(r-1)\sqrt[4]{28}} = \frac{1}{\sqrt[4]{7}\,(\sqrt[4]{4}-1)}$$

$$\Rightarrow \quad \frac{r}{(r-1)}\frac{1}{\sqrt[4]{4}} = \frac{1}{(\sqrt[4]{4}-1)}$$

Let $\sqrt[4]{4} = \alpha$, we get

$$\Rightarrow \quad \frac{r}{(r-1)\,\alpha} = \frac{1}{\alpha - 1}$$

$$\Rightarrow \quad r\alpha - r = r\alpha - \alpha \Rightarrow r = \alpha \Rightarrow r = \sqrt[4]{4}$$

Now, $(1 + r^2 + r^4)^2 = (1 + (\sqrt[4]{4})^2 + (\sqrt[4]{4})^4)^2$

$$= (1 + 4^{1/2} + 4)^2 = (1 + 2 + 4)^2 = (7)^2$$

$$= 49$$

55. Let $a = 10 + D$ ...(i)

$b = 10 + 2D$ ...(ii)

$ab = 10 + 3D$ ...(iii)

On substituting the values of a and b in Eq. (iii), we get

$$(10 + D)(10 + 2D) = (10 + 3D)$$

$$\Rightarrow \quad 2D^2 + 27D + 90 = 0$$

$$\therefore \quad D = -6,\, D = -\frac{15}{2}$$

$$\therefore \quad a_1 = 10 - 6 = 4,$$

$$a_2 = 10 - \frac{15}{2} = \frac{5}{2}$$

and $b_1 = 10 - 12 = -2,\, b_2 = 10 - 15 = -5$

Now, $\left(\frac{2a_1a_2 + b_1b_2}{100}\right) = \left(\frac{2 \times 10 + 10}{100}\right) = 0.3$

56. Given equation, $Ax^3 + Bx^2 + Cx + D = 0$ ...(i)

where, $A \neq 0$

Let roots are α, β, γ, then $\beta = \frac{\alpha + \gamma}{2}$ ...(ii)

Given relation, $2B^3 + \lambda\, ABC + \mu\, A^2D = 0$ ...(iii)

From Eq. (i), $\alpha + \beta + \gamma = -\frac{\beta}{A}$

$$\Rightarrow \quad 3\beta = -\frac{B}{A} \quad \text{[from Eq. (ii)]}$$

$$\Rightarrow \quad \beta = -\frac{B}{3A}$$

Now, β satisfy Eq. (i), so

$$A\left(\frac{-B}{3A}\right)^3 + B\left(\frac{-B}{3A}\right)^2 + C\left(\frac{-B}{3A}\right) + D = 0$$

$$\Rightarrow \quad \frac{-B^3}{27A^2} + \frac{B^3}{9A^2} - \frac{BC}{3A} + D = 0$$

$$\Rightarrow \quad \frac{2}{27}\frac{B^3}{A^2} - \frac{BC}{3A} + D = 0$$

$$\Rightarrow \quad 2B^3 - 9\,ABC + 27\,DA^2 = 0$$

Compare with Eq. (iii), we get

$$\lambda = -9,\, \mu = 27$$

$$2\lambda + \mu^2 = -18 + 27^2$$

$$= -18 + 729 = 711$$

57. Let $P = \lim_{n \to \infty}\left(\frac{1}{1+x} + \frac{2}{1+x^2} + \frac{2^2}{1+x^4} + \ldots \text{ upto } n \text{ terms}\right)$

$$= \lim_{n \to \infty} \sum_{r=0}^{n}\left(\frac{2^r}{1 + x^{2^r}} + \frac{2^r}{1 - x^{2^r}} - \frac{2^r}{1 - x^{2^r}}\right)$$

$$= \lim_{n \to \infty} \sum_{r=0}^{n}\left(\frac{2^{r+1}}{1 - x^{2^{r+1}}} - \frac{2^r}{1 - x^{2^r}}\right)$$

$$= \lim_{n \to \infty}\left(\frac{2^{n+1}}{1 - x^{2^{n+1}}} - \frac{1}{1-x}\right)$$

$$= \lim_{n \to \infty} \frac{\dfrac{2^{n+1}}{x^{2^{n+1}}}}{\dfrac{1}{x^{2^{n+1}}} - 1} - \frac{1}{1-x} = 0 - \frac{1}{1-x}$$

$$= \frac{1}{x-1} = \frac{1}{x - \lambda} \quad \text{[given]}$$

$$\therefore \quad \lambda = 1$$

$$\Rightarrow \quad 10\lambda = 10$$

58. Let number of AP be $(a - d), a, (a + d)$.

According to the question,

$(a - d)^2, a^2, (a + d)^2$ are in GP.

$$\therefore \quad (a^2)^2 = (a - d)^2 (a + d)^2$$

$$\Rightarrow \quad a^4 = (a^2 - d^2)^2$$

$$\Rightarrow \quad a^4 = a^4 + d^4 - 2a^2d^2$$

$$\Rightarrow \quad a^2(a^2 - 2d^2) = 0$$

$$\Rightarrow \quad a \neq 0, \text{ so } a^2 = 2d^2$$

$$\Rightarrow \quad a = \pm\sqrt{2}d \quad \text{...(i)}$$

Let common ratio of GP be r.

$$\therefore \quad r^2 = \frac{(a + d)^2}{(a - d)^2}$$

$$\Rightarrow \quad r^2 = \frac{a^2 + d^2 + 2ad}{a^2 + d^2 - 2ad}$$

$$\Rightarrow \quad r^2 = \frac{2d^2 + d^2 + 2\sqrt{2}d^2}{2d^2 + d^2 - 2\sqrt{2}\,d^2}$$

[from Eq. (i) for $a = \sqrt{2}\,d$]

$$\Rightarrow \quad r^2 = \frac{(3 + 2\sqrt{2})\,d^2}{(3 - 2\sqrt{2})\,d^2}$$

$$\Rightarrow \quad r^2 = \frac{(3 + 2\sqrt{2})(3 + 2\sqrt{2})}{9 - 8}$$

$$\Rightarrow \quad r^2 = (3 + 2\sqrt{2})^2$$

$$\Rightarrow \quad r^2 = (3 + \sqrt{8})^2$$

$$\therefore \quad r = \pm(3 + \sqrt{8})$$

$$\Rightarrow \quad r = 3 + \sqrt{8} \quad [\because r \text{ is positive}]$$

Similarly, for $a = -\sqrt{2}\,d$, we get

$$r = \pm(3 - \sqrt{8})$$

$$\Rightarrow \quad r = (3 - \sqrt{8}) \quad [\because r \text{ is positive}]$$

Compare r with $3 \pm \sqrt{k}$, we get

$$k = 8$$

$$\therefore \quad \left[\frac{k^2}{3}\right] = \left[\frac{64}{3}\right] = 21$$

59. Since, a, b, c, d are in AP.

So, $b - a = c - b = d - c = D$ [common difference]

$$\therefore \quad d = a + 3D \Rightarrow a - d = -3D$$

and $\quad d = b + 2D \Rightarrow b - d = -2D$

Also, $\quad c = a + 2D \Rightarrow c - a = 2D$

$$\therefore \quad 2(a - b) + k(b - c)^2 + (c - a)^3$$

$$= 2(a - d) + (b - d)^2 + (c - d)^3$$

$$\Rightarrow -2D + kD^2 + (2D)^3 = -6D + 4D^2 - D^3$$

$$\Rightarrow \quad 9D^2 + (k - 4)D + 4 = 0$$

Since, D is real

$$\therefore \quad (k - 4)^2 - 4(4)(9) \ge 0$$

$$\Rightarrow \quad k^2 - 8k - 128 \ge 0$$

$$\Rightarrow \quad (k - 16)(k + 8) \ge 0$$

$$\Rightarrow \quad k \in [-\infty, -8] \cup [16, \infty)$$

So, smallest positive value of k is 16.

60. The ball is dropped from the height, $h = 80$ m

So, initially it travels the distance of 80 m.

Then, rebounds to x% of its previous height.

So, it rebounds by the distance of $\frac{80x}{100}$ m from the same height it drops again.

It continues like this till it comes to rest.

$\therefore$ Total distance travel is given by

$$320 = 80 + \left(2 \times \frac{80x}{100} + 2 \times \frac{80x^2}{(100)^2} + \dots\right)$$

$$\Rightarrow \quad 4 = 1 + \frac{2x}{100} + \frac{2x^2}{(100)^2} + \dots$$

$$\Rightarrow \quad 3 = \frac{\frac{2x}{100}}{1 - \frac{x}{100}} \Rightarrow 3 = \frac{2x}{100 - x} \Rightarrow x = 60$$

61. $S_k = \dfrac{k}{1 - \dfrac{1}{k+1}} = k + 1$

$$\therefore \quad \sum_{k=1}^{10} S_k = \sum_{k=1}^{10} (k + 1) = \frac{10(10+1)}{2} + 10 = 65$$

62. **(A)** a, b, c, d are in AP. [a, b, c, d are positive real numbers]

By AM > GM, for a, b, c

$$b > \sqrt{ac} \Rightarrow b^2 > ac \quad \text{...(i)}$$

Now, applying for b, c, d

$$c > \sqrt{bd} \Rightarrow c^2 > bd \quad \text{...(ii)}$$

From Eqs. (i) and (ii), we get

$$b^2c^2 > (ac)(bd) \Rightarrow bc > ad$$

Again, applying AM > HM for a, b, c

$$b > \frac{2}{\frac{1}{a} + \frac{1}{c}} \Rightarrow \frac{1}{a} + \frac{1}{c} > \frac{2}{b} \quad \text{...(iii)}$$

For last 3 terms b, c, d

$$c > \frac{2}{\frac{1}{b} + \frac{1}{d}} \Rightarrow \frac{1}{b} + \frac{1}{d} > \frac{2}{c} \quad \text{...(iv)}$$

From Eqs. (iii) and (iv), we get

$$\frac{1}{a} + \frac{1}{c} + \frac{1}{b} + \frac{1}{d} > \frac{2}{b} + \frac{2}{c}$$

$$\Rightarrow \quad \frac{1}{a} + \frac{1}{d} > \frac{1}{b} + \frac{1}{c}$$

(B) a, b, c, d are in GP.

For a, b, c applying AM > GM,

$$\Rightarrow \quad \frac{a + c}{2} > b \Rightarrow a + c > 2b \quad \text{...(i)}$$

Similarly, for b, c, d

$$b + d > 2c \quad \text{...(ii)}$$

From Eqs. (i) and (ii), we get

$$a + b + c + d > 2b + 2c \Rightarrow a + d > b + c$$

Now, applying GM > HM for $a, b\ c$

$$b > \frac{2ac}{a + c}$$

$$\Rightarrow \quad \frac{1}{c} + \frac{1}{a} > \frac{2}{c} \quad \text{...(iii)}$$

Similarly, for b, c, d, we get

$$\frac{1}{d} + \frac{1}{b} > \frac{2}{c} \quad \text{...(iv)}$$

On adding Eqs. (iii) and (iv), we get

$$\frac{1}{a} + \frac{1}{b} + \frac{1}{c} + \frac{1}{d} > 2\left(\frac{1}{b} + \frac{1}{c}\right)$$

$$\Rightarrow \quad \frac{1}{a} + \frac{1}{d} > \frac{1}{b} + \frac{1}{c}$$

(C) a, b, c, d are in HP.

Applying AM > HM for a, b, c

$$\frac{a + c}{2} > b \Rightarrow a + c > 2b \quad \text{...(i)}$$

Similarly, for last 3 terms b, c, d

$$\Rightarrow \quad b + d > 2c \quad \text{...(ii)}$$

On adding Eqs. (i) and (ii), we get

$$a + b + c + d > 2b + 2c$$

$$\Rightarrow \quad a + d > b + c$$

Again, applying GM > HM for a, b, c

$$\sqrt{ac} > b$$

$$\Rightarrow \quad ac > b^2 \quad \text{...(iii)}$$

Similarly, for b, c, d

$$\Rightarrow \quad bd > c^2 \quad \text{...(iv)}$$

On multiplying Eqs. (iii) and (iv), we get

$$abcd > b^2c^2$$

$$ad > bc$$

(D) $\frac{1}{a}, \frac{1}{b}, \frac{1}{c}, \frac{1}{d}$ are in G.P.

$\therefore \quad \frac{1}{a} \times \frac{1}{d} = \frac{1}{b} \times \frac{1}{c}$

$\Rightarrow \quad ad = bc$

63. (A) $a_1, a_2, a_3, \ldots, a_n, \ldots$ are in AP

and $\quad a_1 = \frac{5}{2}, a_{10} = 16$

$\therefore \quad a_1 + a_2 + \ldots + a_n = 110$

$\Rightarrow \quad \frac{n}{2}(a_1 + a_n) = 110$

$\Rightarrow \quad \frac{n}{2}\left[\frac{5}{2} + \frac{5}{2} + (n-1)d\right] = 110 \quad \ldots(\text{i})$

Now, $d = \frac{a_{10} - a_1}{10 - 1} = \frac{16 - \frac{5}{2}}{9} = \frac{27}{9 \times 2} = \frac{3}{2} \quad \ldots(\text{ii})$

From Eqs. (i) and (ii), we get

$\frac{n}{2}\left[5 + (n-1)\frac{3}{2}\right] = 110$

$\Rightarrow \quad 5n + (n^2 - n)\frac{3}{2} = 220$

$\Rightarrow \quad 3n^2 + 7n - 440 = 0$

$\Rightarrow \quad 3n^2 + 40n - 33n - 440 = 0$

$\Rightarrow \quad n(3n + 40) - 11(3n + 40) = 0$

$\Rightarrow \quad (3n + 40)(n - 11) = 0$

So, $\quad n = -\frac{40}{3}$ or $n = 11$

$\therefore \quad n = 11 \quad [n \in N]$

(B) Let first angle $= a$ [in degrees]

Common difference $= d$ [in degrees]

Number of sides $n = 9$

$\therefore$ Sum of interior angles $= (n-2) \times 180°$

$\Rightarrow \quad \frac{n}{2}[2a + (n-1)d] = (n-2) \times 180°$

$\Rightarrow \quad \frac{9}{2}(2a + 8d) = 7 \times 180° \Rightarrow a + 4d = 140°$

and largest angle $T_9 = a + 8d < 180°$

$\Rightarrow \quad 4d < 40$

$\Rightarrow \quad d < 10$

$\therefore \quad d = 9$

(C) Given increasing GP,

$a_1, a_2, \ldots, a_n, \ldots$

where $\quad a_6 = 4a_4$

$a_1 r^5 = 4a_1 r^3 \quad$ [r is the common ratio]

$\Rightarrow \quad r^2 = 4$

$\Rightarrow \quad r = 2 \quad [\because$ increasing GP]

and $\quad a_9 - a_7 = 192$

$a_1(r^8 - r^6) = 192$

$a_1(256 - 64) = 192$

$a_1 = \frac{192}{192}$

$a_1 = 1$

Then, $a_2 = 2, a_3 = 4$ and $a_4 + a_5 + \ldots + a_n = 1016$

$(a_1 + a_2 + \ldots + a_n) - (a_1 + a_2 + a_3) = 1016$

$\frac{1(2^n - 1)}{2 - 1} = 1016 + 7$

$2^n = 1023 + 1 = 1024 = 2^{10}$

$\therefore \quad n = 10$

(D) Given, α and β are root of $x^2 - 8x + 4 = 0$.

$\therefore \quad \alpha\beta = 4$

Also, $\alpha, a_1, a_2, \ldots, a_5, \beta$ are in GP.

$\therefore a_1 a_2 a_3 a_4 a_5 = (\sqrt{\alpha\beta})^5$

Now, $\sum_{i=1}^{5} \log_2 a_i = \log_2 a_1 + \log_2 a_2 + \log_2 a_3 + \log_2 a_4 + \log_2 a_5$

$= \log_2(a_1 a_2 \ldots a_5)$

$= \log_2(\sqrt{\alpha\beta})^5 = 5\log_2\sqrt{4} = 5$

64. (A) $b + c = 20$ and $a + d = 20$

$\Rightarrow a + b + c + d = 40 \quad \left[\because \frac{b+c}{2} = 10 \text{ and } \frac{a+d}{2} = 10, \text{ as } a, b, 10, c, d \text{ are in AP}\right]$

(B) Sides are $2, 2r, 2r^2$

Now, $(2r^2)^2 = 4r^2 + 4 \Rightarrow r^4 - r^2 - 1 = 0$

$\Rightarrow \quad r^2 = \frac{1 + \sqrt{5}}{2} \Rightarrow 2r^2 = 1 + \sqrt{5}$

$\Rightarrow \quad a^2 + b^2 = 26$

(C) $a + ar + ar^2 = 70$

Now, $4a, 5ar, 4ar^2$ are in AP

$\Rightarrow \quad 5r - 4 = 4r^2 - 5r$

$\Rightarrow \quad 5r = 2(r^2 + 1)$

So, $\quad ar + a\left(\frac{5r}{2}\right) = 70$

$\Rightarrow \quad ar = 20$

$\Rightarrow$ GP is 40, 20, 10

(D) $\cos 60° = \frac{4 + 9 - c_1^2}{12}$

$\Rightarrow \quad c_1^2 = 7 \Rightarrow c_1 = \sqrt{7}$

other side is $\cos 120° = \frac{4 + 9 - c_2^2}{12}$

$\Rightarrow \quad c_2^2 = 19 \Rightarrow c_2 = \sqrt{19}$

Perimeter $= 2(\sqrt{7} + \sqrt{19})$

$\therefore a = 7$ and $b = 19$

Now, AM of a, b and 4 is

$\frac{7 + 19 + 4}{3} = 10$

65. **(A)** $4a^2 + 9b^2 + 16c^2 = 2(3ab + 6bc + 4ca)$

$$(2a)^2 + (3b)^2 + (4c)^2 - (2a)(3b)(4c) - (2a)(4c) = 0$$

$$\frac{1}{2}\{(2a - 3b)^2 + (3b - 4c)^2 + (4c - 2a)^2\} = 0$$

$\Rightarrow$ $2a - 3b = 0$ and $3b - 4c = 0$

and $4c - 2a = 0 \Rightarrow 2a = 3b$

and $3b = 4c$ and $4c = 2a$

$\Rightarrow$ $a = \dfrac{3}{2}b$ and $b = \dfrac{4}{3}c$ and $c = \dfrac{1}{2}a$

$\Rightarrow$ $a = \dfrac{3}{2}b$ and $b = \dfrac{4}{3}c$ and $c = \dfrac{3}{4}b$

So, a, b, c are $\dfrac{3}{2}b, b, \dfrac{3}{4}b$

Reciprocal of the terms $\dfrac{2}{3b}, \dfrac{1}{b}, \dfrac{4}{3b}$, which is in AP.

So, these a, b, c are in HP.

(B) $17a^2 + 13b^2 + 5c^2 = 3ab + 15bc + 5ca$

$\Rightarrow$ $34a^2 + 26a^2 + 10c^2 - 6ab - 30bc - 10ca = 0$

$\Rightarrow$ $(3a - b)^2 + (5b - 3c)^2 + (c - 5a)^2 = 0$

$\Rightarrow$ $3a - b = 0$ and $5b - 3c = 0$ and $c - 5a = 0$

$\Rightarrow$ $\dfrac{a}{1} = \dfrac{b}{3} = \dfrac{c}{5} = \lambda$ [say]

$\therefore$ $a = \lambda, b = 3\lambda, c = 5\lambda$

Hence, a, b, c are in AP.

(C) $a^2 + 9b^2 + 25c^2 = abc\left(\dfrac{15}{a} + \dfrac{5}{b} + \dfrac{3}{c}\right)$

$\Rightarrow$ $(a)^2 + (3b)^2 + (5c)^2 - 15bc - 5ac - 3ab = 0$

$\Rightarrow$ $\dfrac{1}{2}\{(a - 3b)^2 + (3b - 5c)^2 + (5c - a)^2\} = 0$

$\Rightarrow$ $a - 3b = 0$ and $3b - 5c = 0$ and $5c - a = 0$

$\Rightarrow$ $a = 3b$ and $3b = 5c$ and $5c = a$

$\Rightarrow$ $a = 3b$ and $b = \dfrac{5}{3}c$ and $c = \dfrac{a}{5}$

$\Rightarrow$ $a = 3b$ and $b = \dfrac{5}{3}c$ and $c = \dfrac{3}{5}b$

So, a, b, c are of the form $3b, b, \dfrac{3b}{5}$.

Reciprocal of $3b, b, \dfrac{3b}{5}$ are $\dfrac{1}{3b}, \dfrac{1}{b}, \dfrac{5}{3b}$, which are in AP.

$$\left[\because \frac{1}{b} - \frac{1}{3b} = \frac{2}{3b} \text{ and } \frac{5}{3b} - \frac{1}{b} = \frac{2}{3b}\right]$$

$\therefore$ a, b, c are in HP.

(D) $(a^2 + b^2 + c^2)p^2 - 2p(ab + bc + ca) + a^2 + b^2 + c^2 \le 0$

$\Rightarrow$ $(a^2p^2 + b^2 - 2abp) + (b^2p^2 + c^2 - 2pbc)$
$+ (c^2p^2 + a^2 - 2acp) \le 0$

$\Rightarrow$ $(ap - b)^2 + (bp - c)^2 + (cp - a)^2 \le 0$

$\Rightarrow$ $(ap - b)^2 + (bp - c)^2 + (cp - a)^2 = 0$

$\Rightarrow$ $ap - b = 0$ and $bp - c = 0$ and $cp - a = 0$

$\Rightarrow$ $p = \dfrac{b}{a}$ and $p = \dfrac{c}{b}$ and $p = \dfrac{a}{c}$ $\Rightarrow$ $\dfrac{b}{a} = \dfrac{c}{b} = \dfrac{a}{c}$

$\Rightarrow a, b, c$ are in GP.

66. **Method I** $S = 77 + 757 + 7557 + \ldots + \overbrace{75\ldots.57}^{98}$

GP

$$S = (70+7)+(700+50+7)+(7000+550+7)+(70000+5550+7)$$

GP

$$\ldots\ldots + (\underbrace{70000\ldots\ldots0}_{99} + \underbrace{5555\ldots\ldots550}_{98} + 7$$

$\Rightarrow S = 7(10 + 10^2 + 10^3 + \ldots + 10^{99})$

$$+ 50(1 + 11 + 111 + \ldots + \overbrace{111\ldots\ldots1}^{98}) + (\underbrace{7 + 7 + 7\ldots + 7}_{99})$$

$$\Rightarrow S = 7\left(\frac{10^{99} - 1}{9}\right) + \frac{50}{9}[(10 - 1) + (10^2 - 1)$$

$$+ (10^3 - 1) + \ldots + (10^{98} - 1)] + 7 \times 99$$

$$= 7 \times \left(\frac{10^{99} - 1}{9}\right) + \frac{50}{9}\left[10\left(\frac{10^{98} - 1}{9}\right) - 98\right] + 7 \times 99$$

$$= \frac{7 \times 10^{100}}{9} - \frac{70}{9} + \frac{50}{9}\left[\frac{10^{99} - 1 - 9}{9} - 98\right] + 7 \times 99$$

$$= \frac{7 \times 10^{100}}{9} - \frac{70}{9} + \frac{50}{9}[\overbrace{1111\ldots.1}^{99} - 99] + 7 \times 99$$

$$= \frac{7 \times 10^{100} - 70 + \overbrace{5555\ldots.50}^{99}}{9} - 550 + 693$$

$$= \frac{\overbrace{75555\ldots.5}^{99} - 70 + 143 \times 9}{9}$$

$$= \frac{\overbrace{75555\ldots.57}^{99} + 1210}{9} = \frac{\overbrace{7555\ldots.57}^{99} + m}{n} \quad \text{(Given)}$$

$\therefore m = 1210$ and $n = 9$

Hence, $m + n = 1210 + 9 = 1219$

Method II 1st difference $\longrightarrow$

680 6800 68000

$$S = 77 + 757 + 7557 + \ldots\ldots + \overbrace{7555\ldots\ldots57}^{98})$$

We observe that Ist difference of given series is 680, 6800, 68000, ... which are in GP.

As we know that (by technique), if 1st difference is in GP, then the general term is $T_n = \alpha(r)^n + \beta$, where r is the common ratio.

From above GP i.e. 680, 6800, 68000, ... its common ratio = 10.

$\therefore$ $T_n = \alpha(10)^n + \beta$ ...(i)

If $n = 1$ then $T_1 = 10\alpha + \beta = 77$ (given) i.e. first term of S.

If $n = 2$ then $T_2 = 100\alpha + \beta = 757$ (given) i.e. second term of S.

On solving T_1 and T_2, we get

$$\alpha = \frac{68}{9} \text{ and } \beta = \frac{13}{9}$$

Now, according to given data in question, we have

$S = \dfrac{\overbrace{7555\ldots57}^{99} + m}{n}$ which takes the form (in general term) is

$$S = \frac{T_{100} + m}{n} = \frac{(\alpha \cdot 10^{100} + \beta) + m}{n} \quad \ldots\text{(ii)}$$

Now, $S = \sum_{n=1}^{99} T_n$ [from Eq. (i)]

$$= \sum_{n=1}^{99} (\alpha(10)^n + \beta) = \alpha \sum_{n=1}^{99} 10^n + \sum_{n=1}^{99} \beta$$

$$= \alpha \left[\frac{10(10^{99} - 1)}{9} \right] + 99\beta$$

$$= \alpha \left(\frac{10^{100}}{9} - \frac{10}{9} \right) + 99\beta = \frac{\alpha \cdot 10^{100}}{9} - \frac{10\alpha}{9} + 99\beta$$

$$= \frac{\alpha(10^{100}) + \beta}{9} - \frac{\beta}{9} - \frac{10\alpha}{9} + 99\beta$$

$$= \frac{T_{100}}{9} - \frac{13}{81} - \frac{10}{9} \times \frac{68}{9} + 99 \times \frac{13}{9} = \frac{T_{100} + 1210}{9} \quad \text{...(iii)}$$

From Eqs. (ii) and (iii), we get

$$m = 1210 \text{ and } n = 9$$

$\therefore$ $m + n = 1219$

67. Since, $a_1, a_2, a_3, \ldots$, is an arithmetic progression with $a_1 = 7$ and a common difference is 8.

Thus, $a_n = 7 + (n-1)8$

and $T_1 = 3$ (given)

and $T_{n+1} = T_n + a_n$

$\therefore$ $T_n = T_{n-1} + a_{n-1}$

$\vdots$

$T_2 = T_1 + a_1$

$\therefore$ $T_{n+1} = (T_{n-1} + a_{n-1}) + a_n$

$= (T_{n-2} + a_{n-2}) + a_{n-1} + a_n$

$\vdots$

$T_{n+1} = T_1 + a_1 + a_2 + \ldots + a_{n-1} + a_n$

$= T_1 + \frac{n}{2}[2(7) + (n-1) \cdot 8]$

$= T_1 + n(4n + 3)$

$\therefore$ $T_{n+1} = 3 + n(4n+3)$ ...(i)

For $n = 19$, $T_{20} = 3 + 19(79) = 1504$

and $n = 29$,

$T_{30} = 3 + 29(119) = 3454$

Thus, option (c) is true.

Now, $\sum_{k=1}^{20} T_k = 3 + \sum_{k=2}^{20} T_k = 3 + \sum_{k=1}^{19} (3 + 4n^2 + 3n)$

$$= 3 + 3(19) + \frac{4(19)(20)(39)}{6} + \frac{3(19)(20)}{2}$$

$$= 3 + 57 + 9880 + 570 = 10510$$

Thus, option (b) is also true.

Similarly, $\sum_{k=1}^{30} T_k = 3 + \sum_{k=1}^{29} (4n^2 + 3n + 3) = 35615$

68. Since, $l_1, l_2, l_3, \ldots, l_{100}$ are consecutive terms of an arithmetic progression with common difference d_1 and also given, $w_1, w_2, \ldots, w_{100}$ are consecutive terms of another arithmetic progression with common difference d_2 with $d_1 d_2 = 10$.

Now, $A_{51} - A_{50} = 1000$ [given]

$\Rightarrow l_{51}w_{51} - l_{50}w_{50} = 1000$

[given, l_i be the length, w_i be the width and area is A_i]

$\Rightarrow$ $(a + 50d_1)(b + 50d_2) - (a + 49d_1)(b + 49d_2) = 1000$

$\Rightarrow$ $ab + 50d_1 b + 50d_2 a + 2500 d_1 d_2$

$- ab - 49bd_1 - 49ad_2 - 2401\, d_1 d_2 = 1000$

$\Rightarrow$ $bd_1 + ad_2 + 99d_1 d_2 = 1000$

Since, $d_1 d_2 = 10$

So, $bd_1 + ad_2 = 1000 - 990 = 10$ ...(i)

Now, $A_{100} - A_{90}\; l_{100}w_{100} - l_{90}w_{90} = (a + 99d_1)(b + 99d_2)$

$- (a + 89d_1)(b + 89d_2)$

$= ab + 99d_1 b + 99d_2 a + 99^2 d_1 d_2 - ab - 89bd_1 - 89ad_2 - 89^2 d_1 d_2$

$= 10(bd_1 + ad_2) + (99^2 - 89^2)\, d_1 d_2$

$= 10 \cdot (10) + 1880 \cdot d_1 d_2$ [by Eq. (i)]

$= 100 + (1880) \cdot (10)$

$= 100 + 18800$

$= 18900$

69. For real numbers y_1, y_2, y_3, the quantities $3^{y_1}, 3^{y_2}$ and 3^{y_3} are positive real numbers, so according to the AM-GM inequality, we have

$$\frac{3^{y_1} + 3^{y_2} + 3^{y_3}}{3} \geq (3^{y_1} \cdot 3^{y_2} \cdot 3^{y_3})^{1/3}$$

$$\Rightarrow \quad 3^{y_1} + 3^{y_2} + 3^{y_3} \geq 3(3^{y_1} \cdot 3^{y_2} \cdot 3^{y_3})^{1/3}$$

On applying logarithm with base 3, we get

$$\log_3(3^{y_1} + 3^{y_2} + 3^{y_3}) \geq \left[1 + \frac{1}{3}(y_1 + y_2 + y_3) \right]$$

$$= 1 + 3 = 4 \quad \{\because y_1 + y_2 + y_3 = 9\}$$

$\therefore$ $m = 4$

Now, for positive real numbers x_1, x_2 and x_3, according to AM-GM inequality, we have

$$\frac{x_1 + x_2 + x_3}{3} \geq (x_1 x_2 x_3)^{\frac{1}{3}}$$

On applying logarithm with base 3, we get

$$\log_3 \left(\frac{x_1 + x_2 + x_3}{3} \right) \geq \frac{1}{3}(\log_3 x_1 + \log_3 x_2 + \log_3 x_3)$$

$$\Rightarrow \quad 1 \geq \frac{1}{3}(\log_3 x_1 + \log_3 x_2 + \log_3 x_3)$$

$[\because x_1 + x_2 + x_3 = 9]$

$\therefore$ $M = 3$

Now, $\log_2(m^3) + \log_3(M^2) = 3\log_2(4) + 2\log_3(3) = 6 + 2 = 8$

70. Given arithmetic progression of positive integers terms $a_1, a_2, a_3, \ldots$ having common difference '2' and geometric progression of positive integers terms $b_1, b_2, b_3, \ldots$ having common ratio '2' with $a_1 = b_1 = c$, such that

$2(a_1 + a_2 + a_3 + \ldots + a_n) = b_1 + b_2 + b_3 + \ldots + b_n$

$\Rightarrow$ $2 \times \frac{n}{2}[2c + (n-1)2] = c\left(\frac{2^n - 1}{2 - 1} \right)$

$\Rightarrow$ $2nc + 2n^2 - 2n = 2^n \cdot c - c$

$\Rightarrow$ $c[2^n - 2n - 1] = 2n^2 - 2n$

$\because$ $c \in N \Rightarrow 2n^2 - 2n \geq 2^n - 2n - 1$

$\Rightarrow$ $2n^2 + 1 \geq 2^n \Rightarrow n \leq 6$

and also $c > 0 \Rightarrow n > 2$

$\therefore$ The possible value of n are 3, 4, 5, 6.

So, at $n=3$, $c=\dfrac{(2\times 9)-6}{8-6-1}=12$

At $n=4$, $c=\dfrac{32-8}{16-8-1}=\dfrac{24}{9}=\dfrac{8}{3}\notin N$

At $n=5$, $c=\dfrac{50-10}{32-10-1}=\dfrac{40}{21}\notin N$

and at, $n=6$, $c=\dfrac{72-12}{64-12-1}=\dfrac{60}{51}\notin N$

$\therefore$ There is only one possible value of c.

Exercise 3 - Challenging Problems

1. $a\neq 1, b\neq 0$ and $a\neq b$

Let $S=(a+b)+(a^2+ab+b^2)$
$+(a^3+a^2b+ab^2+b^3)+\ldots+n$ terms

$$=\frac{1}{(a-b)}[(a^2-b^2)+(a^3-b^3)+(a^4-b^4)+\ldots+n\text{ terms}]$$

$$=\frac{1}{(a-b)}[a^2(1+a+\ldots+n\text{ terms})-b^2(1+b+b^2+\ldots+n\text{ terms})]$$

$$=\frac{1}{(a-b)}\left[a^2\cdot\frac{1\cdot(a^n-1)}{(a-1)}-b^2\cdot\frac{1\cdot(b^n-1)}{(b-1)}\right]$$

$$=\frac{1}{(a-b)}\left[a^2\frac{(1-a^n)}{(1-a)}-b^2\frac{(1-b^n)}{(1-b)}\right]$$

2. $a=S_n=\dfrac{a(r^n-1)}{r-1}$ ...(i)

$$b=S_{2n}-S_n=\frac{a(r^{2n}-1)}{(r-1)}-\frac{a(r^n-1)}{(r-1)}=\frac{a(r^n-1)}{(r-1)}(r^n)\quad\text{...(ii)}$$

$$c=S_{3n}-S_{2n}=\frac{a(r^{3n}-1)}{(r-1)}-\frac{a(r^{2n}-1)}{(r-1)}$$

$$=\frac{a(r^n-1)}{(r-1)}(r^{2n}+r^n+1-r^n-1)=\frac{a(r^n-1)}{(r-1)}\cdot(r^n)^2\quad\text{...(iii)}$$

From Eqs. (i), (ii) and (iii), $b^2=ac$, so a, b, c are in GP.

3. (i) $\dfrac{1}{1^2}+\dfrac{1}{2^2}+\dfrac{1}{3^2}+\ldots+\infty=\dfrac{\pi^2}{6}$ ...(i)

$$\therefore\ \frac{1}{1^2}+\frac{1}{3^2}+\frac{1}{5^2}+\ldots+\infty$$

$$=\left(\frac{1}{1^2}+\frac{1}{2^2}+\frac{1}{3^2}+\frac{1}{4^2}+\ldots+\infty\right)-\left(\frac{1}{2^2}+\frac{1}{4^2}+\frac{1}{6^2}+\ldots+\infty\right)$$

$$=\frac{\pi^2}{6}-\frac{1}{4}\frac{\pi^2}{6}=\frac{3}{4}\times\frac{\pi^2}{6}=\frac{\pi^2}{8}$$

(ii) $1-\dfrac{1}{2^2}+\dfrac{1}{3^2}-\dfrac{1}{4^2}+\ldots+\infty=\left(\dfrac{1}{1^2}-\dfrac{1}{3^3}+\ldots\right)-\dfrac{1}{2^2}\left(\dfrac{1}{1^2}-\dfrac{1}{2^2}+\ldots+\infty\right)$

$$=\frac{\pi^2}{8}-\frac{1}{4}\times\frac{\pi^2}{6}=\frac{\pi^2}{12}\quad\text{[by part (i)]}$$

4. $t_1=1$ and $t_r-t_{r-1}=2^{r-1}, r\geq 2$

$$t_2-t_1=2$$
$$t_3-t_2=2^2$$
$$t_4-t_3=2^3$$
$$\vdots\quad\vdots\quad\vdots$$
$$t_n-t_{n-1}=2^{n-1}$$

Addiing columnwise, we get

$$t_n-t_1=2+2^2+\ldots+2^{n-1}$$
$$t_n=1+2+2^2+\ldots+2^{n-1}$$
$$t_n=\frac{1\cdot(2^n-1)}{2-1}\Rightarrow t_n=2^n-1$$

So, $\displaystyle\sum_{r=1}^{n}t_r=t_1+t_2+\ldots+t_n=(2-1)+(2^2-1)+\ldots+(2^n-1)$

$$=(2+2^2+\ldots+2^n)-n=\frac{2\cdot(2^n-1)}{(2-1)}-n=2^{n+1}-2-n$$
$$=2^{n+1}-n-2$$

5. (i) $I_n=\displaystyle\int_0^{\pi}\frac{\sin 2nx}{\sin x}dx=\int_0^{\pi}\frac{\sin 2n(\pi-x)}{\sin x}dx$

$$=\int_0^{\pi}\frac{\sin(2n\pi-2nx)}{\sin x}dx$$

$$I_n=-\int_0^{\pi}\frac{\sin 2nx}{\sin x}dx$$

$$I_n=-I_n\Rightarrow 2I_n=0$$
$$\Rightarrow\quad I_n=0$$

$\therefore$ $I_1=I_2=I_3=\ldots=0$

which is a constant series.

$\therefore$ This series is AP with common difference 0 and first term 0.

(ii) $I_n=\displaystyle\int_0^{\pi}\frac{\sin^2 nx}{\sin^2 x}dx$

Let $f(x)=\dfrac{\sin^2 nx}{\sin^2 x}$

Hence, $f(\pi-x)=f(x)$

So, $I_n=2\displaystyle\int_0^{\pi/2}\frac{\sin^2 nx}{\sin^2 x}dx$

Now, $I_{n+1}+I_{n-1}-2I_n$

$$=2\int_0^{\pi/2}\left\{\frac{(\sin^2(n+1)x-\sin^2 nx)}{\sin^2 x}+\frac{(\sin^2(n-1)x-\sin^2 nx)}{\sin^2 x}\right\}dx$$

$$=2\int_0^{\pi/2}\frac{\sin(2n+1)x\sin x-\sin(2n-1)x\sin x}{\sin^2 x}dx$$

$$=2\int_0^{\pi/2}\frac{\sin(2n+1)x-\sin(2n-1)x}{\sin x}dx$$

$$=2\int_0^{\pi/2}\frac{2\cos 2nx\sin x}{\sin x}dx$$

$$=4\int_0^{\pi/2}\cos 2nx\,dx=\frac{4}{2n}[\sin 2nx]_0^{\pi/2}=\frac{2}{n}\cdot 0=0$$

$\therefore$ $I_{n+1}+I_{n-1}=2I_n$ $\therefore I_1, I_2, I_3,\ldots$ are in AP.

6. Let a, b, c (unequal number) are in HP

$$\therefore \quad b = \frac{2ac}{a+c}$$

$$\Rightarrow \quad \frac{b}{2} = \frac{ac}{a+c} = \lambda \quad \text{[say]}$$

$$\Rightarrow \quad b = 2\lambda \text{ and } ac = \lambda(a+c) \quad \text{...(i)}$$

Now, a^2, b^2, c^2 are in AP

$$\text{So,} \quad b^2 = \frac{a^2 + c^2}{2} \Rightarrow 2b^2 = a^2 + c^2$$

$$\Rightarrow \quad 2(2\lambda)^2 = (a+c)^2 - 2ac$$

$$\Rightarrow \quad (a+c)^2 - 2\lambda(a+c) - 8\lambda^2 = 0$$

$$\Rightarrow \quad (a + c - 4\lambda)(a + c + 2\lambda) = 0$$

$$\Rightarrow \quad a + c = 4\lambda \text{ or } a + c = -2\lambda$$

Case I If $a + c = 4\lambda$

$$\therefore \quad ac = 4\lambda^2 \quad \text{[from Eq. (i)]}$$

$$\Rightarrow \quad (a-c)^2 = (a+c)^2 - 4ac$$

$$\Rightarrow \quad (a-c)^2 = 16\lambda^2 - 16\lambda^2$$

$$\Rightarrow \quad (a-c)^2 = 0 \Rightarrow a = c$$

Let given that a, b, c are distinct, so $a + c = 4\lambda$ is not valid.

Case II If $a + c = -2\lambda$

$$\Rightarrow \quad ac = -2\lambda^2 \quad \text{[from Eq. (i)]}$$

$$\therefore \quad (a-c)^2 = (a+c)^2 - 4ac$$

$$\Rightarrow \quad (a-c)^2 = 4\lambda^2 + 8\lambda^2 \Rightarrow (a-c) = \pm 2\sqrt{3}\lambda \quad \text{...(ii)}$$

$$\text{If} \quad a - c = 2\sqrt{3}\lambda, \quad \text{...(iii)}$$

$$\text{then} \quad a + c = 2\lambda$$

From Eqs. (ii) and (iii), we get

$$a = (\sqrt{3} - 1)\lambda \text{ and } c = -(1 + \sqrt{3})\lambda$$

$$\therefore \quad a : b : c = (\sqrt{3} - 1)\lambda : 2\lambda : -(\sqrt{3} + 1)\lambda$$

$$a : b : c = (\sqrt{3} - 1) : 2 : -(\sqrt{3} + 1)$$

$$\Rightarrow \quad a : b : c = (1 - \sqrt{3}) : -2 : (\sqrt{3} + 1)$$

$$\text{If} \quad a - c = -2\sqrt{3}\lambda, \quad \text{...(iv)}$$

$$\text{then} \quad a + c = -2\lambda \quad \text{...(v)}$$

From Eqs. (iv) and (v), we get

$$a = -(\sqrt{3} + 1)\lambda \text{ and } c = (\sqrt{3} - 1)\lambda$$

$$\therefore \quad a : b : c = -(\sqrt{3} + 1)\lambda : 2\lambda : (\sqrt{3} - 1)\lambda$$

$$\Rightarrow \quad a : b : c = (1 + \sqrt{3}) : -2 : (1 - \sqrt{3})$$

7. $a_1, a_2, a, \ldots, a_n$ are in AP with $a_1 = 0$ and common difference d

$$[d \neq 0]$$

$$\therefore a_2 = d, a_3 = 2d, \ldots, a_n = (n-1)d$$

$$\text{LHS} = \frac{a_3}{a_2} + \frac{a_4}{a_3} + \frac{a_5}{a_4} + \ldots + \frac{a_n}{a_{n-1}} - a_2\left(\frac{1}{a_2} + \frac{1}{a_3} + \ldots + \frac{1}{a_{n-2}}\right)$$

$$= \frac{1}{a_2}(a_3 - a_2) + \frac{1}{a_3}(a_4 - a_2) + \ldots + \frac{(a_{n-1} - a_2)}{a_{n-2}} + \frac{a_n}{a_{n-1}}$$

$$= \frac{1}{d}(2d - d) + \frac{1}{2d}(3d - d) + \ldots + \frac{[(n-2)d - d]}{(n-3)d} + \frac{(n-1)d}{(n-2)d}$$

$$= [1 + 1 + \ldots + (n-3) \text{ times}] + \frac{n-1}{n-2}$$

$$= (n-3) + \frac{(n-1)}{n-2} = (n-3) + \frac{(n-2)+1}{(n-2)}$$

$$= (n-3) + 1 + \frac{1}{n-2} = n - 2 + \frac{1}{n-2}$$

$$= \frac{a(n-2)d}{d} + \frac{d}{(n-2)d} = \frac{a_{n-1}}{a_2} + \frac{a_2}{a_{n-1}} = \text{RHS}$$

8. $\theta_1, \theta_2, \theta_3, \ldots, \theta_n$ are in AP.

$$\text{So,} \quad \theta_2 - \theta_1 = \theta_3 - \theta_2 = \ldots = \theta_n - \theta_{n-1} = d$$

$$\therefore \text{LHS} = \sin d\,[\sec\theta_1 \sec\theta_2 + \sec\theta_2 \sec\theta_3 + \ldots + \sec\theta_{n-1} \sec\theta_n]$$

$$= \sin d\left[\frac{1}{\cos\theta_1 \cos\theta_2} + \frac{1}{\cos\theta_2 \cos\theta_3} + \ldots + \frac{1}{\cos\theta_{n-1}\cos\theta_n}\right]$$

$$= \frac{\sin d}{\cos\theta_1 \cos\theta_2} + \frac{\sin d}{\cos\theta_2 \cos\theta_3} + \ldots + \frac{\sin d}{\cos\theta_{n-1}\cos\theta_n}$$

$$= \frac{\sin(\theta_2 - \theta_1)}{\cos\theta_1 \cos\theta_2} + \frac{\sin(\theta_3 - \theta_2)}{\cos\theta_2 \cos\theta_3} + \ldots + \frac{\sin(\theta_n - \theta_{n-1})}{\cos\theta_{n-1}\cos\theta_n}$$

$$= (\tan\theta_2 - \tan\theta_1) + (\tan\theta_3 - \tan\theta_2) + \ldots + (\tan\theta_n - \tan\theta_{n-1})$$

$$= \tan\theta_n - \tan\theta_1 = \text{RHS}$$

9. $S = \sum_{n=0}^{\infty} \frac{2^n}{a^{2^n} + 1}, (a > 1)$

$$S_n = \sum_{n=0}^{n} \frac{2^n}{a^{2^n} + 1}$$

$$= \frac{1}{a+1} + \frac{2}{a^2+1} + \frac{4}{a^4+1} + \frac{8}{a^8+1} + \ldots + \frac{2^n}{a^{2^n}+1}$$

$$= \frac{1}{1+a} + \frac{2}{1+a^2} + \frac{4}{1+a^4} + \frac{8}{1+a^8} + \ldots + \frac{2^n}{1+a^{2^n}}$$

$$= \left(-\frac{1}{1-a} + \frac{1}{1-a}\right) + \frac{1}{1+a} + \frac{2}{1+a^2} + \frac{4}{1+a^4} + \ldots + \frac{2^n}{1+a^{2^n}}$$

$$= \frac{1}{a-1} + \left(\frac{1}{1-a} + \frac{1}{1+a}\right) + \frac{2}{1+a^2} + \frac{4}{1+a^4} + \ldots + \frac{2^n}{1+a^{2^n}}$$

$$= \frac{1}{a-1} + \left(\frac{2}{1-a^2} + \frac{2}{1+a^2}\right) + \frac{4}{1+a^4} + \ldots + \frac{2^n}{1+a^{2^n}}$$

$$\vdots \qquad \vdots \qquad \vdots \qquad \vdots$$

$$S_n = \frac{1}{a-1} + \frac{2^{n+1}}{1 - a^{2^{n+1}}}$$

$$S = \lim_{n\to\infty} S_n = \lim_{n\to\infty}\left(\frac{1}{a-1} + \frac{2^{n+1}}{1 - a^{2^{n+1}}}\right)$$

$$= \lim_{n\to\infty}\left(\frac{1}{a-1} + \frac{\frac{2^{n+1}}{a^{2^{n+1}}}}{\frac{1}{a^{2^{n+1}}} - 1}\right) = \frac{1}{a-1} + \frac{0}{0-1} = \frac{1}{a-1}$$

10. $T_n = \tan^{-1}\left(\frac{2^{n-1}}{1+2^{2n-1}}\right) = \tan^{-1}\left(\frac{2^{n-1}}{1+2^n\cdot 2^{n-1}}\right)$

$$= \tan^{-1}\left(\frac{2^n - 2^{n-1}}{1+2^n\cdot 2^{n-1}}\right) = \tan^{-1}2^n - \tan^{-1}2^{n-1}$$

$$S_n = T_1 + T_2 + \ldots + T_n$$

$$= (\tan^{-1}2^1 - \tan^{-1}2^0) + (\tan^{-1}2^2 - \tan^{-1}2^1) + \ldots + (\tan^{-1}2^n - \tan^{-1}2^{n-1})$$

$$= (\tan^{-1}2^n - \tan^{-1}1)$$

$$S_n = \tan^{-1}2^n - \frac{\pi}{4}$$

$$S = \lim_{n\to\infty} S_n = \lim_{n\to\infty}\left(\tan^{-1}2^n - \frac{\pi}{4}\right) = \frac{\pi}{2} - \frac{\pi}{4} = \frac{\pi}{4}$$

11. Let d_1, d_2 and d_3 be the common differences of the 3 arithmetic progressions.

$\therefore \quad S_i = \frac{n}{2}[2\times a + (n-1)\,d_i],\ \forall\ i = 1, 2, 3$

$\Rightarrow \quad S_i = \frac{n}{2}[2 + (n-1)\,d_i]$

$\Rightarrow \quad S_i = n + \frac{n(n-1)}{2}d_i \Rightarrow d_i = \frac{2(S_i - n)}{n(n-1)}$

Given that d_1, d_2, d_3 are in HP.

$\therefore \quad \frac{1}{d_1}, \frac{1}{d_2}, \frac{1}{d_3}$ are in AP.

$\therefore \quad \frac{2}{d_2} = \frac{1}{d_1} + \frac{1}{d_3}$

$\Rightarrow \quad \frac{2}{\frac{2(S_2-n)}{n(n-1)}} = \frac{1}{\frac{2(S_1-n)}{n(n-1)}} + \frac{1}{\frac{2(S_3-n)}{n(n-1)}}$

$\Rightarrow \quad \frac{2}{S_2-n} = \frac{1}{S_1-n} + \frac{1}{S_3-n}$

$\Rightarrow \quad \frac{2}{S_2-n} = \frac{S_3+S_1-2n}{(S_1-n)(S_3-n)}$

$\Rightarrow 2[S_1S_3 - (S_1+S_3)\,n + n^2] = (S_2-n)(S_1+S_3-2n)$

$\Rightarrow 2S_1S_3 - 2(S_1+S_3)\,n + 2n^2 = S_1S_2 + S_2S_3 - 2nS_2 - n(S_1+S_3) + 2n^2$

$\Rightarrow \quad 2S_1S_3 - S_2S_3 - S_1S_2 = n(S_1 + S_3 - 2S_2)$

$\Rightarrow \quad n = \frac{(2S_1S_3 - S_2S_3 - S_1S_2)}{(S_1 - 2S_2 + S_3)}$

12. Let their ages be a, ar, ar^2.

After 3 yr, their ages will be $a+3$, $ar+3$, ar^2+3.

Given, $2(a+3) = ar^2 + 3$ ...(i)

Let x rupees be the sum of the money divided.

And let $y = a + ar + ar^2$ ...(ii)

Then, $y + 9 = a + 3 + (ar+3) + (ar^2+3)$

We have, $\quad \frac{x(a+3)}{(y+9)} = \frac{xa}{y} + 105$

$\Rightarrow \quad x\left(\frac{a+3}{y+9} - \frac{a}{y}\right) = 105$ ...(iii)

Also, $\quad \frac{x(ar+3)}{(y+9)} = \frac{xar}{y} + 15$

$\Rightarrow \quad x\left[\frac{ar+3}{y+9} - \frac{ar}{y}\right] = 15$ ...(iv)

On dividing Eq. (iii) by Eq. (iv), we get

$$\frac{y(a+3) - a(y+9)}{y(ar+3) - ar(y+9)} = 7$$

$\Rightarrow \quad \frac{y-3a}{y-3ar} = 7$

$\Rightarrow \quad 6y = 21ar - 3a$

$\Rightarrow \quad y = \frac{a(7r-1)}{2}$

From Eq. (ii),

$$\frac{a(7r-1)}{2} = a + ar + ar^2$$

$\Rightarrow \quad 5ar = 3a + 2ar^2$ ...(v)

From Eqs. (i) and (ii), we get

$$a = 12,\ r = \frac{3}{2}$$

Let ages of these friends are $12, 12\times\frac{3}{2}, 12\times\left(\frac{3}{2}\right)^2$ i.e. 12, 18, 27.

"The definition of a good mathematical problem is the mathematics it generates rather than the problem itself.*

–Andrew Wiles

4 Logarithms

Learning Milestones

- Definition
- Properties of Logarithm
- Properties of Monotonocity of Logarithm
- Graphs of Logarithmic Functions
- Characteristic
- Mantissa

Practice Milestone - JEE Main Pattern

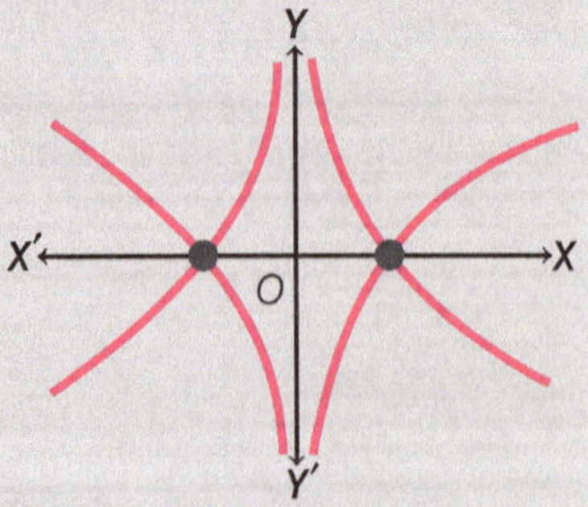

4.1 Definition

The logarithm of any positive number, whose base is a number (>0) different from 1, is the index or the power to which the base must be raised in order to obtain the given number.

i.e. if $a^x = b$ (where $a > 0, \neq 1$), then x is called the logarithm of b to the base a and we write $\log_a b = x$, clearly $b > 0$.

Thus, $\log_a b = x \Leftrightarrow a^x = b, a > 0, a \neq 1$ and $b > 0$.

If $a = 10$, then we write $\log b$ rather than $\log_{10} b$. If $a = e$, we write $\ln b$ rather than $\log_e b$.

Here, 'e' is called as **Napier's base** and has numerical value equal to 2.7182. Also, $\log_{10} e$ is known as **Napierian constant**.

i.e. $\quad \log_{10} e = 0.4343$

$\therefore \quad \ln b = 2.303 \log_{10} b$

$$\left[\text{since, } \ln b = \log_{10} b \times \log_e 10 = \frac{1}{\log_{10} e} \times \log_{10} b = \frac{1}{0.4343} \log_{10} b = 2.303 \log_{10} b\right]$$

Remember

(i) $\log 2 = \log_{10} 2 = 0.3010$

(ii) $\log 3 = \log_{10} 3 = 0.4771$

(iii) $\ln 2 = 2.303 \log 2 = 0.693$

(iv) $\ln 10 = 2.303$

- **Corollary I** From the definition of the logarithm of the number b to the base a, we have an identity

$$a^{\log_a b} = b, a > 0, a \neq 1 \text{ and } b > 0$$

which is known as the **Fundamental Logarithmic Identity**.

- **Corollary II** The function defined by $f(x) = \log_a x, a > 0, a \neq 1$ is called logarithmic function. Its domain is $(0, \infty)$ and range is R (set of all real numbers).

- **Corollary III** $a^x > 0, \forall x \in R$

(i) If $a > 1$, then a^x is monotonically increasing.

e.g. $5^{2.7} > 5^{2.5}, 3^{222} > 3^{111}$

(ii) If $0 < a < 1$, then a^x is monotonically decreasing.

e.g. $\left(\frac{1}{5}\right)^{2.7} < \left(\frac{1}{5}\right)^{2.5}, (0.7)^{222} < (0.7)^{212}$

- **Corollary IV**

(i) If $a > 1$, then $a^{-\infty} = 0$

$\therefore \quad \log_a 0 = -\infty$ (if $a > 1$)

(ii) If $0 < a < 1$, then $a^{\infty} = 0$

$\therefore \quad \log_a 0 = +\infty$ (if $0 < a < 1$)

- **Corollary V**

(i) $\log_a b \to \infty$, if $a > 1, b \to \infty$

(ii) $\log_a b \to -\infty$, if $0 < a < 1, b \to \infty$

JEE Focus Points

Concept Inside Video

- If $x < 0$, $a > 0$ and $a \neq 1$, then $\log_a x$ is an imaginary.
- If $a > 1$, $\log_a x = \begin{cases} +\text{ve}, & x > 1 \\ 0, & x = 1 \\ -\text{ve}, & 0 < x < 1 \end{cases}$

  and if $0 < a < 1$, $\log_a x = \begin{cases} +\text{ve}, & 0 < x < 1 \\ 0, & x = 1 \\ -\text{ve}, & x > 1 \end{cases}$
- $\log_a 1 = 0$ $(a > 0, a \neq 1)$

  $\log_a a = 1$ $(a > 0, a \neq 1)$ and $\log_{(1/a)} a = -1$ $(a > 0, a \neq 1)$

Example 1. Find the value of the following :

(i) $\log_9 27$ (ii) $\log_{3\sqrt{2}} 324$

(iii) $\log_{1/9}(27\sqrt{3})$ (iv) $\log_{(5+2\sqrt{6})}(5-2\sqrt{6})$

(v) $\log_{0.2} 0.008$ (vi) $2^{2\log_4 5}$

(vii) $(0.4)^{-\log_{2.5}\left\{\frac{1}{3}+\frac{1}{3^2}+\frac{1}{3^3}+\dots\right\}}$ (viii) $(0.05)^{\log_{\sqrt{20}}(0.\bar{3})}$

Sol. (i) Let $\quad x = \log_9 27$

$\Rightarrow \quad 9^x = 27 \Rightarrow 3^{2x} = 3^3 \Rightarrow 2x = 3$

$\therefore \quad x = \frac{3}{2}$

(ii) Let $\quad x = \log_{3\sqrt{2}} 324$

$\Rightarrow (3\sqrt{2})^x = 324 = 2^2 \cdot 3^4 \Rightarrow (3\sqrt{2})^x = (3\sqrt{2})^4$

$\therefore \quad x = 4$

(iii) Let $\quad x = \log_{1/9}(27\sqrt{3})$

$\Rightarrow \left(\frac{1}{9}\right)^x = 27\sqrt{3} \Rightarrow 3^{-2x} = 3^{7/2} \Rightarrow -2x = 7/2$

$\therefore \quad x = -\frac{7}{4}$

(iv) $\because (5 + 2\sqrt{6})(5 - 2\sqrt{6}) = 1$

or $\quad 5 + 2\sqrt{6} = \frac{1}{5 - 2\sqrt{6}}$ ...(i)

Now, let $x = \log_{(5+2\sqrt{6})}(5 - 2\sqrt{6})$

$= \log_{1/(5-2\sqrt{6})} 5 - 2\sqrt{6} = -1$ [from Eq. (i)]

(v) Let $x = \log_{0.2} 0.008$

$\Rightarrow (0.2)^x = 0.008$

$\Rightarrow (0.2)^x = (0.2)^3 \Rightarrow x = 3$

(vi) Let $x = 2^{2\log_4 5} = 4^{\log_4 5} = 5$

(vii) Let $x = (0.4)^{-\log_{2.5}\left\{\frac{1}{3}+\frac{1}{3^2}+\frac{1}{3^3}+\ldots\right\}}$

$$= \left(\frac{4}{10}\right)^{-\log_{2.5}\left\{\frac{\frac{1}{3}}{1-\frac{1}{3}}\right\}} = \left(\frac{2}{5}\right)^{-\log_{2.5}\left(\frac{1}{2}\right)}$$

$$= \left(\frac{5}{2}\right)^{\log_{5/2}\left(\frac{1}{2}\right)} = \frac{1}{2}$$

(viii) Let $x = (0.05)^{\log_{\sqrt{20}}(0.\bar{3})} = (0.05)^{\log_{\sqrt{20}}(\lambda)}$ ...(i)

where, $\lambda = 0.\bar{3}$

Then, $\lambda = 0.33333\ldots$ ...(ii)

$\Rightarrow 10\lambda = 3.33333\ldots$ ...(iii)

On subtracting Eq. (ii) from Eq. (iii), we get

$$9\lambda = 3 \Rightarrow \lambda = \frac{1}{3}$$

Now, from Eq. (i),

$$x = (0.05)^{\log_{\sqrt{20}}\left(\frac{1}{3}\right)}$$

$$= \left(\frac{1}{20}\right)^{\log_{(20)^{1/2}}(3)^{-1}} = \left(\frac{1}{20}\right)^{-\frac{1}{1/2}\log_{20} 3}$$

$$= 20^{(2\log_{20} 3)} = 20^{\log_{20} 3^2} = 3^2 = 9$$

Example 2. Find the value of the following:

(i) $\log_{\tan 45^\circ}\cot 30^\circ$

(ii) $\log_{(\sec^2 60^\circ - \tan^2 60^\circ)}\cos 60^\circ$

(iii) $\log_{(\sin^2 30^\circ + \cos^2 30^\circ)} 1$

(iv) $\log_{30} 1$

Sol. (i) Here, base $= \tan 45^\circ = 1$

$\therefore$ log is not defined.

(ii) Here, base $= \sec^2 60^\circ - \tan^2 60^\circ = 1$

$\therefore$ log is not defined.

(iii) $\because \log_{(\sin^2 30^\circ + \cos^2 30^\circ)} 1 = \log_1 1 \neq 1$

$\because$ Here, base = 1

$\therefore$ log is not defined.

(iv) $\log_{30} 1 = 0$

Example 3. If $\log_3 y = x$ and $\log_2 z = x$, then prove that $72^x = y^2 z^3$.

Sol. We have, $\log_3 y = x$ and $\log_2 z = x$

$\Rightarrow y = 3^x$ and $z = 2^x$

Now, $72^x = (2^3 \times 3^2)^x$

$= (2^x)^3 (3^x)^2 = y^2 z^3$

Example 4. If $\log_4 5 = x$ and $\log_5 6 = y$, then show that $\log_2 3 = 2xy - 1$.

Sol. We have, $\log_4 5 = x$ and $\log_5 6 = y$

$\Rightarrow 5 = 4^x$ and $6 = 5^y$

$\Rightarrow 6 = (4^x)^y$

$\Rightarrow 6 = 4^{xy}$

$\Rightarrow 2 \times 3 = 2^{2xy}$

$\Rightarrow 3 = 2^{2xy-1}$

$\Rightarrow \log_2 3 = 2xy - 1$

Example 5. If $\frac{\log_{10} a}{2} = \frac{\log_{10} b}{3} = \frac{\log_{10} c}{5}$, then prove that $bc = a^4$.

Sol. We have, $\frac{\log_{10} a}{2} = \frac{\log_{10} b}{3} = \frac{\log_{10} c}{5} = \lambda$

$\Rightarrow \log_{10} a = 2\lambda$, $\log_{10} b = 3\lambda$ and $\log_{10} c = 5\lambda$

$\Rightarrow a = 10^{2\lambda}$, $b = 10^{3\lambda}$ and $c = 10^{5\lambda}$

Now, $bc = 10^{3\lambda} \times 10^{5\lambda}$

$= 10^{8\lambda}$

$= (10^{2\lambda})^4$

$= a^4$

4.2 Properties of Logarithms

Let m and n be arbitrary positive numbers, $a > 0, a \neq 1$, $b > 0, b \neq 1$ and α, β be any real numbers, then

PROPERTY 1

(i) $\log_a(mn) = \log_a m + \log_a n$

(ii) In general, $\log_a(x_1 x_2 x_3 \ldots x_n)$

$$= \log_a x_1 + \log_a x_2 + \log_a x_3 + \ldots + \log_a x_n$$

[where $x_1, x_2, x_3, \ldots, x_n > 0$]

Or

$$\log_a\left(\prod_{i=1}^{n} x_i\right) = \sum_{i=1}^{n}\log_a x_i, \forall x_i > 0, i \in N$$

(iii) $\log_a\left(\frac{m}{n}\right) = \log_a m - \log_a n$

(iv) $\log_a m^\alpha = \alpha \log_a m$

Example 6. If a, b and c are positive real numbers, then the value of $(ab)^{\log\left(\frac{a}{b}\right)} \times (bc)^{\log\left(\frac{b}{c}\right)} \times (ca)^{\log\left(\frac{c}{a}\right)}$ is

(a) 0 (b) –1

(c) 1 (d) None of these

Sol. (c) Let $A = (ab)^{\log\left(\frac{a}{b}\right)} \times (bc)^{\log\left(\frac{b}{c}\right)} \times (ca)^{\log\left(\frac{c}{a}\right)}$

$$\therefore \log A = \log [(ab)^{\log\left(\frac{a}{b}\right)} \times (bc)^{\log\left(\frac{b}{c}\right)} \times (ca)^{\log\left(\frac{c}{a}\right)}]$$

$$= \log\left(\frac{a}{b}\right) \log (ab) + \log\left(\frac{b}{c}\right) \log (bc) + \log\left(\frac{c}{a}\right) \log (ca)$$

$$= (\log a - \log b)(\log a + \log b) + (\log b - \log c)(\log b + \log c) + (\log c - \log a)(\log c + \log a)$$

$$= 0$$

$$\therefore \quad A = 1$$

Example 7. If $a = \log 2$, $b = \log 3$, $c = \log 7$ and $6^x = 7^{x+4}$, then x is equal to

(a) $\frac{4b}{c+a-b}$ (b) $\frac{4c}{a+b-c}$

(c) $\frac{4b}{c-a-b}$ (d) $\frac{4a}{a+b-c}$

Sol. (b) We have, $6^x = 7^{x+4}$

$$\Rightarrow \quad x \log 6 = (x+4) \log 7$$

$$\Rightarrow \quad x = \frac{4 \log 7}{\log 6 - \log 7} = \frac{4 \log 7}{\log (2 \times 3) - \log 7} = \frac{4 \log 7}{\log 2 + \log 3 - \log 7} = \frac{4c}{a+b-c}$$

Example 8. If $\frac{\log x}{2a+3b-5c} = \frac{\log y}{2b+3c-5a} = \frac{\log z}{2c+3a-5b}$, then the value of xyz is

(a) 0 (b) 1

(c) −1 (d) 2

Sol. (b) We have, $\frac{\log x}{2a+3b-5c} = \frac{\log y}{2b+3c-5a} = \frac{\log z}{2c+3a-5b}$

$$\Rightarrow \frac{\log x}{2a+3b-5c} = \frac{\log y}{2b+3c-5a} = \frac{\log z}{2c+3a-5b} = \frac{\log x + \log y + \log z}{0}$$

$$\Rightarrow \quad \log x + \log y + \log z = 0$$

$$\Rightarrow \quad \log (xyz) = 0$$

$$\Rightarrow \quad xyz = 1$$

Example 9. If a, b and c are three consecutive positive integers, then the value of $\log (1 + ca)$ is equal to

(a) $\log\left(\frac{b}{2}\right)$ (b) $\log b$

(c) $2 \log b$ (d) $\log (2b)$

Sol. (c) We have, a, b and c are three consecutive positive integers.

$\therefore \quad b = a+1, c = a+2$

$\therefore 2b = 2a + 2 = a + a + 2 = a + c$

Now, $\log (1 + ca) = \log (1 + (a+2)a)$

$$= \log (1 + a^2 + 2a) = \log (a+1)^2 = 2 \log (a+1) = 2 \log b$$

PROPERTY 2

(i) $\log_b a = \frac{1}{\log_a b}$

(ii) $\log_b a = \frac{\log_c a}{\log_c b}$ [base changing theorem]

(iii) $\log_b a \times \log_a b = 1$

(vi) $\log_b a \times \log_c b \times \log_a c = 1$

(v) $\log_y x \times \log_z y \times \log_a z = \log_a x$

Example 10. If $\log_3 a \times \log_a x = 4$, then find the value of x.

Sol. We have, $\log_3 a \times \log_a x = 4$

$$\Rightarrow \quad \log_3 x = 4$$

$$\Rightarrow \quad x = 3^4$$

$$\Rightarrow \quad x = 81$$

Example 11. Prove that $\frac{\log_2 24}{\log_{96} 2} - \frac{\log_2 192}{\log_{12} 2} = 3$.

Sol. LHS $= \frac{\log_2 24}{\log_{96} 2} - \frac{\log_2 192}{\log_{12} 2}$

$$= \log_2 24 \times \log_2 96 - \log_2 192 \times \log_2 12$$

Now, let $12 = \lambda$, then

$$\text{LHS} = \log_2 2\lambda \times \log_2 8\lambda - \log_2 16\lambda \times \log_2 \lambda$$

$$= (\log_2 2 + \log_2 \lambda)(\log_2 8 + \log_2 \lambda) - (\log_2 16 + \log_2 \lambda)\log_2 \lambda$$

$$= (\log_2 2 + \log_2 \lambda)(\log_2 2^3 + \log_2 \lambda) - (\log_2 2^4 + \log_2 \lambda)\log_2 \lambda$$
$$= (1 + \log_2 \lambda)(3\log_2 2 + \log_2 \lambda) - (4\log_2 2 + \log_2 \lambda)\log_2 \lambda$$
$$= (1 + \log_2 \lambda)(3 + \log_2 \lambda) - \log_2 \lambda (4 + \log_2 \lambda)$$
$$= 3$$
$$= \text{RHS}$$

Example 12. Solve for a, λ, if

$$\log_\lambda a \cdot \log_5 \lambda \cdot \log_\lambda 25 = 2.$$

Sol. Here, $\lambda > 0, \lambda \neq 1$

We have, $\log_\lambda a \cdot \{\log_5 \lambda \cdot \log_\lambda 25\} = 2$

$\Rightarrow \quad (\log_\lambda a)\{\log_5 25\} = 2$

$\Rightarrow \quad (\log_\lambda a)\{\log_5 5^2\} = 2$

$\Rightarrow \quad (\log_\lambda a)\{2\log_5 5\} = 2$

$\Rightarrow \quad (\log_\lambda a)\{2\} = 2$

$\therefore \quad \log_\lambda (a) = 1$ or $a = \lambda$

PROPERTY 3

(i) $a^{\log_a n} = n$

(ii) $e^{\ln a} = a$

(iii) $a^{\log_b x} = x^{\log_b a}$

Remark $x^y = a^{y \log_a x}$

Example 13. If $x = 27$ and $y = \log_3 4$, then x^y is equal to

(a) $\frac{3}{4}$ (b) $\frac{4}{3}$ (c) 16 (d) 64

Sol. (d) We have, $x = 27$ and $y = \log_3 4$

Now, $x^y = (27)^{\log_3 4}$

$= 4^{\log_3 27} = 4^{\log_3 3^3}$

$= 4^{3 \log_3 3} = 4^3 = 64$

Example 14. The value of $x^{\log_x a \times \log_a y \times \log_y z}$ is

(a) a (b) x
(c) y (d) z

Sol. (d) We have, $\log_x a \times \log_a y \times \log_y z = \log_x z$

Now, $x^{\log_x a \times \log_a y \times \log_y z} = x^{\log_x z}$

$= z$ [using Property 6 (i)]

PROPERTY 4

Some extra properties

(i) $\log_{a^k} x = \frac{1}{k}\log_a x,\ a > 0, a \neq 1, x > 0$

(ii) $\log_a x^{2k} = 2k \log_a |x|,\ a > 0, a \neq 1, k \in I$

(iii) $\log_{a^{2k}} x = \frac{1}{2k}\log_{|a|} x,\ x > 0, a > 0, a \neq \pm 1$ and $k \in I \sim \{0\}$

(iv) $\log_{a^\alpha} x^\beta = \frac{\beta}{\alpha}\log_a x,\ x > 0, a > 0, a \neq 1, \alpha \neq 0$

(v) $\log_a x^2 \neq 2\log_a x,\ a > 0, a \neq 1$

Since, domain of $\log_a (x^2)$ is $R \sim \{0\}$ and domain of $\log_a x$ is $(0, \infty)$ are not same.

(vi) $a^{\log_b a} = \sqrt{a}$, if $b = a^2, a > 0, b > 0, b \neq 1$

(vii) $a^{\log_b a} = a^2$, if $b = \sqrt{a}, a > 0, b > 0, b \neq 1$

Example 15. The solution of $5^{\log_a x} + 5x^{\log_a 5} = 3\ (a > 0)$, is

(a) $2^{\log_a 5}$ (b) $2^{-\log_a 5}$
(c) $2^{-\log_5 a}$ (d) $2^{\log_5 a}$

Sol. (c) We have, $5^{\log_a x} + 5x^{\log_a 5} = 3$

$\Rightarrow \quad x^{\log_a 5} + 5x^{\log_a 5} = 3$

$\Rightarrow \quad 6 \times x^{\log_a 5} = 3$

$\Rightarrow \quad x^{\log_a 5} = \frac{1}{2}$

$\Rightarrow \quad x = (2^{-1})^{\frac{1}{\log_a 5}} \Rightarrow x = 2^{-\log_5 a}$

Example 16. Prove that $a^{\sqrt{\log_a b}} - b^{\sqrt{\log_b a}} = 0$.

Sol. $\because \quad a^{\sqrt{(\log_a b)}} = a^{\sqrt{\log_a b} \times \sqrt{\log_a b} \times \sqrt{\log_b a}}$

$= a^{\log_a b \cdot \sqrt{(\log_b a)}}$

$= b^{\sqrt{\log_b a}}$ [by property 6 (i)]

Hence, $a^{\sqrt{(\log_a b)}} - b^{\sqrt{(\log_b a)}} = 0$

Example 17. If $4^{\log_{16} 4} + 9^{\log_3 9} = 10^{\log_x 83}$, find x.

Sol. $\because \quad 4^{\log_{16} 4} = \sqrt{4} = 2$ [by extra property (vi)]

and $9^{\log_3 9} = 9^2 = 81$ [by extra property (vii)]

$\therefore \quad 4^{\log_{16} 4} + 9^{\log_3 9} = 2 + 81 = 83 = 10^{\log_x 83}$

$\Rightarrow \quad \log_{10} 83 = \log_x 83$

$\therefore \quad x = 10$

4.3 Properties of Monotonocity of Logarithm

1. Constant Base

(i) $\log_a x > \log_a y \Leftrightarrow \begin{cases} x > y > 0, \text{ if } a > 1 \\ 0 < x < y, \text{ if } 0 < a < 1 \end{cases}$

(ii) $\log_a x < \log_a y \Leftrightarrow \begin{cases} 0 < x < y, \text{ if } a > 1 \\ x > y > 0, \text{ if } 0 < a < 1 \end{cases}$

(iii) $\log_a x > p \Leftrightarrow \begin{cases} x > a^p, \text{ if } a > 1 \\ 0 < x < a^p, \text{ if } 0 < a < 1 \end{cases}$

(iv) $\log_a x < p \Leftrightarrow \begin{cases} 0 < x < a^p, \text{ if } a > 1 \\ x > a^p, \text{ if } 0 < a < 1 \end{cases}$

2. Variable Base

(i) $\log_x a$ is defined, if $a > 0, x > 0, x \neq 1$.

(ii) If $a > 1$, then $\log_x a$ is monotonically decreasing in $(0, 1) \cup (1, \infty)$.

(iii) If $0 < a < 1$, then $\log_x a$ is monotonically increasing in $(0, 1) \cup (1, \infty)$.

JEE Focus Points

- If $a > 1, p > 1$, then $\log_a p > 0$
- If $0 < a < 1, p > 1$, then $\log_a p < 0$
- If $a > 1, 0 < p < 1$, then $\log_a p < 0$
- If $p > a > 1$, then $\log_a p > 1$
- If $a > p > 1$, then $0 < \log_a p < 1$
- If $0 < a < p < 1$, then $0 < \log_a p < 1$
- If $0 < p < a < 1$, then $\log_a p > 1$

4.4 Graphs of Logarithmic Functions

1. **Graph of $y = \log_a x$, if $a > 1$ and $x > 0$**

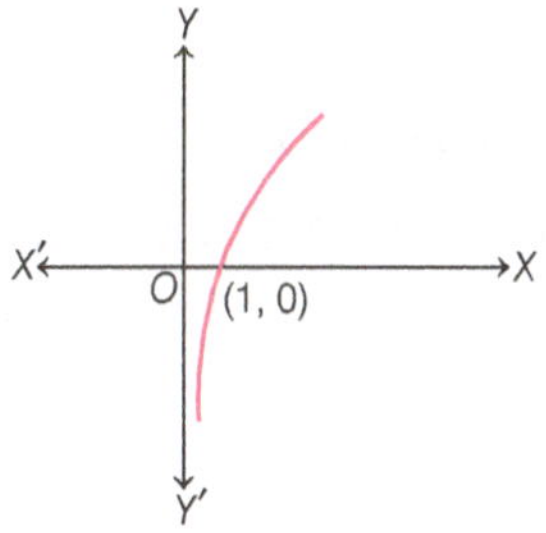

2. **Graph of $y = \log_a x$, if $0 < a < 1$ and $x > 0$**

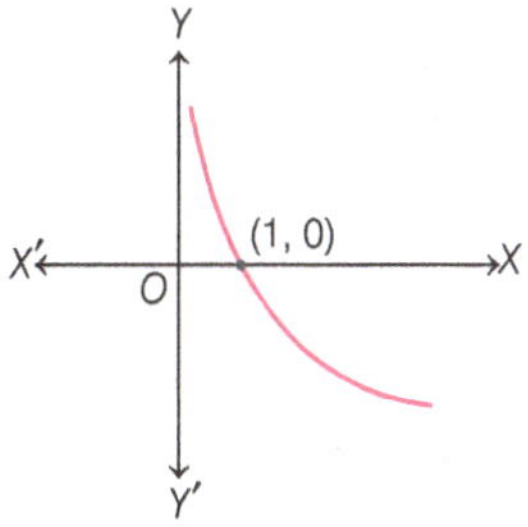

3. **Graph of $y = \log_a |x|$**

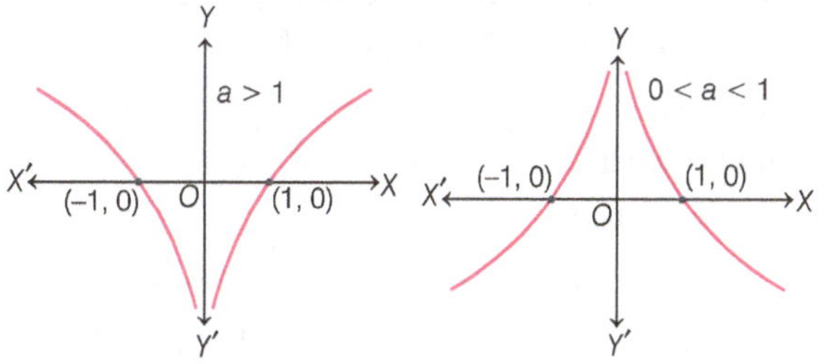

Graphs are symmetrical about Y-axis.

4. **Graph of $y = |\log_a |x||$**

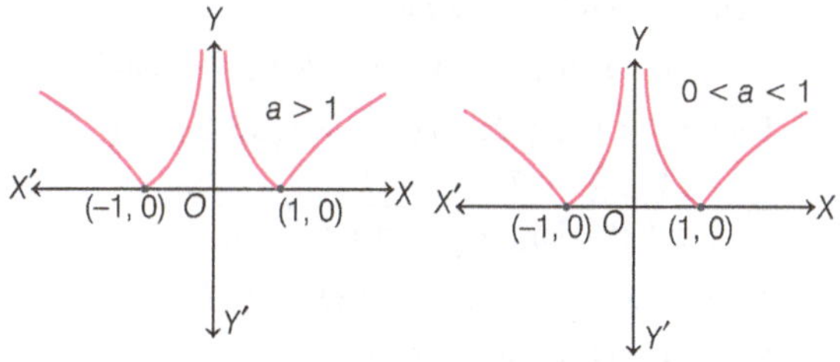

Graphs are same in both cases i.e. $a > 1$ and $0 < a < 1$.

5. **Graph of $|y| = \log_a |x||$**

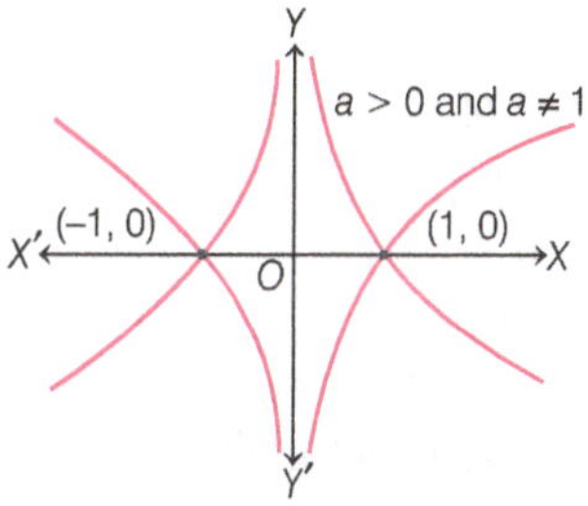

6. **Graph of $y = \log_a [x]$, $a > 1$ and $x \geq 1$**

(where $[\cdot]$ denotes the greatest integer function)

Since, when $1 \leq x < 2, [x] = 1 \Rightarrow \log_a [x] = 0$

when $2 \leq x < 3, [x] = 2 \Rightarrow \log_a [x] = \log_a 2$

when $3 \leq x < 4, [x] = 3 \Rightarrow \log_a [x] = \log_a 3$ and so on.

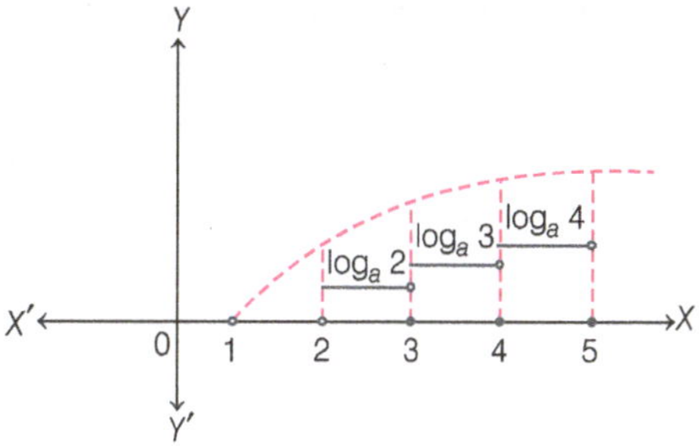

Example 18. Arrange in ascending order $\log_2(x), \log_3(x), \log_e(x), \log_{10}(x)$, if

(i) $x > 1$

(ii) $0 < x < 1$.

Sol. $\because 2 < e < 3 < 10$

(i) For $x > 1$, $\log_x 2 < \log_x e < \log_x 3 < \log_x 10$

$$\Rightarrow \frac{1}{\log_2(x)} < \frac{1}{\log_e(x)} < \frac{1}{\log_3(x)} < \frac{1}{\log_{10}(x)}$$

$$\Rightarrow \log_2(x) > \log_e(x) > \log_3(x) > \log_{10}(x)$$

Hence, ascending order is

$$\log_{10}(x) < \log_3(x) < \log_e(x) < \log_2(x)$$

(ii) For $0 < x < 1$, $\log_x 2 > \log_x e > \log_x 3 > \log_x 10$

$$\Rightarrow \frac{1}{\log_2(x)} > \frac{1}{\log_e(x)} > \frac{1}{\log_3(x)} > \frac{1}{\log_{10}(x)}$$

$\therefore \log_2(x) < \log_e(x) < \log_3(x) < \log_{10}(x)$

which is in ascending order.

Example 19. If $\log 11 = 1.0414$, prove that $10^{11} > 11^{10}$.

Sol. $\because \log 10^{11} = 11 \log 10 = 11$

and $\log 11^{10} = 10 \log 11$

$= 10 \times 1.0414$

$= 10.414$

It is clear that $11 > 10.414$

$\Rightarrow \log 10^{11} > \log 11^{10}$ [$\because$ here, base = 10]

$\Rightarrow 10^{11} > 11^{10}$

Example 20. If $\log_2(x-2) < \log_4(x-2)$, find the interval in which x lies.

Sol. Here, $x - 2 > 0$

$\Rightarrow x > 2$ ...(i)

and $\log_2(x-2) < \log_{2^2}(x-2) = \frac{1}{2}\log_2(x-2)$

$\Rightarrow \log_2(x-2) < \frac{1}{2}\log_2(x-2)$

$\Rightarrow \frac{1}{2}\log_2(x-2) < 0$

$\Rightarrow \log_2(x-2) < 0$

$\Rightarrow x - 2 < 2^0$

$\Rightarrow x - 2 < 1$

$\Rightarrow x < 3$ ...(ii)

From Eqs. (i) and (ii), we get

$$2 < x < 3 \text{ or } x \in (2, 3)$$

Example 21. Prove that $\log_n(n+1) > \log_{(n+1)}(n+2)$ for any natural number $n > 1$.

Sol. Since, $\frac{n+1}{n} = 1 + \frac{1}{n} > 1 + \frac{1}{n+1} = \left(\frac{n+2}{n+1}\right)$

For $n > 1$,

$$\log_n\left(\frac{n+1}{n}\right) > \log_{n+1}\left(\frac{n+1}{n}\right) > \log_{n+1}\left(\frac{n+2}{n+1}\right)$$

$\Rightarrow \log_n(n+1) - \log_n n > \log_{(n+1)}(n+2) - \log_{(n+1)}(n+1)$

$\Rightarrow \log_n(n+1) - 1 > \log_{(n+1)}(n+2) - 1$

$\therefore \log_n(n+1) > \log_{(n+1)}(n+2)$ **Hence proved.**

How to Find Minimum Value of

$\lambda_1 \log_a x + \lambda_2 \log_x a, a > 0, x > 0, a \neq 1, x \neq 1$ and $\lambda_1, \lambda_2 \in R_+$

$\because$ AM $\geq$ GM

$$\Rightarrow \frac{\lambda_1 \log_a x + \lambda_2 \log_x a}{2} \geq \sqrt{(\lambda_1 \log_a x)(\lambda_2 \log_x a)} = \sqrt{\lambda_1 \lambda_2}$$

$$\Rightarrow \lambda_1 \log_a x + \lambda_2 \log_x a \geq 2\sqrt{\lambda_1 \lambda_2}$$

Hence, the minimum value of $\lambda_1 \log_a x + \lambda_2 \log_x a$ is $2\sqrt{\lambda_1 \lambda_2}$.

Example 22. Find the least value of the expression $2\log_{10} x - \log_x 0.01$, where $x > 0, x \neq 1$.

Sol. Let $P = 2\log_{10} x - \log_x 0.01 = 2\log_{10} x - \log_x(10^{-2})$

$= 2(\log_{10} x + \log_x 10)$

$\geq 2 \cdot 2 = 4$ [by above article]

$\therefore P \geq 4$

Hence, the least value of P is 4.

Example 23. Which is smaller 2 or $(\log_\pi 2 + \log_2 \pi)$?

Sol. Let $P = \log_\pi 2 + \log_2 \pi > 2$ [by above article] [$\because \pi \neq 2$]

$\therefore P > 2$

$\Rightarrow (\log_\pi 2 + \log_2 \pi) > 2$

Hence, the smaller number is 2.

4.5 Characteristic and Mantissa

The integral part of a logarithm is called the **characteristic** and the fractional part (decimal part) is called **mantissa**.

i.e. $\log N$ = Integer + Fractional or decimal part (+ve)

↓ Characteristic ↓ Mantissa

The mantissa of log of a number is always kept positive.

i.e. if $\log 564 = 2.751279$, then 2 is the characteristic and 0.751279 is the mantissa of the given number 564.

And if $\log 0.00895 = -2.0481769 = -2 - 0.0481769$

$$= (-2-1) + (1 - 0.0481769)$$

$$= -3 + 0.9518231$$

Hence, -3 is the characteristic and 0.9518231 (not 0.0481769) is mantissa of log 0.00895.

In short, $-3 + 0.9518231$ is written as $\bar{3}.9518231$.

JEE Focus Points

Concept Inside Video

- If $N > 1$, the characteristic of $\log N$ will be one less than the number of digits in the integral part of N.

  e.g. If $\log 235.68 = 2.3723227$

  Here, $N = 235.68$

  $\therefore$ Number of digits in the integral part of $N = 3$

  $\Rightarrow$ Characteristic of $\log 235.68 = N - 1 = 3 - 1 = 2$
- If $0 < N < 1$, the characteristic of $\log N$ is negative and numerically it is one greater than the number of zeroes immediately after the decimal part in N.

  e.g. If $\log 0.0000279 = \bar{5}.4456042$

  Here, four zeroes immediately after the decimal point in the number 0.0000279 is $(\overline{4+1})$, i.e. $\bar{5}$.
- If the characteristics of $\log N$ be n, then number of digits in N is $(n+1)$ (Here, $N > 1$).
- If the characteristics of $\log N$ be $-n$, then there exists $(n-1)$ number of zeroes after decimal part of N (here, $0 < N < 1$).

Example 24. If $\log 2 = 0.301$ and $\log 3 = 0.477$, find the number of digits in 6^{20}.

Sol. Let $P = 6^{20} = (2 \times 3)^{20}$

$$\therefore \quad \log P = 20 \log(2 \times 3) = 20\{\log 2 + \log 3\}$$

$$= 20\{0.301 + 0.477\}$$

$$= 20 \times 0.778 = 15.560$$

Since, the characteristic of $\log P$ is 15, therefore the number of digits in P will be $15 + 1$, i.e. 16.

Example 25. Find the number of zeroes between the decimal point and first significant digit of $(0.036)^{16}$, where $\log 2 = 0.301$ and $\log 3 = 0.477$.

Sol. Let $P = (0.036)^{16}$

$$\Rightarrow \quad \log P = 16 \log (0.036)$$

$$= 16 \log\left(\frac{36}{1000}\right)$$

$$= 16 \log\left(\frac{2^2 \cdot 3^2}{1000}\right)$$

$$= 16\{\log 2^2 + \log 3^2 - \log 10^3\}$$

$$= 16\{2\log 2 + 2\log 3 - 3\}$$

$$= 16\{2 \times 0.301 + 2 \times 0.477 - 3\}$$

$$= 16\{1.556 - 3\}$$

$$= 24.896 - 48$$

$$= -48 + 24 + 0.896$$

$$= -24 + 0.896$$

$$= \overline{24} + 0.896$$

$\therefore$ The required number of zeroes $= 24 - 1$

$$= 23$$

Example 26. If $\log_{10} 7 = 0.8451$, then find the position of the first significant figure of 7^{-20}.

Sol. Let $x = 7^{-20}$

$$\therefore \quad \log x = -20 \log 7$$

$$= -20 \times 0.8451$$

$$= -16.9020$$

$$= -17 + 1 - 0.9020$$

$$= -17 + 0.0980$$

$$= \overline{17} + 0.0980$$

Hence, the position of first significant figure is 17th.

JEE Pattern EXAMPLES

Single Option Correct Type Questions

Example 1 *If $0 \le a \le x$, then the minimum value of $\log_a x + \log_x x$ is*

(a) 1 (b) 2 (c) 0 (d) −1

Sol. (b) We have, $0 \le a \le x \Rightarrow \log_a x \ge 1$

$\Rightarrow \log_a x + \log_x x \ge 1 + \log_x x$

$\Rightarrow \log_a x + \log_x x \ge 1 + 1 \Rightarrow \log_a x + \log_x x \ge 2$

Example 2 *If* $\dfrac{1}{\log_2 a} + \dfrac{1}{\log_4 a} + \dfrac{1}{\log_8 a} + \dfrac{1}{\log_{16} a} + \dots + \dfrac{1}{\log_{2^n} a} = \dfrac{n(n+1)}{\lambda}$, *then λ equals to*

(a) $\log_2 a$ (b) $\log_a 4$ (c) $\log_2 a^2$ (d) $\log_4 a$

Sol. (c) We have,

$$\frac{1}{\log_2 a} + \frac{1}{\log_4 a} + \frac{1}{\log_8 a} + \frac{1}{\log_{16} a} + \dots \frac{1}{\log_{2^n} a} = \frac{n(n+1)}{\lambda}$$

$$\Rightarrow \log_a 2 + \log_a 4 + \log_a 8 + \log_a 16 + \dots + \log_a 2^n = \frac{n(n+1)}{\lambda}$$

$$\Rightarrow \log_a 2 + 2\log_a 2 + 3\log_a 2 + 4\log_a 2 + \dots + n\log_a 2 = \frac{n(n+1)}{\lambda}$$

$$\Rightarrow \log_a 2\,[1 + 2 + 3 + 4 + \dots + n] = \frac{n(n+1)}{\lambda}$$

$$\Rightarrow \log_a 2 \times \frac{n(n+1)}{2} = \frac{n(n+1)}{\lambda}$$

$$\Rightarrow \frac{1}{2}\log_a 2 = \frac{1}{\lambda}$$

$$\Rightarrow \lambda = \frac{2}{\log_a 2} = 2\log_2 a = \log_2 a^2$$

Example 3 *If $\log_{ax} x, \log_{bx} x, \log_{cx} x$ are in HP, where a, b, c and x belonging to $(1, \infty)$, then a, b, c are in*

(a) AP (b) GP

(c) HP (d) None of these

Decoding the Question

If three numbers a, b and c are in HP, then $b = \dfrac{2ac}{a+c}$ and in GP, then $b^2 = ac$

Sol. (b) We have, $\log_{ax} x, \log_{bx} x, \log_{cx} x$ are in HP.

$\log_x ax, \log_x bx, \log_x cx$ are in AP.

$\log_x a + 1, \log_x b + 1, \log_x c + 1$ are in AP.

$\log_x a, \log_x b, \log_x c$ are in AP.

$\Rightarrow 2\log_x b = \log_x a + \log_x c$

$\Rightarrow \log_x b^2 = \log_x ac$

$\Rightarrow b^2 = ac$

$\therefore a, b, c$ are in GP.

Example 4 *The number of solutions of $\log_2(x+5) = 6 - x$ is*

(a) 0 (b) 1 (c) 2 (d) 3

Sol. (b) We have, $\log_2(x+5) = 6 - x$

$\Rightarrow x + 5 = 2^{6-x}$

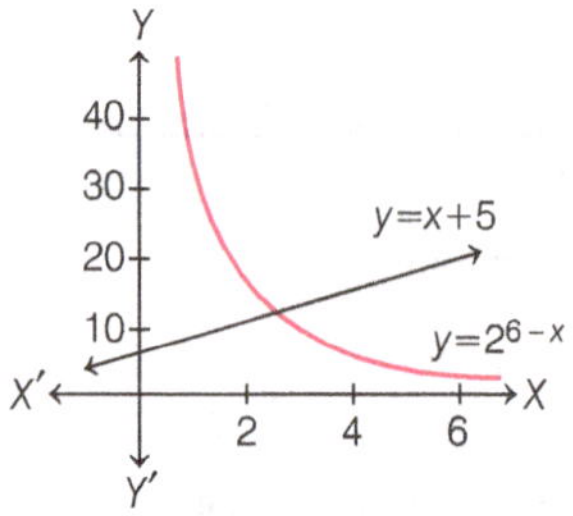

We observe that the two curves intersect at exactly one point.

Hence, the given equation has exactly one solution.

Example 5 *The solution set of $\log_2 |4 - 5x| > 2$, is*

(a) $\left(\dfrac{8}{5}, \infty\right)$ (b) $\left(\dfrac{4}{5}, \dfrac{8}{5}\right)$

(c) $(-\infty, 0) \cup \left(\dfrac{8}{5}, \infty\right)$ (d) None of these

Sol. (c) We have, $\log_2 |4 - 5x| > 2$

$\Rightarrow \log_2 |4 - 5x| > \log_2 4 \Rightarrow |4 - 5x| > 4$

$[\because \log_a x > \log_a y \Rightarrow x > y, \text{ if } a > 1]$

$\Rightarrow 4 - 5x < -4$ or $4 - 5x > 4$

$\Rightarrow x > \dfrac{8}{5}$ or $x < 0 \Rightarrow x \in (-\infty, 0) \cup \left(\dfrac{8}{5}, \infty\right)$

Example 6 *If* $\log_{0.04}(x-1) \ge \log_{0.2}(x-1)$, *then* $x \in$

(a) (1, 2] (b) $(-\infty, 2]$

(c) $[2, \infty)$ (d) None of these

Sol. (c) We have, $\log_{0.04}(x-1) \ge \log_{0.2}(x-1)$

$$\Rightarrow \log_{(0.2)^2}(x-1) \ge \log_{0.2}(x-1)$$

$$\Rightarrow \frac{1}{2}\log_{0.2}(x-1) \ge \log_{0.2}(x-1)$$

$$\Rightarrow \frac{1}{2}\log_{0.2}(x-1) \le 0$$

$$\Rightarrow \log_{0.2}(x-1) \le 0$$

$$\Rightarrow x-1 \ge (0.2)^0$$

$$\Rightarrow x-1 \ge 1 \Rightarrow x \ge 2$$

Example 7 *The expression* $\log_2 5 - \sum_{k=1}^{4}\log_2\left(\sin\left(\frac{k\pi}{5}\right)\right)$ *reduces to* $\frac{p}{q}$, *where p and q are co-prime, the value of* p^2+q^2 *is*

(a) 13 (b) 17 (c) 26 (d) 29

Sol. (b) Let $p = \log_2 5 - \sum_{k=1}^{4}\log_2\left(\sin\left(\frac{k\pi}{5}\right)\right)$

$$= \log_2 5 - \left\{\log_2\left(\sin\left(\frac{\pi}{5}\right)\right) + \log_2\left(\sin\left(\frac{2\pi}{5}\right)\right) + \log_2\left(\sin\left(\frac{3\pi}{5}\right)\right) + \log_2\left(\sin\left(\frac{4\pi}{5}\right)\right)\right\}$$

$$= \log_2 5 - \log_2\left\{\sin\frac{\pi}{5}\cdot\sin\frac{2\pi}{5}\cdot\sin\frac{3\pi}{5}\cdot\sin\frac{4\pi}{5}\right\}$$

$$= \log_2 5 - \log_2\left\{\sin^2\left(\frac{\pi}{5}\right)\cdot\sin^2\left(\frac{2\pi}{5}\right)\right\}$$

$$= \log_2 5 - \log_2\left\{\frac{(1-\cos 72^\circ)(1-\cos 144^\circ)}{4}\right\}$$

$$= \log_2 5 - \log_2\left\{\frac{(1-\sin 18^\circ)(1+\cos 36^\circ)}{4}\right\}$$

$$= \log_2 5 - \log_2\left\{\frac{\left(1-\frac{\sqrt{5}-1}{4}\right)\left(1+\frac{\sqrt{5}+1}{4}\right)}{4}\right\}$$

$$= \log_2 5 - \log_2\left\{\frac{(5-\sqrt{5})(5+\sqrt{5})}{64}\right\}$$

$$= \log_2 5 - \log_2\left(\frac{5}{16}\right)$$

$$= \log_2\left(5\times\frac{16}{5}\right)$$

$$= \log_2 2^4 = \frac{4}{1} = \frac{p}{q} \quad \text{[given]}$$

$\therefore$ $p = 4, q = 1$

Hence, $p^2+q^2 = 4^2+1^2 = 17$

Example 8 *If* $3 \le a \le 2015, 3 \le b \le 2015$ *such that* $\log_a b + 6\log_b a = 5$, *the number of ordered pairs (a, b) of integers is*

(a) 48 (b) 50 (c) 52 (d) 54

Sol. (c) Let $x = \log_a b$ ...(i)

$$\Rightarrow x + \frac{6}{x} = 5$$

$$\Rightarrow x^2 - 5x + 6 = 0$$

$$\Rightarrow x = 2, 3$$

From Eq. (i), we get

$$\log_a b = 2, 3$$

$$\Rightarrow b = a^2 \text{ or } a^3$$

The pairs (a, b) are

$(3, 3^2), (4, 4^2), (5, 5^2), (6, 6^2), \ldots, (44, 44^2)$ and $(3, 3^3), (4, 4^3), (5, 5^3), \ldots, (12, 12^3)$.

Hence, there are $42 + 10 = 52$ pairs.

Example 9 *The lengths of the sides of a triangle are* $\log_{10} 12, \log_{10} 75$ *and* $\log_{10} n$, *where* $n \in N$. *If a and b are the least and greatest values of n respectively, the value of* $b-a$ *is divisible by*

(a) 221 (b) 222 (c) 223 (d) 224

Sol. (c) In a triangle,

$$\log_{10} 12 + \log_{10} 75 > \log_{10} n$$

$$\Rightarrow n < 12 \times 75 = 900$$

$$\therefore n < 900 \quad \text{...(i)}$$

and $\log_{10} 12 + \log_{10} n > \log_{10} 75$

$$\Rightarrow n > \frac{75}{12} = \frac{25}{4}$$

$$\therefore n > \frac{25}{4} \quad \text{...(ii)}$$

From Eqs. (i) and (ii), we get

$$\frac{25}{4} < n < 900$$

$$\therefore n = 7, 8, 9, 10, \ldots, 899$$

Hence, $a = 7, b = 899$

$\therefore$ $b - a = 892 = 4 \times 223$

Hence, $b - a$ is divisible by 223.

Example 10 *If* $5\log_{abc}(a^3+b^3+c^3) = 3\lambda\left(\frac{1+\log_3(abc)}{\log_3(abc)}\right)$ *and* $(abc)^{a+b+c} = 1$ *and* $\lambda = \frac{m}{n}$, *where m and n are relative primes, the value of* $|m+n| + |m-n|$ *is*

(a) 8 (b) 10 (c) 12 (d) 14

Sol. (b) $\because$ $(abc)^{a+b+c} = 1 = (abc)^0$

$$\therefore a+b+c = 0 \Rightarrow a^3+b^3+c^3 = 3abc$$

Now, LHS $= 5\log_{abc}(a^3+b^3+c^3) = 5\log_{abc}(3abc)$ ...(i)

and RHS $= 3\lambda\left(\dfrac{1+\log_3(abc)}{\log_3(abc)}\right) = 3\lambda\left(\dfrac{\log_3(3abc)}{\log_3(abc)}\right)$

$= 3\lambda \log_{abc}(3abc)$ ...(ii)

From Eqs. (i) and (ii), we get

$$5\log_{abc}(3abc) = 3\lambda \log_{abc}(3abc)$$

$\therefore \quad \lambda = \dfrac{5}{3} = \dfrac{m}{n}$ [given]

$\Rightarrow \quad m = 5, n = 3$

Hence, $|m+n| + |m-n| = 8 + 2 = 10$

Example 11 *If*

$$a^{\log_b c} = 3 \cdot 3^{\log_4 3} \cdot 3^{\log_4 3^{\log_4 3}} \cdot 3^{\log_4 3^{\log_4 3^{\log_4 3}}} \ldots \infty,$$

where a, b, c ∈ Q, the value of abc is

(a) 9 (b) 12 (c) 16 (d) 20

Sol. (c) $a^{\log_b c} = 3^{1+\log_4 3+(\log_4 3)^2+(\log_4 3)^3+\ldots\infty}$

$= 3^{1/(1-\log_4 3)} = 3^{1/\log_4(4/3)} = 3^{\log_{4/3} 4}$

$\therefore \quad a = 3, b = \dfrac{4}{3}, c = 4$

Hence, $abc = 3 \cdot \dfrac{4}{3} \cdot 4 = 16$

Example 12 *Number of real roots of equation*

$$3^{\log_3(x^2-4x+3)} = (x-3) \text{ is}$$

(a) 0 (b) 1 (c) 2 (d) infinite

Sol. (a) $\because \quad 3^{\log_3(x^2-4x+3)} = (x-3)$ ...(i)

Eq. (i) is defined, if $x^2-4x+3>0$

$\Rightarrow \quad (x-1)(x-3)>0$

$\Rightarrow \quad x<1$ or $x>3$ ...(ii)

Eq. (i) reduces to $x^2-4x+3 = x-3$

$\Rightarrow \quad x^2-5x+6=0$

$\therefore \quad x = 2, 3$ ...(iii)

From Eqs. (ii) and (iii), we get $x \in \phi$

$\therefore$ Number of real roots = 0

Example 13 *If* $\log_6 a + \log_6 b + \log_6 c = 6$, *where a, b, c ∈ N and a, b, c are in GP and b − a is a square of an integer, then the value of a + b − c is*

(a) 21 (b) 15

(c) 9 (d) 3

Sol. (b) $\because \quad \log_6 a + \log_6 b + \log_6 c = 6$

$\Rightarrow \quad \log_6(abc) = 6$

$\Rightarrow \quad abc = 6^6$

$\Rightarrow \quad b^3 = 6^6$ $[\because b^2 = ac]$

$\Rightarrow \quad b = 36$

Also, $b - a = 36 - a$ is a square for $a = 35, 32, 27, 20, 11$

Now, $c = \dfrac{b^2}{a} = \dfrac{36^2}{a}$ is an integer for $a = 27$

$\therefore \quad a = 27, b = 36, c = 48$

Hence, $a + b - c = 27 + 36 - 48 = 15$

Example 14 *If* $x = \log_{2a}\left(\dfrac{bcd}{2}\right), y = \log_{3b}\left(\dfrac{acd}{3}\right), z = \log_{4c}\left(\dfrac{abd}{4}\right)$ *and* $w = \log_{5d}\left(\dfrac{abc}{5}\right)$ *and* $\dfrac{1}{x+1} + \dfrac{1}{y+1} + \dfrac{1}{z+1} + \dfrac{1}{w+1} = \log_{abcd} N + 1$, *the value of N is*

(a) 40 (b) 80 (c) 120 (d) 160

Decoding the Question

We know that $\log_a a = 1$

$$\log_b a = \frac{1}{\log_a b}$$

$$\log(a \cdot b \cdot c) = \log a + \log b + \log c$$

Sol. (c) $\because \quad x = \log_{2a}\left(\dfrac{bcd}{2}\right)$

$\Rightarrow \quad x + 1 = \log_{2a}\left(\dfrac{2abcd}{2}\right) = \log_{2a}(abcd)$

$\therefore \quad \dfrac{1}{x+1} = \log_{abcd} 2a$

Similarly, $\dfrac{1}{y+1} = \log_{abcd} 3b$, $\dfrac{1}{z+1} = \log_{abcd} 4c$

and $\dfrac{1}{w+1} = \log_{abcd} 5d$

$\therefore \quad \dfrac{1}{x+1} + \dfrac{1}{y+1} + \dfrac{1}{z+1} + \dfrac{1}{w+1} = \log_{abcd}(2a \cdot 3b \cdot 4c \cdot 5d)$

$= \log_{abcd}(120abcd)$

$= \log_{abcd} 120 + 1$

$= \log_{abcd} N + 1$ [given]

Hence, $N = 120$

Example 15 *The equation*

$$(\log_{10} x + 2)^3 + (\log_{10} x - 1)^3 = (2\log_{10} x + 1)^3 \text{ has}$$

(a) one solution (b) two solutions

(c) three solutions (d) four solutions

Sol. (c) Let $\log_{10} x + 2 = a$ and $\log_{10} x - 1 = b$

$\therefore \quad a + b = 2\log_{10} x + 1$, then given equation reduces to

$$a^3 + b^3 = (a+b)^3$$

$\Rightarrow \quad 3ab(a+b) = 0$

$\Rightarrow \quad a = 0$ or $b = 0$ or $a + b = 0$

$\Rightarrow \quad \log_{10} x + 2 = 0$ or $\log_{10} x - 1 = 0$

or $\quad 2\log_{10} x + 1 = 0$

$\Rightarrow \quad x = 10^{-2}$ or $x = 10$ or $x = 10^{-1/2}$

Hence, $x = \dfrac{1}{100}$ or $x = 10$ or $x = \dfrac{1}{\sqrt{10}}$

Numerical Value Type Questions

Example 16 *If* $a^x = b, b^y = c, c^z = a, x = \log_b a^{k_1}$, $y = \log_c b^{k_2}, z = \log_a c^{k_3}$, *then minimum value of* $k_1 + 2k_2 + 4k_3$ *is ....*

Sol. (6) We have, $a = c^z = b^{yz} = a^{xyz}$

$\therefore \quad xyz = 1$

Also, $xyz = \log_b a^{k_1} \cdot \log_c b^{k_2} \cdot \log_a c^{k_3}$

$\Rightarrow \quad xyz = k_1 k_2 \cdot k_3 \log_b a \log_c b \log_a c$

$\Rightarrow \quad 1 = k_1 k_2 k_3$

Now, $\quad$ AM $\geq$ GM

$$\Rightarrow \frac{k_1 + 2k_2 + 4k_3}{3} \geq (k_1 \cdot 2k_2 \cdot 4k_3)^{\frac{1}{3}}$$

$$\Rightarrow k_1 + 2k_2 + 4k_3 \geq 3(8)^{\frac{1}{3}}$$

$$\Rightarrow k_1 + 2k_2 + 4k_3 \geq 6$$

Example 17 *The number of zeroes coming immediately after the decimal point in the value of* $(0.2)^{25}$ *is (take* $\log_{10} 2 = 0.30103$) ....

Sol. (17) Let $x = (0.2)^{25}$

$\Rightarrow \log_{10} x = 25 \log_{10} 0.2$

$\Rightarrow \log_{10} x = 25(\log_{10} 2 - 1)$

$\Rightarrow \log_{10} x = 25 \times (0.30103 - 1) = -17.47425$

$\therefore$ There are 17 zeroes immediately after the decimal point.

Example 18 *If* $[x]$ *denotes the greatest integer less than or equal to x, then the value of* $[\log_{10} 6730.4]$ *is ....*

Sol. (3) We have, $10^3 < 6730.40 < 10^4$

$\Rightarrow \quad 3 < \log_{10} 6730.40 < 4$

$\Rightarrow \quad [\log_{10} 6730.40] = 3$

Example 19 *If* x_1 *and* x_2 *are the solutions of the equation* $x^{\log_{10} x} = 100x$ *such that* $x_1 > 1$ *and* $x_2 < 1$, *the value of* $\frac{x_1 x_2}{2}$ *is ....*

Sol. (5) $\because \quad x^{\log_{10} x} = 100x$

Taking logarithm on both sides on base 10, then we get

$\log_{10} x \cdot \log_{10} x = \log_{10} 100 + \log_{10} x$

$\Rightarrow \quad (\log_{10} x)^2 - \log_{10} x - 2 = 0$

$\Rightarrow \quad (\log_{10} x - 2)(\log_{10} x + 1) = 0$

$\therefore \quad \log_{10} x = 2, -1$

$\Rightarrow \quad x = 10^2, 10^{-1}$

$\therefore \quad x_1 = 100, x_2 = \frac{1}{10}$

$\therefore \quad \frac{x_1 x_2}{2} = 5$

Example 20 *If* $(31.6)^a = (0.0000316)^b = 100$, *the value of* $\frac{1}{a} - \frac{1}{b}$ *is ....*

Sol. (3) $\because \quad (31.6)^a = (0.0000316)^b = 100$

$\Rightarrow \quad a \log_{10}(31.6) = b \log_{10}(0.0000316) = \log_{10} 100$

$\Rightarrow \quad a \log_{10}(31.6) = b \log_{10}(31.6 \times 10^{-6}) = 2$

$\Rightarrow \quad a \log_{10}(31.6) = b \log_{10}(31.6) - 6b = 2$

$\Rightarrow \quad \frac{2}{a} = \log_{10}(31.6)$

and $\quad \frac{2}{b} = \log_{10}(31.6) - 6$

$\therefore \quad \frac{2}{a} - \frac{2}{b} = 6$

$\Rightarrow \quad \frac{1}{a} - \frac{1}{b} = 3$

EXERCISE

JEE Main Pattern

Single Option Correct Type Questions

1. If $a^2 + b^2 - c^2 = 0$, then $\frac{1}{\log_{c+a} b} + \frac{1}{\log_{c-a} b}$ is equal to

(a) 1 (b) 2 (c) −1 (d) −2

2. If $n = 2024!$, then $\sum_{x=1}^{2024} \log_n x$ is equal to

(a) 1 (b) 0 (c) 2024 (d) −1

3. If [.] denotes the GIF, then the value of n, if $[\log_2 1] + [\log_2 2] + [\log_2 3] + \ldots + [\log_2 n] = 1538$, $n \in N$ is

(a) 252 (b) 253 (c) 254 (d) 255

4. If $x^{\log_x (3-x)^2} = 25$, then x is equal to

(a) −2, 8 (b) −2
(c) 8 (d) None of these

5. If $\log_{10} 2 = 0.3010\ldots$, the number of digits in the number 2000^{2000} is

(a) 6601 (b) 6602 (c) 6603 (d) 6604

6. There exist a positive number λ, such that $\log_2 x + \log_4 x + \log_8 x = \log_\lambda x$, for all positive real numbers x. If $\lambda = \sqrt[b]{a}$, where $a, b \in N$, the smallest possible value of $(a + b)$ is equal to

(a) 12 (b) 63 (c) 65 (d) 75

7. If a, b and c are the three real solutions of the equation

$$x^{\log_{10}^2 x + \log_{10} x^3 + 3} = \frac{2}{\frac{1}{\sqrt{x+1}-1} - \frac{1}{\sqrt{x+1}+1}}$$

where, $a > b > c$, then a, b, c are in

(a) AP (b) GP
(c) HP (d) $a^{-1} + b^{-1} = c^{-1}$

8. If $f(n) = \prod_{i=2}^{n-1} \log_i (i+1)$, the value of $\sum_{k=1}^{100} f(2^k)$ equals

(a) 5010 (b) 5050 (c) 5100 (d) 5049

9. If $\log_3 27 \cdot \log_x 7 = \log_{27} x \cdot \log_7 3$, the least value of x, is

(a) 7^{-3} (b) 3^{-7} (c) 7^3 (d) 3^7

10. If $x = \log_5 (1000)$ and $y = \log_7 (2058)$, then

(a) $x > y$ (b) $x < y$
(c) $x = y$ (d) None of these

11. If $\log_5 120 + (x-3) - 2\log_5 (1 - 5^{x-3}) = -\log_5 (0.2 - 5^{x-4})$, then x is

(a) 1 (b) 2 (c) 3 (d) 4

12. If $x_n > x_{n-1} > \ldots > x_2 > x_1 > 1$, the value of

$$\log_{x_1} \log_{x_2} \log_{x_3} \ldots \log_{x_n} x_n^{x_{n-1}^{\cdot^{\cdot^{x_1}}}}$$ is

(a) 0 (b) 1
(c) 2 (d) undefined

13. If $\frac{x(y+z-x)}{\log x} = \frac{y(z+x-y)}{\log y} = \frac{z(x+y-z)}{\log z}$, then $x^y y^x = z^y y^z$ is equal to

(a) $z^x x^z$ (b) $x^z y^x$ (c) $x^y y^z$ (d) $x^x y^y$

14. If $y = a^{\frac{1}{1-\log_a x}}$ and $z = a^{\frac{1}{1-\log_a y}}$, then x is equal to

(a) $a^{\frac{1}{1+\log_a z}}$ (b) $a^{\frac{1}{2+\log_a z}}$
(c) $a^{\frac{1}{1-\log_a z}}$ (d) $a^{\frac{1}{2-\log_a z}}$

15. If $\log_{0.3} (x-1) < \log_{0.09} (x-1)$, then x lies in the interval

(a) $(-\infty, 1)$ (b) $(1, 2)$
(c) $(2, \infty)$ (d) None of these

16. The value of $a^x - b^y$ is (where $x = \sqrt{\log_a b}$ and $y = \sqrt{\log_b a}$, $a > 0$, $b > 0$ and $a, b \neq 1$)

(a) 1 (b) 2 (c) 0 (d) −1

17. If $x = 1 + \log_a bc$, $y = 1 + \log_b ca$, $z = 1 + \log_c ab$, then $\frac{xyz}{xy + yz + zx}$ is equal to

(a) 0 (b) 1 (c) −1 (d) 2

18. The value of $a^{\frac{\log_b (\log_b N)}{\log_b a}}$ is

(a) $\log_a N$ (b) $\log_b N$ (c) $\log_N a$ (d) $\log_N b$

19. The value of $49^A + 5^B$, where $A = 1 - \log_7 2$ and $B = -\log_5 4$ is

(a) 10.5 (b) 11.5 (c) 12.5 (d) 13.5

20. The number of real values of the parameter λ for which $(\log_{16} x)^2 - \log_{16} x + \log_{16} \lambda = 0$ with real coefficients will have exactly one solution is

(a) 1 (b) 2 (c) 3 (d) 4

21. The number of roots of the equation $x^{\log_x (x+3)^2} = 16$ is
(a) 1 (b) 0 (c) 2 (d) 4

22. The point on the graph $y = \log_2 \log_6 \{2^{\sqrt{(2x+1)}} + 4\}$, whose y-coordinate is 1 is
(a) (1, 1) (b) (6,1)
(c) (8, 1) (d) (12, 1)

23. Given, $\log 2 = 0.301$ and $\log 3 = 0.477$, then the number of digits before decimal in $3^{12} \times 2^8$ is
(a) 7 (b) 8
(c) 9 (d) 11

24. The number of solution(s) for the equation $2\log_x a + \log_{ax} a + 3\log_{a^2 x} a = 0$, is
(a) one (b) two
(c) three (d) four

25. Let $a = \log_3 \log_3 2$ and an integer k satisfying $1 < 2^{(-k+3^{-a})} < 2$, then k equals to
(a) 0 (b) 1
(c) 2 (d) 3

26. Let (x_0, y_0) be solution of the following equations $(2x)^{\ln 2} = (3y)^{\ln 3}$ and $3^{\ln x} = 2^{\ln y}$, then x_0 is
(a) $\frac{1}{6}$ (b) $\frac{1}{3}$
(c) $\frac{1}{2}$ (d) 6

27. If $3^x = 4^{x-1}$, then x is not equal to
(a) $\frac{2\log_3 2}{2\log_3 2 - 1}$ (b) $\frac{2}{2 - \log_2 3}$
(c) $\frac{1}{1 - \log_4 3}$ (d) $\frac{2\log_2 3}{2\log_2 3 - 1}$

Numerical Value Type Questions

28. The value of
$$6 + \log_{3/2}\left(\frac{1}{3\sqrt{2}}\sqrt{4 - \frac{1}{3\sqrt{2}}\sqrt{4 - \frac{1}{3\sqrt{2}}\sqrt{4 - \frac{1}{3\sqrt{2}}\cdots}}}\right)$$
is ....

29. If $x, y \in R^+$ and $\log_{10}(2x) + \log_{10} y = 2$ and $\log_{10} x^2 - \log_{10}(2y) = 4$ and $x + y = \frac{m}{n}$, where m and n are relative prime, the value of $m - 3n^6$ is ....

30. A line $x = \lambda$ intersects the graph of $y = \log_5 x$ and $y = \log_5(x+4)$. The distance between the points of intersection is 0.5. Given $\lambda = a + \sqrt{b}$, where a and b are integers, the value of $(a+b)$ is ....

31. If the left hand side of the equation $a(b-c)x^2 + b(c-a)xy + c(a-b)y^2 = 0$ is a perfect square, the value of
$$\left\{\frac{\log(a+c) + \log(a-2b+c)}{\log(a-c)}\right\}^2, (a, b, c \in R^+, a > c)$$ is ......

32. Number of integers satisfying the inequality $\left(\frac{1}{3}\right)^{\frac{|x+2|}{2-|x|}} > 9$ is ....

33. If $x > 2$ is a solution of the equation $|\log_{\sqrt{3}} x - 2| + |\log_3 x - 2| = 2$, then the value of x is ....

34. Number of integers satisfying the inequality $\log_2 \sqrt{x} - 2\log_{1/4}^2 x + 1 > 0$, is ....

35. The value of $b(> 0)$ for which the equation $2\log_{1/25}(bx + 28) = -\log_5(12 - 4x - x^2)$ has coincident roots, is ....

36. The value of $\frac{2^{\log_{2^{1/4}} 2} - 3^{\log_{27} 125} - 4}{7^{4\log_{49} 2} - 3}$ is ....

37. If x_1 and x_2 $(x_2 > x_1)$ are the integral solutions of the equation $(\log_5 x)^2 + \log_{5x}\left(\frac{5}{x}\right) = 1$, the value of $|x_2 - 4x_1|$ is ......

38. If $x = \log_\lambda a = \log_a b = \frac{1}{2}\log_b c$ and $\log_\lambda c = nx^{n+1}$, the value of n is ....

Answer Key

1. (b)	2. (a)	3. (d)	4. (c)	5. (c)	6. (d)	7. (b)	8. (b)	9. (a)	10. (a)
11. (a)	12. (b)	13. (a)	14. (c)	15. (c)	16. (c)	17. (b)	18. (b)	19. (c)	20. (b)
21. (b)	22. (d)	23. (c)	24. (b)	25. (b)	26. (c)	27. (d)	28. (4)	29. (9)	30. (6)
31. (4)	32. (3)	33. (9)	34. (3)	35. (4)	36. (7)	37. (1)	38. (2)		

Solutions

1. We have, $\frac{1}{\log_{c+a} b} + \frac{1}{\log_{c-a} b} = \log_b(c+a) + \log_b(c-a)$

$$= \log_b(c^2 - a^2)$$
$$= \log_b b^2$$
$$[\because a^2 + b^2 - c^2 = 0 \Rightarrow c^2 - a^2 = b^2]$$
$$= 2$$

2. We have, $\sum_{x=1}^{2024} \log_n x = \log_n 1 + \log_n 2 + \log_n 3 + \ldots + \log_n 2024$

$$= \log_n(1 \cdot 2 \cdot 3 \cdot 4 \ldots 2024)$$
$$= \log_n 2024!$$
$$= \log_n n \qquad [\because n = 2024!]$$
$$= 1$$

3. We know that if $2^{r-1} \le k < 2^r$

$\Rightarrow \quad r - 1 \le \log_2 k < r$

$\Rightarrow \quad [\log_2 k] = r - 1$

We have, $[\log_2 1] + [\log_2 2] + [\log_2 3] + [\log_2 4] + [\log_2 5] + \ldots + [\log_2 n] = 1538$

$\Rightarrow [\log_2 2^0] + \sum_{k=2}^{2^2-1}[\log_2 k] + \sum_{k=2^2}^{2^3-1}[\log_2 k] + \sum_{k=2^3}^{2^4-1}[\log_2 k] + \ldots = 1538$

$\Rightarrow \quad 0 + \sum_{k=2}^{2^2-1} 1 + \sum_{k=2^2}^{2^3-1} 2 + \sum_{k=2^3}^{2^4-1} 3 + \sum_{k=2^4}^{2^5-1} 4 + \ldots = 1538$

$\Rightarrow \quad 0 + 1 \times 2 + 2 \times 2^2 + 3 \times 2^3 + 4 \times 2^4 + \ldots = 1538$

We observe that

$0 + 1 \times 2 + 2 \times 2^2 + 3 \times 2^3 + 4 \times 2^4 + 5 \times 2^5 + 6 \times 2^6 + 7 \times 2^7$

$$= 0 + 2 + 8 + 24 + 64 + 160 + 384 + 896$$
$$= 1538$$

$\therefore \quad n = 1 + 2 + 2^2 + 2^3 + 2^4 + 2^5 + 2^6 + 2^7$

$$= 1\left(\frac{2^8 - 1}{2 - 1}\right) = 255$$

4. We have, $x^{\log_x (3-x)^2} = 25$

$\Rightarrow \quad (3 - x)^2 = 25, x > 0, x \ne 1$

$\Rightarrow \quad 3 - x = \pm 5, x > 0, x \ne 1$

$\Rightarrow \quad x = -2, 8, x > 0, x \ne 1$

$\therefore \quad x = 8$

5. $\log_{10} 2 = 0.3010$

Let $\quad y = 2000^{2000}$

$$\log_{10} y = 2000 \log_{10} 2000$$
$$= 2000 \times (\log_{10} 2 + 3)$$
$$= 2000 \times 3.3010 = 6602$$

So, the number of digits in $2000^{2000} = 6602 + 1 = 6603$

6. $\because \lambda > 0$ and $\lambda \ne 1$ and $x > 0$

$$\log_2 x + \log_4 x + \log_8 x = \log_\lambda x$$

$\Rightarrow \quad \log_2 x + \frac{1}{2}\log_2 x + \frac{1}{3}\log_2 x = \log_\lambda x$

$\Rightarrow \quad \frac{11}{6}\log_2 x = \log_\lambda x$

$\Rightarrow \quad \frac{11}{6\log_x 2} = \frac{1}{\log_x \lambda}$

$\Rightarrow \quad 11\log_x \lambda - 6\log_x 2 = 0$

$\Rightarrow \quad \log_x\left(\frac{\lambda^{11}}{2^6}\right) = 0 \Rightarrow \frac{\lambda^{11}}{2^6} = 1$

$\Rightarrow \quad \lambda^{11} = 2^6 \Rightarrow \lambda = 2^{6/11}$

$\Rightarrow \quad \lambda = (2^6)^{1/11} \qquad \ldots(i)$

Given that, $\lambda = \sqrt[b]{a}$ and $a, b \in N$

$\Rightarrow \quad \lambda = a^{\frac{1}{b}} \qquad \ldots(ii)$

From Eqs. (i) and (ii), we get

$$a = 2^6 \text{ and } b = 11$$

$\Rightarrow \quad a + b = 64 + 11 = 75$

7. $x^{\log_{10}^2 x + \log_{10} x^3 + 3} = \dfrac{2}{\dfrac{1}{\sqrt{x+1} - 1} - \dfrac{1}{\sqrt{x+1} + 1}} \qquad \ldots(i)$

Given, a, b and c are real solution of Eq. (i) and $a > b > c$ and for Eq. (i) to be defined $x > 0, x > -1 \Rightarrow x > 0$

From Eq. (i), $x^{\log_{10}^2 x + 3\log_{10} x + 3} = \frac{2x}{2}$

On taking logarithm both sides on base 10, then

$$(\log_{10}^2 x + 3\log_{10} x + 3)\log_{10} x = \log_{10} x$$

$\Rightarrow (\log_{10}^2 x + 3\log_{10} x + 2)\log_{10} x = 0$

$\Rightarrow (\log_{10} x + 1)(\log_{10} x + 2)\log_{10} x = 0$

$\therefore \quad \log_{10} x = -2, -1, 0$

$\therefore \quad x = 10^{-2}, 10^{-1}, 10^0$

$$x = \frac{1}{100}, \frac{1}{10}, 1$$

So, a, b, c can take values $a = 1, b = \frac{1}{10}, c = \frac{1}{100} \qquad (\because a > b > c)$

$\therefore a, b$ and c are in GP.

8. $f(n) = \prod_{i=2}^{n-1} \frac{\log(i+1)}{\log(i)} = \frac{\log(n)}{\log(2)} = \log_2 n$

$\therefore \quad f(2^k) = k$

Then, $\sum_{k=1}^{100} f(2^k) = \sum_{k=1}^{100} k = \frac{100 \cdot (100 + 1)}{2} = 5050$

9. $\log_3 27 \cdot \log_x 7 = \log_{27} x \cdot \log_7 3$ ... (i)

Eq. (i) valid for $x > 0, x \neq 1$

On solving Eq. (i),

$$\log_3(3^3) \cdot \log_x 7 = \frac{1}{3}\log_3 x \cdot \log_7 3$$

$\Rightarrow \quad 9 \cdot \log_x 7 = \log_7 x$

$\Rightarrow \quad 9 = (\log_7 x)^2$

$\Rightarrow \quad \log_7 x = \pm 3$

$\Rightarrow \quad x = 7^3 \text{ or } x = 7^{-3}$

Then, the least value of x is $\frac{1}{7^3}$ i.e. 7^{-3}.

10. $\because \; x = \log_5(5^3 \times 8) = 3 + \log_5 8$

$\Rightarrow \quad x - 3 = \log_5 8$ ...(i)

and $\quad y = \log_7(7^3 \times 6) = 3 + \log_7 6$

$\Rightarrow \quad y - 3 = \log_7 6$ ...(ii)

$\because \quad 8 > 6$ and $7 > 5$

$\Rightarrow \quad \log 8 > \log 6$ and $\log 7 > \log 5$

or $\quad (\log 8)(\log 7) > (\log 6)(\log 5)$

$\Rightarrow \quad \log_5 8 > \log_7 6$

$\Rightarrow \quad x - 3 > y - 3$ [from Eqs. (i) and (ii)]

$\therefore \quad x > y$

11. $\because \; \log_5 120 + (x-3) - 2\log_5(1 - 5^{x-3}) = -\log_5(0.2 - 5^{x-4})$

$\Rightarrow \quad \log_5(5 \times 24) + (x-3)$

$$= \log_5(1 - 5^{x-3})^2 - \log_5\left(\frac{1 - 5^{x-3}}{5}\right)$$

$\Rightarrow \quad 1 + \log_5 24 + (x-3) = \log_5 \{5 \cdot (1 - 5^{x-3})\}$

$\Rightarrow \quad 1 + \log_5(24 \cdot 5^{x-3}) = 1 + \log_5(1 - 5^{x-3})$

$\Rightarrow \quad 24 \cdot 5^{x-3} = 1 - 5^{x-3}$

$\Rightarrow \quad 25 \cdot 5^{x-3} = 1$

$\Rightarrow \quad 5^{x-1} = 5^0$

$\therefore \quad x - 1 = 0$

$\Rightarrow \quad x = 1$

12. Given, $x_n > x_{n-1} > \cdots > x_2 > x_1 > 1$

$\therefore \; \log_{x_1} \log_{x_2} \log_{x_3} \cdots \log_{x_n} x_n^{x_{n-1}^{\cdot^{\cdot^{x_1}}}}$

$= \log_{x_1} \log_{x_2} \log_{x_3} \cdots \log x_{n-1}^{x_{n-2}^{\cdot^{\cdot^{x_1}}}}$

$= \log_{x_1} x_1 = 1$ $[\because \log_a a = 1]$

13. Let $\frac{x(y+z-x)}{\log x} = \frac{y(z+x-y)}{\log y} = \frac{z(x+y-z)}{\log z} = \frac{1}{n}$

Then, $\quad \log x = nx(y + z - x)$ ...(i)

$\log y = ny(z + x - y)$ ...(ii)

and $\quad \log z = nz(x + y - z)$ ...(iii)

$\therefore \; y \log x + x \log y = y \log z + z \log y$

$= z \log x + x \log z$

$\Rightarrow \quad \log(x^y \cdot y^x) = \log(y^z \cdot z^y) = \log(x^z \cdot z^x)$

$\Rightarrow \quad x^y \cdot y^x = y^z \cdot z^y = z^x \cdot x^z$

14. $\because \; y = a^{\frac{1}{1-\log_a x}} \Rightarrow \log_a y = \frac{1}{1 - \log_a x}$ ...(i)

and $\quad z = a^{\frac{1}{1-\log_a y}}$

or $\quad \log_a z = \frac{1}{1 - \log_a y}$ ...(ii)

From Eqs. (i) and (ii), we get

$$\log_a z = \frac{1}{1 - \left(\frac{1}{1 - \log_a x}\right)} = 1 - \frac{1}{\log_a x}$$

$\Rightarrow \quad \frac{1}{\log_a x} = (1 - \log_a z) \Rightarrow \log_a x = \frac{1}{(1 - \log_a z)}$

$\therefore \quad x = a^{\frac{1}{1-\log_a z}}$

15. $\log_{0.3}(x-1) < \log_{0.09}(x-1)$ ...(i)

Eq. (i) defined for $x > 1$, ...(ii)

$\Rightarrow \quad \log_{0.3}(x-1) - \log_{(0.3)^2}(x-1) < 0$

$\Rightarrow \quad \log_{0.3}(x-1) - \frac{1}{2}\log_{0.3}(x-1) < 0$

$\Rightarrow \quad \frac{1}{2}\log_{0.3}(x-1) < 0$

$\Rightarrow \quad \log_{0.3}(x-1) < 0$

$\Rightarrow \quad (x-1) > (0.3)^0$

[$\because$ base of log is lie in (0, 1)]

$\Rightarrow \quad x > 2$ ...(iii)

From Eqs. (ii) and (iii), we get

$x > 2 \Rightarrow x \in (2, \infty)$

16. $\because \; a^x = a^{\sqrt{\log_a b}}$

$= a^{\sqrt{\log_a b}\sqrt{\log_a b}\sqrt{\log_b a}} = a^{\log_a b \sqrt{\log_b a}}$

$= (a^{\log_a b})^{\sqrt{\log_b a}}$ $[\because x^{mn} = (x^m)^n]$

$= b^{\sqrt{\log_b a}} = b^y$

$\therefore \; a^x - b^y = 0$

17. $\because \; x = 1 + \log_a bc = \log_a a + \log_a bc = \log_a(abc)$

$\therefore \quad \frac{1}{x} = \log_{abc} a$ ...(i)

Similarly, $\quad \frac{1}{y} = \log_{abc} b$ ...(ii)

and $\quad \frac{1}{z} = \log_{abc} c$ ...(iii)

On adding Eqs. (i), (ii) and (iii), we get

$$\frac{1}{x} + \frac{1}{y} + \frac{1}{z} = \log_{abc} abc = 1$$

$\Rightarrow \quad \frac{xy + yz + zx}{xyz} = 1 \text{ or } \frac{xyz}{xy + yz + zx} = 1$

18. $a^{\frac{\log_b(\log_b N)}{\log_b a}} = a^{\log_a(\log_b N)} = \log_b N$

19. Since, $\quad A = 1 - \log_7 2$

$\Rightarrow \quad A = \log_7 7 - \log_7 2$

$$A = \log_7 \frac{7}{2} \Rightarrow 7^A = \frac{7}{2} \Rightarrow 49^A = \frac{49}{4}$$

and $$B = -\log_5 4 = \log_5 \left(\frac{1}{4}\right) \Rightarrow 5^B = \frac{1}{4}$$

$$\therefore \quad 49^A + 5^B = \frac{49}{4} + \frac{1}{4} = \frac{50}{4} = 12.5$$

20. $(\log_{16} x)^2 - \log_{16} x + \log_{16} \lambda = 0$ ...(i)

Eq. (i) defined for $x > 0, \lambda > 0$ $\left(\log_{16} x - \frac{1}{2}\right)^2 - \frac{1}{4} + \log_{16} \lambda = 0$

For exactly one solution,

$$\log_{16} x - \frac{1}{2} = 0$$

$$\therefore \quad -\frac{1}{4} + \log_{16} \lambda = 0$$

$$\Rightarrow \quad \log_{16} \lambda = \frac{1}{4}$$

or $$\lambda = (16)^{1/4} = 2$$

21. $x^{\log_x (x+3)^2} = 16$ ...(i)

From Eq. (i), $x > 0$ and $x \neq 1$ ... (ii)

By Eq. (i), $(x+3)^2 = 16$

$$\Rightarrow \quad x + 3 = \pm 4$$

$$\Rightarrow \quad x = 1 \text{ or } x = -7$$

From Eq. (ii), no values of x satisfy Eq. (i).

$\therefore$ Number of roots = 0

22. Given, $y = \log_2 \log_6 (2^{\sqrt{2x+1}} + 4)$ ...(i)

From Eq. (i) to be defined,

$$2x + 1 > 0 \Rightarrow x > -\frac{1}{2} \quad \text{... (ii)}$$

We find value of x for which $y = 1$

$$\therefore \quad 1 = \log_2 \log_6 (2^{\sqrt{2x+1}} + 4)$$

$$\Rightarrow \quad \log_6 (2^{\sqrt{2x+1}} + 4) = 2$$

$$\Rightarrow \quad 2^{\sqrt{2x+1}} + 4 = 36$$

$$\Rightarrow \quad 2^{\sqrt{2x+1}} = 32 = 2^5$$

$$\Rightarrow \quad \sqrt{2x+1} = 5$$

$$\Rightarrow \quad 2x + 1 = 25$$

$$\Rightarrow \quad x = 12$$

So, required point is (12, 1).

23. Given that, $\log 2 = 0.301$

$$\log 3 = 0.477$$

Let $$y = 3^{12} \times 2^8$$

$$\log y = 12 \log 3 + 8 \log 2$$
$$= 12 \times (0.477) + 8(0.301)$$
$$= 8.132$$

So, number of digits before decimal in $3^{12} \times 2^8 = 8 + 1$
$= 9$

24. Given, equation $2 \log_x a + \log_{ax} a + 3 \log_{a^2 x} a = 0$ ...(i)

$$\Rightarrow \quad \frac{2}{\log_a x} + \frac{1}{1 + \log_a x} + \frac{3}{2 + \log_a x} = 0 \quad \text{...(ii)}$$

Let $\log_a x = t$

Then, Eq. (ii),

$$\frac{2}{t} + \frac{1}{1+t} + \frac{3}{2+t} = 0$$

$$\Rightarrow \quad 6t^2 + 11t + 4 = 0$$

$$\Rightarrow \quad t = -\frac{4}{3} \text{ or } -\frac{1}{2}$$

So, $$x = a^{-4/3} \text{ or } x = a^{-1/2}$$

Two value of x possible for which Eq. (i) is defined and satisfy.

25. $\because$ $a = \log_3 \log_3 2$

$$\Rightarrow \quad 3^a = \log_3 2$$

$$\therefore \quad 3^{-a} = \log_2 3$$

Now, $$1 < 2^{-k + 3^{-a}} < 2^1$$

$$\Rightarrow \quad 2^0 < 2^{-k + 3^{-a}} < 2^1$$

$$\therefore \quad 0 < -k + 3^{-a} < 1$$

$$\Rightarrow \quad 0 < -k + \log_2 3 < 1$$

$$\Rightarrow \quad 0 > k - \log_2 3 > -1$$

$$\Rightarrow \quad \log_2 3 - 1 < k < \log_2 3$$

$$\therefore \quad k = 1$$

26. $\because (2x)^{\ln 2} = (3y)^{\ln 3}$

Taking log with base e on both sides, then

$$\ln 2 (\ln 2 + \ln x) = \ln 3 (\ln 3 + \ln y) \quad \text{...(i)}$$

and $$3^{\ln x} = 2^{\ln y}$$

Taking log with base e on both sides, then

$$\ln x \cdot \ln 3 = \ln y \cdot \ln 2 \quad \text{...(ii)}$$

From Eqs. (i) and (ii), we get

$$\ln 2 (\ln 2 + \ln x) = \ln 3 \left(\ln 3 + \frac{\ln x \cdot \ln 3}{\ln 2}\right)$$

$$\Rightarrow \quad \ln x \left(\frac{(\ln 3)^2}{\ln 2} - \ln 2\right) = -((\ln 3)^2 - (\ln 2)^2)$$

$$\therefore \quad \ln x = -\ln 2 = \ln \left(\frac{1}{2}\right) \Rightarrow x = \frac{1}{2}$$

$$\therefore \quad x_0 = \frac{1}{2}$$

27. $(3/4)^x = 1/4$

Taking log with base 2

$$\Rightarrow \quad x(\log_2 3 - 2) = -2$$

$$\therefore \quad x = \frac{2}{2 - \log_2 3} = \frac{1}{1 - \log_4 3}$$

and taking log with base 3

$$\Rightarrow \quad x(1 - \log_3 4) = -2 \log_3 2$$

$$\therefore \quad x = \frac{2 \log_3 2}{2 \log_3 2 - 1}$$

28. Let $S = \frac{1}{3\sqrt{2}}\sqrt{4 - \frac{1}{3\sqrt{2}}\sqrt{4 - \frac{1}{3\sqrt{2}}\sqrt{4 - \frac{1}{3\sqrt{2}} \dots \infty}}}$

$\Rightarrow \quad S = \frac{1}{3\sqrt{2}}\sqrt{4 - S}$

or $\quad (3\sqrt{2}\, S)^2 = 4 - S$

$\Rightarrow \quad 18S^2 + S - 4 = 0$

$\Rightarrow \quad (9S - 4)(2S + 1) = 0$

$\therefore \quad 9S - 4 = 0 \qquad [\because 2S + 1 \neq 0]$

or $\quad S = \frac{4}{9} = \left(\frac{3}{2}\right)^{-2}$

$\Rightarrow \quad \log_{3/2} S = -2 \Rightarrow 6 + \log_{3/2} S = 6 - 2 = 4$

Hence,

$$6 + \log_{3/2}\left(\frac{1}{3\sqrt{2}}\sqrt{4 - \frac{1}{3\sqrt{2}}\sqrt{4 - \frac{1}{3\sqrt{2}}\sqrt{4 - \frac{1}{3\sqrt{2}} \dots}}}\right) = 4$$

29. $\log_{10}(2x) + \log_{10} y = 2 \Rightarrow 2xy = 10^2 \qquad \text{...(i)}$

and $\quad \log_{10} x^2 - \log_{10} 2y = 4$

$\Rightarrow \quad \frac{x^2}{2y} = 10^4 \qquad \text{...(ii)}$

From Eqs. (i) and (ii), $x^3 = 10^6$

$\Rightarrow \quad x = 100$

From Eq. (i), $\quad y = \frac{1}{2}$

$\therefore \quad x + y = 100 + \frac{1}{2} = \frac{201}{2} = \frac{m}{n} \qquad \text{[given]}$

$\therefore \quad m = 201 \text{ and } n = 2$

$\Rightarrow \quad m - 3n^6 = 201 - 3(2)^6 = 201 - 192 = 9$

30. Solving, $x = \lambda$ and $y = \log_5 x$, we get

$A \equiv (\lambda, \log_5 \lambda), \lambda > 0$

and solving $x = \lambda$ and $y = \log_5(x + 4)$, we get

$B \equiv \{\lambda, \log_5(\lambda + 4)\}, \lambda > -4$

Given, $\quad AB = 0.5$

$\Rightarrow \quad \log_5(\lambda + 4) - \log_5 \lambda = 0.5$

$\Rightarrow \quad \frac{\lambda + 4}{\lambda} = (5)^{1/2} = \sqrt{5}$

$\Rightarrow \quad \lambda = \frac{4}{\sqrt{5} - 1} = 4\frac{(\sqrt{5} + 1)}{4}$

$= 1 + \sqrt{5} = a + \sqrt{b} \qquad \text{[given]}$

$\therefore \quad a = 1 \text{ and } b = 5$

Then, $\quad a + b = 1 + 5 = 6$

31. $\therefore \; a(b - c)x^2 + b(c - a)xy + c(a - b)y^2 = 0, y \neq 0 \qquad \text{...(i)}$

$$a(b - c)\left(\frac{x}{y}\right)^2 + b(c - a)\left(\frac{x}{y}\right) + c(a - b) = 0$$

Let $\quad \frac{x}{y} = X$

$\Rightarrow \quad a(b - c)X^2 + b(c - a)X + c(a - b) = 0$

$\because \quad a(b - c) + b(c - a) + c(a - b) = 0$

$\therefore \quad X = 1$

$\because$ Eq. (i) is perfect square.

$\therefore$ Roots are equal.

$\therefore \quad 1 \times 1 = \frac{c(a - b)}{a(b - c)}$

$\Rightarrow \quad b = \frac{2ac}{a + c} \qquad \text{...(ii)}$

Now, $\log(a + c) + \log(a - 2b + c)$

$= \log\{(a + c)^2 - 2b(a + c)\}$

$= \log\{(a + c)^2 - 4ac\} \qquad \text{[from Eq. (ii)]}$

$= \log(a - c)^2 = 2\log(a - c)$

$\Rightarrow \quad \frac{\log(a + c) + \log(a - 2b + c)}{\log(a - c)} = 2$

$\therefore \quad \left\{\frac{\log(a + c) + \log(a - 2b + c)}{\log(a - c)}\right\}^2 = 4$

32. According to the question, $x \in I$

Given equation, $\left(\frac{1}{3}\right)^{\frac{|x+2|}{2-|x|}} > 9 \qquad [x \neq \pm 2] \text{...(i)}$

$\Rightarrow \quad -3^{\frac{|x+2|}{-2-|x|}} > 3^2$

$\Rightarrow \quad -\frac{|x + 2|}{2 - |x|} > 2$

$\Rightarrow \quad \frac{|x + 2|}{|x| - 2} - 2 > 0$

$\Rightarrow \quad \frac{|x + 2| - 2|x| + 4}{|x| - 2} > 0 \qquad \text{...(ii)}$

Case I If $x < -2$, $\frac{-x - 2 + 2x + 4}{-x - 2} > 0$

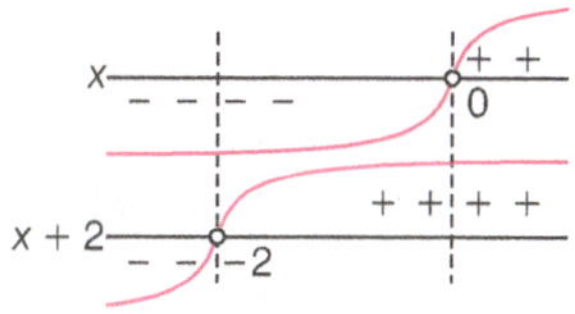

$\frac{x + 2}{-(x + 2)} > 0 \Rightarrow -1 > 0$

which is not possible.

Case II $-2 < x < 0$, then Eq. (ii)

$\Rightarrow \quad \frac{x + 2 + 2x + 4}{-x - 2} > 0 \Rightarrow \frac{3x + 6}{-(x + 2)} > 0$

$\frac{-3(x + 2)}{(x + 2)} > 0 \Rightarrow -3 > 0$

which is not possible.

Case III When $x > 0$

From Eq. (ii),

$\frac{x + 2 - 2x + 4}{x - 2} > 0 \Rightarrow \frac{-x + 6}{x - 2} > 0$

$\frac{x - 6}{x - 2} < 0 \Rightarrow 2 < x < 6$

So, the integer values of $x = 3, 4, 5$

So, the number of integer values of x is 3.

33. $x > 2$

$$|\log_{\sqrt{3}} x - 2| + |\log_3 x - 2| = 2$$
$$|2\log_3 x - 2| + |\log_3 x - 2| = 2$$
$$2|\log_3 x - 1| + |\log_3 x - 2| = 2$$

Let $\log_3 x = y$ ...(i)

Then, Eq. (i) $\Rightarrow 2|y-1| + |y-2| = 2$ ...(ii)

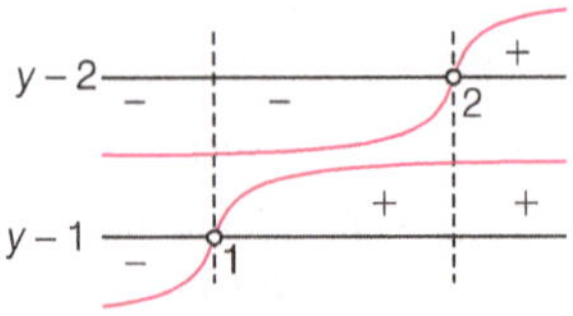

Case I $y < 1$, then $x < 3$

Eq. (ii) becomes $-2y + 2 - y + 2 = 2$

$$-3y = -2 \Rightarrow y = \frac{2}{3}$$

$$\log_3 x = \frac{2}{3} \quad \text{[from Eq. (i)]}$$

$$\Rightarrow \quad x = 3^{2/3}$$

which is less than 2, so not acceptable.

Case II $1 < y < 2$, then $3 < x < 9$

From Eq. (ii), $2(y-1) - (y-2) = 2$

$\Rightarrow \quad y = 2$

$\Rightarrow \quad \log_3 x = 2$

$\therefore \quad x = 3^2 = 9$ [impossible]

Case III $y \geq 2$, then $x \geq 9$

From Eq. (ii), $2(y-1) + (y-2) = 2$

$\therefore \quad y = 2 \Rightarrow \log_3 x = 2$

$\therefore \quad x = 9$ [acceptable]

34. Given equation is

$$\log_2 \sqrt{x} - 2\log_{1/4}^2 x + 1 > 0 \quad \text{...(i)}$$

From Eq. (i), $x > 0$

Eq. (i) $\Rightarrow \dfrac{1}{2}\log_2 x - \dfrac{2}{(-2)^2}\log_2^2 x + 1 > 0$

$\Rightarrow \quad \dfrac{1}{2}\log_2 x - \dfrac{1}{2}\log_2^2 x + 1 > 0$

$\Rightarrow \quad (\log_2 x)^2 - (\log_2 x) - 2 < 0$

$\Rightarrow \quad (\log_2 x - 2)(\log_2 x + 1) < 0$

$\Rightarrow \quad -1 < \log_2 x < 2$

$\Rightarrow \quad 2^{-1} < x < 2^2$

$\Rightarrow \quad \dfrac{1}{2} < x < 4$

$\Rightarrow \quad x \in I, \ \text{so} \ x = 1, 2, 3$

So, number of integer value of x is 3.

35. Given that, $b > 0$

$$2\log_{1/25}(bx + 28) = -\log_5(12 - 4x - x^2) \quad \text{...(i)}$$

$$\frac{2}{(-2)}\log_5(bx + 28) = -\log_5(12 - 4x - x^2)$$

$\Rightarrow \quad bx + 28 = 12 - 4x - x^2$

and $\quad bx + 28 > 0$

and $\quad 12 - 4x - x^2 > 0$

$\Rightarrow \quad x^2 + (4 + b)x + 16 = 0$ ...(ii)

and $\quad x > \dfrac{-28}{b}$ and $-6 < x < 2$

Since, Eq. (i) has coincident roots, so discriminant Eq. (ii) is zero.

$$(4 + b)^2 - 64 = 0$$
$$b + 4 = \pm 8$$
$$b = 4 \ \text{or} \ b = -12$$

Since, $\quad b > 0$ so $b = 4$

for this value $x > -7$ and $-6 < x < 2$.

36. $$\frac{2^{\log_{2^{1/4}} 2} - 3^{\log_{27} 125} - 4}{7^{4\log_{49} 2} - 3} = \frac{2^{4\log_2 2} - 3^{\log_{3^3} 5^3} - 4}{7^{4\log_{7^2} 2^1} - 3}$$

$$= \frac{2^4 - 5 - 4}{7^{2\log_7 2} - 3} = \frac{16 - 9}{2^2 - 3} = 7$$

37. $(\log_5 x)^2 + \log_{5x}\left(\dfrac{5}{x}\right) = 1, \ x > 0, \ x \neq \dfrac{1}{5}$

$$\Rightarrow \quad (\log_5 x)^2 + \frac{\log_5\left(\frac{5}{x}\right)}{\log_5(5x)} = 1 \Rightarrow (\log_5 x)^2 + \frac{1 - \log_5 x}{1 + \log_5 x} = 1$$

Let $\log_5 x = t$, then

$$t^2 + \frac{1 - t}{1 + t} = 1$$

$\Rightarrow \quad t^3 + t^2 - 2t = 0$

$\Rightarrow \quad t(t + 2)(t - 1) = 0$

$\Rightarrow \quad t = -2, 0, 1$

$\Rightarrow \quad x = 5^{-2}, 5^0, 5^1$

$\Rightarrow \quad x = \dfrac{1}{25}, 1, 5$

$x_1, x_2 \in I$

$\therefore \quad x_1 = 1, x_2 = 5$

$\therefore \quad |x_2 - 4x_1| = |5 - 4| = 1$

38. Given, $x = \log_\lambda a = \log_a b = \dfrac{1}{2}\log_b c$ and $\log_\lambda c = nx^{n+1}$

$x = \log_\lambda a = \log_a b = \log_b \sqrt{c}$ and $\log_\lambda c = nx^{n+1}$ ...(i)

From Eq. (i), $\log_\lambda a \times \log_a b \times \log_b \sqrt{c} = x^3$

$$\log_\lambda \sqrt{c} = x^3, \frac{1}{2}\log_\lambda c = x^3$$

$$\log_\lambda c = 2x^3$$

Compare with $\quad \log_\lambda c = nx^{n+1}$

$\Rightarrow \quad n = 2$

Mathematics is a place where you can do things which you can't do in the real world.

-Marcus du Sautoy

5

Permutations and Combinations

Learning Milestones

Milestone 1 Fundamental Principle of Counting

- Fundamental Principle of Counting
- Factorial Notation
- Divisibility Test
- Principle of Inclusion and Exclusion

Milestone 2 Permutation

- Permutation
- Number of Permutations Under Certain Conditions
- Circular Permutation
- Restricted Circular Permutations
- Rank in a Dictionary
- Gap Method

Milestone 3 Combination

- Combination
- Restricted Combinations
- Combination from Identical Objects
- Arrangements in Groups
- Multinomial Theorem
- Geometrical Problem

Practice Milestones

Practice Milestone 1- JEE Main Pattern
Practice Milestone 2 - JEE Advanced Pattern
Practice Milestone 3 - Challenging Problems

Milestone 1 Fundamental Principle of Counting

- Fundamental Principle of Counting • Factorial Notation • Divisibility Test
- Principle of Inclusion and Exclusion

In everyday life, we need to know about the number of ways of doing certain work from given number of available options. e.g. Three persons A, B and C are applying for a job in which only one post is vacant. Clearly, vacant post can be filled either by A or B or C i.e. total number of ways doing this work is three.

Again, let two persons A and B are to be seated in a row, then only two possible ways of arrangement is AB or BA. In two arrangements, persons are same but their order is different. Thus, in arranging things, order of things is important.

5.1 Fundamental Principle of Counting

(i) Multiplication Principle

If an operation can be performed in 'm' different ways, following which a second operation can be performed in 'n' different ways, then the two operations in succession can be performed in $m \times n$ ways. This can be extended to any finite number of operations.

Example 1. A hall has 12 gates. In how many ways can a man enter the hall through one gate and come out through a different gate?

Sol. Since, there are 12 ways of entering into the hall. After entering into the hall, the man come out through a different gate in 11 ways.

Hence, by the fundamental principle of multiplication, total number of ways is $12 \times 11 = 132$ ways.

Example 2. There are three stations A, B and C, five routes for going from station A to station B and four routes for going from station B to station C. Find the number of different ways through which a person can go from A to C via B.

Sol. Since, there are five routes for going from A to B and four routes for going from B to C.

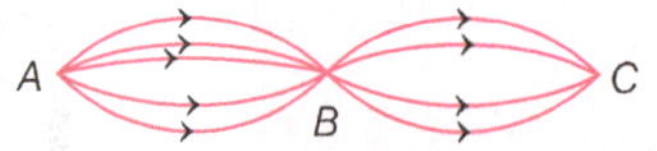

Hence, by the fundamental principle of multiplication, total number of different ways

$= 5 \times 4$ [i.e. A to B and then B to C]

$= 20$ ways

(ii) Addition Principle

If an operation can be performed in 'm' different ways and another operation, which is independent of the first operation, can be performed in 'n' different ways. Then, either of the two operations can be performed in $(m + n)$ ways. This can be extended to any finite number of mutually exclusive operation.

Example 3. There are 25 students in a class in which 15 boys and 10 girls. The class teacher select either a boy or a girl for monitor of the class. In how many ways the class teacher can make this selection?

Sol. Since, there are 15 ways to select a boy, so there are 10 ways to select a girl.

Hence, by the fundamental principle of addition, either a boy or a girl can be performed in $15 + 10 = 25$ ways.

Example 4. There are 4 students for Physics, 6 students for Chemistry and 7 students for Mathematics gold medal. In how many ways one of these gold medals be awarded?

Sol. The Physics, Chemistry and Mathematics student's gold medal can be awarded in 4, 6 and 7 ways, respectively.

Hence, by the fundamental principle of addition, number ways of awarding one of the three gold medals.

$= 4 + 6 + 7 = 17$ ways.

Example 5. Find the number of 4 letter words, with or without meaning, which can be formed out of the letters of the word PLACE, where the repetition of the letters is not allowed.

Sol. We have to form 4 letter words from the letters of the word PLACE.

There are five letters i.e. P, L, A, C, E. It is given that repetition is not allowed.

First place can be filled in 5 different ways by anyone 5 letters P, L, A, C, E.

Following which, second place can be filled by remaining 4 letters in 4 different ways, following which the third place can be filled by remaining 3 letters in 3 different ways and last place by remaining 2 letters in 2 different ways.

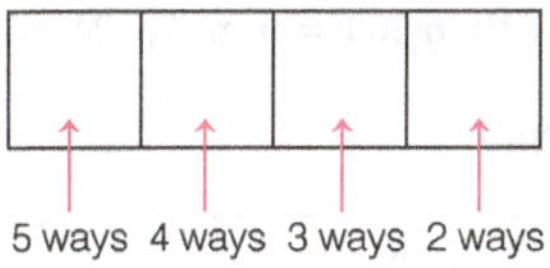

$\therefore$ Required number of words $= 5 \times 4 \times 3 \times 2$
$= 120$

Example 6. Total number of n digit numbers $(n > 1)$, in which no two consecutive digits are same.

Sol.

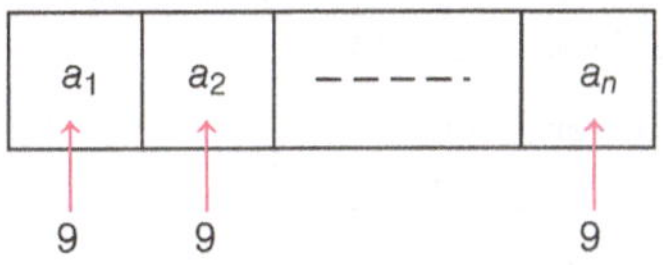

Place a_1 can be filled in 9 ways as digit 0 can not be used.

Place a_2 can be filled in 9 ways as 0 can be used but digit of place a_1 can not be used.

Similarly, each of the remaining places can be filled in 9 ways.

$\therefore$ Total number of such numbers $= 9 \times 9 \times 9 \ldots n$ times $= 9^n$

5.2 Factorial Notation

Let n be a positive integer. Then, the continued product of first 'n' natural numbers is called factorial n, to be denoted by $n!$ or $\underline{|n}$

i.e. $n! = n(n-1)(n-2)\ldots 3 \cdot 2 \cdot 1$

Example 7. Find n, if $(n+2)! = 60 \times (n-1)!$.

Sol. $\because (n+2)! = (n+2)(n+1)n(n-1)!$

$$\Rightarrow \quad \frac{(n+2)!}{(n-1)!} = (n+2)(n+1)n$$

$$\Rightarrow \quad 60 = (n+2)(n+1)n \qquad \text{[given]}$$

$$\Rightarrow \quad 5 \times 4 \times 3 = (n+2) \times (n+1) \times n$$

$$\therefore \quad n = 3$$

JEE Focus Points

- $n! = n(n-1)! = n(n-1)(n-2)!$
- $0! = 1! = 1$
- $(2n)! = 2^n n![1 \cdot 3 \cdot 5 \ldots (2n-1)]$
- $\dfrac{n!}{r!} = n(n-1)(n-2)\ldots(r+1)$ $\quad [r < n]$
- $\dfrac{n!}{(n-r)!} = n(n-1)(n-2)\ldots(n-r+1)$ $\quad [r < n]$
- $\dfrac{1}{n!} + \dfrac{1}{(n+1)!} = \dfrac{\lambda}{(n+2)!}$, then $\lambda = (n+2)^2$
- If $x! = y! \Rightarrow x = y$ or $x = 0, y = 1$ or $x = 1, y = 0$
- $(m+n)! \neq m! + n!$
- $(mn)! \neq m!\,n!$

Example 8. Evaluate $\sum_{r=1}^{n} r \times r!$.

Sol. We have, $\sum_{r=1}^{n} r \times r! = \sum_{r=1}^{n} \{(r+1)-1\} r! = \sum_{r=1}^{n} (r+1)! - r!$

$$= (n+1)! - 1!$$

[put $r = n$ in $(r+1)!$ and $r = 1$ is $r!$]

$$= (n+1)! - 1$$

Example 9. Find the remainder when $\sum_{r=1}^{n} r!$ is divided by 15, if $n \geq 5$.

Sol. Let $N = \sum_{r=1}^{n} r! = 1! + 2! + 3! + 4! + 5! + 6! + 7! + \ldots + n!$

$$= (1! + 2! + 3! + 4!) + (5! + 6! + 7! + \ldots + n!)$$

$$= 33 + (5! + 6! + 7! + \ldots + n!)$$

$$\Rightarrow \frac{N}{15} = \frac{33}{15} + \frac{(5! + 6! + 7! + \ldots + n!)}{15}$$

$$= 2 + \frac{3}{15} + \text{Integer} \qquad \text{[as 5!, 6!, ... are divisible by 15]}$$

$$= \frac{3}{15} + \text{Integer}$$

Hence, remainder is 3.

Exponent of prime p in $n!$

Exponent of prime p in $n!$ is denoted by $E_p(n!)$, where p is prime number and n is a natural number. The last integer amongst 1, 2, 3, ..., $(n-1)$, n which is divisible by p is $\left[\dfrac{n}{p}\right]p$, where $[\cdot]$ denotes the greatest integer function.

$$\therefore \quad E_p(n!) = E_p(1 \cdot 2 \cdot 3 \ldots (n-1) \cdot n)$$

$$= E_p\left(p \cdot 2p \cdot 3p \ldots (n-1)p \cdot \left[\frac{n}{p}\right] p\right)$$

[because the remaining natural numbers from 1 to n are not divisible by p]

$$= \left[\frac{n}{p}\right] + E_p\left(1\cdot 2\cdot 3 \ldots \left[\frac{n}{p}\right]\right) \quad \ldots(i)$$

Now, the last integer amongst 1, 2, 3, ..., $\left[\frac{n}{p}\right]$ which is divisible by p is $\left[\frac{\frac{n}{p}}{p}\right] = \left[\frac{n}{p^2}\right]$. Now, from Eq. (i), we get

$$E_p(n!) = \left[\frac{n}{p}\right] + E_p\left(p, 2p, 3p, \ldots, \left[\frac{n}{p^2}\right]p\right)$$

[because the remaining natural numbers from 1 to $\left[\frac{n}{p}\right]$ are not divisible by p]

$$\therefore \quad E_p(n!) = \left[\frac{n}{p}\right] + \left[\frac{n}{p^2}\right] + E_p\left(1\cdot 2\cdot 3 \ldots \left[\frac{n}{p^2}\right]\right)$$

Similarly, we get

$$E_p(n!) = \left[\frac{n}{p}\right] + \left[\frac{n}{p^2}\right] + \left[\frac{n}{p^3}\right] + \ldots + \left[\frac{n}{p^s}\right]$$

where, s is the largest natural number, such that

$$p^s \le n < p^{s+1}$$

Example 10. Find the exponent of 3 in 100!.

Sol. In terms of prime factors 100! can be written as $2^a \cdot 3^b \cdot 5^c \cdot 7^d \ldots$

Now, $b = E_3(100!)$

$$= \left[\frac{100}{3}\right] + \left[\frac{100}{3^2}\right] + \left[\frac{100}{3^3}\right] + \left[\frac{100}{3^4}\right] + \ldots$$

$= 33 + 11 + 3 + 1 + 0 + \ldots$

$= 48$

Hence, exponent of 3 is 48.

Example 11. Prove that 33! is divisible by 2^{19} and what is the largest integer n such that 33! is divisible by 2^n?

Sol. In terms of prime factors, 33! can be written as $2^a \cdot 3^b \cdot 5^c \cdot 7^d \cdot \ldots$

Now, $E_2(33!) = \left[\frac{33}{2}\right] + \left[\frac{33}{2^2}\right] + \left[\frac{33}{2^3}\right] + \left[\frac{33}{2^4}\right] + \left[\frac{33}{2^5}\right] + \ldots$

$= 16 + 8 + 4 + 2 + 1 + 0 + \ldots$

$= 31$

Hence, the exponent of 2 in 33! is 31.

Now, 33! is divisible by 2^{31} which is also divisible by 2^{19}.

$\therefore$ Largest value of n is 31.

Example 12. Find the number of zeroes at the end of 100!.

Sol. In terms of prime factors, 100! can be written as $2^a \cdot 3^b \cdot 5^c \cdot 7^d \ldots$

Now, $E_2(100!) = \left[\frac{100}{2}\right] + \left[\frac{100}{2^2}\right] + \left[\frac{100}{2^3}\right] + \left[\frac{100}{2^4}\right] + \left[\frac{100}{2^5}\right] + \left[\frac{100}{2^6}\right]$

$= 50 + 25 + 12 + 6 + 3 + 1$

$= 97$

and $E_5(100!) = \left[\frac{100}{5}\right] + \left[\frac{100}{5^2}\right]$

$= 20 + 4 = 24$

$\therefore \quad 100! = 2^{97} \cdot 3^b \cdot 5^{24} \cdot 7^d \ldots$

$= 2^{73} \cdot 3^b \cdot (2 \times 5)^{24} \cdot 7^d \ldots$

$= 2^{73} \cdot 3^b \cdot (10)^{24} \cdot 7^d \ldots$

Hence, number of zeroes at the end of 100! is 24 or exponent of 10 in 100! = min (97, 24) = 24.

Alternate Solution

Number of zeroes at the end of 100!

$= E_5(100!)$

$= \left[\frac{100}{5}\right] + \left[\frac{100}{5^2}\right] + \ldots$

$= 20 + 4 + 0 + \ldots$

$= 24$

Example 13. For how many positive integral values of n does $n!$ end with precisely 25 zeroes?

Sol. $\because$ Number of zeroes at the end of $n! = 25$ [given]

$\Rightarrow \quad E_5(n!) = 25$

$\Rightarrow \quad \left[\frac{n}{5}\right] + \left[\frac{n}{25}\right] + \left[\frac{n}{125}\right] + \ldots = 25$

It's easy to see that $n = 105$ is the smallest satisfactory value of n. The next four values of n will also work (i.e. $n = 106$, 107, 108, 109). Hence, the answer is 5.

Example 14. Find the exponent of 80 in 180!.

Sol. $\because 80 = 2^4 \times 5$

$\therefore \quad E_2(180!) = \left[\frac{180}{2}\right] + \left[\frac{180}{2^2}\right] + \left[\frac{180}{2^3}\right] + \left[\frac{180}{2^4}\right] + \left[\frac{180}{2^5}\right] + \left[\frac{180}{2^6}\right] + \left[\frac{180}{2^7}\right] + \ldots$

$= 90 + 45 + 22 + 11 + 5 + 2 + 1$

$= 176$

and $E_5(180!) = \left[\frac{180}{5}\right] + \left[\frac{180}{5^2}\right] + \left[\frac{180}{5^3}\right] + \ldots$

$= 36 + 7 + 1 + 0 + \ldots$

$= 44$

Now, exponent of 16 in 180! is $\left[\frac{176}{4}\right] = 44$, where $[\cdot]$ denotes the greatest integer function.

Hence, the exponent of 80 in 180! is 44.

5.3 Divisibility Test

In decimal system, all numbers are formed by the digits 0, 1, 2, 3, ..., 9.

If ***a b c d e*** is a five-digit number in decimal system, then we can write that.

$\boldsymbol{abcde} = 10^4 \cdot a + 10^3 \cdot b + 10^2 \cdot c + 10 \cdot d + e.$

Number ***a b c d e*** will be divisible

(1) **by 2**, if e is divisible by 2.

(2) **by 4**, if $2d + e$ is divisible by 4.

(3) **by 8**, if $4c + 2d + e$ is divisible by 8.

(4) **by 2^t**, if number formed by last t digits is divisible by 2^t.

e.g. Number 820101280 is divisible by 2^5 because 01280 is divisible by 2^5.

(5) **by 5**, if $e = 0$ or 5.

(6) **by 5^t**, if number formed by last t digits is divisible by 5^t.

e.g. Number 1128375 is divisible by 5^3 because 375 is divisible by 5^3.

(7) **by 3**, if $a + b + c + d + e$ (sum of digits) is divisible by 3.

(8) **by 9**, if $a + b + c + d + e$ is divisible by 9.

(9) **by 6**, if e = even and $a + b + c + d + e$ is divisible by 3.

(10) **by 18**, if $e =$ even and $a + b + c + d + e$ is divisible by 9.

(11) **by 7**, if $abcd - 2e$ is divisible by 7.

e.g. Number 6552 is divisible by 7 because $655 - 2 \times 2 = 651 = 93 \times 7$ is divisible by 7.

(12) **by 11**, if $\underbrace{a + c + e}_{\text{Sum of digits at odd places}} - \underbrace{(b + d)}_{\text{Sum of digits at even places}}$ is divisible by 11.

e.g. Number 15222163 is divisible by 11 because $(1 + 2 + 2 + 6) - (5 + 2 + 1 + 3) = 0$ is divisible by 11.

(13) **by 13,** if $abcd + 4e$ is divisible by 13.

e.g. Number 1638 is divisible by 13 because $163 + 4 \times 8 = 195 = 15 \times 13$ is divisible by 13.

5.4 Principle of Inclusion and Exclusion

1. If A and B are finite sets, from the Venn diagram (i), it is clear that

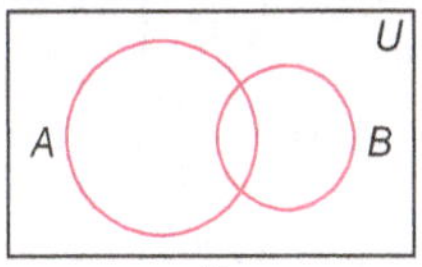

(i)

$$n(A \cup B) = n(A) + n(B) - n(A \cap B)$$

and $n(A' \cap B') = n(U) - n(A \cup B)$

2. If A, B and C are three finite sets, then from the Venn diagram (ii), it is clear that

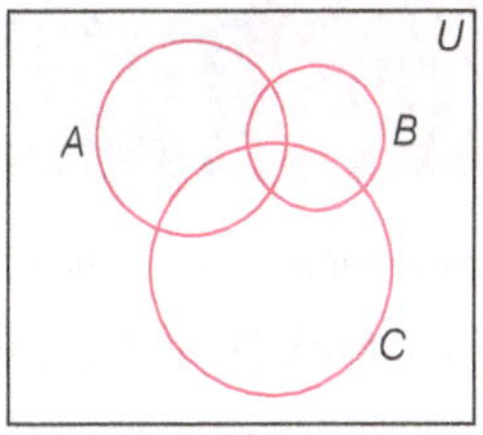

(ii)

$$n(A \cup B \cup C) = n(A) + n(B) + n(C) - n(A \cap B) - n(B \cap C) - n(C \cap A) + n(A \cap B \cap C)$$

and $n(A' \cap B' \cap C') = n(U) - n(A \cup B \cup C)$

JEE Focus Points

If $A_1, A_2, A_3, \ldots, A_n$ are finite sets, then

$n(A_1 \cup A_2 \cup \ldots \cup A_n)$

$= \Sigma n(A_i) - \Sigma n(A_i \cap A_j) + \Sigma n(A_i \cap A_j \cap A_k) - \ldots + (-1)^n \, \Sigma n(A_1 \cap A_2 \cap \ldots \cap A_n)$

Concept Inside Video

and $n(A'_1 \cap A'_2 \cap \ldots \cap A'_n) = n(U) - n(A_1 \cup A_2 \cup \ldots \cup A_n)$.

e.g. The number of positive integers from 1 to 1000, which are not divisible by 2, 3 or 5 is $n(A'_2 \cap A'_3 \cap A'_5)$.

$\therefore n(A'_2 \cap A'_3 \cap A'_5) = n(U) - n(A_2 \cup A_3 \cup A_5)$

[$\because$ here, $n(U) = 1000$]

$= 1000 - 734 = 266$

Example 15. Find the number of positive integers from 1 to 1000, which are divisible by atleast 2, 3 or 5.

Sol. Let A_k be the set of positive integers from 1 to 1000, which is divisible by k.

Obviously, we have to find $n(A_2 \cup A_3 \cup A_5)$.

If [·] denotes the greatest integer function, then

$$n(A_2) = \left[\frac{1000}{2}\right] = [500] = 500$$

$$n(A_3) = \left[\frac{1000}{3}\right] = [333.33] = 333$$

$$n(A_5) = \left[\frac{1000}{5}\right] = [200] = 200$$

$$n(A_2 \cap A_3) = \left[\frac{1000}{6}\right] = [166.67] = 166$$

$$n(A_3 \cap A_5) = \left[\frac{1000}{15}\right] = [66.67] = 66$$

$$n(A_2 \cap A_5) = \left[\frac{1000}{10}\right] = [100] = 100$$

and $n(A_2 \cap A_3 \cap A_5) = \left[\frac{1000}{30}\right] = [33.33] = 33$

From Principle of Inclusion and Exclusion

$$n(A_2 \cup A_3 \cup A_5) = n(A_2) + n(A_3) + n(A_5) - n(A_2 \cap A_3) - n(A_3 \cap A_5) - n(A_2 \cap A_5) + n(A_2 \cap A_3 \cap A_5)$$

$$= 500 + 333 + 200 - 166 - 66 - 100 + 33$$

$$= 734$$

Hence, the number of positive integers from 1 to 1000, which are divisible by atleast 2, 3 or 5 is 734.

Milestone Practice 5.1

1. Find the number of ordered pairs (x, y) such that $x < 4 < y$ and $x, y \in \{1, 2, 3, \ldots, 10\}$.
2. In how many ways can 4 persons stand in a queue?
3. In how many ways 10 different balls can be put in 2 different boxes?
4. There are n keys and corresponding them n locks. Each lock gets opened by only one key which is made for it. Find the maximum number of trials required to open the locks.
5. Find the number of 5 digits that can be formed with the digits 0, 1, 2, 3, 4 if the digits can be repeated in any number.
6. Find the value of $1 \cdot 1! + 2 \cdot 2! + 3 \cdot 3! + \ldots + 50 \cdot 50!$
7. If $\frac{n!}{2!(n-2)!} : \frac{n!}{4!(n-4)!} = 2:1$, then find $n^2 - 2n - 10$.
8. Find the remainder when $1! + 2! + 3! + 4! + \ldots + n!$ is divided by 15, in $n \geq 5$.
9. Find the exponent of 80 in 200!.

Answer Key

1. 18	2. 24	3. 1024	4. $\frac{n(n+1)}{2}$
5. 2500	6. $51! - 1$	7. 5	8. 3
9. 49			

For Detailed Solution

Milestone 2 Permutation

• Permutation • Number of Permutations Under Certain Conditions • Circular Permutation
• Restricted Circular Permutations • Rank in a Dictionary • Gap Method

5.5 Permutation

Each of the different arrangements which can be made by taking some or all of a number of things is called a permutation. In permutation, order of the arrangement is important.

Important Results

1. The number of permutations of n different things, taking r at a time is denoted by ^nP_r or $P(n, r)$ or $A(n, r)$, then

$$^nP_r = n(n-1)(n-2)\ldots(n-r+1) = \frac{n!}{(n-r)!}$$

where, $n \in N, r \in W$ and $0 \le r \le n$.

Proof LHS $= {}^nP_r =$ Number of ways of filling up r vacant places simultaneously from n different things

1	2	3	----	r
↓	↓	↓		↓
n ways	$(n-1)$ ways	$(n-2)$ ways		$(n-r+1)$ ways

$$= n(n-1)(n-2)\ldots(n-r+1)$$

$$= \frac{\dfrac{n(n-1)(n-2)\ldots(n-r+1)\times(n-r)}{(n-r-1)(n-r-2)\ldots3\times2\times1}}{(n-r)!}$$

$$= \frac{n!}{(n-r)!} = \text{RHS}$$

JEE SPIKE

(i) The number of permutations of n different things taken all at a time $= {}^nP_n = n!$

(ii) $^nP_0 = 1, {}^nP_1 = n$ and $^nP_{n-1} = {}^nP_n = n!$

(iii) $^nP_r = n({}^{n-1}P_{r-1}) = n(n-1)({}^{n-2}P_{r-2})$
$= n(n-1)(n-2)({}^{n-3}P_{r-3})$
$= \ldots$

(iv) $^{n-1}P_r = (n-r)\,{}^{n-1}P_{r-1}$

(v) $\dfrac{^nP_r}{^nP_{r-1}} = (n-r+1)$

Example 16. If $^{56}P_{r+6} : {}^{54}P_{r+3} = 30800:1$, find $^rP_2$.

Sol. We have, $\dfrac{^{56}P_{r+6}}{^{54}P_{r+3}} = \dfrac{30800}{1}$

$\Rightarrow (56)(55)\dfrac{^{54}P_{r+4}}{^{54}P_{r+3}} = \dfrac{30800}{1}$ [from note (iii)]

$\Rightarrow \dfrac{^{54}P_{r+4}}{^{54}P_{r+3}} = 10$

$\Rightarrow 54-(r+4)+1 = 10$ [from note (v)]

$r = 41$

$\therefore {}^rP_2 = {}^{41}P_2$

$= 41 \cdot 40 = 1640$

Example 17. If $^{n+5}P_{n+1} = \dfrac{11(n-1)}{2} \cdot {}^{n+3}P_n$, find n.

Sol. We have,

$$\frac{^{n+5}P_{n+1}}{^{n+3}P_n} = \frac{11(n-1)}{2}$$

$\Rightarrow \dfrac{(n+5)(n+4)\cdot{}^{n+3}P_{n-1}}{^{n+3}P_n} = \dfrac{11(n-1)}{2}$ [from note (iii)]

$\Rightarrow \dfrac{(n+5)(n+4)}{(n+3-n+1)} = \dfrac{11(n-1)}{2}$ [from note (v)]

$\Rightarrow (n+5)(n+4) = 22(n-1)$

$\Rightarrow n^2 - 13n + 42 = 0$

$\Rightarrow (n-6)(n-7) = 0$

$\therefore n = 6, 7$

Example 18. If $^{m+n}P_2 = 90$ and $^{m-n}P_2 = 30$, find the values of m and n.

Sol. $\because {}^{m+n}P_2 = 90 = 10 \times 9 = {}^{10}P_2$

$\therefore m + n = 10$ ...(i)

and $^{m-n}P_2 = 30 = 6 \times 5 = {}^6P_2$

$\therefore m - n = 6$ ...(ii)

From Eqs. (i) and (ii), we get

$m = 8$ and $n = 2$

JEE SCANNER

Example Similar to PYQ Asked in JEE Main 2023

If ${}^{2n+1}P_{n-1} : {}^{2n-1}P_n = 3:5$, then the value of $n^2 + n + 1$ is ....

Sol. (21) We have,

$${}^{2n+1}P_{n-1} : {}^{2n-1}P_n = 3:5$$

$$\Rightarrow \quad \frac{{}^{2n+1}P_{n-1}}{{}^{2n-1}P_n} = \frac{3}{5}$$

$$\Rightarrow \quad \frac{(2n+1)!}{(n+2)!} \times \frac{(n-1)!}{(2n-1)!} = \frac{3}{5}$$

$$\Rightarrow \quad \frac{(2n+1)(2n)}{(n+2)(n+1)(n)} = \frac{3}{5}$$

$$\Rightarrow \quad 10(2n+1) = 3(n+2)(n+1)$$

$$\Rightarrow \quad 3n^2 - 11n - 4 = 0$$

$$\Rightarrow \quad (n-4)(3n+1) = 0$$

$$\Rightarrow \quad n = 4, -\frac{1}{3}$$

$$\therefore \quad n = 4 \, [n \in W]$$

Now, $n^2 + n + 1 = 16 + 4 + 1 = 21$

Skill Builder

For Sol.

If ${}^{2n}P_3 : {}^{n}P_2 = 20:1$, then the value of $n^2 + 2n + 10$ is ....

■ **For more practice** See Q.1 and Q.2 of Milestone 5.2.

Example 19. Find the value of r, if

(i) ${}^{11}P_r = 990$

(ii) ${}^{8}P_5 + 5 \cdot {}^{8}P_4 = {}^{9}P_r$

(iii) ${}^{22}P_{r+1} : {}^{20}P_{r+2} = 11:52$

Sol. (i) $\because {}^{11}P_r = 990 = 11 \times 10 \times 9 = {}^{11}P_3$

$\therefore \quad r = 3$

(ii) $\because \quad {}^{8}P_5 + 5 \cdot {}^{8}P_4 = {}^{9}P_r$

$$\Rightarrow \quad {}^{8}P_4 \left(\frac{{}^{8}P_5}{{}^{8}P_4} + 5 \right) = {}^{9}P_r$$

$$\Rightarrow \quad {}^{8}P_4 \, (8 - 5 + 1 + 5) = {}^{9}P_r \quad \text{[from note (v)]}$$

$$\Rightarrow \quad 9 \cdot {}^{8}P_4 = {}^{9}P_r$$

$$\Rightarrow \quad {}^{9}P_5 = {}^{9}P_r \quad \text{[from note (iii)]}$$

$$\therefore \quad r = 5$$

(iii) $\because \quad {}^{22}P_{r+1} : {}^{20}P_{r+2} = 11:52$

$$\Rightarrow \quad \frac{{}^{22}P_{r+1}}{{}^{20}P_{r+2}} = \frac{11}{52}$$

$$\Rightarrow \quad \frac{22 \cdot 21 \cdot {}^{20}P_{r-1}}{(19-r)\cdot(20-r)\cdot(21-r)\cdot {}^{20}P_{r-1}} = \frac{11}{52}$$

[from note (iii) and (iv)]

$$\Rightarrow \quad (21-r)\cdot(20-r)\cdot(19-r) = 52 \times 2 \times 21$$

$$= 14 \times 13 \times 12$$

$$\therefore \quad r = 7$$

Example 20. Prove that

$${}^{1}P_1 + 2 \cdot {}^{2}P_2 + 3 \cdot {}^{3}P_3 + \ldots + n \cdot {}^{n}P_n = {}^{n+1}P_{n+1} - 1.$$

Sol. LHS $= {}^{1}P_1 + 2 \cdot {}^{2}P_2 + 3 \cdot {}^{3}P_3 + \ldots + n \cdot {}^{n}P_n$

$$= \sum_{r=1}^{n} r \cdot {}^{r}P_r = \sum_{r=1}^{n} \{(r+1) - 1)\} \cdot {}^{r}P_r$$

$$= \sum_{r=1}^{n} \{(r+1) \cdot {}^{r}P_r - {}^{r}P_r)\}$$

$$= \sum_{r=1}^{n} ({}^{r+1}P_{r+1} - {}^{r}P_r) \quad \text{[from note (iii)]}$$

$$= {}^{n+1}P_{n+1} - {}^{1}P_1 = {}^{n+1}P_{n+1} - 1$$

$= \text{RHS}$

Example 21. Determine the number of permutations of the letters of the word 'SIMPLETON' taken all at a time.

Sol. There are 9 letters in the word 'SIMPLETON' and all the 9 letters are different. Hence, the number of permutations taking all the letters at a time

$$= {}^{9}P_9 = 9! = 362880$$

Example 22. How many different signals can be given using any number of flags from 4 flags of different colours?

Sol. The signals can be made by using one or more flags at a time. Hence, by the fundamental principle of addition, the total number of signals

$$= {}^{4}P_1 + {}^{4}P_2 + {}^{4}P_3 + {}^{4}P_4$$

$$= 4 + (4 \times 3) + (4 \times 3 \times 2) + (4 \times 3 \times 2 \times 1)$$

$$= 4 + 12 + 24 + 24 = 64$$

Example 23. Find the total number of 9-digit numbers which have all different digits.

Sol. Number of digits are 10 (0, 1, 2, 3, 4, 5, 6, 7, 8, 9)

Total number of 9-digit numbers $= {}^{10}P_9$

Out of these, the number of numbers having zero at the first place $= {}^{9}P_8$

Hence, required number of numbers $= {}^{10}P_9 - {}^9P_8$

$$= 10 \times {}^9P_8 - {}^9P_8$$
$$= 9 \times {}^9P_8$$
$$= 9 \times \frac{9!}{1!}$$
$$= 9 \times 9!$$

Note Total number of n digit numbers $(1 \le n \le 10)$, which have all different digits $= {}^{10}P_n - {}^9P_{n-1}$

JEE SCANNER

Example Similar to PYQ Asked in JEE Main 2023

A 5-digit number divisible by 3 is to be formed using the numbers 0, 1, 2, 3, 4 and 5 without repetition, then the total number of ways in which this can be done is ....

Sol. (216) A number will be divisible by 3, if sum of the digits in number be divisible by 3.

Here, $0 + 1 + 2 + 3 + 4 + 5 = 15$, which is divisible by 3. Therefore, the digit that can be left out, while the sum still is multiple of 3, is either 0 or 3.

If 0 left out

Then, possible numbers $= {}^5P_5 = 5! = 120$

If 3 left out

Then, possible numbers $= {}^5P_5 - {}^4P_4 = 5! - 4! = 120 - 24 = 96$

Hence, required total numbers $= 120 + 96 = 216$

Skill Builder

A 5-digit number is formed by the digits 1, 2, 3, 4, 5 without repetition, then the number of the numbers, thus formed divisible by 4, is ....

For Sol.

- **For more practice** See Q.3 of Milestone Practice 5.2.

Example 24. Find the number of permutations of letters *a b c d e f g* taken all together if neither *'beg'* nor *'cad'* pattern appear.

Sol. The total number of permutations without any restriction is 7!

$$n(U) = 7! = 5040$$

Let $n(A)$ be the number of permutations in which *'beg'* pattern always appears

$$\underline{b\,e\,g}\,a\,c\,d\,f$$

i.e. $n(A) = 5! = 120$

and let $n(B)$ be the number of permutations in which *'cad'* pattern always appears

$$\underline{c\,a\,d}\,b\,e\,f\,g$$

i.e. $n(B) = 5! = 120$

Now, $n(A \cap B)$ = Number of permutations in which *'beg'* and *'cad'* pattern appear

$$\underline{b\,e\,g}\,\underline{c\,a\,d}\,f$$

i.e. $n(A \cap B) = 3! = 6$

Hence, the number of permutations in which *'beg'* and *'cad'* patterns do not appear is $n(A' \cap B')$.

or $n(A' \cap B') = n(U) - n(A \cup B)$

$$= n(U) - [n(A) + n(B) - n(A \cap B)]$$
$$= 5040 - 120 - 120 + 6$$
$$= 4806$$

2. The number of permutations of n things taken all at a time, p are alike of one kind, q are alike of second kind and r are alike of a third kind and the rest $n - (p + q + r)$ are all different is $\frac{n!}{p!q!r!}$

Proof Let the required number of permutations be x. Since, p different things can be arranged among themselves in $p!$ ways, therefore if we replace p identical things by p different things, which are also different from the rest of things, the number of permutations will become $x \times p!$

Again, if we replace q identical things by q different things, the number of permutations will become $(x \times p!) \times q!$

Again, if we replace r identical things by r different things, the number of permutations will become $(x \times p! \times q!) \times r!$. Now, all the n things are different and therefore, number of permutations should be $n!$.

Thus, $x \times p! \times q! \times r! = n!$

$$\therefore \quad x = \frac{n!}{p!q!r!}$$

The above theorem can be extended further i.e. if there are n things taken all at a time, p_1 are alike of one kind, p_2 are alike of second kind, p_3 are alike of third kind, ..., p_r are alike of rth kind such that $p_1 + p_2 + p_3 + \ldots + p_r = n$, the number of permutations of these n things is $\frac{n!}{p_1!\,p_2!\,p_3!\ldots p_r!}$.

Example 25. How many words can be formed with the letters of the word 'ARIHANT' by rearranging them?

Sol. Here, total letters 7, in which 2A's but the rest are different. Hence, the number of words formed $= \frac{7!}{2!} = 2520$

Example 26. Find the number of permutations of the letters of the words 'DADDY DID A DEADLY DEED'.

Sol. Here, total letters 19, in which 9D 's, 3A's, 2Y's, 3E's and rest occur only once.

$\therefore$ Required number of permutations $= \frac{19!}{9! \times 3! \times 2! \times 3!}$

Example 27. How many words can be formed with the letters of the words
(i) HIGH SCHOOL and
(ii) INTERMEDIATE by rearranging them?

Sol. (i) Here, total letters are 10, in which 3H's and 2O's, but the rest are different. Hence, the number of words formed $= \dfrac{10!}{3!\,2!}$

(ii) Here, total letters are 12, in which 2I's, 2T's and 3E's but the rest are different. Hence, the number of words formed $= \dfrac{12!}{2!\,2!\,3!}$

Note [for remember]
High School = 10 th class = Total number of letters are 10
Intermediate = 12 th class
= Total number of letters are 12

3. The number of permutations of n different things taken r at a time when each thing may be repeated any number of times is n^r.

Proof Since, the number of permutations of n different things taken r at a time = Number of ways in which r blank places can be filled by n different things.

Clearly, the first place can be filled in n ways. Since, each thing may be repeated, the second place can be filled in n ways. Similarly, each of the 3rd, 4th, ..., rth place can be filled in n ways.

By multiplication principle, the number of permutations of n different things taken r at a time when each thing may be repeated any number of times

$$= n \times n \times n \times \ldots \times r \text{ factors} = n^r$$

Corollary When $r = n$

i.e. the number of permutations of n different things, taken all at a time, when each thing may be repeated any number of times in each arrangements is n^n.

Example 28. A child has four pockets and three marbles. In how many ways can the child put the marbles in its pockets?

Sol. The first marble can be put into the pocket in 4 ways, so can the second. Thus, the number of ways in which the child can put the marbles $= 4 \times 4 \times 4 = 4^3 = 64$ ways

Example 29. There are m men and n monkeys $(n > m)$. If a man have any number of monkeys. In how many ways may every monkey have a master?

Sol. The first monkey can select his master by m ways and after that the second monkey can select his master again by m ways, so can the third and so on.

All monkeys can select master $= m \times m \times m \ldots$ upto n factors $= (m)^n$ ways

Example 30. How many four digit numbers can be formed by using the digits 1, 2, 3, 4, 5, 6, 7, if atleast one digit is repeated ?

Sol. The numbers that can be formed when repetition of digits is allowed are $7^4 = 2401$.

The numbers that can be formed when all the digits are distinct when repetition is not allowed are ${}^7P_4 = 840$.

Therefore, the numbers that can be formed when atleast one digit is repeated $= 7^4 - {}^7P_4$
$= 2401 - 840 = 1561$

Example 31. In how many ways can 4 prizes be distributed among 5 students, if no student gets all the prizes?

Sol. The number of ways in which the 4 prizes can be given away to the 5 students, if a student can get any number of prizes $= 5^4 = 625$.

Again, the number of ways in which a student gets all the 4 prizes = 5, since there are 5 students and any one of them may get all the four prizes.
Therefore, the required number of ways in which a student does not get all the prizes $= 625 - 5 = 620$.

Example 32. Find the number of n-digit numbers, which contain the digits 2 and 7, but not the digits 0, 1, 8, 9.

Sol. The total number without any restrictions containing digits 2, 3, 4, 5, 6, 7 is $n(U) = 6^n$.

The total number of numbers that contain 3, 4, 5, 6, 7 is $n(A) = 5^n$.

The total number of numbers that contain 2, 3, 4, 5, 6 is $n(B) = 5^n$.

The total number of numbers that contain 3, 4, 5, 6 is $n(A \cap B) = 4^n$.

The total number of numbers that do not contain digits 2 and 7 is $n(A \cup B)$

i.e., $n(A \cup B) = n(A) + n(B) - n(A \cap B)$
$= 5^n + 5^n - 4^n = 2(5^n) - 4^n$

Hence, the total number of numbers that contain 2 and 7 is $n(A' \cap B')$

$\therefore\ n(A' \cap B') = n(U) - n(A \cup B) = 6^n - 2 \cdot (5^n) + 4^n$

Example 33. Show that the total number of permutations of n different things taken not more than r at a time, when each thing may be repeated any number of times is $\dfrac{n(n^r - 1)}{(n-1)}$.

Sol. Given, total different things $= n$

The number of permutations of n things taken one at a time $= {}^nP_1 = n$, now if we taken two at a time (repetition is allowed), then first place can be filled by n ways and second place can again be filled in n ways.

$\therefore$ The number of permutations of n things taken two at a time
$= {}^nP_1 \times {}^nP_1 = n \times n = n^2$

Similarly, the number of permutations of n things taken three at a time $= n^3$

$\vdots \quad \vdots \quad \vdots \quad \vdots \quad \vdots$

The number of permutations of n things taken r at a time $= n^r$.

Hence, the total number of permutations

$$= n + n^2 + n^3 + \dots + n^r$$

$$= \frac{n(n^r - 1)}{(n-1)} \qquad \text{[sum of } r \text{ terms of a GP]}$$

5.6 Number of Permutations Under Certain Conditions

(i) Number of permutations of n different things, taken r at a time, when a particular thing is to be always included in each arrangement, is $r \cdot {}^{n-1}P_{r-1}$

Corollary Number of permutations of n different things, taken r at a time, when p particular things is to be always included in each arrangement, is

$$p!(r-(p-1))^{n-p}P_{r-p}.$$

(ii) Number of permutations of n different things, taken r at a time, when a particular thing is never taken in each arrangement, is

$$^{n-1}P_r.$$

(iii) Number of permutations of n different things, taken all at a time, when m specified things always come together, is

$$m! \times (n-m+1)!$$

(iv) Number of permutations of n different things, taken all at a time, when m specified things never come together, is

$$n! - m! \times (n-m+1)!$$

Example 34. How many permutations can be made out of the letters of the word 'TRIANGLE' ? How many of these will begin with T and end with E ?

Sol. The word 'TRIANGLE' has eight different letters, which can be arranged themselves in 8! ways.

$\therefore$ Total number of permutations $= 8! = 40320$

Again, when T is fixed at the first place and E at the last place, the remaining six can be arranged themselves in $6!$ ways.

$\therefore$ The number of permutations which begin with T and end with E $= 6! = 720$.

Example 35. In how many ways can the letters of the word 'INSURANCE' be arranged, so that the vowels are never separate?

Sol. The word 'INSURANCE' has nine different letters, combine the vowels into one bracket as (IUAE) and treating them as one letter we have six letters viz.

(IUAE) N S R N C and these can be arranged among themselves in $\frac{6!}{2!}$ ways and four vowels within the bracket can be arranged themselves in $4!$ ways.

$\therefore$ Required number of words $= \frac{6!}{2!} \times 4! = 8640$

Example 36. How many words can be formed with the letters of the word 'PATALIPUTRA' without changing the relative positions of vowels and consonants?

Sol. The word 'PATALIPUTRA' has eleven letters, in which 2P's, 3A's, 2T's, 1L, 1U, 1R and 1I. Vowels are AAIUA.

These vowels can be arranged themselves in $\frac{5!}{3!} = 20$ ways.

The consonants are PTLPTR these consonants can be arranged themselves in $\frac{6!}{2!2!} = 180$ ways

$\therefore$ Required number of words $= 20 \times 180 = 3600$ ways.

Example 37. Find the number of permutations that can be had from the letters of the word 'OMEGA'

(i) O and A occuping end places.
(ii) E being always in the middle.
(iii) Vowels occuping odd places.
(iv) Vowels being never together.

Sol. There are five letters in the word 'OMEGA'.

(i) When O and A occuping end places

i.e. M E G (OA)

The first three letters (M, E, G) can be arranged themselves by $3! = 6$ ways and last two letters (O, A) can be arranged themselves by $2! = 2$ ways.

$\therefore$ Total number of such words $= 6 \times 2 = 12$ ways.

(ii) When E is the fixed in the middle, then there are four places left to be filled by four remaining letters O, M, G and A and this can be done in $4!$ ways.

$\therefore$ Total number of such words $= 4! = 24$ ways.

(iii) Three vowels (O, E, A) can be arranged in the odd places in $3!$ ways (1st, 3rd and 5th) and the two consonants (M, G) can be arranged in the even places in $2!$ ways (2nd and 4th)

$\therefore$ Total number of such words $= 3! \times 2! = 12$ ways.

(iv) Total number of words $= 5! = 120$

Combine the vowels into one bracket as (OEA) and treating them as one letter, we have

(OEA), M, G and these can be arranged themselves in $3!$ ways and three vowels with in the bracket can be arranged themselves in $3!$ ways.

$\therefore$ Number of ways when vowels come together

$$= 3! \times 3! = 36 \text{ ways.}$$

Hence, number of ways when vowels being never together $= 120 - 36 = 84$ ways.

JEE SCANNER

Example Similar to PYQ Asked in JEE Main 2023

How many different words can be formed by using all the letters of the word ALLAHABAD in which both L do not come together?

Sol. (5880) There are 9 letters in the word 'ALLAHABAD' out of which 4 are A's, 2 are L's and the rest are all distinct.

$\therefore$ Total number of words $= \dfrac{9!}{4!\,2!} = 7560$

Now, considering both L together and treating them as one letter we have 8 letters out of which A repeats 4 times and others are distinct.

$\therefore$ Such number of words $= \dfrac{8!}{4!} \times \dfrac{2!}{2!} = 1680$

Hence, the number of words in which both L do not come together = Total number of words − Number of words in which both L come together.

$= 7560 - 1680$

$= 5880$

Skill Builder

The number of arrangements of the letters of the word 'INDEPENDENCE' in which all vowels never occur together is ...

For Sol.

■ **For more practice** See Q.6 of Milestone Practice 5.2.

5.7 Circular Permutations

(i) Arrangements round a circular table

Consider five persons A, B, C, D and E on the circumference of a circular table in order which has no head now, shifting A, B, C, D and E one position in anti-clockwise direction, we will get arrangements as follows :

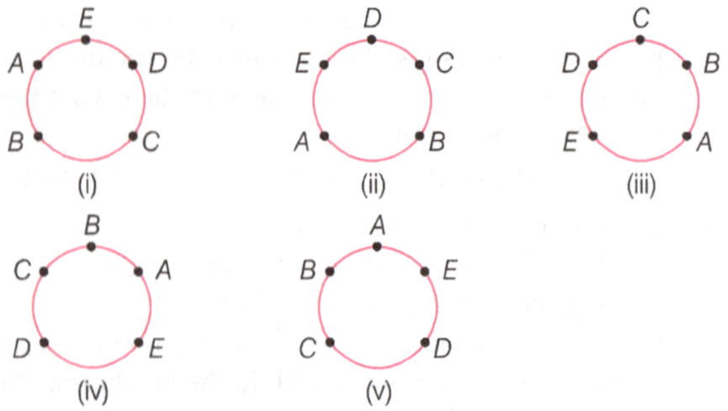

We see that if 5 persons are sitting at a round table, they can be shifted five times and five different arrangements. Thus, obtained will be the same, because anti-clockwise order of A, B, C, D and E does not change.

But if A, B, C, D and E are sitting in a row and they are shifted in such an order that the last occupies the place of first, then the five arrangements will be different. Thus, if there are 5 things, then for each circular arrangement number of linear arrangements is 5. Similarly, if n different things are arranged along a circle for each circular arrangement number of linear arrangements is n.

Therefore, the number of linear arrangements of n different things $= n \times$ number of circular arrangements of n different things.

(ii) Arrangements of beads or flowers (all different) around a circular necklace or garland

Consider five beads A, B, C, D and E in a necklace or five flowers A, B, C, D and E in a garland, etc. If the necklace or garland on the left is turned over, we obtain the arrangement on the right i.e. anti-clockwise and clockwise order of arrangement is not different we will get arrangements as follows:

We see that arrangements in figures are not different.

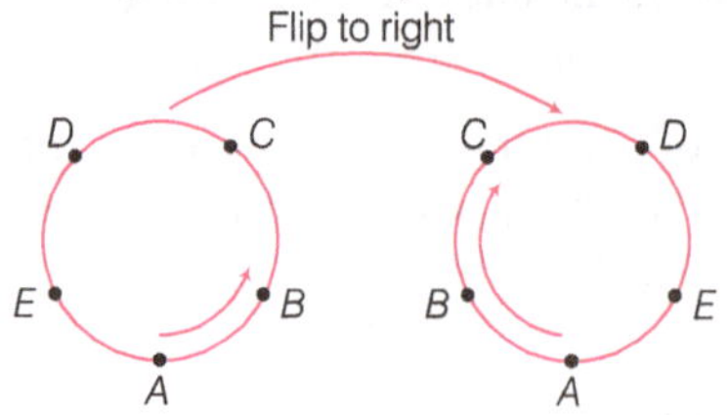

Then, the number of circular permutations of n different things taken all at a time is $\frac{1}{2}(n-1)!$, if clockwise and anti-clockwise orders are taken as not different.

Example 38. Find the number of ways in which 12 different beads can be arranged to form a necklace.

Sol. 12 different beads can be arranged among themselves in a circular order in $(12-1)! = 11!$ ways. Now, in the case of necklace, there is no distinction between clockwise and anti-clockwise arrangements. So, the required number of arrangements $= \frac{1}{2}(11!)$.

Example 39. Consider 21 different pearls on a necklace. How many ways can the pearls be placed in on this necklace such that 3 specific pearls always remain together?

Sol. After fixing the places of three pearls, treating 3 specific pearls = 1 unit. So, we have now 18 pearls + 1 unit = 19 and the number of arrangement will be $(19-1)! = 18!$

Also, the number of ways of 3 pearls can be arranged between themselves is $3! = 6$.

Since, there is no distinction between the clockwise and anti-clockwise arrangements.

So, the required number of arrangements $= \frac{1}{2} 18! \cdot 6 = 3(18!)$.

5.8 Restricted Circular Permutations

***Case* I** If clockwise and anti-clockwise orders are taken as different, then the number of circular permutations of n different things taken r at a time.

$$= \frac{^nP_r}{r} = \frac{1}{r} \cdot \frac{n!}{(n-r)!}$$

Example 40. In how many ways can 24 persons be seated round a table, if there are 13 sets ?

Sol. In case of circular table, the clockwise and anti-clockwise orders are different, the required number of circular permutations $= \frac{^{24}P_{13}}{13} = \frac{24\,!}{13 \times 11\,!}$.

$\Rightarrow n\,! = n \times$ number of circular arrangements of n different things

$\Rightarrow$ Number of circular arrangements of n different things

$$= \frac{n\,!}{n} = (n-1)\,!$$

Hence, the number of circular permutations of n different things taken all at a time is $(n-1)\,!$, if clockwise and anti-clockwise orders are taken as different.

Example 41. Find the number of ways in which three Americans, two British, one Chinese, one Dutch and one Egyptian can sit on a round table so that persons of the same nationality are separated.

Sol. The total number of persons without any restrictions is

$$n(U) = (8-1)!$$
$$= 7! = 5040$$

When, three Americans (A_1, A_2, A_3) are sit together,

$$n(A) = 5! \times 3!$$
$$= 720$$

When, two British (B_1, B_2) are sit together,

$$n(B) = 6! \times 2!$$
$$= 1440$$

When, three Americans (A_1, A_2, A_3) and two British (B_1, B_2) are sit together, $n(A \cap B) = 4! \times 3! \times 2!$

$$= 288$$

$$\therefore \quad n(A \cup B) = n(A) + nB) - n(A \cap B)$$
$$= 720 + 1440 - 288$$
$$= 1872$$

Hence, $\quad n(A \cap B') = n(U) - n(A \cup B)$

$$= 5040 - 1872$$
$$= 3168$$

Example 42. In how many different ways can five boys and five girls form a circle such that the boys and girls alternate?

Sol. After fixing up one boy on the table, the remaining can be arranged in 4 ! ways but boys and girls are to alternate. There will be 5 places, one place each between two boys these five places can be filled by 5 girls in 5 ! ways.

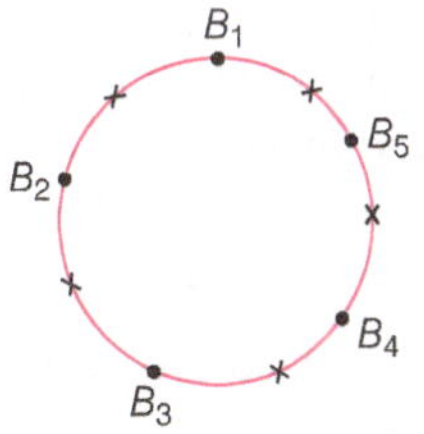

Hence, by the principle of multiplication, the required number of ways $= 4\,! \times 5\,! = 2880$.

Example 43. 20 persons were invited to a party. In how many ways can they and the host be seated at a circular table ? In how many of these ways will two particular persons be seated on either side of the host?

Sol. I Part Total persons on the circular table

$$= 20 \text{ guest} + 1 \text{ host}$$
$$= 21$$

They can be seated in $(21-1)\,! = 20\,!$ ways.

II Part After fixing the places of three persons (1 host + 2 persons).

Treating (1 host + 2 persons) = 1 unit, so we have now {(remaining 18 persons + 1 host) = 19} and the number of arrangement will be $(19-1)\,! = 18\,!$ also these two particular persons can be seated on either side of the host in $2\,!$ ways.

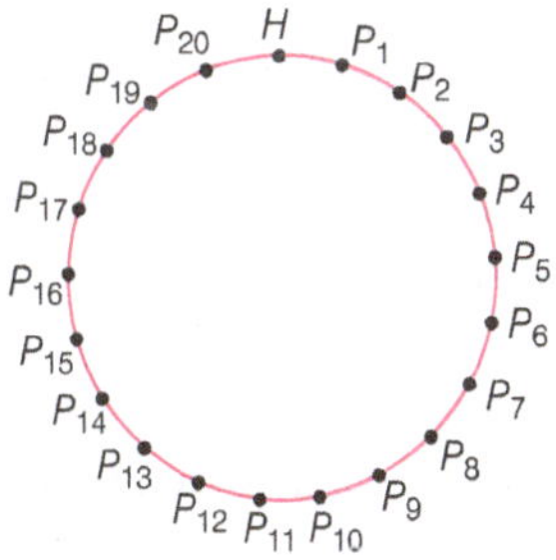

Hence, the number of ways of seating 21 persons on the circular table such that two particular persons be seated on either side of the host $= 18\,! \times 2\,! = 2 \times 18\,!$

***Case* II** If clockwise and anti-clockwise orders are taken as not different, then the number of circular permutations of n different things taken r at a time $= \frac{^nP_r}{2r} = \frac{1}{2r} \cdot \frac{n!}{(n-r)!}$

5.9 Rank in a Dictionary

The dictionary format means words are arranged in alphabetical formal.

JEE SCANNER

Example Similar to PYQ Asked in JEE Main 2023

All letters of the word UMANG are written in all possible orders and these words are written as in a dictionary with serial numbers. Then, find the serial number of the word UMANG.

Sol. The letters in alphabetical order are A, G, M, N, U

$\therefore$ The first word is AGMNU

Number of words beginning with $A = 4! = 24$

Number of words beginning with $G = 4! = 24$

Number of words beginning with $M = 4! = 24$

Number of words beginning with $N = 4! = 24$

Number of words beginning with $UA = 3! = 6$

Number of words beginning with $UG = 3! = 6$

Number of words beginning with $UMAG = 1! = 1$

Number of words beginning with $UMANG = 1$

$\therefore$ Rank of the word

UMANG $= 24 + 24 + 24 + 24 + 6 + 6 + 1 + 1 = 110$

Skill Builder

All letters of the word ZENITH are written in all possible orders and these words are written as in a dictionary with serial numbers. The serial number of the word ZENITH is ....

For Sol.

■ **For more practice** See Q.11 of Milestone Practice 5.2.

Example 44. If letters of the word SURITI are arranged as in dictionary, find its rank.

Sol. The letters in alphabetical order are I, I, R, S, T, U

$\therefore$ The first word is IIRSTU

Number of words beginning with I $= 5! = 120$

Number of words beginning with R $= \frac{5!}{2!} = 60$

Number of words beginning with SI $= 4! = 24$

Number of words beginning with SR $= \frac{4!}{2!} = 12$

Number of words beginning with ST $= \frac{4!}{2!} = 12$

Number of words beginning with SUI $= 3! = 6$

Number of words beginning with SURII $= 1! = 1$

Number of words beginning with SURITI $= 1$

$\therefore$ Rank of the word SURITI

$= 120 + 60 + 24 + 12 + 12 + 6 + 1 + 1 = 236$

5.10 Gap Method

[when particular objects are never together]

Example 45. There are 10 candidates for an examination out of which 4 are appearing in Mathematics and remaining 6 are appearing in different subjects. In how many ways can they be seated in a row so that no two Mathematics candidates are together?

Sol. In this method, first arrange the remaining candidates.

Here, remaining candidates = 6

$$\times 0 \times 0 \times 0 \times 0 \times 0 \times 0 \times$$

$\times$: Places available for Mathematics candidates

0 : Places for others

Remaining candidates can be arranged in $6!$ ways.

There are seven places available for Mathematics candidates so that no two Mathematics candidates are together.

Now, four candidates can be placed in these seven places in ${}^7P_4$ ways.

Hence, the total number of ways $= 6! \times {}^7P_4 = 720 \times 840$

$= 604800$

Example 46. In how many ways can 7 plus (+) and 5 minus (–) signs be arranged in a row so that no two minus (–) signs are together?

Sol. In this method, first arrange the plus (+) signs.

Here, minus (–) signs = 5

$$0 + 0 + 0 + 0 + 0 + 0 + 0 + 0$$

We can put minus (–) sign in any of the 8 places in the above arrangement i.e., we have to select 5 places out of 8 which can be done is ${}^8C_5$ ways

$= {}^8C_3$ ways

$= 56$ ways

Example 47. Find the number of ways in which 5 girls and 5 boys can be arranged in a row, if no two boys are together.

Sol. In this example, there is no condition for arranging the girls. Now, 5 girls can be arranged in $5!$ ways.

$$\times G \times G \times G \times G \times G \times$$

When girls are arranged, six gaps are generated as shown above with '$\times$'.

Now, boys must occupy the places with '$\times$' marked, so that no two boys are together.

Therefore, five boys can be arranged in these six gaps in ${}^6P_5$ ways.

Hence, total number of arrangement is $5! \times {}^6P_5$.

Example 48. Find the number of ways in which 5 girls and 5 boys can be arranged in a row, if boys and girls are alternate.

Sol. First five girls can be arranged in 5 ! ways

i.e. $\times G \times G \times G \times G \times G$ or $G \times G \times G \times G \times G \times$

Now, if girls and boys are alternate, then boys can occupy places with '$\times$' as shows above.

Hence, total number of arrangements is

$$5! \times 5! + 5! \times 5! = 2 \times (5!)^2$$

Use of Set Theory

A set is well defined collection of distinct objects.

Subset

If every element of a set A is also an element of a set B, then A is called the subset B, we write

$$A \subset B \Leftrightarrow \{x \in A \Rightarrow x \in B\}$$

Union

The union of two sets A and B is the set of all those elements which are either in A or in B or in both. This set is denoted by $A \cup B$ or $A + B$.

Symbolically, $A \cup B = \{x : x \in A \text{ or } x \in B\}$

Intersection

The intersection of two sets A and B is the set of all elements which are common in A and B. This set is denoted by $A \cap B$ or AB.

Symbolically, $A \cap B = \{x : x \in A \text{ and } x \in B\}$

Example 49. A is a set containing n elements. A subset P_1 of A is chosen. The set A is reconstructed by replacing the elements of P_1. Next, a subset P_2 of A is chosen and again the set is reconstructed by replacing the elements of P_2. In this way $m\,(>1)$ subsets $P_1, P_2, \ldots, P_m$ of A are chosen. Find the number of ways of choosing $P_1, P_2, \ldots, P_m$, so that

(i) $P_1 \cap P_2 \cap P_3 \cap \ldots \cap P_m = \phi$

(ii) $P_1 \cup P_2 \cup P_3 \cup \ldots \cup P_m = A$

Sol. Let $A = \{a_1, a_2, a_3, \ldots, a_n\}$

(i) For each a_i $(1 \le i \le n)$, we have either $a \in P_j$ or $a_i \notin P_j$ $(1 \le j \le m)$. i.e. there are 2^m choices in which $a_i (1 \le i \le n)$ may belong to the P_j's.

Out of these, there is only one choice, in which $a_i \in P_j$ for all $j = 1, 2, \ldots, m$ which is not favourable for $P_1 \cap P_2 \cap P_3 \cap \ldots \cap P_m$ to be ϕ. Thus, $a_i \notin P_1 \cap P_2 \cap \ldots \cap P_m$ in $(2^m - 1)$ ways. Since, there are n elements in the set A, the total number of choices is $(2^m - 1)^n$.

(ii) There is exactly one choice, in which, $a_i \in P_j$, for all $j = 1, 2, 3, \ldots, m$ which is not favourable for $P_1 \cup P_2 \cup P_3 \cup \ldots \cup P_m$ to be equal to A. Thus, a_i can belong to $P_1 \cup P_2 \cup P_3 \cup \ldots \cup P_m$ in $(2^m - 1)$ ways.

Since, there are n elements in the set A, the number of ways in which $P_1 \cup P_2 \cup P_3 \cup \ldots \cup P_m$ can be equal to A is $(2^m - 1)^n$.

JEE SCANNER

Example Similar to PYQ Asked in JEE Main 2023

The sum of all five digit numbers that can be formed using the digits 1, 2, 3, 4 and 5 (repetition of digits not allowed), is

(a) 3999860 (b) 3999940

(c) 3999760 (d) 3999960

Sol. (d) Required sum $= (5-1)!\,(1+2+3+4+5)\left(\dfrac{10^5 - 1}{9}\right)$

$= 24 \cdot 15 \cdot 11111 = 3999960$

Alternate Solution

Since, one of the numbers formed with the 5 digits a, b, c, d and e is $10^4 a + 10^3 b + 10^2 c + 10d + e$;

Hence, $10^4 a$ will occur altogether in 4 ! ways similarly each of $10^4 b, 10^4 c, 10^4 d, 10^4 e$ will occur in 4 ! ways.

Hence, if all the numbers formed with the digits be written one below the other, thus

$$10^4 \cdot a + 10^3 \cdot b + 10^2 \cdot c + 10 \cdot d + e$$
$$10^4 \cdot b + 10^3 \cdot c + 10^2 \cdot d + 10 \cdot e + a$$
$$10^4 \cdot c + 10^3 \cdot d + 10^2 \cdot e + 10 \cdot a + b$$
$$10^4 \cdot d + 10^3 \cdot e + 10^2 \cdot a + 10 \cdot b + c$$
$$10^4 \cdot e + 10^3 \cdot a + 10^2 \cdot b + 10 \cdot c + d$$

Hence, the required sum

$= 4! \times (a + b + c + d + e) \times (10^4 + 10^3 + 10^2 + 10 + 1)$

$= 4! \times (1 + 2 + 3 + 4 + 5)(11111)$

$= 3999960$

Skill Builder

For Sol.

The sum of all the numbers that can be formed with the digits 2, 3, 4, 5 taken all at a time is

(a) 93334 (b) 93324 (c) 93354 (d) 93344

■ **For more practice** See Q.12 of Milestone Practice 5.2.

Example 50. A is a set containing n elements. A subset P of A is chosen. The set A is reconstructed by replacing the elements of P. A subset of A is again chosen. Find the number of ways of choosing P and Q, so that

(i) $P \cap Q$ contains exactly r elements.

(ii) $P \cap Q$ contains exactly 2 elements.

(iii) $P \cap Q = \phi$

Sol. Let $A = \{a_1, a_2, a_3, \ldots, a_n\}$

(i) The r elements in P and Q such that $P \cap Q$ can be chosen out of n is ${}^nC_r$ ways a general element of A must satisfy one of the following possibilities [here, general element be $a_i (1 \le i \le n)$]

(i) $a_i \in P$ and $a_i \in Q$ (ii) $a_i \in P$ and $a_i \notin Q$

(iii) $a_i \notin P$ and $a_i \in Q$ (iv) $a_i \notin P$ and $a_i \notin Q$

Let $a_1, a_2, ..., a_r \in P \cap Q$
There is only one choice each of them (i.e. (i) choice) and three choices (ii), (iii) and (iv) for each of remaining $(n-r)$ elements.
Hence, number of ways of remaining elements $= 3^{n-r}$
Hence, number of ways in which $P \cap Q$ contains exactly r elements $= {}^nC_r \times 3^{n-r}$

(i) Put $r = 2$, then ${}^nC_2 \times 3^{n-2}$
(ii) Put $r = 0$, then ${}^nC_0 \times 3^n = 3^n$

Sum of digits

Case-1 The sum of the digits in the unit's place of all numbers formed with the help of $a_1, a_2, ..., a_n$ taken all at a time is $(n-1)!(a_1 + a_2 + ... + a_n)$
(repetition of digits not allowed)

Case-2 The sum of all digit numbers that can be formed using the digits $a_1, a_2, ..., a_n$ (repetition of digits not allowed) is $= (n-1)!(a_1 + a_2 + ... + a_n)\dfrac{(10^n - 1)}{9}$

Example 51. Find the sum of the digits in the unit's place of all numbers formed with the help of 3, 4, 5, 6 taken all at a time.

Sol. Sum of the digits in the unit's place

$$= (4-1)!(3+4+5+6)$$
$$= 6 \times 18$$
$$= 108$$

Milestone Practice 5.2

1. If ${}^9P_5 + 5 \cdot {}^9P_4 = {}^{10}P_r$, find r.
2. If $P(2n-1, n) : P(2n+1, n-1) = 22 : 7$, find the value of $n^2 - 10$.
3. How many 5 digit numbers divisible by 4 can be formed by using the digits 1, 2, 3, 4, 5, 6. Iff repetition of digits is not allowed.
4. Ten different letters of an alphabet are given words with five letters are formed from these given letters. Determine the number of words which have atleast one letter repeated.
5. Find the number of permutations of all the letters of the word 'MATHEMATICS' which starts with consonants only.
6. Find the number of arrangements of the letters of the word SALOON, if two O's do not occur together.
7. How many words can be formed by using all the letters of the word ALLAHABAD in which vowels occupy the even positions?
8. If the different permutations of the word, 'EXAMINATION' are listed as in a dictionary, how many items are there in the list before the first word starting with E.
9. How many ways are there to seat n married couples $(n \geq 3)$ around a table such that men and women are alternate and each women is not adjacent to her husband?
10. Find the rank of the word 'PENCIL'.
11. The letters of the word 'CODES' are written in all possible ways and these words are arranged as in a dictionary in a series. Then, find the serial number of the word SEDOC.
12. Find the sum of all 6 digit numbers that can be formed using the digits 2, 3, 4, 5, 6, 7, (repetition of digits not allowed).

Answer Key

1. 5	2. 90	3. 192	4. 69760
5. 3175200	6. 240	7. 60	8. 907200
9. $(n-1)!(n!-2)$	10. 643	11. 112	12. 359999640

For Detailed Solution

Milestone 3 Combination

• Combination • Restricted Combinations • Combinations from Identical Objects • Arrangements in Groups • Multinomial Theorem • Geometrical Problems

5.11 Combination

Each of the different groups or selections which can be made by some or all of a number of given things without reference to the order of the things in each group is called a combination.

Important Result

(1) The number of combinations of n different things taken r at a time is denoted by ^nC_r or $C(n, r)$ or $\binom{n}{r}$.

Then,

$$^nC_r = \frac{n!}{r!\,(n-r)!} \qquad [0 \le r \le n]$$

$$= \frac{^nP_r}{r!}$$

$$= \frac{n(n-1)(n-2)\dots(n-r+1)}{r(r-1)(r-2)\dots 2\cdot 1}, n \in N \text{ and } r \in W$$

Proof Let the number of combinations of n different things taken r at a time be ^nC_r.

Now, each combination consists of r different things and these r things can be arranged among themselves in $r!$ ways.

Thus, for one combination of r different things, the number of arrangements is $r!$.

Hence, for ^nC_r combinations, number of arrangements is

$$r! \times {^nC_r} \qquad \text{...(i)}$$

But number of permutations of n different things taken r at a time is ^nP_r. ...(ii)

From Eqs. (i) and (ii), we get

$$r! \times {^nC_r} = {^nP_r} = \frac{n!}{(n-r)!}$$

$$\therefore \quad {^nC_r} = \frac{n!}{r!(n-r)!}, r \in W \text{ and } n \in N$$

JEE Focus Points

- ^nC_r is a natural number.
- $^nC_r = 0$, if $r > n$
- $^nC_0 = {^nC_n} = 1$, $^nC_1 = n$
- $^nP_r = {^nC_r}$, if $r = 0$ or 1
- $^nC_r = {^nC_{n-r}}$
- If $^nC_x = {^nC_y} \Rightarrow x = y$ or $x + y = n$
- $^nC_r + {^nC_{r-1}} = {^{n+1}C_r}$ [Pascal's rule]
- $^nC_r = \frac{n}{r} \cdot {^{n-1}C_{r-1}}$
- $n \cdot {^{n-1}C_{r-1}} = (n-r+1) \cdot {^nC_{r-1}}$
- $\frac{^nC_r}{^nC_{r-1}} = \frac{n-r+1}{r}$
- (a) If n is even, ^nC_r is greatest for $r = \frac{n}{2}$

  (b) If n is odd, ^nC_r is greatest for $r = \frac{n-1}{2}$ or $\frac{n+1}{2}$
- $^nC_0 + {^nC_1} + {^nC_2} + \dots + {^nC_n} = 2^n$
- $^nC_0 + {^nC_2} + {^nC_4} + \dots = {^nC_1} + {^nC_3} + {^nC_5} + \dots = 2^{n-1}$
- $^{2n+1}C_0 + {^{2n+1}C_1} + {^{2n+1}C_2} + \dots + {^{2n+1}C_n} = 2^{2n}$
- $^nC_n + {^{n+1}C_n} + {^{n+2}C_n} + {^{n+3}C_n} + \dots + {^{2n-1}C_n} = {^{2n}C_{n+1}}$

Example 52. If $^{15}C_{3r} = {^{15}C_{r+3}}$, find $^rC_2$.

Sol. We have, $\quad ^{15}C_{3r} = {^{15}C_{r+3}}$

$\Rightarrow \quad 3r = r + 3$ or $3r + r + 3 = 15$

$\Rightarrow \quad 2r = 3$ or $4r = 12$

$\Rightarrow \quad r = \frac{3}{2}$ or $r = 3$

but $r \in W$, so that $\quad r \ne \frac{3}{2}$

$\therefore \quad r = 3$

Then, $\quad ^rC_2 = {^3C_2} = {^3C_1} = 3$

JEE SCANNER

Example Similar to PYQ Asked in JEE Main 2023

If ${}^{2n}C_3 : {}^nC_3 = 11:1$, find the value of $(n^2 + 2n):(n^2 - 3n + 1)$

Sol. We have, $${}^{2n}C_3 : {}^nC_3 = 11:1$$

$$\Rightarrow \frac{{}^{2n}C_3}{{}^nC_3} = \frac{11}{1}$$

$$\Rightarrow \frac{2n(2n-1)(2n-2)}{3.2.1} \times \frac{3.2.1}{n(n-1)(n-2)} = 11$$

$$\Rightarrow \frac{4(2n-1)}{n-2} = 11$$

$$\Rightarrow 8n - 4 = 11n - 22$$

$$\Rightarrow 3n = 18$$

$$\Rightarrow n = 6$$

$$\therefore (n^2 + 2n):(n^2 - 3n + 1) = (36 + 12):(36 - 18 + 1) = 48:19$$

Skill Builder

If ${}^{2n}C_2 : {}^nC_2 = 9:2$, find the value of $(n^2 - 3):(n^2 + n + 4)$.

For Sol.

- **For more practice** See Q.1 of Milestone Practice 5.3.

Example 53. If ${}^nC_9 = {}^nC_7$, find n.

Sol. We have, ${}^nC_9 = {}^nC_7 \Rightarrow n = 9 + 7$ $[\because 9 \neq 7]$

$\therefore$ $n = 16$

Example 54. Prove that

$$\binom{n}{r} + 2\binom{n}{r-1} + \binom{n}{r-2} = \binom{n+2}{r}$$

Sol. $\therefore \binom{n}{r} = {}^nC_r$

$$\therefore \text{LHS} = \binom{n}{r} + 2\binom{n}{r-1} + \binom{n}{r-2}$$

$$= {}^nC_r + 2\,{}^nC_{r-1} + {}^nC_{r-2}$$

$$= ({}^nC_r + {}^nC_{r-1}) + ({}^nC_{r-1} + {}^nC_{r-2})$$

$$= {}^{n+1}C_r + {}^{n+1}C_{r-1} = {}^{n+2}C_r$$

$$= \binom{n+2}{r} = \text{RHS}$$

Example 55. If ${}^{n+1}C_{r+1} : {}^nC_r : {}^{n-1}C_{r-1} = 11:6:3$, find the values of n and r.

Sol. Here, $$\frac{{}^{n+1}C_{r+1}}{{}^nC_r} = \frac{11}{6}$$

$$\Rightarrow \frac{n+1}{r+1} \cdot \frac{{}^nC_r}{{}^nC_r} = \frac{11}{6} \qquad \left[\because {}^nC_r = \frac{n}{r} \cdot {}^{n-1}C_{r-1}\right]$$

$$\Rightarrow \frac{n+1}{r+1} = \frac{11}{6}$$

$$\Rightarrow 6n + 6 = 11r + 11$$

$$\Rightarrow 6n - 11r = 5 \qquad \text{...(i)}$$

and $$\frac{{}^nC_r}{{}^{n-1}C_{r-1}} = \frac{6}{3}$$

$$\Rightarrow \frac{n}{r} \cdot \frac{{}^{n-1}C_{r-1}}{{}^{n-1}C_{r-1}} = \frac{6}{3} \qquad \left[\because {}^nC_r = \frac{n}{r} \cdot {}^{n-1}C_{r-1}\right]$$

$$\Rightarrow \frac{n}{r} = 2$$

$$\Rightarrow n = 2r \qquad \text{...(ii)}$$

On solving Eqs. (i) and (ii), we get $n = 10$ and $r = 5$.

Example 56. If ${}^nC_{r-1} = 36$, ${}^nC_r = 84$ and ${}^nC_{r+1} = 126$, find r.

Sol. Here, $$\frac{{}^nC_r}{{}^nC_{r-1}} = \frac{84}{36}$$

$$\Rightarrow \frac{n-r+1}{r} = \frac{7}{3} \qquad \left[\because \frac{{}^nC_r}{{}^nC_{r-1}} = \frac{n-r+1}{r}\right]$$

$$\Rightarrow 3n - 3r + 3 = 7r$$

$$\Rightarrow 10r - 3n = 3 \qquad \text{...(i)}$$

and $$\frac{{}^nC_{r+1}}{{}^nC_r} = \frac{n-(r+1)+1}{(r+1)} = \frac{126}{84} \qquad \left[\because \frac{{}^nC_r}{{}^nC_{r-1}} = \frac{n-r+1}{r}\right]$$

$$\Rightarrow \frac{n-r}{r+1} = \frac{3}{2}$$

$$\Rightarrow 2n - 2r = 3r + 3$$

$$\Rightarrow 5r - 2n = -3$$

or $$10r - 4n = -6 \qquad \text{...(ii)}$$

On subtracting Eq. (ii) from Eq. (i), we get

$$n = 9$$

From Eq. (i), we get

$$10r - 27 = 3$$

$$\Rightarrow 10r = 30$$

$$\therefore r = 3$$

Example 57. Prove that product of r consecutive positive integers is divisible by $r!$.

Sol. Let r consecutive positive integers be (m), $(m+1), (m+2), \dots, (m+r-1)$, where $m \in N$.

$\therefore$ Product $= m(m+1)(m+2)\dots(m+r-1)$

$$= \frac{(m-1)!\, m(m+1)(m+2)\dots(m+r-1)}{(m-1)!}$$

$$= \frac{(m+r-1)!}{(m-1)!} = \frac{r! \cdot (m+r-1)!}{r!(m-1)!}$$

$[\because {}^{m+r-1}C_r$ is natural number$]$

$$= r! \cdot {}^{m+r-1}C_r,$$

which is divisible by $r!$.

Example 58. Evaluate

$$^{47}C_4 + \sum_{j=0}^{3} {}^{50-j}C_3 + \sum_{k=0}^{5} {}^{56-k}C_{53-k}.$$

Sol. We have, $^{47}C_4 + \sum_{j=0}^{3} {}^{50-j}C_3 + \sum_{k=0}^{5} {}^{56-k}C_{53-k}$

$$= {}^{47}C_4 + \sum_{j=0}^{3} {}^{50-j}C_3 + \sum_{k=0}^{5} {}^{56-k}C_3 \quad [\because {}^nC_r = {}^nC_{n-r}]$$

$$= {}^{47}C_4 + ({}^{50}C_3 + {}^{49}C_3 + {}^{48}C_3 + {}^{47}C_3) + ({}^{56}C_3 + {}^{55}C_3 + {}^{54}C_3 + {}^{53}C_3 + {}^{52}C_3 + {}^{51}C_3)$$

$$= {}^{47}C_4 + {}^{47}C_3 + {}^{48}C_3 + {}^{49}C_3 + {}^{50}C_3 + {}^{51}C_3 + {}^{52}C_3 + {}^{53}C_3 + {}^{54}C_3 + {}^{55}C_3 + {}^{56}C_3$$

$$= ({}^{47}C_4 + {}^{47}C_3) + {}^{48}C_3 + {}^{49}C_3 + {}^{50}C_3 + {}^{51}C_3 + {}^{52}C_3 + {}^{53}C_3 + {}^{54}C_3 + {}^{55}C_3 + {}^{56}C_3$$

$$= {}^{48}C_4 + {}^{48}C_3 + {}^{49}C_3 + {}^{50}C_3 + {}^{51}C_3 + \dots + {}^{56}C_3 \quad [\because {}^nC_r + {}^nC_{r-1} = {}^{n+1}C_r]$$

$$= {}^{49}C_4 + {}^{49}C_3 + {}^{50}C_3 + \dots + {}^{56}C_3$$

$$\vdots \quad \vdots \quad \vdots \quad \vdots \quad \vdots$$

$$= {}^{56}C_4 + {}^{56}C_3 = {}^{57}C_4$$

Example 59. Prove that the greatest value of $^{2n}C_r \ (0 \le r \le 2n)$ is $^{2n}C_n$ (for $1 \le r \le n$).

Sol. We have,

$$\frac{^{2n}C_r}{^{2n}C_{r-1}} = \frac{2n - r + 1}{r} \quad \left[\because \frac{^nC_r}{^nC_{r-1}} = \frac{n-r+1}{r}\right]$$

$$= \frac{2(n-r) + (r+1)}{r}$$

$$= \frac{1 + 2(n-r) + 1}{r} > 1$$

$$\Rightarrow \quad \frac{^{2n}C_r}{^{2n}C_{r-1}} > 1 \quad [\text{for } 1 \le r \le n]$$

$$\therefore \quad {}^{2n}C_{r-1} < {}^{2n}C_r$$

On putting $r = 1, 2, 3, \dots, n$, then

$$^{2n}C_0 < {}^{2n}C_1, \ {}^{2n}C_1 < {}^{2n}C_2, \dots, {}^{2n}C_{n-1} < {}^{2n}C_n$$

On combining all inequalities, we get

$$\Rightarrow \ {}^{2n}C_0 < {}^{2n}C_1 < {}^{2n}C_2 < {}^{2n}C_3 < \dots < {}^{2n}C_{n-1} < {}^{2n}C_n$$

but $^{2n}C_r = {}^{2n}C_{2n-r}$, it follows that

$$^{2n}C_{2n} < {}^{2n}C_{2n-1} < {}^{2n}C_{2n-2} < {}^{2n}C_{2n-3} < \dots < {}^{2n}C_{n+1} < {}^{2n}C_n$$

Hence, the greatest value of $^{2n}C_r$ is $^{2n}C_n$.

JEE SCANNER

Example Similar to PYQ Asked in JEE Main 2023

The value of $\sum_{j=1}^{5} {}^{52-j}C_3$ is

(a) $^{52}C_3 - {}^{47}C_4$ (b) $^{52}C_4 - {}^{47}C_4$
(c) $^{52}C_4 - {}^{47}C_3$ (d) None of these

Sol. (b) Let $S = \sum_{j=1}^{5} {}^{52-j}C_3$

$$= {}^{51}C_3 + {}^{50}C_3 + {}^{49}C_3 + {}^{48}C_3 + {}^{47}C_3$$

$$\therefore \ S + {}^{47}C_4 = {}^{47}C_4 + {}^{47}C_3 + {}^{48}C_3 + {}^{49}C_3 + {}^{50}C_3 + {}^{51}C_3$$

$$\Rightarrow S + {}^{47}C_4 = {}^{48}C_4 + {}^{48}C_3 + {}^{49}C_3 + {}^{50}C_3 + {}^{51}C_3$$

$$= {}^{49}C_4 + {}^{49}C_3 + {}^{50}C_3 + {}^{51}C_3$$

$$= {}^{50}C_4 + {}^{50}C_3 + {}^{51}C_3 = {}^{51}C_4 + {}^{51}C_3 = {}^{52}C_4$$

$$\therefore \quad S = {}^{52}C_4 - {}^{47}C_4$$

Skill Builder

For Sol.

The value of $\sum_{j=0}^{6} {}^{49-j}C_4$ is

(a) $^{50}C_5 - {}^{43}C_5$ (b) $^{50}C_5 - {}^{43}C_4$
(c) $^{50}C_4 - {}^{43}C_4$ (d) None of these

■ **For more practice** See Q.3 of Milestone Practice 5.3.

Example 60. Thirty six games were played in a football tournament with each team playing once against each other. How many teams were there?

Sol. Let the number of teams be n.

Then, number of matches to be played is

$$^nC_2 = 36$$

$$\Rightarrow \quad {}^nC_2 = \frac{9 \times 8}{1 \times 2} = {}^9C_2$$

$$\Rightarrow \quad n = 9$$

Example 61. If there are 12 persons in a party, and if each two of them shake hands with each other, how many handshakes happen in the party?

Sol. When two persons shake hands, it is counted as one hand-shake, not two.

So, total number of handshake is same as the number of ways of selecting 2 persons among 12 persons

$$\therefore \text{Total handshakes} = {}^{12}C_2 = \frac{12 \times 11}{2 \times 1} = 66$$

5.12 Restricted Combinations

(i) The number of selections (combinations) of r objects out of n different objects, when

(a) k particular things are always included $= {}^{n-k}C_{r-k}$.

(b) k particular things are never included $= {}^{n-k}C_r$.

(ii) The number of combinations of r things out of n different things, such that k particular things are not together in any selection $= {}^nC_r - {}^{n-k}C_{r-k}$.

(iii) The number of combinations of n different objects taking r at a time when, p particular objects are always included and q particular objects are always excluded $= {}^{n-p-q}C_{r-p}$.

Concept Inside Video

JEE Focus Points

- The number of selections of r consecutive things out of n things in a row $= n - r + 1$.
- The number of selections of r consecutive things out of n things along a circle $= \begin{cases} n, \text{ if } r < n \\ 1, \text{ if } r = n \end{cases}$

Example 62. In how many ways can a cricket, eleven players by chosen out of a batch 15 players, if

(i) a particular is always chosen.

(ii) a particular player is never chosen?

Sol. (i) Since, particular player is always chosen. It means that $11 - 1 = 10$ players are selected out of the remaining $15 - 1 = 14$ players.

$\therefore$ Required number of ways $= {}^{14}C_{10} = {}^{14}C_4$

$$= \frac{14 \cdot 13 \cdot 12 \cdot 11}{1 \cdot 2 \cdot 3 \cdot 4} = 1001$$

(ii) Since, particular player is never chosen. It means that 11 players are selected out of the remaining $15 - 1 = 14$ players.

$\therefore$ Required number of ways $= {}^{14}C_{11} = {}^{14}C_3$

$$= \frac{14 \cdot 13 \cdot 12}{1 \cdot 2 \cdot 3} = 364$$

Example 63. How many different selections of 6 books can be made from 11 different books, if

(i) two particular books are always selected?

(ii) two particular books are never selected?

Sol. (i) Since, two particular books are always selected. It means that $6 - 2 = 4$ books are selected out of the remaining $11 - 2 = 9$ books.

$\therefore$ Required number of ways $= {}^9C_4 = \dfrac{9 \cdot 8 \cdot 7 \cdot 6}{1 \cdot 2 \cdot 3 \cdot 4} = 126$

(ii) Since, two particular books are never selected. It means that 6 books are selected out of the remaining $11 - 2 = 9$ books.

$\therefore$ Required number of ways $= {}^9C_6$

$$= {}^9C_3 = \frac{9 \cdot 8 \cdot 7}{1 \cdot 2 \cdot 3} = 84$$

Example 64. A person tries to form as many different parties as he can, out of his 20 friends. Each party should consist of the same number. How many friends should be invited at a time? In how many of these parties would the same friends be found?

Sol. Let the person invite r number of friends at a time. Then, the number of parties are ${}^{20}C_r$, which is maximum, when $r = 10$.

If a particular friend will be found in p parties, then p is the number of combinations out of 20 in which this particular friend must be included. Therefore, we have to select 9 more from 19 remaining friends.

Hence, $p = {}^{19}C_9$

(2) The number of ways (or combinations) of n different things selecting atleast one of them is $2^n - 1$. This can also be stated as the total number of combinations of n different things.

Proof For each things, there are two possibilities, whether it is selected or not selected.

Hence, the total number of ways is given by total possibilities of all the things which is equal to

$2 \times 2 \times 2 \times \ldots \times n$ factors $= 2^n$

But, this includes one case in which nothing is selected.

Hence, the total number of ways of selecting one or more of n different things $= 2^n - 1$

Alternate Solution

Number of ways of selecting one, two, three, ..., n things from n different things are ${}^nC_1, {}^nC_2, {}^nC_3, \ldots, {}^nC_n$, respectively.

Hence, the total number of ways or selecting atleast one thing is

${}^nC_1 + {}^nC_2 + {}^nC_3 + \ldots + {}^nC_n$

$$= ({}^nC_0 + {}^nC_1 + {}^nC_2 + \ldots + {}^nC_n) - {}^nC_0$$

$$= 2^n - 1$$

Example 65. Mohan has 8 friends, in how many ways he invite one or more of them to dinner?

Sol. Mohan select one or more than one of his 8 friends. So, required number of ways

$$= {}^8C_1 + {}^8C_2 + {}^8C_3 + \ldots + {}^8C_8$$

$$= 2^8 - 1 = 255$$

Example 66. A question paper consists of two sections having respectively, 3 and 5 questions. The following note is given on the paper "It is not necessary to attempt all the questions one question from each section is compulsory". In how many ways can a candidate select the questions?

Sol. Here, we have two sections A and B (say), the section A has 3 questions and section B has 5 questions and one question from each section is compulsory, according to the given direction.

$\therefore$ Number of ways selecting one or more than one question from section A is $2^3 - 1 = 7$

and number of ways selecting one or more than one question from section B is $2^5 - 1 = 31$

Hence, by the principle of multiplication, the required number of ways in which a candidate can select the questions

$$= 7 \times 31 = 217$$

Example 67. A student is allowed to select atleast one and atmost n books from a collection of $(2n+1)$ books. If the total number of ways in which he can select a book is 63, find the value of n.

Sol. Given, student select atleast one and atmost n books from a collection of $(2n + 1)$ books. It means that he select one book or two books or three books or ... or n books. Hence, by the given hypothesis.

$$^{2n+1}C_1 + {}^{2n+1}C_2 + {}^{2n+1}C_3 + \ldots + {}^{2n+1}C_n = 63 \quad \ldots\text{(i)}$$

Also, the sum of binomial coefficients, is

$$^{2n+1}C_0 + {}^{2n+1}C_1 + \ldots + {}^{2n+1}C_n + {}^{2n+1}C_{n+1} + \ldots + {}^{2n+1}C_{n+1}$$

$$= (1+1)^{2n+1} = 2^{2n+1}$$

$$\Rightarrow \quad ^{2n+1}C_0 + 2({}^{2n+1}C_1 + {}^{2n+1}C_2 + \ldots + {}^{2n+1}C_n) + {}^{2n+1}C_{2n+1} = 2^{2n+1} \quad [\because {}^nC_r = C_{n-r}]$$

$$\Rightarrow \quad 1 + 2 \times 63 + 1 = 2^{2n+1} \Rightarrow 128 = 2^{2n+1}$$

$$\Rightarrow \quad 2^7 = 2^{2n+1} \Rightarrow 7 = 2n + 1$$

$$\therefore \quad n = 3$$

Example 68. There are three books of Physics, four of Chemistry and five of Mathematics. How many different collections can be made such that each collection consists of

(i) one book of each subject,

(ii) atleast one book of each subject,

(iii) atleast one book of Mathematics.

Sol. (i) $^3C_1 \times {}^4C_1 \times {}^5C_1 = 3 \times 4 \times 5 = 60$

(ii) $(2^3 - 1) \times (2^4 - 1) \times (2^5 - 1) = 7 \times 15 \times 31 = 3255$

(iii) $(2^5 - 1) \times 2^7 = 31 \times 128 = 3968$

5.13 Combinations from Identical Objects

(i) The number of combinations of n identical objects taking r objects $(r \le n)$ at a time $= 1$.

(ii) The number of combinations of zero or more objects from n identical objects $= n + 1$.

(iii) The total number of combinations of atleast one out of $a_1 + a_2 + a_3 + \ldots + a_n$ objects, where a_1 are alike of one kind, a_2 are alike of second kind, a_3 are alike of third kind, ..., a_n are alike of nth kind

$$= (a_1 + 1)(a_2 + 1)(a_3 + 1)\ldots(a_n + 1) - 1$$

Example 69. How many selections of atleast one red ball from a bag containing 4 red balls and 5 black balls, balls of the same colour being identical?

Sol. Number of selections of atleast one red ball from 4 identical red balls = 4

Number of selections of any number of black balls from 5 identical black balls = 5 + 1 = 6

$\therefore$ Required number of selections of balls $= 4 \times 6 = 24$

Example 70. There are p copies each of n different books. Find the number of ways in which a non-empty selection can be made from them.

Sol. Since, copies of the same book are identical.

$\therefore$ Number of selections of any number of copies of a book is $p + 1$. Similarly, in the case for each book.

Therefore, total number of selections is $(p + 1)^n$.

But this includes a selection, which is empty i.e., zero copy of each book. Excluding this, the required number of non-empty selections is $(p + 1)^n - 1$.

Example 71. There are 4 oranges, 5 apples and 6 mangoes in a fruit basket and all fruits of the same kind are identical. In how many ways can a person make a selection of fruits from among the fruits in the basket?

Sol. Zero or more oranges can be selected out of 4 identical oranges = 4 + 1 = 5 ways.

Similarly, for apples number of selection = 5 + 1 = 6 ways and mangoes can be selected in 6 + 1 = 7 ways.

$\therefore$ The total number of selections when all the three kinds of fruits are selected $= 5 \times 6 \times 7$

$$= 210$$

But in one of these selection number of each kind of fruit is zero and hence this selection must be excluded.

$\therefore$ Required number $= 210 - 1$

$$= 209$$

Combinations when both Identical and Distinct Objects are Present

The number of combinations (selections) of one or more objects out of $a_1 + a_2 + a_3 + \ldots + a_n$ objects, where a_1 are alike of one kind, a_2 are alike of second kind, a_3 are alike of third kind, ..., a_n are alike of nth kind and k are distinct.

$$= \{(a_1+1)(a_2+1)(a_3+1)\cdots(a_n+1)\}$$
$$({}^kC_0 + {}^kC_1 + {}^kC_2 + \ldots + {}^kC_k) - 1$$
$$= \{(a_1+1)(a_2+1)(a_3+1)\ \ldots\ (a_n+1)\}2^k - 1$$

Example 72. Find the number of ways in which one or more letters can be selected from the letters
AAAAA BBBB CCC DD EFG.

Sol. Here, $5A$'s are alike, $4\ B$'s are alike, $3\ C$'s are alike, $2D$'s are alike and E, F, G are different.

$\therefore$ Total number of combinations

$$= (5+1)(4+1)(3+1)(2+1)2^3 - 1$$
$$= 6 \cdot 5 \cdot 4 \cdot 3 \cdot 8 - 1 = 2879$$

[excluding the case, when no letter is selected]

Explanation Selection from $(AAAAA)$ can be made by 6 ways such include no A, include one A, include two A, include three A, include four A, include five A. Similarly, selections from $(BBBB)$ can be made in 5 ways, selections from (CCC) can be made in 4 ways, selections from (DD) can be made in 3 ways and from E, F, G can be made in $2 \times 2 \times 2$ ways.

Number of Divisors of *N*

Every natural number N can always be put in the form $N = p_1^{\alpha_1} \cdot p_2^{\alpha_2} \cdot p_3^{\alpha_3} \ldots p_k^{\alpha_k}$, where $p_1, p_2, p_3, \ldots, p_k$ are distinct primes and $\alpha_1, \alpha_2, \alpha_3, \ldots, \alpha_k \in W$.

(i) The total number of divisors of N including 1 and N
$= (\alpha_1+1)(\alpha_2+1)(\alpha_3+1)\ldots(\alpha_k+1)$

(ii) The total number of divisors of N excluding 1 and N
$= (\alpha_1+1)(\alpha_2+1)(\alpha_3+1)\ldots(\alpha_k+1) - 2$

(iii) The total number of divisors of N excluding either 1 or $N = (\alpha_1+1)(\alpha_2+1)(\alpha_3+1)\ldots(\alpha_k+1) - 1$

(iv) Sum of all divisors $= (p_1^0 + p_1^1 + p_1^2 + p_1^3 + \ldots + p_1^{\alpha_1})$
$(p_2^0 + p_2^1 + p_2^2 + p_2^3 + \ldots + p_2^{\alpha_2}) \ldots$
$(p_k^0 + p_k^1 + p_k^2 + p_k^3 + \ldots + p_k^{\alpha_k})$

$$= \left(\frac{1 - p_1^{\alpha_1+1}}{1 - p_1}\right) \cdot \left(\frac{1 - p_2^{\alpha_2+1}}{1 - p_2}\right) \ldots \left(\frac{1 - p_k^{\alpha_k+1}}{1 - p_k}\right)$$

(v) Sum of proper divisors (excluding 1 and the expression itself) = Sum of all divisors $-(N+1)$

(vi) The number of even divisors of N are possible only, if $p_1 = 2$, otherwise there is no even divisor.
$\therefore$ Required number of **even** divisors
$$= \alpha_1(\alpha_2+1)(\alpha_3+1) + \ldots + (\alpha_k+1)$$

(vii) The number of **odd** divisors of N

***Case* I** If $p_1 = 2$, the number of odd divisors
$$= (\alpha_2+1)(\alpha_3+1)\ldots(\alpha_k+1)$$

***Case* II** If $p_1 \neq 2$, the number of odd divisors
$$= (\alpha_1+1)(\alpha_2+1)(\alpha_3+1)\ldots(\alpha_k+1)$$

(viii) The number of ways in which N can be resolved as a product of two factors

$$= \begin{cases} \frac{1}{2}(\alpha_1+1)(\alpha_2+1)\ldots(\alpha_k+1), & \text{if } N \text{ is not a perfect square.} \\ \frac{1}{2}\{(\alpha_1+1)(\alpha_2+1)\ldots(\alpha_k+1)+1\}, & \text{if } N \text{ is a perfect square.} \end{cases}$$

(ix) The number of ways in which a composite number N can be resolved into two factors which are relatively prime (or coprime) to each other is equal to 2^{n-1}, where n is the number of different factors (or different primes) in N.

Example 73. Find the number of proper factors of the number 38808. Also, find sum of all these divisors.

Sol. The number $38808 = 2^3 \cdot 3^2 \cdot 7^2 \cdot 11$

Hence, the total number of proper factors (excluding 1 and itself i.e., 38808)

$$= (3+1)(2+1)(2+1)(1+1) - 2$$
$$= 72 - 2 = 70$$

And sum of all these divisors (proper)

$$= (2^0 + 2^1 + 2^2 + 2^3)(3^0 + 3^1 + 3^2)$$
$$(7^0 + 7^1 + 7^2)(11^0 + 11^1) - 1 - 38808$$
$$= (15)(13)(57)(12) - 38809$$
$$= 133380 - 38809$$
$$= 94571$$

Example 74. Find the number of even proper divisors of the number 1008.

Sol. $\because 1008 = 2^4 \times 3^2 \times 7^1$

$\therefore$ Required number of even proper divisors

= Total number of selections of atleast one 2 and any number of 3's or 7's.

$$= 4 \times (2+1) \times (1+1) - 1$$
$$= 23$$

Example 75. Find the number of odd proper divisors of the number 35700. Also, find sum of the odd proper divisors.

Sol. $\because 35700 = 2^2 \times 3^1 \times 5^2 \times 7^1 \times 17^1$

$\therefore$ Required number of odd proper divisors

= Total number of selections of zero 2 and any number of 3's or 5's or 7's or 17's

$= (1+1)(2+1)(1+1)(1+1) - 1 = 23$

$\therefore$ The sum of odd proper divisors

$= (3^0 + 3^1)(5^0 + 5^1 + 5^2)(7^0 + 7^1)(17^0 + 17^1) - 1$

$= 4 \times 31 \times 8 \times 18 - 1$

$= 17856 - 1$

$= 17855$

Example 76. If $N = 10800$, find

(i) the number of divisors of the form $4m + 2, \forall\, m \in W$.

(ii) the number of divisors which are multiple of 10.

(iii) the number of divisors which are multiple of 15.

Sol. We have, $N = 10800 = 2^4 \times 3^3 \times 5^2$

(i) $\because (4m+2) = 2(2m+1)$, in any divisor of the form $4m+2$, 2 should be exactly 1.

So, the number of divisors of the form

$(4m+2) = 1 \times (3+1) \times (2+1) = 1 \times 4 \times 3 = 12$

(ii) $\therefore$ The required number of proper divisors

= Total number of selections of atleast one 2 and one 5 from 2, 2, 2, 2, 3, 3, 3, 5, 5

$= 4 \times (3+1) \times 2 = 32$

(iii) $\therefore$ The required number of proper divisors

= Total number of selections of atleast one 3 and one 5 from 2, 2, 2, 2, 3, 3, 3, 5, 5

$= (4+1) \times 3 \times 2 = 30$

Example 77. Find the number of divisors of the number $N = 2^3 \cdot 3^5 \cdot 5^7 \cdot 7^9 \cdot 9^{11}$. Which are perfect square?

Sol. $\because N = 2^3 \cdot 3^5 \cdot 5^7 \cdot 7^9 \cdot 9^{11}$

$= 2^3 \cdot 3^5 \cdot 5^7 \cdot 7^9 \cdot 3^{22}$

$= 2^3 \cdot 3^{27} \cdot 5^7 \cdot 7^9$

For perfect square of N, each prime factor must occur even number of times.

2 can be taken in 2 ways (i.e., 2^0 or 2^2)

3 can be taken in 14 ways (i.e., 3^0 or 3^2 or 3^4 or 3^6 or 3^8 or 3^{10} or 3^{12} or 3^{14} or 3^{16} or 3^{18} or 3^{20} or 3^{22} or 3^{24} or 3^{26})

5 can taken in 4 ways (i.e., 5^0 or 5^2 or 5^4 or 5^6)

and 7 can taken in 5 ways

(i.e. 7^0 or 7^2 or 7^4 or 7^4 or 7^6 or 7^8)

Hence, total divisors which are perfect squares

$= 2 \times 14 \times 4 \times 5 = 560$

Example 78. In how many ways the number 10800 can be resolved as a product of two factors?

Sol. Let $N = 10800 = 2^4 \times 3^3 \times 5^2$

Here, N is not a perfect square [$\because$ power of 3 is odd]

Hence, the number of ways $= \frac{1}{2}(4+1)(3+1)(2+1) = 30$

Example 79. In how many ways the number 18900 can be split in two factors which are relatively prime (or coprime)?

Sol. Let $N = 18900 = 2^2 \cdot 3^3 \cdot 5^2 \cdot 7^1$

Relatively prime or coprime Two numbers not necessarily prime are said to be relatively prime or coprime, if their HCF (highest common factor) is one as 2, 3, 5, 7 are relatively prime numbers.

$\therefore \quad n = 4$ [number of different primes in N]

Hence, number of ways in which a composite number N can be resolved into two factors which are relatively prime or coprime $= 2^{4-1} = 2^3 = 8$

Division of Objects Into Groups

(a) Division of Objects Into Groups of Unequal Size

Theorem : Number of ways in which $(m+n)$ distinct objects can be divided into two unequal groups containing m and n objects is $\frac{(m+n)!}{m!\,n!}$.

Proof The number of ways in which $(m+n)$ distinct objects are divided into two groups of the size m and n

= The number of ways m objects are selected out of $(m+n)$ objects to form one of the group, which can be done in ${}^{m+n}C_m$ ways. The other group of n objects is formed by the remaining n objects.

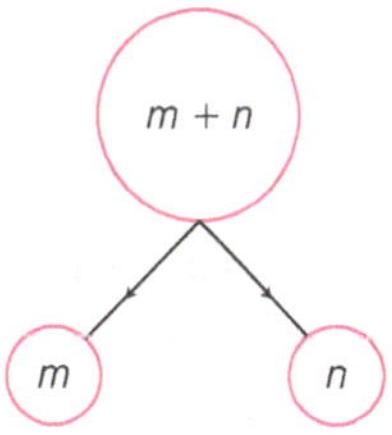

(Tree diagram)

$= {}^{m+n}C_m \cdot {}^nC_n = \frac{(m+n)}{m!\,n!}$

Corollary I The number of ways to distribute $(m+n)$ distinct objects among 2 persons in the groups containing m and n objects

= (Number of ways to divide) $\times$ (Number of groups)

$= \frac{(m+n)}{m!\,n!} \times 2!$

***Corollary* II** The number of ways in which $(m+n+p)$ distinct objects can be divided into three unequal groups containing m, n and p objects, is

$$^{m+n+p}C_m \cdot {}^{n+p}C_n \cdot {}^{p}C_p = \frac{(m+n+p)!}{m!\,n!\,p!}$$

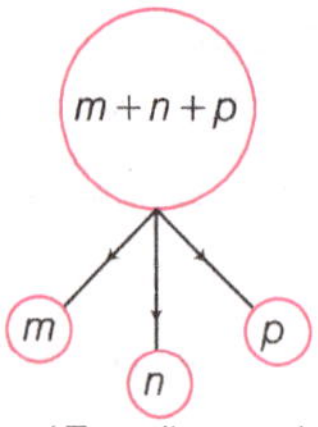

(Tree diagram)

***Corollary* III** The number of ways to distribute $(m+n+p)$ distinct objects among 3 persons in the groups containing m, n and p objects

= (Number of ways to divide) × (Number of groups)

$$= \frac{(m+n+p)!}{m!\,n!\,p!} \times 3!$$

***Corollary* IV** The number of ways in which $(x_1 + x_2 + x_3 + \cdots + x_n)$ distinct objects can be divided into n unequal groups containing x_1, $x_2, x_3, \ldots, x_n$ objects, is

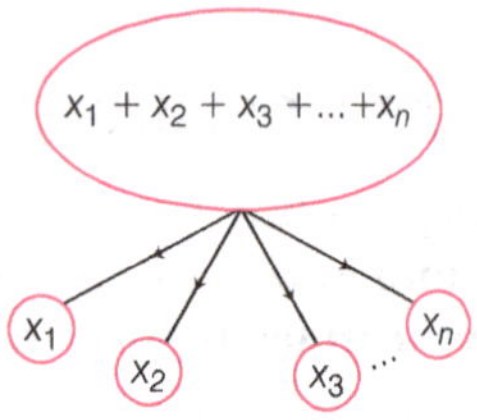

(Tree diagram)

$$\frac{(x_1 + x_2 + x_3 + \cdots + x_n)!}{x_1!\,x_2!\,x_3!\cdots x_n!}.$$

***Corollary* V** The number of ways to distribute $(x_1 + x_2 + x_3 + \ldots + x_n)$ distinct objects among n persons in the groups containing $x_1, x_2, \ldots, x_n$ objects

= (Number of ways to divide) × (Number of groups)

$$= \frac{(x_1 + x_2 + x_3 + \ldots + x_n)!}{x_1!\,x_2!\,x_3!\ldots x_n!} \times n!$$

(b) Division of Objects Into Groups of Equal Size

The number of ways in which mn distinct objects can be divided equally into m groups, each containing n objects and

(i) If order of groups is not important is

$$\left(\frac{(mn)!}{(n!)^m}\right) \times \frac{1}{m!}.$$

(ii) If order of groups is important is

$$\left(\frac{(mn)!}{(n!)^m} \times \frac{1}{m!}\right) \times m! = \frac{(mn)!}{(n!)^m}.$$

JEE SPIKE

Division of $14n$ objects into 6 groups of $2n, 2n, 2n, 2n, 3n, 3n$,

size is $\dfrac{\left(\dfrac{(14n)!}{(2n)!\,(2n)!\,(2n)!\,(2n)!\,(3n)!\,(3n)!}\right)}{4!\,2!}$

$$= \frac{(14n)}{((2n)!)^4\,((3n)!)^2} \times \frac{1}{4!\,2!}$$

Concept Inside Video

Now, the distribution ways of these 6 groups among 6 persons is

$$\frac{(14n)!}{[(2n)!)]^4\,[(3n)!]^2} \times \frac{1}{4!\,2!} \times 6! = \frac{(14n)!}{[(2n)!]^4\,[(3n)!]^2} \times 15$$

Example 80. In how many ways can a pack of 52 cards be

(i) distributed equally among four players in order?

(ii) divided into four groups of 13 cards each?

(iii) divided into four sets, three of them having 17 cards each and fourth just one card?

Sol. (i) Here, order of group is important, then the numbers of ways in which 52 different cards can be divided equally into 4 players is $\dfrac{52!}{4!\,(13!)^4} \times 4! = \dfrac{52!}{(13!)^4}$.

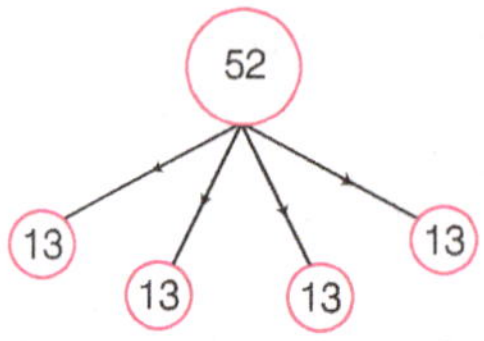

(Tree diagram)

(ii) Here, order of group is not important, then the number of ways in which 52 different cards can be divided equally into 4 groups is $\dfrac{52!}{4!\,(13!)^4}$.

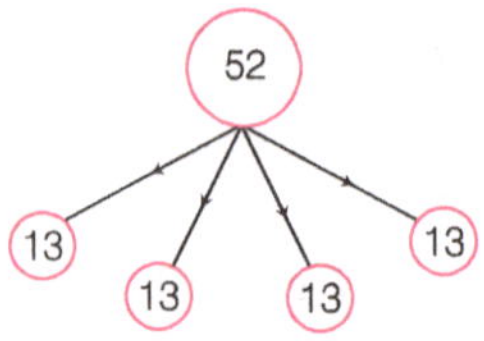

(Tree diagram)

(iii) First, we divide 52 cards into two sets which contains 1 and 51 cards respectively, is $\dfrac{52!}{1!\,51!}$.

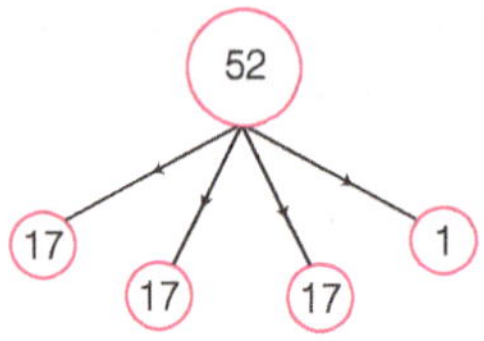

Now, 51 cards can be divided equally in three sets each contains 17 cards (here order of sets is not important) in $\dfrac{51!}{3!\,(17!)^3}$ ways.

Hence, the required number of ways

$$= \frac{52!}{1!\,51!} \times \frac{51!}{3!(17!)^3}$$

$$= \frac{52!}{1!\,3!(17!)^3}$$

$$= \frac{52!}{(17!)^3\,3!}$$

Example 81. In how many ways can 12 different balls be divided between 2 boys, one receiving 5 and the other 7 balls? Also, in how many ways can these 12 balls be divided into groups of 5, 4 and 3 balls, respectively?

Sol. I Part Here, order is important, then the number of ways in which 12 different balls can be divided between two boys which contains 5 and 7 balls respectively, is

$$= \frac{12!}{5!\,7!} \times 2!$$

$$= \frac{12 \cdot 11 \cdot 10 \cdot 9 \cdot 8 \cdot 7!}{(5 \cdot 4 \cdot 3 \cdot 2 \cdot 1)7!} \cdot 2$$

$$= 1584$$

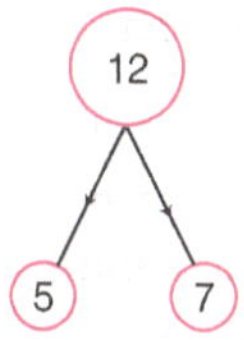

(Tree diagram)

Alternate Solution

First boy can be given 5 balls out of 12 balls in ${}^{12}C_5$. Second boy can be given 7 balls out of 7 balls (i.e., $12 - 5 = 7$) but there order is important boys interchange by (2 types), then required number of ways

$$= {}^{12}C_5 \times {}^{7}C_7 \times 2!$$

$$= \frac{12!}{5!\,7!} \times 1 \times 2!$$

$$= \frac{12! \times 2}{5! \times 7!} = \frac{12 \cdot 11 \cdot 10 \cdot 9 \cdot 8 \cdot 7! \cdot 2}{5 \cdot 4 \cdot 3 \cdot 2 \cdot 1 \cdot 7!}$$

$$= 1584$$

II Part Here, order is not important, then the number of ways in which 12 different balls can be divided into three groups of 5,4 and 3 balls respectively, is

$$= \frac{12!}{5!\,4!\,3!} = \frac{12 \cdot 11 \cdot 10 \cdot 9 \cdot 8 \cdot 7 \cdot 6 \cdot 5!}{5! \cdot 4 \cdot 3 \cdot 2 \cdot 1 \cdot 3 \cdot 2 \cdot 1}$$

$$= 27720$$

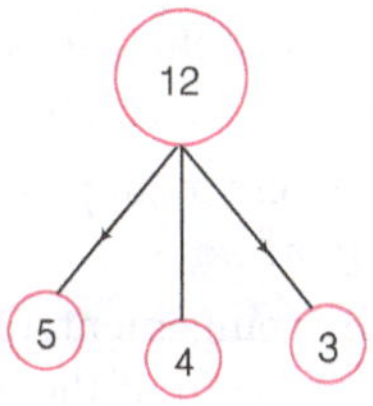

(Tree diagram)

Example 82. In how many ways can 16 different books be distributed among three students A, B, C so that B gets 1 more than A and C get 2 more than B?

Sol. Let A gets n books, then B gets $n + 1$ and C gets $n + 3$.

Now, $n + (n + 1) + (n + 3) = 16$

$\Rightarrow \quad 3n = 12$

$\therefore \quad n = 4$

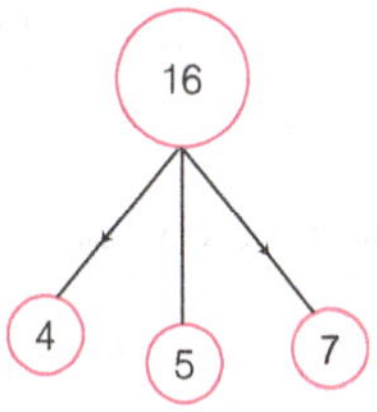

(Tree diagram)

$\Rightarrow$ A, B, C gets 4, 5 and 7 books, respectively.

Hence, the total number of ways for the required distribution $= \dfrac{16!}{4!\,5!\,7!}$

5.14 Arrangement in Groups

(a) The number of ways in which n different things can be arranged into r different groups is

$$r(r+1)(r+2)\ldots(r+n-1) \text{ or } n!\cdot{}^{n-1}C_{r-1}$$

according as blank groups are or are not admissible.

Proof

(i) Let n letters $a_1, a_2, a_3, \ldots, a_n$ be written in a row in any order. All the arrangements of the letters in r groups, blank groups being admissible, can be obtained thus, place among the letters $(r - 1)$ marks of partition and arrange the $(n + r - 1)$ things (consisting of letters and marks) in all possible orders.

Since, $(r - 1)$ of the things are alike, the number of different arrangements is

$$\frac{(n+r-1)!}{(r-1)!} = r(r+1)(r-2)\ldots(r+n-1).$$

(ii) All the arrangements of the letters in r groups, none of the groups being blank, can be obtained as follows:

(I) Arrange the letters in all possible orders. This can be done in $n!$ ways.

(II) In every such arrangement, place $(r-1)$ marks of partition in $(r-1)$ out of the $(n-1)$ spaces between the letters. This can be done in ${}^{n-1}C_{r-1}$ ways.

Hence, the required number is $n! \cdot {}^{n-1}C_{r-1}$.

Example 83. In how many ways 5 different balls can be arranged into 3 different boxes so that no box remains empty?

Sol. The required number of ways $= 5! \cdot {}^{5-1}C_{3-1} = 5! \cdot {}^4C_2$

$$= (120) \cdot \left(\frac{4 \cdot 3}{1 \cdot 2}\right) = 720$$

Alternate Solution

Each box must contain atleast one ball, since no box remains empty. Boxes can have balls in the following systems :

Box	I	II	III
Number of balls	1	1	3

Or

Box	I	II	III
Number of balls	1	2	2

All 5 balls can be arranged by 5! ways and boxes can be arranged in each system by $\frac{3!}{2!}$.

Hence, required number of ways $= 5! \times \frac{3!}{2!} + 5! \times \frac{3!}{2!}$

$= 120 \times 3 + 120 \times 3 = 720$

(b) The number of ways in which n different things can be distributed into r different groups is

$$r^n - {}^rC_1(r-1)^n + {}^rC_2(r-2)^n - \ldots + (-1)^{r-1} \cdot {}^rC_{r-1}$$

Or

$$\sum_{p=0}^{r} (-1)^p \cdot {}^rC_p \cdot (r-p)^n$$

Or

Coefficient of x^n in $n!(e^x - 1)^r$.

Here, blank groups are not allowed.

Proof In any distribution, denote the groups by $g_1, g_2, g_3, \ldots, g_r$ and consider the distributions in which blanks are allowed.

The total number of these is r^n.

The number in which g_1 is blank, is $(r-1)^n$.

Therefore, the number in which g_1 is not blank, is

$$r^n - (r-1)^n$$

of these last, the number in which g_2 is blank, is

$$(r-1)^n - (r-2)^n$$

Therefore, the number in which g_1, g_2 are not blank, is

$$r^n - 2(r-1)^n + (r-2)^n$$

of these last, the number in which g_3 is blank, is

$$(r-1)^n - 2(r-2)^n + (r-3)^n$$

Therefore, the number in which g_1, g_2, g_3 are not blank, is

$$r^n - 3(r-1)^n + 3(r-2)^n - (r-3)^n$$

This process can be continued as far as we like and it is obvious that the coefficients are formed as in a binomial expansion.

Hence, the number of distributions in which no one of x assigned groups is blank, is

$$r^n - {}^xC_1(r-1)^n + {}^xC_2(r-2)^n - \ldots + (-1)^x(r-x)^n$$

when $x = r$, then

$$r^n - {}^rC_1(r-1)^n + {}^rC_2(r-2)^n - \ldots + (-1)^{r-1} \cdot {}^rC_{r-1}$$
$$(r-(r-1))^n + (-1)^r \cdot {}^rC_r(r-r)^n$$

Or

$$r^n - {}^rC_1(r-1)^n + {}^rC_2(r-2)^n - \ldots + (-1)^{r-1} \cdot {}^rC_{r-1}$$

Alternate method

By Principle of Inclusion and Exclusion

Let A_i denotes the set of distribution of things, if ith group gets nothing. Then, $n(A_i) = (r-1)^n$

[as n things can be distributed among $(r-1)$ groups in $(r-1)^n$ ways]

Then, $n(A_i \cap A_j)$ represents number of distribution ways in which groups i and j get no object. Then, $n(A_i \cap A_j) = (r-2)^n$

Also, $\quad n(A_i \cap A_j \cap A_k) = (r-3)^n$

This process can be continued, then the required number is

$$n(A_1' A_2' \cap \ldots \cap A_r')$$
$$= n(U) - n(A_1 \cup A_2 \cup \ldots \cup A_r)$$
$$= r^n - \left\{\sum n(A_i) - \sum n(A_i \cap A_j) + \sum n(A_i \cap A_j \cap A_k) \ldots + (-1)^n \sum n(A_1 \cap A_2 \cap \ldots \cap A_r)\right\}$$
$$= r^n - \{{}^rC_1(r-1)^n - {}^rC_2(r-2)^n + {}^rC_3(r-3)^n - \ldots + (-1)^r \cdot {}^rC_{r-1}\}$$
$$= r^n - {}^rC_1(r-1)^n + {}^rC_2(r-2)^n - {}^rC_3(r-3)^n + \ldots + (-1)^{r-1} \cdot {}^rC_{r-1} \cdot 1$$

Note Coefficient of x^r in $e^{px} = \frac{p^r}{r!}$.

Example 84. In how many ways 5 different balls can be distributed into 3 boxes so that no box remains empty?

Sol. The required number of ways

$$= 3^5 - {}^3C_1(3-1)^5 + {}^3C_2(3-2)^5 - {}^3C_3(3-3)^5$$
$$= 243 - 96 + 3 - 0$$
$$= 150$$

Or

Coefficient of x^5 in $5!(e^x - 1)^3$

$$= \text{Coefficient of } x^5 \text{ in } 5!(e^{3x} - 3e^{2x} + 3e^x - 1)$$
$$= 5!\left(\frac{3^5}{5!} - 3 \times \frac{2^5}{5!} + 3 \times \frac{1}{5!}\right)$$
$$= 3^5 - 3 \cdot 2^5 + 3$$
$$= 243 - 96 + 3$$
$$= 150$$

Example 85. In how many ways can 5 different books be tied up in three bundles?

Sol. The required number of ways $= \frac{1}{3!}(3^5 - {}^3C_1 \cdot 2^5 + {}^3C_2 \cdot 1^5)$

$$= \frac{150}{6}$$
$$= 25$$

Example 86. If $n(A) = 5$ and $n(B) = 3$, find number of onto mappings from A to B.

Sol. We know that in onto mapping, each image must be assigned atleast one pre-image.

This is equivalent to number of ways in which 5 different balls (pre-images) can be distributed in 3 different boxes (images), if no box remains empty. The total number of onto mappings from A to B

$$= 3^5 - {}^3C_1(3-1)^5 + {}^3C_2(3-2)^5$$
$$= 243 - 96 + 3 = 150$$

(c) The number of ways in which n identical things can be distributed into r different groups is

$$^{n+r-1}C_{r-1} \text{ or } {}^{n-1}C_{r-1}$$

According, as blank groups are or are not admissible.

Proof

If blank groups are not allowed Any such distribution can be effected as follows:

Place the n things in a row and put marks of partition in a selection of $(r-1)$ out of the $(n-1)$ spaces between them. This can be done in $^{n-1}C_{r-1}$.

If blank groups are allowed The number of distribution is the same as that of $(n+r)$ things of the same sort into r groups with no blank groups. For such a distribution can be effected thus, put one of the $(n+r)$ things into each of the r groups and distribute the remaining n things into r groups, blank lots being allowed. Hence, the required number is $^{n+r-1}C_{r-1}$.

Alternate method

The number of distribution of n identical things into r different groups is the coefficient of x^n in $(1 + x + x^2 + \ldots + \infty)^r$ or in $(x + x^2 + x^3 + \ldots + \infty)^r$ according as blank groups are or are not allowed.

These expressions are respectively equal to $(1-x)^{-r}$ and $x^r(1-x)^{-r}$

Hence, coefficient of x^n in two expressions are $^{n+r-1}C_{r-1}$ and $^{n-1}C_{r-1}$, respectively.

Example 87. In how many ways 5 identical balls can be distributed into 3 different boxes so that no box remains empty?

Sol. The required number of ways $= {}^{5-1}C_{3-1}$

$$= {}^4C_2 = \frac{4 \cdot 3}{1 \cdot 2} = 6$$

Alternate Solution

Each box must contain atleast one ball, since no box remains empty. Boxes can have balls in the following systems.

Box	I	II	III
Number of balls	1	1	3

Or

Box	I	II	III
Number of balls	1	2	2

Here, balls are identical but boxes are different the number of combinations will be 1 in each systems.

$\therefore$ Required number of ways $= 1 \times \frac{3!}{2!} + 1 \times \frac{3!}{2!}$

$$= 3 + 3$$
$$= 6$$

Example 88. Four boys picked up 30 mangoes. In how many ways can they divide them, if all mangoes be identical?

Sol. Clearly, 30 mangoes can be distributed among 4 boys such that each boy can receive any number of mangoes.

Hence, total number of ways $= {}^{30+4-1}C_{4-1}$

$$= {}^{33}C_3$$
$$= \frac{33 \cdot 32 \cdot 31}{1 \cdot 2 \cdot 3}$$
$$= 5456$$

Example 89. Find the positive number of solutions of $x+y+z+w=20$ under the following conditions.

(i) Zero value of x, y, z and w are included.

(ii) Zero values are excluded.

Sol. (i) Since, $x+y+z+w=20$

Here, $x \geq 0, y \geq 0, z \geq 0, w \geq 0$

The number of solutions of the given equation in this case is same as the number of ways of distributing 20 things among 4 different groups.

Hence, total number of solutions $= {}^{20+4-1}C_{4-1}$

$$= {}^{23}C_3 = \frac{23 \cdot 22 \cdot 21}{1 \cdot 2 \cdot 3} = 1771$$

(ii) Since, $x+y+z+w=20$ ...(i)

Here, $x \geq 1, y \geq 1, z \geq 1, w \geq 1$

or $x-1 \geq 0, y-1 \geq 0, z-1 \geq 0, w-1 \geq 0$

Let $x_1 = x-1 \Rightarrow x = x_1+1$

$y_1 = y-1 \Rightarrow y = y_1+1$

$z_1 = z-1 \Rightarrow z = z_1+1$

$w_1 = w-1 \Rightarrow w = w_1+1$

Then, from Eq. (i), we get

$$x_1+1+y_1+1+z_1+1+w_1+1=20$$

$\Rightarrow$ $x_1+y_1+z_1+w_1=16$

and $x_1 \geq 0, y_1 \geq 0, z_1 \geq 0, w_1 \geq 0$

Hence, total number of solutions $= {}^{16+4-1}C_{4-1}$

$$= {}^{19}C_3 = \frac{19 \cdot 18 \cdot 17}{1 \cdot 2 \cdot 3} = 57 \cdot 17 = 969$$

JEE SCANNER

Example Similar to PYQ Asked in JEE Main 2023

The number of integral solutions are there to $x+y+z+t=29$, when $x \geq 1, y > 1, z \geq 3$ and $t \geq 0$ is ......

Sol. (2600) Since, $x+y+z+t=29$ ...(i)

and x, y, z, t are integers.

$\therefore$ $x \geq 1, y \geq 2, z \geq 3, t \geq 0$

$\Rightarrow$ $x-1 \geq 0, y-2 \geq 0, z-3 \geq 0, t \geq 0$

Let $x_1 = x-1, x_2 = y-2, x_3 = z-3$

or $x = x_1+1, y = x_2+2, z = x_3+3$ and then $x_1 \geq 0, x_2 \geq 0, x_3 \geq 0, t \geq 0$.

From Eq. (i), we get

$x_1+1+x_2+2+x_3+3+t=29 \Rightarrow x_1+x_2+x_3+t=23$

Hence, total number of solutions $= {}^{23+4-1}C_{4-1}$

$$= {}^{26}C_3 = \frac{26 \cdot 25 \cdot 24}{1 \cdot 2 \cdot 3} = 2600$$

Skill Builder

The number of integral solutions are there to the system of equations $x_1+x_2+x_3+x_4+x_5=20$ and $x_1+x_2=15$, when $x_k \geq 0$ is ....

For Sol.

■ **For more practice** See Q.9 of Milestone Practice 5.3.

Example 90. Find the number of non-negative integral solutions of $3x+y+z=24$.

Sol. We have, $3x+y+z=24$ and given $x \geq 0, y \geq 0, z \geq 0$

Let $x = k$

$\therefore$ $y+z=24-3k$ ...(i)

Here, $24 \geq 24-3k \geq 0$ $[\because x \geq 0]$

Hence, $0 \leq k \leq 8$

The total number of integral solutions of Eq. (i) is

$${}^{24-3k+2-1}C_{2-1} = {}^{25-3k}C_1 = 25-3k$$

Hence, the total number of solutions of the original equation

$$= \sum_{k=0}^{8}(25-3k) = 25\sum_{k=0}^{8}1 - 3\sum_{k=0}^{8}k$$

$$= 25 \cdot 9 - 3 \cdot \frac{8 \cdot 9}{2} = 225 - 108 = 117$$

(d) The number of ways in which n identical things can be distributed into r groups so that no group contains less than l things and more than m things $(l < m)$ is coefficient of x^{n-lr} in the expansion of $(1-x^{m-l+1})^r(1-x)^{-r}$.

Proof Required number of ways

= Coefficient of x^n in the expansion of

$$(x^l + x^{l+1} + x^{l+2} + \ldots + x^m)^r$$

[$\because$ no group contains less than l things and more than m things, here r groups]

= Coefficient of x^n in the expansion of

$$x^{lr}(1+x+x^2+\ldots+x^{m-l})^r$$

= Coefficient of x^{n-lr} in the expansion of

$$(1+x+x^2+\ldots+x^{m-l})^r$$

= Coefficient of x^{n-lr} in the expansion of

$$\left(\frac{1 \cdot (1-x^{m-l+1})}{(1-x)}\right)^r$$

[sum of $m-l+1$ terms of GP]

= Coefficient of x^{n-lr} in the expansion of

$$(1-x^{m-l+1})^r(1-x)^{-r}$$

Example 91. In how many ways can three persons, each throwing a single dice once, make a sum of 15 ?

Sol. Number on the faces of the dice are 1, 2, 3, 4, 5, 6 (least number 1, greatest number 6)

Here, $l=1, m=6, r=3$ and $n=15$

$\therefore$ Required number of ways = Coefficient of $x^{15-1\times3}$ in the expansion of $(1-x^6)^3(1-x)^{-3}$.

= Coefficient of x^{12} in the expansion of

$$(1-3x^6+3x^{12})(1+{}^3C_1x+{}^4C_2x^2+\ldots+{}^8C_6x^6+\ldots+{}^{14}C_{12}x^{12}+\ldots)$$

$$= {}^{14}C_{12} - 3 \times {}^8C_6 + 3 = {}^{14}C_2 - 3 \times {}^8C_2 + 3$$

$$= 91 - 84 + 3 = 10$$

Example 92. In how many ways in which an examiner can assign 30 marks to 8 questions, giving not less than 2 marks to any question?

Sol. If examiner given marks any seven questions 2 (each) marks, then marks on remaining questions given by examiner $= -7 \times 2 + 30 = 16$

If x_i are the marks assigned to ith question, then $x_1 + x_2 + x_3 + \ldots + x_8 = 30$ and $2 \le x_i \le 16$ for $i = 1, 2, 3, \ldots, 8$.

Here, $l = 2, m = 16, r = 8$ and $n = 30$

$\therefore$ Required number of ways

$= $ Coefficient of $x^{30 - 2\times 8}$ in the expansion of $(1 - x^{16-2+1})^8(1-x)^{-8}$

$= $ Coefficient of x^{14} in the expansion of $(1 - x^{15})^8(1 + {}^8C_1 x + {}^9C_2 x^2 + \ldots + {}^{21}C_{14} x^{14} + \ldots)$

$= $ Coefficient of x^{14} in the expansion of $(1 + {}^8C_1 x + {}^9C_2 x^2 + \ldots + {}^{21}C_{14} x^{14} + \ldots)$

$= {}^{21}C_{14} = {}^{21}C_7$

JEE SPIKE

Coefficient of x^r in the expansion of $(1 - x)^{-n}$ is ${}^{n+r-1}C_r$.

(e) If a group has n things in which p are identical, then the number of ways of selecting r things from a group is

$$\sum_{r=0}^{r} {}^{n-p}C_r \text{ or } \sum_{r=r-p}^{r} {}^{n-p}C_r, \text{according as } r \le p \text{ or } r \ge p.$$

Example 93. A bag has contains 23 balls in which 7 are identical. Then, find the number of ways of selecting 12 balls from bag.

Sol. Here, $n = 23, p = 7, r = 12 \quad (r > p)$

$\therefore$ Required number of selections $= \sum_{r=5}^{12} {}^{16}C_r$

$$= {}^{16}C_5 + {}^{16}C_6 + {}^{16}C_7 + {}^{16}C_8 + {}^{16}C_9 + {}^{16}C_{10} + {}^{16}C_{11} + {}^{16}C_{12}$$

$$= ({}^{16}C_5 + {}^{16}C_6) + ({}^{16}C_7 + {}^{16}C_8) + ({}^{16}C_9 + {}^{16}C_{10}) + ({}^{16}C_{11} + {}^{16}C_{12})$$

$$= {}^{17}C_6 + {}^{17}C_8 + {}^{17}C_{10} + {}^{17}C_{12} \quad [\because {}^nC_r + {}^nC_{r-1} = {}^{n+1}C_r]$$

$$= {}^{17}C_{11} + {}^{17}C_9 + {}^{17}C_{10} + {}^{17}C_{12} \quad [\because {}^nC_r = {}^nC_{n-r}]$$

$$= ({}^{17}C_{11} + {}^{17}C_{12}) + ({}^{17}C_9 + {}^{17}C_{10})$$

$$= {}^{18}C_{12} + {}^{18}C_{10} = {}^{18}C_6 + {}^{18}C_8$$

Derangements Any change in the order of the things in a group is called a derangement.

Or

When 'n' things are to be placed at 'n' specific places but none of them is placed on its specified position, then we say that the 'n' things are deranged.

Or

Assume $a_1, a_2, a_3, \ldots, a_n$ be n distinct things, such that their positions are fixed in a row. If we now rearrange $a_1, a_2, a_3, \ldots, a_n$ in such a way that no one occupy its original position, then such an arrangement is called a derangement.

Consider 'n' letters and 'n' corresponding envelops. The number of ways in which letters can be placed in the envelopes (one letter in each envelope) so that no letter is placed in correct envelope is

$$n!\left(1 - \frac{1}{1!} + \frac{1}{2!} - \frac{1}{3!} + \ldots + (-1)^n \frac{1}{n!}\right)$$

Proof n letters are denoted by 1, 2, 3, ..., n. Let A_i denote the set of distribution of letters in envelopes (one letter in each envelop) so that the i th letter is placed in the corresponding envelope, then

$$n(A_i) = 1 \times (n-1)!$$

[$\because$ the remaining $(n-1)$ letters can be placed in $(n-1)$ envelopes is $(n-1)!$]

and $n(A_i \cap A_j) = 1 \times 1 \times (n-2)!$ [$\because$ i and j can be placed in their corresponding envelopes and remaining $(n-2)$ letters can be placed in $(n-2)$ envelopes in $(n-2)!$ way]

Also, $n(A_i \cap A_j \cap A_k) = 1 \times 1 \times 1 \times (n-3)!$

Hence, the required number is

$$n(A_1' \cap A_2' \cap A_3' \cap \ldots \cap A_n')$$

$$= n(U) - n(A_1 \cup A_2 \cup A_3 \cup \ldots \cup A_n)$$

$$= n! - \{\sum n(A_i) - \sum n(A_i \cap A_j) + \sum n(A_i \cap A_j \cap A_k) - \ldots + (-1)^n \sum n(A_1 \cap A_2 \cap A_3 \cap \ldots \cap A_n)$$

$$= n! - \{{}^nC_1 \times (n-1)! - {}^nC_2 \times (n-2)! + {}^nC_3 \times (n-3)! - \ldots + (-1)^{n-1} \times {}^nC_n \times 1!\}$$

$$= n! - \left\{\frac{n \times (n-1)!}{1!} - \frac{n(n-1)}{2!} \times (n-2)! + \frac{n(n-1)(n-2)}{3!} \times (n-3)! - \ldots + (-1)^{n-1} \times 1\right\}$$

$$= n! - \left\{\frac{n!}{1!} - \frac{n!}{2!} + \frac{n!}{3!} - \ldots + (-1)^n \cdot 1\right\}$$

$$= n!\left[1 - \frac{1}{1!} + \frac{1}{2!} - \frac{1}{3!} + \ldots + \frac{(-1)^n}{n!}\right]$$

Maha Short-cut Method

If $$D_n = n!\left[1 - \frac{1}{1!} + \frac{1}{2!} - \frac{1}{3!} + \ldots + \frac{(-1)^n}{n!}\right]$$

Then, $\boldsymbol{D_{n+1} = (n+1)D_n + (-1)^{n+1}, \forall\, x \in N}$

and $\boldsymbol{D_{n+1} = n(D_n + D_{n-1}), \forall\, x \in N - \{1\}}$

where, $D_1 = 0$

For $n = 1$, from result I

$$D_2 = 2D_1 + (-1)^2 = 0 + 1 = 1$$

For $n = 2$, from result I

$$D_3 = 3D_2 + (-1)^3 = 3 \times 1 - 1 = 2$$

For $n = 3$, from result I

$$D_4 = 4D_3 + (-1)^4 = 4 \times 2 + 1 = 9$$

For $n = 4$, from result I

$$D_5 = 5D_4 + (-1)^5 = 5 \times 9 - 1 = 44$$

For $n = 5$, from result I

$$D_6 = 6D_5 + (-1)^6 = 6 \times 44 + 1 = 265$$

Note $D_1 = 0, D_2 = 1, D_3 = 2, D_4 = 9, D_5 = 44, D_6 = 265$ [Remember]

JEE SPIKE

If r things go to wrong place out of n things, then $(n - r)$ things go to original place (here $r < n$).

If D_n = Number of ways, if all n things go to wrong places and D_r = Number of ways, if r things go to wrong places.

If r goes to wrong places out of n, then $(n - r)$ go to correct places.

Then, $D_n = {}^nC_{n-r}\, D_r$,

where $D_r = r!\left(1 - \frac{1}{1!} + \frac{1}{2!} - \frac{1}{3!} + \ldots + (-1)^r \frac{1}{r!}\right)$

Concept Inside Video

If atleast p things go to wrong places, then $D_n = \sum_{r=p}^{n} {}^nC_{n-r} \cdot D_r$

Example 94. A person writes letters to six friends and addresses the corresponding envelopes. In how many ways can the letters be placed in the envelopes so that

(i) atleast two of them are in the wrong envelopes?

(ii) all the letters are in the wrong envelopes?

Sol. (i) The number of ways in which atleast two of them in the wrong envelopes

$$= \sum_{r=2}^{6} {}^6C_{6-r} \cdot D_r$$

$$= {}^6C_4 \times D_2 + {}^6C_3 \times D_3 + {}^6C_2 \times D_4 + {}^6C_1 \times D_5 + {}^6C_0 \times D_6$$

$$= 15D_2 + 20D_3 + 15D_4 + 6D_5 + D_6 \quad \text{[from note]}$$

$$= 15 \times 1 + 20 \times 2 + 15 \times 9 + 6 \times 44 + 265 = 719$$

(ii) The number of ways in which all letters be placed in wrong envelopes $= D_6 = 265$ [from note]

5.15 Multinomial Theorem

(i) If there are l objects of one kind, m objects of second kind, n objects of third kind and so on, then the number of ways of choosing r objects out of these objects (i.e. $l + m + n + \ldots$) is the coefficient of x^r in the expansion of

$$(1 + x + x^2 + x^3 + \ldots + x^l)(1 + x + x^2 + \ldots + x^m)(1 + x + x^2 + \ldots + x^n)$$

Further, if one object of each kind is to be included, then the number of ways of choosing r objects out of these objects (i.e. $l + m + n + \ldots$) is the coefficient of x^r in the expansion of

$$(x + x^2 + x^3 + \ldots + x^l)(x + x^2 + x^3 + \ldots + x^m)(x + x^2 + x^3 + \ldots + x^n)\ldots$$

(ii) If there are l objects of one kind, m objects of second kind, n objects of third kind and so on, then the number of possible arrangements/permutations of r objects out of these objects (i.e. $l + m + n + \ldots$) is the coefficient of x^r in the expansion of

$$r!\left(1 + \frac{x}{1!} + \frac{x^2}{2!} + \ldots + \frac{x^l}{l!}\right)\left(1 + \frac{x}{1!} + \frac{x^2}{2!} + \ldots + \frac{x^m}{m!}\right)\left(1 + \frac{x}{1!} + \frac{x^2}{2!} + \ldots + \frac{x^n}{n!}\right)\ldots$$

Different Cases of Multinomial Theorem

***Case* I If upper limit of a variable is more than or equal to the sum required, then the upper limit of that variable can be taken as infinite.**

Example 95. In how many ways the sum of upper faces of four distinct die can be five?

Sol. Here, the number of required ways will be equal to the number of solutions of $x_1 + x_2 + x_3 + x_4 = 5$ i.e., $1 \le x_i \le 6$ for $i = 1, 2, 3, 4$.

Since, upper limit is 6, which is greater than required sum, so upper limit taken as infiite. So, number of solutions is equal to coefficient of α^5 in the expansion of

$$(1 + \alpha + \alpha^2 + \ldots + \infty)^4$$

$$= \text{Coefficient of } \alpha^5 \text{ in the expansion of } (1 - \alpha)^{-4}$$

$$= \text{Coefficient of } \alpha^5 \text{ in the expansion of } (1 + {}^4C_1\alpha + {}^5C_2\alpha^2 + \ldots)$$

$$= {}^8C_5 = {}^8C_3 = \frac{8 \cdot 7 \cdot 6}{1 \cdot 2 \cdot 3} = 56$$

***Case* II If the upper limit of a variable is less than the sum required and the lower limit of all variables is non-negative, then the upper limit of that variable is that given in the problem.**

Example 96. In an examination, the maximum marks each of three papers is 50 and the maximum marks for the fourth paper is 100. Find the number of ways in which the candidate can score 60% marks in aggregate.

Sol. Aggregate of marks = $50 \times 3 + 100 = 250$

$\therefore$ 60% of the aggregate $= \frac{60}{100} \times 250 = 150$

Let the marks scored by the candidate in four papers be x_1, x_2, x_3 and x_4. Here, the number of required ways will be equal to the number of solutions of $x_1 + x_2 + x_3 + x_4 = 150$ i.e. $0 \le x_1, x_2, x_3 \le 50$ and $0 \le x_4 \le 100$.

Since, the upper limit is 100 < required sum (150).

The number of solutions of the equation is equal to coefficient of α^{150} in the expansion of

$(\alpha^0 + \alpha^1 + \alpha^2 + \ldots + \alpha^{50})^3 (\alpha^0 + \alpha^1 + \alpha^2 + \ldots + \alpha^{100})$

= Coefficient of α^{150} in the expansion of

$$(1 - \alpha^{51})^3 (1 - \alpha^{101})(1 - \alpha)^{-4}$$

= Coefficient of α^{150} in the expansion of

$$(1 - 3\alpha^{51} + 3\alpha^{102})(1 - \alpha^{101})(1 + {}^4C_1\alpha + {}^5C_2\alpha^2 + \ldots + \infty)$$

= Coefficient of α^{150} in the expansion of

$$(1 - 3\alpha^{51} - \alpha^{101} + 3\alpha^{102})(1 + {}^4C_1\alpha + {}^5C_2\alpha^2 + \ldots + \infty)$$

$= {}^{153}C_{150} - 3 \times {}^{102}C_{99} - {}^{52}C_{49} + 3 \times {}^{51}C_{48}$

$= {}^{153}C_3 - 3 \times {}^{102}C_3 - {}^{52}C_3 + 3 \times {}^{51}C_3 = 110551$

Very Important Trick

On multiplying $p_0 + p_1\alpha + p_2\alpha^2 + p_3\alpha^3 + \ldots + p_n\alpha^n$ by $(1 + \alpha)$, we get

$$p_0 + (p_0 + p_1)\alpha + (p_1 + p_2)\alpha^2 + (p_2 + p_3)\alpha^3 + \ldots + (p_{n-2} + p_{n-1})\alpha^{n-1} + (p_{n-1} + p_n)\alpha^n + p_n\alpha^{n+1}$$

i.e. we just add coefficient of α^r with coefficient of α^{r-1} (i.e. previous term) to get coefficient α^r in product.

Now, coefficient of $\alpha^r = p_{r-1} + p_r$

On multiplying $p_0 + p_1\alpha + p_2\alpha^2 + p_3\alpha^3 + \ldots + p_n\alpha^n$ by $(1 + \alpha + \alpha^2)$, we get

$$p_0 + (p_0 + p_1)\alpha + (p_0 + p_1 + p_2)\alpha^2 + (p_1 + p_2 + p_3)\alpha^3 + (p_2 + p_3 + p_4)\alpha^4 + \ldots$$

i.e. to find coefficient of α^r in product and add this with 2 preceding coefficients.

Now, coefficient of $\alpha^r = p_{r-2} + p_{r-1} + p_r$

Similarly, in product of $p_0 + p_1\alpha + p_2\alpha^2 + \ldots$ with $(1 + \alpha + \alpha^2 + \alpha^3)$, the coefficient of α^r in product will be

$$\underbrace{p_{r-3} + p_{r-2} + p_{r-1}}_{\text{3 preceding coefficients}} + p_r$$

and in product of $p_0 + p_1\alpha + p_2\alpha^2 + \ldots$ with $(1 + \alpha + \alpha^2 + \alpha^3 + \alpha^4)$, the coefficient of α^r in product will be $\underbrace{p_{r-4} + p_{r-3} + p_{r-2} + p_{r-1}}_{\text{4 preceding coefficients}} + p_r$

Finally, in product of $p_0 + p_1\alpha + p_2\alpha^2 + \ldots$ with $(1 + \alpha + \alpha^2 + \alpha^3 + \ldots + \text{upto } \infty)$, the coefficient of α^r in product will be $\underbrace{p_0 + p_1 + p_2 + \ldots + p_{r-1}}_{\text{all preceding coefficients}} + p_r$

Example 97. Find the coefficient of α^6 in the product $(1 + \alpha + \alpha^2)(1 + \alpha + \alpha^2)(1 + \alpha + \alpha^2 + \alpha^3)(1 + \alpha)(1 + \alpha)(1 + \alpha)$.

Sol. The given product can be written as

$(1 + \alpha + \alpha^2)(1 + \alpha + \alpha^2)(1 + \alpha + \alpha^2 + \alpha^3)(1 + \alpha)^3$

or $(1 + \alpha + \alpha^2)(1 + \alpha + \alpha^2)(1 + \alpha + \alpha^2 + \alpha^3)(1 + 3\alpha + 3\alpha^2 + \alpha^3)$

Multiplying Synthetically

1	α	α^2	α^3	α^4	α^5	α^6	...
1	3	3	1	0	0	0	

... on multiplying by $1 + \alpha + \alpha^2 + \alpha^3 \rightarrow$ To each coefficient add 3 preceding coefficients.

1	4	7	8	7	4	1	...

...on multiplying by $1 + \alpha + \alpha^2 \rightarrow$ To each coefficient add 2 preceding coefficients.

1	5	12	19	22	19	12	...

...on multiplying by $1 + \alpha + \alpha^2 \rightarrow$ To each coefficient add 2 preceding coefficients.

...	...	...	...	...	...	53	...

Hence, required coefficient is 53.

Example 98. Find the number of different selections of 5 letters which can be made from 5*A*'s, 4*B* 's, 3*C*'s, 2*D*'s and 1*E*'s.

Sol. All selections of 5 letters are given by 5th degree terms in

$(1 + A + A^2 + A^3 + A^4 + A^5)(1 + B + B^2 + B^3 + B^4)(1 + C + C^2 + C^3)(1 + D + D^2)(1 + E)$

$\therefore$ Number of 5 letter selections

= Coefficient of α^5 in $(1 + \alpha + \alpha^2 + \alpha^3 + \alpha^4 + \alpha^5)(1 + \alpha + \alpha^2 + \alpha^3 + \alpha^4)(1 + \alpha + \alpha^2 + \alpha^3)(1 + \alpha + \alpha^2)(1 + \alpha)$

Multiplying synthetically

1	α	α^2	α^3	α^4	$\alpha^5 \ldots$	
1	1	1	1	1	1	
						$\times 1+\alpha+\alpha^2+\alpha^3+\alpha^4$
1	2	3	4	5	5 ...	
						$\times 1+\alpha+\alpha^2+\alpha^3$
1	3	6	10	14	17 ...	
						$\times 1+\alpha+\alpha^2$
1	4	10	19	30	41 ...	
						$\times 1+\alpha$
1	5	14	29	49	71	

Hence, required coefficient is 71.

Example 99. Find the number of combinations and permutations of 4 letters taken from the word EXAMINATION.

Sol. There are 11 letters A, A, E, I, I, N, N, X, M, T, O.

Then, number of combinations

$= \text{Coefficient of } x^4 \text{ in } (1+x+x^2)^3(1+x)^5$

[$\because$ 2A's, 2I 's, 2N's, 1E, 1X, 1M, 1T and 1O]

$= \text{Coefficient of } x^4 \text{ in } \{(1+x)^3 + x^6 + 3(1+x)^2x^2 + 3(1+x)x^4\}(1+x)^5$

$= \text{Coefficient of } x^4 \text{ in}$

$\{(1+x)^8 + x^6(1+x)^5 + 3x^2(1+x)^7 + 3x^4(1+x)^6\}$

$= {}^8C_4 + 0 + 3\cdot{}^7C_2 + 3 = \dfrac{8\cdot7\cdot6\cdot5}{1\cdot2\cdot3\cdot4} + 3\cdot\dfrac{7\cdot6}{1\cdot2} + 3 = 70 + 63 + 3$

$= 136$

and number of permutations

$= \text{Coefficient of } x^4 \text{ in } 4!\left(1+\dfrac{x}{1!}+\dfrac{x^2}{2!}\right)^3\left(1+\dfrac{x}{1!}\right)^5$

$= \text{Coefficient of } x^4 \text{ in } 4!\left(1+x+\dfrac{x^2}{2}\right)^3(1+x)^5$

$= \text{Coefficient of } x^4 \text{ in}$

$4!\left\{(1+x)^3 + \dfrac{x^6}{8} + \dfrac{3}{2}(1+x)^2x^2 + \dfrac{3}{4}x^4(1+x)\right\}(1+x)^5$

$= \text{Coefficient of } x^4 \text{ in}$

$4!\left\{(1+x)^8 + \dfrac{x^6}{8}(1+x)^5 + \dfrac{3}{2}x^2(1+x)^7 + \dfrac{3}{4}x^4(1+x)^6\right\}$

$= 4!\left\{{}^8C_4 + 0 + \dfrac{3}{2}\cdot{}^7C_2 + \dfrac{3}{4}\right\}$

$= 24\left\{\dfrac{8\cdot7\cdot6\cdot5}{1\cdot2\cdot3\cdot4} + \dfrac{3}{2}\cdot\dfrac{7\cdot6}{1\cdot2} + \dfrac{3}{4}\right\}$

$= 8\cdot7\cdot6\cdot5 + 6(3\cdot7\cdot6) + 6\cdot3$

$= 1680 + 756 + 18$

$= 2454$

Alternate Solution

There are 11 letters: A, A, I, I, N, N, E, X, M, T, O

The following cases arise:

***Case I* All letters different** The required number of choosing 4 different letters from 8 different (A, I, N, E, X, M, T, O) types of the letters $= {}^8C_4 = \dfrac{8\cdot7\cdot6\cdot5}{1\cdot2\cdot3\cdot4} = 70$

and number of permutations $= {}^8P_4 = 8\cdot7\cdot6\cdot5 = 1680$

***Case II* Two alike of one type and two alike of another type** This must be 2 A's, 2 I's or 2I's, 2N's, or 2N's, 2A's.

$\therefore$ Number of selections $= {}^3C_2 = 3$

e.g. [for arrangements]

A	A	I	I

and number of permutations $= 3\cdot\dfrac{4!}{2!2!} = 18$

***Case III* Two alike and two different** This must be 2 A's or 2 I's or 2N's and for each case 7 different letters.

e.g. for 2A's, 7 differents's are I, N, E, X, M, T, O

e.g. [for arrangements]

A	X	A	O

$\therefore$ Number of selections $= {}^3C_1 \times {}^7C_2 = 3 \times \dfrac{7\times6}{1\times2} = 63$

and number of permutations $= 63\cdot\dfrac{4!}{2!} = 756$

From Case I, II and III

The required number of combinations $= 70 + 3 + 63 = 136$

and number of permutations $= 1680 + 18 + 756 = 2454$

Number of Solutions with the Help of Multinomial Theorem

***Case* I** If the equation $\alpha + 2\beta + 3\gamma + \ldots + q\theta = n$ ...(i)

(a) If zero included, the number of solutions of Eq. (i)

$= \text{Coefficient of } x^n \text{ in } (1+x+x^2+\ldots)$

$(1+x^2+x^4+\ldots)(1+x^3+x^6+\ldots)\ldots$

$(1+x^q+x^{2q}+\ldots)$

$= \text{Coefficient of } x^n \text{ in}$

$(1-x)^{-1}(1-x^2)^{-1}(1-x^3)^{-1}\ldots(1-x^q)^{-1}$

(b) If zero excluded, then the number of solutions of Eq. (i)

$= \text{Coefficient of } x^n \text{ in } (x+x^2+x^3+\ldots)$

$(x^2+x^4+x^6+\ldots)(x^3+x^6+x^9+\ldots)$

$\ldots(x^q+x^{2q}+\ldots)$

$= \text{Coefficient of } x^n \text{ in } x^{1+2+3+\ldots+q}(1-x)^{-1}$

$(1-x^2)^{-1}(1-x^3)^{-1}\ldots(1-x^q)^{-1}$

$= \text{Coefficient of } x^{n-\frac{q(q+1)}{2}} \text{ in}$

$(1-x)^{-1}(1-x^2)^{-1}(1-x^3)^{-1}\ldots(1-x^q)^{-1}$

Example 100. Find the number of non-negative integral solutions of $x_1 + x_2 + x_3 + 4x_4 = 20$.

Sol. Number of non-negative integral solutions of the given equation

$= \text{Coefficient of } x^{20} \text{ in } (1-x)^{-1}(1-x)^{-1}(1-x)^{-1}(1-x^4)^{-1}$

$= \text{Coefficient of } x^{20} \text{ in } (1-x)^{-3}(1-x^4)^{-1}$

$= \text{Coefficient of } x^{20} \text{ in } (1 + {}^3C_1 + {}^4C_2 x^2 + {}^5C_3 x^3 + {}^6C_4 x^4 + \dots + {}^{10}C_8 x^8 + \dots + {}^{14}C_{12} x^{12} + \dots + {}^{18}C_{16} x^{16} + \dots + {}^{22}C_{20} x^{20} + \dots)(1 + x^4 + x^8 + x^{12} + x^{16} + x^{20} + \dots)$

$= 1 + {}^6C_4 + {}^{10}C_8 + {}^{14}C_{12} + {}^{18}C_{16} + {}^{22}C_{20}$

$= 1 + {}^6C_2 + {}^{10}C_2 + {}^{14}C_2 + {}^{18}C_2 + {}^{22}C_2$

$= 1 + \left(\frac{6\cdot5}{1\cdot2}\right) + \left(\frac{10\cdot9}{1\cdot2}\right) + \left(\frac{14\cdot13}{1\cdot2}\right) + \left(\frac{18\cdot17}{1\cdot2}\right) + \left(\frac{22\cdot21}{1\cdot2}\right)$

$= 1 + 15 + 45 + 91 + 153 + 231$

$= 536$

Example 101. Find the number of positive unequal integral solutions of the equation $x + y + z + w = 20$.

Sol. We have, $x + y + z + w = 20$ ...(i)

Assume $x < y < z < w$. Here, $x, y, z, w \geq 1$

Now, let $x = x_1, y - x = x_2, z - y = x_3$ and $w - z = x_4$

$\therefore \quad x = x_1, y = x_1 + x_2, z = x_1 + x_2 + x_3$

and $\quad w = x_1 + x_2 + x_3 + x_4$

From Eq. (i), $4x_1 + 3x_2 + 2x_3 + x_4 = 20$

Then, $x_1, x_2, x_3, x_4 \geq 1$

$\because \quad 4x_1 + 3x_2 + 2x_3 + x_4 = 20$ ...(ii)

$\therefore$ Number of positive integral solutions of Eq. (ii)

$= \text{Coefficient of } x^{20-10} \text{ in } (1-x^4)^{-1}(1-x^3)^{-1}(1-x^2)^{-1}(1-x)^{-1}$

$= \text{Coefficient of } x^{10} \text{ in } (1-x^4)^{-1}(1-x^3)^{-1}(1-x^2)^{-1}(1-x)^{-1}$

$= \text{Coefficient of } x^{10} \text{ in } (1 + x^4 + x^8 + x^{12} + \dots) \times (1 + x^3 + x^6 + x^9 + x^{12} + \dots) \times (1 + x^2 + x^4 + x^6 + x^8 + x^{10} + \dots) \times (1 + x + x^2 + x^3 + x^4 + x^5 + x^6 + x^7 + x^8 + x^9 + x^{10} + \dots)$

$= \text{Coefficient of } x^{10} \text{ in } (1 + x^3 + x^6 + x^9 + x^4 + x^7 + x^{10} + x^8) \times (1 + x^2 + x^4 + x^6 + x^8 + x^{10})(1 + x + x^2 + x^3 + x^4 + x^5 + x^6 + x^7 + x^8 + x^9 + x^{10})$ [neglecting higher powers]

$= \text{Coefficient of } x^{10} \text{ in } (1 + x^2 + x^4 + x^6 + x^8 + x^{10} + x^3 + x^5 + x^7 + x^9 + x^6 + x^8 + x^{10} + x^9 + x^4 + x^6 + x^8 + x^{10} + x^7 + x^9 + x^{10} + x^8 + x^{10})(1 + x + x^2 + x^3 + x^4 + x^5 + x^6 + x^7 + x^8 + x^9 + x^{10})$ [neglecting higher powers]

$= 1+1+1+1+1+1+1+1+1+1+1+1+1+1+1+1+1+1+1+1+1+1+1$

$= 23$

But x, y, z and w can be arranged in ${}^4P_4 = 4!$

$= 24$

Hence, required number of solutions $= (23)(24)$

$= 552$

Example 102. In how many ways can 15 identical blankets be distributed among six beggars, such that everyone gets atleast one blanket and two particular beggars get equal blankets and another three particular beggars get equal blankets.

Sol. The number of ways of distributing blankets is equal to the number of solutions of the equation $3x + 2y + z = 15$, where $x \geq 1, y \geq 1, z \geq 1$ which is equal to coefficient of α^{15} in

$(\alpha^3 + \alpha^6 + \alpha^9 + \alpha^{12} + \alpha^{15} + \dots) \times (\alpha^2 + \alpha^4 + \alpha^6 + \alpha^8 + \alpha^{10} + \alpha^{12} + \alpha^{14} + \dots) \times (\alpha + \alpha^2 + \alpha^3 + \dots + \alpha^{15} + \dots)$

$= \text{Coefficient of } \alpha^9 \text{ in } (1 + \alpha^3 + \alpha^6 + \alpha^9) \times (1 + \alpha^2 + \alpha^4 + \alpha^6 + \alpha^8) \times (1 + \alpha + \alpha^2 + \alpha^3 + \alpha^4 + \alpha^5 + \alpha^6 + \alpha^7 + \alpha^8 + \alpha^9)$ [neglecting higher powers]

$= \text{Coefficient of } \alpha^9 \text{ in } (1 + \alpha^2 + \alpha^4 + \alpha^6 + \alpha^8 + \alpha^3 + \alpha^5 + \alpha^7 + \alpha^9 + \alpha^6 + \alpha^8 + \alpha^9) \times (1 + \alpha + \alpha^2\ \alpha^3 + \alpha^4 + \alpha^5 + \alpha^6 + \alpha^7 + \alpha^8 + \alpha^9)$ [neglecting higher powers]

$= 1+1+1+1+1+1+1+1+1+1+1+1 = 12$

***Case* II** If the inequation

$$x_1 + x_2 + x_3 + \dots + x_m \leq n \quad \text{...(i)}$$

[when the required sum is not fixed]

In this case, we introduce a dummy variable x_{m+1}.

So that, $x_1 + x_2 + x_3 + \dots + x_m + x_{m+1} = n,$

$$x_{m+1} \geq 0 \quad \text{...(ii)}$$

Here, the number of solutions of Eqs. (i) and (ii) will be same.

Example 103. Find the number of positive integral solutions of the inequation $3x+y+z\leq 30$.

Sol. Let dummy variable w, then

$$3x+y+z+w=30,\ w\geq 0 \quad \text{...(i)}$$

Now, let $a=x-1, b=y-1, c=z-1, d=w$, then

$$3a+b+c+d=25, \quad \text{...(ii)}$$

where $a, b, c, d\geq 0$

$\therefore$ Number of positive integral solutions of Eq. (i)

= Number of non-negative integral solutions of Eq. (ii)

= Coefficient of α^{25} in $(1+\alpha^3+\alpha^6+\ldots)(1+\alpha+\alpha^2+\ldots)^3$

= Coefficient of α^{25} in $(1+\alpha^3+\alpha^6+\ldots)(1-\alpha)^{-3}$

= Coefficient of α^{25} in

$$(1+\alpha^3+\alpha^6+\ldots)(1+{}^3C_1\alpha+{}^4C_2\alpha^2+\ldots)$$

$= {}^{27}C_{25}+{}^{24}C_{22}+{}^{21}C_{19}+{}^{18}C_{16}+{}^{15}C_{13}+{}^{12}C_{10}+{}^{9}C_{7}+{}^{6}C_{4}+{}^{3}C_{1}$

$= {}^{27}C_{2}+{}^{24}C_{2}+{}^{21}C_{2}+{}^{18}C_{2}+{}^{15}C_{2}+{}^{12}C_{2}+{}^{9}C_{2}+{}^{6}C_{2}+{}^{3}C_{1}$

$=351+276+210+153+105+66+36+15+3$

$=1215$

Example 104. In how many ways can we get a sum of atmost 15 by throwing six distinct die?

Sol. Let x_1, x_2, x_3, x_4, x_5 and x_6 be the number that appears on the six dice.

The number of ways = Number of solutions of the inequation

$$x_1+x_2+x_3+x_4+x_5+x_6\leq 15$$

Introducing a dummy variable $x_7 (x_7\geq 0)$, the inequation becomes an equation

$$x_1+x_2+x_3+x_4+x_5+x_6+x_7=15$$

Here, $1\leq x_i\leq 6$ for $i=1, 2, 3, 4, 5, 6$ and $x_7\geq 0$.

Therefore, number of solutions

= Coefficient of x^{15} in $(x+x^2+x^3+x^4+x^5+x^6)^6 \times(1+x+x^2+\ldots)$

= Coefficient of x^9 in $(1-x^6)^6(1-x)^{-7}$

= Coefficient of x^9 in $(1-6x^6)(1+{}^7C_1x+{}^8C_2x^2+\ldots)$ [neglecting higher powers]

$={}^{15}C_9-6\times {}^9C_3$

$={}^{15}C_6-6\times {}^9C_3$

$=5005-504$

$=4501$

***Case* III** If the inequation $x_1+x_2+x_3+\ldots+x_n\geq n$ [when the values of $x_1, x_2, \ldots, x_n$ are restricted]

In this case, first find the number of solutions of $x_1+x_2+x_3+\ldots+x_n\leq n-1$ and then subtract it from the total number of solutions.

Example 105. In how many ways can we get a sum greater than 15 by throwing six distinct dice?

Sol. Let x_1, x_2, x_3, x_4, x_5 and x_6 be the number that appears on the six dice.

The number of ways = Number of solutions of the inequation

$$x_1+x_2+x_3+x_4+x_5+x_6>15$$

Here, $1\leq x_i\leq 6, i=1, 2, 3, 4, 5, 6$

Total number of cases $=6^6=2^6\times 3^6=64\times 729=46656$

and number of ways to get the sum less than or equal to 15, which is 4501 [from Example 104]

Hence, the number of ways to get a sum greater than 15 is $46656-4501=42155$

***Case* IV** If the equation $x_1x_2x_3\ldots x_n=2^{\alpha_1}\cdot 3^{\alpha_2}\cdot 5^{\alpha_3}\ldots$ where $\alpha_1, \alpha_2, \alpha_3, \ldots$ are natural numbers.

In this case, number of positive integral solutions $(x_1, x_2, x_3, \ldots, x_n)$ are

$$({}^{\alpha_1+n-1}C_{n-1})({}^{\alpha_2+n-1}C_{n-1})({}^{\alpha_3+n-1}C_{n-1})\ldots$$

Example 106. Find the total number of positive integral solutions for (x, y, z) such that $xyz=24$.

Sol. $\because$ $xyz=24=2^3\times 3^1$

Hence, total number of positive integral solutions

$$=({}^{3+3-1}C_{3-1})({}^{1+3-1}C_{3-1})$$
$$={}^5C_2\times {}^3C_2=30$$

Alternate Solution

$\because$ $xyz=24=2^3\times 3^1$

Now, consider three boxes x, y, z.

3 can be put in any of the three boxes.

Also, 2, 2, 2 can be distributed in the three boxes in ${}^{3+3-1}C_{3-1}={}^5C_2=10$ ways.

Hence, the total number of positive integral solutions

= The number of distributions which is given by $3\times 10=30$.

5.16 Geometrical Problems

(a) If there are n points in a plane out of these points no three are in the same line except m points which are collinear, then

(i) total number of different lines obtained by joining these n points is ${}^nC_2-{}^mC_2+1$.

(ii) total number of different triangles formed by joining these n points is ${}^nC_3-{}^mC_3$.

(iii) total number of different quadrilateral formed by joining these n points is

$${}^nC_4-({}^mC_3\cdot{}^nC_1+{}^mC_4\cdot{}^nC_0).$$

Example 107. There are 10 points in a plane out of these points no three are in the same straight line except 4 points which are collinear. How many
(i) straight lines
(ii) triangles
(iii) quadrilateral, by joining them?

Sol. (i) Required number of straight lines

$$= {}^{10}C_2 - {}^4C_2 + 1$$
$$= \frac{10\cdot 9}{1\cdot 2} - \frac{4\cdot 3}{1\cdot 2} + 1$$
$$= 45 - 6 + 1 = 40$$

(ii) Required number of triangles

$$= {}^{10}C_3 - {}^4C_3$$
$$= \frac{10\cdot 9\cdot 8}{1\cdot 2\cdot 3} - {}^4C_1$$
$$= 120 - 4 = 116$$

(iii) Required number of quadrilaterals

$$= {}^{10}C_4 - ({}^4C_3\cdot {}^6C_1 + {}^4C_4\cdot {}^6C_0)$$
$$= \frac{10\cdot 9\cdot 8\cdot 7}{1\cdot 2\cdot 3\cdot 4} - ({}^4C_1\cdot {}^6C_1 + 1.1)$$
$$= 210 - (4\times 6 + 1) = 210 - 25 = 185$$

(b) If there are n points in a plane out of these points no any three are collinear, then
(i) Total points of intersection of the lines joining these n points $= {}^pC_2$, where $p = {}^nC_2$
(ii) If n points are the vertices of a polygon, then total number of diagonals $= {}^nC_2 - n = \frac{n(n-3)}{2}$

Example 108. How many number of points of intersection of n straight lines, if n satisfies
$${}^{n+5}P_{n+1} = \frac{11(n-1)}{2} \times {}^{n+3}P_n \text{ ?}$$

Sol. We have,
$${}^{n+5}P_{n+1} = \frac{11(n-1)}{2} \times {}^{n+3}P_n$$
$$\Rightarrow \frac{(n+5)!}{4!} = \frac{11(n-1)}{2} \times \frac{(n+3)!}{3!}$$
$$\Rightarrow \frac{(n+5)(n+4)}{4} = \frac{11(n-1)}{2}$$
$$\Rightarrow n^2 - 13n + 42 = 0$$
$$\Rightarrow (n-6)(n-7) = 0$$
$$\Rightarrow n = 6 \text{ or } n = 7$$

The number of points of intersection of lines is ${}^6C_2$ or ${}^7C_2$
$$= 15 \text{ or } 21$$

Example 109. The interior angles of a regular polygon measure 150° each. Then, find the number of diagonals of the polygon.

Sol. Each exterior angle = 30°

$$\therefore \text{ Number of sides} = \frac{360^\circ}{30^\circ} = \frac{360^\circ \times \frac{\pi}{180^\circ}}{30^\circ \times \frac{\pi}{180^\circ}} = 12$$
$$\therefore \text{ Number of diagonals} = {}^{12}C_2 - 12$$
$$= 66 - 12$$
$$= 54$$

Example 110. In a polygon the number of diagonals is 77. Find the number of sides of the polygon.

Sol. Let number of sides of the polygon $= n$, then
$${}^nC_2 - n = 77$$
$$\Rightarrow \frac{n(n-1)}{2} - n = 77$$
$$\Rightarrow \frac{n(n-3)}{2} = \frac{14\times 11}{2}$$
we get, $n = 14$

(c) n straight lines are drawn in a plane such that no two of them are parallel and no three of them are concurrent. Then, number of parts into which these lines divides the plane is equal to
$$1 + \sum_{k=1}^{n} k, \text{ i.e. } \frac{(n^2 + n + 2)}{2}$$

Example 111. If n lines are drawn in a plane such that no two of them are parallel and no three of them are concurrent, such that these lines divide the plane in 67 parts, then find number of different points at which these lines will cut.

Sol. Given number of straight lines $= n$, then
$$1 + \sum_{k=1}^{n} k = 67 \Rightarrow \frac{n^2 + n + 2}{2} = 67$$
$$\Rightarrow n^2 + n - 132 = 0 \Rightarrow (n+12)(n-11) = 0$$
$$\therefore n = 11, n \neq -12$$
Hence, required number of points $= {}^nC_2 = {}^{11}C_2$
$$= \frac{11\cdot 10}{2} = 55$$

(d) If m parallel lines in a plane are intersected by a family of other n parallel lines. Then, total number of parallelograms so formed
$$= {}^mC_2 \cdot {}^nC_2 \text{ i.e. } \frac{mn(m-1)(n-1)}{4}$$

Example 112. Find the number of rectangles in a chess board, which are not a square.

Sol. Number of rectangles $= {}^9C_2 \times {}^9C_2 = (36)^2 = 1296$

Number of squares $= 8\times 8 + 7\times 7 + 6\times 6 + \ldots + 1\times 1 = 204$

$\therefore$ Required number $= 1296 - 204 = 1092$

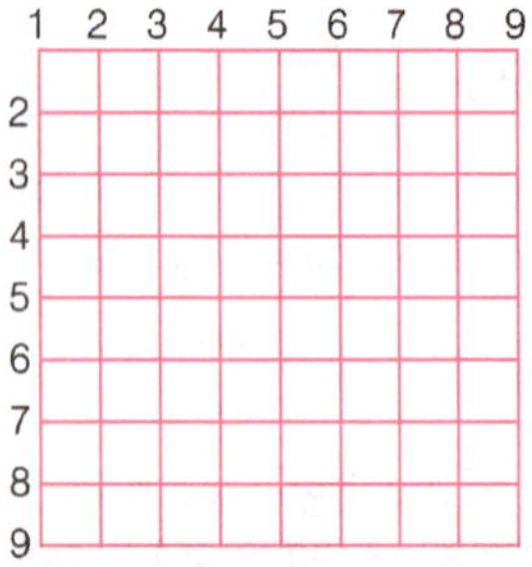

Square can be formed as follows :

To form the smallest square, select any two consecutive lines from the given (here 9) vertical and horizontal lines. This can be done in 8×8 ways (1-2, 2-3, 3-4, ..., 8-9)

Again, to form the square consists of four small squares, select the lines as follows (1-3, 2-4, 3-5,..., 7-9) from both vertical and horizontal lines, thus 7×7 squares are obtained. Proceed in the same way.

(e) Number of Rectangles and Squares

(i) Number of rectangles of any size in a square of $n \times n$ is $\sum_{r=1}^{n} r^3$ and number of squares of any size is $\sum_{r=1}^{n} r^2$.

(ii) In a rectangle of $n \times p$ $(n < p)$ number of rectangles of any size is $\frac{np}{4}(n+1)(p+1)$ and number of squares of any size is

$$\sum_{r=1}^{n} (n+1-r)(p+1-r).$$

Example 113. Find the number of rectangles excluding squares from a rectangle of size 9×6.

Sol. Here, $n = 6$ and $p = 9$

$\therefore$ Number of rectangles excluding square

$$= \frac{6 \cdot 9}{4}(6+1)(9+1) - \sum_{r=1}^{6}(7-r)(10-r)$$

$$= 945 - \sum_{r=1}^{6}(70 - 17r + r^2) = 945 - 154 = 791$$

(f) If there are n rows, first row has α_1 squares, 2nd row has α_2 squares, 3rd row has α_3 squares, ... and nth row has α_n squares. If we have to filled up the squares with β X_s such that each row has atleast one X. The number of ways = Coefficient of x^{β} in

$$({}^{\alpha_1}C_1 x + {}^{\alpha_1}C_2 x^2 + \ldots + {}^{\alpha_1}C_{\alpha_1} x^{\alpha_1})$$
$$\times ({}^{\alpha_2}C_1 x + {}^{\alpha_2}C_2 x^2 + \ldots + {}^{\alpha_2}C_{\alpha_2} x^{\alpha_2})$$
$$\times ({}^{\alpha_3}C_1 x + {}^{\alpha_3}C_2 x^2 + \ldots + {}^{\alpha_3}C_{\alpha_3} x^{\alpha_3}) \times$$
$$\ldots \times ({}^{\alpha_n}C_1 x + {}^{\alpha_n}C_2 x^2 + \ldots + {}^{\alpha_n}C_{\alpha_n} x^{\alpha_n})$$

Example 114. Six X 's have to be placed in the squares of the figure below, such that each row contains atleast one X. In how many different ways can this be done?

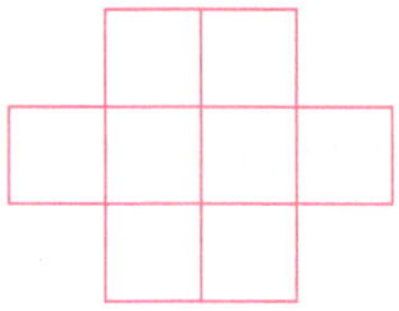

Sol. The required number of ways

$$= \text{Coefficient of } x^6 \text{ in } ({}^2C_1 x + {}^2C_2 x^2)({}^4C_1 x + {}^4C_2 x^2 + {}^4C_3 x^3 + {}^4C_4 x^4)({}^2C_1 x + {}^2C_2 x^2)$$

$$= \text{Coefficient of } x^3 \text{ in } (2+x)^2 (4 + 6x + 4x^2 + x^3)$$

$$= \text{Coefficient of } x^3 \text{ in } (4 + 4x + x^2)(4 + 6x + 4x^2 + x^3)$$

$$= 4 + 16 + 6$$

$$= 26$$

Alternate Solution

In the given figure there are 8 squares and we have to place 6 X's this can be done in ${}^8C_6 = {}^8C_2 = \frac{8 \cdot 7}{1 \cdot 2} = 28$ ways

But these include the possibility that either headed row or lowest row may not have any X. These two possibilities are to be excluded.

$\therefore$ Required number of ways $= 28 - 2 = 26$

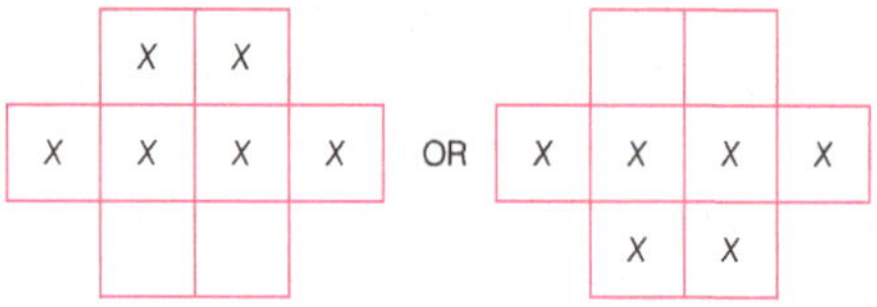

Example 115. In how many ways the letters of the word DIPESH can be placed in the squares of the adjoining figure so that no row remains empty?

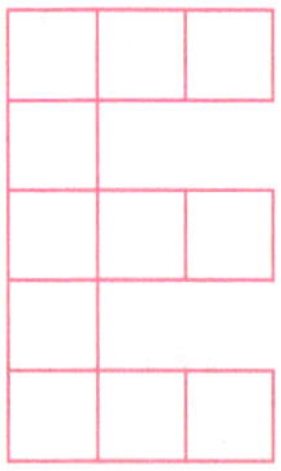

Sol. If all letters are same, then number of ways

$$= \text{Coefficient of } x^6 \text{ in } ({}^3C_1 x + {}^3C_2 x^2 + {}^3C_3 x^3)^3 ({}^1C_1 x)^2$$

$$= \text{Coefficient of } x \text{ in } (3 + 3x + x^2)^3$$

$$= \text{Coefficient of } x \text{ in } (3 + 3x)^3$$

[neglecting higher degree term]

$$= 27 \times {}^3C_1$$

$$= 81$$

But in DIPESH all letters are different.

$\therefore$ Required number of ways $= 81 \times 6!$

Milestone Practice 5.3

1. If ${}^{n+2}C_8 : {}^{n-2}P_4 = 57:16$, find the value of $(n+1):(n-2)$.
2. If ${}^{15}C_{3r} : {}^{15}C_{r+1} = 11:3$, find the value of r.
3. Find the value of $\sum_{r=0}^{10} {}^{40+r}C_{10+r}$.
4. A committee of 5 is to be formed out of 6 jents and 4 ladies. In how many ways this can be done, when
   (a) atleast two ladies are included?
   (b) atmost two ladies are included?
5. Find the number of ways in which the number 300300 can be split into two factors which are relatively prime.
6. In how many ways can 8 different books be distributed among 3 students if each receives at least 2 books?
7. Consider the equation $\frac{2}{x}+\frac{5}{y}=\frac{1}{3}$, $x, y \in N$.
   Find the number of solutions of the equation.
8. Find the number of non-negative integral solutions of $x_1 + x_2 + x_3 + 4x_4 = 20$.
9. Find the total numbers of integral solutions of the equation $x+y+z+t=35$, where $x \geq 2$, $y \geq 3$, $z \geq 4$, and $t \geq 0$
10. Find the number of ways in which 5 letters can be placed in 10 marked envelopes, so that no letter is in the right envelope.
11. Find the number of seven letters word that can be formed by using the letters of the word SUCCESS, so that the two C are together but no two S are together.
12. Find the maximum number of points of intersection of 7 straight lines and 5 circles when 3 straight lines are parallel and 2 circles are concentric.

Answer Key

1. 20 : 17	2. 3	3. $S = {}^{51}C_{20} - {}^{40}C_9$	4. (a) 186 (b) 186
5. 32	6. 2940	7. 12	8. 536
9. ${}^{29}C_3$	10. 44	11. 24	12. 106

For Detailed Solution

JEE Pattern EXAMPLES

Single Correct Option Type Questions

Example 1 *The number of zeroes at the end in product $5^6 \cdot 6^7 \cdot 7^8 \cdot 8^9 \cdot 9^{10} \ldots 30^{31}$, is*

(a) 135 (b) 136
(c) 137 (d) 138

Sol. (c) Let $S = 5^6 \cdot 6^7 \cdot 7^8 \ldots (30)^{31}$

$$= [5^6 \times 10^{11} \times 15^{16} \times 20^{21} \times 25^{26} \times 30^{31}] \times \text{some integers.}$$

$\therefore E_5(S) = 6 + 11 + 16 + 21 + 26 + 26 + 31$
$= 137$

$\therefore$ Number of zeroes $= 137$

Example 2 *The number of pairs of parallel diagonals in a regular polygon of 10 sides, is*

(a) 40 (b) 45
(c) 50 (d) 55

Sol. (b) Fix a vertex, say A,

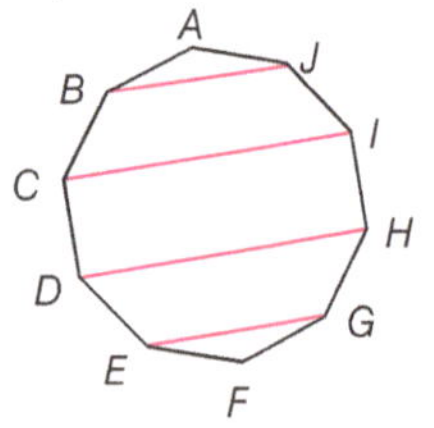

There are 4 parallel diagonals. There are 5 such sets, since the number of vertices are 10.
$\therefore$ Number of such diagonals $= {}^4C_2 \times 5 = 30$
Now, fix a side AB

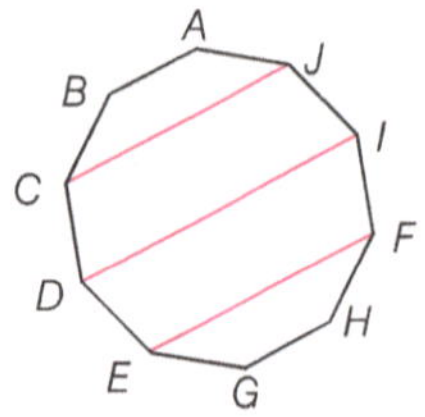

There are 3 parallel diagonals CJ, DI, EF and 5 such sets.

$\therefore$ Number of such diagonals $= {}^3C_2 \times 5 = 15$

So, required number of diagonals $= 30 + 15 = 45$

Example 3 *Number of permutations of the word PANCHKULA, where A and U are separated, is*

(a) $21 \times 7!$ (b) $21 \times 6!$ (c) $20 \times 7!$ (d) $20 \times 6!$

Sol. (a) **Case I** All A, U, A are separated.
First arrange P, N, C, H, K, L in 6!
Seven gaps are formed.

$$\times P \times N \times C \times H \times K \times L \times$$

A, U, A are arranged in these gaps in ${}^7C_3 \times \frac{3!}{2!}$ ways.

$\therefore$ Number of such words $= 6! \times {}^7C_3 \times \frac{3!}{2!}$

Case II AA are together but separated from U.
So, we need two places for AA and U.
$\therefore$ Number of such words $= 6! \times {}^7C_2 \times 2!$

So, required number of words

$$= 6! \times {}^7C_3 \times \frac{3!}{2!} + 6! \times {}^7C_2 \times 2!$$

$$= 6! \times \frac{7 \times 6 \times 5}{3 \times 2 \times 1} \times \frac{3!}{2!} + 6! \times \frac{7 \times 6}{2 \times 1} \times 2!$$

$$= 7! \times 15 + 7! \times 6 = 21 \times 7!$$

Example 4 *Number of words formed using all the letters of the word 'EXAMINATION' if alike letters are never adjacent, is*

(a) $275 \times 8!$ (b) $\frac{275}{2} \times 8!$
(c) $\frac{275}{4} \times 8!$ (d) None of these

Sol. (c) We have word, 'EXAMINATION'.
Letters are E, X, (AA), M, (I, I), (N, N), T, O
P = Set of words in which (AA) are together.
Q = Set of words in which (EE) are together.
R = Set of words in which (NN) are together.

$$\therefore n(P \cup Q \cup R) = n(P) + n(Q) + n(R) - n(P \cap Q) - n(Q \cap R) - n(R \cap P) + n(P \cap Q \cap R)$$

$$= \frac{10!}{2!2!} + \frac{10!}{2!2!} + \frac{10!}{2!2!} - \frac{9!}{2!} - \frac{9!}{2!} - \frac{9!}{2!} + 8!$$

$\therefore$ Required number of words $= n(P' \cap Q' \cap R')$

$$= n(P \cup Q \cup R)' = n(U) - n(P \cup Q \cup R)$$

$$= \frac{11!}{2!2!2!} - 3 \times \frac{10!}{2!2!} + 3 \times \frac{9!}{2!} - 8! = \frac{275}{4} \times 8!$$

Example 5 *If all the permutation of the letters in the word OBJECT are arranged in alphabetical order as in a dictionary, then 717th word is*

(a) TOJECB (b) TOEJBC (c) TOCJEB (d) TOJCBE

Sol. (d) The order of letters of the word 'OBJECT' is BCEJOT.

Words starting with B = 5!

Words starting with C = 5!

Words starting with E = 5!

Words starting with J = 5!

Words starting with O = 5!

Words starting with TB = 4!

Words starting with TC = 4!

Words starting with TE = 4!

Words starting with TJ = 4!

Words starting with TOB = 3!

Words starting with TOC = 3!

Words starting with TOE = 3!

Words starting with TOJB = 2!

Words starting with TOJC = 2!

∴ Total number of words = 718

Hence, 717th word is TOJCBE.

Example 6 *Number of words of 4 letters that can be formed with the letters of the word IIT JEE, is*

(a) 42 (b) 82 (c) 102 (d) 142

Sol. (c) There are 6 letters I, I, E, E, T, J

The following cases arise:

***Case* I** All letters are different

$$^4P_4 = 4! = 24$$

***Case* II** Two alike and two different

$$^2C_1 \times {}^3C_2 \times \frac{4!}{2!} = 72$$

***Case* III** Two alike of one kind and two alike of another kind

$$^2C_2 \times \frac{4!}{2!\,2!} = 6$$

Hence, number of words = 24 + 72 + 6 = 102

Alternate Solution

Number of words = Coefficient of x^4 in $4!\left(1 + \frac{x}{1!} + \frac{x^2}{2!}\right)^2 (1 + x)^2$

$= $ Coefficient of x^4 in $6[(1 + x)^2 + 1]^2 (1 + x)^2$

$= $ Coefficient of x^4 in $6[(1 + x)^6 + 2(1 + x)^4 + (1 + x)^2]$

$= 6[{}^6C_4 + 2 \cdot {}^4C_4 + 0] = 6(15 + 2) = 102$

Example 7 *Let y be element of the set $A = \{1, 2, 3, 5, 6, 10, 15, 30\}$ and x_1, x_2, x_3 be integers such that $x_1 x_2 x_3 = y$, the number of positive integral solutions of $x_1 x_2 x_3 = y$, is*

(a) 27 (b) 64 (c) 81 (d) 256

Sol. (b) Number of solutions of the given equations is the same as the number of solutions of the equation

$$x_1\, x_2\, x_3\, x_4 = 30 = 2 \times 3 \times 5$$

Here, x_4 is infact a dummy variable.

If $x_1\, x_2\, x_3 = 15$, then $x_4 = 2$ and if $x_1 x_2\, x_3 = 5$, then $x_4 = 6$, etc.

Thus, $\quad x_1\, x_2\, x_3\, x_4 = 2 \times 3 \times 5$

Each of 2, 3 and 5 will be factor of exactly one of x_1, x_2, x_3, x_4 in 4 ways.

∴ Required number = $4^3 = 64$

Example 8 *The number of positive integer solutions of $a + b + c = 60$, where a is a factor of b and c, is*

(a) 184 (b) 200 (c) 144 (d) 270

Sol. (c) ∵ a is a factor of b and $c \Rightarrow a$ divides 60

∴ $\quad a = 1, 2, 3, 4, 5, 6, 10, 12, 15, 30 \quad [\because a \neq 60]$

and $b = ma$, $c = na$, when $m, n \geq 1$

∵ $\quad a + b + c = 60$

$\Rightarrow \quad a + ma + na = 60 \Rightarrow m + n = \left(\frac{60}{a} - 1\right)$

∴ Number of solutions $= {}^{\frac{60}{a} - 1 - 1}C_{2-1} = \left(\frac{60}{a} - 2\right)$

Hence, total number of solutions for all values of a

$= 58 + 28 + 18 + 13 + 10 + 8 + 4 + 3 + 2 + 0 = 144$

Example 9 *The number of times the digit 3 will be written when listing the integers from 1 to 1000, is*

(a) 269 (b) 271 (c) 300 (d) 302

Sol. (c) Since, 3 does not occur in 1000. So, we have to count the number of times 3 occurs, when we list the integers from 1 to 999.

Any number between 1 and 999 is of the form xyz, where $0 \leq x, y, z \leq 9$.

Let us first count the number in which 3 occurs exactly once. Since, 3 can occur at one place in ${}^3C_1$ ways, there are ${}^3C_1 \times 9 \times 9 = 243$ such numbers. Next 3 can occur in exactly two places in ${}^3C_2 \times 9 = 27$ such numbers. Lastly, 3 can occur in all three digits in one number only. Hence, the number of times, 3 occurs is $1 \times 243 + 2 \times 27 + 3 \times 1 = 300$

Example 10 *Number of points having position vector $a\hat{\mathbf{i}} + b\hat{\mathbf{j}} + c\hat{\mathbf{k}}$, where $a, b, c \in \{1, 2, 3, 4, 5\}$ such that $2^a + 3^b + 5^c$ is divisible by 4, is*

(a) 70 (b) 140 (c) 210 (d) 280

Sol. (a) ∵ $2^a + 3^b + 5^c = 2^a + (4 - 1)^b + (4 + 1)^c$

$= 2^a + 4k + (-1)^b + (1)^c \quad [k = \text{constant}]$

$= 2^a + 4k + (-1)^b + 1$

I. $a = 1$, $b =$ even, $c =$ any number

II. $a \neq 1$, $b =$ odd, $c =$ any number

∴ Required number of ways $= 1 \times 2 \times 5 + 4 \times 3 \times 5 = 70$

[∵ even numbers = 2, 4; odd numbers = 1, 3, 5 and any numbers = 1, 2, 3, 4, 5]

Example 11 *Number of positive unequal integral solutions of the equation $x + y + z = 12$ is*

(a) 21 (b) 42
(c) 63 (d) 84

Sol. (b) We have, $x + y + z = 12$ ...(i)

Assume $x < y < z$.

Here, $x, y, z \geq 1$

$\therefore$ Solutions of Eq. (i) are

(1, 2, 9), (1, 3, 8), (1, 4, 7), (1, 5, 6), (2, 3, 7), (2, 4, 6) and (3, 4, 5).

Number of positive integral solutions of Eq. (i) = 7 but x, y, z can be arranged in $3! = 6$

Hence, required number of solutions $= 7 \times 6 = 42$

Example 12 *12 boys and 2 girls are to be seated in a row such that there are atleast 3 boys between the 2 girls. The number of ways this can be done is $\lambda \times 12!$, the value of λ is*

(a) 55 (b) 110
(c) 20 (d) 45

Sol. (b) Let P = Number of ways, 12 boys and 2 girls are seated in a row

$= 14! = 14 \times 13 \times 12!$

$= 182 \times 12!$

P_1 = Number of ways, the girls can sit together

$= (14 - 2 + 1) \times 2! \times 12!$

$= 26 \times 12!$

P_2 = Number of ways, one boy sits between the girls

$= (14 - 3 + 1) \times 2! \times 12!$

$= 24 \times 12!$

P_3 = Number of ways, two boys sit between the girls

$= (14 - 4 + 1) \times 2! \times 12!$

$= 22 \times 12!$

$\therefore$ Required number of ways $= (182 - 26 - 24 - 22) \times 12!$

$= 110 \times 12!$

$= \lambda \times 12!$ [given]

$\therefore \qquad \lambda = 110$

Example 13 *Let N be a natural number. If its first digit (from the left) is deleted, it gets reduced to $\frac{N}{29}$. The sum of all the digits of N is*

(a) 14 (b) 17
(c) 23 (d) 29

Sol. (a) Let $N = a_n \, a_{n-1} \, a_{n-2} \dots a_3 \, a_2 \, a_1 \, a_0$

$$= a_0 + 10a_1 + 10^2 a_2 + \dots + 10^{n-1} a_{n-1} + 10^n a_n \quad \text{...(i)}$$

Then, $\frac{N}{29} = a_{n-1} \, a_{n-2} \, a_{n-3} \dots a_3 \, a_2 \, a_1 \, a_0$

$$= a_0 + 10a_1 + 10^2 a_2 + \dots + 10^{n-2} a_{n-2} + 10^{n-1} a_{n-1}$$

or $N = 29(a_0 + 10a_1 + 10^2 a_2 + \dots + 10^{n-2} a_{n-2} + 10^{n-1} a_{n-1})$ ...(ii)

From Eqs. (i) and (ii), we get

$$10^n \cdot a_n = 28(a_0 + 10a_1 + 10^2 a_2 + \dots + 10^{n-1} a_{n-1})$$

$\Rightarrow$ 28 divides $10^n \cdot a_n$

$\Rightarrow \quad a_n = 7, n \geq 2$

$\Rightarrow \quad 5^2 = a_0 + 10a_1$

The required N is 725 or 7250 or 72500, etc.

$\therefore$ The sum of the digits is 14.

JEE SCANNER

Example 14 Similar to PYQ Asked in JEE Main 2024

All the letters of the word 'EXAMPLE' are written in all possible ways with or without meaning of and hence words as in a dictionary. The serial number of the word 'EXAMPLE' is ....

Sol. (1344) The alphabet in series of word 'EXAMPLE' is

A, E, E, L, M, P, X

Words starting with A = 6!

Words starting with EA = 5!

Words starting with EE = 5!

Words starting with EL = 5!

Words starting with EM = 5!

Words starting with EP = 5!

Words starting with EXAE = 3!

Words starting with EXAL = 3!

Words starting with EXAME = 2!

Words starting with EXAML = 2!

Words starting with EXAMPE = 1!

Words starting with EXAMPLE = 1!

$\therefore$ Total $= 720 + 5 \times 5! + 3 \times 3! + 2 \times 2! + 1 + 1!$

$= 720 + 600 + 18 + 4 + 2 = 1344$

Thus, the serial number of word EXAMPLE is 1344.

Skill Builder

All the letters of the word 'CHALK' are written in all possible ways with or without meaning of and hence words as in dictionary. The serial number of the word 'CHALK' is ....

For Sol.

Example 15 *If the number of ways of selecting n cards out of unlimited number of cards bearing the number 0, 9, 3, so that they cannot be used to write the number 903 is 93, then n is equal to*

(a) 3 (b) 4 (c) 5 (d) 6

Sol. (c) We cannot write 903.

If in the selection of n cards, we get either

(9 or 3), (9 or 0), (0 or 3), (only 0), (only 3) or (only 9).

For (9 or 3) can be selected $= 2 \times 2 \times 2 \times \ldots \times n$ factors $= 2^n$

Similarly, (9 or 0) or (0 or 3) can be selected $= 2^n$

In the above selection (only 0) or (only 3) or (only 9) is repeated twice.

$\therefore$ Total ways $= 2^n + 2^n + 2^n - 3 = 93$

$\Rightarrow \quad 3 \cdot 2^n = 96 \Rightarrow 2^n = 32 = 2^5$

$\therefore \quad n = 5$

JEE SCANNER

Example 16 Similar to PYQ Asked in JEE Main 2024

Number of ways of arranging 10 identical books into 4 identical shelves, where any number of shelves may remain empty is equal to

(a) 9 (b) 18 (c) 17 (d) 23

Sol. (d) 3 Shelves empty : $(10,0,0,0) \rightarrow 1$ way

2 Shelves empty : (9,1,0,0), (8,2,0,0), (7,3,0,0), (6,4,0,0), (5,5,0,0) $\rightarrow$ 5 ways

1 Shelf empty : (8, 1, 1, 0), (7, 2, 1, 0), (6, 3, 1, 0), (6, 2, 2, 0), (5, 3, 2, 0), (5, 4, 1, 0), (4, 4, 2, 0), (4, 3, 3, 0) $\rightarrow$ 8 ways

0 Shelf empty : (7, 1, 1, 1), (6, 2, 1, 1), (5, 3, 1, 1), (5, 2, 2, 1), (4, 3, 2, 1), (4, 2, 2, 2), (4, 4, 1, 1), (3, 3, 2, 2), (3, 3, 3, 1) $\rightarrow$ 9 ways

Total $= (1 + 5 + 8 + 9)$ ways $= 23$ ways

Skill Builder

Number of ways of arranging 6 identical books into 3 identical shelves, where any number of shelves may remain empty is equal to

(a) 4 (b) 5 (c) 7 (d) 9

For Sol.

More than One Correct Option Type Questions

Example 17 *A person has 10 friends among whom two are married to each other. Person wishes to invite five of them for a party. If the married couples refuse to attend separately, then the number of different ways in which person can invite five friends, is*

(a) ${}^8C_5$ (b) $2 \times {}^8C_3$

(c) ${}^{10}C_5 - 2 \times {}^8C_4$ (d) None of these

Sol. (*b*, *c*) The number of ways of inviting with the couple not included $= {}^8C_5$

The number of ways of inviting with the couple included $= {}^8C_3$

$\therefore$ The required number of ways $= {}^8C_5 + {}^8C_3$

$$= {}^8C_3 + {}^8C_3 = 2 \times {}^8C_3$$

Again, $${}^{10}C_5 - 2 \times {}^8C_4 = \frac{10!}{5!5!} - 2 \times \frac{8!}{4!4!} = \frac{8!}{4!4!}\left[\frac{10 \times 9}{5 \times 5} - 2\right]$$

$$= \frac{8!}{4!4!}\left[\frac{8}{5}\right] = \frac{8! \times 8}{5! \times 3! \times 4}$$

$$= 2 \times {}^8C_3$$

Example 18 *If* ${}^{2n+1}P_{n-1} : {}^{2n-1}P_n = 3:5$, *then*

(a) $n = 3$ (b) $n = 4$

(c) $n^2 - 7n + 12 = 0$ (d) $n^2 - 4n + 3 = 0$

Sol. (b, c) We have,

$${}^{2n+1}P_{n-1} : {}^{2n-1}P_n = 3:5$$

$$\Rightarrow \quad \frac{(2n+1)!}{(n+2)!} \times \frac{(n-1)!}{(2n-1)!} = \frac{3}{5}$$

$$\Rightarrow \quad \frac{(2n+1)(2n)}{(n+2)(n+1)(n)} = \frac{3}{5}$$

$$\Rightarrow \quad 10(2n+1) = 3(n+2)(n+1)$$

$$\Rightarrow \quad 3n^2 - 11n - 4 = 0$$

$$\Rightarrow \quad (n-4)(3n+1) = 0 \Rightarrow n = 4$$

Also, $n = 4$

$$\Rightarrow \quad n^2 - 7n + 12 = 0$$

Example 19 *For the number* $N = 3960$,

(a) Number of divisors = 48

(b) Number of even divisors = 36

(c) Number of proper divisors = 44

(d) Sum of all divisors = 14040

Sol. (a, b, d) We have, $N = 3960 = 2^3 \times 3^2 \times 5 \times 11$

$\therefore$ Number of divisors $= (3+1)(2+1)(1+1)(1+1)$

$$= 4 \times 3 \times 2 \times 2 = 48$$

Number of even divisors $= (2+1)(2+1)(1+1)(1+1)$

$$= 3 \times 3 \times 2 \times 2 = 36$$

Number of proper divisors $= 48 - 2 = 46$

and sum of divisors $= (2^0 + 2^1 + 2^2 + 2^3)(3^0 + 3^1 + 3^2)(5^0 + 5^1)(11^0 + 11^1)$

$$= 15 \times 13 \times 6 \times 12 = 14040$$

Example 20 *In a plane, there are two families of lines $y = x + r, y = -x + r$, where $r \in \{0, 1, 2, 3, 4\}$. The number of squares of diagonals of the length 2 formed by the lines is*

(a) 9 (b) 16 (c) $\frac{3}{2} \cdot {}^4C_2$ (d) ${}^5C_2 + {}^3P_2$

Sol. (a, c) There are two sets of five parallel lines at equal distances. Clearly, lines like l_1, l_3, m_1 and m_3 form a square whose diagonal's length is 2.

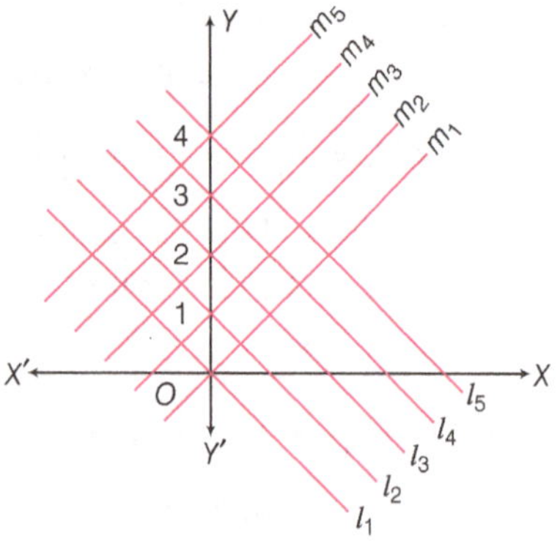

$\therefore$ The number of required squares $= 3 \times 3 = 9 = \frac{3}{2} \cdot {}^4C_2$

[$\because$ choices are $(l_1, l_2), (l_2, l_4)$ and (l_3, l_5) for one set, etc.]

Example 21 *Number of ways in which three numbers in AP can be selected from 1, 2, 3, ..., n, is*

(a) $\left(\frac{n-1}{2}\right)^2$, if n is even (b) $\frac{n(n-2)}{4}$, if n is even

(c) $\frac{(n-1)^2}{4}$, if n is odd (d) $\frac{n(n+1)}{2}$, if n is odd

Sol. (b, c) If a, b, c are in AP, then $a + c = 2b$

a and c both are odd or both are even.

***Case* I** If n is even

Let $n = 2m$ in which m are even and m are odd numbers.

$\therefore$ Number of ways $= {}^mC_2 + {}^mC_2 = 2 \cdot {}^mC_2 = 2 \cdot \frac{m(m-1)}{2}$

$$= \frac{n}{2}\left(\frac{n}{2} - 1\right) = \frac{n(n-2)}{4} \qquad [\because n = 2m]$$

***Case* II** If n is odd

Let $n = 2m + 1$ in which m are even and $m + 1$ are odd numbers.

$\therefore$ Number of ways $= {}^mC_2 + {}^{m+1}C_2$

$$= \frac{m(m-1)}{2} + \frac{(m+1)m}{2} = m^2 = \frac{(n-1)^2}{4}$$

$[\because n = 2m + 1]$

Example 22 *If n objects are arranged in a row, then number of ways of selecting three of these objects so that no two of them are next to each other, is*

(a) ${}^{n-2}C_3$ (b) ${}^{n-3}C_3 + {}^{n-3}C_2$

(c) $\frac{(n-2)(n-3)(n-4)}{6}$ (d) ${}^nC_2$

Sol. (a, b, c) Let a_0 be the number of objects to the left of the first object chosen, a_1 be the number of objects between the first and the second, a_2 be the number of objects between the second and the third and a_3 be the number of objects to the right of the third object. Then,

$$a_0, a_3 \ge 0 \text{ and } a_1, a_2 \ge 1$$

Also, $a_0 + a_1 + a_2 + a_3 = n - 3$

Let $a = a_0 + 1, b = a_3 + 1$, then $a \ge 1, b \ge 1$ such that $a + a_1 + a_2 + b = n - 1$

The total number of positive integral solutions of this equation is ${}^{n-1-1}C_{4-1} = {}^{n-2}C_3 = {}^{n-3}C_3 + {}^{n-3}C_2$

$$= \frac{(n-2)(n-3)(n-4)}{1 \cdot 2 \cdot 3}$$

Example 23 *Given that the divisors of $n = 3^p \cdot 5^q \cdot 7^r$ are of the form $4\lambda + 1, \lambda \ge 0$. Then,*

(a) $p + r$ is always even (b) $p + q + r$ is even or odd

(c) q can be any integer (d) if p is even, then r is odd

Sol. (a, b, c)

$\because$ $3^p = (4-1)^p = 4\lambda_1 + (-1)^p$,

$5^q = (4+1)^q = 4\lambda_2 + 1$

and $7^r = (8-1)^r = 8\lambda_3 + (-1)^r$

Hence, both p and r must be odd or both must be even. Thus, $p + r$ is always even. Also, $p + q + r$ can be odd or even.

Example 24 *Number of ways in which 15 identical coins can be put into 6 different bags*

(a) is coefficient of x^{15} in $x^6(1 + x + x^2 + \ldots \infty)^6$, if no bag remains empty

(b) is coefficient of x^{15} in $(1 - x)^{-6}$

(c) is same as number of the integral solutions of $a + b + c + d + e + f = 15$

(d) is same as number of non-negative integral solutions of $\sum_{i=1}^{6} x_i = 15$

Sol. (a, b, d) Let bags be x_1, x_2, x_3, x_4, x_5 and x_6, then $x_1 + x_2 + x_3 + x_4 + x_5 + x_6 = 15$.

$\therefore$ For no bags remains empty, number of ways

$= $ Coefficient of x^{15} in $(x^1 + x^2 + x^3 + \ldots \infty)^6$

$= $ Coefficient of x^{15} in $x^6(1 + x + x^2 + \ldots \infty)^6$

$= $ Coefficient of x^9 in $(1 - x)^{-6}$

In option (c), it is not mentioned that solution is positive integral.

Passage Based Questions

Passage I

(Ex. Nos. 25 to 26)

All the letters of the word 'AGAIN' be arranged and the words thus formed are known as 'Simple Words'. Further two new types of words are defined as follows:

(i) **Smart word** All the letters of the word 'AGAIN' are being used, but vowels can be repeated as many times as we need.

(ii) **Dull word** All the letters of the word 'AGAIN' are being used, but consonants can be repeated as many times as we need.

Example 25 *If a vowel appears in between two similar letters, the number of simple words is*

(a) 12 (b) 6

(c) 36 (d) 14

Example 26 Number of 7 letter smart words is

(a) 1500 (b) 1050

(c) 1005 (d) 150

Sol. (25 to 26)

25. (b)

N	A-I-A	G

$\therefore$ Required number of simple words $= 3! = 6$

26. (b)

A	G	A	I	N	A	A
					I	I
					A	I

$\therefore$ Number of 7 letter smart words

$$= \frac{7!}{4!} + \frac{7!}{2!\,3!} + \frac{7!}{3!\,2!}$$

$$= 210 + 420 + 420 = 1050$$

Passage II

(Ex. Nos. 27 to 28)

Consider a polygon of sides n which satisfies the equation $3 \cdot {}^nP_4 = {}^{n-1}P_5$.

Example 27 *Rajdhani express travelling from Delhi to Mumbai has n stations enroute. Number of ways in which a train can be stopped at 3 stations if no two of the stopping stations are consecutive, is*

(a) 20 (b) 35

(c) 56 (d) 84

Example 28 *Number of quadrilaterals that can be formed using the vertices of a polygon of sides 'n' if exactly 1 side of the quadrilateral is common with side of the n-gon, is*

(a) 96 (b) 100 (c) 150 (d) 156

Sol. (27 to 28)

$\because \quad 3 \cdot {}^nP_4 = {}^{n-1}P_5$

It is clear that $n \geq 6$.

$\therefore \; 3 \cdot n(n-1)(n-2)(n-3) = (n-1)(n-2)(n-3)(n-4)(n-5)$

$\Rightarrow \quad (n-1)(n-2)(n-3)(n^2 - 12n + 20) = 0$

$\Rightarrow \quad (n-1)(n-2)(n-3)(n-10)(n-2) = 0$

$\therefore \quad n = 10, n \neq 1, 2, 3 \quad [\because n \geq 6]$

$\Rightarrow \quad n = 10$

27. (d) Let a_0 be the number of stations to the left of the station I chosen, a_1 be the number of stations between the station I and station II, a_2 be the number of stations between the station II and station III and a_3 be the number of stations to the right of the third station.

Then,

$$a_0, a_3 \geq 0 \text{ and } a_1, a_2 \geq 1$$

Also, $a_0 + a_1 + a_2 + a_3 = n + 1 - 3$

Let $a = a_0 + 1, b = a_3 + 1$, then $a, b \geq 1$ such that

$$a + a_1 + a_2 + b = n$$

$\therefore$ Required number of ways $= {}^{n-1}C_{4-1} = {}^9C_3$ [here, $n = 10$]

$= 84$

28. (c) Number of quadrilaterals of which exactly one side is the side of the n-gon

$$= n \times {}^{n-4}C_2 = 10 \times {}^6C_2 = 150 \quad [\because n = 10]$$

Stem Based Questions

Stem I

(Ex. Nos. 29 and 30)

Consider the number $N = 2016$.

Example 29 Number of cyphers at the end of ${}^NC_{N/2}$ is ...

Example 30 Sum of all even divisors of the number N is ...

Sol. (29 and 30)

29. (2) $\because \quad {}^NC_{N/2} = {}^{2016}C_{1008} = \dfrac{(2016)!}{[(1008)!]^2}$

$$E_5(2016!) = \left[\frac{2016}{5}\right] + \left[\frac{2016}{5^2}\right] + \left[\frac{2016}{5^3}\right] + \left[\frac{2016}{5^4}\right]$$

$$= 403 + 80 + 16 + 3 = 502$$

and $\quad E_5(1008!) = \left[\frac{1008}{5}\right] + \left[\frac{1008}{5^2}\right] + \left[\frac{1008}{5^3}\right] + \left[\frac{1008}{5^4}\right]$

$$= 201 + 40 + 8 + 1$$

$$= 250$$

Hence, the number of cyphers at the end of ${}^{2016}C_{1008}$

$$= 502 - 250 - 250 = 2$$

30. (6448) $\because \quad N = 2016 = 2^5 \cdot 3^2 \cdot 7^1$

$\therefore$ Sum of all even divisors of the number N

$$= (2 + 2^2 + 2^3 + 2^4 + 2^5)(1 + 3 + 3^2)(1 + 7^1)$$

$$= 6448$$

Single Integer Answer Type Questions

Example 31 *If* $\binom{18}{r-2}+2\binom{18}{r-1}+\binom{18}{r}\geq\binom{20}{13}$, *then the number of values of r are ....*

Sol. (7) We have, $\binom{18}{r-2}+2\binom{18}{r-1}+\binom{18}{r}\geq\binom{20}{13}$

It means that $^{18}C_{r-2}+2\cdot{}^{18}C_{r-1}+{}^{18}C_r\geq{}^{20}C_{13}$

$\Rightarrow\ ({}^{18}C_{r-2}+{}^{18}C_{r-1})+({}^{18}C_{r-1}+{}^{18}C_r)\geq{}^{20}C_7$

$\Rightarrow\ {}^{19}C_{r-1}+{}^{19}C_r\geq{}^{20}C_7$

$\Rightarrow\ {}^{20}C_r\geq{}^{20}C_7$

or $\ {}^{20}C_r\geq{}^{20}C_{13}$

$\Rightarrow\ 7\leq r\leq 13$

$\therefore\ r=7,8,9,10,11,12,13$

Hence, the number of values of r are 7.

Example 32 *If* λ *be the number of 3-digit numbers are of the form xyz with* $x<y$, $z<y$ *and* $x\neq 0$, *the value of* $\frac{\lambda}{30}$ *is ....*

Sol. (8) Since, $x\geq 1$, then $y\geq 2$ $\quad[\because x<y]$

If $y=n$, then x takes values form 1 to $n-1$ and z can take the values from 0 to $n-1$ (i.e. n values).

Thus, for each values of $y(2\leq y\leq 9)$, x and z take $n(n-1)$ values.

Hence, the 3-digit numbers are of the form xyz

$$=\sum_{n=2}^{9}n(n-1)=\sum_{n=1}^{9}n(n-1)$$

$[\because$ at $n=1$, $n(n-1)=0]$

$$=\sum_{n=1}^{9}n^2-\sum_{n=1}^{9}n$$

$$=\frac{9(9+1)(18+1)}{6}-\frac{9(9+1)}{2}$$

$$=285-45$$

$$=240=\lambda \quad \text{[given]}$$

$$\therefore\quad \frac{\lambda}{30}=8$$

Example 33 *If total number of runs scored in n matches is* $\left(\frac{n+1}{4}\right)(2^{n+1}-n-2)$, *where* $n>1$ *and the runs scored in the kth match are given by* $k\cdot 2^{n+1-k}$, *where* $1\leq k\leq n$. *Then, value of n is ....*

Sol. (7) Given, runs scored in kth match $=k\cdot 2^{n+1-k}$, $1\leq k\leq n$

and runs scored in n matches

$$=\frac{n+1}{4}(2^{n+1}-n-2)$$

$$\therefore\ \sum_{k=1}^{n}k\cdot 2^{n+1-k}=\frac{n+1}{4}(2^{n+1}-n-2)$$

$$\Rightarrow 2^{n+1}\left[\sum_{k=1}^{n}\frac{k}{2^k}\right]=\frac{n+1}{4}(2^{n+1}-n-2)$$

$$\Rightarrow 2^{n+1}\left[\frac{1}{2}+\frac{2}{2^2}+\frac{3}{2^3}+\ldots+\frac{n}{2^n}\right]=\frac{n+1}{4}(2^{n+1}-n-2) \quad \text{...(i)}$$

Let $\quad S=\frac{1}{2}+\frac{2}{2^2}+\frac{3}{2^3}+\ldots+\frac{n}{2^n} \quad$ ...(ii)

$\therefore\quad \frac{1}{2}S=\frac{1}{2^2}+\frac{2}{2^3}+\frac{3}{2^4}+\ldots+\frac{n-1}{2^n}+\frac{n}{2^{n+1}} \quad$ ...(iii)

On subtracting Eq. (iii) from Eq. (ii), we get

$$\frac{1}{2}S=\frac{1}{2}+\frac{1}{2^2}+\frac{1}{2^3}+\ldots+\frac{1}{2^n}-\frac{n}{2^{n+1}}$$

$$\Rightarrow\quad \frac{1}{2}S=\frac{\frac{1}{2}\left(1-\frac{1}{2^n}\right)}{1-\frac{1}{2}}-\frac{n}{2^{n+1}}$$

$$\Rightarrow\quad S=2\left[1-\frac{1}{2^n}-\frac{n}{2^{n+1}}\right] \quad \text{...(iv)}$$

From Eqs. (i) and (iv), we get

$$2\cdot 2^{n+1}\left[1-\frac{1}{2^n}-\frac{n}{2^{n+1}}\right]=\frac{n+1}{4}[2^{n+1}-n-2]$$

$$\Rightarrow\quad 2[2^{n+1}-2-n]=\frac{n+1}{4}[2^{n+1}-2-n]$$

$$\Rightarrow\quad \frac{n+1}{4}=2$$

$$\Rightarrow\quad n=7$$

Example 34 *Words of length 10 are formed using the letters A, B, C, D, E, F, G, H, I, J. Let x be the number of such words where no letter is repeated; and let y be the number of such words where exactly one letter is repeated twice and no other letter is repeated. Then,* $\frac{y}{9x}$ *is equal to ....*

Sol. (5) $\quad x=10\,!$

$$y={}^{10}C_1\times{}^{9}C_8\times\frac{10!}{2!}=10\times 9\times\frac{10!}{2}$$

$$\Rightarrow\ \frac{y}{9x}=\frac{10}{2}=5$$

Example 35 *Let n be the number of ways in which 5 boys and 5 girls can stand in a queue in such a way that all the girls stand consecutively in the queue. Let m be the number of ways in which 5 boys and 5 girls can stand in a queue in such a way that exactly four girls stand consecutively in the queue. Then, the value of m/n is ....*

Sol. (5) Here, ___ B_1___ B_2 ___ B_3 ___ B_4 ___ B_5 ___

Out of 5 girls, 4 girls are together and 1 girl is separate. Now, to select 2 positions out of 6 positions between boys = ${}^6C_2$ ...(i)

4 girls are to be selected out of 5 = ${}^5C_4$ ...(ii)

Now, 2 groups of girls can be arranged in 2! ways. ...(iii)

Also, the group of 4 girls and 5 boys is arranged in $4! \times 5!$ ways. ...(iv)

Now, total number of ways

$$= {}^6C_2 \times {}^5C_4 \times 2! \times 4! \times 5!$$

[from Eqs. (i), (ii), (iii) and (iv)]

$\therefore \quad m = {}^6C_2 \times {}^5C_4 \times 2! \times 4! \times 5!$

and $\quad n = 5! \times 6!$

$$\Rightarrow \quad \frac{m}{n} = \frac{{}^6C_2 \times {}^5C_4 \times 2! \times 4! \times 5!}{6! \times 5!}$$

$$= \frac{15 \times 5 \times 2 \times 4!}{6 \times 5 \times 4!} = 5$$

Numerical Value Type Questions

Example 36 *There are 720 permutations of the digits 1, 2, 3, 4, 5, 6. Suppose these permutations are arranged from smallest to largest numerical values, beginning from 123456 and ending with 654321. Then, the last two digit of the number at 267th position is ....*

Sol. (46) Number of numbers beginning with $1 = 5! = 120$

Number of numbers beginning with $2 = 5! = 120$

Number of numbers beginning with $31 = 4! = 24$

Number of numbers beginning with $3214 = 2! = 2$

266

$\therefore$ The number at 267th position = 321546

So, last two digits of required number is 46.

Example 37 *The number of 5 digit numbers which are divisible by 4, with digits from the set {1, 2, 3, 4, 5} and the repetition of digits is allowed, is ....*

Sol. (625) A number is divisible by 4 if last two digit number is divisible by 4.

$\therefore$ Last two digit number divisible by 4 from 1, 2, 3, 4, 5 are 12, 24, 32, 44, 52

$\therefore$ The number of 5 digit number which are divisible by 4, from the digit 1, 2, 3, 4, 5 and digit is repeated is

$$5 \times 5 \times 5 \times (5 \times 1) = 625$$

Example 38 *Let $n_1 < n_2 < n_3 < n_4 < n_5$ be positive integers such that $n_1 + n_2 + n_3 + n_4 + n_5 = 20$. The number of such distinct arrangements $(n_1, n_2, n_3, n_4, n_5)$ is p, then 45p is equal to ....*

> **Decoding the Question**
> Reduce the equation into a new equation, where sum of variables is less. Then, find the number of arrangement.

Sol. (7) As, $n_1 \geq 1, n_2 \geq 2, n_3 \geq 3, n_4 \geq 4, n_5 \geq 5$

Let $n_1 - 1 = x_1 \geq 0, n_2 - 2 = x_2 \geq 0, \ldots, n_5 - 5 = x_5 \geq 0$

$\Rightarrow$ New equation will be

$$x_1 + 1 + x_2 + 2 + \ldots + x_5 + 5 = 20$$

$$\Rightarrow \quad x_1 + x_2 + x_3 + x_4 + x_5 = 20 - 15 = 5$$

Now, $\quad x_1 \leq x_2 \leq x_3 \leq x_4 \leq x_5$

x_1	x_2	x_3	x_4	x_5
0	0	0	0	5
0	0	0	1	4
0	0	0	2	3
0	0	1	1	3
0	0	1	2	2
0	1	1	1	2
1	1	1	1	1

So, 7 possible cases will be there.

$\therefore \quad p = 7$

Now, $45p = 315$

Example 39 *Eighteen guests have to be seated half on each side of a long table. Four particular guests desire to sit on one particular side and three other on the other side. If the number of ways in which the sitting arrangements can be made is $({}^aP_b \times {}^aP_c \times (d)!)$, then $a + b + c + d$ is equal to*

Sol. (27) Let the two sides be A and B. Assume that four particular guests wish to sit on side A. Four guests who wish to sit on side A can be accommodated on nine chairs in ${}^9P_4$ ways and three guests who wish to sit on side B can be accommodated in ${}^9P_3$ ways. Now, the remaining guests are left who can sit on 11 chairs on both the sides of the table in (11!) ways. Hence, the total number of ways in which 18 persons can be seated $= {}^9P_4 \times {}^9P_3 \times (11)!$.

$$= {}^aP_b \times {}^aP_c \times d! \quad \text{[given]}$$

By comparing, we get

$$a = 9, b = 4, c = 3 \text{ and } d = 11$$

$\therefore a + b + c + d = 9 + 4 + 3 + 11 = 27$

Example 40 *A man X has 7 friends, 4 of them are ladies and 3 are men. His wife Y also has 7 friends, 3 of them are ladies and 4 are men. Assume X and Y have no common friends. Then, the total number of ways in which X and Y together can throw a party inviting 3 ladies and 3 men, so that 3 friends of each of X and Y are in this party, is ....*

Sol. (485) Given, X has 7 friends, 4 of them are ladies and 3 are men, while Y has 7 friends, 3 of them are ladies and 4 are men.

$\therefore$ Total number of required ways

$$= {}^3C_3 \times {}^4C_0 \times {}^4C_0 \times {}^3C_3 + {}^3C_2 \times {}^4C_1 \times {}^4C_1 \times {}^3C_2 + {}^3C_1 \times {}^4C_2 \times {}^4C_2 \times {}^3C_1 + {}^3C_0 \times {}^4C_3 \times {}^4C_3 \times {}^3C_0$$

$= 1 + 144 + 324 + 16 = 485$

Example 41 *Let $S = \{1, 2, 3, \ldots, 9\}$. For $k = 1, 2, \ldots, 5$, let N_k be the number of subsets of S, each containing five elements out of which exactly k are odd. Then, $N_1 + N_2 + N_3 + N_4 + N_5$ is equal to ....*

Sol. (126) $N_i = {}^5C_k \times {}^4C_{5-k}$

$$N_1 = 5 \times 1 = 5$$
$$N_2 = 10 \times 4 = 40$$
$$N_3 = 10 \times 6 = 60$$
$$N_4 = 5 \times 4 = 20$$
$$N_5 = 1$$
$$N_1 + N_2 + N_3 + N_4 + N_5 = 126$$

Matching Type Questions

Example 42 *Match the Column I with Column II.*

Column I		Column II	
(A)	The sum of the factors of 8! which are odd and are the form $3\lambda + 2, \lambda \in N$, is	(p)	384
(B)	The number of divisors of $n = 2^7 \cdot 3^5 \cdot 5^3$ which are the form $4\lambda + 1, \lambda \in N$, is	(q)	240
(C)	Total number of divisors of $n = 2^5 \cdot 3^4 \cdot 5^{10} \cdot 7^6$ which are the form $4\lambda + 2, \lambda \geq 1$, is	(r)	11
(D)	Total number of divisors of $n = 3^5 \cdot 5^7 \cdot 7^9$ which are the form $4\lambda + 1, \lambda \geq 0$, is	(s)	40

Sol. (A) → s; (B) → r; (C) → p; (D) → q

(A) Here, $8! = 2^7 \cdot 3^2 \cdot 5^1 \cdot 7^1$

So, the odd factors are 1, 3, 5, 7, 35 of which 5 and 35 are of the form $3\lambda + 2$.

∴Sum is 40.

(B) Number of odd numbers $= (5 + 1)(3 + 1) = 24$

Required number $= 12$, but 1 is included.

∴ Required number of numbers $= 12 - 1 = 11$ of the form $4\lambda + 1$.

(C) Here, $4\lambda + 2 = 2(2\lambda + 1)$

∴ Total divisors $= 1 \cdot 5 \cdot 11 \cdot 7 - 1 = 384$

[∵ one is subtracted because there will be case when selected powers of 3, 5 and 7 are zero]

(D) Here, any positive integer power of 5 will be in the form of $4\lambda + 1$ when even powers of 3 and 7 will be in the form of $4\lambda + 1$ and odd powers of 3 and 7 will be in the form of $4\lambda - 1$.

∴ Required divisors $= 8(3 \cdot 5 + 3 \cdot 5) = 240$

Example 43 *Match the Column I with Column II.*

Column I		Column II	
(A)	Four dice (six faced) are rolled. The number of possible outcomes in which atleast one die shows 2, is	(p)	210
(B)	Let A be the set of 4-digit numbers $a_1a_2a_3a_4$, where $a_1 > a_2 > a_3 > a_4$. Then, $n(A)$ is equal to	(q)	480
(C)	The total number 3-digit numbers, the sum of whose digits is even, is equal to	(r)	671
(D)	The number of 4-digit numbers that can be formed from the digits 0, 1, 2, 3, 4, 5, 6, 7, so that each number contains digit 1, is	(s)	450

Sol. (A) → r; (B) → p; (C) → s; (D) → q

(A) The number of possible outcomes with 2 on atleast one die = The total number of outcomes with 2 on atleast one die = (The total number of outcomes) – (The number of outcomes in which 2 does not appear on any dice)
$= 6^4 - 5^4 = 1296 - 625 = 671$

(B) Any selection of four digits from the 10 digits 0, 1, 2, 3,..., 9 gives one number. So, the required number of numbers is ${}^{10}C_4$ i.e. 210.

(C) Let the number be $n = pqr$. Since, $p + q + r$ is even, p can be filled in 9 ways and q can be filled in 10 ways.

r can be filled in number of ways depending upon what is the sum of p and q.

If $(p + q)$ is odd, then r can be filled with any one of five odd digits.

If $(p + q)$ is even, then r can be filled with any one of five even digits.

In any case, r can be filled in five ways.

Hence, total number of numbers is $9 \times 10 \times 5 = 450$

(D) After fixing 1 at one position out of 4 places, 3 places can be filled by ${}^7P_3$ ways. But for some numbers whose fourth digit is zero, such type of ways is ${}^6P_2$. Therefore, total number of ways is ${}^7P_3 + {}^6P_2 = 480$

EXERCISE 1

JEE Main Pattern

Single Option Correct Type Questions

1. The total number of integers n, such that $2 \leq n \leq 2000$ and HCF of n and 36 is 1, is

(a) 333 (b) 444 (c) 555 (d) 666

2. The number of ordered pairs (x, y) if $x, y \in \{0, 1, 2, 3, \ldots. 10\}$ and $|x - y| > 5$, is

(a) 25 (b) 30 (c) 35 (d) 40

3. Sum of the series $\sum_{r=1}^{n} (r^2 + 1) r!$, is

(a) $(n+1)!$ (b) $(n+2)! - 1$ (c) $n(n+1)!$ (d) $n!$

4. The exponent of 12 is 100!, is

(a) 24 (b) 46 (c) 47 (d) 48

5. Five different digits from the set of numbers {1, 2, 3, 4, 5, 6, 7} are written in random order. Then, the number of numbers that can be formed using 5 different digits from this set if the number is divisible by 9, is

(a) 240 (b) 200 (c) 160 (d) 120

6. There are m points on one straight line AB and n points on another straight line AC, none of them being A. The number of triangles can be formed with these points is

(a) $\frac{mn}{2}(m + n - 2)$ (b) $\frac{mn}{2}(m + n - 1)$

(c) $\frac{mn}{2}(m + n)$ (d) $\frac{mn}{2}(m + n + 1)$

7. The number 24! is divisible by

(a) 6^{24} (b) 24^7 (c) 12^{12} (d) 48^{10}

8. The sum of all the numbers of four different digits that can be made by using the digits 0, 1, 2 and 3 is

(a) 26664 (b) 39996

(c) 38664 (d) None of these

9. If ${}^nC_3 + {}^nC_4 > {}^{n+1}C_3$, then

(a) $n > 6$ (b) $n > 7$ (c) $n < 6$ (d) $n < 7$

10. The number of ways in which we can select four numbers from 1 to 30 so as to exclude every selection of four consecutive numbers is

(a) 27378 (b) 27405

(c) 27399 (d) None of these

11. Total number of words that can be formed using all letters of the word BRIJESH that neither begins with I nor ends with B is equal to

(a) 3720 (b) 4920 (c) 3600 (d) 4800

12. The number of words of four letters containing equal number of vowels and consonants, where repetition is allowed, is

(a) 105^2 (b) 210×243

(c) 105×243 (d) 150×21^2

13. Number of ways in which ₹ 18 can be distributed amongst four persons, such that nobody receives less than ₹ 3 is

(a) 4^2 (b) 2^4 (c) 4! (d) 84

14. The number of ways to fill each of the four cells of the table with a distinct natural number, such that the sum of the numbers is 10 and the sums of the numbers placed diagonally are equal, is

(a) 4 (b) 8 (c) 24 (d) 6

15. In how many ways can a team of 6 horses be selected out of a stud of 16, so that there shall to always be three out of $A\ B\ C\ A'\ B'\ C'$ but never AA', BB' or CC' together.

(a) 840 (b) 1260

(c) 960 (d) 720

16. A lady gives a dinner party to 5 guests to be selected from nine friends. The number of ways of forming the party of 5, given that two of the friends will not attend the party together, is

(a) 56 (b) 126

(c) 91 (d) None of these

17. If a, b, c and d are odd natural numbers, such that $a + b + c + d = 20$, the number of values of the ordered quadruplet (a, b, c, d) is

(a) 165 (b) 455

(c) 310 (d) None of these

18. If $l =$ LCM of 8!, 10! and 12! and $h =$ HCF of 8!, 10! and 12!, then $\frac{l}{h}$ is equal to

(a) 132 (b) 11800

(c) 11880 (d) None of these

19. The number of positive integers satisfying the inequality ${}^{n+1}C_{n-2} - {}^{n+1}C_{n-1} \leq 100$ is

(a) 9 (b) 8

(c) 5 (d) None of these

20. The number of ways in which a score of 11 can be made from a through by three persons, each throwing a single die once, is
(a) 45 (b) 18 (c) 27 (d) 68

21. In a plane there are 37 straight lines, of which 13 pass through the point A and 11 pass through the point B. Besides, no three lines pass through one point, no line passes through both points A and B and no two are parallel, the number of intersection points the lines have, is
(a) 535 (b) 601 (c) 728 (d) 963

22. If a denotes the number of permutations of $x+2$ things taken all at a time, b the number of permutations of x things taken 11 at a time and c the number of permutations of $x-11$ things taken all at a time such that $a = 182bc$, the value of x is
(a) 15 (b) 12 (c) 10 (d) 18

23. If the permutations of a, b, c, d and e taken all together are written down in alphabetical order as in dictionary and numbered, the rank of the permutation *debac* is
(a) 90 (b) 91 (c) 92 (d) 93

24. A set containing n elements. A subset P of A is chosen. The set A is reconstructed by replacing the element of P. A subset Q of A is again chosen the number of ways of choosing P and Q, so that $P \cap Q = \phi$, is
(a) $2^{2n} - {}^{2n}C_n$ (b) 2^n
(c) $2^n - 1$ (d) 3^n

25. The straight lines I_1, I_2, I_3 are parallel and lie in the same plane. A total number of m points on I_1 ; n points on I_2 ; k points on I_3, the maximum number of triangles formed with vertices at these points is
(a) ${}^{m+n+k}C_3$ (b) ${}^{m+n+k}C_3 - {}^mC_3 - {}^nC_3 - {}^kC_3$
(c) ${}^mC_3 + {}^nC_3 + {}^kC_3$ (d) None of these

26. Let A be a set of $n (\geq 3)$ distinct elements. The number of triplets (x, y, z) of the set A in which atleast two coordinates are equal to
(a) ${}^nP_3$ (b) $n^3 - {}^nP_3$ (c) $3n^2 - 2n$ (d) $3n^2(n-1)$

27. The total number of five-digit numbers of different digits in which the digit in the middle is the largest, is
(a) $2^2 \cdot 3^2 \cdot 7^2$ (b) $2^3 \cdot 3 \cdot 7^3$ (c) $2^2 \cdot 3^3 \cdot 7^2$ (d) $2^3 \cdot 3^2 \cdot 7^3$

Numerical Value Type Questions

28. T_n denotes the number of triangles which can be formed using the vertices of a regular polygon of n sides. If $T_{n+1} - T_n = 21$, then the value of n is ....

29. The number of divisors of the form $4n + 2 (n \geq 0)$ of the integer 240, is ....

30. If ${}^nP_r = {}^nP_{r+1}$ and ${}^nC_r = {}^nC_{r-1}$, then the value of $n + r$ is ....

31. If the number of ways in which we can get a score of 11 by throwing three dice is 3λ, then the value of λ is ....

32. There are six periods in each working day of a school. If the number of ways in which 5 subjects can be arranged if each subject is allotted at least one period and no period remains vacant is $2^a \times 3^b \times 5^c$, then $a + b + c$ is equal to ....

33. If the number of ways of selection of atleast one vowel and one consonant from the word TRIPLE is x, then heighest prime factor of x is ....

34. The number of integral solutions of $x + y + z = 0$, with $x \geq -5$, $y \geq -5$, $z \geq -5$ is 17λ, then the value of λ is ....

35. If $PQRS$ is a convex quadrilateral with 3, 4, 5 and 6 points marked on sides PQ, QR, RS and PS, respectively. If the number of triangles with vertices on difference sides is x, then number of proper divisor of x is equal to ....

36. A person has n friends. The minimum value of n so that person can invite a different pair of friends everyday for four weeks in a row is ....

37. There are n distinct white and n distinct black balls. If the number of ways of arranging them in a row so that neighbouring balls are of different colours is 1152, then the value of n is ....

38. The ten's digit of $1! + 2! + 3! + \ldots + 97!$ is ....

39. The exponent of 7 in ${}^{100}C_{50}$ is ....

40. Let P_n denotes the number of ways in which three people can be selected out of n people sitting in a row, in two of them are consecutive. If $P_{n+1} - P_n = 15$, the value of n is ....

41. If the letters of the word are arranged as in a dictionary. m and n are the rank of the words BULBUL and NANNU respectively, then the value of $m - 4n$ is ....

42. An n-digit number is a positive number with exactly n-digits. Nine hundred distinct n-digit numbers are to be formed using only the three digits 2, 5 and 7. The smallest value of n for which this is possible, is ....

Previous Year Questions

43. Number of ways of arranging 8 identical books into 4 identical shelves, where any number of shelves may remain empty is equal to **[Single Correct Type, 2024 Main]**
(a) 12 (b) 16 (c) 15 (d) 18

44. Let $\alpha = \dfrac{(4!)!}{(4!)^{3!}}$ and $\beta = \dfrac{(5!)!}{(5!)^{4!}}$. Then,
[Single Correct Type, 2024 Main]
(a) $\alpha \in N$ and $\beta \in N$ (b) $\alpha \notin N$ and $\beta \notin N$
(c) $\alpha \in N$ and $\beta \notin N$ (d) $\alpha \notin N$ and $\beta \in N$

45. If all the words with or without meaning made using all the letters of the word 'NAGPUR' are arranged as in a dictionary, then the word at 315th position in this arrangement is **[Single Correct Type, 2024 Main]**
(a) NRAGUP (b) NRAPUG
(c) NRAPGU (d) NRAGPU

46. The number of ways five alphabets can be chosen from the alphabets of the word MATHEMATICS, where the chosen alphabets are not necessarily distinct, is equal to **[Single Correct Type, 2024 Main]**
(a) 177 (b) 181 (c) 179 (d) 175

47. If n is the number of ways five different employees can sit into four indistinguishable offices where any office may have any number of persons including zero, then n is equal to **[Single Correct Type, 2024 Main]**
(a) 51 (b) 43 (c) 53 (d) 47

48. The number of ways in which 21 identical apples can be distributed among three children such that each child gets at least 2 apples, is **[Single Correct Type, 2024 Main]**
(a) 130 (b) 406 (c) 136 (d) 142

49. Let $0 \le r \le n$. If ${}^{n+1}C_{r+1} : {}^{n}C_{r} : {}^{n-1}C_{r-1} = 55:35:21$, then $2n + 5r$ is equal to **[Single Correct Type, 2024 Main]**
(a) 62 (b) 60 (c) 50 (d) 55

50. If for some m, n: ${}^6C_m + 2({}^6C_{m+1}) + {}^6C_{m+2} > {}^8C_3$ and ${}^{n-1}P_3 : {}^nP_4 = 1:8$, then ${}^nP_{m+1} + {}^{n+1}C_m$ is equal to **[Single Correct Type, 2024 Main]**
(a) 372 (b) 376 (c) 380 (d) 384

51. ${}^{n-1}C_r = (k^2 - 8)\,{}^nC_{r+1}$ if and only if **[Single Correct Type, 2024 Main]**
(a) $2\sqrt{2} < k \le \sqrt{3}$ (b) $2\sqrt{3} < k \le 3\sqrt{2}$
(c) $2\sqrt{2} < k < 2\sqrt{3}$ (d) $2\sqrt{3} < k < 3\sqrt{3}$

52. The number of triangles whose vertices are at the vertices of a regular octagon but none of whose sides is a side of the octagon is **[Single Correct Type, 2024 Main]**
(a) 16 (b) 56 (c) 24 (d) 48

53. All the letters of the word "GTWENTY" are written in all possible ways with or without meaning and these words are written as in a dictionary. The serial number of the word "GTWENTY" is .... **[Numerical Value Type, 2024 Main]**

54. The number of 3-digit numbers, formed using the digits 2, 3, 4, 5 and 7. When the repetition of digits is not allowed and which are not divisible by 3 is equal to .... **[Numerical Value Type, 2024 Main]**

55. The total number of words (with or without meaning) that can be formed out of the letters of the word 'DISTRIBUTION' taken four at a time, is equal to .... **[Numerical Value Type, 2024 Main]**

56. The total number of three-digit numbers, divisible by 3, which can be formed using the digits 1, 3, 5, 8, if repetition of digits is allowed, is **[Single Correct Type, 2023 Main]**
(a) 22 (b) 18 (c) 20 (d) 21

57. The number of five digit numbers, greater than 40000 and divisible by 5, which can be formed using the digits 0, 1, 3, 5, 7 and 9 without repetition, is equal to **[Single Correct Type, 2023 Main]**
(a) 72 (b) 132 (c) 96 (d) 120

58. The number of arrangements of the letters of the word "INDEPENDENCE" in which all the vowels always occur together is **[Single Correct Type, 2023 Main]**
(a) 16800 (b) 33600 (c) 18000 (d) 14800

59. All words, with or without meaning, are made using all the letters of the word MONDAY. These words are written as in a dictionary with serial numbers. The serial number of the word MONDAY is **[Single Correct Type, 2023 Main]**
(a) 327 (b) 328 (c) 324 (d) 326

60. If the number of words, with or without meaning, which can be made using all the letters of the word MATHEMATICS in which C and S do not come together, is $(6!)k$, then k is equal to **[Single Correct Type, 2023 Main]**
(a) 5670 (b) 1890 (c) 945 (d) 2835

61. All the letters of the word PUBLIC are written in all possible orders and these words are written as in a dictionary with serial numbers. Then, the serial number of the word PUBLIC is **[Single Correct Type, 2023 Main]**
(a) 576 (b) 578 (c) 580 (d) 582

62. The value of $\dfrac{1}{1!50!} + \dfrac{1}{3!48!} + \dfrac{1}{5!46!} + \ldots + \dfrac{1}{49!2!} + \dfrac{1}{51!1!}$ is **[Single Correct Type, 2023 Main]**
(a) $\dfrac{2^{51}}{50!}$ (b) $\dfrac{2^{51}}{51!}$ (c) $\dfrac{2^{50}}{51!}$ (d) $\dfrac{2^{50}}{50!}$

63. If ${}^{2n+1}P_{n-1} : {}^{2n-1}P_n = 11:21$, then $n^2 + n + 15$ is equal to **[Single Correct Type, 2023 Main]**
(a) 45 (b) 50 (c) 56 (d) 52

64. The number of triplets (x, y, z), where x, y, z are distinct non-negative integers satisfying $x + y + z = 15$, is **[Single Correct Type, 2023 Main]**
(a) 136 (b) 80
(c) 114 (d) 92

65. Let the number of elements in sets A and B be five and two respectively. Then, the number of subsets of $A \times B$ each having at least 3 and at most 6 elements is **[Single Correct Type, 2023 Main]**
(a) 782 (b) 792
(c) 752 (d) 772

66. The number of ways, in which 5 girls and 7 boys can be seated at a round table so that no two girls sit together, is **[Single Correct Type, 2023 Main]**

(a) $7(360)^2$ (b) $7(720)^2$ (c) 720 (d) $126(5!)^2$

67. Eight persons are to be transported from city A to city B in three cars of different makes. If each car can accommodate at most three persons, then the number of ways, in which they can be transported, is **[Single Correct Type, 2023 Main]**

(a) 1680 (b) 3360 (c) 1120 (d) 560

68. If ${}^{2n}C_3 : {}^nC_3 = 10:1$, then the ratio $(n^2+3n):(n^2-3n+4)$ is **[Single Correct Type, 2023 Main]**

(a) 27:11 (b) 2:1 (c) 65:37 (d) 35:16

69. If $({}^{30}C_1)^2 + 2({}^{30}C_2)^2 + 3({}^{30}C_3)^2 + \ldots + 30({}^{30}C_{30})^2 = \dfrac{\alpha 60!}{(30!)^2}$, then α is equal to **[Single Correct Type, 2023 Main]**

(a) 30 (b) 60
(c) 10 (d) 15

70. Total numbers of 3-digit numbers that are divisible by 6 and can be formed by using the digits 1, 2, 3, 4, 5 with repetition, is .... **[Numerical Value Type, 2023 Main]**

71. The sum of all the four-digit numbers that can be formed using all the digits 2, 1, 2, 3 is equal to .... **[Numerical Value Type, 2023 Main]**

72. The number of permutations of the digits 1, 2, 3, ..., 7 without repetition, which neither contain the string 153 nor the string 2467, is .... **[Numerical Value Type, 2023 Main]**

73. Let the digits a, b, c be in AP. Nine-digit numbers are to be formed using each of these three digits thrice such that three consecutive digits are in AP at least once. How many such numbers can be formed? **[Numerical Value Type, 2023 Main]**

74. The number of 4-letter words, with or without meaning, each consisting of 2 vowels and 2 consonants, which can be formed from the letters of the word UNIVERSE without repetition is...... . **[Numerical Value Type, 2023 Main]**

75. Let 5-digit numbers be constructed using the digits 0, 2, 3, 4, 7, 9 with repetition allowed and are arranged in ascending order with serial numbers. Then, the serial number of the number 42923 is .... **[Numerical Value Type, 2023 Main]**

76. If all the six digit numbers $x_1\, x_2\, x_3\, x_4\, x_5\, x_6$ with $0 < x_1 < x_2 < x_3 < x_4 < x_5 < x_6$ are arranged in the increasing order, then the sum of the digits in the 72th number is .... **[Numerical Value Type, 2023 Main]**

77. Number of 4-digit numbers (the repetition of digits is allowed) which are made using the digits 1, 2, 3 and 5 and are divisible by 15, is equal to .... **[Numerical Value Type, 2023 Main]**

78. Five digit numbers are formed using the digits 1, 2, 3, 5, 7 with repetitions and are written in descending order with serial numbers. e.g. the number 77777 has serial number 1. Then, the serial number of 35337 is .... **[Numerical Value Type, 2023 Main]**

79. A person forgets his 4-digit ATM pin code. But he remembers that in the code all the digits are different, the greatest digit is 7 and the sum of the first two digits is equal to the sum of the last two digits. Then, the maximum number of trials necessary to obtain the correct code is .... **[Numerical Value Type, 2023 Main]**

80. Some couples participated in a mixed doubles badminton tournament. If the number of matches played, so that no couple played in a match is 840, then the total number of persons, who participated in the tournament, is .... **[Numerical Value Type, 2023 Main]**

81. Let R be a relation from the set $\{1, 2, 3, \ldots, 60\}$ to itself such that $R = \{(a, b) : b = pq$, where $p, q \geq 3$ are prime numbers$\}$. Then, the number of elements in R, is **[Single Correct Type, 2022 Main]**

(a) 600 (b) 660 (c) 540 (d) 720

82. The total number of 5-digit numbers, formed by using the digits 1, 2, 3, 5, 6, 7 without repetition, which are multiple of 6, is **[Single Correct Type, 2022 Main]**

(a) 36 (b) 48 (c) 60 (d) 72

83. The number of bijective functions $f:\{1, 3, 5, 7, \ldots, 99\} \to \{2, 4, 6, 8, \ldots, 100\}$, such that $f(3) \geq f(9) \geq f(15) \geq (21) \geq \ldots \geq f(99)$, is .... **[Single Correct Type, 2022 Main]**

(a) ${}^{50}P_{17}$ (b) ${}^{50}P_{33}$
(c) $33! \times 17!$ (d) $50!/2$

84. A class contains b boys and g girls. If the number of ways of selecting 3 boys and 2 girls from the class is 168, then $b + 3g$ is equal to .... **[Numerical Value Type, 2022 Main]**

85. Let S be the set of all passwords which are six to eight characters long, where each character is either an alphabet from $\{A, B, C, D, E\}$ or a number from $\{1, 2, 3, 4, 5\}$ with the repetition of characters allowed. If the number of passwords in S whose atleast one character is a number from $\{1, 2, 3, 4, 5\}$ is $\alpha \times 5^6$, then α is equal to .... **[Numerical Value Type, 2022 Main]**

86. The number of 5- digit natural numbers, such that the product of their digits is 36, is .... **[Numerical Value Type, 2022 Main]**

87. The letters of the word 'MANKIND' are written in all possible orders and arranged in serial order as in an English dictionary. Then, the serial number of the word 'MANKIND' is .... **[Numerical Value Type, 2022 Main]**

88. The number of 6-digit numbers made by using the digits 1, 2, 3, 4, 5, 6, 7 without repetition and which are multiple of 15 is .... **[Numerical Value Type, 2022 Main]**

89. The total number of four-digit numbers such that each of the first three digits is divisible by the last digit is equal to .... **[Numerical Value Type, 2022 Main]**

90. Let $b_1b_2b_3b_4$ be a 4-element permutation with $b_i \in \{1, 2, 3, ..., 100\}$ for $1 \le i \le 4$ and $b_i \ne b_j$ for $i \ne j$, such that either b_1, b_2, b_3 are consecutive integers or b_2, b_3, b_4 are consecutive integers. Then, the number of such permutations $b_1b_2b_3b_4$ is equal to ......
[Numerical Value Type, 2022 Main]

91. The total number of three-digit numbers, with one digit repeated exactly two times, is ....
[Numerical Value Type, 2022 Main]

92. In an examination, there are 5 multiple choice questions with 3 choices, out of which exactly one is correct. There are 3 marks for each correct answer, –2 marks for each wrong answer and 0 mark if the question is not attempted. Then, the number of ways a student appearing in the examination gets 5 marks is .... **[Numerical Value Type, 2022 Main]**

93. Team *A* consists of 7 boys and *n* girls and Team *B* has 4 boys and 6 girls. If a total of 52 single matches can be arranged between these two teams when a boy plays against a boy and a girl plays against a girl, then *n* is equal to **[Single Correct Type, 2021 Main]**
(a) 6 (b) 5 (c) 4 (d) 2

94. The sum of all the 4-digit distinct numbers that can be formed with the digits 1, 2, 2 and 3 is
[Single Correct Type, 2021 Main]
(a) 26664 (b) 122664
(c) 122234 (d) 22264

95. A scientific committee is to be formed from 6 Indians and 8 foreigners, which includes at least 2 Indians and double the number of foreigners as Indians. Then, the number of ways, the committee can be formed, is
[Single Correct Type, 2021 Main]
(a) 1050 (b) 1625 (c) 560 (d) 575

96. The total number of positive integral solutions (x, y, z), such that $xyz = 24$ is **[Single Correct Type, 2021 Main]**
(a) 36 (b) 24 (c) 45 (d) 30

97. If the sides *AB*, *BC* and *CA* of a ΔABC have 3, 5 and 6 interior points respectively, then the total number of triangles that can be constructed using these points as vertices, is equal to **[Single Correct Type, 2021 Main]**
(a) 364 (b) 240 (c) 333 (d) 360

98. Consider a rectangle *ABCD* having 5, 7, 6, 9 points in the interior of the line segments *AB*, *CD*, *BC*, *DA*, respectively. Let α be the number of triangles having these points from different sides as vertices and β be the number of quadrilaterals having these points from different sides as vertices. Then, $(\beta - \alpha)$ is equal to
[Single Correct Type, 2021 Main]
(a) 795 (b) 1173 (c) 1890 (d) 717

99. The number of six letter words (with or without meaning), formed using all the letters of the word 'VOWELS', so that all the consonants never come together, is .... **[Numerical Value Type, 2021 Main]**

100. The sum of all 3-digit numbers less than or equal to 500, that are formed without using the digit 1 and they all are multiple of 11, is .... **[Numerical Value Type, 2021 Main]**

101. If ${}^1P_1 + 2\cdot{}^2P_2 + 3\cdot{}^3P_3 + \ldots + 15\cdot{}^{15}P_{15} = {}^qP_r - s, 0 \le s \le 1$, then ${}^{q+s}C_{r-s}$ is equals to ....
[Numerical Value Type, 2021 Main]

102. The number of 3-digit even numbers, formed by the digits 0, 1, 3, 4, 6, 7, if the repetition of digits is not allowed, is .... **[Numerical Value Type, 2021 Main]**

103. If the digits are not allowed to repeat in any number formed by using the digits 0, 2, 4, 6, 8, then the number of all numbers greater than 10000 is equal to ....
[Numerical Value Type, 2021 Main]

104. The missing value in the following figure is
[Numerical Value Type, 2021 Main]

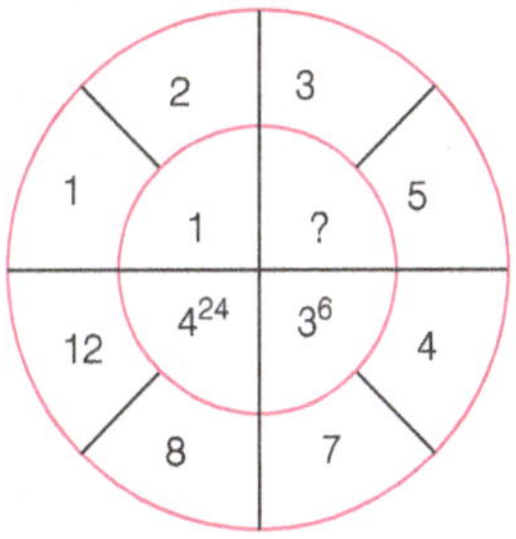

105. The number of times the digit 3 will be written when listing the integers from 1 to 1000 is ....
[Numerical Value Type, 2021 Main]

106. The total number of 4-digit numbers whose greatest common divisor with 18 is 3, is ....
[Numerical Value Type, 2021 Main]

107. The total number of two digit numbers *n*, such that $3^n + 7^n$ is a multiple of 10, is ....
[Numerical Value Type, 2021 Main]

108. The total number of numbers, lying between 100 and 1000 that can be formed with the digits 1, 2, 3, 4, 5, if the repetition of digits is not allowed and numbers are divisible by either 3 or 5, is ....
[Numerical Value Type, 2021 Main]

109. The students $S_1, S_2, \ldots, S_{10}$ are to be divided into 3 groups A, B and C such that each group has at least one student and the group C has at most 3 students. Then, the total number of possibilities of forming such groups is .... **[Numerical Value Type, 2021 Main]**

110. The value of $(2 \cdot {}^1P_0 - 3 \cdot {}^2P_1 + 4 \cdot {}^3P_2 - \ldots$ up to 51th term) + $(1! - 2! + 3! - \ldots$ up to 51 th term) is equal to **[Single Correct Type, 2020 Main]**

(a) $1 - 51(51)!$ (b) $1 + (51)!$
(c) $1 + (52)!$ (d) 1

111. If the number of five-digit numbers with distinct digits and 2 at the 10th place is 336 k, then k is equal to **[Single Correct Type, 2020 Main]**

(a) 8 (b) 7
(c) 4 (d) 6

112. Total number of 6-digit numbers in which only and all the five digits 1, 3, 5, 7 and 9 appear, is **[Single Correct Type, 2020 Main]**

(a) 6! (b) $\frac{5}{2}(6!)$
(c) $\frac{1}{2}(6!)$ (d) 5^6

113. There are 3 sections in a question paper and each section contains 5 questions. A candidate has to answer a total of 5 questions, choosing at least one question from each section. Then, the number of ways, in which the candidate can choose the questions, is **[Single Correct Type, 2020 Main]**

(a) 3000 (b) 1500 (c) 2255 (d) 2250

114. Let $n > 2$ be an integer. Suppose that there are n Metro stations in a city located along a circular path. Each pair of stations is connected by a straight track only. Further, each pair of nearest stations is connected by blue line, whereas all remaining pairs of stations are connected by red line. If the number of red lines in 99 times the number of blue lines, then the value of n is **[Single Correct Type, 2020 Main]**

(a) 201 (b) 200 (c) 101 (d) 199

EXERCISE 2 — JEE Advanced Pattern

Single Option Correct Type Questions

1. The total number of words that can be formed using all letters of the word 'RITESH' that neither begins with I nor ends with R, is

(a) 504 (b) 480 (c) 600 (d) 720

2. A man has three friends. The number of ways he can invite one friend everyday for dinner on six successive nights, so that no friend is invited more than three times, is

(a) 360 (b) 420 (c) 170 (d) 510

3. The number of three digit numbers of the form xyz such that $x < y$, $z \le y$ and $x \ne 0$, is

(a) 240 (b) 244 (c) 276 (d) 285

4. The letters of the word 'MEERUT' are arranged in all possible ways as in a dictionary, then the rank of the word 'MEERUT' is

(a) 119 (b) 120 (c) 121 (d) 122

5. The number of ways in which 10 candidates $A_1, A_2, \ldots, A_{10}$ can be ranked so that A_1 is always above A_2, is

(a) 10! (b) $\frac{10!}{2}$
(c) 9! (d) None of these

6. Let A be the set of four digit numbers $a_1a_2\,a_3a_4$, where $a_1 > a_2 > a_3 > a_4$, then $n(A)$ is

(a) 126 (b) 84
(c) 210 (d) None of these

7. The number of distinct rational numbers x such that $0 < x < 1$ and $x = \frac{p}{q}$, where $p, q \in \{1, 2, 3, 4, 5, 6\}$ is

(a) 15 (b) 13 (c) 12 (d) 11

8. The total number of integral solutions of $xyz = 24$ is

(a) 30 (b) 36
(c) 90 (d) 120

9. If $ABCD$ is a convex quadrilateral with 3, 4, 5 and 6 points, marked on sides AB, BC, CD and DA respectively, then the number of triangles with vertices on different sides, is

(a) 220 (b) 270
(c) 282 (d) 342

10. The number of ways can a team of six horses be selected out of a stud of 16, so that there shall always be three out of A, B, C, D, E, F but never AD, BE or CF together, is

(a) 720 (b) 840
(c) 960 (d) 1260

11. The number of polynomials of the form $x^3 + ax^2 + bx + c$ that are divisible by $x^2 + 1$, where a, $b, c \in \{1, 2, 3, 4, 5, 6, 7, 8, 9, 10\}$, is
(a) 10 (b) 15 (c) 5 (d) 8

12. Let $x_1, x_2, x_3, \ldots, x_k$ be the divisors of positive integer 'n' (including 1 and n). If $x_1 + x_2 + \ldots + x_k = 75$, then $\sum_{i=1}^{k} \frac{1}{x_i}$ is equal to
(a) $\frac{k^2}{75}$ (b) $\frac{75}{k}$ (c) $\frac{n^2}{75}$ (d) $\frac{75}{n}$

13. The total number of functions 'f' from the set $\{1, 2, 3\}$ into the set $\{1, 2, 3, 4, 5\}$ such that $f(i) \le f(j), \forall\, i < j$, is
(a) 35 (b) 30 (c) 50 (d) 60

14. Ten persons numbered 1, 2, 3, ..., 10 play a chess tournament, each player playing against every player exactly one game. It is known that no game ends in a draw. Let $w_1, w_2, w_3, \ldots, w_{10}$ be the number of games won by player 1, 2, 3, ..., 10 respectively and $l_1, l_2, l_3, \ldots, l_{10}$ be the number of games lost by the players 1, 2, 3, ..., 10 respectively, then
(a) $\Sigma w_i^2 = 81 - \Sigma l_i^2$ (b) $\Sigma w_i^2 = 81 + \Sigma l_i^2$
(c) $\Sigma w_i^2 = \Sigma l_i^2$ (d) None of these

15. In the next world cup of cricket there will be 12 teams, divided equally in two groups. Teams of each group will play a match against each other. From each group 3 top teams will qualify for the next round. In this round each team will play against others once. Four top teams of this round will qualify for the semi- final round, where each team will play against the others once. Two top teams of this round will go to the final round, where they will play the best of three matches. The minimum number of matches in the next world cup will be
(a) 54 (b) 53 (c) 38 (d) 37

16. The total number of positive integral solution of $15 < x_1 + x_2 + x_3 \le 20$ is equal to
(a) 685 (b) 785 (c) 1125 (d) 1575

17. The number of ways in which 17 persons depart from railway station in 2 cars and 2 autos, given that 2 particular persons depart by the same car (4 persons can sit in a car and 3 persons can sit in an auto) is
(a) $\frac{15!}{2!4!(3!)^3}$ (b) $\frac{16!}{(2!)^2 4!(3!)^3}$
(c) $\frac{17!}{2!4!(3!)^3}$ (d) $\frac{15!}{4!(3!)^3}$

18. The total number of 6 digit natural numbers that can be made with the digits 1, 2, 3, 4, if all digits are to appear in the same number at least once is
(a) 1560 (b) 840
(c) 1080 (d) 480

19. If all the words formed from the letters of the word HORROR are arranged in the opposite order as they are in a dictionary, then the rank of the word HORROR is
(a) 56 (b) 57 (c) 58 (d) 59

20. If ${}^{n-1}C_r = (k^2 - 3)^n C_{r+1}$, then k belongs to
(a) $[-\sqrt{3}, \sqrt{3}]$ (b) $[-\infty, -2)$
(c) $(2, \infty)$ (d) $(\sqrt{3}, 2]$

More than One Correct Option Type Questions

21. Number of ways in which 200 people can be divided in 100 couples is
(a) $\frac{(200)!}{2^{100}(100)!}$ (b) $1 \times 3 \times 5 \times \ldots \times 199$
(c) $\frac{101}{2} \times \frac{102}{2} \times \ldots \times \frac{200}{2}$ (d) $\frac{(200)!}{(100)!}$

22. If a 7-digit number made up of all distinct digits 8, 7, 6, 4, 2, x and y is divisible by 3, then
(a) maximum value of $x - y$ is 9.
(b) maximum value of $x + y$ is 12.
(c) minimum value of xy is 0.
(d) minimum value of $x + y$ is 3.

23. Number of points of intersection of n straight lines if n satisfies ${}^{n+5}P_{n+1} = \frac{11(n-1)}{2} \times {}^{n+3}P_n$ is
(a) 15 (b) 28 (c) 21 (d) 10

24. If $P = 21(21^2 - 1^2)(21^2 - 2^2)(21^2 - 3^2)\ldots(21^2 - 10^2)$, then P is divisible by
(a) 22! (b) 21!
(c) 19! (d) 20!

25. Number of ways in which 30 identical things are distributed among six persons is
(a) ${}^{17}C_5$ if each gets odd number of things
(b) ${}^{16}C_{11}$ if each gets odd number of things
(c) ${}^{14}C_5$ if each gets even number of things (excluding 0)
(d) ${}^{15}C_{10}$ if each gets even number of things (excluding 0)

26. If $300! = 3^m \times$ an integer, then
(a) $m = 148$
(b) $m = 150$
(c) It is equivalent to number of n in $150! = 2^{n-2} \times$ an integer
(d) $m = {}^{150}C_2$

27. If $102! = 2^\alpha \cdot 3^\beta \cdot 5^\gamma \cdot 7^\delta \ldots$, then
(a) $\alpha = 98$ (b) $\beta = 2\gamma + 1$
(c) $\alpha = 2\beta$ (d) $2\gamma = 3\delta$

28. The number of ways of choosing triplet (x, y, z) such that $z \ge \max\{x, y\}$ and $x, y, z \in \{1, 2, 3, \ldots, n, n+1\}$, is
(a) ${}^{n+1}C_3 + {}^{n+2}C_3$ (b) $\frac{n(n+1)(2n+1)}{6}$
(c) $1^2 + 2^2 + 3^2 + \ldots + n^2$ (d) $2({}^{n+2}C_3) - {}^{n+1}C_2$

29. Let n be 4-digit integer in which all the digits are different. If x is the number of odd integers and y is the number of even integers, then

(a) $x < y$ (b) $x > y$
(c) $x + y = 4500$ (d) $|x - y| = 56$

30. Let $S = \{1, 2, 3, \ldots, n\}$. If X denotes the set of all subsets of S containing exactly two elements, then the value of $\sum_{A \in X} (\text{min. } A)$ is given by

(a) ${}^{n+1}C_3$ (b) ${}^{n}C_3$
(c) $\frac{n(n^2-1)}{6}$ (d) $\frac{n(n^2-3n+2)}{6}$

31. Let $p = 2520$, x = number of divisors of p which are multiple of 6, y = number of divisors of p which are multiple of 9, then
(a) $x = 12$ (b) $x = 24$ (c) $y = 12$ (d) $y = 16$

32. If N denotes the number of ways of selecting r objects out of n distinct objects $(r \geq n)$ with unlimited repetition but with each object included atleast once in selection, then N is
(a) ${}^{r-1}C_{r-n}$ (b) ${}^{r-1}C_n$ (c) ${}^{r-1}C_{n-1}$ (d) ${}^{r-1}C_{r-n-1}$

33. There are three teams x, $x+1$ and y childrens and total number of childrens in the teams is 24. If two childrens of the same team do not fight,then
(a) maximum number of fights is 190
(b) maximum number of fights is 191
(c) maximum number of fights occur when $x = 7$
(d) maximum number of fights occur when $x = 8$

34. Let N denotes the number of ways in which $3n$ letters can be selected from $2n$ A's, $2nB$'s and $2nC$'s. Then,
(a) $3 \mid (N-1)$ (b) $n \mid (N-1)$
(c) $(n+1) \mid (N-1)$ (d) $3n(n+1) \mid (N-1)$

35. If $\alpha = x_1x_2x_3$ and $\beta = y_1y_2y_3$ are two 3-digit numbers, then the number of pairs of α and β can be formed so that α can be subtracted from β without borrowing, is
(a) $2! \times 10! \times 10!$ (b) $(45)(55)^2$
(c) $3^2 \cdot 5^3 \cdot 11^2$ (d) 136125

Passage Based Questions

Passage I
(Q. Nos. 36 and 37)

- Consider the word W = TERRORIST.

36. Number of four letter words that can be made using only the letters from the word W, if each word must contains atleast one vowel, is
(a) 588 (b) 504 (c) 294 (d) 600

37. Number of arrangements of the word W, if R's as well as T's are separated, is
(a) 9860 (b) 1080 (c) 10200 (d) 11400

Passage II
(Q. Nos. 38 and 39)

- Different words are formed by arranging the letters of the word 'SUCCESS'.

38. The number of words in which no two C's and no two S's are together, is
(a) 120 (b) 96 (c) 24 (d) 180

39. The number of words in which the consonants appear in alphabetic order, is
(a) 42 (b) 40 (c) 420 (d) 480

Passage III
(Q. Nos. 40 and 41)

- Let $f(n)$ denotes the number of different ways, the positive integer n can be expressed as the sum of the 1's and 2's. e.g. $f(4) = 5$
i.e. $4 = 1+1+1+1$
$= 1+1+2 = 1+2+1 = 2+1+1 = 2+2$

40. The value of $f\{f(6)\}$ is
(a) 376 (b) 377 (c) 321 (d) 370

41. The number of solutions of the equation $f(n) = n$, where $n \in N$ is
(a) 1 (b) 2 (c) 3 (d) 4

Stem Based Questions

Stem I
(Q. Nos. 42 and 43)

- Different words are being formed by arranging the letters of the word 'ARRANGE'.

42. The number of words in which neither two R's nor two A's come together, is ....

43. The rank of the word 'ARRANGE' in the dictionary is ....

Stem II
(Q. Nos. 44 and 45)

- Let $S(n)$ denotes the number of ordered pairs (x, y) satisfying $\frac{1}{x} + \frac{1}{y} = \frac{1}{n}$, $\forall\, x, y, n \in N$.

44. $S(6) + S(7)$ equals ....

45. $\sum_{r=1}^{10} S(r)$ equals ....

Single Integer Type Questions

46. If a, b, c are three natural numbers in AP such that $a+b+c=21$ and if possible number of ordered triplet (a, b, c) is λ, then the vlaue of $(\lambda - 5)$ is ....

47. If 2λ is the number of ways of selecting 3 member subset of $\{1, 2, 3, \ldots, 29\}$, so that the numbers form of a GP with integer common ratio, then the value of λ is ....

48. In a certain test, there are n questions. In this test, 2^{n-k} students gave wrong answers to atleast k questions, where $k = 1, 2, 3, \ldots, n$. If the total number of wrong answers given is 127, then the value of n is ....

49. A 7-digit number made up of all distinct digits 8, 7, 6, 4, 2, x and y, is divisible by 3. The, possible number of ordered pair (x, y) is ....

50. There are five points A, B, C, D and E. No three points are collinear and no four are concyclic. If the line AB intersects of the circles drawn throught the five points. The number of points of intersection on the line apart from A and B is

Numerical Value Type Questions

51. The number of three-digit numbers having only two consecutive digits identical is ....

52. The number of ways in which a person can walk up a stairway which has 7 steps if he can take 1 or 2 steps up the stairs at a time is ....

53. A debate club consists of 6 girls and 4 boys. A team of 4 members is to be selected from this club including the selection of a captain (from among these 4 members) for the team. If the team has to include atmost one boy, the number of ways of selecting the team is ....

54. The total number of ways in which 5 balls of different colours can be distributed among 3 persons so that each person gets at least one ball, is ....

55. If r, s, t are prime numbers and p, q are the positive integers such that LCM of p, q is $r^2s^4t^2$, then the number of ordered pairs (p, q) is ....

Matching Type Questions

56. Match the following.

	Column I		Column II
(A)	${}^{n+4}C_{n+1} - {}^{n+3}C_n = 15(n+2)$, then n equals	(p)	19
(B)	$11 \cdot {}^nP_4 = 20 \cdot {}^{n-2}P_4$, then n equals	(q)	27
(C)	${}^{2n}C_3 = 11 \cdot {}^nC_3$, then n equals	(r)	16
(D)	${}^{n+2}C_8 : {}^{n-2}P_4 = 57 : 16$, then n equals	(s)	6

57. Match the following.

	Column I		Column II
(A)	Number of increasing permutations of m symbols are there from the n set numbers $(a_1, a_2, \ldots, a_n)$, where the order among the numbers, is given by $a_1 < a_2 < a_3 < \ldots < a_{m-1} < a_m$ is	(p)	n^m
(B)	There are m men and n monkeys. Number of ways in which every monkey has a master, if a man can have any number of monkeys is	(q)	${}^mC_n$
(C)	Number of ways in which r red balls and $(m-1)$ green balls can be arranged in a line, so that no two red balls are together is (balls of the same colour are alike)	(r)	${}^nC_m$
(D)	Number of ways in which 'm' different toys can be distributed in n children, if every child may received any number of toys is	(s)	m^n

58. Match the following.

	Column I		Column II
(A)	Number of straight lines joining any two of 10 points of which four point are collinear is	(p)	30
(B)	Maximum number of points of intersection of 10 straight lines in the plane is	(q)	60
(C)	Maximum number of points of intersection of 6 circles in the plane is	(r)	40
(D)	Maximum number of points of intersection of 6 parabolas is	(s)	45

59. Consider a 6×6 chessboard. Then, match the following columns.

	Column I		Column II
(A)	Number of rectangles is	(p)	${}^{10}C_5$
(B)	Number of squares is	(q)	441
(C)	Number of ways three squares can be selected, if they are not in same row or column is	(r)	91
(D)	In how many ways eleven '+' sign can be arranged in the squares, if no row remains empty	(s)	2400

60. 5 balls are to be placed in 3 boxes. Each box can hold all the 5 balls. Number of ways in which the balls can be placed so that no box remain empty, if

	Column I		Column II
(A)	balls are identical but boxes are different	(p)	2
(B)	balls are different but boxes are identical	(q)	25
(C)	balls as well as boxes are identical	(r)	50
(D)	balls as well as boxes are identical but boxes kept in a row	(s)	6

Previous Year Questions

61. Let X be the set of all five digit numbers formed using 1, 2, 2, 2, 4, 4, 0. For example, 22240 is in X while 02244 and 44422 are not in X. Suppose that each element of X has an equal chance of being chosen. Let p be the conditional probability that an element chosen at random is a multiple of 20, given that it is a multiple of 5. Then, the value of $38p$ is equal to ....

[Numerical Value Type, 2023 Adv.]

62. The number of 4-digit integers in the closed interval [2022, 4482] formed by using the digits 0, 2, 3, 4, 6, 7 is......... . **(2022 Adv.)**

63. Let $S_1 = \{(i, j, k): i, j, k \in \{1, 2, ..., 10\}\}$

$S_2 = \{(i, j): 1 \le i < j + 2 \le 10, i, j \in \{1, 2, ..., 10\}\}$,

$S_3 = \{(i, j, k, l): 1 \le i < j < k < l, i, j, k, l \in \{1, 2, ..., 10\}\}$

and $S_4 = \{(i, j, k, l): i, j, k$ and l are distinct elements in $\{1, 2, ..., 10\}\}$. If the total number of elements in the set S_r is n_r, $r = 1, 2, 3, 4$, then which of the following statements is (are) true? **[More Than One Correct, 2021 Adv.]**

(a) $n_1 = 1000$ (b) $n_2 = 44$

(c) $n_3 = 220$ (d) $\frac{n_4}{12} = 420$

64. In a hotel, four rooms are available. Six persons are to be accommodated in these four rooms in such a way that each of these rooms contains at least one person and at most two persons. Then the number of all possible ways in which this can be done is ....

[Numerical Value Type, 2020 Adv.]

65. For non-negative integers s and r, let

$$\binom{s}{r} = \begin{cases} \frac{s!}{r!(s-r)!}, & \text{if } r \le s, \\ 0, & \text{if } r > s \end{cases}$$

For positive integers m and n, let $g(m, n) = \sum_{p=0}^{m+n} \frac{f(m, n, p)}{\binom{n+p}{p}}$

where for any non-negative integer p,

$$f(m, n, p) = \sum_{i=0}^{p} \binom{m}{i}\binom{n+i}{p}\binom{p+n}{p-i}.$$

Then, which of the following statements is/are true?

[More Than One Correct, 2020 Adv.]

(a) $g(m, n) = g(n, m)$ for all positive integers m, n

(b) $g(m, n+1) = g(m+1, n)$ for all positive integers m, n

(c) $g(2m, 2n) = 2g(m, n)$ for all positive integers m, n

(d) $g(2m, 2n) = (g(m, n))^2$ for all positive integers m, n

66. An engineer is required to visit a factory for exactly four days during the first 15 days of every month and it is mandatory that no two visits take place on consecutive days. Then the number of all possible ways in which such visits to the factory can be made by the engineer during 1-15 June 2021 is ....

[Numerical Value Type, 2020 Adv.]

67. Five persons A, B, C, D and E are seated in a circular arrangement. If each of them is given a hat of one of the three colours red, blue and green, then the number of ways of distributing the hats such that the persons seated in adjacent seats get different coloured hats is .... **[Numerical Value Type, 2019 Adv.]**

EXERCISE 3

Challenging Problems

1. Given that ${}^nC_{n-r} + 3\,{}^nC_{n-r+1} + 3\,{}^nC_{n-r+2} + {}^nC_{n-r+3} = {}^xC_r$, find x.

2. Solve the equation $3\,{}^{x+1}C_2 + P_2 x = 4\,{}^xA_2, x \in N$.

3. How many positive terms are there in the sequence (x_n) if $x_n = \frac{195}{4P_n} - \frac{{}^{n+3}A_3}{P_{n+1}}, n \in N$?

4. In how many different ways can a set A of $3n$ elements be partitioned into 3 subsets of equal number of elements ? (The subsets P, Q, R form a partition if $P \cup Q \cup R = A, P \cap R = \phi, Q \cap R = \phi, R \cap P = \phi$.)

5. There are n straight lines in a plane, no two of which are parallel and no three passes through the same point. Their point of intersection are joined. Show that the number of fresh lines thus introduced, is $\frac{1}{8}n(n-1)(n-2)(n-3)$.

6. A train is going from Cambridge to London stops at nine intermediate stations. Six persons enter the train during the journey with six different tickets. How many different sets of tickets they have had?

7. A tea party is arranged for 16 people along two sides of a large table with 8 chairs on each side. Four men sit on one particular side and two on the other side. In how many ways can they be seated?

8. Prove that ${}^{n-1}C_3 + {}^{n-1}C_4 > {}^nC_3$ if $n > 7$.

9. In how many ways, we can choose two teams of mixed double for a tennis tournament from four couples such that if any couple participates, then it is in the same team?

10. 6 balls marked as 1, 2, 3, 4, 5 and 6 are kept in a box. Two players A and B start to take out 1 ball at a time from the box one after another without replacing the ball till the game is over. The number marked on the ball is added each time to the previous sum to get the sum of numbers marked on the balls taken out. If this sum is even, then 1 point is given to the player. The first player to get 2 points is declared winner. At the start of the game, the sum is 0. If A starts to take out the ball, find the number of ways in which the game can be won.

Answer Key

Exercise 1

1. (d)	2. (b)	3. (c)	4. (d)	5. (a)	6. (c)	7. (b)	8. (c)	9. (a)	10. (a)
11. (a)	12. (d)	13. (d)	14. (b)	15. (c)	16. (c)	17. (a)	18. (c)	19. (b)	20. (c)
21. (a)	22. (b)	23. (d)	24. (d)	25. (b)	26. (b)	27. (c)	28. (7)	29. (4)	30. (5)
31. (9)	32. (7)	33. (5)	34. (8)	35. (10)	36. (8)	37. (4)	38. (1)	39. (0)	40. (8)
41. (3)	42. (7)	43. (c)	44. (a)	45. (c)	46. (c)	47. (a)	48. (c)	49. (c)	50. (a)
51. (a)	52. (a)	53. (553)	54. (36)	55. (3734)	56. (a)	57. (d)	58. (a)	59. (a)	60. (a)
61. (d)	62. (c)	63. (a)	64. (c)	65. (b)	66. (d)	67. (a)	68. (b)	69. (d)	70. (16)
71. (26664)	72. (4898)	73. (1260)	74. (432)	75. (2997)	76. (32)	77. (21)	78. (1436)	79. (72)	80. (16)
81. (b)	82. (d)	83. (b)	84. (17)	85. (7073)	86. (180)	87. (1492)	88. (360)	89. (1086)	90. (18915)
91. (243)	92. (40)	93. (c)	94. (a)	95. (b)	96. (d)	97. (c)	98. (d)	99. (576)	100. (7744)
101. (136)	102. (52)	103. (96)	104. (4)	105. (300)	106. (1000)	107. (45)	108. (32)	109. (31650)	110. (c)
111. (a)	112. (b)	113. (d)	114. (a)						

Exercise 2

1. (a)	2. (d)	3. (c)	4. (d)	5. (b)	6. (c)	7. (d)	8. (d)	9. (d)	10. (c)
11. (a)	12. (d)	13. (a)	14. (c)	15. (b)	16. (a)	17. (d)	18. (a)	19. (c)	20. (d)
21. (a,b,c)	22. (a,b,c,d)	23. (a,c)	24. (b,c,d)	25. (a,c)	26. (a)	27. (a,b,c,d)	28. (a,b,c,d)	29. (a,d)	30. (a,c)
31. (b,d)	32. (a,c)	33. (b,c)	34. (d)	35. (b,c,d)	36. (a)	37. (c)	38. (b)	39. (a)	40. (b)
41. (c)	42. (660)	43. (342)	44. (12)	45. (48)	46. (8)	47. (6)	48. (7)	49. (8)	50. (8)
51. (162)	52. (21)	53. (380)	54. (150)	55. (225)	56. A→q, B→r, C→s, D→p		57. A→r, B→s, C→q, D→p		
58. A→r, B→s, C→p, D→q			59. A→q, B→r, C→s, D→p		60. A→s, B→q, C→p, D→s		61. (38)	62. (569)	63. (a,b,d)
64. (1080)	65. (a,b,c,d)	66. (495)	67. (30)						

Solutions

Exercise 1 - JEE Main Pattern

1. We have, $36 = 2^2 \times 3^2$

If HCF $(n, 36) = 1$, then n should not be divisible by 2 or 3.

The number of integers in the range [2, 2000] that are divisible by 2 is 1000 [2, 4, 6, ..., 2000]

The number of integers in the range [2, 2000] that are divisible by 3 is 666 [3, 6, 9, ..., 1998]

The number of integers in the range [2, 2000] that are divisible by 6 is 333 [6, 12, 18, ..., 1998]

$\therefore$ Total number of integers divisible by 2 or 3

$$= 1000 + 666 - 333 = 1333$$

$\therefore$ Required number of numbers $= 1999 - 1333$

$$= 666$$

2. When $x - y > 5$, we have following cases

x	y	Number of cases
6	0	1
7	0, 1	2
8	0, 1, 2	3
9	0, 1, 2, 3	4
10	0, 1, 2, 3, 4	5
	Total	15

Similarly, we have 15 cases for $x - y < -5$

$\therefore$ Required number of ordered pairs $= 30$

3. We have,

$$\sum_{r=1}^{n}(r^2+1)r! = \sum_{r=1}^{n}[(r+2)(r+1)-3(r+1)+2]r!$$

$$= \sum_{r=1}^{n}[(r+2)! - 3(r+1)! + 2r!]$$

$$= \sum_{r=1}^{n}[(r+2)! - (r+1)!] - 2\sum_{r=1}^{n}[(r+1)! - r!]$$

$$= [(n+2)! - 2!] - 2[(n+1)! - 1]$$

$$= (n+2)! - 2(n+1)!$$

$$= (n+1)![n+2-2]$$

$$= n(n+1)!$$

4. We have, $12 = 2^2 \times 3$ and $100! = 2^a \cdot 3^b \cdot 5^c \cdot \ldots$

Now, $a = E_2(100!)$

$$= \left[\frac{100}{2}\right] + \left[\frac{100}{2^2}\right] + \left[\frac{100}{2^3}\right] + \left[\frac{100}{2^4}\right] + \left[\frac{100}{2^5}\right] + \left[\frac{100}{2^6}\right]$$

$$= 50 + 25 + 12 + 6 + 3 + 1$$

$$= 97$$

$b = E_3(100!)$

$$= \left[\frac{100}{3}\right] + \left[\frac{100}{3^2}\right] + \left[\frac{100}{3^3}\right] + \left[\frac{100}{3^4}\right]$$

$$= 33 + 11 + 3 + 1 = 48$$

$\therefore$ $100! = 2^{97} \times 3^{48} \times 5^c \times \ldots$

$$= (2^2 \times 3)^{48} \times 2 \times 5^c \times \ldots$$

$$= 12^{48} \times 2 \times 5^c \times \ldots$$

$\therefore$ $E_{12}(100!) = 48$

5. Sum of given digits $= 1 + 2 + 3 + 4 + 5 + 6 + 7 = 28$

Two digits have to be taken out.

If the number formed by remaining 5 digits is divisible by 9, then the sum of digits must be divisible by 9.

If x and y are such numbers.

Then, $x + y = 10$

$\therefore$ $x = 3, y = 7$ or $x = 4, y = 6$

Number comprises the digits {1, 2, 4, 5, 6} or {1, 2, 3, 5, 7}

$\therefore$ Required numbers $= 2 \times 5! = 240$

6.

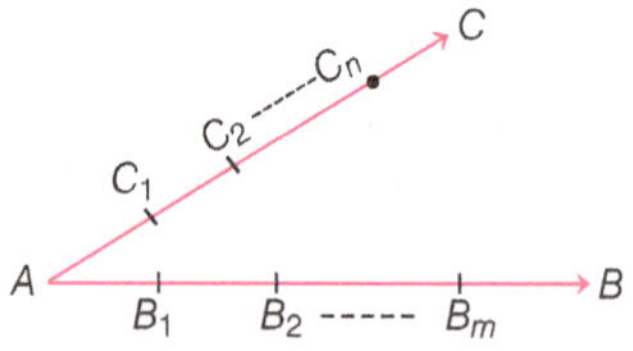

A triangle can be constructed in the following ways :

(i) By taking two points on AB and one on AC

(ii) By taking one point on AB and two on AC

(iii) By taking one point on AB, one point on AC and third point as vertex A

$\therefore$ Number of required triangles $= {}^mC_2 \times {}^nC_1 + {}^mC_1 \times {}^nC_2 + {}^mC_1 \times {}^nC_1 \times {}^1C_1$

$$= \frac{m(m-1)n}{2} + \frac{mn(n-1)}{2} + mn$$

$$= \frac{mn(m+n)}{2}$$

7. We have,

$$E_2(24!) = \left[\frac{24}{2}\right] + \left[\frac{24}{2^2}\right] + \left[\frac{24}{2^3}\right] + \left[\frac{24}{2^4}\right]$$

$$= 12 + 6 + 3 + 1$$

$$= 22$$

$$E_3(24!) = \left[\frac{24}{3}\right] + \left[\frac{24}{3^2}\right]$$

$$= 8 + 2$$

$$= 10$$

$\therefore \quad 24! = 2^{22} \times 3^{10} \times \text{some integers (say } \lambda)$

$= 2^{7 \times 3} \times 3^{10} \times 2 \times \lambda$

$= (2^3 \times 3)^7 \times 3^3 \times 2 \times \lambda$

$= (24)^7 \times 3^3 \times 2 \times \lambda$

$\therefore$ 24! is divisible by 24^7.

8. We have,

Required sum = (sum of all the numbers formed by the digits 0, 1, 2, 3) – (sum of all the numbers having 0 at thousand place)

$= [(0+1+2+3) \times (4-1)! \times 1111] - [(1+2+3)(3-1)! \times 111]$

$= 6 \times 6 \times 1111 - 6 \times 2 \times 111$

$= 39996 - 1332$

$= 38664$

9. We have,

$${}^nC_3 + {}^nC_4 > {}^{n+1}C_3$$

$$\Rightarrow \quad {}^{n+1}C_4 > {}^{n+1}C_3$$

$$\Rightarrow \quad \frac{{}^{n+1}C_4}{{}^{n+1}C_3} > 1$$

$$\Rightarrow \quad \frac{n-2}{4} > 1$$

$$\Rightarrow \quad n > 6$$

10. The number of ways of selecting four numbers from 1 to 30 without any restriction is ${}^{30}C_4$. The number of ways of selecting four consecutive.

[i.e. (1, 2, 3, 4), (2, 3, 4, 5), ..., (27, 28, 29, 30)] number is 27.

$\therefore$Required number of ways = ${}^{30}C_4 - 27$

$$= \frac{30 \times 29 \times 28 \times 27}{4 \times 3 \times 2 \times 1} - 27$$

$$= 27378$$

11. Total number of words without any restriction = 7!

Total number of words starting with I = 6!

Total number of words ending with B = 6!

Total number of words starting with I and ending with B = 5!

$\therefore$Required number words = 7! – 6! – 6! + 5!

$= 7! - 2 \times 6! + 5!$

$= 5![42 - 12 + 1]$

$= 120 \times 31$

$= 3720$

12. Let us first select two places for vowels, which can be selected from 4 places in ${}^4C_2$ ways. Now, these places can be filled by vowels in $5 \times 5 = 25$ ways (repetition is allowed).
The remaining two places can be filled by consonants in 21×21 ways.

$\therefore$ Required number of words = ${}^4C_2 \times 25 \times 21 \times 21$

$= 150 \times 21^2$

13. Let x_1, x_2, x_3, x_4 be the amount distributed to four persons.

Then, $\quad x_1 + x_2 + x_3 + x_4 = 18$

and $\quad x_1, x_2, x_3, x_4 \geq 3$

$\Rightarrow \quad x_i - 3 \geq 0, i = 1, 2, 3, 4$

Let $\quad y_i = x_i - 3$

Now, $\quad x_1 + x_2 + x_3 + x_4 = 18$

$\Rightarrow \quad y_1 + y_2 + y_3 + y_4 = 6$

$\therefore$Total number of required ways

= Number of non-negative integral solution of above equation

$= {}^{6+4-1}C_{4-1}$

$= {}^9C_3$

$$= \frac{9 \times 8 \times 7}{3 \times 2 \times 1}$$

$= 84$

14. The natural numbers are 1, 2, 3, 4. Clearly, in one diagonal we have to place 1, 4 and in the other 2, 3.

2	4
1	3

(i)

4	3
2	1

(ii)

The number of ways in (i) = $2! \times 2! = 4$

The number of ways in (ii) = $2! \times 2! = 4$

$\therefore$Total number of ways = 4 + 4 = 8

15. 16 Horses → $ABCA'B'C'$; 10 others

The number of ways is ${}^{10}C_3 \times$ number of ways of choosing out of $ABCA'B'C'$, so that AA', BB' or CC' are not together

$= {}^{10}C_3$ (one from each of pairs AA', BB' and CC')

$= {}^{10}C_3 \times 8$

$$= \frac{10 \times 9 \times 8}{3 \times 2 \times 1} \times 8 = 960$$

16. ${}^9C_5 - {}^{9-2}C_{5-2} = {}^9C_4 - {}^7C_3$

$= 126 - 35 = 91$

17. Let $a = 2x - 1, b = 2y - 1, c = 2z - 1, d = 2w - 1$

where, $\quad x, y, z, w \in N$

Then, $\quad a + b + c + d = 20$

$\Rightarrow \quad x + y + z + w = 12$

$\therefore$ Number of ordered quadruplet = ${}^{12-1}C_{4-1}$

$= {}^{11}C_3$

$$= \frac{11 \cdot 10 \cdot 9}{1 \cdot 2 \cdot 3} = 165$$

18. l = LCM of 8!, 10! and 12! = 12!

and h = HCF of 8!, 10! and 12! = 8!

$$\therefore \quad \frac{l}{h} = \frac{12!}{8!} = 12 \cdot 11 \cdot 10 \cdot 9 = 11880$$

19. $${}^{n+1}C_{n-2} - {}^{n+1}C_{n-1} \leq 100$$

$$\Rightarrow \quad {}^{n+1}C_3 - {}^{n+1}C_2 \leq 100$$

$$\Rightarrow \quad \frac{(n+1)n(n-1)}{6} - \frac{(n+1)n}{2} \leq 100$$

$$\Rightarrow \quad n(n+1)(n-4) \leq 600$$

It is true for $n = 2, 3, 4, 5, 6, 7, 8, 9$

20. Required number of ways

$$= \text{Coefficient of } x^{11} \text{ in } (x + x^2 + x^3 + x^4 + x^5 + x^6)^3$$
$$= \text{Coefficient of } x^8 \text{ in } (1 + x + x^2 + x^3 + x^4 + x^5)^3$$
$$= \text{Coefficient of } x^8 \text{ in } (1 - x^6)^3(1 - x)^{-3}$$
$$= \text{Coefficient of } x^8 \text{ in } (1 - 3x^6 + 3x^{12} - x^{18}) \quad (1 + {}^3C_1 x + \dots)$$
$$= {}^{10}C_8 - 3 \times {}^4C_2 = 45 - 18 = 27$$

21. $\because$ 13 lines pass through A and 11 lines pass through B.

$\therefore$ Number of intersection points

$$= {}^{37}C_2 - {}^{13}C_2 - {}^{11}C_2 + 2 \quad [\because \text{two points } A \text{ and } B]$$
$$= 535$$

22. $\because \quad a = 182bc$

$\Rightarrow \quad (x + 2)! = 182 \times {}^xP_{11} \times (x - 11)!$

$\Rightarrow \quad (x + 2)! = 182 \times x!$

$\Rightarrow \quad (x + 2)(x + 1) = 14 \times 13$

$\therefore \quad x = 12$

23. The letters in alphabetical order are *abcde*

$a \to 4! = 24$	$db \to 3! = 6$
$b \to 4! = 24$	$dc \to 3! = 6$
$c \to 4! = 24$	$dea \to 2! = 2$
$da \to 3! = 6$	$debac \to 1$

$\therefore$ The rank of *debac* $= 24 + 24 + 24 + 6 + 6 + 6 + 2 + 1 = 93$

24. Let $A = \{a_1, a_2, a_3, \dots, a_n\}$

(i) $a_i \in P, a_i \in Q$ (ii) $a_i \in P, a_i \notin Q$

(iii) $a_i \notin P, a_i \in Q$ (iv) $a_i \notin P, a_i \notin Q$, where $1 \le i \le n$

$\because P \cap Q = \phi$ [cases in favour 3 i.e. (ii), (iii), (iv)]

$\therefore$ Required number of ways $= 3^n$

25. Total points on all three lines $= m + n + k$

$\therefore$ Maximum number of triangles $= {}^{m+n+k}C_3 - {}^mC_3 - {}^nC_3 - {}^kC_3$

26. Required number of triplets = Total number of triplets without restrictions – Number of triplets with all different coordinates

$$= n^3 - {}^nP_3$$

27. Let middle largest digit be r, then digits available for remaining four places are 0, 1, 2, 3, ..., $r - 1$.

Number of ways filling remaining four places

$$= \sum_{r=4}^{9} ({}^rP_4 - {}^{r-1}P_3) = \sum_{r=4}^{9} (r - 1) \times {}^{r-1}P_3$$
$$= 3 \times {}^3P_3 + 4 \times {}^4P_3 + 5 \times {}^5P_3 + 6 \times {}^6P_3 + 7 \times {}^7P_3 + 8 \times {}^8P_3$$
$$= 5292 = 2^2 \cdot 3^3 \cdot 7^2$$

28. We have, $\quad T_n = {}^nC_3$

$\therefore \quad T_{n+1} - T_n = 21$

$\Rightarrow \quad {}^{n+1}C_3 - {}^nC_3 = 21$

$\Rightarrow \quad {}^nC_2 + {}^nC_3 - {}^nC_3 = 21$

$\Rightarrow \quad {}^nC_2 = 21$

$\Rightarrow \quad \dfrac{n(n-1)}{2} = 21$

$\Rightarrow \quad n(n - 1) = 7 \times 6$

$\therefore \quad n = 7$

29. We have,

$$240 = 2^4 \times 3 \times 5$$

and $\quad 4n + 2 = 2(2n + 1)$

$\quad = 2 \times$ an odd natural number

$\therefore$ Number of divisors of the form $4n + 2$

= Number of ways of selecting one 2 and any number of 3 and 5

$= 1 \times (1 + 1) \times (1 + 1)$

$= 4$

30. We have, $\quad {}^nP_r = {}^nP_{r+1}$

$\Rightarrow \quad \dfrac{n!}{(n-r)!} = \dfrac{n!}{(n-r-1)!}$

$\Rightarrow \quad n - r = 1 \quad$ ...(i)

Also, $\quad {}^nC_r = {}^nC_{r-1}$

$\Rightarrow \quad r + r - 1 = n$

$\Rightarrow \quad n - 2r = -1 \quad$ ...(ii)

On solving Eqs. (i) and (ii), we get

$$n = 3, r = 2$$

$\therefore \quad n + r = 5$

31. Dice is marked with numbers 1, 2, 3, 4, 5, 6. If the sum of dice in three throw is 11, then observations must be (1, 4, 6), (1, 5, 5), (2, 3, 6), (2, 4, 5), (3, 3, 5), (3, 4, 4).

We can get these observation in $3! + \dfrac{3!}{2!} + 3! + 3! + \dfrac{3!}{2!} + \dfrac{3!}{2!} = 27$ ways.

$\therefore \quad \lambda = 9$

32. Let the five subjects are a, b, c, d, e. Since, number of subjects are less than the number of periods, any one of the five subjects will occur twice.

If subject a occurs twice, then six subjects can be arranged in

$$\frac{6!}{2!} = 360$$

So, total number of ways $= 5 \times 360 = 1800$

$= 2^3 \times 3^2 \times 5^2$

$\therefore \quad a = 3, b = 2, c = 2$

$\Rightarrow \quad a + b + c = 7$

33. We have consonants T, R, P, L and vowels I, E.

Number of ways of selecting atleast one consonant

$$= 2^4 - 1 = 15$$

Number of ways of selecting atleast one vowel $= 2^2 - 1 = 3$

$\therefore$ Required number of selections, $x = 15 \times 3$

$= 45 = 3^2 \times 5$

$\therefore$ Height prime factor of $x = 5$

34. Let $x_1 = x+5, y_1 = y+5, z_1 = z+5$.

Then, $x_1, y_1, z_1 \geq 0$ and $x+y+z=0$

$\therefore \quad x_1 + y_1 + z_1 = 15$

So, number of solutions $= {}^{15+3-1}C_{3-1}$

$= {}^{17}C_2$

$= \dfrac{17 \times 16}{2}$

$= 17 \times 8$

$\therefore \quad \lambda = 8$

35. Total number of triangles

= Number of triangles with vertices on sides PQ, QR, RS or QR, RS, PS or RS, PS, PQ or PS, PQ, QR

$= {}^3C_1 \times {}^4C_1 \times {}^5C_1 + {}^4C_1 \times {}^5C_1 \times {}^6C_1 + {}^5C_1 \times {}^6C_1 \times {}^3C_1 + {}^6C_1 \times {}^3C_1 \times {}^4C_1$

$= 60 + 120 + 90 + 72$

$= 342$

$\therefore \quad x = 342$

$= 2 \times 3^2 \times 19$

$\therefore$ Number of proper divisor of x

$= (1+1)(2+1)(1+1) - 2$

$= 12 - 2$

$= 10$

36. We have, ${}^nC_2 = 4 \times 7$

$\Rightarrow \quad \dfrac{n(n-1)}{2} = 28$

$\Rightarrow \quad n(n-1) = 56$

$\Rightarrow \quad n(n-1) = 8 \times 7$

$\therefore \quad n = 8$

37. Number of arrangement $= 2 \times n! \times n!$

$\therefore \quad 2 \times (n!)^2 = 1152$

$\Rightarrow \quad (n!)^2 = 576$

$\Rightarrow \quad n! = 24$

$\therefore \quad n = 4$

38. For $n \geq 10$, the number of zeros in $n! \geq 2$

$\therefore \quad 1! + 2! + 3! + 4! + \ldots + 97! = \ldots 13$

$\therefore$ Ten's digit = 1

39. $\because \quad {}^{100}C_{50} = \dfrac{100!}{(50!)^2}$

$\therefore \quad E_7(100!) = \left[\dfrac{100}{7}\right] + \left[\dfrac{100}{7^2}\right] = 14 + 2 = 16$

and $\quad E_7(50!) = \left[\dfrac{50}{7}\right] + \left[\dfrac{50}{7^2}\right] = 7 + 1 = 8$

$\therefore \; E_7$ in $({}^{100}C_{50}) = 16 - 2 \times 8 = 0$

40. ${}^{n-1}C_3 - {}^{n-2}C_3 = 15 \qquad [\because P_n = {}^{n-2}C_3]$

$\Rightarrow \quad n = 8$

41. For BULBUL, the letters in alphabetical order are BBLLUU

BB $\rightarrow \dfrac{4!}{2!2!} = 6 \qquad$ BULBLU $\rightarrow 1$

BL $\rightarrow \dfrac{4!}{2!} = 12 \qquad$ BULBUL $\rightarrow 1$

BU $\rightarrow \dfrac{3!}{2!} = 3$

$\therefore \quad m = 6 + 12 + 3 + 1 + 1 = 23$

For NANNU

The letters in alphabetical order are ANNNU

A $\rightarrow \dfrac{4!}{3!} = 4 \qquad$ NANNU $\rightarrow 1$

$\therefore \quad n = 4 + 1 = 5$

Hence, $m - 4n = 23 - 20 = 3$

42. Each of the n digits can be anyone of the three 2, 5 or 7.

$\therefore$ The number of n-digit numbers is 3^n.

$\Rightarrow \quad 3^n > 900$

$\Rightarrow \quad n = 7, 8, 9 \ldots$

Hence, smallest value of n is 7.

43. 8 identical objects into 4 identical shelves, where any number of shelves may remain empty is given by

0008, 0017, 0026, 0035, 0044 = 5

$$\left.\begin{matrix} 0 & 1 & 1 & 6 \\ 0 & 1 & 2 & 5 \\ 0 & 1 & 3 & 4 \\ 0 & 2 & 2 & 4 \\ 0 & 2 & 3 & 3 \end{matrix}\right] = 5$$

$$\left.\begin{matrix} 1 & 1 & 1 & 5 \\ 1 & 1 & 2 & 4 \\ 1 & 1 & 3 & 3 \\ 1 & 2 & 2 & 3 \end{matrix}\right] = 4$$

$$2 \quad 2 \quad 2 \quad 2] = 1$$

Total = 15

44. Let 24 distinct objects are divided into 6 groups of 4 objects on each group.

Number of ways of formation of group $= \dfrac{24!}{(4!)^6 \cdot 6!} \in N$

Similarly, let 120 distinct objects are divided into 24 groups of 5 objects in each group.

$\therefore$Number of ways of formation of groups $= \dfrac{(120)!}{(5!)^{24} \cdot 24!} \in N$

Hence, $\alpha \in N$ and $\beta \in N$.

45. NAGPUR can be arranged alphabetically as A G N P R U

Now, we need to find 315th word

So, total words starting with

A = A 5 4 3 2 1 = 5! = 120

Total words starting with

G = G 5 4 3 2 1 = 5! = 120

Total words starting with

N = N 5 4 3 2 1 = 5! = 120

Total words = 120 + 120 + 120 = 360

So, 315th words starts with N.

Now, words with N as first letter, and A as second letter

= N A 4 3 2 1 = 4! = 24

G as second letter = N G 4 3 2 1 = 4! = 24

P as second letter = N P 4 3 2 1 = 4! = 24

Total words so far = 240 + 24 × 3 = 312

So, we have to find next 3 words

⇒ N R A G P U

⇒ N R A G U P

⇒ N R A P G U → 315th words

46. AA, MM, TT, H, I, C, S, E

(a) All distinct $= {}^8C_5 = \frac{8\cdot 7\cdot 6}{3\cdot 2\cdot 1} = 56$

(b) 2 same 1st kind, 2 same 2nd kind, 1 different

$= {}^3C_2 \times {}^6C_1 = 3 \times 6 = 18$

(c) 2 same, 3 different $= {}^3C_1 \times {}^7C_4 = 3 \times \frac{7\cdot 6\cdot 5}{3\cdot 2\cdot 1} = 105$

Hence, the total = 56 + 18 + 105 = 179

47. Since, office are identical so we can distributes in following ways.

I	II	III	IV	
0	0	0	5	1 = 1
0	0	1	4	$\frac{5!}{4!1!} = 5$
0	1	1	3	$\frac{5!}{3!2!} = 10$
0	1	2	2	$\frac{5!}{2!2!.2!} = 15$
1	1	1	2	$\frac{5!}{1!1!1!2!} \times \frac{1}{3!} = 10$
0	0	2	3	$\frac{5!}{3!2!} = 10$

∴ Total 1 + 5 + 10 + 15 + 10 + 10 = 51

48. Remaining apples after distributing 2 apples to each of three child = 21 − 6 = 15

Number of ways $= {}^{15+3-1}C_{3-1}$

$= {}^{17}C_2 = \frac{17 \times 16}{2}$

$= 17 \times 8 = 136$

49. Given, $\frac{{}^{n+1}C_{r+1}}{{}^nC_r} = \frac{55}{35}$ ...(i)

and $\frac{{}^nC_r}{{}^{n-1}C_{r-1}} = \frac{35}{21}$ ...(ii)

Now, by using property

$${}^nC_r = \frac{n}{r}\,{}^{n-1}C_{r-1}$$

By Eq. (i), $\frac{n+1}{r+1} \times \frac{{}^nC_r}{{}^nC_r} = \frac{55}{35}$

$\Rightarrow \frac{n+1}{r+1} = \frac{11}{7}$

$\Rightarrow 7n + 7 = 11r + 11$

$\Rightarrow 7n = 11r + 4$ ...(iii)

By Eq. (ii), $\frac{n}{r}\frac{{}^{n-1}C_{r-1}}{{}^{n-1}C_{r-1}} = \frac{35}{21}$

$\Rightarrow \frac{n}{r} = \frac{5}{3} \Rightarrow 3n = 5r$ ...(iv)

By Eqs. (iii) and (iv),

$n = 10$ and $r = 6$

$\Rightarrow 2n + 5r = 2 \times 10 + 5 \times 6 = 50$

50. **Decoding the Question**

Use, ${}^nC_r + {}^nC_{r-1} = {}^{n+1}C_r$

Given, ${}^6C_m + 2({}^6C_{m+1}) + {}^6C_{m+2} > {}^8C_3$

$\Rightarrow ({}^6C_m + {}^6C_{m+1}) + ({}^6C_{m+1} + {}^6C_{m+2}) > {}^8C_3$

$\Rightarrow {}^7C_{m+1} + {}^7C_{m+2} > {}^8C_3$

$\Rightarrow {}^8C_{m+2} > {}^8C_3$

$\Rightarrow m = 2$

and $\frac{{}^{n-1}P_3}{{}^nP_4} = \frac{1}{8} \Rightarrow \frac{\frac{(n-1)!}{(n-4)!}}{\frac{n!}{(n-4)!}} = \frac{1}{8} \Rightarrow \frac{1}{n} = \frac{1}{8} \Rightarrow n = 8$

$\therefore {}^nP_{m+1} + {}^{n-1}C_m = {}^8P_3 + {}^9C_2$

$= 8 \times 7 \times 6 + \frac{9 \times 8}{2}$

$= 336 + 36 = 372$

51. Given, ${}^{n-1}C_r = (k^2 - 8)\,{}^nC_{r+1}$ ...(i)

$\Rightarrow {}^{n-1}C_r = (k^2 - 8)\frac{n}{r+1}\cdot {}^{n-1}C_r \quad \left[\because {}^nC_r = \frac{n}{r}\,{}^{n-1}C_{r-1}\right]$

$\Rightarrow \frac{1}{k^2 - 8} = \frac{n}{r+1}$ ...(ii)

From Eq. (i) to defined ${}^nC_{r+1}$,

$$n \geq r + 1 \Rightarrow \frac{n}{r+1} \geq 1$$

$\Rightarrow \frac{1}{k^2 - 8} \geq 1$

$\Rightarrow \frac{1 - (k^2 - 8)}{k^2 - 8} \geq 0$

$\Rightarrow \frac{k^2 - 9}{k^2 - 8} \leq 0$

$$\Rightarrow \quad \frac{(k-3)(k+3)}{(k-2\sqrt{2})(k+2\sqrt{2})} \le 0$$

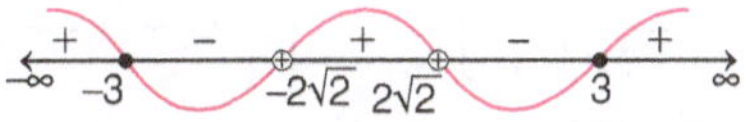

$\Rightarrow \; k \in [-3, -2\sqrt{2}) \cup (2\sqrt{2}, 3]$

So, $k \in (2\sqrt{2}, \sqrt{3}]$ [by given option]

52. Total triangle formed with vertices of octagon = ${}^8C_3$

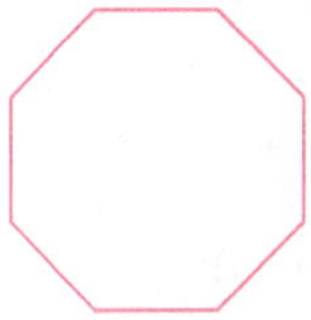

Now, one condition is given that no side of triangle coincides with side of octagon.

Case I Number of triangle with all sides coincides with octagon = 0

Case II Number of triangle with 2 sides coincides with octagon = ${}^8C_1$

[∵ from one vertex two adjacent sides are originating]

Case III Number of triangle with 1 side coincides with octagon = ${}^8C_1 \times {}^4C_1$

[∵ when we select one side, we have to leave adjacent sides also of selected side, so remaining vertices will be 4]

∴ Total triangles with no sides coinciding with octagon is

$$= {}^8C_3 - 0 - {}^8C_1 - {}^8C_1 \times {}^4C_1$$

$$= 56 - (0 + 8 + 32) = 16$$

53. Given, word GTWENTY

Words start with E $= \frac{6!}{2!} = 360$

Words start with GE $= \frac{5!}{2!} = 60$

Words start with GN $= \frac{5!}{2!} = 60$

Words start with GTE = 4! = 24

Words start with GTN = 4! = 24

Words start with GTT = 4! = 24

∴ Serial number of the word GTWENTY

= 360 + 60 + 60 + 24 + 24 + 24 + 1

= 553

Alternate Solution

Increasing Position of letters in the word	G	T	W	E	N	T	Y
	2	4	5	1	3	4	6
	6 !	5 !	4 !	3 !	2 !	1 !	0 !

$$= \frac{1 \times 6!}{2!} + \frac{2 \times 5!}{2!} + \frac{3 \times 4!}{1!} + 0 + 0 + 0 + 0 + 1$$

= 360 + 120 + 72 + 1 = 553

54. Given digits = 2, 3, 4, 5, 7

Total 3-digit numbers = ${}^5C_3 \times 3! = 60$

Now, 3-digit numbers that are divisible by 3

234, 237, 345, 357

↓ ↓ ↓ ↓

3! + 3! + 3! + 3! = 24

Hence, three digit numbers that are not divisible by 3

= Total – Divisible by 3

= 60 – 24 = 36

55. DISTRIBUTION

3I, 2T, 1D, 1S, 1R, 1B, 1U, 1O, 1N

Number of word taken 4 at time.

Case	Number of words
All are different	${}^9C_4 \times 4! = 3024$
1 Pair + 2 different	$2 \times {}^2C_1 \times {}^8C_2 \times \frac{4!}{2!} = 672$
2 Pairs	${}^2C_2 \times \frac{4!}{2!2!} = 6$
1 triplet + 1 Different	${}^1C_1 \times {}^8C_1 \times \frac{4!}{3!} = 32$
Total	**3734**

56. **I** All three digits are alike

111, 333, 555, 888 ⟶ 4

II 2 digits are alike

$558 \longrightarrow \frac{3!}{2!} = 3;\; 885 \longrightarrow \frac{3!}{2!} = 3$

III All three digits are different

1, 3, 5 ⟶ 6; 1, 3, 8 ⟶ 6

∴ Total numbers = 22

57. Since, number is divisible by 5, so units digit can be 0 or 5.

Case 1 Units digit = 0

Since number is greater than 40000 and digits can't be repeated, the leading digit has only 3 options (5 or 7 or 9)

Remaining digits can be filled in 4 and 3 and 2 ways.

Number of ways = 4! × 3

Case 2 Units digit = 5

Here, leading digit has 2 options

(7 or 9). Remaining digits can be filled in 4 and 3 and 2 ways.

So, number of ways = 4! × 2

Total numbers = 4! × 3 + 4! × 2 = 120

58. Vowels – I, EEEE

Consonants – N, D, P, N, D, N, C

Number of ways in which vowels are always occur together

$$= \frac{8!}{3! \times 2!} \times \frac{5!}{4!} = 16800$$

59. First arrange the letters of the word MONDAY in alphabetical order i.e. ADMNOY

$A-----=5!$

$D-----=5!$

Ⓜ $A----=4!$

Ⓜ $D----=4!$

ⓂⓃ$----=4!$

ⓂⓄ $A---=3!$

ⓂⓄ $D---=3!$

ⓂⓄⓃ $A--=2!$

ⓂⓄⓃⒹⒶⓎ $=327$

Rank $=327$

60. Total number of words $=\dfrac{11!}{2!2!2!}$

C and S come together in $\dfrac{10!}{2!2!2!}\times 2!$ words

$\therefore$ Required number of words $=\dfrac{11!}{(2!)^3}-\dfrac{10!}{(2!)^2}$

$$=\frac{10!}{(2!)^2}\left(\frac{11}{2}-1\right)$$

$$=\frac{10!\times 9}{8}$$

$$=10\times 9\times 8\times 7\times 6!\times\frac{9}{8}$$

$$=6!\times 5670$$

$\Rightarrow \quad k=5670$

61. Given, word is PUBLIC and alphabetical order of letter is BCILPU, so number of words start with letter,

B - - - - - is $5!=120$

C - - - - - is $5!=120$

I - - - - - is $5!=120$

L - - - - - is $5!=120$

PB - - - - is $4!=24$

PC - - - - is $4!=24$

PI - - - - is $4!=24$

PL - - - - is $4!=24$

PUBC - - is $2!=2$

PUBI - - is $2!=2$

PUBLC - is $1!=1$

PUBLIC - is $1!=1$

$\therefore$ Serial number of the word PUBLIC

$=4\times 120+4\times 24+2\times 2+2=582$

62. We have, $\dfrac{1}{1!\,50!}+\dfrac{1}{3!\,48!}+\dfrac{1}{5!\,46!}+\ldots+\dfrac{1}{49!\,2!}+\dfrac{1}{51!\,1!}$

$$=\frac{1}{1!\,50!}+\frac{1}{3!\,48!}+\frac{1}{5!\,46!}+\ldots+\frac{1}{49!\,2!}+\frac{1}{51!\,0!}$$

$[\because 0!=1!=1]$

$$=\frac{1}{51!}\left[\frac{51!}{1!\,50!}+\frac{51!}{3!\,48!}+\frac{51!}{5!\,46!}+\ldots+\frac{51!}{49!\,2!}+\frac{51!}{51!\,0!}\right]$$

$$=\frac{1}{51!}({}^{51}C_1+{}^{51}C_3+\ldots+{}^{51}C_{51})$$

$$=\frac{1}{51!}\left(\frac{2^{51}}{2}\right)\quad\left[\because {}^nC_1+{}^nC_3+\ldots+{}^nC_n=\frac{2^n}{2}\right]$$

$$=\frac{2^{50}}{51!}$$

63. We have, ${}^{2n+1}P_{n-1}:{}^{2n-1}P_n=11:21$

$$\Rightarrow \frac{{}^{2n+1}P_{n-1}}{{}^{2n-1}P_n}=\frac{11}{21}$$

$$\Rightarrow \frac{\dfrac{(2n+1)!}{(n+2)!}}{\dfrac{(2n-1)!}{(n-1)!}}=\frac{11}{21}$$

$$\Rightarrow \frac{(2n+1)(2n)}{(n+2)(n+1)n}=\frac{11}{21}$$

$$\Rightarrow 42(2n+1)=11(n+2)(n+1)$$

$$\Rightarrow 11n^2-51n-20=0$$

$$\Rightarrow (n-5)(11n+4)=0$$

$$\Rightarrow n=5,-\frac{4}{11}$$

$$\Rightarrow n=5\quad\left[\because n\neq-\frac{4}{11}\right]$$

$\therefore \quad n^2+n+15=5^2+5+15=45$

64. We have, $x+y+z=15$

Total number of solution $={}^{15+3-1}C_{3-1}$

$$={}^{17}C_2$$

$$=\frac{17\times 16}{2}$$

$$=136$$

Now consider the case when $x=y\neq z$

x	y	z
1	1	13

i.e. $\dfrac{3!}{2!}=3$

Other cases are

2	2	11
3	3	9
7	7	1
4	4	7
6	6	3
0	0	15

$\therefore$ Total number of solution when

$$x=y\neq z=7\times\frac{3!}{2!}=21$$

Now consider the case when $x=y=z$

i.e. | 5 | 5 | 5 | $=1$

$\therefore$ Total number of solution in which

$$x=y=z=1$$

$\therefore$ Required answer $=136-21-1=114$

65. Given, $n(A) = 5$ and $n(B) = 2$

Then, $n(A \times B) = 5 \times 2 = 10$

$\therefore$ Number of subsets $= {}^{10}C_3 + {}^{10}C_4 + {}^{10}C_5 + {}^{10}C_6$

$= 120 + 210 + 252 + 210 = 792$

66. Given that, number of boys = 7

Number of girls = 5

Number of ways boys can sit $= (7-1)! = 6! = 720$

There are 7 gaps after sitting of boys in which 5 girls to sit.

Total number of ways $= 720 \times {}^7C_5 \cdot 5!$

$$= 720 \times \frac{7 \times 6}{1 \times 2} \times 120$$

$$= 7 \times 6 \times 3 \times 120 \times 120 = 126\,(5\,!)^2$$

67. Let C_1, C_2 and C_3 be the three cars in which 8 person are to be transported from city A to city B.

$$\begin{matrix} C_1 & C_2 & C_3 \\ \downarrow & \downarrow & \downarrow \\ 3 & 3 & 2 \end{matrix}$$

Let the number of person transported in cars C_1, C_2 and C_3 are 3, 3 and 2 respectively.

There are total $\frac{8!}{3!\,3!\,2!}$ group.

$\therefore$ They can travel $\frac{8!}{3!3!2!} \times 3$ ways or 1680 ways.

68. We have, ${}^{2n}C_3 : {}^nC_3 = 10 : 1$

$$\Rightarrow \frac{{}^{2n}C_3}{{}^nC_3} = \frac{10}{1}$$

$$\Rightarrow \frac{(2n)!}{3!(2n-3)!} \times \frac{3!(n-3)!}{n!} = \frac{10}{1}$$

$$\Rightarrow \frac{(2n)(2n-1)(2n-2)}{(n)(n-1)(n-2)} = \frac{10}{1}$$

$$\Rightarrow 4n^2 - 6n + 2 = 5(n^2 - 3n + 2)$$

$$\Rightarrow n^2 - 9n + 8 = 0$$

$$\Rightarrow (n-8)(n-1) = 0$$

$$\Rightarrow n = 8\ (n = 1 \text{ not valid})$$

$$\therefore \frac{n^2 + 3n}{n^2 - 3n + 4} = \frac{88}{44} = \frac{2}{1} = 2 : 1$$

69. Given, $({}^{30}C_1)^2 + 2({}^{30}C_2)^2 + 3({}^{30}C_3)^2 + \dots + 30({}^{30}C_{30})^2$

Let, $S = 0\,({}^{30}C_0)^2 + 1({}^{30}C_1)^2 + 2({}^{30}C_2)^2 + \dots + 30({}^{30}C_{30})^2$ ...(i)

or $S = 30({}^{30}C_{30})^2 + 29({}^{30}C_{29})^2 + \dots + 0({}^{30}C_0)^2$ ...(ii)

On adding Eqs. (i) and (ii), we get

$2S = 30\,\{({}^{30}C_0)^2 + ({}^{30}C_1)^2 + \dots + ({}^{30}C_{30})^2\}$ $[\because {}^nC_r = {}^nC_{n-r}]$

$\therefore S = 15\,\{{}^{30}C_0 \cdot {}^{30}C_{30} + {}^{30}C_1 \cdot {}^{30}C_{29} + \dots + {}^{30}C_{30} \cdot {}^{30}C_0\}$

$S = 15\,\{{}^{60}C_{30}\}$

$$S = 15 \times \frac{60!}{(30!)\,(30!)} = \alpha \cdot \frac{60!}{(30!)^2}$$

$\therefore \alpha = 15$

70. For 3-digit number to be divisible by 6, unit digit should be even and sum of digit is divisible by 3.

(2, 1, 3), (2, 3, 4), (2, 5, 5), (2, 2, 5), (2, 2, 2), (4, 1, 1), (4, 4, 1), (4, 4, 4), (4, 3, 5)

$(2, 1, 3) \Rightarrow 132, 312$

$(2, 3, 4) \Rightarrow 342, 432, 324, 234$

$(2, 5, 5) \Rightarrow 552$

$(2, 2, 5) \Rightarrow 522, 252$

$(2, 2, 2) \Rightarrow 222$

$(4, 1, 1) \Rightarrow 114$

$(4, 4, 1) \Rightarrow 414, 144$

$(4, 4, 4) \Rightarrow 444$

$(4, 3, 5) \Rightarrow 354, 534$

Required number is 16.

71. We have, four digits are 2, 1, 2, 3

Total numbers when 1 is at unit digit $= \frac{3!}{2!} = 3$

Total number when 2 is at unit digit $= 3! = 6$

Total numbers when 3 is at unit digit $= \frac{3!}{2!} = 3$

Sum of digits at unit place $= 3 \times 1 + 6 \times 2 + 3 \times 3 = 24$

$\therefore$ Required sum $= 24 \times 1000 + 24 \times 100 + 24 \times 10 + 24 \times 1$

$= 24 \times 1111 = 26664$

72. Given that digits are 1, 2, 3, 4, 5, 6, 7

Total permutations = 7!

Let p = Number which can taking string 153

q = Number which containing string 2467

$\therefore$ $n(p) = 5! \times 1 \Rightarrow n(q) = 4! \times 1$

$n(p \cap q) = 2!$

$\therefore$ $n(p \cup q) = n(p) + n(q) - n(p \cap q)$

$= 5! + 4! - 2! = 120 + 24 - 2 = 142$

$\therefore$ n (neither string 143 nor string 2467)

$= 7! - 142 = 5040 - 142 = 4898$

73. Taking a consecutive 3-place as a group out of nine, we have 7 places to fill now which can be chosen in ${}^7C_1 = 7$ ways ...(i)

In the group, digits a, b, c can be placed as $a\ b\ c$ or $c\ b\ a$ i.e. in 2 ways ...(ii)

In remaining 6 places, $2a$'s, $2b$'s and $2c$'s have to be permuted which can be done in $\frac{6!}{2!\,2!\,2!}$ ways ...(iii)

(Permutation of alike objects)

So, total numbers that can be formed $= 7 \times 2 \times \frac{6!}{2!\,2!\,2!} = 1260$

74. Given word is UNIVERSE

Here vowels are E, I, U and consonants are N, R, S, V

$\therefore$ Required number of 4-letters words, with or without meaning, each consisting of 2 vowels and 2 consonants

$= {}^3C_2 \times {}^4C_2 \times 4!$

$= {}^3C_1 \times {}^4C_2 \times 24$ $[\because {}^nC_r = {}^nC_{n-r}]$

$= 3 \times 6 \times 24 = 432$

75. Number starting with 2 and 3 $= 2 \times 6^4$

Number starting with 40 $= 6^3$

Number starting with 420, 422, 423, 424, 427 $= 5 \times 6^2$

Number starting with 4290 $= 6$

Next numbers are 42920, 42922, 42923

So, the serial number of 42923 $= 2 \times 6^4 + 6^3 + 5 \times 6^2 + 6 + 3$

$= 2997$

76. Let numbers are

1, 2, 3, 4, 5, 6, 7, 8, 9

Now, total number of numbers starting with 1 (fix on first place) $= {}^8C_5 = \dfrac{8!}{5!3!} = 56$

Now, fix 2, 3 on first and second place.

So, total number of numbers starting with 2, 3 $= {}^6C_4 = 15$

Total number $= 56 + 15 = 71$

Now, 72 number will be 245678

So, the sum of 72 numbers digits $= 2 + 4 + 5 + 6 + 7 + 8 = 32$

77. **Decoding the Question**

For number to be divisible by 15, last digit of number should be 5 and the sum of digits must be divisible by 3.

If last place is fixed by 5.

So, possible combinations are shown below,

1 2 1 5	2 3 5 5	3 5 5 5
Total=3	Total=6	Total=3
2 2 3 5	1 1 5 5	3 3 1 5
Total=3	Total=3	Total=3

Hence, total number of 4-digits numbers which are also divisible by 15 $= 3 + 6 + 3 + 3 + 3 + 3 = 21$

78. We have, 5-digit numbers formed using 1, 2, 3, 5, 7 with repetitions and written in decreasing order.

Numbers starting with 7 .... $= 5^4$

Numbers starting with 5 .... $= 5^4$

Numbers starting with $3 \cdot 7$ ... $= 5^3$

Numbers starting with $3 \cdot 5 \cdot 7$ .. $= 5^2$

Numbers starting with $3 \cdot 5 \cdot 5$ .. $= 5^2$

Numbers starting with $3 \cdot 5 \cdot 3 \cdot 7$. $= 5^1$

Numbers starting with $3 \cdot 5 \cdot 3 \cdot 5$. $= 5^1$

Number starting with $3 \cdot 5 \cdot 3 \cdot 3 \cdot 7 = 5^0$

$\therefore$ Serial number of 3 5 3 3 7 $= 2 \cdot 5^4 + 5^3 + 2 \cdot 5^2 + 2 \cdot 5^1 + 5^0$

$= 1436$

79. According to condition $a + b = c + d$

If sum is 3 $\rightarrow$ (0, 3) (1, 2) [Not posible]

If sum is 4 $\rightarrow$ (0, 4) (1, 3) [Not posible]

If sum is 5 $\rightarrow$ (0, 5) (1, 4) (2, 3) [Not posible]

If sum is 6 $\rightarrow$ (0, 6) (1, 5) (2, 4) [Not posible]

If sum is 7 $\rightarrow$ (0, 7) (1, 6) (2, 5) (3, 4)

If sum is 8 $\rightarrow$ (1, 7) (2, 6) (3, 5)

If sum is 9 $\rightarrow$ (2, 7) (3, 6) (4, 5)

If sum is 10 $\rightarrow$ (3, 7) (4, 6)

If sum is 11 $\rightarrow$ (4, 7), (5, 6)

Now, total trials

$= 4 \times {}^3C_1 \times 2! + 4 \times {}^2C_1 \times 2! + 4 \times {}^2C_1 \times 2! + 4 \times {}^1C_1 \times 2! + 4 \times {}^1C_1 \times 2!$

$= 24 + 16 + 16 + 8 + 8$

$= 72$

80. Let 'n' be the total number of couples who participated in the tournament t.

According to question,

$$2 \times {}^nC_2 \times {}^{n-2}C_2 = 840$$

$$\Rightarrow \quad {}^nC_2 \times {}^{n-2}C_2 = 420$$

$$\Rightarrow \quad \frac{n!}{2!(n-2)!} \times \frac{n-2!}{(n-4)!2!} = 420$$

$$\Rightarrow \quad \frac{n(n-1)(n-2)(n-3)}{4} = 420$$

Putting $n = 8$ satisfies the equation.

So, $n = 8$

$\therefore$ Total players $= 2n = 2 \times 8 = 16$

81. Now, number of possible values of $a = 60$, for $b = pq$,

If $p = 3$, then $q = 3, 5, 7, 11, 13, 17, 19$.

So, total cases $= 7$

If $p = 5$, then $q = 5, 7, 11$.

So, total cases $= 3$

If $p = 7$, then $q = 7$.

So, total case $= 1$

Therefore, total cases $= 60(7 + 3 + 1) = 660$

82. Number should be multiple of 6 and it should be even.

Total sum $= 1 + 2 + 3 + 5 + 6 + 7 = 24$

The number removed should be in 2 types.

Excluding 3 $\rightarrow$ 2 ways $= 4! \times 2 = 48$

Excluding 6 $\rightarrow$ 1 way $= 4! = 24$

Total cases $= 48 + 24 = 72$

83. $f : \{1, 3, 5, 7, ..., 99\} \rightarrow \{2, 4, 6, 8, ..., 100\}$,

Let $f : A \rightarrow B$,

where $A = \{1, 3, 5, 7, ..., 99\}$ and $B = \{2, 4, 6, ..., 100\}$

As number of elements in A and B is 50.

$\therefore$ Total possibilities $= 50$

Such that $f(3) \geq f(9) \geq f(15) \geq (21) \geq ... \geq f(99)$

We have, AP = 3, 9, 15, 21, ..., 99

Here, $a_n = 99$, $a_1 = 3$ and $d = 6$

$a_n = a + (n-1)d \Rightarrow 99 = 3 + (n-1)6$

$\Rightarrow \quad n = 17$

Hence, number of bijective function $= {}^{50}C_{17} \times 33! = {}^{50}P_{33}$

84. Number of ways of selecting 3 boys from b boys $= {}^bC_3$

Number of ways of selecting 2 girls from g girls $= {}^gC_2$

Number of ways of selecting 3 boys and 2 girls from the class $= 168$

$$^bC_3 \times {^gC_2} = 168$$

$$\Rightarrow \quad \frac{b(b-1)(b-2)}{6} \times \frac{g(g-1)}{2} = 168$$

$$\Rightarrow \quad b(b-1)(b-2) \times g(g-1) = 168 \times 6 \times 2$$

$$\Rightarrow \quad b(b-1)(b-2) \times g(g-1) = 2016$$

As b and g are natural number, so make factor of 206

$$b(b-1)(b-2) \times g(g-1) = 6 \times 7 \times 8 \times 3 \times 2$$

$$\Rightarrow \quad b = 8 \text{ and } g = 3$$

$$\therefore \quad b + 3g = 8 + 3 \times 3 = 8 + 9 = 17$$

85. $\because$ Required number of password

$= $ Total number of character from {1, 2, 3, 4, 5}.

$= (10^6 - 5^6) + (10^7 - 5^7) + (10^8 - 5^8)$

$= 10^6(1 + 10 + 100) - 5^6(1 + 5 + 25)$

$= 10^6 \times 111 - 5^6 \times 31$

$= 5^6(2^6 \times 111 - 31) = 5^6 \times 7073$

$\therefore \alpha = 7073$

86. Factors of 36 is 1, 2, 3, 4, 6, 9, 12, 18, 36 or $1 \times 2^2 \times 3^2$

Case I When digits are (1, 2, 2, 3, 3).

The number of such combinations is $\frac{5!}{2!\,2!} = \frac{5 \times 4 \times 3}{1 \times 2} = 30$

Case II When digits are (1, 4, 3, 3, 1).

The number of such combination is $\frac{5!}{2!\,2!} = \frac{5 \times 4 \times 3}{1 \times 2} = 30$

Case III When digits are (1, 9, 2, 2, 1).

The number of such combinations $= \frac{5!}{2!\,2!} = 30$

Case IV When digits are (1, 4, 9, 1, 1).

The number of such combination is $5!/3! = 20$

Case V When digits are (1, 2, 3, 6, 1).

The number of such combination is $\frac{5!}{2!} = 5 \times 4 \times 3 = 60$

Case VI When digits are (1, 6, 6, 1, 1).

The number of such combination is $\frac{5!}{3!\,2!} = 10$

$\therefore$ The total number of combinations are

$30 + 30 + 30 + 20 + 60 + 10 = 180$

87. The letters of the word 'MANKIND' are written in all possible order and arranged in serial order as in an english dictionary.

Represent serial order in dictionary	⑤ M	① A	⑥ N	④ K	③ I	⑥ N	② D
	$\frac{4}{2!}$	0	$\frac{3}{2!}$	2	1	1	0
	×	×	×	×	×	×	×
	6!	5!	4!	3!	2!	1!	0!
Outcomes	1440	0	36	12	2	1	10

Thus, the serial number of the word

MANKIND is $(1440 + 0 + 36 + 12 + 2 + 1) + 1$

$= 1491 + 1 = 1492$

88. Given digits are 1, 2, 3, 4, 5, 6, 7.

Total positions are 6 with fixed unit digit.

. . . . ⇓ 5

The sum of digits 1, 2, 3, 4, 5, 6, 7 is 28. So, only 1, 4 and 7 can be removed.

If 1 is removed, then the total number of numbers are 5!. Similarly, for 4 and 7.

Total number of ways $= 5! \times 3 = 360$

89. **Decoding the Question**

Assume 4-digit number is *abcd* and make cases for $d = 1$ to 9 and solve further using multiplication principle of counting.

Let the four digit number be *abcd*.

It is given that a, b and c should be divisible by d.

Numbers a, b, c and d are chosen from 0, 1, 2, 3, 4, 5, 6, 7, 8, 9.

| a | b | c |

Number of such numbers

$d=1$ | 9 | 10 | 10 | = 900 [$\because$ first entry cannot be zero]

$d=2$ | 4 | 5 | 5 | = 100

$d=3$ | 3 | 4 | 4 | = 48

$d=4$ | 2 | 3 | 3 | = 18

$d=5$ | 1 | 2 | 2 | = 4

$d=6, 7, 8, 9$ | 1 | 2 | 2 | ×4 = 16

Required total number $= 900 + 100 + 48 + 18 + 4 + 16$

$= 1086$

90. $b_i \in \{1, 2, 3, \ldots, 100\}$

Let $P = $ Set when b_1, b_2, b_3 are consecutive

$n(P) = 97 + 97 + 97 + \ldots\ldots$ (98 times)

$= 97 \times 98$

Similarly, $Q = $ Set when b_2, b_3, b_4 are consecutive

$n(Q) = 97 \times 98$

$n(P \cap Q) = 97$

$n(P \cup Q) = n(P) + n(Q) - n(P \cap Q)$

$= 97 \times 98 + 97 \times 98 - 97$

$= 97(98 + 98 - 1)$

$= 97(195) = 18915$

Hence, the number of required permutations is 18915.

91. **Case I** When all the digits are non-zero. Let the three digit be x, x and y, where $x, y \neq 0$, then the number of formation of three digit number would be

$$^9C_2 \times 2! \times \frac{3!}{2!} = 216$$

Case II When non-repeated digit would be zero, then total number of such three-digit numbers are $^9C_1 \times 2! = 18$

Case III When the repeated digit would be zero.

The total number of such three digit number are ${}^9C_1 = 9$

$\therefore$ The required number of three digit numbers are $216 + 18 + 9 = 243$.

92. Let the student marks 'x' correct answers and 'y' incorrect.

So, $3x - 2y = 5$ and $x + y \le 5$ where $x, y \in W$.

Thus, only possible solution is $(x, y) = (3, 2)$

The student can mark correct answer by only one choice but for incorrect answers there are two choices. So, total number of ways a student appearing in the examination gets 5 marks is

$$ {}^5C_3 (1)^3 \cdot (2)^2 = \frac{5!}{3! \times 2!} \times 1 \times 4 = 40 $$

93. Number of matches when a girl plays against a girl $= n \times 6 = 6n$

Number of matches when a boy plays against a boy $= 7 \times 4 = 28$

According to the question, $28 + 6n = 52 \Rightarrow n = 4$

94. Given, digits are $= 1, 2, 2, 3$

$\therefore$ Total distinct numbers $= 4!/2! = 12$

1 at unit place $\Rightarrow$ Number of such numbers $= \frac{3!}{2!} = 3$

2 at unit place $\Rightarrow$ Number of such numbers $= 3! = 6$

3 at unit place $\Rightarrow$ Number of such numbers $= 3!/2! = 3$

$\therefore$ Sum of digits at unit place is

$$ 3 \times 1 + 6 \times 2 + 3 \times 3 = 24 $$

Hence, sum of all 4 digit such numbers

$$ = (3 + 12 + 9)(10^3 + 10^2 + 10 + 1) $$
$$ = 26664 $$

95. **Decoding the Question**

(i) Number of ways to select r persons out of n persons $= {}^nC_r$

(ii) Add the number of ways possible in each of the cases.

Given,

Number of Indians = 6

Number of foreigners = 8

Committee of at least 2 Indians and double number of foreigners is to be formed. Hence, the required cases are

$$ (2I, 4F) + (3I, 6F) + (4I, 8F) $$
$$ = {}^6C_2 \times {}^8C_4 + {}^6C_3 \times {}^8C_6 + {}^6C_4 \times {}^8C_8 $$
$$ = (15 \times 70) + (20 \times 28) + (15 \times 1) $$
$$ = 1050 + 560 + 15 = 1625 $$

96. Given, $xyz = 24 \Rightarrow xyz = 2^3 \cdot 3^1$

Let $x = 2^{a_1} \cdot 3^{b_1}$,

$y = 2^{a_2} \cdot 3^{b_2}$,

$z = 2^{a_3} \cdot 3^{b_3}$

where, $a_1, a_2, a_3 \in \{0, 1, 2, 3\}$

$b_1, b_2, b_3 \in \{0, 1\}$

Case I $a_1 + a_2 + a_3 = 3$

$\therefore$ Non-negative solution $= {}^{3+3-1}C_{3-1} = {}^5C_2 = 10$

Case II $b_1 + b_2 + b_3 = 1$

$\therefore$ Non-negative solution $= {}^{1+3-1}C_{3-1} = {}^3C_2 = 3$

$\therefore$ Total solutions $= 10 \times 3 = 30$

97. **Method (I)** (Proper Method)

Whenever we construct a triangle, we must require three non-collinear points.

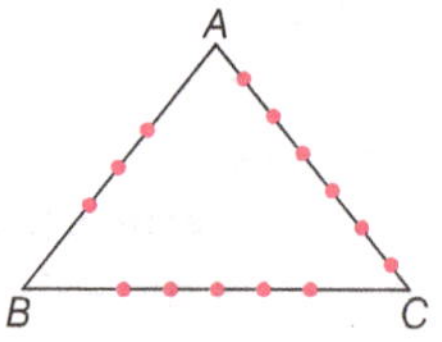

$\therefore$ Total number of triangles using the points 3, 5 and 6 which are on the sides AB, BC and CA

= Either taking (one point from AB, BC and CA)

or (one point from AB and two points from BC)

or (one point from BC and two points from AB)

or (one point from AB and two points from AC)

or (one point from AC and two points from AB)

or (one point from BC and two points from AC)

or (one point from AC and two points from BC)

$\Rightarrow$ Total number of triangles

$$ = ({}^3C_1 \times {}^5C_1 \times {}^6C_1) + ({}^3C_1 \times {}^5C_2) + ({}^5C_1 \times {}^3C_2) + ({}^3C_1 \times {}^6C_2) + ({}^6C_1 \times {}^3C_2) + ({}^5C_1 \times {}^6C_2) + ({}^6C_1 \times {}^5C_2) $$
$$ = 90 + 30 + 15 + 45 + 18 + 75 + 60 $$
$$ = 333 $$

Method (II) (Direct Method)

Total number of points $= 3 + 5 + 6 = 14$

Then, when we construct a triangle, we must select 3 points out of 14 but these points never be collinear.

$\therefore$ Total number of triangles formed $= {}^{14}C_3 - {}^3C_3 - {}^5C_3 - {}^6C_3$
$$ = 333 $$

98. **Decoding the Question**

In a rectangle of $n \times p$ $(n < p)$, numbers of rectangles of any size is ${}^{n+1}C_2$ or $\frac{np}{4}(n+1)(p+1)$ and number of square of any size is $\sum_{r=1}^{n} (n + 1 - r)(p + 1 - r)$.

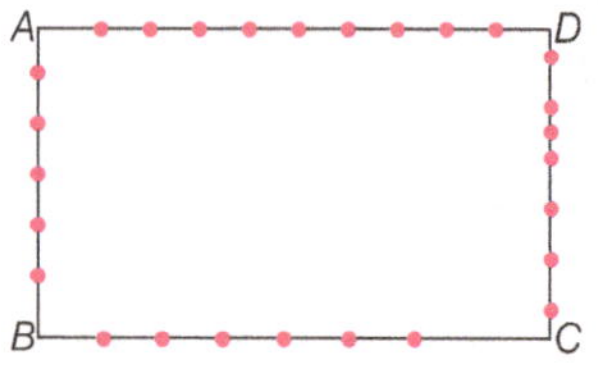

Number of triangles that can be formed from the points on 3 of the sides.

$${}^5C_1{}^7C_1{}^6C_1 + {}^5C_1{}^7C_1{}^9C_1 + {}^5C_1{}^6C_1{}^9C_1 + {}^6C_1{}^7C_1{}^9C_1$$

$$= 210 + 315 + 270 + 378$$

$$\Rightarrow \quad \alpha = 1173$$

Number of quadrilaterals that can be formed by taking one point from each of the four vertex

$${}^5C_1{}^7C_1{}^6C_1{}^9C_1 = 5 \times 6 \times 7 \times 9$$

$$= 1890$$

$$\Rightarrow \quad \beta = 1890$$

$$\therefore \quad \beta - \alpha = 1890 - 1173$$

$$= 717$$

99. VOWELS (2 Vowel + 4 consonant)

All consonants must not be together

Total possibility of formation of 6 letter word = 6!

The number of arrangement when all the consonant comes together = 3! × 4!

Number of arrangement when all the consonant never come together

$= \text{Total} - \text{All consonant together} = 6! - 3!\,4!$

$= 576$

100. Multiples of 11 such that they are of 3-digit and less than 500.

110, 121, 132, ..., 495

$$n = \frac{495 - 110}{11} + 1 = 36$$

$$S = \frac{36}{2}(110 + 495) = 10890$$

Again, multiplies of 11 which are 3-digits, less than 500 and having 1 at hundred's place are 110, 121, 132, ..., 198

$$n_1 = \left(\frac{198 - 110}{11}\right) + 1 = 9$$

$$S_1 = \frac{9}{2}(110 + 198) = 1386$$

The multiply of 11 which are of 3-digits, less than 500 and having 1 at ten's place are 319, 418

$$\therefore \quad S_2 = 319 + 418 = 737$$

The multiple of 11 which are 3-digits, less than 500 and having 1 at unit place are 231, 341, 451

$$\therefore \quad S_3 = 231 + 341 + 451 = 1023$$

$\therefore$ Required sum $= S - S_1 - S_2 - S_3$

$= 7744$

101. ${}^1P_1 + 2 \cdot {}^2P_2 + 3 \cdot {}^3P_3 + \dots + 15 \cdot {}^{15}P_{15}$

$$= 1! + 2 \cdot 2! + 3 \cdot 3! + \dots + 15 \cdot 15!$$

$$= \Sigma r \cdot r! = \Sigma (r + 1 - 1) r!$$

$$= \Sigma [(r+1)! - r!]$$

$$= (2! - 1!) + (3! - 2!) + \dots (15! - 14!) + (16! - 15!)$$

$$= (16! - 1!) = {}^{16}P_{16} - 1$$

$$q = r = 16, s = 1$$

$${}^{q+s}C_{r-s} = {}^{17}C_{15} = 136$$

102. **Case I** When 0 is at unit place

Total number $= 5 \times 4 = 20$

Case II When 4 or 6 are at unit place

Total numbers $= 4 \times 4 \times 2 = 32$

[0 cannot be come at hundredth place]

$\therefore$ Total number of required $= 20 + 32 = 52$

103. 0, 2, 4, 6, 8

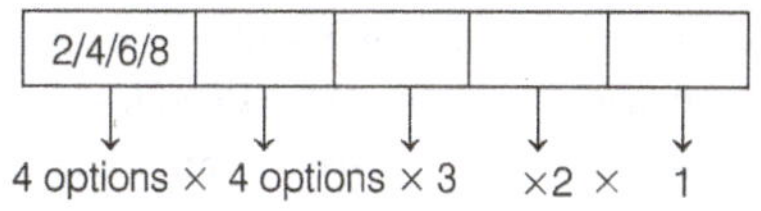

$\therefore$ Total $= 4 \times 4 \times 3 \times 2 \times 1 = 96$

104. As, we observe the pattern

Inside number $= (\text{difference})^{(\text{difference})!}$

i.e. $1 = (2-1)^{(2-1)!}$, $4^{24} = (12-8)^{(12-8)!}$, $3^6 = (7-4)^{(7-4)!}$

$\therefore \; ? = (5-3)^{(5-3)!}$

$\therefore$ Required number $= 2^{2!} = 4$

105. Let the number be xyz, $0 \le x, y, z \le 9$

Case I '3' appears only one time

$$\Rightarrow \quad {}^3C_1 \times 9 \times 9 = 243$$

Case II '3' appears two times

$$\Rightarrow \quad {}^3C_2 \times 2 \times 9 = 54$$

Case III '3' appears three times

$$\Rightarrow \quad {}^3C_3 \times 3 = 3$$

$\therefore$ Total $= 243 + 54 + 3 = 300$

106. Let x be four digit number, then $gcd(x, 18) = 3$

This implies x is divisible by 3 but not divisible by 2 and 9.

The 4-digit numbers which is an odd multiple of 3 are 1005, 1011, 1017, ... 9999

These are 1500 in counting i.e. total number of 4-digit numbers which is odd multiple of 3 are 1500.

Now, The 4-digit numbers which is an odd multiple of 9 are, 1017, 1035, ...9999

These, are total 500.

Then, required 4-digit numbers $= 1500 - 500 = 1000$

107. We can write, $7^n = (10-3)^n$ or $7^n = 10K + (-3)^n$

(using expansion)

$$\therefore 7^n + 3^n = 10K + (-3)^n + 3^n = \begin{cases} 10K, & n = \text{odd} \\ 10K + 2 \cdot 3^n, & n = \text{even} \end{cases}$$

This implies $n = \text{odd}$

$n = 11, 13, 15, \dots 99$ (since, n is two digit number)

$\therefore$ Total possible n are 45.

108. Given, digits $= \{1, 2, 3, 4, 5\}$

Numbers divisible by 3 (sum of digits divisible by 3).

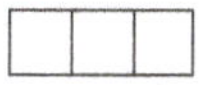

Case I When sum is 12 $\to$ 3, 4, 5 $\to 3! = 6$

Case II When sum is 9 $\to$ 2, 3, 4 $\to 3! = 6$

Case III When sum is 9 → 1, 3, 5 → $3! = 6$

Case IV When sum is 6 → 1, 2, 3 → $3! = 6$

So, total numbers divisible by $3 = 6 \times 4 = 24$

Numbers divisible by 5 (ending with 5)

$$\boxed{}\boxed{}\boxed{5} = 4 \times 3 = 12$$

4×3 ↑ 1

So, total numbers divisible by $5 = 12$

Numbers divisible by 15, are 135, 315, 345, 435

i.e. total 4 numbers are divisible by both 3 and 5. i.e. divisible by 15.

Hence, the required numbers which are divisible by 3 or 5

$$= 24 + 12 - 4 = 32$$

109. Given, total students = 10

Number of groups = 3 (i.e. A, B and C)

Each group has atleast one student but group C has atmost 3 students.

∴ There are 3 cases depending on number of students in group C.

Case I C has 1 student, then $\left.\begin{matrix} A \\ B \end{matrix}\right] \leftarrow 9$ students

$\therefore$ Number of ways $= {}^{10}C_1 \times [2^9 - 2]$

Case II C has 2 students, then $\left.\begin{matrix} A \\ B \end{matrix}\right] \leftarrow 8$ Students.

$\therefore$ Number of ways $= {}^{10}C_2 \times [2^8 - 2]$

Case III C has 3 students, then $\left.\begin{matrix} A \\ B \end{matrix}\right] \leftarrow 7$ Students.

$\therefore$ Number of ways $= {}^{10}C_3 \times [2^7 - 2]$

$\therefore$ Required number of possibilities

$$= {}^{10}C_1(2^9 - 2) + {}^{10}C_2(2^8 - 2) + {}^{10}C_3(2^7 - 2)$$

$$= 2^7[{}^{10}C_1 \times 4 + {}^{10}C_2 \times 2 + {}^{10}C_3] - 20 - 90 - 240$$

$$= (128 \times 250) - 350$$

$$= 31650$$

110. We have, $(2 \cdot {}^1P_0 - 3 \cdot {}^2P_1 + 4 \cdot {}^3P_2 - \ldots$ upto 51th terms)

$+ (1! - 2! + 3! - 4! + \ldots$ upto 51th terms)

$$= 2! - 3! + 4! - \ldots - 51! + 52! + 1! - 2! + 3! + \ldots + 51!$$

$$= 1 + 52!$$

111. It is given that the 10th place of 5 digit number with distinct digits is '2', then the ten thousand place, thousand place, hundred place and unit place we can fill in 8, 8, 7 and 6 ways only.

$$\underset{8}{\_}\ \underset{8}{\_}\ \underset{7}{\_}\ \underset{1}{2}\ \underset{6}{\_}$$

So, required number of five digit numbers is

$8 \times 8 \times 7 \times 6 = 336\, k$ (given)

$$\Rightarrow \quad k = \frac{8 \times 8 \times 7 \times 6}{336} = \frac{8 \times 8 \times 7}{56} = 8$$

112. To make 6-digit numbers from given digits 1, 3, 5, 7 and 9, we must repeat a digit and we can done the same in ${}^5C_1$ ways.

Now, the arrangement of these 6-digits in which two are identical is $\frac{6!}{2!}$.

So, required numbers of 6-digit numbers $= {}^5C_1 \frac{6!}{2!} = \frac{5}{2}(6!)$

113. As each section has 5 questions, so number of ways to select 5 questions are $S_1 \quad S_2 \quad S_3$

$$\begin{matrix} S_1 \rightarrow \\ S_2 \rightarrow \\ S_3 \rightarrow \end{matrix} \begin{bmatrix} 1 & 1 & 3 \\ 1 & 3 & 1 \\ 3 & 1 & 1 \end{bmatrix}$$

and

$$\begin{matrix} S_1 \rightarrow \\ S_2 \rightarrow \\ S_3 \rightarrow \end{matrix} \begin{bmatrix} 1 & 2 & 2 \\ 2 & 1 & 2 \\ 2 & 2 & 1 \end{bmatrix}$$

∴ Total number of selection of 5 questions

$$= 3 \times ({}^5C_1 \times {}^5C_1 \times {}^5C_3) + 3 \times ({}^5C_1 \times {}^5C_2 \times {}^5C_2)$$

$$= 3(5 \times 5 \times 10) + 3(5 \times 10 \times 10)$$

$$= 750 + 1500 = 2250$$

114. According to the given question,

Number of blue lines $= n$

and number of red lines $= {}^nC_2 - n$

$\because \quad {}^nC_2 - n = 99n$

$$\Rightarrow \quad \frac{n(n-1)}{2} = 100n \Rightarrow n - 1 = 200 \Rightarrow n = 201$$

Exercise 2 - JEE Advanced Pattern

1. Required number of words $= 6! - 5! - 5! + 4! = 504$

2. Let x, y, z be the friends and a, b, c denote the case when x is invited a times, y is invited b times and z is invited c times. Now, we have the following possibilities $(a, b, c) = (1, 2, 3)$ or $(2, 2, 2)$ or $(3, 3, 0)$ [grouping of 6 days of week]

Hence, the total number of ways

$$= \frac{6!}{1!\,2!\,3!} \times 3! + \frac{6!}{2!\,2!\,2!} \times \frac{3!}{3!} + \frac{6!}{3!\,3!\,0!} \times \frac{3!}{2!}$$

$$= 360 + 90 + 60 = 510$$

3. If $y = n$, then x takes values from 1 to $n - 1$ and z can take values from 0 to n (i.e. $(n + 1)$ values). Thus, for each value of y $(2 \le y \le 9)$, x and z take $(n - 1)(n + 1)$ values.

Hence, the 3-digit numbers are of the form xyz

$$= \sum_{x=2}^{9} (n-1)(n+1)$$

$$= \sum_{x=2}^{9} (n^2 - 1) = 276$$

4. The letters in alphabetical order are EEMRTU

E → $5! = 120$

MEERTU → $1! = 1$

MEERUT → 1

$\therefore$ Rank of MEERUT $= 120 + 1 + 1 = 122$

5. The candidates can be ranked in 10! ways. In half of these ways, A_1 is above A_2 and in another half, A_2 is above A_1. So, required number of ways $= \frac{10!}{2}$.

6. Any selection of four digits from the ten digits 0, 1, 2, 3, ..., 9 gives one number.

So, the required number of numbers $= {}^{10}C_4 = 210$

7. As $0 < x < 1$, we have $p < q$

The number of rational numbers $= 5 + 4 + 3 + 2 + 1 = 15$

When p, q have a common factor, we get some rational numbers which are not different from those already counted.

There are 4 such numbers $\frac{2}{4}, \frac{2}{6}, \frac{3}{6}, \frac{4}{6}$.

$\therefore$ The required number of rational numbers $= 15 - 4 = 11$

8. We have, $24 = 2 \times 3 \times 4 = 2 \times 2 \times 6$

$= 1 \times 6 \times 4 = 1 \times 3 \times 8$

$= 1 \times 2 \times 12 = 1 \times 1 \times 24$

The number of positive integral solutions of $xyz = 24$ is

$$3! + \frac{3!}{2!} + 3! + 3! + 3! + \frac{3!}{2!} = 30$$

and number of integral solutions having two negative factors is ${}^3C_2 \times 30 = 90$.

Hence, number of integral solutions $= 30 + 90 = 120$

9. Total number of triangles = Number of triangles with vertices on sides $[(AB, BC, CD) + (AB, BC, DA) + (AB, CD, DA) + (BC, CD, DA)]$

$= {}^3C_1 \times {}^4C_1 \times {}^5C_1 + {}^3C_1 \times {}^4C_1 \times {}^6C_1 + {}^3C_1 \times {}^5C_1 \times {}^6C_1 + {}^4C_1 \times {}^5C_1 \times {}^6C_1$

$= 60 + 72 + 90 + 120 = 342$

10. $\because$ 16 horses = 10 horses + (A, B, C, D, E, F)

$\therefore$ The number of ways $= {}^{10}C_3 \times$ (Number of ways of choosing out of A, B, C, D, E, F, so that AD, BE and CF are not together)

$= {}^{10}C_3 \times$ (One from each of pairs AD, BE, CF)

$= {}^{10}C_3 \times {}^2C_1 \times {}^2C_1 \times {}^2C_1 = 960$

11. We have, $i^3 + ai^2 + bi + c = 0$

and $(-i)^3 + a(-i)^2 + b(-i) + c = 0$

$\Rightarrow$ $(c - a) + (b - 1)i = 0$

and $(c - a) - i(b - 1) = 0 \Rightarrow b = 1, a = c$

Thus, total number of such polynomials $= {}^{10}C_1 = 10$

12. $$\sum_{i=1}^{k} \frac{1}{x_i} = \frac{1}{x_1} + \frac{1}{x_2} + \ldots + \frac{1}{x_k} = \frac{\sum_{i=1}^{k} x_i}{n} = \frac{75}{n}$$

[as LCM of $x_1, x_2, x_3, \ldots, x_k$ is n]

13. Let '1' be associated with 'r', $r \in \{1, 2, 3, 4, 5\}$, then '2' can be associated with $r, r + 1, \ldots, 5$.

Let '2' be associated with 'j' then 3 can be associated with j, $j + 1, \ldots, 5$. Thus, required number of functions

$$\sum_{r=1}^{5} \left(\sum_{j=r}^{5} (6 - j) \right) = \sum_{r=1}^{5} \frac{(6 - r)(7 - r)}{2} = 35$$

14. Clearly, each player will play 9 games.

$\therefore$ Total number of games $= {}^{10}C_2 = 45$

Clearly, $w_i + l_i = 9$ and $\Sigma w_i = \Sigma l_i = 45$

$\Rightarrow$ $w_i = 9 - l_i \Rightarrow w_i^2 = 81 - 18 l_i + l_i^2$

$\Rightarrow$ $\Sigma w_i^2 = \Sigma 81 - 18 \Sigma l_i + \Sigma l_i^2$

$= 81 \times 10 - 18 \times 45 + \Sigma l_i^2 = \Sigma l_i^2$

15. The number of matches in the first round $= {}^6C_2 + {}^6C_2 = 30$

The number of matches in the next round $= {}^6C_2 = 15$

and the number of matches in the semi-final round $= {}^4C_2 = 6$

$\therefore$ The required number of matches $= 30 + 15 + 6 + 2 = 53$

[$\because$ for 'best of three' atleast two matches are played]

16. We have, $15 < x_1 + x_2 + x_3 \le 20$

$\Rightarrow$ $x_1 + x_2 + x_3 = 16 + r, r = 0, 1, 2, 3, 4$

Now, the number of positive integral solution of $x_1 + x_2 + x_3 = 16 + r$ is equal to ${}^{13+r+3-1}C_{13+r}$

i.e. ${}^{15+r}C_{13+r} = {}^{15+r}C_2$

$\therefore$ Total number of solutions

$= \sum_{r=0}^{4} {}^{15+r}C_2$

$= {}^{15}C_2 + {}^{16}C_2 + {}^{17}C_2 + {}^{18}C_2 + {}^{19}C_2$

$= \frac{1}{2}[15 \times 14 + 16 \times 15 + 17 \times 16 + 18 \times 17 + 19 \times 18]$

$= 685$

17. Make 1 group of 2 persons, 1 group of 4 persons, and 3 groups of 3 persons among 15 persons (except 2 particular persons).

Hence, the number of ways by grouping method is $\frac{15!}{2!4!(3!)^3 3!}$

Now, we add those two persons in the group of 2 persons and thus the number of arrangements of these groups into cars and autos is

$$\frac{15!}{2!4!(3!)^3 3!} \times 2! \times 3! = \frac{15!}{4!(3!)^3}$$

18. There can be two types of numbers.

(i) Anyone of the digits 1, 2, 3, 4 appears thrice and the remaining digits only once, i.e., of the type 1, 2, 3, 4, 4, 4, etc. Number of ways selection of digit which appears thrice is ${}^4C_1$

Then, the number of numbers of this type is $(6!/3!) \times {}^4C_1 = 480$

(ii) Any two of the digits 1, 2, 3, 4 appears twice and the remaining two only once, i.e. of the type 1, 2, 3, 3, 4, 4 etc. The number of ways of selection of two digits which appear twice is ${}^4C_2$. Then, the number of numbers of this type is $[6!/(2!2!) \times {}^4C_2] = 1080$.

$\therefore$ Required number of numbers $= 480 + 1080 = 1560$

19. Order of letters in opposite direction is R, R, R, O, O, H

Words starting with R $= \frac{5!}{2!2!} = 30$

Words starting with O $= \frac{5!}{3!} = 20$

Words starting with HR $= \frac{4!}{2!2!} = 6$

Next word will be HORRRO, HORROR

So, Rank of word HORROR $= 30 + 20 + 6 + 1 + 1 = 58$

20. We have, $k^2 - 3 = \frac{^{n-1}C_r}{^nC_{r+1}}, 0 \le r \le n-1$

$\Rightarrow \quad k^2 - 3 = \frac{(n-1)!}{r!(n-4-1)!} \times \frac{(n-r-1)!(r+1)!}{n!}$

$\Rightarrow \quad k^2 - 3 = \frac{r+1}{n}$

$\Rightarrow \quad \frac{1}{n} \le k^2 - 3 \le 1 \, [\because 0 \le r \le n-1 \Rightarrow 1 \le r+1 \le n]$

$\Rightarrow \quad 3 < k^2 \le 4 \Rightarrow k \in (\sqrt{3}, 2]$

21. Required number of ways $= \frac{(200)!}{\underbrace{2!2!..2!}_{100 \text{ times}}(100)!} = \frac{(200)!}{100!2^{100}}$

$= 1 \times 3 \times 5 \times \ldots \times 199$

$= \frac{101}{2} \times \frac{102}{2} \times \ldots \times \frac{200}{2}$

$\left[\because \frac{(2n)!}{2^n \cdot n!} = 1 \cdot 3 \cdot 5 \ldots (2n-1)\right]$

22. We have, 8, 7, 6, 4, 2, x and y

Any number is divisible by 3 if sum of digits is divisible by 3.

$\therefore$ $x + y + 27$ is divisible by 3

Now, x, y can take values from 0, 1, 3, 5. 9.

Possible pairs are (5, 1), (3, 0), (9, 0), (9, 3) and (1, 5), (0, 3), (0, 9), (3, 9).

23. We have, $^{n+5}P_{n+1} = \frac{11(n-1)}{2} \times {}^{n+3}P_n$

$\Rightarrow \quad \frac{(n+5)!}{4!} = \frac{11(n-1)}{2} \times \frac{(n+3)!}{3!}$

$\Rightarrow \quad (n+5)(n+4) = 22(n-1)$

$\therefore \quad n = 6 \text{ or } 7$

So, number of points of intersection of lines is $^6C_2$ or $^7C_2$

i.e. 15 or 21.

24. We have,

$P = 21(21+1)(21-1)(21+2)(21-2)\ldots(21+10)(21-10)$

$= (21-10)(21-9)\ldots(21-1)21(21+1)(21+2)\ldots(21+10)$

$= 11 \times 12 \times 13 \times \ldots \times 30 \times 31$

which is divisible by 21!, 20!, 19!.

25. Let person p_i get x_i number of things such that

$x_1 + x_2 + x_3 + x_4 + x_5 + x_{10} = 30$

If x_i is odd or $x_i = 2\lambda_i + 1, \lambda_i \ge 0$, then

$2(\lambda_1 + \lambda_2 + \lambda_3 + \lambda_4 + \lambda_5 + \lambda_6) + 6 = 30$

$\Rightarrow \quad \lambda_1 + \lambda_2 + \lambda_3 + \lambda_4 + \lambda_5 + \lambda_6 = 12$

Then, number of solutions is $^{12+6-1}C_{6-1} = {}^{17}C_5$

If x_i is even or $x_i = 2\lambda_i, \lambda_i \ge 1$, then

$2(\lambda_1 + \lambda_2 + \lambda_3 + \lambda_4 + \lambda_5 + \lambda_6) = 30$

$\lambda_1 + \lambda_2 + \lambda_3 + \lambda_4 + \lambda_5 + \lambda_6 = 15$

Then, number of solutions is $^{15-1}C_{6-1} = {}^{14}C_5$

26. $E_3(300!) = \left[\frac{300}{3}\right] + \left[\frac{300}{3^2}\right] + \left[\frac{300}{3^3}\right] + \left[\frac{300}{3^4}\right] + \left[\frac{300}{3^5}\right]$

$= 100 + 33 + 11 + 3 + 1 = 148$

$\therefore \quad m = 148$

and $E_2(150!) = \left[\frac{150}{2}\right] + \left[\frac{150}{2^2}\right] + \left[\frac{150}{2^3}\right] + \ldots + \left[\frac{150}{2^7}\right]$

$= 75 + 37 + 18 + 9 + 4 + 2 + 1 = 146$

$\therefore \quad n - 2 = 146 \Rightarrow n = 148$

27. $\because E_2(102!) = 98, E_3(102!) = 49,$

$E_5(102!) = 24$ and $E_7(102!) = 16$

$\therefore \alpha = 98, \beta = 49, \gamma = 24$ and $\delta = 16$

28. Triplets with

(i) $x = y < z$ (ii) $x < y < z$ (iii) $y < x < z$

can be chosen in $^{n+1}C_2, {}^{n+1}C_3, {}^{n+1}C_3$ ways.

$\therefore \quad {}^{n+1}C_2 + {}^{n+1}C_3 + {}^{n+1}C_3 = {}^{n+2}C_3 + {}^{n+1}C_3$

$= 2({}^{n+2}C_3) - {}^{n+1}C_2$

$= \frac{n(n+1)(2n+1)}{6}$

29. **When x is odd.**

Unit's place filled by 1, 3, 5, 7, 9.

$\therefore \quad x = 8 \times 8 \times 7 \times 5 = 2240$

When x is even.

Unit's place filled by 0, 2, 4, 6, 8.

$\therefore \quad y = 8 \times 8 \times 7 \times 4 + 9 \times 8 \times 7 \times 1 = 2296$

$\Rightarrow \quad x < y$ and $|x - y| = 56$

30. $\sum_{A \in X} \min A$

$\sum_{r=1}^{n-1} r(n-r) = n\sum_{r=1}^{n-1} r - \sum_{r=1}^{n-1} r^2$

$= \frac{n(n-1)n}{2} - \frac{(n-1)n(2n-1)}{6}$

$= \frac{(n+1) \cdot n \cdot (n-1)}{1 \cdot 2 \cdot 3} = {}^{n+1}C_3 = \frac{n(n^2-1)}{6}$

31. $\because \quad p = 2520 = 2^3 \cdot 3^2 \cdot 5^1 \cdot 7^1$

$= 6 \cdot 2^2 \cdot 3^1 \cdot 5^1 \cdot 7^1 = 9 \cdot 2^3 \cdot 5^1 \cdot 7^1$

$\therefore \quad x = (2+1)(1+1)(1+1)(1+1) = 24$

and $\quad y = (3+1)(1+1)(1+1) = 16.$

32. $\because x_1 + x_2 + x_3 + \ldots + x_n = r, \forall x_i \ge 1, (1 \le i \le n)$

Total number of such solutions $= {}^{r-1}C_{n-1} = {}^{r-1}C_{r-n}$

33. $\because \; x + x + 1 + y = 24 \Rightarrow y = 23 - 2x$

Let N = Total number of fights subject to the condition that any two children of one team do not fight.

$\therefore \quad N = {}^{24}C_2 - ({}^xC_2 + {}^{x+1}C_2 + {}^yC_2)$

$= {}^{24}C_2 - ({}^xC_2 + {}^{x+1}C_2 + {}^{23-2x}C_2)$

$= 23 - 3x^2 + 45x$

$\therefore \quad \frac{dN}{dx} = 0 - 6x + 45$

For maximum or minimum, put $\frac{dN}{dx} = 0 \Rightarrow x = 7.5$

$\Rightarrow \quad x = 7 \quad [\because x \in I]$

Now, $\frac{d^2N}{dx^2} < 0$

$\therefore$ N will be maximum when $x = 7$

and $N = 23 - 3(7)^2 + 45 \times 7 = 191$

34. $\because x + y + z = 3n$

$\Rightarrow N =$ Coefficient of α^{3n} in $(1 + \alpha + \alpha^2 + \ldots + \alpha^{2n})^3$

$=$ Coefficient of α^{3n} in $(1 - \alpha^{2n+1})^3 (1 - \alpha)^{-3}$

$=$ Coefficient of α^{3n} in $(1 - 3\alpha^{2n+1})\ (1 + {}^3C_1 \alpha + \ldots)$

$= {}^{3n+2}C_{3n} - 3 \cdot {}^{n+1}C_{n-1}$

$= {}^{3n+2}C_2 - 3 \cdot {}^{n+1}C_2 = 3n^2 + 3n + 1$

$\therefore N - 1 = 3n(n + 1)$

35. Since, α can be subtracted from β without borrowing, if $y_i \geq x_i$, for $i = 1, 2, 3$.

Let $x_i = \lambda$

If $i = 1$, then $\lambda = 1, 2, 3, \ldots, 9$

and if $i = 2$ and 3, then $\lambda = 0, 1, 2, 3, \ldots, 9$

Hence, total number of ways of choosing the pair α, β

$$= \left(\sum_{\lambda=1}^{9} (10 - \lambda)\right)\left(\sum_{\lambda=0}^{9} (10 - \lambda)\right)^2 = (45)(55)^2$$

36. There are 9 letters

T, T, R, R, R, E, O, I, S

$\lambda =$ Number of four lettered words (no restriction)

$=$ Coefficient of x^4 in

$$4!\left(1 + \frac{x}{1!} + \frac{x^2}{2!}\right)\left(1 + \frac{x}{1!} + \frac{x^2}{2!} + \frac{x^3}{3!}\right)(1 + x)^4 = 626$$

$\mu =$ Number of four lettered words (no vowels)

$=$ Coefficient of x^4 in

$$4!\left(1 + \frac{x}{1!} + \frac{x^2}{2!}\right)\left(1 + \frac{x}{1!} + \frac{x^2}{2!} + \frac{x^3}{3!}\right)(1 + x) = 38$$

$\therefore$ Required ways (atleast one vowel) $= 626 - 38 = 588$

37. × E × T T × O × I × S ×

Number of ways having TT together and RRR separated

$= {}^6C_3 \times 5! = 2400$

Hence, number of arrangements of the word W, if R's as well as T's are separated $= 12600 - 2400 = 10200$

38. × U × C × C × E ×

There are five available places for three SSS.

$\therefore$ Total number of ways no two S's together $= {}^5C_3 \times \frac{4!}{2!} = 120$

Hence, number of words having CC separated and SSS separated $= 120 - 24 = 96$

39. Total number of ways $= \frac{7!}{2!3!} = 420$

Consonants in SUCCESS are S, C, C, S, S

Number of ways arranging consonants $= \frac{5!}{2!3!} = 10$

Hence, number of words in which consonants appear in alphabetic order $= \frac{420}{10} = 42$

40. $\because f(6) = {}^6C_0 + {}^5C_1 + {}^4C_2 + {}^3C_3 = 13$

$\therefore f\{f(6)\} = f(13) = {}^{13}C_0 + {}^{12}C_1 + {}^{11}C_2 + {}^{10}C_3 + {}^9C_4 + {}^8C_5 + {}^7C_6$

$= 1 + 12 + 55 + 120 + 126 + 56 + 7 = 377$

41. $\because f(1) = {}^1C_0 = 1,\ f(2) = {}^2C_0 + {}^1C_1 = 2,\ f(3) = {}^3C_0 + {}^2C_1 = 3,$

$f(4) = 5$ [given]

and $f(5) = {}^5C_0 + {}^4C_1 + {}^3C_2 = 8$

Thus, we say that $f(n) > n$ for $n = 4, 5, 6, \ldots$

Hence, number of solutions for $f(n) = n$ is 3.

42. The number of ways in which two A's are together

i.e. × A A × N × G × E × is ${}^5C_2 \times 4! = 240$

Hence, number of ways in which neither two R's no two A's come together $= 900 - 240 = 660$

43. The letters in alphabetical order are AAEGNRR

AA $\to \frac{5!}{2!} = 60$ARA $\to 4! = 24$

AE $\to \frac{5!}{2!} = 60$ ARE $\to 4! = 24$

AG $\to \frac{5!}{2!} = 60$ARG $\to 4! = 24$

AN $\to \frac{5!}{2!} = 60$ARN $\to 4! = 24$

ARRAE $\to 2! = 2$ ARRAG $\to 2! = 2$

ARRANEG $\to 1$ ARRANGE $\to 1$

$\therefore$ Rank in dictionary

$= 60 + 60 + 60 + 60 + 24 + 24 + 24 + 24 + 2 + 2 + 1 + 1 = 342$

Sol. (Q. Nos. 44-45)

$$\frac{1}{x} + \frac{1}{y} = \frac{1}{n} \Rightarrow (x - n)(y - n) = n^2$$

$\therefore \quad x = n + \lambda,\ y = n + \frac{n^2}{\lambda}$, where λ is divisor of n^2.

The number of integral solutions (x, y) is equal to the number of divisors of n^2.

If $n = 3, n^2 = 9 = 3^2$, then the equation has 3 solutions.

$(x, y) = (4, 12), (6, 6), (12, 4)$

44. $\because \quad 6^2 = 2^2 \cdot 3^2$

$\Rightarrow \quad S(6) = 3 \times 3 = 9$ and $7^2 \Rightarrow S(7) = 3$

$\therefore \quad S(6) + S(7) = 12$

Also, $8^2 = 2^6$

$\Rightarrow \quad S(8) = 7$ and $9^2 = 3^4 \quad \Rightarrow S(9) = 5$

$\therefore \quad S(8) + S(9) = 12$

$\Rightarrow \quad S(6) + S(7) = S(8) + S(9) = 12$

45. $\because \quad 1^2 \to S(1) = 1,\ 2^2 \to S(2) = 3,\ 3^2 \to S(3) = 3,$

$4^2 \to 2^4 \to S(4) = 5,\ 5^2 \to S(5) = 3,\ S(6) = 9$

$S(7) = 3,\ S(8) = 7,\ S(9) = 5$ and $S(10) = 9$ [from above]

$$\therefore \sum_{r=1}^{10} S(r) = S(1) + S(2) + S(3) + S(4) + S(5) + S(6) + S(7) + S(8) + S(9) + S(10)$$

$= 1 + 3 + 3 + 5 + 3 + 9 + 3 + 7 + 5 + 9 = 48$

46. $a+b+c=21 \Rightarrow 3b=21 \Rightarrow b=7$ $[\because a+c=2b]$

$\Rightarrow \quad a+b+c=21 \Rightarrow a+c=14$

$\Rightarrow \quad \lambda = {}^{14-1}C_{2-1} = {}^{13}C_1 = 13$

Hence, $\lambda - 5 = 13 - 5 = 8$

47. 2λ = Number of selecting 3 member subsets of $\{1, 2, 3, \ldots, 29\}$ which are in GP with common ratio (2 or 3 or 4 or 5).

$$= \left[\frac{29}{2^2}\right] + \left[\frac{29}{3^2}\right] + \left[\frac{29}{4^2}\right] + \left[\frac{29}{5^2}\right]$$

$$= 7 + 3 + 1 + 1 = 12$$

$\therefore \quad \lambda = 6$

48. The number of students answering exactly $i (1 \le i \le n-1)$ questions wrongly is $2^{n-i} - 2^{n-i-1}$. The number of students answering all n questions wrongly is 2^0.

Hence, the total number of wrong answers

$$\sum_{i=1}^{n-1} i(2^{n-i} - 2^{n-i-1}) + n(2^0) = 127$$

$\Rightarrow 2^{n-1} + 2^{n-2} + 2^{n-3} + \ldots + 2^1 + 2^0 = 127$

$\Rightarrow \quad 2^n - 1 = 127 \Rightarrow 2^n = 128 = 2^7$

$\therefore \quad n = 7$

49. The sum of digits is divisible by 3.

i.e. $8+7+6+4+2+x+y$ or $27+x+y$ is divisible by 3.

$\therefore$ $x+y$ must be divisible by 3.

Then, possible ordered pairs are

(0, 3), (3, 0), (1, 5), (5, 1), (0, 9), (9, 0), (3, 9), (9, 3)

$\therefore$ Number of ordered pairs = 8

50. Number of circles through ACD, ACE, ADE intersect the line $AB = 3$

and number of circles through BCD, BCE, BDE intersect the line $AB = 3$

and number of circles through CDE intersects the line $AB = 2$

Hence, number of points of intersection $= 3 + 3 + 2 = 8$

51. When two consecutive digits are 11, 22 ..., 99, then such numbers $= 9 \times 9 = 81$

a	a	

When two consecutive digits are 00, then such numbers $= 9 \times 1 = 9$

	0	0

When two consecutive digits are 11, 22, ..., 99, then such numbers $= 8 \times 9 = 72$

	a	a

$\therefore$ Total number of numbers $= 81 + 9 + 72 = 162$

52. If x denotes the number of times he can take unit step and y denote the number of times he can take 2 steps, then

$$x + 2y = 7$$

We must have $x = 1, 3, 5$

If $x = 1$, the step will be 1222

$\therefore$ Number of ways $= \frac{4!}{3!} = 4$

If $x = 3$, the steps will be 11122

$\therefore$ Number of ways $= \frac{5!}{2!3!} = 10$

If $x = 5$, the steps will be 111112

$\therefore$ Number of ways $= {}^6C_1 = 6$

If $x = 7$, the steps will be 1111111

$\therefore$ Number of ways $= {}^7C_0 = 1$

$\therefore$ Total number of ways = 21

53. We have, 6 girls and 4 boys. To select 4 members (atmost one boy)

i.e. (1 boy and 3 girls) or (4 girls) $= {}^6C_3 \cdot {}^4C_1 + {}^6C_4$ ...(i)

Now, selection of captain from 4 members $= {}^4C_1$ ...(ii)

$\therefore$ Number of ways to select 4 members (including the selection of a captain, from these 4 members) $= ({}^6C_3 \cdot {}^4C_1 + {}^6C_4)\, {}^4C_1$

$= (20 \times 4 + 15) \times 4 = 380$

54. **Case I**

A	B	C
1	1	3

Case II

A	B	C
1	2	2

Number of ways to distribute 5 balls

$$= \left({}^5C_1 \cdot {}^4C_1 \cdot {}^3C_3 \times \frac{3!}{2!}\right) + \left({}^5C_1 \cdot {}^4C_2 \cdot {}^2C_2 \times \frac{3!}{2!}\right)$$

$$= 60 + 90 = 150$$

55. Since, r, s, t are prime numbers.

$\therefore$ Selection of p and q are as under

p	q	**Number of ways**
r^0	r^2	1 way
r^1	r^2	1 way
r^2	r^0, r^1, r^2	3 ways

$\therefore$ Total number of ways to select, $r = 5$

Selection of s as under

s^0	s^4	1 way
s^1	s^4	1 way
s^2	s^4	1 way
s^3	s^4	1 way
s^4	s^0, s^1, s^2, s^3, s^4	5 ways

$\therefore$ Total number of ways to select $s = 9$

Similarly, the number of ways to select $t = 5$

$\therefore$ Total number of ways $= 5 \times 9 \times 5 = 225$

56. (A) ${}^{n+4}C_{n+1} - {}^{n+3}C_n = 15(n+2)$

$\Rightarrow \quad {}^{n+3}C_{n+1} + {}^{n+3}C_n - {}^{n+3}C_n = 15(n+2)$

$\Rightarrow \quad {}^{n+3}C_{n+1} = 15(n+2)$

$\Rightarrow \quad {}^{n+3}C_2 = 15(n+2)$

$\Rightarrow \quad \frac{(n+3)}{2} = 15$

$\Rightarrow \quad n = 27$

(B) $11 \cdot {}^nP_4 = 20 \cdot {}^{n-2}P_4$

$\Rightarrow 11.n(n-1)(n-2)(n-3) = 20(n-2)(n-3)(n-4)(n-5)$

$\Rightarrow \quad 11n(n-1) = 20(n-4)(n-5) \quad [\because n \neq 2, 3]$

$\Rightarrow \quad 9n^2 - 169n + 400 = 0$

$\therefore \quad n = 16 \Rightarrow n \neq \frac{25}{9}$

(C) ${}^{2n}C_3 = 11 \cdot {}^nC_3$

$\Rightarrow \quad \frac{2n(2n-1)(2n-2)}{1 \cdot 2 \cdot 3} = \frac{11 \cdot n(n-1)(n-2)}{1 \cdot 2 \cdot 3}$

$\therefore \quad n = 6$

(D) ${}^{n+2}C_8 : {}^{n-2}P_4 = 57 : 16 \Rightarrow \frac{{}^{n+2}C_8}{{}^{n-2}P_4} = \frac{57}{16}$

$\Rightarrow \quad \frac{(n+2)}{8} \cdot \frac{n+1}{7} \cdot \frac{(n)}{6} \cdot \frac{(n-1)}{5} \cdot \frac{{}^{n-2}C_4}{{}^{n-2}P_4} = \frac{57}{16}$

$\Rightarrow \quad (n+2)(n+1)\,n(n-1) = 21 \cdot 20 \cdot 19 \cdot 18$

$\therefore \quad n = 19$

57. (A) $\frac{{}^nP_m}{m!} = {}^nC_m$

(B) Required ways $= \underbrace{m \times m \times m \times \ldots \times m}_{n \text{ times}} = m^n$

(C) $\times G \times G \times G \times G \times \ldots \times G \times$

Here, number of gaps for red balls $= m - 1 + 1 = m$

$\therefore$ Required ways $= {}^mC_n$

(D) Required ways $= \frac{n \times n \times n \times \ldots \times n}{m \text{ times}} = n^m$

58. (A) Required lines $= {}^{10}C_2 - {}^4C_2 + 1 = 40$

(B) Maximum number of points $= {}^{10}C_2 = 45$

(C) Maximum number of points $= {}^6C_2 \times 2 = 30$

(D) Maximum number of points $= {}^6C_2 \times 4 = 60$

59. (A) Number of rectangles $= {}^7C_2 \times {}^7C_2 = 441$

[select two vertical and two horizontal lines]

(B) Number of squares $= 1^2 + 2^2 + 3^2 + 4^2 + 5^2 + 6^2 = 91$

(C) First square can be selected in 36 ways, second square can be selected in $(36 - 6 - 5) = 25$ ways and third square can be selected in $(25 - 5 - 4) = 16$ ways.

$\therefore$ Required ways $= 36 \times 25 \times 15 = 2400$

(D) $a_1 + a_2 + a_3 + a_4 + a_5 + a_6 = 11$

where, $a_1, a_2, a_3, a_4, a_5, a_6, \geq 1$

$\therefore$ Required ways $= {}^{11-1}C_{6-1} = {}^{10}C_5$

60. (A) $\boxed{3|1|1}$ or $\boxed{2|1|1}$ Required ways

$= 1 \times 1 \times 1 \times \frac{3!}{2!} + 1 \times 1 \times 1 \times \frac{3!}{2!} = 6$

(B) $\boxed{3|1|1}$ or $\boxed{2|1|1}$ Required ways

$= \frac{{}^5C_3 \times {}^2C_1 \times {}^1C_1}{2} + \frac{{}^5C_2 \times {}^3C_2 \times {}^1C_1}{2} = 25$

(C) $\boxed{3|1|1}$ or $\boxed{2|1|1}$ Required ways $= 1 \times 1 \times 1 + 1 \times 1 \times 1 = 2$

(D) $\boxed{3|1|1}$ or $\boxed{2|1|1}$ Required ways $= 3 + 3 = 6$

61. Number of five-digit numbers divisible by 5 (_ _ _ 0) _ _ _ _ 0

Number of element in X which are multiple of 5.

$\underbrace{- - - -}_{1,\,2,\,2,\,2 \text{ (fixed)}}$ 0 $\longrightarrow \frac{4!}{3!} = 4$

$\underbrace{- - - -}_{1,\,4,\,2,\,2 \text{ (fixed)}}$ 0 $\longrightarrow \frac{4!}{2!} = 12$

$\underbrace{- - - -}_{4,\,2,\,2,\,2 \text{ (fixed)}}$ 0 $\longrightarrow \frac{4!}{3!} = 4$

$\underbrace{- - - -}_{2,\,2,\,4,\,4 \text{ (fixed)}}$ 0 $\longrightarrow \frac{4!}{2!2!} = 6$

$\underbrace{- - - -}_{1,\,2,\,4,\,4 \text{ (fixed)}}$ 0 $\longrightarrow \frac{4!}{2!} = 12$

Total = 38

62. Counting integer starting from 2.

Case I If zero on 2nd place

i.e. 2 0 2 _ (5) $\rightarrow$ 5 cases

on 2 0 _ _ (4, 6) $\rightarrow$ 24 cases

Case II If non-zero number on 2nd place.

i.e. 2 _ _ _ (5, 6, 6) = 180 cases

Counting integer starting from 3.

i.e. 3 _ _ _ (6, 6, 6) = 216 cases

Counting integer starting from 4.

Case I If 0, 2, or 3 on 2nd place, then

i.e. 4 _ _ _ (3, 6, 6) = 108 cases

Case II If 4 on 2nd place, then

i.e. 4 4 _ _ (6, 6) = 36 cases

$\therefore$ Thus, total number of 4-digit integers in the closed interval [2022, 4482] formed by using the above digits is

$5 + 24 + 180 + 216 + 108 + 36 = 569$

Thus, the required number is 569.

63. Number of elements in $n_1 = 10 \times 10 \times 10 = 1000$

Number of elements in $n_2 = 9(J=8) + 8(J=7) + 7(J=6) + 6(J=5) + 5(J=4) + 4(J=3) + 3(J=2) + 2(J=1) = 44$

Number of elements in $n_3 = {}^{10}C_4 = 210$

Number of elements in $n_4 = {}^{10}P_4 = 210 \times 4! = 5040$

Now, $\frac{n_4}{12} = \frac{5040}{12} = 420$

So, options (a), (b), (d) are correct.

64. The groups of persons can be made only in 2, 2, 1, 1

$\therefore$ So, the number of required ways is equal to number of ways to distribute the 6 distinct objects in group sizes 1, 1, 2 and 2

$= \frac{6!}{(2!)^2\,(1!)^2\,(2!)\,(2!)}(4!)$

$= 360 \times 3 = 1080$

65. According to condition $a + b = c + d$

If sum is $3 \rightarrow (0, 3)\ (1, 2)$ [not possible]
If sum is $4 \rightarrow (0, 4)\ (1, 3)$ [not possible]
If sum is $5 \rightarrow (0, 5)\ (1, 4)\ (2, 3)$ [not possible]
If sum is $6 \rightarrow (0, 6)\ (1, 5)\ (2, 4)$ [not possible]
If sum is $7 \rightarrow (0, 7)\ (1, 6)\ (2, 5)\ (3, 4)$
If sum is $8 \rightarrow (1, 7)\ (2, 6)\ (3, 5)$
If sum is $9 \rightarrow (2, 7)\ (3, 6)\ (4, 5)$
If sum is $10 \rightarrow (3, 7)\ (4, 6)$
If sum is $11 \rightarrow (4, 7), (5, 6)$
Now total trials

$$4 \times {}^3C_1 \times 2! + 4 \times {}^2C_1 \times 2! +$$
$$4 \times {}^2C_1 \times 2! + 4 \times {}^1C_1 \times 2! +$$
$$4 \times {}^1C_1 \times 2! = 24 + 16 + 16 + 8 + 8 = 72$$

66. Let the engineer visits the factory first time after x_1 days to 1 June, second time after x_2 days to first visit and so on.

$\therefore\ x_1 + x_2 + x_3 + x_4 + x_5 = 11$

where $x_1, x_5 \ge 0$ and $x_2, x_3, x_4 \ge 1$ according to the requirement of the question.

Now, let $x_2 = a + 1$, $x_3 = b + 1$ and $x_4 = c + 1$ where $a, b, c \ge 0$

$\therefore$ New equation will be

$$x_1 + a + b + c + x_5 = 8$$

Now, the number of all possible ways in which the engineer can made visits is equals to the non-negative integral solution of equation

$x_1 + a + b + c + x_5 = 8$, and it is equal to

$$^{8+5-1}C_{5-1} = {}^{12}C_4$$
$$= \frac{12 \times 11 \times 10 \times 9}{4 \times 3 \times 2} = 495$$

67. Given that, no two persons sitting adjacent in circular arrangement, have hats of same colour. So, only possible combination due to circular arrangement is $2 + 2 + 1$.

So, there are following three cases of selecting hats are

$2R + 2B + 1G$ or $2B + 2G + 1R$ or
$2G + 2R + 1B$.

To distribute these 5 hats first we will select a person which we can done in $^5C_1$ ways and distribute that hat which is one of it's colour. And, now the remaining four hats can be distributed in two ways.

So, total ways will be $3 \times {}^5C_1 \times 2$

$$= 3 \times 5 \times 2 = 30$$

Exercise 3 - Challenging Problems

1. We have, $^nC_{n-r} + 3\,^nC_{n-r+1} + 3\,^nC_{n-r+2} + {}^nC_{n-r+3} = {}^xC_r$

$$\Leftrightarrow ({}^nC_{n-r} + {}^nC_{n-r+1}) + 2({}^nC_{n-r+1} + {}^nC_{n-r+2}) + ({}^nC_{n-r+2} + {}^nC_{n-r+3}) = {}^xC_r$$
$$\Leftrightarrow {}^{n+1}C_{n-r+1} + 2.{}^{n+1}C_{n-r+2} + {}^{n+1}C_{n-r+3} = {}^xC_r$$
$$\Leftrightarrow ({}^{n+1}C_{n-r+1} + {}^{n+1}C_{n-r+2}) + ({}^{n+1}C_{n-r+2} + {}^{n+1}C_{n-r+3}) = {}^xC_r$$
$$\Leftrightarrow {}^{n+2}C_{n-r+2} + {}^{n+2}C_{n-r+3} = {}^xC_r$$
$$\Leftrightarrow {}^{n+3}C_{n-r+3} = {}^xC_r$$
$$\Leftrightarrow {}^{n+3}C_r = {}^xC_r \qquad [\because {}^nC_r = {}^nC_{n-r}]$$

Hence, $x = n + 3$

2. We have, $3\,^{x+1}C_2 + P_2 \cdot x = 4\,^xA_2$

$$\Leftrightarrow \frac{3(x+1)x}{1 \cdot 2} + 2!x = 4 \cdot x(x-1)$$
$$\Leftrightarrow 3x^2 + 3x + 4x = 8x^2 - 8x$$
$$\Leftrightarrow 5x^2 - 15x = 0$$
$$\Leftrightarrow 5x(x-3) = 0$$
$$\therefore x \ne 0 \qquad [\because x \in N]$$

Hence, $x = 3$ is the solution of the given equation.

3. We have, $x_n = \frac{195}{4P_n} - \frac{^{n+3}A_3}{P_{n+1}}$

$$\therefore\ x_n = \frac{195}{4 \cdot n!} - \frac{(n+3)(n+2)(n+1)}{(n+1)!}$$
$$= \frac{195}{4 \cdot n!} - \frac{(n+3)(n+2)}{n!}$$
$$= \frac{195 - 4n^2 - 20n - 24}{4 \cdot n!} = \frac{171 - 4n^2 - 20n}{4 \cdot n!}$$

$\because\ x_n$ is positive.

$$\therefore\ \frac{171 - 4n^2 - 20n}{4 \cdot n!} > 0 \Rightarrow 4n^2 + 20n - 171 < 0$$

which is true for $n = 1, 2, 3, 4$

Hence, the given sequence (x_n) has 4 positive terms.

4. The required number of ways = The number of ways in which $3n$ different things can be divided in 3 equal groups = The number of ways to distribute $3n$ different things equally among three persons $= \frac{3n!}{3!(n!)^3} = \frac{3n!}{6(n!)^3}$

5. Let AB be any one of n straight lines and suppose it is intersected by some other straight line CD at P.

Then, it is clear that AB contains $(n-1)$ of the points of intersection because it is intersected by the remaining $(n-1)$ straight lines in $(n-1)$ different points. So, the aggregate number of points contained in the n straight lines is $n(n-1)$. But in making up this aggregate, each point has evidently been counted twice. For instance, the point P has been counted once among the points situated on AB and again among those on CD.

Hence, the actual number of points $= \frac{n(n-1)}{2}$

Now, we have to find the number of new lines formed by joining these points. The number of new lines passing through P is evidently equal to the number of points lying outside the lines AB and CD for getting a new line joining P with each of these points only.

Since, each of the lines AB and CD contained $(n-2)$ points besides the point P, the number of points situated on AB and CD

$$= 2(n-2) - 1 = (2n-3)$$

$\therefore$ The number of points outside AB and CD

$$= \frac{n(n-1)}{2} - (2n-3)$$

The number of new lines passing through P and similarly through each other points.

$\therefore$ The aggregate number of new lines passing through the points

$$= \frac{n(n-1)}{2}\left\{\frac{n(n-1)}{2} - (2n-3)\right\}$$

But in making up this aggregate, every new line is counted twice. For instance, if Q is one of the points outside AB and CD, the line PQ is counted once among the lines passing through P and again among these passing through Q.

Hence, actual number of fresh lines introduced

$$= \frac{1}{2}\left[\frac{n(n-1)}{2}\left\{\frac{n(n-1)}{2} - (2n-3)\right\}\right]$$

6. 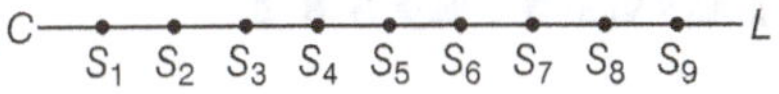

For S_1, 9 different tickets are available, one for each of the remaining 9 stations, similarly at S_2, 8 different tickets are available and so on.

Thus, total number of different tickets

$$= 9 + 8 + 7 + 6 + 5 + 4 + 3 + 2 + 1 = 45$$

So, the six different tickets must be any six of these 45 and there are evidently as many different sets of 6 tickets as there are combinations of 45 things taken 6 at a time.

Hence, the required number $= {}^{45}C_6$.

7. There are 8 chairs on each side of the table. Let sides be represented by A and B. Let four persons sit on side A, then number of ways arranging 4 persons on 8 chairs on side $A = {}^8P_4$ and then two persons sit on side B, then number of ways arranging 2 persons on 8 chairs on side $B = {}^8P_2$ and arranging the remaining 10 persons in remaining 10 chairs in 10! ways.

Hence, the total number of ways in which the persons can be arranged $= {}^8P_4 \times {}^8P_2 \times 10! = \dfrac{8!\cdot 8!\, 10!}{4!\, 6!}$

8. We have,

$$ {}^{n-1}C_3 + {}^{n-1}C_4 > {}^nC_3 \qquad [\because {}^nC_r + {}^nC_{r-1} = {}^{n+1}C_r]$$

$$\Leftrightarrow \quad {}^nC_4 > {}^nC_3$$

$$\Leftrightarrow \quad \frac{n!}{4!(n-4)!} > \frac{n!}{3!(n-3)!}$$

$$\Leftrightarrow \quad \frac{1}{4(n-4)!} > \frac{1}{(n-3)(n-4)!} \qquad [\because m! = m(m-1)!]$$

$$\Leftrightarrow \quad n-3 > 4 \Leftrightarrow n > 7$$

9. ***Case* I When no couple is chosen**

We can choose 2 men in ${}^4C_2 = 6$ ways and hence two teams can be formed in $2\times 6 = 12$ ways.

***Case* II When only one couple is chosen**

A couple can be chosen in ${}^4C_1 = 4$ ways and the other team can be chosen in ${}^3C_1 \times {}^2C_1 = 6$ ways. Hence, two teams can be formed in $4\times 6 = 24$ ways.

***Case* III When two couples are chosen**

Then team can be chosen in ${}^4C_2 = 6$ ways. Hence, total ways $= 12 + 24 + 6 = 42$.

10. Denoting A_1, B_1, A_2 and B_2 for their taking out the ball, a chart is made to denote the winner.

S. No.		A_1	B_1	A_2	B_2	Number of ways
1.	**Points** Number on the ball sum	1 Even (1 of 3) Even	1 Even (1 of 2) Even	0 Odd (1 of 3) Odd	2 Odd (1 of 2) Even	${}^3C_1\times{}^2C_1\times{}^3C_1\times{}^2C_1 = 36$
2.	**Points** Number on the ball sum	−1 Odd (1 of 3) Odd	1 Odd (1 of 2) Even	0 Even (1 of 3) Even	2 Even (1 of 2) Even	${}^3C_1\times{}^2C_1\times{}^3C_1\times{}^2C_1 = 36$
3.	**Points** Number on the ball sum	1 Even (1 of 3) Even	2 Odd (1 of 3) Odd	0 Odd (1 of 3) Even		${}^3C_1\times{}^3C_1\times{}^2C_1 = 18$
4.	**Points** Number on the ball sum	1 Even (1 of 3) Even	1 Even (1 of 2) Even	2 Even (1 of 1) Even		${}^3C_1\times{}^2C_1\times{}^1C_1 = 6$

$\therefore$ Total number of ways in which the game can be won when A starts the game $= 36 + 36 + 18 + 6 = 96$

> *A Mathematician is a build man in a dark room looking for a black cat which is not there.*
>
> **–Charles Darwin**

6

Binomial Theorem

Learning Milestones

Milestone 1 Binomial Theorem and Its Properties

- Binomial Theorem For Positive Integral Index
- Middle Term
- Greatest Term
- Trinomial Expansion

Milestone 2 Some Important Theorems

- Two Important Theorems
- Divisibility Problems
- Use of Complex Numbers in Binomial Theorem
- Multinomial Theorem
- Use of Differentiation
- Use of Integration
- Binomial Inside Binomial
- Sum of the Series

Practice Milestones

Practice Milestone 1- JEE Main Pattern

Practice Milestone 2 - JEE Advanced Pattern

Practice Milestone 3 - Challenging Problems

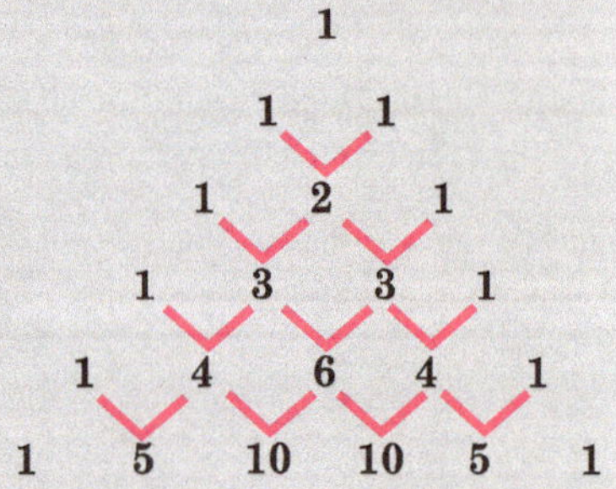

Milestone 1 Binomial Theorem and Its Properties

• Binomial Theorem For Positive Integral Index • Middle Term • Greatest Term • Trinomial Expansion

An algebraic expression consisting of two dissimilar terms with positive or negative sign between them is called a binomial expressions.

e.g. $x+a, x^2a-\frac{a}{x}, \frac{p}{x^2}-\frac{q}{x^4}, 5-x,$

$(x^2+1)^{1/3}-\frac{1}{\sqrt{(x^3+1)}}$, etc. are called binomial expressions.

6.1 Binomial Theorem for Positive Integral Index

If $x, a \in C$ and $n \in N$, then

$$(x+a)^n = {}^nC_0\, x^{n-0}\, a^0 + {}^nC_1\, x^{n-1} a^1 + {}^nC_2\, x^{n-2}\, a^2 + \ldots$$
$$+ {}^nC_r\, x^{n-r}\, a^r + \ldots + {}^nC_{n-1}\, x^1\, a^{n-1} + {}^nC_n\, x^0\, a^n \quad \ldots\text{(i)}$$

or $\quad (x+a)^n = \sum_{r=0}^{n} {}^nC_r\, x^{n-r}\, a^r$

Hence, ${}^nC_0, {}^nC_1, {}^nC_2, \ldots, {}^nC_n$ are called binomial coefficients.

Pascal's Triangle

Coefficients of binomial expansion can also be easily determined by Pascal's triangle.

$(x+a)^0$	1
$(x+a)^1$	1 1
$(x+a)^2$	1 2 1
$(x+a)^3$	1 3 3 1
$(x+a)^4$	1 4 6 4 1
$(x+a)^5$	1 5 10 10 5 1

Pascal triangle gives the direct binomial coefficients.

e.g. $(x+a)^4 = 1\cdot x^4 + 4\cdot x^3\cdot a + 6\cdot x^2\cdot a^2 + 4\cdot x\cdot a^3 + 1\cdot a^4$

$= x^4 + 4x^3a + 6x^2a^2 + 4xa^3 + a^4$

JEE Focus Points

- An algebraic expression consisting of three dissimilar terms is called a trinomial.
  e.g. $a+2b+c, x-2y+3z, 2\alpha-\frac{3}{\beta}+\gamma$, etc. are called the trinomials.

Concept Inside Video

- In general, expressions consisting more than two dissimilar terms are known as multinomial expressions.
- In each term, the degree is n and the coefficient of $x^{n-r}\, a^r$ is equal to the number of ways $\underbrace{x, x, x, \ldots, x}_{(n-r)\text{ times}}, \underbrace{a, a, a, \ldots, a}_{r\text{ times}}$ can be arranged, which is given by $\frac{n!}{(n-r)!\,r!} = {}^nC_r$

  e.g. $(x+a)^5 = \frac{5!}{5!\,0!}x^5a^0 + \frac{5!}{4!\,1!}x^4a + \frac{5!}{3!\,2!}x^3a^2 + \frac{5!}{2!\,3!}x^2a^3 + \frac{5!}{1!\,4!}xa^4 + \frac{5!}{0!\,5!}x^0a^5$

  $= {}^5C_0\,x^5 + {}^5C_1\,x^4a + {}^5C_2\,x^3a^2 + {}^5C_3\,x^2a^3 + {}^5C_4\,xa^4 + {}^5C_5\,a^5$

- Let $S = (x+a)^n = \sum_{r=0}^{n} {}^nC_r\, x^{n-r}\, a^r$

  Replacing r by $n-r$, we have

  $S = (x+a)^n = \sum_{r=0}^{n} {}^nC_{n-r}\, x^{n-(n-r)}\, a^{n-r}$

  $= \sum_{r=0}^{n} {}^nC_{n-r}\, x^r\, a^{n-r}$

  $= {}^nC_n\, a^n + {}^nC_{n-1}\, a^{n-1}\, x + {}^nC_{n-2}\, a^{n-2}\, x^2 + \ldots + {}^nC_0\, x^n$

  Thus, replacing r by $n-r$, we are infact writing the binomial expansion in reverse order.

How to Construct a Pascal's Triangle

Binomial coefficients in the expansion of $(x+a)^3$ are

	1	3	3	1	
	1	3	3		1
	1	(1+3)	(3+3)	(3+1)	1
Then,	1	4	6	4	1

are the binomial coefficients in the expansion of $(x+a)^4$.

Example 1. Expand $\left(x+\frac{1}{x}\right)^4$ by binomial theorem.

Sol. Using binomial theorem, we get

$$\left(x+\frac{1}{x}\right)^4 = {}^4C_0(x)^4\left(\frac{1}{x}\right)^0 + {}^4C_1(x)^3\left(\frac{1}{x}\right)^1 + {}^4C_2(x)^2\left(\frac{1}{x}\right)^2 + {}^4C_3(x)^1\left(\frac{1}{x}\right)^3 + {}^4C_4(x)^0\left(\frac{1}{x}\right)^4$$

$$= {}^4C_0x^4 + {}^4C_1\frac{x^3}{x} + {}^4C_2\frac{x^2}{x^2} + {}^4C_3\frac{x}{x^3} + {}^4C_4\frac{1}{x^4}$$

$$= x^4 + 4x^2 + 6 + \frac{4}{x^2} + \frac{1}{x^4}$$

Some Important Points

1. Replacing a by $(-a)$ in Eq. (i), we get

$$(x-a)^n = {}^nC_0\, x^{n-0}\, a^0 - {}^nC_1\, x^{n-1}\, a^1 + {}^nC_2\, x^{n-2}\, a^2 - \dots + \dots + (-1)^r\, {}^nC_r\, x^{n-r}\, a^r + \dots + (-1)^n\, {}^nC_n\, x^0\, a^n \quad \dots\text{(ii)}$$

or $\quad (x-a)^n = \sum_{r=0}^{n} (-1)^r\, {}^nC_r\, x^{n-r}\, a^r$

2. On adding Eqs. (i) and (ii), we get

$$(x+a)^n + (x-a)^n = 2\{{}^nC_0\, x^{n-0}\, a^0 + {}^nC_2\, x^{n-2}\, a^2 + {}^nC_4\, x^{n-4}\, a^4 + \dots\}$$

$$= 2\ \{\text{Sum of terms at odd places}\}$$

The last term is ${}^nC_n\, a^n$ or ${}^nC_{n-1}\, x\, a^{n-1}$, according as n is even or odd, respectively.

3. On subtracting Eq. (ii) from Eq. (i), we get

$$(x+a)^n - (x-a)^n = 2\{{}^nC_1\, x^{n-1}\, a^1 + {}^nC_3\, x^{n-3}\, a^3 + {}^nC_5\, x^{n-5}\, a^5 + \dots\}$$

$$= 2\ \{\text{Sum of terms at even places}\}$$

The last term is ${}^nC_{n-1}\, x\, a^{n-1}$ or ${}^nC_n\, a^n$, according as n is even or odd, respectively.

4. Replacing x by 1 and a by x in Eq. (i), we get

$$(1+x)^n = {}^nC_0\, x^0 + {}^nC_1\, x^1 + {}^nC_2\, x^2 + \dots + {}^nC_r\, x^r + \dots + {}^nC_{n-1}\, x^{n-1} + {}^nC_n\, x^n \quad \dots\text{(iii)}$$

or $\quad (1+x)^n = \sum_{r=0}^{n} {}^nC_r\, x^r$

5. Replacing x by $(-x)$ in Eq. (iii), we get

$$(1-x)^n = {}^nC_0\, x^0 - {}^nC_1\, x^1 + {}^nC_2\, x^2 - \dots + (-1)^r\, {}^nC_r\, x^r + \dots + {}^nC_n(-1)^n\, x^n$$

or $\quad (1-x)^n = \sum_{r=0}^{n} (-1)^r\, {}^nC_r\, x^r$

Example 2. Expand $\left(2a-\frac{3}{b}\right)^5$ by binomial theorem.

Sol. Using binomial theorem, we get

$$\left(2a-\frac{3}{b}\right)^5 = {}^5C_0\,(2a)^{5-0}\left(-\frac{3}{b}\right)^0 + {}^5C_1(2a)^{5-1}\left(-\frac{3}{b}\right)^1 + {}^5C_2\,(2a)^{5-2}\left(-\frac{3}{b}\right)^2 + {}^5C_3\,(2a)^{5-3}\left(-\frac{3}{b}\right)^3 + {}^5C_4\,(2a)^{5-4}\left(-\frac{3}{b}\right)^4 + {}^5C_5\,(2a)^{5-5}\left(-\frac{3}{b}\right)^5$$

$$= {}^5C_0\,(2a)^5 - {}^5C_1\,(2a)^4\left(\frac{3}{b}\right) + {}^5C_2\,(2a)^3\left(\frac{3}{b}\right)^2 - {}^5C_3\,(2a)^2\left(\frac{3}{b}\right)^3 + {}^5C_4\,(2a)^1\left(\frac{3}{b}\right)^4 - {}^5C_5\left(\frac{3}{b}\right)^5$$

$$= 32a^5 - \frac{240\,a^4}{b} + \frac{720\,a^3}{b^2} - \frac{1080\,a^2}{b^3} + \frac{810\,a}{b^4} - \frac{243}{b^5}$$

Example 3. Using binomial theorem evaluate $(999)^4$.

Sol. We have,

$$(999)^4 = (1000-1)^4$$

$$= {}^4C_0(1000)^4 - {}^4C_1(1000)^3 + {}^4C_2(1000)^2 - {}^4C_3(1000)^1 + {}^4C_4(1000)^0$$

$$= 1000000000000 - 4\times 1000000000 + 6\times 1000000 - 4\times 1000 + 1$$

$$= 1000000000000 - 4000000000 + 6000000 - 4000 + 1$$

$$= 996005996001$$

Example 4. The degree of the polynomial

$$(x+\sqrt{x^2-1})^6 + (x-\sqrt{x^2-1})^6 \text{ is}$$

(a) 4 (b) 5
(c) 6 (d) None of these

Sol. (c) Let $\sqrt{(x^2-1)} = a$

Then, $(x+a)^6 + (x-a)^6$

$$= 2\{{}^6C_0\, x^{6-0}\, a^0 + {}^6C_2\, x^{6-2}\, a^2 + {}^6C_4\, x^{6-4}\, a^4 + {}^6C_6\, x^{6-6}\, a^6\}$$

$$= 2\{x^6 + 15x^4a^2 + 15x^2a^4 + a^6\} \quad \text{[from point (2)]}$$

$$= 2\{x^6 + 15x^4(x^2-1) + 15x^2(x^2-1)^2 + (x^2-1)^3\} \quad [\because a = \sqrt{x^2-1}]$$

$$= 2(32x^6 - 48x^4 + 18x^2 - 1)$$

So, degree = 6

Example 5. In the expansion of $(x+a)^n$, if sum of odd terms is P and sum of even terms is Q, prove that

(i) $P^2 - Q^2 = (x^2-a^2)^n$

(ii) $4\,PQ = (x+a)^{2n} - (x-a)^{2n}$

Sol. $\because (x+a)^n = {}^nC_0\, x^{n-0}a^0 + {}^nC_1\, x^{n-1}a^1 + {}^nC_2\, x^{n-2}a^2 + {}^nC_3\, x^{n-3}a^3 + \ldots + \ldots + {}^nC_n\, x^{n-n}a^n$

$= ({}^nC_0\, x^n + {}^nC_2\, x^{n-2}a^2 + {}^nC_4\, x^{n-4}a^4 + \ldots) + ({}^nC_1\, x^{n-1}a^1 + {}^nC_3\, x^{n-3}a^3 + {}^nC_5\, x^{n-5}a^5 + \ldots)$

$= P + Q$ (given) ...(i)

and $(x-a)^n = {}^nC_0\, x^{n-0}a^0 - {}^nC_1\, x^{n-1}a^1 + {}^nC_2\, x^{n-2}a^2 - {}^nC_3\, x^{n-3}a^3 + \ldots + {}^nC_n\, x^{n-n}a^n$

$= ({}^nC_0\, x^n + {}^nC_2\, x^{n-2}a^2 + {}^nC_4\, x^{n-4}a^4 + \ldots) - ({}^nC_1\, x^{n-1}a + {}^nC_3\, x^{n-3}a^3 + {}^nC_5\, x^{n-5}a^5 + \ldots)$

$= P - Q$ (given) ...(ii)

(i) $P^2 - Q^2 = (P+Q)(P-Q)$

$= (x+a)^n \cdot (x-a)^n$

$= (x^2 - a^2)^n$ [from Eqs. (i) and (ii)]

(ii) $(x+a)^{2n} - (x-a)^{2n} = [(x+a)^n]^2 - [(x-a)^n]^2$

$= (P+Q)^2 - (P-Q)^2$

$= 4PQ$ [from Eqs. (i) and (ii)]

Example 6. Show that $(101)^{50} > (100)^{50} + (99)^{50}$.

Sol. Since, $(101)^{50} - (99)^{50} = (100+1)^{50} - (100-1)^{50}$

$= 2\{{}^{50}C_1 (100)^{49} + {}^{50}C_3 (100)^{47} + {}^{50}C_5 (100)^{45} + \ldots\}$

$= 2 \times {}^{50}C_1 (100)^{49} + 2\{{}^{50}C_3 (100)^{47} + {}^{50}C_5 (100)^{45} + \ldots\}$

$= (100)^{50} + (\text{a positive number}) > (100)^{50}$

Hence, $(101)^{50} - (99)^{50} > (100)^{50}$

$\Rightarrow (101)^{50} > (100)^{50} + (99)^{50}$

Example 7. If $a_n = \sum_{r=0}^{n} \frac{1}{{}^nC_r}$, then find the value of $\sum_{r=0}^{n} \frac{r}{{}^nC_r}$.

Sol. Let $P = \sum_{r=0}^{n} \frac{r}{{}^nC_r}$ ...(i)

Replacing r by $(n-r)$ in Eq. (i), we get

$P = \sum_{r=0}^{n} \frac{(n-r)}{{}^nC_{n-r}}$

$= \sum_{r=0}^{n} \frac{(n-r)}{{}^nC_r}$ $[\because {}^nC_r = {}^nC_{n-r}]$ ...(ii)

On adding Eqs. (i) and (ii), we get

$2P = \sum_{r=0}^{n} \frac{n}{{}^nC_r} = n \sum_{r=0}^{n} \frac{1}{{}^nC_r} = na_n$ [given]

$\therefore P = \frac{n}{2} a_n$

Hence, $\sum_{r=0}^{n} \frac{r}{{}^nC_r} = \frac{n}{2} a_n$

Properties of Binomial Expansion $(x+a)^n$

(i) This expansion has $(n+1)$ terms.

(ii) Since, ${}^nC_r = {}^nC_{n-r}$, we have

${}^nC_0 = {}^nC_n = 1$

${}^nC_1 = {}^nC_{n-1} = n$

${}^nC_2 = {}^nC_{n-2} = \frac{n(n-1)}{2!}$ and so on.

(iii) In any term, the suffix of C is equal to the index of a and the index of $x = n -$ (suffix of C).

(iv) In each term, sum of the indices of x and a is equal to n.

JEE Focus Points

- ${}^nC_r$ can also be represented by $C(n, r)$ or $\binom{n}{r}$.
- ${}^nC_x = {}^nC_y$, then either $x = y$ or $n = x + y$. So, ${}^nC_r = {}^nC_{n-r} = \frac{n!}{r!\,(n-r)!}$
- ${}^nC_r + {}^nC_{r-1} = {}^{n+1}C_r$
- $\frac{{}^nC_r}{{}^nC_{r-1}} = \frac{n-r+1}{r}$
- ${}^nC_r = \frac{n}{r} \cdot {}^{n-1}C_{r-1}$

Example 8. Find the number of dissimilar terms in the expansion of $(1 - 3x + 3x^2 - x^3)^{33}$.

Sol. $(1 - 3x + 3x^2 - x^3)^{33} = [(1-x)^3]^{33} = (1-x)^{99}$

Therefore, number of dissimilar terms in the expansion of $(1 - 3x + 3x^2 - x^3)^3$ is 100.

Example 9. Find the value of $\sum_{r=1}^{n} \frac{r \cdot {}^nC_r}{{}^nC_{r-1}}$.

Sol. $\because \frac{{}^nC_r}{{}^nC_{r-1}} = \frac{n-r+1}{r}$

$\therefore \frac{r \cdot {}^nC_r}{{}^nC_{r-1}} = (n-r+1)$

$\therefore \sum_{r=1}^{n} \frac{r \cdot {}^nC_r}{{}^nC_{r-1}} = \sum_{r=1}^{n} (n-r+1)$

$= \sum_{r=1}^{n} (n+1) - \sum_{r=1}^{n} r$

$= (n+1) \sum_{r=1}^{n} 1 - (1+2+3+\ldots+n)$

$= (n+1) \cdot n - \frac{n(n+1)}{2} = \frac{n(n+1)}{2}$

Example 10. Let C_r stands for ${}^nC_r$, prove that

$$(C_0 + C_1)(C_1 + C_2)(C_2 + C_3)\dots(C_{n-1} + C_n) = \frac{(n+1)^n}{n!}(C_0 C_1 C_2 \dots C_{n-1}).$$

Sol. LHS $= (C_0 + C_1)(C_1 + C_2)(C_2 + C_3)\dots(C_{n-1} + C_n)$

$$= \prod_{r=1}^{n}(C_{r-1} + C_r) = \prod_{r=1}^{n}({}^{n+1}C_r) \quad [\because {}^nC_r + {}^nC_{r-1} = {}^{n+1}C_r]$$

$$= \prod_{r=1}^{n}\left(\frac{n+1}{r}\right){}^nC_{r-1} \quad \left[\because {}^nC_r = \frac{n}{r}\cdot{}^{n-1}C_{r-1}\right]$$

$$= \prod_{r=1}^{n}(n+1)\cdot\prod_{r=1}^{n}\frac{1}{r}\cdot\prod_{r=1}^{n}C_{r-1}$$

$$= (n+1)^n\cdot\frac{1}{n!}\cdot(C_0C_1C_2\dots C_{n-1})$$

$$= \frac{(n+1)^n}{n!}(C_0\,C_1\,C_2\dots C_{n-1}) = \text{RHS}$$

Example 11. Find the sum of the series

$$\sum_{r=0}^{n}(-1)^r\,{}^nC_r\left\{\frac{1}{2^r} + \frac{3^r}{2^{2r}} + \frac{7^r}{2^{3r}} + \frac{15^r}{2^{4r}} + \dots \text{upto } m \text{ terms}\right\}.$$

Sol. $\because (1-x)^n = \sum_{r=0}^{n}(-1)^r\,{}^nC_r\,x^r$ ...(i)

Let $$P = \sum_{r=0}^{n}(-1)^r\,{}^nC_r\left\{\left(\frac{1}{2}\right)^r + \left(\frac{3}{4}\right)^r + \left(\frac{7}{8}\right)^r + \left(\frac{15}{16}\right)^r + \dots \text{upto } m \text{ terms}\right\}$$

$$= \sum_{r=0}^{n}(-1)^r\,{}^nC_r\cdot\left(\frac{1}{2}\right)^r + \sum_{r=0}^{n}(-1)^r\,{}^nC_r\cdot\left(\frac{3}{4}\right)^r + \sum_{r=0}^{n}(-1)^r\,{}^nC_r\cdot\left(\frac{7}{8}\right)^r + \sum_{r=0}^{n}(-1)^r\,{}^nC_r\cdot\left(\frac{15}{16}\right)^r + \dots \text{upto } m \text{ terms}$$

$$= \left(1-\frac{1}{2}\right)^n + \left(1-\frac{3}{4}\right)^n + \left(1-\frac{7}{8}\right)^n + \left(1-\frac{15}{16}\right)^n + \dots \text{upto } m \text{ terms}$$

$$= \left(\frac{1}{2}\right)^n + \left(\frac{1}{2}\right)^{2n} + \left(\frac{1}{2}\right)^{3n} + \left(\frac{1}{2}\right)^{4n} + \dots \text{upto } m \text{ terms}$$

$$= \frac{\left(\frac{1}{2}\right)^n\left[1-\left\{\left(\frac{1}{2}\right)^n\right\}^m\right]}{1-\left(\frac{1}{2}\right)^n}$$

$$= \frac{(2^{mn}-1)}{2^{mn}(2^n-1)}$$

General Term

The term ${}^nC_r\,x^{n-r}\,a^r$ is the $(r+1)$ th term from beginning in the expansion of $(x+a)^n$. It is usually called the general term and it is denoted by T_{r+1}.

i.e. $\quad T_{r+1} = {}^nC_r\,x^{n-r}\,a^r$

Example 12. Find the 7th term in the expansion of $\left(4x - \frac{1}{2\sqrt{x}}\right)^{13}$.

Sol. Seventh term, $T_7 = T_{6+1} = {}^{13}C_6\,(4x)^{13-6}\left(-\frac{1}{2\sqrt{x}}\right)^6$

$$= {}^{13}C_6\cdot 4^7\cdot x^7\cdot\frac{1}{2^6\cdot x^3}$$

$$= {}^{13}C_6\cdot 2^8\cdot x^4$$

Example 13. Find the coefficient of x^8 in the expansion of $\left(x^2 - \frac{1}{x}\right)^{10}$.

Sol. Here, $T_{r+1} = {}^{10}C_r\,(x^2)^{10-r}\left(-\frac{1}{x}\right)^r$

$$= {}^{10}C_r\,x^{20-2r}\cdot(-1)^r\cdot\frac{1}{x^r}$$

$$= {}^{10}C_r\,(-1)^r\cdot x^{20-3r} \quad \text{...(i)}$$

Now, in order to find out the coefficient of x^8, $20-3r$ must be 8. i.e. $20 - 3r = 8$

$\therefore \quad r = 4$

Hence, putting $r = 4$ in Eq. (i), we get

Required coefficient $= (-1)^4\cdot{}^{10}C_4 = \frac{10\cdot 9\cdot 8\cdot 7}{1\cdot 2\cdot 3\cdot 4} = 210$

Example 14. Find the term independent of x in the expansion of $\left(\frac{3}{2}x^2 - \frac{1}{3x}\right)^9$.

Sol. Here, $T_{r+1} = {}^9C_r\left(\frac{3}{2}x^2\right)^{9-r}\left(-\frac{1}{3x}\right)^r$

$$= (-1)^r\cdot{}^9C_r\cdot\left(\frac{3}{2}\right)^{9-r}\cdot\left(\frac{1}{3}\right)^r\cdot x^{18-3r} \quad \text{...(i)}$$

If this term is independent of x, then the index of x must be zero, i.e. $18 - 3r = 0 \Rightarrow r = 6$

Therefore, $(r+1)$ th term, i.e. 7th term is independent of x and its value by putting $r = 6$ in Eq. (i),

$$= (-1)^6\cdot{}^9C_6\cdot\left(\frac{3}{2}\right)^3\cdot\left(\frac{1}{3}\right)^6 = {}^9C_3\cdot\frac{1}{2^3\cdot 3^3}$$

$$= \frac{9\cdot 8\cdot 7}{(1\cdot 2\cdot 3)\,2^3\cdot 3^3} = \frac{7}{18}$$

JEE SCANNER

Example Similar to PYQ Asked in JEE Main 2023

If the coefficient of x^7 in the expansion of $\left(ax^2+\frac{1}{bx}\right)^{11}$ is equal to the coefficient of x^{-7} in the expansion of $\left(ax-\frac{1}{bx^2}\right)^{11}$, a and b are positive real numbers, then the relation between a and b is equal to

(a) $ab=1$ (b) $ab=-1$ (c) $ab=2$ (d) $ab=5$

Sol. (a) For $\left(ax^2+\frac{1}{bx}\right)^{11}$, $T_{r+1}={}^{11}C_r\,(ax^2)^{11-r}\left(\frac{1}{bx}\right)^r$

$$={}^{11}C_r\cdot\frac{a^{11-r}}{b^r}\cdot x^{22-3r} \quad \text{...(i)}$$

Now, in order to find out the coefficient of x^7, $22-3r$ must be 7, i.e. $22-3r=7 \Rightarrow r=5$

Hence, on putting $r=5$ in Eq. (i), we get

Required coefficient $={}^{11}C_5\cdot\frac{a^6}{b^5}$

For $\left(ax-\frac{1}{bx^2}\right)^{11}$, $T_{R+1}={}^{11}C_R\,(ax)^{11-R}\left(-\frac{1}{bx^2}\right)^R$

$$={}^{11}C_R\,(a)^{11-R}\left(-\frac{1}{b}\right)^R\cdot x^{11-3R}$$

$$=(-1)^R\cdot{}^{11}C_R\cdot\frac{a^{11-R}}{b^R}\cdot x^{11-3R} \quad \text{...(ii)}$$

Now, in order to find out the coefficient of x^{-7}, $11-3R$ must be -7. i.e. $11-3R=-7 \Rightarrow R=6$.

Hence, on putting $R=6$ in Eq. (ii), we get

Required coefficient $=(-1)^6\cdot{}^{11}C_6\cdot\frac{a^5}{b^6}={}^{11}C_5\cdot\frac{a^5}{b^6}$ $[\because {}^nC_r={}^nC_{n-r}]$

Also given, coefficient of x^7 in

$\left(ax^2+\frac{1}{bx}\right)^{11}$ = coefficient of x^{-7} in $\left(ax-\frac{1}{bx^2}\right)^{11}$

$\Rightarrow {}^{11}C_5\cdot\frac{a^6}{b^5}={}^{11}C_5\cdot\frac{a^5}{b^6} \Rightarrow ab=1$

which is the required relation between a and b.

Skill Builder

For Sol.

The coefficient of x^8 in the expansion of $\left(ax^4+\frac{1}{bx^4}\right)^{12}$ is equal to coefficient of x^{-8} in the expansion of $\left(ax^4-\frac{1}{bx^4}\right)^{12}$, *a* and *b* are positive real numbers, then the relation between *a* and *b* is equal to

(a) $a^2b^2=2$ (b) $a^2b^2=1$
(c) $a^2b^2=-1$ (d) $a^2b^2=-2$

- **For more practice** See Q.9 of Milestone Practice 6.1.

Example 15. The coefficient of the term independent of x in the expansion of $(1+x+2x^3)\left(\frac{3}{2}x^2-\frac{1}{3x}\right)^9$, is

(a) $\frac{1}{3}$ (b) $\frac{19}{54}$ (c) $\frac{17}{54}$ (d) $\frac{1}{4}$

Sol. (c) We have,

$$(1+x+2x^3)\left(\frac{3}{2}x^2-\frac{1}{3x}\right)^9$$

$$=(1+x+2x^3)\left[\sum_{r=0}^{9}{}^9C_r\left(\frac{3}{2}x^2\right)^{9-r}\left(\frac{-1}{3x}\right)^r\right]$$

$$=(1+x+2x^3)\left[\sum_{r=0}^{9}{}^9C_r\left(\frac{3}{2}\right)^{9-r}\left(\frac{-1}{3}\right)^r\cdot x^{18-3r}\right]$$

$$=\left[\sum_{r=0}^{9}{}^9C_r\left(\frac{3}{2}\right)^{9-r}\left(-\frac{1}{3}\right)^r x^{18-3r}\right]$$

$$+\left[\sum_{r=0}^{9}{}^9C_r\left(\frac{3}{2}\right)^{9-r}\left(-\frac{1}{3}\right)^r x^{19-3r}\right]$$

$$+2\left[\sum_{r=0}^{9}{}^9C_r\left(\frac{3}{2}\right)^{9-r}\left(\frac{-1}{3}\right)^r x^{21-3r}\right]$$

So, for independent of x,

$$18-3r=0,\ 19-3r=0,\ 21-3r=0$$

$\Rightarrow$ $r=6$, $r=$ not possible, $r=7$

$\therefore$ Coefficient of term independent of x

$$={}^9C_6\left(\frac{3}{2}\right)^3\left(-\frac{1}{3}\right)^6+2\times{}^9C_7\left(\frac{3}{2}\right)^2\left(\frac{-1}{3}\right)^7=\frac{7}{18}-\frac{2}{27}=\frac{17}{54}$$

Example 16. The coefficient of x^5 in the expansion of $(1+x)^{21}+(1+x)^{22}+\ldots+(1+x)^{30}$ is

(a) ${}^{51}C_5$ (b) ${}^{31}C_6-{}^{21}C_6$
(c) ${}^9C_5$ (d) ${}^{30}C_6+{}^{20}C_6$

Sol. (b) We have,

$$(1+x)^{21}+(1+x)^{22}+\ldots+(1+x)^{30}$$

$$=(1+x)^{21}\left[\frac{(1+x)^{10}-1}{1+x-1}\right]$$

$$=\frac{1}{x}[(1+x)^{31}-(1+x)^{21}]$$

$\therefore$ Coefficient of x^5 = Coefficient of x^6 in

$$[(1+x)^{31}-(1+x)^{21}]={}^{31}C_6-{}^{21}C_6$$

$(p+1)$th Term From End in the Expansion of $(x+a)^n$

$(p+1)$ th term from end in the expansion of $(x+a)^n$

$=(p+1)$ th term from beginning in the expansion of $(a+x)^n$

$={}^nC_p\,a^{n-p}\,x^p$

JEE SCANNER

Example Similar to PYQ Asked in JEE Main 2023

If the fifth term from the beginning and the fifth term from the end in the expansion of $\left(\sqrt[4]{2}+\frac{1}{\sqrt[4]{3}}\right)^n$ are equal, then n is ....

Sol. (8) In the expansion $\left(\sqrt[4]{2}+\frac{1}{\sqrt[4]{3}}\right)^n$, the fifth term from the beginning and the fifth term from the end are

$${}^nC_4(\sqrt[4]{2})^{n-4}\left(\frac{1}{\sqrt[4]{3}}\right)^4 \text{ and } {}^nC_{n-4}(\sqrt[4]{2})^4\left(\frac{1}{\sqrt[4]{3}}\right)^{n-4}, \text{ respectively.}$$

According to the question,

$${}^nC_4(\sqrt[4]{2})^{n-4}\left(\frac{1}{\sqrt[4]{3}}\right)^4 = {}^nC_{n-4}(\sqrt[4]{2})^4\left(\frac{1}{\sqrt[4]{3}}\right)^{n-4}$$

$$\Rightarrow \quad 2^{\frac{n-4}{4}} \times 3^{\frac{-4}{4}} = 2^{\frac{4}{4}} \times 3^{\frac{-(n-4)}{4}} \qquad [\because {}^nC_r = {}^nC_{n-r}]$$

$$\Rightarrow \quad (2\times 3)^{\frac{n-4}{4}-\frac{4}{4}} = 1$$

$$\Rightarrow \quad \frac{n-8}{4} = 0$$

$$\Rightarrow \quad n = 8$$

Skill Builder

If the seventh term from the beginning and end in the binomial expansion of $\left(\sqrt[3]{2}+\frac{1}{\sqrt[3]{3}}\right)^n$ are equal, then n is ....

For Sol.

- **For more practice** See Q.11 of Milestone Practice 6.1.

Example 17. Find the 4th term from the end in the expansion of $\left(\frac{x^3}{2}-\frac{2}{x^2}\right)^7$.

Sol. 4th term from the end in the expansion of $\left(\frac{x^3}{2}-\frac{2}{x^2}\right)^7$

= 4th term from beginning in the expansion of $\left(-\frac{2}{x^2}+\frac{x^3}{2}\right)^7$

$$= {}^7C_3\left(-\frac{2}{x^2}\right)^{7-3}\left(\frac{x^3}{2}\right)^3 = \frac{7\cdot 6\cdot 5}{1\cdot 2\cdot 3}\cdot\frac{2^4}{x^8}\cdot\frac{x^9}{2^3} = 70x$$

Example 18. Find the $(n+1)$th term from the end in the expansion of $\left(2x-\frac{1}{x}\right)^{3n}$.

Sol. $(n+1)$th term from the end in the expansion of $\left(2x-\frac{1}{x}\right)^{3n}$

$= (n+1)$ th term from beginning in the expansion of $\left(-\frac{1}{x}+2x\right)^{3n}$

$$= T_{n+1} = {}^{3n}C_n\left(-\frac{1}{x}\right)^{3n-n}(2x)^n = {}^{3n}C_n\cdot 2^n\cdot x^{-n}$$

How to Find Free from Radical Terms or Rational Terms in the Expansion of $(a^{1/p}+b^{1/q})^N, \forall\ a, b \in$ Prime Numbers

First, find $\quad T_{r+1} = {}^NC_r\,(a^{1/p})^{N-r}\,(b^{1/q})^r$

$\therefore \quad T_{r+1} = {}^NC_r\cdot a^{(N-r)/p}\cdot b^{r/q}$

By inspection, putting the values of $0\le r\le N$, when indices of a and b are integers.

JEE Focus Points

- If indices of a and b are positive integers. Then, free from radical terms = Terms which are integers
  $\therefore$ Number of non-integral terms
  = Total terms − Number of integral terms
- If indices of a and b both are not positive integers. Then, free from radical terms
  = Rational terms − Integral terms
- Number of irrational terms
  = Total terms − Number of rational terms

Example 19. Find the number of terms in the expansion of $(\sqrt[4]{9}+\sqrt[6]{8})^{500}$ which are integers.

Sol. Since, $(\sqrt[4]{9}+\sqrt[6]{8})^{500} = (9^{1/4}+8^{1/6})^{500}$

$= (3^{1/2}+2^{1/2})^{500}$

$[\because a, b \in \text{prime numbers}]$

$\therefore$ General term, $T_{r+1} = {}^{500}C_r\,(3^{1/2})^{500-r}\cdot(2^{1/2})^r$

$= {}^{500}C_r\cdot 3^{\frac{500-r}{2}}\cdot 2^{r/2}$

$= {}^{500}C_r\cdot 3^{250-r/2}\cdot 2^{r/2}$

Now, $\quad 0\le r\le 500$

For $r = 0, 2, 4, 6, 8, \ldots, 500$, indices of 3 and 2 are positive integers.

Hence, number of terms which are integers $= 250+1 = 251$

JEE SCANNER

Example Similar to PYQ Asked in JEE Main 2021

The sum of all rational terms in the expansion of $(3^{1/5}+2^{1/3})^{15}$ is equal to ....

Sol. (59) The general term in the expansion of $(3^{1/5}+2^{1/3})^{15}$ is

$$T_{r+1} = {}^{15}C_r\,(3^{1/5})^{15-r}\cdot(2^{1/3})^r$$

$$= {}^{15}C_r \cdot 3^{3-\frac{r}{5}} \cdot 2^{\frac{r}{3}}$$

Now, $0 \le r \le 15$

For $r = 0, 15$

Rational terms are T_{0+1} and T_{15+1}.

Then, $T_{0+1} = {}^{15}C_0 \cdot 3^3 \cdot 2^0 = 27$

and $T_{15+1} = {}^{15}C_{15} \cdot 3^0 \cdot 2^5 = 32$

$\therefore$ Sum of all rational terms $= 27 + 32 = 59$

Skill Builder

The sum of all rational terms in the expansion of $(2^{1/4}+3^{1/5})^{20}$ is equal to ......

For Sol.

- **For more practice** See Q.12 of Milestone Practice 6.1.

Example 20. Find the number of irrational terms in the expansion of $(\sqrt[8]{5}+\sqrt[6]{2})^{100}$.

Sol. Since, $(\sqrt[8]{5}+\sqrt[6]{2})^{100} = (5^{1/8}+2^{1/6})^{100}$

$\therefore$ General term, $T_{r+1} = {}^{100}C_r\,(5^{1/8})^{100-r}\,(2^{1/6})^r$

$$= {}^{100}C_r\,(5)^{(100-r)/8}\cdot(2)^{r/6}$$

As, 2 and 5 are coprime.

$\therefore$ T_{r+1} will be rational, if $(100-r)$ is a multiple of 8 and r is a multiple of 6.

Also, $0 \le r \le 100$

$\therefore$ $r = 0, 6, 12, 18, \ldots, 96$

Now, $100 - r = 4, 10, 16, \ldots, 100$ ...(i)

and $100 - r = 0, 8, 16, 24, \ldots, 100$ ...(ii)

The common terms in Eqs. (i) and (ii) are 16, 40, 64 and 88.

$\therefore$ $r = 84, 60, 36, 12$ gives rational terms.

$\therefore$ The number of irrational terms $= 101 - 4 = 97$

Problems Regarding Three/Four Consecutive Terms or Coefficients

(i) If consecutive coefficients are given

In this case, divide consecutive coefficients pairwise, we get equations and then solve them.

Example 21. Let n be a positive integer. If the coefficients of rth, $(r+1)$th and $(r+2)$th terms in the expansion of $(1+x)^n$ are in AP, then find the relation between n and r.

Sol. $\because$ $T_r = T_{(r-1)+1} = {}^nC_{r-1}\,x^{r-1}$

$T_{r+1} = {}^nC_r\,x^r$ and $T_{r+2} = T_{(r+1)+1} = {}^nC_{r+1}\,x^{r+1}$

$\therefore$ Coefficients of rth, $(r+1)$th and $(r+2)$th terms in the expansion of $(1+x)^n$ are ${}^nC_{r-1}, {}^nC_r, {}^nC_{r+1}$.

$\because$ Given, ${}^nC_{r-1}, {}^nC_r, {}^nC_{r+1}$ are in AP and $n \ge r+1$.

$\therefore$ $\dfrac{{}^nC_{r-1}}{{}^nC_r}, 1, \dfrac{{}^nC_{r+1}}{{}^nC_r}$ are also in AP.

$\Rightarrow$ $\dfrac{r}{n-r+1}, 1, \dfrac{n-r}{r+1}$ are in AP.

$$\Rightarrow 1 - \frac{r}{n-r+1} = \frac{n-r}{r+1} - 1 \Rightarrow \frac{n-2r+1}{n-r+1} = \frac{n-2r-1}{r+1}$$

$$\Rightarrow nr - 2r^2 + r + n - 2r + 1$$
$$= n^2 - 2nr - n - nr + 2r^2 + r + n - 2r - 1$$
$$\Rightarrow n^2 - 4nr + 4r^2 = n + 2 \Rightarrow (n-2r)^2 = n+2$$

Example 22. If a, b, c and d are any four consecutive coefficients in the expansion of $(1+x)^n$, then prove that

(i) $\dfrac{a}{a+b} + \dfrac{c}{c+d} = \dfrac{2b}{b+c}$.

(ii) $\left(\dfrac{b}{b+c}\right)^2 > \dfrac{ac}{(a+b)(c+d)}$, if $x > 0$.

Sol. Let a, b, c and d be the coefficients of the r th, $(r+1)$th, $(r+2)$th and $(r+3)$th terms respectively, in the expansion of $(1+x)^n$. Then,

$$T_r = T_{r-1+1} = {}^nC_{r-1}\,x^{r-1}$$

$\therefore$ $a = {}^nC_{r-1}$ ...(i)

$\because$ $T_{r+1} = {}^nC_r\,x^r$

$\therefore$ $b = {}^nC_r$ ...(ii)

$\because$ $T_{r+2} = T_{(r+1)+1} = {}^nC_{r+1}\,x^{r+1}$

$\therefore$ $c = {}^nC_{r+1}$ ....(iii)

and $T_{r+3} = T_{(r+2)+1} = {}^nC_{r+2}\,x^{r+2}$

$\therefore$ $d = {}^nC_{r+2}$ ...(iv)

From Eqs. (i) and (ii), we get

$$a + b = {}^nC_{r-1} + {}^nC_r = {}^{n+1}C_r$$
$$= \frac{n+1}{r}\cdot{}^nC_{r-1} = \left(\frac{n+1}{r}\right)a$$

$\therefore$ $\dfrac{a}{a+b} = \dfrac{r}{n+1}$ ...(v)

From Eqs. (ii) and (iii), we get

$$b + c = {}^nC_r + {}^nC_{r+1} = {}^{n+1}C_{r+1}$$
$$= \left(\frac{n+1}{r+1}\right){}^nC_r = \left(\frac{n+1}{r+1}\right)b$$

$\therefore$ $\dfrac{b}{b+c} = \dfrac{r+1}{n+1}$ ...(vi)

From Eqs. (iii) and (iv), we get

$$c+d={}^nC_{r+1}+{}^nC_{r+2}={}^{n+1}C_{r+2}$$

$$=\left(\frac{n+1}{r+2}\right){}^nC_{r+1}=\left(\frac{n+1}{r+2}\right)c$$

$$\therefore \quad \frac{c}{c+d}=\frac{r+2}{n+1} \qquad \text{...(vii)}$$

From Eqs. (v), (vi) and (vii), we get

$$\frac{a}{a+b},\frac{b}{b+c} \text{ and } \frac{c}{c+d} \text{ are in AP.}$$

(i) $\dfrac{a}{a+b}+\dfrac{c}{c+d}=2\left(\dfrac{b}{b+c}\right)$ or $\dfrac{a}{a+b}+\dfrac{c}{c+d}=\dfrac{2b}{b+c}$

(ii) AM > GM

$$\therefore \quad \left(\frac{b}{b+c}\right)>\sqrt{\left(\frac{a}{a+b}\right)\left(\frac{c}{c+d}\right)}$$

$$\Rightarrow \quad \left(\frac{b}{b+c}\right)^2>\frac{ac}{(a+b)(c+d)}$$

(ii) If consecutive terms are given

In this case, divide consecutive terms pairwise. i.e.

If four consecutive terms are $T_r, T_{r+1}, T_{r+2}, T_{r+3}$.

Then, find $\dfrac{T_{r+1}}{T_r},\dfrac{T_{r+2}}{T_{r+1}},\dfrac{T_{r+3}}{T_{r+2}} \Rightarrow \lambda_1,\lambda_2,\lambda_3$ (say).

Then, divide λ_2 by λ_1 and λ_3 by λ_2 and solve.

Example 23. If the 2nd, 3rd and 4th terms in the expansion of $(x+y)^n$ are 240, 720 and 1080 respectively, find x, y and n.

Sol. Given, $T_2=T_{1+1}={}^nC_1\cdot x^{n-1}\cdot y=240$ ...(i)

$$T_3=T_{2+1}={}^nC_2\cdot x^{n-2}\cdot y^2=720 \qquad \text{...(ii)}$$

and $T_4=T_{3+1}={}^nC_3\cdot x^{n-3}\cdot y^3=1080$ ...(iii)

On dividing Eq. (ii) by Eq. (i), we get

$$\frac{{}^nC_2\cdot x^{n-2}\cdot y^2}{{}^nC_1\cdot x^{n-1}\cdot y}=\frac{720}{240}$$

$$\Rightarrow \quad \left(\frac{n-2+1}{2}\right)\cdot\frac{y}{x}=3$$

$$\Rightarrow \quad \frac{y}{x}=\frac{6}{n-1} \qquad \text{...(iv)}$$

Also, dividing Eq. (iii) by Eq. (ii), we get

$$\frac{{}^nC_3\cdot x^{n-3}\cdot y^3}{{}^nC_2\cdot x^{n-2}\cdot y^2}=\frac{1080}{720}$$

$$\Rightarrow \quad \left(\frac{n-3+1}{3}\right)\cdot\frac{y}{x}=\frac{3}{2}$$

$$\Rightarrow \quad \frac{y}{x}=\frac{9}{2(n-2)} \qquad \text{...(v)}$$

From Eqs. (iv) and (v), we get

$$\frac{6}{n-1}=\frac{9}{2(n-2)}$$

$$\Rightarrow \quad 12n-24=9n-9 \Rightarrow 3n=15$$

$$\therefore \quad n=5$$

From Eq. (iv), we get

$$y=\frac{3}{2}x \qquad \text{...(vi)}$$

From Eqs. (i) and (vi), we get

$$^5C_1\cdot x^4\cdot y=240$$

$$\Rightarrow \quad 5\cdot x^4\cdot\frac{3}{2}x=240$$

$$\therefore \quad x^5=32=2^5 \Rightarrow x=2$$

From Eq. (vi), we get

$$y=3$$

Hence, $x=2, y=3$ and $n=5$

6.2 Middle Terms

The middle term depends upon the value of n.

(i) **When n is even** The total number of terms in the expansion of $(x+a)^n$ is $n+1$ (odd). So, there is only one middle term, i.e., $\left(\dfrac{n}{2}+1\right)$th term is the middle term. It is given by $T_{n/2+1}={}^nC_{n/2}\,x^{n/2}\,a^{n/2}$

(ii) **When n is odd** The total number of terms in the expansion of $(x+a)^n$ is $n+1$ (even). So, there are two middle terms, i.e., $\left(\dfrac{n+1}{2}\right)$th and $\left(\dfrac{n+3}{2}\right)$th are two middle terms. They are given by

$$T_{\frac{n+1}{2}}=T_{\left(\frac{n-1}{2}\right)+1}={}^nC_{\frac{n-1}{2}}\cdot x^{\frac{n+1}{2}}\cdot a^{\frac{n-1}{2}}$$

and
$$T_{\frac{n+3}{2}}=T_{\left(\frac{n+1}{2}\right)+1}={}^nC_{\frac{n+1}{2}}\cdot x^{\frac{n-1}{2}}\cdot a^{\frac{n+1}{2}}$$

Example 24. Find the middle term in the expansion of $\left(\dfrac{a}{x}+bx\right)^{12}$.

Sol. The number of terms in the expansion of $\left(\dfrac{a}{x}+bx\right)^{12}$ is 13 (odd), its middle term is $\left(\dfrac{12}{2}+1\right)$th, i.e., 7th term.

$$\therefore \text{ Required term, } T_7=T_{6+1}={}^{12}C_6\left(\frac{a}{x}\right)^6(bx)^6$$

$$={}^{12}C_6\,a^6\,b^6=924\,a^6\,b^6$$

Example 25. Find the middle term in the expansion of $\left(3x-\frac{x^3}{6}\right)^9$.

Sol. The number of terms in the expansion of $\left(3x-\frac{x^3}{6}\right)^9$ is 10 (even). So, there are two middle terms, i.e. $\left(\frac{9+1}{2}\right)$th and $\left(\frac{9+3}{2}\right)$th terms. They are given by T_5 and T_6.

$$\therefore \quad T_5 = T_{4+1} = {}^9C_4\,(3x)^5\left(-\frac{x^3}{6}\right)^4$$

$$= \frac{9\cdot8\cdot7\cdot6}{1\cdot2\cdot3\cdot4}\cdot3^5\,x^5\cdot\frac{x^{12}}{6^4} = \frac{189}{8}x^{17}$$

$$\text{and } T_6 = T_{5+1} = {}^9C_5\,(3x)^4\left(-\frac{x^3}{6}\right)^5 = -\,{}^9C_4\cdot3^4\cdot x^4\cdot\frac{x^{15}}{6^5}$$

$$= -\frac{9\cdot8\cdot7\cdot6}{1\cdot2\cdot3\cdot4}\cdot3^4\cdot\frac{x^{19}}{6^5} = -\frac{21}{16}x^{19}$$

Example 26. Show that the middle term in the expansion of $(1+x)^{2n}$ is $\frac{1\cdot3\cdot5\ldots(2n-1)}{n!}\cdot2^n\,x^n$, n being a positive integer.

Sol. The number of terms in the expansion of $(1+x)^{2n}$ is $2n+1$ (odd), its middle term is $(n+1)$th term.

$\therefore$ Required term $= T_{n+1}$

$$= {}^{2n}C_n\,x^n = \frac{2n!}{n!\,n!}x^n = \frac{(1\cdot2\cdot3\cdot4\ldots(2n-1)\cdot2n)}{n!\,n!}x^n$$

$$= \frac{\{1\cdot3\cdot5\ldots(2n-1)\}\{2\cdot4\cdot6\ldots2n\}}{n!\,n!}x^n$$

$$= \frac{\{1\cdot3\cdot5\ldots(2n-1)\}\,2^n\,(1\cdot2\cdot3\ldots n)}{n!\,n!}x^n$$

$$= \frac{\{1\cdot3\cdot5\ldots(2n-1)\}\,2^n\,n!}{n!\,n!}x^n$$

$$= \frac{1\cdot3\cdot5\ldots(2n-1)}{n!}2^n\,x^n$$

6.3 Greatest Term

If T_r and T_{r+1} are the rth and $(r+1)$th terms in the expansion of $(x+a)^n$, then

$$\frac{T_{r+1}}{T_r} = \frac{{}^nC_r\cdot x^{n-r}\cdot a^r}{{}^nC_{r-1}\cdot x^{n-r+1}\cdot a^{r-1}} = \left(\frac{n-r+1}{r}\right)\cdot\frac{a}{x}$$

Let numerically, T_{r+1} be the greatest term in the above expansion.

Then, $T_{r+1}\ge T_r$ or $\frac{T_{r+1}}{T_r}\ge1 \Rightarrow \left(\frac{n-r+1}{r}\right)\left|\frac{a}{x}\right|\ge1$

[$\because a$ may be (+ ve) or (– ve)]

$$\text{or} \qquad r \le \frac{(n+1)}{\left(1+\left|\frac{x}{a}\right|\right)} \qquad \ldots\text{(i)}$$

Now, on substituting values of n, x and a in Eq. (i), we get

$$r \le m+f \text{ or } r\le m$$

where, $\quad m\in N$ and $0<f<1$

In the first case, T_{m+1} is the greatest term, while in the second case, T_m and T_{m+1} are the greatest terms and both are equal (numerically).

Shortcut Method

To find the greatest term (numerically) in the expansion of $(x+a)^n$.

$$\text{Now,} \quad (x+a)^n = a^n\left(1+\frac{x}{a}\right)^n$$

$$\text{Calculate} \quad m = \frac{\left|\frac{x}{a}\right|(n+1)}{\left(\left|\frac{x}{a}\right|+1\right)}$$

Case I If $m\in$ Integer, then T_m and T_{m+1} are the greatest terms and both are equal (numerically).

Case II If $m\notin$ Integer, then $T_{[m]+1}$ is the greatest term, where $[\cdot]$ denotes the greatest integer function.

Example 27. Find numerically the greatest term in the expansion of $(2+3x)^9$, when $x=3/2$.

Sol. Let T_{r+1} be the greatest term in the expansion of $(2+3x)^9$, we have

$$\frac{T_{r+1}}{T_r} = \left(\frac{9-r+1}{r}\right)\left|\frac{3x}{2}\right| = \left(\frac{10-r}{r}\right)\left|\frac{3}{2}\times\frac{3}{2}\right| = \frac{90-9r}{4r}$$

[$\because x=3/2$]

$$\therefore \qquad \frac{T_{r+1}}{T_r}\ge1 \Rightarrow \frac{90-9r}{4r}\ge1 \Rightarrow 90\ge13r$$

$$\therefore \qquad r\le\frac{90}{13}=6\frac{12}{13} \text{ or } r\le6\frac{12}{13}$$

$\therefore$ Maximum value of r is 6.

So, greatest term $= T_{6+1} = {}^9C_6\,(2)^{9-6}\,(3x)^6$

$$= {}^9C_3\cdot2^3\cdot\left(3\times\frac{3}{2}\right)^6$$

$$= \frac{9\cdot8\cdot7}{1\cdot2\cdot3}\cdot\frac{2^3\cdot3^{12}}{2^6} = \frac{7\times3^{13}}{2}$$

Alternate Solution

Since, $(2+3x)^9 = 2^9\left(1+\frac{3x}{2}\right)^9$

Now, $m = \dfrac{(9+1)\left|\frac{3x}{2}\right|}{\left|\frac{3x}{2}\right|+1} = \dfrac{10\times\frac{9}{4}}{\frac{9}{4}+1}$ [$\because x = 3/2$]

$= \frac{90}{13} = 6\frac{12}{13} \ne$ Integer

$\therefore$ The greatest term in the expansion is

$T_{[m]+1} = T_{6+1}$ in $(2+3x)^9$

$= {}^9C_6\,(2)^{9-6}\,(3x)^6 = {}^9C_3 \cdot 2^3 \cdot \left(\frac{3^2}{2}\right)^6$ [$\because x = 3/2$]

$= \frac{9\cdot 8\cdot 7}{1\cdot 2\cdot 3}\cdot\frac{3^{12}}{2^3} = \frac{7\times 3^{13}}{2}$

Example 28. Find numerically the greatest term in the expansion of $(3-5x)^{11}$, when $x=\frac{1}{5}$.

Sol. Let T_{r+1} be the greatest term in the expansion of $(3-5x)^{11}$, we have

$$\frac{T_{r+1}}{T_r} = \left(\frac{11-r+1}{r}\right)\left|-\frac{5x}{3}\right|$$

$$= \left(\frac{12-r}{r}\right)\left|-\frac{1}{3}\right| = \frac{12-r}{3r} \qquad [\because x = 1/5]$$

$\therefore \quad \frac{T_{r+1}}{T_r} \ge 1 \Rightarrow \frac{12-r}{3r} \ge 1 \Rightarrow 12 \ge 4r$

$\therefore \quad r \le 3 \Rightarrow r = 2, 3$

So, the greatest terms are T_{2+1} and T_{3+1}.

$\therefore$ Greatest term (when $r=2$) $= T_{2+1} = {}^{11}C_2\,(3)^9\,(-5x)^2$

$$= \frac{11\cdot 10}{1\cdot 2}\cdot 3^9\cdot(1)^2 = 55\times 3^9 \qquad [\because x = 1/5]$$

and greatest term (when $r=3$) $= T_{3+1}$

$$= \left|{}^{11}C_3\,(3)^8\,(-5x)^3\right| = \left|{}^{11}C_3\,(3)^8\,(-1)^3\right| \qquad [\because x = 1/5]$$

$$= {}^{11}C_3\cdot 3^8 = \frac{11\cdot 10\cdot 9}{1\cdot 2\cdot 3}\cdot 3^8 = 55\times 3^9$$

From above, we say that the values of both greatest terms are equal.

Greatest Coefficient

(i) If n is even, then greatest coefficient is ${}^nC_{n/2}$.

(ii) If n is odd, then greatest coefficients are ${}^nC_{(n-1)/2}$ and ${}^nC_{(n+1)/2}$.

Example 29. Show that, if the greatest term in the expansion of $(1+x)^{2n}$ has also the greatest coefficient, then x lies between $\frac{n}{n+1}$ and $\frac{n+1}{n}$.

Sol. In the expansion of $(1+x)^{2n}$, the middle term is $\left(\frac{2n}{2}+1\right)$th i.e., $(n+1)$th term, we know that from binomial expansion, middle term has greatest coefficient.

[$\because$ Terms $T_1, T_2, T_3, \ldots, T_n, T_{n+1}, T_{n+2}, \ldots$]

$\therefore \quad T_n < T_{n+1} > T_{n+2}$

$\Rightarrow \quad \frac{T_{n+1}}{T_n} = \frac{{}^{2n}C_n\cdot x^n}{{}^{2n}C_{n-1}\cdot x^{n-1}} = \frac{2n-n+1}{n}\cdot x$

$\Rightarrow \quad \frac{T_{n+1}}{T_n} > 1$ or $\frac{n+1}{n}\cdot x > 1$

or $\quad x > \frac{n}{n+1}$ ...(i)

and $\quad \frac{T_{n+2}}{T_{n+1}} = \frac{{}^{2n}C_{n+1}\,x^{n+1}}{{}^{2n}C_n\,x^n} = \frac{2n-(n+1)+1}{n+1}\cdot x$

$= \frac{n}{n+1}\cdot x$

$\Rightarrow \quad \frac{T_{n+2}}{T_{n+1}} < 1$

$\Rightarrow \quad \frac{n}{n+1}\cdot x < 1$ or $x < \frac{n+1}{n}$ ...(ii)

From Eqs. (i) and (ii), we get

$$\frac{n}{n+1} < x < \frac{n+1}{n}$$

Important Properties of the Binomial Coefficients

In the binomial expansion of $(1+x)^n$. Let us denote the coefficients ${}^nC_0, {}^nC_1, {}^nC_2, \ldots, {}^nC_r, \ldots, {}^nC_n$ by $C_0, C_1, C_2, \ldots, C_r, \ldots, C_n$, respectively.

(i) **The coefficients of the terms equidistant from the beginning and the end are equal.**

The $(r+1)$th term from the beginning in the expansion of $(1+x)^n$ is ${}^nC_r\,x^r$.

$\therefore$ The coefficient of the $(r+1)$th term from the beginning is ${}^nC_r$ and the $(r+1)$th term from the end in the expansion of $(1+x)^n = (r+1)$ th term from the beginning in the expansion of $(x+1)^n = {}^nC_r\,x^{n-r}$

$\therefore$ The coefficient of the $(r+1)$th term from the end is ${}^nC_r$.

Hence, the coefficients of $(r+1)$th term from the beginning and the end are equal.

(ii) **The sum of the binomial coefficients in the expansion of $(1+x)^n$**

$\because \quad (1+x)^n = {}^nC_0 + {}^nC_1\,x + {}^nC_2\,x^2 + {}^nC_3\,x^3 + \ldots + {}^nC_n\,x^n$

Putting $x=1$, we get

$$2^n = {}^nC_0 + {}^nC_1 + {}^nC_2 + \ldots + {}^nC_n$$

or $C_0 + C_1 + C_2 + \ldots + C_n = 2^n$

$\therefore$ Sum of binomial coefficients $= 2^n$

(iii) **The sum of the coefficients of the odd terms = The sum of the coefficients of the even terms**

$\because \ (1+x)^n = {}^nC_0 + {}^nC_1\, x + {}^nC_2\, x^2 + {}^nC_3\, x^3 + \ldots + {}^nC_n\, x^n$

Putting $x=-1$, we get

$$0 = {}^nC_0 - {}^nC_1 + {}^nC_2 - {}^nC_3 + {}^nC_4 - {}^nC_5 + \ldots$$

or $\ {}^nC_1 + {}^nC_3 + {}^nC_5 + \ldots = {}^nC_0 + {}^nC_2 + {}^nC_4 + \ldots$

Since, the sum of all the coefficients is 2^n, therefore each side is equal to $\frac{2^n}{2}$ i.e. 2^{n-1}.

Hence, $C_1 + C_3 + C_5 + \ldots = C_0 + C_2 + C_4 + \ldots = 2^{n-1}$

6.4 Trinomial Expansion

For $n \in N, (1+x+x^2)^n = \sum_{r=0}^{2n} a_r x^r$

$$= a_0 + a_1 x + a_2 x^2 + \ldots + a_n x^n + \ldots + a_{2n} x^{2n} \quad \ldots(i)$$

There are $(2n+1)$ terms. The middle coefficient is a_n which is also the greatest.

$$a_0 = a_{2n}, a_1 = a_{2n-1}, \ldots, a_r = a_{2n-r}$$

The coefficients of $(1+x+x^2)^n$ for $n = 0, 1, 2, \ldots$ can be arranged in a triangle.

```
                1
             1  1  1
          1  2  3  2  1
       1  3  6  7  6  3  1
    1  4 10 16 19 16 10  4  1
 1  5 15 30 45 51 45 30 15  5  1
 .  .  .  .  .  .  .  .  .  .  .
```

i.e., The rows contains the coefficients for $n = 0, 1, 2, 3, \ldots$.

Each entry other than two entries at the ends is the sum of three entries above it.

$$15 = 1 + 4 + 10,$$

$$30 = 16 + 10 + 4, \text{ etc.}$$

Putting $x=1$ and $x=-1$ in Eq. (i), we get

$$a_0 + a_1 + a_2 + a_3 + \ldots + a_{2n} = 3^n$$

[sum of all coefficients] ...(ii)

and $\ a_0 - a_1 + a_2 - a_3 + \ldots + a_{2n} = 1 \quad \ldots$(iii)

On adding Eqs. (ii) and (iii), we get

$$a_0 + a_2 + a_4 + \ldots + a_{2n} = \frac{3^n + 1}{2}$$

[sum of coefficients of even powers of x]

On subtracting Eq. (iii) from Eq. (ii), we get

$$a_1 + a_3 + a_5 + \ldots + a_{2n-1} = \frac{3^n - 1}{2}$$

[sum of coefficients of odd powers of x]

Putting $x = i(\sqrt{-1})$ in Eq. (i), we get

$$a_0 + a_1 i + a_2 i^2 + a_3 i^3 + a_4 i^4 + a_5 i^5 + \ldots + a_{2n} i^{2n} = i^n$$

$\Rightarrow \quad (a_0 - a_2 + a_4 - \ldots) + i(a_1 - a_3 + a_5 - \ldots) = i^n$

$$(a_0 - a_2 + a_4 - \ldots) + i(a_1 - a_3 + a_5 - \ldots)$$

$$= \left(\cos\frac{\pi}{2} + i\sin\frac{\pi}{2}\right)^n$$

$$= \cos\left(\frac{n\pi}{2}\right) + i\sin\left(\frac{n\pi}{2}\right)$$

On comparing real and imaginary parts, we get

$$a_0 - a_2 + a_4 - \ldots = \cos\left(\frac{n\pi}{2}\right)$$

and $$a_1 - a_3 + a_5 - \ldots = \sin\left(\frac{n\pi}{2}\right)$$

Putting $x = \omega$ and ω^2 (cube roots of unity) in Eq. (i), we get

$$a_0 + a_1\omega + a_2\omega^2 + a_3\omega^3 + a_4\omega^4 + \ldots = 0 \quad \ldots(iv)$$

and $\ a_0 + a_1\omega^2 + a_2\omega^4 + a_3\omega^6 + a_4\omega^8 + \ldots = 0 \quad \ldots$(v)

On adding Eqs. (ii), (iv) and (v) and then dividing by 3, we get

$$a_0 + a_3 + a_6 + \ldots = 3^{n-1}$$

JEE Focus Points

For $n \in N$, $(1+x+x^2)^n = \sum_{r=0}^{2n} a_r x^r$

- $a_1 + a_4 + a_7 + \ldots = a_2 + a_5 + a_8 + \ldots = 3^{n-1}$
- $a_0 + a_4 + a_8 + \ldots = \frac{1}{4}\left\{3^n + 1 + 2\cos\left(\frac{n\pi}{2}\right)\right\}$
- $a_1 + a_5 + a_9 + \ldots = \frac{1}{4}\left\{3^n - 1 + 2\sin\left(\frac{n\pi}{2}\right)\right\}$
- $a_0 + a_6 + a_{12} + \ldots = \frac{1}{6}\left\{3^n + 1 + 2^{n+1}\cos\left(\frac{n\pi}{3}\right)\right\}$
- $\sum_{r=1}^{2n} r \cdot a_r = n \cdot 3^n$
- $\sum_{r=1}^{2n} (-1)^{r-1} \cdot r \cdot a_r = -n$

Example 30. Find the sum of coefficients in the expansion of the binomial $(5p-4q)^n$, where n is a positive integer.

Sol. Putting $p=q=1$ in $(5p-4q)^n$,

the required sum of coefficients $=(5-4)^n=1^n=1$

Example 31. In the expansion of $(3^{-x/4}+3^{5x/4})^n$, if the sum of binomial coefficients is 64 and the term with the greatest binomial coefficient exceeds the third by $(n-1)$, find the value of x.

Sol. Given sum of the binomial coefficients in the expansion of $(3^{-x/4}+3^{5x/4})^n=64$

Then, putting $3^{-x/4}=3^{5x/4}=1$

$\therefore \quad (1+1)^n=64 \Rightarrow 2^n=2^6$

$\therefore \quad n=6$

We know that, middle term has the greatest binomial coefficients. Here, $n=6$

$\therefore$ Middle term $=\left(\dfrac{n}{2}+1\right)$th term $=$ 4th term $=T_4$

and given that $T_4=(n-1)+T_3$

$$\Rightarrow \quad T_{3+1}=(6-1)+T_{2+1}$$

$$\Rightarrow \quad {}^6C_3(3^{-x/4})^3(3^{5x/4})^3=5+{}^6C_2(3^{-x/4})^4(3^{5x/4})^2$$

$$\Rightarrow \quad 20\cdot 3^{3x}=5+15\cdot 3^{3x/2}$$

Let $\quad 3^{3x/2}=t$

$$\therefore \quad 20t^2=5+15t$$

$$\Rightarrow \quad 4t^2-3t-1=0 \Rightarrow (4t+1)(t-1)=0$$

$$\therefore \quad t=1,\ t\neq -\frac{1}{4} \Rightarrow 3^{3x/2}=1=3^0$$

$$\therefore \quad \frac{3x}{2}=0 \text{ or } x=0$$

Example 32. Find the values of

(i) $\dfrac{1}{(n-1)!}+\dfrac{1}{(n-3)!3!}+\dfrac{1}{(n-5)!5!}+\dots$

(ii) $\dfrac{1}{12!}+\dfrac{1}{10!2!}+\dfrac{1}{8!4!}+\dots+\dfrac{1}{12!}$

Sol. (i) $\because 1!=1$

$\therefore$ The given series can be written as

$$\frac{1}{(n-1)!\,1!}+\frac{1}{(n-3)!\,3!}+\frac{1}{(n-5)!\,5!}+\dots \quad \text{...(i)}$$

$\because$ Sum of values of each terms in factorial are equal.

i.e. $(n-1)+1=(n-3)+3=(n-5)+5=\dots=n$

From Eq. (i),

$$\frac{1}{n!}\left[\frac{n!}{(n-1)!\,1!}+\frac{n!}{(n-3)!\,3!}+\frac{n!}{(n-5)!\,5!}+\dots\right]$$

$$=\frac{1}{n!}({}^nC_1+{}^nC_3+{}^nC_5+\dots)=\frac{2^{n-1}}{n!}$$

(ii) $\because \quad 0!=1$

$\therefore$ The given series can be written as

$$\frac{1}{12!0!}+\frac{1}{10!\,2!}+\frac{1}{8!\,4!}+\dots+\frac{1}{0!\,12!} \quad \text{...(ii)}$$

$\because$ Sum of values of each terms in factorial are equal

i.e., $\quad 12+0=10+2=8+4=\dots=12$

From Eq. (ii), $\dfrac{1}{12!}\left[\dfrac{12!}{12!\,0!}+\dfrac{12!}{10!\,2!}+\dfrac{12!}{8!\,4!}+\dots+\dfrac{12!}{0!\,12!}\right]$

$$=\frac{1}{12!}({}^{12}C_0+{}^{12}C_2+{}^{12}C_4+\dots+{}^{12}C_{12})=\frac{2^{12-1}}{12!}=\frac{2^{11}}{12!}$$

Example 33. Prove that the sum of the coefficients in the expansion of $(1+x-3x^2)^{2163}$ is -1.

Sol. Putting $x=1$ in $(1+x-3x^2)^{2163}$, the required sum of coefficients $=(1+1-3)^{2163}=(-1)^{2163}=-1$

Example 34. If the sum of the coefficients in the expansion of $(\alpha x^2-2x+1)^{35}$ is equal to the sum of the coefficients in the expansion of $(x-\alpha y)^{35}$, find the value of α.

Sol. Given, sum of the coefficients in the expansion of $(\alpha x^2-2x+1)^{35}$

= Sum of the coefficients in the expansion of $(x-\alpha y)^{35}$

Putting $x=y=1$, we get

$$(\alpha-1)^{35}=(1-\alpha)^{35}$$

$$\Rightarrow \quad (\alpha-1)^{35}=-(\alpha-1)^{35}$$

$$\Rightarrow \quad 2(\alpha-1)^{35}=0$$

$$\Rightarrow \quad \alpha-1=0$$

$$\therefore \quad \alpha=1$$

Example 35. If $(1+x-2x^2)^{20}=\sum_{r=0}^{40}a_rx^r$, then find the value of $a_1+a_3+a_5+\dots+a_{39}$.

Sol. $\because \quad (1+x-2x^2)^{20}=\sum_{r=0}^{40}a_rx^r \quad \text{...(i)}$

Putting $x=1$, we get $0=\sum_{r=0}^{40}a_r$

or $\quad a_0+a_1+a_2+a_3+a_4+a_5+\dots+a_{39}+a_{40}=0 \quad \text{...(ii)}$

Putting $x=-1$ in Eq. (i), we get

$$(-2)^{20}=\sum_{r=0}^{40}(-1)^r a_r$$

or $a_0-a_1+a_2-a_3+a_4-a_5+\dots-a_{39}+a_{40}=2^{20} \quad \text{...(iii)}$

On subtracting Eq. (iii) from Eq. (ii), we get

$$2[a_1+a_3+a_5+\dots+a_{39}]=-2^{20}$$

or $\quad a_1+a_3+a_5+\dots+a_{39}=-2^{19}$

Milestone Practice 6.1

1. Simplify the expression
$\alpha^5 + 10\alpha^4\beta + 40\alpha^3\beta^2 + 80\alpha^2\beta^3 + 80\alpha\beta^4 + 32\beta^5$

2. If $x = \dfrac{[18^3 + 7^3 + 3 \times 18 \times 7 \times 25]}{[3^6 + 6 \times 243 \times 2 + 15 \times 81 \times 4 + 20 \times 27 \times 8 + 15 \times 9 \times 16 + 6 \times 3 \times 32 + 64]}$,
then find $x^{10} - 1$.

3. Prove that $\sum_{r=0}^{n} {}^nC_r 3^r = 4^n$

4. Using binomial theorem, evaluate $(102)^6$.

5. Find the 6th term in the expansion of $\left(\dfrac{4x}{5} - \dfrac{5}{2x}\right)^9$.

6. Find the 4th term from the end in the expansion of $\left(\dfrac{3}{x^2} - \dfrac{x^3}{6}\right)^7$.

7. Find the middle term in the expansion of $\left(\dfrac{2}{3}x^2 - \dfrac{3}{2x}\right)^{20}$.

8. The coefficient of x^3 in the expansion of $\left(ax^3 + \dfrac{1}{bx^3}\right)^{15}$ is equal to the coefficient of x^{-3} in the expansion of $\left(ax^3 - \dfrac{1}{bx^3}\right)^{15}$, a and b are positive real numbers, then prove that $ab = 1$.

9. If the 6th term in the expansion of $\left(\dfrac{1}{x^{8/3}} + x^2\log_{10}^{x}\right)^8$ is 5600, then find the value of x.

10. In $\left(\sqrt[3]{5} + \dfrac{1}{\sqrt[3]{7}}\right)^n$, if the 9th term from the beginning and the ninth term from the end are equal, find n.

11. Find the sum of all rational terms in the expansion of $\left(4^{\frac{1}{3}} + 5^{\frac{1}{4}}\right)^{12}$

12. Find the value of a so that the term independent of x in $\left(\sqrt{x} + \dfrac{a}{x^2}\right)^{10}$ is 405.

13. If the middle term in the binomial expansion of $\left(\dfrac{1}{x} + x\sin x\right)^{10}$ is equal to $\dfrac{63}{8}$, find the value of x.

14. If $x = \dfrac{1}{3}$, find the greatest term in the expansion of $(1 + 4x)^8$.

Answer Key

1. $(\alpha + 2\beta)^5$
2. 0
4. 1126162419264
5. $-\dfrac{5040}{x}$
6. $\dfrac{35}{48}x^6$
7. ${}^{20}C_{10}x^{10}$
9. 10
10. 16
11. 381
12. ± 3
13. $n\pi + (-1)^n\dfrac{\pi}{6}, n \in Z$
14. $56\left(\dfrac{4}{3}\right)^5$

For Detailed Solution

Milestone 2 Some Important Theorems

• Two Important Theorems • Divisibility Problems • Use of Complex Numbers in Binomial Theorem • Multinomial Theorem • Use of Differentiation • Use of Integration • Binomial Inside Binomial • Sum of the Series

6.5 Two Important Theorems

Theorem 1 If $(\sqrt{P}+Q)^n = I + f$, where I and n are positive integers, n being odd and $0 \le f < 1$, then show that $(I+f)f = k^n$, where $P - Q^2 = k > 0$ and $\sqrt{P} - Q < 1$.

Proof Given, $\sqrt{P} - Q < 1$

$\therefore \quad 0 < (\sqrt{P} - Q)^n < 1$

Now, let $(\sqrt{P}-Q)^n = f'$,

where $\quad 0 < f' < 1$

Also $\quad I + f = (\sqrt{P}+Q)^n \quad$ ...(i)

$0 \le f < 1 \quad$ ...(ii)

$f' = (\sqrt{P}-Q)^n \quad$ ...(iii)

and $\quad 0 < f' < 1 \quad$ ...(iv)

On subtracting Eq. (iii) from Eq. (i), we get

$$I + f - f' = (\sqrt{P}+Q)^n - (\sqrt{P}-Q)^n$$

$$= 2[{}^nC_1 (\sqrt{P})^{n-1} \cdot Q + {}^nC_3 (\sqrt{P})^{n-3} \cdot Q^3 + \ldots]$$

$$= 2\,(\text{integer})$$

$$= \text{Even integer} \quad \text{...(v)}$$

[Since, n is odd, RHS contains even powers of $\sqrt{P}$, so RHS is an even integer]

$\therefore$ LHS is also an integer.

$\because$ I is an integer.

$\therefore$ $(f - f')$ is also an integer.

$\Rightarrow \quad f - f' = 0 \quad [\because -1 < (f - f') < 1]$

or $\quad f = f'$

From Eq. (v), I is an even integer and

$$(I+f)f = (I+f)f'$$

$$= (\sqrt{P}+Q)^n (\sqrt{P}-Q)^n$$

$$= (P - Q^2)^n$$

$$= k^n$$

JEE SPIKE

If n is even integer, then $(\sqrt{P}+Q)^n + (\sqrt{P}-Q)^n = I + f + f'$

Since, LHS and I are integers.

$\therefore \quad (f + f')$ is also an integer.

$\Rightarrow \quad f + f' = 1 \quad [\because 0 < (f + f') < 2]$

$\therefore \quad f' = 1 - f$

Hence, $\quad (I+f)(1-f) = (I+f)f'$

$= (\sqrt{P}+Q)^n (\sqrt{P}-Q)^n$

$= (P - Q^2)^n = k^n$

Concept Inside Video

Theorem 2 If $(P+\sqrt{Q})^n = I + f$, where I and n are positive integers and $0 \le f < 1$, show that $(I+f)(1-f) = k^n$, where $P^2 - Q = k > 0$ and $P - \sqrt{Q} < 1$.

Proof Given, $P - \sqrt{Q} < 1 \quad \therefore \quad 0 < (P-\sqrt{Q})^n < 1$

Now, let $(P-\sqrt{Q})^n = f'$, where $0 < f' < 1$

Also, $\quad I + f = (P+\sqrt{Q})^n \quad$ ...(i)

$0 \le f < 1 \quad$ ...(ii)

$f' = (P-\sqrt{Q})^n \quad$ ...(iii)

and $\quad 0 < f' < 1 \quad$ ...(iv)

On adding Eqs. (i) and (iii), we get

$$I + f + f' = (P+\sqrt{Q})^n + (P-\sqrt{Q})^n$$

$$= 2[{}^nC_0 P^n + {}^nC_2 P^{n-2} (\sqrt{Q})^2 + {}^nC_4 P^{n-4} (\sqrt{Q})^4 + \ldots]$$

$$= 2\,(\text{integer}) = \text{Even integer} \quad \text{...(v)}$$

[Since, RHS contains even power of $\sqrt{Q}$, so RHS is an even integer]

$\therefore$ LHS is also an integer. $\quad [\because I$ is an integer$]$

$\Rightarrow$ $f + f'$ is also an integer.

$\therefore \quad f + f' = 1 \quad [\because 0 < (f + f') < 2]$

or $\quad f' = 1 - f$

From Eq. (v), I = even integer $-$ 1 = odd integer and

$$(I+f)(1-f) = (I+f)f' = (P+\sqrt{Q})^n (P-\sqrt{Q})^n$$

$$= (P^2 - Q)^n = k^n$$

Example 36. Show that the integral part of $(5+2\sqrt{6})^n$ is odd, where n is natural number.

Sol. $(5+2\sqrt{6})^n$ can be written as $(5+\sqrt{24})^n$

Now, let $I+f=(5+\sqrt{24})^n$ ...(i)

$0 \le f < 1$ ...(ii)

and let $f'=(5-\sqrt{24})^n$ ...(iii)

$0 < f' < 1$ ...(iv)

On adding Eqs. (i) and (iii), we get

$$I+f+f'=(5+\sqrt{24})^n+(5-\sqrt{24})^n$$

$$I+1=2p, \forall\ p \in N$$

$$= \text{Even integer} \quad \text{[from theorem 2]}$$

$\therefore$ $I=2p-1=$ Odd integer

Example 37. Show that the integral part of $(5\sqrt{5}+11)^{2n+1}$ is even, where $n \in N$.

Sol. $(5\sqrt{5}+11)^{2n+1}$ can be written as $(\sqrt{125}+11)^{2n+1}$

Now, let $I+f=(\sqrt{125}+11)^{2n+1}$ ...(i)

$0 \le f < 1$ ...(ii)

and let $f'=(\sqrt{125}-11)^{2n+1}$ ...(iii)

$0 < f' < 1$ ...(iv)

On subtracting Eq. (iii) from Eq. (i), we get

$$I+f-f'=(\sqrt{125}+11)^{2n+1}-(\sqrt{125}-11)^{2n+1}$$

$$I+0=2p, \forall\ p \in N$$

$$= \text{Even integer} \quad \text{[from theorem 1]}$$

$\therefore$ $I=2p=$ Even integer

Example 38. Let $R=(6\sqrt{6}+14)^{2n+1}$ and $f=R-[R]$, where $[\cdot]$ denotes the greatest integer function. Find the value of Rf, $n \in N$.

Sol. $(6\sqrt{6}+14)^{2n+1}$ can be written as $(\sqrt{216}+14)^{2n+1}$ and given that $f=R-[R]$

and $R=(6\sqrt{6}+14)^{2n+1}$

$=(\sqrt{216}+14)^{2n+1}$

$\therefore$ $[R]+f=(\sqrt{216}+14)^{2n+1}$ ...(i)

$0 \le f < 1$ ...(ii)

Let $f'=(\sqrt{216}-14)^{2n+1}$ ...(iii)

$0 < f' < 1$ ...(iv)

On subtracting Eq. (iii) from Eq. (i), we get

$$[R]+f-f'=(\sqrt{216}+14)^{2n+1}-(\sqrt{216}-14)^{2n+1}$$

$$[R]+0=2p, \forall\ p \in N = \text{Even integer [from theorem 1]}$$

$\therefore$ $f-f'=0$ or $f=f'$

Now, $Rf=Rf'$

$=(\sqrt{216}+14)^{2n+1}(\sqrt{216}-14)^{2n+1}$

$=(216-196)^{2n+1}$

$=(20)^{2n+1}$

Example 39. If $(7+4\sqrt{3})^n=s+t$, where n and s are positive integers and t is a proper fraction, show that $(1-t)(s+t)=1$.

Sol. $(7+4\sqrt{3})^n$ can be written as $(7+\sqrt{48})^n$

$\therefore$ $s+t=(7+\sqrt{48})^n$ ...(i)

$0 < t < 1$ ...(ii)

Now, let $t'=(7-\sqrt{48})^n$ ...(iii)

$0 < t' < 1$ ...(iv)

On adding Eqs. (i) and (iii), we get

$$s+t+t'=(7+\sqrt{48})^n+(7-\sqrt{48})^n$$

$$s+1=2p, \forall\ p \in N = \text{Even integer} \quad \text{[from theorem 2]}$$

$\therefore$ $t+t'=1$ or $1-t=t'$

Then, $(1-t)(s+t)=t'(s+t)=(7-\sqrt{48})^n(7+\sqrt{48})^n$ [from Eqs. (i) and (iii)]

$=(49-48)^n=(1)^n=1$

Example 40. If $x=(8+3\sqrt{7})^n$, where n is a natural number, prove that the integral part of x is an odd integer and also show that $x-x^2+x[x]=1$, where $[\cdot]$ denotes the greatest integer function.

Sol. $(8+3\sqrt{7})^n$ can be written as $(8+\sqrt{63})^n$

$\therefore$ $x=[x]+f$

or $[x]+f=(8+\sqrt{63})^n$ ...(i)

$0 \le f < 1$ ...(ii)

Now, let $f'=(8-\sqrt{63})^n$ ...(iii)

$0 < f' < 1$ ...(iv)

On adding Eqs. (i) and (iii), we get

$$[x]+f+f'=(8+\sqrt{63})^n+(8-\sqrt{63})^n$$

$$[x]+1=2p, \forall\ p \in N = \text{Even integer}$$

[from theorem 2]

$\therefore$ $[x]=2p-1=$ Odd integer

i.e., Integral part of $x=$ Odd integer

$\because$ $f+f'=1 \Rightarrow 1-f=f'$ ...(v)

LHS $=x-x^2+x[x]=x-x(x-[x])=x-xf$ $[\because x=[x]+f]$

$=x(1-f)=xf'$ [from Eq.(v)]

$=(8+\sqrt{63})^n(8-\sqrt{63})^n$ [from Eqs.(i) and (iii)]

$=(64-63)^n$

$=(1)^n=1=$ RHS

JEE SPIKE

If $x=[x]+f$ and $0<f'<1$ and if $[x]+f+f'=$ Integer, then addition and if $[x]+f-f'=$ Integer, the subtraction and values of $(f+f')$ and $(f-f')$ are 1 and 0, respectively.

6.6 Divisibility Problems

Type I

(i) $(x^n - a^n)$ is divisible by $(x - a)$, $\forall\, n \in N$.

(ii) $(x^n + a^n)$ is divisible by $(x + a)$, $\forall\, n \in$ Only odd natural numbers.

JEE SCANNER

Example Similar to PYQ Asked in JEE Main 2023

If $1992^{1998} - 1955^{1998} - 1938^{1998} + 1901^{1998}$ is divisible by n, then n is equal to ....

Sol. (1998) Let $P = 1992^{1998} - 1955^{1998} - 1938^{1998} + 1901^{1998}$

$$= \underbrace{(1992^{1998} - 1955^{1998})}_{\substack{\text{divisible by } (1992-1955)\\ \text{i.e. } 37}} - \underbrace{(1938^{1998} - 1901^{1998})}_{\substack{\text{divisible by } (1938-1901)\\ \text{i.e. } 37}}$$

$\therefore$ P is divisible by 37.

Also, $P = \underbrace{(1992^{1998} - 1938^{1998})}_{\substack{\text{divisible by } (1992-1938)\\ \text{i.e. } 54}} - \underbrace{(1955^{1998} - 1901^{1998})}_{\substack{\text{divisible by } (1955-1901)\\ \text{i.e. } 54}}$

$\therefore$ P is also divisible by 54.

Hence, P is divisible by 37×54, i.e. 1998.

$\therefore$ $n = 1998$

Skill Builder

If $72^{1002} - 66^{1002} - 55^{1002} + 49^{1002}$ is divisible by n, then n is equal to ....

For Sol.

■ **For more practice** See Q. 2 of Milestone Practice 6.2.

Example 41. Prove that $2222^{5555} + 5555^{2222}$ is divisible by 7.

Sol. We have, $2222^{5555} + 5555^{2222}$

$$= (2222^{5555} + 4^{5555}) + (5555^{2222} - 4^{2222}) - (4^{5555} - 4^{2222}) \quad \text{...(i)}$$

The number $(2222^{5555} + 4^{5555})$ is divisible by

$$2222 + 4 = 2226 = 7 \times 318,$$

which is divisible by 7 and the number $(5555^{2222} - 4^{2222})$ is divisible by

$$5555 - 4 = 5551 = 7 \times 793,$$

which is divisible by 7 and the number $(4^{5555} - 4^{2222}) = 4^{2222}(4^{3333} - 1) = 4^{2222}(64^{1111} - 1^{1111})$ is divisible by $64 - 1 = 63 = 7 \times 9$, which is divisible by 7.

Therefore, each brackets of Eq. (i) are divisible by 7.

Hence, $2222^{5555} + 5555^{2222}$ is divisible by 7.

Type II To show that an Expression is Divisible by An Integer

Solution Process

(i) If a, p, n and r are positive integers, first of all write $a^{pn+r} = a^{pn} \cdot a^r = (a^p)^n \cdot a^r$

(ii) If we will show that the given expression is divisible by c. Then, expression $a^p = \{1 + (a^p - 1)\}$, if some power of $(a^p - 1)$ has c as a factor.

or $a^p = \{2 + (a^p - 2)\}$, if some power of $(a^p - 2)$ has c as a factor.

or $a^p = \{3 + (a^p - 3)\}$, if some power of $(a^p - 3)$ has c as a factor.

$\vdots \quad \vdots \quad \vdots \quad \vdots \quad \vdots \quad \vdots$

or $a^p = \{k + (a^p - k)\}$, if some power of $(a^p - k)$ has c as a factor.

Example 42. If n is any positive integer, show that $2^{3n+3} - 7n - 8$ is divisible by 49.

Sol. Given expression

$$= 2^{3n+3} - 7n - 8 = 2^{3n} \cdot 2^3 - 7n - 8$$
$$= 8^n \cdot 8 - 7n - 8 = 8(1+7)^n - 7n - 8$$
$$= 8(1 + {}^nC_1 \cdot 7 + {}^nC_2 \cdot 7^2 + \dots + {}^nC_n \cdot 7^n) - 7n - 8$$
$$= 8 + 56n + 8({}^nC_2 \cdot 7^2 + \dots + {}^nC_n \cdot 7^n) - 7n - 8$$
$$= 49n + 8({}^nC_2 \cdot 7^2 + \dots + {}^nC_n \cdot 7^n)$$
$$= 49\{n + 8({}^nC_2 + \dots + {}^nC_n \cdot 7^{n-2})\}$$

Hence, $2^{3n+3} - 7n - 8$ is divisible by 49.

Example 43. If 10^n divides the number $101^{100} - 1$, find the greatest value of n.

Sol. We have, $101^{100} - 1 = (1 + 100)^{100} - 1$

$$= 1 + {}^{100}C_1 \cdot 100 + {}^{100}C_2 \cdot 100^2 + \dots + {}^{100}C_{100}\, 100^{100} - 1$$
$$= {}^{100}C_1 \cdot 100 + {}^{100}C_2 \cdot 100^2 + \dots + {}^{100}C_{100} \cdot 100^{100}$$
$$= (100)(100) + {}^{100}C_2 \cdot 100^2 + \dots + {}^{100}C_{100} \cdot 100^{100}$$
$$= (100)^2 [1 + {}^{100}C_2 + \dots + 100^{98}]$$
$$= 100^2\, k, \text{ where } k \text{ is a positive integer}$$

Therefore, $101^{100} - 1$ is divisible by 100^2 i.e., 10^4.

$\therefore \quad n = 4$

How to Find Remainder by Using Binomial Theorem

If a, p, n and r are positive integers, then to find the remainder when a^{pn+r} is divided by b, we adjust power of a to a^{pn+r} which is very close to b, say with difference 1 i.e. $b \pm 1$.

Also, the remainder is always positive. When number of the type $5n-2$ is divided by 5, then we have

$$5)\,5n-2\,(n$$
$$\underline{\;\;5n\;\;}$$
$$\underline{-2}$$

We can write $-2=-2-3+3=-5+3$

or $\dfrac{5n-2}{5}=\dfrac{5n-5+3}{5}=n-1+\dfrac{3}{5}$

Hence, the remainder is 3.

Example 44. If 7^{103} is divided by 25, find the remainder.

Sol. We have, $7^{103}=7\cdot 7^{102}=7\cdot(7^2)^{51}=7\,(49)^{51}=7\,(50-1)^{51}$

$=7\,[(50)^{51}-{}^{51}C_1\,(50)^{50}+{}^{51}C_2\,(50)^{49}-\ldots-1]$

$=7\,[(50)^{51}-{}^{51}C_1\,(50)^{50}+{}^{51}C_2\,(50)^{49}-\ldots+{}^{51}C_{50}\,(50)]-7-18+18$

$=7\,[50\,((50)^{50}-{}^{51}C_1(50)^{49}+{}^{51}C_2(50)^{48}-\ldots+{}^{51}C_{50})]-25+18$

$=7\,[50k]-25+18$, where k is an integer.

$=25\,[14k-1]+18=25p+18$ [where p is an integer]

Now, $\dfrac{7^{103}}{25}=p+\dfrac{18}{25}$. Hence, the remainder is 18.

Example 45. Find the remainder, when $5^{5^{5^{\cdots^{5}}}}$ (24 times 5) is divided by 24.

Sol. Here, $5^{5^{5^{\cdots^{5}}}}$ (23 times 5) is an odd natural number.

Let $5^{5^{5^{\cdots^{5}}}}$ (23 times 5) $=2m+1$

Now, let $x=5^{5^{5^{\cdots^{5}}}}$ (24 times 5) $=5^{2m+1}=5\cdot 5^{2m}$, where m is a natural number.

$\therefore\quad x=5\cdot(5^2)^m=5\,(24+1)^m$

$=5\,[{}^mC_0\,(24)^m+{}^mC_1\,(24)^{m-1}+\ldots+{}^mC_{m-1}\,(24)+1]$

$=5\,(24k+1)=24\,(5k)+5$, where k is positive integer

$\therefore\quad \dfrac{x}{24}=5k+\dfrac{5}{24}$

Hence, the remainder is 5.

Example 46. If 7 divides $32^{32^{32}}$, then find the remainder.

Sol. We have, $32=2^5$

$\therefore\quad 32^{32}=(2^5)^{32}=2^{160}=(3-1)^{160}$

$={}^{160}C_0\,(3)^{160}-{}^{160}C_1\,(3)^{159}+\ldots-{}^{160}C_{159}\,(3)+1$

$=3\,(3^{159}-{}^{160}C_1\,(3)^{158}+\ldots-{}^{160}C_{159})+1$

$=3m+1,\ m\in I^+$

Now, $32^{32^{32}}=32^{3m+1}=2^{5\,(3m+1)}=2^{15m+5}$

$=2^2\cdot 2^{3\,(5m+1)}=4\,(8)^{5m+1}=4\,(7+1)^{5m+1}$

$=4[\,{}^{5m+1}C_0\,(7)^{5m+1}+{}^{5m+1}C_1\,(7)^{5m}+{}^{5m+1}C_2\,(7)^{5m-1}+\ldots+{}^{5m+1}C_{5m}\,(7)+1]$

$=4[7\,({}^{5m+1}C_0(7)^{5m}+{}^{5m+1}C_1(7)^{5m-1}+\ldots+{}^{5m+1}C_{5m})+1]$

$=4\,[7k+1]$, where k is positive integer

$=28k+4$

$\therefore\quad \dfrac{32^{32^{32}}}{7}=4k+\dfrac{4}{7}$

Hence, the remainder is 4.

How to Find Last Digit, Last Two Digits, Last Three Digits, ... and so on.

If a, p, n and r are positive integers, then a^{pn+r} is adjust of the form $(10k\pm1)^m$, where k and m are positive integers. For last digit, take 10 common. For last two digits, take 100 common, for last three digits, take 1000 common , ... and so on.

i.e. $(10k\pm1)^m=(10k)^m+{}^mC_1\,(10k)^{m-1}\,(\pm1)+{}^mC_2\,(10k)^{m-2}\,(\pm1)^2+\ldots+{}^mC_{m-2}\,(10k)^2\,(\pm1)^{m-2}+{}^mC_{m-1}(10k)\,(\pm1)^{m-1}+(\pm1)^m$

For last digit $=10\lambda+(\pm1)^m$

For last two digits $=100\mu+{}^mC_{m-1}\,(10k)\,(\pm1)^{m-1}+(\pm1)^m$

For last three digits $=1000\nu+{}^mC_{m-2}(10k)^2(\pm1)^{m-2}+{}^mC_{m-1}\,(10k)\,(\pm1)^{m-1}+(\pm1)^m$ and so on where $\lambda,\mu,\nu\in I$.

Example 47. Find the last two digits of 3^{400}.

Sol. We have, $3^{400}=(3^2)^{200}=(9)^{200}=(10-1)^{200}$

$=(10)^{200}-{}^{200}C_1\,(10)^{199}+{}^{200}C_2\,(10)^{198}-{}^{200}C_3\,(10)^{197}+\ldots+{}^{200}C_{198}\,(10)^2-{}^{200}C_{199}\,(10)+1$

$=100\mu-{}^{200}C_{199}\,(10)+1$, where $\mu\in I$

$=100\mu-{}^{200}C_1\,(10)+1=100\mu-2000+1$

$=100\,(\mu-20)+1=100\,p+1$, where p is an integer.

Hence, the last two digits of 3^{400} is $00+1=01$.

Example 48. If the number is 17^{256}, find the

(i) last digit.

(ii) last two digits.

(iii) last three digits of 17^{256}.

Sol. Since, $17^{256}=(17^2)^{128}=(289)^{128}=(290-1)^{128}$

$\therefore\ 17^{256}={}^{128}C_0\,(290)^{128}-{}^{128}C_1\,(290)^{127}+{}^{128}C_2\,(290)^{126}-{}^{128}C_3\,(290)^{125}+\ldots-{}^{128}C_{125}\,(290)^3+{}^{128}C_{126}\,(290)^2-{}^{128}C_{127}\,(290)+1$

(i) **For last digit**

$$17^{256} = 290[{}^{128}C_0 (290)^{127} - {}^{128}C_1(290)^{126} + {}^{128}C_2 (290)^{125} - \dots - {}^{128}C_{127} (1)] + 1$$
$$= 10(k) + 1, \text{ where } k \text{ is an integer.}$$

$\therefore$ Last digit $= 0 + 1 = 1$

(ii) **For last two digits,**

$$17^{256} = (290)^2 [{}^{128}C_0 (290)^{126} - {}^{128}C_1 (290)^{125} + {}^{128}C_2 (290)^{124} - \dots + {}^{128}C_{126} (1)] - {}^{128}C_{127} (290) + 1$$
$$= 100m - {}^{128}C_{127} (290) + 1, \text{ where } m \text{ is an integer.}$$
$$= 100m - {}^{128}C_1 (290) + 1 = 100m - 128 \times 290 + 1$$
$$= 100m - 128 \times (300 - 10) + 1$$
$$= 100(m - 384) + 1281$$
$$= 100n + 1281, \text{ where } n \text{ is an integer.}$$

$\therefore$ Last two digits $= 00 + 81 = 81$

(iii) **For last three digits,**

$$17^{256} = (290)^3 [{}^{128}C_0 (290)^{125} - {}^{128}C_1 (290)^{124} + {}^{128}C_2 (290)^{123} - \dots - {}^{128}C_{125} (1)] + {}^{128}C_{126} (290)^2 - {}^{128}C_{127} (290) + 1$$
$$= 1000m + {}^{128}C_{126} (290)^2 - {}^{128}C_{127} (290) + 1$$

where, m is an integer

$$= 1000m + {}^{128}C_2 (290)^2 - {}^{128}C_1 (290) + 1$$
$$= 1000m + \frac{(128)(127)}{2}(290)^2 - 128 \times 290 + 1$$
$$= 1000m + (128)(127)(290)(145) - (128)(290) + 1$$
$$= 1000m + (128)(290)(127 \times 145 - 1) + 1$$
$$= 1000m + (128)(290)(18414) + 1$$
$$= 1000m + 683527680 + 1$$
$$= 1000m + 683527000 + 680 + 1$$
$$= 1000(m + 683527) + 681$$

$\therefore$ Last three digits $= 000 + 681 = 681$

Two Important Results

(i) $2 \le \left(1 + \frac{1}{n}\right)^n < 3, n \ge 1, n \in N$

(ii) If $n > 6$, then $\left(\frac{n}{3}\right)^n < n! < \left(\frac{n}{2}\right)^n$

Example 49. Find the positive integer just greater than $(1 + 0.0001)^{10000}$.

Sol. $(1 + 0.0001)^{10000} = \left(1 + \frac{1}{10000}\right)^{10000}$

We know that, $2 \le \left(1 + \frac{1}{n}\right)^n < 3,\ n \ge 1,\ n \in N$ [Result (i)]

Hence, positive integer just greater than $(1 + 0.0001)^{10000}$ is 3.

Example 50. Find the greater number in 300! and $\sqrt{300^{300}}$.

Sol. Since, $(100)^{150} > 3^{150}$

$$\Rightarrow (100)^{150} \cdot (100)^{150} > 3^{150} \cdot (100)^{150}$$
$$\Rightarrow (100)^{300} > (300)^{150}$$
$$\text{or} \quad (100)^{300} > \sqrt{300^{300}} \quad \dots(i)$$

Using result (ii), $\left(\frac{n}{3}\right)^n < n!$

Putting $n = 300$, we get

$$(100)^{300} < 300! \quad \dots(ii)$$

From Eqs. (i) and (ii), we get

$$\sqrt{300^{300}} < (100)^{300} < 300!$$
$$\Rightarrow \sqrt{300^{300}} < 300!$$

Hence, the greater number is 300 !.

Example 51. Find the greater number in 100^{100} and (300)!.

Sol. Using Result (ii),

We know that, $\left(\frac{n}{3}\right)^n < n!$

Putting $n = 300$, we get

$$(100)^{300} < (300)! \quad \dots(i)$$

But $$(100)^{100} < (100)^{300} \quad \dots(ii)$$

From Eqs. (i) and (ii), we get

$$(100)^{100} < (100)^{300} < (300)!$$
$$\Rightarrow (100)^{100} < (300)!$$

Hence, the greater number is (300) !.

6.7 Use of Complex Numbers in Binomial Theorem

If $\theta \in R, n \in N$ and $i = \sqrt{-1}$, then

$$(\cos\theta + i\sin\theta)^n = {}^nC_0 (\cos\theta)^{n-0} (i\sin\theta)^0 + {}^nC_1 (\cos\theta)^{n-1} (i\sin\theta)^1 + {}^nC_2 (\cos\theta)^{n-2} (i\sin\theta)^2 + {}^nC_3 (\cos\theta)^{n-3} (i\sin\theta)^3 + \dots$$

or $$\cos n\theta + i\sin n\theta = \cos^n\theta + i \cdot {}^nC_1 (\cos\theta)^{n-1} \sin\theta - {}^nC_2 (\cos\theta)^{n-2} \sin^2\theta - i \cdot {}^nC_3 (\cos\theta)^{n-3} \sin^3\theta + \dots$$

On comparing real and imaginary parts, we get

$$\cos n\theta = \cos^n\theta - {}^nC_2 (\cos\theta)^{n-2} \sin^2\theta - {}^nC_4 (\cos\theta)^{n-4} \sin^4\theta - \dots$$

and $$\sin n\theta = {}^nC_1 (\cos\theta)^{n-1} \sin\theta - {}^nC_3 (\cos\theta)^{n-3} \sin^3\theta + {}^nC_5 (\cos\theta)^{n-5} \sin^5\theta - \dots$$

Example 52. If $(1+x)^n = C_0 + C_1 x + C_2 x^2 + C_3 x^3 + C_4 x^4 + \ldots$, find the values of

(i) $C_0 - C_2 + C_4 - C_6 + \ldots$

(ii) $C_1 - C_3 + C_5 - C_7 + \ldots$

(iii) $C_0 + C_3 + C_6 + \ldots$

Sol. $\because (1+x)^n = C_0 + C_1 x + C_2 x^2 + C_3 x^3 + C_4 x^4 + C_5 x^5 + \ldots$

On putting $x = i$, where $i = \sqrt{-1}$, then

$$(1+i)^n = C_0 + C_1 i + C_2 i^2 + C_3 i^3 + C_4 i^4 + C_5 i^5 + \ldots$$
$$= (C_0 - C_2 + C_4 - \ldots) + i(C_1 - C_3 + C_5 - \ldots) \quad \ldots(\text{i})$$

Also, $(1+i)^n = \left[\sqrt{2}\left(\frac{1}{\sqrt{2}} + \frac{i}{\sqrt{2}}\right)\right]^n$

$$= 2^{n/2}\left(\cos\frac{\pi}{4} + i \sin\frac{\pi}{4}\right)^n$$
$$= 2^{n/2}\left(\cos\frac{n\pi}{4} + i \sin\frac{n\pi}{4}\right) \quad \ldots(\text{ii})$$

From Eqs. (i) and (ii), we get

$$(C_0 - C_2 + C_4 - \ldots) + i(C_1 - C_3 + C_5 - \ldots) = 2^{n/2}\cos\left(\frac{n\pi}{4}\right) + i \cdot 2^{n/2}\sin\left(\frac{n\pi}{4}\right)$$

On comparing real and imaginary parts, we get

$$C_0 - C_2 + C_4 - \ldots = 2^{n/2}\cos\left(\frac{n\pi}{4}\right) \quad [\text{part (i)}]$$
$$C_1 - C_3 + C_5 - \ldots = 2^{n/2}\sin\left(\frac{n\pi}{4}\right) \quad [\text{part (ii)}]$$

We have, $(1+x)^n = C_0 + C_1 x + C_2 x^2 + C_3 x^3 + C_4 x^4 + C_5 x^5 + C_6 x^6 + \ldots$

Putting $x = 1, \omega, \omega^2$ (cube roots of unity) and adding, we get

$$3(C_0 + C_3 + C_6 + \ldots) = 2^n + (1+\omega)^n + (1+\omega^2)^n$$
$$= 2^n + (-\omega^2)^n + (-\omega)^n$$
$$= 2^n + (-1)^n(\omega^{2n} + \omega^n)$$
$$= 2^n + (-1)^n\left\{e^{\frac{4\pi i n}{3}} + e^{\frac{2\pi i n}{3}}\right\}$$
$$= 2^n + (-1)^n \cdot e^{n\pi i} \cdot 2\cos\left(\frac{n\pi}{3}\right)$$
$$= 2^n + (-1)^n \cdot (-1)^n \cdot 2\cos\left(\frac{n\pi}{3}\right)$$
$$= 2^n + (-1)^{2n} \cdot 2\cos\left(\frac{n\pi}{3}\right)$$
$$= 2^n + 2\cos\left(\frac{n\pi}{3}\right)$$
$$\therefore \quad C_0 + C_3 + C_6 + \ldots = \frac{1}{3}\left\{2^n + 2\cos\left(\frac{n\pi}{3}\right)\right\}$$

Example 53. Find the value of

$${}^{4n}C_0 + {}^{4n}C_4 + {}^{4n}C_8 + \ldots + {}^{4n}C_{4n}.$$

Sol. $\because 4 - 0 = 8 - 4 = \ldots = 4$

$\therefore$ Four roots of unity $(1)^{1/4}$ are $1, -1, i, -i$, we have

$$(1+x)^{4n} = {}^{4n}C_0 + {}^{4n}C_1 x + {}^{4n}C_2 x^2 + {}^{4n}C_3 x^3 + \ldots$$

Putting $x = 1, -1, i, -i$ and then adding, we get

$$4({}^{4n}C_0 + {}^{4n}C_4 + {}^{4n}C_8 + \ldots) = 2^{4n} + 0 + (1+i)^{4n} + (1-i)^{4n}$$
$$= 2^{4n} + (2i)^{2n} + (-2i)^{2n}$$
$$= 2^{4n} + 2^{2n}(-1)^n + 2^{2n}(-1)^n$$
$$= 2^{4n} + (-1)^n \cdot 2^{2n+1}$$
$$\therefore \quad {}^{4n}C_0 + {}^{4n}C_4 + {}^{4n}C_8 + \ldots = 2^{4n-2} + (-1)^n \cdot 2^{2n-1}$$

JEE Focus Points

Concept Inside Video

If $(1+x)^n = C_0 + C_1 x + C_2 x^2 + C_3 x^3 + \ldots + C_n x^n$, then

- $C_0 + C_4 + C_8 + C_{12} + \ldots = \frac{1}{2}\left\{2^{n-1} + 2^{n/2}\cos\left(\frac{n\pi}{4}\right)\right\}$
- $C_1 + C_5 + C_9 + C_{13} + \ldots = \frac{1}{2}\left\{2^{n-1} + 2^{n/2}\sin\left(\frac{n\pi}{4}\right)\right\}$
- $C_0 + C_6 + C_{12} + \ldots = \frac{1}{3}\left\{2^{n-1}\cos\left(\frac{n\pi}{4}\right) + 3^{n/2}\cos\left(\frac{n\pi}{6}\right)\right\}$

6.8 Multinomial Theorem

If n is a positive integer and $x_1, x_2, x_3, \ldots, x_k \in C$, then the coefficient of $x_1^{a_1} \cdot x_2^{a_2} \cdot x_3^{a_3} \ldots x_k^{a_k}$ in the expansion of $(x_1 + x_2 + x_3 + \ldots + x_k)^n$ is $\sum \frac{n!}{(a_1!)(a_2!)(a_3!)\ldots(a_k!)}$, where, $a_1, a_2, a_3, \ldots, a_k$ are all non-negative integers such that $a_1 + a_2 + a_3 + \ldots + a_k = n$.

In Particular

(i) $(a+b+c)^n = \sum \frac{n!}{(\alpha!)(\beta!)(\gamma!)} a^\alpha b^\beta c^\gamma$ such that $\alpha + \beta + \gamma = n$

(ii) $(a+b+c+d)^n = \sum \frac{n!}{(\alpha!)(\beta!)(\gamma!)(\delta!)} a^\alpha b^\beta c^\gamma d^\delta$ such that $\alpha + \beta + \gamma + \delta = n$

Example 54. Find the coefficient of $a^4 b^3 c^2 d$ in the expansion of $(a - b + c - d)^{10}$.

Sol. The coefficient of $a^4 b^3 c^2 d$ in the expansion of

$$(a - b + c - d)^{10} \text{ is } (-1)^4 \frac{10!}{4!\,3!\,2!\,1!} = 12600$$

[powers of b and d are 3 and 1 $\therefore (-1)^3(-1)$]

Example 55. Find the coefficient of $a^3b^4c^5$ in the expansion of $(bc+ca+ab)^6$.

Sol. In this case, write $a^3b^4c^5 = (ab)^x (bc)^y (ca)^z$

$\therefore \quad a^3b^4c^5 = a^{z+x} \cdot b^{x+y} \cdot c^{y+z}$

$\Rightarrow \quad z+x=3, x+y=4, y+z=5$

On adding all, we get $2(x+y+z)=12$

$\therefore \quad x+y+z=6$

Then, $x=1, y=3, z=2$

Therefore, the coefficient of $a^3b^4c^5$ in the expansion of $(bc+ca+ab)^6$ or the coefficient of $(ab)^1(bc)^3(ca)^2$ in the expansion of $(bc+ca+ab)^6$ is $\frac{6!}{1!3!2!}$, i.e. 60.

Alternate Solution

Coefficient of $a^3b^4c^5$ in the expansion of $(bc+ca+ab)^6$

$= $ Coefficient of $a^3b^4c^5$ in the expansion of $(abc)^6\left(\frac{1}{a}+\frac{1}{b}+\frac{1}{c}\right)^6$

$= $ Coefficient of $\left(\frac{1}{a}\right)^3\left(\frac{1}{b}\right)^2\left(\frac{1}{c}\right)^1$ in the expansion

of $\left(\frac{1}{a}+\frac{1}{b}+\frac{1}{c}\right)^6$ is $\frac{6!}{3!2!1!}=60$

Number of Distinct or Dissimilar Terms in the Multinomial Expansion

Statement The number of distinct or dissimilar terms in the multinomial expansion of $(x_1+x_2+x_3+\ldots+x_k)^n$ is ${}^{n+k-1}C_{k-1}$.

Proof We have, $(x_1+x_2+x_3+\ldots+x_k)^n$

$$=\sum \frac{n!}{(\alpha_1!)(\alpha_2!)(\alpha_3!)\ldots(\alpha_k!)} x_1^{\alpha_1} x_2^{\alpha_2} x_3^{\alpha_3} \ldots x_k^{\alpha_k}$$

where, $\alpha_1, \alpha_2, \alpha_3, \ldots, \alpha_k$ are non-negative integers such that

$$\alpha_1+\alpha_2+\alpha_3+\ldots+\alpha_k=n \quad \ldots(i)$$

Here, the number of terms in the expansion of

$(x_1+x_2+x_3+\ldots+x_k)^n$

= The number of non-negative integral solutions of the Eq. (i)

$= {}^{n+k-1}C_{k-1}$

Example 56. Find the total number of distinct or dissimilar terms in the expansion of $(x+y+z+w)^n$, $n \in N$.

Sol. The total number of distinct or dissimilar terms in the expansion of $(x+y+z+w)^n$ is

$$= {}^{n+4-1}C_{4-1} = {}^{n+3}C_3$$

$$= \frac{(n+3)(n+2)(n+1)}{1\cdot 2\cdot 3}$$

$$= \frac{(n+1)(n+2)(n+3)}{6}$$

Greatest Coefficient in Multinomial Expansion

The greatest coefficient in the expansion of $(x_1+x_2+x_3+\ldots+x_k)^n$ is $\frac{n!}{(q!)^{k-r}((q+1)!)^r}$, where q is the quotient and r is the remainder when n is divided by k

i.e. $\quad k)\,n\,(q$

$\quad\quad \overline{r}$

Example 57. Find the greatest coefficient in the expansion of $(a+b+c+d)^{15}$.

Sol. Here, $n=15$ and $k=4$ [$\because$ a, b, c, d are four terms]

$4)\,15\,(3$

$\quad 12$

$\quad \overline{3}$

$\therefore \quad q=3$ and $r=3$

Hence, greatest coefficient $= \frac{15!}{(3!)^1(4!)^3}$

Coefficient of x^r in Multinomial Expansion

If n is a positive integer and $a_1, a_2, a_3, \ldots, a_k \in C$, then coefficient of x^r in the expansion of $(a_1+a_2x+a_3x^2+\ldots+a_kx^{k-1})^n$, is

$$\sum \frac{n!}{(\alpha_1!)(\alpha_2!)(\alpha_3!)\ldots(\alpha_k!)} a_1^{\alpha_1} a_2^{\alpha_2} a_3^{\alpha_3} \ldots a_k^{\alpha_k}$$

where, $\alpha_1, \alpha_2, \alpha_3, \ldots, \alpha_k$ are non-negative integers such that

$$\alpha_1+\alpha_2+\alpha_3+\ldots+\alpha_k=n$$

and $\quad \alpha_2+2\alpha_3+3\alpha_4+\ldots+(k-1)\alpha_k=r$

Example 58. Find the coefficient of x^7 in the expansion of $(1+3x-2x^3)^{10}$.

Sol. Coefficient of x^7 in the expansion of $(1+3x-2x^3)^{10}$ is

$$= \sum \frac{10!}{\alpha!\,\beta!\,\gamma!} (1)^\alpha (3)^\beta (-2)^\gamma$$

where, $\alpha+\beta+\gamma=10$ and $\beta+3\gamma=7$

The possible values of α, β and γ are given below

α	β	γ
3	7	0
5	4	1
7	1	2

$\therefore$ Coefficient of x^7

$$= \frac{10!}{3!7!0!}(1)^3(3)^7(-2)^0 + \frac{10!}{5!4!1!}(1)^5(3)^4(-2)^1 + \frac{10!}{7!1!2!}(1)^7(3)^1(-2)^2$$

$= 262440 - 204120 + 4320$
$= 62640$

6.9 Use of Differentiation

This method applied only when the numericals occur as the product of the binomial coefficients, if

$$(1+x)^n = C_0 + C_1 x + C_2 x^2 + C_3 x^3 + \dots + C_n x^n$$

Solution Process

(i) If last term of the series leaving the plus or minus sign is m, then divide m by n. If q is the quotient and r is the remainder.

i.e. $m = nq + r$ or $n)\,m\,(q$, $\underline{nq}$, $\underline{r}$

Then, replace x by x^q in the given series and multiplying both sides of the expression by x^r.

(ii) After this, differentiate both sides w.r.t. x and put $x = 1$ or -1 or $i (i = \sqrt{-1})$, etc. According to the given series.

(iii) If product of two numericals (or square of numericals) or three numericals (or cube of numericals), then differentiate twice or thrice.

Example 59. If $(1+x)^n = C_0 + C_1 x + C_2 x^2 + \dots + C_n x^n$, prove that $C_1 + 2C_2 + 3C_3 + \dots + nC_n = n \cdot 2^{n-1}$.

Sol. Here, last term of $C_1 + 2C_2 + 3C_3 + \dots + nC_n$ is nC_n i.e., n and last term with positive sign.

Then, $n = n \cdot 1 + 0$ or $n)\,n\,(1$, $\underline{n}$, $\underline{0}$

Here, $q = 1$ and $r = 0$

Then, the given series is

$$(1+x)^n = C_0 + C_1 x + C_2 x^2 + C_3 x^3 + \dots + C_n x^n$$

Differentiating both sides w.r.t. x, we get

$$n(1+x)^{n-1} = 0 + C_1 + 2C_2 x + 3C_3 x^2 + \dots + nC_n x^{n-1}$$

Putting $x = 1$, we get

$$n \cdot 2^{n-1} = C_1 + 2C_2 + 3C_3 + \dots + nC_n$$

or $\quad C_1 + 2C_2 + 3C_3 + \dots + nC_n = n \cdot 2^{n-1}$

Example 60. If $(1+x)^n = C_0 + C_1 x + C_2 x^2 + \dots + C_n x^n$, prove that

$$C_0 + 2C_1 + 3C_2 + \dots + (n+1)C_n = (n+2)2^{n-1}.$$

Sol. Here, last term of $C_0 + 2C_1 + 3C_2 + \dots + (n+1)C_n$ is $(n+1)C_n$ i.e. $(n+1)$ and last term with positive sign.

and $\quad n + 1 = n \cdot 1 + 1$

or $\quad n)\,n+1\,(1$, $\underline{-n}$, $\underline{1}$

Here, $q = 1$ and $r = 1$

The given series is

$$(1+x)^n = C_0 + C_1 x + C_2 x^2 + \dots + C_n x^n$$

Now, replacing x by x^1 and multiplying both sides by x, we get

$$x(1+x)^n = C_0 x + C_1 x^2 + C_2 x^3 + \dots + C_n x^{n+1}$$

Differentiating both sides w.r.t. x, we get

$$x \cdot n(1+x)^{n-1} + (1+x)^n \cdot 1 = C_0 + 2C_1 x + 3C_2 x^2 + \dots + (n+1)C_n x^n$$

Putting $x = 1$, we get

$$n(2)^{n-1} + 2^n = C_0 + 2C_1 + 3C_2 + \dots + (n+1)C_n$$

or $\quad C_0 + 2C_1 + 3C_2 + \dots + (n+1)C_n = (n+2)2^{n-1}$

Example 61. If $(1+x)^n = C_0 + C_1 x + C_2 x^2 + \dots + C_n x^n$, prove that $C_0 + 3C_1 + 5C_2 + \dots + (2n+1)C_n = (n+1)2^n$.

Sol. Here, last term of $C_0 + 3C_1 + 5C_2 + \dots + (2n+1)C_n$ is $(2n+1)C_n$ i.e. $(2n+1)$ and last term with positive sign.

Then, $\quad 2n + 1 = n \cdot 2 + 1$

or $\quad n)\,2n+1\,(2$, $\underline{-2n}$, $\underline{1}$

Here, $q = 2$ and $r = 1$

The given series is

$$(1+x)^n = C_0 + C_1 x + C_2 x^2 + \dots + C_n x^n$$

Now, replacing x by x^2, we get

$$(1+x^2)^n = C_0 + C_1 x^2 + C_2 x^4 + \dots + C_n x^{2n}$$

On multiplying both sides by x^1, we get

$$x(1+x^2)^n = C_0 x + C_1 x^3 + C_2 x^5 + \dots + C_n x^{2n+1}$$

On differentiating both sides w.r.t. x, we get

$$x \cdot n(1+x^2)^{n-1} \cdot 2x + (1+x^2)^n \cdot 1 = C_0 + 3C_1 x^2 + 5C_2 x^4 + \dots + (2n+1)C_n x^{2n}$$

Putting $x = 1$, we get

$$n \cdot 2^{n-1} \cdot 2 + 2^n = C_0 + 3C_1 + 5C_2 + \dots + (2n+1)C_n$$

or $\quad C_0 + 3C_1 + 5C_2 + \dots + (2n+1)C_n = (n+1)2^n$

Example 62. If $(1+x)^n = C_0 + C_1 x + C_2 x^2 + \ldots + C_n x^n$, prove that
$1^2 \cdot C_1 + 2^2 \cdot C_2 + 3^2 \cdot C_3 + \ldots + n^2 \cdot C_n = n(n+1)2^{n-2}$.

Sol. Here, last term of $1^2 \cdot C_1 + 2^2 \cdot C_2 + 3^2 \cdot C_3 + \ldots + n^2 \cdot C_n$ is $n^2 \cdot C_n$ i.e., n^2. Linear factors of n^2 are n and n; [start always with greater factor] and last term with positive sign.

and $n = n \cdot 1 + 0$ or $n)\,n\,(1$
$$\begin{array}{r} -n \\ \hline 0 \end{array}$$

Here, $q = 1$ and $r = 0$. Then, the given series is
$$(1+x)^n = C_0 + C_1 x + C_2 x^2 + C_3 x^3 + \ldots + C_n x^n$$
On differentiating both sides w.r.t. x, we get
$$n(1+x)^{n-1} = C_1 + 2C_2 x + 3C_3 x^2 + \ldots + n\,C_n x^{n-1} \quad \ldots(i)$$
and in last term, numerical is $n\,C_n$ i.e., n and power of $(1+x)$ is $n-1$.

Then, $n = (n-1) \cdot 1 + 1$ or $n-1)\,n\,(1$
$$\begin{array}{r} n-1 \\ -\;+ \\ \hline 1 \end{array}$$

Here, $q = 1$ and $r = 1$

Now, multiplying both sides by x in Eq. (i), then
$$nx(1+x)^{n-1} = C_1 x + 2C_2 x^2 + 3C_3 x^3 + \ldots + n\,C_n x^n$$
Differentiating on both sides w.r.t. x, we get
$$n\{x \cdot (n-1)(1+x)^{n-2} + (1+x)^{n-1} \cdot 1\}$$
$$= C_1 \cdot 1 + 2^2 C_2 x + 3^2 C_3 x^2 + \ldots + n^2 C_n x^{n-1}$$
Putting $x = 1$, we get
$$n\{1 \cdot (n-1) \cdot 2^{n-2} + 2^{n-1}\} = 1^2 \cdot C_1 + 2^2 \cdot C_2 + 3^2 \cdot C_3 + \ldots + n^2 \cdot C_n$$
or $1^2 \cdot C_1 + 2^2 \cdot C_2 + 3^2 \cdot C_3 + \ldots + n^2 \cdot C_n = n(n+1)2^{n-2}$

Alternate Solution

LHS $= 1^2 \cdot C_1 + 2^2 \cdot C_2 + 3^2 \cdot C_3 + \ldots + n^2 \cdot C_n$
$$= \sum_{r=1}^{n} r^2 \cdot {}^nC_r = \sum_{r=1}^{n} r^2 \cdot \frac{n}{r} \cdot {}^{n-1}C_{r-1}$$
$$\left[\because {}^nC_r = \frac{n}{r} \cdot {}^{n-1}C_{r-1}\right]$$
$$= n\sum_{r=1}^{n} r \cdot {}^{n-1}C_{r-1} = n\sum_{r=1}^{n} \{(r-1)+1\} \cdot {}^{n-1}C_{r-1}$$
$$= n\sum_{r=1}^{n} (r-1) \cdot {}^{n-1}C_{r-1} + n\sum_{r=1}^{n} {}^{n-1}C_{r-1}$$
$$= n\sum_{r=1}^{n} (n-1) \cdot {}^{n-2}C_{r-2} + n\sum_{r=1}^{n} {}^{n-1}C_{r-1}$$
$$= n(n-1)\sum_{r=1}^{n} {}^{n-2}C_{r-2} + n\sum_{r=1}^{n} {}^{n-1}C_{r-1}$$
$$= n(n-1)(0 + {}^{n-2}C_0 + {}^{n-2}C_1 + {}^{n-2}C_2 + \ldots + {}^{n-2}C_{n-2}) + n({}^{n-1}C_0 + {}^{n-1}C_1 + {}^{n-1}C_2 + \ldots + {}^{n-1}C_{n-1})$$
$$= n(n-1) \cdot 2^{n-2} + n \cdot 2^{n-1} = n(n+1)2^{n-2} = \text{RHS}$$

Example 63. If $(1+x)^n = C_0 + C_1 x + C_2 x^2 + \ldots + C_n x^n$, prove that $(1 \cdot 2)\,C_2 + (2 \cdot 3)\,C_3 + \ldots + \{(n-1) \cdot n\}\,C_n = n(n-1)2^{n-2}$.

Sol. Here, last term of
$(1 \cdot 2)\,C_2 + (2 \cdot 3)\,C_3 + \ldots + \{(n-1) \cdot n\}\,C_n$ is $(n-1)n\,C_n$ i.e. $(n-1)\,n$

[start with greater factor here greater factor is n] and last term with positive sign, then $n = n \cdot 1 + 0$

or $n)\,n\,(1$
$$\begin{array}{r} -n \\ \hline 0 \end{array}$$

Here, $q = 1$ and $r = 0$

The given series is
$$(1+x)^n = C_0 + C_1 x + C_2 x^2 + C_3 x^3 + \ldots + C_n x^n$$
Differentiating on both sides w.r.t. x, we get
$$n(1+x)^{n-1} = 0 + C_1 + 2C_2 x + 3C_3 x^2 + \ldots + n\,C_n x^{n-1}$$
Again, differentiating on both sides w.r.t. x, we get
$$n(n-1)(1+x)^{n-2} = 0 + 0 + (1 \cdot 2)\,C_2 + (2 \cdot 3)\,C_3 x + \ldots + \{(n-1) \cdot n\}\,C_n x^{n-2}$$
Putting $x = 1$, we get
$$n(n-1)(1+1)^{n-2} = (1 \cdot 2)\,C_2 + (2 \cdot 3)\,C_3 + \ldots + \{(n-1)\,n\} \cdot C_n$$
or $(1 \cdot 2)\,C_2 + (2 \cdot 3)\,C_3 + \ldots + \{(n-1)\,n\} \cdot C_n = n(n-1)2^{n-2}$

Example 64. If $(1+x)^n = C_0 + C_1 x + C_2 x^2 + C_3 x^3 + \ldots + C_n x^n$, prove that
$C_0 - 2C_1 + 3C_2 - 4C_3 + \ldots + (-1)^n (n+1)\,C_n = 0$.

Sol. Numerical value of last term of
$C_0 - 2C_1 + 3C_2 - 4C_3 + \ldots + (-1)^n (n+1)\,C_n$ is $(n+1)\,C_n$ i.e. $(n+1)$, then
$n + 1 = n \cdot 1 + 1$ or $n)\,n+1\,(1$
$$\begin{array}{r} -n \\ \hline 1 \end{array}$$

Here, $q = 1$ and $r = 1$

The given series is
$$(1+x)^n = C_0 + C_1 x + C_2 x^2 + C_3 x^3 + \ldots + C_n x^n$$
On multiplying both sides by x, we get
$$x(1+x)^n = C_0 x + C_1 x^2 + C_2 x^3 + C_3 x^4 + \ldots + C_n x^{n+1}$$
On differentiating both sides w.r.t. x, we get
$$x \cdot n(1+x)^{n-1} + (1+x)^n \cdot 1 = C_0 + 2C_1 x + 3C_2 x^2 + 4C_3 x^3 + \ldots + (n+1)\,C_n x^n$$
Putting $x = -1$, we get
$$0 = C_0 - 2C_1 + 3C_2 - 4C_3 + \ldots + (-1)^n (n+1)\,C_n$$
or $\quad C_0 - 2C_1 + 3C_2 - 4C_3 + \ldots + (-1)^n (n+1)\,C_n = 0$

Example 65. If $(1+x)^n = C_0 + C_1 x + C_2 x^2 + C_3 x^3 + \ldots + C_n x^n$ prove that $C_1 - 2C_2 + 3C_3 - \ldots + (-1)^{n-1} n C_n = 0.$

Sol. Numerical value of last term of

$C_1 - 2C_2 + 3C_3 - \ldots + (-1)^{n-1} n C_n$ is nC_n i.e., n, then

and $\quad n = n \cdot 1 + 0$ or $n) n (1$
$$\begin{array}{r} -n \\ \hline 0 \end{array}$$

Here, $q = 1$ and $r = 0$

The given series is

$$(1+x)^n = C_0 + C_1 x + C_2 x^2 + C_3 x^3 + \ldots + C_n x^n$$

On differentiating both sides w.r.t. x, we get

$$n(1+x)^{n-1} = 0 + C_1 + 2C_2 x + 3C_3 x^2 + \ldots + n C_n x^{n-1}$$

Putting $\quad x = -1$, we get

$$0 = C_1 - 2C_2 + 3C_3 - \ldots + (-1)^{n-1} n C_n$$

or $\quad C_1 - 2C_2 + 3C_3 - \ldots + (-1)^{n-1} n C_n = 0$

Example 66. If $(1+x)^n = C_0 + C_1 x + C_2 x^2 + C_3 x^3 + \ldots + C_n x^n$, prove that $C_0 - 3C_1 + 5C_2 - \ldots + (-1)^n (2n+1) C_n = 0.$

Sol. The numerical value of last term of

$C_0 - 3C_1 + 5C_2 - \ldots + (-1)^n (2n+1) C_n$ is $(2n+1) C_n$

i.e. $\quad (2n+1)$

and $\quad 2n + 1 = 2 \cdot n + 1$ or $n) 2n + 1 (2$
$$\begin{array}{r} -2n \\ \hline 1 \end{array}$$

Here, $q = 2$ and $r = 1$

The given series is

$(1+x)^n = C_0 + C_1 x + C_2 x^2 + C_3 x^3 + \ldots + C_n x^n$ now,

replacing x by x^2, then we get

$$(1+x^2)^n = C_0 + C_1 x^2 + C_2 x^4 + \ldots + C_n x^{2n}$$

On multiplying both sides by x, we get

$$x(1+x^2)^n = C_0 x + C_1 x^3 + C_2 x^5 + \ldots + C_n x^{2n+1}$$

On differentiating both sides w.r.t. x, we get

$$x \cdot n(1+x^2)^{n-1} 2x + (1+x^2)^n \cdot 1 = C_0 + 3C_1 x^2 + 5C_2 x^4 + \ldots + (2n+1) C_n x^{2n}$$

Putting $x = i$ in both sides, we get

$$0 + 0 = C_0 - 3C_1 + 5C_2 - \ldots + (2n+1)(-1)^n C_n$$

or $\quad C_0 - 3C_1 + 5C_2 - \ldots + (-1)^n (2n+1) C_n = 0$

Alternate Solution

I. $\text{LHS} = C_0 - 3C_1 + 5C_2 - \ldots + (-1)^n (2n+1) C_n$

$= C_0 - (1+2) C_1 + (1+4) C_2 - \ldots + (-1)^n (1+2n) C_n$

$= (C_0 - C_1 + C_2 - \ldots + (-1)^n C_n) - 2(C_1 - 2C_2 + \ldots + (-1)^{n-1} n \cdot C_n)$

$= (1-1)^n - 2 \cdot 0$ [from Example 65]

$= 0 = \text{RHS}$

II. $\text{LHS} = C_0 - 3C_1 + 5C_2 - \ldots + (-1)^n (2n+1) C_n$

$= \sum_{r=1}^{n} (-1)^r (2r+1)\, {}^nC_r$

$= \sum_{r=1}^{n} (-1)^r [2r \cdot {}^nC_r + {}^nC_r]$

$= 2 \sum_{r=1}^{n} n \cdot {}^{n-1}C_{r-1} + \sum_{r=1}^{n} (-1)^r \cdot {}^nC_r$

$= 2n(1-1)^{n-1} + (1-1)^n = 0 + 0 = 0 = \text{RHS}$

6.10 Use of Integration

This method is applied only when the numericals occur as the denominator of the binomial coefficient.

Solution Process

If $(1+x)^n = C_0 + C_1 x + C_2 x^2 + C_3 x^3 + \ldots + C_n x^n$, then integrate both sides between the suitable limits which gives the required series.

1. If the sum contains $C_0, C_1, C_2, \ldots, C_n$ are all positive signs, then integrate between limits 0 to 1.
2. If the sum contains alternate signs (i.e., +, −), then integrate between limits −1 to 0.
3. If the sum contains odd coefficients (i.e., $C_0, C_2, C_4, \ldots$), then integrate between −1 to +1.
4. If the sum contains even coefficients (i.e., $C_1, C_3, C_5, \ldots$), then subtracting (2) from (1) and then dividing by 2.
5. If in denominator of binomial coefficient product of two numericals, then integrate two times first times taken limits between 0 to x and second times take suitable limits.

Example 67. If $(1+x)^n = C_0 + C_1 x + C_2 x^2 + \ldots + C_n x^n$, prove that

$$C_0 + \frac{C_1}{2} + \frac{C_2}{3} + \ldots + \frac{C_n}{n+1} = \frac{2^{n+1} - 1}{n+1}.$$

Sol. $\because \quad (1+x)^n = C_0 + C_1 x + C_2 x^2 + \ldots + C_n x^n \quad \ldots \text{(i)}$

Integrating both sides of Eq. (i) within limits 0 to 1, then we get

$$\int_0^1 (1+x)^n \, dx = \int_0^1 (C_0 + C_1 x + C_2 x^2 + \ldots + C_n x^n) \, dx$$

$$\left[\frac{(1+x)^{n+1}}{n+1}\right]_0^1 = \left[C_0 x + \frac{C_1 x^2}{2} + \frac{C_2 x^3}{3} + \ldots + \frac{C_n x^{n+1}}{n+1}\right]_0^1$$

$$\Rightarrow \quad \frac{2^{n+1} - 1}{n+1} = C_0 + \frac{C_1}{2} + \frac{C_2}{3} + \ldots + \frac{C_n}{n+1}$$

or $\quad C_0 + \dfrac{C_1}{2} + \dfrac{C_2}{3} + \ldots + \dfrac{C_n}{n+1} = \dfrac{2^{n+1} - 1}{n+1}$

Example 68. If $(1+x)^n = C_0 + C_1 x + C_2 x^2 + C_3 x^3 + \ldots + C_n x^n$, prove that
$$C_0 - \frac{C_1}{2} + \frac{C_2}{3} - \ldots + (-1)^n \frac{C_n}{n+1} = \frac{1}{n+1}.$$

Sol. $\because (1+x)^n = C_0 + C_1 x + C_2 x^2 + \ldots + C_n x^n$ ...(i)

Integrating on both sides of Eq. (i) within limits – 1 to 0, then we get
$$\int_{-1}^{0} (1+x)^n \, dx = \int_{-1}^{0} (C_0 + C_1 x + C_2 x^2 + \ldots + C_n x^n) \, dx$$
$$\Rightarrow \left[\frac{(1+x)^n}{n+1}\right]_{-1}^{0} = \left[C_0 x + \frac{C_1 x^2}{2} + \frac{C_2 x^3}{3} + \ldots + \frac{C_n x^{n+1}}{n+1}\right]_{-1}^{0}$$
$$\Rightarrow \frac{1-0}{n+1} = 0 - \left(-C_0 + \frac{C_1}{2} - \frac{C_2}{3} + \ldots + (-1)^{n+1} \frac{C_n}{n+1}\right)$$
$$\Rightarrow \frac{1}{n+1} = C_0 - \frac{C_1}{2} + \frac{C_2}{3} - \ldots + (-1)^{n+2} \frac{C_n}{n+1}$$
$$\Rightarrow \frac{1}{n+1} = C_0 - \frac{C_1}{2} + \frac{C_2}{3} - \ldots + (-1)^n \frac{C_n}{n+1}$$
$$[\because (-1)^{n+2} = (-1)^n (-1)^2 = (-1)^n]$$
Hence, $C_0 - \frac{C_1}{2} + \frac{C_2}{3} - \ldots + (-1)^n \frac{C_n}{n+1} = \frac{1}{n+1}$

Example 69. If $(1+x)^n = C_0 + C_1 x + C_2 x^2 + C_3 x^3 + \ldots + C_n x^n$, prove that
$$\frac{C_0}{1} + \frac{C_2}{3} + \frac{C_4}{5} + \ldots = \frac{2^n}{n+1}.$$

Sol. $\because (1+x)^n = C_0 + C_1 x + C_2 x^2 + C_3 x^3 + C_4 x^4 + \ldots + C_n x^n$ ...(i)

Integrating on both sides of Eq. (i) within limits – 1 to 1, then we get
$$\int_{-1}^{1} (1+x)^n \, dx = \int_{-1}^{1} (C_0 + C_1 x + C_2 x^2 + C_3 x^3 + C_4 x^4 + \ldots + C_n x^n) \, dx$$
$$= \int_{-1}^{1} (C_0 + C_2 x^2 + C_4 x^4 + \ldots) dx + \int_{-1}^{1} (C_1 x + C_3 x^3 + \ldots) dx$$
$$= 2\int_{0}^{1} (C_0 + C_2 x^2 + C_4 x^4 + \ldots) \, dx + 0$$
[by property of definite integral]
[since, second integral contains odd function]
$$\Rightarrow \left[\frac{(1+x)^{n+1}}{n+1}\right]_{-1}^{1} = 2\left[\left(C_0 x + \frac{C_2 x^3}{3} + \frac{C_4 x^5}{5} + \ldots\right)\right]_0^1$$
$$\Rightarrow \frac{2^{n+1}}{n+1} = 2\left(C_0 + \frac{C_2}{3} + \frac{C_4}{5} + \ldots\right)$$
or $C_0 + \frac{C_2}{3} + \frac{C_4}{5} + \ldots = \frac{2^n}{n+1}$

Example 70. If $(1+x)^n = C_0 + C_1 x + C_2 x^2 + C_3 x^3 + \ldots + C_n x^n$, prove that $\frac{C_1}{2} + \frac{C_3}{4} + \frac{C_5}{6} + \ldots = \frac{2^n - 1}{n+1}$.

Sol. We know that, from Examples (67) and (68)
$$C_0 + \frac{C_1}{2} + \frac{C_2}{3} + \frac{C_3}{4} + \frac{C_4}{5} + \frac{C_5}{6} + \ldots = \frac{2^{n+1} - 1}{n+1} \quad \ldots(i)$$
and $$C_0 - \frac{C_1}{2} + \frac{C_2}{3} - \frac{C_3}{4} + \frac{C_4}{5} - \frac{C_5}{6} + \ldots = \frac{1}{n+1} \quad \ldots(ii)$$
On subtracting Eq. (ii) from Eq. (i), we get
$$2\left(\frac{C_1}{2} + \frac{C_3}{4} + \frac{C_5}{6} + \ldots\right) = \frac{2^{n+1} - 2}{n+1}$$
On dividing each sides by 2, we get
$$\frac{C_1}{2} + \frac{C_3}{4} + \frac{C_5}{6} + \ldots = \frac{2^n - 1}{n+1}$$

Example 71. If $(1+x)^n = C_0 + C_1 x + C_2 x^2 + \ldots + C_n x^n$, prove that
$$3C_0 + 3^2 \frac{C_1}{2} + \frac{3^3 C_2}{3} + \frac{3^4 C_3}{4} + \ldots + \frac{3^{n+1} C_n}{n+1} = \frac{4^{n+1} - 1}{n+1}.$$

Sol. $\because (1+x)^n = C_0 + C_1 x + C_2 x^2 + C_3 x^3 + \ldots + C_n x^n$ ...(i)

Integrating on both sides of Eq. (i) within limits 0 to 3, we get
$$\int_0^3 (1+x)^n dx = \int_0^3 (C_0 + C_1 x + C_2 x^2 + C_3 x^3 + \ldots + C_n x^n) dx$$
$$\Rightarrow \left[\frac{(1+x)^{n+1}}{n+1}\right]_0^3 = \left[C_0 x + \frac{C_1 x^2}{2} + \frac{C_2 x^3}{3} + \frac{C_3 x^4}{4} + \ldots + \frac{C_n x^{n+1}}{n+1}\right]_0^3$$
$$\Rightarrow \frac{4^{n+1} - 1}{n+1} = 3C_0 + \frac{3^2 C_1}{2} + \frac{3^3 C_2}{3} + \frac{3^4 C_3}{4} + \ldots + \frac{3^{n+1} C_n}{n+1}$$
Hence,
$$3C_0 + \frac{3^2 C_1}{2} + \frac{3^3 C_2}{3} + \frac{3^4 C_3}{4} + \ldots + \frac{3^{n+1} C_n}{n+1} = \frac{4^{n+1} - 1}{n+1}$$

Alternate Solution

I. $$\text{LHS} = 3C_0 + \frac{3^2 C_1}{2} + \frac{3^3 C_2}{3} + \frac{3^4 C_3}{4} + \ldots + \frac{3^{n+1} C_n}{n+1}$$
$$= 3 \cdot 1 + \frac{3^2 \cdot n}{2} + \frac{3^3 \cdot n(n-1)}{1 \cdot 2 \cdot 3} + \frac{3^4 \cdot n(n-1)(n-2)}{1 \cdot 2 \cdot 3 \cdot 4} + \ldots + \frac{3^{n+1}}{n+1}$$
$$= \frac{1}{(n+1)}\left[3 \cdot (n+1) + \frac{3^2 (n+1) n}{1 \cdot 2} + \frac{3^3 (n+1) n(n-1)}{1 \cdot 2 \cdot 3} + \frac{3^4 (n+1) n(n-1)(n-2)}{1 \cdot 2 \cdot 3 \cdot 4} + \ldots + 3^{n+1}\right]$$
Put $n + 1 = N$, then
$$\text{LHS} = \frac{1}{N}\left[3N + \frac{3^2 N(N-1)}{2!} + \frac{3^3 N(N-1)(N-2)}{3!} + \frac{3^4 N(N-1)(N-2)(N-3)}{4!} + \ldots + 3^N\right]$$

$$= \frac{1}{N}[{}^NC_1(3) + {}^NC_2(3)^2 + {}^NC_3(3)^3 + \ldots + {}^NC_N(3)^N]$$

$$= \frac{1}{N}[{}^NC_0 + {}^NC_1(3) + {}^NC_2(3)^2 + {}^NC_3(3)^3 + \ldots + {}^NC_N(3)^N - {}^NC_0]$$

$$= \frac{1}{N}\{(1+3)^N - 1\} = \frac{4^N - 1}{N} = \frac{4^{n+1}-1}{n+1} = \text{RHS}$$

II. $\text{LHS} = 3C_0 + 3^2\frac{C_1}{2} + \frac{3^3 C_2}{3} + \frac{3^4 C_3}{4} + \ldots + \frac{3^{n+1}C_n}{n+1}$

$$= \sum_{r=0}^{n} \frac{3^{r+1}\cdot {}^nC_r}{(r+1)} = \sum_{r=0}^{n} \frac{3^{r+1}\cdot {}^{n+1}C_{r+1}}{(n+1)} \qquad \left[\because \frac{{}^{n+1}C_{r+1}}{n+1} = \frac{{}^nC_r}{r+1}\right]$$

$$= \frac{1}{(n+1)}\sum_{r=0}^{n} {}^{n+1}C_{r+1}\cdot 3^{r+1}$$

$$= \frac{1}{(n+1)}({}^{n+1}C_1\cdot 3 + {}^{n+1}C_2\cdot 3^2 + {}^{n+1}C_3\cdot 3^3 + \ldots + {}^{n+1}C_{n+1}\cdot 3^{n+1})$$

$$= \frac{1}{(n+1)}[(1+3)^{n+1} - {}^{n+1}C_0] = \frac{4^{n+1}-1}{n+1} = \text{RHS}$$

Example 72. If $(1+x)^n = C_0 + C_1x + C_2x^2 + \ldots + C_nx^n$, show that

$$\frac{2^2}{1\cdot 2}C_0 + \frac{2^3}{2\cdot 3}C_1 + \frac{2^4}{3\cdot 4}C_2 + \ldots + \frac{2^{n+2}C_n}{(n+1)(n+2)} = \frac{3^{n+2}-2n-5}{(n+1)(n+2)}.$$

Sol. Given, $(1+x)^n = C_0 + C_1x + C_2x^2 + C_3x^3 + \ldots + C_nx^n$ ...(i)

Integrating both sides of Eq. (i) within limits 0 to x, we get

$$\int_0^x (1+x)^n\,dx = \int_0^x (C_0 + C_1x + C_2x^2 + \ldots + C_nx^n)\,dx$$

$$\Rightarrow \left[\frac{(1+x)^{n+1}}{n+1}\right]_0^x = \left[C_0x + \frac{C_1x^2}{2} + \frac{C_2x^3}{3} + \ldots + \frac{C_nx^{n+1}}{n+1}\right]_0^x$$

$$\Rightarrow \frac{(1+x)^{n+1}-1}{(n+1)} = C_0x + \frac{C_1x^2}{2} + \frac{C_2x^3}{3} + \ldots + \frac{C_nx^{n+1}}{n+1} \quad \text{...(ii)}$$

Again, integrating both sides of Eq. (ii) within limits 0 to 2, we get

$$\int_0^2 \frac{(1+x)^{n+1}-1}{(n+1)}\,dx = \int_0^2\left(C_0x + \frac{C_1x^2}{2} + \frac{C_2x^3}{3} + \ldots + \frac{C_nx^{n+1}}{n+1}\right)dx$$

$$\Rightarrow \frac{1}{(n+1)}\left(\frac{(1+x)^{n+2}}{n+2} - x\right)\Bigg]_0^2 = \left[\frac{C_0x^2}{1\cdot 2} + \frac{C_1x^3}{2\cdot 3} + \frac{C_2x^4}{3\cdot 4} + \ldots + \frac{C_nx^{n+2}}{(n+1)(n+2)}\right]_0^2$$

$$\Rightarrow \frac{1}{(n+1)}\left\{\frac{3^{n+2}}{n+2} - 2 - \frac{1}{n+2}\right\} = \frac{2^2}{1\cdot 2}C_0 + \frac{2^3}{2\cdot 3}C_1 + \frac{2^4}{3\cdot 4}C_2 + \ldots + \frac{2^{n+2}C_n}{(n+1)(n+2)}$$

Hence, $\frac{2^2}{1\cdot 2}C_0 + \frac{2^3}{2\cdot 3}C_1 + \frac{2^4}{3\cdot 4}C_2 + \ldots + \frac{2^{n+2}C_n}{(n+1)(n+2)}$

$$= \frac{3^{n+2}-2n-5}{(n+1)(n+2)}$$

When Each Term in Summation Contains the Product of Two Binomial Coefficients or Square of Binomial Coefficients

Solution Process

1. **If difference of the lower suffixes of binomial coefficients in each term is same.**

   i.e. ${}^nC_0\,{}^nC_2 + {}^nC_1\cdot{}^nC_3 + {}^nC_2\cdot{}^nC_4 + \ldots$

   Here, $2-0 = 3-1 = 4-2 = \ldots = 2$

   ***Case* I If each term of series is positive, then**

   $$(1+x)^n = C_0 + C_1x + C_2x^2 + \ldots + C_nx^n \quad \text{...(i)}$$

   Interchanging 1 and x, we get

   $$(x+1)^n = C_0x^n + C_1x^{n-1} + C_2x^{n-2} + \ldots + C_n \quad \text{...(ii)}$$

   Then, multiplying Eqs. (i) and (ii) and equate the coefficients of suitable power of x on both sides.

   Replacing x by $\frac{1}{x}$ in Eq. (i), then we get

   $$\left(1+\frac{1}{x}\right)^n = C_0 + \frac{C_1}{x} + \frac{C_2}{x^2} + \ldots + \frac{C_n}{x^n} \quad \text{...(iii)}$$

   Then, multiplying Eqs. (i) and (iii) and equate the coefficients of suitable power of x on both sides.

Example 73. If $(1+x)^n = C_0 + C_1x + C_2x^2 + C_3x^3 + \ldots + C_nx^n$, prove that

$$C_0C_r + C_1C_{r+1} + C_2C_{r+2} + \ldots + C_{n-r}C_n = \frac{2n!}{(n-r)!(n+r)!}$$

Sol. Here, differences of lower suffixes of binomial coefficients in each term is r.

i.e. $r - 0 = r+1-1 = r+2-2 = \ldots = n-(n-r) = r$

Given,

$$(1+x)^n = C_0 + C_1x + C_2x^2 + \ldots + C_{n-r}x^{n-r} + \ldots + C_nx^n \quad \text{...(i)}$$

Now, $(x+1)^n = C_0x^n + C_1x^{n-1} + C_2x^{n-2} + \ldots + C_rx^{n-r} + C_{r+1}x^{n-r-1} + C_{r+2}x^{n-r-2} + \ldots + C_n$ ...(ii)

On multiplying Eqs. (i) and (ii), we get

$$(1+x)^{2n} = (C_0 + C_1x + C_2x^2 + \dots + C_{n-r}x^{n-r} + \dots + C_nx^n) \times (C_0x^n + C_1x^{n-1} + C_2x^{n-2} + \dots + C_rx^{n-r} + C_{r+1}x^{n-r-1} + C_{r+2}x^{n-r-2} + \dots + C_n) \quad \dots(iii)$$

Now, coefficient of x^{n-r} on LHS of Eq. (iii) $= {}^{2n}C_{n-r}$

$$= \frac{2n!}{(n-r)!(n+r)!}$$

and coefficient of x^{n-r} on RHS of Eq. (iii)

$$= C_0C_r + C_1C_{r+1} + C_2C_{r+2} + \dots + C_{n-r}C_n$$

But Eq. (iii) is an identity, therefore coefficient of x^{n-r} in RHS = coefficient of x^{n-r} in LHS.

$$\Rightarrow C_0C_r + C_1C_{r+1} + C_2C_{r+2} + \dots + C_{n-r}C_n = \frac{2n!}{(n-r)!(n+r)!}$$

Alternate Solution

Given,

$$(1+x)^n = C_0 + C_1x + C_2x^2 + \dots + C_rx^r + C_{r+1}x^{r+1} + C_{r+2}x^{r+2} + \dots + C_{n-r}x^{n-r} + \dots + C_nx^n \quad \dots(i)$$

Now, $$\left(1+\frac{1}{x}\right)^n = C_0 + \frac{C_1}{x} + \frac{C_2}{x^2} + \dots + \frac{C_r}{x^r} + \frac{C_{r+1}}{x^{r+1}} + \frac{C_{r+2}}{x^{r+2}} + \dots + \frac{C_{n-r}}{x^{n-r}} + \dots + \frac{C_n}{x^n} \quad \dots(ii)$$

On multiplying Eqs. (i) and (ii), we get

$$\frac{(1+x)^{2n}}{x^n} = (C_0 + C_1x + C_2x^2 + \dots + C_rx^r + C_{r+1}x^{r+1} + C_{r+2}x^{r+2} + \dots + C_{n-r}x^{n-r} + \dots + C_nx^n) \times \left(C_0 + \frac{C_1}{x} + \frac{C_2}{x^2} + \dots + \frac{C_r}{x^r} + \frac{C_{r+1}}{x^{r+1}} + \frac{C_{r+2}}{x^{r+2}} + \dots + \frac{C_{n-r}}{x^{n-r}} + \dots + \frac{C_n}{x^n}\right) \quad \dots(iii)$$

Now, coefficient of $\frac{1}{x^r}$ in RHS

$$= (C_0C_r + C_1C_{r+1} + C_2C_{r+2} + \dots + C_{n-r}C_n)$$

$\therefore$ Coefficient of $\frac{1}{x^r}$ in LHS = Coefficient of x^{n-r} in

$$(1+x)^{2n} = {}^{2n}C_{n-r} = \frac{2n!}{(n-r)!(n+r)!}$$

But Eq. (iii) is an identity,

therefore coefficient of $\frac{1}{x^r}$ in RHS = coefficient of $\frac{1}{x^r}$ in LHS.

$$\Rightarrow C_0C_r + C_1C_{r+1} + C_2C_{r+2} + \dots + C_{n-r}C_n = \frac{2n!}{(n-r)!(n+r)!}$$

Example 74. If $(1+x)^n = C_0 + C_1x + C_2x^2 + \dots + C_nx^n$, prove that

$$C_0^2 + C_1^2 + C_2^2 = \frac{2n!}{n!n!} = \frac{1\cdot3\cdot5\dots(2n-1)}{n!}\cdot 2^n.$$

Sol. Given, $(1+x)^n = C_0 + C_1x + C_2x^2 + \dots + C_nx^n \quad \dots(i)$

Now, $(x+1)^n = C_0x^n + C_1x^{n-1} + C_2x^{n-2} + \dots + C_n \quad \dots(ii)$

On multiplying Eqs. (i) and (ii), we get

$$(1+x)^{2n} = (C_0 + C_1x + C_2x^2 + \dots + C_nx^n) \times (C_0x^n + C_1x^{n-1} + C_2x^{n-2} + \dots + C_n) \quad \dots(iii)$$

Now, coefficient of x^n in RHS

$$= C_0^2 + C_1^2 + C_2^2 + \dots + C_n^2$$

And coefficient of x^n in LHS $= {}^{2n}C_n = \frac{2n!}{n!n!}$

$$= \frac{1\cdot2\cdot3\cdot4\cdot5\dots(2n-1)2n}{n!n!} = \frac{1\cdot3\cdot5\dots(2n-1)2^n n!}{n!n!}$$

But Eq. (iii) is an identity, therefore coefficient of x^n in RHS = coefficient of x^n in LHS.

$$\Rightarrow C_0^2 + C_1^2 + C_2^2 + \dots + C_n^2 = \frac{2n!}{n!n!} = \frac{1\cdot3\cdot5\cdot\dots\cdot(2n-1)}{n!}\cdot 2^n$$

***Case* II If terms of the series alternately positive and negative, then**

$$(1-x)^n = C_0 - C_1x + C_2x^2 - \dots + (-1)^n C_nx^n \quad \dots(i)$$

$$\text{and } (x+1)^n = C_0x^n + C_1x^{n-1} + C_2x^{n-2} + \dots + C_n \quad \dots(ii)$$

Then, multiplying Eqs. (i) and (ii) and equate the coefficient of suitable power of x on both sides.

Or

Replacing x by $\frac{1}{x}$ in Eq. (i), we get

$$\left(1-\frac{1}{x}\right)^n = C_0 - \frac{C_1}{x} + \frac{C_2}{x^2} - \dots + (-1)^n\frac{C_n}{x^n} \quad \dots(iii)$$

Then, multiplying Eqs. (i) and (iii) and equate the coefficient of suitable power of x on both sides.

Example 75. Prove that

$$({}^{2n}C_0)^2 - ({}^{2n}C_1)^2 + ({}^{2n}C_2)^2 - \dots + ({}^{2n}C_{2n})^2 = (-1)^n \cdot {}^{2n}C_n.$$

Sol. Since, $(1-x)^{2n} = {}^{2n}C_0 - {}^{2n}C_1x + {}^{2n}C_2x^2 - \dots + (-1)^{2n}\cdot{}^{2n}C_{2n}x^{2n}$

or $(1-x)^{2n} = {}^{2n}C_0 - {}^{2n}C_1x + {}^{2n}C_2x^2 - \dots + {}^{2n}C_{2n}x^{2n} \quad \dots(i)$

and $(x+1)^{2n} = {}^{2n}C_0x^{2n} + {}^{2n}C_1x^{2n-1} + {}^{2n}C_2x^{2n-2} + \dots + {}^{2n}C_{2n} \quad \dots(ii)$

On multiplying Eqs. (i) and (ii), we get

$$(x^2-1)^{2n} = ({}^{2n}C_0 - {}^{2n}C_1 x + {}^{2n}C_2 x^2 - \dots + {}^{2n}C_{2n} x^{2n})$$
$$\times({}^{2n}C_0 x^{2n} + {}^{2n}C_1 x^{2n-1} + {}^{2n}C_2 x^{2n-2} + \dots + {}^{2n}C_{2n}) \quad \dots\text{(iii)}$$

Now, coefficient of x^{2n} in RHS

$$= ({}^{2n}C_0)^2 - ({}^{2n}C_1)^2 + ({}^{2n}C_2)^2 - \dots + ({}^{2n}C_{2n})^2$$

Now, LHS can also be written as $(1-x^2)^{2n}$.

$\therefore$ General term in LHS, $T_{r+1} = {}^{2n}C_r(-x^2)^r$

Putting $r=n$, we get $T_{n+1} = (-1)^n \cdot {}^{2n}C_n x^{2n}$

$\Rightarrow$ Coefficient of x^{2n} in LHS $= (-1)^n \cdot {}^{2n}C_n$

But Eq. (iii) is an identity, therefore coefficient of x^{2n} in RHS = coefficient of x^{2n} in LHS

$$\Rightarrow ({}^{2n}C_0)^2 - ({}^{2n}C_1)^2 + ({}^{2n}C_2)^2 - \dots + ({}^{2n}C_{2n})^2 = (-1)^n \cdot {}^{2n}C_n$$

Alternate Solution

Since, $(1+x)^{2n} = {}^{2n}C_0 + {}^{2n}C_1 x + {}^{2n}C_2 x^2 + \dots + {}^{2n}C_{2n}x^{2n}$ ...(i)

and $\left(1-\frac{1}{x}\right)^{2n} = {}^{2n}C_0 - \frac{{}^{2n}C_1}{x} + \frac{{}^{2n}C_2}{x^2} - \dots + \frac{{}^{2n}C_{2n}}{x^{2n}}$ ...(ii)

On multiplying Eqs. (i) and (ii), we get

$$\frac{(x^2-1)^{2n}}{x^{2n}} = ({}^{2n}C_0 + {}^{2n}C_1 x + {}^{2n}C_2 x^2 + \dots + {}^{2n}C_{2n} x^{2n})$$
$$\times\left({}^{2n}C_0 - \frac{{}^{2n}C_1}{x} + \frac{{}^{2n}C_2}{x^2} - \dots + \frac{{}^{2n}C_{2n}}{x^{2n}}\right) \dots\text{(iii)}$$

Now, constant term in RHS

$$= ({}^{2n}C_0)^2 - ({}^{2n}C_1)^2 + ({}^{2n}C_2)^2 - \dots + ({}^{2n}C_{2n})^2$$

Constant term in LHS = Constant term in $\frac{(x^2-1)^{2n}}{x^{2n}}$

= Coefficient of x^{2n} in $(x^2-1)^{2n}$

= Coefficient of x^{2n} in $(1-x^2)^{2n}$

$= {}^{2n}C_n(-1)^n = (-1)^n \cdot {}^{2n}C_n$

But Eq. (iii) is an identity, therefore the constant term in RHS = constant term in LHS.

$$\Rightarrow ({}^{2n}C_0)^2 - ({}^{2n}C_1)^2 + ({}^{2n}C_2)^2 - \dots + ({}^{2n}C_{2n})^2 = (-1)^n \cdot {}^{2n}C_n$$

Example 76. If $(1+x)^n = C_0 + C_1 x + C_2 x^2 + \dots + C_n x^n$, prove that $C_0^2 - C_1^2 + C_2^2 - \dots + (-1)^n \cdot C_n^2 = 0$ or $(-1)^{n/2} \cdot \frac{n!}{(n/2)!(n/2)!}$, according as n is odd or even.

Also, evaluate $C_0^2 - C_1^2 + C_2^2 - \dots + (-1)^n \cdot C_n^2$ for $n = 10$ and $n = 11$

Sol. Since, $(1-x)^n = C_0 - C_1 x + C_2 x^2 - \dots + (-1)^n C_n x^n$ ...(i)

and $(x+1)^n = C_0 x^n + C_1 x^{n-1} + C_2 x^{n-2} + \dots + C_n$ ...(ii)

On multiplying Eqs. (i) and (ii), we get

$$(1-x^2)^n = \{C_0 - C_1 x + C_2 x^2 - \dots + (-1)^n C_n x^n\}$$
$$\times(C_0 x^n + C_1 x^{n-1} + C_2 x^{n-2} + \dots + C_n) \dots\text{(iii)}$$

Now, coefficient of x^n in RHS

$$= C_0^2 - C_1^2 + C_2^2 - \dots + (-1)^n C_n^2$$

General term in LHS $= T_{r+1} = {}^nC_r(-x^2)^r = {}^nC_r(-1)^r x^{2r}$

Putting $2r = n$, we get $r = n/2$

$\therefore$ $T_{(n/2)+1} = {}^nC_{n/2}(-1)^{n/2} x^n$

$\therefore$ Coefficient of x^n in LHS $= {}^nC_{n/2}(-1)^{n/2}$

$$= (-1)^{n/2} \cdot \frac{n!}{(n/2)!(n/2)!}$$

$$= \begin{cases} 0, & \text{if } n \text{ is odd} \\ (-1)^{n/2}\dfrac{n!}{(n/2)!(n/2)!}, & \text{if } n \text{ is even} \end{cases}$$

$$\left[\because \left(\frac{\text{odd}}{2}\right)! = \infty\right]$$

But Eq. (iii) is an identity, therefore coefficient of x^n in RHS = coefficient of x^n in LHS.

$$\Rightarrow C_0^2 - C_1^2 + C_2^2 - \dots + (-1)^n C_n^2 = \begin{cases} 0, & \text{if } n \text{ is odd} \\ (-1)^{n/2}\dfrac{n!}{(n/2)!(n/2)!}, & \text{if } n \text{ is even} \end{cases}$$

Now, for $n = 10$,

$$C_0^2 - C_1^2 + C_2^2 - \dots + C_{10}^2 = (-1)^{10/2}\frac{10!}{5!5!} = -252$$

[$\because$ 10 is even]

and from $n = 11$,

$$C_0^2 - C_1^2 + C_2^2 - \dots - C_{11}^2 = 0$$

[$\because$ 11 is odd]

2. If sum of the lower suffixes of binomial coefficients in each term is same.

i.e., $C_0C_n + C_1C_{n-1} + C_2C_{n-2} + \dots + C_nC_0$

Here, $0 + n = 1 + (n-1) = 2 + (n-2) = \dots = n + 0 = n$

***Case* I** If each term of series is positive, then

$$(1+x)^m = C_0 + C_1 x + C_2 x^2 + \dots + C_m x^m \quad \dots\text{(i)}$$

and $\quad (1+x)^n = C_0 + C_1 x + C_2 x^2 + \dots + C_n x^n$ ...(ii)

Then, multiplying Eqs. (i) and (ii) and equate the coefficient of suitable power of x on both sides.

Example 77. Prove that

$${}^{m+n}C_r = {}^mC_r + {}^mC_{r-1}\,{}^nC_1 + {}^mC_{r-2}\,{}^nC_2 + \dots + {}^nC_r$$

if $r < m$, $r < n$ and m, n, r are positive integers.

Sol. Here, sum of lower suffixes of binomial coefficients in each term is r.

i.e. $\quad r = r-1+1 = r-2+2 = \dots = r = r$

Since,

$$(1+x)^m = {}^mC_0 + {}^mC_1 x + \dots + {}^mC_{r-2}x^{r-2} + {}^mC_{r-1}x^{r-1} + {}^mC_r x^r + \dots + {}^mC_m x^m \dots\text{(i)}$$

and $(1+x)^n = {}^nC_0 + {}^nC_1 x + {}^nC_2 x^2 + \dots + {}^nC_r x^r + \dots + {}^nC_n x^n$ ...(ii)

On multiplying Eqs. (i) and (ii), we get

$$(1+x)^{m+n} = ({}^mC_0 + {}^mC_1 x + \dots + {}^mC_{r-2}x^{r-2} + {}^mC_{r-1}x^{r-1} + {}^mC_r x^r + \dots + {}^mC_m x^m) \times ({}^nC_0 + {}^nC_1 x + {}^nC_2 x^2 + \dots + {}^nC_r x^r + \dots + {}^nC_n x^n) \quad \text{...(iii)}$$

Now, coefficient of x^r in RHS

$$= {}^mC_r \cdot {}^nC_0 + {}^mC_{r-1} \cdot {}^nC_1 + {}^mC_{r-2} \cdot {}^nC_2 + \dots + {}^mC_0 \cdot {}^nC_r$$

$$= {}^mC_r + {}^mC_{r-1} \cdot {}^nC_1 + {}^mC_{r-2} \cdot {}^nC_2 + \dots + {}^nC_r$$

Coefficient of x^r in LHS $= {}^{m+n}C_r$

But Eq. (iii) is an identity, therefore coefficient of x^r in LHS = coefficient of x^r in RHS.

$$\Rightarrow \quad {}^{m+n}C_r = {}^mC_r + {}^mC_{r-1} \cdot {}^nC_1 + {}^mC_{r-2} \cdot {}^nC_2 + \dots + {}^nC_r$$

***Case* II** If terms of the series alternately positive and negative, then

$$(1-x)^n = C_0 - C_1 x + C_2 x^2 - \dots + (-1)^n C_n x^n \quad \text{...(i)}$$

and $(1+x)^n = C_0 + C_1 x + C_2 x^2 + \dots + C_n x^n$ ...(ii)

Then, multiplying Eqs. (i) and (ii) and equate the coefficient of suitable power of x on both sides.

Example 78. If $(1+x)^n = C_0 + C_1 x + C_2 x^2 + \dots + C_n x^n$, prove that

$C_0 C_n - C_1 C_{n-1} + C_2 C_{n-2} - \dots + (-1)^n C_n C_0 = 0$ or $(-1)^{n/2} \dfrac{n!}{(n/2)!(n/2)!}$, according as n is odd or even.

Sol. Given, $(1+x)^n = C_0 + C_1 x + C_2 x^2 + \dots + C_{n-2} x^{n-2} + C_{n-1} x^{n-1} + C_n x^n$ ...(i)

and $(1-x)^n = C_0 - C_1 x + C_2 x^2 - \dots + (-1)^n C_n x^n$ ...(ii)

On multiplying Eqs. (i) and (ii), we get

$$(1-x^2)^n = (C_0 + C_1 x + C_2 x^2 + \dots + C_{n-2} x^{n-2} + C_{n-1} x^{n-1} + C_n x^n) \times (C_0 - C_1 x + C_2 x^2 - \dots + (-1)^n C_n x^n) \quad \text{...(iii)}$$

Now, coefficient of x^n in RHS

$$= C_0 C_n - C_1 C_{n-1} + C_2 C_{n-2} - \dots + (-1)^n C_n C_0$$

Now, general term in LHS,

$$T_{r+1} = {}^nC_r (-x^2)^r = (-1)^r \cdot {}^nC_r x^{2r}$$

Putting $2r = n$, we get

$$r = n/2$$

Now, $T_{n/2+1} = (-1)^{n/2} \cdot {}^nC_{n/2} x^n$

$\therefore$ Coefficient of x^n in LHS $= (-1)^{n/2} \cdot {}^nC_{n/2}$

$$= (-1)^{n/2} \cdot \frac{n!}{(n/2)!(n/2)!}$$

$$= \begin{cases} 0 & \text{if } n \text{ is odd} \\ (-1)^{n/2} \cdot \dfrac{n!}{(n/2)!(n/2)!}, & \text{if } n \text{ is even} \end{cases}$$

But Eq. (iii) is an identity, therefore the coefficient of x^n in RHS = coefficient of x^n in LHS.

$$\Rightarrow C_0 C_n - C_1 C_{n-1} + C_2 C_{n-2} - \dots + (-1)^n C_n C_0 = \begin{cases} 0, & \text{if } n \text{ is odd} \\ (-1)^{n/2} \cdot \dfrac{n!}{(n/2)!(n/2)!}, & \text{if } n \text{ is even} \end{cases}$$

***Case* III** If each term is the product of two binomial coefficient divided or multiplied by an integer, then integrating or differentiating by preceeding method. Then, multiplying two series and equate the coefficient of suitable power of x on both sides.

Example 79. If $(1+x)^n = C_0 + C_1 x + C_2 x^2 + C_3 x^3 + \dots + C_n x^n$, prove that

$$C_1^2 + 2C_2^2 + 3C_3^2 + \dots + nC_n^2 = \frac{(2n-1)!}{((n-1)!)^2}.$$

Sol. Given, $(1+x)^n = C_0 + C_1 x + C_2 x^2 + C_3 x^3 + \dots + C_n x^n$

Differentiating both sides w.r.t. x, we get

$$n(1+x)^{n-1} = 0 + C_1 + 2C_2 x + 3C_3 x^2 + \dots + nC_n x^{n-1}$$

$$\Rightarrow n(1+x)^{n-1} = C_1 + 2C_2 x + 3C_3 x^2 + \dots + nC_n x^{n-1} \quad \text{...(i)}$$

and $(x+1)^n = C_0 x^n + C_1 x^{n-1} + C_2 x^{n-2} + C_3 x^{n-3} + \dots + C_n$ ...(ii)

On multiplying Eqs. (i) and (ii), then we get

$$n(1+x)^{2n-1} = (C_1 + 2C_2 x + 3C_3 x^2 + \dots + nC_n x^{n-1}) \times (C_0 x^n + C_1 x^{n-1} + C_2 x^{n-2} + C_3 x^{n-3} + \dots + C_n) \quad \text{...(iii)}$$

Now, coefficient of x^{n-1} on RHS

$$= C_1^2 + 2C_2^2 + 3C_3^2 + \dots + nC_n^2$$

and coefficient of x^{n-1} on LHS

$$= n \cdot {}^{2n-1}C_{n-1} = n \cdot \frac{(2n-1)!}{(n-1)!\,n!}$$

$$= \frac{(2n-1)!}{(n-1)!(n-1)!} = \frac{(2n-1)!}{\{((n-1)!)^2\}}$$

But Eq. (iii) is an identity, therefore the coefficient of x^{n-1} in RHS = coefficient of x^{n-1} in LHS.

$$\Rightarrow \quad C_1^2 + 2C_2^2 + 3C_3^2 + \dots + nC_n^2 = \frac{(2n-1)!}{\{(n-1)!\}^2}$$

Example 80. If $(1+x)^n = C_0 + C_1 x + C_2 x^2 + \dots + C_n x^n$, prove that $C_0^2 + \dfrac{C_1^2}{2} + \dfrac{C_2^2}{3} + \dots + \dfrac{C_n^2}{n+1} = \dfrac{(2n+1)!}{\{(n+1)!\}^2}$.

Sol. Given, $(1+x)^n = C_0 + C_1 x + C_2 x^2 + \dots + C_n x^n$

Integrating both sides w.r.t. x within limits 0 to x, we get

$$\int_0^x (1+x)^n\,dx = \int_0^x (C_0 + C_1 x + C_2 x^2 + \dots + C_n x^n)\,dx$$

$$\frac{(1+x)^{n+1} - 1}{(1+n)} = C_0 x + \frac{C_1 x^2}{2} + \frac{C_2 x^3}{3} + \dots + \frac{C_n x^{n+1}}{n+1} \quad \text{...(i)}$$

and $(x+1)^n = C_0 x^n + C_1 x^{n-1} + C_2 x^{n-2} + \dots + C_n$ ...(ii)

Multiplying Eqs. (i) and (ii), we get

$$\frac{1}{(n+1)}\{(1+x)^{2n+1}-(1+x)^n\}$$

$$=\left(C_0x+\frac{C_1x^2}{2}+\frac{C_2x^3}{3}+\ldots+\frac{C_nx^{n+1}}{n+1}\right)$$

$$\times(C_0x^n+C_1x^{n-1}+C_2x^{n-2}+\ldots+C_n)\quad\ldots\text{(iii)}$$

Now, coefficient of x^{n+1} in RHS of Eq. (iii)

$$=C_0^2+\frac{C_1^2}{2}+\frac{C_2^2}{3}+\ldots+\frac{C_n^2}{n+1}$$

and coefficient of x^{n+1} in LHS of Eq. (iii)

$$=\frac{1}{(n+1)}\{{}^{2n+1}C_{n+1}-0\}$$

$$=\frac{1}{(n+1)}\cdot\frac{(2n+1)!}{(n+1)!\,n!}$$

$$=\frac{(2n+1)!}{(n+1)!\,(n+1)!}$$

$$=\frac{(2n+1)!}{\{(n+1)!\}^2}$$

But Eq. (iii) is an identity, therefore coefficient of x^{n+1} in RHS of Eq. (iii) = coefficient of x^{n+1} in LHS of Eq. (iii).

$$\Rightarrow\ C_0^2+\frac{C_1^2}{2}+\frac{C_2^2}{3}+\ldots+\frac{C_n^2}{n+1}=\frac{(2n+1)!}{\{(n+1)!\}^2}$$

6.11 Binomial Inside Binomial

The upper suffices of binomial coefficients are different but lower suffices are same.

Example 81. Evaluate $\sum_{r=0}^{n}{}^{n+r}C_n$.

Sol. $\sum_{r=0}^{n}{}^{n+r}C_n={}^nC_n+{}^{n+1}C_n+{}^{n+2}C_n+\ldots+{}^{2n}C_n$

= Coefficient of x^n in

$$[(1+x)^n+(1+x)^{n+1}+(1+x)^{n+2}+\ldots+\ldots+(1+x)^{2n}]$$

$$=\text{Coefficient of } x^n \text{ in}\left[\frac{(1+x)^n[(1+x)^{n+1}-1]}{(1+x)-1}\right]$$

$$=\text{Coefficient of } x^{n+1}\text{ in }[(1+x)^{2n+1}-(1+x)^n]$$

$$={}^{2n+1}C_{n+1}-0={}^{2n+1}C_n$$

Example 82. If $(1+x)^n=C_0+C_1x+C_2x^2+\ldots+C_nx^n$, prove that

$$C_0\cdot{}^{2n}C_n-C_1\cdot{}^{2n-2}C_n+C_2\cdot{}^{2n-4}C_n-\ldots=2^n$$

Sol. LHS $=C_0\cdot{}^{2n}C_n-C_1\cdot{}^{2n-2}C_n+C_2\cdot{}^{2n-4}C_n-\ldots$

= Coefficient of x^n in

$$[C_0(1+x)^{2n}-C_1(1+x)^{2n-2}+C_2(1+x)^{2n-4}-\ldots]$$

= Coefficient of x^n in

$$[C_0((1+x)^2)^n-C_1[(1+x)^2]^{n-1}+C_2[(1+x)^2]^{n-2}-\ldots]$$

= Coefficient of x^n in $[[(1+x)^2-1]^n]$

= Coefficient of x^n in $(2x+x^2)^n$

= Constant term in $(2+x)^n$

$=2^n=$ RHS

Example 83. If $(1+x)^n=C_0+C_1x+C_2x^2+C_3x^3+\ldots+C_nx^n$, prove that

$$C_0\cdot{}^{2n}C_n-C_1\cdot{}^{2n-1}C_n+C_2\cdot{}^{2n-2}C_n-C_3\cdot{}^{2n-3}C_n+\ldots+(-1)^nC_n\cdot{}^nC_n=1$$

Sol. LHS $=C_0\cdot{}^{2n}C_n-C_1\cdot{}^{2n-1}C_n+C_2\cdot{}^{2n-2}C_n-C_3\cdot{}^{2n-3}C_n+\ldots+(-1)^nC_n\cdot{}^nC_n$

= Coefficient of x^n in

$$[C_0(1+x)^{2n}-C_1(1+x)^{2n-1}+C_2(1+x)^{2n-2}-C_3(1+x)^{2n-3}+\ldots+(-1)^nC_n\cdot(1+x)^n]$$

= Coefficient of x^n in

$$(1+x)^n[C_0(1+x)^n-C_1(1+x)^{n-1}+C_2(1+x)^{n-2}-C_3(1+x)^{n-3}+\ldots+(-1)^nC_n\cdot 1]$$

= Coefficient of x^n in $(1+x)^n[((1+x)-1)^n]$

= Coefficient of x^n in $(1+x)^n\cdot x^n$

= Constant term in $(1+x)^n$

$=1=$ RHS

6.12 Sum of the Series

***Case* I When *i* and *j* are independent.**

In this summation, three types of terms occur, when $i<j$, $i=j$ and $i>j$,

i.e. $$\sum_{i=0}^{n}\sum_{j=0}^{n}a_i\,a_j=\sum_{i=0}^{n}\left\{a_i\left(\sum_{j=0}^{n}a_j\right)\right\}$$

$$=\sum_{i=0}^{n}a_i\sum_{j=0}^{n}a_j=\left(\sum_{i=0}^{n}a_i\right)^2\text{ or }\left(\sum_{j=0}^{n}a_j\right)^2$$

***Corollary* I** $$\sum_{i=0}^{n}\sum_{j=0}^{n}{}^nC_i\,{}^nC_j=\left(\sum_{i=0}^{n}{}^nC_i\right)^2$$

$$=(2^n)^2=2^{2n}$$

Example 84. If $(1+x)^n=C_0+C_1x+C_2x^2+\ldots+C_nx^n$, find the values of the following.

(i) $\sum_{i=0}^{n}\sum_{j=0}^{n}(C_i+C_j)$

(ii) $\sum_{i=0}^{n}\sum_{j=0}^{n}(i+j)\,C_i\,C_j$

Sol. (i) $\sum_{i=0}^{n}\sum_{j=0}^{n}(C_i+C_j)=\sum_{i=0}^{n}\sum_{j=0}^{n}C_i+\sum_{i=0}^{n}\sum_{j=0}^{n}C_j$

$$=\sum_{j=0}^{n}\left(\sum_{i=0}^{n}C_i\right)+\sum_{i=0}^{n}\left(\sum_{j=0}^{n}C_j\right)$$

$$=\sum_{j=0}^{n}(2^n)+\sum_{i=0}^{n}(2^n)=(n+1)\cdot 2^n+(n+1)\cdot 2^n$$

$$=2(n+1)2^n=(n+1)2^{n+1}$$

(ii) $\sum_{i=0}^{n}\sum_{j=0}^{n}(i+j)C_iC_j=\sum_{i=0}^{n}\sum_{j=0}^{n}iC_iC_j+\sum_{i=0}^{n}\sum_{j=0}^{n}jC_iC_j$

$$=\sum_{i=0}^{n}iC_i\left(\sum_{j=0}^{n}C_j\right)+\sum_{j=0}^{n}jC_j\left(\sum_{i=0}^{n}C_i\right)$$

$$=\sum_{i=0}^{n}iC_i(2^n)+\sum_{j=0}^{n}jC_j(2^n)$$

$$=2^n\sum_{i=0}^{n}i\,{}^nC_i+2^n\sum_{j=0}^{n}j\,{}^nC_j$$

$$=2^n\sum_{i=0}^{n}i\cdot\frac{n}{i}\cdot{}^{n-1}C_{i-1}+2^n\sum_{j=0}^{n}j\cdot\frac{n}{j}\cdot{}^{n-1}C_{j-1}$$

$$=n\cdot 2^n\sum_{i=0}^{n}{}^{n-1}C_{i-1}+n\cdot 2^n\sum_{j=0}^{n}{}^{n-1}C_{j-1}$$

$$=n\cdot 2^n\cdot 2^{n-1}+n\cdot 2^n\cdot 2^{n-1}$$

$$=n\cdot 2\cdot 2^{2n-1}=n\cdot 2^{2n}$$

***Case* II When *i* and *j* are dependent.**

In this summation, when $i<j$ is equal to the sum of the terms when $i>j$, if a_i and a_j are symmetrical. So, in this case

$$\sum_{i=0}^{n}\sum_{j=0}^{n}a_i\,a_j=\sum_{0\le i<j\le n}\sum a_i\,a_j+\sum_{i=j}\sum a_ia_j+\sum_{0\le j<i\le n}\sum a_ia_j$$

$$=2\sum_{0\le i<j\le n}\sum a_i\,a_j+\sum_{i=j}\sum a_i\,a_j$$

$$\Rightarrow\sum_{0\le i<j\le n}\sum a_i\,a_j=\frac{\sum_{i=0}^{n}\sum_{j=0}^{n}a_i\,a_j-\sum_{i=j}\sum a_i\,a_j}{2}$$

When a_i and a_j are not symmetrical, we find the sum by listing all the terms.

***Corollary* I**

$$\sum_{0\le i<j\le n}\sum {}^nC_i\,{}^nC_j=\frac{\sum_{i=0}^{n}\sum_{j=0}^{n}{}^nC_i{}^nC_j-\sum_{i=j}\sum {}^nC_i\cdot{}^nC_j}{2}$$

$$=\frac{(2^n)^2-\sum_{i=0}^{n}({}^nC_i)^2}{2}=\frac{2^{2n}-{}^{2n}C_n}{2}=2^{2n-1}-\frac{2n!}{2(n!)^2}$$

Example 85. If $(1+x)^n=C_0+C_1x+C_2x^2+\ldots+C_nx^n$, find the values of the following.

(i) $\sum_{0\le i<j\le n}\sum C_i$ (ii) $\sum_{0\le i<j\le n}\sum jC_i$ (iii) $\sum_{i\ne j}\sum C_i\,C_j$

(iv) $\sum_{0\le i\le j\le n}\sum C_i\,C_j$ (v) $\sum_{0\le i<j\le n}\sum (C_i\pm C_j)^2$

(vi) $\sum_{0\le i<j\le n}\sum (i+j)\,C_i\,C_j$ (vii) $\sum_{0\le i<j\le n}\sum (i\cdot j)\,C_i\,C_j$

Sol. (i) $\sum_{0\le i<j\le n}\sum C_i=\frac{\left(\sum_{i=0}^{n}\sum_{j=0}^{n}C_i\right)-\sum_{i=j}\sum C_i}{2}$

$$=\frac{(n+1)\sum_{i=0}^{n}C_i-\sum_{i=0}^{n}C_i}{2}=n\cdot 2^{n-1}$$

(ii) Here, j and C_i are not symmetrical.

$$\sum_{0\le i<j\le n}\sum j\,C_i=\sum_{r=0}^{n-1}{}^nC_r\,\{(r+1)+(r+2)+(r+3)+\ldots+n\}$$

$$=\sum_{r=0}^{n-1}{}^nC_r\cdot\frac{(n-r)(n+r+1)}{2}$$

$$=\frac{1}{2}\sum_{r=0}^{n-1}{}^nC_r\,(n^2-r^2+n-r)$$

$$=\frac{1}{2}(n^2+n)\sum_{r=0}^{n-1}{}^nC_r-\frac{1}{2}\sum_{r=0}^{n-1}r\cdot{}^nC_r-\frac{1}{2}\sum_{r=0}^{n-1}r^2\cdot{}^nC_r$$

$$=\frac{1}{2}(n^2+n)(2^n-1)-\frac{1}{2}\cdot n\cdot(2^{n-1}-1)-\frac{1}{2}\cdot n\,[(n-1)(2^{n-2}-1)+2^{n-1}-1]$$

$$=n(3n+1)\cdot 2^{n-3}$$

(iii) Here, $i\ne j$ i.e., $i>j$ or $i<j$

But C_i and C_j are symmetrical.

$$\therefore\ \sum_{i\ne j}\sum C_i\,C_j=2\sum_{0\le i<j\le n}\sum C_i\,C_j$$

$$=2\left(\frac{2^{2n}-{}^{2n}C_n}{2}\right)\quad\text{[from corollary I]}$$

$$=2^{2n}-{}^{2n}C_n$$

(iv) $\sum_{0\le i\le j\le n}\sum C_iC_j=\sum_{0\le i<j\le n}\sum C_iC_j+\sum_{i=j}\sum C_iC_j$

$$=\frac{1}{2}(2^{2n}-{}^{2n}C_n)+{}^{2n}C_n\quad\text{[from corollary I]}$$

$$=\frac{1}{2}(2^{2n}+{}^{2n}C_n)$$

(v) $\sum_{0\le i<j\le n}\sum (C_i\pm C_j)^2=\sum_{0\le i<j\le n}\sum (C_i^2+C_j^2\pm 2\,C_iC_j)$

$$=\sum_{0\le i<j\le n}\sum (C_i^2+C_j^2)\pm 2\sum_{0\le i<j\le n}\sum C_i\,C_j$$

$$\because\ \sum_{0\le i<j\le n}\sum (C_i^2+C_j^2)=\frac{\sum_{i=0}^{n}\sum_{j=0}^{n}(C_i^2+C_j^2)-2\sum_{i=0}^{n}C_i^2}{2}$$

$$=\frac{\sum_{i=0}^{n}\left(\sum_{j=0}^{n}C_i^2+\sum_{j=0}^{n}C_j^2\right)-2\cdot{}^{2n}C_n}{2}$$

$$= \frac{\sum_{i=0}^{n} ((n+1)\,C_i^2 + {}^{2n}C_n) - 2\cdot{}^{2n}C_n}{2}$$

$$= \frac{(n+1)\sum_{i=0}^{n} C_i^2 + {}^{2n}C_n \sum_{i=0}^{n} 1 - 2\cdot{}^{2n}C_n}{2}$$

$$= \frac{(n+1)\cdot{}^{2n}C_n + {}^{2n}C_n\cdot(n+1) - 2\cdot{}^{2n}C_n}{2}$$

$$= n\cdot{}^{2n}C_n$$

$$\therefore \sum_{0\le i<j\le n}\sum (C_i \pm C_j)^2 = n\cdot{}^{2n}C_n \pm (2^{2n} - {}^{2n}C_n)$$

[from corollary 1]

$$= (n \mp 1)\,{}^{2n}C_n \pm 2^{2n}$$

(vi) $\sum_{0\le i<j\le n}\sum (i+j)C_iC_j$

Let $P = \sum_{0\le i<j\le n}\sum (i+j)\,C_i\,C_j$ ...(i)

Replacing i by $n-i$ and j by $n-j$ in Eq. (i), then we get

$$P = \sum_{0\le i<j\le n}\sum (n-i+n-j)\,C_{n-i}\,C_{n-j}$$

[∵ sum of binomial expansion does not change if we replace r by $n-r$]

$$P = \sum_{0\le i<j\le n}\sum (2n-i-j)\,C_i\,C_j$$

[$\because {}^nC_r = {}^nC_{n-r}$] ...(ii)

On adding Eqs. (i) and (ii), we get

$$2P = 2n\sum_{0\le i<j\le n}\sum C_i\,C_j$$

or $P = n\sum_{0\le i<j\le n}\sum C_i\,C_j = \frac{n}{2}(2^{2n} - {}^{2n}C_n)$

[from corollary I]

(vii) $\sum_{0\le i<j\le n}\sum (i\cdot j)\,C_i\,C_j = \sum_{0\le i<j\le n}\sum (i\,{}^nC_i)(j\cdot{}^nC_j)$

$$= n^2\sum_{0\le i<j\le n}\sum {}^{n-1}C_{i-1}\,{}^{n-1}C_{j-1}$$

$$= n^2\left[\frac{2^{2(n-1)} - {}^{2n-2}C_{n-1}}{2}\right]$$ [from corollary I]

$$= n^2\left(2^{2n-3} - \frac{1}{2}\cdot{}^{2n-2}C_{n-1}\right)$$

Milestone Practice 6.2

1. Find the greatest integer less than or equal to $(\sqrt{2}+1)^6$.
2. Show that $2092^{51} - 2055^{51} + 2038^{51} + 2001^{51}$ is divisible by 37 and 1998 both.
3. Show that $2^{4n+4} - 15n - 16$, where $n \in N$ is divisible by 225.
4. Find the remainder when $1690^{2608} + 2608^{1690}$ is divided by 7.
5. Find the sum of ${}^{17}C_0 + {}^{17}C_1 + {}^{17}C_2 + \ldots + {}^{17}C_8$.
6. Find the sum of the coefficient of all integral powers of x in the expansion of $(1+2\sqrt{x})^{40}$.
7. If the sum of the coefficient in the expansion of $(\alpha^2x^2 - 3\alpha x + 2)^{51}$ is zero, then find the value of α.
8. If the number of terms in the expansion of $(x+y+z)^n$ are 36, then find the value of n.
9. If $x = 3\,{}^nC_0 - 8\,{}^nC_1 + 13\,{}^nC_2 - 18\,{}^nC_3 + \ldots$, then find x.
10. Prove that
$$\frac{{}^nC_1}{1} - \frac{{}^nC_2}{2} + \frac{{}^nC_3}{3} - \frac{{}^nC_4}{4} + \ldots + \frac{(-1)^{n-1}}{n}\,{}^nC_n = 1 + \frac{1}{2} + \frac{1}{3} + \ldots + \frac{1}{n}$$
11. Find the sum of $1\times 2\times {}^nC_1 + 2\times 3\times {}^nC_2 + \ldots + n(n+1)\times {}^nC_n$.
12. If $x + y = 1$, prove that
$$\sum_{r=0}^{n} r\,{}^nC_r x^r y^{n-r} = nx.$$
13. Find $\sum_{r=0}^{n} {}^{n+r}C_r$.

Answer Key

1. 197
4. 1
5. 2^{16}
6. $\frac{3^{40}+1}{2}$
7. 1, 2
8. 7
9. 0
11. $n(n+3)\times 2^{n-2}$
13. ${}^{2n+1}C_{n+1}$

For Detailed Solution

JEE Pattern EXAMPLES

Single Option Correct Type Questions

Example 1 *If T_6 is the 6th term of the expansion $\left(2x^2 - \frac{1}{3x^2}\right)^{10}$, then $[T_6]$ is, where $[\cdot]$ denotes greatest integer function.*

(a) 33 (b) 34 (c) – 33 (d) – 34

Sol. (d) We have, $\left(2x^2 - \frac{1}{3}x^2\right)^{10}$

$\therefore \quad T_6 = T_{5+1}$

$$= {}^{10}C_5(2x^2)^{10-5}\left(\frac{-1}{3x^2}\right)^5 = {}^{10}C_5 \times \frac{2^5}{(-3)^5} \times \frac{x^{10}}{x^{10}}$$

$$= -\frac{10\times9\times8\times7\times6}{5\times4\times3\times2\times1} \times \frac{32}{243} = -\frac{896}{27}$$

$\therefore [T_6] = -34$

Example 2 *The term in $\left(\sqrt[3]{\frac{a}{\sqrt{b}}} + \sqrt{\frac{b}{\sqrt[3]{a}}}\right)^{21}$ which has the same power of a and b is*

(a) 9th (b) 10th (c) 11th (d) 12th

Sol. (b) We have, $T_{r+1} = {}^{21}C_r\left(\sqrt[3]{\frac{a}{\sqrt{b}}}\right)^{21-r}\left(\sqrt{\frac{b}{\sqrt[3]{a}}}\right)^r$

$$= {}^{21}C_r a^{7-\frac{r}{3}-\frac{r}{6}} \cdot b^{\frac{1}{2}r-\frac{7}{2}+\frac{1}{6}r}$$

$$= {}^{21}C_r a^{7-\frac{1}{2}r} \cdot b^{\frac{2}{3}r-\frac{7}{2}}$$

For same power of a and b,

$$7 - \frac{1}{2}r = \frac{2}{3}r - \frac{7}{2}$$

$\Rightarrow \quad 7 + \frac{7}{2} = \frac{2}{3}r + \frac{1}{2}r$

$\Rightarrow \quad \frac{21}{2} = \frac{7}{6}r$

$\Rightarrow \quad r = 9$

$\therefore T_{10}$ is required term.

JEE SCANNER

Example 3 Similar to PYQ Asked in JEE Main 2024

If the term independent of x in the expansion of $\left(ax - \frac{1}{x}\right)^{10}$ is – 8064, then a^3 is equal to

(a) 8 (b) 27

(c) 64 (d) 216

Sol. (a) General term of expansion $\left(ax - \frac{1}{x}\right)^{10}$

$$= {}^{10}C_r(ax)^{10-r}\left(\frac{-1}{x}\right)^r$$

$$= {}^{10}C_r a^{10-r}(-1)^r \cdot x^{10-r-r}$$

For term independent of x, we have,

$$10 - r - r = 0$$

$\Rightarrow \quad 2r = 10$

$\Rightarrow \quad r = 5$

$\therefore \quad {}^{10}C_5 a^{10-5}(-1)^5 = -8064$ [given]

$\Rightarrow \quad \frac{10!}{5!5!}a^5 \cdot (-1) = -8064$

$\Rightarrow \quad \frac{10\times9\times8\times7\times6}{5\times4\times3\times2} \cdot a^5 = 8064$

$\Rightarrow \quad a^5 = 32 \Rightarrow a^5 = 2^5$

$\therefore \quad a = 2$

Thus, $a^3 = 2^3 = 8$

Skill Builder

If the term independent of x in the expansion of $\left(\sqrt{\frac{x}{a}} + \sqrt{\frac{3}{x}}\right)^{10}$ is 252, then a^2 is equal to

(a) 4 (b) 9

(c) 16 (d) 25

For Sol.

Example 4 *The remainder when 7^{103} is divided by 25 is*

(a) 16 (b) 17 (c) 18 (d) 19

Sol. (c) We have,

$$7^{103} = 7 \times 7^{102}$$
$$= 7 \times (49)^{51}$$
$$= 7(50-1)^{51}$$
$$= 7\,[{}^{51}C_0 50^{51} - {}^{51}C_1 50^{50} + \ldots - {}^{51}C_{51} 50^0]$$
$$= 7\,[25k - 1]$$
$$= 7 \cdot 25k - 7 - 25 + 25$$
$$= 25(7k-1) + 18$$

$\therefore$ Remainder $= 18$

Example 5 *The coefficient of x^4 in the expansion of $(1+x+x^2+x^3)^{11}$ is*

(a) 900 (b) 945 (c) 990 (d) 1025

Sol. (c) We have,

$$(1 + x + x^2 + x^3)^{11}$$
$$= [(1+x) + x^2(1+x)]^{11}$$
$$= [(1+x)(1+x^2)]^{11}$$
$$= (1+x)^{11}(1+x^2)^{11}$$
$$= (1 + {}^{11}C_1 x + {}^{11}C_2 x^2 + {}^{11}C_3 x^3 + {}^{11}C_4 x^4 + \ldots)(1 + {}^{11}C_1 x^2 + {}^{11}C_2 x^4 + \ldots)$$

$\therefore$ Coefficient of $x^4 = {}^{11}C_2 + {}^{11}C_1 \times {}^{11}C_2 + {}^{11}C_4$

$$= \frac{11 \times 10}{2 \times 1} + \frac{11 \times 11 \times 10}{2 \times 1} + \frac{11 \times 10 \times 9 \times 8}{4 \times 3 \times 2 \times 1}$$
$$= 55 + 605 + 330$$
$$= 990$$

Example 6 *The value of*

$${}^{10}C_1(x-1)^2 - {}^{10}C_2(x-2)^2 + {}^{10}C_3(x-3)^2 + \ldots - {}^{10}C_{10}(x-10)^2 \text{ is}$$

(a) x^8 (b) x^6 (c) x^4 (d) x^2

Sol. (d) Let $S = {}^{10}C_1(x-1)^2 - {}^{10}C_2(x-2)^2 + {}^{10}C_3(x-3)^2 + \ldots - {}^{10}C_{10}(x-10)^2$

$$= \sum_{r=1}^{10} (-1)^{r+1}\, {}^{10}C_r (x-r)^2$$
$$= \sum_{r=1}^{10} (-1)^{r+1}\, {}^{10}C_r (x^2 - 2xr + r^2)$$
$$= x^2 \sum_{r=1}^{10} (-1)^{r+1}\, {}^{10}C_r - 2x \sum_{r=1}^{10} (-1)^{r+1}\, {}^{10}C_r r + \sum_{r=1}^{10} (-1)^{r+1}\, {}^{10}C_r r^2$$
$$= x^2 \sum_{r=1}^{10} (-1)^{r+1}\, {}^{10}C_r - 2x(0) + 0$$
$$= x^2({}^{10}C_1 - {}^{10}C_2 + {}^{10}C_3 - {}^{10}C_4 + \ldots - {}^{10}C_{10})$$
$$= x^2(1)$$
$$= x^2$$

JEE SCANNER

Example 7 Similar to PYQ Asked in JEE Main 2024

If the constant term in the expansion of $\left(\sqrt{\frac{x}{3}} + \frac{\sqrt{3}}{2x^2}\right)^{10}$, $x \neq 0$ is $\frac{\alpha}{12}$, then $\frac{\alpha^3}{5}$ is equal to

(a) 64 (b) 81 (c) 25 (d) 169

Sol. (c) For $\left(\sqrt{\frac{x}{3}} + \frac{\sqrt{3}}{2x^2}\right)^{10}$, then general term is

$$T_{r+1} = {}^{10}C_r \left(\sqrt{\frac{x}{3}}\right)^{10-r} \cdot \left(\frac{\sqrt{3}}{2x^2}\right)^r$$
$$= {}^{10}C_r (\sqrt{3})^{r-10} \cdot (\sqrt{3})^r \cdot 2^{-r} \cdot x^{\frac{10-r}{2} - 2r}$$
$$= {}^{10}C_r (\sqrt{3})^{2r-10} \cdot 2^{-r} x^{\frac{10-5r}{2}}$$

For Constant term

$$\frac{10-5r}{2} = 0$$
$$\Rightarrow \quad r = 2$$

Thus, $T_3 = {}^{10}C_2 3^{\left(\frac{4-10}{2}\right)} \cdot 2^{-2}$

$$= \frac{10!}{2!8!} 3^{-3} \cdot 2^{-2}$$
$$= \frac{10 \times 9}{2} \times \frac{1}{3^3 \times 2^2}$$
$$= \frac{5 \times 2 \times 3^2}{2 \times 3^3 \times 2^2} = \frac{5}{3 \times 2^2} = \frac{5}{12}$$

On comparing, $\alpha = 5$

Thus, $\frac{\alpha^3}{5} = \frac{5^3}{5} = 5^2 = 25$

Skill Builder

If the constant term in the expansion of $\left(2x^2 - \frac{3}{x^3}\right)^{25}$, $x \neq 0$ is ${}^{25}C_a 2^b \cdot 3^c$, then $a + b + c$ is equal to

(a) 15 (b) 20
(c) 45 (d) 35

For Sol.

Example 8 If $\binom{2n+1}{0}+\binom{2n+1}{3}+\binom{2n+1}{6}+\ldots=170$, then n equals

(a) 2 (b) 4 (c) 6 (d) 8

Sol. (b) $\because (1+x)^{2n+1} = {}^{2n+1}C_0 + {}^{2n+1}C_1x + {}^{2n+1}C_2x^2 + {}^{2n+1}C_3x^3 + {}^{2n+1}C_4x^4 + {}^{2n+1}C_5x^5 + {}^{2n+1}C_6x^6 + \ldots$

Putting $x = 1, \omega, \omega^2$ (where ω is cube root of unity) and adding, we get

$$2^{2n+1} + (1+\omega)^{2n+1} + (1+\omega^2)^{2n+1} = 3({}^{2n+1}C_0 + {}^{2n+1}C_3 + {}^{2n+1}C_6 + \ldots)$$

$$\Rightarrow \quad 2^{2n+1} - \omega^{2(2n+1)} - \omega^{2n+1} = 3({}^{2n+1}C_0 + {}^{2n+1}C_3 + {}^{2n+1}C_6 + \ldots)$$

$[\because 1+\omega+\omega^2=0]$

$$\Rightarrow \quad {}^{2n+1}C_0 + {}^{2n+1}C_3 + {}^{2n+1}C_6 + \ldots = \frac{1}{3}(2^{2n+1} - \omega^{2(2n+1)} - \omega^{2n+1})$$

$$\Rightarrow \quad \binom{2n+1}{0}+\binom{2n+1}{3}+\binom{2n+1}{6}+\ldots = \frac{1}{3}(2^{2n+1} - \omega^{2(2n+1)} - \omega^{2n+1})$$

$$\Rightarrow \quad 170 = \frac{1}{3}(2^{2n+1} - \omega^{2(2n+1)} - \omega^{2n+1})$$

For $n = 4$, $170 = \frac{1}{3}(512 - 1 - 1) = 170$ $[\because \omega^3 = 1]$

Hence, $n = 4$

Example 9 $({}^mC_0 + {}^mC_1 - {}^mC_2 - {}^mC_3) + ({}^mC_4 + {}^mC_5 - {}^mC_6 - {}^mC_7) + \ldots = 0$ if and only if for some positive integer k, m is equal to

(a) $4k$ (b) $4k+1$ (c) $4k-1$ (d) $4k+2$

Decoding the Question

The Demoivre's theorem states that for any real number x,
$(\cos x + i\sin x)^n = \cos(nx) + i\sin(nx)$

Sol. (c) If $\theta \in R$ and $i = \sqrt{-1}$, then $(\cos\theta + i\sin\theta)^m$

$$= {}^mC_0(\cos\theta)^m + {}^mC_1(\cos\theta)^{m-1}(i\sin\theta) + {}^mC_2(\cos\theta)^{m-2}(i\sin\theta)^2 + \ldots + {}^mC_m(i\sin\theta)^m$$

$$(\cos m\theta + i\sin m\theta) = [{}^mC_0(\cos\theta)^m - {}^mC_2(\cos\theta)^{m-2}\cdot\sin^2\theta + {}^mC_4(\cos\theta)^{m-4}\sin^4\theta - \ldots] + i[{}^mC_1(\cos\theta)^{m-1}\cdot\sin\theta - {}^mC_3(\cos\theta)^{m-3}\sin^3\theta + \ldots]$$

[using Demoivre's theorem]

Comparing real and imaginary parts, we get

$$\cos m\theta = {}^mC_0(\cos\theta)^m - {}^mC_2(\cos\theta)^{m-2}\sin^2\theta + {}^mC_4(\cos\theta)^{m-4}\sin^4\theta - \ldots \quad \ldots(i)$$

$$\sin m\theta = {}^mC_1(\cos\theta)^{m-1}\cdot\sin\theta - {}^mC_3(\cos\theta)^{m-3}\cdot\sin^3\theta + \ldots \quad \ldots(ii)$$

On adding Eqs. (i) and (ii), we get

$$\cos m\theta + \sin m\theta = {}^mC_0(\cos\theta)^m + {}^mC_1(\cos\theta)^{m-1}\cdot\sin\theta - {}^mC_2(\cos\theta)^{m-2}\sin^2\theta - {}^mC_3(\cos\theta)^{m-3}\sin^3\theta + {}^mC_4(\cos\theta)^{m-4}\sin^4\theta + \ldots \sin\left(m\theta + \frac{\pi}{4}\right)$$

$$= (\cos\theta)^m\left\{\begin{array}{l}{}^mC_0 + {}^mC_1\tan\theta - {}^mC_2\tan^2\theta - {}^mC_3\tan^3\theta \\ + {}^mC_4\tan^4\theta + {}^mC_5\tan^5\theta - \ldots\end{array}\right\}$$

Putting $\theta = \frac{\pi}{4}$, $\sqrt{2}\sin\left(\frac{(m+1)\pi}{4}\right) = \frac{1}{2^{m/2}}$

$$\left\{\begin{array}{l}({}^mC_0 + {}^mC_1 - {}^mC_2 - {}^mC_3) + ({}^mC_4 + {}^mC_5 - {}^mC_6 - {}^mC_7) \\ + \ldots + ({}^mC_{m-3} + {}^mC_{m-2} - {}^mC_{m-1} - {}^mC_m)\end{array}\right\}$$

$\because ({}^mC_0 + {}^mC_1 - {}^mC_2 - {}^mC_3) + ({}^mC_4 + {}^mC_5 - {}^mC_6 - {}^mC_7) + \ldots = 0$ [given]

$$\therefore \quad \sin\left(\frac{(m+1)\pi}{4}\right) = 0 \Rightarrow \frac{(m+1)\pi}{4} = k\pi$$

or $\quad m = 4k - 1, \forall k \in I$

Example 10 If coefficient of x^n in the expansion of $(1+x)^{101}(1-x+x^2)^{100}$ is non-zero, then n cannot be of the form

(a) $3\lambda + 1$ (b) 3λ (c) $3\lambda + 2$ (d) None of these

Sol. (c) $\because (1+x)^{101}(1-x+x^2)^{100} = (1+x)((1+x)(1-x+x^2))^{100}$

$$= (1+x)(1+x^3)^{100}$$

$$= (1+x)(1 + {}^{100}C_1x^3 + {}^{100}C_2x^6 + {}^{100}C_3x^9 + \ldots + \ldots + {}^{100}C_{100}x^{300})$$

Clearly, in this expression x^3 will present if $n = 3\lambda$ or $n = 3\lambda + 1$. So, n cannot be of the form $3\lambda + 2$.

Example 11 The sum $\sum_{i=0}^{m}\binom{10}{i}\binom{20}{m-i}$, (where $\frac{p}{q} = 0$, if $p < q$) is maximum when m is

(a) 5 (b) 10 (c) 15 (d) 20

Sol. (c) $\sum_{i=0}^{m}\binom{10}{i}\binom{20}{m-i} = \sum_{i=0}^{m} {}^{10}C_i\,{}^{20}C_{m-i}$

$$= {}^{10}C_0\cdot{}^{20}C_m + {}^{10}C_1\cdot{}^{20}C_{m-1} + {}^{10}C_2\cdot{}^{20}C_{m-2} + \ldots + {}^{10}C_m\cdot{}^{20}C_0$$

= Coefficient of x^m in the expansion of product $(1+x)^{10}(1+x)^{20}$

= Coefficient of x^m in the expansion of $(1+x)^{30} = {}^{30}C_m$

To get maximum value of the given sum, ${}^{30}C_m$ should be maximum. Which is so, when $m = \frac{30}{2} = 15$

Example 12 If ${}^{n-1}C_r = (k^2 - 3)\cdot{}^nC_{r+1}$ then k belongs to

(a) $(-\infty, -2]$ (b) $[2, \infty)$ (c) $[-\sqrt{3}, \sqrt{3}]$ (d) $(\sqrt{3}, 2]$

Sol. (d) $\because \quad {}^{n-1}C_r = (k^2-3)\cdot{}^nC_{r+1}$

$$\Rightarrow \quad k^2 - 3 = \frac{{}^{n-1}C_r}{{}^nC_{r+1}} = \frac{r+1}{n} \quad \ldots(i)$$

$$\Rightarrow \quad 0 \le r \le n-1$$

$$\Rightarrow \quad 1 \le r+1 \le n$$

$$\Rightarrow \quad \frac{1}{n} \le \frac{r+1}{n} \le 1$$

$$\Rightarrow \quad \frac{1}{n} \le (k^2-3) \le 1$$

$$\Rightarrow \quad 3 + \frac{1}{n} \le k^2 \le 4 \quad \text{or} \quad 3 < k^2 \le 4 \quad [\text{here, } n \ge 2]$$

$$\therefore \quad k \in [-2, \sqrt{3}) \cup (\sqrt{3}, 2]$$

Example 13 *The coefficient of x^{50} in the series $\sum_{r=1}^{101} rx^{r-1}(1+x)^{101-r}$ is*

(a) ${}^{100}C_{50}$ (b) ${}^{101}C_{50}$

(c) ${}^{102}C_{50}$ (d) ${}^{103}C_{50}$

Sol. (c) Let $S = \sum_{r=1}^{101} rx^{r-1}(1+x)^{101-r}$

$$= (1+x)^{100} + 2x(1+x)^{99} + 3x^2(1+x)^{98} + \ldots + 101x^{100}$$

$$S = (1+x)^{100}\left\{1 + 2\left(\frac{x}{1+x}\right) + 3\left(\frac{x}{1+x}\right)^2 + \ldots + 101\left(\frac{x}{1+x}\right)^{100}\right\} \quad \ldots(i)$$

$$\therefore \frac{Sx}{(1+x)} = (1+x)^{100}\left\{\left(\frac{x}{1+x}\right) + 2\left(\frac{x}{1+x}\right)^2 + 3\left(\frac{x}{1+x}\right)^3 + \ldots + 101\left(\frac{x}{1+x}\right)^{101}\right\} \quad \ldots(ii)$$

On subtracting Eq. (ii) from Eq. (i), then we get

$$\frac{S}{(1+x)} = (1+x)^{100}\left\{1 + \left(\frac{x}{1+x}\right) + \left(\frac{x}{1+x}\right)^2 + \ldots + \left(\frac{x}{1+x}\right)^{100} - 101\left(\frac{x}{1+x}\right)^{101}\right\}$$

$$= (1+x)^{100}\left\{\frac{1\cdot\left(1 - \left(\frac{x}{1+x}\right)^{101}\right)}{1 - \left(\frac{x}{1+x}\right)} - 101\left(\frac{x}{1+x}\right)^{101}\right\}$$

$$\therefore \quad S = (1+x)^{102} - x^{101}(1+x) - 101x^{101}$$

and coefficient of x^{50} in $S = {}^{102}C_{50}$.

Example 14 *The largest integer λ such that 2^{λ} divides $3^{2^n} - 1$, $n \in N$ is*

(a) $n-1$ (b) n

(c) $n+1$ (d) $n+2$

Sol. (d) $\because 3^{2^n} - 1 = (4-1)^{2^n} - 1$

$$= (4^{2^n} - {}^{2^n}C_1 \cdot 4^{2^n-1} + {}^{2^n}C_2 \cdot 4^{2^n-2} - \ldots - {}^{2^n}C_{2^n-1} \cdot 4 + 1) - 1$$

$$= 4^{2^n} - 2^n \cdot 4^{2^n-1} + \frac{2^n(2^n-1)}{2} \cdot 4^{2^n-2} - \ldots - 2^n \cdot 4$$

$$= 2^{n+2}(2^{2^{n+1}-n-2} - 2^{2^{n+1}-4} + \ldots - 1)$$

$$= 2^{n+2}k,$$

where $k = (2^{2^{n+1}-n-2} - 2^{2^{n+1}-4} + \ldots - 1)$ is an integer.

Hence, $3^{2^n} - 1$ is divisible by 2^{n+2}

$\Rightarrow \quad \lambda = n+2$

Example 15 *The last term in the binomial expansion of $\left(\sqrt[3]{2} - \frac{1}{\sqrt{2}}\right)^n$ is $\left(\frac{1}{3\sqrt[3]{9}}\right)^{\log_3 8}$, then the 5th term from beginning is*

(a) ${}^{10}C_6$ (b) $2\,{}^{10}C_4$

(c) $\frac{1}{2}\cdot{}^{10}C_4$ (d) None of these

Sol. (a) Since, last term in the expansion of $\left(\sqrt[3]{2} - \frac{1}{\sqrt{2}}\right)^n$

$$= \left(\frac{1}{3\cdot\sqrt[3]{9}}\right)^{\log_3 8}$$

$$\Rightarrow \quad {}^nC_n \cdot \left(-\frac{1}{\sqrt{2}}\right)^n = \left(\frac{1}{3\cdot\sqrt[3]{9}}\right)^{\log_3 8}$$

$$\Rightarrow \quad (-1)^n \cdot \left(\frac{1}{2}\right)^{n/2} = \left(\frac{1}{3^{5/3}}\right)^{\log_3 8}$$

$$= (3^{-5/3})^{\log_3 2^3}$$

$$= 3^{-\frac{5}{3}\times 3\times \log_3 2}$$

$$= 3^{-5\log_3 2} = 3^{\log_3 2^{-5}} = 2^{-5} = \left(\frac{1}{2}\right)^5$$

$$\Rightarrow \quad (-1)^n \cdot \left(\frac{1}{2}\right)^{n/2} = \left(\frac{1}{2}\right)^5$$

$\therefore \quad n = 10$

Now, 5th term from beginning $= {}^{10}C_4(\sqrt[3]{2})^6\left(-\frac{1}{\sqrt{2}}\right)^4$

$$= {}^{10}C_4 \cdot 2^2 \cdot \frac{1}{2^2} = {}^{10}C_4 = {}^{10}C_6$$

Example 16 *If $f(x) = \sum_{r=1}^{n}\{r^2({}^nC_r - {}^nC_{r-1}) + (2r+1)\,{}^nC_r\}$* and $f(30) = 30(2)^{\lambda}$, then the value of λ is

(a) 3 (b) 4 (c) 5 (d) 6

Sol. (c) Here, $f(x) = \sum_{r=1}^{n}\{r^2({}^nC_r - {}^nC_{r-1}) + (2r+1)\,{}^nC_r\}$

$$= \sum_{r=1}^{n}(r^2 + 2r + 1)\,{}^nC_r - r^2 \cdot {}^nC_{r-1}$$

$$= \sum_{r=1}^{n}((r+1)^2 \cdot {}^nC_r - r^2 \cdot {}^nC_{r-1})$$

$$= (n+1)^2 \cdot {}^nC_n - 1^2 \cdot {}^nC_0$$

$$= (n+1)^2 - 1 = (n^2 + 2n)$$

$\therefore \quad f(30) = (30)^2 + 2(30) = 960$

$= 30 \times 32$

$= 30(2)^5 = 30(2)^{\lambda}$ [given]

Hence, $\lambda = 5$

More than One Correct Option Type Questions

Example 17 *If in the expansion of $(a+b)^n$, the first three terms of the expansion are 729, 7290 and 30375, respectively then*

(a) $a=3$ (b) $b=5$
(c) $n=6$ (d) None of these

Sol. (a,b,c) We have,

$$T_1 = {}^nC_0 a^{n-0} b^0 = a^n = 729 \quad \text{...(i)}$$

$$T_2 = {}^nC_1 a^{n-1} b^1 = n a^{n-1} b = 7290 \quad \text{...(ii)}$$

and $$T_3 = {}^nC_2 a^{n-2} b^2 = \frac{n(n-1)}{2} a^{n-2} b^2 = 30375 \quad \text{...(iii)}$$

On dividing Eq. (ii) by Eq. (i), we get

$$\frac{nb}{a} = 10 \quad \text{...(iv)}$$

On dividing Eq. (iii) by Eq. (ii), we get

$$\frac{(n-1)b}{a} = \frac{25}{3} \quad \text{...(v)}$$

From Eqs. (iv) and (v), we have

$$\frac{n}{n-1} = \frac{6}{5}$$

$$\Rightarrow \quad n = 6$$

Substituting $n=6$ in Eq. (i), we get

$$a^6 = 729$$

$$\Rightarrow \quad a = 3$$

Substituting $a=3$, $n=6$ in Eq (iv), we get

$$\frac{6b}{3} = 10$$

$$\Rightarrow \quad b = 5$$

Example 18 *For the number* $\dfrac{5^{99}}{13}$,

(a) Integral part is even (b) Integral part is odd
(c) Fractional part is $\dfrac{8}{13}$ (d) Remainder is 8

Sol. (b,c,d) We have,

$$5^{99} = 5 \times 5^{98} = 5 \times 25^{49} = 5(26-1)^{49}$$
$$= 5[{}^{49}C_0 26^{49} - {}^{49}C_1 26^{48} + {}^{49}C_2 26^{47} - \ldots + {}^{49}C_{48} 26 - {}^{49}C_{49}]$$
$$= 5(26k-1) = 130k - 5$$
$$= 130k - 13 + 8 = 13(10k-1) + 8$$

Hence, remainder is 8.

Integral part $= 10k - 1 =$ odd and fractional part $= \dfrac{8}{13}$

Example 19 *The middle term in the expansion of* $\left(\dfrac{x}{2}+2\right)^8$ *is 1120, then $x \in R$ is equal to*

(a) -2 (b) 3 (c) -3 (d) 2

Decoding the Question

In the expansion $(x+a)^n$ or $(x-a)^n$, if n is even, then the middle term is $\left(\dfrac{n}{2}+1\right)$th term, if n is odd, then the middle term is $\left(\dfrac{n+1}{2}\right)$th term and $\left(\dfrac{n+3}{2}\right)$th term.

Sol. (a,d) We have, $n = 8$ (even), so

$$\text{Middle term} = \left(\frac{n}{2}+1\right)\text{th term} = 5\text{th term}$$

Now, according to the question

$$T_5 = 1120$$

$$\Rightarrow \quad {}^8C_4 \left(\frac{x}{2}\right)^4 (2)^4 = 1120 \Rightarrow {}^8C_4 x^4 = 1120$$

$$\Rightarrow \quad \frac{8\times7\times6\times5}{4\times3\times2\times1} x^4 = 1120 \Rightarrow x^4 = 16 \Rightarrow x = \pm 2$$

Example 20 *Let* $a_n = \left(1+\dfrac{1}{n}\right)^n$. *Then for each $n \in N$*

(a) $a_n \ge 2$ (b) $a_n < 3$ (c) $a_n < 4$ (d) $a_n < 2$

Sol. (a,b,c) $\because$ $a_n = \left(1+\dfrac{1}{n}\right)^n = {}^nC_0 + {}^nC_1 \cdot \left(\dfrac{1}{n}\right) + \sum_{r=2}^{n} {}^nC_r \left(\dfrac{1}{n}\right)^r$

$$= 2 + \sum_{r=2}^{n} {}^nC_r \left(\frac{1}{n}\right)^r$$

$\therefore$ $a_n \ge 2$ for all $n \in N$

Also, $\lim_{n\to\infty} \left(1+\dfrac{1}{n}\right)^n = e = 2.7182\ldots$

$\therefore$ $a_n < e$

Finally, $2 \le a_n < e$

Example 21 *Let* $S_n(x) = \sum_{k=0}^{n} {}^nC_k \sin(kx)\cos((n-k)x)$, *then*

(a) $S_5\left(\dfrac{\pi}{2}\right) = 16$ (b) $S_7\left(\dfrac{-\pi}{2}\right) = 64$
(c) $S_{50}(\pi) = 0$ (d) $S_{51}(-\pi) = -2^{50}$

Sol. (a,b,c) $\because$ $S_n(x) = \sum_{k=0}^{n} {}^nC_k \sin(kx)\cos((n-k)x)$ ...(i)

Replace k by $n-k$ in Eq. (i), then

$$S_n(x) = \sum_{k=0}^{n} {}^nC_{n-k} \sin((n-k)x)\cos(kx)$$

or $$S_n(x) = \sum_{k=0}^{n} {}^nC_k \sin((n-k)x)\cos(kx) \quad \text{...(ii)}$$

On adding Eqs. (i) and (ii), we get

$$2S_n(x) = \sum_{k=0}^{n} {}^nC_k \cdot \sin(nx) = 2^n \cdot \sin(nx)$$

$$\Rightarrow \quad S_n(x) = 2^{n-1} \cdot \sin(nx)$$

$$\therefore \quad S_5\left(\frac{\pi}{2}\right) = 2^4 \cdot \sin\left(\frac{5\pi}{2}\right) = 16,$$

$$S_7\left(-\frac{\pi}{2}\right) = 2^6 \cdot \sin\left(-\frac{7\pi}{2}\right) = 2^6 \times -1 \times -1 = 64$$

$$S_{50}(\pi) = 2^{49} \cdot \sin(50\pi) = 0$$

and $$S_{51}(-\pi) = 2^{50} \cdot \sin(-51\pi) = 0$$

Example 22 *If $a+b=k$, when $a, b>0$ and $S(k,n)=\sum_{r=0}^{n} r^2({}^nC_r)a^r\cdot b^{n-r}$, then*

(a) $S(1,3)=3(3a^2+ab)$ (b) $S(2,4)=16(4a^2+ab)$

(c) $S(3,5)=25(5a^2+ab)$ (d) $S(4,6)=36(6a^2+ab)$

Decoding the Question

For the coefficients $C_0, C_1, \ldots, C_n$ of $(1+x)^n$, we know that

$$\frac{{}^nC_r}{{}^{n-1}C_{r-1}}=\frac{n}{r}$$

Sol. (a,b) $\because\ S(k,n)=\sum_{r=0}^{n} r^2\cdot({}^nC_r)a^r\cdot b^{n-r}$

$$=b^n\sum_{r=0}^{n} r^2\cdot\left(\frac{n}{r}\cdot{}^{n-1}C_{r-1}\right)\cdot\left(\frac{a}{b}\right)^r$$

$$=nb^n\sum_{r=0}^{n}((r-1)+1)^{n-1}C_{r-1}\cdot\left(\frac{a}{b}\right)^r$$

$$=nb^n\sum_{r=0}^{n}((n-1)\cdot{}^{n-2}C_{r-2}+{}^{n-1}C_{r-1})\left(\frac{a}{b}\right)^r$$

$$=nb^n\cdot(n-1)\cdot\left(\frac{a}{b}\right)^2\sum_{r=0}^{n}{}^{n-2}C_{r-2}\left(\frac{a}{b}\right)^{r-2}+nb^n\cdot\left(\frac{a}{b}\right)\sum_{r=0}^{n}{}^{n-1}C_{r-1}\left(\frac{a}{b}\right)^{r-1}$$

$$=nb^n\cdot(n-1)\left(\frac{a}{b}\right)^2\left(1+\frac{a}{b}\right)^{n-2}+nb^n\cdot\left(\frac{a}{b}\right)\cdot\left(1+\frac{a}{b}\right)^{n-1}$$

$$=n(n-1)a^2k^{n-2}+nak^{n-1}$$

$$=n^2a^2k^{n-2}+nak^{n-2}(k-a)=n^2a^2k^{n-2}+nabk^{n-2}$$

$\therefore\quad S(1,3)=9a^2+3ab=3(3a^2+ab)\qquad[\because\ a+b=k]$

$S(2,4)=16(4a^2+ab),\ S(3,5)=135(5a^2+ab)$

$S(4,6)=1536(6a^2+ab)$

Example 23 *The value of x, for which the ninth term in the expansion of $\left\{\frac{\sqrt{10}}{(\sqrt{x})^{5\log_{10}x}}+x\cdot x^{\frac{1}{2\log_{10}x}}\right\}^{10}$ is 450 is equal to*

(a) 10 (b) 10^2 (c) $\sqrt{10}$ (d) $10^{-2/5}$

Sol. (b,d) Let $\log_{10}x=\lambda\Rightarrow x=10^\lambda$ ...(i)

Given, $T_9=450$

$$\Rightarrow\ {}^{10}C_8\cdot\left(\frac{\sqrt{10}}{10^{\frac{5\lambda^2}{2}}}\right)^2\cdot(10^\lambda\cdot10^{1/2})^8=450$$

$$\Rightarrow\ {}^{10}C_2\cdot\frac{10}{10^{5\lambda^2}}\cdot10^{8\lambda}\cdot10^4=450\Rightarrow10^{8\lambda+4-5\lambda^2}=1=10^0$$

$$\Rightarrow\ 8\lambda+4-5\lambda^2=0\Rightarrow\ 5\lambda^2-8\lambda-4=0$$

$$\Rightarrow\ \lambda=2,-2/5$$

$$\Rightarrow\ x=10^2,10^{-2/5}\qquad\text{[from Eq. (i)]}$$

Example 24 *For a positive integer n, if the expansion of $\left(\frac{5}{x^2}+x^4\right)$ has a term independent of x, then n can be*

(a) 18 (b) 27 (c) 36 (d) 45

Sol. (a,b,c,d) Let $(r+1)$th term of $\left(\frac{5}{x^2}+x^4\right)^n$ be independent of x.

We have, $T_{r+1}={}^nC_r\left(\frac{5}{x^2}\right)^{n-r}(x^4)^r={}^nC_r\cdot5^{n-r}\cdot x^{6r-2n}$

For this term to be independent of x,

$$6r-2n=0\text{ or }n=3r$$

For $r=6, 9, 12, 15,$

$$n=18, 27, 36, 45$$

Passage Based Questions

Passage I

(Ex. Nos. 25 to 26)

Consider $(1+x+x^2)^n=\sum_{r=0}^{2n}a_r\,x^r$, where $a_0, a_1, a_2, \ldots, a_{2n}$ are real numbers and n is a positive integer.

Example 25 *The value of $\sum_{r=0}^{n-1}a_{2r}$ is*

(a) $\frac{3^n-2a_{2n}-1}{4}$ (b) $\frac{3^n-2a_{2n}+1}{4}$

(c) $\frac{3^n+2a_{2n}-1}{4}$ (d) $\frac{3^n+2a_{2n}+1}{4}$

Sol. (b) Given,

$$(1+x+x^2)^n=a_0+a_1x+a_2x^2+\ldots+a_{2n}x^{2n}\quad\text{...(i)}$$

$$\sum_{r=0}^{n-1}a_{2r}=a_0+a_2+\ldots+a_{n-1}\quad\text{...(ii)}$$

Now, put $x=1$ and $x=-1$ in Eq. (i), we get

$$3^n=a_0+a_1+a_2+\ldots+a_n+\ldots+a_{2n}\quad\text{...(iii)}$$

$$1=a_0-a_1+a_2-a_3+\ldots+a_n+\ldots+a_{2n}\quad\text{...(iv)}$$

On adding Eqs. (iii) and (iv), we get

$$2(a_0+a_2+a_4+\ldots+a_{n-1}+a_n+\ldots+a_{2n})=3^n+1$$

$$\Rightarrow\ 2[2(a_0+a_2+a_4+\ldots+a_{n-1})+a_{2n})=3^n+1$$

$[\because\ a_r=a_{2n-r}]$

$$\therefore\ a_0+a_2+a_4+\ldots+a_{n-1}=\frac{3^n-2a_{2n}+1}{4}$$

$$\Rightarrow\ \sum_{r=0}^{n-1}a_{2r}=\frac{3^n-2a_{2n}+1}{4}$$

Example 26 *The value of $\sum_{r=1}^{n}a_{2r-1}$ is*

(a) $\frac{3^n-1}{2}$ (b) $\frac{3^n-1}{4}$ (c) $\frac{3^n+1}{2}$ (d) $\frac{3^n+1}{4}$

Sol. (b) On subtracting Eq. (iv) from Eq. (iii), we get

$$2(a_1 + a_3 + a_5 + \dots + a_{n-1} + a_{n+1} + \dots + a_{2n-1}) = 3^n - 1$$

$$\Rightarrow \quad 2[2(a_1 + a_3 + a_5 + \dots + a_{2n-1}] = 3^n - 1 \qquad [\because a_r = a_{2n-r}]$$

$$\therefore \quad a_1 + a_3 + a_5 + \dots + a_{2n-1} = \frac{3^n - 1}{4}$$

$$\Rightarrow \quad \sum_{r=1}^{n} a_{2r-1} = \frac{3^n - 1}{4}$$

Stem Based Questions

Stem I

(Ex. Nos. 27 to 28)

Let
$$S = \sum_{r=1}^{30} \frac{{}^{30+r}C_r\,(2r-1)}{{}^{30}C_r\,(30+r)},$$

$$K = \sum_{r=0}^{30} ({}^{30}C_r)^2$$

and
$$G = \sum_{r=0}^{60} (-1)^r\,({}^{60}C_r)^2$$

Example 27 *The value of $(G - S)$ is ....*

(a) 0 (b) 1 (c) 2^{30} (d) 2^{60}

Sol. (b) $\because S = \sum_{r=1}^{30} \frac{{}^{30+r}C_r(2r-1)}{{}^{30}C_r(30+r)}$

$$= \sum_{r=0}^{30} \frac{{}^{30+r}C_r}{{}^{30}C_r}\left(1 - \frac{30-r+1}{30+r}\right)$$

$$= \sum_{r=0}^{30} \left[\frac{{}^{30+r}C_r}{{}^{30}C_r} - \frac{{}^{30+r}C_r}{{}^{30}C_r} \cdot \frac{30-r+1}{30+r}\right]$$

$$= \sum_{r=0}^{30} \left[\frac{{}^{30+r}C_r}{{}^{30}C_r} - \frac{\frac{30+r}{r} \cdot {}^{29+r}C_{r-1}}{{}^{30}C_r} \cdot \frac{30-r+1}{30+r}\right]$$

$$= \sum_{r=0}^{30} \left[\frac{{}^{30+r}C_r}{{}^{30}C_r} + \frac{{}^{29+r}C_{r-1}}{{}^{30}C_{r-1}}\right] \qquad \left[\because \frac{{}^nC_r}{{}^nC_{r-1}} = \frac{n-r+1}{r}\right]$$

For $r = 30$,

$$\frac{31-r}{r} \cdot {}^{30}C_r = {}^{30}C_{r-1} = \frac{{}^{30+30}C_{30}}{{}^{30}C_{30}} - \frac{{}^{29+1}C_0}{{}^{30}C_0} = {}^{60}C_{30} - 1$$

$$K = \sum_{r=1}^{30} ({}^{30}C_r)^2 = {}^{60}C_{30}$$

and $G = \sum_{r=0}^{60} (-1)^r\,({}^{60}C_r)^2$

$$= ({}^{60}C_0)^2 - ({}^{60}C_1)^2 + ({}^{60}C_2)^2 - \dots + ({}^{60}C_{60}) = {}^{60}C_{30}$$

$[\because n = 60$ is even$]$

$$\therefore \quad K = G$$

$$G - S = {}^{60}C_{30} - ({}^{60}C_{30} - 1) = 1$$

Example 28 *The value of $(SK - SG)$ is ....*

(a) 0 (b) 1 (c) 2^{30} (d) 2^{60}

Sol. (a) $SK - SG = S(K - G) = S(G - G) = 0 \qquad [\because K = G]$

Single Integer Answer Type Questions

Example 29 *The digit at unit's place in $2^{9^{100}}$ is ....*

Sol. (2) $\because \; 9^{100} = (2 \cdot 4 + 1)^{100} = 4n + 1$ [say]

[where n is positive integer]

$$\therefore \quad 2^{9^{100}} = 2^{4n+1} = 2^{4n} \cdot 2 = (16)^n \cdot 2$$

The digit at unit's place in $(16)^n = 6$.

$\therefore$ The digit at unit's place in $(16)^n \cdot 2 = 2$

Example 30 *If $(1+x)^n = \sum_{r=0}^{n} a_r x^r$, $b_r = 1 + \frac{a_r}{a_{r-1}}$ and $\prod_{r=1}^{n} b_r = \frac{(101)^{100}}{100!}$, then the value of $\frac{n}{20}$ is*

Sol. (5) Here, $a_r = {}^nC_r$

$$\therefore \quad b_r = 1 + \frac{a_r}{a_{r-1}} = 1 + \frac{{}^nC_r}{{}^nC_{r-1}}$$

$$= 1 + \frac{n-r+1}{r} = \frac{(n+1)}{r}$$

$$\Rightarrow \quad \prod_{r=1}^{n} b_r = \prod_{r=1}^{n} \frac{(n+1)}{r}$$

$$= \frac{(n+1)}{1} \cdot \frac{(n+1)}{2} \cdot \frac{(n+1)}{3} \dots \frac{(n+1)}{n} = \frac{(n+1)^n}{n!}$$

$$= \frac{(101)^{100}}{100!} \qquad \text{[given]}$$

$$\therefore \quad n = 100 \Rightarrow \frac{n}{20} = 5$$

Example 31 *Let m be the smallest positive integer such that the coefficient of x^2 in the expansion of $(1+x)^2 + (1+x)^3 + \dots + (1+x)^{49} + (1+mx)^{50}$ is $(3n+1)$ ${}^{51}C_3$ for some positive integer n. Then, the value of n is*

Sol. (5) Coefficient of x^2 in the expansion of

$$\{(1+x)^2 + (1+x)^3 + \dots + (1+x)^{49} + (1+mx)^{50}\} = (3n+1)^{51}C_3$$

$$\Rightarrow \quad {}^2C_2 + {}^3C_2 + {}^4C_2 + \dots + {}^{49}C_2 + {}^{50}C_2 \cdot m^2 = (3n+1) \cdot {}^{51}C_3$$

$$\Rightarrow \quad {}^{50}C_3 + {}^{50}C_2 m^2 = (3n+1) \cdot {}^{51}C_3$$

$$[\because {}^rC_r + {}^{r+1}C_r + \dots + {}^nC_r = {}^{n+1}C_{r+1}]$$

$$\Rightarrow \quad \frac{50 \times 49 \times 48}{3 \times 2 \times 1} + \frac{50 \times 49}{2} \times m^2 = (3n+1)\frac{51 \times 50 \times 49}{3 \times 2 \times 1}$$

$$\Rightarrow \quad m^2 = 51n + 1$$

$\therefore$ Minimum value of m^2 for which $(51n+1)$ is integer (perfect square) for $n=5$.

$\therefore \quad m^2 = 51\times 5+1$

$\Rightarrow \quad m^2 = 256$

$\Rightarrow \quad m = 16$ and $n = 5$

Hence, the value of n is 5.

Example 32 *The coefficient of x^9 in the expansion of $(1+x)(1+x^2)(1+x^3)\ldots(1+x^{100})$ is*

Sol. (8) Coefficient of x^9 in the expansion of

$(1+x)(1+x^2)(1+x^3)\ldots(1+x^{100}) =$ Terms having x^9

$$= [1^{99}\cdot x^9, 1^{98}\cdot x\cdot x^8, 1^{98}\cdot x^2\cdot x^7, 1^{98}\cdot x^3\cdot x^6, 1^{98}\cdot x^4\cdot x^5, 1^{97}\cdot x\cdot x^2\cdot x^6, 1^{97}\cdot x\cdot x^3\cdot x^5, 1^{97}\cdot x^2\cdot x^3\cdot x^4]$$

$\therefore$ Coefficient of $x^9 = 8$

Example 33 *The coefficients of three consecutive terms of $(1+x)^{n+5}$ are in the ratio $5:10:14$. Then, n is equal to*

Sol. (6) Let the three consecutive terms in $(1+x)^{n+5}$ be t_r, t_{r+1}, t_{r+2} having coefficients

$${}^{n+5}C_{r-1}, {}^{n+5}C_r, {}^{n+5}C_{r+1}.$$

Given, ${}^{n+5}C_{r-1} : {}^{n+5}C_r : {}^{n+5}C_{r+1} = 5:10:14$

$$\therefore \quad \frac{{}^{n+5}C_r}{{}^{n+5}C_{r-1}} = \frac{10}{5} \text{ and } \frac{{}^{n+5}C_{r+1}}{{}^{n+5}C_r} = \frac{14}{10}$$

$$\Rightarrow \quad \frac{n+5-(r-1)}{r} = 2$$

$$\text{and} \quad \frac{n-r+5}{r+1} = \frac{7}{5}$$

$\Rightarrow \quad n-r+6 = 2r$

and $\quad 5n-5r+25 = 7r+7$

$\Rightarrow \quad n+6 = 3r$ and $5n+18 = 12r$

$$\therefore \quad \frac{n+6}{3} = \frac{5n+18}{12}$$

$\Rightarrow \quad 4n+24 = 5n+18 \Rightarrow n = 6$

Numerical Value Type Questions

Example 34 *The total number of different terms in the product $({}^{101}C_0 - {}^{101}C_1x + {}^{101}C_2x^2 - \ldots - {}^{101}C_{101}x^{101})$ $(1+x+x^2+\ldots+x^{100})^{101}$ is ......*

Sol. (102) We have, $({}^{101}C_0 - {}^{101}C_1x + {}^{101}C_2x^2 - \ldots - {}^{101}C_{101}x^{101})(1+x+x^2+\ldots+x^{100})^{101}$

$$= (1-x)^{101}\left(\frac{1-x^{101}}{1-x}\right)^{101}$$

$$= (1-x^{101})^{101}$$

$\therefore$ Number of different terms $= 102$

JEE SCANNER

Example 35 Similar to PYQ Asked in JEE Main 2024

If the second, third and fourth terms in the expansion of $(x+y)^n$ are 4320, 5400 and 3000 respectively, then $n^2+x^2+y^2$ is equal to ....

Sol. (77) We know,

$$T_2 = {}^nC_1x^{n-1}y$$

$$\Rightarrow \quad n\cdot x^{n-1}\cdot y = 4320 \quad \ldots\text{(i)}$$

$$T_3 = {}^nC_2x^{n-2}\cdot y^2$$

$$\Rightarrow \quad \frac{n(n-1)}{2}\cdot x^{n-2}\cdot y^2 = 5400 \quad \ldots\text{(ii)}$$

$$\text{Now,} \quad \frac{T_2}{T_3} = \frac{4320}{5400}$$

$$\Rightarrow \quad \frac{2nx^{n-1}\cdot y}{n(n-1)\cdot x^{n-2}y^2} = \frac{432}{540}$$

$$\Rightarrow \quad \frac{x}{y} = \frac{2}{5}(n-1) \quad \ldots\text{(iii)}$$

$$\text{Now,} \quad T_4 = {}^nC_3x^{n-3}y^3$$

$$\Rightarrow \quad \frac{n(n-1)(n-2)}{6}\cdot x^{n-3}\cdot y^3 = 3000 \quad \ldots\text{(iv)}$$

$$\text{Now,} \quad \frac{T_3}{T_4} = \frac{5400}{3000}$$

$$\Rightarrow \quad \frac{6n(n-1)\cdot x^{n-2}y^2}{2\cdot n(n-1)(n-2)x^{n-3}\cdot y^3} = \frac{9}{5}$$

$$\Rightarrow \quad \frac{3x}{(n-2)y} = \frac{9}{5}$$

$$\Rightarrow \quad \frac{x}{y} = \frac{3}{5}(n-2) \quad \ldots\text{(v)}$$

From Eqs. (iii) and (v), we get

$$\frac{2}{5}(n-1) = \frac{3}{5}(n-2)$$

$\Rightarrow \quad 2n-2 = 3n-6$

$\Rightarrow \quad n = 4$

$$\text{Hence,} \quad \frac{x}{y} = \frac{2}{5}(4-1) = \frac{2}{5}\times 3 = \frac{6}{5}$$

$\therefore \quad x = 6, y = 5, n = 4$

$$\therefore \quad n^2+x^2+y^2 = 4^2+6^2+5^2$$

$$= 16+36+25$$

$$= 77$$

Skill Builder

If the first, second and third terms in the expansion of $(a+b)^n$ are 1, 14 and 84 respectively, then $6(a^2+b^3+n)$ is equal to ....

For Sol.

Example 36 *Coefficient of x^{11} in the expansion of $(1+x^2)^4(1+x^3)^7(1+x^4)^{12}$ is ....*

Sol. (1113) Coefficient of x^r in $(1+x)^n$ is ${}^nC_r$.

In this type of questions, we find different composition of terms where product will give us x^{11}.

Now, consider

Coefficient of x^{11} in expansion of $(1+x^2)^4(1+x^3)^7(1+x^4)^{12}$ is

(coefficient of x^a) $\times$ (coefficient of x^b) $\times$ (coefficient of x^c)

such that $a+b+c=11$

Here, $a=2m$, $b=3n$ and $c=4p$

$\therefore 2m+3n+4p=11$

Case I $m=0, n=1, p=2$

Case II $m=1, n=3, p=0$

Case III $m=2, n=1, p=1$

Case IV $m=4, n=1, p=0$

$\therefore$ Required coefficient

$$= {}^4C_0 \times {}^7C_1 \times {}^{12}C_2 + {}^4C_1 \times {}^7C_3 \times {}^{12}C_0 + {}^4C_2 \times {}^7C_1 \times {}^{12}C_1 + {}^4C_4 \times {}^7C_1 \times {}^{12}C_0$$

$$= 462 + 140 + 504 + 7$$

$$= 1113$$

Example 37 *The term independent of x in expansion of $\left(\dfrac{x+1}{x^{2/3}-x^{1/3}+1} - \dfrac{x-1}{x-x^{1/2}}\right)^{10}$ is ....*

Sol. (210) $\left[\dfrac{x+1}{x^{2/3}-x^{1/3}+1} - \dfrac{(x-1)}{x-x^{1/2}}\right]^{10}$

$$= \left[\frac{(x^{1/3})^3+1^3}{x^{2/3}-x^{1/3}+1} - \frac{\{(\sqrt{x})^2-1\}}{\sqrt{x}(\sqrt{x}-1)}\right]^{10}$$

$$= \left[\frac{(x^{1/3}+1)(x^{2/3}+1-x^{1/3})}{x^{2/3}-x^{1/3}+1} - \frac{\{(\sqrt{x})^2-1\}}{\sqrt{x}(\sqrt{x}-1)}\right]^{10}$$

$$= \left[(x^{1/3}+1) - \frac{(\sqrt{x}+1)}{\sqrt{x}}\right]^{10}$$

$$= (x^{1/3} - x^{-1/2})^{10}$$

$\therefore$ The general term is

$$T_{r+1} = {}^{10}C_r (x^{1/3})^{10-r}(-x^{-1/2})^r$$

$$= {}^{10}C_r (-1)^r x^{\frac{10-r}{3} - \frac{r}{2}}$$

For independent of x, put

$$\frac{10-r}{3} - \frac{r}{2} = 0 \Rightarrow 20 - 2r - 3r = 0$$

$\Rightarrow \quad 20 = 5r \Rightarrow r = 4$

$\therefore \quad T_5 = {}^{10}C_4 (-1)^4$

$$= \frac{10 \times 9 \times 8 \times 7}{4 \times 3 \times 2 \times 1} = 210$$

Example 38 *The largest value of x for which the 4th term in the expansion of $\left(5^{2/5 \log_5 \sqrt{4^x+44}} + \dfrac{1}{5^{\log_5 \sqrt[3]{2^{x-1}+7}}}\right)^8$ is 336, is ....*

Sol. (1) Given, $\left(5^{2/5 \log_5 \sqrt{4^x+44}} + \dfrac{1}{5^{\log_5 \sqrt[3]{2^{x-1}+7}}}\right)^8$

$$= \left(\sqrt{(4^x+44)^{2/5}} + \frac{1}{\sqrt[3]{2^{x-1}+7}}\right)^8$$

$$= \left((4^x+44)^{1/5} + \frac{1}{(2^{x-1}+7)^{1/3}}\right)^8$$

Now, $T_4 = T_{3+1} = {}^8C_3\{(4^x+44)^{1/5}\}^{8-3} \dfrac{1}{\{(2^{x-1}+7)^{1/3}\}^3}$

Given, $336 = {}^8C_3\left(\dfrac{4^x+44}{2^{x-1}+7}\right)$

Let $2^x = y \Rightarrow 336 = {}^8C_3\left(\dfrac{y^2+44}{\left(\frac{y}{2}\right)+7}\right)$

or $\quad 336 = \dfrac{8 \times 7 \times 6}{3 \times 2 \times 1}\left(\dfrac{2(y^2+44)}{y+14}\right)$

$\Rightarrow \quad y^2 - 3y + 2 = 0 \Rightarrow y = 2$ or $x = 1$

Example 39 *If the coefficient of x^8 in $\left(ax^2 + \dfrac{1}{bx}\right)^{13}$ is equal to the coefficient of x^{-8} in $\left(ax - \dfrac{1}{bx^2}\right)^{13}$, then the value of $ab+3$ is ....*

Sol. (2) The general term in $\left(ax^2 + \dfrac{1}{bx}\right)^{13}$ is

$$T_{r+1} = {}^{13}C_r (ax^2)^{13-r}\left(\frac{1}{bx}\right)^r$$

$$= {}^{13}C_r (a)^{13-r}(b)^{-r}(x)^{26-3r}$$

For coefficient of x^8, put $26 - 3r = 8$

$\Rightarrow \quad r = 6$

$\therefore \quad T_7 = {}^{13}C_6 (a)^{13-6}(b)^{-6}x^8 = {}^{13}C_6 a^7 \cdot b^{-6} \cdot x^8$

Now, in $\left(ax - \dfrac{1}{bx^2}\right)^{13}$, the general term

$$T'_{r+1} = {}^{13}C_r (ax)^{13-r}\left(-\frac{1}{bx^2}\right)^r$$

$$= {}^{13}C_r (a)^{13-r}(b)^{-r}(x)^{13-3r}(-1)^r$$

For coefficient of x^{-8}, put $13 - 3r = -8$

$\Rightarrow \quad r = 7$

$\therefore \quad T_8' = (-1)^7\, {}^{13}C_7 (a)^{13-7} (b)^{-7} (x)^{-8}$

$= (-1)^7\, {}^{13}C_7 (a)^6 (b)^{-7} \cdot x^{-8}$

Given, $T_7 = T_8' \Rightarrow {}^{13}C_6 \cdot a^7 \cdot b^{-6} = -\,{}^{13}C_7 \cdot a^6 \cdot b^{-7}$

$\Rightarrow \quad \frac{a^7}{a^6} = -\frac{b^6}{b^7}$

$\Rightarrow \quad a = -\frac{1}{b} \Rightarrow ab + 1 = 0 \Rightarrow ab + 3 = 2$

Matching Type Questions

Example 40 *Match the following columns.*

	Column I		Column II
(A)	If m and n are the numbers of rational terms in the expansions of $(\sqrt{2} + 3^{1/5})^{10}$ and $(\sqrt{3} + 5^{1/8})^{256}$ respectively, then	(p)	$n - m = 5$
(B)	If m and n are the numbers of irrational terms in the expansions of $(2^{1/2} + 3^{1/5})^{40}$ and $(5^{1/10} + 2^{1/6})^{100}$ respectively, then	(q)	$m + n = 17$
(C)	If m and n are the numbers of rational terms in the expansions of $(1 + \sqrt{2} + 3^{1/3})^6$ and $(1 + \sqrt[3]{2} + \sqrt[5]{3})^{15}$ respectively, then	(r)	$n - m = 31$
(D)	If number of rational terms in the expansion of $(3^{1/4} + 7^{1/6})^{144}$ and $(\sqrt{2} + 5^{1/3})^{20}$ is m and n respectively, then	(s)	$m + n = 35$
		(t)	$n - m = 59$

Sol. (A) → (r, s); (B) → (t); (C) → (p); (D) → (q)

(A) $\because \; (\sqrt{2} + 3^{1/5})^{10} = (2^{1/2} + 3^{1/5})^{10}$

$\therefore \quad T_{r+1} = {}^{10}C_r \cdot 2^{\frac{10-r}{2}} \cdot 3^{\frac{r}{5}}$

For rational terms, $r = 0, 10$ $\quad [\because 0 \le r \le 10]$

$\therefore$ Number of rational terms = 2

i.e. $\quad m = 2$ and $(\sqrt{3} + 5^{1/8})^{256} = (3^{1/2} + 5^{1/8})^{256}$

$\therefore \; T_{R+1} = {}^{256}C_R \cdot 3^{\frac{256-R}{2}} \cdot 5^{R/8}$

For rational terms, $r = 0, 8, 16, 24, 32, \ldots, 256$ $\quad [\because 0 \le r \le 256]$

$\therefore$ Number of rational terms = 1 + 32 = 33

i.e. $n = 33 \Rightarrow m + n = 35$ (s) and $n - m = 31$

(B) T_{r+1} in $(2^{1/3} + 3^{1/5})^{40} = {}^{40}C_r \cdot 2^{\frac{40-r}{3}} \cdot 3^{r/5}$

For rational terms, $r = 10, 25, 40$ $\quad [\because 0 \le r \le 40]$

$\because$ Number of rational terms = 3

$\therefore$ Number of irrational terms

= Total terms – Number of rational terms

= 41 – 3 = 38 i.e. $m = 38$

and T_{R+1} in $(5^{1/10} + 2^{1/6})^{100} = {}^{100}C_R \cdot 5^{\frac{100-R}{10}} \cdot 2^{R/6}$

rational terms, $R = 0, 30, 60, 90$ $\quad [\because 0 \le R \le 100]$

$\because$ Number of rational terms = 4

$\therefore$ Number of irrational terms = 101 – 4 = 97

i.e. $n = 97 \Rightarrow m + n = 135, n - m = 97 - 38 = 59$

(C) $\because \; (1 + \sqrt{2} + 3^{1/3})^6 = (1 + 2^{1/2} + 3^{1/3})^6$

$$= \sum_{\alpha+\beta+\gamma=6} \frac{6!}{\alpha!\,\beta!\,\gamma!} (1)^\alpha (2^{1/2})^\beta (3^{1/3})^\gamma$$

$$= \sum_{\alpha+\beta+\gamma=6} \frac{6!}{\alpha!\,\beta!\,\gamma!} 2^{\beta/2} \cdot 3^{\gamma/3}$$

Values of (α, β, γ) for rational terms are

(0, 0, 6), (1, 2, 3), (3, 0, 3), (0, 6, 0), (2, 4, 0), (4, 2, 0), (6, 0, 0).

$\therefore$ Number of rational terms = 7 i.e., $m = 7$

and $(1 + \sqrt[3]{2} + \sqrt[5]{3})^{15} = (1 + 2^{1/3} + 3^{1/5})^{15}$

$$= \sum_{\alpha+\beta+\gamma=15} \frac{15!}{\alpha!\,\beta!\,\gamma!} (1)^\alpha (2^{1/3})^\beta (3^{1/5})^\gamma$$

$$= \sum_{\alpha+\beta+\gamma=15} \frac{15!}{\alpha!\,\beta!\,\gamma!} 2^{\beta/3} \cdot 3^{\gamma/5}$$

of (α, β, γ) for rational terms are

(5, 0, 10), (2, 3, 10), (10, 0, 5), (7, 3, 5), (4, 6, 5), (1, 9, 5), (15, 0, 0), (12, 3, 0), (9, 6, 0), (6, 9, 0), (3, 12, 0), (15, 0, 0).

$\therefore$ Number of rational terms = 12 i.e. $n = 12$

Hence, $m + n = 19$ and $n - m = 5$

(D) T_{r+1} in $\left(3^{\frac{1}{4}} + 7^{\frac{1}{6}}\right)^{144} = {}^{144}C_r\, 3^{\frac{1}{4}(144-r)} \cdot 7^{\frac{r}{6}}$

$= {}^{144}C_r\, 3^{36 - \frac{r}{4}} \cdot 7^{\frac{r}{6}}$

For rational terms, $r = 0, 12, 24, 36, \ldots, 144$

$\therefore \quad m = 13$

and T_{R+1} in $\left(2^{\frac{1}{2}} + 5^{\frac{1}{3}}\right)^{20} = {}^{20}C_r\, 2^{\frac{20-r}{2}} \cdot 5^{\frac{r}{3}} = {}^{20}C_r\, 2^{10 - \frac{r}{2}} \cdot 5^{\frac{r}{3}}$

For rational terms, $r = 0, 6, 12, 18$

$\therefore \quad n = 4$

$\therefore \quad m + n = 13 + 4 = 17$

and $m - n = 13 - 4 = 9$

Example 41 *If* $(1 + x)^n = \sum_{r=0}^{n} C_r\, x^r$, *match the following.*

	Column I		Column II
(A)	If $S = \sum_{r=0}^{n} \lambda\, C_r$ and values of S are a, b, c for $\lambda = 1, r, r^2$ respectively, then	(p)	$a = b + c$
(B)	If $S = \sum_{r=0}^{n} (-1)^r\, \lambda\, C_r$ and values of S are a, b, c for $\lambda = 1, r, r^2$ respectively, then	(q)	$a + b = c + 2$

(C)	If $S = \sum_{r=0}^{n} \frac{\lambda C_r}{(r+1)}$ and values of S are a, b, c for $\lambda = 1, r, r^2$ respectively, then	(r)	$a^3 + b^3 + c^3 = 3abc$
(D)	If $S = \sum_{r=0}^{n} (\lambda - 1) C_r$ and values of S are a, b, c for $\lambda = 1, r, r^2$ respectively, then	(s)	$b^{c-a} + (c-a)^b = 1$
		(t)	$a + c = 4b$

Sol. (A) → (p, q); (B) → (p, r, t); (C) → (s, t); (D) → (s)

(A) For $\lambda = 1$, $a = \sum_{r=0}^{n} C_r = 2^n$

For $\lambda = r$, $b = \sum_{r=0}^{n} r\, C_r = \sum_{r=0}^{n} r \cdot \frac{n}{r} \cdot {}^{n-1}C_{r-1}$

$$= n \sum_{r=0}^{n} {}^{n-1}C_{r-1} = n \cdot 2^{n-1}$$

and for $\lambda = r^2$, $c = \sum_{r=0}^{n} r^2\, C_r = \sum_{r=0}^{n} r^2 \cdot \frac{n}{r} \cdot {}^{n-1}C_{r-1}$

$$= n \sum_{r=0}^{n} r \cdot {}^{n-1}C_{r-1} = n \sum_{r=1}^{n} r \cdot {}^{n-1}C_{r-1}$$

$$= n \left[\sum_{r=1}^{n} \{(r-1)+1\}^{n-1}C_{r-1} \right]$$

$$= n \left[\sum_{r=1}^{n} (r-1) \cdot {}^{n-1}C_{r-1} + \sum_{r=1}^{n} {}^{n-1}C_{r-1} \right]$$

$$= n \left[\sum_{r=1}^{n} (r-1) \frac{(n-1)}{(r-1)} \cdot {}^{n-2}C_{r-2} + 2^{n-1} \right]$$

$$= n \left[(n-1) \sum_{r=1}^{n} {}^{n-2}C_{r-2} + 2^{n-1} \right]$$

$$= n\,[(n-1) \cdot 2^{n-2} + 2^{n-1}] = n(n+1)\,2^{n-2}$$

For $n = 1$, $a = 2$, $b = 1$, $c = 1$ and for $n = 2$, $a = 4$, $b = 4$, $c = 6$ $\Big\}$ $a = b + c$, $a + b = c + 2$

(B) For $\lambda = 1$, $a = \sum_{r=0}^{n} (-1)^r \cdot C_r = 0$

For $\lambda = r$, $b = \sum_{r=0}^{n} (-1)^r \cdot r \cdot C_r = \sum_{r=0}^{n} (-1)^r \cdot r \cdot \frac{n}{r} {}^{n-1}C_{r-1}$

$$= n \sum_{r=1}^{n} (-1)^r \cdot {}^{n-1}C_{r-1} = n(1-1)^{n-1} = 0$$

and for $\lambda = r^2$, $c = \sum_{r=0}^{n} (-1)^r \cdot r^2 \cdot C_r$

$$= \sum_{r=0}^{n} (-1)^r \cdot r^2 \cdot \frac{n}{r} \cdot {}^{n-1}C_{r-1}$$

$$= n \sum_{r=0}^{n} (-1)^r \cdot r \cdot {}^{n-1}C_{r-1}$$

$$= n \sum_{r=0}^{n} (-1)^r \{(r-1)+1\}\, {}^{n-1}C_{r-1}$$

$$= n \sum_{r=0}^{n} (-1)^r (r-1)\, {}^{n-1}C_{r-1} + n \sum_{r=0}^{n} (-1)^r \cdot {}^{n-1}C_{r-1}$$

$$= 0 + 0 = 0$$

$\therefore$ $a = b = c = 0 \Rightarrow a = b + c$

$\Rightarrow$ $a^3 + b^3 + c^3 = 3abc \Rightarrow a + c = 4b$

(C) For $\lambda = 1$, $a = \sum_{r=0}^{n} \frac{C_r}{(r+1)} = \frac{1}{(n+1)} \sum_{r=0}^{n} \left(\frac{n+1}{r+1}\right) \cdot {}^nC_r$

$$= \frac{1}{(n+1)} \sum_{r=0}^{n} {}^{n+1}C_{r+1} = \frac{1}{n+1}(2^{n+1} - 1) = \frac{2^{n+1}-1}{n+1}$$

For $\lambda = r$, $b = \sum_{r=0}^{n} \frac{r \cdot C_r}{(r+1)} = \sum_{r=0}^{n} \left(1 - \frac{1}{r+1}\right) C_r$

$$= 2^n - \left(\frac{2^{n+1}-1}{n+1}\right) = \frac{(n-1)\,2^n + 1}{n+1}$$

For $\lambda = r^2$, $c = \sum_{r=0}^{n} \frac{r^2 \cdot C_r}{(r+1)} = \sum_{r=0}^{n} \left((r-1) + \frac{1}{r+1}\right) C_r$

$$= \sum_{r=0}^{n} r \cdot C_r - \sum_{r=0}^{n} C_r + \sum_{r=0}^{n} \frac{C_r}{r+1}$$

$$= n \cdot 2^{n-1} - 2^n + \frac{2^{n+1}-1}{n+1}$$

$$= \frac{(n^2 - n + 2)\,2^{n-1} - 1}{(n+1)}$$

For $n = 1$, $a = \frac{3}{2}, b = \frac{1}{2}, c = \frac{1}{2}$ and for $n = 2$, $a = \frac{7}{3}, b = \frac{5}{3}, c = \frac{7}{3}$; $\Big\}$ $a + c = 4b$, $b^{c-a} + (c-a)^b = 1$

(D) For $\lambda = 1$, $a = \sum_{r=0}^{n} (1-1)\, C_r = 0$

For $\lambda = r$, $b = \sum_{r=0}^{n} (r-1)\, C_r = \sum_{r=0}^{n} {}^rC_r - \sum_{r=0}^{n} C_r$

$$= \sum_{r=0}^{n} r \cdot \frac{n}{r}\, {}^{n-1}C_{r-1} - 2^n$$

$$= n \cdot 2^{n-1} - 2^n = 2^{n-1}(n-2)$$

For $\lambda = r^2$, $C = \sum_{r=0}^{n} (r^2 - 1) C_r = \sum_{r=0}^{n} r^2\, C_r - \sum_{r=0}^{n} C_r$

$$= \sum_{r=0}^{n} r^2 \cdot \frac{n}{r}\, {}^{n-1}C_{r-1} - 2^n$$

$$= n \sum_{r=0}^{n} r \cdot {}^{n-1}C_{r-1} - 2^n$$

$$= n \sum_{r=1}^{n} ((r-1)+1)^{n-1}C_{r-1} - 2^n$$

$$= n \left[\sum_{r=1}^{n} (r-1) \cdot \frac{n-1}{r-1} \cdot {}^{n-2}C_{r-2} + \sum_{r=1}^{n} {}^{n-1}C_{r-1} \right] - 2^n$$

$$= n \cdot [(n-1) \cdot 2^{n-2} + 2^{n-1}] - 2^n = n(n+1) \cdot 2^{n-2} - 2^n$$

For $n = 1$, $a = 0$, $b = -1$, $c = -1$

For $n = 2$, $a = 0$, $b = 0$, $c = 2$

$\therefore$ $b^{c-a} + (c-a)^b = 1$

EXERCISE 1

JEE Main Pattern

Single Option Correct Type Questions

1. If $\sum_{r=0}^{n} {}^nC_r(-1)^r[i^r+i^{2r}+i^{3r}+i^{4r}]=2^n+2^{n/2+1}f(n)$, then

(a) $f(1)=\frac{-1}{\sqrt{2}}$ (b) $f(1)=\frac{1}{\sqrt{2}}$

(c) $f(2)=\frac{1}{2}$ (d) $f(2)=\frac{-1}{2}$

2. The coefficient of x^{13} in the expansion of $(1-x)^5(1+x+x^2+x^3)^4$, is

(a) 1 (b) 2

(c) 3 (d) 4

3. The coefficient of x^n in $\left(1+\frac{x}{1!}+\frac{x^2}{2!}+\ldots+\frac{x^n}{n!}\right)^2$ is

(a) $n!$ (b) $\frac{2^n}{n!}$ (c) $\frac{n!}{2^n}$ (d) 2^n

4. The greatest coefficient in the expansion of $\left(1+\frac{2x}{3}\right)^{15}$ is

(a) ${}^{15}C_5\left(\frac{2}{3}\right)^5$ (b) ${}^{15}C_6\left(\frac{2}{3}\right)^6$

(c) ${}^{15}C_7\left(\frac{2}{3}\right)^7$ (d) ${}^{15}C_8\left(\frac{2}{3}\right)^8$

5. In the expansion of $(1+x)^n$, 7th and 8th terms are equal, then the value of $\left(\frac{7}{x}+6\right)^n$ is

(a) n^n (b) $(n-1)^n$

(c) n^2 (d) $(n-1)^2$

6. If $(1+2x+3x^2)^{10}=a_0+a_1x+a_2x^2+\ldots+a_{20}x^{20}$, then a_1 is equal to

(a) 10 (b) 20

(c) 210 (d) None of these

7. The term independent of a in the expansion of $\left(1+\sqrt{a}+\frac{1}{\sqrt{a}-1}\right)^{-30}$ is

(a) ${}^{30}C_{20}$ (b) ${}^{30}C_{10}$

(c) ${}^{30}C_5$ (d) None of these

8. If $(5+2\sqrt{6})^n=I+f$, where $I\in N, n\in N$ and $0\le f<1$, then I equals

(a) $\frac{1}{f}-f$ (b) $\frac{1}{1+f}-f$ (c) $\frac{1}{1-f}-f$ (d) $\frac{1}{1-f}+f$

9. The coefficient of the middle term in the binomial expansion, in powers of x, of $(1+\alpha x)^4$ and $(1-\alpha x)^6$ is same, if α equals to

(a) $\frac{3}{5}$ (b) $\frac{10}{3}$ (c) $\frac{-3}{10}$ (d) $\frac{-5}{3}$

10. The remainder left out when $8^{2n}-(62)^{2n+1}$ is divided by 9, is

(a) 0 (b) 2 (c) 7 (d) 8

11. The coefficient of x^9 in the expansion of $(1+x)(1+x^2)(1+x^3)\ldots(1+x^{100})$ is

(a) 2 (b) 6 (c) 9 (d) 8

12. The coefficient of $a^3b^4c^2$ in the expansion of $(2a-3b+4c)^9$ is

(a) 12063600 (b) 13063680

(c) 11063680 (d) 12063680

13. The term independent of x in the expansion of $(2^x+2^{-x}+\log_e e^{x+2})^{30}$ is

(a) ${}^{30}C_{10}$ (b) ${}^{60}C_{10}$ (c) ${}^{30}C_{20}$ (d) ${}^{60}C_{30}$

14. $\sum_{0\le i\le j\le 10}({}^{10}C_j)({}^jC_i)=$

(a) 2^{10} (b) 3^{10} (c) $2^{10}-1$ (d) $3^{10}-1$

15. The value of $\frac{{}^nC_0}{n}+\frac{{}^nC_1}{n+1}+\frac{{}^nC_2}{n+2}+\ldots+\frac{{}^nC_n}{2n}$ is equal to

(a) $\int_0^1 x^{n-1}(1-x)^n dx$ (b) $\int_1^2 x^n(x-1)^{n-1}dx$

(c) $\int_1^2 x^{n-1}(1+x)^n dx$ (d) $\int_0^1 (1-x)^n x^{n-1}dx$

16. The last two digits of the number 19^{9^4} is

(a) 19 (b) 29 (c) 39 (d) 81

17. If the second term in the expansion of $\left(\sqrt[13]{a}+\frac{a}{\sqrt{a^{-1}}}\right)^n$ is $14a^{5/2}$, the value of $\frac{{}^nC_3}{{}^nC_2}$ is

(a) 4 (b) 3 (c) 12 (d) 6

18. If $6^{83}+8^{83}$ is divided by 49, the remainder is

(a) 0 (b) 14 (c) 35 (d) 42

19. The sum of all the rational terms in the expansion of $(3^{1/4}+4^{1/3})^{12}$ is

(a) 91 (b) 251 (c) 273 (d) 283

20. Last four digits of the number $N=7^{100}-3^{100}$ is

(a) 2000 (b) 4000
(c) 6000 (d) 8000

21. If 5^{99} is divided by 13, the remainder is

(a) 2 (b) 4 (c) 6 (d) 8

22. The value of $\left\{\frac{3^{2003}}{28}\right\}$, where $\{.\}$ denotes the fractional part function is

(a) 17/28 (b) 19/28 (c) 23/28 (d) 5/28

23. The value of $\sum_{r=0}^{20} r(20-r)({}^{20}C_r)^2$ is equal to

(a) $400\ {}^{37}C_{20}$ (b) $400\ {}^{40}C_{19}$
(c) $400\ {}^{38}C_{19}$ (d) $400\ {}^{38}C_{20}$

24. If $(3+x^{2008}+x^{2009})^{2010}=a_0+a_1x+a_2x^2+\ldots+a_nx^n$, the value of $a_0-\frac{a_1}{2}-\frac{a_2}{2}+a_3-\frac{a_4}{2}-\frac{a_5}{2}+a_6-\ldots$ is

(a) 1 (b) 2^{2010} (c) 5^{2010} (d) 3^{2010}

25. The total number of terms which depend on the value of x in the expansion of $\left(x^2-2+\frac{1}{x^2}\right)^n$ is

(a) $2n+1$ (b) $2n$ (c) $n+1$ (d) n

26. The coefficient of x^{10} in the expansion of $(1+x^2-x^3)^8$, is

(a) 420 (b) 476 (c) 532 (d) 588

27. The number of real negative terms in the binomial expansion of $(1+ix)^{4n-2}$, $n\in N, n>0, i=\sqrt{-1}$, is

(a) n (b) $n+1$ (c) $n-1$ (d) $2n$

28. $\sum_{p=1}^{n}\sum_{m=p}^{n}\binom{n}{m}\binom{m}{p}$ is equal to

(a) 3^n (b) 2^n (c) 3^n+2^n (d) 3^n-2^n

29. The largest real value of x, such that $\sum_{r=0}^{4}\left(\frac{5^{4-r}}{(4-r)!}\right)\left(\frac{x^r}{r!}\right)=\frac{8}{3}$ is

(a) $2\sqrt{2}-5$ (b) $2\sqrt{2}+5$
(c) $-2\sqrt{2}-5$ (d) $-2\sqrt{2}+5$

Numerical Value Type Questions

30. The number of terms which are free from radical signs in the expansion of $(y^{1/5}+x^{1/10})^{55}$ is ....

31. If the sum of the numerical coefficients in the expansion of $\left(1+\frac{x}{3}+\frac{2y}{3}\right)^{12}$ is 1024λ, then the value of λ is ....

32. If the three consecutive coefficients in the expansion of $(1+x)^n$ are 28, 56, 70, then the value of n is ....

33. If the constant term in the binomial expansion of $\left(x^2-\frac{1}{x}\right)^n$, $n\in N$ is 15, then the value of n is ....

34. The remainder if $1+2+2^2+2^3+\ldots+2^{1999}$ is divided by 5 is ....

35. Largest real value for x such that $\sum_{k=0}^{4}\left(\frac{3^{4-k}}{(4-k)!}\right)\left(\frac{x^k}{k!}\right)=\frac{32}{3}$ is ....

36. If the second term of the expansion $\left[a^{1/13}+\frac{a}{\sqrt{a^{-1}}}\right]^n$ is $14a^{5/2}$, then the value of $\frac{{}^nC_3}{{}^nC_2}$ is ....

37. Least positive integer just greater than $(1+0.00002)^{50000}$ is ....

38. If fractional part of $\frac{2^{4n}}{15}$ is $\frac{a}{15}$, then the value of a is ....

39. If ${}^{10}C_0+({}^{10}C_0+{}^{10}C_1)+({}^{10}C_0+{}^{10}C_1+{}^{10}C_2)+\ldots+({}^{10}C_0+{}^{10}C_1+{}^{10}C_2+\ldots+{}^{10}C_9)=a\times b^c$, then $a+b-c$ is equal to ....

40. The remainder when $\left(\sum_{r=1}^{5}{}^{20}C_{2r-1}\right)^6$ is divided by 11 is ....

41. For integer $n>1$, the digit at unit's place in the number $\sum_{r=0}^{100} r!+2^{2^n}$ is ....

42. If $(1+x+x^2+x^3)^n=\sum_{r=0}^{3n}a_rx^r$ and $\sum_{r=0}^{3n}a_r=k$ and if $\sum_{r=0}^{3n}r\,a_r=\frac{\lambda nk}{2}$, the value of λ is ....

43. The number of rational terms in the expansion of $\left(\sqrt[3]{4}+\frac{1}{\sqrt[4]{6}}\right)^{20}$ is ....

44. If $2^{2006}+2006$ is divided by 7, the remainder is ....

45. The last two digits of the natural number 19^{9^4} is ab, the value of $b-3a$ is ....

Previous Year Questions

46. If the term independent of x in the expansion of $\left(\sqrt{a}x^2+\frac{1}{2x^3}\right)^{10}$ is 105, then a^2 is equal to **[Single Correct Type, 2024 Main]**

(a) 6 (b) 4 (c) 2 (d) 9

47. Let m and n be the coefficients of seventh and thirteenth terms respectively in the expansion of $\left\{\frac{1}{3}x^{1/3}+\frac{1}{2x^{2/3}}\right\}^{18}$. Then, $\left(\frac{n}{m}\right)^{1/3}$ is **[Single Correct Type, 2024 Main]**

(a) $\frac{9}{4}$ (b) $\frac{1}{9}$ (c) $\frac{4}{9}$ (d) $\frac{1}{4}$

48. If A denotes the sum of all the coefficients in the expansion of $(1-3x+10x^2)^n$ and B denotes the sum of all the coefficient in the expansion of $(1+x^2)^n$, then **[Single Correct Type, 2024 Main]**

(a) $B=A^3$ (b) $A=3B$ (c) $3A=B$ (d) $A=B^3$

49. Suppose $2-p, p, 2-\alpha, \alpha$ are the coefficients of four consecutive terms in the expansion of $(1+x)^n$. Then, the value of $p^2-\alpha^2+6\alpha+2p$ equals **[Single Correct Type, 2024 Main]**

(a) 8 (b) 6 (c) 10 (d) 4

50. If the coefficients of x^4, x^5 and x^6 in the expansion of $(1+x)^n$ are in the arithmetic progression, then the maximum value of n is **[Single Correct Type, 2024 Main]**

(a) 21 (b) 14 (c) 7 (d) 28

51. If the constant term in the expansion of $(1+2x-3x^3)\left(\frac{3}{2}x^2-\frac{1}{3x}\right)^9$ is p, then $108p$ is equal to .... **[Numerical Value Type, 2024 Main]**

52. If the coefficient of x^{30} in the expansion of $\left(1+\frac{1}{x}\right)^6(1+x^2)^7(1-x^3)^8; x\neq 0$ is α, then $|\alpha|$ equals .... **[Numerical Value Type, 2024 Main]**

53. Let the coefficient of x^r in the expansion of $(x+3)^{n-1}+(x+3)^{n-2}(x+2)+(x+3)^{n-3}(x+2)^2+\ldots+(x+2)^{n-1}$ be α_r. If $\sum_{r=0}^{n}\alpha_r=\beta^n-\gamma^n, \beta, \gamma\in N$, then the value of $\beta^2+\gamma^2$ equals .... **[Numerical Value Type, 2024 Main]**

54. Fractional part of the number $\frac{4^{2022}}{15}$ is equal to **[Single Correct Type, 2023 Main]**

(a) $\frac{8}{15}$ (b) $\frac{1}{15}$ (c) $\frac{14}{15}$ (d) $\frac{4}{15}$

55. $25^{190}-19^{190}-8^{190}+2^{190}$ is divisible by **[Single Correct Type, 2023 Main]**

(a) 14 but not by 34 (b) 34 but not by 14
(c) neither 14 nor 34 (d) both 14 and 34

56. If a_r is the coefficient of x^{10-r} in the Binomial expansion of $(1+x)^{10}$, then $\sum_{r=1}^{10}r^3\left(\frac{a_r}{a_{r-1}}\right)^2$ is equal to **[Single Correct Type, 2023 Main]**

(a) 1210 (b) 4895 (c) 3025 (d) 5445

57. Among the statements :

(S1) $2023^{2022}-1999^{2022}$ is divisible by 8.

(S2) $13(13)^n-12n-13$ is divisible by 144 for infinitely many $n\in N$. **[Single Correct Type, 2023 Main]**

(a) both (S1) and (S2) are incorrect
(b) only (S2) is correct
(c) both (S1) and (S2) are correct
(d) only (S1) is correct

58. If the coefficient of x^{15} in the expansion of $\left(ax^3+\frac{1}{bx^{\frac{1}{3}}}\right)^{15}$ is equal to the coefficient of x^{-15} in the expansion of $\left(ax^{\frac{1}{3}}-\frac{1}{bx^3}\right)^{15}$, where a and b are positive real numbers, then for each such ordered pair (a, b) **[Single Correct Type, 2023 Main]**

(a) $ab=1$ (b) $a=b$ (c) $a=3b$ (d) $ab=3$

59. Let $(a+bx+cx^2)^{10}=\sum_{i=0}^{20}p_ix^i$, $a, b, c\in N$. If $p_1=20$ and $p_2=210$, then $2(a+b+c)$ is equal to **[Single Correct Type, 2023 Main]**

(a) 15 (b) 12 (c) 8 (d) 6

60. The number of integral terms in the expansion of $\left(3^{\frac{1}{2}}+5^{\frac{1}{4}}\right)^{680}$ is equal to .... **[Numerical Value Type, 2023 Main]**

61. 50th root of a number x is 12 and 50th root of another number y is 18. Then, the remainder obtained on dividing $(x+y)$ by 25 is .... **[Numerical Value Type, 2023 Main]**

62. The constant term in the expansion of $\left(2x+\frac{1}{x^7}+3x^2\right)^5$ .... **[Numerical Value Type, 2023 Main]**

63. The remainder, when $(2021)^{2022}+(2022)^{2021}$ is divided by 7 is **[Single Correct Type, 2022 Main]**

(a) 0 (b) 1 (c) 2 (d) 6

64. Let $n \geq 5$ be an integer. If $9^n - 8n - 1 = 64\alpha$ and $6^n - 5n - 1 = 25\beta$, then $\alpha - \beta$ is equal to **[Single Correct Type, 2022 Main]**

(a) $1 + {}^nC_2(8-5) + {}^nC_3(8^2 - 5^2) + \ldots + {}^nC_n(8^{n-1} - 5^{n-1})$
(b) $1 + {}^nC_3(8-5) + {}^nC_4(8^2 - 5^2) + \ldots + {}^nC_n(8^{n-2} - 5^{n-2})$
(c) ${}^nC_3(8-5) + {}^nC_4(8^2 - 5^2) + \ldots + {}^nC_n(8^{n-2} - 5^{n-2})$
(d) ${}^nC_4(8-5) + {}^nC_5(8^2 - 5^2) + \ldots + {}^nC_n(8^{n-3} - 5^{n-3})$

65. The coefficient of x^{101} in the expression $(5+x)^{500} + x(5+x)^{499} + x^2(5+x)^{498} + \ldots + x^{500}, x > 0$, is **[Single Correct Type, 2022 Main]**

(a) ${}^{501}C_{101}(5)^{399}$ (b) ${}^{501}C_{101}(5)^{400}$
(c) ${}^{501}C_{100}(5)^{400}$ (d) ${}^{500}C_{101}(5)^{399}$

66. Consider the sequence $a_1, a_2, a_3, \ldots$ such that $a_1 = 1$, $a_2 = 2$ and $a_{n+2} = \dfrac{2}{a_{n+1}} + a_n$ for $n = 1, 2, 3, \ldots$ If

$$\left(\frac{a_1 + \frac{1}{a_2}}{a_3}\right) \cdot \left(\frac{a_2 + \frac{1}{a_3}}{a_4}\right) \cdot \left(\frac{a_3 + \frac{1}{a_4}}{a_5}\right) \cdots \left(\frac{a_{30} + \frac{1}{a_{31}}}{a_{32}}\right)$$

$= 2^{\alpha}({}^{61}C_{31})$, then α is equal to **[Single Correct Type, 2022 Main]**

(a) -30 (b) -31 (c) -60 (d) -61

67. If the constant term in the expansion of $\left(3x^3 - 2x^2 + \dfrac{5}{x^5}\right)^{10}$ is $2^k \cdot l$, where l is an odd integer, then the value of k is equal to **[Single Correct Type, 2022 Main]**

(a) 6 (b) 7 (c) 8 (d) 9

68. Let the coefficients of the middle terms in the expansion of $\left(\dfrac{1}{\sqrt{6}} + \beta x\right)^4$, $(1 - 3\beta x)^2$ and $\left(1 - \dfrac{\beta}{2}x\right)^6$, $\beta > 0$, respectively form the first three terms of an AP. If d is the common difference of this AP, then $50 - \dfrac{2d}{\beta^2}$ is equal to .... **[Numerical Value Type, 2022 Main]**

69. If the fourth term in the expansion of $(x + x^{\log_2 x})^7$ is 4480, then the value of x, where $x \in N$ is equal to **[Single Correct Type, 2021 Main]**

(a) 2 (b) 4 (c) 3 (d) 1

70. If the coefficients of x^7 in $\left(x^2 + \dfrac{1}{bx}\right)^{11}$ and x^{-7} in $\left(x - \dfrac{1}{bx^2}\right)^{11}$, $b \neq 0$, are equal, then the value of b is equal to **[Single Correct Type, 2021 Main]**

(a) 2 (b) -1 (c) 1 (d) -2

71. Let $[x]$ denote greatest integer less than or equal to x. If for $n \in N$, $(1 - x + x^3)^n = \sum_{j=0}^{3n} a_j x^j$, then $\sum_{j=0}^{\left[\frac{3n}{2}\right]} a_{2j} + 4 \sum_{j=0}^{\left[\frac{3n-1}{2}\right]} a_{2j+1}$ is equal to **[Single Correct Type, 2021 Main]**

(a) 2 (b) 2^{n-1}
(c) 1 (d) n

72. A possible value of 'x', for which the ninth term in the expansion of $\left\{3^{\log_3\sqrt{25^{x-1}+7}} + 3^{\left(-\frac{1}{8}\right)\log_3(5^{x-1}+1)}\right\}^{10}$ is equal to 180, is **[Single Correct Type, 2021 Main]**

(a) 0 (b) -1
(c) 2 (d) 1

73. The ratio of the coefficient of the middle term in the expansion of $(1+x)^{20}$ and the sum of the coefficients of two middle terms in expansion of $(1+x)^{19}$ is .... **[Numerical Value Type, 2021 Main]**

74. The number of elements in the set $\{n \in \{1, 2, 3, \ldots, 100\} : (11)^n > (10)^n + (9)^n\}$ is .... **[Numerical Value Type, 2021 Main]**

75. Let $\alpha > 0, \beta > 0$ be such that $\alpha^3 + \beta^2 = 4$. If the maximum value of the term independent of x in the binomial expansion of $\left(\alpha x^{\frac{1}{9}} + \beta x^{-\frac{1}{6}}\right)^{10}$ is $10k$, then k is equal to **[Single Correct Type, 2020 Main]**

(a) 84 (b) 176
(c) 352 (d) 336

76. The coefficient of x^7 in the expression $(1+x)^{10} + x(1+x)^9 + x^2(1+x)^8 + \ldots + x^{10}$ is **[Single Correct Type, 2020 Main]**

(a) 420 (b) 330
(c) 210 (d) 120

77. The natural number m, for which the coefficient of x in the binomial expansion of $\left(x^m + \dfrac{1}{x^2}\right)^{22}$ is 1540, is .... **[Numerical Value Type, 2020 Main]**

78. If sum of the coefficients of all even powers of x in the product $(1 + x + x^2 + \ldots + x^{2n})(1 - x + x^2 - x^3 + \ldots + x^{2n})$ is 61, then n is equal to .... **[Numerical Value Type, 2020 Main]**

EXERCISE 2

JEE Advanced Pattern

Single Option Correct Type Questions

1. The sum of rational terms in $(\sqrt{2}+\sqrt[3]{3}+\sqrt[6]{5})^{10}$, is

(a) 11792 (b) 1260
(c) 126 (d) None of these

2. If $(1+x-3x^2)^{2145}=a_0+a_1x+a_2x^2+\ldots$, then $a_0-a_1+a_2-a_3+\ldots$ ends with

(a) 1 (b) 3 (c) 7 (d) 9

3. In the expansion of $\left(\sqrt{\frac{q}{p}}+\sqrt[10]{\frac{p^7}{q^3}}\right)^n$, there is a term similar to pq, then that term is equal to

(a) $45pq$ (b) $120\,pq$ (c) $210\,pq$ (d) $252\,pq$

4. Let $(5+2\sqrt{6})^n=I+f$, where $n, I \in N$ and $0<f<1$, then the value of $f^2-f+I\cdot f-I$, is

(a) a natural number (b) a negative integer
(c) a prime number (d) an irrational number

5. If $x+\frac{1}{x}=1$ and $p=x^{4000}+\frac{1}{x^{4000}}$ and q is the digit at unit place in the number $2^{2^n}+1$, $n\in N$ and $n>1$, then $p+q$, is

(a) 8 (b) 6
(c) 7 (d) None of these

6. If the number of terms in $\left(x+1+\frac{1}{x}\right)^n$ $(n\in I^+)$ is 401, then n is greater than

(a) 201 (b) 200
(c) 199 (d) None of these

7. $\sum_{r=0}^{n-1}\frac{{}^nC_r}{{}^nC_r+{}^nC_{r+1}}$ is equal to

(a) $\frac{n}{2}$ (b) $\frac{n+1}{2}$ (c) $\frac{n(n+1)}{2}$ (d) $\frac{n(n-1)}{2(n+1)}$

8. The largest term in the expansion of $\left(\frac{b}{2}+\frac{b}{2}\right)^{100}$ is

(a) b^{100} (b) $\left(\frac{b}{2}\right)^{100}$

(c) ${}^{100}C_{50}\left(\frac{b}{2}\right)^{100}$ (d) ${}^{100}C_{50}b^{100}$

9. If the fourth term of $\left(\sqrt{x^{\left(\frac{1}{1+\log x}\right)}}+\sqrt[12]{x}\right)^6$ is equal to 200 and $x>1$, x is equal to

(a) $10\sqrt{2}$ (b) 10 (c) 10^4 (d) $\frac{10}{\sqrt{2}}$

10. The coefficient of x^m in $(1+x)^m+(1+x)^{m+1}+\ldots+(1+x)^n$, $m\le n$, is

(a) ${}^{n+1}C_{m+1}$ (b) ${}^{n-1}C_{m-1}$
(c) ${}^nC_m$ (d) ${}^nC_{m+1}$

11. The number of values of 'r' satisfying the equation ${}^{39}C_{3r-1}-{}^{39}C_{r^2}={}^{39}C_{r^2-1}-{}^{39}C_{3r}$ is

(a) 1 (b) 2 (c) 3 (d) 4

12. The sum $S={}^{20}C_2+2\cdot{}^{20}C_3+3\cdot{}^{20}C_4+\ldots+19\cdot{}^{20}C_{20}$ is equal to

(a) $1+5\cdot 2^{20}$ (b) $1+2^{21}$ (c) $1+9\cdot 2^{20}$ (d) 2^{20}

13. The remainder, if $1+2+2^2+2^3+\ldots+2^{1999}$ is divided by 5, is

(a) 0 (b) 1 (c) 2 (d) 3

14. Coefficient of $\frac{1}{x}$ in the expansion of $(1+x)^n(1+1/x)^n$ is

(a) $\frac{n!}{(n-1)!(n+1)!}$ (b) $\frac{2n!}{(n-1)!(n+1)!}$

(c) $\frac{n!}{(2n-1)!(2n+1)!}$ (d) $\frac{2n!}{(2n-1)!(2n+1)!}$

15. If $(3+x^{2008}+x^{2009})^{2010}=a_0+a_1x+a_2x^2+\ldots+a_nx^n$, then the value of $a_0-\frac{1}{2}a_1-\frac{1}{2}a_2+a_3-\frac{1}{2}a_4-\frac{1}{2}a_5+a_6-\ldots$ is

(a) 3^{2010} (b) 1
(c) 2^{2010} (d) None of these

16. The value of $\sum_{r=2}^{10}{}^rC_2\cdot{}^{10}C_r$ is

(a) 10460 (b) 11240 (c) 11520 (d) 12640

17. In the expansion of $\left(\frac{1}{x^2} - x^3\right)^n$, $n \in N$, if the sum of the coefficients of x^5 and x^{10} is 0, then n is
(a) 25 (b) 20
(c) 15 (d) 10

18. The value of $\sum_{r=0}^{50} (-1)^r \frac{^{50}C_r}{r+2}$ is equal to
(a) $\frac{1}{2550}$ (b) $\frac{1}{2600}$
(c) $\frac{1}{2652}$ (d) None of these

More than One Correct Option Type Questions

19. If the middle term in the expansion of $\left(x^2 + \frac{1}{x}\right)^n$ is $924x^6$, then
(a) $n = 10$
(b) $n = 12$
(c) Sum of all binomial coefficient $= 2^{10}$
(d) Sum of all binomial coefficient $= 2^{12}$

20. For 27^{27},
(a) last digit is 3 (b) second last digit is 0
(c) third last digit is 8 (d) None of these

21. The sum of the coefficient in the expansion of $(1 + ax - 2x^2)^n$ is
(a) positive, when $a < 1$, $n = 2k$, $k \in N$
(b) negative, when $a < 1$, $n = 2k + 1$, $k \in N$
(c) positive, when $a > 1$, $n \in N$
(d) zero, when $a = 1$

22. In the expansion of $(7^{1/3} + 11^{1/9})^{6561}$,
(a) there are exactly 730 rational terms
(b) there are exactly 5832 irrational terms
(c) the term which involves greatest binomial coefficients is irrational.
(d) the term which involves greatest binomial coefficients is rational.

23. If n is a positive integer and $(3\sqrt{3} + 5)^{2n+1} = \alpha + \beta$, where α is an integer and $0 < \beta < 1$, then
(a) α is an even integer
(b) $(\alpha + \beta)^2$ is divisible by 2^{2n+1}
(c) the integer just below $(3\sqrt{3} + 5)^{2n+1}$ divisible by 3
(d) α is divisible by 10

24. If $(8 + 3\sqrt{7})^n = P + F$, where P is an integer and F is a proper fraction, then
(a) P is an odd integer
(b) P is an even integer
(c) $F(P + F) = 1$
(d) $(1 - F)(P + F) = 1$

25. The value of x for which the 6th term in the expansion of $\left\{2^{\log_2\sqrt{(9^{x-1}+7)}} + \frac{1}{2^{\left(\frac{1}{5}\right)\log_2(3^{x-1}+1)}}\right\}^7$ is 84, is
(a) 4 (b) 3 (c) 2 (d) 1

26. Consider the binomial expansion of $\left(\sqrt{x} + \frac{1}{2\cdot\sqrt[4]{x}}\right)^n$, $n \in N$, where the terms of the expansion are written in decreasing powers of x. If the coefficients of the first three terms form an arithmetic progression, then the statement(s) which hold good is /are
(a) Total number of terms in the expansion of the binomial is 8
(b) Number of terms in the expansion with integral power of x is 3
(c) There is no term in the expansion which is independent of x
(d) Fourth and fifth are the middle terms of the expansion

27. Let $(1 + x^2)^2 (1 + x)^n = a_0 + a_1x + a_2x^2 + \dots$, if a_1, a_2 and a_3 are in AP, the value of n is
(a) 2 (b) 3 (c) 4 (d) 7

28. If $(1 + x)^n = C_0 + C_1x + C_2x^2 + C_3x^3 + \dots + C_nx^n$, then $C_0 - (C_0 + C_1) + (C_0 + C_1 + C_2) - (C_0 + C_1 + C_2 + C_3) + \dots + (-1)^{n-1}(C_0 + C_1 + C_2 + \dots + C_{n-1})$, when n is even integer is
(a) a positive value (b) a negative value
(c) divisible by 2^{n-1} (d) divisible by 2^n

29. If $f(n) = \sum_{i=0}^{n} \binom{30}{30-i}\binom{20}{n-i}$, then
(a) maximum value of $f(n)$ is $^{50}C_{25}$
(b) $f(0) + f(1) + f(2) + \dots + f(50) = 2^{50}$
(c) $f(n)$ is always divisible by 50
(d) $f^2(0) + f^2(1) + f^2(2) + \dots + f^2(50) = {}^{100}C_{50}$

30. If the middle term of $\left(x + \frac{1}{x}\sin^{-1}x\right)^8$ is equal to $\frac{630}{16}$, the values of x is/are
(a) $-\frac{\pi}{3}$ (b) $-\frac{\pi}{6}$ (c) $\frac{\pi}{6}$ (d) $\frac{\pi}{3}$

31. If $b^2 < ac$, the sum of the coefficients in the expansion of $(a\alpha^2x^2 + 2b\alpha x + c)^n$, $(a, b, c, \alpha \in R, n \in N)$, is
(a) + ve, if $a > 0$ (b) + ve, if $c > 0$
(c) − ve, if $a < 0$, n is odd (d) + ve, if $c < 0$, n is even

32. In the expansion of $\left(x^2 + 1 + \frac{1}{x^2}\right)^n$, $n \in N$, then
(a) number of terms $= 2n + 1$
(b) term independent of $x = 2^{n-1}$
(c) coefficient of $x^{2n-1} = n$
(d) coefficient of $x^2 = n$

33. The coefficient of the $(r+1)$th term of $\left(x+\frac{1}{x}\right)^{20}$, when expanded in the descending powers of x, is equal to the coefficient of the 6th term of $\left(x^2+2+\frac{1}{x^2}\right)^{10}$ when expanded in ascending powers of x. The value of r is

(a) 5 (b) 6

(c) 14 (d) 15

Passage Based Questions

Passage I

(Q. Nos. 34 and 35)

- Consider $(1+x+x^2)^n = \sum_{r=0}^{2n} a_r x^r$, where $a_0, a_1, a_2, \ldots, a_{2n}$ are real numbers and n is a positive integer.

34. The value of $\sum_{r=0}^{n-1} a_r$ is

(a) $\frac{-3^n - a_n}{2}$ (b) $\frac{3^n - a_n}{2}$ (c) $\frac{a_n - 3^n}{2}$ (d) $\frac{3^n + a_n}{2}$

35. If n is even, the value of $\sum_{r=0}^{n/2-1} a_{2r}$ is

(a) $\frac{3^n - 1 + a_n}{2}$ (b) $\frac{3^n - 1 - a_n}{4}$

(c) $\frac{3^n + 1 + a_n}{2}$ (d) $\frac{3^n + 1 - 2a_n}{4}$

Passage II

(Q. Nos. 36 and 37)

- If $(1+x+2x^2)^{20} = a_0 + a_1 x + a_2 x^2 + \ldots + a_{40} x^{40}$.

36. The value of $a_0 + a_2 + a_4 + \ldots + a_{38}$ is

(a) $2^{19}(2^{19}-1)$ (b) $2^{20}(2^{19}-1)$

(c) $2^{19}(2^{20}-1)$ (d) $2^{20}(2^{20}-1)$

37. The value of $a_1 + a_3 + a_5 + \ldots + a_{37}$ is

(a) $2^{19}(2^{19}-20)$ (b) $2^{19}(2^{20}-21)$

(c) $2^{19}(2^{19}-21)$ (d) $2^{19}(2^{19}-19)$

Passage III

(Q. Nos. 38 and 39)

- Suppose, m divided by n, then quotient q and remainder r

i.e. $n)\,m\,(q$

$\quad\;\; \underline{-}$

$\quad\;\; \underline{r}$

or $m = nq + r$, $\forall\, m, n, q, r \in I$ and $n \neq 0$

38. If a is the remainder when 5^{40} is divided by 11 and b is the remainder when 2^{2011} is divided by 17, the value of $a+b$ is

(a) 7 (b) 8 (c) 9 (d) 10

39. If $19^{93} - 13^{99}$ is divided by 162, the remainder is

(a) 8 (b) 4 (c) 1 (d) 0

Passage IV

(Q. Nos. 40 and 41)

- Consider the binomial expansion $R = (1+2x)^n = I + f$, where I is the integral part of R and f is the fractional part of R, $n \in N$. Also, the sum of coefficients of R is 2187.

40. The value of $(n + Rf)$ for $x = \frac{1}{\sqrt{2}}$ is

(a) 7 (b) 8 (c) 9 (d) 10

41. If ith term is the greatest term for $x = 1/3$, then i equals

(a) 4 (b) 5 (c) 6 (d) 7

Passage V

(Q. Nos. 42 and 43)

- If $(x+a_1)(x+a_2)(x+a_3)\ldots(x+a_n) = x^n + S_1 x^{n-1} + S_2 x^{n-2} + \ldots + S_n$ where, $S_1 = \sum_{i=1}^{n} a_i$, $S_2 = \sum\sum_{1 \le i < j \le n} a_i a_j$, $S_3 = \sum\sum\sum_{1 \le i < j < k \le n} a_i a_j a_k$ and so on.

42. If $(1+x)^n = C_0 + C_1 x + C_2 x^2 + \ldots + C_n x^n$, the coefficient of x^n in the expansion of $(x+C_0)(x+3C_1)(x+5C_2)\ldots(x+(2n+1)C_n)$, is

(a) $n \cdot 2^n$ (b) $(n+1) \cdot 2^n$

(c) $n \cdot 2^{n+1}$ (d) $n \cdot 2^n + 1$

43. If $(1+x)^n = C_0 + C_1 x + C_2 x^2 + \ldots + C_n x^n$, the coefficient of x^{n-1} in the expansion of $(x+C_0)(x+C_1)(x+C_2)\ldots(x+C_n)$ is

(a) $2^{2n-1} - \frac{1}{2}\,{}^{2n}C_{n-1}$ (b) $2^{2n-1} - \frac{1}{2}\,{}^{2n}C_n$

(c) $2^{2n-1} - \frac{1}{2}\,{}^{2n+1}C_n$ (d) $2^{2n-1} - \frac{1}{2}\,{}^{2n+1}C_{n-1}$

Stem Based Questions

Stem I

(Q. Nos. 44 and 45)

- Let us consider the binomial expression

$$A = \left(x^2 + \frac{3}{x}\right)^m \text{ and } B = \left(\frac{5x}{2} + \frac{x^{-2}}{2}\right)^n$$

Sum of coefficients of expansion of B is 6561. The difference of the coefficient of third term to the second term in the expansion of A is equal to 117.

44. The value of m is ....

45. If n^m is divided by 7, the remainder is ....

Stem II

(Q. Nos. 46 and 47)

- Let us consider the binomial expression $(1+x)^n = \sum_{r=0}^{n} a_r\, x^r$, where a_4, a_5 and a_6 are in AP, $(n<10)$. Consider another binomial expression of $A = (\sqrt[3]{2} + \sqrt[4]{3})^{13n}$, the expression of A contains some rational terms $T_{a_1}, T_{a_2}, T_{a_3}, \ldots, T_{a_m}$ $(a_1 < a_2 < a_3 < \ldots < a_m)$.

46. The value of $\sum_{i=1}^{n} a_i$ is ....

47. The value of a_m is ....

Single Integer Type Questions

48. If $\dfrac{\left[\begin{array}{l} {}^nC_r + 4\cdot {}^nC_{r+1} + 6\cdot {}^nC_{r+2} \\ \quad + 4\cdot {}^nC_{r+3} + {}^nC_{r+4} \end{array}\right]}{\left[\begin{array}{l} {}^nC_r + 3\cdot {}^nC_{r+1} + 3\cdot {}^nC_{r+2} \\ \quad + {}^nC_{r+3} \end{array}\right]} = \dfrac{n+\lambda}{r+\lambda}$, the value of λ is ....

49. The value of

$$99^{50} - 99\cdot 98^{50} + \frac{99\cdot 98}{1\cdot 2}(97)^{50} - \ldots + 99 \text{ is } \ldots\ldots\ldots$$

50. If the greatest term in the expansion of $(1+x)^{2n}$ has the greatest coefficient if and only if $x \in \left(\frac{10}{11}, \frac{11}{10}\right)$ and the fourth term in the expansion of $\left(\lambda x + \frac{1}{x}\right)^m$ is $\frac{n}{4}$, the value of $m\lambda$ is ....

51. If the value of $(n+2)\cdot {}^nC_0 \cdot 2^{n+1} - (n+1)\cdot {}^nC_1 \cdot 2^n + n\cdot {}^nC_2 \cdot 2^{n-1} - \ldots$ is equal to $k(n+1)$, the value of k is ....

52. If $(1+x+x^2+\ldots+x^9)^4 (x+x^2+x^3+\ldots+x^9) = \sum_{r=1}^{45} a_r\, x^r$ and the value of $a_2 + a_6 + a_{10} + \ldots + a_{42}$ is λ, the sum of all digits of λ is ....

Numerical Value Type Questions

53. Remainder when $6^{83} + 8^{63}$ is divided by 49 is ....

54. The constant term in the expansion of $(\log_{10}(x^{\log_{10}^x} - \log_{x^2} 100)^{12}$ is ....

55. The value of $\sum_{r=0}^{3} {}^8C_r\,({}^5C_{r+1} - {}^4C_r)$ is ....

56. The sum of the series

$$\frac{{}^{101}C_1}{{}^{101}C_0} + 2\times\frac{{}^{101}C_2}{{}^{101}C_1} + 3\times\frac{{}^{101}C_3}{{}^{101}C_2} + \ldots + 101\times\frac{{}^{101}C_{101}}{{}^{101}C_{100}} \text{ is } \ldots\ldots$$

57. Let $a = 3^{\frac{1}{223}} + 1$ and for all $n \geq 3$, let $f(n) = {}^nC_0\cdot a^{n-1} - {}^nC_1\cdot a^{n-2} + {}^nC_2\cdot a^{n-3} - \ldots + (-1)^{n-1}\cdot {}^nC_{n-1}\cdot a^0$. If the value of $f(2007) + f(2008) = 3^k$, where $k \in N$, then the value of k is ....

Matching Type Questions

58. Match the following columns.

Column I		Column II
(A) If $\binom{18}{r-2} + 2\binom{18}{r-1} + \binom{18}{r} \geq \binom{20}{13}$, then the values of r is /are	(p)	5
(B) The digit in the unit's place of the number $183! + 3^{183}$ is less than	(q)	6
(C) If the 4th term in the expansion of $\left(ax + \frac{1}{x}\right)^n$ is $5/2$, then na is less than	(r)	7
(D) If $(1+ax)^n = 1 + 8x + 24x^2 + \ldots$, then the sum of values of a and n are	(s)	8
	(t)	9

59. Match the following columns.

Column I		Column II
(A) The sum of binomial coefficients of terms containing power of x more than x^{30} in $(1+x)^{61}$ is divisible by	(p)	2^{31}
(B) The sum of binomial coefficients of rational terms in the expansion of $(1+\sqrt{3})^{62}$ is divisible by	(q)	2^{58}
(C) If $\left(x + \frac{1}{x} + x^2 + \frac{1}{x^2}\right)^{31} = a_0\, x^{-62} + a_1\, x^{-61} + a_2\, x^{-60} + \ldots + a_{124}\, x^{62}$, then $a_1 + a_3 + a_5 + \ldots + a_{123}$ is divisible by	(r)	2^{59}
(D) The sum of coefficients of terms of degree 13 in the expansion of $(1+x)^{11}(1+y^2-z)^{10}$ is ${}^{10}C_m$, then the value of m^{29} is	(s)	2^{60}
	(t)	2^{61}

60. Match the following columns.

	Column I		Column II
(A)	If $11^n + 21^n$ is divisible by 16, then n can be	(p)	4
(B)	The remainder, when 3^{37} is divided by 80, is less than	(q)	5
(C)	In the expansion of $(1 + x)^{29}$ coefficient of $(r + 1)$th term is equal to that of $(r + k)$th term, then the value of k cannot be	(r)	6
(D)	If the ratio of 2nd and 3rd terms in the expansion of $(a + b)^n$ is equal to ratio of 3rd and 4th terms in the expansion of $(a + b)^{n+3}$, then n is less than	(s)	7

Previous Year Questions

61. Let a and b be two non-zero real numbers. If the coefficient of x^5 in the expansion of $\left(ax^2 + \frac{70}{27bx}\right)^4$ is equal to the coefficient of x^{-5} in the expansion of $\left(ax - \frac{1}{bx^2}\right)^7$, then the value of $2b$ is ....

[Numerical Value Type, 2023 Adv.]

62. Suppose $\det \begin{bmatrix} \sum_{k=0}^{n} k & \sum_{k=0}^{n} {}^nC_k k^2 \\ \sum_{k=0}^{n} {}^nC_k k & \sum_{k=0}^{n} {}^nC_k 3^k \end{bmatrix} = 0$ holds for some positive integer n. Then $\sum_{k=0}^{n} \frac{{}^nC_k}{k+1}$ equals ....

[Numerical Value Type, 2023 Adv.]

63. For non-negative integers s and r, let

$$\binom{s}{r} = \begin{cases} \dfrac{s!}{r!(s-r)!} & \text{if } r \le s, \\ 0 & \text{if } r > s \end{cases}$$

For positive integers m and n, let

$$g(m, n) = \sum_{p=0}^{m+n} \frac{f(m, n, p)}{\binom{n+p}{p}}$$

where for any non-negative integer p,

$$f(m, n, p) = \sum_{i=0}^{p} \binom{m}{i} \binom{n+i}{p} \binom{p+n}{p-i}.$$

Then which of the following statements is/are TRUE?

[Single Correct Type, 2020 Adv.]

(a) $g(m, n) = g(n, m)$ for all positive integers m, n
(b) $g(m, n + 1) = g(m + 1, n)$ for all positive integers m, n
(c) $g(2m, 2n) = 2g(m, n)$ for all positive integers m, n
(d) $g(2m, 2n) = (g(m, n))^2$ for all positive integers m, n

EXERCISE 3

Challenging Problems

1. Determine the value of x in the expression of $(x + x^{\log_{10} x})^5$, if the third term in the expansion is 1000000.

2. Prove that, if p is a prime number greater than 2, the difference $[(2+\sqrt{5})^p] - 2^{p+1}$ is divisible by p, where $[.]$ denotes greatest integer.

3. If $(1+x)^n = C_0 + C_1 x + C_2 x^2 + \ldots + C_n x^n$, find the value of $\sum\sum_{0 \le i < j \le n} (i+j)(C_i + C_j + C_i C_j)$.

4. Prove the identity
$$\frac{1}{{}^{2n+1}C_r} + \frac{1}{{}^{2n+1}C_{r+1}} = \frac{2n+2}{2n+1} \cdot \frac{1}{{}^{2n}C_r},$$
use it to prove $\displaystyle\sum_{r=1}^{r=2n-1} \frac{(-1)^{r-1} r}{{}^{2n}C_r} = \frac{n}{n+1}$.

5. Let $a_0, a_1, a_2, \ldots$ are the coefficients in the expansion of $(1 + x + x^2)^n$ arranged order of x. Find the value of $a_r - {}^nC_1 a_{r-1} + {}^nC_r a_{r-2} - \ldots + (-1)^r \, {}^nC_r a_0$, where r is not divisible by 3.

6. Let $f(x) = a_0 + a_1 x + a_2 x^2 + \ldots + a_{2n} x^{2n}$ and
$$g(x) = b_0 + b_1 x + b_2 x^2 + \ldots + b_{n-1} x^{n-1} + x^n + x^{n+1} + \ldots + x^{2n}.$$
If $f(x) = g(x+1)$, find a_n in terms of n.

7. Show that $\dfrac{C_0}{1} - \dfrac{C_1}{4} + \dfrac{C_2}{7} - \ldots + (-1)^n \dfrac{C_n}{3n+1}$
$$= \frac{3^n \cdot n!}{1 \cdot 4 \cdot 7 \ldots (3n+1)},$$ where C_r stands for ${}^nC_r$.

Answer Key

Exercise 1

1. (b)	2. (d)	3. (b)	4. (b)	5. (a)	6. (b)	7. (d)	8. (c)	9. (c)	10. (b)
11. (d)	12. (b)	13. (d)	14. (b)	15. (b)	16. (a)	17. (a)	18. (c)	19. (d)	20. (d)
21. (d)	22. (b)	23. (d)	24. (b)	25. (b)	26. (b)	27. (a)	28. (d)	29. (a)	30. (6)
31. (4)	32. (8)	33. (6)	34. (0)	35. (1)	36. (4)	37. (3)	38. (1)	39. (3)	40. (3)
41. (0)	42. (3)	43. (3)	44. (1)	45. (6)	46. (b)	47. (c)	48. (d)	49. (*)	50. (b)
51. (54)	52. (678)	53. (25)	54. (b)	55. (b)	56. (a)	57. (c)	58. (a)	59. (b)	60. (171)
61. (23)	62. (1080)	63. (a)	64. (c)	65. (a)	66. (c)	67. (d)	68. (57)	69. (a)	70. (c)
71. (a)	72. (d)	73. (1)	74. (96)	75. (d)	76. (b)	77. (13)	78. (30)		

Exercise 2

1. (a)	2. (b)	3. (d)	4. (b)	5. (b)	6. (c)	7. (a)	8. (c)	9. (b)	10. (a)
11. (b)	12. (c)	13. (a)	14. (b)	15. (c)	16. (c)	17. (c)	18. (c)	19. (b,d)	20. (a,b,c)
21. (b,c,d)	22. (a,b,c)	23. (a,d)	24. (a,d)	25. (c,d)	26. (b,c)	27. (b,c)	28. (b,c)	29. (a,b,d)	30. (a,d)
31. (a,b,c)	32. (a,c)	33. (a,d)	34. (b)	35. (d)	36. (c)	37. (b)	38. (c)	39. (d)	40. (b)
41. (a)	42. (b)	43. (b)	44. (6)	45. (1)	46. (127)	47. (89)	48. (4)	49. (0)	50. (3)
51. (4)	52. (9)	53. (35)	54. (495)	55. (220)	56. (5151)	57. (9)			

58. (A) → (r,s,t); (B) → (s,t); (C) → (p,q,r,s,t); (D) → (q)

59. (A) → (p,q,r,s); (B) → (p,q,r,s,t); (C) → (p,q,r,s,t); (D) → (q)

60. (A) → (q,s); (B) → (p,q,r,s); (C) → (q,s); (D) → (r,s)

61. (3) 62. (6.20) 63. (d)

Solutions

Exercise 1 - JEE Main Pattern

1. We have,

$$\sum_{r=0}^{n} {}^nC_r(-1)^r [i^r + i^{2r} + i^{3r} + i^{4r}]$$

$$= \sum_{r=0}^{n} {}^nC_r(-1)^r[i^r + (-1)^r + (-i)^r + 1^r]$$

$$= \sum_{r=0}^{n} {}^nC_r[(-i)^r + 1^r + i^r + (-1)^r]$$

$$= (1-i)^n + (1+1)^n + (1+i)^n + (1-1)^n$$

$$= (\sqrt{2})^n\left(\frac{1}{\sqrt{2}} - \frac{i}{\sqrt{2}}\right)^n + (\sqrt{2})^n\left(\frac{1}{\sqrt{2}} + \frac{i}{\sqrt{2}}\right)^n + 2^n$$

$$= (\sqrt{2})^n\left(\cos\frac{\pi}{4} - i\sin\frac{\pi}{4}\right)^n + (\sqrt{2})^n\left(\cos\frac{\pi}{4} + i\sin\frac{\pi}{4}\right)^n + 2^n$$

$$= (\sqrt{2})^n\left(\cos\frac{n\pi}{4} - i\sin\frac{n\pi}{4}\right) + (\sqrt{2})^n\left(\cos\frac{n\pi}{4} + i\sin\frac{n\pi}{4}\right) + 2^n$$

$$= 2(\sqrt{2})^n\cos\frac{n\pi}{4} + 2^n$$

$$= 2^n + 2^{\frac{n}{2}+1}\cos\frac{n\pi}{4}$$

$$\therefore f(n) = \cos\frac{n\pi}{4}$$

Now, $f(1) = \cos\frac{\pi}{4} = \frac{1}{\sqrt{2}}$ and $f(2) = \cos\frac{\pi}{2} = 0$

2. We have,

$$(1-x)^5(1+x+x^2+x^3)^4$$

$$= (1-x)^5((1+x)(1+x^2))^4$$

$$= (1-x)^5(1+x)^4(1+x^2)^4$$

$$= (1-x)(1-x^2)^4(1+x^2)^4$$

$$= (1-x)(1-x^4)^4$$

$$= (1-x)(1-4x^4+6x^8-4x^{12}+x^{16})$$

$\therefore$ Coefficient of $x^{13} = (-1)(-4) = 4$

3. We have,

$$\left(1 + \frac{x}{1!} + \frac{x^2}{2!} + \ldots + \frac{x^n}{n!}\right)^2$$

$$= \left(1 + \frac{x}{1!} + \frac{x^2}{2!} + \ldots + \frac{x^n}{n!}\right)\left(1 + \frac{x}{1!} + \frac{x^2}{2!} + \ldots + \frac{x^n}{n!}\right)$$

$\therefore$ Coefficient of

$$x^n = 1 \times \frac{1}{n!} + \frac{1}{1!} \times \frac{1}{(n-1)!} + \frac{1}{2!} \times \frac{1}{(n-2)!} + \ldots + \frac{1}{n!}$$

$$= \frac{1}{n!}\left(\frac{n!}{n!} + \frac{n!}{1!(n-1)!} + \frac{n!}{2!(n-2)!} + \ldots + \frac{n!}{n!}\right)$$

$$= \frac{1}{n!}({}^nC_0 + {}^nC_1 + {}^nC_2 + \ldots + {}^nC_n)$$

$$= \frac{2^n}{n!}$$

4. Greatest coefficient is equal to the greatest term when $x = 1$.

For $x = 1$,

$$\frac{T_{r+1}}{T_r} = \frac{15-r+1}{r} \times \frac{2}{3}$$

Let $\frac{T_{r+1}}{T_r} \geq 1$

$$\Rightarrow \quad \frac{15-r+1}{r} \times \frac{2}{3} \geq 1$$

$$\Rightarrow \quad 32 - 2r \geq 3r$$

$$\Rightarrow \quad 5r \leq 32$$

$$\Rightarrow \quad r \leq \frac{32}{5}$$

So, for greatest coefficient, $r = 6$.

Hence, 7th term has the greatest coefficient and its value is ${}^{15}C_6(2/3)^6$.

5. We have,

$$T_7 = T_8$$

$$\Rightarrow \quad {}^nC_6x^6 = {}^nC_7x^7$$

$$\Rightarrow \quad x = \frac{{}^nC_6}{{}^nC_7}$$

$$\Rightarrow \quad x = \frac{7}{n-6}$$

$$\Rightarrow \quad \frac{7}{x} + 6 = n$$

$$\therefore \quad \left(\frac{7}{x} + 6\right)^n = n^n$$

6. We have,

$$(1 + 2x + 3x^2)^{10}$$

$\therefore$ a_1 = coefficient of x in $(1 + 2x + 3x^2)^{10}$

= Coefficient of x in $((1 + 2x) + 3x^2)^{10}$

= Coefficient of x in $({}^{10}C_0(1+2x)^{10} + {}^{10}C_1(1+2x)^9(3x^2)\ldots)$

= Coefficient of x in ${}^{10}C_0(1+2x)^{10}$

$= {}^{10}C_0 \times 2 \times {}^{10}C_1$

$= 20$

7. We have, $\left(1+\sqrt{a}+\dfrac{1}{\sqrt{a}-1}\right)^{-30}$

$$=\left(\frac{a-1+1}{\sqrt{a}-1}\right)^{-30}$$
$$=\left(\frac{a}{\sqrt{a}-1}\right)^{-30}$$
$$=\left(\frac{\sqrt{a}-1}{a}\right)^{30}$$
$$=\frac{1}{a^{30}}(1-\sqrt{a})^{30}$$
$$=\frac{1}{a^{30}}[{}^{30}C_0-{}^{30}C_1\sqrt{a}+{}^{30}C_2(\sqrt{a})^2-\ldots+{}^{30}C_{30}(\sqrt{a})^{30}]$$

∴ There is no term independent of a.

8. Let $G=(5-2\sqrt{6})^n$

Then, $I+f+G=(5+2\sqrt{6})^n+(5-2\sqrt{6})^n$

$\Rightarrow\quad I+f+G=2[{}^nC_0 5^n(2\sqrt{6})^0+{}^nC_2 5^{n-2}(2\sqrt{6})^2+\ldots]$

$\Rightarrow\quad I+f+G=$ An even integer

$\Rightarrow\quad f+G=1$ ...(i)

Now, $\quad I+f=(5+2\sqrt{6})^n$

$\Rightarrow\quad I=(5+2\sqrt{6})^n-f$

$\Rightarrow\quad I=\dfrac{1}{(5-2\sqrt{6})^n}-f$

$\Rightarrow\quad I=\dfrac{1}{1-f}-f$ [from Eq. (i)]

9. We have, in the expansion of $(1+\alpha x)^4$,

Middle term $={}^4C_2(\alpha x)^2=6\alpha^2x^2$

In the expansion of $(1-\alpha x)^6$,

Middle term $={}^6C_3(-\alpha x)^3=-20\alpha^3x^3$

Now, according to the question

$$6\alpha^2=-20\alpha^3$$

$\Rightarrow\quad \alpha=0,\dfrac{-3}{10}$

10. We have, $8^{2n}-(62)^{2n+1}$

$$=64^n-(62)^{2n+1}$$
$$=(63+1)^n-(63-1)^{2n+1}$$
$$=(1+63)^n+(1-63)^{2n+1}$$
$$=[1+{}^nC_1\times 63+{}^nC_2\times(63)^2+\ldots+{}^nC_n\times(63)^n]$$
$$+[1-{}^{2n+1}C_1\times 63+{}^{2n+1}C_2(63)^2+\ldots+(-1)^{2n+1}(63)^{2n+1}]$$
$$=2+63[{}^nC_1+{}^nC_2\times 63+\ldots+{}^nC_n\times(63)^{n-1}]$$
$$+(-{}^{2n+1}C_1+{}^{2n+1}C_2\times 63+\ldots+(-1)^{2n+1}(63)^{2n}]$$
$$=2+\text{Multiple of }63$$

∴ Required remainder = 2

11. We observe that, x^9 can be formed in the following 8 ways: $x^{9+0}, x^{1+8}, x^{2+7}, x^{3+6}, x^{4+5}, x^{1+3+5}, x^{1+2+6}, x^{2+3+4}$ and coefficient in each case is 1.

∴Coefficient of $x^9=1+1+1+\ldots+1$ (8 times) $=8$

12. The general term in the expansion $(2a-3b+4c)^9$

$$=\frac{9!}{p!q!r!}2^p(-3)^q4^ra^pb^qc^r=\frac{9!}{p!q!r!}(2a)^p(-3b)^q(4c)^r$$

∴ Coefficient of $a^3b^4c^2=\dfrac{9!}{3!4!2!}\cdot 2^3\cdot(-3)^4\cdot 4^2$

$$=1260\times 10368=13063680$$

13. We have, $(2^x+2^{-x}+\log_e e^{x+2})^{30}$

$$=(2^x+2^{-x}+x+2)^{30}$$
$$=((2^{x/2}+2^{-x/2})^2+x)^{30}$$

∴ The term independent of x occurs in ${}^{30}C_0(2^{x/2}+2^{-x/2})^{60}$

$$={}^{30}C_0\times{}^{60}C_{30}$$
$$={}^{60}C_{30}$$

14. $\displaystyle\sum_{0\le i\le j\le 10}({}^{10}C_j)({}^jC_i)$

$$={}^{10}C_0{}^0C_0+{}^{10}C_1({}^1C_0+{}^1C_1)+{}^{10}C_2({}^2C_0+{}^2C_1+{}^2C_2)+\ldots$$
$$+{}^{10}C_{10}({}^{10}C_0+{}^{10}C_1+\ldots+{}^{10}C_{10})$$
$$={}^{10}C_0+{}^{10}C_1(2)+{}^{10}C_2(2^2)+{}^{10}C_3(2^3)+\ldots+{}^{10}C_{10}(2^{10})$$
$$=(1+2)^{10}$$
$$=3^{10}$$

15. Let $\quad S=\dfrac{{}^nC_0}{n}+\dfrac{{}^nC_1}{n+1}+\dfrac{{}^nC_2}{n+2}+\ldots+\dfrac{{}^nC_n}{2n}$

$$={}^nC_0\int_0^1x^{n-1}dx+{}^nC_1\int_0^1x^ndx+\ldots+{}^nC_n\int_0^1x^{2n-1}dx$$
$$=\int_0^1[{}^nC_0x^{n-1}+{}^nC_1x^n+\ldots+{}^nC_nx^{2n-1}]dx$$
$$=\int_0^1x^{n-1}(1+x)^n\,dx$$
$$=\int_1^2x^n(x-1)^{n-1}\,dx$$

16. ∵ $19^{9^4}=(20-1)^{9^4}=(20-1)^{6561}$

$$=-1+(6561)\times 20+\text{multiple of }100$$
$$=-1+20+\text{multiple of }100$$
$$=19+\text{multiple of }100$$

∴ Last two digits of the number 19^{9^4} is 19.

17. $T_2={}^nC_1(\sqrt[13]{a})^{n-1}\left(\dfrac{a}{\sqrt{a^{-1}}}\right)^1=14a^{5/2}$ [given]

$\Rightarrow\quad n(a)^{\frac{n-1}{13}}a^{1+\frac{1}{2}}=14a^{5/2}$

$\Rightarrow\quad na^{\frac{n-1}{13}}a^{3/2}=14a^{5/2}$

When we put $n=14$, then it satisfies the above equation

∴ $\quad\dfrac{{}^nC_3}{{}^nC_2}=\dfrac{{}^{14}C_3}{{}^{14}C_2}=\dfrac{14-3+1}{3}=4$

18. $6^{83}+8^{83}=(7-1)^{83}+(7+1)^{83}$

$$=2(7^{83}+{}^{83}C_2\cdot 7^{81}+{}^{83}C_4\cdot 7^{79}+\dots+{}^{83}C_{80}7^3+{}^{83}C_{82}7)$$

$$=2\{49m+{}^{83}C_{82}\cdot 7\}$$

where, m is an integer

$$=98m+2\cdot{}^{83}C_1\cdot 7=98m+2\cdot 83\cdot 7$$

$$=98m+2(77+6)\cdot 7=49(2m+22)+84$$

$$=49(2m+22)+49+35$$

$$=49(2m+23)+35=49n+35$$

where n is an integer.

Hence, the remainder is 35.

19. In the expansion of $(3^{1/4}+2^{2/3})^{12}$, the general term is

$$T_{r+1}={}^{12}C_r(3^{1/4})^{12-r}(2^{2/3})^r={}^{12}C_r 3^{3-\frac{r}{4}}2^{\frac{2r}{3}}$$

Now, $0\le r\le 12$

$\therefore$ $r=0, 12$

Rational terms are T_{0+1} and T_{12+1}

Now, $T_1={}^{12}C_0 3^3 2^0=27$

$\Rightarrow$ $T_{13}={}^{12}C_{12}3^0\cdot 2^8=256$

$\therefore$ Required sum $=T_1+T_{13}$

$$=27+256=283$$

20. $N=7^{100}-3^{100}=(7^2)^{50}-(3^2)^{50}$

$$=(50-1)^{50}-(10-1)^{50}$$

$$=[(50)^{50}-{}^{50}C_1(50)^{49}+{}^{50}C_2(50)^{48}-{}^{50}C_3(50)^{47}+\dots+{}^{50}C_{48}(50)^2-{}^{50}C_{49}(50)+1]$$

$$-[10^{50}-{}^{50}C_1\cdot 10^{49}+{}^{50}C_2(10)^{48}-{}^{50}C_3(10)^{47}+\dots+{}^{50}C_{48}(10)^2-{}^{50}C_{49}(10)+1]$$

$$=[10^4m-{}^{50}C_{47}(50)^3+{}^{50}C_{48}(50)^2-{}^{50}C_{49}(50)+1]$$

$$-[10^4n-{}^{50}C_{47}(10)^3+{}^{50}C_{48}(10)^2-{}^{50}C_{49}(10)+1]$$

when m and n are integers.

$$=10^4p-{}^{50}C_3[(50)^3-(10)^3]+{}^{50}C_2[(50)^2-(10)^2]-{}^{50}C_1[(50)-(10)]$$

When p is an integer.

$$=10^4p-124\times 196\times 10^5+294\times 10^4-2000=10^4q-2000$$

When q is an integer.

$$=10^4q-10^4+10^4-2000=10^4(q-1)+8000$$

$\therefore$ Last four digits $=0000+8000=8000$

21. Let $P=5^{99}=5\times 5^{98}=5(25)^{49}=5(26-1)^{49}$

$$=5[{}^{49}C_0(26)^{49}-{}^{49}C_1(26)^{48}+{}^{49}C_2(26)^{47}-\dots+{}^{49}C_{48}(26)-{}^{49}C_{49}\cdot 1]$$

$=5\times 26k-5$, when k is an integer.

$$\therefore\ \frac{P}{13}=10k-\frac{5}{13}=10k-1+\frac{8}{13}$$

Hence, the remainder is 8.

22. $$\frac{3^{2003}}{28}=\frac{3^2\times 3^{2001}}{28}=\frac{9}{28}(3^3)^{667}=\frac{9}{28}(28-1)^{667}$$

$$=\frac{9}{28}\{(28)^{667}-{}^{667}C_1(28)^{666}+{}^{667}C_2(28)^{665}-\dots+{}^{667}C_{666}(28)-1\}$$

$=9k-\frac{9}{28}$, where k is an integer.

$$=(9k-1)+\frac{19}{28}$$

or $$\left\{\frac{3^{2003}}{28}\right\}=\left\{(9k-1)+\frac{19}{28}\right\}=\frac{19}{28}$$

23. $$\sum_{r=0}^{20} r(20-r)\times({}^{20}C_r)^2$$

$$=\sum_{r=0}^{20} r\times{}^{20}C_r(20-r)\times{}^{20}C_{20-r}=\sum_{r=0}^{20}20\cdot{}^{19}C_{r-1}\times 20\times{}^{19}C_{19-r}$$

$$=400\sum_{r=0}^{20}{}^{19}C_{r-1}\times{}^{19}C_{19-r}$$

$=400\times$ Coefficient of x^{18} in $(1+x)^{19}(1+x)^{19}$

$$=400\times{}^{38}C_{18}=400\times{}^{38}C_{20}$$

24. Given, $(3+x^{2008}+x^{2009})^{2010}=a_0+a_1x+a_2x^2+\dots+a_nx^n$

On putting $x=\omega$ and ω^2 respectively, we get

$$(3+\omega^{2008}+\omega^{2009})^{2010}=a_0+a_1\omega+a_2\omega^2+a_3\omega^3+\dots$$

or $$(3+\omega+\omega^2)^{2010}=a_0+a_1\omega+a_2\omega^2+a_3\omega^3+\dots$$

or $$2^{2010}=a_0+a_1\omega+a_2\omega^2+a_3\omega^3+a_4\omega^4+a_5\omega^5+a_6\omega^6+\dots \quad \text{...(i)}$$

and $[3+(\omega^2)^{2008}+(\omega^2)^{2009}]^{2010}$

$$=a_0+a_1\omega^2+a_2\omega^4+a_3\omega^6+a_4\omega^8+a_5\omega^{10}+a_6\omega^{12}+\dots$$

or $(3+\omega^2+\omega)^{2010}$

$$=a_0+a_1\omega^2+a_2\omega^4+a_3\omega^6+a_4\omega^8+a_5\omega^{10}+a_6\omega^{12}+\dots$$

$$\Rightarrow 2^{2010}=a_0+a_1\omega^2+a_2\omega^4+a_3\omega^6+a_4\omega^8+a_5\omega^{10}+a_6\omega^{12} \quad \text{...(ii)}$$

On adding Eqs. (i) and (ii), we get

$$2\times 2^{2010}=2a_0+a_1(\omega+\omega^2)+a_2(\omega^2+\omega^4)+a_3(\omega^3+\omega^6)+a_4(\omega^4+\omega^8)+a_5(\omega^5+\omega^{10})+a_6(\omega^6+\omega^{12})+\dots$$

$$=2a_0-a_1-a_2+2a_3-a_4-a_5+2a_6-\dots$$

$$\Rightarrow\quad 2^{2010}=a_0-\frac{1}{2}a_1-\frac{1}{2}a_2+a_3-\frac{1}{2}a_4-\frac{1}{2}a_5+a_6-\dots$$

25. Now, $$\left(x^2-2+\frac{1}{x^2}\right)^n=\frac{(x^4-2x^2+1)^n}{x^{2n}}=\frac{(x^2-1)^{2n}}{x^{2n}}$$

$\therefore$ Total number of terms that are dependent of x is equal to number of terms in the expansion of $(x^2-1)^{2n}$ that have degree of x different from $2n$, which is given by $(2n+1)-1=2n$.

26. Given expansion can be rewritten as $[1+x^2(1-x)]^8$

$$={}^8C_0+{}^8C_1x^2(1-x)+{}^8C_2x^4(1-x)^2+{}^8C_3x^6(1-x)^3+{}^8C_4x^8(1-x)^4+{}^8C_5x^{10}(1-x)^5+\dots$$

There are only two terms, which we get the coefficient of x^{10}.

$\therefore$ Coefficient of $x^{10}={}^8C_4$[Coefficient of x^2 in $(1-x)^4$] $+{}^8C_5$[Coefficient of x^0 in $(1-x)^5$]

$$={}^8C_4({}^4C_2)+{}^8C_5(1)$$

$$=({}^8C_4)({}^4C_2)+{}^8C_3=(70)(6)+56=476$$

27. $(1+ix)^{4n-2} = {}^{4n-2}C_0 + {}^{4n-2}C_1(ix) + {}^{4n-2}C_2(ix)^2 + \cdots + {}^{4n-2}C_{4n-2}(ix)^{4n-2}$

Here, we see that Ist negative term is T_3 and the next term is T_7 and the last negative term is T_{4n-1}.

Now, $3, 7, \cdots, 4n-1$

It is an AP.

$\because \quad l = a + (N-1)d$

$\therefore \quad 4n - 1 = 3 + (N-1)4$

$\Rightarrow \quad n - 1 = N - 1 \Rightarrow N = n$

28. $\because \quad \binom{n}{m}\binom{m}{p} = \dfrac{n!}{m!(n-m)!} \times \dfrac{m!}{p!(m-p)!}$

$$= \frac{n!}{(n-m)!\,p!(m-p)!} = \binom{n}{p}\binom{n-p}{m-p}$$

$$\therefore \sum_{p=1}^{n}\sum_{m=p}^{n}\binom{n}{m}\binom{m}{p} = \sum_{p=1}^{n}\sum_{m=p}^{n}\binom{n}{p}\binom{n-p}{m-p}$$

$$= \sum_{p=1}^{n}\binom{n}{p}\sum_{m=p}^{n}\binom{n-p}{m-p}$$

$$= \sum_{p=1}^{n}\binom{n}{p}\sum_{t=0}^{n-p}\binom{n-p}{t} \quad [\text{where, } t = m-p]$$

$$= 2^n \sum_{p=1}^{n}\binom{n}{p} 2^{n-p}$$

$$= 2^n \sum_{p=1}^{n}\binom{n}{p}\frac{1}{2^p} = 2^n\left[\left(1+\frac{1}{2}\right)^n - 1\right] = 3^n - 2^n$$

29. Given, $\displaystyle\sum_{r=0}^{4} \frac{5^{4-r}}{(4-r)!}\left(\frac{x^r}{r!}\right) = \frac{8}{3}$

$\Rightarrow \quad \dfrac{(5+x)^4}{4!} = \dfrac{8}{3}$

$\Rightarrow \quad (5+x)^4 = 64 = (2\sqrt{2})^4 \Rightarrow 5 + x = \pm 2\sqrt{2}$

$\therefore \quad x = 2\sqrt{2} - 5$ or $x = -2\sqrt{2} - 5$

Hence, largest real value of x is $2\sqrt{2} - 5$.

30. For $(y^{1/5} + x^{1/10})^{55}$,

$$T_{r+1} = {}^{55}C_r (y^{1/5})^{55-r}(x^{1/10})^r = {}^{55}C_r y^{11-\frac{r}{5}} x^{\frac{r}{10}}$$

For T_{r+1} to be free from radical signs, $\dfrac{r}{5}$ and $\dfrac{r}{10}$ must be integers.

Also, $0 \le r \le 55$

$\therefore \; r = 0, 10, 20, 30, 40, 50$

So, required number of terms is 6.

31. The sum of the numerical coefficients is obtained by putting $x = 1, y = 1$.

$\therefore$ Required sum $= \left(1 + \dfrac{1}{3} + \dfrac{2}{3}\right)^{12}$

$= 2^{12}$

$= 2^{10} \times 2^2$

$= 1024 \times 4$

$\therefore \quad \lambda = 4$

32. Let the three consecutive coefficients are

${}^nC_{r-1} = 28, {}^nC_r = 56, {}^nC_{r+1} = 70$

$\therefore \quad \dfrac{{}^nC_r}{{}^nC_{r-1}} = \dfrac{n-r+1}{r} = \dfrac{56}{28} = 2$

and $\dfrac{{}^nC_{r+1}}{{}^nC_r} = \dfrac{n-r}{r+1} = \dfrac{70}{56} = \dfrac{5}{4}$

$\therefore \quad n + 1 = 3r$ and $4n - 5 = 9r$

$\Rightarrow \quad \dfrac{4n-5}{n+1} = 3$

$\Rightarrow \quad n = 8$

33. We have, $T_{r+1} = {}^nC_r (x^2)^{n-r}\left(\dfrac{-1}{x}\right)^r$

$= {}^nC_r (-1)^r x^{2n-3r}$

For constant term,

$2n - 3r = 0$

$\Rightarrow \quad r = \dfrac{2n}{3}$

$\therefore$ Constant term $= {}^nC_{\frac{2n}{3}}(-1)^{2n/3}$

$\therefore \quad {}^nC_{\frac{2n}{3}}(-1)^{2n/3} = 15$

$\Rightarrow \quad {}^nC_{\frac{2n}{3}}(-1)^{2n/3} = {}^6C_4$

$\therefore \quad n = 6$

34. We have, $1 + 2 + 2^2 + 2^3 + \ldots + 2^{1999}$

$= \dfrac{1(2^{2000} - 1)}{2 - 1}$

$= 2^{2000} - 1$

$= 4^{1000} - 1$

$= (1-5)^{1000} - 1$

$= 1 - {}^{1000}C_1 5 + {}^{1000}C_2 5^2 - {}^{1000}C_3 5^3 + \ldots + {}^{1000}C_{1000} 5^{1000} - 1$

$= 5k$

So, remainder $= 0$

35. We have,

$$\sum_{k=0}^{4}\left(\frac{3^{4-k}}{(4-k)!}\right)\left(\frac{x^k}{4!}\right)$$

$$= \sum_{k=0}^{4}\left(\frac{4!}{(4-k)!k!} \times 3^{4-k}\cdot x^k \cdot \frac{1}{4!}\right)$$

$$= \sum_{k=0}^{4}\frac{{}^4C_k 3^{4-k} x^k}{4!} = \frac{(3+x)^k}{4!}$$

According to the question,

$\dfrac{(3+x)^k}{4!} = \dfrac{32}{3}$

$\Rightarrow \quad (3+x)^k = 256$

$\Rightarrow \quad x + 3 = 4$

$\Rightarrow \quad x = 1$

36. We have,

$$T_2 = {}^nC_1 (a^{1/13})^{n-1} \cdot a\sqrt{a} = 14a^{5/2}$$

$$\Rightarrow \quad na^{\frac{n-1}{13}} = 14a$$

$$\Rightarrow \quad na^{\frac{n-14}{13}} = 14$$

$$\Rightarrow \quad \frac{n-14}{13} = 0$$

$$\Rightarrow \quad n = 14$$

$$\therefore \quad \frac{{}^nC_3}{{}^nC_2} = \frac{{}^{14}C_3}{{}^{14}C_2}$$

$$= \frac{14 \times 13 \times 12}{3 \times 2 \times 1} \times \frac{2 \times 1}{14 \times 13} = 4$$

37. We have,

$$(1 + 0 \cdot 00002)^{50000} = \left(1 + \frac{1}{50000}\right)^{50000}$$

We know that,

$$2 \le \left(1 + \frac{1}{n}\right)^n < 3, \forall\, n \ge 1$$

∴Least integer is 3.

38. We have,

$$\frac{2^{4n}}{15} = \frac{(2^4)^n}{15}$$

$$= \frac{16^n}{15}$$

$$= \frac{(15+1)^n}{15}$$

$$= \frac{{}^nC_0 15^n + {}^nC_1 15^{n-1} + \ldots + {}^nC_{n-1} 15 + {}^nC_n}{15}$$

$$= \frac{15\lambda + 1}{15}$$

$$\therefore \text{Fractional part} = \frac{1}{15}$$

So, $a = 1$

39. We have,

$$ {}^{10}C_0 + ({}^{10}C_0 + {}^{10}C_1) + ({}^{10}C_0 + {}^{10}C_1 + {}^{10}C_2) + \ldots + ({}^{10}C_0 + {}^{10}C_1 + \ldots + {}^{10}C_9)$$

$$= 10 \times {}^{10}C_0 + 9 \times {}^{10}C_1 + 8 \times {}^{10}C_2 + \ldots + {}^{10}C_9$$

$$= {}^{10}C_1 + 2 \times {}^{10}C_2 + 3 \times {}^{10}C_3 + \ldots + 10 \times {}^{10}C_{10}$$

$$= \sum_{r=1}^{10} r \cdot {}^{10}C_r$$

$$= 10 \sum_{r=1}^{10} {}^9C_{r-1}$$

$$= 10 \times 2^9$$

$\therefore a = 10, b = 2, c = 9$

So, $a + b - c = 3$

40. Let $S = \left(\sum_{r=1}^{5} {}^{20}C_{2r-1}\right)^6$

Now, ${}^{20}C_1 + {}^{20}C_3 + {}^{20}C_5 + \ldots + {}^{20}C_{19} = 2^{19}$

Again, ${}^{20}C_1 = {}^{20}C_{19}$, ${}^{20}C_3 = {}^{20}C_{17}$ and so on

$\therefore\ 2({}^{20}C_1 + {}^{20}C_3 + \ldots + {}^{20}C_9) = 2^{19}$

$$\Rightarrow \quad \sum_{r=1}^{5} {}^{20}C_{2r-1} = 2^{18}$$

$$\therefore \quad S = (2^{18})^6 = 2^{108} = 8(2^5)^{21}$$

$$= 8(33-1)^{21} = 8(33k - 1)$$

$$= 8 \times 33k - 8 + 11 - 11 = 11(24k - 1) + 3$$

So, required remainder = 3

41. The unit digit of 2^{2^n} is always 6 for $n > 1$.

Now, $\sum_{r=0}^{100} r! = 0! + 1! + 2! + 3! + 4! + 10(k); k \in N$

$$= 1 + 1 + 2 + 6 + 24 + 10k = 34 + 10k$$

$\therefore$ Unit digit of $\sum_{r=0}^{100} r! + 2^{2^n}$

$$= \text{Unit place of } \sum_{r=0}^{100} r! + \text{Unit place of } 2^{2^n}$$

$= 4 + 0 + 6 = 10$, its unit place is 0.

42. Given, $\sum_{r=0}^{3n} a_r x^r = (1 + x + x^2 + x^3)^n$

It is clear that a_r is the coefficient of x^r in the expansion of $(1 + x + x^2 + x^3)^n$.

On replacing x by $\frac{1}{x}$ in the given equation, we get

$$\sum_{r=0}^{3n} a_r \left(\frac{1}{x}\right)^r = \frac{(1 + x + x^2 + x^3)^n}{x^{3n}}$$

Here, a_r represents the coefficient of 3^{3n-r} in $(1 + x + x^2 + x^3)^n$.

Thus, $\quad a_r = a_{3n-r}$ ...(i)

Let $\quad I = \sum_{r=0}^{3n} r \times a_r = \sum_{r=0}^{3n} (3n - r)\, a_{3n-r}$

[replacing r by $3n - r$]

$$= \sum_{r=0}^{3n} (3n - r)\, a_r \quad \text{[from Eq. (i)]}$$

$$= 3n \sum_{r=0}^{3n} - \sum_{r=0}^{3n} r a_r$$

$$\Rightarrow \quad 2I = 3nk \Rightarrow I = \frac{3nk}{2}$$

$$\therefore \quad \lambda = 3$$

43. We have, $T_{r+1} = {}^{20}C_r \cdot 4^{\frac{20-r}{3}} \cdot 6^{-r/4}$

$$= {}^{20}C_r \cdot 2^{\frac{40-2r}{3}} \cdot 2^{-r/4} \cdot 3^{-r/4}$$

$$= {}^{20}C_r \cdot 2^{\frac{160-11r}{12}} \cdot 3^{-r/4}$$

For rational terms, $\frac{r}{4}$ and $\frac{160-11r}{12}$ must be integers and

$0 \le r \le 20$.

$\therefore \quad \frac{r}{4}$ is an integer.

$\Rightarrow \quad r = 0, 4, 8, 12, 16, 20$

Clearly, for $r = 8$, 16 and 20, $\frac{160-11r}{12}$ is also an integer.

$\therefore$ The number of rational terms is 3.

44. We have, $2^{2006} = 2^2 (2^3)^{668}$

$$= 4(1+7)^{668} = 4(1+7k) = 4 + 28k$$

$\therefore \ 2^{2006} + 2006 = 4 + 28k + 7 \times (286) + 4$

Hence, remainder is 1.

45. We have, $19^{9^4} = (20-1)^{6561}$

$$= (20)^{6561} - {}^{6561}C_1 (20)^{6560} + {}^{6561}C_2 (20)^{6559}$$

$$- \ldots - {}^{6561}C_{6559} (20)^2 + {}^{6561}C_{6560} (20)^2 - 1$$

$$= 1000\,k - {}^{6561}C_2 (400) + {}^{6561}C_1 (20) - 1$$

where, k is an integer.

$$= 1000p + 6561 \times 20 - 1 = 1000p + 131220 - 1$$

where, p is an integer.

$$= 1000p + 131219$$

$\therefore \quad ab = 19$ i.e. $a = 1, b = 9$

Hence, $b - 3a = 9 - 3 = 6$

46. $\left(\sqrt{a}x^2 + \frac{1}{2x^3}\right)^{10}$

General term $= {}^{10}C_r (\sqrt{a}x^2)^{10-r} \left(\frac{1}{2x^3}\right)^r$

$\therefore$ For the term independent of x

$\Rightarrow \ 2(10-r) - 3r = 0 \Rightarrow r = 4$

Put $r = 4$,

$${}^{10}C_4 (\sqrt{a}x^2)^6 \left(\frac{1}{2x^3}\right)^4 = \frac{10\cdot 9\cdot 8\cdot 7}{4\cdot 3\cdot 2\cdot 1} \times a^3 \times \frac{1}{2^4} = 210a^3 \times \frac{1}{16}$$

Now, $210a^3 \times \frac{1}{16} = 105 \Rightarrow a^3 = 8 \Rightarrow a^2 = 4$

47. We have,

$$\left(\frac{1}{3}x^{1/3} + \frac{1}{2x^{2/3}}\right)^{18}$$

Given, coefficients of $T_7 = m$

and coefficients of $T_{13} = n$

Now, $$\frac{m}{n} = \frac{{}^{18}C_6 \left(\frac{1}{3}\right)^{12} \cdot \left(\frac{1}{2}\right)^6}{{}^{18}C_{12} \left(\frac{1}{3}\right)^6 \cdot \left(\frac{1}{2}\right)^{12}} \qquad [\because {}^nC_r = {}^nC_{n-r}]$$

$$\Rightarrow \left(\frac{m}{n}\right)^{1/3} = \left(\frac{1}{3^{12}} \times 3^6 \times \frac{1}{2^6} \times 2^{12}\right)^{1/3} = \left(\frac{2^6}{3^6}\right)^{1/3} = \frac{4}{9}$$

$$\therefore \quad \left(\frac{m}{n}\right)^{1/3} = \frac{4}{9}$$

48. Given, A = Sum of all the coefficients in the expansion of $(1 - 3x + 10x^2)^n$

B = Sum of all the coefficient in the expansion of $(1 + x^2)^n$.

Put $x = 1$ in $(1 - 3x + 10x^2)^n$ to get A and in similar way you can find B also.

So, $A = (8)^n$ and $B = 2^n$

Hence, $A = (2^n)^3 = B^3$

49. Binomial coefficients of 4 consecutive terms of $(1 + x)^n$ are ${}^nC_r, {}^nC_{r+1}, {}^nC_{r+2}, {}^nC_{r+3}$, respectively.

Given, $\quad {}^nC_r = 2 - p, {}^nC_{r+2} = 2 - \alpha$,

$${}^nC_{r+1} = p, \quad {}^nC_{r+3} = \alpha$$

$\therefore \quad {}^nC_r + {}^nC_{r+1} = 2$

and ${}^nC_{r+2} + {}^nC_{r+3} = 2$

$\Rightarrow \quad {}^{n+1}C_{r+1} = 2$

and $\quad {}^{n+1}C_{r+3} = 2$

$\therefore \quad {}^{n+1}C_{r+1} = {}^{n+1}C_{r+3}$

$\Rightarrow \quad r + 1 + r + 3 = n + 1$

$\Rightarrow \quad 2r + 4 = n + 1$

$\Rightarrow \quad n = 2r + 3$

Now, ${}^{n+1}C_{r+1} = 2$

$${}^{2r+4}C_{r+1} = 2$$

Not such value possible.

50. For $(1 + x)^n$

Coefficient of $x^4 \Rightarrow {}^nC_4$

Coefficient of $x^5 = {}^nC_5$

Coefficient of $x^6 = {}^nC_6$

$\because \quad {}^nC_4, {}^nC_5, {}^nC_6 \to$ AP

$\Rightarrow \ 2 \cdot {}^nC_5 = {}^nC_4 + {}^nC_6$

$$2 \times \frac{n!}{(n-5)!\,5!} = \frac{n!}{(n-4)!\,4!} + \frac{n!}{(n-6)!\,6!}$$

$$\Rightarrow \quad \frac{2}{(n-5)\cdot 5} = \frac{1}{(n-4)(n-5)} + \frac{1}{6 \times 5}$$

$\Rightarrow \ n^2 - 21n + 98 = 0$

$\Rightarrow \quad n = 14, 7$

$\therefore$ Maximum value of $n = 14$

51. **Decoding the Question**

General term of Binomial expansion $(a + b)^n$ is

$$T_{r+1} = {}^nC_r a^{n-r} b^r.$$

We have, $(1 + 2x - 3x^2)\left(\frac{3}{2}x^2 - \frac{1}{3x}\right)^9$

Here, general term of $\left(\frac{3}{2}x^2 - \frac{1}{3x}\right)^9$

$$= {}^9C_r \left(\frac{3}{2}x^2\right)^{9-r} (-1)^r \left(\frac{1}{3x}\right)^r$$

$$= {}^9C_r \frac{(3)^{9-r}}{(2)^{9-r}} (x^2)^{9-r} (-1)^r (3x)^{-r}$$

$$= {}^9C_r \frac{3^{9-2r}}{2^{9-r}} (-1)^r x^{18-3r}$$

For constant term, put $18 - 3r = 0 \Rightarrow r = 6$

On putting $r = 6$, we get

Coefficient of $x^0 = {}^9C_6 \frac{1}{216} x^0 = \frac{7}{18} x^0$

On putting $r = 7$, we get

Coefficient of $x^{-3} = {}^9C_7 \frac{3^{-5}}{2^2} (-1)^7 x^{-3}$

$$= -{}^9C_7 \frac{1}{3^5 \cdot 2^2} x^{-3}$$

$$= -\frac{1}{27} x^{-3}$$

$$\therefore (1 + 2x - 3x^3)\left(\frac{7}{18} x^0 - \frac{1}{27} x^{-3}\right)$$

Constant term $= \frac{7}{18} + \frac{3}{27}$

$$= \frac{7+2}{18} = \frac{1}{2}$$

$$\therefore \quad p = \frac{1}{2}$$

$$\therefore \quad 108p = 108 \times \frac{1}{2} = 54$$

52. Coefficient of x^{30} in

$$\frac{(x+1)^6 (1+x^2)^7 (1-x^3)^8}{x^6}$$

Coefficient of x^{36} in $(1+x)^6 (1+x^2)^7 (1-x^3)^8$

General term,

$${}^6C_{r_1} \, {}^7C_{r_2} \, {}^8C_{r_3} (-1)^{r_3} x^{r_1 + 2r_2 + 3r_3}$$

$$r_1 + 2r_2 + 3r_3 = 36$$

Case I

r_1	r_2	r_3
0	6	8
2	5	8
4	4	8
6	3	8

$r_1 + 2r_2 = 12$ [taking $r_3 = 8$]

Case II

r_1	r_2	r_3
1	7	7
3	6	7
5	5	7

$r_1 + 2r_2 = 15$ [taking $r_3 = 7$]

Case III

r_1	r_2	r_3
4	7	6
6	6	6

$r_1 + 2r_2 = 18$ [taking $r_3 = 6$]

Coefficient $= 7 + (15 \times 21) + (15 \times 35) + (35)$
$- (6 \times 8) - (20 \times 7 \times 8) - (6 \times 21 \times 8)$
$+ (15 \times 28) + (7 \times 28)$

$$= -678 = \alpha$$

Hence, $|\alpha| = 678$

53. $(x+3)^{n-1} + (x+3)^{n-2}(x+2)$
$+ (x+3)^{n-3}(x+2)^2 + \ldots + (x+2)^{n-1}$

$$= (x+3)^{n-1} \left[\frac{\left(\frac{x+2}{x+3}\right)^n - 1}{\frac{x+2}{x+3} - 1}\right]$$

$$= (x+3)^{n-1} \left[\frac{\frac{(x+2)^n}{(x+3)^n} - 1}{\frac{-1}{x+3}}\right]$$

$$= (x+3)^n - (x+2)^n$$

Coefficient of $x^r = {}^nC_r 3^r - {}^nC_r 2^r = \alpha_r$

$$\sum_{r=0}^{n} \alpha_r = \sum_{r=0}^{n} {}^nC_r 3^r - \sum_{r=0}^{n} {}^nC_r 2^r$$

$$= (1+3)^n - (1+2)^n$$

$$= 4^n - 3^n = \beta^n - \gamma^n$$

$$\beta = 4, \gamma = 3, \beta^2 + \gamma^2 = 25$$

54. $\frac{4^{2022}}{15} = \frac{4^{2(1011)}}{15}$

$$= \frac{(16)^{1011}}{15} = \frac{(15+1)^{1011}}{15}$$

$$= \frac{15K + 1}{15}$$

$$\therefore \left\{\frac{4^{2022}}{15}\right\} = \left\{\frac{15K+1}{15}\right\} = \frac{1}{15}$$

55. $\because (x^n - a^n)$ is divisible by $(x - a)$.

$\therefore (25^{190} - 19^{190})$ is divisible by $(25 - 19)$ i.e., 6

and $(8^{190} - 2^{190})$ is divisible by $(8 - 2) = 6$

$\Rightarrow (25^{190} - 19^{190}) - (8^{190} - 2^{190})$ is divisible by 6

Again, $(25^{190} - 8^{190})$ is divisible by $(25 - 8) = 17$

and $(19^{190} - 2^{190})$ is divisible by $(19 - 2) = 17$

$\Rightarrow (25^{190} - 8^{190}) - (19^{190} - 2^{190})$ is divisible by 17.

$\Rightarrow$ The given value is divisible by 6 as well as 17.

Hence, this it is divisible by 2, 3, 17, 34 but not divisible by 14.

56. In the expansion of $(1+x)^{10}$

$$T_{r+1} = {}^{10}C_r\, x^{10-r} = {}^{10}C_r\, x^{10-r}$$

Coefficient of $x^{10-r} = a_r = {}^{10}C_r$

We know that $\dfrac{{}^nC_r}{{}^nC_{r-1}} = \dfrac{n-r+1}{r}$

$$\frac{a_r}{a_{r-1}} = \frac{{}^{10}C_r}{{}^{10}C_{r-1}} = \frac{10-r+1}{r} = \frac{11-r}{r}$$

Now, $\displaystyle\sum_{r=1}^{10} r^3\left(\frac{a_r}{a_{r-1}}\right)^2 = \sum_{r=1}^{10} r^3\left(\frac{11-r}{r}\right)^2$

$$= \sum_{r=1}^{10} r(r^2 - 22r + 121)$$

$$= \sum_{r=1}^{10} r^3 - 22\sum_{r=1}^{10} r^2 + 121\sum_{r=1}^{10} r$$

$$= \left[\frac{10(10+1)}{2}\right]^2 - 22\left[\frac{10\times(10+1)(20+1)}{6}\right] + 121\times\frac{10\times(10+1)}{2}$$

$$= 1210$$

Alternate Solution

$$\sum_{r=1}^{10} r^3\left(\frac{a_r}{a_{r-1}}\right)^2 = \sum_{r=1}^{10} r^3\left(\frac{{}^{10}C_r}{{}^{10}C_{r-1}}\right)^2$$

$$= \sum_{r=1}^{10} r^3 \times \frac{(11-r)^2}{r^2} = \sum_{r=1}^{10} r(11-r)^2$$

$$= \sum_{r=1}^{10} (r^2 - 22r + 121)r$$

$$= \sum_{r=1}^{10} (r^3 - 22r^2 + 121r)$$

we will get 1210.

57. We have,

$S1: (2023)^{2022} - (1999)^{2022}$

$$= (1999+24)^{2022} - (1999)^{2022}$$

$$= {}^{2022}C_0\,(1999)^{2022}(24)^0 + {}^{2022}C_1\,(1999)^{2021}(24)^1 + {}^{2022}C_2(1999)^{2020}(24)^2 + \dots - (1999)^{2022}$$

$$= {}^{2022}C_1\,(1999)^{2021}(24) + {}^{2022}C_2(1999)^{2022}(24)^2 + \dots$$

$$= 24\left({}^{2022}C_1(1999)^{2021} + {}^{2022}C_2(1999)^{2022}(24) + \dots\right)$$

$\Rightarrow$ $S1$ is divisible by 24.

Now, $S2: 13(13)^n - 12n - 13$

Here, $13^n = (1+12)^n$

$$= 1 + {}^nC_1 12 + {}^nC_2(12)^2 + {}^nC_3(12)^3 + \dots \text{ upto } n \text{ terms.}$$

$\therefore$ $S2: 13\,(1 + {}^nC_1(12) + {}^nC_2(12)^2 + {}^nC_3(12)^3 + \dots) - 12n - 13$

$$= 13 + 156n + 13\,({}^nC_2(12)^2 + {}^nC_3(12)^3 + \dots) - 12n - 13$$

$$= 144n + 144\times 13\,({}^nC_2 + {}^nC_3(12) + \dots)$$

$$144(n + 13({}^nC_2 + {}^nC_3(12)\dots)$$

$\Rightarrow$ $S2$ is divisible by 144 for infinitely many $n \in N$.

58. Now, general term in the expansion of $\left(ax^3 + \dfrac{1}{bx^{1/3}}\right)^{15}$ is

$$T_{r+1} = {}^{15}C_r\,.\,(ax^3)^{15-r}\left(\frac{1}{bx^{1/3}}\right)^r$$

$$= {}^{15}C_r\,.\,(a)^{15-r}.(x)^{45-3r}\,.\,(b)^{-r}(x)^{-r/3}$$

For coefficient of x^{15}, we put

$$45 - 3r - \frac{r}{3} = 15$$

$\Rightarrow$ $30 = \dfrac{10r}{3}$

$\Rightarrow$ $r = 9$

So, coefficient of x^{15} in $\left(ax^3 + \dfrac{1}{bx^{1/3}}\right)^{15} = {}^{15}C_9\, a^6 b^{-9}$ ...(i)

Again, we find general term in $\left(ax^{1/3} - \dfrac{1}{bx^3}\right)^{15}$ is

$$T_{r+1} = {}^{15}C_r\,.\,(ax^{\frac{1}{3}})^{15-r}.\left(-\frac{1}{bx^3}\right)^r$$

$\Rightarrow$ $T_{r+1} = {}^{15}C_r\,.\,(a)^{15-r}\,.\,(x)^{\frac{15-r}{3}}\,.\,(-1)^r.\,(b)^{-r}\,.\,(x)^{-3r}$

For coefficient of x^{-15}, we get

$$5 - \frac{r}{3} - 3r = -15 \Rightarrow \frac{10r}{3} = 20$$

$\Rightarrow$ $r = 6$

$\therefore$ Coefficient of x^{-15} in $\left(ax^{\frac{1}{3}} - \dfrac{1}{bx^3}\right)^{15}$

$$= {}^{15}C_6\,.\,a^9 \times b^{-6} \times (-1)^6$$

$$= {}^{15}C_6\,.\,a^9 b^{-6}$$ ...(ii)

According to the question,

Eq. (i) = Eq. (ii)

$\Rightarrow$ ${}^{15}C_9\, a^6.\, b^{-9} = {}^{15}C_6\,.\,a^9 b^{-6}$

$\Rightarrow$ $a^6 b^6 = a^9 b^9$

$\Rightarrow$ $a^3 b^3 = 1$, where $a, b > 0$

$\Rightarrow$ $ab = 1$

59. $(a + bx + cx^2)^{10} = p_0 + p_1 x + p_2 x^2 + \dots + p_{20} x^{20} = \displaystyle\sum_{i=0}^{20} p_i x^i$

Coefficient of x

$\Rightarrow$ $20 = \dfrac{10!\, a^9\, (bx)^1\, (cx^2)^0}{9!\,1!}$

$$20 = 10a^9\, b^1 \Rightarrow a = 1, b = 2$$

Coefficient of $x^2 = \dfrac{10!\, a^9 \times (cx^2)^1}{9!\,1!} + \dfrac{10!\,(a^8)(bx)^2(cx^2)^0}{8!\,2!}$

$$= 10c + 180 = 210$$

$$10c = 30$$

$\Rightarrow$ $c = 3$

$$2(a+b+c) = 2(1+2+3)$$

$$= 2(6) = 12$$

60. We have, $\left(3^{\frac{1}{2}}+5^{\frac{1}{4}}\right)^{680}$

General term of the expansion $\left(3^{\frac{1}{2}}+5^{\frac{1}{4}}\right)^{680}$

$$={}^{680}C_r(3^{1/2})^{680-r}(5^{1/4})^r$$

$$={}^{680}C_r\times 3^{\frac{680-r}{2}}\times 5^{\frac{r}{4}}$$

The term will be integral if r is a multiple of 4.

$\therefore$ $r=0,4,8,12,\ldots,680$ (which is an AP)

$$680=0+(n-1)4$$

$$n=\frac{680}{4}+1=171$$

61. We have,

$$x^{1/50}=12 \Rightarrow x=12^{50}$$

And $y^{1/50}=18 \Rightarrow y=18^{50}$

So, $x+y=12^{50}+18^{50}$

$$=(12^2)^{25}+(18^2)^{25}$$

$$=(144)^{25}+(324)^{25}$$

$$=(150-6)^{25}+(325-1)^{25}$$

$\because$ 150 and 325 is divisible by 25.

$$=25K-(6^{25}+1)$$

$$=25K-[(5+1)^{25}+1]$$

$$=25K-25K_1-(1+1)=25K_2-2$$

So, when $x+y$ is dividing by 25

Then, remainder $=25-2=23$

62. $\left(2x+\frac{1}{x^7}+3x^2\right)^5$

General term is

$$\frac{5!(2x)^{n_1}(x^{-7})^{n_2}(3x^2)^{n_3}}{n_1!n_2!n_3!}=\frac{5!2^{n_1}3^{n_3}}{n_1!n_2!n_3!}x^{n_1-7n_2+2n_3}$$

For constant term, $n_1-7n_2+2n_3=0$

$\Rightarrow n_1+2n_3=7n_2$ and $n_1+n_2+n_3=5$

Only possible, when $n_1=1, n_2=1, n_3=3$

Constant term $=\dfrac{5!\cdot 2^1\cdot 3^3}{1!1!3!}$

$$=5\times4\times2\times27=40\times27=1080$$

63. Let $N=(2021)^{2022}+(2022)^{2021}$

Nearest multiple of 7 is 2023.

$\therefore$ $N=(2023-2)^{2022}+(2023-1)^{2021}$

$$=(7\lambda-2)^{2022}+(7\lambda_1-1)^{2021}$$

$$=[(7\lambda-2)^3]^{674}+(7\lambda_1)^{2021}-2021$$

$$(7\lambda_1)^{2020}+\ldots-1=(7\lambda_2-1)^{674}+(7\lambda_3-1]$$

$$=(7\lambda_4+1)+(7\lambda_5-1)$$

$$=7(\lambda_4+\lambda_5)=7\lambda_6$$

$\therefore$ N is multiple of 7, hence remainder is 0.

64. $9^n-8n-1=64\alpha$

and $6^n-5n-1=25\beta$

$$9^n=(1+8)^n={}^nC_0+{}^nC_18^1+{}^nC_28^2+{}^nC_38^3+{}^nC_48^4+\ldots$$

$$\Rightarrow \frac{9^n-8n-1}{64}={}^nC_2+{}^nC_38+{}^nC_48^2+\ldots$$

$$\Rightarrow \alpha={}^nC_2+{}^nC_38+{}^nC_48^2+\ldots$$

Similarly, $\beta={}^nC_2+{}^nC_35+{}^nC_45^2+\ldots$

$$\therefore \alpha-\beta={}^nC_3(8-5)+{}^nC_4(8^2-5^2)+\ldots+{}^nC_n(8^{n-2}-5^{n-2})$$

65. The given expression forms a GP with common ratio

$$\left(\frac{x}{5+x}\right) \qquad [\because r>1]$$

$$\frac{x^{500}\frac{[(x+5)^{501}-x^{501}]}{x^{501}}}{\frac{5}{x}}\left(\frac{5+x}{x}\right)$$

$\Rightarrow$ Coefficient of x^{101} in expression

$$\frac{1}{5}[(x+5)^{501}-x^{501}]$$

$$=\frac{1}{5}\times{}^{501}C_{101}\times5^{501-101}$$

$$={}^{501}C_{101}\times5^{399}$$

66. $a_1=1, a_2=2, a_{n+2}=\dfrac{2}{a_{n+1}}+a_n$

$$\Rightarrow a_{n+2}\cdot a_{n+1}-a_{n+1}\cdot a_n=2$$

$$a_3\cdot a_2-a_2\cdot a_1=2$$

$$a_4\cdot a_3-a_3\cdot a_2=2$$

$$a_5\cdot a_4-a_4\cdot a_3=2$$

....

....

$\therefore$ The series $a_1\cdot a_2, a_2\cdot a_3, a_3\cdot a_4, a_4\cdot a_5, \ldots$

$\Rightarrow 1\cdot2, 2\cdot2, 2\cdot3, 2\cdot4, \ldots$

Now, $\displaystyle\prod_{n=1}^{n=30}\left(\frac{a_n+\frac{1}{a_{n+1}}}{a_{n+2}}\right)$

$$=\prod_{n=1}^{n=30}\left(\frac{a_{n+2}-\frac{1}{a_{n+1}}}{a_{n+2}}\right)$$

$$=\prod_{n=1}^{30}\left(1-\frac{1}{a_{n+2}\cdot a_{n+1}}\right)$$

$$=\left(1-\frac{1}{2\cdot2}\right)\cdot\left(1-\frac{1}{2\cdot3}\right)\cdot\left(1-\frac{1}{2\cdot4}\right)\ldots\left(1-\frac{1}{2\cdot31}\right)$$

$$\Rightarrow \frac{3\cdot5\cdot7\cdot\ldots 61}{2^{30}(2\cdot3\cdot4\cdot\ldots31)}=\frac{2^{-60}\cdot61!}{31!\,30!}$$

$$=2^{-60}\cdot{}^{61}C_{30}$$

$\therefore$ $\alpha=-60$

67. Given, constant term in the expansion of $\left(3x^3-2x^2+\frac{5}{x^5}\right)^{10}$ is $2^k \cdot l$, where l is odd integer.

General term, $T_{r+1}=\frac{10!}{r_1!r_2!r_3!}(3x^3)^{r_1}(-2x^2)^{r_2}\left(\frac{5}{x^5}\right)^{r_3}$

$=\frac{10!}{r_1!r_2!r_3!}(3)^{r_1}(-2)^{r_2}(5)^{r_3}(x)^{3r_1+2r_2-5r_3}$

For constant term,

$$3r_1+2r_2-5r_3=0 \quad \text{...(i)}$$

and $$r_1+r_2+r_3=10 \quad \text{...(ii)}$$

From Eq. (i) – Eq (ii) × 2, we get

$$r_1-(5+2)r_3=-20$$

$\Rightarrow$ $r_1+20=7r_3$

$\Rightarrow$ $r_1=1, r_3=3$ and $r_2=6$

$\therefore$ Constant term $=\frac{10!}{(1)!(6)!(3)!}(3)^1(-2)^6(5)^3$

$=\frac{10\cdot9\cdot8\cdot7}{3\cdot2}\times3\times2^6\times5^3$

$=2^9\times3^2\times5^4\times7^1=2^k\times l$

Hence, $k=9$

68. There are total 5 terms in the expansion of $\left(\frac{1}{\sqrt{6}}+\beta x\right)^4$.

Middle terms is 3rd term, $T_3={}^4C_2\left(\frac{1}{\sqrt{6}}\right)^2(\beta x)^2$

Coefficient of the middle terms of this expansion $=\beta^2$

There are 3 terms in the expansion of $(1-3\beta x)^2$.

Middle term $(T_2)={}^2C_1(-3\beta x)=-6\beta x$

Coefficient of second terms of this expansion $=-6\beta$

There are 7 terms in the expansion $\left(1-\frac{\beta x}{2}\right)^6$.

Middle terms is 4th term $T_4={}^6C_3\left(-\frac{\beta}{2}x\right)^3$

Coefficient of 4th term of this expansion $=-20\frac{\beta^3}{8}=-\frac{5\beta^3}{2}$

The three terms of AP are $\beta^2, -6\beta, \frac{-5}{2}\beta^3$.

$\therefore$ $2(-6\beta)=\beta^2-\frac{5\beta^3}{2}$

$\Rightarrow$ $-12\beta=\beta^2-\frac{5\beta^3}{2}$

$\Rightarrow$ $-24\beta=2\beta^2-5\beta^3$

$\Rightarrow$ $5\beta^2-2\beta-24=0$ $\quad[\because \beta\neq0]$

$\Rightarrow$ $5\beta^2-12\beta+10\beta-24=0$

$\Rightarrow$ $\beta=\frac{12}{5}, \beta\neq-2$

$\therefore$ $d=-6\beta-\beta^2=-\beta(6+\beta)$

$=-\frac{12}{5}\left[6+\frac{12}{5}\right]$

$=-\frac{12}{5}\left(\frac{42}{5}\right)=-\frac{504}{25}$

$\Rightarrow$ $50-\frac{2d}{\beta^2}=50-\frac{2\left(-\frac{504}{25}\right)}{\frac{144}{25}}=50+7=57$

69. $T_{r+1}={}^nC_r(x^{\log_2 x})^{n-r}x^r$

$T_4={}^7C_3(x^{\log_2 x})^4x^3$

$=35x^{4\log_2 x}x^3$

$35x^{3+4\log_2 x}=4480$

$x^{3+4\log_2 x}=128=2^7$

Taking log on both sides,

$(3+4\log_2 x)(\log_2 x)=7$

$\Rightarrow$ $4(\log_2 x)^2+3\log_2 x-7=0$

$\Rightarrow$ $(\log_2 x-1)(4\log_2 x+7)=0$

$\Rightarrow$ $\log_2 x=1$ $\quad[\because x\in N]$

$\therefore$ $x=2$

70. Coefficient of x^7 in $\left(x^2+\frac{1}{bx}\right)^{11}$

General term $={}^{11}C_r x^{3r-11}b^{r-11}$

$\Rightarrow$ $3r-11=7\Rightarrow r=6$

$\therefore$ Coefficient of $x^7={}^{11}C_6b^{-5}$

Now, coefficient of x^{-7} in $\left(x-\frac{1}{bx^2}\right)^{11}$.

General term $={}^{11}C_r\left(\frac{-1}{b}\right)^{11-r}x^{3r-22}$

$\Rightarrow$ $3r-22=-7\Rightarrow r=5$

Coefficient $={}^{11}C_5\left(\frac{-1}{b}\right)^6={}^{11}C_5b^{-6}$

Now, according to the question,

$${}^{11}C_6b^{-5}={}^{11}C_5b^{-6}\Rightarrow b=1$$

71. Given, $(1-x+x^3)^n=\sum_{j=0}^{3n}a_j x^j$

$$(1-x+x^3)^n=a_0+a_1x+a_2x^2+\ldots+a_{3n}x^{3n}$$

Putting $x=1$,

$$1=a_0+a_1+a_2+\ldots+a_{3n} \quad \text{...(i)}$$

Putting $x=-1$,

$$1=a_0-a_1+a_2-a_3+\ldots(-1)^{3n}a_{3n} \quad \text{...(ii)}$$

Adding Eqs. (i) and (ii), we get

$$a_0+a_2+a_4+\ldots=1$$

On subtracting Eq. (ii) from Eq. (i), we get

$$a_1+a_3+a_5+\ldots=0$$

Now, $\sum_{j=0}^{\left[\frac{3n}{2}\right]}a_{2j}+4\sum_{j=0}^{\left[\frac{3n-1}{2}\right]}a_{2j}+1=[a_0+a_2+a_4+\ldots]+4[a_1+a_3+a_5+\ldots]+1$

$=1+4\times0+1=2$

72. We have, $\left\{3^{\log_3\sqrt{25^{x-1}+7}}+3^{-\frac{1}{8}\cdot\log_3(5^{x-1}+1)}\right\}^{10}$

$$=\left\{\sqrt{25^{x-1}+7}+(5^{x-1}+1)^{\frac{-1}{8}}\right\}^{10}$$

Ninth term in the expansion is 180.

So, $^{10}C_8(\sqrt{25^{x-1}+7})^{10-8}\cdot\left[(5^{x-1}+1)^{\frac{-1}{8}}\right]^8=180$

$\Rightarrow \quad {}^{10}C_8(25^{x-1}+7)(5^{x-1}+1)^{-1}=180$

$\Rightarrow \quad 45(25^{x-1}+7)(5^{x-1}+1)^{-1}=180$

$\Rightarrow \quad \dfrac{25^{x-1}+7}{5^{x-1}+1}=4$

Let $\quad 5^{x-1}=t$

$\Rightarrow \quad \dfrac{t^2+7}{t+1}=4$

$\Rightarrow \quad t^2-4t+3=0$

$\Rightarrow \quad t=3$ or $t=1$

When $t=3$

$5^{x-1}=3$

$\Rightarrow \quad x=\log_5 15$

When $\quad t=1$

$5^{x-1}=1 \qquad [t=5^{x-1}]$

$\Rightarrow \quad x=1$

73. Coefficient of middle term of $(1+x)^{20}$ is $^{20}C_{10}$.

Coefficient of middle term of $(1+x)^{19}$ is $^{19}C_9$ and $^{19}C_{10}$

According to the question,

$$\left(\frac{^{20}C_{10}}{^{19}C_9+{}^{19}C_{10}}\right)=\frac{^{20}C_{10}}{^{20}C_{10}}=1$$

74. $\quad 11^n>10^n+9^n$

$\Rightarrow 11^n-9^n>10^n$

$\Rightarrow (10+1)^n-(10-1)^n>10^n$

$\{(10+1)^n-(10-1)^n={}^nC_0 10^n+{}^nC_1 10^{n-1}+{}^nC_2 10^{n-2}+\ldots$

$-\{{}^nC_0 10^n-{}^nC_1 10^{n-1}\ldots\}$

$\Rightarrow 2({}^nC_1 10^{n-1}+{}^nC_3 10^{n-3}\ldots)>10^n$

For $n=1 \Rightarrow 2.1 \ngtr 10$

For $n=2 \Rightarrow 2(2) \ngtr 100$

For $n=3 \Rightarrow 2(3\cdot 10^2+1) \ngtr 1000$

For $n=4$

$2({}^4C_1 10^4+{}^4C_3 10^1)=8080 \ngtr 10^4$

For, $n=5$

$\Rightarrow 2({}^5C_1 10^4+{}^5C_3 10^2+{}^5C_5)>10^5$

Hence, $n\in\{5, 6, 7, \ldots\ldots 100\}$

$\therefore$ Number of elements $=96$

75. **Decoding the Question**

Use the inequality AM ≥ GM

$$\frac{\alpha^3+\beta^2}{2}\ge\sqrt{\alpha^3\beta^2}$$
$$\alpha^6\beta^4\le 16$$

$\because$ The general term in the expansion of binomial is

$$T_{r+1}={}^{10}C_r\,\alpha^{10-r}\beta^r x^{\left(\frac{20-2r-3r}{18}\right)}$$

For the term independent of x,

$20-2r-3r=0 \Rightarrow r=4$

So, the value of the term independent of x is

$^{10}C_4\,\alpha^6\beta^4=210\alpha^6\beta^4$

Now, it is given that $\alpha>0, \beta>0$, such that $\alpha^3+\beta^2=4$, so according to AM-GM inequality, we have

$$\frac{\alpha^3+\beta^2}{2}\ge\sqrt{\alpha^3\beta^2}$$

$\Rightarrow \quad \alpha^6\beta^4\le 16$

It is given that, the maximum value of

$210\alpha^6\beta^4=10k$

$\Rightarrow \quad 210\times 16=10k\Rightarrow k=336$

76. The above expression is geometric series having first term,

$a=(1+x)^{10}$

common ratio, $r=\dfrac{x}{1+x}$ and number of terms, $n=11 \qquad [\because r<1]$

$$=\frac{(1+x)^{10}\left(\dfrac{(1+x)^{11}-x^{11}}{(1+x)^{11}}\right)}{\dfrac{1+x-x}{1+x}}$$

$=(1+x)^{11}-x^{11}$

The coefficient of x^7 in the given expression $=$ coefficient of x^7 in the expansion of $(1+x)^{11}$

$={}^{11}C_7=11\times 10\times 3=330$

77. The general term (i.e. $(r+1)$th term) in the expansion of binomial $\left(x^m+\dfrac{1}{x^2}\right)^{22}$ is

$$T_{r+1}={}^{22}C_r(x^m)^{22-r}x^{-2r}$$

$\because$ The coefficient $^{22}C_r=1540 \qquad$ [given]

$\Rightarrow \quad r=3$ or 19

at $\quad r=3,$

$\Rightarrow \quad 19\,m=7 \Rightarrow m=\dfrac{7}{19}\notin N$

Now, at $r=19,$

$\Rightarrow \quad 3m=39\Rightarrow m=13\in N$

So, the natural value of $m=13$.

78. Let $(1+x+x^2+\ldots+x^{2n})$

$(1-x+x^2-x^3+\ldots+x^{2n})$

$=a_0+a_1x+a_2x^2+\ldots+a_{4n}x^{4n}$

On putting $x = 1$, we get

$$\underbrace{(1+1+1+\ldots+1)}_{(2n+1)\text{ terms}}\underbrace{(1-1+1-1+\ldots+1)}_{(2n+1)\text{ terms}} = a_0 + a_1 + a_2 + \ldots + a_{4n}$$

$\Rightarrow (2n+1) = a_0 + a_1 + a_2 + \ldots + a_{4n}$ ...(i)

Similarly, on putting $x = -1$, we get

$$\underbrace{(1-1+1-1+\ldots+1)}_{(2n+1)\text{ terms}}\underbrace{(1+1+1+\ldots+1)}_{(2n+1)\text{ terms}} = a_0 - a_1 + a_2 - a_3 + \ldots + a_{4n}$$

$\Rightarrow (2n+1) = a_0 - a_1 + a_2 - a_3 \ldots + a_{4n}$ ...(ii)

On adding Eqs. (i) and (ii), we get

$$2(a_0 + a_2 + a_4 + \ldots + a_{4n}) = 2(2n+1)$$

$\Rightarrow \quad a_0 + a_2 + a_4 + \ldots + a_{4n} = 2n+1$

$\Rightarrow$ Sum of coefficients of all even powers of x in the product $(1 + x + x^2 + \ldots + x^{2n})(1 - x + x^2 - x^3 + \ldots + x^{2n})$

$$= 2n + 1 = 61 \quad \text{[given]}$$

$\Rightarrow \quad 2n = 60 \Rightarrow n = 30$

Exercise 2 - JEE Advanced Pattern

1. General term of given expression $= \dfrac{10!}{\alpha!\beta!\gamma!} 2^{\alpha/2}\cdot 3^{\beta/3}\cdot 5^{\gamma/6}$ ...(i)

α, β, γ satisfying two following property

$$0 \le \alpha, \beta, \gamma \le 10; \alpha + \beta + \gamma = 10$$

$\therefore \quad \alpha = 0, 2, 4, 6, 8, 10; \beta = 0, 3, 6; \gamma = 0, 6$

Hence, possible pairs of $(\alpha, \beta, \gamma) = (4, 6, 0); (4, 0, 6); (10, 0, 0)$

$\therefore$ There exists three rational terms.

So, sum of rational terms $= \dfrac{10!}{4!6!}\cdot 2^2 \cdot 3^2 + \dfrac{10!}{4!6!} 2^2 \cdot 5^1 + \dfrac{10!}{10!} 2^5$

$= 11792$

2. We have, $(1 + x - 3x^2)^{2145} = a_0 + a_1 x + a_2 x^2 + \cdots$

On putting $x = -1$, we get

$$a_0 - a_1 + a_2 - \ldots = (-3)^{2145}$$

But we know that, $3^1 = 3, 3^2 = 9, 3^3 = 27, 3^4 = 81$

$\therefore \quad a_0 - a_1 + a_2 + \ldots = [(-3)^4]^{536}(-3)^1$

$\therefore \quad$ End digit of $(-3)^{2145}$

$=$ End digit of $[(-3)^4]^{536} \times$ End digit of $(-3)^1$

$= 1 \times 3 = 3$

3. We have,

$$T_{r+1} = {}^nC_r\left(\sqrt{\frac{q}{p}}\right)^{n-r}\left(\sqrt[10]{\frac{p^7}{q^3}}\right)^r = {}^nC_r (q)^{\frac{n-r}{2} - \frac{3r}{10}} \times (p)^{\frac{r-n}{2} + \frac{7r}{10}}$$

$$= {}^nC_r \cdot q^{\frac{5n-8r}{10}} \cdot p^{\frac{12r-5n}{10}}$$

For coefficient of pq, we put

$$\frac{5n - 8r}{10} = 1, \frac{12r - 5n}{10} = 1$$

$\Rightarrow \quad 5n - 8r - 10 = 0, 12r - 5n - 10 = 0$

$\Rightarrow \quad r = 5, n = 10$

$\therefore \quad T_6 = {}^{10}C_5\, pq = 252\, pq$

4. We have, $(5 + 2\sqrt{6})^n = (5 + \sqrt{24})^n$

Now, let $\quad I + f = (5 + \sqrt{24})^n$ ...(i)

$0 \le f < 1$ ...(ii)

and $\quad f' = (5 - \sqrt{24})^n$ ...(iii)

$0 < f' < 1$ ...(iv)

On adding Eqs. (i) and (iii), we get

$I + f + f' = 2k$ (even integer)

$\Rightarrow \quad f + f' = 1 \Rightarrow f' = 1 - f$

$\therefore \quad f^2 - f + If - I = f(f-1) + I(f-1)$

$= (f-1)(I+f)$

$= -(1-f)(I+f) = -f'(I+f)$

$= -(5-\sqrt{24})^n (5+\sqrt{24})^n$

$= -(25-24)^n = -1$

$=$ a negative integer

5. Given, $\quad x + \dfrac{1}{x} = 1 \Rightarrow x^2 - x + 1 = 0$

$\Rightarrow (x+\omega)(x+\omega^2) = 0$

$\Rightarrow \quad x = -\omega, -\omega^2$

$\therefore \quad p = (-\omega)^{4000} + \dfrac{1}{(-\omega)^{4000}} = \omega^{4000} + \dfrac{1}{\omega^{4000}}$

$= \omega + \dfrac{1}{\omega} = \dfrac{\omega^2 + 1}{\omega} = -\dfrac{\omega}{\omega} = -1$

Also, for $\quad x = -\omega^2, p = -1$

For $\quad n > 1, 2^n = 4k, k \in N$

$\therefore \quad 2^{2^n} = 2^{4k} = (16)^k =$ last digit number is 6

Now, $q =$ unit digit at unit place in the number $(2^{2^n} + 1)$

$= 6 + 1 = 7$

$\therefore p + q = -1 + 7 = 6$

6. Now, $\left(x + 1 + \dfrac{1}{x}\right)^n = \dfrac{(1 + x + x^2)^n}{x^n}$

Since, $(1 + x + x^2)^n$ is of the form

$a_0 + a_1 x + a_2 x^2 + \cdots + a_{2n} x^{2n}$ which contains $2n + 1$ terms.

$\therefore \quad 2n + 1 = 401 \Rightarrow 2n = 400 \Rightarrow n = 200$

which is greater than 199.

7. We have, $\displaystyle\sum_{r=0}^{n-1} \frac{{}^nC_r}{{}^nC_r + {}^nC_{r+1}} = \sum_{r=0}^{n-1} \frac{{}^nC_r}{{}^{n+1}C_{r+1}}$

$$= \sum_{r=0}^{n-1} \frac{{}^nC_r}{\frac{n+1}{r+1}\,{}^nC_r} = \sum_{r=0}^{n-1} \frac{r+1}{n+1}$$

$$= \frac{1}{n+1}[1 + 2 + \cdots + n]$$

$$= \frac{n(n+1)}{2(n+1)} = \frac{n}{2}$$

8. Here, $n = 100$, so the total number of terms is 101.

$\therefore$ Largest term $=$ Middle term $=$ 51th term

$$= {}^{100}C_{50}\left(\frac{b}{2}\right)^{50}\left(\frac{b}{2}\right)^{50} = {}^{100}C_{50}\left(\frac{b}{2}\right)^{100}$$

9. We have, $T_4 = {}^6C_3 \left(\sqrt{x^{\left(\frac{1}{1+\log x}\right)}}\right)^3 (x^{1/12})^3$

$= 200$ [given]

$\Rightarrow \quad 20\left(x^{\frac{3}{2(1+\log x)}}\right) x^{1/4} = 200$

$\Rightarrow \quad x^{\frac{3}{2(1+\log x)}+\frac{1}{4}} = 10$

On taking logarithm on base 10, we get

$$\left[\frac{3}{2(1+\log x)} + \frac{1}{4}\right] \log x = 1$$

$\Rightarrow \quad \dfrac{(6+1+\log x)\log x}{4(1+\log x)} = 1$

$\Rightarrow \quad (\log x)^2 + 3\log x - 4 = 0$

$\Rightarrow \quad (\log x + 4)(\log x - 1) = 0$

$\Rightarrow \quad \log x = -4, 1$

$\therefore \quad x = 10^{-4}, 10$

But $\quad x > 1$

$\therefore \quad x = 10$

10. $\because (1+x)^m + (1+x)^{m+1} + \cdots + (1+x)^n$

$$= \frac{(1+x)^m\{(1+x)^{n-m+1} - 1\}}{(1+x)-1} = \frac{(1+x)^{n+1} - (1+x)^m}{x}$$

$\therefore$ Coefficient of x^m in

$(1+x)^m + (1+x)^{m+1} + \cdots + (1+x)^n$

or coefficient of x^m in $\dfrac{(1+x)^{n+1} - (1+x)^m}{x}$

or coefficient of x^{m+1} in $(1+x)^{n+1} - (1+x)^m$

$$= {}^{n+1}C_{m+1} - 0 = {}^{n+1}C_{m+1}$$

11. We have, ${}^{39}C_{3r-1} + {}^{39}C_{3r} = {}^{39}C_{r^2} + {}^{39}C_{r^2-1}$

$\Rightarrow \quad {}^{40}C_{3r} = {}^{40}C_{r^2}$

$\Rightarrow \quad 3r = r^2$ or $40 - 3r = r^2$

$\Rightarrow \quad r = 0, 3$ or $r^2 + 3r - 40 = 0$

$\Rightarrow \quad (r+8)(r-5) = 0$

$\Rightarrow \quad r = 0, 3, 5, -8$

But $r = 0, -8$ do not satisfy the given equation

$\therefore \quad r = 3, 5$

12. We have, $(1+x)^{20} = {}^{20}C_0 + {}^{20}C_1\, x + {}^{20}C_2\, x^2 + \cdots + {}^{20}C_{20}\, x^{20}$

On dividing by x, we get

$$\frac{(1+x)^{20}}{x} = \frac{{}^{20}C_0}{x} + {}^{20}C_1 + {}^{20}C_2 x + {}^{20}C_3 x^2 + \cdots + {}^{20}C_{20}\, x^{19}$$

On differentiating w.r.t. x, we get

$$\frac{20(1+x)^{19}\cdot x - (1+x)^{20}}{x^2} = -\frac{{}^{20}C_0}{x^2} + 0 + {}^{20}C_2$$

$$+ 2\cdot{}^{20}C_3 x + \cdots + 19\cdot{}^{20}C_{20}\, x^{18}$$

On putting $x = 1$, we get

$$20(2)^{19} - (2)^{20} = -\frac{1}{1} + {}^{20}C_2 + 2\cdot{}^{20}C_3 + \cdots + 19\cdot{}^{20}C_{20}$$

$\therefore \quad {}^{20}C_2 + 2\cdot{}^{20}C_3 + \cdots + 19\cdot{}^{20}C_{20} = 1 + 10\cdot 2^{20} - 2^{20} = 1 + 9\cdot 2^{20}$

13. We have, $S = \dfrac{1(2^{2000} - 1)}{2-1} = 2^{2000} - 1 = (2^2)^{1000} - 1$

$= (5-1)^{1000} - 1$

$= (5^{1000} - {}^{1000}C_1\cdot 5^{999} + {}^{1000}C_2\cdot 5^{998} \cdots$

$+ {}^{1000}C_{998}\cdot 5^2 - {}^{1000}C_{999}\cdot 5 + 1) - 1$

$= 5(5^{999} - {}^{1000}C_1\cdot 5^{998} + {}^{1000}C_2\cdot 5^{997} - \cdots - {}^{1000}C_{999})$

$\therefore$ Remainder is 0.

14. Now, $(1+x)^n\left(1+\dfrac{1}{x}\right)^n = \dfrac{(1+x)^{2n}}{x^n}$

$\therefore$ Coefficient of x^{-1} in $(1+x)^n\left(1+\dfrac{1}{x}\right)^n$

$$= \text{Coefficient of } x^{n-1} \text{ in } (1+x)^{2n} = {}^{2n}C_{n-1} = \frac{(2n)!}{(n-1)!\,(n+1)!}$$

15. We have,

$(3 + x^{2008} + x^{2009})^{2010} = a_0 + a_1 x + a_2 x^2 + \ldots + a_n x^n$

Put $x = \omega$

$(3 + \omega^{2008} + \omega^{2009})^{2010} = a_0 + a_1\omega + a_2\omega^2 + \ldots$

$\Rightarrow \quad (3 + \omega + \omega^2)^{2010} = a_0 + a_1\omega + a_2\omega^2 + \ldots$

$\Rightarrow \quad 2^{2010} = a_0 + a_1\omega + a_2\omega^2 + \ldots$ ...(i)

Put $x = \omega^2$,

$(3 + \omega^{4016} + \omega^{4018})^{2010} = a_0 + a_1\omega^2 + a_2\omega^4 + \ldots$

$\Rightarrow \quad (3 + \omega^2 + \omega)^{2010} = a_0 + a_1\omega^2 + a_2\omega^4 + \ldots$

$\Rightarrow \quad 2^{2010} = a_0 + a_1\omega^2 + a_2\omega + \ldots$ ...(ii)

On adding Eqs. (i) and (ii), we get

$$2 \times 2^{2010} = 2a_0 - a_1 - a_2 + 2a_3 - a_4 - a_5 + 2a_6 - \ldots$$

$\Rightarrow \quad 2^{2010} = a_0 - \dfrac{1}{2}a_1 - \dfrac{1}{2}a_2 + a_3 - \dfrac{1}{2}a_4 - \dfrac{1}{2}a_5 + a_6 - \ldots$

16. (c) We have,

$$\sum_{r=2}^{10} {}^rC_2 \cdot {}^{10}C_r$$

$$= \sum_{r=2}^{10} \frac{r(r-1)}{2} \times \frac{10!}{r!(10-r)!}$$

$$= \frac{1}{2}\sum_{r=2}^{10} \frac{10!}{(r-2)!\,(10-r)!}$$

$$= \frac{10\times 9}{2}\sum_{r=2}^{10} \frac{8!}{(r-2)!(10-r)!}$$

$$= \frac{10\times 9}{2}\sum_{r=2}^{10} {}^8C_{r-2}$$

$= 45 \times 2^8$

$= 11520$

17. For $\left(\frac{1}{x^2}-x^3\right)^n$, $T_{r+1}={}^nC_r\left(\frac{1}{x^2}\right)^{n-r}(-x^3)^r={}^nC_r(-1)^r x^{5r-2n}$

For x^5, $5r-2n=5$

$$\Rightarrow \quad r=\frac{5+2n}{5}=\frac{2n}{5}+1$$

For x^{10}, $5r-2n=10$

$$\Rightarrow \quad r=\frac{2n}{5}+2$$

$\therefore$ n should be multiple of 5

So, $n=5k$

Now, according to the question

$$-{}^{5k}C_{2k+1}+{}^{5k}C_{2k+2}=0$$

$$\Rightarrow \quad \frac{5k!}{(2k+1)!(3k-1)!}=\frac{5k!}{(2k+2)!(3k-2)!}$$

$$\Rightarrow \quad \frac{1}{3k-1}=\frac{1}{2k+2}$$

$$\Rightarrow \quad k=3$$

$$\therefore \quad n=15$$

18. We know that

$$(1-x)^n=\sum_{r=0}^{n}{}^nC_r(-1)^r x^r$$

$$\Rightarrow \quad x(1-x)^n=\sum_{r=0}^{n}(-1)^r\,{}^nC_r x^{r+1}$$

$$\Rightarrow \quad \int_0^1 x(1-x)^n=\sum_{r=0}^{n}(-1)^r\frac{{}^nC_r}{r+2}$$

$$\Rightarrow \quad \sum_{r=0}^{n}(-1)^r\frac{{}^nC_r}{r+2}=\int_0^1 x(1-x)^n\,dx$$

$$=\int_0^1(1-x)x^n dx$$

$$=\int_0^1 x^n-x^{n+1}\,dx$$

$$=\left[\frac{x^{n+1}}{n+1}-\frac{x^{n+2}}{n+2}\right]_0^1$$

$$=\frac{1}{n+1}-\frac{1}{n+2}$$

$$=\frac{1}{(n+1)(n+2)}$$

$$\therefore \quad \sum_{r=0}^{50}(-1)^r\frac{{}^{50}C_r}{r+2}=\frac{1}{51\times 52}=\frac{1}{2652}$$

19. Since, there is only one middle term, so n is even.

$\therefore$ Middle term $=\left(\frac{n}{2}+1\right)$th term

$$=T_{\frac{n}{2}+1}$$

$$={}^nC_{\frac{n}{2}}(x^2)^{n/2}\left(\frac{1}{x}\right)^{n/2}$$

$$={}^nC_{\frac{n}{2}}x^{n/2}$$

Now, according to the question

$${}^nC_{\frac{n}{2}}x^{n/2}=924x^6$$

$$\therefore \quad \frac{n}{2}=6$$

$$\Rightarrow \quad n=12$$

Also, sum of all binomial coefficient $=(1+1)^{12}=2^{12}$

20. We have,

$$27^{27}=3^{81}=3\times 3^{80}=3\times 9^{40}$$
$$=3\times(10-1)^{40}$$
$$=3[10^{40}-{}^{40}C_1 10^{39}+\ldots+{}^{40}C_{38}10^2-{}^{40}C_{39}10+1]$$
$$=3[1000\lambda-400+1]$$
$$=3[1000\lambda-399]$$

$\therefore$ Last 3 digits is 803.

21. We have, $(1+ax-2x^2)^n$

$\therefore$ Sum of coefficients $=(1+a-2)^n=(a-1)^n$

If $a>1$, then for $n\in N$

$$(a-1)^n>0$$

If $a<1$, then for $n=2k+1$, $k\in N$

$$(a-1)^n<0$$

If $a=1$, then $(a-1)^n=0$

22. We have,

$$T_{r+1}={}^{6561}C_r 7^{\frac{6561-r}{3}}\cdot 11^{\frac{r}{9}}$$

For, term free of radical sign,

$r=$ multiple of 9

$=0, 9, 18, 27, \ldots, 6561$

Hence, there are 730 rational terms.

The greatest binomial coefficients are

${}^{6561}C_{\frac{6561-1}{2}}$ and ${}^{6561}C_{\frac{6561+1}{2}}={}^{6561}C_{3280}$ and ${}^{6561}C_{3281}$

Now, 3280 and 3281 are not multiple of 3, hence both terms involving greatest binomial coefficients are irrational.

23. $(3\sqrt{3}+5)^{2n+1}=(\sqrt{27}+5)^{2n+1}$

Now, let $\alpha+\beta=(\sqrt{27}+5)^{2n+1}$ ...(i)

$0<\beta<1$ ...(ii)

and let $\beta'=(\sqrt{27}-5)^{2n+1}$ ...(iii)

$0<\beta'<1$ ...(iv)

On subtracting Eq. (iii) from Eq. (i), we get

$$\alpha+\beta-\beta'=(\sqrt{27}+5)^{2n+1}-(\sqrt{27}-5)^{2n+1} \quad \text{...(v)}$$

$$\Rightarrow \quad \alpha+0=2p \text{ (even integer)}, \forall\, p\in N$$

$$\Rightarrow \quad \alpha=2p=\text{even integer}$$

Also, from Eq. (v), we get

$$\alpha=(\sqrt{27}+5)^{2n+1}-(\sqrt{27}-5)^{2n+1}$$

divisible by $(\sqrt{27}+5)-(\sqrt{27}-5)$

i.e. divisible by 10.

24. We have, $(8+3\sqrt{7})^n=(8+\sqrt{63})^n$

Now, let $P+F=(8+\sqrt{63})^n$ ...(i)

$0<F<1$ ...(ii)

and let $F'=(8-\sqrt{63})^n$ ...(iii)

$0<F'<1$ ...(iv)

On adding Eqs. (i) and (iii), we get

$P+F+F'=(8+\sqrt{63})^n+(8-\sqrt{63})^n$ ...(v)

$\Rightarrow \quad P+1=2p$ (even integer), $\forall p\in N$

$\Rightarrow \quad P=2p-1=$ odd integer

$\therefore \quad F'=1-F$

$\therefore \quad (1-F)(P+F)=F'(P+F)=(8-\sqrt{63})^n(8+\sqrt{63})^n$

$=(64-63)^n=1^n=1$

25. We have, 6th term in the expansion of

$$\left\{2^{\log_2\sqrt{(9^{x-1}+7)}}+\frac{1}{2^{(1/5)\log_2(3^{x-1}+1)}}\right\}^7$$

or $\left\{\sqrt{(9^{x-1}+7)}+\dfrac{1}{(3^{x-1}+1)^{1/5}}\right\}^7$ is $T_6=T_{5+1}$

$$={}^7C_5(\sqrt{9^{x-1}+7})^2\left\{\frac{1}{(3^{x-1}+1)^{1/5}}\right\}^5$$

$$={}^7C_2\cdot\frac{(9^{x-1}+7)}{(3^{x-1}+1)}=21\cdot\frac{(9^{x-1}+7)}{(3^{x-1}+1)}=84 \quad \text{[given]}$$

$\Rightarrow (9^{x-1}+7)=4(3^{x-1}+1)$

Let $3^{x-1}=\lambda$, then

$\lambda^2-4\lambda+3=0$

or $\quad (\lambda-3)(\lambda-1)=0$

$\therefore \quad \lambda=3,1$

$\Rightarrow \quad 3^{x-1}=3^1,3^0$

or $\quad x-1=1,0$ or $x=2,1$

26. $\left(\sqrt{x}+\dfrac{1}{2\cdot\sqrt[4]{x}}\right)^n$ or $\left(x^{1/2}+\dfrac{1}{2}x^{-1/4}\right)^n$

$$={}^nC_0\cdot x^{\frac{n}{2}}+{}^nC_1\cdot\left(\frac{1}{2}\right)\cdot x^{\frac{2n-3}{4}}+{}^nC_2\cdot\left(\frac{1}{2}\right)^2\cdot x^{\frac{n-3}{2}}+\cdots$$

According to the question,

${}^nC_0, {}^nC_1\left(\dfrac{1}{2}\right), {}^nC_2\left(\dfrac{1}{2}\right)^2$ are in AP.

$\therefore \quad {}^nC_1={}^nC_0+{}^nC_2\left(\dfrac{1}{2}\right)^2 \Rightarrow n=1+\dfrac{n(n-1)}{4\cdot 2}$

$\Rightarrow \quad n^2-9n+8=0 \Rightarrow (n-8)(n-1)=0$

$\therefore \quad n=8, n\neq 1$

Option (a) Number of terms $=8+1=9$

Option (b) Now, $T_{r+1}={}^8C_r\cdot x^{4-\frac{r}{2}}\cdot\left(\dfrac{1}{2}\right)^r\cdot x^{-\frac{r}{4}}$

$\because \quad 0\le r\le 8$

For integral powers of x, $r=0,4,8$

$\therefore$ Number of terms in the expansion with integral power of x is 3.

Option (c) From option (b),

$$T_{r+1}={}^8C_r\cdot x^{4-\frac{3r}{4}}\cdot\left(\frac{1}{2}\right)^r$$

For independent of x,

$$4-\frac{3r}{4}=0 \Rightarrow r=\frac{16}{3}\notin W$$

$\therefore$ No terms in the given expansion which is independent of x.

Option (d) Middle term is

$$T_5={}^8C_4\cdot x\cdot\left(\frac{1}{2}\right)^4$$

i.e. only one middle term.

27. We have,

Coefficient of x, x^2 and x^3 in $(1+x^2)^2(1+x)^n$

i.e., values of a_1, a_2 and a_3 in $(1+2x^2+x^4)(1+x)^n$

$\Rightarrow \quad a_1={}^nC_1$, $a_2={}^nC_2+2$ and $a_3={}^nC_3+2\,{}^nC_1$

According to the question,

$2a_2=a_1+a_3$

$\Rightarrow \quad 2({}^nC_2+2)={}^nC_1+({}^nC_3+2\,{}^nC_1)$

$\Rightarrow \quad \left[2\dfrac{n(n-1)}{2}\right]+4=3n+\dfrac{n(n-1)(n-2)}{6}$

$\Rightarrow \quad n^3-9n^2+26n-24=0$

$\Rightarrow \quad (n-2)(n^2-7n+12)=0$

$\Rightarrow \quad (n-2)(n-3)(n-4)=0$

$\Rightarrow \quad n=2,3,4$

Hence, $n=3,4$ $\quad [n\neq 2, \because {}^nC_3$ is not defined]

28. We have, $C_0-(C_0+C_1)+(C_0+C_1+C_2)-(C_0+C_1+C_2+C_3)+\cdots(-1)^{n-1}(C_0+C_1+\cdots+C_{n-1})$

For even integer, take $n=2m$, we get

$=C_0-(C_0+C_1)+(C_0+C_1+C_2)-(C_0+C_1+C_2+C_3)+\cdots-(C_0+C_1+\cdots+C_{2m-1})$

$=-(C_1+C_3+C_5+\cdots+C_{2m-1})$

$=-(C_1+C_3+C_5+\cdots+C_{n-1})$ $\quad [\because n=2m]$

$=-2^{n-1}$

29. We have, $f(n)=\sum_{i=0}^{n}\binom{30}{30-i}\binom{20}{n-i}=\sum_{i=0}^{n}\binom{30}{i}\binom{20}{n-i}={}^{50}C_n$

$\therefore f(n)$ is greatest, when $n=25$

$\therefore$ Maximum value of $f(n)$ is ${}^{50}C_{25}$.

Also, $\quad f(0)+f(1)+\cdots+f(50)$

$={}^{50}C_0+{}^{50}C_1+{}^{50}C_2+\cdots+{}^{50}C_{50}=2^{50}$

Also, ${}^{50}C_n$ is not divisible by 50 for any n as 50 is not a prime number.

$$\sum_{n=0}^{50}(f(n))^2=({}^{50}C_0)^2+({}^{50}C_1)^2+\cdots+({}^{50}C_{50})^2={}^{100}C_{50}$$

30. Here, n is even, so middle term is $\left(\frac{8}{2}+1\right)$th, i.e. 5th term.

$\therefore \quad T_5 = {}^8C_4(x)^4\left(\frac{\sin^{-1}x}{x}\right)^4 = \frac{630}{16}$ [given]

$\Rightarrow \quad 70(\sin^{-1}x)^4 = \frac{630}{16} \Rightarrow (\sin^{-1}x)^4 = \frac{9}{16}$

$\Rightarrow \quad (\sin^{-1}x)^2 = \frac{3}{4} \Rightarrow \sin^{-1}x = \pm\frac{\sqrt{3}}{2}$

$\Rightarrow \quad x = -\frac{\pi}{3}, \frac{\pi}{3}$ $\left[\because \sin^{-1}x \in \left(-\frac{\pi}{2}, \frac{\pi}{2}\right)\right]$

31. Sum of coefficients $= (a\alpha^2 + 2b\alpha + c)^n$

Let $f(\alpha) = a\alpha^2 + 2b\alpha + c$

Now, $D = 4b^2 - 4ac = 4(b^2 - ac) < 0$

$\therefore \quad f(\alpha) < 0$ or $f(\alpha) > 0, \forall \alpha \in R$

If $a > 0$, then $f(\alpha) > 0$

$\Rightarrow (a\alpha^2 + 2b\alpha + c)^n > 0$

If $c > 0$, i.e. $f(0) > 0 \Rightarrow f(\alpha) > 0$

$\Rightarrow \quad (a\alpha^2 + 2b\alpha + c)^n > 0$

If $a < 0$, then $f(\alpha) < 0$

$\Rightarrow (a\alpha^2 + 2b\alpha + c)^n < 0$, if n is odd

If $c < 0$, then $f(0) < 0 \Rightarrow f(\alpha) < 0$

$\Rightarrow (a\alpha^2 + 2b\alpha + c)^n > 0$, if n is even.

32. $\because \left(x^2 + 1 + \frac{1}{x^2}\right)^n = \frac{(1 + x^2 + x^4)^n}{x^{2n}}$

$= \frac{a_0 + a_1x^2 + a_2x^4 + \ldots + a_{2n}x^{4n}}{x^{2n}}$

$\therefore$ Number of terms $= 2n + 1$

Term independent of $x = a_n =$ Constant term in $\left(x^2 + 1 + \frac{1}{x^2}\right)^n$

$=$ Coefficient of x^{2n} in $(1 + x^2 + x^4)^n$

$=$ Coefficient of x^n in $(1 + x + x^2)^n$

$= \frac{d^n}{dx^n}(1 + x + x^2)^n \neq 2^{n-1}$

Coefficient of x^{2n-2} in $\left(x^2 + 1 + \frac{1}{x^2}\right)^n$

$=$ Coefficient of x^{4n-2} in $(1 + x^2 + x^4)^n$

$=$ Coefficient of x^{2n-1} in $(1 + x + x^2)^n$

Now, let $(1 + x + x^2)^n = \lambda_0 + \lambda_1 x + \lambda_2 x^2 + \ldots + \lambda_{2n-1}x^{2n-1} + \lambda_{2n}x^{2n}$

On replacing x by $\frac{1}{x}$, we get

$$\left(1 + \frac{1}{x} + \frac{1}{x^2}\right)^n = \lambda_0 + \frac{\lambda_1}{x} + \frac{\lambda_2}{x^2} + \ldots + \frac{\lambda_{2n-1}}{x^{2n-1}} + \frac{\lambda_{2n}}{x^{2n}}$$

or $\quad (1 + x + x^2)^n = \lambda_{2n} + \lambda_{2n-1}x + \ldots + \lambda_1 x^{2n-1} + \lambda_0 x^{2n}$

On differentiating both sides w.r.t. x, we get

$$n(1 + x + x^2)^{n-1}\cdot(1 + 2x) = \lambda_{2n-1} + \ldots + 2n\lambda_0 x^{2n-1}$$

On putting $x = 0$, we get $\lambda_{2n-1} = n$

Hence, coefficient of $x^{2n-1} = n$

and coefficient of x^2 in $\left(x^2 + 1 + \frac{1}{x^2}\right)^n$

$=$ Coefficient of x^{2n+2} in $(1 + x^2 + x^4)^n$

$=$ Coefficient of x^{n+1} in $(1 + x + x^2)^n$

$= \frac{d^{n+1}}{dx^{n+1}}(1 + x + x^2)^n \neq n$

33. Now, $\left(x + \frac{1}{x}\right)^{20} = {}^{20}C_0x^{20} + {}^{20}C_1x^{18} + {}^{20}C_2x^{16} + {}^{20}C_3x^{14} + \ldots + {}^{20}C_9x^2 + {}^{20}C_{10} + {}^{20}C_{11}x^{-2} + \ldots + {}^{20}C_{20}x^{-20}$

$T_{r+1} = {}^{20}C_r \cdot x^{20-2r}$ ...(i)

and $\left(x^2 + 2 + \frac{1}{x^2}\right)^{10} = \left(\frac{1}{x} + x\right)^{20}$

$= {}^{20}C_0x^{-20} + {}^{20}C_1x^{-18} + {}^{20}C_2x^{-16} + \ldots + {}^{20}C_{10} + {}^{20}C_{11}x^2 + {}^{20}C_{12}x^4 + \ldots + {}^{20}C_{20}x^{20}$

$\therefore \quad T_6 = T_{5+1} = {}^{20}C_5x^{-10}$ ...(ii)

According to the question, ${}^{20}C_r = {}^{20}C_5$

$\therefore \quad r = 5$ or $20 = r + 5 \Rightarrow r = 5, 15$

Sol. (34 and 35)

34. We have, $(1 + x + x^2)^n = \sum_{r=0}^{2n} a_r x^r$ ...(i)

On replacing x by $\frac{1}{x}$, we get

$$\left(1 + \frac{1}{x} + \frac{1}{x^2}\right)^n = \sum_{r=0}^{2n} a_r\left(\frac{1}{x}\right)^r$$

$\Rightarrow \quad (1 + x + x^2)^n = \sum_{r=0}^{2n} a_r x^{2n-r}$ ...(ii)

From Eqs. (i) and (ii), we get

$$\sum_{r=0}^{2n} a_r x^r = \sum_{r=0}^{2n} a_r x^{2n-r}$$

Equating the coefficient of x^{2n-r} on both sides, we get

$a_{2n-r} = a_r$ ...(iii)

$0 \le r \le 2n$

On putting $r = 0, 1, 2, 3, \ldots, n-1, n$, we get

$a_{2n} = a_0$

$a_{2n-1} = a_1$

$a_{2n-2} = a_2$

$a_{2n-3} = a_3$

$\vdots \quad \vdots \quad \vdots$

$a_{n+1} = a_{n-1}, a_n = a_n$

Then, $a_0 + a_1 + a_2 + \ldots + a_{n-1} = a_{n+1} + a_{n+2} + \ldots + a_{2n}$ ...(iv)

and on putting $x = 1$ in Eq. (i), we get

$$\sum_{r=0}^{2n} a_r = 3^n$$

$\Rightarrow (a_0 + a_1 + a_2 + \ldots + a_{n-1}) + a_n + (a_{n+1} + a_{n+2} + \ldots + a_{2n}) = 3^n$

From Eq.(iv), we get

$$2(a_0 + a_1 + a_2 + \ldots + a_{n-1}) = 3^n - a_n$$

or $$\sum_{r=0}^{n-1} a_r = \frac{(3^n - a_n)}{2}$$

35. On putting $x = 1$ and $x = -1$ in Eq. (i), we get

$$3^n = a_0 + a_1 + a_2 + \ldots + a_{2n} \quad \ldots\text{(v)}$$

$$1 = a_0 - a_1 + a_2 - a_3 + \ldots + a_{2n} \quad \ldots\text{(vi)}$$

On adding and subtracting Eqs. (v) and (vi), we get

$$\frac{3^n + 1}{2} = (a_0 + a_2 + \ldots + a_{2n}) \quad \ldots\text{(vii)}$$

$$\frac{3^n - 1}{2} = (a_1 + a_3 + a_5 + \ldots + a_{2n-1}) \quad \ldots\text{(viii)}$$

Also, $a_r = a_{2n-r}$

Put $r = 0, 2, 4, 6, \ldots, n-1$

$$a_0 = a_{2n}, a_2 = a_{2n-2}, a_4 = a_{2n-4}, \ldots a_{n-1} = a_{n+1}$$

From Eq. (vii), we get

$$\frac{3^n + 1}{2} = 2(a_0 + a_2 + \ldots + a_{n-2}) + a_n$$

$$\frac{3^n + 1 - 2a_n}{4} = a_0 + a_2 + \ldots + a_{n-1}$$

Sol. (36 and 37)

Given, $(1 + x + 2x^2)^{20} = a_0 + a_1x + a_2x^2 + \ldots + a_{40}x^{40}$

On putting $x = 1$ and $x = -1$ respectively, we get

$$a_0 + a_1 + a_2 + \ldots + a_{40} = 4^{20} = 2^{40} \quad \ldots\text{(i)}$$

and $$a_0 - a_1 + a_2 - \ldots + a_{40} = 2^{20} \quad \ldots\text{(ii)}$$

From Eqs. (i) and (ii), we get

$$a_0 + a_2 + a_4 + \ldots + a_{38} + a_{40} = 2^{19}(2^{20} + 1) \quad \ldots\text{(iii)}$$

and $$a_1 + a_3 + a_5 + \ldots + a_{37} + a_{39} = 2^{19}(2^{20} - 1) \quad \ldots\text{(iv)}$$

Also, replacing x by $\frac{1}{x}$ in given expression, we get

$$\left(1 + \frac{1}{x} + \frac{2}{x^2}\right)^{20} = a_0 + \frac{a_1}{x} + \frac{a_2}{x^2} + \ldots + \frac{a_{38}}{x^{38}} + \frac{a_{39}}{x^{39}} + \frac{a_{40}}{x^{40}}$$

$$\Rightarrow \quad (2 + x + x^2)^{20} = a_0x^{40} + a_1x^{39} + \ldots + a_{38}x^2 + a_{39}x + a_{40} \quad \ldots\text{(v)}$$

On putting $x = 0$, we get $a_{40} = 2^{20}$ ...(vi)

On differentiating both sides of Eq. (v) w.r.t. x and put $x = 0$, we get

$$a_{39} = 20(2)^{19} \quad \ldots\text{(vii)}$$

36. $a_0 + a_2 + a_4 + \ldots + a_{38} + a_{40} = 2^{19}(2^{20} + 1)$ [from Eq. (iii)]

$$\Rightarrow \quad a_0 + a_2 + a_4 + \ldots + a_{38} = 2^{19}(2^{20} + 1) - a_{40}$$

$$= 2^{19}(2^{20} + 1) - 2^{20} \quad \text{[from Eq. (vi)]}$$

$$= 2^{19}(2^{20} - 1)$$

37. $a_1 + a_3 + a_5 + \ldots + a_{37} + a_{39} = 2^{19}(2^{20} - 1)$ [from Eq. (iv)]

$$\Rightarrow \quad a_1 + a_3 + a_5 + \ldots + a_{37} = 2^{19}(2^{20} - 1) - a_{39}$$

$$= 2^{19}(2^{20} - 1) - 20(2)^{19} \quad \text{[from Eq. (vii)]}$$

$$= 2^{19}(2^{20} - 21)$$

Sol. (38 and 39)

38. $5^{40} = (5^2)^{20} = (22 + 3)^{20} = 22\lambda + 3^{20}, \lambda \in N$

Also, $3^{20} = (3^2)^{10} = (11 - 2)^{10} = 11\mu + 2^{10}, \mu \in N$

Now, $2^{10} = 1024 = 11 \times 93 + 1$

$\therefore$ Remainder, $a = 1$

Also, $2^{2011} = 2^3(2^4)^{502} = 2^3(17 - 1)^{502}$

$$= 8[(17)^{502} - {}^{502}C_1(17)^{501} + \ldots - {}^{502}C_{501}(17) + 1]$$

$$= 8(17\lambda + 1), \lambda \in N = 8 \times 17\lambda + 8$$

$\therefore$ Remainder, $b = 8$

Hence, $a + b = 1 + 8 = 9$

39. $19^{93} - 13^{99} = \text{(odd number)} - \text{(odd number)} = \text{even number}$

$\therefore$ $19^{93} - 13^{99}$ is divisible by 2.

Now, $19^{93} - 13^{99} = (18 + 1)^{93} - (12 + 1)^{99}$

$$= [(18)^{93} + {}^{93}C_1(18)^{92} + {}^{93}C_2(18)^{91} \ldots + \ldots + {}^{93}C_{92}(18) + 1] - [(12)^{99} + {}^{99}C_1(12)^{98} + {}^{99}C_2(12)^{97} + \ldots + {}^{99}C_{98}(12) + 1]$$

$$= (18)^2\lambda + {}^{93}C_1 \times 18 - (12)^2\mu - {}^{99}C_1(12)$$

When λ and μ are integers

$$= (18)^2\lambda - (12)^2\mu + 486$$

$$= 81 \times 4\lambda - 12^2({}^{99}C_2 + 12 \cdot {}^{99}C_3) + 81p + 486$$

$$= 81 \text{ (integer), where } p \text{ is an integer.}$$

But 2 and 81 are co-prime.

$\therefore$ $19^{93} - 13^{99}$ is divisible by 162.

Sol. (40 and 41)

Here, $(1 + 2)^n = 2187$

$$3^n = 2187 = 3^7 \Rightarrow n = 7$$

At $x = \frac{1}{\sqrt{2}}$, $R = (\sqrt{2} + 1)^7 = I + f$

40. Let $f' = (\sqrt{2} - 1)^7, 0 < f' < 1$

$\therefore$ $Rf' = (\sqrt{2} + 1)^7(\sqrt{2} - 1)^7 = (1)^7 = 1$

$\therefore$ $(n + Rf) = 7 + 1 = 8$

41. Here, $m = \left|\frac{(n+1)(x)}{1+x}\right|$

$$= \left|\frac{(7+1)\left(2 \times \frac{1}{3}\right)}{1 + 2 \times \frac{1}{3}}\right| = -\frac{8 \times \frac{2}{3}}{\frac{5}{3}} = \frac{16}{5} = 3.2$$

$$T_{[m]+1} = T_{3+1} = T_4$$

Sol. (42 and 43)

42. $(x + C_0)(x + 3 \cdot C_1)(x + 5 \cdot C_2) + \ldots \{x + (2n + 1) \cdot C_n\}$

$$= x^{n+1} + x^n\{C_0 + 3 \cdot C_1 + 5 \cdot C_2 + \ldots + (2n + 1) \cdot C_n\}$$

$\therefore$ Coefficient of $x^n = C_0 + 3 \cdot C_1 + 5 \cdot C_2 + \ldots + (2n + 1) \cdot C_n$

$$= (C_0 + C_1 + C_2 + \ldots + C_n) + 2\{C_1 + 2 \cdot C_2 + \ldots n \cdot C_n\}$$

$$= 2^n + 2\left\{n + 2 \cdot \frac{n(n-1)}{2} + \ldots + n\right\}$$

$$= 2^n + 2n\left\{1 + (n-1) + \frac{(n-1)(n-2)}{1\cdot 2} + \ldots + 1\right\}$$

$$= 2^n + 2n\{^{n-1}C_0 + {}^{n-1}C_1 + {}^{n-1}C_2 + \ldots + {}^{n-1}C_{n-1}\}$$

$$= 2^n + 2n(1+1)^{n-1} = 2^n + n\cdot 2^n = (n+1)2^n$$

43. $(x + C_0)(x + C_1)(x + C_2) + \ldots + (x + C_n)$

$$= x^{n+1} + \left(\sum_{r=0}^{n} C_r\right)^n x^n + \left(\sum_{0\le i}\sum_{j\le n} C_iC_j\right)x^{n-1} + \ldots$$

$\therefore$ Coefficient of x^{n-1} in $\sum_{0\le i\le j\le n}\sum C_iC_j$

$$= \frac{1}{2}\left[\left(\sum_{r=0}^{n} C_r\right)^2 - \left(\sum_{r=0}^{n} C_r^2\right)\right] = \frac{1}{2}\{2^{2n} - {}^{2n}C_n\}$$

$$= 2^{2n-1} - \frac{1}{2}\cdot{}^{2n}C_n$$

Sol. (44 and 45)

Since, sum of coefficient of B is 6561.

$\therefore \quad \left(\frac{5}{2} + \frac{1}{2}\right)^n = 6561$

$\Rightarrow \quad 3^n = 6561 \Rightarrow 3^n = 3^8$

$\therefore \quad n = 8$

44. Coefficient $(T_3 - T_2) = 117$

$$^mC_2 3^2 - {}^mC_1 3^1 = 117 \Rightarrow m = 6$$

45. $n^m = 8^6 = (1+7)^6 = (1 + 7k)$

Hence, remainder is 1.

Sol. (46 and 47)

$\because a_4, a_5, a_6$ i.e. $^nC_4, {}^nC_5, {}^nC_6$ are in AP, then

$$2\cdot{}^nC_5 = {}^nC_4 + {}^nC_6$$

$\Rightarrow \quad 2 = \frac{^nC_4}{^nC_5} + \frac{^nC_6}{^nC_5} = \frac{5}{n-5+1} + \frac{n-6+1}{6}$

$\Rightarrow \quad 2 = \frac{5}{n-4} + \frac{n-5}{6}$

$\Rightarrow \quad 12n - 48 = 30 + n^2 - 9n + 20$

$\Rightarrow \quad n^2 - 21n + 98 = 0 \Rightarrow n = 7, 14$

Hence, $\quad n = 7 \quad [\because n < 10]$

Also, $\quad A = (\sqrt[3]{2} + \sqrt[4]{3})^{13n} = (2^{1/3} + 3^{1/4})^{91}$

$\therefore \quad T_{r+1} = {}^{91}C_r(2^{1/3})^{91-r}\cdot(3^{1/4})^r$

$$= {}^{91}C_r\cdot 2^{\frac{91-r}{3}}\cdot 3^{r/4} \quad \ldots(i)$$

46. $\sum_{i=1}^{n} a_i = \sum_{i=1}^{7} a_i = a_1 + a_2 + a_3 + \ldots + a_7$

$$= {}^7C_1 + {}^7C_2 + {}^7C_3 + \ldots + {}^7C_7 = 2^7 - 1 = 127$$

47. From Eq. (i), we get

$$0 \le r \le 91$$

For rational terms, $r = 4, 16, 28, 40, 52, 64, 76, 88$

Rational terms are $T_5, T_{17}, T_{29}, T_{41}, T_{53}, T_{65}, T_{77}, T_{89}$

$\therefore \quad a_m = 89$

48. $^nC_r + 4\cdot{}^nC_{r+1} + 6\cdot{}^nC_{r+2} + 4\cdot{}^nC_{r+3} + {}^nC_{r+4}$

$$= ({}^nC_r + {}^nC_{r+1}) + 3({}^nC_{r+1} + {}^nC_{r+2}) + 3({}^nC_{r+2} + {}^nC_{r+3}) + ({}^nC_{r+3} + {}^nC_{r+4})$$

$$= {}^{n+1}C_{r+1} + 3\cdot{}^{n+1}C_{r+2} + 3\cdot{}^{n+1}C_{r+3} + {}^{n+1}C_{r+4}$$

$$= ({}^{n+1}C_{r+1} + {}^{n+1}C_{r+2}) + 2({}^{n+1}C_{r+2} + {}^{n+1}C_{r+3}) + ({}^{n+1}C_{r+3} + {}^{n+1}C_{r+4})$$

$$= {}^{n+2}C_{r+2} + 2\cdot{}^{n+2}C_{r+3} + {}^{n+2}C_{r+4}$$

$$= ({}^{n+2}C_{r+2} + {}^{n+2}C_{r+3}) + ({}^{n+2}C_{r+3} + {}^{n+2}C_{r+4})$$

$$= {}^{n+3}C_{r+3} + {}^{n+3}C_{r+4}$$

$$= {}^{n+4}C_{r+4} = \frac{n+4}{r+4}\,{}^{n+3}C_{r+3}$$

Similarly, $^nC_r + 3\cdot{}^nC_{r+1} + 3\cdot{}^nC_{r+2} + {}^nC_{r+3} = {}^{n+3}C_{r+3}$

$\therefore \quad \frac{n+4}{r+4} = \frac{n+\lambda}{r+\lambda} \Rightarrow \lambda = 4$

49. $99^{50} - 99\cdot 98^{50} + \frac{99\cdot 98}{1\cdot 2}(97)^{50} - \ldots + 99$

$$= 99^{50} - {}^{99}C_1(98)^{50} + {}^{99}C_2(97)^{50} - \ldots + {}^{99}C_{98}\cdot 1$$

$$= {}^{99}C_0(99)^{50} - {}^{99}C_1(99-1)^{50} + {}^{99}C_2(99-2)^{50} - \ldots + {}^{99}C_{98}(99-98)^{50} - {}^{99}C_{99}(99-99)^{50}$$

$$= (99)^{50}\{{}^{99}C_0 - {}^{99}C_1 + {}^{99}C_2 - \ldots + {}^{99}C_{98} - {}^{99}C_{99}\} + {}^{50}C_1(99)^{49}\{{}^{99}C_1 - 2\cdot{}^{99}C_2 + 3\cdot{}^{99}C_3 - \ldots\}$$

$$= 0 + 0 = 0$$

50. $\because$ Greatest term in the expansion of $(1+x)^{2n}$ has the greatest coefficient.

$\therefore \quad T_{n+1} = {}^{2n}C_n x^n \quad$ (greatest term)

$\therefore \quad T_n < T_{n+1} > T_{n+2}$

$\Rightarrow \quad {}^{2n}C_{n-1}\cdot x^{n-1} < {}^{2n}C_n\cdot x^n > {}^{2n}C_{n+1}\cdot x^{n+1}$

$\Rightarrow \quad \frac{^{2n}C_{n-1}}{^{2n}C_n}\cdot\frac{1}{x} < 1 > \frac{^{2n}C_{n+1}}{^{2n}C_n}\cdot x$

$\Rightarrow \quad \frac{n}{n+1}\cdot\frac{1}{x} < 1 > \frac{n}{n+1}x$

$\Rightarrow \quad x > \frac{n}{n+1}$ and $x < \frac{n+1}{n}$

i.e., $\quad x \in \left(\frac{n}{n+1}, \frac{n+1}{n}\right)$

Given, $\quad x \in \left(\frac{10}{11}, \frac{11}{10}\right)$

$\therefore \quad n = 10$

Also, T_4 in $\left(\lambda x + \frac{1}{x}\right)^m = {}^mC_3(\lambda x)^{m-3}\left(\frac{1}{x}\right)^3 = \frac{n}{4} \quad$ [given]

$$^mC_3\cdot\lambda^{m-3}\cdot x^{m-6} = \frac{n}{4} \quad \text{[given]}$$

$$= \frac{10}{4} \quad [\because n = 10]$$

$$= \frac{5}{2}$$

Put $m - 6 = 0$, we get

$$m = 6$$

$$\therefore \quad {}^6C_3 \cdot \lambda^3 = \frac{5}{2}$$

$$\Rightarrow \quad \lambda^3 = \frac{5}{2} \times \frac{1}{20} = \frac{1}{8} = \left(\frac{1}{2}\right)^3$$

$$\therefore \quad \lambda = \frac{1}{2}$$

Hence, $m\lambda = 6 \times \frac{1}{2} = 3$

51. We know that, $(x-1)^n = {}^nC_0x^n - {}^nC_1x^{n-1} + {}^nC_2x^{n-2} - \dots$

$$\therefore \quad x^2(x-1)^n = {}^nC_0x^{n+2} - {}^nC_1x^{n+1} + {}^nC_2\,x^n - \dots$$

On differentiating w.r.t. x, we get

$$2x\,(x-1)^n + x^2 \cdot n(x-1)^{n-1}$$

$$= (n+2)\,{}^nC_0\,x^{n+1} - (n+1)\,{}^nC_1x^n + n \cdot {}^nC_2\,x^{n-1} - \dots$$

On putting $x = 2$, we get

$$(n+2)\,{}^nC_0\,2^{n+1} - (n+1) \cdot {}^nC_1 \cdot 2^n + n \cdot {}^nC_2 2^{n-1} - \dots$$

$$= 4 + 4n = 4\,(1+n)$$

$$\therefore \quad k = 4$$

52. On putting $x = 1, -1, i, -i$ in the given expression, we get

$$10^4 \times 9 = a_1 + a_2 + a_3 + a_4 + \dots + a_{45} \qquad \text{...(i)}$$

$$0 = -a_1 + a_2 - a_3 + a_4 + \dots - a_{45} \qquad \text{...(ii)}$$

$$(1+i)^4 \cdot i = a_1 i - a_2 - a_3 i + a_4 + \dots$$

$$\Rightarrow \quad -i\,(2i)^2 = -a_1 i + a_2 + a_3 i - a_4 - \dots$$

$$\Rightarrow \quad 4i = -a_1 i + a_2 + a_3 i - a_4 - \dots \qquad \text{...(iii)}$$

$$\text{and} \quad -4i = a_1 i + a_2 - a_3 i - a_4 - \dots \qquad \text{...(iv)}$$

On adding Eqs. (i), (ii), (iii) and (iv), we get

$$4\,(a_2 + a_6 + a_{10} + a_{14} + \dots + a_{42}) = 9 \times 10^4$$

or $\quad a_2 + a_6 + a_{10} + \dots + a_{42} = 22500 = \lambda \qquad$ [given]

$\therefore$ Required sum $= 2 + 2 + 5 + 0 + 0 = 9$

53. We have, $6^{83} + 8^{63}$

$$= (1+7)^{83} + (7-1)^{83}$$

$$= (1+7)^{83} - (1-7)^{83}$$

$$= 2[{}^{83}C_1 \times 7 + {}^{83}C_3 \times 7^3 + \dots + {}^{83}C_{83} \times 7^{83}]$$

$$= 2 \times 7 \times 83 + 49I, \text{ where } I \in Z$$

Now, $14 \times 83 = 1162$

$$\therefore \quad \frac{1162}{49} = 23\frac{35}{49}$$

$\therefore$ Remainder $= 35$

54. We have, $\left(\log_{10}(x^{\log_{10}^x} - \log_{x^2} 100\right)^{12}$

$$= \left((\log x)^2 - \frac{1}{\log x}\right)^{12}$$

$$\therefore \quad T_{r+1} = {}^{12}C_r\,((\log x)^2)^{12-r} \cdot \left(\frac{-1}{\log x}\right)^r$$

$$= {}^{12}C_r(\log x)^{24-3r}(-1)^r$$

For constant term, $24 - 3r = 0 \Rightarrow r = 8$

$$\therefore \quad \text{Constant term} = {}^{12}C_8$$

$$= {}^{12}C_4$$

$$= \frac{12 \times 11 \times 10 \times 9}{4 \times 3 \times 2 \times 1} = 495$$

55. We have, $\sum_{r=0}^{3} {}^8C_r({}^5C_{r+1} - {}^4C_r)$

$$= \sum_{r=0}^{3} ({}^8C_r \times {}^4C_{r+1})$$

$$= {}^8C_0 \times {}^4C_1 + {}^8C_1 \times {}^4C_2 + {}^8C_2 \times {}^4C_3 + {}^8C_3 \times {}^4C_4$$

$$= \text{Coefficient of } x^3 \text{ in } (1+x)^4(1+x)^8$$

$$= \text{Coefficient of } x^3 \text{ in } (1+x)^{12}$$

$$= {}^{12}C_3$$

$$= \frac{12 \times 11 \times 10}{3 \times 2 \times 1} = 220$$

56. We have,

$$T_r = r\frac{{}^{101}C_r}{{}^{101}C_{r-1}}$$

$$= \frac{r(101 - r + 1)}{r}$$

$$= 102 - r$$

$$\therefore \quad S_n = \sum_{r=1}^{101}(102 - r)$$

$$= 101 + 100 + 99 + \dots + 2 + 1$$

$$= 5151$$

57. $f(n) = {}^nC_0(a)^{n-1} - {}^nC_1(a)^{n-2} + {}^nC_2(a)^{n-3}$

$$+ \dots + (-1)^{n-1}\,{}^nC_{n-1}a^0$$

$$+ (-1)^n \cdot {}^nC_n \cdot \left(\frac{1}{a}\right) - (-1)^n \cdot {}^nC_n \cdot \left(\frac{1}{a}\right)$$

$$= \frac{1}{a}({}^nC_0a^n - {}^nC_1a^{n-1} + {}^nC_2a^{n-2}$$

$$+ \dots + (-1)^n\,{}^nC_n) - (-1)^n \cdot {}^nC_n\left(\frac{1}{a}\right)$$

$$= \frac{1}{a}\{(a-1)^n - (-1)^n\,{}^nC_n\}$$

$$= \frac{1}{a}\{(3^{\frac{n}{223}} - (-1)^n)\}$$

$$f(n) = \frac{3^{\frac{n}{223}} - (-1)^n}{(3^{\frac{1}{223}} + 1)} \qquad [\text{since, } a = 1 + 3^{1/223}]$$

$$\Rightarrow \quad f(2007) = \frac{3^{\frac{2007}{223}} + 1}{3^{\frac{1}{223}} + 1}$$

$$\Rightarrow \quad f(2008) = \frac{3^{\frac{2008}{223}} - 1}{3^{\frac{1}{223}} + 1}$$

$\Rightarrow \quad f(2007)+f(2008)=\dfrac{3^{\frac{2007}{223}}+3^{\frac{2008}{223}}}{3^{\frac{1}{223}}+1}$

$=\dfrac{3^9+3^{9+\frac{1}{223}}}{3^{\frac{1}{223}}+1}=3^9\dfrac{(1+3^{\frac{1}{223}})}{(1+3^{\frac{1}{223}})}=3^9$

$\Rightarrow \quad 3^9=3^k$, then $k=9$

58. (A) Given, $\binom{18}{r-2}+2\binom{18}{r-1}+\binom{18}{r}\geq\binom{20}{13}$

$\Rightarrow \binom{18}{r-2}+\binom{18}{r-1}+\binom{18}{r-1}+\binom{18}{r}\geq\binom{20}{13}$

$\Rightarrow \binom{19}{r-1}+\binom{19}{r}\geq\binom{20}{13}$

$\Rightarrow \binom{20}{r}\geq\binom{20}{7} \Rightarrow 7\leq r\leq 13$

$\therefore \quad r=7,8,9,10,11,12,13$

(B) The unit digit of 183! is 0.

Now, $3^{183}=(3^4)^{45}(3)^3$

Unit digit of 3^{183} = Unit digit of $(81)^{45}\times$ Unit digit of 27

$=1\times 7=7$

$\therefore$ Unit digit of $183!+3^{183}=0+7=7$

which is less than 8 and 9.

(C) $T_4={}^nC_3\,(ax)^{n-3}\left(\dfrac{1}{x}\right)^3=\dfrac{5}{2}$

$\Rightarrow \quad {}^nC_3\,a^{n-3}x^{n-6}=\dfrac{5}{2} \Rightarrow n=6$ and $a=\dfrac{1}{2}$

$\therefore \quad na=6\times\dfrac{1}{2}=3$

(D) Given, $(1+ax)^n=1+8x+24x^2+\dots$

$\Rightarrow 1+n\cdot ax+\dfrac{n(n-1)}{1\cdot 2}a^2x^2+\dots=1+8x+24x^2+\dots$

On comparing the coefficients of x and x^2, we get

$na=8$ and $\dfrac{n(n-1)}{1\cdot 2}a^2=24$

$\Rightarrow \quad na(n-1)a=48$

$\Rightarrow \quad 8(8-a)=48$

$\Rightarrow \quad 8-a=6$

$\Rightarrow \quad a=2$

$\Rightarrow \quad n=4$

$\therefore \quad a+n=2+4=6$

59. (A) The coefficient of power of x more than x^{30} in $(1+x)^{61}$ is

${}^{61}C_{31}+{}^{61}C_{32}+\dots+{}^{61}C_{61}$

We know that, $(1+1)^{61}={}^{61}C_0+{}^{61}C_1+{}^{61}C_2+\dots+{}^{61}C_{61}$

$\Rightarrow \quad 2^{61}=2({}^{61}C_{31}+{}^{61}C_{32}+\dots+{}^{61}C_{61})$

$\Rightarrow \quad {}^{61}C_{31}+{}^{61}C_{32}+\dots+{}^{61}C_{61}=2^{60}$

Hence, 2^{60} is divisible by $2^{31},2^{58},2^{59},2^{60}$.

(B) General term is, $T_{r+1}={}^{62}C_r(\sqrt{3})^r={}^{62}C_r3^{r/2}$

For rational term = r should be multiple of 2.

i.e. $\quad r=0,2,4,6,\dots,62$

$\therefore$ Required sum $=T_1+T_3+\dots+T_{63}$

$={}^{62}C_0+{}^{62}C_2+\dots+{}^{62}C_{62}=2^{62-1}=2^{61}$

Hence, 2^{61} is divisible by $2^{31},2^{58},2^{59},2^{60},2^{61}$.

(C) Put $x=1$ and $x=-1$ in given expression, then we get

$4^{31}=a_0+a_1+a_2+a_3+\dots+a_{124}$ ...(i)

and $\quad 2^{31}=a_0-a_1+a_2-a_3+\dots+a_{124}$ ...(ii)

On subtracting Eq. (ii) from Eq. (i), we get

$2^{62}-2^{31}=2(a_1+a_3+\dots+a_{123})$

$\Rightarrow \quad 2^{31}(2^{31}-1)=(a_1+a_3+\dots+a_{123})$

$\therefore a_1+a_3+\dots+a_{123}$ is divisible by $2^{31},2^{58},2^{59},2^{60},2^{61}$.

(D) Required sum of coefficient

= Coefficient of t^{13} in $(1+t)^{11}(1+t^2-t)^{10}$

= Coefficient of t^{13} in $(1+t)(1+t^3)^{10}$

= Coefficient of t^{13} in $[(1+t^3)^{10}+t(1+t^3)^{10}]$

= Coefficient of t^{12} in $(1+t^3)^{10}$

$={}^{10}C_4$

$\therefore m=4$

Thus, $m^{29}=4^{29}=(2^2)^{29}=2^{58}$

60. (A) $(11)^n+(21)^n=(16-5)^n+(16+5)^n$

$=2[{}^nC_0(16)^n+{}^nC_2(16)^{n-2}(5)^2$
$+{}^nC_4(16)^{n-4}(5)^4+{}^nC_6(16)^{n-6}(5)^6+\dots]$

Hence, given expression is divisible by 16, if $n=1,3,5,7$

(B) $3^{37}=(3^4)^9\cdot 3=(81)^9\cdot 3=3(80+1)^9]$

$=3[{}^9C_1(80)^8+{}^9C_2(80)^7+\dots+1]$

$\therefore$ Remainder of 3^{37} is 3.

(C) $\quad T_{r+1}=T_{r+k}\Rightarrow {}^{29}C_r={}^{29}C_{r+k-1}$

$\Rightarrow \quad 29-r=r+k-1$

$\Rightarrow \quad 30=2r+k \quad [\because r\leq 29]$

For even values of k, i.e., $k=0,2,4,6,8,\dots,28,$

(D) Given, $\dfrac{T_2}{T_3}=\dfrac{T'_3}{T'_4}$

$\Rightarrow \quad \dfrac{{}^nC_1(a)^{n-1}(b)^1}{{}^nC_2(a)^{n-2}(b)^2}=\dfrac{{}^{n+3}C_2(a)^{n+1}(b)^2}{{}^{n+3}C_3(a)^n(b)^3}$

$\Rightarrow \quad \dfrac{{}^nC_1}{{}^nC_2}\times\dfrac{a}{b}=\dfrac{{}^{n+3}C_2}{{}^{n+3}C_3}\cdot\dfrac{a}{b}$

$\Rightarrow \quad \dfrac{{}^nC_2}{{}^nC_1}=\dfrac{{}^{n+3}C_3}{{}^{n+3}C_2}$

$\Rightarrow \quad \dfrac{n-2+1}{2}=\dfrac{n+3-3+1}{3}$

$\Rightarrow \quad 3n-3=2n+2$

$\therefore \quad n=5$

61. General term in the expansion of $\left(ax^2+\dfrac{70}{27bx}\right)^4$ is

$T_{r+1}={}^4C_r(a\cdot x^2)^{4-r}\cdot\left(\dfrac{70}{27bx}\right)^r$

$\Rightarrow \quad T_{r+1}={}^4C_r\cdot(a)^{4-r}\cdot\dfrac{(70)^r}{(27b)^r}\times x^{8-3r}$ ...(i)

According to the question, $8-3r=5$ (exponent of x)

$\Rightarrow \quad 8-5=3r \Rightarrow r=1$

Again, we have to find general term in the expansion of $\left(ax-\frac{1}{bx^2}\right)^7$ is

$$T_{r+1}={}^7C_r\cdot(ax)^{7-r}\cdot\left(-\frac{1}{bx^2}\right)^r$$

$$\Rightarrow \quad T_{r+1}={}^7C_r\,(a)^{7-r}\cdot\left(-\frac{1}{b}\right)^r\cdot(x)^{7-3r} \quad \text{...(ii)}$$

According to the question, $7-3r=-5$

$\Rightarrow \quad 7+5=3r\Rightarrow r=4$

So, coefficient of x^{-5} = coefficient of x^5 (given in question)

$$\Rightarrow \quad {}^7C_4\cdot a^3\left(-\frac{1}{b}\right)^4={}^4C_1\,a^3\cdot\frac{70}{27b}$$

[after putting $r=1$ in Eq. (i) and $r=4$ in Eq. (ii)]

$$\Rightarrow \quad \frac{35a^3}{b^4}=\frac{280a^3}{27b} \quad (\because a,b\neq 0)$$

$$\Rightarrow \quad b^3=\frac{35\times 27}{280}\Rightarrow b=\frac{3}{2}$$

$\therefore \quad 2b=3$

62. It is given that

$$\begin{vmatrix}\sum_{k=0}^{n}k & \sum_{k=0}^{n}{}^nC_k k^2\\ \sum_{k=0}^{n}{}^nC_k .k & \sum_{k=0}^{n}{}^nC_k 3^k\end{vmatrix}=0$$

$$\Rightarrow \quad \begin{vmatrix}\frac{n(n+1)}{2} & n(n+1)2^{n-2}\\ n.2^{n-1} & 4^n\end{vmatrix}=0$$

$$\left[\because \sum_{k=0}^{n}k=\frac{n(n+1)}{2},\ \sum_{k=0}^{n}{}^nC_k k=n.2^{n-1},\ \sum_{k=0}^{n}{}^nC_k k^2=n(n+1)2^{n-2} \text{ and } \sum_{k=0}^{n}{}^nC_k 3^k=4^n\right]$$

$$\Rightarrow \quad \frac{n(n+1)}{2}4^n-n^2(n+1)\,2^{2n-3}=0$$

$$\Rightarrow \quad \frac{4^n}{2}-n\frac{4^{n-1}}{2}=0\Rightarrow n=4$$

$$\therefore \quad \sum_{k=0}^{n}\frac{{}^nC_k}{k+1}=\sum_{k=0}^{4}\frac{{}^4C_k}{k+1}=\frac{1}{5}\sum_{k=0}^{4}{}^5C_{k+1}=\frac{1}{5}(2^5-1)$$

$$=\frac{1}{5}(32-1)=31/5=6.20$$

63. Since, $f(m,n,p)=\sum_{i=0}^{p}\binom{m}{i}\binom{n+i}{p}\binom{p+n}{p-i}$

$$=\sum_{i=0}^{p}\frac{m!}{i!(m-i)!}\times\frac{(n+i)!}{p!(n+i-p)!}\times\frac{(p+n)!}{(p-i)!(n+i)!}$$

$$=\frac{(n+p)!}{p!}\sum_{i=0}^{p}{}^mC_i\frac{1}{(p-i)!(n+i-p)!}$$

$$=\frac{(n+p)!}{n!p!}\sum_{i=0}^{p}{}^mC_i\times{}^nC_{p-i}={}^{n+p}C_p\ {}^{m+n}C_p$$

Since, $g(m,n)=\sum_{p=0}^{m+n}\frac{f(m,n,p)}{\binom{n+p}{p}}=\sum_{p=0}^{m+n}\left(\frac{{}^{n+p}C_p\times{}^{m+n}C_p}{{}^{n+p}C_p}\right)$

$$=\sum_{p=0}^{m+n}{}^{m+n}C_p=2^{m+n}$$

$\therefore \quad g(m,n)=g(n,m)=2^{m+n}$,

and $g(m,n+1)=2^{m+n+1}=g(m+1,n)$

and $g(2m;2n)=2^{2(m+n)}=(2^{(m+n)})^2=(g(m,n))^2$

Exercise 3 - Challenging Problems

1. We have, $10000=T_3=T_{2+1}={}^5C_2\,x^{(5-2)}(x^{\log_{10}x})^2$

$$\Rightarrow \quad 100000=x^3\cdot x^{2\log_{10}x}=x^{3+2\log_{10}x}$$

$$\Rightarrow 3+2\log_{10}x=\log_x 100000=5\log_x 10=\frac{5}{\log_{10}x}$$

$$\Rightarrow 2(\log_{10}x)^2+3\log_{10}x-5=0$$

Put $\log_{10}x=y$, we get

$$2y^2+3y-5=0\ \Rightarrow\ y=-\frac{5}{2}\text{ or }1$$

$$\therefore \quad \log_{10}x=-\frac{5}{2}\text{ or }1$$

$$\Rightarrow \quad x=10\text{ or }10^{-5/2}$$

2. Let $(2+\sqrt{5})^p$ or $(\sqrt{5}+2)^p=I+f$ ...(i)

$$0\le f<1 \quad \text{...(ii)}$$

$$(\sqrt{5}-2)^p=f' \quad \text{...(iii)}$$

and $\quad 0<f'<1$ ...(iv)

On subtracting Eq. (iii) from Eq. (i), we get

$$I+f-f'=(\sqrt{5}+2)^p-(\sqrt{5}-2)^p$$

$$=2\{{}^pC_1(\sqrt{5})^{p-1}\cdot 2^1+{}^pC_3(\sqrt{5})^{p-3}\cdot 2^3+\ldots+{}^pC_p(\sqrt{5})^0 2^p\}$$

[$\because$ integer value of $f-f'=0$]

$\therefore \quad [(\sqrt{5}+2)^p]+0-2^{p+1}$

$$=2\{{}^pC_1(\sqrt{5})^{p-1}\cdot 2+{}^pC_3(\sqrt{5})^{p-3}\cdot 2^3+\ldots+{}^pC_{p-2}(\sqrt{5})^2\cdot 2^{p-2}\}$$

$=p\lambda=p$ (integer)

$\therefore \quad [(\sqrt{5}+2)^p]-2^{p+1}$ is divisible by P.

3. $P=\sum\sum_{0\le i<j\le n}(i+j)(C_i+C_j+C_iC_j)$ ...(i)

Replacing i by $n-i$ and j by $n-j$ in Eq. (i), we get

$$P=\sum\sum_{0\le i<j\le n}(n-i+n-j)(C_{n-i}+C_{n-j}+C_{n-i}C_{n-j})$$

$$=\sum\sum_{0\le i<j\le n}(2n-i-j)(C_i+C_j+C_iC_j)[\because {}^nC_r={}^nC_{n-r}] \quad \text{...(ii)}$$

On adding Eqs. (i) and (ii), then we get

$$2P=2n\sum\sum_{0\le i<j\le n}(C_i+C_j+C_iC_j)$$

$$\therefore \quad P=n\sum\sum_{0\le i<j\le n}(C_i+C_j)+n\sum\sum_{0\le i<j\le n}C_iC_j$$

$$=n\cdot n(C_0+C_1+C_2+\ldots+C_n)+\frac{n}{2}(2^{2n}-{}^{2n}C_n)$$

$$= n^2 \cdot 2^n + n \cdot 2^{2n-1} - \frac{n}{2} \cdot {}^{2n}C_n$$

$$= n^2 \cdot 2^n + n\left\{2^{2n-1} - \frac{2n!}{2(n!)^2}\right\}$$

4. $$\text{LHS} = \frac{1}{{}^{2n+1}C_r} + \frac{1}{{}^{2n+1}C_{r+1}}$$

$$= \frac{(2n+1-r)!\,r!}{(2n+1)!} + \frac{(2n-r)!\,(r+1)!}{(2n+1)!}$$

$$= (2n-r)!\,(r)!\left[\frac{(2n+1-r)+r+1}{(2n+1)!}\right]$$

$$= \frac{(2n-r)!\,(r)!(2n+2)}{(2n+1)\,(2n)!} = \frac{2n+2}{2n+1} \cdot \frac{1}{{}^{2n}C_r}$$

Now, $$\sum_{r=1}^{2n-1} \frac{(-1)^{r-1} \cdot r}{{}^{2n}C_r} = \sum_{r=1}^{2n-1} (-1)^{r-1} \left(\frac{2n+1}{2n+2}\right) \left[\frac{1}{{}^{2n+1}C_r} + \frac{1}{{}^{2n+1}C_{r+1}}\right] \times r$$

$$= \left(\frac{2n+1}{2n+2}\right) \sum_{r=1}^{2n-1} (-1)^{r-1} \left(\frac{1}{{}^{2n+1}C_r} + \frac{1}{{}^{2n+1}C_{r+1}}\right) \times r$$

$$= \left(\frac{2n+1}{2n+2}\right)\left[\left(\frac{1}{{}^{2n+1}C_1} + \frac{1}{{}^{2n+1}C_2}\right) - 2\left(\frac{1}{{}^{2n+1}C_2} + \frac{1}{{}^{2n+1}C_3}\right) + 3\left(\frac{1}{{}^{2n+1}C_3} + \frac{1}{{}^{2n+1}C_4}\right) - 4\left(\frac{1}{{}^{2n+1}C_4} + \frac{1}{{}^{2n+1}C_5}\right) + \dots + (2n-1)\left(\frac{1}{{}^{2n+1}C_{2n-1}} + \frac{1}{{}^{2n+1}C_{2n}}\right)\right]$$

$$= \left(\frac{2n+1}{2n+2}\right)\left[\frac{1}{{}^{2n+1}C_1} - \frac{1}{{}^{2n+1}C_2} + \frac{1}{{}^{2n+1}C_3} - \frac{1}{{}^{2n+1}C_4} + \dots + \frac{(2n-1)}{{}^{2n+1}C_{2n}}\right]$$

$$= \left(\frac{2n+1}{2n+2}\right)\left[\frac{1}{{}^{2n+1}C_1} - \frac{1}{{}^{2n+1}C_2} + \frac{1}{{}^{2n+1}C_3} - \frac{1}{{}^{2n+1}C_4} + \dots - \frac{1}{{}^{2n+1}C_{2n}} + \frac{2n}{{}^{2n+1}C_{2n}}\right]$$

$$= \left(\frac{2n+1}{2n+2}\right)\left[\left(\frac{1}{{}^{2n+1}C_1} - \frac{1}{{}^{2n+1}C_{2n}}\right) - \left(\frac{1}{{}^{2n+1}C_2} - \frac{1}{{}^{2n+1}C_{2n-1}}\right) + \dots + \frac{2n}{{}^{2n+1}C_{2n}}\right]$$

$$= \left(\frac{2n+1}{2n+2}\right)\left[0 + \frac{2n}{{}^{2n+1}C_{2n}}\right] = \left(\frac{2n+1}{2n+2}\right)\left(\frac{2n}{2n+1}\right)$$

$$= \frac{2n}{2n+2} = \frac{n}{n+1}$$

5. Given, $$(1 + x + x^2)^n = a_0 + a_1 x + a_2 x^2 + \dots + a_{r-2} x^{r-2} + a_{r-1} x^{r-1} + a_r x^r + \dots + a_{2n} x^{2n} \quad \dots \text{(i)}$$

and $$(1-x)^n = {}^nC_0 - {}^nC_1 x + {}^nC_2 x^2 - \dots + (-1)^r\, {}^nC_r x^r + \dots + (-1)^n\, {}^nC_n \quad \dots \text{(ii)}$$

On multiplying Eqs. (i) and (ii) and equating coefficient of x^r on both sides, we get

Coefficient of x^r in $(1-x^3)^n$

$$= {}^nC_0\, a_r - {}^nC_1 a_{r-1} + {}^nC_2 a_{r-2} - \dots + (-1)^r\, {}^nC_r a_r$$

Since, r is not a multiple of 3, therefore the expression $(1-x^3)^n$ does not contain x^r in any term.

$\therefore$ Coefficient of x^r in $(1-x^3)^n = 0$

Hence, $a_r - {}^nC_1\, a_{r-1} + {}^nC_2\, a_{r-2} - \dots + (-1)^r\, {}^nC_r\, a_0 = 0$

6. Given, $f(x) = g(x+1)$

$$\therefore a_0 x^0 + a_1 x + a_2 x^2 + \dots + a_{2n} x^{2n}$$
$$= b_0 + b_1(x+1) + b_2(x+1)^2 + \dots + b_{n-1}(x+1)^{n-1} + (x+1)^n + (x+1)^{n+1} + (x+1)^{n+2} + \dots + (x+1)^{2n}$$

Equating coefficient of x^n on both sides, we get

$$a_n = {}^nC_n + {}^{n+1}C_n + \dots + {}^{2n}C_n$$
$$= {}^{n+1}C_{n+1} + {}^{n+1}C_n + \dots + {}^{2n}C_n \qquad [\because {}^nC_n = {}^{n+1}C_{n+1}]$$
$$= {}^{n+2}C_{n+1} + \dots + {}^{2n}C_n = {}^{2n}C_{n+1} + {}^{2n}C_n \qquad [\because {}^nC_r + {}^nC_{r-1} = {}^{n+1}C_r]$$
$$= {}^{2n+1}C_{n+1}$$

7. $(1-x^3)^n = C_0 - C_1 x^3 + C_2 x^6 - C_3 x^9 + \dots + (-1)^n C_n x^{3n}$

Then, $\int_0^1 (1-x^3)^n\, dx$

$$= \int_0^1 (C_0 - C_1 x^3 + C_2 x^6 - \dots + (-1)^n C_n (x^{3n}))\, dx$$

$$= \left[\frac{C_0 x}{1} - \frac{C_1 x^4}{4} + \frac{C_2 x^7}{7} - \dots + (-1)^n \frac{C_n x^{3n+1}}{3n+1}\right]_0^1$$

$$= \frac{C_0}{1} - \frac{C_1}{4} + \frac{C_2}{7} - \dots + (-1)^n \frac{C_n}{3n+1}$$

Let $I_n = \int_0^1 (1-x^3)^n \cdot 1\, dx$

$$= [(1-x^3)^n \cdot x]_0^1 - \int_0^1 n(1-x^3)^{n-1} \cdot (-3x^2) \cdot x\, dx$$

$$= 0 - 3n \int_0^1 (1-x^3)^{n-1} (1 - x^3 - 1)\, dx$$

$$= -3n(I_n - I_{n-1})$$

$$\Rightarrow I_n = \frac{3n}{(3n+1)} I_{n-1}; \quad I_{n-1} = \frac{3(n-1)}{(3n-2)} I_{n-2}$$

$$I_{n-2} = \frac{3(n-2)}{(3n-5)} I_{n-3}$$

$$\vdots \qquad \vdots \qquad \vdots$$

$$I_3 = \frac{3 \cdot 3}{10} I_2; \quad I_2 = \frac{3 \cdot 2}{7} I_1; \quad I_1 = \frac{3 \cdot 1}{4} I_0 = \frac{3 \cdot 1}{3}(1)$$

$$\therefore \quad I_n = \frac{(3 \cdot 1)(3 \cdot 2)(3 \cdot 3) \dots (3 \cdot n)}{1 \cdot 4 \cdot 7 \cdot 10 \dots (3n+1)} \cdot 1 = \frac{3^n \cdot n!}{1 \cdot 4 \cdot 7 \cdot 10 \dots (3n+1)}$$

Hence, $$\frac{C_0}{1} - \frac{C_1}{4} + \frac{C_2}{7} - \dots + (-1)^n \frac{C_n}{3n+1} = \frac{3^n \cdot n!}{1 \cdot 4 \cdot 7 \dots (3n+1)}$$

7

> *Mathematics may not teach us to add love or subtract hate, but it gives us hope that every problem has a solution.*
>
> **-Philip J. Davis**

Matrices

Learning Milestones

Milestone 1 Types and Algebra of Matrices
- Definition
- Types of Matrices
- Algebra of Matrices
- Product of Two Matrices
- Various Kind of Matrices

Milestone 2 Transpose, Singular and Non-singular Matrices
- Transpose of a Matrix
- Expansion of Determinant
- Singular and Non-singular Matrices

Milestone 3 Adjoint and Inverse of a Matrix
- Minors and Cofactors
- Adjoint of a Matrix
- Inverse of a Matrix (Reciprocal Matrix)
- Matrix Polynomial

Milestone 4 Eigen Values and Cayley-Hamilton Theorem
- Solutions of Linear Simultaneous Equation Using Matrix Method
- Eigen Values or Characteristics Roots and Characteristics Vectors of a Square Matrix
- Cayley-Hamilton Theorem

$$\begin{bmatrix} a_{11} & a_{12} & \cdots & a_{1n} \\ a_{21} & a_{22} & \cdots & a_{2n} \\ a_{31} & a_{33} & \cdots & a_{3n} \\ \vdots & \vdots & & \vdots \\ a_{m1} & a_{m2} & \cdots & a_{mn} \end{bmatrix}$$

Practice Milestones

Practice Milestone 1- JEE Main Pattern
Practice Milestone 2 - JEE Advanced Pattern
Practice Milestone 3 - Challenging Problems

Milestone 1 Types and Algebra of Matrices

• Definition • Types of Matrices • Algebra of Matrices • Product of Two Matrices • Various Kind of Matrices

7.1 Definition

A set of mn numbers (real or complex) arranged in the form of a rectangular array having m rows and n columns is called a matrix of order $m \times n$ or an $m \times n$ matrix (which is read as m by n matrix).

An $m \times n$ matrix is usually written as

$$\begin{bmatrix} a_{11} & a_{12} & a_{13} & \cdots & a_{1n} \\ a_{21} & a_{22} & a_{23} & \cdots & a_{2n} \\ a_{31} & a_{32} & a_{33} & \cdots & a_{3n} \\ \cdots & \cdots & \cdots & \cdots & \cdots \\ \cdots & \cdots & \cdots & \cdots & \cdots \\ a_{m_1} & a_{m_2} & a_{m_3} & \cdots & a_{mn} \end{bmatrix}$$

In a compact form the above matrix is represented by $[a_{ij}]$, $i = 1, 2, 3, \ldots, m$, $j = 1, 2, 3, \ldots, n$ or simply by $[a_{ij}]_{m \times n}$, where the symbols a_{ij} represent any numbers (a_{ij} lies in the ith row (from top) and jth column (from left)).

Notations A matrix is denoted by capital letter such as $A, B, C, \ldots, X, Y, Z$.

JEE Focus Points

- A matrix may be represented by the symbols $[a_{ij}]$, (a_{ij}), $||a_{ij}||$ or by a single capital letter A (say).
$$A = [a_{ij}]_{m \times n} \text{ or } (a_{ij})_{m \times n} \text{ or } ||a_{ij}||$$
Generally, the first system is adopted.
- The numbers $a_{11}, a_{12}, \ldots$ etc of rectangular array are called the elements or entries of the matrix.
- A matrix is essentially an arrangement of elements and has no value.
- The plural of matrix is matrices.

Example 1. If a matrix has 12 elements, what are the possible orders it can have? What will be the possible orders if it has 7 elements?

Sol. We know that if a matrix is of order $m \times n$, it has mn elements. Thus, to find all possible orders of a matrix with 12 elements, we will find all ordered pairs of natural numbers, whose product is 12.

Thus, all possible ordered pairs are (1, 12), (12, 1), (2, 6), (6, 2), (3, 4), (4, 3).

Hence, possible orders are 1×12, 12×1, 2×6, 6×2, 3×4 and 4×3.

If the matrix has 7 elements, then the possible orders will be 1×7 and 7×1.

Example 2. Construct a 2×3 matrix $A = [a_{ij}]$, whose elements are given by

(i) $a_{ij} = \dfrac{(i+2j)^2}{2}$.

(ii) $a_{ij} = \dfrac{1}{2}|2i - 3j|$.

(iii) $a_{ij} = \begin{cases} i - j, & i \geq j \\ i + j, & i < j \end{cases}$

(iv) $a_{ij} = \left[\dfrac{i}{j}\right]$,

where $[\cdot]$ denotes the greatest integer function.

Sol. We have, $A = \begin{bmatrix} a_{11} & a_{12} & a_{13} \\ a_{21} & a_{22} & a_{23} \end{bmatrix}_{2 \times 3}$

(i) Since, $a_{ij} = \dfrac{(i+2j)^2}{2}$, therefore

$$a_{11} = \frac{(1+2)^2}{2} = \frac{9}{2},\ a_{12} = \frac{(1+4)^2}{2} = \frac{25}{2},$$

$$a_{13} = \frac{(1+6)^2}{2} = \frac{49}{2},\ a_{21} = \frac{(2+2)^2}{2} = 8,$$

$$a_{22} = \frac{(2+4)^2}{2} = 18 \text{ and } a_{23} = \frac{(2+6)^2}{2} = 32$$

Hence, the required matrix, $A = \begin{bmatrix} \frac{9}{2} & \frac{25}{2} & \frac{49}{2} \\ 8 & 18 & 32 \end{bmatrix}$.

(ii) Since, $a_{ij} = \dfrac{1}{2}|2i - 3j|$, therefore

$$a_{11} = \frac{1}{2}|2-3| = \frac{1}{2}|-1| = \frac{1}{2},$$

$$a_{12} = \frac{1}{2}|2-6| = \frac{1}{2}|-4| = \frac{4}{2} = 2,$$

$$a_{13} = \frac{1}{2}|2-9| = \frac{1}{2}|-7| = \frac{7}{2},$$

$$a_{21} = \frac{1}{2}|4-3| = \frac{1}{2}|1| = \frac{1}{2},$$

$$a_{22} = \frac{1}{2}|4-6| = \frac{1}{2}|-2| = \frac{2}{2} = 1$$

and $$a_{23} = \frac{1}{2}|4-9| = \frac{1}{2}|-5| = \frac{5}{2}$$

Hence, the required matrix is $A = \begin{bmatrix} \frac{1}{2} & 2 & \frac{7}{2} \\ \frac{1}{2} & 1 & \frac{5}{2} \end{bmatrix}$.

(iii) Since, $a_{ij} = \begin{cases} i-j, & i \geq j \\ i+j, & i < j \end{cases}$, therefore

$$a_{11} = 1-1 = 0, a_{12} = 1+2 = 3, a_{13} = 1+3 = 4,$$
$$a_{21} = 2-1 = 1, a_{22} = 2-2 = 0 \text{ and } a_{23} = 2+3 = 5$$

Hence, the required matrix is $A = \begin{bmatrix} 0 & 3 & 4 \\ 1 & 0 & 5 \end{bmatrix}$.

(iv) Since, $a_{ij} = \left[\frac{i}{j}\right]$, therefore $[\because [x] \leq x]$

$$a_{11} = \left[\frac{1}{1}\right] = [1] = 1, a_{12} = \left[\frac{1}{2}\right] = [0.5] = 0,$$
$$a_{13} = \left[\frac{1}{3}\right] = [0.33] = 0, a_{21} = \left[\frac{2}{1}\right] = [2] = 2$$

and $$a_{22} = \left[\frac{2}{2}\right] = [1] = 1 \text{ and } a_{23} = \left[\frac{2}{3}\right] = [0.67] = 0$$

Hence, the required matrix is $A = \begin{bmatrix} 1 & 0 & 0 \\ 2 & 1 & 0 \end{bmatrix}$

7.2 Types of Matrices

1. Row Matrix

A matrix is said to be row matrix or row vector, if it contains only one row, i.e. a matrix $A = [a_{ij}]_{m \times n}$ is said to be row matrix, if $m = 1$.

e.g. (i) $A = [a_{11} \quad a_{12} \quad a_{13} \quad \dots \quad a_{1n}]_{1 \times n}$

(ii) $B = [3 \quad 5 \quad -7 \quad 9]_{1 \times 4}$

are called row matrices.

2. Column Matrix

A matrix is said to be column matrix or column vector, if it contains only one column, i.e., a matrix $A = [a_{ij}]_{m \times n}$ is said to be column matrix, if $n = 1$.

e.g.

(i) $A = \begin{bmatrix} a_{11} \\ a_{21} \\ a_{31} \\ \vdots \\ a_{mn} \end{bmatrix}_{m \times 1}$ (ii) $B = \begin{bmatrix} 7 \\ 0 \\ -8 \\ 2 \\ 1 \end{bmatrix}_{5 \times 1}$

are called column matrices.

3. Rectangular Matrix

A matrix is said to be rectangular matrix, if the number of rows and the number of columns are not equal i.e., a matrix $A = [a_{ij}]_{m \times n}$ is called a rectangular matrix, iff $m \neq n$.

e.g.

(i) $A = \begin{bmatrix} 1 & 3 & 4 & 5 \\ 2 & 0 & -3 & 8 \\ 7 & 4 & 2 & 5 \end{bmatrix}_{3 \times 4}$ (ii) $B = \begin{bmatrix} 2 & -3 \\ 3 & 0 \\ 4 & 8 \end{bmatrix}_{3 \times 2}$

are called rectangular matrices.

4. Square Matrix

A matrix is said to be a square matrix, if the number of rows and the number of columns are equal i.e., a matrix $A = [a_{ij}]_{m \times n}$ is called a square matrix, iff $m = n$.

e.g.

(i) $A = \begin{bmatrix} a_{11} & a_{12} & a_{13} \\ a_{21} & a_{22} & a_{23} \\ a_{31} & a_{32} & a_{33} \end{bmatrix}_{3 \times 3}$ (ii) $B = \begin{bmatrix} a & b \\ c & d \end{bmatrix}_{2 \times 2}$

are called square matrices.

5. Diagonal Matrix

A square matrix is said to be a diagonal matrix, if all its non-diagonal elements are zero.

Thus, $A = [a_{ij}]_{n \times n}$ is called a diagonal matrix, if $a_{ij} = 0$, when $i \neq j$.

e.g.

(i) $A = [2]$ (ii) $B = \begin{bmatrix} -1 & 0 \\ 0 & 2 \end{bmatrix}$

(iii) $C = \begin{bmatrix} 3 & 0 & 0 \\ 0 & 5 & 0 \\ 0 & 0 & 7 \end{bmatrix}$

are diagonal matrices of order 1, 2 and 3, respectively. A diagonal matrix of order n having $d_1, d_2, d_3, \dots, d_n$ as diagonal elements may be denoted by diag $(d_1, d_2, d_3, \dots, d_n)$.

Thus, $A = $ diag (2), $B = $ diag (–1, 2) and $C = $ diag (3, 5, 7).

JEE Focus Points

- No element of principal diagonal in a diagonal matrix is zero.
- Minimum number of zero in a diagonal matrix is given by $n(n-1)$, where n is order of matrix.

6. Scalar Matrix

A diagonal matrix is said to be a scalar matrix, if its diagonal elements are equal. Thus, $A = [a_{ij}]_{n \times n}$ is called scalar matrix, if

$$a_{ij} = \begin{cases} 0, \text{ if } i \neq j \\ k, \text{ if } i = j \end{cases}, \text{ where } k \text{ is scalar.}$$

e.g.

(i) $[7]$ (ii) $\begin{bmatrix} 2 & 0 \\ 0 & 2 \end{bmatrix}$ (iii) $\begin{bmatrix} 5 & 0 & 0 \\ 0 & 5 & 0 \\ 0 & 0 & 5 \end{bmatrix}$

are scalar matrices of order 1, 2 and 3, respectively. They can be written as diag (7), diag (2, 2) and diag (5, 5, 5), respectively.

7. Unit or Identity Matrix

A diagonal matrix is said to be an identity matrix, if its diagonal elements are equal to 1.

Thus, $A = [a_{ij}]_{n \times n}$ is called unit or identity matrix, if

$$a_{ij} = \begin{cases} 0, \text{ if } i \neq j \\ 1, \text{ if } i = j \end{cases}$$

A unit matrix of order n is denoted by I_n or I.

e.g.

(i) $I_1 = [1]$ (ii) $I_2 = \begin{bmatrix} 1 & 0 \\ 0 & 1 \end{bmatrix}$ (iii) $I_3 = \begin{bmatrix} 1 & 0 & 0 \\ 0 & 1 & 0 \\ 0 & 0 & 1 \end{bmatrix}$

are identity matrices of order 1, 2 and 3, respectively.

8. Singleton Matrix

A matrix is said to be singleton matrix, if it has only one element i.e. a matrix $A = [a_{ij}]_{m \times n}$ is said to be singleton matrix, if $m = n = 1$.

e.g. $[3], [k], [-2]$ are singleton matrices.

9. Triangular Matrix

A square matrix is called a triangular matrix, if its each element above or below the principal diagonal is zero. It is of two types:

(a) **Upper Triangular Matrix** A square matrix in which all elements below the principal diagonal are zero is called an upper triangular matrix i.e. a matrix $A = [a_{ij}]_{n \times n}$ is said to be an upper triangular matrix, if $a_{ij} = 0$, when $i > j$.

e.g.

(i) $\begin{bmatrix} 3 & -2 & 4 & 1 \\ 0 & 2 & -3 & 2 \\ 0 & 0 & 7 & 5 \\ 0 & 0 & 0 & 8 \end{bmatrix}_{4 \times 4}$

(ii) $\begin{bmatrix} a_{11} & a_{12} & a_{13} & a_{14} & a_{15} \\ 0 & a_{22} & a_{23} & a_{24} & a_{25} \\ 0 & 0 & a_{33} & a_{34} & a_{35} \\ 0 & 0 & 0 & a_{44} & a_{45} \\ 0 & 0 & 0 & 0 & a_{55} \end{bmatrix}_{5 \times 5}$

are upper triangular matrices.

(b) **Lower Triangular Matrix** A square matrix in which all elements above the principal diagonal are zero is called a lower triangular matrix i.e. a matrix $A = [a_{ij}]_{n \times n}$ is said to be a lower triangular matrix, if $a_{ij} = 0$, when $i < j$.

e.g.

(i) $\begin{bmatrix} 7 & 0 & 0 \\ 5 & 4 & 0 \\ 2 & 3 & 4 \end{bmatrix}_{3 \times 3}$ (ii) $\begin{bmatrix} 10 & 0 & 0 & 0 \\ 8 & 9 & 0 & 0 \\ 5 & 6 & 7 & 0 \\ 1 & 2 & 3 & 4 \end{bmatrix}_{4 \times 4}$

are lower triangular matrices.

JEE SPIKE

Minimum number of zeroes in a triangular matrix is given by $\frac{n(n-1)}{2}$, where n is order of matrix.

10. Horizontal Matrix

A matrix is said to be horizontal matrix, if the number of rows is less than the number of columns i.e. a matrix $A = [a_{ij}]_{m \times n}$ is said to horizontal matrix, iff $m < n$.

e.g. $A = \begin{bmatrix} 2 & 3 & 4 & 5 \\ 8 & 9 & 7 & -2 \\ 2 & -2 & -3 & 4 \end{bmatrix}_{3 \times 4}$ is a horizontal matrix.

[$\because$ number of rows (3) < number of columns (4)]

11. Vertical Matrix

A matrix is said to be vertical matrix, if the number of rows is greater than the number of columns i.e. a matrix $A=[a_{ij}]_{m\times n}$ is said to vertical matrix, iff $m>n$.

e.g. $A=\begin{bmatrix} 2 & 3 & 4 \\ 0 & -1 & 7 \\ 3 & 5 & 4 \\ 2 & 7 & 9 \\ -1 & 2 & -5 \end{bmatrix}_{5\times 3}$ is a vertical matrix.

[$\because$ number of rows (5) > number of columns (3)]

12. Null Matrix or Zero Matrix

A matrix is said to be null matrix or zero matrix, if all elements are zero i.e., a matrix $A=[a_{ij}]_{m\times n}$ is said to be a zero or null matrix, iff $a_{ij}=0, \forall\, i, j$. It is denoted by O.

e.g.

(i) $O_{2\times 3}=\begin{bmatrix} 0 & 0 & 0 \\ 0 & 0 & 0 \end{bmatrix}$ (ii) $O_{3\times 3}=\begin{bmatrix} 0 & 0 & 0 \\ 0 & 0 & 0 \\ 0 & 0 & 0 \end{bmatrix}$

are null matrices.

13. Sub-Matrix

A matrix which is obtained from a given matrix by deleting any number of rows and number of columns is called a sub-matrix of the given matrix.

e.g. $\begin{bmatrix} 3 & 4 \\ -2 & 5 \end{bmatrix}$ is a sub-matrix of $\begin{bmatrix} 8 & 9 & 5 \\ 2 & 3 & 4 \\ 3 & -2 & 5 \end{bmatrix}$.

7.3 Algebra of Matrices

Equal Matrices

Two matrices are said to be equal, if

(i) they are of the same order i.e., if they have same number of rows and columns.

(ii) the elements in the corresponding positions of the two matrices are equal.

Thus, if $A=[a_{ij}]_{m\times n}$, $B=[b_{ij}]_{p\times q}$, then $A=B$, iff

(i) $m=p, n=q$ (ii) $a_{ij}=b_{ij}, \forall\, i, j$

e.g. If $A=\begin{bmatrix} -1 & 2 & 4 \\ 3 & 0 & 5 \end{bmatrix}_{2\times 3}$ and $B=\begin{bmatrix} a & b & c \\ d & e & f \end{bmatrix}_{2\times 3}$

are equal matrices, then

$a=-1, b=2, c=4, d=3, e=0, f=5$

Example 3. If $\begin{bmatrix} x+3 & 2y+x \\ z-1 & 4w-8 \end{bmatrix}=\begin{bmatrix} -x-1 & 0 \\ 3 & 2w \end{bmatrix}$, then find the value of $|x+y|+|z+w|$.

Sol. As the given matrices are equal so their corresponding elements are equal.

$$x+3=-x-1 \Rightarrow 2x=-4$$

$\therefore$ $x=-2$ ...(i)

$2y+x=0$

$\Rightarrow$ $2y-2=0$ [from Eq. (i)]

$\Rightarrow$ $y=1$ ...(ii)

$z-1=3$

$\Rightarrow$ $z=4$ ...(iii)

$4w-8=2w$

$\Rightarrow$ $2w=8$

$\therefore$ $w=4$ ...(iv)

Hence, $|x+y|+|z+w|=|-2+1|+|4+4|=1+8=9$

Example 4. If $\begin{bmatrix} 2\alpha+1 & 3\beta \\ 0 & \beta^2-5\beta \end{bmatrix}=\begin{bmatrix} \alpha+3 & \beta^2+2 \\ 0 & -6 \end{bmatrix}$, find the equation whose roots are α and β.

Sol. The given matrices will be equal, iff

$$2\alpha+1=\alpha+3 \Rightarrow \alpha=2$$

$$3\beta=\beta^2+2 \Rightarrow \beta^2-3\beta+2=0$$

$\therefore$ $\beta=1, 2$

and $\beta^2-5\beta=-6$ ...(i)

$\Rightarrow$ $\beta^2-5\beta+6=0$

$\therefore$ $\beta=2, 3$ ...(ii)

From Eqs. (i) and (ii), we get

$$\beta=2 \Rightarrow \alpha=2, \beta=2$$

$\therefore$ Required equation is $x^2-(2+2)x+2\cdot 2=0$

$\Rightarrow$ $x^2-4x+4=0$

Addition of Matrices

Let A, B be two matrices, each of order $m\times n$. Then, their sum $A+B$ is a matrix of order $m\times n$ and is obtained by adding the corresponding elements of A and B.

Thus, if $A=[a_{ij}]_{m\times n}$ and $B=[b_{ij}]_{m\times n}$, then $A+B=[a_{ij}+b_{ij}]_{m\times n}, \forall\, i, j$

Example 5. Given, $A=\begin{bmatrix} 1 & 3 & 5 \\ -2 & 0 & 2 \\ 0 & 4 & -3 \end{bmatrix}$, $B=\begin{bmatrix} 0 & 3 \\ -2 & 0 \\ 0 & -4 \end{bmatrix}$

and $C=\begin{bmatrix} 4 & 1 & -2 \\ 3 & 2 & 1 \\ 2 & -1 & 7 \end{bmatrix}$. Find (which ever defined)

(i) $A+B$. (ii) $A+C$.

Sol. (i) Given, A is a matrix of the type 3×3 and B is a matrix of the type 3×2.

Since, A and B are not of the same type.

$\therefore$ Sum $A + B$ is not defined.

(ii) As A and C are two matrices of the same type, therefore the sum $A + C$ is defined.

$$\therefore A + C = \begin{bmatrix} 1 & 3 & 5 \\ -2 & 0 & 2 \\ 0 & 4 & -3 \end{bmatrix} + \begin{bmatrix} 4 & 1 & -2 \\ 3 & 2 & 1 \\ 2 & -1 & 7 \end{bmatrix}$$

$$= \begin{bmatrix} 1+4 & 3+1 & 5-2 \\ -2+3 & 0+2 & 2+1 \\ 0+2 & 4-1 & -3+7 \end{bmatrix} = \begin{bmatrix} 5 & 4 & 3 \\ 1 & 2 & 3 \\ 2 & 3 & 4 \end{bmatrix}$$

Example 6. Given that $M = \begin{bmatrix} 2 & 0 & 1 \\ -1 & 1 & 0 \\ 3 & 2 & 5 \end{bmatrix}$, $N = \begin{bmatrix} 0 & -1 & 2 \\ 7 & 1 & -1 \\ 0 & 1 & -2 \end{bmatrix}$ and $P = \begin{bmatrix} 0 & 2 & 4 \\ 0 & -1 & 3 \\ 2 & 1 & 0 \end{bmatrix}$, then find $M + N - P$.

Sol. $M + N = \begin{bmatrix} 2 & -1 & 3 \\ 6 & 2 & -1 \\ 3 & 3 & 3 \end{bmatrix}$

$$M + N - P = \begin{bmatrix} 2 & -1 & 3 \\ 6 & 2 & -1 \\ 3 & 3 & 3 \end{bmatrix} - \begin{bmatrix} 0 & 2 & 4 \\ 0 & -1 & 3 \\ 2 & 1 & 0 \end{bmatrix} = \begin{bmatrix} 2 & -3 & -1 \\ 6 & 3 & -4 \\ 1 & 2 & 3 \end{bmatrix}$$

Properties of Matrix Addition

Property 1 Addition of matrices is commutative,

i.e. $A + B = B + A$

where A and B are any two $m \times n$ matrices, i.e. matrices of the same order.

Property 2 Addition of matrices is associative

i.e. $(A + B) + C = A + (B + C)$

where A, B and C are any three matrices of the same order $m \times n$ (say).

Property 3 Existence of additive identity

i.e. $A + O = A = O + A$

where A be any $m \times n$ matrix and O be the $m \times n$ null matrix. The null matrix O is the identity element for matrix addition.

Property 4 Existence of additive inverse

If A be any $m \times n$ matrix, then there exists another $m \times n$ matrix B, such that $A + B = O = B + A$

where O is the $m \times n$ null matrix.

Here, the matrix B is called the additive inverse of the matrix A or the negative of A.

Property 5 Cancellation laws

If A, B and C are matrices of the same order $m \times n$ (say),

then $A + B = A + C \Rightarrow B = C$ [left cancellation law]

and $B + A = C + A \Rightarrow B = C$ [right cancellation law]

Scalar Multiplication

Let $A = [a_{ij}]_{m \times n}$ be a matrix and k be any number called a scalar. Then, the matrix obtained by multiplying every element of A by k is called the scalar multiple of A by k and is denoted by kA.

Thus, $kA = [ka_{ij}]_{m \times n}$

Properties of Scalar Multiplication

If $A = [a_{ij}]_{m \times n}$, $B = [b_{ij}]_{m \times n}$ are two matrices and k, l are scalars , then

(i) $k(A + B) = kA + kB$ (ii) $(k + l)A = kA + lA$

(iii) $(kl)A = k(lA) = l(kA)$ (iv) $(-k)A = -(kA) = k(-A)$

(v) $1A = A, (-1)A = -A$

Example 7. Determine the matrix A,

when $A = 4\begin{bmatrix} 1 & 2 & 3 \\ -1 & -2 & -3 \\ 4 & 2 & 6 \end{bmatrix} + 2\begin{bmatrix} 5 & 4 & 1 \\ 3 & 2 & 4 \\ 3 & 8 & 2 \end{bmatrix}$.

Sol. $A = \begin{bmatrix} 4 & 8 & 12 \\ -4 & -8 & -12 \\ 16 & 8 & 24 \end{bmatrix} + \begin{bmatrix} 10 & 8 & 2 \\ 6 & 4 & 8 \\ 6 & 16 & 4 \end{bmatrix}$

$$= \begin{bmatrix} 4+10 & 8+8 & 12+2 \\ -4+6 & -8+4 & -12+8 \\ 16+6 & 8+16 & 24+4 \end{bmatrix} = \begin{bmatrix} 14 & 16 & 14 \\ 2 & -4 & -4 \\ 22 & 24 & 28 \end{bmatrix}$$

Example 8. If $A = \begin{bmatrix} 0 & 2 \\ 3 & -4 \end{bmatrix}$ and $kA = \begin{bmatrix} 0 & 3a \\ 2b & 24 \end{bmatrix}$, then find the value of $b - a - k$.

Sol. We have, $A = \begin{bmatrix} 0 & 2 \\ 3 & -4 \end{bmatrix} \Rightarrow kA = \begin{bmatrix} 0 & 2k \\ 3k & -4k \end{bmatrix}$

But $kA = \begin{bmatrix} 0 & 3a \\ 2b & 24 \end{bmatrix}$

$\therefore \begin{bmatrix} 0 & 2k \\ 3k & -4k \end{bmatrix} = \begin{bmatrix} 0 & 3a \\ 2b & 24 \end{bmatrix}$

$\Rightarrow 2k = 3a, 3k = 2b, -4k = 24$

$\Rightarrow k = -6, a = -4, b = -9$

Hence, $b - a - k = -9 - (-4) - (-6)$

$= -9 + 4 + 6 = 1$

Subtraction of Matrices

Let A, B be two matrices, each of order $m \times n$. Then, their subtraction $A - B$ is a matrix of order $m \times n$ and is obtained by subtracting the corresponding elements of A and B. Thus, if $A = [a_{ij}]_{m \times n}$ and $B = [b_{ij}]_{m \times n}$,

then $\quad A - B = [a_{ij} - b_{ij}]_{m \times n}, \forall\, i, j$

e.g. $\quad$ If $A = \begin{bmatrix} 2 & 3 \\ 4 & 5 \\ 6 & 7 \end{bmatrix}$ and $B = \begin{bmatrix} a & b \\ c & d \\ e & f \end{bmatrix}$,

then $\quad A - B = \begin{bmatrix} 2 & 3 \\ 4 & 5 \\ 6 & 7 \end{bmatrix} - \begin{bmatrix} a & b \\ c & d \\ e & f \end{bmatrix} = \begin{bmatrix} 2-a & 3-b \\ 4-c & 5-d \\ 6-e & 7-f \end{bmatrix}$

Example 9. Given, $A = \begin{bmatrix} 1 & 2 & -3 \\ 5 & 0 & 2 \\ 1 & -1 & 1 \end{bmatrix}$ and $B = \begin{bmatrix} 3 & -1 & 2 \\ 4 & 2 & 5 \\ 2 & 0 & 3 \end{bmatrix}$.

Find the matrix C such that $A + 2C = B$.

Sol. Given, $A + 2C = B$

$$2C = B - A = \begin{bmatrix} 3 & -1 & 2 \\ 4 & 2 & 5 \\ 2 & 0 & 3 \end{bmatrix} - \begin{bmatrix} 1 & 2 & -3 \\ 5 & 0 & 2 \\ 1 & -1 & 1 \end{bmatrix}$$

$$= \begin{bmatrix} 3-1 & -1-2 & 2+3 \\ 4-5 & 2-0 & 5-2 \\ 2-1 & 0+1 & 3-1 \end{bmatrix}$$

$$\therefore \quad 2C = \begin{bmatrix} 2 & -3 & 5 \\ -1 & 2 & 3 \\ 1 & 1 & 2 \end{bmatrix} \Rightarrow C = \frac{1}{2}\begin{bmatrix} 2 & -3 & 5 \\ -1 & 2 & 3 \\ 1 & 1 & 2 \end{bmatrix}$$

$$\therefore \quad C = \begin{bmatrix} 1 & -3/2 & 5/2 \\ -1/2 & 1 & 3/2 \\ 1/2 & 1/2 & 1 \end{bmatrix}$$

Example 10. Solve the following equations for X and Y.

$$2X - Y = \begin{bmatrix} 3 & -3 & 0 \\ 3 & 3 & 2 \end{bmatrix}, 2Y + X = \begin{bmatrix} 4 & 1 & 5 \\ -1 & 4 & -4 \end{bmatrix}$$

Sol. Given, $\quad 2X - Y = \begin{bmatrix} 3 & -3 & 0 \\ 3 & 3 & 2 \end{bmatrix}$

On multiplying both sides by 2, we get

$$4X - 2Y = 2\begin{bmatrix} 3 & -3 & 0 \\ 3 & 3 & 2 \end{bmatrix};$$

$$4X - 2Y = \begin{bmatrix} 6 & -6 & 0 \\ 6 & 6 & 4 \end{bmatrix} \quad \text{...(i)}$$

also given $\quad X + 2Y = \begin{bmatrix} 4 & 1 & 5 \\ -1 & 4 & -4 \end{bmatrix} \quad$ ...(ii)

Adding Eqs. (i) and (ii), we get

$$5X = \begin{bmatrix} 6 & -6 & 0 \\ 6 & 6 & 4 \end{bmatrix} + \begin{bmatrix} 4 & 1 & 5 \\ -1 & 4 & -4 \end{bmatrix}$$

$$= \begin{bmatrix} 6+4 & -6+1 & 0+5 \\ 6-1 & 6+4 & 4-4 \end{bmatrix} = \begin{bmatrix} 10 & -5 & 5 \\ 5 & 10 & 0 \end{bmatrix}$$

$$\therefore \quad X = \frac{1}{5}\begin{bmatrix} 10 & -5 & 5 \\ 5 & 10 & 0 \end{bmatrix}$$

$$\Rightarrow \quad X = \begin{bmatrix} 2 & -1 & 1 \\ 1 & 2 & 0 \end{bmatrix}$$

Putting the value of X in Eq. (ii), we get

$$\begin{bmatrix} 2 & -1 & 1 \\ 1 & 2 & 0 \end{bmatrix} + 2Y = \begin{bmatrix} 4 & 1 & 5 \\ -1 & 4 & -4 \end{bmatrix}$$

$$\Rightarrow \quad 2Y = \begin{bmatrix} 4 & 1 & 5 \\ -1 & 4 & -4 \end{bmatrix} - \begin{bmatrix} 2 & -1 & 1 \\ 1 & 2 & 0 \end{bmatrix}$$

$$= \begin{bmatrix} 4-2 & 1+1 & 5-1 \\ -1-1 & 4-2 & -4-0 \end{bmatrix} = \begin{bmatrix} 2 & 2 & 4 \\ -2 & 2 & -4 \end{bmatrix}$$

$$\therefore \quad Y = \begin{bmatrix} 1 & 1 & 2 \\ -1 & 1 & -2 \end{bmatrix}$$

Hence, $\quad X = \begin{bmatrix} 2 & -1 & 1 \\ 1 & 2 & 0 \end{bmatrix}$

and $\quad Y = \begin{bmatrix} 1 & 1 & 2 \\ -1 & 1 & -2 \end{bmatrix}$

JEE SPIKE

If two matrices A and B are of the same order, then only their addition and subtraction is possible and these matrices are said to be **conformable** for addition or subtraction.

On the other hand, if the matrices A and B are of different orders, then their addition and subtraction is not possible and these matrices are called **non-conformable** for addition and subtraction.

7.4 Product of Two Matrices

Multiplication

Conformable for Multiplication

A and B be two matrices are said to be conformable for the product AB, if the number of columns in A (called the pre-factor) is equal to the number of rows in B (called the post-factor) otherwise non-conformable for multiplication. Thus,

(i) AB is defined, if number of columns in A = number of rows in B.

(ii) BA is defined, if number of columns in B = number of rows in A.

Multiplication of Matrices

Let $A=[a_{ij}]_{m\times n}$ and $B=[b_{ij}]_{n\times p}$ be two matrices, then the product AB is defined as the matrix $C=[C_{ij}]_{m\times p}$,

where $C_{ij}=\sum_{j=1}^{n} a_{ij}\, b_{jk}, 1\le i\le m, 1\le k\le p$

$$=a_{i1}\, b_{1k}+a_{i2}\, b_{2k}+a_{i3}\, b_{3k}+\ldots+a_{in}\, b_{nk}$$

i.e., (i, k) th entry of the product AB is the sum of the product of the corresponding elements of the ith row of A (pre-factor) and kth column of B (post-factor).

Example 11. If $A=\begin{bmatrix}0 & 1 & 2\\ 1 & 2 & 3\\ 2 & 3 & 4\end{bmatrix}$ and $B=\begin{bmatrix}1 & -2\\ -1 & 0\\ 2 & -1\end{bmatrix}$, obtain the product AB and explain why BA is not defined?

Sol. Here, the number of columns in $A=3=$ the number of rows in B.

Therefore, the product AB is defined.

$$AB=\begin{bmatrix}0 & 1 & 2\\ 1 & 2 & 3\\ 2 & 3 & 4\end{bmatrix}\begin{matrix}R_1\\ R_2\\ R_3\end{matrix}\times\overset{\begin{matrix}C_1 & C_2\end{matrix}}{\begin{bmatrix}1 & -2\\ -1 & 0\\ 2 & -1\end{bmatrix}}$$

R_1, R_2, R_3 are rows of A and C_1, C_2 are columns of B.

$$\therefore\quad AB=\begin{bmatrix}R_1C_1 & R_1C_2\\ R_2C_1 & R_2C_2\\ R_3C_1 & R_3C_2\end{bmatrix}_{3\times 2}$$

$$\begin{bmatrix}\begin{bmatrix}0 & 1 & 2\end{bmatrix}\begin{bmatrix}1\\ -1\\ 2\end{bmatrix} & \begin{bmatrix}0 & 1 & 2\end{bmatrix}\begin{bmatrix}-2\\ 0\\ -1\end{bmatrix}\\ \begin{bmatrix}1 & 2 & 3\end{bmatrix}\begin{bmatrix}1\\ -1\\ 2\end{bmatrix} & \begin{bmatrix}1 & 2 & 3\end{bmatrix}\begin{bmatrix}-2\\ 0\\ -1\end{bmatrix}\\ \begin{bmatrix}2 & 3 & 4\end{bmatrix}\begin{bmatrix}1\\ -1\\ 2\end{bmatrix} & \begin{bmatrix}2 & 3 & 4\end{bmatrix}\begin{bmatrix}-2\\ 0\\ -1\end{bmatrix}\end{bmatrix}_{3\times 2}$$

$$=\begin{bmatrix}0\times 1+1\times(-1)+2\times 2 & 0\times(-2)+1\times 0+2\times(-1)\\ 1\times 1+2\times(-1)+3\times 2 & 1\times(-2)+2\times 0+3\times(-1)\\ 2\times 1+3\times(-1)+4\times 2 & 2\times(-2)+3\times 0+4\times(-1)\end{bmatrix}_{3\times 2}$$

$$=\begin{bmatrix}0-1+4 & 0+0-2\\ 1-2+6 & -2+0-3\\ 2-3+8 & -4+0-4\end{bmatrix}_{3\times 2}$$

$$=\begin{bmatrix}3 & -2\\ 5 & -5\\ 7 & -8\end{bmatrix}_{3\times 2}$$

Since, the number of columns of B is 2 and the number of rows of A is 3, BA is not defined $(\because 2\ne 3)$.

JEE SCANNER

Example Similar to PYQ Asked in JEE Main 2023

Let α and β be real numbers. Consider a 3×3 matrix A such that $A^2=4A+\alpha I$. If $A^4=28A+\beta I$, then

(a) $\alpha=\frac{9}{2}$
(b) $\alpha=\frac{7}{2}$
(c) $\beta=-\frac{207}{4}$
(d) $\beta=\frac{182}{9}$

Sol. (c) We have, $\alpha,\beta\in R$ and A is a 3×3 matrix such that

$$A^2=4A+\alpha I \quad \ldots(i)$$

and $$A^4=28A+\beta I \quad \ldots(ii)$$

Consider $A^4=A^2\cdot A^2=(4A+\alpha I)(4A+\alpha I)$

$$=16A^2+8\alpha A+\alpha^2 I$$

From Eq (i), $A^4=16(4A+\alpha I)+8\alpha A+\alpha^2 I$

$$=64A+16\alpha I+8\alpha A+\alpha^2 I$$

$$=(64+8\alpha)A+(16\alpha+\alpha^2)I \quad \ldots(iii)$$

From Eqs. (ii) and (iii), we get

$$64+8\alpha=28 \text{ and } 16\alpha+\alpha^2=\beta$$

$$\alpha=-\frac{9}{2} \text{ and } \beta=\alpha^2+16\alpha$$

$$\therefore\quad \beta=\left(-\frac{9}{2}\right)^2+16\left(-\frac{9}{2}\right)=\frac{-207}{4}$$

Skill Builder

Let α and β be real numbers. Consider a 3×3 matrix P such that $P^2=2P+\alpha I$ and $P^4=16P+\beta I$, then α, β is equal to

(a) 2, 12
(b) 4, 3
(c) 4, 2
(d) 2, 3

For Sol.

■ **For more practice** See Q.7 of Milestone Practice 7.1.

Example 12. If $A=\begin{bmatrix}0 & -\tan(\alpha/2)\\ \tan(\alpha/2) & 0\end{bmatrix}$ and I is a 2×2 unit matrix, prove that

$$I+A=(I-A)\begin{bmatrix}\cos\alpha & -\sin\alpha\\ \sin\alpha & \cos\alpha\end{bmatrix}.$$

Sol. Since, $I=\begin{bmatrix}1 & 0\\ 0 & 1\end{bmatrix}$ and given $A=\begin{bmatrix}0 & -\tan(\alpha/2)\\ \tan(\alpha/2) & 0\end{bmatrix}$

$$\therefore\quad I+A=\begin{bmatrix}1 & -\tan(\alpha/2)\\ \tan(\alpha/2) & 1\end{bmatrix} \quad \ldots(i)$$

$$\text{RHS}=(I-A)\begin{bmatrix}\cos\alpha & -\sin\alpha\\ \sin\alpha & \cos\alpha\end{bmatrix}$$

$$= \begin{bmatrix} 1 & \tan(\alpha/2) \\ -\tan(\alpha/2) & 1 \end{bmatrix} \begin{bmatrix} \cos\alpha & -\sin\alpha \\ \sin\alpha & \cos\alpha \end{bmatrix}$$

$$= \begin{bmatrix} 1 & \tan(\alpha/2) \\ -\tan(\alpha/2) & 1 \end{bmatrix} \begin{bmatrix} \dfrac{1-\tan^2(\alpha/2)}{1+\tan^2(\alpha/2)} & \dfrac{-2\tan(\alpha/2)}{1+\tan^2(\alpha/2)} \\ \dfrac{2\tan(\alpha/2)}{1+\tan^2(\alpha/2)} & \dfrac{1-\tan^2(\alpha/2)}{1+\tan^2(\alpha/2)} \end{bmatrix}$$

Let $\tan(\alpha/2) = \lambda$, then

$$\text{RHS} = \begin{bmatrix} 1 & \lambda \\ -\lambda & 1 \end{bmatrix} \begin{bmatrix} \dfrac{1-\lambda^2}{1+\lambda^2} & \dfrac{-2\lambda}{1+\lambda^2} \\ \dfrac{2\lambda}{1+\lambda^2} & \dfrac{1-\lambda^2}{1+\lambda^2} \end{bmatrix}$$

$$= \begin{bmatrix} \dfrac{1-\lambda^2+2\lambda^2}{1+\lambda^2} & \dfrac{-2\lambda+\lambda(1-\lambda^2)}{1+\lambda^2} \\ \dfrac{-\lambda(1-\lambda^2)+2\lambda}{1+\lambda^2} & \dfrac{2\lambda^2+1-\lambda^2}{1+\lambda^2} \end{bmatrix}$$

$$= \begin{bmatrix} \dfrac{1+\lambda^2}{1+\lambda^2} & \dfrac{-\lambda(1+\lambda^2)}{1+\lambda^2} \\ \dfrac{\lambda(1+\lambda^2)}{1+\lambda^2} & \dfrac{1+\lambda^2}{1+\lambda^2} \end{bmatrix}$$

$$= \begin{bmatrix} 1 & -\lambda \\ \lambda & 1 \end{bmatrix}$$

$$= \begin{bmatrix} 1 & -\tan(\alpha/2) \\ \tan(\alpha/2) & 1 \end{bmatrix} \quad [\because \lambda = \tan(\alpha/2)]$$

$$= I + A \quad \text{[from Eq. (i)]}$$

$$= \text{LHS}$$

Pre-multiplication and Post-multiplication of Matrices

The matrix AB is the matrix B pre-multiplied by A and the matrix BA is the matrix B post-multiplied by A.

Properties of Multiplication of Matrices

Property 1 Multiplication of matrices is not commutative i.e. $AB \neq BA$

Property 2 Matrix multiplication is associative if conformability assumed. i.e. $A(BC) = (AB)C$

Property 3 Matrix multiplication is distributive with respect to addition. i.e. $A(B+C) = AB + AC$, whenever both sides of equality are defined.

Property 4 If A is an $m \times n$ matrix, then $I_m A = A = A I_n$.

Property 5 If product of two matrices is a zero matrix, it is not necessary that one of the matrices is a zero matrix.

e.g.

(i) $$\begin{bmatrix} 1 & 1 \\ 2 & 2 \end{bmatrix} \times \begin{bmatrix} -1 & 1 \\ 1 & -1 \end{bmatrix} = \begin{bmatrix} 1\cdot(-1)+1.1 & 1\cdot1+1\cdot(-1) \\ 2\cdot(-1)+2.1 & 2\cdot1+2\cdot(-1) \end{bmatrix} = \begin{bmatrix} 0 & 0 \\ 0 & 0 \end{bmatrix} = O$$

(ii) $$\begin{bmatrix} 0 & 0 \\ 1 & 0 \end{bmatrix} \times \begin{bmatrix} 0 & 0 \\ 0 & 1 \end{bmatrix} = \begin{bmatrix} 0\cdot0+0\cdot0 & 0\cdot0+0\cdot1 \\ 1\cdot0+0\cdot0 & 1\cdot0+0\cdot1 \end{bmatrix} = \begin{bmatrix} 0 & 0 \\ 0 & 0 \end{bmatrix} = O$$

None of the matrices on the LHS is a null matrix whereas their product is a null matrix.

Property 6 Multiplication of a matrix A by a null matrix conformable with A for multiplication.

e.g. If $A = \begin{bmatrix} 3 & 4 \\ 5 & 6 \\ 7 & 8 \end{bmatrix}_{3\times2}$ and $O = \begin{bmatrix} 0 & 0 & 0 \\ 0 & 0 & 0 \end{bmatrix}_{2\times3}$,

then $AO = \begin{bmatrix} 0 & 0 & 0 \\ 0 & 0 & 0 \\ 0 & 0 & 0 \end{bmatrix}_{3\times3}$, which is a 3×3 null matrix.

Property 7 Multiplication of a matrix by itself

The product of $A\,A\,A \dots m$ times $= A^m$ and $(A^m)^n = A^{mn}$

JEE Focus Points

- If I be unit matrix, then $I^2 = I^3 = \dots = I^m = I \ (m \in I_+)$
- If A and B are two matrices of the same order, then
  - (i) $(A+B)^2 = A^2 + AB + BA + B^2$
  - (ii) $(A-B)^2 = A^2 - AB - BA + B^2$
  - (iii) $(A+B)(A-B) = A^2 - AB + BA - B^2$
  - (iv) $A(-B) = (-A)(B) = -AB$

Example 13. If $A = \begin{bmatrix} 1 & 2 \\ -2 & 3 \end{bmatrix}$, $B = \begin{bmatrix} 2 & 1 \\ 2 & 3 \end{bmatrix}$ and $C = \begin{bmatrix} -3 & 1 \\ 2 & 0 \end{bmatrix}$, verify that $(AB)C = A(BC)$ and $A(B+C) = AB + AC$.

Sol. We have, $AB = \begin{bmatrix} 1 & 2 \\ -2 & 3 \end{bmatrix} \times \begin{bmatrix} 2 & 1 \\ 2 & 3 \end{bmatrix}$

$$= \begin{bmatrix} 1\cdot2+2\cdot2 & 1\cdot1+2\cdot3 \\ (-2)\cdot2+3\cdot2 & (-2)\cdot1+3\cdot3 \end{bmatrix} = \begin{bmatrix} 6 & 7 \\ 2 & 7 \end{bmatrix}$$

$$BC = \begin{bmatrix} 2 & 1 \\ 2 & 3 \end{bmatrix} \times \begin{bmatrix} -3 & 1 \\ 2 & 0 \end{bmatrix} = \begin{bmatrix} 2\cdot(-3)+1\cdot2 & 2\cdot1+1\cdot0 \\ 2\cdot(-3)+3\cdot2 & 2\cdot1+3\cdot0 \end{bmatrix}$$

$$= \begin{bmatrix} -6+2 & 2+0 \\ -6+6 & 2+0 \end{bmatrix} = \begin{bmatrix} -4 & 2 \\ 0 & 2 \end{bmatrix}$$

$$AC=\begin{bmatrix}1 & 2\\ -2 & 3\end{bmatrix}\times\begin{bmatrix}-3 & 1\\ 2 & 0\end{bmatrix}=\begin{bmatrix}1\cdot(-3)+2\cdot 2 & 1\cdot 1+2\cdot 0\\ (-2)\cdot(-3)+3\cdot 2 & (-2)\cdot 1+3\cdot 0\end{bmatrix}$$

$$=\begin{bmatrix}-3+4 & 1+0\\ 6+6 & -2+0\end{bmatrix}=\begin{bmatrix}1 & 1\\ 12 & -2\end{bmatrix}$$

$$B+C=\begin{bmatrix}2 & 1\\ 2 & 3\end{bmatrix}+\begin{bmatrix}-3 & 1\\ 2 & 0\end{bmatrix}=\begin{bmatrix}2-3 & 1+1\\ 2+2 & 3+0\end{bmatrix}=\begin{bmatrix}-1 & 2\\ 4 & 3\end{bmatrix}$$

Now, $(AB)C=\begin{bmatrix}6 & 7\\ 2 & 7\end{bmatrix}\times\begin{bmatrix}-3 & 1\\ 2 & 0\end{bmatrix}=\begin{bmatrix}-18+14 & 6+0\\ -6+14 & 2+0\end{bmatrix}$

$$=\begin{bmatrix}-4 & 6\\ 8 & 2\end{bmatrix} \quad \text{...(i)}$$

$$A(BC)=\begin{bmatrix}1 & 2\\ -2 & 3\end{bmatrix}\times\begin{bmatrix}-4 & 2\\ 0 & 2\end{bmatrix}$$

$$=\begin{bmatrix}-4+0 & 2+4\\ 8+0 & -4+6\end{bmatrix}=\begin{bmatrix}-4 & 6\\ 8 & 2\end{bmatrix} \quad \text{...(ii)}$$

Thus, from Eqs. (i) and (ii), we get $(AB)C=A(BC)$

Now, $A(B+C)=\begin{bmatrix}1 & 2\\ -2 & 3\end{bmatrix}\times\begin{bmatrix}-1 & 2\\ 4 & 3\end{bmatrix}=\begin{bmatrix}-1+8 & 2+6\\ 2+12 & -4+9\end{bmatrix}$

$$=\begin{bmatrix}7 & 8\\ 14 & 5\end{bmatrix} \quad \text{...(iii)}$$

and $AB+AC=\begin{bmatrix}6 & 7\\ 2 & 7\end{bmatrix}+\begin{bmatrix}1 & 1\\ 12 & -2\end{bmatrix}=\begin{bmatrix}6+1 & 7+1\\ 2+12 & 7-2\end{bmatrix}$

$$=\begin{bmatrix}7 & 8\\ 14 & 5\end{bmatrix} \quad \text{...(iv)}$$

Thus, from Eqs. (iii) and (iv), we get

$A(B+C)=AB+AC$

Trace of a Matrix

The sum of all diagonal elements of a square matrix $A=[a_{ij}]_{n\times n}$ (say) is called the **trace** of a matrix A and is denoted by Tr (A).

Thus, $\text{Tr}(A)=\sum_{i=1}^{n} a_{ii}=a_{11}+a_{22}+a_{33}+\ldots+a_{nn}$

e.g. If $A=\begin{bmatrix}2 & -7 & 9\\ 0 & 3 & 2\\ 8 & 9 & 4\end{bmatrix}$, then $\text{Tr}(A)=2+3+4=9$

Properties of Trace of a Matrix

Let $A=[a_{ij}]_{n\times n}$, $B=[b_{ij}]_{n\times n}$ and k is a scalar, then

(i) $\text{Tr}(kA)=k\cdot\text{Tr}(A)$

(ii) $\text{Tr}(A\pm B)=\text{Tr}(A)\pm\text{Tr}(B)$

(iii) $\text{Tr}(AB)=\text{Tr}(BA)$

(iv) $\text{Tr}(I_n)=n$

(v) $\text{Tr}(AB)\neq\text{Tr}(A)\,\text{Tr}(B)$

Example 14. If matrices $X=\begin{bmatrix}2 & -1\\ 5 & 0\end{bmatrix}$, $Y=\begin{bmatrix}-1 & 3\\ -1 & 4\end{bmatrix}$, then find Tr $(3X+Y)$.

Sol. $\text{Tr}(3X+Y)=\text{Tr}(3X)+\text{Tr}(Y)=3\text{Tr}(X)+\text{Tr}(Y)$

$=3(2+0)+3$

$=6+3=9$

Example 15. If matrix $M=\begin{bmatrix}-1 & 1 & 2\\ 3 & 0 & 1\\ -2 & 2 & -1\end{bmatrix}$, then find $\text{Tr}\left(\frac{M}{2}\right)$.

Sol. $\text{Tr}\left(\frac{M}{2}\right)=\frac{1}{2}\text{Tr}(M)=\frac{1}{2}(-1+0-1)=-1$

7.5 Various Kinds of Matrices

Idempotent Matrix

A square matrix A is called idempotent provided it satisfies the relation $A^2=A$.

Note $A^n=A$, $\forall\, n\geq 2$, $n\in N$.

Example 16. Show that the matrix $A=\begin{bmatrix}2 & -2 & -4\\ -1 & 3 & 4\\ 1 & -2 & -3\end{bmatrix}$ is idempotent.

Sol. $A^2=A\cdot A=\begin{bmatrix}2 & -2 & -4\\ -1 & 3 & 4\\ 1 & -2 & -3\end{bmatrix}\times\begin{bmatrix}2 & -2 & -4\\ -1 & 3 & 4\\ 1 & -2 & -3\end{bmatrix}$

$$=\begin{bmatrix}2\cdot 2+(-2)\cdot(-1)+(-4)\cdot 1 & 2\cdot(-2)+(-2)\cdot 3+(-4)\cdot(-2) & 2\cdot(-4)+(-2)\cdot 4+(-4)\cdot(-3)\\ (-1)\cdot 2+3\cdot(-1)+4\cdot 1 & (-1)\cdot(-2)+3\cdot 3+4\cdot(-2) & (-1)\cdot(-4)+3\cdot 4+4\cdot(-3)\\ 1.2+(-2)\cdot(-1)+(-3)\cdot 1 & 1\cdot(-2)+(-2)\cdot 3+(-3)\cdot(-2) & 1\cdot(-4)+(-2)\cdot 4+(-3)\cdot(-3)\end{bmatrix}$$

$$=\begin{bmatrix}2 & -2 & -4\\ -1 & 3 & 4\\ 1 & -2 & -3\end{bmatrix}=A$$

Hence, the matrix A is idempotent.

Periodic Matrix

A square matrix A is called periodic, if $A^{k+1}=A$, where k is a positive integer. If k is the least positive integer for which $A^{k+1}=A$, then k is said to be **period** of A. For $k=1$, we get $A^2=A$ and we called it to be **idempotent matrix.**

Nilpotent Matrix

A square matrix A is called nilpotent matrix of order k provided it satisfies the relation $A^k = O$ and $A^{k-1} \neq O$, where k is positive integer and O is null matrix and k is the order of the nilpotent matrix A.

Example 17. Show that $\begin{bmatrix} 1 & 1 & 3 \\ 5 & 2 & 6 \\ -2 & -1 & -3 \end{bmatrix}$ is nilpotent matrix of order 3.

Sol. Let $A = \begin{bmatrix} 1 & 1 & 3 \\ 5 & 2 & 6 \\ -2 & -1 & -3 \end{bmatrix}$

$$\therefore A^2 = A \cdot A = \begin{bmatrix} 1 & 1 & 3 \\ 5 & 2 & 6 \\ -2 & -1 & -3 \end{bmatrix} \times \begin{bmatrix} 1 & 1 & 3 \\ 5 & 2 & 6 \\ -2 & -1 & -3 \end{bmatrix}$$

$$= \begin{bmatrix} 1+5-6 & 1+2-3 & 3+6-9 \\ 5+10-12 & 5+4-6 & 15+12-18 \\ -2-5+6 & -2-2+3 & -6-6+9 \end{bmatrix}$$

$$= \begin{bmatrix} 0 & 0 & 0 \\ 3 & 3 & 9 \\ -1 & -1 & -3 \end{bmatrix}$$

$$\therefore A^3 = A^2 \cdot A = \begin{bmatrix} 0 & 0 & 0 \\ 3 & 3 & 9 \\ -1 & -1 & -3 \end{bmatrix} \times \begin{bmatrix} 1 & 1 & 3 \\ 5 & 2 & 6 \\ -2 & -1 & -3 \end{bmatrix}$$

$$= \begin{bmatrix} 0+0+0 & 0+0+0 & 0+0+0 \\ 3+15-18 & 3+6-9 & 9+18-27 \\ -1-5+6 & -1-2+3 & -3-6+9 \end{bmatrix}$$

$$= \begin{bmatrix} 0 & 0 & 0 \\ 0 & 0 & 0 \\ 0 & 0 & 0 \end{bmatrix} = O$$

$\therefore \quad A^3 = O$

i.e. $\quad A^k = O$

Here, $\quad k = 3$

Hence, the matrix A is nilpotent of order 3.

Example 18. Show that matrix $\begin{bmatrix} ab & b^2 \\ -a^2 & -ab \end{bmatrix}$ is nilpotent. Also, find its index.

Sol. $A = \begin{bmatrix} ab & b^2 \\ -a^2 & -ab \end{bmatrix}$

$$A^2 = \begin{bmatrix} ab & b^2 \\ -a^2 & -ab \end{bmatrix}\begin{bmatrix} ab & b^2 \\ -a^2 & -ab \end{bmatrix} = \begin{bmatrix} 0 & 0 \\ 0 & 0 \end{bmatrix}$$

$\therefore$ A is nilpotent of order 2.

Involutory Matrix

A square matrix A is called involutory provided it satisfies the relation $A^2 = I$, where I is identity matrix.

Example 19. Show that the matrix $A = \begin{bmatrix} -5 & -8 & 0 \\ 3 & 5 & 0 \\ 1 & 2 & -1 \end{bmatrix}$ is involutory.

Sol. $A^2 = A \cdot A = \begin{bmatrix} -5 & -8 & 0 \\ 3 & 5 & 0 \\ 1 & 2 & -1 \end{bmatrix} \times \begin{bmatrix} -5 & -8 & 0 \\ 3 & 5 & 0 \\ 1 & 2 & -1 \end{bmatrix}$

$$= \begin{bmatrix} 25-24+0 & 40-40+0 & 0+0+0 \\ -15+15+0 & -24+25+0 & 0+0+0 \\ -5+6-1 & -8+10-2 & 0+0+1 \end{bmatrix}$$

$$= \begin{bmatrix} 1 & 0 & 0 \\ 0 & 1 & 0 \\ 0 & 0 & 1 \end{bmatrix} = I$$

Hence, the given matrix A is involutory.

Example 20. If $A = \begin{bmatrix} i & -i \\ -i & i \end{bmatrix}, B = \begin{bmatrix} 1 & -1 \\ -1 & 1 \end{bmatrix}, i = \sqrt{-1}$, then prove that $A^8 = 128B$.

Sol. $A = i\begin{bmatrix} 1 & -1 \\ -1 & 1 \end{bmatrix} = iB$

$A^2 = i^2B^2 = -B^2$ ...(i)

Now, $B^2 = \begin{bmatrix} 1 & -1 \\ -1 & 1 \end{bmatrix}\begin{bmatrix} 1 & -1 \\ -1 & 1 \end{bmatrix}$

$$= \begin{bmatrix} 2 & -2 \\ -2 & 2 \end{bmatrix}$$

$$= 2\begin{bmatrix} 1 & -1 \\ -1 & 1 \end{bmatrix} = 2B$$

$B^2 = 2B$ ...(ii)

From Eqs. (i) and (ii), we get

$$A^2 = -2B$$

On squaring both sides,

$$A^4 = 4B^2 = 4(2B) = 8B$$

Again, on squaring both sides,

$$A^8 = 64B^2 = 64 \times 2B$$

$$A^8 = 128B$$

Milestone Practice 7.1

1. If $\begin{bmatrix} x-y & z \\ 2x-y & w \end{bmatrix} = \begin{bmatrix} -1 & 4 \\ 0 & 5 \end{bmatrix}$, then find $x+y+z+w$.

(a) 9 (b) 10 (c) 11 (d) 12

2. The number of square matrices of order 5 with entries from the set {0, 1} such that the sum are all elements in each row is 1 and sum of all the elements in each column is also 1, is

(a) 225 (b) 120 (c) 150 (d) 125

3. Let $A = \begin{bmatrix} a & b & c \\ p & q & r \\ x & y & z \end{bmatrix}$ and $B = \begin{bmatrix} 4x & 2a & -p \\ 4y & 2b & -q \\ 4z & 2c & -r \end{bmatrix}$.

If $\det(A) = 2$, then $\det(B)$ is equal to

(a) -8 (b) 8 (c) -16 (d) 16

4. Let $M = [a_{ij}]_{3\times 3}$, where $a_{ij} \in \{-1, 1\}$. Then, maximum possible value of $\det(M)$ is

(a) 3 (b) 4
(c) 5 (d) 6

5. If $A = \begin{bmatrix} \cos\theta & \sin\theta \\ -\sin\theta & \cos\theta \end{bmatrix}$, then $A^2 = I$ is true for

(a) $\theta = 0$ (b) $\theta = \frac{\pi}{4}$
(c) $\theta = \frac{\pi}{2}$ (d) None of these

6. Let $A = \begin{bmatrix} 0 & \alpha \\ 0 & 0 \end{bmatrix}$ and $(A+I)^{50} - 50A = \begin{bmatrix} a & b \\ c & d \end{bmatrix}$, the value of $a+b+c+d$, is

(a) 1 (b) 2
(c) 4 (d) None of these

7. Let a and b be real numbers. Consider a 3×3 matrix A such that $A^2 = 5A + \alpha I$ and $A^4 = 17A + \beta I$, then 25β is equal to

(a) 3834 (b) -3834
(c) 2813 (d) 1784

8. Let matrix A of order 3 be such that $A^2 = 2A - I$, where I is an identity matrix of order 3. Then, $n \in N$ and $n \geq 2$, A^n is equal to

(a) $nA-(n-1)I$ (b) $nA-I$
(c) $2^{n-1}A-(n-1)I$ (d) $2^{n-1}A-I$

9. Let $A = \begin{bmatrix} 1 & 0 \\ 1/2 & 1 \end{bmatrix}$ if $A^n = \begin{bmatrix} 1 & 0 \\ 50 & 1 \end{bmatrix}$, then value of n

(a) 10 (b) 50 (c) 100 (d) 200

10. Let $A = [a_{ij}]$ be a 2×2 matrix, where

$$a_{ij} = \begin{cases} 2, & \text{if} \quad i = j \\ 1, & \text{if} \quad |i-j| = 1 \\ 0, & \text{otherwise} \end{cases} \text{ and } A^2 - \lambda A + 3I = 0,$$

then value of λ is

(a) 4 (b) 8
(c) 1 (d) 2

11. If $A = \begin{bmatrix} -1 & 3/2 \\ -1/2 & 1/2 \end{bmatrix}$, then A^3 is equal to

(a) $2I$ (b) I (c) $\frac{I}{4}$ (d) $\frac{I}{8}$

12. If $A = \begin{bmatrix} 1 & 0 \\ 1/2 & 1 \end{bmatrix}$, then A^{100} is equal to

(a) $\begin{bmatrix} 1 & 0 \\ 25 & 0 \end{bmatrix}$ (b) $\begin{bmatrix} 1 & 0 \\ 50 & 1 \end{bmatrix}$
(c) $\begin{bmatrix} 1 & 0 \\ (1/2)^{100} & 1 \end{bmatrix}$ (d) None of these

13. If the product of n matrices $\begin{bmatrix} 1 & 1 \\ 0 & 1 \end{bmatrix}\begin{bmatrix} 1 & 2 \\ 0 & 1 \end{bmatrix}\begin{bmatrix} 1 & 3 \\ 0 & 1 \end{bmatrix} \cdots \begin{bmatrix} 1 & n \\ 0 & 1 \end{bmatrix}$ is equal to the matrix $\begin{bmatrix} 1 & 378 \\ 0 & 1 \end{bmatrix}$, the value of n is equal to

(a) 26 (b) 27 (c) 377 (d) 378

14. If the value of $\prod_{k=1}^{50} \begin{bmatrix} 1 & 2k-1 \\ 0 & 1 \end{bmatrix}$ is equal to $\begin{bmatrix} 1 & y \\ 0 & 1 \end{bmatrix}$, then y is equal to

(a) 62500 (b) 2500
(c) 1250 (d) 12500

15. If $A = \begin{bmatrix} 1 & 2 \\ 2 & 3 \end{bmatrix}$ and $A^2 - \lambda A - I_2 = O$, then λ is equal to

(a) -4 (b) -2 (c) 2 (d) 4

Answer Key

1. (d)	2. (b)	3. (c)	4. (b)	5. (a)
6. (b)	7. (b)	8. (a)	9. (c)	10. (a)
11. (d)	12. (b)	13. (b)	14. (b)	15. (d)

For Detailed Solution

Milestone 2 Transpose, Singular and Non-Singular Matrices

• Transpose of a Matrix • Expansion of Determinant • Singular and Non-singular Matrices

7.6 Transpose of a Matrix

Let $A=[a_{ij}]_{m\times n}$ be any given matrix, then the matrix obtained by interchanging the rows and columns of A is called the transpose of A. Transpose of the matrix A is denoted by A' or A^T or A^t. In other words, if $A=[a_{ij}]_{m\times n}$, then $A'=[a_{ji}]_{n\times m}$.

e.g. If $A=\begin{bmatrix}2 & 3 & 4 & 5\\ -2 & -1 & 4 & 8\\ 7 & 5 & 3 & 1\end{bmatrix}_{3\times 4}$, then $A'=\begin{bmatrix}2 & -2 & 7\\ 3 & -1 & 5\\ 4 & 4 & 3\\ 5 & 8 & 1\end{bmatrix}_{4\times 3}$

Properties of Transpose Matrices

If A' and B' denote the transpose of A and B respectively, then

(i) $(A')'=A$

(ii) $(A\pm B)'=A'\pm B'$; A and B are conformable for matrix addition.

(iii) $(kA)'=kA'$; k is a scalar.

(iv) $(AB)'=B'A'$; A and B are conformable for matrix product AB.

In general, $(A_1A_2A_3\ldots A_{n-1}A_n)'=A'_n\ A'_{n-1}\cdots A'_3\ A'_2\ A'_1$ (reversal law for transpose).

Note $I'=I$, where I is an identity matrix.

Example 21. If $A=\begin{bmatrix}\cos\theta & -\sin\theta\\ \sin\theta & \cos\theta\end{bmatrix}$, then the values of θ satisfying the equation $A^T+A=I_2$ is

(a) $2n\pi\pm\dfrac{\pi}{3}$ (b) $n\pi+\dfrac{\pi}{6}$ (c) $2n\pi$ (d) $n\pi$

Sol. (a) Given, $A=\begin{bmatrix}\cos\theta & -\sin\theta\\ \sin\theta & \cos\theta\end{bmatrix}$; $A^T=\begin{bmatrix}\cos\theta & \sin\theta\\ -\sin\theta & \cos\theta\end{bmatrix}$

We have, $A^T+A=I_2$

$$\Rightarrow \begin{bmatrix}\cos\theta & \sin\theta\\ -\sin\theta & \cos\theta\end{bmatrix}+\begin{bmatrix}\cos\theta & -\sin\theta\\ \sin\theta & \cos\theta\end{bmatrix}=\begin{bmatrix}1 & 0\\ 0 & 1\end{bmatrix}$$

$$\Rightarrow \begin{bmatrix}2\cos\theta & 0\\ 0 & 2\cos\theta\end{bmatrix}=\begin{bmatrix}1 & 0\\ 0 & 1\end{bmatrix}$$

On comparing both sides, we get $2\cos\theta=1$

$$\Rightarrow \cos\theta=\frac{1}{2}=\cos\left(\frac{\pi}{3}\right) \Rightarrow \theta=2n\pi\pm\frac{\pi}{3}$$

JEE SCANNER

Example Similar to PYQ Asked in JEE Main 2023

Let $P=\begin{bmatrix}3 & 1\\ -1 & 3\end{bmatrix}$, $A=\begin{bmatrix}1 & 0\\ 1 & 1\end{bmatrix}$ and $Q=PAP^T$. Then, $a+b+c+d$ is

(a) 2004 (b) 2003
(c) 2007 (d) 2005

Sol. (b) Given, $A=\begin{bmatrix}1 & 0\\ 1 & 1\end{bmatrix}$ and $P=\begin{bmatrix}3 & 1\\ -1 & 3\end{bmatrix}$

$$\Rightarrow A^2=\begin{bmatrix}1 & 0\\ 2 & 1\end{bmatrix}\Rightarrow A^3=\begin{bmatrix}1 & 0\\ 3 & 1\end{bmatrix}$$

$$\therefore A^n=\begin{bmatrix}1 & 0\\ n & 1\end{bmatrix}$$

$$PP^T=\begin{bmatrix}3 & 1\\ -1 & 3\end{bmatrix}\begin{bmatrix}3 & -1\\ 1 & 3\end{bmatrix}=\begin{bmatrix}10 & 0\\ 0 & 10\end{bmatrix}=10I$$

Now, $10^{2001}\begin{bmatrix}a & b\\ c & d\end{bmatrix}=P^TQ^{2001}P$

$=P^T(PAP^T)(PAP^T)(PAP^T)\ldots(PAP^T)P$

$=10\,IA\,10\,IA\,10\,I\ \ldots.\ 10\,IA\,10\,I=10^{2001}\ A^{2001}$

$$\Rightarrow \begin{bmatrix}a & b\\ c & d\end{bmatrix}=A^{2001}=\begin{bmatrix}1 & 0\\ 2001 & 1\end{bmatrix}$$

$\therefore\ a=1, b=0, c=2001, d=1$

$\Rightarrow a+b+c+d=1+0+2001+1=2003$

Skill Builder

Let $P=\begin{bmatrix}\dfrac{\sqrt{8}}{3} & \dfrac{1}{3}\\ -\dfrac{1}{3} & \dfrac{\sqrt{8}}{3}\end{bmatrix}$, $A=\begin{bmatrix}1 & 1\\ 0 & 1\end{bmatrix}$ and $Q=PAP^T$.

If $P^TQ^{1993}P=\begin{bmatrix}a & b\\ c & d\end{bmatrix}$, then $2a+b-4c-d$ is

(a) 1993 (b) 1995 (c) 1994 (d) 1992

For Sol.

■ **For more practice** See Q.1 of Milestone Practice 7.2.

Example 22. Let $A = BB^T + CC^T$, where $B = \begin{bmatrix} \cos\theta \\ \sin\theta \end{bmatrix}, C = \begin{bmatrix} \sin\theta \\ -\cos\theta \end{bmatrix}$, $\theta \in R$, then A is

(a) $\begin{bmatrix} 0 & 0 \\ 0 & 0 \end{bmatrix}$ (b) $\begin{bmatrix} 0 & 1 \\ 1 & 0 \end{bmatrix}$

(c) $\begin{bmatrix} 1 & 0 \\ 0 & 1 \end{bmatrix}$ (d) $\begin{bmatrix} 0 & 0 \\ 0 & 1 \end{bmatrix}$

Sol. (c) $A = BB^T + CC^T$

$$= \begin{bmatrix} \cos\theta \\ \sin\theta \end{bmatrix} [\cos\theta \ \sin\theta] + \begin{bmatrix} \sin\theta \\ -\cos\theta \end{bmatrix} [\sin\theta \ \ -\cos\theta]$$

$$= \begin{bmatrix} \cos^2\theta & \cos\theta\sin\theta \\ \sin\theta\cos\theta & \sin^2\theta \end{bmatrix} + \begin{bmatrix} \sin^2\theta & -\sin\theta\cos\theta \\ -\sin\theta\cos\theta & \cos^2\theta \end{bmatrix}$$

$$= \begin{bmatrix} 1 & 0 \\ 0 & 1 \end{bmatrix}$$

Symmetric Matrix

A square matrix $A = [a_{ij}]_{n \times n}$ is said to be symmetric if $A' = A$ i.e. $a_{ij} = a_{ji}, \forall i, j$.

e.g. If $A = \begin{bmatrix} a & h & g \\ h & b & f \\ g & f & c \end{bmatrix}$, then $A' = \begin{bmatrix} a & h & g \\ h & b & f \\ g & f & c \end{bmatrix}$

Here, A is symmetric matrix as $A' = A$.

Skew-Symmetric Matrix

A square matrix $A = [a_{ij}]_{n \times n}$ is said to be skew-symmetric matrix, if $A' = -A$,

i.e. $a_{ij} = -a_{ji}, \forall i, j$. (the pair of conjugate elements are additive inverse of each other)

Now, if we put $i = j$, we have $a_{ii} = -a_{ii}$.

Therefore, $2a_{ii} = 0$ or $a_{ii} = 0, \forall i$'s.

This means that all the diagonal elements of a skew-symmetric matrix are zero, but not the converse.

e.g. If $A = \begin{bmatrix} 0 & h & g \\ -h & 0 & f \\ -g & -f & 0 \end{bmatrix}$, then

$$A' = \begin{bmatrix} 0 & -h & -g \\ h & 0 & -f \\ g & f & 0 \end{bmatrix} = -\begin{bmatrix} 0 & h & g \\ -h & 0 & f \\ -g & -f & 0 \end{bmatrix}$$

$$= -A$$

Here, A is skew-symmetric matrix as $A' = -A$.

JEE SCANNER

Example Similar to PYQ Asked in JEE Main 2023

Let A be a symmetric matrix such that $|A| = 4$ and $\begin{bmatrix} 1 & 2 \\ 3 & 4 \end{bmatrix} A = \begin{bmatrix} 2 & 1 \\ \alpha & \beta \end{bmatrix}$. If the sum of the diagonal elements of A is S, then $\frac{\alpha\beta}{S}$ is equal to

(a) $\frac{7}{25}$ (b) $\frac{18}{25}$ (c) $\frac{13}{25}$ (d) $\frac{11}{25}$

Sol. (b) Let A be a symmetric matrix i.e. $A = \begin{bmatrix} a & c \\ c & b \end{bmatrix}$

Such that $|A| = 4 \Rightarrow ab - c^2 = 4$

and $\begin{bmatrix} 1 & 2 \\ 3 & 4 \end{bmatrix} A = \begin{bmatrix} 2 & 1 \\ \alpha & \beta \end{bmatrix} \Rightarrow \begin{bmatrix} 1 & 2 \\ 3 & 4 \end{bmatrix} \begin{bmatrix} a & c \\ c & b \end{bmatrix} = \begin{bmatrix} 2 & 1 \\ \alpha & \beta \end{bmatrix}$

$\Rightarrow \begin{bmatrix} a + 2c & c + 2b \\ 3a + 4c & 3c + 4b \end{bmatrix} = \begin{bmatrix} 2 & 1 \\ \alpha & \beta \end{bmatrix}$

$\Rightarrow$ $a + 2c = 2, c + 2b = 1$

$3a + 4c = \alpha$ and $3c + 4b = \beta$

On solving $a + 2c = 2$ and $c + 2b = 1$, we get $a = 4b$

Now, $ab - c^2 = 4 \Rightarrow 4b \times b - c^2 = 4$

$\Rightarrow$ $4b^2 - c^2 = 4 \Rightarrow 4b^2 - (1 - 2b)^2 = 4$

$\Rightarrow 4b^2 - (1 + 4b^2 - 4b) = 4 \Rightarrow -1 + 4b = 4$

$\Rightarrow$ $4b = 5 \Rightarrow b = \frac{5}{4}$

and $c = 1 - 2b = 1 - 2\left(\frac{5}{4}\right) = 1 - \frac{5}{2} = \frac{-3}{2}$

and $a + 2c = 2 \Rightarrow a + 2\left(-\frac{3}{2}\right) = 2 \Rightarrow a = 5$

$\therefore$ $A = \begin{bmatrix} 5 & \frac{-3}{2} \\ \frac{-3}{2} & \frac{5}{4} \end{bmatrix}$

Given, $a + b = S \Rightarrow S = \frac{25}{4}$

Now, $\alpha = 3a + 4c = 3(5) + 4\left(-\frac{3}{2}\right) = 9$

and $\beta = 3c + 4b = 3\left(-\frac{3}{2}\right) + 4\left(\frac{5}{4}\right) = \frac{1}{2}$

$\therefore$ $\frac{\alpha\beta}{S} = 9 \times \frac{1}{2} \times \frac{4}{25} = \frac{18}{25}$

Skill Builder

Let A be a symmetric matrix such that $|A| = 3$ and $\begin{bmatrix} 1 & 3 \\ 3 & 2 \end{bmatrix} A = \begin{bmatrix} 3 & 1 \\ \alpha & \beta \end{bmatrix}$. If the sum of the diagonal elements of A is $2S$, then $\frac{\alpha\beta}{S}$ is

For Sol.

(a) -8 (b) -7 (c) -6 (d) -9

■ **For more practice** See Q.18 of Milestone Practice 7.2.

JEE Focus Points

Concept Inside Video

- Maximum number of distinct entries in any symmetric matrix of order n is $\frac{n(n+1)}{2}$.
- For any square matrix A with real number entries, then $A + A'$ is a symmetric matrix.
  Proof $(A + A')' = A' + (A')' = A' + A = A + A'$
- Trace of a skew-symmetric matrix is always 0.
- For any square matrix A with real number entries, then $A - A'$ is a skew-symmetric matrix.
  Proof $(A - A')' = A' - (A')' = A' - A = -(A - A')$
- Every square matrix can be uniquely expressed as the sum of a symmetric and a skew-symmetric matrix.
  i.e. If A is a square matrix, then we can write
  $$A = \frac{1}{2}(A + A') + \frac{1}{2}(A - A')$$

Properties of Symmetric and Skew-Symmetric Matrices

(i) If A be a square matrix, then AA' and $A'A$ are symmetric matrices.

(ii) All positive integral powers of a symmetric matrix are symmetric, because $(A^n)' = (A')^n$.

(iii) All positive odd integral powers of a skew-symmetric matrix are skew-symmetric and positive even integral powers of a skew-symmetric matrix are symmetric, because $(A^n)' = (A')^n$.

(iv) If A be a symmetric matrix and B be a square matrix of order that of A, then $-A, kA, A', A^{-1}, A^n$ and $B'AB$ are also symmetric matrices, where $n \in N$ and k is a scalar.

(v) If A be a skew-symmetric matrix, then

(a) A^{2n} is a symmetric matrix for $n \in N$.

(b) A^{2n+1} is a skew-symmetric matrix for $n \in N$.

(c) kA is a skew-symmetric matrix, where k is scalar.

(d) $B'AB$ is also skew-symmetric matrix, where B is a square matrix of order that of A.

(vi) If A and B are two symmetric matrices, then

(a) $A \pm B, AB + BA$ are symmetric matrices.

(b) $AB - BA$ is a skew-symmetric matrix

(c) AB is a symmetric matrix, iff $AB = BA$
(where A and B are square matrices of same order)

(vii) If A and B are two skew-symmetric matrices, then

(a) $A \pm B, AB - BA$ are skew-symmetric matrices.

(b) $AB + BA$ is a symmetric matrix.
(where A and B are square matrices of same order)

(viii) If A be a skew-symmetric matrix and C is a column matrix, then $C'AC$ is a zero matrix, where $C'AC$ is conformable.

Example 23. If M is 3×3 skew symmetric matrix, then find Tr(M).

Sol. For skew symmetric matrix all diagonal elements are zero.
Hence, $\text{Tr}(M) = 0$

Example 24. If A and B are symmetric matrices, then matrix ABA is

(a) symmetric matrix

(b) skew-symmetric matrix

(c) diagonal matrix

(d) scalar matrix

Sol. (a) We have, $(ABA)^T = A^T B^T A^T = ABA$
$[\because A^T = A, B^T = B]$

$\Rightarrow$ ABA symmetric matrix.

Example 25. Number of 3×3 real matrices $A = [a_{ij}]$ such that $a_{ij} + a_{ji} = 0, \forall\, i, j = 1, 2, 3$ and $|a_{ij}| \in \{0, 1, 2, 3, 4, 5, 6, 7, 8, 9\}$ is equal to

(a) 6856 (b) 6857

(c) 6858 (d) 6859

Sol. (d) Given matrix A is skew-symmetric matrix.
$\because$ Diagonal entries are zero. Other pair of corresponding entries each can be chosen 19 ways.
$\therefore$ Number of such matrices $= 19 \times 19 \times 19 = 6859$

Example 26. If the maximum number of distinct elements in a symmetric matrix of order n is 45, then the value of n is

(a) 9 (b) 10 (c) 15 (d) 16

Sol. (a) Maximum number of elements in a symmetric matrix,
$$\frac{n(n+1)}{2} = 45$$
$$\Rightarrow \quad n(n+1) = 90 \Rightarrow n = 9$$

Orthogonal Matrix

A square matrix A is said to be orthogonal matrix, iff $AA' = I$, where I is an identity matrix.

JEE Focus Points

- If $AA' = I$, then $A^{-1} = A$.
- If A and B are orthogonal, then AB is also orthogonal.
- If A is orthogonal, then A^{-1} and A' are also orthogonal.

Example 27. If matrix $\begin{bmatrix} 0 & 2b & c \\ a & b & -c \\ a & -b & c \end{bmatrix}$ is orthogonal matrix, then

(a) a^2, b^2, c^2 are in AP. (b) a^2, b^2, c^2 are in GP.
(c) b^2, c^2, a^2 are in AP. (d) b^2, c^2, a^2 are in GP.

Sol. (c) Let $A = \begin{bmatrix} 0 & 2b & c \\ a & b & -c \\ a & -b & c \end{bmatrix}$, then

$$A^T = \begin{bmatrix} 0 & a & a \\ 2b & b & -b \\ c & -c & c \end{bmatrix}$$

Since, A is orthogonal, then

$$AA^T = I$$

$$\Rightarrow \begin{bmatrix} 0 & 2b & c \\ a & b & -c \\ a & -b & c \end{bmatrix}\begin{bmatrix} 0 & a & a \\ 2b & b & -b \\ c & -c & c \end{bmatrix} = \begin{bmatrix} 1 & 0 & 0 \\ 0 & 1 & 0 \\ 0 & 0 & 1 \end{bmatrix}$$

Equating the corresponding elements

$$4b^2 + c^2 = 1, 2b^2 - c^2 = 0, a^2 + b^2 + c^2 = 1$$

After solving, we get

$$a^2 = \frac{1}{2}, b^2 = \frac{1}{6}, c^2 = \frac{1}{3}$$

Here, $a^2 + b^2 = \frac{1}{2} + \frac{1}{6}$

$$= \frac{3+1}{6} = \frac{4}{6} = \frac{2}{3} = 2c^2$$

$\Rightarrow a^2, c^2, b^2$ are in AP.

Determinant of Square Matrix

Let $A = [a_{ij}]_{n \times n}$ be a matrix. The determinant formed by the elements of A is said to be the determinant of matrix A. This is denoted by $|A|$.

7.7 Expansion of Determinant

(i) Expansion of Two Order

$$\begin{vmatrix} a_1 & b_1 \\ a_2 & b_2 \end{vmatrix} = \begin{vmatrix} a_1 & \\ & b_2 \end{vmatrix} - \begin{vmatrix} & b_1 \\ a_2 & \end{vmatrix} = a_1 b_2 - b_1 a_2$$

e.g. $$\begin{vmatrix} 5 & -4 \\ -3 & 2 \end{vmatrix} = \begin{vmatrix} 5 & \\ & 2 \end{vmatrix} - \begin{vmatrix} & -4 \\ -3 & \end{vmatrix} = 10 - 12 = -2$$

(ii) Expansion of Third Order

(a) *With respect to first row.*

$$\begin{vmatrix} a_1 \cdots & b_1 \cdots & c_1 \\ a_2 & b_2 & c_2 \\ a_3 & b_3 & c_3 \end{vmatrix} = a_1 \begin{vmatrix} b_2 & c_2 \\ b_3 & c_3 \end{vmatrix} - b_1 \begin{vmatrix} a_2 & c_2 \\ a_3 & c_3 \end{vmatrix} + c_1 \begin{vmatrix} a_2 & b_2 \\ a_3 & b_3 \end{vmatrix}$$

$$= a_1 (b_2 c_3 - b_3 c_2) - b_1 (a_2 c_3 - a_3 c_2) + c_1 (a_2 b_3 - a_3 b_2)$$

(b) *With respect to second column.*

$$\begin{vmatrix} a_1 & b_1 & c_1 \\ & \vdots & \\ a_2 & b_2 & c_2 \\ & \vdots & \\ a_3 & b_3 & c_3 \end{vmatrix} = -b_1 \begin{vmatrix} a_2 & c_2 \\ a_3 & c_3 \end{vmatrix} + b_2 \begin{vmatrix} a_1 & c_1 \\ a_3 & c_3 \end{vmatrix} - b_3 \begin{vmatrix} a_1 & c_1 \\ a_2 & c_2 \end{vmatrix}$$

$$= -b_1 (a_2 c_3 - a_3 c_2) + b_2 (a_1 c_3 - a_3 c_1) - b_3 (a_1 c_2 - a_2 c_1)$$

Example 28. The value of the determinant $\begin{vmatrix} 1 & 2 & 4 \\ 3 & 4 & 9 \\ 2 & -1 & 6 \end{vmatrix}$ is

(a) 11 (b) −11 (c) 6 (d) 0

Sol. (b) On expanding the determinant along the first row

$$\Delta_1 = 1\begin{vmatrix} 4 & 9 \\ -1 & 6 \end{vmatrix} - 2\begin{vmatrix} 3 & 9 \\ 2 & 6 \end{vmatrix} + 4\begin{vmatrix} 3 & 4 \\ 2 & -1 \end{vmatrix}$$

$$= 1(24 + 9) - 2(18 - 18) + 4(-3 - 8)$$

$$= 33 - 0 - 44 = -11$$

Example 29. If $\Delta = \begin{vmatrix} 1 & \sin\theta & 1 \\ -\sin\theta & 1 & \sin\theta \\ -1 & -\sin\theta & 1 \end{vmatrix}$, then

(a) $1 \le \Delta \le 2$ (b) $2 \le \Delta \le 4$
(c) $1 \le \Delta \le 5$ (d) $0 \le \Delta \le 4$

Sol. (b) Given, $\Delta = \begin{vmatrix} 1 & \sin\theta & 1 \\ -\sin\theta & 1 & \sin\theta \\ -1 & -\sin\theta & 1 \end{vmatrix}$

On expanding along first row, we get

$$\Delta = 1\begin{vmatrix} 1 & \sin\theta \\ -\sin\theta & 1 \end{vmatrix} - \sin\theta \begin{vmatrix} -\sin\theta & \sin\theta \\ -1 & 1 \end{vmatrix} + 1\begin{vmatrix} -\sin\theta & 1 \\ -1 & -\sin\theta \end{vmatrix}$$

$$= (1 + \sin^2\theta) - \sin\theta(-\sin\theta + \sin\theta) + (\sin^2\theta + 1)$$

$$= 2(1 + \sin^2\theta)$$

Again, $0 \le \sin^2\theta \le 1$

$\Rightarrow \quad 1 \le (1+\sin^2\theta) \le 1+1 \Rightarrow 2 \le 2(1+\sin^2\theta) \le 4$

$\therefore \quad 2 \le \Delta \le 4$

Properties of the Determinant of a Matrix

If A and B are square matrices of same order, then

(i) $|A|$ exists $\Leftrightarrow A$ is a square matrix.

(ii) $|A'| = |A|$

(iii) $|AB| = |A||B|$ and $|AB| = |BA|$

(iv) If A is skew-symmetric matrix of even order, then $|A|$ is a perfect square.

(v) $|kA| = k^n|A|$, where n is order of A and k is scalar.

(vi) $|A^n| = |A|^n$, where $n \in N$

(vii) If $A = \text{diag}(a_1, a_2, a_3, \ldots, a_n)$, then $|A| = a_1 \cdot a_2 \cdot a_3 \ldots a_n$

Example 30. If $A = \begin{bmatrix} a & b & c \\ b & c & a \\ c & a & b \end{bmatrix}$, $abc = 1$, $A^T A = I$, then find the value of $a^3 + b^3 + c^3$ is

(a) 2, −1 (b) 2, 4

(c) −2, 4 (d) 2, −4

Sol. (b) $\because \quad A^T A = I$

$\Rightarrow \quad |A^T A| = |I|$

$\Rightarrow \quad |A^T||A| = 1$

$\Rightarrow \quad |A||A| = 1 \quad [\because |A^T| = |A|]$

$\Rightarrow \quad |A| = \pm 1$

$\Rightarrow \quad \begin{vmatrix} a & b & c \\ b & c & a \\ c & a & b \end{vmatrix} = \pm 1$

$\Rightarrow \quad 3abc - (a^3 + b^3 + c^3) = \pm 1$

or $\quad 3 - (a^3 + b^3 + c^3) = \pm 1 \quad [\because abc = 1]$

or $\quad a^3 + b^3 + c^3 = 3 \pm 1 = 2$ or 4

Example 31. If M is a square matrix of order 3 satisfying $M^T M = 4I$ and $|M| = 8$, then the value of $|M - 2I|$ is equal to

(a) 2 (b) 4 (c) 16 (d) 0

Sol. (d) $|M - 2I| = \left|M - \frac{1}{2}M^T M\right| = \frac{1}{2^3}|2M - M^T M|$

$= \frac{1}{8}|2I - M^T||M| = |(2I)^T - M^T|$

$= |2I - M| = (-1)^3|M - 2I| = -|M - 2I|$

$= |M - 2I| = 0 \Rightarrow |M - 2I| = 0$

7.8 Singular and Non-Singular Matrices

A square matrix A is said to be a singular, if $|A| = 0$ and a square matrix A is said to be non-singular, if $|A| \ne 0$.

e.g.

(i) $A = \begin{bmatrix} 1 & 2 & 3 \\ -1 & 0 & 2 \\ 2 & 4 & 6 \end{bmatrix}$ is a singular matrix. Since, $|A| = 0$.

(ii) $A = \begin{bmatrix} 2 & 3 \\ 4 & 5 \end{bmatrix}$ is a non-singular matrix.

Since, $|A| = 10 - 12$

$= -2 \ne 0$

Example 32. If $\omega \ne 1$ is a complex cube root of unity, then prove that

$$\begin{bmatrix} 1+2\omega^{2017}+\omega^{2018} & \omega^{2018} & 1 \\ 1 & 1+\omega^{2018}+2\omega^{2017} & \omega^{2017} \\ \omega^{2017} & \omega^{2018} & 2+\omega^{2017}+2\omega^{2018} \end{bmatrix}$$ is singular.

Sol. Let $A = \begin{bmatrix} 1+2\omega^{2017}+\omega^{2018} & \omega^{2018} & 1 \\ 1 & 1+\omega^{2018}+2\omega^{2017} & \omega^{2017} \\ \omega^{2017} & \omega^{2018} & 2+\omega^{2017}+2\omega^{2018} \end{bmatrix}$

$\because \quad \omega^3 = 1$

$\Rightarrow \quad \omega^{2017} = \omega$

and $\quad \omega^{2018} = \omega^2$, then

$$A = \begin{bmatrix} 1+2\omega+\omega^2 & \omega^2 & 1 \\ 1 & 1+\omega^2+2\omega & \omega \\ \omega & \omega^2 & 2+\omega+2\omega^2 \end{bmatrix}$$

$$= \begin{bmatrix} \omega & \omega^2 & 1 \\ 1 & \omega & \omega \\ \omega & \omega^2 & -\omega \end{bmatrix} \quad [\because 1+\omega+\omega^2 = 0]$$

Now, $|A| = \begin{vmatrix} \omega & \omega^2 & 1 \\ 1 & \omega & \omega \\ \omega & \omega^2 & -\omega \end{vmatrix} = \omega \begin{vmatrix} \omega & \omega & 1 \\ 1 & 1 & \omega \\ \omega & \omega & -\omega \end{vmatrix} = 0$

$[\because C_1 = C_2]$

Thus, $|A| = 0$.

Hence, A is singular matrix.

Example 33. Number of the real values of x for which the matrix $\begin{bmatrix} x+1 & 3 & 5 \\ 1 & x+3 & 5 \\ 1 & 3 & x+5 \end{bmatrix}$ is non-singular, is

(a) 0 (b) 2 (c) 4 (d) infinite

Sol. (d) Let $A = \begin{bmatrix} x+1 & 3 & 5 \\ 1 & x+3 & 5 \\ 1 & 3 & x+5 \end{bmatrix}$

$$\therefore \quad |A| = \begin{vmatrix} x+1 & 3 & 5 \\ 1 & x+3 & 5 \\ 1 & 3 & x+5 \end{vmatrix}$$

On applying $C_1 \to C_1 + C_2 + C_3$, then

$$|A| = \begin{vmatrix} x+9 & 3 & 5 \\ x+9 & x+3 & 5 \\ x+9 & 3 & x+5 \end{vmatrix}$$

On applying $R_2 \to R_2 - R_1$ and $R_3 \to R_3 - R_1$, then

$$|A| = \begin{vmatrix} x+9 & 3 & 5 \\ 0 & x & 0 \\ 0 & 0 & x \end{vmatrix} = x^2(x+9)$$

$\because$ A is non-singular.

$$\therefore \quad |A| \neq 0 \Rightarrow x^2(x+9) \neq 0$$

$$\therefore \quad x \neq 0, -9$$

Hence, $x \in R - \{0, -9\}$.

Example 34. Let $M = \begin{bmatrix} x & 2x & 3x \\ f(x) & g(x) & h(x) \\ 0 & 1 & 1 \end{bmatrix}$ be a singular matrix. If $f(x) = \ln(e^x + 1)$ and $g(x) = \ln(e^x - 1)$, then the value of $h'(\ln 3)$ is equal to

(a) $\frac{9}{8}$ (b) $\frac{9}{4}$

(c) 3 (d) 6

Sol. (b) Given, $M = \begin{bmatrix} x & 2x & 3x \\ f(x) & g(x) & h(x) \\ 0 & 1 & 1 \end{bmatrix}$

On applying $C_1 \to C_1 + C_2$, we get

$$M = \begin{bmatrix} 3x & 2x & 3x \\ f(x)+g(x) & g(x) & h(x) \\ 1 & 1 & 1 \end{bmatrix}$$

$$\Rightarrow \quad |M| = \begin{vmatrix} 3x & 2x & 3x \\ f(x)+g(x) & g(x) & h(x) \\ 1 & 1 & 1 \end{vmatrix} = 0$$

$$\Rightarrow \quad h(x) = f(x) + g(x)$$

$$\Rightarrow \quad h'(x) = f'(x) + g'(x) = \frac{e^x}{e^x+1} + \frac{e^x}{e^x-1}$$

$$h'(\ln 3) = \frac{3}{4} + \frac{3}{2} = \frac{9}{4}$$

Milestone Practice 7.2

1. Let $P=\begin{bmatrix}4 & 3\\ -3 & 4\end{bmatrix}$, $A=\begin{bmatrix}1 & 0\\ 1 & 1\end{bmatrix}$ and $Q=PAP^T$. If $P^TQ^{1003}P=5^{2006}\begin{bmatrix}a & b\\ c & d\end{bmatrix}$, then $2a+b+c-2d$ is equal to

(a) 2006 (b) 1003 (c) 1004 (d) 2004

2. If A and B are symmetric matrices, then ABA is

(a) symmetric matrix (b) skew-symmetric matrix
(c) diagonal matrix (d) scalar matrix

3. If A is a skew-symmetric matrix and n is odd positive integer, then A^n is

(a) a skew-symmetric matrix. (b) a symmetric matrix.
(c) a diagonal matrix. (d) None of these.

4. If A is symmetric as well as skew-symmetric matrix, then A is

(a) diagonal matrix (b) null matrix
(c) triangular matrix (d) None of these

5. If A is square matrix order 3, then $|(A-A')^{2015}|$ is

(a) $|A|$ (b) $|A'|$ (c) 0 (d) A

6. The maximum number of different elements required to form a symmetric matrix of order 6 is

(a) 15 (b) 17 (c) 19 (d) 21

7. If A and B are square matrices of order 3×3 such that A is an orthogonal matrix and B is a skew-symmetric matrix, then which of the following statement is true?

(a) $|AB|=1$ (b) $|AB|=0$ (c) $|AB|=-1$ (d) $|AB|=2$

8. If A is a 3×3 matrix and $\det(3A)=k\{\det(A)\}$, k is equal to

(a) 9 (b) 6 (c) 1 (d) 27

9. If A is non-singular matrix satisfying $A=AB-BA$, then which one of the following holds true, where $\det(M)=|M|$.

(a) $|B|=0$ (b) $B=0$
(c) $|A|=1$ (d) $|B+I|=|B-I|$

10. If A is a square matrix such that $A^2=A$, then $\det(A)$ is equal to

(a) 0 or 1 (b) -2 or 2 (c) -3 or 3 (d) 1 or -1

11. Let $A=\begin{bmatrix}\beta & -1\\ 1 & 2\beta\end{bmatrix}$ and $\det(A^4)=16$, then the product of all possible real values of β equals

(a) $\frac{1}{2}$ (b) $-\frac{1}{2}$ (c) 0 (d) 2

12. If $A_i=\begin{bmatrix}2^{-i} & 3^{-i}\\ 3^{-i} & 2^{-i}\end{bmatrix}$, then $\sum_{i=1}^{\infty}\det(A_i)$ is equal to

(a) $\frac{3}{4}$ (b) $\frac{5}{24}$ (c) $\frac{5}{4}$ (d) $\frac{7}{144}$

13. If $AB=A$ and $BA=B$, then

(a) $B=I$ (b) $A=I$ (c) $A^2=-A$ (d) $B^2=B$

14. The values of x for which the given matrix $\begin{bmatrix}-x & x & 2\\ 2 & x & -x\\ x & -2 & -x\end{bmatrix}$ will be non-singular are

(a) $-2\le x\le 2$ (b) for all x other than 2 and -2
(c) $x\ge 2$ (d) $x\le -2$

15. Let $A=[a_{ij}]$ be 3×3 order matrix and $B=[b_{ij}]$ be 3×3 order matrix such that b_{ij} is the sum of elements of ith row of A except a_{ij}. If $\det(A)=4$, then the value of $\det(B)$ is equal to

(a) 2 (b) 4 (c) 6 (d) 8

16. Let matrix $M(x)=\begin{bmatrix}0 & x-a & x-b\\ x+a & 0 & x-c\\ x+b & x+c & 0\end{bmatrix}$, then matrix $M(0)\cdot(M(0))^T$, $(a, b, c\ne 0)$ is

(a) Null matrix (b) Skew-symmetric matrix
(c) Orthogonal matrix (d) Symmetric matrix

17. If A is skew-symmetrix matrix of order 3 and X be another matrix of same order, then $|XA+AX^T|$ is equal to, where $|P|$ denotes $\det(P)$ is

(a) $|X+X^T|$ (b) $|A+X|$ (c) $|A-X|$ (d) zero

18. Let A be a symmetric matrix such that $|A|=2$ and $\begin{bmatrix}3 & 1\\ 4 & 5\end{bmatrix}A=\begin{bmatrix}1 & 3\\ \alpha & \beta\end{bmatrix}$. If the sum of the diagonal elements of A is S, $\frac{\alpha^2\beta}{S}=\frac{m}{n}$, then find $m+n$.

Answer Key

1. (b)	2. (a)	3. (a)	4. (b)	5. (c)
6. (d)	7. (b)	8. (d)	9. (d)	10. (a)
11. (b)	12. (b)	13. (d)	14. (b)	15. (d)
16. (d)	17. (d)	18. (81)		

For Detailed Solution

Milestone 3 Adjoint and Inverse of a Matrix

• Minors and Cofactors • Adjoint of a Matrix • Inverse of a Matrix (Reciprocal Matrix) • Matrix Polynomial

7.9 Minors and Cofactors

Let $$\Delta = \begin{vmatrix} a_{11} & a_{12} & a_{13} & \cdots & a_{1n} \\ a_{21} & a_{22} & a_{23} & \cdots & a_{2n} \\ a_{31} & a_{32} & a_{33} & \cdots & a_{3n} \\ \cdots & \cdots & \cdots & \cdots & \cdots \\ a_{n1} & a_{n2} & a_{n3} & \cdots & a_{nn} \end{vmatrix}$$

be a determinant of order n, $n \geq 2$, then the determinant of order $n-1$ obtained from the determinant Δ after deleting the ith row and jth column is called the **minor of the element a_{ij}** and it is usually denoted by M_{ij}, where $i = 1, 2, 3, \ldots, n$ and $j = 1, 2, 3, \ldots, n$.

If M_{ij} is the minor of the element a_{ij} in the determinant Δ, then $(-1)^{i+j} M_{ij}$ is called the **cofactor of the element a_{ij}**. It is usually denoted by C_{ij}.

Thus, $$C_{ij} = (-1)^{i+j} M_{ij}$$

$$= \begin{cases} M_{ij}, & \text{if } i+j \text{ is an even integer} \\ -M_{ij}, & \text{if } i+j \text{ is an odd integer} \end{cases}$$

Example 35. Find the determinants of minors and cofactors of the determinant $\begin{vmatrix} 2 & 3 & 4 \\ 7 & 2 & -5 \\ 8 & -1 & 3 \end{vmatrix}$.

Sol. Here, $M_{11} = \begin{vmatrix} 2 & -5 \\ -1 & 3 \end{vmatrix} = 6 - 5 = 1$

[delete 1st row and 1st column]

$\therefore \quad C_{11} = (-1)^{1+1} M_{11} = M_{11} = 1$

$M_{12} = \begin{vmatrix} 7 & -5 \\ 8 & 3 \end{vmatrix} = 21 + 40 = 61$

[delete 1st row and 2nd column]

$\therefore \quad C_{12} = (-1)^{1+2} M_{12} = -M_{12} = -61$

$M_{13} = \begin{vmatrix} 7 & 2 \\ 8 & -1 \end{vmatrix} = -7 - 16 = -23$

[delete 1st row and 3rd column]

$\therefore \quad C_{13} = (-1)^{1+3} M_{13} = M_{13} = -23$

$M_{21} = \begin{vmatrix} 3 & 4 \\ -1 & 3 \end{vmatrix}$ [delete 2nd row and 1st column]

$= 9 + 4 = 13$

$\therefore \quad C_{21} = (-1)^{2+1} M_{21} = -M_{21} = -13$

$M_{22} = \begin{vmatrix} 2 & 4 \\ 8 & 3 \end{vmatrix}$ [delete 2nd row and 2nd column]

$= 6 - 32 = -26$

$\therefore \quad C_{22} = (-1)^{2+2} M_{22} = M_{22} = -26$

$M_{23} = \begin{vmatrix} 2 & 3 \\ 8 & -1 \end{vmatrix}$ [delete 2nd row and 3rd column]

$= -2 - 24 = -26$

$\therefore \quad C_{23} = (-1)^{2+3} M_{23} = -M_{23} = 26$

$M_{31} = \begin{vmatrix} 3 & 4 \\ 2 & -5 \end{vmatrix}$ [delete 3rd row and 1st column]

$= -15 - 8 = -23$

$\therefore \quad C_{31} = (-1)^{3+1} M_{31} = M_{31} = -23$

$M_{32} = \begin{vmatrix} 2 & 4 \\ 7 & -5 \end{vmatrix}$ [delete 3rd row and 2nd column]

$= -10 - 28 = -38$

$\therefore \quad C_{32} = (-1)^{3+2} M_{32} = -M_{32} = 38$

and $M_{33} = \begin{vmatrix} 2 & 3 \\ 7 & 2 \end{vmatrix} = 4 - 21 = -17$

[delete 3rd row and 3rd column]

$\therefore \quad C_{33} = (-1)^{3+3} M_{33} = M_{33} = -17$

Hence, the determinants of minors and cofactors are

$$M = \begin{vmatrix} 1 & 61 & -23 \\ 13 & -26 & -26 \\ -23 & -38 & -17 \end{vmatrix} \text{ and } C = \begin{vmatrix} 1 & -61 & -23 \\ -13 & -26 & 26 \\ -23 & 38 & -17 \end{vmatrix},$$

respectively.

JEE Focus Points

Concept Inside Video

- The sum of products of the elements of any row or column with their corresponding cofactors is equal to the value of the determinant.

i.e. $\Delta = a_{11}C_{11} + a_{12}C_{12} + a_{13}C_{13}$
$= a_{11}C_{11} + a_{21}C_{21} + a_{31}C_{31}$
$= a_{21}C_{21} + a_{22}C_{22} + a_{23}C_{23} = a_{12}C_{12} + a_{22}C_{22} + a_{32}C_{32}$
$= a_{31}C_{31} + a_{32}C_{32} + a_{33}C_{33} = a_{13}C_{13} + a_{23}C_{23} + a_{33}C_{33}$

Now, value of n order determinant

$$\Delta = \begin{vmatrix} a_{11} & a_{12} & a_{13} & \cdots & \cdots & a_{1n} \\ a_{21} & a_{22} & a_{23} & \cdots & \cdots & a_{2n} \\ a_{31} & a_{32} & a_{33} & \cdots & \cdots & a_{3n} \\ \cdots & \cdots & \cdots & \cdots & \cdots & \cdots \\ \cdots & \cdots & \cdots & \cdots & \cdots & \cdots \\ a_{n1} & a_{n2} & a_{n3} & \cdots & \cdots & a_{nn} \end{vmatrix}$$

$= a_{11}C_{11} + a_{12}C_{12} + a_{13}C_{13} + \ldots + a_{1n}C_{1n}$

(when expanded along first row)

- The sum of the product of element of any row (or column) with corresponding cofactors of another row (or column) is equal to zero.

i.e. $a_{11}C_{21} + a_{12}C_{22} + a_{13}C_{23} = 0,$
$a_{11}C_{13} + a_{21}C_{23} + a_{31}C_{33} = 0$, etc.

- If the value of a n order determinant is Δ, then the value of the determinant formed by the cofactors of corresponding elements of the given determinant is given by

$$\Delta^c = \Delta^{n-1}$$

i.e., in case of second order determinant

$$\Delta^c = \Delta$$

and third order determinant $\Delta^c = \Delta^2$.

7.10 Adjoint of a Matrix

Let $A = [a_{ij}]$ be a square matrix of order n and let C_{ij} be cofactor of a_{ij} in A. Then, the transpose of the matrix of cofactors of elements of A is called the adjoint of A and is denoted by adj (A).

Thus, $\text{adj}(A) = [C_{ij}]'$

$\Rightarrow \quad (\text{adj } A)_{ij} = C_{ji} = \text{Cofactor of } a_{ji} \text{ in } A$

i.e. if $\quad A = \begin{bmatrix} a_{11} & a_{12} & a_{13} \\ a_{21} & a_{22} & a_{23} \\ a_{31} & a_{32} & a_{33} \end{bmatrix}$, then

$$\text{adj } A = \begin{bmatrix} C_{11} & C_{12} & C_{13} \\ C_{21} & C_{22} & C_{23} \\ C_{31} & C_{32} & C_{33} \end{bmatrix}' = \begin{bmatrix} C_{11} & C_{21} & C_{31} \\ C_{12} & C_{22} & C_{32} \\ C_{13} & C_{23} & C_{33} \end{bmatrix},$$

where C_{ij} denotes the cofactor of a_{ij} in A.

Example 36. Find the adjoint of matrix $A = \begin{bmatrix} 2 & 3 \\ 1 & 4 \end{bmatrix}$.

Sol. Shortcut method :

$$\text{Adj } A = \begin{bmatrix} 4 & -3 \\ -1 & 2 \end{bmatrix}$$

[for 2×2 matrix interchange diagonal elements and change sign of other diagonal]

Example 37. Find the adjoint of the matrix

$$A = \begin{bmatrix} 1 & 2 & 3 \\ 0 & 5 & 0 \\ 2 & 4 & 3 \end{bmatrix}.$$

Sol. If C be the matrix of cofactors of the element in $|A|$, then

$$C = \begin{bmatrix} C_{11} & C_{12} & C_{13} \\ C_{21} & C_{22} & C_{23} \\ C_{31} & C_{32} & C_{33} \end{bmatrix}$$

$$= \begin{bmatrix} \begin{vmatrix} 5 & 0 \\ 4 & 3 \end{vmatrix} & -\begin{vmatrix} 0 & 0 \\ 2 & 3 \end{vmatrix} & \begin{vmatrix} 0 & 5 \\ 2 & 4 \end{vmatrix} \\ -\begin{vmatrix} 2 & 3 \\ 4 & 3 \end{vmatrix} & \begin{vmatrix} 1 & 3 \\ 2 & 3 \end{vmatrix} & -\begin{vmatrix} 1 & 2 \\ 2 & 4 \end{vmatrix} \\ \begin{vmatrix} 2 & 3 \\ 5 & 0 \end{vmatrix} & -\begin{vmatrix} 1 & 3 \\ 0 & 0 \end{vmatrix} & \begin{vmatrix} 1 & 2 \\ 0 & 5 \end{vmatrix} \end{bmatrix} = \begin{bmatrix} 15 & 0 & -10 \\ 6 & -3 & 0 \\ -15 & 0 & 5 \end{bmatrix}$$

$$\Rightarrow \quad \text{adj } A = C' = \begin{bmatrix} 15 & 6 & -15 \\ 0 & -3 & 0 \\ -10 & 0 & 5 \end{bmatrix}$$

Properties of Adjoint Matrix

Property 1 If A be a square matrix order n, then

$$A(\text{adj } A) = (\text{adj } A)A = |A| I_n$$

i.e. the product of a matrix and its adjoint is commutative.

Deductions of Property 1

Deduction 1 If A be a square singular matrix of order n, then $\quad A(\text{adj} A) = (\text{adj} A)\, A = O \quad$ [null matrix]

Since, for singular matrix, $|A| = 0$.

Deduction 2 If A be a square non-singular matrix of order n, then $\quad |\text{adj } A| = |A|^{n-1}$

Since, for non-singular matrix, $|A| \neq 0$.

Proof $\because \quad A(\text{adj } A) = |A| I_n$

On taking determinant both sides, then

$$|A(\text{adj } A)| = ||A| I_n|$$

$\Rightarrow \quad |A||\text{adj } A| = |A|^n |I_n| = |A|^n \quad [\because |I_n| = 1]$

$\Rightarrow \quad |\text{adj } A| = |A|^{n-1} \quad [\because |A| \neq 0]$

$$\text{adj}(0) = 0, \ \text{adj}(I) = I$$

Property 2 If A and B are square matrices of order n, then

$$\text{adj}(AB) = (\text{adj } B)(\text{adj } A)$$

Deduction $\text{adj}(M^2) = (\text{adj } M)^2$

In general, $\text{adj}A^m = (\text{adj}A)^m$

Property 3 If A is a square matrix of order n, then

$$(\text{adj } A)' = \text{adj } A'$$

Property 4 If A be a square non-singular matrix of order n, then $\text{adj}(\text{adj}A) = |A|^{n-2} A$

Proof $\because$ $A(\text{adj } A) = |A| I_n$ ...(i)

Replace A by adj A, then

$$(\text{adj } A)(\text{adj}(\text{adj } A)) = |\text{adj } A| I_n$$
$$= |A|^{n-1} I_n \quad [\because |\text{adj } A| = |A|^{n-1}]$$
$$= I_n |A|^{n-1}$$

Pre-multiplying both sides by matrix A, then

$$A(\text{adj } A)(\text{adj}(\text{adj } A)) = AI_n |A|^{n-1} = A|A|^{n-1}$$

$\Rightarrow$ $|A| I_n(\text{adj}(\text{adj}A)) = A|A|^{n-1}$

$\Rightarrow$ $(\text{adj}(\text{adj } A)) = A|A|^{n-2}$

or $\text{adj}(\text{adj } A) = |A|^{n-2} A$

Property 5 If A be a square non-singular matrix of order n, then

$$|\text{adj}(\text{adj } A)| = |A|^{(n-1)^2}$$

Proof $\because$ $\text{adj}(\text{adj } A) = |A|^{n-2} A$

On taking determinant both sides, then

$$|\text{adj}(\text{adj } A)| = ||A|^{n-2} A|$$
$$= |A|^{n(n-2)} |A| \quad [\because |kA| = k^n |A|]$$
$$= |A|^{n^2-2n+1} = |A|^{(n-1)^2}$$

JEE SPIKE

In general, $|\underbrace{\text{adj}(\text{adj}(\text{adj} \dots (\text{adj } A)))}_{\text{adj } m \text{ times}}| = |A|^{(n-1)^m}$

Property 6 If A be a square matrix of order n and k is a scalar, then

$$\text{adj}(kA) = k^{n-1} \cdot (\text{adj } A)$$

Proof $\because$ $A(\text{adj } A) = |A| I_n$ ...(i)

Replace A by kA, then

$$kA(\text{adj}(kA)) = |kA| I_n = k^n |A| I_n$$

$\Rightarrow$ $A(\text{adj}(kA)) = k^{n-1}|A| I_n$

$$= k^{n-1} A(\text{adj } A) \quad \text{[from Eq. (i)]}$$

Hence, $\text{adj}(kA) = k^{n-1}(\text{adj } A)$

Property 7 Adjoint of a diagonal matrix is a diagonal matrix.

i.e. If $A = \begin{bmatrix} a & 0 & 0 \\ 0 & b & 0 \\ 0 & 0 & c \end{bmatrix}$, then $\text{adj } A = \begin{bmatrix} bc & 0 & 0 \\ 0 & ca & 0 \\ 0 & 0 & ab \end{bmatrix}$

Note $\text{adj}(I_n) = I_n$.

Example 38. If $A = \begin{bmatrix} -1 & 1 & 1 \\ 1 & -1 & 1 \\ 1 & 1 & -1 \end{bmatrix}$, then find the values of

(i) $|A||\text{adj } A|$ (ii) $|\text{adj}(\text{adj}(\text{adj } A))|$

(iii) $|\text{adj}(3A)|$ (iv) $\text{adj}(\text{adj } A)$

Sol. $\because$ $A = \begin{bmatrix} -1 & 1 & 1 \\ 1 & -1 & 1 \\ 1 & 1 & -1 \end{bmatrix}$

$\therefore |A| = (-1)(1-1) - (1)(-1-1) + (1)(1+1) = 4 \neq 0$

$\Rightarrow$ A is non-singular.

(i) $|A||\text{adj } A| = |A||A|^2$ $[\because n = 3]$

$$= |A|^3 = 4^3 = 64$$

(ii) $|\text{adj}(\text{adj}(\text{adj } A))| = |A|^{(3-1)^3} = |A|^8 = 4^8 = 2^{16}$

(iii) $|\text{adj}(3A)| = |3^2 \text{ adj } A| = (3^2)^3 |\text{adj } A|$

$$= 3^6 |A|^2 = 729 \times 4^2 = 11664$$

(iv) $\text{adj}(\text{adj}A) = |A|^2 A = 16A$

Example 39. Let $A = [a_{ij}]_{3 \times 3}$ be such that $a_{ij} = \begin{cases} 3, \text{ when } i = j \\ 0, \ i \neq j \end{cases}$, then $\left\{ \dfrac{\det(\text{adj}(\text{adj}A))}{5} \right\}$ is equal to

(where $\{\cdot\}$ denotes fractional part)

(a) $\dfrac{2}{5}$ (b) $\dfrac{1}{5}$

(c) $\dfrac{2}{3}$ (d) $\dfrac{1}{3}$

Sol. (b) $A = \begin{bmatrix} 3 & 0 & 0 \\ 0 & 3 & 0 \\ 0 & 0 & 3 \end{bmatrix}$

Now, $|\text{adj}(\text{adj } A)| = (|A|^2)^2 = |A|^4 = (27)^4$

Now, $\left\{ \dfrac{(27)^4}{5} \right\} = \left\{ \dfrac{(25+2)^4}{5} \right\} = \dfrac{1}{5}$

Example 40. Let M be the square matrix of order 3, if $|M| = 2$, then the value of $|\text{adj } M^3|$ is

(a) 2^3 (b) 2^6 (c) 0 (d) 2^9

Sol. (b) $|\text{adj } M^3| = |M^3|^2$ [from property $|\text{adj } A| = |A|^{n-1}$]

$$= |M|^6 = 2^6$$

Example 41. If the adjoint of 3×3 matrix M is $\begin{bmatrix} 1 & 4 & 4 \\ 2 & 1 & 7 \\ 1 & 1 & 3 \end{bmatrix}$, then possible value of det (M) is

(a) ± 2 (b) ± 1 (c) ± 3 (d) ± 5

Sol. (a) $|\text{adj } M| = |M|^2$ [$\because$ order of M is 3×3]

$$|M|^2 = \begin{vmatrix} 1 & 4 & 4 \\ 2 & 1 & 7 \\ 1 & 1 & 3 \end{vmatrix}$$

$$|M|^2 = 1(3-7) - 4(6-7) + 4(2-1)$$

$$= -4 + 4 + 4 = 4$$

$\therefore$ $|M| = \pm 2$

Example 42. The value of k ($k \in R$) such that det (adj (adj$A$)) $= 16$, where $A = \begin{bmatrix} k & 1 & 2 \\ 0 & -1 & 1 \\ 4 & 1 & 1 \end{bmatrix}$ is equal to

(a) 5, 7 (b) 2, 7

(c) 5, 2 (d) 5, 3

Sol. (a) $|\text{adj}(\text{adj } A)| = |A|^{2^2} = |A|^4 = 16$

$\Rightarrow$ $|A| = \pm 2$

Now, $|A| = k(-1-1) - 1(0-4) + 2(0+4)$

$= -2k + 4 + 8 = 12 - 2k$

$\Rightarrow$ $12 - 2k = \pm 2$

$\therefore$ $2k = 12 \pm 2 = 14, 10 \Rightarrow k = 7, 5$

7.11 Inverse of a Matrix (Reciprocal Matrix)

A square matrix A (non-singular) of order n is said to be invertible, if there exists a square matrix B of the same order such that $AB = I_n = BA$,

then B is called the inverse (reciprocal) of A and is denoted by A^{-1}. Thus, $A^{-1} = B \Leftrightarrow AB = I_n = BA$

We have, $A(\text{adj } A) = |A| I_n$

$\Rightarrow$ $A^{-1} A(\text{adj } A) = A^{-1} I_n |A|$

$\Rightarrow$ $I_n(\text{adj } A) = A^{-1} |A| I_n$

$\therefore$ $A^{-1} = \dfrac{\text{adj } A}{|A|}$; provided $|A| \neq 0$

JEE SPIKE

The necessary and sufficient condition for a square matrix A to be invertible is that $|A| \neq 0$.

Properties of Inverse of a Matrix

Property 1 (Uniqueness of inverse) Every invertible matrix possesses a unique inverse.

Proof Let A be an invertible matrix of order $n \times n$. Let B and C be two inverses of A.

Then, $AB = BA = I_n$ ...(i)

and $AC = CA = I_n$ ...(ii)

Now, $AB = I_n$

$\Rightarrow$ $C(AB) = CI_n$ [pre-multiplying by C]

$\Rightarrow$ $(CA)B = CI_n$ [by associativity]

$\Rightarrow$ $I_n B = CI_n$ [$\because CA = I_n$ by Eq. (ii)]

$\Rightarrow$ $B = C$

Hence, an invertible matrix possesses a unique inverse.

Property 2 (Reversal law) If A and B are invertible matrices of order $n \times n$, then AB is invertible and $(AB)^{-1} = B^{-1}A^{-1}$.

Proof It is given that A and B are invertible matrices.

$|A| \neq 0$ and $|B| \neq 0 \Rightarrow |A||B| \neq 0$

$\Rightarrow$ $|AB| \neq 0$

Hence, AB is an invertible matrix.

Now, $(AB)(B^{-1}A^{-1}) = A(BB^{-1})A^{-1}$ [by associativity]

$= (AI_n)A^{-1}$ [$\because BB^{-1} = I_n$]

$= AA^{-1}$ [$\because AI_n = A$]

$= I_n$ [$\because AA^{-1} = I_n$]

Also, $(B^{-1}A^{-1})(AB) = B^{-1}(A^{-1}A)B$ [by associativity]

$= B^{-1}(I_n B)$ [$\because A^{-1}A = I_n$]

$= B^{-1}B$ [$\because I_n B = B$]

$= I_n$ [$\because B^{-1}B = I_n$]

Thus, $(AB)(B^{-1}A^{-1}) = I_n = (B^{-1}A^{-1})(AB)$

Hence, $(AB)^{-1} = B^{-1}A^{-1}$

Property 3 Let A be an invertible matrix of order n, then A' is also invertible and $(A')^{-1} = (A^{-1})'$.

Proof $\because$ A is invertible matrix

$\therefore$ $|A| \neq 0 \Rightarrow |A'| \neq 0$ [$\because |A| = |A'|$]

Hence, A^{-1} is also invertible.

Now, $AA^{-1} = I_n = A^{-1}A$

$\Rightarrow$ $(AA^{-1})' = (I_n)' = (A^{-1}A)'$

$\Rightarrow$ $(A^{-1})'A' = I_n = A'(A^{-1})'$

[by reversal law for transpose]

$\Rightarrow$ $(A')^{-1} = (A^{-1})'$ [by definition of inverse]

Property 4 Let A be an invertible matrix of order n and $k \in N$, then

$$(A^k)^{-1} = (A^{-1})^k = A^{-k}$$

Proof We have,

$$(A^k)^{-1} = (\underbrace{A \times A \times A \times \ldots \times A}_{\text{repeat } k \text{ times}})^{-1}$$

$$= \underbrace{A^{-1} \times A^{-1} \times A^{-1} \times \ldots \times A^{-1}}_{\text{repeat } k \text{ times}}$$

[by reversal law for inverse]

$$= (A^{-1})^k = A^{-k}$$

Property 5 Let A be an invertible matrix of order n, then $(A^{-1})^{-1} = A$.

Proof We have, $A^{-1}A = I_n$

$\therefore$ Inverse of $A^{-1} = A$

$\Rightarrow$ $(A^{-1})^{-1} = A$

Note $I_n^{-1} = I_n$ as $I_n^{-1}\ I_n = I_n$

Property 6 Let A be an invertible matrix of order n, then $|A^{-1}| = \dfrac{1}{|A|}$.

Proof $\because$ A is invertible, then $|A| \neq 0$.

Now, $AA^{-1} = I_n = A^{-1}A$

$\Rightarrow$ $|AA^{-1}| = |I_n|$

$\Rightarrow$ $|A||A^{-1}| = 1$ $[\because |AB| = |A||B| \text{ and } |I_n| = 1]$

$\Rightarrow$ $|A^{-1}| = \dfrac{1}{|A|}$ $[\because |A| \neq 0]$

Property 7 Inverse of a non-singular diagonal matrix is a diagonal matrix.

i.e. If $A = \begin{bmatrix} a & 0 & 0 \\ 0 & b & 0 \\ 0 & 0 & c \end{bmatrix}$ and $|A| \neq 0$, then $A^{-1} = \begin{bmatrix} \frac{1}{a} & 0 & 0 \\ 0 & \frac{1}{b} & 0 \\ 0 & 0 & \frac{1}{c} \end{bmatrix}$

JEE SPIKE

The inverse of a non-singular square matrix A of order 2 is obtained by interchanging the diagonal elements and changing signs of off-diagonal elements and dividing by $|A|$.

e.g. If $A = \begin{bmatrix} a & b \\ c & d \end{bmatrix}$ and $|A| = (ad - bc) \neq 0$, then

$$A^{-1} = \frac{1}{(ad - bc)} \begin{bmatrix} d & -b \\ -c & a \end{bmatrix}$$

Concept Inside Video

JEE SCANNER

Example Similar to PYQ Asked in JEE Main 2023

Let A be a 3×3 matrix such that $|\text{adj}(\text{adj}(\text{adj } A))| = 15^4$. Then, $|A^{-1}\text{adj } A|$ is equal to

(a) $5\sqrt{3}$ (b) $\sqrt{15}$ (c) $\sqrt{7}$ (d) $\sqrt{3}$

Sol. (b) Given, $|\text{adj}(\text{adj}(\text{adj } A))| = 15^4$

$\Rightarrow$ $|A|^{(n-1)^3} = 15^4$

$\Rightarrow$ $|A|^8 = 15^4$ $[\because n = 3]$

$\Rightarrow$ $|A|^2 = 15 \Rightarrow |A| = \sqrt{15}$

$\therefore$ $|A^{-1}\text{adj } A| = |A^{-1}||\text{adj } A|$

$= \dfrac{1}{|A|}|A|^{n-1}$

$= \dfrac{1}{|A|} \cdot |A|^2 = |A| = \sqrt{15}$

Skill Builder

Let A be a 3×3 matrix such that $|\text{adj}(\text{adj}(\text{adj } A))| = 4^{16}$. Then, $|A^{-1}\text{adj } A| + |A|$ is equal to

(a) 34 (b) 36

(c) 32 (d) 31

For Sol.

■ **For more practice** See Q.13 of Milestone Practice 7.3.

Example 43. Compute the inverse of the matrix

$$A = \begin{bmatrix} 0 & 1 & 2 \\ 1 & 2 & 3 \\ 3 & 1 & 1 \end{bmatrix}.$$

Sol. We have, $A = \begin{bmatrix} 0 & 1 & 2 \\ 1 & 2 & 3 \\ 3 & 1 & 1 \end{bmatrix}$

Then, $|A| = \begin{vmatrix} 0 & 1 & 2 \\ 1 & 2 & 3 \\ 3 & 1 & 1 \end{vmatrix}$

$= 0 \cdot (2 - 3) - 1(1 - 9) + 2(1 - 6)$

$= -2 \neq 0$

$\therefore$ A^{-1} exists.

Now, cofactors along $R_1 = -1, 8, -5$

cofactors along $R_2 = 1, -6, 3$

cofactors along $R_3 = -1, 2, -1$

Let C is a matrix of cofactors of the elements in $|A|$

$\therefore$ $C = \begin{bmatrix} -1 & 8 & -5 \\ 1 & -6 & 3 \\ -1 & 2 & -1 \end{bmatrix}$

$$\therefore \quad \text{adj } A = C' = \begin{bmatrix} -1 & 1 & -1 \\ 8 & -6 & 2 \\ -5 & 3 & -1 \end{bmatrix}$$

$$\text{Hence,} \quad A^{-1} = \frac{\text{adj } A}{|A|} = -\frac{1}{2}\begin{bmatrix} -1 & 1 & -1 \\ 8 & -6 & 2 \\ -5 & 3 & -1 \end{bmatrix}$$

$$= \begin{bmatrix} \frac{1}{2} & -\frac{1}{2} & \frac{1}{2} \\ -4 & 3 & -1 \\ \frac{5}{2} & -\frac{3}{2} & \frac{1}{2} \end{bmatrix}$$

Example 44. If A and B are symmetric non-singular matrices of same order, $AB = BA$ and $A^{-1}B^{-1}$ exist, then prove that $A^{-1}B^{-1}$ is symmetric.

Sol. $\because \quad A' = A, B' = B$

and $\quad |A| \neq 0, |B|' \neq 0$

$\therefore \quad (A^{-1}B^{-1})' = (B^{-1})'(A^{-1})'$ [by reversal law of transpose]

$= (B')^{-1}(A')^{-1}$ [by property 3]

$= B^{-1}A^{-1}$ [$\because A' = A$ and $B' = B$]

$= (AB)^{-1}$ [by reversal law of inverse]

$= (BA)^{-1}$ [$\because AB = BA$]

$= A^{-1}B^{-1}$ [by reversal law of inverse]

Hence, $A^{-1}B^{-1}$ is symmetric.

Example 45. If A, B and C are three non-singular square matrices of order 3 satisfying the equation $A^2 = A^{-1}$ and let $B = A^8$ and $C = A^2$, then find the value of det $(B - C)$.

Sol. $\because \quad B = A^8 = (A^2)^4 = (A^{-1})^4$ [$\because A^{-1} = A^2$]

$= (A^4)^{-1} = (A^{2\cdot 2})^{-1}$

$= ((A^2)^2)^{-1} = ((A^2)^{-1})^2 = ((A^{-1})^{-1})^2 = A^2 = C$

So, $\quad B = C \Rightarrow B - C = 0$

$\therefore \quad \det(B - C) = 0$

Example 46. If matrix $A = \begin{bmatrix} 1 & 2 & -2 \\ -2 & 2 & 1 \\ 2 & 1 & 2 \end{bmatrix}$, then A^{-1} is equal to

(a) A (b) A^T (c) $\frac{A}{9}$ (d) $\frac{A^T}{9}$

Sol. $A = 3\begin{bmatrix} 1/3 & 2/3 & -2/3 \\ -2/3 & 2/3 & 1/3 \\ 2/3 & 1/3 & 2/3 \end{bmatrix} = 3Q$, Q is orthogonal.

$$\therefore \quad A^{-1} = (3Q)^{-1} = \frac{1}{3}Q^T = \frac{1}{3}\left(\frac{A}{3}\right)^T = \frac{1}{9}A^T$$

7.12 Matrix Polynomial

Let $f(x) = a_0 x^m + a_1 x^{m-1} + a_2 x^{m-2} + \ldots + a_{m-1}x + a_m$ be a polynomial in x and let $A = [a_{ij}]_{n \times n}$, then expression of the form

$f(A) = a_0 A^m + a_1 A^{m-1} + a_2 A^{m-2} + \ldots + a_{m-1} A + a_m I_n$ is called a matrix polynomial.

Thus, to obtain $f(A)$ replace x by A in $f(x)$ and the constant term is multiplied by the identity matrix of order equal to that of A.

e.g. If $f(x) = x^2 - 7x + 32$ is a polynomial in x and A is a square matrix of order 3, then $f(A) = A^2 - 7A + 32 I_3$ is a matrix polynomial.

JEE Focus Points

- The polynomial equation $f(x) = 0$ is satisfied by the matrix

$$A = [a_{ij}]_{n \times n}, \text{ then } f(A) = 0.$$

- Let $A = [a_{ij}]_{n \times n}$ satisfies the equation

$$a_0 + a_1 x + a_2 x^2 + \ldots + a_r x^r = 0,$$

then A is invertible of $a_0 \neq 0$, $|A| = 0$ and its inverse is given by

$$A^{-1} = \frac{1}{a_0}(a_1 I_n + a_2 A + \ldots + a_r A^{r-1}).$$

Concept Inside Video

Example 47. If A and B are square matrices of order 3 such that $|A| = -2$ and $|B| = 1$, then det $(A^{-1}$ adj $(B^{-1}) \cdot$ adj $(A^{-1}))$ is equal to

(a) 8 (b) −8 (c) $\frac{1}{8}$ (d) $-\frac{1}{8}$

Sol. (d) $\det(A^{-1} \text{ adj}(B^{-1}) \cdot \text{adj}(A^{-1}))$

$$= |A^{-1}||\text{adj} B^{-1}||\text{adj} A^{-1}| = |A^{-1}||B^{-1}|^2|A^{-1}|^2$$

$$= \frac{1}{|A|} \times \frac{1}{|B|^2} \times \frac{1}{|A|^2} = \frac{1}{-2} \times \frac{1}{1} \times \frac{1}{(-2)^2} = -\frac{1}{8}$$

Example 48. If A is matrix of order 3 such that $|A| = 5$ and $B = \text{adj } A$, then $||A^{-1}|(AB)^T|$ is equal to

(a) 5 (b) 1

(c) 25 (d) $\frac{1}{25}$

Sol. (b) $\because \quad |A^{-1}| = \frac{1}{|A|} = \frac{1}{5}$,

$|(AB)^T| = |AB| = |A||B|$

$= 5|\text{adj } A| = 5^3$

Now, $\quad ||A^{-1}|(AB)^T| = \left|\frac{1}{5}(AB)^T\right|$

$= \frac{1}{5^3}|AB| = 1$

JEE SCANNER

Example Similar to PYQ Asked in JEE Main 2023

If $A = \begin{bmatrix} 1 & 6 \\ \lambda & 12 \end{bmatrix}$, $A^{-1} = \alpha A + \beta I$ *and* $\alpha + \beta = -3$ *and* $\alpha^2 + \beta^2 - \lambda^2 = \dfrac{m}{n}$, *then* $m - n$ *is ....*

Sol. (181) Characteristic equation is $|A - xI| = 0$

$$\Rightarrow \quad \begin{vmatrix} 1-x & 6 \\ \lambda & 12-x \end{vmatrix} = 0$$

$$\Rightarrow \quad x^2 - 13x + 12 - 6\lambda = 0$$

$$\Rightarrow \quad A^2 - 13A + (12 - 6\lambda)I = 0$$

$$\Rightarrow \quad (12 - 6\lambda)I = -A^2 + 13A$$

$$\Rightarrow \quad (12 - 6\lambda)A^{-1} = -A(AA^{-1}) + 13A \cdot A^{-1}$$

$$\Rightarrow \quad A^{-1} = \left(\frac{-1}{12 - 6\lambda}\right)A + \left(\frac{13}{12 - 6\lambda}\right)I$$

$$\Rightarrow \quad \alpha = \frac{-1}{12 - 6\lambda} \text{ and } \beta = \frac{13}{12 - 6\lambda}$$

$$\because \quad \alpha + \beta = -3 \quad \text{(given)}$$

$$\Rightarrow \quad \frac{-1}{12 - 6\lambda} + \frac{13}{12 - 6\lambda} = -3$$

$$\Rightarrow \quad \frac{12}{12 - 6\lambda} = -3 \Rightarrow \lambda = \frac{8}{3}$$

$$\therefore \quad \alpha = \frac{-1}{12 - 16} = \frac{1}{4}$$

and

$$\beta = \frac{13}{12 - 16} = \frac{-13}{4}$$

$$\therefore \quad \alpha^2 + \beta^2 - \lambda^2 = \left(\frac{1}{4}\right)^2 + \left(\frac{-13}{4}\right)^2 - \left(\frac{8}{3}\right)^2$$

$$= \frac{170}{16} - \frac{64}{9} = \frac{1530 - 1024}{144} = \frac{253}{72}$$

$$\therefore \quad m = 253, n = 72$$

$$\Rightarrow \quad m - n = 181$$

Skill Builder

If $A = \begin{bmatrix} 1 & 2 \\ \beta & 3 \end{bmatrix}$, $A^{-1} = \lambda A + \gamma I$ and $\lambda + \gamma = 3$, then $\lambda^2 + \gamma^2 + \beta^2$ is equal to ....

For Sol.

■ **For more practice** See Q.10 of Milestone Practice 7.3.

Example 49. If $A = \begin{bmatrix} 3 & 1 \\ 2 & 1 \end{bmatrix}$, then find the value of $|a| + |b|$ such that $A^2 + aA + bI = O$. Hence, find A^{-1}.

Sol. We have, $A = \begin{bmatrix} 3 & 1 \\ 2 & 1 \end{bmatrix}$, then $|A| = \begin{vmatrix} 3 & 1 \\ 2 & 1 \end{vmatrix} = 3 - 2 = 1 \neq 0$

$\therefore$ A^{-1} exists.

Now, $$A^2 = A \cdot A = \begin{bmatrix} 3 & 1 \\ 2 & 1 \end{bmatrix}\begin{bmatrix} 3 & 1 \\ 2 & 1 \end{bmatrix} = \begin{bmatrix} 11 & 4 \\ 8 & 3 \end{bmatrix}$$

Since, $A^2 + aA + bI = O$

$$\Rightarrow \quad \begin{bmatrix} 11 & 4 \\ 8 & 3 \end{bmatrix} + a\begin{bmatrix} 3 & 1 \\ 2 & 1 \end{bmatrix} + b\begin{bmatrix} 1 & 0 \\ 0 & 1 \end{bmatrix} = \begin{bmatrix} 0 & 0 \\ 0 & 0 \end{bmatrix}$$

$$\Rightarrow \quad \begin{bmatrix} 11 + 3a + b & 4 + a \\ 8 + 2a & 3 + a + b \end{bmatrix} = \begin{bmatrix} 0 & 0 \\ 0 & 0 \end{bmatrix}$$

On equating the corresponding elements, we get

$$11 + 3a + b = 0 \quad \text{...(i)}$$

$$4 + a = 0 \quad \text{...(ii)}$$

$$8 + 2a = 0 \quad \text{...(iii)}$$

$$3 + a + b = 0 \quad \text{...(iv)}$$

From Eqs. (ii) and (iv), we get $a = -4$ and $b = 1$

$$\therefore \quad |a| + |b| = |-4| + |1| = 4 + 1 = 5$$

As $$A^2 + aA + bI = O$$

$$\Rightarrow \quad A^2 - 4A + I = O$$

$$\Rightarrow \quad I = 4A - A^2$$

$$\Rightarrow \quad IA^{-1} = (4A - A^2)A^{-1}$$

$$\Rightarrow \quad A^{-1} = 4(AA^{-1}) - A(AA^{-1})$$

$$= 4I - AI = 4I - A$$

$$= 4\begin{bmatrix} 1 & 0 \\ 0 & 1 \end{bmatrix} - \begin{bmatrix} 3 & 1 \\ 2 & 1 \end{bmatrix}$$

$$= \begin{bmatrix} 4 & 0 \\ 0 & 4 \end{bmatrix} - \begin{bmatrix} 3 & 1 \\ 2 & 1 \end{bmatrix}$$

$$\therefore \quad A^{-1} = \begin{bmatrix} 1 & -1 \\ -2 & 3 \end{bmatrix}$$

Example 50. $A = \begin{bmatrix} 2 & 3 \\ 1 & 2 \end{bmatrix}$ show that $A^2 - 4A + I = 0$, hence find A^{-1}.

Sol. $$A^2 = \begin{bmatrix} 2 & 3 \\ 1 & 2 \end{bmatrix}\begin{bmatrix} 2 & 3 \\ 1 & 2 \end{bmatrix} = \begin{bmatrix} 7 & 12 \\ 4 & 7 \end{bmatrix}$$

$$A^2 - 4A + I = \begin{bmatrix} 7 & 12 \\ 4 & 7 \end{bmatrix} - \begin{bmatrix} 8 & 12 \\ 4 & 8 \end{bmatrix} + \begin{bmatrix} 1 & 0 \\ 0 & 1 \end{bmatrix}$$

$$= \begin{bmatrix} 0 & 0 \\ 0 & 0 \end{bmatrix} = 0$$

Multiplying by A^{-1}, we get

$$A^2A^{-1} - 4AA^{-1} + A^{-1} = 0$$

$$\therefore \quad A^{-1} = 4I - A = \begin{bmatrix} 2 & -3 \\ -1 & 2 \end{bmatrix}$$

Example 51. A square matrix P satisfies $P^2 = I - P$, where I is identity matrix. If $P^n = 5I - 8P$, then n is

(a) 4 (b) 5
(c) 6 (d) 7

Sol. (c) $P^2 = I - P$

$P^3 = P - P^2 = 2P - I$

$P^4 = 2I - 3P$

$P^5 = -3I + 5P$

$P^6 = 5I - 8P$

$\therefore \quad n = 6$

Example 52. If for matrix $A = \begin{bmatrix} \cos\theta & 2\sin\theta \\ \sin\theta & \cos\theta \end{bmatrix}$, $A^{-1} = A^T$, then the number of possible value (s) of θ in $[0, 2\pi]$ is

(a) 2 (b) 3 (c) 1 (d) 4

Sol. (b) $\begin{bmatrix} \cos\theta & 2\sin\theta \\ \sin\theta & \cos\theta \end{bmatrix}\begin{bmatrix} \cos\theta & \sin\theta \\ 2\sin\theta & \cos\theta \end{bmatrix} = \begin{bmatrix} 1 & 0 \\ 0 & 1 \end{bmatrix}$

$$\begin{bmatrix} \cos^2\theta + 4\sin^2\theta & 3\sin\theta\cos\theta \\ 3\sin\theta\cos\theta & \sin^2\theta + \cos^2\theta \end{bmatrix} = \begin{bmatrix} 1 & 0 \\ 0 & 1 \end{bmatrix}$$

$\Rightarrow \quad \sin\theta = 0$

$\therefore \quad \theta = 0, \pi, 2\pi$

Milestone Practice 7.3

1. If $A = \begin{bmatrix} -1 & -2 & -2 \\ 2 & 1 & -2 \\ 2 & -2 & 1 \end{bmatrix}$, then adj A equals to

(a) A (b) A^T (c) $3A$ (d) $3A^T$

2. If A is a 3×3 matrix and B is its adjoint such that $|B| = 64$, then $|A|$ is equal to

(a) 64 (b) ± 64 (c) ± 8 (d) 18

3. For any 2×2 matrix A, if $A(\text{adj } A) = \begin{bmatrix} 10 & 0 \\ 0 & 10 \end{bmatrix}$, then $|A|$ is equal to

(a) 0 (b) 10 (c) 20 (d) 100

4. If A is a singular matrix, then adj A is

(a) singular (b) non-singular
(c) symmetric (d) not defined

5. If $A = \begin{bmatrix} 1 & 2 & -1 \\ -1 & 1 & 2 \\ 2 & -1 & 1 \end{bmatrix}$, then det (adj (adj A)) is

(a) 14^4 (b) 14^3 (c) 14^2 (d) 14

6. If $k \in R_0$, then det (adj (kI_n)) is equal to

(a) k^{n-1} (b) $k^{n(n-1)}$
(c) k^n (d) k

7. Let matrix $A = \begin{bmatrix} x & y & -z \\ 1 & 2 & 3 \\ 1 & 1 & 2 \end{bmatrix}$, where $x, y, z \in N$, if det $\cdot$ (adj (adj A)) $= 2^8 \cdot 3^4$, then number of such matrices A is

(a) 220 (b) 45
(c) 55 (d) 110

8. If $A^{-1} = \begin{bmatrix} \sin^2\alpha & 0 & 0 \\ 0 & \sin^2\beta & 0 \\ 0 & 0 & \sin^2\gamma \end{bmatrix}$,

$B^{-1} = \begin{bmatrix} \cos^2\alpha & 0 & 0 \\ 0 & \cos^2\beta & 0 \\ 0 & 0 & \cos^2\gamma \end{bmatrix}$,

where α, β, γ are any real

and $C = (A^{-5} + B^{-5}) + 5A^{-1}B^{-1}$
$(A^{-3} + B^{-3}) + 10A^{-2}B^{-2}(A^{-1} + B^{-1})$, then $|C|$ is equal to

(a) 0 (b) 1
(c) 2 (d) 3

9. If $A = \begin{bmatrix} \cos x & \sin x & 0 \\ -\sin x & \cos x & 0 \\ 0 & 0 & 1 \end{bmatrix} = f(x)$, then A^{-1} is equal to

(a) $f(-x)$ (b) $f(x)$
(c) $-f(x)$ (d) $-f(-x)$

10. $A = \begin{bmatrix} 1 & 5 \\ \lambda & 10 \end{bmatrix}$, $A^{-1} = \alpha A + \beta I$ and $\alpha + \beta = -2$, then $4\alpha^2 + \beta^2 + \lambda^2$ is equal to

(a) 14 (b) 12
(c) 19 (d) 10

11. If $A=\begin{bmatrix}0 & 1 & -1\\ 2 & 1 & 3\\ 3 & 2 & 1\end{bmatrix}$, then $(A(\text{adj}\,A)\,A^{-1})\,A$ is equal to

(a) $\begin{bmatrix}-6 & 0 & 0\\ 0 & -6 & 0\\ 0 & 0 & -6\end{bmatrix}$ (b) $\begin{bmatrix}0 & \frac{1}{6} & -\frac{1}{6}\\ \frac{1}{3} & \frac{1}{6} & \frac{1}{2}\\ \frac{1}{2} & \frac{1}{3} & \frac{1}{6}\end{bmatrix}$

(c) $2\begin{bmatrix}3 & 0 & 0\\ 0 & 3 & 0\\ 0 & 0 & 3\end{bmatrix}$ (d) $2\begin{bmatrix}1 & 0 & 0\\ 0 & 1 & 0\\ 0 & 0 & 1\end{bmatrix}$

12. A is an involutory matrix given by $A=\begin{bmatrix}0 & 1 & -1\\ 4 & -3 & 4\\ 3 & -3 & 4\end{bmatrix}$, then the inverse of $\frac{A}{2}$ will be

(a) $2A$ (b) $\frac{A^{-1}}{2}$ (c) $\frac{A}{2}$ (d) A^2

13. If A and B are square matrices of order 3 such that $|A|=-2$, $|B|=1$, then $\det\cdot(A^{-1}\text{adj}\,(B^{-1}).\,\text{adj}\,(2A^{-1}))$ is equal to

(a) 8 (b) −8

(c) 1 (d) −1

14. A square non-singular matrix A satisfies the equation $x^2-x+2=0$, then A^{-1} is equal to

(a) $I-A$ (b) $(I-A)/2$

(c) $I+A$ (d) $(I+A)/2$

15. If $A^2-A+I=0$, then A^{-1} is equal to

(a) A (b) $A+I$

(c) $I-A$ (d) $A-I$

16. If M be the square matrix of order 3 such that $|M|=2$, then $\left|\text{adj}\left(\frac{M}{2}\right)\right|$ equals to

(a) $\frac{1}{2}$ (b) $\frac{1}{4}$

(c) $\frac{1}{8}$ (d) $\frac{1}{16}$

17. If $A=\begin{bmatrix}1 & 0 & 0\\ 0 & 1 & 0\\ a & b & -1\end{bmatrix}$ and where I is the unit matrix of order 3, then $A^2+2A^4+4A^6$ is equal to

(a) $7A^8$ (b) $7A^7$ (c) $8I$ (d) $6I$

18. If $\begin{bmatrix}2 & 0 & 7\\ 0 & 1 & 0\\ 1 & -2 & 1\end{bmatrix}^{-1}=\begin{bmatrix}-x & 14x & 7x\\ 0 & 1 & 0\\ x & -4x & -2x\end{bmatrix}$, then x is equal to

(a) $\frac{1}{5}$ (b) $\frac{1}{4}$ (c) $\frac{1}{3}$ (d) $\frac{1}{2}$

19. Let $A=\begin{bmatrix}a & 0 & 1\\ 0 & b & 2\\ -1 & 0 & c\end{bmatrix}$, where a, b, c positive integers. If $\text{tr}\,(A)=7$, then differences between greatest and least values of $|A|$ is

(a) 6 (b) 7

(c) 8 (d) 9

20. If A and P are square matrics of order 2 such that $P+P^T=0$ and $2A+P=4I$, then least value of det. (A) is

(a) 4 (b) 5

(c) $\frac{16}{5}$ (d) $\frac{17}{4}$

Answer Key

1. (d)	2. (c)	3. (b)	4. (a)	5. (a)
6. (a)	7. (c)	8. (b)	9. (a)	10. (a)
11. (c)	12. (a)	13. (b)	14. (b)	15. (c)
16. (a)	17. (a)	18. (a)	19. (d)	20. (a)

For Detailed Solution

Milestone 4 Eigen Values and Cayley-Hamilton Theorem

• Solutions of Linear Simultaneous Equation Using Matrix Method • Eigen Values or Characteristics Roots and Characteristics Vectors of a Square Matrix • Cayley-Hamilton Theorem

7.13 Solutions of Linear Simultaneous Equations Using Matrix Method

Let us consider a system of n linear equations in n unknowns say $x_1, x_2, x_3, \ldots, x_n$ given as below

$$\left.\begin{aligned} a_{11}x_1 + a_{12}x_2 + a_{13}x_3 + \ldots + a_{1n}x_n &= b_1 \\ a_{21}x_1 + a_{22}x_2 + a_{23}x_3 + \ldots + a_{2n}x_n &= b_2 \\ a_{31}x_1 + a_{32}x_2 + a_{33}x_3 + \ldots + a_{3n}x_n &= b_3 \\ \ldots \quad \ldots \ldots \ldots \ldots \ldots \ldots & \ldots \\ \ldots \quad \ldots \ldots \ldots \ldots \ldots \ldots & \ldots \\ a_{n1}x_1 + a_{n2}x_2 + a_{n3}x_3 + \ldots + a_{nn}x_n &= b_n \end{aligned}\right\} \quad \ldots(i)$$

If $b_1 = b_2 = b_3 = \ldots = b_n = 0$, then the system of Eq.(i) is called a system of homogeneous linear equations and if atleast one of $b_1, b_2, b_3, \ldots, b_n$ is non-zero, then it is called a system of non-homogeneous linear equation.

We write the above system of Eq. (i) in the matrix form as

$$\begin{bmatrix} a_{11} & a_{12} & a_{13} & \ldots & a_{1n} \\ a_{21} & a_{22} & a_{23} & \ldots & a_{2n} \\ a_{31} & a_{32} & a_{33} & \ldots & a_{3n} \\ \ldots & \ldots & \ldots & \ldots & \ldots \\ \ldots & \ldots & \ldots & \ldots & \ldots \\ a_{n1} & a_{n2} & a_{n3} & \ldots & a_{nn} \end{bmatrix} \begin{bmatrix} x_1 \\ x_2 \\ x_3 \\ \ldots \\ \ldots \\ x_n \end{bmatrix} = \begin{bmatrix} b_1 \\ b_2 \\ b_3 \\ \ldots \\ \ldots \\ b_n \end{bmatrix} \Rightarrow AX = B \quad \ldots(ii)$$

where $A = \begin{bmatrix} a_{11} & a_{12} & a_{13} & \ldots & a_{1n} \\ a_{21} & a_{22} & a_{23} & \ldots & a_{2n} \\ a_{31} & a_{32} & a_{33} & \ldots & a_{3n} \\ \ldots & \ldots & \ldots & \ldots & \ldots \\ \ldots & \ldots & \ldots & \ldots & \ldots \\ a_{n1} & a_{n2} & a_{n3} & \ldots & a_{nn} \end{bmatrix}$,

$$X = \begin{bmatrix} x_1 \\ x_2 \\ x_3 \\ \ldots \\ \ldots \\ x_n \end{bmatrix} \text{ and } B = \begin{bmatrix} b_1 \\ b_2 \\ b_3 \\ \ldots \\ \ldots \\ b_n \end{bmatrix}$$

Pre-multiplying Eq. (ii) by A^{-1}, we get

$$A^{-1}(AX) = A^{-1}B \Rightarrow (A^{-1}A)X = A^{-1}B$$

$$\Rightarrow \quad IX = A^{-1}B$$

$$\Rightarrow \quad X = A^{-1}B = \frac{(\text{adj } A)B}{|A|}$$

Types of Equations

(1) **When system of equations is non-homogeneous**

(i) If $|A| \neq 0$, then the system of equations is consistent and has a unique solution given by $X = A^{-1}B$.

(ii) If $|A| = 0$ and $(\text{adj}A) \cdot B \neq 0$, then the system of equations is inconsistent and has no solution.

(iii) If $|A| = 0$ and $(\text{adj}A) \cdot B = O$, then the system of equations is consistent and has an infinite number of solutions.

(2) **When system of equations is homogeneous**

(i) If $|A| \neq 0$, then the system of equations has only trivial solution and it has one solution.

(ii) If $|A| = 0$, then the system of equations has non-trivial solution and it has infinite solutions.

(iii) If number of equations < number of unknowns, then it has non-trivial solution.

Example 53. Solve the system of equations $x + 2y + 3z = 1$, $2x + 3y + 2z = 2$ and $3x + 3y + 4z = 1$ with the help of matrix inversion.

Sol. We have,

$$x + 2y + 3z = 1,$$
$$2x + 3y + 2z = 2$$
and $$3x + 3y + 4z = 1$$

The given system of equations in the matrix form are written as below.

$$\begin{bmatrix} 1 & 2 & 3 \\ 2 & 3 & 2 \\ 3 & 3 & 4 \end{bmatrix} \begin{bmatrix} x \\ y \\ z \end{bmatrix} = \begin{bmatrix} 1 \\ 2 \\ 1 \end{bmatrix}$$

$$AX = B \Rightarrow X = A^{-1}B \qquad \text{...(i)}$$

where $A = \begin{bmatrix} 1 & 2 & 3 \\ 2 & 3 & 2 \\ 3 & 3 & 4 \end{bmatrix}, X = \begin{bmatrix} x \\ y \\ z \end{bmatrix}$ and $B = \begin{bmatrix} 1 \\ 2 \\ 1 \end{bmatrix}$

$$|A| = 1(12-6) - 2(8-6) + 3(6-9)$$
$$= 6 - 4 - 9$$
$$= -7 \neq 0$$

$\therefore$ A^{-1} exists and has unique solution.

Let C be the matrix of cofactors of elements in $|A|$.

Now, cofactors along $R_1 = 6, -2, -3$

cofactors along $R_2 = 1, -5, 3$

and cofactors along $R_3 = -5, 4, -1$

$$\therefore \quad C = \begin{bmatrix} 6 & -2 & -3 \\ 1 & -5 & 3 \\ -5 & 4 & -1 \end{bmatrix}$$

$$\therefore \quad \text{adj } A = C^T$$

$$\Rightarrow \quad \text{adj } A = \begin{bmatrix} 6 & -2 & -3 \\ 1 & -5 & 3 \\ -5 & 4 & -1 \end{bmatrix}^T = \begin{bmatrix} 6 & 1 & -5 \\ -2 & -5 & 4 \\ -3 & 3 & -1 \end{bmatrix}$$

$$\Rightarrow \quad A^{-1} = \frac{\text{adj } A}{|A|} = -\frac{1}{7}\begin{bmatrix} 6 & 1 & -5 \\ -2 & -5 & 4 \\ -3 & 3 & -1 \end{bmatrix} = \begin{bmatrix} -\frac{6}{7} & -\frac{1}{7} & \frac{5}{7} \\ \frac{2}{7} & \frac{5}{7} & -\frac{4}{7} \\ \frac{3}{7} & -\frac{3}{7} & \frac{1}{7} \end{bmatrix}$$

From Eq. (i), $X = A^{-1}B$

$$\Rightarrow \quad \begin{bmatrix} x \\ y \\ z \end{bmatrix} = \begin{bmatrix} -\frac{6}{7} & -\frac{1}{7} & \frac{5}{7} \\ \frac{2}{7} & \frac{5}{7} & -\frac{4}{7} \\ \frac{3}{7} & -\frac{3}{7} & \frac{1}{7} \end{bmatrix}\begin{bmatrix} 1 \\ 2 \\ 1 \end{bmatrix} = \begin{bmatrix} -\frac{3}{7} \\ \frac{8}{7} \\ -\frac{2}{7} \end{bmatrix}$$

Hence, $x = -\frac{3}{7}, y = \frac{8}{7}$ and $z = -\frac{2}{7}$ is the required solution.

Example 54. Solve the system of equations $x + 3y - 2z = 0$, $2x - y + 4z = 0$ and $x - 11y + 14z = 0$.

Sol. We have,
$$x + 3y - 2z = 0$$
$$2x - y + 4z = 0$$
$$x - 11y + 14z = 0$$

The given system of equations in the matrix form can be written as below.

$$\begin{bmatrix} 1 & 3 & -2 \\ 2 & -1 & 4 \\ 1 & -11 & 14 \end{bmatrix}\begin{bmatrix} x \\ y \\ z \end{bmatrix} = \begin{bmatrix} 0 \\ 0 \\ 0 \end{bmatrix}$$

$$AX = O \qquad \text{...(i)}$$

where $A = \begin{bmatrix} 1 & 3 & -2 \\ 2 & -1 & 4 \\ 1 & -11 & 14 \end{bmatrix}, X = \begin{bmatrix} x \\ y \\ z \end{bmatrix}$ and $O = \begin{bmatrix} 0 \\ 0 \\ 0 \end{bmatrix}$

$$\therefore \quad |A| = 1(-14+44) - 3(28-4) - 2(-22+1)$$
$$= 30 - 72 + 42$$
$$= 0$$

and therefore the system has a non-trivial solution. Now, we may write first two of the given equations

$$x + 3y = 2z$$

and
$$2x - y = -4z$$

Solving these equations in terms of z, we get

$$x = -\frac{10}{7}z \text{ and } y = \frac{8}{7}z$$

Putting $x = -\frac{10}{7}z$ and $y = \frac{8}{7}z$ in third equation of the given system,

we get, LHS $= -\frac{10}{7}z - \frac{88}{7}z + 14z = 0 =$ RHS

Now, if $z = 7k$, then

$$x = -10k \text{ and } y = 8k$$

Hence, $x = -10k$, $y = 8k$ and $z = 7k$ (where k is arbitrary) are the required solutions.

Example 55. Solve the system of equations $2x + 3y - 3z = 0$, $3x - 3y + z = 0$ and $3x - 2y - 3z = 0$.

Sol. We have,
$$2x + 3y - 3z = 0$$
$$3x - 3y + z = 0$$
$$3x - 2y - 3z = 0$$

The given system of equations in the matrix form can be written as below.

$$\begin{bmatrix} 2 & 3 & -3 \\ 3 & -3 & 1 \\ 3 & -2 & -3 \end{bmatrix}\begin{bmatrix} x \\ y \\ z \end{bmatrix} = \begin{bmatrix} 0 \\ 0 \\ 0 \end{bmatrix}$$

$$AX = O \qquad \text{...(i)}$$

where $A = \begin{bmatrix} 2 & 3 & -3 \\ 3 & -3 & 1 \\ 3 & -2 & -3 \end{bmatrix}, X = \begin{bmatrix} x \\ y \\ z \end{bmatrix}$ and $O = \begin{bmatrix} 0 \\ 0 \\ 0 \end{bmatrix}$

$$\therefore \quad |A| = 2(9+2) - 3(-9-3) - 3(-6+9)$$
$$= 22 + 36 - 9$$
$$= 49 \neq 0$$

Hence, the equations have a unique trivial solution $x = 0$, $y = 0$ and $z = 0$ only.

JEE SCANNER

Example Similar to PYQ Asked in JEE Main 2024

The system of equations $x+y+z=6$, $x+2y+3z=10$ and $x+3y+\lambda z=14$ has unique solution, if

(a) $\lambda \neq 5$ (b) $\lambda \neq 0$

(c) $\lambda - 3 \neq 0$ (d) $\lambda \neq 2$

Sol. (a) The given system of equations are

$$x+y+z=6$$
$$x+2y+3z=10$$
$$x+3y+\lambda z=14$$

Let $A = \begin{bmatrix} 1 & 1 & 1 \\ 1 & 2 & 3 \\ 1 & 3 & \lambda \end{bmatrix}$

The system of equations has unique solution if $|A| \neq 0$

$$\begin{vmatrix} 1 & 1 & 1 \\ 1 & 2 & 3 \\ 1 & 3 & \lambda \end{vmatrix} \neq 0$$

$\Rightarrow 1(2\lambda - 9) - 1(\lambda - 3) + 1(3-2) \neq 0$

$\Rightarrow \quad 2\lambda - 9 - \lambda + 3 + 1 \neq 0$

$\Rightarrow \quad \lambda - 5 \neq 0$

$\Rightarrow \quad \lambda \neq 5$

Skill Builder

The system of equations $x+y+7z=3$, $2x+5y+\lambda z=6$ and $x+2y+3z=3$ has unique solution, if

(a) $\lambda \neq 2$ (b) $\lambda \neq 3$

(c) $\lambda \neq 7$ (d) $\lambda \neq 5$

For Sol.

■ **For more practice** See Q.2 of Milestone Practice 7.4.

Example 56. The system $AX = B$ of n equations in n unknowns has infinitely many solutions, if

(a) $|A| \neq 0$

(b) $|A| = 0$, (adj A) $B \neq 0$

(c) $|A| = 0$, (adj A) $B = 0$

(d) $|A| \neq 0$, (adj A) $B = 0$

Sol. (c) Here, $AX = B$

$\Rightarrow \quad (\text{adj}A)\, AX = (\text{adj}A)\, B$

$\Rightarrow \quad |A|\, X = (\text{adj}A)\, B$

Clearly, if the system has infinite solutions, $|A| = 0$

$\Rightarrow \quad (\text{adj}A)\, B = 0$

Example 57. The system of equations $x+y+z=8$, $x-y+2z=6$, $3x+5y-7z=14$ has

(a) a unique solution (b) infinite many solutions

(c) No solution (d) None of these

Sol. (a) $AX = B$, $A = \begin{bmatrix} 1 & 1 & 1 \\ 1 & -1 & 2 \\ 3 & 5 & -7 \end{bmatrix}$

Here, $|A| = 18 \neq 0$,

So, system has unique solution.

7.14 Eigen Values or Characteristic Roots and Characteristic Vectors of a square matrix

Let X be any non-zero vector satisfying

$$AX = \lambda X \quad \text{...(i)}$$

where, λ is any scalar, then λ is said to be eigen value or characteristic root of square matrix A and the vector X is called eigen vector or characteristic vector of matrix A.

Now, from Eq. (i), we have

$$(A - \lambda I)\, X = O$$

Since, $X \neq O$, we deduce that the matrix $(A - \lambda I)$ is singular, so that its determinant is 0

i.e. $\quad |A - \lambda I| = 0 \quad$ ...(ii)

is called characteristic equation of matrix A.

If A be $n \times n$ matrix, then equation $|A - \lambda I| = 0$ reduces to polynomial equation of nth from degree in λ, which given n values of λ i.e. matrix A will have n characteristic roots or eigen values.

Important Properties of Eigen Values

(i) Any square matrix A and its transpose A^T have the same eigen values.

(ii) The sum of the eigen values of a matrix is equal to the trace of the matrix.

(iii) The product the eigen values of a matrix A is equal to the determinant of A.

(iv) If $\lambda_1, \lambda_2, \lambda_3, \lambda_4, \ldots, \lambda_n$ are the eigen values of A, then the eigen values of

(a) kA are $k\lambda_1, k\lambda_2, k\lambda_3, k\lambda_4, \ldots, k\lambda_n$.

(b) A^m are $\lambda_1^m, \lambda_2^m, \lambda_3^m, \lambda_4^m, \ldots, \lambda_n^m$.

(c) A^{-1} are $\frac{1}{\lambda_1}, \frac{1}{\lambda_2}, \frac{1}{\lambda_3}, \frac{1}{\lambda_4}, \ldots, \frac{1}{\lambda_n}$.

Example 58. Let matrix $A = \begin{bmatrix} 4 & 6 & 6 \\ 1 & 3 & 2 \\ -1 & -4 & -3 \end{bmatrix}$, find the non-zero column vector X such that $AX = \lambda X$ for some scalar λ.

Sol. The characteristic equation is $|A-\lambda I|=0$

$$\Rightarrow \begin{vmatrix} 4-\lambda & 6 & 6 \\ 1 & 3-\lambda & 2 \\ -1 & -4 & -3-\lambda \end{vmatrix}=0$$

$$\Rightarrow \lambda^3-4\lambda^2-\lambda+4=0$$

or $$(\lambda+1)(\lambda-1)(\lambda-4)=0$$

The eigen values are $\lambda=-1, 1, 4$

If $\lambda=-1$, we get

$$5x+6y+6z=0,\ x+4y+2z=0$$

and $-x-4y-2z=0$

Giving $$\frac{x}{6}=\frac{y}{2}=\frac{z}{-7},\ X=\begin{bmatrix} 6 \\ 2 \\ -7 \end{bmatrix}$$

If $\lambda=1$, we get $3x+6y+6z=0,\ x+2y+2z=0$

and $-x-4y-4z=0$

Giving, $$\frac{x}{0}=\frac{y}{1}=\frac{z}{-1},\ X=\begin{bmatrix} 0 \\ 1 \\ -1 \end{bmatrix}$$

If $\lambda=4$, we get

$$0\cdot x+6y+6z=0,\ x-y+2z=0$$

and $$-x-4y-7z=0$$

Giving, $$\frac{x}{3}=\frac{y}{1}=\frac{z}{-1},\ X=\begin{bmatrix} 3 \\ 1 \\ -1 \end{bmatrix}$$

Hence, column vector, $X=\begin{bmatrix} 6 \\ 2 \\ -7 \end{bmatrix}, \begin{bmatrix} 0 \\ 1 \\ -1 \end{bmatrix}, \begin{bmatrix} 3 \\ 1 \\ -1 \end{bmatrix}$.

Example 59. Show that the characteristic roots of an idempotent matrix are either zero or unity.

Sol. Let A be an idempotent matrix, then

$$A^2=A \quad \text{...(i)}$$

If λ be an eigen value of the matrix A corresponding to eigen vector X, so that

$$AX=\lambda X \quad \text{...(ii)}$$

where $X\neq 0$

From Eq. (ii), $A(AX)=A(\lambda X)$

$\Rightarrow (AA)X=\lambda(AX)$

$\Rightarrow A^2X=\lambda(\lambda X)$ [from Eq. (ii)]

$\Rightarrow AX=\lambda^2 X$ [from Eq. (i)]

$\Rightarrow \lambda X=\lambda^2 X$ [from Eq. (ii)]

$\Rightarrow (\lambda-\lambda^2)X=0$

$\Rightarrow \lambda-\lambda^2=0$ [$\because X\neq 0$]

$\therefore \lambda=0$

or $\lambda=1$

Example 60. If $3, -2$ are the eigen values of a non-singular matrix A and $|A|=4$, find the eigen values of adj (A).

Sol. $\because A^{-1}=\dfrac{\text{adj } A}{|A|}$, if λ is eigen value of A, then λ^{-1} is eigen value of A^{-1}.

Thus, for $\text{adj}(A)X=(A^{-1}X)|A|=|A|\lambda^{-1}I$

Thus, eigen value corresponding to $\lambda=3$ is $\dfrac{4}{3}$ and corresponding to $\lambda=-2$ is $\dfrac{4}{-2}=-2$.

Example 61. Let A be 3×3 matrix given by $A=(a_{ij})_{3\times 3}$. If for every column vector X satisfies $X'OX=0$ and $a_{12}=2008$, $a_{13}=2010$ and $a_{23}=-2012$, then value of $a_{21}+a_{31}+a_{32}$ is equal to

(a) -6

(b) 2006

(c) -2006

(d) 0

Sol. (c) Let $X=\begin{bmatrix} x_1 \\ x_2 \\ x_3 \end{bmatrix}$, then

$$[x_1, x_2, x_3]\begin{bmatrix} a_{11} & a_{12} & a_{13} \\ a_{21} & a_{22} & a_{23} \\ a_{31} & a_{32} & a_{33} \end{bmatrix}\begin{bmatrix} x_1 \\ x_2 \\ x_3 \end{bmatrix}=0$$

$$\Rightarrow a_{11}x_1^2+a_{22}x_2^2+a_{33}x_3^2+(a_{12}+a_{21})x_1x_2 + (a_{13}+a_{31})x_1x_3+(a_{23}+a_{32})x_2x_3=0$$

It is true for every x_1, x_2, x_3

$\therefore a_{11}=a_{22}=a_{33}=0,\ a_{12}+a_{21}=0,\ a_{31}+a_{13}=0,\ a_{23}+a_{32}=0$

$\Rightarrow A$ is a skew-symmetric matrix.

$a_{21}=-2008,\ a_{31}=-2010,\ a_{32}=2012$

$\therefore a_{21}+a_{31}+a_{32}=-2006$

7.15 Cayley-Hamilton Theorem

Every square matrix A satisfies its characteristic equation $|A-\lambda I|=0$

i.e. $a_0\lambda^n+a_1\lambda^{n-1}+a_2\lambda^{n-2}+\ldots+a_n=0$

$\therefore$ By Cayley-Hamilton theorem

$$a_0A^n+a_1A^{n-1}+a_2A^{n-2}+\ldots+a_nI=O$$

$$\Rightarrow A^{-1}=-\left\{\frac{a_0}{a_n}A^{n-1}+\frac{a_1}{a_n}A^{n-2}+\frac{a_2}{a_n}A^{n-3}+\ldots+\frac{a_{n-1}}{a_n}I\right\}$$

Example 62. Find the characteristic equation of the matrix $A=\begin{bmatrix}2 & 1\\3 & 2\end{bmatrix}$ and hence find its inverse using Cayley-hamilton theorem.

Sol. Characteristic equation is

$$|A-\lambda I|=0$$

$$\Rightarrow \begin{bmatrix}2-\lambda & 1\\3 & 2-\lambda\end{bmatrix}=0$$

$$\Rightarrow (2-\lambda)^2-3=0$$

$$\Rightarrow \lambda^2-4\lambda+1=0$$

$\therefore$ By Cayley-hamilton theorem,

$$A^2-4A+I=O \text{ or } I=4A-A^2$$

Multiplying by A^{-1}, we get

$$A^{-1}=4A^{-1}A-A^{-1}AA$$

$$=4I-IA=4I-A$$

$$=4\begin{bmatrix}1 & 0\\0 & 1\end{bmatrix}-\begin{bmatrix}2 & 1\\3 & 2\end{bmatrix}$$

$$=\begin{bmatrix}2 & -1\\-3 & 2\end{bmatrix}$$

Use of Binomial Theorem

If A and B are of same order square matrices such that $AB=BA$, then $(n\in N)$

(i) $(A+B)^n={}^nC_0A^nB^0+{}^nC_1A^{n-1}B+{}^nC_2A^{n-2}B^2+\ldots+{}^nC_nA^0B^n$

(ii) $(I+A)^n=I+{}^nC_1A+{}^nC_2A^2+\ldots+{}^nC_nA^n$

Example 63. Let $A=\begin{bmatrix}1 & 2 & 0\\0 & 2 & 0\\0 & -1 & 2\end{bmatrix}$ be a given matrix. If $P=A^4+8A$ and $Q=-5A^3+8A^2-10A$, then

(a) $\text{tr}(P+Q)=5$

(b) $\text{tr}(P+Q)=0$

(c) $\det(P+Q)=18$

(d) $\det(P+Q)=32$

Sol. (d) $|A-xI|=0$

$$\Rightarrow \begin{vmatrix}1-x & 2 & 0\\0 & 2-x & 0\\0 & -1 & 2-x\end{vmatrix}=0$$

$$\Rightarrow x^3-5x^2+8x-4=0$$

$$\Rightarrow A^3-5A^2+8A-4I=0$$

$$\Rightarrow A^4-5A^3+8A^2-4A=0 \quad \ldots\text{(i)}$$

$$\Rightarrow P+Q=A^4-5A^3+8A^2-2A=2A \quad \text{[by Eq. (i)]}$$

$\therefore$ $\text{tr}(P+Q)=10$ and $|P+Q|=|2A|=32$

Example 64. Let $A=\begin{bmatrix}a & x & p\\y & q & b\\r & c & z\end{bmatrix}$ and $B=\begin{bmatrix}0 & 0 & 1\\0 & 1 & 0\\1 & 0 & 0\end{bmatrix}$

where a,b,c,x,y,z,p,q,r are natural numbers.
If $\text{tr}(AB+AB^3+AB^5+\ldots+AB^{19})=210$, then number of ordered triplets (p,q,r) is

(a) 175 (b) 190 (c) 210 (d) 225

Sol. (b) $AB=\begin{bmatrix}a & x & p\\y & q & b\\r & c & z\end{bmatrix}\begin{bmatrix}0 & 0 & 1\\0 & 1 & 0\\1 & 0 & 0\end{bmatrix}=\begin{bmatrix}p & x & a\\b & q & y\\z & c & r\end{bmatrix}$

$$\therefore \quad AB=AB^3=\ldots=AB^{19}=\begin{bmatrix}p & x & a\\b & q & y\\z & c & r\end{bmatrix}$$

$$\Rightarrow \text{tr}(AB+AB^3+\ldots+AB^{19})=210$$

$$\therefore \quad 10(p+q+r)=210$$

$$\Rightarrow \quad p+q+r=21$$

Number of ordered triplet $={}^{21-1}C_{3-1}={}^{20}C_2=190$

Example 65. If $A=\begin{bmatrix}1 & 2\\0 & 1\end{bmatrix}$, $P=\begin{bmatrix}\cos\theta & \sin\theta\\-\sin\theta & \cos\theta\end{bmatrix}$, $Q=P^TAP$, then $PQ^{2014}P^T$ is equal to

(a) $\begin{bmatrix}1 & 2^{2014}\\0 & 1\end{bmatrix}$ (b) $\begin{bmatrix}1 & 4028\\0 & 1\end{bmatrix}$

(c) $(P^T)^{2013}A^{2014}P^{2013}$ (d) $P^TA^{2014}P$

Sol. (b) $P\cdot P^T=\begin{bmatrix}\cos\theta & \sin\theta\\-\sin\theta & \cos\theta\end{bmatrix}\begin{bmatrix}\cos\theta & -\sin\theta\\\sin\theta & \cos\theta\end{bmatrix}$

$$=\begin{bmatrix}1 & 0\\0 & 1\end{bmatrix}=I$$

$$A^n=(I+M)^n=I+{}^nC_1M+{}^nC_2M^2+\ldots$$

where $I=\begin{bmatrix}1 & 0\\0 & 1\end{bmatrix}$ and $M=\begin{bmatrix}0 & 2\\0 & 0\end{bmatrix}$,

then $M^2=0$

$$\therefore \quad A^n=I+{}^nC_1M+0$$

$$=\begin{bmatrix}1 & 0\\0 & 1\end{bmatrix}+\begin{bmatrix}0 & 2n\\0 & 0\end{bmatrix}$$

$$=\begin{bmatrix}1 & 2n\\0 & 1\end{bmatrix}$$

$$PQ^{2014}P^T=P(P^TAP)(P^TAP)\ldots(P^TAP)P^T$$

$$=IAIA\ldots AI$$

$$=A^{2014}$$

$$=\begin{bmatrix}1 & 4028\\0 & 1\end{bmatrix}$$

Milestone Practice 7.4

1. If the system of equations $ax + y = 1$, $x + 2y = 3$, $2x + 3y = 5$ are consistent, then a is given by

(a) 0 (b) 1
(c) 2 (d) None of these

2. The system of equations $x + y + z = 2$, $2x + y - z = 3$, $3x + 2y + \lambda z = 4$ has unique solution if

(a) $\lambda \neq 0$ (b) $-1 < \lambda < 1$
(c) $\lambda = 0$ (d) $-2 < \lambda < 2$

3. The value of a for which the following system of equations $a^3x + (a+1)^3y + (a+2)^3z = 0$, $ax + (a+1)y + (a+2)z = 0$, $x + y + z = 0$ has a non-trivial solution is equal to

(a) 2 (b) 1
(c) 0 (d) –1

4. The number of solutions of the set of equations $\frac{2x^2}{a^2} - \frac{y^2}{b^2} - \frac{z^2}{c^2} = 0$, $-\frac{x^2}{a^2} + \frac{2y^2}{b^2} - \frac{z^2}{c^2} = 0$, $-\frac{x^2}{a^2} - \frac{y^2}{b^2} + \frac{2z^2}{c^2} = 0$ is

(a) unique solution (b) no solution
(c) infinitely many solutions (d) two solutions

5. Let $A = \begin{bmatrix} x & y & z \\ y & z & x \\ z & x & y \end{bmatrix}$, x, y and z real numbers such that $x + y + z > 0$ and $xyz = 2$, if $A^2 = I$. Then, value of $x^3 + y^3 + z^3$ is

(a) 5 (b) 7
(c) –5 (d) –7

6. Let $A = \begin{bmatrix} 0 & 1 & 0 \\ 1 & 0 & 0 \\ 0 & 0 & 1 \end{bmatrix}$, then the number of 3×3 matrices B with entries from set {1, 2, 3, 4, 5} and satisfying $AB = BA$ is

(a) 3125 (b) 3175 (c) 3225 (d) 3025

7. If $A = \begin{bmatrix} -2 & 3 \\ -1 & 1 \end{bmatrix}$, then A^3 is equal to

(a) $2A$ (b) A (c) $2I$. (d) I

8. If $A = \begin{bmatrix} 2 & 2 & 1 \\ 1 & 3 & 1 \\ 1 & 2 & 2 \end{bmatrix}$ and the sum of eigen values of A is m and product of eigen values of A is n, then $m + n$ is equal to

(a) 10 (b) 12 (c) 14 (d) 16

9. If $A = \begin{bmatrix} 1 & 2 \\ -1 & 4 \end{bmatrix}$ and θ be the angle between the two non-zero column vectors X such that $AX = \lambda X$ for some scalar λ, then $9\sec^2\theta$ is equal to

(a) 13 (b) 12 (c) 11 (d) 10

10. If A is matrix of order 3 such that $|A| = 5$ and $b = \text{adj } A$, then the value of $||A^{-1}|(AB)^T|$ is equal to

(a) 5 (b) 1 (c) 25 (d) $\frac{1}{25}$

11. Let M be a 3×3 matrix satisfying $M^3 = 0$. Then, which of the following statements are not true?

(a) $\left|\frac{1}{2}M^2 + M + I\right| \neq 0$ (b) $\left|\frac{1}{2}M^2 - M + I\right| = 0$
(c) $\left|\frac{1}{2}M^2 + \frac{M}{2} + I\right| \neq 0$ (d) $\left|\frac{1}{2}M^2 - \frac{M}{2} + I\right| \neq 0$

Answer Key

1. (a)	2. (a)	3. (d)	4. (c)	5. (b)
6. (a)	7. (d)	8. (b)	9. (d)	10. (b)
11. (b)				

For Detailed Solution

JEE Pattern
EXAMPLES

Single Option Correct Type Questions

Example 1 *If A is a square matrix of order 2 such that* $A\begin{bmatrix}1\\-1\end{bmatrix}=\begin{bmatrix}-1\\2\end{bmatrix}$ *and* $A^2\begin{bmatrix}1\\-1\end{bmatrix}=\begin{bmatrix}1\\0\end{bmatrix}$. *The sum of elements and product of elements of A are S and P, then S + P is*

(a) −1 (b) 2 (c) 4 (d) 5

Sol. (d) Let $A=\begin{bmatrix}a & b\\c & d\end{bmatrix}$

From first part, $A\begin{bmatrix}1\\-1\end{bmatrix}=\begin{bmatrix}-1\\2\end{bmatrix}$ ...(i)

$\Rightarrow \begin{bmatrix}a & b\\c & d\end{bmatrix}\begin{bmatrix}1\\-1\end{bmatrix}=\begin{bmatrix}-1\\2\end{bmatrix}$

or $a-b=-1$ ...(ii)

and $c-d=2$ ...(iii)

From second part,

$$A^2\begin{bmatrix}1\\-1\end{bmatrix}=\begin{bmatrix}1\\0\end{bmatrix} \Rightarrow A\left(A\begin{bmatrix}1\\-1\end{bmatrix}\right)=\begin{bmatrix}1\\0\end{bmatrix}$$

From Eq. (i), we get

$$A\begin{bmatrix}-1\\2\end{bmatrix}=\begin{bmatrix}1\\0\end{bmatrix} \Rightarrow \begin{bmatrix}a & b\\c & d\end{bmatrix}\begin{bmatrix}-1\\2\end{bmatrix}=\begin{bmatrix}1\\0\end{bmatrix}$$

or $-a+2b=1$ ...(iv)

and $-c+2d=0$ ...(v)

From Eqs. (ii) and (iv), we get

$a=-1, b=0$

and from Eqs. (iii) and (v), we get

$c=4, d=2$

$\therefore$ $S=a+b+c+d=5$

and $P=abcd=0$

Hence, $S+P=5$

Example 2 *If P is an orthogonal matrix and* $Q=PAP^T$ *and* $B=P^TQ^{1000}P$, *then* B^{-1} *is, where A is involutory matrix*

(a) A (b) A^{1000}
(c) I (d) None of these

Decoding the Question

We know that two matrix are orthogonal if its transpose is equal to its inverse matrix i.e. $AA^T=I \Rightarrow A^T=A^{-1}$.

Sol. (c) Given, P is orthogonal

$\therefore$ $P^TP=I$ ...(i)

and $Q=PAP^T$ ...(ii)

Now, $B=P^TQ^{1000}P=P^T(PAP^T)^{1000}P$ [from Eq. (ii)]

$=P^TPAP^T(PAP^T)^{999}P$

$=IAP^T\cdot PAP^T(PAP^T)^{998}P$

$=AIAP^T(PAP^T)^{998}P$

$=A^2P^TPAP^T(PAP^T)^{997}P$

$=A^2IAP^T(PAP^T)^{997}P$

$=A^3P^T(PAP^T)^{997}P$

... ...

$=A^{1000}P^TP=A^{1000}=I$ [$\because$ A is involutory]

Hence, $B^{-1}=I^{-1}=I$

Example 3 *If matrix* $A=\begin{bmatrix}a & x & y\\x & b & z\\y & z & c\end{bmatrix}$, *where* $a, b, c, x, y, z \in \{1, 2, 3, 4, 5, 6\}$ *and also a, b, c, x, y, z are distinct, then the number of A with trace equal to 10 are*

(a) $3\,(3!)^2$ (b) $2(3!)^2$ (c) $(3!)^2$ (d) $(3!)^3$

Sol. (a) $\text{Tr}(A)=a+b+c=10,\ a\neq b\neq c$

It may be (1, 3, 6), (1, 4, 5), (2, 3, 5)

Number of matrices $=3!\times 3!\times 3$

[arrangement of diagonal elements, arrangement non-diagonal elements]

$=3(3!)^2$

Example 4 *Let* $M=\begin{bmatrix}0 & i\\i & 0\end{bmatrix}$, *where* $i=\sqrt{-1}$ *and I be identity matrix of order 2. Then,* $I+M+M^2+M^3+\ldots+M^{2010}$ *is equal to*

(a) $\begin{bmatrix}0 & 0\\0 & 0\end{bmatrix}$ (b) $\begin{bmatrix}0 & i\\i & 0\end{bmatrix}$ (c) $\begin{bmatrix}1 & i\\i & 1\end{bmatrix}$ (d) $\begin{bmatrix}-1 & 0\\0 & -1\end{bmatrix}$

Sol. (b) $M=\begin{bmatrix}0 & i\\ i & 0\end{bmatrix}$, $M^2=MM=\begin{bmatrix}-1 & 0\\ 0 & -1\end{bmatrix}$,

$$M^3=\begin{bmatrix}0 & -i\\ -i & 0\end{bmatrix}, M^4=\begin{bmatrix}1 & 0\\ 0 & 1\end{bmatrix}=I$$

So, $I+M+M^2+M^3=\begin{bmatrix}0 & 0\\ 0 & 0\end{bmatrix}$

$$\therefore\ I+M+M^2+M^3+\ldots+M^{2010}$$
$$=(1+M+M^2+M^3)+M^4(1+M+M^2+M^3)+\ldots+M^{2008}(I+M+M^2)$$
$$=0+0+\ldots M^{2008}\cdot M \quad [\because I+M+M^2=M]$$
$$=M^{2009}=M$$

Example 5 *If $A=\begin{bmatrix}1 & 1\\ 1 & 1\end{bmatrix}$ and $\det(A^n-I)=1-\lambda^n, n\in N$, then the value of λ, is*

(a) 1 (b) 2 (c) 3 (d) 4

Sol. (*b*) $\because\quad A=\begin{bmatrix}1 & 1\\ 1 & 1\end{bmatrix}$

$$\therefore\quad A^2=\begin{bmatrix}2 & 2\\ 2 & 2\end{bmatrix}=2\begin{bmatrix}1 & 1\\ 1 & 1\end{bmatrix}=2A$$

$$\Rightarrow\quad A^3=A^2\cdot A=2A^2=2^2A$$

Similarly, $A^n=2^{n-1}A$

$$\therefore\quad A^n-I=\begin{bmatrix}2^{n-1} & 2^{n-1}\\ 2^{n-1} & 2^{n-1}\end{bmatrix}-\begin{bmatrix}1 & 0\\ 0 & 1\end{bmatrix}=\begin{bmatrix}2^{n-1}-1 & 2^{n-1}\\ 2^{n-1} & 2^{n-1}-1\end{bmatrix}$$

$$\Rightarrow\quad \det(A^n-I)=(2^{n-1}-1)^2-(2^{n-1})^2$$
$$=1-2^n$$
$$=1-\lambda^n \quad \text{[given]}$$
$$\therefore\quad \lambda=2$$

Example 6 *If $\omega(\neq 1)$ is a cube root of unity and matrix $A=\begin{bmatrix}1 & 1 & 1\\ 1 & \omega & \omega^2\\ 1 & \omega^2 & \omega\end{bmatrix}$, then A^{-1} is equal to*

(a) $\begin{bmatrix}1 & \omega & \omega^2\\ \omega^2 & 1 & \omega\\ \omega & \omega^2 & 1\end{bmatrix}$ (b) $\frac{1}{3}\begin{bmatrix}1 & 1 & 1\\ 1 & \omega^2 & \omega\\ 1 & \omega & \omega^2\end{bmatrix}$

(c) $\begin{bmatrix}1 & \omega & \omega^2\\ 1 & \omega^2 & \omega\\ 1 & 1 & 1\end{bmatrix}$ (d) $3\begin{bmatrix}1 & \omega & \omega^2\\ 1 & \omega^2 & \omega\\ 1 & 1 & 1\end{bmatrix}$

> **Decoding the Question**
> The sum of the cube roots of unity is zero
> i.e. $1+\omega+\omega^2=0$ and $\omega^3=1$

Sol. (b) $|A|=\begin{vmatrix}1 & 1 & 1\\ 1 & \omega & \omega^2\\ 1 & \omega^2 & \omega\end{vmatrix}=3(\omega^2-\omega)$

$$\text{adj}(A)=\begin{bmatrix}\omega^2-\omega & \omega^2-\omega & \omega^2-\omega\\ \omega^2-\omega & \omega-1 & 1-\omega^2\\ \omega^2-\omega & 1-\omega^2 & \omega-1\end{bmatrix}^T$$

$$A^{-1}=\frac{\text{adj}(A)}{|A|}=\frac{1}{3}\begin{bmatrix}1 & 1 & 1\\ 1 & 1/\omega & -\frac{1+\omega}{\omega}\\ 1 & -\frac{1+\omega}{\omega} & \frac{1}{\omega}\end{bmatrix}=\frac{1}{3}\begin{bmatrix}1 & 1 & 1\\ 1 & \omega^2 & \omega\\ 1 & \omega & \omega^2\end{bmatrix}$$

$[\because 1+\omega+\omega^2=0, \omega^3=1]$

Example 7 *For a matrix $A=\begin{bmatrix}1 & 2r-1\\ 0 & 1\end{bmatrix}$, the value of $\sum_{r=1}^{50}\begin{bmatrix}1 & 2r-1\\ 0 & 1\end{bmatrix}$ is equal to*

(a) $\begin{bmatrix}1 & 100\\ 0 & 1\end{bmatrix}$ (b) $\begin{bmatrix}1 & 4950\\ 0 & 1\end{bmatrix}$

(c) $\begin{bmatrix}1 & 5050\\ 0 & 1\end{bmatrix}$ (d) $\begin{bmatrix}1 & 2500\\ 0 & 1\end{bmatrix}$

Sol. (d) $\sum_{r=1}^{50}\begin{bmatrix}1 & 2r-1\\ 0 & 1\end{bmatrix}=\begin{bmatrix}1 & 1+3+5+\ldots+99\\ 0 & 1\end{bmatrix}$

$$=\begin{bmatrix}1 & (50)^2\\ 0 & 1\end{bmatrix}=\begin{bmatrix}1 & 2500\\ 0 & 1\end{bmatrix}$$

Example 8 *If $A_1, A_2, A_3, \ldots, A_{2n-1}$ are n skew-symmetric matrices of same order, then $B=\sum_{r=1}^{n}(2r-1)(A_{2r-1})^{2r-1}$ will be*

(a) symmetric
(b) skew-symmetric
(c) neither symmetric nor skew-symmetric
(d) data not adequate

Sol. (b) $\because\ B=A_1+3A_3^3+5A_5^5+\ldots\ +(2n-1)(A_{2n-1})^{2n-1}$

$$\therefore\ B^T=(A_1+3A_3^3+5A_5^5+\ldots+(2n-1)(A_{2n-1})^{2n-1})^T$$
$$=A_1^T+3(A_3^T)^3+5(A_5^T)^5+\ldots+(2n-1)(A_{2n-1}^T)^{2n-1}$$
$$=-A_1+3(-A_3)^3+5(-A_5)^5+\ldots+(2n-1)(-A_{2n-1})^{2n-1}$$
$$=-(A_1+3A_3^3+5A_5^5+\ldots+(2n-1)A_{2n-1}^{2n-1})$$
$$=-B$$

Hence, B is skew-symmetric.

Example 9 *Elements of a matrix A of order* 10×10 *are defined as* $a_{ij} = \omega^{i+j}$ *(where* ω *is cube root of unity), then trace* (A) *of the matrix is*

(a) 0 (b) 1 (c) 3 (d) None of these

Sol. (d) $\text{Tr}(A) = \sum_{i=j=1}^{10} a_{ij} = \sum_{i=j=1}^{10} \omega^{i+j} = \sum_{i=1}^{10} \omega^{2i}$

$= \omega^2 + \omega^4 + \omega^6 + \omega^8 + \ldots + \omega^{20}$

$= (\omega^2 + \omega + 1) + (\omega^2 + \omega + 1) + (\omega^2 + \omega + 1) + \omega^{20}$

$= 0 + 0 + 0 + \omega^2 = \omega^2$

JEE SCANNER

Example 10 Similar to PYQ Asked in JEE Main 2024

Let $\alpha \in (0, \infty)$ *and* $A = \begin{bmatrix} 2 & 1 & 2 \\ 1 & 0 & 1 \\ 0 & \alpha & 0 \end{bmatrix}$. *If* $\det(adj(2A - A^T) \cdot adj(A - 2A^T)) = 2^8$, *then* $(\det(A))^2$ *is equal to*

(a) 4 (b) 0 (c) 8 (d) 9

Sol. (b) $|\text{adj}(A - 2A^T)(2A - A^T)| = 2^8$

$|(A - 2A^T)(2A - A^T)| = 2^4$

$\Rightarrow \quad |A - 2A^T||2A - A^T| = \pm 16$ ...(i)

Now, $(A - 2A^T)^T = A^T - 2A$

$\Rightarrow \quad |(A - 2A^T)^T| = |A^T - 2A|$

$\Rightarrow \quad |A - 2A^T| = A^T - 2A$

Then, Eq. (i) becomes,

$|A - 2A^T|^2 = 16 \Rightarrow |A - 2A^T| = \pm 4$

$$\left|\begin{bmatrix} 2 & 1 & 2 \\ 1 & 0 & 1 \\ 0 & \alpha & 0 \end{bmatrix} - 2\begin{bmatrix} 2 & 1 & 0 \\ 1 & 0 & \alpha \\ 2 & 1 & 0 \end{bmatrix}\right| = \pm 4 \Rightarrow \begin{vmatrix} -2 & -1 & 2 \\ -1 & 0 & 1-2\alpha \\ -4 & \alpha - 2 & 0 \end{vmatrix} = \pm 4$$

$\Rightarrow \quad 4(1 - \alpha^2) = \pm 4 \Rightarrow \alpha = 0 \text{ or } \alpha = \pm\sqrt{2}$

$\because \alpha \in (0, \infty) \quad \therefore \alpha = \sqrt{2}$

Thus, $|A| = \begin{vmatrix} 2 & 1 & 2 \\ 1 & 0 & 1 \\ 0 & \sqrt{2} & 0 \end{vmatrix} = 0 \Rightarrow |A|^2 = 0$

Skill Builder

Let $\alpha \in (1, \infty)$ and $A = \begin{bmatrix} 1 & 2 & 1 \\ 0 & 0 & 1 \\ \alpha & 0 & 2 \end{bmatrix}$. If $\det(\text{adj}(2A - A^T) \cdot \text{adj}(A - 2A^T)) = 2^8$, then $(\det A)^2$ is equal to

For Sol.

(a) $\frac{100}{49}$ (b) $\frac{10}{7}$ (c) $\frac{2}{49}$ (d) $\frac{3}{70}$

Example 11 *If A and B are square symmetric matrices of order 3 such that* $2(A + B) = A^T + B^T + 3I$ *and* $AA^T = 4I$, *then* $\det(12A^{-1} - BA^T + I)$ *is equal to*

(a) 125 (b) 25 (c) 255 (d) 175

Sol. (a) $A + B = 3I$

$\Rightarrow \quad AA^T + BA^T = 3A^T$

$\Rightarrow \quad AA^T = 3A^T - BA^T$

$\Rightarrow \quad 4I = 3A^T - BA^T$

$\Rightarrow \quad 12A^{-1} - BA^T + I = 5I$

$\therefore \quad |12A^{-1} - BA^T + I| = 125$

More than One Correct Option Type Questions

Example 12 *If matrix M is a square matrix, then*

(a) MM^T is symmetric matrix.

(b) MM^T is skew-symmetric matrix.

(c) M^TM is symmetric matrix.

(d) M^TM is skew-symmetric matrices.

Sol. (a, c) Given, M is a square matrix.

Using properties of symmetric matrix,

If M be a square matrix, then MM^T and M^TM are symmetric matrices.

Example 13 *If* $A = [a_{ij}]_{n \times n}$ *and f is a function, we define* $f(A) = [f(a_{ij})]_{n \times n}$. *Let* $A = \begin{bmatrix} \frac{\pi}{2} - \theta & \theta \\ -\theta & \frac{\pi}{2} - \theta \end{bmatrix}$, *then*

(a) $\sin A$ is invertible. (b) $\sin A = \cos A$

(c) $\sin A$ is orthogonal. (d) $\sin 2A = 2\sin A \cos A$

Sol. (*a, c*) $\sin A = \begin{bmatrix} \cos\theta & \sin\theta \\ -\sin\theta & \cos\theta \end{bmatrix}$

and $\cos\theta = \begin{bmatrix} \sin\theta & \cos\theta \\ \cos\theta & \sin\theta \end{bmatrix}$

$\therefore |\sin A| = \cos^2\theta + \sin^2\theta = 1 \neq 0$

Hence, $\sin A$ is invertible.

Also, $(\sin A)(\sin A)^T = \begin{bmatrix} \cos\theta & \sin\theta \\ -\sin\theta & \cos\theta \end{bmatrix}\begin{bmatrix} \cos\theta & -\sin\theta \\ \sin\theta & \cos\theta \end{bmatrix}$

$= \begin{bmatrix} 1 & 0 \\ 0 & 1 \end{bmatrix} = I$

Hence, $\sin A$ is orthogonal.

Also, $2\sin A\cos A = 2\begin{bmatrix} \cos\theta & \sin\theta \\ -\sin\theta & \cos\theta \end{bmatrix}\begin{bmatrix} \sin\theta & \cos\theta \\ \cos\theta & \sin\theta \end{bmatrix}$

$= 2\begin{bmatrix} \sin 2\theta & 1 \\ \cos 2\theta & 0 \end{bmatrix}$

$\neq \sin 2A$

Example 14 *Let A and B are two square idempotent matrices such that $AB \pm BA$ is a null matrix, the value of $\det(A-B)$ can be equal*

(a) -1 (b) 0

(c) 1 (d) 2

Sol. (a,b,c) $\because \quad (A-B)^2 = A^2 - AB - BA + B^2$

$$= A + B \quad [\because AB + BA = 0 \text{ and } A^2 = A,\ B^2 = B]$$

$\therefore \quad |A - B|^2 = |A + B| \quad \ldots(\text{i})$

and $\quad (A+B)^2 = A^2 + AB + BA + B^2$

$$= A + B \quad [\because AB + BA = 0 \text{ and } A^2 = A,\ B^2 = B]$$

$\Rightarrow \quad |A + B|^2 = |A + B|$

$\Rightarrow \quad |A + B|(|A + B| - 1) = 0$

$\therefore \quad |A + B| = 0, 1$

From Eq. (i),

$$|A - B|^2 = 0, 1$$

$\Rightarrow \quad |A - B| = 0, \pm 1$

or $\quad \det(A - B) = 0, -1, 1$

Example 15 *Let* $A = \begin{bmatrix} 1 & 0 & 0 \\ 2 & 1 & 0 \\ 4 & 2 & 1 \end{bmatrix}$ *and $B = [b_{ij}]$ is a 3×3 matrix such that $A^{100} - B = I$, then*

(a) $b_{32} = b_{21}$

(b) B is lower triangular matrix

(c) B is upper triangular matrix

(d) $b_{21} = 100$

Sol. (a,b) Let $\quad D = A - I$

$$= \begin{bmatrix} 1 & 0 & 0 \\ 2 & 1 & 0 \\ 4 & 2 & 1 \end{bmatrix} - \begin{bmatrix} 1 & 0 & 0 \\ 0 & 1 & 0 \\ 0 & 0 & 1 \end{bmatrix} = \begin{bmatrix} 0 & 0 & 0 \\ 2 & 0 & 0 \\ 4 & 2 & 0 \end{bmatrix}$$

$$(I + D)^{100} = I + {}^{100}C_1 \cdot D + {}^{100}C_2 D^2 + {}^{100}C_3 D^3 + \ldots + {}^{100}C_{100} D^{100}$$

$$D^2 = \begin{bmatrix} 0 & 0 & 0 \\ 2 & 0 & 0 \\ 4 & 2 & 0 \end{bmatrix}\begin{bmatrix} 0 & 0 & 0 \\ 2 & 0 & 0 \\ 4 & 2 & 0 \end{bmatrix} = \begin{bmatrix} 0 & 0 & 0 \\ 0 & 0 & 0 \\ 4 & 0 & 0 \end{bmatrix}$$

Similarly, $D^3 = D^2 \cdot D = \begin{bmatrix} 0 & 0 & 0 \\ 0 & 0 & 0 \\ 4 & 0 & 0 \end{bmatrix}\begin{bmatrix} 0 & 0 & 0 \\ 2 & 0 & 0 \\ 4 & 2 & 0 \end{bmatrix}$

$\Rightarrow \quad D^3 = \begin{bmatrix} 0 & 0 & 0 \\ 0 & 0 & 0 \\ 0 & 0 & 0 \end{bmatrix}$

$\Rightarrow \quad A = I + D$

$\Rightarrow \quad A^{100} = (I + D)^{100} = I + 100 \cdot D + 4950 D^2 + 0 + \ldots + 0$

$$= I + 100D + 4950D^2$$

$\Rightarrow \quad B = A^{100} - I = 100D + 4950\, D^2$

$$= 100\begin{bmatrix} 0 & 0 & 0 \\ 2 & 0 & 0 \\ 4 & 2 & 0 \end{bmatrix} + 4950\begin{bmatrix} 0 & 0 & 0 \\ 0 & 0 & 0 \\ 4 & 0 & 0 \end{bmatrix} = \begin{bmatrix} 0 & 0 & 0 \\ 200 & 0 & 0 \\ 20200 & 200 & 0 \end{bmatrix}$$

Example 16 *Let* $A = \begin{bmatrix} a & b & 1 \\ 2 & 1 & 3 \\ 1 & c & 2 \end{bmatrix}$ *and $3A^{-1} = 5A - A^2$. Then,*

(a) $|A| = 3$ (b) $|A| = -3$

(c) $\text{tr}(A) = 5$ (d) $\text{tr}(A) = a + b + c$

Sol. (b,c,d) $3I = 5A^2 - A^3$

$\Rightarrow \quad A^3 - 5A^2 + 3I = 0$

$$\text{tr}(A) = 5 = a + 3,\ a = 2$$

$$|A| = -3,\ 4 + 2c + 3b - 1 - 6c - 4b = -3$$

$$b + 4c = 6 \text{ and } a + 2 + 2a - 2b - 1 - 3c = 0$$

$\therefore \quad 2b + 3c = 7,\ 2b + 8c = 12,\ c = 1 \text{ and } b = 2$

Example 17 *Let A be a square matrix of order such that*

$[\text{adj}\ \{\text{adj}\ (\text{adj}(A))\}] = \begin{bmatrix} 16 & 0 & 4 \\ 5 & 4 & 0 \\ 1 & 4 & 3 \end{bmatrix}$ *and $\det(A)$ is positive.*

Then, which of the following must be correct?

(a) $8\,\text{tr}(A^{-1}) = 23$ (b) $8\,\text{tr}(A^{-1}) = 35$

(c) $|\text{adj}\ A| = 4$ (d) $|\text{adj}\ A| = 2$

Decoding the Question

We will use the property

$$\text{adj}\ (\text{adj}A) = |A|^{n-2} \cdot A$$

$\therefore \quad [\text{adj}(\text{adj}(\text{adj}(A)))] = |\text{adj}\,A|^{n-2}\, \text{adj}A = (|A|^{n-1})^{n-2} \text{adj}A$

Sol. (a,c) $|\text{adj}\,(\text{adj}\,(\text{adj}A))| = |A|^8 = 256 \Rightarrow |A| = 2$

$$\text{adj}\,(\text{adj}\,(\text{adj}\ A)) = |\text{adj}A|\,(\text{adj}A) = 4(\text{adj}A) = \begin{bmatrix} 16 & 0 & 4 \\ 5 & 4 & 0 \\ 1 & 4 & 3 \end{bmatrix}$$

$$\text{adj}A = \begin{bmatrix} 4 & 0 & 1 \\ 5/4 & 1 & 0 \\ 1/4 & 1 & 3/4 \end{bmatrix} \Rightarrow A^{-1} = \begin{bmatrix} 2 & 0 & 1/2 \\ 5/8 & 1/2 & 0 \\ 1/8 & 1/2 & 3/8 \end{bmatrix}$$

Passage Based Questions

Passage I

(Ex. Nos. 18 to 19)

If $A_0 = \begin{bmatrix} 2 & -2 & -4 \\ -1 & 3 & 4 \\ 1 & -2 & -3 \end{bmatrix}$ and $B_0 = \begin{bmatrix} -4 & -3 & -3 \\ 1 & 0 & 1 \\ 4 & 4 & 3 \end{bmatrix}$ and

$B_n = \text{adj}(B_{n-1}), n \in N$ and I is an identity matrix of order 3.

Example 18 *$\det(A_0 + A_0^2 B_0^2 + A_0^3 + A_0^4 B_0^4 + \ldots$ upto 12 terms) is equal to*

(a) 1200 (b) −960 (c) 0 (d) −9600

Example 19 *For a variable matrix X, the equation $A_0 X = B_0$ will have*

(a) unique solution (b) infinite solution
(c) finitely many solution (d) no solution

Sol. (Ex. Nos 18 to 19)

$\because \quad A_0 = \begin{bmatrix} 2 & -2 & -4 \\ -1 & 3 & 4 \\ 1 & -2 & -3 \end{bmatrix} \Rightarrow |A_0| = 0$

and $\text{adj} B_0 = \begin{bmatrix} -4 & 1 & 4 \\ -3 & 0 & 4 \\ -3 & 1 & 3 \end{bmatrix}^T = \begin{bmatrix} -4 & -3 & -3 \\ 1 & 0 & 1 \\ 4 & 4 & 3 \end{bmatrix} = B_0$

$\because \quad B_n = \text{adj}(B_{n-1}), n \in N$

$\therefore \quad B_1 = \text{adj}(B_0) = B_0$

$\Rightarrow \quad B_2 = \text{adj}(B_1) = \text{adj}(B_0) = B_0,$

Similarly, $B_3 = B_0, B_4 = B_0, \ldots$

$\therefore \quad B_n = B_0, \forall\, n \in N$

18. (c) $\det(A_0 + A_0^2 B_0^2 + A_0^3 + A_0^4 B_0^4 + \ldots$ upto 12 terms)

$= \det$

$\det[A_0(I + A_0 B_0^2 + A_0^2 + A_0^3 B_0^4 + \ldots \text{upto 12 terms})]$

$= |A_0|(I + A_0 B_0^2 + A_0^2 + A_0^3 B_0^4 + \ldots$ upto 12 terms)

$= 0$ $\quad [\because |A_0| = 0]$

19. (d) $\because |A_0| = 0$

$\Rightarrow A_0^{-1}$ is not possible.

Hence, the system of equation $A_0 X = B_0$ has no solution.

Passage II

(Ex. Nos. 20 to 21)

Consider two 3×3 matrices A and B satisfying $A = \text{adj } B - B^T$, and $B = \text{adj } A - A^T$

Example 20 *If A is a non-singular matrix, then $(\det A)^2 + (\det B)^2$ is equal to*

(a) 16 (b) 48 (c) 64 (d) 128

Example 21 *The value of $|\text{adj}(2B^{-1})|$ is equal to*

(a) 1 (b) 16
(c) 64 (d) 128

Sol. (Ex. Nos. 20 to 21)

20. (d) $A = \text{adj } B - B^T$ ...(i)

$B = \text{adj } A - A^T$ ...(ii)

$A^T = (\text{adj} B)^T - B$

$\text{adj } A = \text{adj } B^T$, since A is non-singular.

$\Rightarrow$ B is non-singular.

$\Rightarrow \quad A = B^T$ or $A = -B^T$

If $\quad A = B^T$

$\Rightarrow \quad \text{adj} B = 2A$ [using Eq. (i)]

$\Rightarrow \quad |B|^2 = 8|B|$ $\quad [\because |kc| = k^n |c|$, n is order of matrix]

$\Rightarrow \quad |B| = 8$ and $|A| = 8$

$\Rightarrow \quad |A|^2 + |B|^2 = 64 + 64 = 128$

21. (a) $|\text{adj}(2B^{-1})| = \dfrac{(2^3)^2}{8^2} = \dfrac{64}{64} = 1$

Stem Based Questions

Stem I

(Ex. Nos. 22 to 23)

If α and β are the roots of the equation

$$[1\ 25]\begin{bmatrix} 0 & 1/2 \\ -1 & 1/2 \end{bmatrix}^5 \begin{bmatrix} 1 & -1 \\ 2 & 0 \end{bmatrix}^{10} \begin{bmatrix} 0 & 1/2 \\ -1 & 1/2 \end{bmatrix}^5 \begin{bmatrix} x^2 - 5x + 20 \\ x + 2 \end{bmatrix} = [40]$$

Example 22 *Value of $(1-\alpha)(1-\beta)$ is ………*

Example 23 *Value of $\alpha\beta$ …… .*

Sol. (Ex. Nos 22 to 23)

Let $A = \begin{bmatrix} 0 & 1/2 \\ -1 & 1/2 \end{bmatrix}$ and $B = \begin{bmatrix} 1 & -1 \\ 2 & 0 \end{bmatrix}$

Here, $\quad AB = I = BA$

$A^5 B^{10} A^5 = A^5 B^5 B^5 A^5 = I^5 I^5 = I$

$\Rightarrow \quad [1\ 25]\begin{bmatrix} x^2 - 5x + 20 \\ x + 2 \end{bmatrix} = [40]$

$\Rightarrow \quad x^2 + 20x + 30 = 0$

$\Rightarrow \quad \alpha + \beta = -20$

$\Rightarrow \quad \alpha\beta = 30, (1-\alpha)(1-\beta) = 1 - (\alpha + \beta) + \alpha\beta$

$= 1 - (-20) + 30$

$= 51$

22. (51) **23.** (30)

Single Integer Answer Type Questions

Example 24 *Let A be a 3×3 diagonal matrix which commutes with every 3×3 matrix. If $\det(A)=8$, then tr (A) is*

Sol. (6) Let $A=\begin{bmatrix}\alpha & 0 & 0\\ 0 & \beta & 0\\ 0 & 0 & \gamma\end{bmatrix}$

$$\therefore \begin{bmatrix}\alpha & 0 & 0\\ 0 & \beta & 0\\ 0 & 0 & \gamma\end{bmatrix}\begin{bmatrix}a & h & g\\ h & b & f\\ g & f & c\end{bmatrix}=\begin{bmatrix}a & h & g\\ h & b & f\\ g & f & c\end{bmatrix}\begin{bmatrix}\alpha & 0 & 0\\ 0 & \beta & 0\\ 0 & 0 & \gamma\end{bmatrix}$$

$$\Rightarrow \alpha=\beta=\gamma$$

$$\therefore A=\begin{bmatrix}\alpha & 0 & 0\\ 0 & \alpha & 0\\ 0 & 0 & \alpha\end{bmatrix}$$

$$\Rightarrow \det(A)=\alpha^3=8 \quad \text{[given]}$$

$$\therefore \alpha=2$$

$$\therefore A=\begin{bmatrix}2 & 0 & 0\\ 0 & 2 & 0\\ 0 & 0 & 2\end{bmatrix}$$

$$\Rightarrow \text{tr } A=2+2+2=6$$

Example 25 *Let A and B be two non-singular matrices such that $A\neq I$, $B^3=I$ and $AB=BA^2$, where I is the identity matrix, the least value of k such that $A^k=I$ is*

Sol. (7) Given, $AB=BA^2$

$$\Rightarrow B=A^{-1}BA^2 \text{ and } B^3=I$$
$$\Rightarrow (A^{-1}BAA)(A^{-1}BAA)(A^{-1}BAA)=I$$
$$\Rightarrow (A^{-1}BA)(BA)(BAA)=I \quad [\because A^{-1}A=I]$$
$$\Rightarrow A^{-1}B(AB)(AB)AA=I$$
$$\Rightarrow A^{-1}B(BA^2)(BA^2)AA=I \quad [\because AB=BA^2]$$
$$\Rightarrow A^{-1}BBA(AB)A^4=I$$
$$\Rightarrow A^{-1}BBA(BA^2)A^4=I \quad [\because AB=BA^2]$$
$$\Rightarrow A^{-1}BB(AB)A^6=I$$
$$\Rightarrow A^{-1}BB(BA^2)A^6=I \quad [\because AB=BA^2]$$
$$\Rightarrow A^{-1}B^3A^8=I$$
$$\Rightarrow (A^{-1}I)A^8=I \quad [\because B^3=I]$$
$$\Rightarrow A^{-1}A^8=I$$
$$\Rightarrow A^7=I=A^k \quad [\because A^k=I]$$
$$\Rightarrow A^k=A^7$$

$\therefore$ Least value of k is 7.

Example 26 *If M is the matrix $\begin{bmatrix}1 & -3\\ -1 & 1\end{bmatrix}$, then*

$$M-\frac{1}{3}M^2+\frac{1}{9}M^3\dots+\left(-\frac{1}{3}\right)^n M^{n+1}+\dots\infty=\frac{3}{13}\begin{bmatrix}1 & \alpha\\ \beta & 1\end{bmatrix},$$

then $\left|\frac{\alpha}{\beta}\right|$ is equal to ....

Sol. (3) Let $N=M-\frac{M^2}{3}+\frac{M^3}{9}-\frac{M^4}{27}+\dots\infty \quad$ ...(i)

$$\Rightarrow \frac{-MN}{3}=\frac{-M^2}{3}+\frac{M^3}{9}-\frac{M^4}{27}+\dots\infty \quad \text{...(ii)}$$

On subtracting Eq. (ii) from Eq. (i), we get

$$\left(I+\frac{M}{3}\right)N=M$$

$$\Rightarrow N=\begin{bmatrix}3 & -9\\ -3 & 3\end{bmatrix}\begin{bmatrix}4 & -3\\ -1 & 4\end{bmatrix}^{-1}=\frac{1}{13}\begin{bmatrix}3 & -27\\ -9 & 3\end{bmatrix}=\frac{3}{13}\begin{bmatrix}1 & -9\\ -3 & 1\end{bmatrix}$$

$\therefore \alpha=-9$ and $\beta=-3$

$$\Rightarrow \left|\frac{\alpha}{\beta}\right|=\left|\frac{-9}{-3}\right|=3$$

Example 27 *If* $\begin{vmatrix}2bc-a^2 & c^2 & b^2\\ c^2 & 2ca-b^2 & a^2\\ b^2 & a^2 & 2ab-c^2\end{vmatrix}$ $=(a^3+b^3+c^3+kabc)^2$, *then find the value of k.*

Sol. (−3) We have, $\begin{vmatrix}2bc-a^2 & c^2 & b^2\\ c^2 & 2ca-b^2 & a^2\\ b^2 & a^2 & 2ab-c^2\end{vmatrix}$

$$=\begin{vmatrix}a & b & c\\ b & c & a\\ c & a & b\end{vmatrix}\times\begin{vmatrix}-a & c & b\\ -b & a & c\\ -c & b & a\end{vmatrix}=\begin{vmatrix}a & b & c\\ b & c & a\\ c & a & b\end{vmatrix}\begin{vmatrix}a & b & c\\ b & c & a\\ c & a & b\end{vmatrix}=\begin{vmatrix}a & b & c\\ b & c & a\\ c & a & b\end{vmatrix}^2$$

$$=[a(bc-a^2)+b(ac-b^2)+c(ab-c^2)]^2$$
$$=[a^3+b^3+c^3-3abc]^2$$

$\therefore k=-3$

Example 28 *Let $A=\begin{bmatrix}\sqrt{3} & 1 & 0\\ 1 & -\sqrt{3} & 0\\ 0 & 0 & 2\end{bmatrix}$ and $d=\det(2A^T+AA^T+\text{adj } A)$, then $\sqrt{d}$ is ....*

Sol. (8) Given, $A=\begin{bmatrix}\sqrt{3} & 1 & 0\\ 1 & -\sqrt{3} & 0\\ 0 & 0 & 2\end{bmatrix}$

$$A^T=\begin{bmatrix}\sqrt{3} & 1 & 0\\ 1 & -\sqrt{3} & 0\\ 0 & 0 & 2\end{bmatrix}$$

$$\Rightarrow \quad AA^T = \begin{bmatrix} \sqrt{3} & 1 & 0 \\ 1 & -\sqrt{3} & 0 \\ 0 & 0 & 2 \end{bmatrix} \begin{bmatrix} \sqrt{3} & 1 & 0 \\ 1 & -\sqrt{3} & 0 \\ 0 & 0 & 2 \end{bmatrix}$$

$$= \begin{bmatrix} 4 & 0 & 0 \\ 0 & 4 & 0 \\ 0 & 0 & 4 \end{bmatrix} = 4 \begin{bmatrix} 1 & 0 & 0 \\ 0 & 1 & 0 \\ 0 & 0 & 1 \end{bmatrix} = 4I$$

$$\Rightarrow \quad A^T = 4A^{-1} = \frac{4\operatorname{adj}A}{|A|}$$

$$\because \quad |A| = \sqrt{3}(-2\sqrt{3}) - 1(2) = -6 - 2 = -8$$

$$\Rightarrow \quad A^T = \frac{4\operatorname{adj}A}{-8} \Rightarrow 2A^T + \operatorname{adj}A = 0$$

$$\because \quad d = |2A^T + AA^T + \operatorname{adj}A|$$

$$= |0 + 4I| = |4I|$$

$$= 4^3 |I| = 64$$

$$\therefore \quad \sqrt{d} = \sqrt{64} = 8$$

Numerical Value Type Questions

Example 29 *$D = \begin{bmatrix} 1 & 0 & 0 \\ 0 & 2 & 0 \\ 0 & 0 & 3 \end{bmatrix}$ and $P = \begin{bmatrix} 7 & 0 & 2 \\ 0 & 1 & 0 \\ 2 & 0 & 5 \end{bmatrix}$ consider matrix $M = P^{-1}DP$, then $\det(M^2 + M)$ is equal to ....*

Sol. (144) Given, $D = \begin{bmatrix} 1 & 0 & 0 \\ 0 & 2 & 0 \\ 0 & 0 & 3 \end{bmatrix}$ and $P = \begin{bmatrix} 7 & 0 & 2 \\ 0 & 1 & 0 \\ 2 & 0 & 5 \end{bmatrix}$

Now, $\det(M^2 + M)$

$$= \det[(P^{-1}DP)(P^{-1}DP) + P^{-1}DP]$$

$$= \det(P^{-1}D^2P + P^{-1}DP) = \det(P^{-1}(D^2 + D)P]$$

$$= \det(P^{-1}P)\det(D^2 + D)$$

$$= \det(I)\det(D)\det(D + I)$$

$$= 1^3(1\cdot 2\cdot 3)(2\cdot 3\cdot 4) = 144$$

Example 30 *Let E and M be 3×3 matrices satisfying of equations $EM^T = (EM)^T = 20I$ and $(E+M)^T = 17(E-M)^T$, where I identify matrix of order 3. If $E^2 + M^2 = \frac{a}{b}I$, where a and b are co-prime, then the value of $a + b$ is equal to ....*

Sol. (743) $(EM)^T = 20I$

On taking transpose both sides, we get

$$EM = 20I \quad \text{...(i)}$$

$$(E+M)^T = 17(E-M)^T$$

$$\Rightarrow \quad E^T + M^T = 17(E^T - M^T)$$

$$\Rightarrow \quad 16E^T = 18M^T$$

$$\Rightarrow \quad 16E = 18M \quad \text{...(ii)}$$

On solving Eqs. (i) and (ii), we get

$$E = \pm \frac{3\sqrt{10}}{2} I, \; M = \pm \frac{4\sqrt{10}}{3} I$$

$$E^2 + M^2 = \frac{725}{18} I$$

$$\Rightarrow \quad a + b = 743$$

JEE SCANNER

Example 31 Similar to PYQ Asked in JEE Main 2024

If $A = \begin{bmatrix} 2 & 1 \\ -1 & 2 \end{bmatrix}$, $B = \begin{bmatrix} 0 & 1 \\ 1 & 1 \end{bmatrix}$, $C = ABA^T$ and $X = A^TC^2A$, then $\frac{\det X}{125}$ is equal to ....

Sol. (125) Given, $A = \begin{bmatrix} 2 & 1 \\ -1 & 2 \end{bmatrix} \Rightarrow A^T = \begin{bmatrix} 2 & -1 \\ 1 & 2 \end{bmatrix}$

and $B = \begin{bmatrix} 0 & 0 \\ 1 & 1 \end{bmatrix}$

Thus, $AA^T = \begin{bmatrix} 2 & 1 \\ -1 & 2 \end{bmatrix}\begin{bmatrix} 2 & -1 \\ 1 & 2 \end{bmatrix} = \begin{bmatrix} 5 & 0 \\ 0 & 5 \end{bmatrix} = 5I$

$$C = ABA^T$$

$$C^2 = (ABA^T)(ABA^T)$$

$$= ABA^TABA^T$$

$$= AB5IBA^T$$

$$= 5ABBA^T$$

$$= 5AB^2A^T$$

Now, $X = A^TC^2A$

$$= 5A^TAB^2A^TA$$

$$= 5 \cdot 5IB^2 \cdot 5I$$

$$= 125B^2I$$

$$= 125\begin{bmatrix} 1 & 1 \\ 1 & 2 \end{bmatrix} \quad \left[\because B^2 = \begin{bmatrix} 0 & 1 \\ 1 & 1 \end{bmatrix}\begin{bmatrix} 0 & 1 \\ 1 & 1 \end{bmatrix} = \begin{bmatrix} 1 & 1 \\ 1 & 2 \end{bmatrix}\right]$$

$$= \begin{bmatrix} 125 & 125 \\ 125 & 250 \end{bmatrix}$$

$$\therefore \quad \det X = 15625$$

Thus, $\frac{\det X}{125} = 125$

Skill Builder

If $A = \begin{bmatrix} \sqrt{5} & -1 \\ 1 & \sqrt{5} \end{bmatrix}$ and $B = \begin{bmatrix} 1 & 0 \\ 0 & 1 \end{bmatrix}$, $C = ABA^T$ and $X = A^TC^2A$, then $(\det X)^{\frac{1}{2}}$ is equal to ......

For Sol.

Example 32 $A=\begin{bmatrix}0&1\\3&0\end{bmatrix}$ *and* $(A^8+A^6+A^4+A^2+I)\cdot V=\begin{bmatrix}0\\11\end{bmatrix}$ *(where I is the 2×2 identity matrix), then the product of all elements of matrix V is ....*

Sol. (0) $A=\begin{bmatrix}0&1\\3&0\end{bmatrix}$

$$\Rightarrow A^2=A\cdot A=\begin{bmatrix}0&1\\3&0\end{bmatrix}\begin{bmatrix}0&1\\3&0\end{bmatrix}=\begin{bmatrix}3&0\\0&3\end{bmatrix}$$

$$\Rightarrow A^4=A^2\cdot A^2=\begin{bmatrix}3&0\\0&3\end{bmatrix}\begin{bmatrix}3&0\\0&3\end{bmatrix}=\begin{bmatrix}3^2&0\\0&3^2\end{bmatrix}$$

$$\Rightarrow A^8=\begin{bmatrix}3^4&0\\0&3^4\end{bmatrix}$$

and $A^6=A^4\cdot A^2=\begin{bmatrix}3^2&0\\0&3^2\end{bmatrix}\begin{bmatrix}3&0\\0&3\end{bmatrix}=\begin{bmatrix}3^3&0\\0&3^3\end{bmatrix}$

Let $V=\begin{bmatrix}x\\y\end{bmatrix}$

$$A^8+A^6+A^4+A^2+I$$

$$=\begin{bmatrix}81&0\\0&81\end{bmatrix}+\begin{bmatrix}27&0\\0&27\end{bmatrix}+\begin{bmatrix}9&0\\0&9\end{bmatrix}+\begin{bmatrix}3&0\\0&3\end{bmatrix}+\begin{bmatrix}1&0\\0&1\end{bmatrix}$$

$$=\begin{bmatrix}121&0\\0&121\end{bmatrix}$$

$$(A^8+A^6+A^4+A^2+I)V=\begin{bmatrix}0\\11\end{bmatrix}$$

or $\begin{bmatrix}121&0\\0&121\end{bmatrix}\begin{bmatrix}x\\y\end{bmatrix}=\begin{bmatrix}0\\11\end{bmatrix}$

or $\begin{bmatrix}121x\\121y\end{bmatrix}=\begin{bmatrix}0\\11\end{bmatrix}$

$\Rightarrow$ $x=0$ and $y=\frac{1}{11}$

$\Rightarrow$ $V=\begin{bmatrix}x\\y\end{bmatrix}=\begin{bmatrix}0\\1/11\end{bmatrix}$

Thus, product of all elements of $V=0\times\frac{1}{11}=0$

Example 33 *Let* $A=\begin{bmatrix}1&0&0\\1&0&1\\0&1&0\end{bmatrix}$ *satisfies* $A^n=A^{n-2}+A^2-I$*, then trace of* A^{50} *equals ....*

Sol. (3) $A^2=\begin{bmatrix}1&0&0\\1&0&1\\0&1&0\end{bmatrix}\begin{bmatrix}1&0&0\\1&0&1\\0&1&0\end{bmatrix}=\begin{bmatrix}1&0&0\\1&1&0\\1&0&1\end{bmatrix}$

Given, $A^n=A^{n-2}+A^2-I$

$\Rightarrow$ $A^{50}=A^{48}+A^2-I$

Further $A^{48}=A^{46}+A^2-I$

$A^{46}=A^{44}+A^2-I$

$\vdots \quad \vdots \quad \vdots \quad \vdots$

$A^4=A^2+A^2-I$

On adding all

$A^{50}=25A^2-24I$

$$\Rightarrow A^{50}=25\begin{bmatrix}1&0&0\\1&1&0\\1&0&1\end{bmatrix}-24\begin{bmatrix}1&0&0\\0&1&0\\0&0&1\end{bmatrix}$$

$$\Rightarrow A^{50}=\begin{bmatrix}1&0&0\\25&1&0\\25&0&1\end{bmatrix}$$

Hence, trace of $A^{50}=1+1+1=3$

Matching Type Questions

Example 34 *Match the following columns.*

Column I		Column II
(A) If A is a square matrix of order 3 and det $(A)=3$, then det $(6A^{-1})$ is divisible by	(p)	3
(B) If A is a square matrix of order 3 and det $(A)=\frac{1}{4}$, then det [adj (adj (2A))] is divisible by	(q)	4
(C) If A and B are square matrices of odd order and $(A+B)^2=A^2+B^2$, if det $(A)=2$, then det(B) is divisible by	(r)	5
(D) A square matrix A of order 3 satisfies $A^2=I-A$. If $A^n=5I-8A$, then n is divisible by	(s)	6

Sol. (A) $\to$ (p, q, s); (B) $\to$(q); (C) $\to$(p, q, r, s); (D) $\to$(p, s)

(A) $\det(6A^{-1})=6^3\det(A^{-1})=\frac{216}{\det(A)}=\frac{216}{3}=72$

(B) $\det[\text{adj}(\text{adj}(2A))]=[\det(2A)]^4$

$=[2^3\det(A)]^4=2^{12}[\det(A)]^4$

$=2^{12}\left(\frac{1}{4}\right)^4=2^4=16$

(C) $\because$ $(A+B)^2=A^2+AB+BA+B^2$

$\Rightarrow$ $A^2+B^2=A^2+AB+BA+B^2$ $\quad[\because (A+B)^2=A^2+B^2]$

$\Rightarrow$ $AB+BA=O \Rightarrow AB=-BA$

$\therefore$ $\det(AB)=\det(-BA)=-\det(BA)$

$\Rightarrow$ $\det(A)\cdot\det(B)=-\det(B)\cdot\det(A)$

$\Rightarrow$ $2\det(A)\cdot\det(B)=0$

$\Rightarrow$ $4\det(B)=0$ $\quad[\because \det(A)=2]$

$\therefore$ $\det(B)=0$

(D) $\because A^3 = A^2A = (I-A)A = A - A^2$
$= A-(I-A) = 2A - I$

Now, $A^4 = A^3A = A^2 \cdot A^2$
$= (I-A)(I-A)$
$= I - A - A + A^2 = I - 2A + (I-A)$
$= I - 2A + I - A = 2I - 3A$

Similarly, $A^5 = 5A - 3I$
$A^6 = 5I - 8A$

Thus, $n = 6$

$\therefore$ n is divisible by 3, 6.

Example 35 *Match the following columns.*

	Column I		Column II
(A)	If $\begin{bmatrix}1 & 2 & a\\0 & 1 & 4\\0 & 0 & 1\end{bmatrix}^n = \begin{bmatrix}1 & 18 & 2007\\0 & 1 & 36\\0 & 0 & 1\end{bmatrix}$, then $(n+a)$ is divisible by	(p)	4
(B)	If A is a square matrix of order 3 such that $\lvert A\rvert = a$, $B = \text{adj}(A)$ and $\lvert B\rvert = b$, then $(ab^2 + a^2b + 1)\lambda$ is divisible by, where $\frac{1}{2}\lambda = \frac{a}{b} + \frac{a^2}{b^3} + \frac{a^3}{b^5} + \ldots$ upto ∞ and $a = 3$	(q)	9
(C)	Let $A = \begin{bmatrix}a & b & c\\p & q & r\\1 & 1 & 1\end{bmatrix}$ and $B = A^2$. If $(a-b)^2 + (p-q)^2 = 25$, $(b-c)^2 + (q-r)^2 = 36$ and $(c-a)^2 + (r-p)^2 = 49$, then det $\left(\frac{B}{2}\right)$ is divisible by	(r)	10
(D)	Let M be a 3×3 matrix satisfying $M\begin{bmatrix}0\\1\\0\end{bmatrix} = \begin{bmatrix}-1\\2\\3\end{bmatrix}$, $M\begin{bmatrix}1\\-1\\0\end{bmatrix} = \begin{bmatrix}1\\1\\-1\end{bmatrix}$, and $M\begin{bmatrix}1\\1\\1\end{bmatrix} = \begin{bmatrix}0\\0\\12\end{bmatrix}$, then the sum of the diagonal entries of M is	(s)	12
		(t)	15

Sol. (A) → (p, r); (B) → (t); (C) → (p, q, s); (D) → (q)

(A) $\because \quad A = \begin{bmatrix}1 & 2 & a\\0 & 1 & 4\\0 & 0 & 1\end{bmatrix}$

$\therefore \quad A^2 = \begin{bmatrix}1 & 2 & a\\0 & 1 & 4\\0 & 0 & 1\end{bmatrix}\begin{bmatrix}1 & 2 & a\\0 & 1 & 4\\0 & 0 & 1\end{bmatrix} = \begin{bmatrix}1 & 4 & 2a+8\\0 & 1 & 8\\0 & 0 & 1\end{bmatrix}$

$\Rightarrow \quad A^3 = \begin{bmatrix}1 & 4 & 2a+8\\0 & 1 & 8\\0 & 0 & 1\end{bmatrix}\begin{bmatrix}1 & 2 & a\\0 & 1 & 4\\0 & 0 & 1\end{bmatrix} = \begin{bmatrix}1 & 6 & 3a+24\\0 & 1 & 12\\0 & 0 & 1\end{bmatrix}$

Similarly, we get

$$A^n = \begin{bmatrix}1 & 2n & na + 8\sum_{r=0}^{n-1} r\\0 & 1 & 4n\\0 & 0 & 1\end{bmatrix} = \begin{bmatrix}1 & 18 & 2007\\0 & 1 & 36\\0 & 0 & 1\end{bmatrix} \quad \text{[given]}$$

$\Rightarrow \quad 2n = 18 \Rightarrow n = 9$

$\therefore \quad na + 8\sum_{r=0}^{n-1} r = 2007 \Rightarrow 9a + 8\sum_{r=0}^{8} r = 2007$

$\Rightarrow \quad 9a + 8\cdot\left(\frac{8\times 9}{2}\right) = 2007$

$\Rightarrow \quad 9a = 2007 - 288 = 1719$

$\therefore \quad a = 191$

Hence, $n + a = 9 + 191 = 200$

(B) $B = \text{adj } A$

$\Rightarrow \quad b = \lvert B\rvert = \lvert \text{adj} A\rvert = \lvert A\rvert^2 = a^2 = 9$

$\Rightarrow \quad a = 3, b = 9$

and $\frac{1}{2}\lambda = \frac{3}{9} + \frac{3^2}{9^3} + \frac{3^3}{9^5} + \ldots + \infty$

$$= \frac{1}{3} + \frac{1}{81} + \frac{1}{27\times 81} + \ldots + \infty = \frac{\frac{1}{3}}{1-\frac{1}{27}} = \frac{9}{26}$$

$\Rightarrow \quad \lambda = \frac{9}{13}$

Now, $(ab^2 + a^2b + 1)\lambda = (3\times 81 + 9\times 9 + 1)\times\frac{9}{13} = 225$

(C) $\det(A) = \begin{vmatrix}a & b & c\\p & q & r\\1 & 1 & 1\end{vmatrix} = \begin{vmatrix}a & p & 1\\b & q & 1\\c & r & 1\end{vmatrix} = 2\times\frac{1}{2}\begin{vmatrix}a & p & 1\\b & q & 1\\c & r & 1\end{vmatrix}$

$= 2 \times$ Area of the triangle with vertices $(a, p), (b, q)$ and (c, r) with sides 5, 6, 7

$= 2\times\sqrt{s(s-a)(s-b)(s-c)} = 2\times 6\sqrt{6} = 12\sqrt{6}$

Hence, $\det\left(\frac{B}{2}\right) = \left(\frac{1}{2}\right)^3 \det(B) = \frac{1}{8}\det(A^2)$

$= \frac{1}{8}(\det A)^2 = \frac{1}{8}(12\sqrt{6})^2 = 108$

(D) Let $M = \begin{bmatrix}a & b & c\\d & e & f\\g & h & i\end{bmatrix}$

$M\begin{bmatrix}0\\1\\0\end{bmatrix} = \begin{bmatrix}-1\\2\\3\end{bmatrix}$

$\Rightarrow \quad b = -1, e = 2, h = 3$

$$M\begin{bmatrix}1\\-1\\0\end{bmatrix}=\begin{bmatrix}1\\1\\-1\end{bmatrix}$$

$\Rightarrow \quad a=0, d=3, g=2$

$$M\begin{bmatrix}1\\1\\1\end{bmatrix}=\begin{bmatrix}0\\0\\12\end{bmatrix}\Rightarrow g+h+i=12\Rightarrow i=7$$

Therefore, sum of diagonal elements = 9

Example 36 *Matrices A, B and C has order 3×3, then match the following columns.*

	Column I		Column II
(A)	If $\|A\|=2$, A has order 3×3, then $\|2A^{-1}\|$ is equal to	(p)	1
(B)	If $\|A\|=\frac{1}{8}$ (A has order 3×3), then $\|\text{adj}(\text{adj}2A)\|$ is equal to	(q)	4
(C)	If $(A+B)^2=A^2+B^2$ and $\|A\|=2$, then $\|B\|$ is equal to	(r)	24
(D)	If $\|A\|=2, \|B\|=3$ and $\|C\|=4$, then $\|ABC\|$ is equal to	(s)	0

Sol. (A) → (q), (B) → (p), (C) → (s), (D) → (r)

(A) $|A|=2, n=3$

$$|2A^{-1}|=2^3|A^{-1}|$$
$$=2^3\times\frac{1}{|A|}$$
$$=\frac{2^3}{2}$$
$$=2^2=4$$

(B) $|A|=\frac{1}{8}, n=3$

$$|\text{adj}\ (\text{adj}\ 2A)|=|(2A)|^{(n-1)^2}=|2A|^4$$
$$=2^{12}|A|^4$$
$$=2^{12}\times\left(\frac{1}{8}\right)^4$$
$$=2^{12}\times\frac{1}{(2^3)^4}$$
$$=\frac{2^{12}}{2^{12}}=1$$

(C) $(A+B)^2=A^2+B^2$

$$|A+B|^2=|A|^2+|B|^2$$
$$\Rightarrow |A|^2+|B|^2+2|A||B|=|A|^2+|B|^2$$
$$\Rightarrow \quad 2|A||B|=0$$
$$\Rightarrow \quad |B|=0$$

(D) Given, $|A|=2, |B|=3, |C|=4$

$$\because \quad |ABC|=|A||B|C|$$
$$=2\times 3\times 4$$
$$=24$$

EXERCISE 1

JEE Main Pattern

Single Option Correct Type Questions

1. If both $A - \frac{1}{2}I$ and $A + \frac{1}{2}I$ are orthogonal matrices, then
   (a) A is orthogonal.
   (b) A is skew-symmetric matrix of even order.
   (c) $A^2 = \frac{3}{4}I$
   (d) None of the above

2. If matrix $M = \begin{bmatrix} 0 & 2 \\ \lambda & -1 \end{bmatrix}$ satisfies $M(M^3 + 3I) = 2I$, then value of λ is
   (a) $\frac{1}{2}$ (b) $-\frac{1}{2}$
   (c) 0 (d) 1

3. If A and B are two square matrices such that $B = -A^{-1}BA$, then $(A+B)^2$ is equal to
   (a) O (b) $A^2 + B^2$
   (c) $A^2 + 2AB + B^2$ (d) $A + B$

4. If matrix $A = [a_{ij}]_{3\times 3}$, matrix $B = [b_{ij}]_{3\times 3}$, where $a_{ij} + a_{ji} = 0$ and $b_{ij} - b_{ji} = 0$, then $A^4 \cdot B^3$ is
   (a) skew-symmetric matrix (b) singular
   (c) symmetric (d) zero matrix

5. Let A be a $n \times n$ matrix such that $A^n = \alpha A$, where α is a real number different from 1 and -1. The matrix $A + I_n$ is
   (a) singular (b) invertible
   (c) scalar matrix (d) None of these

6. If $A = \begin{bmatrix} \frac{-1+i\sqrt{3}}{2i} & \frac{-1-i\sqrt{3}}{2i} \\ \frac{1+i\sqrt{3}}{2i} & \frac{1-i\sqrt{3}}{2i} \end{bmatrix}$, $i = \sqrt{-1}$ and $f(x) = x^2 + 2$, then $f(A)$ equals to
   (a) $\begin{bmatrix} 1 & 0 \\ 0 & 1 \end{bmatrix}$ (b) $\left(\frac{3-i\sqrt{3}}{2}\right)\begin{bmatrix} 1 & 0 \\ 0 & 1 \end{bmatrix}$
   (c) $\left(\frac{5-i\sqrt{3}}{2}\right)\begin{bmatrix} 1 & 0 \\ 0 & 1 \end{bmatrix}$ (d) $(2+i\sqrt{3})\begin{bmatrix} 1 & 0 \\ 0 & 1 \end{bmatrix}$

7. The number of solutions of the matrix equation $X^2 = I$ other than I is
   (a) 0 (b) 1
   (c) 2 (d) more than 2

8. If $P = \begin{bmatrix} \cos\frac{\pi}{6} & \sin\frac{\pi}{6} \\ -\sin\frac{\pi}{6} & \cos\frac{\pi}{6} \end{bmatrix}$, $A = \begin{bmatrix} 1 & 1 \\ 0 & 1 \end{bmatrix}$ and $Q = PAP^T$, then $P^T Q^{2007} P$ is equal to
   (a) $\begin{bmatrix} 1 & \sqrt{3}/2 \\ 0 & 2007 \end{bmatrix}$ (b) $\begin{bmatrix} 1 & 2007 \\ 0 & 1 \end{bmatrix}$
   (c) $\begin{bmatrix} \sqrt{3}/2 & 2007 \\ 0 & 1 \end{bmatrix}$ (d) $\begin{bmatrix} \sqrt{3}/2 & -1/2 \\ 1 & 2007 \end{bmatrix}$

9. If $f(\theta) = \begin{bmatrix} \cos^2\theta & \cos\theta\sin\theta & -\sin\theta \\ \cos\theta\sin\theta & \sin^2\theta & \cos\theta \\ \sin\theta & -\cos\theta & 0 \end{bmatrix}$, then $f\left(\frac{\pi}{7}\right)$ is
   (a) symmetric
   (b) skew-symmetric
   (c) singular
   (d) non-singular

10. If A and B are two non-singular matrices of the same order such that $B^r = I$ for some positive integer $r > 1$. Then, $A^{-1}B^{r-1}A - A^{-1}B^{-1}A$ is equal to
    (a) I (b) $2I$
    (c) 0 (d) $-I$

11. If $A = \begin{bmatrix} \cos\theta & \sin\theta \\ \sin\theta & -\cos\theta \end{bmatrix}$, $B = \begin{bmatrix} 1 & 0 \\ -1 & 1 \end{bmatrix}$, $C = ABA^T$, then $A^T C^n A$, $n \in I^+$ equals to
    (a) $\begin{bmatrix} -n & 1 \\ 1 & 0 \end{bmatrix}$ (b) $\begin{bmatrix} 1 & -n \\ 0 & 1 \end{bmatrix}$
    (c) $\begin{bmatrix} 0 & 1 \\ 1 & -n \end{bmatrix}$ (d) $\begin{bmatrix} 1 & 0 \\ -n & 1 \end{bmatrix}$

12. Number of symmetric matrices of order 3 with all the entries from the set {0, 1, 2, ..., 9} is
    (a) 9^{10} (b) 10^6
    (c) 10^9 (d) 6^{10}

13. If A and B are different matrices satisfying $A^3 = B^3$ and $A^2B = B^2A$, then
    (a) det $(A^2 + B^2)$ must be zero.
    (b) det $(A - B)$ must be zero.
    (c) det $(A^2 + B^2)$ as well as det $(A - B)$ must be zero.
    (d) atleast one of det $(A^2 + B^2)$ or det $(A - B)$ must be zero.

14. If A is a skew-symmetric matrix of order 2 and B, C are matrices $\begin{bmatrix} 1 & 4 \\ 2 & 9 \end{bmatrix}$, $\begin{bmatrix} 9 & -4 \\ -2 & 1 \end{bmatrix}$ respectively, then $A^3(BC) + A^5(B^2C^2) + A^7(B^3C^3) + \ldots + A^{2n+1}(B^nC^n)$, is

(a) a symmetric matrix (b) a skew-symmetric matrix
(c) an identity matrix (d) None of these

15. If $A = \begin{bmatrix} a & b & c \\ x & y & z \\ p & q & r \end{bmatrix}$, $B = \begin{bmatrix} q & -b & y \\ -p & a & -x \\ r & -c & z \end{bmatrix}$ and if A is invertible, then which of the following is not true?

(a) $|A| = |B|$
(b) $|A| = -|B|$
(c) $|\text{adj } A| = |\text{adj } B|$
(d) A is invertible $\Leftrightarrow B$ is invertible

16. Let three matrices $A = \begin{bmatrix} 2 & 1 \\ 4 & 1 \end{bmatrix}$, $B = \begin{bmatrix} 3 & 4 \\ 2 & 3 \end{bmatrix}$ and $C = \begin{bmatrix} 3 & -4 \\ -2 & 3 \end{bmatrix}$, then $\text{tr}(A) + \text{tr}\left(\frac{ABC}{2}\right) + \text{tr}\left(\frac{A(BC)^2}{4}\right) + \text{tr}\left(\frac{A(BC)^3}{8}\right) + \ldots + \infty$ equals to

(a) 4 (b) 9 (c) 12 (d) 6

17. If A is non-singular and $(A - 2I)(A - 4I) = O$, then $\frac{1}{6}A + \frac{4}{3}A^{-1}$ is equal to

(a) O (b) I
(c) $2I$ (d) $6I$

18. If $A = \begin{bmatrix} 0 & 1 & 2 \\ 1 & 2 & 3 \\ 3 & a & 1 \end{bmatrix}$ and $A^{-1} = \begin{bmatrix} 1/2 & -1/2 & 1/2 \\ -4 & 3 & b \\ 5/2 & -3/2 & 1/2 \end{bmatrix}$, then

(a) $a = 1, b = -1$ (b) $a = 2, b = -\frac{1}{2}$
(c) $a = -1, b = 1$ (d) $a = \frac{1}{2}, b = \frac{1}{2}$

19. Given the matrix $A = \begin{bmatrix} x & 3 & 2 \\ 1 & y & 4 \\ 2 & 2 & z \end{bmatrix}$. If $xyz = 60$ and $8x + 4y + 3z = 20$, then $A(\text{adj } A)$ is equal to

(a) $64I$ (b) $88I$
(c) $68I$ (d) $34I$

Numerical Value Type Questions

20. A and B are two square matrices such that $A^2B = BA$ and if $(AB)^{10} = A^k \cdot B^{10}$, then k is equal to ....

21. The set of natural number is divided into array of rows and columns in the form of matrices as $A_1 = [1]$, $A_2 = \begin{bmatrix} 2 & 3 \\ 4 & 5 \end{bmatrix}$, $A_3 = \begin{bmatrix} 6 & 7 & 8 \\ 9 & 10 & 11 \\ 12 & 13 & 14 \end{bmatrix}$ and so on.

Let the $\text{tr}(A_{10}) = \lambda$, then λ is equal to ....

22. Let $M = [a_{ij}]_{3\times3}$, where $a_{ij} \in \{-1, 1\}$. Then, the maximum possible value of $\det |M|$ is ....

23. Let M be a square matrix of order 3 whose element is real numbers and $\text{adj}(\text{adj}(\text{adj } A)) = \begin{bmatrix} 16 & 0 & -3 \\ 0 & 4 & 0 \\ 0 & 3 & 4 \end{bmatrix}$. Then, the value of $\text{tr}(A^{-1})$ is equal to ....

24. Let $M = \begin{bmatrix} a & -360 \\ b & c \end{bmatrix}$, where a, b and c are integers, then the smallest positive value of b such that $M^2 = 0$ is ....

25. Let $A = \begin{bmatrix} -3 & 0 & 2 \\ 1 & x & 5 \\ -2 & 0 & x^2 \end{bmatrix}$, $B = \begin{bmatrix} 2 \\ b \\ 1 \end{bmatrix}$ and $C = [3 \;\; 5 \;\; 1]$. Then, the number of integral values of b for which $\text{tr}(ABC) \le -18, \forall x \in R$ is ....

26. Let M be 3×3 matrix with entries from the set $\{0, 1, 2\}$. Then, the maximum number of such matrices, for which the sum of diagonal elements of M^TM is 7 is ....

27. If $A = \begin{bmatrix} 1 & 1 & 1 \\ 0 & 1 & 1 \\ 0 & 0 & 1 \end{bmatrix}$ and $M = A + A^2 + A^3 + \ldots + A^{20}$, then the sum of all the elements of matrix M is equal to ....

28. If M is a square matrix of order 3 satisfying $M^TM = 4I$ and $|M| = 8$, where $\det(M^T) = |M|$, then the value of $|M - 2I|$ is equal to ....

Previous Year Questions

29. Consider the matrix $f(x) = \begin{bmatrix} \cos x & -\sin x & 0 \\ \sin x & \cos x & 0 \\ 0 & 0 & 1 \end{bmatrix}$.

Given below are two statements.

Statement I $f(-x)$ is the inverse of the matrix $f(x)$.

Statement II $f(x)f(y) = f(x + y)$.

In the light of the above statements, choose the correct answer from the options given below.

[Single Correct Type, 2024 Main]

(a) Statement I is true but Statement II is false.
(b) Both Statement I and Statement II are true.
(c) Both Statement I and Statement II are false.
(d) Statement I is false but Statement II is true.

30. The values of α, for which $\begin{vmatrix} 1 & \frac{3}{2} & \alpha+\frac{3}{2} \\ 1 & \frac{1}{3} & \alpha+\frac{1}{3} \\ 2\alpha+3 & 3\alpha+1 & 0 \end{vmatrix}=0$,

lie in the interval **[Single Correct Type, 2024 Main]**

(a) $(-2, 1)$ (b) $(-3, 0)$ (c) $\left(-\frac{3}{2}, \frac{3}{2}\right)$ (d) $(0, 3)$

31. Let A be a square matrix such that $AA^T = I$. Then, $\frac{1}{2}A[(A+A^T)^2+(A-A^T)^2]$ is equal to

[Single Correct Type, 2024 Main]

(a) $A^2 + A^T$ (b) $A^3 + A^T$
(c) $A^2 + I$ (d) $A^3 + I$

32. Let $R=\begin{bmatrix} x & 0 & 0 \\ 0 & y & 0 \\ 0 & 0 & z \end{bmatrix}$ be a non-zero 3×3 matrix, where

$x\sin\theta = y\sin\left(\theta+\frac{2\pi}{3}\right) = z\sin\left(\theta+\frac{4\pi}{3}\right) \neq 0, \theta\in(0.2\pi)$.

For a square matrix M, let trace (M) denote the sum of all the diagonal entries of M.

Then, among the statements :

Statement I Trace $(R)=0$

Statement II If trace (adj (adj (R))) = 0, then R has exactly one non-zero entry.

[Single Correct Type, 2024 Main]

(a) Only Statement I is true.
(b) Neither Statement I nor II is true.
(c) Both I and II are true.
(d) Only Statement II is true.

33. Let A be a 3×3 real matrix such that

$A\begin{bmatrix}1\\0\\1\end{bmatrix}=2\begin{bmatrix}1\\0\\1\end{bmatrix}, A\begin{bmatrix}-1\\0\\1\end{bmatrix}=4\begin{bmatrix}-1\\0\\1\end{bmatrix}, A\begin{bmatrix}0\\1\\0\end{bmatrix}=2\begin{bmatrix}0\\1\\0\end{bmatrix}$

Then, the system $(A-3I)\begin{bmatrix}x\\y\\z\end{bmatrix}=\begin{bmatrix}1\\2\\3\end{bmatrix}$ has

[Single Correct Type, 2024 Main]

(a) exactly two solutions (b) unique solution
(c) infinitely many solutions (d) no solution

34. Let $A=\begin{bmatrix} 2 & a & 0 \\ 1 & 3 & 1 \\ 0 & 5 & b \end{bmatrix}$. If $A^3 = 4A^2 - A - 21I$, where I is the identity matrix of order 3×3. Then, $2a+3b$ is equal to

[Single Correct Type, 2024 Main]

(a) -10 (b) -9
(c) -13 (d) -12

35. Let $B=\begin{bmatrix} 1 & 3 \\ 1 & 5 \end{bmatrix}$ and A be a 2×2 matrix such that $AB^{-1}=A^{-1}$. If $BCB^{-1}=A$ and $C^4+\alpha C^2+\beta I=O$, then $2\beta-\alpha$ is equal to **[Single Correct Type, 2024 Main]**

(a) 8 (b) 10 (c) 16 (d) 2

36. Let $A=\begin{bmatrix} 1 & 2 \\ 0 & 1 \end{bmatrix}$ and

$B=I+\text{adj}(A)+(\text{adj}\,A)^2+\ldots+(\text{adj}\,A)^{10}$. Then, the sum of all the elements of the matrix B is

[Single Correct Type, 2024 Main]

(a) -88 (b) -124 (c) -110 (d) 22

37. If A is a square matrix of order 3 such that $\det(A)=3$ and $\det(\text{adj}(-4\,\text{adj}(-3\,\text{adj}(3\text{adj}(2A)^{-1}))))=2^m 3^n$, then $m+2n$ is equal to **[Single Correct Type, 2024 Main]**

(a) 3 (b) 4 (c) 6 (d) 2

38. Let A and B be two square matrices of order 3 such that $|A|=3$ and $|B|=2$. Then, $|A^TA(\text{adj}(2A))^{-1}$ $(\text{adj}(4B))(\text{adj}(AB))^{-1}AA^T|$ is equal to

[Single Correct Type, 2024 Main]

(a) 32 (b) 108 (c) 81 (d) 64

39. Let $A=\begin{bmatrix} 2 & 0 & 1 \\ 1 & 1 & 0 \\ 1 & 0 & 1 \end{bmatrix}$, $B=[B_1, B_2, B_3]$, where B_1, B_2, B_3 be column matrics and $AB_1=\begin{bmatrix}1\\0\\0\end{bmatrix}$, $AB_2=\begin{bmatrix}2\\3\\0\end{bmatrix}$, $AB_3=\begin{bmatrix}3\\2\\1\end{bmatrix}$. If $\alpha=|B|$ and β is the sum of all the diagonal elements of B, then $\alpha^3+\beta^3$ is equal to ....

[Numerical Value Type, 2024 Main]

40. Let A be a 2×2 real matrix and I be the identity matrix of order 2. If the roots of the equation $|A-xI|=0$ be -1 and 3, then the sum of the diagonal elements of the matrix A^2 is .... **[Numerical Value Type, 2024 Main]**

41. Let A be a 2×2 symmetric matrix such that $A\begin{bmatrix}1\\1\end{bmatrix}=\begin{bmatrix}3\\7\end{bmatrix}$ and the determinant of A be 1. If $A^{-1}=\alpha A+\beta I$, where I is an identity matrix of order 2×2, then $\alpha+\beta$ equals....... .

[Numerical Value Type, 2024 Main]

42. Let $A=I_2-2MM^T$, where M is a real matrix of order 2×1 such that the relation $M^TM=I_1$ holds. If λ is a real number such that the relation $AX=\lambda X$ holds for some non- zero real matrix X of order 2×1, then the sum of squares of all possible values of λ is equal to ....

[Numerical Value Type, 2024 Main]

43. Let A be a non-singular matrix of order 3. If $\det(3\text{adj}(2\text{adj}((\det A)A)))=3^{-13}\cdot2^{-10}$ and $\det(3\,\text{adj}(2A))=2^m\cdot3^n$, then $|3m+2n|$ is equal to ....

[Numerical Value Type, 2024 Main]

44. Let A be a 3×3 matrix and $\det(A) = 2$. If $n = \det(\underbrace{\text{adj}(\text{adj}(\ldots(\text{adj } A))))}_{2024\text{-times}}$, then the remainder when n is divided by 9 is equal to .... **[Numerical Value Type, 2024 Main]**

45. Let $A = [a_{ij}]_{2 \times 2}$, where $a_{ij} \neq 0$ for all i, j and $A^2 = I$. Let a be the sum of all diagonal elements of A and $b = |A|$. Then, $3a^2 + 4b^2$ is equal to **[Single Correct Type, 2023 Main]**
(a) 7 (b) 14 (c) 3 (d) 4

46. Let α and β be real numbers. Consider a 3×3 matrix A such that $A^2 = 3A + \alpha I$. If $A^4 = 21A + \beta I$, then **[Single Correct Type, 2023 Main]**
(a) $\alpha = 1$ (b) $\alpha = 4$ (c) $\beta = 8$ (d) $\beta = -8$

47. The number of square matrices of order 5 with entries from the set {0, 1}, such that the sum of all the elements in each row is 1 and the sum of all the elements in each column is also 1, is **[Single Correct Type, 2023 Main]**
(a) 120 (b) 125 (c) 225 (d) 150

48. Let $P = \begin{bmatrix} \frac{\sqrt{3}}{2} & \frac{1}{2} \\ -\frac{1}{2} & \frac{\sqrt{3}}{2} \end{bmatrix}$, $A = \begin{bmatrix} 1 & 1 \\ 0 & 1 \end{bmatrix}$ and $Q = PAP^T$. If $P^T Q^{2007} P = \begin{bmatrix} a & b \\ c & d \end{bmatrix}$, then $2a + b - 3c - 4d$ is equal to **[Single Correct Type, 2023 Main]**
(a) 2007 (b) 2004 (c) 2005 (d) 2006

49. Let A be a 2×2 matrix with real entries such that $A^T = \alpha A + I$, where $\alpha \in R - \{-1, 1\}$. If $\det(A^2 - A) = 4$, then the sum of all possible values of α is equal to **[Single Correct Type, 2023 Main]**
(a) 5/2 (b) 2 (c) 3/2 (d) 0

50. If P is a 3×3 real matrix such that $P^T = aP + (a-1)I$, where $a > 1$, then **[Single Correct Type, 2023 Main]**
(a) P is a singular matrix (b) $|\text{Adj } P| = 1$
(c) $|\text{Adj } P| > 1$ (d) $|\text{Adj } P| = 1/2$

51. Let A be a 3×3 matrix such that $|\text{adj}(\text{adj}(\text{adj } A))| = 12^4$. Then, $|A^{-1}\text{adj } A|$ is equal to **[Single Correct Type, 2023 Main]**
(a) 12 (b) 1 (c) $2\sqrt{3}$ (d) $\sqrt{6}$

52. Let for $A = \begin{bmatrix} 1 & 2 & 3 \\ \alpha & 3 & 1 \\ 1 & 1 & 2 \end{bmatrix}$, $|A| = 2$. If $|2 \text{ adj}(2 \text{ adj}(2A))| = 32^n$. Then, $3n + \alpha$ is equal to **[Single Correct Type, 2023 Main]**
(a) 10 (b) 11 (c) 12 (d) 9

53. Let $A = \begin{bmatrix} m & n \\ p & q \end{bmatrix}$, $d = |A| \neq 0$ and $|A - d(\text{adj } A)| = 0$. Then, **[Single Correct Type, 2023 Main]**
(a) $1 + d^2 = (m+q)^2$ (b) $1 + d^2 = m^2 + q^2$
(c) $(1+d)^2 = m^2 + q^2$ (d) $(1+d)^2 = (m+q)^2$

54. Let A be a $n \times n$ matrix such that $|A| = 2$. If the determinant of the matrix Adj $(2 \cdot \text{adj}(2A^{-1}))$ is 2^{84}, then n is equal to .... **[Numerical Value Type, 2023 Main]**

55. Let $A = \begin{bmatrix} 1 & 2 \\ -2 & -5 \end{bmatrix}$. Let $\alpha, \beta, \in R$ be such that $\alpha A^2 + \beta A = 2I$. Then, $\alpha + \beta$ is equal to **[Single Correct Type, 2022 Main]**
(a) -10 (b) -6 (c) 6 (d) 10

56. Let A and B be any two 3×3 symmetric and skew-symmetric matrices, respectively. Then, which of the following is not true? **[Single Correct Type, 2022 Main]**
(a) $A^4 - B^4$ is a symmetric matrix.
(b) $AB - BA$ is a symmetric matrix.
(c) $B^5 - A^5$ is a skew-symmetric matrix.
(d) $AB + BA$ is a skew-symmetric matrix.

57. Let $A = \begin{bmatrix} 0 & -2 \\ 2 & 0 \end{bmatrix}$. If M and N are two matrices given by $M = \sum_{k=1}^{10} A^{2k}$ and $N = \sum_{k=1}^{10} A^{2k-1}$, then MN^2 is **[Single Correct Type, 2022 Main]**
(a) a non-identity symmetric matrix
(b) a skew-symmetric matrix
(c) neither symmetric nor skew-symmetric matrix
(d) an identity matrix

58. Let $A = \begin{bmatrix} 4 & -2 \\ \alpha & \beta \end{bmatrix}$. If $A^2 + 4A + 18I = 0$, then $\det(A)$ is equal to **[Single Correct Type, 2022 Main]**
(a) -18 (b) 18
(c) -50 (d) 50

59. Let A be a matrix of order 3×3 and $\det(A) = 2$. Then, det $(\det(A) \text{ adj } (5 \text{ adj } (A^3)))$ is equal to **[Single Correct Type, 2022 Main]**
(a) 512×10^6 (b) 256×10^6
(c) 1024×10^6 (d) 256×10^{11}

60. Let A be a 3×3 invertible matrix. If $|\text{adj}(24A)| = |\text{adj}(3\text{adj}(2A))|$, then $|A|^2$ is equal to **[Single Correct Type, 2022 Main]**
(a) 6^6 (b) 2^{12} (c) 2^6 (d) 1

61. Let $S = \{\sqrt{n} : 1 \le n \le 50 \text{ and } n \text{ is odd}\}$. Let $a \in S$ and $A = \begin{bmatrix} 1 & 0 & a \\ -1 & 1 & 0 \\ -a & 0 & 1 \end{bmatrix}$. If $\sum_{a \in S} \det(\text{adj } A) = 100\lambda$, then λ is equal to **[Single Correct Type, 2022 Main]**
(a) 218 (b) 221 (c) 663 (d) 1717

62. Let $X = \begin{bmatrix} 1 \\ 1 \\ 1 \end{bmatrix}$ and $A = \begin{bmatrix} -1 & 2 & 3 \\ 0 & 1 & 6 \\ 0 & 0 & -1 \end{bmatrix}$. For $k \in N$, if $X' A^k X = [33]$, then k is equal to .... **[Numerical Value Type, 2022 Main]**

63. Let $A=\begin{bmatrix}1+i & 1\\ -i & 0\end{bmatrix}$, where $i=\sqrt{-1}$. Then, the number of elements in the set $\{n\in\{1,2,\ldots,100\}: A^n=A\}$ is ....

[Numerical Value Type, 2022 Main]

64. Let $A=\begin{bmatrix}2 & -2\\ 1 & -1\end{bmatrix}$ and $B=\begin{bmatrix}-1 & 2\\ -1 & 2\end{bmatrix}$. Then, the number of elements in the set $\{(n, m): n, m\in\{1, 2, \ldots, 10\}$ and $nA^n+mB^m=I\}$ is ....

[Numerical Value Type, 2022 Main]

65. Let S be the set containing all 3×3 matrices with entries from $\{-1, 0, 1\}$. The total number of matrices $A\in S$ such that the sum of all the diagonal elements of A^TA is 6, is ....

[Numerical Value Type, 2022 Main]

66. The number of matrices $A=\begin{bmatrix}a & b\\ c & d\end{bmatrix}$, where a, b, c and d $\in\{-1,0,1,2,3,\ldots,10\}$, such that $A=A^{-1}$, is ....

[Numerical Value Type, 2022 Main]

67. Let $X=\begin{bmatrix}0 & 1 & 0\\ 0 & 0 & 1\\ 0 & 0 & 0\end{bmatrix}$, $Y=\alpha I+\beta X+\gamma X^2$ and $Z=\alpha^2 I-\alpha\beta X+(\beta^2-\alpha\gamma)X^2, \alpha, \beta, \gamma\in R$. If $Y^{-1}=\begin{bmatrix}1/5 & -2/5 & 1/5\\ 0 & 1/5 & -2/5\\ 0 & 0 & 1/5\end{bmatrix}$, then $(\alpha-\beta+\gamma)^2$ is equal to ....

[Numerical Value Type, 2022 Main]

68. Let $A=\begin{bmatrix}1 & 0 & 0\\ 0 & 1 & 1\\ 1 & 0 & 0\end{bmatrix}$. Then, $A^{2025}-A^{2020}$ is equal to

[Single Correct Type, 2021 Main]

(a) A^6-A (b) A^5 (c) A^5-A (d) A^6

69. Let A be a symmetric matrix of order 2 with integer entries. If the sum of the diagonal elements of A^2 is 1, then the possible number of such matrices is

[Single Correct Type, 2021 Main]

(a) 4 (b) 1 (c) 6 (d) 12

70. If $A=\begin{bmatrix}\frac{1}{\sqrt{5}} & \frac{2}{\sqrt{5}}\\ \frac{-2}{\sqrt{5}} & \frac{1}{\sqrt{5}}\end{bmatrix}$, $B=\begin{bmatrix}1 & 0\\ i & 1\end{bmatrix}$, $i=\sqrt{-1}$, and $Q=A^TBA$, then the inverse of the matrix $AQ^{2021}A^T$ is equal to

[Single Correct Type, 2021 Main]

(a) $\begin{bmatrix}\frac{1}{\sqrt{5}} & -2021\\ 2021 & \frac{1}{\sqrt{5}}\end{bmatrix}$ (b) $\begin{bmatrix}1 & 0\\ -2021i & 1\end{bmatrix}$

(c) $\begin{bmatrix}1 & 0\\ 2021i & 1\end{bmatrix}$ (d) $\begin{bmatrix}1 & -2021i\\ 0 & 1\end{bmatrix}$

71. Let $A=\begin{bmatrix}1 & 2\\ -1 & 4\end{bmatrix}$. If $A^{-1}=\alpha I+\beta A, \alpha, \beta\in R$, I is a 2×2 identity matrix, then $4(\alpha-\beta)$ is equal to

[Single Correct Type, 2021 Main]

(a) 5 (b) $\frac{8}{3}$

(c) 2 (d) 4

72. Let $A=\begin{bmatrix}0 & 1 & 0\\ 1 & 0 & 0\\ 0 & 0 & 1\end{bmatrix}$. Then, the number of 3×3 matrices B with entries from the set $\{1, 2, 3, 4, 5\}$ and satisfying $AB=BA$ is .... **[Numerical Value Type, 2021 Main]**

73. Let I be an identity matrix of order 2×2 and $P=\begin{bmatrix}2 & -1\\ 5 & -3\end{bmatrix}$. Then, the value of $n\in N$ for which $P^n=5I-8P$ is equal to .... **[Numerical Value Type, 2021 Main]**

74. Let $A=\begin{bmatrix}a & b\\ c & d\end{bmatrix}$ and $B=\begin{bmatrix}\alpha\\ \beta\end{bmatrix}\neq\begin{bmatrix}0\\ 0\end{bmatrix}$, such that $AB=B$ and $a+d=2021$, then the value of $ad-bc$ is equal to .... **[Numerical Value Type, 2021 Main]**

75. Let $A=\begin{bmatrix}x & y & z\\ y & z & x\\ z & x & y\end{bmatrix}$, where x, y and z are real numbers, such that $x+y+z>0$ and $xyz=2$. If $A^2=I_3$, then the value of $x^3+y^3+z^3$ is ....

[Numerical Value Type, 2021 Main]

76. Let A be a 3×3 real matrix. If $\det(2\text{Adj}(2\text{ Adj}(\text{Adj}(2A))))=2^{41}$, then the value of $\det(A^2)$ equal ....

[Numerical Value Type, 2021 Main]

77. Let M be any 3×3 matrix with entries from the set $\{0, 1, 2\}$. The maximum number of such matrices, for which the sum of diagonal elements of M^TM is seven, is ....

[Numerical Value Type, 2021 Main]

78. If the matrices $A=\begin{bmatrix}1 & 1 & 2\\ 1 & 3 & 4\\ 1 & -1 & 3\end{bmatrix}$, $B=\text{adj}A$ and $C=3A$, then $\frac{|\text{adj } B|}{|C|}$ is equal to **[Single Correct Type, 2020 Main]**

(a) 16 (b) 2 (c) 8 (d) 72

79. Let α be a root of the equation $x^2+x+1=0$ and the matrix $A=\frac{1}{\sqrt{3}}\begin{bmatrix}1 & 1 & 1\\ 1 & \alpha & \alpha^2\\ 1 & \alpha^2 & \alpha^4\end{bmatrix}$, then the matrix A^{31} is equal to **[Single Correct Type, 2020 Main]**

(a) A^3 (b) I_3 (c) A^2 (d) A

EXERCISE 2
JEE Advanced Pattern

Single Option Correct Type Questions

1. For a, b, c, $A = \begin{bmatrix} a^2 & 6 & 8 \\ 3 & b^2 & 9 \\ 4 & 5 & c^2 \end{bmatrix}$ and $B = \begin{bmatrix} 2a & 3 & 5 \\ 2 & 2b & 6 \\ 1 & 4 & 2c-3 \end{bmatrix}$.

   If $\text{tr}(A) = \text{tr}(B)$, then the value of $\frac{1}{a} + \frac{1}{b} + \frac{1}{c}$ is equal to

   (a) 1 (b) 2 (c) 3 (d) 4

2. Let $M = \begin{bmatrix} x & 2x & 3x \\ f(x) & g(x) & h(x) \\ 0 & 1 & 1 \end{bmatrix}$ be a singular matrix. If $f(x) = \ln(e^x + 1)$ and $g(x) = \ln(e^x - 1)$, then $h'(\ln 3)$

   (a) $\frac{9}{8}$ (b) $\frac{9}{4}$ (c) 3 (d) 6

3. If matrix $A = \begin{bmatrix} 1 & 2 \\ 3 & 4 \end{bmatrix}$, then $8A^{-4}$ is equal to

   (a) $145A^{-1} + 27I$ (b) $145A^{-1} - 27I$
   (c) $27I - 145A^{-1}$ (d) $29A^{-1} + 9I$

4. Let A be a square matrix of order 3. If $\det(A) = 2$, then the value of $\det(\text{adj } A^3)$ is equal to

   (a) 2^3 (b) 2^6 (c) 2^9 (d) 2^{12}

5. Let M be a column matrix such that $A = \frac{MM^T}{M^TM}$, then matrix A is

   (a) idempotent (b) symmetric
   (c) involutry (d) None of these

6. Let three matrices $A = \begin{bmatrix} 2 & 1 \\ 4 & 1 \end{bmatrix}$, $B = \begin{bmatrix} 3 & 4 \\ 2 & 3 \end{bmatrix}$, $C = \begin{bmatrix} 3 & -4 \\ -2 & 3 \end{bmatrix}$.

   Then, $\text{tr}(A) + \text{tr}\left(\frac{ABC}{2}\right) + \text{tr}\left(\frac{A(BC)^2}{4}\right) + \text{tr}\left(\frac{A(BC)^3}{8}\right) + \dots \infty$ is equal to

   (a) 6 (b) 9
   (c) 12 (d) None of these

7. If $A = [a_{ij}]_{n \times n}$, where $a_{ij} = i^{100} + j^{100}$, then $\lim_{n \to \infty} \left(\frac{\sum_{i=1}^{n} \text{Tr}(A)}{n^{101}} \right)$ is equal to

   (a) $\frac{1}{50}$ (b) $\frac{1}{101}$ (c) $\frac{2}{101}$ (d) $\frac{3}{101}$

8. If $A = \begin{bmatrix} 1 & -1 & 0 \\ -1 & 1 & 1 \\ 0 & 1 & 1 \end{bmatrix}$, then $A^{-1} + A^2$ is equal to

   (a) $3A - I$ (b) $3A + I$ (c) $2A - I$ (d) $2A + I$

9. If A is a 2×2 matrix such that $A\begin{bmatrix} 1 \\ -1 \end{bmatrix} = \begin{bmatrix} -1 \\ 2 \end{bmatrix}$ and $A^2\begin{bmatrix} 1 \\ -1 \end{bmatrix} = \begin{bmatrix} 1 \\ 0 \end{bmatrix}$, then the sum of the elements of A is

   (a) -1 (b) 0 (c) 2 (d) 5

10. How many 2×3 matrices M with entries from $\{0, 1, 2\}$ are there for which the sum of the diagonal entries of M^TM is 5?

    (a) 198 (b) 126 (c) 135 (d) 162

11. If $\begin{bmatrix} 2 & -1 \\ 1 & 0 \\ -3 & 4 \end{bmatrix} A = \begin{bmatrix} -1 & -8 & -10 \\ 1 & -2 & -5 \\ 9 & 22 & 15 \end{bmatrix}$, then sum of all the elements of matrix A is

    (a) 0 (b) 1 (c) 2 (d) -3

12. If $\begin{bmatrix} \cos\frac{2\pi}{7} & -\sin\frac{2\pi}{7} \\ \sin\frac{2\pi}{7} & \cos\frac{2\pi}{7} \end{bmatrix}^k = \begin{bmatrix} 1 & 0 \\ 0 & 1 \end{bmatrix}$, then the least positive integral value of k is

    (a) 3 (b) 6 (c) 7 (d) 14

13. If $P = \begin{bmatrix} \frac{\sqrt{3}}{2} & \frac{1}{2} \\ \frac{-1}{2} & \frac{\sqrt{3}}{2} \end{bmatrix}$; $A = \begin{bmatrix} 1 & 1 \\ 0 & 1 \end{bmatrix}$ and $Q = PAP^T$, then $P^TQ^{2005}P$ is equal to

    (a) $\begin{bmatrix} 1 & 2005 \\ 0 & 1 \end{bmatrix}$ (b) $\begin{bmatrix} 1 & 2005 \\ 2005 & 1 \end{bmatrix}$

    (c) $\begin{bmatrix} 1 & 0 \\ 2005 & 1 \end{bmatrix}$ (d) $\begin{bmatrix} 1 & 0 \\ 0 & 1 \end{bmatrix}$

14. Let $A = \begin{bmatrix} 0 & 1 \\ 1 & 0 \end{bmatrix}$ and $B = \sum_{r=1}^{2017} A^r$, then $|B|$ is equal to

    (a) 2017 (b) -2017 (c) 0 (d) 2015

15. If A is a matrix such that $A^2 = A$. If $(I + A)^n = I + \lambda A$, $n \in N$, then λ is equal to

(a) 2^n (b) $2^n - 2$

(c) $2^n - 1$ (d) n

More than One Correct Option Type Questions

16. If A and B are two orthogonal matrices of order n and $|A| + |B| = 0$, then which of the following must be true, where $\det(M) = |M|$

(a) $|A + B| = |A| + |B|$

(b) $|A + B| = 0$

(c) A and B both are singular.

(d) $A + B = 0$

17. Let M be 3×3 matrix satisfying $M^3 = 0$, then which of the following statement (s) are true?

(a) $\left|\frac{1}{2}M^2 + M + I\right| \neq 0$ (b) $\left|\frac{1}{2}M^2 - M + I\right| = 0$

(c) $\left|\frac{1}{2}M^2 + M + I\right| = 0$ (d) $\left|\frac{1}{2}M^2 - M + I\right| \neq 0$

18. If matrix $M = \begin{bmatrix} 1 & 0 & 0 \\ 1 & 0 & 1 \\ 0 & 1 & 0 \end{bmatrix}$, then

(a) $M^3 - M^2 = M - I$ (b) $|M^{2010} - I| = 0$

(c) $M^{50} = \begin{bmatrix} 1 & 0 & 0 \\ 25 & 1 & 0 \\ 25 & 0 & 1 \end{bmatrix}$ (d) $M^{50} = \begin{bmatrix} 1 & 1 & 0 \\ 25 & 1 & 0 \\ 25 & 0 & 1 \end{bmatrix}$

19. Let $A = [a_{ij}]_{3 \times 3}$ be a matrix such that $a_{ij} = 0 \; \forall \; i \neq j$ and $a_{ij} > 0, \forall \; i = j$. If adj A satisfies the equation $x^3 - 9x^2 + px - 27 = 0$, $p \in R$, then

(a) $\text{tr}(A) = 3\sqrt{3}$ (b) $|\text{adj}(\text{adj } A)| = 3^6$

(c) $\text{tr}(A^{-1}) = \frac{1}{3\sqrt{3}}$ (d) $|A| = 3\sqrt{3}$

20. Let $A = \begin{bmatrix} 1 & 2 & 0 \\ 0 & 2 & 0 \\ 0 & -1 & 2 \end{bmatrix}$ be a given matrix. If $P = A^4 + 8A$, $Q = -5A^3 + 8A^2 - 10A$, then

(a) $\text{tr}(P + Q) = 10$

(b) $\text{tr}(P + Q) = 0$

(c) $|P + Q| = 8$

(d) $|P + Q| = 32$

21. Let A and B are two matrices such that $AB = BA$, then for every $n \in N$

(a) $A^n B = BA^n$

(b) $(AB)^n = A^n B^n$

(c) $(A + B)^n = {}^nC_0 A^n + {}^nC_1 A^{n-1} B + \ldots + {}^nC_n B^n$

(d) $A^{2n} - B^{2n} = (A^n - B^n)(A^n + B^n)$

22. Let $A = \begin{bmatrix} 1 & 2 & 2 \\ 2 & 1 & 2 \\ 2 & 2 & 1 \end{bmatrix}$. Then,

(a) $A^2 - 4A - 5I_3 = O$ (b) $A^{-1} = \frac{1}{5}(A - 4I_3)$

(c) A^3 is invertible. (d) A^2 is invertible.

23. Let M be a 3×3 matrix satisfying $M\begin{bmatrix} 1 \\ 0 \\ 0 \end{bmatrix} = \begin{bmatrix} -1 \\ 2 \\ 3 \end{bmatrix}$, $M\begin{bmatrix} 0 \\ 1 \\ 0 \end{bmatrix} = \begin{bmatrix} 1 \\ 1 \\ -1 \end{bmatrix}$ and $M\begin{bmatrix} 0 \\ 0 \\ 1 \end{bmatrix} = \begin{bmatrix} 0 \\ -1 \\ 2 \end{bmatrix}$, then

(a) $\text{tr}(M) = 2$

(b) sum of all elements in $M = 6$.

(c) $|M| = -8$

(d) Number of distinct elements in M is 6.

24. Defined as $B_P = A^P(\text{adj}(\text{adj} \ldots (\text{adj } A)))$ where $p \in N$ and $|A| = 2$, then following statements is (are) true?

(a) $\text{tr}(B_1) = 4$ (b) $|B_2| = 8$

(c) $\sum_{p=1}^{\infty} |B_p^{-1}| = 1$ (d) $\text{adj}(\text{adj } B_2) = A^3$

Passage Based Questions

Passage I

(Q. Nos. 25 and 26)

■ 3×3 matrices are formed using the elements from the set $\{-3, -2, -1, 0, 1, 2, 3\}$, then

25. Number of matrices that are skew-symmetric matrices or scalar matrices is

(a) $7^7 - 7^4$ (b) $7^7 - 7^3$ (c) $7^3 + 6$ (d) $7^4(7^3 - 6)$

26. Number of matrices each of whose trace is atleast 7 is

(a) $7^9 - 7^7$ (b) $5(7^6)$ (c) $10(7^6)$ (d) 7^7

Passage II

(Q. Nos. 27 and 28)

■ Let $A = \begin{bmatrix} a & b & c \\ b & c & a \\ c & a & b \end{bmatrix}$ is an orthogonal matrix and $abc = \lambda (< 0)$.

27. The value of $a^2b^2 + b^2c^2 + c^2a^2$, is

(a) 2λ (b) -2λ (c) λ^2 (d) $-\lambda$

28. The value of $a^3 + b^3 + c^3$, is

(a) λ (b) 2λ

(c) 3λ (d) None of these

Passage III
(Q. Nos. 29 and 30)

- A and B are square matrices such that $\det(A)=1$, $BB^T=I$, $\det(B)>0$ and $A(\text{adj } A+\text{adj. } B)=B$.

29. The value of $\det(A+B)$ is
(a) 2 (b) -1 (c) 4 (d) 1

30. AB^{-1} is equal to
(a) A^TB^{-1} (b) $A^{-1}B^{-1}$
(c) $B^{-1}A$ (d) B^TA^{-1}

Passage IV
(Q. Nos. 31 and 32)

- If A is a symmetric matrix, B is a skew-symmetric matrix, $(A+B)^{-1}$ and $(A-B)^{-1}$ exist and $C=(A+B)^{-1}(A-B)$, then

31. $C^T(A+B)C$ is equal to
(a) $A+B$ (b) $A-B$ (c) A (d) B

32. $C^T(A-B)C$ is equal to
(a) $A+B$ (b) $A-B$ (c) A (d) B

Stem Based Questions

Stem I
(Q. Nos. 33 and 34)

- Let A be the square matrix of order 3 satisfies the matrix equation $A^3-6A^2+7A-8I=0$ and $B=A-2I$ $\det(A)=8$, then

33. The value of $\det(\text{adj}(I-2A^{-1}))$ is equal to ....

34. If $\text{adj}\left(\left(\frac{B}{2}\right)^{-1}\right)=\left(\frac{m}{n}\right)B$, then least value of $(m+n)$, where $m, n \in N$ is ......

Stem II
(Q. Nos. 35 and 36)

- Consider, two 3×3 matrices A and B satisfying $A=\text{adj}(B)-B^T$ and $B=\text{adj}(A)-A^T$. Also, given that A is a non-singular matrix.
(where P^T denotes transpose of matrix P)

35. $|A|+|B|$ is equal to ....

36. If $AB+BA=KI$, then K is equal to ....

Single Integer Type Questions

37. Let A, B, C, D be (not necessarily) real matrices such that $A^T=BCD$; $B^T=CDA$; $C^T=DAB$ and $D^T=ABC$ for the matrix $S=ABCD$, the least value of k such that $S^k=S$ is ....

38. If $A=\begin{bmatrix}1 & \tan x\\ -\tan x & 1\end{bmatrix}$ and a function $f(x)$ is defined as $f(x)=\det(A^TA^{-1})$ and if $f(f(f(f\dots f(x))))$ is $(n\geq2)\ \lambda$, the value of 2^λ is ....

39. Consider two matrices $B=\begin{bmatrix}1 & 0\\ 0 & -1\end{bmatrix}$ and $C=\begin{bmatrix}0 & 1\\ -1 & 0\end{bmatrix}$. If matrix $A=\sum_{n=1}^{100}(B^n+C^n)$, then absolute value of $\det(A)$ is equal to ....

40. Let A be a 3×3 matrix given by $A=[a_{ij}]$. If for every column vector X, $X^TAX=O$ and $a_{23}=-1008$, the sum of the digits of a_{32} is ....

41. Let A be the set of all 3×3 skew-symmetric matrices whose entries are either -2, 0 or 2. If there are exactly three 0's, three 1's, and three (-2)'s, then the number of such matrices is ....

42. If A is an idempotent matrix and I is an identity matrix of the same order, then the value of n, such that $(A+I)^n=I+127\,A$ is ....

43. If matrix $M=\begin{bmatrix}a^3+1 & a^2b & a^2c\\ ab^2 & b^3+1 & b^2c\\ ac^2 & bc^2 & c^3+1\end{bmatrix}$, then number of triplets (a, b, c) of positive integer for which satisfying $\det(M)=11$, is ....

44. If $A=\begin{bmatrix}0 & 1\\ 3 & 0\end{bmatrix}$ and $(A^8+A^6+A^4+A^2+I)V=\begin{bmatrix}0\\ 11\end{bmatrix}$, where V is a vertical vector and I is the 2×2 identity matrix and if λ is sum of all elements of vertical vector V, the value of 11λ is ....

45. Let A be a square matrix of order 3 whose elements are real numbers and $\text{adj}(\text{adj}(\text{adj } A))=\begin{bmatrix}16 & 0 & -3\\ 0 & 4 & 0\\ 0 & 3 & 4\end{bmatrix}$. Then, absolute value of $\text{tr}(A^{-1})$ is ....

Numerical Value Type Questions

46. If A is an idempotent matrix satisfying, $(I-0.4A)^{-1}=I-\alpha A$, where I is the unit matrix of the same order as that of A, then the value of $|9\alpha|^2$ is equal to ....

47. Let $A=\begin{bmatrix}x^3+1 & x+5 & 3x+2\\ y+1 & -6x^2+2 & z-1\\ 2 & 3 & 9x+6\end{bmatrix}$ and $|A|=3$.

If $f(x)=\text{tr}(B^{-1})$ and $B=\text{adj}(A)$, then global maximum value of $f(x)$ in $x\in[0, b]$ is ....

48. Let A be the set of all 3×3 symmetric materics all of, where entries either 0 or 1. Five of these entries are 1 and four of them 0 each. If n is number of such matrices, then n is equal to ....

49. Let $P=\begin{bmatrix}1 & 0 & 0\\ 4 & 1 & 0\\ 16 & 4 & 1\end{bmatrix}$ and I be the identity matrix of order 3. If $Q=[q_{ij}]$ is a matrix such that $P^{50}-Q=I$, then $\dfrac{q_{31}+q_{32}}{q_{21}}$ is equal to ....

50. Let matrix $A=\begin{bmatrix}x & y & -z\\ 1 & 2 & 3\\ 1 & 1 & 2\end{bmatrix}$, where $x, y, z \in N$.

If $\det[\text{adj}(\text{adj } A)]=2^8\cdot3^4$, then the number of such matrices is ....

51. Let A_n and B_n be square matrices of order 3 which are defined as $A_n=[a_{ij}]$ and $B_n=[b_{ij}]$, where $a_{ij}=\dfrac{2i+j}{3^{2n}}$, $b_{ij}=\dfrac{3i-j}{2^{2n}}, \forall\, i, j, 1\le i, j\le 3$.

If $p=\lim\limits_{n\to\infty} \text{tr}(3A_1+3^2A_2+3^3A_3+\ldots 3^nA_n)$

$q=\lim\limits_{n\to\infty} \text{tr}(2B+2^2B_2+2^3B_3+\ldots+2^2B_n)$, then $p+q$ is equal to ....

Matching Type Questions

52. Suppose a square matrix A of order 2 which has its elements as 0, 1, 2 and 4. Let N denotes the number of such matrices.

	Column I		Column II
(A)	Possible non-negative value of $\|A\|$	(p)	2
(B)	Sum of values of determinants corresponding to N matrices is	(q)	4
(C)	If absolute values of $\|A\|$ least, then possible values of $\|(\text{adj}(\text{adj})(\text{adj})A)\|$	(r)	− 2
(D)	If $\|A\|$ is greatest, then $\|4A^{-1}\|=$	(s)	0
		(t)	8

53. If A is non-singular matrix of order $n\times n$,

	Column I		Column II
(A)	adj (A^{-1}) is	(p)	$A(\det A)^{n-2}$
(B)	det (adj (A^{-1})) is	(q)	$(\det A)^{n-1}$ (adj A)
(C)	adj (adj A) is	(r)	$\dfrac{\text{adj (adj } A)}{(\det A)^{n-1}}$
(D)	adj (A det (A)) is	(s)	$(\det A)^{1-n}$
		(t)	$\dfrac{A}{(\det A)}$

54. Match the following columns.

	Column I		Column II
(A)	If A is a diagonal matrix of order 3×3 is commutative with every square matrix of order 3×3 under multiplication and tr $(A)=12$, then $\|A\|$ is divisible by	(p)	3
		(q)	4
(B)	Let $a,b,c\in R^+$ and the system of equations $(1-a)x+y+z=0$, $x+(1-b)y+z=0$, $x+y+(1-c)z=0$ has infinitely many solutions. If λ be the minimum value of $a\,b\,c$, then λ is divisible by	(r)	6
(C)	Let $A=[a_{ij}]_{3\times3}$ be a matrix whose elements are distinct integers from 1, 2, 3, ..., 9. The matrix is formed so that the sum of the numbers is every row, column and each diagonal is a multiple of 9. If number of all such possible matrices is λ, then λ is divisible by	(s)	8
(D)	If the equations $x+y=1$, $(c+2)x+(c+4)y=6$, $(c+2)^2x+(c+4)^2y=36$ are consistent and c_1, c_2 $(c_1>c_2)$ are two values of c, then $c_1\,c_2$ is divisible by	(t)	9

55. Match the following columns.

	Column I		Column II
(A)	If $M_r = \begin{bmatrix} r-1 & \frac{1}{r} \\ 1 & \frac{1}{(r-1)^2} \end{bmatrix}$ and $\lvert M_r \rvert$ is the corresponding determinant, then $\lim_{n \to \infty} (\lvert M_2 \rvert + \lvert M_3 \rvert + \dots \lvert M_n \rvert) =$	(p)	0
(B)	If $(A+B)^2 = A^2 + B^2$ and $\lvert A \rvert = 2$, then $\lvert B \rvert =$ (where A and B are matrices of odd order)	(q)	1
(C)	If $A = \begin{bmatrix} 3 & 1 \\ -1 & 1 \end{bmatrix}$ and a matrix C is defined as $C = (BAB^{-1})(B^{-1}A^TB)$, where $\lvert C \rvert = K^2 (K \in N)$, then $K =$	(r)	2
(D)	If $A = \begin{bmatrix} 1 & 1 \\ -1 & 1 \end{bmatrix}$ and $A^4 = -\lambda I$, then $\lambda - 2$ is equal to	(s)	4

Previous Year Questions

56. Let $M = [a_{ij}]$, $i, j \in \{1, 2, 3\}$ be the 3×3 matrix such that $a_{ij} = 1$ if $j+1$ is divisible by i, otherwise $a_{ij} = 0$, then which of the following statements is (are) true?

[More than Correct Type, 2023 Adv.]

(a) M is invertible.

(b) There exists a non-zero column matrix $\begin{bmatrix} a_1 \\ a_2 \\ a_3 \end{bmatrix}$ such that $M \begin{bmatrix} a_1 \\ a_2 \\ a_3 \end{bmatrix} = \begin{bmatrix} -a_1 \\ -a_2 \\ -a_3 \end{bmatrix}$

(c) The set $\{X \in R^3 : MX = 0\} \neq \{0\}$, where $O = \begin{bmatrix} 0 \\ 0 \\ 0 \end{bmatrix}$

(d) The matrix $(M - 2I)$ is invertible, where I is identify matrix.

57. Let $R = \left\{ \begin{bmatrix} a & 3 & b \\ c & 2 & d \\ 0 & 5 & 0 \end{bmatrix}; a, b, c, d \in \{0, 3, 5, 7, 11, 13, 17, 19\} \right\}$.

Then, the number of invertible matrices in R is ....

[Numerical Value Type, 2023 Adv.]

58. Let β be a real number consider the matrix

$A = \begin{bmatrix} \beta & 0 & 1 \\ 2 & 1 & -2 \\ 3 & 1 & -2 \end{bmatrix}$. If $A^7 - (\beta - 1) A^6 - \beta A^5$ is a singular matrix, then the value of 9β is ....

[Numerical Value Type, 2022 Adv.]

59. If $M = \begin{bmatrix} \frac{5}{2} & \frac{3}{2} \\ -\frac{3}{2} & -\frac{1}{2} \end{bmatrix}$, then which of the following matrices is equal to M^{2022}?

[Single Correct Type, 2022 Adv.]

(a) $\begin{bmatrix} 3034 & 3033 \\ -3033 & -3032 \end{bmatrix}$

(b) $\begin{bmatrix} 3034 & -3033 \\ 3033 & -3032 \end{bmatrix}$

(c) $\begin{bmatrix} 3033 & 3032 \\ -3032 & -3031 \end{bmatrix}$

(d) $\begin{bmatrix} 3032 & 3031 \\ -3031 & -3030 \end{bmatrix}$

60. For any 3×3 matrix M let $\lvert M \rvert$ denotes the determinant of M. Let I be the 3×3 identity matrix. Let E and F be the 3×3 matrics such that $(I - EF)$ is invertible. If $G = (I - EF)^{-1}$, then which of the following statements is (are) true?

[More than Correct Type, 2021 Adv.]

(a) $\lvert FE \rvert = \lvert I - FE \rvert \lvert FGE \rvert$

(b) $(I - FE)(I + FGE) = I$

(c) $EFG = GEF$

(d) $(I - FE)(I - FGE) = I$

61. Let M be a 3×3 invertible matrix with real entries and let I denote the 3×3 identity matrix. If $M^{-1} = \text{adj}(\text{adj } M)$, then which of the following is (are) always true?

[More than Correct Type, 2020 Adv.]

(a) $M = I$

(b) $\det(M) = 1$

(c) $M^2 = I$

(d) $(\text{adj } M)^2 = I$

62. The trace of a square matrix is defined to the sum of its diagonal entries. If A is a 2×2 matrix such that the trace of A is 3 and the trace of A^3 is -18, then the value of the determinant of A is ...... **[Numerical Value Type, 2020 Adv.]**

EXERCISE 3
Challenging Problems

1. If $A^n = 0$, then evaluate

   (i) $I + A + A^2 + A^3 + \ldots + A^{n-1}$

   (ii) $I - A + A^2 - A^3 + \ldots + (-1)^{n-1} A^{n-1}$ for odd 'n',

   where I is the identity matrix having the same order of A.

2. If A is idempotent matrix, then show that
$$(A + I)^n = I + (2^n - 1)A, \forall\, n \in N,$$
   where I is the identity matrix having the same order of A.

3. If S is a real skew-symmetric matrix, the show that $I - S$ is non-singular and matrix
$A = (I + S)(I - S)^{-1} = (I - S)^{-1}(I + S)$ is orthogonal.

4. Let A and B be matrices of order n. Prove that if $(I - AB)$ is invertible, $(I - BA)$ is also invertible and $(I - BA)^{-1} = I + B(I - AB)^{-1} A$, where I be the identity matrix of order n.

5. Let A, B, C be $n \times n$ real matrices that are pairwise commutative and $ABC = 0$. Prove that
$|A^3 + B^3 + C^3|\,|A + B + C| \geq 0$, where $|M| = \det(M)$.

6. Let $A = \begin{bmatrix} 3 & a & -1 \\ 2 & 5 & c \\ b & 8 & 2 \end{bmatrix}$ is symmetric and
$B = \begin{bmatrix} d & 3 & a \\ b-a & e & -2b-c \\ -2 & 6 & -f \end{bmatrix}$ is skew-symmetric, find AB.

   If AB is symmetric or skew-symmetric or neither of them. Justify your answer.

7. If B, C are square matrices of order n and if $A = B + C$, $BC = CB$, $C^2 = 0$, show that for any positive integer p, $A^{p+1} = B^p[B + (p+1)C]$.

8. Construct an orthogonal matrix using the skew-symmetric matrix $A = \begin{bmatrix} 0 & 2 \\ -2 & 0 \end{bmatrix}$.

9. Let A be a $n \times n$ matrix such that $A^n = \alpha A$, where α is a real number different from 1 and -1. Prove that matrix $A + I_n$ is invertiable.

10. Find the product of two matrices
$$A = \begin{bmatrix} \cos^2\theta & \cos\theta\sin\theta \\ \cos\theta\sin\theta & \sin^2\theta \end{bmatrix},$$
$$B = \begin{bmatrix} \cos^2\phi & \cos\phi\sin\phi \\ \cos\phi\sin\phi & \sin^2\phi \end{bmatrix}$$
   Show that AB is the zero matrix if θ and ϕ differ by an odd multiple of $\frac{\pi}{2}$.

11. By the method matrix inversion, solve the system
$$\begin{bmatrix} 1 & 1 & 1 \\ 2 & 5 & 7 \\ 2 & 1 & -1 \end{bmatrix} \begin{bmatrix} x & u \\ y & v \\ z & w \end{bmatrix} = \begin{bmatrix} 9 & 2 \\ 52 & 15 \\ 0 & -1 \end{bmatrix}$$

12. Let $A, B. U, V$ and X be the matrices defined as follows.
$$A = \begin{bmatrix} a & 1 & 0 \\ 1 & b & d \\ 1 & b & c \end{bmatrix}, B = \begin{bmatrix} a & 1 & 1 \\ 0 & d & c \\ f & g & h \end{bmatrix}, U = \begin{bmatrix} f \\ g \\ h \end{bmatrix}, V = \begin{bmatrix} a^2 \\ 0 \\ 0 \end{bmatrix}, X = \begin{bmatrix} x \\ y \\ z \end{bmatrix}$$
   If $AX = U$ has infinitely many solutions, show that $BX = V$ cannot have a unique solution. If $afd \neq 0$, show that $BX = V$ has no solution.

Answer Key

Exercise 1

1. (b)	2. (a)	3. (b)	4. (d)	5. (b)	6. (d)	7. (d)	8. (b)	9. (d)	10. (c)
11. (d)	12. (b)	13. (d)	14. (b)	15. (a)	16. (d)	17. (b)	18. (a)	19. (c)	20. (35)
21. (3355)	22. (4)	23. (3)	24. (10)	25. (5)	26. (540)	27. (2020)	28. (0)	29. (b)	30. (b)
31. (b)	32. (b)	33. (b)	34. (c)	35. (b)	36. (a)	37. (b)	38. (d)	39. (28)	40. (10)
41. (5)	42. (2)	43. (14)	44. (7)	45. (d)	46. (d)	47. (a)	48. (c)	49. (a)	50. (b)
51. (c)	52. (b)	53. (d)	54. (5)	55. (d)	56. (c)	57. (a)	58. (b)	59. (a)	60. (c)
61. (b)	62. (10)	63. (25)	64. (1)	65. (5376)	66. (50)	67. (100)	68. (a)	69. (a)	70. (b)
71. (d)	72. (3125)	73. (6)	74. (2020)	75. (7)	76. (4)	77. (540)	78. (c)	79. (a)	

Exercise 2

1. (c)	2. (b)	3. (c)	4. (b)	5. (b)	6. (a)	7. (c)	8. (a)	9. (d)	10. (a)
11. (b)	12. (c)	13. (a)	14. (b)	15. (c)	16. (a,b)	17. (a,d)	18. (a,b,c)	19. (a,b,d)	20. (a,d)
21. (a,c,d)	22. (a,b,c,d)	23. (a,b,c)	24. (a,b,d)	25. (c)	26. (c)	27. (b)	28. (d)	29. (d)	30. (c)
31. (a)	32. (b)	33. (1.56)	34. (7)	35. (16)	36. (8)	37. (3)	38. (2)	39. (0)	40. (9)
41. (8)	42. (7)	43. (3)	44. (1)	45. (3)	46. (36)	47. (21)	48. (12)	49. (103)	50. (55)

51. (21)
52. (A) → (p,q,t); (B) → (s); (C) → (p); (D) → (p)
53. (A) → (r,t); (B) → (s); (C) → (p); (D) → (q)
54. (A) → (q,s); (B) → (p,t); (C) → (p,q,r,s); (D) → (q,s)
55. (A) → (q); (B) → (p); (C) → (s); (D) → (r)
56. (b,c)
57. (3780)
58. (3)
59. (a)
60. (a,b,c)
61. (b,c,d)
62. (5)

Solutions

Exercise 1 - JEE Main Pattern

1. $\because \quad \left(A-\frac{1}{2}I\right)\left(A-\frac{1}{2}I\right)^T = I \quad \text{...(i)}$

and $\left(A+\frac{1}{2}I\right)\left(A+\frac{1}{2}I\right)^T = I \quad \text{...(ii)}$

$\Rightarrow \quad \left(A-\frac{1}{2}I\right)\left(A^T-\frac{I}{2}\right) = I$

and $\left(A+\frac{1}{2}I\right)\left(A^T+\frac{1}{2}I\right) = I$

$\Rightarrow \quad A + A^T = 0$ [subtracting the two results]

$\Rightarrow \quad A^T = -A$

$\therefore$ A is skew-symmetric matrix.

From first result, we get

$$AA^T = \frac{3}{4}I \Rightarrow A^2 = -\frac{3}{4}I$$

$\therefore \quad |A^2| = \left|-\frac{3}{4}I\right|$

$\therefore \quad |A|^2 = \left(-\frac{3}{4}\right)^n$

$\Rightarrow n$ is even.

2. Given, matrix $M = \begin{bmatrix} 0 & 2 \\ \lambda & -1 \end{bmatrix}$ satisfies

$$M(M^3 + 3I) = 2I$$

$\Rightarrow \quad M^4 + 3MI - 2I = 0$

$\Rightarrow \quad M^4 + 3M - 2I = 0$

$\because \quad M^2 = \begin{bmatrix} 0 & 2 \\ \lambda & -1 \end{bmatrix}\begin{bmatrix} 0 & 2 \\ \lambda & -1 \end{bmatrix} = \begin{bmatrix} 2\lambda & -2 \\ -\lambda & 2\lambda+1 \end{bmatrix}$

$$M^4 = M^2 \cdot M^2 = \begin{bmatrix} 2\lambda & -2 \\ -\lambda & 2\lambda+1 \end{bmatrix}\begin{bmatrix} 2\lambda & -2 \\ -\lambda & 2\lambda+1 \end{bmatrix}$$

$$= \begin{bmatrix} 4\lambda^2+2\lambda & -8\lambda-2 \\ -4\lambda^2-\lambda & 4\lambda^2+6\lambda+1 \end{bmatrix}$$

Now, $M^4 + 3M - 2I = 0$

$\Rightarrow \begin{bmatrix} 4\lambda^2+2\lambda & -8\lambda-2 \\ -4\lambda^2-\lambda & 4\lambda^2+6\lambda+1 \end{bmatrix} + \begin{bmatrix} 0 & 6 \\ 3\lambda & -3 \end{bmatrix} - \begin{bmatrix} 2 & 0 \\ 0 & 2 \end{bmatrix} = \begin{bmatrix} 0 & 0 \\ 0 & 0 \end{bmatrix}$

$\Rightarrow \quad \begin{bmatrix} 4\lambda^2+2\lambda-2 & -8\lambda+4 \\ -4\lambda^2+2\lambda & 4\lambda^2+6\lambda-4 \end{bmatrix} = \begin{bmatrix} 0 & 0 \\ 0 & 0 \end{bmatrix}$

On compairing both sides, we get

$$-8\lambda + 4 = 0$$

$\Rightarrow \quad -8\lambda = -4$

$\Rightarrow \quad \lambda = \frac{1}{2}$

3. $\because \quad B = -A^{-1}BA$

$\Rightarrow \quad AB = -BA$

$\Rightarrow \quad AB + BA = 0$

Now, $\quad (A+B)^2 = (A+B)(A+B)$

$= A^2 + AB + BA + B^2$

$= A^2 + 0 + B^2$

$= A^2 + B^2$

4. Since, A is skew-symmetric.

$\therefore \quad |A| = 0$

$\Rightarrow \quad |A^4B^3| = |A^4||B^3| = |A|^4|B|^3 = 0$

5. Let $\quad B = A + I_n$

$\therefore \quad A = B - I_n$

Given, $\quad A^n = \alpha A$

$\Rightarrow \quad (B - I_n)^n = \alpha(B - I_n)$

$\Rightarrow \quad B^n - {}^nC_1B^{n-1} + {}^nC_2B^{n-2} + \ldots + (-1)^n I_n$

$= \alpha B - \alpha I_n$

$\Rightarrow \quad B(B^{n-1} - {}^nC_1B^{n-2} + {}^nC_2B^{n-3} + \ldots - \alpha I_n)$

$= [(-1)^{n+1} - \alpha] I_n \neq 0 \quad [\because \alpha \neq \pm 1]$

Hence, B is invertible.

6. $\because \quad \omega = \frac{-1+i\sqrt{3}}{2}$ and $\omega^2 = \frac{-1-i\sqrt{3}}{2}$

Also, $\omega^3 = 1$ and $\omega + \omega^2 = -1$

Thus, $A = \begin{bmatrix} -i\omega & -i\omega^2 \\ i\omega^2 & i\omega \end{bmatrix}$

$\therefore \quad A^2 = \begin{bmatrix} -i\omega & -i\omega^2 \\ i\omega^2 & i\omega \end{bmatrix}\begin{bmatrix} -i\omega & -i\omega^2 \\ i\omega^2 & i\omega \end{bmatrix} = \begin{bmatrix} -\omega^2+\omega & 0 \\ 0 & -\omega^2+\omega \end{bmatrix}$

Now, $f(A) = A^2 + 2I = \begin{bmatrix} -\omega^2+\omega & 0 \\ 0 & -\omega^2+\omega \end{bmatrix} + \begin{bmatrix} 2 & 0 \\ 0 & 2 \end{bmatrix}$

$$= \begin{bmatrix} -\omega^2+\omega+2 & 0 \\ 0 & -\omega^2+\omega+2 \end{bmatrix}$$

$$= (-\omega^2+\omega+2)^2\begin{bmatrix} 1 & 0 \\ 0 & 1 \end{bmatrix} = (2+i\sqrt{3})\begin{bmatrix} 1 & 0 \\ 0 & 1 \end{bmatrix}$$

7. $\because \quad X^2 = I \Rightarrow (X^{-1}X)X = X^{-1}I$

$\Rightarrow \quad IX = X^{-1}$

$\Rightarrow \quad X = X^{-1}$

which is self invertible involutory matrix.

There are many such matrices which are inverse of their own.

8. We have, $P^T = P^{-1}$ $\quad [\because PP^T = I]$

Now, $Q = PAP^T = PAP^{-1}$

$\therefore \quad Q^{2007} = PA^{2007}P^{-1}$

$\therefore \quad P^TQ^{2007}P = P^{-1}(PA^{2007}P^{-1})\,P$

$$= A^{2007} = \begin{bmatrix} 1 & 2007 \\ 0 & 1 \end{bmatrix}$$

$$\left[\because A^2 = \begin{bmatrix} 1 & 2 \\ 0 & 1 \end{bmatrix}, A^3 = \begin{bmatrix} 1 & 3 \\ 0 & 1 \end{bmatrix}, \dots\right]$$

9. $\because$

$$|f(\theta)| = \begin{vmatrix} \cos^2\theta & \cos\theta\sin\theta & -\sin\theta \\ \cos\theta\sin\theta & \sin^2\theta & \cos\theta \\ \sin\theta & -\cos\theta & 0 \end{vmatrix}$$

On multiplying in R_3 by $\cos\theta$ and then take common $\cos\theta$ from C_1, then

$$|f(\theta)| = \begin{vmatrix} \cos\theta & \cos\theta\sin\theta & -\sin\theta \\ \sin\theta & \sin^2\theta & \cos\theta \\ \sin\theta & -\cos^2\theta & 0 \end{vmatrix}$$

Applying $R_2 \to R_2 - R_3$, we get

$$|f(\theta)| = \begin{vmatrix} \cos\theta & \cos\theta\sin\theta & -\sin\theta \\ 0 & 1 & \cos\theta \\ \sin\theta & -\cos^2\theta & 0 \end{vmatrix}$$

Applying $C_2 \to C_2 - \sin\theta\, C_1$, then

$$|f(\theta)| = \begin{vmatrix} \cos\theta & 0 & -\sin\theta \\ 0 & 1 & \cos\theta \\ \sin\theta & -1 & 0 \end{vmatrix} = 1$$

$\therefore \quad f\left(\dfrac{\pi}{7}\right)$ is non-singular matrix.

10. Given, $B^r = I \Rightarrow B^rB^{-1} = IB^{-1}$

$\Rightarrow \quad B^{r-1} = B^{-1}$

$\therefore \quad A^{-1}B^{r-1}A = A^{-1}B^{-1}A$

$\Rightarrow A^{-1}B^{r-1}A - A^{-1}B^{-1}A = 0$

11. Here, $A = \begin{bmatrix} \cos\theta & \sin\theta \\ \sin\theta & -\cos\theta \end{bmatrix}$

$\Rightarrow \quad AA^T = I$

$\because \quad C = ABA^T$

$\Rightarrow \quad A^TC = BA^T$

Now, $A^TC^nA = A^TC\cdot C^{n-1}A$

$= BA^TC^{n-1}A$

$= BA^TC\,C^{n-2}A$

$= B^2A^TC^{n-2}A$

$\dots \quad \dots \quad \dots$

$= B^{n-1}A^TCA = B^{n-1}(BA^T)\,A$

$$= B^nA^TA = B^nI = B^n = \begin{bmatrix} 1 & 0 \\ -n & 1 \end{bmatrix}$$

12. Let symmetric matrix of order 3×3 is $\begin{bmatrix} a & x & y \\ x & b & z \\ y & z & c \end{bmatrix}$.

Thus, x can be filled in 10 ways, y can be filled in 10 ways, z can be filled in 10 ways elements of diagonal can be filled in 10^3ways.

Thus, total number of matrix formed which are symmetric is

$$10^3 \times 10^3 = 10^6$$

13. $\because \quad A^3 - A^2B = B^3 - B^2A$

$\Rightarrow \quad A^2(A-B) = B^2(B-A)$

or $\quad (A^2 + B^2)(A-B) = 0$

or $\det(A^2 + B^2)\cdot\det(A-B) = 0$

Either $\det(A^2+B^2) = 0$ or $\det(A-B) = 0$

14. Let $A = \begin{bmatrix} 0 & a \\ -a & 0 \end{bmatrix}$,

$$BC = \begin{bmatrix} 1 & 4 \\ 2 & 9 \end{bmatrix}\begin{bmatrix} 9 & -4 \\ -2 & 1 \end{bmatrix} = \begin{bmatrix} 1 & 0 \\ 0 & 1 \end{bmatrix} = I$$

$\therefore \; B^2C^2 = (BC)^2 = I^2 = I$

Similarly, $B^2C^2 = B^3C^3 = \dots = B^nC^n = I$

Let $\quad D = A^3(BC) + A^5(B^2C^2) + A^7(B^3C^3) + \dots + A^{2n+1}(B^nC^n)$

$= A^3 + A^5 + A^7 + \dots + A^{2n+1}$

$= A(A^2 + A^4 + A^6 + \dots + A^{2n})$

Let $\quad A = \begin{bmatrix} 0 & a \\ -a & 0 \end{bmatrix}$

$\Rightarrow \quad A^2 = \begin{bmatrix} -a^2 & 0 \\ 0 & -a^2 \end{bmatrix} = -a^2I$

$\therefore \quad D = IA(-a^2 + a^4 - a^6 + \dots + (-1)^n a^{2n}) \quad [a > 0]$

$= A(-a^2 + a^4 - a^6 + \dots + (-1)^n a^{2n})$

Hence, D is skew-symmetric.

15. $\because \quad |B| = \begin{vmatrix} q & -b & y \\ -p & a & -x \\ r & -c & z \end{vmatrix}$

Applying $R_2 \to (-1)\,R_2$, then

$$|B| = \begin{vmatrix} q & -b & y \\ p & -a & x \\ r & -c & z \end{vmatrix}$$

Applying $C_2 \to (-1)\,C_2$, then

$$|B| = \begin{vmatrix} q & b & y \\ p & a & x \\ r & c & z \end{vmatrix} = |B^T| = \begin{vmatrix} q & p & r \\ b & a & c \\ y & x & z \end{vmatrix}$$

$$= -\begin{vmatrix} b & a & c \\ q & p & r \\ y & x & z \end{vmatrix} \quad [R_1 \leftrightarrow R_2]$$

$$= \begin{vmatrix} b & a & c \\ y & x & z \\ q & p & r \end{vmatrix} \quad [R_2 \leftrightarrow R_3]$$

$$= -\begin{vmatrix} a & b & c \\ x & y & z \\ p & q & r \end{vmatrix} = -|A| \quad [C_1 \leftrightarrow C_2]$$

$\Rightarrow \quad |B| = -|A|$

Also, $|\text{adj } B| = |B|^2 = |A|^2 = |\text{adj } A|$ [$\because |A| \neq 0$, then $|B| \neq 0$]

16. $\because BC = \begin{bmatrix} 3 & 4 \\ 2 & 3 \end{bmatrix}\begin{bmatrix} 3 & -4 \\ -2 & 3 \end{bmatrix} = \begin{bmatrix} 1 & 0 \\ 0 & 1 \end{bmatrix} = I$

$$\therefore \quad \text{tr}(A) + \text{tr}\left(\frac{ABC}{2}\right) + \text{tr}\left(\frac{A(BC)^2}{4}\right) + \text{tr}\left(\frac{A(BC)^3}{8}\right) + \dots$$

$$= \text{tr}(A) + \text{tr}\left(\frac{A}{2}\right) + \text{tr}\left(\frac{A}{2^2}\right) + \text{tr}\left(\frac{A}{2^3}\right) + \dots \text{upto } \infty$$

$$= \text{tr}(A) + \frac{1}{2}\text{tr}(A) + \frac{1}{2^2}\text{tr}(A) + \dots \text{upto } \infty$$

$$= \frac{\text{tr}(A)}{1 - \left(\frac{1}{2}\right)} = 2\,\text{tr}(A) = 2(2+1) = 6$$

17. We have,

$$(A - 2I)(A - 4I) = O$$

$\Rightarrow \quad A^2 - 4A - 2A + 8I^2 = O$

$\Rightarrow \quad A^2 - 6A + 8I = O$

$\Rightarrow \quad A^{-1}(A^2 - 6A + 8I) = A^{-1}O$

$\Rightarrow \quad A - 6I + 8A^{-1} = O$

$\Rightarrow \quad \frac{1}{6}A + \frac{4}{3}A^{-1} = I$

18. We have, $\quad AA^{-1} = I$

$$\Rightarrow \begin{bmatrix} 0 & 1 & 2 \\ 1 & 2 & 3 \\ 3 & a & 1 \end{bmatrix}\begin{bmatrix} \frac{1}{2} & -\frac{1}{2} & \frac{1}{2} \\ -4 & 3 & b \\ \frac{5}{2} & -\frac{3}{2} & \frac{1}{2} \end{bmatrix} = \begin{bmatrix} 1 & 0 & 0 \\ 0 & 1 & 0 \\ 0 & 0 & 1 \end{bmatrix}$$

$$\Rightarrow \begin{bmatrix} 1 & 0 & b+1 \\ 0 & 1 & 2(b+1) \\ 4(1-a) & 3(a-1) & ab+2 \end{bmatrix} = \begin{bmatrix} 1 & 0 & 0 \\ 0 & 1 & 0 \\ 0 & 0 & 1 \end{bmatrix}$$

On comparing, we get

$$b + 1 = 0, ab + 2 = 1, a - 1 = 0$$

$\therefore \quad a = 1, b = -1$

19. $\because \quad A(\text{adj } A) = |A|\, I \quad \dots(\text{i})$

Now, $\quad |A| = \begin{vmatrix} x & 3 & 2 \\ 1 & y & 4 \\ 2 & 2 & z \end{vmatrix}$

$= x(yz - 8) - 3(z - 8) + 2(2 - 2y)$

$= xyz - (8x + 4y + 3z) + 28$

$= 60 - 20 + 28$

$= 68$

From Eq. (i), $A(\text{adj } A) = 68I$

20. $(AB)^2 = AB \cdot AB = A \cdot A^2B \cdot B = A^3B^2$

$(AB)^3 = (AB)^2AB = A^3B^2 \cdot AB = A^7B^3$

$(AB)^4 = (AB)^3AB = A^7B^3 \cdot AB = A^{15} \cdot B^4$

$\Rightarrow \quad (AB)^{10} = A^{35}B^{10}$

$\Rightarrow \quad K = 35$

21. First element of $A_{10} = 286$ (10th of square 1, 2, 6, 15, ...)

Trace of $A_{10} = 286 + 297 + 308 + \dots + 385 = 3355$

22. Let $M = \begin{bmatrix} a & b & c \\ d & e & f \\ g & h & i \end{bmatrix}$.

Then, $|M| = a(ei - fh) - b(di - gf) + c(dh - eg)$

for maximum, $a = 1, c = 1, b = -1$ and $d = e = h = i = 1$

and $g = f = -1$

So, $|M| = 4$

23. $\because \quad \text{adj}(\text{adj } A) = |A|^{n-2} A$

$\Rightarrow \quad \text{adj}(\text{adj}(\text{adj } A)) = |\text{adj } A|^{n-2}\,\text{adj} A = (|A|^{n-1})^{n-2}\text{adj} A$

On putting $n = 3$, we get

$\Rightarrow \quad \text{adj}(\text{adj}(\text{adj} A)) = |A|^2\,\text{adj} A$

$$= \begin{bmatrix} 16 & 0 & -3 \\ 0 & 4 & 0 \\ 0 & 3 & 4 \end{bmatrix} \quad \dots(\text{i})$$

On taking determinant both sides, we get

$$|\text{adj}(\text{adj}(\text{adj} A))| = |A|^6\,|A|^2 = 256$$

$\Rightarrow \quad |A|^8 = 2^8 \Rightarrow |A| = \pm 2$

$$\text{adj } A = \frac{1}{4}\begin{bmatrix} 16 & 0 & -3 \\ 0 & 4 & 0 \\ 0 & 3 & 4 \end{bmatrix} = \begin{bmatrix} 4 & 0 & -3/4 \\ 0 & 1 & 0 \\ 0 & 3/4 & 1 \end{bmatrix} \quad [\text{from Eq. (i)}]$$

$$\because \quad A^{-1} = \frac{\text{adj} A}{|A|} = \pm\begin{bmatrix} 2 & 0 & -3/8 \\ 0 & 1/2 & 0 \\ 0 & 3/8 & 1/2 \end{bmatrix}$$

$\therefore \quad \text{trace}(A^{-1}) = 3$

24. Given, $\quad M = \begin{bmatrix} a & -360 \\ b & c \end{bmatrix}$

$$M^2 = \begin{bmatrix} a & -360 \\ b & c \end{bmatrix}\begin{bmatrix} a & -360 \\ b & c \end{bmatrix}$$

$$= \begin{bmatrix} a^2 - 360b & -360a - 360c \\ ab + bc & -360b + c^2 \end{bmatrix}$$

$\because \quad M^2 = 0$

$$\Rightarrow \begin{bmatrix} a^2 - 360b & -360(a+c) \\ ab + bc & c^2 - 360b \end{bmatrix} = \begin{bmatrix} 0 & 0 \\ 0 & 0 \end{bmatrix}$$

On comparing both sides, we get

$$a^2 - 360b = 0 \text{ or } c^2 - 360b = 0$$

$$\Rightarrow \quad b = \frac{a^2}{360} = \frac{c^2}{360}$$

For a, $a = \sqrt{360b}$, where a and b are integers.

So, minimum possible value of b is 10.

25. Given, $A = \begin{bmatrix} -3 & 0 & 2 \\ 1 & x & 5 \\ -2 & 0 & x^2 \end{bmatrix}, B = \begin{bmatrix} 2 \\ b \\ 1 \end{bmatrix}$ and $C = [3 \quad 5 \quad 1]$

$$AB = \begin{bmatrix} -3 & 0 & 2 \\ 1 & x & 5 \\ -2 & 0 & x^2 \end{bmatrix} \begin{bmatrix} 2 \\ b \\ 1 \end{bmatrix} = \begin{bmatrix} -4 \\ 7+xb \\ -4+x^2 \end{bmatrix}$$

$$ABC = \begin{bmatrix} -4 \\ 7+xb \\ -4+x^2 \end{bmatrix} [3 \quad 5 \quad 1]$$

$$= \begin{bmatrix} -12 & -20 & -4 \\ 21+3xb & 35+5xb & 7+xb \\ -12+3x^2 & -20+5x^2 & -4+x^2 \end{bmatrix}$$

$\because$ $\text{tr}(ABC) = -12+35+5xb+x^2-4$

$= x^2+5xb+19 \le -18$

$= x^2+5xb \le -37$

$\Rightarrow$ $x^2+5xb+37 \le 0$

Now, $D^2 - 4ac > 0$

$\Rightarrow$ $25b^2 - 148 > 0$

$\Rightarrow$ $25b^2 > 148$

$\Rightarrow$ $b^2 > 5.92$

$\therefore$ b can be 0, 1, 2, – 1, – 2.

$\therefore$ Total number of integral value of b is 5.

26. Let $M = \begin{bmatrix} a & b & c \\ d & e & f \\ g & h & i \end{bmatrix}$, then

$$M^T = \begin{bmatrix} a & d & g \\ b & e & h \\ c & f & i \end{bmatrix}$$

$$M^TM = \begin{bmatrix} a & d & g \\ b & e & h \\ c & f & i \end{bmatrix} \begin{bmatrix} a & b & c \\ d & e & f \\ g & h & i \end{bmatrix}$$

$$= \begin{bmatrix} a^2+d^2+g^2 & ab+de+gh & ac+df+gi \\ ab+de+gh & b^2+e^2+h^2 & bc+ef+hi \\ ac+df+gi & bc+ef+hi & c^2+f^2+i^2 \end{bmatrix}$$

$\because$ Sum of diagonal elements of $M^TM = 7$

$\Rightarrow$ $a^2+b^2+c^2+d^2+e^2+f^2+g^2+h^2+i^2 = 7$

Case I Seven (1's) and Two (0's)

$\Rightarrow$ ${}^9C_2 = 36$

Case II One (2's) and three (1's) and five (0's)

$\Rightarrow$ ${}^9C_1 \times {}^8C_3 \times {}^5C_5 = 504$

$\therefore$ Maximum number of such matrices is $36 + 504 = 540$

27. Given, $A = \begin{bmatrix} 1 & 1 & 1 \\ 0 & 1 & 1 \\ 0 & 0 & 1 \end{bmatrix}$

$$\Rightarrow \quad A^n = \begin{bmatrix} 1 & n & \frac{n(n+1)}{2} \\ 0 & 1 & n \\ 0 & 0 & 1 \end{bmatrix}$$

$\because$ $M = A + A^2 + A^3 + \ldots + A^{20}$

$$\Rightarrow \quad M = \begin{bmatrix} \sum_{n=1}^{20} 1 & \sum_{n=1}^{20} n & \sum_{n=1}^{20} \frac{n(n+1)}{2} \\ 0 & \sum_{n=1}^{20} 1 & \sum_{n=1}^{20} n \\ 0 & 0 & \sum_{n=1}^{20} 1 \end{bmatrix}$$

$$\therefore \quad M = \begin{bmatrix} 20 & 210 & 1540 \\ 0 & 20 & 210 \\ 0 & 0 & 20 \end{bmatrix}$$

$\therefore$ Sum of all the elements of matrix M

$= 20+210+1540+20+210+20$

$= 2020$

28. $\because$ $(M-2I)^T = M^T - 2I^T = M^T - 2I$

$= M^T - \frac{2M^TM}{4}$ $\quad [\because M^TM = 4I]$

$= M^T - \frac{M^TM}{2}$

$= M^T\left(I - \frac{M}{2}\right)$

On taking determinant both sides, we get

$|(M-2I)^T| = |M^T| \left| I - \frac{M}{2} \right|$

$\Rightarrow$ $|M-2I| = |M| \left| I - \frac{M}{2} \right|$ $\quad [\because |A^T| = |A|]$

$\Rightarrow$ $|M-2I| = \frac{1}{(-2)^3} |M| \, |M-2I|$

$\Rightarrow$ $|M-2I| = -\frac{1}{8} \times 8 |M-2I|$

$\Rightarrow$ $|M-2I| + |M-2I| = 0$

$\Rightarrow$ $|M-2I| = 0$

29. Use the formulas in following manner

first use $\cos x \cos y \pm \sin x \sin y = \cos(x \pm y)$, then use $\sin x \cos y \pm \sin y \cos x = \sin(x \pm y)$

Given, $f(x) = \begin{bmatrix} \cos x & -\sin x & 0 \\ \sin x & \cos x & 0 \\ 0 & 0 & 1 \end{bmatrix}$

So, $f(-x) = \begin{bmatrix} \cos x & \sin x & 0 \\ -\sin x & \cos x & 0 \\ 0 & 0 & 1 \end{bmatrix}$

Now, $f(x)\cdot f(-x)=\begin{bmatrix}\cos x & -\sin x & 0\\ \sin x & \cos x & 0\\ 0 & 0 & 1\end{bmatrix}\begin{bmatrix}\cos x & \sin x & 0\\ -\sin x & \cos x & 0\\ 0 & 0 & 1\end{bmatrix}$

$$\begin{bmatrix}\cos^2 x+\sin^2 x+0 & \sin x\cos x-\sin x\cos x+0 & 0+0+0\\ \sin x\cos x-\cos x\sin x+0 & \sin^2 x+\cos^2 x+0 & 0+0+0\\ 0+0+0 & 0+0+0 & 0+0+1\end{bmatrix}$$

$$=\begin{bmatrix}1 & 0 & 0\\ 0 & 1 & 0\\ 0 & 0 & 1\end{bmatrix}=1$$

This shows that $f(-x)$ is the inverse of the matrix $f(x)$.

So, Statement I is true.

Now, $f(x)\cdot f(y)=\begin{bmatrix}\cos x & -\sin x & 0\\ \sin x & \cos x & 0\\ 0 & 0 & 1\end{bmatrix}\begin{bmatrix}\cos y & -\sin y & 0\\ \sin y & \cos y & 0\\ 0 & 0 & 1\end{bmatrix}$

$$\Rightarrow \quad f(x)\cdot f(y)=\begin{bmatrix}\cos(x+y) & -\sin(x+y) & 0\\ \sin(x+y) & \cos(x+y) & 0\\ 0 & 0 & 1\end{bmatrix}$$

$$\Rightarrow \quad f(x)\cdot f(y)=f(x+y)$$

So, Statement II is also true.

30. Given determinant is

$$\begin{vmatrix}1 & 3/2 & \alpha+3/2\\ 1 & 1/3 & \alpha+1/3\\ 2\alpha+3 & 3\alpha+1 & 0\end{vmatrix}=0$$

$$\Rightarrow \left(\alpha+\frac{3}{2}\right)\left[3\alpha+1-\frac{2\alpha}{3}-1\right]-\left(\alpha+\frac{1}{3}\right)\left[3\alpha+1-3\alpha-\frac{9}{2}\right]=0$$

$$\Rightarrow \left(\alpha+\frac{3}{2}\right)\left[\frac{7\alpha}{3}\right]-\left(\alpha+\frac{1}{3}\right)\left[-\frac{7}{2}\right]=0$$

$$\Rightarrow \frac{7\alpha^2}{3}+\frac{7\alpha}{2}+\frac{7}{2}\alpha+\frac{7}{6}=0$$

$$\Rightarrow \frac{7\alpha^2}{3}+7\alpha+\frac{7}{6}=0$$

$$\Rightarrow 14\alpha^2+42\alpha+7=0$$

$$\Rightarrow 2\alpha^2+6\alpha+1=0$$

$$\Rightarrow \alpha=\frac{-6\pm\sqrt{36-4\times2\times1}}{2\times2}$$

$$\Rightarrow \alpha=\frac{-6\pm\sqrt{28}}{4}$$

$$\Rightarrow \alpha=\frac{-3\pm\sqrt{7}}{2}$$

$$=\frac{-3\pm2.65}{2} \qquad [\because \sqrt{7}=2.645]$$

$$\Rightarrow \alpha=(-0.175)\text{ or }(-2.82)\in(-3,0)$$

31. We have,

$$AA^T=I$$

$$\frac{1}{2}A[(A+A^T)^2+(A-A^T)^2]=\frac{1}{2}A[A^2+(A^T)^2+2AA^T+A^2+(A^T)^2-2AA^T]$$

$$=\frac{1}{2}A[2A^2+2(A^T)^2]=A^3+A^T$$

32. Consider A is a non-singular matrix, then use adj (adj A) $=|A|^{n-2}A$

Given, $R=\begin{bmatrix}x & 0 & 0\\ 0 & y & 0\\ 0 & 0 & z\end{bmatrix}$,

$$x\sin\theta=y\sin\left(\theta+\frac{2\pi}{3}\right)=z\sin\left(\theta+\frac{4\pi}{3}\right)\neq0$$

$$\because \sin\theta+\sin\left(\theta+\frac{2\pi}{3}\right)+\sin\left(\theta+\frac{4\pi}{3}\right)$$

$$=\sin\theta+\sin\theta\cos\frac{2\pi}{3}+\cos\theta\sin\frac{2\pi}{3}+\sin\theta\cos\frac{4\pi}{3}+\cos\theta\sin\frac{4\pi}{3}=0,\ \forall\theta\in R$$

$$\therefore \quad \frac{1}{x}+\frac{1}{y}+\frac{1}{z}=0$$

$$\Rightarrow \quad xy+yz+zx=0$$

Statement I $\operatorname{tr}(R)=0$

$$x+y+z=0$$

and $\quad xy+yz+zx=0$

$\Rightarrow \quad x+y+z=0$, which is not possible.

$\therefore$ Statement I is false.

Statement II $\operatorname{tr}[\operatorname{adj}(\operatorname{adj} R)]=0$

$\because \quad \operatorname{adj}(\operatorname{adj} R)=|R|R$

$\therefore \quad \operatorname{tr}(\operatorname{adj}(\operatorname{adj} R))=\operatorname{tr}(|R|R)$

$$=|R|(x+y+z)$$

$$=xyz(x+y+z)\neq0$$

$\therefore$ Statement II is false.

33. Let $A=\begin{bmatrix}a_1 & b_1 & c_1\\ a_2 & b_2 & c_2\\ a_3 & b_3 & c_3\end{bmatrix}$

Given, $A\begin{bmatrix}1\\0\\1\end{bmatrix}=2\begin{bmatrix}1\\0\\1\end{bmatrix}$

$$\begin{bmatrix}a_1 & b_1 & c_1\\ a_2 & b_2 & c_2\\ a_3 & b_3 & c_3\end{bmatrix}\begin{bmatrix}1\\0\\1\end{bmatrix}=\begin{bmatrix}2\\0\\2\end{bmatrix}$$

$$\Rightarrow \quad \begin{bmatrix}a_1+c_1\\ a_2+c_2\\ a_3+c_3\end{bmatrix}=\begin{bmatrix}2\\0\\2\end{bmatrix}$$

$$a_1 + c_1 = 2 \quad \text{...(i)}$$
$$a_2 + c_2 = 0 \quad \text{...(ii)}$$
$$a_3 + c_3 = 2 \quad \text{...(iii)}$$

and $A\begin{bmatrix} -1 \\ 0 \\ 1 \end{bmatrix} = 4\begin{bmatrix} -1 \\ 0 \\ 1 \end{bmatrix}$

$$\begin{bmatrix} a_1 & b_1 & c_1 \\ a_2 & b_2 & c_2 \\ a_3 & b_3 & c_3 \end{bmatrix}\begin{bmatrix} -1 \\ 0 \\ 1 \end{bmatrix} = \begin{bmatrix} -4 \\ 0 \\ 4 \end{bmatrix}$$

$$\Rightarrow \begin{bmatrix} -a_1 + c_1 \\ -a_2 + c_2 \\ -a_3 + c_3 \end{bmatrix} = \begin{bmatrix} -4 \\ 0 \\ 4 \end{bmatrix}$$

$$-a_1 + c_1 = -4 \quad \text{...(iv)}$$
$$-a_2 + c_2 = 0 \quad \text{...(v)}$$
$$-a_3 + c_3 = 4 \quad \text{...(vi)}$$

From Eqs. (i) and (iv), we get

$$c_1 = -1, a_1 = 3$$

From Eqs. (ii) and (v), we get

$$a_2 = 0, c_2 = 0$$

From Eqs. (iii) and (vi), we get

$$a_3 = -1, c_3 = 3$$

Also, $A\begin{bmatrix} 0 \\ 1 \\ 0 \end{bmatrix} = 2\begin{bmatrix} 0 \\ 1 \\ 0 \end{bmatrix}$

$$\Rightarrow \begin{bmatrix} a_1 & b_1 & c_1 \\ a_2 & b_2 & c_2 \\ a_3 & b_3 & c_3 \end{bmatrix}\begin{bmatrix} 0 \\ 1 \\ 0 \end{bmatrix} = \begin{bmatrix} 0 \\ 2 \\ 0 \end{bmatrix}$$

$$\Rightarrow \begin{bmatrix} b_1 \\ b_2 \\ b_3 \end{bmatrix} = \begin{bmatrix} 0 \\ 2 \\ 0 \end{bmatrix}$$

$$b_1 = 0, b_2 = 2, b_3 = 0$$

$$A = \begin{bmatrix} 3 & 0 & -1 \\ 0 & 2 & 0 \\ -1 & 0 & 3 \end{bmatrix}$$

Now, $A - 3I = \begin{bmatrix} 3 & 0 & -1 \\ 0 & 2 & 0 \\ -1 & 0 & 3 \end{bmatrix} - \begin{bmatrix} 3 & 0 & 0 \\ 0 & 3 & 0 \\ 0 & 0 & 3 \end{bmatrix}$

$$= \begin{bmatrix} 0 & 0 & -1 \\ 0 & -1 & 0 \\ -1 & 0 & 0 \end{bmatrix}$$

$$(A - 3I)\begin{bmatrix} x \\ y \\ z \end{bmatrix} = \begin{bmatrix} 1 \\ 2 \\ 3 \end{bmatrix} \Rightarrow \begin{bmatrix} 0 & 0 & -1 \\ 0 & -1 & 0 \\ -1 & 0 & 0 \end{bmatrix}\begin{bmatrix} x \\ y \\ z \end{bmatrix} = \begin{bmatrix} 1 \\ 2 \\ 3 \end{bmatrix}$$

$$\Rightarrow \begin{bmatrix} -z \\ -y \\ -x \end{bmatrix} = \begin{bmatrix} 1 \\ 2 \\ 3 \end{bmatrix}$$

$$x = -3, y = -2, z = -1$$

It is an unique solution.

34.

> **Decoding the Question**
>
> Use, if A is 3×3 matrices, then
>
> $$A^3 - \text{Tr}(A)(A)^2 + \Sigma A_{ii}(A) + |A| I = 0$$
>
> where A_{ii} = cofactor of a_{ii} to solve the questions.

$$A = \begin{bmatrix} 2 & a & 0 \\ 1 & 3 & 1 \\ 0 & 5 & b \end{bmatrix}$$

and $A^3 = 4A^2 - A - 21I$

So, $x^3 - 4x^2 + x + 21 = 0$ is the characteristic equation of matrix A.

So, sum of roots $= T_r(A)$

$$\Rightarrow \quad -(-4) = 2 + 3 + b$$
$$\Rightarrow \quad 5 + b = 4 \Rightarrow b = -1 \quad \text{...(i)}$$

Product of roots $= |A|$

$$\Rightarrow \quad -21 = 2(3b - 5) - a(b)$$

Put $b = -1$ from Eq. (i),

$$-21 = 2(-8) + a$$
$$\Rightarrow \quad a = -21 + 16 = -5$$

Therefore, $2a + 3b = 2(-5) + 3(-1) = -13$

35. $B = \begin{bmatrix} 1 & 3 \\ 1 & 5 \end{bmatrix}$

$BCB^{-1} = A$ and $(BCB^{-1})(BCB^{-1}) = A^2$

$$BC^2B^{-1} = A^2 \quad \text{...(i)}$$

and $AB^{-1} = A^{-1}$

$$B^{-1} = A^{-1} \cdot A^{-1}$$

(pre multiply by A^{-1})

In Eq. (i) Pre multiply of B^{-1} and post multiply by B, we get

$$C^2 = B^{-1}AAB = A^{-1}A^{-1} \cdot AAB$$
$$C^2 = B$$

$\therefore \quad C^4 + \alpha C^2 + \beta I = 0$

$\Rightarrow \quad B^2 + \alpha B + \beta I = 0$

Now, $|B - \lambda I| = 0$,

which is characteristics equation of B.

$$\Rightarrow \begin{vmatrix} 1-\lambda & 3 \\ 1 & 5-\lambda \end{vmatrix} = 0$$

$$\Rightarrow \quad 5 + \lambda^2 - 6\lambda - 3 = 0$$
$$\lambda^2 - 6\lambda + 2 = 0$$
$$\therefore \quad B^2 - 6B + 2I = 0$$
$$\alpha = -6, \beta = 2$$
$$\therefore \quad 2\beta - \alpha = 4 + 6 = 10$$

36. $A = \begin{bmatrix} 1 & 2 \\ 0 & 1 \end{bmatrix} \Rightarrow \text{adj } A = \begin{bmatrix} 1 & -2 \\ 0 & 1 \end{bmatrix}$

$$(\text{adj } A)^2 = \begin{bmatrix} 1 & -4 \\ 0 & 1 \end{bmatrix}$$

$$\vdots \quad \vdots \quad \vdots$$

$$(\text{adj } A)^{10} = \begin{bmatrix} 1 & -20 \\ 0 & 1 \end{bmatrix}$$

$\therefore B = I + \text{adj} A + (\text{adj } A)^2 + \ldots + (\text{adj } A)^{10}$

$$= \begin{bmatrix} 1 & 0 \\ 0 & 1 \end{bmatrix} + \begin{bmatrix} 1 & -2 \\ 0 & 1 \end{bmatrix} + \begin{bmatrix} 1 & -4 \\ 0 & 1 \end{bmatrix} + \ldots \begin{bmatrix} 1 & -20 \\ 0 & 1 \end{bmatrix} = \begin{bmatrix} 11 & -110 \\ 0 & 11 \end{bmatrix}$$

Sum of elements of $B = -88$

37. According to the question,

$|A| = 3$, where A is matrix of order 3

and given $|\text{adj}(-4 \text{ adj}(-3 \text{ adj}(3 \text{ adj}((2A)^{-1}))))| = 2^m 3^n$

Now, LHS $\Rightarrow |-4 \text{ adj}(-3 \text{ adj}(3 \text{ adj}((2A)^{-1})))|^{3-1}$

$[\because |\text{adj } A| = |A|^{n-1}]$

$= (-4)^6 |\text{adj}(-3 \text{ adj}(3 \text{ adj}((2A)^{-1})))|^2$

$= 4^6 |-3 \text{ adj}(3 \text{ adj}((2A)^{-1}))|^4$

$= 4^6 \cdot (-3)^{3 \cdot 4} |\text{adj}(3 \text{ adj}((2A)^{-1}))|^4$

$= 4^6 \cdot 3^{12} |3 \text{ adj}((2A)^{-1})|^8$

$= 4^6 \cdot 3^{12} \cdot 3^{24} |\text{adj}(2A^{-1})|^8$

$= 4^6 \cdot 3^{36} |2A^{-1}|^{16} = 4^6 \cdot 3^{36} \dfrac{1}{|2A|^{16}}$

$= 2^{12} \cdot 3^{36} \times \dfrac{1}{2^{48} |A|^{16}} = 2^{12} \cdot 3^{36} \times \dfrac{1}{2^{48} \cdot 3^{16}}$

$= \dfrac{3^{20}}{2^{36}} = 2^{-36} \cdot 3^{20} = 2^m \cdot 3^n = \text{RHS}$

On comparing, we get

$m = -36, n = 20$

$\Rightarrow \quad m + 2n = -36 + 2 \times 20 = 4$

38. Given, $|A| = 3, |B| = 2$

$\therefore |A^T A (\text{adj}(2A))^{-1} (\text{adj}(4B)) (\text{adj}(AB))^{-1} A A^T|$

$= |A^T| |A| |\text{adj}(2A)^{-1}| |\text{adj}(4B)| |(\text{adj}(AB))^{-1}| |A| |A^T|$

$= 3 \times 3 \times \dfrac{1}{|\text{adj}(2A)|} |4^{3-1} \text{adj}(B)| \times \dfrac{1}{|\text{adj}(AB)|} \times 3 \times 3$

$= 3^4 \times \dfrac{1}{|2^{3-1} \text{adj}(A)|} \times 4^2 \times |\text{adj}(B)| \times \left| \dfrac{1}{\text{adj}(B) \cdot \text{adj}(A)} \right|$

$= 3^4 \times \dfrac{1}{(2^2)^3 |\text{adj}(A)|} \times (4^2)^3 \times |B|^{3-1} \times \dfrac{1}{|B|^{3-1} |A|^{3-1}}$

$= \dfrac{3^4}{2^6 \times 3^{3-1}} \times 4^6 \times 2^2 \times \dfrac{1}{2^2 \times 3^2}$

$= \dfrac{3^4}{2^6 \times 3^2} \times 2^{12} \times 2^2 \times \dfrac{1}{2^2 \times 3^2} = 2^6 = 64$

39. Given, $A = \begin{bmatrix} 2 & 0 & 1 \\ 1 & 1 & 0 \\ 1 & 0 & 1 \end{bmatrix}$ and $B = [B_1, B_2, B_3]$

Let $B_1 = \begin{bmatrix} x_1 \\ y_1 \\ z_1 \end{bmatrix}, B_2 = \begin{bmatrix} x_2 \\ y_2 \\ z_2 \end{bmatrix}, B_3 = \begin{bmatrix} x_3 \\ y_3 \\ z_3 \end{bmatrix}$

Since, $AB_1 = \begin{bmatrix} 1 \\ 0 \\ 0 \end{bmatrix}$ [given]

$\Rightarrow \begin{bmatrix} 2 & 0 & 1 \\ 1 & 1 & 0 \\ 1 & 0 & 1 \end{bmatrix} \begin{bmatrix} x_1 \\ y_1 \\ z_1 \end{bmatrix} = \begin{bmatrix} 1 \\ 0 \\ 0 \end{bmatrix} \Rightarrow x_1 = 1, y_1 = -1, z_1 = -1$

and $AB_2 = \begin{bmatrix} 2 \\ 3 \\ 0 \end{bmatrix}$ [given]

$\Rightarrow \begin{bmatrix} 2 & 0 & 1 \\ 1 & 1 & 0 \\ 1 & 0 & 1 \end{bmatrix} \begin{bmatrix} x_2 \\ y_2 \\ z_2 \end{bmatrix} = \begin{bmatrix} 2 \\ 3 \\ 0 \end{bmatrix} \Rightarrow x_2 = 2, y_2 = 1, z_2 = -2$

and $AB_3 = \begin{bmatrix} 3 \\ 2 \\ 1 \end{bmatrix} \Rightarrow \begin{bmatrix} 2 & 0 & 1 \\ 1 & 1 & 0 \\ 1 & 0 & 1 \end{bmatrix} \begin{bmatrix} x_3 \\ y_3 \\ z_3 \end{bmatrix} = \begin{bmatrix} 3 \\ 2 \\ 1 \end{bmatrix}$

$\Rightarrow \quad x_3 = 2, y_3 = 0, z_3 = -1$

Hence, $B = \begin{bmatrix} 1 & 2 & 2 \\ -1 & 1 & 0 \\ -1 & -2 & -1 \end{bmatrix} \Rightarrow |B| = 3$

According to the question,

$\alpha = |B| = 3$

and $\beta =$ Sum of all the diagonal elements of $B = 1$

Thus, $\alpha^3 + \beta^3 = 27 + 1 = 28$

40. Let $A = \begin{bmatrix} a & b \\ c & d \end{bmatrix}$

$\therefore |A - xI| = \begin{vmatrix} a - x & b \\ c & d - x \end{vmatrix} = 0$

$\Rightarrow \quad x^2 - (a + d)x + ad - bc = 0$

Sum of roots $= a + d = -1 + 3 = 2$ ...(i)

and product of roots $= ad - bc = (-1)(3) = -3$ ...(ii)

Now, $A^2 = \begin{bmatrix} a & b \\ c & d \end{bmatrix} \begin{bmatrix} a & b \\ c & d \end{bmatrix} = \begin{bmatrix} a^2 + bc & b(a + d) \\ c(a + d) & d^2 + bc \end{bmatrix}$

$\therefore$ Trace of $A^2 = tr(A^2) = a^2 + d^2 + 2bc = (a + d)^2 - 2(ad - bc)$

$= 4 + 6 = 10$ [using Eqs. (i) and (ii)]

41. Let $A = \begin{bmatrix} a & b \\ b & d \end{bmatrix}$

$\begin{bmatrix} a & b \\ b & d \end{bmatrix} \begin{bmatrix} 1 \\ 1 \end{bmatrix} = \begin{bmatrix} 3 \\ 7 \end{bmatrix}$ and $|A| = 1$

$ad - b^2 = 1, a + b = 3, b + d = 7$

$a = 3 - b, d = 7 - b$

Now, $ad - b^2 = 1$

$(3 - b)(7 - b) - b^2 = 1 \Rightarrow 21 - 10b = 1$

$\therefore \quad b = 2, a = 1$ and $d = 5$

$\therefore \quad A = \begin{bmatrix} 1 & 2 \\ 2 & 5 \end{bmatrix}$

$A^{-1} = \alpha A + \beta I \Rightarrow \begin{bmatrix} 5 & -2 \\ -2 & 1 \end{bmatrix} = \begin{bmatrix} \alpha & 2\alpha \\ 2\alpha & 5\alpha \end{bmatrix} + \begin{bmatrix} \beta & 0 \\ 0 & \beta \end{bmatrix}$

$\alpha + \beta = 5 \Rightarrow 2\alpha = -2$

$\alpha = -1, \beta = 6$

$\therefore \quad \alpha + \beta = 5$

42. We have, $A = I_2 - 2MM^T$

$\Rightarrow \quad A^2 = (I_2 - 2MM^T)(I_2 - 2MM^T)$

$= I_2 - 2MM^T - 2MM^T + 4MM^T \cdot MM^T$

$= I_2 - 4MM^T + 4\,MM^T$

$\therefore \quad A^2 = I_2$

Now, $AX = \lambda X \Rightarrow A^2X = \lambda AX \Rightarrow X = \lambda(\lambda X)$

or $X = \lambda^2 X \Rightarrow X(\lambda^2 - 1) = 0$

$\Rightarrow \quad \lambda^2 = 1$

$\Rightarrow \quad \lambda = \pm 1$

So, sum of square of all possible value 2.

43. $|3\,\text{adj}(2\,\text{adj}(|A|A)| = |3\,\text{adj}(2|A|^2\,\text{adj}A|$

$= |3 \cdot 2^2 |A|^4\,\text{adj}(\text{adj}A)|$

$= 2^6 \cdot 3^3 |A|^{12} |A|^4$

$= 2^6 \cdot 3^3 \cdot |A|^{16}$

$= 2^{-10} \cdot 3^{-13}$ [given]

So, $|A|^{16} = 2^{-16} \cdot 3^{-16}$

$\Rightarrow \quad |A| = 2^{-1} \cdot 3^{-1}$ ...(i)

Now, $|3\,\text{adj}(2A)| = |3 \cdot 2^2\,\text{adj}(A)|$

$= 2^6 \cdot 3^3 |A|^2 = 2^m \cdot 3^n$ [given]

$\Rightarrow \quad 2^6 \cdot 3^3 \cdot 2^{-2} \cdot 3^{-2} = 2^m \cdot 3^n$ [from Eq. (i)]

$\Rightarrow \quad 2^m \cdot 3^n = 2^4\, 3^1$

$\therefore \quad m = 4, n = 1$

Hence, $|3m + 2n| = |12 + 2|$

$= |14| = 14$

44. For a 3×3 matrix

$$|\text{adj}\,A| = |A|^2$$

$$\underbrace{|\text{adj}(\text{adj}(\text{adj}\ldots(\text{adj}\,A)))|}_{2024\text{ times}} = |A|^{2^{2024}}$$

$$= 2^{2^{2024}}$$

$\therefore \quad 2^2 2^{2022} = 4(8)^{674} = 4(9-1)^{674}$

$\Rightarrow \quad 2^{2024} = 4(\text{mod}\,9)$

$\Rightarrow \quad 2^{2024} = 9m + 4,$

where m is even.

$\Rightarrow \quad 2^{9m+4} = 16 \cdot (2^3)^{3m} = 16(\text{mod}\,9) \equiv 7$

45. Given, $A^2 = I$ and $b = |A|$

Let $A = \begin{bmatrix} a_1 & b_1 \\ a_2 & b_2 \end{bmatrix}$

$\therefore \quad A^2 = \begin{bmatrix} a_1 & b_1 \\ a_2 & b_2 \end{bmatrix}\begin{bmatrix} a_1 & b_1 \\ a_2 & b_2 \end{bmatrix}$

$= \begin{bmatrix} a_1^2 + b_1a_2 & a_1b_1 + b_1b_2 \\ a_1a_2 + a_2b_2 & b_1a_2 + b_2^2 \end{bmatrix}$

$= \begin{bmatrix} 1 & 0 \\ 0 & 1 \end{bmatrix}$ $[\because A^2 = I]$

By equality of matrices, we get

$a_1a_2 + a_2b_2 = 0$ and $a_1b_1 + b_1b_2 = 0$

$\Rightarrow \quad a_2(a_1 + b_2) = 0$ and $b_1(a_1 + b_2) = 0$

$\Rightarrow \quad a_1 + b_2 = 0$ [since, $b_1, a_2 \neq 0$]

$\Rightarrow$ Sum of diagonal elements $= 0$

$\Rightarrow \quad a = 0$

Now, $A^2 = I$

$\Rightarrow \quad |A^2| = 1$

$\Rightarrow \quad |A|^2 = 1$ $[\because |A^n| = |A|^n]$

$\Rightarrow \quad b^2 = 1$ $[\because |A| = b]$

$\therefore \quad 3a^2 + 4b^2 = 3(0) + 4(1) = 4$

46. We have, $\alpha, \beta \in R$ and 3×3 matrix

A such that $A^2 = 3A + \alpha I$ ... (i)

and $A^4 = 21A + \beta I$ ... (ii)

Consider $A^4 = A^2 \cdot A^2$

$= (3A + \alpha I)(3A + \alpha I)$ [from Eq. (i)]

$= 9A^2 + 6\alpha A + \alpha^2 I$

From Eq. (i),

$A^4 = 9(3A + \alpha I) + 6\alpha A + \alpha^2 I$

$= (27 + 6\alpha)AI + (\alpha^2 + 9\alpha)I$ ...(iii)

From Eqs. (ii) and (iii), we get

$21A + \beta I = (27 + 6\alpha)A + (\alpha^2 + 9\alpha I)$

$\Rightarrow \quad (\beta - \alpha^2 - 9\alpha)I = (6 + 6\alpha)A$

For a general 3×3 matrix A, we get

$6 + 6\alpha = 0 \Rightarrow 6\alpha = -6$

$\Rightarrow \quad \alpha = -1$ ...(iv)

and $\beta - \alpha^2 - 9\alpha = 0$

$\Rightarrow \quad \beta = \alpha^2 + 9\alpha = (-1)^2 + 9(-1)$

$= 1 - 9 = -8$

$\therefore \quad \beta = -8$

47. Given the order of the matrix is 5.

$\because$ Sum of each row as well as each column = 1

It means, if the first position of each row or column is 1, then remaining position contains 0. Also, the position of 1 in each row or column is as per the permutation law.

Hence, number of ways $= 5 \times 4 \times 3 \times 2 \times 1$

$= 120$ ways

48. Given, $A = \begin{bmatrix} 1 & 1 \\ 0 & 1 \end{bmatrix}, P = \begin{bmatrix} \frac{\sqrt{3}}{2} & \frac{1}{2} \\ \frac{-1}{2} & \frac{\sqrt{3}}{2} \end{bmatrix}$

$\Rightarrow \quad A^2 = \begin{bmatrix} 1 & 2 \\ 0 & 1 \end{bmatrix}, P^T = \begin{bmatrix} \frac{\sqrt{3}}{2} & \frac{-1}{2} \\ \frac{1}{2} & \frac{\sqrt{3}}{2} \end{bmatrix}$

$\Rightarrow \quad A^3 = \begin{bmatrix} 1 & 2 \\ 0 & 1 \end{bmatrix}\begin{bmatrix} 1 & 1 \\ 0 & 1 \end{bmatrix} = \begin{bmatrix} 1 & 3 \\ 0 & 1 \end{bmatrix}$

$\therefore \quad A^n = \begin{bmatrix} 1 & n \\ 0 & 1 \end{bmatrix}$

$$PP^T = \begin{bmatrix} \frac{\sqrt{3}}{2} & \frac{1}{2} \\ \frac{-1}{2} & \frac{\sqrt{3}}{2} \end{bmatrix} \begin{bmatrix} \frac{\sqrt{3}}{2} & -\frac{1}{2} \\ \frac{1}{2} & \frac{\sqrt{3}}{2} \end{bmatrix} = \begin{bmatrix} 1 & 0 \\ 0 & 1 \end{bmatrix} = I$$

Now, $\begin{bmatrix} a & b \\ c & d \end{bmatrix} = P^T Q^{2007} P$

$= P^T(PAP^T)(PAP^T)(PAP^T)\dots(PAP^T)P$

$= IAIA \dots IAI = A^{2007}$

$\Rightarrow \begin{bmatrix} a & b \\ c & d \end{bmatrix} = \begin{bmatrix} 1 & 2007 \\ 0 & 1 \end{bmatrix} \quad \left[\because A^n = \begin{bmatrix} 1 & n \\ 0 & 1 \end{bmatrix}\right]$

On comparing both sides,

$a = 1, b = 2007, c = 0, d = 1$

$\therefore \ 2a + b - 3c - 4d = 2005$

49. We have, $A^T = \alpha A + I$,

where A is 2×2 matrix and $\alpha \in R - \{-1, 1\}$

$(A^T)^T = \alpha A^T + I$

$\Rightarrow \quad A = \alpha A^T + I$

$\Rightarrow \quad A = \alpha(\alpha A + I) + I \quad [\because A^T = \alpha A + I]$

$\Rightarrow \quad A = \alpha^2 A + (\alpha + 1) I$

$\Rightarrow \quad A(1 - \alpha^2) = (\alpha + 1) I$

$\Rightarrow \quad A = \dfrac{(\alpha + 1)}{(1 - \alpha)(1 + \alpha)} I$

$\Rightarrow \quad A = \dfrac{1}{1 - \alpha} I \quad \dots(i)$

$\Rightarrow \quad |A| = \dfrac{1}{(1 - \alpha)^2} \quad \dots(ii)$

Also, $\quad |A^2 - A| = 4$

$|A||A - I| = 4$

$\Rightarrow \quad \dfrac{1}{(1-\alpha)^2} \left| \left(\dfrac{1}{1-\alpha} - 1 \right) I \right| = 4$

$\Rightarrow \quad \dfrac{1}{(1-\alpha)^2} \left| \left(\dfrac{\alpha}{1-\alpha} \right) I \right| = 4$

$\Rightarrow \quad \dfrac{1}{(1-\alpha)^2} \times \dfrac{\alpha^2}{(1-\alpha)^2} = 4$

$\Rightarrow \quad \dfrac{\alpha^2}{(1-\alpha)^4} = 4 \Rightarrow \dfrac{\alpha}{(1-\alpha)^2} = \pm 2$

$\Rightarrow \quad 2(1-\alpha)^2 = \pm \alpha$

If $2(1-\alpha)^2 = \alpha$, then $2\alpha^2 - 5\alpha + 2 = 0$

Sum of all values of $\alpha = \dfrac{5}{2}$

$\left[\because \text{Sum of zero} = \dfrac{-\text{Coefficient of } x}{\text{Coefficient of } x^2}\right]$

If $2(1-\alpha)^2 = -\alpha$, then $2\alpha^2 - 3\alpha + 2 = 0$

No real value of α.

Hence, sum of all values of $\alpha = \dfrac{5}{2}$

50. Given that $P^T = aP + (a-1)I \quad \dots(i)$

$\Rightarrow \quad (P^T)^T = aP^T + (a-1)I^T$

$\Rightarrow \quad P = aP^T + (a-1)I \quad \dots(ii)$

$[\because (A^T)^T = A \text{ and } I^T = I]$

From Eq. (i), putting the value of P^T in Eq. (ii), we get

$P = a[aP + (a-1)I] + (a-1)I$

$\Rightarrow \quad P = a^2 P + a(a-1)I + (a-1)I$

$\Rightarrow \quad (1 - a^2)P = (a-1)(a+1)I \Rightarrow (1 - a^2)P = (a^2 - 1)I$

$\therefore \quad P = -I$

So, $\quad \text{adj} P = I \Rightarrow |\text{adj } P| = 1$

51. For 3×3 matrix, $n = 3$

Given, $|\text{adj}(\text{adj}(\text{adj } A))| = 12^4$

$\Rightarrow \quad |A|^{(n-1)^3} = 12^4 \Rightarrow |A|^{2^3} = 12^4$

$\Rightarrow \quad |A|^8 = 12^4 \Rightarrow |A| = \sqrt{12} = 2\sqrt{3}$

$\therefore \quad |A| = 2\sqrt{3}$

$\therefore \ |A^{-1} \text{adj } A| = \left| \dfrac{1}{|A|} \right| . |\text{adj } A| = \dfrac{|A|^2}{|A|} = |A| = 2\sqrt{3}$

52. Given, $A = \begin{bmatrix} 1 & 2 & 3 \\ \alpha & 3 & 1 \\ 1 & 1 & 2 \end{bmatrix}$ and $|A| = 2$

$\therefore \quad |A| = \begin{vmatrix} 1 & 2 & 3 \\ \alpha & 3 & 1 \\ 1 & 1 & 2 \end{vmatrix} = 1(5) + 2(1 - 2\alpha) + 3(\alpha - 3) = -\alpha - 2$

Given, $|A| = 2 \Rightarrow -\alpha - 2 = 2$

$\Rightarrow \quad -\alpha = 4 \Rightarrow \alpha = -4$

Now, $|2 \text{ adj}(2 \text{ adj}(2A)| = 2^3 |\text{adj}(2 \text{ adj}(2A)|$

$= 8|\text{adj}(2 \cdot 2^2 \text{ adj}(A)|$

$= 8|\text{adj}(2^3 \text{ adj} A)| = 8|2^6 \text{adj}(\text{adj } A)|$

$= 8 \cdot (2^6)^3 |\text{adj}(\text{adj } A)|$

$= 2^3 \cdot 2^{18} \cdot |A|^4$

$[\because |\text{adj}(\text{adj } A)| = |A|^{(n-1)^2}]$

$= 2^3 \cdot 2^{18} \cdot 2^4$

$= 2^{25} = (2^5)^5 = (32)^5 = (32)^n \quad$ [given]

So, $\quad n = 5$

and $\quad \alpha = -4$

Thus, $3n + \alpha = 3 \times 5 - 4 = 15 - 4 = 11$

53. Given, $\quad A = \begin{bmatrix} m & n \\ p & q \end{bmatrix}$

$d = |A| \neq 0 \quad \dots(i)$

and $|A - d(\text{adj } A)| = 0 \quad \dots(ii)$

Now, $A - d(\text{adj } A) = \begin{bmatrix} m & n \\ p & q \end{bmatrix} - d \begin{bmatrix} q & -n \\ -p & m \end{bmatrix}$

$= \begin{bmatrix} m - qd & n(1+d) \\ p(1+d) & q - md \end{bmatrix}$

From Eq. (ii), $\begin{vmatrix} m-qd & n(1+d) \\ p(1+d) & q-md \end{vmatrix}=0$

$\Rightarrow \quad (m-qd)(q-md)-np(1+d)^2=0$

$\Rightarrow \quad mq-m^2d-q^2d+mqd^2-np(1+d)^2=0$

$\Rightarrow \quad (mq-np)+d^2(mq-np)-d(m^2+q^2+2np)=0$

$\Rightarrow \quad d+d^3-d((m+q)^2-2d)=0 \quad [\because d=mq-np]$

$\Rightarrow \quad 1+d^2=(m+q)^2-2d$

$\Rightarrow \quad (1+d)^2=(m+q)^2$

54. **Decoding the Question**

(i) If A is a non-singular matrix of order n, then $|\text{adj } A|=|A|^{n-1}$

(ii) $|A^{-1}|=|A|^{-1}$

(iii) $|kA|=k^n|A|$, where A is a matrix of order n.

We have, $|\text{adj}(2\text{ adj}(2A^{-1}))|=2^{84}$

$\Rightarrow \quad |2\text{ adj}(2A^{-1})|^{n-1}=2^{84}$

$\Rightarrow \quad (2^n|\text{adj}(2A^{-1})|^{n-1}=2^{84}$

$\Rightarrow \quad 2^{n(n-1)}(|2A^{-1}|^{(n-1)})^{n-1}=2^{84}$

$\Rightarrow \quad 2^{n(n-1)}(2^n|A^{-1}|)^{(n-1)^2}=2^{84}$

$\Rightarrow \quad 2^{n(n-1)}\left(2^n\dfrac{1}{|A|}\right)^{(n-1)^2}=2^{84}$

$\Rightarrow \quad 2^{n(n-1)}\left(\dfrac{2^n}{2}\right)^{(n-1)^2}=2^{84}$

$\Rightarrow \quad 2^{n(n-1)+(n-1)^3}=2^{84}$

$\Rightarrow \quad n(n-1)+(n-1)^3=84$

$\Rightarrow \quad (n-1)[n+n^2-2n+1]=84$

$\Rightarrow \quad (n-1)(n^2-n+1)=84$

$\Rightarrow \quad n=5$

55. $A=\begin{bmatrix} 1 & 2 \\ -2 & -5 \end{bmatrix}$

Characteristic equation of A is

$|A-\lambda I|=0$

$\Rightarrow \quad \begin{vmatrix} 1-\lambda & 2 \\ -2 & -5-\lambda \end{vmatrix}=0$

$\Rightarrow \quad \lambda^2+4\lambda-1=0$

$\therefore \quad A^2+4A-I=0$

$\Rightarrow \quad 2A^2+8A=2I$

$\Rightarrow \quad \alpha=2,\beta=8$

$\therefore \quad \alpha+\beta=10$

56. Given, A and B are any two 3×3 symmetric and skew-symmetric matrix, respectively.

$\Rightarrow \quad A^T=A,\ B^T=-B$

Let $\quad C=A^4-B^4$

$C^T=(A^4-B^4)^T=(A^4)^T-(B^4)^T$

$=(A^T)^4-(B^T)^4$

$=A^4-(-B)^4 \quad [\because A^T=A \text{ and } B^T=-B]$

$=A^4-B^4 \quad [\because (-B)^4=B^4]$

$=C$

$\therefore$ C is a symmetric matrix.

Let $\quad D=AB-BA$

$D^T=(AB-BA)^T=(AB)^T-(BA)^T$

$=B^TA^T-A^TB^T \quad [\because (AB)^T=B^TA^T]$

$=-BA+AB \quad [\because A^T=A \text{ and } B^T=-B]$

$=D$

$\therefore$ D is a symmetric matrix.

Let $\quad E=B^5-A^5$

$E^T=(B^5-A^5)^T=(B^5)^T-(A^5)^T$

$=(B^T)^5-(A^T)^5=(-B)^5-A^5 [\because A^T=A, B^T=-B]$

$=-B^5-A^5=-[B^5+A^5]\neq -E$

$\therefore$ E is neither symmetric nor skew-symmetric.

Let $\quad F=AB+BA$

$F^T=(AB+BA)^T=(AB)^T+(BA)^T$

$=B^TA^T+A^TB^T=-BA-AB$

$=-(AB+BA)=-F$

$\therefore$ F is a skew-symmetric.

57. $\because \quad A=\begin{bmatrix} 0 & -2 \\ 2 & 0 \end{bmatrix}$

$\therefore \quad A^2=\begin{bmatrix} -4 & 0 \\ 0 & -4 \end{bmatrix}=-4I$

$A^3=A^2\cdot A$

$=\begin{bmatrix} -4 & 0 \\ 0 & -4 \end{bmatrix}\begin{bmatrix} 0 & -2 \\ 2 & 0 \end{bmatrix}=\begin{bmatrix} 0 & 8 \\ -8 & 0 \end{bmatrix}=-4A$

$M=\sum_{k=1}^{10}(A^2)^k$

$=[(-4)+(-4)^2+\ldots+(-4)^{10}]I$

$=-4\lambda I$, which is symmetric,

where $\lambda=[1+(-4)+(-4)^2+\ldots+(-4)^9]$

$N=\sum_{k=1}^{10}A^{2k-1}$

$=A[1+(-4)+(-4)^3+\ldots+(-4)^9]$

$=\lambda A$, which is skew-symmetric

Now, N^2 is symmetric.

$MN=(-4\lambda I)(\lambda A)$

$=-4\lambda^2A=NM$

$MN^2=(MN)N=(NM)N \quad [\because MN=NM]$

$=N(MN)=N(NM)=N^2M$

Hence, MN^2 is non-identity symmetric matrix.

58. $A=\begin{bmatrix}4 & -2\\ \alpha & \beta\end{bmatrix}$ satisfies

$$A^2+4A+18I=0$$

Characteristic equation of A is

$$A^2-(T_r(A))A+|A|I=0$$

Comparing this with given equation, we get

$$|A|=18$$

59. Given, $|A|=2$

Now, $||A|\ \text{adj}\ (5\ \text{adj}\ A^3)|=|5^2\cdot|A|\cdot\text{adj}\ (\text{adj}\ A^3)|$

$$=25^3\cdot|A|^3\cdot|\text{adj}\ (A)^3|^2$$
$$=25^3\cdot 2^3\cdot|A^3|^4$$
$$=25^3\cdot 2^3\cdot 2^{12}=(25\times 2\times 2)^3\times 2^9$$
$$=10^6\cdot 512=512\times 10^6$$

60. $|\text{adj}\ (24A)|=|\ \text{adj}3\ (\text{adj}\ 2A)|$

$\Rightarrow\quad |24A|^2=|\ 3\text{adj}\ (2A)|^2\qquad [\because |\text{adj}A|=|A|^{n-1}]$

$\Rightarrow\quad ((24)^3\ |A|)^2=(3^3\ |\text{adj}(2A)|)^2=3^6\ (|2A|^2)^2$

$\Rightarrow\quad ((24)^3\ |A|)^2=3^6\cdot 2^{12}\cdot|A|^4$

$\Rightarrow\quad (24)^6\cdot|A|^2=3^6\cdot 2^{12}\cdot|A|^4$

$\Rightarrow\quad |A|^2=\dfrac{(24)^6}{3^6\cdot 2^{12}}=\dfrac{3^6\cdot 2^{18}}{3^6\cdot 2^{12}}=2^6$

61. Let $S=\{\sqrt{n}, 1\le n\le 50$ and n is odd$\}$

$$=\{1,\sqrt{3},\sqrt{5},\sqrt{7},\sqrt{9},\ldots,\sqrt{49}\}$$

Also given, $A=\begin{bmatrix}1 & 0 & a\\ -1 & 1 & 0\\ -a & 0 & 1\end{bmatrix}$

$\Rightarrow\quad \det A=1(1)-0+a(a)=a^2+1$

So, $\det \text{adj}\ A=|A|^{3-1}=|A|^2=(a^2+1)^2$

$\therefore\ \sum_{a\in S}\det(\text{adj}\ A)=\sum_{a\in S}(a^2+1)^2$

$$=(1+1)^2+(3+1)^2+(5+1)^2+\ldots+(49+1)^2$$
$$=2^2(1^2+2^2+3^2+\ldots+25^2)$$
$$=4.\frac{25\cdot(25+1)\ (2\cdot 25+1)}{6}$$

$\Rightarrow\quad 100\cdot 221=100\ \lambda\qquad$ [given]

Thus, $\quad\lambda=221$

62. Given, $\quad X=\begin{bmatrix}1\\1\\1\end{bmatrix}, A=\begin{bmatrix}-1 & 2 & 3\\ 0 & 1 & 6\\ 0 & 0 & -1\end{bmatrix}$

$$A^2=\begin{bmatrix}1 & 0 & 6\\ 0 & 1 & 0\\ 0 & 0 & 1\end{bmatrix}, A^3=\begin{bmatrix}-1 & 2 & -3\\ 0 & 1 & 6\\ 0 & 0 & -1\end{bmatrix}$$

$$A^4=\begin{bmatrix}1 & 0 & 12\\ 0 & 1 & 0\\ 0 & 0 & 1\end{bmatrix}, A^5=\begin{bmatrix}-1 & 2 & -9\\ 0 & 1 & 6\\ 0 & 0 & -1\end{bmatrix}$$

$$A^6=\begin{bmatrix}1 & 0 & 18\\ 0 & 1 & 0\\ 0 & 0 & 1\end{bmatrix}$$

When k is even, $A^k=\begin{bmatrix}1 & 0 & 3k\\ 0 & 1 & 0\\ 0 & 0 & 1\end{bmatrix}$

$X'A^kX=33$

$\Rightarrow[1\quad 1\quad 1]\begin{bmatrix}1 & 0 & 3k\\ 0 & 1 & 0\\ 0 & 0 & 1\end{bmatrix}\begin{bmatrix}1\\1\\1\end{bmatrix}=[33]$

$\Rightarrow\quad [1\quad 1\quad 1]\begin{bmatrix}1+3k\\1\\1\end{bmatrix}=[33]$

$\Rightarrow\quad 1+3k+1+1=33$

$\Rightarrow\quad k=10$

When k is odd.

$$X'A^kX=[33]\Rightarrow X'A\cdot A^{k-1}X=[33]$$

$$[1\quad 1\quad 1]\begin{bmatrix}-1 & 2 & 3\\ 0 & 1 & 6\\ 0 & 0 & -1\end{bmatrix}$$
$$\begin{bmatrix}1 & 0 & 3(k-1)\\ 0 & 1 & 0\\ 0 & 0 & 1\end{bmatrix}\begin{bmatrix}1\\1\\1\end{bmatrix}=[33]$$

$\Rightarrow\quad -3k+2+3+8=33\ \Rightarrow k=\dfrac{-20}{3}\notin N$

Hence, $k=10, n\in N$

63. Given, $A=\begin{bmatrix}1+i & 1\\ -i & 0\end{bmatrix}$

$\therefore\quad A^2=\begin{bmatrix}1+i & 1\\ -i & 0\end{bmatrix}\begin{bmatrix}1+i & 1\\ -i & 0\end{bmatrix}$

$$=\begin{bmatrix}i & 1+i\\ 1-i & -i\end{bmatrix}$$

$$A^4=\begin{bmatrix}i & 1+i\\ 1-i & -i\end{bmatrix}\begin{bmatrix}i & 1+i\\ 1-i & -i\end{bmatrix}=I$$

So, $A^5=A, A^9=A$ and so on.

Clearly, $n=1,5,9,\ldots,97$

Number of values of $n=25$

64. Given, $\quad A=\begin{bmatrix}2 & -2\\ 1 & -1\end{bmatrix}$

$\Rightarrow\quad A^2=\begin{bmatrix}2 & -2\\ 1 & -1\end{bmatrix}\begin{bmatrix}2 & -2\\ 1 & -1\end{bmatrix}=\begin{bmatrix}2 & -2\\ 1 & -1\end{bmatrix}$

$\therefore\quad A^n=A,\forall\ n\in N$

$$B^2=\begin{bmatrix}-1 & 2\\ -1 & 2\end{bmatrix}\begin{bmatrix}-1 & 2\\ -1 & 2\end{bmatrix}=\begin{bmatrix}-1 & 2\\ -1 & 2\end{bmatrix}$$

$\therefore\quad B^m=B,\forall\ m\in N$

Now, $nA^n + mB^m = I$

$$n\begin{bmatrix}2 & -2\\1 & -1\end{bmatrix} + m\begin{bmatrix}-1 & 2\\-1 & 2\end{bmatrix} = \begin{bmatrix}1 & 0\\0 & 1\end{bmatrix} \quad [\because A^n = A \text{ and } B^m = B]$$

$$= \begin{bmatrix}2n - m & -2n + 2m\\n - m & -n + 2m\end{bmatrix} = \begin{bmatrix}1 & 0\\0 & 1\end{bmatrix}$$

$\Rightarrow$ $2n - m = 1, -n + 2m = 1$ and $n - m = 0 \Rightarrow m = n$

On putting $m = n$ in equation $2n - m = 1$, we get

$$2n - n = 1 \Rightarrow n = 1$$

$\therefore$ $(m, n) = (1, 1)$

Hence, the number of element in set is 1.

65. Let $A = \begin{bmatrix}a_1 & b_1 & c_1\\a_2 & b_2 & c_2\\a_3 & b_3 & c_3\end{bmatrix}, A^T = \begin{bmatrix}a_1 & a_2 & a_3\\b_1 & b_2 & b_3\\c_1 & c_2 & c_3\end{bmatrix}$

$\therefore$ $A^TA = \begin{bmatrix}a_1 & a_2 & a_3\\b_1 & b_2 & b_3\\c_1 & c_2 & c_3\end{bmatrix}\begin{bmatrix}a_1 & b_1 & c_1\\a_2 & b_2 & c_2\\a_3 & b_3 & c_3\end{bmatrix}$

Trace $(A^TA) = a_1^2 + b_1^2 + c_1^2 + a_2^2 + b_2^2 + c_2^2 + a_3^2 + b_3^2 + c_3^2$

Given, trace $(A^TA) = 6$

So, total number of such matrices is ${}^9C_6 \times 2^6 = 5376$

66. Given, $A = \begin{bmatrix}a & b\\c & d\end{bmatrix}$

$$|A| = \begin{vmatrix}a & b\\c & d\end{vmatrix} = ad - bc$$

A^{-1} exist if $ad - bc \neq 0$

If $A = A^{-1}$, then $A^2 = I$

$$\begin{bmatrix}a & b\\c & d\end{bmatrix}\begin{bmatrix}a & b\\c & d\end{bmatrix} = \begin{bmatrix}1 & 0\\0 & 1\end{bmatrix}$$

$$\Rightarrow \begin{bmatrix}a^2 + bc & ab + bd\\ac + cd & bc + d^2\end{bmatrix} = \begin{bmatrix}1 & 0\\0 & 1\end{bmatrix}$$

$$\Rightarrow \begin{bmatrix}a^2 + bc & b(a + d)\\c(a + d) & bc + d^2\end{bmatrix} = \begin{bmatrix}1 & 0\\0 & 1\end{bmatrix}$$

$$ab + bd = 0 \quad \text{...(i)}$$
$$ac + cd = 0 \quad \text{...(ii)}$$
$$a^2 + bc = 1 \quad \text{...(iii)}$$
$$bc + d^2 = 1 \quad \text{...(iv)}$$

On subtracting Eq. (iv) from Eq. (iii), we get

$$a^2 - d^2 = 0$$
$$(a + d)(a - d) = 0$$
$$\Rightarrow a + d = 0 \text{ or } a - d = 0$$

Case I When, $a + d = 0$ or $a = -d$

(a, d) can be $(-1, 1), (0, 0)$ and $(1, -1)$

(a) When, $(a, d) = (-1, 1)$

$$a^2 + bc = 1$$
$$1 + bc = 1$$
$$bc = 0$$

When, $b = 0$, then possibility of c is 12.

When, $c = 0$, then possibility of b is 12.

$\therefore$ Total number of possibility $= 24 - 1 = 23$

as $(0, 0)$ is repeated.

(b) When, $(a, d) = (0, 0)$

$$a^2 + bc = 1 \Rightarrow bc = 1$$

Possible value of (b, c) is $(1, 1), (-1, -1)$

(c) When, $(a, d) = (1, -1)$

There are 23 possible value

Case II When $a - d = 0$, then $a = d$

From Eq. (ii),

$$ac + cd = 0 \Rightarrow 2ac = 0$$
$$a \neq 0, c = 0$$

From Eq. (i),

$$d \neq 0, b = 0$$

From Eq. (iii),

$$a^2 = 1 \Rightarrow a = \pm 1$$

There are only 2 possible values.

Total number of possible values $= 23 + 23 + 2 + 2 = 50$

67. Given, $X = \begin{bmatrix}0 & 1 & 0\\0 & 0 & 1\\0 & 0 & 0\end{bmatrix}, Y = \alpha I + \beta X + \gamma X^2$

$$Z = \alpha^2 I - \alpha\beta X + (\beta^2 - \alpha\gamma)X^2$$

$$Y^{-1} = \begin{bmatrix}\frac{1}{5} & \frac{-2}{5} & \frac{1}{5}\\0 & \frac{1}{5} & \frac{-2}{5}\\0 & 0 & \frac{1}{5}\end{bmatrix}$$

To find $(\alpha - \beta + \gamma)^2$

From given value of X

$$X^2 = \begin{bmatrix}0 & 0 & 1\\0 & 0 & 0\\0 & 0 & 0\end{bmatrix}$$

Let $Y = \begin{bmatrix}\alpha & \beta & \gamma\\0 & \alpha & \beta\\0 & 0 & \alpha\end{bmatrix}$

Then, $Z = \alpha^2 I - \alpha\beta X + (\beta^2 - \alpha\gamma)X^2$

$$= \alpha^2\begin{bmatrix}1 & 0 & 0\\0 & 1 & 0\\0 & 0 & 1\end{bmatrix} - \alpha\beta\begin{bmatrix}0 & 1 & 0\\0 & 0 & 1\\0 & 0 & 0\end{bmatrix} + (\beta^2 - \alpha\gamma)\begin{bmatrix}0 & 0 & 1\\0 & 0 & 0\\0 & 0 & 0\end{bmatrix}$$

$$= \begin{bmatrix}\alpha^2 & -\alpha\beta & \beta^2 - \alpha\gamma\\0 & \alpha^2 & -\alpha\beta\\0 & 0 & \alpha^2\end{bmatrix}$$

Let $Y \cdot Y^{-1} = I \begin{bmatrix}\alpha & \beta & \gamma\\0 & \alpha & \beta\\0 & 0 & \alpha\end{bmatrix}\begin{bmatrix}\frac{1}{5} & \frac{-2}{5} & \frac{1}{5}\\0 & \frac{1}{5} & \frac{-2}{5}\\0 & 0 & \frac{1}{5}\end{bmatrix} = \begin{bmatrix}1 & 0 & 0\\0 & 1 & 0\\0 & 0 & 1\end{bmatrix}$

$$\frac{\alpha}{5} = 1 \Rightarrow \alpha = 5$$

$$\therefore \quad -\frac{2}{5}\alpha + \frac{\beta}{5} = 0 \Rightarrow \frac{\beta}{5} = \frac{2}{5}\alpha$$

$$\beta = 10$$

and $\quad \dfrac{\alpha}{5} - \dfrac{2}{5}\beta + \dfrac{\gamma}{5} = 0$

$$\Rightarrow \quad \frac{5}{5} - \frac{2}{5} \times 10 + \frac{\gamma}{5} = 0$$

$$\Rightarrow \quad 1 - 4 + \frac{\gamma}{5} = 0 \Rightarrow \gamma = 15$$

$$\therefore \quad (\alpha - \beta + \gamma)^2 = (5 - 10 + 15)^2 = 100$$

68. $A = \begin{bmatrix} 1 & 0 & 0 \\ 0 & 1 & 1 \\ 1 & 0 & 0 \end{bmatrix}$

Now, $A^2 = \begin{bmatrix} 1 & 0 & 0 \\ 0 & 1 & 1 \\ 1 & 0 & 0 \end{bmatrix}\begin{bmatrix} 1 & 0 & 0 \\ 0 & 1 & 1 \\ 1 & 0 & 0 \end{bmatrix} = \begin{bmatrix} 1 & 0 & 0 \\ 1 & 1 & 1 \\ 1 & 0 & 0 \end{bmatrix}$

$$A^3 = \begin{bmatrix} 1 & 0 & 0 \\ 1 & 1 & 1 \\ 1 & 0 & 0 \end{bmatrix}\begin{bmatrix} 1 & 0 & 0 \\ 0 & 1 & 1 \\ 1 & 0 & 0 \end{bmatrix} = \begin{bmatrix} 1 & 0 & 0 \\ 2 & 1 & 1 \\ 1 & 0 & 0 \end{bmatrix}$$

$$A^4 = \begin{bmatrix} 1 & 0 & 0 \\ 2 & 1 & 1 \\ 1 & 0 & 0 \end{bmatrix}\begin{bmatrix} 1 & 0 & 0 \\ 0 & 1 & 1 \\ 1 & 0 & 0 \end{bmatrix} = \begin{bmatrix} 1 & 0 & 0 \\ 3 & 1 & 1 \\ 1 & 0 & 0 \end{bmatrix}$$

$$\vdots \qquad \vdots \qquad \vdots$$

$$A^n = \begin{bmatrix} 1 & 0 & 0 \\ n-2 & 1 & 1 \\ 1 & 0 & 0 \end{bmatrix}\begin{bmatrix} 1 & 0 & 0 \\ 0 & 1 & 1 \\ 1 & 0 & 0 \end{bmatrix} = \begin{bmatrix} 1 & 0 & 0 \\ n-1 & 1 & 1 \\ 1 & 0 & 0 \end{bmatrix}$$

$$A^{2025} - A^{2020} = \begin{bmatrix} 1 & 0 & 0 \\ 2024 & 1 & 1 \\ 1 & 0 & 0 \end{bmatrix} - \begin{bmatrix} 1 & 0 & 0 \\ 2019 & 1 & 1 \\ 1 & 0 & 0 \end{bmatrix} = \begin{bmatrix} 0 & 0 & 0 \\ 5 & 0 & 0 \\ 0 & 0 & 0 \end{bmatrix}$$

Now, $A^6 - A = \begin{bmatrix} 1 & 0 & 0 \\ 5 & 1 & 1 \\ 1 & 0 & 0 \end{bmatrix} - \begin{bmatrix} 1 & 0 & 0 \\ 0 & 1 & 1 \\ 1 & 0 & 0 \end{bmatrix} = \begin{bmatrix} 0 & 0 & 0 \\ 5 & 0 & 0 \\ 0 & 0 & 0 \end{bmatrix}$

$$\therefore \; A^{2025} - A^{2020} = A^6 - A$$

69. Let A be the matrix as follows,

$A = \begin{bmatrix} a & b \\ b & c \end{bmatrix}$, since A is symmetric matrix.

Now, $A^2 = \begin{bmatrix} a & b \\ b & c \end{bmatrix}\begin{bmatrix} a & b \\ b & c \end{bmatrix} = \begin{bmatrix} a^2 + b^2 & ab + bc \\ ab + bc & b^2 + c^2 \end{bmatrix}$

Given that the sum of diagonal entries of A^2 is 1.

i.e. $\quad a^2 + b^2 + b^2 + c^2 = 1$ or $a^2 + 2b^2 + c^2 = 1$

Case I $a = 0$

Then, $2b^2 + c^2 = 1$

(a) $c = 0$ gives, $b^2 = \dfrac{1}{2}$ or $b = \pm\dfrac{1}{\sqrt{2}}$

$\therefore a = 0, b = 1/\sqrt{2}, c = 0$

$a = 0, b = -1/\sqrt{2}, c = 0$ [2 matrices]

(b) $b = 0$, gives $c^2 = 1$ or $c = \pm 1$

$\therefore a = 0, b = 0, c = 1$ and $a = 0, b = 0, c = -1$ (2 matrices)

Case II $b = 0$, then $a^2 + c^2 = 1$

(a) $a = 0$, then $c = \pm 1$

$a = 0, b = 0, c = 1$ and $a = 0, b = 0, c = -1$

This is repeated case.

(b) $c = 0$, then $a = \pm 1$

$a = 1, b = 0, c = 0$ and $a = -1, b = 0, c = 0$

Again, 2 matrices.

Thus, only acceptable matrices are as follows

$$A = \begin{bmatrix} 0 & 0 \\ 0 & 1 \end{bmatrix}, \begin{bmatrix} 0 & 0 \\ 0 & -1 \end{bmatrix}, \begin{bmatrix} 1 & 0 \\ 0 & 0 \end{bmatrix}, \begin{bmatrix} -1 & 0 \\ 0 & 0 \end{bmatrix}$$

Then, possible number of such matrices are 4.

70. $AA^T = \begin{bmatrix} \frac{1}{\sqrt{5}} & \frac{2}{\sqrt{5}} \\ \frac{-2}{\sqrt{5}} & \frac{1}{\sqrt{5}} \end{bmatrix}\begin{bmatrix} \frac{1}{\sqrt{5}} & \frac{-2}{\sqrt{5}} \\ \frac{2}{\sqrt{5}} & \frac{1}{\sqrt{5}} \end{bmatrix}$

$$AA^T = \begin{bmatrix} 1 & 0 \\ 0 & 1 \end{bmatrix} = I$$

Now, $Q^2 = A^TBAA^TBA$

$\Rightarrow \quad Q^2 = A^TB^2A$

Again, $Q^3 = (A^TBA)(A^TB^2A) = A^TB^3A$

Similarly, $Q^{2021} = A^TB^{2021}A$

$$\Rightarrow \quad AQ^{2021}A^T = A(A^TB^{2021}A)A^T$$
$$= (AA^T)\, B^{2021}(AA^T)$$
$$= B^{2021}$$

As, $B = \begin{bmatrix} 1 & 0 \\ i & 1 \end{bmatrix} \Rightarrow B^2 = \begin{bmatrix} 1 & 0 \\ 2i & 1 \end{bmatrix}$,

Similarly, $B^{2021} = \begin{bmatrix} 1 & 0 \\ 2021\,i & 1 \end{bmatrix}$

$$(B^{2021})^{-1} = \frac{\operatorname{adj}(B^{2021})}{|B^{2021}|}$$
$$= \begin{bmatrix} 1 & 0 \\ -2021\,i & 1 \end{bmatrix}$$

71. Given, $\quad A = \begin{bmatrix} 1 & 2 \\ -1 & 4 \end{bmatrix}$

$$A^{-1} = \alpha I + \beta A, \alpha, \beta \in R$$

Now, $\quad A^{-1} = \dfrac{\operatorname{adj} A}{|A|}$

If $X = \begin{bmatrix} a & b \\ c & d \end{bmatrix}$, then $\operatorname{adj} X = \begin{bmatrix} d & -b \\ -c & a \end{bmatrix}$

Similarly, adj A $= \begin{bmatrix} 4 & -2 \\ 1 & 1 \end{bmatrix}$

$$|A| = 4 - (-2) = 6$$

$$\therefore \quad A^{-1} = \frac{1}{6}\begin{bmatrix} 4 & -2 \\ 1 & 1 \end{bmatrix}$$

Now, $A^{-1} = \alpha I + \beta A$

$$= \begin{bmatrix} \alpha & 0 \\ 0 & \alpha \end{bmatrix} + \begin{bmatrix} \beta & 2\beta \\ -\beta & 4\beta \end{bmatrix}$$

$$= \begin{bmatrix} \alpha+\beta & 2\beta \\ -\beta & \alpha+4\beta \end{bmatrix}$$

$$\Rightarrow \begin{bmatrix} \alpha+\beta & 2\beta \\ -\beta & \alpha+4\beta \end{bmatrix} = \begin{bmatrix} \frac{2}{3} & -\frac{1}{3} \\ \frac{1}{6} & \frac{1}{6} \end{bmatrix}$$

$\therefore \quad \beta = -\frac{1}{6}$ and $\alpha + \beta = \frac{2}{3}$

$\Rightarrow \quad \alpha = \frac{4}{6} + \frac{1}{6} = \frac{5}{6}$

$\therefore \quad 4(\alpha - \beta) = 4\left(\frac{5}{6} + \frac{1}{6}\right) = 4$

72. $A = \begin{bmatrix} 0 & 1 & 0 \\ 1 & 0 & 0 \\ 0 & 0 & 1 \end{bmatrix}, B = \begin{bmatrix} a_1 & a_2 & a_3 \\ b_1 & b_2 & b_3 \\ c_1 & c_2 & c_3 \end{bmatrix}$

$\because \quad AB = BA$ [given]

$$\Rightarrow \begin{bmatrix} b_1 & b_2 & b_3 \\ a_1 & a_2 & a_3 \\ c_1 & c_2 & c_3 \end{bmatrix} = \begin{bmatrix} a_2 & a_1 & a_3 \\ b_2 & b_1 & b_3 \\ c_2 & c_1 & c_3 \end{bmatrix}$$

$\Rightarrow b_1 = a_2,\ b_2 = a_1,\ b_3 = a_3$ and $c_1 = c_2$

$$\therefore \quad B = \begin{bmatrix} a_1 & a_2 & a_3 \\ a_2 & a_1 & a_3 \\ c_1 & c_1 & c_3 \end{bmatrix}$$

Number of distinct elements in B is 5

and according to question,

$a_{ij} \in \{1, 2, 3, 4, 5\}$.

So, number of matrices $= 5 \times 5 \times 5 \times 5 \times 5 = 3125$

73. $P = \begin{bmatrix} 2 & -1 \\ 5 & -3 \end{bmatrix}$

Now, $P^n = 5I - 8P = \begin{bmatrix} 5 & 0 \\ 0 & 5 \end{bmatrix} - \begin{bmatrix} 16 & -8 \\ 40 & -24 \end{bmatrix}$

$\Rightarrow \quad P^n = \begin{bmatrix} -11 & 8 \\ -40 & 29 \end{bmatrix}$ ... (i)

Now, $P^2 = \begin{bmatrix} -1 & 1 \\ -5 & 4 \end{bmatrix}$

Again, $P^3 = P \cdot P^2 = \begin{bmatrix} 3 & -2 \\ 10 & -7 \end{bmatrix}$

Now, $P^6 = P^3 \cdot P^3 = \begin{bmatrix} 3 & -2 \\ 10 & -7 \end{bmatrix}\begin{bmatrix} 3 & -2 \\ 10 & -7 \end{bmatrix}$

$\Rightarrow \quad P^6 = \begin{bmatrix} -11 & 8 \\ -40 & 29 \end{bmatrix} = P^n$ [From Eq. (i)]

$\therefore \quad n = 6$

74. Method I

Given, $A = \begin{bmatrix} a & b \\ c & d \end{bmatrix}, B = \begin{bmatrix} \alpha \\ \beta \end{bmatrix} \neq \begin{bmatrix} 0 \\ 0 \end{bmatrix}$ i.e. $B \neq 0$ and $AB = B$

$\Rightarrow AB - B = 0 \Rightarrow B(A - I) = 0$

$\Rightarrow \quad |(A - I)B| = 0$

$\because \quad B \neq 0$

$\therefore \quad |A - I| = 0$

$$\Rightarrow \begin{vmatrix} (a-1) & b \\ c & (d-1) \end{vmatrix} = 0$$

$\Rightarrow \quad (a-1)(d-1) - bc = 0$

$\Rightarrow \quad ad - (a+d) + 1 - bc = 0$

$\Rightarrow \quad ad - 2021 + 1 - bc = 0$ $[\because a + d = 2021]$

$\Rightarrow \quad ad - bc = 2020$

Method II

Given, $A = \begin{bmatrix} a & b \\ c & d \end{bmatrix}, B = \begin{bmatrix} \alpha \\ \beta \end{bmatrix}$

$AB = B$

$$\Rightarrow \begin{bmatrix} a & b \\ c & d \end{bmatrix}\begin{bmatrix} \alpha \\ \beta \end{bmatrix} = \begin{bmatrix} \alpha \\ \beta \end{bmatrix} \Rightarrow \begin{bmatrix} a\alpha + b\beta \\ c\alpha + d\beta \end{bmatrix} = \begin{bmatrix} \alpha \\ \beta \end{bmatrix}$$

$\Rightarrow \quad a\alpha + b\beta = \alpha$

$\Rightarrow \quad \alpha(a-1) = -b\beta$ ...(i)

and $\quad c\alpha + d\beta = \beta \Rightarrow c\alpha = \beta(1-d)$ ... (ii)

On dividing Eq. (i) by Eq. (ii), we get

$$\frac{a-1}{c} = \frac{-b}{1-d}$$

$\Rightarrow \quad (a-1)(1-d) = -bc$

$\Rightarrow \quad a - 1 - ad + d = -bc$

$\Rightarrow \quad a + d - 1 = ad - bc$

$\Rightarrow \quad 2021 - 1 = ad - bc$

$\Rightarrow \quad ad - bc = 2020$

75. Here, $A = \begin{bmatrix} x & y & z \\ y & z & x \\ z & x & y \end{bmatrix}$

$$\therefore \quad |A| = \begin{vmatrix} x & y & z \\ y & z & x \\ z & x & y \end{vmatrix}$$

$$= -(x^3 + y^3 + z^3 - 3xyz)$$

Also, $A^2 = I_3$

$|A^2| = |I_3| = 1$

$\Rightarrow \quad |A|^2 = 1$

$\therefore \quad (-(x^3 + y^3 + z^3 - 3xyz))^2 = 1$

$\Rightarrow \quad x^3 + y^3 + z^3 - 3xyz = 1$ $[\because x + y + z > 0]$

$\Rightarrow \quad x^3 + y^3 + z^3 = 1 + 3xyz$

$= 1 + 3(2) = 7$ $[\because xyz = 2]$

76. We have, A is a square matrix of 3×3.

Now, 2 adj(2adj (adj (2A)))

$= 2\text{adj}(2\text{adj}(2^{3-1}\text{adj}A))$ $\quad [\because \text{adj}(KA) = K^{n-1}\text{adj}A]$

$= 2\text{adj}(2\text{adj}(4\text{adj}A))$

$= 2\text{adj}(2 \times 4^{3-1}\text{adj adj}A)$

$= 2\text{adj}(32\text{ adjadj}A)$

$= 2 \times 32^{3-1}\text{adjadjadj}A$

$= 2^{11}\text{adjadjadj}A$

$= 2^{11}\text{adj}(|A|^{3-2}A)$

$= 2^{11}\text{adj}(|A|A)$

$= 2^{11} \times |A|^{3-1}\text{adj}A = 2^{11} \times |A|^2\text{adj}A$

Now, $|2\text{adj}(2\text{adj}(\text{adj}(2A)))| = 2^{41}$

$\Rightarrow \quad |2^{11} \times |A|^2\text{adj}A| = 2^{41}$

$\Rightarrow \quad (2^{11})^3(|A|^2)^3|\text{adj}A| = 2^{41}$

$\Rightarrow \quad 2^{33}|A|^6|A|^{3-1} = 2^{41}$

$\Rightarrow \quad |A|^8 = 2^8$

$\Rightarrow \quad |A| = \pm 2$

Now, $|A^2| = |A|^2 = (\pm 2)^2 = 4$

77. Given, M is a 3×3 matrix.

Let $M = \begin{bmatrix} a & b & c \\ d & e & f \\ g & h & i \end{bmatrix}$, then $M^TM = \begin{bmatrix} a & d & g \\ b & e & h \\ c & f & i \end{bmatrix} \times \begin{bmatrix} a & b & c \\ d & e & f \\ g & h & i \end{bmatrix}$

Sum of diagonal elements

$= a^2 + b^2 + c^2 + d^2 + e^2 + f^2 + g^2 + h^2 + i^2 = 7 \quad \ldots(\text{i})$

According to the question, the entries are {0, 1, 2}. $[\because M^TM = 7]$

i.e. $\{a, b, c, \ldots, h, i\} = \{0, 1, 2\}$

So, for Eq. (i) to be true, there are two cases.

Case I When 7-1's are there and 2-0's are there.

$\Rightarrow \; {}^9C_7 \times {}^2C_2 = 36$ ways of arrangements.

Case II When 1-2's is there, 3-1's and 5-0's are there.

${}^9C_1 \times {}^8C_3 \times {}^5C_5 = 9 \times \dfrac{8!}{3!5!} \times 1$

$= 504$ ways of arrangements.

$\therefore$ Total possible arrangements $= 36 + 504$

$= 540$

78. Given matrices, $A = \begin{bmatrix} 1 & 1 & 2 \\ 1 & 3 & 4 \\ 1 & -1 & 3 \end{bmatrix}$ $B = \text{adj}(A)$ and $C = 3A$

Now, $\quad |\text{adj}(B)| = |\text{adj}(\text{adj}(A))|$ $\quad [\because B = \text{adj}(A)]$

and $|\text{adj}(\text{adj}(A))| = |A|^{(n-1)^2}$,

where n is the order of square matrix A.

$\therefore \; |\text{adj}(\text{adj}(A))| = |A|^{(3-1)^2} = |A|^4$

and $\quad |C| = |3A| = 3^3|A| = 27|A|$

$\because \quad |KA| = K^n|A|$,

where K is a scalar and n is the order of square matrix A.

$\therefore \quad \dfrac{|\text{adj}B|}{|C|} = \dfrac{|A|^4}{27|A|} = \dfrac{|A|^3}{27}$

$\because \quad |A| = \begin{vmatrix} 1 & 1 & 2 \\ 1 & 3 & 4 \\ 1 & -1 & 3 \end{vmatrix} = 1(9+4) - 1(3-4) + 2(-1-3)$

$= 13 + 1 - 8 = 6$

So, $\dfrac{|\text{adj}B|}{|C|} = \dfrac{|A|^3}{27} = \dfrac{6^3}{27} = 2^3 = 8$

79. It is given that α is the root of equation $x^2 + x + 1 = 0$, so $\alpha^2 + \alpha + 1 = 0$ and $\alpha^3 = 1$.

Now, matrix $A = \dfrac{1}{\sqrt{3}}\begin{bmatrix} 1 & 1 & 1 \\ 1 & \alpha & \alpha^2 \\ 1 & \alpha^2 & \alpha^4 \end{bmatrix}$

$= \dfrac{1}{\sqrt{3}}\begin{bmatrix} 1 & 1 & 1 \\ 1 & \alpha & \alpha^2 \\ 1 & \alpha^2 & \alpha \end{bmatrix}$ $\quad [\because \alpha^3 = 1]$

$\therefore \; A^2 = \left(\dfrac{1}{\sqrt{3}}\right)^2\begin{bmatrix} 1 & 1 & 1 \\ 1 & \alpha & \alpha^2 \\ 1 & \alpha^2 & \alpha \end{bmatrix}\begin{bmatrix} 1 & 1 & 1 \\ 1 & \alpha & \alpha^2 \\ 1 & \alpha^2 & \alpha \end{bmatrix}$

$= \dfrac{1}{3}\begin{bmatrix} 1+1+1 & 1+\alpha+\alpha^2 & 1+\alpha^2+\alpha \\ 1+\alpha+\alpha^2 & 1+\alpha^2+\alpha^4 & 1+\alpha^3+\alpha^3 \\ 1+\alpha^2+\alpha & 1+\alpha^3+\alpha^3 & 1+\alpha^4+\alpha^2 \end{bmatrix}$

$= \dfrac{1}{3}\begin{bmatrix} 3 & 0 & 0 \\ 0 & 0 & 3 \\ 0 & 3 & 0 \end{bmatrix}$ $\quad [\because \alpha^3 = 1 \text{ and } \alpha^2 + \alpha + 1 = 0]$

$= \begin{bmatrix} 1 & 0 & 0 \\ 0 & 0 & 1 \\ 0 & 1 & 0 \end{bmatrix}$

$\therefore \; A^4 = A^2 \cdot A^2$

$= \begin{bmatrix} 1 & 0 & 0 \\ 0 & 0 & 1 \\ 0 & 1 & 0 \end{bmatrix}\begin{bmatrix} 1 & 0 & 0 \\ 0 & 0 & 1 \\ 0 & 1 & 0 \end{bmatrix} = \begin{bmatrix} 1 & 0 & 0 \\ 0 & 1 & 0 \\ 0 & 0 & 1 \end{bmatrix} = I$

$\therefore \; A^8 = I = A^{16} = A^{20} = A^{24} = A^{28}$

$\because A^{31} = A^{28} \cdot A^3 = I \cdot A^3 = A^3$

$\Rightarrow A^{31} = A^3$

Exercise 2 - JEE Advanced Pattern

1. $a^2 + b^2 + c^2 = 2a + 2b + 2c - 3$

$\Rightarrow (a-1)^2 + (b-1)^2 + (c-1)^2 = 0$

$\Rightarrow \quad a = b = c = 1$

$\Rightarrow \quad \dfrac{1}{a} + \dfrac{1}{b} + \dfrac{1}{c} = 3$

2. Given, $M = \begin{bmatrix} x & 2x & 3x \\ f(x) & g(x) & h(x) \\ 0 & 1 & 1 \end{bmatrix}$ is a singular matrix and

$f(x) = \ln(e^x + 1)$ and $g(x) = \ln(e^x - 1)$

Applying $C_2 \to C_2 - C_3$

$$\Rightarrow M = \begin{bmatrix} x & -x & 3x \\ f(x) & g(x)-h(x) & h(x) \\ 0 & 0 & 1 \end{bmatrix}$$

Since, M is a singular matrix.

$\therefore \quad |M| = 0$

$\Rightarrow x[g(x)-h(x)+f(x)] = 0 \Rightarrow h(x) = f(x)+g(x)$

$\Rightarrow \quad h(x) = \ln(e^x+1)+\ln(e^x-1)$

$\Rightarrow \quad h(x) = \ln(e^{2x}-1)$

On differentiating both sides w.r.t. x, we get

$$h'(x) = \frac{2e^{2x}}{e^{2x-1}}$$

For $x = \ln 3$, we have

$$h'(\ln 3) = \frac{2e^{2\ln 3}}{e^{2\ln 3}-1} = \frac{9}{4}$$

3. $A = \begin{vmatrix} 1 & 2 \\ 3 & 4 \end{vmatrix}$

$$|A - \lambda I| = 0$$

$$\Rightarrow \begin{vmatrix} 1-\lambda & 2 \\ 3 & 4-\lambda \end{vmatrix} = 0$$

$\Rightarrow \quad (1-\lambda)(4-\lambda)-6 = 0$

$\Rightarrow \quad 4-5\lambda+\lambda^2-6 = 0$

$\Rightarrow \quad \lambda^2-5\lambda-2 = 0$

$\Rightarrow \quad A^2-5A-2I = 0$

$\Rightarrow \quad A^{-2} = \frac{1}{2}(I-5A^{-1})$

$\Rightarrow \quad A^{-4} = \frac{1}{4}(I-5A^{-1})^2$

$= \frac{1}{4}[I-10A^{-1}+25A^{-2}]$

$= \frac{1}{4}[I-10A^{-1}+\frac{25}{2}(I-5A^{-1})]$

$= \frac{1}{4}\left[\frac{27}{2}I-10A^{-1}-\frac{125}{2}A^{-1}\right]$

$= \frac{1}{4}\left[\frac{27I-145A^{-1}}{2}\right]$

$= \frac{1}{8}[27I-145A^{-1}]$

$\Rightarrow \quad 8A^{-4} = 8 \times \frac{1}{8}[27I-145A^{-1}]$

$= 27I-145A^{-1}$

4. A is a square matrix of order 3 such that

$|A| = 2$

We know that $\quad A^{-1} = \frac{\text{adj}A}{|A|} \Rightarrow |A^{-1}| = \frac{|\text{adj}A|}{|A|^3}$

$\Rightarrow \quad \frac{1}{|A|} = \frac{|\text{adj}A|}{|A|^3} \quad \left[\because |A^{-1}| = \frac{1}{|A|}\right]$

$\Rightarrow \quad |\text{adj } A| = |A|^2$

$\Rightarrow \quad |(\text{adj } A^3)| = (|A^3|^2) = |A|^6 = 2^6$

5. Let $M = \begin{bmatrix} a \\ b \\ c \end{bmatrix}$, then $M^T = [a \quad b \quad c]$

$$\Rightarrow MM^T = \begin{bmatrix} a \\ b \\ c \end{bmatrix}[a \quad b \quad c] = \begin{bmatrix} a^2 & ab & ac \\ ab & b^2 & bc \\ ac & bc & c^2 \end{bmatrix}$$

and $\quad M^TM = [a \quad b \quad c]\begin{bmatrix} a \\ b \\ c \end{bmatrix} = [a^2+b+c^2]$

$$\text{Now, } A = \frac{MM^T}{M^TM} = \frac{1}{(a^2+b^2+c^2)}\begin{bmatrix} a^2 & ab & ac \\ ab & b^2 & bc \\ ac & bc & c^2 \end{bmatrix}$$

$A^T = A$

$\therefore \quad A$ is symmetric matrix.

6. Given, $\quad A = \begin{bmatrix} 2 & 1 \\ 4 & 1 \end{bmatrix}, B = \begin{bmatrix} 3 & 4 \\ 2 & 3 \end{bmatrix}, C = \begin{bmatrix} 3 & -4 \\ -2 & 3 \end{bmatrix}$

Now, $\quad BC = \begin{bmatrix} 3 & 4 \\ 2 & 3 \end{bmatrix}\begin{bmatrix} 3 & -4 \\ -2 & 3 \end{bmatrix} = \begin{bmatrix} 1 & 0 \\ 0 & 1 \end{bmatrix}$ ...(i)

Let $S = \text{tr}(A) + \text{tr}\left(\frac{ABC}{2}\right) + \text{tr}\left(\frac{A(BC)^2}{4}\right) + \text{tr}\left(\frac{A(BC)^3}{8}\right) + \ldots \infty$

$\therefore \quad S = \text{tr}(A) + \text{tr}\left(\frac{A}{2}\right) + \text{tr}\left(\frac{A}{4}\right) + \ldots \infty$ [using Eq. (i)]

$\because \quad \text{tr}(A) = 2+1 = 3$

$\Rightarrow \quad S = 3 + \frac{3}{2} + \frac{3}{4} + \ldots \infty$

The sum of infinite terms of a GP series is

$$S_\infty = \frac{a}{1-r}$$

$$\therefore \quad S_\infty = S = \frac{3}{\left(1-\frac{1}{2}\right)} = 6$$

7. We have, $\quad a_{ij} = i^{100} + j^{100}$

$$\Rightarrow \text{Tr}(A) = \sum_{i=j} a_{ij} = i^{100} + i^{100} = 2i^{100}$$

$$\therefore \lim_{n\to\infty}\left(\frac{\text{Tr}(A)}{n^{101}}\right) = \lim_{n\to\infty}\left(\frac{\sum_{i=1}^{n}(2i^{100})}{n^{101}}\right)$$

$$= 2\lim_{n\to\infty}\sum_{i=1}^{n}\left(\frac{i}{n}\right)^{100}\cdot\frac{1}{n} = 2\int_0^1 x^{100}dx = \frac{2}{101}$$

8. Given, $A = \begin{bmatrix} 1 & -1 & 0 \\ -1 & 1 & 1 \\ 0 & 1 & 1 \end{bmatrix}$

$$|A - \lambda I| = 0$$

$$\Rightarrow \begin{vmatrix} 1-\lambda & -1 & 0 \\ -1 & 1-\lambda & 1 \\ 0 & 1 & 1-\lambda \end{vmatrix} = 0$$

$\Rightarrow (1-\lambda)((1-\lambda)^2-1)+1(\lambda-1)=0$

$\Rightarrow \quad -\lambda^3+3\lambda^2-\lambda-1=0$

$\Rightarrow \quad A^3-3A^2+A+I=0$

Multiplying by A^{-1} on both sides, we get

$$A^2-3A+I+A^{-1}=0$$

$\Rightarrow \quad A^{-1}+A^2=3A-I$

9. $A\begin{bmatrix}1\\-1\end{bmatrix}=\begin{bmatrix}-1\\2\end{bmatrix}$ ...(i)

and $A^2\begin{bmatrix}1\\-1\end{bmatrix}=\begin{bmatrix}1\\0\end{bmatrix}$ ...(ii)

Let A be given by $A=\begin{bmatrix}a & b\\c & d\end{bmatrix}$ the first equation gives

$a-b=-1$ ...(iii)

$c-d=2$ ...(iv)

For the second equation

$$A^2\begin{bmatrix}1\\-1\end{bmatrix}=A\left(A\begin{bmatrix}1\\-1\end{bmatrix}\right)=A\left(\begin{bmatrix}-1\\2\end{bmatrix}\right)=\begin{bmatrix}1\\0\end{bmatrix}$$

This gives

$-a+2b=1$ ...(v)

$-c+2d=0$ ...(vi)

On adding Eqs. (iii) and (v), we get

$$b=0 \text{ and } a=-1$$

On adding Eqs. (iv) and (vi), we get

$$d=2 \text{ and } c=4$$

So, the sum of $a+b+c+d=5$

10. Let $M=\begin{bmatrix}a & b & c\\d & e & f\\g & h & i\end{bmatrix}$

$\therefore tr(M^TM)=a^2+b^2+c^2+d^2+e^2+f^2+g^2+h^2+i^2$

$=5$, where entries are $\{0, 1, 2\}$

only two cases are possible

Case I Five entries are 1 and other four are 0.

$\therefore$ Number of matrices $={}^9C_5\times 1!=126$

Case II One entry is 2, one entry is 1 and others are 0.

$\therefore$ Number of matrices $={}^9C_2\times 2!=72$

So, total number of matrices $=126+72=198$

11. Since, the product matrix is 3×3 matrix and the pre multiple of A is a 3×2 matrix, therefore A is 2×3 matrix. Let

$A=\begin{bmatrix}l & m & n\\x & y & z\end{bmatrix}$, then the given equation becomes

$$\begin{bmatrix}2 & -1\\1 & 0\\-3 & 4\end{bmatrix}\begin{bmatrix}l & m & n\\x & y & z\end{bmatrix}=\begin{bmatrix}-1 & -8 & -10\\1 & -2 & -5\\9 & 22 & 15\end{bmatrix}$$

or $\begin{bmatrix}2l-x & 2m-y & 2n-z\\l & m & n\\-3l+4x & -3m+4y & -3n+4z\end{bmatrix}=\begin{bmatrix}-1 & -8 & -10\\1 & -2 & -5\\9 & 22 & 15\end{bmatrix}$

or $2l-x=-1, 2m-y=-8, 2n-z=-10$

$l=1, m=-2, n=-5$

$\Rightarrow \quad x=3, y=4, z=0, l=1, m=-2, n=-5$

$\Rightarrow \quad A=\begin{bmatrix}l & m & n\\x & y & z\end{bmatrix}=\begin{bmatrix}1 & -2 & -5\\3 & 4 & 0\end{bmatrix}$

$\therefore$ Sum of all the elements of matrix A is

$$1-2-5+3+4+0=1$$

12. We know that

$$\begin{bmatrix}\cos\theta & -\sin\theta\\\sin\theta & \cos\theta\end{bmatrix}^n=\begin{bmatrix}\cos n\theta & -\sin n\theta\\\sin n\theta & \cos n\theta\end{bmatrix}$$

$$\begin{bmatrix}\cos\frac{2\pi}{7} & -\sin\frac{2\pi}{7}\\\sin\frac{2\pi}{7} & \cos\frac{2\pi}{7}\end{bmatrix}^k=\begin{bmatrix}\cos\frac{2k\pi}{7} & -\sin\frac{2k\pi}{7}\\\sin\frac{2k\pi}{7} & \cos\frac{2k\pi}{7}\end{bmatrix}$$

$$=\begin{bmatrix}1 & 0\\0 & 1\end{bmatrix}, \text{ if } k=7m,$$

where $m\in N$.

Hence, the least value of k is 7.

13. $PP^T=\begin{bmatrix}\frac{\sqrt3}{2} & \frac12\\-\frac12 & \frac{\sqrt3}{2}\end{bmatrix}\begin{bmatrix}\frac{\sqrt3}{2} & -\frac12\\\frac12 & \frac{\sqrt3}{2}\end{bmatrix}=\begin{bmatrix}1 & 0\\0 & 1\end{bmatrix}=I$

Also, $\quad Q=PAP^T$

$\therefore P^TQ^{2005}P=P^T[(PAP^T)(PAP^T)\text{.... 2005 times}]P$

$=(P^TP)A(P^TP)A(P^TP)\dots(P^TP)$

$=I\cdot A^{2005}$

$=A^{2005}$

$\because \quad A=\begin{bmatrix}1 & 1\\0 & 1\end{bmatrix}$;

$A^2=\begin{bmatrix}1 & 1\\0 & 1\end{bmatrix}\begin{bmatrix}1 & 1\\0 & 1\end{bmatrix}=\begin{bmatrix}1 & 2\\0 & 1\end{bmatrix}$

$\therefore \quad A^3=\begin{bmatrix}1 & 2\\0 & 1\end{bmatrix}\begin{bmatrix}1 & 1\\0 & 1\end{bmatrix}=\begin{bmatrix}1 & 3\\0 & 1\end{bmatrix}$

Similarly, $A^{2005}=\begin{bmatrix}1 & 2005\\0 & 1\end{bmatrix}$

$\therefore \quad P^TQ^{2005}P=\begin{bmatrix}1 & 2005\\0 & 1\end{bmatrix}$

14. $\because A+I=\begin{bmatrix}1 & 1\\1 & 1\end{bmatrix}$

$(A+I)^2=2(A+I)$

$\Rightarrow \quad A^2=I, A^3=A, A^4=I, A^5=A, \dots$

$\therefore \sum_{r=1}^{2017}A^r=\underbrace{(A+A+\dots+A)}_{1009\text{ times}}+\underbrace{(I+I+\dots+I)}_{1008\text{ times}}$

$=1009A+1008I$

$=\begin{bmatrix}1008 & 1009\\1009 & 1008\end{bmatrix}$

$|B|=(1008)^2-(1009)^2=-2017$

15. $\because (I + A)^n = I + {}^nC_1 A + {}^nC_2 A^2 + \ldots + {}^nC_n A^n$

$$= I + ({}^nC_1 + {}^nC_2 + {}^nC_3 + \ldots + {}^nC_n)\,A$$

$$= I + (2^n - 1)A$$

$\because (I + A)^n = I + \lambda A$ [given]

$\therefore \quad \lambda = 2^n - 1, n \in N$

16. $A^{-1} = A^T, B^{-1} = B^T$ [$\because$ A and B are orthogonal matrices]

$\Rightarrow A^T A = AA^T = I$

and $B^T B = BB^T = I$

$|A| + |B| = 0$ [given]

$\Rightarrow \quad |A| = -|B| \Rightarrow |A||B| = -1 = |AB|$

Now, $A + B = AI + BI$

$$= ABB^T + BAA^T = A(B^T + A^T)B$$

$\therefore \quad |A + B| = |A(B^T + A^T)B| = |A||B^T + A^T||B|$

$$= |AB||(B + A)^T| = -|A + B|$$

$\Rightarrow \quad 2|A + B| = 0 \Rightarrow |A + B| = 0$

and $|A + B| = |A| \pm |B|$

$\therefore \quad |A + B| = |A| + |B|$

17. Given, $M^3 = 0$,

Consider $M = \begin{bmatrix} 0 & 1 & 0 \\ 0 & 0 & 1 \\ 0 & 0 & 0 \end{bmatrix}$ which satisfies $M^3 = 0$

Now, $\dfrac{M^2}{2} + M + I = \begin{bmatrix} 0 & 0 & 1/2 \\ 0 & 0 & 0 \\ 0 & 0 & 0 \end{bmatrix} + \begin{bmatrix} 0 & 1 & 0 \\ 0 & 0 & 1 \\ 0 & 0 & 0 \end{bmatrix} + \begin{bmatrix} 1 & 0 & 0 \\ 0 & 1 & 0 \\ 0 & 0 & 1 \end{bmatrix}$

$$= \begin{bmatrix} 1 & 1 & 1/2 \\ 0 & 1 & 1 \\ 0 & 0 & 1 \end{bmatrix}$$

$\therefore \quad \left|\dfrac{M^2}{2} + M + I\right| = 1 \neq 0$

Now, $\dfrac{M^2}{2} - M + I = \begin{bmatrix} 0 & 0 & 1/2 \\ 0 & 0 & 0 \\ 0 & 0 & 0 \end{bmatrix} - \begin{bmatrix} 0 & 1 & 0 \\ 0 & 0 & 1 \\ 0 & 0 & 0 \end{bmatrix} + \begin{bmatrix} 1 & 0 & 0 \\ 0 & 1 & 0 \\ 0 & 0 & 1 \end{bmatrix}$

$$= \begin{bmatrix} 1 & -1 & 1/2 \\ 0 & 1 & -1 \\ 0 & 0 & 1 \end{bmatrix}$$

$\therefore \quad \left|\dfrac{M^2}{2} - M + I\right| = 1 \neq 0$

18. Given, $M = \begin{bmatrix} 1 & 0 & 0 \\ 1 & 0 & 1 \\ 0 & 1 & 0 \end{bmatrix}$

$$M^2 = \begin{bmatrix} 1 & 0 & 0 \\ 1 & 0 & 1 \\ 0 & 1 & 0 \end{bmatrix}\begin{bmatrix} 1 & 0 & 0 \\ 1 & 0 & 1 \\ 0 & 1 & 0 \end{bmatrix} = \begin{bmatrix} 1 & 0 & 0 \\ 1 & 1 & 0 \\ 1 & 0 & 1 \end{bmatrix}$$

$$M^3 = \begin{bmatrix} 1 & 0 & 0 \\ 1 & 1 & 0 \\ 1 & 0 & 1 \end{bmatrix}\begin{bmatrix} 1 & 0 & 0 \\ 1 & 0 & 1 \\ 0 & 1 & 0 \end{bmatrix} = \begin{bmatrix} 1 & 0 & 0 \\ 2 & 0 & 1 \\ 1 & 1 & 0 \end{bmatrix}$$

$$M^4 = \begin{bmatrix} 1 & 0 & 0 \\ 2 & 0 & 1 \\ 1 & 1 & 0 \end{bmatrix}\begin{bmatrix} 1 & 0 & 0 \\ 1 & 0 & 1 \\ 0 & 1 & 0 \end{bmatrix} = \begin{bmatrix} 1 & 0 & 0 \\ 2 & 1 & 0 \\ 2 & 0 & 1 \end{bmatrix}$$

$\therefore \quad M^3 - M^2 = \begin{bmatrix} 1 & 0 & 0 \\ 2 & 0 & 1 \\ 1 & 1 & 0 \end{bmatrix} - \begin{bmatrix} 1 & 0 & 0 \\ 1 & 1 & 0 \\ 1 & 0 & 1 \end{bmatrix} = \begin{bmatrix} 0 & 0 & 0 \\ 1 & -1 & 1 \\ 0 & 1 & -1 \end{bmatrix}$

$$M - I = \begin{bmatrix} 1 & 0 & 0 \\ 1 & 0 & 1 \\ 0 & 1 & 0 \end{bmatrix} - \begin{bmatrix} 1 & 0 & 0 \\ 0 & 1 & 0 \\ 0 & 0 & 1 \end{bmatrix} = \begin{bmatrix} 0 & 0 & 0 \\ 1 & -1 & 1 \\ 0 & 1 & -1 \end{bmatrix}$$

Now, $\quad M^{2010} = \begin{bmatrix} 1 & 0 & 0 \\ 1005 & 1 & 0 \\ 1005 & 0 & 1 \end{bmatrix}$

$\Rightarrow \quad M^{2010} - I = \begin{bmatrix} 1 & 0 & 0 \\ 1005 & 1 & 0 \\ 1005 & 0 & 1 \end{bmatrix} - \begin{bmatrix} 1 & 0 & 0 \\ 0 & 1 & 0 \\ 0 & 0 & 1 \end{bmatrix} = \begin{bmatrix} 0 & 0 & 0 \\ 1005 & 0 & 0 \\ 1005 & 0 & 0 \end{bmatrix}$

$\therefore \quad |M^{2010} - I| = 0$

and $\quad M^{50} = \begin{bmatrix} 1 & 0 & 0 \\ 25 & 1 & 0 \\ 25 & 0 & 1 \end{bmatrix}$

19. Consider $A = \begin{bmatrix} a_1 & 0 & 0 \\ 0 & a_2 & 0 \\ 0 & 0 & a_3 \end{bmatrix}$, adj $A = \begin{bmatrix} a_2 a_3 & 0 & 0 \\ 0 & a_1 a_3 & 0 \\ 0 & 0 & a_1 a_2 \end{bmatrix}$

Let $C =$ adj A satisfy $x^3 - 9x^2 + px - 27 = 0$

$\therefore \quad \text{tr}(C) = 9$ and $|C| = 27$

$\Rightarrow \quad |\text{adj } A| = 27 \Rightarrow |A|^2 = 27 \Rightarrow |A| = 3\sqrt{3}$

Also, $\quad |\text{adj}\,(\text{adj } A)| = |A|^4 = 3^6$

Now, $\quad \text{tr}(\text{adj } A) = 9$ [given]

$\Rightarrow a_1 a_2 + a_2 a_3 + a_3 a_1 = 9$ ...(i)

and $\quad |A| = a_1 a_2 a_3 = 3\sqrt{3}$ ...(ii)

$\Rightarrow \quad \dfrac{1}{a_1} + \dfrac{1}{a_2} + \dfrac{1}{a_3} = \dfrac{9}{3\sqrt{3}} = \sqrt{3} = \text{tr}(A^{-1})$

Also, GM of $a_1 a_2, a_3$ is $\sqrt{3}$ and HM of $a_1 a_2 a_3$ is $\sqrt{3}$.

$\Rightarrow \quad \text{tr}(A) = 3\sqrt{3}$

20. $\quad |A - \lambda I| = 0$

$\Rightarrow \quad \begin{vmatrix} 1-\lambda & 2 & 0 \\ 0 & 2-\lambda & 0 \\ 0 & -1 & 2-\lambda \end{vmatrix} = 0$

$\Rightarrow \quad (1-\lambda)(2-\lambda)(2-\lambda) = 0$

$\Rightarrow \quad \lambda^3 - 5\lambda^2 + 8\lambda - 4 = 0$

$\Rightarrow \quad A^3 - 5A^2 + 8A - 4I = 0$

$\Rightarrow \quad A^4 - 5A^3 + 8A^2 - 4A = 0$

$\Rightarrow \quad A^4 - 5A^3 + 8A^2 - 2A = 2A$ ...(i)

$\because \quad P = A^4 + 8A$ and $Q = -5A^3 + 8A^2 - 10A$ [given]

$\Rightarrow P + Q = A^4 - 5A^3 + 8A^2 - 2A$

$\therefore \; P + Q = 2A$ [from Eq. (i)]

$\therefore \quad \text{tr}(P + Q) = 2\,\text{tr}(A) = 2 \times 5 = 10$

and $\quad |P + Q| = |2A| = 2^3 |A| = 8 \times 4 = 32$

21. $\because A^2B = A(AB) = A(BA) = (AB)A = (BA)A = BA^2$

Similarly, $A^3B = BA^3$

In general, $A^nB = BA^n, \forall n \ge 1$

and $(A+B)^n = {}^nC_0A^n + {}^nC_1A^{n-1}B + {}^nC_2A^{n-2}B^2 + \ldots + {}^nC_nB^n$

Also, $(A^n - B^n)(A^n + B^n) = A^nA^n + A^nB^n - B^nA^n - B^nB^n$

$= A^{2n} - B^{2n}$ $\quad [\because AB = BA]$

22. $A^2 = \begin{bmatrix} 1 & 2 & 2 \\ 2 & 1 & 2 \\ 2 & 2 & 1 \end{bmatrix}\begin{bmatrix} 1 & 2 & 2 \\ 2 & 1 & 2 \\ 2 & 2 & 1 \end{bmatrix} = \begin{bmatrix} 9 & 8 & 8 \\ 8 & 9 & 8 \\ 8 & 8 & 9 \end{bmatrix}$

We have, $A^2 - 4A - 5I_3$

$$= \begin{bmatrix} 9 & 8 & 8 \\ 8 & 9 & 8 \\ 8 & 8 & 9 \end{bmatrix} - 4\begin{bmatrix} 1 & 2 & 2 \\ 2 & 1 & 2 \\ 2 & 2 & 1 \end{bmatrix} - 5\begin{bmatrix} 1 & 0 & 0 \\ 0 & 1 & 0 \\ 0 & 0 & 1 \end{bmatrix} = O$$

or $5I_3 = A^2 - 4A = A(A - 4I_3)$

or $I_3 = A \cdot \frac{1}{5}(A - 4I_3)$ or $A^{-1} = \frac{1}{5}(A - 4I_3)$

Note that $|A| = 5$.

Since, $|A^3| = |A|^3 = 5^3 \ne 0$, A^3 is invertible.

Similarly, A^2 is invertible.

23. Let $M = \begin{bmatrix} a_{11} & a_{12} & a_{13} \\ a_{21} & a_{22} & a_{23} \\ a_{31} & a_{32} & a_{33} \end{bmatrix}$ be the given matrix.

Now, $\begin{bmatrix} a_{11} & a_{12} & a_{13} \\ a_{21} & a_{22} & a_{23} \\ a_{31} & a_{32} & a_{33} \end{bmatrix}\begin{bmatrix} 1 \\ 0 \\ 0 \end{bmatrix} = \begin{bmatrix} -1 \\ 2 \\ 3 \end{bmatrix} \Rightarrow a_{11} = -1, a_{21} = 2, a_{31} = 3$

and $\begin{bmatrix} a_{11} & a_{12} & a_{13} \\ a_{21} & a_{22} & a_{23} \\ a_{31} & a_{32} & a_{33} \end{bmatrix}\begin{bmatrix} 0 \\ 1 \\ 0 \end{bmatrix} = \begin{bmatrix} 1 \\ 1 \\ -1 \end{bmatrix} \Rightarrow a_{12} = 1, a_{22} = 1, a_{32} = -1$

and $\begin{bmatrix} a_{11} & a_{12} & a_{13} \\ a_{21} & a_{22} & a_{23} \\ a_{31} & a_{32} & a_{33} \end{bmatrix}\begin{bmatrix} 0 \\ 0 \\ 1 \end{bmatrix} = \begin{bmatrix} 0 \\ -1 \\ 2 \end{bmatrix} \Rightarrow a_{13} = 0, a_{23} = -1, a_{33} = 2$

$\therefore \text{tr}(M) = a_{11} + a_{22} + a_{33} = -1 + 1 + 2 = 2$

and sum of all elements $= -1 + 2 + 3 + 1 + 1 - 1 + 0 - 1 + 2 = 6$

$\therefore \quad M = \begin{bmatrix} -1 & 1 & 0 \\ 2 & 1 & -1 \\ 3 & -1 & 2 \end{bmatrix}$

$\Rightarrow \quad |M| = -1(2-1) - 1(4+3) = -1 - 7 = -8$

24. Given, $\quad B_P = A^P(\text{adj}(\text{adj} \ldots (\text{adj } A)))$

$\Rightarrow \quad B_1 = A(\text{adj} A) = |A| I_2$

$\therefore \quad \text{tr}(B_1) = 2|A| = 4$

$B_2 = A^2|\text{adj}(\text{adj}A))$

$\Rightarrow \quad B_2 = A^2 \cdot |A|^{n-2} A$

$= A^3 |A|^{2-2} = A^3$

$\therefore \quad \det(B_2) = |A|^3 = 8$

Now, $\sum_{p=1}^{\infty} \det(B_P^{-1}) = |B_1^{-1}| + |B_2^{-1}| + B_3^{-1}| + \ldots + \infty$

$= \frac{1}{|A|^2} + \frac{1}{|A|^3} + \frac{1}{|A|^4} + \ldots + \infty$

$= \frac{1}{4} + \frac{1}{8} + \frac{1}{16} + \ldots + \infty$

$= \frac{1/4}{1 - \frac{1}{2}} = \frac{1}{2} \ne 1$

and $\quad \text{adj}(\text{adj } B_2) = |B_2|^{n-2} B_2$

$= B_2$ $\quad [\because n = 2]$

$\Rightarrow \quad \text{adj}(\text{adj } B_2) = A^3$

Sol. (Q. Nos. 25 and 26)

25. Let A be a skew-symmetric matrix $= \begin{bmatrix} 0 & x & y \\ -x & 0 & z \\ -y & -z & 0 \end{bmatrix}$. x, y, z each can be filled in 7 ways corresponding to each of x, y, z other places can be filled in 1 ways.

$\therefore \quad n(A) = 7^3$

B be a scalar matrix, then $n(B) = 7$

$\therefore \quad n(A \cap B) = 1$ $\quad$ [all entries are zero]

$\therefore \quad n(A \cup B) = n(A) + n(B) - n(A \cap B)$

$= 7^3 + 7 - 1 = 7^3 + 6$

26. Let a, b and c are trace elements.

Trace		Trace elements
9	:	3, 3, 3
8	:	3, 3, 2
7	:	3, 2, 2 or 3, 3, 1

$\therefore$ Number of matrices each of whose trace is atleast

$$7 = 1(7^6) + 3(7^6) + 6(7^6) = 10(7^6)$$

Sol. (Q. Nos. 27 and 28)

Here, $A = \begin{bmatrix} a & b & c \\ b & c & a \\ c & a & b \end{bmatrix}$ is orthogonal.

$\therefore \quad AA^T = I$

$\Rightarrow \quad \begin{bmatrix} a & b & c \\ b & c & a \\ c & a & b \end{bmatrix}\begin{bmatrix} a & b & c \\ b & c & a \\ c & a & b \end{bmatrix} = I$

$$\begin{bmatrix} a^2+b^2+c^2 & ab+bc+ca & ab+bc+ca \\ ab+bc+ca & a^2+b^2+c^2 & ab+bc+ca \\ ab+bc+ca & ab+bc+ca & a^2+b^2+c^2 \end{bmatrix} = \begin{bmatrix} 1 & 0 & 0 \\ 0 & 1 & 0 \\ 0 & 0 & 1 \end{bmatrix}$$

$\because \quad a^2 + b^2 + c^2 = 1$ $\quad$ ...(i)

$ab + bc + ca = 0$ $\quad$ ...(ii)

$(a+b+c)^2 = (c^2 + b^2 + a^2) + 2(ab + bc + ca)$

$(a+b+c)^2 = 1 + 0 = a + b + c = \pm 1$ $\quad$ ...(iii)

27. $\because a^2b^2 + b^2c^2 + c^2a^2 = (ab + bc + ca)^2 - 2abc(a + b + c)$

$= 0 - 2abc(\pm 1) = \mp 2\lambda$ $\quad [\because abc = \lambda]$

$= -2\lambda$ $\quad [\because \lambda < 0]$

28. $\because a^3+b^3+c^3-3abc=(a+b+c)(a^2+b^2+c^2-ab-bc-ca)$

$\Rightarrow a^3+b^3+c^3-3\lambda=(\pm 1)(1-0)$ [from Eqs. (i), (ii) and (iii) and $abc=\lambda$]

$\Rightarrow a^3+b^3+c^3=3\lambda\pm 1$

Sol. (Q. Nos. 29 and 30)

29. $BB^T=I$

$\therefore |BB^T|=1$

$\Rightarrow |B||B^T|=1 \Rightarrow |B|=1$

$A(\text{adj}\cdot A+\text{adj}\cdot B)=B$

$\Rightarrow |A|I+A\times \text{adj } B=B$

$\Rightarrow I+A\times \text{adj } B=B$

$\Rightarrow I\times B+A\times(\text{adj } B)\times B=B^2$

$\Rightarrow B+A|B|I=B^2 \Rightarrow B+A=B^2$ ...(i)

$\Rightarrow |A+B|=|B^2|=1$

30. $B+A=B^2$ [from Eq. (i) in Q.29]

$\Rightarrow B^TB+B^TA=B^TB^2$

$\Rightarrow I+B^TA=B \Rightarrow B^TA=B-I$ ...(ii)

Now, from Eq. (i), we get

$B^2-B=A \Rightarrow B(B-I)=A$

Multiplying both sides by B^{-1}, we get

$\Rightarrow B-I=AB^{-1}$ ...(iii)

So, from Eqs. (ii) and (iii), we get

$AB^{-1}=B^TA$

$\Rightarrow AB^{-1}=B^{-1}A$ [$\because BB^T=I$ then $B^T=B^{-1}$]

Sol. (Q. Nos. 31 and 32)

Given, $A=A^T$

$B=-B^T$

$(A+B)\neq 0, (A-B)\neq 0$

$C=(A+B)^{-1}(A-B)$

$(A+B)C=(A+B)(A+B)^{-1}(A-B)$

$(A+B)C=A-B$ ...(i)

$A-B=A^T+B^T=(A+B)^T$ ...(ii)

$(A-B)^T-((A+B)^T)^T=A+B$ ...(iii)

31. $C^T(A+B)C=C^T[(A+B)C]$

$=C^T(A-B)$ [from Eq. (i)]

$=C^T(A+B)^T$ [from Eq. (ii)]

$=[(A+B)C]^T$

$=(A-B)^T$ [from Eq. (i)]

$=A+B$ [from Eq. (iii)]

32. $C^T(A-B)C=[C^T(A+B)^T]C$ [from Eq. (ii)]

$=[(A+B)C]^TC$

$=(A-B)^TC$ [from Eq. (i)]

$=(A+B)C$ [from Eq. (iii)]

$=A-B$ [from Eq. (i)]

33. Given that $B=A-2I$ ...(i)

and $A^3-6A^2+7A-8I=0$

$\therefore (A-2I)^3=5A$ ...(ii)

$\therefore B^3=5A$

$\Rightarrow |B^3|=|5A|=5^3|A|=5^3\times 8$

$\Rightarrow |B|=10$

Now, from Eq. (i), we get

$A^{-1}B=I-2A^{-1}$

$\therefore |\text{adj}(I-2A^{-1})|=|I-2A^{-1}|^2$

$$\Rightarrow |A^{-1}B|^2=\left(\frac{|B|}{|A|}\right)^2=\left(\frac{5}{4}\right)^2=\frac{25}{16}=1.56$$

34. $$\text{adj}\left(\left(\frac{B}{2}\right)^{-1}\right)=\left(\text{adj}\left(\frac{B}{2}\right)\right)^{-1}=\frac{\text{adj}\left(\text{adj}\frac{B}{2}\right)}{\left|\text{adj}\frac{B}{2}\right|}$$

$$=\frac{\left|\frac{B}{2}\right|\frac{B}{2}}{\left|\frac{B}{2}\right|^2}=\frac{\frac{B}{2}}{\left|\frac{B}{2}\right|}=\frac{4B}{|B|}=\frac{2B}{5}$$

$$\therefore \text{adj}\left(\left(\frac{B}{2}\right)^{-1}\right)=\left(\frac{m}{n}\right)B$$

$\Rightarrow m=2, n=5$

$\Rightarrow m+n=2+5=7$

Sol. (Q.Nos. 35 and 36)

35. (16) Given, $A+B^T=\text{adj } B$

$\Rightarrow A^T+B=(\text{adj} B)^T$ ...(i)

and $B+A^T=\text{adj } A$ ...(ii)

From Eqs. (i) and (ii), we get

$(\text{adj } B)^T=\text{adj } A$

$\Rightarrow |B|^2=|A|^2 \Rightarrow |B|=\pm|A|$

If $|B|=|A| \Rightarrow (B^{-1})^T=A^{-1}=(B^T)^{-1} \Rightarrow A=B^T$

$\therefore \text{adj } B=2B^T$

$\Rightarrow |B|^2=2^3|B|$

$\Rightarrow |B|=8, |A|=8$

$\therefore |A|+|B|=8+8=16$

36. (8) If $|B|=-|A|$

$\Rightarrow (-B^{-1})^T=A^{-1}=(-B^T)^{-1}$

$\Rightarrow A=-B^T$

$\therefore \text{adj } B=0$, which is not possible.

Now, $A=B^T$

$\text{adj } B=2A$

$(\text{adj } B)B=2AB=|B|I \Rightarrow AB=4I$

Also, $B \text{ adj } B=2BA=|B|I$

$\Rightarrow BA=4I$

$\therefore AB+BA=8I$

$\Rightarrow K=8$

37. $S = ABCD = A(BCD) = AA^T$ ...(i)

$\therefore \quad S^3 = (ABCD)(ABCD)(ABCD)$

$= (ABC)(DAB)(CDA)(BCD)$

$= D^T C^T B^T A^T = (BCD)^T A^T$

$= (A^T)^T A^T = AA^T = S$

$\Rightarrow \quad S^3 = S$

Hence, the least value of k is 3.

38. $\because \quad A = \begin{bmatrix} 1 & \tan x \\ -\tan x & 1 \end{bmatrix}$

$\therefore \quad \det A = \begin{vmatrix} 1 & \tan x \\ -\tan x & 1 \end{vmatrix} = (1 + \tan^2 x) = \sec^2 x$

$\Rightarrow \det A^T = \det A = \sec^2 x$

Now, $f(x) = \det(A^T A^{-1}) = (\det A^T)(\det A^{-1})$

$= (\det A^T)(\det A)^{-1} = \dfrac{\det A^T}{\det A} = 1$

$\therefore \quad \lambda = \underbrace{f(f(f(f \ldots f(x))))}_{n \text{ times}} = 1$ $[\because f(x) = 1]$

Hence, $2^\lambda = 2^1 = 2$

39. Given, $B = \begin{bmatrix} 1 & 0 \\ 0 & -1 \end{bmatrix}$

$B^2 = \begin{bmatrix} 1 & 0 \\ 0 & -1 \end{bmatrix}\begin{bmatrix} 1 & 0 \\ 0 & -1 \end{bmatrix} = \begin{bmatrix} 1 & 0 \\ 0 & 1 \end{bmatrix} = I$

$B^3 = \begin{bmatrix} 1 & 0 \\ 0 & 1 \end{bmatrix}\begin{bmatrix} 1 & 0 \\ 0 & -1 \end{bmatrix} = \begin{bmatrix} 1 & 0 \\ 0 & -1 \end{bmatrix} = B$

$\therefore \quad B^1 = B^3 = \ldots = B^{99} = B$

and $\quad B^2 = B^4 = \ldots = B^{100} = I$

Now, $\quad C = \begin{bmatrix} 0 & 1 \\ -1 & 0 \end{bmatrix}$

$C^2 = \begin{bmatrix} 0 & 1 \\ -1 & 0 \end{bmatrix}\begin{bmatrix} 0 & 1 \\ -1 & 0 \end{bmatrix} = \begin{bmatrix} -1 & 0 \\ 0 & -1 \end{bmatrix} = -I$

and $\quad C^3 = C^2 C = -I \cdot C = -C$

$C^1 = C, C^2 = -I, C^3 = -C, C^4 = I$

and $\quad C^5 = C, C^6 = -I \ldots$

$\sum_{n=1}^{100} B^n = B + B^2 + B^3 + \ldots + B^{100}$

$= [B + B^3 + \ldots + B^{99}] + [B^2 + B^4 + \ldots + B^{100}]$

$= 50B + 50I = 50[B + I]$

$= 50\left[\begin{bmatrix} 1 & 0 \\ 0 & -1 \end{bmatrix} + \begin{bmatrix} 1 & 0 \\ 0 & 1 \end{bmatrix}\right] = 50\begin{bmatrix} 2 & 0 \\ 0 & 0 \end{bmatrix}$

and $\quad \sum_{n=1}^{100} C^n = 25 \sum_{n=1}^{4} C^n$

$= 25[C - I - C + I] = 25(0) = 0$

$\therefore \quad A = \sum_{n=1}^{100} (B^n + C^n) = 50\begin{bmatrix} 2 & 0 \\ 0 & 0 \end{bmatrix}$

and $\quad |A| = 50(0) = 0$

40. Let $X = \begin{bmatrix} x_1 \\ x_2 \\ x_3 \end{bmatrix}$ and given $X^T AX = O$

$\Rightarrow \quad [x_1 \; x_2 \; x_3]\begin{bmatrix} a_{11} & a_{12} & a_{13} \\ a_{21} & a_{22} & a_{23} \\ a_{31} & a_{32} & a_{33} \end{bmatrix}\begin{bmatrix} x_1 \\ x_2 \\ x_3 \end{bmatrix} = O$

$\Rightarrow \quad [x_1 \; x_2 \; x_3]\begin{bmatrix} a_{11}x_1 + a_{12}x_2 + a_{13}x_3 \\ a_{21}x_1 + a_{22}x_2 + a_{23}x_3 \\ a_{31}x_1 + a_{32}x_2 + a_{33}x_3 \end{bmatrix} = O$

$\Rightarrow a_{11}x_1^2 + a_{12}x_1x_2 + a_{13}x_1x_3 + a_{21}x_1x_2 + a_{22}x_2^2 + a_{23}x_2x_3$
$+ a_{31}x_1x_3 + a_{32}x_2x_3 + a_{33}x_3^2 = 0$

$\Rightarrow a_{11}x_1^2 + a_{22}x_2^2 + a_{33}x_3^2 + (a_{12} + a_{21})x_1x_2 + (a_{23} + a_{32})x_2x_3$
$+ (a_{31} + a_{13})x_3x_1 = 0$

it is true for every x_1, x_2, x_3, then

$a_{11} = a_{22} = a_{33} = 0$ and $a_{12} = -a_{21}, a_{23} = -a_{32}, a_{13} = -a_{31}$

Now, as $a_{23} = -1008 \Rightarrow a_{32} = 1008$

$\therefore$ Sum of digits $= 1 + 0 + 0 + 8 = 9$

41. In a skew-symmetric matrix, diagonal elements are zero.

Also, $a_{ij} + a_{ji} = 0$

Hence, number of matrices $= 2 \times 2 \times 2 = 8$

42. $\because$ A is idempotent matrix

$\therefore \quad A^2 = A$

$\Rightarrow \quad A = A^2 = A^3 = A^4 = A^5 = \ldots$ ...(i)

Now, $(A + I)^n = (I + A)^n$

$= I + {}^nC_1 A + {}^nC_2 A^2 + {}^nC_3 A^3 + \ldots + {}^nC_n A^n$

$= I + ({}^nC_1 + {}^nC_2 + {}^nC_3 + \ldots + {}^nC_n) A$ [from Eq.(i)]

$\Rightarrow \quad (A + I)^n = I + (2^n - 1)A$ ...(ii)

Given that

$(A + I)^n = I + 127 A$ ...(iii)

From Eqs (ii) and (iii), we get

$2^n - 1 = 127 \Rightarrow 2^n = 128 = 2^7$

$\therefore \quad n = 7$

43. Given, $M = \begin{bmatrix} a^3 + 1 & a^2 b & a^2 c \\ ab^2 & b^3 + 1 & b^2 c \\ ac^2 & bc^2 & c^3 + 1 \end{bmatrix}$

$|M| = (a^3 + 1)((b^3 + 1)(c^3 + 1) - b^3c^3) - a^2b(ab^2(c^3 + 1) - ab^2c^3)$
$+ a^2c(ab^3c^2 - ac^2(b^3 + 1))$

$= (a^3 + 1)(b^3c^3 + b^3 + c^3 + 1 - b^3c^3) - a^2b(ab^2c^3 + ab^2 - ab^2c^3)$
$+ a^2c(ab^3c^2 - ab^3c^2 - ac^2)$

$= (a^3 + 1)(b^3 + c^3 + 1) - a^2b(ab^2) + a^2c(-ac^2)$

$= a^3b^3 + a^3c^3 + a^3 + b^3 + c^3 + 1 - a^3b^3 - a^3c^3$

$= a^3 + b^3 + c^3 + 1$

$\because \quad |M| = 11$ [given]

$\therefore \quad a^3 + b^3 + c^3 + 1 = 11 \Rightarrow a^3 + b^3 + c^3 = 10$

Possible numbers are (1, 1, 2).

$\therefore$ Number of triplets (a, b, c) is 3.

44. $\because \quad A=\begin{bmatrix}0 & 1\\ 3 & 0\end{bmatrix}$

$\therefore \quad A^2 = A\cdot A = \begin{bmatrix}0 & 1\\ 3 & 0\end{bmatrix}\begin{bmatrix}0 & 1\\ 3 & 0\end{bmatrix}=\begin{bmatrix}3 & 0\\ 0 & 3\end{bmatrix}=3I$

$\Rightarrow \quad A^4=(A^2)^2=9I,\ A^6=27I,\ A^8=81I$

Now, $(A^8+A^6+A^4+A^2+I)V=(121)IV=(121)V$ ...(i)

Given, $(A^8+A^6+A^4+A^2+I)V=\begin{bmatrix}0\\ 11\end{bmatrix}$ ...(ii)

From Eqs.(i) and (ii), $(121)V=\begin{bmatrix}0\\ 11\end{bmatrix} \Rightarrow V=\begin{bmatrix}0\\ \frac{1}{11}\end{bmatrix}$

$\therefore$ Sum of elements of $V=0+\frac{1}{11}=\frac{1}{11}=\lambda$ [given]

$\therefore \quad 11\lambda=1$

45. $\text{adj}(\text{adj } A)=|A|^{n-2}A$

$\Rightarrow \text{adj}(\text{adj}(\text{adj } A))=|\text{adj } A|^{n-2}\text{adj}A$

$=(|A|^{n-1})^{n-2}\text{adj } A$

Put $n=3$,

$\Rightarrow \text{adj}(\text{adj}(\text{adj } A))=A^2\text{adj } A=\begin{bmatrix}16 & 0 & -3\\ 0 & 4 & 0\\ 0 & 3 & 4\end{bmatrix}$ ...(i)

On taking determinant both sides, we get

$|\text{adj}(\text{adj}(\text{adj } A))|=|A|^6|A|^2=256=|A|^8=2^8$

$\Rightarrow \quad |A|=\pm 2$

$\therefore \quad \text{adj } A=\frac{1}{4}\begin{bmatrix}16 & 0 & -3\\ 0 & 4 & 0\\ 0 & 3 & 4\end{bmatrix}$

$=\begin{bmatrix}4 & 0 & -3/4\\ 0 & 1 & 0\\ 0 & 3/4 & 1\end{bmatrix}$ [from Eq. (i)]

$\therefore \quad A^{-1}=\frac{\text{adj } A}{|A|}=\pm\begin{bmatrix}2 & 0 & -3/8\\ 0 & 1/2 & 0\\ 0 & 3/8 & 1/2\end{bmatrix}$

$\therefore \text{tr}(A^{-1})=3$

46. Given, $A^2=A$

Now, $I=(I-0.4A)(I-\alpha A)$

$=I-I\alpha A-0.4AI+0.4\alpha A^2$

$=I-A\alpha-0.4A+0.4\alpha A$

$=I-A(0.4+\alpha)+0.4\alpha A$

$\Rightarrow \quad 0.4\alpha=0.4+\alpha$

$\Rightarrow \quad \alpha=-2/3$

$\Rightarrow \quad |9\alpha|=6$

$\Rightarrow \quad |9\alpha|^2=(6)^2=36$

47. Given, $A=\begin{bmatrix}x^3+1 & x+5 & 3x+2\\ y+1 & -6x^2+2 & z-1\\ 2 & 3 & 9x+6\end{bmatrix}$ and $|A|=3$

$\because \quad B=\text{adj}(A)$

$B^{-1}=\frac{\text{adj}(B)}{|B|}=\frac{\text{adj}(\text{adj } A)}{|\text{adj } A|}=\frac{|A|^{n-2}A}{||A|^{n-1}|}=\frac{3\cdot A}{3^2}$

$\therefore \quad B^{-1}=\frac{1}{3}A=\frac{1}{3}\begin{bmatrix}x^3+1 & x+5 & 3x+2\\ y+1 & -6x^2+2 & z-1\\ 2 & 3 & 9x+6\end{bmatrix}$

$\because \quad f(x)=\text{tr}(B^{-1})$

$=\frac{1}{3}[x^3+1-6x^2+2+9x+6]$

$=\frac{1}{3}[x^3-6x^2+9x+9]$

$f'(x)=\frac{1}{3}[3x^2-12x+9]=x^2-4x+3$

Put $f'(x)=0$

$\Rightarrow \quad x^2-4x+3=0$

$\Rightarrow \quad x-3=0$ or $x-1=0 \Rightarrow x=3$ or 1

and $f''(x)=2x-4$

$f''(1)=2-4=-2<0$, maximum

$f''(3)=6-4=2>0$, minimum

$f(1)=\frac{1}{3}(1-6+9+9)=\frac{13}{3}$

$f(0)=\frac{9}{3}=3$

$f(6)=\frac{1}{3}[216-216+54+9]=\frac{63}{3}=21$

48. Each element of set A is 3×3 symmetric matrix with five of its entries as 1 and four of its entries as 0, we can keep in diagonal either 2 zero and one 1 or no zero and three 1.

So, that the left over zeroes and ones are even in number.

Hence, taking 2 zeroes and one 1 in diagonal the possible cases are $\frac{3!}{2!}\times\frac{3!}{2!}=9$

and taking 3 ones in diagonal the possible cases are $1\times\frac{3!}{2!}=3$

$\therefore$ Total elements A can have $=9+3=12$.

49. Given, $P=\begin{bmatrix}1 & 0 & 0\\ 4 & 1 & 0\\ 16 & 4 & 1\end{bmatrix}$

$\Rightarrow \quad P^2=\begin{bmatrix}1 & 0 & 0\\ 4 & 1 & 0\\ 16 & 4 & 1\end{bmatrix}\begin{bmatrix}1 & 0 & 0\\ 4 & 1 & 0\\ 16 & 4 & 1\end{bmatrix}=\begin{bmatrix}1 & 0 & 0\\ 8 & 1 & 0\\ 48 & 8 & 1\end{bmatrix}$

$=\begin{bmatrix}1 & 0 & 0\\ 4\times 2 & 1 & 0\\ 16(1+2) & 4\times 2 & 1\end{bmatrix}$

$\Rightarrow \quad P^3=\begin{bmatrix}1 & 0 & 0\\ 8 & 1 & 0\\ 48 & 8 & 1\end{bmatrix}\begin{bmatrix}1 & 0 & 0\\ 4 & 1 & 0\\ 16 & 4 & 1\end{bmatrix}$

$=\begin{bmatrix}1 & 0 & 0\\ 12 & 1 & 0\\ 96 & 12 & 1\end{bmatrix}=\begin{bmatrix}1 & 0 & 0\\ 4\times 3 & 1 & 0\\ 16(1+2+3) & 4\times 3 & 1\end{bmatrix}$

Similarly, $P^{50} = \begin{bmatrix} 1 & 0 & 0 \\ 4\times 50 & 1 & 0 \\ 16(1+2+3+\ldots+50) & 4\times 50 & 1 \end{bmatrix}$

$\Rightarrow \quad P^{50} = \begin{bmatrix} 1 & 0 & 0 \\ 200 & 1 & 0 \\ 20400 & 200 & 1 \end{bmatrix}$

$\because \quad P^{50} - Q = I$

$\Rightarrow \begin{bmatrix} 1 & 0 & 0 \\ 200 & 1 & 0 \\ 20400 & 200 & 1 \end{bmatrix} - \begin{bmatrix} q_{11} & q_{12} & q_{13} \\ q_{21} & q_{22} & q_{23} \\ q_{31} & q_{32} & q_{33} \end{bmatrix} = \begin{bmatrix} 1 & 0 & 0 \\ 0 & 1 & 0 \\ 0 & 0 & 1 \end{bmatrix}$

$\Rightarrow \quad 200 - q_{21} = 0$

$\Rightarrow \quad q_{21} = 200$

$\Rightarrow \quad 200 - q_{32} = 0$

$\Rightarrow \quad q_{32} = 200$

$\Rightarrow \quad 20400 - q_{31} = 0$

$\Rightarrow \quad q_{31} = 20400$

$\therefore \quad \dfrac{q_{31} + q_{32}}{q_{21}} = \dfrac{20400 + 200}{200} = 103$

50. Given, $A = \begin{bmatrix} x & y & -z \\ 1 & 2 & 3 \\ 1 & 1 & 2 \end{bmatrix}$

and $\det(\text{adj}(\text{adj } A)) = 2^8 3^4$

$\Rightarrow \quad |A|^{(n-1)^2} = 2^8 \times 3^4$

$\Rightarrow \quad |A|^4 = 2^8 \times 3^4 \quad [\because \text{order of matrix} = n = 3]$

$\Rightarrow \quad |A|^4 = (2^2 \times 3)^4$

$\Rightarrow \quad |A| = 12$

$\Rightarrow \begin{vmatrix} x & y & -z \\ 1 & 2 & 3 \\ 1 & 1 & 2 \end{vmatrix} = 12 \Rightarrow x + y + z = 12$

If $x_1 + x_2 + \ldots + x_n = m$, then number of solutions are ${}^{m-1}C_{n-1}$.

Here, $m = 12$ and $n = 3$

$\therefore$Number of solutions for $x + y + z = 12$ is ${}^{11}C_2 = 55$.

Hence, 55 such matrices are possible.

51. Given, A_n and B_n be square matrix of order such that

$A_n = [a_{ij}]$ and $B_n = [b_{ij}]$

where, $a_{ij} = \dfrac{2i + j}{3^{2n}}$ and $b_{ij} = \dfrac{3i - j}{2^{2n}}, 1 \le i, j \le 3$

$\therefore \quad a_{11} = \dfrac{3}{3^{2n}}, a_{12} = \dfrac{4}{3^{2n}}, a_{13} = \dfrac{5}{3^{2n}}$

$a_{21} = \dfrac{5}{3^{2n}}, a_{22} = \dfrac{6}{3^{2n}}, a_{23} = \dfrac{7}{3^{2n}}$

$a_{31} = \dfrac{7}{3^{2n}}, a_{32} = \dfrac{8}{3^{2n}}, a_{33} = \dfrac{9}{3^{2n}}$

$\therefore \quad A_n = \dfrac{1}{3^{2n}} \begin{bmatrix} 3 & 4 & 5 \\ 5 & 6 & 7 \\ 7 & 8 & 9 \end{bmatrix}$

Now, $b_{11} = \dfrac{2}{2^{2n}}, b_{12} = \dfrac{1}{2^{2n}}, b_{13} = 0$

$b_{21} = \dfrac{5}{2^{2n}}, b_{22} = \dfrac{4}{2^{2n}}, b_{23} = \dfrac{3}{2^{2n}}$

$b_{31} = \dfrac{8}{2^{2n}}, b_{32} = \dfrac{7}{2^{2n}}, b_{33} = \dfrac{6}{2^{2n}}$

$\therefore \quad B_n = \dfrac{1}{2^{2n}} \begin{bmatrix} 2 & 1 & 0 \\ 5 & 4 & 3 \\ 8 & 7 & 6 \end{bmatrix}$

$\because \quad P = \lim_{n\to\infty} \text{tr}(3A_1 + 3^2 A_2 + 3^3 A_3 + \ldots)$

$= \lim_{n\to\infty} 18\left(\dfrac{3}{3^2} + \dfrac{3^2}{3^4} + \dfrac{3^3}{3^6} + \ldots\right)$

$= 18 \times \dfrac{\frac{3}{3^2}}{1 - \frac{1}{3}} \quad \left[\because \text{sum of infinity term in GP is } \dfrac{a}{1-r}\right]$

$= 18 \times \dfrac{1}{3\left(1 - \frac{1}{3}\right)} = 9$

and $\quad q = \lim_{n\to\infty} \text{tr}(2B_1 + 2^2 B_2 + 2^3 B_3 + \ldots)$

$= \lim_{n\to\infty} 12\left(\dfrac{2}{2^2} + \dfrac{2^2}{2^4} + \ldots\right) = 12 \times \dfrac{1}{2\left(1 - \frac{1}{2}\right)} = 12$

$\therefore \; p + q = 9 + 12 = 21$

52. **(A)** Possible non-negative value of $|A|$ is

$1\times 2 = 2, -1\times 2 = -2, 1\times 4 = 4, -1\times 4 = -4$

$2\times 4 = 8, -2\times 4 = -8$

$\therefore$ Possible values are 2, 4, 8.

(B) Sum $= 2 + (-2) + 4 + (-4) + 8 + (-8) = 0$

(C) Absolute least value of $|A| = 2$

$\therefore \quad |\text{adj } A| = |A|^{n-1} = |A|^{2-1} = |A|$

$\Rightarrow |\text{adj}(\text{adj}(\text{adj } A))| = |\text{adj}(\text{adj } A)|^{2-1}$

$= |\text{adj}(\text{adj} A)|$

$= |\text{adj } A|$

$= |A| = |-2| = 2$

(D) $|4A^{-1}| = 4^2 |A^{-1}|$

$= 16 \times \dfrac{1}{|A|} = \dfrac{16}{8} = 2 \quad [\because \text{greatest value of } |A| = 8]$

53. **(A)** $\text{adj}(A^{-1}) = (A^{-1})^{-1} \det(A^{-1}) = \dfrac{A}{\det(A)}$

Also, $\dfrac{\text{adj}(\text{adj } A)}{(\text{adj } A)^{n-1}} = \dfrac{A[\det(A)]^{n-2}}{(\det A)^{n-1}} = \dfrac{A}{\det(A)}$

(B) $\det(\text{adj}(A^{-1})) = (\det A^{-1})^{n-1}$

$= \dfrac{1}{(\det A)^{n-1}} = (\det A)^{1-n}$

(C) $\text{adj}[\text{adj } A] = A(\det A)^{n-2}$

(D) $\text{adj}(A \det A) = (\det A)^{n-1}(\text{adj } A)$

54. **(A)** A diagonal matrix is commutative with every square matrix, if it is scalar matrix, so every diagonal element is 4.

Therefore, $|A| = \begin{vmatrix} 4 & 0 & 0 \\ 0 & 4 & 0 \\ 0 & 0 & 4 \end{vmatrix} = 64$

(B) $\begin{vmatrix} 1-a & 1 & 1 \\ 1 & 1-b & 1 \\ 1 & 1 & 1-c \end{vmatrix} = 0$

Applying $R_1 \to R_1 - R_3$ and $R_2 \to R_2 - R_3$, then

$$\begin{vmatrix} -a & 0 & c \\ 0 & -b & c \\ 1 & 1 & 1-c \end{vmatrix} = 0$$

$\Rightarrow \quad -a(-b + bc - c) - 0 + c(b) = 0$

$$ab + bc + ca = abc \quad \text{...(i)}$$

Now, $\quad AM \geq GM$

$\Rightarrow \quad \dfrac{ab + bc + ca}{3} \geq (ab \cdot bc \cdot ca)^{\frac{1}{3}}$

$\Rightarrow \quad \dfrac{abc}{3} \geq (abc)^{\frac{2}{3}}$ [from Eq. (i)]

$\Rightarrow \quad (abc)^{\frac{1}{3}} \geq 3$

$\therefore \quad abc \geq 27$

Hence, $\quad \lambda = 27$

(C) $\because \quad A = \begin{bmatrix} a_{11} & a_{12} & a_{13} \\ a_{21} & a_{22} & a_{23} \\ a_{31} & a_{32} & a_{33} \end{bmatrix}$

Given, $\displaystyle\sum_{k=1}^{3} a_{ik} = 9\lambda_i, \forall\, i \in \{1, 2, 3\}$;

$\displaystyle\sum_{k=1}^{3} a_{kj} = 9\mu_j, \forall\, j \in \{1, 2, 3\}$ and

$a_{11} + a_{22} + a_{33} = 9v$; where $\lambda_i, \mu_j, v \in \{1, 2\}$

Following types of matrices are possible:

$A = \begin{bmatrix} 1 & & \\ & 3 & \\ & & 5 \end{bmatrix}; B = \begin{bmatrix} 2 & & \\ & 3 & \\ & & 4 \end{bmatrix}; C = \begin{bmatrix} 7 & & \\ & 3 & \\ & & 8 \end{bmatrix};$

$D = \begin{bmatrix} 6 & & \\ & 3 & \\ & & 9 \end{bmatrix}; E = \begin{bmatrix} 1 & & \\ & 6 & \\ & & 2 \end{bmatrix}; F = \begin{bmatrix} 3 & & \\ & 6 & \\ & & 9 \end{bmatrix};$

$G = \begin{bmatrix} 4 & & \\ & 6 & \\ & & 8 \end{bmatrix}; H = \begin{bmatrix} 5 & & \\ & 6 & \\ & & 7 \end{bmatrix}; I = \begin{bmatrix} 1 & & \\ & 9 & \\ & & 8 \end{bmatrix};$

$J = \begin{bmatrix} 2 & & \\ & 9 & \\ & & 7 \end{bmatrix}; K = \begin{bmatrix} 3 & & \\ & 9 & \\ & & 6 \end{bmatrix}; L = \begin{bmatrix} 4 & & \\ & 9 & \\ & & 5 \end{bmatrix}$

Now, if we interchange 1 and 5 to obtain

$$A_1 = \begin{bmatrix} 5 & 4 & 9 \\ 7 & 3 & 8 \\ 6 & 2 & 1 \end{bmatrix}$$

Also, $\quad A^T = \begin{bmatrix} 1 & 8 & 9 \\ 2 & 3 & 4 \\ 6 & 7 & 5 \end{bmatrix}$ and $A_1^T = \begin{bmatrix} 5 & 7 & 6 \\ 4 & 3 & 2 \\ 9 & 8 & 1 \end{bmatrix}$

Then, from A we get four matrices A, A_1, A^T, A_1^T.

Similarly, from $B, C, D, \ldots, K, L$ we get 4 matrices.

Thus, total $12 \times 4 = 48$ matrices. Hence, $\lambda = 48$.

(D) For consistent, $\begin{vmatrix} 1 & 1 & 1 \\ c+2 & c+4 & 6 \\ (c+2)^2 & (c+4)^2 & 36 \end{vmatrix} = 0$

Applying $C_2 \to C_2 - C_1$, we get

$$\begin{vmatrix} 1 & 0 & 1 \\ c+2 & 2 & 6 \\ (c+2)^2 & 4c+12 & 36 \end{vmatrix} = 0$$

$\Rightarrow \quad 2\begin{vmatrix} 1 & 0 & 1 \\ c+2 & 1 & 6 \\ (c+2)^2 & 2c+6 & 36 \end{vmatrix} = 0$

$\Rightarrow \quad -12c - 0 + 1[(c+2)(2c+6) - (c+2)^2] = 0$

$\Rightarrow \quad c^2 - 6c + 8 = 0$

$\Rightarrow \quad c = 2, 4$

$\therefore \quad c_1 = 4, c_2 = 2$

$\Rightarrow \quad c_1^{c_2} = 4^2 = 16$

55. **(A)** $|M_r| = \dfrac{1}{r-1} - \dfrac{1}{r}$

$\displaystyle\lim_{n \to \infty} \sum_{r=2}^{n} \left(\frac{1}{r-1} - \frac{1}{r}\right)$

$\displaystyle= \lim_{n \to \infty} \left[\left(\frac{1}{1} - \frac{1}{2}\right) + \left(\frac{1}{2} - \frac{1}{3}\right) + \ldots + \left(\frac{1}{n-1} - \frac{1}{n}\right)\right]$

$= 1 - 0 = 1$

(B) $(A + B)^2 = A^2 + B^2$

$\Rightarrow \quad AB + BA = O \Rightarrow AB = -BA$

$\Rightarrow \quad |AB| = |-BA| \Rightarrow |A||B| = -|B||A|$

[A and B are odd ordered matrices]

$\Rightarrow \quad |B| = -|B|$

$\Rightarrow \quad |B| = 0$

(C) $K^2 = |C| = (\det \cdot A)^2 = 4^2 \Rightarrow k = 4$

(D) $A^4 = -4I \Rightarrow \lambda = 4 \Rightarrow \lambda - 2 = 2$

56. Given, $M_{ij} = (a_{ij})$, where $i, j \in \{1, 2, 3\}$

and $\quad a_{ij} = \begin{cases} 1, \text{ if } & j+1 \text{ is divisible by } i \\ 0, & \text{otherwise} \end{cases}$

So, $M = \begin{bmatrix} 1 & 1 & 1 \\ 1 & 0 & 1 \\ 0 & 1 & 0 \end{bmatrix}$

Now, determinant of $M = |M| = 1(-1) - 1(-1) + 0$

[expanding along (C_1)] $= 0$

So, M is singular matrix

i.e. M is non-invertible matrix.

Now, $M\begin{bmatrix}a_1\\a_2\\a_3\end{bmatrix}=\begin{bmatrix}-a_1\\-a_2\\-a_3\end{bmatrix}$

$$\Rightarrow \begin{bmatrix}1&1&1\\1&0&1\\0&1&0\end{bmatrix}\begin{bmatrix}a_1\\a_2\\a_3\end{bmatrix}=\begin{bmatrix}-a_1\\-a_2\\-a_3\end{bmatrix}$$

$$\Rightarrow \begin{bmatrix}a_1+a_2+a_3\\a_1+0+a_3\\0+a_2+0\end{bmatrix}=\begin{bmatrix}-a_1\\-a_2\\-a_3\end{bmatrix}$$

$$\Rightarrow a_1+a_2+a_3=-a_1 \quad \text{...(i)}$$

$$a_1+a_3=-a_2$$

$$\Rightarrow a_1+a_2+a_3=0 \quad \text{...(ii)}$$

$$a_2=-a_3$$

$$\Rightarrow a_2+a_3=0 \quad \text{...(iii)}$$

Putting the value of $a_1+a_2+a_3$ from Eq. (ii) in Eq. (i), we get

$a_1=0$ and $a_2+a_3=0$ [from Eq. (iii)]

Hence, infinite solutions exists, i.e. there exists a column matrix with infinite possibilities.

Also, $MX=0$

$$\Rightarrow \begin{bmatrix}1&1&1\\1&0&1\\0&1&0\end{bmatrix}\begin{bmatrix}x\\y\\z\end{bmatrix}=\begin{bmatrix}0\\0\\0\end{bmatrix}$$

$$\Rightarrow \begin{bmatrix}x+y+z\\x+0+z\\0+y+0\end{bmatrix}=\begin{bmatrix}0\\0\\0\end{bmatrix}\Rightarrow \left.\begin{matrix}x+y+z=0\\x+z=0\\y=0\end{matrix}\right\}$$

So, infinite solutions.

Again, $M-2I=\begin{bmatrix}1&1&1\\1&0&1\\0&1&0\end{bmatrix}-2\begin{bmatrix}1&0&0\\0&1&0\\0&0&1\end{bmatrix}=\begin{bmatrix}-1&1&1\\1&-2&1\\0&1&-2\end{bmatrix}$

$\therefore |M-2I|$ = determinant value of $(M-2I)$

$$=-I(3)-1(-2-1)=-3+3=0$$

i.e. $(M-2I)$ is singular matrix and hence it is non-invertible matrix.

57. $\because |R|=-5\begin{vmatrix}a&b\\c&d\end{vmatrix}$

$|R|$ can be zero in the following cases

(i) Two of a, b, c and d are zeroes which can be (a and b), (b and d), (d and c) or (c and a) 4×7^2 ways $=196$

(ii) Any three of a, b, c and d are zeroes $={}^4C_3\times7=28$

(iii) All four of a, b, c and d are zeroes $\rightarrow 1$

(iv) All four of a, b, c and d are non-zero but same number $\rightarrow 7$

(v) When two are alike and 2 other are alike (non-zero) $={}^7C_2\times2\times2=84$

$\therefore$ Number of invertible matrices

$$=8^4-196-28-1-7-84=3780$$

58. Given, $A=\begin{bmatrix}\beta&0&1\\2&1&-2\\3&1&-2\end{bmatrix}$

$$\therefore \quad |A|=-1 \quad \text{...(i)}$$

For $A^7-(\beta-1)A^6-\beta A^5$ to be singular.

$$|A^5||(A^2-(\beta-1)A-\beta|=0$$

$$\Rightarrow |A^5||A+I||A-\beta I|=0$$

As, $|A|\neq0$

$$\Rightarrow |A+I|=0 \text{ or } |A-\beta I|=0$$

$$\Rightarrow \begin{bmatrix}\beta+1&0&1\\2&2&-2\\3&1&-1\end{bmatrix}=0$$

$\because \quad -1\neq0$

$$\Rightarrow |A+I|\neq0$$

$$\therefore \quad |A-\beta I|=\begin{vmatrix}0&0&1\\2&1-\beta&-2\\3&1&-2-\beta\end{vmatrix}=0$$

$$\Rightarrow 2-3(1-\beta)=0$$

$$\Rightarrow 2-3+3\beta=0$$

$$\Rightarrow 3\beta=1$$

$$\Rightarrow \beta=\frac{1}{3}$$

$$\therefore \quad 9\beta=3$$

59. $M=\begin{bmatrix}\frac{5}{2}&\frac{3}{2}\\-\frac{3}{2}&-\frac{1}{2}\end{bmatrix}=\begin{bmatrix}1+\frac{3}{2}&0+\frac{3}{2}\\0-\frac{3}{2}&1-\frac{2}{2}\end{bmatrix}$

$$M=\begin{bmatrix}1&0\\0&1\end{bmatrix}+\begin{bmatrix}\frac{3}{2}&\frac{3}{2}\\-\frac{3}{2}&\frac{-3}{2}\end{bmatrix}$$

$$=\begin{bmatrix}1&0\\0&1\end{bmatrix}+\frac{3}{2}\begin{bmatrix}1&1\\-1&-1\end{bmatrix}$$

$$I=\begin{bmatrix}1&0\\0&1\end{bmatrix}$$

Let $A=\begin{bmatrix}1&1\\-1&-1\end{bmatrix}$

$$\Rightarrow M=I+\frac{3}{2}A;\ M^2=\left[I+\frac{3}{2}A\right]$$

$$=I^2+\frac{9}{4}A^2+2\cdot\frac{3}{2}A\cdot I$$

$$M^2=I+\frac{9}{4}A^2+3A$$

$$A^2=\begin{bmatrix}1&1\\-1&-1\end{bmatrix}\begin{bmatrix}1&1\\-1&-1\end{bmatrix}=\begin{bmatrix}0&0\\0&0\end{bmatrix}$$

So, $M^2=I+3A$

$$M^4=I^2+9A^2+6A=I+6A \quad [\because A^2=O]$$

Similarly, $M^{2022}=I+3033A=\begin{bmatrix}1&0\\0&1\end{bmatrix}+\begin{bmatrix}3033&3033\\-3033&-3033\end{bmatrix}$

$$=\begin{bmatrix}3034&3033\\-3033&-3032\end{bmatrix}$$

60. Given, $G=(I-EF)^{-1}$

$$\Rightarrow \quad G(I-EF)=(I-EF)G=I \qquad \text{...(i)}$$

(a) Now, $|I-FE||FGE|$

$$=|FGE-FEFGE|$$
$$=|FGE-F(G-I)E| \qquad \text{[from Eq. (i)]}$$
$$=|FGE-FGE+FE|$$
$$=|FE|$$

(b) $(I-FE)(I+FGE)$

$$=I+FGE-FE-FEFGE$$
$$=I+FGE-FE-F(G-I)E \text{ [from Eq. (i)]}$$
$$=I+FGE-FE-FGE+FE$$
$$=I$$

(c) From Eq. (i), we have

$$G(I-EF)=(I-EF)G$$
$$\Rightarrow \quad G-GEF=G-EFG$$
$$\Rightarrow \quad GEF=EFG$$

(d) $(I-FE)(I-FGE)$

$$=I-FGE-FE+FEFGE$$
$$=I-FGE-FE+F(G-I)E$$
$$=I-FGE-FE+FGE-FE$$
$$=I-2FE$$
$$\neq I$$

61. Given, $\quad M^{-1}=\text{adj}(\text{adj } M)$

$$=|M|^{3-2}M$$
$$=|M|M$$

Now, $\quad M\cdot M^{-1}=|M|M^2$

$$\Rightarrow \quad I=|M|^5 \qquad [\because M \text{ is } 3\times 3 \text{ matrix}]$$
$$\Rightarrow \quad |M|=|I|=I$$

Now, $\quad \det(M^{-1})=M$

$$\Rightarrow \quad M^2=I$$

and $\quad M^{-1}=\dfrac{\text{adj } M}{|M|} \Rightarrow \text{adj } M=M$

$$\therefore \quad (\text{adj } M)^2=M^2=I$$

62. Let $A=\begin{bmatrix} a & b \\ c & d\end{bmatrix}$ is a 2×2 matrix.

$$A^2=\begin{bmatrix} a^2+bc & ab+bd \\ ac+dc & bc+d^2\end{bmatrix}$$

and $A^3=\begin{bmatrix} a^3+2abc+bdc & a^2b+abd+b^2c+bd^2 \\ a^2c+adc+bc^2+d^2c & abc+2bcd+d^3\end{bmatrix}$

Given, $\text{tr}(A)=3$

$$\Rightarrow \quad a+d=3$$

and $\quad \text{tr}(A^3)=-18$

$$\Rightarrow \quad a^3+d^3+3abc+3bcd=-18$$
$$\Rightarrow \quad a^3+d^3+3bc(a+d)=-18$$
$$\Rightarrow \quad a^3+d^3+9bc=-18$$
$$\Rightarrow \quad (a+d)((a+d)^2-3ad)+9bc=-18$$
$$\Rightarrow \quad 3(9-3ad)+9bc=-18$$
$$\Rightarrow \quad ad-bc=5 \Rightarrow |A|=5$$

Exercise 3 - Challenging Problems

1. (i) $A^n=0 \Rightarrow A^n-I=-I$

$$\Rightarrow \quad A^n-I^n=-I$$
$$\Rightarrow \quad I^n-A^n=I$$
$$\Rightarrow \quad (I-A)(I+A+A^2+A^3+\ldots+A^{n-1})=I$$
$$\Rightarrow \quad (I+A+A^2+A^3+\ldots+A^{n-1})$$
$$=(I-A)^{-1}I=(I-A)^{-1}$$

(ii) $A^n=0 \Rightarrow A^n+I=I$

$$\Rightarrow \quad A^n+I^n=I$$
$$\Rightarrow \quad I^n+A^n=I$$
$$\Rightarrow \quad (I+A)(I-A+A^2-A^3+\ldots+A^{n-1})=I$$

$[\because n \text{ is odd}]$

$$\Rightarrow I-A+A^2-A^3+\ldots+A^{n-1}$$
$$=(I+A)^{-1}I=(I+A)^{-1}$$

2. $\because A$ is idempotent matrix

$$\therefore \quad A^2=A,$$

similarly $A=A^2=A^3=A^4=\ldots=A^n \qquad \text{...(i)}$

Now, $\quad (A+I)^n=(I+A)^n$

$$=I+{}^nC_1A+{}^nC_2A^2+{}^nC_3A^3+\ldots+{}^nC_nA^n$$
$$=I+({}^nC_1+{}^nC_2+{}^nC_3+\ldots+{}^nC_n)A$$

[from Eq. (i)]

$$=I+(2^n-1)A$$

Hence, $(A+I)^n=I+(2^n-1)A,\ \forall\, n\in N.$

3. $\because S$ is skew-symmetric matrix

$$\therefore \quad S^T=-S \qquad \text{...(i)}$$

First we will show that $I-S$ is non-singular. The equality $|I-S|=0 \Rightarrow I$ is a characteristic root of the matrix S but this is not possible, for a real skew-symmetric matrix can have zero or purely imaginary numbers as its characteristic roots.

Thus, $|I-S|\neq 0$ i.e. $I-S$ is non-singular.

We have,

$$A^T=\{(I+S)(I-S)^{-1}\}^T$$
$$=\{(I-S)^{-1}(I+S)\}^T$$
$$=((I-S)^{-1})^T(I+S)^T$$
$$=(I+S)^T\{(I-S)^{-1}\}^T$$
$$=((I-S)^T)^{-1}(I+S)^T$$
$$=(I+S)^T((I-S)^T)^{-1}$$
$$=(I^T-S^T)^{-1}(I^T+S^T)$$
$$=(I^T+S^T)(I^T-S^T)^{-1}$$
$$=(I+S)^{-1}(I-S)$$
$$=(I-S)(I+S)^{-1} \qquad \text{[from Eq. (i)]}$$

$$\therefore \quad A^TA=(I+S)^{-1}(I-S)(I+S)(I-S)^{-1}$$
$$=(I-S)(I+S)^{-1}(I-S)^{-1}(I+S)$$
$$=(I+S)^{-1}(I+S)(I-S)(I-S)^{-1}$$
$$=(I-S)(I-S)^{-1}(I+S)^{-1}(I+S)$$
$$=I\cdot I=I\cdot I=I=I$$

Hence, A is orthogonal.

4. Here, $I - BA = BIB^{-1} - BABB^{-1} = B(I - AB)B^{-1}$ ...(i)

Hence, $|I - BA| = |B||I - AB||B^{-1}|$

$$= |B||I - AB|\frac{1}{|B|}$$

$$= |I - AB|$$

If $|I - AB| \neq 0$, then $|I - BA| \neq 0$

i.e. if $(I - AB)$ is invertible, then $(I - BA)$ is also invertible.

Now, $(I - BA)[I + B(I - AB)^{-1}A]$

$$= (I - BA) + (I - BA)B(I - AB)^{-1}A \text{ [using Eq. (i)]}$$

$$= (I - BA) + B(I - AB)B^{-1}B(I - AB)^{-1}A$$

$$= (I - BA) + B(I - AB)(I - AB^{-1})A$$

$$= (I - BA) + BA$$

$$= I$$

Hence, $(I - BA)^{-1} = I + B(I - AB)^{-1}A$.

5. $A^3 + B^3 + C^3 = (A + B + C)$

$(A + \omega B + \omega^2 C)(A + \omega^2 B + \omega C)$,

where $\omega\ (\neq 1)$ cube root of unity.

$A^3 + B^3 + C^3 = (A + B + C)$

$(A + \omega B + \omega^2 C)\overline{(A + \omega B + \omega^2 C)}$

Hence, $|A^3 + B^3 + C^3||A + B + C|$

$$= |A + B + C|^2 |A + \omega B + \omega^2 C| \times |A + \omega B + \omega^2 C|$$

$\therefore |A^3 + B^3 + C^3||A + B + C|$

$$= |A + B + C|^2 |A + \omega B + \omega^2 C|^2 \geq 0$$

6. $\because$ A is symmetric

$\therefore$ $c = 8, b = -1$ and $a = 2$ ...(i)

and B is skew-symmetric

$\therefore$ $d = e = f = 0$ and $2b + c = 6, a = 2, b - a = -3$ ...(ii)

From Eqs. (i) and (ii), we get

$a = 2, b = -1, c = 8, d = 0, e = 0, f = 0$

$$\therefore \quad A = \begin{bmatrix} 3 & 2 & -1 \\ 2 & 5 & 8 \\ -1 & 8 & 2 \end{bmatrix} \text{ and } B = \begin{bmatrix} 0 & 3 & 2 \\ -3 & 0 & -6 \\ -2 & 6 & 0 \end{bmatrix}$$

$$\Rightarrow AB = \begin{bmatrix} -4 & 3 & -6 \\ -31 & 54 & -26 \\ -28 & 9 & -50 \end{bmatrix}$$

which neither symmetric nor skew-symmetric.

7. $\because$ $A = B + C$

$\Rightarrow A^{p+1} = (B + C)^{p+1}$

$$= {}^{p+1}C_0 B^{p+1} + {}^{p+1}C_1 B^p C + {}^{p+1}C_2 B^{p-1}C^2 + \ldots + {}^{p+1}C_{p+1}C^{p+1}$$

$$= B^{p+1} + {}^{p+1}C_1 B^p C + 0 + 0 + \ldots$$

$[\because C^2 = 0 \Rightarrow C^2 = C^3 = \ldots = 0]$

$$= B^p[B + (p + 1)C]$$

Hence, $A^{p+1} = B^p[B + (p + 1)C]$

8. $\because$ $A = \begin{bmatrix} 0 & 2 \\ -2 & 0 \end{bmatrix} \Rightarrow I - A = \begin{bmatrix} 1 & -2 \\ 2 & 1 \end{bmatrix}$

$$\Rightarrow (I - A)^{-1} = \frac{1}{5}\begin{bmatrix} 1 & 2 \\ -2 & 1 \end{bmatrix} \text{ and } (I + A) = \begin{bmatrix} 1 & 2 \\ -2 & 1 \end{bmatrix}$$

Let B be the orthogonal matrix from a skew-symmetric matrix A, then

$$B = (I - A)^{-1}(I + A)$$

$$= \frac{1}{5}\begin{bmatrix} 1 & 2 \\ -2 & 1 \end{bmatrix}\begin{bmatrix} 1 & 2 \\ -2 & 1 \end{bmatrix}$$

$$= \frac{1}{5}\begin{bmatrix} -3 & 4 \\ -4 & -3 \end{bmatrix} = \begin{bmatrix} -\frac{3}{5} & \frac{4}{5} \\ -\frac{4}{5} & -\frac{3}{5} \end{bmatrix}$$

9. Let $B = A + I$

$\therefore$ $A = B - I$

$\Rightarrow$ $(B - I)^n = \alpha(B - I)$

$\Rightarrow$ $B^n - {}^nC_1 \cdot B^{n-1} + {}^nC_2 B^{n-2} + \ldots + (-1)^n I = \alpha B - \alpha I$

$B^n - {}^nC_1 B^{n-1} + {}^nC_2 B^{n-2} + \ldots + (-1)^{n-1}B - \alpha B$

$$= -\alpha I - (-1)^n I$$

Thus, $B(B^n - {}^nC_1 B^{n-2} + {}^nC_2 B^{n-3} \ldots (-1)^{n-1}I - \alpha I)$

$$= ((-1)^{n+1} - \alpha)I$$

which clearly means B is invertible.

Since, $(-1)^{n+1} - \alpha \neq 0$

10. $AB = \begin{bmatrix} \cos^2\theta & \cos\theta\sin\theta \\ \cos\theta\sin\theta & \sin^2\theta \end{bmatrix}\begin{bmatrix} \cos^2\phi & \cos\phi\sin\phi \\ \cos\phi\sin\phi & \sin^2\phi \end{bmatrix}$

$$= \begin{bmatrix} \cos^2\theta\cos^2\phi + \cos\theta\cos\phi\sin\theta\sin\phi & \cos^2\theta\cos\phi\sin\phi + \sin^2\phi\sin\theta\cos\theta \\ \cos^2\phi\cos\theta\sin\theta + \sin^2\theta\sin\phi\cos\phi & \cos\theta\cos\phi\sin\theta\sin\phi + \sin^2\theta\sin^2\phi \end{bmatrix}$$

$$= \begin{bmatrix} \cos\theta\cos\phi(\cos\theta\cos\phi + \sin\theta\sin\phi) & \cos\phi\sin\phi(\cos\theta\cos\phi + \sin\theta\sin\phi) \\ \sin\theta\cos\phi(\cos\theta\cos\phi + \sin\theta\sin\phi) & \sin\theta\sin\phi(\cos\theta\cos\phi + \sin\theta\sin\phi) \end{bmatrix}$$

$$= \begin{bmatrix} \cos\theta\cos\phi\cos(\theta - \phi) & \cos\theta\sin\phi\cos(\theta - \phi) \\ \sin\theta\cos\phi\cos(\theta - \phi) & \sin\theta\sin\phi\cos(\theta - \phi) \end{bmatrix}$$

Clearly, AB is the zero matrix, if $\cos(\theta \sim \phi) = 0$ i.e. $\theta - \phi$ is an odd multiple of $\frac{\pi}{2}$.

11. We have, $\begin{bmatrix} 1 & 1 & 1 \\ 2 & 5 & 7 \\ 2 & 1 & -1 \end{bmatrix}\begin{bmatrix} x & u \\ y & v \\ z & w \end{bmatrix} = \begin{bmatrix} 9 & 2 \\ 52 & 15 \\ 0 & -1 \end{bmatrix}$

or $AX = B$

or $X = A^{-1}B$ ...(i)

Where, $A = \begin{bmatrix} 1 & 1 & 1 \\ 2 & 5 & 7 \\ 2 & 1 & -1 \end{bmatrix}, X = \begin{bmatrix} x & u \\ y & v \\ z & \omega \end{bmatrix}$ and $B = \begin{bmatrix} 9 & 2 \\ 52 & 15 \\ 0 & -1 \end{bmatrix}$

$\therefore \quad |A| = 1(-5-7) - 1(-2-14) + 1(2-10)$
$= -12 + 16 - 8 = -4 \neq 0$

Let C be the matrix of cofactors of elements of $|A|$.

$$\therefore \quad C = \begin{bmatrix} C_{11} & C_{12} & C_{13} \\ C_{21} & C_{22} & C_{23} \\ C_{31} & C_{32} & C_{33} \end{bmatrix}$$

$$= \begin{bmatrix} \begin{vmatrix} 5 & 7 \\ 1 & -1 \end{vmatrix} & -\begin{vmatrix} 2 & 7 \\ 2 & -1 \end{vmatrix} & \begin{vmatrix} 2 & 5 \\ 2 & 1 \end{vmatrix} \\ -\begin{vmatrix} 1 & 1 \\ 1 & -1 \end{vmatrix} & \begin{vmatrix} 1 & 1 \\ 2 & -1 \end{vmatrix} & -\begin{vmatrix} 1 & 1 \\ 2 & 1 \end{vmatrix} \\ \begin{vmatrix} 1 & 1 \\ 5 & 7 \end{vmatrix} & -\begin{vmatrix} 1 & 1 \\ 2 & 7 \end{vmatrix} & \begin{vmatrix} 1 & 1 \\ 2 & 5 \end{vmatrix} \end{bmatrix}$$

$$= \begin{bmatrix} -12 & 16 & -8 \\ 2 & -3 & 1 \\ 2 & -5 & 3 \end{bmatrix}$$

$$\therefore \text{ adj } A = C' = \begin{bmatrix} -12 & 2 & 2 \\ 16 & -3 & -5 \\ -8 & 1 & 3 \end{bmatrix}$$

$$\therefore \quad A^{-1} = \frac{\text{adj } A}{|A|} = -\frac{1}{4}\begin{bmatrix} -12 & 2 & 2 \\ 16 & -3 & -5 \\ -8 & 1 & 3 \end{bmatrix}$$

$$\text{Now, } A^{-1}B = -\frac{1}{4}\begin{bmatrix} -12 & 2 & 2 \\ 16 & -3 & -5 \\ -8 & 1 & 3 \end{bmatrix} \times \begin{bmatrix} 9 & 2 \\ 52 & 15 \\ 0 & -1 \end{bmatrix}$$

$$= -\frac{1}{4}\begin{bmatrix} -4 & 4 \\ -12 & -8 \\ -20 & -4 \end{bmatrix} = \begin{bmatrix} 1 & -1 \\ 3 & 2 \\ 5 & 1 \end{bmatrix}$$

From Eq. (i), $\quad X = A^{-1}B$

$$\Rightarrow \quad \begin{bmatrix} x & u \\ y & v \\ z & w \end{bmatrix} = \begin{bmatrix} 1 & -1 \\ 3 & 2 \\ 5 & 1 \end{bmatrix}$$

On equating the corresponding elements, we have

$x = 1, u = -1$
$y = 3, v = 2$
$z = 5, w = 1$

12. $AX = U$ has infinite many solutions

$\Rightarrow \quad |A| = 0 = |A_1| = |A_2| = |A_3|$

Now, $\quad |A| = 0$

$$\Rightarrow \quad \begin{vmatrix} a & 1 & 0 \\ 1 & b & d \\ 1 & b & c \end{vmatrix} = 0 \Rightarrow (ab-1)(c-d) = 0$$

$\Rightarrow \quad ab = 1$ or $c = d \quad$ ...(i)

and $\quad |A_1| = 0$

$$\Rightarrow \quad \begin{vmatrix} f & 1 & 0 \\ g & b & d \\ h & b & c \end{vmatrix} = 0$$

$\Rightarrow \quad fb(c-d) - gc + hd = 0$

$\Rightarrow \quad fb(c-d) = gc - hd \quad$ ...(ii)

$\Rightarrow \quad |A_2| = 0$

$$\Rightarrow \quad \begin{vmatrix} a & f & 0 \\ 1 & g & d \\ 1 & h & c \end{vmatrix} = 0$$

$\Rightarrow \quad a(gc - dh) - f(c-d) = 0$

$\Rightarrow \quad a(gc - dh) = f(c-d) \quad$ ...(iii)

$|A_3| = 0$

$$\Rightarrow \quad \begin{vmatrix} a & 1 & f \\ 1 & b & g \\ 1 & b & h \end{vmatrix} = 0$$

$\Rightarrow \quad (h-g)(ab-1) = 0$

$\Rightarrow \quad h = g$ or $ab = 1 \quad$ ...(iv)

Taking $c = d \Rightarrow h = g$ and $ab \neq 1 \quad$ [from Eqs. (i), (ii) and (iv)]

Now, taking $BX = V$,

$$\text{Then,} \quad |B| = \begin{vmatrix} a & 1 & 1 \\ 0 & d & c \\ f & g & h \end{vmatrix} = 0$$

[$\because$ In view of $c = d$ and $g = h$, c_2 and c_3 are identical]

$\Rightarrow \quad BX = V$ has no unique solution.

$$\text{and} \quad |B_1| = \begin{vmatrix} a^2 & 1 & 1 \\ 0 & d & c \\ 0 & g & h \end{vmatrix} = 0 \quad [\because c = d, g = h]$$

$$|B_2| = \begin{vmatrix} a & a^2 & 1 \\ 0 & 0 & c \\ f & 0 & h \end{vmatrix} = a^2fc = a^2df \quad [\because c = d]$$

$$\text{and} \quad |B_3| = \begin{vmatrix} a & 1 & a^2 \\ 0 & d & 0 \\ f & g & 0 \end{vmatrix} = -a^2df$$

If $a^2df \neq 0$, then $|B_2| = |B_3| \neq 0$

Hence, no solution exist.

"

The important thing to remember about Mathematics is not to be frightened.

-Richard Dawkins

8

Determinants

Learning Milestones

Milestone 1 Determinant

- Definition of Determinant
- Expansion of Determinant
- Sarrus Rule for Expansion

Milestone 2 Properties of Determinant

- Minors and Cofactors
- Use of Determinants in Coordinate Geometry
- Properties of Determinants

Milestone 3 Solving a System of Linear Equations

- Largest Value of a Third Order Determinant
- Multiplication of Two Determinants of the Same Order
- System of Linear Equations
- Cramer's Rule
- Nature of Solutions of System of Linear Equations
- System of Homogeneous Linear Equations

Milestone 4 Differentiation and Integration of Determinant

- Differentiation of Determinant
- Integration of Determinant
- Use of Σ in Determinant

$a_1x+b_1y+c_1z=d_1$

$a_2x+b_2y+c_2z=d_2$

$a_3x+b_3y+c_3z=d_3$

Practice Milestones

Practice Milestone 1- JEE Main Pattern

Practice Milestone 2 - JEE Advanced Pattern

Practice Milestone 3 - Challenging Problems

Milestone 1 Determinant

• Definition of Determinant • Expansion of Determinant • Sarrus Rule for Expansion

Determinants were invented independently by **Gabriel Cramer**, whose now well-known rule for solving linear system was published in 1750, although not in present day notation. The now-standard "Vertical line notation", i.e. "| |" was given in 1841 by **Arthur Cayley**. The working knowledge of determinants is a basic necessity for a student. Determinants have wide applications in Engineering, Science, Economics, Social science, etc.

8.1 Definition of Determinant

Consider the system of two homogeneous linear equations

$$a_1 x + b_1 y = 0 \quad \text{...(i)}$$

$$a_2 x + b_2 y = 0 \quad \text{...(ii)}$$

in the two variables x and y.

From these equations, we obtain

$$-\frac{a_1}{b_1} = \frac{y}{x} = -\frac{a_2}{b_2} \Rightarrow \frac{a_1}{b_1} = \frac{a_2}{b_2} \Rightarrow a_1 b_2 - a_2 b_1 = 0$$

The result $a_1 b_2 - a_2 b_1$ is represented by $\begin{vmatrix} a_1 & b_1 \\ a_2 & b_2 \end{vmatrix}$

which is known as determinant of order two. The quantities a_1, b_1, a_2 and b_2 are called constituents or elements of the determinant and $a_1 b_2 - a_2 b_1$ is called its value.

The horizontal lines are called rows and vertical lines are called columns. Here, this determinant consists two rows and two columns.

e.g. The value of the determinant

$$\begin{vmatrix} 2 & 3 \\ 4 & -5 \end{vmatrix} = 2 \times (-5) - 3 \times 4 = -10 - 12 = -22$$

Now, let us consider the system of three homogeneous linear equations

$$a_1 x + b_1 y + c_1 z = 0 \quad \text{...(i)}$$

$$a_2 x + b_2 y + c_2 z = 0 \quad \text{...(ii)}$$

$$a_3 x + b_3 y + c_3 z = 0 \quad \text{...(iii)}$$

On solving Eqs. (ii) and (iii) for x, y and z by cross-multiplication, we get

$$\frac{x}{b_2 c_3 - b_3 c_2} = \frac{y}{c_2 a_3 - c_3 a_2}$$

$$= \frac{z}{a_2 b_3 - a_3 b_2} = k \quad \text{[say]}$$

$\Rightarrow \quad x = k(b_2 c_3 - b_3 c_2), y = k(c_2 a_3 - c_3 a_2)$

and $\quad z = k(a_2 b_3 - a_3 b_2)$

On putting these values of x, y and z in Eq. (i), we get

$$a_1(b_2 c_3 - b_3 c_2) + b_1(c_2 a_3 - c_3 a_2) + c_1(a_2 b_3 - a_3 b_2) = 0$$

or $\quad a_1(b_2 c_3 - b_3 c_2) - b_1(c_3 a_2 - c_2 a_3)$

$$+ c_1(a_2 b_3 - a_3 b_2) = 0 \quad \text{...(iv)}$$

or $\quad a_1 \begin{vmatrix} b_2 & c_2 \\ b_3 & c_3 \end{vmatrix} - b_1 \begin{vmatrix} a_2 & c_2 \\ a_3 & c_3 \end{vmatrix} + c_1 \begin{vmatrix} a_2 & b_2 \\ a_3 & b_3 \end{vmatrix} = 0 \quad \text{...(v)}$

Usually this is written as $\begin{vmatrix} a_1 & b_1 & c_1 \\ a_2 & b_2 & c_2 \\ a_3 & b_3 & c_3 \end{vmatrix} = 0$

Here, the expression $\begin{vmatrix} a_1 & b_1 & c_1 \\ a_2 & b_2 & c_2 \\ a_3 & b_3 & c_3 \end{vmatrix}$ consisting of three rows and three columns, is called determinant of order three.

The quantities $a_1, b_1, c_1, a_2, b_2, c_2, a_3, b_3$ and c_3 are called constituents or elements of the determinant.

JEE Focus Points

- A determinant is generally denoted by D or Δ.
- A determinant of the nth order consists of n rows and n columns and its expansion contains $n!$ terms.
- A determinant of nth order consists of n rows and n columns.
  $\therefore$ Number of constituents in determinant $= n^2$
- In a determinant the horizontal lines counting from top to bottom 1st, 2nd, 3rd, ... respectively, known as rows and denoted by $R_1, R_2, R_3, \ldots$ and vertical lines from left to right 1st, 2nd, 3rd, ... respectively, known as columns and denoted by $C_1, C_2, C_3, \ldots$.
- Shape of every determinant is square.
- Sign system for order 2, order 3, order 4, ... are given by

$$\begin{vmatrix} + & - \\ - & + \end{vmatrix}, \begin{vmatrix} + & - & + \\ - & + & - \\ + & - & + \end{vmatrix}, \begin{vmatrix} + & - & + & - \\ - & + & - & + \\ + & - & + & - \\ - & + & - & + \end{vmatrix}, \ldots$$

8.2 Expansion of Determinant

(i) Expansion of two order

$$\begin{vmatrix} a_1 & b_1 \\ a_2 & b_2 \end{vmatrix} = \begin{vmatrix} a_1 \searrow & \\ & b_2 \end{vmatrix} - \begin{vmatrix} & b_1 \\ a_2 \nearrow & \end{vmatrix} = a_1 b_2 - b_1 a_2$$

e.g.
$$\begin{vmatrix} 4 & -4 \\ -2 & 5 \end{vmatrix} = \begin{vmatrix} 4 \searrow & \\ & 5 \end{vmatrix} - \begin{vmatrix} & -4 \\ -2 \nearrow & \end{vmatrix}$$
$$= 20 - 8 = 12$$

(ii) Expansion of third order

(a) With respect to first row.

$$\begin{vmatrix} a_1 \cdots & b_1 \cdots & c_1 \\ a_2 & b_2 & c_2 \\ a_3 & b_3 & c_3 \end{vmatrix} = a_1 \begin{vmatrix} b_2 & c_2 \\ b_3 & c_3 \end{vmatrix} - b_1 \begin{vmatrix} a_2 & c_2 \\ a_3 & c_3 \end{vmatrix} + c_1 \begin{vmatrix} a_2 & b_2 \\ a_3 & b_3 \end{vmatrix}$$

$$= a_1 (b_2 c_3 - b_3 c_2) - b_1 (a_2 c_3 - a_3 c_2) + c_1 (a_2 b_3 - a_3 b_2)$$

(b) With respect to second column.

$$\begin{vmatrix} a_1 & b_1 & c_1 \\ & \vdots & \\ a_2 & b_2 & c_2 \\ & \vdots & \\ a_3 & b_3 & c_3 \end{vmatrix} = -b_1 \begin{vmatrix} a_2 & c_2 \\ a_3 & c_3 \end{vmatrix} + b_2 \begin{vmatrix} a_1 & c_1 \\ a_3 & c_3 \end{vmatrix} - b_3 \begin{vmatrix} a_1 & c_1 \\ a_2 & c_2 \end{vmatrix}$$

$$= -b_1 (a_2 c_3 - a_3 c_2) + b_2 (a_1 c_3 - a_3 c_1) - b_3 (a_1 c_2 - a_2 c_1)$$

JEE SPIKE

A determinant can be expanded along any of its row or column. Value of the determinant remains same in any of the cases.

Example 1. Find the value of the determinant $\begin{vmatrix} 2 & 3 & 5 \\ 4 & 3 & 2 \\ -2 & 2 & 1 \end{vmatrix}$.

Sol. Expanding the determinant along the first row

$$\Delta_1 = 2\begin{vmatrix} 3 & 2 \\ 2 & 1 \end{vmatrix} - 3\begin{vmatrix} 4 & 2 \\ -2 & 1 \end{vmatrix} + 5\begin{vmatrix} 4 & 3 \\ -2 & 2 \end{vmatrix}$$
$$= 2(3-4) - 3(4+4) + 5(8+6) = -2 - 24 + 70 = 44$$

and expanding the determinant along third column

$$\Delta_2 = 5\begin{vmatrix} 4 & 3 \\ -2 & 2 \end{vmatrix} - 2\begin{vmatrix} 2 & 3 \\ -2 & 2 \end{vmatrix} + 1\begin{vmatrix} 2 & 3 \\ 4 & 3 \end{vmatrix}$$
$$= 5(8+6) - 2(4+6) + (6-12) = 70 - 20 - 6 = 44$$

and expanding the determinant along second column

$$\Delta_3 = -3\begin{vmatrix} 4 & 2 \\ -2 & 1 \end{vmatrix} + 3\begin{vmatrix} 2 & 5 \\ -2 & 1 \end{vmatrix} - 2\begin{vmatrix} 2 & 5 \\ 4 & 2 \end{vmatrix}$$
$$= -3(4+4) + 3(2+10) - 2(4-20)$$
$$= -24 + 36 + 32 = 44$$

Hence, $\Delta_1 = \Delta_2 = \Delta_3$

JEE SCANNER

Example Similar to PYQ Asked in JEE Main 2021

If $\Delta = \begin{vmatrix} 1 & \sin\theta & 1 \\ -\sin\theta & 1 & \sin\theta \\ -1 & -\sin\theta & 1 \end{vmatrix}$, *then maximum value of* Δ *is*

(a) 3 (b) 4 (c) 2 (d) 6

Sol. (b) Given, $\Delta = \begin{vmatrix} 1 & \sin\theta & 1 \\ -\sin\theta & 1 & \sin\theta \\ -1 & -\sin\theta & 1 \end{vmatrix}$

Expanding along first row, we get

$$\Delta = 1\begin{vmatrix} 1 & \sin\theta \\ -\sin\theta & 1 \end{vmatrix} - \sin\theta\begin{vmatrix} -\sin\theta & \sin\theta \\ -1 & 1 \end{vmatrix} + 1\begin{vmatrix} -\sin\theta & 1 \\ -1 & -\sin\theta \end{vmatrix}$$

$$= (1+\sin^2\theta) - \sin\theta(-\sin\theta + \sin\theta) + 1(\sin^2\theta + 1)$$
$$= 2(1+\sin^2\theta)$$

$\because 0 \le \sin^2\theta \le 1$

$\Rightarrow 1 \le 1 + \sin^2\theta \le 2$

$\Rightarrow 2 \le 2(1+\sin^2\theta) \le 4$

$\therefore$ The maximum value of Δ is 4.

Skill Builder

The maximum value of $\Delta = \begin{vmatrix} 1 & 1 & 1 \\ 1 & 1+\sin\theta & 1 \\ 1 & 1 & 1+\cos\theta \end{vmatrix}$ is

(a) $\frac{1}{2}$ (b) $\frac{3}{2}$

(c) 2 (d) 1

For Sol.

■ **For more practice** See Q.6 of Milestone Practice 8.1.

Example 2. If $\Delta = \begin{vmatrix} 1 & \cos\theta & 1 \\ -\cos\theta & 1 & \cos\theta \\ -1 & -\cos\theta & 1 \end{vmatrix}$, then what is the maximum and minimum value of Δ?

Sol. Given, $\Delta = \begin{vmatrix} 1 & \cos\theta & 1 \\ -\cos\theta & 1 & \cos\theta \\ -1 & -\cos\theta & 1 \end{vmatrix}$

Expanding along first row, we get

$$\Delta = 1\begin{vmatrix} 1 & \cos\theta \\ -\cos\theta & 1 \end{vmatrix} - \cos\theta\begin{vmatrix} -\cos\theta & \cos\theta \\ -1 & 1 \end{vmatrix} + 1\begin{vmatrix} -\cos\theta & 1 \\ -1 & -\cos\theta \end{vmatrix}$$

$$= (1 + \cos^2\theta) - \cos\theta(-\cos\theta + \cos\theta) + 1(\cos^2\theta + 1)$$

$$= 2(1 + \cos^2\theta)$$

Since, $0 \le \cos^2\theta \le 1$

$\Rightarrow \quad 1 \le 1 + \cos^2\theta \le 2$

$\Rightarrow \quad 2 \le 2(1 + \cos^2\theta) \le 4$

Therefore, $\Delta_{max} = 4, \Delta_{\min} = 2$

8.3 Sarrus Rule for Expansion

Sarrus gave a rule for a determinant of order 3.

Rule Write down the three rows of the Δ and rewrite the first two rows. The three diagonals sloping down to the right given the three terms and the three diagonals sloping down to the left also given the three terms.

If $\quad \Delta = \begin{vmatrix} a_1 & b_1 & c_1 \\ a_2 & b_2 & c_2 \\ a_3 & b_3 & c_3 \end{vmatrix}$

Rule

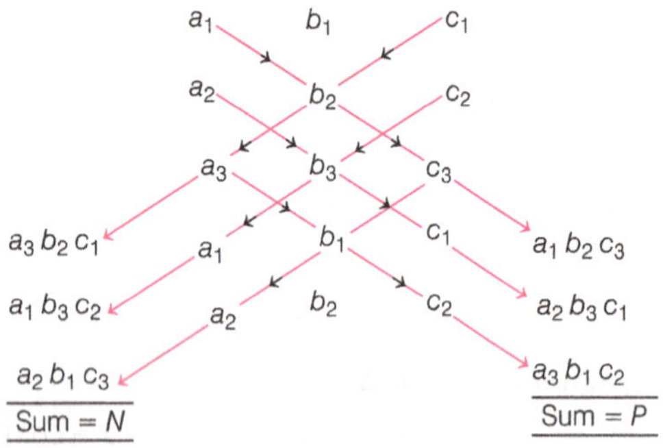

$\therefore \quad \Delta = P - N$

Example 3. Use the Sarrus rule, to find the value of $\begin{vmatrix} 4 & -2 & 3 \\ 5 & -1 & -1 \\ 6 & 2 & 1 \end{vmatrix}$.

Sol. Let $\Delta = \begin{vmatrix} 4 & -2 & 3 \\ 5 & -1 & -1 \\ 6 & 2 & 1 \end{vmatrix}$.

Using Sarrus rule, we have

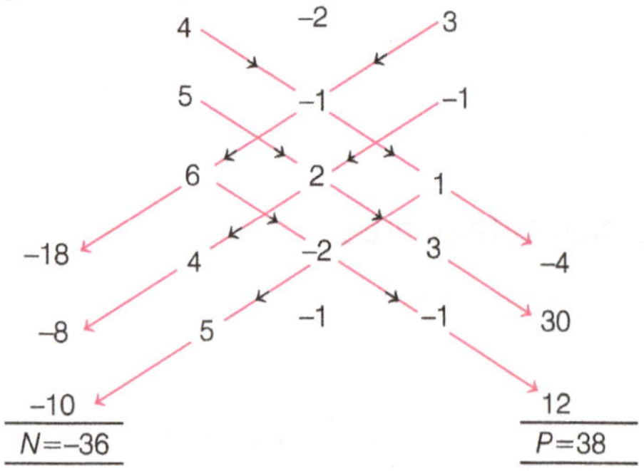

$\therefore \quad \Delta = P - N = 38 + 36 = 74$

Example 4. If $a, b, c \in R$, find the number of real roots of the equation $\begin{vmatrix} 2x & c & -b \\ -c & 2x & a \\ b & -a & 2x \end{vmatrix} = 0$

Sol. Let $\Delta = \begin{vmatrix} 2x & c & -b \\ -c & 2x & a \\ b & -a & 2x \end{vmatrix}$

Rule

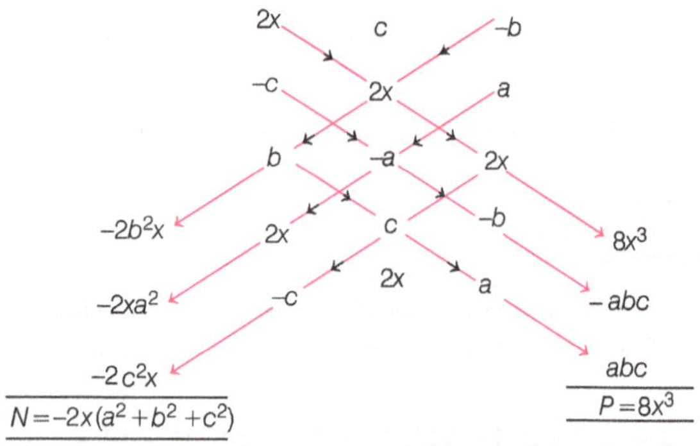

$\therefore \quad \Delta = P - N$

$$= 8x^3 + 2x(a^2 + b^2 + c^2) = 0 \qquad \text{[given]}$$

$\therefore \quad x = 0 \text{ or } 4x^2 = -(a^2 + b^2 + c^2)$

$\Rightarrow \quad x = 0 \text{ or } x = \pm\frac{i}{2}\sqrt{(a^2 + b^2 + c^2)}$, where $i = \sqrt{-1}$

Hence, number of real roots is one.

Milestone Practice 8.1

1. Sum of real roots of the equation $\begin{vmatrix} 1 & 4 & 20 \\ 1 & -2 & 5 \\ 1 & 2x & 5x^2 \end{vmatrix} = 0$ is

(a) -2 (b) -1
(c) 0 (d) 1

2. If $\begin{vmatrix} 6i & -3i & 1 \\ 4 & 3i & -1 \\ 20 & 3 & i \end{vmatrix} = x + iy, i = \sqrt{-1}$, then

(a) $x = 3, y = 1$ (b) $x = 1, y = 3$
(c) $x = 0, y = 3$ (d) $x = 0, y = 0$

3. If $p\lambda^4 + q\lambda^3 + r\lambda^2 + s\lambda + t$
$= \begin{vmatrix} \lambda^2 + 3\lambda & \lambda - 1 & \lambda + 3 \\ \lambda^2 + 1 & 2 - \lambda & \lambda - 3 \\ \lambda^2 - 3 & \lambda + 4 & 3\lambda \end{vmatrix}$, then t is equal to

(a) 7 (b) 14
(c) 21 (d) 28

4. If one root of the equation
$\begin{vmatrix} 7 & 6 & x^2 - 13 \\ 2 & x^2 - 13 & 2 \\ x^2 - 13 & 3 & 7 \end{vmatrix} = 0$ is $x = 2$, the sum of all other five roots is

(a) $2\sqrt{15}$ (b) -2
(c) $\sqrt{20} + \sqrt{15} - 2$ (d) None of these

5. If A, B and C are the angles of a non-right angled ΔABC, the value of $\begin{vmatrix} \tan A & 1 & 1 \\ 1 & \tan B & 1 \\ 1 & 1 & \tan C \end{vmatrix}$ is

(a) 0 (b) 1
(c) 2 (d) 3

6. If $\Delta = \begin{vmatrix} 1 & 3\cos\theta & 1 \\ \sin\theta & 1 & 3\cos\theta \\ 1 & \sin\theta & 1 \end{vmatrix}$, the maximum value of Δ is

(a) -10 (b) $-\sqrt{10}$
(c) $\sqrt{10}$ (d) 10

7 If the value of the determinant $\begin{vmatrix} a & 1 & 1 \\ 1 & b & 1 \\ 1 & 1 & c \end{vmatrix}$ is positive, then $(a, b, c > 0)$

(a) $abc > 1$
(b) $abc > -8$
(c) $abc < -8$
(d) $abc > -2$

Answer Key

1. (d)	2. (d)	3. (c)	4. (b)	5. (c)	6. (d)	7. (b)

For Detailed Solution

Milestone 2 Properties of Determinant

• Minors and Cofactors • Use of Determinants in Coordinate Geometry • Properties of Determinants

8.4 Minors and Cofactors

Let $$\Delta = \begin{vmatrix} a_{11} & a_{12} & a_{13} & \cdots & a_{1n} \\ a_{21} & a_{22} & a_{23} & \cdots & a_{2n} \\ a_{31} & a_{32} & a_{33} & \cdots & a_{3n} \\ \cdots & \cdots & \cdots & \cdots & \cdots \\ a_{n1} & a_{n2} & a_{n3} & \cdots & a_{nn} \end{vmatrix}$$

be a determinant of order n, $n \geq 2$, then the determinant of order $n-1$ obtained from the determinant Δ after deleting the ith row and jth column is called the **minor of the element a_{ij}** and it is usually denoted by M_{ij}, where $i = 1, 2, 3, \ldots, n$ and $j = 1, 2, 3, \ldots, n$.

If M_{ij} is the minor of the element a_{ij} in the determinant Δ, then $(-1)^{i+j} M_{ij}$ is called the **cofactor of the element a_{ij}**.

It is usually denoted by C_{ij}.

Thus, $$C_{ij} = (-1)^{i+j} M_{ij} = \begin{cases} M_{ij}, & \text{if } i+j \text{ is an even integer} \\ -M_{ij}, & \text{if } i+j \text{ is an odd integer} \end{cases}$$

(i) Let $\Delta = \begin{vmatrix} a_{11} & a_{12} \\ a_{21} & a_{22} \end{vmatrix}$, then

$$M_{11} = |a_{22}| = a_{22},\ M_{12} = |a_{21}| = a_{21},$$
$$M_{21} = |a_{12}| = a_{12},\ M_{22} = |a_{11}| = a_{11} \text{ and}$$
$$C_{11} = (-1)^{1+1} M_{11} = a_{22},$$
$$C_{12} = (-1)^{1+2} M_{12} = -a_{21},$$
$$C_{21} = (-1)^{2+1} M_{21} = -a_{12}$$
$$\text{and } C_{22} = (-1)^{2+2} M_{22} = a_{11}$$

(ii) Let $\Delta = \begin{vmatrix} a_{11} & a_{12} & a_{13} \\ a_{21} & a_{22} & a_{23} \\ a_{31} & a_{32} & a_{33} \end{vmatrix}$

Determinants of minors and cofactors are

$$\Delta^M = \begin{vmatrix} M_{11} & M_{12} & M_{13} \\ M_{21} & M_{22} & M_{23} \\ M_{31} & M_{32} & M_{33} \end{vmatrix},\ \Delta^c = \begin{vmatrix} C_{11} & C_{12} & C_{13} \\ C_{21} & C_{22} & C_{23} \\ C_{31} & C_{32} & C_{33} \end{vmatrix}$$

where,

$$M_{11} = \begin{vmatrix} a_{22} & a_{23} \\ a_{32} & a_{33} \end{vmatrix}, C_{11} = (-1)^{1+1} M_{11} = M_{11}$$

$$M_{12} = \begin{vmatrix} a_{21} & a_{23} \\ a_{31} & a_{33} \end{vmatrix}, C_{12} = (-1)^{1+2} M_{12} = -M_{12}$$

$$M_{13} = \begin{vmatrix} a_{21} & a_{22} \\ a_{31} & a_{32} \end{vmatrix}, C_{13} = (-1)^{1+3} M_{13} = M_{13}$$

$$M_{21} = \begin{vmatrix} a_{12} & a_{13} \\ a_{32} & a_{33} \end{vmatrix}, C_{21} = (-1)^{2+1} M_{21} = -M_{21}$$

$$M_{22} = \begin{vmatrix} a_{11} & a_{13} \\ a_{31} & a_{33} \end{vmatrix}, C_{22} = (-1)^{2+2} M_{22} = M_{22}$$

$$M_{23} = \begin{vmatrix} a_{11} & a_{12} \\ a_{31} & a_{32} \end{vmatrix}, C_{23} = (-1)^{2+3} M_{23} = -M_{23}$$

$$M_{31} = \begin{vmatrix} a_{12} & a_{13} \\ a_{22} & a_{23} \end{vmatrix}, C_{31} = (-1)^{3+1} M_{31} = M_{31}$$

$$M_{32} = \begin{vmatrix} a_{11} & a_{13} \\ a_{21} & a_{23} \end{vmatrix}, C_{32} = (-1)^{3+2} M_{32} = -M_{32}$$

$$M_{33} = \begin{vmatrix} a_{11} & a_{12} \\ a_{21} & a_{22} \end{vmatrix}, C_{33} = (-1)^{3+3} M_{33} = M_{33}$$

Important Results for Cofactors

1. The sum of products of the elements of any row or column with their corresponding cofactors is equal to the value of the determinant.

   i.e. $\Delta = a_{11} C_{11} + a_{12} C_{12} + a_{13} C_{13}$
   $= a_{11} C_{11} + a_{21} C_{21} + a_{31} C_{31}$
   $= a_{21} C_{21} + a_{22} C_{22} + a_{23} C_{23} = a_{12} C_{12} + a_{22} C_{22} + a_{32} C_{32}$
   $= a_{31} C_{31} + a_{32} C_{32} + a_{33} C_{33} = a_{13} C_{13} + a_{23} C_{23} + a_{33} C_{33}$

   Now, value of n order determinant

$$\Delta = \begin{vmatrix} a_{11} & a_{12} & a_{13} & \cdots & \cdots & a_{1n} \\ a_{21} & a_{22} & a_{23} & \cdots & \cdots & a_{2n} \\ a_{31} & a_{32} & a_{33} & \cdots & \cdots & a_{3n} \\ \cdots & \cdots & \cdots & \cdots & \cdots & \cdots \\ \cdots & \cdots & \cdots & \cdots & \cdots & \cdots \\ a_{n1} & a_{n2} & a_{n3} & \cdots & \cdots & a_{nn} \end{vmatrix}$$
$$= a_{11} C_{11} + a_{12} C_{12} + a_{13} C_{13} + \ldots + a_{1n} C_{1n}$$

(when expanded along first row)

2. The sum of the product of element of any row (or column) with corresponding cofactors of another row (or column) is equal to zero.

   i.e. $a_{11}C_{21} + a_{12}C_{22} + a_{13}C_{23} = 0$,
   $a_{11}C_{13} + a_{21}C_{23} + a_{31}C_{33} = 0$, etc.

3. If the value of a n order determinant is Δ, then the value of the determinant formed by the cofactors of corresponding elements of the given determinant is given by

   $$\Delta^c = \Delta^{n-1}$$

   i.e. in case of second order determinant

   $$\Delta^c = \Delta$$

   and third order determinant $\Delta^c = \Delta^2$.

Example 5. Find the minors and co-factors of the determinant $\begin{vmatrix} 1 & 2 & 3 \\ 4 & 7 & 9 \\ 3 & 2 & 5 \end{vmatrix}$. Also, find the determinant using co-factors.

Sol. Here, $M_{11} = \begin{vmatrix} 7 & 9 \\ 2 & 5 \end{vmatrix} = 35 - 18 = 17$

$\therefore \quad C_{11} = (-1)^{1+1} M_{11} = M_{11} = 17$

$M_{12} = \begin{vmatrix} 4 & 9 \\ 3 & 5 \end{vmatrix} = 20 - 27 = -7$

$\therefore \quad C_{12} = (-1)^{1+2} M_{12} = -M_{12} = 7$

$M_{13} = \begin{vmatrix} 4 & 7 \\ 3 & 2 \end{vmatrix} = 8 - 21 = -13$

$\therefore \quad C_{13} = (-1)^{1+3} M_{13} = M_{13} = -13$

$M_{21} = \begin{vmatrix} 2 & 3 \\ 2 & 5 \end{vmatrix} = 10 - 6 = 4$

$\therefore \quad C_{21} = (-1)^{2+1} M_{21} = -M_{21} = -4$

$M_{22} = \begin{vmatrix} 1 & 3 \\ 3 & 5 \end{vmatrix} = 5 - 9 = -4$

$\therefore \quad C_{22} = (-1)^{2+2} M_{22} = M_{22} = -4$

$M_{23} = \begin{vmatrix} 1 & 2 \\ 3 & 2 \end{vmatrix} = 2 - 6 = -4$

$C_{23} = (-1)^{2+3} M_{23} = -M_{23} = 4$

$M_{31} = \begin{vmatrix} 2 & 3 \\ 7 & 9 \end{vmatrix} = 18 - 21 = -3$

$C_{31} = (-1)^{3+1} M_{31} = M_{31} = -3$

$M_{32} = \begin{vmatrix} 1 & 3 \\ 4 & 9 \end{vmatrix} = 9 - 12 = -3$

$C_{32} = (-1)^{3+2} M_{32} = -M_{32} = 3$

$M_{33} = \begin{vmatrix} 1 & 2 \\ 4 & 7 \end{vmatrix} = 7 - 8 = -1$

$\therefore \quad C_{33} = (-1)^{3+3} M_{33} = M_{33} = -1$

Now, $\Delta = a_{11}C_{11} + a_{12}C_{12} + a_{13}C_{13}$
$= 1 \times 17 + 2 \times 7 + 3 \times (-13)$
$= 17 + 14 - 39 = -8$

Goyal's Method for Cofactors

(Direct Method)

This method applied only for third order determinant.

Method If $\quad \Delta = \begin{vmatrix} a_1 & a_2 & a_3 \\ b_1 & b_2 & b_3 \\ c_1 & c_2 & c_3 \end{vmatrix}$

***Step* I** Write down the three rows of the Δ and rewrite first two rows.

i.e.
$$\begin{matrix} a_1 & a_2 & a_3 \\ b_1 & b_2 & b_3 \\ c_1 & c_2 & c_3 \\ a_1 & a_2 & a_3 \\ b_1 & b_2 & b_3 \end{matrix}$$

***Step* II** Alter Step I, rewrite first two columns.

i.e.
$$\begin{matrix} a_1 & a_2 & a_3 & a_1 & a_2 \\ b_1 & b_2 & b_3 & b_1 & b_2 \\ c_1 & c_2 & c_3 & c_1 & c_2 \\ a_1 & a_2 & a_3 & a_1 & a_2 \\ b_1 & b_2 & b_3 & b_1 & b_2 \end{matrix}$$

***Step* III** After step II, deleting first row and first column, then we get all cofactors i.e.

$$\begin{matrix} b_2 & \times & b_3 & \times & b_1 & \times & b_2 \\ c_2 & \times & c_3 & \times & c_1 & \times & c_2 \\ a_2 & \times & a_3 & \times & a_1 & \times & a_2 \\ b_2 & & b_3 & & b_1 & & b_2 \end{matrix}$$

or $\quad \Delta^c = \begin{vmatrix} b_2c_3 - b_3c_2 & b_3c_1 - b_1c_3 & b_1c_2 - b_2c_1 \\ c_2a_3 - c_3a_2 & c_3a_1 - c_1a_3 & c_1a_2 - c_2a_1 \\ a_2b_3 - a_3b_2 & a_3b_1 - a_1b_3 & a_1b_2 - a_2b_1 \end{vmatrix}$

Example 6. Find the determinant of cofactors of the determinant $\begin{vmatrix} 1 & 3 & 3 \\ -4 & 3 & 6 \\ 4 & -7 & 9 \end{vmatrix}$ by Direct Method.

Sol. Let $\Delta = \begin{vmatrix} 1 & 3 & 3 \\ -4 & 3 & 6 \\ 4 & -7 & 9 \end{vmatrix}$

***Step* I** Write down the three rows of the Δ and rewrite first two rows.

i.e.
$$\begin{matrix} 1 & 3 & 3 \\ -4 & 3 & 6 \\ 4 & -7 & 9 \\ 1 & 3 & 3 \\ -4 & 3 & 6 \end{matrix}$$

***Step* II** After step I, rewrite first two columns

$$\text{i.e.} \quad \begin{array}{ccccc} 1 & 3 & 3 & 1 & 3 \\ -4 & 3 & 6 & -4 & 3 \\ 4 & -7 & 9 & 4 & -7 \\ 1 & 3 & 3 & 1 & 3 \\ -4 & 3 & 6 & -4 & 3 \end{array}$$

***Step* III** After Step II, deleting first row and first column, then we get all cofactors i.e.,

$$\begin{array}{cccc} 3 & 6 & -4 & 3 \\ -7 & 9 & 4 & -7 \\ 3 & 3 & 1 & 3 \\ 3 & 6 & -4 & 3 \end{array}$$

$$\text{or} \quad \Delta^c = \begin{vmatrix} 69 & 60 & 16 \\ -48 & -3 & 19 \\ 9 & -18 & 15 \end{vmatrix}$$

Example 7. If the value of a third order determinant is 12, find the value of the square of the determinant formed by the cofactors.

Sol. Here, $n = 3$ and $\Delta = 12$

$\therefore \quad (\Delta^c)^2 = (\Delta^2)^2 = \Delta^4 = 12^4 = 20736$

8.5 Use of Determinants in Coordinate Geometry

(i) Area of triangle whose vertices are $(x_1, y_1), (x_2, y_2)$ and (x_3, y_3) is given by

$$\Delta = \frac{1}{2} \begin{vmatrix} x_1 & y_1 & 1 \\ x_2 & y_2 & 1 \\ x_3 & y_3 & 1 \end{vmatrix}$$

(ii) If points $(x_1, y_1), (x_2, y_2)$ and (x_3, y_3) are collinear, then

$$\begin{vmatrix} x_1 & y_1 & 1 \\ x_2 & y_2 & 1 \\ x_3 & y_3 & 1 \end{vmatrix} = 0$$

(iii) If $a_r x + b_r y + c_r = 0; r = 1, 2, 3$ are the sides of a triangle, then the area of the triangle is given by

$$\Delta = \frac{1}{|2C_1C_2C_3|} \begin{vmatrix} a_1 & b_1 & c_1 \\ a_2 & b_2 & c_2 \\ a_3 & b_3 & c_3 \end{vmatrix}^2$$

where C_1, C_2 and C_3 are the cofactors of the elements c_1, c_2 and c_3 respectively, in the determinant

$$\begin{vmatrix} a_1 & b_1 & c_1 \\ a_2 & b_2 & c_2 \\ a_3 & b_3 & c_3 \end{vmatrix}$$

(iv) Equation of straight line passing through two points (x_1, y_1) and (x_2, y_2) is

$$\begin{vmatrix} x & y & 1 \\ x_1 & y_1 & 1 \\ x_2 & y_2 & 1 \end{vmatrix} = 0$$

(v) If three lines $a_r x + b_r y + c_r = 0;\ r = 1, 2, 3$ are concurrent, then

$$\begin{vmatrix} a_1 & b_1 & c_1 \\ a_2 & b_2 & c_2 \\ a_3 & b_3 & c_3 \end{vmatrix} = 0$$

(vi) If $ax^2 + 2hxy + by^2 + 2gx + 2fy + c = 0$ represents a pair of straight lines, then

$$\begin{vmatrix} a & h & g \\ h & b & f \\ g & f & c \end{vmatrix} = 0$$

(vii) Equation of circle through three non-collinear points $(x_1, y_1), (x_2, y_2)$ and (x_3, y_3) is given by

$$\begin{vmatrix} x^2 + y^2 & x & y & 1 \\ x_1^2 + y_1^2 & x_1 & y_1 & 1 \\ x_2^2 + y_2^2 & x_2 & y_2 & 1 \\ x_3^2 + y_3^2 & x_3 & y_3 & 1 \end{vmatrix} = 0$$

Some Useful Operations

(i) The interchange of ith row and jth row is denoted by $R_i \leftrightarrow R_j$. (In case of column $C_i \leftrightarrow C_j$)

(ii) The addition of m times the elements of jth row to the corresponding elements of ith row is denoted by $R_i \to R_i + mR_j$. (In case of column $C_i \to C_i + mC_j$)

(iii) The addition of m times the elements of jth row and n times the elements of k th row to the corresponding elements of ith row is denoted by

$$R_i \to R_i + mR_j + nR_k.$$

(In case of column $C_i \to C_i + mC_j + nC_k$)

JEE SCANNER

Example Similar to PYQ Asked in JEE Main 2021

Let the area of triangle with vertices $A(1,\alpha)$, $B(\alpha,0)$, and $C(0,\alpha)$ be 6 sq units. If the points $(-\alpha,\alpha)$, $(\alpha,-\alpha)$ and (α,β) are collinear, then β is

(a) 3, −3

(b) 2, −2

(c) 12, −12

(d) 6, 2

Sol. (c) Given that the area of triangle whose vertices are $A(1,\alpha)$, $B(\alpha,0)$, $C(0,\alpha)$ is 6 sq units.

Thus, $\frac{1}{2}\begin{vmatrix} 1 & \alpha & 1 \\ \alpha & 0 & 1 \\ 0 & \alpha & 1 \end{vmatrix} = 6$

$\Rightarrow \left| 1(-\alpha) - \alpha(\alpha - 0) + 1(\alpha^2) \right| = 12$

$\Rightarrow \quad \left| -\alpha - \alpha^2 + \alpha^2 \right| = 12$

$\Rightarrow \quad \alpha = \pm 12$

Take $\alpha = 12$

Thus, $(-12, 12)$, $(12, -12)$, $(12, \beta)$ are collinear.

Then, $\begin{vmatrix} -12 & 12 & 1 \\ 12 & -12 & 1 \\ 12 & \beta & 1 \end{vmatrix} = 0$

$\Rightarrow -12(-12-\beta) - 12(12-12) + 1(12\beta + 144) = 0$

$\Rightarrow \quad 144 + 12\beta + 12\beta + 144 = 0$

$\Rightarrow \quad \beta = -12$

Take $\alpha = -12$

Thus, $(12, -12)$, $(-12, 12)$, $(-12, \beta)$ are collinear.

Then, $\begin{vmatrix} 12 & -12 & 1 \\ -12 & 12 & 1 \\ -12 & \beta & 1 \end{vmatrix} = 0$

$\Rightarrow 12(12-\beta) + 12(-12+12) + 1(-12\beta + 144) = 0$

$\Rightarrow \quad 144 - 12\beta - 12\beta + 144 = 0$

$\Rightarrow \quad \beta = 12$

$\therefore \quad \beta = 12, -12$

Skill Builder

Let the area of triangle with vertices $A(\alpha, 1)$, $\beta(0,\alpha)$ and $C(\alpha, 0)$ be 2 sq units. If the points $(\alpha, -\alpha)$, $(-\alpha, \alpha)$ and (α^2, β) are collinear, then 2β is

(a) 16 (b) −32

(c) 8 (d) −8

For Sol.

■ **For more practice** See Q.3 of Milestone Practice 8.2.

8.6 Properties of Determinants

We shall establish certain properties of a determinant of the third order but reader should note that these are capable of application to a determinant of any order.

● **Property I The value of a determinant remains unaltered when rows are changed into corresponding columns and columns are changed into corresponding rows.**

Proof Let $\Delta = \begin{vmatrix} a_1 & b_1 & c_1 \\ a_2 & b_2 & c_2 \\ a_3 & b_3 & c_3 \end{vmatrix}$

Expanding the determinant along the first row, then

$$\Delta = a_1(b_2c_3 - b_3c_2) - b_1(a_2c_3 - a_3c_2) + c_1(a_2b_3 - a_3b_2)$$

$$= a_1(b_2c_3 - b_3c_2) - a_2(b_1c_3 - b_3c_1) + a_3(b_1c_2 - b_2c_1)$$

$$= \begin{vmatrix} a_1 & a_2 & a_3 \\ b_1 & b_2 & b_3 \\ c_1 & c_2 & c_3 \end{vmatrix}$$

$$= \Delta',$$

where Δ' be the value of the determinant when rows of determinant Δ are changed into corresponding columns.

● **Property II If any two rows (or two columns) of a determinant are interchanged, then the sign of determinant is changed and the numerical value remains unaltered.**

Proof Let $\Delta = \begin{vmatrix} a_1 & b_1 & c_1 \\ a_2 & b_2 & c_2 \\ a_3 & b_3 & c_3 \end{vmatrix}$

Expanding the determinant along the first row, then

$$\Delta = a_1(b_2c_3 - b_3c_2) - b_1(a_2c_3 - a_3c_2) + c_1(a_2b_3 - a_3b_2)$$

$$= -a_2(b_1c_3 - b_3c_1) + b_2(a_1c_3 - a_3c_1) - c_2(a_1b_3 - a_3b_1)$$

$$= -[a_2(b_1c_3 - b_3c_1) - b_2(a_1c_3 - a_3c_1) + c_2(a_1b_3 - a_3b_1)]$$

$$= -\begin{vmatrix} a_2 & b_2 & c_2 \\ a_1 & b_1 & c_1 \\ a_3 & b_3 & c_3 \end{vmatrix} \quad [\text{by } R_1 \leftrightarrow R_2]$$

Hence, $\begin{vmatrix} a_1 & b_1 & c_1 \\ a_2 & b_2 & c_2 \\ a_3 & b_3 & c_3 \end{vmatrix} = -\begin{vmatrix} a_2 & b_2 & c_2 \\ a_1 & b_1 & c_1 \\ a_3 & b_3 & c_3 \end{vmatrix}$

Property III **If two rows (or columns) of a determinant are identical, then the value of the determinant is zero.**

Proof Let $\Delta = \begin{vmatrix} a_1 & b_1 & c_1 \\ a_2 & b_2 & c_2 \\ a_1 & b_1 & c_1 \end{vmatrix} = -\begin{vmatrix} a_1 & b_1 & c_1 \\ a_2 & b_2 & c_2 \\ a_1 & b_1 & c_1 \end{vmatrix} = -\Delta$ [by $R_1 \leftrightarrow R_3$]

$\Rightarrow \quad 2\Delta = 0$

$\therefore \quad \Delta = 0$

Property IV **If the elements of any row (or any column) of a determinant be each multiplied by the same factor k, then the value of the determinant is multiplied by k.**

Proof Let $\Delta = \begin{vmatrix} a_1 & b_1 & c_1 \\ a_2 & b_2 & c_2 \\ a_3 & b_3 & c_3 \end{vmatrix} = a_1 C_{11} + b_1 C_{12} + c_1 C_{13}$

Then, $\begin{vmatrix} ka_1 & kb_1 & kc_1 \\ a_2 & b_2 & c_2 \\ a_3 & b_3 & c_3 \end{vmatrix} = ka_1 C_{11} + kb_1 C_{12} + kc_1 C_{13}$

[where C_{11}, C_{12} and C_{13} are the cofactors of a_1, b_1 and c_1 in Δ]

$= k(a_1 C_{11} + b_1 C_{12} + c_1 C_{13}) = k\Delta$

Property V **If every element of some column (or row) is the sum of two items, then the determinant is equal to the sum of two determinants; one containing the first term in place of each sum, the other only the second term. The remaining elements of both determinants are the same as in the given determinant i.e.**

$$\begin{vmatrix} a_1 + x & b_1 & c_1 \\ a_2 + y & b_2 & c_2 \\ a_3 + z & b_3 & c_3 \end{vmatrix} = \begin{vmatrix} a_1 & b_1 & c_1 \\ a_2 & b_2 & c_2 \\ a_3 & b_3 & c_3 \end{vmatrix} + \begin{vmatrix} x & b_1 & c_1 \\ y & b_2 & c_2 \\ z & b_3 & c_3 \end{vmatrix}$$

Proof Let $\Delta = \begin{vmatrix} a_1 + x & b_1 & c_1 \\ a_2 + y & b_2 & c_2 \\ a_3 + z & b_3 & c_3 \end{vmatrix}$

Expanding the determinant along first column, then

$$\Delta = (a_1 + x)\begin{vmatrix} b_2 & c_2 \\ b_3 & c_3 \end{vmatrix} - (a_2 + y)\begin{vmatrix} b_1 & c_1 \\ b_3 & c_3 \end{vmatrix} + (a_3 + z)\begin{vmatrix} b_1 & c_1 \\ b_2 & c_2 \end{vmatrix}$$

$$= a_1\begin{vmatrix} b_2 & c_2 \\ b_3 & c_3 \end{vmatrix} - a_2\begin{vmatrix} b_1 & c_1 \\ b_3 & c_3 \end{vmatrix} + a_3\begin{vmatrix} b_1 & c_1 \\ b_2 & c_2 \end{vmatrix} + x\begin{vmatrix} b_2 & c_2 \\ b_3 & c_3 \end{vmatrix} - y\begin{vmatrix} b_1 & c_1 \\ b_3 & c_3 \end{vmatrix} + z\begin{vmatrix} b_1 & c_1 \\ b_2 & c_2 \end{vmatrix}$$

$$= \begin{vmatrix} a_1 & b_1 & c_1 \\ a_2 & b_2 & c_2 \\ a_3 & b_3 & c_3 \end{vmatrix} + \begin{vmatrix} x & b_1 & c_1 \\ y & b_2 & c_2 \\ z & b_3 & c_3 \end{vmatrix}$$

JEE Focus Points

- $\begin{vmatrix} a_1 + b_1 + c_1 & d_1 + e_1 & f_1 \\ a_2 + b_2 + c_2 & d_2 + e_2 & f_2 \\ a_3 + b_3 + c_3 & d_3 + e_3 & f_3 \end{vmatrix}$
$= \begin{vmatrix} a_1 & d_1 & f_1 \\ a_2 & d_2 & f_2 \\ a_3 & d_3 & f_3 \end{vmatrix} + \begin{vmatrix} a_1 & e_1 & f_1 \\ a_2 & e_2 & f_2 \\ a_3 & e_3 & f_3 \end{vmatrix} + \begin{vmatrix} b_1 & d_1 & f_1 \\ b_2 & d_2 & f_2 \\ b_3 & d_3 & f_3 \end{vmatrix} + \begin{vmatrix} b_1 & e_1 & f_1 \\ b_2 & e_2 & f_2 \\ b_3 & e_3 & f_3 \end{vmatrix} + \begin{vmatrix} c_1 & d_1 & f_1 \\ c_2 & d_2 & f_2 \\ c_3 & d_3 & f_3 \end{vmatrix} + \begin{vmatrix} c_1 & e_1 & f_1 \\ c_2 & e_2 & f_2 \\ c_3 & e_3 & f_3 \end{vmatrix}$
- If each element of first row of a determinant consists of algebraic sum of p elements, second row consists of algebraic sum of q elements, third row consists of algebraic sum of r elements and so on. Then, given determinant is equivalent to the sum of $p \times q \times r \times \ldots$ other determinants in each of which the elements consists of single term.

Property VI **The value of the determinant does not change, if the elements of any row (or column) are increased or diminished by equimultiples of the corresponding elements of any other row (or column) of the determinant.**

i.e. $\begin{vmatrix} a_1 + mb_1 + nc_1 & b_1 & c_1 \\ a_2 + mb_2 + nc_2 & b_2 & c_2 \\ a_3 + mb_3 + nc_3 & b_3 & c_3 \end{vmatrix} = \begin{vmatrix} a_1 & b_1 & c_1 \\ a_2 & b_2 & c_2 \\ a_3 & b_3 & c_3 \end{vmatrix}$

Proof $\begin{vmatrix} a_1 + mb_1 + nc_1 & b_1 & c_1 \\ a_2 + mb_2 + nc_2 & b_2 & c_2 \\ a_3 + mb_3 + nc_3 & b_3 & c_3 \end{vmatrix}$

$$= \begin{vmatrix} a_1 & b_1 & c_1 \\ a_2 & b_2 & c_2 \\ a_3 & b_3 & c_3 \end{vmatrix} + m\begin{vmatrix} b_1 & b_1 & c_1 \\ b_2 & b_2 & c_2 \\ b_3 & b_3 & c_3 \end{vmatrix} + n\begin{vmatrix} c_1 & b_1 & c_1 \\ c_2 & b_2 & c_2 \\ c_3 & b_3 & c_3 \end{vmatrix}$$

$$= \begin{vmatrix} a_1 & b_1 & c_1 \\ a_2 & b_2 & c_2 \\ a_3 & b_3 & c_3 \end{vmatrix} + m \cdot 0 + n \cdot 0 = \begin{vmatrix} a_1 & b_1 & c_1 \\ a_2 & b_2 & c_2 \\ a_3 & b_3 & c_3 \end{vmatrix}$$

Property VII **If each element on one side or other side or both side of the principal diagonal of determinant is zero, then the value of the determinant is the product of the diagonal element.**

i.e. $\begin{vmatrix} a & 0 & 0 \\ f & b & 0 \\ e & d & c \end{vmatrix} = \begin{vmatrix} a & i & h \\ 0 & b & g \\ 0 & 0 & c \end{vmatrix} = \begin{vmatrix} a & 0 & 0 \\ 0 & b & 0 \\ 0 & 0 & c \end{vmatrix} = abc$

Proof Let $\Delta = \begin{vmatrix} a\cdots & 0\cdots & 0 \\ f & b & 0 \\ e & d & c \end{vmatrix}$

Expanding along R_1, we get $a\begin{vmatrix} b & 0 \\ d & c \end{vmatrix} = a(bc) = abc$

Property VIII If determinant Δ becomes zero on putting $x=\alpha$, then we say that $(x-\alpha)$ is a factor of Δ.

i.e. if $\Delta = \begin{vmatrix} x & 5 & 2 \\ x^2 & 9 & 4 \\ x^3 & 16 & 8 \end{vmatrix}$

At $x=2, \Delta=0$ [because C_1 and C_3 are identical at $x=2$]

and at $x=0, \Delta=0$ [because all elements of C_1 are zero]

Hence, $(x-0)$ and $(x-2)$ are the factors of Δ.

JEE Focus Points

- It should be noted that while applying operations on determinant that atleast one row (or column) must remain unchanged.
- Maximum number of operations at a time = order – 1
- It should be noted that, if the row (or column) which is changed by multiplied a non-zero number, then the determinant will be divided by that number.

Example 8. Evaluate $\begin{vmatrix} 10 & 11 & 20 \\ 12 & 13 & 24 \\ 9 & 10 & 18 \end{vmatrix}$.

Sol. Let $\Delta = \begin{vmatrix} 10 & 11 & 20 \\ 12 & 13 & 24 \\ 9 & 10 & 18 \end{vmatrix}$

Applying $C_3 \to C_3 - 2C_1$, then

$$\Delta = \begin{vmatrix} 10 & 11 & 0 \\ 12 & 13 & 0 \\ 9 & 10 & 0 \end{vmatrix} = 0 \quad [\because \text{all elements of } C_3 \text{ are zero}]$$

$\therefore \quad \Delta = 0$

Example 9. Prove that $\begin{vmatrix} \alpha & \beta & \gamma \\ \theta & \phi & \psi \\ \lambda & \mu & \nu \end{vmatrix} = \begin{vmatrix} \beta & \mu & \phi \\ \alpha & \lambda & \theta \\ \gamma & \nu & \psi \end{vmatrix}$.

Sol. LHS $= \begin{vmatrix} \alpha & \beta & \gamma \\ \theta & \phi & \psi \\ \lambda & \mu & \nu \end{vmatrix} = \begin{vmatrix} \alpha & \theta & \lambda \\ \beta & \phi & \mu \\ \gamma & \psi & \nu \end{vmatrix}$

[interchanging rows and columns]

$$= (-1)\begin{vmatrix} \alpha & \lambda & \theta \\ \beta & \mu & \phi \\ \gamma & \nu & \psi \end{vmatrix} \quad [C_2 \leftrightarrow C_3]$$

$$= (-1)^2\begin{vmatrix} \beta & \mu & \phi \\ \alpha & \lambda & \theta \\ \gamma & \nu & \psi \end{vmatrix} \quad [R_1 \leftrightarrow R_2]$$

$$= \begin{vmatrix} \beta & \mu & \phi \\ \alpha & \lambda & \theta \\ \gamma & \nu & \psi \end{vmatrix} = \text{RHS}$$

Example 10. Using the properties of determinant and without expanding, prove that $\begin{vmatrix} \alpha & \alpha+\beta & \alpha+\gamma \\ \beta & \beta+\gamma & \beta+\alpha \\ \gamma & \gamma+\alpha & \gamma+\beta \end{vmatrix}$

$$= (\alpha+\beta+\gamma)[-\gamma^2-\alpha^2-\beta^2+\alpha\beta+\beta\gamma+\gamma\alpha].$$

Sol. Let LHS $= \Delta = \begin{vmatrix} \alpha & \alpha+\beta & \alpha+\gamma \\ \beta & \beta+\gamma & \beta+\alpha \\ \gamma & \gamma+\alpha & \gamma+\beta \end{vmatrix}$

Applying $C_2 \to C_2 - C_1$ and $C_3 \to C_3 - C_1$, then

$$\Delta = \begin{vmatrix} \alpha & \beta & \gamma \\ \beta & \gamma & \alpha \\ \gamma & \alpha & \beta \end{vmatrix}$$

Applying $C_1 \to C_1 + C_2 + C_3$, then

$$\Delta = \begin{vmatrix} \alpha+\beta+\gamma & \beta & \gamma \\ \alpha+\beta+\gamma & \gamma & \alpha \\ \alpha+\beta+\gamma & \alpha & \beta \end{vmatrix} = (\alpha+\beta+\gamma)\begin{vmatrix} 1 & \beta & \gamma \\ 1 & \gamma & \alpha \\ 1 & \alpha & \beta \end{vmatrix}$$

Applying $R_2 \to R_2 - R_1$ and $R_3 \to R_3 + R_1$, then

$$\Delta = (\alpha+\beta+\gamma)\begin{vmatrix} 1 & \beta & \gamma \\ 0 & \gamma-\beta & \alpha-\gamma \\ 2 & \alpha+\beta & \beta+\gamma \end{vmatrix}$$

$$= (\alpha+\beta+\gamma)[1(\gamma^2-\beta^2-\alpha^2+\alpha\gamma-\alpha\beta+\beta\gamma) + 2(\alpha\beta-\beta\gamma-\gamma^2+\beta\gamma)]$$

$$= (\alpha+\beta+\gamma)[-\gamma^2-\alpha^2-\beta^2+\alpha\beta+\beta\gamma+\gamma\alpha] = \text{RHS}$$

Example 11. Without expanding as far as possible, prove that $\begin{vmatrix} 1 & 1 & 1 \\ x & y & z \\ x^3 & y^3 & z^3 \end{vmatrix} = (x-y)(y-z)(z-x)(x+y+z)$.

Sol. Let $\Delta = \begin{vmatrix} 1 & 1 & 1 \\ x & y & z \\ x^3 & y^3 & z^3 \end{vmatrix}$

for $x=y, \Delta=0$ [$\because C_1$ and C_2 are identical]

Hence, $(x-y)$ is a factor of Δ. Similarly, $(y-z)$ and $(z-x)$ are factors of Δ. But Δ is a homogeneous expression of the 4 th degree in x, y and z.

There must be one more factor of the 1st degree in x, y and z say $k(x+y+z)$, where k is a constant.

Let $\Delta = k(x-y)(y-z)(z-x)(x+y+z)$

On putting $x=0, y=1$ and $z=2$, then

$$\begin{vmatrix} 1 & 1 & 1 \\ 0 & 1 & 2 \\ 0 & 1 & 8 \end{vmatrix} = k(0-1)(1-2)(2-0)(0+1+2)$$

$\Rightarrow \quad 1\cdot(8-2) = k(-1)(-1)(2)(3)$

$\therefore \quad k = 1$

$\Rightarrow \quad \Delta = (x-y)(y-z)(z-x)(x+y+z) = \text{RHS}$

Example 12. Solve for x, $\begin{vmatrix} 2x-1 & 3x & 4x \\ 5x+4 & 6x+1 & 8x+2 \\ 6x-1 & 9x & 12x \end{vmatrix} = 8$.

Sol. Given, $\begin{vmatrix} 2x-1 & 3x & 4x \\ 5x+4 & 6x+1 & 8x+2 \\ 6x-1 & 9x & 12x \end{vmatrix} = 8$

Applying $R_3 \to R_3 - 3R_1$, then

$$\begin{vmatrix} 2x-1 & 3x & 4x \\ 5x+4 & 6x+1 & 8x+2 \\ 2 & 0 & 0 \end{vmatrix} = 8$$

Expanding along 3rd row, we get

$$2\begin{vmatrix} 3x & 4x \\ 6x+1 & 8x+2 \end{vmatrix} = 8$$

$$\Rightarrow \quad 2[3x(8x+2) - 4x(6x+1)] = 8$$

$$\Rightarrow \quad 2[24x^2 + 6x - 24x^2 - 4x] = 8 \Rightarrow 2[2x] = 8$$

$$\Rightarrow \quad 4x = 8 \Rightarrow x = 2$$

JEE SCANNER

Example Similar to PYQ Asked in JEE Main 2024

The value of α, for which $\begin{vmatrix} 1 & 5 & \alpha+5 \\ 1 & 2 & \alpha+2 \\ 2\alpha+5 & 3\alpha+2 & 0 \end{vmatrix} = 0$ *is*

(a) $-2 \pm 2\sqrt{3}$ (b) $-2 \pm \sqrt{3}$
(c) $-3 \pm \sqrt{2}$ (d) $2 + \sqrt{2}$

Sol. (b) Given, $\begin{vmatrix} 1 & 5 & \alpha+5 \\ 1 & 2 & \alpha+2 \\ 2\alpha+5 & 3\alpha+2 & 0 \end{vmatrix} = 0$

Applying $C_3 \to C_3 - C_2$, we get

$$\begin{vmatrix} 1 & 5 & \alpha \\ 1 & 2 & \alpha \\ 2\alpha+5 & 3\alpha+2 & -3\alpha-2 \end{vmatrix} = 0$$

Expanding along R_1, we get

$$-3\alpha^2 - 8\alpha - 4 + 10\alpha^2 + 40\alpha + 10 - \alpha^2 - 8\alpha = 0$$

$$\Rightarrow \quad 6\alpha^2 + 24\alpha + 6 = 0$$

$$\Rightarrow \quad \alpha^2 + 4\alpha + 1 = 0 \Rightarrow \alpha = -2 \pm \sqrt{3}$$

Skill Builder

The value of a, for which

$$\begin{vmatrix} 4a & 6a+2 & 8a+1 \\ 6a+2 & 9a+3 & 12a \\ 8a+1 & 12a & 16a+2 \end{vmatrix} = 0 \text{ is}$$

For Sol.

(a) $\frac{11}{97}$ (b) $\frac{-11}{97}$ (c) $\frac{19}{97}$ (d) $\frac{-19}{97}$

■ **For more practice** See Q.8 of Milestone Practice 8.2.

Example 13. Solve for x,

$$\begin{vmatrix} x^2+a^2 & ab & ac \\ ab & x^2+b^2 & bc \\ ac & bc & x^2+c^2 \end{vmatrix} = 0$$

Sol. Let LHS $= \Delta = \begin{vmatrix} x^2+a^2 & ab & ac \\ ab & x^2+b^2 & bc \\ ac & bc & x^2+c^2 \end{vmatrix}$

On taking common a, b and c form R_1, R_2 and R_3 respectively, then

$$\Delta = \frac{1}{abc}\begin{vmatrix} \frac{x^2}{a}+a & b & c \\ a & \frac{x^2}{b}+b & c \\ a & b & \frac{x^2}{c}+c \end{vmatrix}$$

Applying $R_3 \to R_3 - R_1$ and $R_2 \to R_2 - R_1$, then

$$\Delta = \frac{1}{abc}\begin{vmatrix} \frac{x^2}{a}+a & b & c \\ \frac{-x^2}{a} & \frac{x^2}{b} & 0 \\ \frac{-x^2}{a} & 0 & \frac{x^2}{c} \end{vmatrix}$$

Applying $R_3 \to R_3 - R_2$, then

$$\Delta = \frac{1}{abc}\begin{vmatrix} \frac{x^2}{a}+a & b & c \\ \frac{-x^2}{a} & \frac{x^2}{b} & 0 \\ 0 & \frac{-x^2}{b} & \frac{x^2}{c} \end{vmatrix}$$

Now, applying $C_2 \to bC_2$ and $C_3 \to cC_3$, then we get

$$\Delta = \frac{1}{a}\begin{vmatrix} \frac{x^2}{a}+a & b^2 & c^2 \\ \frac{-x^2}{a} & x^2 & 0 \\ 0 & -x^2 & x^2 \end{vmatrix}$$

Now, applying $C_2 \to C_2 + C_3$, then we get

$$\Delta = \frac{1}{a}\begin{vmatrix} \frac{x^2}{a}+a & b^2+c^2 & c^2 \\ \frac{-x^2}{a} & x^2 & 0 \\ 0 & 0 & x^2 \end{vmatrix}$$

$$= \frac{1}{a}\left[x^2\left\{x^2 \times \left(\frac{x^2}{a}+a\right) + \frac{x^2}{a}(b^2+c^2)\right\}\right]$$

$$= \frac{x^2}{a}\left[\frac{x^4}{a} + ax^2 + \frac{x^2b^2}{a} + \frac{x^2c^2}{a}\right] = \frac{x^4}{a^2}[x^2 + a^2 + b^2 + c^2]$$

Now, since LHS = 0

$\therefore \quad \dfrac{x^4}{a^2}[x^2+a^2+b^2+c^2]=0$

$\Rightarrow \quad x^4=0$ or $x^2+a^2+b^2+c^2=0$

$\Rightarrow \quad x=0$ or $x^2=-a^2-b^2-c^2$

$\Rightarrow \quad x=0$ or $x=\pm i\sqrt{a^2+b^2+c^2}$, where $i=\sqrt{-1}$.

Example 14. If a, b and c are all different and if $\begin{vmatrix} b^2+c^2 & ab & ac \\ ba & c^2+a^2 & bc \\ ca & cb & a^2+b^2 \end{vmatrix}=1$, then prove that $abc=\dfrac{1}{2}$.

Sol. Let $\Delta=\begin{vmatrix} b^2+c^2 & ab & ac \\ ba & c^2+a^2 & bc \\ ca & cb & a^2+b^2 \end{vmatrix}$

On multiplying R_1, R_2 and R_3 by a, b and c respectively, then

$$\Delta=\frac{1}{abc}\begin{vmatrix} a(b^2+c^2) & a^2b & a^2c \\ b^2a & b(c^2+a^2) & b^2c \\ c^2a & c^2b & c(a^2+b^2) \end{vmatrix}$$

$$=\frac{abc}{abc}\begin{vmatrix} b^2+c^2 & a^2 & a^2 \\ b^2 & c^2+a^2 & b^2 \\ c^2 & c^2 & a^2+b^2 \end{vmatrix}$$

Applying $R_1 \to R_1+R_2+R_3$, then

$$\Delta=2\begin{vmatrix} (b^2+c^2) & (a^2+c^2) & (a^2+b^2) \\ b^2 & c^2+a^2 & b^2 \\ c^2 & c^2 & a^2+b^2 \end{vmatrix}$$

Applying $R_2 \to R_2-R_1$ and $R_3 \to R_3-R_1$, then

$$\Delta=2\begin{vmatrix} b^2+c^2 & a^2+c^2 & a^2+b^2 \\ -c^2 & 0 & -a^2 \\ -b^2 & -a^2 & 0 \end{vmatrix}$$

Applying $R_1 \to R_1+R_2+R_3$, we get

$$\Delta=2\begin{vmatrix} 0 & c^2 & b^2 \\ -c^2 & 0 & -a^2 \\ -b^2 & -a^2 & 0 \end{vmatrix}$$

$$\Delta=2[-c^2(0-a^2b^2)+b^2(a^2c^2-0)]$$

$$=2[a^2b^2c^2+a^2b^2c^2]=4a^2b^2c^2 \quad \text{...(i)}$$

Since, given that $\Delta=1$

$\therefore \quad 4a^2b^2c^2=1 \Rightarrow a^2b^2c^2=\dfrac{1}{4} \Rightarrow abc=\dfrac{1}{2}$

Milestone Practice 8.2

1. If λ and μ are the cofactors of 3 and -2 respectively, in the determinant $\begin{vmatrix} 1 & 0 & -2 \\ 3 & -1 & 2 \\ 4 & 5 & 6 \end{vmatrix}$, the value of $\lambda + \mu$ is

(a) 5 (b) 7 (c) 9 (d) 11

2. An equilateral triangle has each of its sides of length 4 cm. If $(x_r, y_r)(r = 1, 2, 3)$ are its vertices, the value of $\begin{vmatrix} x_1 & y_1 & 1 \\ x_2 & y_2 & 1 \\ x_3 & y_3 & 1 \end{vmatrix}^2$ is

(a) 192 (b) 768
(c) 1024 (d) 128

3. If the area of triangle with vertices $P(2, \alpha)$, $Q(2\alpha, 0)$ and $R(0, \alpha)$ be 8 sq units. if the points $(\alpha, -2\alpha)$, $(-\alpha, \alpha)$ and (α, β) are collinear, then positive integral value of β is

(a) 16 (b) 14
(c) 17 (d) 12

4. If the lines $ax + y + 1 = 0$, $x + by + 1 = 0$ and $x + y + c = 0$ (a, b and c being distinct and different from 1) are concurrent, the value of $\frac{a}{a-1} + \frac{b}{b-1} + \frac{c}{c-1}$ is

(a) 0 (b) 1
(c) 2 (d) 3

5. If $p + q + r = 0 = a + b + c$, the value of the determinant $\begin{vmatrix} pa & qb & rc \\ qc & ra & pb \\ rb & pc & qa \end{vmatrix}$ is

(a) 0 (b) $pa + qb + rc$
(c) 1 (d) None of these

6. If p, q and r are in AP, the value of determinant
$$\begin{vmatrix} a^2 + 2^{n+1} + 2p & b^2 + 2^{n+2} + 3q & c^2 + p \\ 2^n + p & 2^{n+1} + q & 2q \\ a^2 + 2^n + p & b^2 + 2^{n+1} + 2q & c^2 - r \end{vmatrix}$$ is

(a) 1 (b) 0
(c) $a^2b^2c^2 - 2^n$ (d) $(a^2 + b^2 + c^2) - 2^n q$

7. If $\begin{vmatrix} x & 3 & 6 \\ 3 & 6 & x \\ 6 & x & 3 \end{vmatrix} = \begin{vmatrix} 2 & x & 7 \\ x & 7 & 2 \\ 7 & 2 & x \end{vmatrix} = \begin{vmatrix} 4 & 5 & x \\ 5 & x & 4 \\ x & 4 & 5 \end{vmatrix} = 0$, then x is equal to

(a) 0 (b) -9
(c) 3 (d) None of these

8. The value of x for which $\begin{vmatrix} -x & x & 2 \\ 2 & x & -x \\ x & -2 & -x \end{vmatrix} = 0$ is

(a) ± 2 (b) ± 3
(c) ± 5 (d) ± 7

9. If $a + b + c = 0$, the one root of $\begin{vmatrix} a - x & c & b \\ c & b - x & a \\ b & a & c - x \end{vmatrix} = 0$ is

(a) 1 (b) 2
(c) $a^2 + b^2 + c^2$ (d) 0

10. If $a^2 + b^2 + c^2 = -2$ and
$$f(x) = \begin{vmatrix} 1 + a^2x & (1 + b^2)x & (1 + c^2)x \\ (1 + a^2)x & 1 + b^2x & (1 + c^2)x \\ (1 + a^2)x & (1 + b^2)x & 1 + c^2x \end{vmatrix}$$, the $f(x)$ is a polynomial of degree

(a) 0 (b) 1
(c) 2 (d) 3

11. If a, b, c, d, e and f are in GP, the value of $\begin{vmatrix} a^2 & d^2 & x \\ b^2 & e^2 & y \\ c^2 & f^2 & z \end{vmatrix}$, is

(a) depends on x and y
(b) depends on x and z
(c) depends on y and z
(d) independent of x, y and z

Answer Key

1. (c)	2. (a)	3. (a)	4. (c)	5. (a)	6. (b)
7. (b)	8. (a)	9. (d)	10. (c)	11. (d)	

For Detailed Solution

Milestone 3 Solving a System of Linear Equations

- Largest Value of a Third Order Determinant • Multiplication of Two Determinants of the Same Order
- System of Linear Equations • Cramer's Rule • Nature of Solutions of System of Linear Equations
- System of Homogeneous Linear Equations

8.7 Largest Value of a Third Order Determinant

Example 15. Find the largest value of a third order determinant whose elements are 0 or 1.

Sol. Let $\Delta = \begin{vmatrix} a_1 & b_1 & c_1 \\ a_2 & b_2 & c_2 \\ a_3 & b_3 & c_3 \end{vmatrix}$

$$\Delta = a_1(b_2c_3 - b_3c_2) - b_1(a_2c_3 - a_3c_2) + c_1(a_2b_3 - a_3b_2)$$
$$= (a_1b_2c_3 + a_2b_3c_1 + a_3b_1c_2) - (b_1c_3a_2 + b_2c_1a_3 + b_3c_2a_1)$$

Since, each element of Δ is either 0 or 1, therefore the value of the Δ cannot exceed 3. But to attain this value, each expression with a positive sign must equal 1, while those with a negative sign must be 0.

However, if $a_1b_2c_3 = a_2b_3c_1 = a_3b_1c_2 = 1$, every element of the determinant must be 1, making its value zero.

Thus, noting that

$$\begin{vmatrix} 0 & 1 & 1 \\ 1 & 0 & 1 \\ 1 & 1 & 0 \end{vmatrix} = 2$$

The largest value of Δ is 2.

Example 16. Find the largest value of a third order determinant, whose elements are 1 or −1.

Sol. Let $\Delta = \begin{vmatrix} a_1 & b_1 & c_1 \\ a_2 & b_2 & c_2 \\ a_3 & b_3 & c_3 \end{vmatrix}$

$$\therefore \Delta = a_1(b_2c_3 - b_3c_2) - b_1(a_2c_3 - a_3c_2) + c_1(a_2b_3 - a_3b_2)$$
$$= (a_1b_2c_3 + a_2b_3c_1 + a_3b_1c_2) - (b_1c_3a_2 + b_2c_1a_3 + b_3c_2a_1)$$

Since, each element of Δ is either 1 or −1, therefore the value of the Δ cannot exceed 6. But it can be 6 only if

$$a_1b_2c_3 = a_2b_3c_1 = a_3b_1c_2 = 1 \quad \text{...(i)}$$

and $$b_1c_3a_2 = b_2c_1a_3 = b_3c_2a_1 = -1 \quad \text{...(ii)}$$

In the first case, the product of the nine elements of the determinant equals 1, while it is −1 in the second case, so the two cannot occur simultaneously i.e., the determinant cannot equal 6. The following determinant satisfies the given conditions and equals the largest value

$$\begin{vmatrix} -1 & 1 & 1 \\ 1 & -1 & 1 \\ 1 & 1 & -1 \end{vmatrix} = -1(1-1) - 1(-1-1) + 1(1+1) = 4$$

8.8 Multiplication of Two Determinants of the Same Order

Let the two determinants of third order be

$$\Delta_1 = \begin{vmatrix} a_1 & b_1 & c_1 \\ a_2 & b_2 & c_2 \\ a_3 & b_3 & c_3 \end{vmatrix}$$

and $$\Delta_2 = \begin{vmatrix} \alpha_1 & \beta_1 & \gamma_1 \\ \alpha_2 & \beta_2 & \gamma_2 \\ \alpha_3 & \beta_3 & \gamma_3 \end{vmatrix}$$

Let Δ be their product.

Method of Multiplication (Row by Row)

Take the first row of Δ_1 and the first row of Δ_2 i.e., a_1, b_1, c_1 and $\alpha_1, \beta_1, \gamma_1$ multiplying the corresponding elements and add. The result is $a_1\alpha_1 + b_1\beta_1 + c_1\gamma_1$ is the first element of first row of Δ.

Now, similar product first row of Δ_1 and second row of Δ_2 gives $a_1\alpha_2 + b_1\beta_2 + c_1\gamma_2$ is the second element of first row of Δ and the product of first row of Δ_1 and third row of Δ_2 gives $a_1\alpha_3 + b_1\beta_3 + c_1\gamma_3$ is the third element of first row of Δ. The second row and third row of Δ is obtained by multiplying second row and third row of Δ_1 with 1st, 2nd, 3rd row of Δ_2 in the above manner.

Hence, $\Delta = \Delta_1 \times \Delta_2 = \begin{vmatrix} a_1 & b_1 & c_1 \\ a_2 & b_2 & c_2 \\ a_3 & b_3 & c_3 \end{vmatrix} \times \begin{vmatrix} \alpha_1 & \beta_1 & \gamma_1 \\ \alpha_2 & \beta_2 & \gamma_2 \\ \alpha_3 & \beta_3 & \gamma_3 \end{vmatrix}$

$$= \begin{vmatrix} a_1\alpha_1 + b_1\beta_1 + c_1\gamma_1 & a_1\alpha_2 + b_1\beta_2 + c_1\gamma_2 & a_1\alpha_3 + b_1\beta_3 + c_1\gamma_3 \\ a_2\alpha_1 + b_2\beta_1 + c_2\gamma_1 & a_2\alpha_2 + b_2\beta_2 + c_2\gamma_2 & a_2\alpha_3 + b_2\beta_3 + c_2\gamma_3 \\ a_3\alpha_1 + b_3\beta_1 + c_3\gamma_1 & a_3\alpha_2 + b_3\beta_2 + c_3\gamma_2 & a_3\alpha_3 + b_3\beta_3 + c_3\gamma_3 \end{vmatrix}$$

Multiplication can also be performed row by column or column by row or column by column as required in the problem.

Example 17. Evaluate

$\Delta = \begin{vmatrix} 1 & -1 & 0 \\ 2 & 3 & 4 \\ 0 & 1 & 2 \end{vmatrix} \times \begin{vmatrix} 2 & 2 & -4 \\ -4 & 2 & -4 \\ 2 & -1 & 5 \end{vmatrix}$ using the concept of multiplication of determinants. If $\Delta = x$, then find x.

Sol. Let $\Delta = \begin{vmatrix} 1 & -1 & 0 \\ 2 & 3 & 4 \\ 0 & 1 & 2 \end{vmatrix} \times \begin{vmatrix} 2 & 2 & -4 \\ -4 & 2 & -4 \\ 2 & -1 & 5 \end{vmatrix}$

$$= \begin{vmatrix} 2-2+0 & -4-2+0 & 2+1+0 \\ 4+6-16 & -8+6-16 & 4-3+20 \\ 0+2-8 & 0+2-8 & 0-1+10 \end{vmatrix}$$

$$= \begin{vmatrix} 0 & -6 & 3 \\ -6 & -18 & 21 \\ -6 & -6 & 9 \end{vmatrix}$$

Applying $R_2 \to R_2 - R_3$, then

$$\Delta = \begin{vmatrix} 0 & -6 & 3 \\ 0 & -12 & 12 \\ 6 & -6 & 9 \end{vmatrix}$$

Now, applying $R_3 \to \frac{1}{6}R_3$, $R_2 \to \frac{1}{12}R_2$, we get

$$\Delta = \begin{vmatrix} 0 & -6 & 3 \\ 0 & -1 & 1 \\ 1 & -1 & \frac{3}{2} \end{vmatrix}$$

Expand along C_1, we get

$$\Delta = 1(-6+3) = -3$$

Now, $\Delta = x$

$\therefore \quad x = -3$

Example 18. If $ax_1^2 + by_1^2 + cz_1^2 = ax_2^2 + by_2^2 + cz_2^2 = ax_3^2 + by_3^2 + cz_3^2 = d$, $ax_2x_3 + by_2y_3 + cz_2z_3 = ax_3x_1 + by_3y_1 + cz_3z_1 = ax_1x_2 + by_1y_2 + cz_1z_2 = f$, then prove that $\begin{vmatrix} x_1 & y_1 & z_1 \\ x_2 & y_2 & z_2 \\ x_3 & y_3 & z_3 \end{vmatrix} = (d-f)\left\{\frac{(d+2f)}{abc}\right\}^{1/2}$.

Sol. Let LHS $= \Delta = \begin{vmatrix} x_1 & y_1 & z_1 \\ x_2 & y_2 & z_2 \\ x_3 & y_3 & z_3 \end{vmatrix}$

$$\therefore \Delta^2 = \Delta \times \Delta = \begin{vmatrix} x_1 & y_1 & z_1 \\ x_2 & y_2 & z_2 \\ x_3 & y_3 & z_3 \end{vmatrix} \times \begin{vmatrix} x_1 & y_1 & z_1 \\ x_2 & y_2 & z_2 \\ x_3 & y_3 & z_3 \end{vmatrix}$$

$$= \frac{1}{abc}\begin{vmatrix} x_1 & y_1 & z_1 \\ x_2 & y_2 & z_2 \\ x_3 & y_3 & z_3 \end{vmatrix} \times \begin{vmatrix} ax_1 & by_1 & cz_1 \\ ax_2 & by_2 & cz_2 \\ ax_3 & by_3 & cz_3 \end{vmatrix}$$

$$= \frac{1}{abc}\begin{vmatrix} ax_1^2 + by_1^2 + cz_1^2 & ax_1x_2 + by_1y_2 + cz_1z_2 & ax_3x_1 + by_3y_1 + cz_3z_1 \\ ax_1x_2 + by_1y_2 + cz_1z_2 & ax_2^2 + by_2^2 + cz_2^2 & ax_2x_3 + by_2y_3 + cz_2z_3 \\ ax_3x_1 + by_3y_1 + cz_3z_1 & ax_2x_3 + by_2y_3 + cz_2z_3 & ax_3^2 + by_3^2 + cz_3^2 \end{vmatrix}$$

[multiplying row by row]

$$= \frac{1}{abc}\begin{vmatrix} d & f & f \\ f & d & f \\ f & f & d \end{vmatrix} \quad \text{[given]}$$

Applying $C_1 \to C_1 + C_2 + C_3$, then

$$= \frac{1}{abc}\begin{vmatrix} d+2f & f & f \\ d+2f & d & f \\ d+2f & f & d \end{vmatrix} = \frac{(d+2f)}{abc}\begin{vmatrix} 1 & f & f \\ 1 & d & f \\ 1 & f & d \end{vmatrix}$$

Applying $R_2 \to R_2 - R_1$ and $R_3 \to R_3 - R_1$, then

$$= \frac{(d+2f)}{abc}\begin{vmatrix} 1 & f & f \\ 0 & d-f & 0 \\ 0 & 0 & d-f \end{vmatrix}$$

$$= \frac{(d+2f)}{abc}(d-f)^2$$

$$\therefore \Delta = (d-f)\left\{\frac{d+2f}{abc}\right\}^{1/2} = \text{RHS}$$

An Important Property

If A_1, B_1 and $C_1, \ldots$ are respectively the cofactors of the elements a_1, b_1 and $c_1, \ldots$ of the determinant.

$$\Delta = \begin{vmatrix} a_1 & b_1 & c_1 \\ a_2 & b_2 & c_2 \\ a_3 & b_3 & c_3 \end{vmatrix}, \Delta \neq 0, \text{ then } \begin{vmatrix} A_1 & B_1 & C_1 \\ A_2 & B_2 & C_2 \\ A_3 & B_3 & C_3 \end{vmatrix} = \Delta^2$$

Proof Consider

$$\begin{vmatrix} a_1 & b_1 & c_1 \\ a_2 & b_2 & c_2 \\ a_3 & b_3 & c_3 \end{vmatrix} \times \begin{vmatrix} A_1 & B_1 & C_1 \\ A_2 & B_2 & C_2 \\ A_3 & B_3 & C_3 \end{vmatrix}$$

$$= \begin{vmatrix} a_1A_1 + b_1B_1 + c_1C_1 & a_1A_2 + b_1B_2 + c_1C_2 & a_1A_3 + b_1B_3 + c_1C_3 \\ a_2A_1 + b_2B_1 + c_2C_1 & a_2A_2 + b_2B_2 + c_2C_2 & a_2A_3 + b_2B_3 + c_2C_3 \\ a_3A_1 + b_3B_1 + c_3C_1 & a_3A_2 + b_3B_2 + c_3C_2 & a_3A_3 + b_3B_3 + c_3C_3 \end{vmatrix}$$

[multiplying row by row]

$$= \begin{vmatrix} \Delta & 0 & 0 \\ 0 & \Delta & 0 \\ 0 & 0 & \Delta \end{vmatrix} = \Delta^3 \quad \left[\text{as } a_iA_j + b_iB_j + c_iC_j = \begin{cases} \Delta, & i = j \\ 0, & i \neq j \end{cases}\right]$$

$$\Rightarrow \Delta \begin{vmatrix} A_1 & B_1 & C_1 \\ A_2 & B_2 & C_2 \\ A_3 & B_3 & C_3 \end{vmatrix} = \Delta^3 \text{ or } \begin{vmatrix} A_1 & B_1 & C_1 \\ A_2 & B_2 & C_2 \\ A_3 & B_3 & C_3 \end{vmatrix} = \Delta^2 \ [\because \Delta \neq 0]$$

Note Let $\Delta \neq 0$ and Δ^c denotes the determinant formed by the cofactors of Δ and n is order of determinant, then

$$\Delta^c = \Delta^{n-1}$$

This is known as power cofactor formula.

Example 19. Show that

$$\begin{vmatrix} x & a & x+a \\ y & b & y+b \\ z & c & z+c \end{vmatrix}^2 = \begin{vmatrix} bz - cy & -az + cx & ay - bx \\ bz - cy & -az + cx & ay - bx \\ -bz + cy & az - cz & -ay + bx \end{vmatrix}.$$

Sol. Let $\Delta(x) = \begin{vmatrix} x & a & x+a \\ y & b & y+b \\ z & c & z+c \end{vmatrix}$

Cofactors of 1st row of Δ are

$bz - cy, bz - cy, -bz + cy$

Cofactors of 2nd row of Δ are

$-az + cx, -az + cx, az - cx$

Cofactors of 3rd row of Δ are

$ay - bx, ay - bx, -ay + bx$

Hence, the determinant of the cofactors of Δ is

$$\Delta^c = \begin{vmatrix} bz - cy & bz - cy & -bz + cy \\ -az + cx & -az + cx & az - cx \\ ay - bx & ay - bx & -ay + bx \end{vmatrix}$$

Interchanging rows into columns, we get

$$\Delta^c = \begin{vmatrix} bz - cy & -az + cx & ay - bx \\ bz - cy & -az + cx & ay - bx \\ -bz + cy & az - cx & -ay + bx \end{vmatrix}$$

$$= \begin{vmatrix} x & a & x+a \\ y & b & y+b \\ z & c & z+c \end{vmatrix}^2 \quad [\because \Delta^c = \Delta^2]$$

Example 20. Prove the following by multiplication of determinants and power cofactor formula

$$\begin{vmatrix} 0 & c & b \\ c & 0 & a \\ b & a & 0 \end{vmatrix}^2 = \begin{vmatrix} b^2 + c^2 & ab & ac \\ ab & c^2 + a^2 & bc \\ ac & bc & a^2 + b^2 \end{vmatrix}$$

$$= \begin{vmatrix} -a^2 & ab & ac \\ ab & -b^2 & bc \\ ac & bc & -c^2 \end{vmatrix} = 4a^2b^2c^2.$$

Sol. Let $\Delta = \begin{vmatrix} 0 & c & b \\ c & 0 & a \\ b & a & 0 \end{vmatrix}$.

Expanding along R_1, then

$\Delta = 0 - c(0 - ab) + b(ac - 0) = 2abc$

$$\therefore \begin{vmatrix} 0 & c & b \\ c & 0 & a \\ b & a & 0 \end{vmatrix}^2 = \Delta^2 = (2abc)^2 = 4a^2b^2c^2 \quad \ldots(\text{i})$$

Also,

$$\begin{vmatrix} 0 & c & b \\ c & 0 & a \\ b & a & 0 \end{vmatrix}^2 = \begin{vmatrix} 0 & c & b \\ c & 0 & a \\ b & a & 0 \end{vmatrix} \times \begin{vmatrix} 0 & c & b \\ c & 0 & a \\ b & a & 0 \end{vmatrix}$$

$$= \begin{vmatrix} b^2 + c^2 & ab & ac \\ ab & c^2 + a^2 & bc \\ ac & bc & a^2 + b^2 \end{vmatrix} \quad \ldots(\text{ii})$$

[multiplying row by row]

and

$$\Delta^c = \begin{vmatrix} -a^2 & ab & ac \\ ab & -b^2 & bc \\ ac & bc & -c^2 \end{vmatrix}$$

$$= \Delta^{3-1} = \Delta^2$$

$$= \begin{vmatrix} 0 & c & b \\ c & 0 & a \\ b & a & 0 \end{vmatrix}^2 \quad \ldots(\text{iii})$$

From Eqs. (i), (ii) and (iii), we get

$$\begin{vmatrix} 0 & c & b \\ c & 0 & a \\ b & a & 0 \end{vmatrix}^2 = \begin{vmatrix} b^2+c^2 & ab & ac \\ ab & c^2+a^2 & bc \\ ac & bc & a^2+b^2 \end{vmatrix}$$

$$= \begin{vmatrix} -a^2 & ab & ac \\ ab & -b^2 & bc \\ ac & bc & -c^2 \end{vmatrix}$$

$$= 4a^2b^2c^2$$

Express a Determinant Into Product of Two Determinants

Consider the determinant $\begin{vmatrix} a_1\alpha_1+b_1\beta_1 & a_1\alpha_2+b_1\beta_2 \\ a_2\alpha_1+b_2\beta_1 & a_2\alpha_2+b_2\beta_2 \end{vmatrix}$

Let $\Delta = \begin{vmatrix} a_1\alpha_1+b_1\beta_1 & a_1\alpha_2+b_1\beta_2 \\ a_2\alpha_1+b_2\beta_1 & a_2\alpha_2+b_2\beta_2 \end{vmatrix}$

By the property of determinant, Δ can be written as

$$\Delta = \begin{vmatrix} a_1\alpha_1 & a_1\alpha_2+b_1\beta_2 \\ a_2\alpha_1 & a_2\alpha_2+b_2\beta_2 \end{vmatrix} + \begin{vmatrix} b_1\beta_1 & a_1\alpha_2+b_1\beta_2 \\ b_2\beta_1 & a_2\alpha_2+b_2\beta_2 \end{vmatrix}$$

$$= \begin{vmatrix} a_1\alpha_1 & a_1\alpha_2 \\ a_2\alpha_1 & a_2\alpha_2 \end{vmatrix} + \begin{vmatrix} a_1\alpha_1 & b_1\beta_2 \\ a_2\alpha_1 & b_2\beta_2 \end{vmatrix} + \begin{vmatrix} b_1\beta_1 & a_1\alpha_2 \\ b_2\beta_1 & a_2\alpha_2 \end{vmatrix} + \begin{vmatrix} b_1\beta_1 & b_1\beta_2 \\ b_2\beta_1 & b_2\beta_2 \end{vmatrix}$$

$$= \alpha_1\alpha_2\begin{vmatrix} a_1 & a_1 \\ a_2 & a_2 \end{vmatrix} + \alpha_1\beta_2\begin{vmatrix} a_1 & b_1 \\ a_2 & b_2 \end{vmatrix} + \beta_1\alpha_2\begin{vmatrix} b_1 & a_1 \\ b_2 & a_2 \end{vmatrix} + \beta_1\beta_2\begin{vmatrix} b_1 & b_1 \\ b_2 & b_2 \end{vmatrix}$$

$$= 0 + \alpha_1\beta_2\begin{vmatrix} a_1 & b_1 \\ a_2 & b_2 \end{vmatrix} - \beta_1\alpha_2\begin{vmatrix} a_1 & b_1 \\ a_2 & b_2 \end{vmatrix} + 0$$

$$= \begin{vmatrix} a_1 & b_1 \\ a_2 & b_2 \end{vmatrix}(\alpha_1\beta_2 - \alpha_2\beta_1)$$

$$= \begin{vmatrix} a_1 & b_1 \\ a_2 & b_2 \end{vmatrix} \times \begin{vmatrix} \alpha_1 & \beta_1 \\ \alpha_2 & \beta_2 \end{vmatrix}$$

$$\therefore \begin{vmatrix} a_1\alpha_1+b_1\beta_1 & a_1\alpha_2+b_1\beta_2 \\ a_2\alpha_1+b_2\beta_1 & a_2\alpha_2+b_2\beta_2 \end{vmatrix} = \begin{vmatrix} a_1 & b_1 \\ a_2 & b_2 \end{vmatrix} \times \begin{vmatrix} \alpha_1 & \beta_1 \\ \alpha_2 & \beta_2 \end{vmatrix}$$

Example 21. Prove that

$$\begin{vmatrix} x_1+y_1b_1 & x_1+y_1b_2 & x_1+y_1b_3 \\ x_2+y_2b_1 & x_2+y_2b_2 & x_2+y_2b_3 \\ x_3+y_3b_1 & x_3+y_3b_2 & x_3+y_3b_3 \end{vmatrix} = 0$$

Sol. LHS $= \begin{vmatrix} x_1+y_1b_1 & x_1+y_1b_2 & x_1+y_1b_3 \\ x_2+y_2b_1 & x_2+y_2b_2 & x_2+y_2b_3 \\ x_3+y_3b_1 & x_3+y_3b_2 & x_3+y_3b_3 \end{vmatrix}$

$$= \begin{vmatrix} 0 & x_1 & y_1 \\ 0 & x_2 & y_2 \\ 0 & x_3 & y_3 \end{vmatrix} \times \begin{vmatrix} a_1 & 1 & b_1 \\ a_2 & 1 & b_2 \\ a_3 & 1 & b_3 \end{vmatrix} \quad \text{[row by row]}$$

$$= 0 \times \begin{vmatrix} a_1 & 1 & b_1 \\ a_2 & 1 & b_2 \\ a_3 & 1 & b_3 \end{vmatrix} = 0 = \text{RHS}$$

Example 22. Prove that

$$\begin{vmatrix} 2 & \alpha+\beta+\gamma+\delta & \alpha\beta+\gamma\delta \\ \alpha+\beta+\gamma+\delta & 2(\alpha+\beta)(\gamma+\delta) & \alpha\beta(\gamma+\delta)+\gamma\delta(\alpha+\beta) \\ \alpha\beta+\gamma\delta & \alpha\beta(\gamma+\delta)+\gamma\delta(\alpha+\beta) & 2\alpha\beta\gamma\delta \end{vmatrix} = 0.$$

Sol. LHS $= \begin{vmatrix} 2 & \alpha+\beta+\gamma+\delta & \alpha\beta+\gamma\delta \\ \alpha+\beta+\gamma+\delta & 2(\alpha+\beta)(\gamma+\delta) & \alpha\beta(\gamma+\delta)+\gamma\delta(\alpha+\beta) \\ \alpha\beta+\gamma\delta & \alpha\beta(\gamma+\delta)+\gamma\delta(\alpha+\beta) & 2\alpha\beta\gamma\delta \end{vmatrix}$

$$= \begin{vmatrix} 1 & 1 & 0 \\ \alpha+\beta & \gamma+\delta & 0 \\ \alpha\beta & \gamma\delta & 0 \end{vmatrix} \times \begin{vmatrix} 1 & 1 & 0 \\ \gamma+\delta & \alpha+\beta & 0 \\ \gamma\delta & \alpha\beta & 0 \end{vmatrix} \quad \text{[row by row]}$$

$$= 0 \times 0 = 0 = \text{RHS}$$

Example 23. Evaluate the value of

$$\Delta = \begin{vmatrix} \sin(A+x) & \sin(A+y) & \sin(A+z) \\ \sin(B+x) & \sin(B+y) & \sin(B+z) \\ \sin(C+x) & \sin(C+y) & \sin(C+z) \end{vmatrix}.$$

Sol. Let $\Delta = \begin{vmatrix} \sin(A+x) & \sin(A+y) & \sin(A+z) \\ \sin(B+x) & \sin(B+y) & \sin(B+z) \\ \sin(C+x) & \sin(C+y) & \sin(C+z) \end{vmatrix}$

$$= \begin{vmatrix} \sin A\cos x+\cos A\sin x & \sin A\cos y+\cos A\sin y & \sin A\cos z+\cos A\sin z \\ \sin B\cos x+\cos B\sin x & \sin B\cos y+\cos B\sin y & \sin B\cos z+\cos B\sin z \\ \sin C\cos x+\cos C\sin x & \sin C\cos y+\cos C\sin y & \sin C\cos z+\cos C\sin z \end{vmatrix}$$

$$= \begin{vmatrix} \sin A & \cos A & 0 \\ \sin B & \cos B & 0 \\ \sin C & \cos C & 0 \end{vmatrix} \times \begin{vmatrix} \cos x & \sin x & 0 \\ \cos y & \sin y & 0 \\ \cos z & \sin z & 0 \end{vmatrix} = 0 \times 0$$

$\therefore \quad \Delta = 0$

Example 24. If α, β and γ are real numbers, without expanding at any stage, prove that

$$\begin{vmatrix} 1 & \cos(\beta-\alpha) & \cos(\gamma-\alpha) \\ \cos(\alpha-\beta) & 1 & \cos(\gamma-\beta) \\ \cos(\alpha-\gamma) & \cos(\beta-\gamma) & 1 \end{vmatrix} = 0.$$

Sol. $$\text{LHS} = \begin{vmatrix} 1 & \cos(\beta-\alpha) & \cos(\gamma-\alpha) \\ \cos(\alpha-\beta) & 1 & \cos(\gamma-\beta) \\ \cos(\alpha-\gamma) & \cos(\beta-\gamma) & 1 \end{vmatrix}$$

$$= \begin{vmatrix} \cos(\alpha-\alpha) & \cos(\beta-\alpha) & \cos(\gamma-\alpha) \\ \cos(\alpha-\beta) & \cos(\beta-\beta) & \cos(\gamma-\beta) \\ \cos(\alpha-\gamma) & \cos(\beta-\gamma) & \cos(\gamma-\gamma) \end{vmatrix}$$

$$= \begin{vmatrix} \cos\alpha & \sin\alpha & 0 \\ \cos\beta & \sin\beta & 0 \\ \cos\gamma & \sin\gamma & 0 \end{vmatrix} \times \begin{vmatrix} \cos\alpha & \sin\alpha & 0 \\ \cos\beta & \sin\beta & 0 \\ \cos\gamma & \sin\gamma & 0 \end{vmatrix}$$

$$= 0 \times 0 = 0 = \text{RHS}$$

Example 25. If $a, b, c, x, y, z \in R$, prove that

$$\begin{vmatrix} (a-x)^2 & (b-x)^2 & (c-x)^2 \\ (a-y)^2 & (b-y)^2 & (c-y)^2 \\ (a-z)^2 & (b-z)^2 & (c-z)^2 \end{vmatrix} = \begin{vmatrix} (1+ax)^2 & (1+bx)^2 & (1+cx)^2 \\ (1+ay)^2 & (1+by)^2 & (1+cy)^2 \\ (1+az)^2 & (1+bz)^2 & (1+cz)^2 \end{vmatrix}.$$

Sol. $$\text{LHS} = \begin{vmatrix} (a-x)^2 & (b-x)^2 & (c-x)^2 \\ (a-y)^2 & (b-y)^2 & (c-y)^2 \\ (a-z)^2 & (b-z)^2 & (c-z)^2 \end{vmatrix}$$

$$= \begin{vmatrix} a^2-2ax+x^2 & b^2-2bx+x^2 & c^2-2cx+x^2 \\ a^2-2ay+y^2 & b^2-2by+y^2 & c^2-2cy+y^2 \\ a^2-2az+z^2 & b^2-2bz+z^2 & c^2-2cz+z^2 \end{vmatrix}$$

$$= \begin{vmatrix} 1 & 2x & x^2 \\ 1 & 2y & y^2 \\ 1 & 2z & z^2 \end{vmatrix} \times \begin{vmatrix} a^2 & -a & 1 \\ b^2 & -b & 1 \\ c^2 & -c & 1 \end{vmatrix} \quad \text{[row by row]}$$

$$= \begin{vmatrix} 1 & 2x & x^2 \\ 1 & 2y & y^2 \\ 1 & 2z & z^2 \end{vmatrix} \times (-1)(-1) \begin{vmatrix} 1 & a & a^2 \\ 1 & b & b^2 \\ 1 & c & c^2 \end{vmatrix}$$

[$C_1 \leftrightarrow C_3$ and taking (-1) common from second determinant]

$$= \begin{vmatrix} 1 & 2x & x^2 \\ 1 & 2y & y^2 \\ 1 & 2z & z^2 \end{vmatrix} \times \begin{vmatrix} 1 & a & a^2 \\ 1 & b & b^2 \\ 1 & c & c^2 \end{vmatrix}$$

$$= \begin{vmatrix} 1+2ax+a^2x^2 & 1+2bx+b^2x^2 & 1+2cx+c^2x^2 \\ 1+2ay+a^2y^2 & 1+2by+b^2y^2 & 1+2cy+c^2y^2 \\ 1+2az+a^2z^2 & 1+2bz+b^2z^2 & 1+2cz+c^2z^2 \end{vmatrix}$$

[multiplying row by row]

$$= \begin{vmatrix} (1+ax)^2 & (1+bx)^2 & (1+cx)^2 \\ (1+ay)^2 & (1+by)^2 & (1+cy)^2 \\ (1+az)^2 & (1+bz)^2 & (1+cz)^2 \end{vmatrix} = \text{RHS}$$

8.9 System of Linear Equations

(i) Consistent equations *Definite and unique solution* [Intersecting lines]

A system of (linear) equations is said to be consistent, if it has atleast one solution.

Let $a_1x + b_1y + c_1 = 0$ and $a_2x + b_2y + c_2 = 0$,

then $\dfrac{a_1}{a_2} \neq \dfrac{b_1}{b_2}$

$\Rightarrow$ Given system are consistent.

e.g. System of equations $\left.\begin{matrix} x+y=2 \\ x-y=6 \end{matrix}\right\}$ is consistent

because it has a solution $x = 4, y = -2$. Here, two lines intersect at one point.

i.e., intersecting lines.

(ii) Inconsistent equations *No solution* [Parallel lines]

A system of (linear) equations is said to be inconsistent, if it has no solution.

Let $a_1x + b_1y + c_1 = 0$ and $a_2x + b_2y + c_2 = 0$, then

$\dfrac{a_1}{a_2} = \dfrac{b_1}{b_2} \neq \dfrac{c_1}{c_2}$

$\Rightarrow$ Given equations are inconsistent.

e.g. System of equations $\left.\begin{matrix} x+y=2 \\ 2x+2y=5 \end{matrix}\right\}$ is inconsistent

because it has no solution i.e. there is no value of x and y which satisfy both the equations. Here, the two lines are parallel.

(iii) Dependent equations *Infinite solutions* [Identical lines]

A system of (linear) equations is said to be dependent, if it has infinite solutions.

Let $a_1x + b_1y + c_1 = 0$ and $a_2x + b_2y + c_2 = 0$, then

$\dfrac{a_1}{a_2} = \dfrac{b_1}{b_2} = \dfrac{c_1}{c_2} \Rightarrow$ Given equations are dependent.

e.g. System of equations $\left.\begin{matrix} x+2y=3 \\ 2x+4y=6 \end{matrix}\right\}$ is dependent

because it has infinite solutions i.e. there are infinite values of x and y satisfy both the equations. Here, the two lines are identical.

8.10 Cramer's Rule

System of Linear Equations in Two Variables

Let us consider a system of equations be

$$\left.\begin{array}{l} a_1x+b_1y+c_1=0 \\ a_2x+b_2y+c_2=0 \end{array}\right\}, \text{ where } \frac{a_1}{a_2} \neq \frac{b_1}{b_2}$$

On solving by cross-multiplication, we get

$$\frac{x}{(b_1c_2-b_2c_1)}=\frac{y}{(c_1a_2-c_2a_1)}=\frac{1}{(a_1b_2-a_2b_1)}$$

or $$\frac{x}{\begin{vmatrix} b_1 & c_1 \\ b_2 & c_2 \end{vmatrix}}=\frac{y}{\begin{vmatrix} c_1 & a_1 \\ c_2 & a_2 \end{vmatrix}}=\frac{1}{\begin{vmatrix} a_1 & b_1 \\ a_2 & b_2 \end{vmatrix}}$$

or $$x=\frac{\begin{vmatrix} b_1 & c_1 \\ b_2 & c_2 \end{vmatrix}}{\begin{vmatrix} a_1 & b_1 \\ a_2 & b_2 \end{vmatrix}}, y=\frac{\begin{vmatrix} c_1 & a_1 \\ c_2 & a_2 \end{vmatrix}}{\begin{vmatrix} a_1 & b_1 \\ a_2 & b_2 \end{vmatrix}}$$

System of Linear Equations in Three Variables

Let us consider a system of linear equations be

$$a_1x+b_1y+c_1z=d_1 \quad \text{...(i)}$$
$$a_2x+b_2y+c_2z=d_2 \quad \text{...(ii)}$$
$$a_3x+b_3y+c_3z=d_3 \quad \text{...(iii)}$$

Here, $$\Delta=\begin{vmatrix} a_1 & b_1 & c_1 \\ a_2 & b_2 & c_2 \\ a_3 & b_3 & c_3 \end{vmatrix}, \Delta_1=\begin{vmatrix} d_1 & b_1 & c_1 \\ d_2 & b_2 & c_2 \\ d_3 & b_3 & c_3 \end{vmatrix},$$

$$\Delta_2=\begin{vmatrix} a_1 & d_1 & c_1 \\ a_2 & d_2 & c_2 \\ a_3 & d_3 & c_3 \end{vmatrix} \text{ and } \Delta_3=\begin{vmatrix} a_1 & b_1 & d_1 \\ a_2 & b_2 & d_2 \\ a_3 & b_3 & d_3 \end{vmatrix}$$

If $\Delta \neq 0$, then

$$\Delta_1=\begin{vmatrix} d_1 & b_1 & c_1 \\ d_2 & b_2 & c_2 \\ d_3 & b_3 & c_3 \end{vmatrix}=\begin{vmatrix} a_1x+b_1y+c_1z & b_1 & c_1 \\ a_2x+b_2y+c_2z & b_2 & c_2 \\ a_3x+b_3y+c_3z & b_3 & c_3 \end{vmatrix}$$

Applying $C_1 \to C_1 - yC_2 - zC_3$, then

$$\Delta_1=\begin{vmatrix} a_1x & b_1 & c_1 \\ a_2x & b_2 & c_2 \\ a_3x & b_3 & c_3 \end{vmatrix}=x\begin{vmatrix} a_1 & b_1 & c_1 \\ a_2 & b_2 & c_2 \\ a_3 & b_3 & c_3 \end{vmatrix}=x\Delta$$

$\therefore$ $$x=\frac{\Delta_1}{\Delta}, \text{ where } \Delta \neq 0$$

Similarly, $\Delta_2 = y\Delta$ and $\Delta_3 = z\Delta$

$\therefore$ $$y=\frac{\Delta_2}{\Delta} \text{ and } z=\frac{\Delta_3}{\Delta}$$

Thus, $$x=\frac{\Delta_1}{\Delta}, y=\frac{\Delta_2}{\Delta}, z=\frac{\Delta_3}{\Delta}, \text{ where } \Delta \neq 0 \quad \text{...(iv)}$$

The rule given in Eq. (iv) to find the values of x, y and z is called the **CRAMER'S RULE.**

JEE Focus Points

- Δ_i is obtained by replacing elements of ith columns by d_1, d_2, d_3, where $i = 1, 2, 3$.
- Cramer's rule can be used only when $\Delta \neq 0$.

8.11 Nature of Solution of System of Linear Equations

Let us consider a system of linear equations be

$$a_1x+b_1y+c_1z=d_1$$
$$a_2x+b_2y+c_2z=d_2$$
$$a_3x+b_3y+c_3z=d_3$$

Now, there are two cases arise

***Case* I** If $\Delta \neq 0$

In this case, $x=\frac{\Delta_1}{\Delta}, y=\frac{\Delta_2}{\Delta}, z=\frac{\Delta_3}{\Delta}$

Then, system will have unique finite solutions and so equations are **consistent**.

***Case* II** If $\Delta = 0$

(a) **When atleast one of $\Delta_1, \Delta_2, \Delta_3$ be non-zero**

(i) Let $\Delta_1 \neq 0$, then from $\Delta_1 = x\Delta$ will not be satisfied for any value of x because $\Delta = 0$ and $\Delta_1 \neq 0$ and hence no value of x is possible.

(ii) Let $\Delta_2 \neq 0$, then from $\Delta_2 = y\Delta$ will not be satisfied for any value of y because $\Delta = 0$ and $\Delta_2 \neq 0$ and hence no value of y is possible.

(iii) Let $\Delta_3 \neq 0$, then from $\Delta_3 = z\Delta$ will not be satisfied for any value of z because $\Delta = 0$ and $\Delta_3 \neq 0$ and hence no value of z is possible.

Thus, if $\Delta = 0$ and any of $\Delta_1, \Delta_2, \Delta_3$ is non-zero. Then, the system has no solution i.e., equations are **inconsistent.**

(b) **When $\Delta_1 = \Delta_2 = \Delta_3 = 0$**

In this case, $\left.\begin{array}{l} \Delta_1 = x\Delta \\ \Delta_2 = y\Delta \\ \Delta_3 = z\Delta \end{array}\right\}$ will be true for all values of x, y and z.

But, since $a_1x + b_1y + c_1z = d_1$, therefore only two of x, y and z will be independent and third will be dependent on the other two.

Thus, the system will have infinite number of solutions i.e. equations are **consistent**.

JEE Focus Points

- If $\Delta \neq 0$, the system will have unique finite solution and so equations are consistent.
- If $\Delta = 0$ and atleast one of $\Delta_1, \Delta_2, \Delta_3$ be non-zero, then the system has no solution i.e. equations are inconsistent.
- If $\Delta = \Delta_1 = \Delta_2 = \Delta_3 = 0$, the equations will have infinite number of solutions i.e. equations are consistent.

Concept Inside Video

Example 26. Solve the following system of equations by Cramer's rule.

$$x + y = 5 \text{ and } 3x - 4y = 9$$

Sol. Here, $\Delta = \begin{vmatrix} 1 & 1 \\ 3 & -4 \end{vmatrix} = -4 - 3 = -7 \neq 0$

$$\Delta_1 = \begin{vmatrix} 5 & 1 \\ 9 & -4 \end{vmatrix} = -20 - 9 = -29$$

and $\Delta_2 = \begin{vmatrix} 1 & 5 \\ 3 & 9 \end{vmatrix} = 9 - 15 = -6$

Then, by Cramer's rule

$$x = \frac{\Delta_1}{\Delta} = \frac{-29}{-7} = \frac{29}{7} \text{ and } y = \frac{\Delta_2}{\Delta} = \frac{-6}{-7} = \frac{6}{7}$$

$\therefore \quad x = \frac{29}{7}, y = \frac{6}{7}$

Example 27. Solve the following system of equations by Cramer's rule.

$$2x - y + 3z = 9,\ x + y + z = 6,\ x - y + z = 2$$

Sol. Here, $\Delta = \begin{vmatrix} 2 & -1 & 3 \\ 1 & 1 & 1 \\ 1 & -1 & 1 \end{vmatrix} = 2(1+1) + 1(1-1) + 3(-1-1)$

$= 4 + 0 - 6 = -2$

$$\Delta_1 = \begin{vmatrix} 9 & -1 & 3 \\ 6 & 1 & 1 \\ 2 & -1 & 1 \end{vmatrix} = 9(1+1) + 1(6-2) + 3(-6-2)$$

$= 18 + 4 - 24 = -2$

$$\Delta_2 = \begin{vmatrix} 2 & 9 & 3 \\ 1 & 6 & 1 \\ 1 & 2 & 1 \end{vmatrix} = 2(6-2) - 9(1-1) + 3(2-6)$$

$= 8 - 0 - 12 = -4$

$$\Delta_3 = \begin{vmatrix} 2 & -1 & 9 \\ 1 & 1 & 6 \\ 1 & -1 & 2 \end{vmatrix} = 2(2+6) + 1(2-6) + 9(-1-1)$$

$= 16 - 4 - 18 = -6$

Thus, by Cramer's rule,

$$x = \frac{\Delta_1}{\Delta}, y = \frac{\Delta_2}{\Delta} \text{ and } z = \frac{\Delta_3}{\Delta}$$

$\Rightarrow \quad x = \frac{-2}{-2} = 1, y = \frac{-4}{-2} = 2 \text{ and } z = \frac{-6}{-2} = 3$

$\therefore \quad x = 1, y = 2, z = 3$

JEE SCANNER

Example Similar to PYQ Asked in JEE Main 2024

If the system of equations $x + 2y - z = \alpha$, $3x + 9y + \beta z = -2$, $5x + 2y + z = 1$ has infinitely many solutions, then $3\alpha - 4\beta$ is

(a) -24 (b) 20 (c) -40 (d) 21

Sol. (b) Given system of equations has infinitely many solutions so, $\Delta = 0$

$$\Rightarrow \begin{vmatrix} 1 & 2 & -1 \\ 3 & 9 & \beta \\ 5 & 2 & 1 \end{vmatrix} = 0$$

$\Rightarrow \quad (9 - 2\beta) - 2(3 - 5\beta) - 1(6 - 45) = 0$

$\Rightarrow \quad 9 - 2\beta - 6 + 10\beta - 6 + 45 = 0$

$\Rightarrow \quad 8\beta + 42 = 0 \Rightarrow \beta = \frac{-21}{4}$

For infinite solutions, $\Delta_x = \Delta_y = \Delta_z = 0$

So, $\Delta_x = \begin{vmatrix} \alpha & 2 & -1 \\ -2 & 9 & -21/4 \\ 1 & 2 & 1 \end{vmatrix} = 0 \Rightarrow \alpha = -\frac{1}{3}$

$\therefore \quad 3\alpha - 4\beta = 3\left(\frac{-1}{3}\right) - 4\left(\frac{-21}{4}\right) = 20$

Skill Builder

For Sol.

If the system of equations $2x + 3y + z = \alpha$, $x - 2y + \beta z = 4$, $2x + 4y - z = -1$ has infinitely many solutions, then $16\alpha + 4\beta$ is

(a) 32 (b) 40 (c) 36 (d) 38

- **For more practice** See Q.9 of Milestone Practice 8.3.

Example 28. For what values of p and q, the system of equations $x + y + z = 6$, $x + 2y + 3z = 10$ and $x + 2y + pz = q$ has

(i) unique solution?

(ii) an infinitely many solutions?

(iii) no solution?

Sol. Given equations are

$$x + y + z = 6$$

$\Rightarrow \quad x + 2y + 3z = 10$

$$x + 2y + pz = q$$

$$\therefore \quad \Delta = \begin{vmatrix} 1 & 1 & 1 \\ 1 & 2 & 3 \\ 1 & 2 & p \end{vmatrix} = (p-3)$$

$$\Delta_1 = \begin{vmatrix} 6 & 1 & 1 \\ 10 & 2 & 3 \\ q & 2 & p \end{vmatrix}$$

$$= 6(2p-6) - 1(10p-3q) + (20-2q)$$

$$= 2p + q - 16$$

$$\Delta_2 = \begin{vmatrix} 1 & 6 & 1 \\ 1 & 10 & 3 \\ 1 & q & p \end{vmatrix}$$

$$= 1(10p-3q) - 6(p-3) + 1(q-10) = 4p - 2q + 8$$

$$\text{and } \Delta_3 = \begin{vmatrix} 1 & 1 & 6 \\ 1 & 2 & 10 \\ 1 & 2 & q \end{vmatrix}$$

$$= 1(2q-20) - 1(q-10) + 6(2-2) = q - 10$$

(i) For unique solution, $\Delta \neq 0 \Rightarrow p \neq 3, q \in R$

(ii) For infinitely many solutions, $\Delta = \Delta_1 = \Delta_2 = \Delta_3 = 0$

$\therefore \quad p = 3, q = 10$

(iii) For no solution, $\Delta = 0$ and atleast one of $\Delta_1, \Delta_2, \Delta_3$ is non-zero is $p = 3$ and $q \neq 10$.

Condition for Consistency of Three Linear Equations in Two Unknowns

Let us consider a system of linear equations in x and y

$$a_1 x + b_1 y + c_1 = 0 \quad \text{...(i)}$$

$$a_2 x + b_2 y + c_2 = 0 \quad \text{...(ii)}$$

$$a_3 x + b_3 y + c_3 = 0 \quad \text{...(iii)}$$

will be consistent, the values of x and y obtained from any two equations satisfy the third equation.

On solving Eqs. (ii) and (iii) by Cramer's rule, we have

$$\frac{x}{\begin{vmatrix} b_2 & c_2 \\ b_3 & c_3 \end{vmatrix}} = \frac{y}{\begin{vmatrix} c_2 & a_2 \\ c_3 & a_3 \end{vmatrix}} = \frac{1}{\begin{vmatrix} a_2 & b_2 \\ a_3 & b_3 \end{vmatrix}}$$

These values of x and y will satisfy Eq. (i), then

$$a_1 \begin{vmatrix} b_2 & c_2 \\ b_3 & c_3 \end{vmatrix} + b_1 \begin{vmatrix} c_2 & a_2 \\ c_3 & a_3 \end{vmatrix} + c_1 \begin{vmatrix} a_2 & b_2 \\ a_3 & b_3 \end{vmatrix} = 0$$

$$\Rightarrow \quad a_1 \begin{vmatrix} b_2 & c_2 \\ b_3 & c_3 \end{vmatrix} - b_1 \begin{vmatrix} a_2 & c_2 \\ a_3 & c_3 \end{vmatrix} + c_1 \begin{vmatrix} a_2 & b_2 \\ a_3 & b_3 \end{vmatrix} = 0$$

$$\therefore \quad \begin{vmatrix} a_1 & b_1 & c_1 \\ a_2 & b_2 & c_2 \\ a_3 & b_3 & c_3 \end{vmatrix} = 0$$

which is the required condition.

JEE SPIKE

For consistency of three linear equations in two knowns, the number of solution is one.

Example 29. Find the value of λ, if the following equations are consistent

$$x + y - 3 = 0$$

$$(1+\lambda)x + (2+\lambda)y - 8 = 0$$

$$x - (1+\lambda)y + (2+\lambda) = 0$$

Sol. The given equations in two unknowns are consistent, then

$$\begin{vmatrix} 1 & 1 & -3 \\ (1+\lambda) & (2+\lambda) & -8 \\ 1 & -(1+\lambda) & (2+\lambda) \end{vmatrix} = 0$$

Applying $C_2 \to C_2 - C_1$ and $C_3 \to C_3 + 3C_1$, then

$$\begin{vmatrix} 1 & \cdots & 0 & \cdots & 0 \\ \vdots & & & & \\ (1+\lambda) & & 1 & & (3\lambda-5) \\ \vdots & & & & \\ 1 & & -(2+\lambda) & & (5+\lambda) \end{vmatrix} = 0$$

Expanding along R_1, then

$$1 \cdot \begin{vmatrix} 1 & 3\lambda - 5 \\ -(2+\lambda) & (5+\lambda) \end{vmatrix} = 0$$

$$\Rightarrow \quad (5+\lambda) + (2+\lambda)(3\lambda-5) = 0$$

$$\Rightarrow \quad 3\lambda^2 + 2\lambda - 5 = 0 \text{ or } (3\lambda+5)(\lambda-1) = 0$$

$$\therefore \quad \lambda = 1, -5/3$$

8.12 System of Homogeneous Linear Equations

Let us consider a system of homogeneous linear equations in three unknown x, y and z be

$$a_1 x + b_1 y + c_1 z = 0 \quad \text{...(i)}$$

$$a_2 x + b_2 y + c_2 z = 0 \quad \text{...(ii)}$$

$$a_3 x + b_3 y + c_3 z = 0 \quad \text{...(iii)}$$

Here, $\Delta = \begin{vmatrix} a_1 & b_1 & c_1 \\ a_2 & b_2 & c_2 \\ a_3 & b_3 & c_3 \end{vmatrix}$

***Case* I** If $\Delta \neq 0$, then $x = 0, y = 0, z = 0$ is the only solution of above system. This solution is called a **Trivial solution**.

***Case* II** If $\Delta = 0$, atleast one of x, y and z is non-zero. This solution is called a **Non-trivial solution**.

Explanation From Eqs. (ii) and (iii), we get

$$\frac{x}{(b_2 c_3 - b_3 c_2)} = \frac{y}{(c_2 a_3 - c_3 a_2)} = \frac{z}{(a_2 b_3 - a_3 b_2)}$$

or $$\frac{x}{\begin{vmatrix} b_2 & c_2 \\ b_3 & c_3 \end{vmatrix}} = \frac{y}{\begin{vmatrix} c_2 & a_2 \\ c_3 & a_3 \end{vmatrix}} = \frac{z}{\begin{vmatrix} a_2 & b_2 \\ a_3 & b_3 \end{vmatrix}} = k[\text{say}]\ (\neq 0)$$

$$\therefore \quad x = k\begin{vmatrix} b_2 & c_2 \\ b_3 & c_3 \end{vmatrix}, y = k\begin{vmatrix} c_2 & a_2 \\ c_3 & a_3 \end{vmatrix}$$

and $$z = k\begin{vmatrix} a_2 & b_2 \\ a_3 & b_3 \end{vmatrix}$$

On putting these values of x, y and z in Eq. (i), we get

$$a_1\left\{k\begin{vmatrix} b_2 & c_2 \\ b_3 & c_3 \end{vmatrix}\right\} + b_1\left\{k\begin{vmatrix} c_2 & a_2 \\ c_3 & a_3 \end{vmatrix}\right\} + c_1\left\{k\begin{vmatrix} a_2 & b_2 \\ a_3 & b_3 \end{vmatrix}\right\} = 0$$

$$\Rightarrow \quad a_1\begin{vmatrix} b_2 & c_2 \\ b_3 & c_3 \end{vmatrix} - b_1\begin{vmatrix} a_2 & c_2 \\ a_3 & c_3 \end{vmatrix} + c_1\begin{vmatrix} a_2 & b_2 \\ a_3 & b_3 \end{vmatrix} = 0$$

$[\because k \neq 0]$

or $$\begin{vmatrix} a_1 & b_1 & c_1 \\ a_2 & b_2 & c_2 \\ a_3 & b_3 & c_3 \end{vmatrix} = 0$$

or $$\Delta = 0$$

This is the condition for system have **Non-trivial solution.**

JEE Focus Points

- If $\Delta \neq 0$, the given system of equations has unique solution for all its variables, then the given equations are said to have Trivial solution.
- If $\Delta = 0$, the given system of equations has no solution or infinite solutions for all its variables, then the given equations are said to have Non-trivial solution.

Concept Inside Video

Example 30. Find all values of λ for which the equations

$$(\lambda - 1)x + (3\lambda + 1)y + 2\lambda z = 0$$
$$(\lambda - 1)x + (4\lambda - 2)y + (\lambda + 3)z = 0$$
$$2x + (3\lambda + 1)y + 3(\lambda - 1)z = 0$$

possess non-trivial solution and find the ratios $x : y : z$, where λ has the smallest of these values.

Sol. The given system of linear equations has non-trivial solution, then we must have

$$\begin{vmatrix} \lambda - 1 & 3\lambda + 1 & 2\lambda \\ \lambda - 1 & 4\lambda - 2 & \lambda + 3 \\ 2 & 3\lambda + 1 & 3(\lambda - 1) \end{vmatrix} = 0$$

Applying $R_2 \to R_2 - R_1$ and $R_3 \to R_3 - R_1$, then

$$\begin{vmatrix} \lambda - 1 & 3\lambda + 1 & 2\lambda \\ 0 & \lambda - 3 & -\lambda + 3 \\ 3 - \lambda & 0 & \lambda - 3 \end{vmatrix} = 0$$

Applying $C_3 \to C_3 + C_2$, then

$$\begin{vmatrix} \lambda - 1 & 3\lambda + 1 & 5\lambda + 1 \\ 0 & \lambda - 3 & 0 \\ 3 - \lambda & 0 & \lambda - 3 \end{vmatrix} = 0$$

Expanding along R_2, we get

$$(\lambda - 3)\begin{vmatrix} \lambda - 1 & 5\lambda + 1 \\ 3 - \lambda & \lambda - 3 \end{vmatrix} = 0$$

$$\Rightarrow \quad (\lambda - 3)[(\lambda - 1)(\lambda - 3) - (3 - \lambda)(5\lambda + 1)] = 0$$

$$\Rightarrow \quad (\lambda - 3)^2 \cdot 6\lambda = 0$$

$$\therefore \quad \lambda = 0, 3$$

Here, smallest value of λ is 0.

$\therefore$ The first two equations can be written as

$$x - y = 0 \text{ and } x + 2y - 3z = 0.$$

Using Cramer's rule, we get

$$\frac{x}{\begin{vmatrix} -1 & 0 \\ 2 & -3 \end{vmatrix}} = \frac{y}{\begin{vmatrix} 0 & 1 \\ -3 & 1 \end{vmatrix}} = \frac{z}{\begin{vmatrix} 1 & -1 \\ 1 & 2 \end{vmatrix}}$$

$$\Rightarrow \quad \frac{x}{3} = \frac{y}{3} = \frac{z}{3} \Rightarrow \frac{x}{1} = \frac{y}{1} = \frac{z}{1}$$

$$\therefore \quad x : y : z = 1 : 1 : 1$$

Example 31. Given, $x = cy + bz$, $y = az + cx$ and $z = bx + ay$, where x, y and z are not all zero, prove that $a^2 + b^2 + c^2 + 2abc = 1$.

Sol. The given equation can be rewritten as

$$x - cy - bz = 0$$
$$-cx + y - az = 0$$
$$-bx - ay + z = 0$$

Since, x, y and z are not all zero, the system will have non-trivial solution, if

$$\begin{vmatrix} 1 & -c & -b \\ -c & 1 & -a \\ -b & -a & 1 \end{vmatrix} = 0$$

Applying $C_2 \to C_2 + cC_1$ and $C_3 \to C_3 + bC_1$, then

$$\begin{vmatrix} 1 & 0 & 0 \\ -c & 1 - c^2 & -a - bc \\ -b & -a - bc & 1 - b^2 \end{vmatrix} = 0$$

Expanding along R_1, we get

$$1\begin{vmatrix} 1 - c^2 & -a - bc \\ -a - bc & 1 - b^2 \end{vmatrix} = 0$$

$$\Rightarrow \quad (1 - c^2)(1 - b^2) - (a + bc)^2 = 0$$

$$\Rightarrow \quad 1 - b^2 - c^2 + b^2c^2 - a^2 - b^2c^2 - 2abc = 0$$

$$\Rightarrow \quad a^2 + b^2 + c^2 + 2abc = 1$$

Milestone Practice 8.3

1. Number of second order determinants which have maximum values whose each entry is either –1 or 1 is equal to

(a) 2 (b) 4 (c) 6 (d) 8

2. Minimum value of a second order determinant whose each entry is either 1 or 2 is equal to

(a) 0 (b) –1 (c) –2 (d) –3

3. If $l_i^2 + m_i^2 + n_i^2 = 1, (i = 1, 2, 3)$ and $l_i l_j + m_i m_j + n_i n_j = 0, (i \neq j; i, j = 1, 2, 3)$ and $\Delta = \begin{vmatrix} l_1 & m_1 & n_1 \\ l_2 & m_2 & n_2 \\ l_3 & m_3 & n_3 \end{vmatrix}$, then

(a) $|\Delta| = 3$ (b) $|\Delta| = 2$ (c) $|\Delta| = 1$ (d) $|\Delta| = 0$

4. Let $\Delta_0 = \begin{vmatrix} a_{11} & a_{12} & a_{13} \\ a_{21} & a_{22} & a_{23} \\ a_{31} & a_{32} & a_{33} \end{vmatrix}$ and Δ_1 denotes the determinant formed by the cofactors of elements of Δ_0 and Δ_2 denote the determinant formed by the cofactors of Δ_1 and so on. Δ_n denotes the determinant formed by the cofactors of Δ_{n-1}, the determinant value of Δ_n is

(a) Δ_0^{2n} (b) $\Delta_0^{2^n}$ (c) $\Delta_0^{n^2}$ (d) Δ_0^2

5. If $\begin{vmatrix} 1 & x & x^2 \\ x & x^2 & 1 \\ x^2 & 1 & x \end{vmatrix} = 3$, then the value of

$\begin{vmatrix} x^3 - 1 & 0 & x - x^4 \\ 0 & x - x^4 & x^3 - 1 \\ x - x^4 & x^3 - 1 & 0 \end{vmatrix}$, is

(a) 6 (b) 9 (c) 18 (d) 27

6. The value of the determinant

$\begin{vmatrix} (a_1 - b_1)^2 & (a_1 - b_2)^2 & (a_1 - b_3)^2 & (a_1 - b_4)^2 \\ (a_2 - b_1)^2 & (a_2 - b_2)^2 & (a_2 - b_3)^2 & (a_2 - b_4)^2 \\ (a_3 - b_1)^2 & (a_3 - b_2)^2 & (a_3 - b_3)^2 & (a_3 - b_4)^2 \\ (a_4 - b_1)^2 & (a_4 - b_2)^2 & (a_4 - b_3)^2 & (a_4 - b_4)^2 \end{vmatrix}$, is

(a) depends on $a_i, i = 1, 2, 3, 4$

(b) depends on $b_i, i = 1, 2, 3, 4$

(c) depends on $c_i, i = 1, 2, 3, 4$

(d) 0

7. Value of $\begin{vmatrix} 1 + x_1 & 1 + x_1 x & 1 + x_1 x^2 \\ 1 + x_2 & 1 + x_2 x & 1 + x_2 x^2 \\ 1 + x_3 & 1 + x_3 x & 1 + x_3 x^2 \end{vmatrix}$ depends upon

(a) only x (b) only x_1

(c) only x_2 (d) None of these

8. If the system of linear equations $x + y + z = 6$, $x + 2y + 3z = 14$ and $2x + 5y + \lambda z = \mu$ $(\lambda, \mu \in R)$ has a unique solution, then

(a) $\lambda \neq 8$ (b) $\lambda = 8$ and $\mu \neq 36$

(c) $\lambda = 8$ and $\mu = 36$ (d) None of these

9. The given system of equations $a + b + 2c = x$, $3a + 2b - yc = 4$, $2a - b + c = -2$ has infinitely many solutions, then $4x - y$ is

(a) 16 (b) 14 (c) 13 (d) 11

10. The system of equations $ax - y - z = a - 1$, $x - ay - z = a - 1$, $x - y - az = a - 1$ has no solution, if a is

(a) either –2 or 1 (b) –2

(c) 1 (d) 2

11. The system of equations $x + 2y - 4z = 3$, $2x - 3y + 2z = 5$ and $x - 12y + 16z = 1$ has

(a) inconsistent solution (b) unique solution

(c) infinitely many solutions (d) None of these

12. If $c < 1$ and the system of equations $x + y - 1 = 0$, $2x - y - c = 0$ and $-bx + 3by - c = 0$ is consistent, then the possible real values of b are

(a) $b \in \left(-3, \frac{3}{4}\right)$ (b) $b \in \left(-\frac{3}{2}, 4\right)$

(c) $b \in \left(-\frac{3}{4}, 3\right)$ (d) None of these

13. The equations $x + 2y = 3$, $y - 2x = 1$ and $7x - 6y + a = 0$ are consistent for

(a) $a = 7$ (b) $a = 1$

(c) $a = 11$ (d) None of these

14. Values of k for which the system of equations $x + ky + 3z = 0$, $kx + 2y + 2z = 0$ and $2x + 3y + 4z = 0$ possesses non-trivial solution

(a) $\left\{2, \frac{5}{4}\right\}$ (b) $\left\{-2, \frac{5}{4}\right\}$

(c) $\left\{2, -\frac{5}{9}\right\}$ (d) $\left\{-2, -\frac{5}{4}\right\}$

Answer Key

1. (b)	2. (d)	3. (c)	4. (a)	5. (b)	6. (d)	7. (d)
8. (a)	9. (c)	10. (b)	11. (c)	12. (c)	13. (a)	14. (a)

For Detailed Solution

Milestone 4 Differentiation and Integration of Determinant

• Differentiation of Determinant • Integration of Determinant • Use of Σ in Determinant

8.13 Differentiation of Determinant

Let $\Delta(x)$ be a determinant of order n. If we write $\Delta(x)=[C_1\ C_2\ C_3 \ldots C_n]$, where $C_1, C_2, C_3, \ldots, C_n$ denotes 1st, 2nd, 3rd, ..., nth columns respectively, then

$$\Delta'(x)=[C_1'\ C_2\ C_3 \cdots C_n]+[C_1\ C'_2\ C_3 \cdots C_n] +[C_1\ C_2\ C_3' \cdots C_n]+\cdots+[C_1\ C_2\ C_3 \cdots C_n']$$

$$=\Sigma\,[C_1{}'\ C_2\ C_3 \cdots C_n]$$

where C_i' denotes the column which contains the derivative of all the functions in the ith column C_i. Also, if

$$\Delta(x)=\begin{bmatrix} R_1 \\ R_2 \\ R_3 \\ \vdots \\ R_n \end{bmatrix}$$

where $R_1, R_2, R_3, \ldots, R_n$ denote 1st, 2nd, 3rd, ..., nth rows respectively, then

$$\Delta'(x)=\begin{bmatrix} R_1' \\ R_2 \\ R_3 \\ \vdots \\ R_n \end{bmatrix}+\begin{bmatrix} R_1 \\ R_2' \\ R_3 \\ \vdots \\ R_n \end{bmatrix}+\begin{bmatrix} R_1 \\ R_2 \\ R_3' \\ \vdots \\ R_n \end{bmatrix}+\cdots+\begin{bmatrix} R_1 \\ R_2 \\ R_3 \\ \vdots \\ R_n' \end{bmatrix}=\Sigma\begin{bmatrix} R_1' \\ R_2 \\ R_3 \\ \vdots \\ R_n \end{bmatrix}$$

where R'_i denotes the row which contains the derivative of all the functions in the ith row R_i.

Corollary I **For $n=2$,**

$$\Delta(x)=[C_1\ C_2], \text{ then } \Delta'(x)=[C_1'\ C_2]+[C_1\ C_2']$$

Also, if $\Delta(x)=\begin{bmatrix} R_1 \\ R_2 \end{bmatrix}$, then $\Delta'(x)=\begin{bmatrix} R'_1 \\ R_2 \end{bmatrix}+\begin{bmatrix} R_1 \\ R'_2 \end{bmatrix}$

e.g. Let $\Delta(x)=\begin{vmatrix} a_1(x) & b_1(x) \\ a_2(x) & b_2(x) \end{vmatrix}$, then

$$\Delta'(x)=\begin{vmatrix} a_1'(x) & b_1'(x) \\ a_2(x) & b_2(x) \end{vmatrix}+\begin{vmatrix} a_1(x) & b_1(x) \\ a_2'(x) & b_2'(x) \end{vmatrix}$$

[derivative according to row wise]

Corollary II **For $n=3$,** $\Delta(x)=[C_1\ C_2\ C_3]$, then

$$\Delta'(x)=[C_1'\ C_2\ C_3]+[C_1\ C_2'\ C_3]+[C_1\ C_2\ C_3']$$

Also, if $\Delta(x)=\begin{bmatrix} R_1 \\ R_2 \\ R_3 \end{bmatrix}$, then $\Delta'(x)=\begin{bmatrix} R'_1 \\ R_2 \\ R_3 \end{bmatrix}+\begin{bmatrix} R_1 \\ R'_2 \\ R_3 \end{bmatrix}+\begin{bmatrix} R_1 \\ R_2 \\ R'_3 \end{bmatrix}$

e.g. Let $\Delta(x)=\begin{vmatrix} a_1(x) & a_2(x) & a_3(x) \\ b_1(x) & b_2(x) & b_3(x) \\ c_1(x) & c_2(x) & c_3(x) \end{vmatrix}$, then

$$\Delta'(x)=\begin{vmatrix} a_1'(x) & a_2'(x) & a'_3(x) \\ b_1(x) & b_2(x) & b_3(x) \\ c_1(x) & c_2(x) & c_3(x) \end{vmatrix}+\begin{vmatrix} a_1(x) & a_2(x) & a_3(x) \\ b_1'(x) & b_2'(x) & b_3'(x) \\ c_1(x) & c_2(x) & c_3(x) \end{vmatrix}+\begin{vmatrix} a_1(x) & a_2(x) & a_3(x) \\ b_1(x) & b_2(x) & b_3(x) \\ c_1'(x) & c_2'(x) & c_3'(x) \end{vmatrix}$$

[derivative according to row wise]

JEE Focus Points

Concept Inside Video

- In a third order determinant, if two rows (columns) consist functions of x and third row (column) is constant,

  let $\Delta(x)=\begin{vmatrix} a_1(x) & a_2(x) & a_3(x) \\ b_1(x) & b_2(x) & b_3(x) \\ c_1 & c_2 & c_3 \end{vmatrix}$, then

  $$\Delta'(x)=\begin{vmatrix} a_1'(x) & a_2'(x) & a_3'(x) \\ b_1(x) & b_2(x) & b_3(x) \\ c_1 & c_2 & c_3 \end{vmatrix}+\begin{vmatrix} a_1(x) & a_2(x) & a_3(x) \\ b_1'(x) & b_2'(x) & b'_3(x) \\ c_1 & c_2 & c_3 \end{vmatrix}$$

- In a third order determinant, if only one row (column) consists functions of x and other rows (columns) are constant, let

  $\Delta(x)=\begin{vmatrix} a_1(x) & a_2(x) & a_3(x) \\ b_1 & b_2 & b_3 \\ c_1 & c_2 & c_3 \end{vmatrix}$, then $\Delta'(x)=\begin{vmatrix} a_1'(x) & a_2'(x) & a_3'(x) \\ b_1 & b_2 & b_3 \\ c_1 & c_2 & c_3 \end{vmatrix}$

  and in general

  $$\frac{d^n}{dx^n}\{\Delta(x)\}=\begin{vmatrix} \frac{d^n}{dx^n}\{a_1(x)\} & \frac{d^n}{dx^n}\{a_2(x)\} & \frac{d^n}{dx^n}\{a_3(x)\} \\ b_1 & b_2 & b_3 \\ c_1 & c_2 & c_3 \end{vmatrix}$$

Important Derivatives (Committed to Memory)

If a and b are constants and $n \in N$, then

1. if $y=(ax+b)^n$, then $\dfrac{d^n y}{dx^n}=n!a^n$
2. if $y=\sin(ax+b)$, then $\dfrac{d^n y}{dx^n}=\sin\left(\dfrac{n\pi}{2}+ax+b\right)\cdot a^n$
3. if $y=\cos(ax+b)$, then $\dfrac{d^n y}{dx^n}=\cos\left(\dfrac{n\pi}{2}+ax+b\right)\cdot a^n$

Example 32. If $f(x)=\begin{vmatrix}\sin x & \cos x & \sin x\\ \cos x & -\sin x & \cos x\\ x & 1 & 1\end{vmatrix}$, find the value of $2^{f'(0)}+\{f'(1)\}^2$.

Sol. $f'(x)=\begin{vmatrix}\cos x & -\sin x & \cos x\\ \cos x & -\sin x & \cos x\\ x & 1 & 1\end{vmatrix}+\begin{vmatrix}\sin x & \cos x & \sin x\\ -\sin x & -\cos x & -\sin x\\ x & 1 & 1\end{vmatrix}$

$$+\begin{vmatrix}\sin x & \cos x & \sin x\\ \cos x & -\sin x & \cos x\\ 1 & 0 & 0\end{vmatrix}$$

[derivative according to rowwise]

$$=0+0+1\begin{vmatrix}\cos x & \sin x\\ -\sin x & \cos x\end{vmatrix}=\cos^2 x+\sin^2 x=1$$

$\therefore\ f'(x)=1 \Rightarrow f'(0)=1$ and $f'(1)=1$

$\Rightarrow\ 2^{f'(0)}+\{f'(1)\}^2=2^1+1^2=3$

Example 33. Let

$$g(\theta)=\begin{vmatrix}1+\cos^2\theta & \sin^2\theta & 4\sin 4\theta\\ \cos^2\theta & 1+\sin^2\theta & 4\sin 4\theta\\ \cos^2\theta & \sin^2\theta & 1+4\sin 4\theta\end{vmatrix},$$

then find the value of $g'\left(\dfrac{\pi}{2}\right)$

Sol. Given, $g(\theta)=\begin{vmatrix}1+\cos^2\theta & \sin^2\theta & 4\sin 4\theta\\ \cos^2\theta & 1+\sin^2\theta & 4\sin 4\theta\\ \cos^2\theta & \sin^2\theta & 1+4\sin 4\theta\end{vmatrix}$

$$\therefore\quad g'(\theta)=\begin{vmatrix}-2\cos\theta\sin\theta & 2\sin\theta\cos\theta & 16\cos 4\theta\\ \cos^2\theta & 1+\sin^2\theta & 4\sin 4\theta\\ \cos^2\theta & \sin^2\theta & 1+4\sin 4\theta\end{vmatrix}$$

$$+\begin{vmatrix}1+\cos^2\theta & \sin^2\theta & 4\sin 4\theta\\ -2\cos\theta\sin\theta & 2\sin\theta\cos\theta & 16\cos 4\theta\\ \cos^2\theta & \sin^2\theta & 1+4\sin 4\theta\end{vmatrix}$$

$$+\begin{vmatrix}1+\cos^2\theta & \sin^2\theta & 4\sin 4\theta\\ \cos^2\theta & 1+\sin^2\theta & 4\sin 4\theta\\ -2\cos\theta\sin\theta & 2\sin\theta\cos\theta & 16\cos 4\theta\end{vmatrix}$$

[derivative along rowwise]

$$=\begin{vmatrix}-\sin 2\theta & \sin 2\theta & 16\cos 4\theta\\ \cos^2\theta & 1+\sin^2\theta & 4\sin 4\theta\\ \cos^2\theta & \sin^2\theta & 1+4\sin 4\theta\end{vmatrix}$$

$$+\begin{vmatrix}1+\cos^2\theta & \sin^2\theta & 4\sin 4\theta\\ -\sin 2\theta & \sin 2\theta & 16\cos 4\theta\\ \cos^2\theta & \sin^2\theta & 1+4\sin 4\theta\end{vmatrix}$$

$$+\begin{vmatrix}1+\cos^2\theta & \sin^2\theta & 4\sin 4\theta\\ \cos^2\theta & 1+\sin^2\theta & 4\sin 4\theta\\ -\sin 2\theta & \sin 2\theta & 16\cos 4\theta\end{vmatrix}$$

$$\Rightarrow g'\left(\frac{\pi}{2}\right)=\begin{vmatrix}0 & 0 & 16\\ 0 & 2 & 0\\ 0 & 1 & 1\end{vmatrix}+\begin{vmatrix}1 & 1 & 0\\ 0 & 0 & 16\\ 0 & 1 & 1\end{vmatrix}+\begin{vmatrix}1 & 1 & 0\\ 0 & 1 & 0\\ 0 & 0 & 16\end{vmatrix}$$

$$=16(0-0)+1(0-16)-1(0-0)+16(1-0)$$
$$=0-16-0+16=0$$

JEE SCANNER

Example Similar to PYQ Asked in JEE Main 2022

Let $f(x)=\begin{vmatrix}a & -1 & 0\\ ax & a & -1\\ ax^2 & ax & a\end{vmatrix}$. Then the sum of all the values of a for $2f'(3)-f'(2)+50=0$ is

(a) -4 (b) 4 (c) 6 (d) 8

Sol. (a) Given, $f(x)=\begin{vmatrix}a & -1 & 0\\ ax & a & -1\\ ax^2 & ax & a\end{vmatrix}=a\begin{vmatrix}1 & -1 & 0\\ x & a & -1\\ x^2 & ax & a\end{vmatrix}$

$$=a[1(a^2+ax)+1(ax+x^2)]$$
$$=a[a^2+2ax+x^2]=a(x+a)^2$$

$\Rightarrow\quad f(x)=a(x+a)^2$

$f'(x)=2a(x+a)$

As, $\quad 2f'(3)-f'(2)+50=0$

$\Rightarrow\ 2\times 2a(3+a)-2a(2+a)+50=0$

$\Rightarrow\ 12a+4a^2-4a-2a^2+50=0$

$\Rightarrow\ 2a^2+8a+50=0 \Rightarrow a=-2\pm\sqrt{21}i$

$\therefore\ $ Sum $=-4$

Skill Builder

If $f(x)=\begin{vmatrix}1 & -a & -1\\ x & a & 0\\ x^2 & ax & a\end{vmatrix}$ and $f'(x)=64$, then $24a$ is equal to

(a) ± 163 (b) ± 164 (c) ± 192 (d) ± 191

For Sol.

■ **For more practice** See Q.1 of Milestone Practice 8.4.

Example 34. Let α be a repeated root of a quadratic equation $f(x)=0$ and $A(x)$, $B(x)$ and $C(x)$ be polynomials of degree 3, 4, and 5 respectively, show that $\begin{vmatrix} A(x) & B(x) & C(x) \\ A(\alpha) & B(\alpha) & C(\alpha) \\ A'(\alpha) & B'(\alpha) & C'(\alpha) \end{vmatrix}$ is divisible by $f(x)$, where prime ($'$) denotes the derivatives.

Sol. Since, α is a repeated root of the quadratic equation $f(x)=0$, then $f(x)$ can be written as

$$f(x)=a(x-\alpha)^2,$$

where a is some non-zero constant.

Let
$$g(x)=\begin{vmatrix} A(x) & B(x) & C(x) \\ A(\alpha) & B(\alpha) & C(\alpha) \\ A'(\alpha) & B'(\alpha) & C'(\alpha) \end{vmatrix}$$

$g(x)$ is divisible by $f(x)$, if it is divisible by $(x-\alpha)^2$

i.e. $g(\alpha)=0$ and $g'(\alpha)=0$.

As, $A(x)$, $B(x)$ and $C(x)$ are polynomials of degree 3, 4 and 5, respectively.

$\therefore$ Degree of $g(x)\geq 2$

Now,
$$g(\alpha)=\begin{vmatrix} A(\alpha) & B(\alpha) & C(\alpha) \\ A(\alpha) & B(\alpha) & C(\alpha) \\ A'(\alpha) & B'(\alpha) & C'(\alpha) \end{vmatrix}=0$$

[$\because R_1$ and R_2 are identical]

Also,
$$g'(x)=\begin{vmatrix} A'(x) & B'(x) & C'(x) \\ A(\alpha) & B(\alpha) & C(\alpha) \\ A'(\alpha) & B'(\alpha) & C'(\alpha) \end{vmatrix}$$

$$\therefore\quad g'(\alpha)=\begin{vmatrix} A'(\alpha) & B'(\alpha) & C'(\alpha) \\ A(\alpha) & B(\alpha) & C(\alpha) \\ A'(\alpha) & B'(\alpha) & C'(\alpha) \end{vmatrix}=0$$

[$\because R_1$ and R_3 are identical]

This implies that $f(x)$ divides $g(x)$.

Example 35. Find the coefficient of x in the determinant

$$\begin{vmatrix} (1+x)^{a_1b_1} & (1+x)^{a_1b_2} & (1+x)^{a_1b_3} \\ (1+x)^{a_2b_1} & (1+x)^{a_2b_2} & (1+x)^{a_2b_3} \\ (1+x)^{a_3b_1} & (1+x)^{a_3b_2} & (1+x)^{a_3b_3} \end{vmatrix}.$$

Sol. We know that, if $f(x)$ be a polynomial, then coefficient of x^n in $f(x)=\dfrac{1}{n!}f^n(0)$.

Let
$$f(x)=\begin{vmatrix} (1+x)^{a_1b_1} & (1+x)^{a_1b_2} & (1+x)^{a_1b_3} \\ (1+x)^{a_2b_1} & (1+x)^{a_2b_2} & (1+x)^{a_2b_3} \\ (1+x)^{a_3b_1} & (1+x)^{a_3b_2} & (1+x)^{a_3b_3} \end{vmatrix}$$

$$\therefore\quad f'(x)=\begin{vmatrix} a_1b_1(1+x)^{a_1b_1-1} & a_1b_2(1+x)^{a_1b_2-1} & a_1b_3(1+x)^{a_1b_3-1} \\ (1+x)^{a_2b_1} & (1+x)^{a_2b_2} & (1+x)^{a_2b_3} \\ (1+x)^{a_3b_1} & (1+x)^{a_3b_2} & (1+x)^{a_3b_3} \end{vmatrix}$$
$$+\begin{vmatrix} (1+x)^{a_1b_1} & (1+x)^{a_1b_2} & (1+x)^{a_1b_3} \\ a_2b_1(1+x)^{a_2b_1-1} & a_2b_2(1+x)^{a_2b_2-1} & a_2b_3(1+x)^{a_2b_3-1} \\ (1+x)^{a_3b_1} & (1+x)^{a_3b_2} & (1+x)^{a_3b_3} \end{vmatrix}$$
$$+\begin{vmatrix} (1+x)^{a_1b_1} & (1+x)^{a_1b_2} & (1+x)^{a_1b_3} \\ (1+x)^{a_2b_1} & (1+x)^{a_2b_2} & (1+x)^{a_2b_3} \\ a_3b_1(1+x)^{a_3b_1-1} & a_3b_2(1+x)^{a_3b_2-1} & a_3b_3(1+x)^{a_3b_3-1} \end{vmatrix}$$

$$\therefore\quad f'(0)=\begin{vmatrix} a_1b_1 & a_1b_2 & a_1b_3 \\ 1 & 1 & 1 \\ 1 & 1 & 1 \end{vmatrix}+\begin{vmatrix} 1 & 1 & 1 \\ a_2b_1 & a_2b_2 & a_2b_3 \\ 1 & 1 & 1 \end{vmatrix}+\begin{vmatrix} 1 & 1 & 1 \\ 1 & 1 & 1 \\ a_3b_1 & a_3b_2 & a_3b_3 \end{vmatrix}$$
$$=0+0+0=0$$

$\therefore$ Coefficient of x in $f(x)=\dfrac{f'(0)}{1!}=0$

Alternate Solution

Let
$$\begin{vmatrix} (1+x)^{a_1b_1} & (1+x)^{a_1b_2} & (1+x)^{a_1b_3} \\ (1+x)^{a_2b_1} & (1+x)^{a_2b_2} & (1+x)^{a_2b_3} \\ (1+x)^{a_3b_1} & (1+x)^{a_3b_2} & (1+x)^{a_3b_3} \end{vmatrix}=A+Bx+Cx^2+\cdots$$

On differentiating both sides w.r.t. x and then put $x=0$ in both sides, we get

$$B=\begin{vmatrix} a_1b_1 & a_1b_2 & a_1b_3 \\ 1 & 1 & 1 \\ 1 & 1 & 1 \end{vmatrix}+\begin{vmatrix} 1 & 1 & 1 \\ a_2b_1 & a_2b_2 & a_2b_3 \\ 1 & 1 & 1 \end{vmatrix}+\begin{vmatrix} 1 & 1 & 1 \\ 1 & 1 & 1 \\ a_3b_1 & a_3b_2 & a_3b_3 \end{vmatrix}$$
$$=0+0+0=0$$

Hence, coefficient of x in given determinant is 0.

Example 36. If $\Delta(x)=\begin{vmatrix} \alpha+x & \theta+x & \lambda+x \\ \beta+x & \phi+x & \mu+x \\ \gamma+x & \psi+x & \nu+x \end{vmatrix}$, show that $\Delta''(x)=0$ and $\Delta(x)=\Delta(0)+Sx$, where S denotes the sum of all the cofactors of all elements in $\Delta(0)$ and dash denotes the derivative.

Sol. We have,
$$\Delta'(x)=\begin{vmatrix} 1 & \theta+x & \lambda+x \\ 1 & \phi+x & \mu+x \\ 1 & \psi+x & \nu+x \end{vmatrix}+\begin{vmatrix} \alpha+x & 1 & \lambda+x \\ \beta+x & 1 & \mu+x \\ \gamma+x & 1 & \nu+x \end{vmatrix}$$
$$+\begin{vmatrix} \alpha+x & \theta+x & 1 \\ \beta+x & \phi+x & 1 \\ \gamma+x & \psi+x & 1 \end{vmatrix}$$

Applying $C_2 \to C_2 - xC_1$ and $C_3 \to C_3 - xC_1$ in first, $C_1 \to C_1 - xC_2$ and $C_3 \to C_3 - xC_2$ in second and $C_1 \to C_1 - xC_3$ and $C_2 \to C_2 - xC_3$ in third, then

$$\Delta'(x) = \begin{vmatrix} 1 & \theta & \lambda \\ 1 & \phi & \mu \\ 1 & \psi & \nu \end{vmatrix} + \begin{vmatrix} \alpha & 1 & \lambda \\ \beta & 1 & \mu \\ \gamma & 1 & \nu \end{vmatrix} + \begin{vmatrix} \alpha & \theta & 1 \\ \beta & \phi & 1 \\ \gamma & \psi & 1 \end{vmatrix}$$

$$\left[\text{sum of all cofactors in } \Delta(0), \text{ where } \Delta(0) = \begin{vmatrix} \alpha & \theta & \lambda \\ \beta & \phi & \mu \\ \gamma & \psi & \nu \end{vmatrix}\right]$$

$\therefore \quad \Delta''(x) = 0 \quad [\because S \text{ is constant}]$

Since, $\Delta'(x) = S$

On integrating $\Delta(x) = Sx + C \quad \therefore \Delta(0) = 0 + C$

Hence, $\Delta(x) = Sx + \Delta(0)$

Example 37. If $f(x) = \begin{vmatrix} x^n & \sin x & \cos x \\ n! & \sin\left(\frac{n\pi}{2}\right) & \cos\left(\frac{n\pi}{2}\right) \\ \pi & \pi^2 & \pi^3 \end{vmatrix}$, then find the value of $\frac{d^n}{dx^n}\{f(x)\}$ at $x = 0$, $n \in I$.

Sol. $$\frac{d^n}{dx^n}\{f(x)\} = \begin{vmatrix} \frac{d^n}{dx^n}(x^n) & \frac{d^n}{dx^n}(\sin x) & \frac{d^n}{dx^n}(\cos x) \\ n! & \sin\left(\frac{n\pi}{2}\right) & \cos\left(\frac{n\pi}{2}\right) \\ \pi & \pi^2 & \pi^3 \end{vmatrix}$$

$$= \begin{vmatrix} n! & \sin\left(\frac{n\pi}{2} + x\right) & \cos\left(\frac{n\pi}{2} + x\right) \\ n! & \sin\left(\frac{n\pi}{2}\right) & \cos\left(\frac{n\pi}{2}\right) \\ \pi & \pi^2 & \pi^3 \end{vmatrix}$$

$$\therefore \frac{d^n}{dx^n}\{f(x)\} \text{ at } (x = 0) = \begin{vmatrix} n! & \sin\left(\frac{n\pi}{2}\right) & \cos\left(\frac{n\pi}{2}\right) \\ n! & \sin\left(\frac{n\pi}{2}\right) & \cos\left(\frac{n\pi}{2}\right) \\ \pi & \pi^2 & \pi^3 \end{vmatrix}$$

$= 0 \quad [\because R_1 \text{ and } R_2 \text{ are identical}]$

8.14 Integration of a Determinant

Let $$\Delta(x) = \begin{vmatrix} f(x) & g(x) & h(x) \\ p & q & r \\ l & m & n \end{vmatrix}$$

where p, q, r, l, m and n are constants, then

$$\int_a^b \Delta(x)\,dx = \begin{vmatrix} \int_a^b f(x)dx & \int_a^b g(x)dx & \int_a^b h(x)\,dx \\ p & q & r \\ l & m & n \end{vmatrix}$$

JEE SPIKE

If in a determinant, the elements of more than one columns or rows are functions of x, then the integration can be done only after evaluation or expansion of the determinant.

Example 38. If $\Delta(x) = \begin{vmatrix} x & x^2 & x^4 \\ 4 & 5 & 8 \\ 3 & 2 & 9 \end{vmatrix}$, then find $\int_0^1 \Delta(x)dx$.

Sol. $$\int_0^1 \Delta(x)dx = \begin{vmatrix} \int_0^1 xdx & \int_0^1 x^2dx & \int_0^1 x^4dx \\ 4 & 5 & 8 \\ 3 & 2 & 9 \end{vmatrix}$$

$$= \begin{vmatrix} \left[\frac{x^2}{2}\right]_0^1 & \left[\frac{x^3}{3}\right]_0^1 & \left[\frac{x^5}{5}\right]_0^1 \\ 4 & 5 & 8 \\ 3 & 2 & 9 \end{vmatrix}$$

$$= \begin{vmatrix} 1/2 & 1/3 & 1/5 \\ 4 & 5 & 8 \\ 3 & 2 & 9 \end{vmatrix}$$

Applying $R_3 \to R_3 - 6R_1$, we get

$$= \begin{vmatrix} 1/2 & 1/3 & 1/5 \\ 4 & 5 & 8 \\ 0 & 0 & 39/5 \end{vmatrix}$$

Applying $C_3 \to 5C_3$, we get

$$= \begin{vmatrix} 1/2 & 1/3 & 1 \\ 4 & 5 & 40 \\ 0 & 0 & 39 \end{vmatrix}$$

$$= 39\left(\frac{5}{2} - \frac{4}{3}\right)$$

$$= \frac{91}{2}$$

$$\therefore \int_0^1 \Delta(x)dx = \frac{91}{2}$$

Example 39. If $f(x) = \begin{vmatrix} \sin^5 x & \ln \sin x & \frac{\sqrt{\sin x}}{\sqrt{\sin x} + \sqrt{\cos x}} \\ n & \sum_{k=1}^{n} k & \prod_{k=1}^{n} k \\ \frac{8}{15} & \frac{\pi}{2}\ln\left(\frac{1}{2}\right) & \frac{\pi}{4} \end{vmatrix}$,

then find the value of $\int_0^{\pi/2} f(x)\,dx$.

Sol. $\int_0^{\pi/2} f(x)\,dx$

$$= \begin{vmatrix} \int_0^{\pi/2} \sin^5 x\,dx & \int_0^{\pi/2} \ln\sin x\,dx & \int_0^{\pi/2} \frac{\sqrt{\sin x}}{\sqrt{\sin x}+\sqrt{\cos x}} \\ n & \sum_{k=1}^{n} k & \prod_{k=1}^{n} k \\ \frac{8}{15} & \frac{\pi}{2}\ln\left(\frac{1}{2}\right) & \frac{\pi}{4} \end{vmatrix},$$

$$= \begin{vmatrix} \frac{4}{5}\cdot\frac{2}{3} & -\frac{\pi}{2}\ln 2 & \frac{\pi}{4} \\ n & \sum_{k=1}^{n} k & \prod_{k=1}^{n} k \\ \frac{8}{15} & \frac{\pi}{2}\ln\left(\frac{1}{2}\right) & \frac{\pi}{4} \end{vmatrix} \quad \text{[by Walli's formula]}$$

$$= \begin{vmatrix} \frac{8}{15} & \frac{\pi}{2}\ln\left(\frac{1}{2}\right) & \frac{\pi}{4} \\ n & \sum_{k=1}^{n} k & \prod_{k=1}^{n} k \\ \frac{8}{15} & \frac{\pi}{2}\ln\left(\frac{1}{2}\right) & \frac{\pi}{4} \end{vmatrix} = 0 \quad \text{[since } R_1 \text{ and } R_3 \text{ are identical]}$$

Example 40. Let

$$f(x) = \begin{vmatrix} \sec x & \cos x & \sec^2 x + \cot x \operatorname{cosec} x \\ \cos^2 x & \cos^2 x & \operatorname{cosec}^2 x \\ 1 & \cos^2 x & \cos^2 x \end{vmatrix}, \text{ then find}$$

the value of $\int_0^{\pi/2} f(x)\,dx$.

Sol. Applying $C_2 \to C_2 - \cos^2 x\, C_1$, then

$$f(x) = \begin{vmatrix} \sec x & 0 & \sec^2 x + \cot x \operatorname{cosec} x \\ \cos^2 x & \cos^2 x - \cos^4 x & \operatorname{cosec}^2 x \\ 1 & 0 & \cos^2 x \end{vmatrix}$$

[expanding along C_2]

$$= (\cos^2 x - \cos^4 x)\begin{vmatrix} \sec x & \sec^2 x + \cot x \operatorname{cosec} x \\ 1 & \cos^2 x \end{vmatrix}$$

$$= (\cos^2 x - \cos^4 x)(\cos x - \sec^2 x - \cot x \operatorname{cosec} x)$$

$$= \cos^2 x (1 - \cos^2 x)\left(\cos x - \frac{1}{\cos^2 x} - \frac{\cos x}{\sin^2 x}\right)$$

$$= \cos^2 x \sin^2 x \left(\cos x - \frac{1}{\cos^2 x} - \frac{\cos x}{\sin^2 x}\right)$$

$$= \cos^3 x \sin^2 x - \sin^2 x - \cos^3 x$$

$$= -\cos^3 x (1 - \sin^2 x) - \sin^2 x$$

$$f(x) = -\cos^5 x - \sin^2 x$$

$$\therefore \int_0^{\pi/2} f(x)\,dx = -\int_0^{\pi/2} \cos^5 x\,dx - \int_0^{\pi/2} \sin^2 x\,dx$$

$$= -\left(\frac{4}{5}\cdot\frac{2}{3}\cdot 1\right) - \left(\frac{1}{2}\cdot\frac{\pi}{2}\right) = -\left(\frac{8}{15} + \frac{\pi}{4}\right)$$

[by Walli's formula]

8.15 Use of Σ in Determinant

If $\Delta(r) = \begin{vmatrix} f(r) & g(r) & h(r) \\ a & b & c \\ a_1 & b_1 & c_1 \end{vmatrix}$

where a, b, c, a_1, b_1 and c_1 are constants, independent of r, then

$$\sum_{r=1}^{n} \Delta(r) = \begin{vmatrix} \sum_{r=1}^{n} f(r) & \sum_{r=1}^{n} g(r) & \sum_{r=1}^{n} h(r) \\ a & b & c \\ a_1 & b_1 & c_1 \end{vmatrix}$$

JEE SPIKE

If in a determinant, the elements of more than one columns or rows are function of r, then the Σ can be done only after evaluation or expansion of the determinant.

Example 41. Let n be a positive integer and

$$\Delta_r = \begin{vmatrix} 2r-1 & {}^nC_r & 1 \\ n^2-1 & 2^n & n+1 \\ \cos^2 n^2 & \cos^2 n & \cos^2(n+1) \end{vmatrix}, \text{ prove that}$$

$\sum_{r=0}^{n} \Delta_r = 0.$

Sol. We have, $\Delta_r = \begin{vmatrix} 2r-1 & {}^nC_r & 1 \\ n^2-1 & 2^n & n+1 \\ \cos^2(n^2) & \cos^2 n & \cos^2(n+1) \end{vmatrix}$

$$\therefore \quad \sum_{r=0}^{n} \Delta_r = \begin{vmatrix} \sum_{r=0}^{n}(2r-1) & \sum_{r=0}^{n} {}^nC_r & \sum_{r=0}^{n} 1 \\ n^2-1 & 2^n & n+1 \\ \cos^2(n^2) & \cos^2 n & \cos^2(n+1) \end{vmatrix}$$

Now, $\sum_{r=0}^{n}(2r-1) = 2\sum_{r=0}^{n} r - \sum_{r=0}^{n} 1$

$$= 2(0+1+2+3+\ldots+n) - \underbrace{(1+1+1+\ldots+1)}_{(n+1)\text{ times}}$$

$$= \frac{2n(n+1)}{2} - (n+1)$$

$$= (n+1)(n-1)$$

$$= n^2 - 1$$

$$\sum_{r=0}^{n} \Delta_r = \begin{vmatrix} n^2-1 & 2^n & n+1 \\ n^2-1 & 2^n & n+1 \\ \cos^2(n^2) & \cos^2 n & \cos^2(n+1) \end{vmatrix} = 0$$

[since R_1 and R_2 are identical]

Example 42. Let n be a positive integer and

$$\Delta_r = \begin{vmatrix} r^2+r & r+1 & r-2 \\ 2r^2+3r-1 & 3r & 3r-3 \\ r^2+2r+3 & 2r-1 & 2r-1 \end{vmatrix}$$ and

$\sum_{r=1}^{n} \Delta_r = an^2+bn+c$, find the value of $a+b+c$.

Sol. We have, $\Delta_r = \begin{vmatrix} r^2+r & r+1 & r-2 \\ 2r^2+3r-1 & 3r & 3r-3 \\ r^2+2r+3 & 2r-1 & 2r-1 \end{vmatrix}$

Applying $R_2 \to R_2 - (R_1 + R_3)$, then

$$\Delta_r = \begin{vmatrix} r^2+r & r+1 & r-2 \\ \vdots & & \\ -4 \quad \dots & 0 \quad \dots & 0 \\ \vdots & & \\ r^2+2r+3 & 2r-1 & 2r-1 \end{vmatrix}$$

Expanding along R_2, we get

$$= 4 \begin{vmatrix} r+1 & r-2 \\ 2r-1 & 2r-1 \end{vmatrix}$$

$$= 4[(r+1)(2r-1) - (r-2)(2r-1)]$$

$$= 24r - 12$$

Now, $\sum_{r=1}^{n} \Delta_r = 24 \sum_{r=1}^{n} r - 12 \sum_{r=1}^{n} 1$

$$= 24 \frac{n(n+1)}{2} - 12n$$

$$= 12n(n+1-1)$$

$$= 12n^2$$

$$= an^2 + bn + c \qquad \text{[given]}$$

For $n = 1$, we have

$$a + b + c = 12$$

Milestone Practice 8.4

1. If $f(x) = \begin{vmatrix} x & x^2 & x^3 \\ 1 & 2 & 3 \\ 0 & 1 & x \end{vmatrix}$, $f'(1)$ is equal to

(a) -1 (b) 0 (c) 1 (d) 2

2. Let $f(x) = \begin{vmatrix} \sec x & x^2 & x \\ 2\sin x & x^3 & 2x^2 \\ \tan 3x & x^2 & x \end{vmatrix}$, $\lim_{x \to 0} \frac{f(x)}{x^4}$ is equal to

(a) 0 (b) -1 (c) 2 (d) 3

3. Let $\begin{vmatrix} x & 2 & x \\ x^2 & x & 6 \\ x & x & 6 \end{vmatrix} = Ax^4 + Bx^3 + Cx^2 + Dx + E$, the value of $5A + 4B + 3C + 2D + E$ is equal to

(a) -16 (b) -11 (c) 0 (d) 16

4. Let $f(x) = \begin{vmatrix} x^3 & \sin x & \cos x \\ 6 & -1 & 0 \\ p & p^2 & p^3 \end{vmatrix}$, where p is a constant.

Then $\frac{d^3}{dx^3}\{f(x)\}$ at $x = 0$ is

(a) p (b) $p + p^2$
(c) $p + p^3$ (d) independent of p

5. If $y = \sin mx$, the value of the determinant $\begin{vmatrix} y & y_1 & y_2 \\ y_3 & y_4 & y_5 \\ y_6 & y_7 & y_8 \end{vmatrix}$, where $y_n = \frac{d^n y}{dx^n}$, is

(a) m^2 (b) m^3
(c) m^9 (d) None of these

6. Let $f(x) = \begin{vmatrix} 2\cos^2 x & \sin 2x & -\sin x \\ \sin 2x & 2\sin^2 x & \cos x \\ \sin x & -\cos x & 0 \end{vmatrix}$, the value of $\int_0^{\pi/2} \{f(x) + f'(x)\}\, dx$, is

(a) $\frac{\pi}{2}$ (b) π (c) $\frac{3\pi}{2}$ (d) 2π

7. If $f(x) = \begin{vmatrix} \cos x & e^{x^2} & 2x\cos^2\left(\frac{x}{2}\right) \\ x^2 & \sec x & \sin x + x^3 \\ 1 & 2 & x + \tan x \end{vmatrix}$, the value of $\int_{-\pi/2}^{\pi/2} (x^2+1)[f(x) + f''(x)]\, dx$, is

(a) -1 (b) 0 (c) 1 (d) 2

8. If $\Delta_k = \begin{vmatrix} 1 & n & n \\ 2k & n^2+n+1 & n^2+n \\ 2k-1 & n^2 & n^2+n+1 \end{vmatrix}$ and $\sum_{k=1}^{n} \Delta_k = 56$, then n is equal to

(a) 4 (b) 6
(c) 8 (d) 7

Answer Key

1. (c) 2. (b) 3. (b) 4. (d) 5. (d) 6. (b) 7. (b) 8. (d)

For Detailed Solution

JEE Pattern EXAMPLES

Single Option Correct Type Questions

Example 1 *If* $(x_1 - x_2)^2 + (y_1 - y_2)^2 = a^2$, $(x_2 - x_3)^2 + (y_2 - y_3)^2 = b^2$ *and* $(x_3 - x_1)^2 + (y_3 - y_1)^2 = c^2$ *and* $k\begin{vmatrix} x_1 & y_1 & 1 \\ x_2 & y_2 & 1 \\ x_3 & y_3 & 1 \end{vmatrix}^2 = (a+b+c)(b+c-a)(c+a-b)(a+b-c)$, *the value of k is*

(a) 1 (b) 2

(c) 4 (d) 8

Sol. (c) Consider the triangle with vertices $B(x_1, y_1)$, $C(x_2, y_2)$ and $A(x_3, y_3)$

$$AB = c,\ BC = a \text{ and } CA = b$$

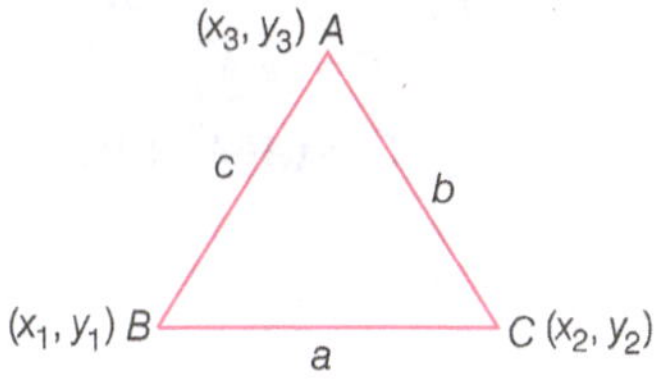

$$\therefore \quad \text{Area of } \Delta ABC = \frac{1}{2}\begin{vmatrix} x_1 & y_1 & 1 \\ x_2 & y_2 & 1 \\ x_3 & y_3 & 1 \end{vmatrix} \quad \text{...(i)}$$

Also, area of $\Delta ABC = \sqrt{s(s-a)(s-b)(s-c)}$, ...(ii)

where $2s = a + b + c$

From Eqs. (i) and (ii), we get

$$\frac{1}{2}\begin{vmatrix} x_1 & y_1 & 1 \\ x_2 & y_2 & 1 \\ x_3 & y_3 & 1 \end{vmatrix} = \sqrt{s(s-a)(s-b)(s-c)}$$

On squaring and simplifying, we get

$$4\begin{vmatrix} x_1 & y_1 & 1 \\ x_2 & y_2 & 1 \\ x_3 & y_3 & 1 \end{vmatrix}^2 = (a+b+c)(b+c-a)(c+a-b)(a+b-c)$$

Hence, the value of k is 4.

Example 2 *If a, b and c are complex numbers, the determinant* $\Delta = \begin{vmatrix} 0 & -b & -c \\ \bar{b} & 0 & -a \\ \bar{c} & \bar{a} & 0 \end{vmatrix}$ *is*

(a) a non-zero real number (b) purely imaginary

(c) 0 (d) None of these

> **Decoding the Question**
> Use, $z + \bar{z} = 0$ i.e. z is purely real and $z - \bar{z} = 0$ i.e. z is purely imaginary, where $z = x + iy$ is a complex number.

Sol. (b) We observe that,

$$\bar{\Delta} = \begin{vmatrix} 0 & -\bar{b} & -\bar{c} \\ b & 0 & -\bar{a} \\ c & a & 0 \end{vmatrix}$$

$$\Rightarrow \quad \bar{\Delta} = \begin{vmatrix} 0 & b & c \\ -\bar{b} & 0 & a \\ -\bar{c} & -\bar{a} & 0 \end{vmatrix}$$

[interchanging rows and columns]

$$= -\begin{vmatrix} 0 & -b & -c \\ \bar{b} & 0 & -a \\ \bar{c} & \bar{a} & 0 \end{vmatrix}$$

[taking (– 1) common from each row]

$$\Rightarrow \quad \bar{\Delta} = -\Delta$$

Hence, Δ is purely imaginary.

Example 3 *The equation*

$$\begin{vmatrix} (1+x)^2 & (1-x)^2 & -(2+x^2) \\ 2x+1 & 3x & 1-5x \\ x+1 & 2x & 2-3x \end{vmatrix} + \begin{vmatrix} (1+x)^2 & 2x+1 & x+1 \\ (1-x)^2 & 3x & 2x \\ 1-2x & 3x-2 & 2x-3 \end{vmatrix} = 0 \text{ has}$$

(a) no real solution

(b) 4 real solutions

(c) two real and two non-real solutions

(d) infinite number of solutions, real or non-real

Sol. (d) Interchanging rows and columns in first determinant, then

$$\begin{vmatrix} (1+x)^2 & 2x+1 & x+1 \\ (1-x)^2 & 3x & 2x \\ -(2+x^2) & 1-5x & 2-3x \end{vmatrix} + \begin{vmatrix} (1+x)^2 & 2x+1 & x+1 \\ (1-x)^2 & 3x & 2x \\ 1-2x & 3x-2 & 2x-3 \end{vmatrix} = 0$$

$$\Rightarrow \begin{vmatrix} (1+x)^2 & 2x+1 & x+1 \\ (1-x)^2 & 3x & 2x \\ -(1+x)^2 & -2x-1 & -x-1 \end{vmatrix} = 0$$

Applying $R_3 \to R_3 + R_1$, then

$$\Rightarrow \begin{vmatrix} (1+x)^2 & 2x+1 & x+1 \\ (1-x)^2 & 3x & 2x \\ 0 & 0 & 0 \end{vmatrix} = 0$$

$$\Rightarrow \qquad 0 = 0$$

which is true for all values of x.

Hence, given equation has infinite number of solutions, real or non-real.

Example 4 *If X, Y and Z are positive numbers such that Y and Z have respectively 1 and 0 at their unit's place and*

$$\Delta = \begin{vmatrix} X & 4 & 1 \\ Y & 0 & 1 \\ Z & 1 & 0 \end{vmatrix}$$

If $(\Delta + 1)$ is divisible by 10, then X has at its unit's place

(a) 0 (b) 1 (c) 2 (d) 3

Sol. (c) Let $X = 10x + \lambda$, $Y = 10y + 1$ and $Z = 10z$, where $x, y, z \in N$, then

$$\Delta = \begin{vmatrix} X & 4 & 1 \\ Y & 0 & 1 \\ Z & 1 & 0 \end{vmatrix} = \begin{vmatrix} 10x+\lambda & 4 & 1 \\ 10y+1 & 0 & 1 \\ 10z & 1 & 0 \end{vmatrix}$$

$$= \begin{vmatrix} 10x & 4 & 1 \\ 10y & 0 & 1 \\ 10z & 1 & 0 \end{vmatrix} + \begin{vmatrix} \lambda & 4 & 1 \\ 1 & 0 & 1 \\ 0 & 1 & 0 \end{vmatrix}$$

$$= 10 \begin{vmatrix} x & 4 & 1 \\ y & 0 & 1 \\ z & 1 & 0 \end{vmatrix} + (1 - \lambda)$$

$\Rightarrow \Delta + 1 = 10k + (2 - \lambda)$,

where $k = \begin{vmatrix} x & 4 & 1 \\ y & 0 & 1 \\ z & 1 & 0 \end{vmatrix}$.

It is given that $(\Delta + 1)$ is divisible by 10. Therefore, $2 - \lambda = 0$ i.e. $\lambda = 2$.

$\therefore \qquad X = 10x + 2$

$\Rightarrow$ 2 is at unit's place of X.

Example 5 *The number of distinct values of a 2×2 determinant whose entries are from the set $\{-1, 0, 1\}$, is*

(a) 3 (b) 4 (c) 5 (d) 6

Decoding the Question

Write the entries of 2×2 determinant using given set, then find determinant.

Sol. (c) Possible values are $-2, -1, 0, 1, 2$

i.e. $\begin{vmatrix} 1 & 0 \\ -1 & 1 \end{vmatrix} = 1$, $\begin{vmatrix} 1 & -1 \\ 0 & 0 \end{vmatrix} = 0$, $\begin{vmatrix} 0 & 1 \\ 1 & -1 \end{vmatrix} = -1$,

$\begin{vmatrix} 1 & -1 \\ 1 & 1 \end{vmatrix} = 2$, $\begin{vmatrix} -1 & 1 \\ 1 & 1 \end{vmatrix} = -2$

JEE SCANNER

Example 6 Similar to PYQ Asked in JEE Main 2024

Let $A = \begin{bmatrix} \sqrt{3} & 1 \\ -1 & \sqrt{3} \end{bmatrix}$, $B = \begin{bmatrix} 1 & 1 \\ 0 & 1 \end{bmatrix}$, $C = ABA^T$ and $X = A^T C^2 A$, then det X is equal to

(a) 4096 (b) 4036 (c) 4063 (d) 4069

Sol. (a) Given, $A = \begin{bmatrix} \sqrt{3} & 1 \\ -1 & \sqrt{3} \end{bmatrix}$ and $B = \begin{bmatrix} 1 & 1 \\ 0 & 1 \end{bmatrix}$

$$A^T = \begin{bmatrix} \sqrt{3} & -1 \\ 1 & \sqrt{3} \end{bmatrix}, AA^T = \begin{bmatrix} \sqrt{3} & 1 \\ -1 & \sqrt{3} \end{bmatrix}\begin{bmatrix} \sqrt{3} & -1 \\ 1 & \sqrt{3} \end{bmatrix} = \begin{bmatrix} 4 & 0 \\ 0 & 4 \end{bmatrix} = 4I$$

$$C = ABA^T$$

$$C^2 = (ABA^T)(ABA^T)$$

$$C^2 = AB\,4IBA^T$$

$$= 4\,AB^2A^T$$

$$\because \quad X = A^T C^2 A$$

$$= 4A^T AB^2 A^T A = 64B^2$$

$$X = 64\begin{bmatrix} 1 & 2 \\ 0 & 1 \end{bmatrix}$$

$$\left[\because B^2 = \begin{bmatrix} 1 & 1 \\ 0 & 1 \end{bmatrix}\begin{bmatrix} 1 & 1 \\ 0 & 1 \end{bmatrix} = \begin{bmatrix} 1 & 2 \\ 0 & 1 \end{bmatrix}\right]$$

$$|X| = 64 \times 64 = 4096$$

Skill Builder

Let $A = \begin{bmatrix} 2 & 1 \\ -1 & 2 \end{bmatrix}$, $B = \begin{bmatrix} 0 & 1 \\ 1 & 1 \end{bmatrix}$, $C = ABA^T$ and $X = A^T C^2 A$, then det X is equal to

(a) 31250

(b) 15625

(c) 125

(d) 250

For Sol.

Example 7 *If* $f(x)=\begin{vmatrix}(1+x)^a & (1+2x)^b & 1\\ 1 & (1+x)^a & (1+2x)^b\\ (1+2x)^b & 1 & (1+x)^a\end{vmatrix}$;

a, b being positive integers, then

(a) constant term in $f(x)$ is 4

(b) coefficient of x in $f(x)$ is 0

(c) constant term in $f(x)$ is $(a-b)$

(d) constant term in $f(x)$ is $(a+b)$

Sol. (b) Let $\begin{vmatrix}(1+x)^a & (1+2x)^b & 1\\ 1 & (1+x)^a & (1+2x)^b\\ (1+2x)^b & 1 & (1+x)^a\end{vmatrix}$

$$= A + Bx + Cx^2 + \ldots$$

Put $x = 0$, then $A = 0$

On differentiating both sides w.r.t. x and then put $x = 0$

$$\begin{vmatrix}a & 2b & 0\\ 1 & 1 & 1\\ 1 & 1 & 1\end{vmatrix}+\begin{vmatrix}1 & 1 & 1\\ 0 & a & 2b\\ 1 & 1 & 1\end{vmatrix}+\begin{vmatrix}1 & 1 & 1\\ 1 & 1 & 1\\ 2b & 0 & a\end{vmatrix}=B$$

$\therefore \quad 0 + 0 + 0 = B$

$\Rightarrow \quad B = 0$

Hence, constant term in $f(x)$ is zero and coefficient of x in $f(x)$ is 0.

Example 8 *If* $f_j = \sum_{i=0}^{2} a_{ij}\, x^i,\ j=1,2,3$ *and* f_j' *and* f_j'' *are denoted by* $\dfrac{df_j}{dx}$ *and* $\dfrac{d^2 f_j}{dx^2}$ *respectively, then*

$g(x)=\begin{vmatrix}f_1 & f_2 & f_3\\ f_1' & f_2' & f_3'\\ f_1'' & f_2'' & f_3''\end{vmatrix}$ *is*

(a) a constant (b) a linear in x

(c) a quadratic in x (d) a cubic in x

Sol. (a) $\because g'(x)=\begin{vmatrix}f_1' & f_2' & f_3'\\ f_1' & f_2' & f_3'\\ f_1'' & f_2'' & f_3''\end{vmatrix}+\begin{vmatrix}f_1 & f_2 & f_3\\ f_1'' & f_2'' & f_3''\\ f_1'' & f_2'' & f_3''\end{vmatrix}+\begin{vmatrix}f_1 & f_2 & f_3\\ f_1' & f_2' & f_3'\\ f_1''' & f_2''' & f_3'''\end{vmatrix}$

$= 0 + 0 + 0$ [$\because f_j$ is a quadratic function]

$\therefore \quad g(x) = c =$ constant

Example 9 *Let* $\Delta_a=\begin{vmatrix}(a-1) & n & 6\\ (a-1)^2 & 2n^2 & 4n-2\\ (a-1)^3 & 3n^3 & 3n^2-3n\end{vmatrix}$,

the value of $\sum_{a=1}^{n}\Delta_a$ *is*

(a) 0 (b) $\dfrac{(n-1)n}{2}$

(c) $\dfrac{(n-1)n^2}{2}$ (d) $\dfrac{(n-1)n(2n-1)}{3}$

> **Decoding the Question**
>
> Use, $\sum_{r=1}^{n} r=\dfrac{n(n+1)}{2}$, $\sum_{r=1}^{n} r^2=\dfrac{n(n+1)(2n+1)}{6}$ and $\sum_{r=1}^{n} r^3=\left(\dfrac{n(n+1)}{2}\right)^2$.

Sol. (a) $\sum_{a=1}^{n}\Delta_a=\begin{vmatrix}\sum_{a=1}^{n}(a-1) & n & 6\\ \sum_{a=1}^{n}(a-1)^2 & 2n^2 & 4n-2\\ \sum_{a=1}^{n}(a-1)^3 & 3n^3 & 3n^2-3n\end{vmatrix}$

$$=\begin{vmatrix}\dfrac{(n-1)n}{2} & n & 6\\ \dfrac{(n-1)n(2n-1)}{6} & 2n^2 & 4n-2\\ \dfrac{(n-1)^2n^2}{4} & 3n^3 & 3n^2-3n\end{vmatrix}$$

$$=\frac{(n-1)n^2}{2}\begin{vmatrix}1 & 1 & 6\\ \dfrac{2n-1}{3} & 2n & 4n-2\\ \dfrac{(n-1)n}{2} & 3n^2 & 3n^2-3n\end{vmatrix}$$

[taking $\dfrac{(n-1)n}{2}$ and n common from C_1 and C_2 respectively]

Applying $C_3 \to C_3 - 6C_1$, then

$$\sum_{a=1}^{n}\Delta_a=\frac{(n-1)n^2}{2}\begin{vmatrix}1 & 1 & 0\\ \dfrac{2n-1}{3} & 2n & 0\\ \dfrac{(n-1)n}{2} & 3n^2 & 0\end{vmatrix}=0$$

Example 10 *If* $\Delta(x)=\begin{vmatrix}1 & \cos x & 1-\cos x\\ 1+\sin x & \cos x & 1+\sin x-\cos x\\ \sin x & \sin x & 1\end{vmatrix}$,

then $\int_0^{\pi/2}\Delta(x)\,dx$ *is equal to*

(a) $-\dfrac{1}{2}$ (b) 0 (c) $\dfrac{1}{4}$ (d) $\dfrac{1}{2}$

Sol. (a) Applying $C_3 \to C_3 + C_2 - C_1$, then

$$\Delta(x)=\begin{vmatrix}1 & \cos x & 0\\ 1+\sin x & \cos x & 0\\ \sin x & \sin x & 1\end{vmatrix}$$

$$=1(\cos x-\cos x-\cos x\sin x)=-\frac{1}{2}\sin 2x$$

$$\therefore \int_0^{\pi/2}\Delta(x)dx=-\frac{1}{2}\int_0^{\pi/2}\sin 2x\,dx$$

$$=\frac{1}{4}[\cos 2x]_0^{\pi/2}=\frac{1}{4}(-1-1)=-\frac{1}{2}$$

Example 11 *Number of values of a for which the system of equations $a^2x+(2-a)y=4+a^2$ and $ax+(2a-1)y=a^5-2$ possess no solution, is*

(a) 0
(b) 1
(c) 2
(d) infinite

> **Decoding the Question**
> If $\Delta = 0$ and atleast one of the determinant Δ_1, Δ_2 is non-zero, then the given system of linear equation is inconsistent i.e. having no solution.

Sol. (c) $\because \Delta = \begin{vmatrix} a^2 & 2-a \\ a & 2a-1 \end{vmatrix} = a^2(2a-1)-a(2-a) = 2a(a+1)(a-1)$

For no solution, $\Delta = 0$

$\therefore \quad a = -1, 0, 1$

$\Rightarrow \quad \Delta_1 = \begin{vmatrix} 4+a^2 & 2-a \\ a^5-2 & 2a-1 \end{vmatrix}$

Values of Δ_1 at $a=-1, 0, 1$ are $-6, 0, 6$ respectively and

$$\Delta_2 = \begin{vmatrix} a^2 & 4+a^2 \\ a & a^5-2 \end{vmatrix}$$

Values of Δ_2 at $a=-1, 0, 1$ are $2, 0, -6$, respectively.

For no solution,

$\Delta = 0$ and atleast one of Δ_1, Δ_2 is non-zero.

$\therefore \quad a = -1, 1$

More than One Correct Option Type Questions

Example 12 *The determinant* $\begin{vmatrix} a^2 & a^2-(b-c)^2 & bc \\ b^2 & b^2-(c-a)^2 & ca \\ c^2 & c^2-(a-b)^2 & ab \end{vmatrix}$ *is divisible by*

(a) $a+b+c$
(b) $(a+b)(b+c)(c+a)$
(c) $a^2+b^2+c^2$
(d) $(a-b)(b-c)(c-a)$

Sol. (a,c,d) Applying $C_2 \to C_2 - C_1 - 2C_3$, then

$$\begin{vmatrix} a^2 & -(b^2+c^2) & bc \\ b^2 & -(c^2+a^2) & ca \\ c^2 & -(a^2+b^2) & ab \end{vmatrix} = -\begin{vmatrix} a^2 & b^2+c^2 & bc \\ b^2 & c^2+a^2 & ca \\ c^2 & a^2+b^2 & ab \end{vmatrix}$$

Applying $C_2 \to C_2 + C_1$, then

$$= -\begin{vmatrix} a^2 & a^2+b^2+c^2 & bc \\ b^2 & a^2+b^2+c^2 & ca \\ c^2 & a^2+b^2+c^2 & ab \end{vmatrix}$$

Applying $R_2 \to R_2 - R_1$ and $R_3 \to R_3 - R_1$, then

$$= -\begin{vmatrix} a^2 & a^2+b^2+c^2 & bc \\ b^2-a^2 & 0 & c(a-b) \\ c^2-a^2 & 0 & -b(c-a) \end{vmatrix}$$

$$= (a^2+b^2+c^2)\begin{vmatrix} -(a+b)(a-b) & c(a-b) \\ (c+a)(c-a) & -b(c-a) \end{vmatrix}$$

$$= (a-b)(c-a)(a^2+b^2+c^2)\begin{vmatrix} -(a+b) & c \\ c+a & -b \end{vmatrix}$$

Applying $C_1 \to C_1 - C_2$, then

$$= (a-b)(c-a)(a^2+b^2+c^2)\begin{vmatrix} -(a+b+c) & c \\ (a+b+c) & -b \end{vmatrix}$$

$$= (a-b)(b-c)(c-a)(a+b+c)(a^2+b^2+c^2)$$

Example 13 *The value of θ lying between $-\frac{\pi}{4}$ and $\frac{\pi}{2}$ and $0 \le A \le \frac{\pi}{2}$ and satisfying the equation*

$$\begin{vmatrix} 1+\sin^2 A & \cos^2 A & 2\sin 4\theta \\ \sin^2 A & 1+\cos^2 A & 2\sin 4\theta \\ \sin^2 A & \cos^2 A & 1+2\sin 4\theta \end{vmatrix} = 0, \text{ are}$$

(a) $A=\frac{\pi}{4}, \theta=-\frac{\pi}{8}$ (b) $A=\frac{3\pi}{8}=\theta$

(c) $A=\frac{\pi}{5}, \theta=-\frac{\pi}{8}$ (d) $A=\frac{\pi}{6}, \theta=\frac{3\pi}{8}$

Sol. (a, b, c, d)

$$\because \begin{vmatrix} 1+\sin^2 A & \cos^2 A & 2\sin 4\theta \\ \sin^2 A & 1+\cos^2 A & 2\sin 4\theta \\ \sin^2 A & \cos^2 A & 1+2\sin 4\theta \end{vmatrix} = 0$$

Applying $R_2 \to R_2 - R_1$ and $R_3 \to R_3 - R_1$, then

$$\begin{vmatrix} 1+\sin^2 A & \cos^2 A & 2\sin 4\theta \\ -1 & 1 & 0 \\ -1 & 0 & 1 \end{vmatrix} = 0$$

Applying $C_1 \to C_1 + C_2$, then

$$\begin{vmatrix} 2 & \cos^2 A & 2\sin 4\theta \\ 0 & 1 & 0 \\ -1 & 0 & 1 \end{vmatrix} = 0$$

$\Rightarrow \quad 1(2+2\sin 4\theta) = 0$

$\therefore \quad \sin 4\theta = -1$

$\Rightarrow \quad 4\theta = (2n-1)\frac{\pi}{2}$

$\Rightarrow \quad \theta = (2n-1)\frac{\pi}{8}$

For $n = 0, 2$, then

$$\theta = -\frac{\pi}{8}, \frac{3\pi}{8} \text{ and } A \in R$$

Example 14 *The digits A, B, C are such that the three digit numbers A88, 6B8, 86C are divisible by 72, the determinant* $\begin{vmatrix} A & 6 & 8 \\ 8 & B & 6 \\ 8 & 8 & C \end{vmatrix}$ *is divisible by*

(a) 72 (b) 144 (c) 288 (d) 216

Sol. (a, b, c) $\because$ $A88, 6B8, 86C$ are divisible by 72.

$\therefore$ $A88, 6B8, 86C$ are also divisible by 9.

$\Rightarrow$ $A+8+8, 6+B+8, 8+6+C$

are divisible by 9, then $A=2, B=4, C=4$

$$\text{Let } \Delta = \begin{vmatrix} A & 6 & 8 \\ 8 & B & 6 \\ 8 & 8 & C \end{vmatrix} = \begin{vmatrix} 2 & 6 & 8 \\ 8 & 4 & 6 \\ 8 & 8 & 4 \end{vmatrix}$$

$$= 2(16-48) - 6(32-48) + 8(64-32) = 288$$

Hence, Δ is divisible by 72, 144 and 288.

Example 15 *If p, q, r and s are in AP and*

$$f(x) = \begin{vmatrix} p+\sin x & q+\sin x & p-r+\sin x \\ q+\sin x & r+\sin x & -1+\sin x \\ r+\sin x & s+\sin x & s-q+\sin x \end{vmatrix}$$

such that $\int_0^1 f(x)\,dx = -2$, *the common difference of the AP can be*

(a) -1 (b) 1/2 (c) 1 (d) 2

Sol. (a, c) $\because$ $f(x) = \frac{1}{2}\begin{vmatrix} p+\sin x & q+\sin x & p-r+\sin x \\ 2q+2\sin x & 2r+2\sin x & -2+2\sin x \\ r+\sin x & s+\sin x & s-q+\sin x \end{vmatrix}$

Applying $R_2 \to R_2 - (R_1 + R_3)$, then

$$f(x) = \frac{1}{2}\begin{vmatrix} p+\sin x & q+\sin x & p-r+\sin x \\ 0 & 0 & -2 \\ r+\sin x & s+\sin x & s-q+\sin x \end{vmatrix}$$

[$\because 2q = p+r, 2r = q+s$ and $p+s = q+r$]

$$= -\frac{(-2)}{2}\begin{vmatrix} p+\sin x & q+\sin x \\ r+\sin x & s+\sin x \end{vmatrix}$$

Applying $C_2 \to C_2 - C_1$, then

$$f(x) = \begin{vmatrix} p+\sin x & D \\ p+2D+\sin x & D \end{vmatrix}$$

[where D = common difference]

$$= D[p+\sin x - p - 2D - \sin x] = -2D^2$$

and $\int_0^1 f(x)\,dx = -2$

$\Rightarrow$ $\int_0^1 (-2D^2)\,dx = -2$

$\Rightarrow$ $-2D^2 = -2$

$\therefore$ $D^2 = 1$

$\Rightarrow$ $D = \pm 1$

Example 16 *If the system of equations* $a^2x - by = a^2 - b$ *and* $bx - b^2y = 2 + 4b$ *possess an infinite number of solutions, the possible values of a and b are*

(a) $a=1, b=-1$ (b) $a=1, b=-2$
(c) $a=-1, b=-1$ (d) $a=-1, b=-2$

Decoding the Question

For infinite number of solutions, we have to solve for $\Delta = 0$ and $\Delta_1 = \Delta_2 = 0$, then find the values of a and b.

Sol. (a, b, c, d) Here, $\Delta = \begin{vmatrix} a^2 & -b \\ b & -b^2 \end{vmatrix} = -a^2b^2 + b^2 = -(a^2-1)b^2$

If $\Delta = 0$, then $a^2 = 1, b = 0$

Now, $\Delta_1 = \begin{vmatrix} a^2-b & -b \\ 2+4b & -b^2 \end{vmatrix}$

For $a^2 = 1$,

$$\Delta_1 = \begin{vmatrix} 1-b & -b \\ 2+4b & -b^2 \end{vmatrix} = b(b+1)(b+2)$$

and $\Delta_2 = \begin{vmatrix} a^2 & a^2-b \\ b & 2+4b \end{vmatrix}$

For $a^2 = 1$,

$$\Delta_2 = \begin{vmatrix} 1 & 1-b \\ b & 2+4b \end{vmatrix} = (b+1)(b+2)$$

For infinite number of solutions, $\Delta = \Delta_1 = \Delta_2 = 0$

$\therefore$ $a^2 = 1, b = -1, -2$

$\Rightarrow$ $a = \pm 1, b = -1, b = -2$

Passage Based Questions

Passage I

(Ex. Nos. 17 and 18)

Consider the system of equations

$$2x + ay + 6z = 8;\quad x + 2y + bz = 5$$
$$x + y + 3z = 4$$

Example 17 *The system has unique solution, if*

(a) $a=2, b=3$ (b) $a=2, b\neq 3$
(c) $a\neq 2, b=3$ (d) $a\neq 2, b\neq 3$

Example 18 *The system has infinite solutions, if*

(a) $a=2, b\in R$ (b) $a=3, b\in R$
(c) $a\in R, b=2$ (d) $a\in R, b=3$

Sol. (Q.Nos. 17 and 18)

$$\Delta = \begin{vmatrix} 2 & a & 6 \\ 1 & 2 & b \\ 1 & 1 & 3 \end{vmatrix} = 2(6-b) - a(3-b) + 6(1-2)$$

$$= ab - 3a - 2b + 6 = (a-2)(b-3)$$

$$\Delta_1 = \begin{vmatrix} 8 & a & 6 \\ 5 & 2 & b \\ 4 & 1 & 3 \end{vmatrix} = 8(6-b) - a(15-4b) + 6(5-8)$$

$$= 4ab - 15a - 8b + 30 = (a-2)(4b-15)$$

$$\Delta_2 = \begin{vmatrix} 2 & 8 & 6 \\ 1 & 5 & b \\ 1 & 4 & 3 \end{vmatrix} = 0 \quad [\because R_1 = 2R_3]$$

$$\Delta_3 = \begin{vmatrix} 2 & a & 8 \\ 1 & 2 & 5 \\ 1 & 1 & 4 \end{vmatrix} = 2(8-5) - a(4-5) + 8(1-2)$$

$$= 6 + a - 8 = a - 2$$

17. (d) The system has unique solution, if

$$\Delta \neq 0$$

$$\Rightarrow \quad (a-2)(b-3) \neq 0$$

$$\Rightarrow \quad a \neq 2, b \neq 3$$

18. (a) The system has infinite solution, if

$$\Delta = \Delta_1 = \Delta_2 = \Delta_3 = 0$$

$$\Rightarrow \quad a - 2 = 0$$

or $\quad a = 2, b \in R$

Passage II

(Ex. Nos. 19 and 20)

Let ${}^xC_i$, ${}^{x^2}C_i$ and ${}^{x^3}C_i (i = 1, 2, 3)$ be Binomial coefficients, where $x \in N$ and $f(x) = 12 \begin{vmatrix} {}^xC_1 & {}^xC_2 & {}^xC_3 \\ {}^{x^2}C_1 & {}^{x^2}C_2 & {}^{x^2}C_3 \\ {}^{x^3}C_1 & {}^{x^3}C_2 & {}^{x^3}C_3 \end{vmatrix}$, then

Example 19 *$f(x)$ is a polynomial of degree*

(a) 6 (b) 10
(c) 14 (d) 18

Example 20 *If $f(x) = (x-1)^m x^n (x+1)^p$, where m, n, $p \in N$, then the value of $\sum mn$ is*

(a) 32 (b) 43
(c) 44 (d) 56

Sol. (Q.Nos. 19 and 20)

$$\because \quad f(x) = 12 \begin{vmatrix} {}^xC_1 & {}^xC_2 & {}^xC_3 \\ {}^{x^2}C_1 & {}^{x^2}C_2 & {}^{x^2}C_3 \\ {}^{x^3}C_1 & {}^{x^3}C_2 & {}^{x^3}C_3 \end{vmatrix}$$

$$= 12 \begin{vmatrix} x & \frac{x(x-1)}{2} & \frac{x(x-1)(x-2)}{6} \\ x^2 & \frac{x^2(x^2-1)}{2} & \frac{x^2(x^2-1)(x^2-2)}{6} \\ x^3 & \frac{x^3(x^3-1)}{2} & \frac{x^3(x^3-1)(x^3-2)}{6} \end{vmatrix}$$

Taking x, x^2 and x^3 common from R_1, R_2 and R_3, then

$$f(x) = x \cdot x^2 \cdot x^3 \begin{vmatrix} 1 & (x-1) & (x-1)(x-2) \\ 1 & (x^2-1) & (x^2-1)(x^2-2) \\ 1 & (x^3-1) & (x^3-1)(x^3-2) \end{vmatrix}$$

$$= x^6(x-1)^2 \begin{vmatrix} 1 & 1 & x-2 \\ 1 & x+1 & (x+1)(x^2-2) \\ 1 & x^2+x+1 & (x^2+x+1)(x^3-2) \end{vmatrix}$$

Applying $R_1 \to R_1 - R_2$ and $R_3 \to R_3 - R_2$, then

$$f(x) = x^6(x-1)^2 \begin{vmatrix} 0 & -x & x(3-x-x^2) \\ 1 & x+1 & (x+1)(x^2-2) \\ 0 & x^2 & x^2(x^2+x^3-3) \end{vmatrix}$$

Expanding along C_1, then

$$= -x^6(x-1)^2 \begin{vmatrix} -x & x(3-x-x^2) \\ x^2 & x^2(x^2+x^3-3) \end{vmatrix}$$

$$= -x^9(x-1)^2 \begin{vmatrix} -1 & 3-x-x^2 \\ 1 & x^2+x^3-3 \end{vmatrix}$$

$$= -x^9(x-1)^2(-x^2-x^3+3-3+x+x^2)$$

$$= x^{10}(x-1)^2(x^2-1)$$

$$= x^{10}(x-1)^3(x+1)$$

19. (c) $f(x)$ is a polynomial of degree 14.

20. (b) Here, $m = 3, n = 10$ and $p = 1$

$$\therefore \sum mn = mn + np + pm = 30 + 10 + 3 = 43$$

Stem Based Questions

Stem I

(Ex. Nos. 21 and 22)

Let $\Delta \neq 0$ and Δ^c denotes the determinant of cofactors, then $\Delta^c = \Delta^{n-1}$, where $n (\geq 1)$ is the order of Δ.

Example 21 *If a, b, c are the roots of the equation $x^3 - 3x^2 + 3x + 7 = 0$, then the value of*

$$\begin{vmatrix} 2bc - a^2 & c^2 & b^2 \\ c^2 & 2ac - b^2 & b^2 \\ b^2 & a^2 & 2ab - c^2 \end{vmatrix}$$ *is ....*

Example 22 *Suppose a, b, $c \in R$, $a + b + c > 0$, $A = bc - a^2$, $B = ca - b^2$, $C = ab - c^2$ and $\begin{vmatrix} A & B & C \\ B & C & A \\ C & A & B \end{vmatrix} = 49$, then $\begin{vmatrix} a & b & c \\ b & c & a \\ c & a & b \end{vmatrix}$ is equal to ....*

Sol. (Q.Nos. 21 and 22)

21. (0) From given equations, we have

$$x = -1, 1 - 2\omega, 1 - 2\omega^2$$

$$\therefore a = -1, b = 1 - 2\omega, c = 1 - 2\omega^2, \text{ where } \omega = e^{i\frac{2\pi}{3}}$$

$$\begin{vmatrix} 2bc - a^2 & c^2 & b^2 \\ c^2 & 2ac - b^2 & a^2 \\ b^2 & a^2 & 2ab - c^2 \end{vmatrix} = \begin{vmatrix} a & b & c \\ b & c & a \\ c & a & b \end{vmatrix}^2$$

$$= (a^3 + b^3 + c^3 - 3abc)^2$$

$$= (a + b + c)^2 (a^2 + b^2 + c^2 - ab - bc - ca)^2$$

$$= \frac{1}{4}(a + b + c)^2 \{(a - b)^2 + (b - c)^2 + (c - a)^2\}$$

$$= \frac{9}{4}\{8(\omega - 1)^2 (1 + \omega + \omega^2)\}$$

$$= 0$$

22. (7) $\because$ $$\begin{vmatrix} A & B & C \\ B & C & A \\ C & A & B \end{vmatrix} = \begin{vmatrix} bc - a^2 & ca - b^2 & ab - c^2 \\ ca - b^2 & ab - c^2 & bc - a^2 \\ ab - c^2 & bc - a^2 & ca - b^2 \end{vmatrix}$$

$$= \begin{vmatrix} a & b & c \\ b & c & a \\ c & a & b \end{vmatrix}^2$$

$$= 49$$

$$\Rightarrow \begin{vmatrix} a & b & c \\ b & c & a \\ c & a & b \end{vmatrix} = 7$$

Single Integer Answer Type Questions

Example 23 *If* $\Delta_r = \begin{vmatrix} r & r-1 \\ r-1 & r \end{vmatrix}$, *where r is a natural number, the value of* $\sqrt[10]{\sum_{r=1}^{1024} \Delta_r}$ *is ....*

Sol. (4) $\because$ $$\Delta_r = r^2 - (r - 1)^2$$

$$\therefore \sum_{r=1}^{1024} \Delta_r = (1024)^2 - (1 - 1)^2 = (1024)^2 = 2^{20}$$

$$\Rightarrow \sqrt[10]{\sum_{r=1}^{1024} \Delta_r} = 2^2 = 4$$

Example 24 *If P, Q and R are the angles of a triangle, the value of* $\begin{vmatrix} \tan P & 1 & 1 \\ 1 & \tan Q & 1 \\ 1 & 1 & \tan R \end{vmatrix}$ *is ....*

Sol. (2) $$\begin{vmatrix} \tan P & 1 & 1 \\ 1 & \tan Q & 1 \\ 1 & 1 & \tan R \end{vmatrix} = \tan P(\tan Q \tan R - 1)$$

$$-1(\tan R - 1) + 1(1 - \tan Q)$$

$$= \tan P \tan Q \tan R - (\tan P + \tan Q + \tan R) + 2$$

$$= 0 + 2$$

[$\because$ In ΔPQR, $\tan P + \tan Q + \tan R = \tan P \tan Q \tan R$]

$$= 2$$

JEE SCANNER

Example 25 Similar to PYQ Asked in JEE Main 2024

Let $A = \begin{bmatrix} 2 & 0 & 0 \\ 0 & a & b \\ 0 & b & a \end{bmatrix}$ *and* $|2A|^4 = 2^{20}$, *where* $a, b \in z$.

Then, 4ab is equal to ....

Sol. (3) We have, $|2A|^4 = 2^{20} \Rightarrow |2A| = 2^5 \Rightarrow 8|A| = 2^5 \Rightarrow |A| = 2^2$

Also, $$A = \begin{bmatrix} 2 & 0 & 0 \\ 0 & a & b \\ 0 & b & a \end{bmatrix} \Rightarrow |A| = 2(a^2 - b^2) = 2^2$$

$$\Rightarrow (a - b)(a + b) = 2 \Rightarrow a - b = 1 \text{ and } a + b = 2$$

$$\Rightarrow a = \frac{3}{2} \text{ and } \frac{1}{2}$$

$$\therefore 4ab = 4 \times \frac{3}{2} \times \frac{1}{2} = 3$$

Skill Builder

Let $A = \begin{bmatrix} 3 & 0 & 0 \\ 0 & x & y \\ 0 & y & x \end{bmatrix}$ and $|3A|^2 = 3^{14}$,

where $x, y \in z$, Then, $x - y$ is equal to ......

For Sol.

Example 26 *Let P be a matrix of order* 3×3 *such that all the entries in P are from the set* $\{-1, 0, 1\}$. *Then, the maximum possible values of the determinant of P is ....*

Sol. (4) $$\det(P) = \begin{vmatrix} a_1 & a_2 & a_3 \\ b_1 & b_2 & b_3 \\ c_1 & c_2 & c_3 \end{vmatrix}$$

$$= (a_1b_2c_3 + a_2b_3c_1 + a_3b_1c_2) - (a_3b_2c_1 + a_1b_3c_2 + a_2b_1c_3)$$

$$= x - y$$

where, $x = a_1b_2c_3 + a_2b_3c_1 + a_3b_1c_2$

and $y = a_3b_2c_1 + a_1b_3c_2 + a_2b_1c_3$

Now, $x \le 3$ and $y \ge -3$

If we consider $\det(P) = 6$, then

$$a_1b_2c_3 = a_2b_3c_1 = a_3b_1c_2 = 1$$

and $$a_3b_2c_1 = a_1b_3c_2 = a_2b_1c_3 = -1,$$

which is contradiction.

So, next possibility is 5 for which one of the terms must be zero but that will make two terms zero.

Hence, greatest value of determinant is 4.

Numerical Value Type Questions

Example 27 *A determinant of second order is made with the elements 0 and 1. The number of determinants with non-negative values is ....*

Sol. (13) The number of determinants that can be made with 0 and $1 = 2 \times 2 \times 2 \times 2 = 16$

and there are only three determinants of second order with negative values

i.e. $\begin{vmatrix} 1 & 1 \\ 1 & 0 \end{vmatrix}, \begin{vmatrix} 0 & 1 \\ 1 & 1 \end{vmatrix}, \begin{vmatrix} 0 & 1 \\ 1 & 0 \end{vmatrix}$

Therefore, number of determinants with non-negative values $= 16 - 3 = 13$

Example 28 *If α and β are the roots of the equations $x^2 - 2x + 4 = 0$, then the value of* $\begin{vmatrix} \Sigma\alpha & \Sigma\alpha^2 & \Sigma\alpha^3 \\ \Sigma\alpha^2 & \Sigma\alpha^3 & \Sigma\alpha^4 \\ \Sigma\alpha^3 & \Sigma\alpha^4 & \Sigma\alpha^5 \end{vmatrix}$ *is ...*

Decoding the Question

First, find the roots of quadratic equation, $ax^2 + bx + c = 0$ by formula $x = \frac{-b \pm \sqrt{b^2 - 4ac}}{2a}$, then find the value of determinant by using given data.

Sol. (0) Given, $x^2 - 2x + 4 = 0$

$\therefore \quad x = 1 \pm i\sqrt{3}$

$\therefore \quad \alpha = 1 + i\sqrt{3}$

and $\quad \beta = 1 - i\sqrt{3}$

$\Rightarrow \quad \alpha = -2\left(\frac{-1 - i\sqrt{3}}{2}\right)$

and $\quad \beta = -2\left(\frac{-1 + i\sqrt{3}}{2}\right)$

$\alpha = -2\omega^2$ and $\beta = -2\omega$, where ω is the cube root of unity.

$$\Sigma\alpha = \alpha + \beta = -2(\omega^2 + \omega) = -2(-1) = 2$$

$$\Sigma\alpha^2 = \alpha^2 + \beta^2 = 4\omega^4 + 4\omega^2 = 4(\omega + \omega^2) = 4(-1) = -4$$

$$\Sigma\alpha^3 = \alpha^3 + \beta^3 = -8\omega^6 - 8\omega^3 = -8 - 8 = -16$$

$$\Sigma\alpha^4 = \alpha^4 + \beta^4 = 16\omega^8 + 16\omega^4 = 16(\omega^2 + \omega)$$

$$= 16(-1) = -16$$

and $\Sigma\alpha^5 = \alpha^5 + \beta^5 = -32\omega^{10} - 32\omega^5$

$$= -32(\omega + \omega^2) = -32(-1) = 32$$

Let $\Delta = \begin{vmatrix} \Sigma\alpha & \Sigma\alpha^2 & \Sigma\alpha^3 \\ \Sigma\alpha^2 & \Sigma\alpha^3 & \Sigma\alpha^4 \\ \Sigma\alpha^3 & \Sigma\alpha^4 & \Sigma\alpha^5 \end{vmatrix} = \begin{vmatrix} 2 & -4 & -16 \\ -4 & -16 & -16 \\ -16 & -16 & 32 \end{vmatrix}$

$$= 2(-4)(-16)\begin{vmatrix} 1 & -2 & -8 \\ 1 & 4 & 4 \\ 1 & 1 & -2 \end{vmatrix}$$

$$= 128\begin{vmatrix} 1 & -2 & -8 \\ 1 & 4 & 4 \\ 1 & 1 & -2 \end{vmatrix}$$

Applying $R_2 \to R_2 - R_1$ and $R_3 \to R_3 - R_1$, then

$$\Delta = 128\begin{vmatrix} 1 & -2 & -8 \\ 0 & 6 & 12 \\ 0 & 3 & 6 \end{vmatrix}$$

Expanding along C_1, we get

$$\Delta = 128 \cdot 1 \cdot \begin{vmatrix} 6 & 12 \\ 3 & 6 \end{vmatrix} = 128(36 - 36) = 0$$

Example 29 *Let S be the sum of all possible determinants of order 2 having 0, 1, 2 and 3 as their elements. Find the common root α of the equations*

$$x^2 + ax + [m+1] = 0, \; x^2 + bx + [m+4] = 0$$

and $x^2 - cx + [m+15] = 0$,

such that $\alpha > S$, where $a + b + c = 0$ and

$$m = \lim_{n \to \infty} \frac{1}{n} \sum_{r=1}^{2n} \frac{r}{\sqrt{(n^2 + r^2)}}$$

and [.] denotes the greatest integer function.

Sol. (3) Let α be a common root of the given equations, then

$$\alpha^2 + a\alpha + [m+1] = 0$$

$$\Rightarrow \quad \alpha^2 + a\alpha + [m] + 1 = 0 \quad \text{...(i)}$$

$$\alpha^2 + b\alpha + [m+4] = 0$$

$$\Rightarrow \quad \alpha^2 + b\alpha + [m] + 4 = 0 \quad \text{...(ii)}$$

and $\quad \alpha^2 - c\alpha + [m + 15] = 0$

$$\Rightarrow \quad \alpha^2 - c\alpha + [m] + 15 = 0 \quad \text{...(iii)}$$

On adding Eqs. (i) and (ii) and subtracting Eq. (iii), we get

$$\alpha^2 + (a + b + c)\alpha + [m] - 10 = 0$$

$$\alpha^2 + 0 + [m] - 10 = 0 \quad [\because a + b + c = 0]$$

$$\Rightarrow \quad \alpha^2 + [m] - 10 = 0 \quad \text{...(iv)}$$

Also, $\quad m = \lim_{n \to \infty} \frac{1}{n} \sum_{r=1}^{2n} \frac{r}{\sqrt{n^2 + r^2}}$

$$= \lim_{n \to \infty} \sum_{r=1}^{2n} \frac{1}{n} \cdot \frac{r/n}{\sqrt{1 + (r/n)^2}} = \int_0^2 \frac{x}{\sqrt{(1 + x^2)}} dx$$

$$[\sqrt{(1 + x^2)}]_0^2 = \sqrt{5} - 1$$

Now, $\quad [m] = [\sqrt{5} - 1] = 1$

From Eq. (iv), we get

$$\alpha^2 + 1 - 10 = 0 \Rightarrow \alpha^2 = 9$$

$\therefore \quad \alpha = \pm 3$

Now, number of determinants of order 2 having

$$0, 1, 2, 3 = 4! = 24$$

Let $\Delta_1 = \begin{vmatrix} a_1 & a_2 \\ a_3 & a_4 \end{vmatrix}$ be one such determinant and their exists another determinant.

Let $\Delta_2 = \begin{vmatrix} a_3 & a_4 \\ a_1 & a_2 \end{vmatrix}$ [obtained on interchanging R_1 and R_2]

such that $\Delta_1 + \Delta_2 = 0$

$\because S =$ Sum of all the 24 determinants $= 0$

Since, $\alpha > S$

$\Rightarrow \alpha > 0$

$\therefore \alpha = 3$

Example 30 *Let k be a positive real number and*

$$A = \begin{bmatrix} 2k-1 & 2\sqrt{k} & 2\sqrt{k} \\ 2\sqrt{k} & 1 & -2k \\ -2\sqrt{k} & 2k & -1 \end{bmatrix} \text{ and } B = \begin{bmatrix} 0 & 2k-1 & \sqrt{k} \\ 1-2k & 0 & 2\sqrt{k} \\ -\sqrt{k} & -2\sqrt{k} & 0 \end{bmatrix}.$$

If $\det(\text{adj } A) + \det(\text{adj } B) = 10^6$, *then k is equal to ....*

Sol. (4.5) $|A| = (2k+1)^3$ and $|B| = 0$

[since, B is a skew-symmetric matrix of order 3]

$\Rightarrow \det(\text{adj } A) = |A|^{3-1}$

$$= \{(2k+1)^3\}^2 = 10^6$$

$\Rightarrow \quad 2k + 1 = 10$ or $2k = 9 \Rightarrow k = 4.5$

Example 31 *For a real number* α, *if the system*

$$\begin{vmatrix} 1 & \alpha & \alpha^2 \\ \alpha & 1 & \alpha \\ \alpha^2 & \alpha & 1 \end{vmatrix} \begin{bmatrix} x \\ y \\ z \end{bmatrix} = \begin{bmatrix} 1 \\ -1 \\ 1 \end{bmatrix}$$ *of linear equations has infinitely many solutions, then* $1 + \alpha + \alpha^2$ *is equal to ....*

Sol. (1) Since, the system of equations has infinitely many solutions.

$$\begin{vmatrix} 1 & \alpha & \alpha^2 \\ \alpha & 1 & \alpha \\ \alpha^2 & \alpha & 1 \end{vmatrix} = 0$$

$\Rightarrow 1(1-\alpha^2) - \alpha(\alpha - \alpha^3) + \alpha^2(\alpha^2 - \alpha^2) = 0$

$\Rightarrow \quad (1-\alpha^2) - \alpha^2 + \alpha^4 = 0$

$\Rightarrow \quad (\alpha^2 - 1)^2 = 0 \Rightarrow \alpha = \pm 1$

For $\alpha = 1$, we get

$$x + y + z = 1 \text{ and } x + y + z = -1$$

Hence, system has no solution.

For $\alpha = -1$, all three equations become $x - y + z = 1$, which represents coincident planes.

$\therefore \quad 1 + \alpha + \alpha^2 = 1$

Matching Type Questions

Example 32 *Let* $f(x)$ *denotes the determinant*

$$f(x) = \begin{vmatrix} x^2 & 2x & 1+x^2 \\ x^2+1 & x+1 & 1 \\ x & -1 & x-1 \end{vmatrix}.$$

On expansion $f(x)$ *is seen to be a 4th degree polynomial given by* $f(x) = a_0x^4 + a_1x^3 + a_2x^2 + a_3x + a_4$.
Using differentiation of determinant or otherwise match the entries in ***Column*** I *with one or more entries of the elements of* ***Column*** II.

Column I			Column II
(A)	$a_0^2 + a_1$ is divisible by	(p)	2
(B)	$a_2^2 + a_4$ is divisible by	(q)	3
(C)	$a_0^2 + a_2$ is divisible by	(r)	4
(D)	$a_4^2 + a_3^2 + a_1^2$ is divisible by	(s)	5

Sol. (A) → (p, s); (B) → (p, r); (C) → (p, q); (D) → (q)

$$\because \quad f(x) = \begin{vmatrix} x^2 & 2x & 1+x^2 \\ x^2+1 & x+1 & 1 \\ x & -1 & x-1 \end{vmatrix}$$

Applying $C_1 \to C_1 - C_3$, then

$$f(x) = \begin{vmatrix} -1 & 2x & 1+x^2 \\ x^2 & x+1 & 1 \\ 1 & -1 & x-1 \end{vmatrix}$$

Expanding along R_1, then

$$f(x) = -(x^2 - 1 + 1) - 2x(x^3 - x^2 - 1) + (1 + x^2)(-x^2 - x - 1)$$

$$= -3x^4 + x^3 - 3x^2 + x - 1 \quad \text{...(i)}$$

According to the question, we get

$$f(x) = a_0x^4 + a_1x^3 + a_2x^2 + a_3x + a_4 \quad \text{...(ii)}$$

From Eqs. (i) and (ii), we get

$a_0 = -3,$

$a_1 = 1,$

$a_2 = -3,$

$a_3 = 1,$

$a_4 = -1$

(A) $a_0^2 + a_1 = (-3)^2 + 1 = 9 + 1 = 10 = 2 \times 5$

(B) $a_2^2 + a_4 = (-3)^2 - 1 = 9 - 1$

$= 8 = 2 \times 4$

(C) $a_0^2 + a_2 = (-3)^2 - 3 = 9 - 3$

$= 6 = 2 \times 3$

(D) $a_4^2 + a_3^2 + a_1^2 = (-1)^2 + (1)^2 + (1)^2 = 1 + 1 + 1 = 3$

Example 33 *Suppose a, b and c are distinct and x, y and z are connected by the system of equations $x+ay+a^2z=a^3$, $x+by+b^2z=b^3$ and $x+cy+c^2z=c^3$.*

	Column I		Column II
(A)	For $x=1$, $y=2$ and $z=3$, $(a+b+c)^{-(ab+bc+ca)}$ is divisible by	(p)	3
(B)	For $x=4$, $y=3$ and $z=2$, $(ab+bc+ca)^{abc}$ is divisible by	(q)	6
(C)	For $x=6$, $y=4$ and $z=2$, $(abc)^{a+b+c}$ is divisible by	(r)	9
(D)	For $x=3$, $y=2$ and $z=3$, $(a+b+c)^{abc}$ is divisible by	(s)	12

Sol. (A) → (p, r) (B) → (p, r); (C) → (p, q, r, s); (D) → (p, r)

$a \neq b \neq c$

$$\Delta = \begin{vmatrix} 1 & a & a^2 \\ 1 & b & b^2 \\ 1 & c & c^2 \end{vmatrix} = (a-b)(b-c)(c-a)$$

$$\Delta_1 = \begin{vmatrix} a^3 & a & a^2 \\ b^3 & b & b^2 \\ c^3 & c & c^2 \end{vmatrix}$$

$$= \begin{vmatrix} a & a^2 & a^3 \\ b & b^2 & b^3 \\ c & c^2 & c^3 \end{vmatrix} = abc \begin{vmatrix} 1 & a & a^2 \\ 1 & b & b^2 \\ 1 & c & c^2 \end{vmatrix}$$

$$= abc(a-b)(b-c)(c-a)$$

$$\Delta_2 = \begin{vmatrix} 1 & a^3 & a^2 \\ 1 & b^3 & b^2 \\ 1 & c^3 & c^2 \end{vmatrix}$$

$$= -\begin{vmatrix} 1 & a^2 & a^3 \\ 1 & b^2 & b^3 \\ 1 & c^2 & c^3 \end{vmatrix}$$

$$= -(a-b)(b-c)(c-a)(ab+bc+ca)$$

and $\Delta_3 = \begin{vmatrix} 1 & a & a^3 \\ 1 & b & b^3 \\ 1 & c & c^3 \end{vmatrix} = (a-b)(b-c)(c-a)(a+b+c)$

By Cramer's rule, we get

$$x = \frac{\Delta_1}{\Delta} = abc$$

$$y = \frac{\Delta_2}{\Delta} = -(ab+bc+ca),$$

$$z = \frac{\Delta_3}{\Delta} = a+b+c$$

(A) $(a+b+c)^{-(ab+bc+ca)} = z^y = 3^2 = 9$,

which is divisible by 3 and 9.

(B) $(ab+bc+ca)^{abc} = (-y)^x = (-3)^4 = 81$,

which is divisible by 3 and 9.

(C) $(abc)^{a+b+c} = x^z = 6^2 = 36$,

which is divisible by 3, 6, 9 and 12.

(D) $(a+b+c)^{abc} = z^x = 3^3 = 27$,

which is divisible by 3 and 9.

EXERCISE 1

JEE Main Pattern

Single Option Correct Type Questions

1. If $\Delta(x) = \begin{vmatrix} x & 1+x^2 & x^3 \\ \log_e(1+x^2) & e^x & \sin x \\ \cos x & \tan x & \sin^2 x \end{vmatrix}$, then

(a) $\Delta(x)$ is divisible by x (b) $\Delta(x) = 0$
(c) $\Delta'(x) = 0$ (d) None of these

2. If a, b and c are sides of a triangle and

$\begin{vmatrix} a^2 & b^2 & c^2 \\ (a+1)^2 & (b+1)^2 & (c+1)^2 \\ (a-1)^2 & (b-1)^2 & (c-1)^2 \end{vmatrix} = 0$, then

(a) ΔABC is an equilateral triangle
(b) ΔABC is a right angled isosceles triangle
(c) ΔABC is an isosceles triangle
(d) None of the above

3. If $f(x) = a + bx + cx^2$ and α, β and γ are the roots of the equation $x^3 = 1$, then $\begin{vmatrix} a & b & c \\ b & c & a \\ c & a & b \end{vmatrix}$ is equal to

(a) $f(\alpha) + f(\beta) + f(\gamma)$
(b) $f(\alpha)\, f(\beta) + f(\beta)\, f(\gamma) + f(\gamma)\, f(\alpha)$
(c) $f(\alpha)\, f(\beta)\, f(\gamma)$
(d) $-f(\alpha)\, f(\beta)\, f(\gamma)$

4. When the determinant $\begin{vmatrix} \cos 2x & \sin^2 x & \cos 4x \\ \sin^2 x & \cos 2x & \cos^2 x \\ \cos 4x & \cos^2 x & \cos 2x \end{vmatrix}$ is expanded in powers of $\sin x$, the constant term in that expression is

(a) 1 (b) 0 (c) -1 (d) 2

5. If [ ] denotes the greatest integer less than or equal to the real number under consideration and $-1 \le x < 0, 0 \le y < 1, 1 \le z < 2$, the value of the determinant

$\begin{vmatrix} [x]+1 & [y] & [z] \\ [x] & [y]+1 & [z] \\ [x] & [y] & [z]+1 \end{vmatrix}$ is

(a) $[x]$ (b) $[y]$
(c) $[z]$ (d) None of these

6. If A, B and C are angles of a triangle, the value of

$\begin{vmatrix} e^{2iA} & e^{-iC} & e^{-iB} \\ e^{-iC} & e^{2iB} & e^{-iA} \\ e^{-iB} & e^{-iA} & e^{2iC} \end{vmatrix}$ is (where $i = \sqrt{-1}$)

(a) 1 (b) -1
(c) -2 (d) -4

7. If $\begin{vmatrix} x^n & x^{n+2} & x^{2n} \\ 1 & x^a & a \\ x^{n+5} & x^{a+6} & x^{2n+5} \end{vmatrix} = 0, \forall\, x \in R$, where $n \in N$, the value of a is

(a) n (b) $n-1$
(c) $n+1$ (d) None of these

8. If $a_1 b_1 c_1, a_2 b_2 c_2$ and $a_3 b_3 c_3$ are three digit even natural numbers and $\Delta = \begin{vmatrix} c_1 & a_1 & b_1 \\ c_2 & a_2 & b_2 \\ c_3 & a_3 & b_3 \end{vmatrix}$, then Δ is

(a) divisible by 2 but not necessarily by 4
(b) divisible by 4 but not necessarily by 8
(c) divisible by 8
(d) None of the above

9. If a, b and c are sides of ΔABC such that

$\begin{vmatrix} c & b\cos B + c\beta & a\cos A + b\alpha + c\gamma \\ a & c\cos B + a\beta & b\cos A + c\alpha + a\gamma \\ b & a\cos B + b\beta & c\cos A + a\alpha + b\gamma \end{vmatrix} = 0$

$\left(\text{where } \alpha, \beta, \gamma \in R^+ \text{ and } \angle A, \angle B, \angle C \ne \frac{\pi}{2}\right)$, ΔABC is

(a) an isosceles (b) an equilateral
(c) can't say (d) None of these

10. If x_1, x_2 and y_1, y_2 are the roots of the equations $3x^2 - 18x + 9 = 0$ and $y^2 - 4y + 2 = 0$, the value of the determinant $\begin{vmatrix} x_1x_2 & y_1y_2 & 1 \\ x_1 + x_2 & y_1 + y_2 & 2 \\ \sin(\pi x_1 x_2) & \cos(\pi/2y_1y_2) & 1 \end{vmatrix}$ is

(a) 0 (b) 1
(c) 2 (d) None of these

11. If the value of $\Delta = \begin{vmatrix} {}^{10}C_4 & {}^{10}C_5 & {}^{11}C_m \\ {}^{11}C_6 & {}^{11}C_7 & {}^{12}C_{m+2} \\ {}^{12}C_8 & {}^{12}C_9 & {}^{13}C_{m+4} \end{vmatrix}$ is equal to zero, then m is equal to

(a) 6 (b) 4
(c) 5 (d) None of these

12. If $f(x)$, $g(x)$ and $h(x)$ are polynomials of degree 4 and $\begin{vmatrix} f(x) & g(x) & h(x) \\ a & b & c \\ p & q & r \end{vmatrix} = mx^4 + nx^3 + rx^2 + sx + t$ be an identity in x, then

$$\begin{vmatrix} f'''(0) - f''(0) & g'''(0) - g''(0) & h'''(0) - h''(0) \\ a & b & c \\ p & q & r \end{vmatrix}$$

is equal to

(a) $2(3n + r)$ (b) $3(2n - r)$
(c) $3(2n + r)$ (d) $2(3n - r)$

13. If $\begin{vmatrix} 1 & 1 & 1 \\ a & b & c \\ a^3 & b^3 & c^3 \end{vmatrix} = (a-b)(b-c)(c-a)(a+b+c)$, where a, b and c are all different, then the determinant

$$\begin{vmatrix} 1 & 1 & 1 \\ (x-a)^2 & (x-b)^2 & (x-c)^2 \\ (x-b)(x-c) & (x-c)(x-a) & (x-a)(x-b) \end{vmatrix}$$ vanishes

when

(a) $a + b + c = 0$ (b) $x = \frac{1}{3}(a + b + c)$
(c) $x = \frac{1}{2}(a + b + c)$ (d) $x = a + b + c$

14. Let $a, b, c \in R$ such that no two of them are equal and satisfy $\begin{vmatrix} 2a & b & c \\ b & c & 2a \\ c & 2a & b \end{vmatrix} = 0$, the equation $24ax^2 + 4bx + c = 0$ has

(a) atleast one root in $\left[0, \frac{1}{2}\right]$
(b) atleast one root in $\left[-\frac{1}{2}, \frac{1}{2}\right]$
(c) atleast one root in $[-1, 0]$
(d) atleast two roots in $[0, 2]$

15. The number of positive integral solution of the equation $\begin{vmatrix} x^3+1 & x^2y & x^2z \\ xy^2 & y^3+1 & y^2z \\ xz^2 & yz^2 & z^3+1 \end{vmatrix} = 11$ is

(a) 0 (b) 3 (c) 6 (d) 12

16. If $f(x) = ax^2 + bx + c$, $a, b, c \in R$ and equation $f(x) - x = 0$ has imaginary roots α, β γ and δ be the roots of $f(f(x)) - x = 0$, then $\begin{vmatrix} 2 & \alpha & \delta \\ \beta & 0 & \alpha \\ \gamma & \beta & 1 \end{vmatrix}$ is

(a) 0
(b) purely real
(c) purely imaginary
(d) None of the above

17. If $(1 + ax + bx^2)^4 = a_0 + a_1x + a_2x^2 + \ldots + a_8x^8$, where $a, b, a_0, a_1, \ldots, a_8 \in R$ such that $a_0 + a_1 + a_2 \neq 0$ and $\begin{vmatrix} a_0 & a_1 & a_2 \\ a_1 & a_2 & a_0 \\ a_2 & a_0 & a_1 \end{vmatrix} = 0$, then

(a) $a = \frac{3}{4}, b = \frac{5}{8}$ (b) $a = \frac{1}{4}, b = \frac{5}{32}$
(c) $a = 1, b = \frac{2}{3}$ (d) None of these

18. Given, $f(x) = \log_{10} x$ and $g(x) = e^{\pi ix}$.

If $\phi(x) = \begin{vmatrix} f(x) \cdot g(x) & (f(x))^{g(x)} & 1 \\ f(x^2) \cdot g(x^2) & (f(x^2))^{g(x^2)} & 0 \\ f(x^3) \cdot g(x^3) & (f(x^3))^{g(x^3)} & 1 \end{vmatrix}$, the value of $\phi(10)$, is

(a) 1 (b) 2
(c) 0 (d) None of these

19. If a, b and c are non-zero real numbers and if the equations $(a-1)x = y + z$, $(b-1)y = z + x$, $(c-1)z = x + y$ has a non-trivial solution, then $ab + bc + ca$ equals to

(a) $a + b + c$ (b) abc
(c) 1 (d) None of these

20. The set of equations $\lambda x - y + (\cos\theta)z = 0$, $3x + y + 2z = 0$, $(\cos\theta)x + y + 2z = 0$, $0 \le \theta \le 2\pi$, has non-trivial solution(s)

(a) for no value of λ and θ
(b) for all value of λ and θ
(c) for all values of λ and only two values of θ
(d) for only one value of λ and all values of θ

21. If A is a 3×3 matrix and $|A| = 2$, then $|2\,\text{adj}(3A\,|A^3|)|$ is equal to

(a) $3^3 6^{12}$ (b) $3^3 6^{15}$
(c) $2^3 6^{18}$ (d) $3^3 6^{18}$

22. If the system of equations $2x + ay + 6z = 6$, $x + 2y + 3z = b$ and $2x - 5y + 2z = 8$ has infinitely many solutions, then $a - b$ is equal to

(a) 1 (b) 2
(c) -1 (d) 3

Numerical Value Type Questions

23. If $(1+ax+bx^2)^4 = a_0 + a_1x + a_2x^2 + \ldots + a_8x^8$, where $a, b, a_0, a_1, \ldots, a_8 \in R$ such that $a_0 + a_1 + a_2 \neq 0$ and $\begin{vmatrix} a_0 & a_1 & a_2 \\ a_1 & a_2 & a_0 \\ a_2 & a_0 & a_1 \end{vmatrix} = 0$, then the value of $5\dfrac{a}{b}$ is ....

24. Let $a+b+c=S$ and $\begin{vmatrix} S+c & a & b \\ c & S+a & b \\ c & a & S+b \end{vmatrix} = 532$, the value of S is ....

25. Let $a, b, c \in R$ not all are equal and $\Delta_1 = \begin{vmatrix} a & b & c \\ b & c & a \\ c & a & b \end{vmatrix}$ and $\Delta_2 = \begin{vmatrix} a+2b & b+3c & c+4a \\ b+2c & c+3a & a+4b \\ c+2a & a+3b & b+4c \end{vmatrix}$, then $\dfrac{\Delta_2}{\Delta_1}$ is equal to ....

26. $A = \begin{bmatrix} 1 & \tan x \\ -\tan x & 1 \end{bmatrix}$ and $f(x)$ is defined as $f(x) = \det(A^TA^{-1})$, then the value of $\underbrace{f(f(f(\ldots f(x))))}_{n \text{ times}}$ is $(n \geq 2)$ ....

27. Let P, Q and R be invertible matrices of order 3 such that $A = PQ^{-1}, B = QR^{-1}$ and $C = RP^{-1}$, then the value of det $(ABC + BCA + CAB)$ is equal to ....

28. The equation $\begin{bmatrix} 1 & 2 & 2 \\ 1 & 3 & 4 \\ 3 & 4 & k \end{bmatrix} \begin{bmatrix} x \\ y \\ z \end{bmatrix} = \begin{bmatrix} 0 \\ 0 \\ 0 \end{bmatrix}$ has a solution for (x, y, z) besides $(0, 0, 0)$, then the value of k is ....

29. The sum of values of p for which the equation $x+y+z=1$, $x+2y+4z=p$ and $x+4y+10z=p^2$ have a solution, is ....

30. If $\begin{vmatrix} x & x+y & x+y+z \\ 2x & 3x+2y & 4x+3y+2z \\ 3x & 6x+3y & 10x+6y+3z \end{vmatrix} = 64$, then the value of x is ....

31. If $x=31, y=32$ and $z=33$, then the value of $\begin{vmatrix} (x^2+1)^2 & (xy+1)^2 & (xz+1)^2 \\ (xy+1)^2 & (y^2+1)^2 & (yz+1)^2 \\ (xz+1)^2 & (yz+1)^2 & (z^2+1)^2 \end{vmatrix}$ is ....

32. Let $A = [a_{ij}]_{3\times3}, B = [b_{ij}]_{3\times3}$ and $C = [c_{ij}]_{3\times3}$ be any three matrices, where $b_{ij} = 3^{i-j} \cdot a_{ij}$ and $c_{ij} = 4^{i-j} \cdot b_{ij}$. If det $A = 2$, then det (BC) is equal to ....

Previous Year Questions

33. Let $\alpha\beta \neq 0$ and $A = \begin{bmatrix} \beta & \alpha & 3 \\ \alpha & \alpha & \beta \\ -\beta & \alpha & 2\alpha \end{bmatrix}$.

If $B = \begin{bmatrix} 3\alpha & -9 & 3\alpha \\ -\alpha & 7 & -2\alpha \\ -2\alpha & 5 & -2\beta \end{bmatrix}$ is the matrix of co-factors of the elements of A, then det(AB) is equal to

[Single Correct Type, 2024 Main]

(a) 64 (b) 343
(c) 125 (d) 216

34. Let $A = \begin{bmatrix} 1 & 0 & 0 \\ 0 & \alpha & \beta \\ 0 & \beta & \alpha \end{bmatrix}$ and $|2A|^3 = 2^{21}$ where, $\alpha, \beta \in Z$.

Then, a value of α is **[Single Correct Type, 2024 Main]**

(a) 3 (b) 5
(c) 9 (d) 17

35. If $\alpha \neq a, \beta \neq b, \gamma \neq c$ and $\begin{vmatrix} \alpha & b & c \\ a & \beta & c \\ a & b & \gamma \end{vmatrix} = 0$, then $\dfrac{a}{\alpha - a} + \dfrac{b}{\beta - b} + \dfrac{\gamma}{\gamma - c}$ is equal to

[Single Correct Type, 2024 Main]

(a) 0 (b) 3
(c) 2 (d) 1

36. Let $A = \begin{bmatrix} 2 & 1 & 2 \\ 6 & 2 & 11 \\ 3 & 3 & 2 \end{bmatrix}$ and $P = \begin{bmatrix} 1 & 2 & 0 \\ 5 & 0 & 2 \\ 7 & 1 & 5 \end{bmatrix}$. The sum of the prime factors of $|P^{-1}AP - 2I|$ is equal to

[Single Correct Type, 2024 Main]

(a) 27 (b) 26
(c) 23 (d) 66

37. If the system of equation $x+4y-z=\lambda$, $7x+9y+\mu z=-3$, $5x+y+2z=-1$ has infinitely many solutions, then $(2\mu+3\lambda)$ is equal to

[Single Correct Type, 2024 Main]

(a) −2 (b) −3
(c) 2 (d) 3

38. If the system of equations

$$x + (\sqrt{2}\sin\alpha)y + (\sqrt{2}\cos\alpha)z = 0,$$
$$x + (\cos\alpha)y + (\sin\alpha)z = 0$$
and $$x + (\sin\alpha)y - (\cos\alpha)z = 0$$

has a non-trivial solution, then $\alpha \in \left(0, \dfrac{\pi}{2}\right)$ is equal to

[Single Correct Type, 2024 Main]

(a) $\dfrac{3\pi}{4}$ (b) $\dfrac{11\pi}{24}$ (c) $\dfrac{7\pi}{24}$ (d) $\dfrac{5\pi}{24}$

39. Let $\lambda, \mu \in R$. If the system of equations

$$3x+5y+\lambda z=3, 7x+11y-9z=2$$

and $97x+155y-189z=\mu$

has infinitely many solutions, then $\mu+2\lambda$ is equal to

[Single Correct Type, 2024 Main]

(a) 27 (b) 24

(c) 22 (d) 25

40. Let A be a 3×3 real matrix such that

$$A\begin{bmatrix}1\\0\\1\end{bmatrix}=2\begin{bmatrix}1\\0\\1\end{bmatrix}, A\begin{bmatrix}-1\\0\\1\end{bmatrix}=4\begin{bmatrix}-1\\0\\1\end{bmatrix}, A\begin{bmatrix}0\\1\\0\end{bmatrix}=2\begin{bmatrix}0\\1\\0\end{bmatrix}$$

Then, the system $(A-3I)\begin{bmatrix}x\\y\\z\end{bmatrix}=\begin{bmatrix}1\\2\\3\end{bmatrix}$ has

[Single Correct Type, 2024 Main]

(a) exactly two solutions

(b) unique solution

(c) infinitely many solutions

(d) no solution

41. Consider the system of linear equations $x+y+z=5$, $x+2y+\lambda^2 z=9$, $x+3y+\lambda z=\mu$, where $\lambda, \mu \in R$. Then, which of the following statement is not correct?

[Single Correct Type, 2024 Main]

(a) System has unique solution, if $\lambda \neq 1$ and $\mu \neq 13$

(b) System is inconsistent, if $\lambda=1$ and $\mu \neq 13$

(c) System has infinite number of solutions, if $\lambda=1$ and $\mu=13$

(d) System is consistent, if $\lambda \neq 1$ and $\mu=13$

42. Let A be a 2×2 symmetric matrix such that

$A\begin{bmatrix}1\\1\end{bmatrix}=\begin{bmatrix}3\\7\end{bmatrix}$ and the determinant of A be 1.

If $A^{-1}=\alpha A+\beta I$, where I is an identity matrix of order 2×2, then $\alpha+\beta$ equals....... .

[Numerical Value Type, 2024 Main]

43. If the system of equations

$2x+7y+\lambda z=3$, $3x+2y+5z=4$ and $x+\mu y+32z=-1$

has infinitely many solutions, then $(\lambda-\mu)$ is equal to ....

[Numerical Value Type, 2024 Main]

44. Let $\alpha\beta\gamma=45$, $\alpha, \beta, \gamma \in R$. If $x(\alpha,1,2)+y(1,\beta,2)+z(2,3,\gamma)=(0,0,0)$ for some $x, y, z \in R$, $xyz \neq 0$, then $6\alpha+4\beta+\gamma$ is equal to ....

[Numerical Value Type, 2024 Main]

45. Let $A=\begin{bmatrix}2&0&1\\1&1&0\\1&0&1\end{bmatrix}$, $B=[B_1, B_2, B_3]$, where B_1, B_2, B_3 be column matrics and $AB_1=\begin{bmatrix}1\\0\\0\end{bmatrix}$, $AB_2=\begin{bmatrix}2\\3\\0\end{bmatrix}$, $AB_3=\begin{bmatrix}3\\2\\1\end{bmatrix}$. If $\alpha=|B|$ and β is the sum of all the diagonal elements of B, then $\alpha^3+\beta^3$ is equal to ....

[Numerical Value Type, 2024 Main]

46. If $\begin{vmatrix}x+1&x&x\\x&x+\lambda&x\\x&x&x+\lambda^2\end{vmatrix}=\frac{9}{8}(103x+81)$, then $\lambda, \frac{\lambda}{3}$ are the roots of the equation **[Single Correct Type, 2023 Main]**

(a) $4x^2+24x+27=0$ (b) $4x^2-24x+27=0$

(c) $4x^2+24x-27=0$ (d) $4x^2-24x-27=0$

47. Let α be a root of the equation $(a-c)x^2+(b-a)x+(c-b)=0$, where a, b, c are distinct real numbers such that the matrix $\begin{bmatrix}\alpha^2&\alpha&1\\1&1&1\\a&b&c\end{bmatrix}$ is singular. Then, the value of $\frac{(a-c)^2}{(b-a)(c-b)}+\frac{(b-a)^2}{(a-c)(c-b)}+\frac{(c-b)^2}{(a-c)(b-a)}$ is

[Single Correct Type, 2023 Main]

(a) 6 (b) 9 (c) 12 (d) 3

48. If A is a 3×3 matrix and $|A|=2$, then $|3\operatorname{adj}(|3A|A^2)|$ is equal to **[Single Correct Type, 2023 Main]**

(a) $3^{12}\cdot6^{10}$ (b) $3^{12}\cdot6^{11}$

(c) $3^{11}\cdot6^{10}$ (d) $3^{10}\cdot6^{11}$

49. Let $A=\begin{bmatrix}2&1&0\\1&2&-1\\0&-1&2\end{bmatrix}$. If $|\operatorname{adj}(\operatorname{adj}(\operatorname{adj}2A))|=(16)^n$, then n is equal to **[Single Correct Type, 2023 Main]**

(a) 8 (b) 10

(c) 12 (d) 9

50. Let $x, y, z>1$ and $A=\begin{bmatrix}1&\log_x y&\log_x z\\\log_y x&2&\log_y z\\\log_z x&\log_z y&3\end{bmatrix}$. Then, $|\operatorname{adj}(\operatorname{adj}A^2)|$ is equal to **[Single Correct Type, 2023 Main]**

(a) 6^4 (b) 4^8 (c) 2^8 (d) 2^4

51. Let the determinant of a square matrix A of order m be $m-n$, where m and n satisfy $4m+n=22$ and $17m+4n=93$. If $\det(n\,\text{adj}(\text{adj}(mA)))=3^a5^b6^c$, then $a+b+c$ is equal to **[Single Correct Type, 2023 Main]**
(a) 101 (b) 96 (c) 109 (d) 84

52. Let $B=\begin{bmatrix}1 & 3 & \alpha\\ 1 & 2 & 3\\ \alpha & \alpha & 4\end{bmatrix}$, $\alpha>2$ be the adjoint of a matrix A and $|A|=2$. Then, $[\alpha\ -2\alpha\ \alpha]\,B\begin{bmatrix}\alpha\\ -2\alpha\\ \alpha\end{bmatrix}$ is equal to
[Single Correct Type, 2023 Main]
(a) 32 (b) 16 (c) -16 (d) 0

53. For the system of linear equations $\alpha x+y+z=1$, $x+\alpha y+z=1$, $x+y+\alpha z=\beta$, which one of the following statements is not correct ? **[Single Correct Type, 2023 Main]**
(a) It has no solution, if $\alpha=-2$ and $\beta=1$
(b) $x+y+z=\frac{3}{4}$, if $\alpha=2$ and $\beta=1$
(c) It has infinitely many solutions, if $\alpha=1$ and $\beta=1$
(d) It has infinitely many solutions, if $\alpha=2$ and $\beta=-1$

54. Let S denote the set of all real values of λ such that the system of equations
$\lambda x+y+z=1$, $x+\lambda y+z=1$ and $x+y+\lambda z=1$
is inconsistent, then $\sum_{\lambda\in S}(|\lambda|^2+|\lambda|)$ is equal to **[Single Correct Type, 2023 Main]**
(a) 12 (b) 6 (c) 4 (d) 2

55. For $\alpha,\beta\in R$, suppose the system of linear equations $x-y+z=5$, $2x+2y+\alpha z=8$ and $3x-y+4z=\beta$ has infinitely many solutions. Then, α and β are the roots of **[Single Correct Type, 2023 Main]**
(a) $x^2+14x+24=0$ (b) $x^2+18x+56=0$
(c) $x^2-18x+56=0$ (d) $x^2-10x+16=0$

56. If the system of equations
$$2x+y-z=5,\ 2x-5y+\lambda z=\mu,\ x+2y-5z=7$$
has infinitely many solutions, then $(\lambda+\mu)^2+(\lambda-\mu)^2$ is equal to **[Single Correct Type, 2023 Main]**
(a) 920 (b) 904 (c) 916 (d) 912

57. For the system of linear equations
$2x-y+3z=5$, $3x+2y-z=7$, $4x+5y+\alpha z=\beta$
which of the following is not correct? **[Single Correct Type, 2023 Main]**
(a) The system has infinitely many solutions for $\alpha=-5$ and $\beta=9$
(b) The system has a unique solution for $\alpha\neq-5$ and $\beta=8$
(c) The system has infinitely many solutions for $\alpha=-6$ and $\beta=9$
(d) The system is inconsistent for $\alpha=-5$ and $\beta=8$

58. If the system of equations
$x+y+az=b$, $2x+5y+2z=6$ and $x+2y+3z=3$
has infinitely many solutions, then $2a+3b$ is equal to **[Single Correct Type, 2023 Main]**
(a) 23 (b) 25 (c) 28 (d) 20

59. For the system of linear equations
$x+y+z=6$, $\alpha x+\beta y+7z=3$ and $x+2y+3z=14$, which of the following is not true?
[Single Correct Type, 2023 Main]
(a) If $\alpha=\beta=7$, then the system has no solution
(b) There is a unique point (α,β) on the line $x+2y+18=0$ for which the system has infinitely many solutions
(c) If $\alpha=\beta$ and $\alpha\neq7$, then the system has a unique solution
(d) For every point $(\alpha,\beta)\neq(7,7)$ on the line $x-2y+7=0$, the system has infinitely many solutions

60. Let the system of linear equations
$x+y+kz=2$, $2x+3y-z=1$ and $3x+4y+2z=k$
have infinitely many solutions. Then, the system
$(k+1)x+(2k-1)y=7$ and $(2k+1)x+(k+5)y=10$ has
[Single Correct Type, 2023 Main]
(a) no solution
(b) unique solution satisfying $x-y=1$
(c) unique solution satisfying $x+y=1$
(d) infinitely many solutions

61. If the system of equations
$$x+2y+3z=3,\ 4x+3y-4z=4$$
and $8x+4y-\lambda z=9+\mu$
has infinitely many solutions, then the ordered pair (λ,μ) is equal to **[Single Correct Type, 2023 Main]**
(a) $\left(-\frac{72}{5},-\frac{21}{5}\right)$ (b) $\left(\frac{72}{5},-\frac{21}{5}\right)$
(c) $\left(-\frac{72}{5},\frac{21}{5}\right)$ (d) $\left(\frac{72}{5},\frac{21}{5}\right)$

62. Consider the following system of equations
$\alpha x+2y+z=1$, $2\alpha x+3y+z=1$, $3x+\alpha y+2z=\beta$
for some $\alpha,\beta\in R$. Then, which of the following is not correct.
[Single Correct Type, 2023 Main]
(a) It has a solution, $\forall\alpha\neq1$ and $\beta=2$
(b) It has no solution, if $\alpha=-1$ and $\beta\neq2$
(c) It has no solution, for $\alpha=3$ and $\beta\neq2$
(d) It has no solution, for $\alpha=-1$ and $\beta\in R$

63. Let S be the set of values of λ, for which the system of equations $6\lambda x-3y+3z=4\lambda^2$, $2x+6\lambda y+4z=1$ and $3x+2y+3\lambda z=\lambda$ has no solution. Then, $12\sum_{\lambda\in S}|\lambda|$ is equal to ....
[Numerical Value Type, 2023 Main]

64. Let A be a 2×2 matrix with $\det(A)=-1$ and $\det((A+I)(\text{adj}(A)+I))=4$. Then, the sum of the diagonal elements of A can be **[Single Correct Type, 2022 Main]**
(a) -1 (b) 2 (c) 1 (d) $-\sqrt{2}$

65. Let A and B be two 3×3 non-zero real matrices such that AB is a zero matrix. Then,

[Single Correct Type, 2022 Main]

(a) the system of linear equation $AX = 0$ has a unique solution
(b) the system of linear equations $AX = 0$ has infinitely many solutions
(c) B is an invertible matrix
(d) Adj (A) is an invertible matrix

66. The number of real values of λ, such that the system of linear equations

$$2x - 3y + 5z = 9,\ x + 3y - z = -18$$

and $3x - y + (\lambda^2 - |\lambda|)z = 16$

has no solutions, is **[Single Correct Type, 2022 Main]**

(a) 0 (b) 1
(c) 2 (d) 4

67. If the system of linear equations

$$2x + 3y - z = -2,\ x + y + z = 4$$

and $x - y + |\lambda|z = 4\lambda - 4$

where $\lambda \in R$, has no solution, then

[Single Correct Type, 2022 Main]

(a) $\lambda = 7$ (b) $\lambda = -7$
(c) $\lambda = 8$ (d) $\lambda^2 = 1$

68. The system of equations

$$-kx + 3y - 14z = 25,\ -15x + 4y - kz = 3$$

and $-4x + y + 3z = 4$ is consistent for all k in the set

[Single Correct Type, 2022 Main]

(a) R (b) $R - \{-11, 13\}$
(c) $R - \{13\}$ (d) $R - \{-11, 11\}$

69. The number of values of α for which the system of equations

$$x + y + z = \alpha,\ \alpha x + 2\alpha y + 3z = -1 \text{ and } x + 3\alpha y + 5z = 4$$

is inconsistent, is **[Single Correct Type, 2022 Main]**

(a) 0 (b) 1 (c) 2 (d) 3

70. The ordered pair (a, b), for which the system of linear equations $3x - 2y + z = b$, $5x - 8y + 9z = 3$, $2x + y + az = -1$ has no solution, is

[Single Correct Type, 2022 Main]

(a) $\left(3, \frac{1}{3}\right)$ (b) $\left(-3, \frac{1}{3}\right)$ (c) $\left(-3, -\frac{1}{3}\right)$ (d) $\left(3, -\frac{1}{3}\right)$

71. The value of $\begin{vmatrix} (a+1)(a+2) & a+2 & 1 \\ (a+2)(a+3) & a+3 & 1 \\ (a+3)(a+4) & a+4 & 1 \end{vmatrix}$ is

[Single Correct Type, 2021 Main]

(a) $(a + 2)(a + 3)(a + 4)$ (b) -2
(c) $(a + 1)(a + 2)(a + 3)$ (d) 0

72. Let $A = \begin{bmatrix} 2 & 3 \\ a & 0 \end{bmatrix}$, $a \in R$ be written as $P + Q$, where P is a symmetric matrix and Q is skew-symmetric matrix. If $\det(Q) = 9$, then the modulus of the sum of all possible values of determinant of P is equal to

[Single Correct Type, 2021 Main]

(a) 36 (b) 24 (c) 45 (d) 18

73. The solutions of the equation

$$\begin{vmatrix} 1+\sin^2 x & \sin^2 x & \sin^2 x \\ \cos^2 x & 1+\cos^2 x & \cos^2 x \\ 4\sin 2x & 4\sin 2x & 1+4\sin 2x \end{vmatrix}$$

$= 0, (0 < x < \pi)$, are **[Single Correct Type, 2021 Main]**

(a) $\frac{\pi}{12}, \frac{\pi}{6}$ (b) $\frac{\pi}{6}, \frac{5\pi}{6}$ (c) $\frac{5\pi}{12}, \frac{7\pi}{12}$ (d) $\frac{7\pi}{12}, \frac{11\pi}{12}$

74. If $A = \begin{bmatrix} 0 & \sin\alpha \\ \sin\alpha & 0 \end{bmatrix}$ and $\det\left(A^2 - \frac{1}{2}I\right) = 0$, then a possible value of α is **[Single Correct Type, 2021 Main]**

(a) $\frac{\pi}{2}$ (b) $\frac{\pi}{3}$ (c) $\frac{\pi}{4}$ (d) $\frac{\pi}{6}$

75. The maximum value of

$$f(x) = \begin{vmatrix} \sin^2 x & 1+\cos^2 x & \cos 2x \\ 1+\sin^2 x & \cos^2 x & \cos 2x \\ \sin^2 x & \cos^2 x & \sin 2x \end{vmatrix},\ x \in R \text{ is}$$

[Single Correct Type, 2021 Main]

(a) $\sqrt{7}$ (b) $\frac{3}{4}$ (c) $\sqrt{5}$ (d) 5

76. Let $A(a, 0)$, $B(b, 2b + 1)$ and $C(0, b)$, $b \neq 0, |b| \neq 1$, be points such that the area of ΔABC is 1 sq. unit, then the sum of all possible values of a is

[Single Correct Type, 2021 Main]

(a) $\frac{-2b}{b+1}$ (b) $\frac{2b}{b+1}$ (c) $\frac{2b^2}{b+1}$ (d) $\frac{-2b^2}{b+1}$

77. Let the area of the triangle with vertices $A(1, \alpha)$, $B(\alpha, 0)$ and $C(0, \alpha)$ be 4 sq units. If the points $(\alpha, -\alpha)$, $(-\alpha, \alpha)$ and (α^2, β) are collinear, then β is equal to

[Single Correct Type, 2021 Main]

(a) 64 (b) -8 (c) -64 (d) 512

78. Let A and B be two 3×3 real matrices such that $(A^2 - B^2)$ is invertible matrix. If $A^5 = B^5$ and $A^3B^2 = A^2B^3$, then the value of the determinant of the matrix $A^3 + B^3$ is equal to

[Single Correct Type, 2021 Main]

(a) 2 (b) 4
(c) 1 (d) 0

79. If the following system of linear equations
$$2x + y + z = 5,\ x - y + z = 3 \text{ and } x + y + az = b$$
has no solution, then **[Single Correct Type, 2021 Main]**

(a) $a = -\frac{1}{3}$ and $b \neq \frac{7}{3}$ (b) $a \neq \frac{1}{3}$ and $b = \frac{7}{3}$

(c) $a \neq -\frac{1}{3}$ and $b = \frac{7}{3}$ (d) $a = \frac{1}{3}$ and $b \neq \frac{7}{3}$

80. Let the system of linear equations
$$4x + \lambda y + 2z = 0,\ 2x - y + z = 0$$
$$\mu x + 2y + 3z = 0,\ \lambda, \mu \in R.$$
has a non-trivial solution. Then which of the following is true ? **[Single Correct Type, 2021 Main]**

(a) $\mu = 6,\ \lambda \in R$ (b) $\lambda = 2,\ \mu \in R$

(c) $\lambda = 3, \mu \in R$ (d) $\mu = -6,\ \lambda \in R$

81. The following system of linear equations
$$2x + 3y + 2z = 9,\ \ 3x + 2y + 2z = 9 \text{ and } x - y + 4z = 8$$
[Single Correct Type, 2021 Main]

(a) does not have any solution

(b) has a unique solution

(c) has infinitely many solutions

(d) has a solution (α, β, γ) satisfying $\alpha + \beta^2 + \gamma^3 = 12$

82. Let A and B be 3×3 real matrices, such that A is symmetric matrix and B is skew-symmetric matrix. Then, the system of linear equations $(A^2B^2 - B^2A^2)X = O$, where X is a 3×1 column matrix of unknown variables and O is a 3×1 null matrix, has **[Single Correct Type, 2021 Main]**

(a) no solution

(b) exactly two solutions

(c) infinitely many solutions

(d) a unique solution

83. The value of $k \in R$, for which the following system of liner equations $3x - y + 4z = 3$, $x + 2y - 3z = -2$ and $6x + 5y + kz = -3$ has infinitely many solutions, is **[Single Correct Type, 2021 Main]**

(a) 3 (b) −5

(c) 5 (d) −3

84. Let $A = \begin{bmatrix} i & -i \\ -i & i \end{bmatrix}$, $i = \sqrt{-1}$. Then, the system of linear equations $A^8 \begin{bmatrix} x \\ y \end{bmatrix} = \begin{bmatrix} 8 \\ 64 \end{bmatrix}$ has **[Single Correct Type, 2021 Main]**

(a) a unique solution (b) infinitely many solutions

(c) no solution (d) exactly two solutions

85. Consider the following system of equations
$$x + 2y - 3z = a,\ 2x + 6y - 11z = b \text{ and } x - 2y + 7z = c$$
where, a, b and c are real constants. Then, the system of equations **[Single Correct Type, 2021 Main]**

(a) has a unique solution, when $5a = 2b + c$

(b) has infinite number of solutions when $5a = 2b + c$

(c) has no solution for all a, b and c

(d) has a unique solution for all a, b and c

86. The system of linear equations
$3x - 2y - kz = 10$, $2x - 4y - 2z = 6$ and $x + 2y - z = 5m$ is inconsistent, if **[Single Correct Type, 2021 Main]**

(a) $k \neq 3,\ m \neq 4/5$ (b) $k = 3,\ m = 4/5$

(c) $k = 3,\ m \neq 4/5$ (d) $k \neq 3,\ m \in R$

87. If $A = \begin{bmatrix} 2 & 3 \\ 0 & -1 \end{bmatrix}$, then the value of
$[\det(A^4) + \det[A^{10} - (\text{adj }(2A))^{10}]$ is equal to …… . **[Numerical Value Type, 2021 Main]**

88. If the system of linear equations $2x + y - z = 3$, $x - y - z = \alpha$ and $3x + 3y + \beta z = 3$ has infinitely many solution, then $\alpha + \beta - \alpha\beta$ is equal to ……… **[Numerical Value Type, 2021 Main]**

89. If $a + x = b + y = c + z + 1$, where a, b, c, x, y, z are non-zero distinct real numbers, then $\begin{vmatrix} x & a+y & x+a \\ y & b+y & y+b \\ z & c+y & z+c \end{vmatrix}$ is equal to **[Single Correct Type, 2020 Main]**

(a) $y(b - a)$ (b) $y(a - b)$

(c) 0 (d) $y(a - c)$

90. If $\Delta = \begin{vmatrix} x-2 & 2x-3 & 3x-4 \\ 2x-3 & 3x-4 & 4x-5 \\ 3x-5 & 5x-8 & 10x-17 \end{vmatrix} = Ax^3 + Bx^2 + Cx + D$, then $B + C$ is equal to **[Single Correct Type, 2020 Main]**

(a) −1 (b) 1 (c) −3 (d) 9

91. The sum of distinct values of λ for which the system of equations $(\lambda - 1)x + (3\lambda + 1)y + 2\lambda z = 0$, $(\lambda - 1)x + (4\lambda - 2)y + (\lambda + 3)z = 0$ and $2x + (3\lambda + 1)y + 3(\lambda - 1) = 0$ has non-zero solutions, is ……… **[Numerical Value Type, 2020 Main]**

EXERCISE 2

JEE Advanced Pattern

Single Option Correct Type Questions

1. If $f(x) = a + bx + cx^2$ and α, β, γ are the roots of the equation $x^3 = 1$, then $\begin{vmatrix} a & b & c \\ b & c & a \\ c & a & b \end{vmatrix}$ is equal to
   (a) $f(\alpha) + f(\beta) + f(\gamma)$
   (b) $f(\alpha) \cdot f(\beta) + f(\beta) \cdot f(\gamma) + f(\gamma) \cdot f(\alpha)$
   (c) $f(\alpha) \cdot f(\beta) \cdot f(\gamma)$
   (d) $-f(\alpha) \cdot f(\beta) \cdot f(\gamma)$

2. Let $P = [a_{ij}]$ be a 3×3 matrix and $Q = [b_{ij}]$, where $b_{ij} = 3^{i+j} \cdot a_{ij}$ for $1 \le i, j \le 6$. If the determinant of P is 6, then the determinant of the matrix Q is
   (a) $3^{10} \times 11$ (b) $3^{11} \times 6$ (c) 3^{12} (d) $3^{13} \times 2$

3. If $\begin{vmatrix} x-6 & 3x & 3x \\ 3x & x-6 & 3x \\ 3x & 3x & x-6 \end{vmatrix} = (A + Bx)(2x - A)^2$, then the ordered pair (A, B) is equal to
   (a) $(6, 7)$ (b) $(-4, -5)$ (c) $(-4, 3)$ (d) $(-6, 7)$

4. Let a, b and c be such that $b(a + c) \neq 0$. If
$$\begin{vmatrix} a & a+1 & a-1 \\ -b & b+1 & b-1 \\ c & c-1 & c+1 \end{vmatrix} + \begin{vmatrix} a+1 & b+1 & c-1 \\ a-1 & b-1 & c+1 \\ (-1)^{n+2}a & (-1)^{n+1}b & (-1)^n c \end{vmatrix} = 0,$$
then the value of n is
   (a) zero (b) an even integer
   (c) an odd integer (d) an integer

5. If $f(\theta) = \begin{vmatrix} a^2 + (b^2 + c^2)\cos\theta & ab(1-\cos\theta) & ca(1-\cos\theta) \\ ab(1-\cos\theta) & b^2 + (c^2 + a^2)\cos\theta & bc(1-\cos\theta) \\ ca(1-\cos\theta) & bc(1-\cos\theta) & c^2 + (a^2 + b^2)\cos\theta \end{vmatrix}$

   Then, evaluate $\int_0^{\pi/2} f(\theta)\, d\theta$
   (a) $a^2 + (b^2 + c^2)\frac{\pi}{4}$ (b) $(a^2 + b^2 + c^2)^3 \frac{\pi}{4}$
   (c) $(a^2 + b^2 + c^2)\frac{\pi}{6}$ (d) $a^2 - (b^2 + c^2)\frac{\pi}{6}$

6. The number of values of k, for which the system of equations $(k + 1)x + 8y = 4k$ and $kx + (k + 3)y = 3k - 1$ has no solution, is
   (a) 1 (b) 2
   (c) 3 (d) None of these

7. If [ ] denotes the greatest integer less than or equal to the real number under considerations, and $0 \le x < 1, 1 \le y < 2, 2 \le z < 3$, then the value of the determinant $\begin{vmatrix} [x]+1 & [y] & [z] \\ [x] & [y]+1 & [z] \\ [x] & [y] & [z]+1 \end{vmatrix}$ is
   (a) $[x]+1$ (b) $\frac{1}{4}[y]$
   (c) $2[z]$ (d) None of these

8. If $a = \cos\theta + i\sin\theta$, $b = \cos 2\theta - i\sin 2\theta$, $c = \cos 3\theta + i\sin 3\theta$ and if $\begin{vmatrix} a & b & c \\ b & c & a \\ c & a & b \end{vmatrix} = 0$, then
   (a) $\theta = 2k\pi, k \in Z$ (b) $\theta = (2k + 1)\pi, k \in Z$
   (c) $\theta = (4k + 1)\pi, k \in Z$ (d) None of these

9. The value of $\begin{vmatrix} \log_5 729 & \log_3 5 \\ \log_5 27 & \log_9 25 \end{vmatrix} \begin{vmatrix} \log_5 9 & \log_5 9 \\ \log_{27} 5 & \log_3 5 \end{vmatrix}$ is
   (a) 4 (b) $\frac{1}{4}$ (c) 5 (d) $\frac{1}{5}$

10. If $A = \begin{bmatrix} 0 & x \\ y & 0 \end{bmatrix}$ and $A^3 + A = O$, then sum of possible values of xy is
    (a) 0 (b) -1 (c) 1 (d) 2

11. If $\Delta_r = \begin{vmatrix} 2^{r-1} & 2 \cdot 3^{r-1} & 4 \cdot 5^{r-1} \\ x & y & z \\ 2^n - 1 & 3^n - 1 & 5^n - 1 \end{vmatrix}$, then $\sum_{r=1}^{n} \Delta_r$ is equal to
    (a) 0 (b) 1 (c) 2 (d) 3

12. The value of $\begin{vmatrix} {}^xC_1 & {}^xC_2 & {}^xC_3 \\ {}^yC_1 & {}^yC_2 & {}^yC_3 \\ {}^zC_1 & {}^zC_2 & {}^zC_3 \end{vmatrix} = A(x - y)(y - z)(z - x)$.

    Then, the value of $\frac{12A}{xyz}$ is
    (a) 0 (b) 1 (c) 2 (d) 3

13. If $\begin{vmatrix} x^2+x & x+1 & x-2 \\ 2x^2+3x-1 & 3x & 3x-3 \\ x^2+2x+3 & 2x-1 & 2x-1 \end{vmatrix} = xA+B$, where A and B are determinants of 3×3 square matrices not involving x, then the value of $A+B$ is

(a) 10 (b) 14
(c) 12 (d) 24

14. If $f(x)=\begin{vmatrix} x^n & \sin x & -\cos x \\ n! & \sin\left(\frac{n\pi}{2}\right) & \cos\left(\frac{n\pi}{2}\right) \\ a & a^2 & a^3 \end{vmatrix}$, where a is a constant, then $\frac{d^n}{dx^n}\{f(x)\}$ at $x=0$ for $n=2m+1$, is

(a) 0 (b) -1
(c) 1 (d) None of these

15. The system of linear equations $5x+y-z=2$, $x-z=2$ and $3x+3y+az=5$ has unique solution, when

(a) $a\neq 3$ (b) $a\neq 4$
(c) $a\neq 9$ (d) $a\neq 5$

16. The system of linear equations
$2x+3\lambda y-z=0$, $\lambda x-2y-z=0$ and $x+2y-\lambda z=0$,
where $\lambda\in R$ has a non-trivial solution for

(a) exactly one value of λ
(b) exactly two values of λ
(c) exactly three values of λ
(d) infinitely many values of λ

17. Let $f(x)=\begin{vmatrix} \sec x & \cos x & \sec^2 x+\cot x \operatorname{cosec} x \\ \cos^2 x & \cos^2 x & \operatorname{cosec}^2 x \\ 1 & \cos^2 x & \cos^2 x \end{vmatrix}$,

then $\int_0^{\pi/2} f(x)\,dx$ is equal to

(a) $-\left(\frac{\pi}{4}+\frac{8}{15}\right)$ (b) $-\frac{\pi}{4}+\frac{8}{15}$
(c) $\frac{\pi}{4}+\frac{2}{15}$ (d) $-\left(\frac{\pi}{4}+\frac{2}{15}\right)$

18. Let $A=[a_{ij}]$ be a 3×3 matrix, where

$$a_{ij}=\begin{cases} 1, & \text{if } i=j \\ -x, & \text{if } |i-j|=1 \\ 2x+1, & \text{otherwise} \end{cases}$$

Let a function $f:R\to R$ be defined as $f(x)=\det(A)$.

Then, $\frac{f_{\min}}{f_{\max}}$ is equal to

(a) $-\frac{20}{27}$ (b) $-\frac{30}{7}$
(c) -4 (d) $-\frac{27}{5}$

More than One Correct Option Type Questions

19. The determinant $\Delta=\begin{vmatrix} a^2+x^2 & ab & ac \\ ab & b^2+x^2 & bc \\ ac & bc & c^2+x^2 \end{vmatrix}$ is divisible by

(a) x (b) x^2
(c) x^3 (d) x^4

20. The value of the determinant
$\begin{vmatrix} \sqrt{6} & 2i & 3+\sqrt{6} \\ \sqrt{12} & \sqrt{3}+\sqrt{8}i & 3\sqrt{2}+\sqrt{6}i \\ \sqrt{18} & \sqrt{2}+\sqrt{12}i & \sqrt{27}+2i \end{vmatrix}$, is (where $i=\sqrt{-1}$)

(a) complex (b) real
(c) irrational (d) rational

21. If $D_k=\begin{vmatrix} 2^{k-1} & \frac{1}{k(k+1)} & \sin k\theta \\ x & y & z \\ 2^n-1 & \frac{n}{n+1} & \frac{\sin\left(\frac{n+1}{2}\right)\theta \sin\frac{n}{2}\theta}{\sin\frac{\theta}{2}} \end{vmatrix}$, then $\sum_{k=1}^{n} D_k$ is equal to

(a) 0 (b) independent of n
(c) independent of θ (d) independent of x, y and z

22. The determinant $\begin{vmatrix} a & b & a\alpha+b \\ b & c & b\alpha+c \\ a\alpha+b & b\alpha+c & 0 \end{vmatrix}$ is equal to zero, if

(a) a, b and c are in AP
(b) a, b, c, are in GP
(c) a, b and c are in HP
(d) $(x-\alpha)$ is a factor of $ax^2+2bx+c$

23. Let $f(x)=\begin{vmatrix} 2\cos x & 1 & 0 \\ 1 & 2\cos x & 1 \\ 0 & 1 & 2\cos x \end{vmatrix}$, then

(a) $f\left(\frac{\pi}{3}\right)=-1$ (b) $f'\left(\frac{\pi}{3}\right)=\sqrt{3}$
(c) $\int_0^{\pi} f(x)dx=0$ (d) $\int_{-\pi}^{\pi} f(x)\,dx=0$

24. If $\Delta(x)=\begin{vmatrix} x^2-5x+3 & 2x-5 & 3 \\ 3x^2+x+4 & 6x+1 & 9 \\ 7x^2-6x+9 & 14x-6 & 21 \end{vmatrix}$
$=ax^3+bx^2+cx+d$, then

(a) $a=0$ (b) $b=0$
(c) $c=0$ (d) $d=47$

25. If a, b and c are the sides of a triangle and A, B and C are the angles opposite to a, b and c respectively, then

$$\Delta = \begin{vmatrix} a^2 & b\sin A & c\sin A \\ b\sin A & 1 & \cos A \\ c\sin A & \cos A & 1 \end{vmatrix}$$ is independent of

(a) a (b) b
(c) c (d) A, B, C

26. Let $f(a, b) = \begin{vmatrix} a & a^2 & 0 \\ 1 & (2a+b) & (a+b)^2 \\ 0 & 1 & (2a+3b) \end{vmatrix}$, then

(a) $(a+b)$ is a factor of $f(a, b)$
(b) $(a+2b)$ is a factor of $f(a, b)$
(c) $(2a+b)$ is a factor of $f(a, b)$
(d) a is a factor of $f(a, b)$

27. If $f(x) = \begin{vmatrix} \sec^2 x & 1 & 1 \\ \cos^2 x & \cos^2 x & \operatorname{cosec}^2 x \\ 1 & \cos^2 x & \cot^2 x \end{vmatrix}$, then

(a) $\int_{-\pi/4}^{\pi/4} f(x)\, dx = \frac{1}{16}(3\pi + 8)$
(b) $f'\left(\frac{\pi}{2}\right) = 0$
(c) maximum value of $f(x)$ is 1
(d) minimum value of $f(x)$ is 0

28. If $\begin{vmatrix} a & a+x^2 & a+x^2+x^4 \\ 2a & 3a+2x^2 & 4a+3x^2+2x^4 \\ 3a & 6a+3x^2 & 10a+6x^2+3x^4 \end{vmatrix}$

$$= a_0 + a_1 x + a_2 x^2 + a_3 x^3 + a_4 x^4 + a_5 x^5 + a_6 x^6 + a_7 x^7$$

and $f(x) = +a_0 x^2 + a_3 x + a_6$, then
(a) $f(x) \geq 0, \forall x \in R$ if $a > 0$
(b) $f(x) = 0$, only if $a = 0$
(c) $f(x) = 0$, has two equal roots
(d) $f(x) = 0$, has more than two root if $a = 0$

29. If $\Delta(x) = \begin{vmatrix} 4x-4 & (x-2)^2 & x^3 \\ 8x-4\sqrt{2} & (x-2\sqrt{2})^2 & (x+1)^3 \\ 12x-4\sqrt{3} & (x-2\sqrt{3})^2 & (x-1)^3 \end{vmatrix}$, then

(a) term independent of x in $\Delta(x) = 16(5-\sqrt{2}-\sqrt{3})$
(b) coefficient of x in $\Delta(x) = 48(1+\sqrt{2}-\sqrt{3})$
(c) coefficient of x in $\Delta(x) = 16(5+\sqrt{2}-\sqrt{3})$
(d) coefficient of x in $\Delta(x)$ is divisible by 16

30. If

$$f(x) = \begin{vmatrix} 3 & 3x & 3x^2+2a^2 \\ 3x & 3x^2+2a^2 & 3x^3+6a^2x \\ 3x^2+2a^3 & 3x^3+6a^2x & 3x^4+12a^2x^2+2a^4 \end{vmatrix},$$

then
(a) $f'(x) = 0$
(b) $y = f(x)$ is a straight line parallel to X-axis
(c) $\int_0^2 f(x)\, dx = 32a^4$
(d) None of the above

31. If $a > b > c$ and the system of equations $ax + by + cz = 0$, $bx + cy + az = 0$, $cx + ay + bz = 0$ has a non-trivial solution, then both the roots of the quadratic equation $at^2 + bt + c$, are
(a) real (b) of opposite sign
(c) positive (d) complex

32. The values of λ and b for which the equations $x + y + z = 3$, $x + 3y + 2z = 6$ and $x + \lambda y + 3z = b$ have
(a) a unique solution, if $\lambda \neq 5, b \in R$
(b) no solution, if $\lambda \neq 5, b = 9$
(c) infinite many solution, $\lambda = 5, b = 9$
(d) None of the above

33. Let λ and α be real. Let S denote the set of all values of λ for which the system of linear equations

$$\lambda x + (\sin\alpha) y + (\cos\alpha) z = 0$$
$$x + (\cos\alpha) y + (\sin\alpha) z = 0$$
$$-x + (\sin\alpha) y - (\cos\alpha) z = 0$$

has a non-trivial solution, then S contains
(a) $(-1, 1)$ (b) $[-\sqrt{2}, -1]$
(c) $[1, \sqrt{2}]$ (d) $(-2, 2)$

Passage Based Questions

Passage I

(Q. Nos. 34 and 35)

- Consider the system of equations
$$x + y + z = 5;\ x + 2y + 3z = 9;\ x + 3y + \lambda z = \mu$$
The system is called smart, brilliant, good and lazy according as it has solution, unique solution, infinitely many solutions and no solution, respectively.

34. The system is smart, if
(a) $\lambda \neq 5$ or $\lambda = 5$ and $\mu = 13$
(b) $\lambda \neq 5$ and $\mu = 13$
(c) $\lambda \neq 5$ and $\mu \neq 13$
(d) $\lambda \neq 5$ or $\lambda = 5$ and $\mu \neq 13$

35. The system is good, if

(a) $\lambda \neq 5$ or $\lambda = 5$ and $\mu = 13$
(b) $\lambda = 5$ and $\mu = 13$
(c) $\lambda = 5$ and $\mu \neq 13$
(d) $\lambda \neq 5$, μ is any real number

Passage II

(Q. Nos. 36 and 37)

- If $\Delta = \begin{vmatrix} a_{11} & a_{12} & a_{13} \\ a_{21} & a_{22} & a_{23} \\ a_{31} & a_{32} & a_{33} \end{vmatrix}$ and $C_{ij} = (-1)^{i+j} M_{ij}$, where M_{ij} is a determinant obtained by deleting ith row and jth column, then $\begin{vmatrix} C_{11} & C_{12} & C_{13} \\ C_{21} & C_{22} & C_{23} \\ C_{31} & C_{32} & C_{33} \end{vmatrix} = \Delta^2$.

36. If $\begin{vmatrix} 1 & x & x^2 \\ x & x^2 & 1 \\ x^2 & 1 & x \end{vmatrix} = 5$ and $\Delta = \begin{vmatrix} x^3-1 & 0 & x-x^4 \\ 0 & x-x^4 & x^3-1 \\ x-x^4 & x^3-1 & 0 \end{vmatrix}$, then sum of digits of Δ^2, is

(a) 7 (b) 8
(c) 13 (d) 11

37. Suppose $a, b, c \in R$, $a+b+c>0$, $A = bc - a^2$, $B = ca - b^2$ and $C = ab - c^2$ and $\begin{vmatrix} A & B & C \\ B & C & A \\ C & A & B \end{vmatrix} = 49$, then the value of $a^3 + b^3 + c^3 - 3abc$, is

(a) −7 (b) 7
(c) −2401 (d) 2401

Passage III

(Q. Nos. 38 and 39)

- If α, β, γ are the roots of $x^3 + 2x^2 - x - 3 = 0$

38. If the absolute value of the expression $\frac{\alpha-1}{\alpha+2} + \frac{\beta-1}{\beta+2} + \frac{\gamma-1}{\gamma+2}$ can be expressed as $\frac{m}{n}$, where m and n are co-prime, the value of $\begin{vmatrix} m & n^2 \\ m-n & m+n \end{vmatrix}$, is

(a) 17 (b) 27
(c) 37 (d) 47

39. If $a = \alpha^2 + \beta^2 + \gamma^2$, $b = \alpha\beta + \beta\gamma + \gamma\alpha$, the value of $\begin{vmatrix} a & b & b \\ b & a & b \\ b & b & a \end{vmatrix}$, is

(a) 14 (b) 49
(c) 98 (d) 196

Passage IV

(Q. Nos. 40 and 41)

- Let $\Delta = \begin{vmatrix} -bc & b^2+bc & c^2+bc \\ a^2+ac & -ac & c^2+ac \\ a^2+ab & b^2+ab & -ab \end{vmatrix}$ and the equation $x^3 - px^2 + qx - r = 0$ has roots a, b, c, where $a, b, c \notin R^+$.

40. The value of Δ is

(a) $\leq 9r^3$ (b) $\geq 27r^2$ (c) $\leq 27r^2$ (d) $\geq 81r^3$

41. If $\Delta = 27$ and $a^2 + b^2 + c^2 = 2$, then the value of $\sum a^2 b$, is

(a) $3(2\sqrt{2} - p)$ (b) $3(2\sqrt{2} - r)$
(c) $3(2\sqrt{2} - q)$ (d) $3(2\sqrt{2} - p - q)$

Stem Based Questions

Stem I

(Q. Nos. 42 and 43)

- Suppose $f(x)$ is a function satisfying the following conditions
 (i) $f(0) = 2$, $f(1) = 1$
 (ii) $f(x)$ has a minimum value at $x = \frac{5}{2}$
 (iii) For all x,
 $f'(x) = \begin{vmatrix} 2ax & 2ax-1 & 2ax+b+1 \\ b & b+1 & -1 \\ 2(ax+b) & 2ax+2b+1 & 2ax+b \end{vmatrix}$.

42. The value of $f(2) + f(3)$ is ....

43. The number of solutions of the equation $f(x) + 1 = 0$ is ...

Stem II

(Q. Nos. 44 and 45)

- If $\begin{vmatrix} x & e^{x-1} & (x-1)^3 \\ x - \ln x & \cos(x-1) & (x-1)^2 \\ \tan x & \sin^2 x & \cos^2 x \end{vmatrix} = a_0 + a_1(x-1) + a_2(x-1)^2 + \ldots$

44. The value of $\cos^{-1}(a_1)$, is ....

45. The value of $\lim_{x \to a_0} (\sin x)^x$ is ....

Stem III

(Q. Nos. 46 and 47)

- If $\Delta n = \begin{vmatrix} a^2+n & ab & ac \\ ab & b^2+n & bc \\ ac & bc & c^2+n \end{vmatrix}$, $n \in N$ and the equation $x^3 - \lambda x^2 + 11x - 6 = 0$ has roots a, b, c and a, b, c are in AP.

46. The value of $\sum_{r=1}^{7} \Delta_n$ is ....

47. The value of $\sum_{r=1}^{30} \left(\frac{27\Delta_r - \Delta_{3r}}{27r^2}\right)$ is ....

Single Integer Type Questions

48. If $\begin{vmatrix} 3^2+k & 4^2 & 3^2+3+k \\ 4^2+k & 5^2 & 4^2+4+k \\ 5^2+k & 6^2 & 5^2+5+k \end{vmatrix} = 0$,

the value of $\sqrt{2^k\sqrt{2^k\sqrt{2^k\ldots\infty}}}$ is ....

49. Let α, β and γ are three distinct roots of

$\begin{vmatrix} x-1 & -6 & 2 \\ -6 & x-2 & -4 \\ 2 & -4 & x-6 \end{vmatrix} = 0$, the value of $\left(\frac{1}{\alpha}+\frac{1}{\beta}+\frac{1}{\gamma}\right)^{-1}$

is ....

50. If $\begin{vmatrix} x & e^{x-1} & (x-1)^3 \\ x-\ln x & \cos(x-1) & (x-1)^2 \\ \tan x & \sin^2 x & \cos^2 x \end{vmatrix} = \sum_{r=0}^{n} a_r (x-1)^r$,

the value of $(2^{a_0} + 3^{a_1})^{a_1+1}$ is ....

51. If $\begin{vmatrix} 1 & \cos\alpha & \cos\beta \\ \cos\alpha & 1 & \cos\gamma \\ \cos\beta & \cos\gamma & 1 \end{vmatrix} = \begin{vmatrix} 0 & \cos\alpha & \cos\beta \\ \cos\alpha & 0 & \cos\gamma \\ \cos\beta & \cos\gamma & 0 \end{vmatrix}$,

$\cos^2\alpha + \cos^2\beta + \cos^2\gamma$ is equal to ....

52. Let $f(a, b, c) = \begin{vmatrix} (b+c)^2 & a^2 & a^2 \\ b^2 & (c+a)^2 & b^2 \\ c^2 & c^2 & (a+b)^2 \end{vmatrix}$, the

greatest integer $n \in N$ such that $(a+b+c)^n$ divides $f(a, b, c)$ is ....

53. If $0 \le \theta \le \pi$ and the system of equations $x = (\sin\theta)\,y + (\cos\theta)\,z$, $y = z + (\cos\theta)\,x$ and $z = (\sin\theta)\,x + y$ has a non-trivial solution, then $\frac{8\theta}{\pi}$ is equal to ....

54. The value of the determinant $\begin{vmatrix} 1 & 1 & 1 & 1 \\ 1 & 2 & 3 & 4 \\ 1 & 3 & 6 & 10 \\ 1 & 4 & 10 & 20 \end{vmatrix}$ is ....

55. If a, b, c and d are the roots of the equation $x^4 + 2x^3 + 4x^2 + 8x + 16 = 0$, the value of the

determinant $\begin{vmatrix} 1+a & 1 & 1 & 1 \\ 1 & 1+b & 1 & 1 \\ 1 & 1 & 1+c & 1 \\ 1 & 1 & 1 & 1+d \end{vmatrix}$ is ....

56. If $a \ne 0, b \ne 0, c \ne 0$ and $\begin{vmatrix} 1+a & 1 & 1 \\ 1+b & 1+2b & 1 \\ 1+c & 1+c & 1+3c \end{vmatrix} = 0$,

the value of $|a^{-1} + b^{-1} + c^{-1}|$ is equal to ....

57. If the system of equations

$$ax + hy + g = 0;\ hx + by + f = 0$$

and $ax^2 + 2hxy + by^2 + 2gx + 2fy + c + \lambda = 0$ has a unique solution and $\frac{abc + 2fgh - af^2 - bg^2 - ch^2}{h^2 - ab} = 8$,

the value of λ is ....

Numerical Value Type Questions

58. If $f(x) = \begin{vmatrix} (1+x)^{11} & (1+x)^{12} & (1+x)^{13} \\ (1+x)^{21} & (1+x)^{22} & (1+x)^{23} \\ (1+x)^{31} & (1+x)^{32} & (1+x)^{33} \end{vmatrix}$, then the

coefficient of x in $f(x) = 0$ is ....

59. The system of equations

$$\alpha x + y + z = \alpha - 1,$$
$$x + \alpha y + z = \alpha - 1$$
and $$x + y + \alpha z = \alpha - 1$$

has no solution, if α is ....

60. If $a_1, a_2, a_3, \ldots, a_n, \ldots$ are in GP, then the determinant

$\Delta = \begin{vmatrix} \log a_n & \log a_{n+1} & \log a_{n+2} \\ \log a_{n+3} & \log a_{n+4} & \log a_{n+5} \\ \log a_{n+6} & \log a_{n+7} & \log a_{n+8} \end{vmatrix}$ is equal to ....

61. If $\alpha, \beta \ne 0$ and $f(n) = \alpha^n + \beta^n$ and

$\begin{vmatrix} 3 & 1+f(1) & 1+f(2) \\ 1+f(1) & 1+f(2) & 1+f(3) \\ 1+f(2) & 1+f(3) & 1+f(4) \end{vmatrix} = k(1-\alpha)^2(1-\beta)^2(\alpha-\beta)^2$,

then k^2 is equal to ....

62. If $\begin{vmatrix} (1+\alpha)^2 & (1+2\alpha)^2 & (1+3\alpha)^2 \\ (2+\alpha)^2 & (2+2\alpha)^2 & (2+3\alpha)^2 \\ (3+\alpha)^2 & (3+2\alpha)^2 & (3+3\alpha)^2 \end{vmatrix} = -512\alpha$, then the

sum of square values of α is ....

63. If S is the set of distinct values of a and b for which the following system of linear equations

$$x+y+z=1$$
$$x+ay+z=1$$
$$ax+by+z=0$$

has no solution, then the value of $a+b$ is ....

Matching Type Questions

64. Match the following columns.

Column I		Column II
(A) If a,b,c are three complex numbers such that $a^2+b^2+c^2=0$ and $\begin{vmatrix} b^2+c^2 & ab & ac \\ ab & c^2+a^2 & bc \\ ac & bc & a^2+b^2 \end{vmatrix}=\lambda a^2b^2c^2$, then λ is divisible by	(p)	2
(B) If $a,b,c \in R$ and $\begin{vmatrix} a & a+b & a+b+c \\ 2a & 5a+2b & 7a+5b+2c \\ 3a & 7a+3b & 9a+7b+3c \end{vmatrix}=-1024$, then a is divisible by	(q)	3
(C) Let $\Delta(x)=\begin{vmatrix} x-1 & 2x^2-5 & x^3-1 \\ 2x^2+5 & 2x+2 & x^3+3 \\ x^3-1 & x+1 & 3x^2-2 \end{vmatrix}$ and $ax+b$ be the remainder, when $\Delta(x)$ is divided by x^2-1, then $4a+2b$ is divisible by	(r)	4
(D) If $\Delta(x)=\begin{vmatrix} (a^x+a^{-x})^2 & (a^x-a^{-x})^2 & 1 \\ (a^y+a^{-y})^2 & (a^y-a^{-y})^2 & 1 \\ (a^z+a^{-z})^2 & (a^z-a^{-z})^2 & 1 \end{vmatrix}$, where $a, b, c, x, y, z \in Z$. Then Δ is equal to	(s)	5
	(t)	0

65. Match the following columns.

Column I		Column II
(A) Let $f_1(x)=x+a_1$, $f_2(x)=x^2+b_1x+b_2$, $x_1=2$, $x_2=3$ and $x_3=5$ and $\Delta=\begin{vmatrix} 1 & 1 & 1 \\ f_1(x_1) & f_1(x_2) & f_1(x_3) \\ f_2(x_1) & f_2(x_2) & f_2(x_3) \end{vmatrix}$, then Δ is	(p)	Even number
(B) If $\lvert a_1-b_1\rvert=6$ and $f(x)=\begin{vmatrix} 1 & b_1 & a_1 \\ 1 & b_1 & 2a_1-x \\ 1 & 2b_1-x & a_1 \end{vmatrix}$, then the minimum value of $f(x)$ is	(q)	Prime number
(C) If coefficient of x in $f(x)=\begin{vmatrix} x-2 & (x-1)^2 & x^3 \\ x-1 & x^2 & (x+1)^3 \\ x & (x+1)^2 & (x+2)^3 \end{vmatrix}$ is λ, then $\lvert\lambda\rvert$ is	(r)	Odd number
(D) If $f(x)=\lambda$, where $f(x)=\begin{vmatrix} 1 & \cos(\beta-\alpha) & \cos(\gamma-\alpha) \\ \cos(\alpha-\beta) & 1 & \cos(\gamma-\beta) \\ \cos(\alpha-\gamma) & \cos(\beta-\gamma) & 1 \end{vmatrix}$, then λ is	(s)	Composite number
	(t)	Perfect number

66. Match the following columns.

Column I		Column II
(A) If $\begin{vmatrix} x^2+3x & x-1 & x+3 \\ x^2+1 & 2+3x & x-3 \\ x^2-3 & x+4 & 3x \end{vmatrix}$ $=ax^4+bx^3+cx^2+dx+e$, then $e+a$ is divisible by	(p)	2
(B) If $\begin{vmatrix} x-1 & 5x & 7 \\ x^2-1 & x-1 & 8 \\ 2x & 3x & 0 \end{vmatrix}=ax^3+bx^2+cx+d$, then $(c+a-3)$ is divisible by	(q)	3
(C) If $\begin{vmatrix} x^3+4x & x+3 & x-2 \\ x-2 & 5x & x-1 \\ x-3 & x+2 & 4x \end{vmatrix}$ $=ax^5+bx^4+cx^3+dx^2+ex+f$, then $(f+e)$ is divisible by	(r)	5
(D) If $\Delta=\begin{vmatrix} 1+a^2-b^2 & 2ab & -2b \\ 2ab & 1-a^2+b^2 & 2a \\ 2b & -2a & 1-a^2-b^2 \end{vmatrix}$ $=(p+a^2+b^2)^q$, then $p+q$ is divisible by	(s)	6
	(t)	7

Previous Year Questions

67. Let α, β and γ be real numbers. Consider the following system of linear equation $x+2y+z=7$, $x+\alpha z=11$ and $2x-3y+\beta z=\gamma$.
Match each entry in **List-I** to the correct entries in **List-II.**

	List-I		List-II
(P)	If $\beta=\frac{1}{2}(7\alpha-3)$ and $\gamma=28$, then the system has	(1)	a unique solution
(Q)	If $\beta=\frac{1}{2}(7\alpha-3)$ and $\gamma\neq 28$, then the system has	(2)	no solution
(R)	If $\beta\neq\frac{1}{2}(7\alpha-3)$ where $\alpha=1$ and $\gamma\neq 28$, then the system has	(3)	infinitely many solutions
(S)	If $\beta\neq\frac{1}{2}(7\alpha-3)$ where $\alpha=1$ and $\gamma=28$, then the system has	(4)	$x=11, y=-2$ and $z=0$ as a solution
		(5)	$x=-15, y=4$ and $z=0$ as a solution

[Matching Type, 2023 Adv.]

The correct option is

	P	Q	R	S		P	Q	R	S
(a)	3	2	1	4	(b)	3	2	5	4
(c)	2	1	4	5	(d)	2	1	1	3

68. Let $|M|$ denote the determinant of a square matrix M.
Let $g:\left[0,\frac{\pi}{2}\right]\to R$ be the function defined by

$$g(\theta)=\sqrt{f(\theta)-1}+\sqrt{f\left(\frac{\pi}{2}-\theta\right)-1}$$

where, $$f(\theta)=\frac{1}{2}\begin{vmatrix}1 & \sin\theta & 1\\ -\sin\theta & 1 & \sin\theta\\ -1 & -\sin\theta & 1\end{vmatrix}+\begin{vmatrix}\sin\pi & \cos(\theta+\pi/4) & \tan(\theta-\pi/4)\\ \sin(\theta-4/\pi) & -\cos\pi/2 & \log_e(4/\pi)\\ \cot(\theta+4/\pi) & \log_e(\pi/4) & \tan\pi\end{vmatrix}$$

Let $p(x)$ be a quadratic polynomial whose roots are the maximum and minimum values of the function $g(\theta)$, and $p(2)=2-\sqrt{2}$. Then, which of the following is/are TRUE ?

[More than One Option Correct, 2022 Adv.]

(a) $p\left(\frac{3+\sqrt{2}}{4}\right)<0$ (b) $p\left(\frac{1+3\sqrt{2}}{4}\right)>0$

(c) $p\left(\frac{5\sqrt{2}-1}{4}\right)>0$ (d) $p\left(\frac{5-\sqrt{2}}{4}\right)<0$

69. Let p, q and r be non-zero real numbers that are, respectively, the 10th, 100th and 1000th terms of an Harmonic progression. Consider the system of linear equations

$$x+y+z=1,\ 10x+100y+1000z=0$$

and $$qrx+pry+pqz=0$$

[Matching Type, 2022 Adv.]

	List I		List II
I.	If $\frac{q}{r}=10$, then the system of linear equations has	P.	$x=0, y=\frac{10}{9}, z=-\frac{1}{9}$ as a solution
II.	If $\frac{p}{r}\neq 100$, then the system of linear equations has	Q.	$x=\frac{10}{9}, y=-\frac{1}{9}, z=0$ as a solution
III.	If $\frac{p}{q}\neq 10$, then the system of linear equations has	R.	infinitely many solutions
IV.	If $\frac{p}{q}=10$, then the system of linear equations has	S.	no solution
		T.	atleast one solution

	I	II	III	IV		I	II	III	IV
(a)	R	S	S	R	(b)	P	Q	R	S
(c)	S	P	R	Q	(d)	S	R	S	R

▪ **Question Stem** (Q. Nos. 70-72)

Let α, β and γ be real numbers such that the system of linear equations $x+2y+3z=\alpha$, $4x+5y+6z=\beta$ and $7x+8y+9z=\gamma-1$ is consistent.
Let $|M|$ represent the determinant of the matrix

$$M=\begin{bmatrix}\alpha & 2 & \gamma\\ \beta & 1 & 0\\ -1 & 0 & 1\end{bmatrix}.$$

Let P be the plane containing all those (α, β, γ) for which the above system of linear equations is consistent, and D be the square of the distance of the point (0, 1, 0) from the plane P. **[Stem Type, 2021 Adv.]**

70. The value of $|M|$ is ....

71. The value of D is ....

72. Let P be a matrix of order 3×3 such that all the entries in P are from the set $\{-1, 0, 1\}$. Then, the maximum possible value of the determinant of P is ....

EXERCISE 3
Challenging Problems

1. Prove that $\begin{vmatrix} b+c & c & b \\ c & c+a & a \\ b & a & a+b \end{vmatrix} = 4abc.$

2. Prove that $\begin{vmatrix} a-b-c & 2a & 2a \\ 2b & b-c-a & 2b \\ 2c & 2c & c-a-b \end{vmatrix} = (a+b+c)^3.$

3. Find the value of determinant $\begin{vmatrix} \sqrt{13}+\sqrt{3} & 2\sqrt{5} & \sqrt{5} \\ \sqrt{15}+\sqrt{26} & 5 & \sqrt{10} \\ 3+\sqrt{65} & \sqrt{15} & 5 \end{vmatrix}.$

4. Find the value of the determinant $\begin{vmatrix} bc & ca & ab \\ p & q & r \\ 1 & 1 & 1 \end{vmatrix}$, where a, b and c respectively are the pth, qth and rth terms of a harmonic progression.

5. Without expanding the determinant at any stage, prove that $\begin{vmatrix} -5 & 3+5i & \frac{3}{2}-4i \\ 3-5i & 8 & 4+5i \\ \frac{3}{2}+4i & 4-5i & 9 \end{vmatrix}$ has a purely real value.

6. Prove without expanding that $\begin{vmatrix} ah+bg & g & ab+ch \\ bf+ba & f & hb+bc \\ af+bc & c & bg+fc \end{vmatrix} = a \begin{vmatrix} ah+bg & a & h \\ bf+ba & h & b \\ af+bc & g & f \end{vmatrix}.$

7. If A, B and C are the angles of a triangle and

$$\begin{vmatrix} 1 & 1 & 1 \\ 1+\sin A & 1+\sin B & 1+\sin C \\ \sin A+\sin^2 A & \sin B+\sin^2 B & \sin C+\sin^2 C \end{vmatrix} = 0,$$

then prove that ΔABC must be isosceles.

8. Prove that $\begin{vmatrix} \beta\gamma & \beta\gamma'+\beta'\gamma & \beta'\gamma' \\ \gamma\alpha & \gamma\alpha'+\gamma'\alpha & \gamma'\alpha' \\ \alpha\beta & \alpha\beta'+\alpha'\beta & \alpha'\beta' \end{vmatrix}$
$= (\alpha\beta'-\alpha'\beta)(\beta\gamma'-\beta'\gamma)(\gamma\alpha'-\gamma'\alpha).$

9. If $y = \frac{u}{v}$, where u and v are functions of x, show that

$$v^3 \frac{d^2y}{dx^2} = \begin{vmatrix} u & v & 0 \\ u' & v & v \\ u'' & v'' & 2v' \end{vmatrix}.$$

10. Show that the determinant $\Delta(x)$ is given by $\Delta(x) = \begin{vmatrix} \sin(x+\alpha) & \cos(x+\alpha) & a+x\sin\alpha \\ \sin(x+\beta) & \cos(x+\beta) & b+x\sin\beta \\ \sin(x+\gamma) & \cos(x+\gamma) & c+x\sin\gamma \end{vmatrix}$. is independent of x.

11. Evaluate $\begin{vmatrix} {}^xC_1 & {}^xC_2 & {}^xC_3 \\ {}^yC_1 & {}^yC_2 & {}^yC_3 \\ {}^zC_1 & {}^zC_2 & {}^zC_3 \end{vmatrix}.$

12. (i) Find maximum value of

$$f(x) = \begin{vmatrix} 1+\sin^2 x & \cos^2 x & 4\sin 2x \\ \sin^2 x & 1+\cos^2 x & 4\sin 2x \\ \sin^2 x & \cos^2 x & 1+4\sin 2x \end{vmatrix}.$$

(ii) Let A, B and C be the angles of a triangle, such that $A \geq B \geq C$.

Find the minimum value of Δ, where

$$\Delta = \begin{vmatrix} \sin^2 A & \sin A\cos A & \cos^2 A \\ \sin^2 B & \sin B\cos B & \cos^2 B \\ \sin^2 C & \sin C\cos C & \cos^2 C \end{vmatrix}.$$

13. If $f(x) = \begin{vmatrix} x^2-4x+6 & 2x^2+4x+10 & 3x^2-2x+16 \\ x-2 & 2x+2 & 3x-1 \\ 1 & 2 & 3 \end{vmatrix}$,

then find the value of $\int_{-3}^{3} \frac{x^2 \sin x}{1+x^6} f(x)dx.$

14. If $Y = sX$ and $Z = tX$ all the variables beings functions of x, then prove that $\begin{vmatrix} X & Y & Z \\ X_1 & Y_1 & Z_1 \\ X_2 & Y_2 & Z_2 \end{vmatrix} = X^3 \begin{vmatrix} s_1 & t_1 \\ s_2 & t_2 \end{vmatrix}$,

where suffixes denote the order of differentiation with respect to x.

15. If f, g and h are differentiable functions of x and $\Delta = \begin{vmatrix} f & g & h \\ (xf)' & (xg)' & (xh)' \\ (x^2f)'' & (x^2g)'' & (x^2h)'' \end{vmatrix}$, then prove that $\Delta' = \begin{vmatrix} f & g & h \\ f' & g' & h' \\ (x^3f'')' & (x^3g'')' & (x^3h'')' \end{vmatrix}$.

16. If $|a_1| > |a_2| + |a_3|, |b_2| > |b_1| + |b_3|$ and $|c_3| > |c_1| + |c_2|$, then show that $\begin{vmatrix} a_1 & a_2 & a_3 \\ b_1 & b_2 & b_3 \\ c_1 & c_2 & c_3 \end{vmatrix} \neq 0$.

17. Show that $\begin{vmatrix} (a-a_1)^{-2} & (a-a_1)^{-1} & a_1^{-1} \\ (a-a_2)^{-2} & (a-a_2)^{-1} & a_2^{-1} \\ (a-a_3)^{-2} & (a-a_3)^{-1} & a_3^{-1} \end{vmatrix} = \pm \dfrac{a^2 \Pi(a_i - a_j)}{\Pi a_i \Pi(a-a_i)^2}$. Write out the terms of the product in the numerator and give the resulting expression its correct sign.

18. Show that in general there are three values of t for which the following system of equations has a non-trivial solution $(a-t)x + by + cz = 0$, $bx + (c-t)y + az = 0$ and $cx + ay + (b-t)z = 0$. Express the product of these values of t in the form of a determinant.

19. Eliminates

(i) a, b and c

(ii) x, y, z from the equations

$$-a + \frac{by}{z} + \frac{cz}{y} = 0, \quad -b + \frac{cz}{x} + \frac{ax}{z} = 0$$

and $$-c + \frac{ax}{y} + \frac{by}{x} = 0.$$

20. If x, z and y are not all zero and if

$ax + by + cz = 0, \; bx + cy + az = 0$

and $cx + ay + bz = 0$, then

prove that $x : y : z = 1 : 1 : 1$ or $1 : \omega : \omega^2$ or $1 : \omega^2 : \omega$.

Answer Key

Exercise 1

1. (a)	2. (c)	3. (d)	4. (c)	5. (c)	6. (d)	7. (c)	8. (a)	9. (b)	10. (a)
11. (c)	12. (d)	13. (b)	14. (a)	15. (b)	16. (b)	17. (b)	18. (c)	19. (b)	20. (a)
21. (b)	22. (a)	23. (8)	24. (6)	25. (25)	26. (1)	27. (27)	28. (2)	29. (3)	30. (4)
31. (8)	32. (4)	33. (d)	34. (b)	35. (a)	36. (b)	37. (b)	38. (d)	39. (d)	40. (b)
41. (a)	42. (5)	43. (38)	44. (55)	45. (28)	46. (b)	47. (d)	48. (c)	49. (b)	50. (c)
51. (b)	52. (c)	53. (b)	54. (b)	55. (c)	56. (c)	57. (c)	58. (a)	59. (d)	60. (c)
61. (b)	62. (c)	63. (24)	64. (b)	65. (b)	66. (c)	67. (b)	68. (d)	69. (b)	70. (c)
71. (b)	72. (a)	73. (d)	74. (c)	75. (c)	76. (d)	77. (c)	78. (d)	79. (d)	80. (a)
81. (b)	82. (c)	83. (b)	84. (c)	85. (b)	86. (c)	87. (16)	88. (5)	89. (b)	90. (c)
91. (3)									

Exercise 2

1. (d)	2. (d)	3. (d)	4. (c)	5. (b)	6. (c)	7. (c)	8. (a)	9. (a)	10. (b)
11. (a)	12. (b)	13. (c)	14. (a)	15. (c)	16. (a)	17. (a)	18. (d)	19. (a,b,c,d)	20. (b,d)
21. (a,b,c,d)	22. (b,d)	23. (a,c,d)	24. (a,b,c)	25. (a,b,c,d)	26. (a,b,d)	27. (a,b,c,d)	28. (a,c,d)	29. (a,b,d)	30. (a,b)
31. (a,b)	32. (a,c)	33. (a,b,c)	34. (a)	35. (b)	36. (c)	37. (b)	38. (c)	39. (d)	40. (b)
41. (b)	42. (1)	43. (0)	44. ($\pi/2$)	45. (1)	46. (14^3)	47. (280)	48. (2)	49. (9)	50. (2)
51. (1)	52. (3)	53. (6)	54. (1)	55. (8)	56. (3)	57. (8)	58. (0)	59. (−2)	60. (0)

61. (1) 62. (32) 63. (2) 64. (A) → (p,r); (B) → (p,r); (C) → (p,q,s); (D) → (t)

65. (A) → (p,s,t); (B) → (r,s); (C) → (p,q,s); (D) → (p) 66. (A) → (r); (B) → (r,t); (C) → (p,q,s); (D) → (p)

67. (a) 68. (a,c) 69. (a) 70. (1) 71. (1.5) 72. (4)

Solutions

Exercise 1 - JEE Main Pattern

1. Let $\Delta(x) = \begin{vmatrix} x & 1+x^2 & x^3 \\ \log_e(1+x^2) & e^x & \sin x \\ \cos x & \tan x & \sin^2 x \end{vmatrix}$

$$= a + bx + cx^2 + \ldots$$

On putting $x = 0$, we get

$$\begin{vmatrix} 0 & 1 & 0 \\ 0 & 1 & 0 \\ 1 & 0 & 0 \end{vmatrix} = a$$

$\therefore$ $\qquad 0 = a$

or $\qquad a = 0$, then

$$\Delta(x) = bx + cx^2 + \ldots$$

Hence, $\Delta(x)$ is divisible by x.

2. Given, $\begin{vmatrix} a^2 & b^2 & c^2 \\ (a+1)^2 & (b+1)^2 & (c+1)^2 \\ (a-1)^2 & (b-1)^2 & (c-1)^2 \end{vmatrix} = 0$

$$\Rightarrow \begin{vmatrix} a^2 & b^2 & c^2 \\ a^2+2a+1 & b^2+2b+1 & c^2+2c+1 \\ a^2-2a+1 & b^2-2b+1 & c^2-2c+1 \end{vmatrix} = 0$$

Applying $R_2 \to R_2 - R_3$, then

$$\begin{vmatrix} a^2 & b^2 & c^2 \\ 4a & 4b & 4c \\ a^2-2a+1 & b^2-2b+1 & c^2-2c+1 \end{vmatrix} = 0$$

Applying $R_3 \to R_3 - R_1 + \frac{1}{2}R_2$, then

$$4\begin{vmatrix} a^2 & b^2 & c^2 \\ a & b & c \\ 1 & 1 & 1 \end{vmatrix} = 0$$

$$\Rightarrow -\begin{vmatrix} 1 & 1 & 1 \\ a & b & c \\ a^2 & b^2 & c^2 \end{vmatrix} = 0 \qquad [\because R_1 \leftrightarrow R_3]$$

$$\Rightarrow \begin{vmatrix} 1 & 1 & 1 \\ a & b & c \\ a^2 & b^2 & c^2 \end{vmatrix} = 0$$

$\Rightarrow \qquad (a-b)(b-c)(c-a) = 0$

$\therefore \qquad a-b=0$ or $b-c=0$ or $c-a=0$

$\Rightarrow \qquad a=b$ or $b=c$ or $c=a$

Hence, ΔABC is an isosceles triangle.

3. $\because \begin{vmatrix} a & b & c \\ b & c & a \\ c & a & b \end{vmatrix} = -(a^3+b^3+c^3-3abc)$

$$= -(a+b+c)(a+b\omega+c\omega^2)(a+b\omega^2+c\omega)$$

[where ω is cube roots of unity]

$$= -f(\alpha)f(\beta)f(\gamma) \qquad [\because \alpha = 1, \beta = \omega, \gamma = \omega^2]$$

4. Let $\Delta = \begin{vmatrix} \cos 2x & \sin^2 x & \cos 4x \\ \sin^2 x & \cos 2x & \cos^2 x \\ \cos 4x & \cos^2 x & \cos 2x \end{vmatrix}$

$$= \begin{vmatrix} 1-2\sin^2 x & \sin^2 x & 1-8\sin^2 x(1-\sin^2 x) \\ \sin^2 x & 1-2\sin^2 x & 1-\sin^2 x \\ 1-8\sin^2 x(1-\sin^2 x) & 1-\sin^2 x & 1-2\sin^2 x \end{vmatrix}$$

The required constant term is $\begin{vmatrix} 1 & 0 & 1 \\ 0 & 1 & 1 \\ 1 & 1 & 1 \end{vmatrix}$

Applying $C_3 \to C_3 - C_1$, then

$$\begin{vmatrix} 1 & 0 & 0 \\ 0 & 1 & 1 \\ 1 & 1 & 0 \end{vmatrix} = 1(0-1) = -1$$

5. $\because \quad -1 \le x < 0 \Rightarrow [x] = -1$

$0 \le y < 1 \Rightarrow [y] = 0$

$1 \le z < 2 \Rightarrow [z] = 1$

Let $\Delta = \begin{vmatrix} [x]+1 & [y] & [z] \\ [x] & [y]+1 & [z] \\ [x] & [y] & [z]+1 \end{vmatrix} = \begin{vmatrix} 0 & 0 & 1 \\ -1 & 1 & 1 \\ -1 & 0 & 2 \end{vmatrix}$

Expanding along C_2, then

$$\Delta = \begin{vmatrix} 0 & 1 \\ -1 & 2 \end{vmatrix} = 1 = [z]$$

6. $\because$ In a triangle $A+B+C = \pi$ and $e^{\pi} = \cos\pi + i\sin\pi = -1$

$$e^{i(B+C)} = e^{i(\pi - A)} = e^{i\pi} \cdot e^{-iA} = -e^{-iA}$$

$\Rightarrow \qquad e^{-i(B+C)} = -e^{iA}$

Similarly, $\qquad e^{-i(A+B)} = -e^{iC}$

and $\qquad e^{-i(C+A)} = -e^{iB}$

Taking e^{iA}, e^{iB}, e^{iC} common from R_1, R_2 and R_3 respectively, we get

$$\Delta = e^{iA} \cdot e^{iB} \cdot e^{iC} \begin{vmatrix} e^{iA} & e^{-i(A+C)} & e^{-i(A+B)} \\ e^{-i(B+C)} & e^{iB} & e^{-i(A+B)} \\ e^{-i(B+C)} & e^{-i(A+C)} & e^{iC} \end{vmatrix}$$

$$= e^{i\pi}\begin{vmatrix} e^{iA} & -e^{iB} & -e^{iC} \\ -e^{iA} & e^{iB} & -e^{iC} \\ -e^{iA} & -e^{iB} & e^{iC} \end{vmatrix}$$

Taking e^{iA}, e^{iB}, e^{iC} common from C_1, C_2 and C_3 respectively, we get

$$\Delta = (-1)\,e^{iA}\cdot e^{iB}\cdot e^{iC}\begin{vmatrix} 1 & -1 & -1 \\ -1 & 1 & -1 \\ -1 & -1 & 1 \end{vmatrix}$$

$$= (-1)\,e^{i\pi}\begin{vmatrix} 1 & -1 & -1 \\ -1 & 1 & -1 \\ -1 & -1 & 1 \end{vmatrix}$$

$$= (-1)(-1)\begin{vmatrix} 1 & -1 & -1 \\ -1 & 1 & -1 \\ -1 & -1 & 1 \end{vmatrix} = \begin{vmatrix} 1 & -1 & -1 \\ -1 & 1 & -1 \\ -1 & -1 & 1 \end{vmatrix}$$

Applying $C_2 \to C_2 + C_1$ and $C_3 \to C_3 + C_1$, then

$$\Delta = \begin{vmatrix} 1 & 0 & 0 \\ -1 & 0 & -2 \\ -1 & -2 & 0 \end{vmatrix} = 1(0-4) = -4$$

7. Taking x^5 common from R_3, then

$$x^5\begin{vmatrix} x^n & x^{n+2} & x^{2n} \\ 1 & x^a & a \\ x^n & x^{a+1} & x^{2n} \end{vmatrix} = 0, \forall\, x \in R$$

$$\Rightarrow \quad a + 1 = n + 2 \Rightarrow a = n + 1$$

8. As $a_1 b_1 c_1$, $a_2 b_2 c_2$ and $a_3 b_3 c_3$ are even natural numbers each of c_1, c_2, c_3 is divisible by 2.

Let $c_i = 2\lambda_i$ for $i = 1, 2, 3$ and $\lambda_i \in N$, then

$$\Delta = \begin{vmatrix} 2\lambda_1 & a_1 & b_1 \\ 2\lambda_2 & a_2 & b_2 \\ 2\lambda_3 & a_3 & b_3 \end{vmatrix} = 2\begin{vmatrix} \lambda_1 & a_1 & b_1 \\ \lambda_2 & a_2 & b_2 \\ \lambda_3 & a_3 & b_3 \end{vmatrix} = 2m$$

where m is some natural number. Thus, Δ is divisible by 2. That Δ may not be divisible by 4 can be seen by taking the three numbers as 112, 122 and 134.

$$\Delta = \begin{vmatrix} 2 & 1 & 1 \\ 2 & 1 & 2 \\ 4 & 1 & 3 \end{vmatrix} = 2(3-2) - 1(6-8) + 1(2-4) = 2$$

which is divisible by 2 but not by 4.

9. Let $\Delta = \begin{vmatrix} c & b\cos B + c\beta & a\cos A + b\alpha + c\gamma \\ a & c\cos B + a\beta & b\cos A + c\alpha + a\gamma \\ b & a\cos B + b\beta & c\cos A + a\alpha + b\gamma \end{vmatrix}$

Applying $C_2 \to C_2 - \beta C_1$ and $C_3 \to C_3 - \gamma C_1$, then

$$\Delta = \begin{vmatrix} c & b\cos B & a\cos A + b\alpha \\ a & c\cos B & b\cos A + c\alpha \\ b & a\cos B & c\cos A + a\alpha \end{vmatrix}$$

Applying $C_3 \to C_3 - \alpha \sec B\, C_2$, then

$$\Delta = \begin{vmatrix} c & b\cos B & a\cos A \\ a & c\cos B & b\cos A \\ b & a\cos B & c\cos A \end{vmatrix} = \cos A \cos B \begin{vmatrix} c & b & a \\ a & c & b \\ b & a & c \end{vmatrix}$$

Applying $C_1 \leftrightarrow C_3$, then $\Delta = -\cos A \cos B \begin{vmatrix} a & b & c \\ b & c & a \\ c & a & b \end{vmatrix}$

$$= \cos A \cos B\,(a+b+c)\cdot\frac{1}{2}[(a-b)^2 + (b-c)^2 + (c-a)^2]$$

Given, $\cos A \neq 0$, $\cos B \neq 0$ and $a + b + c \neq 0$

$\because \quad \Delta = 0$

$\therefore \quad (a-b)^2 + (b-c)^2 + (c-a)^2 = 0$

which is independent, when $a - b = 0$, $b - c = 0$ and $c - a = 0$

i.e. $\quad a = b = c$

Hence, ΔABC is an equilateral.

10. Here, $\left.\begin{aligned} x_1 + x_2 = 6,\ x_1 x_2 = 3 \\ \text{and } y_1 + y_2 = 4,\ y_1 y_2 = 2 \end{aligned}\right\}$ ...(i)

Let $\Delta = \begin{vmatrix} x_1 x_2 & y_1 y_2 & 1 \\ x_1 + x_2 & y_1 + y_2 & 2 \\ \sin(\pi x_1 x_2) & \cos\left(\dfrac{\pi}{2y_1 y_2}\right) & 1 \end{vmatrix}$

$$= \begin{vmatrix} 3 & 2 & 1 \\ 6 & 4 & 2 \\ \sin 3\pi & \cos\left(\dfrac{\pi}{4}\right) & 1 \end{vmatrix} \quad \text{[from Eq. (i)]}$$

Applying $R_2 \to R_2 - 2R_1$, then $\Delta = \begin{vmatrix} 3 & 2 & 1 \\ 0 & 0 & 0 \\ 0 & \dfrac{1}{\sqrt{2}} & 1 \end{vmatrix} = 0$

11. $\because \Delta = \begin{vmatrix} {}^{10}C_4 & {}^{10}C_5 & {}^{11}C_m \\ {}^{11}C_6 & {}^{11}C_7 & {}^{12}C_{m+2} \\ {}^{12}C_8 & {}^{12}C_9 & {}^{13}C_{m+4} \end{vmatrix}$

Applying $C_2 \to C_2 + C_1$ and use Pascal's rule $({}^nC_r + {}^nC_{r-1} = {}^{n+1}C_r)$, then

$$\Delta = \begin{vmatrix} {}^{10}C_4 & {}^{11}C_5 & {}^{11}C_m \\ {}^{11}C_6 & {}^{12}C_7 & {}^{12}C_{m+2} \\ {}^{12}C_8 & {}^{13}C_9 & {}^{13}C_{m+4} \end{vmatrix} = 0 \quad \text{[given]}$$

$\therefore \quad m = 5$

12. Let $F(x) = \begin{vmatrix} f(x) & g(x) & h(x) \\ a & b & c \\ p & q & r \end{vmatrix} = mx^4 + nx^3 + rx^2 + sx + t$ ...(i)

On differentiating twice and thrice of Eq. (i) w.r.t. x, then

$$F''(x) = \begin{vmatrix} f''(x) & g''(x) & h''(x) \\ a & b & c \\ p & q & r \end{vmatrix}$$

$$= 12mx^2 + 6nx + 2r \quad \text{...(ii)}$$

$$F'''(x) = \begin{vmatrix} f'''(x) & g'''(x) & h'''(x) \\ a & b & c \\ p & q & r \end{vmatrix} = 24mx + 6n \quad \text{...(iii)}$$

On putting $x = 0$ in Eqs. (ii) and (iii), we get

$$\begin{vmatrix} f''(0) & g''(0) & h''(0) \\ a & b & c \\ p & q & r \end{vmatrix} = 2r \qquad \text{...(iv)}$$

and
$$\begin{vmatrix} f'''(0) & g'''(0) & h'''(0) \\ a & b & c \\ p & q & r \end{vmatrix} = 6n \qquad \text{...(v)}$$

Now, subtracting Eq. (iv) from Eq. (v), we get

$$\begin{vmatrix} f'''(0) - f''(0) & g'''(0) - g''(0) & h'''(0) - h''(0) \\ a & b & c \\ p & q & r \end{vmatrix}$$

$$= 6n - 2r = 2(3n - r)$$

13. Let $\Delta = \begin{vmatrix} 1 & 1 & 1 \\ a & b & c \\ a^3 & b^3 & c^3 \end{vmatrix}$

Taking a, b, c common from C_1, C_2, C_3, then $\Delta = abc \begin{vmatrix} \frac{1}{a} & \frac{1}{b} & \frac{1}{c} \\ 1 & 1 & 1 \\ a^2 & b^2 & c^2 \end{vmatrix}$

On multiplying in R_1 by abc, then

$$\Delta = \begin{vmatrix} bc & ca & ab \\ 1 & 1 & 1 \\ a^2 & b^2 & c^2 \end{vmatrix} = -\begin{vmatrix} 1 & 1 & 1 \\ bc & ca & ab \\ a^2 & b^2 & c^2 \end{vmatrix} \qquad [R_1 \leftrightarrow R_2]$$

$$= \begin{vmatrix} 1 & 1 & 1 \\ a^2 & b^2 & c^2 \\ bc & ca & ab \end{vmatrix} \qquad [R_2 \leftrightarrow R_3]$$

$$= (a - b)(b - c)(c - a)(a + b + c)$$

Now, $D = \begin{vmatrix} 1 & 1 & 1 \\ (x-a)^2 & (x-b)^2 & (x-c)^2 \\ (x-b)(x-c) & (x-c)(x-a) & (x-a)(x-b) \end{vmatrix}$

$$= (b - a)(c - b)(a - c)(3x - a - b - c)$$

Now, given that a, b and c are all different, then $D = 0$

$\therefore \quad 3x - a - b - c = 0 \Rightarrow x = \frac{1}{3}(a + b + c)$

14. Given, determinant

$$2a(bc - 4a^2) - b(b^2 - 2ac) + c(2ab - c^2) = 0$$

$\Rightarrow \quad -[(2a)^3 + b^3 + c^3 - 3 \cdot 2a \cdot b \cdot c] = 0$

$\Rightarrow \quad \frac{1}{2}(2a + b + c)[(2a - b)^2 + (b - c)^2 + (c - 2a)^2] = 0$

$\Rightarrow \quad 2a + b + c = 0 \qquad \text{...(i)} \; [\because b \neq c]$

Let $\quad f(x) = 8ax^3 + 2bx^2 + cx + d$

$\therefore f(0) = d$ and $f\left(\frac{1}{2}\right) = a + \frac{b}{2} + \frac{c}{2} + d = \frac{2a + b + c}{2} + d$

$$= \frac{0}{2} + d = d \qquad \text{[from Eq. (i)]}$$

$\Rightarrow \quad f(0) = f\left(\frac{1}{2}\right)$

So, $f(x)$ satisfies Rolle's theorem and hence $f'(x) = 0$ has atleast one root in $\left[0, \frac{1}{2}\right]$.

15. Given, $\begin{vmatrix} x^3 + 1 & x^2y & x^2z \\ xy^2 & y^3 + 1 & y^2z \\ xz^2 & yz^2 & z^3 + 1 \end{vmatrix} = 11$

Taking x, y, z common from C_1, C_2, C_3 respectively, then

$$\Rightarrow \quad xyz \begin{vmatrix} \frac{x^3+1}{x} & x^2 & x^2 \\ y^2 & \frac{y^3+1}{y} & y^2 \\ z^2 & z^2 & \frac{z^3+1}{z} \end{vmatrix} = 11$$

On multiplying R_1 by x, R_2 by y and R_3 by z, we get

$$\Rightarrow \quad \begin{vmatrix} x^3 + 1 & x^3 & x^3 \\ y^3 & y^3 + 1 & y^3 \\ z^3 & z^3 & z^3 + 1 \end{vmatrix} = 11$$

Applying $R_1 \to R_1 + R_2 + R_3$, then

$$\begin{vmatrix} x^3 + y^3 + z^3 + 1 & x^3 + y^3 + z^3 + 1 & x^3 + y^3 + z^3 + 1 \\ y^3 & y^3 + 1 & y^3 \\ z^3 & z^3 & z^3 + 1 \end{vmatrix} = 11$$

Applying $C_2 \to C_2 - C_1$ and $C_3 \to C_3 - C_1$, then

$$\begin{vmatrix} x^3 + y^3 + z^3 + 1 & 0 & 0 \\ y^3 & 1 & 0 \\ z^3 & 0 & 1 \end{vmatrix} = 11$$

$\Rightarrow \quad x^3 + y^3 + z^3 + 1 = 11$

$\Rightarrow \quad x^3 + y^3 + z^3 = 10$

Therefore, the ordered triplets are (2, 1, 1), (1, 2, 1) and (1, 1, 2).

16. $\because f(x) - x = 0$ has imaginary roots.

Then, $\quad f(x) - x > 0$ or $f(x) - x < 0, \forall x \in R$

for $\quad f(x) - x > 0, \forall x \in R,$

then $\quad f[f(x)] - f(x) > 0, \forall x \in R$

On adding, we get

$$f[f(x)] - x > 0, \forall x \in R$$

Similarly, $f[f(x)] - x < 0, \forall x \in R$

Thus, roots of the equation $f[f(x)] - x = 0$ are imaginary

Let $\quad z = \begin{vmatrix} 2 & \alpha & \delta \\ \beta & 0 & \alpha \\ \gamma & \beta & 1 \end{vmatrix}$

Then, $\quad \bar{z} = \begin{vmatrix} 2 & \bar{\alpha} & \bar{\delta} \\ \bar{\beta} & 0 & \bar{\alpha} \\ \bar{\gamma} & \bar{\beta} & 1 \end{vmatrix} = \begin{vmatrix} 2 & \beta & \gamma \\ \alpha & 0 & \beta \\ \delta & \alpha & 1 \end{vmatrix} = \begin{vmatrix} 2 & \alpha & \delta \\ \beta & 0 & \alpha \\ \gamma & \beta & 1 \end{vmatrix} = z$

Hence, z is purely real.

17. On putting $x = 0$, we get $a_0 = 1$

On differentiating both sides w.r.t. x and putting $x = 0$, we get

$$a_1 = 4a$$

On differentiating again w.r.t. x and putting $x = 0$, we get

$$2a_2 = 12a^2 + 8b$$

or $\quad a_2 = 6a^2 + 4b$

Also, given $\begin{vmatrix} a_1 & a_1 & a_2 \\ a_0 & a_2 & a_0 \\ a_2 & a_0 & a_1 \end{vmatrix} = 0$

$\Rightarrow \quad -(a_0^3 + a_1^3 + a_2^3 - 3a_0a_1a_2) = 0$

$\Rightarrow \quad \frac{1}{2}(a_0 + a_1 + a_2)[(a_0 - a_1)^2 + (a_1 - a_2)^2 + (a_2 - a_0)^2] = 0$

$\because \quad a_0 + a_1 + a_2 \neq 0$

$\therefore \quad (a_0 - a_1)^2 + (a_1 - a_2)^2 + (a_2 - a_0)^2 = 0$

$\Rightarrow \quad a_0 - a_1 = 0, a_1 - a_2 = 0, a_2 - a_0 = 0$

$\therefore \quad a_0 = a_1 = a_2$

$\Rightarrow \quad 1 = 4a = 6a^2 + 4b$

$\Rightarrow \quad a = \frac{1}{4}$ and $b = \frac{5}{32}$

18. $\because f(x) = \log_{10} x$ and $g(x) = e^{\pi i x}$

$\therefore \quad f(10) = \log_{10} 10 = 1$

and $\quad g(10) = e^{10\pi i} = (-1)^{10} = 1$

$f(10^2) = \log_{10} 10^2 = 2$

and $\quad g(10^2) = e^{100\pi i} = (-1)^{100} = 1$

$f(10^3) = \log_{10} 10^3 = 3$

and $\quad g(10^3) = e^{1000\pi i} = (-1)^{1000} = 1$

Given, $\phi(x) = \begin{vmatrix} f(x)\cdot g(x) & (f(x))^{g(x)} & 1 \\ f(x^2)\cdot g(x^2) & (f(x^2))^{g(x^2)} & 0 \\ f(x^3)\cdot g(x^3) & (f(x^3))^{g(x^3)} & 1 \end{vmatrix}$

$\therefore \quad \phi(10) = \begin{vmatrix} f(10)\cdot g(10) & [f(10)]^{g(10)} & 1 \\ f(10^2)\cdot g(10^2) & [f(10^2)]^{g(10^2)} & 0 \\ f(10^3)\cdot g(10^3) & [f(10^3)]^{g(10^3)} & 1 \end{vmatrix}$

$= \begin{vmatrix} 1 & 1 & 1 \\ 2 & 2 & 0 \\ 3 & 3 & 1 \end{vmatrix} = 0$

19. The given equations can be written as

$(a-1)x - y - z = 0,$

$-x + (b-1)y - z = 0$

and $\quad -x - y + (c-1)z = 0$

For non-trivial solution

$\begin{vmatrix} a-1 & -1 & -1 \\ -1 & b-1 & -1 \\ -1 & -1 & c-1 \end{vmatrix} = 0$

Applying $C_1 \to C_1 - C_3$ and $C_2 \to C_2 - C_3$, then

$\begin{vmatrix} a & 0 & -1 \\ 0 & b & -1 \\ -c & -c & c-1 \end{vmatrix} = 0$

Expanding along R_1, then

$\Rightarrow \quad a(bc - b - c) - 0 - 1(0 + bc) = 0$

$\Rightarrow \quad ab + bc + ca = abc$

20. For non-trivial solution $\begin{vmatrix} \lambda & -1 & \cos\theta \\ 3 & 1 & 2 \\ \cos\theta & 1 & 2 \end{vmatrix} = 0$

Applying $R_3 \to R_3 - R_2$, then

$\begin{vmatrix} \lambda & -1 & \cos\theta \\ 3 & 1 & 2 \\ \cos\theta - 3 & 0 & 0 \end{vmatrix} = 0$

Expanding along R_3, then

$\Rightarrow \quad (\cos\theta - 3)(-2 - \cos\theta) = 0$

$\Rightarrow \quad (\cos\theta - 3)(2 + \cos\theta) = 0$

$\cos\theta = 3, -2$

$\cos\theta \in [-1, 1]$

$\therefore \quad \cos\theta \neq 3, -2$

No value of λ and θ.

Hence, $\begin{vmatrix} \lambda & -1 & \cos\theta \\ 3 & 1 & 2 \\ \cos\theta & 1 & 2 \end{vmatrix} > 0$ only trivial solution is possible.

21. Given that A is 3×3 matrix and $|A| = 2$

Now, $|2\,\text{adj}(3A|A^3|)| = 2^3\,|\text{adj}(|3A|A^3)|$

$= 2^3\,|\text{adj}(54A^3)|$

$= 2^3\,|54A^3|^2 = 2^3(54^3)^2 \times |A|^6$

$= 2^3 \times (54)^6 \times 2^6 \qquad [\because |A| = 2]$

$\Rightarrow \quad 2^3 \times (3^3 \times 2)^6 \times 2^6 = 2^{3+6+6} \times 3^{18} = 2^{15} \times 3^{18} = 6^{15} \times 3^3$

22. Given system of equations,

$2x + ay + 6z = 6,$

$x + 2y + 3z = b$

and $\quad 2x - 5y + 2z = 8$

Since, given system of equation has infinitely many solutions

$\therefore \quad D = 0$ and $D_1 = D_2 = D_3 = 0$

Here, $\quad D = \begin{vmatrix} 2 & a & 6 \\ 1 & 2 & 3 \\ 2 & -5 & 2 \end{vmatrix} = 0$

$\Rightarrow 2(4 + 15) - a(2 - 6) + 6(-5 - 4) = 0$

$\Rightarrow \quad 38 + 4a - 54 = 0 \Rightarrow a = 4$

and $D_1 = \begin{vmatrix} 6 & 4 & 6 \\ b & 2 & 3 \\ 8 & -5 & 2 \end{vmatrix}$

$\Rightarrow 6(4 + 15) - 4(2b - 24) + 6(-5b - 16) = 0$

$\Rightarrow \quad 114 - 8b + 96 - 30b - 96 = 0$

$\Rightarrow \quad b = 3$

$\therefore \quad a - b = 4 - 3 = 1$

23. Putting $x = 0$, $a_0 = 1$

$(1 + ax + bx^2)^4 = (1 + ax + bx^2)(1 + ax + bx^2)$

$(1 + ax + bx^2)(1 + ax + bx^2)$

Clearly, $a_0 = 1$, $a_1 =$ Coefficient of $x = a + a + a + a = 4a$

and $a_2 =$ Coefficient of $x^2 = 4b + 6a^2$

Now, $\Delta = -(a_0^3 + a_1^3 + a_2^3 - 3a_0a_1a_2)$

$\because \quad a_0 + a_1 + a_2 \neq 0$

$\therefore \quad a_0 = a_1 = a_2$

$$1 = 4a = 6a^2 + 4b \Rightarrow a = \frac{1}{4} \text{ and } b = \frac{5}{32}$$

Hence, $5\frac{a}{b} = 5\frac{1}{4} \times \frac{32}{5} = 8$

24. Given that $\begin{vmatrix} S+c & a & b \\ c & S+a & b \\ c & a & S+b \end{vmatrix} = 532$

Applying $C_1 \to C_1 + C_2 + C_3$, we get

$$(a+b+c+S)\begin{vmatrix} 1 & a & b \\ 1 & S+a & b \\ 1 & a & S+b \end{vmatrix} = 532$$

Applying $R_1 \to R_1 - R_2$ and $R_2 \to R_2 - R_3$, we get

$$2S\begin{vmatrix} 0 & -S & 0 \\ 0 & S & -S \\ 1 & a & S+b \end{vmatrix} = 532$$

$\Rightarrow \quad 2S^3 = 532$

$\Rightarrow \quad S^3 = 216 \Rightarrow S = 6$

25. $\Delta_2 = \begin{vmatrix} a & b+3c & c+4a \\ b & c+3a & a+4b \\ c & a+3b & b+4c \end{vmatrix} + 2\begin{vmatrix} b & b+3c & c+4a \\ c & c+3a & a+4b \\ a & a+3b & b+4c \end{vmatrix}$

$\Delta' \qquad\qquad \Delta''$

Applying $C_3 \to C_3 - 4C_1$ in Δ' and $C_2 \to C_2 - C_1$ in Δ'', we get

$$\Delta_2 = \begin{vmatrix} a & b+3c & c \\ b & c+3a & a \\ c & a+3b & b \end{vmatrix} + 2\times3\begin{vmatrix} b & c & c+4a \\ c & a & a+4b \\ a & b & b+4c \end{vmatrix}$$

Applying $C_2 \to C_2 - 3C_3$ in Δ' and $C_3 \to C_3 - C_2$ in Δ'', we get

$$\Delta_2 = \begin{vmatrix} a & b & c \\ b & c & a \\ c & a & b \end{vmatrix} + 6\begin{vmatrix} b & c & 4a \\ c & a & 4b \\ a & b & 4c \end{vmatrix}$$

$$= \begin{vmatrix} a & b & c \\ b & c & a \\ c & a & b \end{vmatrix} + 24\begin{vmatrix} a & b & c \\ b & c & a \\ c & a & b \end{vmatrix}$$

$$= 25\begin{vmatrix} a & b & c \\ b & c & a \\ c & a & b \end{vmatrix} = 25\Delta_1 \Rightarrow \frac{\Delta_2}{\Delta_1} = 25$$

26. $A = \begin{bmatrix} 1 & \tan x \\ -\tan x & 1 \end{bmatrix}$

Hence, $\det A = \sec^2 x$

$\therefore \quad \det A^T = \sec^2 x$

Now, $\quad f(x) = \det(A^T A^{-1}) = (\det A^T)(\det A^{-1})$

$= (\det A^T)(\det A)^{-1}$

$= \dfrac{\det(A^T)}{\det(A)} = 1$

Hence, $\quad f(x) = 1$

27. We have, $A = PQ^{-1}$, $B = QR^{-1}$ and $C = RP^{-1}$

$\therefore \quad ABC = I$, $BCA = I$ and $CAB = I$

$\therefore \quad \det(ABC + BCA + CAB) = \det(3I)$

$= 3^3 \times \det(I) = 27$

28. $\begin{vmatrix} 1 & 2 & 2 \\ 1 & 3 & 4 \\ 3 & 4 & k \end{vmatrix} = 0$

$\Rightarrow 1(3k-16) - 2(k-12) + 2(4-9) = 0$

$\Rightarrow \quad 3k - 16 - 2k + 24 - 10 = 0$

$\Rightarrow \quad k = 2$

29. Given, $\quad x + y + z = 1 \quad$ ...(i)

$x + 2y + 4z = p \quad$ ...(ii)

and $\quad x + 4y + 10z = p^2 \quad$ ...(iii)

$$\Delta = \begin{vmatrix} 1 & 1 & 1 \\ 1 & 2 & 4 \\ 1 & 4 & 10 \end{vmatrix}$$

Applying $R_1 \to R_1 - R_2$ and $R_2 \to R_2 - R_3$, we get

$$\begin{vmatrix} 0 & -1 & -3 \\ 0 & -2 & -6 \\ 1 & 4 & 10 \end{vmatrix} = 0$$

Since, $\Delta = 0$ solution is not unique.

The system will have infinite solutions,

if $\Delta_1 = 0, \Delta_2 = 0, \Delta_3 = 0$

$$\Delta_1 = \begin{vmatrix} 1 & 1 & 1 \\ p & 2 & 4 \\ p^2 & 4 & 10 \end{vmatrix} = 0$$

Applying $C_3 \to C_3 - C_2$, we get

$$\Delta_1 = \begin{vmatrix} 1 & 1 & 0 \\ p & 2 & 2 \\ p^2 & 4 & 6 \end{vmatrix} = 0$$

$\Rightarrow \quad 1(12-8) - 1(6p - 2p^2) = 0$

$\Rightarrow \quad 4 - 6p + 2p^2 = 0 \Rightarrow 2(p^2 - 3p + 2) = 0$

$\Rightarrow \quad p^2 - 3p + 2 = 0 \Rightarrow p = 1 \text{ or } 2$

$\therefore$ Sum $= 1 + 2 = 3$

30. $\Delta = \begin{vmatrix} x & x+y & x+y+z \\ 2x & 3x+2y & 4x+3y+2z \\ 3x & 6x+3y & 10x+6y+3z \end{vmatrix}$

$$= \begin{vmatrix} x & x & x \\ 2x & 3x & 4x \\ 3x & 6x & 10x \end{vmatrix} + \begin{vmatrix} 0 & y & y+z \\ 0 & 2y & 3y+2z \\ 0 & 3y & 6y+3z \end{vmatrix}$$

$$= x^3\begin{vmatrix} 1 & 1 & 1 \\ 2 & 3 & 4 \\ 3 & 6 & 10 \end{vmatrix} + 0$$

On solving, we get

$x^3(6 - 8 + 3) = 64 \quad$ [given]

$\Rightarrow \quad x^3 = 64$

or $\quad x = 4$

31. $\begin{vmatrix} (x^2+1)^2 & (xy+1)^2 & (xz+1)^2 \\ (xy+1)^2 & (y^2+1)^2 & (yz+1)^2 \\ (xz+1)^2 & (yz+1)^2 & (z^2+1)^2 \end{vmatrix}$

$$= \begin{vmatrix} 1 & x & x^2 \\ 1 & y & y^2 \\ 1 & z & z^2 \end{vmatrix} \begin{vmatrix} 1 & 1 & 1 \\ 2x & 2y & 2z \\ x^2 & y^2 & z^2 \end{vmatrix} = 2(x-y)^2(y-z)^2(z-x)^2$$

Putting $x = 31$, $y = 32$ and $z = 33$, we get

$$= 2(1)^2(1)^2(2)^2 = 8$$

32. $\det B = \begin{vmatrix} a_{11} & \dfrac{a_{12}}{3} & \dfrac{a_{13}}{3^2} \\ 3a_{21} & a_{22} & \dfrac{a_{23}}{3} \\ 9a_{31} & 3a_{32} & a_{33} \end{vmatrix} = 3 \times 9 \begin{vmatrix} a_{11} & \dfrac{a_{12}}{3} & \dfrac{a_{13}}{3^2} \\ a_{21} & \dfrac{a_{22}}{3} & \dfrac{a_{23}}{9} \\ a_{31} & \dfrac{a_{32}}{3} & \dfrac{a_{33}}{9} \end{vmatrix}$

$$= \begin{vmatrix} a_{11} & a_{12} & a_{13} \\ a_{21} & a_{22} & a_{23} \\ a_{31} & a_{32} & a_{33} \end{vmatrix}$$

[multiplying C_2 by 3 and C_3 by 9]

$$= \det A = 2$$

Similarly, $\det C = \det A = 2$

$\therefore \quad \det(BC) = (\det B)(\det C) = 2 \times 2 = 4$

33. Given, $A = \begin{bmatrix} \beta & \alpha & 3 \\ \alpha & \alpha & \beta \\ -\beta & \alpha & 2\alpha \end{bmatrix}$

$$B = \begin{bmatrix} 3\alpha & -9 & -3\alpha \\ -\alpha & 7 & -2\alpha \\ -2\alpha & 5 & -2\beta \end{bmatrix} = \text{cofactor matrix of } A$$

$A_{21} = \text{cofactor of } a_{21}$

$2\alpha^2 - 3\alpha = \alpha$

$\alpha = 0, 2$ (accept)

Now, $2\alpha^2 - \alpha\beta = 3\alpha$

$\alpha = 2, \beta = 1$

$\therefore \quad |AB| = |A||B| = |A| \cdot |A|^2 = |A|^3$

Now, $|A| = \begin{vmatrix} 1 & 2 & 3 \\ 2 & 2 & 1 \\ -1 & 2 & 4 \end{vmatrix} = 6$

$\therefore$ Required value $= 6^3 = 216$

34. We have, $|2A|^3 = 2^{21}$

$\Rightarrow \quad |2A| = 2^7 \Rightarrow 8|A| = 2^7 \Rightarrow |A| = 2^4$

Also, $A = \begin{bmatrix} 1 & 0 & 0 \\ 0 & \alpha & \beta \\ 0 & \beta & \alpha \end{bmatrix}$

$\Rightarrow \quad |A| = \alpha^2 - \beta^2 = 2^4$

$\Rightarrow \quad (\alpha - \beta)(\alpha + \beta) = 16$

$\Rightarrow \quad \alpha - \beta = 2$ and $\alpha + \beta = 8$

$\Rightarrow \quad \alpha = 5$ and $\beta = 3$

35. $\begin{vmatrix} \alpha & b & c \\ a & \beta & c \\ a & b & \gamma \end{vmatrix} = 0$

$\Rightarrow \alpha(\beta\gamma - bc) - b(a\gamma - ac) + c(ab - a\beta) = 0$

$\Rightarrow \alpha\beta\gamma - bc\alpha - ba\gamma + abc + abc - ca\beta = 0$

$\Rightarrow \gamma(\alpha - a)(\beta - b) - b(\alpha - a)(c - \gamma) + a(b - \beta)(c - \gamma) = 0$

Divide and multiply by $(\alpha - a)(\beta - b)(\gamma - c)$, we get

$$\frac{\gamma}{(\gamma - c)} + \frac{b}{(\beta - b)} + \frac{a}{(\alpha - a)} = 0$$

Alternate Solution

Applying $R_1 \to R_1 - R_2$, $R_2 \to R_2 - R_3$,

$$\begin{vmatrix} \alpha - a & b - \beta & 0 \\ 0 & \beta - b & c - \gamma \\ a & b & \gamma \end{vmatrix} = 0$$

$\Rightarrow \quad (\alpha - a)[\gamma(\beta - b) - b(c - \gamma)] - (b - \beta)[-a(c - \gamma)] = 0$

$\Rightarrow \gamma(\alpha - a)(\beta - b) - b(\alpha - a)(c - \gamma) + a(b - \beta)(c - \gamma) = 0$

Divide and multiply by $(\alpha - a)(\beta - b)(\gamma - c)$, we get

$$\frac{\gamma}{(\gamma - c)} + \frac{b}{(\beta - b)} + \frac{a}{(\alpha - a)} = 0$$

36. $A = \begin{bmatrix} 2 & 1 & 2 \\ 6 & 2 & 11 \\ 3 & 3 & 2 \end{bmatrix}$ and $P = \begin{bmatrix} 1 & 2 & 0 \\ 5 & 0 & 2 \\ 7 & 1 & 5 \end{bmatrix}$

Let $B = P^{-1}AP - 2I$

Pre multiply by P, $PB = AP - 2P$ $\quad [\because PP^{-1} = I$ and $PI = P]$

Post multiply by P^{-1}, $PBP^{-1} = A - 2I$

Now, $\quad |PBP^{-1}| = |A - 2I|$

$$|P| \cdot |B| \cdot |P^{-1}| = \begin{vmatrix} 2-2 & 1 & 2 \\ 6 & 2-2 & 11 \\ 3 & 3 & 2-2 \end{vmatrix}$$

$$|P| \cdot |B| \cdot \frac{1}{|P|} = \begin{vmatrix} 0 & 1 & 2 \\ 6 & 0 & 11 \\ 3 & 3 & 0 \end{vmatrix}$$

$|B| = -1(-33) + 2(18)$ $\quad$ [expand w.r.t. R_1]

$\Rightarrow \quad |P^{-1}AP - 2I| = 33 + 36 = 69$

Prime factors of 69 is 3 and 23

$\therefore \quad$ Sum $= 3 + 23 = 26$

37. Given system of equations has infinitely many solutions.

So, $\quad \Delta = 0$

$$\Rightarrow \quad \begin{vmatrix} 1 & 4 & -1 \\ 7 & 9 & \mu \\ 5 & 1 & 2 \end{vmatrix} = 0$$

$\Rightarrow \quad (18 - \mu) - 4(14 - 5\mu) - 1(-38) = 0$

$\Rightarrow \quad 18 - \mu - 56 + 20\mu + 38 = 0 \Rightarrow \mu = 0$

$\Delta_x = \Delta_y = \Delta_z = 0$ $\quad$ [for infinite solutions]

So, $\quad \Delta_x = \begin{vmatrix} \lambda & 4 & -1 \\ -3 & 9 & 0 \\ -1 & 1 & 2 \end{vmatrix} = 0$

$\Rightarrow \quad \lambda(18) - 4(-6) - 1(-3 + 9) = 0$

$\Rightarrow \quad 18\lambda = -24 + 6 = -18 \Rightarrow \lambda = -1$

Therefore, $2\mu + 3\lambda = -3$

38. For non-trivial solution

$$\begin{vmatrix} 1 & \sqrt{2}\sin\alpha & \sqrt{2}\cos\alpha \\ 1 & \sin\alpha & -\cos\alpha \\ 1 & \cos\alpha & \sin\alpha \end{vmatrix} = 0$$

$\Rightarrow 1 - \sqrt{2}\sin\alpha(\sin\alpha + \cos\alpha) + \sqrt{2}\cos\alpha(\cos\alpha - \sin\alpha) = 0$

[expanding along R_1]

$\Rightarrow \quad 1 + \sqrt{2}\cos 2\alpha - \sqrt{2}\sin 2\alpha = 0$

$\Rightarrow \quad \cos 2\alpha - \sin 2\alpha = -1/\sqrt{2}$

$\Rightarrow \quad \cos(2\alpha + \pi/4) = -1/2$

$\Rightarrow \quad 2\alpha + \dfrac{\pi}{4} = 2n\pi \pm \dfrac{2\pi}{3}, n \in I$

$\Rightarrow \quad \alpha + \dfrac{\pi}{8} = n\pi \pm \dfrac{\pi}{3}, n \in I$

For $n = 0, \alpha = \dfrac{\pi}{3} - \dfrac{\pi}{8} = \dfrac{5\pi}{24}$

39. Given system of equations

$3x + 5y + \lambda z = 3$ ...(i)

$7x + 11y - 9z = 2$ ...(ii)

$97x + 155y - 189z = \mu$ ...(iii)

On solving Eq. (i) $\times 31$ – Eq. (iii), we get

$-4x + (31\lambda + 189)z = 93 - \mu$ ...(iv)

On solving Eq. (ii) $\times 155$ – Eq. (iii) $\times 11$, we get,

$1085x + 1705y - 1395z = 310$

$1067x + 1705y - 2079z = 11\mu$

$\quad - \quad - \quad + \quad -$

$18x + 684z = 310 - 11\mu$ ...(v)

Again, Eq. (iv) $\times 9$ + Eq. (v) $\times 2$, we get

$-36x + 9(31\lambda + 189)z = 9(93 - \mu)$

$36x + 1368z = 2(310 - 11\mu)$

$(279\lambda + 3069)z = 1457 - 31\mu$

For infinite solution

$\lambda = \dfrac{-3069}{279} = \dfrac{-341}{31}$ and $\mu = \dfrac{1457}{31}$

Hence, $\mu + 2\lambda = \dfrac{1457 - 682}{31} = \dfrac{775}{31} = 25$

Alternate Solution

Since, the system of equations has infinitely many solutions

So, $\Delta = 0, \Delta x = 0, \Delta y = 0$ and $\Delta z = 0$

$$\therefore \begin{vmatrix} 3 & 5 & \lambda \\ 7 & 11 & -9 \\ 97 & 155 & -189 \end{vmatrix}$$

$\Rightarrow 3(11 \times (-189) + 9 \times 155) - 5(7 \times (-189)) + 9(97)) + \lambda(7 \times 155 - 97 \times 11) = 0$

$\Rightarrow \quad -2052 + 2250 + 18\lambda = 0$

$\Rightarrow \quad \lambda = \dfrac{-198}{18} = -11$ and $\begin{vmatrix} 3 & 5 & 3 \\ 7 & 11 & 2 \\ 97 & 155 & \mu \end{vmatrix} = 0$

$\Rightarrow 3(11\mu - 310) - 5(7\mu - 194) + 3(7 \times 155 - 97 \times 11) = 0$

$\Rightarrow \quad 33\mu - 930 - 35\mu + 970 + 54 = 0$

$\Rightarrow \quad -2\mu = -94 \Rightarrow \mu = 47$

Hence, $\mu + 2\lambda = 47 - 22 = 25$

40. Let $A = \begin{bmatrix} a_1 & b_1 & c_1 \\ a_2 & b_2 & c_2 \\ a_3 & b_3 & c_3 \end{bmatrix}$

Given, $\quad A\begin{bmatrix} 1 \\ 0 \\ 1 \end{bmatrix} = 2\begin{bmatrix} 1 \\ 0 \\ 1 \end{bmatrix}$

$\Rightarrow \begin{bmatrix} a_1 & b_1 & c_1 \\ a_2 & b_2 & c_2 \\ a_3 & b_3 & c_3 \end{bmatrix}\begin{bmatrix} 1 \\ 0 \\ 1 \end{bmatrix} = \begin{bmatrix} 2 \\ 0 \\ 2 \end{bmatrix}$

$\Rightarrow \begin{bmatrix} a_1 + c_1 \\ a_2 + c_2 \\ a_3 + c_3 \end{bmatrix} = \begin{bmatrix} 2 \\ 0 \\ 2 \end{bmatrix}$

$a_1 + c_1 = 2$ ...(i)

$a_2 + c_2 = 0$ ...(ii)

$a_3 + c_3 = 2$ ...(iii)

and $\quad A\begin{bmatrix} -1 \\ 0 \\ 1 \end{bmatrix} = 4\begin{bmatrix} -1 \\ 0 \\ 1 \end{bmatrix}$

$\begin{bmatrix} a_1 & b_1 & c_1 \\ a_2 & b_2 & c_2 \\ a_3 & b_3 & c_3 \end{bmatrix}\begin{bmatrix} -1 \\ 0 \\ 1 \end{bmatrix} = \begin{bmatrix} -4 \\ 0 \\ 4 \end{bmatrix}$

$\Rightarrow \begin{bmatrix} -a_1 + c_1 \\ -a_2 + c_2 \\ -a_3 + c_3 \end{bmatrix} = \begin{bmatrix} -4 \\ 0 \\ 4 \end{bmatrix}$

$-a_1 + c_1 = -4$ ...(iv)

$-a_2 + c_2 = 0$ ...(v)

$-a_3 + c_3 = 4$ ...(vi)

From Eqs. (i) and (iv), we get

$c_1 = -1, a_1 = 3$

From Eqs. (ii) and (v), we get

$a_2 = 0, c_2 = 0$

From Eqs. (iii) and (vi), we get

$a_3 = -1, c_3 = 3$

Also, $\quad A\begin{bmatrix} 0 \\ 1 \\ 0 \end{bmatrix} = 2\begin{bmatrix} 0 \\ 1 \\ 0 \end{bmatrix}$

$\Rightarrow \begin{bmatrix} a_1 & b_1 & c_1 \\ a_2 & b_2 & c_2 \\ a_3 & b_3 & c_3 \end{bmatrix}\begin{bmatrix} 0 \\ 1 \\ 0 \end{bmatrix} = \begin{bmatrix} 0 \\ 2 \\ 0 \end{bmatrix}$

$\Rightarrow \begin{bmatrix} b_1 \\ b_2 \\ b_3 \end{bmatrix} = \begin{bmatrix} 0 \\ 2 \\ 0 \end{bmatrix}$

$b_1 = 0, b_2 = 2, b_3 = 0$

$A = \begin{bmatrix} 3 & 0 & -1 \\ 0 & 2 & 0 \\ -1 & 0 & 3 \end{bmatrix}$

$$\text{Now, } A-3I = \begin{bmatrix} 3 & 0 & -1 \\ 0 & 2 & 0 \\ -1 & 0 & 3 \end{bmatrix} - \begin{bmatrix} 3 & 0 & 0 \\ 0 & 3 & 0 \\ 0 & 0 & 3 \end{bmatrix}$$

$$= \begin{bmatrix} 0 & 0 & -1 \\ 0 & -1 & 0 \\ -1 & 0 & 0 \end{bmatrix}$$

$$(A-3I)\begin{bmatrix} x \\ y \\ z \end{bmatrix} = \begin{bmatrix} 1 \\ 2 \\ 3 \end{bmatrix}$$

$$\Rightarrow \begin{bmatrix} 0 & 0 & -1 \\ 0 & -1 & 0 \\ -1 & 0 & 0 \end{bmatrix}\begin{bmatrix} x \\ y \\ z \end{bmatrix} = \begin{bmatrix} 1 \\ 2 \\ 3 \end{bmatrix}$$

$$\begin{bmatrix} -z \\ -y \\ -x \end{bmatrix} = \begin{bmatrix} 1 \\ 2 \\ 3 \end{bmatrix}$$

$$x=-3,\ y=-2,\ z=-1$$

It is a unique solution.

41. Given, system is $x+y+z=5$,

$$x+2y+\lambda^2 z = 9,$$

and $x+3y+\lambda z = \mu$

where $\lambda, \mu \in R$.

For unique solution $\Rightarrow \Delta \neq 0$

$$\Delta = \begin{vmatrix} 1 & 1 & 1 \\ 1 & 2 & \lambda^2 \\ 1 & 3 & \lambda \end{vmatrix} \neq 0$$

$$2\lambda^2 - \lambda - 1 \neq 0 \Rightarrow \lambda \neq 1, -\frac{1}{2}$$

$$\Delta_x = \begin{vmatrix} 5 & 1 & 1 \\ 9 & 2 & \lambda^2 \\ \mu & 3 & \lambda \end{vmatrix}$$

$$= 10\lambda - 15\lambda^2 - 9\lambda + \mu\lambda^2 + 27 - 2\mu$$

$$= -15\lambda^2 + \lambda + \mu\lambda^2 - 2\mu + 27$$

If $\lambda = 1$, $\Delta_x = -15+1+\mu-2\mu+27 = 13-\mu$

$\Rightarrow \quad \Delta_x = 0, \mu = 13$

$$\Delta_y = \begin{vmatrix} 1 & 5 & 1 \\ 1 & 9 & \lambda^2 \\ 1 & \mu & \lambda \end{vmatrix}$$

$$= 4\lambda + 5\lambda^2 - \lambda^2\mu + \mu - 9$$

If $\lambda = 1$ $\Delta_y = 0$

$$\Delta_z = \begin{vmatrix} 1 & 1 & 5 \\ 1 & 2 & 9 \\ 1 & 3 & \mu \end{vmatrix}$$

$$= 1(2\mu - 27) - 1(\mu - 9) + 5(1) = \mu - 13$$

$\because \ \Delta_z = 0 \Rightarrow \mu = 13$

$\therefore$ Infinite solution $\Rightarrow \lambda = 1$ and $\mu = 13$

For no solution $\Rightarrow \lambda = \frac{-1}{2}, 1$ and $\mu \neq 13$

For unique solution $\Rightarrow \lambda \neq 1$ and $\mu \neq 13$

42. Let $A = \begin{bmatrix} a & b \\ b & d \end{bmatrix}$

$$\begin{bmatrix} a & b \\ b & d \end{bmatrix}\begin{bmatrix} 1 \\ 1 \end{bmatrix} = \begin{bmatrix} 3 \\ 7 \end{bmatrix} \text{ and } |A| = 1$$

$$ad - b^2 = 1,\ a+b=3,\ b+d=7$$

$$a = 3-b,\ d = 7-b$$

Now, $\quad ad - b^2 = 1$

$\Rightarrow \quad (3-b)(7-b) - b^2 = 1$

$\Rightarrow \quad 21 - 10b = 1$

$\therefore \quad b = 2, a = 1$ and $d = 5$

$\therefore \quad A = \begin{bmatrix} 1 & 2 \\ 2 & 5 \end{bmatrix}$

$$A^{-1} = \alpha A + \beta I$$

$$\Rightarrow \begin{bmatrix} 5 & -2 \\ -2 & 1 \end{bmatrix} = \begin{bmatrix} \alpha & 2\alpha \\ 2\alpha & 5\alpha \end{bmatrix} + \begin{bmatrix} \beta & 0 \\ 0 & \beta \end{bmatrix}$$

$$\alpha + \beta = 5 \Rightarrow 2\alpha = -2$$

$$\alpha = -1, \beta = 6$$

$\therefore \quad \alpha + \beta = 5$

43. For infinitely many solution

$$D = D_x = D_y = D_z = 0$$

$$D_z = \begin{vmatrix} 2 & 7 & 3 \\ 3 & 2 & 4 \\ 1 & \mu & -1 \end{vmatrix} = 0 \Rightarrow \mu = -39$$

$$D = \begin{vmatrix} 2 & 7 & \lambda \\ 3 & 2 & 5 \\ 1 & -39 & 32 \end{vmatrix} = 0 \Rightarrow \lambda = -1$$

$\Rightarrow \quad \lambda - \mu = 38$

44. Given, $\alpha\beta\gamma = 45$ and $\alpha, \beta, \gamma \in R$

$\Rightarrow \quad x(\alpha, 1, 2) + y(1, \beta, 2) + z(2, 3, \gamma) = (0, 0, 0)$

$x, y, z \in R$, $xyz \neq 0$

$\Rightarrow \quad \alpha x + y + 2z = 0$

$\Rightarrow \quad x + \beta y + 3z = 0$

$\Rightarrow \quad 2x + 2y + \gamma z = 0$

$\Rightarrow \quad xyz \neq 0$

$\Rightarrow$ non-trivial solution

$$\begin{vmatrix} \alpha & 1 & 2 \\ 1 & \beta & 3 \\ 2 & 2 & \gamma \end{vmatrix} = 0$$

$\Rightarrow \alpha(\beta\gamma - 6) - 1(\gamma - 6) + 2(2 - 2\beta) = 0$

$\Rightarrow \quad \alpha\beta\gamma - 6\alpha - \gamma + 6 + 4 - 4\beta = 0$

$\Rightarrow \quad 6\alpha + 4\beta + \gamma = 55$

45. Given, $A = \begin{bmatrix} 2 & 0 & 1 \\ 1 & 1 & 0 \\ 1 & 0 & 1 \end{bmatrix}$ and $B = [B_1, B_2, B_3]$

Let $B_1 = \begin{bmatrix} x_1 \\ y_1 \\ z_1 \end{bmatrix}$, $B_2 = \begin{bmatrix} x_2 \\ y_2 \\ z_2 \end{bmatrix}$, $B_3 = \begin{bmatrix} x_3 \\ y_3 \\ z_3 \end{bmatrix}$

Since, $AB_1 = \begin{bmatrix} 1 \\ 0 \\ 0 \end{bmatrix}$ [given]

$\Rightarrow \begin{bmatrix} 2 & 0 & 1 \\ 1 & 1 & 0 \\ 1 & 0 & 1 \end{bmatrix} \begin{bmatrix} x_1 \\ y_1 \\ z_1 \end{bmatrix} = \begin{bmatrix} 1 \\ 0 \\ 0 \end{bmatrix}$

$\Rightarrow \quad x_1 = 1, y_1 = -1, z_1 = -1$

and $AB_2 = \begin{bmatrix} 2 \\ 3 \\ 0 \end{bmatrix}$ [given]

$\Rightarrow \begin{bmatrix} 2 & 0 & 1 \\ 1 & 1 & 0 \\ 1 & 0 & 1 \end{bmatrix} \begin{bmatrix} x_2 \\ y_2 \\ z_2 \end{bmatrix} = \begin{bmatrix} 2 \\ 3 \\ 0 \end{bmatrix}$

$\Rightarrow \quad x_2 = 2, y_2 = 1, z_2 = -2$

and $AB_3 = \begin{bmatrix} 3 \\ 2 \\ 1 \end{bmatrix}$

$\Rightarrow \begin{bmatrix} 2 & 0 & 1 \\ 1 & 1 & 0 \\ 1 & 0 & 1 \end{bmatrix} \begin{bmatrix} x_3 \\ y_3 \\ z_3 \end{bmatrix} = \begin{bmatrix} 3 \\ 2 \\ 1 \end{bmatrix} \Rightarrow x_3 = 2, y_3 = 0, z_3 = -1$

Hence, $B = \begin{bmatrix} 1 & 2 & 2 \\ -1 & 1 & 0 \\ -1 & -2 & -1 \end{bmatrix} \Rightarrow |B| = 3$

According to the question,

$$\alpha = |B| = 3$$

and $\beta =$ Sum of all the diagonal elements of $B = 1$

Thus, $\alpha^3 + \beta^3 = 27 + 1 = 28$

46. Given, $\begin{vmatrix} x+1 & x & x \\ x & x+\lambda & x \\ x & x & x+\lambda^2 \end{vmatrix} = \frac{9}{8}(103x + 81)$

Here, we can substitute any value of x.

Hence, put $x = 0$

Then, $\begin{vmatrix} 1 & 0 & 0 \\ 0 & \lambda & 0 \\ 0 & 0 & \lambda^2 \end{vmatrix} = \frac{9}{8} \times 81 \Rightarrow \lambda^3 = \frac{3^6}{2^3}$

$\Rightarrow \quad \lambda = \frac{3^2}{2} = \frac{9}{2}$

$\Rightarrow \quad \lambda = \frac{9}{2} \Rightarrow \frac{\lambda}{3} = \frac{3}{2}$

If λ, $\lambda/3$ are roots then, quadratic equation will be

$$x^2 - \left(\lambda + \frac{\lambda}{3}\right)x + \frac{\lambda^2}{3} = 0$$

$\Rightarrow \quad x^2 - \left(\frac{12}{2}\right)x + \frac{27}{4} = 0$

$\Rightarrow \quad x^2 - 6x + \frac{27}{4} = 0$

or $\quad 4x^2 - 24x + 27 = 0$

47. Given quadratic equation is $(a - c)x^2 + (b - a)x + (c - b) = 0$

and the matrix $\begin{bmatrix} \alpha^2 & \alpha & 1 \\ 1 & 1 & 1 \\ a & b & c \end{bmatrix}$ is singular.

So, its determinant value will be zero.

i.e. $\Delta = 0 \Rightarrow \begin{vmatrix} \alpha^2 & \alpha & 1 \\ 1 & 1 & 1 \\ a & b & c \end{vmatrix} = 0$

$\Rightarrow \alpha^2(c - b) - \alpha(c - a) + (b - a) = 0$

i.e. when we put $\alpha = 1$, then the given matrix will be singular.

Now, $\frac{(a-c)^2}{(b-a)(c-b)} + \frac{(b-a)^2}{(a-c)(c-b)} + \frac{(c-b)^2}{(a-c)(b-a)}$

$$= \frac{(c-a)^2}{(a-b)(b-c)} + \frac{(a-b)^2}{(b-c)(c-a)} + \frac{(b-c)^2}{(a-b)(c-a)}$$

$$= \frac{(c-a)^3 + (a-b)^3 + (b-c)^3}{(a-b)(b-c)(c-a)}$$

Here, we use the formula $x^3 + y^3 + z^3 = 3xyz$, when $x + y + z = 0$ i.e. here $(c - a) + (a - b) + (b - c) = 0$.

So, $(c-a)^3 + (a-b)^3 + (b-c)^3 = 3(c-a)(a-b)(b-c)$

Hence, required expression will become

$$\frac{3(a-b)(b-c)(c-a)}{(a-b)(b-c)(c-a)} = 3$$

Alternate Solution

$\frac{(a-c)^2}{(b-a)(c-b)} + \frac{(b-a)^2}{(a-c)(c-b)} + \frac{(c-b)^2}{(a-c)(b-a)}$

$$= \frac{(a-c)^3 + (b-a)^2 + (c-b)^3}{(-a+b)(c-b)(a-c)}$$

Here, $(a - c) + (b - a) + (c - b) = 0$.

Now, using the result $x^3 + y^3 + z^3 = 3xyz$ when $(x + y + z) = 0$, we get

$$(a-c)^3 + (b-a)^3 + (c-b)^3 = 3(a-c)(b-a)(c-b)$$

Hence, required expression will become

$$\frac{3(a-c)(b-a)(c-b)}{(b-a)(c-b)(a-c)} = 3$$

48. Given that A is 3×3 matrix and $|A| = 2$

Now, $|3\,\text{adj}(|3A|\,A^2)| = 3^3|\,\text{adj}(|3A|\,A^2)|$

$= 3^3|\text{adj}(54A^2)|$ $\quad [\because |kA| = k^3|A|]$

$= 3^3\,|54A^2|^2 = 3^3 \times (54^3)^2 \times |A|^4$

$= 3^3 \times (54)^6 \times 2^4$ $\quad [\because |A| = 2 \text{ (given)}]$

$= 3^3 \times (3^3 \times 2)^6 \times 2^4$

$= 3^{11} \times 3^{10} \times 2^{10} = 3^{11} \times 6^{10}$

49. $|\text{adj}(\text{adj}(\text{adj}\,2A))| = |2A|^{(n-1)^3}$

$= |2A|^8$

$= (2^3\,|A|)^8$

$= 2^{24}\,|A|^8$

Now, $A = \begin{bmatrix} 2 & 1 & 0 \\ 1 & 2 & -1 \\ 0 & -1 & 2 \end{bmatrix}$

$|A| = 4$

$\therefore |\text{adj}(\text{adj}(\text{adj} 2A))| = 2^{24} \cdot 4^8 = 2^{24} \cdot 2^{16}$

$= 2^{40} = (16)^{10} = (16)^n$ [given]

$\therefore \quad n = 10$

50. **Decoding the Question**

By using the change of base formula, the logarithmic expression "$\log_a x$" can be written as,

$\dfrac{\log_b x}{\log_b a}$, where $a, b, x > 0$ and $a, b \neq 1$.

Given, $A = \begin{bmatrix} 1 & \log_x y & \log_x z \\ \log_y x & 2 & \log_y z \\ \log_z x & \log_z y & 3 \end{bmatrix}$

$$|A| = \begin{vmatrix} 1 & \dfrac{\log y}{\log x} & \dfrac{\log z}{\log x} \\ \dfrac{\log x}{\log y} & 2 & \dfrac{\log z}{\log y} \\ \dfrac{\log x}{\log z} & \dfrac{\log y}{\log z} & 3 \end{vmatrix}$$

Expanding along R_1

$$|A| = 1(6-1) - \frac{\log y}{\log x}\left(\frac{3\log x}{\log y} - \frac{\log x}{\log y}\right) + \frac{\log z}{\log x}\left(\frac{\log x}{\log z} - \frac{2\log x}{\log z}\right)$$

$|A| = 5 - 2 - 1 = 2$

We know that, $|\text{adj}(\text{adj}(A))| = |A|^{(n-1)^2}$

So, $|\text{adj}(\text{adj}A^2)| = |A^2|^{(3-1)^2} = |A^2|^4 = |A|^8 = 2^8$

51. $|A| = m - n$

and $4m + n = 22 \Rightarrow n = 22 - 4m$

Also, $17m + 4n = 93$

$17m + 88 - 16m = 93$

$\Rightarrow \quad m = 5$

$\therefore \quad n = 22 - 4 \times 5 = 2$

$|A| = m - n = 5 - 2 = 3$

$\det(n \text{ adj}(\text{adj}(mA))) = 3^a 5^b 6^c$

$= n^m [\det(mA)]^{(m-1)^2}$

$= n^m (m^m \det(A))^{(m-1)^2}$

$= n^m \cdot m^{m(m-1)^2} (|A|)^{(m-1)^2}$

$\because n = 2, m = 5$ and $|A| = 3$

$\therefore 2^5 \cdot 5^{5(5-1)^2} (3)^{(5-1)^2} = 2^5 \cdot 5^{5 \times 4^2} (3)^{4^2} = 2^5 \cdot 5^{80} (3)^{16}$

$= 2^5 \times 3^5 \times 3^{11} \times 5^{80} = (6)^5 \times (3)^{11} \times (5)^{80}$

$= 3^{11} \times 5^{80} \times 6^5 = 3^a 5^b 6^c$

$\Rightarrow a = 11, b = 80, c = 5$

$a + b + c = 11 + 80 + 5 = 96$

52. Given, $B = \begin{bmatrix} 1 & 3 & \alpha \\ 1 & 2 & 3 \\ \alpha & \alpha & 4 \end{bmatrix}, \alpha > 2$

Since, B is adjoint of matrix A, then

$|B| = |\text{adj } A| = |A|^{3-1} = (2)^2 = 4$

So, $\begin{vmatrix} 1 & 3 & \alpha \\ 1 & 2 & 3 \\ \alpha & \alpha & 4 \end{vmatrix} = 4$

$\Rightarrow 1(8 - 3\alpha) - 3(4 - 3\alpha) + \alpha(\alpha - 2\alpha) = 4$

$\Rightarrow \quad 8 - 3\alpha - 12 + 9\alpha + \alpha^2 - 2\alpha^2 = 4$

$\Rightarrow \quad -\alpha^2 + 6\alpha - 8 = 0$

$\therefore \quad \alpha = 2, 4$

Since, $\alpha > 2$ so only $\alpha = 4$

Thus, $[\alpha, -2\alpha \quad \alpha] \; B \begin{bmatrix} \alpha \\ -2\alpha \\ \alpha \end{bmatrix} = [4 \; -8 \; 4] \begin{bmatrix} 1 & 3 & 4 \\ 1 & 2 & 3 \\ 4 & 4 & 4 \end{bmatrix} \begin{bmatrix} 4 \\ -8 \\ 4 \end{bmatrix}$

$= -16$

53. **Decoding the Question**

Let $AX = B$ be a system of m linear equations in n variables.

If $|A| \neq 0$, then the system is consistent and has unique solution.

If $|A| = 0$ and $(\text{adj } A) B = 0$, then system is consistent and has infinite number of solutions.

If $|A| = 0$ and $(\text{adj } A) B \neq 0$, then system is inconsistent and has no solutions.

We have, $\alpha x + y + z = 1$

$x + \alpha y + z = 1$

$x + y + \alpha z = \beta$

$\therefore \quad D = \begin{vmatrix} \alpha & 1 & 1 \\ 1 & \alpha & 1 \\ 1 & 1 & \alpha \end{vmatrix}$

$= \alpha(\alpha^2 - 1) - 1(\alpha - 1) + 1(1 - \alpha)$

$= (\alpha - 1)^2 (\alpha + 2)$

Now, if $D = 0 \Rightarrow (\alpha - 1)^2(\alpha + 2) = 0 \Rightarrow \alpha = 1, -2$

So, at $\alpha = 1, \beta = 1$,

all equations become same.

Hence, system has infinite solution.

Again, at $\alpha = -2, \beta = 1, D = 0$

So, system has no solution.

On adding all equations, we have

$(2 + \alpha)x + (2 + \alpha)y + (2 + \alpha)z = \beta + 2$

$\Rightarrow \quad x + y + z = \dfrac{\beta + 2}{\alpha + 2}$

When $\alpha = 2, \quad \beta = 1$

$x + y + z = \dfrac{3}{4}$

54. **Decoding the Question**

The system is inconsistent, if at least one of the determinants, D_x, D_y or D_z has a value not equal to zero and the denominator determinant has a value of zero.

We have, $\lambda x + y + z = 1$

$x + \lambda y + z = 1$

$x + y + \lambda z = 1$

$$\therefore \quad D = \begin{vmatrix} \lambda & 1 & 1 \\ 1 & \lambda & 1 \\ 1 & 1 & \lambda \end{vmatrix}$$

$$= \lambda(\lambda^2 - 1) - 1(\lambda - 1) + 1(1 - \lambda) = (\lambda - 1)^2(\lambda + 2)$$

Now, when $D = 0$

$\Rightarrow (\lambda - 1)^2(\lambda + 2) = 0 \Rightarrow \lambda = 1, -2$

But when $\lambda = 1$, all the equations becomes identical, so system will have infinite solution.

So, for inconsistency, $\lambda = -2$

$$\therefore \sum_{\lambda \in S} (|\lambda|^2 + |\lambda|) = |-2|^2 + |-2| = 4 + 2 = 6$$

55. Given that system of linear equations,

$x - y + z = 5,\ 2x + 2y + \alpha z = 8$

and $3x - y + 4z = \beta$

has infinitely many solution, then

$$\Delta = \Delta_x = \Delta_y = \Delta_z = 0$$

$$\Delta = \begin{vmatrix} 1 & -1 & 1 \\ 2 & 2 & \alpha \\ 3 & -1 & 4 \end{vmatrix} = 0$$

$$8 + \alpha + 8 - 3\alpha - 8 = 0 \Rightarrow \alpha = 4$$

$$\Delta_z = \begin{vmatrix} 1 & -1 & 5 \\ 2 & 2 & 8 \\ 3 & -1 & \beta \end{vmatrix} = 0$$

$4\beta = 56 \Rightarrow \beta = 14 \Rightarrow \alpha = 4$ and $\beta = 14$

So, equation is

$$x^2 - (\alpha + \beta) + \alpha \cdot \beta = 0$$

$$\Rightarrow \quad x^2 - 18x + 56 = 0$$

56. Given system of equations are

$2x + y - z = 5$

$2x - 5y + \lambda z = \mu$

$x + 2y - 5z = 7$

has infinitely many solutions.

$$\text{So,} \quad D = \begin{vmatrix} 2 & 1 & -1 \\ 2 & -5 & \lambda \\ 1 & 2 & -5 \end{vmatrix} = 0$$

$\Rightarrow 2(25 - 2\lambda) + 1(\lambda + 10) - 1(4 + 5) = 0$

$\Rightarrow 50 - 4\lambda + \lambda + 10 - 9 = 0$

$\Rightarrow 3\lambda = 51 \Rightarrow \lambda = 17$

$$\text{and} \quad D_3 = \begin{vmatrix} 2 & 1 & 5 \\ 2 & -5 & \mu \\ 1 & 2 & 7 \end{vmatrix} = 0$$

$\Rightarrow 2(-35 - 2\mu) - 1(14 - \mu) + 5(4 + 5) = 0$

$\Rightarrow -70 - 4\mu - 14 + \mu + 45 = 0$

$\Rightarrow 3\mu = -39 \Rightarrow \mu = -13$

Thus, $(\lambda + \mu)^2 + (\lambda - \mu)^2 = 2(\lambda^2 + \mu^2) = 2(17^2 + 13^2)$

$= 2(289 + 169) = 2(458) = 916$

57. Given system of linear equation is

$2x - y + 3z = 5$

$3x + 2y - z = 7$

$4x + 5y + \alpha z = \beta$

$$\text{Now, } \Delta = \begin{vmatrix} 2 & -1 & 3 \\ 3 & 2 & -1 \\ 4 & 5 & \alpha \end{vmatrix} = 7(\alpha + 5)$$

So, this system of equation has unique solution if $\alpha \neq -5$

$$\text{and } \Delta_1 = \begin{vmatrix} 5 & -1 & 3 \\ 7 & 2 & -1 \\ \beta & 5 & \alpha \end{vmatrix} = 17\alpha - 5\beta + 130$$

$$\text{and } \Delta_2 = \begin{vmatrix} 2 & 5 & 3 \\ 3 & 7 & -1 \\ 4 & \beta & \alpha \end{vmatrix} = -11\beta + \alpha + 104$$

$$\text{and } \Delta_3 = \begin{vmatrix} 2 & -1 & 5 \\ 3 & 2 & 7 \\ 4 & 5 & \beta \end{vmatrix} = 7(\beta - 9)$$

For infinitely many solutions,

$$\Delta = \Delta_1 = \Delta_2 = \Delta_3 = 0$$

So, $\Delta = 0 \Rightarrow 7(\alpha + 5) = 0 \Rightarrow \alpha = -5$

$\Delta_3 = 0 \Rightarrow 7(\beta - 9) = 0 \Rightarrow \beta = 9$

and $\beta = 8$ and $\Delta_3 \neq 0$

And, if $\alpha = -5$ then $\Delta = 0$, then system of linear equation is in consistent.

58. Given, system of equations

$x + y + az = b$

$2x + 5y + 2z = 6$

and $x + 2y + 3z = 3$

Since, given system of equation has infinitely many solutions.

$\therefore \quad D = 0$ and $D_1 = D_2 = D_3 = 0$

$$\text{Here,} \quad D = \begin{vmatrix} 1 & 1 & a \\ 2 & 5 & 2 \\ 1 & 2 & 3 \end{vmatrix} = 0$$

$\Rightarrow 1(15 - 4) - 1(6 - 2) + a(4 - 5) = 0$

$\Rightarrow -a + 11 - 4 = 0 \Rightarrow a = 7$

$$\text{and} \quad D_1 = \begin{vmatrix} b & 1 & a \\ 6 & 5 & 2 \\ 3 & 2 & 3 \end{vmatrix} = 0$$

$\Rightarrow b(15 - 4) - 1(18 - 6) + a(12 - 15) = 0$

$\Rightarrow 11b - 12 - 3a = 0$

$\Rightarrow 11b - 12 - 21 = 0 \quad [\because a = 7]$

$\Rightarrow 11b - 33 = 0 \Rightarrow b = 3$

$\therefore 2a + 3b = 2(7) + 3(3) = 14 + 9 = 23$

59. We have,

$$x + y + z = 6$$
$$\alpha x + \beta y + 7z = 3$$
$$x + 2y + 3z = 14$$

$$\therefore \quad A = \begin{bmatrix} 1 & 1 & 1 \\ \alpha & \beta & 7 \\ 1 & 2 & 3 \end{bmatrix}$$

$$|A| = 1(3\beta - 14) - 1(3\alpha - 7) + 1(2\alpha - \beta)$$
$$= 2\beta - \alpha - 7$$

Now, if $\alpha = \beta$

and $\alpha \neq 7$, then

$$|A| = 2\alpha - \alpha - 7 = \alpha - 7 \neq 0$$

So, system has unique solution.

If $\alpha = \beta = 7$, then $|A| = 0$. Also, system of equations are

$x + y + z = 6$,

$$7x + 7y + 7z = 3$$

$$\Rightarrow \quad x + y + z = \frac{3}{7}$$

and, $\quad x + 2y + 3z = 14$

Since, first and second equation contradict each other.

So, system has no solution.

Again, $(\alpha, \beta) \neq (7, 7)$ on the line $x - 2y + 7 = 0$, $|A| \neq 0$.

So, system has unique solution.

So, option (d) is false.

Alternate Solution

Given equations are

$$x + y + z = 6 \quad \text{...(i)}$$
$$\alpha x + \beta y + 7z = 3 \quad \text{...(ii)}$$
$$x + 2y + 3z = 14 \quad \text{...(iii)}$$

On solving Eqs. (i) and (iii), we get

$$x = -2 + z \text{ and } y = 8 - 2z$$

Now, put the value of x and y in Eq. (ii), we get

$$\alpha(-2 + z) + \beta(8 - 2z) + 7z = 3$$

$$\Rightarrow \quad (\alpha - 2\beta + 7)z = 2\alpha - 8\beta + 3$$

So, equations have unique solution if

$$\alpha - 2\beta + 7 \neq 0$$

And equations have no solution, if

$$\alpha - 2\beta + 7 = 0 \text{ and } 2\alpha - 8\beta + 3 \neq 0$$

Hence, for every point $(\alpha, \beta) \neq (7, 7)$ on the line $x - 2y + 7 = 0$, the system has infinitely many solutions.

60. Given system of linear equations

$$\left.\begin{aligned} x + y + kz &= 2 \\ 2x + 3y - z &= 1 \\ 3x + 4y + 2z &= k \end{aligned}\right\} \quad \text{... (i)}$$

Also, given another system of linear equations is

$$\left.\begin{aligned} (k+1)x + (2k-1)y &= 7 \\ (2k+1)x + (k+5)y &= 10 \end{aligned}\right\} \quad \text{... (ii)}$$

Since, system (i) have infinitely many solutions.

So, $\quad \Delta = 0$

$$\Rightarrow \quad \begin{vmatrix} 1 & 1 & k \\ 2 & 3 & -1 \\ 3 & 4 & 2 \end{vmatrix} = 0$$

$$\Rightarrow 1(6 + 4) - 1(4 + 3) + k(8 - 9) = 0$$

$$\Rightarrow \quad k = 3$$

For this value of k, system (ii) will become

$$4x + 5y = 7 \quad \text{... (iii)}$$
$$7x + 8y = 10 \quad \text{... (iv)}$$

Clearly, they have a unique solution.

Subtract Eq. (iii) from Eq. (iv), we get

$$3x + 3y = 3 \Rightarrow x + y = 1$$

61. **Decoding the Question**

The system of an equation has infinitely many solutions when the lines are coincident and they have the same y-intercept.

If $AX = B$ be a system of m linear equation in n variable.

If $|A| = 0$ and adj $A \cdot B = 0$, then system is consistent and has infinite number of solutions.

We have,

$$x + 2y + 3z = 3$$
$$4x + 3y - 4z = 4$$
$$8x + 4y - \lambda z = 9 + \mu$$

For infinitely many solutions,

$|A| = 0$ and $(\text{adj } A) \cdot B = 0$ in the form $AX = B$.

$$\therefore \quad \begin{vmatrix} 1 & 2 & 3 \\ 4 & 3 & -4 \\ 8 & 4 & -\lambda \end{vmatrix} = 0$$

$$\Rightarrow 1(-3\lambda + 16) - 2(-4\lambda + 32) + 3(16 - 24) = 0$$

$$\Rightarrow \quad -3\lambda + 16 + 8\lambda - 64 - 24 = 0$$

$$\Rightarrow \quad 5\lambda - 72 = 0 \Rightarrow \lambda = \frac{72}{5}$$

$$\text{adj } A = \begin{bmatrix} A_{11} & A_{12} & A_{13} \\ A_{21} & A_{22} & A_{23} \\ A_{31} & A_{32} & A_{33} \end{bmatrix}^T = \begin{bmatrix} A_{11} & A_{21} & A_{31} \\ A_{12} & A_{22} & A_{32} \\ A_{13} & A_{23} & A_{33} \end{bmatrix},$$

where A_{ij} are cofactors.

$$\because \quad A = \begin{bmatrix} 1 & 2 & 3 \\ 4 & 3 & -4 \\ 8 & 4 & -\frac{72}{5} \end{bmatrix}$$

$$\therefore \quad (\text{adj } A)B = \begin{bmatrix} -\frac{136}{5} & \frac{204}{5} & -17 \\ \frac{128}{5} & -\frac{192}{5} & 16 \\ -8 & 12 & -5 \end{bmatrix} \cdot \begin{bmatrix} 3 \\ 4 \\ 9 + \mu \end{bmatrix} = 0$$

From 3rd row expansion,

$$-24 + 48 - 45 - 5\mu = 0 \Rightarrow -21 - 5\mu = 0$$

$$\Rightarrow \quad \mu = -\frac{21}{5}$$

62. **Decoding the Question**

Let $AX = B$ be a system of n linear equation in n variables then

(i) If $|A| \neq 0$, then the system of equations is consistent and has a unique solution

(ii) If $|A| = 0$ and $(\text{adj } A)B = 0$, then the system of equations is consistent and has infinitely many solutions.

(iii) If $|A| = 0$ and $(\text{adj } A)B \neq 0$, then the system of equations is inconsistent i.e. having no solution.

We have,

$$\left.\begin{aligned} \alpha x + 2y + z &= 1 \\ 2\alpha x + 3y + z &= 1 \\ 3x + \alpha y + 2z &= \beta \end{aligned}\right\} \quad \dots \text{(i)}$$

Let $A = \begin{bmatrix} \alpha & 2 & 1 \\ 2\alpha & 3 & 1 \\ 3 & \alpha & 2 \end{bmatrix}, X = \begin{bmatrix} x \\ y \\ z \end{bmatrix}, B = \begin{bmatrix} 1 \\ 1 \\ \beta \end{bmatrix}$

So, we have $AX = B$

For $|A| \neq 0$, we have a unique solution

i.e. $\begin{vmatrix} \alpha & 2 & 1 \\ 2\alpha & 3 & 1 \\ 3 & \alpha & 2 \end{vmatrix} \neq 0$

$$\alpha(3\cdot 2 - \alpha \cdot 1) - 2(2\alpha \cdot 2 - 3 \cdot 1) + 1(2\alpha \cdot \alpha - 3 \cdot 3) \neq 0$$

$\Rightarrow \quad \alpha^2 - 2\alpha - 3 \neq 0$

$\Rightarrow \quad (\alpha + 1)(\alpha - 3) \neq 0$

$\Rightarrow \quad \alpha \neq -1, 3$

i.e. the system of equations has a solution, $\forall \alpha \in R - \{-1, 3\}$.

For no solution, $|A| = 0$ and $\text{adj}(A) \cdot B \neq 0$

i.e. $\alpha = -1, 3$ and $\text{adj}(A) \cdot B \neq 0$

For $\alpha = -1$, $A = \begin{bmatrix} -1 & 2 & 1 \\ -2 & 3 & 1 \\ 3 & -1 & 2 \end{bmatrix}$

and $\quad \text{adj}(A) = [\text{Co-factor matrix}]$

$$= \begin{bmatrix} 7 & 7 & -7 \\ -5 & -5 & 5 \\ -1 & -1 & 1 \end{bmatrix}$$

Now, $\text{adj}(A) \cdot B = \begin{bmatrix} 7 & 7 & -7 \\ -5 & -5 & 5 \\ -1 & -1 & 1 \end{bmatrix} \begin{bmatrix} 1 \\ 1 \\ \beta \end{bmatrix} = \begin{bmatrix} 14 - 7\beta \\ -10 + 5\beta \\ -2 + \beta \end{bmatrix}$

For $\beta = 2$, $\text{adj}(A) \cdot B = 0$

So, it will have no solution, $\forall \beta \neq 2$.

For $\alpha = 3$,

$$A = \begin{bmatrix} 3 & 2 & 1 \\ 6 & 3 & 1 \\ 3 & 3 & 2 \end{bmatrix}$$

$\Rightarrow \quad \text{adj}(A) = [\text{Co-factor matrix}]$

$$= \begin{bmatrix} 3 & -9 & 9 \\ -1 & 3 & -3 \\ -1 & 3 & -3 \end{bmatrix}$$

Now, $\text{adj}(A) \cdot B = \begin{bmatrix} 3 & -9 & 9 \\ -1 & 3 & -3 \\ -1 & 3 & -3 \end{bmatrix} \begin{bmatrix} 1 \\ 1 \\ \beta \end{bmatrix} = \begin{bmatrix} -6 + 9\beta \\ 2 - 3\beta \\ 2 - 3\beta \end{bmatrix}$

For any value of β, $\text{adj}(A) \cdot B \neq 0$

$\therefore$ It will have no solution.

63. We have, the given system of equation has no solution.

$\Rightarrow \quad \Delta = 0$

i.e. $\begin{vmatrix} 6\lambda & -3 & 3 \\ 2 & 6\lambda & 4 \\ 3 & 2 & 3\lambda \end{vmatrix} = 0$

$\Rightarrow 6\lambda(18\lambda^2 - 8) + 3(6\lambda - 12) + 3(4 - 18\lambda) = 0$

$\Rightarrow \quad 18\lambda^3 - 14\lambda - 4 = 0$

$\Rightarrow \quad (\lambda - 1)(3\lambda + 1)(3\lambda + 2) = 0$

$\Rightarrow \quad \lambda = 1, -\frac{1}{3}, -\frac{2}{3}$

$$12 \sum_{\lambda \in S} |\lambda| = 12\left[|1| + \left|-\frac{1}{3}\right| + \left|-\frac{2}{3}\right|\right]$$

$$= 12\left[1 + \frac{1}{3} + \frac{2}{3}\right] = 24$$

64. Given, $|A| = -1$ and $|(A + I)(\text{adj } A + I)| = 4$

Now, Let $A = \begin{bmatrix} a & b \\ c & d \end{bmatrix}$, $\text{adj } A = \begin{bmatrix} d & -b \\ -c & a \end{bmatrix}$

As, $\quad |A| = -1, ad - bc = -1$

$\Rightarrow \quad |(A + I)(\text{adj } A + I)| = 4$

$\Rightarrow \quad |A \text{ adj } A + \text{adj } A + A + I| = 4$

$\Rightarrow \quad ||A| I + \text{adj } A + A + I| = 4 \qquad [\because A \text{ adj } A = |A| I_n]$

$\Rightarrow \quad |-I + \text{adj } A + A + I| = 4 \qquad [\because |A| = -1]$

$\Rightarrow \quad |\text{adj } A + A| = 4$

$\Rightarrow \quad \begin{vmatrix} d + a & 0 \\ 0 & a + d \end{vmatrix} = 4$

$\Rightarrow \quad (a + d)^2 = 4 \Rightarrow a + d = \pm 2$

65. A and B are 3×3 non-zero real matrices.

So, $AB = 0 \qquad |A|\,|B| = 0$

$|A| = 0 \qquad |B| = 0$

If $|A| \neq 0$, $B = 0$ but B is a non-zero matrix so not possible.

If $|B| \neq 0$, $A = 0$ but A is a non-zero matrix so not possible.

So, only possible value is $|A| = |B| = 0$

$\Rightarrow AX = 0$ has infinitely many solutions.

66. **Decoding the Question**

To find the roots of quadratic equation by formula

$$x = \frac{-b \pm \sqrt{b^2 - 4ac}}{2a}$$

(general equation $ax^2 + bx + c = 0$)

The given system of linear equation is

$$\left.\begin{aligned} 2x - 3y + 5z &= 9 \\ x + 3y - z &= -18 \\ 3x - y + (\lambda^2 - |\lambda|)z &= 16 \end{aligned}\right\} \quad \dots \text{(i)}$$

Now, $\Delta = \begin{vmatrix} 2 & -3 & 5 \\ 1 & 3 & -1 \\ 3 & -1 & \lambda^2 - |\lambda| \end{vmatrix}$

$= 2(3\lambda^2 - 3|\lambda| - 1) + 3(\lambda^2 - |\lambda| + 3) + 5(-1-9)$

$= 9|\lambda|^2 - 9|\lambda| - 43$

For no solution of system Eq. (i), we get

$\Delta = 0 \Rightarrow 9|\lambda|^2 - 9|\lambda| - 43 = 0$

$\Rightarrow |\lambda| = \dfrac{9 \pm \sqrt{(-9)^2 + 4\cdot 9\cdot 43}}{2\cdot 9}$

Clearly from above we see that there are 2 values of $|\lambda|$ out of which one is positive and other is negative.

Thus, we get 2 values of λ satisfy the system of equation such that system has no solutions.

67. The system of given equation has no solution,

$$\Delta = \begin{vmatrix} 2 & 3 & -1 \\ 1 & 1 & 1 \\ 1 & -1 & |\lambda| \end{vmatrix} = 0 \Rightarrow |\lambda| = 7$$

But at $\lambda = 7$, $D_x = D_y = D_z = 0$

$P_1 : 2x + 3y - z = -2$

$P_2 : x + y + z = 4$

$P_3 : x - y + |\lambda| z = 4\lambda - 4$

So, clearly $5P_2 - 2P_1 = P_3$, so at $\lambda = 7$, system of equation is having infinite solutions.

So, $\lambda = -7$ is correct answer.

68. The given system of equations is consistent if $\Delta \neq 0$

$$\begin{vmatrix} -k & 3 & -14 \\ -15 & 4 & -k \\ -4 & 1 & 3 \end{vmatrix} \neq 0$$

$\Rightarrow -k(12 + k) - 3(-45 - 4k) - 14(-15 + 16) \neq 0$

$\Rightarrow \quad -k^2 + 121 \neq 0$

$\Rightarrow \quad k^2 \neq 121$

$\Rightarrow \quad k \neq -11$ or 11

Hence, the system is consistent if

$k \in R - \{-11, 11\}$

69. The given system of equation is

$x + y + z = \alpha$

$\alpha x + 2\alpha y + 3z = -1$

$x + 3\alpha y + 5z = 4$ is inconsistent if $\Delta = 0$

Where, $\Delta = \begin{vmatrix} 1 & 1 & 1 \\ \alpha & 2\alpha & 3 \\ 1 & 3\alpha & 5 \end{vmatrix} = 0$

$= 1(10\alpha - 9\alpha) - 1(5\alpha - 3) + 1(3\alpha^2 - 2\alpha)$

$= 3\alpha^2 - 6\alpha + 3 = 0 = (\alpha - 1)^2 = 0$

Hence, the value of 'α' is 1.

70. Given, equations are

$3x - 2y + z = b$

$5x - 8y + 9z = 3$

$2x + y + az = -1$

For no solutions, $\Delta = 0$ and atleast one of $\Delta_x, \Delta_y, \Delta_z \neq 0$.

$$\Delta = \begin{vmatrix} 3 & -2 & 1 \\ 5 & -8 & 9 \\ 2 & 1 & a \end{vmatrix} = 0$$

$\Rightarrow 3(-8a - 9) + 2(5a - 18) + 5 + 16 = 0 \Rightarrow a = -3$

If $\quad \Delta_z = \begin{vmatrix} 3 & -2 & b \\ 5 & -8 & 3 \\ 2 & 1 & -1 \end{vmatrix} = 0$

$\Rightarrow 3(8 - 3) + 2(-5 - 6) + b(5 + 16) = 0$

$\Rightarrow \quad 15 - 22 + 21b = 0 \Rightarrow b = \dfrac{1}{3}$

i.e. for $b \neq \dfrac{1}{3}$, there are no solution.

Thus, $(a, b) \equiv (-3, -1/3)$.

71. Let $A = \begin{vmatrix} (a+1)(a+2) & a+2 & 1 \\ (a+2)(a+3) & a+3 & 1 \\ (a+3)(a+4) & a+4 & 1 \end{vmatrix}$

Expanding along C_3, we get

$A = [(a+4)(a+2)(a+3) - (a+3)(a+3)(a+4)]$

$\quad -1[(a+1)(a+2)(a+4) - (a+2)(a+3)(a+4)]$

$\quad +1[(a+1)(a+2)(a+3) - (a+2)(a+2)(a+3)]$

$= -(a+4)(a+3) + 2(a+2)(a+4) - (a+2)(a+3)$

$= (a+4)[-a-3+2a+4] - (a+2)(a+3)$

$= (a+4)(a+1) - (a+2)(a+3)$

$= a^2 + 5a + 4 - a^2 - 5a - 6 = -2$

72. $A = \begin{bmatrix} 2 & 3 \\ a & 0 \end{bmatrix}, A^T = \begin{bmatrix} 2 & a \\ 3 & 0 \end{bmatrix}$

$A = \dfrac{A + A^T}{2} + \dfrac{A - A^T}{2}$

Let $\quad P = \dfrac{A + A^T}{2}$ and $Q = \dfrac{A - A^T}{2}$

$Q = \begin{pmatrix} 0 & \dfrac{3-a}{2} \\ \dfrac{a-3}{2} & 0 \end{pmatrix}$

Det $(Q) = 9$, $0 - \left(\dfrac{3-a}{2}\right)\left(\dfrac{a-3}{2}\right) = 9$

$\Rightarrow \quad \left(\dfrac{a-3}{2}\right)^2 = 9$

$\Rightarrow \quad (a-3)^2 = 36 \Rightarrow a - 3 = \pm 6$

$\Rightarrow \quad a = 9, -3$

$P = \begin{bmatrix} 2 & \dfrac{a+3}{2} \\ \dfrac{a+3}{2} & 0 \end{bmatrix}$

$P = \begin{bmatrix} 2 & 6 \\ 6 & 0 \end{bmatrix}$ or $\begin{bmatrix} 2 & 0 \\ 0 & 0 \end{bmatrix}$

$|P| = -36$ or 0

$\therefore \quad |-36 + 0| = 36$

73. Given, $\begin{vmatrix} 1+\sin^2 x & \sin^2 x & \sin^2 x \\ \cos^2 x & 1+\cos^2 x & \cos^2 x \\ 4\sin 2x & 4\sin 2x & 1+4\sin 2x \end{vmatrix} = 0 \, (0 < x < \pi)$

Expanding along R_1,

$(1+\sin^2 x)[(1+\cos^2 x)(1+4\sin 2x)-4\cos^2 x\sin 2x]-\sin^2 x$
$[\cos^2 x(1+4\sin 2x)-4\cos^2 x\sin 2x]+\sin^2 x[4\cos^2 x\sin 2x$
$-4\sin 2x(1+\cos^2 x)]=0$

$\Rightarrow (1+\sin^2 x)[1+4\sin 2x+\cos^2 x+4\sin 2x\cos^2 x$
$-4\cos^2 x\sin 2x]-\sin^2 x[\cos^2 x+4\sin 2x\cos^2 x$
$-4\cos^2 x\sin 2x]+\sin^2 x[4\cos^2 x\sin 2x-4\sin 2x$
$-4\sin 2x\cos^2 x]=0$

$\Rightarrow (1+\sin^2 x)[1+4\sin 2x+\cos^2 x]-\sin^2 x[\cos^2 x]$
$-4\sin^2 x\sin 2x=0$

$\Rightarrow 1+4\sin 2x+\cos^2 x+\sin^2 x+4\sin^2 x\sin 2x$
$+\sin^2 x\cos^2 x-\sin^2 x\cos^2 x-4\sin^2 x\sin 2x=0$

$\Rightarrow \quad 2+4\sin 2x=0$

$\Rightarrow \quad \sin 2x=-\frac{1}{2} \Rightarrow 2x=\pi+\frac{\pi}{6}, 2\pi-\frac{\pi}{6}$

$\Rightarrow \quad 2x=\frac{7\pi}{6}, \frac{11\pi}{6} \Rightarrow x=\frac{7\pi}{12}, \frac{11\pi}{12}$

74. $A=\begin{bmatrix} 0 & \sin\alpha \\ \sin\alpha & 0 \end{bmatrix}$ and $\det\left(A^2-\frac{1}{2}I\right)=0$

$A^2=\begin{bmatrix} 0 & \sin\alpha \\ \sin\alpha & 0 \end{bmatrix}\begin{bmatrix} 0 & \sin\alpha \\ \sin\alpha & 0 \end{bmatrix}$

$A^2=\begin{bmatrix} \sin^2\alpha & 0 \\ 0 & \sin^2\alpha \end{bmatrix}$

$\frac{I}{2}=\begin{bmatrix} 1/2 & 0 \\ 0 & 1/2 \end{bmatrix}$

Now, $\left[A^2-\frac{I}{2}\right]=\begin{bmatrix} \sin^2\alpha-1/2 & 0 \\ 0 & \sin^2\alpha-1/2 \end{bmatrix}$

$\because \quad \det\left[A^2-\frac{1}{2}I\right]=0$

$\Rightarrow \begin{vmatrix} \sin^2\alpha-1/2 & 0 \\ 0 & \sin^2\alpha-1/2 \end{vmatrix}=0$

$\Rightarrow \quad \left[\sin^2\alpha-\frac{1}{2}\right]^2=0 \Rightarrow \sin\alpha=\pm\frac{1}{\sqrt{2}}$

$\Rightarrow \quad \alpha=\frac{\pi}{4}$ is one possibility.

75. **Decoding the Question**

If $f(\theta)=A\sin\theta+B\cos\theta$, then the range of $f(\theta)$ will be
$-\sqrt{A^2+B^2}\le f(\theta)\le\sqrt{A^2+B^2}$

Given, $f(x)=\begin{vmatrix} \sin^2 x & 1+\cos^2 x & \cos 2x \\ 1+\sin^2 x & \cos^2 x & \cos 2x \\ \sin^2 x & \cos^2 x & \sin 2x \end{vmatrix}$

Expanding along R_1

$f(x)=\sin^2 x(\cos^2 x\sin 2x-\cos^2 x\cos 2x)-(1+\cos^2 x)$
$[(1+\sin^2 x)\sin 2x-\sin^2 x\cos 2x]$
$+\cos 2x[\cos^2 x+\cos^2 x\sin^2 x-\cos^2 x\sin^2 x]$

$f(x)=\sin^2 x\cos^2 x(\sin 2x-\cos 2x)-(1+\cos^2 x)$
$[\sin 2x+\sin^2 x(\sin 2x-\cos 2x)]+\cos 2x\cos^2 x$

$f(x)=\sin^2 x\cos^2 x(\sin 2x-\cos 2x)$
$-\sin 2x-\sin^2 x(\sin 2x-\cos 2x)$
$-\cos^2 x\sin 2x-\cos^2 x\sin^2 x(\sin 2x-\cos 2x)$
$+\cos 2x\cos^2 x$

$f(x)=-\sin 2x-\sin^2 x(\sin 2x-\cos 2x)-\cos^2 x(\sin 2x-\cos 2x)$

$f(x)=-\sin 2x-(\sin^2 x+\cos^2 x)(\sin 2x-\cos 2x)$

$f(x)=-\sin 2x-\sin 2x+\cos 2x$

$f(x)=-(2\sin 2x-\cos 2x)$

As, we know that, if $f(\theta)=A\sin\theta+B\cos\theta$

Then, $-\sqrt{A^2+B^2}\le f(\theta)\le\sqrt{A^2+B^2}$

Here, we have, $f(x)=2\sin 2x-\cos 2x$

$-\sqrt{2^2+1^2}\le f(x)\le\sqrt{2^2+1^2}$

$-\sqrt{5}\le f(x)\le\sqrt{5}$

So, maximum value of $f(x)$ is $\sqrt{5}$.

76. $A(a, 0), B(b, 2b+1), C(0, b)$

Area of $\Delta ABC=\frac{1}{2}\begin{vmatrix} a & 0 & 1 \\ b & 2b+1 & 1 \\ 0 & b & 1 \end{vmatrix}=\pm 1$

$\Rightarrow \quad \frac{1}{2}[a(b+1)+b^2]=\pm 1$

$\Rightarrow \quad a=\frac{2-b^2}{b+1}$ or $\frac{-2-b^2}{b+1}$

Sum of all possible values of $a=\frac{-2b^2}{b+1}$

77. Given that the area of triangle whose vertices are $A(1, \alpha)$ $B(\alpha, 0)$, $C(0, \alpha)$ is 4 $(\text{unit})^2$.

Thus, $\frac{1}{2}\begin{vmatrix} 1 & \alpha & 1 \\ \alpha & 0 & 1 \\ 0 & \alpha & 1 \end{vmatrix}=4$

$\Rightarrow \quad |1(0-\alpha)-\alpha(\alpha)+\alpha^2|=8 \Rightarrow \alpha=\pm 8$

Take, $\alpha=8$

Thus, $(8, -8)$, $(-8, 8)$ and $(64, \beta)$ are collinear.

Then, $\begin{vmatrix} 8 & -8 & 1 \\ -8 & 8 & 1 \\ 64 & \beta & 1 \end{vmatrix}=0$

$\Rightarrow \quad 8(8-\beta)+8(-8-64)+1(-8\beta-512)=0$

$\Rightarrow \quad 8-\beta-72-\beta-64=0$

[divided both side by 8]

$\Rightarrow \quad -2\beta=128 \Rightarrow \beta=-64$

Similarly, take $\alpha=-8$, then also $\beta=-64$.

Hence, the value of β is -64.

78. Let $C = A^2 - B^2, |C| \neq 0$ $[\because C$ is invertible matrix, $|C| \neq 0]$

Now, $A^5 = B^5$ ...(i)

and $A^3B^2 = A^2B^3$ ...(ii)

Subtracting Eq. (ii) from Eq. (i),

$$A^5 - A^3B^2 = B^5 - A^2B^3$$

$\Rightarrow$ $A^3(A^2 - B^2) = B^3(B^2 - A^2)$

$\Rightarrow$ $A^3(A^2 - B^2) + B^3(A^2 - B^2) = 0$

$\Rightarrow$ $(A^3 + B^3)(A^2 - B^2) = 0$

Multiplying inverse of $(A^2 - B^2)$ on both sides

$$A^3 + B^3 = 0$$

79. $\Delta = \begin{vmatrix} 2 & 1 & 1 \\ 1 & -1 & 1 \\ 1 & 1 & a \end{vmatrix}$

$= 2(-a-1) - 1(a-1) + (1+1) = 1 - 3a$

$\Delta_3 = \begin{vmatrix} 2 & 1 & 5 \\ 1 & -1 & 3 \\ 1 & 1 & b \end{vmatrix} = 2(-b-3) - 1(b-3) + 5(1+1)$

$= 7 - 3b$

Now, $z = \dfrac{\Delta_3}{\Delta}$

If $\Delta = 0$ and $\Delta_3 \neq 0$, then no solution

$1 - 3a = 0$

$\Rightarrow$ $7 - 3b \neq 0$

$\Rightarrow$ $a = \dfrac{1}{3}, b \neq \dfrac{7}{3}$

80. Given, system of linear equations

$$4x + \lambda y + 2z = 0$$
$$2x - y + z = 0$$
$$\mu x + 2y + 3z = 0$$

For non-trivial solution, $\Delta = 0$

$$\begin{vmatrix} 4 & \lambda & 2 \\ 2 & -1 & 1 \\ \mu & 2 & 3 \end{vmatrix} = 0$$

$\Rightarrow 4(-3-2) - \lambda(6-\mu) + 2(4+\mu) = 0$

$\Rightarrow$ $-\lambda(6-\mu) - 2(6-\mu) = 0$

$\Rightarrow$ $(6-\mu)(\lambda+2) = 0$

$\Rightarrow$ $\lambda = -2$ and $\mu \in R$ or $\mu = 6$

and $\lambda \in R$.

81. The given system of equations is non-homogeneous and it can be written

As, $\begin{bmatrix} 2 & 3 & 2 \\ 3 & 2 & 2 \\ 1 & -1 & 4 \end{bmatrix} \begin{bmatrix} x \\ y \\ z \end{bmatrix} = \begin{bmatrix} 9 \\ 9 \\ 8 \end{bmatrix}$

i.e. $AX = B$

Now, $|A| = 2(8+2) - 3(12-2) + 2(-3-2)$

$= 20 - 30 - 10 = -20 \neq 0$

$\because |A| \neq 0$, then this system have unique solution.

82. Given, A be a 3×3 matrix.

A is symmetric and B is skew-symmetric.

$\therefore$ $A^T = A, B^T = -B$

Let $A^2B^2 - B^2A^2 = P$

$P^T = (A^2B^2 - B^2A^2)^T$

$= (A^2B^2)^T - (B^2A^2)^T = (B^2)^T(A^2)^T - (A^2)^T(B^2)^T$

$= B^2A^2 - A^2B^2 = -(A^2B^2 - B^2A^2) = -P$

$\Rightarrow$ $P^T = -P$

P is skew-symmetric.

$\therefore$ $|P| = 0$

Hence, $PX = 0$ have infinite solutions.

83. Given system of equation can be written in form $AX = B$, where A is 3×3, X is 3×1 and B is 3×1 matrix as follows.

$$\begin{bmatrix} 3 & -1 & 4 \\ 1 & 2 & -3 \\ 6 & 5 & k \end{bmatrix} \begin{bmatrix} x \\ y \\ z \end{bmatrix} = \begin{bmatrix} 3 \\ -2 \\ -3 \end{bmatrix}$$

This system of linear equation has infinitely many solutions when $|A| = 0$

i.e. $\begin{vmatrix} 3 & -1 & 4 \\ 1 & 2 & -3 \\ 6 & 5 & k \end{vmatrix} = 0$

$\Rightarrow$ $3(2k+15) + (k+18) + 4(5-12) = 0$

$\Rightarrow$ $6k + 45 + k + 18 + 20 - 48 = 0$

$\Rightarrow$ $7k + (35) = 0 \Rightarrow 7k = -35$

$\therefore$ $k = -5$

84. Let $= A \begin{bmatrix} i & -i \\ -i & i \end{bmatrix}$

$A^2 = A \cdot A = \begin{bmatrix} i & -i \\ -i & i \end{bmatrix} \begin{bmatrix} i & -i \\ -i & i \end{bmatrix}$

$= \begin{bmatrix} i^2 + i^2 & -i^2 - i^2 \\ -i^2 - i^2 & i^2 + i^2 \end{bmatrix}$

$= \begin{bmatrix} -2 & 2 \\ 2 & -2 \end{bmatrix} A^4 = \begin{bmatrix} -2 & 2 \\ 2 & -2 \end{bmatrix} \begin{bmatrix} -2 & 2 \\ 2 & -2 \end{bmatrix}$

$= \begin{bmatrix} 4+4 & -4-4 \\ -4-4 & 4+4 \end{bmatrix} = \begin{bmatrix} 8 & -8 \\ -8 & 8 \end{bmatrix}$

Similarly, $A^8 = A^4 \cdot A^4$

$= \begin{bmatrix} 8 & -8 \\ -8 & 8 \end{bmatrix} \begin{bmatrix} 8 & -8 \\ -8 & 8 \end{bmatrix}$

$= \begin{bmatrix} 64+64 & -64-64 \\ -64-64 & 64+64 \end{bmatrix} = \begin{bmatrix} 128 & -128 \\ -128 & 128 \end{bmatrix}$

Now, $A^8 \begin{bmatrix} x \\ y \end{bmatrix} = \begin{bmatrix} 8 \\ 64 \end{bmatrix} \Rightarrow \begin{bmatrix} 128 & -128 \\ -128 & 128 \end{bmatrix} \begin{bmatrix} x \\ y \end{bmatrix} = \begin{bmatrix} 8 \\ 64 \end{bmatrix}$

$\Rightarrow 128x - 128y = 8 \Rightarrow x - y = \dfrac{1}{16}$ ...(i)

and $-128x + 128y = 64 \Rightarrow x - y = -\dfrac{1}{2}$ ...(ii)

From Eqs. (i) and (ii), we get these two lines are parallel. So, there will be no solution.

85. Given, system of equation can be written as $AX = B$, where

$$A = \begin{bmatrix} 1 & 2 & -3 \\ 2 & 6 & -11 \\ 1 & -2 & 7 \end{bmatrix}, X = \begin{bmatrix} x \\ y \\ z \end{bmatrix}, B = \begin{bmatrix} a \\ b \\ c \end{bmatrix}$$

Then, $|A| = \begin{vmatrix} 1 & 2 & -3 \\ 2 & 6 & -11 \\ 1 & -2 & 7 \end{vmatrix} = 1(42-22) - 2(14+11) - 3(-4-6)$

$= 20 - 50 + 30 = 0$

$$|A_1| = \begin{vmatrix} a & 2 & -3 \\ b & 6 & -11 \\ c & -2 & 7 \end{vmatrix}$$

$= a(42-22) - 2(7b+11c) - 3(-2b-6c)$

$= 20a - 8b - 4c = 4(5a - 2b - c)$

$$|A_2| = \begin{vmatrix} 1 & a & -3 \\ 2 & b & -11 \\ 1 & c & 7 \end{vmatrix}$$

$= 1(7b + 11c) - a(14+11) - 3(2c - b)$

$= -25a + 10b + 5c = -5(5a - 2b - c)$

$$|A_3| = \begin{vmatrix} 1 & 2 & a \\ 2 & 6 & b \\ 1 & -2 & c \end{vmatrix} = -10a + 4b + 2c = -2(5a - 2b - c)$$

For infinite solution,

$|A| = |A_1| = |A_2| = |A_3| = 0$

$\Rightarrow \quad 5a - 2b - c = 0$

$\Rightarrow \quad 5a = 2b + c$

86. Given, $3x - 2y - kz = 10$

$2x - 4y - 2z = 6$

$x + 2y - z = 5m$

Condition for inconsistency $\Rightarrow \Delta = 0$

and at least one of the $\Delta_x, \Delta_y, \Delta_z$ is non-zero.

Now, $\Delta = \begin{vmatrix} 3 & -2 & -k \\ 2 & -4 & -2 \\ 1 & 2 & -1 \end{vmatrix}$

$= 3(4+4) + 2(-2+2) - k(4+4) = 24 - 8k$

Now, $\Delta = 0$

$\therefore \quad 24 - 8k = 0 \Rightarrow k = \frac{24}{8} = 3$

$$\Delta_x = \begin{vmatrix} 10 & -2 & -k \\ 6 & -4 & -2 \\ 5m & 2 & -1 \end{vmatrix}$$

$= 10(4+4) + 2(-6+10m) - 3(12+20m)$

$= 32 - 40m = 8(4 - 5m)$

$$\Delta_y = \begin{vmatrix} 3 & 10 & -k \\ 2 & 6 & -2 \\ 1 & 5m & -1 \end{vmatrix}$$

$= 3(-6+10m) - 10(-2+2) - 3(10m-6) = 0$

$$\Delta_z = \begin{vmatrix} 3 & -2 & 10 \\ 2 & -4 & 6 \\ 1 & 2 & 5m \end{vmatrix}$$

$= 3(-20m - 12) + 2(10m - 6) + 10(4+4)$

$= -40m + 32 = 8(4 - 5m)$

Here, either Δ_x or $\Delta_z \neq 0$

$\Rightarrow \quad 8(4 - 5m) \neq 0 \Rightarrow m \neq 4/5$

Hence, the required values are $k = 3, m \neq 4/5$.

87. If $A = \begin{bmatrix} 2 & 3 \\ 0 & -1 \end{bmatrix}$

$\det(A^4) + \det[A^{10} - [\text{adj}(2A)]^{10}]$

$$A \cdot A = \begin{bmatrix} 2 & 3 \\ 0 & -1 \end{bmatrix}\begin{bmatrix} 2 & 3 \\ 0 & -1 \end{bmatrix} = \begin{bmatrix} 4 & 3 \\ 0 & 1 \end{bmatrix}$$

$$A = \begin{bmatrix} 2 & 3 \\ 0 & -1 \end{bmatrix}, A^2 = \begin{bmatrix} 4 & 3 \\ 0 & 1 \end{bmatrix}$$

$A^3 = A^2 \cdot A$

$$= \begin{bmatrix} 4 & 3 \\ 0 & 1 \end{bmatrix}\begin{bmatrix} 2 & 3 \\ 0 & -1 \end{bmatrix} = \begin{bmatrix} 8 & 9 \\ 0 & -1 \end{bmatrix}$$

$A^4 = A^3 \cdot A$

$$= \begin{bmatrix} 8 & 9 \\ 0 & -1 \end{bmatrix}\begin{bmatrix} 2 & 3 \\ 0 & -1 \end{bmatrix} = \begin{bmatrix} 16 & 15 \\ 0 & 1 \end{bmatrix}$$

$$A^n = \begin{bmatrix} 2^n & 2^n - (-1)^n \\ 0 & (-1)^n \end{bmatrix}$$

$$A^{10} = \begin{bmatrix} 2^{10} & 2^{10} - 1 \\ 0 & 1 \end{bmatrix} \Rightarrow 2A = \begin{bmatrix} 4 & 6 \\ 0 & -2 \end{bmatrix}$$

$$\text{adj}(2A) = \begin{bmatrix} -2 & -6 \\ 0 & 4 \end{bmatrix}$$

$$\text{adj}(2A) = -2\begin{bmatrix} 1 & 3 \\ 0 & -2 \end{bmatrix}$$

$$\left[\because x = \begin{pmatrix} a & b \\ c & d \end{pmatrix} \text{ and adj}(x) = \begin{pmatrix} d & -b \\ -c & a \end{pmatrix}\right]$$

$$[\text{adj}(2A)]^2 = 4\begin{pmatrix} 1 & 3 \\ 0 & -2 \end{pmatrix}\begin{pmatrix} 1 & 3 \\ 0 & -2 \end{pmatrix} = 4\begin{bmatrix} 1 & -3 \\ 0 & 4 \end{bmatrix}$$

$$[\text{adj}(2A)]^3 = 4\begin{bmatrix} 1 & -3 \\ 0 & 4 \end{bmatrix} \times (-2)\begin{bmatrix} 1 & 3 \\ 0 & -2 \end{bmatrix}$$

$$= -8\begin{bmatrix} 1 & 9 \\ 0 & -8 \end{bmatrix} (\text{adj}(2A))^n$$

$$= (-2)^n \begin{bmatrix} 1 & (-1)^n[2^n - (-1)^n] \\ 0 & (-1)^n 2^n \end{bmatrix}$$

$$[\text{adj}(2A)]^{10} = 2^{10}\begin{bmatrix} 1 & -(2^{10} - 1) \\ 0 & 2^{10} \end{bmatrix}$$

Now, $A^{10} - [\text{adj}(2A)]^{10} = \begin{bmatrix} 2^{10} & 2^{10} - 1 \\ 0 & 1 \end{bmatrix} - \begin{bmatrix} 2^{10} & -(2^{20} - 2^{10}) \\ 0 & 2^{20} \end{bmatrix}$

$$= \begin{bmatrix} 0 & 2 \cdot 2^{10} - 2^{20} - 1 \\ 0 & 1 - 2^{20} \end{bmatrix}$$

$\det|A^{10} - \text{adj}(2A)^{10}| = 0$

$\therefore \quad \det(A^4) + \det[A^{10} - \text{adj}(2A)^{10}] = 16$

88. Given, system of equation

$$2x + y - z = 3,$$
$$x - y - z = \alpha$$
and $$3x + 3y + \beta z = 3$$

has infinitely many solutions, if $\Delta = 0$, $\Delta_1 = \Delta_2 = \Delta_3 = 0$

Now, $$\Delta = \begin{vmatrix} 2 & 1 & -1 \\ 1 & -1 & -1 \\ 3 & 3 & \beta \end{vmatrix} = 0$$

$\Rightarrow$ $2(-\beta + 3) - 1(\beta + 3) - 1(3 + 3) = 0$

$\Rightarrow$ $\beta = -1$

$$\Delta_1 = \begin{vmatrix} 3 & 1 & -1 \\ \alpha & -1 & -1 \\ 3 & 3 & -1 \end{vmatrix} = 0$$

$\Rightarrow 3(1 + 3) - 1(-\alpha + 3) - 1(3\alpha + 3) = 0$

$\Rightarrow$ $12 + \alpha - 3 - 3\alpha - 3 = 0$

$\Rightarrow$ $\alpha = 3$

Also, $$\Delta_2 = \begin{vmatrix} 2 & 3 & -1 \\ 1 & \alpha & -1 \\ 3 & 3 & -1 \end{vmatrix} = 0$$

$\Rightarrow$ $2(-\alpha + 3) - 3(-1 + 3) - 1(3 - 3\alpha) = 0$

$\Rightarrow$ $\alpha = 3$ and $\Delta_3 = \begin{vmatrix} 2 & 1 & 3 \\ 1 & -1 & \alpha \\ 3 & 3 & 3 \end{vmatrix} = 0$

$\Rightarrow$ $2(-3 - 3\alpha) - 1(3 - 3\alpha) + 3(3 + 3) = 0$

$\Rightarrow$ $-3\alpha + 9 = 0$

$\Rightarrow$ $\alpha = 3$

$\therefore$ $\alpha = 3, \beta = -1$

So, $\alpha + \beta - \alpha\beta = 3 - 1 - 3(-1) = 5$

89. Given determinant,

$$D = \begin{vmatrix} x & a+y & x+a \\ y & b+y & y+b \\ z & c+y & z+c \end{vmatrix}$$

$$= \begin{vmatrix} x & a+y & x \\ y & b+y & y \\ z & c+y & z \end{vmatrix} + \begin{vmatrix} x & a+y & a \\ y & b+y & b \\ z & c+y & c \end{vmatrix}$$

$$= 0 + \begin{vmatrix} x & a & a \\ y & b & b \\ z & c & c \end{vmatrix} + \begin{vmatrix} x & y & a \\ y & y & b \\ z & y & c \end{vmatrix} = y\begin{vmatrix} x & 1 & a \\ y & 1 & b \\ z & 1 & c \end{vmatrix}$$

Applying $C_1 \to C_1 + C_3$, we get

$$D = y\begin{vmatrix} x+a & 1 & a \\ y+b & 1 & b \\ z+c & 1 & c \end{vmatrix}$$

It is given that $a + x = b + y = c + z + 1 = \lambda$ (let), so

$$D = y\begin{vmatrix} \lambda & 1 & a \\ \lambda & 1 & b \\ \lambda - 1 & 1 & c \end{vmatrix}$$

Applying $R_1 \to R_1 - R_3$ and $R_2 \to R_2 - R_3$, we get

$$D = y\begin{vmatrix} 1 & 0 & a-c \\ 1 & 0 & b-c \\ \lambda - 1 & 1 & c \end{vmatrix}$$

$$= y(-1)[(b - c) - (a - c)] = y(a - b)$$

90. Given determinant is

$$\Delta = \begin{vmatrix} x-2 & 2x-3 & 3x-4 \\ 2x-3 & 3x-4 & 4x-5 \\ 3x-5 & 5x-8 & 10x-17 \end{vmatrix}$$

Expanding along R_1

$$\Delta = (x-2)[(3x-4)(10x-17) - (4x-5)(5x-8)] - (2x-3)$$
$$[(2x-3)(10x-17) - (4x-5)(3x-5)]$$
$$+ (3x-4)[(2x-3)(5x-8) - (3x-4)(3x-5)]$$

$$\Delta = (x-2)[30x^2 - 91x + 68 - 20x^2 + 57x - 40]$$
$$- (2x-3)[20x^2 - 64x + 51 - 12x^2 + 35x - 25]$$
$$+ (3x-4)[10x^2 - 31x + 24 - 9x^2 + 27x - 20]$$

$$\Delta = (x-2)[10x^2 - 34x + 28] - (2x-3)[8x^2 - 29x + 26]$$
$$+ (3x-4)[x^2 - 4x + 4]$$

$$\Delta = 2(x-2)[5x^2 - 17x + 14] - (2x-3)(x-2)(8x-13)$$
$$+ (3x-4)(x-2)^2$$

$$\Delta = 2(x-2)^2(5x-7) - (2x-3)(x-2)(8x-13) + (3x-4)(x-2)^2$$

$$\Delta = (x-2)^2[10x - 14 + 3x - 4] - (2x-3)(x-2)(8x-13)$$

$$\Delta = (x-2)^2(13x - 18) - (2x-3)(x-2)(8x-13)$$

$$\Delta = (x-2)[(x-2)(13x-18) - (2x-3)(8x-13)]$$

$$\Delta = (x-2)[-3x^2 + 6x - 3] = -3x^3 + 12x^2 - 15x + 6$$

$$= Ax^3 + Bx^2 + Cx + D \qquad \text{[given]}$$

On comparing the coefficient of different terms, we get

$$A = -3, B = 12, C = -15 \text{ and } D = 6$$

$\therefore$ $B + C = -3$

91. Given system of equations

$$(\lambda - 1)x + (3\lambda + 1)y + 2\lambda z = 0$$
$$(\lambda - 1)x + (4\lambda - 2)y + (\lambda + 3)z = 0$$

and $2x + (3\lambda + 1)y + 3(\lambda - 1)z = 0$ has non-zero solutions.

So, $$\Delta = 0 \Rightarrow \begin{vmatrix} \lambda - 1 & 3\lambda + 1 & 2\lambda \\ \lambda - 1 & 4\lambda - 2 & \lambda + 3 \\ 2 & 3\lambda + 1 & 3(\lambda - 1) \end{vmatrix} = 0$$

$\Rightarrow (\lambda - 1)[6(2\lambda - 1)(\lambda - 1) - (\lambda + 3)(3\lambda + 1)]$
$- (3\lambda + 1)[3(\lambda - 1)^2 - 2(\lambda + 3)]$
$+ 2\lambda[(\lambda - 1)(3\lambda + 1) - 2(4\lambda - 2)] = 0$

$\Rightarrow (\lambda - 1)[12\lambda^2 - 18\lambda + 6 - 3\lambda^2 - 10\lambda - 3]$
$- (3\lambda + 1)[3\lambda^2 - 6\lambda + 3 - 2\lambda - 6]$
$+ 2\lambda[3\lambda^2 - 2\lambda - 1 - 8\lambda + 4] = 0$

$\Rightarrow \lambda[9\lambda^2 - 28\lambda + 3 - 9\lambda^2 + 24\lambda + 9 + 6\lambda^2$
$- 20\lambda + 6] - 1[12\lambda^2 - 36\lambda] = 0$

$\Rightarrow$ $\lambda[6\lambda^2 - 36\lambda + 54] = 0$

$\Rightarrow$ $\lambda(\lambda - 3)^2 = 0$

$\Rightarrow$ $\lambda = 0, 3, 3$

$\therefore$ Sum of distinct values of λ is 3.

Exercise 2 - JEE Advanced Pattern

1. Given, $f(x) = a + bx + cx^2$

and let α, β, γ are $1, \omega, \omega^2$ respectively and we know $\omega^3 = 1$.

Also, $1 + \omega + \omega^2 = 0$

So, $f(\alpha) = f(1) = a + b + c$

$f(\beta) = f(\omega) = a + b\omega + c\omega^2$

and $f(\gamma) = f(\omega^2) = a + b\omega^2 + c\omega$

Now, $\begin{vmatrix} a & b & c \\ b & c & a \\ c & a & b \end{vmatrix}$

$= 3abc - a^3 - b^3 - c^3$

$= -(a+b+c)(a^2 + b^2 + c^2 - ab - bc - ca)$

$= -(a+b+c)\{a^2 + b^2 + c^2 + (-1)ab + (-1)bc + (-1)ca\}$

$= -(a+b+c)\{a^2 + b^2 + c^2 + (\omega + \omega^2)ab + (\omega + \omega^2)bc + (\omega + \omega^2)ca\}$

$= -(a+b+c)(a + b\omega + c\omega^2)(a + b\omega^2 + c\omega)$

$= -f(1)\, f(\omega)\, f(\omega^2)$

$= -f(\alpha)\, f(\beta)\, f(\gamma)$

2. $P = [a_{ij}] = \begin{bmatrix} a_{11} & a_{12} & a_{13} \\ a_{21} & a_{22} & a_{23} \\ a_{31} & a_{32} & a_{33} \end{bmatrix}$

and $Q = [b_{ij}] = \begin{bmatrix} 9a_{11} & 27a_{12} & 81a_{13} \\ 27a_{21} & 81a_{22} & 243a_{23} \\ 81a_{31} & 243a_{32} & 729a_{33} \end{bmatrix}$ $[\because b_{ij} = 3^{i+j} \cdot a_{ij}]$

$\therefore\ |Q| = 3^{12} \begin{vmatrix} a_{11} & a_{12} & a_{13} \\ a_{21} & a_{22} & a_{23} \\ a_{31} & a_{32} & a_{33} \end{vmatrix} = 3^{12} \cdot |P| = 3^{12} \times 6 = 3^{13} \times 2$

3. $\Delta = \begin{vmatrix} x-6 & 3x & 3x \\ 3x & x-6 & 3x \\ 3x & 3x & x-6 \end{vmatrix}$

Applying $C_1 \to C_1 + C_2 + C_3$, we get

$\Delta = \begin{vmatrix} 7x-6 & 3x & 3x \\ 7x-6 & x-6 & 3x \\ 7x-6 & 3x & x-6 \end{vmatrix}$

Applying $R_1 \to R_1 - R_2$ and $R_2 \to R_2 - R_3$, we get

$\Delta = \begin{vmatrix} 0 & 2x+6 & 0 \\ 0 & -2x-6 & 2x+6 \\ 7x-6 & 3x & x-6 \end{vmatrix}$

Expanding along C_1, we get

$\Delta = (2x+6)^2 (7x-6)$

$\therefore\ A = -6$ and $B = 7$

Hence, $(A, B) = (-6, 7)$

4. $\begin{vmatrix} a & a+1 & a-1 \\ -b & b+1 & b-1 \\ c & c-1 & c+1 \end{vmatrix} + (-1)^n \begin{vmatrix} a+1 & b+1 & c-1 \\ a-1 & b-1 & c+1 \\ a & -b & c \end{vmatrix}$

$= \begin{vmatrix} a & a+1 & a-1 \\ -b & b+1 & b-1 \\ c & c-1 & c+1 \end{vmatrix} + (-1)^n \begin{vmatrix} a+1 & a-1 & a \\ b+1 & b-1 & -b \\ c-1 & c+1 & c \end{vmatrix}$

[since, $\det(A) = \det(A^T)$]

$= \begin{vmatrix} a & a+1 & a-1 \\ -b & b+1 & b-1 \\ c & c-1 & c+1 \end{vmatrix} + (-1)^{n+2} \begin{vmatrix} a & a+1 & a-1 \\ -b & b+1 & b-1 \\ c & c-1 & c+1 \end{vmatrix}$

This is equal to zero only, if $n + 2$ is odd i.e. n is an odd integer.

5. Applying $C_1 = aC_1, C_2 \to bC_2$ an $C_3 \to cC_3$, we get

$f(\theta) = \dfrac{1}{abc} \begin{vmatrix} a^3 + a(b^2 + c^2)\cos\theta & ab^2(1-\cos\theta) & c^2a(1-\cos\theta) \\ a^2b(1-\cos\theta) & b^3 + b(c^2 + a^2)\cos\theta & c^2b(1-\cos\theta) \\ a^2c(1-\cos\theta) & b^2c(1-\cos\theta) & c^3 + c(a^2 + b^2)\cos\theta \end{vmatrix}$

$= \dfrac{abc}{abc} \begin{vmatrix} a^2 + (b^2 + c^2)\cos\theta & b^2(1-\cos\theta) & c^2(1-\cos\theta) \\ a^2(1-\cos\theta) & b^2 + (c^2 + a^2)\cos\theta & c^2(1-\cos\theta) \\ a^2(1-\cos\theta) & b^2(1-\cos\theta) & c^2 + (a^2 + b^2)\cos\theta \end{vmatrix}$

Applying $C_1 \to C_1 + C_2 + C_3$, we get

$f(\theta) = (a^2 + b^2 + c^2) \begin{vmatrix} 1 & b^2(1-\cos\theta) & c^2(1-\cos\theta) \\ 1 & b^2 + (c^2 + a^2)\cos\theta & c^2(1-\cos\theta) \\ 1 & b^2(1-\cos\theta) & c^2 + (a^2 + b^2)\cos\theta \end{vmatrix}$

Applying $R_2 \to R_2 - R_1$ and $R_3 \to R_3 - R_1$, we get

$= (a^2 + b^2 + c^2) \begin{vmatrix} 1 & b^2(1-\cos\theta) & c^2(1-\cos\theta) \\ 0 & (a^2 + b^2 + c^2)\cos\theta & 0 \\ 0 & 0 & (a^2 + b^2 + c^2)\cos\theta \end{vmatrix}$

$= (a^2 + b^2 + c^2)^3 \cos^2\theta$

$\therefore\ \displaystyle\int_0^{\frac{\pi}{2}} f(\theta)\, d\theta = \int_0^{\frac{\pi}{2}} (a^2 + b^2 + c^2)^3 \cos^2\theta\, d\theta$

$= (a^2 + b^2 + c^2)^3 \displaystyle\int_0^{\frac{\pi}{2}} \cos^2\theta\, d\theta = (a^2 + b^2 + c^2)^3 \cdot \frac{\pi}{4}$

6. For no solution, $|\Delta| = 0$ and Δ_1 or $\Delta_2 \neq 0$

Now, $|\Delta| = \begin{vmatrix} k+1 & 8 \\ k & k+3 \end{vmatrix} = 0 \Rightarrow k = 1, 3$

Now, $\Delta_1 = \begin{vmatrix} 4k & 8 \\ 3k-1 & k+3 \end{vmatrix}$

$= 4k(k+3) - 8(3k-1) = 4k^2 + 12k - 24k + 8$

$= 4k^2 - 12k + 8 = 4(k^2 - 3k + 2) = 4(k-2)(k-1)$

Since, $\Delta_1 \neq 0 \Rightarrow k \neq 1, 2$

$\therefore\ k = 3$

7. $\because 0 \le x < 1 \quad \therefore [x] = 0$

$1 \le y < 2 \quad \therefore [y] = 1$

$2 \le z < 3 \quad \therefore [z] = 2$

Hence, the given determinant is

$$\begin{vmatrix} 1 & 1 & 2 \\ 0 & 2 & 2 \\ 0 & 1 & 3 \end{vmatrix} = 6 - 2 = 4 = 2 \times 2 = 2[z]$$

8. $$\Delta = \begin{vmatrix} a & b & c \\ b & c & a \\ c & a & b \end{vmatrix}$$

$$= -(a+b+c)(a^2+b^2+c^2-ab-bc-ca)$$

$$= -\frac{1}{2}(a+b+c)[(a-b)^2+(b-c)^2+(c-a)^2] = 0$$

$\Rightarrow a+b+c=0$ or $a=b=c$

If $a+b+c=0$, we have

$\cos\theta + \cos 2\theta + \cos 3\theta = 0$ and $\sin\theta - \sin 2\theta + \sin 3\theta = 0$

or $\cos 2\theta (2\cos\theta + 1) = 0$ and $\sin 2\theta (1 - 2\cos\theta) = 0$ ...(i)

which is not possible as $\cos 2\theta = 0$ gives $\sin 2\theta \ne 0$,

$\cos\theta \ne \frac{1}{2}$ and $\cos\theta = -\frac{1}{2}$ gives $\sin 2\theta \ne 0, \cos\theta \ne \frac{1}{2}$.

Therefore, Eq. (i) does not hold simultaneously. Therefore,

$a+b+c \ne 0 \Rightarrow a=b=c$

$\therefore \quad e^{i\theta} = e^{-2i\theta} = e^{3i\theta}$

which is satisfied only $e^{i\theta} = 1$ i.e. $\cos\theta = 1, \sin\theta = 0$.

So, $\theta = 2k\pi, k \in Z$.

9. Let $$\Delta_1 = \begin{vmatrix} \log_5 729 & \log_3 5 \\ \log_5 27 & \log_9 25 \end{vmatrix} = \begin{vmatrix} \log_5 3^6 & \log_3 5 \\ \log_5 3^3 & \log_{3^2} 5^2 \end{vmatrix}$$

$$= \begin{vmatrix} 6\log_5 3 & \log_3 5 \\ 3\log_5 3 & \frac{2}{2}\log_3 5 \end{vmatrix}$$

$$= 6\log_5 3 \cdot \log_3 5 - 3\log_5 3 \cdot \log_3 5 = 6 - 3 = 3$$

and $$\Delta_2 = \begin{vmatrix} \log_5 9 & \log_5 9 \\ \log_{27} 5 & \log_3 5 \end{vmatrix} = \begin{vmatrix} \log_5 3^2 & \log_5 3^2 \\ \log_{3^3} 5 & \log_3 5 \end{vmatrix}$$

$$= \begin{vmatrix} 2\log_5 3 & 2\log_5 3 \\ \frac{1}{3}\log_3 5 & \log_3 5 \end{vmatrix}$$

$$= 2\log_5 3 \log_3 5 - \frac{2}{3}\log_5 3 \log_3 5 = 2 - \frac{2}{3} = \frac{4}{3}$$

$\therefore \Delta_1 \Delta_2 = 3 \times \frac{4}{3} = 4$

10. $A^3 + A = O$

$\Rightarrow \quad A(A^2 + I) = O$

$\Rightarrow \quad |A(A^2+I)| = O \Rightarrow |A| = 0$ or $|A^2 + I| = O$

If $|A| = 0$, then $xy = 0$

$$A^2 + I = \begin{bmatrix} 0 & x \\ y & 0 \end{bmatrix}\begin{bmatrix} 0 & x \\ y & 0 \end{bmatrix} + \begin{bmatrix} 1 & 0 \\ 0 & 1 \end{bmatrix}$$

$$= \begin{bmatrix} xy & 0 \\ 0 & xy \end{bmatrix} + \begin{bmatrix} 1 & 0 \\ 0 & 1 \end{bmatrix} = \begin{bmatrix} xy+1 & 0 \\ 0 & xy+1 \end{bmatrix}$$

$\Rightarrow \quad |A^2 + I| = 0$

$\Rightarrow \quad (xy+1)^2 = 0 \Rightarrow xy = -1$

So, sum of possible values of xy is -1.

11. Using the properties of determinants, we have

$$\sum_{r=1}^{n} \Delta_r = \begin{vmatrix} \sum_{r=1}^{n} 2^{r-1} & \sum_{r=1}^{n} 2\cdot 3^{r-1} & \sum_{r=1}^{n} 4\cdot 5^{r-1} \\ x & y & z \\ 2^n - 1 & 3^n - 1 & 5^n - 1 \end{vmatrix}$$

Now, $$\sum_{r=1}^{n} 2^{r-1} = 1 + 2 + 2^2 + \ldots + 2^{n-1}$$

$$= \frac{1\cdot(2^n - 1)}{2-1} = 2^n - 1$$

$$\sum_{r=1}^{n} 2\cdot 3^{r-1} = 2[1 + 3 + 3^2 + \ldots + 3^{n-1}] = 3^n - 1$$

and $$\sum_{r=1}^{n} 4\cdot 5^{r-1} = 4[1 + 5 + 5^2 + \ldots + 5^{n-1}] = 5^n - 1$$

$$\therefore \quad \sum_{r=1}^{n} \Delta_r = \begin{vmatrix} 2^n - 1 & 3^n - 1 & 5^n - 1 \\ x & y & z \\ 2^n - 1 & 3^n - 1 & 5^n - 1 \end{vmatrix} = 0$$

[$\because R_1$ and R_3 are identical]

12. $$\Delta = \begin{vmatrix} {}^xC_1 & {}^xC_2 & {}^xC_3 \\ {}^yC_1 & {}^yC_2 & {}^yC_3 \\ {}^zC_1 & {}^zC_2 & {}^zC_3 \end{vmatrix} = \begin{vmatrix} x & \frac{x(x-1)}{2} & \frac{x(x-1)(x-2)}{6} \\ y & \frac{y(y-1)}{2} & \frac{y(y-1)(y-2)}{6} \\ z & \frac{z(z-1)}{2} & \frac{z(z-1)(z-2)}{6} \end{vmatrix}$$

Taking x, y, z common from R_1, R_2 and R_3 respectively and then taking $\frac{1}{2}$ and $\frac{1}{6}$ common from C_2 and C_3 respectively, we have

$$\Delta = \frac{xyz}{12}\begin{vmatrix} 1 & x-1 & x^2 - 3x + 2 \\ 1 & y-1 & y^2 - 3y + 2 \\ 1 & z-1 & z^2 - 3z + 2 \end{vmatrix}$$

Applying $C_2 \to C_2 + C_1$ and $C_3 \to C_3 - 2C_1$

$$= \frac{xyz}{12}\begin{vmatrix} 1 & x & x^2 - 3x \\ 1 & y & y^2 - 3y \\ 1 & z & z^2 - 3z \end{vmatrix}$$

$$= \frac{xyz}{12}\begin{vmatrix} 1 & x & x^2 \\ 1 & y & y^2 \\ 1 & z & z^2 \end{vmatrix} \quad \text{[applying } C_3 \to C_3 + 3C_2]$$

$$= \frac{xyz}{12}(x-y)(y-z)(z-x)$$

On comparing, we get

$$A = \frac{xyz}{12}$$

$$\therefore \quad \frac{12A}{xyz} = \frac{xyz}{xyz} = 1$$

13. $\Delta = \begin{vmatrix} x^2+x & x+1 & x-2 \\ 2x^2+3x-1 & 3x & 3x-3 \\ x^2+2x+3 & 2x-1 & 2x-1 \end{vmatrix}$

Applying $R_2 \to R_2 - (R_1 + R_3)$, we get

$$\Delta = \begin{vmatrix} x^2+x & x+1 & x-2 \\ -4 & 0 & 0 \\ x^2+2x+3 & 2x-1 & 2x-1 \end{vmatrix}$$

Applying $R_1 \to R_1 + \frac{x^2}{4}R_2$ and $R_3 \to R_3 + \frac{x^2}{4}R_2$, we get

$$\Delta = \begin{vmatrix} x & x+1 & x-2 \\ -4 & 0 & 0 \\ 2x+3 & 2x-1 & 2x-1 \end{vmatrix} = \begin{vmatrix} x & x+1 & x-2 \\ -4 & 0 & 0 \\ 3 & -3 & 3 \end{vmatrix}$$

[applying $R_3 \to R_3 - 2R_1$]

$$= x\begin{vmatrix} 1 & 1 & 1 \\ -4 & 0 & 0 \\ 3 & -3 & 3 \end{vmatrix} + \begin{vmatrix} 0 & 1 & -2 \\ -4 & 0 & 0 \\ 3 & -3 & 3 \end{vmatrix} = xA + B,$$

where $A = \begin{vmatrix} 1 & 1 & 1 \\ -4 & 0 & 0 \\ 3 & -3 & 3 \end{vmatrix}$ and $B = \begin{vmatrix} 0 & 1 & -2 \\ -4 & 0 & 0 \\ 3 & -3 & 3 \end{vmatrix}$

Now, $A = -(-4)(3+3) = 4 \times 6 = 24$

and $B = -1(-12-0) - 2(12-0) = 12 - 24 = -12$

Thus, $A + B = 24 - 12 = 12$

14. $\frac{d^n}{dx^n} f(x) = \begin{vmatrix} n! & \sin\left(x + \frac{n\pi}{2}\right) & -\cos\left(x + \frac{n\pi}{2}\right) \\ n! & \sin\left(\frac{n\pi}{2}\right) & \cos\frac{n\pi}{2} \\ a & a^2 & a^3 \end{vmatrix}$

$$\Rightarrow \frac{d^n}{dx^n} f(x) = \begin{vmatrix} n! & \sin\left(\frac{n\pi}{2}\right) & -\cos\left(\frac{n\pi}{2}\right) \\ n! & \sin\frac{n\pi}{2} & \cos\frac{n\pi}{2} \\ a & a^2 & a^3 \end{vmatrix} \quad \text{[at } x = 0\text{]}$$

$$= \begin{vmatrix} n! & \sin\left(\frac{n\pi}{2}\right) & 0 \\ n! & \sin\left(\frac{n\pi}{2}\right) & 0 \\ a & a^2 & a^3 \end{vmatrix} = 0$$

15. Given, system of equations are

$5x + y - z = 2$; $x - z = 2$ and $3x + 3y + az = 5$

For unique solution, $\Delta \neq 0$

$$\begin{vmatrix} 5 & 1 & -1 \\ 1 & 0 & -1 \\ 3 & 3 & a \end{vmatrix} \neq 0$$

$\Rightarrow \quad 5(0+3) - 1(a+3) - 1(3-0) \neq 0$

$\Rightarrow \quad 15 - a - 3 - 3 \neq 0 \Rightarrow a \neq 9$

16. System has non-trivial solution.

$$\therefore \quad \begin{vmatrix} 2 & 3\lambda & -1 \\ \lambda & -2 & -1 \\ 1 & 2 & -\lambda \end{vmatrix} = 0$$

$\Rightarrow \quad 2(2\lambda + 2) - 3\lambda(-\lambda^2 + 1) - 1(2\lambda + 2) = 0$

$\Rightarrow \quad 4(\lambda + 1) + 3\lambda(\lambda^2 - 1) - 2(\lambda + 1) = 0$

$\Rightarrow 4(\lambda + 1) + 3\lambda(\lambda - 1)(\lambda + 1) - 2(\lambda + 1) = 0$

$\Rightarrow \quad (\lambda + 1)[4 + 3\lambda^2 - 3\lambda - 2] = 0$

$\Rightarrow \quad (\lambda + 1)(3\lambda^2 - 3\lambda + 2) = 0$

$\Rightarrow \quad (\lambda + 1) = 0, \ \lambda = \frac{3 \pm \sqrt{9 - 24}}{6}$

$\Rightarrow \quad \lambda = -1 \qquad [\because \lambda \in R]$

17. Applying $R_1 \to R_1 - \sec x \, R_3$, we get

$$f(x) = \begin{vmatrix} 0 & 0 & \sec^2 x + \cot x \operatorname{cosec} x - \cos x \\ \cos^2 x & \cos^2 x & \operatorname{cosec}^2 x \\ 1 & \cos^2 x & \cos^2 x \end{vmatrix}$$

$= (\sec^2 x + \cot x \operatorname{cosec} x - \cos x)(\cos^4 x - \cos^2 x)$

$= \left(1 + \frac{\cos^3 x}{\sin^2 x} - \cos^3 x\right) \cdot (\cos^2 x - 1)$

$= -\sin^2 x \left(\frac{\sin^2 x + \cos^3 x - \cos^3 x \sin^2 x}{\sin^2 x}\right)$

$= -(\sin^2 x + \cos^5 x)$

$\Rightarrow \quad \int_0^{\pi/2} f(x)\, dx = -\int_0^{\pi/2} (\sin^2 x + \cos^5 x)\, dx$

$= -\left(\frac{1}{2} \cdot \frac{\pi}{2} + \frac{4 \cdot 2}{5 \cdot 3 \cdot 1}\right) = -\left(\frac{\pi}{4} + \frac{8}{15}\right)$

18. $a_{ij} = \begin{cases} 1, & i = j \\ -x, & |i - j| = 1 \\ 2x + 1, & \text{otherwise} \end{cases}$

$A = [a_{ij}]$ be 3×3 matrix.

$$\therefore \quad A = \begin{bmatrix} 1 & -x & 2x+1 \\ -x & 1 & -x \\ 2x+1 & -x & 1 \end{bmatrix}$$

$|A| = (1 - x^2) - x(-2x^2 - x + x) + (2x + 1)(x^2 - 2x - 1)$

$|A| = 4x^3 - 4x^2 - 4x$

$\Rightarrow \quad f'(x) = 12x^2 - 8x - 4$

$\Rightarrow \quad f'(x) = 0$

$\Rightarrow \quad 4(3x^2 - 2x - 1) = 0 \Rightarrow (x - 1)(3x + 1) = 0$

+   –   +

–1/3   1

$\Rightarrow \quad x = 1, -\frac{1}{3}$

At $f(1) \to$ minimum

$f\left(-\frac{1}{3}\right) \to$ maximum

$$f(1) = 4(1^3 - 1^2 - 1) = -4$$

$$f\left(-\frac{1}{3}\right) = \frac{20}{27}$$

$$\therefore \quad \frac{f_{\min}}{f_{\max}} = \frac{-4}{20/27} = \frac{-4 \times 27}{20} = \frac{-27}{5}$$

19. $\because \Delta = \begin{vmatrix} a^2 + x^2 & ab & ac \\ ab & b^2 + x^2 & bc \\ ac & bc & c^2 + x^2 \end{vmatrix}$

Taking a, b, c common from R_1, R_2, R_3 respectively, then

$$\Delta = abc \begin{vmatrix} \frac{a^2 + x^2}{a} & b & c \\ a & \frac{b^2 + x^2}{b} & c \\ a & b & \frac{c^2 + x^2}{c} \end{vmatrix}$$

On multiplying C_1, C_2, C_3 by a, b, c respectively, then

$$\Delta = \begin{vmatrix} a^2 + x^2 & b^2 & c^2 \\ a^2 & b^2 + x^2 & c^2 \\ a^2 & b^2 & c^2 + x^2 \end{vmatrix}$$

Now, applying $C_1 \to C_1 + C_2 + C_3$, then

$$\Delta = \begin{vmatrix} x^2 + a^2 + b^2 + c^2 & b^2 & c^2 \\ x^2 + a^2 + b^2 + c^2 & b^2 + x^2 & c^2 \\ x^2 + a^2 + b^2 + c^2 & b^2 & c^2 + x^2 \end{vmatrix}$$

Applying $R_2 \to R_2 - R_1$ and $R_3 \to R_3 - R_1$, then

$$\Delta = \begin{vmatrix} x^2 + a^2 + b^2 + c^2 & b^2 & c^2 \\ 0 & x^2 & 0 \\ 0 & 0 & x^2 \end{vmatrix}$$

$$= x^4 (x^2 + a^2 + b^2 + c^2)$$

20. Let $\Delta = \begin{vmatrix} \sqrt{6} & 2i & 3 + \sqrt{6} \\ \sqrt{12} & \sqrt{3} + \sqrt{8}\, i & 3\sqrt{2} + \sqrt{6}\, i \\ \sqrt{18} & \sqrt{2} + \sqrt{12}\, i & \sqrt{27} + 2i \end{vmatrix}$

Applying $R_2 \to R_2 - \sqrt{2}\, R_1$ and $R_3 \to R_3 - \sqrt{3}\, R_1$, then

$$\Delta = \begin{vmatrix} \sqrt{6} & 2i & 3+\sqrt{6} \\ 0 & \sqrt{3} & -2\sqrt{3}+6i \\ 0 & \sqrt{2} & -3\sqrt{2}+2i \end{vmatrix}$$

Expanding along C_1, we get

$$= \sqrt{6} \begin{vmatrix} \sqrt{3} & -2\sqrt{3} + \sqrt{6i} \\ \sqrt{2} & -3\sqrt{2} + 2i \end{vmatrix}$$

$$= \sqrt{6}\, [-3\sqrt{6} + 2i\sqrt{3} + 2\sqrt{6} - 2i\sqrt{3}]$$

$$= \sqrt{6}\, (-\sqrt{6}) = -6 \qquad \text{[real and rational]}$$

21. $\sum_{k=1}^{n} 2^{k-1} = 1 + 2 + 2^2 + \ldots + 2^{n-1} = 2^n - 1$

$$\sum_{k=1}^{n} \frac{1}{k(k+1)} = \sum_{k=1}^{n} \left(\frac{1}{k} - \frac{1}{k+1}\right) = \frac{1}{1} - \frac{1}{n+1} = \frac{n}{n+1}$$

and $\sum_{k=1}^{n} \sin k\theta = \dfrac{\sin\left(\frac{n+1}{2}\right)\theta \sin\left(\frac{n\theta}{2}\right)}{\sin\left(\frac{\theta}{2}\right)}$

Given, $D_k = \begin{vmatrix} 2^{k-1} & \frac{1}{k(k+1)} & \sin k\theta \\ x & y & z \\ 2^n - 1 & \frac{n}{n+1} & \frac{\sin\left(\frac{n+1}{2}\right)\theta \sin\left(\frac{n\theta}{2}\right)}{\sin\left(\frac{\theta}{2}\right)} \end{vmatrix}$

$$\therefore \sum_{k=1}^{n} D_k = \begin{vmatrix} \sum_{k=1}^{n} 2^{k-1} & \sum_{k=1}^{n} \frac{1}{k(k+1)} & \sum_{k=1}^{n} \sin k\theta \\ x & y & z \\ 2^n - 1 & \frac{n}{n+1} & \frac{\sin\left(\frac{n+1}{2}\right)\theta \sin\left(\frac{n\theta}{2}\right)}{\sin\left(\frac{\theta}{2}\right)} \end{vmatrix}$$

$$= \begin{vmatrix} 2^n - 1 & \frac{n}{n+1} & \frac{\sin\left(\frac{n+1}{2}\right)\theta \sin\left(\frac{n\theta}{2}\right)}{\sin\left(\frac{\theta}{2}\right)} \\ x & y & z \\ 2^n - 1 & \frac{n}{n+1} & \frac{\sin\left(\frac{n+1}{2}\right)\theta \sin\left(\frac{n\theta}{2}\right)}{\sin\left(\frac{\theta}{2}\right)} \end{vmatrix} = 0$$

22. We have, $\begin{vmatrix} a & b & a\alpha + b \\ b & c & b\alpha + c \\ a\alpha + b & b\alpha + c & 0 \end{vmatrix} = 0$

Applying $C_3 \to C_3 - \alpha C_1 - C_2$, then

$$\begin{vmatrix} a & b & 0 \\ b & c & 0 \\ aa + b & ba + c & -(a\alpha^2 + 2b\alpha + c) \end{vmatrix} = 0$$

Expanding along C_3, we get

$$-(a\alpha^2 + 2b\alpha + c)(ac - b^2) = 0$$

$$\Rightarrow \quad (a\alpha^2 + 2b\alpha + c)(b^2 - ac) = 0$$

$$\Rightarrow \quad b^2 - ac = 0 \text{ or } a\alpha^2 + 2b\alpha + c = 0$$

i.e. a, b and c are in GP or $(x - \alpha)$ is a factor of $ax^2 + 2bx + c = 0$.

23. $\because \ f(x)=\begin{vmatrix} 2\cos x & 1 & 0 \\ 1 & 2\cos x & 1 \\ 0 & 1 & 2\cos x \end{vmatrix}$

$= 2\cos x(4\cos^2 x - 1) - 1(2\cos x - 0) + 0$

$= 2\cos x(4\cos^2 x - 1 - 1) = 4\cos x(2\cos^2 x - 1)$

$= 4\cos x \cos 2x = 2(\cos 3x + \cos x)$

Option (a)

$$f\left(\frac{\pi}{3}\right) = 2\left(\cos\frac{3\pi}{3} + \cos\frac{\pi}{3}\right) = 2\left(-1 + \frac{1}{2}\right) = -1$$

Option (b)

$f'(x) = 2(-3\sin 3x - \sin x)$

$\therefore \quad f'\left(\frac{\pi}{3}\right) = 2\left(-3\sin\pi - \sin\frac{\pi}{3}\right) = 2\left(0 - \frac{\sqrt{3}}{2}\right) = -\sqrt{3}$

Option (c)

$$\int_0^{\pi} f(x)\,dx = 2\int_0^{\pi}(\cos 3x + \cos x)\,dx = 2\left[\frac{\sin 3x}{3} + \sin x\right]_0^{\pi}$$

$= 2[(0+0) - (0+0)] = 0$

Option (d)

$$\int_{-\pi}^{\pi} f(x)dx = 2\int_{-\pi}^{\pi}(\cos 3x + \cos x)\,dx = 4\int_0^{\pi}(\cos 3x + \cos x)\,dx$$

$= 0$ [from option (c)]

24. $\because \Delta(x) = \begin{vmatrix} x^2 - 5x + 3 & 2x - 5 & 3 \\ 3x^2 + x + 4 & 6x + 1 & 9 \\ 7x^2 - 6x + 9 & 14x - 6 & 21 \end{vmatrix}$

Applying $R_2 \to R_2 - 3R_1$ and $R_3 \to R_3 - 7R_1$, then

$= \begin{vmatrix} x^2 - 5x + 3 & 2x - 5 & 3 \\ 16x - 5 & 16 & 0 \\ 29x - 12 & 29 & 0 \end{vmatrix}$

Expanding along C_3, we get $= 3\begin{vmatrix} 16x - 5 & 16 \\ 29x - 12 & 29 \end{vmatrix}$

Applying $C_1 \to C_1 - xC_2$, then

$\Delta(x) = 3\begin{vmatrix} -5 & 16 \\ -12 & 29 \end{vmatrix} = 3(-145 + 192)$

$= 3 \times 47$

$= 141 = ax^3 + bx^2 + cx + d$ [given]

$\therefore \ a = 0, b = 0, c = 0, d = 141$

25. $\because \Delta = \begin{vmatrix} a^2 & b\sin A & c\sin A \\ b\sin A & 1 & \cos A \\ c\sin A & \cos A & 1 \end{vmatrix}$

Taking common a from both R_1 and C_1, then

$$\Delta = \begin{vmatrix} 1 & \frac{b\sin A}{a} & \frac{c\sin A}{a} \\ \frac{b\sin A}{a} & 1 & \cos A \\ \frac{c\sin A}{a} & \cos A & 1 \end{vmatrix} = \begin{vmatrix} 1 & \sin B & \sin C \\ \sin B & 1 & \cos A \\ \sin C & \cos A & 1 \end{vmatrix}$$

[by sine rule]

Applying $C_2 \to C_2 - \sin B\, C_1$ and $C_3 \to C_3 - \sin C\, C_1$, then

$$\Delta = \begin{vmatrix} 1 & 0 & 0 \\ \sin B & 1 - \sin^2 B & \cos A - \sin B \sin C \\ \sin C & \cos A - \sin B \sin C & 1 - \sin^2 C \end{vmatrix}$$

Expanding along R_1, then

$$\Delta = \begin{vmatrix} \cos^2 B & \cos[\pi - (B + C)] - \sin B \sin C \\ \cos[\pi - (B + C)] - \sin B \sin C & \cos^2 C \end{vmatrix}$$

$[\because A + B + C = \pi]$

$$= \begin{vmatrix} \cos^2 B & -\cos(B + C) - \sin B \sin C \\ -\cos(B + C) - \sin B \sin C & \cos^2 C \end{vmatrix}$$

$$= \begin{vmatrix} \cos^2 B & -\cos B \cos C \\ -\cos B \cos C & \cos^2 C \end{vmatrix}$$

$= \cos^2 B \cos^2 C - \cos^2 B \cos^2 C = 0$

26. $\because \ f(a, b) = \begin{vmatrix} a & a^2 & 0 \\ 1 & (2a + b) & (a + b)^2 \\ 0 & 1 & (2a + 3b) \end{vmatrix}$

Applying $C_2 \to C_2 - aC_1$, then

$$f(a, b) = \begin{vmatrix} a & 0 & 0 \\ 1 & (a + b) & (a + b)^2 \\ 0 & 1 & (2a + 3b) \end{vmatrix}$$

Expanding along R_1, then

$$f(a, b) = a\begin{vmatrix} (a + b) & (a + b)^2 \\ 1 & (2a + 3b) \end{vmatrix}$$

$$= a(a + b)\begin{vmatrix} 1 & (a + b) \\ 1 & (2a + 3b) \end{vmatrix}$$

$= a(a + b)(2a + 3b - a - b)$

$= a(a + b)(a + 2b)$

27. $\because \quad f(x) = \begin{vmatrix} \sec^2 x & 1 & 1 \\ \cos^2 x & \cos^2 x & \operatorname{cosec}^2 x \\ 1 & \cos^2 x & \cot^2 x \end{vmatrix}$

Applying $C_2 \to C_2 - \cos^2 x\, C_1$, then

$$f(x) = \begin{vmatrix} \sec^2 x & 0 & 1 \\ \cos^2 x & \cos^2 x - \cos^4 x & \operatorname{cosec}^2 x \\ 1 & 0 & \cot^2 x \end{vmatrix}$$

Expanding along C_2, then

$$f(x) = \sin^2 x \cos^2 x\begin{vmatrix} \sec^2 x & 1 \\ 1 & \cot^2 x \end{vmatrix}$$

$= \sin^2 x \cos^2 x(\operatorname{cosec}^2 x - 1)$

$= \sin^2 x \cos^2 x \cot^2 x$

$= \cos^4 x$

Option (a)

$$\int_{-\pi/4}^{\pi/4} f(x)\,dx = \int_{-\pi/4}^{\pi/4} \cos^4 x\,dx = 2\int_0^{\pi/4} \cos^4 x\,dx$$

$$= 2\int_0^{\pi/4} \left(\frac{1+\cos 2x}{2}\right)^2 dx$$

$$= 2 \times \frac{1}{2}\int_0^{\pi/2} \left(\frac{1+\cos x}{2}\right)^2 dx$$

$$= \frac{1}{4}\int_0^{\pi/2} (1 + 2\cos x + \cos^2 x)\,dx$$

$$= \frac{1}{4}\int_0^{\pi/2} 1 \cdot dx + \frac{1}{2}\int_0^{\pi/2} \cos x\,dx + \frac{1}{4}\int_0^{\pi/2} \cos^2 x\,dx$$

$$= \frac{1}{4}\left(\frac{\pi}{2} - 0\right) + \frac{1}{2}(\sin x)_0^{\pi/2} + \frac{1}{4}\cdot\frac{1}{2}\cdot\frac{\pi}{2}$$

$$= \frac{\pi}{8} + \frac{1}{2}(1-0) + \frac{\pi}{16} = \frac{1}{16}(2\pi + 8 + \pi) = \frac{1}{16}(3\pi + 8)$$

Option (b)

$\because \quad f'(x) = 4\cos^3 x \cdot (-\sin x)$

$\therefore \quad f'\left(\frac{\pi}{2}\right) = 0$

Option (c) and (d)

$\because \quad 0 \le \cos^4 x \le 1$

$\because$ Maximum value of $f(x)$ is 1.

and minimum value of $f(x)$ is 0.

28. Let $\Delta = \begin{vmatrix} a & a+x^2 & a+x^2+x^4 \\ 2a & 3a+2x^2 & 4a+3x^2+2x^4 \\ 3a & 6a+3x^2 & 10a+6x^2+3x^4 \end{vmatrix}$

Applying $R_2 \to R_2 - 2R_1$ and $R_3 \to R_3 - 3R_1$, then

$$\Delta = \begin{vmatrix} a & a+x^2 & a+x^2+x^4 \\ 0 & a & 2a+x^2 \\ 0 & 3a & 7a+3x^2 \end{vmatrix}$$

Applying $R_3 \to R_3 - 3R_2$, then

$$\Delta = \begin{vmatrix} a & a+x^2 & a+x^2+x^4 \\ 0 & a & 2a+x^2 \\ 0 & 0 & a \end{vmatrix}$$

$$= a^3 = a_0 + a_1 x + a_2 x^2 + a_3 x^3 + a_4 x^4 + a_5 x^5 + a_6 x^6 + a_7 x^7 \quad \text{[given]}$$

$\therefore \quad a_0 = a^3, a_1 = 0, a_2 = 0, a_3 = 0, a_4 = 0, a_5 = 0, a_6 = 0, a_7 = 0$

and $\quad f(x) = a_0 x^2 + a_3 x + a_6 = a^3 x^2$

Option (a) $f(x) \ge 0 \Rightarrow a^3 x^2 \ge 0$

If $a^3 > 0$, then $x^2 \ge 0$

$\therefore \quad a > 0, x \in R$

Option (b) If $a = 0$, then $f(x) = 0$

and If $x = 0$, then $f(x) = 0$

$\therefore$ Option (b) is false.

Option (c) $f(x) = 0 \Rightarrow a^3 x^2 = 0$ or $x^2 = 0$

$\therefore \quad x = 0, 0$

Option (d) For $a = 0$, $f(x) = 0$ is an identity, then it has more than two roots.

29. Let $\Delta(x) = \begin{vmatrix} 4x-4 & (x-2)^2 & x^3 \\ 8x-4\sqrt{2} & (x-2\sqrt{2})^2 & (x+1)^3 \\ 12x-4\sqrt{3} & (x-2\sqrt{3})^2 & (x-1)^3 \end{vmatrix}$

$$= a_0 + a_1 x + a_2 x^2 + \dots \quad \text{...(i)}$$

On putting $x = 0$ in Eq. (i), then

$$\begin{vmatrix} -4 & 4 & 0 \\ -4\sqrt{2} & 8 & 1 \\ -4\sqrt{3} & 12 & -1 \end{vmatrix} = a_0$$

or $\quad a_0 = -4(-8-12) - 4(4\sqrt{2} + 4\sqrt{3})$

$= 16(5 - \sqrt{2} - \sqrt{3})$

$=$ term independent of x in Δ.

Also, on differentiating Eq. (i) w.r.t. x and then put $x = 0$, we get

$$\begin{vmatrix} 4 & -4 & 0 \\ -4\sqrt{2} & 8 & 1 \\ -4\sqrt{3} & 12 & -1 \end{vmatrix} + \begin{vmatrix} -4 & 4 & 0 \\ 8 & -4\sqrt{2} & 3 \\ -4\sqrt{3} & 12 & -1 \end{vmatrix} + \begin{vmatrix} -4 & 4 & 0 \\ -4\sqrt{2} & 8 & 1 \\ 12 & -4\sqrt{3} & 3 \end{vmatrix} = a_1$$

$\therefore \quad a_1 = 4(-8-12) + 4(4\sqrt{2} + 4\sqrt{3})$

$\quad - 4(4\sqrt{2} - 36) - 4(-8 + 12\sqrt{3})$

$\quad - 4(24 + 4\sqrt{3}) - 4(-12\sqrt{2} - 12)$

$= 48 + 48\sqrt{2} - 48\sqrt{3}$

$= 48(1 + \sqrt{2} - \sqrt{3})$

$=$ Coefficient of x in $\Delta(x)$

30. $\because \quad f(x) = \begin{vmatrix} 3 & 3x & 3x^2+2a^2 \\ 3x & 3x^2+2a^2 & 3x^3+6a^2x \\ 3x^2+2a^2 & 3x^3+6a^2x & 3x^4+12a^2x^2+2a^4 \end{vmatrix}$

Applying $C_3 \to C_3 - xC_2$ and $C_2 \to C_2 - xC_1$, then

$$f(x) = \begin{vmatrix} 3 & 0 & 2a^2 \\ 3x & 2a^2 & 4a^2x \\ 3x^2+2a^2 & 4a^2x & 6a^2x^2+2a^4 \end{vmatrix}$$

Applying $C_3 \to C_3 - xC_2$, then

$$= \begin{vmatrix} 3 & 0 & 2a^2 \\ 3x & 2a^2 & 2a^2x \\ 3x^2+2a^2 & 4a^2x & 2a^2x^2+2a^4 \end{vmatrix}$$

$$= 4a^4 \begin{vmatrix} 3 & 0 & 1 \\ 3x & 1 & x \\ 3x^2+2a^2 & 2x & x^2+a^2 \end{vmatrix}$$

Applying $C_1 \to C_1 - 3C_3$, then

$$f(x) = 4a^4 \begin{vmatrix} 0 & 0 & 1 \\ 0 & 1 & x \\ -a^2 & 2x & x^2+a^2 \end{vmatrix}$$

Expanding along C_1, we get

$$= 4a^4 [-a^2 (0-1)] = 4a^6$$

$\therefore \quad f'(x) = 0$

i.e. $y = f(x)$ is a straight line parallel to X-axis.

31. $\because a > b > c$ and given equations are

$$ax + by + cz = 0,$$
$$bx + cy + az = 0$$

and $$cx + ay + bz = 0$$

For non-trivial solution

$$\begin{vmatrix} a & b & c \\ b & c & a \\ c & a & b \end{vmatrix} = 0$$

$\Rightarrow \quad 3abc - (a^3 + b^3 + c^3) = 0$

$\therefore \quad a + b + c = 0$

If α and β be the roots of $at^2 + bt + c = 0$

$\therefore \quad \alpha + \beta = -\dfrac{b}{a}$ and $\alpha\beta = \dfrac{c}{a}$

and $D = b^2 - 4ac = (-a-c)^2 - 4ac = (a-c)^2 > 0$

For opposite sign $|\alpha - \beta| > 0$

$\Rightarrow \quad (\alpha - \beta)^2 > 0 \Rightarrow (\alpha + \beta)^2 - 4\alpha\beta > 0$

$\Rightarrow \quad \dfrac{b^2}{a^2} - \dfrac{4c}{a} > 0 \Rightarrow (-a-c)^2 - 4ac > 0$

$\Rightarrow \quad (a-c)^2 > 0$, true

Hence, the roots are real and have opposite sign.

32. Here, $\Delta = \begin{vmatrix} 1 & 1 & 1 \\ 1 & 3 & 2 \\ 1 & \lambda & 3 \end{vmatrix} = 1(9 - 2\lambda) - 1(3-2) + 1(\lambda - 3)$

$$= -(\lambda - 5)$$

$$\Delta_1 = \begin{vmatrix} 3 & 1 & 1 \\ 6 & 3 & 2 \\ b & \lambda & 3 \end{vmatrix} = 3(9 - 2\lambda) - 1(18 - 2b) + 1(6\lambda - 3b)$$

$$= -(b - 9)$$

$$\Delta_2 = \begin{vmatrix} 1 & 3 & 1 \\ 1 & 6 & 2 \\ 1 & b & 3 \end{vmatrix} = 1$$

$$(18 - 2b) - 3(3-2) + 1(b-6) = -(b-9)$$

and $\Delta_3 = \begin{vmatrix} 1 & 1 & 3 \\ 1 & 3 & 6 \\ 1 & \lambda & b \end{vmatrix} = 1$

$$(3b - 6\lambda) - 1(b-6) + 3(\lambda - 3) = (2b - 3\lambda - 3)$$

Aliter (a) for unique solution $\Delta \neq 0$

i.e. $\quad \lambda \neq 5, b \in R$

Aliter (b) for no solution

$\Delta = 0$ and atleast one of $\Delta_1, \Delta_2, \Delta_3$ is non-zero

$\therefore \quad \lambda = 5, b \neq 9$

Aliter (c) For infinite many solution

$$\Delta = \Delta_1 = \Delta_2 = \Delta_3 = 0$$

$\therefore \quad \lambda = 5, b = 9$

33. For non-trivial solutions

$$\begin{vmatrix} \lambda & \sin\alpha & \cos\alpha \\ 1 & \cos\alpha & \sin\alpha \\ -1 & \sin\alpha & -\cos\alpha \end{vmatrix} = 0$$

Expanding along C_1, we get

$\Rightarrow \quad \lambda(-\cos^2\alpha - \sin^2\alpha) - 1(-\sin\alpha\cos\alpha - \sin\alpha\cos\alpha)$
$\qquad -1(\sin^2\alpha - \cos^2\alpha) = 0$

$\Rightarrow \quad -\lambda + \sin 2\alpha + \cos 2\alpha = 0$

$\Rightarrow \quad \lambda = (\sin 2\alpha + \cos 2\alpha)$

$\because \quad -\sqrt{2} \le \sin 2\alpha + \cos 2\alpha \le \sqrt{2}$

$\therefore \quad -\sqrt{2} \le \lambda \le \sqrt{2}$

$\Rightarrow \quad S = [-\sqrt{2}, \sqrt{2}]$

Sol. (Q. Nos. 34 and 35)

$$\Delta = \begin{vmatrix} 1 & 1 & 1 \\ 1 & 2 & 3 \\ 1 & 3 & \lambda \end{vmatrix} = (\lambda - 5),$$

$$\Delta_1 = \begin{vmatrix} 5 & 1 & 1 \\ 9 & 2 & 3 \\ \mu & 3 & \lambda \end{vmatrix} = (\lambda + \mu - 18),$$

$$\Delta_2 = \begin{vmatrix} 1 & 5 & 1 \\ 1 & 9 & 3 \\ 1 & \mu & \lambda \end{vmatrix} = (4\lambda - 2\mu + 6)$$

and $\Delta_3 = \begin{vmatrix} 1 & 1 & 5 \\ 1 & 2 & 9 \\ 1 & 3 & \mu \end{vmatrix} = (\mu - 13)$

34. The system is smart, if

$$\Delta \neq 0 \Rightarrow \lambda \neq 5$$

or $\quad \Delta = \Delta_1 = \Delta_2 = \Delta_3 = 0$

$\Rightarrow \quad \lambda = 5$ and $\mu = 13$

35. The system is good, if

$$\Delta = \Delta_1 = \Delta_2 = \Delta_3 = 0$$

$\Rightarrow \quad \lambda = 5$ and $\mu = 13$

Sol. (Q. Nos. 36 and 37)

$$\because \begin{vmatrix} bc - a^2 & ca - b^2 & ab - c^2 \\ ca - b^2 & ab - c^2 & bc - a^2 \\ ab - c^2 & bc - a^2 & ca - b^2 \end{vmatrix} = \begin{vmatrix} a & b & c \\ b & c & a \\ c & a & b \end{vmatrix}^2 \quad \text{...(i)}$$

For $a = 1, b = x$ and $c = x^2$

$$\begin{vmatrix} x^3 - 1 & 0 & x - x^4 \\ 0 & x - x^4 & x^3 - 1 \\ x - x^4 & x^3 - 1 & 0 \end{vmatrix} = \begin{vmatrix} 1 & x & x^2 \\ x & x^2 & 1 \\ x^2 & 1 & x \end{vmatrix}^2$$

$\therefore \quad \Delta = 5^2 = 25$

36. $\because \Delta^2 = (25)^2 = 625$

Sum of digits of $\Delta^2 = 6 + 2 + 5 = 13$

37. From Eq. (i), we get

$$\begin{vmatrix} A & B & C \\ B & C & A \\ C & A & B \end{vmatrix} = \begin{vmatrix} a & b & c \\ b & c & a \\ c & a & b \end{vmatrix}^2$$

$$\Rightarrow \quad 49 = \begin{vmatrix} a & b & c \\ b & c & a \\ c & a & b \end{vmatrix}^2$$

$$\Rightarrow \quad \begin{vmatrix} a & b & c \\ b & c & a \\ c & a & b \end{vmatrix} = \pm 7$$

$$\Rightarrow \quad -(a^3 + b^3 + c^3 - 3abc) = \pm 7$$

$$\Rightarrow \quad a^3 + b^3 + c^3 - 3abc = \mp 7$$

$$\therefore \quad a^3 + b^3 + c^3 - 3abc = 7 \qquad [\because a + b + c > 0]$$

Sol. (Q. Nos. 38 and 39)

38. Let $x = \dfrac{\alpha - 1}{\alpha + 2} \Rightarrow \alpha = \dfrac{2x + 1}{1 - x}$

$\because$ α is a root of $x^3 + 2x^2 - x - 3 = 0$

$$\Rightarrow \quad \alpha^3 + 2\alpha^2 - \alpha - 3 = 0$$

$$\Rightarrow \quad \left(\frac{2x+1}{1-x}\right)^3 + 2\left(\frac{2x+1}{1-x}\right)^2 - \left(\frac{2x+1}{1-x}\right) - 3 = 0$$

$$\Rightarrow \quad x^3 + 6x^2 + 21x - 1 = 0 \qquad \text{...(i)}$$

Hence, $\dfrac{\alpha - 1}{\alpha + 2}, \dfrac{\beta - 1}{\beta + 2}$ and $\dfrac{\gamma - 1}{\gamma + 2}$ are the roots of Eq. (i), then

$$\frac{\alpha - 1}{\alpha + 2} + \frac{\beta - 1}{\beta + 2} + \frac{\gamma - 1}{\gamma + 2} = -6$$

$$\therefore \quad \left|\frac{\alpha - 1}{\alpha + 2} + \frac{\beta - 1}{\beta + 1} + \frac{\gamma - 1}{\gamma + 2}\right| = \frac{6}{1} = \frac{m}{n}$$

$$\Rightarrow \quad m = 6 \text{ and } n = 1,$$

then $\begin{vmatrix} m & n^2 \\ m - n & m + n \end{vmatrix} = \begin{vmatrix} 6 & 1 \\ 5 & 7 \end{vmatrix} = 42 - 5 = 37$

39. $\because \begin{vmatrix} a & b & b \\ b & a & b \\ b & b & a \end{vmatrix} = \begin{vmatrix} \alpha & \beta & \gamma \\ \beta & \gamma & \alpha \\ \gamma & \alpha & \beta \end{vmatrix}^2 = (\alpha^3 + \beta^3 + \gamma^3 - 3\alpha\beta\gamma)^2$

$$= (\alpha + \beta + \gamma)^2[(\alpha + \beta + \gamma)^2 - 3(\alpha\beta + \beta\gamma + \gamma\alpha)]^2$$

$$= (-2)^2[(-2)^2 + 3]^2$$

$$= 4 \times 49 = 196$$

Sol. (Q. Nos. 40 and 41)

Multiplying R_1, R_2, R_3 by a, b, c respectively and then taking a, b, c common from C_1, C_2, C_3, we get

$$\Delta = \begin{vmatrix} -bc & ab + ac & ac + ab \\ ab + bc & -ac & bc + ab \\ ac + bc & bc + ac & -ab \end{vmatrix}$$

Applying $C_2 \to C_2 - C_1$ and $C_3 \to C_3 - C_1$ and then taking $(ab + bc + ca)$ from C_2 and C_3, we get

$$\Delta = (ab + bc + ca)^2 \begin{vmatrix} -bc & 1 & 1 \\ ab + bc & -1 & 0 \\ ac + bc & 0 & -1 \end{vmatrix}$$

Applying $R_1 \to R_1 + R_2 + R_3$, we get

$$= (ab + bc + ca)^2 \begin{vmatrix} ab + bc + ca & 0 & 0 \\ ab + bc & -1 & 0 \\ ac + bc & 0 & -1 \end{vmatrix}$$

$$= (ab + bc + ca)^3 \begin{vmatrix} -1 & 0 \\ 0 & -1 \end{vmatrix}$$

$$= (ab + bc + ca)^3$$

Also, a, b and c are the roots of

$$x^3 - px^2 + qx - r = 0$$

$$\because \quad a + b + c = p, ab + bc + ca = q, abc = r$$

$$\Rightarrow \quad \Delta = q^3 \qquad \text{...(i)}$$

40. $\because$ AM $\geq$ GM

$$\Rightarrow \quad \left(\frac{ab + bc + ca}{3}\right) \geq (ab \cdot bc \cdot ca)^{1/3}$$

$$\Rightarrow \quad \frac{q}{3} \geq (r^2)^{1/3}$$

$$\Rightarrow \quad q^3 \geq 27r^2$$

$$\text{or} \quad \Delta \geq 27r^2 \qquad \text{[from Eq. (i)]}$$

41. $\because \quad \Delta = 27$

$$\Rightarrow \quad q^3 = 27$$

$$\therefore \quad q = 3$$

or $\quad ab + bc + ca = 3$ and $a^2 + b^2 + c^2 = 2$

$$\therefore \quad \sum a^2 b = a^2 b + a^2 c + b^2 a + b^2 c + c^2 a + c^2 b$$

$$= (a + b + c)(ab + bc + ca) - 3abc$$

$$= 3p - 3r = 6\sqrt{2} - 3r$$

$$[\because (a + b + c)^2 = a^2 + b^2 + c^2 + 2(ab + bc + ca)]$$

$$= 3(2\sqrt{2} - r) \qquad [\therefore p^2 = 8 \Rightarrow p = 2\sqrt{2}]$$

Sol. (Q. Nos. 42 and 43)

$$\because \quad f'(x) = \begin{vmatrix} 2ax & 2ax - 1 & 2ax + b + 1 \\ b & b + 1 & -1 \\ 2(ax + b) & 2ax + 2b + 1 & 2ax + b \end{vmatrix}$$

Applying $C_2 \to C_2 - C_1$ and $C_3 \to C_3 - C_1$, then

$$f'(x) = \begin{vmatrix} 2ax & -1 & b + 1 \\ b & 1 & -1 - b \\ 2ax + 2b & 1 & -b \end{vmatrix}$$

Applying $R_3 \to R_3 - R_1$, then

$$f'(x) = \begin{vmatrix} 2ax & -1 & b + 1 \\ b & 1 & -1 - b \\ 2b & 2 & -2b - 1 \end{vmatrix}$$

Applying $R_3 \to R_3 - 2R_2$, then

$$f'(x) = \begin{vmatrix} 2ax & -1 & b + 1 \\ b & 1 & -1 - b \\ 0 & 0 & 1 \end{vmatrix}$$

$$\Rightarrow \quad f'(x) = (2ax + b)$$

$$\therefore \quad f(x) = ax^2 + bx + c$$

$$f(0) = 2 \Rightarrow c = 2 \qquad \text{...(i)}$$

and $\quad f(1)=1 \Rightarrow a+b+2=1 \Rightarrow a+b=-1 \qquad \text{...(ii)}$

Also, $\quad f'\left(\frac{5}{2}\right)=0 \Rightarrow 5a+b=0 \qquad \text{...(iii)}$

From Eqs. (ii) and (iii), we get

$$a=\frac{1}{4} \text{ and } b=-\frac{5}{4}$$

$$\therefore \quad f(x)=\frac{x^2}{4}-\frac{5x}{4}+2$$

42. $\because f(2)+f(3)=\left(\frac{4}{4}-\frac{10}{4}+2\right)+\left(\frac{9}{4}-\frac{15}{4}+2\right)=1$

43. $\because f(x)+1=0 \Rightarrow \frac{x^2}{4}-\frac{5x}{4}+3=0$

$$\because \quad D=\frac{25}{16}-3$$

$$=-\frac{23}{16}<0$$

$\therefore$ Number of solutions = 0

Sol. (Q. Nos. 44 to 45)

Put $x=1$ on both sides, we get

$$\begin{vmatrix} 1 & 1 & 0 \\ 1 & 1 & 0 \\ \tan 1 & \sin^2 1 & \cos^2 1 \end{vmatrix}=a_0 \Rightarrow 0=a_0$$

we observe that

$$a_1=f'(1)$$

where $f(x)=\begin{vmatrix} x & e^{x-1} & (x-1)^3 \\ x-\ln x & \cos(x-1) & (x-1)^2 \\ \tan x & \sin^2 x & \cos^2 x \end{vmatrix}$

$$f'(x)=\begin{vmatrix} 1 & e^{x-1} & 3(x-1)^2 \\ x-\ln x & \cos(x-1) & (x-1)^2 \\ \tan x & \sin^2 x & \cos^2 x \end{vmatrix}+\begin{vmatrix} x & e^{x-1} & (x-1)^3 \\ 1-\frac{1}{x} & -\sin(x-1) & 2(x-1) \\ \tan x & \sin^2 x & \cos^2 x \end{vmatrix}+\begin{vmatrix} x & e^{x-1} & (x-1)^3 \\ x-\ln x & \cos(x-1) & (x-1)^2 \\ \sec^2 x & \sin 2x & -\sin 2x \end{vmatrix}$$

$$\Rightarrow f'(1)=\begin{vmatrix} 1 & 1 & 0 \\ 1 & 1 & 0 \\ \tan 1 & \sin^2 1 & \cos^2 1 \end{vmatrix}+\begin{vmatrix} 1 & 1 & 0 \\ 0 & 0 & 0 \\ \tan 1 & \sin^2 1 & \cos^2 1 \end{vmatrix}+\begin{vmatrix} 1 & 1 & 0 \\ 1 & 1 & 0 \\ \sec^2 1 & \sin 2 & -\sin 2 \end{vmatrix}$$

$$=0+0+0=0$$

$$\therefore \quad a_1=0$$

44. $\cos^{-1}(a_1)=\cos^{-1}(0)=\frac{\pi}{2}$

45. Let $P=\lim_{x\to a_0}(\sin x)^x=\lim_{x\to 0}(\sin x)^x$

$\therefore \ln p=\lim_{x\to 0} x\ln\sin x \qquad$ [form $(0\times\infty)$]

$$=\lim_{x\to 0}\frac{\ln\sin x}{1/x}=\lim_{x\to 0}\frac{\cot x}{-1/x^2} \qquad \text{[by } L' \text{ Hospital's Rule]}$$

$$=-\lim_{x\to 0}\frac{x^2}{\tan x}=-1\times 0=0$$

$$\therefore \quad P=e^0=1$$

Sol. (Q. Nos. 46 to 47)

Taking a,b,c common from R_1,R_2,R_3 respectively and then multiplying by a,b,c in C_1,C_2,C_3 respectively, we get

$$\Delta_n=\begin{vmatrix} a^2+n & b^2 & c^2 \\ a^2 & b^2+n & c^2 \\ a^2 & b^2 & c^2+n \end{vmatrix}$$

Applying $C_1 \to C_1+C_2+C_3$, then

$$\Delta_n=\begin{vmatrix} n+a^2+b^2+c^2 & b^2 & c^2 \\ n+a^2+b^2+c^2 & b^2+n & c^2 \\ n+a^2+b^2+c^2 & b^2 & c^2+n \end{vmatrix}$$

Applying $R_2 \to R_2-R_1$ and $R_3 \to R_3-R_1$, then

$$\Delta_n=\begin{vmatrix} n+a^2+b^2+c^2 & b^2 & c^2 \\ 0 & n & 0 \\ 0 & 0 & n \end{vmatrix}$$

$$\Delta_n=n^3+n^2(a^2+b^2+c^2) \qquad \text{...(i)}$$

Also, $a+b+c=\lambda$

$$3b=\lambda \qquad [\because a,b,c \text{ are in AP}]$$

$$\therefore \quad b=\frac{\lambda}{3}$$

Also, b is root of $x^3-\lambda x^2+11x-6=0$

$$\Rightarrow \quad b^3-\lambda b^2+11b-6=0$$

$$\Rightarrow \quad \frac{\lambda^3}{27}-\frac{\lambda^3}{9}+\frac{11\lambda}{3}-6=0$$

$$\Rightarrow \quad 2\lambda^3-99\lambda+162=0$$

$$\because \quad \lambda=6$$

Then, equation becomes $x^3-6x^2+11x-6=0$

$$\therefore \quad x=1,2,3$$

Let $\quad a=1, b=2$ and $c=3$

From Eq. (i), we get

$$\Delta_n=n^3+14n^2$$

$$\therefore \quad \sum_{n=1}^{n}\Delta_n=\frac{n(n+1)(3n^2+59n+28)}{12}$$

46. $\sum_{r=1}^{7}\Delta_r=\frac{7\cdot 8(147+59\cdot 7+28)}{12}=(14)^3$

47. $\because \quad \Delta_r=r^3+14r^2$

$$\therefore \quad \frac{27\Delta_r-\Delta_{3r}}{27r^2}=\frac{28}{3}$$

$$\Rightarrow \quad \sum_{r=1}^{30}\left(\frac{27\Delta_r-\Delta_{3r}}{27r^2}\right)=\frac{28}{3}\times 30=280$$

48. We have, $\begin{vmatrix} 3^2+k & 4^2 & 3^2+3+k \\ 4^2+k & 5^2 & 4^2+4+k \\ 5^2+k & 6^2 & 5^2+5+k \end{vmatrix}=0$

Applying $C_3 \to C_3 - C_1$, then

$$\begin{vmatrix} 3^2+k & 4^2 & 3 \\ 4^2+k & 5^2 & 4 \\ 5^2+k & 6^2 & 5 \end{vmatrix}=0$$

Applying $R_2 \to R_2 - R_1$ and $R_3 \to R_3 - R_1$, then

$$\begin{vmatrix} 9+k & 16 & 3 \\ 7 & 9 & 1 \\ 16 & 20 & 2 \end{vmatrix}=0$$

$\Rightarrow$ $(9+k)(18-20)-16(14-16)+3(140-144)=0$

$\Rightarrow$ $-18-2k+32-12=0$

$\Rightarrow$ $2k=2$

$\therefore$ $k=1$

Now, $\sqrt{2^k\sqrt{2^k\sqrt{2^k}}\ldots\infty}=(2^k)^{\frac{1}{2}+\frac{1}{4}+\frac{1}{8}+\ldots+\infty}$

$$=(2^k)^{\frac{\frac{1}{2}}{1-\frac{1}{2}}}=2^k=2^1=2$$

49. We have, $\begin{vmatrix} x-1 & -6 & 2 \\ -6 & x-2 & -4 \\ 2 & -4 & x-6 \end{vmatrix}=0$

Applying $C_2 \to C_2 + 3C_3$, then

$$\begin{vmatrix} x-1 & 0 & 2 \\ -6 & x-14 & -4 \\ 2 & 3x-22 & x-6 \end{vmatrix}=0$$

Expanding along R_1, then

$(x-1)\{(x-14)(x-6)+4(3x-22)\}-0+2\{-18x+132-2x+28\}=0$

$\Rightarrow$ $(x-1)(x^2-8x-4)+2(-20x+160)=0$

$\Rightarrow$ $x^3-9x^2-36x+324=0$

$\Rightarrow$ $(x-9)(x-6)(x+6)=0$

$\therefore$ $x=9$ or 6 or -6

Now, let $\alpha=9, \beta=6, \gamma=-6$

$\therefore$ $\dfrac{1}{\alpha}+\dfrac{1}{\beta}+\dfrac{1}{\gamma}=\dfrac{1}{9}+\dfrac{1}{6}-\dfrac{1}{6}=\dfrac{1}{9}$

$\therefore$ $\left(\dfrac{1}{\alpha}+\dfrac{1}{\beta}+\dfrac{1}{\gamma}\right)^{-1}=9$

50. We have, $\begin{vmatrix} x & e^{x-1} & (x-1)^3 \\ x-\ln x & \cos(x-1) & (x-1)^2 \\ \tan x & \sin^2 x & \cos^2 x \end{vmatrix}$

$$=a_0+a_1(x-1)+a_2(x-1)^2+\ldots+a_n(x-1)^n \qquad \ldots(i)$$

On putting $x=1$ in Eq. (i), we get

$$\begin{vmatrix} 1 & 1 & 0 \\ 1 & 1 & 0 \\ \tan 1 & \sin^2 1 & \cos^2 1 \end{vmatrix}=a_0+0+0+\ldots$$

$\therefore$ $a_0=0$ [$\because$ R_1 and R_2 are identical]

On differentiating Eq. (i) both sides w.r.t. x, then

$$\begin{vmatrix} 1 & e^{x-1} & 3(x-1)^2 \\ x-\ln x & \cos(x-1) & (x-1)^2 \\ \tan x & \sin^2 x & \cos^2 x \end{vmatrix}+\begin{vmatrix} x & e^{x-1} & (x-1)^3 \\ \left(1-\frac{1}{x}\right) & -\sin(x-1) & 2(x-1) \\ \tan x & \sin^2 x & \cos^2 x \end{vmatrix}+\begin{vmatrix} x & e^{x-1} & (x-1)^3 \\ x-\ln x & \cos(x-1) & (x-1)^2 \\ \sec^2 x & \sin 2x & -\sin 2x \end{vmatrix}$$

$$=0+a_1+2a_2(x-1)+3a_3(x-1)^2+\ldots+na_n(x-1)^{n-1}$$

Now, on putting $x=1$, we get

$$\begin{vmatrix} 1 & 1 & 0 \\ 1 & 1 & 0 \\ \tan 1 & \sin^2 1 & \cos^2 1 \end{vmatrix}+\begin{vmatrix} 1 & 1 & 0 \\ 0 & 0 & 0 \\ \tan 1 & \sin^2 1 & \cos^2 1 \end{vmatrix}+\begin{vmatrix} 1 & 1 & 0 \\ 1 & 1 & 0 \\ \sec^2 1 & \sin 2 & -\sin 2 \end{vmatrix}$$

$$=a_1+0+0+\ldots+0$$

$\therefore a_1=0+0+0=0$

Hence, $(2^{a_0}+3^{a_1})^{a_1+1}=(2^0+3^0)^{0+1}=(1+1)^1=2^1=2$

51. Given, $\begin{vmatrix} 1 & \cos\alpha & \cos\beta \\ \cos\alpha & 1 & \cos\gamma \\ \cos\beta & \cos\gamma & 1 \end{vmatrix}=\begin{vmatrix} 0 & \cos\alpha & \cos\beta \\ \cos\alpha & 0 & \cos\gamma \\ \cos\beta & \cos\gamma & 0 \end{vmatrix}$

$\Rightarrow$ $1(1-\cos^2\gamma)-\cos\alpha(\cos\alpha-\cos\beta\cos\gamma)+\cos\beta(\cos\gamma\cos\alpha-\cos\beta)$

$=0-\cos\alpha(0-\cos\beta\cos\gamma)+\cos\beta(\cos\gamma\cos\alpha-0)$

$\Rightarrow$ $1-\cos^2\alpha-\cos^2\beta-\cos^2\gamma+2\cos\alpha\cos\beta\cos\gamma=2\cos\alpha\cos\beta\cos\gamma$

$\Rightarrow$ $1-\cos^2\alpha-\cos^2\beta-\cos^2\gamma=0$

Hence, $\cos^2\alpha+\cos^2\beta+\cos^2\gamma=1$

52. $\because$ $f(a,b,c)=\begin{vmatrix} (b+c)^2 & a^2 & a^2 \\ b^2 & (c+a)^2 & b^2 \\ c^2 & c^2 & (a+b)^2 \end{vmatrix}$

Applying $C_2 \to C_2 - C_1$ and $C_3 \to C_3 - C_1$, then

$$f(a,b,c)=\begin{vmatrix} (b+c)^2 & a^2-(b+c)^2 & a^2-(b+c)^2 \\ b^2 & (c+a)^2-b^2 & 0 \\ c^2 & 0 & (a+b)^2-c^2 \end{vmatrix}$$

$$=\begin{vmatrix} (b+c)^2 & (a+b+c)(a-b-c) & (a+b+c)(a-b-c) \\ b^2 & (c+a+b)(c+a-b) & 0 \\ c^2 & 0 & (a+b+c)(a+b-c) \end{vmatrix}$$

$$=(a+b+c)^2\begin{vmatrix} (b+c)^2 & a-b-c & a-b-c \\ b^2 & c+a-b & 0 \\ c^2 & 0 & a+b-c \end{vmatrix}$$

Applying $R_1 \to R_1 - (R_2 + R_3)$, then

$$f(a, b, c) = (a+b+c)^2 \begin{vmatrix} 2bc & -2c & -2b \\ b^2 & c+a-b & 0 \\ c^2 & 0 & a+b-c \end{vmatrix}$$

Applying $C_2 \to C_2 + \frac{1}{b} C_1$ and $C_3 \to C_3 + \frac{1}{c} C_1$, then

$$f(a, b, c) = (a+b+c)^2 \begin{vmatrix} 2bc & 0 & 0 \\ b^2 & c+a & \frac{b^2}{c} \\ c^2 & \frac{c^2}{b} & a+b \end{vmatrix}$$

Expanding along R_1, then

$$f(a, b, c) = (a+b+c)^2 [2bc \{(c+a)(a+b) - bc\}]$$
$$= (a+b+c)^2 \{2bc(ac + bc + a^2 + ab - bc)\}$$
$$= 2bc(a+b+c)^2 a(a+b+c)$$
$$= 2abc(a+b+c)^3$$

We get, greatest integer $n \in N$ such that $(a+b+c)^n$ divides $f(a, b, c)$ is 3.

53. The system of equations has a non-trivial solution, then

$$\begin{vmatrix} 1 & -\sin\theta & -\cos\theta \\ -\cos\theta & 1 & -1 \\ -\sin\theta & -1 & 1 \end{vmatrix} = 0$$

Applying $C_3 \to C_3 + C_2$, then

$$\begin{vmatrix} 1 & -\sin\theta & -\sin\theta - \cos\theta \\ -\cos\theta & 1 & 0 \\ -\sin\theta & -1 & 0 \end{vmatrix} = 0$$

Expanding along C_3, then

$$(-\sin\theta - \cos\theta)(\cos\theta + \sin\theta) = 0$$

$\Rightarrow \quad (\sin\theta + \cos\theta)^2 = 0$

$\Rightarrow \quad \sin\theta + \cos\theta = 0$

$\Rightarrow \quad \sin\theta = -\cos\theta$

$\therefore \quad \tan\theta = -1$

$\Rightarrow \quad \theta = \frac{3\pi}{4} \qquad [\because \theta \in [0, \pi]]$

Hence, $\quad \frac{8\theta}{\pi} = 6$

54. Let $\quad \Delta = \begin{vmatrix} 1 & 1 & 1 & 1 \\ 1 & 2 & 3 & 4 \\ 1 & 3 & 6 & 10 \\ 1 & 4 & 10 & 20 \end{vmatrix}$

Applying $R_2 \to R_2 - R_1$, $R_3 \to R_3 - R_1$ and $R_4 \to R_4 - R_1$, then

$$\Delta = \begin{vmatrix} 1 & 1 & 1 & 1 \\ 0 & 1 & 2 & 3 \\ 0 & 2 & 5 & 9 \\ 0 & 3 & 9 & 19 \end{vmatrix}$$

Expanding along C_1, then $\Delta = \begin{vmatrix} 1 & 2 & 3 \\ 2 & 5 & 9 \\ 3 & 9 & 19 \end{vmatrix}$

Applying $R_2 \to R_2 - 2R_1$ and $R_3 \to R_3 - 3R_1$, then $= \begin{vmatrix} 1 & 2 & 3 \\ 0 & 1 & 3 \\ 0 & 3 & 10 \end{vmatrix}$

Expanding along C_1, we get

$$\Delta = 1 \begin{vmatrix} 1 & 3 \\ 3 & 10 \end{vmatrix} = 10 - 9 = 1$$

55. Let $\Delta = \begin{vmatrix} 1+a & 1 & 1 & 1 \\ 1 & 1+b & 1 & 1 \\ 1 & 1 & 1+c & 1 \\ 1 & 1 & 1 & 1+d \end{vmatrix}$

Taking a, b, c, d common from R_1, R_2, R_3 and R_4 respectively, then

$$\Delta = abcd \begin{vmatrix} 1+\frac{1}{a} & \frac{1}{a} & \frac{1}{a} & \frac{1}{a} \\ \frac{1}{b} & 1+\frac{1}{b} & \frac{1}{b} & \frac{1}{b} \\ \frac{1}{c} & \frac{1}{c} & 1+\frac{1}{c} & \frac{1}{c} \\ \frac{1}{d} & \frac{1}{d} & \frac{1}{d} & 1+\frac{1}{d} \end{vmatrix}$$

Applying $R_1 \to R_1 + R_2 + R_3 + R_4$ and taking $\left(1 + \frac{1}{a} + \frac{1}{b} + \frac{1}{c} + \frac{1}{d}\right)$ common, we get

$$\Delta = abcd \left(1 + \frac{1}{a} + \frac{1}{b} + \frac{1}{c} + \frac{1}{d}\right) \begin{vmatrix} 1 & 1 & 1 & 1 \\ \frac{1}{b} & 1+\frac{1}{b} & \frac{1}{b} & \frac{1}{b} \\ \frac{1}{c} & \frac{1}{c} & 1+\frac{1}{c} & \frac{1}{c} \\ \frac{1}{d} & \frac{1}{d} & \frac{1}{d} & 1+\frac{1}{d} \end{vmatrix}$$

Applying $C_2 \to C_2 - C_1$, $C_3 \to C_3 - C_1$ and $C_4 \to C_4 - C_1$, then

$$\Delta = abcd \left(1 + \frac{1}{a} + \frac{1}{b} + \frac{1}{c} + \frac{1}{d}\right) \begin{vmatrix} 1 & 0 & 0 & 0 \\ \frac{1}{b} & 1 & 0 & 0 \\ \frac{1}{c} & 0 & 1 & 0 \\ \frac{1}{d} & 0 & 0 & 1 \end{vmatrix}$$

$$= abcd \left(1 + \frac{1}{a} + \frac{1}{b} + \frac{1}{c} + \frac{1}{d}\right) 1 \cdot 1 \cdot 1$$
$$= abcd + (bcd + acd + abd + abc)$$
$$= \sigma_4 + \sigma_3$$
$$= \frac{16}{1} + \left(-\frac{8}{1}\right) = 8$$

56. Given, $\begin{vmatrix} 1+a & 1 & 1 \\ 1+b & 1+2b & 1 \\ 1+c & 1+c & 1+3c \end{vmatrix} = 0$

Taking a, b, c common from R_1, R_2 and R_3 respectively, then

$$abc \begin{vmatrix} 1+\frac{1}{a} & \frac{1}{a} & \frac{1}{a} \\ 1+\frac{1}{b} & 2+\frac{1}{b} & \frac{1}{b} \\ 1+\frac{1}{c} & 1+\frac{1}{c} & 3+\frac{1}{c} \end{vmatrix} = 0$$

Applying $R_1 \to R_1 + R_2 + R_3$ and taking $\left(3+\frac{1}{a}+\frac{1}{b}+\frac{1}{c}\right)$ common, we get

$$abc\left(3+\frac{1}{a}+\frac{1}{b}+\frac{1}{c}\right) \begin{vmatrix} 1 & 1 & 1 \\ 1+\frac{1}{b} & 2+\frac{1}{b} & \frac{1}{b} \\ 1+\frac{1}{c} & 1+\frac{1}{c} & 3+\frac{1}{c} \end{vmatrix} = 0$$

Applying $C_2 \to C_2 - C_1$ and $C_3 \to C_3 - C_1$, then

$$abc\left(3+\frac{1}{a}+\frac{1}{b}+\frac{1}{c}\right) \begin{vmatrix} 1 & 0 & 0 \\ 1+\frac{1}{2} & 1 & -1 \\ 1+\frac{1}{c} & 0 & 2 \end{vmatrix} = 0$$

Expanding along R_1, we get

$$2\,abc\left(3+\frac{1}{a}+\frac{1}{b}+\frac{1}{c}\right) = 0$$

$\because \quad a \neq 0, b \neq 0, c \neq 0$

$\therefore \quad \frac{1}{a}+\frac{1}{b}+\frac{1}{c} = -3$ or $|a^{-1}+b^{-1}+c^{-1}| = 3$

57. Given equations

$$ax + hy + g = 0, \quad \text{...(i)}$$

$$hx + by + f = 0 \quad \text{...(ii)}$$

and $ax^2 + 2hxy + by^2 + 2gx + 2fy + c + \lambda = 0$ ...(iii)

Eq. (iii), can be written as

$$x(ax + hy + g) + y(hx + by + f) + gx + fy + c + \lambda = 0$$

$\Rightarrow \quad x \cdot 0 + y \cdot 0 + gx + fy + c + \lambda = 0$ [from Eqs. (i) and (ii)]

$\Rightarrow \quad gx + fy + c + \lambda = 0$ ...(iv)

According to the question Eqs. (i), (ii) and (iii) has unique solution. So, Eqs. (i), (ii) and (iv) has unique solution,

then $\begin{vmatrix} a & h & g \\ h & b & f \\ g & f & c+\lambda \end{vmatrix} = 0$

$\Rightarrow a(bc + b\lambda - f^2) - h(ch + h\lambda - fg) + g(hf - bg)$

$\Rightarrow (abc + 2fgh - af^2 - bg^2 - ch^2) = \lambda(h^2 - ab)$

or $\quad \frac{abc + 2fgh - af^2 - bg^2 - ch^2}{h^2 - ab} = \lambda$

According to the question, $\lambda = 8$

58. $\begin{vmatrix} (1+x)^{11} & (1+x)^{12} & (1+x)^{13} \\ (1+x)^{21} & (1+x)^{22} & (1+x)^{23} \\ (1+x)^{31} & (1+x)^{32} & (1+x)^{33} \end{vmatrix} = A_0 + A_1x + A_2x^2 + \ldots$ [let]

On differentiating both sides w.r.t. x and then put $x = 0$, we get

$$\begin{vmatrix} 11 & 12 & 13 \\ 1 & 1 & 1 \\ 1 & 1 & 1 \end{vmatrix} + \begin{vmatrix} 1 & 1 & 1 \\ 21 & 22 & 23 \\ 1 & 1 & 1 \end{vmatrix} + \begin{vmatrix} 1 & 1 & 1 \\ 1 & 1 & 1 \\ 31 & 32 & 33 \end{vmatrix} = 0 + A_1 + 0 + 0 + \ldots$$

$\Rightarrow \quad 0 + 0 + 0 = A_1$

$\therefore \quad A_1 = 0$

$\therefore \quad$ Coefficient of x in $f(x) = 0$

59. For no solution or infinitely many solutions

$$\begin{vmatrix} \alpha & 1 & 1 \\ 1 & \alpha & 1 \\ 1 & 1 & \alpha \end{vmatrix} = 0$$

Applying $C_1 \to C_1 + C_2 + C_3$, then

$$\begin{vmatrix} \alpha+2 & 1 & 1 \\ \alpha+2 & \alpha & 1 \\ \alpha+2 & 1 & \alpha \end{vmatrix} = 0$$

Applying $R_1 \to R_2 - R_1$ and $R_3 \to R_3 - R_1$, then

$$\begin{vmatrix} \alpha+2 & 1 & 1 \\ 0 & \alpha-1 & 0 \\ 0 & 0 & \alpha-1 \end{vmatrix} = 0 \Rightarrow (\alpha-1)^2(\alpha+2) = 0$$

$\therefore \quad \alpha = 1, -2$

For $\alpha = 1$, clearly there an infinitely many solutions and when we put $\alpha = -2$ in given system of equations and adding them together LHS $\neq$ RHS. i.e., no solution.

60. $\because a_1, a_2, a_3, \ldots$ are in GP.

$\therefore$ Using $a_n = a_1 r^{n-1}$, we get the given determinant, as

$$\begin{vmatrix} \log(a_1r^{n-1}) & \log(a_1r^n) & \log(a_1r^{n+1}) \\ \log(a_1r^{n+2}) & \log(a_1r^{n+3}) & \log(a_1r^{n+4}) \\ \log(a_1r^{n+5}) & \log(a_1r^{n+6}) & \log(a_1r^{n+7}) \end{vmatrix}$$

Applying $C_2 \to C_2 - C_1$ and $C_3 \to C_3 - C_1$ and

using $\log m - \log n = \log\left(\frac{m}{n}\right)$, we get

$$\begin{vmatrix} \log(a_1r^{n-1}) & \log r & 2\log r \\ \log(a_1r^{n+2}) & \log r & 2\log r \\ \log(a_1r^{n+5}) & \log r & 2\log r \end{vmatrix} = 0$$

[$\because C_2$ and C_3 are proportional]

$\therefore \Delta = 0$

61. $\because \begin{vmatrix} 3 & 1+f(1) & 1+f(2) \\ 1+f(1) & 1+f(2) & 1+f(3) \\ 1+f(2) & 1+f(3) & 1+f(4) \end{vmatrix}$

$$= \begin{vmatrix} 1+1+1 & 1+\alpha+\beta & 1+\alpha^2+\beta^2 \\ 1+\alpha+\beta & 1+\alpha^2+\beta^2 & 1+\alpha^3+\beta^3 \\ 1+\alpha^2+\beta^2 & 1+\alpha^3+\beta^3 & 1+\alpha^4+\beta^4 \end{vmatrix}$$

$$= \begin{vmatrix} 1 & 1 & 1 \\ 1 & \alpha & \beta \\ 1 & \alpha^2 & \beta^2 \end{vmatrix} \times \begin{vmatrix} 1 & 1 & 1 \\ 1 & \alpha & \beta \\ 1 & \alpha^2 & \beta^2 \end{vmatrix} = \begin{vmatrix} 1 & 1 & 1 \\ 1 & \alpha & \beta \\ 1 & \alpha^2 & \beta^2 \end{vmatrix}^2$$

$$= \{(1-\alpha)(1-\beta)(\alpha-\beta)\}^2 = (1-\alpha)^2(1-\beta)^2(\alpha-\beta)^2$$

So, $k = 1 \Rightarrow k^2 = 1$

62. Applying $R_2 \to R_2 - R_1$ and $R_3 \to R_3 - R_1$, then

$$\begin{vmatrix} (1+\alpha)^2 & (1+2\alpha)^2 & (1+3\alpha)^2 \\ 2\alpha+3 & 4\alpha+3 & 6\alpha+3 \\ 4\alpha+8 & 8\alpha+8 & 12\alpha+8 \end{vmatrix} = -512\alpha$$

Applying $R_3 \to R_3 - 2R_2$, then

$$\begin{vmatrix} (1+\alpha)^2 & (1+2\alpha)^2 & (1+3\alpha)^2 \\ 2\alpha+3 & 4\alpha+3 & 6\alpha+3 \\ 2 & 2 & 2 \end{vmatrix} = -512\alpha$$

Applying $C_2 \to C_2 - \frac{1}{2}(C_1 + C_3)$, then

$$\begin{vmatrix} (1+\alpha)^2 & -\alpha^2 & (1+3\alpha)^2 \\ 2\alpha+3 & 0 & 6\alpha+3 \\ 2 & 0 & 2 \end{vmatrix} = -512\alpha$$

$\Rightarrow \quad \alpha^2(4\alpha + 6 - 12\alpha - 6) = -512\alpha$

$\Rightarrow \quad -8\alpha^3 = -512\alpha$

$\Rightarrow \quad -8\alpha^3 + 512\alpha = 0$

$\Rightarrow \quad -8\alpha(\alpha^2 - 64) = 0$

$\Rightarrow \quad \alpha = 0, \alpha = \pm 4$

$\Rightarrow \quad \alpha^2 = 0, 16, 16$

$\therefore$ Sum = 0 + 16 + 16 = 32

63. $\because \Delta = \begin{bmatrix} 1 & 1 & 1 \\ 1 & a & 1 \\ a & b & 1 \end{bmatrix} = 1(a-b) - 1(1-a) + 1(b-a^2) = -(a-1)^2$

$\Delta_1 = \begin{bmatrix} 1 & 1 & 1 \\ 1 & a & 1 \\ 0 & b & 1 \end{bmatrix} = 1(a-b) - 1(1) + 1(b) = (a-1)$

$\Delta_2 = \begin{bmatrix} 1 & 1 & 1 \\ 1 & 1 & 1 \\ a & 0 & 1 \end{bmatrix} = 1(1) - 1(1-a) + 1(0-a) = 0$

and $\Delta_3 = \begin{bmatrix} 1 & 1 & 1 \\ 1 & a & 1 \\ a & b & 0 \end{bmatrix} = 1(-b) - 1(-a) + 1(b-a^2) = -a(a-1)$

For $a = 1$, $\Delta = \Delta_1 = \Delta_2 = \Delta_3 = 0$

and for $b = 1$ only

$$x + y + z = 1$$
$$x + y + z = 1$$
$$x + y + z = 0$$

i.e. no solution ($\because$ RHS are not equal)

Hence, for no solution $b = 1$ only.

Thus, $a + b = 1 + 1 = 2$

64. (A) $\to$ (p, r); (B) $\to$ (p, r); (C) $\to$ (p, q, s); (D) $\to$ (t)

(A) Using $a^2 + b^2 + c^2 = 0$, we get

$$\Delta = \begin{vmatrix} b^2+c^2 & ab & ac \\ ab & c^2+a^2 & bc \\ ac & bc & a^2+b^2 \end{vmatrix}$$

$$= \begin{vmatrix} -a^2 & ab & ac \\ ab & -b^2 & bc \\ ac & bc & -c^2 \end{vmatrix}$$

$$= abc \begin{vmatrix} -a & a & a \\ b & -b & b \\ c & c & -c \end{vmatrix}$$

[taking a, b, c common from C_1, C_2, C_3 respectively]

Applying $C_2 \to C_2 + C_1$ and $C_3 \to C_3 + C_1$, then

$$\Delta = abc \begin{vmatrix} -a & 0 & 0 \\ b & 0 & 2b \\ c & 2c & 0 \end{vmatrix}$$

$= (abc)(-a)(-4bc)$

$= 4a^2b^2c^2$

$\therefore \quad \lambda = 4$

(B) Let $\quad \Delta = \begin{vmatrix} a & a+b & a+b+c \\ 2a & 5a+2b & 7a+5b+2c \\ 3a & 7a+3b & 9a+7b+3c \end{vmatrix}$

Applying $R_2 \to R_2 - 2R_1$ and $R_3 \to R_3 - 3R_1$, then

$$\Delta = \begin{vmatrix} a & a+b & a+b+c \\ 0 & 3a & 5a+3b \\ 0 & 4a & 6a+4b \end{vmatrix}$$

$$= a \begin{vmatrix} 3a & 5a+3b \\ 4a & 6a+4b \end{vmatrix}$$

$= a(18a^2 + 12ab - 20a^2 - 12ab)$

$= -2a^3$

$= -1024$ [given]

$\Rightarrow \quad a^3 = 512 = 8^3$

$\therefore \quad a = 8$

(C) Let $\Delta(x) = \begin{vmatrix} x-1 & 2x^2-5 & x^3-1 \\ 2x^2+5 & 2x+2 & x^3+3 \\ x^3-1 & x+1 & 3x^2-2 \end{vmatrix}$ ...(i)

According to the question,

$\Delta(x) = (x^2 - 1)P(x) + ax + b$

$\therefore$ $\Delta(1) = a + b$ and $\Delta(-1) = -a + b$ ...(ii)

From Eq. (i), we get

$$\Delta(1) = \begin{vmatrix} 0 & -3 & 0 \\ 7 & 4 & 4 \\ 0 & 2 & 1 \end{vmatrix} = 3(7 - 0) = 21$$

$$\text{and } \Delta(-1) = \begin{vmatrix} -2 & -3 & -2 \\ 7 & 0 & 2 \\ -2 & 0 & 1 \end{vmatrix} = 3(7+4) = 33$$

From Eq. (ii), $a + b = 21$ and $-a + b = 33$, we get

$$a = -6, b = 27$$

$\therefore \quad 4a + 2b = -24 + 54 = 30$

(D) Applying $C_1 \to C_1 - C_2$, we get

$$\Delta = \begin{vmatrix} 4 & (a^x - a^{-x})^2 & 1 \\ 4 & (a^y - a^{-y})^2 & 1 \\ 4 & (a^z - a^{-z})^2 & 1 \end{vmatrix} \quad [\text{using } (a+b)^2 - (a-b)^2 = 4ab]$$

$$= 4\begin{vmatrix} 1 & (a^x - a^{-x})^2 & 1 \\ 1 & (a^y - a^{-y})^2 & 1 \\ 1 & (a^z - a^{-z})^2 & 1 \end{vmatrix}$$

$= 4 \times 0 = 0 \quad [\because C_1$ and C_3 are identical column]

65. (A) → (p, s, t); (B) → (r, s); (C) → (p, q, s); (D) → (p)

(A) $\because \quad \Delta = \begin{vmatrix} 1 & 1 & 1 \\ f_1(x_1) & f_1(x_2) & f_1(x_3) \\ f_2(x_1) & f_2(x_2) & f_2(x_3) \end{vmatrix} = \begin{vmatrix} 1 & 1 & 1 \\ f_1(2) & f_1(3) & f_1(5) \\ f_2(2) & f_2(3) & f_2(5) \end{vmatrix}$

$$= \begin{vmatrix} 1 & 1 & 1 \\ 2+a_1 & 3+a_1 & 5+a_1 \\ 4+2b_1+b_2 & 9+3b_1+b_2 & 25+5b_1+b_2 \end{vmatrix}$$

Applying $C_2 \to C_2 - C_1$ and $C_3 \to C_3 - C_1$, then

$$\Delta = \begin{vmatrix} 1 & 0 & 0 \\ 2+a_1 & 1 & 3 \\ 4+2b_1+b_2 & 5+b_1 & 21+3b \end{vmatrix}$$

$$= \begin{vmatrix} 1 & 3 \\ 5+b_1 & 21+3b_1 \end{vmatrix}$$

$= 21 + 3b_1 - 15 - 3b_1$

$= 6$

(B) $\because f(x) = \begin{vmatrix} 1 & b_1 & a_1 \\ 1 & b_1 & 2a_1 - x \\ 1 & 2b_1 - x & a_1 \end{vmatrix}$

Applying $R_2 \to R_2 - R_1$ and $R_3 \to R_3 - R_1$, then

$$f(x) = \begin{vmatrix} 1 & b_1 & a_1 \\ 0 & 0 & a_1 - x \\ 0 & b_1 - x & 0 \end{vmatrix}$$

$= -(a_1 - x)(b_1 - x)$

$= -x^2 + (a_1 + b_1)x - a_1 b_1$

Minimum value of $f(x) = -\dfrac{D}{4a}$

$$= -\frac{(a_1+b_1)^2 - 4a_1b_1}{4(-1)}$$

$$= \frac{(a_1 - b_1)^2}{4}$$

$$= \frac{36}{4} = 9$$

(C) $\because f(x)$ is a polynomial of degree atmost 6 in x.

If $f(x) = a_0 + a_1x + a_2x^2 + a_3x^3 + a_4x^4 + a_5x^5 + a_6x^6$

$\Rightarrow \lambda = a_1 = f'(0)$

$$= \begin{vmatrix} 1 & 1 & 0 \\ 1 & 0 & 1 \\ 1 & 1 & 8 \end{vmatrix} + \begin{vmatrix} -2 & -2 & 0 \\ -1 & 0 & 1 \\ 0 & 2 & 8 \end{vmatrix} + \begin{vmatrix} -2 & 1 & 0 \\ -1 & 0 & 3 \\ 0 & 1 & 12 \end{vmatrix}$$

$= -8 - 12 + 18 = -2$

$\therefore \quad |\lambda| = 2$

(D) $f(x) = \begin{vmatrix} 1 & \cos(\beta - \alpha) & \cos(\gamma - \alpha) \\ \cos(\alpha - \beta) & 1 & \cos(\gamma - \beta) \\ \cos(\alpha - \gamma) & \cos(\beta - \gamma) & 1 \end{vmatrix}$

$$= \begin{vmatrix} \cos^2\alpha + \sin^2\alpha & \cos\beta\cos\alpha + \sin\beta\sin\alpha & \cos\alpha\cos\gamma + \sin\alpha\sin\gamma \\ (\cos\alpha\cos\beta + \sin\alpha\sin\beta) & \cos^2\beta + \sin^2\beta & \cos\beta\cos\gamma + \sin\beta\sin\gamma \\ (\cos\alpha\cos\gamma + \sin\alpha\sin\gamma) & \cos\beta\cos\gamma + \sin\beta\sin\gamma & \cos^2\gamma + \sin^2\gamma \end{vmatrix}$$

$$= \begin{vmatrix} \cos\alpha & \sin\alpha & 0 \\ \cos\beta & \sin\beta & 0 \\ \cos\gamma & \sin\gamma & 0 \end{vmatrix} \cdot \begin{vmatrix} \cos\alpha & \sin\alpha & 0 \\ \cos\beta & \sin\beta & 0 \\ \cos\gamma & \sin\gamma & 0 \end{vmatrix}$$

$= 0$

66. (A) → (r); (B) → (r, t); (C) → (p, q, s); (D) → (p)

(A) Let $\quad f(x) = \begin{vmatrix} x^2+3x & x-1 & x+3 \\ x^2+1 & 2+3x & x-3 \\ x^2-3 & x+4 & 3x \end{vmatrix}$

$$f(x) = ax^4 + bx^3 + cx^2 + dx + e \quad \text{...(i)}$$

$\therefore \quad e = f(0) = \begin{vmatrix} 0 & -1 & 3 \\ 1 & 2 & -3 \\ -3 & 4 & 0 \end{vmatrix}$

$= 0 + 1(0 - 9) + 3(4 + 6)$

$= 21$

Dividing both sides of Eq. (i) by x^4 i.e. C_1 by x^2, C_2 by x and C_3 by x and then taking $\lim\limits_{x \to \infty}$, we get

$$a = \begin{vmatrix} 1 & 1 & 1 \\ 1 & 3 & 1 \\ 1 & 1 & 3 \end{vmatrix} = 1(8) - 1(2) + 1(-2) = 4$$

Hence, $e + a = 25$

(B) Let $f(x) = \begin{vmatrix} x-1 & 5x & 7 \\ x^2-1 & x-1 & 8 \\ 2x & 3x & 0 \end{vmatrix} = ax^3 + bx^2 + cx + d \quad \text{...(i)}$

$$\therefore \quad c = f'(0) = \begin{vmatrix} 1 & 0 & 7 \\ 0 & -1 & 8 \\ 2 & 0 & 0 \end{vmatrix} + \begin{vmatrix} -1 & 5 & 7 \\ -1 & 1 & 8 \\ 0 & 3 & 0 \end{vmatrix} + \begin{vmatrix} -1 & 0 & 0 \\ -1 & -1 & 0 \\ 0 & 0 & 0 \end{vmatrix}$$

$= 2(0 + 7) - 3(-8 + 7) + 0$

$= 17$

Dividing both sides of Eq. (i) by x^3 i.e. C_1 by x^2, C_2 by x and taking $\lim_{x\to\infty}$, we get

$$a = \begin{vmatrix} 0 & 5 & 7 \\ \vdots & & \\ 1 & \cdots 1 \cdots & 8 \\ \vdots & & \\ 0 & 3 & 0 \end{vmatrix} = -1(0-21) = 21$$

Hence, $c + a - 3 = 35$

(C) Let $g(x) = \begin{vmatrix} x^3+4x & x+3 & x-2 \\ x-2 & 5x & x-1 \\ x-3 & x+2 & 4x \end{vmatrix}$

$$= ax^5 + bx^4 + cx^3 + dx^2 + ex + f$$

$$\therefore \quad f = g(0) = \begin{vmatrix} 0 & 3 & -2 \\ -2 & 0 & -1 \\ -3 & 2 & 0 \end{vmatrix}$$

$$= 0 - 3(0-3) - 2(-4-0) = 17$$

and $e = g'(0) = \begin{vmatrix} 4 & 3 & -2 \\ 1 & 0 & -1 \\ 1 & 2 & 0 \end{vmatrix} + \begin{vmatrix} 0 & 1 & -2 \\ -2 & 5 & -1 \\ -3 & 1 & 0 \end{vmatrix} + \begin{vmatrix} 0 & 3 & 1 \\ -2 & 0 & 1 \\ -3 & 2 & 4 \end{vmatrix}$

$$= 1 - 23 + 11 = -11$$

Hence, $f + e = 17 - 11 = 6$

(D) $\Delta = \begin{vmatrix} 1+a^2-b^2 & 2ab & -2b \\ 2ab & 1-a^2+b^2 & 2a \\ 2b & -2a & 1-a^2-b^2 \end{vmatrix}$

Applying $C_1 \to C_1 + (-b)C_3$ and $C_2 \to C_2 + aC_3$, we get

$$\Delta = \begin{vmatrix} 1+a^2+b^2 & 0 & -2b \\ 0 & 1+a^2+b^2 & 2a \\ b(1+a^2+b^2) & -a(1+a^2+b^2) & 1-a^2-b^2 \end{vmatrix}$$

$$= (1+a^2+b^2)^2 \begin{vmatrix} 1 & 0 & -2b \\ 0 & 1 & 2a \\ b & -a & 1-a^2-b^2 \end{vmatrix}$$

$$= (1+a^2+b^2)^2 \begin{vmatrix} 1 & 0 & 0 \\ 0 & 1 & 2a \\ b & -a & 1-a^2+b^2 \end{vmatrix}$$

[applying $C_3 \to C_3 + 2bC_1$]

$$= (1+a^2+b^2)^3$$

On comparing, we get

$$p = 1, q = 3$$

Then, $p + q = 1 + 3 = 4$, which is divisible by 2.

67. Given system of linear equations,

$$x + 2y + z = 7$$
$$x + 0 \cdot y + \alpha z = 11$$
$$2x - 3y + \beta z = \gamma$$

Now, $\Delta = \begin{vmatrix} 1 & 2 & 1 \\ 1 & 0 & \alpha \\ 2 & -3 & \beta \end{vmatrix} = 0$

$\Rightarrow \quad 3\alpha - 2(\beta - 2\alpha) - 3 = 0$

$\Rightarrow \quad 7\alpha - 2\beta = 3 \Rightarrow \beta = \frac{1}{2}(7\alpha - 3)$

Also, $\Delta x = \begin{vmatrix} 7 & 2 & 1 \\ 11 & 0 & \alpha \\ \gamma & -3 & \beta \end{vmatrix}$, $\Delta y = \begin{vmatrix} 1 & 7 & 1 \\ 1 & 11 & \alpha \\ 2 & \gamma & \beta \end{vmatrix}$

and $\quad \Delta z = \begin{vmatrix} 1 & 2 & 7 \\ 1 & 0 & 11 \\ 2 & -3 & \gamma \end{vmatrix}$

Now, $\Delta x = 21\alpha - 2(11\beta - \alpha\gamma) - 33$

$\Rightarrow \quad \Delta x = 21\alpha - 22\beta + 2\alpha\gamma - 33$

and $\quad \Delta y = 11\beta - \alpha\gamma - 7(\beta - 2\alpha) + \gamma - 22$

$\Rightarrow \quad \Delta y = 14\alpha + 4\beta + \gamma - \alpha\gamma - 22$

and $\quad \Delta z = 33 - 2(\gamma - 22) + 7(-3) = 33 - 2\gamma + 44 - 21 = 56 - 2\gamma$

i.e. if $\gamma = 28$, then $\Delta z = 0$

Options checking

(P) If $\beta = \frac{1}{2}(7\alpha - 3)$ and $\gamma = 2\delta$, then $\Delta = 0$, $\Delta x = \Delta y = \Delta z = 0$.

So, infinitely many solutions.

Also, $x = 11$, $y = -2$ and $z = 0$ will satisfy all the three given equations. Hence, it is a solution.

(Q) If $\beta = \frac{1}{2}(7\alpha - 3)$ and $\gamma \neq 28$, then $\Delta = 0$ but $\Delta z \neq 0$

Hence, no solution.

(R) If $\beta \neq \frac{1}{2}(7\alpha - 3)$, $\alpha = 1$ and $\gamma \neq 28$, then $\Delta \neq 0$ and $\Delta z \neq 0$.

Hence, a unique solution.

(S) If $\beta \neq \frac{1}{2}(7\alpha - 3)$, $\alpha = 1$, $\gamma = 28$, then $\Delta \neq 0$, $\Delta x \neq 0$, $\Delta y \neq 0$ but $\Delta z = 0$

Hence, a unique solution.

$x = 11$, $y = -2$ and $z = 0$ will satisfy all the three equations.

So, finally option (a) is correct.

68. Given that

$$f(\theta) = \frac{1}{2}\begin{vmatrix} 1 & \sin\theta & 1 \\ -\sin\theta & 1 & \sin\theta \\ -1 & -\sin\theta & 1 \end{vmatrix} + \begin{vmatrix} \sin\pi & \cos\left(\theta + \frac{\pi}{4}\right) & \tan\left(\theta - \frac{\pi}{4}\right) \\ \sin\left(\theta - \frac{\pi}{4}\right) & -\cos\frac{\pi}{2} & \log_e\left(\frac{4}{\pi}\right) \\ \cot\left(\theta + \frac{\pi}{4}\right) & \log_e\left(\frac{\pi}{4}\right) & \tan\pi \end{vmatrix}$$

Here, $\cos\left(\theta + \frac{\pi}{4}\right) = -\sin\left(\theta - \frac{\pi}{4}\right)$,

$$\tan\left(\theta - \frac{\pi}{4}\right) = -\cot\left(\theta - \frac{\pi}{4}\right),$$

$$\log_e\left(\frac{4}{\pi}\right) = -\log_e\left(\frac{\pi}{4}\right)$$

and $\quad \sin\pi = -\cos\frac{\pi}{2} = \tan\pi = 0$

So, the second part is skew-symmetric matrix of odd order.
So, its determinant is zero.

Thus, $f(\theta) = \frac{1}{2}\{(1+\sin^2\theta) - \sin\theta\,(0) + 1\,(1+\sin^2\theta)\}$

$\Rightarrow \quad f(\theta) = 1 + \sin^2\theta$

Given, $g(\theta) = \sqrt{f(\theta) - 1} + \sqrt{f\left(\frac{\pi}{2} - \theta\right) - 1}$

$= \sqrt{1+\sin^2\theta - 1} + \sqrt{1 + \cos^2\theta - 1}$

$\Rightarrow \quad g(\theta) = |\sin\theta| + |\cos\theta|$

Thus, clearly, maximum and minimum value of $g(\theta)$ is $\sqrt{2}$ and 1, respectively.

Since, given $p(x)$ be a quadratic polynomial whose roots are maximum and minimum value of the function $g(\theta)$, then $p(x) = a(x-\sqrt{2})(x-1)$, where $a \in R - \{0\}$

But given $p(2) = 2 - \sqrt{2}$, then $a = 1$

$\therefore \quad p(x) = (x - \sqrt{2})(x-1)$

Now, $p\left(\frac{3+\sqrt{2}}{4}\right) = \left(\frac{3-3\sqrt{2}}{4}\right)\left(\frac{\sqrt{2}-1}{4}\right) < 0$

and $p\left(\frac{1+3\sqrt{2}}{4}\right) = \left(\frac{1-\sqrt{2}}{4}\right)\left(\frac{3\sqrt{2}-3}{4}\right) < 0$

and $p\left(\frac{5\sqrt{2}-1}{4}\right) = \left(\frac{\sqrt{2}-1}{4}\right)\left(\frac{5\sqrt{2}-5}{4}\right) > 0$

and $p\left(\frac{5-\sqrt{2}}{4}\right) = \left(\frac{5-5\sqrt{2}}{4}\right)\left(\frac{1-\sqrt{2}}{4}\right) > 0$

69. Let p, q and r be non-zero real number that are, respectively the 10th, 100th, 1000th terms of an Harmonic progression.

So, $p = \frac{1}{a+9d}, q = \frac{1}{a+99d}, r = \frac{1}{a+999d}$

Given, system of linear equations is,

$$x + y + z = 1 \qquad \text{...(i)}$$

$$10x + 100y + 1000z = 0 \qquad \text{...(ii)}$$

$$qrx + pry + pqz = 0 \qquad \text{...(iii)}$$

Now, Eq. (iii) can be written as,

$$\frac{x}{p} + \frac{y}{q} + \frac{z}{r} = 0 \qquad [\because p, q, r \neq 0]$$

Putting the values of p, q and r, we get

$$(a+9d)x + (a+99d)y + (a+999d)z = 0$$

Now, $\Delta = \begin{vmatrix} 1 & 1 & 1 \\ 10 & 100 & 1000 \\ a+9d & a+99d & a+999d \end{vmatrix} = 0$

$\Delta_x = \begin{vmatrix} 1 & 1 & 1 \\ 0 & 100 & 1000 \\ 0 & a+99d & a+999d \end{vmatrix}$

$= 900(d-a)$

$\Delta_y = \begin{vmatrix} 1 & 1 & 1 \\ 10 & 0 & 1000 \\ a+9d & 0 & a+999d \end{vmatrix} = 990(a-d)$

$\Delta_z = \begin{vmatrix} 1 & 1 & 1 \\ 10 & 100 & 0 \\ a+9d & a+99d & 0 \end{vmatrix} = 90(d-a)$

Now, for (I), If $\frac{q}{r} = 10$

$\Rightarrow \quad a = d$

So, $\Delta = \Delta_x = \Delta_y = \Delta_z = 0$

So, Eqs. (i) and (ii) represents non-parallel lines and Eqs. (ii) and (iii) represents same plane.

$\Rightarrow$ Infinitely many solutions.

For (II), If $\frac{p}{r} \neq 100 \Rightarrow a \neq d$

So, $\Delta = 0, \Delta_x = \Delta_y = \Delta_z \neq 0$

This case, get no solution.

For (III), $\frac{p}{q} \neq 10 \Rightarrow a \neq d$

$\therefore$ Also this case no solution.

For (IV), If $\frac{p}{q} = 10 \Rightarrow a = d$

So, infinity many solutions.

70. $7x + 8y + 9z - (\gamma - 1)$

$= A(4x + 5y + 6z - \beta) + B(x + 2y + 3z - \alpha)$

On equating the coefficients,

$$4A + B = 7 \qquad \text{... (i)}$$

$$5A + 2B = 8 \qquad \text{... (ii)}$$

and $\quad -(\gamma - 1) = -A\beta - \alpha B \qquad$ ...(iii)

On solving Eqs. (i) and (ii), we get

$$A = 2 \text{ and } B = -1$$

From Eq. (iii), we get

$$-\gamma + 1 = -2\beta - \alpha(-1)$$

$\Rightarrow \quad \alpha - 2\beta + \gamma = 1 \qquad$ ...(iv)

Now, determinant of

$M = |M| = \begin{vmatrix} \alpha & 2 & \gamma \\ \beta & 1 & 0 \\ -1 & 0 & 1 \end{vmatrix}$

$= \alpha - 2\beta + \gamma = 1 \qquad$ [from Eq. (iv)]

71. Equation of plane P is given by

$$x - 2y + z = 1$$

Hence, perpendicular distance of the point (0, 1, 0) from the plane

$P = \frac{|0 - 2\times 1 + 0 - 1|}{\sqrt{1^2 + (-2)^2 + 1^2}}$

$= \frac{|3|}{\sqrt{6}}$

$\Rightarrow \quad D = \left(\frac{|3|}{\sqrt{6}}\right)^2$

$= \frac{9}{6} = 1.5$

72. Let $\text{Det}(P)=\begin{vmatrix} a_1 & b_1 & c_1 \\ a_2 & b_2 & c_2 \\ a_3 & b_3 & c_3 \end{vmatrix}$

$$=a_1(b_2c_3-b_3c_2)-a_2(b_1c_3-b_3c_1)+a_3(b_1c_2-b_2c_1)$$

Now, maximum value of $\text{Det}(P)=6$

If $a_1=1, a_2=-1, a_3=1,$

$b_2c_3=b_1c_3=b_1c_2=1$

and $b_3c_2=b_3c_1=b_2c_1=-1$

But it is not possible as

$(b_2c_3)(b_3c_1)(b_1c_2)=-1$

and $(b_1c_3)(b_3c_2)(b_2c_1)=1$

i.e. $b_1b_2b_3c_1c_2c_3=1$ and -1

Similar contradiction occurs when

$a_1=1, a_2=1, a_3=1, b_2c_1=b_3c_1=b_1c_2=1$

and $b_3c_2=b_1c_3=b_1c_2=-1$

Now, for value to be 5 one of the terms must be zero but that will make 2 terms zero which means answer cannot be 5

Now, $\begin{vmatrix} 1 & 1 & 1 \\ -1 & 1 & 1 \\ 1 & -1 & 1 \end{vmatrix}=4$

Hence, maximum value is 4.

Exercise 3 - Challenging Problems

1. Let $\Delta=\begin{vmatrix} b+c & c & b \\ c & c+a & a \\ b & a & a+b \end{vmatrix}$

Applying $R_1\to R_1-(R_2+R_3)$, then

$\therefore \quad \Delta=\begin{vmatrix} 0 & -2a & -2a \\ c & c+a & a \\ b & a & a+b \end{vmatrix}$

Taking $(-2a)$ common from R_1, then

$$\Delta=(-2a)\begin{vmatrix} 0 & 1 & 1 \\ c & c+a & a \\ b & a & a+b \end{vmatrix}$$

Applying $C_2\to C_2-C_3$, then

$\therefore \quad \Delta=(-2a)\begin{vmatrix} 0 & 0 & 1 \\ c & c & a \\ b & -b & a+b \end{vmatrix}$

Expanding along R_1, we get

$$\Delta=(-2a)\cdot 1\cdot\begin{vmatrix} c & c \\ b & -b \end{vmatrix}$$

$$=(-2a)(-2bc)$$

Hence, $\Delta=4abc$

2. Let $\Delta=\begin{vmatrix} a-b-c & 2a & 2a \\ 2b & b-c-a & 2b \\ 2c & 2c & c-a-b \end{vmatrix}$

Since, the answer is $(a+b+c)^3$, we shall try to get $(a+b+c)$.

Applying $R_1\to R_1+R_2+R_3$, then

$$\Delta=\begin{vmatrix} a+b+c & a+b+c & a+b+c \\ 2b & b-c-a & 2b \\ 2c & 2c & c-a-b \end{vmatrix}$$

Taking $(a+b+c)$ common from R_1, we get

$$\Delta=(a+b+c)\begin{vmatrix} 1 & 1 & 1 \\ 2b & b-c-a & 2b \\ 2c & 2c & c-a-b \end{vmatrix}$$

Applying $C_1\to C_2-C_1$ and $C_3\to C_3-C_1$

$\therefore \quad \Delta=(a+b+c)\begin{vmatrix} 1 & 0 & 0 \\ 2b & -a-b-c & 0 \\ 2c & 0 & -c-a-b \end{vmatrix}$

[by property, since all elements above leading diagonal are zero]

$$=(a+b+c)\cdot 1\cdot(-a-b-c)\cdot(-c-a-b)$$

Hence, $\Delta=(a+b+c)^3$

3. Let $\Delta=\begin{vmatrix} \sqrt{13}+\sqrt{3} & 2\sqrt{5} & \sqrt{5} \\ \sqrt{15}+\sqrt{26} & 5 & \sqrt{10} \\ 3+\sqrt{65} & \sqrt{15} & 5 \end{vmatrix}$

$$=\begin{vmatrix} \sqrt{3} & 2\sqrt{5} & \sqrt{5} \\ \sqrt{15} & 5 & \sqrt{10} \\ 3 & \sqrt{15} & 5 \end{vmatrix}+\begin{vmatrix} \sqrt{13} & 2\sqrt{5} & \sqrt{5} \\ \sqrt{26} & 5 & \sqrt{10} \\ \sqrt{65} & \sqrt{15} & 5 \end{vmatrix}$$

Taking common from 1st determinant $\sqrt{3}$, $\sqrt{5}$ and $\sqrt{5}$ from C_1, C_2 and C_3 respectively and taking common from 2nd determinant $\sqrt{13}$, $\sqrt{5}$ and $\sqrt{5}$ from C_1, C_3 and C_3 respectively, we get

$$=\sqrt{3}\times\sqrt{5}\times\sqrt{5}\begin{vmatrix} 1 & 2 & 1 \\ \sqrt{5} & \sqrt{5} & \sqrt{2} \\ \sqrt{3} & \sqrt{3} & \sqrt{5} \end{vmatrix}+\sqrt{13}\times\sqrt{5}\times\sqrt{5}\begin{vmatrix} 1 & 2 & 1 \\ \sqrt{2} & \sqrt{5} & \sqrt{2} \\ \sqrt{5} & \sqrt{3} & \sqrt{5} \end{vmatrix}$$

$$=\sqrt{3}\times 5\begin{vmatrix} 1 & 2 & 1 \\ \sqrt{5} & \sqrt{5} & \sqrt{2} \\ \sqrt{3} & \sqrt{3} & \sqrt{5} \end{vmatrix}+0 \qquad [\because C_1 \text{ and } C_3 \text{ are identical}]$$

$$=5\sqrt{3}\begin{vmatrix} 1 & 2 & 1 \\ \sqrt{5} & \sqrt{5} & \sqrt{2} \\ \sqrt{3} & \sqrt{3} & \sqrt{5} \end{vmatrix}$$

Applying $C_2\to C_2-C_1$,

then $\Delta=5\sqrt{3}\begin{vmatrix} 1 & 1 & 1 \\ \sqrt{5} & 0 & \sqrt{2} \\ \sqrt{3} & 0 & \sqrt{5} \end{vmatrix}$

Expanding along C_2, then

$$\Delta=5\sqrt{3}\cdot(-1)\begin{vmatrix} \sqrt{5} & \sqrt{2} \\ \sqrt{3} & \sqrt{5} \end{vmatrix}=-5\sqrt{3}(5-\sqrt{6})$$

$$=-25\sqrt{3}+15\sqrt{2}$$

$$=15\sqrt{2}-25\sqrt{3}$$

4. Given that, a, b and c are p th, q th and r th terms of HP $\Rightarrow \frac{1}{a}, \frac{1}{b}$ and $\frac{1}{c}$ are p th, q th and r th terms of an AP.

Let A and D are the first term and common difference of AP, then

$$\frac{1}{a} = A + (p-1)D \qquad \text{...(i)}$$

$$\frac{1}{b} = A + (q-1)D \qquad \text{...(ii)}$$

$$\frac{1}{c} = A + (r-1)D \qquad \text{...(iii)}$$

Now, given determinant is

$$\Delta = \begin{vmatrix} bc & ca & ab \\ p & q & r \\ 1 & 1 & 1 \end{vmatrix} = abc \begin{vmatrix} \frac{1}{a} & \frac{1}{b} & \frac{1}{c} \\ p & q & r \\ 1 & 1 & 1 \end{vmatrix}$$

On substituting the values of $\frac{1}{a}, \frac{1}{b}$ and $\frac{1}{c}$ from Eqs. (i), (ii) and (iii) In Δ, then

$$\Delta = abc \begin{vmatrix} A+(p-1)D & A+(q-1)D & A+(r-1)D \\ p & q & r \\ 1 & 1 & 1 \end{vmatrix}$$

Applying $R_1 \to R_1 - (A-D)R_3 - DR_2$, then

$$\Delta = abc \begin{vmatrix} 0 & 0 & 0 \\ p & q & r \\ 1 & 1 & 1 \end{vmatrix} = 0$$

5. Let $$z = \begin{vmatrix} -5 & 3+5i & \frac{3}{2}-4i \\ 3-5i & 8 & 4+5i \\ \frac{3}{2}+4i & 4-5i & 9 \end{vmatrix}$$

Then, $$\bar{z} = \begin{vmatrix} -5 & 3-5i & \frac{3}{2}+4i \\ 3+5i & 8 & 4-5i \\ \frac{3}{2}-4i & 4+5i & 9 \end{vmatrix} \qquad \text{[i.e., conjugate of } z\text{]}$$

$$= \begin{vmatrix} -5 & 3+5i & \frac{3}{2}-4i \\ 3-5i & 8 & 4+5i \\ \frac{3}{2}+4i & 4-5i & 9 \end{vmatrix}$$

[interchanging rows into columns]

$\Rightarrow \quad \bar{z} = z$

Hence, z is purely real.

6. $$\text{LHS} = \begin{vmatrix} ah+bg & g & ab+ch \\ bf+ba & f & hb+bc \\ af+bc & c & bg+fc \end{vmatrix}$$

$$= b\begin{vmatrix} ah+bg & g & a \\ bf+ba & f & h \\ af+bc & c & g \end{vmatrix} + c\begin{vmatrix} ah+bg & g & h \\ bf+ba & f & b \\ af+bc & c & f \end{vmatrix}$$

In second determinant, applying $C_1 \to C_1 - bC_2 - aC_3$, then

$$= \begin{vmatrix} ah+bg & bg & a \\ bf+ba & bf & h \\ af+bc & bc & g \end{vmatrix} + c\begin{vmatrix} 0 & g & h \\ 0 & f & b \\ 0 & c & f \end{vmatrix}$$

In first determinant, applying $C_2 \to C_2 - C_1$, then

$$= \begin{vmatrix} ah+bg & -ah & a \\ bf+ba & -ba & h \\ af+bc & -af & q \end{vmatrix} + 0$$

$$= a\begin{vmatrix} ah+bg & a & h \\ bf+ba & h & b \\ af+bc & g & f \end{vmatrix} = \text{RHS}$$

7. Let $$\Delta = \begin{vmatrix} 1 & 1 & 1 \\ 1+\sin A & 1+\sin B & 1+\sin C \\ \sin A+\sin^2 A & \sin B+\sin^2 B & \sin C+\sin^2 C \end{vmatrix}$$

Applying $C_2 \to C_2 - C_1$ and $C_3 \to C_3 - C_1$, then

$$\Delta = \begin{vmatrix} 1 & 0 & 0 \\ 1+\sin A & \sin B-\sin A & \sin C-\sin A \\ \sin A+\sin^2 A & (\sin B-\sin A)(\sin B+\sin A+1) & (\sin C-\sin A)(\sin C+\sin A+1) \end{vmatrix}$$

Expanding along R_1, then

$$\Delta = \begin{vmatrix} \sin B-\sin A & \sin C-\sin A \\ (\sin B-\sin A)(\sin B+\sin A+1) & (\sin C-\sin A)(\sin C+\sin A+1) \end{vmatrix}$$

$$= (\sin B-\sin A)(\sin C-\sin A)\begin{vmatrix} 1 & 1 \\ \sin B+\sin A+1 & \sin C+\sin A+1 \end{vmatrix}$$

$$= (\sin B-\sin A)(\sin C-\sin A)(\sin C-\sin B)$$

But, given $\Delta = 0$

$\therefore \quad (\sin B-\sin A)(\sin C-\sin A)(\sin C-\sin B) = 0$

$\therefore \quad \sin B-\sin A = 0$ or $\sin C-\sin A = 0$

or $\quad \sin C-\sin B = 0$

$\Rightarrow \quad \sin B = \sin A$ or $\sin C = \sin A$ or $\sin C = \sin B$

$B = A$ or $C = A$ or $C = B$

In all the three cases, we will have an isosceles triangle.

8. Let $$\Delta = \begin{vmatrix} \beta\gamma & \beta\gamma'+\beta'\gamma & \beta'\gamma' \\ \gamma'\alpha & \gamma'\alpha'+\gamma\alpha & \gamma\alpha' \\ \alpha\beta & \alpha\beta'+\alpha'\beta & \alpha'\beta' \end{vmatrix}$$

Taking $\beta'\gamma'$, $\gamma'\alpha'$ and $\alpha'\beta'$ common from R_1, R_2 and R_3 respectively, then

$$\Delta = (\beta'\gamma')(\gamma'\alpha')(\alpha'\beta')\begin{vmatrix} \frac{\beta}{\beta'}\frac{\gamma}{\gamma'} & \frac{\beta}{\beta'}+\frac{\gamma}{\gamma'} & 1 \\ \frac{\gamma}{\gamma'}\frac{\alpha}{\alpha'} & \frac{\gamma}{\gamma'}+\frac{\alpha}{\alpha'} & 1 \\ \frac{\alpha}{\alpha'}\frac{\beta}{\beta'} & \frac{\alpha}{\alpha'}+\frac{\beta}{\beta'} & 1 \end{vmatrix}$$

Applying $R_2 \to R_2 - R_1$ and $R_3 \to R_3 - R_1$

Then, $\Delta = (\alpha'\beta'\gamma')^2 \begin{vmatrix} \frac{\beta}{\beta'}\frac{\gamma}{\gamma'} & \frac{\beta}{\beta'}+\frac{\gamma}{\gamma'} & 1 \\ \frac{\gamma}{\gamma'}\left(\frac{\alpha}{\alpha'}-\frac{\beta}{\beta'}\right) & \left(\frac{\alpha}{\alpha'}-\frac{\beta}{\beta'}\right) & 0 \\ \frac{\beta}{\beta'}\left(\frac{\alpha}{\alpha'}-\frac{\gamma}{\gamma'}\right) & \left(\frac{\alpha}{\alpha'}-\frac{\gamma}{\gamma'}\right) & 0 \end{vmatrix}$

$$= (\alpha'\beta'\gamma')^2\left(\frac{\alpha}{\alpha'}-\frac{\beta}{\beta'}\right)\left(\frac{\alpha}{\alpha'}-\frac{\gamma}{\gamma'}\right)\begin{vmatrix} \frac{\beta}{\beta'}\frac{\gamma}{\gamma'} & \frac{\beta}{\beta'}+\frac{\gamma}{\gamma'} & 1 \\ \frac{\gamma}{\gamma'} & 1 & 0 \\ \frac{\beta}{\beta'} & 1 & 0 \end{vmatrix}$$

Expanding along C_3, then

$$\Delta = (\alpha'\beta'\gamma')^2\left(\frac{\alpha}{\alpha'}-\frac{\beta}{\beta'}\right)\left(\frac{\alpha}{\alpha'}-\frac{\gamma}{\gamma'}\right)\left(\frac{\gamma}{\gamma'}-\frac{\beta}{\beta'}\right)$$

$$= (\alpha'\beta'\gamma')^2\left(\frac{\alpha}{\alpha'}-\frac{\beta}{\beta'}\right)\left(\frac{\beta}{\beta'}-\frac{\gamma}{\gamma'}\right)\left(\frac{\gamma}{\gamma'}-\frac{\alpha}{\alpha'}\right)$$

$$= (\alpha'\beta'\gamma')^2 \frac{(\alpha\beta'-\alpha'\beta)(\beta\gamma'-\beta'\gamma)(\gamma\alpha'-\gamma'\alpha)}{(\alpha'\beta'\gamma')^2}$$

Hence, $\Delta = (\alpha\beta'-\alpha'\beta)(\beta\gamma'-\beta'\gamma)(\gamma\alpha'-\gamma'\alpha)$

9. Since, $y = \frac{u}{v}$

$$\therefore \quad \frac{dy}{dx} = \frac{v\frac{du}{dx} - u\frac{dv}{dx}}{v^2} = \frac{vu' - uv'}{v^2} \Rightarrow v^2\frac{dy}{dx} = vu' - uv' \quad \text{...(i)}$$

On differentiating both sides w.r.t. x, we get

$$v^2\frac{d^2y}{dx^2} + \frac{dy}{dx}\cdot 2vv' = (vu'' + u'v') - (uv'' + v'u')$$

$$\Rightarrow \quad v^2\frac{d^2y}{dx^2} + 2vv'\frac{dy}{dx} = vu'' - uv''$$

On multiplying both sides by v, then

$$v^3\frac{d^2y}{dx^2} + 2v'\left(v^2\frac{dy}{dx}\right) = v^2u'' - uvv''$$

$$\Rightarrow \quad v^3\frac{d^2y}{dx^2} + 2v'(vu' - uv') = v^2u'' - uvv'' \quad \text{[from Eq. (i)]}$$

$$\Rightarrow \quad v^3\frac{d^2y}{dx^2} = 2uv^2 - uvv'' - 2vu'v' + v^2u'' \quad \text{...(ii)}$$

and $\begin{vmatrix} v & v & 0 \\ v' & v' & v \\ v'' & v'' & 2v' \end{vmatrix} = u(2v'^2 - vu'') - v(2u'v' - u''v)$

$$= 2uv'^2 - 4vv'' - 2vu'v' + v^2u'' \quad \text{...(iii)}$$

From Eqs. (ii) and (iii), we get

$$v^3\frac{d^2y}{dx^2} = \begin{vmatrix} u & v & 0 \\ u' & v' & v \\ u' & v'' & 2v' \end{vmatrix}$$

10. Here, we have to prove that $\Delta(x)$ is independent of x. So, it is sufficient to prove that $\Delta'(x) = 0$

Now, $\Delta(x) = \begin{vmatrix} \sin(x+\alpha) & \cos(x+\alpha) & a + x\sin\alpha \\ \sin(x+\beta) & \cos(x+\beta) & b + x\sin\beta \\ \sin(x+\gamma) & \cos(x+\gamma) & c + x\sin\gamma \end{vmatrix}$

On differentiating w.r.t. x, we get

$$\Delta'(x) = \begin{vmatrix} \cos(x+\alpha) & \cos(x+\alpha) & a + x\sin\alpha \\ \cos(x+\beta) & \cos(x+\beta) & b + x\sin\beta \\ \cos(x+\gamma) & \cos(x+\gamma) & c + x\sin\gamma \end{vmatrix}$$

$$+ \begin{vmatrix} \sin(x+\alpha) & -\sin(x+\alpha) & a + x\sin\alpha \\ \sin(x+\beta) & -\sin(x+\beta) & b + x\sin\beta \\ \sin(x+\gamma) & -\sin(x+\gamma) & c + x\sin\gamma \end{vmatrix}$$

$$+ \begin{vmatrix} \sin(x+\alpha) & \cos(x+\alpha) & \sin\alpha \\ \sin(x+\beta) & \cos(x+\beta) & \sin\beta \\ \sin(x+\gamma) & \cos(x+\gamma) & \sin\gamma \end{vmatrix}$$

$$= 0 - 0 + \begin{vmatrix} \sin(x+\alpha) & \cos(x+\alpha) & \sin\alpha \\ \sin(x+\beta) & \cos(x+\beta) & \sin\beta \\ \sin(x+\gamma) & \cos(x+\gamma) & \sin\gamma \end{vmatrix}$$

$$= \begin{vmatrix} \sin(x+\alpha) & \cos(x+\alpha) & \sin\alpha \\ \sin(x+\beta) & \cos(x+\beta) & \sin\beta \\ \sin(x+\gamma) & \cos(x+\gamma) & \sin\gamma \end{vmatrix}$$

Applying $C_1 \to C_1 - (\cos x)C_3$ and $C_2 \to C_2 + (\sin x)C_3$, we get

$$\Delta'(x) = \begin{vmatrix} \sin x\cos\alpha & \cos x\cos\alpha & \sin\alpha \\ \sin x\cos\beta & \cos x\cos\beta & \sin\beta \\ \sin x\cos\gamma & \cos x\cos\gamma & \sin\gamma \end{vmatrix}$$

$$= \sin x \cdot \cos x \begin{vmatrix} \cos\alpha & \cos\alpha & \sin\alpha \\ \cos\beta & \cos\beta & \sin\beta \\ \cos\gamma & \cos\gamma & \sin\gamma \end{vmatrix}$$

$= \sin x \cdot \cos x \times 0$ [$\because C_1$ and C_2 are identical]

$= 0$

Thus, $\Delta(x)$ is independent of x.

11. Let $\Delta = \begin{vmatrix} {}^xC_1 & {}^xC_2 & {}^xC_3 \\ {}^yC_1 & {}^yC_2 & {}^yC_3 \\ {}^zC_1 & {}^zC_2 & {}^zC_3 \end{vmatrix} = \begin{vmatrix} x & \frac{x(x-1)}{1\cdot 2} & \frac{x(x-1)(x-2)}{1\cdot 2\cdot 3} \\ y & \frac{y(y-1)}{1\cdot 2} & \frac{y(y-1)(y-2)}{1\cdot 2\cdot 3} \\ z & \frac{z(z-1)}{1\cdot 2} & \frac{z(z-1)(z-2)}{1\cdot 2\cdot 3} \end{vmatrix}$

$$= \frac{xyz}{12}\begin{vmatrix} 1 & x-1 & x^2-3x+2 \\ 1 & y-1 & y^2-3y+2 \\ 1 & z-1 & z^2-3z+2 \end{vmatrix}$$

Applying $C_2 \to C_2 + C_1$, then

$$\Delta = \frac{xyz}{12}\begin{vmatrix} 1 & x & x^2-3x+2 \\ 1 & y & y^2-3y+2 \\ 1 & z & z^2-3z+2 \end{vmatrix}$$

Applying $C_3 \to C_3 + 3C_2 - 2C_1$, then

$$\Delta = \frac{xyz}{12}\begin{vmatrix} 1 & x & x^2 \\ 1 & y & y^2 \\ 1 & z & z^2 \end{vmatrix} = \frac{1}{12}xyz(x-y)(y-z)(z-x)$$

12. (i) $\because$ $f(x)=\begin{vmatrix} 1+\sin^2 x & \cos^2 x & 4\sin 2x \\ \sin^2 x & 1+\cos^2 x & 4\sin 2x \\ \sin^2 x & \cos^2 x & 1+4\sin 2x \end{vmatrix}$

Applying $R_2 \to R_2 - R_1$ and $R_3 \to R_3 - R_1$, then

$$f(x)=\begin{vmatrix} 1+\sin^2 x & \cos^2 x & 4\sin 2x \\ -1 & 1 & 0 \\ -1 & 0 & 1 \end{vmatrix}$$

Applying $C_2 \to C_2 + C_1$, then

$$f(x)=\begin{vmatrix} 1+\sin^2 x & 2 & 4\sin 2x \\ \vdots & & \\ -1 & \dots\ 0\ \dots & 0 \\ \vdots & & \\ -1 & -1 & 1 \end{vmatrix}$$

Expanding along R_2, then

$$f(x)=\begin{vmatrix} 2 & 4\sin 2x \\ -1 & 1 \end{vmatrix}=2+4\sin 2x$$

$\therefore$ Maximum value of

$$f(x)=2+4(1)=6$$

(ii) $\because$ $\Delta=\begin{vmatrix} \sin^2 A & \sin A\cos A & \cos^2 A \\ \sin^2 B & \sin B\cos B & \cos^2 B \\ \sin^2 C & \sin C\cos C & \cos^2 C \end{vmatrix}$

$$=\cos^2 A\cos^2 B\cos^2 C\begin{vmatrix} \tan^2 A & \tan A & 1 \\ \tan^2 B & \tan B & 1 \\ \tan^2 C & \tan C & 1 \end{vmatrix}$$

$$=-\cos^2 A\cos^2 B\cos^2 C\begin{vmatrix} 1 & \tan A & \tan^2 A \\ 1 & \tan B & \tan^2 B \\ 1 & \tan C & \tan^2 C \end{vmatrix}$$

$$=-\cos^2 A\cos^2 B\cos^2 C(\tan A-\tan B)(\tan B-\tan C)(\tan C-\tan A)$$

$$=-\sin(A-B)\sin(B-C)\sin(C-A)$$

$$=\sin(A-B)\sin(B-C)\sin(A-C)\geq 0\quad [\because A\geq B\geq C]$$

$\therefore$ $\Delta \geq 0$

Hence, minimum value of Δ is 0.

13. Let $f(x)=\begin{vmatrix} x^2-4x+6 & 2x^2+4x+10 & 3x^2-2x+16 \\ x-2 & 2x+2 & 3x-1 \\ 1 & 2 & 3 \end{vmatrix}$

On differentiating w.r.t. x, we get

$$f'(x)=\begin{vmatrix} 2x-4 & 4x+4 & 6x-2 \\ x-2 & 2x+2 & 3x-1 \\ 1 & 2 & 3 \end{vmatrix}+\begin{vmatrix} x^2-4x+6 & 2x^2+4x+10 & 3x^2-2x+16 \\ 1 & 2 & 3 \\ 1 & 2 & 3 \end{vmatrix}+\begin{vmatrix} x^2-4x+6 & 2x^2+4x+10 & 3x^2-2x+16 \\ x-2 & 2x+2 & 3x-1 \\ 0 & 0 & 0 \end{vmatrix}$$

$f'(x)=0,\ \forall\ x\in R$ and $f(x)=$ Constant

As, $f(0)=\begin{vmatrix} 6 & 10 & 16 \\ -2 & 2 & -1 \\ 1 & 2 & 3 \end{vmatrix}=2 \therefore f(x)=2$

Now, $I=\int_{-3}^{3}\frac{x^2\sin x}{1+x^6}f(x)\,dx=2\int_{-3}^{3}\frac{x^2\sin x}{1+x^6}dx$

Let $g(x)=\dfrac{x^2\sin x}{1+x^6}$

$\therefore$ $g(-x)=\dfrac{-x^2\sin x}{1+x^6}=-g(x)$

Hence, g is an odd function.

$\therefore$ $I=0$

14. Since, $Y=sX$ and $Z=tX$

$Y_1=sX_1+Xs_1$ ...(i)

$Y_2=sX_2+Xs_2+2X_1s_1$ ...(ii)

$Z_1=tX_1+Xt_1$ ...(iii)

and $Z_2=tX_2+Xt_2+2X_1t_1$ ...(iv)

$$\text{LHS}=\begin{vmatrix} X & Y & Z \\ X_1 & Y_1 & Z_1 \\ X_2 & Y_2 & Z_2 \end{vmatrix}$$

$$=\begin{vmatrix} X & sX & tX \\ X_1 & sX_1+Xs_1 & tX_1+Xt_1 \\ X_2 & sX_2+Xs_2+2X_1s_1 & tX_2+Xt_2+2X_1t_1 \end{vmatrix}$$

[using Eqs. (i), (ii), (iii) and (iv)]

Applying $C_2 \to C_2 - sC_1$ and $C_3 \to C_3 - tC_1$, then

$$=\begin{vmatrix} X & 0 & 0 \\ X_1 & Xs_1 & Xt_1 \\ X_2 & Xs_2+2X_1s_1 & Xt_2+2X_1t_1 \end{vmatrix}$$

Expanding w.r.t. R_1, then

$$=X^2\begin{vmatrix} s_1 & t_1 \\ Xs_2+2X_1s_1 & Xt_2+2X_1t_1 \end{vmatrix}$$

Applying $R_2 \to R_2 - 2X_1R_1$, then

$$=X^2\begin{vmatrix} s_1 & t_1 \\ Xs_2 & Xt_2 \end{vmatrix}=X^3\begin{vmatrix} s_1 & t_1 \\ s_2 & t_2 \end{vmatrix}=\text{RHS}$$

15. Given determinant may be expressed as

$$\Delta=\begin{vmatrix} f & g & h \\ xf'+f & xg'+g & xh'+h \\ (x^2f''+4xf'+2f) & (x^2g''+4xg'+2g) & (x^2h''+4xh'+2h) \end{vmatrix}$$

Now, applying $R_3 \to R_3 - 4R_2 + 2R_1$, then

$$\Delta=\begin{vmatrix} f & g & h \\ xf'+f & xg'+g & xh'+h \\ x^2f'' & x^2g'' & x^2h'' \end{vmatrix}$$

Applying $R_2 \to R_2 - R_1$, then $\Delta = \begin{vmatrix} f & g & h \\ xf' & xg' & xh' \\ x^2f'' & x^2g'' & x^2h'' \end{vmatrix}$

$$\Rightarrow \Delta = x\begin{vmatrix} f & g & h \\ f' & g' & h' \\ x^2f'' & x^2g'' & x^2h'' \end{vmatrix} \Rightarrow \Delta = \begin{vmatrix} f & g & h \\ f' & g' & h' \\ x^3f'' & x^3g'' & x^3h'' \end{vmatrix}$$

$$\therefore \quad \Delta' = \begin{vmatrix} f' & g & h' \\ f' & g' & h' \\ x^3f'' & x^3g'' & x^3h'' \end{vmatrix} + \begin{vmatrix} f & g & h \\ f'' & g'' & h'' \\ x^3f'' & x^3g'' & x^3h'' \end{vmatrix} + \begin{vmatrix} f & g & h \\ f' & g' & h' \\ (x^3f'')' & (x^3g'')' & (x^3h'')' \end{vmatrix}$$

$$= 0 + 0 + \begin{vmatrix} f & g & h \\ f' & g' & h' \\ (x^3f'')' & (x^3g'')' & (x^3h'')' \end{vmatrix}$$

Hence, $\Delta' = \begin{vmatrix} f & g & h \\ f' & g' & h' \\ (x^3f'')' & (x^3g'')' & (x^3h'')' \end{vmatrix}$

16. Let the given determinant be equal to zero. Then, there exist x, y and z not all zero, such that

$$a_1x + a_2y + a_3z = 0, \; b_1x + b_2y + b_3z = 0$$

and $\quad c_1x + c_2y + c_3z = 0$

Assume that, $|x| \ge |y| \ge |z|$ and $x \ne 0$.

Then, from $a_1x = (-a_2y) + (-a_3z)$

$\therefore \quad |a_1x| = |-a_2y - a_3z| \le |a_2y| + |a_3z|$

$\Rightarrow \quad |a_1|\,|x| \le |a_2|\,|y| + |a_3|\,|z|$

But $\quad x \ne 0$ i.e. $|a_1| \le |a_2| + |a_3|$

Similarly, $\quad |b_2| \le |b_1| + |b_3|$

$|c_3| \le |c_1| + |c_2|$

which is contradiction. Hence, the assumption that the determinant is zero must be wrong.

17. LHS $= \begin{vmatrix} (a-a_1)^{-2} & (a-a_1)^{-1} & a_1^{-1} \\ (a-a_2)^{-2} & (a-a_2)^{-1} & a_2^{-1} \\ (a-a_3)^{-2} & (a-a_3)^{-1} & a_3^{-1} \end{vmatrix}$

$$= (a-a_1)^{-2}(a-a_2)^{-2}(a-a_3)^{-2}\begin{vmatrix} 1 & (a-a_1) & a_1^{-1}(a-a_1)^2 \\ 1 & (a-a_2) & a_2^{-1}(a-a_2)^2 \\ 1 & (a-a_3) & a_3^{-1}(a-a_3)^2 \end{vmatrix}$$

Applying $R_2 \to R_2 - R_1$ and $R_3 \to -R_3 - R_1$, then

$$\text{LHS} = \frac{1}{\prod (a-a_i)^2}\begin{vmatrix} 1 & (a-a_1) & a_1^{-1}(a-a_1)^2 \\ 0 & (a_1-a_2) & \dfrac{(a^2-a_1a_2)(a_1-a_2)}{a_1a_2} \\ 0 & (a_1-a_3) & \dfrac{(a^2-a_1a_3)(a_1-a_3)}{a_1a_3} \end{vmatrix}$$

Expanding w.r.t. 1st column, then

$$\text{LHS} = \frac{1}{\prod (a-a_i)^2}\begin{vmatrix} (a_1-a_2) & \dfrac{(a^2-a_1a_2)(a_1-a_2)}{a_1a_2} \\ (a_1-a_3) & \dfrac{(a^2-a_1a_3)(a_1-a_3)}{a_1a_3} \end{vmatrix}$$

$$= \frac{(a_1-a_2)(a_1-a_3)}{\prod (a-a_i)^2}\begin{vmatrix} 1 & \dfrac{a^2-a_1a_2}{a_1a_2} \\ 1 & \dfrac{a^2-a_1a_3}{a_1a_3} \end{vmatrix}$$

$$= \frac{(a_1-a_2)(a_1-a_3)\,a^2(a_2-a_3)}{a_1a_2a_3\prod (a-a_i)^2}$$

$$= \frac{-a^2\prod (a_i-a_j)}{\prod a_i \prod (a-a_i)^2}$$

Numerator $= -a^2(a_1-a_2)(a_2-a_3)(a_3-a_1)$

The resulting expression has negative sign.

18. The given system of equation will have a non-trivial solution in the determinant of coefficients.

$$\therefore \quad \Delta = \begin{vmatrix} a-t & b & c \\ b & c-t & a \\ c & a & b-t \end{vmatrix}$$

$\Delta = 0$ is a cubic equation in t.

So, it has in general three solutions t_1, t_2 and t_3.

Let $\quad \Delta = a_0t^3 + a_1t^2 + a_2t + a_3$

Clearly, $a_0 =$ Coefficient of $t^3 = -1$,

so $t_1t_2t_3 = -\dfrac{a_3}{a_0} = -\dfrac{a_3}{-1} = a_3 =$ Constant term in the expansion of Δ. i.e. Δ (at $t = 0$)

$$\therefore \quad t_1t_2t_3 = a_3 = \begin{vmatrix} a & b & c \\ b & c & a \\ c & a & b \end{vmatrix}$$

19. (i) Eliminating a, b and c from given equations, we obtain

$$\begin{vmatrix} -1 & \dfrac{y}{z} & \dfrac{z}{y} \\ -1 & \dfrac{z}{x} & \dfrac{x}{z} \\ -1 & \dfrac{x}{y} & \dfrac{y}{z} \end{vmatrix} = 0$$

Applying $R_2 \to R_2 - R_1$ and $R_3 \to R_3 - R_1$, then

$$\begin{vmatrix} -1 & \dfrac{y}{z} & \dfrac{z}{y} \\ 0 & \dfrac{z}{x}-\dfrac{y}{z} & \dfrac{x}{z}-\dfrac{z}{y} \\ 0 & \dfrac{x}{y}-\dfrac{y}{z} & \dfrac{y}{x}-\dfrac{z}{y} \end{vmatrix} = 0$$

Expanding along C_1, then

$$-\left(\frac{z}{x}-\frac{y}{x}\right)\left(\frac{y}{x}-\frac{z}{y}\right)+\left(\frac{x}{y}-\frac{y}{z}\right)\left(\frac{x}{z}-\frac{z}{y}\right)=0$$

$$\Rightarrow \quad \frac{yz}{x^2}+\frac{zx}{y^2}+\frac{xy}{z^2}+1=0$$

(ii) To eliminate x, y and z.

Let $\alpha=\frac{y}{z}$, $\beta=\frac{z}{x}$ and $\gamma=\frac{x}{y}$ in the given equations,

$$b\alpha+\frac{c}{\alpha}=a, \quad \text{...(i)}$$

$$c\beta+\frac{a}{\beta}=b \quad \text{...(ii)}$$

and $$a\gamma+\frac{b}{\gamma}=c \quad \text{...(iii)}$$

Also, $\alpha\beta\gamma=1$

From Eqs. (i), (ii) and (iii), we get

$$\left(b\alpha+\frac{c}{\alpha}\right)\left(c\beta+\frac{a}{\beta}\right)\left(a\gamma+\frac{b}{\gamma}\right)=abc$$

$$\Rightarrow 2abc+ac^2\frac{\beta\gamma}{\alpha}+a^2b\frac{\alpha\gamma}{\beta}+b^2c\frac{\alpha\beta}{\gamma}+a^2c\frac{\gamma}{\alpha\beta}+bc^2\frac{\beta}{\gamma\alpha}+ab^2\frac{\alpha}{\beta\gamma}=abc$$

$[\because \alpha\beta\gamma=1]$

$$\Rightarrow \quad ac^2\frac{1}{\alpha^2}+a^2b\frac{1}{\beta^2}+b^2c\frac{1}{\gamma^2}+a^2c\gamma^2+bc^2\beta^2+ab^2\alpha^2=-abc$$

$$\Rightarrow a\left(\frac{c^2}{\alpha^2}+b^2\alpha^2\right)+b\left(\frac{a^2}{\beta^2}+\beta^2c^2\right)+c\left(\frac{b^2}{\gamma^2}+a^2\gamma^2\right)=-abc \quad \text{...(iv)}$$

On squaring Eqs. (i), (ii) and (iii), we get

$$b^2\alpha^2+\frac{c^2}{\alpha^2}=a^2-2bc,\ c^2\beta^2+\frac{a^2}{\beta^2}=b^2-2ca$$

and $$a^2\gamma^2+\frac{b^2}{\gamma^2}=c^2-2ab$$

On putting these values in Eq. (iv), we get

$$a(a^2-2bc)+b(b^2-2ca)+c(c^2-2ab)=-abc$$

$$a^3+b^3+c^3=5abc$$

20. Here, $\Delta=\begin{vmatrix} a & b & c \\ b & c & a \\ c & a & b \end{vmatrix}$. According to the question, x, y and z not all zero.

Hence, the given system of equations has non-trivial solution.

$$\Delta=0$$

$$\begin{vmatrix} a & b & c \\ b & c & a \\ c & a & b \end{vmatrix}=0$$

$$\Rightarrow \quad \frac{1}{2}(a+b+c)[(a-b)^2+(b-c)^2+(c-a)^2]=0$$

$\therefore$ $$a+b+c=0$$

or $$(a-b)^2+(b-c)^2+(c-a)^2=0$$

Case I If $a+b+c=0$

From first two equations,

$$ax+by-(a+b)z=0$$
$$bx-(a+b)y+ax=0$$

[by cross-multiplication law]

$$\therefore \quad \frac{x}{ab-(a+b)^2}=\frac{y}{-b(a+b)-a^2}=\frac{z}{-a(a+b)-b^2}$$

$$\Rightarrow \quad \frac{x}{-(a^2+ab+b^2)}=\frac{y}{-(a^2+ab+b^2)}=\frac{z}{-(a^2+ab+b^2)}$$

$\therefore$ $$x:y:z=1:1:1$$

Case II If $(a-b)^2+(b-c)^2+(c-a)^2=0$

It is possible only, when

$$a-b=0,\ b-c=0$$

and $$c-a=0$$

Then, $$a=b=c$$

In this case all the three equations reduce in the forms

$$x+y+z=0 \quad \text{...(i)}$$

Then, Eq. (i) will be satisfied, if

$$x=k,\ y=k\omega,\ z=k\omega^2$$

or $$x=k,\ y=k\omega^2,\ z=k\omega$$

where ω is the cube root of unity.

Then, $$x:y:z=1:\omega:\omega^2 \text{ or } 1:\omega^2:\omega$$

Hence, combined both cases, we get

$$x:y:z=1:1:1$$

or $$1:\omega:\omega^2$$

or $$1:\omega^2:\omega$$

“

The beauty of Mathematics only shows itself to more patient followers.

-Maryan Mirzakhani

9

Probability

Learning Milestones

Milestone 1 Classical Probability
- Some Basic Definitions
- Mathematical or Priori
- Odds in Favour and Odds Against the Event

Milestone 2 Conditional Probability
- Algebra of Probability
- Conditional Probability
- Independent Events

Milestone 3 Some Important Theorems of Probability
- Total Probability Theorem
- Baye's Theorem or Inverse Probability
- Random Variable and Its Distribution
- Mean and Variance of a Random Variable
- Binomial Theorem on Probability
- Expectation
- Uncountable Uniform Spaces

Practice Milestones

Practice Milestone 1- JEE Main Pattern
Practice Milestone 2 - JEE Advanced Pattern
Practice Milestone 3 - Challenging Problems

Milestone 1 Classical Probability

• Some Basic Definitions • Mathematical or Priori • Odds in Favour and Odds Against the Event

It is the statistical concept that measures the possibility of something to happens.

9.1 Some Basic Definitions

1. Random Experiment

An experiment whose outcome cannot be predicted with certainty, is called a random experiment.

Or

If in each trial of an experiment, which when repeated under identical conditions, the outcome is not unique but the outcome in a trial is one of the several possible outcomes, then such an experiment is known as a random experiment.

e.g.

(i) "Throwing an unbiased die" is a random experiment because when a die is thrown, we cannot say with certainty which one of the numbers 1, 2, 3, 4, 5 and 6 will come up.

(ii) "Tossing of a fair coin" is a random experiment because when a coin is tossed, we cannot say with certainty whether either a head or a tail will come up.

(iii) "Drawing a card from a well-shuffled pack of cards'' is a random experiment.

JEE Focus Points

- A die is a solid cube which has six faces and numbers 1, 2, 3, 4, 5 and 6 marked on the faces, respectively. In throwing or rolling a die, then any one number can be on the uppermost face.
- ➢ A pack of cards consists of 52 cards in 4 suits, i.e (a) Spades (♠) (b) Clubs (♣) (c) Hearts (♥) (d) Diamonds (♦). Each suit consists of 13 cards. Out of these, spades and clubs are black faced cards, while hearts and diamonds are red faced cards. The King, Queen, Jack (or Knave) are called face cards or honour cards.
  - ➢ **Game of bridge** It is played by 4 players, each player is given 13 cards.
  - ➢ **Game of whist** It is played by two pairs of persons.

2. Sample Space

The set of all possible results of a random experiment is called the sample space of that experiment and it is generally denoted by S. Each element of a sample space is called a **sample point.**

Example 1. A coin and a die are tossed together.
(i) Write the sample space.
(ii) How many cases are possible?

Sol. If a coin is tossed, then number of possible cases are $\{H,T\}$ and if a die is rolled, then number of possible cases are $\{1, 2, 3, 4, 5, 6\}$.

Now, according to the question,

(i) Sample space is $\{H_1, H_2, \dots H_6, T_1, T_2, \dots T_6\}$.

(ii) Number of cases = Number of subsets $= 2^{12}$.

Example 2. If three coins are tossed, represent the sample space and the event of getting atleast two heads, then find the number of elements in them.

Sol. Let S be the sample space and E be the event of occurrence of atleast two heads and let H denote the occurrence of head and T denote the occurrence of tail, when one coin is tossed.

Then, $S = \{H, T\} \times \{H, T\} \times \{H, T\}$

$$S = \{(H, H, H), (H, H, T), (H, T, H), (T, H, H), (T, T, H), (T, H, T), (H, T, T), (T, T, T)\}$$

and $E = \{(H, H, H), (H, H, T), (H, T, H), (T, H, H)\}$

Also, $n(S) = 8$ and $n(E) = 4$

3. Elementary Event

An event having only a single sample point is called an elementary or simple event or it is subset of sample space.

e.g. When two coins are tossed, the sample space, $S = \{HH, HT, TH, TT\}$, then the event, $E_1 = \{HH\}$ of getting both the heads is a simple event.

4. Compound Event

If an event has more than one sample point, then it is called a compound event.

Example 3. Two dice are rolled. Let T, R and S be the events of getting all even numbers, all odd numbers and a sum of 12 respectively.

(i) Which events are elementary events?

(ii) Which events are compound events?

Sol. On throwing of two dice, we get

Sample space $(S) = \{(1, 1), (1, 2), (1, 3), (1, 4), (1, 5), (1, 6), (2, 1), (2, 2), (2, 3), (2, 4), (2, 5), (2, 6), (3, 1), (3, 2), (3, 3), (3, 4), (3, 5), (3, 6), (4, 1), (4, 2), (4, 3), (4, 4), (4, 5), (4, 6), (5, 1), (5, 2), (5, 3), (5, 4), (5, 5), (5, 6), (6, 1), (6, 2), (6, 3), (6, 4), (6, 5), (6, 6)\}$

Now, $T = \{(2, 2), (2, 4), (2, 6), (4, 2), (4, 4), (4, 6), (6, 2), (6, 4), (6, 6)\}$

$R = \{(1, 1), (1, 3), (1, 5), (3, 1), (3, 3), (3, 5), (5, 1) (5, 3), (5, 5)\}$

and $S = \{(6, 6)\}$

(i) Since, S consists a single sample point, therefore it is an elementary or simple event.

(ii) Since, both T and R contains more than one sample points, therefore each of them is compound event.

5. Equally likely Events

The given events are said to be equally likely, if none of them is expected to occur in preference to the other.

e.g.

(i) When an unbiased coin is tossed, then occurrence of head or tail are equally likely cases and there is no reason to expect a 'head' or a 'tail' in preference to the other.

(ii) When an unbiased die is thrown, all the six faces 1, 2, 3, 4, 5 and 6 are equally likely to come up. There is no reason to expect 1 or 2 or 3 or 4 or 5 or 6 in preference to the other.

6. Complementary Event

Let E be an event and S be the sample space for a random experiment, then complement of E is denoted by E' or E^c or $\overline{E}$. Clearly, E' means E does not occur.

Thus, E' occurs $\Leftrightarrow E$ does not occur.

e.g. When an unbiased die is thrown,

then the sample space $S = \{1, 2, 3, 4, 5, 6\}$.

If $E = \{1, 4, 6\}$, then $E' = \{2, 3, 5\}$

Example 4. Two dice are thrown once. If the event getting the sum of numbers on the dice less than and equal to 9, then find the complementary event of it.

Sol. On throwing of two dice, we get

Sample space $(S) = \{(1, 1), (1, 2), (1, 3), (1, 4), (1, 5), (1, 6), (2, 1), (2, 2), (2, 3), (2, 4), (2, 5), (2, 6), (3, 1), (3, 2), (3, 3), (3, 4), (3, 5), (3, 6), (4, 1), (4, 2), (4, 3), (4, 4), (4, 5), (4, 6), \ldots\ldots (6, 6)\}$

Let E be the event of getting the sum of numbers on the dice less than and equal to 9.

$\therefore$ E' be the event of getting the sum of number on the dice greater than 9

$= \{(4, 6), (5, 5), (5, 6), (6, 4), (6, 5), (6, 6)\}$

7. Mutually Exclusive Events

A set of events is said to be mutually exclusive, if occurrence of one of them precludes the occurrence of any of the remaining events. If a set of events $E_1, E_2, \ldots, E_n$ are mutually exclusive events.

Then, $E_1 \cap E_2 \cap \ldots \cap E_n = \phi$

e.g. If we thrown an unbiased die,

then the sample space $S = \{1, 2, 3, 4, 5, 6\}$ in which

$E_1 = \{1, 2, 3\}$ = the event of occurrence of a number less than 4 and $E_2 = \{5, 6\}$ = the event of occurrence of a number greater than 4. Clearly, $E_1 \cap E_2 = \phi$

So, E_1 and E_2 are mutually exclusive.

8. Exhaustive Events

A set of events is said to be exhaustive, if the performance of the experiment results in the occurrence of atleast one of them. If a set of events $E_1, E_2, \ldots, E_n$ are exhaustive events.

Then, $E_1 \cup E_2 \cup \ldots \cup E_n = S$

e.g. If we thrown an unbiased die,

then sample space $S = \{1, 2, 3, 4, 5, 6\}$ in which

$E_1 = \{1, 2, 3, 4\}$ = the event of occurrence of a number less than 5

and $E_2 = \{3, 4, 5, 6\}$ = the event of occurrence of a number greater than 2

Then, $E_1 \cup E_2 = \{1, 2, 3, 4, 5, 6\}$ and $E_1 \cap E_2 = \{3, 4\}$

So, $E_1 \cup E_2 = S$ and $E_1 \cap E_2 \neq \phi$

Hence, E_1 and E_2 are exhaustive events.

9. Mutually Exclusive and Exhaustive Events

A set of events is said to be mutually exclusive and exhaustive, if above two conditions are satisfied. If a set of events $E_1, E_2, \ldots, E_n$ are mutually exclusive and exhaustive events.

Then, $E_1 \cup E_2 \cup \ldots \cup E_n = S$

and $E_1 \cap E_2 \cap \ldots \cap E_n = \phi$

e.g. If we thrown an unbiased die, then sample space $S=\{1,2,3,4,5,6\}$ in which

$E_1=\{1,3,5\}$ = the event of occurrence of an odd number

and $E_2=\{2,4,6\}$ = the event of occurrence of an even number

Then, $E_1 \cup E_2=\{1,2,3,4,5,6\}$ and $E_1 \cap E_2=\phi$

So, $E_1 \cup E_2=S$ and $E_1 \cap E_2=\phi$.

Hence, E_1 and E_2 are mutually exclusive and exhaustive events.

Example 5. Four coins are tossed together, consider the following events?

Q: No Tail appears.

R: Exactly two tails appears

T: Atleast three tails appears.

M: Exactly one tail appears so they form a set of mutually exclusive and exhaustive events?

Sol. When four coins are tossed together, we get

Sample space, $S=\{(HHHH),(HTHH),(HTTH),(HTTT),(HHTH),(HHHT),(TTTH),(THTH),(HHTT),(TTHH),(HTHT),(TTTT),(THHH),(THHT),(THTT),(TTHT)\}$

Given, Q = event of getting no tail

$\therefore \quad Q=\{(HHHH)\}$

R = event of getting exactly two tails

$\therefore R=\{(HTTH),(THTH),(HHTT),(TTHH),(HTHT),(THHT)\}$

T = event of getting atleast three tails

$\therefore\ T=\{(HTTT),(TTTH),(TTTT),(THTT),(TTHT)\}$

and M = event of getting exactly one tail.

$\therefore \quad M=\{(HTHH),(HHTH),(HHHT),(THHH)\}$

Clearly, $Q \cap R=\phi, Q \cap T=\phi\ \ R \cap T=\phi,$

$Q \cap M=\phi, R \cap M=\phi$ and $T \cap M=\phi$

So, we can say that Q, R, T and M are mutually exclusive events. [$\because$ Q, R, T and M are pairwise disjoint]

Also, $(Q \cup R \cup T \cup M)=\{(HHHH),(HTTH),(THTH),(HHTT),(TTHH),(HTHT),(THHT),(HTTT),(TTTH),(TTTT),(THTT),(TTHT),(HTHH),(HHTH),(HHHT),(THHH)\}$

$=S$

$\therefore$ Q, R, T and M are exhaustive events.

Hence, Q, R, T and M form a set of mutually exclusive and exhaustive events.

9.2 Mathematical or Priori or Classical Definition of Probability

The probability of an event E to occur is the ratio of the number of cases in its favour to the total number of cases (equally likely).

$$\therefore \quad P(E)=\frac{n(E)}{n(S)}$$

$$=\frac{\text{Number of cases favourable to event } E}{\text{Total number of cases}}$$

JEE Focus Points

Concept Inside Video

- For impossible event ϕ; $P(\phi)=0$
- For sure event S, $P(S)=1$

Relationship between $P(E)$ and $P(E')$

If E is any event and E' be the complement of event E, then $P(E)+P(E')=1$

Proof Let S be the sample space, then

$$E'=S-E \Rightarrow n(E')=n(S)-n(E)$$

$$\Rightarrow \quad \frac{n(E')}{n(S)}=1-\frac{n(E)}{n(S)} \Rightarrow P(E')=1-P(E)$$

i.e. $P(E)+P(E')=1$

- Probability always lies between 0 and 1 i.e. $0 \le P(E) \le 1$
- We use the sign '+' for the operation 'or' and '×' for the operation 'and' in order to solve the problems on definition of probability.

9.3 Odds in Favour and Odds Against the Event

Let S be the sample space. If a is the number of cases favourable to the event E, b is the number of cases favourable to the event E', the **odds in favour** of E are defined by $a:b$ and **odds against** of E are $b:a$.

i.e. odds in favour of event E is

$$\frac{a}{b}=\frac{n(E)}{n(E')}=\frac{\frac{n(E)}{n(S)}}{\frac{n(E')}{n(S)}}=\frac{P(E)}{P(E')} \Rightarrow \frac{P(E')}{P(E)}=\frac{b}{a}$$

$$\Rightarrow \quad \frac{P(E')+P(E)}{P(E)}=\frac{b+a}{a} \Rightarrow \frac{1}{P(E)}=\frac{b+a}{a}$$

$$\Rightarrow \quad P(E)=\frac{a}{a+b} \text{ and } P(E')=\frac{b}{a+b}$$

Example 6. Two dice are thrown simultaneously. What is the probability obtaining a total score less than 11?

Sol. Let S be the sample space and E be the event of obtaining a total less than 11.

Then, $S=\{1,2,3,4,5,6\} \times \{1,2,3,4,5,6\}$

$\Rightarrow n(S)=6 \times 6=36$

Let E' be the event of obtaining a total score greater than or equal to 11.

Also, $\quad E'=\{(5,6),(6,5),(6,6)\};$

$\therefore \quad n(E')=3$

Then, probability of obtaining a total score greater than or equal to 11,

$$P(E') = \frac{n(E')}{n(S)} = \frac{3}{36} = \frac{1}{12}$$

$$\therefore \quad P(E) = 1 - P(E') = 1 - \frac{1}{12} = \frac{11}{12}$$

Hence, required probability is $\frac{11}{12}$.

JEE SCANNER

Example Similar to PYQ Asked in JEE Main 2024

A fair coin is tossed repeatedly until a head is obtained. Let X denote the number of tosses required and let $a = P(X = H_1)$ i.e. getting head at first toss, $b = P(X = H_2)$ i.e. getting head at second toss and $c = P(X = H_3)$ i.e. getting head at third toss. Then, $\frac{b+c}{3a}$ is equal to

(a) $\frac{1}{4}$ (b) $\frac{3}{2}$ (c) $\frac{1}{2}$ (d) $\frac{2}{3}$

Sol. (a) Let H, H_1 and H_2 denote the number of tosses to get head in first, second and third toss respectively.

$$\therefore \quad a = P(X = H_1) = \frac{1}{2}$$

The probability of not getting a 'head' at the first but at second toss is

$$b = P(X = H_2) = \frac{1}{2} \times \frac{1}{2} = \frac{1}{4}$$

The probability of getting a head at the third toss

$$c = P(X = H_3) = \frac{1}{2} \times \frac{1}{2} \times \frac{1}{2} = \frac{1}{8}$$

$$\text{Thus, } \frac{b+c}{3a} = \frac{\frac{1}{8} + \frac{1}{4}}{3(1/2)} = \frac{\frac{1+2}{8}}{3/2} = \frac{3}{8} \times \frac{2}{3} = \frac{1}{4}$$

Skill Builder

A fair die is tossed repeatedly until a six is obtained. Let X denote the number of tosses required. Let the probability $a = P(X = 3)$ and $b = P(X \geq 3)$. Then, the value of $a + b$ is

For Sol.

(a) $\frac{121}{216}$ (b) $\frac{175}{216}$ (c) $\frac{133}{216}$ (d) $\frac{149}{216}$

■ **For more practice** See Q.21 of Milestone Practice 9.1.

Example 7. If a leap year is selected at random, then what is the chance it will contain 53 Sunday?

Decoding the Question

In a leap year 366 days exist i.e. 52 complete week and 2 days more. Use this while solving the question.

Sol. A leap year has 366 days i.e., 52 complete week and two days more. These two days will be two consecutive days of a week. A leap year will have 53 Sundays, if out of the two consecutive days of a week selected at random one is a Sunday.

Let S be the sample space and E be the event that out of the two consecutive days of a week one is Sunday, then

S = {(Sunday, Monday), (Monday, Tuesday), (Tuesday, Wednesday), (Wednesday, Thursday), (Thursday, Friday), (Friday, Saturday), (Saturday, Sunday)};

$$n(S) = 7$$

Of these total 7 outcomes, the favourable outcomes are 2.

$$n(E) = 2$$

Now, required probability, $P(E) = \frac{n(E)}{n(S)} = \frac{2}{7}$

Example 8. A bag contains 8 red and 5 white balls. Three balls are drawn at random. Find the probability that

(i) all the three balls are white.

(ii) all the three balls are red.

(iii) one ball is red and two balls are white.

Sol. Let S be the sample space, E_1 be the event of getting 3 white balls, E_2 be the event of getting 3 red balls and E_3 be the event of getting one red ball and two white balls.

$\therefore$ $n(S)$ = Number of ways of selecting 3 balls out of

$$13(8+5) = {}^{13}C_3 = \frac{13 \cdot 12 \cdot 11}{1 \cdot 2 \cdot 3} = 286$$

(i) $n(E_1)$ = Number of ways of selecting 3 white balls out of 5

$$= {}^5C_3 = {}^5C_2 = \frac{5 \cdot 4}{1 \cdot 2} = 10$$

$$\therefore \quad P\text{ (getting 3 white balls)} = \frac{n(E_1)}{n(S)} = \frac{10}{286} = \frac{5}{143}$$

(ii) $n(E_2)$ = Number of ways of selecting 3 red balls out of 8

$$= {}^8C_3 = \frac{8 \cdot 7 \cdot 6}{1 \cdot 2 \cdot 3} = 56$$

$$\therefore \quad P\text{ (getting 3 red balls)} = \frac{n(E_2)}{n(S)} = \frac{56}{286} = \frac{28}{143}$$

(iii) $n(E_3)$ = Number of ways of selecting 1 red ball out of 8 and 2 white balls out of 5

$$= {}^8C_1 \cdot {}^5C_2 = 8 \cdot 10 = 80$$

$\therefore$ P (getting 1 red and 2 white balls)

$$= \frac{n(E_3)}{n(S)} = \frac{80}{286} = \frac{40}{143}$$

Example 9. Let S be a set consisting of first five prime number. Suppose A and B are two matrices of order 2 each with distinct entries $\in S$. The chance that the matrix AB has atleast one odd entry, is

(a) 90% (b) 84%

(c) 80% (d) 96%

Sol. (d) $S = \{2, 3, 5, 7, 11\}$

Total ways in which A and B can be chosen $= ({}^5C_4 \; 4!)^2$
$= (5!)^2$

$P(E) = 1 - P$ (A and B does not contain the element 2)

$$= 1 - \frac{(4!)^2}{(5!)^2} = 1 - \frac{1}{25} = \frac{24}{25} = 96\%$$

Example 10. A 2×2 matrix is formed with entries from set {0, 1}. The probability it is singular is

(a) $\frac{3}{16}$ (b) $\frac{1}{8}$ (c) $\frac{5}{8}$ (d) $\frac{5}{16}$

Sol. (c) Out of 16 matrices only six are non-singular

$$\begin{bmatrix} 1 & 1 \\ 0 & 1 \end{bmatrix}, \begin{bmatrix} 1 & 1 \\ 1 & 0 \end{bmatrix}, \begin{bmatrix} 0 & 1 \\ 1 & 1 \end{bmatrix}, \begin{bmatrix} 1 & 0 \\ 1 & 1 \end{bmatrix}, \begin{bmatrix} 1 & 0 \\ 0 & 1 \end{bmatrix}, \begin{bmatrix} 0 & 1 \\ 1 & 0 \end{bmatrix}.$$

$\therefore$ Required probability $= 1 - \frac{6}{16} = \frac{5}{8}$

Milestone Practice 9.1

1. A problem in Mathematics is given to three students and their respective probabilities of solving the problem are $\frac{1}{2}, \frac{1}{3}$ and $\frac{1}{4}$. The probability that the problem is solved, is
(a) $\frac{3}{4}$ (b) $\frac{1}{2}$ (c) $\frac{2}{3}$ (d) $\frac{1}{3}$

2. A dice is thrown 3 times and the sum of the 3 numbers thrown is 15. The probability that the first throw was a four, is
(a) $\frac{1}{5}$ (b) $\frac{1}{4}$ (c) $\frac{1}{6}$ (d) $\frac{2}{5}$

3. Three faces of a fair dice are yellow, two faces red and one blue. The dice is tossed three times. The probability that the colours yellow, red and blue appear in the first, second and third toss respectively, is
(a) $\frac{1}{6}$ (b) $\frac{1}{12}$ (c) $\frac{1}{24}$ (d) $\frac{1}{36}$

4. A speaks truth in 75% of cases and B in 80% of cases. The percentage of cases they are likely to contradict each other in stating the same fact, is
(a) 30% (b) 35% (c) 45% (d) 25%

5. An unbiased dice with faces marked 1, 2, 3, 4, 5, 6 is rolled four times. Out of four face values obtained the probability that the minimum face value is not less than 2 and the maximum face value is not greater than 5, is
(a) $\frac{16}{81}$ (b) $\frac{1}{81}$ (c) $\frac{80}{81}$ (d) $\frac{65}{81}$

6. Three numbers are chosen at random without replacement from {1, 2, 3, ..., 10}. The probability that the minimum of the chosen number is 3 or their maximum is 7, is
(a) $\frac{11}{20}$ (b) $\frac{7}{20}$ (c) $\frac{11}{40}$ (d) $\frac{7}{40}$

7. Seven white balls and three black balls are randomly placed in a row. The probability that no two black balls are placed adjacently, is
(a) $\frac{1}{2}$ (b) $\frac{7}{15}$ (c) $\frac{2}{15}$ (d) $\frac{1}{3}$

8. Two numbers are selected randomly from the set $S = \{1, 2, 3, 4, 5, 6\}$ without replacement. The probability that minimum of the two numbers is less than 4, is
(a) $\frac{1}{15}$ (b) $\frac{14}{15}$ (c) $\frac{1}{5}$ (d) $\frac{4}{5}$

9. If $\frac{1+3p}{3}, \frac{1-p}{4}$ and $\frac{1-2p}{2}$ are the probabilities of the three mutually exclusive events, then $p \in$
(a) [0, 1] (b) $\left[0, \frac{1}{2}\right]$ (c) $\left[\frac{1}{3}, 1\right]$ (d) $\left[\frac{1}{3}, \frac{1}{2}\right]$

10. Three identical dice are rolled once. The probability that the same number will appear on each of them, is
(a) $\frac{1}{6}$ (b) $\frac{1}{36}$ (c) $\frac{1}{18}$ (d) $\frac{3}{28}$

11. If the letters of the word ASSASSIN are written down in a row, the probability that no two S's occur together, is
(a) $\frac{1}{35}$ (b) $\frac{1}{21}$ (c) $\frac{1}{14}$ (d) $\frac{1}{28}$

12. A box contains 2 black, 4 white and 3 red balls. One ball is drawn at random from the box and kept aside. From the remaining balls in the box another ball is drawn and kept beside the first. This process is repeated till all the balls are drawn from the box. The probability that the balls drawn from the box are in the sequence 2 black, 4 white and 3 red, is
(a) $\frac{1}{126}$ (b) $\frac{1}{630}$ (c) $\frac{1}{1260}$ (d) $\frac{1}{2520}$

13. If three distinct numbers are chosen randomly from the first 100 natural numbers, then the probability that all three of them are divisible by both 2 and 3, is
(a) $\frac{4}{55}$ (b) $\frac{4}{35}$ (c) $\frac{4}{33}$ (d) $\frac{4}{1155}$

14. There are 2 vans each having numbered seats, 3 in the front and 4 at the back. There are 3 girls and 9 boys to be seated in the vans. The probability of 3 girls sitting together in a back row on adjacent seats, is
(a) $\frac{1}{13}$ (b) $\frac{1}{39}$ (c) $\frac{1}{65}$ (d) $\frac{1}{91}$

15. A and B stand in a ring along with 10 other persons. If the arrangement is at random, then the probability that there are exactly 3 persons between A and B, is

(a) $\frac{1}{11}$ (b) $\frac{2}{11}$ (c) $\frac{3}{11}$ (d) $\frac{4}{11}$

16. The first 12 letters of English alphabet are written down at random in a row. The probability that there are exactly 4 letters between A and B, is

(a) $\frac{7}{33}$ (b) $\frac{7}{66}$ (c) $\frac{7}{99}$ (d) $\frac{5}{33}$

17. Six boys and six girls sit in a row randomly. The probability that the six girls sit together or the boys and girls sit alternately, is

(a) $\frac{3}{308}$ (b) $\frac{1}{100}$ (c) $\frac{2}{205}$ (d) $\frac{4}{407}$

18. If from each of three boxes containing 3 white and 1 black, 2 white and 2 black, 1 white and 3 black balls, one ball is drawn, the probability of drawing 2 white and 1 black ball, is

(a) $\frac{13}{32}$ (b) $\frac{1}{4}$

(c) $\frac{1}{32}$ (d) $\frac{3}{16}$

19. If E be any event in sample space, then maximum value of $3\sqrt{P(E)} + 4\sqrt{P(\overline{E})}$ is

(a) 4 (b) 2

(c) 5 (d) Cannot be determined

20. If the letters of the word MATHEMATICS are arranged arbitrarily, the probability that C comes before E, E before H, H before I and I before S, is

(a) $\frac{3}{10}$ (b) $\frac{1}{20}$ (c) $\frac{1}{120}$ (d) $\frac{1}{720}$

21. A fair die is tossed repeatedly until a six is obtained. Let X denotes the number of tosses required and $a = P(X = 4)$, $b = P(X \geq 4)$. Then, the value of $\frac{b}{a}$ is

(a) 4 (b) 6 (c) 3 (d) 2

Answer Key

1. (a)	2. (a)	3. (d)	4. (b)	5. (a)
6. (c)	7. (b)	8. (d)	9. (d)	10. (b)
11. (c)	12. (c)	13. (d)	14. (d)	15. (b)
16. (b)	17. (a)	18. (a)	19. (c)	20. (c)
21. (b)				

For Detailed Solution

Milestone 2 Conditional Probability

• Algebra of Probability • Conditional Probability • Independent Events

It is the possibility of an event or outcome occurring, based on the occurrence of a previous event or outcome. We will study, conditional probability in detailed in this milestone.

9.4 Algebra of Probability

If A, B and C are any three events, then

(i) $A \cap B$ or AB denotes the event of simultaneous occurrence of both the events A and B.

(ii) $A \cup B$ or $A + B$ denotes the event of occurrence of atleast one of the events A or B.

(iii) $A - B$ denotes the occurrence of event A but not B.

(iv) $\overline{A}$ denotes the not occurrence of event A.

(v) $A \cap \overline{B}$ denotes the occurrence of event A but not B.

(vi) $\overline{A} \cap \overline{B} = \overline{(A \cup B)}$ denotes the occurrence of neither A nor B.

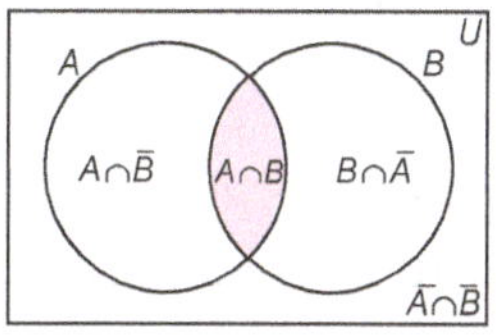

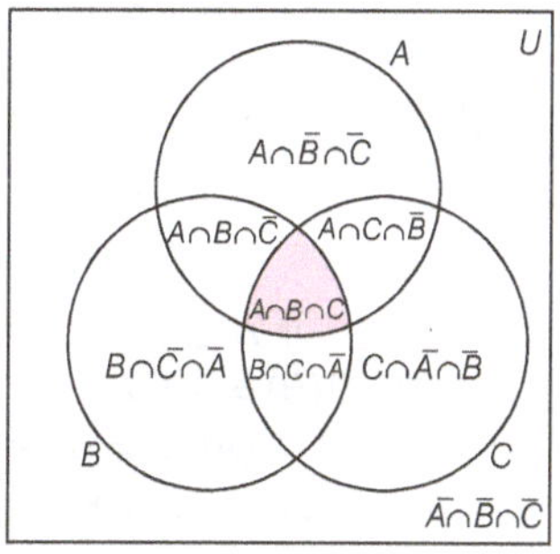

(vii) $A \cup B \cup C$ denotes the occurrence of atleast one event A, B or C.

(viii) $(A \cap \bar{B}) \cup (\bar{A} \cap B)$ denotes the occurrence of exactly one of A and B.

(ix) $A \cap B \cap C$ denotes the occurrence of all three A, B and C.

(x) $(A \cap B \cap \bar{C}) \cup (A \cap \bar{B} \cap C) \cup (\bar{A} \cap B \cap C)$ denotes the occurrence of exactly two of A, B and C.

Important Results

1. If A and B are arbitrary events, then

(a) $P(A \cup B) = P(A) + P(B) - P(A \cap B)$

If A and B are mutually exclusive events, then $A \cap B = \phi$. Hence, $P(A \cap B) = 0$.

$\therefore\ P(A \cup B) = P(A) + P(B)$

(b) P (exactly one of A, B occurs)

$$= P(A \cap \bar{B}) + P(\bar{A} \cap B)$$
$$= P(A) - P(A \cap B) + P(B) - P(A \cap B)$$
$$= P(A) + P(B) - 2P(A \cap B)$$
$$= P(A \cup B) - P(A \cap B)$$

(c) P (neither A nor B)

$$= P(\bar{A} \cap \bar{B}) = P(\overline{A \cup B}) = 1 - P(A \cup B)$$

$P(\bar{A} \cup \bar{B}) = 1 - P(A \cap B)$

2. If A, B and C are three events, then

(a) $P(A \cup B \cup C) = P(A) + P(B) + P(C) - P(A \cap B) - P(B \cap C) - P(C \cap A) + P(A \cap B \cap C)$

If A, B and C are mutually exclusive events, then

$A \cap B = \phi$, $B \cap C = \phi$, $C \cap A = \phi$, $A \cap B \cap C = \phi$

$\Rightarrow P(A \cap B) = 0$, $P(B \cap C) = 0$, $P(C \cap A) = 0$, $P(A \cap B \cap C) = 0$

$\therefore\ P(A \cup B \cup C) = P(A) + P(B) + P(C)$

(b) P (atleast two of A, B, C occur)

$$= P(A \cap B) + P(B \cap C) + P(C \cap A) - 2P(A \cap B \cap C)$$

(c) P (exactly two of A, B, C occur)

$$= P(A \cap B) + P(B \cap C) + P(C \cap A) - 3P(A \cap B \cap C)$$

(d) P (exactly one of A, B, C occur)

$$= P(A) + P(B) + P(C) - 2P(A \cap B) - 2P(B \cap C) - 2P(C \cap A) + 3P(A \cap B \cap C)$$

Example 11. If A, B and C are three events, such that $P(A) = 0.3$, $P(B) = 0.4$, $P(C) = 0.8$, $P(AB) = 0.08$, $P(AC) = 0.28$, $P(ABC) = 0.09$. If $P(A \cup B \cup C) \geq 0.75$, then show that $P(BC)$ lies in the interval $0.23 \leq x \leq 0.48$.

Sol. Let $P(BC) = x$

Since, $P(A \cup B \cup C) = P(A) + P(B) + P(C) - P(AB) - P(BC) - P(CA) + P(ABC)$

$$= 0.3 + 0.4 + 0.8 - 0.08 - x - 0.28 + 0.09 = 1.23 - x$$

But given that $P(A \cup B \cup C) \geq 0.75$ and $P(A \cup B \cup C) \leq 1$

$\therefore\quad 0.75 \leq 1.23 - x \leq 1 \Rightarrow -0.75 \geq -1.23 + x \geq -1$

or $\quad 1.23 - 0.75 \geq x \geq 1.23 - 1$ or $0.23 \leq x \leq 0.48$

Example 12. For a post, three persons A, B and C appear in the interview. The probability of A being selected is twice that of B and the probability of B being selected is thrice that of C. What are the individual probabilities of A, B and C being selected?

Sol. Let E_1, E_2 and E_3 be the events of selection of A, B and C respectively.

Let $\quad P(E_3) = x$

Then, $P(E_2) = 3P(E_3) = 3x$ and $P(E_1) = 2P(E_2) = 6x$

Since, E_1, E_2 and E_3 are mutually exclusive and exhaustive events.

$\therefore\quad P(E_1 \cup E_2 \cup E_3) = P(E_1) + P(E_2) + P(E_3) = 1$

$\therefore\quad P(E_1) + P(E_2) + P(E_3) = 1 \Rightarrow 6x + 3x + x = 1$

$\therefore\quad x = \frac{1}{10}$

Hence, $P(E_1) = 6x = \frac{6}{10} = \frac{3}{5}$, $P(E_2) = 3x = \frac{3}{10}$

and $\quad P(E_3) = x = \frac{1}{10}$

9.5 Conditional Probability

The probability of occurrence of an event E_1, given that E_2 has already occurred is called the conditional probability of occurrence of E_1 on the condition that E_2 has already occurred, it is denoted by $P\left(\frac{E_1}{E_2}\right)$.

Thus, $$P\left(\frac{E_1}{E_2}\right) = \frac{P(E_1 \cap E_2)}{P(E_2)}, \quad [E_2 \neq \phi]$$

$$= \frac{\frac{n(E_1 \cap E_2)}{n(S)}}{\frac{n(E_2)}{n(S)}} = \frac{n(E_1 \cap E_2)}{n(E_2)}$$

Generalised form

If $E_1, E_2, E_3, \ldots, E_n$ are n events such that $E_1 \neq \phi$, $E_1 E_2 \neq \phi$, $E_1 E_2 E_3 \neq \phi$, ..., $E_1 E_2 E_3 \ldots E_{n-1} \neq \phi$, then

$P(E_1 \cap E_2 \cap E_3 \cap \ldots \cap E_n)$

$$= P(E_1) \cdot P\left(\frac{E_2}{E_1}\right) \cdot P\left(\frac{E_3}{E_1 E_2}\right) \cdot P\left(\frac{E_4}{E_1 E_2 E_3}\right) \ldots P\left(\frac{E_n}{E_1 E_2 E_3 \ldots E_{n-1}}\right)$$

JEE SCANNER

Example Similar to PYQ Asked in JEE Main 2023

Two dice are thrown. The probability that the sum of the numbers coming up on them is 9, if it is known that the number 5 always occurs on the first dice is

(a) $\frac{4}{5}$ (b) $\frac{1}{6}$ (c) $\frac{5}{6}$ (d) $\frac{3}{5}$

Sol. (b) Let S be the sample space

$\therefore \quad S = \{1, 2, 3, 4, 5, 6\} \times \{1, 2, 3, 4, 5, 6\}$

$\therefore \quad n(S) = 36$

and let $E_1 \equiv$ The event that the sum of the numbers coming up is 9.

and $E_2 \equiv$ The event of occurrence of 5 on the first dice.

$\therefore \quad E_1 \equiv \{(3, 6), (6, 3), (4, 5), (5, 4)\}$

$\therefore \quad n(E_1) = 4$

and $E_2 = \{(5, 1), (5, 2), (5, 3), (5, 4), (5, 5), (5, 6)\}$

$\therefore \quad n(E_2) = 6$

$E_1 \cap E_2 = \{(5, 4)\}$

$\therefore \quad n(E_1 \cap E_2) = 1$

Now, $P(E_1 \cap E_2) = \frac{n(E_1 \cap E_2)}{n(S)} = \frac{1}{36}$

and $P(E_2) = \frac{n(E_2)}{n(S)} = \frac{6}{36} = \frac{1}{6}$

$\therefore$ Required probability,

$$P\left(\frac{E_1}{E_2}\right) = \frac{P(E_1 \cap E_2)}{P(E_2)} = \frac{\frac{1}{36}}{\frac{1}{6}} = \frac{1}{6}$$

Skill Builder

A bag contains 3 red and 7 black balls. Two balls are drawn at random without replacement. If the second ball is red, then the probability that the first ball is also red, is

For Sol.

(a) $\frac{1}{9}$ (b) $\frac{5}{9}$

(c) $\frac{2}{9}$ (d) $\frac{4}{9}$

▪ **For more practice** See Q.12 of Milestone Practice 9.2.

Example 13. In a class, 30% students fail in English; 20% students fail in Hindi and 10% students fail in English and Hindi both. A student is chosen at random, then what is the probability that he will fail in English, if he has failed in Hindi?

Sol. Let S be the sample space.

If $n(S) = 100$, then

$E_1 \equiv$ The event that the student chosen fail in English

$\therefore n(E_1) = 30$

and $E_2 \equiv$ The event that the student chosen fail in Hindi

$\therefore \quad n(E_2) = 20$ and $n(E_1 \cap E_2) = 10$

$\therefore \quad P(E_2) = \frac{n(E_2)}{n(S)} = \frac{20}{100} = \frac{1}{5}$

and $P(E_1 \cap E_2) = \frac{n(E_1 \cap E_2)}{n(S)} = \frac{10}{100} = \frac{1}{10}$

$\therefore$ Required probability, $P\left(\frac{E_1}{E_2}\right) = \frac{P(E_1 \cap E_2)}{P(E_2)} = \frac{\frac{1}{10}}{\frac{1}{5}} = \frac{1}{2}$

Example 14. If a die is thrown, the probability of occurrence of a number greater than 1, if it is known that only odd numbers can come up, is equal to

(a) $\frac{1}{3}$ (b) $\frac{2}{3}$ (c) $\frac{1}{2}$ (d) $\frac{1}{6}$

Sol. (b) Let S = The sample space = {1, 2, 3, 4, 5, 6}

A = The event of occurrence of an odd number = {1, 3, 5}

B = The event of occurrence of number greater than 1 = {2, 3, 4, 5 6}

Here, $A \cap B = \{3, 5\}$

So that $P\left(\frac{B}{A}\right) = \frac{P(A \cap B)}{P(A)}$

$= \frac{n(A \cap B)}{n(A)} = \frac{2}{3}$

Example 15. A bag contains 5 red marbles and 5 green marbles. One marble is drawn, its colour recorded, and then placed back into the bag. This process is repeated until a green marble is found. Given that the first green marble is found on an odd numbered draw, the probability that it is found on the fifth draws is

(a) $\frac{1}{32}$ (b) $\frac{3}{64}$ (c) $\frac{1}{256}$ (d) $\frac{3}{256}$

Sol. (b) Let S = The event of occurrence of green marble

F = The event of occurrence of red marble

E : Green marbles is drawn on an odd numbers drawn

$P(S) = \frac{1}{2}; \quad P(F) = \frac{1}{2}$

$P(E) = P(S \text{ or } FFS \text{ or } FFFFS \text{ or } \ldots..) = \frac{P(S)}{1 - P(F)\,P(F)}$

$= \frac{1/2}{1 - 1/4} = \frac{2}{3}$

Let A : Green marble is drawn on this 5th draw

$$P(A/E)=\frac{P(A\cap E)}{P(E)}=\frac{P(A)}{P(E)}$$

$$=\frac{1/32}{2/3}=\frac{1}{32}\cdot\frac{3}{2}=\frac{3}{64}$$

9.6 Independent Events

Two events are said to be independent, if the occurrence of one does not depend on the occurrence of the other.

e.g. When an unbiased die is thrown, then the sample space $S=\{1,2,3,4,5,6\}$

Let $E_1=\{1,3,5\}=$ the event of occurrence of an odd number and $E_2=\{2,4,6\}=$ the event of occurrence of an even number.

Clearly, the occurrence of odd number does not depend on the occurrence of even number.

So, E_1 and E_2 are independent events.

There events $E_1E_2E_3$ the independent if and only if

$$P(E_1\cap E_2)=P(E_1)\,P(E_2)$$

$$P(E_2\cap E_3)=P(E_2)\,P(E_3)$$

$$P(E_3\cap E_1)=P(E_3)\,P(E_1)$$

and $P(E_1\cap E_2\cap E_3)=P(E_1)\,P(E_2)\,P(E_3)$

JEE Focus Points

- If E_1 and E_2 are independent events, then
  - E_1 and $\bar{E}_2$ are independent events.
  - $\bar{E}_1$ and E_2 are independent events.
  - $\bar{E}_1$ and $\bar{E}_2$ are independent events.
- If E_1 and E_2 are independent events, then $P\left(\frac{E_2}{E_1}\right)=P(E_2)$
- If E_1 and E_2 are two events such that $E_2\neq\phi$, then $P\left(\frac{E_1}{E_2}\right)+P\left(\frac{\bar{E}_1}{E_2}\right)=1$
- If $E_1, E_2, E_3, \ldots, E_n$ are independent events, then $P(E_1\cup E_2\cup E_3\cup\ldots\cup E_n)=1-P(\bar{E}_1)\cdot P(\bar{E}_2)\cdot P(\bar{E}_3)\ldots P(\bar{E}_n)$
- If E_1, E_2 and E_3 are three events such that $E_1\neq\phi$, $E_1E_2\neq\phi$, then $P(E_1\cap E_2\cap E_3)=P(E_1)\cdot P\left(\frac{E_2}{E_1}\right)\cdot P\left(\frac{E_3}{E_1E_2}\right)$

Example 16. If A and B are independent events, the probability that both A and B occur is $\frac{1}{8}$ and the probability that none of them occurs is $\frac{3}{8}$. Find the probability of the occurrence of A.

Sol. We have,

$$P(A\cap B)=\frac{1}{8}\Rightarrow P(A)\,P(B)=\frac{1}{8} \quad \text{...(i)}$$

[$\because$ A and B are independent]

and $$P(\bar{A}\cap\bar{B})=\frac{3}{8}\Rightarrow P(\bar{A})\,P(\bar{B})=\frac{3}{8}$$

$$\Rightarrow (1-P(A))(1-P(B))=\frac{3}{8}$$

$$\Rightarrow 1-P(A)-P(B)+\frac{1}{8}=\frac{3}{8} \quad \text{[from Eq. (i)]}$$

$$\Rightarrow P(A)+P(B)=\frac{3}{4} \quad \text{...(ii)}$$

The quadratic equation whose roots are $P(A)$ and $P(B)$ is

$x^2-[P(A)+P(B)]x+P(A)\cdot P(B)=0$

$$\Rightarrow x^2-\frac{3}{4}x+\frac{1}{8}=0 \quad \text{[from Eqs. (i) and (ii)]}$$

or $8x^2-6x+1=0$ or $x=\frac{1}{2},\frac{1}{4}$

Hence, $P(A)=\frac{1}{2}$ or $\frac{1}{4}$

Example 17. A bag contain four tickets marked with 112, 121, 211, 222 one ticket is drawn at random from bag. Let E_i $(i=1,2,3)$ denote the event that ith digit on ticket is 2, then

(a) E_1 and E_2 are not independent
(b) E_2 and E_3 are not independent
(c) E_3 and E_1 are not independent
(d) E_1, E_2, E_3 are not independent

Sol. (d) We have, $P(E_i)=\frac{2}{4}=\frac{1}{2}$ for $i=1,2,3$

For $i\neq j$, $P(E_i\cap E_j)=\frac{1}{4}=P(E_j)\,P(E_i)$.

Therefore, E_i, E_j are independent.

Also, $P(E_1\cap E_2\cap E_3)=\frac{1}{4}\neq P(E_1)\,P(E_2)\,P(E_3)$

E_1, E_2, E_3 are not independent.

Example 18. Let E_1, E_2 and E_3 be three independent events associated with a random experiment such that $3P(E_1\cap\bar{E}_2\cap\bar{E}_3)=P(\bar{E}_1\cap E_2\cap\bar{E}_3)=9P(\bar{E}_1\cap\bar{E}_2\cap E_3)$ $=3-3P(E_1\cup E_2\cup E_3)$, where $P(E_1), P(E_2), P(E_3)\neq 1$ and $P(A)$ denotes probability of event A. Then,

$\begin{vmatrix} P(E_1) & P(E_2) & P(E_3)\\ P(E_2) & P(E_3) & P(E_1)\\ P(E_3) & P(E_1) & P(E_2)\end{vmatrix}$ is equal to

(a) $\frac{9}{32}$ (b) $-\frac{9}{32}$ (c) $\frac{5}{37}$ (d) $\frac{7}{19}$

Sol. (b) Let $P(E_1) = a$, $P(E_2) = b$ and $P(E_3) = c$

$$\Rightarrow \quad 3a(1-b)(1-c) = (1-a)\,b\,(1-c) = 9(1-a)(1-b)c = 3(1-a)(1-b)(1-c)$$

$$\Rightarrow \quad \frac{3a}{1-a} = \frac{b}{1-b} = \frac{9c}{1-c} = 3$$

$$\Rightarrow \quad a = \frac{1}{2}, b = \frac{3}{4}, c = \frac{1}{4}$$

$$\text{Now, } \begin{vmatrix} 1/2 & 3/4 & 1/4 \\ 3/4 & 1/4 & 1/2 \\ 1/4 & 1/2 & 3/4 \end{vmatrix} = -\frac{9}{32}$$

Example 19. Events A, B, C satisfy $P(A) = 0.3$, $P(B) = 0.3$ and $P(C) = 0.5$. Events A and B are mutually exclusive. Events A and C are independent and $P(B / C) = 0.2$, $P(A \cup B \cup C)$ equals

(a) 0.95 (b) 0.85 (c) 0.75 (d) 0.65

Sol. (b) Given, $P(A) = 0.3$, $P(B) = 0.3$, $P(C) = 0.5$ and $P\left(\frac{B}{C}\right) = 0.2$

$$\because \quad P(B/C) = \frac{P(B \cap C)}{P(C)}$$

$$\therefore \quad P(B \cap C) = 0.2 P(C) = 0.1$$

$$\text{Now, } P(A \cup B \cup C) = \Sigma P(A) - \Sigma P(A \cap B) + P(A \cap B \cap C)$$
$$= 1.1 - [0 + 0.1 + (0.5)(0.3)] + 0$$
$$= 1.1 - 0.25 = 0.85$$

Example 20. A room has three electric lamps. From a collection of 10 electric bulbs of which 6 are good 3 are selected at random and put in the lamps. The probability that the room is lighted, lies in the interval

(a) (0.4, 0.6) (b) (0.6, 0.8)
(c) (0.8, 0.9) (d) (0.9, 1)

Sol. (d) Total bulbs = 10

Let G = Good bulbs = 6

and D = Defective bulbs = 4

Let E = Room gets lighted

$$P(E) = 1 - P(\overline{E}) = 1 - P\text{ (defective bulbs)}$$

$$= 1 - P(DDDD) = 1 - \frac{{}^4C_3}{{}^{10}C_3} = \frac{29}{30} = 0.96$$

Example 21. If A and B are two independent events such that $P(A \cap B) = \frac{1}{10}$, $P(A \cup B)^c = \frac{2}{5}$, then

(a) $P(A) = \frac{1}{2}$, $P(B) = \frac{1}{3}$ (b) $P(A) = \frac{1}{5}$, $P(B) = \frac{1}{3}$
(c) $P(A) = \frac{1}{2}$, $P(B) = \frac{1}{5}$ (d) $P(A) = \frac{1}{3}$, $P(B) = \frac{1}{2}$

Sol. (c) Let $P(A) = p$, $P(B) = q$

Then, $pq = \frac{1}{10}$ ... (i)

and $(1-p)(1-q) = \frac{2}{5}$ ... (ii)

From Eqs. (i) and (ii), we get

$$p + q = \frac{7}{10} \text{ and } pq = \frac{1}{10}$$

Let $p = \frac{1}{10q}$

Put the value of p in $p + q = \frac{7}{10}$, we get

$$\frac{1}{10q} + q = \frac{7}{10}$$

$$\Rightarrow \quad 10q^2 - 7q + 1 = 0 \Rightarrow 5q(2q-1) - 1(2q-1) = 0$$

$$\Rightarrow \quad (5q-1)(2q-1) = 0 \Rightarrow q = \frac{1}{5} \text{ or } q = \frac{1}{2}$$

When $q = \frac{1}{5}$, then $p = \frac{1}{2} \Rightarrow P(A) = \frac{1}{2}$ and $P(B) = \frac{1}{5}$

When $q = \frac{1}{2}$, then $p = \frac{1}{5} \Rightarrow P(A) = \frac{1}{5}$ and $P(B) = \frac{1}{2}$

Milestone Practice 9.2

1. If $P(A) = 0{\cdot}8$, $P(B) = 0{\cdot}5$, then $P(A \cap B)$ lies in the interval

(a) $[0{\cdot}2, 0{\cdot}5]$ (b) $[0{\cdot}2, 0{\cdot}3]$
(c) $[0{\cdot}3, 0{\cdot}5]$ (d) $[0{\cdot}1, 0{\cdot}5]$

2. If $P(A) = \frac{1}{4}$, $P(B) = \frac{1}{13}$ and $P(A \cap B) = \frac{1}{52}$, then the value of $P(\overline{A} \cap \overline{B})$, is

(a) $\frac{3}{13}$ (b) $\frac{5}{13}$ (c) $\frac{7}{13}$ (d) $\frac{9}{13}$

3. If A and B are independent events such that $P(\overline{A} \cap B) = \frac{2}{15}$ and $P(A \cap \overline{B}) = \frac{1}{6}$, then $P(B)$ is

(a) $\frac{1}{5}$ (b) $\frac{1}{6}$ (c) $\frac{4}{5}$ (d) $\frac{5}{6}$

4. 6 chocolates out of 8 different brands available in the market are chosen. Probability that all the chocolates are of different brands.

(a) $\frac{{}^8C_6}{{}^{13}C_6}$ (b) $\frac{{}^8C_6}{{}^{13}C_8}$
(c) $\frac{{}^8C_6}{8^6}$ (d) None of these

5. If A, B and C are mutually exclusive and exhaustive events associated with a random experiment. If $P(B) = \frac{3}{2}P(A)$ and $P(C) = \frac{1}{2}P(B)$, then $P(A)$ is equal to

(a) $\frac{2}{13}$ (b) $\frac{4}{13}$ (c) $\frac{6}{13}$ (d) $\frac{8}{13}$

6. If A and B are two events such that $P(A \cap B) = \frac{1}{4}$, $P(\bar{A} \cap \bar{B}) = \frac{1}{5}$ and $P(A) = P(B) = p$, then p is equal to

(a) $\frac{17}{40}$ (b) $\frac{19}{40}$ (c) $\frac{21}{40}$ (d) $\frac{23}{40}$

7. If A and B are two events such that $P(A \cup B) = \frac{3}{4}$, $P(A \cap B) = \frac{1}{4}$, $P(\bar{A}) = \frac{2}{3}$. Then, $(\bar{A} \cap B)$ is equal to

(a) $\frac{5}{12}$ (b) $\frac{3}{8}$ (c) $\frac{5}{8}$ (d) $\frac{1}{4}$

8. If $P(B) = \frac{3}{4}$, $P(A \cap B \cap \bar{C}) = \frac{1}{3}$ and $P(\bar{A} \cap B \cap \bar{C}) = \frac{1}{3}$, then $P(B \cap C)$ is equal to

(a) $\frac{1}{12}$ (b) $\frac{1}{6}$

(c) $\frac{1}{15}$ (d) $\frac{1}{9}$

9. If A and B are two events such that $P(A) > 0$ and $P(B) \neq 1$, then $P\left(\frac{\bar{A}}{\bar{B}}\right)$ is equal to

(a) $1 - P\left(\frac{A}{B}\right)$ (b) $1 - P\left(\frac{A}{\bar{B}}\right)$

(c) $\frac{1 - P(A \cup B)}{1 - P(B)}$ (d) $\frac{P(\bar{A})}{P(B)}$

10. If $P(A) = \frac{3}{8}$, $P(B) = \frac{5}{8}$ and $P(A \cup B) = \frac{3}{4}$, then $P\left(\frac{\bar{A}}{\bar{B}}\right)$ is equal to

(a) $\frac{1}{4}$ (b) $\frac{1}{3}$

(c) $\frac{2}{3}$ (d) $\frac{3}{4}$

11. If two events A and B are such that $P(\bar{A}) = 0 \cdot 3$, $P(B) = 0 \cdot 4$ and $P(A \cap \bar{B}) = 0 \cdot 5$, then $P\left(\frac{B}{A \cup \bar{B}}\right)$ is equal to

(a) $\frac{1}{4}$ (b) $\frac{1}{5}$

(c) $\frac{2}{5}$ (d) $\frac{3}{5}$

12. Two dice are thrown. The probability that the number appeared have a sum of 8. If it is known that the second die always exhibits 4, is

(a) $\frac{5}{6}$ (b) $\frac{1}{6}$ (c) $\frac{2}{3}$ (d) $\frac{1}{3}$

13. A and B each throw a fair dice. The probability that A's throw is not greater than B's throw is equal to

(a) $\frac{1}{3}$ (b) $\frac{2}{3}$

(c) $\frac{3}{12}$ (d) $\frac{7}{12}$

14. If a die is thrown, the probability of occurrence of a number greater than 3, if it is known that only prime numbers can come up, is equal to

(a) $\frac{1}{3}$ (b) $\frac{2}{3}$

(c) $\frac{1}{2}$ (d) $\frac{2}{5}$

15. There are m persons sitting in a row. Two of them are selection at random. The probability that the two selected persons are not together is

(a) $\frac{2}{m}$ (b) $1 - \frac{2}{m}$

(c) $\frac{m(m-1)}{(m+1)(m+2)}$ (d) None of these

16. Three ordinary and fair dice are rolled simultaneously. The probability of sum of outcomes being atleast is equal to 8 is equal

(a) $\frac{81}{108}$ (b) $\frac{27}{216}$

(c) $\frac{81}{216}$ (d) $\frac{181}{216}$

17. If the paper of 4 students can be checked by any one of the 7 teachers, then the probability that all the 4 papers are checked by exactly 2 teachers is

(a) $\frac{2}{7}$ (b) $\frac{6}{49}$

(c) $\frac{32}{343}$ (d) None of these

Answer Key

1. (c)	2. (d)	3. (b,c)	4. (c)	5. (b)
6. (c)	7. (a)	8. (a)	9. (c)	10. (c)
11. (a)	12. (b)	13. (d)	14. (a)	15. (b)
16. (d)	17. (b)			

For Detailed Solution

Milestone 3 Some Important Theorems of Probability

• Total Probability Theorem • Baye's Theorem or Inverse Probability • Random Variable and Its Distribution • Mean and Variance of a Random Variable • Binomial Theorem on Probability • Expectation • Uncountable Uniform Spaces

9.7 Total Probability Theorem

Let $E_1, E_2, \ldots, E_n$ be n mutually exclusive and exhaustive events i.e. $E_i \cap E_j = \phi$ for $i \neq j$ and $\bigcup_{i=1}^{n} E_i = S$.

Suppose that $P(E_i) > 0, \forall\, 1 \leq i \leq n$

Then, for any event E

$$P(E) = \sum_{i=1}^{n} P(E_i) \cdot P\left(\frac{E}{E_i}\right)$$

Proof Since, $E_1, E_2, \ldots, E_n$ are disjoint

$\therefore E \cap E_1, E \cap E_2, \ldots, E \cap E_n$ are also disjoint.

Now, $$E = E \cap S = E \cap \left(\bigcup_{i=1}^{n} E_i\right) = \bigcup_{i=1}^{n} (E \cap E_i)$$

$\therefore$ $$P(E) = \sum_{i=1}^{n} P(E \cap E_i) = \sum_{i=1}^{n} P(E_i) \cdot P\left(\frac{E}{E_i}\right)$$

JEE SCANNER

Example Similar to PYQ Asked in JEE Main 2024

Bag A contains 3 red and 2 white balls and bag B contains 2 red and 5 white balls. A bag is selected at random, a ball is drawn and put into the other bag, and then a ball is drawn from that bag. Find the probability that both the balls are drawn are of the same colour.

(a) $\frac{900}{1680}$ (b) $\frac{901}{1680}$ (c) $\frac{3721}{4220}$ (d) $\frac{3740}{4220}$

Sol. (b) Let E_{11} be the event of transferring a red ball from bag A to bag $B = \frac{3}{5}$

Let X be the event of drawing a red ball from bag B,

$P\left(\frac{X}{E_{11}}\right) = \frac{3}{8}$

Let E_{12} be the event of transferring a white ball from bag A to bag $B = \frac{2}{5}$

Let Y be the event of drawing a white ball from bag B,

$P\left(\frac{Y}{E_{12}}\right) = \frac{6}{8}$

Let E_{21} be the event of transferring a red ball from bag B to bag $A = \frac{2}{7}$

Let C be the event of drawing a red ball from bag A,

$P\left(\frac{C}{E_{21}}\right) = \frac{4}{6}$

Let E_{22} be the event of transferring a white ball from bag B to bag $A = \frac{5}{7}$

Let D be the event of drawing a white ball from bag A,

$P\left(\frac{D}{E_{22}}\right) = \frac{3}{6} = \frac{1}{2}$

Hence, required probability,

$$P(E_1) = P(E_{11}) \cdot P\left(\frac{X}{E_{11}}\right) + P(E_{12}) \cdot P\left(\frac{Y}{E_{12}}\right)$$

$$= \frac{3}{5} \times \frac{3}{8} + \frac{2}{5} \times \frac{6}{8} = \frac{9}{40} + \frac{12}{40} = \frac{21}{40}$$

Required probability,

$$P(E_2) = P(E_{21}) \cdot P\left(\frac{C}{E_{21}}\right) + P(E_{22}) \cdot P\left(\frac{D}{E_{22}}\right)$$

$$= \frac{2}{7} \times \frac{4}{6} + \frac{5}{7} \times \frac{3}{6} = \frac{8}{42} + \frac{15}{42} = \frac{23}{42}$$

$$\therefore P(E) = \frac{1}{2} P(E_1) + \frac{1}{2} P(E_2)$$

[$\because$ a bag was picked randomly with equal probability]

$$= 0.5\left(\frac{21}{40} + \frac{23}{42}\right) = \frac{901}{1680}$$

Skill Builder

Three groups A, B and C are competing for positions on the chairman of company X. The probabilities of their winning are 0.6, 0.3, 0.1 respectively. If the group A wins, the probability of introducing a new product is 0.8 and the corresponding probabilities for group B and C are 0.7 and 0.6. The probability that the new product will be introduced, is

(a) 0.61 (b) 0.48 (c) 0.75 (d) 0.21

For Sol.

■ **For more practice** See Q.3 of Milestone Practice 9.3.

Example 22. The probability that certain electronic component fails, when first used is 0.10. If it does not fail immediately, then the probability that it lasts for one year is 0.99. What is the probability that a new component will last for one year?

Sol. Given probability of electronic component fails, when first used = 0.10

i.e. $P(F) = 0.10$

$\therefore \quad P(\bar{F}) = 1 - P(F) = 0.90$

and let $P(Y)$ = Probability of new component to last for one year

$\because \quad P(F) + P(\bar{F}) = 1$

Obviously, the two events are mutually exclusive and exhaustive

$\therefore \quad P\left(\frac{Y}{F}\right) = 0$ and $P\left(\frac{Y}{\bar{F}}\right) = 0.99$

$$\therefore \quad P(Y) = P(F) \cdot P\left(\frac{Y}{F}\right) + P(\bar{F}) . P\left(\frac{Y}{\bar{F}}\right)$$

$$= 0.10 \times 0 + 0.90 \times 0.99$$

$$= 0 + (0.9)(0.99)$$

$$= 0.891$$

Example 23. Three persons A, B and C are contesting for positions on the Board of Directors of a company. The probabilities of their winning are 0.5, 0.3 and 0.2, respectively. If the person A wins, then the probability of introducing a new product is 0.7 and the corresponding probabilities for persons B and C are 0.6 and 0.5, respectively. Find the probability that the new product will be introduced.

Sol. Given, $P(A) = 0.5$, $P(B) = 0.3$ and $P(C) = 0.2$

$\therefore \quad P(A) + P(B) + P(C) = 1$

Then, events A, B, C are exhaustive.

If $P(E)$ = Probability of introducing a new product, then as given

$$P\left(\frac{E}{A}\right) = 0.7, P\left(\frac{E}{B}\right) = 0.6 \text{ and } P\left(\frac{E}{C}\right) = 0.5$$

$$P(E) = P(A) \cdot P\left(\frac{E}{A}\right) + P(B) \cdot P\left(\frac{E}{B}\right) + P(C) \cdot P\left(\frac{E}{C}\right)$$

$$= 0.5 \times 0.7 + 0.3 \times 0.6 + 0.2 \times 0.5$$

$$= 0.35 + 0.18 + 0.10$$

$$= 0.63$$

9.8 Baye's Theorem or Inverse Probability

If an event E can occur only with one of the n mutually exclusive and exhaustive events $E_1, E_2, E_3, \ldots, E_n$ and the probabilities $P(E / E_1), P(E / E_2), \ldots, P(E / E_n)$ are known, then

$$P\left(\frac{E_k}{E}\right) = \frac{P(E_k) \cdot P\left(\frac{E}{E_k}\right)}{\sum_{k=1}^{n} P(E_k) \cdot P\left(\frac{E}{E_k}\right)}$$

Proof The event E occurs with one of the n mutually exclusive and exhaustive events $E_1, E_2, E_3, \ldots, E_n$, then

$$E = EE_1 + EE_2 + EE_3 + \ldots + EE_n$$

$$\Rightarrow \quad P(E) = P(EE_1) + P(EE_2) + P(EE_3) + \ldots + P(EE_n)$$

$$= \sum_{k=1}^{n} P(EE_k) = \sum_{k=1}^{n} P(E_k) \cdot P\left(\frac{E}{E_k}\right)$$

$$\therefore \quad P\left(\frac{E_k}{E}\right) = \frac{P(E_k\ E)}{P(E)} = \frac{P(E_k) \cdot P\left(\frac{E}{E_k}\right)}{\sum_{k=1}^{n} P(E_k) \cdot P\left(\frac{E}{E_k}\right)}$$

Here, the probabilities $P(E_k)$ and $P\left(\frac{E_k}{E}\right)$ are known as **priori** and **posteriori** probabilities, respectively.

Example 24. In a test, an examinee either guesses or copies or knows the answer to a multiple choice question with four choices. The probability that he makes a guess is $\frac{1}{3}$ and the probability that he copies the answer is $\frac{1}{6}$. The probability that his answer is correct given that he copied it is $\frac{1}{8}$. Find the probability that he knew the answer to the question given that he correctly answered it.

Sol. Let E_1 be the event that the answer is guessed, E_2 be the event that the answer is copied, E_3 be the event that the examinee knows the answer and E be the event that the examinee answers correctly.

Given, $P(E_1) = \frac{1}{3}, P(E_2) = \frac{1}{6}$

Assume that events E_1, E_2 and E_3 are exhaustive.

$$\therefore \quad P(E_1) + P(E_2) + P(E_3) = 1$$

$$\therefore \quad P(E_3) = 1 - P(E_1) - P(E_2) = 1 - \frac{1}{3} - \frac{1}{6} = \frac{1}{2}$$

Now, $P\left(\frac{E}{E_1}\right)$ ≡ Probability of getting correct answer by guessing

$= \frac{1}{4}$ [since 4 alternatives]

$P\left(\frac{E}{E_2}\right)$ ≡ Probability of answering correctly by copying

$= \frac{1}{8}$

and $P\left(\frac{E}{E_3}\right) \equiv$ Probability of answering correctly by knowing

$= 1$

Clearly, $\left(\frac{E_3}{E}\right)$ is the event he knew the answer to the question, given that he correctly answered it.

$$\therefore \; P\left(\frac{E_3}{E}\right) = \frac{P(E_3)\cdot P\left(\frac{E}{E_3}\right)}{P(E_1)\cdot P\left(\frac{E}{E_1}\right) + P(E_2)\cdot P\left(\frac{E}{E_2}\right) + P(E_3)\cdot P\left(\frac{E}{E_3}\right)}$$

$$= \frac{\frac{1}{2}\times 1}{\frac{1}{3}\times\frac{1}{4}+\frac{1}{6}\times\frac{1}{8}+\frac{1}{2}\times 1} = \frac{24}{29}$$

JEE SCANNER

Example Similar to PYQ Asked in JEE Main 2024

A die is tossed. If the die shows a 1 or a 2, then one coin is tossed. If die shows 3, then two coins tossed otherwise three coins are tossed. Given that the resulting coin tosses produced no heads. The probability that the die showed 1 or 2 is equal to

(a) $\frac{8}{13}$ (b) $\frac{5}{13}$ (c) $\frac{7}{13}$ (d) $\frac{6}{13}$

Sol. (a) Let $A =$ Event that we have i.e. one, two or three normal coins tossed produced no heads

$B_1 =$ The dice shows up 1 or 2

$B_2 =$ The dice shows up 3

$B_3 =$ The dice shows up 4, 5 or 6

$$P(B_1) = \frac{1}{3};\; P(B_2) = \frac{1}{6};\; P(B_3) = \frac{1}{2}$$

$$P(A/B_1) = \frac{1}{2},\; P(A/B_2) = \frac{1}{2}.\frac{1}{2} = \frac{1}{4}$$

$$P(A/B_3) = \frac{1}{2}.\frac{1}{2}.\frac{1}{2} = \frac{1}{8}$$

$$P\left(\frac{B_1}{A}\right) = \frac{P(B_1)\times P\left(\frac{A}{B_1}\right)}{P(B_1)\times P\left(\frac{A}{B_1}\right) + P(B_2)\times P\left(\frac{A}{B_2}\right) + P(B_3)\times P\left(\frac{A}{B_3}\right)}$$

$$= \frac{\frac{1}{3}\cdot\frac{1}{2}}{\frac{1}{3}\cdot\frac{1}{2}+\frac{1}{6}\cdot\frac{1}{4}+\frac{1}{2}\cdot\frac{1}{8}} = \frac{8}{13}$$

Skill Builder

A bag contains 4 balls. Two balls are drawn at random without replacement and are found to be blue. What is the probability that all balls in the bag are blue?

For Sol.

(a) $\frac{3}{5}$ (b) $\frac{1}{6}$ (c) $\frac{1}{18}$ (d) $\frac{1}{2}$

■ **For more practice** See Q.16 of Milestone Practice 9.3.

9.9 Random Variable and its Distribution

Let S be the sample space associated with a given random experiment. Then, a real valued function X which assigns to each event $w \in S$ to a unique real number $X(w)$ is called a random variable. A random variable is a function that associate a unique numerical value with every outcome of an experiment. The value of the random variable will vary from trial-to-trial as the experiment is repeated. A random variable is usually denoted by the capital letters X, Y, Z, etc.

e.g. A coin is tossed ten times. The random variable X is the number of tails that are noted. X can only take the values 0, 1, 2,..., 10. So, X is a discrete random variable.

There are two types of random variable:

(i) **Discrete random variable** If the range of the real function $X : U \to R$ is a finite set or an infinite set of real numbers, it is called a discrete random variable.

(ii) **Continuous random variable** If the range of X is an interval (a, b) of R, then X is called a continuous random variable.

e.g. In tossing of two coins $S = (HH, HT, TH, TT)$, let X denotes number of heads in tossing of two coins, then

$$X(HH) = 2, X(TH) = 1, X(TT) = 0$$

Probability Distribution

A random variable X takes values $X_1, X_2, \ldots, X_n$ with respective probabilities $P_1, P_2, \ldots, P_n$, then

X	X_1	X_2	$X_3 \ldots$	X_n
$P(X)$	P_1	P_2	$P_3 \ldots$	P_n

is known as the probability distribution of X.

Or

Probability distribution gives the values of the random variable along with the corresponding probabilities.

It satisfies the following conditions:

(i) $0 \le P(x_i) \le 1$ (ii) $\Sigma P(x_i) = 1$

e.g. Probability distribution when two coins are tossed.

Let X denotes the number of heads occurred, then

$P(X = 0) =$ Probability of occurrence of zero head

$$= P(TT) = \frac{1}{2}\cdot\frac{1}{2} = \frac{1}{4}$$

$P(X = 1) =$ Probability of occurrence of one head

$$= P(HT) + P(TH)$$

$$= \frac{1}{2}\cdot\frac{1}{2} + \frac{1}{2}\cdot\frac{1}{2} = \frac{1}{2}$$

$P(X=2)=$ Probability of occurrence of two heads

$$=P(HH)=\frac{1}{2}\cdot\frac{1}{2}=\frac{1}{4}$$

Thus, the probability distribution when two coins are tossed, is as given below:

X	0	1	2
$P(X)$	$\frac{1}{4}$	$\frac{1}{2}$	$\frac{1}{4}$

Example 25. A random variable X has the following probability distribution. Then, the value of

X	0	1	2	3	4	5	6	7
$P(X)$	0	k	$2k$	$2k$	$3k$	k^2	$2k^2$	$7k^2+k$

(i) k (ii) $P(X<3)$ (iii) $P(X>6)$ (iv) $P(0<X<3)$

are respectively

(a) $\frac{1}{10}, \frac{3}{10}, \frac{17}{100}$ and $\frac{3}{10}$
(b) $\frac{1}{10}, \frac{3}{10}, \frac{3}{10}$ and $\frac{17}{100}$
(c) $\frac{17}{100}, \frac{1}{10}, \frac{3}{10}$ and $\frac{3}{10}$
(d) None of these

Sol. (a) (i) It is known that the sum of a probability distribution of random variable is one,

i.e. $\Sigma P(X)=1$, therefore

$$P(0)+P(1)+P(2)+P(3)+P(4)+P(5)+P(6)+P(7)=1$$

$$\Rightarrow 0+k+2k+2k+3k+k^2+2k^2+7k^2+k=1$$

$$\Rightarrow 10k^2+9k-1=0$$

$$\Rightarrow 10k^2+10k-k-1=0$$

$$\Rightarrow 10k(k+1)-1(k+1)=0$$

$$\Rightarrow (k+1)(10k-1)=0$$

$$\Rightarrow k+1=0 \text{ or } 10k-1=0$$

$$\Rightarrow k=-1 \text{ or } k=\frac{1}{10}$$

But $k=-1$ is not possible as the probability of an event is never negative.

$$\therefore \quad k=\frac{1}{10}$$

(ii) $P(X<3)=P(0)+P(1)+P(2)=0+k+2k$

$$=0+\frac{1}{10}+\frac{2}{10}=\frac{3}{10} \qquad \left[\text{put } k=\frac{1}{10}\right]$$

(iii) $P(X>6)=P(7)=7k^2+k$

$$=\frac{7}{100}+\frac{1}{10}=\frac{17}{100} \qquad \left[\text{put } k=\frac{1}{10}\right]$$

(iv) $P(0<X<3)=P(1)+P(2)=k+2k$

$$=\frac{1}{10}+\frac{2}{10}=\frac{3}{10} \qquad \left[\text{put } k=\frac{1}{10}\right]$$

9.10 Mean and Variance of a Random Variable

If X is a discrete random variable which assumes values $x_1, x_2, x_3, \ldots, x_n$ with respective probabilities $p_1, p_2, p_3, \ldots, p_n$, then the mean $\overline{X}$ of X is defined as

$$\overline{X}=p_1x_1+p_2x_2+\ldots+p_nx_n \Rightarrow \overline{X}=\sum_{i=1}^{n} p_i x_i$$

and variance of X is defined as

$$\text{var}(X)=p_1(x_1-\overline{X})^2+p_2(x_2-\overline{X})^2+\ldots+p_n(x_n-\overline{X})^2$$

$$=\sum_{i=1}^{n} p_i(x_i-\overline{X})^2$$

where, $\overline{X}=\sum_{i=1}^{n} p_i x_i$ is the mean of x.

$$\Rightarrow \text{var}(X)=\sum_{i=1}^{n} p_i x_i^2-\left(\sum_{i=1}^{n} p_i x_i\right)^2$$

The square root of the variance gives the standard deviation i.e. $\sqrt{\text{var}(X)}=\sqrt{\sigma^2}=\sigma$

JEE Focus Points

- The mean of a random variable X is also known as its mathematical expectation or expected value and is denoted by $E(X)$.
- The variance and standard deviation of a random variable are always non-negative.
- **Variance** $V(X)=\sigma_x^2=E(X^2)-\{E(X)\}^2$
  where, $E(X^2)=\sum_{i=1}^{n} x_i^2 P(x_i)$
- **Standard Deviation** $\sqrt{V(X)}=\sigma_x=\sqrt{E(X^2)-\{E(X)\}^2}$
- If $Y=aX+b$, then
  (a) $E(Y)=E(aX+b)=aE(X)+b$
  (b) $\sigma_Y^2=V(Y)=a^2V(X)=a^2\sigma_X^2$
  (c) $\sigma_Y=\sqrt{V(Y)}=|a|\sigma_X$
- If $Z=aX^2+bX+c$, then
  $E(Z)=E(aX^2+bX+c)=aE(x)^2+bE(x)+c$

Example 26. A class has 15 students whose ages are 14, 17, 15, 14, 21, 17, 19, 20, 16, 18, 20, 17, 16, 19 and 20 yr. One student is selected in such a manner that each has the same chance of being of chosen and the age X of the selected student is recorded. What is the probability distribution of the random variable X? Mean, variance and standard deviation of X, are respectively

(a) 17.53, 4.8 and 2.19
(b) 2.19, 4.8 and 17.53
(c) 17.53, 2.19 and 4.8
(d) None of these

Sol. (a) Here, total number of students = 15

The age of students in ascending order are 14, 14, 15, 16, 16, 17, 17, 17, 18, 19, 19, 20, 20, 20, 21.

Now, $P(X=14)=\frac{2}{15}, P(X=15)=\frac{1}{15},$

$P(X=16)=\frac{2}{15}, P(X=17)=\frac{3}{15},$

$P(X=18)=\frac{1}{15}, P(X=19)=\frac{2}{15},$

$P(X=20)=\frac{3}{15}, P(X=21)=\frac{1}{15}$

Therefore, the probability distribution of random variable X is as follows:

X	14	15	16	17	18	19	20	21
Number of students	2	1	2	3	1	2	3	1
$P(X)$	$\frac{2}{5}$	$\frac{1}{15}$	$\frac{2}{15}$	$\frac{3}{15}$	$\frac{1}{15}$	$\frac{2}{15}$	$\frac{3}{15}$	$\frac{1}{15}$

The third row gives the probability distribution of X.

$\therefore$ Mean of $X=\Sigma X\ P(X)$

$$=\frac{\left[\begin{array}{r}14\times2+15\times1+16\times2+17\times3+18\times1+19\times2\\+20\times3+21\times1\end{array}\right]}{15}$$

$$=\frac{28+15+32+51+18+38+60+21}{15}=\frac{263}{15}=17.53$$

Variance of $X=\Sigma X^2\ P(X)-(\text{Mean})^2$

$$=\frac{\left[\begin{array}{l}(14)^2\times2+(15)^2\times1+(16)^2\times2+(17)^2\times3\\+(18)^2\times1+(19)^2\times2+(20)^2\times3+(21)^2\times1\end{array}\right]}{15}-\left(\frac{263}{15}\right)^2$$

$$=\frac{\left[\begin{array}{r}392+225+512+867+324+722\\+1200+441\end{array}\right]}{15}-\left(\frac{263}{15}\right)^2$$

$$=\frac{4683}{15}-\left(\frac{263}{15}\right)^2=312.2-307.4=4.8$$

SD of $X=\sqrt{\text{Variance}}=\sqrt{4.8}=2.19$

9.11 Binomial Theorem on Probability

Suppose, a binomial experiment has probability of success p and that of failure q (i.e. $p+q=1$). If E be an event and let X = number of successes i.e. number of times event E occurs in n trials.

Then, the probability of occurrence of event E exactly r times in n trials is denoted by

$P(X=r)$ or $P(r)$ and is given by $P(X=r)$

or $\quad P(r)={}^nC_r\,p^r q^{n-r}$

$\qquad = (r+1)$ th terms in the expansion of $(q+p)^n$

where, $r=0, 1, 2, 3, \ldots, n$.

JEE Focus Points

- The probability of getting atleast k success is
$$P(r\ge k)=\sum_{r=k}^{n}{}^nC_r p^r q^{n-r}.$$
- The probability of getting atmost k success is
$$P(0\le r\le k)=\sum_{r=0}^{k}{}^nC_r p^r q^{n-r}.$$
- The probability distribution of the random variable X is as given below

X	0	1	2	...	r	...	n
$P(X)$	q^n	${}^nC_1\,pq^{n-1}$	${}^nC_2\,p^2q^{n-2}$	...	${}^nC_r\,p^rq^{n-r}$		p^n

- The mean, the variance and the standard deviation of binomial distribution are np, npq, $\sqrt{npq}$.
- Mode of binomial distribution is the value of r when $P(X=r)$ is maximum.
$$(n+1)\,p-1\le r\le(n+1)p$$

Example 27. If on an average, out of 10 ships, one is drowned, then what is the probability that out of 5 ships, atleast 4 reach safely?

Sol. Let p be the probability that a ship reaches safely.

$\therefore\ p=\frac{9}{10}$

$\therefore\ q=$ Probability that a ship is drowned $=1-p=1-\frac{9}{10}$

$\therefore\ q=\frac{1}{10}$

Let X be the random variable, showing the number of ships reaching safely.

Then, P (atleast 4 reaching safely) $=P(X=4$ or $X=5)$

$=P(X=4)+P(X=5)$

$$={}^5C_4\left(\frac{9}{10}\right)^4\left(\frac{1}{10}\right)^{5-4}+{}^5C_5\left(\frac{9}{10}\right)^5\left(\frac{1}{10}\right)^{5-5}$$

$$=\frac{5\times9^4}{10^5}+\frac{9^5}{10^5}=\frac{9^4\times14}{10^5}$$

Example 28. A man takes a step forward with probability 0.4 and backward with probability 0.6. Then, find the probability that at the end of eleven steps he is one step away from the starting point.

Sol. Since, the man is one step away from starting point mean that either

(i) man has taken 6 steps forward and 5 steps backward.

(ii) man has taken 5 steps forward and 6 steps backward.

Taking, movement 1 step forward as success and 1 step backward as failure.

$\therefore\ p=$ Probability of success $=0.4$

and $q=$ Probability of failure $=0.6$

$\therefore$ Required probability $=P(X=6$ or $X=5)$

$=P(X=6)+P(X=5)={}^{11}C_6\,p^6q^5+{}^{11}C_5\,p^5q^6$

$$= {}^{11}C_5(p^6q^5 + p^5q^6)$$

$$= \frac{11\cdot10\cdot9\cdot8\cdot7}{1\cdot2\cdot3\cdot4\cdot5}\{(0\cdot4)^6(0\cdot6)^5 + (0\cdot4)^5(0\cdot6)^6\}$$

$$= \frac{11\cdot10\cdot9\cdot8\cdot7}{1\cdot2\cdot3\cdot4\cdot5}(0\cdot24)^5 = 0\cdot37$$

Hence, the required probability is 0·37.

Example 29. Two coins look similar, but have different probabilities of falling "head". One is a fair coin, with $P(H) = 1/2$, but the other is weighted so that $P(H) = 4/5$. One of the coin is chosen at random and is tossed 10 times, let X denotes the number of heads that of appear, and F is the event that the fair coin was drawn. If $X = 7$ is observed, the probability that the coin was fair, is

(a) $\frac{5^{10}}{5^8 + 8^{10}}$ (b) $\frac{5^8}{5^{10} + 4^{10}}$

(c) $\frac{5^{10}}{5^{10} + 8^7}$ (d) $\frac{5^{10}}{5^{10} + 8^8}$

Sol. (d) A coin randomly selected tossed 10 times, fell head wise 7 times.

B_1 : Coin was a fair coin, $P(B_1) = 1/2$

B_2 : Coin was a weighted coin, $P(B_2) = 4/5$

$$P(A/B_1) = {}^{10}C_7 \cdot \left(\frac{1}{2}\right)^7 \left(\frac{1}{2}\right)^3 = {}^{10}C_3 \frac{1}{2^{10}}$$

$$P(A/B_2) = {}^{10}C_7 \cdot \left(\frac{4}{5}\right)^7 \cdot \left(\frac{1}{5}\right)^3 = {}^{10}C_3 \cdot \frac{4^7}{5^{10}}$$

$$P(B_1/A) = \frac{\frac{1}{2^{10}}}{\frac{1}{2^{10}} + \frac{4^7}{5^{10}}} = \frac{1}{1 + \frac{4^7 \cdot 2^{10}}{5^{10}}} = \frac{5^{10}}{5^{10} + 8^8}$$

Example 30. From a pack of 52 playing cards; half of the cards are randomly removed without looking at them. From the remaining cards, 3 cards are drawn randomly. The probability that all are king.

(a) $\frac{1}{(25)(17)(13)}$ (b) $\frac{1}{(25)(15)(13)}$

(c) $\frac{1}{(52)(17)(13)}$ (d) $\frac{1}{(13)(51)(17)}$

Sol. (a) Let E_1 = "No card is king from removed cards"

E_2 = "1 card is king from removed cards"

E_3 = "2 card is king from removed cards"

E_4 = "3 card is king from removed cards"

F = 3 cards are drawn from pack those are kings.

$$P(F) = \sum_{i=1}^{4} P(E_i) . P\left(\frac{F}{E_i}\right)$$

$$= \frac{{}^{48}C_{26}}{{}^{52}C_{26}} \cdot \frac{{}^4C_3}{{}^{26}C_3} + \frac{{}^{48}C_{25} \cdot {}^4C_1}{{}^{52}C_{26}} \cdot \frac{{}^3C_3}{{}^{26}C_3} + 0 + 0$$

$$= \frac{4}{{}^{52}C_{26} \cdot {}^{26}C_3}({}^{48}C_{26} + {}^{48}C_{25})$$

$$= \frac{4 \times {}^{49}C_{26}}{{}^{52}C_{26} \cdot {}^{26}C_3} = \frac{1}{(13)(17)(25)}$$

9.12 Expectation

If p be the probability of success of a person in any venture and m be the sum of money which he will receive in case of success, the sum of money denoted by pm is called his expectation.

Example 31. A and B throw with one die for a stake of ₹ 11 which is to be won by the player who first throw 6. If A has the first throw, then what are their respective expectations?

Sol. Since, A can win the game at the 1st, 3rd, 5th,..., trials.

Let p be the probability of success and q be the probability of failure, then

$$p = \frac{1}{6} \text{ and } q = \frac{5}{6}$$

$$P(A \text{ wins at the first trial}) = \frac{1}{6}$$

$$P(A \text{ wins at the 3rd trials}) = \frac{5}{6}\cdot\frac{5}{6}\cdot\frac{1}{6}$$

$$P(A \text{ wins at the 5th trials}) = \frac{5}{6}\cdot\frac{5}{6}\cdot\frac{5}{6}\cdot\frac{5}{6}\cdot\frac{1}{6} \text{ and so on.}$$

Therefore, $P(A \text{ wins}) = \frac{1}{6} + \left(\frac{5}{6}\right)^2 \frac{1}{6} + \left(\frac{5}{6}\right)^4 \cdot \frac{1}{6} + \dots\infty$

$$= \frac{\frac{1}{6}}{1 - \left(\frac{5}{6}\right)^2} = \frac{6}{11}$$

Similarly, $P(B \text{ wins}) = \frac{5}{6}\cdot\frac{1}{6} + \left(\frac{5}{6}\right)^3 \frac{1}{6} + \left(\frac{5}{6}\right)^5 \frac{1}{6} + \dots\infty$

$$= \frac{\frac{5}{6}\cdot\frac{1}{6}}{1 - \left(\frac{5}{6}\right)^2} = \frac{5}{11}$$

Hence, expectations of A and B are ₹ $\frac{6}{11} \times 11$ and ₹ $\frac{5}{11} \times 11$, respectively. i.e. Expectations of A and B are ₹ 6 and ₹ 5, respectively.

9.11 Uncountable Uniform Spaces (Geometrical Problems)

Example 32. Two persons A and B agree to meet at a place between 11 to 12 noon. The first one to arrive waits for 20 min and then leave. If the time of their arrival be independent and at random, then what is the probability that A and B meet?

Sol. Let A and B arrive at the place of their meeting x minutes and y minutes after 11 noon.

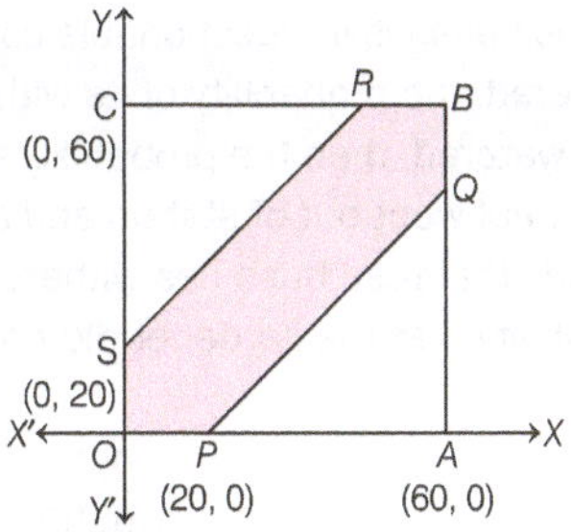

The given condition ⇒ their meeting is possible only if

$$|x - y| \le 20 \quad \text{...(i)}$$

$OABC$ is a square, where $A \equiv (60, 0)$ and $C \equiv (0, 60)$

Considering the equality part of Eq. (i),

i.e. $|x - y| = 20$

∴ The area representing the favourable cases

$= \text{Area } OPQBRSO$

$= \text{Area of square } OABC - \text{Area of } \Delta PAQ - \text{Area of } \Delta SRC$

$= (60)(60) - \frac{1}{2}(40)(40) - \frac{1}{2}(40)(40)$

$= 3600 - 1600 = 2000$ sq units

Total way = Area of square $OABC$

$= (60)(60) = 3600$ sq units

Required probability $= \frac{2000}{3600} = \frac{5}{9}$

Example 33. Two friends visit to a restaurant randomly during 5 pm to 6 pm. Among the two, whoever comes first waits for 15 min and then leaves. The probability that they meet is

(a) $\frac{1}{4}$ (b) $\frac{1}{16}$ (c) $\frac{7}{16}$ (d) $\frac{9}{16}$

Sol. (c) Let the friends come to the restaurant at 5 h, x min and 5 h, y min, respectively, where $x, y \in [0, 60]$

Hence, the sample space consists of all points (x, y) lying in 60×60 square as shown above and for favourable cases, $|x - y| \le 15$, i.e. $-15 \le x - y \le 15$ which is shown by shaded region in the graph shown below :

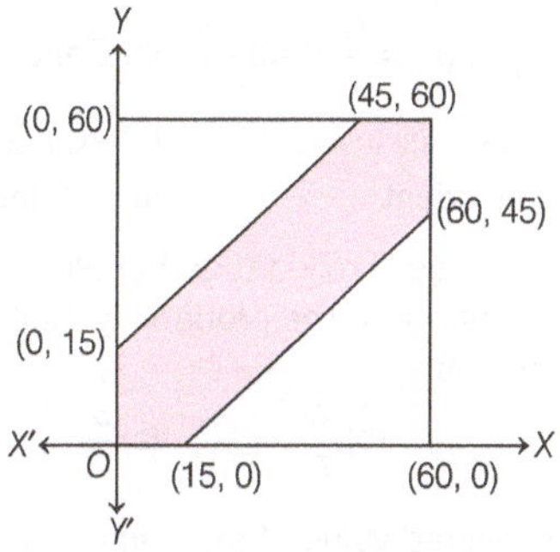

Hence, the probability that they will meet is given by

$$1 - \frac{2 \times \frac{1}{2} \times 45 \times 45}{60 \times 60} = 1 - \left(\frac{3}{4}\right)^2 = \frac{7}{16}$$

Milestone Practice 9.3

1. A bag A contains 3 white and 2 black balls and another bag B contains 2 white and 4 black balls. A bag and a ball out of it are picked at random. The probability that the ball is white, is

(a) $\frac{2}{7}$ (b) $\frac{7}{9}$ (c) $\frac{4}{15}$ (d) $\frac{7}{15}$

2. There are two bags, one of which contains 3 black and 4 white balls, while the other contains 4 black and 3 white balls. A die is cast. If the face 1 or 3 turns up a ball is taken out from the first bag and if any other face turns up, a ball is taken from the second bag. The probability of choosing a black ball, is

(a) $\frac{7}{15}$ (b) $\frac{8}{15}$ (c) $\frac{10}{21}$ (d) $\frac{11}{21}$

3. There are two groups of subjects, one of which consists of 5 Science subjects and 3 Engineering subjects and the other consists of 3 Science and 5 Engineering subjects. An unbiased die is cast. If number 3 or 5 turns up, a subject from group I is selected, otherwise a subject is selected from group II. The probability that an Engineering subject is selected ultimately, is

(a) $\frac{7}{13}$ (b) $\frac{9}{17}$ (c) $\frac{13}{24}$ (d) $\frac{11}{20}$

4. A box contains N coins, of which m are fair and the rest are biased. The probability of getting head when a fair coin is tossed is $\frac{1}{2}$, while it $\frac{2}{3}$ when a biased coin is tossed. A coin is drawn from the box at random and is tossed twice. The first time it shows head and the second time it shows tail. The probability that the coin drawn is fair, is

(a) $\frac{5m}{m + 8N}$ (b) $\frac{3m}{m + 8N}$

(c) $\frac{7m}{m + 8N}$ (d) $\frac{9m}{m + 8N}$

5. A card is lost from a pack of 52 playing cards. From the remainder of the pack, one card is drawn and is found to be a spade. The probability that the missing card is a spade, is

(a) $\frac{2}{17}$ (b) $\frac{3}{17}$ (c) $\frac{4}{17}$ (d) $\frac{5}{17}$

6. A person is known to speak the truth 4 times out of 5. He throws a die and reports that it is an ace. The probability that it is actually an ace, is

(a) $\frac{1}{3}$ (b) $\frac{2}{9}$ (c) $\frac{4}{9}$ (d) $\frac{5}{9}$

7. Events E and F are such that $P(E^C \text{ or } F^C) = 0.25$

$P(E) = \frac{7}{8}, P(F) = \frac{6}{7}$, then events E and F are

(a) mutually exclusive (b) exhaustive
(c) independent (d) nothing can be said

8. A pair of dice is rolled together till a sum of either 5 or 7 is obtained. The probability that 5 comes before 7, is

(a) $\frac{2}{5}$ (b) $\frac{2}{7}$ (c) $\frac{3}{7}$ (d) $\frac{3}{5}$

9. The expected value of the number of points, obtained in a single throw of die, is

(a) $\frac{3}{2}$ (b) $\frac{5}{2}$ (c) $\frac{7}{2}$ (d) $\frac{9}{2}$

10. Two points P and Q are taken at random on a line segment OA of length a. The probability that $PQ > b$, where $0 < b < a$, is

(a) $\frac{b}{a}$ (b) $\frac{b^2}{a^2}$
(c) $\left(\frac{a-b}{a}\right)^2$ (d) $\left(\frac{a-2b}{a-b}\right)^2$

11. Let A and B are two independent events with $P(A) = \frac{1}{2}$ and $P(A \cup B) = \frac{2}{3}$, then the probabilities of the events $P(B)$, $P(A / B)$ and $P(B^C / A)$ are in

(a) AP (b) GP
(c) HP (d) None of these

12. Pal's gardener is not dependable, the probability that he will forget to water the rose bush is 2/3. The rose bush is in questionable condition. Any how if watered, the probability of its withering is 1/2 and if not watered, then the probability of its withering is 3/4. Pal went out of station and after returning he finds that rose bush has withered. The probability that the gardener did not water the rose bush.

(a) 50% (b) 60%
(c) 75% (d) 80%

13. There are 4 machines and it is known that exactly 2 of them are faulty. They are tested, one by one, in a random order till both the faulty machines are identified. Then, the probability that only 2 tests are needed is

(a) $\frac{1}{3}$ (b) $\frac{1}{6}$ (c) $\frac{1}{2}$ (d) $\frac{1}{4}$

14. X and Y are two weak students in mathematics and their chances of solving a problem correctly are 1/8 and 1/12 respectively. They are given a question and they obtain the same answer. If the probability of common mistake is $\frac{1}{1001}$, then probability that the answer was correct is a / b (a and b are coprimes). Then, $|a - b|$ is equal to

(a) 3 (b) 1 (c) 5 (d) 7

15. If $a, b, c \in N$, the probability that $a^2 + b^2 + c^2$ is divisible by 7 is $\frac{m}{n}$ where m, n are relatively prime natural numbers, then $m + n$ is equal to

(a) 3 (b) 2 (c) 7 (d) 8

16. If bag I contains 7 red and 3 yellow balls while another bag II contains 9 red and 5 yellow balls. One ball is drawn at random from one of the bags and it is found to be yellow. The probability that it was drawn from bag II is

(a) $\frac{21}{46}$ (b) $\frac{25}{46}$ (c) $\frac{17}{46}$ (d) $\frac{27}{46}$

Answer Key

1. (d)	2. (d)	3. (c)	4. (d)	5. (c)
6. (c)	7. (c)	8. (a)	9. (c)	10. (c)
11. (a)	12. (c)	13. (a)	14. (b)	15. (d)
16. (b)				

For Detailed Solution

JEE Pattern EXAMPLES

Single Option Correct Type Questions

Example 1 *Let S be a set consisting of first five prime numbers. Suppose A and B are two matrices of order 2 each with distinct entries $\in S$. The chance that the matrix AB has atleast one odd entry, is*

(a) 90% (b) 84% (c) 80% (d) 96%

Decoding the Question

As, AB matrix has atleast one odd entry that means both A and B do not contain 2.

Sol. (d) $S = \{2, 3, 5, 7, 11\}$

Total ways in which A and B can be chosen $= ({}^5C_4 \, . \, 4!)^2$

$= (5!)^2$

$P(E) = 1 - P$ (A and B does not contain the element 2)

$$= 1 - \frac{(4!)^2}{(5!)^2} = 1 - \frac{1}{25} = \frac{24}{25} = 96\%$$

Example 2 *One percent of the population suffers from a certain disease. There is a blood test for this disease, and it is 99% accurate, in other words, the probability that it gives the correct answer is 0.99, regardless of whether the person is sick or healthy. A person takes the blood test, and the result says that he has the disease. The probability that he actually has the disease, is*

(a) 0.99% (b) 25% (c) 50% (d) 75%

Sol. (c) A : Blood result says positive about the disease

B_1 : Person suffers from the disease $= \frac{1}{100}$

B_2 : Person does not suffer $= \frac{99}{100}$

$$P(A / B_1) = \frac{99}{100}; \; P(A / B_2) = \frac{1}{100}$$

$$P(B_1 / A) = \frac{P(B_1) \, . \, P(A / B_1)}{P(B_1) \, . \, P(A / B_1) + P(B_2) \, . \, P(A / B_2)}$$

$$= \frac{\frac{1}{100} \cdot \frac{99}{100}}{\frac{1}{100} \cdot \frac{99}{100} + \frac{99}{100} \cdot \frac{1}{100}} = \frac{99}{2 \times 99} = \frac{1}{2} = 50\%$$

Example 3 *To obtain a gold coin; 6 men, all of different weight, are trying to build a human pyramid as shown in the figure. Human pyramid is called "stable" if some one not in the bottom row is "supported by" each of the two closest people beneath him and no body can be supported by anybody of lower weight. Formation of 'stable' pyramid is the only condition to get a gold coin. What is the probability that they will get gold coin?*

(a) $\frac{1}{45}$ (b) $\frac{2}{45}$ (c) $\frac{4}{45}$ (d) $\frac{1}{15}$

Sol. (a) Total case $= n = 6!$

Favourable case $= m = (3! \times 2!) + (2! \times 2!) = 16$

Probability $= \frac{16}{6!} = \frac{1}{45}$

Example 4 *Two light bulbs are connected in series in a circuit. The probability that an increase in voltage above its rated value will break the circuit if, under these assumptions, the chance that a bulb burns out is 0.4 for each of the two bulbs, is*

(a) 0.64 (b) 0.48 (c) 0.16 (d) 0.8

Sol. (b) P (bulb burns) = 0.4

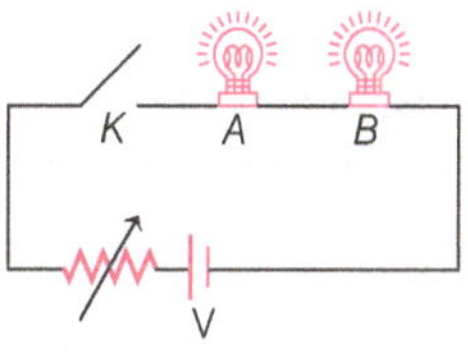

A circuit breaks when A or B burn

Hence, P (circuit breaks)

$= P$ (A burns and B does not burn)

$+ P$ (A does not burn and B burns)

$= (0.4)(0.6) + (0.6)(0.4) = 0.24 + 0.24 = 0.48$

JEE SCANNER

Example 5 Similar to PYQ Asked in JEE Main 2024

Let A and B be two independent events. If the probability that both A and B happen is $\frac{1}{12}$ and the probability that neither A nor B happens is $\frac{1}{2}$. Then, the value of $P(A \cup B)$ is

(a) $\frac{6}{13}$ (b) $\frac{1}{2}$ (c) $\frac{1}{4}$ (d) $\frac{1}{3}$

Sol. (b) Both A and B happen $\Rightarrow P(A \cap B) = \frac{1}{12}$

and neither A nor B happens

$$\Rightarrow \quad P(\bar{A} \cap \bar{B}) = \frac{1}{2}$$

But for independent events, we have

$$P(A \cap B) = P(A) \,.\, P(B)$$

$$\Rightarrow \quad \frac{1}{12} = P(A) \,.\, P(B) \quad \text{...(i)}$$

$$P(\bar{A} \cap \bar{B}) = P(\bar{A}) \,.\, P(\bar{B})$$

$$= \{1 - P(A)\} \,.\, \{1 - P(B)\}$$

$$= 1 - P(A) - P(B) + P(A)\,P(B)$$

$$\Rightarrow \quad P(A) + P(B) = 1 + P(A) \,.\, P(B) - P(\bar{A} \cap \bar{B})$$

$$= 1 + \frac{1}{12} - \frac{1}{2}$$

$$= \frac{12 + 1 - 6}{12}$$

$$= \frac{13 - 6}{12} = \frac{7}{12} \quad \text{...(ii)}$$

On solving Eqs. (i) and (ii), we get

Either $P(A) = \frac{1}{3}$ and $P(B) = \frac{1}{4}$ or $P(A) = \frac{1}{4}$ and $P(B) = \frac{1}{3}$

Thus, $P(A \cup B) = P(A) + P(B) - P(A \cap B)$

$$= \frac{1}{4} + \frac{1}{3} - \frac{1}{12}$$

$$= \frac{6}{12} = \frac{1}{2}$$

Skill Builder

Let A and B be two independent events. The probability that both A and B occur together is 1/6 and the probability that neither of them occur is $\frac{1}{3}$.

Then, the probability of occurrence of A is

(a) $\frac{1}{2}$ (b) $\frac{1}{3}$

(c) Both (a) and (b) (d) None of these

For Sol.

Example 6 *If three fair dice are tossed and the product of the three numbers that appear is even, the probability that the sum of the numbers is also even, is*

(a) $\frac{1}{2}$ (b) $\frac{3}{5}$ (c) $\frac{4}{7}$ (d) $\frac{5}{7}$

Sol. (c) Product of the three numbers appearing is even $\Rightarrow$ atleast one of the throws is even.

Possible cases : $E_1 \equiv$ Exactly one even and 2 odd.

$E_2 \equiv$ Exactly two even and 1 odd.

$E_3 \equiv$ All three even

Now, $P(E_1 \cup E_2 \cup E_3) = 1 - P$ (all three throws are odd)

$$= 1 - \left(\frac{1}{2}\right)\left(\frac{1}{2}\right)\left(\frac{1}{2}\right) = \frac{7}{8}$$

Hence, $P\,(E_1 \text{ or } E_3 \,/\, E_1 \cup E_2 \cup E_3)$

$$= \frac{P(E_1 \cup E_3)}{P(E_1 \cup E_2 \cup E_3)}$$

$$= \frac{P(E_1) + P(E_3) - P(E_1 \cap E_3)}{P(E_1 \cup E_2 \cup E_3)}$$

$$= \frac{3\left(\frac{1}{2} \times \frac{1}{2} \times \frac{1}{2}\right) + \left(\frac{1}{2} \times \frac{1}{2} \times \frac{1}{2}\right) - 0}{\frac{7}{8}}$$

$$= \frac{4}{8}\left(\frac{8}{7}\right) = \frac{4}{7}$$

Example 7 *A random selector can only select one of the nine integer 1, 2, 3, ..., 7, 8, 9 and it makes these selections with equal probability. The probability that after 10 selections, the product of 10 numbers selected will be divisible by 10 is*

(a) $1 - \left[\left(\frac{8}{9}\right)^{10} + \left(\frac{5}{9}\right)^{10} - \left(\frac{4}{9}\right)^{10}\right]$

(b) $1 - \left[\left(\frac{8}{9}\right)^{10} + \left(\frac{5}{9}\right)^{10} + \left(\frac{4}{9}\right)^{10}\right]$

(c) $1 - \left[\left(\frac{8}{9}\right)^{10} - \left(\frac{5}{9}\right)^{10} + \left(\frac{4}{9}\right)^{10}\right]$

(d) $1 - \left[\left(\frac{8}{9}\right)^{10} - \left(\frac{5}{9}\right)^{10} - \left(\frac{4}{9}\right)^{10}\right]$

Sol. (a) $P\,(1, 3, 5, 7, 9) = \left(\frac{5}{9}\right)^{10}$; $P\,(1, 3, 7, 9) = \left(\frac{4}{9}\right)^{10}$;

$P(5) = \left(\frac{5}{9}\right)^{10}\left(\frac{4}{9}\right)^{10}$; $P\,(1, 2, 3, 4, 6, 7, 8, 9) = \left(\frac{8}{9}\right)^{10}$;

$P\,(1, 2, 3, 4, 5, 6, 7, 8, 9) = \left(\frac{8}{9}\right)^{10} + \left(\frac{5}{9}\right)^{10} - \left(\frac{4}{9}\right)^{10}$

$P\,(\text{divided by } 10) = 1 - \left[\left(\frac{8}{9}\right)^{10} + \left(\frac{5}{9}\right)^{10} - \left(\frac{4}{9}\right)^{10}\right]$

JEE SCANNER

Example 8 Similar to PYQ Asked in JEE Main 2024

A is a set containing 4 distinct elements. A non-zero subset P of A is chosen at random. The set A is reconstructed by replacing the elements of P. A non-zero subset Q of A is again chosen at random. If the probability that P and Q have no common elements is given by $p = \frac{m}{n}$, then the least value of $(m + n)$, is

(a) 9 (b) 10 (c) 11 (d) 12

Sol. (c) $n(S) = (2^4 - 1)(2^4 - 1) = (15)(15) = 225$

$$n(A) = {}^4C_1(2^3 - 1) + {}^4C_2(2^2 - 1) + {}^4C_3(2^1 - 1) + {}^4C_4(2^0 - 1)$$
$$= 28 + 18 + 4 = 50$$
$$P(A) = \frac{50}{225} = \frac{2}{9} \Rightarrow m + n = 11$$

Skill Builder

Three numbers are chosen at random without replacement from {1, 2, 3, ..., 10}. The probability that the minimum of the chosen numbers is 3 or their maximum is 7, is

(a) $\frac{1}{2}$ (b) $\frac{1}{3}$

(c) $\frac{1}{4}$ (d) $\frac{11}{40}$

For Sol.

Example 9 *The probability of simultaneously occurrence of atleast one of the two events A and B is p. If the probability that exactly one of A, B occurs is q. The value of $(P(A^c) + P(B^c))$ is equal to*

(a) $2 - 2p + q$ (b) $2 - p + 2q$

(c) $2 + 2p - q$ (d) $2 - 2p - q$

Sol. (a) Given, $P(A) + P(B) - P(A \cap B) = p$ ...(i)

and $P(A \cup B) - P(A \cap B) = q$ ...(ii)

$\Rightarrow P(A \cap B) = p - q$

From Eqs. (i) and (ii),

$$P(A \cup B) = P(A) + P(B) - P(A \cap B)$$
$$\Rightarrow P(A) + P(B) = P(A \cup B) + P(A \cap B)$$
$$= p + p - q = 2p - q \quad \text{... (iii)}$$

Now, $P(A^c) + P(B^c) = 1 - P(A) + 1 - P(B)$
$$= 2 - [P(A) + P(B)] = 2 - 2p + q$$

Example 10 *Events E and F are such that $P(E^c \text{ or } F^c) = 0.25$, $P(E) = \frac{7}{8}$ and $P(F) = \frac{6}{7}$, then the events E and F are*

(a) mutually exclusive (b) exhaustive

(c) independent (d) nothing can be said

Sol. (c) $P(E^c \text{ or } F^c) = \frac{1}{4}$

$$P(E^c) + P(F^c) - P(E^c \cap F^c) = \frac{1}{4}$$
$$P(E^c \cap F^c) = \frac{1}{7} + \frac{1}{8} - \frac{1}{4} = \frac{8 + 7 - 14}{56} = \frac{1}{56}$$

Also, $P(E^c) \cdot P(F^c) = \frac{1}{8} \cdot \frac{1}{7} = \frac{1}{56}$

$\Rightarrow E^c$ and F^c are independent.

Hence, E and F are independent.

$$P(E \cup F) = \frac{7}{8} + \frac{6}{7} - \frac{3}{4} = \frac{49 + 48 - 42}{56} = \frac{55}{56} \neq 1$$

$\therefore$ E and F are not exhaustive.

Example 11 *One hundred management students who read at least one of the three business magazines are surveyed to study the readership pattern. It is found that 80 read Business India, 50 read Business World and 30 read Business Today. Five students read all the three magazines. A student was selected randomly. The probability that he reads exactly two magazines, is*

(a) $\frac{1}{2}$ (b) $\frac{3}{8}$ (c) $\frac{3}{5}$ (d) $\frac{1}{3}$

Sol. (a)

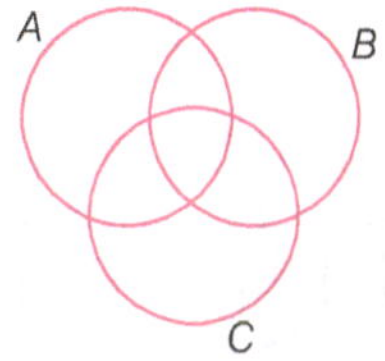

A : Business India, B : Business World, C : Business Today

$n(A) = 80$; $n(B) = 50$; $n(C) = 30$; $n(A \cap B \cap C) = 5$

$$n(E - 2) = \Sigma n(A \cap B) - 3n(A \cap B \cap C) \quad \text{...(i)}$$

Hence, $n(A \cup B \cup C) = \Sigma n(A) - \Sigma n(A \cap B) + n(A \cap B \cap C)$

$$100 = 160 - \Sigma n(A \cap B) + 5$$
$$\Rightarrow \Sigma n(A \cap B) = 165 - 100 = 65$$
$$n(E - 2) = 65 - 15 = 50$$
$$P\text{ (exactly two)} = \frac{50}{100} = \frac{1}{2}$$

Example 12 *An instrument is being tested upon each trial the instrument fails with probability p. After the first failure the instrument is repaired and after the second failure it is considered to be unfit for operation. The chance that the instrument is rejected exactly in the kth trial, is*

(a) $(k - 1)\,p(1 - p)^{k-1}$ (b) $(k - 1)p^2(1 - p)^{k-2}$

(c) $kp(1 - p)^{k-1}$ (d) $kp^2(1 - p)^{k-2}$

Sol. (b) $P(E) = P$ (instrument fails exactly once in first $(k - 1)$ trials and then in the kth trial)

$$= {}^{k-1}C_1 \cdot p(1 - p)^{k-1} \cdot p = (k - 1)p^2(1 - p)^{k-2}$$

JEE SCANNER

Example 13 Similar to PYQ Asked in JEE Main 2024

A bag contains 10 balls, whose colours are either red or green. 6 balls are drawn at random without replacement and it was found that 3 balls are red and other 3 balls are green. The probability that the bag contains equal number of red and green balls is

(a) $\frac{7}{21}$ (b) $\frac{10}{30}$ (c) $\frac{10}{33}$ (d) $\frac{7}{33}$

Sol. (c) Let $E_1 = 3$ red, 7 green; $E_2 = 4$ red, 6 green;

$E_3 = 5$ red, 5 green; $E_4 = 6$ red, 4 green;

$E_5 = 7$ red, 3 green; $A = 3$ red, 3 green ball drawn.

Then, $P(E_1) = P(E_2) = P(E_3) = P(E_4) = P(E_5) = \frac{1}{5}$

Now,

$$P\left(\frac{A}{E_1}\right) = \frac{{}^3C_3\,{}^7C_3}{{}^{10}C_6} = \frac{35}{210} = \frac{1}{6},\quad P\left(\frac{A}{E_2}\right) = \frac{{}^4C_3\,{}^6C_3}{{}^{10}C_6} = \frac{80}{210} = \frac{8}{21}$$

$$P\left(\frac{A}{E_3}\right) = \frac{{}^5C_3\,{}^5C_3}{{}^{10}C_6} = \frac{100}{210} = \frac{10}{21},\quad P\left(\frac{A}{E_4}\right) = \frac{{}^6C_3\,{}^4C_3}{{}^{10}C_6} = \frac{80}{210} = \frac{8}{21}$$

$$P\left(\frac{A}{E_5}\right) = \frac{{}^7C_3\,{}^3C_3}{{}^{10}C_6} = \frac{35}{210} = \frac{1}{6}$$

Required probability $= P\left(\frac{E_3}{A}\right)$

$$\therefore P\left(\frac{E_3}{A}\right) = \frac{P(E_3)\cdot P\left(\frac{A}{E_3}\right)}{P(E_1)\cdot P\left(\frac{A}{E_1}\right) + P(E_2)\cdot P\left(\frac{A}{E_2}\right) + P(E_3)\cdot P\left(\frac{A}{E_3}\right) + P(E_4)\cdot P\left(\frac{A}{E_4}\right) + P(E_5)\cdot P\left(\frac{A}{E_5}\right)}$$

$$= \frac{\frac{1}{5}\times\frac{10}{21}}{\frac{1}{5}\times\frac{1}{6}+\frac{1}{5}\times\frac{8}{21}+\frac{1}{5}\times\frac{10}{21}+\frac{1}{5}\times\frac{8}{21}+\frac{1}{5}\times\frac{1}{6}}$$

$$= \frac{\frac{10}{105}}{\frac{1}{30}+\frac{8}{105}+\frac{10}{105}+\frac{8}{105}+\frac{1}{30}} = \frac{10}{105}\times\frac{210}{66} = \frac{10}{33}$$

Skill Builder

A bag contains 6 balls, whose colours are either white or black. 4 balls are drawn at random without replacement and it was found that 2 balls are white and other 2 balls are black. The probability that the bag contains equal number of while and black balls is

(a) $\frac{2}{7}$ (b) $\frac{2}{5}$

(c) $\frac{3}{7}$ (d) $\frac{3}{4}$

For Sol.

Example 14 *I alternately toss a fair coin and a fair die, until I either toss a head or throw the face two. If I toss the coin first, the probability that I throw the face two before I toss a head, is*

(a) $\frac{1}{7}$ (b) $\frac{7}{12}$ (c) $\frac{5}{12}$ (d) $\frac{5}{7}$

Sol. (a) H : Tossing a Head, $P(H) = \frac{1}{2}$;

A : Event of tossing a 2 with die, $P(A) = \frac{1}{6}$

E : Tossing the face before tossing a head

Now, $P(E) = P(\overline{H} \cap A)$ or $\{(\overline{H} \cap \overline{A})$ and $(\overline{H} \cap A)\}$ or .....)

$$= \left(\frac{1}{2}\cdot\frac{1}{6}\right) + \left(\frac{1}{2}\cdot\frac{5}{6}\right)\cdot\left(\frac{1}{2}\cdot\frac{1}{6}\right) + \ldots$$

$$= \frac{1}{12} + \frac{5}{12}\cdot\frac{1}{12} + \ldots \infty$$

$$\therefore \quad P(E) = \frac{\frac{1}{12}}{1-\frac{5}{12}} = \frac{1}{7}$$

Example 15 *The probability that in a year of 22nd century chosen at random, there will be 53 Sundays, is*

(a) $\frac{3}{28}$ (b) $\frac{2}{28}$ (c) $\frac{7}{28}$ (d) $\frac{5}{28}$

Sol. (d) In the 22nd century, there are 25 leap years viz. 2100, 2104, 2108,..., 2196 and 75 non-leap years.

Consider the following events:

E_1 = Selecting a leap year from 22nd century

E_2 = Selecting a non-leap year from 22nd century

E = There are 53 Sundays in a year of 22nd century

We have, $P(E_1) = \frac{25}{100}$, $P(E_2) = \frac{75}{100}$, $P\left(\frac{E}{E_1}\right) = \frac{2}{7}$ and $P\left(\frac{E}{E_2}\right) = \frac{1}{7}$

Required probability $= P(E) = P((E \cap E_1) \cup (E \cap E_2))$

$$= P(E \cap E_1) + P(E \cap E_2)$$

$$= P(E_1).P\left(\frac{E}{E_1}\right) + P(E_2).P\left(\frac{E}{E_2}\right)$$

$$= \frac{25}{100}\times\frac{2}{7} + \frac{75}{100}\times\frac{1}{7} = \frac{5}{28}$$

Example 16 *In a convex hexagon two diagonals are drawn at random. The probability that the diagonals intersect at an interior point of the hexagon, is*

(a) $\frac{5}{12}$ (b) $\frac{7}{12}$ (c) $\frac{2}{5}$ (d) $\frac{3}{5}$

Sol. (a) We have,

Number of diagonals of a hexagon $= {}^6C_2 - 6 = 9$

$\therefore \quad n(s)$ = Total number of selections of two diagonals

$= {}^9C_2 = 36$

and $n(E)$ = The number of selections of two diagonals which intersect at an interior point

= The number of selections of four vertices

$= {}^6C_4 = 15$

Hence, required probability $= \dfrac{n(E)}{n(S)} = \dfrac{15}{36} = \dfrac{5}{12}$

Example 17 *A natural number x is randomly selected from the set of first 100 natural numbers. The probability that it satisfies the inequality* $x + \dfrac{100}{x} > 50$ *is*

(a) $\dfrac{2}{100}$ (b) $\dfrac{53}{100}$ (c) $\dfrac{54}{100}$ (d) $\dfrac{55}{100}$

Sol. (b) $x^2 - 50x + 100 > 0$

$x > 47.92$

$x \in \{48, 49, \dots, 100\}$

Hence, required probability $= \dfrac{53}{100}$

Example 18 *Two numbers b and c are chosen at random with replacement from the numbers 1, 2, 3, 4, 5, 6, 7, 8 and 9. The probability that* $x^2 + bx + c > 0\ \forall\ x \in R$, *is*

(a) $\dfrac{17}{123}$ (b) $\dfrac{32}{81}$ (c) $\dfrac{82}{125}$ (d) $\dfrac{45}{143}$

Sol. (b) Here, $x^2 + bx + c > 0,\ \forall\ x \in R$

$\therefore \quad D < 0$

$\Rightarrow \quad b^2 < 4c$

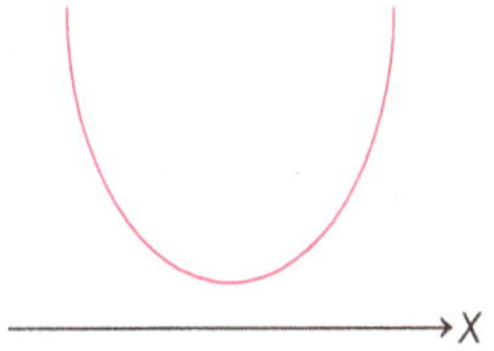

Value of b	Possible values of c		
1	$1 < 4c$	$\Rightarrow c > \dfrac{1}{4} \Rightarrow$	$\{1, 2, 3, 4, 5, 6, 7, 8, 9\}$
2	$4 < 4c$	$\Rightarrow c > 1 \Rightarrow$	$\{2, 3, 4, 5, 6, 7, 8, 9\}$
3	$9 < 4c$	$\Rightarrow c > \dfrac{9}{4} \Rightarrow$	$\{3, 4, 5, 6, 7, 8, 9\}$
4	$16 < 4c$	$\Rightarrow c > 4 \Rightarrow$	$\{5, 6, 7, 8, 9\}$
5	$25 < 4c$	$\Rightarrow c > 6.25 \Rightarrow$	$\{7, 8, 9\}$
6	$36 < 4c$	$\Rightarrow c > 9 \Rightarrow$	Impossible
7	Impossible		
8	Impossible		
9	Impossible		

$n(E)$ = Number of favourable cases $= 9 + 8 + 7 + 5 + 3 = 32$

$n(S)$ = Total ways $= 9 \times 9 = 81$

$\therefore$ Required probability $= \dfrac{n(E)}{n(S)} = \dfrac{32}{81}$

Example 19 *Three dice are thrown. The probability of getting a sum which is a perfect square, is*

(a) $\dfrac{2}{5}$ (b) $\dfrac{9}{20}$ (c) $\dfrac{1}{4}$ (d) None of these

Sol. (d) $n(S)$ = Total number of ways $= 6 \times 6 \times 6 = 216$

The sum of the numbers on three dice varies from 3 to 18 and among these 4, 9 and 16 are perfect squares.

$\therefore n(E)$ = Number of favourable ways

= Coefficient of x^4 in $(x + x^2 + \dots + x^6)^3$ + Coefficient of x^9 in $(x + x^2 + \dots + x^6)^3$ + Coefficient of x^{16} in $(x + x^2 + \dots + x^6)^3$

= Coefficient of x in $(1 + x + \dots + x^5)^3$ + Coefficient of x^6 in $(1 + x + x^2 + \dots + x^5)^3$ + Coefficient of x^{13} in $(1 + x + x^2 + \dots + x^5)^3$

= Coefficient of x in $(1 - x^6)^3(1 - x)^{-3}$ + Coefficient of x^6 in $(1 - x^6)^3(1 - x)^{-3}$ + Coefficient of x^{13} in $(1 - x^6)^3(1 - x)^{-3}$

= Coefficient of x in $(1)(1 + {}^3C_1x + \dots)$ + Coefficient of x^6 in $(1 - 3x^6)(1 + {}^3C_1x + \dots)$ + Coefficient of x^{13} in $(1 - 3x^6 + 3x^{12} + \dots)$; $(1 + {}^3C_1x + \dots)$

$= {}^3C_1 + ({}^8C_6 - 3) + ({}^{15}C_{13} - 3 \times {}^9C_7 + 9)$

$= {}^3C_1 + ({}^8C_2 - 3) + ({}^{15}C_2 - 3 \times {}^9C_2 + 9)$

$= 3 + 25 + 6$

$= 34$

$\therefore$ Required probability $= \dfrac{n(E)}{n(S)} = \dfrac{34}{216} = \dfrac{17}{108}$

Example 20 *A quadratic equation is chosen from the set of all quadratic equations which are unchanged by squaring their roots. The chance that the chosen equation has equal roots, is*

(a) $\dfrac{1}{2}$ (b) $\dfrac{1}{3}$ (c) $\dfrac{1}{4}$ (d) None of these

Sol. (a) Let α and β be the roots of the quadratic equation.

According to the question,

$\alpha + \beta = \alpha^2 + \beta^2$ and $\alpha\beta = \alpha^2\beta^2 \Rightarrow \alpha\beta(\alpha\beta - 1) = 0$

$\Rightarrow \alpha\beta = 1$ or $\alpha\beta = 0$

$\Rightarrow \alpha = 1, \beta = 1; \alpha = \omega, \beta = \omega^2$ [cube roots and unity]

$\alpha = 1, \beta = 0; \alpha = 0, \beta = 0$

$\therefore \quad n(S) =$ Number of quadratic equations which are unchanged by squaring their roots
$= 4$

and $n(E) =$ Number of quadratic equations have equal roots
$= 2$

$\therefore$ Required probability $= \dfrac{n(E)}{n(S)} = \dfrac{2}{4} = \dfrac{1}{2}$

Example 21 *Three-digit numbers are formed using the digits 0, 1, 2, 3, 4, 5 without repetition of digits. If a number is chosen at random, then the probability that the digits either increase or decrease, is*

(a) $\dfrac{1}{10}$ (b) $\dfrac{2}{11}$ (c) $\dfrac{3}{10}$ (d) $\dfrac{4}{11}$

Sol. (c) $n(S) =$ Total number of three digit numbers
$= {}^6P_3 - {}^5P_2 = 120 - 20 = 100$

$n(E) =$ Number of numbers with digits either increase or decrease
$=$ Number of numbers with increasing digits + Number of numbers with decreasing digits
$= {}^5C_3 + {}^6C_3 = 10 + 20 = 30$

$\therefore$ Required probability $= \dfrac{n(E)}{n(S)} = \dfrac{30}{100} = \dfrac{3}{10}$

More than One Correct Option Type Questions

Example 22 *For two given events A and B, $P(A \cap B)$ is*

(a) not less than $P(A) + P(B) - 1$
(b) not greater than $P(A) + P(B)$
(c) equal to $P(A) + P(B) - P(A \cup B)$
(d) equal to $P(A) + P(B) + P(A \cup B)$

Sol. (a, b, c) We know that

$$P(A \cap B) = P(A) + P(B) - P(A \cup B)$$

Also, $P(A \cup B) \le 1$

$\therefore \quad P(A \cap B)_{\text{min.}}$, when, $P(A \cup B)_{\text{max}} = 1$

$\Rightarrow \quad P(A \cap B) \ge P(A) + P(B) - 1$

$\therefore$ Option (a) is true.

Again, $P(A \cup B) \ge 0$

$\therefore \quad P(A \cap B)_{\text{max.}}$, when $P(A \cup B)_{\text{min.}} = 0$

$\Rightarrow \quad P(A \cap B) \le P(A) + P(B)$

$\therefore$ Option (b) is true.

Also, $P(A \cap B) = P(A) + P(B) - P(A \cup B)$

Thus, option (c) is also correct.

Example 23 *If M and N are any two events, then the probability that exactly one of them occurs is*

(a) $P(M) + P(N) - 2P(M \cap N)$
(b) $P(M) + P(N) - P(\overline{M \cup N})$
(c) $P(\overline{M}) + P(\overline{N}) - 2P(\overline{M} \cap \overline{N})$
(d) $P(M \cap \overline{N}) - P(\overline{M} \cap N)$

Sol. (a, c) P(exactly one of M, N occurs)

$$= P\{(M \cap \overline{N}) \cup (\overline{M} \cap N)\}$$
$$= P(M \cap \overline{N}) + P(\overline{M} \cap N)$$
$$= P(M) - P(M \cap N) + P(N) - P(M \cap N)$$
$$= P(M) + P(N) - 2P(M \cap N)$$

Also, P(exactly one of them occurs)

$$= \{1 - P(\overline{M} \cap \overline{N})\}\{1 - P(\overline{M} \cup \overline{N})\}$$
$$= P(\overline{M} \cup \overline{N}) - P(\overline{M} \cap \overline{N})$$
$$= P(\overline{M}) + P(\overline{N}) - 2P(\overline{M} \cap \overline{N})$$

Example 24 *Let p_n denote the probability of getting n heads, when a fair coin is tossed m times. If p_4, p_5, p_6 are in AP, then values of m can be*

(a) 5 (b) 7 (c) 10 (d) 14

Sol. (b, d) $\because \; p_4 = {}^mC_4 \left(\dfrac{1}{2}\right)^4 \left(\dfrac{1}{2}\right)^{m-4} = {}^mC_4 \left(\dfrac{1}{2}\right)^m$

$$p_5 = {}^mC_5 \left(\frac{1}{2}\right)^5 \left(\frac{1}{2}\right)^{m-5} = {}^mC_5 \left(\frac{1}{2}\right)^m$$

and $\quad p_6 = {}^mC_6 \left(\dfrac{1}{2}\right)^6 \left(\dfrac{1}{2}\right)^{m-6} = {}^mC_6 \left(\dfrac{1}{2}\right)^m$

According to the question, p_4, p_5, p_6 are in AP

$\therefore \quad 2p_5 = p_4 + p_6$

$\Rightarrow \quad 2 \times {}^mC_5 \left(\dfrac{1}{2}\right)^m = {}^mC_4 \left(\dfrac{1}{2}\right)^m + {}^mC_6 \left(\dfrac{1}{2}\right)^m$

or $\quad 2 \times {}^mC_5 = {}^mC_4 + {}^mC_6$

or $\quad 2 = \dfrac{{}^mC_4}{{}^mC_5} + \dfrac{{}^mC_6}{{}^mC_5}$

$\Rightarrow \quad 2 = \dfrac{5}{m - 5 + 1} + \dfrac{m - 6 + 1}{6}$

$\Rightarrow \quad 2 = \dfrac{5}{m - 4} + \dfrac{m - 5}{6}$

$\Rightarrow \quad m^2 - 21m + 98 = 0$

$\Rightarrow \quad (m - 14)(m - 7) = 0$

$\Rightarrow \quad m = 7$ or 14

Example 25 *If $A_1, A_2, \ldots, A_n$ are n independent events, such that $P(A_i) = \dfrac{1}{i+1}$, $i = 1, 2, \ldots, n$, then the probability that none of $A_1, A_2, A_3, \ldots, A_n$ occur, is*

(a) $\dfrac{n}{n+1}$ (b) $\dfrac{1}{n+1}$

(c) less than $\dfrac{1}{n}$ (d) greater than $\dfrac{1}{n+2}$

Sol. (b, c, d) $\because A_1, A_2, A_3, \ldots, A_n$ are n independent, then

Required probability $= P(A_1' \cap A_2' \cap A_3' \cap \ldots \cap A_n')$
$= P(A_1').P(A_2').P(A_3') \ldots P(A_n')$

$$= (1 - P(A_1))(1 - P(A_2))(1 - P(A_3)) \dots (1 - P(A_n))$$

$$= \left(1 - \frac{1}{2}\right)\left(1 - \frac{1}{3}\right)\left(1 - \frac{1}{4}\right) \dots \left(1 - \frac{1}{n+1}\right)$$

$$= \frac{1}{2} \times \frac{2}{3} \times \frac{3}{4} \times \dots \times \frac{n}{n+1} = \frac{1}{n+1}$$

$\because \quad n + 2 > n + 1 > n;$

$\therefore \quad \frac{1}{n+2} < \frac{1}{n+1} < \frac{1}{n}$

Example 26 *A and B are two events, such that $P(A \cup B) \geq \frac{3}{4}$ and $\frac{1}{8} \leq P(A \cap B) \leq \frac{3}{8}$, then*

(a) $P(A) + P(B) \leq \frac{11}{8}$ (b) $P(A) \cdot P(B) \leq \frac{3}{8}$

(c) $P(A) + P(B) \geq \frac{7}{8}$ (d) None of these

Sol. (a, c) $\because \quad \frac{3}{4} \leq P(A \cup B) \leq 1$

$\Rightarrow \quad \frac{3}{4} \leq P(A) + P(B) - P(A \cap B) \leq 1$

As the minimum value of $P(A \cap B) = \frac{1}{8}$, we get

$P(A) + P(B) - \frac{1}{8} \geq \frac{3}{4} \Rightarrow P(A) + P(B) \geq \frac{7}{8}$ [alternate (c)]

As the maximum value of $P(A \cap B) = \frac{3}{8}$, we get

$P(A) + P(B) - \frac{3}{8} \leq 1 \Rightarrow P(A) + P(B) \leq \frac{11}{8}$ [alternate (a)]

Example 27 *A, B, C and D cut a pack of 52 cards successively in the order given. If the person who cuts a spade first receives ₹ 350, then the expectations of*

(a) *B* is ₹ 96 (b) *D* is ₹ 54

(c) $(A + C)$ is ₹ 200 (d) $(B - D)$ is ₹ 56

Sol. (a, b, c) Let E be the event of any one cutting a spade in one cut and let S be the sample space, then

$$n(E) = {}^{13}C_1 = 13 \text{ and } n(S) = {}^{52}C_1 = 52$$

$\therefore \quad p = P(E) = \frac{n(E)}{n(S)} = \frac{1}{4}$ and $q = p(\bar{E}) = 1 - p = \frac{3}{4}$

The probability of A winning (when A starts the game)

$$= p + q^4 p + q^8 p + \dots \infty = \frac{p}{1 - q^4} = \frac{\frac{1}{4}}{1 - \left(\frac{3}{4}\right)^4} = \frac{64}{175}$$

$\therefore \quad E(A) = ₹ 350 \times \frac{64}{175} = ₹ 128$

$E(B) = ₹128 \times q = ₹128 \times \frac{3}{4} = ₹ 96$

$E(C) = ₹96 \times q = ₹96 \times \frac{3}{4} = ₹ 72$

and $E(D) = ₹72 \times q = ₹72 \times \frac{3}{4} = ₹ 54$

$\therefore E(A + C) = ₹ 200$ and $E(B - D) = ₹ 42$.

Example 28 *Let X and Y be two events such that $P(X) = \frac{1}{3}$, $P(X/Y) = \frac{1}{2}$ and $P(Y/X) = \frac{2}{5}$. Then,*

(a) $P(Y) = \frac{4}{15}$ (b) $P(X'/Y) = \frac{1}{2}$

(c) $P(X \cup Y) = \frac{2}{5}$ (d) $P(X \cap Y) = \frac{1}{5}$

Sol. (a, b) Given, $P(X) = \frac{1}{3}$, $P\left(\frac{X}{Y}\right) = \frac{P(X \cap Y)}{P(Y)} = \frac{1}{2}$

and $\quad P\left(\frac{Y}{X}\right) = \frac{P(X \cap Y)}{P(X)} = \frac{2}{5}$

So, $\quad P(X \cap Y) = \frac{2}{15}$ and $P(Y) = \frac{4}{15}$

Now, $\quad P\left(\frac{X'}{Y}\right) = \frac{P(Y) - P(X \cap Y)}{P(Y)}$

$$= \frac{\frac{4}{15} - \frac{2}{15}}{\frac{4}{15}} = \frac{1}{2}$$

$$P(X \cup Y) = \frac{1}{3} + \frac{4}{15} - \frac{2}{15} = \frac{7}{15}$$

Example 29 *There are three bags B_1, B_2 and B_3. The bag B_1 contains 5 red and 5 green balls, B_2 contains 3 red and 5 green balls, and B_3 contains 5 red and 3 green balls. Bags B_1, B_2 and B_3 have probabilities $\frac{3}{10}$, $\frac{3}{10}$ and $\frac{4}{10}$ respectively of being chosen. A bag is selected at random and a ball is chosen at random from the bag. Then, which of the following options is/are correct?*

(a) Probability that the chosen ball is green, given that the selected bag is B_3, equals 3/8.

(b) Probability that the selected bag is B_3, given that the chosen ball is green, equals 5/13.

(c) Probability that the chosen ball is green equals $\frac{39}{80}$.

(d) Probability that the selected bag is B_3 and the chosen ball is green equals 3/10.

Decoding the Question

In this question, use conditional probability, total probability and Baye's theorem.

Sol. (a, c) It is given that there are three bags B_1, B_2 and B_3 and probabilities of being chosen B_1, B_2 and B_3 are respectively.

$\therefore \; P(B_1) = \frac{3}{10}$, $P(B_2) = \frac{3}{10}$ and $P(B_3) = \frac{4}{10}$.

5 *R*	3 *R*	5 *R*
5 *G*	5 *G*	3 *G*
B_1	B_2	B_3

Now, probability that the chosen ball is green, given that selected bag is

$$B_3 = P\left(\frac{G}{B_3}\right) = \frac{3}{8}$$

Now, probability that the selected bag is B_3, given that the chosen ball is green

$$\therefore \quad P\left(\frac{B_3}{G}\right) = \frac{P\left(\frac{G}{B_3}\right)P(B_3)}{P\left(\frac{G}{B_1}\right)P(B_1)+P\left(\frac{G}{B_2}\right)P(B_2)+P\left(\frac{G}{B_3}\right)P(B_3)}$$

[by Baye's theorem]

$$= \frac{\left(\frac{3}{8}\times\frac{4}{10}\right)}{\left(\frac{5}{10}\times\frac{3}{10}\right)+\left(\frac{5}{8}\times\frac{3}{10}\right)+\left(\frac{3}{8}\times\frac{4}{10}\right)}$$

$$= \frac{\frac{1}{2}}{\frac{1}{2}+\frac{5}{8}+\frac{1}{2}} = \frac{4}{13}$$

Now, probability that the chosen ball is green

$$= P(G) = P(B_1)P\left(\frac{G}{B_1}\right)+P(B_2)P\left(\frac{G}{B_2}\right)+P(B_3)P\left(\frac{G}{B_3}\right)$$

[by using theorem of total probability]

$$= \left(\frac{3}{10}\times\frac{5}{10}\right)+\left(\frac{3}{10}\times\frac{5}{8}\right)+\left(\frac{4}{10}\times\frac{3}{8}\right)$$

$$= \frac{3}{20}+\frac{3}{16}+\frac{3}{20}$$

$$= \frac{12+15+12}{80}$$

$$= \frac{39}{80}$$

Now, probability that the selected bag is B_3 and the chosen ball is green

$$= P(B_3)\times P\left(\frac{G}{B_3}\right) = \frac{4}{10}\times\frac{3}{8} = \frac{3}{20}$$

Example 30 *A ship is fitted with three engines E_1, E_2 and E_3. The engines function independently of each other with respective probabilities 1/2, 1/4 and 1/4. For the ship to be operational atleast two of its engines must function. Let X denotes the event that the ship is operational and let X_1, X_2 and X_3 denote, respectively the events that the engines E_1, E_2 and E_3 are functioning. Which of the following is/are true?*

(a) $P[X_1^c | X] = 3/16$

(b) P [exactly two engines of the ship are functioning] $= \frac{7}{8}$

(c) $P[X | X_2] = \frac{5}{16}$

(d) $P[X | X_1] = \frac{7}{16}$

Sol. (b, d) **Description of Situation** It is given that ship would work if atleast two of engines must work. If X be event that the ship works. Then, $X \Rightarrow$ either any two of E_1, E_2, E_3 works or all three engines E_1, E_2, E_3 works.

Given, $P(E_1) = \frac{1}{2}$, $P(E_2) = \frac{1}{4}$, $P(E_3) = \frac{1}{4}$

$$\therefore \quad P(X) = \left\{\begin{matrix} P(E_1 \cap E_2 \cap \bar{E}_3) + P(E_1 \cap \bar{E}_2 \cap E_3) \\ + P(\bar{E}_1 \cap E_2 \cap E_3) + P(E_1 \cap E_2 \cap E_3) \end{matrix}\right\}$$

$$= \left(\frac{1}{2}\cdot\frac{1}{4}\cdot\frac{3}{4}+\frac{1}{2}\cdot\frac{3}{4}\cdot\frac{1}{4}+\frac{1}{2}\cdot\frac{1}{4}\cdot\frac{1}{4}+\frac{1}{2}\cdot\frac{1}{4}\cdot\frac{1}{4}\right)$$

$$= \frac{1}{4}$$

Now,

(a) $$P\left(\frac{X_1^c}{X}\right) = P\left(\frac{X_1^c \cap X}{X}\right) = \frac{P(\bar{E}_1 \cap E_2 \cap E_3)}{P(X)} = \frac{\frac{1}{2}\cdot\frac{1}{4}\cdot\frac{1}{4}}{1/4} = \frac{1}{8}$$

(b) P (exactly two engines of the ship are functioning)

$$= \frac{P(E_1 \cap E_2 \cap \bar{E}_3) + P(E_1 \cap \bar{E}_2 \cap E_3) + P(\bar{E}_1 \cap E_2 \cap E_3)}{P(X)}$$

$$= \frac{\frac{1}{2}\cdot\frac{1}{4}\cdot\frac{3}{4}+\frac{1}{2}\cdot\frac{3}{4}\cdot\frac{1}{4}+\frac{1}{2}\cdot\frac{1}{4}\cdot\frac{1}{4}}{\frac{1}{4}} = \frac{7}{8}$$

(c) $$P\left(\frac{X}{X_2}\right) = \frac{P(X \cap X_2)}{P(X_2)}$$

$$= \frac{P \text{ (ship is operating with } E_2 \text{ function)}}{P(X_2)}$$

$$= \frac{P(E_1 \cap E_2 \cap \bar{E}_3) + P(\bar{E}_1 \cap E_2 \cap E_3) + P(E_1 \cap E_2 \cap E_3)}{P(E_2)}$$

$$= \frac{\frac{1}{2}\cdot\frac{1}{4}\cdot\frac{3}{4}+\frac{1}{2}\cdot\frac{1}{4}\cdot\frac{1}{4}+\frac{1}{2}\cdot\frac{1}{4}\cdot\frac{1}{4}}{\frac{1}{4}} = \frac{5}{8}$$

(d) $$P\left(\frac{X}{X_1}\right) = \frac{P(X \cap X_1)}{P(X_1)}$$

$$= \frac{\frac{1}{2}\cdot\frac{1}{4}\cdot\frac{1}{4}+\frac{1}{2}\cdot\frac{3}{4}\cdot\frac{1}{4}+\frac{1}{2}\cdot\frac{1}{4}\cdot\frac{3}{4}}{1/2} = \frac{7}{16}$$

Example 31 *Let E and F be two independent events. The probability that exactly one of them occurs is $\frac{11}{25}$ and the probability of none of them occurring is $\frac{2}{25}$. If $P(T)$ denotes the probability of occurrence of the event T, then*

(a) $P(E) = \frac{4}{5}$, $P(F) = \frac{3}{5}$ (b) $P(E) = \frac{1}{5}$, $P(F) = \frac{2}{5}$

(c) $P(E) = \frac{2}{5}$, $P(F) = \frac{1}{5}$ (d) $P(E) = \frac{3}{5}$, $P(F) = \frac{4}{5}$

Sol. (a, d)

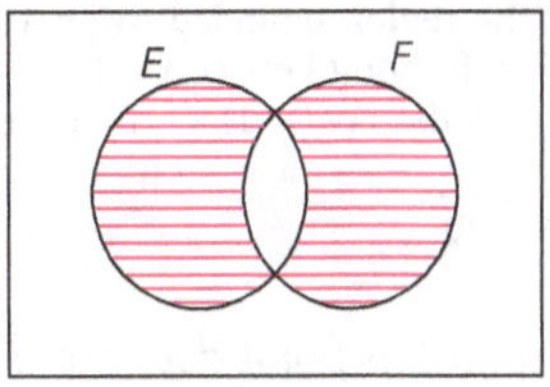

$$P(E \cup F) - P(E \cap F) = \frac{11}{25} \quad \text{...(i) [i.e. only } E \text{ or only } F]$$

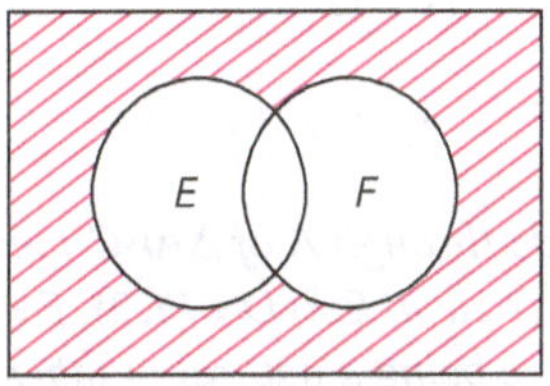

Neither of them occurs $= \frac{2}{25}$

$$\Rightarrow \quad P(\bar{E} \cap \bar{F}) = \frac{2}{25} \quad \text{...(ii)}$$

From Eq. (i), $P(E) + P(F) - 2P(E \cap F) = \frac{11}{25}$ ...(iii)

From Eq. (ii), $(1 - P(E))(1 - P(F)) = \frac{2}{25}$

$$\Rightarrow \quad 1 - P(E) - P(F) + P(E) \cdot P(F) = \frac{2}{25} \quad \text{...(iv)}$$

From Eqs. (iii) and (iv),

$$P(E) + P(F) = \frac{7}{5} \text{ and } P(E) \cdot P(F) = \frac{12}{25}$$

$$\therefore \quad P(E) \cdot \left[\frac{7}{5} - P(E)\right] = \frac{12}{25}$$

$$\Rightarrow \quad (P(E))^2 - \frac{7}{5}P(E) + \frac{12}{25} = 0$$

$$\Rightarrow \quad \left[P(E) - \frac{3}{5}\right]\left[P(E) - \frac{4}{5}\right] = 0$$

$$\therefore \quad P(E) = \frac{3}{5} \text{ or } \frac{4}{5} \Rightarrow P(F) = \frac{4}{5} \text{ or } \frac{3}{5}$$

Passage Based Questions

Passage I

(Ex. Nos. 32 and 33)

Each coefficient in the equation $ax^2 + bx + c = 0$ is determined by throwing an ordinary die.

Example 32 *The probability that roots of quadratic are real and distinct, is*

(a) $\frac{5}{216}$ (b) $\frac{19}{108}$ (c) $\frac{173}{216}$ (d) $\frac{17}{108}$

Sol. (b) For roots of $ax^2 + bx + c = 0$ to be real and distinct,

$$b^2 - 4ac > 0$$

Values of b	Possible values of a and c
1, 2	No values of a and c
3	(1, 1), (1, 2), (2, 1)
4	(1, 1), (1, 2), (2, 1), (1, 3), (3, 1)
5	(1, 1), (1, 2), (2, 1), (1, 3), (3, 1), (2, 2), (1, 4), (4, 1), (1, 5), (5, 1), (2, 3), (3, 2), (1, 6), (6, 1)
6	(1, 1), (1, 2), (2, 1), (1, 3), (3, 1), (2, 2), (1, 4), (4, 1), (1, 5), (5, 1), (2, 3), (3, 2), (1, 6), (6, 1), (2, 4), (4, 2)

If E be the event of favourable cases, then $n(E) = 38$

Total ways, $n(S) = 6 \times 6 \times 6 = 216$

Hence, the required probability, $P_1 = \frac{n(E)}{n(S)} = \frac{38}{216} = \frac{19}{108}$

Example 33 *The probability that roots of quadratic are equal, is*

(a) $\frac{5}{216}$ (b) $\frac{7}{216}$ (c) $\frac{11}{216}$ (d) $\frac{17}{216}$

Sol. (a) For roots of $ax^2 + bx + c = 0$ to be equal $b^2 = 4ac$ i.e. b^2 must be even.

Values of b	Possible values of a and c
2	(1, 1)
4	(2, 2), (1, 4), (4, 1)
6	(3, 3)

If E be the event of favourable cases, then $n(E) = 5$

Total ways, $n(S) = 6 \times 6 \times 6 = 216$

Hence, the required probability, $P_2 = \frac{n(E)}{n(S)} = \frac{5}{216}$

Passage II

(Ex. Nos. 34 and 35)

A box contains n coins. Let $P(E_i)$ be the probability that exactly i out of n coins are biased. If $P(E_i)$ is directly proportional to $i(i+1)$; $1 \le i \le n$.

Example 34 *Proportionality constant k is equal to*

(a) $\frac{3}{n(n^2+1)}$ (b) $\frac{1}{(n^2+1)(n+2)}$

(c) $\frac{3}{n(n+1)(n+2)}$ (d) $\frac{1}{(n+1)(n+2)(n+3)}$

Sol. (c) $\because P(E_i) \propto i(i+1)$

$\Rightarrow P(E_i) = k\,i(i+1)$, where k is proportionality constant.

We have, $P(E_1) + P(E_2) + P(E_3) + \dots + P(E_n) = 1$

[$\because E_1, E_2, \dots, E_n$ are mutually exclusive and exhaustive events]

$$\Rightarrow \sum_{i=1}^{n} P(E_i) = 1 \Rightarrow k\sum_{i=1}^{n}(i^2 + i) = 1 \Rightarrow k\left[\sum n^2 + \sum n\right] = 1$$

$$\Rightarrow k\left[\frac{n(n+1)(2n+1)}{6} + \frac{n(n+1)}{2}\right] = 1$$

$$\therefore \quad k = \frac{3}{n(n+1)(n+2)} \quad \text{...(i)}$$

Example 35 *If P be the probability that a coin selected at random is biased, then $\lim_{x \to \infty} P$ is*

(a) $\frac{1}{4}$ (b) $\frac{3}{4}$ (c) $\frac{3}{5}$ (d) $\frac{7}{8}$

Sol. (b) $\because P = P(E) = \sum_{i=1}^{n} \cdot P(E_i)\, P\left(\frac{E}{E_i}\right)$ ...(ii)

$$= \sum_{i=1}^{n} k\, i(i+1) \cdot \frac{i}{n} = \frac{k}{n}\sum_{i=1}^{n}(i^3 + i^2) = \frac{k}{n}[\sum n^3 + \sum n^2]$$

$$= \frac{k}{n}\left[\left(\frac{n(n+1)}{2}\right)^2 + \frac{n(n+1)(2n+1)}{6}\right]$$

$$= \frac{k(n+1)(n+2)(3n+1)}{12}$$

$$= \frac{3}{n(n+1)(n+2)} \cdot \frac{(n+1)(n+2)(3n+1)}{12} \quad \text{[from Eq. (i)]}$$

$$= \frac{3n+1}{4n} = \frac{3}{4} + \frac{1}{4n}$$

$$\therefore \lim_{n \to \infty} P = \lim_{n \to \infty}\left[\frac{3}{4} + \frac{1}{3n}\right] = \frac{3}{4} + 0 = \frac{3}{4}$$

Stem Based Questions

Stem I

(Ex. Nos. 36 to 37)

Three randomly chosen non-negative integers x, y and z are found to satisfy the equation $x + y + z = 10$.

Example 36 *The probability that z is even, is ....*

Sol. Number of non-negative integer solution $= {}^{10+3-1}C_{3-1} = 66$

We have, $z = 2k, k \geq 0$

$x + y + 2k = 10 \Rightarrow x + y = 10 - 2k$

Now, number of solution $= {}^{11-2k}C_1 = 11 - 2k$

$$\Sigma(11 - 2k) = 11 + 9 + 7 + 5 + 3 + 1 = 36$$

$\therefore$ Required probability $= \frac{6}{11}$

Example 37 *The probability that z is odd, is ....*

Sol. Obtained that the probability of z is even $= \frac{6}{11}$.

Since, probability of z to be odd

$= 1 -$ Probability of z to be even

$= 1 - \frac{6}{11} = \frac{5}{11}$

Stem II

(Ex. Nos. 38 to 39)

Two dice are thrown simultaneously to get the coordinate of a point on XY-plane.

Example 38 *Probability that this point lies inside or on the region bounded by $|x| + |y| = 3$ is ....*

Sol. Any point on or inside the region bounded by $|x| + |y| = 3$ will have x and y coordinate lying between -3 and 3 which will turnup as a throw of a die i.e. (1, 1), (1, 2), (2, 1).

Hence, probability is $\frac{3}{36} = \frac{1}{12}$.

Example 39 *Probability that this point does not lie inside or on the region bounded by $|x| + |y| = 3$, is equal to ....*

Sol. Required probability $= 1 - \frac{1}{12} = \frac{11}{12}$

Single Integer Answer Type Questions

Example 40 *The altitude through A of ΔABC meets BC at D and the circumscribed circle at E. If $D \equiv (2, 3)$, $E \equiv (5, 5)$, the ordinate of the orthocentre being a natural number. If the probability that the orthocentre lies on the lines $y = 1$; $y = 2$; $y = 3$...... $y = 10$ is $\frac{m}{n}$, where m and n are relative primes, the value of $m + n$ is ....*

Sol. (8) Let the orthocentre be $O(x, y)$.

It is clear from the OE is perpendicular bisector of line BC.

$$\therefore \quad OD = DE$$

$$\Rightarrow \sqrt{(x-2)^2 + (y-3)^2} = \sqrt{(5-2)^2 + (5-3)^2}$$

$$\Rightarrow (x-2)^2 + (y-3)^2 = (5-2)^2 + (5-3)^2$$

$$\Rightarrow x^2 + y^2 - 4x - 6y = 0 \Rightarrow x = 2 \pm \sqrt{13 - (y-3)^2}$$

$\Rightarrow y$ can take the values as 1, 2, 3, 4, 5, 6

$\therefore$ Required probability $= \frac{6}{10} = \frac{3}{5} = \frac{m}{n}$ [given]

$\Rightarrow m = 3$ and $n = 5$

$\therefore m + n = 8$

Example 41 *The digits 1, 2, 3, 4, 5, 6, 7, 8 and 9 are written in random order to form a nine digit number. Let p be the probability that this number is divisible by 36, the value of 9p is ....*

Sol. (2) $\because 1 + 2 + 3 + 4 + 5 + 6 + 7 + 8 + 9 = 45$, a number consisting all these digits will be divisible by 9.

Thus, the number will be divisible by 36, if and only if it is divisible by 4. The number formed by its last two digits must be divisible by 4.

The possible values of the last pair to the following:

12, 16, 24, 28, 32, 36, 48, 52, 56, 64, 68, 72, 76, 84, 92, 96.

i.e. There are 16 ways of choosing last two digits.

The remaining digits can be arranged in ${}^7P_7 = 7!$ ways.

Therefore, number of favourable ways $= 16 \times 7!$

and number of total ways $= 9!$

$\therefore$ Required probability, $p = \frac{16 \times 7!}{9!} = \frac{16}{9 \times 8} = \frac{2}{9} \Rightarrow 9p = 2$

Example 42 *Eight players $P_1, P_2, \ldots, P_8$ play a knock-out tournament. It is known that whenever the players P_i and P_j play, the player P_i will win if $i < j$. Assuming that the players are paired at random in each round. If the probability that the player P_4 reaches the final is D, then 35D is equal to ……*

Sol. (4) The number of ways in which $P_1, P_2, \ldots, P_8$ can be paired in four pairs

$$= \frac{1}{4!}[({}^8C_2)({}^6C_2)({}^4C_2)({}^2C_2)]$$

$$= \frac{1}{4!} \times \frac{8!}{2!6!} \times \frac{6!}{2!4!} \times \frac{4!}{2!2!} \times 1$$

$$= \frac{1}{4!} \times \frac{8 \times 7}{2! \times 1} \times \frac{6 \times 5}{2! \times 1} \times \frac{4 \times 3}{2! \times 1} = \frac{8 \times 7 \times 6 \times 5}{2 \cdot 2 \cdot 2 \cdot 2} = 105$$

Now, atleast two players certainly reach the second round between P_1, P_2, P_3 and P_4 can reach in final if exactly two players play against each other between P_1, P_2, P_3 and remaining player will play against one of the players from P_5, P_6, P_7, P_8 and P_4 plays against one of the remaining three from $P_5 \ldots P_8$.

This can be possible in ${}^3C_2 \times {}^4C_1 \times {}^3C_1 = 3 \cdot 4 \cdot 3 = 36$ ways

$\therefore$ Probability that P_4 and exactly one of $P_5 \ldots P_8$ reach second round $= \frac{36}{105} = \frac{12}{35}$

If P_1, P_i, P_4 and P_j, where $i = 2$ or 3 and $j = 5$ or 6 or 7 reach the second round, then they can be paired in 2 pairs in $\frac{1}{2!}({}^4C_2)({}^2C_2) = 3$ ways. But P_4 will reach the final, if P_1 plays against P_i and P_4 plays against P_j.

Hence, the probability that P_4 will reach the final round from the second $= 1/3$

$\therefore$ Probability that P_4 will reach the final is

$$D = \frac{12}{35} \times \frac{1}{3} = \frac{4}{35}.$$

Hence, $35D = 4$

Example 43 *Of the three independent events E_1, E_2 and E_3, the probability that only E_1 occurs is α, only E_2 occurs is β and only E_3 occurs is γ. Let the probability p that none of events E_1, E_2 or E_3 occurs satisfy the equations $(\alpha - 2\beta)$, $p = \alpha\beta$ and $(\beta - 3\gamma)\, p = 2\beta\gamma$. All the given probabilities are assumed to lie in the interval (0, 1). Then, $\frac{\text{probability of occurrence of } E_1}{\text{probability of occurrence of } E_3}$ is equal to …… .*

Decoding the Question

For the events to be independent,

$P(E_1 \cap E_2 \cap E_3) = P(E_1) \cdot P(E_2) \cdot P(E_3)$

$P(E_1 \cap \bar{E}_2 \cap \bar{E}_3) = P(\text{only } E_1 \text{ occurs})$

$= P(E_1) \cdot (1 - P(E_2))\,(1 - P(E_3))$

Use this to solve the question.

Sol. (6) Let x, y and z be probabilities of E_1, E_2 and E_3, respectively.

$\therefore \quad \alpha = x(1-y)(1-z)$ …(i)

$\beta = (1-x) \cdot y(1-z)$ …(ii)

$\gamma = (1-x)(1-y)z$ …(iii)

$\Rightarrow \quad p = (1-x)(1-y)(1-z)$ …(iv)

Given, $(\alpha - 2\beta)p = \alpha\beta$ and $(\beta - 3\gamma)p = 2\beta\gamma$ …(v)

From above equations,

$$x = 2y \text{ and } y = 3z$$

$$\therefore \quad x = 6z \Rightarrow \frac{x}{z} = 6$$

Example 44 *If two events A and B are such that $P(A^c) = 0.3$, $P(B) = 0.4$ and $P(A \cap B^c) = 0.5$, then $4P[B/(A \cup B^c)]$ is equal to ………*

Sol. (1) $\quad P(A^c) = 0.3$ [given]

$\Rightarrow \quad P(A) = 0.7$

$P(B) = 0.4$ [given]

$\Rightarrow \quad P(B^c) = 0.6$

and $\quad P(A \cap B^c) = 0.5$ [given]

Now, $\quad P(A \cup B^c) = P(A) + P(B^c) - P(A \cap B^c)$

$= 0.7 + 0.6 - 0.5 = 0.8$

$$\therefore \quad P[B/(A \cup B^c)] = \frac{P\{B \cap (A \cup B^c)\}}{P(A \cup B^c)}$$

$$= \frac{P\{(B \cap A) \cup (B \cap B^c)\}}{0.8}$$

$$= \frac{P\{(B \cap A) \cup \phi\}}{0.8} = \frac{P(B \cap A)}{0.8}$$

$$= \frac{1}{0.8}[P(A) - P(A \cap B^c)]$$

$$= \frac{0.7 - 0.5}{0.8} = \frac{0.2}{0.8} = \frac{1}{4}$$

Now, $4P[B/(A \cup B^c)] = 4 \times \frac{1}{4} = 1$

Example 45 *A person goes to office either by car, scooter, bus or train probability of which being $\frac{1}{7}, \frac{3}{7}, \frac{2}{7}$ and $\frac{1}{7}$, respectively. Probability that he reaches offices late, if he takes car, scooter, bus or train is $\frac{2}{9}, \frac{1}{9}, \frac{4}{9}$ and $\frac{1}{9}$, respectively. Given that he reached office in time, then 7th times the probability that he travelled by a car is equal to ………*

Sol. (1) As, the statement shows problem is to be related to Baye's law.

Let C, S, B, T be the events when person is going by car, scooter, bus or train, respectively.

$\therefore P(C) = \frac{1}{7}, P(S) = \frac{3}{7}, P(B) = \frac{2}{7}, P(T) = \frac{1}{7}$

Again, L be the event of the person reaching office late.

$\therefore \bar{L}$ be the event of the person reaching office in time.

Then, $P\left(\frac{\bar{L}}{C}\right)=\frac{7}{9}$, $P\left(\frac{\bar{L}}{S}\right)=\frac{8}{9}$, $P\left(\frac{\bar{L}}{B}\right)=\frac{5}{9}$ and $P\left(\frac{\bar{L}}{T}\right)=\frac{8}{9}$

$$\therefore 7P\left(\frac{C}{\bar{L}}\right)=7\left[\frac{P\left(\frac{\bar{L}}{C}\right)\cdot P(C)}{P\left(\frac{\bar{L}}{C}\right)\cdot P(C)+P\left(\frac{\bar{L}}{S}\right)\cdot P(S)+P\left(\frac{\bar{L}}{B}\right)\cdot P(B)+P\left(\frac{\bar{L}}{T}\right)\cdot P(T)}\right]$$

$$=7\left[\frac{\frac{7}{9}\times\frac{1}{7}}{\frac{7}{9}\times\frac{1}{7}+\frac{8}{9}\times\frac{3}{7}+\frac{5}{9}\times\frac{2}{7}+\frac{8}{9}\times\frac{1}{7}}\right]=\frac{1}{7}\times 7=1$$

Example 46 *Three boys and two girls stand in a queue. The probability that the number of boys ahead of every girl is atleast one more than the number of girls ahead of her is P_1, then $2P_1$ is equal to ....*

Sol. (1) Total number of ways to arrange 3 boys and 2 girls are 5!.

According to given condition, following cases may arise.

B	G	G	B	B
G	G	B	B	B
G	B	G	B	B
G	B	B	G	B
B	G	B	G	B

So, number of favourable ways $=5\times 3!\times 2!=60$

$\therefore$ Required probability $(P_1)=\frac{60}{120}=\frac{1}{2}$

Hence, $2P_1=1$

Numerical Value Type Questions

Example 47 *Four fair dice D_1, D_2, D_3 and D_4 each having six faces numbered 1, 2, 3, 4, 5 and 6 are rolled simultaneously. The probability that D_4 shows a number appearing on one of D_1, D_2 and D_3, is D, then $216D$ is equal to ....*

Decoding the Question

As one of the dice shows a number appearing on one of P_1, P_2 and P_3. Thus, three cases arise.

(i) All show same number.

(ii) Number appearing on D_4 appears on any one of D_1, D_2 and D_3.

(iii) Number appearing on D_4 appears on any two of D_1, D_2 and D_3.

Sample space $=6\times 6\times 6\times 6=6^4$

Favourable events = Case I or Case II or Case III

Sol. (91) **Case I** First we should select one number for D_4 which appears on all

i.e. $\quad {}^6C_1\times 1$.

Case II For D_4 there are ${}^6C_1$ ways.

Now, it appears on any one of D_1, D_2 and D_3 i.e. ${}^3C_1\times 1$.

For other two there are 5×5 ways.

$\Rightarrow \quad {}^6C_1\times {}^3C_1\times 1\times 5\times 5$

Case III For D_4 there are ${}^6C_1$ ways now, it appears on any two of D_1, D_2 and D_3

$\Rightarrow \quad {}^3C_2\times 1^2$

For other one there are 5 ways.

$\Rightarrow \quad {}^6C_1\times {}^3C_2\times 1^2\times 5$

Thus, probability $(D)=\frac{{}^6C_1+{}^6C_1\times {}^3C_1\times 5^2+{}^6C_1\times {}^3C_2\times 5}{6^4}$

$=\frac{6(1+75+15)}{6^4}$

$=\frac{91}{216}$

$\therefore 216D=91$

Example 48 *If three distinct numbers are chosen randomly from the first 100 natural numbers, then 1155th times, the probability that all three of them are divisible by both 2 and 3, is ....*

Sol. (4) Since, three distinct numbers are to be selected from first 100 natural numbers.

$\Rightarrow \quad n(S)={}^{100}C_3$

$E_{(\text{favourable events})}$ = All three of them are divisible by both 2 and 3

$\Rightarrow$ Divisible by 6 i.e. {6, 12, 18, ..., 96}

Thus, out of 16 we have to select 3.

$\therefore \quad n(E)={}^{16}C_3$

$\therefore$ Required probability $=1155\times\frac{{}^{16}C_3}{{}^{100}C_3}=4$

Example 49 *If p and q are chosen randomly from the set {1, 2, 3, 4, 5, 6, 7, 8, 9 and 10} with replacement, then the probability that the roots of the equation $x^2+px+q=0$ are real, is equal to ....*

Sol. (0.62) The required probability

$=1-$ (Probability of the event that the roots of $x^2+px+q=0$ are non-real)

The roots of $x^2+px+q=0$ will be non-real if and only if $p^2-4q<0$,

i.e. if $p^2<4q$

The possible values of p and q can be possible according to the following table.

Value of q	Value of p	Number of pairs of p, q
1	1	1
2	1, 2	2
3	1, 2, 3	3
4	1, 2, 3	3
5	1, 2, 3, 4	4
6	1, 2, 3, 4	4
7	1, 2, 3, 4, 5	5
8	1, 2, 3, 4, 5	5
9	1, 2, 3, 4, 5	5
10	1, 2, 3, 4, 5, 6	6

Therefore, the number of possible pairs = 38

Also, the total number of possible pairs is $10 \times 10 = 100$

$\therefore$ The required probability $= 1 - \dfrac{38}{100} = 1 - 0.38 = 0.62$

Example 50 *The probability that at least one of the events A and B occurs is 0.6. If A and B occur simultaneously with probability 0.2, then* $P(\overline{A}) + P(\overline{B})$ *is equal to ....*

Sol. (1.2) Given, $P(A \cup B) = 0.6$, $P(A \cap B) = 0.2$

$$\therefore\ P(\overline{A}) + P(\overline{B}) = [1 - P(A)] + [1 - P(B)]$$
$$= 2 - [P(A) + P(B)]$$
$$= 2 - [P(A \cup B) + P(A \cap B)]$$
$$= 2 - [0.6 + 0.2] = 1.2$$

Example 51 *Two events A and B have probabilities 0.25 and 0.50, respectively. The probability that both A and B occur simultaneously is 0.14. Then, the probability that neither A nor B occurs, is equal to ....*

Sol. (0.39) Given, $P(A) = 0.25$, $P(B) = 0.50$, $P(A \cap B) = 0.14$

$$P(A \cup B) = P(A) + P(B) - P(A \cap B)$$
$$= 0.\ 25 + 0.50 - 0.14 = 0.61$$

Now, $P(\overline{A \cup B}) = 1 - P(A \cup B) = 1 - 0.61 = 0.39$

Example 52 *The minimum number of times a fair coin needs to be tossed, so that the probability of getting atleast two heads is atleast 0.96, is ....*

Sol. (8) Using Binomial distribution,

$$P(X \ge 2) = 1 - P(X = 0) - P(X = 1)$$
$$= 1 - \left(\frac{1}{2}\right)^n - \left[{}^nC_1 \cdot \left(\frac{1}{2}\right) \cdot \left(\frac{1}{2}\right)^{n-1}\right]$$
$$= 1 - \frac{1}{2^n} - {}^nC_1 \cdot \frac{1}{2^n} = 1 - \left(\frac{1+n}{2^n}\right)$$

Given, $P(X \ge 2) \ge 0.96$

$$\therefore\quad 1 - \frac{(n+1)}{2^n} \ge \frac{24}{25} \Rightarrow \frac{n+1}{2^n} \le \frac{1}{25} \Rightarrow n = 8$$

Example 53 *For a biased die the probabilities for the different faces to turn up are given below*

Face	1	2	3	4	5	6
Probability	0.1	0.32	0.21	0.15	0.05	0.17

This die is tossed and you are told that either face 1 or face 2 has turned up. Then, 5th times the probability that it is face 1, is ....

Sol. (0.238) Let A be the event that face 1 turns up and B be the event that face 2 turns up.

$\therefore P(A) = 0.1$, $P(B) = 0.32$

Since, A and B are mutually exclusive.

Thus, $P(A \cup B) = P(A) + P(B) = 0.1 + 0.32 = 0.42$

Now, $P\left(\dfrac{A}{A \cup B}\right) = \dfrac{P(A \cap (A \cup B))}{P(A \cup B)} = \dfrac{P(A)}{P(A \cup B)} = \dfrac{0.1}{0.42} = \dfrac{5}{21}$

$= 0.238$

Example 54 *Numbers are selected at random, one at a time, from the two-digit numbers 00, 01, 02, ..., 99 with replacement. An event E occurs if and only if the product of the two digits of a selected number is 18. If four numbers are selected, then probability that the event E occurs at least 3 times is t. The value of* $25^4 t$ *is equal to ....*

Sol. (97) Let E be the event that product of the two digits is 18, therefore required numbers are 29 , 36, 63 and 92.

Hence, $p = P(E) = \dfrac{4}{100}$

and probability of non-occurrence of E is

$$q = 1 - P(E) = 1 - \frac{4}{100} = \frac{96}{100}$$

Out of the four numbers selected, the probability that the event E occurs atleast 3 times, is given as

$$P = {}^4C_3 p^3 q + {}^4C_4 p^4 = 4\left(\frac{4}{100}\right)^3\left(\frac{96}{100}\right) + \left(\frac{4}{100}\right)^4 = \frac{97}{25^4} = t$$

$$\therefore\ 25^4 t = \frac{97}{25^4} \times 25^4 = 97$$

Example 55 *Suppose the probability for A to win a game against B is 0.4. If A has an option of playing either a 'best of 3 games' or a 'best of 5 games" match against B, which option should choose so that the probability of his winning the match is higher and by how much percent? (no game ends in a draw).*

Sol. (9.82) **Case I** When A plays 3 games against B.

In this case, we have

$$n = 3,\ p = 0.4 \text{ and } q = 0.6$$

Let X denote the number of wins.

Then, $P(X = r) = {}^3C_r (0.4)^r (0.6)^{3-r}$;

$$r = 0, 1, 2, 3$$

$\therefore$ P_1 = Probability of winning the best of 3 games

$= P(X \ge 2) = P(X = 2) + P(X = 3)$

$= {}^3C_2(0.4)^2(0.6)^1 + {}^3C_3(0.4)^3(0.6)^0 = 0.288 + 0.064 = 0.352$

Case II When A plays 5 games against B.

In this case, we have $n = 5$, $p = 0.4$ and $q = 0.6$

Let X denotes the number of wins in 5 games.

Then, $P(X = r) = {}^5C_r(0.4)^r(0.6)^{5-r}$, where $r = 0, 1, 2, \dots, 5$

$\therefore$ P_2 = Probability of winning the best of 5 games

$= P(X \ge 3) = P(X = 3) + P(X = 4) + P(X = 5)$

$= {}^5C_3(0.4)^3(0.6)^2 + {}^5C_4(0.4)^4(0.6) + {}^5C_5(0.4)^5(0.6)^0$

$= 0.2304 + 0.0768 + 0.01024 = 0.31744$

Clearly, $P_1 > P_2$. Therefore, first option i.e. 'best of 3 games' has higher probability of winning the match.

Now, $\dfrac{P_1 - P_2}{P_1} \times 100 = \dfrac{0.352 - 0.31744}{0.352} \times 100 = 9.82\%$

Example 56 *A man takes a step forward with probability 0.4 and backwards with probability 0.6. If the probability that at the end of eleven steps he is one step away from the starting point is ${}^{11}C_6\,(m)^5$, then m is equal to ....*

Sol. (0.367) The man will be one step away from the starting point, if (i) either he is one step ahead or (ii) one step behind the starting point.

The man will be one step ahead at the end of eleven steps, if he moves six steps forward and five steps backward. The probability of this event is ${}^{11}C_6(0.4)^6(0.6)^5$.

The man will be one step behind at the end of eleven steps, if he moves six steps backward and five steps forward.

The probability of this event is ${}^{11}C_6(0.6)^6(0.4)^5$.

$\therefore$ Required probability

$= {}^{11}C_6(0.4)^6(0.6)^5 + {}^{11}C_6(0.6)^6(0.4)^5 = 0.147 + 0.220 = 0.367$

Matching Type Questions

Example 57 *If A and B are two independent events, such that $P(A) = \dfrac{1}{3}$ and $P(B) = \dfrac{1}{4}$.*

	Column I		Column II
(A)	If $P\left(\dfrac{A}{B}\right) = \lambda_1$, then $12\lambda_1$ is	(p)	a prime number
(B)	If $P\left(\dfrac{A}{A \cup B}\right) = \lambda_2$, then $9\lambda_2$ is	(q)	a composite number
(C)	If $P[(A \cap \overline{B}) \cup (\overline{A} \cap B)] = \lambda_3$, then $12\lambda_3$ is	(r)	a natural number
(D)	If $P(\overline{A} \cup B) = \lambda_4$, then $12\lambda_4$ is	(s)	a perfect number

Sol. A $\to$ (q, r); B $\to$ (q, r, s); C $\to$ (p, r); D $\to$ (q, r)

$\because$ A and B are independent events.

$\therefore$ $P(A \cap B) = P(A) \cdot P(B) = \dfrac{1}{12}$,

$P(A \cap \overline{B}) = P(A) \cdot P(\overline{B}) = \dfrac{1}{3} \times \left(1 - \dfrac{1}{4}\right) = \dfrac{1}{4}$,

$P(\overline{A} \cap B) = P(\overline{A}) \cdot P(B) = \left(1 - \dfrac{1}{3}\right) \cdot \dfrac{1}{4} = \dfrac{1}{6}$

(A) $P\left(\dfrac{A}{B}\right) = \dfrac{P(A \cap B)}{P(B)} = \dfrac{\frac{1}{12}}{\frac{1}{4}} = \dfrac{1}{3} = \lambda_1$ [given]

$\therefore$ $12\lambda_1 = 4$ [natural number and composite number]

(B) $P\left(\dfrac{A}{A \cup B}\right) = \dfrac{P(A \cap (A \cup B))}{P(A \cup B)} = \dfrac{P(A)}{P(A \cup B)}$

$= \dfrac{P(A)}{P(A) + P(B) - P(A \cap B)} = \dfrac{\frac{1}{3}}{\frac{1}{3} + \frac{1}{4} - \frac{1}{12}} = \dfrac{2}{3} = \lambda_2$ [given]

$\therefore$ $9\lambda_2 = 6$

[natural number, composite number and perfect number]

(C) $P((A \cap \overline{B}) \cup (\overline{A} \cap B)) = P(A \cap \overline{B}) + P(\overline{A} \cap B)$

$= \dfrac{1}{4} + \dfrac{1}{6} = \dfrac{5}{12} = \lambda_3$ [given]

$\therefore$ $12\lambda_3 = 5$

[prime number and natural number]

(D) $P(\overline{A} \cup B) = P(\overline{A}) + P(B) - P(\overline{A} \cap B)$

$= \left(1 - \dfrac{1}{3}\right) + \dfrac{1}{4} - \dfrac{1}{6} = \dfrac{3}{4} = \lambda_4$ [given]

$\therefore$ $12\lambda_4 = 9$ [natural number and composite number]

Example 58 *Two dice are thrown simultaneously the probability of getting*

	Column I		Column II
(A)	A sum of atleast 10	(p)	$\dfrac{1}{2}$
(B)	An even number as the first term	(q)	$\dfrac{11}{36}$
(C)	The product a perfect square	(r)	$\dfrac{1}{6}$
(D)	Atleast one of the two number as 4	(s)	$\dfrac{2}{9}$

Sol. A $\to$ (r); B $\to$ (p); C $\to$ (s); D $\to$ (q)

(A) A sum atleast 10 = [(6, 4), (4, 6), (5, 5), (6, 5), (5, 6), (6, 6)]

$p = \dfrac{6}{36} = \dfrac{1}{6}$

(B) Getting even number sum $= \dfrac{18}{36} = \dfrac{1}{2}$

(C) Getting product of two numbers be a perfect square

(1, 1), (1, 4), (2, 2), (4, 1), (3, 3), (4, 4), (5, 5), (6, 6)

$p = \dfrac{8}{36} = \dfrac{2}{9}$

(D) Getting at least one of two number as 4.

$p = \dfrac{11}{36}$

EXERCISE 1

JEE Main Pattern

Single Option Correct Type Questions

1. There are two vans each having numbered seats, 3 in the front and 4 at the back. There are 3 girls and 9 boys to be seated in the vans. The probability of 3 girls sitting together in a back row on adjacent seats, is
(a) $\frac{1}{13}$ (b) $\frac{1}{39}$ (c) $\frac{1}{65}$ (d) $\frac{1}{91}$

2. A positive integer N is selected so as to be $100 < N < 200$. Then, the probability that it is divisible by 4 or 7, is
(a) $\frac{7}{33}$ (b) $\frac{17}{33}$ (c) $\frac{32}{99}$ (d) $\frac{34}{99}$

3. Three different numbers are selected at random from the set $A = \{1, 2, 3, \ldots, 10\}$. The probability that the product of two of the numbers is equal to third, is
(a) $\frac{3}{4}$ (b) $\frac{1}{40}$ (c) $\frac{1}{8}$ (d) $\frac{39}{40}$

4. The numbers $1, 2, 3, \ldots, n$ are arranged in a random order. Then, the probability that the digits $1, 2, 3, \ldots, k (k < n)$ appears as neighbours in that order, is
(a) $\frac{1}{n!}$ (b) $\frac{k!}{n!}$
(c) $\frac{(n-k)!}{n!}$ (d) $\frac{(n-k+1)!}{n!}$

5. Four identical dice are rolled once. The probability that atleast three different numbers appear on them, is
(a) $\frac{13}{42}$ (b) $\frac{17}{42}$ (c) $\frac{23}{42}$ (d) $\frac{25}{42}$

6. Two small squares on a chess board are chosen at random. Then, the probability that they have a common side, is
(a) $\frac{1}{3}$ (b) $\frac{1}{9}$ (c) $\frac{1}{18}$ (d) $\frac{5}{18}$

7. A letter is known to have come from CHENNAI, JAIPUR, NAINITAL, DUBAI and MUMBAI. On the post mark only two consecutive letters AI are legible. Then, the probability that it come from MUMBAI, is
(a) $\frac{42}{319}$ (b) $\frac{84}{403}$ (c) $\frac{39}{331}$ (d) $\frac{42}{331}$

8. Let a die is loaded in such a way that prime number faces are twice as likely to occur as a non-prime number faces. Then, the probability that an odd number will be show up when the die is tossed, is
(a) $\frac{1}{3}$ (b) $\frac{2}{3}$ (c) $\frac{4}{9}$ (d) $\frac{5}{9}$

9. One ticket is selected at random from 100 tickets numbered 00, 01, 02, ..., 99.
Suppose, X and Y are the sum and product of the digit found on the ticket $P(X = 7/Y = 0)$ is given by
(a) $\frac{2}{3}$ (b) $\frac{2}{19}$
(c) $\frac{1}{50}$ (d) None of these

10. If a bag contains 50 tickets, numbered $1, 2, 3, \ldots, 50$ of which five are drawn at random and arranged in ascending order of magnitude $(x_1 < x_2 < x_3 < x_4 < x_5)$. The probability that $x_3 = 30$, is
(a) $\frac{{}^{20}C_2 \times {}^{29}C_2}{{}^{50}C_5}$ (b) $\frac{{}^{20}C_2}{{}^{50}C_5}$
(c) $\frac{{}^{29}C_2}{{}^{50}C_5}$ (d) None of these

11. Three six faced dice are tossed together, then the probability that exactly two of the three numbers are equal, is
(a) $\frac{165}{216}$ (b) $\frac{177}{216}$ (c) $\frac{51}{216}$ (d) $\frac{90}{216}$

12. A book contains 1000 pages. A page is chosen at random. The probability that the sum of the digits of the marked number on the page is equal to 9, is
(a) $\frac{23}{500}$ (b) $\frac{11}{200}$
(c) $\frac{7}{100}$ (d) None of these

13. A bag contains four tickets numbered 00, 01, 10 and 11. Four tickets are chosen at random with replacement, then the probability that sum of the numbers on the tickets is 23, is
(a) $\frac{3}{32}$ (b) $\frac{1}{64}$ (c) $\frac{5}{256}$ (d) $\frac{7}{256}$

14. Fifteen coupons are numbered 1 to 15. Seven coupons are selected at random, one at a time with replacement. Then, the probability that the largest number appearing on a selected coupon be 9, is

(a) $\left(\frac{1}{15}\right)^7$ (b) $\left(\frac{8}{15}\right)^7$

(c) $\left(\frac{3}{5}\right)^7$ (d) None of these

15. A box contains tickets numbered 1 to 20. 3 tickets are drawn from the box with replacement. The probability that the largest number on the tickets is 7, is

(a) $\frac{7}{20}$ (b) $1-\left(\frac{7}{20}\right)^3$

(c) $\frac{2}{19}$ (d) None of these

16. An unbiased die with faces marked 1, 2, 3, 4, 5 and 6 is rolled four times. Out of four face values obtained, then the probability that the minimum face value is not less than 2 and the maximum face value is not greater than 5, is

(a) $\frac{16}{81}$ (b) $\frac{1}{81}$ (c) $\frac{80}{81}$ (d) $\frac{65}{81}$

17. A bag contains four tickets marked with numbers 112, 121, 211 and 222. One ticket is drawn at random from the bag. Let $E_i (i = 1, 2, 3)$ denote the event that ith digit on the ticket is 2. Then, which of the following is not true?

(a) E_1 and E_2 are independent
(b) E_2 and E_3 are independent
(c) E_3 and E_1 are independent
(d) E_1, E_2 and E_3 are independent

18. Two positive real numbers x and y satisfying $x \le 1$ and $y \le 1$ are chosen at random. The probability that $x + y \le 1$, given that $x^2 + y^2 \le 1/4$, is

(a) $\frac{8-\pi}{16-\pi}$ (b) $\frac{4-\pi}{16-\pi}$

(c) $\frac{4-\pi}{8-\pi}$ (d) None of these

19. If the sides of a triangle are decided by the throw of a single dice thrice, the probability that triangle is of maximum area given that it is an isosceles triangle, is

(a) $\frac{1}{7}$ (b) $\frac{1}{27}$

(c) $\frac{1}{14}$ (d) None of these

20. A and B are persons standing in corner square as shown in the figure. They start to move on same time with equal speed, if A can move only in East or South direction and B can move only in North or West direction. If in each step they reach in next square and their choice of direction are equality. If it is given that A and B meet in shaded region, then the probability that they have met in the top most shaded square, is

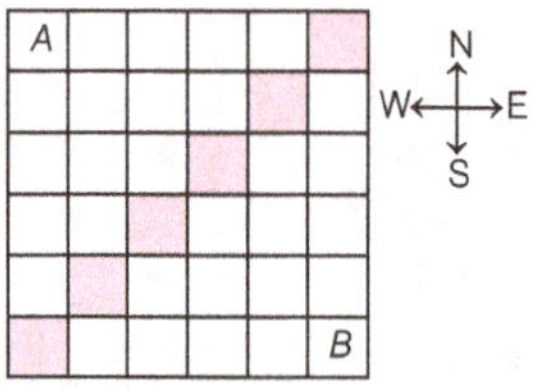

(a) $\frac{1}{6}$ (b) $\frac{{}^5C_2}{{}^{10}C_3}$ (c) $\frac{1}{{}^{10}C_5}$ (d) $\frac{1}{2^5 \times 6}$

Numerical Value Type Questions

21. Seven digit numbers are formed using digits 1, 2, 3, 4, 5, 6, 7, 8, 9 without repetition. The probability of selecting a number such that product of any 5 consecutive digits is divisible by either 5 or 7 is P. Then, $12P$ is equal to ......

22. Mr. A writes an article. The article originally is error free. Each day Mr. B introduces one new error into the article. At the end of the day, Mr. A checks the article and has $\frac{2}{3}$ chance of catching each individual error still in the article. After 3 days, the probability that the article is error free can be expressed as $\frac{p}{q}$, where p and q are relatively prime positive integers. Let $\lambda = q - p$, then the sum of the digit of λ is ....

23. India and Australia play a series of 7 one-days matches. Each team has equal probability of winning a match. No match ends in a draw. If the probability that India wins atleast three consecutive matches can be expressed as $\frac{p}{q}$, where p and q are relatively prime positive integers. Then, unit digit of p is ....

24. The minimum number of tosses of a pair of dice so that the probability of getting the sum of the digits on the dice equal to 7 on at least one toss is greater than 0.95 is .... ($\log_{10} 2 = 0.3010$; $\log_{10} 3 = 0.4771$)

25. A bag contains $(n+1)$ coins. It is known that one is a rigged coin and n of them are normal coins. A coin was taken out and tossed. If the chance that the coins show up the face head is $\frac{7}{12}$, then the value of n is equal to ....

26. Sita and Gita both have a pair of tetrahedral dice, whose faces are marked as 1, 2, 3 and 4, the lowest face being regarded as the outcome. They throw their dice simultaneously. If $P = \frac{a}{b}$ be the probability expressed in lowest term, that the sum of the numbers on their dice is different, then the sum of the digits of value $(a+b)$ is ......

27. Two cards are drawn at random from a pack of playing cards. If the odds against that one card is a heart and the other is an ace, are $m : 2$, then the value of m is ....

28. Three balls are marked 1, 2 and 3. They are placed in a bowl and a ball is drawn, its number is recorded and the ball is returned to the bowl. The process is replaced two more times. If the sum of the three numbers is 6, then $P=\frac{a}{b}$ is the probability (express in lowest form) that the ball numbered 2 was drawn all the three times, then the value of $(a+b)$ is ....

Previous Year Questions

29. If an unbiased dice is rolled thrice, then the probability of getting a greater number in the ith roll than the number obtained in the $(i-1)$th roll, $i=2, 3$, is equal to **[Single Correct Type, 2024 Main]**

(a) $\frac{3}{54}$ (b) $\frac{1}{54}$ (c) $\frac{2}{54}$ (d) $\frac{5}{54}$

30. The coefficients a, b and c in the quadratic equation $ax^2+bx+c=0$ are from the set (1, 2, 3, 4,5, 6). If the probability of this equation having one real root bigger than the other is p, then $216p$ equals **[Single Correct Type, 2024 Main]**

(a) 57 (b) 38 (c) 76 (d) 19

31. A coin is biased so that a head is twice as likely to occur as a tail. If the coin is tossed 3 times, then the probability of getting two tails and one head is **[Single Correct Type, 2024 Main]**

(a) $\frac{1}{27}$ (b) $\frac{2}{9}$ (c) $\frac{2}{27}$ (d) $\frac{1}{9}$

32. A fair die is thrown until 2 appears. Then, the probability that 2 appears in even number of throws, is **[Single Correct Type, 2024 Main]**

(a) $\frac{5}{11}$ (b) $\frac{1}{6}$ (c) $\frac{5}{6}$ (d) $\frac{6}{11}$

33. Let the sum of two positive integers be 24. If the probability, that their product is not less than 3/4 times their greatest possible product is $\frac{m}{n}$, where gcd $(m, n)=1$, then $n-m$ equals **[Single Correct Type, 2024 Main]**

(a) 8 (b) 10 (c) 11 (d) 9

34. Two integers x and y are chosen with replacement from the set $[0, 1, 2, 3, \ldots, 10]$. Then, the probability that $|x-y|\geq 5$, is **[Single Correct Type, 2024 Main]**

(a) $\frac{62}{121}$ (b) $\frac{30}{121}$ (c) $\frac{60}{121}$ (d) $\frac{31}{121}$

35. Let Ajay will not appear in JEE exam with probability $p=\frac{2}{7}$, while both Ajay and Vijay will appear in the exam with probability $q=\frac{1}{5}$. Then, the probability, that Ajay will appear in the exam and Vijay will not appear is **[Single Correct Type, 2024 Main]**

(a) $\frac{18}{35}$ (b) $\frac{9}{35}$ (c) $\frac{24}{35}$ (d) $\frac{3}{35}$

36. An integer is chosen at random from the integers 1, 2, 3, ..., 50. The probability that the chosen integer is a multiple of atleast one of 4, 6 and 7 is **[Single Correct Type, 2024 Main]**

(a) $\frac{8}{25}$ (b) $\frac{9}{50}$ (c) $\frac{14}{25}$ (d) $\frac{21}{50}$

37. Three urns A, B and C contain 7 red, 5 black; 5 red, 7 black and 6 red, 6 black balls, respectively. One of the urn is selected at random and a ball is drawn from it. If the ball drawn is black, then the probability that it is drawn from urn A is **[Single Correct Type, 2024 Main]**

(a) $\frac{4}{17}$ (b) $\frac{5}{16}$ (c) $\frac{5}{18}$ (d) $\frac{7}{18}$

38. A company has two plants A and B to manufacture motorcycles. 60% motorcycles are manufactured at plant A and the remaining are manufactured at plant B. 80% of the motorcycles manufactured at plant A are rated of the standard quality, while 90% of the motorcycles manufactured at plant B are rated of the standard quality. A motorcycle picked up randomly from the total production is found to be of the standard quality. If p is the probability that it was manufactured at plant B, then $126p$ is **[Single Correct Type, 2024 Main]**

(a) 66 (b) 56
(c) 64 (d) 54

39. Bag A contains 3 white, 7 red balls and Bag B contains 3 white, 2 red balls. One bag is selected at random and a ball is drawn from it. The probability of drawing the ball from the bag A, if the ball drawn is white, is **[Single Correct Type, 2024 Main]**

(a) $\frac{1}{4}$ (b) $\frac{1}{3}$ (c) $\frac{3}{10}$ (d) $\frac{1}{9}$

40. Let a, b and c denote the outcome of three independent rolls of a fair tetrahedral die, whose four faces are marked 1, 2, 3, 4. If the probability that $ax^2+bx+c=0$ has all real roots is $\frac{m}{n}$, $gcd(m,n)=1$, then $m+n$ is equal to .... **[Numerical Value Type, 2024 Main]**

41. Three balls are drawn at random from a bag containing 5 blue and 4 yellow balls. Let the random variables X and Y, respectively denote the number of blue and yellow balls. If $\overline{X}$ and $\overline{Y}$ are the means of X and Y respectively. Then, $7\overline{X}+4\overline{Y}$ is equal to .... **[Numerical Value Type, 2024 Main]**

42. In a tournament, a team plays 10 matches with probabilities of winning and losing each match as $\frac{1}{3}$ and $\frac{2}{3}$ respectively. Let x be the number of matches that the team wins and y be the number of matches that team loses. If the probability $P(|x-y|\leq 2)$ is p, then $3^9 p$ equals .... **[Numerical Value Type, 2024 Main]**

43. A fair die is tossed repeatedly until a six is obtained. Let X denote the number of tosses required and let $a = P(X = 3)$, $b = P(X \geq 3)$ and $c = P(X \geq 6 \mid X > 3)$. Then, $\frac{b+c}{a}$ is equal to .... **[Numerical Value Type, 2024 Main]**

44. Three dice are rolled. If the probability of getting different numbers on the three dice is $\frac{p}{q}$, where p and q are co-prime, then $q - p$ is equal to **[Single Correct Type, 2023 Main]**

(a) 4 (b) 3 (c) 1 (d) 2

45. A bag contains 6 white and 4 black balls. A die is rolled once and the number of balls equal to the number obtained on the die are drawn from the bag at random. The probability that all the balls drawn are white is **[Single Correct Type, 2023 Main]**

(a) $\frac{9}{50}$ (b) $\frac{1}{4}$ (c) $\frac{11}{50}$ (d) $\frac{1}{5}$

46. Let the probability of getting head for a biased coin be $\frac{1}{4}$. It is tossed repeatedly until a head appears. Let N be the number of tosses required. If the probability that the equation $64x^2 + 5Nx + 1 = 0$ has no real root is $\frac{p}{q}$, where p and q are co-prime, then $q - p$ is equal to .... **[Numerical Value Type, 2023 Main]**

47. 25% of the population are smokers. A smoker has 27 times more chances to develop lung cancer than a non smoker. A person is diagnosed with lung cancer and the probability that this person is a smoker is $k/10$. Then, the value of k is .... **[Numerical Value Type, 2023 Main]**

48. The probability, that in a randomly selected 3-digit number at least two digits are odd, is **[Single Correct Type, 2022 Main]**

(a) $\frac{19}{36}$ (b) $\frac{15}{36}$ (c) $\frac{13}{36}$ (d) $\frac{23}{36}$

49. The probability that a relation R from $\{x, y\}$ to $\{x, y\}$ is both symmetric and transitive is equal to **[Single Correct Type, 2022 Main]**

(a) $\frac{5}{16}$ (b) $\frac{9}{16}$ (c) $\frac{11}{16}$ (d) $\frac{13}{16}$

50. The probability that a randomly chosen one-one function from the set $\{a, b, c, d\}$ to the set $\{1, 2, 3, 4, 5\}$ satisfies $f(a) + 2f(b) - f(c) = f(d)$ is **[Single Correct Type, 2022 Main]**

(a) $\frac{1}{24}$ (b) $\frac{1}{40}$ (c) $\frac{1}{30}$ (d) $\frac{1}{20}$

51. In an examination, there are 10 true-false type questions. Out of 10, a student can guess the answer of 4 questions correctly with probability 3/4 and the remaining 6 questions correctly with probability 1/4. If the probability that the student guesses the answers of exactly 8 questions correctly out of 10 is $\frac{27k}{4^{10}}$, then k is equal to .... **[Numerical Value Type, 2022 Main]**

52. Let A and B be independent events such that $P(A) = p$ and $P(B) = 2p$. The largest value of p, for which P (exactly one of A, B occurs) $= \frac{5}{9}$, is **[Single Correct Type, 2021 Main]**

(a) $\frac{1}{3}$ (b) $\frac{2}{9}$ (c) $\frac{4}{9}$ (d) $\frac{5}{12}$

53. Four dice are thrown simultaneously and the numbers shown on these dice are recorded in 2×2 matrices. The probability that such formed matrices have all different entries and are non singular, is **[Single Correct Type, 2021 Main]**

(a) $\frac{45}{162}$ (b) $\frac{23}{81}$ (c) $\frac{22}{81}$ (d) $\frac{43}{162}$

54. An electric instrument consists of two units. Each unit must function independently for the instrument to operate. The probability that the first unit functions is 0.9 and that of the second unit is 0.8. The instrument is switched on and it fails to operate. If the probability that only the first unit failed and second unit is functioning is P, then $98\,P$ is equal to .... **[Numerical Value Type, 2021 Main]**

55. Let there be three independent events E_1, E_2 and E_3. The probability that only E_1 occurs is α, only E_2 occurs is β and only E_3 occurs is γ. Let p denote the probability of none of events occur that satisfies the equations $(\alpha - 2\beta)p = \alpha\beta$ and $(\beta - 3\gamma)p = 2\beta\gamma$.

All the given probabilities are assumed to lie in the interval (0, 1). Then, $\frac{\text{probability of occurrence of } E_1}{\text{probability of occurrence of } E_3}$ is equal to .... **[Numerical Value Type, 2021 Main]**

56. Let A and B be two independent events such that $P(A) = \frac{1}{3}$ and $P(B) = \frac{1}{6}$. Then, which of the following is TRUE? **[Single Correct Type, 2020 Main]**

(a) $P(A/(A \cup B)) = \frac{1}{4}$ (b) $P(A'/B') = \frac{1}{3}$

(c) $P(A/B') = \frac{1}{3}$ (d) $P(A/B) = \frac{2}{3}$

57. A random variable X has the following probability distribution

X	1	2	3	4	5
$P(X)$	K^2	$2K$	K	$2K$	$5K^2$

Then, $P(X > 2)$ is equal to **[Single Correct Type, 2020 Main]**

(a) $\frac{1}{6}$ (b) $\frac{23}{36}$ (c) $\frac{1}{36}$ (d) $\frac{7}{12}$

58. The probability of a man hitting a target is 1/10. The least number of shots required, so that the probability of his hitting the target at least once is greater than 1/4, is .... **[Numerical Value Type, 2020 Main]**

EXERCISE 2

JEE Advanced Pattern

Single Option Correct Type Questions

1. If the integers m and n are chosen at random between 1 and 100, then the probability that a number of the form $7^m + 7^n$ is divisible by 5, equals

(a) $\frac{1}{4}$ (b) $\frac{1}{7}$ (c) $\frac{1}{8}$ (d) $\frac{1}{49}$

2. Seven white balls and three black balls are randomly placed in a row. The probability that no two black balls are placed adjacently, equals

(a) $\frac{1}{2}$ (b) $\frac{7}{15}$ (c) $\frac{2}{15}$ (d) $\frac{1}{3}$

3. Three of the six vertices of a regular hexagon are chosen at random. The probability that the triangle with three vertices is equilateral, equals

(a) $\frac{1}{2}$ (b) $\frac{1}{5}$ (c) $\frac{1}{10}$ (d) $\frac{1}{20}$

4. Three identical dice are rolled. The probability that the same number will appear on each of them, is

(a) $\frac{1}{6}$ (b) $\frac{1}{36}$ (c) $\frac{1}{18}$ (d) $\frac{3}{28}$

5. For three events A, B and C, if P(exactly one of A or B occurs) = P(exactly one of B or C occurs) = P (exactly one of C or A occurs) $= \frac{1}{4}$ and P (all the three events occur simultaneously) $= \frac{1}{16}$, then the probability that atleast one of the events occurs, is

(a) $\frac{7}{32}$ (b) $\frac{7}{16}$ (c) $\frac{7}{64}$ (d) $\frac{3}{16}$

6. If $P(B) = \frac{3}{4}$, $P(A \cap B \cap \overline{C}) = \frac{1}{3}$ and $P(\overline{A} \cap B \cap \overline{C}) = 1/3$, then $P(B \cap C)$ is equal to

(a) $\frac{1}{12}$ (b) $\frac{1}{6}$ (c) $\frac{1}{15}$ (d) $\frac{1}{9}$

7. If E and F are events with $P(E) \leq P(F)$ and $P(E \cap F) > 0$, then which one is not correct?

(a) occurrence of E $\Rightarrow$ occurrence of F

(b) occurrence of F $\Rightarrow$ occurrence of E

(c) non-occurrence of E $\Rightarrow$ non-occurrence of F

(d) None of the above

8. For the three events A, B and C, P(exactly one of the events A or B occurs) = P(exactly one of the events B or C occurs) = P(exactly one of the events C or A occurs) $= p$ and P(all the three events occurs simultaneously) $= p^2$, where $0 < p < \frac{1}{2}$. Then, the probability of atleast one of the three events A, B and C occurring is

(a) $\frac{3p + 2p^2}{2}$ (b) $\frac{p + 3p^2}{4}$ (c) $\frac{p + 3p^2}{2}$ (d) $\frac{3p + 2p^2}{4}$

9. A bag contains 4 red and 6 black balls. A ball is drawn at random from the bag, its colour is observed and this ball along with two additional balls of the same colour are returned to the bag. If now a ball is drawn at random from the bag, then the probability that this drawn ball is red, is

(a) $\frac{3}{10}$ (b) $\frac{2}{5}$ (c) $\frac{1}{5}$ (d) $\frac{3}{4}$

10. Three randomly chosen non-negative integers x, y and z are found to satisfy the equation $x + y + z = 10$. Then, the probability that z is even, is

(a) $\frac{36}{55}$ (b) $\frac{6}{11}$ (c) $\frac{1}{2}$ (d) $\frac{5}{11}$

11. Let two fair six-faced dice A and B be thrown simultaneously. If E_1 is the event that die A shows up four, E_2 is the event that die B shows up two and E_3 is the event that the sum of numbers on both dice is odd, then which of the following statements is not true?

(a) E_1 and E_2 are independent

(b) E_2 and E_3 are independent

(c) E_1 and E_3 are independent

(d) E_1, E_2 and E_3 are independent

12. A computer producing factory has only two plants T_1 and T_2. Plant T_1 produces 20% and plant T_2 produces 80% of the total computers produced. 7% of computers produced in the factory turn out to be defective. It is known that P(computer turns out to be defective, given that it is produced in plant T_1) $= 10P$ (computer turns out to be defective, given that it is produced in plant T_2), where $P(E)$ denotes the probability of an event E. A computer produced in the factory is randomly selected and it does not turn out to be defective. Then, the probability that it is produced in plant T_2, is

(a) $\frac{36}{73}$ (b) $\frac{47}{79}$ (c) $\frac{78}{93}$ (d) $\frac{75}{83}$

13. Let A and B be two events such that $P(\overline{A \cup B}) = \frac{1}{6}$, $P(A \cap B) = \frac{1}{4}$ and $P(\overline{A}) = \frac{1}{4}$, where $\overline{A}$ stands for the complement of the event A. Then , the events A and B are
(a) independent but not equally likely
(b) independent and equally likely
(c) mutually exclusive and independent
(d) equally likely but not independent

14. A signal which can be green or red with probability $\frac{4}{5}$ and $\frac{1}{5}$ respectively, is received by station A and then transmitted to station B. The probability of each station receiving the signal correctly is $\frac{3}{4}$. If the signal received at station B is green, then the probability that the original signal green is
(a) $\frac{3}{5}$ (b) $\frac{6}{7}$ (c) $\frac{20}{23}$ (d) $\frac{9}{20}$

15. Let E^c denotes the complement of an event E. If E, F, G are pairwise independent events with $P(G) > 0$ and $P(E \cap F \cap G) = 0$. Then, $P(E^c \cap F^c \mid G)$ equals
(a) $P(E^c) + P(F^c)$ (b) $P(E^c) - P(F^c)$
(c) $P(E^c) - P(F)$ (d) $P(E) - P(F^c)$

16. One Indian and four American men and their wives are to be seated randomly around a circular table. Then, the conditional probability that Indian man is seated adjacent to his wife given that each American man is seated adjacent to his wife, is
(a) $\frac{1}{2}$ (b) $\frac{1}{3}$ (c) $\frac{2}{5}$ (d) $\frac{1}{5}$

More than One Correct Option Type Questions

17. If E and F are independent events such that $0 < P(E) < 1$ and $0 < P(F) < 1$, then
(a) E and F are mutually exclusive
(b) E and $\overline{F}$ (complement of the event F) are independent
(c) $\overline{E}$ and $\overline{F}$ are independent
(d) $P(E / F) + P(\overline{E} / F) = 1$

18. For any two events A and B in a sample space
(a) $P\left(\frac{A}{B}\right) \geq \frac{P(A) + P(B) - 1}{P(B)}$, $P(B) \neq 0$, is always true
(b) $P(A \cap \overline{B}) = P(A) - P(A \cap B)$, does not hold
(c) $P(A \cup B) = 1 - P(\overline{A})\, P(\overline{B})$, if A and B are independent
(d) $P(A \cup B) = 1 - P(\overline{A})\, P(\overline{B})$, if A and B are disjoint

19. Let E and F be two independent events. Then, the probability that both E and F happens is $\frac{1}{12}$ and the probability that neither E nor F happens is $\frac{1}{2}$. Then,
(a) $P(E) = 1/3,\ P(F) = 1/4$ (b) $P(E) = 1/2,\ P(F) = 1/6$
(c) $P(E) = 1/6,\ P(F) = 1/2$ (d) $P(E) = 1/4,\ P(F) = 1/3$

20. Let X be a set containing n elements. If two subsets A and B of X are picked at random, then the probability that A and B have same number of elements, is
(a) $\frac{{}^{2n}C_n}{2^{2n}}$ (b) $\frac{1}{{}^{2n}C_n}$
(c) $\frac{1 \cdot 3 \cdot 5 \ldots (2n-1)}{2^n \cdot (n!)}$ (d) $\frac{3^n}{4^n}$

21. The probabilities that a student passes in Mathematics, Physics and Chemistry are m, p and c, respectively. In these subjects, the student has a 75% chance of passing in atleast one, a 50% chance of passing in atleast two and a 40% chance of passing in exactly two. Which of the following relations are true?
(a) $p + m + c = 19/20$ (b) $p + m + c = 27/20$
(c) $pmc = 1/10$ (d) $pmc = 1/4$

22. $(n \geq 5)$ persons are sitting in a row. Three of these are selected at random, the probability that no two of the selected persons are sit together, is
(a) $\frac{{}^{n-3}P_2}{{}^{n}P_2}$ (b) $\frac{{}^{n-3}C_2}{{}^{n}C_2}$
(c) $\frac{(n-3)(n-4)}{n(n-1)}$ (d) $\frac{{}^{n-3}C_2}{{}^{n}P_2}$

23. Given that $x \in [0, 1]$ and $y \in [0, 1]$. Let A be the event of (x, y) satisfying $y^2 \leq x$ and B be the event of (x, y) satisfying $x^2 \leq y$, then not true, is
(a) $P(A \cap B) = \frac{1}{3}$
(b) A and B are exhaustive
(c) A and B are mutually exclusive
(d) A and B are independent

24. There are three bags, B_1, B_2 and B_3. The bag B_1 contains 5 red and 5 green balls, B_2 contains 3 red and 5 green balls and B_3 contains 5 red and 3 green balls. Bags B_1, B_2 and B_3 have probabilities $\frac{3}{10}$, $\frac{3}{10}$ and $\frac{4}{10}$ respectively of being chosen. A bag is selected at random and a ball is chosen at random from the bag. Then, which of the following options is/are correct?
(a) Probability that the selected bag is B_3 and the chosen ball is green equals $\frac{3}{10}$
(b) Probability that the chosen ball is green, given that the selected bag is B_3, equals $\frac{3}{8}$
(c) Probability that the selected bag is B_3, given that the chosen ball is green, equals $\frac{5}{13}$
(d) Probability that the chosen ball is green equals $\frac{39}{80}$

25. If $\bar{E}$ and $\bar{F}$ are the complementary events of E and F respectively and if $0 < P(F) < 1$, then
(a) $P(E/F) + P(\bar{E}/F) = 1$ (b) $P(E/F) + P(E/\bar{F}) = 1$
(c) $P(\bar{E}/F) + P(E/\bar{F}) = 1$ (d) $P(E/\bar{F}) + P(\bar{E}/\bar{F}) = 1$

Passage Based Questions

Passage I

(Q. Nos. 26 and 27)

- If p and q are chosen randomly from the set $\{1, 2, 3, 4, 5, 6, 7, 8, 9, 10\}$ with replacement.

26. The probability that roots of $x^2 + px + q = 0$ are real and distinct, is
(a) 0.38 (b) 0.03 (c) 0.59 (d) 0.89

27. The probability that roots of $x^2 + px + q = 0$ are equal, is
(a) 0.58 (b) 0.55 (c) 0.38 (d) 0.03

Passage II

(Q. Nos. 28 and 29)

- A cube having all of its sides painted is cut to be two horizontal, two vertical and other two planes, so as to form 27 cubes all having the same dimensions of these cubes, a cube is selected at random.

28. If P_1 be the probability that the cube selected having atleast one of its sides painted, then the value of $27P_1$, is
(a) 14 (b) 18 (c) 22 (d) 26

29. If P_2 be the probability that the cube selected has two sides painted, then the value of $27P_2$, is
(a) 3 (b) 8 (c) 12 (d) 17

Passage III

(Q. Nos. 30 and 31)

- A JEE aspirant estimates that she will be successful with an 80% chance, if she studies 10 h per day with a 60% chance, if she studies 7 h per day and with a 40% chance if she studies 4 h per day. She further believes that she will study 10 h, 7 h and 4 h per day with probabilities 0.1, 0.2, and 0.7, respectively.

30. The probability that she will be successful, is
(a) 0.28 (b) 0.38 (c) 0.48 (d) 0.58

31. Given that she is successful, the chances that she studied for 4 h, is
(a) $\frac{1}{12}$ (b) $\frac{5}{12}$ (c) $\frac{7}{12}$ (d) $\frac{11}{12}$

Passage IV

(Q. Nos. 32 and 33)

- Football teams T_1 and T_2 have to play two games against each other. It is assumed that the outcomes of the two games are independent. The probabilities of T_1 winning, drawing and losing a game against T_2 are $\frac{1}{2}, \frac{1}{6}$ and $\frac{1}{3}$, respectively. Each team gets 3 points for a win, 1 point for a draw and 0 point for a loss in a game. Let X and Y denote the total points scored by teams T_1 and T_2, respectively, after two games.

32. $P(X > Y)$ is
(a) $\frac{1}{4}$ (b) $\frac{5}{12}$ (c) $\frac{1}{2}$ (d) $\frac{7}{12}$

33. $P(X = Y)$ is
(a) $\frac{11}{36}$ (b) $\frac{1}{3}$ (c) $\frac{13}{36}$ (d) $\frac{1}{2}$

Stem Based Questions

Stem I

(Q. Nos. 34 and 35)

- Let A and B be two events such that $P(B/A) = \frac{2}{5}, P(A/B) = \frac{1}{7}$ and $P(A \cap B) = \frac{1}{9}$. Consider

34. $P(A' \cup B)$ is equal to ....

35. $P(A' \cap B')$ is equal to ....

Stem II

(Q. Nos. 36 and 37)

- Box I contains three cards bearing numbers 1, 2, 3 ; box II contains five cards bearing numbers 1, 2, 3, 4, 5; and box III contains seven cards bearing numbers 1, 2, 3, 4, 5, 6, 7. A card is drawn from each of the boxes. Let x_i be the number on the card drawn from the ith box $i = 1, 2, 3$.

36. The probability that $x_1 + x_2 + x_3$ is odd, is ....

37. The probability that x_1, x_2 and x_3 are in an arithmetic progression, is ....

Single Integer Type Questions

38. A bag contains $(n+1)$ coins. It is known that one of these coins shows heads on both sides, whereas the other coins are fair. One coin is selected at random and tossed. If the probability that the toss result in heads is $\frac{7}{12}$, then the value of n is ....

39. A determinant of the second order is made with the elements 0 and 1. If $\frac{m}{n}$ be the probability that the determinant made is non-negative, where m and n are relative primes, then the value of $n - m$ is ....

40. Three students appear in an examination of Mathematics. The probabilities of their success are $\frac{1}{3}, \frac{1}{4}$ and $\frac{1}{5}$, respectively. If the probability of success of atleast two is $\frac{\lambda}{12}$, then the value of λ is ....

41. A die is rolled three times, if p be the probability of getting a large number than the previous number, then the value of $54p$ is ....

42. In a multiple choice question, there are five alternative answers of which one or more than one are correct. A candidate will get marks on the question, if he ticks all the correct answers. If he decides to tick answers at random, then the least number of choices should he be allowed, so that the probability of his getting marks on the question exceeds $\frac{1}{8}$ is ....

43. There are n different objects $1, 2, 3, \ldots, n$ distributed at random in n places marked $1, 2, 3, \ldots, n$. If p be the probability that atleast three of the objects occupy places corresponding to their number, then the value of $6p$ is ....

44. A sum of money is rounded off to the nearest rupee, if $\left(\frac{m}{n}\right)^2$ be the probability that the round off error is atleast ten paise, where m and n are positive relative primes, then the value of $(n - m)$ is ....

45. A special die is so constructed that the probabilities of throwing 1, 2, 3, 4, 5 and 6 are $(1-k)/6, (1+2k)/6, (1-k)/6, (1+k)/6, (1-2k)/6$ and $(1+k)/6$, respectively. If two such dice are thrown and the probability of getting a sum equal to lies between $\frac{1}{9}$ and $\frac{2}{9}$, then the integral value of k is ....

46. Seven digits from the numbers 1, 2, 3, 4, 5, 6, 7, 8 and 9 are written in random order. If the probability that this seven-digit number divisible by 9 is p, then the value of $18p$ is ....

47. 8 players $P_1, P_2, P_3, \ldots, P_8$ play a knock out tournament. It is known that all the players are of equal strength. The tournament is held in three rounds where the players are paired at random in each round. If it is given that P_1 wins in the third round. If p be the probability that P_2 loses in the second round, then the value of $7p$ is ....

Numerical Value Type Questions

48. If 12 identical balls are to be placed in 3 different boxes, then the probability that one of the boxes contains exactly 3 balls, is $Q\frac{(2)^{11}}{3^{12}}$. The value of Q is equal to ......

49. If the letters of the word 'ASSASSIN' we written down at random in a row, then the probability that no two S'S occure together is p. The value of $8750\,p$ is equal to ......

50. If $\frac{1+3p}{3}, \frac{1-p}{4}$ and $\frac{1-2p}{2}$ are the probabilities of three mutually exclusive events, then the set of all values of p is $a \le p \le b$. The value of $69a + 64b$ is equal to ....

51. One hundred identical coins, each with probability p, of showing up heads are tossed once. If $0 < p < 1$ and the probability of heads showing on 50 coins is equal to that of heads showing on 50 coins, then the value of $\left(\frac{404}{5}\right)p$ is equal to ....

Matching Type Questions

52. Match the following columns.

	Column I		Column II
(A)	If $P(\overline{A}) = 0.3$, $P(B) = 0.4$ and $P(A\overline{B}) = 0.5$ and $P[B/(A \cup \overline{B})] = \lambda_1$, then $\frac{1}{\lambda_1}$ is	(p)	A prime number
(B)	The coefficient of a quadratic equation $ax^2 + bx + c = 10 (a \ne b \ne c)$ are chosen from first three prime numbers, then the probability that roots of the equation are real is λ_2, then $\frac{1}{\lambda_2}$ is	(q)	A composite number
(C)	A fair coin is tossed repeatedly. If tail appears on first four tosses, then the probability of head appearing on the fifth toss is λ_3, then $\frac{1}{\lambda_3}$ is	(r)	A natural number
(D)	Three persons A, B and C are to speak at a function along with 6 other persons. If the persons speak in random order, then the probability that A speaks before B and B speaks before C is λ_4, then $\frac{1}{\lambda_4}$ is	(s)	A perfect number

53. A and B are two events, such that $P(A) = \frac{3}{5}$ and $P(B) = \frac{2}{3}$

Column I		Column II	
(A)	$P(A \cap B) \in$	(p)	$\left[\frac{2}{3}, 1\right]$
(B)	$P(A \cup B) \in$	(q)	$\left[\frac{4}{9}, 1\right]$
(C)	$P(A / B) \in$	(r)	$\left[\frac{2}{5}, \frac{9}{10}\right]$
(D)	$P(B / A) \in$	(s)	$\left[\frac{4}{15}, \frac{3}{5}\right]$

54. Three players A, B and C alternatively throw a die in that order, the first player to throw a 6 being deemed the winner. A's die is fair whereas B and C throw dice with probabilities p_1 and p_2 respectively, of throwing a 6.

Column I		Column II	
(A)	If $p_1 = \frac{1}{5}, p_2 = \frac{1}{4}$ and probability that A wins the game is $\frac{1}{\lambda_1}$, then λ_1 is divisor of	(p)	6
(B)	If $p_1 = \frac{1}{5}, p_2 = \frac{1}{4}$ and probability that C wins the game is $\frac{1}{\lambda_2}$, then λ_2 is divisor of	(q)	8
(C)	If $P(A \text{ wins}) = P(B \text{ wins})$ and $\frac{1}{p_1} = \lambda_3$, then λ_3 is divisor of	(r)	12
(D)	If game is equiprobable to all the three players and $\frac{1}{p_1} = \lambda_4$, then λ_4 is divisor of	(s)	15

Previous Year Questions

55. Let $X = \left\{(x, y) \in Z \times Z : \frac{x^2}{8} + \frac{y^2}{20} < 1 \text{ and } y^2 < 5x\right\}$.

Three distinct points P, Q and R are randomly chosen from X. Then, the probability that P, Q and R form a triangle whose area is a positive integer, is

[Single Correct Type, 2023 Adv.]

(a) $\frac{71}{220}$ (b) $\frac{73}{220}$ (c) $\frac{79}{220}$ (d) $\frac{83}{220}$

56. Consider an experiment of tossing a coin repeatedly until the outcomes of two consecutive tosses are same. If the probability of a random toss resulting in head is $\frac{1}{3}$, then the probability that the experiment stops with head is **[Single Correct Type, 2023 Adv.]**

(a) $\frac{1}{3}$ (b) $\frac{5}{21}$ (c) $\frac{4}{21}$ (d) $\frac{2}{7}$

57. Two players P_1 and P_2, play a game against each other. In every round of the game, each player rolls a fair die once, where the six faces of the die have six distinct numbers. Let x and y denote the readings on the die rolled by P_1 and P_2, respectively. If $x > y$, then P_1 scores 5 points and P_2 scores 0 point. If $x = y$, then each player scores 2 points. If $x < y$, then P_1 scores 0 point and P_2 scores 5 points. Let X_i and Y_i be the total scores of P_1 and P_2 respectively, after playing the i th round. **[Matching Type, 2022 Adv.]**

List-I		List-II	
I.	Probability of $(X_2 \geq Y_2)$ is	P.	$\frac{3}{8}$
II.	Probability of $(X_2 > Y_2)$ is	Q.	$\frac{11}{16}$
III.	Probability of $(X_3 = Y_3)$ is	R.	$\frac{5}{16}$
IV.	Probability of $(X_3 > Y_3)$ is	S.	$\frac{355}{864}$
		T.	$\frac{77}{432}$

The correct option is

(a) I → (Q); II → (R); III → (T); IV → (S)
(b) I → (Q); II → (R); III → (T); IV → (T)
(c) I → (P); II → (R); III → (Q); IV → (S)
(d) I → (P); II → (R); III → (Q); IV → (T)

58. In a study about a pandemic, data of 900 persons was collected. It was found that

190 persons had symptom of fever, 220 persons had symptom of cough, 220 persons had symptom of breathing problem, 330 persons had symptom of fever or cough or both, 350 persons had symptom of cough or breathing problem or both, 340 persons had symptom of fever or breathing problem or both, 30 persons had all three symptoms (fever, cough and breathing problem)

If a person is chosen randomly from these 900 persons, then the probability that the person has at most one symptom is .... **[Numerical Value Type, 2022 Adv.]**

59. Consider three sets $E_1 = \{1, 2, 3\}$, $F_1 = \{1, 3, 4\}$ and $G_1 = \{2, 3, 4, 5\}$. Two elements are chosen at random, without replacement, from the set E_1 and let S_1 denote the set of these chosen elements. Let $E_2 = E_1 - S_1$ and $F_2 = F_1 \cup S_1$. Now, two elements are chosen at random, without replacement, from the set F_2 and let S_2 denote the set of these chosen elements.

Let $G_2 = G_1 \cup S_2$. Finally, two elements are chosen at random, without replacement, from the set G_2 and let S_3 denote the set of these chosen elements.

Let $E_3 = E_2 \cup S_3$. Given that, $E_1 = E_3$, let p be the conditional probability of the event $S_1 = \{1, 2\}$. Then, the value of p is **[More than One Option Correct, 2021 Adv.]**

(a) $\frac{1}{5}$ (b) $\frac{3}{5}$ (c) $\frac{1}{2}$ (d) $\frac{2}{5}$

60. Let E, F and G be three events having probabilities $P(E)=\frac{1}{8}$, $P(F)=\frac{1}{6}$ and $P(G)=\frac{1}{4}$, and let $P(E\cap F\cap G)=\frac{1}{10}$. For any event H, if H^C denotes its complement, then which of the following statements is (are) true? **[More than One Option Correct, 2021 Adv.]**

(a) $P(E\cap F\cap G^C)\le\frac{1}{40}$ (b) $P(E^C\cap F\cap G)\le\frac{1}{15}$

(c) $P(E\cup F\cup G)\le\frac{13}{24}$ (d) $P(E^C\cap F^C\cap G^C)\le\frac{5}{12}$

61. A number is chosen at random from the set $\{1,2,3,\ldots,2000\}$. Let p be the probability that the chosen number is a multiple of 3 or a multiple of 7. Then, the value of $500p$ is ____. **[Numerical Value Type, 2021 Adv.]**

EXERCISE 3 — Challenging Problems

1. A five digit number is formed by the digits 1, 2, 3, 4 and 5 without repetition. Find the probability that the number formed is divisible by 4.

2. A dice is rolled three times, then find the probability of getting a large number than the previous number.

3. A car is parked among N cars standing in a row but not at either end. On his return, the owner finds that exactly r of the N places are still occupied. What is the probability that both the places neighbouring his car are empty?

4. Two teams A and B play a tournament. The first one to win $(n+1)$ games win the series. The probability that A wins a game is p and that B wins a game is q (no ties). Find the probability that A wins the series. Hence or otherwise prove that $\sum_{r=0}^{n} {}^{n+1}C_r\cdot\frac{1}{2^{n+r}}=1$.

5. An artillery target may be either at point I with probability $\frac{8}{9}$ or at point II with probability $\frac{1}{9}$. We have 21 shells each of which can be fired either at point I or II. Each shell may hit the target independently of the other shell with probability $\frac{1}{2}$. How many shells must be fired at point I to hit the target with maximum probability?

6. There are 6 red and 8 green balls in a bag. 5 balls are drawn at random and placed in a red box. The remaining balls are placed in a green box. What is the probability that the number of red balls in the green box plus the number of green balls in the red box is not a prime number?

7. An urn contains 'a' green and 'b' pink balls $k\ (< a, b)$ balls are drawn and laid a side, their colour being ignored. Then, one more ball is drawn. Find the probability that it is green.

8. A fair coin is tossed 12 times. Find the probability that two heads do not occur consecutively.

9. Given that $x+y=2a$, where a is constant and that all values of x between 0 and $2a$ are equally likely, then show that the chance that $xy>\frac{3}{4}a^2$, is $\frac{1}{2}$.

10. A chess game between Kamsky and Anand is won by whoever first wins a out of 2 games. Kamsky's chance of winning, drawing or loosing a particular game are 2. The games are independent and $p+q+r=1$. Prove that the probability that Kamsky wins the match is $\frac{p^2(p+3r)}{(p+r)^3}$.

11. Of three independent events, the chance that only the first occurs is a, the other that only the second occurs is b and the chance of only third occurs is c. Show that the cases of three events are respectively $a/(a+x)$, $b/(b+x)$, $c/(c+x)$, where x is a root of the equation $(a+x)(b+x)(c+x)=x^2$.

12. A is a set containing n elements. A subset P of A is chosen at random and the set A is reconstructed by replacing the elements of P. Another subset Q of A is now chosen at random. Find the probability that $P\cup Q$ contains exactly r elements, with $1\le r\le n$.

13. An electric component manufactured by 'RASU electronics' is tested for its defectiveness by a sophisticated testing device. Let A denote the even "the device is defective" and B the event "the testing device reveals the component to be defective." Suppose, $P(A) = \alpha$ and $P(B/A) = P(B'/A') = 1 - \alpha$, where $0 < \alpha < 1$. Show that the probability that the component is not defective, given that the testing device reveals it to be defective is independent of α.

14. A bag contains n white and n red balls. Pairs of balls are drawn without replacement until the bag is empty. Show that the probability that each pair consists of one white and one red ball is $2^n / ({}^{2n}C_n)$.

15. If m things are distributed among 'a' men and 'b' women, then show that the probability that the number of things received by men is odd, is $\frac{1}{2}\frac{\{(b+a)^m - (b-a)^m\}}{(b+a)^m}$.

Answer Key

Exercise 1

1. (d)	2. (d)	3. (b)	4. (d)	5. (d)	6. (c)	7. (b)	8. (d)	9. (b)	10. (a)
11. (d)	12. (b)	13. (a)	14. (c)	15. (d)	16. (a)	17. (d)	18. (a)	19. (b)	20. (c)
21. (7)	22. (7)	23. (7)	24. (17)	25. (5)	26. (117)	27. (49)	28. (8)	29. (d)	30. (b)
31. (b)	32. (a)	33. (b)	34. (b)	35. (a)	36. (d)	37. (c)	38. (d)	39. (b)	40. (19)
41. (17)	42. (8288)	43. (12)	44. (a)	45. (d)	46. (27)	47. (9)	48. (a)	49. (a)	50. (d)
51. (479)	52. (d)	53. (d)	54. (28)	55. (6)	56. (c)	57. (b)	58. (3)		

Exercise 2

1. (a)	2. (b)	3. (c)	4. (b)	5. (b)	6. (a)	7. (c)	8. (a)	9. (b)	10. (b)
11. (d)	12. (c)	13. (a)	14. (c)	15. (c)	16. (c)	17. (b,c,d)	18. (a,c)	19. (a,d)	20. (a,c)
21. (b,c)	22. (a,b,c)	23. (b,c,d)	24. (b,d)	25. (a,d)	26. (c)	27. (d)	28. (d)	29. (c)	30. (c)
31. (c)	32. (b)	33. (c)	34. (5/6)	35. (1/18)	36. (53/105)	37. (11/105)	38. (5)	39. (3)	40. (2)
41. (5)	42. (4)	43. (1)	44. (1)	45. (0)	46. (2)	47. (2)	48. (55)	49. (625)	50. (55)

51. (51) 52. (A) → (q,r), (B) → (p,r), (C) → (p,r), (D) → (q,r,s) 53. (A) → (s), (B) → (p), (C) → (r), (D) → (q)

54. (A) → (p,r,s), (B) → (p,r,s), (C) → (s), (D) → (q,r) 55. (b) 56. (b) 57. (a) 58. (0.8) 59. (a) 60. (a,b,c)

61. (214)

Solutions

Exercise 1 - JEE Main Pattern

1. 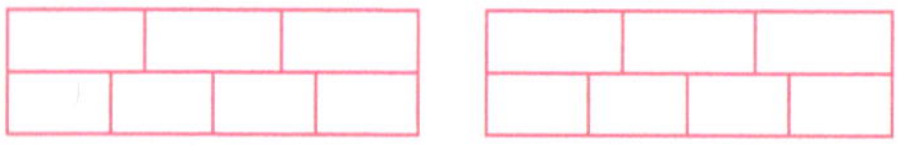

$n(S) = $ Number of total ways $= {}^{14}P_{12} = \dfrac{14!}{2!} = 7 \times 13!$

The girls can be seated together in the back seats leaving a corner seat in $4 \times 3! = 24$ ways and the boys can be seated in the remaining 11 seats in ${}^{11}P_9 = \dfrac{11!}{2!} = \dfrac{1}{2} \times 11!$ ways.

$\therefore n(E) = $ Number of favourable ways $= 24 \times \dfrac{1}{2} \times 11! = 12!$

The required probability $= \dfrac{n(E)}{n(S)} = \dfrac{12!}{7 \times 13!} = \dfrac{1}{91}$

2. Let us consider two events

A : Numbers divisible by 4.

B : Numbers divisible by 7.

We have, $A = \{104, 108, \ldots, 196\}$

$\Rightarrow n(A) = 24$

$B = \{105, 112, \ldots, 196\}$

$n(B) = 14$ and $A \cap B = \{112, 140, 168, 196\}$

$\Rightarrow n(A \cap B) = 4$

Let $n(E) = $ Number of favourable ways

$n(A \cup B) = n(A) + n(B) - n(A \cap B) = 34$

$n(S) = $ Total number of ways $= 99$

$\therefore$ Required probability $= \dfrac{n(E)}{n(S)} = \dfrac{34}{99}$

3. $n(S) = $ Total number of ways $= {}^{10}C_3 = \dfrac{10 \cdot 9 \cdot 8}{1 \cdot 2 \cdot 3} = 120$

The product of two numbers is equal to third number, the favourable cases are 2, 3, 6; 2, 4, 8; 2, 5, 10.

$\therefore n(E) = $ The number of favourable cases $= 3$

$\therefore$ Required probability $= \dfrac{n(E)}{n(S)} = \dfrac{3}{120} = \dfrac{1}{40}$

4. $n(S) = $ Total number of ways $= {}^{n}P_n = n!$

Considering digits $1, 2, 3, 4, \ldots, k$ as one digit, we have $(n - k + 1)$ digits which can be arranged $= (n - k + 1)!$

$\therefore n(E) = $ Number of favourable ways $= (n - k + 1)!$

Hence, required probability $= \dfrac{n(E)}{n(S)} = \dfrac{(n-k+1)!}{n!}$

5. Let a, b, c and d be four different numbers out of $\{1, 2, 3, 4, 5, 6\}$.

$\Rightarrow (a, a, a, a)$ can appear in ${}^{6}C_1 = 6$ ways

$\Rightarrow (a, a, a, b)$ can appear in $2 \times {}^{6}C_2 = 30$ ways

$\Rightarrow (a, a, b, b)$ can appear in ${}^{6}C_2 = 15$ ways

$\Rightarrow (a, a, b, c)$ can appear in $3 \times {}^{6}C_3 = 60$ ways

$\Rightarrow (a, b, c, d)$ can appear in ${}^{6}C_4 = 15$ ways

$\therefore$ Required probability $= \dfrac{60 + 15}{6 + 30 + 15 + 60 + 15} = \dfrac{75}{126} = \dfrac{25}{42}$

6. Total number of ways to choose two squares

$= {}^{64}C_2 = \dfrac{64 \cdot 63}{2} = 32 \cdot 63$

For favourable ways we must chosen two consecutive small squares for any row or any columns.

$\therefore$ Number of favourable ways $= 7 \cdot 8 + 8 \cdot 7 = 2 \cdot 8 \cdot 7$

$\therefore$ Required probability $= \dfrac{2 \cdot 8 \cdot 7}{32 \cdot 63} = \dfrac{1}{18}$

7. In the word MUMBAI, there are 5 adjacent pairs of letters of which only one gives AI.

$\therefore$ Required probability $= \dfrac{\frac{1}{5}}{\frac{1}{6} + \frac{1}{5} + \frac{1}{7} + \frac{1}{4} + \frac{1}{5}} = \dfrac{84}{403}$

8. Numbers on die are 1, 2, 3, 4, 5, 6.

Prime numbers are 2, 3, 5 and non-prime numbers are 1, 4, 6.

Now, let weight assigned to non-prime numbers is λ, then weight assigned to prime number is 2λ.

$\therefore \lambda + 2\lambda + 2\lambda + \lambda + 2\lambda + \lambda = 1$

$\Rightarrow \lambda = \dfrac{1}{9}$

$\therefore$ Probability that an odd number 1 or 3 or 5 will be show up when the die is tossed.

$\lambda + 2\lambda + 2\lambda = 5\lambda = \dfrac{5}{9}$

9. We have, $(X = 7) = \{07, 16, 25, 34, 43, 52, 61, 70\}$

and $(Y = 0) = \{00, 01, 02, \ldots, 10, 20, 30, \ldots, 90\}$

Thus, $(X = 7) \cap (Y = 0) = \{07, 70\}$

$\therefore P\left(\dfrac{X = 7}{Y = 0}\right) = \dfrac{P\{(X = 7) \cap (Y = 0)\}}{P(Y = 0)} = \dfrac{2}{19}$

10. $n(S) = $ Total number of ways $= {}^{50}C_5$

Now, x_3 is fixed to be 30 and x_1, x_2 (two numbers) are to be chosen from first 29 numbers and x_4, x_5 (two numbers) from last 20 numbers are to be chosen.

$\therefore n(E) = $ Number of favourable ways $= {}^{29}C_2 \times {}^{20}C_2$

Hence, required probability $= \dfrac{n(E)}{n(S)} = \dfrac{{}^{29}C_2 \times {}^{20}C_2}{{}^{50}C_5}$

11. $n(S)$ = Total number of ways $= 6^3 = 216$

$n(E)$ = Number of favourable ways $= 2 \times {}^6C_2 \times \frac{3!}{2!} = 90$

$\therefore$ Required probability $= \frac{n(E)}{n(S)} = \frac{90}{216}$

12. $n(S)$ = Total number of ways $= 1000$

The favourable cases that the sum of the digits of the marked number on the page is equal to 9 are one digit number or two digits numbers or three digits numbers, if three digit number is abc. Then, $a + b + c = 9$; $0 \le a, b, c \le 9$

$\therefore \quad n(E)$ = Number of favourable ways

= Number of solutions of the equation

$= {}^{9+3-1}C_{3-1} = {}^{11}C_2 = 55$

$\therefore$ Required probability $= \frac{n(E)}{n(S)} = \frac{55}{1000} = \frac{11}{200}$

13. $n(S)$ = The total number of ways of choosing the tickets

$= 4 \times 4 \times 4 \times 4 = 256$

$n(E)$ = The number of ways in which the sum can be 23

= Coefficient of x^{23} in $(1 + x + x^{10} + x^{11})^4$

= Coefficient of x^{23} in $(1 + x)^4 + (1 + x^{10})^4$

= Coefficient of x^{23} in $(1 + 4x + 6x^2 + 4x^3 + x^4)$

$\times (1 + 4x^{10} + 6x^{20})$

$= 4 \times 6 = 24$

The probability of required event $= \frac{n(E)}{n(S)} = \frac{24}{256} = \frac{3}{32}$

14. Total coupons = 15

$1 \le$ selected coupon number ≤ 9 i.e. 1, 2, 3, 4, 5, 6, 7, 8, 9

$\therefore$ Probability of one selected coupon $= \frac{9}{15} = \frac{3}{5}$

Hence, the required probability

$$= \left(\frac{3}{5}\right) \times \left(\frac{3}{5}\right) \times \ldots \times 7 \text{ times} = \left(\frac{3}{5}\right)^7$$

15. Let X denote the largest number on the 3 tickets drawn.

We have, $P(X \le 7) = \left(\frac{7}{20}\right)^3$ and $P(X \le 6) = \left(\frac{6}{20}\right)^3$

Thus, $P(X = 7) = P(X \le 7) - P(X \le 6) = \left(\frac{7}{20}\right)^3 - \left(\frac{6}{20}\right)^3$

16. Total number = 6 (i.e. 1, 2, 3, 4, 5, 6)

Favourable number = 2, 3, 4, 5 = 4

Probability of favourable number in one draw $= \frac{4}{6} = \frac{2}{3}$

$\therefore$ Required probability $= \left(\frac{2}{3}\right)^4 = \frac{16}{81}$

17. We have, $P(E_i) = \frac{2}{4} = \frac{1}{2}$ for $i = 1, 2, 3$

Also, for $i \ne j$, $P(E_i \cap E_j) = \frac{1}{4} = P(E_i)\, P(E_j)$

Therefore, E_i and E_j are independent for $i \ne j$.

Also, $P(E_1 \cap E_2 \cap E_3) = \frac{1}{4} \ne P(E_1) P(E_2) P(E_3)$

$\therefore E_1, E_2$ and E_3 are not independent.

18. Required probability $= \frac{\text{Area of strips region}}{\text{Area of dotted region}}$

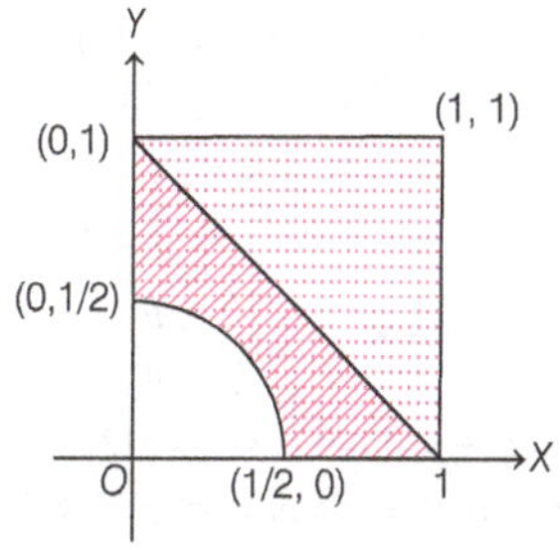

$$= \frac{\frac{1}{2} \times 1 \times 1 - \frac{1}{4} \times \pi \left(\frac{1}{2}\right)^2}{1 \times 1 - \frac{1}{4} \times \pi \left(\frac{1}{2}\right)^2} = \frac{8 - \pi}{16 - \pi}$$

19. When the two equal sides are 1 each, then third side could be only 1.

When the two equal sides are 2 each, then third side can take values 1, 2, 3.

When two equal sides are 3 each, then third side can take values 1, 2, 3, 4, 5. When the two equal sides are 4 each, then third side can take values 1, 2, 3, 4, 5, 6 same in the case when two equal sides are 5 and 6.

$\therefore$ Total number of triangles $= 1 + 3 + 5 + 6 + 6 + 6 = 27$

Required probability $= \frac{1}{27}$

20. Required probability

$$= \frac{\left(\frac{1}{2}\right)^5 \times \left(\frac{1}{2}\right)^5}{\left(\sum_{r=0}^{5} {}^5C_r \left(\frac{1}{2}\right)^r \left(\frac{1}{2}\right)^{5-r}\right)^2} = \frac{1}{\left(\sum_{r=0}^{5} {}^5C_r\right)^2} = \frac{1}{{}^{10}C_5}$$

21. Digits = 9{1, 2, 3, 4, 5, 7, 6, 8, 9}

Total cases of making 7 digits number $= {}^9C_7 \times 7!$

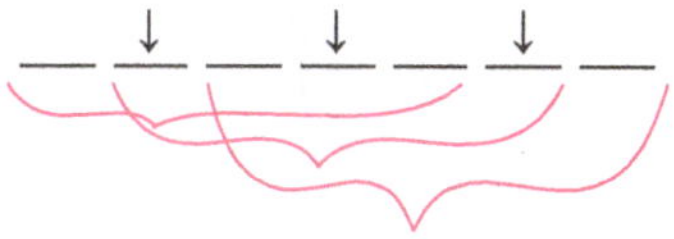

$\Rightarrow$ 3 ways to select five consecutive digits from seven digit number.

Favourable cases $= ({}^7C_3 \times 3! \times {}^6C_4 \times 4!)$

Then, probability $(P) = 1 - \frac{{}^7C_3 \times 3! \times {}^6C_4 \times 4!}{{}^9C_7 \times 7!}$

$$= 1 - \frac{7 \times 6 \times 5 \times 3 \times 2 \times 1 \times 6 \times 5 \times 4 \times 3 \times 2 \times 1 \times 2 \times 1}{3 \times 2 \times 1 \times 2 \times 1 \times 9 \times 8 \times 7 \times 6 \times 5 \times 4 \times 3 \times 2 \times 1}$$

$$= 1 - \frac{5}{12} = \frac{7}{12}$$

Hence, $12P = 7$

22. In 3 days, total error made by Mr. $B = 3$

Suppose, error on day $1 = A$

error on day $2 = B$

error on day $3 = C$

$\therefore$ Probability (Article to be error free)

$$= \left[\frac{2}{3} + \frac{1}{3} \times \frac{2}{3} + \frac{1}{3} \times \frac{1}{3} \times \frac{2}{3}\right]\left[\frac{2}{3} + \frac{1}{3} \times \frac{2}{3}\right]\left[\frac{2}{3}\right]$$

$$= \left(\frac{18 + 6 + 2}{27}\right)\left(\frac{6 + 2}{9}\right) \times \frac{2}{3}$$

$$= \frac{26}{27} \times \frac{8}{9} \times \frac{2}{3} = \frac{416}{729} = \frac{p}{q}$$

$\because \quad \lambda = q - p = 729 - 416 = 313$

Therefore, the sum of digits of $\lambda = 3 + 1 + 3 = 7$.

23. Atleast 3 = Exactly 3 + Exactly 4 + Exactly 5 + Exactly 6 + Exactly 7

So, total cases $= 2^7 = 128$

and favourable cases $\Rightarrow$

Exactly 7 = WWWWWWW $\Rightarrow$ 1 case

Exactly 6 = L WWWWWW, WWWWWWL $\Rightarrow$ 2 cases

Exactly 5 = 5 cases

Exactly 4 = 12 cases

Exactly 3 = 27 cases

$\therefore$ Total favourable cases $= 1 + 2 + 5 + 12 + 27 = 47$

$\therefore$ Probability $(P) = \frac{47}{128} = \frac{p}{q}$

So, $p = 47$ and unit digit of $p = 7$

24. $n(S) = 36$

Let E be the event of getting the sum of digits on the dice equal to 7.

Then, $n(E) = 6$ i.e. $\{(1, 6), (2, 5), (3, 4), (4, 3), (5, 2), (6, 1)\}$

Then, $P(E) = \frac{6}{36} = \frac{1}{6} = p$

and $P(E') = 1 - P(E) = 1 - \frac{1}{6} = \frac{5}{6} = q$

Now, probability of not throwing the sum 7 in first m trials $= q^m$

Therefore, $p = 1 - q^m = 1 - \left(\frac{5}{6}\right)^m$

According to the question,

$$1 - \left(\frac{5}{6}\right)^m > 0.95$$

$$\Rightarrow \quad \left(\frac{5}{6}\right)^m < 0.05$$

$$\Rightarrow \quad m(\log 5 - \log 6) < \log(1) - \log(20)$$

$$\Rightarrow \quad m < \frac{-\log(20)}{\log 5 - \log 6}$$

$$\Rightarrow \quad m > 16.44$$

Hence, the minimum number of tosses are 17.

25. The probability of getting a head on the rigged coin = 1

The probability of getting a head on the fair coin $= \frac{1}{2}$

$\because$ Out of $(n + 1)$ coins, there is 1 rigged coin and n fair coins. Hence, if one coin is drawn, it can either be a rigged coin or a fair coin.

Therefore, the required probability is

$$= \frac{1}{n + 1} \times 1 + \frac{n}{n + 1} \times \frac{1}{2}$$

$$= \frac{n + 2}{2(n + 1)} = \frac{7}{12}$$

$$\Rightarrow \quad \frac{n + 2}{n + 1} = \frac{7}{6}$$

$$\Rightarrow \quad 6n + 12 = 7n + 7$$

$$\Rightarrow \quad n = 5$$

26. $\because P$ (different numbers) $= 1 - P$ (same numbers)

Sum of digits	Sita	Gita	Number of ways
8	(4, 4)	(4, 4)	$1 \times 1 = 1$
7	(4, 3), (3, 4)	(4, 3), (3, 4)	$2 \times 2 = 4$
6	(3, 3), (2, 4), (4, 2)	(3, 3), (2, 4), (4, 2)	$3 \times 3 = 9$
5	(1, 4), (2, 3), (4, 1), (3, 2)	(1, 4), (2, 3) (4, 1), (3, 2)	$4 \times 4 = 16$
4	(2, 2), (3, 1), (1, 3)	(2, 2), (3, 1), (1, 3)	$3 \times 3 = 9$
3	(1, 2), (2, 1)	(1, 2), (2, 1)	$2 \times 2 = 4$
2	(1, 1)	(1, 1)	$1 \times 1 = 1$

$$\therefore P \text{ (same numbers)} = \frac{(1 + 4 + 9 + 16 + 9 + 4 + 1)}{4^4}$$

$$= \frac{2(1 + 4 + 9 + 8)}{4 \times 4 \times 4 \times 4} = \frac{22}{2 \times 64} = \frac{11}{64}$$

$$\therefore P \text{ (different numbers)} = 1 - \frac{11}{64} = \frac{53}{64} = \frac{a}{b}$$

Then, $a + b = 53 + 64 = 117$

27. Odds against = Probability of event not happening : Probability of event happening

Probability of event happening $= \frac{{}^{13}C_1 \times {}^4C_1}{{}^{52}C_2}$

$$= \frac{13 \times 4 \times 2}{52 \times 51} = \frac{2}{51}$$

$\therefore$ Probability of event not happening $= 1 - \frac{2}{51}$

$$= \frac{49}{51}$$

Therefore, odds against $= \frac{49}{51} : \frac{2}{51}$

$$= 49 : 2 = m : 2$$

Then, $\quad m = 49$

28. Since, the sum of the noted numbers are 6 the number on balls are either 1, 2, 3 or 2, 2, 2

So, total number of cases $= 3! + 1$

$\downarrow$ for (1, 2, 3)

$= 7$

Therefore, required probability $= \frac{1}{7} = \frac{a}{b}$

Hence, $a + b = 1 + 7 = 8$

29. Favourable cases $= {}^6C_3$

Total outcomes $= 6^3$

$\therefore$ Probability of getting greater number than previous are

$$= \frac{{}^6C_3}{6^3} = \frac{20}{216} = \frac{5}{54}$$

30. Given, $ax^2 + bx + c = 0$

One root bigger than other

$\therefore$ Roots are real and distinct

$$D > 0 \Rightarrow b^2 - 4ac > 0$$

$b = 3$, then $(a, c) = (1, 1), (1, 2), (2, 1)$

$b = 4$, then $(a, c) = (1, 1), (1, 2), (2, 1)\ (1, 3), (3, 1)$

$b = 5$, then $(a, c) = (1, 1), (1, 2), (2, 1)\ (1, 3), (3, 1), (1, 4), (4, 1), (1, 5), (5, 1), (1, 6), (6, 1), (2, 3), (3, 2), (2, 2)$

$b = 6$, then $(a, c) = (1, 1), (1, 2), (2, 1)\ (1, 3), (3, 1), (1, 4), (4, 1), (1, 5), (5, 1), (1, 6), (6, 1), (2, 3), (3, 2), (2, 2), (2, 4), (4, 2)$.

Favourable cases = 38

$$\therefore \quad p = \frac{38}{6 \times 6 \times 6} \Rightarrow 216p = 38$$

31. Let probability of tail $= \frac{1}{3}$

Probability of head $= \frac{2}{3}$

Two tails and one head $= TTH, THT, HTT$

Probability of getting 2 tails and 1 head

$$= \left(\frac{1}{3} \times \frac{1}{3} \times \frac{2}{3}\right) + \left(\frac{1}{3} \times \frac{2}{3} \times \frac{1}{3}\right) + \left(\frac{2}{3} \times \frac{1}{3} \times \frac{1}{3}\right) = \frac{2}{9}$$

32. We have, $P(2) = \frac{1}{6}$ and $P(\overline{2}) = \frac{5}{6}$

$\therefore P$[2 obtained on even numbered toss]

$$= \frac{5}{6} \times \frac{1}{6} + \left(\frac{5}{6}\right)^3 \times \frac{1}{6} + \left(\frac{5}{6}\right)^5 \times \frac{1}{6} + \ldots$$

$$= \frac{\frac{5}{6} \times \frac{1}{6}}{1 - \left(\frac{5}{6}\right)^2} = \frac{5}{36} \times \frac{36}{11} = \frac{5}{11}$$

33. Let the numbers be x and y.

So, $x + y = 24$; $x, y \in N$ and $x \cdot y \geq \frac{3}{4}$ (maximum product)

Maximum product will be found,

When $x = y = \frac{24}{2} = 12$

So, $xy \geq \frac{3}{4}(12 \times 12) \Rightarrow xy \geq \frac{3}{4} \times 144 \Rightarrow xy \geq 108$

Possible cases are

x	y	xy
1	23	23
2	22	44
⋮	⋮	⋮
6	18	108
⋮	⋮	⋮
11	13	143
12	12	144
13	11	143
⋮	⋮	⋮
18	6	108

$\therefore$ Total combination = 13

So, $P(xy \geq 108) = \frac{13}{23} = \frac{m}{n}$

So, $n - m = 23 - 13 = 10$

34. Since, x and y each can take values from 0 to 10, so the total number of ways of selecting x and y is $11 \times 11 = 121$.

Now, $|x - y| > 5 \Rightarrow x - y < -5$ or $x - y > 5$

When $x - y > 5$, we have following cases

When $x = 0, y = 0 \rightarrow 1$ case

$x = 7, y = 0, 1 \rightarrow 2$ cases

$x = 8, y = 0, 1, 2, \rightarrow 3$ cases

$x = 9, y = 0, 1, 2, 3 \rightarrow 4$ cases

$x = 10, y = 0, 1, 2, 3, 4 \rightarrow 5$ cases

Hence, the total number of cases 15.

Similarly, we have 15 cases for $x - y < 5$.

There are 30 pairs values of x and y satisfying these two inequalities. So, favourable number of ways is 30.

Hence, required probability is $\frac{30}{121}$.

35. Given, Ajay will not appear in exam $P(\overline{A}) = \frac{2}{7} \Rightarrow P(A) = \frac{5}{7}$

and both Ajay and Vijay will appear in the exam with probability $P(A \cap V) = \frac{1}{5} = P(A) \cdot P(V)$

[$\because P(A)$ and $P(V)$ are independent]

$$\therefore \quad P(A) \cdot P(V) = \frac{1}{5} \Rightarrow P(V) = \frac{7}{25} \qquad \left[\because P(A) = \frac{5}{7}\right]$$

Now, probability that Ajay will appear in the exam and Vijay will not appear

$$P(A \cap \overline{V}) = P(A)P(\overline{V})$$

$$= \frac{5}{7} \times \left(1 - \frac{7}{25}\right) \qquad [\because P(\overline{A}) = -P(A)]$$

$$= \frac{18}{35}$$

36. **Decoding the Question**

Use the formula to get final result

$n(A \cup B \cup C) = n(A) + n(B) + n(C) - n(A \cap B) - n(B \cap C) - n(C \cap A) + n(A \cap B \cap C)$

$U = \{1, 2, 3, \ldots, 50\}$

A = Set of integers which is multiple of 4

B = Set of integers which is multiple of 6

C = Set of integers which is multiple of 7

$$n(A) = 12$$
$$n(B) = 8$$
$$n(C) = 7$$
$$n(A \cap B) = 4$$
$$n(B \cap C) = 1$$
$$n(C \cap A) = 1$$
$$n(A \cap B \cap C) = 0$$

$$\therefore \quad n(A \cup B \cup C) = n(A) + n(B) + n(C) - n(A \cap B) - n(B \cap C) - n(C \cap A) + n(A \cap B \cap C)$$
$$= 12 + 8 + 7 - 4 - 1 - 1 + 0 = 21$$

$\therefore$ Required probability $= \dfrac{21}{50}$

37.

A	B	C
7 Red, 5 Black	5 Red, 7 Black	6 Red, 6 Black

Now, if ball drawn is black, then probability that it is chosen

$$\text{from urn } A = \frac{\frac{1}{3} \times \frac{5}{12}}{\frac{1}{3} \times \frac{5}{12} + \frac{1}{3} \times \frac{7}{12} + \frac{1}{3} \times \frac{6}{12}} = \frac{\frac{5}{36}}{\frac{5}{36} + \frac{7}{36} + \frac{6}{36}} = \frac{5}{18}$$

38. Let $E_1 \to$ Motorcycle produced at plant A

$E_2 \to$ Motorcycle produced at plant B

$A \to$ Motorcycle of standard quality

So, according to the question,

$$P(E_1) = 0.6; \; P(E_2) = 0.4$$
$$P(A / E_1) = 0.8; \; P(A / E_2) = 0.9$$

So, by Bayes theorem, probability of motorcycle produced at B and of standard quality

$$P(E_2 / A) = \frac{P(E_2)\, P(A / E_2)}{P(E_1)\, P(A / E_1) + P(E_2)\, P(A / E_2)}$$
$$= \frac{0.4 \times 0.9}{0.6 \times 0.8 + 0.4 \times 0.9} = \frac{36}{84} = \frac{3}{7}$$

$$\therefore \quad p = \frac{3}{7}$$

and $\quad 126p = 126 \times \dfrac{3}{7} = 54$

39. Use having formula, $P(E_i / A) = \dfrac{P(E_i) P(A / E_i)}{\sum_{i=1}^{n} P(E_i) P(A / E_i)}$,

$i = 1, 2, \ldots, n$

E_1 = Bag A is selected

E_2 = Bag B is selected

A	B
3 W, 7 R	3 W, 2 R

E = Drawing ball from bag is white.

According to the question, we have to find $P\left[\dfrac{E_1}{E}\right]$

Using Baye's theorem,

$$P\left(\frac{E_1}{E}\right) = \frac{P(E_1) \cdot P\left(\frac{E}{E_1}\right)}{P(E_1).P\left(\frac{E}{E_1}\right) + P(E_2)P\left(\frac{E}{E_2}\right)}$$
$$= \frac{\frac{1}{2} \times \frac{3}{10}}{\frac{1}{2} \times \frac{3}{10} + \frac{1}{2} \times \frac{3}{5}} = \frac{3}{3 + 6} = \frac{1}{3}$$

40. $a, b, c \in \{1, 2, 3, 4\}$

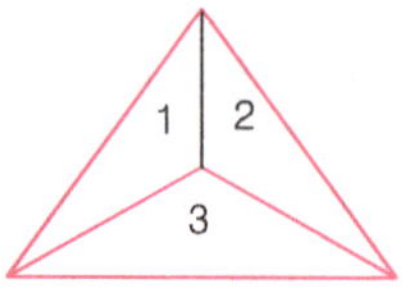

Tetrahedral dice

Now, $ax^2 + bx + c = 0$ has all real roots, if $D \geq 0$.

$\Rightarrow \quad b^2 - 4ac \geq 0$

Let $b = 1 \Rightarrow 1 - 4ac \geq 0$ (not feasible)

$b = 2 \Rightarrow 4 - 4ac \geq 0 \Rightarrow 1 \geq ac \Rightarrow a = 1, c = 1$

$b = 3 \Rightarrow 9 - 4ac \geq 0 \Rightarrow \dfrac{9}{4} \geq ac$

$\Rightarrow (a = 1, c = 1), (a = 1, c = 2), (a = 2, c = 1)$

$b = 4 \Rightarrow 16 - 4ac \geq 0 \quad \Rightarrow 4 \geq ac$

$\Rightarrow (a = 1, c = 2), (a = 2, c = 1), (a = 1, c = 3)$

$(a = 3, c = 1), (a = 1, c = 4), (a = 4, c = 1), (a = 2, c = 2)$

$\therefore$ Required probability $= \dfrac{12}{4 \times 4 \times 4} = \dfrac{3}{16} = \dfrac{m}{n}$ [given]

$\therefore \quad m + n = 19$

41.

Probability	Blue balls
$\dfrac{{}^5C_0 \cdot {}^4C_3}{{}^9C_3}$	0
$\dfrac{{}^5C_1 \cdot {}^4C_2}{{}^9C_3}$	1
$\dfrac{{}^5C_2 \cdot {}^4C_1}{{}^9C_3}$	2
$\dfrac{{}^5C_3 \cdot {}^4C_0}{{}^9C_3}$	3
0	4
0	5

$$7\overline{X} = \frac{({}^5C_0 \cdot {}^4C_3 \times 0) + {}^5C_1 \cdot {}^4C_2 + {}^5C_2 \cdot {}^4C_1 \times 2 + {}^5C_3 \cdot {}^4C_0 \times 3}{{}^9C_3} \times 7$$

$$= \frac{30 + 80 + 30}{84} \times 7 = \frac{35}{3}$$

Probability	Yellow balls
$\frac{{}^5C_3 \cdot {}^4C_0}{{}^9C_3}$	0
$\frac{{}^5C_2 \cdot {}^4C_1}{{}^9C_3}$	1
$\frac{{}^5C_1 \cdot {}^4C_2}{{}^9C_3}$	2
$\frac{{}^5C_0 \cdot {}^4C_3}{{}^9C_3}$	3
0	4

$$4\overline{Y} = \frac{0 + {}^5C_2 \cdot {}^4C_1 + {}^5C_1 \cdot {}^4C_2 \times 2 + {}^5C_0 \cdot {}^4C_3 \times 3}{{}^9C_3} \times 4$$

$$= \frac{40 + 60 + 12}{84} \times 4 = \frac{112}{21} = \frac{16}{3}$$

Then, $7\overline{X} + 4\overline{Y} = \frac{35}{3} + \frac{16}{3} = 17$

42. $P(W) = \frac{1}{3}, P(L) = \frac{2}{3}$

$x =$ Number of matches that team wins

$y =$ Number of matches that team loses

$|x - y| \le 2$ and $x + y = 10$

$|x - y| = 0, 1, 2\ x, y \in N$

Case 1 $|x - y| = 0 \Rightarrow x = y$

$\because \quad x + y = 10 \Rightarrow x = y = 5$

$\therefore P(|x - y| = 0) = {}^{10}C_5 \left(\frac{1}{3}\right)^5 \left(\frac{2}{3}\right)^5$ ...(i)

Case 2 $|x - y| = 1 \Rightarrow x - y = \pm 1$

+1	−1
$x - y = 1$	$x - y = -1$
$x + y = 10$	$x + y = 10$
$x = \frac{11}{2}$	$x = \frac{9}{2}$
NP	NP

Case 3 $|x - y| = 2$

$x - y = \pm 2$

+2	−2
$x + y = 10$	$x + y = 10$
$x - y = 2$	$x - y = -2$
$x = 6$	$x = 4$
$y = 4$	$y = 6$

$\therefore P(|x - y| = 2) = {}^{10}C_6 \left(\frac{1}{3}\right)^6 \left(\frac{2}{3}\right)^4 + {}^{10}C_4 \left(\frac{1}{3}\right)^4 \left(\frac{2}{3}\right)^6$ ...(ii)

Required probability

$$= {}^{10}C_5 \left(\frac{1}{3}\right)^5 \left(\frac{2}{3}\right)^5 + {}^{10}C_6 \left(\frac{1}{3}\right)^6 \left(\frac{2}{3}\right)^4 + {}^{10}C_4 \left(\frac{1}{3}\right)^4 \left(\frac{2}{3}\right)^6$$

$$P = \frac{{}^{10}C_5\, 2^5}{3^{10}} + \frac{{}^{10}C_6\, 2^4}{3^{10}} + \frac{{}^{10}C_4\, 2^6}{3^{10}}$$

$$\Rightarrow 3^9 P = \frac{1}{3}({}^{10}C_5 2^5 + {}^{10}C_6 2^4 + {}^{10}C_4 2^6) = 8288$$

43. $a = P(X = 3) = \frac{5}{6} \times \frac{5}{6} \times \frac{1}{6} = \frac{25}{216}$

and $\quad b = P(X \ge 3)$

$$= \frac{5}{6} \times \frac{5}{6} \times \frac{1}{6} + \left(\frac{5}{6}\right)^3 \times \frac{1}{6} + \left(\frac{5}{6}\right)^4 \times \frac{1}{6} + \dots$$

$$= \frac{\frac{25}{216}}{1 - \frac{5}{6}} = \frac{25}{216} \times \frac{6}{1} = \frac{25}{36}$$

$$P(X \ge 6) = \left(\frac{5}{6}\right)^5 \times \frac{1}{6} + \left(\frac{5}{6}\right)^6 \times \frac{1}{6} + \dots$$

$$= \frac{\left(\frac{5}{6}\right)^5 \times \frac{1}{6}}{1 - \frac{5}{6}} = \left(\frac{5}{6}\right)^5$$

$$c = \frac{\left(\frac{5}{6}\right)^5}{\left(\frac{5}{6}\right)^3} = \frac{25}{36}$$

Hence, $\frac{b + c}{a} = \frac{\left(\frac{5}{6}\right)^2 + \left(\frac{5}{6}\right)^2}{\left(\frac{5}{6}\right)^2 \times \frac{1}{6}} = 12$

44. Total number of outcomes $= 6 \times 6 \times 6$

$= 216$

Number of outcomes getting different numbers on the three dice are

$${}^6P_3 = \frac{6!}{3!} = 120$$

$\therefore$ Required probability $= \frac{120}{216} = \frac{5}{9}$

$\therefore \quad p = 5$ and $q = 9$

$\therefore \quad q - p = 9 - 5 = 4$

45. 6 − White, 4 − Black $\rightarrow$ Total number of balls $= 10$

Probability getting all the balls drawn are white is

$$= \frac{1}{6} \times \frac{{}^6C_1}{{}^{10}C_1} + \frac{1}{6} \times \frac{{}^6C_2}{{}^{10}C_2} + \frac{1}{6} \frac{{}^6C_3}{{}^{10}C_3} + \frac{1}{6} \frac{{}^6C_4}{{}^{10}C_4} + \frac{1}{6} \frac{{}^6C_5}{{}^{10}C_5} + \frac{1}{6} \times \frac{{}^6C_6}{{}^{10}C_6}$$

$$= \frac{1}{6} \times \frac{6}{10} + \frac{1}{6} \times \frac{15}{45} + \frac{1}{6} \times \frac{20}{120} + \frac{1}{6} \times \frac{15}{210} + \frac{1}{6} \times \frac{6}{252} + \frac{1}{6} \times \frac{1}{210}$$

$$= \frac{1}{6}\left[\frac{3}{5} + \frac{1}{3} + \frac{1}{6} + \frac{1}{14} + \frac{1}{42} + \frac{1}{210}\right] = \frac{1}{6} \times \frac{6}{5} = \frac{1}{5}$$

46. Given, $P(H)=\frac{1}{4}$ then, $P(T)=1-\frac{1}{4}=\frac{3}{4}$

If N = number of tosses required when the process is repeated until a head appears.

Then, probability $=\frac{1}{4}+\left(\frac{3}{4}\right)\left(\frac{1}{4}\right)+\left(\frac{3}{4}\right)^2\left(\frac{1}{4}\right)+\ldots+\left(\frac{3}{4}\right)^{N-1}\left(\frac{1}{4}\right)$

$$P=\frac{1}{4}\left[1+\frac{3}{4}+\left(\frac{3}{4}\right)^2+\ldots+\left(\frac{3}{4}\right)^{N-1}\right]$$

$$P=\frac{1}{4}\left\{\frac{1\cdot\left\{1-\left(\frac{3}{4}\right)^N\right\}}{1-\frac{3}{4}}\right\}\Rightarrow P=1-\left(\frac{3}{4}\right)^N$$

Now, quadratic equation $64x^2-5Nx+1=0$ has no real root

$\Rightarrow \quad D<0$

$25N^2-4\times64<0$

$\Rightarrow \quad (5N)^2<(16)^2 \Rightarrow 5N<16$

$\Rightarrow \quad N<\frac{16}{5}\Rightarrow N<3.2$

Then, $p=1-\left(\frac{3}{4}\right)^3$; $p=1-\frac{27}{64}=\frac{37}{64}$

Hence, $p=37, q=64$

$q-p=64-37=27$

47. Probability of a person being a smoker = 25%

$$P(S)=\frac{25}{100}\Rightarrow P(S)=\frac{1}{4}$$

So, probability of a person being non smoker

$$=P(N)=1-\frac{1}{4}=\frac{3}{4}$$

And probability of a smoker to get a lung cancer

$$=P\left(\frac{L}{S}\right)$$

$\because$ Probability of a non-smoker to get a lung cancer $=P\left(\frac{L}{N}\right)$

and $P\left(\frac{L}{S}\right)=27P\left(\frac{L}{N}\right)$ and $P\left(\frac{S}{L}\right)=\frac{k}{10}$

$$P\left(\frac{S}{L}\right)=\frac{P(S)\cdot P\left(\frac{L}{S}\right)}{P(L)}=\frac{k}{10}$$

Where, $P(L)=P(N)\cdot P\left(\frac{L}{N}\right)+P(S)\cdot P\left(\frac{L}{S}\right)$

$$=\frac{3}{4}P\left(\frac{L}{N}\right)+\frac{1}{4}\left\{27P\left(\frac{L}{N}\right)\right\}$$

So, $\quad P(L)=\frac{30}{4}P\left(\frac{L}{N}\right)$

So, $P\left(\frac{S}{L}\right)=\dfrac{\frac{1}{4}\left\{27P\left(\frac{L}{N}\right)\right\}}{\frac{30}{4}P\left(\frac{L}{N}\right)}=\frac{k}{10}\Rightarrow P\left(\frac{S}{L}\right)=\frac{9}{10}=\frac{k}{10}\Rightarrow k=9$

48. Required cases = Total ways − all digits even − exactly one digit odd

Total ways = 900 ways

All digits even $=4\times5\times5=100$ ways

One digit odd $=\underset{\text{odd}}{5}\times5\times5=125$ ways

$4\times\underset{\text{odd}}{5}\times5=100$ ways

$4\times5\times\underset{\text{odd}}{5}=100$ ways

$\therefore$ Required probability $=\frac{900-425}{900}=\frac{19}{36}$

49. R is relation from $\{x, y\}$ to $\{x, y\}$.

Total number of relation $=2^{2\times2}=16$

The relation which are symmetric as well as transitive are $\phi, \{(x, x)\}, \{(y, y)\}, \{(x, x), (y, y)\}$ and $\{(x, x), (y, y), (x, y), (y, x)\}$.

$\therefore$ Required probability $=\frac{5}{16}$

50. Number of one-one function from $\{a, b, c, d\}$ to set $\{1, 2, 3, 4, 5\}$ is

$${}^5P_4=120$$

$\therefore \quad n(S)=120$

The required possible set of value $(f(a), f(b), f(c), f(d))$ such that $f(a)+2f(b)-f(c)=f(d)$ are

(5,1,3,4), (5,1,4,3), (4,2,3,5), (4,2,5,3), (1,3,2,5) and (1,3,5,2)

$\therefore \quad n(E)=6$

$\therefore$ Required probability $=\frac{n(E)}{n(S)}=\frac{6}{120}=\frac{1}{20}$

51. Required probability

$$={}^4C_2\left(\frac{3}{4}\right)^2\left(\frac{1}{4}\right)^2\left(\frac{1}{4}\right)^6+{}^6C_2\left(\frac{3}{4}\right)^2\left(\frac{1}{4}\right)^4\left(\frac{3}{4}\right)^4+{}^4C_1\,{}^6C_1\left(\frac{3}{4}\right)\left(\frac{1}{4}\right)\left(\frac{3}{4}\right)^3\left(\frac{1}{4}\right)^5$$

$$=\frac{1}{4^{10}}[6\times9+15\times9^3+24\times9^2]$$

$$=\frac{27}{4^{10}}\times479=\frac{27}{4^{10}}k$$

Thus, the value of k is 479.

52. P(Exactly one out of A or B occurs) $=\frac{5}{9}$

$$P(A\cap\bar{B})+P(\bar{A}\cap B)=\frac{5}{9}$$

$$P(A)P(\bar{B})+P(\bar{A})P(B)=\frac{5}{9}$$

[$\because$ A and B are independent events]

$\therefore \quad p(1-2p)+(1-p)2p=\frac{5}{9}$

$\Rightarrow \quad 9p-18p^2+18p-18p^2=5$

$\Rightarrow \quad 36^2p-27p+5=0$

$\Rightarrow \quad (3p-1)(12p-5)=0$

$\Rightarrow \quad p=\frac{1}{3}$ or $p=\frac{5}{12}\Rightarrow p_{\max}=\frac{5}{12}$

53. Let $A = \begin{vmatrix} a & b \\ c & d \end{vmatrix}, |A| = ad - bc$

$n(s) = 6 \times 6 \times 6 \times 6 = 6^4$

For non-singular matrix $|A| \neq 0 \Rightarrow ad \neq bc$

Now, a, b, c and d should be different.

If $ad = bc \Rightarrow \frac{a}{b} = \frac{c}{d}$

If $a = 1, \frac{1}{2} = \frac{3}{6}$ and $\frac{1}{3} = \frac{2}{6}$

So, $\{a, b, c, d\} = \{1, 2, 3, 6\}$ or $\{1, 3, 2, 6\}$

If $a = 2$

$\frac{2}{1} = \frac{6}{3}, \frac{2}{3} = \frac{4}{6}, \frac{2}{4} = \frac{3}{6} = \frac{1}{2}, \frac{2}{6} = \frac{1}{3}$

So, $\{a, b, c, d\} = \{2, 1, 6, 3\}, \{2, 3, 4, 6\}, \{2, 4, 3, 6\}, \{2, 4, 1, 2\}, \{2, 6, 1, 3\}$

If $a = 3$, $\frac{3}{1} = \frac{6}{2}, \frac{3}{2} = \frac{6}{4}, \frac{3}{6} = \frac{1}{2}$

$\{a, b, c, d\} = \{3, 1, 6, 2\}, \{3, 2, 6, 4\}, \{3, 6, 1, 2\}$

If $a = 4, \frac{4}{2} = \frac{6}{3}, \frac{4}{6} = \frac{2}{3},$

$\{a, b, c, d\} = \{4, 2, 6, 3\}, \{4, 6, 2, 3\}$

If $a = 5 \Rightarrow$ Not possible

If $a = 6, \frac{6}{2} = \frac{3}{1}, \frac{6}{3} = \frac{2}{1}, \frac{6}{4} = \frac{3}{2}, \frac{6}{3} = \frac{4}{2}$

$\{a, b, c, d\} = \{6, 2, 3, 1\}, \{6, 3, 2, 1\}, \{6, 4, 3, 2\}, \{6, 3, 4, 2\}$

So, $n(\overline{E}) = 2 + 5 + 3 + 2 + 0 + 4 = 16$

So, $n(E) = {}^6C_4 4! - 16$

Probability $= \frac{{}^6C_4 4! - 16}{6^4} = \frac{43}{162}$

54. $P(A) =$ Probability of first unit to function

and $P(B) =$ Probability of second unit to function

$P(A) = 0.9, P(\overline{A}) = 0.1$

$P(B) = 0.8, P(\overline{B}) = 0.2$

$AB \to$ Operate

$A\overline{B} \to$ Not operate

$\overline{A}\ B \to$ Not operate

$\overline{A}\ \overline{B} \to$ Not operate

According to question, first failed and second functioning, given that instrument has failed, So according to Bayes theorem

$\therefore \quad P = \frac{P(\overline{A}) \cdot P(B)}{P(A)\ P(\overline{B}) + P(\overline{A})P(B) + P(\overline{A})\ P(\overline{B})}$

$= \frac{(0.1 \times 0.8)}{(0.9 \times 0.2) + (0.1 \times 0.8) + (0.1 \times 0.2)} = \frac{8}{28}$

$\therefore\ 98P = \frac{8}{28} \times 98 = 28$

55. **Decoding the Question**

(i) $P(X) = p \Rightarrow P(\overline{X}) = 1 - p$

(ii) If A, B, C are independent events, then

P (only A occurs) $= P(A\overline{B}\,\overline{C}) = P(A) \cdot P(\overline{B}) \cdot P(\overline{C})$

Similarly, for $P(B)$ and $P(C)$

and P(none occurs) $= P(\overline{A}) \cdot P(\overline{B}) \cdot P(\overline{C})$.

Let $P(E_1) = x, P(E_2) = y, P(E_3) = z$

Then, $(1 - x)(1 - y)(1 - z) = p$ ...(A)

Probability of only $E_1 = P(E_1 \cap \overline{E}_2 \cap \overline{E}_3)$

$\alpha = x(1 - y)(1 - z)$ ...(B)

Similarly, $\beta = (1 - x)\ y(1 - z)$ ...(C)

$\gamma = (1 - x)(1 - y)z$ ...(D)

On dividing Eq. (A) by Eq. (B), we get

$\frac{p}{\alpha} = \frac{1 - x}{x} \Rightarrow xp = \alpha - \alpha x \Rightarrow x = \frac{\alpha}{\alpha + p}$

Similarly, $y = \frac{\beta}{\beta + p} \Rightarrow z = \frac{\gamma}{\gamma + p}$

$\frac{P(E_1)}{P(E_3)} = \frac{x}{z} = \left(\frac{\alpha}{\alpha + p}\right) \times \left(\frac{\gamma + p}{\gamma}\right)$

$\frac{x}{z} = \left(\frac{\alpha}{\gamma}\right)\left(\frac{\gamma + p}{\alpha + p}\right) = \left(\frac{1 + p/\gamma}{1 + p/\alpha}\right)$

Also given, $p = \frac{\alpha\beta}{\alpha - 2\beta} = \frac{2\beta\gamma}{\beta - 3\gamma}$

$\alpha p - 2\beta p = \alpha\beta \Rightarrow \frac{\alpha p}{\alpha + 2p} = \beta$ ...(i)

$\beta p - 3p\gamma = 2\beta\gamma$

$\Rightarrow \quad \beta(p - 2\gamma) = 3p\gamma \Rightarrow \beta = \frac{3p\gamma}{p - 2\gamma}$ ...(ii)

From Eqs. (i) and (ii), we get

$\frac{\alpha p}{\alpha + 2p} = \frac{3p\gamma}{p - 2\gamma}$

$\Rightarrow \quad \frac{1}{1 + 2\left(\frac{p}{\alpha}\right)} = \frac{3}{\left(\frac{p}{\gamma}\right) - 2}$

$\Rightarrow \quad (p/\gamma) - 2 = 3 + 6(p/\alpha)$

$\Rightarrow \quad \frac{p}{\gamma} = 5 + 6\left(\frac{p}{\alpha}\right)$

$\therefore \quad \frac{x}{z} = \frac{1 + p/\gamma}{1 + p/\alpha} = \frac{1 + 5 + 6(p/\alpha)}{1 + p/\alpha}$

$= 6\left(\frac{1 + p/\alpha}{1 + p/\alpha}\right)$

$= 6$

56. It is given that A and B are two independent events such that $P(A) = \frac{1}{3}$ and $P(B) = 1/6$, then

$P(A \cap B) = P(A) \cdot P(B) = \frac{1}{18}$

Now, $P(A|(A \cup B)) = \frac{P(A \cap (A \cup B))}{P(A \cup B)}$

$= \frac{P(A)}{P(A) + P(B) - P(A \cap B)}$

$= \frac{\frac{1}{3}}{\frac{1}{3} + \frac{1}{6} - \frac{1}{18}} = \frac{\frac{1}{3}}{\frac{6 + 3 - 1}{18}} = \frac{6}{8} = \frac{3}{4}$

and $$P(A'|B') = \frac{P(A' \cap B')}{P(B')}$$
$$= \frac{P((A \cup B)')}{P(B')} = \frac{1 - P(A \cup B)}{1 - P(B)}$$
$$= \frac{1 - \frac{6+3-1}{18}}{1 - \frac{1}{6}} = \frac{\frac{10}{18}}{\frac{5}{6}} = \frac{2}{3}$$

and $$P(A|B') = \frac{P(A \cap B')}{P(B')}$$
$$= \frac{P(A) \cdot P(B')}{P(B')} = P(A) = \frac{1}{3}$$

and $$P(A|B) = \frac{P(A \cap B)}{P(B)}$$
$$= \frac{P(A)P(B)}{P(B)} = \frac{1}{3}$$

57. Given probability distribution for a random variable X is

X	1	2	3	4	5
$P(X)$	K^2	$2K$	K	$2K$	$5K^2$

Then, $P(X > 2) = 1 - \{P(X = 1) + P(X = 2)\}$
$= 1 - K^2 - 2K$

$\therefore \quad \sum_{X=1}^{5} P(X) = 1$

$\Rightarrow \quad 6K^2 + 5K = 1 \Rightarrow 6K(K+1) - 1(K+1) = 0$

$\Rightarrow \quad K = \frac{1}{6}, -1 \qquad [\because P(X) \geq 0, \text{ so } K \not< 0]$

$\Rightarrow \quad K = \frac{1}{6}$

$\therefore \quad P(X > 2) = 1 - \frac{1}{36} - \frac{2}{6} = \frac{36 - 1 - 12}{36} = \frac{23}{36}$

Time Saving Technique

$\sum_{X=1}^{5} P(x) = 1$

$6K^2 + 5K = 1 \Rightarrow K = 1/6, -1$

We take, $K = 1/6$

$P(X > 2) = 1 - [P(X = 1) + P(X = 2)]$

$= 1 - \left(\frac{1}{36} + \frac{2}{6}\right) = \frac{23}{36}$

58. Let probability of hitting a target, $p = \frac{1}{10}$

So, probability of not hitting a target, $q = \frac{9}{10}$

So, probability of not hitting target in n trials $= \left(\frac{9}{10}\right)^n$

$\therefore$ Probability of hitting target at least one $= 1 - \left(\frac{9}{10}\right)^n > \frac{1}{4}$

$\Rightarrow \quad (0.9)^n < 0.75$

$\therefore$ Least number of shots required $= n_{\min} = 3$

Exercise 2 - JEE Advanced Pattern

1. $7^1 = 7, 7^2 = 49, 7^3 = 343, 7^4 = 2401, \ldots$

Therefore, for $7^r, r \in N$ the number ends at unit place $7, 9, 3, 1, 7, \ldots$

$\therefore$ $7^m + 7^n$ will be divisible by 5 if it end at 5 or 0.

But it cannot end at 5. Also for end at 0.

For this m and n should be as follows

	m	n
1	$4r$	$4r-2$
2	$4r-1$	$4r-3$
3	$4r-2$	$4r$
4	$4r-3$	$4r-1$

For any given value of m, there will be 25 values of n.

Hence, the probability of the required event is

$$\frac{100 \times 25}{100 \times 100} = \frac{1}{4}$$

2. The number of ways of placing 3 black balls without any restriction is ${}^{10}C_3$.

Since, we have total 10 places of putting 10 balls in a row.

Now, the number of ways in which no two black balls put together is equal to the number of ways of choosing 3 places marked '—' out of eight places.

—W—W—W—W—W—W—W—

This can be done in ${}^8C_3$ ways.

$\therefore$ Required probability $= \frac{{}^8C_3}{{}^{10}C_3} = \frac{8 \times 7 \times 6}{10 \times 9 \times 8} = \frac{7}{15}$

3. Three vertices out of 6 can be chosen in ${}^6C_3$ ways.

So, total ways $= {}^6C_3 = 20$

Only two equilateral triangles can be formed ΔAEC and ΔBFD.

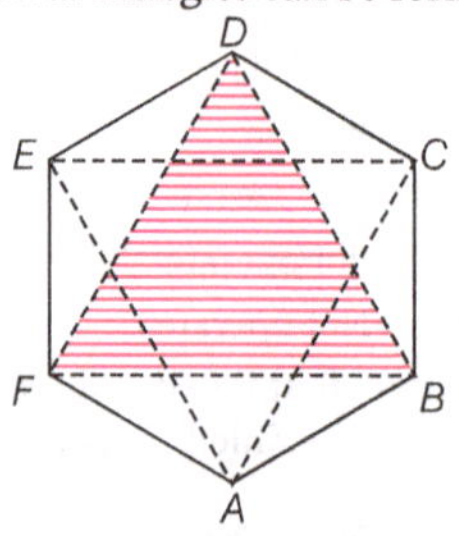

$\therefore$ Favourable ways $= 2$

So, required probability $= \frac{2}{20} = \frac{1}{10}$

4. Since, three dice are rolled.

$\therefore$ Total number of cases

$S = 6 \times 6 \times 6 = 216$

and the same number appear on each of them $= {}^6C_1 = 6$

$\therefore$ Required probability $= \frac{6}{216} = \frac{1}{36}$

5. We have, P (exactly one of A or B occurs)

$= P(A \cup B) - P(A \cap B)$

$= P(A) + P(B) - 2P(A \cap B)$

According to the question,

$$P(A) + P(B) - 2P(A \cap B) = \frac{1}{4} \quad \text{...(i)}$$

$$P(B) + P(C) - 2P(B \cap C) = \frac{1}{4} \quad \text{...(ii)}$$

and $$P(C) + P(A) - 2P(C \cap A) = \frac{1}{4} \quad \text{...(iii)}$$

On adding Eqs. (i), (ii) and (iii), we get

$$2[P(A) + P(B) + P(C) - P(A \cap B) - P(B \cap C) - P(C \cap A)] = \frac{3}{4}$$

$$\Rightarrow P(A) + P(B) + P(C) - P(A \cap B) - P(B \cap C) - P(C \cap A) = \frac{3}{8}$$

$\therefore P$ (atleast one event occurs)

$$= P(A \cup B \cup C)$$

$$= P(A) + P(B) + P(C) - P(A \cap B) - P(B \cap C) - P(C \cap A) + P(A \cap B \cap C)$$

$$= \frac{3}{8} + \frac{1}{16} = \frac{7}{16} \quad \left[\because P(A \cap B \cap C) = \frac{1}{16}\right]$$

6. Given, $P(B) = \frac{3}{4}$, $P(A \cap B \cap \bar{C}) = \frac{1}{3}$

and $P(\bar{A} \cap B \cap \bar{C}) = \frac{1}{3}$

which can be shown in Venn diagram.

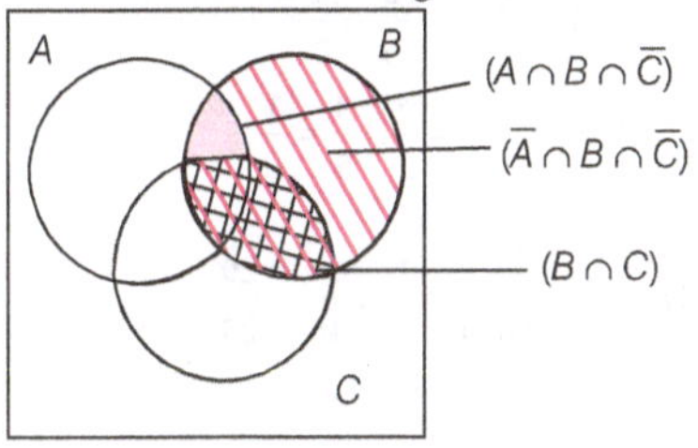

$$\therefore P(B \cap C) = P(B) - \{P(A \cap B \cap \bar{C}) + P(\bar{A} \cap B \cap \bar{C})\}$$

$$= \frac{3}{4} - \left(\frac{1}{3} + \frac{1}{3}\right) = \frac{3}{4} - \frac{2}{3} = \frac{1}{12}$$

7. It is given that

$$P(E) \le P(F) \Rightarrow E \subseteq F \quad \text{...(i)}$$

and $$P(E \cap F) > 0 \Rightarrow E \subset F \quad \text{...(ii)}$$

(a) occurrence of $E \Rightarrow$ occurrence of F [from Eq. (i)]

(b) occurrence of $F \Rightarrow$ occurrence of E [from Eq. (ii)]

(c) non-occurrence of $E \Rightarrow$ occurrence of F

Hence, option (c) is not correct. [From Eq. (i)]

8. We know that

P (exactly one of A or B occurs) $= P(A) + P(B) - 2P(A \cap B)$

$$\therefore \quad P(A) + P(B) - 2P(A \cap B) = p \quad \text{...(i)}$$

Similarly, $$P(B) + P(C) - 2P(B \cap C) = p \quad \text{...(ii)}$$

and $$P(C) + P(A) - 2P(C \cap A) = p \quad \text{...(iii)}$$

On adding Eqs. (i), (ii) and (iii), we get

$$2[P(A) + P(B) + P(C) - P(A \cap B) - P(B \cap C) - P(C \cap A)] = 3p$$

$$\Rightarrow P(A) + P(B) + P(C) - P(A \cap B) - P(B \cap C) - P(C \cap A) = \frac{3p}{2} \quad \text{...(iv)}$$

It also given that

$$P(A \cap B \cap C) = p^2 \quad \text{...(v)}$$

$\therefore$ P(at least one of the events A, B, and C occurs)

$$= P(A) + P(B) + P(C) - P(A \cap B) - P(B \cap C) - P(C \cap A) + P(A \cap B \cap C)$$

$$= \frac{3p}{2} + p^2 \quad \text{[from Eqs. (iv) and (v)]}$$

$$= \frac{3p + 2p^2}{2}$$

9. Let E_1 = Event that first ball drawn is red

E_2 = Event that first ball drawn is black

A = Event that second ball drawn is red

$$P(E_1) = \frac{4}{10}, P\left(\frac{A}{E_1}\right) = \frac{6}{12}$$

$$\Rightarrow \quad P(E_2) = \frac{6}{10}, P\left(\frac{A}{E_2}\right) = \frac{4}{12}$$

By law of total probability

$$P(A) = P(E_1) \times P\left(\frac{A}{E_1}\right) + P(E_2) \times P\left(\frac{A}{E_2}\right)$$

$$= \frac{4}{10} \times \frac{6}{12} + \frac{6}{10} \times \frac{4}{12} = \frac{24 + 24}{120} = \frac{48}{120} = \frac{2}{5}$$

10. We know that total number of ways of dividing n identical things among r persons $= {}^{n+r-1}C_{r-1}$

Total number of non-negative solutions of $x + y + z = 10$ are ${}^{12}C_2 = 66$

If z is even, then there can be following cases arise

$z = 0 \Rightarrow$ Number of ways of solving $x + y = 10 \Rightarrow {}^{11}C_1$

$z = 2 \Rightarrow$ Number of ways of solving $x + y = 8 \Rightarrow {}^{9}C_1$

$z = 4 \Rightarrow$ Number of ways of solving $x + y = 6 \Rightarrow {}^{7}C_1$

$z = 6 \Rightarrow$ Number of ways of solving $x + y = 4 \Rightarrow {}^{5}C_1$

$z = 8 \Rightarrow$ Number of ways of solving $x + y = 2 \Rightarrow {}^{3}C_1$

$z = 10 \Rightarrow$ Number of ways of solving $x + y = 0 \Rightarrow 1$

$\therefore$ Total ways when z is even $= 11 + 9 + 7 + 5 + 3 + 1 = 36$

$\therefore$ Required probability $= \frac{36}{66} = \frac{6}{11}$

11. Clearly, $E_1 = \{(4,1),(4,2),(4,3),(4,4),(4,5),(4,6)\}$

$E_2 = \{(1, 2),(2, 2),(3, 2),(4, 2),(5, 2),(6, 2)\}$

and $E_3 = \{(1, 2), (1, 4), (1, 6), (2, 1), (2, 3), (2, 5), (3, 2), (3, 4), (3, 6), (4, 1), (4, 3), (4, 5), (5, 2), (5, 4), (5, 6), (6, 1), (6, 3), (6, 5)\}$

$$\Rightarrow \quad P(E_1) = \frac{6}{36} = \frac{1}{6}, \ P(E_2) = \frac{6}{36} = \frac{1}{6} \text{ and } P(E_3) = \frac{18}{36} = \frac{1}{2}$$

Now, $P(E_1 \cap E_2) = P$ (getting 4 on die A and 2 on die B)

$$= \frac{1}{36} = P(E_1) \cdot P(E_2)$$

$P(E_2 \cap E_3) = P$ (getting 2 on die B and sum of numbers on both dice is odd)

$$= \frac{3}{36} = P(E_2) \cdot P(E_3)$$

$P(E_1 \cap E_3) = P$ (getting 4 on die A and sum of numbers on both dice is odd)

$$= \frac{3}{36} = P(E_1) \cdot P(E_3)$$

and $P(E_1 \cap E_2 \cap E_3) = P$ [getting 4 on die A, 2 on die B and sum of numbers is odd]

$$= P(\text{impossible event}) = 0$$

Hence, E_1, E_2 and E_3 are not independent.

12. Let $x = P$ (computer turns out to be defective, given that it is produced in plant T_2)

$$\Rightarrow \quad x = P\left(\frac{D}{T_2}\right) \quad \text{...(i)}$$

where, $D =$ Defective computer

$\therefore$ P (computer turns out to be defective given that is produced in plant T_1)

$$= 10x$$

$$\text{i.e.} \quad P\left(\frac{D}{T_1}\right) = 10x \quad \text{...(ii)}$$

Also, $\quad P(T_1) = \frac{20}{100}$ and $P(T_2) = \frac{80}{100}$

Given, P (defective computer) $= \frac{7}{100}$ i.e. $P(D) = \frac{7}{100}$

Using law of total probability,

$$P(D) = P(T_1) \cdot P\left(\frac{D}{T_1}\right) + P(T_2) \cdot P\left(\frac{D}{T_2}\right)$$

$$\therefore \quad \frac{7}{100} = \left(\frac{20}{100}\right) \cdot 10x + \left(\frac{80}{100}\right) \cdot x$$

$$\Rightarrow \quad 7 = (280)\,x \Rightarrow x = \frac{1}{40} \quad \text{...(iii)}$$

$$\therefore \quad P\left(\frac{D}{T_2}\right) = \frac{1}{40} \text{ and } P\left(\frac{D}{T_1}\right) = \frac{10}{40}$$

$$\Rightarrow \quad P\left(\frac{\overline{D}}{T_2}\right) = 1 - \frac{1}{40} = \frac{39}{40}$$

$$\text{and} \quad P\left(\frac{\overline{D}}{T_1}\right) = 1 - \frac{10}{40} = \frac{30}{40} \quad \text{...(iv)}$$

Using Baye's theorem,

$$P\left(\frac{T_2}{\overline{D}}\right) = \frac{P(T_2 \cap \overline{D})}{P(T_1 \cap \overline{D}) + P(T_2 \cap \overline{D})}$$

$$= \frac{P(T_2) \cdot P\left(\frac{\overline{D}}{T_2}\right)}{P(T_1) \cdot P\left(\frac{\overline{D}}{T_1}\right) + P(T_2) \cdot P\left(\frac{\overline{D}}{T_2}\right)}$$

$$= \frac{\frac{80}{100} \cdot \frac{39}{40}}{\frac{20}{100} \cdot \frac{30}{40} + \frac{80}{100} \cdot \frac{39}{40}} = \frac{78}{93}$$

13. Given, $P(\overline{A \cup B}) = \frac{1}{6}$, $P(A \cap B) = \frac{1}{4}$, $P(\overline{A}) = \frac{1}{4}$

$$\therefore \quad P(A \cup B) = 1 - P(\overline{A \cup B}) = 1 - \frac{1}{6} = \frac{5}{6}$$

$$\text{and} \quad P(A) = 1 - P(\overline{A}) = 1 - \frac{1}{4} = \frac{3}{4}$$

$$\therefore \quad P(A \cup B) = P(A) + P(B) - P(A \cap B)$$

$$\frac{5}{6} = \frac{3}{4} + P(B) - \frac{1}{4} \Rightarrow P(B) = \frac{1}{3}$$

$\Rightarrow$ A and B are not equally likely

$$P(A \cap B) = P(A) \cdot P(B) = \frac{1}{4}$$

So, events are independent.

14. From the tree diagram, it follows that

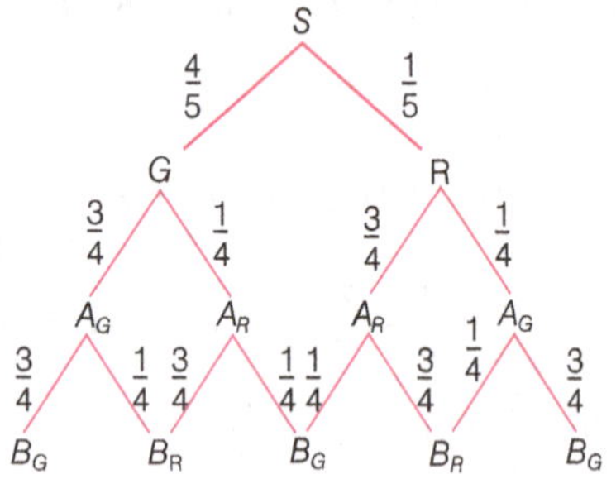

$$P(B_G) = \frac{46}{80}$$

$$P(B_G | G) = \frac{10}{16} = \frac{5}{8}$$

$$P(B_G \cap G) = \frac{5}{8} \times \frac{4}{5} = \frac{1}{2}$$

$$\therefore \quad P(G | B_G) = \frac{\frac{1}{2}}{P(B_G)} = \frac{1}{2} \times \frac{80}{46} = \frac{20}{23}$$

15. $$P\left(\frac{E^c \cap F^c}{G}\right) = \frac{P(E^c \cap F^c \cap G)}{P(G)}$$

$$= \frac{P(G) - P(E \cap G) - P(G \cap F)}{P(G)}$$

$$= \frac{P(G)[1 - P(E) - P(F)]}{P(G)} \quad [\because P(G) \neq 0]$$

$$= 1 - P(E) - P(F) = P(E^c) - P(F)$$

16. Let $E =$ event when each American man is seated adjacent to his wife

and $A =$ event when Indian man is seated adjacent to his wife

Now, $n(A \cap E) = (4!) \times (2!)^5$

Even when each American man is seated adjacent to his wife.

Again, $n(E) = (5!) \times (2!)^4$

$$\therefore \quad P\left(\frac{A}{E}\right) = \frac{n(A \cap E)}{n(E)} = \frac{(4!) \times (2!)^5}{(5!) \times (2!)^4} = \frac{2}{5}$$

Alternate Solution

Fixing four American couples and one Indian man in between any two couples, we have

5 different ways in which his wife can be seated, of which 2 cases are favourable.

$\therefore$ Required probability $= \frac{2}{5}$

17. E and F are independent events. Then,

$$P(E \cap F) = P(E) \cdot P(F) \quad \text{...(i)}$$

Option (a) is obviously not true. So, check for options (b), (c) and (d)

$$\begin{aligned} P(E \cap \bar{F}) &= P(E) - P(E \cap F) \\ &= P(E) - P(E) \cdot P(F) \quad \text{[from Eq. (i)]} \\ &= P(E)[1 - P(F)] \\ &= P(E) \cdot P(\bar{F}) \end{aligned}$$

$\therefore$ E and $\bar{F}$ are independent events.

Now, $$\begin{aligned} P(\bar{E} \cap \bar{F}) &= P(\overline{E \cup F}) \\ &= 1 - P(E \cup F) \\ &= 1 - [P(E) + P(F) - P(E \cap F)] \\ &= [1 - P(E)] - P(F) + P(E) \cdot P(F) \\ &= P(\bar{E}) - P(F)[1 - P(E)] \\ &= P(\bar{E})[1 - P(F)] = P(\bar{E}) \cdot P(\bar{F}) \end{aligned}$$

$\therefore$ $\bar{E}$ and $\bar{F}$ are independent events.

Again, $$P\left(\frac{E}{F}\right) + P\left(\frac{\bar{E}}{F}\right) = \frac{P(E \cap F)}{P(F)} + \frac{P(\bar{E} \cap F)}{P(F)}$$

$$= \frac{P(E) \cdot P(F)}{P(F)} + \frac{P(\bar{E}) \cdot P(F)}{P(F)}$$

$$= P(E) + P(\bar{E}) = 1$$

18. We know that $P(A \cap B) \geq P(A) + P(B) - 1$ ...(i)

$$P\left(\frac{A}{B}\right) = \frac{P(A \cap B)}{P(B)} \quad [P(B) \neq 0]$$

$$\Rightarrow \quad P\left(\frac{A}{B}\right) \geq \frac{P(A) + P(B) - 1}{P(B)} \quad \text{[from Eq. (i)]}$$

Option (a) is true.

$$P(A \cap \bar{B}) = P(A) - P(A \cap B)$$

Option (b) is not true.

$$P(A \cup B) = P(A) + P(B) - P(A \cap B)$$

If A and B are independent events, then $P(A \cap B) = P(A) \cdot P(B)$.

Then, $$\begin{aligned} P(A \cup B) &= P(A) + P(B) - P(A) \cdot P(B) \\ &= P(A) + P(B)[1 - P(A)] + 1 - 1 \\ &= 1 + P(B)\, P(\bar{A}) - P(\bar{A}) \quad [\because P(\bar{A}) = 1 - P(A)] \\ &= 1 + P(\bar{A})[P(B) - 1] = 1 - P(\bar{A}) \cdot P(\bar{B}) \end{aligned}$$

Option (c) is true.

If A and B are disjoint, then $P(A \cap B) = 0$.

Then, $P(A \cup B) = 1 - P(\bar{A})P(\bar{B})$ does not hold.

19. E and F are two independent events

$$P(E \cap F) = P(E) \cdot P(F) \quad \text{...(i)}$$

$$P(E \cap F) = \frac{1}{12} \quad \text{...(ii)}$$

$$P(\bar{E} \cap \bar{F}) = \frac{1}{2}$$

$$\Rightarrow \quad 1 - P(E \cup F) = \frac{1}{2}$$

$$\Rightarrow \quad P(E) + P(F) - P(E \cap F) = \frac{1}{2}$$

$$\Rightarrow \quad P(E) + P(F) - \frac{1}{12} = \frac{1}{2}$$

$$\Rightarrow \quad P(E) + P(F) = \frac{1}{2} + \frac{1}{12}$$

$$\Rightarrow \quad P(E) + P(F) = \frac{7}{12} \quad \text{...(iii)}$$

From Eqs. (i) and (ii), we get,

$$P(E) \cdot P(F) = \frac{1}{12} \Rightarrow P(E) = \frac{1}{12P(F)}$$

Put this value in Eq. (iii) we get

$$P(F) + \frac{1}{12P(F)} = \frac{7}{12}$$

Let $$P(F) = x$$

Then, $$x + \frac{1}{12x} = \frac{7}{12}$$

$$\Rightarrow \quad \frac{12x^2 + 1}{12x} = \frac{7}{12}$$

$$\Rightarrow \quad 12x^2 - 7x + 1 = 0$$

$$\Rightarrow \quad 12x^2 - 4x - 3x + 1 = 0$$

$$\Rightarrow \quad 4x(3x - 1) - 1(3x - 1) = 0$$

$$\Rightarrow \quad (3x - 1)(4x - 1) = 0$$

$$\Rightarrow \quad x = \frac{1}{3} \text{ or } \frac{1}{4}$$

$$\therefore \quad P(E) = \frac{1}{4}, P(F) = \frac{1}{3} \text{ or } P(E) = \frac{1}{3}, P(F) = \frac{1}{4}$$

20. Total number of subset of set contain n elements $= 2^n$

Number of ways choosing A and $B = 2^n \cdot 2^n = 2^{2n}$.

The number of subset of x which contains exactly r elements $= {}^nC_r$

$\therefore$ The number of ways of choosing A and B, so that they have the same number of elements

$$= ({}^nC_0)^2 + ({}^nC_1)^2 + \ldots + ({}^nC_n)^2 = {}^{2n}C_n$$

$$= \frac{1 \cdot 2 \cdot 3 \ldots (2n-1)(2n)}{n!\, n!} = \frac{2^n(1 \cdot 3 \cdot 5 \ldots (2n-1))}{n!}$$

$$\therefore \text{ Required probability} = \frac{{}^{2n}C_n}{2^{2n}} \text{ or } \frac{1 \cdot 3 \cdot 5 \ldots (2n-1)}{2^n(n!)}$$

21. According to the question,

$$(m + p + c) - mp - mc - pc + mpc = \frac{3}{4} \quad \text{...(i)}$$

$$mp(1 - c) + mc(1 - p) + pc(1 - m) = \frac{2}{5}$$

or $$mp + mc + pc - 3mpc = \frac{2}{5} \quad \text{...(ii)}$$

Also, $$mp + pc + mc - 2mpc = \frac{1}{2} \quad \text{...(iii)}$$

From Eqs. (ii) and (iii), we get

$$mpc = \frac{1}{2} - \frac{2}{5} = \frac{1}{10}$$

$$\therefore \quad mp + mc + pc = \frac{2}{5} + \frac{3}{10} = \frac{7}{10}$$

$$m + p + c = \frac{3}{4} + \frac{7}{10} - \frac{1}{10} = \frac{27}{20}$$

22. Favourable number of cases $= {}^{n-3}P_2$

Total number of cases $= {}^{n}P_2$

$$\therefore \text{ Required probability} = \frac{{}^{n-3}P_2}{{}^{n}P_2} = \frac{{}^{n-3}C_2 \times 2!}{{}^{n}C_2 \times 2!} = \frac{{}^{n-3}C_2}{{}^{n}C_2}$$

$$= \frac{\frac{(n-3)(n-4)}{2 \times 1}}{\frac{n(n-1)}{2 \times 1}} = \frac{(n-3)(n-4)}{n(n-1)}$$

23. $A =$ The event of (x, y) belonging to the area $OEBAO$

$B =$ The event of (x, y) belonging to the area $ODBCO$

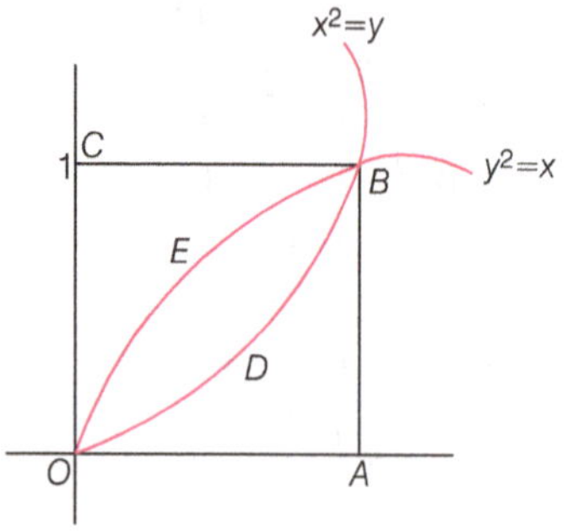

$$\therefore \quad P(A) = \frac{\text{area of } OEBAO}{\text{area of } OABCO} = \frac{\int_0^1 \sqrt{x}\, dx}{1 \times 1} = \frac{2}{3}$$

$$\text{and} \quad P(B) = \frac{\text{area of } ODBCO}{\text{area of } OABCO} = \frac{\int_0^1 \sqrt{y}\, dy}{1 \times 1} = \frac{2}{3}$$

$$\text{and } P(A \cap B) = \frac{\text{area of } ODBEO}{\text{area of } OABCO} = \frac{\int_0^1 \sqrt{x}\, dx - \int_0^1 x^2 dx}{1 \times 1} = \frac{1}{3}$$

$\therefore P(A) + P(B) = \frac{2}{3} + \frac{2}{3} \neq 1.$

So, A and B are not exhaustive,

$$P(A) \cdot P(B) = \frac{2}{3} \cdot \frac{2}{3} \neq \frac{1}{3}.$$

So, A and B are not independent

and $P(A \cup B) = 1$, $P(A) + P(B) \neq P(A \cup B)$.

So, A and B are not mutually exclusive.

24.

B_1	B_2	B_3
R-5	R-3	R-5
G-5	G-5	G-3

$\because P(B_1) = \frac{3}{10}, P(B_2) = \frac{3}{10}, P(B_3) = \frac{4}{10}$

$$P\left(\frac{G}{B_1}\right) = \frac{5}{10}, P\left(\frac{G}{B_2}\right) = \frac{5}{8}, P\left(\frac{G}{B_3}\right) = \frac{3}{8}$$

(a) $P(B_3 \cap G) = P(B_3) P\left(\frac{G}{B_3}\right) = \frac{4}{10} \times \frac{3}{8} = \frac{3}{20}$

$\therefore$ Option (a) is not true.

(b) $P\left(\frac{G}{B_3}\right) = \frac{3}{8}$

$\therefore$ Option (b) is true.

(c) $\because P\left(\frac{B_3}{G}\right) = \frac{P(G/B_3)P(B_3)}{P(B/B_1)P(B_1) + P(G/B_2) + P(G/B_3)P(B_3)}$

$$= \frac{\frac{3}{8} \times \frac{4}{10}}{\frac{5}{10} \times \frac{3}{10} + \frac{5}{8} \times \frac{3}{10} + \frac{3}{8} \times \frac{4}{10}}$$

$$= \frac{\frac{12}{80}}{\frac{15}{100} + \frac{15}{80} + \frac{12}{80}}$$

$$= \frac{12}{80} \times \frac{400}{60 + 75 + 60}$$

$$= \frac{60}{195} = \frac{4}{13}$$

$\therefore$ Option (c) is not true.

(d) $P(G) = P\left(\frac{G}{B_1}\right) P(B_1) + P\left(\frac{G}{B_2}\right)$

$$P(B_2) + P\left(\frac{G}{B_3}\right) P(B_3) = \frac{5}{10} \times \frac{3}{10} + \frac{5}{8} \times \frac{3}{10} + \frac{3}{8} \times \frac{4}{10}$$

$$= \frac{60 + 75 + 60}{400} = \frac{195}{400} = \frac{39}{80}$$

$\therefore$ Option (d) is true.

25. (a) $P(E/F) + P(\bar{E}/F) = \frac{P(E \cap F)}{P(F)} + \frac{P(\bar{E} \cap F)}{P(F)}$

$$= \frac{P(E \cap F) + P(\bar{E} \cap F)}{P(F)}$$

$$= \frac{P(F)}{P(F)} = 1$$

Therefore, option (a) is correct.

(b) $P(E/F) + P(E/\bar{F}) = \frac{P(E \cap F)}{P(F)} + \frac{P(E \cap \bar{F})}{P(\bar{F})}$

$$= \frac{P(E \cap F)}{P(F)} + \frac{P(E \cap \bar{F})}{1 - P(F)} \neq 1$$

Therefore, option (b) is not correct.

(c) $P(\bar{E}/F) + P(E/\bar{F}) = \frac{P(\bar{E} \cap F)}{P(F)} + \frac{P(E \cap \bar{F})}{P(\bar{F})}$

$$= \frac{P(\bar{E} \cap F)}{P(F)} + \frac{P(E \cap \bar{F})}{1 - P(F)} \neq 1$$

Therefore, option (c) is not correct.

(d) $P(E/\bar{F}) + P(\bar{E}/\bar{F}) = \frac{P(E \cap \bar{F})}{P(\bar{F})} + \frac{P(\bar{E} \cap \bar{F})}{P(\bar{F})}$

$$= \frac{P(E \cap \bar{F}) + P(\bar{E} \cap \bar{F})}{P(\bar{F})}$$

$$= \frac{P(\bar{F})}{P(\bar{F})} = 1$$

Therefore, option (d) is correct.

Sol. (26 and 27)

26. Roots of $x^2 + px + q = 0$ are real and distinct, if $p^2 > 4q$.

Value of p	Possible values of q
1	No value
2	No value
3	1, 2
4	1, 2, 3
5	1, 2, 3, 4, 5, 6
6	1, 2, 3,..., 8
7	1, 2, 3,..., 10
8	1, 2, 3,..., 10
9	1, 2, 3,..., 10
10	1, 2, 3,..., 10

∴ Number of favourable ways

$$= 2 + 3 + 6 + 8 + 10 + 10 + 10 + 10 = 59$$

and total ways $= 10 \times 10 = 100$

Hence, the required probability $= \frac{59}{100} = 0.59$

27. Roots of $x^2 + px + q = 0$ are equal, if $p^2 = 4q$

i.e. p^2 must be even.

Value of p	Possible values of q
2	1
4	4
6	9
8	No value
10	No value

∴ Number of favourable ways $= 1 + 1 + 1 = 3$

and total ways $= 10 \times 10 = 100$

Hence, the required probability $= \frac{3}{100} = 0.03$

Sol. (28 and 29)

28. The number of cubes having atleast one side painted is

$9 + 9 + 3 + 3 + 1 + 1 = 26$ and total cubes $= 27$

∴ Required probability, $P_1 = \frac{26}{27} \Rightarrow 27P_1 = 26$

29. The number of cubes having two sides painted is

$4 + 4 + 1 + 1 + 1 + 1 = 12$ and total cubes $= 27$

∴ Required probability, $P_2 = \frac{12}{27} \Rightarrow 27P_2 = 12$

Sol. (30 and 31)

30. A : She gets a success

E_1 : She studies 10 h

∴ $P(E_1) = 0.1$

E_2 : She studies 7 h

∴ $P(E_2) = 0.2$

and E_3 : She studies 4 h

∴ $P(E_3) = 0.7$

and $P\left(\frac{A}{E_1}\right) = 0.80$, $P\left(\frac{A}{E_2}\right) = 0.60$ and $P\left(\frac{A}{E_3}\right) = 0.40$

$$\therefore \quad P(A) = P(E_1) \cdot P\left(\frac{A}{E_1}\right) + P(E_2) \cdot P\left(\frac{A}{E_2}\right) + P(E_3) \cdot P\left(\frac{A}{E_3}\right)$$

$$= 0.1 \times 0.80 + 0.2 \times 0.60 + 0.7 \times 0.40 = 0.48$$

31. $$P\left(\frac{E_3}{A}\right) = \frac{P(E_3 \cap A)}{P(A)} = \frac{P(E_3) \cdot P\left(\frac{A}{E_3}\right)}{P(A)} = \frac{0.7 \times 0.40}{0.48} = \frac{7}{12}$$

Sol. (32 and 33)

32. Here, $P(X > Y) = P(T_1 \text{win})\, P(T_1 \text{ win}) + P(T_1 \text{ win})\, P(\text{draw}) + P(\text{draw})\, P(T_1 \text{ win})$

$$= \left(\frac{1}{2} \times \frac{1}{2}\right) + \left(\frac{1}{2} \times \frac{1}{6}\right) + \left(\frac{1}{6} \times \frac{1}{2}\right) = \frac{5}{12}$$

33. $P[X = Y] = P(\text{draw}) \cdot P(\text{draw}) + P(T_1 \text{ win})\, P(T_2 \text{ win}) + P(T_2 \text{ win}) \cdot P(T_1 \text{ win})$

$$= \left(\frac{1}{6} \times \frac{1}{6}\right) + \left(\frac{1}{2} \times \frac{1}{3}\right) + \left(\frac{1}{3} \times \frac{1}{2}\right) = \frac{13}{36}$$

Sol. (34 and 35)

Given, $P\left(\frac{B}{A}\right) = \frac{2}{5}$, $P\left(\frac{A}{B}\right) = \frac{1}{7}$ and $P(A \cap B) = 1/9$

$$\therefore \quad P\left(\frac{B}{A}\right) = \frac{P(B \cap A)}{P(A)}$$

$$\Rightarrow \quad P(A) = \frac{P(B \cap A)}{P\left(\frac{B}{A}\right)} = \frac{1/9}{2/5} = \frac{5}{18}$$

Similarly, $P(B) = \frac{P(B \cap A)}{P\left(\frac{A}{B}\right)} = \frac{1/9}{1/7} = \frac{7}{9}$

34. $P(A' \cup B) = 1 - P(A - B)$

$$= 1 - P(A) + P(A \cap B)$$

$$= 1 - \frac{5}{18} + \frac{1}{9} = \frac{18 - 5 + 2}{18} = \frac{15}{18} = \frac{5}{6}$$

35. $P(A' \cap B') = P(A \cup B)'$

$$= 1 - P(A \cup B)$$

$$= 1 - P(A) - P(B) + P(A \cap B)$$

$$= 1 - \frac{5}{18} - \frac{7}{9} + \frac{1}{9} = \frac{18 - 5 - 14 + 2}{18} = \frac{1}{18}$$

Sol. (36 and 37)

36. As, $x_1 + x_2 + x_3$ is odd.

So, all may be odd or one of them is odd and other two are even.

∴ Required probability

$$= \frac{{}^2C_1 \times {}^3C_1 \times {}^4C_1 + {}^1C_1 \times {}^2C_1 \times {}^4C_1 + {}^2C_1 \times {}^2C_1 \times {}^3C_1 + {}^1C_1 \times {}^3C_1 \times {}^3C_1}{{}^3C_1 \times {}^5C_1 \times {}^7C_1}$$

$$= \frac{24 + 8 + 12 + 9}{105} = \frac{53}{105}$$

37. Since, x_1, x_2, x_3 are in AP.

$\therefore \quad x_1 + x_3 = 2x_2$

So, $x_1 + x_3$ should be even number.

Either both x_1 and x_3 are odd or both are even.

$\therefore$ Required probability $= \dfrac{{}^2C_1 \times {}^4C_1 + {}^1C_1 \times {}^3C_1}{{}^3C_1 \times {}^5C_1 \times {}^7C_1} = \dfrac{11}{105}$

38. $\dfrac{7}{12} = \dfrac{1}{(n+1)} \cdot 1 + \dfrac{n}{(n+1)} \cdot \dfrac{1}{2}$

$\Rightarrow \dfrac{7}{6} = \dfrac{(n+2)}{(n+1)} \Rightarrow n = 5$

39. Let S be the sample space, then

$n(S) =$ Total number of determinants that can be made with 0 and $1 = 2 \times 2 \times 2 \times 2 = 16$

$\because \begin{vmatrix} a & b \\ c & d \end{vmatrix}$, each element can be replaced by two types i.e., 0 and 1

and let E be the event that the determinant made is non-negative.

Also, E' be the event that the determinant is negative.

$\therefore \quad E' = \left\{ \begin{vmatrix} 1 & 1 \\ 1 & 0 \end{vmatrix}, \begin{vmatrix} 0 & 1 \\ 1 & 1 \end{vmatrix}, \begin{vmatrix} 0 & 1 \\ 1 & 0 \end{vmatrix} \right\}$

$\therefore \quad P(E') = 3$

then $P(E') = \dfrac{n(E')}{n(S)} = \dfrac{3}{16}$

Hence, the required probability,

$P(E) = 1 - P(E')$

$= 1 - \dfrac{3}{16} = \dfrac{13}{16} = \dfrac{m}{n}$ [given]

$\Rightarrow \quad m = 13$ and $n = 16$, then $n - m = 3$

40. Let E_1, E_2 and E_3 be the events that first, second and third student get success. Then,

$$P(E_1) = \frac{1}{3}, P(E_2) = \frac{1}{4} \text{ and } P(E_3) = \frac{1}{5}$$

Given, probability of success of atleast two $= \dfrac{\lambda}{12}$

$\Rightarrow P(E_1 \cap E_2 \cap \bar{E}_3) + P(\bar{E}_1 \cap E_2 \cap E_3)$
$+ P(E_1 \cap \bar{E}_2 \cap E_3) + P(E_1 \cap E_2 \cap E_3) = \dfrac{\lambda}{12}$

$\Rightarrow P(E_1) \cdot P(E_2) \cdot P(\bar{E}_3) + P(\bar{E}_1) \cdot P(E_2) \cdot P(E_3)$
$+ P(E_1) \cdot P(\bar{E}_2) \cdot P(E_3) + P(E_1) \cdot P(E_2) \cdot P(E_3) = \dfrac{\lambda}{12}$

$\Rightarrow \dfrac{1}{3} \cdot \dfrac{1}{4} \cdot \dfrac{4}{5} + \dfrac{2}{3} \cdot \dfrac{1}{4} \cdot \dfrac{1}{5} + \dfrac{1}{3} \cdot \dfrac{3}{4} \cdot \dfrac{1}{5} + \dfrac{1}{3} \cdot \dfrac{1}{4} \cdot \dfrac{1}{5} = \dfrac{\lambda}{12} \Rightarrow \dfrac{10}{60} = \dfrac{\lambda}{12}$

$\therefore \quad \lambda = 2$

41. Let S be the sample space and E be the event of getting a large number than the previous number.

$\therefore \quad n(S) = 6 \times 6 \times 6 = 216$

Now, we count the number of favourable ways. Obviously, the second number has to be greater than 1. If the second number is $i (i > 1)$, then the number of favourable ways $= (i-1) \times (6-i)$

$\therefore \quad n(E) =$ Total number of favourable ways

$= \sum_{i=1}^{6} (i-1) \times (6-i)$

$= 0 + 1 \times 4 + 2 \times 3 + 3 \times 2 + 4 \times 1 + 5 \times 0$

$= 4 + 6 + 6 + 4 = 20$

Therefore, the required probability,

$P(E) = \dfrac{n(E)}{n(S)} = \dfrac{20}{216}$

$= \dfrac{5}{54} = p$ [given]

$\therefore \quad 54p = 5$

42. The number of ways to answer a question $= 2^5 - 1 = 31$.

i.e., In 31 ways only one correct.

Let number of choices $= n$

Now, according to the question,

$$\frac{n}{31} > \frac{1}{8}$$

$\Rightarrow \quad n > \dfrac{31}{8} \Rightarrow n > 3.8$

$\therefore$ Least value of $n = 4$

43. Let E_i denote the event that the ith object goes to the ith place, we have

$$P(E_i \cap E_j \cap E_k) = \frac{(n-3)!}{n!} \text{ for } i < j < k$$

Since, we can choose 3 places out of n is ${}^nC_3$ ways, the probability of the required event is

$$p = {}^nC_3 \cdot \frac{(n-3)!}{n!} = \frac{n!}{3!(n-3)!} \cdot \frac{(n-3)!}{n!} = \frac{1}{6}$$

$\therefore \quad 6p = 1$

44. The sample space is

$S = \{-0.50, -0.49, -0.48, \ldots, -0.01, 0.00, 0.01, \ldots, 0.49\}$

Let E be the event that the round off error is atleast 10 paise, then E' is the event that the round off error is atmost a paise.

$\therefore \quad E' = \{-0.09, -0.08, \ldots, -0.01, 0.00, 0.01, \ldots, 0.09\}$

$\therefore \quad n(E') = 19$ and $n(S) = 100$

$\therefore \quad P(E') = \dfrac{n(E')}{n(S)} = \dfrac{19}{100}$

$\therefore$ Required probability, $P(E) = 1 - P(E') = 1 - \dfrac{19}{100}$

$= \dfrac{81}{100} = \left(\dfrac{m}{n}\right)^2$

$\therefore \quad m = 9$ and $n = 10$

$\Rightarrow \quad n - m = 1$

45. Let E_1, E_2, E_3, E_4, E_5 and E_6 be the events of occurrence of 1, 2, 3, 4, 5 and 6 on the dice respectively and let E be the event of getting a sum of numbers equal to 9.

$\therefore \quad P(E_1) = \dfrac{1-k}{6}; P(E_2) = \dfrac{1+2k}{6}; P(E_3) = \dfrac{1-k}{6};$

$P(E_4) = \dfrac{1+k}{6}; P(E_5) = \dfrac{1-2k}{6}; P(E_6) = \dfrac{1+k}{6}$

and $\dfrac{1}{9} \le P(E) \le \dfrac{2}{9}$

Then, $E \equiv \{(3,6),(6,3),(4,5),(5,4)\}$

Hence, $P(E) = P(E_3E_6) + P(E_6E_3) + P(E_4E_5) + P(E_5E_4)$

$$= P(E_3)P(E_6) + P(E_6)P(E_3) + P(E_4)P(E_5) + P(E_5)P(E_4)$$

$$= 2P(E_3)P(E_6) + 2P(E_4)P(E_5)$$

[since E_1, E_2, E_3, E_4, E_5 and E_6 are independent]

$$= 2\left(\frac{1-k}{6}\right)\left(\frac{1+k}{6}\right) + 2\left(\frac{1+k}{6}\right)\left(\frac{1-2k}{6}\right)$$

$$= \frac{1}{18}[2 - k - 3k^2]$$

Since, $\frac{1}{9} \le P(E) \le \frac{2}{9}$

$\Rightarrow \quad \frac{1}{9} \le \frac{1}{18}[2-k-3k^2] \le \frac{2}{9}$

$\Rightarrow \quad 2 \le 2 - k - 3k^2 \le 4$

$\Rightarrow \quad 2 \le 2 - k - 3k^2$ and $2 - k - 3k^2 \le 4$

$\Rightarrow \quad 3k\left(k + \frac{1}{3}\right) \le 0$ and $3k^2 + k + 2 \ge 0$

$\Rightarrow \quad -\frac{1}{3} \le k \le 0$ and $k \in R$

$\therefore \quad -\frac{1}{3} \le k \le 0$

Hence, integral value of k is 0.

46. Let $a_1, a_2, a_3, a_4, a_5, a_6$ and a_7 be the seven digits and the remaining two be a_8 and a_9.

Let $a_1 + a_2 + a_3 + a_4 + a_5 + a_6 + a_7 = 9k, k \in I$ ...(i)

Also, $a_1 + a_2 + a_3 + a_4 + \dots + a_9 = 1 + 2 + 3 + 4 + \dots + 9$

$$= \frac{9 \times 10}{2} = 45 \quad \text{...(ii)}$$

On subtracting Eq. (i) from Eq. (ii), we get

$$a_8 + a_9 = 45 - 9k \quad \text{...(iii)}$$

Since, $a_1 + a_2 + a_3 + a_4 + \dots + a_9$ and $a_1 + a_2 + \dots + a_7$ are divisible by 9, if and only if $a_8 + a_9$ is divisible by 9. Let S be the sample space and E be the event that the sum of the digits a_8 and a_9 is divisible by 9.

$\because \quad a_8 + a_9 = 45 - 9k$

Maximum value of $a_8 + a_9 = 17$ and minimum value of

$a_8 + a_9 = 3$

$\therefore \quad 3 \le 45 - 9k \le 17$

$\Rightarrow \quad -42 \le -9k \le -28 \Rightarrow \frac{42}{9} \le k \ge \frac{28}{9}$ or $\frac{28}{9} \le k \ge \frac{42}{9}$

Hence, $k = 4$ [$\because$ k is positive integer]

$\therefore$ From Eq. (iii), we get

$$a_8 + a_9 = 45 - 9 \times 4$$

$\therefore \quad a_8 + a_9 = 9$

Now, possible pair of (a_8, a_9) can be $\{(1,8),(2,7),(3,6),(4,5)\}$

$\therefore \quad E = \{(1,8),(2,7),(3,6),(4,5)\}$

$n(E) = 4$ and $n(S) = {}^9C_2 = 36$

$\therefore$ Required probability, $P(E) = \frac{n(E)}{n(S)} = \frac{4}{36} = \frac{1}{9} = p$ [given]

$\therefore \quad 18p = 2$

47. Let A be the event of P_1 winning in third round and B be the event of P_2 winning in first round but loosing in second round.

We have, $P(A) = \frac{1}{{}^8C_1} = \frac{1}{8}$

$P(B \cap A)$ = Probability of both P_1 and P_2 winning in first round $\times$ Probability of P_1 winning and P_2 loosing in second round $\times$ Probability of P_1 winning in third round

$$= \frac{{}^{8-2}C_{4-2}}{{}^8C_4} \times \frac{{}^{4-2}C_{2-1}}{{}^4C_2} \times \frac{{}^{2-1}C_{1-1}}{{}^2C_1}$$

$$= \frac{{}^6C_2}{{}^8C_4} \times \frac{{}^2C_1}{{}^4C_2} \times \frac{{}^1C_0}{{}^2C_1} = \frac{1}{28}$$

Hence, $P\left(\frac{B}{A}\right) = \frac{P(B \cap A)}{P(A)} = \frac{\frac{1}{28}}{\frac{1}{8}} = \frac{2}{7} = p$ [given]

$\therefore \quad 7p = 2$

48. We have mentioned that boxes are different and one particular box has 3 balls.

Then, number of ways $= \frac{{}^{12}C_3 \times 2^9}{3^{12}} = \frac{55}{3}\left(\frac{2}{3}\right)^{11} = 55\left(\frac{2^{11}}{3^{12}}\right)$

$\therefore \quad Q = 55$

49. Total number of ways to arrange 'ASSASSIN' is $\frac{8!}{4! \cdot 2!}$.

First we fix the position ⊗A⊗A⊗I⊗N⊗.

Number of ways in which no two S's occur together

$$= \frac{4!}{2!} \times {}^5C_4$$

$\therefore$ Required probability $= \frac{4! \times 5 \times 4! \times 2!}{2! \times 8!} = \frac{1}{14}$

Here, $P = \frac{1}{14}$

$\therefore 8750P = 8750 \times \frac{1}{14} = 625$

50. Since, $\frac{1+3p}{3}, \frac{1-p}{4}$ and $\frac{1-2p}{2}$ are the probability of mutually exclusive events.

$\therefore \quad \frac{1+3p}{3} + \frac{1-p}{4} + \frac{1-2p}{2} \le 1$

$\Rightarrow \quad 4 + 12p + 3 - 3p + 6 - 12p \le 12$

$\Rightarrow \quad 13 - 3p \le 12$

$\Rightarrow \quad p \ge \frac{1}{3}$ ...(i)

and $\quad 0 \le \frac{1+3p}{3} \le 1, 0 \le \frac{1-p}{4} \le 1, 0 \le \frac{1-2p}{2} \le 1$

$\Rightarrow \quad 0 \le 1 + 3p \le 3, \ 0 \le 1 - p \le 4, \ 0 \le 1 - 2p \le 2$

$\Rightarrow \quad -\frac{1}{3} \le p \le \frac{2}{3}, 1 \ge p \ge -3, \frac{1}{2} \ge p \ge -\frac{1}{2}$ ...(ii)

From Eqs. (i) and (ii),

$$\frac{1}{3} \le p \le \frac{1}{2}$$

Here, $a = \frac{1}{3}, b = \frac{1}{2}$

$\therefore \quad 69a + 64b = \frac{69}{3} + \frac{64}{2} = 23 + 32 = 55$

51. Let X be the number of coins showing heads. Let X be a binomial variate with parameters $n = 100$ and p.

Since, $P(X = 50) = P(X = 51)$

$\Rightarrow \quad {}^{100}C_{50}p^{50}(1-p)^{50} = {}^{100}C_{51}(p)^{51}(1-p)^{49}$

$\Rightarrow \quad \frac{(100)!}{(50!)(50!)} \cdot \frac{(51!) \times (49!)}{100!} = \frac{p}{1-p}$

$\Rightarrow \quad \frac{p}{1-p} = \frac{51}{50}$

$\Rightarrow \quad p = \frac{51}{101}$

Now, $\left(\frac{405}{5}\right)P = \frac{405}{5} \times \frac{51}{101} = 51$

52. **(A)** $P(\bar{A}) = 0.3 \Rightarrow P(A) = 1 - P(\bar{A}) = 0.7, P(B) = 0.4,$

$\Rightarrow \quad 0.5 = 0.7 - P(AB)$

$\therefore \quad P(AB) = 0.2$

$\Rightarrow P\left[\frac{B}{(A \cup \bar{B})}\right] = \frac{P[B \cap (A \cup \bar{B})]}{P(A \cup \bar{B})} = \frac{P(A \cap B)}{P(A) + P(\bar{B}) - P(A\bar{B})}$

$= \frac{0.2}{0.7 + 0.6 - 0.5} = \frac{1}{4} = \lambda_1$ [given]

$\therefore \quad \frac{1}{\lambda_1} = 4$ [composite number and natural number]

(B) First three prime numbers are 2, 3 and 5.

For roots to be real $D \ge 0$

Thus, real roots are obtained by $b = 5, a = 2, c = 3$

and $b = 5, a = 3, c = 2$

i.e. two ways.

Total ways of choosing $a, b, c = 3 \times 2 \times 1 = 6$

$\therefore$ Required probability $= \frac{2}{6} = \frac{1}{3} = \lambda_2$ [given]

$\therefore \quad \frac{1}{\lambda_2} = 3$

[prime number and natural number]

(C) Here, tossing of the coin is an independent event. Thus, the result of 5th trial is independent of outcome of previous trials.

$\therefore \quad \lambda_3 = \frac{1}{2} \Rightarrow \frac{1}{\lambda_3} = 2$

[prime number and natural number]

(D) Clearly, $n(S) = {}^9P_9 = 9!$

Now, 3 positions out of 9 positions can be chosen in ${}^9C_3$ ways and at these positions A, B and C can speak in required order, further remaining 6 persons can speak in 6! ways.

$\therefore$ Required probability $= \frac{{}^9C_3 \times 6!}{9!}$

$= \frac{9! \times 6!}{3! \times 6! \times 9!} = \frac{1}{6} = \lambda_4$ [given]

$\therefore \quad \frac{1}{\lambda_4} = 6$

[a composite number, a natural number and a perfect number]

53. **(A)** $\frac{3}{5} \ge P(A \cap B) \ge P(A) + P(B) - 1 = \frac{3}{5} + \frac{2}{3} - 1 = \frac{4}{15}$

$\therefore \quad \frac{3}{5} \ge P(A \cap B) \ge \frac{4}{15} \Rightarrow P(A \cap B) \in \left[\frac{4}{15}, \frac{3}{5}\right]$

(B) $\because P(A \cup B) = P(A) + P(B) - P(A \cap B)$

$= \frac{3}{5} + \frac{2}{3} - P(A \cap B) = \frac{19}{15} - P(A \cap B)$

$\Rightarrow \quad \frac{2}{3} \le P(A \cup B) \le 1 \quad \left[\because P(A \cap B) \in \left[\frac{4}{15}, \frac{3}{5}\right]\right]$

$\therefore \quad P(A \cup B) \in \left[\frac{2}{3}, 1\right]$

(C) $P\left(\frac{A}{B}\right) = \frac{P(A \cap B)}{P(B)} = \frac{3}{2}P(A \cap B)$

$\Rightarrow \quad \frac{2}{5} \le P\left(\frac{A}{B}\right) \le \frac{9}{10} \quad \left[\because P(A \cap B) \in \left[\frac{4}{15}, \frac{3}{5}\right]\right]$

$\therefore \quad P\left(\frac{A}{B}\right) \in \left[\frac{2}{5}, \frac{9}{10}\right]$

(D) $P\left(\frac{B}{A}\right) = \frac{P(B \cap A)}{P(A)} = \frac{5}{3}P(A \cap B)$

$\Rightarrow \quad \frac{4}{9} \le P\left(\frac{B}{A}\right) \le 1 \quad \left[\because P(A \cap B) \in \left[\frac{4}{15}, \frac{3}{5}\right]\right]$

$\therefore \quad P\left(\frac{B}{A}\right) \in \left[\frac{4}{9}, 1\right]$

54. Let $q_1 = 1 - p_1$ and $q_2 = 1 - p_2$

(A) $\because$ A can win the game at the 1st, 4th, 7th,... trials.

$\therefore P(A \text{ wins}) = \frac{1}{6} + \frac{5}{6}(q_1)(q_2)\left(\frac{1}{6}\right) + \left(\frac{5}{6}\right)^2(q_1)^2(q_2)^2\left(\frac{1}{6}\right) + \dots$

$= \frac{\frac{1}{6}}{1 - \frac{5}{6}q_1q_2} = \frac{1}{6 - 5q_1q_2} = \frac{1}{6 - 5\left(\frac{4}{5}\right)\left(\frac{3}{4}\right)} = \frac{1}{\lambda_1}$ [given]

$\therefore \quad \lambda_1 = 3$

(B) $P(C \text{ wins}) = \frac{5}{6} \cdot q_1 \cdot p_2 + \left(\frac{5}{6}\right)^2 \cdot q_1^2 \cdot q_2 p_2 + \dots$

$= \frac{\frac{5}{6}q_1 \cdot p_2}{1 - \frac{5}{6}q_1q_2} = \frac{5q_1p_2}{6 - 5q_1q_2} = \frac{5 \times \frac{4}{5} \times \frac{1}{4}}{6 - 5 \times \frac{4}{5} \times \frac{3}{4}} = \frac{1}{3}$

$= \frac{1}{\lambda_2}$ [given]

$\therefore \quad \lambda_2 = 3$

(C) $\because$ $P(A \text{ wins}) = P(B \text{ wins})$

$$\Rightarrow \frac{1}{6-5q_1q_2} = \frac{5p_1}{6-5q_1q_2}$$

$$\therefore \quad p_1 = \frac{1}{5} = \frac{1}{\lambda_3} \quad \text{[given]}$$

$$\therefore \quad \lambda_3 = 5$$

(D) $P(A \text{ wins}) = P(B \text{ wins}) = P(C \text{ wins})$

$$\Rightarrow \frac{1}{6-5q_1q_2} = \frac{5p_1}{6-5q_1q_2} = \frac{5q_1p_2}{6-5q_1q_2}$$

$$\Rightarrow 1 = 5p_1 = 5q_1p_2$$

$$\Rightarrow p_1 = \frac{1}{5}, \frac{1}{p_2} = 5q_1 = 5\left(1-\frac{1}{5}\right) = 4 = \lambda_4 \quad \text{[given]}$$

$$\therefore \quad \lambda_4 = 4$$

55. Given inequations are $\frac{x^2}{8} + \frac{y^2}{20} < 1$ and $y^2 < 5x$.

Now, solving its corresponding equation i.e. on solving $\frac{x^2}{8} + \frac{y^2}{20} = 1$ and $y^2 = 5x$, we get

$$\frac{x^2}{8} + \frac{5x}{20} = 1 \Rightarrow \frac{x^2}{8} + \frac{x}{4} = 1 \Rightarrow x^2 + 2x = 8$$

$$\Rightarrow x^2 + 2x - 8 = 0$$

$$\Rightarrow (x-2)(x+4) = 0 \Rightarrow x = 2, -4$$

Here, $x = -4$ (rejected) because area bounded by these curves lies in positive direction of X-axis.

So, $x = 2$ only acceptable.

$\therefore$ Corresponding y values are $\pm\sqrt{10}$.

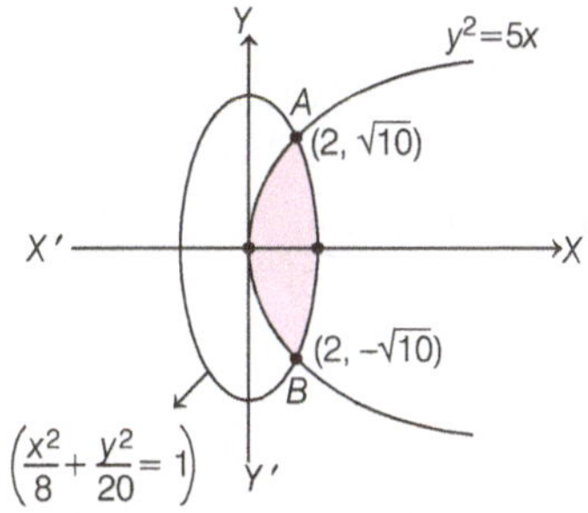

Let $A \equiv (2, \sqrt{10})$ and $B \equiv (2, -\sqrt{10})$, $\frac{x^2}{8} + \frac{y^2}{20} = 1$

The points inside region are

{(1, 1), (1, 0), (1, – 1), (1, 2), (1, – 2), (2, 1), (2, – 1), (2, 3), (2, – 3), (2, – 2), (2, 2), (2, 0)}

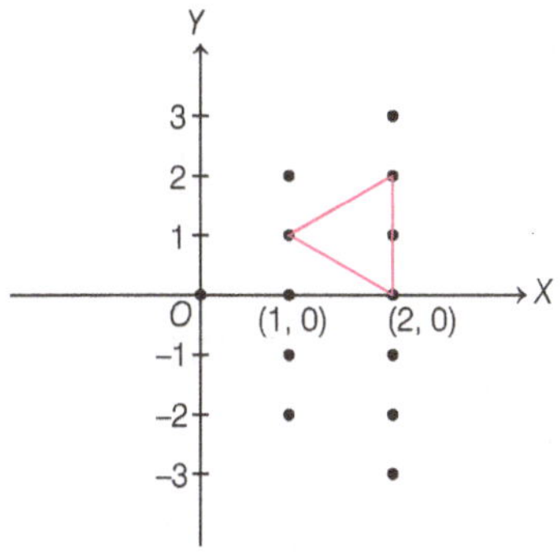

Total number of ways to select three points

$$= {}^{12}C_3 = \frac{12!}{3!\,9!} = \frac{12 \times 11 \times 10 \times 9!}{3 \times 2 \times 9!} = 220 = n(S),$$

where S = sample space

Now, selecting 3 points on which

2 points are either $x = 1$ or $x = 2$ but distance between them is even.

Case I Triangles with base length = 2

$$n(E) = 3 \times 7 + 5 \times 5 = 46,$$

where E = favourable event

Case II Triangle with base length = 4

$$n(E) = 1 \times 7 + 3 \times 5 = 22$$

Case III Triangles with base length = 6

$$n(E) = 1 \times 5 = 5$$

Hence, $P(E) = \frac{n(E)}{n(S)} = \frac{46 + 22 + 5}{220} = \frac{73}{220}$

56. Given, $P(H) = \frac{1}{3}$

$$\therefore \quad P(T) = \frac{2}{3}$$

According to question, possible cases are

HH	or	*THH*
HTHH		*THTHH*
HTHTHH		*THTHTHH*
HTHTHTHH		*THTHTHTHH*
⋮		⋮
and so on		and so on

Hence, required probability

$P(HH$ or $HTHH$ or $HTHTHH$ or $HTHTHTHH$ ...)

+ P (THH or $THTHH$ or $THTHTHH$ or $THTHTHTHH$ ...)

$$= \frac{\frac{1}{3} \times \frac{1}{3}}{1 - \frac{2}{3} \times \frac{1}{3}} + \frac{\frac{2}{3} \times \frac{1}{3} \times \frac{1}{3}}{1 - \frac{2}{3} \times \frac{1}{3}}$$

[there is two sum of infinite GP's, so using $S_\infty = \frac{a}{1-r}$]

$$= \frac{\frac{1}{9}}{\frac{7}{9}} + \frac{\frac{2}{27}}{\frac{7}{9}} = \frac{1}{7} + \frac{2}{21} = \frac{3+2}{21} = \frac{5}{21}$$

57. Since, $P(X_i > Y_i) + P(X_i < Y_i) + P(X_i = Y_i) = 1$

and $\quad P(X_i > Y_i) = P(X_i < Y_i) = P$

For $i = 2$,

$$P(X_2 = Y_2) = 2P(x > y) \cdot P(x < y) + (P(x = y))^2$$

$$= 2 \cdot \frac{{}^6C_2}{{}^{36}C_1} \times \frac{{}^6C_2}{{}^{36}C_1} + \left(\frac{{}^6C_1}{{}^{36}C_1}\right)^2$$

$$= \frac{25}{72} + \frac{1}{36} = \frac{27}{72} = \frac{3}{8}$$

and $P(X_2 > Y_2) = \frac{1}{2}\left(1 - \frac{3}{8}\right) = \frac{5}{16}$

$\therefore \quad P(X_2 \geq Y_2) = \frac{5}{16} + \frac{3}{8} = \frac{11}{16}$

$\therefore$ (I) $\to$ (Q),

(II) $\to$ (R)

For $i = 3$,

$P(X_3 = Y_3) = 6P(x > y) \cdot P(x < y)\, P(x = y) + [P(x = y)]^3$

$$= 6 \cdot \frac{^6C_2}{36} \cdot \frac{^6C_2}{36} \cdot \frac{^6C_1}{36} + \left(\frac{^6C_1}{36}\right)^2$$

$$= 6 \cdot \frac{15}{36} \cdot \frac{15}{36} \cdot \frac{15}{36} + \frac{225}{1296} = \frac{231}{1296} = \frac{77}{432}$$

$\therefore$ (III) $\to$ T

and $P(X_3 > Y_3) = \frac{1}{2}\left(1 - \frac{77}{432}\right)$

$$= \frac{1}{2} \cdot \left(\frac{432 - 77}{432}\right) = \frac{355}{864}$$

$\therefore$ (IV) $\to$ S

58. Let F, C and B be the set of people having symptoms of fever, cough and breathing problem, respectively.

Here, we have $n(F) = 190$,

$n(B) = 220$

and $n(C) = 220$

Also, $n(F \cup C) = 330$,

$n(C \cup B) = 350$,

$n(F \cup B) = 340$

and $n(F \cap C \cap B) = 30$

So, $n(F \cap C) = n(F) + n(C) - n(F \cup C) = 80$

Similarly, $n(F \cap B) = 70$

and $n(C \cap B) = 90$

By Venn diagram, we can better understand.

Here,

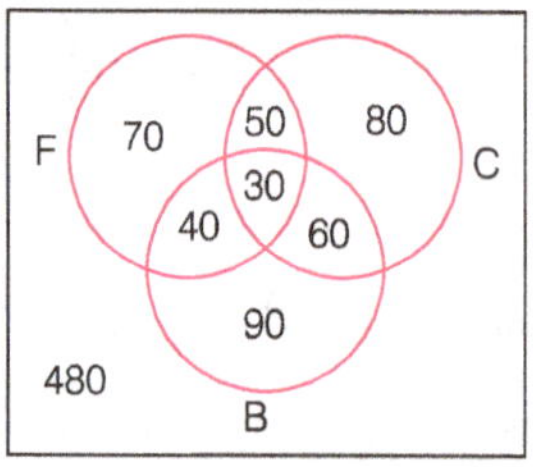

Number of people having at most one symptom

$= 70 + 80 + 90 + 480$

$= 720$

Required probability $= \frac{720}{900} = 0.8$

59.

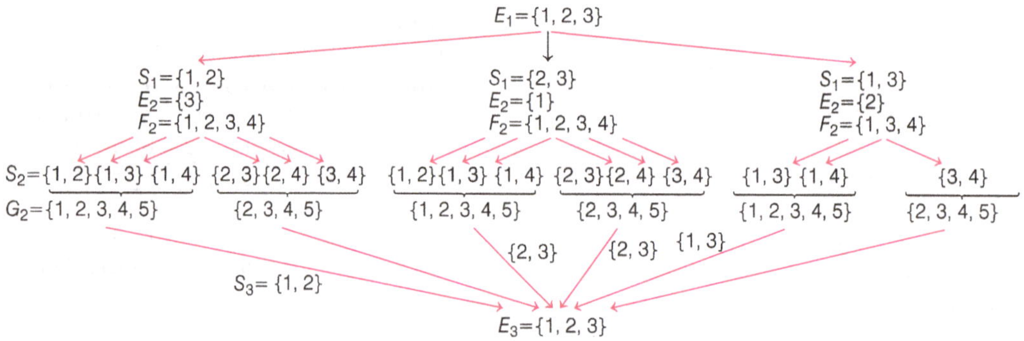

To find Probability

$$P = \frac{P(S_1 \cap (E_1 = E_3))}{P(E_1 = E_3)} = \frac{P(A_{1,2})}{P(A)}$$

where, $P(A) = P(A_{1,2}) + P(A_{1,3}) + P(A_{2,3})$

Also, $A_{1,2}$ represents 1, 2 chosen at start and similarly others.

Now, $P(A_{1,2}) = \frac{1}{3} \times \frac{1 \times {}^3C_1}{^4C_2} \times \frac{1}{^5C_2}$

$$= \frac{1}{3} \times \frac{3}{6} \times \frac{1}{10} = \frac{1}{3} \times \frac{1}{2} \times \frac{1}{10}$$

$$P(A_{1,3}) = \frac{1}{3} \times \frac{1 \times {}^2C_1}{^4C_2} \times \frac{1}{^5C_2} = \frac{1}{3} \times \frac{2}{3} \times \frac{1}{10}$$

$$P(A_{2,3}) = \frac{1}{3} \times \left[\frac{^3C_2 \times 1}{^4C_2} \times \frac{1}{^4C_2} + \frac{1 \times {}^3C_1}{^4C_2} \times \frac{1}{^5C_2}\right]$$

$$= \frac{1}{3} \times \left[\frac{3}{6} \times \frac{1}{6} + \frac{3}{6} \times \frac{1}{10}\right]$$

$$= \frac{1}{3}\left[\frac{1}{2} \times \frac{1}{6} + \frac{1}{2} \times \frac{1}{10}\right]$$

$$P(A) = \frac{1}{3}\left[\frac{1}{2} \times \frac{1}{10} + \frac{1}{2} \times 0 + \frac{1}{2} \times \frac{1}{10} + \frac{1}{2} \times \frac{1}{6} + \frac{2}{3} \times \frac{1}{10} + \frac{1}{3} \times 0\right]$$

$$= \frac{1}{3}\left[\frac{1}{4}\right] = \frac{1}{12}$$

$$\therefore \text{Required probability} = \frac{\frac{1}{3}\left(\frac{1}{2} \times \frac{1}{10}\right)}{1/12} \qquad \left[\because P = \frac{P(A_{1,2})}{P(A)}\right]$$

$$= \frac{1}{60} \times \frac{12}{1} = \frac{1}{5}$$

60. **For option (a)**

$P(E \cap F \cap G^C) = P(E \cap F) - P(E \cap F \cap G)$

$\leq P(E) - P(E \cap F \cap G)$

$= \frac{1}{8} - \frac{1}{10} = \frac{1}{40}$

For option (b)

$P(E^C \cap F \cap G) = P(F \cap G) - P(E \cap F \cap G) \leq P(F) - P(E \cap F \cap G)$

$= \frac{1}{6} - \frac{1}{10} = \frac{1}{15}$

For option (c)

$P(E \cup F \cup G) \leq P(E) + P(F) + P(G)$

$= \frac{1}{8} + \frac{1}{6} + \frac{1}{4} = \frac{3+4+6}{24} = \frac{13}{24}$

For option (d)

$P(E^C \cap F^C \cap G^C) = 1 - P(E \cup F \cup G) \geq 1 - 13/24$

$P(E^C \cap F^C \cap G^C) \geq \frac{11}{24} > \frac{5}{12}$

61. Given, set $= \{1, 2, 3, \ldots, 2000\}$

Let E_1 = Event that it is a multiple of $3 = \{3, 6, 9, \ldots, 1998\}$

$\therefore \quad n(E_1) = 666$

and E_2 = Event that it is a multiple of $7 = \{7, 14, \ldots, 1995\}$

$\therefore \quad n(E_2) = 285$

$E_1 \cap E_2$ = multiple of $21 = \{21, 42, \ldots, 1995\}$

$n(E_1 \cap E_2) = 95$

$\therefore \ P(E_1 \cup E_2) = P(E_1) + P(E_2) - P(E_1 \cap E_2)$

$P(E_1 \cup E_2) = \frac{666 + 285 - 95}{2000} = \frac{856}{2000} = p$ [given]

Hence, $500p = 500 \times \frac{856}{2000} = \frac{856}{4} = 214$

Exercise 3 - Challenging Problems

1. Let S be the sample space, then

$n(S)$ = Total number of numbers of five digits formed with the digits 1, 2, 3, 4 and 5 without repetition

$= {}^5P_5 = 5! = 120$

We know that, a number is divisible by 4 if the last two digits of the number is divisible by 4.

Then, for divisible by 4, last two digits 12 or 24 or 32 or 52.

Let E be the event that the number formed is divisible by 4.

$\therefore \quad n(E) = 3! \times 4 = 24$

$\therefore$ Required probability, $P(E) = \frac{n(E)}{n(S)} = \frac{24}{120} = \frac{1}{5}$

2. Let S be the sample space and E be the event of getting a large number than the previous number.

$\therefore \quad n(S) = 6 \times 6 \times 6 = 216$

Now, we count the number of favourable ways. Obviously, the second number has to be greater than 1. If the second number is $i (i > 1)$, then the number of favourable ways $= (i-1) \times (6-i)$

$\therefore \ n(E)$ = Total number of favourable ways

$= \sum_{i=1}^{6} (i-1) \times (6-i)$

$= 0 + 1 \times 4 + 2 \times 3 + 3 \times 2 + 4 \times 1 + 5 \times 0$

$= 4 + 6 + 6 + 4 = 20$

Therefore, the required probability,

$P(E) = \frac{n(E)}{n(S)} = \frac{20}{216} = \frac{5}{54}$

3. Finding r cars in N places, there are $(r-1)$ cars other than his own in $(N-1)$ places.

$\therefore$ Total number of ways $= {}^{N-1}C_{r-1} = \frac{(n-1)!}{(r-1)!(N-r)!}$

Now, the $(r-1)$ cars must be parked in $N-3$ places (because neighbouring slots are empty).

$\therefore$ Number of favourable ways $= {}^{N-3}C_{r-1} = \frac{(N-3)!}{(r-1)!(N-r-2)!}$

$\therefore$ Required probability $= \frac{\text{Favourable ways}}{\text{Total ways}}$

$= \frac{(N-3)!}{(r-1)!(N-r-2)!} \times \frac{(r-1)!(N-r)!}{(N-1)!}$

$= \frac{(N-r)(N-r-1)}{(N-1)(N-2)}$

4. A wins the series in $(n+r+1)$ games (say). He wins the $(n+r+1)$ th game and n out of the first $(n+r)$ games.

$\therefore \quad P(A) = \sum_{r=0}^{n} ({}^{n+r}C_n)\, q^r p^{n+1}$ [where $p + q = 1$]

Similarly, $\quad P(B) = \sum_{r=0}^{n} ({}^{n+r}C_n)\, q^{n+1} p^r$

Now, $P(A) + P(B) = 1$

$\therefore \quad \sum_{r=0}^{n} [q^r p^{n+1} + q^{n+1} p^r]\, {}^{n+r}C_n = 1$

Now, put $p = q = \frac{1}{2}$

$\therefore \quad \sum_{r=0}^{n} {}^{n+r}C_n \left[\frac{1}{2^{n+r+1}} + \frac{1}{2^{n+r+1}}\right] = 1$

$\Rightarrow \quad \sum_{r=0}^{n} ({}^{n+r}C_n) \frac{1}{2^{n+r}} = 1$

5. Let A denotes the event that the target is hit when x shells are fired at point I.

Let $E_1 (E_2)$ denote the event.

We have, $P(E_1) = \frac{8}{9}$, $P(E_2) = \frac{1}{9} \Rightarrow P\left(\frac{A}{E_1}\right) = 1 - \left(\frac{1}{2}\right)^x$

and $\quad P\left(\frac{A}{E_2}\right) = 1 - \left(\frac{1}{2}\right)^{21-x}$

Now, $\quad P(A) = \frac{8}{9}\left[1 - \left(\frac{1}{2}\right)^x\right] + \frac{1}{9}\left[1 - \left(\frac{1}{2}\right)^{21-x}\right]$

$$\Rightarrow \quad \frac{dP(A)}{dx} = \frac{8}{9}\left[\left(\frac{1}{2}\right)^x \log 2\right] + \frac{1}{9}\left[-\left(\frac{1}{2}\right)^{21-x} \log 2\right]$$

Now, we must have $\frac{dP(A)}{dx} = 0 \Rightarrow x = 12$

Also, $\frac{d^2P(A)}{dx^2} < 0$

Hence, $P(A)$ is maximum where $x = 12$.

6. The composition of the balls in the red box and in the green box and the sum suggested in the problem may be one of the following

Red box		Green box		Sum of Green in Red and Red in Green
Red	Green	Green	Red	
0	5	3	6	11
1	4	4	5	9
2	3	5	4	7
3	2	6	3	5
4	1	7	2	3
5	0	8	1	1

Of these the 2nd and the last correspond to the sum being not a prime number.

Hence, the required probability

$$= \frac{{}^6C_1 \times {}^8C_4 \times {}^6C_5 \times {}^8C_0}{{}^{14}C_5} = \frac{420 + 6}{2002} = \frac{213}{1001}$$

7. Let E_i denote the event that out of the first k balls drawn, i balls are green. Let A denote the event that $(k+1)$th ball drawn is also green.

We have, now $P(E_i) = \frac{{}^aC_i \times {}^bC_{k-i}}{{}^{a+b}C_k}$

Here, $0 \le i \le k$ and $P\left(\frac{A}{E_i}\right) = \frac{a-i}{a+b-k}$

Now, $\quad P(A) = \sum_{j=0}^{k} \frac{{}^aC_j \times {}^bC_{k-j}}{{}^{a+b}C_k} \times \frac{a-j}{a+b-k}$

Also, $(1+x)^{a-1}(1+x)^b$

$$= [{}^{a-1}C_0 + {}^{a-1}C_1 x + \ldots + {}^{a-1}C_{a-1}x^{a-1}] \times [{}^bC_0 + {}^bC_1 x + \ldots + {}^bC_b x^b]$$

$$\Rightarrow \sum_{j=0}^{n} ({}^{a-1}C_j)({}^bC_{k-j}) = \text{coefficient of } x^k$$

Hence, $\quad P(A) = \frac{a}{a+b}$

8. Total number of outcomes $= 2 \times 2 \times 2 \ldots 12$ times $= 4096$

Let a_n denote the number of outcomes in which two consecutive heads do not occur when the fair coin is tossed n times.

$\Rightarrow \quad a_1 = 2, a_2 = 3$

For $n \ge 3$, if the last outcome is T, then we cannot have two consecutive heads in the first $(n-1)$ tosses. This can happen in a_{n-1} ways. If the last outcome is H, we must have T the $(n-1)$th toss and we cannot have two consecutive heads in the first $(n-2)$ tosses. This can happen in a_{n-2} ways.

$\Rightarrow \quad a_n = a_{n-1} + a_{n-2}$ for $n \ge 3$

$\Rightarrow \quad a_{10} = 144, a_{11} = 233 \Rightarrow \alpha_{12} = 377$

Hence, the required probability is $\frac{377}{4096}$.

9. Let PQ be a diameter of a circle with centre O and radius a. Take a point A at random in PQ.

Let, $AP = x$, $AQ = y$, then $x + y = 2a$ and all values of x between 0 and $2a$ are equally likely.

Draw the ordinate AB, then $AB^2 = AP, AQ = xy$

If P', Q' are the mid-points of OP, OQ, the ordinates at these points are equal to $a\sqrt{\frac{3}{4}}$.

Hence, $AB > a\sqrt{\frac{3}{4}}$ if and only if, A lies in $P'Q'$.

Hence, the chance that $xy > \frac{3}{4}a^2$ is $\frac{A'B'}{AB}$ i.e. $\frac{1}{2}$.

10. (i) Kamsky wins one of the first n games and draws the remaining [$(n-1)$

(ii) Kamsky wins exactly one of the first n games and draws the remaining] $n-2$. We have,

$$P(i) = {}^nP_1 pq^{n-1} \text{ and } P(ii) = {}^nP_2\, pq^{n-2} r$$

$\Rightarrow$ The probability that Kamsky wins this match is

$$\sum_{n=1}^{\infty} p^2[nq^{n-1} + n(n-1)\, rq^{n-2}]$$

$$= p^2 \sum_{n=1}^{\infty} nq^{n-1} + p^2 r \sum_{n=1}^{\infty} n(n-1)\, q^{n-2}$$

Differentiating both sides w.r.t. q, we get

$$\sum_{n=1}^{\infty} nq^{n-1} = \frac{1}{(1-q)^2} \text{ and } \sum_{n=1}^{\infty} n(n-1)\, q^{n-2} = \frac{2}{(1-q)^3}$$

Thus, the probability that Kamsky wins the match is

$$\frac{p^2}{(1-q)^2} + \frac{2p^2 r}{(1-q)^3} = \frac{p^2(p+3r)}{(p+r)^3}$$

because $p + q + r = 1$.

11. Let A, B and C be three independent events having probabilities p, q and r, respectively.

Then, according to the question, we have

P (only the first occurs) $= P(A \cap \bar{B} \cap \bar{C})$

[$\because$ A, B, C are independent]

$= P(A) \cdot P(\bar{B}) \cdot P(\bar{C})$

$= p(1-q)(1-r) = a$ ...(i)

P (only the second occurs) $= P(\bar{A} \cap B \cap \bar{C})$

$= P(\bar{A}) \cdot P(B) \cdot P(\bar{C})$

$= (1-p)\, q(1-r) = b$ ...(ii)

and P (only the third occurs) $= P(\bar{A} \cap \bar{B} \cap C)$

$= P(\bar{A}) \cdot P(\bar{B}) \cdot P(C)$

$= (1-p)(1-q)\, r = c$ ...(iii)

Multiplying Eqs. (i), (ii) and (iii), then

$$pqr\, \{(1-p)(1-q)(1-r)\}^2 = abc$$

or $$\frac{abc}{pqr} = [(1-p)(1-q)(1-r)]^2 = x^2 \quad \text{[say] ...(iv)}$$

$$(1-p)(1-q)(1-r) = x \quad \text{...(v)}$$

Dividing Eq. (i) by Eq. (v), then

$$\frac{p}{1-p} = \frac{a}{x} \quad \text{or} \quad px = a - ap$$

$$\therefore \quad p = \frac{a}{(a+x)}$$

Similarly, $q = \dfrac{b}{b+x}$ and $r = \dfrac{c}{c+x}$

Replacing the values of p, q and r in Eq. (iv), then

$$\left\{\left(1 - \frac{a}{a+x}\right)\left(1 - \frac{b}{b+x}\right)\left(1 - \frac{c}{c+x}\right)\right\}^2 = x^2$$

$$\Rightarrow \quad \frac{(x^3)^2}{(a+x)^2 (b+x)^2 (c+x)^2} = x^2$$

$$\Rightarrow \quad \frac{x^3}{(a+x)(b+x)(c+x)} = x$$

or $$(a+x)(b+x)(c+x) = x^2$$

Hence, x is a root of the equation $(a+x)(b+x)(c+x) = x^2$

12. Let $A = \{a_1, a_2, \dots, a_n\}$

For each $a_i \in A\ (1 \le i \le n)$, we have the following choices.

(i) $a_i \in P$ and $a_i \in Q$ (ii) $a_i \in P$ and $a_i \notin Q$

(iii) $a_i \notin P$ and $a_i \in Q$ (iv) $a_i \notin P$ and $a_i \notin Q$

Therefore, for one element a_i of A, total number of cases is 4.

Let S be the sample space

$$\therefore \quad n(S) = 4^n$$

and number of cases in which $a_i \in P \cup Q$ is 3, since case $4 \notin P \cup Q$ and let E be the event of favourable cases, then

$n(E) =$ number of ways in which exactly r elements of A will belong to $P \cup Q$

$$= {}^nC_r (3)^r\, 1^{n-r} = {}^nC_r 3^r$$

$\therefore$ Required probability, $P(E) = \dfrac{n(E)}{n(S)} = \dfrac{{}^nC_r 3^r}{4^n}$

13. Given that $P(A) = \alpha$, $P(B/A) = P(B'/A') = 1 - \alpha$

Thus, $P(A') = 1 - P(A) = 1 - \alpha$

and $P(B/A') = 1 - P(B'/A') = 1 - (1-\alpha) = \alpha$ ...(i)

$$\therefore \quad P(A'/B) = \frac{P(A' \cap B)}{P(B)}$$

$$= \frac{P(B) - P(A \cap B)}{P(B)} = \frac{P(B) - P(A) \cdot P(B/A)}{P(B)}$$

$$\left[\because P\left(\frac{B}{A}\right) = \frac{P(A \cap B)}{P(A)}\right]$$

$$= \frac{P(B) - \alpha(1-\alpha)}{P(B)} \quad \text{...(ii)}$$

But $P(B) = P(A) \cdot P(B/A) + P(A') \cdot P(B/A')$

$= \alpha(1-\alpha) + (1-\alpha) \cdot \alpha$ [from Eq. (i)]

$= 2\alpha(1-\alpha)$ ...(3)

Putting the value of $P(B)$ from Eq. (iii) in Eq. (ii), then

$$P\left(\frac{A'}{B}\right) = \frac{2\alpha(1-\alpha) - \alpha(1-\alpha)}{2\alpha(1-\alpha)} = \frac{\alpha(1-\alpha)}{2\alpha(1-\alpha)} = \frac{1}{2}$$

which is independent of α.

14. Let S be the sample space and E be the event that each of the n pairs of balls drawn consists of one white and one red ball.

$$\therefore \quad n(S) = ({}^{2n}C_2)({}^{2n-2}C_2)({}^{2n-4}C_2)\dots({}^4C_2)({}^2C_2)$$

$$= \left\{\frac{(2n)(2n-1)}{1 \cdot 2}\right\}\left\{\frac{(2n-2)(2n-3)}{1 \cdot 2}\right\}\left\{\frac{(2n-4)(2n-5)}{1 \cdot 2}\right\} \dots \left\{\frac{4 \cdot 3}{1 \cdot 2}\right\}\left\{\frac{2 \cdot 1}{1 \cdot 2}\right\}$$

$$= \frac{1 \cdot 2 \cdot 3 \cdot 4 \dots (2n-1)\, 2n}{2^n} = \frac{2n!}{2^n}$$

and $n(E) = ({}^nC_1\, {}^nC_1)({}^{n-1}C_1\, {}^{n-1}C_1)({}^{n-2}C_1\, {}^{n-2}C_1) \dots ({}^2C_1\, {}^2C_1)({}^1C_1\, {}^1C_1)$

$$= n^2 \cdot (n-1)^2 \cdot (n-2)^2 \dots 2^2 \cdot 1^2$$

$$= [1 \cdot 2 \cdot 3 \dots (n-1)\, n]^2 = (n!)^2$$

$\therefore$ Required probability,

$$P(E) = \frac{n(E)}{n(S)} = \frac{(n!)^2}{(2n)!/2^n} = \frac{2^n}{\frac{2n!}{(n!)^2}} = \frac{2^n}{{}^{2n}C_n}$$

15. Let p be the probability that any one thing is received by a men and q be the probability that any one thing is received by a women.

$$\therefore \quad p = \frac{a}{a+b} \text{ and } q = \frac{b}{a+b}$$

Clearly, $p + q = 1$ i.e. $q = 1 - p$

Out of m things, if r are received by a men, then the rest $(m-r)$ will be received by women.

The probability for this to happen is given by

$$P(r) = {}^mC_r p^r q^{m-r} \quad [r = 0, 1, \dots, m]$$

The probability P that odd number of things are received by men is given by

$$P = P(1) + P(3) + P(5) + \dots$$

$$= {}^mC_1 pq^{m-1} + {}^mC_3 p^3 q^{m-3} + {}^mC_5 p^5 q^{m-5} + \dots \quad \text{...(i)}$$

We know that,

$$(q+p)^m = q^m + {}^mC_1 q^{m-1} p + {}^mC_2 q^{m-2} p^2 + \dots + p^m \quad \text{...(ii)}$$

and $$(q-p)^m = q^m - {}^mC_1 q^{m-1} p + {}^mC_2 q^{m-2} p^2 - \dots + (-1)^m p^m \quad \text{...(iii)}$$

Subtracting Eq.(iii) from Eq. (ii), then

$$(q+p)^m - (q-p)^m = 2\{{}^mC_1 q^{m-1} p + {}^mC_3 q^{m-3} p^3 + \dots\}$$

$= 2P$ [from Eq. (i)]

$$\therefore \quad P = \frac{1}{2}\{(q+p)^m - (q-p)^m\}$$

$$= \frac{1}{2}\left\{1 - \left(\frac{b-a}{b+a}\right)^m\right\} = \frac{1}{2}\left\{\frac{(b+a)^m - (b-a)^m}{(b+a)^m}\right\}$$

> *Statistics may be rightly called the science of average and their estimates.*
>
> **-A.L. Bowley & A.L. Boddington**

10 Statistics

Learning Milestones

Milestone 1 Measures of Central Tendecy

- Mean (Arithmetic Mean)
- Geometric Mean
- Harmonic Mean
- Median
- Mode
- Relation between Mean, Mode and Median

Milestone 2 Measures of Dispersion

- Range
- Mean Deviation
- Standard Deviation
- Variance

$$\sum_{i=1}^{n}$$

Practice Milestones

Practice Milestone 1- JEE Main Pattern
Practice Milestone 2 - JEE Advanced Pattern
Practice Milestone 3 - Challenging Problems

Milestone 1 Measures of Central Tendency

- Mean (Arithmetic Mean) • Geometric Mean • Harmonic Mean • Median • Mode
- Relation between Mean, Mode and Median

Introduction

We have already learnt, in the previous classes about the collection of data and how we can tabulate them in frequency distribution-simple distribution, ungrouped and grouped frequency distributions, continuous and discrete distribution and cumulative frequency distribution. We are also familiar with the terms like class, limits, class boundaries, class marks etc.

Now, in this chapter, we will extend our study in which we use our previous knowledge to find the measures of central tendency and measures of dispersion.

Measure of Central Tendency

It is difficult to analyse and grasp knowledge from a large data set, for make it easy the necessity for average arises. Central tendency is the statistical measure which represent a single value for the entire distribution. It provide an accurate description of the entire data set. Average value of the data set generally lies in the central part of the distribution.

10.1 Mean (Arithmetic Mean)

Mean of a distribution is the sum of the values of all the observations divided by number of observations.

Mean of Ungrouped or Individual Data

If $x_1, x_2, \ldots x_n$ are n observations, then their mean can be calculated by the following two methods.

(a) **Direct Method**

$$\text{Mean}(\bar{x}) = \frac{x_1 + x_2 + \ldots + x_n}{n} = \frac{\sum_{i=1}^{n} x_i}{n} = \frac{1}{n}\sum_{i=1}^{n} x_i$$

(b) **Shortcut Method**

$$\text{Mean}(\bar{x}) = A + \frac{1}{n}\sum_{i=1}^{n} d_i$$

where A = Assumed mean

[∵ middle value or value with maximum frequency is mostly considered as assumed mean]

d_i = Deviation from assumed mean $= x_i - A$

Example 1. If the mean of the number $24 + x$, $27 + x$, $85 + x$, $103 + x$, $151 + x$ is 78, then the mean of $30 + x$, $21 + x$, $84 + x$, $104 + x$, $41 + x$ is

(a) 56 (b) 75 (c) 82 (d) 80

Sol. (a) Given,

$$78 = \frac{(24 + x) + (27 + x) + (85 + x) + (103 + x) + (151 + x)}{5}$$

$$78 \times 5 = 390 + 5x$$

$$\Rightarrow \quad 390 - 390 = 5x \Rightarrow x = 0$$

Therefore, the mean of given observations is

$$\bar{x} = \frac{(30 + x) + (21 + x) + (84 + x) + (104 + x) + (41 + x)}{5}$$

$$\bar{x} = \frac{280 + 5x}{5} = \frac{280 + 0}{5} = 56$$

Example 2. If a variable X is expressed as a linear function of two variates U and V in the form $X = aU + bV$, then the mean $\overline{X}$ of X is

(a) $a\overline{U} + b\overline{V}$ (b) $\overline{U} + \overline{V}$

(c) $b\overline{U} + a\overline{V}$ (d) None of these

Sol. (a) We have, $\Sigma X = a\Sigma U + b\Sigma V$

$$\overline{X} = \frac{1}{n}\Sigma X = a \cdot \frac{1}{n}\Sigma U + b \cdot \frac{1}{n}\Sigma V = a\overline{U} + b\overline{V}$$

Mean of Grouped Data/Mean of Discrete Frequency Distribution and Continuous Frequency Distribution

If $x_1, x_2, x_3 \ldots, x_n$ are n observations whose corresponding frequencies are $f_1, f_2, f_3 \ldots, f_n$, then their mean can be calculated by the following two methods.

(a) **Direct method**

$$\bar{x} = \frac{x_1 f_1 + x_2 f_2 + \ldots + x_n f_n}{f_1 + f_2 + \ldots + f_n} = \frac{\sum_{i=1}^{n} f_i x_i}{\sum_{i=1}^{n} f_i}$$

(b) **Shortcut method**

$$\bar{x} = A + \sum_{i=1}^{n} f_i d_i, \text{ where } A = \text{Assumed mean}$$

and $\quad d_i$ = Deviation from assumed mean $= x_i - A$

In continuous frequency distribution, x_i is taken as mid-point (class mark) of respective classes. Apart from the above mentioned methods for grouped data, we can use step deviation method for finding mean of continuous frequency distribution.

(c) **Step-deviation method**

When length of the given class intervals in a grouped data is same, then mean can be obtained by the following formula

$$\bar{x} = A + \left(\frac{\Sigma f_i u_i}{\Sigma f_i}\right) \times h$$

where, $A =$ Assumed mean, $u_i = \dfrac{x_i - A}{h}$

$f_i =$ Frequency and $h =$ Width of class interval

Combined Mean

If set of N_1 observations has mean $\bar{X}_1$ and set of N_2 observations has mean $\bar{X}_2$, then their combined mean is $\dfrac{N_1\bar{X}_1 + N_2\bar{X}_2}{N_1 + N_2}$.

Weighted Arithmetic Mean

If $w_1, w_2, \ldots, w_n$ are the weights assigned to the values $x_1, x_2, \ldots, x_n$ respectively, then their weighted arithmetic mean $(\bar{x}_w)$ is

$$\bar{x}_w = \frac{w_1x_1 + w_2x_2 + w_3x_3 + \ldots + w_nx_n}{w_1 + w_2 + w_3 + \ldots + w_n} = \frac{\sum_{i=1}^{n} w_i x_i}{\sum_{i=1}^{n} w_i}$$

JEE Focus Points

- The arithmetic mean does not depend on the choice of (assumed mean).
- Mean is dependent on change of scale, i.e. if we add, subtract, multiply, or divide each origin and observation by x, then new mean can be obtained by adding, subtracting, multiplying or dividing original mean by x respectively.
- Sum of deviations of observation from their mean is equal to 0 i.e. $\sum_{i=1}^{n} (x_i - \bar{x}) = 0$.
- Sum of the squares of deviations from the mean is minimum, i.e. $\sum_{i=1}^{n} (x_i - \bar{x})^2$ is minimum.

Example 3. If the arithmetic mean of the numbers $x_1, x_2, \ldots x_n$ is $\bar{x}$, then the arithmetic mean of the numbers $ax_1 + b, ax_2 + b, ax_3 + b, + \ldots + ax_n + b$, where a and b are two constants, would be

(a) $\bar{x}$ (b) $na\bar{x} + nb$ (c) $a\bar{x}$ (d) $a\bar{x} + b$

Sol. (d) As mean is dependent on change of scale.

New mean (mean of $ax_1 + b, ax_2 + b, \ldots ax_n + b$)

$= a$ (old mean) $+ b = a\bar{x} + b$

Example 4. The mean for the following observation is

x	1	1/2	1/3	1/4	1/5	1/6
f	1	2	3	4	5	6

(a) $\dfrac{3}{7}$ (b) $\dfrac{4}{7}$ (c) $\dfrac{2}{7}$ (d) $\dfrac{1}{7}$

Sol. (c) Mean for discrete frequency distribution is given by

$$\bar{x} = \frac{\sum_{i=1}^{n} f_i x_i}{\sum_{i=1}^{n} f_i}$$

$$\bar{x} = \frac{1 \times 1 + 2 \times \frac{1}{2} + 3 \times \frac{1}{3} + 4 \times \frac{1}{4} + 5 \times \frac{1}{5} + 6 \times \frac{1}{6}}{1 + 2 + 3 + 4 + 5 + 6}$$

$$\bar{x} = \frac{1+1+1+1+1+1}{1+2+3+4+5+6} = \frac{6}{21} \Rightarrow \bar{x} = \frac{2}{7}$$

Example 5. The arithmetic mean of the marks from the following distribution table is 28. The value of x is

Marks	0-10	10-20	20-30	30-40	40-50	50-60
Number of students	12	18	27	x	$x-3$	6

(a) 20 (b) 17 (c) 18 (d) 12

Sol. (a)

Marks	Class marks (x_i)	f_i	$f_i x_i$
0-10	5	12	60
10-20	15	18	270
20-30	25	27	675
30-40	35	x	$35x$
40-50	45	$x-3$	$45x - 135$
50-60	55	6	330
Total		$2x + 60$	$1200 + 80x$

$$\text{Mean } (\bar{x}) = \frac{\sum_{i=1}^{n} f_i x_i}{\sum_{i=1}^{n} f_i} = \frac{1200 + 80x}{2x + 60} = 28 \quad \text{[given]}$$

$\Rightarrow \quad 1200 + 80x = 28(2x + 60)$

$\Rightarrow \quad 24x = 480 \Rightarrow x = \dfrac{480}{24}$

$\therefore \quad x = 20$

Example 6. The mean height of 30 male workers in a factory is 61 cm and the mean height of 35 female workers in the same factory is 58 cm. The combined mean height of 65 workers in the factory is

(a) 51.47 (b) 59.38 (c) 58.47 (d) 60.38

Sol. (b) $N_1 = 30, N_2 = 35, \overline{X}_1 = 61$ cm, $\overline{X}_2 = 58$ cm

$$\therefore \quad \overline{X} = \frac{N_1\overline{X}_1 + N_2\overline{X}_2}{N_1 + N_2} = \frac{30 \times 61 + 35 \times 58}{30 + 35} = \frac{3860}{65}$$

$= 59.38$ cm

$\therefore$ Combined mean height of 65 workers in the factory is 59.38 cm.

Example 7. A student obtained 65%, 90% and 95% in three subjects. If the marks of another subject is added, then the average cannot be less than

(a) 61% (b) 62.5% (c) 62.3% (d) 61.5%

Sol. (b) Marks obtained from three subjects out of 300 is

$65 + 90 + 95 = 250$

If the marks of another subject is added, then the marks will be ≥ 250 out of 400.

$\therefore$ Minimum average marks $= \dfrac{250}{400} = 62.5\%$

[when marks in the fourth subject = 0]

10.2 Geometric Mean (GM)

(a) **For ungrouped data**

If $x_1, x_2, \ldots, x_n$ are n observations, none of them being 0, then geometric mean is given by $\text{GM} = (x_1 \cdot x_2, \ldots x_n)^{1/n}$

or $\text{GM} = \text{anti-log}\left(\dfrac{\log x_1 + \log x_2 + \ldots + \log x_n}{n}\right)$

(b) **For grouped data**

Geometric mean of n observations $x_1, x_2, \ldots, x_n$ whose corresponding frequencies are $f_1, f_2, \ldots, f_n$ is given by

$$\text{GM} = (x_1^{f_1} \cdot x_2^{f_2} \ldots x_n^{f_n})^{1/N}, \text{ where } N = \sum_{i=1}^{n} f_i$$

or $$\text{GM} = \text{anti-log}\left(\frac{\sum_{i=1}^{n} f_i \log x_i}{N}\right)$$

Value of x are taken to be the values corresponding to the mid-points of class intervals.

(c) **Combined Geometric Mean**

If $G_1, G_2, \ldots, G_k$ are GM of k series of sizes $n_1, n_2 \ldots, n_k$, then GM of combined series is given by

$$\log G = \frac{n_1 \log G_1 + n_2 \log G_2 + \ldots + n_k \log G_k}{n_1 + n_2 + \ldots + n_k}$$

$$= \frac{1}{N} \sum_{i=1}^{k} n_i \log G_i$$

where, $N = n_1 + n_2 + \ldots + n_k$

Example 8. The geometric mean of the numbers $2, 2^2, 2^3 \ldots, 2^n$ is

(a) $2^{2/n}$ (b) $2^{\frac{n-1}{2}}$ (c) $2^{n/2}$ (d) $2^{\frac{n+1}{2}}$

Sol. (d) $\text{GM} = (2 \cdot 2^2 \cdot 2^3 \ldots 2^n)^{1/n}$

$$= 2^{\frac{1+2+3+\ldots+n}{n}} = 2^{\frac{n(n+1)}{2n}} = 2^{\frac{n+1}{2}}$$

Example 9. The geometric mean G of the product of n series of data, with geometric means $G_1, G_2, \ldots, G_n$ respectively, then G is equal to

(a) $\log G_1 + \log G_2 + \ldots + \log G_n$

(b) $G_1 \cdot G_2 \ldots G_n$

(c) $\log G_1 \cdot \log G_2 \ldots \log G_n$

(d) None of the above

Sol. (b) Let $x_1, x_2, \ldots, x_n$ be the variates corresponding to n sets of data, each having same number of observations say k and x be their product.

Then, $x = x_1 \cdot x_2, \ldots x_n$

i.e. $\log x = \log x_1 + \log x_2 + \ldots + \log x_n$

or $$\frac{\Sigma \log x}{k} = \frac{\Sigma \log x_1}{k} + \frac{\Sigma \log x_2}{k} + \ldots + \frac{\Sigma \log x_n}{k}$$

or $$\log G = \log G_1 + \log G_2 + \ldots + \log G_n$$

$\Rightarrow$ $$G = G_1 \cdot G_2 \ldots G_n$$

10.3 Harmonic Mean (HM)

(a) **For ungrouped data**

The harmonic mean of n non-zero observations $x_1, x_2 \ldots, x_n$ is

$$\text{HM} = \frac{n}{\frac{1}{x_1} + \frac{1}{x_2} + \ldots + \frac{1}{x_n}}$$

(b) **For grouped data**

The harmonic mean of n non-zero observations $x_1, x_2, \ldots, x_n$ with respective frequencies $f_1, f_2 \ldots, f_n$ is given by

$$\text{HM} = \frac{f_1 + f_2 + \ldots + f_n}{\frac{f_1}{x_1} + \frac{f_2}{x_2} + \ldots + \frac{f_n}{x_n}} = \frac{\sum_{i=1}^{n} f_i}{\sum_{i=1}^{n} \frac{f_i}{x_i}}$$

Example 10. The harmonic mean of $\frac{1}{2}, \frac{2}{3}, \frac{3}{4}, \frac{4}{5}$ with frequencies 1, 2, 3, 4 respectively, is

(a) $\frac{5}{7}$ (b) $\frac{4}{7}$

(c) $\frac{3}{7}$ (d) $\frac{2}{7}$

Sol. (a) We know that

$$\text{Harmonic mean} = \frac{\sum_{i=1}^{n} f_i}{\sum_{i=1}^{n} \frac{f_i}{x_i}}$$

$$\therefore \quad \sum_{i=1}^{n} f_i = 1+2+3+4 = 10$$

and
$$\sum_{i=1}^{n} \frac{f_i}{x_i} = \frac{1}{1/2} + \frac{2}{2/3} + \frac{3}{3/4} + \frac{4}{4/5}$$
$$= 2+3+4+5$$
$$= 14$$

$$\therefore \text{Harmonic mean} = \frac{10}{14} = \frac{5}{7}$$

10.4 Median

Median is the middle value in the distribution when the values are arranged in ascending or descending order.

(a) **For individual data**

Let n be number of observations, then median can be calculated by the following steps

(i) Arrange the data in ascending or descending order.

(ii) • If n is odd, then

$$\text{Median} = \text{Value of } \frac{1}{2}(n+1)\text{th observation}$$

• It n is even, then

$$\text{Median} = \text{Mean of the } \left(\frac{n}{2}\right)\text{th and } \left(\frac{n}{2}+1\right)\text{th observation}$$

(b) **For discrete frequency data**

The following listed steps should be followed to find median of the discrete frequency distribution.

(i) Arrange the values of the variate in ascending or descending order.

(ii) Prepare a cumulative frequency table.

(iii) Find $\frac{N}{2}$, where $N = \Sigma f_i$ and find the cumulative frequency is just greater than or equal to $\frac{N}{2}$, the corresponding value of x is median.

(c) **For continuous data set**

Following are the steps to find median of continuous data set

(i) Prepare a cumulative frequency table.

(ii) Find the median class, whose cumulative frequency is just greater than or equal to $\frac{N}{2}$.

(iii) Median is given by

$$\text{Median} = l + \frac{\left(\frac{N}{2}\right) - cf}{f} \times h$$

where, l = lower limit of median class
N = Total frequency
f = Frequency of the median class
h = Width of the median class
cf = Cumulative frequency of the class preceding the median class.

JEE Focus Points

- Median divides the distribution in two equal halves.
- Median is 'positional' average. It is measure of position rather than of magnitude.
- Extreme value do not affect the median as strongly as they affect the mean.
- Sum of absolute value of deviations from the median is minimum i.e. $|x_i - M|$ is minimum.

Example 11. The median of a set of 13 distinct observations is 18. If each of the last six observations of set is increased by 2, then the median of the new set

(a) is increased by 2
(b) is decreased by 2
(c) is two times the original median
(d) remains the same as that of the original set

Sol. (d) Since, $n = 13$, median term $= \left(\frac{13+1}{2}\right)$th = 7th term

Now, the last six observations are increased by 2. Since, the median is the 7th observation, which remains unchanged, there will be no change in median.

Example 12. Calculate the median for the following distribution.

Class	5-10	10-15	15-20	20-25	25-30
Frequency	5	6	15	10	14

(a) 15 (b) 20 (c) 19.66 (d) 15.33

Sol. (c)

Class	Frequency	cf
5-10	5	5
10-15	6	11
15-20	15	26
20-25	10	36
25-30	14	50
Total	50	

Here, $N = 50$

$$\frac{N}{2} = \frac{50}{2} = 25$$

Median class corresponding to 26 is 15-20.

In which $l = 15$, $cf = 11$, $f = 15$, $h = 5$

$$\text{Median} = l + \frac{\left(\frac{N}{2} - cf\right)}{f} \times h = 15 + \frac{(25-11)}{15} \times 5 = 15 + \frac{14}{15} \times 5$$

$$= 19.66$$

Example 13. If a variable takes the discrete values $\alpha - 3, \alpha - 10, \alpha - \frac{5}{2}, \alpha + 3, \alpha - 2, \alpha + \frac{1}{2}, \alpha + 5, \alpha + 7 \ (\alpha > 0)$, then median is

(a) $\alpha - \frac{3}{4}$ (b) $\alpha + 3$ (c) $\alpha - 2$ (d) $\alpha + \frac{1}{2}$

Sol. (a) Arrange the data as follows

$$\alpha - 10, \alpha - 3, \alpha - \frac{5}{2}, \alpha - 2, \alpha + \frac{1}{2}, \alpha + 3, \alpha + 5, \alpha + 7$$

$$\text{Median} = \frac{1}{2}[\text{Value of 4th term} + \text{Value of 5th term}]$$

$$= \frac{1}{2}\left[\alpha - 2 + \alpha + \frac{1}{2}\right] = \frac{1}{2}\left[2\alpha - \frac{3}{2}\right] = \alpha - \frac{3}{4}$$

JEE SCANNER

Example Similar to PYQ asked in JEE Main 2019

The mean and the median of the following ten numbers in increasing order 8, 20, 24, 27, 32, x, 40, 65, 68, y are 40 and 33 respectively, then $\frac{y}{x}$ is equal to

(a) $\frac{41}{17}$ (b) $\frac{31}{16}$ (c) $\frac{21}{17}$ (d) $\frac{51}{16}$

Sol. (a) Ten numbers in increasing order are

8, 20, 24, 27, 32, x, 40, 65, 68, y

$$\text{Mean} = \frac{\Sigma x_i}{n} = \frac{x + y + 284}{10} = 40 \Rightarrow x + y = 116$$

$$\text{Median} = \frac{T_5 + T_6}{2} = 33 \Rightarrow \frac{32 + x}{2} = 33$$

$\Rightarrow$ $x = 34$ and $y = 82$

Hence, $\frac{y}{x} = \frac{82}{34} = \frac{41}{17}$

Skill Builder

The mean and the median of the following ten numbers in increasing order 10, 12, 18, 20, 28, x, 35, 42, y, 60 are 31 and 30 respectively, then the value of xy is equal to

(a) 1694 (b) 1785

(c) 1696 (d) 1796

For Sol.

- **For more practice** See Q.10 of Milestone Practice 10.1.

10.5 Mode

An observation with maximum frequency is called the mode. More than one mode is possible when more than one value have the same maximum frequency. In this situation, the data is called multimodal.

Mode for Continuous Frequency Distribution

It is not possible to determine the mode by looking at the frequencies in a continuous frequency distribution.

In continuous frequency distribution, we locate a modal class i.e. class with maximum frequency.

Mode can be found by the given formula

$$\text{Mode} = l + \left[\frac{f_1 - f_0}{2f_1 - f_0 - f_2}\right] \times i$$

where, l = Lower limit of modal class

f_1 = Frequency of modal class

f_0 = Frequency of the class preceding the modal class

f_2 = Frequency of the class succeeding the modal class

i = Length of modal class

JEE Focus Points

- Mode is not affected by the presence of extremely large or small items.
- Mode can be found for both numerical and non-numerical data.

Example 14. A set of number consists of three 4's, five 5's, six 6's, eight 8's and seven 10's. The mode of this set of number is

(a) 6 (b) 7 (c) 8 (d) 10

Sol. (c) Mode of the data is 8 as it is repeated maximum number of times.

10.6 Relationship between Mean, Mode and Median

A distribution can be symmetric and skewed. In symmetric distribution, frequencies are distributed on both side of the centre point of the frequency curve i.e. distribution will have a skewness equal to zero.

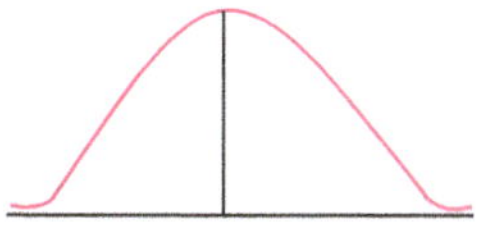

Mean = Mode = Median

For positively skewed distribution

Skewed to right

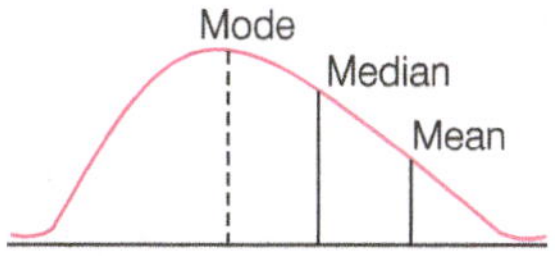

Mean > Median > Mode

For negatively skewed distribution

Skewed to left

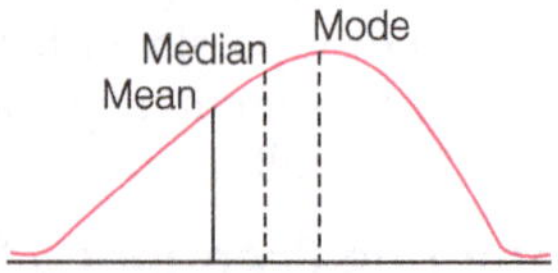

Mean $<$ Median $<$ Mode

For moderately asymmetric distribution, we have

$$\text{Mean} - \text{Mode} = 3\,(\text{Mean} - \text{Median})$$

$$\Rightarrow \quad \text{Mode} = 3\,\text{Median} - 2\,\text{Mean}$$

This formula is known as empirical formula.

Example 15. The mode of a moderately asymmetrical distribution whose median is $8x$ and mean is $9x$ is

(a) $8x$ (b) $7x$ (c) $6x$ (d) $5x$

Sol. (c) For moderately skewed distribution

$$\text{Mode} = 3\,\text{Median} - 2\,\text{Mean} = 3\times 8x - 2\times 9x$$
$$= 24x - 18x = 6x$$
$$\Rightarrow \quad \text{Mode} = 6x$$

Milestone Practice 10.1

1. The mean of the series $x_1, x_2 \ldots x_n$ is $\bar{x}$. If x_2 is replaced by λ, then the new mean is

(a) $\bar{x} - x_2 + \lambda$ (b) $\dfrac{\bar{x} - x_2 + \lambda}{n}$

(c) $\dfrac{(n-1)\bar{x} + \lambda}{n}$ (d) $\dfrac{n\bar{x} - x_2 + \lambda}{n}$

2. If for some $x \in R$, then frequency distribution of the marks obtained by 20 students in a test is

Marks	2	3	5	7
Frequency	$(x+1)^2$	$2x-5$	x^2-3x	x

Then, the mean of the marks is

(a) 3.2 (b) 2.8 (c) 3 (d) 4.8

3. The mean of a set of observations is $\bar{x}$. If each observation is divided by $\beta, \beta \neq 0$ and then decreased by 20, then the mean of new set is

(a) $\dfrac{\bar{x}}{\beta}$ (b) $\dfrac{\bar{x}+20}{\beta}$ (c) $\dfrac{\bar{x}+20\beta}{\beta}$ (d) $\dfrac{\bar{x}}{\beta} - 20$

4. The mean of n terms is $\bar{x}$. If the first term is increased by 1, second by 2 and so on, then the new mean is

(a) $\bar{x} - n$ (b) $\bar{x} + \dfrac{n}{2}$

(c) $\bar{x} + \dfrac{n+1}{2}$ (d) None of these

5. If the sum of the deviations of 50 observations from 30 is 50, then the mean of these observations is

(a) 50 (b) 30 (c) 51 (d) 31

6. If the average of the numbers 148, 146, 144, 142, ... in AP, be 125, then the total numbers in the series will be

(a) 18 (b) 24 (c) 30 (d) 48

7. If the mean of n observations $1^2, 2^2, 3^2, \ldots, n^2$ is $\dfrac{46n}{11}$, then n is equal to

(a) 11 (b) 12 (c) 23 (d) 22

8. If the sum of deviations of a number of observations about 4 is 30 and that about 3 is 40. Then, mean of the observations is

(a) 7 (b) 10

(c) 11 (d) None of these

9. In a set of $2n$ distinct observations, each of the observations below the median of all the observations is increased by 5 and each of the remaining observations is decreased by 3. Then, the mean of the new set of observations

(a) increases by 1 (b) decreases by 1

(c) decreases by 2 (d) increases by 2

10. The mean and the median of the following eight numbers in increasing order 20, 24, 32, 40, x, 55, 70 and y are 45 and 42 respectively, then value of $\dfrac{x}{y}$ is

(a) $\dfrac{49}{75}$ (b) $\dfrac{44}{75}$

(c) $\dfrac{41}{75}$ (d) $\dfrac{47}{75}$

Answer Key

1. (d)	2. (b)	3. (d)	4. (c)	5. (d)
6. (b)	7. (a)	8. (a)	9. (a)	10. (b)

For Detailed Solution

Milestone 2 Measures of Dispersion

• Range • Mean deviation • Standard deviation • Variance

The measure of central tendency do not tell us anything about scatteredness or variability of the data. It only reveal one characterstic of data i.e. the point of central tendency.

e.g. The following data representing marks obtained by sections A and B in a mathematics test out of 20 as follows

1, 2, 3, 4, 6, 7, 8, 10, 19, 20 and 5, 5, 5, 6, 8, 9, 9, 9, 14, 10

Both the data have same arithmetic mean i.e. 8. But both the data had a wide difference. A section has some dull students and some bright students. Whereas B section has average students. Such variation in the data is called dispersion.

Dispersion gives an idea about the extent to which individual items vary from one another and the central value. A measure of dispersion from the mean gives us the information about how closed the observed value are from the mean.

10.7 Range

Range is the simplest method of measurement of dispersion. If L and S are largest and smallest observations of the distribution. Then,

$$\text{Range} = L - S$$

(Difference between the two extreme observations)

$$\text{Coefficient of range} = \frac{L - S}{L + S}$$

For grouped frequency distribution

Range = Upper limit of highest class − Lower limit of lower class

10.8 Mean deviation

It is the arithmetic mean of deviations of observations from the central value (mean or median).

For ungrouped or individual series

The mean deviation from average A (usually mean or median) of n observation i.e. $x_1, x_2 \dots x_n$ is

$$\text{MD} = \frac{\sum_{i=1}^{n} |x_i - A|}{n} = \frac{\sum_{i=1}^{n} |d_i|}{n}$$

where, $d_i = x_i - A$

For grouped distribution

The mean deviation from average A (mean or median) of n observation i.e. $x_1, x_2 \dots x_n$ where corresponding frequencies $f_1, f_2 \dots f_n$ is

$$\text{MD} = \frac{\sum_{i=1}^{n} f_i |x_i - A|}{\sum_{i=1}^{n} f_i} = \frac{\sum_{i=1}^{n} f_i |d_i|}{\sum_{i=1}^{n} f_i}$$

$$\text{Coefficient of MD} = \frac{\text{Mean deviation}}{\text{Corresponding average}}$$

Example 16. The mean deviation about median of the following distribution is

Size	20	21	22	23	24
Frequency	5	4	5	1	5

(a) 2.25 (b) 1.25 (c) 1.5 (d) 3.5

Sol. (b)

Size	Frequency (f_i)	cf	$d_i = \lvert x_i - M\rvert$	$f_i d_i$
20	5	5	2	10
21	4	9	1	4
22	5	14	0	0
23	1	15	1	1
24	5	20	2	10
Total	$\Sigma f_i = 20$			25

$$\text{Now, median} = \frac{\left[\left(\frac{20}{2}\right)\text{th} + \left(\frac{20}{2}+1\right)\text{th}\right]}{2} = \frac{10\text{th} + 11\text{th}}{2}$$

$$= \frac{22+22}{2} = 22$$

$$\therefore \quad \text{MD} = \frac{\Sigma f_i d_i}{\Sigma f_i} = \frac{25}{20} = 1.25$$

JEE SCANNER

Example Similar to PYQ Asked in JEE Main 2023

Let S be the set of all values of x_i for which the mean deviation about mean of 50 consecutive positive integers $x_i, x_2 \ldots x_{50}$ is $\frac{25}{2}$. Then, S is

(a) ϕ (b) {99} (c) N (d) {9}

Sol. (c) Let x_i be any natural number

$x_i, x_i + 1, \ldots, x_i + 49$ are values of x_i's.

$$\bar{x} = \frac{x_i + (x_i + 1) + (x_i + 2) + \ldots + (x_i + 49)}{50}$$

$$= \frac{50x_i + (1 + 2 + \ldots + 49)}{50} = x_i + \frac{49 \times 50}{2 \times 50} = x_i + \frac{49}{2}$$

$$\text{Mean deviation about mean} = \sum_{i=1}^{50} \frac{|x_i - \bar{x}|}{50}$$

$$= \frac{2\left(\frac{49}{2} + \frac{47}{2} + \ldots + \frac{1}{2}\right)}{50}$$

$$= \frac{1 + 3 + \ldots + 49}{50}$$

$$= \frac{\frac{25}{2}(1 + 49)}{50} = \frac{25}{2}$$

So, it is true for all natural numbers.

Skill Builder

Let A be the set of all values of x_i for which the mean deviation about mean of 42 consecutive positive integers $x_1, x_2, \ldots, x_{42}$ is $\frac{21}{2}$, then A is

(a) N (b) Z
(c) ϕ (d) {10}

For Sol.

■ **For more practice** See Q.2 of Milestone Practice 10.2.

Example 17. Find the mean deviation from mean for the following data

Classes	Frequency
10-20	3
20-30	8
30-40	14
40-50	19
50-60	7
60-70	6
70-80	3

Sol. We construct the following table

Classes	x_i	f_i	$f_i x_i$	$\lvert x_i - \bar{x} \rvert$	$f_i \lvert x_i - \bar{x} \rvert$
10-20	15	3	45	28.16	84.48
20-30	25	8	200	18.16	145.28
30-40	35	14	490	8.16	114.24
40-50	45	19	855	1.84	34.96
50-60	55	7	385	11.84	82.88
60-70	65	6	390	21.84	131.04
70-80	75	3	225	31.84	95.52
		$\Sigma f_i = 60$	$\Sigma f_i x_i = 2590$		$\Sigma f_i \lvert x_i - \bar{x} \rvert = 688.4$

Therefore, $\bar{x} = \frac{\Sigma f_i x_i}{\Sigma f_i} = \frac{2590}{60} = 43.16$

and $\text{MD} = \frac{\Sigma f_i |x_i - \bar{x}|}{\Sigma f_i} = \frac{688.4}{60}$

$= 11.47$

10.9 Standard Deviation

It is the square root of the arithmetic average of the square of the deviations from the mean. It is denoted by σ.

For Individual series

If $x_1, x_2 \ldots x_n$ are n observations, then

$$\text{SD}(\sigma) = \sqrt{\frac{\sum_{i=1}^{n} (x_i - \bar{x})^2}{n}} \quad \text{or} \quad (\sigma) = \sqrt{\frac{\sum_{i=1}^{n} x_i^2}{n} - (\bar{x})^2}$$

or $$\sigma = \sqrt{\frac{1}{n}\sum_{i=1}^{n} d_i^2 - \left(\frac{1}{n}\sum_{i=1}^{n} d_i\right)^2}$$

where, $d_i = x_i - \bar{x}$

For grouped distribution

Standard deviation of n observations $x_1, x_2 \ldots x_n$ having frequencies $f_1, f_2 \ldots f_n$ respectively, is

$$\sigma = \sqrt{\frac{\sum_{i=1}^{n} f_i (x_i - \bar{x})^2}{N}}$$

or $$\sigma = \frac{\sum_{i=1}^{n} f_i x_i^2}{N} - (\bar{x})^2$$

or $$\sigma = \sqrt{\frac{1}{N}\left(\sum_{i=1}^{n} f_i d_i^2\right) - \frac{1}{N^2}\left(\sum_{i=1}^{n} f_i d_i\right)^2}$$

where, $d_i = x_i - \bar{x}$ and $N = \Sigma f_i$

JEE Focus Points

- It is independent of change of origin but dependent of change of scale.
- Let $\bar{x}_1$ is the mean and σ_1 is the standard deviation of series having n_1 observations and $\bar{x}_2$ is the mean and σ_2 is the standard deviation of series having n_2 observations.

  Combined mean $(\bar{x})$ of two series is given by

  $$\bar{x} = \frac{n_1\bar{x}_1 + n_2\bar{x}_2}{n_1 + n_2}$$

  and combined standard deviation of two series is given by

  $$\sigma = \sqrt{\frac{n_1(\sigma_1^2 + d_1^2) + n_2(\sigma_2^2 + d_2^2)}{n_1 + n_2}}$$

  or $\sigma = \sqrt{\frac{n_1\sigma_1^2 + n_2\sigma_2^2}{n_1 + n_2} + \frac{n_1 n_2(\bar{x}_1 - \bar{x}_2^2)}{(n_1 + n_2)^2}}$

  where, $d_i = \bar{x}_1 - \bar{x}$ and $d_2 = \bar{x}_2 - \bar{x}$

Concept Inside Video

Example 18. If $\sum_{i=1}^{n}(x_i - a) = n$ and $\sum_{i=1}^{n}(x_i - a)^2 = na$, $(n, a > 1)$, then the standard deviation of n observations

(a) $a - 1$ (b) $n\sqrt{a-1}$ (c) $\sqrt{n(a-1)}$ (d) $\sqrt{a-1}$

Sol. (d) It is given that $\sum_{i=1}^{n}(x_i - a) = n$ and $\sum_{i=1}^{n}(x_i - a)^2 = na$, $(n, a > 1)$

$\therefore$ Standard deviation of n observations

$$= \sqrt{\frac{\sum_{i=1}^{n}(x_i - a)^2}{n} - \left(\frac{\sum_{i=1}^{n}(x_i - a)}{n}\right)^2} = \sqrt{\frac{na}{n} - \left(\frac{n}{n}\right)^2} = \sqrt{a-1}$$

Example 19. The scores of a batsman in 9 matches were as follows 30, 70, 48, 42, 35,46, 54, 44, 27. Compute the standard deviation.

Sol.

Variable (x_i)	$x_i - \bar{x} = x_i - 44$	$(x_i - \bar{x})^2$
30	−14	196
70	26	676
48	4	16
42	− 2	4
35	− 9	81
46	2	4
54	10	100
44	0	0
27	− 17	289
Total		1366

Here, $\bar{x} = \frac{30 + 70 + 48 + 42 + 35 + 46 + 54 + 44 + 27}{9} = 44$

Standard deviation, $\sigma = \sqrt{\frac{1}{n}\Sigma(x_i - \bar{x})^2} = \sqrt{\frac{1}{9} \times 1366}$

$= \sqrt{151.77} = 12.31$

JEE SCANNER

Example Similar to PYQ Asked in JEE Main 2023

Let $4 = x_1 < x_2 < \ldots < x_5$ be in an AP with common difference d. If the standard deviation of $x_1, x_2 \ldots x_5$ is 5 and mean is $\bar{x}$, then $\bar{x} + x_2$ is equal to

(a) $\frac{15}{\sqrt{2}} + 4$ (b) $\frac{15}{\sqrt{2}} + 8$ (c) $\frac{15}{\sqrt{2}} + 6$ (d) $\frac{15}{\sqrt{2}} + 2$

Sol. (b) $4 = x_1 < x_2 < \ldots < x_5$

$4, 4 + d, 4 + 2d, \ldots, 4 + 4d$

$0, d, 2d, \ldots, 4d$ are in AP.

$$\bar{x} = \frac{4 + 4 + d + 4 + 2d + 4 + 3d + 4 + 4d}{5} = \frac{20 + 10d}{5} = 4 + 2d$$

$$\sigma = \sqrt{\frac{\Sigma(x_1 - \bar{x})^2}{n}}$$

$$\Rightarrow \quad 5 = \sqrt{\frac{(2d)^2 + (d)^2 + (0)^2 + (d)^2 + (2d)^2}{5}}$$

$$\Rightarrow \quad 25 = \frac{10d^2}{5} \Rightarrow d = \frac{5}{\sqrt{2}}$$

$$\Rightarrow \bar{x} + x_2 = 4 + 2d + 4 + d = 3d + 8 = 3 \times \frac{5}{\sqrt{2}} + 8 = \frac{15}{\sqrt{2}} + 8$$

Skill Builder

Let $6 = x_1 < x_2 < \ldots < x_5$ be in an AP with common difference d. If the standard deviation of $x_1, x_2, \ldots, x_5$ is 8 and mean is $\bar{x}$, then $x_1 + x_2$ is equal to

(a) $10 + \sqrt{2}$ (b) $12 + 3\sqrt{2}$

(c) $12 + 4\sqrt{2}$ (d) $10 + 2\sqrt{2}$

For Sol.

- **For more practice** See Q.5 of Milestone Practice 10.2.

Example 20. Find the standard deviation for the following data

Height (in cm)	138	142	146	150	154
Number of students	3	15	8	19	5

Sol. h = Common difference of values of $x = 4$

Let us take assumed mean as $A = 150$

x_i	f_i	$d_i = \frac{x_i - 150}{4}$	$f_i d_i$	$f_i d_i^2$
138	3	− 3	− 9	27
142	15	− 2	− 30	60
146	8	− 1	− 8	8
150	19	0	0	0
154	5	1	5	5
Total	50		− 42	100

Here, $N = 50$, $h = 4$, $\Sigma f_i d_i = -42$, $\Sigma f_i d_i^2 = 100$

Standard deviation, $\sigma = h\sqrt{\frac{1}{N}\Sigma f_i d_i^2 - \left(\frac{1}{N}\Sigma f_i d_i\right)^2}$

$$= 4\sqrt{\frac{1}{50}\times 100 - \left(\frac{1}{50}\times -42\right)^2} = 4\sqrt{2 - 0.7056} = 4.55$$

Example 21. Calculate the standard deviation for the following distribution

Marks	20-30	30-40	40-50	50-60	60-70
Number of Students	5	4	3	13	15

Sol. Let us take assumed mean as $A = 45$ and $h = 10$

Class interval	Mid-values (x_i)	Step deviations $u_i = \frac{x_i - A}{h}$	Frequency f_i	$f_i\, u_i$	$f_i\, u_i^2$
20-30	25	− 2	5	−10	20
30-40	35	− 1	4	− 4	4
40-50	45	0	3	0	0
50-60	55	1	13	13	13
60-70	65	2	15	30	60
Total			$N = 40$	29	97

$$\text{SD} = \sigma = h \times \sqrt{\frac{\Sigma f_i\, u_i^2}{N} - \left(\frac{\Sigma f_i\, u_i}{N}\right)^2} = 10\times\sqrt{\frac{97}{40} - \left(\frac{29}{40}\right)^2}$$

$$= 10\times\sqrt{2.425 - 0.525} = 10\times\sqrt{1.9} = 13.7$$

10.10 Variance

The square of standard deviation is called the variance and it is denoted by σ^2 or var (x)

$$\text{Var}(x) = \sigma^2 = (\text{standard deviation})^2$$

Example 22. The mean and variance of 8 observations are 10 and 13.5, respectively. If 6 of these observation are 5, 7, 10, 12, 14, 15, then the absolute difference of the remaining two observations is

(a) 9 (b) 3 (c) 7 (d) 5

Sol. (c) Let remaining two observations be x and y, so

$$\text{Mean} = \frac{5+7+10+12+14+15+x+y}{8} = 10$$

$\Rightarrow \quad x + y = 80 - 63 \Rightarrow x + y = 17 \quad$ ...(i)

and variance

$$= \frac{25+49+100+144+196+225+x^2+y^2}{8} - 100 = 13.5$$

$\Rightarrow \quad \frac{739 + x^2 + y^2}{8} = 113.5 \Rightarrow x^2 + y^2 = 908 - 739$

$\Rightarrow \quad x^2 + y^2 = 169 \quad$ ...(ii)

From Eqs. (i) and (ii), we get $x = 12$ and $y = 5$

$\therefore \quad |x - y| = |12 - 5| = 7$

JEE SCANNER

Example Similar to PYQ Asked in JEE Main 2023

The mean and variance of 6 observations are 8 and 17, respectively. If one observation 8 is omited, a and b respectively mean and variance of remaining 5 observation, then $a+5b-100$ equal to

(a) 10 (b) 64 (c) 36 (d) 289

Sol. (a) $\frac{x_1 + x_2 + \ldots + x_6}{6} = 8 \Rightarrow \frac{x_1 + x_2 + \ldots + x_5 + 8}{6} = 8$

$\Rightarrow \quad x_1 + x_2 + \ldots + x_5 = 40$

$\therefore \quad \frac{x_1 + x_2 + \ldots + x_5}{5} = \frac{40}{5} = 8 = a$

$$\frac{\Sigma x_i^2}{6} - 8^2 = 17$$

$$\Sigma x_i^2 = 6\times 17 + (64\times 6) = 486$$

$\Rightarrow \quad x_1^2 + x_2^2 + \ldots + x_5^2 = 486 - 64$

$\Rightarrow \quad x_1^2 + x_2^2 + \ldots + x_5^2 = 422$

$$b = \frac{x_1^2 + x_2^2 + \ldots + x_5^2}{5} - 8^2 = \frac{422}{5} - 64 = \frac{102}{5}$$

$$a + 5b - 100 = 8 + 5\times\frac{102}{5} - 100$$

$$= 8 + 102 - 100 = 8 + 2 = 10$$

$\therefore \quad a + 5b - 100 = 10$

Skill Builder

The mean and variance of 5 observation are 10 and 23, respectively. If one observation 6 is omitted, p and q respectively mean and variance of remaining 4 observation, then $p + 4q$ equal to

(a) 104 (b) 106
(c) 102 (d) 108

For Sol.

■ **For more practice** See Q.9 of Milestone Practice 10.2.

Example 23. For a group of 200 candidates the mean and standard deviation were found to be 40 and 15, respectively. Later on it was found that the score 43 was misread as 34. Find the correct mean and variance.

Sol. Given, $n = 200$, $\bar{x} = 40$, $\sigma^2 = (15)^2 = 225$

$\therefore \quad \bar{x} = \frac{\Sigma x_i}{n} \Rightarrow \Sigma x_i = n\bar{x}$

$\Rightarrow \Sigma x_i = 200 \times 40 = 8000$

Now, corrected Σx_i = Incorrect Σx_i − (Sum of incorrect values) + (Sum of correct values)

$$= 8000 - 34 + 43 = 8009$$

$\therefore$ Corrected mean $= \dfrac{\text{Corrected } \Sigma x_i}{n}$

$= \dfrac{8009}{200} = 40.045$

and $\sigma^2 = (15)^2 = 225$

$\Rightarrow \quad 225 = \dfrac{\Sigma x_i^2}{200} - \left(\dfrac{\Sigma x_i}{200}\right)^2$

$\Rightarrow \quad 225 = \dfrac{\Sigma x_i^2}{200} - \left(\dfrac{8000}{200}\right)^2$

$\Rightarrow \quad 225 = \dfrac{\Sigma x_i^2}{200} - 1600$

$\Rightarrow \quad \Sigma x_i^2 = 200\,(1600 + 225)$

$= 365000$

$\Rightarrow$ Incorrect $\Sigma x_i^2 = 365000$

Corrected Σx_i^2 = (Incorrect Σx_i^2) − (Sum of square of incorrect value) + (Sum of square of correct value)

Corrected $\Sigma x_i^2 = 365000 - (34)^2 + (43)^2$

$= 365693$

So, correct variance

$= \dfrac{\text{Corrected } \Sigma x_i^2}{200} - \left(\dfrac{\text{Corrected } \Sigma x_i}{200}\right)^2$

$= \dfrac{365693}{200} - \left(\dfrac{8009}{200}\right)^2$

$= 1828.465 - 1603.602$

$= 224.863$

Coefficient of Variation

The absolute measure of dispersion cannot be used for the purpose of comparing the variability of two or more series with same mean.

To compare the dispersion of two or more series with different units, it is necessary to compute their coefficient of variation (CV).

$$CV = \frac{\sigma}{\bar{x}} \times 100, \ \bar{x} \neq 0$$

where, σ = Standard deviation, $\bar{x}$ = Mean

CV is used for comparing uniformity, homogeneity variability stability and consistency of two.

The series with greater CV is said to be more variable than the other.

The series with lesser CV is said to be more consistent, uniform, highly stable, etc. than the other.

Comparison of the two series with same mean

Let σ_1 and σ_2 be the standard deviation of series Ist and IInd respectively and $\bar{x}$ be the mean of the two series.

Then, $\quad$ CV (Ist series) $= \dfrac{\sigma_1}{\bar{x}} \times 100$

and $\quad$ CV (IInd series) $= \dfrac{\sigma_2}{\bar{x}} \times 100$

From above, it is clear that CVs can be compared on the basis of values of σ_1 and σ_2 only.

CV is best measure of comparing variability of the two series. It can be used for comparing the consistency of the price of shares of two or more companies.

Example 24. The following are some particulars of the distribution of weights of boys and girls in a class :

	Boys	Girls
Number	100	50
Mean weight	60 kg	45 kg
Variance	9	4

Which of the distribution is more variable?

Sol. In order to compare the variability of boys and girls, we have to calculate their coefficients of variation. Let σ_1 and σ_2 denoted the standard deviation of boys and girls, respectively.

Further, let $\bar{x}_1$ and $\bar{x}_2$ be the mean weight of boys and girls.

We have,

$\bar{x}_1 = 60, \quad \bar{x}_2 = 45$

$\sigma_1^2 = 9, \quad \sigma_2^2 = 4$

$\sigma_1 = 3, \quad \sigma_2 = 2$

Now, coefficient of variation of boys

$= \dfrac{\sigma_1}{\bar{x}_1} \times 100$

$= \dfrac{3}{60} \times 100 = 5$

and coefficient of variation of girls

$= \dfrac{\sigma_2}{\bar{x}_2} \times 100$

$= \dfrac{2}{45} \times 100 = 4.44$

Clearly, coefficient of variation of boys is greater than coefficient of girls.

So, boys more variable than girls.

Milestone Practice 10.2

1. Following are the marks obtained by 9 students in a Mathematics test 50, 69, 20, 33, 53, 39, 40, 65, 59. The mean deviation from the median is
(a) 9 (b) 10.5 (c) 12.67 (d) 14.76

2. Let S be the set of all values of x_i for which the mean deviation about mean of 80 consecutive positive integers $x_1, x_2, \ldots, x_{80}$ is 20, then S is
(a) ϕ (b) N
(c) Z (d) R

3. If the standard deviation of the numbers 2, 3, a and 11 is 3.5, then which of the following is true?
(a) $3a^2 - 26a + 55 = 0$ (b) $3a^2 - 32a + 84 = 0$
(c) $3a^2 - 34a + 91 = 0$ (d) $3a^2 - 23a + 44 = 0$

4. Mean and standard deviation of 100 observations were found to be 40 and 10, respectively. If at the time of calculation two observations were wrongly taken as 30 and 70 in place of 3 and 27, respectively, find the correct standard deviation.
(a) 10.20 (b) 10.24
(c) 10.29 (d) 10.27

5. Let $10 = x_1 < x_2 < \ldots < x_5$ be in an AP with common difference d. If the standard deviation of $x_1, x_2, \ldots\ldots, x_5$ is 14 and mean is $\bar{x}$, then $\bar{x} + x_2 + x_4$ is
(a) $20 + \sqrt{98}$ (b) $20 + 6\sqrt{98}$
(c) $20 + 4\sqrt{98}$ (d) $20 + 9\sqrt{98}$

6. If for a distribution $\Sigma(x - 5) = 3, \Sigma(x - 5)^2 = 43$ and the total number of items is 18, find the mean and standard deviation.
(a) 94, 1.53 (b) 5.17, 1.53
(c) 93, 1.55 (d) None of these

7. The mean and variance of n values of a variable x are 0 nd σ^2, respectively. If the variable $y = x^2$, then mean of y is
(a) σ (b) σ^2
(c) 1 (d) None of these

8. The variance of the numbers 2, 3, 11 and x is $\frac{49}{4}$.
Find the value of x.
(a) $6, \frac{14}{3}$ (b) $6, \frac{14}{5}$
(c) $6, \frac{16}{3}$ (d) None of these

9. The mean and variance of 8 observations are 16 and 25, respectively. If one observation 9 is omitted, p and q respectively are mean and variance of remaining 7 observations, then $p + 7q$ is
(a) 151 (b) 161
(c) 148 (d) 131

10. Coefficient of variation of two distributions are 50 and 60 and their arithmetic means are 30 and 25 respectively. Difference of their standard deviation is
(a) 0
(b) 1
(c) 1.5
(d) 2.5

Answer Key

1. (c)	2. (b)	3. (b)	4. (b)	5. (b)
6. (b)	7. (b)	8. (a)	9. (b)	10. (a)

For Detailed Solution

JEE Pattern EXAMPLES

Single Option Correct Type Questions

Example 1 *If the mean of the set of numbers $x_1, x_2, \dots, x_n$ is $\bar{x}$, then the mean of the numbers $x_i + 2i, 1 \le i \le n$ is*

(a) $\bar{x} + 2n$ (b) $\bar{x} + n + 1$
(c) $\bar{x} + 2$ (d) $\bar{x} + n$

Sol. (b) $\bar{x} = \frac{1}{n}\sum_{i=1}^{n} x_i$

$$\Rightarrow \sum_{i=1}^{n} x_i = n\bar{x}$$

$$\text{Let } M = \frac{1}{n}\sum_{i=1}^{n}(x_i + 2i) = \frac{1}{n}\sum_{i=1}^{n} x_i + \frac{2(1+2+\dots+n)}{n}$$

$$\Rightarrow M = \frac{1}{n}n\bar{x} + 2\frac{n(n+1)}{2n}$$

$$\therefore M = \bar{x} + (n+1)$$

Example 2 *The mean of a set of observations is $\bar{x}$. If each observation is divided by, $\alpha \ne 0$ and then is increased by 10, then the mean of the new set is*

(a) $\frac{\bar{x}}{\alpha}$ (b) $\frac{\bar{x}+10}{\alpha}$ (c) $\frac{\bar{x}+10\alpha}{\alpha}$ (d) $\alpha\bar{x} + 10$

Sol. (c) Let $x_1, x_2, x_3, \dots x_n$ be n observations. Then,

$$\bar{x} = \frac{1}{n}\sum_{i=1}^{n} x_i$$

$$\therefore \text{ New mean, } \bar{X} = \frac{1}{n}\sum_{i=1}^{n}\left(\frac{x_i}{\alpha} + 10\right)$$

$$= \frac{1}{\alpha}\left(\frac{1}{n}\sum_{i=1}^{n} x_i\right) + \frac{1}{n}\cdot(10n)$$

$$= \frac{1}{\alpha}\bar{x} + 10 = \frac{\bar{x} + 10\alpha}{\alpha}$$

Example 3 *The mean of n observations is $\bar{x}$. If one observation x_{n+1} is added, then the mean remains same. The value of x_{n+1} is*

(a) 0 (b) 1 (c) n (d) $\bar{x}$

Sol. (d) Let $x_1, x_2, x_3, \dots, x_n$ be n observations.

$$\therefore \bar{x} = \frac{\sum x_i}{n} \quad \text{...(i)}$$

$$\text{New mean} = \frac{\sum x_i + x_{n+1}}{n+1}$$

$$\text{According to the question, } \bar{x} = \frac{\sum x_i + x_{n+1}}{n+1}$$

$$\Rightarrow (n+1)\bar{x} = n\bar{x} + x_{n+1} \Rightarrow x_{n+1} = \bar{x}$$

Example 4 *In a class of 100 students, the average amount of pocket money is ₹ 35 per student. If the average is ₹ 25 for girls and ₹ 50 for boys, then the number of girls in the class is*

(a) 20 (b) 40 (c) 60 (d) 80

Sol. (c) Let the number of girls in the class $= y$

$\therefore$ Number of boys in the class $= 100 - y$

Now, $\bar{x}_1 = 25,\ n_1 = y,\ \bar{x}_2 = 50,\ n_2 = 100 - y$

and $\bar{x} = 35,\ n_1 + n_2 = 100$

$$\therefore 35 = \frac{25 \times y + 50 \times (100 - y)}{100}$$

$$\Rightarrow 3500 = 25y + 5000 - 50y \Rightarrow 25y = 1500 \Rightarrow y = 60$$

$\therefore$ Number of girls in the class $= 60$

Example 5 *The average salary of male employees in a firm was ₹ 520 and that of females was ₹ 420. The mean salary of all the employees was ₹ 500. The percentage of male employees is*

(a) 80% (b) 60% (c) 40% (d) 20%

Sol. (a) Since, $\bar{x}_1 = 520, \bar{x}_2 = 420$ and $\bar{x} = 500$

$$\text{Also, we know } \bar{x} = \frac{n_1\bar{x}_1 + n_2\bar{x}_2}{n_1 + n_2}$$

$$\Rightarrow 500(n_1 + n_2) = 520n_1 + 420n_2$$

$$\Rightarrow 20n_1 = 80n_2 \Rightarrow n_1 : n_2 = 4 : 1$$

Hence, the percentage of male employees in the firm

$$= \left(\frac{4}{4+1}\right) \times 100 = 80\%$$

JEE SCANNER

Example 6 Similar to PYQ Asked in JEE Main 2024

Let the median and mean deviation about the median of 7 observation 70, 25, 30, 90, 10, a, b be 70 and $\frac{185}{7}$ respectively. Then, the mean deviation about the mean of these 7 observations is

(a) $\frac{180}{7}$ (b) $\frac{200}{7}$ (c) $\frac{185}{7}$ (d) $\frac{190}{7}$

Sol. (b) Given, median = 70

Observations in increasing order are

10, 25, 30, 70, a, b, 90

Mean deviation about median

$$= \frac{60 + 45 + 40 + 0 - 70 + a - 70 + b + 20}{7}$$

$$\Rightarrow \quad \frac{a+b+25}{7} = \frac{185}{7} \Rightarrow a + b = 160 \quad \text{...(i)}$$

$$\text{Mean} = \frac{10 + 25 + 30 + 70 + a + b + 90}{7}$$

$$= \frac{225 + 160}{7} \quad [\because a + b = 160]$$

$$= \frac{385}{7} = 55$$

Mean deviation about mean

$$= \frac{45+30+25+15+a-55+b-55+35}{7}$$

$$= \frac{a+b+40}{7} = \frac{160+40}{7} = \frac{200}{7}$$

Skill Builder

Let the median and mean deviation about the median of 5 observations 115, 120, 140, a, b be 140 and 15 respectively. Then, the mean deviation about the mean of these 5 observations is

(a) 16.6 (b) 15.6

(c) 14.6 (d) 17.6

For Sol.

Example 7 *Let G_1 and G_2 be the ... geometric means of two ... series $x_1, x_2, \dots, x_n; y_1, y_2, \dots, y_n$. If G is the geometric mean of $\frac{x_i}{y_i}, i = 1, 2, \dots, n$. Then, G is equal to*

(a) $G_1 - G_2$ (b) $\frac{\log G_1}{\log G_2}$ (c) $\frac{G_1}{G_2}$ (d) $\log\left(\frac{G_1}{G_2}\right)$

Decoding the Question

If $x_1, x_2, \dots, x_n$ be n positive observations, then their geometric mean is defined as

$$G = (x_1 \cdot x_2 \cdot \dots \cdot x_n)^{1/n}$$

Sol. (c) Given, $G_1 = (x_1 \cdot x_2 \dots x_n)^{1/n}$ and $G_2 = (y_1 \cdot y_2 \dots y_n)^{1/n}$

$$\therefore \quad G = \left(\frac{x_1}{y_1} \cdot \frac{x_2}{y_2} \dots \frac{x_n}{y_n}\right)^{1/n} = \frac{(x_1 \cdot x_2 \dots x_n)^{1/n}}{(y_1 \cdot y_2 \dots y_n)^{1/n}} = \frac{G_1}{G_2}$$

Example 8 *If SD of X is S, then SD of the variable $\mu = \frac{aX + b}{c}$, where a, b and c are constants, is*

(a) $\left|\frac{c}{a}\right|\sigma$ (b) $\left|\frac{a}{c}\right|\sigma$ (c) $\left|\frac{b}{c}\right|\sigma$ (d) $\frac{c^2}{a^2}\sigma$

Sol. (b) We know that

$$\text{var}(aX + b) = a^2 \text{var}(X)$$

$$\therefore \quad \text{var}\left(\frac{aX + b}{c}\right) = \left(\frac{a}{c}\right)^2 \text{var}(X) = \frac{a^2}{c^2}\sigma^2$$

$$\therefore \quad \text{SD} = \sqrt{\text{var}\left(\frac{aX + b}{c}\right)} = \left|\frac{a}{c}\right|\sigma$$

Example 9 *Let $x_1, x_2, \dots, x_n$ be n observations. Let $w_i = lx_i + k$ for $i = 1, 2, \dots, n$, where l and k are constants. If the mean of x_i's is 48 and their standard deviation is 12, the mean of w_i's is 55 and standard deviation of w_i's is 15, the values of l and k should be*

(a) $l = 1.25, k = -5$ (b) $l = -1.25, k = 5$

(c) $l = 2.5, k = -5$ (d) $l = 2.5, k = 5$

Sol. (a) Given, $w_i = lx_i + k$

$$M(x_i) = \bar{x} = 48, \sigma(x_i) = 12$$

$$M(\overline{w}) = 55 \text{ and } \sigma(w) = 15$$

$$M(w_i) = lM(x_i) + M(k)$$

$$55 = l \times 48 + k \quad \text{...(i)}$$

and $\sigma(w_i) = l\sigma(x_i) + \sigma(k)$

$\Rightarrow \quad 15 = l(12) + 0$

$\Rightarrow \quad l = \frac{15}{12} = 1.25$

$\therefore$ From Eq. (i), $55 = 1.25 \times 48 + k$

$\Rightarrow \quad k = 55 - 60$

$\therefore \quad k = -5$

Example 10 *Consider the numbers 1, 2, 3, 4, 5, 6, 7, 8, 9, 10. If 1 is added to each number, then variance of the numbers so obtained is*

(a) 6.5 (b) 2.87

(c) 3.87 (d) 8.25

Sol. (d) We know SD of first 10 natural number is 2.87.

i.e. $\sigma = 2.87$

Variance, $\sigma^2 = 8.24$

We know that variance is independent of change of origin. Hence, after adding 1 on each observation new variance will same i.e. 8.25.

Example 11 *If the standard deviation of the numbers $-1, 0, 1, k$ is $\sqrt{5}$ where $k > 0$, then k is equal to*

(a) $2\sqrt{\frac{10}{3}}$ (b) $2\sqrt{6}$ (c) $4\sqrt{\frac{5}{3}}$ (d) $\sqrt{6}$

Decoding the Question

If $x_1, x_2 \ldots x_n$ are n observation, then standard deviation

$$= \sqrt{\frac{1}{n}\sum_{i=1}^{n} x_i^2 - \left(\frac{1}{n}\sum_{i=1}^{n} x_i\right)^2}$$

Sol. (b) Given observations are $-1, 0, 1$ and k.

Also, standard deviation of these four observations $= \sqrt{5}$

$$\therefore \sqrt{\frac{(-1)^2 + (0)^2 + (1)^2 + k^2}{4} - \left(\frac{-1+0+1+k}{4}\right)^2} = \sqrt{5}$$

$$\Rightarrow \frac{2+k^2}{4} - \frac{k^2}{16} = 5 \quad \text{[squaring both sides]}$$

$$\Rightarrow \frac{8+4k^2-k^2}{16} = 5 \Rightarrow \frac{8+3k^2}{16} = 5$$

$$\Rightarrow 8 + 3k^2 = 80 \Rightarrow 3k^2 = 72$$

$$\Rightarrow k^2 = 24 \Rightarrow k = 2\sqrt{6} \text{ or } -2\sqrt{6}$$

$$\Rightarrow k = 2\sqrt{6} \quad [\because k > 0]$$

Example 12 *The mean of five observations is 5 and their variance is 9.20. If three of the given five observations are 1, 3 and 8, then a ratio of other two observations is*

(a) 4 : 9 (b) 6 : 7 (c) 10 : 3 (d) 5 : 8

Sol. (a) Let 1, 3, 8, x and y be the five observations.

Then, $\quad$ mean $\bar{x} = \dfrac{\Sigma x_i}{n}$

$$\Rightarrow \bar{x} = \frac{1+3+8+x+y}{5} = 5 \quad \text{(given)}$$

$$\Rightarrow x + y = 25 - 12 = 13$$

$$\Rightarrow x + y = 13 \quad \text{...(i)}$$

and $\quad$ variance $= \sigma^2 = \dfrac{\Sigma(x_i - \bar{x})^2}{n}$

$$= \frac{\left[\begin{array}{l}(1-5)^2 + (3-5)^2 + (8-5)^2 \\ \quad + (x-5)^2 + (y-5)^2\end{array}\right]}{5} = 9.2 \text{ (given)}$$

$$\Rightarrow 16 + 4 + 9 + (x^2 - 10x + 25) + (y^2 - 10y + 25) = 46$$

$$\Rightarrow x^2 + y^2 - 10(x+y) = 46 - 79$$

$$\Rightarrow x^2 + y^2 - 10 \times 13 = -33 \quad [\because x + y = 13]$$

$$\Rightarrow x^2 + y^2 = 97 \quad \text{...(ii)}$$

Let $\quad \dfrac{y}{x} = t \Rightarrow y = xt$

On putting $y = xt$ in Eq. (i), we get

$$x(1+t) = 13$$

$$\Rightarrow x^2(1+t)^2 = 169 \quad \text{...(iii)}$$

On putting $y = xt$ in Eq. (ii), we get

$$x^2(1+t^2) = 97 \quad \text{... (iv)}$$

On dividing Eq. (iii) by Eq. (iv), we get

$$\frac{x^2(1+t)^2}{x^2(1+t^2)} = \frac{169}{97}$$

$$\Rightarrow 97(t^2 + 2t + 1) = 169(1 + t^2)$$

$$\Rightarrow (169 - 97)t^2 - 194t + (169 - 97) = 0$$

$$\Rightarrow 36t^2 - 97t + 36 = 0$$

$$\Rightarrow (4t - 9)(9t - 4) = 0$$

$$\Rightarrow t = \frac{9}{4} \text{ or } t = \frac{4}{9}$$

Example 13 *The mean of the data set comprising of 16 observations is 16. If one of the observation valued 16 is deleted and three new observations valued 3, 4 and 5 are added to the data, then the mean of the resultant data is*

(a) 16.8 (b) 16.0 (c) 15.8 (d) 14.0

Sol. (d) Given, $\dfrac{x_1 + x_2 + x_3 + \ldots + x_{16}}{16} = 16$

$$\Rightarrow \sum_{i=1}^{16} x_i = 16 \times 16$$

Sum of new observations

$$= \sum_{i=1}^{18} y_i = (16 \times 16 - 16) + (3 + 4 + 5) = 252$$

Number of observations = 18

$$\therefore \text{New mean} = \frac{\sum_{i=1}^{18} y_i}{18} = \frac{252}{18} = 14$$

Example 14 *If $\sum_{i=1}^{9}(x_i - 5) = 9$ and $\sum_{i=1}^{9}(x_i - 5)^2 = 45$, then the standard deviation of the 9 items $x_1, x_2, \ldots, x_9$ is*

(a) 9 (b) 4 (c) 2 (d) 3

Sol. (c) We have, $\sum_{i=1}^{9}(x_1 - 5) = 9$ and $\sum_{i=1}^{9}(x_1 - 5)^2 = 45$

$$\text{SD} = \sqrt{\frac{\sum_{i=1}^{9}(x_1 - 5)^2}{9} - \left(\frac{\sum_{i=1}^{9}(x_1 - 5)}{9}\right)^2}$$

$$\Rightarrow \text{SD} = \sqrt{\frac{45}{9} - \left(\frac{9}{9}\right)^2} = \sqrt{5 - 1} = \sqrt{4} = 2$$

Example 15 *The mean and the variance of five observations are 4 and 5.20, respectively. If three of the observations are 3, 4 and 4, then the absolute value of the difference of the other two observations, is*

(a) 1 (b) 7 (c) 5 (d) 3

Sol. (b) Given, mean $\bar{x} = 4$

variance $\sigma^2 = 5.20$

and numbers of observation $n = 5$

Let $x_1 = 3$, $x_2 = 4$, $x_3 = 4$ and x_4, x_5 be the five observations

So, $\sum_{i=1}^{5} x_i = 5 \cdot \bar{x} = 5 \times 4 = 20$

$\Rightarrow \quad x_1 + x_2 + x_3 + x_4 + x_5 = 20$

$\Rightarrow \quad 3 + 4 + 4 + x_4 + x_5 = 20$

$\Rightarrow \quad x_4 + x_5 = 9 \quad$ ...(i)

Now, variance, $\sigma^2 = \dfrac{\sum_{i=1}^{5} x_i^2}{5} - (\bar{x})^2$

$\Rightarrow \quad \dfrac{x_1^2 + x_2^2 + x_3^2 + x_4^2 + x_5^2}{5} - (4)^2 = 5.20$

$\Rightarrow \quad \dfrac{9 + 16 + 16 + x_4^2 + x_5^2}{5} = 16 + 5.20$

$\Rightarrow \quad 41 + x_4^2 + x_5^2 = 5 \times 21.20$

$\Rightarrow \quad x_4^2 + x_5^2 = 106 - 41 \Rightarrow x_4^2 + x_5^2 = 65 \quad$ ...(ii)

$\because \quad (x_4 + x_5)^2 = x_4^2 + x_5^2 + 2x_4x_5$

$\therefore \quad 81 = 65 + 2x_4x_5 \quad$ [from Eqs. (i) and (ii)]

$\Rightarrow \quad 16 = 2x_4x_5$

$\Rightarrow \quad x_4x_5 = 8 \quad$ ...(iii)

Now, $(|x_4 - x_5|)^2 = x_4^2 + x_5^2 - 2x_4x_5$

$= 65 - 16 \quad$ [from Eqs. (ii) and (iii)]

$= 49$

$\Rightarrow \quad |x_4 - x_5| = 7$

Example 16 *All the students of a class performed poorly in Mathematics. The teacher decided to give grace marks of 10 to each of the students. Which of the following statistical measures will not change even after the grace marks were given?*

(a) Mean (b) Median

(c) Mode (d) Variance

Decoding the Question

Variance remain unchanged, if observations are added or subtracted by a fixed number, whereas mean, median and mode will increase by that number.

Sol. (d) If initially all marks were x_i, then

$$\sigma_1^2 = \frac{\sum (x_i - \bar{x})^2}{N}$$

Now, each is increased by 10.

$$\therefore \quad \sigma_2^2 = \frac{\sum [(x_i + 10) - (\bar{x} + 10)]^2}{N} = \sigma_1^2$$

So, variance will not change whereas mean, median and mode will increase by 10.

More than One Correct Option Type Questions

Example 17 *The mean and standard deviation of the data 3, 5, 7, x, y are 5 and 2 respectively, then x and y are roots of the equation*

(a) $x^2 - 10x - 19$ (b) $x^2 - 10x + 19$

(c) $4x^2 - 40x - 76$ (d) $4x^2 - 40x + 76$

Sol. (b,d) Given, mean $= \dfrac{3+5+7+x+y}{5} = 5$

$\Rightarrow \quad 5+3+7+x+y = 25$

$\Rightarrow \quad x + y = 25 - 15 = 10$

$$\text{SD} = \sqrt{\frac{5^2 + 3^2 + 7^2 + x^2 + y^2}{5} - 5^2} = 2$$

$$= \frac{x^2 + y^2 + 83}{5} - 25 = 4 \Rightarrow x^2 + y^2 = 62$$

$\Rightarrow \quad (x+y)^2 - 2xy = 62 \Rightarrow xy = 19$

$\therefore$ Equation is $x^2 - 10x + 19$

Example 18 *If the standard deviation of the numbers 3, 5, x and 13 is 4.5, then which of the following is/are true?*

(a) $3x^2 - 42x + 47 = 0$ (b) $3x^2 + 42x - 47 = 0$

(c) $1.5x^2 - 21x + 47 = 0$ (d) $6x^2 - 84x + 94 = 0$

Sol. (a,d) Given, standard deviation of 4 numbers is 4.5.

$\Rightarrow \quad \dfrac{\sum x_i^2}{4} - (\bar{x})^2 = (4.5)^2$

$\Rightarrow \quad \dfrac{9 + 25 + x^2 + 169}{4} - \left(\dfrac{21 + x}{4}\right)^2 = (4.5)^2$

$\Rightarrow \quad \dfrac{203 + x^2}{4} - \dfrac{441 + 42x + x^2}{16} = (4.5)^2$

$\Rightarrow \quad \dfrac{812 + 4x^2 - 441 - 42x - x^2}{16} = 20.25$

$\Rightarrow \quad 3x^2 - 42x + 371 = 324$

$\Rightarrow \quad 3x^2 - 42x + 47 = 0$

Example 19 *The mean and variance of 7 observations are 8 and 16, respectively. If five observations are 2, 4, 10, 12, 14, then the difference of remaining two observations, is/are*

(a) 2 (b) −2 (c) 1 (d) 4

Sol. (a, b) $\bar{x} = \dfrac{2+4+10+12+14+x+y}{7} = 8$

$\Rightarrow \quad 42 + x + y = 56 \Rightarrow x + y = 14$

$$\sigma^2 = \frac{\sum x_i^2}{n} - \left(\frac{\sum x_i}{n}\right)^2$$

$$16 = \frac{4+16+100+144+196+x^2+y^2}{7} - (8)^2$$

$\Rightarrow \quad 16 + 64 = \dfrac{460 + x^2 + y^2}{7}$

$$\Rightarrow \quad x^2+y^2=100 \quad \text{...(i)}$$

$$\Rightarrow \quad xy=48 \quad \text{...(ii)}$$

On solving Eqs. (i) and (ii), we get

$$x=6 \text{ and } y=8$$

or $\quad y=6$ and $x=8$

$$x-y=2 \text{ or } x-y=-2$$

Passage Based Questions

Passage I

(Ex. Nos. 20 and 21)

If out of 7 observations, five are 2, 4, 10, 12, 14. The mean and variance of these seven observations are 8 and 16, respectively.

Example 20 *Sum of remaining two is*

(a) 12 (b) 14 (c) 26 (d) 18

Example 21 *Product of remaining two is*

(a) 36 (b) 48 (c) 34 (d) 32

Sol. (Q.Nos. (20 and 21)

Let 7 observations be $x_1, x_2, x_3, x_4, x_5, x_6, x_7$.

$$\bar{x}=8$$

$$\Rightarrow \quad \sum_{i=1}^{7} x_i = 56 \quad \text{...(i)}$$

Also, $\sigma^2=16$

$$\Rightarrow \quad 16=\frac{1}{7}\left(\sum_{i=1}^{7} x_i^2\right)-(\bar{x})^2$$

$$\Rightarrow \quad 16=\frac{1}{7}\left(\sum_{i=1}^{7} x_i^2\right)-64$$

$$\Rightarrow \quad \sum_{i=1}^{7} x_i^2 = 560 \quad \text{...(ii)}$$

From Eq. (i), we get

$$x_1+x_2\ldots+x_7=56 \Rightarrow x_6+x_7=14$$

From Eq. (ii), we get

$$x_6^2+x_7^2=100$$

On solving them, we get

$$x_6=8 \text{ or } 6 \text{ and } x_7=6 \text{ or } 8$$

20. (b) Sum of two observations $= x_6+x_7=6+8=14$

21. (b) $x_6 \times x_7 = 6\times 8=48$

Stem Based Questions

Stem I

(Ex. Nos. 22 and 23)

If $A=\{x\in N: 1\le x\le 17\}$ and $B=\{ax+b: x\in X$ and $a, b\in R, a>0\}$. Mean and variance of Y are 17 and 216, respectively.

Example 22 *$a\times b$ is equal to ....*

Example 23 *$a-b$ is equal to ....*

Sol. (Q.Nos. 22 and 23)

$$B(\bar{x})=a\bar{x}+b=\frac{a(1+2+3+\ldots+17)}{17}+b=17$$

$$\frac{a\cdot(17\cdot 18)}{17\cdot 2}+b=17$$

$$9a+b=17 \quad \text{...(i)}$$

$$\sigma A^2=\frac{\sum x^2}{n}-\left(\frac{\sum x}{n}\right)^2$$

$$=\frac{1^2+2^2+\ldots+17^2}{17}-\left(\frac{1+2+\ldots+17}{17}\right)^2$$

$$=\frac{17\times 18\times 35}{6\times 17}-\left(\frac{17\times 18}{2\times 17}\right)^2$$

$$=105-81=24$$

$$\therefore \quad \sigma B^2=a^2\sigma A^2=a^2\cdot 24=216$$

$$a^2=\frac{216}{24}=9$$

$$\Rightarrow \quad a=3$$

$$b=17-27$$

$$\Rightarrow \quad b=-10$$

22. (–30) $a\times b=3\times(-10)=-30$

23. (13) $a-b=3-(-10)=13$

Single Integer Answer Type Questions

Example 24 *Let the mean of the data be 5.*

x	1	3	5	7	9
Frequency (f)	4	24	28	a	8

If m be the mean deviation about mean, then a – 5 m is equal to ......

Sol. (8) Given, mean = 5

$$\bar{x}=\frac{\Sigma f_i x_i}{\Sigma f_i}=5$$

$$\Rightarrow \quad \frac{4+72+140+7a+72}{64+a}=5$$

$$\Rightarrow \quad 288+7a=320+5a$$

$$\Rightarrow \quad 2a=32$$

$$\Rightarrow \quad a=16$$

$$m=\text{MD of } \bar{x}=\frac{\Sigma f_i|x_i-\bar{x}|}{\Sigma f_i}$$

$$=\frac{4\times 4+24\times 2+28\times 0+16\times 2+8\times 4}{64+16}$$

$$m=\frac{128}{80}=\frac{8}{5}$$

$$\therefore \quad a-5m=16-5\times\frac{8}{5}=8$$

Example 25 *Consider the following frequency distribution*

Class	0-6	6-12	12-18	18-24	24-30
Frequency	a	b	12	9	5

If mean $\frac{309}{22}$ *and median* $=14$, *then* $|a-b|$ *is equal to ......*

Sol. (2)

Class	f_i	x_i	$f_i x_i$	cf
0-6	a	3	$3a$	a
6-12	b	9	$9b$	$a+b$
12-18	12	15	180	$a+b+12$
18-24	9	21	189	$a+b+21$
24-30	5	27	135	$a+b+26$
	$N=(26+a+b)$		$(504+3a+9b)$	

$$\text{Mean} = \frac{504+3a+9b}{26+a+b} = \frac{309}{22}$$

$$\Rightarrow \quad 243a+111b = 3054$$

$$\Rightarrow \quad 81a+37b = 1018 \quad \text{...(i)}$$

Median class is $12-18$.

$$\text{Now, median} = 12 + \frac{\left(\frac{a+b+26}{2}\right)-(a+b)}{12} \times 6 = 14$$

$$\Rightarrow \quad \frac{a+b+26-2a-2b}{2} = 4$$

$$\Rightarrow \quad a+b = 18 \quad \text{...(ii)}$$

On solving Eqs. (i) and (ii), we get

$$a = 8 \text{ and } b = 10$$

$$\therefore \quad |a-b| = 2$$

Example 26 *Let the mean and variance of 8 numbers* $x, y, 10, 12, 6, 12, 4, 8$ *be 9 and 9.25. If* $x > y$, *then* $|x-y|$ *is equal to ......*

Sol. (6) Mean = 9

$$\Rightarrow \quad \frac{x+y+12+6+4+8+12+10}{8} = 9 \Rightarrow x+y = 20 \quad \text{...(i)}$$

Variance = 9.25

$$\frac{x^2+y^2+12^2+6^2+4^2+8^2+12^2+10^2}{8} - 9^2 = 9.25$$

$$\Rightarrow \quad x^2+y^2 = 218 \quad \text{...(ii)}$$

On eliminating y from Eqs. (i) and (ii), we get

$$x^2+(20-x)^2 = 218$$

$$\Rightarrow \quad x^2-20x+91 = 0$$

$$\Rightarrow \quad x = 7, 13$$

$$x = 13, y = 7 \ (x > y)$$

$$\therefore \quad |x-y| = 6$$

Example 27 *If the mean and variance of the frequency distribution are 9 and 15.08 respectively, then the value of* $\alpha^2-\beta^2+\frac{\alpha}{\beta}$ *is ......*

x_i	2	4	6	8	10	12	14	16
f_i	4	4	α	15	8	β	4	5

Sol. (1)

x_i	f_i	x_i^2	$f_i x_i$	$f_i x_i^2$
2	4	4	8	16
4	4	16	16	64
6	α	36	6α	36α
8	15	64	120	960
10	8	100	80	800
12	β	144	12β	144β
14	4	196	56	784
16	5	256	80	1280
	$\Sigma f_i = 40 + \alpha + \beta$		$\Sigma f_i x_i = 360 + 6\alpha + 12\beta$	$\Sigma f_i x_i^2 = 3904 + 36\alpha + 144\beta$

Given, mean = 9

$$\Rightarrow \quad \frac{\Sigma f_i x_i}{\Sigma f_i} = 9 \Rightarrow \frac{360+6\alpha+12\beta}{40+\alpha+\beta} = 9$$

$$\Rightarrow \quad 360+6\alpha+12\beta = 9(40+\alpha+\beta)$$

$$\Rightarrow \quad 3\beta = 3\alpha$$

$$\Rightarrow \quad \alpha = \beta \quad \text{...(i)}$$

Variance = 15.08

$$\Rightarrow \quad \frac{\Sigma f_i x_i^2}{\Sigma f_i} - \left(\frac{\Sigma f_i x_i}{\Sigma f_i}\right)^2 = 15.08$$

$$\Rightarrow \quad \frac{3904+36\alpha+144\beta}{40+\alpha+\beta} - (9)^2 = 15.08$$

$$\Rightarrow \quad \frac{3904+180\alpha}{40+2\alpha} = 81+15.08$$

$$\Rightarrow \quad 3904+180\alpha = 96.08(40+2\alpha)$$

$$\Rightarrow \quad 3904+180\alpha = 3843.2+192.16\,\alpha$$

$$\Rightarrow \quad 60.8 = 12.16\,\alpha$$

$$\Rightarrow \quad \alpha = \beta = 5$$

$$\therefore \quad \alpha^2-\beta^2+\frac{\alpha}{\beta} = 25-25+\frac{5}{5} = 1$$

Example 28 *If the mean deviation about mean of the numbers 1, 2, 3, ... n, where n is odd, is* $\left(\frac{n+1}{n}\right)$, *then n is equal to ......*

Sol. (5) Mean deviation of first n natural number $= \dfrac{n^2-1}{4n}$

$$\Rightarrow \quad \frac{n^2-1}{4n} = \frac{n+1}{n} \Rightarrow n^2 - 1 = 4n + 4$$

$$\Rightarrow \quad n^2 - 4n - 5 = 0 \Rightarrow n^2 - 5n + n - 5 = 0$$

$$\Rightarrow \quad n = 5, -1$$

$$\therefore \quad n = 5, \text{ as } n \neq -1$$

Numerical Value Type Questions

Example 29 *Consider the data on x taking the values 0, 2, 4, 8, ..., 2^n with frequencies ${}^nC_0, {}^nC_1, {}^nC_2, \ldots {}^nC_n$, respectively. If the mean of this data is $\dfrac{59048}{2^n}$, then n is equal to ......*

Sol. (10) Mean $= \dfrac{\Sigma x_i f_i}{\Sigma f_i}$

$$= \frac{{}^nC_0(0) + {}^nC_1(2) + {}^nC_2(2^2) + \ldots + {}^nC_n(2^n)}{{}^nC_0 + {}^nC_1 + {}^nC_2 + \ldots + {}^nC_n}$$

$$= \frac{{}^nC_1(2) + {}^nC_2(2^2) + {}^nC_3(2^3) + \ldots + {}^nC_n(2^n)}{2^n}$$

$\because \quad (1+x)^n = {}^nC_0 + {}^nC_1 x + {}^nC_2 x^2 + .. + {}^nC_n x^n$

At $x = 2$, we get

$$3^n = 1 + {}^nC_1(2) + {}^nC_2(2^2) + \ldots + {}^nC_n(2^n)$$

$$\Rightarrow \quad {}^nC_1(2) + {}^nC_2(2^2) + \ldots + {}^nC_n(2^n) = 3^n - 1$$

$$\therefore \quad \text{Mean} = \frac{3^n - 1}{2^n} = \frac{59048}{2^n}$$

$$\Rightarrow \quad 3^n = 59049 = 3^{10} \Rightarrow n = 10$$

Example 30 *The marks obtained by 40 students are grouped in a frequency table in class intervals of 10 marks each. The mean and the variance obtained from this distribution are found to be 40 and 49, respectively. It was later discovered that two observations belonging to the class interval (21 - 30) were included in the class interval (31- 40) by mistake. The variance after correcting the error is ....*

Sol. (49.25) Given, $n = 40, \bar{x} = 40$, $\text{var}(x) = 49$

$$\Rightarrow \quad \bar{x} = \frac{\Sigma f_i x_i}{40} = 40$$

$$\Rightarrow \quad \Sigma f_i x_i = 1600$$

Also, $\text{var}(x) = 49$

$$\Rightarrow \quad \frac{1}{40} \Sigma f_i (x_i - 40)^2 = 49$$

$$\therefore \quad 49 = \frac{1}{40} (\Sigma x_i^2 f_i) - 2 \Sigma x_i f_i + 40 \Sigma f_i$$

$$\Rightarrow \quad 49 = \frac{1}{40} (\Sigma x_i^2 f_i) - 2(1600) + 40 \times 40$$

$$\therefore \quad \Sigma x_i^2 f_i = 1649 \times 40$$

Let (21-30) and (31-40) denote the kth and $(k+1)$ th class intervals, respectively.

Then, if before correction f_k and f_{k+1} are frequencies of those intervals, then after correction (2 observations are shifted from (31-40) to (21-30)), frequency of k th interval becomes $f_k + 2$ and frequency of $(k+1)$ th interval becomes $f_{k+1} - 2$

$$\therefore \quad \bar{x}_{\text{new}} = \frac{1}{40} \left\{ \sum_{\substack{i=1 \\ i \neq k, k+1}}^{40} f_i x_i + (f_k + 2) x_k + (f_{k+1} - 2) x_{k+1} \right\}$$

$$\Rightarrow \quad \bar{x}_{\text{new}} = \frac{1}{40} \left\{ \sum_{i=1}^{40} f_i x_i \right\} + \frac{2}{40} \{(x_k - x_{k+1})\}$$

$$= \frac{1}{40} \sum_{i=1}^{40} f_i x_i + \frac{1}{20}(-10) = 39.5$$

Variance (new)

$$= \frac{1}{40} [\sum_{i=1}^{40} f_i (x_i - 39.5)^2 + f_k (x_k - 39.5)^2$$

$$+ f_{k+1} (x_{k+1} - 39.5)^2 \text{ where } i \neq k, k+1]$$

$$= \frac{1}{40} [\Sigma (f_i x_i^2 - 79 f_i x_i + (39.5)^2 f_i)]$$

$$= \frac{1}{40} \sum_{i=1}^{40} f_i \cdot x_i^2 - 79 \left(\frac{1}{40}\right) \sum_{i=1}^{40} f_i x_i + (39.5)^2 \cdot \frac{1}{40} \sum_{i=1}^{40} f_i$$

$$= 1649 - 3160 + 1560.25 = 49.25$$

Example 31 *In calculating the mean and variance of 10 readings, a student wrongly used the figure 52 for the correct figure of 25. He obtained the mean and variance as 45.0 and 16.0 respectively. Determine the correct mean and variance.*

Sol. (42.3, 43.81) Mean $= \dfrac{\Sigma x_i}{N} \Rightarrow 45 = \dfrac{\Sigma x_i}{10}$

$$\therefore \quad \Sigma x_i = 450$$

Correct $\Sigma x_i = 450 - 52 + 25 = 423$

$$\therefore \quad \text{Correct mean} = \frac{423}{10} = 42.3$$

$$\text{Variance} = \frac{\Sigma x_i^2}{N} - \left(\frac{\Sigma x_i}{N}\right)^2 \Rightarrow 16 = \frac{\Sigma x_i^2}{10} - (45)^2$$

$$\Rightarrow \quad \Sigma x_i^2 = (16 + 2025) \times 10 = 20410$$

$$\therefore \quad \text{Correct } \Sigma x_i^2 = 20410 - (52)^2 + (25)^2$$

$$= 20410 - 2704 + 625$$

$$= 18331$$

$$\therefore \quad \text{Correct variance} = \frac{18331}{10} - (42.3)^2$$

$$= 1833.1 - 1789.29 = 43.81$$

Example 32 *The mean of the data set comprising of 16 observations is 16. If one of the observations valued 16 is deleted and three new observations valued 3,4 and 5 added to the data, then the mean of the resultant data is equal to ......*

Sol. (14) Given, $\frac{x_1 + x_2 + x_3 + \ldots + x_{16}}{16} = 16 \Rightarrow \sum_{i=1}^{16} x_i = 16 \times 16$

Sum of new observations $= \sum_{i=1}^{18} y_i$

$= (16 \times 16 - 16) + (3 + 4 + 5) = 252$

Number of observations = 18

$\therefore$ New mean $= \frac{\sum_{i=1}^{18} y_i}{18} = \frac{252}{18} = 14$

Example 33 *If the median and range of four numbers $\{x, y, 2x + y, x - y\}$, where $0 < y < x < 2y$, are 5 and 14 respectively, then the mean of the number is ......*

Sol. (7) Since, $0 < y < x < 2y$

$\therefore \quad y > \frac{x}{2} \Rightarrow x - y < \frac{x}{2}$

$\therefore \quad x - y < y < x < 2x + y$

Hence, median $= \frac{y + x}{2} = 5$

$\Rightarrow \quad x + y = 10 \quad \ldots(i)$

And range $= (2x + y) - (x - y) = x + 2y$

But range = 14

$\therefore \quad x + 2y = 14 \quad \ldots(ii)$

From Eqs. (i) and (ii), we get

$x = 6$ and $y = 4$

$$\text{Mean} = \frac{(x - y) + y + x + (2x + y)}{4}$$

$$= \frac{4x + y}{4} = x + \frac{y}{4} = 6 + \frac{4}{4} = 6 + 1 = 7$$

Matching Type Questions

Example 34 *Consider the given data with frequency distribution*

x_i	2	6	9	8	3	5
f_i	2	5	3	4	4	2

Match each entry in Column I to the correct enteries in Column II

Column I		Column II	
(A)	The mean of the above data is	(p)	2
(B)	The median of above data is	(q)	1.95
(C)	The mean deviation about mean of the above data is	(r)	6
(D)	The mean deviation about the median of the above data is	(s)	5.75
		(t)	16.5

Sol. (A) → (s); (B) → (r); (C) → (p); (D) → (q);

First of all arrange x_i in increasing order and write corresponding frequencies prepare a table.

x_i	f_i	$f_i x_i$	cf	$\|x_i - \text{mean}\|$	$f_i \|x_i - \text{mean}\|$	$\|x_i - \text{median}\|$	$f_i \|x_i - \text{median}\|$
2	2	4	2	3.75	7.5	4	8
3	4	12	6	2.75	11	3	12
5	2	10	8	0.75	1.5	1	2
6	5	30	13	0.25	1.25	0	0
8	4	32	17	2.25	9	2	8
9	3	27	20	3.25	9.75	3	9
Total	20	115			40		39

(P) Mean $(\overline{X}) = \frac{\Sigma f_i x_i}{\Sigma f_i} = \frac{115}{20} = 5.75$

(Q) Median $= \left(\frac{20}{2}\right)$th observation = 10th observation = 6

(R) Mean deviation about mean $= \frac{\Sigma f_i \,|x_i - \text{mean}|}{\Sigma f_i} = \frac{40}{20} = 2$

(S) Mean deviation about median $= \frac{\Sigma f_i |x_i - \text{median}|}{\Sigma f_i} = \frac{39}{20} = 1.95$

EXERCISE 1

JEE Main Pattern

Single Option Correct Type Questions

1. The mean and the median of the following ten numbers in increasing order 10, 22, 26, 29, 34, x, 42, 67, 70, y are 42 and 35 respectively, then $\frac{y}{x}$ is equal to
(a) $\frac{7}{3}$ (b) $\frac{7}{2}$ (c) $\frac{8}{3}$ (d) $\frac{9}{4}$

2. The mean of a set of 30 observations is 75. If each other observation is multiplied by a non-zero number λ and then each of them is decreased by 25, their mean remains the same. Then, λ is equal to
(a) $\frac{10}{3}$ (b) $\frac{4}{3}$ (c) $\frac{1}{3}$ (d) $\frac{2}{3}$

3. The mean age of 25 teachers in a school is 40 yr. A teacher retires at the age of 60 yr and a new teacher is appointed in his place. If now the mean age of the teachers in this school is 39 yr, then the age (in years) of the newly appointed teacher is
(a) 25 (b) 30 (c) 35 (d) 40

4. If the median and the range of four numbers $\{x, y, 2x+y, x-y\}$, where $0 < y < x < 2y$, are 10 and 28 respectively, then the mean of the numbers is
(a) 18 (b) 10 (c) 5 (d) 14

5. In a college of 300 students every student reads 5 newspapers and every newspaper is read by 60 students. The number of newspapers is
(a) at least 30 (b) at most 20
(c) exactly 25 (d) None of these

6. The variance of first 50 even natural numbers is
(a) $\frac{833}{4}$ (b) 833 (c) 437 (d) $\frac{437}{4}$

7. If both the mean and the standard deviation of 50 observations $x_1, x_2, \dots, x_{50}$ are equal to 16, then the mean of $(x_1-4)^2, (x_2-4)^2, \dots, (x_{50}-4)^2$ is
(a) 480 (b) 400 (c) 380 (d) 525

8. The mean and the variance of five observations are 4 and 5.20, respectively. If three of the observations are 3, 4 and 4, then the absolute value of the difference of the other two observations, is
(a) 1 (b) 7
(c) 5 (d) 3

9. If $\sum_{i=1}^{9}(x_i-5)=9$ and $\sum_{i=1}^{9}(x_i-5)^2=45$, then the standard deviation of the 9 items $x_1, x_2, \dots, x_9$ is
(a) 9 (b) 4 (c) 2 (d) 3

10. If the sum of the deviations of 50 observations from 30 is 50, then the mean of these observations is
(a) 50 (b) 30 (c) 51 (d) 31

11. In a group of data, there are n observations, $x_1, x_2, \dots, x_n$. If $\sum_{i=1}^{n}(x_i+1)^2=9n$ and $\sum_{i=1}^{n}(x_i-1)^2=5n$, the standard deviation of the data is
(a) 2 (b) $\sqrt{7}$ (c) 5 (d) $\sqrt{5}$

12. 5 students of a class have an average height 150 cm and variance 18 cm^2. A new student, whose height is 156 cm, joined them. The variance (in cm^2) of the height of these six students is
(a) 16 (b) 22 (c) 20 (d) 18

13. The AM of n observations is M. If the sum of $(n-4)$ observations is a, then the mean of remaining four observations is
(a) $\frac{nM-a}{4}$ (b) $\frac{nM+a}{2}$ (c) $\frac{nM-a}{2}$ (d) $nM+a$

14. The AM of ${}^{2n+1}C_0, {}^{2n+1}C_1, {}^{2n+1}C_2, \dots, {}^{2n+1}C_n$ is
(a) $\frac{2^n}{n}$ (b) $\frac{2^n}{n+1}$ (c) $\frac{2^{2n}}{n}$ (d) $\frac{2^{2n}}{(n+1)}$

15. If a variable takes values 0, 1, 2, ..., n with frequencies q^n, $\frac{n}{1}q^{n-1}p, \frac{n(n-1)}{1\cdot 2}q^{n-2}p^2, \dots p^n$, where $p+q=1$, then the mean is
(a) np (b) nq (c) $n(p+q)$ (d) None of these

16. The outcome of each of 30 items was observed 10 items gave an outcome $\frac{1}{2}-d$ each, 10 items gave outcome $\frac{1}{2}$ each and the remaining 10 items gave outcome $\frac{1}{2}+d$ each. If the variance of this outcome data is $\frac{4}{3}$, then $|d|$ equals
(a) $\frac{2}{3}$ (b) $\frac{\sqrt{5}}{2}$ (c) $\sqrt{2}$ (d) 2

17. The mean life of a sample of 60 bulbs was 650 h and the standard deviation was 8 h. A second sample of 80 bulbs has a mean life of 660 h and standard deviation 7 h. Find the over all standard deviation.

(a) 8.97 (b) 8.98
(c) 8.94 (d) None of these

18. If harmonic mean of first 5 observations is $\frac{5}{2}$ and harmonic mean of another 5 observations is $\frac{9}{2}$, then harmonic mean of all 10 observations is

(a) 7 (b) $\frac{45}{14}$
(c) $\frac{101}{36}$ (d) None of these

Numerical Value Type Questions

19. The first of two samples has 100 items with mean 15 and SD = 3. It the whole group has 250 items with mean 15.6 and SD = $\sqrt{13.44}$, then the SD of the second group is ......

20. The batsman scores sums in 10 innings 38, 70, 48, 34,42, 55, 46, 63, 54 and 44, then the deviation from median is ......

21. If $\sum_{i=1}^{18}(x_i-8)=9$ and $\sum_{i=1}^{18}(x_i-8)^2=45$, then the standard deviation of $x_1, x_2, \ldots, x_{18}$ is equal to ....

22. For two data sets, each of size 5, the variance are given to be 4 and 5 and the corresponding means are given to be 2 and 4, respectively. The variance of the combined data set is ......

Previous Year Questions

23. If the variance of the frequency distribution

x	c	$2c$	$3c$	$4c$	$5c$	$6c$
f	2	1	1	1	1	1

is 160, then the value of $c \in N$ is **[Single Correct Type, 2024 Main]**

(a) 8 (b) 5
(c) 6 (d) 7

24. The frequency distribution of the age of students in a class of 40 students is given below

Age	15	16	17	18	19	20
Number of Students	5	8	5	12	x	y

If the mean deviation about the median is 1.25, then $4x+5y$ is equal to **[Single Correct Type, 2024 Main]**

(a) 44 (b) 43
(c) 46 (d) 47

25. The mean and standard deviation of 20 observations are found to be 10 and 2, respectively. On rechecking, it was found that an observation by mistake was taken 8 instead of 12. The correct standard deviation is **[Single Correct Type, 2024 Main]**

(a) 1.8 (b) $\sqrt{3.96}$ (c) $\sqrt{3.86}$ (d) 1.94

26. Let $\alpha, \beta \in R$. Let the mean and the variance of 6 observations $-3, 4, 7, -6, \alpha, \beta$ be 2 and 23, respectively. The mean deviation about the mean of these 6 observations is **[Single Correct Type, 2024 Main]**

(a) $\frac{16}{3}$ (b) $\frac{14}{3}$ (c) $\frac{11}{3}$ (d) $\frac{13}{3}$

27. Let the mean and the variance of 6 observations $a, b, 68, 44, 48, 60$ be 55 and 194, respectively. If $a > b$, then $a+3b$ is **[Single Correct Type, 2024 Main]**

(a) 180 (b) 190 (c) 200 (d) 210

28. Let $a_1, a_2, \ldots, a_{10}$ be 10 observations such that $\sum_{k=1}^{10} a_k = 50$ and $\sum_{\forall k<j} a_k \cdot a_j = 1100$. Then, the standard deviation of $a_1, a_2, \ldots, a_{10}$ is equal to **[Single Correct Type, 2024 Main]**

(a) 10 (b) $\sqrt{5}$
(c) 5 (d) $\sqrt{115}$

29. Consider 10 observations $x_1, x_2, \ldots, x_{10}$ such that $\sum_{i=1}^{10}(x_i-\alpha)=2$ and $\sum_{i=1}^{10}(x_i-\beta)^2=40$, where α, β are positive integers. Let the mean and the variance of the observations be $\frac{6}{5}$ and $\frac{84}{25}$, respectively. Then, $\frac{\beta}{\alpha}$ is equal to **[Single Correct Type, 2024 Main]**

(a) 2 (b) 1 (c) $\frac{3}{2}$ (d) $\frac{5}{2}$

30. Let the median and the mean deviation about the median of 7 observations 170, 125, 230, 190, 210, a, b be 170 and $\frac{205}{7}$, respectively. Then, the mean deviation about the mean of these 7 observations is **[Single Correct Type, 2024 Main]**

(a) 32 (b) 28
(c) 30 (d) 31

31. If the mean and variance of five observations are $\frac{24}{5}$ and $\frac{194}{25}$ respectively and the mean of the first four observations is $\frac{7}{2}$, then the variance of the first four observations is equal to **[Single Correct Type, 2024 Main]**

(a) $\frac{4}{5}$ (b) $\frac{77}{12}$ (c) $\frac{5}{4}$ (d) $\frac{105}{4}$

32. Let $a, b, c \in N$ and $a < b < c$. Let the mean, the mean deviation about the mean and the variance of the 5 observations 9, 25, a, b, c be 18, 4 and $\frac{136}{5}$, respectively. Then, $2a + b - c$ is equal to ....

[Numerical Value Type, 2024 Main]

33. The variance σ^2 of the data

x_i	0	1	5	6	10	12	17
f_i	3	2	3	2	6	3	3

is .... **[Numerical Value Type, 2024 Main]**

34. If the mean and variance of the data 65, 68, 58, 44, 48, 45, 60, α, β, 60 where, $\alpha > \beta$, are 56 and 66.2 respectively, then $\alpha^2 + \beta^2$ is equal to ....

[Numerical Value Type, 2024 Main]

35. The mean and standard deviation of 15 observations were found to be 12 and 3, respectively. On rechecking it was found that an observation was read as 10 in place of 12. If μ and σ^2 denote the mean and variance of the correct observations respectively, then $15(\mu + \mu^2 + \sigma^2)$ is equal to .... **[Numerical Value Type, 2024 Main]**

36. Two dice A and B are rolled. Let the numbers obtained on A and B be α and β, respectively. If the variance of $\alpha - \beta$ is $\frac{p}{q}$, where p and q are coprime, then the sum of the positive divisors of p is equal to

[Single Correct Type, 2023 Main]

(a) 36 (b) 72
(c) 48 (d) 31

37. Let the mean and variance of 12 observations be 9/2 and 4 respectively. Later on, it was observed that two observations were considered as 9 and 10 instead of 7 and 14 respectively. If the correct variance is $\frac{m}{n}$, where m and n are coprime. then $m + n$ is equal to

[Single Correct Type, 2023 Main]

(a) 316 (b) 315
(c) 314 (d) 317

38. The mean and variance of a set of 15 numbers are 12 and 14 respectively. The mean and variance of another set of 15 numbers are 14 and σ^2 respectively. If the variance of all the 30 numbers in the two sets is 13, then σ^2 is equal to **[Single Correct Type, 2023 Main]**

(a) 9 (b) 11
(c) 10 (d) 12

39. The mean and variance of 5 observations are 5 and 8, respectively. If 3 observations are 1, 3, 5, then the sum of cubes of the remaining two observations is

[Single Correct Type, 2023 Main]

(a) 1216 (b) 1072
(c) 1792 (d) 1456

40. The mean and standard deviation of 10 observations are 20 and 8 respectively. Later on, it was observed that one observation was recorded as 50 instead of 40. Then, the correct variance is **[Single Correct Type, 2023 Main]**

(a) 11 (b) 14 (c) 13 (d) 12

41. Let the mean of 6 observations 1, 2, 4, 5, x and y be 5 and their variance be 10. Then, their mean deviation about the mean is equal to **[Single Correct Type, 2023 Main]**

(a) $\frac{10}{3}$ (b) 3 (c) $\frac{7}{3}$ (d) $\frac{8}{3}$

42. Let μ be the mean and σ be the standard deviation of the distribution

x_i	0	1	2	3	4	5
f_i	$k+2$	$2k$	k^2-1	k^2-1	k^2+1	$k-3$

where $\Sigma f_i = 62$. If $[x]$ denotes the greatest integer $\le x$, then $[\mu^2 + \sigma^2]$ is equal to **[Single Correct Type, 2023 Main]**

(a) 8 (b) 9 (c) 7 (d) 6

43. Let S be the set of all values of a_1 for which the mean deviation about the mean of 100 consecutive positive integers $a_1, a_2, a_3, \ldots, a_{100}$ is 25. Then, S is

[Single Correct Type, 2023 Main]

(a) N (b) $\{9\}$ (c) ϕ (d) $\{99\}$

44. The mean and variance of 7 observations are 8 and 16, respectively. If one observation 14 is omitted and a and b are respectively mean and variance of remaining 6 observations, then $a + 3b - 5$ is equal to

[Single Correct Type, 2023 Main]

(a) 37 (b) 40 (c) 45 (d) 42

45. Let $X = \{11, 12, 13, \ldots, 40, 41\}$ and $Y = \{61, 62, 63, \ldots, 90, 91\}$ be the two sets of observations. If $\bar{x}$ and $\bar{y}$ are their respective means and σ^2 is the variance of all the observations in $X \cup Y$, then $|\bar{x} + \bar{y} - \sigma^2|$ is equal to **[Single Correct Type, 2023 Main]**

(a) 603 (b) 605 (c) 601 (d) 608

46. The mean and variance of the marks obtained by the students in a test are 10 and 4, respectively. Later, the marks of one of the students in increased from 8 to 12. If the new mean of the marks is 10.2, then their new variance is equal to **[Single Correct Type, 2023 Main]**

(a) 4.04 (b) 4.08 (c) 3.92 (d) 3.96

47. Let sets A and B have 5 elements each. Let the mean of the elements in sets A and B be 5 and 8 respectively and the variance of the elements in sets A and B be 12 and 20 respectively. A new set C of 10 elements is formed by subtracting 3 from each element of A and adding 2 to each element of B. Then, the sum of the mean and variance of the elements of C is

[Single Correct Type, 2023 Main]

(a) 36 (b) 38 (c) 40 (d) 32

48. Let $9 = x_1 < x_2 < \ldots < x_7$ be in an AP with common difference d. If the standard deviation of $x_1, x_2 \ldots, x_7$ is 4 and the mean is $\bar{x}$, then $\bar{x} + x_6$ is equal to **[Single Correct Type, 2023 Main]**

(a) $2\left(9 + \frac{8}{\sqrt{7}}\right)$ (b) $18\left(1 + \frac{1}{\sqrt{3}}\right)$
(c) 34 (d) 25

49. Let the mean and standard deviation of marks of class A of 100 students be respectively 40 and α (> 0) and the mean and standard deviation of marks of class B of n students be respectively 55 and $30 - \alpha$. If the mean and variance of the marks of the combined class of $100 + n$ students are respectively 50 and 350, then the sum of variances of classes A and B is **[Single Correct Type, 2023 Main]**

(a) 650 (b) 450 (c) 500 (d) 900

50. The mean and standard deviation of the marks of 10 students were found to be 50 and 12, respectively. Later, it was observed that two marks 20 and 25 were wrongly read as 45 and 50 respectively. Then, the correct variance is ...... **[Numerical Value Type, 2023 Main]**

51. Let the mean of the data

x	1	3	5	7	9
Frequency (f)	4	24	28	α	8

be 5. If m and σ^2 are respectively the mean deviation about the mean and the variance of the data, then $\frac{3\alpha}{m + \sigma^2}$ is equal to .... **[Numerical Value Type, 2023 Main]**

52. If the mean of the frequency distribution

Class	0-10	10-20	20-30	30-40	40-50
Frequency	2	3	x	5	4

is 28, then its variance is .... **[Numerical Value Type, 2023 Main]**

53. Let the mean and variance of 8 numbers x, y, 10,12, 6, 12, 4, 8 be 9 and 9.25 respectively. If $x > y$, then $3x - 2y$ is equal to .... **[Numerical Value Type, 2023 Main]**

54. If the mean and variance of the frequency distribution

x_i	2	4	6	8	10	12	14	16
f_i	4	4	α	15	8	β	4	5

are 9 and 15.08 respectively, then the value of $\alpha^2 + \beta^2 - \alpha\beta$ is .... **[Numerical Value Type, 2023 Main]**

55. Let $x_1, x_2, x_3, \ldots, x_{20}$ be in geometric progression with $x_1 = 3$ and the common ratio 1/2. A new data is constructed replacing each x_i by $(x_i - i)^2$. If $\bar{x}$ is the mean of new data, then the greatest integer less than or equal to $\bar{x}$ is .... **[Numerical Value Type, 2023 Main]**

56. If the mean deviation about median for the number 3, 5, 7, $2k$, 12, 16, 21, 24 arranged in the ascending order is 6, then the median is **[Single Correct Type, 2022 Main]**

(a) 11.5 (b) 10.5 (c) 12 (d) 11

57. The number of values of $a \in N$ such that the variance of 3, 7, 12, a, $43 - a$ is a natural number is **[Single Correct Type, 2022 Main]**

(a) 0 (b) 2 (c) 5 (d) infinite

58. Let the mean and the variance of 5 observations x_1, x_2, x_3, x_4, x_5 be $\frac{24}{5}$ and $\frac{194}{25}$ respectively. If the mean and variance of the first 4 observation are 7/2 and a respectively, then $(4a + x_5)$ is equal to **[Single Correct Type, 2022 Main]**

(a) 13 (b) 15 (c) 17 (d) 18

59. Suppose, a class has 7 students. The average marks of these students in the mathematics examination is 62, and their variance is 20. A student fails in the examination if he/she gets less than 50 marks, then in worst case, the number of students can fail is **[Single Correct Type, 2022 Main]**

(a) 4 (b) 5 (c) 0 (d) 2

60. The mean and standard deviation of 15 observations are found to be 8 and 3 respectively. On rechecking it was found that, in the observations, 20 was misread as 5. Then, the correct variance is equal to **[Single Correct Type, 2022 Main]**

(a) 17 (b) 15 (c) 19 (d) 14

61. The mean and variance of the data 4, 5, 6, 6, 7, 8, x, y where $x < y$ are 6 and 9/4 respectively. Then, $x^4 + y^2$ is equal to **[Single Correct Type, 2022 Main]**

(a) 162 (b) 320 (c) 674 (d) 420

62. The mean and standard deviation of 50 observations are 15 and 2 respectively. It was found that one incorrect observation was taken such that the sum of correct and incorrect observations is 70. If the correct mean is 16, then the correct variance is equal to **[Single Correct Type, 2022 Main]**

(a) 10 (b) 36 (c) 43 (d) 60

63. The mean of the numbers a, b, 8, 5, 10 is 6 and their variance is 6.8. If M is the mean deviation of the numbers about the mean, then 25 M is equal to **[Single Correct Type, 2022 Main]**

(a) 60 (b) 55
(c) 50 (d) 45

64. Let the mean and the variance of 20 observations $x_1, x_2, \ldots x_{20}$ be 15 and 9, respectively. For $\alpha \in R$, if the mean of $(x_1 + \alpha)^2, (x_2 + \alpha)^2, \ldots, (x_{20} + \alpha)^2$ is 178, then the square of the maximum value of α is equal to .... **[Numerical Value Type, 2022 Main]**

65. The mean and variance of 10 observation were calculated as 15 and 15 respectively by a student who took by mistake 25 instead of 15 for one observation. Then, the correct standard deviation is ....

[Numerical Value Type, 2022 Main]

66. An online exam is attempted by 50 candidates out of which 20 are boys. The average marks obtained by boys is 12 with a variance 2. The variance of marks obtained by 30 girls is also 2. The average marks of all 50 candidates is 15. If μ is the average marks of girls and σ^2 is the variance of marks of 50 candidates, then $\mu + \sigma^2$ is equal to ....

[Numerical Value Type, 2022 Main]

67. Let n be an odd natural number such that the variance of 1, 2, 3, 4, ..., n is 14. Then, n is equal to ....

[Numerical Value Type, 2022 Main]

68. Let the mean and variance of four numbers 3, 7, x and $y(x > y)$ be 5 and 10 respectively. Then, the mean of four numbers $3 + 2x, 7 + 2y, x + y$ and $x - y$ is ....

[Numerical Value Type, 2022 Main]

69. The mean and standard deviation of 40 observations are 30 and 5 respectively. It was noticed that two of these observations 12 and 10 were wrongly recorded. If σ is the standard deviation of the data after omitting the two wrong observations from the data, then $38\sigma^2$ is equal to ....

[Numerical Value Type, 2022 Main]

70. The mean of 10 numbers $7 \times 8, 10 \times 10, 13 \times 12, 16 \times 14, \ldots$ is ....

[Numerical Value Type, 2022 Main]

71. Consider the following frequency distribution

Class	10-20	20-30	30-40	40-50	50-60
Frequency	α	110	54	30	β

If the sum of all frequencies is 584 and median is 45, then $|\alpha - \beta|$ is equal to ....

[Numerical Value Type, 2022 Main]

72. Consider the following frequency distribution

Class	0-6	6-12	12-18	18-24	24-30
Frequency	a	b	12	9	5

If mean $= \frac{309}{22}$ and median $= 14$, then the value $(a - b)^2$ is equal to ....

[Numerical Value Type, 2022 Main]

73. The mean and variance of 7 observations are 8 and 16 respectively. If two observations are 6 and 8, then the variance of the remaining 5 observations is

[Single Correct Type, 2021 Main]

(a) $\frac{92}{5}$ (b) $\frac{134}{5}$

(c) $\frac{536}{25}$ (d) $\frac{112}{5}$

74. The mean and standard deviation of 20 observations were calculated as 10 and 2.5 respectively. It was found that by mistake one data value was taken as 25 instead of 35. If α and $\sqrt{\beta}$ are the mean and standard deviation respectively for correct data, then (α, β) is

[Single Correct Type, 2021 Main]

(a) (11, 26) (b) (10.5, 25) (c) (11, 25) (d) (10.5, 26)

75. Let the mean and variance of the frequency distribution be 6 and 6.8, respectively.

x	$x_1 = 2$	$x_2 = 6$	$x_3 = 8$	$x_4 = 9$
f	4	4	α	β

If x_3 is changed from 8 to 7, then the mean for the new data will be

[Single Correct Type, 2021 Main]

(a) 4 (b) 5 (c) 17/3 (d) 16/3

76. If the mean and variance of the following data :

6, 10, 7, 13, a, 12, b, 12 are 9 and $\frac{37}{4}$ respectively, then $(a - b)^2$ is equal to

[Single Correct Type, 2021 Main]

(a) 24 (b) 12 (c) 32 (d) 16

77. If the mean and variance of six observations 7, 10, 11, 15, a, b are 10 and $\frac{20}{3}$, respectively, then the value of $|a - b|$ is equal to

[Single Correct Type, 2021 Main]

(a) 9 (b) 11 (c) 7 (d) 1

78. The mean of 6 distinct observations is 6.5 and their variance is 10.25. If 4 out of 6 observations are 2, 4, 5 and 7, then the remaining two observations are

[Single Correct Type, 2021 Main]

(a) 10, 11 (b) 3, 18 (c) 8, 13 (d) 1, 20

79. Consider three observations a, b and c, such that $b = a + c$. If the standard deviation of $a + 2, b + 2, c + 2$ is d, then which of the following is true?

[Single Correct Type, 2021 Main]

(a) $b^2 = 3(a^2 + c^2) + 9d^2$ (b) $b^2 = a^2 + c^2 + 3d^2$

(c) $b^2 = 3(a^2 + c^2 + d^2)$ (d) $b^2 = 3(a^2 + c^2) - 9d^2$

80. The first of the two samples in a group has 100 items with mean 15 and standard deviation 3. If the whole group has 250 items with mean 15.6 and standard deviation $\sqrt{13.44}$, then the standard deviation of the second sample is

[Single Correct Type, 2021 Main]

(a) 8 (b) 6 (c) 4 (d) 5

81. Let in a series of $2n$ observations, half of them are equal to a and remaining half are equal to $-a$. Also, by adding a constant b in each of these observations, the mean and standard deviation of new set become 5 and 20, respectively. Then, the value of $a^2 + b^2$ is equal to

[Single Correct Type, 2021 Main]

(a) 425 (b) 650 (c) 250 (d) 925

EXERCISE 2
JEE Advanced Pattern

Single Option Correct Type Questions

1. If $\sum_{i=1}^{9}(x_i-6)=12$ and $\sum_{i=1}^{9}(x_i-6)^2=48$, then the standard deviation of the 9 items $x_1, x_2, \ldots, x_9$ is
(a) 2.41 (b) 2.50
(c) 2.31 (d) 3.12

2. If the sum ofthe deviations of 40 observations from 30 is 40, then the mean of these observations is
(a) 50 (b) 30
(c) 51 (d) 31

3. In a group of data, there are n observations, $x_1, x_2, \ldots, x_n$. If $\sum_{i=1}^{8}(x_i+1)^2=11n$ and $\sum_{i=1}^{n}(x_i-1)^2=7n$, then the standard deviation of the data is
(a) 2 (b) $\sqrt{7}$
(c) 5 (d) $\sqrt{5}$

4. 5 students of a class have an average height 160 cm and variance 19 cm^2. A new student, whose height is 166 cm, joined them. The varaince (in cm^2) of the height of these six students is
(a) 16.42 (b) 22.8
(c) 20.83 (d) 18.80

5. The AM of n observations is P. If the sum of $(n-6)$ observations is a, then the mean of remaining six observations is
(a) $\frac{np-a}{6}$ (b) $\frac{np+a}{3}$
(c) $\frac{np-a}{4}$ (d) $np+a$

6. Consider the frequency distribution, where p is a positive integer

x	p	$2p$	$3p$	$4p$	$5p$	$6p$
f	2	1	1	1	1	1

If the variance is 160, then the value of p is
(a) 7 (b) 6
(c) 8 (d) 9

7. If $\bar{x}_1$ and $\bar{x}_2$ are the means of two distribution such that $\bar{x}_1 > \bar{x}_2$ and $\bar{x}$ is the means of the combined distribution, then
(a) $\bar{x} < \bar{x}_2$ (b) $\bar{x} > \bar{x}_1$
(c) $\bar{x} = \frac{\bar{x}_1+\bar{x}_2}{2}$ (d) $\bar{x}_1 + \bar{x} > \bar{x}_2$

8. The outcome of each 40 items was observed 15 items gave an outcomes $\frac{1}{3}-c$ each, 10 items gave out come $\frac{1}{3}$ each and remaining 15 items gave out come $\frac{1}{3}+C$ each. If the variance of this outcome data is $\frac{6}{5}$, then $[c^2]$ equals, where $[\cdot]$ is greatest integer function.
(a) 2 (b) 1
(c) 3 (d) 4

9. The mean life of a sample of 70 bulbs was 700 h and the standard deviation was 8 h. A second sample of 90 bulbs has a mean life of 710 h and standard deviation 7 h. Find the over all standard deviation.
(a) 8.97 (b) 8.98
(c) 8.95 (d) None of these

10. If harmonic mean of first 10 observative is $\frac{7}{2}$ and harmonic mean of another 10 observation is $\frac{11}{2}$, then harmonic mean of all 20 observative is
(a) $\frac{63}{77}$ (b) $\frac{67}{37}$
(c) $\frac{77}{36}$ (d) $\frac{35}{18}$

More than One Correct Option Type Questions

11. If the mean deviation about the median of the numbers $a, 2a, \ldots, 5a$ is 50, then a is equal to
(a) -4 (b) 4
(c) 14 (d) -14

12. The mean of the numbers $a, b, 8, 5$ and 10 is 6 and the variance is 6.80. Then, which of the following are true?
(a) $a=4$ (b) $b=3$
(c) $a=3$ (d) $b=4$

13. The average marks of boys in a class is 52 and that of girls is 42. The average marks of boys and girls is combined is 50. Then,
(a) percentage of boys = 80%
(b) percentage fo girls = 80%
(c) percentage of girls = 20%
(d) percentage of boys = 20%

14. Consider a data set with the following values 5, 7, 9, 11, 13, then
(a) the variance of the dataset is 8
(b) the mean absolute deviation of the dataset 2.4
(c) the variance of the dataset 1156
(d) the standard deviation of the dataset 152.28

15. Let X and Y be two independentent random variables, each following a normal distribution. $X \sim N(0, 1)$ and $Y \sim N(0, 4)$. Define $Z = X + Y$. Which of the following are correct?
(a) Z follows a normal distribution
(b) Z follows a normal distribution with 0 mean
(c) Z follows a normal distribution with variance 5
(d) Z follows a normal distribution with variance 4

Passage Based Questions

Passage I

(Q. Nos. 16 to 17)

■ There are 60 students in a class. The following is the frequency distribution of the marks obtained by the students in a test

Marks	0	1	2	3	4	5
Frequency	$x-2$	x	x^2	$(x+1)^2$	$2x$	$x+1$

where, x is a positive integer.

16. The mean of the marks is
(a) 2.9 (b) 2.8
(c) 3 (d) None of these

17. The standard deviation of the marks is
(a) 1.14 (b) 1.12
(c) 1.18 (d) None of these

Passage II

(Q. Nos. 18 to 19)

■ In a study on the heights of students in a school, the heights (in inches) of a sample of 10 students were measured as follows

60, 62, 64, 65, 66, 68, 69, 70, 72, 74

18. What is the variance of the heights of these students?
(a) 12.5 (b) 13.2
(c) 16.5 (d) 17.6

19. What is the standard deviation of the heights of these students
(a) 3.5 (b) 4.2
(c) 4.8 (d) 5.6

Stem Based Questions

Stem I

(Q. Nos. 20 to 21)

■ If the standard deviation of $x_1, x_2, \ldots, x_n$ is 3.5.

20. The standard deviation of $-2x_i - 3, -2x_2 - 3, \ldots - 2x_n - 3$ is ....

21. The variance of $-3x_1 - 4, -3x_2 - 4 \ldots -3x_n - 4$ is ....

Stem II

(Q. Nos. 22 to 23)

■ Consider the following data

x	2	3	4	5	6	7
f	4	9	16	14	11	6

22. The standard deviation is ....

23. The variance of data is ....

Single Integer Type Questions

24. If the standard deviation of the data 6, 5, 9, 13, 12, 8, 10 is P, then $[P]$ is ....
[where, $[\cdot]$ is greatest integer function]

25. Consider the following frequency distribution

Class	0-6	6-12	12-18	18-24	24-30
Frequency	a	b	12	9	5

If mean $= \dfrac{309}{22}$ and median $= 14$, then the value $\dfrac{ab}{20}$ is equal to ....

26. The mean age of 25 teachers in a school is 40 yr. A teacher retires at the age of 60 yr and a new teacher is appointed in his place. If the mean age of the teachers in this school now is 39 yr, then the age (in years) of the newly appointed teacher is $7P$, then P is ....

27. Consider the following frequency distribution

Class	10-20	20-30	30-40	40-50	50-60
Frequency	α	110	54	30	β

If the sum of all frequencies is 584 and median is 45, then $\left|\dfrac{\alpha - \beta}{164}\right|$ is equal to ....

28. Consider a set of $3n$ numbers having variance 4. In this set, the mean of first $2n$ numbers is 6 and the mean of the remaining n numbers is 3. A new set is constructed by adding 1 into each of first $2n$ numbers and subtracting 1 from each of the remaining n numbers. If the variance of the new set is k, then $[k]$ is equal to ....

Numerical Value Type Questions

29. An online exam is attempted by 50 candidates out of which 20 are boys. The average marks obtained by boys is 12 with a variance 2. The variance of marks obtained by 30 girls is also 2. The average marks of all 50 candidates is 15. If μ is the average marks of girls and σ^2 is the variance of marks of 50 candidates, then $\mu + \sigma^2$ is equal to ....

30. If the mean and variance of eight numbers 3, 7, 9, 12, 13, 20, x and y be 10 and 25, respectively, then xy is equal to ....

31. If the variance of the terms is an increasing AP, $b_1, b_2, b_3, \ldots, b_{11}$ is 90, then the common difference of this AP is ....

32. The mean of 5 observations is 4.4 and their variance is 8.24. If three of the observations are 1, 2 and 6, then sum of other two observations is ....

33. Let $X_1, X_2, \ldots, X_{18}$ be eighteen observations, such that $\sum_{i=1}^{18}(X_i - \alpha) = 36$ and $\sum_{i=1}^{18}(X_i - \beta)^2 = 90$, where α and β are distinct real numbers. If the standard deviation of these observations is 1, then the value of $|\alpha - \beta|$ is ....

Matching Type Questions

34. Consider the given data with frequency distribution

x_i	0	1	2	3	4	5
f_i	2	4	16	25	8	5

Match each entry Column I to the correct enteries in Column II.

	Column I		Column II
(A)	The mean of the above data	(p)	0.8
(B)	The median of the above data is	(q)	0.85
(C)	The mean deviation about mean of the above data is	(r)	2.8
(D)	The mean deviation about the median of the above data is	(s)	3
		(t)	4

35. Consider the given data with frequency distribution

x_i	1	2	6	3	5
f_i	3	5	7	1	5

Match each entry in Column I to the correct enteries in Column II.

	Column I		Column II
(A)	The GM of mean and median of above data is	(p)	1.71
(B)	The mean of deviation about mean of the above data	(q)	1.86
(C)	The mean deviation about the median of the above data is	(r)	1.78
(D)	The AM of mean deviation about mean and mean deviation about median is	(s)	4.44

EXERCISE 3

Challenging Problems

1. Calculate the mean deviation about the mean of the set of first n natural numbers when n is even natural number.
2. Find the mean and standard deviation of first n terms of an AP, whose first term is a and common difference is d.
3. In calculating the mean and variance of 10 readings, a student wrongly used the figure 52 for the correct figure of 25. He obtained the mean and variance as 45.0 and 16.0 respectively. Determine the correct mean and variance.
4. The mean square deviations of a set of observations $x_1, x_2, \ldots, x_n$ about a point c is defined to be $\frac{1}{n}\sum_{i=1}^{n}(x_i - c)^2$. The mean square deviations about -1 and $+1$ of a set of observations are 7 and 3, respectively. Find the standard deviation of this set of observations.
5. The marks obtained by 40 students are grouped in a frequency table in class intervals of 10 marks each. The mean and the variance obtained from this distribution are found to be 40 and 49, respectively. It was later discovered that two observations belonging to the class interval (21 - 30) were included in the class interval (31 - 40) by mistake. Find the mean and the variance after correcting the error.

Answer Key

Exercise 1

1. (a)	2. (b)	3. (c)	4. (d)	5. (c)	6. (b)	7. (b)	8. (b)	9. (c)	10. (d)
11. (d)	12. (c)	13. (a)	14. (d)	15. (a)	16. (c)	17. (c)	18. (b)	19. (4)	20. (8.6)
21. (1.5)	22. (5.5)	23. (d)	24. (a)	25. (b)	26. (d)	27. (a)	28. (b)	29. (a)	30. (c)
31. (c)	32. (33)	33. (20.0909)	34. (6344)	35. (2521)	36. (c)	37. (d)	38. (c)	39. (b)	40. (c)
41. (d)	42. (a)	43. (a)	44. (a)	45. (a)	46. (d)	47. (b)	48. (c)	49. (c)	50. (269)
51. (8)	52. (151)	53. (25)	54. (25)	55. (142)	56. (d)	57. (a)	58. (b)	59. (c)	60. (a)
61. (b)	62. (c)	63. (a)	64. (4)	65. (2)	66. (25)	67. (13)	68. (12)	69. (238)	70. (398)
71. (164)	72. (4)	73. (c)	74. (d)	75. (c)	76. (d)	77. (d)	78. (a)	79. (d)	80. (c)
81. (a)									

Exercise 2

1. (c)	2. (d)	3. (b)	4. (c)	5. (a)	6. (a)	7. (d)	8. (b)	9. (c)	10. (c)
11. (a,b)	12. (c,d)	13. (a,c)	14. (a,b)	15. (a,b,c)	16. (b)	17. (b)	18. (d)	19. (b)	20. (7)
21. (110.25)	22. (1.38)	23. (1.904)	24. (2)	25. (4)	26. (5)	27. (164)	28. (7)	29. (25)	30. (54)
31. (3)	32. (13)	33. (4)							

34. (A) $\rightarrow$ (r), (B) $\rightarrow$ (s), (C) $\rightarrow$ (q), (D) $\rightarrow$ (p)

35. (A) $\rightarrow$ (s), (B) $\rightarrow$ (q), (C) $\rightarrow$ (p), (D) $\rightarrow$ (r)

Solutions

Exercise 1 - JEE Main Pattern

1. Given ten numbers are

$$10, 22, 26, 29, 34, x, 42, 67, 70, y$$

and their mean = 42

$$\therefore \frac{10 + 22 + 26 + 29 + 34 + x + 42 + 67 + 70 + y}{10} = 42$$

$$\Rightarrow \frac{300 + x + y}{10} = 42$$

$$\Rightarrow x + y = 120 \quad \text{...(i)}$$

and their median (arranged numbers are in increasing order) = 35

$$\Rightarrow \frac{34 + x}{2} = 35 \Rightarrow 34 + x = 70$$

$$\Rightarrow x = 36$$

On substituting $x = 36$ in Eq. (i), we get

$$36 + y = 120 \Rightarrow y = 84$$

$$\therefore \frac{y}{x} = \frac{84}{36} = \frac{7}{3}$$

2. As, mean is a linear operation, so if each observation is multiplied by λ and decreased by 25, then the mean becomes $75\lambda - 25$.

According to the question,

$$75\lambda - 25 = 75 \Rightarrow \lambda = \frac{4}{3}$$

3. Let $\frac{x_1 + x_2 + \ldots + x_{25}}{25} = \bar{x} = 40$

$$\Rightarrow x_1 + x_2 + \ldots + x_{25} = 1000$$

Let A be the age of new teacher.

$$\therefore x_1 + x_2 + \ldots + x_{25} - 60 + A = 39 \times 25$$

$$\Rightarrow 1000 - 60 + A = 975 \Rightarrow A = 975 - 940 = 35$$

4. Since, $0 < y < x < 2y$

$$\therefore y > \frac{x}{2} \Rightarrow x - y < \frac{x}{2}$$

$$\therefore x - y < y < x < 2x + y$$

Hence, median $= \frac{y + x}{2} = 10$

$$\Rightarrow x + y = 20 \quad \text{...(i)}$$

And range $= (2x + y) - (x - y) = x + 2y$

But range = 28

$$\therefore x + 2y = 28 \quad \text{...(ii)}$$

From Eqs. (i) and (ii), we get

$$x = 12, y = 8$$

$$\therefore \text{Mean} = \frac{(x - y) + y + x + (2x + y)}{4}$$

$$= \frac{4x + y}{4} = x + \frac{y}{4} = 12 + \frac{8}{4} = 14$$

5. Let the number of newspapers be n.

Now, according to the question,

$$60n = (300)(5)$$

$$\Rightarrow n = \frac{1500}{60} = 25$$

6. Here, $\bar{X} = \frac{\sum X_i}{n} = \frac{2 + 4 + 6 + 8 + \ldots + 100}{50} = \frac{50 \times 51}{50} = 51$

$[\because \sum 2n = n(n + 1), \text{ here } n = 50]$

Variance, $\sigma^2 = \frac{1}{n}\sum X_i^2 - (\bar{X})^2$

$$= \frac{1}{50}(2^2 + 4^2 + \ldots + 100^2) - (51)^2$$

$$= 833$$

7. It is given that both mean and standard deviation of 50 observations $x_1, x_2, x_3, \ldots, x_{50}$ are equal to 16.

So, $\text{mean} = \frac{\sum x_i}{50} = 16 \quad \text{...(i)}$

and standard deviation $= \sqrt{\frac{\sum x_i^2}{50} - \left(\frac{\sum x_i}{50}\right)^2} = 16$

$$\Rightarrow \frac{\sum x_i^2}{50} - (16)^2 = (16)^2$$

$$\Rightarrow \frac{\sum x_i^2}{50} = 2 \times 256 = 512 \quad \text{...(ii)}$$

Now, mean of $(x_1 - 4)^2, (x_2 - 4)^2, \ldots, (x_{50} - 4)^2$

$$= \frac{\sum (x_i - 4)^2}{50} = \frac{\sum (x_i^2 - 8x_i + 16)}{50}$$

$$= \frac{\sum x_i^2}{50} - 8\left(\frac{\sum x_i}{50}\right) + \frac{16}{50}\sum 1$$

$$= 512 - (8 \times 16) + \left(\frac{16}{50} \times 50\right) \quad \text{[from Eqs. (i) and (ii)]}$$

$$= 512 - 128 + 16$$

$$= 400$$

8. Given mean, $\bar{x} = 4$

variance, $\sigma^2 = 5.20$

and number of observations, $n = 5$

Let $x_1 = 3, x_2 = 4, x_3 = 4$ and x_4, x_5 be the five observations

So, $\sum_{i=1}^{5} x_i = 5 \cdot \bar{x} = 5 \times 4 = 20$

$$\Rightarrow x_1 + x_2 + x_3 + x_4 + x_5 = 20$$

$$\Rightarrow 3 + 4 + 4 + x_4 + x_5 = 20$$

$$\Rightarrow x_4 + x_5 = 9 \quad \text{...(i)}$$

Now, variance $\sigma^2 = \frac{\sum_{i=1}^{5} x_i^2}{5} - (\bar{x})^2$

$\Rightarrow \frac{x_1^2 + x_2^2 + x_3^2 + x_4^2 + x_5^2}{5} - (4)^2 = 5.20$

$\Rightarrow \frac{9 + 16 + 16 + x_4^2 + x_5^2}{5} = 16 + 5.20$

$\Rightarrow 41 + x_4^2 + x_5^2 = 5 \times 21.20$

$\Rightarrow x_4^2 + x_5^2 = 106 - 41$

$\Rightarrow x_4^2 + x_5^2 = 65$ ...(ii)

$\because (x_4 + x_5)^2 = x_4^2 + x_5^2 + 2x_4x_5$

$\therefore 81 = 65 + 2x_4x_5$ [from Eqs. (i) and (ii)]

$\Rightarrow 16 = 2x_4x_5 \Rightarrow x_4x_5 = 8$ ...(iii)

Now, $(|x_4 - x_5|)^2 = x_4^2 + x_5^2 - 2x_4x_5$

$= 65 - 16$ [from Eqs. (ii) and (iii)]

$= 49$

$\Rightarrow |x_4 - x_5| = 7$

9. We have, $\sum_{i=1}^{9}(x_i - 5) = 9$ and $\sum_{i=1}^{9}(x_i - 5)^2 = 45$

$$\text{SD} = \sqrt{\frac{\sum_{i=1}^{9}(x_i - 5)^2}{9} - \left(\frac{\sum_{i=1}^{9}(x_i - 5)}{9}\right)^2}$$

$\Rightarrow \text{SD} = \sqrt{\frac{45}{9} - \left(\frac{9}{9}\right)^2}$

$\Rightarrow \text{SD} = \sqrt{5 - 1} = \sqrt{4} = 2$

10. Let the 50 observations are $x_1, x_2, x_3, \ldots, x_{50}$.

Now, deviations of these observations from 30 are $(x_1 - 30), (x_2 - 30), (x_3 - 30), \ldots, (x_{50} - 30)$

$\because \sum_{i=1}^{50}(x_i - 30) = 50$ [given]

$\Rightarrow \sum_{i=1}^{50} x_i - (30 \times 50) = 50$

$\Rightarrow \sum_{i=1}^{50} x_i = 50(30 + 1) = 50 \times 31$

$\therefore$ Mean of 50 observations $= (\bar{x}) = \frac{\sum_{i=1}^{50} x_i}{50} = 31$

11. We have,

$\sum_{i=1}^{n}(x_i + 1)^2 = 9n$ ...(i)

and $\sum_{i=1}^{n}(x_i - 1)^2 = 5n$ ...(ii)

On subtracting Eq. (ii) from Eq. (i), we get

$\sum_{i=1}^{n}\{(x_i + 1)^2 - (x_i - 1)^2\} = 4n$

$\Rightarrow \sum_{i=1}^{n} 4x_i = 4n \Rightarrow \sum_{i=1}^{n} x_i = n$

$\Rightarrow \frac{\sum_{i=1}^{n} x_i}{n} = 1 \Rightarrow \text{mean}\,(\bar{x}) = 1$

Now, standard deviation

$$= \sqrt{\frac{\sum_{i=1}^{n}(x_i - \bar{x})^2}{n}} = \sqrt{\frac{\sum_{i=1}^{n}(x_i - 1)^2}{n}} = \sqrt{\frac{5n}{n}} = \sqrt{5}$$

12. Let x_1, x_2, x_3, x_4, x_5 be the heights of five students.

Then, we have

Mean, $\bar{x} = \frac{\sum_{i=1}^{5} x_i}{5} = 150 \Rightarrow \sum_{i=1}^{5} x_i = 750$ ...(i)

and variance $= \frac{\sum_{i=1}^{5} x_i^2}{n} - (\bar{x})^2 \Rightarrow \frac{\sum_{i=1}^{5} x_i^2}{5} - (150)^2 = 18$

$\Rightarrow \sum_{i=1}^{5} x_i^2 = 112590$ ...(ii)

Now, new mean $= \frac{\sum_{i=1}^{6} x_i}{6} = \frac{\sum_{i=1}^{5} x_i + 156}{6} = \frac{750 + 156}{6}$

[using Eq. (i)]

$\Rightarrow \bar{x}_{new} = 151$

and new variance $= \frac{\sum_{i=1}^{6} x_i^2}{6} - (\bar{x}_{new})^2$

$= \frac{\sum_{i=1}^{5} x_i^2 + (156)^2}{6} - (151)^2$

$= \frac{112590 + (156)^2}{6} - (151)^2$ [using Eq. (ii)]

$= 22821 - 22801 = 20$

13. Let $x_1, x_2, \ldots, x_n$ be n observations.

$\therefore M = \frac{x_1 + x_2 + x_3 + \ldots + x_n}{n}$

$= \frac{x_1 + x_2 + \ldots + x_{n-4} + x_{n-3} + x_{n-2} + x_{n-1} + x_n}{n}$

$\Rightarrow nM = a + x_{n-3} + x_{n-2} + x_{n-1} + x_n$

$\Rightarrow \frac{nM - a}{4} = \frac{x_{n-3} + x_{n-2} + x_{n-1} + x_n}{4}$

14. ${}^{2n+1}C_0 + {}^{2n+1}C_1 + {}^{2n+1}C_2 + \ldots + {}^{2n+1}C_{2n} + {}^{2n+1}C_{2n+1} = 2^{2n+1}$

Now, ${}^{2n+1}C_0 = {}^{2n+1}C_{2n+1}$,

${}^{2n+1}C_1 = {}^{2n+1}C_{2n} \ldots {}^{2n+1}C_r = {}^{2n+1}C_{2n-r+1}$

So, sum of first $(n+1)$ terms = sum of last $(n+1)$ terms

$$\Rightarrow \ {}^{2n+1}C_0 + {}^{2n+1}C_1 + {}^{2n+1}C_2 + \ldots + {}^{2n+1}C_n = 2^{2n}$$

$$\Rightarrow \ \frac{{}^{2n+1}C_0 + {}^{2n+1}C_1 + {}^{2n+1}C_2 + \ldots + {}^{2n+1}C_n}{n+1} = \frac{2^{2n}}{(n+1)}$$

15. Required mean,

$$\bar{x} = \frac{0\cdot q^n + 1\cdot \frac{n}{1} q^{n-1}p + 2\cdot \frac{n(n-1)}{2!} q^{n-2}p^2 + \ldots + n\cdot p^n}{q^n + \frac{n}{1} q^{n-1}p + \frac{n(n-1)}{2!} q^{n-2}p^2 + \ldots + p^n}$$

$$\Rightarrow \ \bar{x} = \frac{0\cdot {}^nC_0 q^n p^0 + 1\cdot {}^nC_1 q^{n-1}p + \ldots + n\cdot {}^nC_n q^0 p^n}{{}^nC_0 q^n p^0 + {}^nC_1 q^{n-1}p^1 + \ldots + {}^nC_n q^{n-n}p^n}$$

$$\Rightarrow \ \bar{x} = \frac{\sum_{r=0}^{n} r\cdot {}^nC_r q^{n-r}p^r}{\sum_{r=0}^{n} {}^nC_r q^{n-r}p^r} = \frac{\sum_{r=0}^{n} r\cdot \frac{n}{r}\, {}^{n-1}C_{r-1} q^{n-r} p\cdot p^{r-1}}{\sum_{r=0}^{n} {}^nC_r q^{n-r}p^r}$$

$$\Rightarrow \ \bar{x} = \frac{np\left[\sum_{r=1}^{n} {}^{n-1}C_{r-1} p^{r-1} q^{(n-1)-(r-1)}\right]}{\sum_{r=0}^{n} {}^nC_r q^{n-r}p^r}$$

$$\Rightarrow \ \bar{x} = \frac{np(q+p)^{n-1}}{(q+p)^n}$$

$$\therefore \ \bar{x} = np \qquad [\because q + p = 1]$$

16. We know, $\sigma^2 = \frac{\Sigma x^2}{n} - \mu^2$

$$= \frac{10\left(\frac{1}{2} - d\right)^2 + 10 \times \frac{1}{4} + 10\left(\frac{1}{2} + d\right)^2}{30} - \left(\frac{10\left(\frac{1}{2} - d\right) + 10 \times \frac{1}{2} + 10\left(\frac{1}{2} + d\right)}{30}\right)^2 \quad \left[\because \mu = \frac{\Sigma x_i}{n}\right]$$

$$= \frac{20\left(\frac{1}{4} + d^2\right) + 5/2}{30} - \left(\frac{1}{4}\right)$$

$$= \frac{\frac{15}{2} + 20d^2}{30} - \frac{1}{4} = \frac{1}{4} + \frac{2d^2}{3} - \frac{1}{4} = \frac{2}{3}d^2$$

$$\therefore \ \frac{2}{3}d^2 = \frac{4}{3}$$

$$\Rightarrow \ d^2 = 2 \Rightarrow |d| = \sqrt{2}$$

17. Given, $n_1 = 60$, $\bar{x}_1 = 650$, $\sigma_1 = 8$,

$n_2 = 80$, $\bar{x}_2 = 660$, $\sigma_2 = 7$

$$\therefore \text{Combined SD} = \sqrt{\frac{n_1\sigma_1^2 + n_2\sigma_2^2}{n_1 + n_2} + \frac{n_1 n_2 (\bar{x}_1 - \bar{x}_2)^2}{(n_1 + n_2)^2}}$$

$$= \sqrt{\frac{60 \times 64 + 80 \times 49}{60 + 80} + \frac{60 \times 80\,(650 - 660)^2}{(60 + 80)^2}}$$

$$= \sqrt{\frac{3840 + 3920}{140} + \frac{(4800 \times 100)}{(140)^2}}$$

$$= \sqrt{\frac{7760}{140} + \frac{480000}{19600}} = \sqrt{\frac{776}{14} + \frac{4800}{196}}$$

$$= \sqrt{55.42 + 24.49}$$

$$= \sqrt{79.91} = 8.94$$

18. Let H_1 and n_1 are the harmonic mean and number of observations of first group and H_2 and n_2 are the harmonic mean and number of observations of another group.

$\therefore$ By using combined harmonic mean formula, we get

$$\text{Combined harmonic mean} = \frac{n_1 + n_2}{\frac{n_1}{H_1} + \frac{n_2}{H_2}} = \frac{5+5}{\frac{5}{\frac{5}{2}} + \frac{5}{\frac{9}{2}}}$$

$$= \frac{10}{\frac{28}{9}} = \frac{90}{28} = \frac{45}{14}$$

19. We know, $\sigma^2 = \frac{n_1(\sigma_1^2 + d_1^2) + n_2(\sigma_2^2 + d_2^2)}{n_1 + n_2}$

where, $d_1 = m_1 - a$, $d_2 = m_2 - a$, a being the mean of the whole group.

$$\therefore \quad 15.6 = \frac{100 \times 15 + 150 \times m_2}{250}$$

$$\Rightarrow \quad m_2 = 16$$

$$\text{Thus, } 13.44 = \left[\frac{(100 \times 9) + (150 \times \sigma^2) + 100 \times (0.6)^2 + 150 \times (0.4)^2}{250}\right]$$

$$\Rightarrow \quad \sigma = 4$$

20. The ascending order of the given data are

34, 38,42, 44, 46, 48, 54, 55, 63,70.

Hence, median, $M = \frac{46 + 48}{2} = 47$

$$\therefore \text{Median deviation} = \frac{\Sigma |x_i - M|}{n} = \frac{\Sigma |x_i - 47|}{n}$$

$$= \frac{13 + 9 + 5 + 3 + 1 + 1 + 7 + 8 + 16 + 23}{10}$$

$$= \frac{86}{10} = 8.6$$

21. Let $d_i = x_i - 8$

$$\therefore \ \sigma_x^2 = \sigma_d^2 = \frac{1}{18}\Sigma d_i^2 - \left(\frac{1}{8}\Sigma d_i\right)^2 = \frac{1}{18} \times 45 - \left(\frac{9}{18}\right)^2 = \frac{5}{2} - \frac{1}{4} = \frac{9}{4}$$

$$\Rightarrow \sigma_x = 1.5$$

22. $\sigma_x^2 = 4$ and $\sigma_y^2 = 5$

Also, $\bar{x} = 2$ and $\bar{y} = 4$

Now, $\frac{\Sigma x_i}{5} = 2$, $\frac{\Sigma y_i}{5} = 4$

$$\Rightarrow \quad \Sigma x_i = 10, \ \Sigma y_i = 20$$

and $\sigma_x^2 = \left(\frac{1}{5}\Sigma x_i^2\right) - (\bar{x})^2$

$$\Rightarrow \quad \Sigma x_i^2 = 5(4 + 4) \Rightarrow \Sigma x_i^2 = 40$$

and $\sigma^2 y = \left(\frac{1}{5}\sum y_i^2\right) - (\bar{y})^2$

and $\sum y_i^2 = 5(5+16)$

$\Rightarrow \sum y_i^2 = 105$

Combined mean, $\sigma_z^2 = \frac{1}{10}\left(\sum x_i^2 + \sum y_i^2 - \left(\frac{\bar{x}+\bar{y}}{2}\right)\right)^2$

$= \frac{1}{10}(40+105) - 9 = \frac{145-90}{10} = \frac{55}{10} = 5.5$

23.

x	c	$2c$	$3c$	$4c$	$5c$	$6c$
f	2	1	1	1	1	1

$\text{Var}(X) = \frac{\sum f_i x_i^2}{\sum f_i} - \left(\frac{\sum f_i x_i}{\sum f_i}\right)^2$

$160 = \frac{2c^2+4c^2+9c^2+16c^2+25c^2+36c^2}{7} - \left(\frac{2c+2c+3c+4c+5c+6c}{7}\right)^2$

$\Rightarrow 160 = \frac{92c^2}{7} - \frac{484c^2}{49} = \frac{160c^2}{49}$

$\therefore c^2 = 49$

$c = 7$ [taking only positive sign]

24. From given information,

$x + y = 10$ ...(i)

Age (x_i)	f	$\lvert x_i - M\rvert$	$f_i\lvert x_i - M\rvert$
15	5	3	15
16	8	2	16
17	5	1	5
18	12	0	0
19	x	1	x
20	y	2	$2y$

Median $= 18 = M$ (say)

$\therefore \text{MD} = \frac{\sum f_i\lvert x_i - M\rvert}{\sum f_i}$

$\Rightarrow 1.25 = \frac{36 + x + 2y}{40}$

$\Rightarrow x + 2y = 14$ ...(ii)

On solving Eqs. (i) and (ii), we get

$x = 6, y = 4$

Hence, $4x + 5y = 24 + 20 = 44$

25. According to the question,

Mean $(\bar{x}) = 10$ and standard deviation $(\sigma) = 2$

Now, $\bar{x} = \frac{x_1 + x_2 + x_3 + \ldots + x_{20}}{20} = 10$

$\Rightarrow \sum_{i=1}^{20} x_i = 200$

Now, one entry was wrong, taken 8 instead of 12.

So, correct sum $= 200 - 8 + 12 = 204$

Correct mean $= \frac{204}{20} = 10.2$

We know,

Variance, $\sigma^2 = \frac{\sum x_i^2}{n} - (\bar{x})^2 = 4$

$\Rightarrow \frac{\sum x_i^2}{20} - (10)^2 = 4$

$\Rightarrow \sum x_i^2 = 2080$

Now, the correct summation of square of observations

$\Rightarrow \sum x_i^2 = 2080 - 64 + 144 = 2160$

Correct variance,

$\sigma_n^2 = \frac{2160}{20} - (10.2)^2 \Rightarrow \sigma_n^2 = 3.96$

Correct standard deviation, $\sigma_n = \sqrt{3.96}$

26. Given, observations are $-3, 4, 7, -6, \alpha, \beta$

Mean = 2 and variance = 23

$\Rightarrow \frac{-3+4+7+(-6)+\alpha+\beta}{6} = 2$

and $\frac{\sum x_i^2}{n} - (\mu)^2 = 23, \mu = \text{Mean}$

$\Rightarrow \alpha + \beta = 10$ ...(i)

and $\sum x_i^2 = n(23 + \mu^2) = 6 \times (23 + 4) = 27 \times 6$

$\Rightarrow 9 + 16 + 49 + 36 + \alpha^2 + \beta^2 = 162$

$\Rightarrow \alpha^2 + \beta^2 = 52$ ...(ii)

On solving Eqs. (i) and (ii), we get

$\alpha = 4$ and $\beta = 6$

So, mean deviation about mean

$= \frac{\sum\lvert x_i - \bar{x}\rvert}{n}$

$= \frac{\lvert -3-2\rvert + \lvert 4-2\rvert + \lvert 7-2\rvert + \lvert -6-2\rvert + \lvert 4-2\rvert + \lvert 6-2\rvert}{6}$

$= \frac{5+2+5+8+2+4}{6} = \frac{26}{6} = \frac{13}{3}$

27. Mean = 55

$\frac{a+b+68+44+48+60}{6} = 55$

$\Rightarrow a + b + 220 = 330$

$\Rightarrow a + b = 110$ ...(i)

Also, variance = 194

$\sum \frac{(x_i - \bar{x})^2}{n} = 194$

$\sum \frac{(x_i - 55)^2}{6} = 194 \Rightarrow \sum (x_i - 55)^2 = 1164$

$(a-55)^2 + (b-55)^2 + (68-55)^2 + (44-55)^2 + (48-55)^2 + (60-55)^2 = 1164$

$\Rightarrow a^2 - 110a + 3025 + b^2 - 110b + 3025 + 169 + 121 + 49 + 25 = 1164$

$$\Rightarrow \quad a^2 + b^2 - 110(a+b) = -5250$$

$$\Rightarrow \quad a^2 + b^2 - 110 \times 110 = -5250$$

$$\Rightarrow \quad a^2 + b^2 = 6850 \qquad \text{...(ii)}$$

From Eq. (i), $b = 110 - a$ put in Eq. (ii),

$$a^2 + (110-a)^2 = 6850$$

$$\Rightarrow \quad 2a^2 - 220a + 5250 = 0$$

$$\Rightarrow \quad a^2 - 110a + 2625 = 0$$

$$a = 35, 75$$

If $a = 35, b = 75$, not possible as $a > b$.

$$\therefore \quad a + 3b = 35 + 225 = 260$$

28. Given, $\sum_{k=1}^{10} a_k = 50$

$$\Rightarrow \quad a_1 + a_2 + a_3 + \ldots + a_{10} = 50 \qquad \text{...(i)}$$

and $\quad \sum_{\forall k<j} a_k \cdot a_j = 1100 \qquad \text{...(ii)}$

On squaring Eq. (i), we get

$$(a_1 + a_2 + a_3 + \ldots + a_{10})^2 = (50)^2 = 2500$$

$$\Rightarrow \quad \sum_{i=1}^{10} a_i^2 + 2\sum_{k<j} a_k a_j = 2500$$

[when open whole square of LHS and written in Σ notation]

$$\Rightarrow \quad \sum_{i=1}^{10} a_i^2 = 2500 - 2(1100) \qquad \text{[using Eq. (ii)]}$$

$$\Rightarrow \quad \sum_{i=1}^{10} a_i^2 = 300$$

Now, $\text{SD} = \sigma = \sqrt{\frac{\Sigma a_i^2}{10} - \left(\frac{\Sigma a_i}{10}\right)^2} = \sqrt{\frac{300}{10} - \left(\frac{50}{10}\right)^2}$

$$= \sqrt{30 - 25} = \sqrt{5}$$

29. Given that $\overline{X} = \frac{\sum_{i=1}^{10} x_i}{10} = \frac{6}{5}$ and $\frac{x_i^2}{10} - (\overline{x})^2 = \frac{84}{25}$

and $\quad \sum_{i=1}^{10}(x_i - \alpha) = 2, \quad \frac{\sum_{i=1}^{10} x_i^2}{10} - \frac{36}{25} = \frac{84}{25}$

$$\sum_{i=1}^{10} x_i - 10\alpha = 2, \quad \frac{\Sigma x_i^2}{10} = \frac{120}{25}$$

$$\Rightarrow \quad 12 - 10\alpha = 2 \text{ and } \Sigma x_i^2 = 48 \quad \Rightarrow \quad \alpha = 1$$

Now, $\quad \sum_{i=1}^{10}(x_i - \beta)^2 = 40$

$$\Rightarrow \quad \sum_{i=1}^{10} x_i^2 + 10\beta^2 - 2\beta\sum_{i=1}^{10} x_i = 40$$

$$\Rightarrow \quad 48 + 10\beta^2 - 24\beta = 40$$

$$\Rightarrow \quad 10\beta^2 - 24\beta + 8 = 0 \Rightarrow 5\beta^2 - 12\beta + 4 = 0$$

$$\Rightarrow \quad \beta = 2 \text{ or } \beta = \frac{2}{5} \qquad \text{[reject]}$$

$$\therefore \quad \frac{\beta}{\alpha} = \frac{2}{1} = 2$$

30. Given data, 170, 125, 230, 190, 210, a, b

MD about median

$$= \frac{|170-170| + |125-170| + |230-170| + |190-170| + |210-170| + |a-170| + |b-170|}{7}$$

$$\Rightarrow \quad \frac{205}{7} = \frac{0 + 45 + 60 + 20 + 40 + 170 - a + 170 - b}{7}$$

$$\therefore \quad a + b = 300$$

$$\text{Mean} = \frac{170 + 125 + 230 + 190 + 210 + a + b}{7}$$

$$= \frac{170 + 125 + 230 + 190 + 210 + 300}{7}$$

$$= \frac{1225}{7} = 175$$

Mean deviation about mean

$$= \frac{|170-175| + |125-175| + |230-175| + |190-175| + |210-175| + |a-175| + |b-175|}{7}$$

$$= \frac{5 + 50 + 55 + 15 + 35 + 350 - 300}{7}$$

$$= \frac{5 + 50 + 55 + 15 + 35 + 50}{7} = \frac{210}{7} = 30$$

31. $\overline{X} = \frac{24}{5} \Rightarrow \frac{x_1 + x_2 + x_3 + x_4 + x_5}{5} = \frac{24}{5} \Rightarrow \Sigma x_i = 24 \qquad \text{...(i)}$

$$\text{Var}(X) = \frac{194}{25}$$

$$n = 5$$

Mean of first four observation $= \frac{7}{2}$

$$\frac{x_1 + x_2 + x_3 + x_4}{4} = \frac{7}{2}$$

$$x_1 + x_2 + x_3 + x_4 = 14 \qquad \text{...(ii)}$$

By Eqs. (i) and (ii), $x_5 = 10$

Now, $\quad \text{Var}(X) = \frac{194}{25}$

$$\Rightarrow \quad \frac{\Sigma x_i^2}{5} - (\overline{X})^2 = \frac{194}{25}$$

$$\Rightarrow \quad \frac{x_1^2 + x_2^2 + x_3^2 + x_4^2 + x_5^2}{5} - \left(\frac{24}{5}\right)^2 = \frac{194}{25}$$

$$\Rightarrow \quad \frac{x_1^2 + x_2^2 + x_3^2 + x_4^2 + x_5^2}{5} = \frac{194}{25} + \frac{576}{25}$$

$$\Rightarrow \quad x_1^2 + x_2^2 + x_3^2 + x_4^2 = \frac{770}{5} - 100 = \frac{270}{5} = 54$$

$$\text{New variance} = \frac{\sum_{i=1}^{4} x_i^2}{4} - (\overline{X})^2 = \frac{54}{4} - \left(\frac{7}{2}\right)^2 = \frac{5}{4}$$

32. $a, b, c \in N, a < b < c$

$$\overline{X} = \text{Mean} = \frac{9 + 25 + a + b + c}{5} = 18$$

$$a + b + c = 56$$

$$\text{Mean deviation} = \frac{\Sigma |X_i - \overline{X}|}{n} = 4$$

$$\Rightarrow \quad 9 + 7 + |18 - a| + |18 - b| + |18 - c| = 20$$

$$\Rightarrow \quad |18 - a| + |18 - b| + |18 - c| = 4$$

$$\text{Variance} = \frac{\sum |X_i - \overline{X}|^2}{n} = \frac{136}{5}$$

$\Rightarrow\ 81 + 49 + |18 - a|^2 + |18 - b|^2 + |18 - c|^2 = 136$

$\Rightarrow\ (18 - a)^2 + (18 - b)^2 + (18 - c)^2 = 6$

Possible values $(18 - a)^2 = 1, (18 - b)^2 = 1, (18 - c)^2 = 4a < b < c$

So, $18 - a = 1, 18 - b = -1, 18 - c = -2$

$a = 17, b = 19, c = 20$

$\therefore\ 2a + b - c = 2 \times 17 + 19 - 20$

$= 34 + 19 - 20 = 33$

33.

x_i	f_i	$f_i x_i$	$f_i x_i^2$
0	3	0	0
1	2	2	2
5	3	15	75
6	2	12	72
10	6	60	600
12	3	36	432
17	3	51	867
Total	$\sum f_i = 22$	$\sum f_i x_i = 176$	$\sum f_i x_i^2 = 2048$

$$\because\ \text{Var}(\sigma^2) = \left(\frac{\sum f_i x_i^2}{\sum f_i}\right) - \left(\frac{\sum f_i x_i}{\sum f_i}\right)^2$$

$$= \frac{2048}{22} - \left(\frac{176}{22}\right)^2 = \frac{1024}{11} - 64$$

$= 93.0909 - 64 = 29.0909$

34. Given, $\bar{x} = 56$ and $\sigma^2 = 66.2$

$$\text{Variance, } \sigma^2 = \frac{\sum x_i^2}{n} - (\bar{x}_i)^2$$

$$\Rightarrow 66.2 = \frac{65^2 + 68^2 + 58^2 + 44^2 + 48^2 + 45^2 + 60^2 + \alpha^2 + \beta^2 + 60^2}{10} - (56)^2$$

$$\Rightarrow\ 66.2 = \frac{\alpha^2 + \beta^2 + 25678}{10} - (56)^2$$

$\Rightarrow\ 662 + 3136 \times 10 = \alpha^2 + \beta^2 + 25678$

$\Rightarrow\ \alpha^2 + \beta^2 = 6344$

35. Let μ' = incorrect mean,

μ = correct mean [given]

and σ' = standard deviation,

σ = standard deviation (corrected) [given]

Now, we have

$$\mu' = \frac{\sum x_i}{15} = 12 \text{ [given]} \Rightarrow \sum x_i = 180$$

According to the question,

corrected $\sum x_i = 180 - 10 + 12$

$$\Rightarrow\ \mu \text{ (correct mean)} = \frac{182}{15}$$

$$\text{Also, } \sigma' = \sqrt{\frac{\sum x_i^2}{15} - 144} = 3 \Rightarrow \sum x_i^2 = 2295$$

Correct $\Sigma x_i^2 = 2295 - 100 + 144$

$= 2339$

$$\text{Correct variance} = \frac{2339}{15} - \frac{182 \times 182}{15 \times 15}$$

Hence, required value

$= 15(\mu + \mu^2 + \sigma^2)$

$$= 15\left(\frac{182}{15} + \frac{182 \times 182}{15 \times 15} + \frac{2339}{15} - \frac{182 \times 182}{15 \times 15}\right)$$

$$= 15\left(\frac{182}{15} + \frac{2339}{15}\right) = 2521$$

36. Since, $\alpha, \beta \in \{1, 2, 3, 4, 5, 6\}$

$\therefore\ \alpha - \beta \in \{0, 1, 2, 3, 4, 5\}$

$$\text{Mean, } \overline{X} = \frac{0 + 1 + 2 + 3 + 4 + 5}{6} = \frac{5}{2}$$

$$\text{Variance} = \frac{\sum_{i=1}^{n} (x_i - \overline{X})^2}{n} = \frac{\left(0 - \frac{5}{2}\right)^2 + \left(1 - \frac{5}{2}\right)^2 + \ldots + \left(5 - \frac{5}{2}\right)^2}{6}$$

$$= \frac{35}{12} = \frac{p}{q} \quad \text{[given]}$$

i.e. $p = 35$ with divisors $= 1, 5, 7, 35$

Required sum $= 1 + 5 + 7 + 35 = 48$

37. Given, $\dfrac{\sum x}{12} = \dfrac{9}{2}$ and $\dfrac{\sum x^2}{12} - \left(\dfrac{9}{2}\right)^2 = 4$

$\Rightarrow\ \sum x = 54$ and $\sum x^2 = 291$

After correction

$\sum x_{\text{corr.}} = 54 - (9 + 10) + (7 + 14) = 56$

$\sum x_{\text{corr.}}^2 = 291 - (81 + 100) + 49 + 196 = 355$

$$\sigma_{\text{corr.}}^2 = \frac{355}{12} - \left(\frac{56}{12}\right)^2 = \frac{281}{36} = \frac{m}{n}$$

$\therefore\ m + n = 317$

38. We know that if n_1, n_2 are the sizes, $\overline{X}_1, \overline{X}_2$ are the means and σ_1, σ_2 are the standard deriation of the series, then the combine variance of the series is

$$\sigma^2 = \frac{n_1\sigma_1^2 + n_2\sigma_2^2}{n_1 + n_2} + \frac{n_1 \cdot n_2}{(n_1 + n_2)^2}(\overline{X}_1 - \overline{X}_2)^2$$

$$\Rightarrow\ 13 = \frac{15 \times 14 + 15 \times \sigma^2}{15 + 15} + \frac{15 \times 15}{(15 + 15)^2}(12 - 14)^2$$

$$\Rightarrow\ 13 = \frac{14 + \sigma^2}{2} + \frac{1}{4} \times 4$$

$\Rightarrow\ 14 + \sigma^2 = 2 \times 12 \Rightarrow \sigma^2 = 10$

39. Let the remaining two observations be x and y.

$$\text{Then, mean} = \frac{1 + 3 + 5 + x + y}{5} = 5$$

$\Rightarrow\ x + y = 16$ ...(i)

Also, variance $= \dfrac{\sum x_i^2}{N} - (\overline{X})^2$

$\Rightarrow \quad 8 = \dfrac{1^2 + 3^2 + 5^2 + x^2 + y^2}{5} - (5)^2$

$\Rightarrow \quad x^2 + y^2 = 130$ ...(ii)

Now, we know that

$$(x+y)^2 = x^2 + y^2 + 2xy$$

From Eqs. (i) and (ii), we get

$$(16)^2 = 130 + 2xy \Rightarrow xy = 63$$

$\therefore$ Required sum $= x^3 + y^3$

$= (x+y)^3 - 3xy(x+y)$

$= (16)^3 - 3(63)(16)$

$= 4096 - 3024 = 1072$

40. Given, $n = 10, \bar{x} = 20, \sigma_x = 8$

Correct value = 40, Wrong value = 50

$$\bar{x} = \frac{\sum x_i}{n}$$

$$20 = \frac{\sum x_i}{10} \Rightarrow \sum x_i = 200$$

Corrected $\sum x_i = 200 -$ (Wrong value) + Correct value

$= 200 - 50 + 40 = 190$

Corrected mean $= \dfrac{\text{Corrected } \sum x_i}{n} = \dfrac{190}{10} = 19$

$\Rightarrow \quad \sigma_x^2 = \dfrac{\sum x_i^2}{n} - (\bar{x})^2 \Rightarrow (8)^2 = \dfrac{\sum x_i^2}{10} - (20)^2$

$\Rightarrow \quad 64 + 400 = \dfrac{\sum x_i^2}{10} \Rightarrow 464 = \dfrac{\sum x_i^2}{10} \Rightarrow 4640 = \sum x_i^2$

Corrected $\sum x_i^2 = 4640 - (\text{Wrong value})^2 + (\text{Corrected value})^2$

$= 4640 - (50)^2 + (40)^2$

$= 4640 - 2500 + 1600 = 3740$

Corrected variance $= \dfrac{\text{Corrected } \sum x_i^2}{n} - (\text{Corrected mean})^2$

$= \dfrac{3740}{10} - (19)^2 = 374 - 361 = 13$

41. Given observations are 1, 2, 4, 5, x and y

and mean $(\overline{X}) = 5$

and variance $(\sigma^2) = 10$

$\therefore \quad \overline{X} = \text{Mean} = \dfrac{\text{Sum of observations}}{\text{Total observations}}$

$\Rightarrow \quad 5 = \dfrac{1 + 2 + 4 + 5 + x + y}{6}$

$\Rightarrow \quad x + y = 18$ ...(i)

$\therefore \quad$ Variance $= \sigma^2 = \dfrac{\Sigma x_i^2}{n} - (\overline{X})^2$

$10 = \dfrac{1^2 + 2^2 + 4^2 + 5^2 + x^2 + y^2}{6} - (5)^2$

$\Rightarrow \quad 210 = x^2 + y^2 + 46 \Rightarrow x^2 + y^2 = 164$ ...(ii)

On squaring Eq. (i), we get

$$x^2 + y^2 + 2xy = 324$$

From Eq. (ii),

$$2xy + 164 = 324 \Rightarrow 2xy = 160$$

$xy = 80$ ..(iii)

From Eqs. (ii) and (iii), we get

$$x = 10, y = 8 \text{ or } x = 8, y = 10$$

Mean deviation $= \dfrac{\sum |x_i - \overline{X}|}{n}$

$= \dfrac{|1-5| + |2-5| + |4-5| + |5-5| + |10-5| + |8-5|}{6}$

$= \dfrac{4 + 3 + 1 + 0 + 5 + 3}{6} = \dfrac{16}{6} = \dfrac{8}{3}$

Hence, mean deviation about the mean is $\dfrac{8}{3}$.

42. We have, $\sum f_i = 62$

$(K+2) + 2K + (K^2 - 1)) + (K^2 - 1) + (K^2 + 1) + (K - 3) = 62$

$\Rightarrow \quad 3K^2 + 4K - 64 = 0 \Rightarrow (3K + 16)(K - 4) = 0$

$\Rightarrow \quad K = 4$ [rejecting negative value of K]

x_i	0	1	2	3	4	5
f_i	6	8	15	15	17	1

$$\mu = \frac{\sum f_i x_i}{\sum f_i} = \frac{0 + 8 + 30 + 45 + 68 + 5}{62} = \frac{156}{62}$$

and $\sigma^2 = \dfrac{\sum f_i x_i^2}{\sum f_i} - \left(\dfrac{\sum f_i x_i}{\sum f_i}\right)^2$

$= \dfrac{1 \times 8 + 4 \times 15 + 9 \times 15 + 16 \times 17 + 25 \times 1}{62} - \left(\dfrac{156}{62}\right)^2$

$= \dfrac{500}{62} - \left(\dfrac{156}{62}\right)^2 = \dfrac{500}{62} - \mu^2$

$\therefore \quad \sigma^2 + \mu^2 = \dfrac{500}{62}$

Hence, $\quad [\sigma^2 + \mu^2] = 8$

43. Given that mean deviation about mean of 100 consecutive positive integers is 25.

Let first integer be a_1.

Then, $a_2 = a_1 + 1$

$a_3 = a_1 + 2$

$a_4 = a_1 + 3$

....

....

$a_{100} = a_1 + 99$

Now, mean of 100 positive consecutive integers

$$\bar{x} = \frac{a_1 + (a_1 + 1) + (a_1 + 2) + (a_1 + 3)}{100} + \dots (a_1 + 99)$$

$$= \frac{100\, a_1 + (1 + 2 + \dots 99)}{100} = a_1 + 49.5$$

$\therefore \quad \text{MD} = \dfrac{\Sigma |x_i - \bar{x}|}{n} = 25$

$\Rightarrow \dfrac{2(49.5 + 48.5 + \dots 0.5)}{100} = 25 \Rightarrow 2 \times 1250 = 2500$

It is true $\forall\, a_i \in N$

So, set $S = N$

44. Given, mean of 7 observations = 8

and variance of 7 observations = 16

After one observation 14 is omitted, then new mean = a and new variance = b

Let $x_7 = 14$

Now, $\text{Mean} = \dfrac{x_1 + x_2 + x_3 + \ldots + x_7}{7} = 8$

$$\Rightarrow \quad \frac{x_1 + x_2 + x_3 + \ldots + 14}{7} = 8$$

$$\Rightarrow \quad x_1 + x_2 + x_3 + \ldots + x_6 = 42$$

So, $\dfrac{x_1 + x_2 + x_3 + \ldots + x_6}{6} = \dfrac{42}{6} = 7 = a$ [given]

Also, variance $= \dfrac{\Sigma x_i^2}{7} - (8)^2$

Old variance = 16 [given]

$$\Sigma x_i^2 = (16 + 64) \times 7 = 80 \times 7 = 560$$

$$\Rightarrow \quad x_1^2 + x_2^2 + x_3^2 + \ldots + x_6^2 + x_7^2 = 560$$

$$\Rightarrow \quad x_1^2 + x_2^2 + x_3^2 + \ldots + x_6^2 = 560 - (14)^2 = 364$$

$$\therefore \quad b = \frac{x_1^2 + x_2^2 + x_3^2 + \ldots + x_6^2}{6} - (7)^2$$

(new variance) $= \dfrac{364}{6} - 49 = \dfrac{70}{6}$

Hence, $a + 3b - 5 = 7 + 3 \times \dfrac{70}{6} - 5 = 7 + 35 - 5 = 37$

45. Let $X = \{11, 12, \ldots, 40, 41\}$

and $Y = \{61, 62, \ldots, 90, 91\}$ be the two sets of observations.

$$\therefore \quad \overline{X} = \frac{\frac{31}{2}(11 + 41)}{31} = 26 \text{ (Mean of } X)$$

$$\overline{Y} = \frac{\frac{31}{2}(61 + 91)}{31} = 76 \text{ (Mean of } Y)$$

Now, variance (σ^2) of $X \cup Y$ is,

$$\sigma^2 = \frac{\Sigma x_i^2 + \Sigma y_i^2}{62} - \left(\frac{\Sigma x_i + \Sigma y_i}{62}\right)^2$$

$$\sigma^2 = \frac{(11^2 + 12^2 + \ldots + 41^2) + (61^2 + 62^2 + \ldots + 91^2)}{62} - (51)^2$$

$$= 3306 - 2601 = 705$$

$$\therefore \ |\overline{x} + \overline{y} - \sigma^2| = |26 + 76 - 705| = 603$$

46. Given, mean = 10

$$\frac{\sum_{i=1}^{n} x_i}{n} = 10 \Rightarrow \sum_{i=1}^{n} x_i = 10n \quad \ldots\text{(i)}$$

And variance = 4

$$\frac{\Sigma x_i^2}{n} - \left(\frac{\Sigma x_i}{n}\right)^2 = 4 \Rightarrow \Sigma x_i^2 = 104n$$

Now, the marks of one of the students is increased from 8 to 12.

Now, mean = 10.2

$$\frac{\Sigma x_i - 8 + 12}{n} = 10.2$$

$$\Sigma x_i = (10.2)n - 4 \quad \ldots\text{(ii)}$$

From Eqs. (i) and (ii), we get

$$10n = (10.2)n - 4$$

$$0.2n = 4 \Rightarrow n = 20$$

Now, variance $= \dfrac{\Sigma x_i^2 - 8^2 + 12^2}{20} - (10.2)^2 = 104 + 4 - 104.04$

New variance = 3.96

47. We have, $n(A) = n(B) = 5$

Let $A = \{a_1, a_2, a_3, a_4, a_5\}$ and $B = \{b_1, b_2, b_3, b_4, b_5\}$

Mean of element is set $A(a) = 5$

$$a = \frac{\sum_{i=1}^{5} a_i}{5} = 5 \Rightarrow \sum_{i=1}^{5} a_i = 25$$

Mean of element in set $B(b) = 8$

$$b = \frac{\sum_{i=1}^{5} b_i}{5} = 8 \Rightarrow \sum_{i=1}^{5} b_i = 40$$

Variance of element in set $A = 12$

$$\frac{\sum_{i=1}^{5} (a_i)^2}{5} - (a)^2 = 12$$

$$\sum_{i=1}^{5} a_i^2 = (12 + 25) \times 5 = 185$$

Variance of element in set $B = 20$

$$\frac{\sum_{i=1}^{5} b_i^2}{5} - (b)^2 = 20$$

$$\sum_{i=1}^{5} b_i^2 = (20 + 64) \times 5 = 420$$

Let $C = \{C_1, C_2, C_3, C_4, C_5, \ldots C_{10}\}$

Mean of C

$$(c) = \frac{\left(\sum_{i=1}^{5} a_i - 15\right) + \left(\sum_{i=1}^{5} b_i + 10\right)}{10} = \frac{(25 - 15) + (40 + 10)}{10} = 6$$

$$\text{Variance of } C = \frac{\sum_{i=1}^{5} C_i^2}{10} - (c)^2$$

$$= \frac{\sum_{i=1}^{5} (a_i - 3)^2 + \sum_{i=1}^{5} (b_i + 2)^2}{10} - (6)^2$$

$$= \frac{\sum_{i=1}^{5} a_i^2 + \sum_{i=1}^{5} b_i^2 - 6\sum_{i=1}^{5} a_i + 4\sum_{i=1}^{5} b_i + 65}{10} - 36$$

$$= \frac{185 + 420 - 150 + 160 + 65}{10} - 36 = 32$$

Mean + Variance of element of $C = 6 + 32 = 38$

48. We have, $x_1, x_2, x_3, \ldots, x_7$ are in AP with $x_1 = 9$ and common difference $= d$

Now, Mean, $\bar{x} = \frac{\sum_{i=1}^{7} x_i}{7} = \frac{x_1 + x_2 + x_3 + \ldots + x_7}{7}$

$$= \frac{\frac{7}{2}[2x_1 + (7-1)d]}{7} = \frac{1}{2}[2x_1 + 6d]$$

$$= x_1 + 3d = x_4$$

Again, variance $= \frac{\sum_{i=1}^{7}(x_i - \bar{x})^2}{7}$

$$\Rightarrow \quad (4)^2 = \frac{\sum_{i=1}^{7}(x_i - x_4)^2}{7}$$

$$\Rightarrow \quad 16 = \frac{(3d)^2 + (2d)^2 + d^2 + 0 + d^2 + (2d)^2 + (3d)^2}{7}$$

$$\Rightarrow \quad 16 = \frac{28d^2}{7} \Rightarrow d = 2 \quad [\because x_1 < x_2 < x_3 \ldots < x_7]$$

$\therefore \quad \bar{x} = x_1 + 3d = 9 + 3 \times 2 = 15$

and $\quad x_6 = x_1 + 5d = 9 + 5 \times 2 = 19$

So, $\quad \bar{x} + x_6 = 15 + 19 = 34$

49. We have,

	A	B	Combined (A + B)
Mean	$\bar{X}_1 = 40$	$\bar{X}_2 = 55$	$\bar{X}_{12} = 50$
SD	$\sigma_1 = \alpha$	$\sigma_2 = 30 - \alpha$	$\sigma_{12} = 350$
Total number of observation	$n_1 = 100$	$n_2 = n$	$n_{12} = 100 + n$

Now, $\quad \bar{X}_{12} = \frac{n_1\bar{X}_1 + n_2\bar{X}_2}{n_1 + n_2} \Rightarrow 50 = \frac{100 \times 40 + n \times 55}{100 + n}$

$$\Rightarrow \quad 5000 + 50n = 4000 + 55n \Rightarrow n = 200$$

Again, $\quad \sigma_1^2 = \frac{\sum X_{i1}^2}{n_1} - (\bar{X}_1)^2 \Rightarrow \alpha^2 = \frac{\sum X_{i1}^2}{100} - (40)^2$

$$\Rightarrow \quad \sum X_{i1}^2 = (\alpha^2 + 1600) \times 100$$

and $\quad \sigma_2^2 = \frac{\sum X_{i2}^2}{n_2} - (\bar{X}_2)^2$

$$\Rightarrow \quad (30 - \alpha)^2 = \frac{\sum X_{i2}^2}{n} - (55)^2$$

$$\Rightarrow \quad \sum X_{i2}^2 = ((30 - \alpha)^2 + 3025) \times 200 \quad [\because n = 200]$$

Now, $\quad \sigma_{12}^2 = \frac{\sum X_{i1}^2 + \sum X_{i2}^2}{n_1 + n_2} - (\bar{X}_{12})^2$

$$\Rightarrow 350 = \frac{(\alpha^2 + 1600) \times 100 + ((30 - \alpha)^2 + 3025) \times 200}{300} - (50)^2$$

$$\Rightarrow \quad \alpha^2 - 40\alpha + 300 = 0$$

$$\Rightarrow \quad (\alpha - 10)(\alpha - 30) = 0$$

$$\Rightarrow \quad \alpha = 10, 30 \Rightarrow \alpha = 10 \quad [\alpha = 30 \text{ is not possible}]$$

$$\therefore \quad \sigma_1^2 + \sigma_2^2 = \alpha^2 + (30 - \alpha)^2 = (10)^2 + (20)^2 = 500$$

50. Given that the mean and standard deviation of the marks of 10 students were found to be 50 and 12

$$\bar{x} = 50 \text{ and } \sigma = 12 \Rightarrow \sigma^2 = 144$$

Now, $\quad \sum x = 10 \times (\bar{x}) = 10 \times 50 = 500$

$$\sum x_{i(\text{correct})} = 500 + 20 + 25 - 45 - 50 = 450$$

Now, $\quad \frac{\sum x_i^2}{10} - (50)^2 = 144 \quad$ [given]

$$\sum x_{i(\text{correct})}^2 = \{144 + (50)^2\} \times 10 - (45)^2 - (50)^2 + (20)^2 + (25)^2$$

$$= 26440 - 4525 + 1025$$

$$= 26440 - 3500$$

$$\sum x_{i(\text{correct})}^2 = 22940$$

Correct variance $= \frac{\sum (x_{i_\text{correct}})^2}{10} - \left(\frac{\sum x_{i_\text{correct}}}{10}\right)^2$

$$= \frac{22940}{10} - (45)^2 = 2294 - 2025 = 269$$

51. Given, mean = 5

$$\bar{x} = \frac{\sum x_i f_i}{\sum f_i} = 5 \Rightarrow \frac{4 + 72 + 140 + 7\alpha + 72}{64 + \alpha} = 5$$

$$\Rightarrow \quad 288 + 7\alpha = 320 + 5\alpha \Rightarrow 2\alpha = 32 \Rightarrow \alpha = 16$$

$$m = \text{MD about } \bar{x} = \frac{\sum f_i |x_i - \bar{x}|}{\sum f_i}$$

$$= \frac{4 \times 4 + 24 \times 2 + 28 \times 0 + 16 \times 2 + 8 \times 4}{64 + 16}$$

$$m = \frac{128}{80} = \frac{8}{5}$$

$$\sigma^2 = \text{Variance} = \frac{\sum f_i(x_i - \bar{x}_i)^2}{\sum f_i}$$

$$= \frac{4 \times 16 + 24 \times 4 + 28 \times 0 + 16 \times 4 + 8 \times 16}{80} = \frac{352}{80}$$

$$\therefore \quad \frac{3\alpha}{m + \sigma^2} = \frac{3 \times 16}{\frac{8}{5} + \frac{352}{80}} = 8$$

52. Given, mean is 28.

So, $\frac{2 \times 5 + 3 \times 15 + x \times 25 + 5 \times 35 + 4 \times 45}{14 + x} = 28$

$$\Rightarrow \quad \frac{10 + 45 + 25x + 175 + 180}{14 + x} = 28$$

$$\Rightarrow \quad 410 + 25x = 392 + 28x$$

$$\Rightarrow \quad 3x = 18 \Rightarrow x = 6$$

$\therefore$ Variance $= \left(\frac{\sum x_i^2 f_i}{\sum f_i}\right) - (\text{Mean})^2$

$$= \left(\frac{2 \times 5^2 + 3 \times 15^2 + 6 \times 25^2 + 5 \times 35^2 + 4 \times 45^2}{20}\right) - (28)^2$$

$$= \left(\frac{50 + 675 + 3750 + 6125 + 8100}{20}\right) - (28)^2$$

$$= \left(\frac{18720}{20}\right) - (28)^2 = 935 - 784 = 151$$

53. Mean $=9$

$$\Rightarrow \quad \frac{x+y+12+6+4+8+12+10}{8}=9$$

$$\Rightarrow \quad x+y=20 \quad \text{...(i)}$$

Variance $=9.25$

$$\frac{x^2+y^2+12^2+6^2+4^2+8^2+12^2+10^2}{8}-9^2=9.25$$

$$\Rightarrow \quad x^2+y^2=218 \quad \text{...(ii)}$$

Eliminating y from Eqs. (i) and (ii), we get

$$x^2+(20-x)^2=218$$

$$\Rightarrow \quad x^2-20x+91=0$$

$$\Rightarrow \quad x=7, 13$$

$$\Rightarrow \quad x=13, y=7\,(x>y)$$

$$\therefore \quad 3x-2y=39-14=25$$

54.

x_i	f_i	x_i^2	$f_i x_i$	$f_i x_i^2$
2	4	4	8	16
4	4	16	16	64
6	α	36	6α	36α
8	15	64	120	960
10	8	100	80	800
12	β	144	12β	144β
14	4	196	56	784
16	5	256	80	1280
	$\Sigma f_i=40+\alpha+\beta$		$\Sigma f_i x_i=360+6\alpha+12\beta$	$\Sigma f_i x_i^2=3904+36\alpha+144\beta$

Given, mean $=9$

$$\Rightarrow \quad \frac{\Sigma f_i x_i}{\Sigma f_i}=9 \Rightarrow \frac{360+6\alpha+12\beta}{40+\alpha+\beta}=9$$

$$\Rightarrow \quad 360+6\alpha+12\beta=9(40+\alpha+\beta)$$

$$\Rightarrow \quad 3\beta=3\alpha \Rightarrow \alpha=\beta \quad \text{...(i)}$$

variance $=15.08$

$$\Rightarrow \quad \frac{\Sigma f_i x_i^2}{\Sigma f_i}-\left(\frac{\Sigma f_i x_i}{\Sigma f_i}\right)^2=15.08$$

$$\Rightarrow \quad \frac{3904+36\alpha+144\beta}{40+\alpha+\beta}-(9)^2=15.08$$

$$\Rightarrow \quad \frac{3904+180\alpha}{40+2\alpha}=81+15.08$$

$$\Rightarrow \quad 3904+180\alpha=96.08\,(40+2\alpha)$$

$$\Rightarrow \quad 3904+180\alpha=3843.2+192.16\alpha$$

$$\Rightarrow \quad 60.8=12.16\alpha$$

$$\Rightarrow \quad \alpha=5=\beta$$

$$\therefore \alpha^2+\beta^2-\alpha\beta=25+25-25=25$$

55. Since, $x_1, x_2, x_3, \ldots, x_{20}$ are in GP, where $x_1=3$ and r = common ratio $=1/2$

So, $\quad x_1=3 \Rightarrow x_2=\frac{3}{2}$

$$x_3=\frac{3}{2^2} \Rightarrow x_4=\frac{3}{2^3}$$

....

$$x_{20}=\frac{3}{2^{19}}$$

Now, $\displaystyle\sum_{i=1}^{20} x_i=x_1+x_2+x_3+\ldots+x_{20}$

$$=3+\frac{3}{2}+\frac{3}{2^2}+\frac{3}{2^3}+\ldots+\frac{3}{2^{19}}$$

$$=3\left(1+\frac{1}{2}+\frac{1}{2^2}+\frac{1}{2^3}+\ldots+\frac{1}{2^{19}}\right)$$

$$=3\left[\frac{1\left(1-\left(\frac{1}{2}\right)^{20}\right)}{1-\frac{1}{2}}\right]=\frac{3}{1/2}\left(1-\frac{1}{2^{20}}\right)$$

$$\Rightarrow \quad \sum_{i=1}^{20} x_i=6\left(1-\frac{1}{2^{20}}\right) \quad \text{...(i)}$$

According to the question,

$$\bar{x}=\frac{\sum_{i=1}^{20}(x_i-i)^2}{n}=\frac{\sum_{i=1}^{20}x_i^2+\sum_{i=1}^{20}i^2-2\sum_{i=1}^{20}x_i i}{n} \quad \text{...(ii)}$$

From Eq. (i),

$$\sum_{i=1}^{20}(x_i)^2=x_1^2+x_2^2+x_3^2+\ldots x_{20}^2$$

$$=9+\frac{9}{2^2}+\frac{9}{2^4}+\frac{9}{2^6}+\ldots+\frac{9}{2^{38}}$$

$$=9\left[\frac{1-\left(\frac{1}{4}\right)^{20}}{1-\frac{1}{4}}\right]=9\times\frac{4}{3}\left[1-\frac{1}{4^{20}}\right]$$

$$\Rightarrow \quad \sum_{i=1}^{20}(x_i)^2=12\left[1-\left(\frac{1}{2^{40}}\right)\right] \quad \text{...(iii)}$$

and $\displaystyle\sum_{i=1}^{20} i^2=(1)^2+(2)^2+(3)^2+\ldots+(20)^2$

$$=\frac{20\times(20+1)(2\times20+1)}{6}=2870 \quad \text{...(iv)}$$

Also, $\displaystyle\sum_{i=1}^{20} x_i i=3+2.\frac{3}{2}+3.\frac{3}{2^2}+4.\frac{3}{2^3}+5\left(\frac{3}{2^4}\right)+\ldots+20\left(\frac{3}{2^{19}}\right)$

which are in arithmetic co-geometric (AG) series.

Let $z=\displaystyle\sum_{i=1}^{20} x_i i=3+2.\frac{3}{2}+3.\frac{3}{2^2}+4.\frac{3}{2^3}+\ldots+20.\frac{3}{2^{19}}$ ...(v)

$$\frac{1}{2}z=\frac{3}{2}+2.\frac{3}{2^2}+3.\frac{3}{2^3}+\ldots+19.\frac{3}{2^{19}}+20.\frac{3}{2^{20}} \quad \text{...(vi)}$$

On subtracting Eq. (vi) from Eq. (v), we get

$$\left(z-\frac{z}{2}\right)=\left(3+\frac{3}{2}+\frac{3}{2^2}+\frac{3}{2^3}+\frac{3}{2^4}+\ldots+\frac{3}{2^{19}}-20.\frac{3}{2^{20}}\right)$$

$$\Rightarrow \quad \frac{z}{2} = 3\left(1 + \frac{1}{2} + \frac{1}{2^2} + \frac{1}{2^3} + \dots + \frac{1}{2^{19}}\right) - 20.\frac{3}{2^{20}}$$

$$\Rightarrow \quad \frac{z}{2} = 3\left[\frac{1 - \left(\frac{1}{2}\right)^{20}}{1 - \frac{1}{2}}\right] - \frac{60}{2^{20}} = 6\left(1 - \frac{1}{2^{20}}\right) - \frac{60}{2^{20}}$$

$$\Rightarrow \quad z = 6\left(2 - \frac{22}{2^{20}}\right)$$

$$\therefore \quad \sum_{i=1}^{20} x_i i = 6\left(2 - \frac{22}{2^{20}}\right) \quad \text{...(vii)}$$

On putting the values from Eqs. (iii), (iv) and (vii) in Eq. (ii), we get

$$\bar{x} = \frac{12 - \frac{12}{2^{40}} + 2870 - 12\left(2 - \frac{22}{2^{20}}\right)}{20}$$

$$= \frac{2858}{20} + \left(\frac{-12}{2^{40}} + \frac{264}{2^{20}}\right) \times \frac{1}{20}$$

$$\therefore \quad [\bar{x}] = 142$$

56. The given number is 3, 5, 7, $2k$, 12, 16, 21, 24.

Now, mean deviation about median is

$$\sum_{i=1}^{n} \frac{|x_i - M|}{n}$$

And median is $\frac{2k + 12}{2} = k + 6$

According to the question,

$$\sum_{i=1}^{8} \frac{|x_i - M|}{8} = 6$$

$$\Rightarrow \frac{(k+3) + (k+1) + (k-1) + (6-k) + (6-k) + (10-k) + (15-k) + (18-k)}{8} = 6$$

$$\Rightarrow \quad \frac{58 - 2k}{8} = 6$$

$$\Rightarrow \quad k = 5$$

Median is $(5 + 6) = 11$

57. Given, numbers are 3, 7, 12, a, $43 - a$

Mean = 13

$$\text{Variance} = \frac{\sum x_i^2}{n} - (\bar{x})^2$$

$$= \frac{9 + 49 + 144 + a^2 + (43 - a)^2}{5} - 13^2 \in N$$

$$= \frac{202 + 2a^2 - 86a + 1849}{5} - 169$$

$$= \frac{1206 + 2a^2 - 86a}{5}$$

$$= \frac{1205 - 85a}{5} + \frac{2a^2 - a + 1}{5} \in N$$

$$\Rightarrow \quad \frac{2a^2 - a + 1}{5} \in N$$

$\Rightarrow 2a^2 - a + 1 - 5N = 0$ must have solution as natural numbers.

Its $D = 40N - 7$ always has 3 at unit place.

$\Rightarrow$ D cannot be a perfect square.

So, a cannot be integer.

Alternate Solution

$$\text{Mean } (\bar{x}) = \frac{3 + 7 + 12 + \alpha + 43 - a}{5} = 13$$

$$\text{Variance} = \frac{9 + 49 + 144 + a^2 + (43 - a)^2}{5} - (13)^2 \in N$$

$$\Rightarrow \quad \frac{2a^2 - a + 1}{5} \in N$$

$\Rightarrow a^2 - a + 1 - 5n = 0$ must have solution as natural number.

Now, its discriminant $D = 40n - 7$

$\Rightarrow D$ can not be perfect square as all perfect square will be form of $4P$ or $4P + 1$ for $P \in N$.

$\Rightarrow a$ can not be integer.

58. Given,

$$\bar{x} = \frac{\sum x_i}{5} = \frac{24}{5} \quad \text{...(i)}$$

and

$$\sigma^2 = \frac{\sum x_i^2}{5} - (\bar{x})^2 = \frac{194}{25} \quad \text{...(ii)}$$

$$\therefore \quad \sum x_i = 24 \quad \text{[from Eq. (i)]}$$

$$\Rightarrow \quad x_1 + x_2 + x_3 + x_4 + x_5 = 24 \quad \text{...(iii)}$$

and

$$\frac{\sum x_i^2}{5} - \left(\frac{24}{5}\right)^2 = \frac{194}{25} \quad \text{[from Eq. (ii)]}$$

$$\Rightarrow \quad \sum x_i^2 = \frac{194}{5} + \frac{576}{5}$$

$$\Rightarrow \quad \sum x_i^2 = \frac{770}{5} = 154$$

$$\Rightarrow \quad x_1^2 + x_2^2 + x_3^2 + x_4^2 + x_5^2 = 154 \quad \text{...(iv)}$$

$$\because \quad \frac{x_1 + x_2 + x_3 + x_4}{4} = \frac{7}{2}$$

$$\therefore \quad x_1 + x_2 + x_3 + x_4 = 14$$

$$\Rightarrow \quad x_5 = 10 \quad \text{[from Eq. (iii)]}$$

and

$$\frac{x_1^2 + x_2^2 + x_3^2 + x_4^2}{4} - \left(\frac{7}{2}\right)^2 = a$$

$$\Rightarrow \quad x_1^2 + x_2^2 + x_3^2 + x_4^2 = 4a + 49$$

$$\Rightarrow \quad x_5^2 = 154 - (4a + 49) \quad \text{[from Eq. (iv)]}$$

$$\Rightarrow \quad 10^2 = 154 - 4a - 49$$

$$\Rightarrow \quad 100 = 105 - 4a \Rightarrow 4a = 5$$

$$\therefore \quad 4a + x_5 = 5 + 10 = 15$$

59. According to given data,

$$\frac{\sum_{i=1}^{7} (x_i - 62)^2}{7} = 20 \Rightarrow \sum_{i=1}^{7} (x_i - 62)^2 = 140$$

$$\Rightarrow \quad (x_1 - 62)^2 + (x_2 - 62)^2 + \dots + (x_7 - 62)^2 = 140$$

So, for any x_i, $(x_i - 62)^2 \le 140$

$$\Rightarrow \quad x_i > 50, \forall i = 1, 2, 3, \dots, 7$$

So, no student is going to score less than 50.

60. We have, $\dfrac{\sum x_i^2}{15} - 8^2 = 9$

$\Rightarrow \quad \sum x_i^2 = 15 \times 73 = 1095$

Let $\bar{x}_c$ be corrected mean, $\bar{x}_c = 9$

$\sum x_c^2 = 1095 - 25 + 400 = 1470$

Corrected variance $= \dfrac{1470}{15} - (9)^2 = 98 - 81 = 17$

61. According to the question, we have

$\bar{x} = 6$

$\Rightarrow \quad \dfrac{4+5+6+6+7+8+x+y}{8} = 6$

$\Rightarrow \quad x + y = 12 \qquad \text{...(i)}$

and variance $= \dfrac{9}{4}$

$\Rightarrow \quad \dfrac{9}{4} = \dfrac{\sum x_j^2}{n} - (\bar{x})^2$

$\Rightarrow \quad \dfrac{9}{4} = \dfrac{16+25+36+36+49+64+x^2+y^2}{8} - 36$

$\Rightarrow \quad x^2 + y^2 = 80$

$\Rightarrow \quad (x+y)^2 - 2xy = 80$

$\Rightarrow \quad (12)^2 - 80 = 2xy \qquad$ [From Eq. (i)]

$\Rightarrow \quad xy = 32$

Now, $\quad (x-y)^2 = x^2 + y^2 - 2xy = 80 - 2 \times 32 = 16$

$x - y = \pm 4 \qquad \text{...(ii)}$

From Eqs. (i) and (ii), we get

$x + y = 12$

$x - y = 4 \text{ or } x - y = -4$

$\Rightarrow \quad x = 8 \text{ or } x = 4 \text{ or } y = 4, \; y = 8$

So, $\quad x = 4$ and $y = 8 \qquad (\because x < y)$

$\therefore \quad x^4 + y^2 = 256 + 64 = 320$

62. Mean = 15

Standard deviation = 2

Number of observation = 50

Sum of correct and incorrect observation = 70

$(\text{Mean})_c = 16$

Variance = ?

$(\text{Mean})_{\text{incorrect}} = \dfrac{\sum x_i}{50} = 15$

$\Rightarrow \quad (\sum x_i)_{\text{incorrect}} = 750$

$(\text{Mean})_c = \dfrac{(\sum x_i)_c}{50} = 16$

$\Rightarrow \quad (\sum x_i)_c = 800$

$\therefore \quad (\sum x_i)_c - (\sum x_i)_{\text{incorrect}} = 800 - 750 = 50$

If wrong observation was x, then corrected one is $x + 50$

$\Rightarrow \quad x + (x + 50) = 70 \Rightarrow x = 10$

Thus, correct observation = 60

Variance $= \dfrac{\sum x_i^2}{50} - (15)^2 = 2^2 \Rightarrow \dfrac{\sum x_i^2}{50} = 229$

$\Rightarrow \quad (\sum x_i^2)_{\text{incorrect}} = 11450$

Now, $(\sum x_i^2)_{\text{correct}} = 11450 - (10)^2 + (60)^2 = 14950$

Variance of correct set $= \dfrac{14950}{50} - (16)^2 = 299 - 256 = 43$

63. Observations are $a, b, 8, 5, 10$.

Mean, $\quad \mu = \dfrac{a+b+8+5+10}{5} = 6$

$\therefore \quad a + b = 7$

Variance, $\quad \sigma^2 = \dfrac{\Sigma(x_i - \mu)^2}{N}$

$\Rightarrow \quad \sigma^2 = \dfrac{(a-6)^2 + (b-6)^2 + 2^2 + 1^2 + 4^2}{5}$

$\Rightarrow \quad 6.8 \times 5 = a^2 + b^2 - 12a - 12b + 93$

$\Rightarrow \quad a^2 + b^2 = 25 \Rightarrow ab = 12$

$\therefore \quad a = 3, b = 4$

Mean deviation about mean $= \dfrac{\Sigma |x_i - \mu|}{N}$

$M = \dfrac{|3-6| + |4-6| + |8-6| + |5-6| + |10-6|}{5}$

$= \dfrac{3+2+2+1+4}{5} = \dfrac{12}{5}$

$\therefore \quad 25\,M = \dfrac{12}{5} \times 25 = 60$

64. Observations : $x_1, x_2, x_3, \ldots, x_{20}$

Mean, $\quad \dfrac{\sum_{n=1}^{20} x_n}{20} = 15 \Rightarrow \sum_{n=1}^{20} x_n = 300$

Variance, $\quad \dfrac{\sum x_i^2}{20} - \left(\dfrac{\sum x_i}{20}\right)^2 = 9$

$\Rightarrow \quad \dfrac{\sum x_i^2}{20} - (15)^2 = 9$

$\Rightarrow \quad \sum x_i^2 = 20(225 + 9) = 4680$

Mean of $(x_1 + \alpha)^2, (x_2 + \alpha)^2 + \ldots (x_{20} + \alpha)^2$ is 178

$\dfrac{\Sigma (x_i + \alpha)^2}{20} = 178$

$\Rightarrow \quad \sum x_i^2 + 2\alpha \sum x_i + \alpha^2 \Sigma 1 = 3560$

$\Rightarrow \quad 4680 + 2\alpha\,(300) + \alpha^2 \cdot 20 = 3560$

$\Rightarrow \quad \alpha^2 + 30\,\alpha + 56 = 0 \Rightarrow \alpha = -2, -28$

Maximum of $\alpha = -2$

Square of maximum value of $\alpha = 4$

65. Mean $= \dfrac{\sum x_i}{10} = 15,$

variance $= \dfrac{\sum x_i^2}{10} - 225 = 15$

$\Rightarrow \quad \sum x_i = 150$ and $\sum x_i^2 = 2400$

Actual mean $= \dfrac{(\sum x_i) - 25 + 15}{10} = 14$

Actual variance $= \dfrac{(\sum x_i^2) - 625 + 225}{10} - (14)^2 = 200 - 196 = 4$

$\therefore$ Actual standard deviation $= \sqrt{4} = 2$

66. Number of boys = 20

Number of girls = 30

$$\sigma_B^2 = 2, \overline{X}_B = 12, \sigma_G^2 = 2$$

$$\overline{X}_G = \frac{50 \times 15 - 20 \times 12}{30} = \frac{510}{30} = 17 = \mu$$

Variance of 50 candidates

$$\sigma^2 = \frac{20\sigma_B^2 + 30\sigma_G^2}{50} + \frac{20 \cdot 30}{(20+30)^2}(\overline{X}_B - \overline{X}_G)^2$$

$$= \frac{20 \times 2 + 30 \times 2}{50} + \frac{600}{2500} \times 25 = 8$$

$\therefore \quad \mu + \sigma^2 = 17 + 8 = 25$

67. Variance $= \frac{\Sigma x^2}{n} - (\bar{x})^2$ $\quad [\because \bar{x} = \text{means}]$

$$\Rightarrow \quad 14 = \frac{1^2 + 2^2 + 3^3 + \ldots + n^2}{n} - \left(\frac{1+2+3+\ldots+n}{n}\right)^2$$

$$\Rightarrow \quad 14 = \frac{n(n+1)(2n+1)}{6n} - \left(\frac{n(n+1)}{2n}\right)^2$$

$$\Rightarrow \quad 14 = \frac{(n+1)(2n+1)}{6} - \frac{(n+1)^2}{4}$$

$$\Rightarrow \quad 14 = \left(\frac{n+1}{12}\right)[2(2n+1) - 3(n+1)]$$

$$\Rightarrow \quad 168 = (n+1)(n-1)$$

$$\Rightarrow \quad n^2 - 1 = 168$$

$$\Rightarrow \quad n^2 = 169 \Rightarrow n = 13$$

68. Given, mean of 3, 7, x and y is 5.

So, $\quad 3 + 7 + x + y = 20$

$\Rightarrow \quad x + y = 10 \quad$ ...(i)

and variance of 3, 7, x and y is 10

$$\Rightarrow \quad \frac{3^2 + 7^2 + x^2 + y^2}{4} - (5)^2 = 10$$

$\Rightarrow \quad x^2 + y^2 = 82 \quad$ ...(ii)

$\Rightarrow \quad x^2 + (10 - x)^2 = 82 \quad$ [using Eq. (i)]

$\Rightarrow \quad x^2 - 10x + 9 = 0$

$\Rightarrow \quad (x - 9)(x - 1) = 0$

$\Rightarrow \quad x = 1, 9$

$\Rightarrow \quad (x, y) = (9, 1) \quad$ [as $x > y$]

$$\text{Mean} = \frac{3 + 2x + 7 + 2y + x + y + x - y}{4} = \frac{10 + 4x + 2y}{4}$$

$$= \frac{10 + 4(9) + 2(1)}{4}$$

$$= \frac{48}{4} = 12$$

69. Here, $n = 40$, Mean = 30 and $\sigma = 5$

$\because \quad$ Mean $= 30 \Rightarrow \frac{\Sigma x_i}{40} = 30$

$\Rightarrow \quad \Sigma x_i = 1200$

New, $\Sigma x_i = 1200 - 12 - 10 = 1200 - 22 = 1178$

$$\therefore \quad \sigma = \sqrt{\frac{\Sigma x_i^2}{n} - \left(\frac{\Sigma x_i}{n}\right)^2} \Rightarrow 5 = \sqrt{\frac{\Sigma x_i^2}{40} - 900}$$

$\Rightarrow \quad 40(25 + 900) = \Sigma x_i^2$

$\Rightarrow \quad \Sigma x_i^2 = 37000$

New, $\quad \Sigma x_i^2 = 37000 - (12)^2 - (10)^2$

$= 37000 - 144 - 100$

$= 37000 - 244 = 36756$

$$\text{Now,} \quad \sigma = \sqrt{\frac{\text{New } \Sigma x_i^2}{n} - \left(\frac{\text{New } \Sigma x_i}{n}\right)^2}$$

$$\Rightarrow \quad \sigma = \sqrt{\frac{36756}{38} - \left(\frac{1178}{38}\right)^2}$$

$$\Rightarrow \quad \sigma^2 = \frac{36756}{38} - \frac{(1178)^2}{(38)^2}$$

$\Rightarrow \quad 38\sigma^2 = 36756 - 36518$

$\Rightarrow \quad 38\sigma^2 = 238$

70. **For AP** $(7 \times 8), (10 \times 10), (13 \times 12), \ldots\ldots$ 7, 10, 13, ...

$$a_n = 7 + (n-1)3 = 3n + 4$$

For AP 8, 10, 12, ...

$$b_n = 8 + (n-1)2 = 2n + 6$$

So, $\quad T_n = (3n + 4)(2n + 6) = 6n^2 + 26n + 24$

$$\text{Sum, } S_n = \Sigma T_n = 6.\left[\frac{n(n+1)(2n+1)}{6}\right] + 26\left[\frac{n(n+1)}{2}\right] + 24n$$

$$\text{Mean} = \frac{\text{Sum}}{10} = \frac{10 \cdot 11 \cdot 21}{10} + \frac{13 \cdot 10 \cdot 11}{10} + \frac{24 \cdot 10}{10} = 398$$

71. Sum of frequencies = 584

$$\alpha + \beta + 110 + 54 + 30 = 584$$

$$\alpha + \beta = 390$$

Median is at $\frac{584}{2} = 292$th term

$\because$ Median = 45 (lies in class 40 – 50)

$\Rightarrow \quad \alpha + 110 + 54 + 15 = 292$

$\Rightarrow \quad \alpha = 113$

$\Rightarrow \quad \beta = 390 - 113 = 277$

$\Rightarrow \quad \alpha - \beta = 113 - 277 = -164$

$\therefore \quad |\alpha - \beta| = 164$

72.

Class	Frequency	x_i	$f_i x_i$
0-6	a	3	$3a$
6-12	b	9	$9b$
12-18	12	15	180
18-24	9	21	189
24-30	5	27	135
	$\Sigma n = a + b + 26$		$\Sigma f_i x_i = 3a + 9b + 504$

$$\text{Mean} = \frac{\Sigma f_i x_i}{\Sigma n} = \frac{3a + 9b + 504}{a + b + 26} = \frac{309}{22}$$

$\Rightarrow \quad 66a + 198b + 11088 = 309a + 309b + 8034$

$\Rightarrow \quad 243a + 111b = 3054$

$\Rightarrow \quad 81a + 37b = 1018$

$$\text{Median} = 12 + \frac{\frac{a+b+26}{2} - (a+b)}{12} \times 6 = 14$$

$\Rightarrow \quad \frac{a+b}{4} = \frac{9}{2} \Rightarrow a + b = 18$

So, $81a + 37b = 1018$ and $a + b = 18$

$\Rightarrow \quad a = 8$ and $b = 10$

$\therefore \quad (a-b)^2 = 4$

73. Let a, b, c, d and e are 5 remaining observations, $n = 7$, mean $= 8$ and variance $= 16$

Sum of observations $= 7 \times 8 = 56$

Mean of remaining observations $= \frac{56 - 8 - 6}{5} = \frac{42}{5}$

And variance $= \frac{\sum x^2}{n} - (\bar{x})^2 \Rightarrow 16 = \frac{\sum x^2}{7} - 64$

$\Rightarrow \quad \sum x^2 = 560$

$\Rightarrow a^2 + b^2 + c^2 + d^2 + e^2 = 560 - 8^2 - 6^2 = 460$

Variance of 5 remaining observations $= \frac{460}{5} - \left(\frac{42}{5}\right)^2 = \frac{536}{25}$

74. $\bar{x} = \frac{\sum x_i}{20} = 10 \Rightarrow \sum x_i = 200$

$$\sigma^2 = \frac{\sum x_i^2}{20} - 100 = 6.25$$

$$\sum x_i^2 = 20 \times 106.25 = 2125$$

Now, replacing 25 with 35, then

$$\sum x_i - 25 + 35 = 210$$

$$\sum x_i^2 - 25^2 + 35^2 = 2725$$

New mean $= \frac{210}{20} = 10.5 = (\alpha)$

New SD $= \sqrt{\frac{2725}{20} - (10.5)^2}$

SD $= \sqrt{136.25 - 110.25} = \sqrt{26} = \sqrt{\beta}$

$(\alpha, \beta) = (10.5, 26)$

75. Given,

x	$x_1 = 2$	$x_2 = 6$	$x_3 = 8$	$x_4 = 9$
f	4	4	α	β

Mean $= 6 \Rightarrow \frac{8 + 24 + 8\alpha + 9\beta}{8 + \alpha + \beta} = 6 \quad \left[\because \text{Mean} = \frac{\sum f_i x_i}{\sum f_i}\right]$

$\Rightarrow \quad 32 + 8\alpha + 9\beta = 48 + 6\alpha + 6\beta$

$\Rightarrow \quad 2\alpha + 3\beta = 16 \quad$ ...(i)

Also, variance $= 6.8$

$\Rightarrow \quad \frac{4 \times 16 + 4 \times \alpha + 9 \times \beta}{8 + \alpha + \beta} = 6.8$

$$\left[\because \text{Variance} = \frac{\sum f_i (x_i - \bar{x})^2}{\sum f_i}\right]$$

$\Rightarrow \quad 64 + 4\alpha + 9\beta = (8 + \alpha + \beta)\,6.8$

$\Rightarrow \quad 28\alpha - 22\beta = 96$

$\Rightarrow \quad 14\alpha - 11\beta = 48 \quad$ ...(ii)

From Eqs. (i) and (ii), we get

$$\alpha = 5 \text{ and } \beta = 2$$

If x_3 is changed from 8 to 7 then,

x	$x_1 = 2$	$x_2 = 6$	$x_3 = 7$	$x_4 = 9$
f	4	4	5	2

New mean $= \frac{8 + 24 + 35 + 18}{15} = \frac{17}{3}$

76. Given data $= \{6, 10, 7, 13, a, 12, b, 12\}$

Mean $= 9$ and variance $= 37/4$

Now, mean $= \frac{\sum x_i}{n} = \frac{6 + 10 + 7 + 13 + a + 12 + b + 12}{8}$

or $\quad 9 = \frac{60 + a + b}{8}$

$\Rightarrow \quad a + b = 12 \quad$ ...(i)

Variance $= \frac{\sum x_i^2}{n} - \sum\left(\frac{x_i}{n}\right)^2$

$\Rightarrow \quad \frac{37}{4} = \frac{6^2 + 10^2 + 7^2 + 13^2 + a^2 + 12^2 + b^2 + 12^2}{8} - 9^2$

$\Rightarrow \quad \frac{37}{4} = \frac{642 + a^2 + b^2}{8} - 81$

$\Rightarrow \quad 74 = a^2 + b^2 - 6 \Rightarrow a^2 + b^2 = 80 \quad$ ...(ii)

$\therefore \quad (a+b)^2 = a^2 + b^2 + 2ab$

$\quad 2ab = (a+b)^2 - (a^2 + b^2)$

On putting the values from Eqs. (i) and (ii), we get

$$2ab = 12^2 - 80 = 64$$

Now, $\quad (a-b)^2 = a^2 + b^2 - 2ab = 80 - 64 = 16$

77. Given, mean $= 10$

i.e. $\quad \frac{7 + 10 + 11 + 15 + a + b}{6} = 10 \Rightarrow a + b = 17 \quad$ ...(i)

Also, variance $= 20/3$

i.e. $\frac{(7)^2 + (10)^2 + (11)^2 + (15)^2 + a^2 + b^2}{6} - (\text{Mean})^2 = \frac{20}{3}$

$\Rightarrow \quad \frac{495 + a^2 + b^2}{6} - 100 = \frac{20}{3}$

$\Rightarrow \quad a^2 + b^2 = 145 \quad$ ...(ii)

Using Eqs. (i) and (ii), put $b = 17 - a$ in Eq. (ii),

$$a^2 + (17 - a)^2 = 145$$

$\Rightarrow \quad a^2 + 289 + a^2 - 34a = 145$

$\Rightarrow \quad a^2 - 17a + 72 = 0 \Rightarrow (a-9)(a-8) = 0$

$\therefore \quad a = 9$ or $a = 8$

Using $\quad b = 17 - a$

$\therefore \quad b = 8$ or $b = 9$

$\therefore \quad |a - b| = 1$

78. Mean = 6.5

$\therefore$ Total $= 6 \times 6.5 = 39$

Let the remaining two observations be x_1 and x_2

$$\Sigma x_i = 39$$

$$\Rightarrow \quad 2 + 4 + 5 + 7 + x_1 + x_2 = 39$$

$$\Rightarrow \quad x_1 + x_2 = 21$$

$$\text{Variance} = \frac{\Sigma x_i^2}{n} - \Sigma\left(\frac{x_i}{n}\right)^2$$

$$\Rightarrow \quad 10.25 = \frac{\Sigma x_i^2}{6} - 6.5^2$$

$$\therefore \quad \Sigma x_i^2 = 6(10.25 + 42.25)$$

$$= 52.5 \times 6$$

$$\Sigma x_i^2 = 52.5 \times 6$$

$$4 + 16 + 25 + 49 + x_1^2 + x_2^2 = 315$$

$$\Rightarrow \quad x_1^2 + x_2^2 = 221$$

$$\Rightarrow \quad x_1^2 + (21 - x_1)^2 = 221$$

$$\Rightarrow \quad 2x_1^2 - 42x_1 + 441 = 221$$

$$\Rightarrow \quad x_1^2 - 21x_1 + 110 = 0$$

$$\Rightarrow \quad (x_1 - 11)(x_1 - 10) = 0$$

$$\Rightarrow \quad x_1 = 10 \text{ or } 11$$

$$x_2 = 11 \text{ or } 10$$

Remaining two observations are 10 and 11.

79. Given, three observations $= a, b, c$

$$b = a + c$$

Standard deviation $= \sigma$

$$\sigma = \sqrt{\frac{\Sigma(x_i - \mu)^2}{N}}$$

When $x_1 = a + 2$

$$x_2 = b + 2, \quad x_3 = c + 2$$

$$\mu = \frac{(a+2)+(b+2)+(c+2)}{3} = \frac{2b}{3} + 2$$

$$x_1 - \mu = (a + 2) - (2b/3 + 2) = a - 2b/3$$

$$x_2 - \mu = (b + 2) - (2b/3 + 2) = b - 2b/3$$

$$x_3 - \mu = (c + 2) - (2b/3 + 2) = c - 2b/3$$

$$d = \sqrt{\frac{(a - 2b/3)^2 + (b - 2b/3)^2 + (c - 2b/3)^2}{3}}$$

$$3d^2 = a^2 + b^2 + c^2 + \frac{12b^2}{9} - \frac{4}{3}(ab + b^2 + bc)$$

$$\Rightarrow \quad 3d^2 = a^2 + b^2 + c^2 + \frac{4}{3}b^2 - \frac{4}{3}[b(a + c) + b^2]$$

$$\Rightarrow \quad 3d^2 = a^2 + b^2 + c^2 + \frac{4}{3}b^2 - \frac{4}{3}[b \cdot b + b^2]$$

$$\Rightarrow \quad 3d^2 = a^2 + b^2 + c^2 + \frac{4}{3}b^2 - \frac{4}{3} \cdot 2b^2$$

$$\Rightarrow \quad 3d^2 = a^2 + c^2 - \frac{b^2}{3} \Rightarrow b^2 = 3a^2 + 3c^2 - 9d^2$$

80.

Decoding the Question

Suppose we have two sets of data containing n_1 and n_2 observations with means $\bar{X}_1$ and $\bar{X}_2$ and variances S_1^2 and S_2^2. If $\bar{x}_C$ is the combined mean and if S_C^2 is the combined variance of $n_1 + n_2$ observation.

Combined mean $(\bar{x}_C) = \dfrac{n_1 \bar{x}_1 + n_2 \bar{x}_2}{n_1 + n_2}$

Combined standard deviation $= \sqrt{\text{Combined variance}}$

Combined mean = 15.6

$$\Rightarrow \quad \frac{100 \times 15 + 150 \times \bar{x}_B}{250} = 15.6$$

$$\Rightarrow \quad 1500 + 150\bar{x}_B = 3900$$

$$\Rightarrow \quad 150\bar{x}_B = 2400$$

$$\Rightarrow \quad \bar{x}_B = \frac{2400}{150} = 16$$

Combined SD $= \sqrt{13.44}$

$\Rightarrow$ Combined variance $(\sigma^2) = 13.44$

$$\sigma^2 = \frac{\Sigma x_i^2}{n} - (\bar{x})^2$$

$$\Rightarrow \quad 13.44 = \frac{\Sigma x_i^2}{250} - (15.6)^2$$

$$\Rightarrow \quad \Sigma x_i^2 = 64200 \qquad \text{...(i)}$$

For sample A, $\quad 9 = \dfrac{\Sigma(x_i)_A^2}{100} - 225$

$$\Rightarrow \quad \Sigma(x_i)_A^2 = 23400$$

Now, $\quad \Sigma(x_i)_B^2 = 64200 - 23400 = 40800$

$$\text{SD of sample } B = \sqrt{\frac{\Sigma(x_i)_B^2}{n_B} - (\bar{x}_B)^2}$$

$$= \sqrt{\frac{40800}{150} - 256} = 4$$

81. Let observations are denoted by x_i for $1 \le i < 2n$.

$$\therefore \text{Mean}(\bar{x}) = \frac{\Sigma x_i}{2n}$$

$$= \frac{(a + a + a + \dots + a) - (a + a + a + \dots + a)}{2n}$$

$$\Rightarrow \quad \bar{x} = 0$$

and $\quad \sigma_x^2 = \dfrac{\Sigma x_1^2}{2n} - (\bar{x})^2 = \dfrac{\overbrace{a^2 + a^2 + a^2 + \dots + a^2}^{2n \text{ times}}}{2n} - 0 = a^2$

$$\Rightarrow \quad \sigma_x^2 = a^2 \Rightarrow \sigma_x = a$$

According to the question, adding a constant b, then new mean

$$(\bar{y}) = \bar{x} + b = 5$$

$$\Rightarrow \quad 0 + b = 5$$

$$\Rightarrow \quad b = 5$$

and new SD $\quad (\sigma_y) = \sigma_x$ (no change in SD)

$$\Rightarrow \quad \sigma_y = \sigma_x = 20$$

$$\Rightarrow \quad a = 20$$

$$\therefore \quad a^2 + b^2 = 400 + 25 = 425$$

Exercise 2 - JEE Advanced Pattern

1. We have, $\sum_{i=1}^{9}(x_i-6)=12$ and $\sum_{i=1}^{9}(x_i-6)^2=48$

$$\text{SD}=\sqrt{\frac{\sum_{i=1}^{9}(x_i-6)^2}{9}-\left(\frac{\sum_{i=1}^{9}(x_i-6)}{9}\right)^2}$$

$$\Rightarrow \quad \text{SD}=\sqrt{\frac{48}{9}-\left(\frac{12}{9}\right)^2}$$

$$\Rightarrow \quad \text{SD}=\sqrt{\frac{48}{9}-\frac{144}{81}}$$

$$\Rightarrow \quad \text{SD}=\sqrt{\frac{32}{9}}=\frac{4}{3}\times\sqrt{3}=2.31$$

2. Let the 40 observations be

$x_1, x_2, x_3, \ldots, x_{40}$.

Now, deviations of these observations from 30 are

$$(x_i-30),(x_2-30),(x_3-30),\ldots,(x_{40}-30)$$

$$\because \quad \sum_{i=1}^{40}(x_i-30)=40 \qquad \text{[given]}$$

$$\Rightarrow \quad \sum_{i=1}^{40}x_i-(30\times 40)=40$$

$$\Rightarrow \quad \sum_{i=1}^{40}x_i=40(30+1)=40\times 31$$

$\therefore$ Mean of 40 observations $=(\bar{x})$

$$=\frac{\sum_{i=1}^{40}x_i}{40}=31$$

3. We have,

$$\sum_{i=1}^{n}(x_i+1)^2=11n \qquad \text{...(i)}$$

and

$$\sum_{i=1}^{n}(x_i-1)^2=7n \qquad \text{...(ii)}$$

On subtracting Eq. (ii) from Eq. (i), we get

$$\sum_{i=1}^{n}\{(x_i+1)^2-(x_i-1)^2\}=4n$$

$$\Rightarrow \quad \sum_{i=1}^{n}4x_i=4n \Rightarrow \sum_{i=1}^{n}x_i=n$$

$$\Rightarrow \quad \frac{\sum_{i=1}^{n}x_i}{n}=1\Rightarrow \text{mean }(\bar{x})=1$$

Now, standard deviation $=\sqrt{\frac{\sum_{i=1}^{n}(x_i-\bar{x})^2}{n}}=\sqrt{\frac{\sum_{i=1}^{n}(x_i-1)^2}{n}}$

$$=\sqrt{\frac{7n}{n}}=\sqrt{7}$$

4. Let x_1, x_2, x_3, x_4, x_5 be the height of five students.

Then, we have

$$\text{Mean, }\bar{x}=\frac{\sum_{i=1}^{5}x_i}{5}=160 \Rightarrow \sum_{i=1}^{5}x_i=800 \qquad \text{...(i)}$$

and variance $=\frac{\sum_{i=1}^{5}x_i^2}{n}-(\bar{x})^2 \Rightarrow \frac{\sum_{i=1}^{5}x_i^2}{5}-(160)^2=19$

$$\Rightarrow \quad \sum_{i=1}^{5}x_i^2=128095 \qquad \text{...(ii)}$$

Now, new mean $=\frac{\sum_{i=1}^{6}x_i}{6}$

$$=\frac{\sum_{i=1}^{5}x_i+166}{6}=\frac{800+165}{6} \qquad \text{[using Eq. (i)]}$$

$$\Rightarrow \quad \bar{x}_{\text{new}}=161$$

and new variance $=\frac{\sum_{i=1}^{6}x_i^2}{6}-(\bar{x}_{new})^2$

$$=\frac{\sum_{i=1}^{5}x_i^2+(166)^2}{6}-(161)^2$$

$$=\frac{128095+(166)^2}{6}-(161)^2$$

$$=25941.83-25921=20.83 \qquad \text{[using Eq. (ii)]}$$

5. Let $x_1, x_2, \ldots, x_n$ be n observations.

$$P=\frac{x_1+x_2+\ldots+x_n}{n}$$

$$=\frac{x_1+x_2+\ldots+x_{n-5}+x_{n-4}+x_{n-3}+x_{n-2}+x_{n-1}+x_n}{n}$$

$$\Rightarrow np=a+x_{n-5}+x_{n-4}+x_{n-3}+x_{n-2}+x_{n-1}+x_n$$

$$\Rightarrow \frac{np-a}{6}=\frac{x_{n-5}+x_{n-4}+x_{n-3}+x_{n-2}+x_{n-1}+x_n}{6}$$

6.

x_i	f_i	f_ix_i	$f_ix_i^2$
p	2	$2p$	$2p^2$
$2p$	1	$2p$	$4p^2$
$3p$	1	$3p$	$9p^2$
$4p$	1	$4p$	$16p^2$
$5p$	1	$5p$	$25p^2$
$6p$	1	$6p$	$36p^2$
Total	$n=7$	$\sum f_ix_i=22p$	$\sum f_ix_i^2=92p^2$

$$\therefore \quad 6^2=\frac{\Sigma f_ix_i^2}{n}-\left(\frac{\Sigma f_ix_i}{n}\right)^2$$

$$\Rightarrow \quad 160 = \frac{92p^2}{77} - \left(\frac{22p}{7}\right)^2$$

$$\Rightarrow \quad 160 = \frac{92p^2}{7} - \frac{484}{49}p^2$$

$$\Rightarrow \quad 160 = (644 - 484)\frac{p^2}{49}$$

$$\Rightarrow \quad p^2 = 49$$

$$\therefore \quad p = 7$$

7. Let x_1 and x_2 be the number of observation in two groups having means $\bar{x}_1$ and $\bar{x}_2$, respectively.

Then, $\bar{x} = \dfrac{n_1\bar{x}_1 + n_2\bar{x}_2}{n_1 + n_2}$

Now, $\bar{x} - \bar{x}_1 = \dfrac{n_1\bar{x}_1 + n_2\bar{x}_2}{n_1 + n_2} - \bar{x}_1$

$$= \frac{n_2(\bar{x}_2 - \bar{x}_1)}{n_1 + n_2} < 0 \quad [\because \bar{x}_2 < \bar{x}_1]$$

$$\Rightarrow \quad \bar{x} < \bar{x}_1 \quad \text{...(i)}$$

and $\bar{x} - x_2 = \dfrac{n(\bar{x}_1 - \bar{x}_2)}{n_1 + n_2} > 0 \quad [\because \bar{x}_2 < \bar{x}_1]$

$$\Rightarrow \quad \bar{x} > \bar{x}_2 \quad \text{...(ii)}$$

From Eqs. (i) and (ii), we get

$$\bar{x}_1 > \bar{x} > \bar{x}_2$$

8. We know, $6^2 = \dfrac{\sum x^2}{n} - \mu^2$

$$= \frac{15 \times \frac{1}{3} - c + 10 \times \left(\frac{1}{3}\right) + 15\left(\frac{1}{3} + c\right)^2}{40} - \left(\frac{15\left(\frac{1}{3} - c\right) + 10 \times \frac{1}{3} + 15\left(\frac{1}{3} + c\right)}{40}\right)^2$$

$$= \frac{15\left[\frac{1}{9} + c^2 - \frac{2}{C}c + \frac{1}{9} + c^2 + \frac{2}{9}c\right] + \frac{10}{9}}{40} - \left(\frac{1}{9}\right)$$

$$= \frac{30\left[\frac{1}{9} + c^2\right] + \frac{10}{9}}{40} - \frac{1}{9} = \frac{6}{5} \quad \left[\because 6^2 = \frac{6}{5}\right]$$

$$= \frac{\frac{1}{3} + 3c^2 - \frac{1}{9}}{4} = \frac{59}{45}$$

$$= 3c^2 = \frac{236}{45} - \frac{2}{9} = \frac{226}{45}$$

$$\Rightarrow \quad c^2 = 1.67$$

$$\therefore \quad [C^2] = 1$$

9. Given, $n_1 = 70, \bar{x}_1 = 700, \sigma_1 = 8, n_2 = 90, \bar{x}_2 = 710, \sigma_2 = 7$

$$\text{Combined SD} = \sqrt{\frac{n_1\sigma_1^2 + n_2\sigma_2^2}{n_1 + n_2} + \frac{n_1n_2(\bar{x}_1 - \bar{x}_2)^2}{(n_1 + n_2)^2}}$$

$$= \sqrt{\frac{70 \times 64 + 90 \times 49}{70 + 90} + \frac{70 \times 90(700 - 710)^2}{(70 + 90)^2}}$$

$$= \sqrt{\frac{4480 + 4410}{160} + \frac{6300 \times 100}{(160)^2}}$$

$$= \sqrt{55.56 + 24.60}$$

$$= \sqrt{80.16} = 8.95$$

10. Let H_1 and n_1 be the harmonic mean and number of observations of first group and H_2 and n_2 are the harmonic mean and number of observative of another group.

∴ Using combined harmonic mean formula; we get

Combined harmonic mean

$$= \frac{n_1 + n_2}{\frac{n_1}{H_1} + \frac{n_2}{H_2}} = \frac{10 + 10}{\frac{10}{7/2} + \frac{10}{11/2}} = \frac{77}{22 + 14}$$

$$= \frac{77}{36}$$

11. Median of $a, 2a, 3a, 4a, \ldots 50a$ is

$$\frac{25a + 26a}{2} = (25.5)a$$

$$\text{Mean deviation about median} = \frac{\sum_{i=1}^{50} |x_i - \text{Median}|}{n}$$

$$50 = \frac{1}{50}\{2|a|(0.5 + 2.5 + \ldots + 24.5)\}$$

$$\Rightarrow \quad 2500 = 2|a| \cdot \frac{25}{2}(2 \times 0.5 + 2.4 \times 1) = 2|a| \cdot \frac{25}{2}$$

$$\Rightarrow \quad |a| = 4$$

$$\therefore \quad a = \pm 4$$

12. According to the given conditions,

$$6.80 = \left[\frac{(6-a)^2 + (6-b)^2 + (6-8)^2 + (6-5)^2 + (6-10)^2 + (6-6)^2}{5}\right]$$

$$\Rightarrow \quad 34 = (6-a)^2 + (6-b)^2 + 4 + 1 + 16$$

$$\Rightarrow \quad (6-a)^2 + (6-b)^2 = 3^2 + 2^2$$

$$\Rightarrow \quad a = 3 \text{ and } b = 4$$

13. Let the number of boys and girls be x and y.

$\therefore \quad 52x + 42y = 50(x + y)$

$\Rightarrow \quad 52x + 42y = 50x + 50y$

$\Rightarrow \quad 2x = 8y$

$\Rightarrow \quad x = 4y$

∴ Total number of students in the class $= x + y = 4y + y = 5y$

∴ Required percentage of boys $= \left(\dfrac{4y}{5y} \times 100\right)\% = 80\%$

∴ Percentage of girls $= (100 - 80)\% = 20\%$

14. We have, Mean $= \dfrac{5 + 7 + 9 + 11 + 13}{5} = 9$

Now, first calcualte the deviation from the

(a) Mean $-4, -2, 0, 2, 4$

$$\text{Variance} = \frac{(-4)^2 + (-2)^2 + 0^2 + 2^2 + 4^2}{5} = \frac{40}{5} = 8$$

(b) Calculate the mean absolute deviation

$$\text{MAD} = |5-9| + |7-9| + |9-9| + |11-9| + |13-9|$$

$$= \frac{12}{5} = 2.4$$

(c) False

Missprint

(d) Calculate the standard deviation,

$$\text{SD} = \sqrt{\text{variance}} = \sqrt{8} \simeq 2.83$$

15. Given that $X \sim N(0, 1)$ and $Y \sim N(0, 4)$ and they are independent $Z = X + Y$ will follows a normal distribution. Since, the sum of independent normal random. Variable is also normal.

To find the mean and variance of Z,

Mean of Z,

$$E[Z] = E[X] + E[Y] = 0 + 0 = 0$$

Variance of Z,

$$\text{Var}(Z) = \text{Var}(X) + \text{Var}(Y) = 1 + 4 = 5$$

(a) Z follows a normal distribution sum of independent normal random variable is normal

(b) Z follows a normal distribution with zero mean. $[\because E(Z) = 0]$

(c) Z follows a normal distribution with variance 5. $[\because \text{Var}(Z) = 5]$

Sol. (Q.Nos. 16 and 17)

Total number of studnets = 60

$$x - 2 + x + x^2 + (x+1)^2 + 2x + x + 1 = 60$$

$$\Rightarrow \quad 5x - 2 + x^2 + x^2 + 1 + 2x + 1 = 60$$

$$\Rightarrow \quad 2x^2 + 7x = 60$$

$$\Rightarrow \quad 2x^2 + 7x - 60 = 0$$

$$\Rightarrow \quad 2x^2 + 15x - 8x - 60 = 0$$

$$\Rightarrow \quad x(2x + 15) - 4(2x + 15) = 0$$

$$\Rightarrow \quad (2x + 15)(x - 4) = 0$$

$$\Rightarrow \quad x = -\frac{15}{2}, x = 4$$

$$\Rightarrow \quad x = 4 \quad [\because x \text{ is positive}]$$

Marks (x_i)	Frequency (f_i)	x_i^2	$f_i x_i$	$f_i x_i^2$
0	2	0	0	0
1	4	1	4	4
2	16	4	32	64
3	25	9	75	225
4	8	16	32	128
5	5	25	25	125
Total	60		168	546

16. (b) Mean $\bar{x} = \frac{\Sigma f_i x_i}{N} = \frac{168}{60} = 2.8$

17. (b) SD, $\sigma = \sqrt{\frac{\Sigma f_i x_i^2}{N} - (\bar{x})^2} = \sqrt{\frac{546}{60} - (2.8)^2}$

$$= \sqrt{9.1 - 7.84} = \sqrt{1.26} = 1.12$$

Sol. (Q.Nos. 18 and 19)

18. To find the variance, follows these steps

Calculate the mean height,

$$\text{Mean, } \bar{x} = \frac{\sum x}{n}$$

$$\Rightarrow \quad \bar{x} = \frac{670}{10} = 67 \text{ inches}$$

Calculate the square deviation from the mean $(x_i - \bar{x})^2$ for each height x_i is

49, 25, 9, 4, 1, 1, 4, 9, 25, 49

Calculate the variance

$$\text{Variance, } \sigma^2 = \frac{\Sigma(x_i - \bar{x})^2}{n}$$

$$= \frac{49 + 25 + 9 + 4 + 1 + 1 + 4 + 9 + 25 + 49}{10}$$

$$= \frac{176}{10} = 17.6$$

19. Variance $\sigma^2 = 176$

$\therefore$ Standard deviation $= \sqrt{\sigma^2} = \sqrt{17.6} \simeq 4.2$

Sol. (Q.Nos. 20 and 21)

20. Let $d_i = \frac{x_i - A}{h}$, then $\sigma_x = |h|\sigma_d$

$$\text{Now, } -2x_i - 3 = \frac{x_i + \frac{3}{2}}{-\frac{1}{2}}$$

$$\text{Here, } h = -\frac{1}{2}$$

$$\therefore \quad \sigma_d = \frac{1}{|h|}\sigma_x = 2 \times 3.5 = 7$$

21. Let $d_i = \frac{x_i - A}{n}$, then $\sigma_x = |h|\sigma_d$

$$\text{Now, } -3x_i - 4 = \frac{x_i + \frac{4}{3}}{-\frac{1}{3}}$$

$$\text{Here, } h = -\frac{1}{3}$$

$$\therefore \quad \sigma_d = \frac{1}{|h|}\sigma_x = 3 \times 3.5 = 10.5$$

Hence, variance $\sigma_d^2 = 110.25$

Sol. (Q.Nos. 22 and 23)

x_1	f_i	$d_i = x_i - 4$	$f_i d_i$	$f_i d_i^2$
2	4	−2	− 8	16
3	9	−1	− 9	9
4	16	0	0	0
5	14	1	14	14
6	11	2	22	44
7	6	3	18	54
Total	60		$\Sigma f_i d_i = 37$	$\Sigma f_i d_i^2 = 137$

22. $\text{SD} = \sqrt{\frac{\sum f_i d_i^2}{n} - \left(\frac{\sum f_i d_i}{n}\right)^2}$

$= \sqrt{\frac{137}{60} - \left(\frac{37}{60}\right)^2}$

$= \sqrt{2.2833 - (0.616)^2}$

$= \sqrt{2.283 - 0.3794}$

$= \sqrt{1.9037}$

$= 1.38$

23. We know that

Variance, $\sigma^2 = (\text{SD})^2 = (1.38)^2$ [$\because$ SD = 1.38 part(s)]

$\therefore$ Variance = 1.904

24. Given data are 6, 5, 9, 13, 12, 8 and 10

x_i	x_i^2
6	36
5	25
9	81
13	169
12	144
8	64
10	100
$\sum x_i = 63$	$\sum x_i^2 = 619$

$\therefore \quad \text{SD} = \sqrt{\frac{\Sigma x_i^2}{N} - \left(\frac{\Sigma x_i}{N}\right)^2}$

$= \sqrt{\frac{619}{7} - \left(\frac{63}{7}\right)^2}$

$= \sqrt{\frac{7 \times 619 - 3969}{49}} = \sqrt{\frac{364}{49}} = 2.72$

So, $P = 2.72$

Now, $[P] = 2$

25.

Class	Frequency	x_i	$f_i x_i$
0-6	a	3	$3a$
6-12	b	9	$9b$
12-18	12	15	180
18-24	9	21	189
24-30	5	27	135
	$\Sigma n = a + b + 26$		$\Sigma f_i x_i = 3a + 9b + 504$

$\text{Mean} = \frac{\Sigma f_i x_i}{\Sigma n} = \frac{3a + 9b + 504}{a + b + 26} = \frac{309}{22}$

$\Rightarrow \quad 66a + 198b + 11088 = 309a + 309b + 8034$

$\Rightarrow \quad 243a + 111b = 3054$

$\Rightarrow \quad 81a + 37b = 1018$

$\text{Median} = 12 + \frac{\frac{a + b + 26}{2} - (a + b)}{12} \times 6 = 14$

$\Rightarrow \quad \frac{13}{2} - \left(\frac{a + b}{4}\right) = 2$

$\Rightarrow \quad \frac{a + b}{4} = \frac{9}{2}$

$\Rightarrow \quad a + b = 18$

So, $81a + 37b = 1018$

$a + b = 18$

$a = 8$ and $b = 10$

$\therefore \quad \frac{ab}{20} = \frac{8 \times 10}{20} = 4$

26. Given, $n = 25$, $\bar{x} = 40$

$\therefore \quad \bar{x} = \frac{\sum x}{n}$

$\Rightarrow \quad \sum x = 25 \times 40 = 1000$

New sum $= 1000 - 60 + x = 940 + x$

New average $= 39$

$\therefore \quad 39 = \frac{940 + x}{25}$

$\Rightarrow \quad 975 = 940 + x$

$\Rightarrow \quad x = 35$

$\Rightarrow \quad 35 = 7P$

$\Rightarrow \quad P = 5$

27. Sum of frequencies = 584

$\alpha + \beta + 110 + 54 + 30 = 584$

$\alpha + \beta = 390$

Median is at $\frac{584}{2} = 292\text{th}$

$\because$ Median = 45 (lies in class 40 − 50)

$\Rightarrow \quad \alpha + 110 + 54 + 15 = 292$

$\Rightarrow \quad \alpha = 113$

$\Rightarrow \quad \beta = 390 - 113 = 277$

$\Rightarrow \quad \alpha - \beta = 113 - 277 = -164$

$\therefore \quad \left|\frac{\alpha - \beta}{164}\right| = 164$

28. $x : x_1, x_2, x_3, \ldots x_{n+1}, x_{n+2}, \ldots x_{2n}, x_{2n+1} \ldots x_{3n}$

$\frac{1}{3n} \sum_{i=1}^{3n} x_i^2 - (\bar{x})^2 = 4$

$\left[\text{where, } \bar{x} = \frac{n_1 \bar{x}_1 + n_2 \bar{x}_2}{n_1 + n_2} = \frac{2n(6) + n(3)}{3n} = 5\right]$

$\Rightarrow \quad \frac{1}{3n} \sum_{i=1}^{3n} x_i^2 = 25 + 4 = 29$

$\Rightarrow \quad \sum_{i=1}^{3n} = 87n$

$x' : x_1 + 1, x_2 + 1, \ldots, x_{2n} + 1, x_{(2n+1)} - 1 \ldots, x_{3n} - 1$

$\bar{x}' = \frac{2n(6 + 1) + n(3 - 1)}{3n} = \frac{16}{3}$

$$k = \frac{1}{3n}\sum_{i=1}^{3n} x_i^2 - \frac{256}{9}$$

$$= \frac{1}{3n}\left[\sum_{i=1}^{3n} x_i'^2 + 2\sum_{i=1}^{2n} x_i' - 2\sum_{i=2n+1}^{3n} x_i' + 3n\right] - \frac{256}{9}$$

$$= \frac{1}{3n}[87n + 2(12n) - 2\cdot 3n + 3n] - \frac{256}{9}$$

$$\Rightarrow \quad k = 36 - \frac{256}{9} = 7.55$$

Now, $[7.55] = 7$

29. Number of boys = 20

Number of girls = 30

$$\sigma_B^2 = 2, \overline{X}_B = 12, \sigma_G^2 = 2$$

$$\overline{X}_G = \frac{50\times 15 - 20\times 12}{30} = \frac{510}{30} = 17 = \mu$$

Variance of 50 candidates

$$\sigma^2 = \frac{20\sigma_B^2 + 30\sigma_G^2}{50} + \frac{20\cdot 30}{(20+30)^2}(\overline{X}_B - \overline{X}_G)^2$$

$$= \frac{20\times 2 + 30\times 2}{50} + \frac{600}{2500}\times 25 = 8$$

$$\therefore \quad \mu + \sigma^2 = 17 + 8 = 25$$

30. Mean, $\overline{x} = \dfrac{3+7+9+12+13+20+x+y}{8} = 10$

$$\Rightarrow \quad x + y = 16 \quad \text{...(i)}$$

Variance $= \sigma^2 = \dfrac{\Sigma(x_i)^2}{8} - (\overline{x})^2 = 25$

$$\sigma^2 = \frac{9+49+81+144+169+400+x^2+y^2}{8} - 100 = 25$$

$$\Rightarrow \quad x^2 + y^2 = 148 \quad \text{...(ii)}$$

From Eq. (i), $\quad (x+y)^2 = (16)^2 \Rightarrow x^2 + y^2 + 2xy = 256$

Using Eq. (ii), $148 + 2xy = 256 \Rightarrow xy = 54$

31. Variance $= \dfrac{\sum_{i=1}^{11} b_i^2}{11} - \left[\dfrac{\sum_{i=1}^{11} b_i}{11}\right]^2$

Let common difference of AP be d.

$$\frac{\sum_{r=0}^{10}(b_1 + rd)^2}{11} - \left[\frac{\sum_{r=0}^{10}(b_1 + rd)}{11}\right]^2$$

$$= \frac{11b_1^2 + 2b_1 d\left(\frac{10\times 11}{2}\right) + d^2\left(\frac{10\times 11\times 21}{6}\right)}{11} - \left[\frac{11b_1 + \frac{10\times 11}{2}d}{11}\right]^2$$

$$= (b_1^2 + 10b_1 d + 35d^2) - (b_1 + 5d)^2 = 10d^2$$

$\because \quad$ Variance = 90 $\quad$ [given]

$$\Rightarrow \quad 10d^2 = 90 \Rightarrow d = 3$$

32. Let the other two observations be x and y.

Therefore, the series is 1, 2, 6, x and y.

Now, mean $(\overline{x}) = 4.4 = \dfrac{1+2+6+x+y}{5}$

$$\Rightarrow \quad 22 = 9 + x + y \Rightarrow x + y = 13 \quad \text{...(i)}$$

Also, variance $= 8.24 = \dfrac{1}{n}\sum_{i=1}^{5}(x_i - \overline{x})^2$

i.e. $8.24 = \dfrac{1}{5}[(3.4)^2 + (2.4)^2 + (1.6)^2 + x^2 + y^2 - 2\times 4.4(x+y) + 2\times(4.4)^2]$

or $41.20 = 11.56 + 5.76 + 2.56 + x^2 + y^2 - 8.8\times 13 + 38.72$

Therefore, $\quad x^2 + y^2 = 97 \quad$ ...(ii)

But from Eq. (i), we have

$$x^2 + y^2 + 2xy = 169 \quad \text{...(iii)}$$

From Eqs. (ii) and (iii), we have

$$2xy = 72 \quad \text{...(iv)}$$

On subtracting Eq. (iv) from Eq. (ii), we get

$$x^2 + y^2 - 2xy = 97 - 72 \text{ i.e. } (x-y)^2 = 25$$

or $\quad x - y = \pm 5 \quad$ ...(v)

So, from Eqs. (i) and (v), we get

$x = 9$ and $y = 4$, when $x - y = 5$

or $x = 4$ and $y = 9$, when $x - y = -5$

Thus, the remaining observations are 4 and 9.

33. Given, $\sum_{i=1}^{18}[x_i - \alpha] = 36$ and $\sum_{i=1}^{18}|x_i - \beta|^2 = 90$

Now, $\quad \sum_{i=1}^{18}(x_i - \alpha) = 36 \Rightarrow \sum_{i=1}^{18} x_i - 18\alpha = 36$

$$\sum_{i=1}^{18} x_i = 36 + 18\alpha \quad \text{...(i)}$$

Again, $\quad \sum_{i=1}^{18} x_i^2 + 18\beta^2 - 2\beta\sum_{i=1}^{18} x_i = 90$

$$\Rightarrow \quad \sum_{i=1}^{18} x_i^2 + 18\beta^2 - 2\beta(36 + 18\alpha) = 90 \quad \text{[using Eq. (i)]}$$

$$\Rightarrow \quad \sum_{i=1}^{18} x_i^2 = 90 - 18\beta^2 + 2\beta(36 + 18\alpha) \quad \text{...(ii)}$$

Given, standard deviation = 1 i.e. $\sigma^2 = 1$

$$\Rightarrow \quad \frac{\sum_{i=1}^{18} x_i^2}{18} - \left(\frac{\sum_{i=1}^{18} x_i}{18}\right)^2 = 1$$

$$\Rightarrow \quad \frac{1}{18}(90 - 18\beta^2 + 36\alpha\beta + 72\beta) - \left(\frac{36 + 18\alpha}{18}\right)^2 = 1$$

$$\Rightarrow \quad 5 - \beta^2 + 2\alpha\beta + 4\beta - (2+\alpha)^2 = 1$$

$\Rightarrow \quad 5-\beta^2+2\alpha\beta+4\beta-4-\alpha^2+(-4\alpha)=1$

$\Rightarrow \quad -\beta^2+2\alpha\beta+4\beta-\alpha^2-4\alpha=0$

$\Rightarrow \quad \alpha^2+\beta^2+(-2\alpha\beta)-4\beta+4\alpha=0$

$\Rightarrow \quad (\alpha-\beta)^2+4(\alpha-\beta)=0$

$\Rightarrow \quad (\alpha-\beta)(\alpha-\beta+4)=0$

$\Rightarrow \quad \alpha-\beta=-4 \qquad [\because \alpha \neq \beta]$

$\Rightarrow \quad |\alpha-\beta|=|-4|=4$

34. First of all arrange x_i in increasing order and write corresponding frequencies, prepare a table.

x_i	f_i	$x_i f_i$	cf	$\lvert x_i-\bar{x}\rvert$	$f_i\lvert x_i-\bar{x}\rvert$	$\lvert x_i-M\rvert$	$f_i\lvert x_i-M\rvert$
0	2	0	2	2.8	5.6	3	6
1	4	4	6	1.8	7.2	2	8
2	16	32	22	0.8	12.8	1	16
3	25	75	47	0.2	5	0	0
4	8	32	55	1.2	9.6	1	8
5	5	25	60	2.2	11	2	10
Total	60	168					

(A) Mean $(\bar{x})=\dfrac{\Sigma f_i x_i}{\Sigma f_i}=\dfrac{168}{60}=2.8$

(B) Median $=\left(\dfrac{60}{2}\right)$th observation $=$ 30th observation $=3$

(C) Mean deviation about mean $=\dfrac{\Sigma f_i|x_i-\bar{x}|}{\Sigma f_i}$

$=0.85$

(D) Mean deviation about median $=\dfrac{\Sigma f_i|x_i-M|}{\Sigma f_i}$

$=0.8$

35. First of all arrange x_i in increasing order and write corresponding frequency, prepare a table

x_i	f_i	$x_i f_i$	cf	$\lvert x_i-\bar{x}\rvert$	$f_i\lvert x_i-\bar{x}\rvert$	$\lvert x_i-M\rvert$	$f_i\lvert x_i-M\rvert$
1	3	3	3	2.95	8.85	4	12
2	5	10	8	1.95	9.75	3	15
3	1	3	9	0.95	0.95	2	2
5	5	25	14	1.05	5.25	0	0
6	7	42	21	2.05	14.35	1	7
Total	21	83					

(A) Mean $(\bar{x})=\dfrac{\Sigma f_i x_i}{\Sigma f_i}=\dfrac{83}{21}=3.95$

Median $=$ Size of $\left(\dfrac{21+1}{2}\right)$th term $=$ Size of 11th term

Since, the 11th term for under cumulative frequency 14 and the size of the distribution a gainst this cf value is 5.

$\therefore$ Median $=5$

Now, GM of mean and median $=\sqrt{3.95\times 5}=4.44$

(B) Mean deivation about mean $=\dfrac{\Sigma f_i|x_i-\bar{x}|}{\Sigma f_i}$

$=\dfrac{39.15}{21}=1.86$

(C) Mean deviation about median $=\dfrac{\Sigma f_i|x_i-M|}{\Sigma f_i}$

$=\dfrac{36}{4}=1.71$

(D) The AM of mean deviation about mean and mean deviation about median $=\dfrac{1.86+1.71}{2}=1.78$

Exercise 3 - Challenging Problems

1. Since, n is even natural number. Therefore, $n=2m$ for some natural number m.

Let $\bar{X}$ be the mean of first n natural numbers.

Then, $\quad \bar{X}=\dfrac{1+2+3+\ldots+n}{n}$

$=\dfrac{n(n+1)}{2n}=\dfrac{n+1}{2}$

$\Rightarrow \quad \bar{X}=\dfrac{2m+1}{2}=m+\dfrac{1}{2}$

The mean deviation (MD) about mean is given by

$$\text{MD}=\frac{1}{n}\sum_{r=1}^{n}|r-\bar{X}|$$

$$=\frac{1}{2m}\sum_{r=1}^{2m}\left|r-\left(m+\frac{1}{2}\right)\right|$$

$$=\frac{1}{2m}\left[\sum_{r=1}^{m}\left|r-m+\frac{1}{2}\right|+\sum_{r=m+1}^{2m}\left|r-\left|m+\frac{1}{2}\right|\right|\right]$$

$$=\frac{1}{2m}\left[\sum_{r=1}^{m}-\left\{r-\left(m+\frac{1}{2}\right)\right\}+\sum_{r=m+1}^{2m}\left\{r-\left(m+\frac{1}{2}\right)\right\}\right]$$

$$=\frac{1}{2m}\left[-\sum_{r=1}^{m}r+\sum_{r=1}^{m}\left(m+\frac{1}{2}\right)+\sum_{r=m+1}^{2m}r-\sum_{r=m+1}^{2m}\left(m+\frac{1}{2}\right)\right]$$

$$=\frac{1}{2m}\left[\frac{-m(m+1)}{2}+\frac{m(2m+1)}{2}+\frac{m(3m+1)}{2}-\frac{m(2m+1)}{2}\right]$$

$$=\frac{1}{2m}\left[\frac{-m(m+1)}{2}+\frac{m(3m+1)}{2}\right]$$

$$=\frac{m}{4m}(-m-1+3m+1)=\frac{m}{2}=\frac{n}{4}$$

2. The terms of AP are $a, a+d, a+2d, \ldots\ldots a+(n-1)d$.

Let $\bar{X}$ be the mean of these terms.

Then, $\bar{X}=\dfrac{1}{n}(a+a+2d+\ldots\ldots a+(n-1)d)$

$=\dfrac{1}{n}\left[\dfrac{n}{2}(2a+(n-1)d)\right]$

$=a+\dfrac{(n-1)d}{2}$

Let σ be the SD of n terms of the AP then

$$\sigma^2 = \frac{1}{n}\sum_{r=1}^{n}[\{a+(r-1)d\}-\bar{x}]^2$$

$$= \frac{1}{n}\sum_{r=1}^{n}\left[\{a+(r-1)d\}-\left\{a+(n-1)\frac{d}{2}\right\}\right]^2$$

$$= \frac{d^2}{4n}\left[\sum_{r=1}^{n}(2r-2-n+1)^2\right]$$

$$= \frac{d^2}{4n}\left[\sum_{r=1}^{n}2r-(n+1)^2\right]$$

$$= \frac{d^2}{4n}[4r^2-4(n+1)r+(n+1)^2]$$

$$= \frac{d^2}{4n}\left[4\sum_{r=1}^{n}r^2-4(n+1)\sum_{r=1}^{n}r+\sum_{r=1}^{n}(n+1)^2\right]$$

$$= \frac{d^2}{4n}\left[\frac{4n(n+1)(2n+1)}{6}-\frac{4n(n+1)^2}{2}+n(n+1)^2\right]$$

$$= \frac{d^2}{4n}\left\{\frac{2n(n+1)(2n+1)}{3}-n(n+1)^2\right\}$$

$$= \frac{d^2}{12n}n(n+1)\{2(2n+1)-3(n+1)\}$$

$$= \frac{n^2-1}{12}d^2$$

$$\therefore \sigma = d\sqrt{\frac{n^2-1}{12}}$$

3. Mean $= \dfrac{\Sigma x_i}{N} \Rightarrow 45 = \dfrac{\Sigma x_i}{10}$

$\therefore \Sigma x_i = 450$

Correct $\Sigma x_i = 450 - 52 + 25 = 423$

$\therefore$ Correct mean $= \dfrac{423}{10} = 42.3$

Variance $= \dfrac{\Sigma x_i^2}{N} - \left(\dfrac{\Sigma x_i}{N}\right)^2$; $16 = \dfrac{\Sigma x_i^2}{10} - (45)^2$

$\Rightarrow \Sigma x_i^2 = (16 + 2025)\times 10 = 20410$

$\therefore$ Correct $\Sigma x_i^2 = 20410 - (52)^2 + (25)^2$

$= 20410 - 2704 + 625 = 18331$

$\therefore$ Correct variance $= \dfrac{18331}{10} - (42.3)^2$

$= 1833.1 - 1789.29 = 43.81$

4. Mean square deviations $= \dfrac{1}{n}\sum_{i=1}^{n}(x_i - c)^2$, about c.

Also, given that mean square deviation about -1 and $+1$ are 7 and 3, respectively.

$$\Rightarrow \frac{1}{n}\sum_{i=1}^{n}(x_i+1)^2 = 7 \text{ and } \frac{1}{n}\sum_{i=1}^{n}(x_i-1)^2 = 3$$

$$\Rightarrow \sum_{i=1}^{n}x_i^2 + 2\sum_{i=1}^{n}x_i + n = 7n \text{ and } \sum_{i=1}^{n}x_i^2 - 2\sum_{i=1}^{n}x_i + n - 3n$$

$$\Rightarrow \sum_{i=1}^{n}x_i^2 + 2\sum_{i=1}^{n}x_i = 6n \text{ and } \sum_{i=1}^{n}x_i^2 - 2\sum_{i=1}^{n}x_i = 2n$$

$$\Rightarrow \sum_{i=1}^{n}x_i - n \Rightarrow \bar{x} = \frac{\sum_{i=1}^{n}x_i}{n} = 1$$

$$\therefore \text{Standard deviation} = \sqrt{\frac{1}{n}\sum_{i=1}^{n}(x_i-\bar{x})^2}$$

$$= \sqrt{\frac{1}{n}\sum_{i=1}^{n}(x_i-1)^2} = \sqrt{3}$$

5. Given, $n = 40$, $\bar{x} = 40$, $\text{var}(x) = 49$

$$\Rightarrow \bar{x} = \frac{\Sigma f_i x_i}{40} = 40$$

$$\Rightarrow \Sigma f_i x_i = 1600$$

Also, $\text{var}(x) = 49$

$$\Rightarrow \frac{1}{40}\Sigma f_i(x_i - 40)^2 = 49$$

$$\therefore 49 = \frac{1}{40}(\Sigma x_i^2 f_i) - 2\Sigma x_i f_i + 40\Sigma f_i$$

$$\Rightarrow 49 = \frac{1}{40}(\Sigma x_i^2 f_i) - 2(1600) + 40\times 40$$

$$\therefore \Sigma x_i^2 f_i = 1649\times 40$$

Let (21-30) and (31-40) denote the kth and $(k+1)$th class intervals, respectively.

Then, if before correction f_k and f_{k+1} are frequencies of those intervals, then after correction (2 observations are shifted from (31-40) to (21-30)), frequency of kth interval becomes $f_k + 2$ and frequency of $(k+1)$th interval becomes $f_{k+1} - 2$

$$\therefore \bar{x}_{\text{new}} = \frac{1}{40}\left\{\sum_{\substack{i=1\\ i\neq k,\, k+1}}^{40} f_i x_i + (f_k+2)x_k + (f_{k+1}-2)x_{k+1}\right\}$$

$$\Rightarrow \bar{x}_{\text{new}} = \frac{1}{40}\left\{\sum_{i=1}^{40} f_i x_i\right\} + \frac{2}{40}\{(x_k - x_{k+1})\}$$

$$= \frac{1}{40}\sum_{i=1}^{40} f_i x_i + \frac{1}{20}(-10) = 39.5$$

$$\text{Variance (new)} = \frac{1}{40}\Big[\sum_{i=1}^{40} f_i(x_i-39.5)^2 + f_k(x_k-39.5)^2 + f_{k+1}(x_{k+1}-39.5)^2 \quad \text{where } i\neq k, k+1\Big]$$

$$= \frac{1}{40}[\Sigma(f_i x_i^2 - 79 f_i x_i + (39.5)^2 f_i)]$$

$$= \frac{1}{40}\sum_{i=1}^{40} f_i\cdot x_i^2 - 79\left(\frac{1}{40}\right)\sum_{i=1}^{40} f_i x_i + (39.5)^2\cdot\frac{1}{40}\sum_{i=1}^{40} f_i$$

$= 1649 - 3160 + 1560.25$

$= 49.25$

“

I have always been interested in Using Mathematics to make the world work better.

-Alvin E. Roth

11

Sets and Relations

Learning Milestones

Milestone 1 Sets

- Definition of Set
- Representation of Set
- Different Types of Sets
- Laws of Algebra of Sets
- Venn Diagrams (Euler-Venn Diagrams)

Milestone 2 Relations

- Ordered Pair
- Definition of Relation
- Ordered Relation
- Composition of Two Relations

Practice Milestones

Practice Milestone 1- JEE Main Pattern

Practice Milestone 2 - JEE Advanced Pattern

Practice Milestone 3 - Challenging Problems

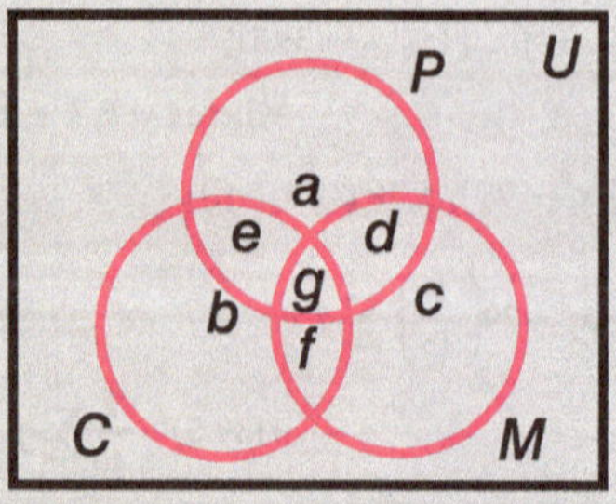

Milestone 1 Sets

- Definition of Set • Representation of Set • Different Types of Sets • Laws of Algebra of Sets
- Venn Diagrams(Euler-Venn Diagrams)

Introduction

The concept of set is fundamental in modern Mathematics. Today this concept is being used in different branches of Mathematics and widely used in the foundation of relations and functions.

The theory of sets was developed by German Mathematician **Georg Cantor** (1845-1918).

11.1 Definition of Set

A set is well-defined collection of distinct objects. Sets are usually denoted by capital letters

$$A, B, C, X, Y, Z, \dots$$

Examples of sets

(i) The set of all complex numbers.

(ii) The set of vowels in the alphabets of English language.

(iii) The set of all natural numbers.

(iv) The set of all triangles in a plane.

(v) The set of all states in India.

(vi) The set of all months in year which has 30 days.

(vii) The set of all stars in space.

Elements of the Set

The elements of the set are denoted by small letters of English alphabets language,

i.e. $a, b, c, x, y, z, \dots$.

If x is an element of a set A, we write $x \in A$ (read as 'x belongs to A').

If x is not an element of A, then we write $x \notin A$ (read as 'x does not belong to A').

e.g. If $A = \{1, 2, 3, 4, 5\}$, then $3 \in A, 6 \notin A$.

11.2 Representation of a Set

There are two methods for representing a set.

1. Tabulation or Roster or Enumeration Method

Under this method, the elements are enclosed in curly brackets or braces { } after separating them by commas.

JEE Focus Points

Concept Inside Video

- The order of writing the elements of a set is immaterial, so $\{a, b, c\}$, $\{b, a, c\}$, $\{c, a, b\}$ all denote the same set.
- An element of a set is not written more than once, i.e. the set $\{1, 2, 3, 4, 3, 3, 2, 1, 2, 1, 4\}$ is identical with the set $\{1, 2, 3, 4\}$.

e.g.

- If A is the set of prime numbers less than 10, then
$$A = \{2, 3, 5, 7\}$$
- If A is the set of all even numbers lying between 2 and 20, then
$$A = \{4, 6, 8, 10, 12, 14, 16, 18\}$$

Example 1. Write the following sets in the roster form

(i) $A = \{x : x$ is a positive integer less than 7 and $x^2 < 49\}$

(ii) $B = \{x : x$ is a whole number less than 10 and $2^x - 1$ is a multiple of 3$\}$

Sol. (i) Given, $x^2 < 49$

$$-7 < x < 7$$

Positive integers lie between -7 and 7 are

$$1, 2, 3, 4, 5, 6$$

$\therefore A = \{1, 2, 3, 4, 5, 6\}$

(ii) We have, $2^x - 1$ is a multiple of 3 and x is less than 10. i.e. 2, 4, 6, 8

$\therefore B = \{2, 4, 6, 8\}$

2. Set Builder Method

Under this method, the stating properties which its elements are to satisfy, then we write

$$A = \{x\, P(x)\} \quad \text{or} \quad A = \{x : P(x)\}$$

and read as 'A is the set of elements x, such that x has the property P'.

Example 2. Write the following sets in the set builder form.

(i) $A = \left\{\frac{1}{2}, \frac{4}{3}, \frac{9}{4}, \frac{16}{5}, \frac{25}{6}\right\}$

(ii) $B = \{A, G, L, X, Y\}$

Sol. (i) We have,

$$\frac{1}{2}, \frac{4}{3}, \frac{9}{4}, \frac{16}{5}, \frac{25}{6} = \frac{n^2}{n+1}$$

$$\therefore A = \left\{x : x = \frac{n^2}{n+1}, 1 \le n \le 5, n \in N\right\}$$

(ii) We have, A, G, L, X, Y

$B = \{x : x$ is letter of word GALAXY$\}$

Some Standard Sets

- N denotes set of all natural numbers $= \{1, 2, 3, \dots\}$.
- Z or I denotes set of all integers
  $= \{\dots, -3, -2, -1, 0, 1, 2, 3, \dots\}$.
- Z_0 or I_0 denotes set of all integers excluding zero
  $= \{\dots, -3, -2, -1, 1, 2, 3, \dots\}$.
- Z^+ or I^+ denotes set of all positive integers
  $= \{1, 2, 3, \dots\} = N$.
- E denotes set of all even integers
  $= \{\dots, -6, -4, -2, 0, 2, 4, 6, \dots\}$.
- O denotes set of all odd integers
  $= \{\dots, -5, -3, -1, 1, 3, 5, \dots\}$.
- W denotes set of all whole numbers $= \{0, 1, 2, 3, \dots\}$.
- Q denotes set of all rational numbers $= \{x : x = p/q$, where p and q are integers and $q \ne 0\}$.
- Q_0 denotes set of all non-zero rational numbers $\{x : x = p/q$, where p and q are integers and $p \ne 0$ and $q \ne 0\}$.
- Q^+ denotes set of all positive rational numbers $= \{x : x = p/q$, where p and q are both positive or negative integers$\}$
- R denotes set of all real numbers.
- R_0 denotes set of all non-zero real numbers.
- R^+ denotes set of all positive real numbers.
- $R - Q$ denotes set of all irrational numbers.
- C denotes set of all complex numbers
  $= \{a + ib : a, b \in R$ and $i = \sqrt{-1}\}$.
- C_0 denotes set of all non-zero complex numbers
  $= \{a + ib : a, b \in R_0$ and $i = \sqrt{-1}\}$.
- N_a denotes set of all natural numbers which are less than or equal to a, where a is positive integer
  $= \{1, 2, 3, \dots, a\}$.

11.3 Different Types of Sets

1. Finite Set

A set having finite number of elements or a definite number of elements is called a finite set.

e.g. (i) $A =$ The set of prime numbers less than 100

(ii) $B = \{x : x$ is months of year$\}$

The number of distinct element in finite set is called the **cardinal number** of S and is denoted by $n(S)$.

2. Infinite set

A set having unlimited number of elements is called an infinite set.

e.g. (i) The set of all natural numbers.

(ii) The set of all point lie on a line.

3. Null Set or Empty Set or Void Set

A set having no element is called a null set or empty set or void set. It is denoted by ϕ or $\{\,\}$.

e.g. (i) $\{x : x \in N, 4 < x < 5\} = \phi$

(ii) $\{x : x \in R, x^2 + 1 = 0\} = \phi$

(iii) $\{x : x^2 = 25, x$ is even number$\} = \phi$

JEE Focus Points

- ϕ is called the null set.
- ϕ is unique.
- ϕ is a subset of every set.
- ϕ is never written within braces i.e., $\{\phi\}$ is not the null set.
- $\{0\}$ is not an empty set as it contains the element 0 (zero).

4. Singleton or Unit Set

A set having one and only one element is called singleton or unit set.

e.g. $\{x : x - 3 = 4\}$ is a singleton set.

Since, $x - 3 = 4$

$\Rightarrow$ $x = 7$

$\therefore$ $\{x : x - 3 = 4\} = \{7\}$

5. Equal Sets

Two sets A and B are said to be equal, if every element of A is an element of B, and every element of B is an element of A. If A and B are equal, we write $A = B$.

It is clear that $A \subseteq B$ and $B \subseteq A$

$\Leftrightarrow$ $A = B$

e.g.

(i) The sets {1, 2, 5} and {5, 2, 1} are equal.

(ii) $\{1, 2, 3\} = \{x : x^3 - 6x^2 + 11x - 6 = 0\}$

6. Equivalent Sets

Two or more sets having the same number of elements are called equivalent sets. Thus, if sets A and B are equivalent, then $n(A) = n(B)$.

e.g. $A = \{x : x^2 - 5x + 6 = 0, x \in R\}$

$B = \{x : x$ is prime factors of $10\}$

Here, $A = \{2, 3\}$ and $B = \{2, 5\}$

$n(A) = n(B)$

$\therefore$ A and B are equivalent sets.

Subset of a Set

If every element of a set A is also an element of a set B, then A is called the subset of B, we write $A \subseteq B$ (read as A is subset of B or A is contained in B).

Thus, $A \subseteq B$

$\Leftrightarrow$ $[x \in A \Rightarrow x \in B]$

Every set is a subset of itself i.e. $A \subseteq A$.

If $A \subseteq B$, $B \subseteq C$, then $A \subseteq C$.

e.g. If $A = \{2, 3, 4\}$ and $B = \{5, 4, 2, 3, 1\}$, then $A \subseteq B$.

The sets $\{a\}, \{b\}, \{a, b\}, \{b, c\}$ are the subsets of the set $\{a, b, c\}$.

Total Number of Subsets

If a set A has n elements, then the number of subsets of $A = 2^n$.

Example 3. Write the letters of the word ALLAHABAD in set form and find the number of subsets in it and write all subsets.

Sol. There are 5 different letters in the word ALLAHABAD i.e. A, L, H, B, D, then set is {A, B, D, H, L}, then number of subsets $= 2^5 = 32$ and all subsets are

ϕ, {A}, {B}, {D}, {H}, {L}, {A, B}, {A, D}, {A, H}, {A, L}, {B, D}, {B, H}, {B, L}, {D, H}, {D, L}, {H, L}, {A, B, D}, {A, B, H}, {A, B, L}, {A, D, H}, {A, D, L}, {A, H, L}, {B, D, H}, {B, D, L}, {B, H, L}, {D, H, L}, {A, B, D, H}, {A, B, D, L}, {B, D, H, L}, {A, D, H, L}, {A, B, H, L}, {A, B, D, H, L}.

Power Set

The set of all the subsets of a given set A is said to be the power set A and is denoted by $P(A)$ or 2^A.

Symbolically, $P(A) = \{x : x \subseteq A\}$

Thus, $x \in P(A) \Leftrightarrow x \subseteq A$.

JEE Focus Points

- ϕ and A are both elements of $P(A)$.
- If $A = \phi$, then $P(\phi) = \{\phi\}$, a singleton but ϕ is a null set.
- If $A = \{a\}$, then $P(A) = \{\phi, \{a\}\}$
  e.g. If $A = \{a, b, c\}$, then
  $P(A)$ or $2^A = \{\phi, \{a\}, \{b\}, \{c\}, \{a, b\}, \{b, c\}, \{c, a\}, \{a, b, c\}\}$
  Also, $n(P(A))$ or $n(2^A) = 2^3 = 8$
- Since, $P(\phi) = \{\phi\}$
  $\therefore$ $P(P(\phi)) = \{\phi, \{\phi\}\}$
  and $P(P(P(\phi))) = \{\phi, \{\phi\}, \{\{\phi\}\}, \{\phi, \{\phi\}\}\}$
- If A has n elements, then $P(A)$ has 2^n elements.

Super Set

The statement $A \subseteq B$ can be rewritten as $B \supseteq A$, then B is called the super set of A and is written as $B \supset A$.

Proper Subset

A set A is said to be proper subset of a set B, if every element of A is an element of B and B has atleast one element which is not an element of A and is denoted by $A \subset B$ (read as "A is a proper subset of B").

e.g.

(i) If $A = \{1, 2, 4\}$ and $B = \{5, 1, 2, 4, 3\}$, then $A \subset B$

Since, $3, 5 \notin A$.

(ii) If $A = \{a, b, c\}$ and $B = \{c, b, a\}$, then $A \not\subset B$ (since, B does not contain any element which is not in A).

(iii) $N \subset I \subset Q \subset R \subset C$

Comparability of Sets

Two sets A and B are said to be comparable, if either $A \subset B$ or $B \subset A$ or $A = B$, otherwise A and B are said to be incomparable.

e.g.

(i) The sets $A = \{1,2,3\}$ and $B = \{1,2,4,6\}$ are incomparable (since $A \not\subset B$ or $B \not\subset A$ or $A \neq B$)

(ii) The sets $A = \{1, 2, 4\}$ and $B = \{1, 4\}$ are comparable (since $B \subset A$).

Interval as Subsets of *R*

The set of all numbers lying between two given real numbers is called an interval in R.

Let a and b be any two real numbers such that $a < b$, then we define the following types of intervals

(i) **Closed interval $[a, b]$**

$[a, b]$ = Closed interval from a to b

$= \{x : x \in R, a \le x \le b\}$

= Set of all real numbers lying between a and b including the end points a and b

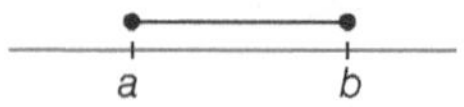

[a, b]

(ii) **Open interval (a, b) or $]a, b[$**

(a, b) = Open interval from a to b

$= \{x : x \in R, a < x < b\}$

= Set of all real numbers lying between a and b, excluding the end point of a and b

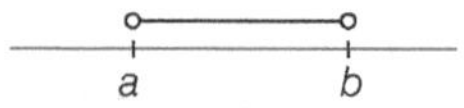

(a, b)

(iii) **Closed open interval $[a, b)$ and open closed interval $(a, b]$**

$[a, b) = \{x : x \in R, a \le x < b\}$

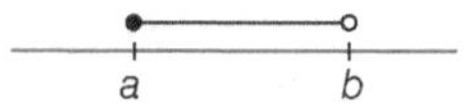

[a, b)

$(a, b] = \{x : x \in R, a < x \le b\}$

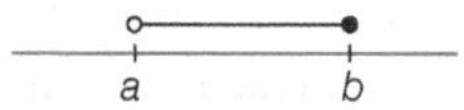

(a, b]

Universal Set

All the sets under consideration are likely to be subsets of a set is called the universal set and is denoted by Ω or S or U.

e.g.

(i) The set of all letters in alphabet of English language $U = \{a, b, c, \ldots, x, y, z\}$ is the universal set of vowels in alphabet of English language.

i.e. $A = \{a, e, i, o, u\}$.

(ii) The set of all integers $I = \{0, \pm 1, \pm 2, \pm 3, \ldots\}$ is the universal set of all even integers.

i.e., $\{0, \pm 2, \pm 4, \pm 6, \ldots\}$

Operation on Sets

1. Union of Sets

The union of two sets A and B is the set of all those elements which are either in A or in B or in both. This set is denoted by $A \cup B$ or $A + B$ (read as 'A union B' or 'A cup B' or 'A join B').

Symbolically, $A \cup B = \{x : x \in A \text{ or } x \in B\}$

or $A \cup B = \{x : x \in A \vee x \in B\}$

Clearly, $x \in A \cup B \Leftrightarrow x \in A$ or $x \in B$

The union of a finite number of sets $A_1, A_2, A_3, \ldots, A_n$ is represented by $A_1 \cup A_2 \cup A_3 \cup \ldots \cup A_n$ or $\bigcup_{i=1}^{n} A_i$.

Symbolically, $\bigcup_{i=1}^{n} A_i = \{x : x \in A_i \text{ for atleast one } i\}$

e.g. (i) If $A = \{1, 2, 3, 4\}$ and $B = \{4, 5, 6\}$, then $A \cup B = \{1, 2, 3, 4, 4, 5, 6\} = \{1, 2, 3, 4, 5, 6\}$

(ii) If $A = \{1,2,3\}$, $B = \{2, 3, 4, 5\}$, $C = \{7, 8\}$, then $A \cup B \cup C = \{1, 2, 3, 4, 5, 7, 8\}$

2. Intersection of Sets

The intersection of two sets A and B is the set of all elements which are common in A and B. This set is denoted by $A \cap B$ or AB (read as 'A intersection B' or 'A cap B' or 'A meet B').

Symbolically, $A \cap B = \{x : x \in A \text{ and } x \in B\}$

or $A \cap B = \{x : x \in A \wedge x \in B\}$

Clearly, $x \in A \cap B \Leftrightarrow x \in A$ and $x \in B$

The intersection of a finite number of sets $A_1, A_2, A_3, \ldots, A_n$ represented by $A_1 \cap A_2 \cap A_3 \cap \ldots \cap A_n$ or $\bigcap_{i=1}^{n} A_i$.

Symbolically, $\bigcap_{i=1}^{n} A_i = \{x : x \in A_i \text{ for all } i\}$

e.g. (i) If $A = \{1, 2, 3\}$ and $B = \{3, 4, 5, 6\}$, then $A \cap B = \{3\}$.

(ii) If $A = \{1, 2, 3\}$, $B = \{2, 3, 4\}$ and $C = \{3, 4, 5\}$, then $A \cap B \cap C = \{3\}$

3. Disjoint Sets

If the two sets A and B have no common element.

i.e., $A \cap B = \phi$, then the two sets A and B are called disjoint or mutually exclusive events.

e.g. If $A = \{a, b, c\}$ and $B = \{1, 2, 3\}$, then $A \cap B = \phi$

Hence, A and B are disjoint sets.

JEE SPIKE

If $S = \{a_1, a_2, a_3, \ldots, a_n\}$, so number of unordered pairs of disjoint sets of S is $\frac{3^n + 1}{2}$.

4. Difference of Sets

If A and B be two given sets, then the set of all those elements of A which do not belong to B is called difference of sets A and B.

It is written as $A - B$. It is also denoted by $A \sim B$ or $\frac{A}{B}$ or $C_A B$ (complement of B in A).

Symbolically, $A - B = \{x : x \in A \text{ and } x \notin B\}$

Clearly, $x \in A - B \Leftrightarrow x \in A$ and $x \notin B$.

5. Symmetric Difference of Two Sets

Let A and B be two sets. The symmetric difference of two sets A and B is the set $(A - B) \cup (B - A)$ or $(A \cup B) - (A \cap B)$ and is denoted by $A \Delta B$ or $A \oplus B$ (A direct sum B).

i.e. $\quad A \oplus B$ or $A \Delta B = (A - B) \cup (B - A)$

and $\quad A \oplus B$ or $A \Delta B = (A \cup B) - (A \cap B)$

e.g.

Let $\quad A = \{1, 2, 3, 4, 5\}$ and $B = \{1, 3, 5, 7\}$,

then $A - B = \{2, 4\}$, $B - A = \{7\}$

$\therefore \quad A \Delta B = (A - B) \cup (B - A)$

$= \{2, 4, 7\}$

6. Complement Set

Let U be the universal set and A be a set, such that $A \subset U$. Then, the complement of A with respect to U is denoted by A' or A^c or $C(A)$ or $U - A$.

Symbolically, A' or A^c or $C(A) = \{x : x \in U \text{ and } x \notin A\}$.

Clearly, $\quad x \in A' \Leftrightarrow x \notin A$.

e.g.

Let $U = \{1, 2, 3, 4, 5, 6, 7\}$ and $A = \{1, 3, 5, 7\}$.

Then, $A' = U - A = \{2, 4, 6\}$

Example 4. Consider the following sets $V = \{a, b, c, d, e, f\}$, $A = \{a, b, c\}$, $B = \{c, d, e, f\}$, $C = \{c, d, e\}$ and $D = \{d, e, f\}$. Evaluate the following sets

(i) $A \cup D$ (ii) $B \cap C$

(iii) $A \cup B \cup C$ (iv) A'

(v) $A \cup (B \cap C)$

Sol. (i) $A \cup D = \{a, b, c, d, e, f\}$

(ii) $B \cap C = \{c, d, e\}$

(iii) $A \cup B \cup C = \{a, b, c, d, e, f\}$

(iv) $A' = \{d, e, f\}$

(v) $B \cap C = \{c, d, e\}$

$\therefore A \cup (B \cap C) = \{a, b, c\} \cup \{c, d, e\}$

$= \{a, b, c, d, e\}$

11.4 Laws of Algebra of Sets

1. **Idempotent Laws**

For any set A,

(i) $\boldsymbol{A \cup A = A}$ (ii) $\boldsymbol{A \cap A = A}$

Proof

(i) Let $x \in A \cup A \Leftrightarrow x \in A$ or $x \in A$

$\Leftrightarrow x \in A$

Hence, $A \cup A = A$

(ii) Let $x \in A \cap A \Leftrightarrow x \in A$ and $x \in A$

$\Leftrightarrow x \in A$

Hence, $A \cap A = A$

2. **Identity Laws**

For any set A,

(i) $\boldsymbol{A \cup \phi = A}$ (ii) $\boldsymbol{A \cap \phi = \phi}$

(iii) $\boldsymbol{A \cup U = U}$ (iv) $\boldsymbol{A \cap U = A}$

Proof

(i) Let $x \in A \cup \phi \Leftrightarrow x \in A$ and $x \in \phi$

$\Leftrightarrow x \in A$

Hence, $A \cup \phi = A$

(ii) Let $x \in A \cap \phi \Leftrightarrow x \in A$ and $x \in \phi$

$\Leftrightarrow x \in \phi$

Hence, $A \cap \phi = \phi$

(iii) Let $x \in A \cup U \Leftrightarrow x \in A$ or $x \in U$

$\Leftrightarrow x \in U$

Hence, $\quad A \cup U = U$

(iv) Let $x \in A \cap U \Leftrightarrow x \in A$ and $x \in U$

$\Leftrightarrow x \in A$

Hence, $A \cap U = A$

3. **Commutative Laws**

For any two sets A and B, we have

(i) $\boldsymbol{A \cup B = B \cup A}$

(ii) $\boldsymbol{A \cap B = B \cap A}$

Proof

(i) Let $x \in A \cup B \Leftrightarrow x \in A$ or $x \in B$

$\Leftrightarrow x \in B$ or $x \in A$

$\Leftrightarrow x \in B \cup A$

$\therefore \quad x \in A \cup B \Leftrightarrow x \in B \cup A$

Hence, $A \cup B = B \cup A$

(ii) Let $x \in A \cap B \Leftrightarrow x \in A$ and $x \in B$

$\Leftrightarrow x \in B$ and $x \in A$

$\Leftrightarrow x \in B \cap A$

$\therefore \quad x \in A \cap B \Leftrightarrow x \in B \cap A$

Hence, $A \cap B = B \cap A$.

4. **Associative Laws**

For any three sets A, B and C, we have

(i) $\boldsymbol{A \cup (B \cup C) = (A \cup B) \cup C}$

(ii) $\boldsymbol{A \cap (B \cap C) = (A \cap B) \cap C}$

Proof

(i) Let $x \in A \cup (B \cup C) \Leftrightarrow x \in A$ or $x \in B \cup C$

$\Leftrightarrow x \in A$ or $(x \in B$ or $x \in C)$

$\Leftrightarrow (x \in A$ or $x \in B)$ or $x \in C$

$\Leftrightarrow x \in A \cup B$ or $x \in C$

$\Leftrightarrow x \in (A \cup B) \cup C$

$\therefore \quad x \in A \cup (B \cup C) \Leftrightarrow x \in (A \cup B) \cup C$

Hence, $A \cup (B \cup C) = (A \cup B) \cup C$.

(ii) Let $x \in A \cap (B \cap C) \Leftrightarrow x \in A$ and $x \in B \cap C$

$\Leftrightarrow x \in A$ and $(x \in B$ and $x \in C)$

$\Leftrightarrow (x \in A$ and $x \in B)$ and $x \in C$

$\Leftrightarrow x \in A \cap B$ and $x \in C$

$\Leftrightarrow x \in (A \cap B) \cap C$

Hence, $A \cap (B \cap C) = (A \cap B) \cap C$.

5. **Distributive Laws**

For any three sets A, B and C, we have

(i) $\boldsymbol{A \cup (B \cap C) = (A \cup B) \cap (A \cup C)}$

(ii) $\boldsymbol{A \cap (B \cup C) = (A \cap B) \cup (A \cap C)}$

Proof

(i) Let $x \in A \cup (B \cap C) \Leftrightarrow x \in A$ or $x \in B \cap C$

$\Leftrightarrow x \in A$ or $(x \in B$ and $x \in C)$

$\Leftrightarrow (x \in A$ or $x \in B)$ and $(x \in A$ or $x \in C)$

$\Leftrightarrow x \in A \cup B$ and $x \in A \cup C$

$\Leftrightarrow x \in [(A \cup B) \cap (A \cup C)]$

$\therefore x \in A \cup (B \cap C) \Leftrightarrow x \in (A \cup B) \cap (A \cup C)$

Hence, $A \cup (B \cap C) = (A \cup B) \cap (A \cup C)$.

(ii) Let $x \in A \cap (B \cup C) \Leftrightarrow x \in A$ and $x \in B \cup C$

$\Leftrightarrow x \in A$ and $(x \in B$ or $x \in C)$

$\Leftrightarrow (x \in A$ and $x \in B)$ or $(x \in A$ and $x \in C)$

$\Leftrightarrow x \in A \cap B$ or $x \in A \cap C$

$\Leftrightarrow x \in (A \cap B) \cup (A \cap C)$

$\therefore x \in A \cap (B \cup C) \Leftrightarrow x \in (A \cap B) \cup (A \cap C)$

Hence, $A \cap (B \cup C) = (A \cap B) \cup (A \cap C)$.

6. For any two sets A and B, we have

(i) $\boldsymbol{P(A) \cap P(B) = P(A \cap B)}$

(ii) $\boldsymbol{P(A) \cup P(B) \subseteq P(A \cup B)}$

where, $P(A)$ is the power set of A.

Proof

(i) Let $x \in P(A) \cap P(B) \Leftrightarrow x \in P(A)$ and $x \in P(B)$

$\Leftrightarrow x \subseteq A$ and $x \subseteq B$

$\Leftrightarrow x \subseteq A \cap B$

$\Leftrightarrow x \in P(A \cap B)$

Hence, $P(A) \cap P(B) = P(A \cap B)$

(ii) Let $x \in P(A) \cup P(B) \Leftrightarrow x \in P(A)$ or $x \in P(B)$

$\Leftrightarrow x \subseteq A$ or $x \subseteq B$

$\Leftrightarrow x \subseteq A \cup B$

$\Leftrightarrow x \in P(A \cup B)$

Hence, $P(A) \cup P(B) \subseteq P(A \cup B)$

7. If A is any set, then $\boldsymbol{(A')' = A}$

Proof Let $x \in (A')' \Leftrightarrow x \notin A' \Leftrightarrow x \in A$

Hence, $(A')' = A$

8. **De-Morgan's Laws**

For any three sets A, B and C, we have

(i) $\boldsymbol{(A \cup B)' = A' \cap B'}$

(ii) $\boldsymbol{(A \cap B)' = A' \cup B'}$

(iii) $\boldsymbol{A - (B \cup C) = (A - B) \cap (A - C)}$

(iv) $\boldsymbol{A - (B \cap C) = (A - B) \cup (A - C)}$

Proof

(i) Let $x \in (A \cup B)' \Leftrightarrow x \notin A \cup B$

$\Leftrightarrow x \notin A$ and $x \notin B$

$\Leftrightarrow x \in A'$ and $x \in B'$

$\Leftrightarrow x \in A' \cap B'$

$\therefore \quad x \in (A \cup B)' \Leftrightarrow x \in A' \cap B'$

Hence, $(A \cup B)' = A' \cap B'$.

(ii) Let $x \in (A \cap B)' \Leftrightarrow x \notin A \cap B$

$\Leftrightarrow x \notin A$ or $x \notin B$

$\Leftrightarrow x \in A'$ or $x \in B'$

$\Leftrightarrow x \in A' \cup B'$

$\therefore \quad x \in (A \cap B)' \Leftrightarrow x \in A' \cup B'$

Hence, $(A \cap B)' = A' \cup B'$.

(iii) Let $x \in A - (B \cup C) \Leftrightarrow x \in A$ and $x \notin B \cup C$

$\Leftrightarrow x \in A$ and $(x \notin B$ and $x \notin C)$

$\Leftrightarrow (x \in A$ and $x \notin B)$ and $(x \in A$ and $x \notin C)$

$\Leftrightarrow x \in (A - B)$ and $x \in (A - C)$

$\Leftrightarrow x \in (A - B) \cap (A - C)$

Hence, $A - (B \cup C) = (A - B) \cap (A - C)$.

(iv) Let $x \in A-(B \cap C) \Leftrightarrow x \in A$ and $x \notin (B \cap C)$

$\Leftrightarrow x \in A$ and $(x \notin B$ or $x \notin C)$

$\Leftrightarrow (x \in A$ and $x \notin B)$ or $(x \in A$ and $x \notin C)$

$\Leftrightarrow x \in (A-B)$ or $x \in (A-C)$

$\Leftrightarrow x \in (A-B) \cup (A-C)$

Hence, $A-(B \cap C)=(A-B) \cup (A-C)$.

Aliter

$$A-(B \cap C)=A \cap (B \cap C)' \quad [\because A-B=A \cap B']$$
$$=A \cap (B' \cup C')$$
$$=(A \cap B') \cup (A \cap C')$$
$$=(A-B) \cup (A-C)$$

More Results on Operations on Sets

For any two sets A and B, we have

1. $\boldsymbol{A \subseteq A \cup B, B \subseteq A \cup B, A \cap B \subseteq A, A \cap B \subseteq B}$

2. $\boldsymbol{A-B=A \cap B'}$

Proof

Let $x \in A-B \Leftrightarrow x \in A$ and $x \notin B$

$\Leftrightarrow x \in A$ and $x \in B'$

$\Leftrightarrow x \in A \cap B'$

Hence, $A-B=A \cap B'$

3. $\boldsymbol{(A-B) \cup B=A \cup B}$

Proof $(A-B) \cup B=(A \cap B') \cup B$

$=(A \cup B) \cap (B' \cup B)$ [from distributive law]

$=(A \cup B) \cap U=A \cup B$

Hence, $(A-B) \cup B=A \cup B$

4. $\boldsymbol{(A-B) \cap B=\phi}$

Proof $(A-B) \cap B=(A \cap B') \cap B$

$=A \cap (B' \cap B)$ [from associative law]

$=A \cap \phi=\phi$

Hence, $(A-B) \cap B=\phi$

5. $\boldsymbol{A \subseteq B \Leftrightarrow B' \subseteq A'}$

Proof Only if part Let $\boldsymbol{A \subseteq B}$ ...(i)

To prove $B' \subseteq A'$

Let $x \in B' \Rightarrow x \notin B$

$\Rightarrow x \notin A$ $[\because A \subseteq B]$

$\Rightarrow x \in A'$

Thus, $x \in B' \Rightarrow x \in A'$ $[\because B \subseteq A]$

Hence, $B' \subseteq A'$ ...(ii)

If part Let $\boldsymbol{B' \subseteq A'}$ ...(iii)

To prove $A \subseteq B$

Let $x \in A \Rightarrow x \notin A'$

$\Rightarrow x \notin B'$ [from Eq.(iii)]

$\Rightarrow x \in B$

Hence, $A \subseteq B$ ...(iv)

From Eqs. (ii) and (iv), we get $A \subseteq B \Leftrightarrow B' \subseteq A'$

6. $\boldsymbol{A-B=B'-A'}$

Proof $A-B=(A \cap B')$

$=B' \cap A=B' \cap (A')'=B'-A'$

Hence, $A-B=B'-A'$

7. $\boldsymbol{(A \cup B) \cap (A \cup B')=A}$

Proof $(A \cup B) \cap (A \cup B')=A \cup (B \cap B')$

[by distributive law]

$=A \cup \phi=A$

Hence, $(A \cup B) \cap (A \cup B')=A$

8. $\boldsymbol{A \cup B=(A-B) \cup (B-A) \cup (A \cap B)}$

Proof $(A-B) \cup (B-A) \cup (A \cap B)$

$=[(A \cup B)-(A \cap B)] \cup (A \cap B)$

$=[(A \cup B) \cap (A \cap B)'] \cup (A \cap B)$

$=[(A \cup B) \cup (A \cap B)] \cap [(A \cap B)' \cup (A \cap B)]$

$=(A \cup B) \cap U=A \cup B$

Hence, $A \cup B=(A-B) \cup (B-A) \cup (A \cap B)$

9. $\boldsymbol{A-(A-B)=A \cap B}$

Proof $A-(A-B)=A-(A \cap B')$

$=A \cap (A \cap B')'$

$=A \cap (A' \cup B)$

$=(A \cap A') \cup (A \cap B)$

$=\phi \cup (A \cap B)=A \cap B$

Hence, $A-(A-B)=A \cap B$

10. $\boldsymbol{A-B=B-A \Leftrightarrow A=B}$

Proof Only if part Let $\boldsymbol{A-B=B-A}$ ...(i)

To prove $A=B$

Let $x \in A \Leftrightarrow (x \in A$ and $x \notin B)$ or $(x \in A$ and $x \in B)$

$\Leftrightarrow x \in (A-B)$ or $x \in (A \cap B)$

$\Leftrightarrow x \in (B-A)$

or $x \in A \cap B$ [from Eq. (i)]

$\Leftrightarrow (x \in B$ and $x \notin A)$ or $(x \in B$ and $x \in A)$

$\Leftrightarrow x \in B$

Hence, $A=B$

If part Let $\boldsymbol{A=B}$

To prove $A-B=B-A$

Now, $A-B=A-A=\phi$ $[\because B=A]$

and $B-A=A-A=\phi$ $[\because B=A]$

$\therefore$ $A-B=B-A$

Hence, $A=B \Rightarrow A-B=B-A$

11. $A \cup B = A \cap B \Leftrightarrow A = B$

Proof Only if part Let $A \cup B = A \cap B$

Now, $x \in A \Rightarrow x \in A \cup B$

$\Rightarrow \quad x \in A \cap B \quad [\because A \cup B = A \cap B]$

$\Rightarrow \quad x \in B$

Thus, $A \subseteq B$ ...(i)

Again, $y \in B \Rightarrow y \in A \cup B$

$\Rightarrow \quad y \in A \cap B \quad [\because A \cup B = A \cap B]$

$\Rightarrow \quad y \in A$

Thus, $B \subseteq A$ ...(ii)

From Eqs. (i) and (ii), we have $A = B$

Thus, $A \cup B = A \cap B \Rightarrow A = B$.

If part Let $A = B$ ...(iii)

To prove $A \cup B = A \cap B$

Now, $A \cup B = A \cup A = A \quad [\because B = A]$ ...(iv)

and $A \cap B = A \cap A = A \quad [\because B = A]$ ...(v)

From Eqs. (iv) and (v), we have $A \cup B = A \cap B$

Hence, $A \cup B = A \cap B \Leftrightarrow A = B$

Example 5. Let A, B and C be three sets such that $A \cup B = A \cup C$ and $A \cap B = A \cap C$. Show that $B = C$.

Sol. Given, $A \cup B = A \cup C$ ...(i)

and $A \cap B = A \cap C$ ...(ii)

To prove $B = C$.

From Eq. (i), $(A \cup B) \cap C = (A \cup C) \cap C$

$\Rightarrow \quad (A \cap C) \cup (B \cap C) = (A \cap C) \cup (C \cup C)$

$\Rightarrow \quad (A \cap B) \cup (B \cap C) = (A \cap C) \cup C$

$[\because A \cap C = A \cap B]$

$\Rightarrow \quad (A \cap B) \cup (B \cap C) = C \quad [\because A \cap C \subseteq C]$

Thus, $C = (A \cap B) \cup (B \cap C)$ ...(iii)

Again, from Eq. (i), $(A \cup B) \cap B = (A \cup C) \cap B$

$\Rightarrow \quad (A \cap B) \cup (B \cap B) = (A \cap B) \cup (C \cap B)$

$\Rightarrow \quad (A \cap B) \cup B = (A \cap B) \cup (B \cap C)$

$\Rightarrow \quad B = (A \cap B) \cup (B \cap C)$

$[\because A \cap B \subseteq B]$

Thus, $B = (A \cap B) \cup (B \cap C)$ ...(iv)

From Eqs. (iii) and (iv), we have $B = C$.

Example 6. Let A and B be any two sets. If for some set X, $A \cap X = B \cap X = \phi$ and $A \cup X = B \cup X$, prove that $A = B$.

Sol. Given, $A \cap X = B \cap X = \phi$ ...(i)

and $A \cup X = B \cup X$ ...(ii)

From Eq. (ii), $A \cap (A \cup X) = A \cap (B \cup X)$

$\Rightarrow \quad A = (A \cap B) \cup (A \cap X)$

$[\because A \subseteq A \cup X \text{ and } A \cap (A \cup X) = A]$

$\Rightarrow \quad A = (A \cap B) \cup \phi \quad [\because A \cap X = \phi]$

$\Rightarrow \quad A = (A \cap B)$

$\Rightarrow \quad A \subseteq B$ ...(iii)

Again, $A \cup X = B \cup X$

$\Rightarrow \quad B \cap (A \cup X) = B \cap (B \cup X)$

$\Rightarrow \quad (B \cap A) \cup (B \cap X) = B$

$[\because B \subseteq B \cup X \text{ and } B \cap (B \cup X) = B]$

$\Rightarrow \quad (B \cap A) \cup \phi = B \quad [\because B \cap X = \phi]$

$\Rightarrow \quad B \cap A = B$

$\Rightarrow \quad B \subseteq A$ ...(iv)

From Eqs. (iii) and (iv), we have $A = B$.

Example 7. If A and B are any two sets, prove that $P(A) = P(B) \Rightarrow A = B$.

Sol. Given, $P(A) = P(B)$ ...(i)

To prove $A = B$

Let $x \in A \Rightarrow$ there exists a subset X of A such that $x \in X$.

Now, $X \subseteq A \Rightarrow X \in P(A)$

$\Rightarrow \quad X \in P(B)$ [from Eq. (i)]

$\Rightarrow \quad X \subseteq B$

$\Rightarrow \quad x \in B \quad [\because x \in X]$

Thus, $x \in A$

$\Rightarrow \quad x \in B$

$\therefore \quad A \subseteq B$ ...(ii)

Let $y \in B \Rightarrow$ there exists a subset Y of B such that $y \in Y$.

Now, $Y \subseteq B \Rightarrow Y \in P(B)$

$\Rightarrow \quad Y \in P(A) \quad [\because P(B) = P(A)]$

$\Rightarrow \quad Y \subseteq A$

$\Rightarrow \quad y \in A \quad [\because y \in Y]$

Thus, $y \in B$

$\Rightarrow \quad y \in A$

$\therefore \quad B \subseteq A$ ...(iii)

From Eqs. (ii) and (iii), we have $A = B$

Use of Sets in Logical Problems

M = Set of students which have Mathematics.

P = Set of students which have Physics.

C = Set of students which have Chemistry.

Applying the different operations on the above sets, then we get following important results.

M' = Set of students which have no Mathematics.

P' = Set of students which have no Physics.

C' = Set of students which have no Chemistry.

$M \cup P$ = Set of students which have atleast one subject Mathematics or Physics.

$P \cup C$ = Set of students which have atleast one subject Physics or Chemistry.

$C \cup M$ = Set of students which have atleast one subject Chemistry or Mathematics.

$M \cap P$ = Set of students which have both subjects Mathematics and Physics.

$P \cap C$ = Set of students which have both subjects Physics and Chemistry.

$C \cap M$ = Set of students which have both subjects Chemistry and Mathematics.

$M \cap P'$ = Set of students which have Mathematics but not Physics.

$P \cap C'$ = Set of students which have Physics but not Chemistry.

$C \cap M'$ = Set of students which have Chemistry but not Mathematics.

$(M \cup P)'$ = Set of students which have not both subjects Mathematics and Physics.

$(P \cup C)'$ = Set of students which have not both subjects Physics and Chemistry.

$(C \cup M)'$ = Set of students which have not both subjects Chemistry and Mathematics.

$(M \cap P \cap C)$ = Set of students which have all three subjects Mathematics, Physics and Chemistry.

$(M \cup P \cup C)$ = Set of all students which have three subjects.

Cardinal Number of Some Sets

If A, B and C are finite sets and U be the finite universal set, then

(i) $n(A') = n(U) - n(A)$

(ii) $n(A \cup B) = n(A) + n(B) - n(A \cap B)$

(iii) $n(A \cup B) = n(A) + n(B)$, if A and B are disjoint non-void sets.

(iv) $n(A \cap B') = n(A) - n(A \cap B)$

(v) $n(A' \cap B') = n(A \cup B)' = n(U) - n(A \cup B)$

(vi) $n(A' \cup B') = n(A \cap B)' = n(U) - n(A \cap B)$

(vii) $n(A - B) = n(A) - n(A \cap B)$

(viii) $n(A \cap B) = n(A \cup B) - n(A \cap B') - n(A' \cap B)$

(ix) $n(A \cup B \cup C) = n(A) + n(B) + n(C) - n(A \cap B) - n(B \cap C) - n(C \cap A) + n(A \cap B \cap C)$

(x) If $A_1, A_2, A_3, \ldots, A_n$ are disjoint sets, then

$$n(A_1 \cup A_2 \cup A_3 \cup \ldots \cup A_n) = n(A_1) + n(A_2) + n(A_3) + \ldots + n(A_n)$$

Example 8. If A and B be two sets containing 6 and 3 elements respectively, what can be the minimum number of elements in $A \cup B$? Also, find the maximum number of elements in $A \cup B$.

Sol. We have, $n(A \cup B) = n(A) + n(B) - n(A \cap B)$,
$n(A \cup B)$ is minimum or maximum according as $n(A \cap B)$ is maximum or minimum, respectively.

***Case* I** If $n(A \cap B)$ is minimum i.e. $n(A \cap B) = 0$ such that

$$A = \{a, b, c, d, e, f\} \text{ and } B = \{g, h, i\}$$

$\therefore \quad n(A \cup B) = n(A) + n(B) = 6 + 3 = 9$

***Case* II** If $n(A \cap B)$ is maximum i.e., $n(A \cap B) = 3$ such that

$$A = \{a, b, c, d, e, f\} \text{ and } B = \{d, a, c\}$$

$\therefore n(A \cup B) = n(A) + n(B) - n(A \cap B) = 6 + 3 - 3 = 6$

Example 9. Suppose $A_1, A_2, \ldots, A_{30}$ are thirty sets each with five elements and $B_1, B_2, \ldots, B_n$ are n sets each with three elements.

Let $\bigcup_{i=1}^{30} A_i = \bigcup_{j=1}^{n} B_j = S$

Assume that each element of S belongs to exactly ten of the A_i's and exactly to nine of the B_j's. Find n.

Sol. Given, A's are thirty sets with five elements each, so

$$\sum_{i=1}^{30} n(A_i) = 5 \times 30 = 150 \quad \ldots\text{(i)}$$

If the m distinct elements in S and each element of S belongs to exactly 10 of the A_i's, so we have

$$\sum_{i=1}^{30} n(A_i) = 10m \quad \ldots\text{(ii)}$$

$\therefore$ From Eqs. (i) and (ii), we get $10m = 150$

$\therefore \quad m = 15 \quad \ldots$(iii)

Similarly, $\sum_{j=1}^{n} n(B_j) = 3n$ and $\sum_{j=1}^{n} n(B_j) = 9m$

$\therefore \quad 3n = 9m \Rightarrow n = \frac{9m}{3} = 3m$

$= 3 \times 15 = 45$ [from Eq. (iii)]

Hence, $n = 45$

Example 10. In a group of 1000 people, there are 750 who can speak Hindi and 400 who can speak Bengali. How many can speak Hindi only? How many can speak Bengali only? How many can speak both Hindi and Bengali?

Sol. Let H and B be the set of those people who can speak Hindi and Bengali respectively, then according to the problem, we have

$$n(H \cup B) = 1000,$$
$$n(H) = 750, n(B) = 400$$

We know that

$$n(H \cup B) = n(H) + n(B) - n(H \cap B)$$
$$1000 = 750 + 400 - n(H \cap B)$$

$\therefore \quad n(H \cap B) = 150$

$\therefore$ Number of people speaking Hindi and Bengali both is 150.

Also, $n(H \cap B') = n(H) - n(H \cap B)$
$= 750 - 150$
$= 600$

Thus, number of people speaking Hindi only is 600.

Again, $n(B \cap H') = n(B) - n(B \cap H)$

$= 400 - 150$

$= 250$

Thus, number of people speaking Bengali only is 250.

Example 11. A survey of 500 television watchers produced the following information, 285 watch football, 195 watch hockey, 115 watch basketball, 45 watch football and basketball, 70 watch football and hockey, 50 watch hockey and basketball, 50 do not watch any of the three games. How many watch all the three games? How many watch exactly one of the three games?

Sol. Let F, H and B be the sets of television watchers who watch Football, Hockey and Basketball, respectively.

Then, according to the problem, we have

$$n(U) = 500,\ n(F) = 285,\ n(H) = 195,$$
$$n(B) = 115,\ n(F \cap B) = 45,$$
$$n(F \cap H) = 70,\ n(H \cap B) = 50$$

and $\quad n(F' \cup H' \cup B') = 50,$

where U is the set of all the television watchers.

Since, $n(F' \cup H' \cup B') = n(U) - n(F \cup H \cup B)$

$\Rightarrow \quad 50 = 500 - n(F \cup H \cup B)$

$\Rightarrow \quad n(F \cup H \cup B) = 450$

We know that,

$$n(F \cup H \cup B) = n(F) + n(H) + n(B) - n(F \cap H) - n(H \cap B) - n(B \cap F) + n(F \cap H \cap B)$$

$\Rightarrow \quad 450 = 285 + 195 + 115 - 70 - 50 - 45 + n(F \cap H \cap B)$

$\therefore \quad n(F \cap H \cap B) = 20$

which is the number of those who watch all the three games. Also, number of persons who watch football only

$= n(F \cap H' \cap B')$

$= n(F) - n(F \cap H) - n(F \cap B) + n(F \cap H \cap B)$

$= 285 - 70 - 45 + 20$

$= 190$

The number of persons who watch hockey only

$= n(H \cap F' \cap B')$

$= n(H) - n(H \cap F) - n(H \cap B) + n(H \cap F \cap B)$

$= 195 - 70 - 50 + 20$

$= 95$

and the number of persons who watch basketball only

$= n(B \cap H' \cap F')$

$= n(B) - n(B \cap H) - n(B \cap F) + n(H \cap F \cap B)$

$= 115 - 50 - 45 + 20 = 40$

Hence, required number of those who watch exactly one of the three games

$= 190 + 95 + 40 = 325$

11.5 Venn Diagrams (Euler-Venn Diagrams)

The diagram drawn to represent sets are called Venn diagrams or Euler Venn diagrams. Here, we represent the universal set U by points within rectangle and the subset A of the set U is represented by the interior of a circle. If a set A is a subset of a set B, then the circle representing A is drawn inside the circle representing B. If A and B are not equal but they have some common elements, then to represent A and B by two intersecting circles.

Venn Diagrams in Different Situations

1. Subset

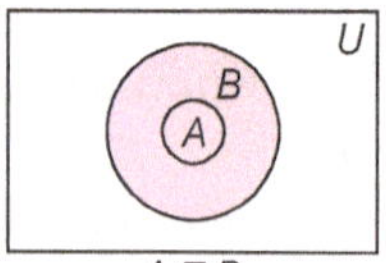

$A \subseteq B$

2. Union of sets

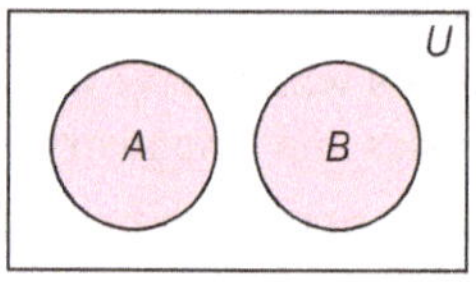

$A \cup B$, when $A \cap B = \phi$

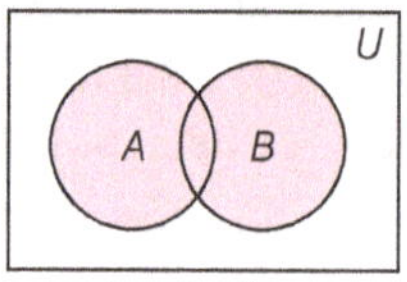

$A \cup B$, when neither $A \subseteq B$ nor $B \subseteq A$

3. Intersection of sets

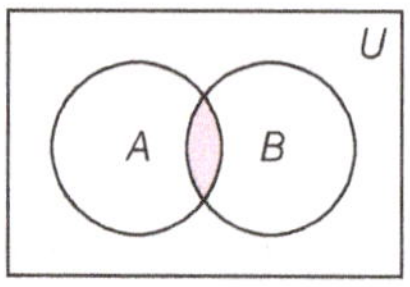

$A \cap B$, when neither $A \subseteq B$ nor $B \subseteq A$

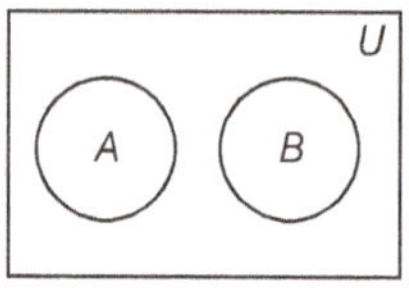

$A \cap B$, when $A \cap B = \phi$ (no shaded one)

4. Difference of sets

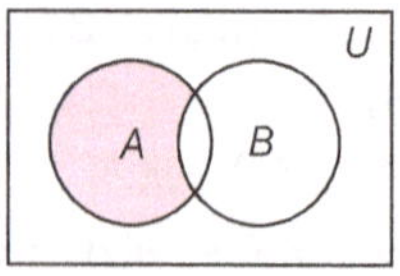

$A - B$, when neither $A \subseteq B$ nor $B \subseteq A$

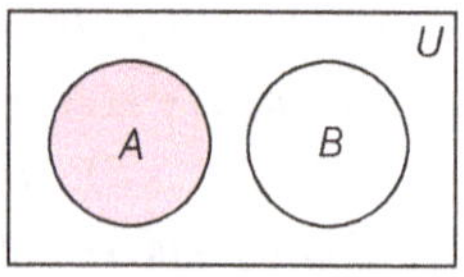

$A - B$, when $A - B = \phi$

5. Complement set

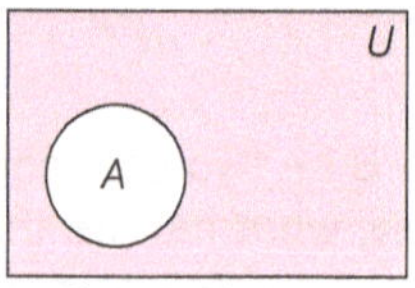

A' = shaded one

6. $A \cup (B \cup C)$ and $(A \cup B) \cup C$

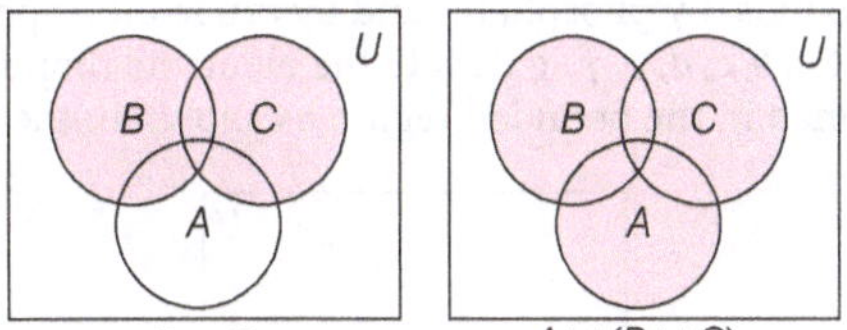

$B \cup C$ $\quad$ $A \cup (B \cup C)$

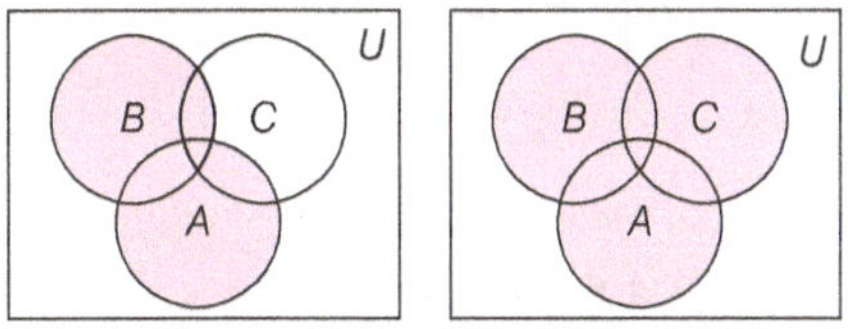

$A \cup B$ $\quad$ $(A \cup B) \cup C$

Hence, $A \cup (B \cup C) = (A \cup B) \cup C$ which is associative law for union.

7. $A \cap (B \cap C)$ and $(A \cap B) \cap C$

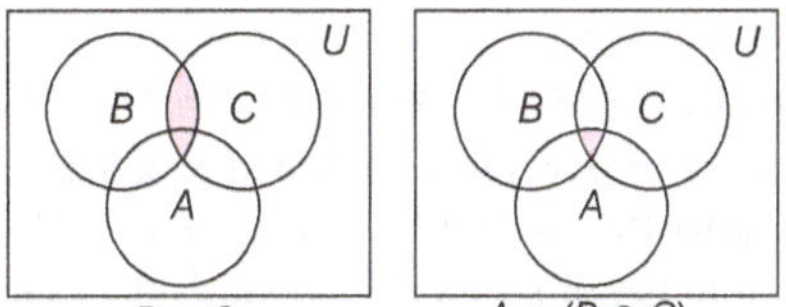

$B \cap C$ $\quad$ $A \cap (B \cap C)$

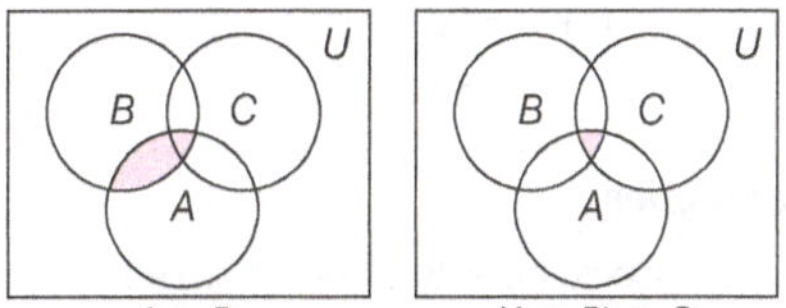

$A \cap B$ $\quad$ $(A \cap B) \cap C$

Hence, $A \cap (B \cap C) = (A \cap B) \cap C$ which is associative law for intersection.

8. Distributive law

(i) $A \cup (B \cap C) = (A \cup B) \cap (A \cup C)$

(ii) $A \cap (B \cup C) = (A \cap B) \cup (A \cap C)$

(i)

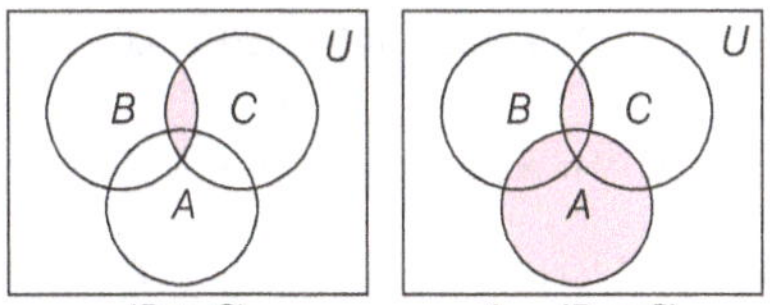

$(B \cap C)$ $\quad$ $A \cup (B \cap C)$

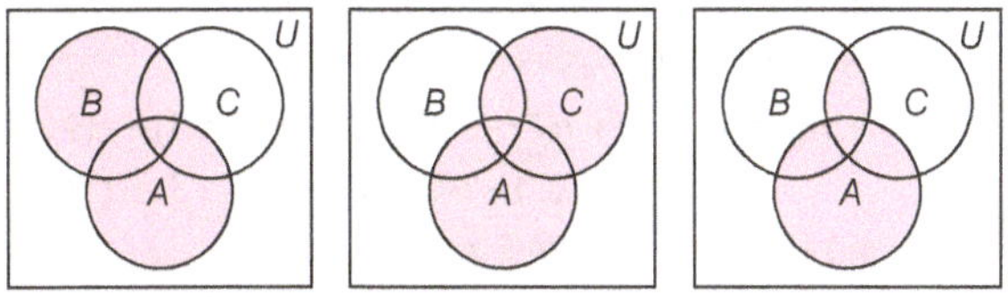

$(A \cup B)$ $\quad$ $(A \cup C)$ $\quad$ $(A \cup B) \cap (A \cup C)$

It is clear from diagrams that

$$A \cup (B \cap C) = (A \cup B) \cap (A \cup C)$$

(ii)

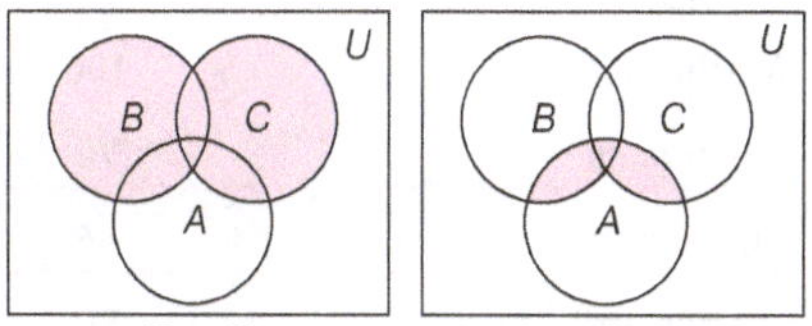

$(B \cup C)$ $\quad$ $A \cap (B \cup C)$

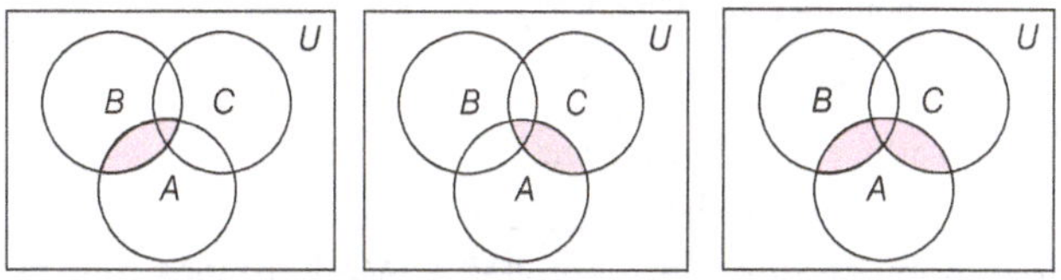

$(A \cap B)$ $\quad$ $(A \cap C)$ $\quad$ $(A \cap B) \cup (A \cap C)$

It is clear from diagrams that

$$A \cap (B \cup C) = (A \cap B) \cup (A \cap C)$$

9. Symmetric difference

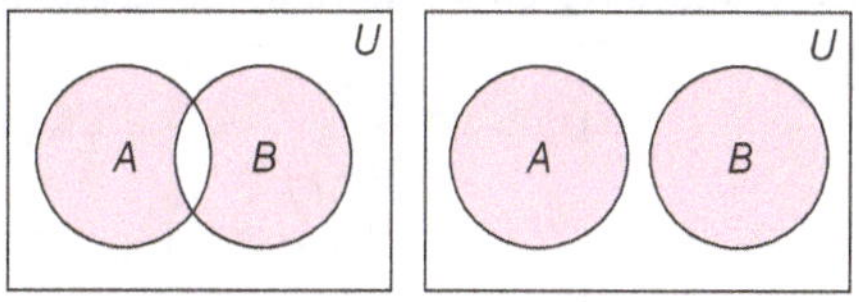

$A \Delta B$, when neither $A \subseteq B$ nor $B \subseteq A$ and $A \cap B \neq \phi$ $\quad$ $A \Delta B$, when $A \cap B = \phi$

JEE SPIKE

Remember with the help of figures.

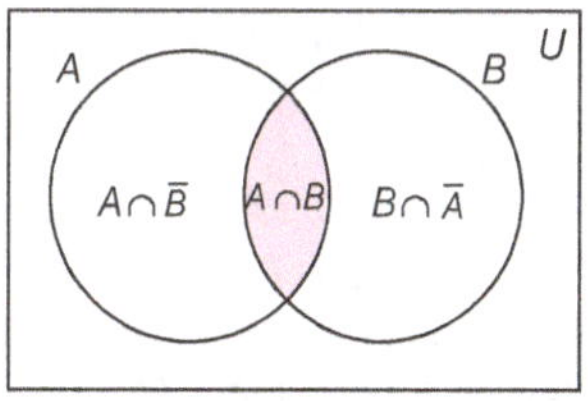

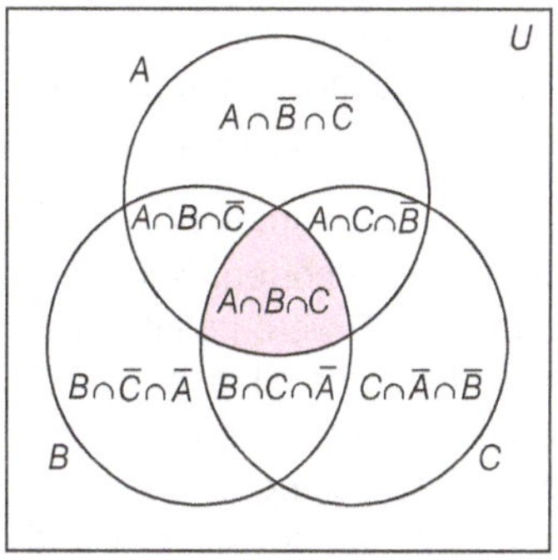

Example 12. A class has 175 students. The following table shows the number of students studying one or more of the following subjects in this case.

Subjects	Number of students
Mathematics	100
Physics	70
Chemistry	46
Mathematics and Physics	30
Mathematics and Chemistry	28
Physics and Chemistry	23
Mathematics, Physics and Chemistry	18

How many students are enrolled in Mathematics alone, Physics alone and Chemistry alone? Are there students who have not offered any one of these subjects?

Sol. Let P, C and M denotes the sets of students studying Physics, Chemistry and Mathematics, respectively.

Let a, b, c, d, e, f, g denote the elements (students) contained in the bounded region as shown in the diagram.

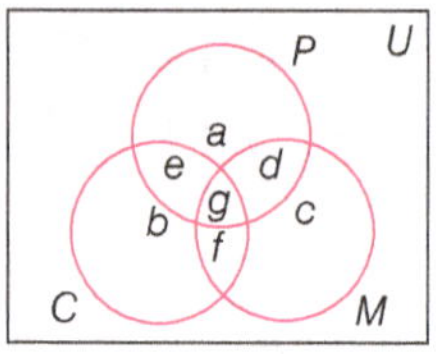

Then, $$a + d + e + g = 70$$
$$c + d + f + g = 100$$
$$b + e + f + g = 46$$
$$d + g = 30$$
$$e + g = 23$$
$$f + g = 28$$
$$g = 18$$

After solving, we get

$$f = 10, e = 5, d = 12, a = 35, b = 13 \text{ and } c = 60$$

$\therefore \quad a + b + c + d + e + f + g = 153$

So, the number of students who have not offered any of these three subjects $= 175 - 153 = 22$

Number of students studying Mathematics only, $c = 60$

Number of students studying Physics only, $a = 35$

Number of students studying Chemistry only, $b = 13$

Example 13. In a pollution study of 1500 Indian rivers the following data were reported. 520 were polluted by sulphur compounds, 335 were polluted by phosphates, 425 were polluted by crude oil, 100 were polluted by both crude oil and sulphur compounds, 180 were polluted by both sulphur compounds and phosphates, 150 were polluted by both phosphates and crude oil and 28 were polluted by sulphur compounds, phosphates and crude oil. How many of the rivers were polluted by atleast one of the three impurities?
How many of the rivers were polluted by exactly one of the three impurities?

Sol. Let S, P and C denote the sets of rivers polluted by sulphur compounds, by phosphates and by crude oil respectively, and let a, b, c, d, e, f, g denote the elements (impurities) contained in the bounded region as shown in the diagram.

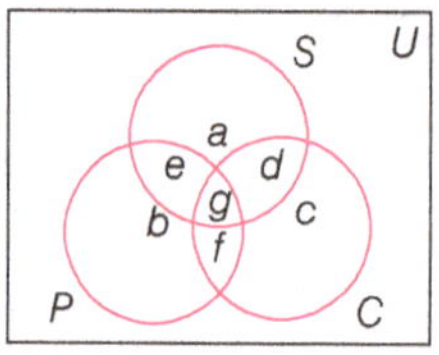

Then, $$a + d + e + g = 520$$
$$c + d + f + g = 425$$
$$b + e + f + g = 335$$
$$d + g = 100$$
$$e + g = 180$$
$$f + g = 150$$
$$g = 28$$

After solving, we get

$$f = 122, e = 152, b = 33, d = 72, c = 203 \text{ and } a = 268$$

The number of rivers were polluted by atleast one of the three impurities $= (a + b + c + d + e + f + g) = 878$

and the number of rivers were polluted by exactly one of the three impurities,

$$a + b + c = 268 + 33 + 203$$
$$= 504$$

Alternate Solution

Let S, P and C denote the sets of rivers polluted by sulphur compounds, by phosphates and by crude oil, respectively.

Then, we are given that

$n(S) = 520, n(P) = 335, n(C) = 425, n(C \cap S) = 100,$
$n(S \cap P) = 180, n(P \cap C) = 150$ and $n(S \cap P \cap C) = 28.$

The number of rivers polluted by atleast one of the three impurities,

$n(S \cup P \cup C)$
$= n(S) + n(P) + n(C) - n(S \cap P)$
$\quad - n(P \cap C) - n(C \cap S) + n(S \cap P \cap C)$
$= 520 + 335 + 425 - 180 - 150 - 100 + 28$
$= 878$

and the number of rivers polluted by exactly one of the three impurities,

$n\{(S \cap P' \cap C') \cup (P \cap C' \cap S') \cup (C \cap P' \cap S')\}$
$= n\{(S \cap (P \cup C)'\} \cup \{P \cap (C \cup S)'\} \cup \{C \cap P \cup S)'\}$
$= n(S \cap (P \cup C)') + n(P \cap (C \cup S)') + n(C \cap (P \cup S)')$
$= n(S) - n(S \cap P) - n(S \cap C)$
$\quad + n(S \cap P \cap C) + n(P) - n(P \cap C) - n(P \cap S) + n(S \cap P \cap C)$
$\quad + n(C) - n(C \cap P) - n(C \cap S) + n(S \cap P \cap C)$
$= n(S) + n(P) + n(C) - 2n(S \cap P) - 2n(S \cap C)$
$\quad - 2n(P \cap C) + 3n(S \cap P \cap C)$
$= 520 + 335 + 425 - 360 - 200 - 300 + 84$
$= 504$

Milestone Practice 11.1

1. If $X = \{4^n - 3n - 1 : n \in N\}$ and $y = \{9(n-1) : n \in N\}$, then $X \cup Y$ equals
   (a) X (b) Y
   (c) N (d) None of these

2. If $N_a = \{an : n \in N\}$, then $N_5 \cap N_7$ equals
   (a) N (b) N_5
   (c) N_7 (d) N_{35}

3. If A and B are two sets, then $A \cap (A \cup B)'$ equals
   (a) A (b) B
   (c) ϕ (d) None of these

4. If A and B are two sets, then $(A - B) \cup (B - A) \cup (A \cap B)$ equals
   (a) $A \cup B$ (b) $A \cap B$
   (c) A (d) B'

5. If $A = \{x : x$ is a multiple of 4$\}$ and $B = \{x : x$ is a multiple of 6$\}$, then $A \subset B$ consists of all multiple of
   (a) 4 (b) 8 (c) 12 (d) 16

6. A set contains $2n + 1$ elements. The number of subsets of this set containing more than n elements equals
   (a) 2^{n-1} (b) 2^n (c) 2^{n+1} (d) 2^{2n}

7. If $A = \{\phi, \{\phi\}\}$, then the power set of A is
   (a) A (b) $\{\phi, \{\phi\}, A\}$
   (c) $\{\phi, \{\phi\}, \{\{\phi\}\}, A\}$ (d) None of these

8. Given $n(U) = 20$, $n(A) = 12$, $n(B) = 9$, $n(A \cap B) = 4$, where U is the universal set, A and B are subsets of U, then $n((A \cup B)')$ equals
   (a) 3 (b) 9
   (c) 11 (d) 17

9. A survey shows that 63% of the Indians like cheese, whereas 76% like apples. If x% of the Indians like both cheese and apples, then x can be
   (a) 40 (b) 65
   (c) 39 (d) None of these

10. In a class of 55 students, the number of students studying different subjects are 23 in Mathematics, 24 in Physics, 19 in Chemistry, 12 in Mathematics and Physics, 9 in Mathematics and Chemistry, 7 in Physics and Chemistry and 4 in all the three subjects. The number of students who have taken exactly one subject is
    (a) 6 (b) 7
    (c) 9 (d) 22

Answer Key

1. (b)	2. (d)	3. (c)	4. (a)	5. (c)
6. (d)	7. (c)	8. (a)	9. (c)	10. (d)

For Detailed Solution

Milestone 2 Relations

• Ordered Pair • Definition of Relation • Ordered Relation • Composition of Two Relations

11.6 Ordered Pair

If A be a set and $a, b \in A$, then the ordered pair of elements a and b in A denoted by (a, b), where a is called the first coordinate and b is called the second coordinate.

Cartesian Product of Two Sets

The cartesian product to two sets A and B is the set of all those ordered pairs whose first coordinate belongs to A and second coordinate belongs to B. This set is denoted by $A \times B$ (read as 'A cross B' or 'product set of A and B').

Symbolically, $A \times B = \{(a, b) : a \in A \text{ and } b \in B\}$

or $\quad A \times B = \{(a, b) : a \in A \wedge b \in B\}$

Thus, $\quad (a, b) \in A \times B \Leftrightarrow a \in A \wedge b \in B$

Similarly, $\quad B \times A = \{(b, a) : b \in B \wedge a \in A\}$

JEE Focus Points

- Ordered pairs (a, b) and (b, a) are different.
- Ordered pairs (a, b) and (c, d) are equal iff $a = c$ and $b = d$.
- $A \times B \neq B \times A$
- If A has p elements and B has q elements, then $A \times B$ has pq elements.
- If $A = \phi$ and $B = \phi$, then $A \times B = \phi$.
- Cartesian product of n sets $A_1, A_2, A_3, \ldots, A_n$ is the set of all ordered n-tuples $(a_1, a_2, \ldots, a_n)$ $a_i \in A_i, i = 1, 2, 3, \ldots, n$ and is denoted by $A_1 \times A_2 \times \ldots \times A_n$ or $\prod_{i=1}^{n} A_i$.

Example 14. If $A = \{1, 2, 3\}$ and $B = \{4, 5\}$, find $A \times B$, $B \times A$ and show that $A \times B \neq B \times A$.

Sol. $A \times B = \{1, 2, 3\} \times \{4, 5\}$

$= \{(1, 4), (1, 5), (2, 4), (2, 5), (3, 4), (3, 5)\}$

and $B \times A = \{4, 5\} \times \{1, 2, 3\}$

$= \{(4, 1), (4, 2), (4, 3), (5, 1), (5, 2), (5, 3)\}$

It is clear that $A \times B \neq B \times A$.

Example 15. If A and B be two sets and $A \times B = \{(3, 3), (3, 4), (5, 2), (5, 4)\}$, find A and B.

Sol. A = First coordinates of all ordered pairs = $\{3, 5\}$

and B = Second coordinates of all ordered pairs = $\{2, 3, 4\}$

Hence, $A = \{3, 5\}$ and $B = \{2, 3, 4\}$

Important Theorems on Cartesian Product

If A, B and C are three sets, then

(i) $A \times (B \cup C) = (A \times B) \cup (A \times C)$

(ii) $A \times (B \cap C) = (A \times B) \cap (A \times C)$

(iii) $A \times (B - C) = (A \times B) - (A \times C)$

(iv) $(A \times B) \cap (S \times T) = (A \cap S) \times (B \cap T)$, where S and T are two sets.

(v) If $A \subseteq B$, then $(A \times C) \subseteq (B \times C)$

(vi) If $A \subseteq B$, then $(A \times B) \cap (B \times A) = A^2$

(vii) If $A \subseteq B$ and $C \subseteq D$, then $A \times C \subseteq B \times D$

Example 16. If A and B are two sets given in such a way that $A \times B$ consists of 6 elements and if three elements of $A \times B$ are (1, 5), (2, 3) and (3, 5), what are the remaining elements?

Sol. Since, $(1, 5), (2, 3), (3, 5) \in A \times B$, then clearly $1, 2, 3 \in A$ and $3, 5 \in B$.

$A \times B = \{1, 2, 3\} \times (3, 5)$

$= (1, 3), (1, 5), (2, 3), (2, 5), (3, 3), (3, 5)$

Hence, the remaining elements are (1, 3), (2, 5), (3, 3).

Introduction of Relation

We use sentences depending upon the relationship of an object to the other object in our daily life such as

(i) 'Ram, Laxman, Bharat, Shatrughan' were the sons of Dashrath.

(ii) 'Sita' was the wife of Ram.

(iii) 'Laxman' was the brother of Ram.

(iv) 'Dashrath' was the father of Ram.

(v) 'Kaushaliya' was the mother of Ram.

If Ram, Laxman, Bharat, Shatrughan, Sita, Kaushaliya and Dashrath are represented by a, b, c, d, e, f and y respectively and A represents the set, then

$$A = \{a, b, c, d, e, f, y\}$$

Here, we see that any two elements of set A are related many ways, i.e. a, b, c, d are sons of y. 'a' is the son of y is represented by aRy.

Similarly, b is the son of y, c is the son of y and d is also son of y are represented as $b\,R\,y$, $c\,R\,y$ and $d\,R\,y$, respectively.

If we write here $y\,R\,a$ it means that y is the son of a which is impossible, since a is the son of y. Hence, y and a cannot be related like this. Its generally represented as $y \not R a$. Hence, we can say that a and y are in definite order. a comes before R and y after R. Therefore, aRy may be represented as a order pair (a, y).

Similarly, bRy, cRy and dRy are represented by $(b, y), (c, y)$ and (d, y), respectively. If all pairs will represented by a set, then we see that first element of each pair is the son of second element. Hence, the set of these pairs may be represented by set R, then

$$R = \{(a, y), (b, y), (c, y), (d, y)\}$$

Symbolically, $R = \{(x, y) : x, y \in A, \text{ where } x \text{ is son of } y\}$

It is clear that R is subset of $A \times A$

i.e. $R \subseteq A \times A$

Corollary In above example, if

$A = \{a, b, c, d\}$ and $B = \{e, f, y\}$, then

$R = \{(x, z) : x \in A, z \in B, \text{ where } x \text{ is son of } z\}$

It is clear that $R \subseteq A \times B$.

11.7 Definition of Relation

A relation (or binary relation) R, from a non-empty set A to another non-empty set B, is a subset of $A \times B$.

i.e. $R \subseteq A \times B$ or $R \subseteq \{(a, b) : a \in A, b \in B\}$

Now, if (a, b) be an element of the relation R, then we write aRb (read as 'a is related to b')

i.e. $(a, b) \in R \Leftrightarrow aRb$

and if (a, b) is not an element of the relation R, then we write $a \not R b$ (read as 'a is not related to b'),

i.e. $(a, b) \notin R \Leftrightarrow a \not R b$.

Domain and Range of Relation

If $R : A \to B$, then domain of R is the set of first elements of the ordered pair (x, y) which belong to R symbolically.

Domain $= \{x : (x, y) \in R, x \in A \text{ for some } y \in B\}$

The range of the relation is the set of the second element of the ordered pairs which belong to R.

Symbolically,

$$\text{Range} : \{y : (x, y) \in R, y \in B \text{ for some } x \in A\}$$

e.g. Let $A = \{1, 2, 3\}$ and $B = \{3, 5, 7\}$, then

$A \times B = \{(1, 3), (1, 5), (1, 7), (2, 3), (2, 5), (2, 7), (3, 3), (3, 5), (3, 7)\}$.

But $R \subseteq A \times B$

i.e. every subset of $A \times B$ is a relation from A to B. If we consider the relation, $R = \{(1, 5), (1, 7), (3, 5), (3, 7)\}$

Then, $1\,R\,5; 1\,R\,7; 3\,R\,5; 3\,R\,7$

Also, $1 \not R\,3; 2 \not R\,3; 2 \not R\,5; 2 \not R\,7; 3 \not R\,3$;

Clearly, Domain $R = \{1, 3\}$ and Range $R = \{5, 7\}$

e.g. Let $A = \{1, 2, 3\}$ and $B = \{4, 5\}$, then number of different relations from A to B is $2^{3 \times 2} = 2^6 = 64$ because A has 3 elements and B has 2 elements.

Example 17. Let $A = \{1, 2, 3, 4, \ldots, 10\}$ and $R = \{(x, y) : x + 2y = 10,\ x,\ y \in A\}$ be a relation in A.

(i) Find R

(ii) Find domain and range of R.

Sol. (i) We have, $(x, y) \in R \Leftrightarrow x + 2y = 10$

$$\Rightarrow \quad y = \frac{10 - x}{2}, \text{ where } x, y \in A$$

$\therefore\ x = 2, y = 4; x = 4, y = 3; x = 6, y = 2;\ x = 8, y = 1$

Also, $y \notin A$ for $x = 1, 3, 5, 7, 9, 10$

$\therefore R = \{(2, 4), (4, 3), (6, 2), (8, 1)\}$

(ii) Domain of $R = \{2, 4, 6, 8\}$

Range of $R = \{4, 3, 2, 1\}$

JEE Focus Points

- Any subset of $A \times A$ is said to be a relation on A.
- If A has m elements and B has n elements, then $A \times B$ has $m \times n$ elements and total number of different relations from A to B is 2^{mn}.
- If $R = A \times B$, then Domain $R = A$ and Range $R = B$.
- The domain as well as range of the empty set (ϕ) is ϕ.
- If $A =$ Dom R and $B =$ Ran R, then we write $B = R[A]$.

Types of Relations from One Set to Another Set

1. Empty Relation

A relation R from A to B is called an empty relation or a void relation from A to B if $R = \phi$.

e.g. Let $A = \{2, 4, 6\}$ and $B = \{7, 11\}$

Let $R = \{(a, b) : a \in A, b \in B \text{ and } a - b \text{ is even}\}$

As, none of the numbers $2 - 7, 2 - 11, 4 - 7, 4 - 11, 6 - 7, 6 - 11$ is an even number, $R = \phi$.

Hence, R is an empty relation.

2. Universal Relation

A relation R from A to B is said to be the universal relation, if $R = A \times B$.

e.g. Let $A = \{1, 2\}$, $B = \{1, 3\}$

and $R = \{(1, 1), (1, 3), (2, 1), (2, 3)\}$

Here, $R = A \times B$

Hence, R is the universal relation from A to B.

Types of Relations on a Set

1. Empty Relation

A relation R on a set A is said to be an empty relation or a void relation, if $R = \phi$.

e.g. Let $A = \{1, 3\}$ and $R = \{(a, b) : a, b \in A$ and $a + b$ is odd$\}$

Hence, R contains no element, therefore R is an empty relation on A.

2. Universal Relation

A relation R on a set A is said to be universal relation on A, if $R = A \times A$.

e.g. Let $A = \{1, 2\}$ and $R = \{(1, 1), (1, 2), (2, 1), (2, 2)\}$

Here, $R = A \times A$

Hence, R is the universal relation on A.

3. Identity Relation

A relation R on a set A is said to be the identity relation on A, if

$$R = \{(a, b) : a \in A, b \in A \text{ and } a = b\}$$

Thus, identity relation, $R = \{(a, a) : \forall\, a \in A\}$

Identity relation on set A is also denoted by I_A.

Symbolically, $I_A = \{(a, a) : a \in A\}$

e.g. Let $A = \{1, 2, 3\}$

Then, $I_A = \{(1, 1), (2, 2), (3, 3)\}$

4. Inverse Relation

If R is a relation from a set A to a set B, then inverse relation of R to be denoted by R^{-1}, is a relation from B to A.

Symbolically, $R^{-1} = \{(b, a) : (a, b) \in R\}$

Thus, $(a, b) \in R \Leftrightarrow (b, a) \in R^{-1}$, $\forall\, a \in A, b \in B$.

$$\text{Dom}(R^{-1}) = \text{Range}(R) \text{ and } \text{Range}(R^{-1}) = \text{Dom}(R)$$

$$(R^{-1})^{-1} = R$$

e.g. If $R = \{(1, 2), (3, 4), (5, 6)\}$, then

$R^{-1} = \{(2, 1), (4, 3), (6, 5)\}$

$\therefore \quad (R^{-1})^{-1} = \{(1, 2), (3, 4), (5, 6)\} = R$

Here, $\text{dom}(R) = \{1, 3, 5\}$, $\text{range}(R) = \{2, 4, 6\}$

and $\text{dom}(R^{-1}) = \{2, 4, 6\}$, $\text{range}(R^{-1}) = \{1, 3, 5\}$

Clearly, $\text{dom}(R^{-1}) = \text{range}(R)$

and $\text{range}(R^{-1}) = \text{dom}(R)$.

Various Types of Relations

1. Reflexive Relation

A relation R on a set A is said to be reflexive, if $a R a, \forall\, a \in A$ i.e. if $(a, a) \in R, \forall\, a \in A$

e.g. Let $A = \{1, 2, 3\}$

$R_1 = \{(1, 1), (2, 2), (3, 3)\}$

$R_2 = \{(1, 1), (2, 2), (3, 3), (1, 2), (2, 1), (1, 3)\}$

and $R_3 = \{(1, 1), (2, 2), (2, 3), (3, 2)\}$

Here, R_1 and R_2 are reflexive relations on A, R_3 is not a reflexive relation on A as $(3, 3) \notin R_3$, i.e. $3 \not{R}_3\, 3$.

JEE SPIKE

The identity relation is always a reflexive relation but a reflexive relation may or may not be the identity relation. It is clear in the above example given, R_1 is both reflexive and identity relation on A but R_2 is a reflexive relation on A but not an identity relation on A.

2. Symmetric Relation

A relation R on a set A is said to be symmetric relation, if

$$a R b \Rightarrow b R a, \forall\, a, b \in A$$

i.e. if $(a, b) \in R \Rightarrow (b, a) \in R, \forall\, a, b \in A$

e.g. Let $A = \{1, 2, 3\}$

$R_1 = \{(1, 2), (2, 1)\}$,

$R_2 = \{(1, 2), (2, 1), (1, 3), (3, 1)\}$

and $R_3 = \{(2, 3), (1, 3), (3, 1)\}$

Here, R_1 and R_2 are symmetric relations on A but R_3 is not a symmetric relation on A because $(2, 3) \in R_3$ but $(3, 2) \notin R_3$.

3. Anti-symmetric Relation

A relation R on a set A is said to be anti-symmetric, if $a R b, b R a \Rightarrow a = b, \forall\, a, b \in A$

i.e. $(a, b) \in R$ and $(b, a) \in R$

$\Rightarrow \quad a = b, \forall\, a, b \in A$

e.g. Let R be the relation in N (natural number) defined by, "x is divisor of y", then R is anti-symmetric because x divides y and y divides $x \Rightarrow x = y$

4. Transitive Relation

A relation R on a set A is said to be a transitive relation, if $a\,R\,b$ and $b\,R\,c \Rightarrow aRc, \forall\, a, b, c \in A$

i.e., $(a, b) \in R$ and $(b, c) \in R \Rightarrow (a, c) \in R, \forall\, a, b, c \in A$

e.g. Let $A = \{1, 2, 3\}$

$$R_1 = \{(1, 2), (2, 3), (1, 3), (3, 2)\}$$
$$R_2 = \{(2, 3), (3, 1)\}$$
$$R_3 = \{(1, 3), (3, 2), (1, 2)\}$$

Then, R_1 is not transitive relation on A because $(2, 3) \in R_1$ and $(3, 2) \in R_1$ but $(2, 2) \notin R_1$. Again, R_2 is not transitive relation on A because $(2, 3) \in R_2$ and $(3, 1) \in R_2$ but $(2, 1) \notin R_2$. Finally R_3 is a transitive relation.

Example 18. Let $A = \{1, 2, 3\}$ and $R = \{(a, b) : a, b \in A,\ a$ divides b and b divides $a\}$. Show that R is an identity relation on A.

Sol. Given, $A = \{1, 2, 3\}$

$a \in A, b \in B$, a divides b and b divides a.

$\Rightarrow \quad a = b$

$\therefore \quad R = \{(a, a), a \in A\} = \{(1, 1), (2, 2), (3, 3)\}$

Hence, R is an identity relation on A.

Example 19. Let $A = \{3, 5\}$, $B = \{7, 11\}$.
Let $R = \{(a, b) : a \in A,\ b \in B,\ a - b$ is even$\}$.
Show that R is an universal relation from A to B.

Sol. Given, $A = \{3, 5\}, B = \{7, 11\}$.

Now, $R = \{(a, b) : a \in A, b \in B$ and $a - b$ is even$\}$
$= \{(3, 7), (3, 11), (5, 7), (5, 11)\}$

Also, $A \times B = \{(3, 7), (3, 11), (5, 7), (5, 11)\}$

Clearly, $R = A \times B$

Hence, R is an universal relation from A to B.

Example 20. Prove that the relation R defined on the set N of natural numbers by $xRy \Leftrightarrow 2x^2 - 3xy + y^2 = 0$ is not symmetric but it is reflexive.

Sol. (i) $2x^2 - 3x \cdot x + x^2 = 0, \forall\, x \in N$.

$\therefore\ x\,R\,x, \forall\, x \in N$, i.e. R is reflexive.

(ii) For $x = 1, y = 2$, $2x^2 - 3xy + y^2 = 0$

$\therefore\ 1R2$

But for $x = 2, y = 1$, $2 \cdot 2^2 - 3 \cdot 2 \cdot 1 + 1^2 = 3 \neq 0$

So, 2 is not related to 1 i.e. $2\not R 1$

$\therefore\ R$ is not symmetric.

Example 21. Let N be the set of natural numbers and relation R on N be defined by $xR\,y \Leftrightarrow x$ divides y, $\forall\, x, y \in N$. Examine whether R is reflexive, symmetric, anti-symmetric or transitive.

Sol. (i) x divides x i.e. $x\,R\,x, \forall\, x \in N$

$\therefore\ R$ is reflexive.

(ii) 1 divides 2 i.e. $1\,R\,2$ but $2 \not R 1$ as 2 does not divides 1.

$\therefore\ R$ is not symmetric.

(iii) x divides y and y divides $x \Rightarrow x = y$

i.e. $x\,Ry$ and $y\,R\,x \Rightarrow x = y$

$\therefore\ R$ is anti-symmetric relation.

(iv) $x\,Ry$ and $y\,Rz \Rightarrow x$ divides y and y divides z.

$\Rightarrow kx = y$ and $k'y = z$, where k, k' are positive integers.

$\Rightarrow\ kk'x = z\ \Rightarrow\ x$ divides $z\ \Rightarrow\ x\,Rz$

$\therefore\ R$ is transitive.

Equivalence Relation

A relation R on a set A is said to be an equivalence relation on A iff

(i) it is reflexive i.e. $(a, a) \in R, \forall\, a \in A$

(ii) it is symmetric i.e. $(a, b) \in R \Rightarrow (b, a) \in R$

(iii) it is transitive i.e. $(a, b) \in R$ and $(b, c) \in R$
$\Rightarrow (a, c) \in R, \forall\, a, b, c \in A$

JEE Focus Points

- If R and S are two equivalence relation on set A, then $R \cap S$ is also an equivalence relation on A.
- The union of two equivalence relation on set is not necessarily an equivalence relation on the set.
- The inverse of an equivalence relation is an equivalence relation.

Example 22. N is the set of natural numbers. The relation R is defined on $N \times N$ as follows

$$(a, b)\,R\,(c, d) \Leftrightarrow a + d = b + c$$

Prove that R is an equivalence relation.

Sol. (i) $(a, b)\,R\,(a, b) \Rightarrow a + b = b + a$

$\therefore\ R$ is reflexive.

(ii) $(a, b)\,R\,(c, d) \Rightarrow a + d = b + c$

$\Rightarrow \quad c + b = d + a \Rightarrow (c, d)\,R\,(a, b)$

$\therefore\ R$ is symmetric.

(iii) $(a, b)\,R\,(c, d)$ and $(c, d)\,R\,(e, f) \Rightarrow a + d = b + c$

and $\quad c + f = d + e$

$\Rightarrow\ a + d + c + f = b + c + d + e$

$\Rightarrow \quad a + f = b + e \Rightarrow (a, b)\,R\,(e, f)$

$\therefore\ R$ is transitive.

Thus, R is an equivalence relation on $N \times N$.

Example 23. A relation R on the set of complex numbers is defined by $z_1\,Rz_2 \Leftrightarrow \dfrac{z_1 - z_2}{z_1 + z_2}$ is real, show that R is an equivalence relation.

Sol. (i) $z_1Rz_1 \Rightarrow \dfrac{z_1 - z_1}{z_1 + z_1}, \forall z_1 \in C\ \Rightarrow\ 0$ is real

$\therefore\ R$ is reflexive.

(ii) $z_1 R z_2 \Rightarrow \dfrac{z_1 - z_2}{z_1 + z_2}$ is real.

$\Rightarrow -\left(\dfrac{z_2 - z_1}{z_1 + z_2}\right)$ is real $\Rightarrow \left(\dfrac{z_2 - z_1}{z_1 + z_2}\right)$ is real

$\Rightarrow z_2 R z_1, \forall z_1, z_2 \in C$

$\therefore$ R is symmetric.

(iii) $\because z_1 R z_2 \Rightarrow \dfrac{z_1 - z_2}{z_1 + z_2}$ is real

$$\Rightarrow \left(\frac{\overline{z_1 - z_2}}{z_1 + z_2}\right) = -\left(\frac{z_1 - z_2}{z_1 + z_2}\right)$$

$$\Rightarrow \left(\frac{\bar{z}_1 - \bar{z}_2}{\bar{z}_1 + \bar{z}_2}\right) + \left(\frac{z_1 - z_2}{z_1 + z_2}\right) = 0$$

$$\Rightarrow 2(z_1\bar{z}_1 - z_2\bar{z}_2) = 0 \Rightarrow |z_1|^2 = |z_2|^2 \quad \text{...(i)}$$

Similarly, $z_2 R z_3 \Rightarrow |z_2|^2 = |z_3|^2$ ...(ii)

From Eqs. (i) and (ii), we get

$$z_1 R z_2, z_2 R z_3$$

$$\Rightarrow |z_1|^2 = |z_3|^2$$

$$\Rightarrow z_1 R z_3$$

$\therefore R$ is transitive.

Hence, R is an equivalence relation.

Equivalence Classes of Equivalence Relation

Let R be an equivalence relation in a non-empty set A.

Let $a \in A$, then the equivalence class of a, denoted by $[a]$ or $\{\bar{a}\}$ is defined as the set of all those points of A which are related to a under the relation R.

Thus, $[a] = \{x \in A : x \; R \; a\}$

JEE Focus Points

- $b \in [a] \Rightarrow a \in [b]$
- $b \in [a] \Rightarrow [a] = [b]$
- Any two equivalence classes are either equal or disjoint

e.g. we consider a very important equivalence relation $x \equiv y \pmod{n}$ iff n divides $(x - y)$: n is fixed positive integer consider $n = 5$, then

$$[0] = \{x : x \equiv 0 \pmod 5\} = \{5p : p \in Z\}$$
$$= \{0, \pm 5, \pm 10, \pm 15 \ldots\}$$
$$[1] = \{x : x \equiv 1 \pmod 5\} = \{x : x - 1 = 5k, k \in Z\}$$
$$= \{5k + 1 : k \in Z\} = \{1, 6, 11, \ldots\}$$

We can easily see that there are only 5 equivalence classes.

$[0], [1], [2], [3]$ and $[4]$, when $n = 5$

11.8 Ordered Relation

A relation R is called ordered, if R is transitive but not an equivalence relation.

Symbolically, $\quad a R b, b R c$

$\Rightarrow \quad a R c, \forall a, b, c \in A$

e.g. Let $R = \{(1, 2), (2, 1), (2, 3), (3, 2), (1, 3), (3, 1)\}$.

Here, R is symmetric.

Since, $(1, 2) \in R \Rightarrow (2, 1) \in R, (2, 3) \in R$

$\Rightarrow \quad (3, 2) \in R$

and R is transitive.

Since, $(1, 2) \in R, (2, 3) \in R$

$\Rightarrow \quad (1, 3) \in R$

and R is not reflexive.

Since, $(1, 1) \notin R, (2, 2) \notin R, (3, 3) \notin R$

Hence, R is not an equivalence relation.

$\therefore$ R is an ordered relation.

Partial Order Relation

A relation R is called partial order relation, if R is reflexive, transitive and anti-symmetric at the same time.

e.g.

Let $\quad R = \{(1, 1), (2, 2), (3, 3), (1, 2), (2, 3), (1, 3)\}$

$\therefore \quad R^{-1} = \{(1, 1), (2, 2), (3, 3), (2, 1), (3, 2), (3, 1)\}$

$R \cap R^{-1} = \{(1, 1), (2, 2), (3,3)\} =$ Identity

$\therefore$ R is anti-symmetric.

It is clear that R is reflexive.

Since, $(1, 1) \in R, (2, 2) \in R, (3, 3) \in R$ and R is transitive.

Since, $(1, 2) \in R$ and $(2, 3) \in R \Rightarrow (1, 3) \in R$

Hence, R is partial order relation.

11.9 Composition of Two Relations

If A, B and C are three sets such that $R \subseteq A \times B$ and $S \subseteq B \times C$, then $(SOR)^{-1} = R^{-1} O S^{-1}$. It is clear that aRb, bSc $\Rightarrow aSORc$.

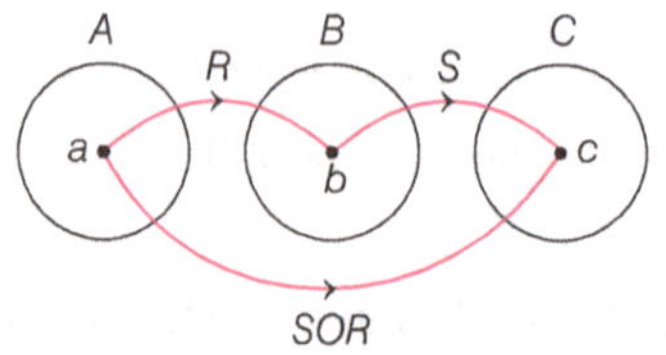

More generally,

$$(R_1 O R_2 O R_3 O \ldots O R_n)^{-1} = R_n^{-1} O \ldots O R_3^{-1} O R_2^{-1} O R_1^{-1}$$

JEE Focus Points

If R is a relation on a set A, then

- R is reflexive $\Rightarrow R^{-1}$ is reflexive.
- R is symmetric $\Rightarrow R^{-1}$ is symmetric.
- R is transitive $\Rightarrow R^{-1}$ is transitive.

Concept Inside Video

JEE SCANNER

Example Similar to PYQ Asked in JEE Main 2023

The minimum number of elements that must be added to the relation $R = \{(a, b), (b, c)\}$ on the set $\{a, b, c\}$ so that it is an equivalence is ....

Sol. Given, $R = \{(a,b),(b,c)\}$

In order to make it equivalence relation as per given set, R must be

$$\{(a, a), (b, b), (c,c), (a, b), (b, a), (b,c), (c,b), (a,c), (c,a)\}$$

Minimum number of elements that must be added $=7$

Skill Builder

The number of equivalence relation in the set {1, 2, 3} containing (1, 2) and (2, 1) is ....

For Sol.

■ **For more practice** See Q.12 of Milestone practice 11.2.

Example 24. Let R be a relation such that $R = \{(1, 4), (3, 7), (4, 5), (4, 6), (7, 6)\}$, find

(i) $R^{-1}OR^{-1}$ and (ii) $(R^{-1}\ OR)^{-1}$.

Sol. (i) We know that, $(ROR)^{-1} = R^{-1}OR^{-1}$

Dom $(R) = \{1, 3, 4, 7\}$

Range $(R) = \{4, 5, 6, 7\}$

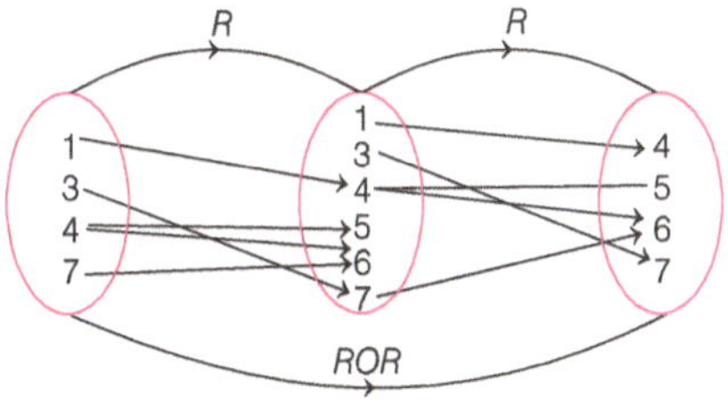

We see that,

$$1 \longrightarrow 4 \longrightarrow 5 \Rightarrow (1, 5) \in ROR$$
$$1 \longrightarrow 4 \longrightarrow 6 \Rightarrow (1, 6) \in ROR$$
$$3 \longrightarrow 7 \longrightarrow 6 \Rightarrow (3, 6) \in ROR$$

$\therefore \quad ROR = \{(1, 5), (1, 6), (3, 6)\}$

Then, $R^{-1}OR^{-1} = (ROR)^{-1}$

$= \{(5, 1), (6, 1), (6, 3)\}$

(ii) We know that, $(R^{-1}OR)^{-1} = R^{-1}O(R^{-1})^{-1} = R^{-1}OR$

Since,

$$R = \{(1, 4), (3, 7), (4, 5), (4, 6), (7, 6)\}$$

$\therefore \quad R^{-1} = \{(4, 1), (7, 3), (5, 4), (6, 4), (6, 7)\}$

$\therefore$ Dom $(R) = \{1, 3, 4, 7\}$, Range $(R) = \{4, 5, 6, 7\}$

Dom $(R^{-1}) = \{4, 5, 6, 7\}$, Range $(R^{-1}) = \{1, 3, 4, 7\}$

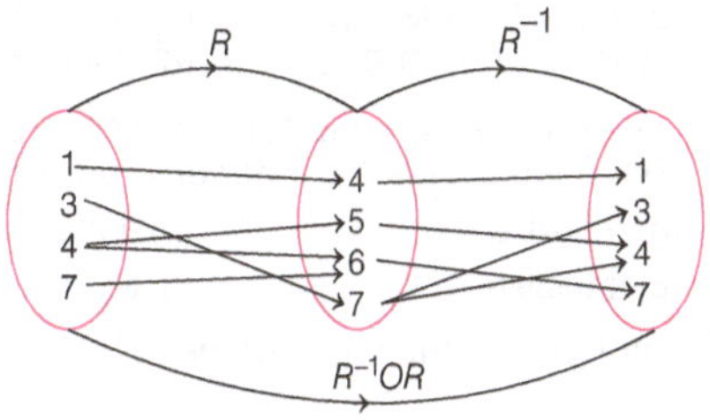

We see that,

$$1 \xrightarrow{R} 4 \xrightarrow{R^{-1}} 1 \Rightarrow (1, 1) \in R^{-1}OR$$
$$3 \xrightarrow{R} 7 \xrightarrow{R^{-1}} 3 \Rightarrow (3, 3) \in R^{-1}OR$$
$$4 \xrightarrow{R} 5 \xrightarrow{R^{-1}} 4 \Rightarrow (4, 4) \in R^{-1}OR$$
$$4 \xrightarrow{R} 6 \xrightarrow{R^{-1}} 4 \Rightarrow (4, 4) \in R^{-1}OR$$
$$4 \xrightarrow{R} 6 \xrightarrow{R^{-1}} 7 \Rightarrow (4, 7) \in R^{-1}OR$$
$$7 \xrightarrow{R} 6 \xrightarrow{R^{-1}} 4 \Rightarrow (7, 4) \in R^{-1}OR$$
$$7 \xrightarrow{R} 6 \xrightarrow{R^{-1}} 7 \Rightarrow (7, 7) \in R^{-1}OR$$

$\therefore \quad R^{-1}OR = \{(1, 1), (3, 3), (4, 4), (7, 7), (4, 7), (7, 4)\}$

Hence, $(R^{-1}OR)^{-1} = R^{-1}OR$

$= \{(1, 1), (3, 3) (4, 4), (7, 7), (4, 7), (7, 4)\}$

Milestone Practice 11.2

1. If $A=\{2,3,5\}$, $B=\{2,5,6\}$, then $(A-B)\times(A\cap B)$ is
(a) $\{(3,2),(3,3),(3,5)\}$
(b) $\{(3,2),(3,5),(3,6)\}$
(c) $\{(3,2),(3,5)\}$
(d) None of these

2. If $n(A)=4$, $n(B)=3$, $n(A\times B\times C)=24$, then $n(C)$ equals
(a) 1
(b) 2
(c) 17
(d) 288

3. The relation R defined on the set of natural numbers as $\{(a,b): a$ differs from b by $3\}$ is given by
(a) $\{(1,4),(2,5),(3,7),\ldots\}$
(b) $\{(4,1),(5,2),(6,3),\ldots\}$
(c) $\{(1,3),(2,6),(3,9),\ldots\}$
(d) None of these

4. Let A be the non-void set of the children in a family. The relation 'x is a brother of y' on A, is
(a) reflexive
(b) anti-symmetric
(c) transitive
(d) equivalence

5. Let $n(A)=n$, then the number of all relations on A, is
(a) 2^n
(b) $2^{n!}$
(c) 2^{n^2}
(d) None of these

6. If $S=\{1,2,3,..,20\}$, $K=\{a,b,c,d\}$, $G=\{b,d,e,f\}$. The number of elements of $(S\times K)\cup(S\times G)$ is
(a) 40
(b) 100
(c) 120
(d) 140

7. The relation R is defined on the set of natural numbers as $\{(a,b): a=2b\}$, then R^{-1} is given by
(a) $\{(2,1)(4,2)(6,3),\ldots\}$
(b) $\{(1,2)(2,4)(3,6),\ldots\}$
(c) R^{-1} is not defined
(d) None of these

8. The relation $R=\{(1,1),(2,2),(3,3),(1,2),(2,3),(1,3)\}$ on set $A=\{1,2,3\}$ is
(a) reflexive but not symmetric
(b) reflexive but not transitive
(c) symmetric and transitive
(d) Neither symmetric nor transitive

9. The number of equivalence relations defined in the set $S=\{a,b,c\}$ is
(a) 5
(b) 3!
(c) 2^3
(d) 3^3

10. If R be a relation from $A=\{1,2,3,4\}$ to $B=\{1,3,5\}$, i.e. $(a,b)\in R \Leftrightarrow a<b$, then ROR^{-1}, is
(a) $\{(1,3),(1,5),(2,3),(2,5),(3,5),(4,5)\}$
(b) $\{(3,1),(5,1),(3,2),(5,2),(5,3),(5,4)\}$
(c) $\{(3,3),(3,5),(5,3),(5,5)\}$
(d) $\{(3,3),(3,4),(4,5)\}$

11. Let A and B be two sets containing 1 element and 3 elements respectively. The number of subsets of $A\times B$ having 2 or more elements is
(a) 1
(b) 2
(c) 4
(d) 8

12. Find the minimum number of elements that must be added to the relation $R=\{(a,b),(b,a)\}$ on the set $\{a,b\}$ so that it is an equivalence relation.
(a) 1
(b) 2
(c) 3
(d) 4

Answer Key

1. (c)	2. (b)	3. (b)	4. (c)	5. (c)
6. (c)	7. (b)	8. (a)	9. (a)	10. (c)
11. (a)	12. (b)			

For Detailed Solution

JEE Pattern EXAMPLES

Single Option Correct Type Questions

Example 1 *Two finite sets have m and n elements. The total number of subsets of the first set is 56 more than the total number of subsets of the second set. The values of m and n are*

(a) 7, 6 (b) 6, 3 (c) 5, 1 (d) 8, 7

Sol. (b) Since, $2^m - 2^n = 56 = 8 \times 7 = 2^3 \times 7$

$\Rightarrow 2^n(2^{m-n} - 1) = 2^3 \times 7$

$\Rightarrow n = 3$ and $2^{m-n} = 8 = 2^3 \Rightarrow n = 3$ and $m - n = 3$

$\Rightarrow n = 3$ and $m - 3 = 3 \Rightarrow n = 3$ and $m = 6$

Example 2 *If $aN = \{ax : x \in N\}$ and $bN \cap cN = dN$, where $b, c \in N$ are relatively prime, then*

(a) $d = bc$ (b) $c = bd$

(c) $b = cd$ (d) None of these

Sol. (a) bN = The set of positive integral multiples of b

cN = The set of positive integral multiples of c

$\therefore bN \cap cN$ = The set of positive integral multiples of bc

$= bcN$ [$\because$ b and c are prime]

$\therefore d = bc$

Example 3 *In a town of 10000 families, it was found that 40% families buy newspaper A, 20% families buy newspaper B and 10% families buy newspaper C, 5% families buy newspapers A and B, 3% buy newspapers B and C and 4% buy newspapers A and C. If 2% families buy all the three newspapers, then number of families which buy A only is*

(a) 3100 (b) 3300 (c) 2900 (d) 1400

Sol. (b) $n(A) = 40\%$ of $10000 = 4000$

$n(B) = 20\%$ of $10000 = 2000$

$n(C) = 10\%$ of $10000 = 1000$

$n(A \cap B) = 5\%$ of $10000 = 500$

$n(B \cap C) = 3\%$ of $10000 = 300$

$n(C \cap A) = 4\%$ of $10000 = 400$

$n(A \cap B \cap C) = 2\%$ of $10000 = 200$

We want to find $n(A \cap B^c \cap C^c) = n[A \cap (B \cup C)^c]$

$= n(A) - n[A \cap (B \cup C)] = n(A) - n[(A \cap B) \cup (A \cap C)]$

$= n(A) - [n(A \cap B) + n(A \cap C) - n(A \cap B \cap C)]$

$= 4000 - [500 + 400 - 200] = 4000 - 700 = 3300$

Example 4 *Let R be the relation on the set R of all real numbers defined by aRb iff $|a - b| \le 1$. Then, R is*

(a) reflexive and symmetric (b) symmetric only

(c) transitive only (d) anti-symmetric only

Sol. (a) $\because |a - a| = 0 < 1 \Rightarrow a\,R\,a, \forall\, a \in R$

$\therefore R$ is reflexive.

Again, $aRb \Rightarrow |a - b| \le 1$

$\Rightarrow |b - a| \le 1 \Rightarrow bRa$

$\therefore R$ is symmetric.

Again, $1\,R\,2$ and $2R1$ but $2 \ne 1$

$\therefore R$ is not anti-symmetric.

Further, $1R2$ and $2R3$ but $1 \not R 3$ [$\because |1 - 3| = 2 > 1$]

$\therefore R$ is not transitive.

Example 5 *The relation R defined on A = {1, 2, 3} by aRb, if $|a^2 - b^2| \le 5$. Which of the following is false?*

(a) $R = \{(1, 1), (2, 2), (3, 3), (2, 1), (1, 2), (2, 3), (3, 2)\}$

(b) $R^{-1} = R$

(c) Domain of $R = \{1, 2, 3\}$

(d) Range of $R = \{5\}$

Sol. (d) Let $a = 1$

Then, $|a^2 - b^2| \le 5 \Rightarrow |1 - b^2| \le 5$

$\Rightarrow |b^2 - 1| \le 5 \Rightarrow b = 1, 2$

Let $a = 2$

Then, $|a^2 - b^2| \le 5$

$\Rightarrow |4 - b^2| \le 5 \Rightarrow |b^2 - 4| \le 5$

$\therefore b = 1, 2, 3$

Let $a = 3$

Then, $|a^2 - b^2| \le 5 \Rightarrow |9 - b^2| \le 5$

$\Rightarrow |b^2 - 9| \le 5 \Rightarrow b = 2, 3$

$\therefore R = \{(1, 1), (1, 2), (2, 1), (2, 2), (2, 3), (3, 2), (3, 3)\}$

$R^{-1} = \{(y, x) : (x, y) \in R\}$

$= \{(1, 1), (2, 1), (1, 2), (2, 2), (3, 2), (2, 3), (3, 3)\} = R$

Domain of $R = \{x : (x, y) \in R\} = \{1, 2, 3\}$

Range of $R = \{y : (x, y) \in R\} = \{1, 2, 3\}$

JEE SCANNER

Example 6 Similar to PYQ Asked in JEE Main 2024

Let R be a relation on $Z \times Z$ defined by $(a, b) R(c, d)$ if and only if $a + d = b + c$. Then, R is

(a) Reflexive, symmetric but not transitive

(b) Reflexive, symmetric and transitive

(c) Symmetric but not reflexive and transitive

(d) Reflexive, transitive but not symmetric

Sol. (b) Relation R defined on $Z \times Z$ such that $(a,b)\ R\ (c, d)$ if and only if $(a + d) = (b + c)$

Now, $(a,b)\ R(a,b)$ because $(a + b) = (b + a)$ holds for each element $(a,b) \in Z \times Z$.

Particularly, $(a, b)\ R(a,b)$.

$\therefore R$ is reflexive.

Now, let $(a, b)\ R(c,d) \Rightarrow a + d = b + c$

$\Rightarrow \quad b + c = a + d$

or $\quad c + b = d + a$

$\Rightarrow \quad (c,d)\ R(a, b)$

$\therefore R$ is symmetric.

Now, let $(a,b)\ R(c, d)$ and $(c,d)\ R(e,f)$

$\Rightarrow \quad a + d = b + c$ and $c + f = d + e$

$\Rightarrow \quad c - d = a - b$ and $c - d = e - f$

$\Rightarrow \quad a - b = e - f$

$\Rightarrow \quad a + f = b + e$

$\Rightarrow \quad (a,b)\ R(e, f)$

$\therefore R$ is transitive.

Skill Builder

For Sol.

Let N denote the set of all natural numbers and R be the relation on $N \times N$ defined by $(a, b) R(c, d)$ if and only if $ad(b + c) = bc(a + d)$, then R is

(a) symmetric, but not reflexive and transitive

(b) transitive but not reflexive and symmetric

(c) symmetric, reflexive but not transitive

(d) reflexive, symmetric and transitive

More than One Correct Option Type Questions

Example 7 *If I is the set of integers and if the relation R is defined over I by aRb, iff $a - b$ is an even integer, $a, b \in I$, the relation R is*

(a) reflexive (b) anti-symmetric

(c) symmetric (d) equivalence

Sol. (a,c,d) $aRb \Leftrightarrow a - b$ is an even integer, $a, b \in I$

$$a - a = 0 \text{ (even integer)}$$

$\therefore \quad (a, a) \in R, \ \forall\, a \in I$

$\therefore$ R is reflexive relation.

Let $(a, b) \in R \Rightarrow (a - b)$ is an even integer.

$\Rightarrow \quad -(b - a)$ is an even integer.

$\Rightarrow \quad (b - a)$ is an even integer.

$\Rightarrow \quad (b, a) \in R$

$\therefore$ R is symmetric relation.

Now, let $(a, b) \in R$ and $(b, c) \in R$

Then, $(a - b)$ is an even integer and $(b - c)$ is an even integer.

So, let $\quad a - b = 2x_1, x_1 \in I$

and $\quad b - c = 2x_2, x_2 \in I$

$\therefore \quad (a - b) + (b - c) = 2(x_1 + x_2)$

$\Rightarrow \quad (a - c) = 2(x_1 + x_2)$

$\Rightarrow \quad a - c = 2x_3$

$\therefore$ $(a - c)$ is an even integer.

$\therefore$ aRb and $bRc \Rightarrow aRc$.

So, R is transitive relation.

Hence, R is an equivalence relation.

A relation R on given set A is said to be anti-symmetric iff $(a, b) \in R$ and $(b, a) \in R$

$\Rightarrow \quad a = b, \forall\, a, b \in A$.

$\therefore$ Given relation is not anti-symmetric relation.

Example 8 *Let $X = \{1, 2, 3, 4, 5\}$ and $Y = \{1, 3, 5, 7, 9\}$. Which of following is/are relations from X to Y?*

(a) $R_1 = \{(x, y) : y = 2 + x, x \in X, y \in Y\}$

(b) $R_2 = \{(1, 1), (2, 1), (3, 3), (4, 3), (5, 5)\}$

(c) $R_3 = \{(1, 1), (1, 3), (3, 5), (3, 7), (5, 7)\}$

(d) $R_4 = \{(1, 3), (2, 5), (2, 4), (7, 9)\}$

Sol. (b,c) $X = \{1, 2, 3, 4, 5\}$ and $Y = \{1, 3, 5, 7, 9\}$

(a) $R_1 = \{(x, y) : y = 2 + x, x \in X, y \in Y\}$

$\Rightarrow R_1 = \{(1, 3), (2, 4), (3, 5), (4, 6), (5, 7)\}$

$R_1 \not\subset x \times y$

(b) $R_2 \subseteq X \times Y$

(c) $R_3 \subseteq X \times Y$

(d) $R_4 \not\subseteq X \times Y \quad$ [$\because$ $(2, 4) \in R_4$ but $4 \notin Y$]

Example 9 *If $A \cup B = A \cup C$ and $A \cap B = A \cap C$, then which of the following is true?*

(a) $B = C$

(b) $A \cup (B \cap C) = (A \cap B) \cap (A \cup C)$

(c) $A \cup (B \cup C) = (A \cup B) \cap (A \cup C)$

(d) $A \cup (B \cap C) = (A \cup B) \cap (A \cup C)$

Sol. (a, d), We have, $B = B \cup (A \cap B)$

$= B \cup (A \cap C) \quad$ [given, $A \cap B = A \cap C$]

$= (A \cup C) \cap (B \cup C) \quad$ [$\because A \cup B = A \cup C$]

$= (A \cap B) \cup C$

$= (A \cap C) \cup C$

$= C$

Passage Based Question

Passage I

(Ex. Nos. 10 and 11)

If $A = \{x : |x| < 2\}$, $B = \{x : |x - 5| \le 2\}$,
$C = \{x : |x| > x\}$ and $D = \{x : |x| < x\}$

Example 10 *The number of integral values in $A \cup B$ is*

(a) 4 (b) 6
(c) 8 (d) 10

Example 11 *The number of integral values in $A \cap C$ is*

(a) 1 (b) 2
(c) 3 (d) 0

Sol. (Ex. Nos. 10 and 11)

$$A = \{x : |x| < 2\} = \{x : -2 < x < 2\} = (-2, 2)$$
$$B = \{x : |x-5| \le 2\} = \{x : -2 \le x - 5 \le 2\}$$
$$= \{x : 3 \le x \le 7\} = [3, 7]$$
$$C = \{x : |x| > x\} = \{x : x < 0\} = (-\infty, 0)$$
and $D = \{x : |x| < x\} = \phi$

10. (c) $A \cup B = (-2, 2) \cup [3, 7]$

Integral values in $A \cup B$ are $-1, 0, 1, 3, 4, 5, 6, 7$.

$\therefore$ Number of integral values in $A \cup B$ is 8.

11. (a) $A \cap C = (-2, 2) \cap (-\infty, 0) = (-2, 0)$

Integral value in $A \cap C$ is -1.

$\therefore$ Number of integral values in $A \cap C$ is 1.

Stem Based Question

Stem I

(Ex. Nos. 12 and 13)

If A, B and C are sets defined as $A = \{x \mid x \in Z^+$ and $x \le 16\}$, $B = \{x \mid x \in Z$ and $-3 < x < 8\}$ and $C = \{x \mid x$ is a prime number$\}$, then

Example 12 *Number of elements belonging to all three sets is ......*

Example 13 *Number of elements belonging to exactly two of A, B and C is ....*

Sol. (Ex. Nos. 12 and 13)

$A = \{x \mid x \in Z^+$ and $x \le 16\} = \{1, 2, 3, ..., 16\}$

$\therefore \quad n(A) = 16$

$B = \{x \mid x \in Z$ and $-3 < x < 8\} = \{-2, -1, 0, 1, 2, ..., 7\}$

$\therefore \quad n(B) = 10$

$C = \{x \mid x$ is a prime number$\}$

$\therefore n(C) = \infty$

Now, $\quad A \cap B = \{1, 2, 3, 4, 5, 6, 7\}$

$\Rightarrow \quad n(A \cap B) = 7$

$B \cap C = \{2, 3, 5, 7\}$

$\Rightarrow \quad n(B \cap C) = 4$

$C \cap A = \{2, 3, 5, 7, 11, 13\}$

$\Rightarrow \quad n(C \cap A) = 6$

12. (4) $A \cap B \cap C = \{2, 3, 5, 7\}$

$\therefore n(A \cap B \cap C) = 4$

13. (5) $n(A \cap B) + n(B \cap C) + n(C \cap A) - 3n(A \cap B \cap C)$

$$= 7 + 4 + 6 - 3 \times 4$$
$$= 17 - 12$$
$$= 5$$

Single Integer Answer Type Questions

Example 14 *Let $\bigcup_{i=1}^{50} X_i = \bigcup_{i=1}^{n} Y_i = T$, where each X_i contains 10 elements and each Y_i contains 5 elements. If each element of the set T is an element of exactly 20 of sets X_i's and exactly 6 of sets Y_i's, then $\frac{n}{10}$ is equal to ....*

Sol. (3) $\bigcup_{i=1}^{50} X_i = \bigcup_{i=1}^{n} Y_i = T$

$\because n(X_i) = 10$ and $n(Y_i) = 5$

So, $\bigcup_{i=1}^{50} X_i = 500$ and $\bigcup_{i=1}^{n} Y_i = 5n$

$$\Rightarrow \quad \frac{500}{20} = \frac{5n}{6}$$
$$\Rightarrow \quad n = 30$$
$$\Rightarrow \quad \frac{n}{10} = 3$$

Example 15 *If $A = \{2, 3\}$, $B = \{4, 5\}$ and $C = \{5, 6\}$, then $n\{(A \times B) \cup (B \times C)\}$ is ....*

Sol. (8) $\because A \times B = \{2, 3\} \times \{4, 5\}$

$$= \{(2, 4), (2, 5), (3, 4), (3, 5)\}$$

and $\quad B \times C = \{4, 5\} \times \{5, 6\}$

$$= \{(4, 5), (4, 6), (5, 5), (5, 6)\}$$

$\therefore \quad (A \times B) \cup (B \times C) = \{(2, 4), (2, 5), (3, 4), (3, 5), (4, 5), (4, 6), (5, 5), (5\ 6)\}$

Now, $n\{(A \times B) \cup (B \times C)\} = 8$

JEE SCANNER

Example 16 Similar to PYQ Asked in JEE Main 2024

The number of elements in the sets $S=\{(x,y,z): x,y,z \in Z,\ 2x+3y+4z=56,\ x,\ y,\ z \geq 0\}$ equals ....

Sol. (80) Given $2x+3y+4z=56$, $x, y, z \geq 0$

$z=0$, $2x+3y=56 \to 10$ cases
$z=1$, $2x+3y=52 \to 9$ cases
$z=2$, $2x+3y=48 \to 9$ cases
$z=3$, $2x+3y=44 \to 8$ cases
$z=4$, $2x+3y=40 \to 7$ cases
$z=5$, $2x+3y=36 \to 7$ cases
$z=6$, $2x+3y=32 \to 6$ cases
$z=7$, $2x+3y=28 \to 5$ cases
$z=8$, $2x+3y=24 \to 5$ cases
$z=9$, $2x+3y=20 \to 4$ cases
$z=10$, $2x+3y=16 \to 3$ cases
$z=11$, $2x+3y=12 \to 3$ cases
$z=12$, $2x+3y=8 \to 2$ cases
$z=13$, $2x+3y=4 \to 1$ case
$z=14$, $2x+3y=0 \to 1$ case

Total $=10+9+9+8+7+7+6+5+5+4+3+3+2+1+1$
$=80$

Skill Builder

The number of elements in the sets $S=\{(x,y,z): x,y,z \in Z,\ x+2y+4z=20,\ x,y,z \geq 0\}$ equals ....

For Sol.

Example 17 *Two finite sets have m and n elements. The total number of subsets of the first set is 48 more than the total number of subsets of the second set. The value of (m – n) is ....*

Sol. (2) As, $2^m - 2^n = 48 = 2^4 \times 3$

$\Rightarrow \quad 2^n(2^{m-n}-1) = 2^4 \times (2^2-1)$
$\Rightarrow \quad n=4$ and $m-n=2$
$\Rightarrow \quad n=4$ and $m=6$

Now, $m-n=6-4=2$

Example 18 *If $S=R$, $A=\{x: -3 \leq x < 7\}$ and $B=\{x: 0 < x < 10\}$ the number of positive integers in $A \Delta B$ is .... (where Δ is symmetric difference of two sets)*

Sol. (3) Here, $A=[-3,7)$, $B=(0,10)$

and $\quad S=(-\infty,\infty)$

$\therefore \quad A-B=[-3,0]$ and $B-A=[7,10)$
$\therefore \quad A \Delta B=(A-B)\cup(B-A)=[-3,0]\cup[7,10)$

$\therefore$ Positive integers are 7, 8, 9.

$\therefore$ Number of positive integers is 3.

Numerical Value Type Questions

Example 19 *Let Z be the set of integers. If $A=\{x \in Z: 2^{(x+2)(x^2-5x+6)}=1\}$ and $B=\{x \in Z: -3 < 2x-1 < 9\}$, then the number of subsets of the set $A \times B$ is 2^λ, then λ is equal to ....*

Sol. (15) Given, set $A=\{x \in Z: 2^{(x+2)(x^2-5x+6)}=1\}$

Consider, $2^{(x+2)(x^2-5x+6)}=1=2^0$

$\Rightarrow \quad (x+2)(x^2-5x+6)=0 \Rightarrow (x+2)(x-3)(x-2)=0$
$\Rightarrow \quad x=-2,2,3 \Rightarrow A=\{-2,2,3\}$

Also, $B=\{x \in Z: -3 < 2x-1 < 9\}$

Consider, $-3 < 2x-1 < 9$, $x \in Z$

$\Rightarrow \quad -2 < 2x < 10, x \in Z \Rightarrow -1 < x < 5, x \in Z$
$\Rightarrow \quad B=\{0,1,2,3,4\}$

So, $A \times B$ has 15 elements.

$\therefore$ Number of subsets of $A \times B = 2^{15}$.

$\therefore \quad \lambda=15$

Example 20 *If $A=\{x \in R: |x-2|>1\}$, $B=\{x \in R: \sqrt{x^2-3}>1\}$ and $C=\{x \in R: |x-4| \geq 2\}$ and Z is the set of all integers, then the number of subsets of the set $(A \cap B \cap C)^C \cap Z$ is ....*

Sol. (256) $A=\{x \in R: |x-2|>1\} \Rightarrow A=(-\infty,1)\cup(3,\infty)$

$B=\{x \in R: \sqrt{x^2-3}>1\} \Rightarrow B=(-\infty,-2)\cup(2,\infty)$
$C=\{x \in R: |x-4| \geq 2\} \Rightarrow C=(-\infty,2]\cup[6,\infty)$

$\Rightarrow \quad A \cap B \cap C=(-\infty,-2)\cup[6,\infty)$
$\Rightarrow \quad (A \cap B \cap C)^C=[-2,6)$

$\therefore \quad (A \cap B \cap C)^C \cap Z=\{-2,-1,0,1,2,3,4,5\}$

Number of subsets of $(A \cap B \cap C)^C \cap Z=2^8=256$

Example 21 *Let $S=\{1,2,3,4\}$, the total number of unordered pair of disjoints subsets of S is equal to ....*

Decoding the Question

Total number of unordered pairs of disjoint subsets of any set containing n elements is equal to $N=\dfrac{3^n+1}{2}$, $n=1,2,\ldots$

Sol. (41) Given, $S=\{1,2,3,4\}$

Let A and B be two disjoint subsets of S.

So, for any element $x \in S$, x is either in A or in B or none.

$\therefore$ Total option $=3^4=81$

Here, $A \neq B$, except when $A=B=\phi$

$\therefore$ $81-1=80$ (ordered pair) are there for which $A \neq B$

Hence, total number of unordered pairs of disjoint subset

$$=\frac{80}{2}+1=41$$

Matching Type Questions

Example 22 *Match the following columns.*

	Column I		Column II
(A)	$R = \{(x, y) : x < y\ ;\ x, y \in N\}$	(p)	Reflexive
(B)	$S = \{(x, y) : x + y = 10\ ;\ x, y \in N\}$	(q)	Symmetric
(C)	$T = \{(x, y) : x = y$ or $x - y = 1\ ;\ x, y \in N\}$	(r)	Transitive
(D)	$U = \{(x, y) : x^y = y^x;\ x, y \in N\}$	(s)	Equivalence

Sol. (A) → (r); (B) → (q); (C) → (p); (D) → (p, q, r, s)

(A) $\because \quad R = \{(x, y) : x < y;\ x, y \in N\}$

$x \not< x$

$\therefore \quad (x, x) \notin R$

So, R is not reflexive.

Now, $(x, y) \in R \Rightarrow x < y \not\Rightarrow y < x$

$\Rightarrow \quad (y, x) \notin R$

$\therefore R$ is not symmetric.

Let $(x, y) \in R$ and $(y, z) \in R$

$\Rightarrow \quad x < y$ and $y < z$

$\Rightarrow \quad x < z$

$\Rightarrow \quad (x, z) \in R$

$\therefore R$ is transitive.

(B) $\because \quad S = \{(x, y) : x + y = 10\ ;\ x, y \in N\}$

$\therefore \quad x + x = 10$

$\Rightarrow \quad 2x = 10$

$\Rightarrow \quad x = 5$

So, each element of N is not related to itself by the relation $x + y = 10$.

$\therefore S$ is not reflexive.

Now, $\quad (x, y) \in S$

$\Rightarrow \quad x + y = 10$

$\Rightarrow \quad y + x = 10$

$\Rightarrow \quad (y, x) \in S$

$\therefore S$ is symmetric relation.

Now, let $(3, 7) \in S$ and $(7, 3) \in S$

$\Rightarrow \quad (3, 3) \notin S$

$\therefore S$ is not transitive.

(C) $\because \quad T = \{(x, y) : x = y$ or $x - y = 1;\ x, y \in N\}$

$\therefore \quad x = x$

So, $\quad (x, x) \in T, \forall\ x \in N$

$\therefore \quad T$ is reflexive.

Let $(3, 2) \in T$ and $3 - 2 = 1$

$\not\Rightarrow \quad 2 - 3 = -1 \Rightarrow (2, 3) \notin T$

$\therefore \quad T$ is not symmetric.

Now, let $(3, 2) \in T$ and $(2, 1) \in T$

$\therefore \quad 3 - 2 = 1$

and $\quad 2 - 1 = 1$

Then, $\quad (3, 1) \notin T \quad [\because 3 - 1 = 2 \neq 1]$

$\therefore \quad T$ is not transitive.

(D) $U = \{(x, y) : x^y = y^x;\ x, y \in N\}$

$\because \quad x^x = x^x$

$\therefore \quad (x, x) \in U$

$\therefore U$ is reflexive.

Now, $\quad (x, y) \in U$

$\Rightarrow \quad x^y = y^x$

$\Rightarrow \quad y^x = x^y$

$\Rightarrow \quad (y, x) \in U$

$\therefore U$ is symmetric.

Now, let $(x, y) \in U$ and $(y, z) \in U$

$\Rightarrow \quad x^y = y^x$

and $\quad y^z = z^y \quad$ ...(i)

Now, $\quad (x^y)^z = (y^x)^z$

$\Rightarrow \quad (x^z)^y = (y^z)^x$

$\Rightarrow \quad (x^z)^y = (z^y)^x \quad$ [using Eq. (i)]

$\Rightarrow \quad (x^z)^y = (z^x)^y$

$\Rightarrow \quad x^z = z^x$

$\Rightarrow \quad (x, z) \in U$

$\therefore \quad U$ is transitive.

Hence, U is an equivalence relation.

EXERCISE 1
JEE Main Pattern

Single Option Correct Type Questions

1. If A and B are two sets, then $A \cap (A \cup B)$ equals
(a) A (b) B
(c) ϕ (d) None of these

2. If R is a relation from a set A to a set B and S is a relation from a set B to set C, then the relation SoR
(a) is from A to C (b) is from C to A
(c) does not exist (d) None of these

3. Let $R = \{(1, 3), (2, 2), (3, 2)\}$ and $S = \{(2, 1), (3, 2), (2, 3)\}$ be two relations on set $A = \{(1, 2, 3)\}$. Then, RoS is equal
(a) $\{(2, 3), (3, 2), (2, 2)\}$ (b) $\{(1, 3), (2, 2), (3, 2), (2, 1), (2, 3)\}$
(c) $\{(3, 2), (1, 3)\}$ (d) $\{(2, 3) (3, 2)\}$

4. If X and Y are two sets, then $X \cap (Y \cap X)'$ equals
(a) X (b) Y
(c) ϕ (d) None of these

5. For real numbers x and y, we write $x R y \Leftrightarrow x - y + \sqrt{2}$ is an irrational number. Then, the relation R is
(a) reflexive (b) symmetric
(c) transitive (d) None of these

6. Let $f(x) = (x+1)^2 - 1, (x \geq -1)$. Then, the set $S = \{x : f(x) = f^{-1}(x)\}$ is
(a) $\left\{0, -1, \frac{-3 + i\sqrt{3}}{2}, \frac{-3 - i\sqrt{3}}{2}\right\}, i = \sqrt{-1}$
(b) $\{0, 1, -1\}$
(c) $\{0, -1\}$
(d) empty

7. The number of elements of the power set of a set containing n elements is
(a) 2^{n-1} (b) 2^n (c) $2^n - 1$ (d) 2^{n+1}

8. Which one of the following is not true?
(a) $A - B \subseteq A$ (b) $B' - A' \subseteq A$
(c) $A \subseteq A - B$ (d) $A \cap B' \subseteq A$

9. If $A = \{1, 2, 3\}$ and $B = \{3, 8\}$, then $(A \cup B) \times (A \cap B)$ is
(a) $\{(3, 1), (3, 2), (3, 3), (3, 8)\}$ (b) $\{(1, 3), (2, 3), (3, 3), (8, 3)\}$
(c) $\{(1, 2), (2, 2), (3, 3), (8, 8)\}$ (d) $\{(8, 3), (8, 2), (8, 1), (8, 8)\}$

10. Let $A = \{p, q, r\}$. Which of the following is not an equivalence relation on A?
(a) $R_1 = \{(p, q), (q, r), (p, r), (p, p)\}$
(b) $R_2 = \{(r, q), (r, p), (r, r), (q, q)\}$
(c) $R_3 = \{(p, p), (q, q), (r, r), (p, q)\}$
(d) None of the above

11. Let $A = \{x : x$ is a multiple of 3$\}$ and $B = \{x : x$ is a multiple of 5$\}$, then $A \cap B$ is given by
(a) $\{3, 6, 9\}$ (b) $\{5, 10, 15, 20, \ldots\}$
(c) $\{15, 30, 45, \ldots\}$ (d) None of these

12. Let $A = \{1, 2, 3\}$, $B = \{3, 4\}$ and $C = \{4, 5, 6\}$, then $A \cup (B \cap C)$ is
(a) $\{3\}$ (b) $\{1, 2, 3, 4\}$
(c) $\{1, 2, 5, 6\}$ (d) $\{1, 2, 3, 4, 5, 6\}$

13. If $A = \{2, 4\}$ and $B = \{3, 4, 5\}$, then $(A \cap B) \times (A \cup B)$ is
(a) $\{(2, 2), (3, 4), (4, 2), (5, 4)\}$
(b) $\{(2, 3), (4, 3), (4, 5)\}$
(c) $\{(2, 4), (3, 4), (4, 4), (4, 5)\}$
(d) $\{(4, 2), (4, 3), (4, 4), (4, 5)\}$

14. Which of the following is the empty set?
(a) $\{x : x$ is a real number and $x^2 - 1 = 0\}$
(b) $\{x : x$ is a real number and $x^2 + 1 = 0\}$
(c) $\{x : x$ is a real number and $x^2 - 9 = 0\}$
(d) $\{x : x$ is a real number and $x^2 = x + 2\}$

15. n/m means that n is factor of m, then the relation f is
(a) reflexive and symmetric
(b) transitive and symmetric
(c) reflexive, transitive and symmetric
(d) reflexive, transitive and not symmetric

16. Let A and B be two non-empty subsets of set X such that A is not a subset of B, then
(a) A is a subset of the complement of B
(b) B is a subset of A
(c) A and B are disjoint
(d) A and the complement of B are non-disjoint

17. Let R be a relation defined by $R = \{(a, b) : a \geq b\}$, where a and b are real numbers, then R is
(a) reflexive, symmetric and transitive
(b) reflexive, transitive but not symmetric
(c) symmetric, transitive but not reflexive
(d) neither transitive, nor reflexive, not symmetric

18. If sets A and B are defined as
$A=\{(x, y): y=e^{x}, x \in R\}$ and $B=\{(x, y): y=x, x \in R\}$.
(a) $B \subset A$
(b) $A \subset B$
(c) $A \cap B=\phi$
(d) $A \cup B$

19. Let R and S be two non-void relations on a set A. Which of the following statement is false?
(a) R and S are transitive $\Rightarrow R \cup S$ is transitive.
(b) R and S are transitive $\Rightarrow R \cap S$ is symmetric.
(c) R and S are symmetric $\Rightarrow R \cup S$ is symmetric.
(d) R and S are reflexive $\Rightarrow R \cap S$ is reflexive.

20. If $X=\{4^{n}-3n-1: n \in N\}$ and $Y=\{9(n-1): n=N\}$, where N is the set of natural numbers, then $X \cup Y$ is equal to
(a) X
(b) Y
(c) N
(d) $Y-X$

21. Let A and B be two sets containing four and two elements, respectively. Then, the number of subsets of the set $A \times B$, each having atleast three elements is
(a) 275
(b) 510
(c) 219
(d) 256

22. Let W denotes the words in the English dictionary. Define the relation R by $R=\{(x, y) \in W \times W\}$ the words x and y have atleast one letter in common, then R is
(a) not reflexive, symmetric and transitive
(b) reflexive, symmetric and not transitive
(c) reflexive, symmetric and transitive
(d) reflexive, not symmetric and transitive

Numerical Value Type Questions

23. Let $S=\{1,2,3,4\}$. The total number of unordered pair of disjoint subsets of S is equal to ....

24. Let A and B be two sets containing 2 elements and 4 elements, respectively. The number of subsets of $A \times B$ having 3 or more elements, is ....

25. In a survey of 200 students of higher secondary school, it was found that 120 studied Mathematics; 90 studies Physics and 70 studied Chemistry; 40 studied Mathematics and Physics; 3 studied Physics and Chemistry; 50 studied Chemistry and Mathematics and 20 studied none of these subjects. The number of students who studied all the three subjects is ....

26. If $n(A)=4$, $n(B)=8$ and $A \subseteq B$, then the number of elements in $A \cup B$ is equal to ....

27. Two finite sets have m and n $(m>n)$ elements. The number of subsets of the first set is 112 more than that of the second set. The value of $mn+m-n$ is ....

28. Let $S=\{1,2,3, \ldots, 100\}$. The number of non-empty subsets A of S such that the product of elements in A is even is $2^{\alpha}-2^{\beta}$, then $\alpha-\beta$ is ....

29. Let $S=\{x \in R: x \geq 0\}$ and $2|\sqrt{x}-3|+\sqrt{x}(\sqrt{x}-6)+6=0$. Then, total number of elements of S is ....

30. Let Z be the set of integers. If
$A=\{x \in Z: 2^{(x+2)(x^{2}-5x+6)}=1)\}$ and
$B=\{x \in Z:-3<2x-1<9\}$, such that number of subsets of the set $A \times B$ is $2^{3\alpha}$, then α is equal to ....

31. Suppose $A_{1}, A_{2}, \ldots A_{30}$ are thirty sets each with five elements and $B_{1}, B_{2}, \ldots B_{n}$ are sets each with three elements. Let $\bigcup_{i=1}^{30} A_{i}=\bigcup_{j=1}^{n} B_{j}=S$. Assume that each element of S belongs to exactly ten of the A_{i}'s and to exactly nine of the B_{j}'s. Then, the value of n is ....

32. Let $R=\{(P, Q): P$ and Q are at the same distance from the origin$\}$ be a relation, such that the equivalence class of $(3,-3)$ is the set $S=\{(x, y): x^{2}+y^{2}=a\sqrt{b}\}$, then ab is equal to ....

33. Given the relation $R=\{(1,3),(3,2),(2,1)\}$ on the set $A=\{1,2,3\}$, the minimum number of ordered pairs which can be added to R to make it an equivalence relation, is ....

Previous Year Questions

34. Let $A=\{n \in[100,700] \cap N: n$ is neither a multiple of 3 nor a multiple of 4$\}$. Then, the number of elements in A is **[Single Correct Type, 2024 Main]**
(a) 300
(b) 280
(c) 310
(d) 290

35. Let $S=\{x \in R:(\sqrt{3}+\sqrt{2})^{x}+(\sqrt{3}-\sqrt{2})^{x}=10\}$. Then, the number of elements in S, is
[Single Correct Type, 2024 Main]
(a) 0
(b) 1
(c) 4
(d) 2

36. Let A and B be two finite sets with m and n elements, respectively. The total number of subsets of the set A is 56 more than the total number of subsets of B. Then, the distance of the point $P(m, n)$ from the point $Q(-2,-3)$ is
[Single Correct Type, 2024 Main]
(a) 6
(b) 10
(c) 4
(d) 8

37. Let a relation R on $N \times N$ be defined as:
$(x_{1}, y_{1}) R(x_{2}, y_{2})$ if and only if $x_{1} \leq x_{2}$ or $y_{1} \leq y_{2}$.
Consider the two statements :
I : R is reflexive but not symmetric.
II : R is transitive
Then, which one of the following is true?
[Single Correct Type, 2024 Main]
(a) Only I is correct.
(b) Only II is correct.
(c) Neither I nor II is correct.
(d) Both I and II are correct.

38. If R is the smallest equivalence relation on the set $\{1, 2, 3, 4\}$ such that $\{(1, 2), (1, 3)\} \subset R$, then the number of elements in R is **[Single Correct Type, 2024 Main]**

(a) 15 (b) 10 (c) 8 (d) 12

39. Let R be a relation on $Z \times Z$ defined by $(a, b) R (c, d)$ if and only if $ad - bc$ is divisible by 5. Then, R is **[Single Correct Type, 2024 Main]**

(a) Reflexive but neither symmetric nor transitive
(b) Reflexive and transitive but not symmetric
(c) Reflexive, symmetric and transitive
(d) Reflexive and symmetric but not transitive

40. Let $S = \{1, 2, 3, ..., 10\}$. Suppose M is the set of all the subsets of S, then the relation $R = \{(A, B) : A \cap B \neq \phi;\ A, B \in M\}$ is **[Single Correct Type, 2024 Main]**

(a) symmetric only
(b) symmetric and reflexive only
(c) reflexive only
(d) symmetric and transitive only

41. Let $A = \{2, 3, 6, 8, 9, 11\}$ and $B = \{1, 4, 5, 10, 15\}$. Let R be a relation on $A \times B$ defined by $(a, b) R (c, d)$ if and only if $3ad - 7bc$ is an even integer. Then, the relation R is **[Single Correct Type, 2024 Main]**

(a) an equivalence relation.
(b) reflexive but not symmetric.
(c) transitive but not symmetric.
(d) reflexive and symmetric but not transitive.

42. Let $A = \{1, 2, 3, 4, 5\}$. Let R be a relation on A defined by xRy if and only if $4x \leq 5y$. Let m be the number of elements in R and n be the minimum number of elements from $A \times A$ that are required to be added to R to make it a symmetric relation. Then, $m + n$ is equal to **[Single Correct Type, 2024 Main]**

(a) 26 (b) 23 (c) 24 (d) 25

43. Let the relations R_1 and R_2 on the set $X = \{1, 2, 3, \ldots, 20\}$ be given by $R_1 = \{(x, y) : 2x - 3y = 2\}$ and $R_2 = \{(x, y) : -5x + 4y = 0\}$. If M and N be the minimum number of elements required to be added in R_1 and R_2, respectively, in order to make the relations symmetric, then $M + N$ equals **[Single Correct Type, 2024 Main]**

(a) 16 (b) 10
(c) 12 (d) 8

44. Consider the relations R_1 and R_2 defined as $aR_1b \Leftrightarrow a^2 + b^2 = 1$ for all $a, b \in R$ and $(a, b) R_2 (c, d) \Leftrightarrow a + d = b + c$ for all $(a, b), (c, d) \in N \times N$. Then, **[Single Correct Type, 2024 Main]**

(a) only R_1 is an equivalence relation
(b) only R_2 is an equivalence relation
(c) R_1 and R_2 both are equivalence relations
(d) neither R_1 nor R_2 is an equivalence relation

45. In a survey of 220 students of a higher secondary school, it was found that atleast 125 and atmost 130 students studied Mathematics; atleast 85 and atmost 95 studied Physics; atleast 75 and atmost 90 studied Chemistry; 30 studied both Physics and Chemistry; 50 studied both Chemistry and Mathematics; 40 studied both Mathematics and Physics and 10 studied none of these subjects. Let m and n respectively be the least and the most number of students who studied all the three subjects. Then, $m + n$ is equal to .... **[Numerical Value Type, 2024 Main]**

46. A group of 40 students appeared in an examination of 3 subjects — Mathematics, Physics and Chemistry. It was found that all students passed in atleast one of the subjects, 20 students passed in Mathematics, 25 students passed in Physics, 16 students passed in Chemistry, atmost 11 students passed in both Mathematics and Physics, atmost 15 students passed in both Physics and Chemistry, atmost 15 students passed in both Mathematics and Chemistry. The maximum number of students passed in all the three subjects is .... **[Numerical Value Type, 2024 Main]**

47. Let $A = \{1, 2, 3, ..., 100\}$. Let R be a relation on A defined by $(x, y) \in R$ if and only if $2x = 3y$. Let R_1 be a symmetric relation on A such that $R \subset R_1$ and the number of elements in R_1 is n. Then, the minimum value of n is .... **[Numerical Value Type, 2024 Main]**

48. Let $A = \{1, 2, 3, 4\}$ and $R = \{(1, 2), (2, 3), (1, 4)\}$ be a relation on A. Let S be the equivalence relation on A such that $R \subset S$ and the number of elements in S is n. Then, the minimum value of n is .... **[Numerical Value Type, 2024 Main]**

49. The number of symmetric relations defined on the set $\{1, 2, 3, 4\}$ which are not reflexive is .... **[Numerical Value Type, 2024 Main]**

50. An organisation awarded 48 medals in event 'A', 25 in event 'B' and 18 in event 'C'. If these medals went to total 60 men and only five men got medals in all the three events, then how many received medals in exactly two of three events? **[Single Correct Type, 2023 Main]**

(a) 10 (b) 9
(c) 21 (d) 15

51. Let $A = \{1, 2, 3, 4, 5, 6, 7\}$. Then, the relation $R = \{(x, y) \in A \times A : x + y = 7\}$ is **[Single Correct Type, 2023 Main]**

(a) reflexive but neither symmetric nor transitive
(b) an equivalence relation
(c) transitive but neither symmetric nor reflexive
(d) symmetric but neither reflexive nor transitive

52. Let $P(S)$ denote the power set of $S = \{1, 2, 3, \ldots, 10\}$. Define the relations R_1 and R_2 on $P(S)$ as AR_1B, if $(A \cap B^c) \cup (B \cap A^c) = \phi$ and AR_2B, if $A \cup B^c = B \cup A^c$, $\forall A, B \in P(S)$. Then, **[Single Correct Type, 2023 Main]**
(a) only R_1 is an equivalence relation
(b) Both R_1 and R_2 are not equivalence relations
(c) only R_2 is an equivalence relation
(d) Both R_1 and R_2 are equivalence relations

53. Let R be a relation defined on N as $a\,R\,b$, if $2a + 3b$ is a multiple of 5, $a, b \in N$. Then, R is
[Single Correct Type, 2023 Main]
(a) symmetric but not transitive
(b) an equivalence relation
(c) transitive but not symmetric
(d) Not reflexive

54. Let $A = \{1, 3, 4, 6, 9\}$ and $B = \{2, 4, 5, 8, 10\}$. Let R be a relation defined on $A \times B$, such that $R = \{(a_1, b_1), (a_2, b_2) : a_1 \le b_2 \text{ and } b_1 \le a_2\}$. Then, the number of elements in the set R is
[Single Correct Type, 2023 Main]
(a) 180 (b) 52 (c) 160 (d) 26

55. Let $A = \{2, 3, 4\}$ and $B = \{8, 9, 12\}$. Then, the number of elements in the relation $R = \{((a_1, b_1), (a_2, b_2)) \in (A \times B, A \times B) : a_1$ divides b_2 and a_2 divides $b_1\}$ is
[Single Correct Type, 2023 Main]
(a) 24 (b) 18 (c) 36 (d) 12

56. Among the relations $S = \{(a, b) : a, b \in R - \{0\}, 2 + \frac{a}{b} > 0\}$ and $T = \{(a, b) : a, b \in R, a^2 - b^2 \in Z\}$, **[Single Correct Type, 2023 Main]**
(a) both S and T are symmetric
(b) T is symmetric but S is not
(c) S is transitive but T is not
(d) neither S nor T is transitive

57. The minimum number of elements that must be added to the relation $R = \{(a, b), (b, c)\}$ on the set $\{a, b, c\}$, so that it becomes symmetric and transitive is
[Single Correct Type, 2023 Main]
(a) 4 (b) 5 (c) 3 (d) 7

58. The relation $R = \{(a, b) : \gcd(a, b) = 1, 2a \ne b, a, b \in Z\}$ is
[Single Correct Type, 2023 Main]
(a) Neither symmetric nor transitive
(b) reflexive but not symmetric
(c) symmetric but not transitive
(d) transitive but not reflexive

59. Let R be a relation on R, given by $R = \{(a, b) : 3a - 3b + \sqrt{7}$ is an irrational number$\}$. Then, R is **[Single Correct Type, 2023 Main]**
(a) an equivalence relation
(b) reflexive and transitive but not symmetric
(c) reflexive and symmetric but not transitive
(d) reflexive but neither symmetric nor transitive

60. Let R be a relation of $N \times N$ defined by $(a, b)\,R\,(c, d)$, if and only if $ad(b - c) = bc(a - d)$. Then, R is
[Single Correct Type, 2023 Main]
(a) transitive but neither reflexive nor symmetric
(b) symmetric and transitive but not reflexive
(c) symmetric but neither reflexive nor transitive
(d) reflexive and symmetric but not transitive

61. The number of elements in the set $\{n \in N : 10 \le n \le 100$ and $3^n - 3$ is a multiple of $7\}$ is ....
[Numerical Value Type, 2023 Main]

62. Let $\lambda \in R$ and let the equation E be $|x|^2 - 2|x| + |\lambda - 3| = 0$. Then, the largest element in the set $S = \{x + \lambda : x$ is an integer solution of $E\}$ is ....
[Numerical Value Type, 2023 Main]

63. Let $A = \{1, 2, 3, 4\}$ and R be a relation on the set $A \times A$ defined by $R = \{((a, b), (c, d)) : 2a + 3b = 4c + 5d\}$. Then the number of elements in R is ....
[Numerical Value Type, 2023 Main]

64. Let $A = \{-4, -3, -2, 0, 1, 3, 4\}$ and $R = \{(a, b) \in A \times A : b = |a|$ or $b^2 = a + 1\}$ be a relation on A. Then, the minimum number of elements, that must be added to the relation R so that it becomes reflexive and symmetric, is .... **[Numerical Value Type, 2023 Main]**

65. The number of relations, on the set $\{1, 2, 3\}$ containing $(1, 2)$ and $(2, 3)$, which are reflexive and transitive but not symmetric, is .... **[Numerical Value Type, 2023 Main]**

66. Let $A = \{0, 3, 4, 6, 7, 8, 9, 10\}$ and R be the relation defined on A such that $R = \{(x, y) \in A \times A : x - y$ is odd positive integer or $x - y = 2\}$. The minimum number of elements that must be added to the relation R, so that it is a symmetric relation, is equal to ....
[Numerical Value Type, 2023 Main]

67. Let $A = \{1, 2, 3, 4, \ldots, 10\}$ and $B = \{0, 1, 2, 3, 4\}$. The number of elements in the relation $R = \{(a, b) \in A \times A : 2(a - b)^2 + 3(a - b) \in B\}$ is ....
[Numerical Value Type, 2023 Main]

68. The minimum number of elements that must be added to the relation $R = \{(a, b), (b, c), (b, d)\}$ on the set $\{a, b, c, d\}$, so that it is an equivalence relation, is ....
[Numerical Value Type, 2023 Main]

69. Let $A = \{x \in R : |x + 1| < 2\}$ and $B = \{x \in R : |x - 1| \ge 2\}$. Then, which one of the following statements is NOT true? **[Single Correct Type, 2022 Main]**
(a) $A - B = (-1, 1)$
(b) $B - A = R - (-3, 1)$
(c) $A \cap B = (-3, -1]$
(d) $A \cup B = R - [1, 3)$

70. Let $S = \left\{ x \in [-6, 3] - \{-2, 2\} : \frac{|x+3| - 1}{|x| - 2} \geq 0 \right\}$ and $T = \{x \in Z : x^2 - 7|x| + 9 \leq 0\}$. Then, the number of elements in $S \cap T$ is **[Single Correct Type, 2022 Main]**

(a) 7 (b) 5 (c) 4 (d) 3

71. Let R be a relation from the set $\{1, 2, 3, \ldots\ldots, 60\}$ to itself such that $R = \{(a, b) : b = pq$, where $p, q \geq 3$ are prime numbers$\}$. Then, the number of elements in R is **[Single Correct Type, 2022 Main]**

(a) 600 (b) 660 (c) 540 (d) 720

72. Let a set $A = A_1 \cup A_2 \cup \ldots \cup A_k$, where $A_i \cap A_j = \phi$ for $i \neq j, 1 \leq i, j \leq k$. Define the relation R from A to A by $R = \{(x, y) : y \in A_i$, if and only if $x \in A_i, 1 \leq i \leq k\}$. Then, R is **[Single Correct Type, 2022 Main]**

(a) reflexive, symmetric but not transitive
(b) reflexive, transitive but not symmetric
(c) reflexive but not symmetric and transitive
(d) an equivalence relation

73. Let $R_1 = \{(a, b) \in N \times N : |a - b| \leq 13\}$ and $R_2 = \{(a, b) \in N \times N : |a - b| \neq 13\}$. Then, on N **[Single Correct Type, 2022 Main]**

(a) Both R_1 and R_2 are equivalence relations
(b) Neither R_1 nor R_2 is an equivalence relation
(c) R_1 is an equivalence relation but R_2 is not
(d) R_2 is an equivalence relation but R_1 is not

74. Let R_1 and R_2 be two relations defined on R by $a R_1 b \Leftrightarrow ab \geq 0$ and $a R_2 b \Leftrightarrow a \geq b$. Then, **[Single Correct Type, 2022 Main]**

(a) R_1 is an equivalence relation but not R_2
(b) R_2 is an equivalence relation but not R_1
(c) Both R_1 and R_2 are equivalence relations
(d) Neither R_1 nor R_2 is an equivalence relation

75. For $\alpha \in N$, consider a relation R on N given by $R = \{(x, y) : 3x + \alpha y$ is a multiple of $7\}$. The relation R is an equivalence relation, if and only if **[Single Correct Type, 2022 Main]**

(a) $\alpha = 14$
(b) α is a multiple of 4
(c) 4 is the remainder when α is divided by 10
(d) 4 is the remainder when α is divided by 7

76. Let $S = \{4, 6, 9\}$ and $T = \{9, 10, 11, \ldots, 1000\}$. If $A = \{a_1 + a_2 + \ldots + a_k : k \in N, a_1, a_2, a_3, \ldots, a_k \in S\}$, then the sum of all the elements in the set $T - A$ is equal to .... **[Numerical Value Type, 2022 Main]**

77. Let $A = \{1, 2, 3, 4, 5, 6, 7\}$ and $B = \{3, 6, 7, 9\}$, Then, the number of elements in the set $\{C \subseteq A : C \cap B \neq \phi\}$ is .... **[Numerical Value Type, 2022 Main]**

78. Let $A : \{1, 2, 3, 4, 5, 6, 7\}$. Define $B = \{T \subseteq A :$ either $1 \notin T$ or $2 \in T\}$ and $C = \{T \subseteq A : T$ the sum of all the elements of T is a prime number$\}$. Then, the number of elements in the set $B \cup C$ is .... **[Numerical Value Type, 2022 Main]**

79. Let $A = \{n \in N : \text{HCF}(n, 45) = 1\}$ and $B = \{2k : k \in \{1, 2, \ldots, 100\}\}$. Then, the sum of all the elements of $A \cap B$ is .... **[Numerical Value Type, 2022 Main]**

80. The sum of all the elements of the set $\{\alpha \in \{1, 2, \ldots, 100\} : \text{HCF}(\alpha, 24) = 1\}$ is .... **[Numerical Value Type, 2022 Main]**

81. Out of all the patients in a hospital 89% are found to be suffering from heart ailment and 98% are suffering from lungs infection. If K% of them are suffering from both ailments, then K can not belong to the set **[Single Correct Type, 2021 Main]**

(a) $\{80, 83, 86, 89\}$ (b) $\{84, 86, 88, 90\}$
(c) $\{79, 81, 83, 85\}$ (d) $\{84, 87, 90, 93\}$

82. Let S_1, S_2 and S_3 be three sets defined as $S_1 = \{z \in C : |z - 1| \leq \sqrt{2}\}$, $S_2 = \{z \in C : \text{Re}((1 - i)z) \geq 1\}$ and $S_3 = \{z \in C : \text{Im}(z) \leq 1\}$. Then, the set $S_1 \cap S_2 \cap S_3$ **[Single Correct Type, 2021 Main]**

(a) has exactly two elements
(b) has infinitely many points
(c) has exactly three elements
(d) is a singleton

83. In a school, there are three types of games to be played. Some of the students play two types of games, but none plays all the three games. Which Venn diagram can justify the above statement? **[Single Correct Type, 2021 Main]**

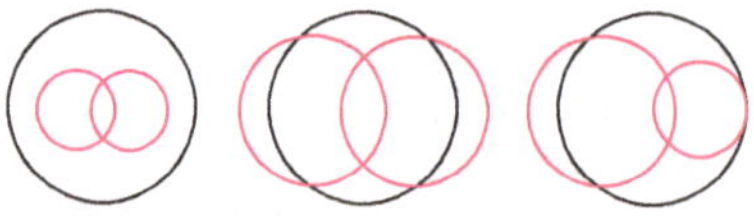

(P) (Q) (R)

(a) P and Q (b) P and R
(c) Q and R (d) None of these

84. Let Z be the set of all integers,

$A = \{(x, y) \in Z \times Z : (x - 2)^2 + y^2 \leq 4\}$,

$B = \{(x, y) \in Z \times Z : x^2 + y^2 \leq 4\}$ and

$C = \{(x, y) \in Z \times Z : (x - 2)^2 + (y - 2)^2 \leq 4\}$

If the total number of relations from $A \cap B$ to $A \cap C$ is 2^P, then the value of P is **[Single Correct Type, 2021 Main]**

(a) 25 (b) 9
(c) 16 (d) 49

85. Let $A = \{(x, y) \in R \times R \mid 2x^2 + 2y^2 - 2x - 2y = 1\}$, $B = \{(x, y) \in R \times R \mid 4x^2 + 4y^2 - 16y + 7 = 0\}$ and $C = \{(x, y) \in R \times R \mid x^2 + y^2 - 4x - 2y + 5 \le r^2\}$. Then, the minimum value of $|r|$ such that $A \cup B \subseteq C$ is equal to **[Single Correct Type, 2021 Main]**

(a) $1 + \sqrt{5}$ (b) $\frac{3 + 2\sqrt{5}}{2}$

(c) $\frac{3 + \sqrt{10}}{2}$ (d) $\frac{2 + \sqrt{10}}{2}$

86. Which of the following is not correct for relation R on the set of real numbers ? **[Single Correct Type, 2021 Main]**

(a) $(x, y) \in R \Leftrightarrow 0 < |x| - |y| \le 1$ is neither transitive nor symmetric.

(b) $(x, y) \in R \Leftrightarrow 0 < |x - y| \le 1$ is symmetric and transitive.

(c) $(x, y) \in R \Leftrightarrow |x| - |y| \le 1$ is reflexive but not symmetric.

(d) $(x, y) \in R \Leftrightarrow |x - y| \le 1$ is reflexive and symmetric.

87. Let $A = \{2, 3, 4, 5, \ldots, 30\}$ and R be an equivalence relation on $A \times A$, defined by $(a, b) = (c, d)$, if and only if $ad = bc$. Then, the number of ordered pairs, which satisfy this equivalence relation with ordered pair (4, 3) is equal to **[Single Correct Type, 2021 Main]**

(a) 5 (b) 6 (c) 8 (d) 7

88. Let N be the set of natural numbers and a relation R on N be defined by $R = \{(x, y) \in N \times N : x^3 - 3x^2y - xy^2 + 3y^3 = 0\}$. Then, the relation R is **[Single Correct Type, 2021 Main]**

(a) symmetric but neither reflexive nor transitive.

(b) reflexive but neither symmetric nor transitive.

(c) reflexive and symmetric, but not transitive.

(d) an equivalence relation.

89. Define a relation R over a class of $n \times n$ real matrices A and B as "ARB, if there exists a non-singular matrix P such that $PAP^{-1} = B$". Then, which of the following is true ? **[Single Correct Type, 2021 Main]**

(a) R is symmetric, transitive but not reflexive.

(b) R is reflexive, symmetric but not transitive.

(c) R is an equivalence relation.

(d) R is reflexive, transitive but not symmetric.

90. Let $R = \{(P, Q) \mid, P$ and Q are at the same distance from the origin$\}$ be a relation, then the equivalence class of $(1, -1)$ is the set **[Single Correct Type, 2021 Main]**

(a) $S = \{(x, y) \mid x^2 + y^2 = 4\}$ (b) $S = \{(x, y) \mid x^2 + y^2 = 1\}$

(c) $S = \{(x, y) \mid x^2 + y^2 = \sqrt{2}\}$ (d) $S = \{(x, y) \mid x^2 + y^2 = 2\}$

91. If $A = \{x \in R : |x - 2| > 1\}$, $B = \{x \in R : \sqrt{x^2 - 3} > 1\}$ and $C = \{x \in R : |x - 4| \ge 2\}$ and Z is the set of all integers, then the number of subsets of the set $(A \cap B \cap C)^C \cap Z$ is .... **[Numerical Value Type, 2021 Main]**

92. Let $A = \{n \in N \mid n^2 \le n + 10000\}$, $B = \{3k + 1 \mid k \in N\}$ and $C = \{2k \mid k \in N\}$, then the sum of all the elements of the set $A \cap (B - C)$ is equal to .... **[Numerical Value Type, 2021 Main]**

93. Let $A = \{n \in N : n$ is a 3-digit number$\}$, $B = \{9k + 2 : k \in N\}$ and $C = \{9k + l : k \in N\}$ for some $l (0 < l < 9)$. If the sum of all the elements of the set $A \cap (B \cup C)$ is 274×400, then l is equal to .... **[Numerical Value Type, 2021 Main]**

94. Let $\bigcup_{i=1}^{50} X_i = \bigcup_{i=1}^{n} Y_i = T$, where each X_i contains 10 elements and each Y_i contains 5 elements. If each element of the set T is an element of exactly 20 of sets X_i's and exactly 6 of sets Y_i's, then n is equal to **[Single Correct Type, 2020 Main]**

(a) 50 (b) 15 (c) 45 (d) 30

95. Consider the two sets $A = \{m \in R :$ both the roots of $x^2 - (m+1)x + m + 4 = 0$ are real$\}$ and $B = [-3, 5)$. Which of the following is not true? **[Single Correct Type, 2020 Main]**

(a) $A - B = (-\infty, -3) \cup [5, \infty)$

(b) $A \cap B = \{-3\}$

(c) $B - A = (-3, 5]$

(d) $A \cup B = R$

96. A survey shows that 63% of the people in a city read newspaper A whereas 76% read newspaper (B). If x% of the people read both the newspapers, then a possible value of x can be **[Single Correct Type, 2020 Main]**

(a) 55 (b) 29

(c) 65 (d) 37

97. Let $X = \{n \in N : 1 \le n \le 50\}$. If $A = \{n \in X : n$ is multiple of 2$\}$ and $B = \{n \in X : n$ is a multiple of 7$\}$, then the number of elements in the smallest subset of X containing both A and B is .... **[Numerical Value Type, 2020 Main]**

EXERCISE 2

JEE Advanced Pattern

Single Option Correct Type Questions

1. Let R and S be two non-void relations on a set A. Which of the following statement is false?
(a) R and S are transitive $\Rightarrow R \cup S$ is transitive
(b) R and S are transitive $\Rightarrow R \cap S$ is symmetric
(c) R and S are symmetric $\Rightarrow R \cup S$ is symmetric
(d) R and S are reflexive $\Rightarrow R \cap S$ is reflexive

2. Two finite sets have m and n $(m > n)$ elements. The number of subsets of the first set is 112 more than that of the second set. The value of mn is
(a) 18 (b) 28 (c) 32 (d) 36

3. Let U be the universal set and $A \cup B \cup C = U$, then $[(A - B) \cup (B - C) \cup (C - A)]'$ equals
(a) $A \cup B \cup C$ (b) $A \cap B \cap C$
(c) $A \cup (B \cap C)$ (d) $A \cap (B \cup C)$

4. Let $S = \{1, 2, 3, 4\}$. The total number of unordered pairs of disjoint subsets of S is equal to
(a) 25 (b) 34 (c) 42 (d) 41

5. In statistical survey of 1003 families of Kolkata it was found that 63 families has neither a radio nor a TV, 794 families has a radio and 187 has TV. The number of families in that group having both a radio and TV is
(a) 36 (b) 41
(c) 32 (d) None of these

6. In a class of 140 students numbered 1 to 140, all even numbered students opted Mathematics course, those whose number is divisible by 3 opted Physics course and those whose number is divisible by 5 opted Chemistry course. Then, the number of students who did not opt for any of the three courses is
(a) 102 (b) 42 (c) 1 (d) 38

7. If $n(A) = 3$, $n(B) = 6$ and $A \subseteq B$, then the number of elements in $A \cup B$ is equal to
(a) 3 (b) 9
(c) 6 (d) None of these

8. If the sets A and B are defined as

$$A = \left\{(x, y) \mid y = \frac{1}{x}, x \neq 0, x \in R\right\}$$

and $B = \{(x, y) \mid y = -x, x \in R\}$, then
(a) $A \cap B = A$ (b) $A \cap B = B$
(c) $A \cap B = \phi$ (d) $A \cup B = A$

9. If $aN = \{ax : x \in N\}$, then the set $4N \cap 6N$ is
(a) $8N$ (b) $10N$
(c) $12N$ (d) None of these

10. $\frac{n}{m}$ means that n is a factor of m, then the relation f is
(a) reflexive and symmetric
(b) transitive and symmetric
(c) reflexive, transitive and symmetric
(d) reflexive, transitive but not symmetric

More than One Correct Option Type Questions

11. Let L be the set of all straight lines in the Euclidean plane. Two lines l_1 and l_2 are said to be related by the relation R iff l_1 is parallel to l_2. Then, the relation R is
(a) reflexive (b) symmetric
(c) transitive (d) equivalence

12. Let $X = \{1, 2, 3, 4, 5\}$ and $Y = \{1, 3, 5, 7, 9\}$. Which of the following is/are relations from X to Y?
(a) $R_1 = \{(x, y) : y = 2 + x, x \in X, y \in Y\}$
(b) $R_2 = \{(1, 1), (2, 1), (3, 3), (4, 3), (5, 5)\}$
(c) $R_3 = \{(1, 1), (1, 3), (3, 5), (3, 7), (5, 7)\}$
(d) $R_4 = \{(1, 3), (2, 5), (2, 4), (7, 9)\}$

13. Let the relation S in the R of real numbers defined as $S = \{(x, y) : x, y \in R \text{ and } x \leq y^3\}$. Which of the following statement is incorrect for relations?
(a) reflexive (b) symmetric
(c) transitive (d) None of these

Passage Based Questions

Passage I

(Q. Nos. 14 and 15)

- R_1 on Z defined by $(a, b) \in R_1$ iff $|a - b| \leq 7$, R_2 on Q defined by $(a, b) \in R_2$ iff $ab = 4$ and R_3 on R defined by $(a, b) \in R_3$ iff $a^2 - 4ab + 3ab^2 = 0$.

14. Relation R_1 is
(a) reflexive and symmetric (b) symmetric and transitive
(c) reflexive and transitive (d) equivalence

15. Relation R_2 is
(a) reflexive (b) symmetric
(c) transitive (d) equivalence

Stem Based Questions

Stem I

(Q. Nos. 16 and 17)

- In a group of children, 35 play football out of which 20 play football only, 22 play hockey; 25 play cricket out of which 11 play cricket only. Out of these 7 play cricket and football but not hockey, 3 play football and hockey but not cricket and 12 play football and cricket both.

16. Number of player who play all the three games, is ....

17. Number of player who play cricket and hockey but not football, is ....

Single Integer Type Questions

18. In a group of 45 students, 22 can speak Hindi only and 12 can speak English only . If $(2\lambda + 1)$ student can speak both Hindi and English, the value of λ is ....

19. If $A = \left\{ x \mid \cos x > -\frac{1}{2} \text{ and } 0 \le x \le \pi \right\}$ and

$B = \left\{ x \mid \sin x > \frac{1}{2} \text{ and } \frac{\pi}{3} \le x \le \pi \right\}$ and if $\pi\lambda \le A \cap B < \pi\mu$, the value of $(\lambda + \mu)$ is ....

20. If $S = R$, $A = \{x : -3 \le x < 7\}$ and $B = \{x : 0 < x < 10\}$, the number of positive integers in $A \Delta B$ is ....

21. Two finite sets have m and n elements. The total number of subsets of the first set is 48 more than the total number of subsets of the second set. The value of $m - n$ is ....

22. If two sets A and B are having 99 elements in common, the number of elements common to each of the sets $A \times B$ and $B \times A$ are $121\lambda^2$, the value of λ is ....

Numerical Value Type Questions

23. The number of reflexive relation are possible in a set $A = \{1, 2, 3\}$ is ....

24. Let X be the set consisting of the first 2025 terms of the arithmetic progression 1, 6, 11, ... and Y be the set consisting of the first 2025 terms of the arithmetic progression 9, 16, 23, ... Then the number of elements in $X \cup Y$ is ....

25. In a certain city, only two newspapers A and B are published. It is known that 25% of the city population read A and 20% read B, while 8% read both. It is also known that 30% of those who read A but not B, look into advertisements and 40% of those who read B not A, look into advertisements while 50% of those who reads both A and B look into the advertisements. If x% of the population read an advertisements. Then, the value of x is ....

26. Given the relation $R = \{(1, 2), (2, 3)\}$ on the set $A = \{1, 2, 3\}$, the minimum number of ordered pairs which can be added to R to make it an equivalence relation, is λ. Then, λ^2 is ....

Matching Type Questions

27. Match the Column I with Column II.

	Column I		Column II
A.	If X and Y are two sets, then $X \cap (X \cup Y)^C$ equal to	p.	C
B.	The set $(A \cap B')' \cup (B \cap C)$ is equal to	q.	ϕ
C.	For sets A and B, $(A \cup B)' \cup (A' \cap B)$ is equal to	r.	$A' \cup B$
D.	Let A, B and C are subsets of set X. Then $(A' + B' \cup C) \cup (B \cap C) \cup (A \cap C)$ is equal to	s.	A'

EXERCISE 3

Challenging Problems

1. If $U = \{x : x^5 - 6x^4 + 11x^3 - 6x^2 = 0\}$, $A = \{x : x^2 - 5x + 6 = 0\}$ and $B = \{x : x^2 - 3x + 2 = 0\}$, then find the value of $n(A \cap B)'$.
2. Let U be the set of all people and $M = \{\text{Males}\}$, $S = \{\text{College students}\}$, $T = \{\text{Teenagers}\}$, $W = \{\text{People having height more than five feet}\}$. Express each of the following in the notation of set theory.
   (i) College student having heights more than five feet.
   (ii) People who are not teenagers and have their height less five feet.
   (iii) All people who are neither males nor teenagers nor college students.
3. The set X consists of all points within and on the unit circle $x^2 + y^2 = 1$, whereas the set Y consists of all points on and inside the rectangular boundary $x = 0$, $x = 1$, $y = -1$ and $y = 1$. Determine $X \cup Y$ and $X \cap Y$. Illustrate your answer by diagrams.
4. Of the members of three athletic team in a certain school, 21 are on the basketball team, 26 on the hockey team and 29 on the football team. 14 play hockey and basketball, 15 play hockey and football, 12 play football and basketball and 8 play all the three games. How many members are there in all?
5. In a survey of population of 450 people, it is found that 205 can speak English, 210 can speak Hindi and 120 people can speak Tamil. If 100 people can speak both Hindi and English; 80 people can speak both English and Tamil, 35 people can speak Hindi and Tamil and 20 people can speak all the three languages, find the number of people who can speak English but not a Hindi or Tamil. Find also the number of people who can speak neither English nor Hindi nor Tamil.
6. A group of 123 workers went to a canteen for cold drinks, ice-cream and tea, 42 workers took ice-cream, 36 tea and 30 cold drinks. 15 workers purchased ice-cream and tea, 10 ice-cream and cold drinks, and 4 cold drinks and tea but not ice-cream, 11 took ice-cream and tea but not cold drinks. Determine how many workers did not purchase anything?
7. R_1 on Z defined by $(a, b) \in R_1$, iff $|a - b| \leq 7$, R_2 on Q defined by $(a, b) \in R_2$, iff $ab = 4$ and R_3 on R defined by $(a, b) \in R_3$, iff $a^2 - 4ab + 3b^2 = 0$. Find whether relation R_1, R_2 and R_3 are reflexive, symmetric and transitive.
8. N is the set of positive integers. The relation R is defined on $N \times N$ as follows:
   $$(a, b)\, R\, (c, d) \Leftrightarrow ad = bc$$
   Prove that R is an equivalence relation.
9. The following relations are defined on the set of real numbers.
   (i) $a\, R\, b \Leftrightarrow |a - b| > 0$
   (ii) $a\, R\, b \Leftrightarrow |a| = |b|$
   (iii) $a\, R\, b \Leftrightarrow |a| \geq |b|$
   (iv) $a\, R\, b \Leftrightarrow 1 + ab > 0$
   (v) $a\, R\, b \Leftrightarrow |a| \leq b$
   Find whether these relations are reflexive, symmetric or transitive.

Answer Key

■ Exercise 1

1. (a)	2. (a)	3. (a)	4. (d)	5. (a)	6. (c)	7. (b)	8. (c)	9. (b)	10. (d)
11. (c)	12. (b)	13. (d)	14. (b)	15. (d)	16. (d)	17. (b)	18. (c)	19. (a)	20. (b)
21. (c)	22. (b)	23. (41)	24. (219)	25. (20)	26. (8)	27. (31)	28. (50)	29. (2)	30. (5)
31. (45)	32. (6)	33. (6)	34. (a)	35. (d)	36. (b)	37. (d)	38. (b)	39. (d)	40. (a)
41. (d)	42. (d)	43. (b)	44. (b)	45. (45)	46. (10)	47. (66)	48. (16)	49. (960)	50. (c)
51. (d)	52. (d)	53. (b)	54. (c)	55. (c)	56. (b)	57. (d)	58. (a)	59. (d)	60. (c)
61. (15)	62. (5)	63. (5)	64. (7)	65. (4)	66. (19)	67. (18)	68. (9)	69. (b)	70. (d)
71. (b)	72. (d)	73. (b)	74. (d)	75. (d)	76. (11)	77. (112)	78. (107)	79. (5264)	80. (1633)
81. (c)	82. (b)	83. (c)	84. (a)	85. (b)	86. (b)	87. (d)	88. (b)	89. (c)	90. (d)
91. (256)	92. (832)	93. (5)	94. (d)	95. (c)	96. (a)	97. (29)			

■ Exercise 2

1. (a)	2. (b)	3. (b)	4. (d)	5. (b)	6. (d)	7. (c)	8. (c)	9. (c)	10. (d)
11. (a,b,c,d)	12. (b,c)	13. (a,b,c)	14. (a)	15. (b)	16. (5)	17. (2)	18. (5)	19. (1)	20. (3)
21. (2)	22. (9)	23. (64)	24. (3761)	25. (13.9)	26. (49)	27. (A) $\rightarrow$ q, (B) $\rightarrow$ r, (C) $\rightarrow$ s, (D) $\rightarrow$ p			

Solutions

Exercise 1 - JEE Main Pattern

1. By Venn diagram,

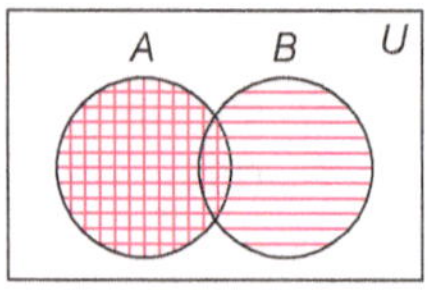

It is clear that $A \cap (A \cup B) = A$

2.

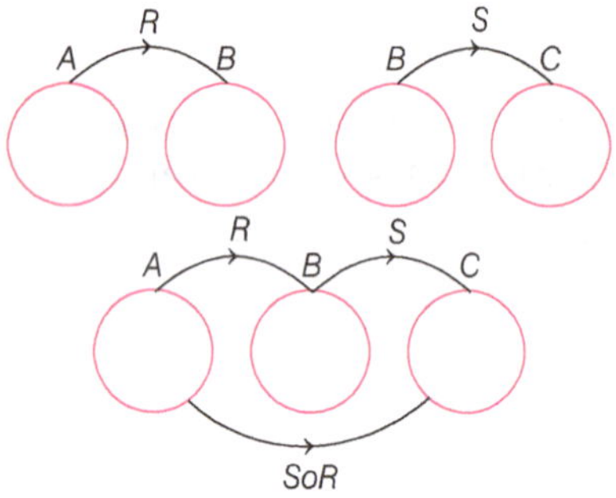

SoR is the relation from A to C.

3. $R = \{(1, 3), (2, 2), (3, 2)\}$

$S = \{(2, 1), (3, 2), (2, 3)\}$

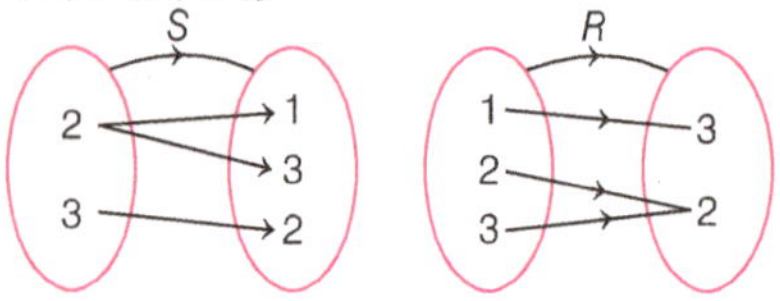

$$RoS = \{(2, 3), (2, 2), (3, 2)\}$$

4. $X \cap (Y \cap X)' = X \cap (Y' \cup X')$

$$= (X \cap Y') \cup (X \cap X')$$

$$= (X \cap Y') \cup \phi = X \cap Y' = X - (X \cap Y)$$

5. $xRy \Leftrightarrow (x - y + \sqrt{2})$ is an irrational number.

Let $(x, x) \in R$.

Then, $x - x + \sqrt{2} = \sqrt{2}$ which is an irrational number.

$\therefore \quad x\,R\,x, \forall\, x \in R$

$\therefore$ R is an reflexive relation.

$x\,R\,y \Rightarrow (x - y + \sqrt{2})$ is an irrational number.

$\Rightarrow -(y - x - \sqrt{2})$ is an irrational number.

$\Rightarrow (y - x - \sqrt{2})$ is an irrational number.

$y\,R\,x \Rightarrow (y - x + \sqrt{2})$ is an irrational number.

So, $xRy \not\Rightarrow yRx$

$\therefore R$ is not a symmetric relation.

Let $(1, 2) \in R$, then $(1 - 2 + \sqrt{2})$ is an irrational number.

$\Rightarrow \qquad (\sqrt{2} - 1)$ is an irrational number.

and $(2, 3) \in R$, then $(2 \;\; - 3 + \sqrt{2})$ is an irrational number.

$\Rightarrow \qquad (\sqrt{2} - 1)$ is an irrational number.

$(1, 3) \in R \Rightarrow (1 - 3 + \sqrt{2})$ is an irrational number.

$\Rightarrow \qquad (\sqrt{2} - 2)$ is an irrational number.

So, $(1, 2) \in R$ and $(2, 3) \in R \not\Rightarrow (1, 3) \in R$ (by any way)

$\therefore$ R is not transitive relation.

6. $f(x) = (x + 1)^2 - 1 \qquad [\because x \geq 1]$

$$= x^2 + 1 + 2x - 1 = x^2 + 2x$$

$$S = \{x : f(x) = f^{-1}(x)\}$$

S is the set of point of intersection of $(y = x)$ and $f(x)$.

Now, solve $\qquad y = x$ and $f(x) = x^2 + 2x$

$$x^2 + 2x = x$$

$$x^2 + x = 0$$

$$x(x + 1) = 0$$

$$x = 0 \text{ or } x = -1$$

7. Let set A contains n elements.

Power set of A is the set of all subsets.

$\therefore$ Number of subsets of $A = {}^nC_o + {}^nC_1 + {}^nC_2 + \ldots + {}^nC_n = 2^n$

$\therefore$ Power set of A contains 2^n elements.

8. By venn diagram, it is clear that

$A - B \subseteq A$ and $B' - A' \subseteq A$ and $A \cap B' \subseteq A$

but $A \not\subseteq A - B$

9. $A = \{1, 2, 3\}$

$$B = \{3, 8\}$$

$$A \cup B = \{1, 2, 3, 8\}$$

$$A \cap B = \{3\}$$

$$(A \cup B) \times (A \cap B) = \{1, 2, 3, 8\} \times \{3\}$$

$$= \{(1, 3), (2, 3), (3, 3)\ (8, 3)\}$$

10. $A = \{p, q, r\}$

$R_1 = \{(p, q), (q, r), (p, r), (p, p)\}$

$(q, q) \notin R_1$, so R_1 is not reflexive relation.

So, R_1 is not an equivalence relation.

$$R_2 = \{(r, q), (r, p), (r, r), (q, q)\}$$

Here, $(p, p) \notin R_2$, so R_2 is not reflexive relation.

So, R_2 is not an equivalence relation.

$$R_3 = \{(p, p), (q, q), (r, r), (p, q)\}$$

R_3 is an reflexive relation.

$$(p, q) \in R_3 \text{ but } (q, p) \notin R_3$$

R_3 is not symmetric relation.

So, R_3 is not equivalence relation.

11. $A = \{x : x \text{ is a multiple of } 3\}$

$A = \{x : x = 3m, m \in N\}$

$B = \{x : x \text{ is a multiple of } 5\}$

$B = \{x : x = 5n, n \in N\}$

$A \cap B = \{x : x \text{ is a multiple of both 3 and 5}\}$

$= \{15, 30, 45, \ldots\}$

12. $A = \{1, 2, 3\}, B = \{3, 4\}, C = \{4, 5, 6\}$

$\Rightarrow \quad B \cap C = \{4\}$

and $A \cup (B \cap C) = \{1, 2, 3, 4\}$

13.
$$A = \{2, 4\}$$
$$B = \{3, 4, 5\}$$
$$A \cap B = \{4\}$$
$$A \cup B = \{2, 3, 4, 5\}$$
$$(A \cap B) \times (A \cup B) = \{(4, 2), (4, 3), (4, 4), (4, 5)\}$$

14.
$$x^2 - 1 = 0 \Rightarrow x = -1, 1$$

$\therefore$ x is real.
$$x^2 + 1 = 0 \Rightarrow x = \pm i$$

$\therefore$ x is not real.
$$x^2 - 9 = 0 \Rightarrow x = \pm 3$$

$\therefore$ x is real.
$$x^2 - x - 2 = 0 \Rightarrow x = 2, -1$$

$\therefore$ x is real.

15. $\frac{n}{m}$ means that n is a factor of m.

So, f is reflexive.

$\because$ A number is a factor of itself.

Now, if n is a factor of m, then m is not a factor of n

$\therefore$ f is not symmetric. Let n is a factor of m and m is a factor of s, then it is true that n is a factor of s.

$\therefore$ f is transitive.

16. Let $X = \{1, 2, 3, 4, 5\}$

$A, B \subset X$

Let $A = \{1, 2\}, B = \{1, 4, 5\}$

So, $A \not\subseteq B$

(a) $B' = \{2, 3\}$

So, $A \neq B'$

So, option (a) is incorrect.

(b) $5 \notin A$

So, $B \not\subseteq A$

So, option (b) is incorrect.

(c) $A \cap B = \{1\} \neq \phi$

So, option (c) is incorrect.

(d) $A \cap B' = \{2\} \neq \phi$

So, A and B' are always non-disjoint.

So, option (d) is correct.

17. $R = \{(a, b) : a \geq b\}$

We know that, $a \geq a$

$\therefore \quad (a, a) \in R, \forall a \in R$

R is a reflexive relation.

Let $(a, b) \in R$

$\Rightarrow \quad a \geq b$

$\not\Rightarrow \quad b \geq a$

$\not\Rightarrow \quad (b, a) \in R$

So, R is not symmetric relation.

Now, let $(a, b) \in R$ and $(b, c) \in R$.

$\Rightarrow \quad a \geq b$ and $b \geq c$

$\Rightarrow \quad a \geq c \Rightarrow (a, c) \in R$

$\therefore$ R is a transitive relation.

18. $A = \{(x, y) : y = e^x, x \in R\}$

$B = \{(x, y) : y = x, x \in R\}$

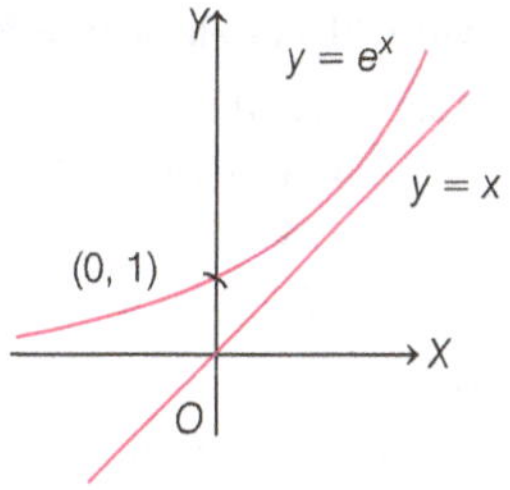

From figure, it can be observed that both the curves have no point of intersection for all $x \in R$.

$\therefore \quad A \cap B = \phi$

19. Let $A = \{1, 2, 3\}, R = \{(1, 1) (1, 2)\}$

and $S = \{(2, 2), (2, 3)\}$

be the transitive relation on A.

Then, $R \cup S = \{(1, 1,) (1, 2)(2, 2) (2, 3)\}$

$R \cup S$ is not transitive, because $(1, 2) \in R \cup S$ and $(2, 3) \in R \cup S$ but $(1, 3) \notin R \cup S$.

20. Since, $4^n - 3n - 1 = (1 + 3)^n - 3n - 1$

$= (1 + {}^nC_1 \cdot 3 + {}^nC_2 \cdot 3^2 + {}^nC_3 \cdot 3^3 + \ldots + {}^nC_n \cdot 3^n) - 3n - 1$

$= 3^2({}^nC_2 + {}^nC_3 \cdot 3 + \ldots + {}^nC_n \cdot 3^{n-2})$

$\Rightarrow 4^n - 3n - 1$ is a multiple of 9 for $n \geq 2$

For $n = 1, 4^n - 3n - 1 = 4 - 3 - 1 = 0$

For $n = 2, 4^n - 3n - 1 = 16 - 6 - 1 = 9$

$\therefore$ $4^n - 3n - 1$ is multiple of 9 for all $n \in N$.

It is clear that X contains elements, which are multiples of 9 and Y contains all multiples of 9.

$\therefore X \subseteq Y$ i.e. $X \cup Y = Y$

21. $n(A) = 4, n(B) = 2 \Rightarrow n(A \times B) = 8$

The number of subsets of $A \times B$ having at least three elements

$= {}^8C_3 + {}^8C_4 + {}^8C_5 + \ldots + {}^8C_8 = 2^8 - ({}^8C_0 + {}^8C_1 + {}^8C_2)$

$= 256 - (1 + 8 + 28) = 219$

22. Clearly, $(x, x) \in R, \forall x \in W$

So, R is reflexive.

Let $(x, y) \in R$, then $(y, x) \in R$ as x and y have atleast one letter in common. So, R is symmetric. But R is not transitive.

e.g. Let x = INDIA, y = MUMBAI and z = JUHU

Then, $(x, y) \in R$ and $(y, z) \in R$ but $(x, z) \notin R$

23. For disjoint sets, $A \cap B = \phi$

Each element in either A or B or neither.

$\therefore$ Total ways $= 3^4 = 81$; $A = B$ iff $A = B = \phi$

Otherwise, A and B are interchangable

$\therefore$ Number of unordered pair for disoint subsets of

$$S = \frac{3^4 + 1}{2} = 41$$

24. Since, $A \times B$ has 8 elements.

$\therefore$ Number of subsets $= 2^8 = 256$

Number of subsets with zero element $= {}^8C_0 = 1$

Number of subsets with one element $= {}^8C_1 = 8$

Number of subsets with one elements $= {}^8C_2 = 28$

Hence, number of subsets of $A \times B$ having 3 or more elements

$$= 256 - (1 + 8 + 28)$$
$$= 256 - 37$$
$$= 219$$

25. $a + e + f + g = 120$ ...(i)

$b + d + f + g = 90$ ...(ii)

$e + f + c + d = 70$ ...(iii)

$g + f = 40$ ...(iv)

$f + d = 30$ ...(v)

$e + f = 50$ ...(vi)

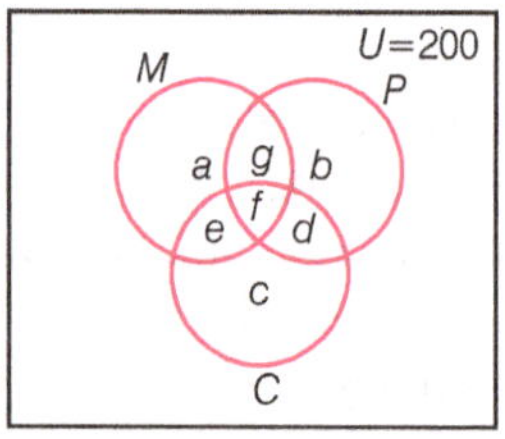

$U - (a + b + c + d + e + f + g) = 20$

$\Rightarrow \quad a + b + c + d + e + f + g = 180$ ...(vii)

From Eqs. (i) and (iv), $a + e = 80$ ...(viii)

From Eqs. (ii) and (iv), $b + d = 50$ ...(ix)

From Eqs. (iii) and (v), $e + c = 40$ ...(x)

from Eqs (viii), (ix) and (x), $a + b + c + d + e + e = 197$ ...(xi)

from (xi), (vii) and (iv), $197 - e + 40 = 180$

$170 - e + 40 = 180$

$e = 210 - 180 = 30$

From Eq. (vi), $e + f = 50$

$\Rightarrow \quad 30 + f = 50$

$\Rightarrow \quad f = 20$

26. Since, $A \subseteq B \Rightarrow A \cup B = B$

$\therefore \ n(A \cup B) = n(B) = 8$ [given]

Hence, the number of elements in $A \cup B$ is 8.

27. According to the question,

$$2^m - 2^n = 112$$

$\Rightarrow \quad 2^n(2^{m-n} - 1) = 2^4 \times 7$

On comparing both sides, we get

$$2^n = 2^4$$

$\Rightarrow \quad n = 4$

and $\quad 2^{m-n} - 1 = 7$

$\Rightarrow \quad 2^{m-n} = 2^3$

$\Rightarrow \quad m - n = 3$

$\Rightarrow \quad m - 4 = 3$

$\therefore \quad m = 7$

$\therefore \quad mn + m - n = 7 \times 4 + 7 - 4$

$= 35 - 4 = 31$

28. Product of two even numbers is always even and product of two odd numbers is always odd.

$\therefore$Number of required subsets

= Total number of subsets

− Total number of subsets having only odd

$= 2^{100} - 2^{50}$

$\Rightarrow \quad 2^{100} - 2^{50} = 2^{\alpha} - 2^{\beta}$

$\Rightarrow \quad \alpha = 100$ and $\beta = 50$ [on comparing both sides]

$\therefore \quad \alpha - \beta = 100 - 50 = 50$

29. **Case I** When $x \in [0, 9]$

$$2(3 - \sqrt{x}) + x - 6\sqrt{x} + 6 = 0$$

$\Rightarrow \quad x - 8\sqrt{x} + 12 = 0$

$\Rightarrow \quad \sqrt{x} = 6, 2$

$\Rightarrow \quad x = 36, 4$

$\therefore \quad x = 4$ $[\because x \in [0, 9]]$

Case II When $x \in [9, \infty)$

$$2(\sqrt{x} - 3) + x - 6\sqrt{x} + 6 = 0$$

$\Rightarrow \quad x - 4\sqrt{x} = 0$

$\Rightarrow \quad x = 16, 0$

$\Rightarrow \quad x = 16$ $[\because x \in [9, \infty)]$

Hence, $x = 4, 16$

$\therefore$ Total number of elements is 2.

30. Given, set $A = \{x \in Z : 2^{(x+2)(x^2 - 5x + 6)} = 1\}$

Consider, $2^{(x+2)(x^2 - 5x + 6)} = 1 = 2^0$

$\Rightarrow \quad (x + 2)(x^2 - 5x + 6) = 0$

$\Rightarrow \quad (x + 2)(x - 3)(x - 2) = 0$

$\Rightarrow \quad x = -2, 2, 3$

$\Rightarrow \quad A = \{-2, 2, 3\}$

Also, $B = \{x \in Z, -3 < 2x - 1 < 9\}$

Consider, $-3 < 2x - 1 < 9, x \in Z$

$\Rightarrow \quad -2 < 2x < 10, x \in Z$

$\Rightarrow -1 < x < 5, x \in Z$

$\Rightarrow \quad B = \{0, 1, 2, 3, 4\}$

So, $A \times B$ has 15 elements.

$\therefore$ Number of subsets of $A \times B = 2^{15} = 2^{3\alpha}$

$$\Rightarrow \quad 3\alpha = 15$$

$$\Rightarrow \quad \alpha = 5$$

31. Given that $\bigcup_{i=1}^{30} A_i = \bigcup_{j=1}^{n} B_j = S$

and each A_i's contain 5 elements.

So, total number of elements in $A_i = 5 \times 30 = 150$.

$\because$ Each element of S belongs to exactly 10 of the A_i's

$$\therefore \quad n(S) = n\left\{\bigcup_{i=1}^{30} A_i\right\} = \frac{150}{10} = 15$$

Now, each B_j's contains 3 elements

So, total number of elements in $B_j = 3 \times n = 3n$

$\because$ Each elements of S belongs to exactly nine of the B_j's

$$\therefore \quad n(S) = n\left\{\bigcup_{j=1}^{n} B_j\right\} = \frac{3n}{9}$$

$$\Rightarrow \quad \frac{3n}{9} = 15$$

$$\Rightarrow \quad n = 45$$

32. Let $P(a, b)$ and $Q(c, d)$ are any two points.

Given, $\quad OP = OQ$

i.e. $\quad \sqrt{a^2 + b^2} = \sqrt{c^2 + d^2}$

Squaring on both sides, we get

$$a^2 + b^2 = c^2 + d^2$$

$$R = \{((a, b), (c, d)) : a^2 + b^2 = c^2 + d^2\}$$

$R(x, y), S(3, -3), OR = OS$ (Equivalence class)

$$\Rightarrow \quad OR = OS$$

$$\Rightarrow \quad \sqrt{x^2 + y^2} = \sqrt{9 + 9}$$

$$\Rightarrow \quad x^2 + y^2 = 18 = 3\sqrt{2} = a\sqrt{b}$$

On comparing, we get $a = 3$ and $b = 2$

$$\therefore \quad ab = 3 \times 2 = 6$$

33. R is reflexive, if it contains (1, 1), (2, 2), (3, 3)

$\because$ $(1, 3) \in R, (3, 2) \in R, (2, 1) \in R$

$\therefore R$ is symmetric if $(3, 1) \in R, (2, 3) \in R, (1, 2) \in R$

Now, $R = \{(1, 1), (2, 2), (3, 3), (1, 3), (3, 2), (2, 1), (3, 1), (2, 3), (1, 2)\}$

$\therefore R$ is transitive.

Thus, R becomes an equivalence relation by adding

(1, 1), (2, 2), (3, 3), (3, 1), (2, 3), (1, 2)

Hence, total number of ordered pair is 6.

34. Total element = 601

(Natural number between [100, 700])

Let set P denotes number multiple of 3 and set Q denotes number multiple of 4.

Now, according to the question, we need

$$n(\bar{P} \cap \bar{Q})$$

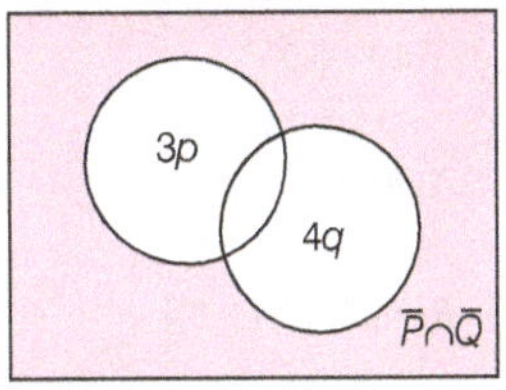

$\Rightarrow$ By De-Morgan's law

$$n(\bar{P} \cap \bar{Q}) = n(\overline{P \cup Q})$$

Now, $\quad n(P) = 200$

$[\because 700 \geq (102 + (n-1)3$ and $700 \geq (100 + (m-1)4)]$

$$n(Q) = 151$$

$n(P \cap Q) = 50 \qquad [\because 700 \geq (104 + (r-1)12)]$

$$\Rightarrow \quad n(P \cup Q) = n(P) + n(Q) - n(P \cap Q) = 200 + 151 - 50 = 301$$

$$\Rightarrow \quad n(\overline{P \cup Q}) = 601 - 301 = 300 = n(\bar{P} \cap \bar{Q})$$

$\therefore$ Number of elements in set A is 300.

35. Given, $(\sqrt{3} + \sqrt{2})^x + (\sqrt{3} - \sqrt{2})^x = 10$

Let $\quad (\sqrt{3} + \sqrt{2})^x = t$

$$\Rightarrow \quad (\sqrt{3} - \sqrt{2})^x = \frac{1}{t}$$

$$\Rightarrow \quad t + \frac{1}{t} = 10$$

$$\Rightarrow \quad t^2 - 10t + 1 = 0$$

$$\Rightarrow \quad t = \frac{10 \pm \sqrt{96}}{2} = 5 \pm 2\sqrt{6}$$

$$\Rightarrow \quad (\sqrt{3} + \sqrt{2})^x = (\sqrt{3} \pm \sqrt{2})^2$$

$$x = \pm 2$$

$\therefore$ Number of solution = 2

36. Given, $n(A) = m$ and $n(B) = n$

$\therefore$ Number of subsets of $A = 2^m$

and number of subsets of $B = 2^n$

According to the question,

$$2^m - 2^n = 56$$

$$\Rightarrow \quad 2^m - 2^n = 2^6 - 2^3$$

$$\Rightarrow \quad m = 6 \text{ and } n = 3$$

So, distance between the points $P(m, n)$, i.e. $P(6, 3)$ and $Q(-2, -3)$ is given by

$$\sqrt{(6+2)^2 + (3+3)^2} = \sqrt{64 + 36} = \sqrt{100} = 10$$

37. $(x_1, y_1)\ R(x_2, y_2) \Rightarrow x_1 \le x_2$ or $y_1 \le y_2$

For $(x_1, y_1), (x_1, y_1)$

$\Rightarrow x_1 \le x_1$ or $y_1 \le y_1$ which is true for all natural number.

$\therefore R$ is reflexive.

$$(1, 1)R(2, 3) \text{ but } ((2, 3), (1, 1)) \notin R$$

$\therefore R$ is not symmetric.

For transitive $x_1 < x_2, y_1 < y_2$

$x_2 < x_3, y_2 < y_3$

$\therefore \quad x_1 < x_3$ and $y_1 < y_3$

R is transitive.

38. $A = \{1, 2, 3, 4\}, \ R = \{(1, 2), (1, 3)\}$

For reflexive,

We need to have (1, 1), (2, 2), (3, 3), (4, 4)

For symmetric $\quad (1, 2) \in R$

$\Rightarrow \quad (2, 1) \in R$

$\Rightarrow \quad (1, 3) \in R$

$\Rightarrow \quad (3, 1) \in R$

$\therefore$ R becomes $\{(1, 1), (2, 2), (3, 3), (4, 4), (1, 2), (2, 1), (1, 3), (3, 1)\}$

Now, (3, 1) and (1, 2) both belongs to R

So, for transitive (3, 2) must be on R.

$\therefore$ (3, 2) must be added.

Again, for symmetric (2, 3) also be an element

$\therefore$ $R = \{(1, 1)\ (2, 2)\ (3, 3)\ (4, 4)\ (1, 2)\ (2, 1)\ (1, 3)\ (3, 1)\ (3, 2)\ (2, 3)\}$

$\therefore$ Number of elements in $R = 10$

39. Given, $(a, b)\ R\ (c, d)$

Such that $ad - bc$ is divisible by 5

For reflexive, $(a, b)\ R\ (a, b)$

$\Rightarrow ab - ba = 0$ which is divisible by 5

$\Rightarrow R$ is reflexive

For symmetric, $(a, b)\ R\ (c, d)$

$\Rightarrow$ $ad - bc$ is divisible by 5

$\Rightarrow$ $-(ad - bc)$ is divisible by 5

$\Rightarrow$ $cb - da$ is divisible by 5

$\Rightarrow$ $(c, d)\ R\ (a, b)$

$\Rightarrow$ R is symmetric

For transitive, $(1, 3)\ R\ (5, 20)$ and $(5, 20)\ R\ (3, 1)$

but (1, 3) is not related to (3, 1)

So, R is not transitive.

40. Given, $S = \{1, 2, 3, 4, \dots, 10\}$

and $\quad R = \{(A, B) : A \cap B \ne \phi ; A, B \in M\}$

To check Reflexivity

M is subset of 'S' as question said.

So, $\quad \phi \in M$

for $\quad \phi \cap \phi = \phi$

$\Rightarrow$ but relation is $A \cap B \ne \phi$

So, it is not reflexive.

To check Symmetricity

$$ARB \Rightarrow A \cap B \ne \phi$$

$$BRA \Rightarrow B \cap A \ne \phi$$

So, it is symmetric.

To check Transitivity

If $\quad A = \{1, 2\}$

$B = \{2, 3\ 4)\}$

$C = \{4, 5, 6)\}$

ARB and BRC but A does not related to C i.e. ARC.

So, it is not transitive.

41. $A = \{2, 3, 6, 8, 9, 11\}$,

$B = \{1, 4, 5, 10, 15\}$

Reflexive $(a, b)\ R\ (a, b)$

So, $3ad - 7bc$

$\Rightarrow 3ab - 7ba = -4ab$ always even

So, it is reflexive

Symmetric If $3ad - 7bc =$ even

Case I odd odd

Case II even even

$(c, d)\ R\ (a, b) \Rightarrow 3bc - 7ad$

So, symmetric relation.

Transitive Set $(3, 4)\ R(6, 4)$ satisfy relation

Set $(6, 4)\ R\ (3, 1)$ satisfy relation

But $(3, 4)\ R\ (3, 1)$ does not satisfy relation

So, it is not transitive. Hence, reflexive and symmetric but not transitive.

42. Given, $A = \{1, 2, 3, 4, 5\}$

Relation R on A is defined as xRy iff $4x \le 5y$

Now, for $x = 1, y \ge \frac{4}{5}$

and for $x = 2, y \ge \frac{8}{5}$ ... so on.

$\therefore R = \{(1, 1), (1, 2), (1, 3), (1, 4), (1, 5), (2, 2), (2, 3), (2, 4), (2, 5),$
$(3, 3), (3, 4), (3, 5), (4, 4), (4, 5), (5, 4), (5, 5)\}$

According to the question, $m = 16$

Now, for R to be symmetric, we will have to add

For $(1, 2) \in R$, (2, 1) has to be added

For $(1, 3) \in R$, (3, 1) has to be added

For $(1, 4) \in R$, (4, 1) has to be added

For $(1, 5) \in R$, (5, 1) has to be added

For $(2, 3) \in R$, (3, 2) has to be added

For $(2, 4) \in R$, (4, 2) has to be added

For $(2, 5) \in R$, (5, 2) has to be added

For $(3, 4) \in R$, (4, 3) has to be added

For $(3, 5) \in R$, (5, 3) has to be added

$n = 9$

$\Rightarrow m + n = 25$

43. According to the question,

Set $X = \{1, 2, 3, \dots, 20\}$

Now, $R_1 = \{(x, y) : 2x - 3y = 2\}$

$$\Rightarrow \quad y = \frac{2x - 2}{3}$$

Here, numerator is always even and denominator is 3, so numerator have to be multiple of 3 to get natural number.

So, $R_1 = \{(4, 2), (7, 4), (10, 6), (13, 8), (16, 10), (19, 12)\}$

Minimum number of elements needs to be added to make

R_1 symmetric $= 6$

So, $M = 6$

Now, $R_2 = \{(x, y) : -5x + 4y = 0\}$

$\Rightarrow \quad y = \dfrac{5}{4}x$

$\Rightarrow x$ must be multiple of 4

$\therefore \quad R_2 = \{(4, 5), (8, 10), (12, 15), (16, 20)\}$

Minimum number of elements needs to be added to make

R_2 symmetric $= 4$

So, $N = 4$

$\therefore \quad M + N = 6 + 4 = 10$

44. We have, $a\, R_1\, b \Leftrightarrow a^2 + b^2 = 1, \forall\, a, b \in R$

For reflexive, $a = b$

$\Rightarrow \quad a^2 + a^2 = 1$

$a = \pm \dfrac{1}{\sqrt{2}}$

$\therefore$ Only $\left(\dfrac{1}{\sqrt{2}}, \dfrac{1}{\sqrt{2}}\right)$ and $\left(-\dfrac{1}{\sqrt{2}}, \dfrac{-1}{\sqrt{2}}\right)$ will be present in R_1.

So, R_1 is not reflexive and not equivalence.

Now, $(a,b)\, R_2 (c, d)$

$\Leftrightarrow a + d = b + c\ \forall\, (a, b), (c,d) \in N \times N$

Checking reflexive, put $a = b = c = d$

$\Rightarrow \quad a + a = a + a$

Which is satisfied $\forall$ ordered pair$\in N \times N$

$\therefore R_2$ is reflexive.

Checking for symmetric.

Let suppose $((a, b), (c,d))$ be in R_2

So, $\quad a + d = b + c \quad$ ...(i)

To check $((c,d), (a, b))$ lies in R_2

Eq. (i) can be written as

$c + b = d + a$

$\therefore R_2$ is symmetric.

Checking for transitive,

Let suppose $((a, b),(c,d))$ and $((c, d), (e, f))$ are in R_2

So, $\quad a + d = b + c \quad$ ...(ii)

and $\quad c + f = d + e \quad$ ...(iii)

Adding Eqs. (ii) and (iii), we get

$a + f = b + e$

$\therefore ((a, b), (e, f))$ also in R_2.

$\therefore R_2$ is also transitive.

So, R_2 is equivalence.

45. According to question,

$125 \le m + 90 - x \le 130$

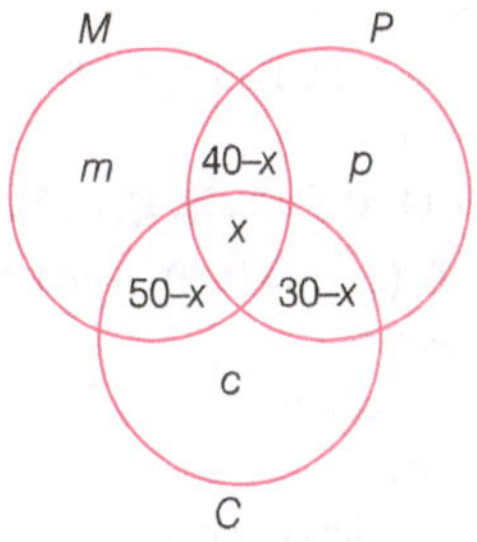

$85 \le p + 70 - x \le 95$

$75 \le c + 80 - x \le 90$

$m + p + c + 120 - 2x = 210$

$\Rightarrow \quad 15 \le x \le 45$

and $\quad 30 - x \ge 0$

$\Rightarrow \quad 15 \le x \le 30$

Hence, $30 + 15 = 45$

46. Given, $n(M \cup P \cup C) = 40$,

We have, $x = n(P \cap M \cap C)$

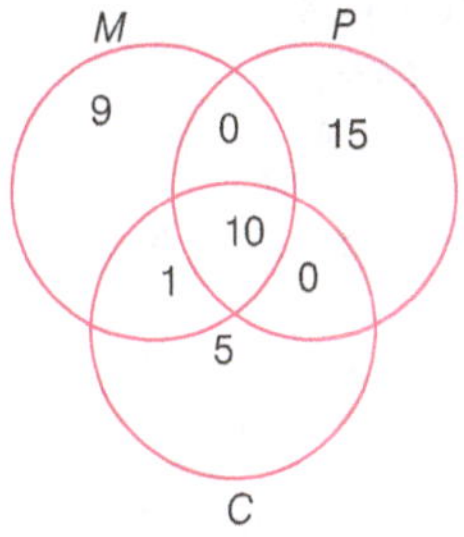

Now, $11 - n(P \cap M \cap C) \ge 0$

$\Rightarrow \quad n(P \cap M \cap C) \le 11$

Which does not satisfy the data.

So, $n(P \cap M \cap C) = 10$

Hence, maximum number of students passed in all the three subjects is 10.

47. $A = \{1, 2, 3, \ldots, 100\}$

$(x, y) \in R$ and $2x = 3y$

Then, $R = \{(3, 2), (6, 4), (9, 6), (12, 8), \ldots, (99, 66)\}$

Number of elements in $R = 33$

R_1 be a symmetric relation on A such that $R \subset R_1$

$\therefore R_1 = \{(3, 2), (2, 3), (6, 4), (4, 6), \ldots (99, 66), (66, 99)\}$

So minimum number of elements in

$R_1 = 66$

So, $\quad n = 66$

48. $A = \{1, 2, 3, 4\}$

$R = \{(1, 2), (2, 3), (1, 4)\}$

Now, for making R to be equivalence we have to make it reflexive, symmetric and transitive.

For reflexive add,

$(1, 1)\ (2, 2)\ (3, 3)\ (4, 4)$

For symmetric add,

$$(2, 1)\ (3, 2)\ (4, 1)$$

R becomes

$\{(1, 1), (2, 2), (3, 3), (4, 4), (1, 2), (2, 1), (2, 3), (3, 2), (1, 4), (4, 1)\}$

For transitive, $(1, 2), (2, 3) \Rightarrow (1, 3)$ so add it.

$(3, 1) \rightarrow$ for symmetric

$(4, 1), (1, 2) = (4, 2)$ so add it

$(2, 4) \rightarrow$ for symmetric

$\therefore$ To make R an equivalence, we have to add all possible doublet

$$n(R) = 4 \times 4 = 16$$

49. Total number of symmetric relation which are no reflective

$$= 2^{\frac{n^2+n}{2}} - 2^{\frac{n^2-n}{2}}$$

$$= 2^{\frac{16+4}{2}} - 2^{\frac{16-4}{2}} = 2^{10} - 2^{6}$$

$$= 1024 - 64 = 960$$

50. We have, $n(A) = 48,$

$n(B) = 25, n(C) = 18$

$n(A \cup B \cup C) = 60$

and $n(A \cap B \cap C) = 5$

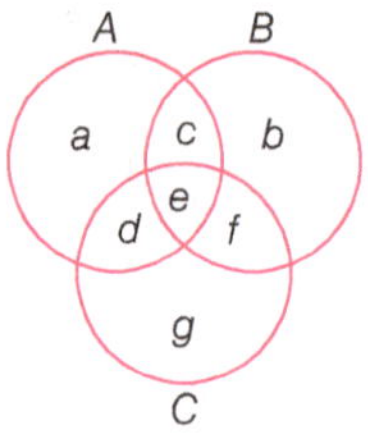

$$e = 5,$$

$$a + c + e + d = 48$$

$\Rightarrow \quad a + c + d = 43 \quad$ ...(i)

$$b + c + e + f = 25$$

$\Rightarrow \quad b + c + f = 20 \quad$ ...(ii)

$$d + e + f + g = 18$$

$\Rightarrow \quad d + f + g = 13 \quad$ ...(iii)

$$a + b + c + d + e + f + g = 60$$

$\Rightarrow \quad a + b + c + d + f + g = 55 \quad$ ...(iv)

Adding Eqs. (i), (ii) and (iii),

$a + b + 2c + 2d + 2f + g = 76 \quad$ ...(v)

Subtract Eq. (iv) from Eq. (v), we get

$$c + d + f = 21$$

$\therefore$ Number of men who received exactly 2 medals $= c + d + f$

$$= 21$$

Alternate Solution

We have, $n(A) = 48$, $n(B) = 25, n(C) = 18$

$n(A \cup B \cup C) = 60$ and $(A \cap B \cap C) = 5$

Number of medals in exactly two of three events

$= n(A) + n(B) + n(C) - n(A \cup B \cup C) - 2n(A \cap B \cap C)$

$= 48 + 25 + 18 - 60 - 2 \times 5 = 21$

51. $x + y = 7$

$$y = 7 - x$$

$$R = \{(1, 6), (2, 5), (3, 4), (4, 3), (5, 2), (6, 1)\}$$

$\because (a, b) \in R \Rightarrow (b, a) \in R$

$\therefore$ Given relation is symmetric but neither reflexive nor transitive.

52. We have, AR_1B

$\Rightarrow (A \cap B^C) \cup (B \cap A^C) = \phi$

$\Rightarrow \quad A \cap B^C = B \cap A^C = \phi \Rightarrow A = B$

So, R_1 is an equivalence relation.

Again, $AR_2B \Rightarrow \; A \cup B^C = B \cup A^C$

$\Rightarrow \quad A^C \cap B = B^C \cap A$

$\Rightarrow \quad A = B$

So, R_2 is an equivalence relation.

53. For reflexive, $aRa \Rightarrow 2a + 3a = 5a$,

It is a multiple of 5, so R is reflexive.

For symmetric,

$bRa \Rightarrow 2b + 3a = 3a + 2b$

$$= \underbrace{(5a + 5b)}_{\text{Multiple of 5}} - \underbrace{(2a + 3b)}_{\text{Multiple of 5}}$$

So, R is symmetric.

For transitive,

$aRb \;\Rightarrow 2a + 3b$ Multiple of 5

$bRc \;\Rightarrow 2b + 3c$ Multiple of 5

$\Rightarrow 2a + 5b + 3c$ Multiple of 5

$$\underbrace{(2a + 3c)}_{\text{Multiple of 5}} + \underbrace{5b}_{\text{Multiple of 5}}$$

So, aRc is transitive.

$\therefore$ An equivalence relation.

54. Given, $A = \{1, 3, 4, 6, 9\}$ and $B = \{2, 4, 5, 8, 10\}$

R is defined on $A \times B$

i.e. $R = \{(a_1, b_1), (a_2, b_2) : a_1 \le b_2 \text{ and } b_1 \le a_2\}$

If $a_1 = 1$, then b_2 can be 2/4/5/8/10

$a_1 = 3$, then b_2 can be 4/5/8/10

$a_1 = 4$, then b_2 can be 4/5/8/10

$a_1 = 6$, then b_2 can be 8/10

$a_1 = 9$, then b_2 can be 10 only

So, number of ways $= 5 + 4 + 4 + 2 + 1 = 16$

Similarly, for $b_1 = 2 \Rightarrow a_2$ can be 3/4/6/9

$b_1 = 4 \;\Rightarrow a_2$ can be 4/6/9

$b_1 = 5 \;\Rightarrow a_2$ can be 6/9

$b_1 = 8 \;\Rightarrow a_2$ can be 9 only

and $b_1 \ne 10$

Thus, number of ways $= 4 + 3 + 2 + 1 = 10$

Finally, number of elements in set R is $16 \times 10 = 160$

55. We have, $A = \{2, 3, 4\}$, $B = \{8, 9, 12\}$

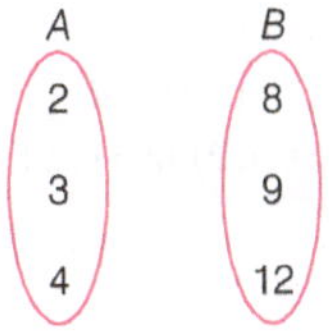

$R = \{((a_1, b_1), (a_2, b_2)) \in (A \times B, A \times B)\ a_1$ divides b_2 and a_2 divides $b_1\}$

2 divides 8 and 12, 3 divides 9 and 12, and 4 divides 8 and 12.

$\therefore$ Each element in A divides exactly 2 element is B.

The number of cases that a_1 divides $b_2 = 3 \times 2 = 6$

[$\because$ Each element has 2 choices]

Similarly, the number of cases that a_2 divides $b_1 = 3 \times 2 = 6$

Hence, the required number of cases $= 6 \times 6 = 36$

56. Let $a = -1, b = 10$.

Then, $2 + \dfrac{a}{b} = 2 - \dfrac{1}{10} = \dfrac{19}{10} > 0$

So, $(-1, 10) \in S$

Now, $a = 10, b = -1$.

Then, $2 + \dfrac{a}{b} = 2 - 10 = -8 < 0$

So, $(10, -1) \notin S$

Hence, S is not symmetric.

We know that

If $a^2 - b^2 \in Z$, then $b^2 - a^2 \in Z$

$\therefore\ (a, b) \in T \Rightarrow (b, a) \in T$

So, T is symmetric.

Again, $a^2 - b^2 \in Z$ and $b^2 - c^2 \in Z$.

$\Rightarrow\ a^2 - b^2 + b^2 - c^2 \in Z$

$\Rightarrow\ a^2 - c^2 \in Z$

$\therefore\ (a, b) \in T, (b, c) \in T \Rightarrow (a, c) \in T$

So, T is transitive.

57. For symmetric

$(a, b), (b, c) \in R$

$\Rightarrow\ (b, a), (c, b) \in R$

For transitive

$(a, b), (b, c) \in R \Rightarrow (a, c) \in R$

Now, symmetric

$\therefore\ (a, c) \in R \Rightarrow (c, a) \in R$

Transitive

$\therefore\ (a, b), (b, a) \in R \Rightarrow (a, a) \in R$

$(b, c), (c, b) \in R \Rightarrow (b, b)$ and $(c, c) \in R$

$\therefore$ Elements to be added so that R becomes symmetric and transitive is $= \{(b, a), (c, b), (a, c), (c, a), (a, a), (b, b), (c, c)\}$

Hence, total number of elements to be added = 7

58. **To check reflexivity**

$(a, a) \Rightarrow \gcd$ of $(a, a) = 1$ and $b = a \neq 2a$, $\forall\ a \in z$. which is true.

To check symmetric

Take, $a = 2$ and $b = 1$

$\Rightarrow\ \gcd(2, 1) = 1$

Also, $2a = 4 \neq b$

Now, when $a = 1, b = 2$, then

$\gcd(1, 2) = 1$

Also, $2a = 2 = b$

Hence, $2a = b$

So, R is not symmetric.

To check transitivity

consider $a = 14$, $b = 19$ and $c = 21$

$\gcd(a, b) = 1$

$\gcd(b, c) = 1$

$\gcd(a, c) = 7$

Hence, R is not transitive.

Finally, R is neither symmetric nor transitive.

59. Now, $3a - 3a + \sqrt{7} = \sqrt{7}$, which is an irrational.

So, $(a, a) \in R$.

Hence, R is reflexive.

Now, take $a = \dfrac{\sqrt{7}}{3}, b = 0$.

Then, $3a - 3b + \sqrt{7} = 2\sqrt{7}$ which is irrational.

$\therefore\ \left(\dfrac{\sqrt{7}}{3}, 0\right) \in R$

Now, if $a = 0, b = \dfrac{\sqrt{7}}{3}$, then $3a - 3b + \sqrt{7} = 0$, which is not irrational.

$\therefore\ \left(0, \dfrac{\sqrt{7}}{3}\right) \notin R$

So, R is not symmetric.

Similarly, $(0, \sqrt{3}) \in R$, $\left(\sqrt{3}, \dfrac{\sqrt{7}}{3}\right) \in R$ but $\left(0, \dfrac{\sqrt{7}}{3}\right) \notin R$.

So, R is not transitive.

60. Now, $ad(b - c) = bc(a - d)$

$\Rightarrow\ \dfrac{b - c}{bc} = \dfrac{a - d}{ad} \Rightarrow \dfrac{1}{a} - \dfrac{1}{b} = \dfrac{1}{d} - \dfrac{1}{c}$

Now, $(a, b)\ R\ (a, b)$

$\Rightarrow\ \dfrac{1}{a} - \dfrac{1}{b} = \dfrac{1}{b} - \dfrac{1}{a}$

which is not true.

So, R is not reflexive.

Again, $(a, b)\ R\ (c, d)$

$\Rightarrow\ \dfrac{1}{a} - \dfrac{1}{b} = \dfrac{1}{d} - \dfrac{1}{c} \Rightarrow \dfrac{1}{c} - \dfrac{1}{d} = \dfrac{1}{b} - \dfrac{1}{a}$

$\Rightarrow\ (c, d)\ R\ (a, b)$

So, R is symmetric.

Again, $(a, b)\ R\ (c, d)$

$\Rightarrow\ \dfrac{1}{a} - \dfrac{1}{b} = \dfrac{1}{d} - \dfrac{1}{c}$ ...(i)

and $(c, d)\ R\ (e, f)$

$\Rightarrow\ \dfrac{1}{c} - \dfrac{1}{d} = \dfrac{1}{f} - \dfrac{1}{e}$ ...(ii)

From Eqs. (i) and (ii), we get

$$\frac{1}{a}-\frac{1}{b}=\frac{1}{e}-\frac{1}{f} \neq (a, b)\ R\ (e, f)$$

So, R is not transitive.

61. We have, $n \in N$

$10 \le n \le 100$ and $3^n - 3$ is a multiple of 7

$\therefore \quad 3^n - 3 = 7k, \forall k \in I$

$3^n = 7k + 3$

Now, $\quad 3 = 3 \pmod 7$

$3^2 = 2 \pmod 7$

$3^3 = -1 \pmod 7$ or $6 \pmod 7$

$3^6 = 1 \pmod 7$

$3^7 = 3 \pmod 7$

Since, $\quad 3^{13} = 3 \pmod 7$

$\vdots$

$\therefore$ n can be 13, 19, ... 97

$\therefore$ Total $n = 15$

62. Given, $\quad |x|^2 - 2|x| + |\lambda - 3| = 0$

$\Rightarrow |x|^2 - 2|x| + 1 + |\lambda - 3| - 1 = 0$

$\Rightarrow \quad (|x| - 1)^2 + |\lambda - 3| = 1$

Since, $\lambda \in R$

At $\lambda = 3$, $x = 0, 2$

At $\lambda = 4$ or 2, $x = 1$ or -1

So, maximum value of $x + \lambda = 5$

Hence, the largest element in the set S is 5.

63. $A = \{1, 2, 3, 4\}$

$R = \{((a, b), (c, d)) : 2a + 3b = 4c + 5d\}$

Let $\alpha = 2a + 3b = 4c + 5d$

Now, $2a = \{2, 4, 6, 8\}, 3b = \{3, 6, 9, 12\}$

$4c = \{4, 8, 12, 16\}, 5d = \{5, 10, 15, 20\}$

$\therefore \quad 2a + 3b = \{5, 8, 11, 14, 7, 10, 13, 16, 9, 12, 15, 18, 11, 14, 17, 20\}$

$= \{5, 7, 8, 9, 10, 11, 12, 13, 14, 15, 16, 17, 18, 20\}$

and $4c + 5d = \{9, 14, 19, 24, 13, 18, 17, 23, 26, 27, 31, 32, 36, 22, 21, 26\}$

$= \{9, 13, 14, 17, 18, 19, 21, 22, 23, 24, 26, 27, 28, 31, 32, 36\}$

Since, $2a + 3b = 4c + 5d$

$\therefore$ Possible values are $\{9, 13, 14, 17, 18\}$

So, pairs of $\{(a, b), (c, d)\} = 5$

$\therefore$ Total number of elements in R is 5.

64. Let $A = \{-4, -3, -2, 0, 1, 3, 4\}$

and $R = \{(a, b) \in A \times A, b = |a|$ or $b^2 = a + 1\}$ be a relation on A.

So, $R = \{(-4, 4), (-3, 3), (3, 3), (4, 4), (0, 0), (3, -2), (0, 1), (1, 1)\}$

This relation R becomes reflexive, if we add only $(-2, -2)$, $(-4, -4)$, $(-3, -3)$ elements and this relation R becomes symmetric, if we add only $(4, -4)$, $(3, -3)$, $(-2, 3)$, $(1, 0)$ elements.

Thus, the required number be 7.

65. Given, set $A = \{1, 2, 3\}$

For relation R to be reflexive

$\Rightarrow \quad (1, 1), (2, 2), (3, 3) \in R$

$\therefore$ $R = \{(1, 1), (2, 2), (3, 3), (1, 2), (2, 3), ...\}$

Since, $(1, 2), (2, 3) \in R$

$\Rightarrow (1, 3) \in R$ to be transitive

$\therefore R_1 = \{(1, 1), (2, , 2), (3, 3), (1, 2), (2, 3), (1, 3)\}$ is a required relation.

Now, $R_2 = \{R_1, (2, 1)\}$ is reflexive, transitive but not symmetric

$R_3 = \{R_1, (3, 2)\}$

and $\quad R_4 = \{R_1, (3, 1), (2, 1)\}$ are total 4 such possible relations

66. $A = \{0, 3, 4, 6, 7, 8, 9, 10\}$

$R = \{(x, y) : x, y \in A, x - y = 2$ or odd positive integer$\}$

$R = \{(6, 4), (8, 6), (9, 7), (10, 8), (3, 0), (7, 0), (9, 0), (4, 3), (6, 3), (8, 3), (10, 3), (7, 4), (9, 4), (7, 6), (9, 6), (8, 7), (10, 7), (9, 8), (10, 9)\}$

To make it symmetric 19 more elements should be added.

67. Given, $A = \{1, 2, 3, 4, ..., 10\}$ and $B = \{0, 1, 2, 3, 4\}$

Now, $2(a-b)^2 + 3(a-b) \in B = (a-b)\{2(a-b) + 3\} \in B$

Since, $(a, b) \in A \times A$

$\therefore \quad a - b = 0 \Rightarrow a = b$

$\Rightarrow$ 10 order pairs $\quad$ [$\because$ A has 10 elements]

and $a - b = -2 \Rightarrow 8$ order pairs

$\{(1, 3), (2, 4), (3, 5), (4, 6), (5, 7), (6, 8), (7, 9), (8, 10)\}$

$\therefore$ Total number of elements in the relation $R = 10 + 8 = 18$

68. Given relation,

$R = \{(a, b), (b, c), (b, d)\}$

and let $\quad A = \{a, b, c, d\}$

For reflexive,

The elements should be (a, a), (b, b), (c, c) and (d, d)

For symmetric,

If $(a, b) \in R \Rightarrow (b, a) \in R$

If $(b, c) \in R \Rightarrow (c, b) \in R$

If $(b, d) \in R \Rightarrow (d, b) \in R$

For transitive,

If $(a, b) \in R$ and $(b, c) \in R$

$\Rightarrow (a, c) \in R \quad$ ...(i)

If $(a, c) \in R \Rightarrow (c, a) \in R$

$\therefore$ Total number $= 4 + 4 + 1 = 9$

69. For set A, $-2 < x + 1 < 2$

$\Rightarrow \quad -3 < x < 1$

$\Rightarrow \quad x \in (-3, 1)$

For set B, $x - 1 \le -2$ or $x - 1 \ge 2$

$\Rightarrow \quad x \le -1$ or $x \ge 3$

$\Rightarrow \quad x \in (-\infty, -1] \cup [3, \infty)$

$A - B = (-1, 1)$

$B - A = R - (-3, 3)$

$A \cap B = (-3, -1]$

$A \cup B = R - [1, 3)$

70. Given, $S = \left\{x \in [-6, 3] - \{-2, 2\} : \frac{|x+3|-1}{|x|-2} \geq 0\right\}$

and $T = \{x \in Z : x^2 - 7|x| + 9 \leq 0\}$

Here, $x^2 - 7|x| + 9 \leq 0$

$\Rightarrow |x|^2 - 7|x| + 9 \leq 0$ $[\because |x|^2 = x^2]$

$$\Rightarrow \left[|x| - \left(\frac{7+\sqrt{49-36}}{2}\right)\right] \leq 0 \left[|x| - \left(\frac{7-\sqrt{49-36}}{2}\right)\right] \leq 0$$

$$\Rightarrow |x| \in \left[\frac{7-\sqrt{13}}{2}, \frac{7+\sqrt{13}}{2}\right]$$

But x an integer,

$|x| = 2, 3, 4, 5$ and $x = \pm 2, \pm 3, \pm 4, \pm 5$

$T = \{\pm 2, \pm 3, \pm 4, \pm 5\}$

$S \cap T \neq \{\pm 2, 4, 5\}$ as $S \notin \{\pm 2, 4, 5\}$

When $x = -3$, then $\frac{|-3+3|-1}{|-3|-2} = \frac{-1}{1} < 0$

When $x = -4$, then $\frac{|-4+3|-1}{|-4|-2} = 0$

When $x = -5$, then $\frac{|-5+3|-1}{|-5|-2} = \frac{1}{3} \geq 0$

When $x = 3$, then $\frac{|3+3|-1}{|3|-2} = 5 \geq 0$

Hence, $S \cap T = \{-5, -4, 3\} \Rightarrow n(S \cap T) = 3$

71. Given, $R = \{(a, b) : b = pq$, where $p, q \geq 3$ are prime numbers$\}$

a can be anything from $\{1, 2, 3, \ldots, 60\}$.

So, total possible values of a are 60.

For $b = pq$

If $p = 3, q = 3, 5, 7, 11, 13, 17, 19$

If $p = 5, q = 5, 7, 11$

If $p = 7, q = 7$

Total possible values of $b = 11$

Total cases $= 60 \times 11 = 660$

72.

> **Decoding the Question**
>
> (i) Recall the definition of symmetric, reflextive and transitive relation.
>
> (ii) A relation is said to be equivalence relation it if is symmetric, reflexive and transitive.

Let $A = \{1, 2, 3\}$

Then, $R = \{(1, 1) (1, 2), (1, 3) (2, 1), (2, 2), (2, 3), (3, 1), (3, 2), (3, 3)\}$

(i) R is reflexive. $[\because (a, a) \in R]$

(ii) R is symmetric. $[\because (a, b) \in R \Rightarrow (b, a) \in R]$

(iii) R is transitive. $[\because (a, b) \in R$ and $(b, c) \in R \Rightarrow (a, c) \in R]$

$\therefore$ R is an equivalence relation.

73. In $R_1 \equiv |2 - 11| = 9 \leq 13$

$\therefore (2, 11) \in R_1$ and $(11, 19) \in R_1$ but $(2, 19) \notin R_1$

$\therefore$ R_1 is not transitive.

Hence, R_1 is not equivalence.

In $R_2 : (13, 3) \in R_2$ and $(3, 26) \in R_2$

but $(13, 26) \notin R_2$ $[\because |13 - 26| = 13]$

$\therefore R_2$ is not transitive.

Hence, R_2 is not equivalence.

74. $R_1 = \{(a, b) : a, b \in R, ab \geq 0\}$

(i) $a \cdot a = a^2 \geq 0 \Rightarrow aR_1a, \forall a \in R$

$\therefore R_1$ is reflexive.

(ii) If $aR_1b \Rightarrow ab \geq 0 \Rightarrow ba \geq 0$;

$\therefore bR_1a$

$\therefore$ R_1 is symmetric.

(iii) If aR_1b and $bR_1c \Rightarrow ab \geq 0$ and $bc \geq 0$

$\therefore (ab)(bc) \geq 0 \Rightarrow (ac)b^2 \geq 0$

Now, if $b \neq 0$, $ac \geq 0$

But, when $b = 0$, ac can be negative. Also, it is not always true that $ac \geq 0$.

$\therefore$ R_1 is not transitive.

$\Rightarrow$ R_1 is not equivalence relation.

Now, $R_2 = \{(a, b) : a, b \in R, a \geq b\}$

(i) $a = a \Rightarrow aR_2a \Rightarrow R_2$ is reflexive.

(ii) If aR_2b, then $a \geq b$, but $b \geq a$ is not true for all $a, b \in R$

e.g. $a = 2, b = 1, 2 > 1$ but $1 < 2$

$\therefore$ R_2 is not symmetric.

$\therefore$ R_2 is not an equivalence relation.

75. For R to be reflexive $\Rightarrow x\,R\,x$

$\Rightarrow$ $3x + \alpha x = 7K$

$\Rightarrow$ $(3 + \alpha)x = 7K$

$\Rightarrow$ $3 + \alpha = 7\lambda$

$\Rightarrow$ $\alpha = 7\lambda - 3 = 7N + 4, K, \lambda, N \in I$

$\therefore$ When, α divided by 7 its leaves remainder as 4.

R to be symmetric $xRy \Rightarrow yRx$

$3x + \alpha y = 7N_1, 3y + \alpha x = 7N_2$

$\Rightarrow$ $(3 + \alpha)(x + y) = 7(N_1 + N_2)$

$= 7N_3$

which holds when $3 + \alpha$ is multiple of 7.

$\therefore$ $\alpha = 7N + 4$

R is be transitive xRy and $yRz \Rightarrow xRz$.

$3x + \alpha y = 7N_1$

and $3y + \alpha z = 7N_2$

and $3x + \alpha z = 7N_3$

$\therefore$ $3x + 7N_2 - 3y = 7N_3$

$\therefore$ $7N_1 - \alpha y + 7N_2 - 3y = 7N_3$

$\therefore$ $7(N_1 + N_2) - (3 + \alpha)y = 7N_4$

$\therefore$ $(3 + \alpha)y = 7N$

which is true again when $3 + \alpha$ divisible by 7, i.e. when α divided by 7, the remainder is 4.

76. $S = \{4, 6, 9\}, T = \{9, 10, 11, \ldots, 1000\}$

$A = \{a_1 + a_2 + \ldots a_k : k \in N, a_1, a_2, a_3 \ldots a_k \in S\}$

$A = \{a; a = 4x + 6y + 9z, \ x, y, z \{0, 1, 2, \ldots\}\}$

$\therefore A = \{9, 10, 12, 13, 14, 15, 16, 17, 18, \ldots\}$

$T - A = \{11\}$

77. Given, $A = \{1, 2, 3, 4, 5, 6, 7\}$ and $B = \{3, 6, 7, 9\}$

Total number of subset of $A = 2^7 = 128$

As, $C \subseteq A$ and $C \cap B = \phi$, so the set C contains only 4 elements i.e. $\{1, 2, 4, 5\}$

$\therefore$ The number of elements in the set $\{C \subseteq A : C \cap B \neq \phi\}$

= Total number of sets − Number of set,

when $C \subseteq A$ and $C \cap B = \phi$

$= 128 - 2^4$

$= 128 - 16 = 112$

78. **Decoding the Question**

According to De-Morgan's first law, the complement of the union of two sets A and B is equal to the intersection of the complement of the sets A and B.

$$(A \cup B)' = A' \cap B'$$

where, A' and B' denotes the complement.

Apply De-Morgan's law,

$$(B \cup C)' = B' \cap C'$$

B' containing subsets of A which do not contains 2 but element 1.

And C' is a set containing subsets of A whose sum of elements is not prime.

So, we need to calculate number of subsets of {3,4,5,6,7} whose sum of elements plus 1 is composite.

Number of 5 elements subset = 1

Number of 4 elements subset = 3 (except selecting 3 or 7)

Number of 3 elements subset = 6 (except selecting {3,4,5} {3,6,7} {4,5,7} or {5,6,7}

Number of such 2 elements subset

= 7 (except selecting {3,7},{4,6} {5,7})

Number of such 1 element subset = 3 (except selecting {4} or {6})

Number of such 0 elements subset = 1

Here, $n(B' \cap C') = 1 + 3 + 6 + 7 + 3 + 1 = 21$

Therefore $n(B \cup C) = 2^7 - 21 = 107$

79. $B = \{2, 4, 6, 8, \ldots, 200\}$ and $45 = 3^2 \cdot 5$

n (multiples of 6) = 33

n (multiples of 10) = 20

n (multiples of 30) = 6

$$\text{Sum} = S_6 = 6\,(1 + 2 + \ldots + 33) = \frac{6\,(33 \times 34)}{2}$$

$$S_{10} = 10\,(1 + 2 + \ldots + 20) = \frac{10\,(20 \times 21)}{2}$$

$$S_{30} = 30\,(1 + 2 + \ldots + 6) = \frac{30\,(6 \times 7)}{2}$$

$$\text{Total sum, } S_{200} = 2\,(1 + 2 + \ldots + 100) = \frac{2(100 \times 101)}{2}$$

Sum of elements of $A \cap B = 2$

$$= 2\left[\frac{100 \times 101}{2} - 3\,\frac{(33 \times 34)}{2} - 5\left(\frac{20 \times 21}{2}\right) + 30\left(6 \times \frac{7}{2}\right)\right]$$

$= 10100 - 3366 - 2100 + 630 = 5264$

Alternate Solution

$$S_6 = \frac{6(33 \times 34)}{2} = 3366$$

$$S_{10} = \frac{10(20 \times 21)}{2} = 2100$$

$$S_{30} = \frac{30(6 \times 7)}{2} = 630$$

$$\therefore \quad S_{200} = \frac{2(100 \times 101)}{2} = 10100$$

Sum of natural numbers up to 100 which are neither divisible by 3 nor by 5.

$= 10100 - 3366 - 2100 + 630 = 5264$

80. **Decoding the Question**

Let $S(\alpha)$ is the sum of all element of the set.

$S(\alpha) = (\Sigma\alpha) - (\Sigma$ multiple of 2$) - (\Sigma$ multiple of 3$)$ $+ \alpha\,(\Sigma$ multiple of 6$)$

Let $S(\alpha)$ is the sum of all elements of the set

$\{\alpha \in \{1, 2, 3, \ldots, 100\};\ \text{HCF}(24, \alpha) = 1\}$

Since, HCF $(24, \alpha) = 1$

$\Rightarrow S(\alpha) = (1 + 2 + 3 \ldots + 100)$

$-S$ (multiple of 3) $- S$(multiple of 2) $+ S$(multiple of 6)

$\Rightarrow S(\alpha) = (1 + 2 + 3 \ldots + 100) - (2 + 4 + 6 + \ldots + 100)$

$- (3 + 6 + 9 + \ldots + 99) + (6 + 12 + 18 + \ldots 96)$

$$\Rightarrow S(\alpha) = \frac{100 \cdot (100 + 1)}{2} - 2 \cdot (1 + 2 + 3 + \ldots + 50)$$

$- 3(1 + 2 + 3 + \ldots + 33) + 6(1 + 2 + 3 + \ldots 16)$

$$= \frac{100 \cdot 101}{2} - 2 \cdot \frac{50 \cdot (50 + 1)}{2} - 3 \cdot \frac{33 \cdot (33 + 1)}{2} + 6 \cdot \frac{16 \cdot (16 + 1)}{2}$$

$= 5050 - 2550 - 1683 + 816$

$= 1633$

81. Let A = Set of patients suffering from heart ailment and

B = Set of patients suffering from lungs infection

Given, $n(A) = 89\%$ and $n(B) = 98\%$

$n(A \cup B) \geq n(A) + n(B) - n(A \cap B)$

$\Rightarrow \quad 100 \geq 89 + 98 - n(A \cap B)$

$\Rightarrow \quad 87 \leq n(A \cap B)$

Also, $\quad n(A \cap B) = \min\{n(A), n(B)\}$

$\Rightarrow \quad n(A \cap B) \leq 89$

$\therefore \quad 87 \leq n\,(A \cap B) \leq 89$

So, $\quad n\,(A \cap B) \notin \{79, 81, 83, 85\}$.

Alternate Solution

$n(A \cup B) \geq n(A) + n(B) - n(A \cap B)$

$\Rightarrow \quad 100 \geq 89 + 98 - n(A \cap B)$

$\Rightarrow \quad 87 \leq n(A \cap B)$

$n(A \cap B) \leq 89$

So, $n(A \cap B) \notin \{79, 81, 83, 85\}$.

82.

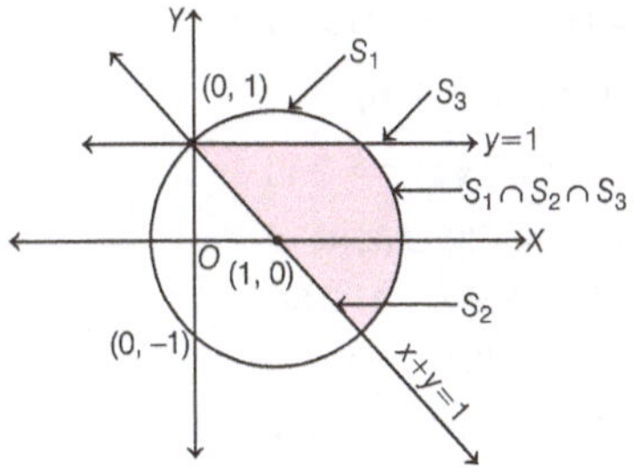

Here, $|z-1| \le \sqrt{2}$, represents a circle S_1 whose centre is $(1, 0)$ and radius $\sqrt{2}$ units and z lies on and inside the circle.

$\text{Re}((1-i)z) \ge 1$, represents

$$S_2 : x + y \ge 1$$

and $\text{Im}(z) \le 1$, represents $S_3 : y \le 1$.

Thus, from figure, $S_1 \cap S_2 \cap S_3$ has infinitely many elements in the shaded region.

83.

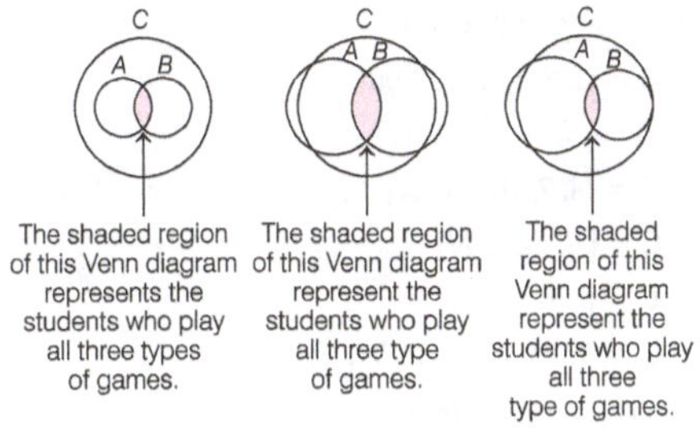

As none plays all the three games, the intersection of all three circles must be zero.

84.

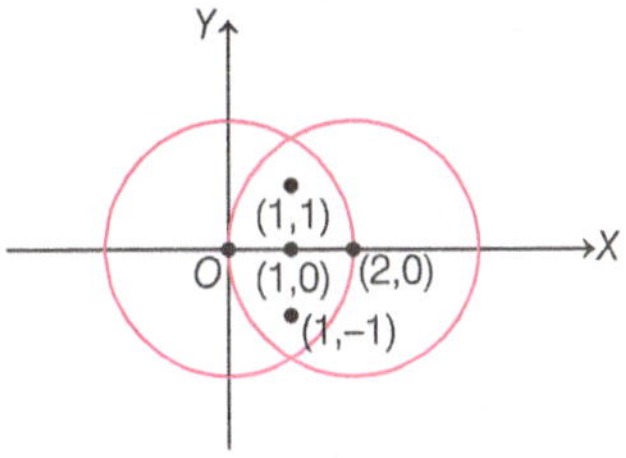

$$(x-2)^2 + y^2 \le 4,\ x^2 + y^2 \le 4$$

and $\quad (x-2)^2 + (y-2)^2 \le 4$

Intersection of A and B is shown by graph as given.

So, $\quad A \cap B = \{(0,0),(1,0),(2,0),(1,1),(1,-1)\}$

$\therefore \quad n(A \cap B) = 5$

Also, intersection of A and C is shown by graph as given.

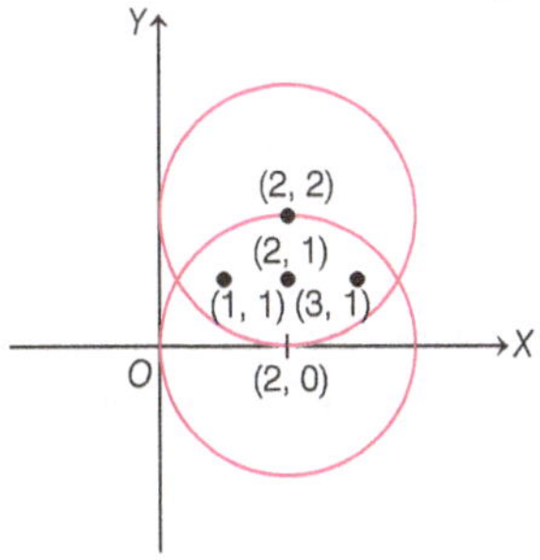

So, $\quad A \cap C = \{(1,1),(2,0),(2,1),(2,2),(3,1)\}$

$\Rightarrow \quad n(A \cap C) = 5$

Number of relations from $(A \cap B)$ to

$$(A \cap C) = 2^{5 \times 5} = 2^{25} = 2^P$$

$\Rightarrow \qquad P = 25$

Time Saving Technique

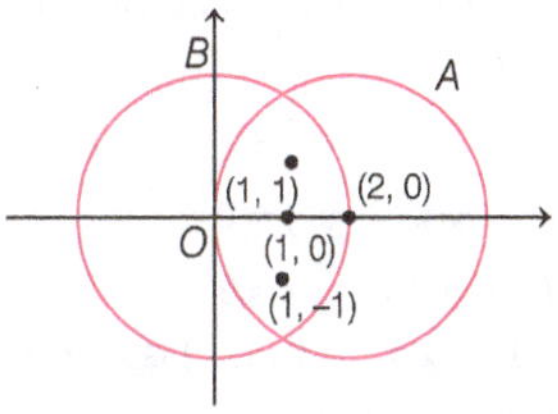

$n(A \cap B) = 5$

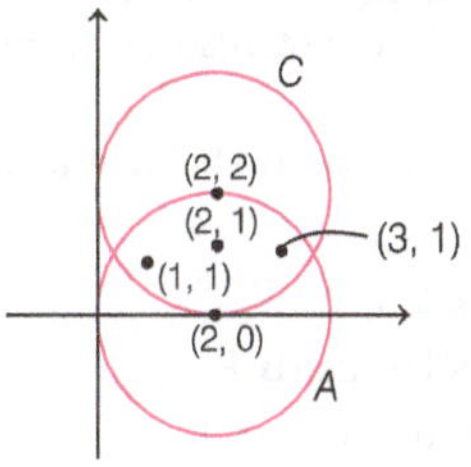

$n(A \cap C) = 5$

$\therefore$ Number of relations from $(A \cap B)$ to $(A \cap C) = 2^{5 \times 5} = 2^{25} = 2^P$

$\Rightarrow \qquad P = 25$

85. Let O be the centre of the circle C. C_1 and C_2 are the centres of circles A and B, respectively.

So, $\quad C_1 = \left(\frac{1}{2}, \frac{1}{2}\right), R_1 = 1$ and $C_2 = (0, 2), R_2 = \frac{3}{2}$

$\quad O = (2, 1)$, radius $r_3 = |r|$

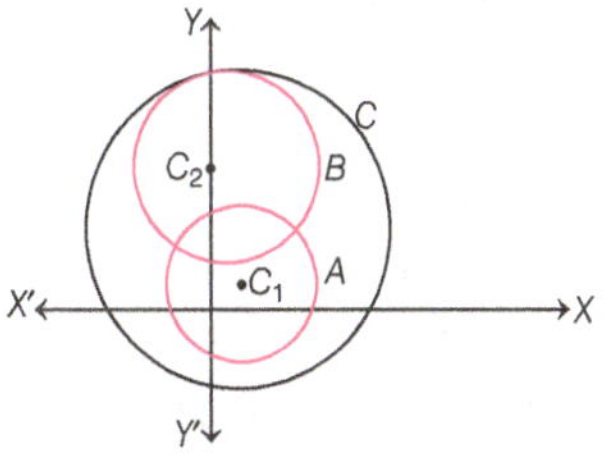

Now, for $A \cup B \subseteq C$, we have

$$r \ge OC_2 + R_2$$

$$= \sqrt{2^2 + 1^2} + \frac{3}{2}$$

$$= \frac{2\sqrt{5} + 3}{2}$$

$$\Rightarrow \ r \ge \frac{2\sqrt{5} + 3}{2}$$

86. According to the question, let's consider option (b), (2, 3) and (3, 4) satisfy $0 < |x - y| \le 1$ but (2, 4) does not satisfy it.

87. $A = \{2, 3, 4, 5, \ldots, 30\}$

$$ad = bc$$

$\therefore \ (a, b) R(4, 3) \Rightarrow 3a = 4b$

$\Rightarrow \quad a = \left(\frac{4}{3}\right) b$

b must be a multiple of 3, b can be (3, 6, 9, ... 30).

Also, a must be less than or equal to 30.

$(a, b) = (4, 3), (8, 6), (12, 9), (16, 12), (20, 15)\ (24, 18), (28, 21)$

$\Rightarrow$ 7 ordered pairs

88. $x^3 - 3x^2y - xy^2 + 3y^3 = 0$

$\Rightarrow x(x^2 - y^2) - 3y(x^2 - y^2) = 0$

$\Rightarrow (x - 3y)(x - y)(x + y) = 0$

Now, $x - x = 0 \Rightarrow x = x, \ \forall (x, x) \in N \times N$

So, R is a reflexive relation.

But not symmetric and transitive relation because, (3, 1) satisfies but (1, 3) does not. Also, (3, 1) and (1, −1) satisfies but (3, −1) does not.

Hence, relation R is reflexive but neither symmetric nor transitive.

89. For reflexive relation,

$\forall (A, A) \in R$ for matrix P.

$\Rightarrow A = PAP^{-1}$ is true for $P = 1$

So, R is reflexive relation.

For symmetric relation,

Let $(A, B) \in R$ for matrix P.

$\Rightarrow \quad A = PBP^{-1}$

After pre-multiply by P^{-1} and post-multiply by P, we get

$$P^{-1}AP = B$$

So, $(B, A) \in R$ for matrix P^{-1}.

So, R is a symmetric relation.

For transitive relation,

Let ARB and BRC

So, $A = PBP^{-1}$ and $B = PCP^{-1}$

Now, $A = P(PCP^{-1})P^{-1}$

$\Rightarrow A = (P)^2 \cdot C \cdot (P^2)^{-1}$

$\therefore (A, C) \in R$ for matrix P^2.

$\therefore R$ is transitive relation.

Hence, R is an equivalence relation.

90. Let $P(a, b)$ and $Q(c, d)$ are any two points.

Given, $OP = OQ$

i.e. $\sqrt{a^2 + b^2} = \sqrt{c^2 + d^2}$

On squaring on both sides, we get

$$a^2 + b^2 = c^2 + d^2 \quad \ldots \text{(i)}$$

$R(x, y), S(1, -1), OR = OS$ (equivalence class)

This gives $OR = \sqrt{x^2 + y^2}$ and $OS = \sqrt{2}$

$\Rightarrow \sqrt{x^2 + y^2} = \sqrt{2} \Rightarrow x^2 + y^2 = 2$ [squaring on both sides]

$\therefore \quad S = \{(x, y) : x^2 + y^2 = 2\}$

91. $A = \{x \in R : |x - 2| > 1\}$

$\Rightarrow A = (-\infty, 1) \cup (3, \infty)$

$B = \{x \in R : \sqrt{x^2 - 3} > 1\}$

$\Rightarrow B = (-\infty, -2) \cup (2, \infty)$

$\Rightarrow C = \{x \in R : |x - 4| \geq 2\}$

$\Rightarrow C = (-\infty, 2] \cup [6, \infty)$

$\Rightarrow A \cap B \cap C = (-\infty, -2) \cup [6, \infty)$

$\Rightarrow (A \cap B \cap C)^C = [-2, 6)$

$\therefore (A \cap B \cap C)^C \cap Z = \{-2, -1, 0, 1, 2, 3, 4, 5\}$

Number of subsets of

$$(A \cap B \cap C)^C \cap Z = 2^8 = 256$$

92. Let $A = \{n \in N \mid n^2 \leq n + 10000\}$

$$n^2 \leq n + 10000$$

$$n^2 - n \leq 10000$$

$\Rightarrow n(n - 1) \leq 100 \times 100$

$\Rightarrow A = \{1, 2, 3, \ldots\ldots, 100\}$ $[\because n \in N]$

Now, $B = \{3k + 1 \mid k \in N\}$

$B = \{4, 7, 10, 13, \ldots\}$

and $C = \{2k \mid k \in N\}$

$C = \{2, 4, 6, 8, \ldots\}$

So, $B - C = \{7, 13, 19, \ldots\ldots, 97, \ldots\}$

So, $A \cap (B - C) = \{7, 13, 19, \ldots\ldots, 97\}$

This form an AP with common difference $(d = 6)$

$\Rightarrow \quad 97 = 7 + (n - 1)6$

$n = \frac{97 - 7}{6} + 1 = 16$ $[\because a_n = a + (n - 1)d]$

Hence, sum $= \frac{16}{2}[7 + 97] = 832$ $\left[\because S_n = \frac{n}{2}(a + l)\right]$

93. Given, $A = \{n \in N : n$ is a 3-digit number$\}$

$B = \{9k + 2 : k \in N\}$

and $C = \{9k + l : k \in N\}$

$\because$ 3 digit number of the form $9k + 2$ are {101, 110, ... 992}

$\Rightarrow \quad \text{Sum} = \frac{100}{2}[101 + 992]$

$$= \frac{100 \times 1093}{2}$$

Similarly, 3-digit number of the form $9k + 5$ are {104, 113, 127, ..., 995}

$\Rightarrow \quad \text{Sum} = \frac{100}{2}[104 + 995] = \frac{100 \times 1099}{2}$

Their sum $= \frac{100 \times 1093}{2} + \frac{100 \times 1099}{2}$

$$= 100 \times 1096 = 400 \times 274$$

Hence, we can say the value of $l = 5$

as the second series of numbers obtained by set C is of the form $9k + 5$.

$\therefore$ Required value of $l = 5$

94. According to the given information number of distinct elements in

$$\bigcup_{i=1}^{50} X_i = \frac{50 \times 10}{20} = 25$$

and number of distinct elements in

$$\bigcup_{i=1}^{n} Y_i = \frac{n \times 5}{6}$$

$\because \quad \bigcup_{i=1}^{50} X_i = \bigcup_{i=1}^{n} Y_i = T$ [given]

$\Rightarrow \quad 25 = \frac{n \times 5}{6}$

$\Rightarrow \quad n = 30$

95. Given sets $A = \{m \in R : \text{both the roots of } x^2 - (m+1)x + m + 4 = 0 \text{ are real}\}$

and $\quad B = [-3, 5)$

$\because$ Roots of $x^2 - (m+1)x + m + 4 = 0$ are real, $m \in R$.

$\therefore \; D \geq 0 \Rightarrow (m+1)^2 - 4(m+4) \geq 0$

$\Rightarrow \quad m^2 - 2m - 15 \geq 0$

$\Rightarrow \quad m^2 - 5m + 3m - 15 \geq 0$

$\Rightarrow \quad m(m-5) + 3(m-5) \geq 0$

$\Rightarrow \quad (m+3)(m-5) \geq 0$

$\Rightarrow \quad m \in (-\infty, -3] \cup [5, \infty)$

$\therefore \quad A = (-\infty, -3] \cup [5, \infty)$

$\therefore \quad A - B = (-\infty, -3) \cup [5, \infty)$

$\quad A \cap B = \{-3\}$,

$\quad B - A = (-3, 5)$

and $\quad A \cup B = R$

96. Let $n(A) =$ Number of people read newspaper $A = 63\%$

$n(B) =$ Number of people read newspaper $B = 76\%$

and $n(A \cap B) =$ Number of people read both $= x\%$

$\because \quad n(A \cup B) = n(A) + n(B) - n(A \cap B)$

and $\quad 76 \leq n(A \cup B) \leq 100$

$\therefore \quad 76 \leq 63 + 76 - x \leq 100$

$\Rightarrow \quad 0 \leq 63 - x \leq 24$

$\Rightarrow \quad 39 \leq x \leq 63$

97. Given, $X = \{n \in N : 1 \leq n \leq 50\}$,

$A = \{n \in X : n \text{ is multiple of } 2\}$

$= \{2, 4, 6, 8, \ldots\ldots, 50\}$

and $\quad B = \{n \in X : n = \text{is multiple of } 7$

$= \{7, 14, 21, 28, 35, 42, 49\}$

$\because$ 14, 28, 42 $\in A$

$\therefore$ Smallest subset of X containing elements of both A and B have elements $= n(A) + n(B) - n(A \cap B)$

$= 25 + 7 - 3$

$= 29$

Exercise 2 - JEE Advanced Pattern

1. Let $A = \{1, 2, 3\}$ and $R = \{(1, 1), (1, 2)\}$

and $S = \{(2, 2), (2, 3)\}$ be the transitive relation on A

Then, $R \cup S = \{(1, 1), (1, 2), (2, 2), (2, 3)\}$

$R \cup S$ is not transitive, because $(1, 2) \in R \cup S$ and $(2, 3) \in R \cup S$ but $(1, 3) \notin R \cup S$

2. According to the question,

$$2^m - 2^n = 112$$

$\Rightarrow \quad 2^n(2^{m-n} - 1) = 2^4 \times 7$

Comparing exponents on both sides, we get

$$2^n = 2^4 \text{ and } 2^{m-n} - 1 = 7$$

Since, $\quad 2^n = 2^4 \Rightarrow n = 4$

Now, $\quad 2^{m-n} = 8$

$\Rightarrow \quad 2^{m-n} = 2^3$

$\Rightarrow \quad m - n = 3$

$\Rightarrow \quad m - 4 = 3$

$\therefore \quad m = 7$

$\therefore \quad mn = 7 \times 4 = 28$

3. $A - B \rightarrow$ Regions 3 and 5

$B - C \rightarrow$ Regions 2 and 6

$C - A \rightarrow$ Regions 4 and 7

$\therefore (A - B) \cup (B - C) \cup (C - A) \rightarrow$ Regions 2, 3, 4, 5, 6, 7

$\therefore [(A - B) \cup (B - C) \cup (C - A)]' \rightarrow$ Regions 1, which is $A \cap B \cap C$.

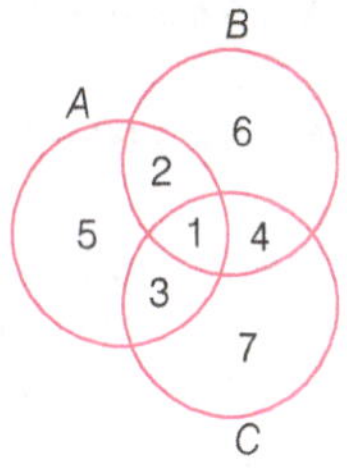

4. $S = \{1, 2, 3, 4\}$

Let A and B be two disjoint subsets of S

Now, for any element $a \in S$, has got three possibilities either, it is in A or B or none.

For every element out of 4 elements there are three choices.

$\therefore$Total options $= 3^4 = 81$

Here, $A \neq B$, except when

$A = B = \phi$

$\therefore 81 - 1 = 80$ (order pairs) are there for which $A \neq B$.

Hence, total number of unordered pairs of disjoint subsets

$$= \frac{80}{2} + 1 = 41$$

5. Let R be the set of families having a radio and T be the set of families having a TV.

Then, $n(R \cup T) =$ Number of families having atleast one of the radio and TV $= 1003 - 63 = 940$

$\therefore \quad n(R) = 794$ and $n(T) = 187$

Let x be the number of families having both a radio and a TV, then number of families who have only radio

$= 794 - x$, number of families who have only TV

$= 187 - x$

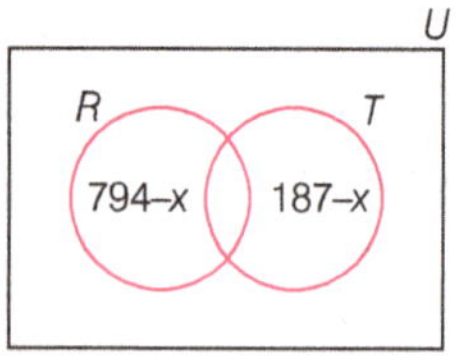

From venn-diagram, $794 - x + x + 187 - x = 940$

$\Rightarrow \quad 981 - x = 940$

$\therefore \quad x = 981 - 940 = 41$

Hence, the required number of families having both a radio and a TV is 41.

6. $P = \{30, 60, 90, 120\}$

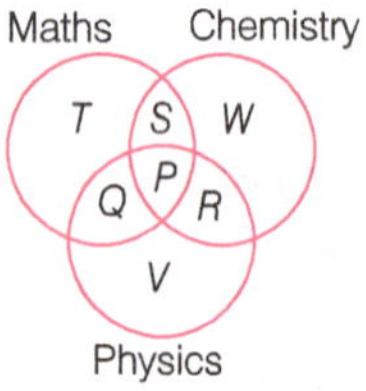

$\Rightarrow n(P) = 4$

$Q = \{6n : n \in N, 1 \le n \le 23\} - P$

$\Rightarrow n(Q) = 19$

$R = \{15n : n \in N, 1 \le n \le 9\} - P$

$\Rightarrow n(R) = 5$

$S = \{10n : n \in N, 1 \le n \le 14\} - P$

$\Rightarrow n(S) = 10$

$n(T) = 70 - n(P) - n(Q) - n(S) = 70 - 33 = 37$

$n(V) = 46 - n(P) - n(Q) - n(R) = 46 - 28 = 18$

$n(W) = 28 - n(P) - n(R) - n(S) = 28 - 19 = 9$

Numbered of required students

$= 140 - (4 + 19 + 5 + 10 + 37 + 18 + 9)$

$= 140 - 102 = 38$

7. Since, $A \subseteq B, A \cup B = B$

So, $n(A \cup B) = n(B) = 6$

8. For $A \cap B$, we have

$$-x = \frac{1}{x} \Rightarrow -x^2 = 1 \Rightarrow x^2 = -1,$$

which is not possible.

$\therefore \quad A \cap B = \phi$

9. $4N = \{4, 8, 12, 16, 20, 24, \dots\}$

and $6N = \{6, 12, 18, 24, \dots\}$

Hence, $4N \cap 6N = \{12, 24, 36, \dots\} = 12N$

10. $\because \frac{n}{m}$ means that n is a factor of m. So, f is reflexive.

$\because$ A number is a factor of itself.

Now, if n is a factor of m, then m is not a factor of n.

$\therefore f$ is not symmetric.

Let n is a factor of m and m is a factor of p, then it is true that n is a factor of p.

$\therefore f$ is transitive.

11. Relation R on the set of all straight lines in the plane is of parallel line.

A line is parallel to itself. So, R is reflexive.

If l_1 is parallel to l_2, then l_2 is parallel to l_1.

$\therefore R$ is symmetric relation. $[l_1, l_2 \in L]$

Let $l_1, l_2, l_3 \in L$

l_1 is parallel to l_2 and l_2 is parallel to l_3.

Then, l_1 is parallel to l_3.

$\therefore R$ is transitive relation.

So, R is an equivalence relation.

12. $X = \{1, 2, 3, 4, 5\}$

$Y = \{1, 3, 5, 7, 9\}$

(a) $R_1 = \{(x, y) : y = 2 + x, x \in X, y \in Y\}$

$R_1 = \{(1, 3), (2, 4), (3, 5), (4, 6), (5, 7)\}$

Here, $(2, 4)$ and $(4, 6) \notin X \times Y$

So, R_1 is not a relation from X to Y.

(b) $R_2 = \{(1, 1), (2, 1), (3, 3) (4, 3), (5, 5)\}$

$R_2 \subseteq X \times Y$

(c) $R_3 = \{(1, 1), (1, 3), (3, 5) (5, 7)\}$

$R_3 \subseteq X \times Y$

(d) $(2, 4) \in R_4$

But $(2, 4) \in X \times Y$

$\therefore R_4$ is not relation from X to Y.

13. Given, $S = \{(x, y) : x, y \in R, x \le y^3\}$

For reflexive

$$\left(\frac{1}{2}, \frac{1}{2}\right) = \frac{1}{2} \not\le \frac{1}{8}$$

$\therefore R$ is not reflexive.

For symmetric

$(1, 2) \equiv 1 \le 8$

But $\quad (2, 1) \equiv 2 \not\le 1$

$\therefore R$ is not symmetric.

For transitive

$(28, 4) \equiv 28 \le 64$

$(4, 3) \equiv 4 \le 27$

$(28, 3) \equiv 28 \not\le 27$

$\therefore R$ is not transitive.

$\therefore R$ is neither reflexive nor symmetric nor transitive.

Sol. (Q. Nos. 14-15)

14. We have, $(a, b) \in R_1$ iff $|a - b| \le 7$, where $a, b \in Z$

Reflexivity Let $a \in Z$

$\Rightarrow \quad a - a = 0$

$\Rightarrow \quad |a - a| \le 7 \Rightarrow 0 \le 7 \Rightarrow (a, a) \in R_1$

$\therefore$ The relation R_1 is reflexive.

Symmetry

$(a, b) \in R_1$

$\Rightarrow \quad |a-b| \le 7 \Rightarrow |-(b-a)| \le 7$

$\Rightarrow \quad |b-a| \le 7 \Rightarrow (b, a) \in R_1$

$\therefore$ The relation R_1 is symmetric.

Transitivity We have $(2, 6), (6, 10) \in R_1$ because

$$|2-6| = 4 \le 7 \text{ and } |6-10| = 4 \le 7$$

Also, $|2-10| = 8 \not\le 7$

$\therefore \quad (2, 10) \notin R_1$

Hence, the relation R_1 is not transitive.

15. We have $(a, b) \in R_2$ iff $ab = 4$, where $a, b \in Q$

Reflexivity $5 \in Q$ and $(5)(5) = 25 \ne 4$

$\therefore \quad (5, 5) \notin R_2$

The relation R_2 is not reflexive.

Symmetry $\quad (a, b) \in R_2$

$\Rightarrow \quad ab = 4 \Rightarrow ba = 4$

$\Rightarrow \quad (b, a) \in R_2$

$\therefore$ The relation R_2 is symmetric.

Transitivity We have $\left(8, \frac{1}{2}\right), \left(\frac{1}{2}, 8\right) \in R_2$ because

$$8\left(\frac{1}{2}\right) = 4 \text{ and } \left(\frac{1}{2}\right)(8) = 4$$

Also, $8(8) = 64 \ne 4$

$\therefore \quad (8, 8) \notin R_2$

$\therefore$ The relation R_2 is not transitive.

Sol. (Q. Nos. 16-17)

Given, $a = 20$ ...(i)

$e + f + g = 15$ ...(ii)

$b + d + f + g = 22$ ...(iii)

$c = 11$ ...(iv)

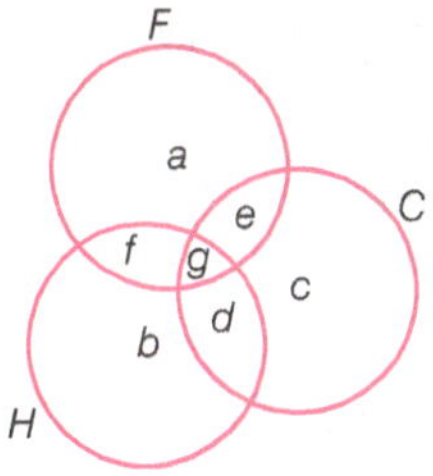

$c + d + e + g = 25$ ...(v)

$\Rightarrow \quad d + e + g = 14$ ...(vi)

$e = 7$ ...(vii)

$f = 3$ ...(viii)

From Eqs. (vii), (viii) and (ix),

$e + g = 12$ ...(ix)

$e = 7, f = 3, g = 5$

From Eq. (vi), $d = 2$

From Eq. (iii) $b + 2 + 3 + 5 = 22$

$\therefore \quad b = 12$

Hence, $a = 20, b = 12, c = 11, d = 2, e = 7, f = 3, g = 5$

16. Number of children play all the three games $= g = 5$

17. Number of children play cricket and hockey but not football $= d = 2$

18. Given, $a = 22, \ c = 12$

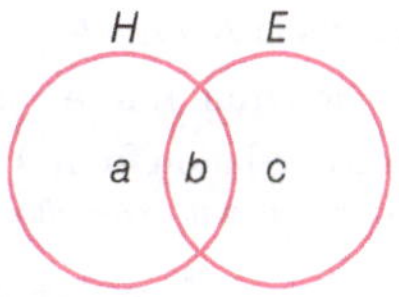

and $\quad a + b + c = 45$

$\Rightarrow \quad 22 + b + 12 = 45$

$\therefore \quad b = 11 = 2\lambda + 1$

$\Rightarrow \quad \lambda = 5$

19. $\therefore \quad \cos x > -\frac{1}{2}$ and $0 \le x \le \pi$

$\Rightarrow \quad -\frac{2\pi}{3} < x < \frac{2\pi}{3}$ and $0 \le x \le \pi$

$\Rightarrow \quad 0 \le x < \frac{2\pi}{3}$

$\therefore \quad A = \left[0, \frac{2\pi}{3}\right]$

Again, $\quad \sin x > \frac{1}{2}$ and $\frac{\pi}{3} \le x \le \pi$

$\Rightarrow \quad \frac{\pi}{6} < x < \frac{5\pi}{6}$ and $\frac{\pi}{3} \le x \le \pi$

$\Rightarrow \quad \frac{\pi}{3} \le x < \frac{5\pi}{6}$

$$B = \left[\frac{\pi}{3}, \frac{5\pi}{6}\right)$$

Now, $\quad A \cap B = \left[\frac{\pi}{3}, \frac{2\pi}{3}\right)$

$$\frac{\pi}{3} \le A \cap B < \frac{2\pi}{3}$$

Here, $\quad \lambda = \frac{1}{3}$ and $\mu = \frac{2}{3}$

$$\lambda + \mu = 1$$

20. Here, $A = [-3, 7), B = (0, 10)$

and $\quad S = (-\infty, \infty)$

$\therefore \quad A - B = [-3, 0]$ and $B - A = [7, 10)$

$\therefore \quad A \Delta B = (A - B) \cup (B - A) = [-3, 0] \cup [7, 10)$

$\therefore$ Positive integers are 7, 8, 9.

Number of positive integers = 3

21. As, $2^m - 2^n = 48 = 16 \times 3 = 2^4 \times 3$

$\Rightarrow \quad 2^n(2^{m-n} - 1) = 2^4 (2^2 - 1)$

$\therefore \quad n = 4$ and $m - n = 2$

$n = 4$ and $m = 6$

Now, $\quad m - n = 2$

22. $n((A \times B) \cap (B \times A)) = n((A \cap B) \times (B \cap A))$

$= n(A \cap B) \cdot n(B \cap A)$

$= n(A \cap B) \cdot n(A \cap B)$

$= 99 \times 99$

$= 121 \times 9^2$

$\therefore \quad \lambda = 9$

23. Given set $A = \{1, 2, 3\}$

Total number of elements in $A \times A = 9$

Total number of reflection from A to $A = 2^9$

Now, number of reflexive relation from A to A

$$= 2^{\text{number of elements in } A\times A \text{ is reflexive}}$$

$$= 2^{n(A\times A) - n(A)} = 2^{9-3} = 2^6 = 64$$

24. Here, $X = \{1, 6, 11, \ldots 10121\}$ $[\because a_n = a + (n-1)d]$

and $Y = \{9, 16, 23, \ldots 14177\}$

$X \cap Y = \{16, 51, 86, \ldots\}$

a_n of $X \cap Y$ is less than 10121.

$\therefore \quad a_n = 16 + (n-1)35 \le 10121$

$\Rightarrow \quad n \le 289.71 \Rightarrow n = 289$

$\therefore n(X \cup Y) = n(X) + n(Y) - n(X \cap Y)$

$= 2025 + 2025 - 289 = 3761$

25. Let C = Set of people who read newspaper A

and D = Set of people who read newspaper B

Given, $n(C) = 25, n(D) = 20$ and $n(C \cap D) = 8$

$\therefore n(C \cap D') = n(C) - n(C \cap D) = 25 - 8 = 17$

But total number of people who read A but not $B = 30\%$

$\therefore$% of people reading newspaper A but not $B = 30\%$ of 17

$$= \frac{30 \times 17}{100} = \frac{51}{10}$$

and $n(C' \cap D) = n(D) - n(C \cap D) = 20 - 8 = 12$

Also, total number of people who read newspaper B but not A $= 40\%$.

$\therefore$% of people reading newspaper B but not $A = 40\%$ of 12

$$= \frac{40 \times 12}{100} = \frac{24}{5}$$

and given total people who read newspaper A and $B = 50\%$

$\therefore$% of people who read newspaper A and $B = 50\%$ of 8

$$= \frac{50 \times 8}{100} = 4$$

$\therefore$Percentage of people reading an advertisement

$$= \left(\frac{51}{10} + \frac{24}{5} + 4\right)\% = 13.9\%$$

$\therefore \quad x = 13.9$

26. $\because$ R is reflexive, if it contains (1, 1), (2, 2), (3, 3)

$\because (1, 2) \in R$ and $(2, 3) \in R$

$\therefore R$ is symmetric, if $(2, 1), (3, 2) \in R$

Now, $R = \{(1, 1), (2, 2), (3, 3), (2, 1), (3, 2), (2, 3), (1, 2)\}$

R will be transitive, if $(3, 1), (1, 3) \in R$

Thus, R becomes an equivalence relation by adding (1, 1), (2, 2), (3, 3), (2, 1), (3, 2), (1, 3), (3, 1).

Hence, the total number of ordered pair is 7.

Here, $\lambda = 7 \therefore \lambda^2 = 49$

27. **(A)** $X \cap (X \cup Y)^C = X \cap (X^C \cap Y^C)$

$= (X \cap X^C) \cap Y^C = \phi \cap Y^C = \phi$

(B) $(A \cap B')' \cup (B \cap C) = (A' \cup (B')') \cup (B \cap C)$

$= (A' \cup B) \cup (C \cap B)$

$= A' \cup (B \cup (C \cap B)) = A' \cup B$

(C) $(A \cup B)' \cup (A' \cap B) = (A' \cap B') \cup (A' \cap B)$

$= (A' \cup A') \cap (A' \cup B) \cap (B' \cup A') \cap (B' \cup B)$

$= A' \cap \{A' \cup (B \cap B')\} \cap U$

$= A' \cap (A' \cup \phi\} \cap U$

$= A' \cap A' \cap U$

$= A' \cap A' \cap U$

$= A' \cap U = A'$

(D) $(A' \cap B' \cap C) \cup (B \cap C) \cup (A \cap C)$

$= [(A \cup B)' \cap C] \cup [(B \cup A) \cap C]$

$= [(A \cup B') \cup (B \cup A)] \cap C$

$= X \cap C$

$= C$

Exercise 3 - Challenging Problems

1. We have, $U = \{x : x^5 - 6x^4 + 11x^3 - 6x^2 = 0\}$

$= \{0, 1, 2, 3\}$

$A = \{x : x^2 - 5x + 6 = 0\} = \{2, 3\}$

and $B = \{x : x^2 - 3x + 2 = 0\} = \{1, 2\}$

$\therefore \quad A \cap B = \{2\}$

Hence, $(A \cap B)' = U - (A \cap B)$

$= \{0, 1, 2, 3\} - \{2\} = \{0, 1, 3\}$

$\therefore \quad n(A \cap B)' = 3$

2. U = Set of all people

M = {Males}

S = {College students}

T = {Teenagers}

W = {People having height more than 5 feet}

(i) College students having heights more than 5 feet $= S \cap W$

(ii) People who are not teenagers and having their heights less than 5 feet $= T' \cap W'$

(iii) All people who are neither males nor teenagers nor college students $= (M \cup T \cup S)'$

3. $X = \{(x, y) : x^2 + y^2 \le 1\}$

$Y = \{(x, y) : 0 \le x \le 1, -1 \le y \le 1\}$

$X \cup Y = \{(x, y) : x^2 + y^2 \le 1 \text{ or } 0 \le x \le 1 \text{ and } -1 \le y \le 1\}$

$X \cap Y = \{(x, y) : x^2 + y^2 \le 1 \text{ and } x \ge 0\}$

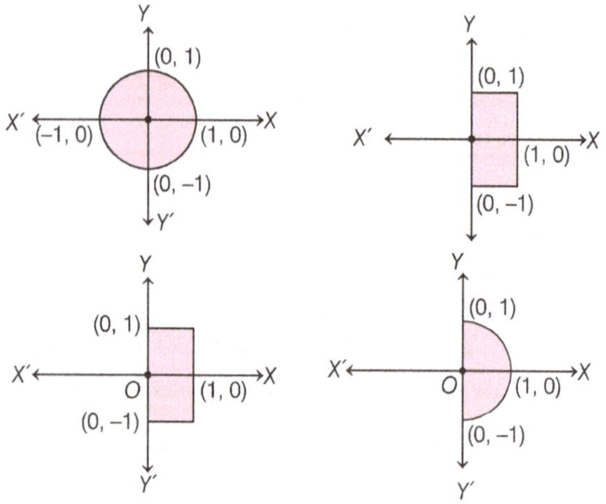

4. $a + f + e + g = 21$ ...(i)

$b + d + f + g = 26$ ...(ii)

$c + d + e + g = 29$ ...(iii)

$f + g = 14$ ...(iv)

$g + d = 15$ ...(v)

$e + g = 12$ ...(vi)

$g = 8$ ...(vii)

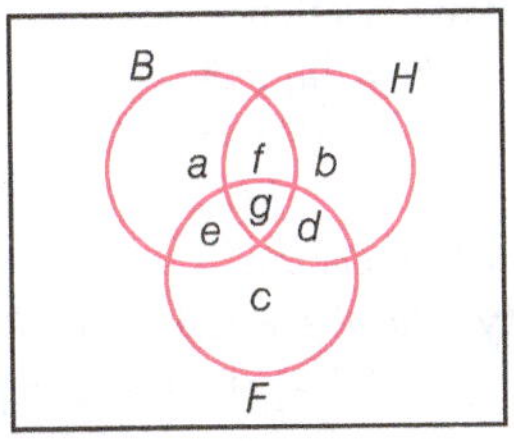

From Eqs. (vii) and (vi), $e = 4$

Form Eqs. (vii) and (v), $d = 7$

From Eqs. (vii) and (iv), $f = 6$

From Eq. (iii), $c + 7 + 4 + 8 = 29 \Rightarrow c = 29 - 19 = 10 = c$

From Eq. (ii), $b + 7 + 6 + 8 = 26 \Rightarrow b = 26 - 21 \Rightarrow b = 5$

From Eq. (i), $a + 6 + 4 + 8 = 21 \Rightarrow a = 21 - 18 \Rightarrow a = 3$

$$n(B) + n(H) + n(F) = a + b + c + d + e + f + g$$
$$= 3 + 5 + 10 + 7 + 4 + 6 + 8 = 43$$

5. $b + e + f + g = 205$ ...(i)

$a + d + f + g = 210$ ...(ii)

$c + d + e + g = 120$ ...(iii)

$f + g = 100$ ...(iv)

$e + g = 800$ ...(v)

$d + g = 35$ ... (vi)

$g = 20$ ...(vii)

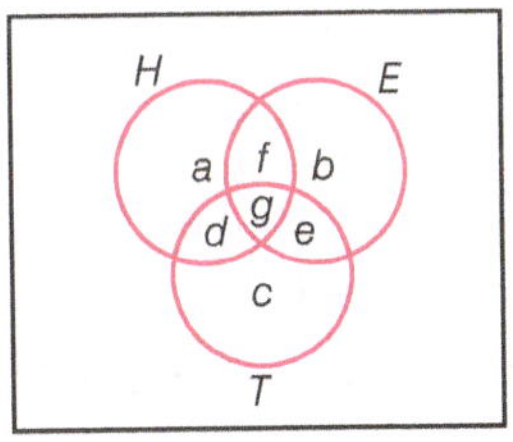

From Eqs. (vi) and (vii), $d = 15$

From Eqs. (vii) and (v), $e = 60$

From Eqs. (vii) and (iv), $f = 80$

From Eq. (i), $b + 60 + 80 + 20 = 205 \Rightarrow b = 205 - 160$

$\Rightarrow b = 45$ = Can speak English but not Hindi or Tamil.

From Eq. (ii) $a + 15 + 80 + 20 = 210$

$\Rightarrow \quad a + 115 = 210 \Rightarrow a = 95$

From Eq. (iii), $c + 15 + 60 + 20 = 120$

$\Rightarrow \quad c = 120 - 95 \Rightarrow c = 25$

People who can speak neither E nor H nor T

$$= 450 - (95 + 45 + 25 + 15 + 60 + 80 + 20)$$
$$= 450 - 340 = 110$$

6. $c + f + g + e = 42$ ...(i)

$b + d + g + e = 36$ ...(ii)

$a + f + d + g = 30$ ...(iii)

$g + e = 15$ ...(iv)

$f + g = 10$ ...(v)

$d = 4$ ...(vi)

$e = 11$ ...(vii)

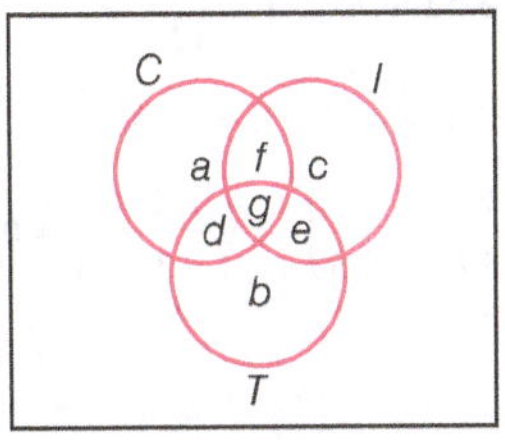

From (iv) and (vii), $g + 11 = 15 \Rightarrow g = 4$ ...(viii)

From (v) and (viii), $f + 4 = 10 \Rightarrow f = 6$ ...(ix)

From (i), $c + 6 + 4 + 11 = 42 \Rightarrow c = 21$ ...(x)

From (ii), $b + 4 + 4 + 11 = 36 \Rightarrow b = 17$ ...(xi)

From (iii), $a + 6 + 4 + 4 = 30 \Rightarrow a = 16$ ...(xii)

Number of required persons

$$= 123 - (16 + 17 + 21 + 4 + 11 + 6 + 4)$$
$$= 123 - 79$$
$$= 44$$

7. We have, $(a, b) \in R_1$, iff $|a - b| \le 7$, where $a, b \in Z$.

For relation R_1

Reflexivity : Let $a \in Z, a - a = 0$

$\Rightarrow \quad |a - a| \le 7 \Rightarrow 0 < 7$

$\Rightarrow \quad (a, a) \in R_1$ (reflexive)

Symmetry : $(a, b) \in R_1 \Rightarrow |a - b| \le 7$

$\Rightarrow \quad |b - a| \le 7 \Rightarrow (b, a) \in R_1$

$\therefore$ R_1 is symmetric.

Transitivity : $(2, 6), (6, 10) \in R_1$ but $(2, 10) \notin R_1$ (not transitive)

We have $(a, b) \in R_2$, iff $ab = 4$, where $a, b \in Q$

For relation R_2

Reflexivity : $5 \in Q$ and $5 \cdot 5 = 25 \ne 4$ (not reflexive)

Symmetry : $(a, b) \in R_2$

$\Rightarrow \quad ab = 4 \Rightarrow ba = 4 \Rightarrow (b, a) \in R_2$

$\therefore$ R_2 is symmetric.

Transitivity : $\left(8, \frac{1}{2}\right), \left(\frac{1}{2}, 8\right) \in R_2$ but $(8, 8) \notin R_2$.

$\therefore$ R_2 is not transitive.

For relation R_3

We have, $(a, b) \in R_3$,

iff $a^2 - 4ab + 3b^2 = 0$, where $a, b \in R$

Reflexivity : $(a, a) \in R_3$

$\because a^2 - 4a \cdot a + 3a^2 = 0$

$\therefore R_3$ is reflexive.

Symmetry : Let $(a, b) \in R_3$

$\Rightarrow \quad a^2 - 4ab + 3b^2 = 0,$

we get $a = b$ and $a = 3b$ and if $(b, a) \in R_3$

$\Rightarrow b^2 - 4ab + 3a^2 = 0$, we get $b = a$ and $b = 3a$.

$\therefore \quad (a, b) \in R_3 \neq (b, a) \in R_3$

$\therefore R_3$ is not symmetry.

Transitivity : We have, $(3, 1)\left(1, \frac{1}{3}\right) \in R_3$

as $3^2 - 4(3)(1) + 3(1)^2 = 9 - 12 + 3 = 0$

and $(1)^2 - 4(1)\left(\frac{1}{3}\right) + 3\left(\frac{1}{3}\right)^2 = 1 - \frac{4}{3} + \frac{1}{3} = 0$

But $\left(3, \frac{1}{3}\right) \notin R_3$

$\because \quad (3)^2 - 4(3)\left(\frac{1}{3}\right) + 3\left(\frac{1}{3}\right)^2 = \frac{16}{3} \neq 0$

$\therefore R_3$ is not transitive.

8. R defined on $N \times N$ such that

$$(a, b)\, R\, (c, d) \Leftrightarrow ad = bc$$

Reflexivity Let $(a, b) \in N \times N$

$\Rightarrow \quad a, b \in N \Rightarrow ab = ba$

$\Rightarrow \quad (a, b)\, R\, (a, b)$

$\therefore R$ is reflexive on, $N \times N$.

Symmetry Let $(a, b), (c, d) \in N \times N$,

then $(a, b)\, R\, (c, d) \Rightarrow ad = bc$

$\Rightarrow \quad cb = da$

$\Rightarrow \quad (c, d)\, R\, (a, b)$

$\therefore R$ is symmetric on $N \times N$.

Transitivity Let $(a, b), (c, d), (e, f) \in N \times N$

Then, $\quad (a, b)\, R\, (c, d) \Rightarrow ad = bc \quad$ ...(i)

$(c, d)\, R\, (e, f) \Rightarrow cf = de \quad$ ...(ii)

From Eqs. (i) and (ii), $(ad)(cf) = (bc)(de)$

$\Rightarrow \quad af = be$

$\Rightarrow \quad (a, b)\, R\, (e, f)$

$\therefore R$ is transitive relation on $N \times N$.

$\therefore R$ is equivalence relation on $N \times N$.

9. (i) $aRb \Leftrightarrow |a - b| > 0$

Reflexivity $a - a = 0$

$\therefore \quad (a, a) \notin R$

$\therefore R$ is not reflexive

Symmetry $(a, b) \in R \Rightarrow |a - b| > 0$

$\Rightarrow \quad |-(b - a) > 0|$

$\Rightarrow \quad |b - a| > 0 \Rightarrow (b, a) \in R$

$\therefore R$ is symmetric relation

Transitivity $(a, b) \in R$ and $(b, c) \in R$

$\Rightarrow \quad |a - b| > 0$ and $|b - c| > 0$

$\Rightarrow \quad |a - b| + |b - c| > 0 \quad$ [by addition]

Now, let $a > b$ and $b > c$, then $a > c$

$|a - b| + |b - c| = a - b + b - c = a - c > 0$

$\Rightarrow \quad |a - c| > 0$

If $a < b$ and $b > c$, then

$|a - b| + |b - c| = -(a - b) + (b - c) = -a + 2b - c$

$\not\Rightarrow \quad |a - c| > 0$

$\therefore R$ is not transitive relation.

(ii) $aRb \Leftrightarrow |a| = |b|$

Reflexivity We have, $|a| = |a|$

$\Rightarrow \quad aRa\ \forall a$

$\therefore R$ is reflecxive relation.

Symmetry $aRb \Rightarrow |a| = |b|$

$\Rightarrow \quad |b| = |a|$

$\Rightarrow \quad bRa$

$\therefore R$ is symmetric relation.

Transitivity $(a, b) \in R$ and $(b, c) \in R$

$\Rightarrow \quad |a| = |b|$ and $|b| = |c|$

$\Rightarrow \quad |a| = |c|$

$\Rightarrow \quad (a, c) \in R$

$\therefore R$ is transitive relation.

(iii) $aRb \Leftrightarrow |a| \geq |b|$

Reflexivity For any $a \in R$, we have $|a| \geq |a|$

So, $\quad aRa\ \forall a$

$\therefore R$ is reflexive relation.

Symmetry $aRb \Rightarrow |a| \geq |b|$

$\Rightarrow \quad |b| \leq |a|$

$\therefore R$ is not symmetric relation.

Transitivity aRb and $bRc \Rightarrow |a| \geq |b|$ and $|b| \geq |c|$

$\Rightarrow \quad |a| \geq |c|$

$\Rightarrow \quad a\, R\, c$

$\therefore R$ is transitive relation.

(iv) $aRb \Leftrightarrow 1 + ab > 0, \forall a, b \in R$

Reflexivity Let $a \notin R \Rightarrow 1 + a \cdot a = 1 + a^2 > 0$

$\Rightarrow \quad (a, a) \in R$

$\therefore R$ is reflexive on R.

Symmetry Let $(a, b) \in R$, then $(a, b) \in R$

$\Rightarrow \quad 1 + ab > 0$

$\Rightarrow \quad 1 + ba > 0$

$\Rightarrow \quad (b, a) \in R$

$\therefore R$ is symmetric on R.

Transitivity We observe that $\left(1, \frac{1}{2}\right) \in R$ and $\left(\frac{1}{2}, -1\right) \in R$ but $(1, -1) \notin R$ because

$$1 + (1)(-1) = 0 \not> 0$$

$\therefore R$ is not transitive on R.

(v) $aRb \Leftrightarrow |a| \leq b$

Reflexivity Let $-1 \in R$, then $|-1| \not\leq (-1)$

$\therefore R$ is not reflexive relation

Symmetry Now, let $-3\, R\, 4$, then $|4| \not\leq -3$

$\Rightarrow \quad 4 \not R -3$

$\therefore R$ is not symmetric relation

Transitivity aRb and $bRc \Rightarrow |a| \leq b$ and $|b| \leq c$

Then, $\quad |a| \leq c \Rightarrow aRc$

$\therefore R$ is transitive relation.